COLLEGES

with Programs or Services for Students with

LEARNING DISABILITIES

MIDGE LIPKIN, Ph.D.

2nd EDITION

© 1993 by Midge Lipkin, Ph.D.

Printed in the United States of America
Second Edition 1993

Prior edition
© 1990, Second printing 1992

Library of Congress Number
93-084224

ISBN 0-9620326-5-4

All inquires should be addressed to:
Schoolsearch
127 Marsh Street
Belmont, Massachusetts 02178

TABLE OF CONTENTS

PREFACE

Radical changes in the post-secondary school education of learning disabled (LD) students have occurred over the last 30 years. Today thousands of LD students are earning high grades in U.S. colleges by using a variety of compensatory skills, classroom aids, and special services. When they graduate, they will enter and succeed in business, industry, and the professions. Yet only a few decades ago most LD students were unable even to matriculate because they could not meet college entrance criteria. Or if admitted, the majority received poor grades or dropped out because they could not handle the work. Educators labeled LD students as dull, lazy, or uninterested and made no effort to discover why they didn't succeed.

This revolution in status was triggered by a chain of events: psychological research, Federal law regarding the public schools, and the rapid development of responsive college-level resources. First, scientists gained a clearer and more compassionate understanding of learning disabilities and how they affect students' performance in the classroom and in life. Diagnostic testing methods were developed to pinpoint students' deficits, and experts evolved teaching techniques to deal with different student learning "styles". These advances were reinforced by passage of Public Law 94-142, the Handicapped Children Act of 1975, which mandated all states to provide compensatory education for LD children through high school.

Under the guidance of Dr. Gertrude Webb, Curry College (Milton, Massachusetts) became, in 1970, the first college to offer a comprehensive program for students with learning disabilities. Then the rapid growth in the number of LD high school graduates with compensatory training (and shrinking college enrollments) put pressure on the academic community to develop LD-responsive resources. Thus, during the 1980's many other U.S. colleges and universities followed Curry's lead by creating LD programs or offering support services.

As a private-practice guidance counselor and author of _The Schoolsearch Guide to Private Schools for Students with Learning Disabilities,_ Dr. Midge Lipkin was uniquely positioned to recognize the need for a single-source, ready-reference guide to LD-responsive colleges during their rapid growth phase. Coping in her own practice with the same lack of an organized information base that had existed before she published her private school guide, she extended her research to cover the hundreds of colleges that were entering the field. This effort culminated, in 1990, in publication of Dr. Lipkin's _The Schoolsearch Guide to Colleges with Programs or Services for Students with Learning Disabilities,_ which detailed and cross-referenced the LD-related facilities of more than 600 colleges. This new edition of the Schoolsearch Guide is not only updated, but expanded to cover many more college resources.

Dr. Lipkin hopes that this book, based on her independent research and analysis, will make the student-college matching task much easier for everyone concerned. She welcomes suggestions from readers on additional college criteria that should be considered for inclusion in future editions of her work.

ACKNOWLEDGMENTS

I would like to thank a number of people who assisted me in making this book possible. My appreciation to Lucky Melanson for her dedication, her long hours of work, and her feeling that no job was neither too large nor too small; Alan Schlingenbaum for his endless hours of teaching me the programs necessary to put this book together; and Virginia Mason for her cover design. A very special thanks to my husband, Alton, my children, Stephen, Deborah, Amy, Peter, Janet, David, and my grandchildren, Todd, Michelle, Margo and Robyn for understanding the magnitude of this project. Without their patience and understanding, this book never would have gone to press.

ABOUT THE AUTHOR

The information in this book was compiled by Dr. Midge Lipkin to fill a critical information gap she encountered in the course of her educational consulting practice. In assisting clients with the school placement process, she found that they needed access to an easily understood, accessible source of data that enabled them to assess, on statistically comparable bases, the merits and possibilities of attending various colleges and universities that accept students with learning disabilities.

Midge Lipkin's current practice focuses on three specialties: neuro-psychological evaluation, therapeutic educational tutoring, and school counseling. As a neuro-psychological evaluator, she conducts in-depth evaluations to determine academic levels and prescribes educational plans to remedy deficits. As a therapeutic educational tutor, she works privately with students with learning disabilities as well as with gifted students who need more academic stimulation.

In recent years, Dr. Lipkin's major emphasis has become school counseling. Through Schoolsearch, she provides direct assistance with all phases of the elementary, secondary school, and college selection and placement process. Starting with a detailed analysis of students' objectives, needs, and credentials, she helps them evaluate potential schools and then guides them through each of the application and follow-up stages.

Dr. Lipkin has more than 30 years experience in the field of education. Some of her professional assignments have been:
- Psychoeducational Advisor, Learning Impairment Training Program, Division of Child Psychiatry, New England Medical Center
- Director of Dorchester Children's Mini School (private day school for emotionally disturbed and learning disabled children)
- Educational Administrator, Dorchester Mental Health, Children's Clinic
- Instructor/Lecturer on teaching of the Learning Disabled
    - Assumption College
    - Boston College
    - Boston University
    - Lesley College
    - Perkins School for the Blind
- Supervisor and Teacher in programs for the learning disabled in the Winchester, Winthrop, Waltham, Sudbury, and Newton, Massachusetts, public school systems

In addition to her Ph.D. in School Administration and Special Education, Lipkin has earned a Certificate for Specific Language Disability from the Massachusetts General Hospital. She also holds a M.A. in Education from Boston University and a B.S. from Lesley College.

Dr. Lipkin is also the author and publisher of The School Search Guide to Private Schools in the Northeast and The Schoolsearch Guide To Colleges With Programs of Services for Students With Learning Disabilities, The School Search Guide To Private Schools For Students With Learning Disabilities.

Chapter 1

INTRODUCTION

SCOPE AND PURPOSE

This edition of <u>The Schoolsearch Guide to Colleges with Programs or Services for Students with Learning Disabilities</u> provides, in an easy-comparison format, detailed information for the 1992-93 academic year on 738 colleges, junior colleges, and community colleges. For these schools, the Guide covers:

- programs, services, and accommodations for students with learning disabilities (LD), and attention deficit disorder/ attention deficit hyperactivity disorder (ADD/ADHD) students; together with

- related key data, such as:
  - admissions procedures and requirements, including LD-responsive modifications;
  - academic curricula and graduation criteria; and
  - sports, recreation, and other campus facilities.

In addition, the Guide lists some 500 other colleges which are known to have an interest in servicing the learning disabled, but which did not reply to the survey.

At first glance, the task of finding a suitable college for a LD and/or ADD/ADHD student might seem relatively easy: every university, college, junior college, and community college that receives Federal funds is barred from discriminating against applicants with learning disabilities by Section 504 of the Rehabilitation Act of 1973. (And almost all colleges rely directly or indirectly to some extent on Federal funds for research, scholarships, student aid, and/or other functions.) But this Federal requirement holds true only <u>if</u> the LD applicants meet the particular admissions criteria the college has set for <u>all</u> new entrants. No school is required to lower its entrance standards so candidates with learning disabilities and/or attention deficit disorders can compete successfully against other high school graduates for admission. Even more important, no college has to modify its curriculum or provide the support services that many LD and ADD/ADHD students need to handle academic work.

For any student, the college selection/admission qualification process can be time-consuming and challenging because it involves matching his/her academic gifts, interests, and goals with different schools' criteria. For LD and ADD/ADHD students (and their parents, educators, and social services consultants), the task can be particularly tedious, frustrating, and confusing because their range of options is even more complicated.

This Guide's unique computerized-format, with cross-reference appendices, is designed to make it relatively easy to find the colleges that offer specific LD and ADD/ADHD resources. Furthermore, as noted above, for each of the 738 colleges that responded, the Guide gives sufficient detail on other factors to enable a student, parent, or guidance counselor to make an informed college choice.

HOW TO USE THIS GUIDE

It's important to read the next three chapters before you attempt to use the Guide to find an appropriate college. Otherwise you might waste a lot of time pouring through pages of data that are not relevant for the particular student who is seeking placement.

The first step in searching for a suitable college is to establish your selection criteria. Chapter 2, Defining the Applicant's Educational Goals and Needs, discusses learning disability and attention deficit disorders, their impact on student performance and life skills, and the need to develop a realistic applicant profile. By filling out Table 4, Applicant's College Search Criteria, you can develop a profile of relevant information that is similar in format to the individual college write-ups and the cross-reference appendices. This format makes it easier to take into account all of the student's qualifications, goals, and needs in evaluating college offerings.

Chapter 3, How to Select and Apply to an Appropriate College, presents a step-by-step review of the college selection and application processes. Hopefully, this chapter will not only clarify and simplify the various steps in the college search process, but also aid the reader to develop a systematic, coordinated approach that takes into account key deadlines.

The heart of the book, of course, is the individual college profiles and the computer-generated cross-reference appendices that make it easy to find desired resources and to compare college offerings. Chapter 4 explains key elements of the Guide's college profile format.

The Guide is a primary data resource. Dr. Lipkin surveyed over 3,000 U.S. schools via a mailed questionnaire, with telephone follow-up for verification The Guide does not rate or rank colleges on the basis of the author's opinion or rely on data from secondary sources. The information contained in each school's profile was provided by its admissions director, LD program director, or some other college official. Each profile also contains a brief statement in the words of the school respondent on what makes its program or services unique. Schoolsearch's primary content contribution has been design of the research instrument which enabled collection of all relevant information in a format that facilitates college-to-college comparison.

Chapter 2. DEFINING THE APPLICANT'S EDUCATIONAL GOALS AND NEEDS

THE KEY QUESTIONS

Before beginning the college search process, any student, parent, or guidance counselor needs to assess the potential applicant's strengths and weaknesses and define related academic and life goals. Each of the colleges listed in this directory offers some unique advantages for the learning disabled (LD) or attention deficit disorder (ADD/ADHD) student. But none of these schools is right for every student. These colleges vary widely in terms of curriculum, campus location, social atmosphere, sports, and recreation programs, as well as in the remedial LD programs or support services/accommodations they offer. So it is important to define the applicant's goals and needs before investigating and comparing the advantages of the various colleges' programs and services.

The key questions the reader needs to answer are:

- Does the student have a learning disability or attention deficit disorder?
  - What kind of disability?
  - How severe is it?

- What special education factors need to be considered in selecting a college?

- What other educational and social services does the student need to obtain from the college to meet his/her life goals?

DEFINING DISABILITY

Learning disabilities and attention deficit disorders are not lay-diagnosed conditions. To qualify for participation in any college-level LD or ADD/ADHD program or to receive related services and accommodations, the student must have a professionally developed evaluation that proves he/she has a learning disability and/or attention deficit disorder. Such an evaluation can be obtained through a public school system or from a private counselor. The specific tests required differ from college to college. A number of the colleges that responded to the survey have listed their test requirements. (In some instances, testing may also be conducted by the college or university itself.)

Learning Disability

Public Law 94-142, the Handicapped Children Act of 1975, mandates all states to provide a free and adequate education for all children, regardless of handicap, through the secondary level. It also contains the official legal definition of "learning disability":

> *Specific learning disability means a disorder in one or more of the basic psychological processes involved in understanding or using language, spoken or written, which may manifest itself in an imperfect ability to listen, think, speak, read, write, spell, or to do mathematical calculations. The term includes such conditions as perceptual handicaps, brain injury, minimal brain dysfunction, dyslexia, and developmental aphasia. The term does not include children who have learning problems that are primarily the result of visual, hearing, or motor handicaps, of mental retardation, of emotional disturbance, or of environmental, cultural, or economic disadvantage.*

Some colleges with programs or services for students with learning disabilities use a broader definition of "learning disability" than specified in P.L. 94-142. But, simply stated, a student is generally deemed to have a learning disability if there is a significant discrepancy between his or her innate cognitive ability and his or her ability to perform in school. The LD student consistently exhibits difficulties in study skills (examples listed in Table 1) and/or underachieves--performs below the level expected in view of his/her apparent intelligence, health, and life circumstances.

3

To be eligible for LD services in the public school system and to qualify for college programs, the student must first undergo a professional evaluation. Field observations, interviews with parents and teachers, and a test battery are correlated to develop a profile for the learning disabled student. (The test battery usually includes a WISC-III, various tests that pinpoint specific learning disabilities, and social/emotional assessment instruments.) The evaluation culminates in an Individual Education Plan (IEP) which specifies the student's long-term educational goals, annual teaching objectives, and the resources to be deployed in working to achieve these goals. P.L.-94-142 requires public school systems to provide this service for adults as well as for kindergartners and older children, but does not require colleges to do so or authorize funding at the college level.

ADD/ADHD

Until October 1991, only students classified as learning disabled were categorized as having an attention deficit disorder (ADD) or an attention deficit hyperactivity disorder (ADHD). Now the Federal Government has accepted a new classification under the umbrella of Special Needs which covers the more than 300,000 students known to have ADD/ADHD without LD. The following definition is proposed by the Professional Group on Attention and Related Disorders (PGRAD):

> *The term "attention deficit disorder" means a disorder in one or more of the basic cognitive processes involved in orienting, focusing, or maintaining attention which results in a marked degree of inattention to academic and social tasks. This disorder may also be manifested in verbal or motor impulsivity and non redundant activity, such as excessive fidgetiness or restlessness. "A marked degree" is defined as a score exceeding the 97th percentile for the child's chronological and mental age as measured by well-standardized methods of assessing school behavior. The disorder frequently manifests itself in developmentally inappropriate degrees of difficulty in listening to and following directions and in organizing, planning, initiating, sustaining, completing, and verifying academic assignments, which require reading, written composition, mathematics, spelling, or handwriting.*

> *Attention deficit disorder must persist over a long period of time (i.e., at least 6 months). When it is observed in children of minority ethnic or cultural backgrounds, it must be assessed in relation to other children of the same background and mental age. To qualify as a disabling condition, the inattention must adversely affect school performance as manifested by a significant discrepancy between general mental ability and academic productivity and/or accuracy.*

Attention deficit disorder is characterized by inattention and impulsivity; attention deficit hyperactivity disorder also includes hyperactivity. Table 2 gives some examples of these three types of behavior. Generally onset before age 7 is specified, as well as duration of more than 6 months. Some of the symptoms exhibited in childhood are masked in adolescence. Those students classified as ADD/ADHD do not meet the criteria for a pervasive developmental disorder, schizophrenia, affective disorder, or severe or profound mental retardation.

<u>Severity of Disorder</u>

Most students with learning disabilities have IEPs and have received ongoing guidance and academic counseling throughout high school. As a result, they and their parents already should be aware of their social and academic strengths and weaknesses. They should have access to a profile of their disabilities, in terms of scope and severity, as well as of the progress they have made in developing compensatory skills and strategies. Any student or parent who needs additional information should consult with the guidance department at their high school or with a private guidance or education counselor.

SPECIAL EDUCATION FACTORS

It is very important to review the student's IEP carefully before selecting a college and not to rely solely on the student's relative success in high school as the basis for choice. Even high I.Q. students without any disabilities can find the move from high school to college academically and socially disastrous. Most colleges expect regular students to be self-motivated and have good, self-disciplined study habits. The level of difficulty of the academic work is much harder than in high school; and the social environment, particularly for students who live on campus, is much more sophisticated and can be quite stressful.

Table 3 lists two types of factors critical for success at the college level-- study habits and personal attributes--that seem to pose problems for most LD and ADD/ADHD students. Few learning disabilities are "cured" so, in addition, each student must continue to exercise compensatory behaviors/strategies to cope with specific deficits. Strategies learned in high school can prove inadequate for the LD or ADD/ADHD student in college without the support of a formal LD program or special services. It is easy to overlook or take for granted the special accommodations (for example, untimed testing or use of a tape recorder for note taking) that the student was permitted in high school and that are necessary if he/she is to keep up with classmates. The applicant needs to find a college(s) that specifically sanctions those accommodations (or equivalents) or offers a full-scale LD program for support, with a faculty advocate to help deal with special problems.

OVERALL COLLEGE SEARCH CRITERIA

Students with learning disabilities are succeeding in every subject from anthropology to zoology at community colleges and prestigious universities across the country. They are participating fully in all other aspects of college life: on-and off-campus sports, drama companies, sororities and fraternities, and the myriad of other activities that make the college experience memorable. It would be a mistake to focus solely on the availability of LD programs and services. After all, one cannot become a member of a ski team in most Florida schools or find at the local community college an esoteric course in archaeology that would lead to a high-prestige field work assignment with a world-renowned scientist. Nothing ventured, nothing gained.

Table 4. Applicant's College Search Criteria, is designed to help the student and his/her advisors develop a search profile that can be easily compared with the resources described in the college write-ups. (Schoolsearch hereby authorizes the reader to make photocopies of the forms in Tables 4-8 for the individual student's use, but does not sanction high-volume replication or reprinting.) Students and parents might find it helpful to review Chapter 4, The College Profile Format, before filling out Table 4.

With this profile in hand, the student can find the colleges that at least meet his/her basic immediate needs. Hopefully these schools will also fill all his/her long-term educational goals. But if not, the student can explore other options (such as college-to-college transfers, attending a LD prep summer school, etc.) that will help him/her to attain these goals.

Table 1. EXAMPLES OF BASIC STUDY SKILLS FOUND DIFFICULT BY STUDENTS WITH LEARNING DISABILITIES

PERCEPTUAL FUNCTIONING

Visual

Discriminating between visual symbols (e,c)
Perceiving spatial orientation
  differences between letters (b and d)
Separating the main part of a
  picture from the background
Proofreading
Remembering letters and words

Auditory

Discriminating between similar sounds
  (bed, bad)
Remembering the sequence of telephone numbers
Remembering the order of letters within words
(aminal for animal)

Visual Construction

Placing letters spatially on a line
Spacing words evenly
Forming even letters

COGNITION

Copying patterns
Forming geometric patterns
Reading own handwriting (both words and numbers)

SPELLING

Remembering sound-symbol association
  (not confusing long and short vowels)
Remembering syllabification and spelling rules
Not reversing, transposing, or cutting
  letters (e.g. , by eliminating vowels or the
  middle of a word)

LANGUAGE (SPOKEN AND WRITTEN)

Understanding what others say
Expressing self clearly and precisely
Responding directly to (non circumventing)
  questions
Retrieving appropriate words when
  speaking and writing
Using parts of speech and punctuation correctly

READING

Decoding and synthesizing words
Associating sounds and symbols
Discriminating between vowel sounds
Reading text aloud in correct order
  (no transposition of words)
Understanding what is read
Identifying the main theme of a story
Sequencing material correctly when
  summarizing reading

MATHEMATICS

Mastering the basic facts
Placing numbers in the right columns
Remembering the sequence of opera-
  tonal processes
Shifting from one process to another
Integrating processes
Solving word problems

ORGANIZATION/GENERAL

Organizing information and ideas
Perceiving cause-and-effect
relationships
Reasoning deductively
Sequencing historical events
Discriminating between important
  and trivial information
Abstracting meaning from metaphors
  e.g. carrying interpretation of proverbs
  beyond literal meaning
Transferring skills/knowledge
  from one field to another
Demonstrating adequate long-and
  short-term memory skill
Acquiring and retaining general
  knowledge

Table 2. EXAMPLES OF ATTENTION DEFICIT DISORDER (ADD)
AND
ATTENTION DEFICIT HYPERACTIVITY DISORDER (ADHD) BEHAVIORS

INATTENTION

Often fails to finish tasks
Often seems not to listen to what is
  said to him/her
Easily distracted by extraneous stimuli
Has difficulty concentrating on school-
  work and other tasks or play activities
requiring sustained attention
Finds it difficult to follow others'
  instructions (not due to opposition
  or failure to comprehend); e.g.,
  doesn't finish assignments
Often loses things necessary for tasks
  or activities at school or at home;
  e.g., toys, pencils, books, assignments

HYPERACTIVITY

Has difficulty remaining seated when
  required to do so
Often fidgets with hands or feet or squirms
  in seat (in adolescents, subjective feeling
  of restlessness)
Has difficulty playing quietly
Often talks excessively
Runs about or climbs on things
Thrashes about in sleep
Is always "on the tracks" as if driven
  by a motor"

IMPULSIVITY

Frequently calls out in class
Often interrupts or intrudes on others
  e.g., butts into other children's games
Often acts before thinking
Has difficulty organizing work (not
  due to cognitive problem)
Often shifts from one uncompleted
  activity to another
Needs a lot of supervision
Often engages in physically dangerous
  activities without considering possible
  consequences (not for the purpose of
  thrill-seeking):e.g. runs into street
  without looking
Has difficulty awaiting turn in games or
  other group situation
Often blurts out answers to question before
  they are completed

Source: Adapted from Quick Reference to the Diagnostic Criteria from DSM-
   III-R, 1987, Washington, D.C.: The American Psychiatric Association,
   1987, Pg. 56-57

Table 3. CRITICAL FACTORS FOR SUCCESSFUL COLLEGE PLACEMENT

STUDY HABITS

Fulfilling course requirements
Remembering assignments and
  assignment details
Advance planning to set and
  meet deadlines
Getting started
Focusing on the task at hand
Taking notes
Outlining and summarizing
Doing related library research
Using the dictionary, thesaurus,
  and other reference books
Completing assignments
Locating completed assignments
Balancing competing course demands
Shifting from one activity to another

PERSONAL ATTRIBUTES

Relating to peers as friends
Working with others
Understanding and dealing with
  others' feelings
Speaking and behaving appropriately
Controlling temper (often subject to
  sudden emotional outbursts)
Relating appropriately to authority
  figures
Following directions
Controlling anxiety about
  performance; e.g., tests

Table 4. APPLICANT'S COLLEGE SEARCH CRITERIA

ACADEMIC GOALS

Courses Leading to Major in _____

Other _____

APPLICANT'S ADMISSIONS PROFILE

SAT/ACT scores _____Untimed_____

HS Course Waivers Required _____

Testing Required _____

Other _____

SPECIFIC LEARNING DISABILITIES/SPECIAL NEEDS

Types	Severity	Types	Severity
_____ Speech/Language	_____	_____ Study Skills	_____
_____ Written Language	_____	_____ Organization/Cognition	_____
_____ Perceptual	_____	_____ Reading	_____
_____ Spelling	_____	_____ Math	_____
_____ Fine Motor	_____	_____ ADD	_____
_____ ADHD	_____		

Other _____

NEED FOR FULL LD PROGRAM? _____

Academic year _____   Summer school _____

Psycho social counseling _____   Support group _____

Faculty advocate _____   Diagnostic testing _____

Remedial tutorial services and accommodations (see next page)

Course reinforcement tutorials _____

REMEDIAL TUTORIAL SERVICES

Tutorials	Group/ Individual	Tutorials	Group/ Individual
Math skills	_____	Word processing	_____
Study skills	_____	Time management	_____
Language arts	_____	Learning strategies	_____
Written expression	_____	Organizational skills	_____

Other _____

ACCOMMODATIONS

Curriculum	Study Aids	Exams
____ Priority registration	____ Typist	____ Oral
____ Math waiver	____ Reader	____ Untimed
____ Foreign language waiver	____ Note taker	____ Take home
____ Course substitution	____ Proof reader	____ With proctor
In Class	____ Text on tape	____ On computer
____ Calculator	____ Early syllabus	____ Extended time
____ Tape recorder	____ Taped handouts	____ On tape
____ Word processor		____ Modified
____ Priority seating		____ Separate room

DESIRED COLLEGE MILIEU

Location _____ Size _____

Student Mix: Male/Female_____ LD/non-LD/ratio _____

Sports/Recreation _____

BUDGET RANGE

Tuition _____ Room and Board _____

LD and ADD/ADHD Services and Facilities _____

SOURCE: Schoolsearch's Colleges for Students With Learning Disabilities, 1993

Chapter 3. HOW TO SELECT AND APPLY TO AN APPROPRIATE COLLEGE

LD ADMISSIONS: SOME REALITY CHECKS

For any student with a learning disability (LD) and/or attention deficit disorder (ADD/ADHD), the college selection and application process can be a real-world test of his/her compensatory skill and strategy training. The keys to a successful college placement are research, analysis, planning, and systematic follow-through--activities which are difficult for many LD and ADD/ADHD students. Furthermore, the admissions procedures for college LD programs are often more time-consuming and more complex than for regular students' curricula. For example, many schools require LD applicants to take special tests, submit statements of deficit, or provide other evidence of the extent and nature of their learning disabilities.

Unfortunately, many LD students assume that they can attend any college or university that has a LD program or offers LD services and also that they can apply at any time. Unlike the public school system, colleges do not have to accept students who don't play by their rules. A student who relies on misconceptions about ease of entry is likely to fail to be admitted to the college of his/her choice. In fact, he/she is unlikely to get into any college if paperwork is incomplete or not submitted on time. It is important to check out the specific LD admissions policy of each college and not make any across-the-board assumptions.

The cautions apply generally whether or not the college has an "open" rather than a "selective" admissions policy or a "rolling" rather than a "fixed" deadline for application submission. In colleges with an open admissions policy, any student with a high school diploma or its equivalent is theoretically eligible to enroll. Many junior colleges and community colleges have open admissions. But some of these schools have a limited number of LD program slots, and others are not staffed to handle all types of learning disabilities.

Selective admissions simply means that a school uses a set of criteria to evaluate each applicant for admission. The criteria may include standardized test scores above a certain percentile or, for example, a 3.5 high school grade point average (GPA). However, students with lower scores should still apply. Most selective admissions schools evaluate each applicant on a variety of factors, so a student whose standardized test scores are below the school's stated cut-off point may still be considered for admission if he or she has strong credentials in other areas, such as class rank, interviews, or recommendations. (Some schools rate themselves as highly selective or most selective and thus may not be as flexible as others are. See Chapter 4 for more information on selectivity.)

A rolling application deadline does not mean that the school welcomes last-minute application filing, but simply that the admissions department makes decisions about applications as they arrive. Schools with rolling admissions may have either a selective or an open admissions policy.

The borderline between colleges that offer full LD programs and those that offer services and/or accommodations is fuzzy. One school's LD program may be another's LD services. Programs usually have staff specially trained to remediate deficits and to assist students to develop compensatory skills. Some programs require students to attend a pre-freshman orientation to acclimate themselves to the rigorous pace of college. An advocate often assists students in course selection and meets with individual professors to help them understand each student's needs. Programs are often diagnostic and prescribe an educational plan for each student. Tutoring is often a key component of LD programs.

Some colleges and universities require LD program students to apply a number of months in advance of the regular application deadline. Many schools require the LD applicant to apply first to the general admissions department, which later refers the application to the LD program if a disability is suspected or if a statement verifying a learning disability is included in the application package. The LD department then determines if the student qualifies for its program and if his/her deficits can be handled. Other colleges require LD applicants to apply directly to the school's LD program. (In this case, students may be judged by different standards from those used for students without learning disabilities.)

In some colleges, services are simply the forms of academic assistance, such as tutoring and counseling, that are offered to the whole student population not just to students with learning disabilities. Others offer services for LD students that focus more on compensating for deficits. Some of the schools with LD services also have learning centers staffed by trained specialists. (There is sometimes a charge for using these services.) A student who applies to a school with LD services will generally be judged by the same standards as all other applicants. Once accepted and enrolled, however, he/she may take advantage of these LD services to succeed in the mainstream academic curriculum.

Many schools with LD programs or services may also offer certain accommodations designed to help students with learning disabilities succeed. Academic adjustments may include schedule modifications; special concessions like take-home tests, oral exams, or notetakers; and special aids, such as tape recorders and word processors. Each school's general policy on these adjustments is listed in its profile. However, the student should be warned that individual instructors and departments may have different policies.

12

THE COLLEGE SELECTION/APPLICATION PROCESS

Pre-Screening Steps

The following section reviews the key steps in the college selection/admission process. The suggested times are designed to eliminate stress, but are, of course, not hard-and-fast deadlines. Also, the accompanying forms/tables are also simply provided as possible aids.

Ideally, the college selection process should start in September of the student's junior year (or even earlier). Before anyone begins to investigate colleges, he/she will find it helpful to draw together a statement of all the applicant's college search criteria--goals, needs, and preferences-for use in assessing schools' suitability. (See Table 4 in Chapter 2.) Then the student should meet with a guidance counselor to:

- Review this statement and confirm or modify the student's need for specific LD and/or ADD/ADHD services and accommodations before and during college,
- Discuss testing requirements,
- Assess his/her high school coursework in light of normal college entrance requirements, and
- Obtain help in instituting any possible remedial action (application to summer school or a private preparatory school, a change in planned junior or senior year curriculum, etc.).

LD students have a number of standardized test options to consider. Many colleges request that students take timed Scholastic Aptitude Tests (SATs) or the American College Test (ACT) well in advance of the college application process. For LD students, a second untimed testing is often suggested. Often a battery of neuroeducational tests (generally to be conducted within the year before application) is requested so that the LD staff can understand better the student's deficits. Among the diagnostic tests that can be required are WAIS-R and the Woodcock-Johnson Psycho-educational Battery.

When the student or parent has revised the statement of applicant's college search criteria (Table 4) to incorporate this new information, he/she should review and prioritize the individual criteria to develop a college profile that pinpoints the features necessary if the student is to have a satisfactory college experience. Everyone's priorities are different. For example, a particular student may require a word processor to function in a classroom, but might be able to do without a calculator or a proof reader, though both would be helpful. Someone whose career goal is professional sports might rate the availability of an athletic program higher than a school's academic curriculum.

Table 5 shows a sample priority check list that might prove helpful. Just fill in the student's own key needs and goals without considering college entrance requirements, funding, etc. (These important factors will be investigated in a later step.) First, rate the student's needs and goals on a scale of 1 to 5:
- Assign #1 ratings to all the needs that must be satisfied.
- Assign #3 ratings to all the important but not essential features.

- Assign #5 ratings to features that would be advantageous for the student but are not critically important.

Then number the #1- and #3 - rated items in order of priority. That is, assign the number 1 to the most important requirement, the number 2 to the next most important, and so on.

Preliminary Screening

The easiest way to make a preliminary screen is to compare the priority check list (Table 5) with the cross-reference appendices at the back of the Guide. Among the cross-reference appendices are tables covering students accepted with these deficits, tutorial services, and academic adjustments (as well as others to be reviewed later).

A worksheet like the one in Table 6 (initial screening list) will make the task easier. Start with the number 1 priority, look it up in the appendix, list all schools that offer that feature, and place check marks in their priority #1 boxes. (When a specific factor is not listed in the appendix, leave the box blank, and go on.) Then look up the next feature, add any new schools, and place check marks in the priority #2 boxes of all schools that offer the feature. Continue this process at least for the first 10 priorities.

If location is a top priority, simple list the names of schools reported in the geographic area--schools are listed by state, the college write-up section-- and fill in the appropriate priority boxes.

The next step is to scan the Guide's college profiles for information on the priority items still to be researched. Most likely these are curriculum, sports, and recreation facilities, which are listed at the end of each write-up. Put check marks in the appropriate blank boxes in Table 6 if the school offers the desired features.

A glance at the completed worksheet will show which schools should first be investigated in depth. The more high-priority check marks, the more likely the college is to offer a positive experience. Transfer the names of the 20 most likely colleges to a set of worksheets like the one shown in Table 7 (college selection worksheet). (Don't throw away Table 6. Further screening may show that these first-choice schools don't meet enough goals, are too expensive, or have too high admissions standards, for example. The process may require looking at a second or a third set of colleges).

If the list has less than 10 college names, recheck the worksheets and discuss the findings with a counselor. The criteria may be too narrow.

Refining the List

Now it's time to take a closer look at the colleges on the preliminary list. With Table 4 to use as an evaluation tool, read the individual college write-ups and complete Table 7 for each of the 20 schools. (As an alternative to copying all that information, make a photocopy of the Schoolsearch write-up.) Make special note on the margins (in red ink so it shows up) where the student's and the college's criteria differ.

An applicant's low test scores or other admissions criteria deficits may appear to be a stumbling block. Review all the rest of the schools on Table 6 against the cross-reference tables on secondary school information and test scores. Identify the ones with open enrollments and the selective colleges with lower entrance requirements. Complete Table 7 or copy the Schoolsearch write-ups for these schools.

In any case, do not give up in despair if the colleges the student likes best seem to have requirements the student cannot meet or don't offer services/accommodations that appear essential. Be realistic, but keep all the student's options open as long as possible. Some schools may make LD program changes in the next academic year that meet the student's needs, and remember that selection usually involves many different factors, not just test scores.

Narrowing the List

Now that the student and/or parent has gained some insight into these colleges' requirements and resources, it is time to narrow (or widen) the number of colleges under active consideration to about ten. Review all the colleges listed on the Table 7 forms and choose:

- three "safe" colleges--community or junior colleges with open enrollment that service students with the particular cluster of disabilities but with a relatively limited curriculum;
- four "likely" colleges--selective colleges that offer needed LD programs and/or services/accommodations and more academic features, but whose admissions criteria appear in line with the student's credentials; and
- three "wish" colleges--more selective colleges that offer the coursework and sports/recreation programs the student desires, may or may not provide the full range of support (services/accommodations) the student needs, and have somewhat higher entrance requirements than the student's record seems likely to meet.

It is now time to confer again (by the middle of the junior year if possible) with the guidance counselor to:

- begin scheduling and preparing for required tests (such as SATs and neuroeducational test),
- review the 10 preliminary college choices;
- discuss the adequacy of the LD and/or ADD/ADHD accommodations and services of the 10 colleges in view of the student's particular deficits and remedial training, and
- if necessary, discuss other options.

Even if a LD student qualifies for a "most selective" or a "highly selective" school, the best choice may be a less competitive college or university that has a more comprehensive LD program which provides counseling, advocacy, testing, remedial and tutorial services, and accommodations. However, LD and ADD/ADHD students who are not heavily dependent on accommodations do have some options that can make it possible for them to attend more selective colleges with limited LD services. The basic concept of these options is that some students can gain enough LD-compensatory training to cope with minimal support in the more rigorous selective colleges' environments. In addition to the usual summer schools and one-year preparatory schools that focus on upgrading the student's academic achievement record are such LD-specific alternatives as attending:

- a community or junior college with a good LD program for two years before transferring to a selective college. (Course credits are unlikely to be fully--if at all--transferable.);
- a private preparatory school that specializes in remedial training in LD skills and strategies for a summer term or for a full year; or
- a special selective-college summer school for LD applicants in the summer following the junior and/or the senior year.

Dr. Midge Lipkin's The Schoolsearch Guide to Private Schools for Students with Learning Disabilities lists many privates schools that offer remedial training. Among these are:

The Achievement School (NC)	Kildonan School (NY)
Brighton Academy (LA)	Lake Michigan Academy (MI)
Carroll School (MA)	Landmark School (MA)
Churchill School (MO)	Landmark West (CA)
The de Paul School (KY)	Pine Ridge (VT)
Gow School (NY)	Trident Academy (SC)

At this point in time only a few colleges are known to offer the summer school option. This is a new field so it would be worthwhile to take the time to query the colleges under consideration to see whether they are planning to add this option. Among the announced summer schools are:

Adelphi College (accepted students only)
Boston College (accepted students only)
Boston University (junior and senior years)
Landmark (only graduated seniors)
Marshall University
University of Massachusetts (accepted students only)
University of Wisconsin-Oshkosh (incoming freshmen)

Note the guidance counselor's comments and recommendations on the Table 7 write-ups for each of the 10 colleges and follow up his/her suggestions about tests, options, and so forth.

Data Collection
Before making his/her final choice of the 5-6 colleges to which he/she will eventually send applications, the student needs to do some "library" and some "field" research. While continuing with the screening process, the applicant should make time to send for more information. Use the Guide to look up the addresses of both the admissions office and the learning disability program of each of the 10 colleges. Send right away for the latest editions of catalogues and other applicant literature so they can be studied before choosing the final college list. (Ask to be put on the colleges' mailing lists to receive the same publications and application forms for the following year as well.) If the colleges' locations are nearby--or the student has a large enough budget--telephone calls would expedite the process.

Now a little field work is in order to assess the 10 colleges' overall environments; The student needs to find out whether he would enjoy both their academic and their social climates. The applicant can learn a lot from college literature that describes campuses and student life, but campus visits and other forms of direct personal contact provide an important, multidimensional information base. A student who is familiar with colleges and/or their students is much more at ease later on in formal admissions interviews, as well as able to make better-informed choices.

Trips should be made to nearby schools while college in session. Contact both the college admissions office and the LD programs administrator (if any) to arrange for a student-led tour or to attend any functions they have planned for potential applicants. If a campus is too distant for a casual visit, ask if the college is planning to hold a recruitment function in your area or, if not, whether any recent alumni/ae live nearby and would be willing to chat with the student about their experiences. Public high schools or local service organizations also occasionally sponsor group college tours.(Ask your guidance counselor.)

It is easy to lose sight of what needs to be done in the initial screening phase when investigating a number of different schools and, even in the final application stage, when focusing on meeting the admissions requirements of the five or six schools on the student's final choice list. Some people find it helpful to keep logs (or diaries) of activities and to review them every month to make sure that deadlines are met, tests are scheduled and conducted on time, and so forth. Table 8 (information gathering/application log) is a simple form that might help in keeping track of college contacts.

Final Selection
By the beginning of the senior year, the student and his/her parents should be familiar enough with the 10 colleges to be able to make informed decisions. At this point, the list should be reduced to 5-6 colleges:

- Two "safe" colleges
- Two "likely" colleges; and
- Two "wish" colleges.

With this combination of colleges, the student should be assured of a placement without cutting off the opportunity to attend a more selective school. Theoretically, it is possible to apply to hundreds of colleges. However, the demands on the student's time for filling out applications and attending interviews and on the parents' pocketbook for application fees make this approach impractical. On the other hand, applying to just one school, even if it's "safe", involves taking the chance of not getting into any school. Too many things can go wrong--all the LD slots may be filled, or an application can be lost in the mail, for example.

The Application Process
At the beginning of the senior year, when the search has yielded five or six final choices and application forms are in hand, schedule another appointment with the guidance counselor to:

- Confirm the suitability of the 5-6 choices;
- Review the applications to make sure that authorization is sent to the high school and testing agency (ies) for submission of all required papers (certification of disability, test scores, references, grade records) at the appropriate times;
- Obtain advice on how to fill out the applications, and
- Discuss financial aid resources, if necessary.

In general, applications are supposed to be filled out by the student applicant without assistance from any parent, counselor, etc. The nature of some learning disabilities is such that some form of accommodation may be necessary, but any departure from the norm should be authorized by the college's admissions office/LD program in advance. Try to obtain at least two copies of each application form so the student can use one as a worksheet. Photocopy the final version for the student's own records so he/she will be prepared to discuss the application's contents in the college interview. Timely submission is essential.

Formal college interviews can usually be scheduled during the early part of the senior year before application submission, but the student should be prepared to answer all the questions on the application form. In general, the best approach is for the applicant to ask questions that demonstrate his/her interest in attending that particular school.

A word about financial aid: the cost of higher education is indeed high--and it continues to rise. Financial aid, however, is available from a variety of sources. Access depends on one's need and one's willingness to search. Colleges' admissions personnel can refer an applicant or a student upon acceptance to the school's financial aid office. High school and private guidance counselors are also a good source of information. Federal funding of compensatory education does not exist at the college level.

Table 5. PRIORITY CHECKLIST

	Priority Value *	Priority Rank
ACADEMIC GOALS		
_____	_____	_____
STUDENTS ACCEPTED WITH THESE DEFICITS		
_____	_____	_____
FULL LD PROGRAM _____	_____	_____
REMEDIAL TUTORIAL SERVICES		
_____	_____	_____
ACCOMMODATIONS		
Curriculum _____	_____	_____
Study Aids _____	_____	_____

Exams _____   _____   _____

In Class _____   _____   _____

COLLEGE MILIEU

Location/Size _____   _____   _____

Sports/Recreation_____   _____   _____

Other_____   _____   _____

*Priority value = 1 - 5.   1=essential;   3=important;   5=advantage but optional

SOURCE: Schoolsearch's Colleges for Students With Learning Disabilities, 1993

Table 6. INITIAL SCREENING LIST

Priority

College	1	2	3	4	5	6	7	8	9	10

_____

_____

_____

_____

_____

_____

Table 7. COLLEGE SELECTION WORKSHEET

College _____

Admissions
Policy/Selectivity _____

Filing Deadline_____

Required Tests_____

LD Types Accepted_____

ADD/ADHD _____

LD
Program _____

LD
Services _____

Accommodations_____

Curriculum
Features _____

Other _____

SOURCE: Schoolsearch's Colleges for Students With Learning Disabilities, 1993

Table 8.   INFORMATION GATHERING/APPLICATION LOG

College/Mail Addresses	Catalogues		College Visit	Application Sent	Interview
	Sent for	Received			
_____	_____	_____	_____	_____	_____
_____	_____	_____	_____	_____	_____
_____	_____	_____	_____	_____	_____
_____	_____	_____	_____	_____	_____

SOURCE: Schoolsearch's Colleges for Students With Learning Disabilities, 1993

Chapter 4. THE COLLEGE PROFILE FORMAT

School profiles are organized by state (in alphabetical order) and within each state by name (also in alphabetical order). Described below are the elements that were considered in preparing the college reports. To save space, for each individual college report, we include only the respondent's affirmative answers. That is, in response to our multi-part query about accommodations, one school might check off untimed exams and leave the other items unchecked. We would only report that the college allowed untimed exams and not that it did not respond to the other items, except indirectly in the cross-reference tables where relevant sections would be left blank.

RATINGS

At the very top of the heading for most schools, two features are headlined: selectivity and service level. This format was adopted to make it easier for students to select suitable colleges.

SELECTIVITY

All colleges were asked to rate their relative selectivity, and to help them make the rating, they were given the following criteria:

Secondary School

	Class Rank	Grades	SAT	ACT	Accepted
Most Selective	Top 10-20%	A/B+	1250-1600	Above 27	40% or less
Highly Selective	Top 20-35%	B+/B	1100-1250	25-17	40-60%
Very Selective	Top 35-50%	B/B-	950-110	23-25	60-75%
Selective	Top 50-65%	B-/C+	800-950	19-23	75-90%
Less Selective	Below 65%	C or less	Below 800	Below 19	Over 90%

The acceptance rates of the most selective schools tend to be low because proportionately large pools of students compete for admission.

SERVICE LEVEL

Colleges were asked to identify their level of service to LD students: accommodation, support, or program. They based their assessments on the following sets of definitions:

ACCOMMODATIONS

The student adjusts to the college.
There is no specific department responsible for LD students.
Students must seek out and arrange any special programs or
   accommodations they require.
Services are available to all students, not only documented LD students.
Students are fully mainstreamed.
Tutoring may be available, but not by LD specialists.

SUPPORT

The college has a structure for providing services to LD students.
A student services or handicapped services office is in charge of
   arrangements for LD students.
There is no LD student advocate.
Documentation of disability is required.
Students are mainstreamed, but with support services offered.
Tutoring may be available, including LD specialists and readers.
Personal tutoring may be an extra cost.
Students may be referred to private LD services in the community.

PROGRAM

The college provides intense support in an LD-specific program.
Staff includes trained LD specialist.
The program has a Director.
Students are required to spend a specific amount of time each week in
   LD center.
Documentation of disability is required.
LD assessment is offered.
There is communication between the LD staff and regular faculty.
A fee is often charged in addition to tuition.
Counseling is available, as well as tutoring.

A separate application to the LD program is required.
There is separate LD orientation.
Special arrangements are often made for course selection.

NAMES, TITLES, ADDRESSES, AND SIZE

Please note that in many cases the Guide lists two different pairs of officials, addresses, and telephone numbers to enable contact with both the admissions office and the LD program (if any). This general information section also presents data on total school and LD enrollment.

ADMISSIONS INFORMATION

The application information section indicates the proportion of applicants who eventually become students, together with key information on regular and LD application deadlines. Under admissions process, each college was asked to describe briefly the application and documentation flow to the point of applicant notification of acceptance/rejection.

Under secondary school information, the most important criteria for admission are rated. Among the factors considered are SAT/ACT scores, class rank, interview, GPA, IQ tests, application, course selection, extracurricular activities, school transcript, personal statement, psychoeducational tests, and recommendations. The relative importance of these factors varies widely.

Under test requirements, the respondents were asked whether:

- standardized tests were waived,
- untimed SAT, ACT, or ACT tests were accepted,
- achievement tests were required,
- WAIS-R was required and the acceptable score range, and
- documentation of LD was required.

In addition, they were asked how current diagnostic testing had to be and what tests they recommended.

Prerequisite high school course requirements (English, math, science, foreign language, and history) are also specified, together with waivers to standard high school courses (such as foreign language and math).

The final section asks for the types of disabilities served. Respondents were queried regarding speech/language, study skills, written language, organizational skills, perceptual skills, reading, spelling, math, and fine motor skills. In addition they were queried about services for ADD with LD, ADD without LD, ADHD with LD, and ADHD without LD.

LD PROGRAMS AND SERVICES

The colleges were asked about the following structural features: program director, special orientation for LD students, syllabus during orientation, LD program (remedial or course reinforcement), student mainstreaming, recommended course credits per semester, time required (or recommended) in learning center, services offered to LD students or to all students, counseling offered on a group or individual basis, and availability of vocational counseling, and support groups.

The next set of features investigated was graduation requirements: course credits, GPA, years to complete degree, math waiver, foreign language waiver, and other requirements.

Staff patterns were questioned: number of staff members (part- or full-time), director, numbers of staff with degrees (BS/BA, MA, PhD), faculty advocate, and whether he/she meets with instructors.

The next feature investigated was the scope of diagnostic testing: ADD, ADHD, IQ, math, personality, organization, handwriting, social skills, perceptual skills, fine motor skills, spoken language, written language, spelling, reading, and study skills.

Under tutoring, the colleges were asked about average size of group tutorials and whether services were rendered by graduates, peers, faculty, LD staff, or teacher trainees. Then they were asked whether tutorials (individual and/or group) were offered in math skills, study skills, language arts, written expression, word processing, time management, learning strategies, and/or organizational skills.

Under academic accommodations, the colleges were asked about curriculum, in-class, study aid, and exam adaptations. Did curriculum modifications include priority registration, math waiver, foreign language waiver, or course substitution? Did in-class modifications include priority seating or use of a calculator, tape recorder, or word processor? Did study aids include a typist, reader, note taker, proof reader, text on tape, early syllabus, or taped handouts? Did exam accommodations include orals, untimed, take-home, with proctor, on computer, extended time, on-tape, modified exam, or separate room?

Under program strengths, each college was asked to provide a brief statement of what makes its program unique. This profile section is a special feature of the Schoolsearch Guide. Each statement was written by an official of the reporting college. The statement sums up the school's philosophy and character and provides prospective students, parents, and guidance counselors with a sense of the school's commitment to students with learning disabilities and the place these students hold in the school's academic and social community.

GENERAL INFORMATION

The "General Information" section of each college or university profile starts with an overview of campus life at the school: ratio of men to women; percentage of foreign students; campus milieu and environs; proximity to transportation and major cities; beaches and ski area; fraternity and sorority life; availability of student housing; and rules regarding cars on campus.

The next section lists the school's accreditation.

Then the colleges were asked to give percentage profiles of the verbal and math SAT/ACT scores for incoming freshmen. Following this, they were asked to give profiles of entering freshmen's standing in their high school classes.

The expenses section includes the cost of tuition, room and board, books (when applicable) and learning disabilities program for the most recent calendar year (1992-93). These numbers are subject to change by schools without notice. Note that at some schools, students enrolled in the LD program may have additional expenses above and beyond the standard tuition costs.

MAJORS

Each college was asked to report the majors that its curriculum supported. In general, the broader the list of majors, the more selective is the admissions policy of the college.

SPORTS

The schools were asked to list both intercollegiate and intramural sports.

STUDENT LIFE ACTIVITIES

Each college was asked to list student organizations and activities that contributed to the quality of the college experience, such as drama groups, student government, newspapers, and specialty clubs.

ACCREDITATION

AABC - American Association of Bible Colleges
AAC - American Association of Colleges
AACSB - American Association of Collegiate Schools of Business
AALS - Association of American Law Schools
AAMS - Association of American Medical Schools
AAUW - American Association of University Women
ABET - Accreditation Board for Engineering and Technology
ABFSE - American Board of Funeral Service Educators
ACE - American Council on Education
ACS - American Chemical Society
AMACAHEA - American Medical Association Committee on Allied Health
       Education & Accreditation
ASBE - Alabama State Board of Education
BRUSNY - Board of Regents University of State of New York
CBHE - Connecticut Board of Higher Education
CBRN - California Board of Registered Nursing
CCA - Career College Association
COEI - Commission on Occupational Education Institutions
CSDE - California State Department of Education
CSWE - Commission of Social Work Education
DEM - Department of Education Massachusetts
EAC - Engineering Accreditation Commission
FRACHE - Federation of Regional Accreditation Commission of Higher
       Education
FSDE - Florida State Department of Education
ICCB - Illinois Community College Board
ICC - Interstate Certification Compact
IDE - Iowa Department of Education
MSDE - Maryland State Department of Education
MBHE - Massachusetts Board of Higher Education
MCCA - Michigan Commission on College Accreditation
MDPI - Michigan Department of Public Instruction
MSACS - Middle States Association of Colleges and Schools
MSCHE - Middle States Commission on Higher Education
MSDE - Minnesota State Department of Education
NACU - National Association for Colleges and Universities
NAM - National Association of Music
NASAD - National Association of Schools of Art and Design
NASM - National Association of Schools of Music
NASDTEC - National Association of State Directors of Teacher
       Education and Certification
NATTS - National Association Trade Technical Schools
NATA - National Athletic Trainers Association
NCA - National Commission of Accreditation
NCATE - National Council for Accreditation of Teacher Education
NCSWE - National Council on Social Work Education
NLN - National League of Nursing
NEASC - New England Association of Schools and Colleges
NJDE - New Jersey Department of Education
NJSBHE - New Jersey State Board of Higher Education
NCDPI - North Carolina Department of Public Instruction
NCACS - North Central Association of Colleges and Schools

NWACS - Northwest Association of Colleges and Schools
OPI - Office of Public Instruction
SCE - School of Continuing Education
SACS - Southern Association of Colleges and Schools
SDI - State Department of Indiana
TCUS - Texas College and University System
USUMC - University Senate of the United Methodist Church
USG - University System of Georgia
UNBN - Utah National Board of Nursing
WACS - Western Association of Colleges and Schools

Selective   **Alabama**
                                                              Program

Auburn University at Montgomery
Taylor Road
Montgomery, Alabama 36193
(205) 244-3000

School Enrollment: **4,690** Male: **1,817** Female: **2,873**
LD Enrollment: **300**

Admissions Contact: **Lee Davis, Director of Admissions**
LD Contact: **Gerri Wolfe, Student Services Coordinator**
Name of Program: **Center for Rehabilitation Resources**
Telephone:**(205) 244-3468**

Admissions

Application Information:
Enrolled:**300**
Applicant must apply **3** months in advance

Secondary School Information
Most Important Criteria For Admissions (1-strongest)

11 SAT/ACT	**9** Application	**3** School transcript
10 Class rank	**7** Course selection	**4** Personal statement
2 Interview	**5** Extra activities	**1** Psychoeducational
8 G.P.A.	Open admission	**6** Recommendations

Test Requirements:
Standardized tests waived: **Yes**
Diagnostic testing waived: **Yes**
Untimed SAT: **Yes** Untimed ACT: **Yes**
Documentation of LD required: **Yes**
Currency of diagnostic testing: **Within last three years**
Tests recommended: **Varies**

Types of Disabilities Served
- Speech/Lang
- Reading
- ADD with LD
- Study skills
- Spelling
- ADD without LD
- Written express
- Math
- ADHD with LD
- Organizational
- Fine Motor
- ADHD without LD
- Perceptual

High School Course Requirements:
Waivers to standard high school courses
Foreign Language : **Yes** Course substitution: **Yes**

Learning Disability Program
Program: Reinforces course work: **Yes**
Students mainstreamed **100** % of the day
Counseling: Individual: **Yes** Group Counseling: **Yes**
Support groups are available:**We Learn Differently (WLD) support group for LD students**

Faculty:
Faculty: **6** Full time: **2** Part time: **4**
LD faculty with: BS/BA: **6** M.A.: **6**
Faculty advocate: **Yes** Meets with instructor: **As needed**

Diagnostic Testing
- ADD
- Personality
- Perceptual skills
- Spelling
- ADHD
- Organization
- Fine motor skills
- Reading
- I.Q.
- Handwriting
- Spoken language
- Study skills
- Math
- Social skills
- Written language

Tutoring:
Average size of group tutorials: **Individual basis**
Services rendered by:
•Graduates •Peers   Faculty   •LD staff   •Teacher trainees

Tutorials

Grp.	Ind.	Tutorials	Grp.	Ind.	Tutorials
	•	Math skills		•	Word processing
	•	Study skills		•	Time management
	•	Language arts		•	Learning strategies
	•	Written express		•	Organizational skills

Academic Accommodations

Curriculum	Study Aids	Exams
• Priority registration	• Typist	• Oral
Math waiver	• Reader	• Untimed
Foreign lang. waiver	• Notetaker	• Take home
Course substitution	• Proof reader	• With proctor
In Class	• Text on tape	• On computer
• Calculators	• Early syllabus	• Extended time
• Tape recorder	• Taped handouts	• On tape
• Word processor		• Modified
• Priority seating		Separate room

Graduation Requirements:
Course credits: **200**

Program Strengths
Our program is an intervention model including the following components: student support services, faculty support services, community resource collaboration, post-secondary network, support group, and work experience. Our staff is composed of peer counselors and a student services coordinator.

General Information:
Auburn University at Montgomery is a 4 year public university. Suburban campus of 20 acres is 10 miles from Montgomery. Ski areas are 500 miles from campus. Beaches are 200 miles from campus. 12 residential halls on campus. Housing is not guaranteed.

Accreditation:SACS

Expenses:
Tuition: In-state: Full year: $476.00 per quarter. Part-time: Per credit:$37.00. Tuition: Out-of-state: Full year: $1,428.00 per quarter. Part-time: Per credit:$111.00. Room and board: $620.00 per quarter

Majors
• AREA STUDIES Urban • BUSINESS Accounting, Business Administration, Business Economics, Business Management, Economics, Finance, Management, Marketing • COMMUNICATIONS Communication, English, Photography, Speech • COMPUTER SCIENCE Data Processing, Programming • EDUCATION Art, Curriculum, Early Childhood, Elementary, Health, Physical, School Psychology, Secondary, Social Studies, Speech/Language • HEALTH SCIENCES Medical Technology, Nursing, Speech/Audiology and Speech • LANGUAGES French, German, Spanish • PREPROFESSIONAL Agriculture, Architecture, Dentistry, Engineering, Forestry, Law, Medicine, Ministry, Pharmacy • SCIENCES Astronomy, Biology, Botany, Chemistry, Marine Biology, Mathematics, Physical Science • SOCIAL SCIENCES Criminal Justice, Government/Political, History, Law Enforcement, Psychology, Sociology • VISUAL AND PERFORM-

Alabama

ING ARTS Art, Art History, Studio Art, Theater

Sports/Activities

• SPORTS RELATED Cheerleading, Pep Band • SPORTS-INTERCOL-LEGIATE Baseball (M), Basketball, Football, Golf, Gymnastics, Racquetball, Soccer, Swimming, Weight Lifting • SPORTS-INTRAMURAL Archery, Badminton, Basketball, Bowling, Ping-Pong, Softball, Swimming, Tennis, Volleyball, Weight Lifting • STUDENT LIFE ACTIVITIES Choral, Debate, Drama Groups, Fraternities, Newspaper, Radio/TV station, Sororities, Student Government, Yearbook

Less Selective   **Alabama**
                                   Services

Chattahoochee Valley Community College
2602 Savage Drive
Phenix City, Alabama 36867
(205) 291-4900

School Enrollment: **2,884** Male: **1,154** Female: **1,730**
LD Enrollment: **4** Male: **1** Female: **3**

Admissions Contact: **Jay Douglas, Chambers Dean of Students**
LD Contact: **Dr. Ann Chard, Dean of Instructions**
Telephone:**(205) 291-4946**

Admissions

Application Information:
Application deadline: **Open**
Rolling Admissions: **Yes**

Secondary School Information
Most Important Criteria For Admissions (1-strongest)

1	SAT/ACT	2 Application	1 School transcript
6	Class rank	1 Course selection	1 Personal statement
1	Interview	1 Extra activities	Psychoeducational
6	G.P.A.	1 Open admission	1 Recommendations

Test Requirements:
Currency of diagnostic testing: **Testing done by college**

Types of Disabilities Served
• Speech/Lang • Reading • ADD with LD
• Study skills • Spelling • ADD without LD
• Written express • Math • ADHD with LD
• Organizational • Fine Motor • ADHD without LD
• Perceptual

Learning Disability Program
Counseling: Individual: **Yes**

Faculty:
Faculty: **10** Full time: **3** Part time: **7**
Faculty advocate: **Yes** Meets with instructor: **once each semester**

Diagnostic Testing
ADD	Personality	Perceptual skills	Spelling
ADHD	Organization	Fine motor skills	Reading
I.Q.	Handwriting	Spoken language	Study skills
Math	Social skills	Written language	

Tutoring:
Average size of group tutorials: **3-4**
Services rendered by:
Graduates Peers •Faculty •LD staff Teacher trainees

Tutorials
Grp.	Ind.	Tutorials	Grp.	Ind.	Tutorials
•	•	Math skills			Word processing
•		Study skills			Time management
		Language arts			Learning strategies
	•	Written express			Organizational skills

Academic Accommodations
Curriculum	Study Aids	Exams
Priority registration	Typist	Oral
Math waiver	Reader	Untimed
Foreign lang. waiver	Notetaker	Take home
Course substitution	• Proof reader	With proctor
In Class	• Text on tape	On computer
• Calculators	Early syllabus	• Extended time
Tape recorder	Taped handouts	On tape
Word processor		Modified
Priority seating		Separate room

General Information:
Chattahoochee Valley Community College is a 2 year public college. Suburban campus of 103 acres is 2 miles from Columbus. Beaches are 300 miles from campus. Housing is not guaranteed.

Accreditation:SACS

Expenses:
Tuition: In-state: Full year: $215.00 per quarter. Part-time: Per credit:$20.00. Tuition: Out-of-state: Full year: $350.00 per quarter.

Majors
• BUSINESS Accounting, Agricultural, Banking, Business Administration, Business Education, Business Management, Fashion Merchandising, Insurance, Real Estate • COMMUNICATIONS Broadcasting, Television/Radio/Film • COMPUTER SCIENCE Data Processing • CRAFTS AND DESIGN Graphic Design • EDUCATION Art, Elementary, Health, Music, Secondary, Special, Speech/Language • ENGINEERING Agricultural • FINE AND PERFORMING ARTS Art, Music, Theater • HEALTH SCIENCES Medical Assistant, Medical Technology, Nursing, Occupational Therapy, Radiological Therapy • LANGUAGES French • PREPROFESSIONAL Engineering, Forestry, Law, Medicine, Pharmacy • SCIENCES Biology, Chemistry, Mathematics • SOCIAL SCIENCES Anthropology, Criminal Justice, Law Enforcement • VOCATIONAL Fire Science, Secretarial, Word Processing

Sports
• SPORTS-INTERCOLLEGIATE Baseball (M), Bowling, Softball (F), Tennis • STUDENT LIFE ACTIVITIES Choral, Drama Groups, Magazine, Music Groups, Musical Theater, Religious Organization, Student Government

Less Selective — **Alabama Services**

Jacksonville State University
700 Pelham Road, North
Jacksonville, Alabama 36265-9982
(205) 782-5781

School Enrollment: **8,200** Male: **4,264** Female: **3,936**
LD Enrollment: **200**

Admissions Contact: **Jerry D. Smith, Ed.D. Director of Admissions**
LD Contact: **Claudia E. McDade, Ph.D. Director**
Name of Program: **Center-Individualized Instruction and Disabled**
Telephone:**(205) 782-5570 Ext. 5098**

Admissions

Application Information:
LD Students Applying: **50** Accepted: **50** Enrolled:**50**
Application deadline: **None**

Secondary School Information
Most Important Criteria For Admissions (1-strongest)

SAT/ACT	Application	School transcript
Class rank	Course selection	Personal statement
Interview	Extra activities	Psychoeducational
G.P.A.	**1** Open admission	Recommendations

Test Requirements:
Untimed ACT: **Yes**

Types of Disabilities Served
- Speech/Lang
- Reading
- ADD with LD
- Study skills
- Spelling
- ADD without LD
- Written express
- Math
- ADHD with LD
- Organizational
- Fine Motor
- ADHD without LD
- Perceptual

High School Course Requirements:

Learning Disability Program
Program: Remedial: **Yes**
Program: Reinforces course work: **Yes**
Students mainstreamed **100** % of the day
Recommended credits per semester: **12**
Counseling: Individual: **Yes** Vocational Counseling: **Yes**
Support groups are available:**Yes**

Faculty:
Faculty: **7** Including Director: **Yes** Full time: **4** Part time: **5**
LD faculty with: BS/BA: **7** M.A.: **5** Ph.D.: **1**
Faculty advocate: **Yes** Meets with instructor: **once a semester**

Diagnostic Testing
ADD	Personality	Perceptual skills	• Spelling
ADHD	Organization	Fine motor skills	• Reading
I.Q.	Handwriting	Spoken language	• Study skills
• Math	• Social skills	• Written language	

Tutoring:
Average size of group tutorials: **3**
Services rendered by:

•Graduates •Peers •Faculty •LD staff Teacher trainees

Tutorials
Grp.	Ind.	Tutorials	Grp.	Ind.	Tutorials
•	•	Math skills		•	Word processing
•	•	Study skills	•	•	Time management
•	•	Language arts	•	•	Learning strategies
•	•	Written express	•		Organizational skills

Academic Accommodations

Curriculum	Study Aids	Exams
Priority registration	Typist	Oral
Math waiver	• Reader	Untimed
Foreign lang. waiver	• Notetaker	Take home
• Course substitution	Proof reader	With proctor
In Class	• Text on tape	On computer
• Calculators	Early syllabus	• Extended time
• Tape recorder	Taped handouts	• On tape
• Word processor		• Modified
Priority seating		Separate room

Graduation Requirements:
Course credits: **128 semester hours** GPA: **2.0 in major** Years to complete degree: **4-5**
Other requirements: **46 hour core curriculum**

Program Strengths
We offer academic support services, state-of-the art instructional technology, and peer tutoring to assist individual students in reaching their highest academic potentials. Since over half of JSU students are serviced yearly, no student is labeled by others who seek Center services. Intensive academic support offered to learning disabled students includes academic advising, advocacy, coordination with funding agencies, assistance in making accommodations, computer-assisted instruction, and tutoring.

General Information:
Jacksonville State University is a 4 year public university. Rural campus 60 miles from Birmingham. Ski areas are 300 miles from campus. Beaches are 300 miles from campus. Housing is not guaranteed. 10 % of students remain on campus for the weekends.

Accreditation:SACS

Expenses:
Tuition: In-state: Full year: $1,420.00. Part-time: Per credit:$60.00. Tuition: Out-of-state: Full year: $2,156.00. Part-time: Per credit:$97.00.
Room and board: $2,570.00

Majors
• BUSINESS Accounting, Business Administration, Business Economics, Business Management, Economics, Finance, Management, Management, Marketing • COMMUNICATION Advertising, Broadcasting, Communication, Creative Writing, English, Journalism, Television/Radio/Film • COMPUTER SCIENCE Data Processing, Programming, Systems Analysis • EDUCATION Art, Curriculum, Early Childhood, Elementary, Health, Music, Physical, Recreation and Youth Leadershi, Science, Secondary, Special • FINE AND PERFORMING ARTS Art, Music, Music Performance, Theater • HEALTH SCIENCES Medical Technology, Nursing, Nutritional/Food, Occupational Therapy • PREPROFESSIONAL Law, Medicine, Recreation, Social Work • SCIENCES Biology, Chemistry, Geography, Mathematics, Physics • SOCIAL SCIENCES Criminal Justice, Government/Political, History, Law Enforcement, Political Science, Psychology, Social Sciences, Sociology • VOCATIONAL Food Service, Home Economics, Secretarial

Sports/Activities
• SPORTS-INTERCOLLEGIATE Baseball (M), Basketball, Football (M),

Alabama

Golf (M), Riflery, Softball (F), Tennis (M), Volleyball • SPORTS-INTRA-MURAL Baseball (M), Basketball, Soccer (M), Softball, Tennis (M), Volleyball

---

Less Selective   **Alabama Services**

Northeast Alabama State Junior College
P.O. Box 159
Rainsville, Alabama 35986
(205) 638-4418

School Enrollment: **1,528** Male: **520** Female: **1,008**

Admissions Contact: **Dr. Joe Burke, Director of Admissions**
LD Contact: **Elaine S. Marshall, ADA Compliance Representative**

Admissions

Application Information:
Separate application:**Yes**
Rolling Admissions: **Yes**

Secondary School Information
Most Important Criteria For Admissions (1-strongest)

SAT/ACT	Application	School transcript
Class rank	Course selection	Personal statement
Interview	Extra activities	Psychoeducational
G.P.A.	Open admission	Recommendations

Test Requirements:
Diagnostic testing waived: **Yes**
Currency of diagnostic testing: **Before or after application**

Types of Disabilities Served
- Speech/Lang
- Study skills
- Written express
- Organizational
- Perceptual
- Reading
- Spelling
- Math
- Fine Motor
- ADD with LD
- ADD without LD
- ADHD with LD
- ADHD without LD

Admissions Process

Open admission based on high school diploma or GED diploma.

Learning Disability Program

Program: Reinforces course work: **Yes**
Students mainstreamed **100** % of the day
Services available for all students: **Yes**
Counseling: Individual: **Yes** Vocational Counseling: **Yes**

Faculty:
Faculty: **1** Full time: **1** M.A.: **1**
Faculty advocate: **Yes** Meets with instructor: **As needed**

Diagnostic Testing

ADD	Personality	Perceptual skills	Spelling
ADHD	Organization	Fine motor skills	• Reading
I.Q.	Handwriting	Spoken language	Study skills
• Math	Social skills	• Written language	

Tutoring:
Services rendered by:
Graduates •Peers •Faculty LD staff Teacher trainees

Tutorials

Grp.	Ind.	Tutorials	Grp.	Ind.	Tutorials
	•	Math skills			Word processing
		Study skills			Time management
		Language arts			Learning strategies
	•	Written express			Organizational skills

Academic Accommodations

Curriculum	Study Aids	Exams
Priority registration	Typist	• Oral
Math waiver	Reader	• Untimed
Foreign lang. waiver	Notetaker	Take home
• Course substitution	Proof reader	With proctor
In Class	• Text on tape	• On computer
Calculators	Early syllabus	• Extended time
• Tape recorder	Taped handouts	• On tape
• Word processor		• Modified
• Priority seating		• Separate room

Graduation Requirements:
Course credits: **96** GPA: **2.0** Years to complete degree: **2+** Language waiver: **Yes**

Program Strengths

LD program is just getting started, but the College responds to student needs and encourages students to disclose needs. Northeast has an established drama program, stage band and chorus, all of which involve a number of students.

General Information:

Northeast Alabama State Junior College is a 2 year public college. Rural campus of 105 acres is 60 miles from Huntsville. Accessible by car. 1% of students are foreign. Housing is not guaranteed.

Accreditation:SACS, CC, NLN

SAT/ACT Scores:
Scores for incoming freshmen: between 20 and 23.

Expenses:
Tuition: In-state: Full year: $273.00 per quarter. Part-time: Per credit:$20.00. Part-time: Per course: $100.00-$273.00. Tuition: Out-of-state: Full year: $455.00 per quarter. Part-time: Per credit:$33.00. Part-time: Per course:$167.00

Majors

• AGRICULTURE Business • ARTS Art History, Art Therapy, Dramatic Arts, Fashion Design, Graphic Arts, Music, Music History, Music Performance, Painting • BUSINESS Accounting, Education, Fashion Merchandising, Human Resources Management, Personnel, Real Estate • COMMUNICATIONS Advertising, Broadcasting, Commercial Design, Commuication, Creative Writing, English, Graphic Design, Journalism, Literature, Public Relations, Speech/Debate/Forensics, Television/Radio/Film • COMPUTER SCIENCE Business Data Programming, Computer Science • EDUCATION Agricultural, Art, Business, Child Development, Early Childhood, Elementary, English, General, Health, Home Economics, Mathematics, Middle School, Music, Music Therapy, Outdoor, Physical, Psychology, Reading, Recreation/Youth Leadership, School Psychology, Science, Secondary, Social Studies, Special, Speech/Language • ENGINEERING Agricultural, Architectural, Environmental/Water Resources, Geological, Mathematical, Systems Analysis • ENVIRONMENTAL CONTROL Water and Wastewater Technolog • HEALTH SCIENCES Medical Laboraotry Technology, Nursing, Occupational Therapy, Pharmaceutical Chemistry, Pharmacology, Physical Therapy, Public Health, Speech Therapy • HUMANITIES Classics, English/Writing/Literature, Fine Arts, Humanities, Liberal Arts , Philosophy, Religion • PRE PROFESSIONAL Agricultural, Architecture, Business, Dentistry, Drafting, Engineering, Fisheries, Industrial Design, Landscaping, Law, Medicine, Ministry, Natu-

ral Resources, Optometry, Pharmacy, Range Management, Recreation, Social Work, Sports Medicine, Urban Design, Veterinarian, Wildlife
• VISUAL AND PERFORMING ARTS Dramatic Arts, Music, Theater
• VOCATIONAL Office Administration, Paralegal, Radiological Technology, Respiratory Therapy Technology, Secretarial, Word Processing

Sports/Activities

• SPORTS-INTRAMURAL Tennis, Volleyball • STUDENT LIFE ACTIVITIES Academic Clubs, Choral, Community Service, Drama Groups, Music Groups, Newspaper, Religious Organization, Student Government, Yearbook

Selective   **Alabama**
Accommodations

Troy State University at Dothan
P.O. Box 8368
Dothan, Alabama 36304
(205) 983-6556

School Enrollment: **2,100** Male: **950** Female: **1,050**
LD Enrollment: **20**

Admissions Contact: **Reta Cordell, Director of Admissions**
LD Contact: **Pamela Williamson, Director of Counseling**
Name of Program: **Instructional Support Program**
Telephone:**(205) 983-6556**

Admissions

Application Information:
LD on admissions committee:**Yes**
Application deadline: **2 weeks before quarter**
Rolling Admissions: **Yes**

Secondary School Information
Most Important Criteria For Admissions (1-strongest)

2 SAT/ACT	**3** Application	**5** School transcript
6 Class rank	**4** Course selection	**11** Personal statement
8 Interview	**9** Extra activities	**7** Psychoeducational
1 G.P.A.	Open admission	**10** Recommendations

Test Requirements:
Untimed SAT: **Yes** Untimed ACT: **Yes**
WAIS-R required: **Yes**
Documentation of LD required: **Yes**
Currency of diagnostic testing: **6 months - 1 year**

Types of Disabilities Served
• Speech/Lang	• Reading	• ADD with LD
• Study skills	• Spelling	• ADD without LD
• Written express	• Math	• ADHD with LD
• Organizational	• Fine Motor	• ADHD without LD
• Perceptual		

High School Course Requirements:
English: **4** Math: **2** Science: **2**

Learning Disability Program
Syllabus available during orientation:**Yes**
Program: Reinforces course work: **Yes**
Program available through:**On going each quarter**
Students mainstreamed **100** % of the day
Recommended credits per semester: **8-12**
Services available for all students: **Yes**
Counseling: Individual: **Yes** Group Counseling: **Yes** Vocational Counseling: **Yes**

Faculty:
Faculty: **5** Full time: **3** Part time: **2**
LD faculty with: BS/BA: **1** M.A.: **4**
Faculty advocate: **Yes** Meets with instructor: **Frequently**

Diagnostic Testing
ADD	• Personality	Perceptual skills	• Spelling
ADHD	Organization	Fine motor skills	• Reading
• I.Q.	Handwriting	Spoken language	• Study skills
• Math	Social skills	• Written language	

Tutoring:
Average size of group tutorials: **3-5**
Services rendered by:
•Graduates •Peers Faculty •LD staff •Teacher trainees

Tutorials
Grp.	Ind.	Tutorials	Grp.	Ind.	Tutorials
•	•	Math skills	•	•	Word processing
	•	Study skills	•	•	Time management
	•	Language arts	•	•	Learning strategies
•	•	Written express	•	•	Organizational skills

Academic Accommodations
Curriculum	Study Aids	Exams
Priority registration	Typist	• Oral
Math waiver	Reader	Untimed
Foreign lang. waiver	Notetaker	Take home
Course substitution	• Proof reader	• With proctor
In Class	• Text on tape	• On computer
Calculators	Early syllabus	• Extended time
• Tape recorder	Taped handouts	• On tape
• Word processor		Modified
• Priority seating		• Separate room

Graduation Requirements:
Course credits: **185 quarter hours** GPA: **2.0** Years to complete degree: **4-7**

Program Strengths
Each student is special. We don't categorize because each student is an individual and we try to serve his or her special needs.

General Information:
Troy State University at Dothan is a 4 year public university. Suburban campus of 275 acres is 2 miles from Dothan. Ski areas are 500+ miles from campus. Beaches are 90 miles from campus. 1% of students are foreign. Housing is not guaranteed.

Accreditation:SACS

Expenses:
Tuition: In-state: Full year: $539.00 per quarter. Part-time: Per credit:$45.00. Tuition: Out-of-state: Full year: $916.00 per quarter. Part-time: Per credit:$78.00.

Alabama

Majors

• BUSINESS Accounting, Business Administration, Business Economics, Business Management, Economics, Finance, Management, Marketing, Personnel • COMPUTER SCIENCE Computer Science, Data Processing, Programming • EDUCATION Early Childhood, Elementary, English, Middle School, School Psychology, Science, Secondary, Social Scien • HEALTH SCIENCES Nursing • PREPROFESSIONAL Law • SCIENCES Biology, Mathematics, Physical Science • SOCIAL SCIENCES Criminal Justice, History, Law Enforcement, Psychology, Social Sciences, Sociology • VOCATIONAL Air Traffic Control, Aircraft Maintenance, Aviation Maintenance, Electronic

Sports

• STUDENT LIFE ACTIVITIES Community Band, Student Government

Transitional   Alabama   Program

UAB - Horizons Program

122 Education Building 901 South 13th Street - UAB St
Birmingham, Alabama 35294-1250
(205) 975-6770-(800) 822-6242

School Enrollment: **40**
LD Enrollment: **20-40**

Admissions Contact: **Jade K. Carter, Ed.D. Director of Admissions**
LD Contact: **Jade K. Carter, Ed.D.**
Name of Program: **Horizons Program**
Telephone:**(205) 975-6770-(800) 822-6242**

Admissions

Secondary School Information

Most Important Criteria For Admissions (1-strongest)

SAT/ACT	Application	School transcript
Class rank	**1** Course selection	**1** Personal statement
1 Interview	Extra activities	**1** Psychoeducational
G.P.A.	Open admission	Recommendations

Test Requirements:

Standardized tests waived: **Yes**
Diagnostic testing waived: **Yes**
Untimed SAT: **Yes** Untimed ACT: **Yes**
WAIS-R required: **Yes**

Types of Disabilities Served

Speech/Lang	Reading	ADD with LD
Study skills	Spelling	ADD without LD
Written express	Math	ADHD with LD
Organizational	Fine Motor	ADHD without LD
Perceptual		

Admissions Process

Students and parents must apply to the Horizons Program separately from UAB admission. Parents, students and recommendation writers must fill out information surveys. All past student records must be forwarded to the Horizons Office. An interview is completed and students are notified of acceptance.

Faculty:
Faculty: **6** Full time: **2** Part time: **4** M.A.: **4** Ph.D.: **1**
Faculty advocate: **Yes** Meets with instructor: **Daily/weekly**

Diagnostic Testing

ADD	Personality	Perceptual skills	Spelling
ADHD	Organization	Fine motor skills	Reading
I.Q.	Handwriting	Spoken language	Study skills
Math	Social skills	Written language	

Tutoring:

Average size of group tutorials: **4-8**
Services rendered by:
•Graduates   Peers   •Faculty   •LD staff   Teacher trainees

Tutorials

Grp.	Ind.	Tutorials	Grp.	Ind.	Tutorials
		Math skills			Word processing
		Study skills			Time management
		Language arts			Learning strategies
		Written express			Organizational skills

Academic Accommodations

Curriculum	Study Aids	Exams
Priority registration	Typist	• Oral
Math waiver	Reader	• Untimed
Foreign lang. waiver	Notetaker	Take home
Course substitution	Proof reader	With proctor
In Class	Text on tape	• On computer
• Calculators	Early syllabus	• Extended time
• Tape recorder	• Taped handouts	• On tape
• Word processor		Modified
• Priority seating		• Separate room

Program Strengths

The Horizons Program is a customized curriculum for students age 17-26 with specific learning disabilities and other mild handicapping conditions. These students participate in a two year program which will result in a Certificate of Program Completion in the student's chosen career area.

General Information:

UAB - Horizons Program is a 2 year university. Urban campus of 265 acres is Accessible by air, train or bus. Ski areas are 90 miles from campus. Beaches are 260 miles from campus. 1 residential halls on campus. Housing is guaranteed.

Accreditation:

Expenses:

Tuition: In-state: Full year: $16,000.00. Tuition: Out-of-state: Full year: $16,000.00. Room and board: $3,500.00

Majors

• AGRICULTURE Landscaping Management • BUSINESS Clerical, Hospital • CAREGIVER Adult Services, Early Childhood

Selective   **Alabama**
                                                  Services

University of Alabama
P.O. Box UA
Tuscaloosa, Alabama 35487-9787
(205) 348-5666

School Enrollment: **18,500** Male: **9,300** Female: **9,200**
LD Enrollment: **70** Male: **42** Female: **28**

Admissions Contact: **Tom Davis, Assistant**
LD Contact: **Warner Moore, Assoc. Dir. Student Services**
Name of Program: **Student Services**
Telephone:**(205) 348-6796**

Admissions

Application Information:
Enrolled:**65**
Separate application:**Yes**
Application deadline: **N/A**

Secondary School Information
Most Important Criteria For Admissions (1-strongest)

2 SAT/ACT	Application	School transcript
Class rank	Course selection	Personal statement
Interview	Extra activities	Psychoeducational
1 G.P.A.	Open admission	Recommendations

Test Requirements:
Untimed SAT: **Yes** Untimed ACT: **Yes**
Documentation of LD required: **Yes**

Types of Disabilities Served
- Speech/Lang
- Study skills
- Written express
- Organizational
- Perceptual
- Reading
- Spelling
- Math
- Fine Motor
- ADD with LD
- ADD without LD
- ADHD with LD
- ADHD without LD

Faculty:
Faculty: **3** Full time: **1** Part time: **2**
Faculty advocate: **Yes**

Diagnostic Testing
ADD	Personality	Perceptual skills	Spelling
ADHD	Organization	Fine motor skills	Reading
I.Q.	Handwriting	Spoken language	Study skills
Math	Social skills	Written language	

Tutoring:
Services rendered by:
•Graduates •Peers Faculty •LD staff Teacher trainees

Tutorials
Grp.	Ind.	Tutorials	Grp.	Ind.	Tutorials
	•	Math skills			Word processing
		Study skills			Time management
	•	Language arts			Learning strategies
		Written express			Organizational skills

Academic Accommodations

Curriculum	Study Aids	Exams
Priority registration	Typist	• Oral
Math waiver	Reader	Untimed
Foreign lang. waiver	Notetaker	Take home
Course substitution	Proof reader	With proctor
In Class	• Text on tape	On computer
• Calculators	Early syllabus	• Extended time
• Tape recorder	Taped handouts	On tape
Word processor		Modified
Priority seating		Separate room

Program Strengths
We don't have a specialized program. We work closely and provide personal attention. We allow for priority registration.

General Information:
University of Alabama is a 4 year public university. Urban campus. of 800 acres is Accessible by air, train or bus. Beaches are 5 hours from campus. 8% of students are foreign. Housing is not guaranteed.20 % of students join fraternities/sororities.

Accreditation:AACSB, ABET, ACEJML, ADA, AHEA, CSWE, FIDER, NASM

Expenses:
Tuition: In-state: Full year: $900.00 per semester. Tuition: Out-of-state: Full year: $2,000.00 per semester. Room and board: $3,200.00

Majors
• AREA STUDIES American, Asian, European, Latin American, Russian/Slavic, Urban • BUSINESS Accounting, Banking, Business Management, Business Statistics, Economics, Finance, Hotel and Restaurant Managemen, Insurance, Investments and Securities, Labor Relations, Management, Marketing, Real Estate, Retail Manufacturing, Travel/Tourism Management • COMMUNICATION Advertising, Broadcasting, Communication, Creative Writing, English, Journalism, Photography, Speech, Television/Radio/Film • COMPUTER SCIENCE Computer Science, Enginee • EDUCATION Art, Early Childhood, Elementary, English, Foreign Language, Health, Mathematics, Middle School, Music, Music Therapy, Physical, School Psychology, Science, Secondary, Social Science, Special, Speech/Language, Vocational • ENGINEERING Aerospace, Chemical, Civil/Environmental, Electrical, Industrial, Mechanical, Metallurgical, Mining/Mineral, Petroleum • FINE AND PERFORMING ARTS Art, Art History, Dance, Music, Studio Art, Theater • HEALTH SCIENCES Communication Disorders, Environmental, Health, Medical Technology, Nursing, Nutritional/Food, Occupational Therapy, Speech Therapy, Speech/Audiology and Speech • LANGUAGES French, German, German, Japanese, Latin, Russian • PHILOSOPHY Classics, English/Writing/Literature, Humanities, Philosophy, Religion • PREPROFESSIONAL Engineering, Law, Medicine, Ministry, Social Work • SCIENCES Archeology, Biochemistry, Biology, Chemistry, Geography, Geology, Marine Biology, Mathematics, Microbiology, Physical Chemistry, Physics • SOCIAL SCIENCES Anthropology, Criminal Justice, Geography, Government/Political, History, International Studies, Library Science, Psychology, Public Relations, Social Sciences, Sociology • VOCATIONAL Electronics Technology, Home Economics, Industrial Design, Textile and Clothing

Sports/Activities
• SPORTS RELATED Baton Twirling, Cheerleading, Drum Major/Majorette, Marching Band, Pep Band, Team Managers • SPORTS-INTERCOLLEGIATE Baseball (M), Basketball, Cross Country, Diving, Football, Golf, Gymnastics (F), Rugby, Swimming, Tennis, Track and Field • SPORTS-INTRAMURAL Badminton, Basketball, Bowling, Fencing, Golf, Karate, Lacrosse, Martial Arts, Racquetball, Sailing, Soccer, Softball, Swimming, Tennis, Track and Field, Volleyball, Water SkiingWeight Lifting, Wrestling (M) • STUDENT LIFE ACTIVITIES Choral, Debate, Drama Groups, Ethnic & Cultural Groups, Fraternities, Jazz Band, Magazine, Music Groups,

Alabama

Newspaper, Radio/TV station, Sororities, Student Government, Symphony Orchestra, Yearbook

Selective	Alabama Program

University of Alabama at Birmingham
UAB Station
Birmingham, Alabama 35294
(205) 934-8221

School Enrollment: **9,004** Male: **4,052** Female: **4,952**
LD Enrollment: **62** Male: **41** Female: **21**

Admissions Contact: **Stella Cocoris, Director of Admissions**
LD Contact: **Dr. Larie Ross-Hunter, Coordinator**
Name of Program: **Handicapped Student Service**
Telephone:**(205) 934-3704**

Admissions

Application Information:
Separate application:**Yes**
Application deadline: **None**
Rolling Admissions: **Yes**

Secondary School Information
Most Important Criteria For Admissions (1-strongest)

1 SAT/ACT	Application	School transcript
Class rank	Course selection	Personal statement
Interview	Extra activities	Psychoeducational
1 G.P.A.	Open admission	Recommendations

Test Requirements:
Diagnostic testing waived: **Yes**
Untimed ACT: **Yes**
Documentation of LD required: **Yes**
Currency of diagnostic testing: **within last three years**
Tests recommended: **Psychologist examination**

Types of Disabilities Served
- Speech/Lang
- Reading
- ADD with LD
- Study skills
- Spelling
- ADD without LD
- Written express
- Math
- ADHD with LD
- Organizational
- Fine Motor
- ADHD without LD
- Perceptual

Admissions Process

Contact Admissions for packet. Apply to Handicapped Student Services after admission.

Learning Disability Program

Program: Reinforces course work: **Yes**
Students mainstreamed **100 %** of the day
Counseling: Individual: **Yes** Vocational Counseling: **Yes**

Faculty:
Faculty: **26** Full time: **4** Part time: **22**
LD faculty with: BS/BA: **26** M.A.: **4** Ph.D.: **2**
Faculty advocate: **Yes** Meets with instructor: **As requested**

Diagnostic Testing
- ADD
- Personality
- Perceptual skills
- Spelling
- ADHD
- Organization•
- Fine motor skills
- Reading
- I.Q.
- Handwriting
- Spoken language
- Study skills
- Math
- Social skills•
- Written language

Tutoring:
Average size of group tutorials: **2-5**
Services rendered by:
•Graduates •Peers •Faculty LD staff Teacher trainees

Tutorials

Grp.	Ind.	Tutorials	Grp.	Ind.	Tutorials
•	•	Math skills	•	•	Word processing
•	•	Study skills	•	•	Time management
•	•	Language arts	•	•	Learning strategies
•	•	Written express	•	•	Organizational skills

Academic Accommodations

Curriculum	Study Aids	Exams
• Priority registration	Typist	• Oral
Math waiver	• Reader	• Untimed
Foreign lang. waiver	• Notetaker	Take home
Course substitution	Proof reader	With proctor
In Class	• Text on tape	On computer
• Calculators	Early syllabus	• Extended time
• Tape recorder	Taped handouts	On tape
• Word processor		Modified
• Priority seating		• Separate room

Program Strengths

Students attending UAB with a documented learning disability are interviewed by the coordinator to determine individual program needs. Assistance is given in securing tutors and books on tape, scribing tests, testing referral, advocating needs such as untimed or oral tests, and individual counseling. A WLD support group meets near the campus.

General Information:

University of Alabama at Birmingham is a 4 year public university. Urban campus of 265 acres is Accessible by air, train or bus. Ski areas are 90 miles from campus. Beaches are 260 miles from campus. 3% of students are foreign. 5 residential halls on campus. Housing is not guaranteed.55 % of students remain on campus for the weekends. 5 % of students join fraternities/sororities.

Accreditation:SACS

SAT/ACT Scores:
Scores for incoming freshmen: **ACT:** 33% below 20. 40% between 20 and 23. 11%between 24 and 25l. 11%between 26 and 28. 5% above 28.

Expenses:
Tuition: In-state: Full year: $1,650.00. Part-time: Per credit:$55.00. Tuition: Out-of-state: Full year: $3,300.00. Part-time: Per credit:$110.00. Room and board: $3,500.00

Majors

- AREA STUDIES African-American, American, Urban, Women's Studies
- BUSINESS Accounting, Banking, Business Administration, Business Education, Business Management, Economics, Finance, Management, Marketing, Personnel, Quantitative Methods, Real Estate
- COMMUNICATION Broadcasting, Commercial Design, English, Journalism, Public Relations • COMPUTER SCIENCE Artificial Intelligence, Data Processing, Programming, Systems Analysis • EDUCATION Art, Curriculum, Early Childhood, Education Leadership, Elementary, Health, Music, Physical, School Psychology, Secondary, Special • ENGINEER-

ING Biomedical, Civil, Electrical, Materials, Mechanical • FINE AND PERFORMING ARTS Art, Art History, Dance, Music, Studio Art, Theater • HEALTH SCIENCES Environmental, Health, Medical Technology, Nursing, Nutritional/Food, Occupational Therapy, Physical Therapy, Radiological Therapy • LANGUAGES French, German, Greek, Latin, Linguistic, Spanish • PHILOSOPHY Philosophy • PREPROFESSIONAL Dentistry, Engineering, Health Administration, Law, Medicine, Optometry, Social Work • SCIENCES Astronomy, Biochemistry, Biology, Chemistry, Earth Science, Ecology, Geology, Marine Biology, Mathematics, Microbiology, Natural Science, Physical Science, Physics, Physiology, Radiology • SOCIAL SCIENCES Anthropology, Criminal Justice, Geography, Gerontology, Government/Political, History, Psychology, Social Sciences, Sociology

Sports/Activities

• SPORTS RELATED Band, Cheerleading, Chess, Dance Team, Pep Band • SPORTS-INTERCOLLEGIATE Baseball (M), Canoeing, Cycling, Football, Horseback Riding, Karate, Martial Arts, Sailing, Scuba • SPORTS-INTRAMURAL Badminton, Basketball, Bowling, Golf, Ping-Pong, Racquetball, Soccer (M), Softball, Squash, Swimming, Tennis, Track and Field (F), Volleyball (F), Water Polo, Wrestling (M) • STUDENT LIFE ACTIVITIES Anthropology Club, Art Guild, Business Club, Cultural/Social Activities, Drama Groups, Ethnic & Cultural Groups, Fraternities, Gaming Society, Jazz Band, Language Clubs, Music Groups, Newspaper, Sororities, Student Government

---

Less Selective **Alabama**

Walker State Technical College

P.O. Drawer K
Sumiton, Alabama 35148
(800) 648-3271

School Enrollment: **1,116** Male: **420** Female: **696**

Admissions Contact: **Paul E. Isaacs, Registrar**

Admissions

Secondary School Information
Most Important Criteria For Admissions (1-strongest)

2 SAT/ACT	**1** Application	**4** School transcript
Class rank	Course selection	Personal statement
Interview	Extra activities	Psychoeducational
3 G.P.A.	Open admission	Recommendations

Test Requirements:
Tests recommended: **ACT-ASSET, ACT, TABE**

Types of Disabilities Served
• Speech/Lang	• Reading	ADD with LD
• Study skills	• Spelling	ADD without LD
• Written express	• Math	ADHD with LD
• Organizational	• Fine Motor	ADHD without LD
• Perceptual		

High School Course Requirements:
English: **4** Math: **2** Science: **1**

Learning Disability Program
Syllabus available during orientation:**Yes**
Program: Remedial: **Yes**
Students mainstreamed **100** % of the day
Services available for all students: **Yes**
Counseling: Individual: **Yes** Group Counseling: **Yes** Vocational Counseling: **Yes**
Support groups are available:**Adult Basic Education and Student Support Services**

Diagnostic Testing
ADD	• Personality	Perceptual skills	• Spelling
ADHD	Organization	Fine motor skills	• Reading
I.Q.	Handwriting	Spoken language	Study skills
• Math	Social skills	• Written language	

Services rendered by:
Graduates   Peers   Faculty   LD staff   Teacher trainees

Tutorials
Grp.	Ind.	Tutorials	Grp.	Ind.	Tutorials
		Math skills			Word processing
		Study skills			Time management
		Language arts			Learning strategies
		Written express			Organizational skills

Academic Accommodations

Curriculum	Study Aids	Exams
Priority registration	Typist	Oral
Math waiver	Reader	Untimed
Foreign lang. waiver	Notetaker	Take home
Course substitution	Proof reader	With proctor
In Class	Text on tape	On computer
Calculators	Early syllabus	Extended time
Tape recorder	Taped handouts	On tape
Word processor		Modified
Priority seating		Separate room

Graduation Requirements:
Course credits: **116** GPA: **2.0** Years to complete degree: **Unlimited**

General Information:
Walker State Technical College is a 2 year public college. 20 miles from Birmingham. Accessible by bus. 1% of students are foreign. Housing is not guaranteed.

Accreditation:SACS, COEI

Expenses:
Tuition: In-state: Full year: $252.00-$351.00. Part-time: Per credit:$21.00 per credit for 1-12 hours. Part-time: Per course: $42.00-$105.00. Tuition: Out-of-state: Full year: $441.00-$614.25. Part-time: Per credit:$36.75. Part-time: Per course:$73.50-$183.75

Majors

• BUSINESS Business Administration, Business Management, Clerical, Secretarial Science • COMPUTER SCIENCE Computer Science • EDUCATION Child Development • ENGINEERING Air Conditioning Technology, Automotive, Computer, Drafting, Electrical, Mining/Mineral • HEALTH SCIENCES Medical Secretary, Nursing, Nursing Assistant, Practical Nursing • PRE PROFESSIONAL • VOCATIONAL Air Conditioning/Heating/Refri, Auto Body, Automobile Technology, Business and Office, Cosmetology, Drafting, Electronics Technology, Legal Secretary, Secretarial, Welding

Sports
• STUDENT LIFE ACTIVITIES Academic Clubs, Student Government

Less Selective
**Alaska
Services**

Sheldon Jackson College
801 Lincoln Street
Sitka, Alaska 99835
(907) 747-5235

School Enrollment: **308** Male: **139** Female: **169**
LD Enrollment: **15** Male: **9** Female: **6**

Admissions Contact: **Kristi Coltharp, Director of Admissions**
LD Contact: **Alice Zellhuber, Director, Service for LD Students**
Name of Program: **Lift-Off Program**
Address: **801 Lincoln St.**
Telephone:**(907) 747-5235**

Admissions

Application Information:
Rolling Admissions: **Yes**

Secondary School Information
Most Important Criteria For Admissions (1-strongest)

SAT/ACT	Application	School transcript
Class rank	Course selection	Personal statement
Interview	Extra activities	Psychoeducational
G.P.A.	Open admission	Recommendations

Test Requirements:
Standardized tests waived: **Yes**

Types of Disabilities Served

Speech/Lang.	• Reading	• ADD with LD
• Study skills	• Spelling	• ADD without LD
• Written express	• Math	• ADHD with LD
• Organizational	• Fine Motor	• ADHD without LD
• Perceptual		

Admissions Process

Student submits application form, fee, and all transcripts of previous education (high school and post-secondary). LD students are asked to submit other pertinent information.

Learning Disability Program

Program: Remedial: **Yes**
Program: Reinforces course work: **Yes**
Students mainstreamed **100** % of the day
Recommended credits per semester: **12**
Time required or recommended in learning center: **Varies**
Services available for all students: **Yes**
Counseling: Individual: **Yes**
Support groups are available:**Yes, Learning Support Group**

Faculty:
Faculty: **1** Full time: **1** Part time: **4** M.A.: **1**
Faculty advocate: **Yes**

Diagnostic Testing

ADD	• Personality	• Perceptual skills	• Spelling
ADHD	Organization•	Fine motor skills	• Reading
• I.Q.	Handwriting	Spoken language	• Study skills
• Math	Social skills	Written language	

Tutoring:
Average size of group tutorials: **1:5**
Services rendered by:

Graduates	•Peers	Faculty	LD staff	Teacher trainees

Tutorials

Grp.	Ind.	Tutorials	Grp.	Ind.	Tutorials
•	•	Math skills	•	•	Word processing
•	•	Study skills	•	•	Time management
•	•	Language arts	•	•	Learning strategies
•	•	Written express	•	•	Organizational skills

Academic Accommodations

Curriculum	Study Aids	Exams
Priority registration	• Typist	• Oral
Math waiver	• Reader	• Untimed
Foreign lang. waiver	Notetaker	• Take home
Course substitution	• Proof reader	With proctor
In Class	• Text on tape	• On computer
• Calculators	Early syllabus	• Extended time
• Tape recorder	Taped handouts	• On tape
• Word processor		Modified
• Priority seating		• Separate room

Graduation Requirements:
Course credits: **130 semester** GPA: **2.0-2 .5 in major** Years to complete degree: **6**
Other requirements: **English Composition, core curriculum in general education requirements.**

Program Strengths
The Lift-Off Program works closely with the Sitka Representative of Alaska State Vocational Rehabilitation Program. During January, a 3-credit Academic Success Course is offered. Additionally, a basic math course (3 credits), two developmental English courses (5 & 2 credits), a Notetaking/Memory Skills course (3 credits) and a College Reading Skills Course (2 credits) are offered.

General Information:
Sheldon Jackson College is a 4 year independent Presbyterian college. Rural campus 800 miles from Seattle or Anchorage. Accessible by plane or ferry. Beaches are 1/2 mile from campus. 1% of students are foreign. 1 residential halls on campus. Housing is not guaranteed.100 % of students remain on campus for the weekends.

Accreditation:NACS

Expenses:
Tuition: In-state: Full year: $6,896.00 per year. Part-time: Per credit:$230.00. Room and board: $4,635.00

Majors
• BUSINESS Business Administration • EDUCATION Elementary, Secondary • HUMANITIES Humanities, Liberal Arts • PRE PROFESSIONAL Fisheries, Forestry, Natural Resources • SCIENCES General, Marine Biology • SOCIAL SCIENCES Social Science

Sports/Activities
• SPORTS-INTERCOLLEGIATE Basketball (F), Basketball (M), Volleyball, Volleyball (F), Volleyball (M), Water Polo • STUDENT LIFE ACTIVITIES Academic Clubs, Drama Groups, Ethnic & Cultural Groups, Musical

Theater, Religious Organization, Student Government, Yearbook

---

Less Selective — Alaska
Services

University of Alaska Anchorage
3211 Providence Drive
Anchorage, Alaska 99508
(907) 786-1525

School Enrollment: **19,614** Male: **11,547** Female: **8,077**

Admissions Contact: **Linda Berg, Smith Director**
LD Contact: **Doran Vaughan, Counselor**
Name of Program: **Disabled Student Services**
Telephone:**(907) 786-1570**

Admissions

Application Information:
Application deadline: **July 1st**
Rolling Admissions: **Yes**

Secondary School Information
Most Important Criteria For Admissions (1-strongest)

SAT/ACT	**1** Application	**2**	School transcript
Class rank	Course selection		Personal statement
Interview	Extra activities		Psychoeducational
1 G.P.A.	**1** Open admission	**2**	Recommendations

Test Requirements:
Standardized tests waived: **Yes**
Untimed SAT: **Yes** Untimed ACT: **Yes**

Types of Disabilities Served
- Speech/Lang
- Study skills
- Written express
- Organizational
- Perceptual
- Reading
- Spelling
- Math
- Fine Motor

ADD with LD
ADD without LD
ADHD with LD
ADHD without LD

Learning Disability Program
Counseling: Individual: **Yes** Vocational Counseling: **Yes**

Diagnostic Testing

ADD	Personality	Perceptual skills	Spelling
ADHD	Organization	Fine motor skills	Reading
I.Q.	Handwriting	Spoken language	Study skills
Math	Social skills	Written language	

Tutoring:
Average size of group tutorials:
Services rendered by:

Graduates	•Peers	Faculty	LD staff	Teacher trainees

Tutorials

Grp.	Ind.	Tutorials	Grp.	Ind.	Tutorials
•	•	Math skills	•	•	Word processing
•	•	Study skills	•	•	Time management
•	•	Language arts	•	•	Learning strategies
•	•	Written express	•	•	Organizational skills

Academic Accommodations

Curriculum	Study Aids	Exams
Priority registration	Typist	• Oral
Math waiver	Reader	Untimed
Foreign lang. waiver	• Notetaker	Take home
Course substitution	Proof reader	With proctor
In Class	• Text on tape	On computer
Calculators	Early syllabus	• Extended time
• Tape recorder	Taped handouts	On tape
• Word processor		Modified
Priority seating		Separate room

Program Strengths
UAA does not have a learning disability program per se. However, we serve a large number of students who have learning disabilities through our disabled student services programs.

General Information:
University of Alaska Anchorage is a 2 and 4 year public University. Urban campus of 300 acres is Anchorage. Accessible by car or bus Ski areas are 45 miles from campus. Housing is not guaranteed.

Accreditation:NWACS

Expenses:
Tuition: In-state: Full year: $1,320.oo. Part-time: Per credit:$55.00. Part-time: Per course: $126.00. Tuition: Out-of-state: Full year: $3,960.00. Room and board: $1,230.00 room only

Majors
• BUSINESS Accounting, Agricultural, Aviation Management, Business Administration, Business Management, Economics, Finance, Management, Marketing, Real Estate • COMMUNICATION Advertising, Broadcasting, English, Journalism, Photography, Television/Radio/Film • COMPUTER SCIENCE Computer Science, Data Processing, Programming, Systems Analysis • EDUCATION Art, Elementary, Music, Physical, Psychology, Secondary, Special • ENGINEERING Civil/Environmental, Petroleum • FINE AND PERFORMING ARTS Art, Dramatic Arts, Music, Music Performance, Theater • HEALTH SCIENCES Dental Assistant, Dental Hygiene, Health, Medical Technology, Nursing • PREPROFESSIONAL Architecture, Engineering, Law, Medicine, Social Work • SCIENCES Biology, Chemistry • SOCIAL SCIENCES Anthropology, Criminal Justice, Government/Political, History, Human Service, Psychology, Sociology • VOCATIONAL Air Conditioning/Heating/Refri, Air Traffic Control, Aircraft Mechanics, Automobile Technology, Aviation Maintenance, Diesel Power Technology, Drafting, Electronics Technology, Fire Science, Fishery Studies, Food Service, Home Economics, Industrial Equipment Maintenan, Paralegal, Piloting, Secretarial, Surveying and Mapping, Welding

Sports/Activities
• SPORTS INTERCOLLEGIATE Cross Country (M), Diving, Figure Skating, Gymnastics (F), Karate, Sailing, Scuba, Skiing - Snow, Squash, Swimming • SPORTS INTRAMURAL Basketball, Ice Hockey (F), Racquetball, Softball, Volleyball • SPORTS RELATED Cheerleading, Chess, Pep Band, Team Managers • STUDENT LIFE ACTIVITIES Concert Band, Debate, Drama Groups, Ethnic & Cultural Groups, Film, Jazz Band, Magazine, Newspaper, Radio/TV station, Religious Organization, Student Government, Symphony Orchestra, Yearbook

Alaska

Selective

Alaska Services

University of Alaska Fairbanks
Fairbanks, Alaska 99775-0060
(907) 474-7822

School Enrollment: **8,910** Male: **3,742** Female: **5,168**

Admissions Contact: **Edna Palmer, Admission Counselor**
LD Contact: **Diane Preston, Cord, Serv.-Students with Disabilities**
Name of Program: **Services for Students with Disabilities**
Address: **Center for Health & Counseling**
Telephone:**(907) 474-7043 TDD 474-7045**

Admissions

Application Information:
Application deadline: **August 1st**
Rolling Admissions: **Yes**

Secondary School Information
Most Important Criteria For Admissions (1-strongest)

SAT/ACT	**1** Application	School transcript
Class rank	**2** Course selection	Personal statement
Interview	Extra activities	Psychoeducational
2 G.P.A.	Open admission	Recommendations

Test Requirements:
Diagnostic testing waived: **Yes**
Documentation of LD required: **Yes**

Types of Disabilities Served
- Speech/Lang
- Study skills
- Written express
- Organizational
- Perceptual
- Reading
- Spelling
- Math
- Fine Motor
- ADD with LD
- ADD without LD
- ADHD with LD
- ADHD without LD

Learning Disability Program
Students mainstreamed **100** % of the day
Counseling: Individual: **Yes**
Support groups are available:**Disabled Students Support Group - open to all campus students with a disability**

Faculty:
Faculty: **2** Including Director: **Yes** Part time: **1** M.A.: **1**
Faculty advocate: **Yes** Meets with instructor: **As needed**

Diagnostic Testing
ADD	Personality	Perceptual skills	Spelling
ADHD	Organization	Fine motor skills	Reading
I.Q.	Handwriting	Spoken language	Study skills
Math	Social skills	Written language	

Tutoring:
Services rendered by:
Graduates •Peers •Faculty LD staff Teacher trainees

Tutorials
Grp.	Ind.	Tutorials	Grp.	Ind.	Tutorials
	•	Math skills		•	Word processing
	•	Study skills		•	Time management
	•	Language arts			Learning strategies
	•	Written express		•	Organizational skills

Academic Accommodations
Curriculum
Priority registration
Math waiver
Foreign lang. waiver
- Course substitution
In Class
- Calculators
- Tape recorder
- Word processor
Priority seating

Study Aids
Typist
- Reader
- Notetaker
- Proof reader
- Text on tape
Early syllabus
Taped handouts

Exams
- Oral
Untimed
- Take home
- With proctor
On computer
- Extended time
On tape
- Modified
- Separate room

Graduation Requirements:
Course credits: **60** GPA: **2.0**
Other requirements: **No grade lower than "C" in courses required for major**

Program Strengths
For students identified as learning disabled we provide specialized tutoring. Our Services for Students with Disabilities Coordinator also provides advocacy and individual counseling. Student aides are available to serve as scribes or note takers. The Coordinator for Disabled Student Services will work with faculty when special accommodations are necessary. We are in the process of developing a program to provide assessment for learning disabilities, special workshops for LD students, and materials for faculty and staff.

General Information:
University of Alaska Fairbanks is a 2 and 4 year public University. Suburban campus of 2,200 acres is 5 miles from Fairbanks. Accessible by bus. Ski areas are 25 miles from campus. Beaches are 350 miles from campus. 3% of students are foreign. Housing is not guaranteed.

Accreditation:NWACS

SAT/ACT Scores:
Scores for incoming freshmen:**Verbal:**57%below 500. 28%between 500 and 599. 13%between 600 and 699. 2%above 700. **Math:**48% below 500. 28% between 500 and 599. 17% between 600 and 699. 7%above 700. **ACT:** 55% below 20. 17% between 20 and 23. 8%between 24 and 25l. 16%between 26 and 28. 4% above 28.

Expenses:
Tuition: In-state: Full year: $1,508.00. Part-time: Per credit:$58.00. Tuition: Out-of-state: Full year: $4,524.00. Part-time: Per credit:$174.00. Room and board: $3,110.00

Majors
• AREA STUDIES Alaska Native Studies • BUSINESS Accounting, Banking, Business Administration, Business Management, Economics, Finance, Marketing, Travel/Tourism Management • COMMUNICATIONS Communication, English, Journalism, Linguistic • COMPUTER SCIENCE Computer Science • EDUCATION Child Development, Elementary, Physical, Secondary • ENGINEERING Civil/Environmental, Electrical, Mechanical, Mining/Mineral, Petroleum • HUMANITIES Humanities • LANGUAGES Eskimo, French, German, Russian, Spanish • PREPROFESSIONAL Engineering, Natural Resources, Social Work • SCIENCES Biology, Chemistry, Earth, General, Geography, Geology, Mathematics, Physics, Statistics, Wildlife Management, Zoology • SOCIAL SCIENCES Anthropology, Criminal Justice, Government/Political, History, Human Service, Psychology, Sociology • VISUAL AND PERFORMING ARTS

Art, Music, Theater • VOCATIONAL Culinary Arts, Diesel Mechanics, Early Childhood Development, Fire Science, Human Services Technology

Sports/Activities

• SPORTS RELATED Pep Band • SPORTS-INTERCOLLEGIATE Basketball, Cross Country, Ice Hockey (M), Riflery, Volleyball (F) • SPORTS-INTRAMURAL Badminton, Baseball, Basketball, Canoeing, Cross Country, Cycling, Fencing, Figure Skating, Golf, Gymnastics, Hand Ball, Judo, Karate, Martial Arts, Racquetball, Riflery, Skiing - Snow, Softball, Swimming, Volleyball, Water Polo, Wrestling • STUDENT LIFE ACTIVITIES Drama Groups, Ethnic & Cultural Groups, Magazine, Music Groups, Musical Theater, Newspaper, Radio/TV station, Religious Organization, Student Government, Symphony Orchestra

Selective   **Arizona Program**

Arizona State University

Tempe, Arizona 85287-0705
(602) 965-7788

School Enrollment: **31,700** Male: **16,500** Female: **15,200**

Admissions Contact: **Susan Clouse, Director of Admissions**
LD Contact: **Deborah Taska**
Name of Program: **Disabled Student Resources**
Telephone:**(602) 965-1234**

Admissions

Application Information:
Application deadline: **April 15th/November 15th**
Applicant must apply **10-12** months in advance
Rolling Admissions: **Yes**

Secondary School Information
Most Important Criteria For Admissions (1-strongest)

1 SAT/ACT	Application	School transcript
1 Class rank	Course selection	Personal statement
Interview	Extra activities	Psychoeducational
1 G.P.A.	Open admission	Recommendations

Test Requirements:
Diagnostic testing waived: **Yes**
Untimed SAT: **Yes** Untimed ACT: **Yes**
WAIS-R required: **Yes**
Currency of diagnostic testing: **2 years**
Tests recommended: **Psycho-Educational Evaluation**

Types of Disabilities Served
- Speech/Lang • Reading • ADD with LD
- Study skills • Spelling • ADD without LD
- Written express • Math • ADHD with LD
- Organizational • Fine Motor • ADHD without LD
- Perceptual

Learning Disability Program
Program: Reinforces course work: **Yes**
Students mainstreamed **100** % of the day
Counseling: Individual: **Yes**

Faculty:
Faculty: **4** Including Director: **Yes** Full time: **3** Part time: **1**
LD faculty with: BS/BA: **2** M.A.: **2**

Diagnostic Testing

ADD	Personality	Perceptual skills	Spelling
ADHD	Organization	Fine motor skills	Reading
I.Q.	Handwriting	Spoken language	Study skills
Math	Social skills	Written language	

Tutoring:
Services rendered by:
•Graduates •Peers Faculty •LD staff Teacher trainees

Tutorials

Grp.	Ind.	Tutorials	Grp.	Ind.	Tutorials
	•	Math skills		•	Word processing
	•	Study skills		•	Time management
		Language arts		•	Learning strategies
	•	Written express		•	Organizational skills

Academic Accommodations

Curriculum	Study Aids	Exams
Priority registration	Typist	• Oral
Math waiver	Reader	Untimed
Foreign lang. waiver	Notetaker	Take home
Course substitution	Proof reader	With proctor
In Class	• Text on tape	On computer
• Calculators	Early syllabus	• Extended time
• Tape recorder	Taped handouts	On tape
• Word processor		Modified
Priority seating		Separate room

Program Strengths
Our learning disability program is part of a larger comprehensive program for disabled students on the Arizona State University campus. Our goal is to assist each of our students to become self-advocating and independent in order to achieve success and happiness academically and throughout life.

General Information:
Arizona State University is a 4 year public university. Urban campus of 600 acres is 10 miles from Phoenix. Accessible by air, train, or bus. Ski areas are 3 hours from campus. Beaches are 8 hours from campus. 3% of students are foreign. Housing is not guaranteed.10 % of students join fraternities/sororities.

Accreditation:NCACS

SAT/ACT Scores:
Scores for incoming freshmen:**Verbal:**64%below 500. 29%between 500 and 599. 6%between 600 and 699. 1%above 700. **Math:**60% below 500. 39% between 500 and 599. 19% between 600 and 699. 2%above 700. **ACT:** 36% below 20. 45% between 20 and 23. 17%between 26 and 28. 2% above 28.

Class Rank:
About 40% of the present freshmen class were in the upper 20% of their high school class. 71% were in the top 40% of their class. 92% were in the top 60% of their class. 99% were in the top 80% of their class.

Expenses:
Tuition: In-state: Full year: $1,478.00. Part-time: Per credit:$77.00. Tuition: Out-of-state: Full year: $6,484.00. Room and board: $3,900.00

Majors
• AREA STUDIES Asian, Latin American, Urban, Women's Studies
• BUSINESS Accounting, Banking, Business Administration, Business Economics, Business Education, Business Management, Economics, Finance, Management, Marketing, Real Estate, Taxation • COMMUNICATIONS Broadcasting, Communication, English, Graphic Design,

Journalism, Photography, Television/Radio/Film • COMPUTER SCIENCE Computer Maintenance, Computer Science, Computer Technology, Hardware Engineer, Programming • CRAFTS AND DESIGN Apparel Design, Ceramics, Crafts • EDUCATION Art, Bilingual, Early Childhood, Elementary, English, Foreign Language, Health, Industrial, Music, Physical, Reading, Science, Secondary, Special • ENGINEERING Aerospace, Biomedical, Bioengineering, Chemical, Civil/Environmental, Engineering Science, Geological, Mechanical, Nuclear • HEALTH SCIENCES Health, Medical Technology, Nursing, Nutritional/Food, Speech Therapy, Speech/Audiology and Speech • HUMANITIES Humanities, Philosophy, Religion • LANGUAGES Chinese, French, German, Italian, Japanese, Russian, Spanish • PREPROFESSIONAL Architecture, Dentistry, Engineering, Law, Medicine, Pharmacy, Pre-Elementary, Recreation, Social Work, Veterinarian • SCIENCES Biology, Botany, Chemistry, Ecology, Geography, Geology, Horticultural, Mathematics, Microbiology, Physics, Physiology, Statistics, Zoology • SOCIAL SCIENCES Anthropology, Criminal Justice, Family Counseling, Government/Political, History, Psychology, Social Sciences, Sociology • VISUAL AND PERFORMING ARTS Art, Art History, Dance, Dramatic Arts, Music, Studio Art, Theater • VOCATIONAL Electronics Technology, Food Service, Home Economics, Interior Design, Jewelry-Metalsmithery, Park/Recreation, Printing/Lithography, Secretarial, Textile and Clothing, Transportation Management

Sports/Activities

• SPORTS RELATED Marching Band • SPORTS-INTERCOLLEGIATE Archery, Badminton, Baseball (M), Basketball, Cross Country, Diving, Football (M), Golf, Gymnastics, Softball (F), Swimming, Tennis, Track and Field, Volleyball (F) • SPORTS-INTRAMURAL Badminton, Basketball, Softball, Tennis, Volleyball • STUDENT LIFE ACTIVITIES Debate, Drama Groups, Ethnic & Cultural Groups, Film, Fraternities, Jazz Band, Newspaper, Radio/TV station, Sororities, Student Government, Symphony Orchestra, Yearbook

Less Selective   **Arizona**
                                        Services

Glendale Community College

6000 West Olive Avenue
Glendale, Arizona 85302
(602) 435-3080

School Enrollment: **19,000** Male: **9,500** Female: **9,500**
LD Enrollment: **75** Male: **39** Female: **36**

Admissions Contact: **Mary Lou Bayless, Asst. Dean Student Serv.**
LD Contact: **Mark Ferris, Director Disabled Student Services**

Admissions

Secondary School Information
Most Important Criteria For Admissions (1-strongest)

SAT/ACT	Application	School transcript
Class rank	Course selection	Personal statement
Interview	Extra activities	Psychoeducational
G.P.A.	Open admission	Recommendations

Test Requirements:
Diagnostic testing waived: **Yes**
Documentation of LD required: **Yes**
Currency of diagnostic testing: **3 years**

Types of Disabilities Served

Speech/Lang	Reading	ADD with LD
Study skills	Spelling	ADD without LD
Written express	Math	ADHD with LD
Organizational	Fine Motor	ADHD without LD
Perceptual		

Admissions Process

Application, transcripts

Diagnostic Testing

ADD	Personality	Perceptual skills	Spelling
ADHD	Organization	Fine motor skills	Reading
I.Q.	Handwriting	Spoken language	Study skills
Math	Social skills	Written language	

Tutoring:
Average size of group tutorials: **1-3**
Services rendered by:

Graduates	•Peers	Faculty	LD staff	Teacher trainees

Tutorials

Grp.	Ind.	Tutorials	Grp.	Ind.	Tutorials
	•	Math skills			Word processing
	•	Study skills		•	Time management
•		Language arts		•	Learning strategies
•		Written express			Organizational skills

Academic Accommodations

Curriculum	Study Aids	Exams
• Priority registration	• Typist	• Oral
Math waiver	• Reader	• Untimed
Foreign lang. waiver	• Notetaker	Take home
Course substitution	Proof reader	• With proctor
In Class	• Text on tape	On computer
• Calculators	Early syllabus	• Extended time
• Tape recorder	Taped handouts	• On tape
• Word processor		Modified
• Priority seating		• Separate room

Graduation Requirements:
Course credits: **64** GPA: **2.0**
Other requirements: **Only AA, AAS, AGS degrees. Also certificates of completion for vocational areas.**

General Information:
Glendale Community College is a 2 year public college. Urban campus of 160 acres is 10 miles from Phoenix. Accessible by bus. Ski areas are 150 miles from campus. Beaches are 350 miles from campus. Housing is not guaranteed.

Accreditation:NCACS

Expenses:
Tuition: In-state: Full year: Part-Time Per credit: $26.00. Tuition: Out-of-state: Full year: Part-Time Per credit: $151.00.

Majors

• AGRICULTURE Business • ARTS Graphic Arts • BUSINESS Accounting, Banking/Finance, Business Administration, Management, Real Estate, Retailing • COMPUTER SCIENCE Computer Science • CRAFTS AND DESIGN Graphic Design, Illustration Design • EDUCATION Early Childhood • HEALTH SCIENCES Nursing • PRE PROFESSIONAL Business, Engineering, Law, Social Work • SCIENCES Earth, Geology • SOCIAL SCIENCES Human Service • VOCATIONAL Air Traffic Control, Automobile Technology, Automotive Service, Business and Office, Drafting, Electronics Technology, Fire Science, Park/Recreation, Word Processing

Sports/Activities

• SPORTS RELATED Cheerleading, Chess, Marching Band • SPORTS-INTERCOLLEGIATE Archery (F), Baseball (M), Basketball (F), Basketball (M), Cross Country (F), Cross Country (M), Football (M), Golf (M), Soccer (M), Softball (F), Tennis (F), Tennis (M), Track and Field (F), Track and Field (M), Volleyball (F) • SPORTS-INTRAMURAL Basketball, Bowling, Golf, Racquetball, Softball, Swimming, Tennis, Volleyball, Weight Lifting • STUDENT LIFE ACTIVITIES Academic Clubs, Choral, Concert Band, Dance, Drama Groups, Ethnic & Cultural Groups, Jazz Band, Music Groups, Musical Theater, Newspaper, Religious Organization, Student Government

---

Selective   **Arizona**
Services

Northern Arizona University

P.O. Box 4084
Flagstaff, Arizona 86011
(602) 523-5511

School Enrollment: **12,578** Male: **5,885** Female: **6,693**
LD Enrollment: **65** Male: **39** Female: **26**

Admissions Contact: **Molly S. Carder, Director of Admissions**
LD Contact: **Jane Mulrooney ,Coordinator**
Name of Program: **Disabled Student Services**
Telephone:**(602) 523-2261**

Admissions

Application Information:
Rolling Admissions: **Yes** Notified when: **As soon as possible**

Secondary School Information
Most Important Criteria For Admissions (1-strongest)

1 SAT/ACT	**2** Application	School transcript
1 Class rank	**2** Course selection	**3** Personal statement
Interview	Extra activities	Psychoeducational
1 G.P.A.	Open admission	Recommendations

Test Requirements:
Diagnostic testing waived: **Yes**
WAIS-R required: **Yes**
Documentation of LD required: **Yes**
Currency of diagnostic testing: **2 years**

Types of Disabilities Served
• Speech/Lang   • Reading   • ADD with LD
• Study skills   • Spelling   • ADD without LD
• Written express • Math   • ADHD with LD
• Organizational • Fine Motor   • ADHD without LD
• Perceptual

Faculty:
Faculty: **2** Part time: **2**
Faculty advocate: **Yes** Meets with instructor: **As needed**

Diagnostic Testing

ADD	Personality	Perceptual skills	Spelling
ADHD	Organization	Fine motor skills	Reading
I.Q.	Handwriting	Spoken language	Study skills
Math	Social skills	Written language	

Tutoring:
Average size of group tutorials: **5-6**
Services rendered by:
Graduates   •Peers   Faculty   •LD staff   Teacher trainees

Tutorials

Grp.	Ind.	Tutorials	Grp.	Ind.	Tutorials
•	•	Math skills			Word processing
•		Study skills			Time management
•	•	Language arts	•		Learning strategies
	•	Written express	•		Organizational skills

Academic Accommodations

Curriculum	Study Aids	Exams
Priority registration	Typist	• Oral
Math waiver	Reader	Untimed
Foreign lang. waiver	• Notetaker	• Take home
Course substitution	• Proof reader	With proctor
In Class	• Text on tape	On computer
Calculators	Early syllabus	• Extended time
• Tape recorder	Taped handouts	On tape
Word processor		• Modified
Priority seating		Separate room

Program Strengths

There is no formal LD program at NAU at this time. Some special services are available on an as-needed basis and include individual and group tutoring in academic areas and study skills. All program services are supplied by volunteers and interns. There is no charge. Approximately 65 students are currently identified as LD. All students must meet the same general admission requirements and exceptions as the general population. Students who may need special services are urged to contact the Disabled Student Coordinator at least 3 months prior to start of the semester.

General Information:

Northern Arizona University is a 4 year public university. Rural campus of 730 acres is 140 miles from Phoenix. Accessible by air, train, or bus. Ski areas are 20 miles from campus. 4% of students are foreign. 21 residential halls on campus. Housing is not guaranteed.60 % of students remain on campus for the weekends. 5 % of students join fraternities/sororities.

Accreditation:Regional

SAT/ACT Scores:
Scores for incoming freshmen:**Verbal:**2%below 500. 3%between 500 and 599. 10%between 600 and 699. 85%above 700. **ACT:** 22% below 20. 50% between 20 and 23. 16%between 24 and 25l. 8%between 26 and 28. 4% above 28.

Class Rank:
About 42% of the present freshmen class were in the upper 20% of their high school class. 34% were in the top 40% of their class. 17% were in the top 60% of their class. 7% were in the top 80% of their class.

Expenses:
Tuition: In-state: Full year: $1,540.00. Part-time: Per credit:$77.00. Tuition: Out-of-state: Full year: $5,916.00. Part-time: Per credit:$244.00. Room and board: $2,700.00.

41

Majors

• AREA STUDIES Latin American • BUSINESS Accounting, Banking, Business Administration, Business Economics, Business Management, Economics, Fashion Merchandising, Finance, Hotel and Restaurant Managemen, International Business, Printing Manufacturing, Travel/Tourism Management • COMMUNICATION Advertising, Broadcasting, Communication, Creative Writing, English, Journalism, Photography, Public Relations, Speech, Television/Radio/Film • COMPUTER SCIENCE Computer Science, Hardware Engineer, Software Engineer, Systems Analysis, Telecommunications • CRAFTS AND DESIGN Ceramics, Illustration Design, Sculpture • EDUCATION Art, Curriculum, Early Childhood, Elementary, English, Health, Industrial, Mathematics, Music, Physical, Science, Secondary, Social Studies, Special, Speech/Language • ENGINEERING Civil/Environmental, Computer, Electrical, Engineering Science, Mechanical • ENVIRONMENTAL CONTROL Energy Conservation • FINE AND PERFORMING ARTS Art, Art History, Dance, Music, Music Performance, Studio Art, Theater • HEALTH SCIENCES Communication Disorders, Dental Hygiene, Medical Technology, Nursing, Nutritional/Food, Physical Therapy, Speech Therapy, Speech/Audiology and Speech • LANGUAGES French, Latin, Spanish • PHILOSOPHY Humanities, Liberal Arts, Philosophy, Religion • PREPROFESSIONAL Dentistry, Engineering, Forestry, Industrial Design, Law, Medicine, Ministry, Pharmacy, Social Work, Veterinarian • SCIENCES Actuarial Technology, Astronomy, Astrophysics, Biochemistry, Biology, Botany, Cell Biology, Earth, Ecology, Geography, Geology, Mathematics, Meteorology, Microbiology, Physical Science, Physics, Statistics, Zoology • SOCIAL SCIENCES Anthropology, Criminal Justice, Geography, Government/Political, History, Law Enforcement, Political Science, Psychology, Public Relations, Social Sciences, Sociology • VOCATIONAL Dental Hygiene, Fashion Design, Food Service, Interior Design, Jewelry-Metalsmithery, Park/Recreation, Printing/Lithography

Sports/Activities

• SPORTS INTERCOLLEGIATE Basketball, Cross Country, Diving (F), Football (M), Rugby, Skiing - Cross Country, Skiing - Snow, Soccer, Softball, Swimming, Tennis, Track and Field, Volleyball (M) • SPORTS INTRAMURAL Archery, Badminton, Basketball, Bowling, Cross Country, Ping-Pong, Racquetball, Soccer, Softball, Swimming, Track and Field, Volleyball, Water Polo • SPORTS RELATED Band, Cheerleading, Chess, Drum Major/Majorette, Marching Band, Pep Band, Team Managers • STUDENT LIFE ACTIVITIES Choral, Concert Band, Dance, Debate, Drama Groups, Ethnic & Cultural Groups, Film, Fraternities, Jazz Band, Magazine, Musical Theater, Radio/TV station, Religious Organization, Sororities

---

Less Selective　　　　　　　　　　**Arizona Services**

Phoenix College

1202 West Thomas Road
Phoenix, Arizona 85013
(602) 285-7500

School Enrollment: **12,372** Male: **5,132** Female: **7,240**

Admissions Contact: **Pat Honzay, Associate Dean of Admissions**
LD Contact: **Ginny Bugh, Program Advisor**

Admissions

Application Information:
Application deadline: **Open**

Secondary School Information

Most Important Criteria For Admissions (1-strongest)

SAT/ACT	Application	School transcript
Class rank	Course selection	Personal statement
Interview	Extra activities	Psychoeducational
G.P.A.	**1** Open admission	Recommendations

Test Requirements:

Untimed SAT: **Yes** Untimed ACT: **Yes** Untimed ACH: **Yes**
WAIS-R required: **Yes**
Documentation of LD required: **Yes**

Types of Disabilities Served

• Speech/Lang	• Reading	• ADD with LD
• Study skills	• Spelling	• ADD without LD
• Written express	• Math	• ADHD with LD
• Organizational	• Fine Motor	• ADHD without LD
• Perceptual		

Learning Disability Program

Counseling: Individual: **Yes**

Faculty:

Faculty: **1** Full time: **1**
Faculty advocate: **Yes** Meets with instructor: **As needed**

Diagnostic Testing

ADD	Personality	Perceptual skills	Spelling
ADHD	Organization	Fine motor skills	Reading
I.Q.	Handwriting	Spoken language	Study skills
Math	Social skills	Written language	

Tutoring:

Services rendered by:
Graduates　•Peers　•Faculty　LD staff　Teacher trainees

Tutorials

Grp.	Ind.	Tutorials	Grp.	Ind.	Tutorials
	•	Math skills		•	Word processing
	•	Study skills	•		Time management
	•	Language arts	•		Learning strategies
	•	Written express	•		Organizational skills

Academic Accommodations

Curriculum	Study Aids	Exams
Priority registration	Typist	• Oral
Math waiver	Reader	Untimed
Foreign lang. waiver	• Notetaker	• Take home
Course substitution	Proof reader	With proctor
In Class	• Text on tape	On computer
• Calculators	Early syllabus	• Extended time
• Tape recorder	Taped handouts	On tape
Word processor		• Modified
Priority seating		Separate room

Program Strengths

We do not have a specific learning disability program but we do have a Special Services Department that can provide tutors, notetakers, test taking accommodations, along with developmental courses in reading, English, and math.

General Information:

Phoenix College is a 2 year public college. Urban campus. Housing is not guaranteed.

Accreditation: Regional

Expenses:
Tuition: In-state: Full year: $576.00. Part-time: Per credit:$24.00. Tuition: Out-of-state: Full year: $3,576.00.

Majors

• BUSINESS Accounting, Banking, Business Administration, Finance, Management, Marketing, Real Estate, Travel/Tourism Management • COMMUNICATIONS Journalism, Photography, Speech • COMPUTER SCIENCE Computer Science, Data Processing, Medical Records Administration, Medical Records Technology • CRAFTS AND DESIGN Graphic Design • EDUCATION Early Childhood, Physical, Teacher Aide • ENGINEERING Civil/Environmental, Engineering Science • ENVIRONMENTAL CONTROL Water and Wastewater Technolog • HEALTH SCIENCES Dental Assistant, Dental Hygiene, Dental Technician, Medical Technology, Nursing • HUMANITIES Liberal Arts • PREPROFESSIONAL Law, Legal Assistant • SCIENCES Behavioral Biology, Natural, Physics • SOCIAL SCIENCES Human Service, Law Enforcement, Law Enforcement, Psychology, Social Sciences • VISUAL AND PERFORMING ARTS Music, Theater • VOCATIONAL Air Condtioning/Heating/Refrig, Automobile Technology, Aviation Administration, Carpentry, Drafting, Fashion Mechandizing, Fire Science, Food Service, Home Economics, Industrial Design, Paralegal, Printing/Lithography, Secretarial, Welding, Word Processing

Sports/Activities

• SPORTS RELATED Marching Band • SPORTS-INTERCOLLEGIATE Archery, Baseball (M), Basketball, Cross Country, Football (M), Golf, Softball (F), Tennis, Volleyball (F), Wrestling (M) • STUDENT LIFE ACTIVITIES Choral, Concert Band, Dance, Drama Groups, Jazz Band, Music Groups, Musical Theater, Newspaper, Radio/TV station, Symphony Orchestra

Less Selective	Arizona Program

Pima Community College

2202 West Anklam Road
Tucson, Arizona 85709-3010
(602) 884-6640

School Enrollment: **9,000** Male: **4,860** Female: **4,140**
LD Enrollment: **70**

Admissions Contact: **Joseph Consentino, Registrar**
LD Contact: **Donald Coleman, Disabled Student Advisor**
Name of Program: **Disabled Student Resources**
Telephone:**(602) 884-6128**

Admissions

Application Information:
Enrolled:**40**
Separate application:**Yes**
Application deadline: **None**
Applicant must apply **3** months in advance
Rolling Admissions: **Yes**

Secondary School Information
Most Important Criteria For Admissions (1-strongest)

SAT/ACT	Application	School transcript
Class rank	Course selection	Personal statement
Interview	Extra activities	Psychoeducational
G.P.A.	Open admission	Recommendations

Test Requirements:
Standardized tests waived: **Yes**
Documentation of LD required: **Yes**
Currency of diagnostic testing: **3 years**
Tests recommended: **None**

Types of Disabilities Served
• Speech/Lang • Reading • ADD with LD
• Study skills • Spelling • ADD without LD
• Written express • Math • ADHD with LD
• Organizational Fine Motor • ADHD without LD
• Perceptual

Learning Disability Program

Program: Remedial: **Yes**
Program: Reinforces course work: **Yes**
Counseling: Individual: **Yes**

Faculty:
Faculty: **3** Including Director: **Yes** Full time: **3**
LD faculty with: BS/BA: **3**
Faculty advocate: **Yes** Meets with instructor: **As needed**

Diagnostic Testing
ADD	Personality	Perceptual skills	• Spelling
ADHD	Organization	Fine motor skills	• Reading
• I.Q.	• Handwriting	Spoken language	• Study skills
• Math	Social skills	• Written language	

Tutoring:
Services rendered by:
Graduates Peers Faculty •LD staff Teacher trainees

Tutorials
Grp.	Ind. Tutorials	Grp.	Ind. Tutorials
	• Math skills		• Word processing
	• Study skills		• Time management
	• Language arts		• Learning strategies
	• Written express		• Organizational skills

Academic Accommodations

Curriculum	Study Aids	Exams
Priority registration	• Typist	• Oral
Math waiver	Reader	Untimed
• Foreign lang. waiver	• Notetaker	Take home
Course substitution	• Proof reader	With proctor
In Class	• Text on tape	On computer
• Calculators	Early syllabus	• Extended time
• Tape recorder	Taped handouts	On tape
• Word processor		• Modified
Priority seating		Separate room

Program Strengths

We serve learning disabled students through tutors, personal counseling, and note-takers. Counseling is available to all students to explain learning disabilities. There also is a support group for the learning disabled.

General Information:

Pima Community College is a 2 year public college. Urban campus of 345 acres is Tucson. Accessible by bus. Housing is not guaranteed.

Accreditation: ACHA

Expenses:
Tuition: In-state: Full year: $264.00. Part-time: Per credit:$22.00.

Arizona

Majors

• BUSINESS Accounting, Banking, Business Education, Business Management, Fashion Merchandising, Hotel and Restaurant Managemen, International Business, Real Estate • COMMUNICATION Advertising, Commercial Design, Communication, Speech, Television/Radio/Film • COMPUTER SCIENCE Data Processing, Hardware Engineer, Programming, Software Engineer • CRAFTS AND DESIGN Graphic Design • EDUCATION Child Development, Early Childhood, Elementary, Physical, Secondary, Special, Speech/Language • ENGINEERING Engineering Science, Industrial, Mechanical • ENVIRONMENTAL CONTROL Water and Wastewater Technolog • FINE AND PERFORMING ARTS Music, Theater • HEALTH SCIENCES Medical Secretary, Medical Technology, Nursing, Nutritional/Food, Physical Therapy • PREPROFESSIONAL Agriculture, Architecture, Dentistry, Engineering, Law, Medicine, Optometry, Pharmacy, Range Management, Social Work, Veterinarian • SCIENCES Biology, Chemistry, Geology, Physics • SOCIAL SCIENCES Anthropology, Criminal Justice, Law Enforcement • VOCATIONAL Air Condtioning/Heating/Refrig, Automobile Technology, Automotive Service, Carpentry, Construction, Dental Hygiene, Drafting, Fire Science, Food Service, Home Economics, Industrial Design, Interior Design, Landscape Architecture, Machinist, Paralegal, Radiological Technology, Respiratory Therapy Technology, Secretarial

Sports/Activities

• SPORTS INTERCOLLEGIATE Baseball (M), Basketball, Bowling, Boxing, Canoeing, Fencing, Golf (M), Gymnastics, Judo, Karate, Martial Arts, Soccer, Softball, Weight Lifting • SPORTS INTRAMURAL Archery, Badminton, Baseball, Basketball, Cross Country, Golf, Hand Ball, Ping-Pong, Racquetball, Softball (F), Swimming, Tennis, Track and Field, Volleyball, Wrestling • SPORTS RELATED Band, Cheerleading, Chess, Pep Band • STUDENT LIFE ACTIVITIES Concert Band, Dance, Debate, Drama Groups, Ethnic & Cultural Groups, Jazz Band, Magazine, Music Groups, Newspaper, Student Government, Yearbook

---

Very Selective   **Arizona**
                                       Program

University of Arizona

S.A.L.T. Program Old Main - Room 117
Tucson, Arizona 85721
(602) 621-1242

School Enrollment: **35,500** Male: **18,500** Female: **17,000**
LD Enrollment: **365** Male: **224** Female: **141**

Admissions Contact: **Lupe Thompson, Admissions Officer**
LD Contact: **Rose Wilhite, Shirley Ramsey ,S.A.L.T. Adms. Coord.**
Name of Program: **S.A.L.T. Program**
Telephone:**(602) 621-1242**

Admissions

Application Information:
LD Students Applying: **350** Accepted: **100** Enrolled:**365**
Application deadline: **Jan. 1 Fall semester; Oct. 1 Spring semester**
Applicant must apply **8** months in advance
Rolling Admissions: **Yes**

Secondary School Information
Most Important Criteria For Admissions (1-strongest)
8 SAT/ACT **11** Application   **2** School transcript
10 Class rank **7** Course selection **4** Personal statement
6 Interview **9** Extra activities **1** Psychoeducational
5 G.P.A.   Open admission **3** Recommendations

Test Requirements:
Untimed SAT: **Yes** Untimed ACT: **Yes**
WAIS-R required: **Yes** Range accepted: **Individual**
Documentation of LD required: **Yes**
Currency of diagnostic testing: **No more than 36**
Tests recommended: **Woodcock-Johnson, Parts I and II**

Types of Disabilities Served
• Speech/Lang   • Reading   • ADD with LD
• Study skills   • Spelling   • ADD without LD
• Written express • Math   • ADHD with LD
• Organizational • Fine Motor   • ADHD without LD
• Perceptual

Admissions Process

Student must apply both to the U of A (contact Lupe Thompson at (602) 621-3237) and to the S.A.L.T. Program. Please contact these departments for specific information.

High School Course Requirements:
English: **4** Math: **3** Science: **2**
Waivers to standard high school courses
Foreign Language : **Yes** Math: **Yes** Course substitution: **Yes**

Learning Disability Program

Special orientation for LD students: **Yes**
Program: Reinforces course work: **Yes**
Program available through:**Year round**
Students mainstreamed **100 %** of the day
Recommended credits per semester: **12-13**
Time required or recommended in learning center: **varies**
Services only for LD students: **Yes**
Counseling: Individual: **Yes** Group Counseling: **Yes** Vocational Counseling: **Yes**
Support groups are available:**Study Skills, socialization skills, "at risk" groups, peer mentor program**

Faculty:
Faculty: **32** Full time: **12** Part time: **20**
LD faculty with: BS/BA: **17** M.A.: **3** Ph.D.: **1**
Meets with instructor: **As needed**

Diagnostic Testing
ADD   Personality   Perceptual skills   Spelling
ADHD   Organization   Fine motor skills   Reading
I.Q.   Handwriting   Spoken language   Study skills
Math   Social skills Written language

Tutoring:
Average size of group tutorials: **any size**
Services rendered by:
•Graduates •Peers   Faculty   •LD staff   Teacher trainees

Tutorials
Grp.	Ind.	Tutorials	Grp.	Ind.	Tutorials
•	•	Math skills	•	•	Word processing
•	•	Study skills	•	•	Time management
•	•	Language arts	•	•	Learning strategies
•	•	Written express	•	•	Organizational skills

Academic Accommodations

Curriculum	Study Aids	Exams
Priority registration	Typist	• Oral
• Math waiver	• Reader	Untimed
• Foreign lang. waiver	Notetaker	• Take home
Course substitution	• Proof reader	• With proctor
In Class	• Text on tape	• On computer
Calculators	Early syllabus	• Extended time
• Tape recorder	Taped handouts	• On tape
Word processor		• Modified
Priority seating		• Separate room

Graduation Requirements:

Course credits: **Varies** GPA: **2.0** Years to complete degree: **None specified** Math waiver: **Yes** Language waiver: **Yes**

Program Strengths

The S.A.L.T. Program is a fee-based enhancement program for college LD students. It includes advocacy and academic counseling, orientation to the University, special test administration, tutoring by S.A.L.T. trained tutors, instruction on and use of computers, instruction in study skills, and tracking of at-risk students. Some tape recorders are available for recovering learners. Ordering texts on tape may also be facilitated through this program.

General Information:

University of Arizona is a 4 year public university. Urban campus of 1 acres is Accessible by air, bus or car. Ski areas are 1 hour from campus. Beaches are 4-8 hours from campus. 8% of students are foreign. 18 residential halls on campus. Housing is not guaranteed.15 % of students join fraternities/sororities.

Accreditation:NCACS

SAT/ACT Scores:

Scores for incoming freshmen:**Verbal:**64.2%below 500. 27.2%between 500 and 599. 7.6%between 600 and 699. .9%above 700. **Math:**39.0% below 500. 35.1% between 500 and 599. 20.7% between 600 and 699. 5.2%above 700. **ACT:** 20.5% below 20. 23.4% between 20 and 23. 28.9%between 24 and 25l. 17.3%between 26 and 28. 9.8% above 28.

Class Rank:

About 51.8% of the present freshmen class were in the upper 20% of their high school class. 80.1% were in the top 40% of their class. 94.0% were in the top 60% of their class. 98.3% were in the top 80% of their class.

Expenses:

Tuition: In-state: Full year: $795.00 per semester. Part-time: Per credit:$80.00. Part-time: Per course: $80.00 times number of units in course. Tuition: Out-of-state: Full year: $3,498.00 per semester. Part-time: Per credit:$289.00. Room and board: $3,400.00 Cost of LD program:Freshmen $1,100.00 per semester; Junior/Senior $300.00 per semester

Majors

• AGRICULTURE Education, Horticultural, Plant Science • AREA STUDIES Jewish/Judaism, Latin American, Mexican/American, Russian/Slavic, Women's Studies • ARTS Art History • BUSINESS Accounting, Business Administration, Business Economics, Economics, Marketing, Personnel • COMMUNICATIONS Communication, Creative Writing, English, Journalism • COMPUTER SCIENCE Computer Science • EDUCATION Art, Early Childhood, Elementary, Health, Home Economics, Music, Physical, Secondary, Social Studies • ENGINEERING Architectural, Chemical, Civil/Environmental, Computer, Electrical, Geological, Industrial, Materials, Mathematical, Mechanical, Mining/Mineral, Nuclear, Physics, Systems Analysis • HEALTH SCIENCES Nursing, Nutritional/Food, Rehabilitation • HUMANITIES Classics, Philosophy • LANGUAGES French, German, Greek, Italian, Latin, Linguistics, Portuguese, Russian, Spanish • SCIENCES Aerospace Science, Agricultural, Animal, Anthropology, Astronomy, Biochemistry, Biology, Chemistry, Earth, Ecol-

ogy, Entomology, Geoscience, Mathematics, Microbiology, Molecular Biology, Physics • SOCIAL SCIENCES • VISUAL AND PERFORMING ARTS Dance, Music, Music Performance, Music Theatre • VOCATIONAL Interior Design, Landscape Architecture

Sports/Activities

• SPORTS RELATED Baton Twirling, Cheerleading, Drum Major/Majorette, Marching Band, Pep Band, Team Managers • SPORTS-INTERCOLLEGIATE Baseball (M), Basketball (F), Basketball (M), Cross Country, Cross Country (F), Cross Country (M), Diving (F), Diving (M), Field Hockey (F), Football (M), Golf (F), Golf (M), Hammer Throw (M), Lacrosse (F), Lacrosse (M), Rugby (M), Soccer (F), Soccer (M), Softball (F), Swimming (F), Swimming (M), Synchronized Swimming, Tennis (F), Tennis (M), Track and Field, Track and Field (F), Track and Field (M), Volleyball (F), Water Polo (M) • SPORTS-INTRAMURAL Badminton, Basketball, Bowling, Cross Country, Diving, Golf, Ping-Pong, Racquetball, Soccer, Softball, Swimming, Tennis, Track and Field, Volleyball, Water Polo, Wrestling (M) • STUDENT LIFE ACTIVITIES Academic Clubs, Dance, Ethnic & Cultural Groups, Film, Fraternities, Music Groups, Newspaper, Political Groups, Radio, Religious Organization, Sororities, Student Government

---

Less Selective

Arkansas Accommodations

Arkansas State University

P.O. Box 1630
State University, Arkansas 72467
(501) 972-3024

School Enrollment: **9,182** Male: **4,003** Female: **5,179**
LD Enrollment: **15**

Admissions Contact: **Leonard McDaniel, Dean of Admission**
LD Contact: **Dr. J. Rice-Mason Asst., Dean of Students**

Admissions

Application Information:
Application deadline: **None**
Rolling Admissions: **Yes**

Secondary School Information
Most Important Criteria For Admissions (1-strongest)

2 SAT/ACT	**1** Application	**3** School transcript
Class rank	Course selection	Personal statement
Interview	Extra activities	Psychoeducational
G.P.A.	**1** Open admission	Recommendations

Test Requirements:
Untimed SAT: **Yes** Untimed ACT: **Yes** Untimed ACH: **Yes**

Types of Disabilities Served
• Speech/Lang	• Reading	• ADD with LD
• Study skills	• Spelling	• ADD without LD
• Written express	• Math	ADHD with LD
• Organizational	• Fine Motor	ADHD without LD
• Perceptual		

Admissions Process

Open admission

45

Arkansas

Learning Disability Program

Counseling: Individual: **Yes**

Faculty:
Faculty advocate: **Yes** Meets with instructor: **As needed**

Diagnostic Testing
ADD	Personality	Perceptual skills	Spelling
ADHD	Organization	Fine motor skills	Reading
I.Q.	Handwriting	Spoken language	Study skills
Math	Social skills	Written language	

Tutoring:
Services rendered by:
•Graduates •Peers •Faculty LD staff Teacher trainees

Tutorials
Grp.	Ind.	Tutorials	Grp.	Ind.	Tutorials
•	•	Math skills			Word processing
•	•	Study skills	•	•	Time management
		Language arts			Learning strategies
		Written express			Organizational skills

Academic Accommodations

Curriculum	Study Aids	Exams
Priority registration	Typist	• Oral
Math waiver	Reader	• Untimed
Foreign lang. waiver	Notetaker	Take home
• Course substitution	Proof reader	• With proctor
In Class	• Text on tape	• On computer
• Calculators	Early syllabus	• Extended time
• Tape recorder	Taped handouts	On tape
• Word processor		• Modified
Priority seating		Separate room

Graduation Requirements:
Course credits: **128** GPA: **2.0** Years to complete degree: **7 years**

Program Strengths

Students with handicaps or disabilities may receive information and counseling through the Office of Student Affairs. The Office of Student Affairs has designated an Assistant Dean of Students to assist disabled students at the University. Students are encouraged to seek assistance with orientation, registration, and making applications for scholarships. Other services provided include making referrals, consultations with faculty/staff, and personal and academic counseling.

General Information:

Arkansas State University is a 4 year public university. Urban campus of 800 acres is 75 miles from Memphis. Accessible by air or bus. Ski areas are 100 miles from campus. 3% of students are foreign. 6 residential halls on campus. Housing is guaranteed.10 % of students join fraternities/sororities.

Accreditation:NCACS

Expenses:
Tuition: In-state: Full year: $2,090.00. Part-time: Per credit:$59.00. Tuition: Out-of-state: Full year: $3,920.00. Part-time: Per credit:$112.00. Room and board: $2,440.00

Majors

• AGRICULTURE Business, Education, Plant Science • ANIMAL SCIENCE Dairy, Poultry • AREA STUDIES African, American, Asian, Black/Afro-American, Caribbean, Ethnic/Cultural, European, Hispanic/American, International Studies, Jewish/Judaism, Latin American, Mexican/American, Middle Eastern, Russian/Slavic, Scandinavian, Urban, Women's Studies • ARTS Art History, Commercial Art, Drafting, Dramatic Arts, Drawing, Film & Video, Graphic Arts, Landscaping, Museum Preservation, Museum Preservation, Music Performance, Painting, Photography, Religious Music, Sculpture, Theater Design • BUSINESS Accounting, Agricultural, Banking, Bookkeeping, Business Administration, Business Economics, Business Education, Business Management, Business Statistics, Clerical, Commercial Art, Data Processing, Economics, Education, Entrepreneur, Finance, Human Resource Development, Insurance, Management, Marketing, Marketing Research, Organizational Behavior, Personnel, Printing Manufacturing, Real Estate, Retail Manufacturing, Secretarial Science, Taxation, Vocational Studies • COMMUNICATION Advertising, Broadcasting, Commercial Design, Communication, English, Graphic Design, Journalism, Literature, Photography, Printing, Public Relations, Television/Radio/Film • COMPUTER SCIENCE Business Data Programming • CRAFTS AND DESIGN Ceramics, Crafts, Enameling, Glass, Graphic Design, Illustration Design, Industrial Design, Jewelry, Printmaking, Sculpture, Textile/Weaving • EDUCATION Adult, Agricultural, Art, Bilingual, Business, Child Development, Early Childhood, Elementary, English, English As A Second Language, Foreign Language, General, Health, Home Economics, Mathematics, Middle School, Music, Outdoor, Physical, Psychology, Reading, Recreation/Youth Leadership, School Psychology, Science, Secondary, Social Studies, Special, Speech/Language, Vocational • ENGINEERING Agricultural, Architectural, Aviation, Civil/Environmental, Computer, Drafting, Electrical, Engineering Science, Environmental/Water Resources, Mathematical, Mechanical, Radio/Television, Systems Analysis, Transportation Logistics • ENVIRONMENTAL CONTROL Air Pollution Control Technolo, Energy Conservation, Sanitation Technology, Solar Heating, Water and Wastewater Technolog • HEALTH SCIENCES Communication Disorders, Dietary Manager, Fitness, Health, Medical Records Technology, Medical Laboratory Technology, Medical Secretary, Nursing, Nursing Assistant, Nutritional/Food, Physical Therapy, Physician's Assistant, Practical Nursing, Public Health, Radiological Therapy, Rehabilitation, Respiratory Therapy, Speech Therapy, Speech/Audiology and Speech, Surgical Technology • HUMANITIES English/Writing/Literature, Fine Arts, Humanities, Liberal Arts , Philosophy, Religion • LANGUAGES Chinese, English, French, German, Japanese, Spanish • MATHEMATICS Actuarial, Applied, Computer, Statistical, Theoretical • PREPROFESSIONAL Agriculture, Architecture, Business, Dentistry, Engineering, Fisheries, Forestry, Law, Legal Assistant, Medicine, Natural Resources, Optometry, Pharmacy, Social Work, Sports Medicine, Veterinarian, Wildlife • RELIGIOUS STUDIES Philosophy, Religious Music • SCIENCES Agricultural, Animal, Anthropology, Applied Mathematics, Archeology, Astronomy, Bacteriology, Biochemistry, Biology, Biomedical, Biophysics, Botany, Microbiology, Physical Science, Poultry, Public Health, Radiology, Soil, Statistics, Zoology • SOCIAL SCIENCES Anthropology, Criminal Justice, Criminology, Family Counseling, Geography, Government/Political, History, Human Service, International Studies, Law Enforcement, Library Science, Political Science, Psychology, Public Relations, Social Sciences, Sociology, Urban and Regional Affair • SPECIAL EDUCATION Deaf/Hearing Impaired, Emotionally Disturbed, Gifted & Talented, Mentally Retarded, Occupational Therapy, Physically Handicapped, Visually Handicapped • VISUAL AND PERFORMING ARTS Art, Art History, Dramatic Arts, Fine Arts, Music, Music Performance, Music Theatre, Studio Art, Theater, Video • VOCATIONAL Aviation Pilot, Aviation Technology, Electronics Technology, Forestry, Legal Secretary, Library Assistant, Office Administration, Printing/Lithography, Radiological Technology, Secretarial, Word Processing

Sports/Activities

• SPORTS INTERCOLLEGIATE Archery (F), Archery (M), Badminton (F), Badminton (M), Basketball (F), Basketball (M), Bowling (F), Bowling (M), Diving (F), Diving (M), Football (M), Golf (F), Golf (M), Gymnastics (F), Gymnastics (M), Hand Ball (M), Ping-Pong (F), Ping-Pong (M), Racquetball (F), Racquetball (M), Riflery, Riflery (F), Scuba, Soccer (F), Soccer (M), Softball (F), Softball (M), Swimming (F), Swimming (M), Tennis (F), Tennis (M), Track and Field (F), Track and Field (M), Volleyball (F), Volleyball (M), Weight Lifting, Weight Lifting (M) • SPORTS INTRAMURAL Archery, Badminton, Basketball, Bowling, Football, Golf, Ping-Pong, Racquetball, Soccer (M), Softball, Swimming, Tennis, Volleyball
• SPORTS RELATED Baton Twirling, Cheerleading, Drill Team, Drum Major/Majorette, Marching Band, Pep Band, Team Managers • STUDENT

LIFE ACTIVITIES Academic Clubs, Choral, Community Service, Concert Band, Dance, Debate, Drama Groups, Ethnic & Cultural Groups, Film, Fraternities, Jazz Band, Magazine, Music Groups, Musical Theater, Newspaper, Orchestra, Political Groups, Radio/TV station, Religious Organization, Sororities, Student Government, Symphony Orchestra, Yearbook

Selective

Arkansas Services

Harding University
900 East Center Box 797
Searcy, Arkansas 72143
(501) 279-4000

School Enrollment: **3,341** Male: **1,528** Female: **1,813**

Admissions Contact: **Mike Williams, Director of Admissions**
LD Contact: **Linda Thompson, Director, Student Support Serv.**
Name of Program: **Student Support Services**
Address: **Box 797,Station A**
Telephone:**(501) 279-4028**

Admissions

Application Information:
LD Students Applying: **25** Accepted: **25**
LD on admissions committee:**Yes**
Rolling Admissions: **Yes**

Secondary School Information
Most Important Criteria For Admissions (1-strongest)

1 SAT/ACT	**1** Application	**1** School transcript
5 Class rank	**4** Course selection	Personal statement
Interview	**6** Extra activities	Psychoeducational
2 G.P.A.	Open admission	**3** Recommendations

Test Requirements:
Untimed SAT: **Yes** Untimed ACT: **Yes**
Documentation of LD required: **Yes**

Types of Disabilities Served
- Speech/Lang
- Study skills
- Written express
- Organizational
- Perceptual
- Reading
- Spelling
- Math
- Fine Motor
- ADD with LD
- ADD without LD
- ADHD with LD
- ADHD without LD

Admissions Process

Admission to Harding University is determined on an individual basis with the following criteria considered: (1) academic preparation, (2) character, (3) educational interests, and (4) academic potential.

High School Course Requirements:
English: **4** Math: **3** Science: **2**

Learning Disability Program

Program: Remedial: **Yes**
Program: Reinforces course work: **Yes**
Students mainstreamed **100** % of the day
Recommended credits per semester: **12-15**
Services available for all students: **Yes**
Counseling: Individual: **Yes** Group Counseling: **Yes** Vocational Counseling: **Yes**

Faculty:
Faculty: **8** Including Director: **Yes** Full time: **6** Part time: **2**
LD faculty with: BS/BA: **1** M.A.: **6**
Faculty advocate: **Yes** Meets with instructor: **As needed**

Diagnostic Testing
- ADD
- ADHD
- I.Q.
- Math
- Personality
- Organization
- Handwriting
- Social skills
- Perceptual skills
- Fine motor skills
- Spoken language
- Written language
- Spelling
- Reading
- Study skills

Tutoring:
Average size of group tutorials: **2-4**
Services rendered by:
- Graduates
- Peers
- Faculty
- LD staff
- Teacher trainees

Tutorials

Grp.	Ind.	Tutorials	Grp.	Ind.	Tutorials
•	•	Math skills	•	•	Word processing
•	•	Study skills	•	•	Time management
•	•	Language arts	•	•	Learning strategies
•	•	Written express	•	•	Organizational skills

Academic Accommodations

Curriculum	Study Aids	Exams
• Priority registration	Typist	• Oral
Math waiver	• Reader	• Untimed
Foreign lang. waiver	• Notetaker	Take home
Course substitution	• Proof reader	• With proctor
In Class	• Text on tape	On computer
Calculators	Early syllabus	• Extended time
• Tape recorder	Taped handouts	On tape
• Word processor		• Modified
Priority seating		• Separate room

Graduation Requirements:
Course credits: **128+** GPA: **1.2**

Program Strengths

We have a remedial/developmental program to remediate basic writing skills, reading skills, elementary algebra, and study skills. This is not specifically for LD students, although several LD students have been placed in the program. We also have a separate Learning Center which offers tutoring, study skills, and help for LD students. The Learning Center is open to all students who desire help.

General Information:

Harding University is a 4 year independent Church of Christ university. Suburban campus of 200 acres is 50 miles from Little Rock. 2.6% of students are foreign. 10 residential halls on campus. Housing is guaranteed.Guaranteed through 4th year. 70 % of students remain on campus for the weekends. 70 % of students join fraternities/sororities.

Accreditation:NCACS

SAT/ACT Scores:
Scores for incoming freshmen: **ACT:** 29% below 20. 34% between 20 and 23. 13%between 24 and 25l. 12%between 26 and 28. 12% above 28.

Expenses:
Tuition: In-state: Full year: Part-time: Per credit: $174.00. Room and board: $3,532.00

Majors

- AREA STUDIES American • BUSINESS Accounting, Business Administration, Business Economics, Business Education, Business Management, Economics, Management, Marketing, Office System, Professional Sales

Arkansas

• COMMUNICATION Advertising, Broadcasting, Communication, English, Journalism, Television/Radio/Film • COMPUTER SCIENCE Computer Science, Data Processing, Programming, Systems Analysis • EDUCATION Art, Early Childhood, Early Childhood, Elementary, Foreign Language, General, Health, Mathematics, Middle School, Music, Physical, Religious, Science, Secondary, Social Science, Social Studies, Special, Speech/Language • FINE AND PERFORMING ARTS Art, Music, Religious Music, Theater • HEALTH SCIENCES Communication Disorders, Medical Technology, Nursing, Nutritional/Food, Speech Therapy, Speech/Audiology and Speech • LANGUAGES French, German, Greek, Hebrew, Spanish • PHILOSOPHY English/Writing/Literature, Humanities, Missions, Religion, Religious Studies, Theological Studies, Youth and Ministry • PREPROFESSIONAL Agriculture, Architecture, Dentistry, Engineering, Law, Medicine, Ministry, Pharmacy, Social Work • SCIENCES Biochemistry, Biology, Chemistry, General Science, Mathematics, Physics • SOCIAL SCIENCES Government/Political, History, Human Resources, International Studies, Psychology, Social Sciences, Sociology • VOCATIONAL Home Economics, Office Administration, Secretarial, Textile and Clothing

Sports/Activities

• SPORTS INTERCOLLEGIATE Baseball, Baseball, Cross Country, Football (M), Softball (F), Tennis (M), Track and Field (M), Track and Field (M), Volleyball (F) • SPORTS INTRAMURAL Archery, Basketball, Bowling, Bowling (F), Football, Ping-Pong, Softball, Softball (F), Swimming, Volleyball • SPORTS RELATED Band, Cheerleading, Drum Major/Majorette, Marching Band, Pep Band, Team Managers • STUDENT LIFE ACTIVITIES Community Service, Debate, Drama Groups, Ethnic & Cultural Groups, Fraternities, Jazz Band, Music Groups, Newspaper, Radio/TV station, Sororities, Student Government, Symphony Orchestra, Yearbook

Selective   **Arkansas**
                                                 Services

Henderson State University
1100 Henderson Street
Arkadelphia, Arkansas 71999-0001
(501) 246-5511

School Enrollment: **3,486** Male: **1,436** Female: **2,050**
LD Enrollment: **13** Male: **7** Female: **6**

Admissions Contact: **Mr. Tom Gattin, Director of Admissions**
LD Contact: **Vickie Faust, Academic Coordinator**
Name of Program: **Student Support Services**
Address: **Box 7603, 1100 Henderson Street**
Telephone:**(501) 246-5511 - Ext. 3038**

Admissions

Application Information:
LD Students Applying: **13** Accepted: **13** Enrolled:**13**

Secondary School Information
Most Important Criteria For Admissions (1-strongest)

SAT/ACT	Application	School transcript
Class rank	Course selection	Personal statement
Interview	Extra activities	Psychoeducational
G.P.A.	Open admission	Recommendations

Test Requirements:
Untimed SAT: **Yes** Untimed ACT: **Yes**
Documentation of LD required: **Yes**

Types of Disabilities Served

Speech/Lang	Reading	ADD with LD
Study skills	Spelling	ADD without LD
Written express	Math	ADHD with LD
Organizational	Fine Motor	ADHD without LD
Perceptual		

Admissions Process

Semi-open admission: ACT Composite 19+ and 2.5 GPA (unconditional admittance). ACT Composite 15-18 (conditional admittance). ACT Composite below 15, must submit supplemental materials for committee approval.

High School Course Requirements:
English: **3** Math: **1** Science: **1**
Waivers to standard high school courses
Course substitution: **Yes**

Learning Disability Program

Students mainstreamed **100** % of the day
Counseling: Individual: **Yes** Group Counseling: **Yes** Vocational Counseling: **Yes**
Support groups are available:**Upon demand**

Faculty:Full time: **1**
Faculty advocate: **Yes**

Diagnostic Testing

ADD •	Personality	Perceptual skills	Spelling
ADHD	Organization	Fine motor skills	• Reading
I.Q.	Handwriting	Spoken language	• Study skills
• Math	Social skills	Written language	

Tutoring:
Average size of group tutorials: **1:1**
Services rendered by:
•Graduates •Peers Faculty LD staff Teacher trainees

Tutorials

Grp.	Ind.	Tutorials	Grp.	Ind.	Tutorials
	•	Math skills		•	Word processing
•		Study skills		•	Time management
		Language arts		•	Learning strategies
	•	Written express		•	Organizational skills

Academic Accommodations

Curriculum	Study Aids	Exams
• Priority registration	• Typist	• Oral
Math waiver	• Reader	Untimed
Foreign lang. waiver	• Notetaker	Take home
Course substitution	• Proof reader	• With proctor
In Class	• Text on tape	On computer
• Calculators	Early syllabus	• Extended time
• Tape recorder	Taped handouts	• On tape
Word processor		• Modified
• Priority seating		• Separate room

Graduation Requirements:
Course credits: **124** GPA: **2.0**

General Information:

Henderson State University is a 4 year public university. Rural campus 67 miles from Little Rock. Accessible by air, train, or bus. Beaches are 7 miles from campus. 1% of students are foreign. 8 residential halls on campus. Housing is not guaranteed.8 % of students join fraternities/sororities.

Accreditation:NCACS, NCATE, NLN

Expenses:
Tuition: In-state: Full year: $660.00. Part-time: Per credit:$57.00. Tuition: Out-of-state: Full year: $1,320.00. Part-time: Per credit:$114.00. Room and board: $1,502.00

Majors

• ARTS Music • BUSINESS Accounting, Business Administration, Business Education, Management, Marketing • COMMUNICATIONS Broadcasting, Communication, English, Journalism, Speech/Debate/Forensic • COMPUTER SCIENCE Computer Science • CRAFTS AND DESIGN Graphic Design • EDUCATION Art, Business, Early Childhood, Elementary, English, Home Economics, Mathematics, Music, Physical, Recreation/Youth Leadership, Science, Secondary, Social Studies, Special • HEALTH SCIENCES Nursing, Speech/Audiology and Speech • HUMANITIES English/Writing/Literature • LANGUAGES French, German, Spanish • MATHEMATICS Computer • SCIENCES Accounting, Biology, Chemistry, Physics • SOCIAL SCIENCES Government/Political, History, Human Service, Political Science, Psychology, Social Sciences, Sociology • SPECIAL EDUCATION Learning Disability, Mentally Retarded • VISUAL AND PERFORMING ARTS Art, Theater

Sports/Activities

• SPORTS RELATED Baton Twirling, Cheerleading, Drill Team, Drum Major/Majorette, Marching Band, Pep Band, Team Managers • SPORTS-INTERCOLLEGIATE Baseball (M), Basketball (F), Basketball (M), Cross Country, Diving, Football (M), Golf, Swimming, Tennis, Track and Field, Volleyball • SPORTS-INTRAMURAL Basketball, Football, Martial Arts, Racquetball, Softball, Volleyball • STUDENT LIFE ACTIVITIES Academic Clubs, Choral, Concert Band, Dance, Debate, Drama Groups, Ethnic & Cultural Groups, Fraternities, Jazz Band, Music Groups, Newspaper, Political Groups, Radio/TV station, Religious Organization, Sororities, Student Government, Yearbook

---

Less Selective **Arkansas**

Accommodations

Southern Arkansas University

SAU Box 1382
Magnolia, Arkansas 71753
(501) 235-4040

School Enrollment: **2,900** Male: **1,375** Female: **1,525**
LD Enrollment: **13**

Admissions Contact: **Mr. S. Whittington, Director of Admissions**
LD Contact: **Dr. Robert Terry, Director**
Name of Program: **Academic Opportunities Program**
Address: **SAU, Box 1250**
Telephone:**(501) 235-4160**

Admissions

Application Information:
Application deadline: **Open**

Secondary School Information
Most Important Criteria For Admissions (1-strongest)

SAT/ACT	Application	School transcript
Class rank	Course selection	Personal statement
Interview	Extra activities	Psychoeducational
G.P.A.	Open admission	Recommendations

Test Requirements:
Untimed SAT: **Yes** Untimed ACT: **Yes**
Documentation of LD required: **Yes**

Types of Disabilities Served
• Speech/Lang	• Reading	• ADD with LD
• Study skills	• Spelling	• ADD without LD
• Written express	• Math	• ADHD with LD
• Organizational	• Fine Motor	• ADHD without LD
• Perceptual		

Learning Disability Program
Services available for all students: **Yes**
Counseling: Individual: **Yes**
Support groups are available:**Supplemental instruction in some courses**

Faculty:
Faculty: **11** Part time: **11**
Faculty advocate: **Yes** Meets with instructor: **As needed**

Diagnostic Testing
ADD	Personality	Perceptual skills	Spelling
ADHD	Organization	Fine motor skills	Reading
I.Q.	Handwriting	Spoken language	Study skills
Math	Social skills	Written language	

Tutoring:
Average size of group tutorials: **Individual**
Services rendered by:
Graduates •Peers •Faculty •LD staff Teacher trainees

Tutorials
Grp.	Ind.	Tutorials	Grp.	Ind.	Tutorials
	•	Math skills		•	Word processing
		Study skills			Time management
		Language arts			Learning strategies
	•	Written express			Organizational skills

Academic Accommodations
Curriculum	Study Aids	Exams
Priority registration	Typist	• Oral
Math waiver	• Reader	Untimed
Foreign lang. waiver	• Notetaker	Take home
• Course substitution	Proof reader	• With proctor
In Class	• Text on tape	On computer
• Calculators	Early syllabus	• Extended time
• Tape recorder	Taped handouts	On tape
• Word processor		• Modified
• Priority seating		Separate room

Graduation Requirements:
Course credits: **125+ field** GPA: **2.0**

Program Strengths
We serve LD students through the Academic Opportunities Program. The AOP Director attempts to educate faculty with LD students enrolled in their classes and secures extended test time and alternate means of testing. We furnish free tutoring and readers. In order to be served, LD students must provide special certification of their disability and recommendations for appropriate accommodations from a psychological examiner.

General Information:
Southern Arkansas University is a 4 year public university. Rural campus of 830 acres is 70 miles from Shreveport, LA. Accessible by bus. 1% of

students are foreign. 6 residential halls on campus. Housing is guaranteed.15 % of students remain on campus for the weekends. 5 % of students join fraternities/sororities.

Accreditation: NCA

SAT/ACT Scores:
Scores for incoming freshmen: **ACT:** 77% below 20. 10% between 20 and 23. 10%between 24 and 251. 2%between 26 and 28. 2% above 28.

Expenses:
Tuition: In-state: Full year: $1,128.00. Part-time: Per credit: $50.00. Tuition: Out-of-state: Full year: $1,758.00. Part-time: Per credit:$76.00. Room and board: $2,100.00

Majors

• BUSINESS Accounting, Agri-business, Business Administration, Business Economics, Business Management, Finance • COMMUNICATIONS Communication, English, Radio/Television, Radio/Television Technology, Speech • EDUCATION Early Childhood, Elementary, Secondary, Special • ENGINEERING Engineering Physics • LANGUAGES French, Spanish • SCIENCES Agricultural, Biology, Chemistry, Mathematics, Political Science • SOCIAL SCIENCES History, Sociology • VISUAL AND PERFORMING ARTS Dramatic Arts, Music • VOCATIONAL Industrial Technology, Secretarial

Sports/Activities

• SPORTS INTERCOLLEGIATE Baseball (M), Basketball, Football (M), Golf, Soccer, Track and Field • SPORTS INTRAMURAL Archery, Badminton, Basketball, Gymnastics, Hand Ball, Ping-Pong, Racquetball, Softball, Swimming, Tennis, Volleyball • SPORTS RELATED Band, Cheerleading, Drill Team, Drum Major/Majorette, Marching Band, Pep Band, Team Managers • STUDENT LIFE ACTIVITIES Drama Groups, Ethnic & Cultural Groups, Fraternities, Jazz Band, Marching BandMusic Groups, Newspaper, Radio/TV station, Religious Organization, Sororities, Student Government, Symphony Orchestra, Yearbook

---

Less Selective   **Arkansas**
                                              Services

University of Arkansas at Pine Bluff
University Drive
Pine Bluff, Arkansas 71601
(501) 541-6542

School Enrollment: **5,100** Male: **1,300** Female: **2,800**

Admissions Contact: **Ms. Kwurly M. Floyd, Acting Adms. Director**
LD Contact: **Aaron Van Wright**
Telephone:**(501) 541-6652**

Admissions

Application Information:
Application deadline: **None**
Rolling Admissions: **Yes**

Secondary School Information
Most Important Criteria For Admissions (1-strongest)

SAT/ACT	Application	School transcript
Class rank	Course selection	Personal statement
Interview	Extra activities	Psychoeducational
G.P.A.	Open admission	Recommendations

Test Requirements:
Untimed SAT: **Yes** Untimed ACT: **Yes**

Types of Disabilities Served

• Speech/Lang	• Reading	• ADD with LD
• Study skills	• Spelling	ADD without LD
• Written express	• Math	• ADHD with LD
• Organizational	• Fine Motor	ADHD without LD
• Perceptual		

Learning Disability Program
Counseling: Individual: **Yes** Group Counseling: **Yes**

Faculty:
Faculty: **6** Full time: **6**
Faculty advocate: **Yes**

Diagnostic Testing

ADD	Personality	Perceptual skills	Spelling
ADHD	Organization	Fine motor skills	Reading
I.Q.	Handwriting	Spoken language	Study skills
Math	Social skills	Written language	

Tutoring:
Services rendered by:
Graduates   •Peers   •Faculty   LD staff   Teacher trainees

Tutorials

Grp.	Ind.	Tutorials	Grp.	Ind.	Tutorials
•	•	Math skills			Word processing
		Study skills			Time management
•	•	Language arts			Learning strategies
		Written express			Organizational skills

Academic Accommodations

Curriculum	Study Aids	Exams
Priority registration	Typist	• Oral
Math waiver	Reader	Untimed
Foreign lang. waiver	• Notetaker	Take home
• Course substitution	Proof reader	With proctor
In Class	Text on tape	On computer
• Calculators	Early syllabus	Extended time
• Tape recorder	Taped handouts	On tape
• Word processor		Modified
Priority seating		Separate room

Program Strengths
We do not offer a special program for learning disabled students. Our staff assists those students who have difficulty with reading, writing, and language skills. We have advisors not advocates.

General Information:
University of Arkansas at Pine Bluff is a 4 year public university. Suburban campus of 300 acres is 5 miles from Pine Bluff. Accessible by bus. Housing is not guaranteed.

Accreditation: NCACS

Expenses:
Tuition: In-state: Full year: $1,260.00. Part-time: Per credit:$66.00. Tuition: Out-of-state: Full year: $2,997.50. Part-time: Per credit:$157.00.

Majors
• AREA STUDIES • BUSINESS Accounting, Agricultural, Business Administration, Business Education, Business Management, Economics • COMMUNICATIONS • COMPUTER SCIENCE Computer Science • EDUCATION Agricultural, Art, Curriculum, Early Childhood, Elementary, English, Industrial, Mathematics, Music, Physical, Science, Secondary, Special • HEALTH SCIENCES Nursing, Nutritional/Food • HUMANI-

TIES English/Writing/Literature, Liberal Arts • LANGUAGES • PRE-PROFESSIONAL Engineering, Social Work • SCIENCES Animal, Biology, Chemistry, Gerontology, Mathematics, Physics • SOCIAL SCIENCES Criminal Justice, Criminology, Human Service, Law Enforcement, Psychology, Social Sciences, Sociology • VISUAL AND PERFORMING ARTS Dramatic Arts, Music • VOCATIONAL Automobile Technology, Fashion Mechandizing, Fishery Studies, Industrial Equipment Maintenan, Park/Recreation, Textile and Clothing

Sports/Activities

• SPORTS RELATED Cheerleading, Drum Major/Majorette, Marching Band, Pep Band • SPORTS-INTERCOLLEGIATE Basketball, Football (M), Tennis, Track and Field, Volleyball (F) • SPORTS-INTRAMURAL Baseball, Basketball, Cross Country, Football (M), Golf, Hand Ball, Racquetball, Soccer (M), Softball, Swimming, Swimming, Tennis, Track and Field, Volleyball, Wrestling (M) • STUDENT LIFE ACTIVITIES Drama Groups, Ethnic & Cultural Groups, Fraternities, Jazz Band, Music Groups, Newspaper, Religious Organization, Sororities, Student Government, Symphony Orchestra, Yearbook

Less Selective	Arkansas Program

University of the Ozarks
415 College Avenue
Clarksville, Arkansas 72830
(501) 754-8715

School Enrollment: **750** Male: **360** Female: **390**
LD Enrollment: **90**
LD Contact: **Dale Jordan, Ph.D. Director**
Name of Program: **Jones Learning Center**
Address: **415 College Avenue**
Telephone:**(501) 754-3839 Ext. 403**

Admissions

Application Information:
Enrolled:**90**
Separate application:**Yes**
LD on admissions committee:**Yes**
Application deadline: **March 15th**
Applicant must apply **12** months in advance
Notified when: **April 15th**

Secondary School Information
Most Important Criteria For Admissions (1-strongest)

SAT/ACT	**4**	Application	**5** School transcript
Class rank	**7**	Course selection	**6** Personal statement
2 Interview		Extra activities	**1** Psychoeducational
G.P.A.		Open admission	**3** Recommendations

Test Requirements:
Diagnostic testing waived: **Yes**
Untimed ACT: **Yes**
WAIS-R required: **Yes** Range accepted: **90+**
Documentation of LD required: **Yes**
Currency of diagnostic testing: **No more than 6 months**
Tests recommended: **Psycho-educational evaluation at our facility**

Types of Disabilities Served
• Speech/Lang
• Study skills
• Written express
• Organizational
• Perceptual
• Reading
• Spelling
• Math
• Fine Motor
• ADD with LD
• ADD without LD
• ADHD with LD
• ADHD without LD

Admissions Process

Complete application, schedule two days for campus visit and testing. Based on interview and tests decision is made as to eligibility.

High School Course Requirements:

Learning Disability Program
Special orientation for LD students: **Yes**
Program: Remedial: **Yes**
Program: Reinforces course work: **Yes**
Services only for LD students: **Yes**
Counseling: Individual: **Yes** Vocational Counseling: **Yes**

Faculty:
Faculty: **23** Including Director: **Yes** Full time: **21** Part time: **2**
LD faculty with: BS/BA: **4** M.A.: **11** Ph.D.: **2**

Diagnostic Testing
ADD	• Personality	• Perceptual skills	• Spelling
ADHD	• Organization	• Fine motor skills	• Reading
• I.Q.	• Handwriting	• Spoken language	• Study skills
• Math	Social skills	• Written language	

Tutoring:
Average size of group tutorials: **5**
Services rendered by:
•Graduates   •Peers   Faculty   •LD staff   Teacher trainees

Tutorials
Grp.	Ind.	Tutorials	Grp.	Ind.	Tutorials
•	•	Math skills	•	•	Word processing
•	•	Study skills	•	•	Time management
•	•	Language arts	•	•	Learning strategies
•	•	Written express	•	•	Organizational skills

Academic Accommodations
Curriculum	Study Aids	Exams
Priority registration	• Typist	• Oral
Math waiver	• Reader	Untimed
• Foreign lang. waiver	• Notetaker	Take home
Course substitution	• Proof reader	• With proctor
In Class	• Text on tape	On computer
• Calculators	Early syllabus	• Extended time
• Tape recorder	• Taped handouts	• On tape
• Word processor		Modified
Priority seating		• Separate room

Graduation Requirements:
Course credits: **133** GPA: **2.0** Years to complete degree: **4-5** Language waiver: **Yes**

Program Strengths
The Jones Learning Center provides a unique opportunity for college-age students who have been diagnosed as having specific learning disabilities. We have designed the Learning Center Program to emphasize the University as a total learning environment. Our college community is small enough to be cohesive, allowing our staff to collaborate more closely to achieve our goals.

General Information:
University of the Ozarks is a 4 year independent Presbyterian university. Rural campus 60 miles from Fort Smith. 3 residential halls on campus. Housing is guaranteed.50 % of students remain on campus for the weekends.

California

Accreditation:NCACS

Expenses:
Tuition: In-state: Full year: $3,400.00. Room and board: $2,330.00 Cost of LD program:$10,750.00

Majors

• BUSINESS Accounting, Business Administration, Business Education, Business Management, Entrepreneur, Marketing • COMMUNICATION Commercial Design, Journalism • EDUCATION Art, Elementary, English, History, Middle School, Physical, Religion, Science, Secondary, Social Studies • HEALTH SCIENCES Medical Technology, Radiological Therapy, Respiratory Therapy • PHILOSOPHY English/Writing/Literature, Liberal Arts, Philosophy, Religion • PREPROFESSIONAL Dentistry, Engineering, Law, Medicine, Ministry, Pharmacy, Veterinarian • SCIENCES Biology, Mathematics, Physical Science, Physiology • SOCIAL SCIENCES Government/Political, History, Psychology, Public Relations, Social Sciences, Sociology • VISUAL AND PERFORMING ARTS Dramatic Arts, Fine Arts, Music, Theater • VOCATIONAL Medical Laboratory Technology, Secretarial

Sports/Activities

• SPORTS-INTERCOLLEGIATE Basketball, Cross Country, Football (M), Golf, Soccer (M), Tennis, Track and Field (F), Track and Field (M) • SPORTS-INTRAMURAL Badminton, Basketball, Football (M), Racquetball, Softball, Tennis, Track and Field (M), Volleyball • STUDENT LIFE ACTIVITIES Choral, Community Service, Concert Band, Drama Groups, Ethnic & Cultural Groups, Jazz Band, Magazine, Music Groups, Musical Theater, Newspaper, Radio/TV station, Religious Organization, Student Government, Yearbook

---

Less Selective	California
	Program

Antelope Valley College
3041 West Avenue K
Lancaster, California 93536
(805) 943-3241

School Enrollment: **11,000** Male: **5,050** Female: **5,950**
LD Enrollment: **175** Male: **70** Female: **105**

Admissions Contact: **Jim McDonald, Admissions Officer**
LD Contact: **David Greenleaf, Prescriptive Learning Instructor**
Name of Program: **Learning Disabilities Program**
Telephone:**(805) 943-3241 Ext. 278**

Admissions

Application Information:
LD Students Applying: **110** Accepted: **80** Enrolled:**80**
Rolling Admissions: **Yes**

Secondary School Information
Most Important Criteria For Admissions (1-strongest)

SAT/ACT	Application	School transcript
Class rank	Course selection	Personal statement
Interview	Extra activities	Psychoeducational
G.P.A.	**1** Open admission	Recommendations

Test Requirements:
Tests recommended: **WAIS-R or Woodcock-Johnson**

Types of Disabilities Served
- Speech/Lang
- Reading
- ADD with LD
- Study skills
- Spelling
- ADD without LD
- Written express
- Math
- ADHD with LD
- Organizational
- Fine Motor
- ADHD without LD
- Perceptual

Learning Disability Program
Program: Reinforces course work: **Yes**
Students mainstreamed **95** % of the day
Counseling: Individual: **Yes**

Faculty:
Faculty: **2** Including Director: **Yes** Full time: **1** Part time: **1**
LD faculty with: BS/BA: **2** M.A.: **1**
Faculty advocate: **Yes** Meets with instructor: **Twice/semester**

Diagnostic Testing

ADD	• Personality	• Perceptual skills	• Spelling
ADHD	• Organization	• Fine motor skills	• Reading
• I.Q.	• Handwriting	• Spoken language	• Study skills
• Math	Social skills	• Written language	

Tutoring:
Services rendered by:
Graduates •Peers •Faculty •LD staff Teacher trainees

Tutorials

Grp.	Ind.	Tutorials	Grp.	Ind.	Tutorials
	•	Math skills		•	Word processing
	•	Study skills			Time management
	•	Language arts			Learning strategies
	•	Written express		•	Organizational skills

Academic Accommodations

Curriculum	Study Aids	Exams
• Priority registration	• Typist	• Oral
Math waiver	• Reader	Untimed
Foreign lang. waiver	• Notetaker	• Take home
Course substitution	• Proof reader	• With proctor
In Class	• Text on tape	• On computer
• Calculators	Early syllabus	• Extended time
• Tape recorder	Taped handouts	On tape
• Word processor		• Modified
• Priority seating		• Separate room

Graduation Requirements:
Course credits: **60** GPA: **2.0**

Program Strengths
Our program is designed to facilitate a student's success, and to that end, we provide a full range of support services.

General Information:
Antelope Valley College is a 2 year public college. Urban campus of 160 acres is 70 miles from Los Angeles. Accessible by air, train or bus. Ski areas are 1 hour from campus. Beaches are 1.5 miles from campus. Housing is not guaranteed.

Accreditation:WACS

Expenses: Part-time: Per credit:$6.00. Part-time: Per credit:$102.00 .

Majors

• BUSINESS Business Administration, Business Management, Economics, Management, Marketing, Real Estate • COMMUNICATIONS English, Journalism, Photography • COMPUTER SCIENCE Computer Science, Data Processing, Programming • CRAFTS AND DESIGN Graphic Design • EDUCATION Early Childhood, Physical, Recreation and Youth Leadershi, Teacher's Aid • ENGINEERING Engineering Science • HEALTH SCIENCES Medical Assistant, Medical Technology, Nursing • HUMANITIES Liberal Arts • PREPROFESSIONAL Agriculture, Architecture, Drafting, Engineering, Forestry, Recreation • SCIENCES Agricultural, Biology, Chemistry, Geography, Mathematics, Natural, Physical Science, Physics, Zoology • SOCIAL SCIENCES Criminal Justice, Government/Political, History, Law Enforcement, Psychology, Social Sciences, Sociology • VISUAL AND PERFORMING ARTS Art, Music • VOCATIONAL Air Conditioning/Heating/Refri, Automobile Technology, Construction, Food Service, Home Economics, Jewelry-Metalsmithery, Office Administration, Secretarial

Sports/Activities

• SPORTS RELATED Pep Band • SPORTS-INTERCOLLEGIATE Baseball (M), Basketball, Cross Country, Football, Golf, Softball (F), Tennis, Track and Field, Volleyball (F) • SPORTS-INTRAMURAL Badminton, Basketball, Volleyball (F) • STUDENT LIFE ACTIVITIES Choral, Concert Band, Dance, Drama Groups, Film, Jazz Band, Music Groups, Musical Theater, Newspaper, Student Government, Symphony Orchestra

Less Selective	California Program

Bakersfield College
1801 Panorama Drive
Bakersfield, California 93305
(805) 395-4557

School Enrollment: **12,200** Male: **5,490** Female: **6,710**
LD Enrollment: **200**

Admissions Contact: **Robert Bruker, Director of Admissions**
LD Contact: **Joyce Kirst/Debbie Shinn, LD Specialists**
Name of Program: **Supportive Services**
Telephone:**(805) 395-4334**

Admissions

Application Information:
LD Students Applying: **200** Accepted: **150** Enrolled:**200**
Rolling Admissions: **Yes**

Secondary School Information
Most Important Criteria For Admissions (1-strongest)

SAT/ACT	**1**	Application	**1**	School transcript
Class rank		Course selection		Personal statement
Interview		Extra activities		Psychoeducational
G.P.A.		Open admission		Recommendations

Test Requirements:
Standardized tests waived: **Yes**
Diagnostic testing waived: **Yes**
Achievement tests required:**1**
Documentation of LD required: **Yes**
Currency of diagnostic testing: **36 months or on site**
Tests recommended: **Woodcock-Johnson Psycho-Educational Battery I and II and Achievement Test such as WRAT - California Norms.**

Types of Disabilities Served
• Speech/Lang • Reading • ADD with LD
• Study skills • Spelling   ADD without LD
• Written express • Math • ADHD with LD
• Organizational • Fine Motor   ADHD without LD
• Perceptual

Admissions Process
Submit application and transcripts - open admission

Learning Disability Program
Special orientation for LD students: **Yes**
Syllabus available during orientation:**Yes**
Program: Remedial: **Yes**
Program: Reinforces course work: **Yes**
Program available through:**August-May**
Students mainstreamed **100** % of the day
Services available for all students: **Yes**
Counseling: Individual: **Yes** Vocational Counseling: **Yes**

Faculty:
Faculty: **12** Full time: **2** Part time: **10** M.A.: **2**
Faculty advocate: **Yes** Meets with instructor: **As needed**

Diagnostic Testing
ADD	Personality	• Perceptual skills	• Spelling
ADHD	Organization	Fine motor skills	• Reading
I.Q.	Handwriting	Spoken language	Study skills
• Math	Social skills	• Written language	

Tutoring:
Average size of group tutorials: **Individualized**
Services rendered by:
  Graduates •Peers •Faculty •LD staff •Teacher trainees

Tutorials
Grp.	Ind.	Tutorials	Grp.	Ind.	Tutorials
•		Math skills	•		Word processing
•		Study skills			Time management
•		Language arts	•	•	Learning strategies
•	•	Written express			Organizational skills

Academic Accommodations
Curriculum	Study Aids	Exams
Priority registration	Typist	• Oral
Math waiver	• Reader	Untimed
Foreign lang. waiver	• Notetaker	Take home
Course substitution	Proof reader	With proctor
In Class	• Text on tape	• On computer
• Calculators	Early syllabus	• Extended time
• Tape recorder	Taped handouts	On tape
• Word processor		Modified
Priority seating		• Separate room

General Information:
Bakersfield College is a 2 year public college. Urban campus 130 miles from Los Angeles. Accessible by air, bus, or train. .1% of students are foreign. Housing is not guaranteed.

Accreditation:WACS

Expenses: Part-time: Per credit:$6.00 to a maximum of $60.00.
Tuition: Out-of-state: Full year: $102.00 per unit to maximum of 15

units. Room and board: $5,500.00 Cost of LD program:None

Majors

• AGRICULTURE • BUSINESS Accounting, Banking/Finance, Business Administration, Economics, Management, Marketing • COMMUNICATIONS Communication, English • EDUCATION Early Childhood, Secondary, Special • ENGINEERING Environmental/Water Resources, Petroleum • HEALTH SCIENCES Medical Laboratory Technology, Nursing, Public Health • HUMANITIES Fine Arts, Philosophy, Religion • PRE PROFESSIONAL Dentistry, Engineering, Law, Medicine, Pharmacy, Veterinarian • SCIENCES Agricultural, Biochemistry, Biology, Chemistry, Computer Science, Geology, Mathematics, Physics • SOCIAL SCIENCES Anthropology, Criminal Justice, History, Political Science, Psychology, Public Relations, Sociology

Sports/Activities

• SPORTS-INTERCOLLEGIATE Baseball (M), Basketball, Cross Country, Diving, Football (M), Golf (M), Softball (F), Swimming, Tennis, Track and Field, Volleyball (F), Wrestling (M)

Selective

California Services

Biola University
13800 Biola Avenue
La Mirada, California 90639
(213) 944-0351

School Enrollment: **2,566** Male: **1,268** Female: **1,298**
LD Enrollment: **6** Male: **3** Female: **3**

Admissions Contact: **Mr. Greg Vaughan, Dean of Admission**
LD Contact: **David Young Dean, Student Relations**
Name of Program: **Disabled Student Services**
Telephone:**(213) 903-4874**

Admissions

Application Information:
Application deadline: **June 1st**

Secondary School Information
Most Important Criteria For Admissions (1-strongest)

2 SAT/ACT	10 Application	6 School transcript
7 Class rank	8 Course selection	3 Personal statement
5 Interview	9 Extra activities	Psychoeducational
1 G.P.A.	Open admission	4 Recommendations

Test Requirements:
Untimed SAT: **Yes**

Types of Disabilities Served
• Speech/Lang • Reading   ADD with LD
• Study skills • Spelling   ADD without LD
• Written express • Math   ADHD with LD
• Organizational • Fine Motor ADHD without LD
• Perceptual

High School Course Requirements:

Learning Disability Program
Counseling: Individual: **Yes** Group Counseling: **Yes**

Faculty:
Faculty: **2** Full time: **2**
Faculty advocate: **Yes**

Diagnostic Testing

ADD	Personality	Perceptual skills	Spelling
ADHD	Organization	Fine motor skills	Reading
I.Q.	Handwriting	Spoken language	Study skills
Math	Social skills	Written language	

Tutoring:
Average size of group tutorials: **10**
Services rendered by:
•Graduates •Peers •Faculty •LD staff Teacher trainees

Tutorials

Grp.	Ind.	Tutorials	Grp.	Ind.	Tutorials
•	•	Math skills	•	•	Word processing
•		Study skills	•	•	Time management
•	•	Language arts	•	•	Learning strategies
•	•	Written express	•	•	Organizational skills

Academic Accommodations

Curriculum	Study Aids	Exams
Priority registration	Typist	• Oral
Math waiver	Reader	Untimed
• Foreign lang. waiver	• Notetaker	• Take home
• Course substitution	Proof reader	With proctor
In Class	• Text on tape	On computer
• Calculators	Early syllabus	• Extended time
• Tape recorder	Taped handouts	On tape
• Word processor		• Modified
Priority seating		Separate room

Program Strengths
It is our commitment to enable physically disabled students to complete an appropriately-adjusted academic program and to graduate. Our services are not unique in themselves. We serve best those who are seeking an undergraduate education in a religiously-oriented, comprehensive university.

General Information:
Biola University is a 4 year independent interdenominational university. Suburban campus of 128 acres is 30 miles from Los Angeles. Accessible by air, train, or bus. Ski areas are 60 miles from campus. Beaches are 15 miles from campus. 7.4% of students are foreign. 10 residential halls on campus. Housing is not guaranteed.30 % of students remain on campus for the weekends.

Accreditation:WASC, ATS, APS, NASM, NLN

SAT/ACT Scores:
Scores for incoming freshmen:**Verbal:**40%below 500. 40%between 500 and 599. 15%between 600 and 699. 5%above 700. **Math:**30% below 500. 50% between 500 and 599. 15% between 600 and 699. 5%above 700.

Expenses:
Tuition: In-state: Full year: $9,172.00. Part-time: Per credit:Part-time: $382.00. Room and board: $3,820.00

Majors
• AREA STUDIES American, Asian, Black/Afro-American, Latin American • BUSINESS Accounting, Business Administration, Business Economics, Business Management, Finance, Management, Marketing • COMMUNICATIONS Broadcasting, Communication, Creative Writing, English, Journalism, Photography, Television/Radio/Film • COMPUTER SCIENCE Data Processing, Programming, Systems Analysis • EDUCA-

TION Art, Curriculum, Early Childhood, Elementary, Middle School, Music, Psychology, Recreation and Youth Leadershi, School Psychology, Secondary, Speech/Language • HEALTH SCIENCES Nursing, Speech Therapy, Speech/Audiology and Speech • HUMANITIES Humanities, Philosophy, Religion • LANGUAGES French, German, Greek, Hebrew, Spanish • PREPROFESSIONAL Engineering, Medicine, Ministry, Recreation, Social Work • SCIENCES Biochemistry, Biology, Botany, Chemistry, Geography, Macrobiology, Marine Biology, Mathematics, Microbiology, Oceanography, Physical Science, Physics • SOCIAL SCIENCES Anthropology, Geography, Government/Political, History, Political Science, Psychology, Social Sciences, Sociology • VISUAL AND PERFORMING ARTS Art, Music, Studio Art, Theater

Sports/Activities

• SPORTS RELATED Band, Cheerleading, Pep Band • SPORTS-INTERCOLLEGIATE Baseball (M), Basketball, Cross Country (M), Soccer (M), Tennis, Track and Field (M), Volleyball (M), Wrestling (M) • SPORTS-INTRAMURAL Archery, Badminton, Football (M), Golf, Racquetball, Softball, Swimming, Volleyball • STUDENT LIFE ACTIVITIES Choral, Concert Band, Drama Groups, Film Production, Jazz Band, Music Ensembles, Music Groups, Musical Theater, Opera, Radio/TV station, Religious Organization, Student Government, Symphony Orchestra, Yearbook

---

Less Selective　　　　　　　　　　　**California Program**

Butte College

3536 Butte Campus Drive
Oronville, California 95965
(916) 895-2361

School Enrollment: **12,369**
LD Enrollment: **150**

Admissions Contact: **Don Gray, Director of Admissions**
LD Contact: **Richard Dunn, LD Specialist**
Name of Program: **Ed. Testing & Learning Center**
Telephone: **(916) 895-2455**

Admissions

Secondary School Information

Most Important Criteria For Admissions (1-strongest)

SAT/ACT	Application	School transcript
Class rank	Course selection	Personal statement
Interview	Extra activities	Psychoeducational
G.P.A.	**1** Open admission	Recommendations

Test Requirements:

Tests recommended: **California Community College Assessment Model**

Types of Disabilities Served

• Speech/Lang	• Reading	• ADD with LD
• Study skills	• Spelling	• ADD without LD
• Written express	• Math	• ADHD with LD
• Organizational	• Fine Motor	• ADHD without LD
• Perceptual		

Learning Disability Program

Program: Remedial: **Yes**
Program: Reinforces course work: **Yes**
Students mainstreamed **100** % of the day

Faculty:

Faculty: **12** Including Director: **Yes** Full time: **2** Part time: **10**
Faculty advocate: **Yes** Meets with instructor: **As needed**

Diagnostic Testing

• ADD	Personality	• Perceptual skills	• Spelling
ADHD	• Organization	Fine motor skills	• Reading
I.Q.	Handwriting	• Spoken language	• Study skills
• Math	Social skills	• Written language	

Tutoring:

Average size of group tutorials: **Individual**
Services rendered by:
　Graduates　•Peers　•Faculty　•LD staff　　Teacher trainees

Tutorials

Grp.	Ind.	Tutorials	Grp.	Ind.	Tutorials
	•	Math skills		•	Word processing
	•	Study skills		•	Time management
	•	Language arts		•	Learning strategies
	•	Written express		•	Organizational skills

Academic Accommodations

Curriculum	Study Aids	Exams
Priority registration	Typist	• Oral
Math waiver	Reader	Untimed
Foreign lang. waiver	• Notetaker	• Take home
Course substitution	• Proof reader	With proctor
In Class	• Text on tape	On computer
• Calculators	Early syllabus	• Extended time
• Tape recorder	Taped handouts	On tape
• Word processor		Modified
Priority seating		Separate room

Program Strengths

Butte Community College is a rural, northern California campus which provides direct services to approximately 150 LD students annually. Eligibility for services is determined by the system-wide California Community College Assessment Model. Eligible students can be served with individualized services and a high tech center featuring computer instruction and personalized computer adaptation.

General Information:

Butte College is a 2 year public college. Rural campus of 960 acres is 16 miles from Chico. Housing is not guaranteed.

Accreditation: Regional

Expenses: Part-time: Per credit:$5.00.　Part-time: Per credit:$96.00.

Majors

• BUSINESS Accounting, Agricultural, Business Administration, Business Management, Economics, Management, Marketing, Real Estate, Travel/Tourism Management • COMMUNICATIONS Advertising, Broadcasting, Commercial Design, Communication, English, Journalism, Photography, Television/Radio/Film • COMPUTER SCIENCE Computer Science, Data Processing, Programming, Telecommunications • CRAFTS AND DESIGN Ceramics, Graphic Design • EDUCATION Art, Bilingual, Child Development, Early Childhood, Health, Industrial, Physical, Vocational • ENGINEERING Civil/Environmental • ENVIRONMENTAL CONTROL Water and Wastewater Technolog • HUMANITIES Humanities, Liberal Arts, Philosophy • LANGUAGES French, German, Italian, Spanish • PREPROFESSIONAL Agriculture, Architecture, Law, Natural Resources • SCIENCES Animal, Astronomy, Biology, Chemistry, Earth, Geography, Horticultural, Mathematics, Physical Science • SOCIAL SCIENCES Anthropology, Criminal Justice, Geography, Government/Political, History,

California

Law Enforcement, Psychology, Social Sciences, Sociology • VISUAL AND PERFORMING ARTS Art, Fine Arts, Studio Art, Theater • VOCATIONAL Automobile Technology, Drafting, Electronics Technology, Fashion Mechandizing, Fire Science, Home Economics, Legal Secretary, Paralegal, Park/Recreation, Respiratory Therapy Technology, Secretarial, Textile and Clothing, Welding, Word Processing

Sports/Activities

• SPORTS RELATED Pep Band • SPORTS-INTERCOLLEGIATE Baseball (M), Basketball, Cross Country, Fencing, Football (M), Golf (M), Softball (F), Tennis, Track and Field, Volleyball (F), Wrestling (M) • STUDENT LIFE ACTIVITIES Concert Band, Film, Jazz Band, Music Ensembles, Music Groups, Newspaper, Radio/TV station, Student Government, Symphony Orchestra

---

Less Selective   **California Services**

Cabrillo College

6500 Soquel Drive
Aptos, California 95003
(408) 479-6220

School Enrollment: **13,500** Male: **5,825** Female: **7,755**
LD Enrollment: **175**

Admissions Contact: **Gloria Garing, Registrar**
LD Contact: **Richard Griffiths, Program Coordinator**
Name of Program: **Learning Skills Program**
Telephone:**(408) 479-6220**

Admissions

Application Information:
Enrolled:**175**
Applicant must apply **3** months in advance

Secondary School Information
Most Important Criteria For Admissions (1-strongest)

SAT/ACT	Application	School transcript
Class rank	Course selection	Personal statement
Interview	Extra activities	Psychoeducational
G.P.A.	Open admission	Recommendations

Test Requirements:
Diagnostic testing waived: **Yes**
Documentation of LD required: **Yes**
Tests recommended: **Woodcock-Johnson Psychoeducational Battery Parts 1 and 2 or WAIS-R**

Types of Disabilities Served
- Speech/Lang
- Study skills
- Written express
- Organizational
- Perceptual
- Reading
- Spelling
- Math
- Fine Motor
- ADD with LD
- ADD without LD
- ADHD with LD
- ADHD without LD

Admissions Process

Complete college application, open to all students 18 years or older - college assessment is required, (waived for LD students), placement is advisory not mandatory.

High School Course Requirements:
Waivers to standard high school courses
Course substitution: **Yes**

Learning Disability Program

Special orientation for LD students: **Yes**
Syllabus available during orientation:**Yes**
Program: Remedial: **Yes**
Program: Reinforces course work: **Yes**
Program available through:**Daily**
Students mainstreamed **100** % of the day
Recommended credits per semester: **Variable**
Counseling: Individual: **Yes** Group Counseling: **Yes** Vocational Counseling: **Yes**
Support groups are available:**LD, ABI (Acquired Brain Injury)**

Faculty:
Faculty: **9** Including Director: **Yes** Full time: **1** Part time: **3**
LD faculty with: BS/BA: **8** M.A.: **5**
Faculty advocate: **Yes** Meets with instructor: **As needed**

Diagnostic Testing
- ADD
- ADHD
- I.Q.
- Math
- Personality
- Organization
- Handwriting
- Social skills
- Perceptual skills
- Fine motor skills
- Spoken language
- Written language
- Spelling
- Reading
- Study skills

Tutoring:
Average size of group tutorials: **5**
Services rendered by:
- Graduates
- Peers
- Faculty
- LD staff
- Teacher trainees

Tutorials

Grp.	Ind.	Tutorials	Grp.	Ind.	Tutorials
•		Math skills	•	•	Word processing
•		Study skills	•		Time management
•	•	Language arts	•		Learning strategies
•	•	Written express	•	•	Organizational skills

Academic Accommodations

Curriculum	Study Aids	Exams
• Priority registration	Typist	• Oral
• Math waiver	• Reader	• Untimed
• Foreign lang. waiver	• Notetaker	• Take home
• Course substitution	• Proof reader	• With proctor
In Class	• Text on tape	• On computer
• Calculators	Early syllabus	• Extended time
• Tape recorder	Taped handouts	On tape
• Word processor		• Modified
Priority seating		• Separate room

Graduation Requirements:
Course credits: **60** GPA: **2.0** Years to complete degree: **2** Math waiver: **Yes**
Language waiver: **Yes**
Other requirements: **Vary according to A.A. or A.S. degree**

Program Strengths
Staff commitment, experience, education, quality of students, mainstream support in college classes.

General Information:
Cabrillo College is a 2 year public college. Suburban campus of 120 acres is 30 miles from San Jose. Accessible by bus. Ski areas are 250 miles from campus. Beaches are 1 mile from campus. 4.5% of students are foreign. Housing is not guaranteed.

Accreditation: WACS, CSDE

Expenses:
Tuition: In-state: Full year: $94.50. Part-time: Per credit:$28.00-$94.50.
Tuition: Out-of-state: Full year: Part-time: Per credit: $101.00. Part-time: Per course:$108.00 Cost of LD program:None

Majors

• AGRICULTURE Horticultural • AREA STUDIES Women's Studies • ARTS Art History, Crafts, Dance, Drafting, Dramatic Arts, Landscaping, Music, Music History, Music Performance, Painting • BUSINESS Accounting, Bookkeeping, Business Administration, Clerical, Data Processing, Economics, Food Management, Secretarial Science • COMMUNICATIONS Communication, Creative Writing, English, Graphic Design, Journalism, Literature, Photography, Speech/Debate/Forensic • COMPUTER SCIENCE Business Data Programming, Computer Science, Computer Technology, Medical Records Technology • ENGINEERING Drafting, Electrical, Engineering Science, Industrial • ENVIRONMENTAL CONTROL Solar Heating • HEALTH SCIENCES Dental Assistant, Dental Hygiene, Dental Technician, Medical Assistant, Medical Secretary, Nursing, Nursing Assistant, Radiological Therapy • HUMANITIES English/Writing/Literature, Humanities, Liberal Arts , Philosophy • LANGUAGES Chinese, English, French, German, Italian, Japanese, Russian, Spanish • MATHEMATICS Actuarial, Statistical, Theoretical • PRE PROFESSIONAL Dentistry, Forestry, Landscaping • RELIGIOUS STUDIES Philosophy • SCIENCES Anthropology, Archeology, Astronomy, Biology, Botany, Chemistry, Ecology, Geology, Horticultural, Physical Chemistry, Physics • SOCIAL SCIENCES Anthropology, Criminal Justice, Geography, History, Law Enforcement, Library Science, Political Science, Psychology, Sociology • VISUAL AND PERFORMING ARTS Art, Art History, Dance, Music, Studio Art, Theater • VOCATIONAL Air Conditioning/Heating/Refri, Business and Office, Culinary Arts, Dental Assistant, Dental Hygiene, Drafting, Electronics Technology, Fire Science, Food Service, Forestry, Home Economics, Industrial Equipment Maintenan, Medical Laboraotry Technology, Plumbing, Radiological Technology, Secretarial, Welding

Sports/Activities

• SPORTS RELATED Cheerleading • SPORTS-INTERCOLLEGIATE Baseball, Baseball (F), Baseball (M), Basketball, Basketball (F), Basketball (M), Cross Country, Cross Country (F), Cross Country (M), Cycling, Diving, Diving (F), Diving (M), Football, Football (M), Golf, Golf (M), Soccer, Soccer (M), Softball, Softball (F), Swimming, Swimming (F), Swimming (M), Tennis, Tennis (F), Tennis (M), Track and Field, Track and Field (F), Track and Field (M), Volleyball, Volleyball (F), Volleyball (M), Water Polo, Water Polo (F), Water Polo (M) • STUDENT LIFE ACTIVITIES Academic Clubs, Choral, Community Service, Dance, Debate, Ethnic & Cultural Groups, Magazine, Political Groups, Religious Organization, Student Government

---

Very Selective | **California**
Services

California State Polytechnic University

3801 West Temple Avenue
Pomona, California 91768
(714) 869-2000

School Enrollment: 20,000
LD Enrollment: 200

Admissions Contact: **Joseph Marshall, Director of Admissions**
LD Contact: **Debra Jakubovitz, Learning Disabilities Specialist**
Name of Program: **Disabled Student Services**
Address: **Cal Poly Pomona 15-126**
Telephone:**(714) 869-3333**

Admissions

Application Information:
Application deadline: **Depends on major**

Secondary School Information
Most Important Criteria For Admissions (1-strongest)

1 SAT/ACT	Application	School transcript
Class rank	Course selection	Personal statement
Interview	Extra activities	Psychoeducational
1 G.P.A.	Open admission	Recommendations

Test Requirements:
Diagnostic testing waived: **Yes**
Untimed SAT: **Yes** Untimed ACT: **Yes**
WAIS-R required: **Yes**
Documentation of LD required: **Yes**
Currency of diagnostic testing: **3 years.**
Tests recommended: **Woodcock-Johnson Revised, WAIS-R**

Types of Disabilities Served

• Speech/Lang	• Reading	• ADD with LD
Study skills	• Spelling	• ADD without LD
• Written express	• Math	• ADHD with LD
Organizational	• Fine Motor	• ADHD without LD
• Perceptual		

Admissions Process

All students apply through the regular admissions process and need to meet same standards. If a course, (e.g. foreign language) is not meet, the student's application may be reviewed by the director of DSS and a probationary admit may be offered.

High School Course Requirements:
English: **4** Math: **3** Science: **1** Foreign Language: **2**
Waivers to standard high school courses
Course substitution: **Yes**

Learning Disability Program

Students mainstreamed **100** % of the day
Recommended credits per semester: **12**
Vocational Counseling: **Yes**
Support groups are available:**Hearing impaired; learning disabled.**

Faculty:
Faculty: **4**
LD faculty with: BS/BA: **1**

Diagnostic Testing

ADD	Personality	• Perceptual skills	• Spelling
ADHD	Organization	Fine motor skills	• Reading
• I.Q.	• Handwriting	Spoken language	Study skills
• Math	Social skills	• Written language	

Tutoring:
Average size of group tutorials: **1:1**
Services rendered by:

Graduates	•Peers	Faculty	LD staff	Teacher trainees

Tutorials

Grp.	Ind.	Tutorials	Grp.	Ind.	Tutorials
	•	Math skills			Word processing
		Study skills		•	Time management
		Language arts		•	Learning strategies
	•	Written express			Organizational skills

California

Academic Accommodations

Curriculum	Study Aids	Exams
• Priority registration	Typist	• Oral
Math waiver	• Reader	Untimed
Foreign lang. waiver	• Notetaker	Take home
Course substitution	Proof reader	• With proctor
In Class	• Text on tape	• On computer
• Calculators	Early syllabus	• Extended time
• Tape recorder	Taped handouts	On tape
Word processor		Modified
• Priority seating		• Separate room

Program Strengths

Workshops are available to all students, regardless of the disability. The purpose of our program is to accommodate the student and to offer suppor services.

General Information:

California State Polytechnic University is a 4 year public university. Suburban campus Ski areas are 25 miles from campus. Beaches are 25 miles from campus. 6 residential halls on campus. Housing is not guaranteed.

Accreditation: WACS, AALR, ABET, CSWE

Expenses:

Tuition: In-state: Full year: $936.00. Part-time: Per credit:$180.00 (less than 6 credits per quarter). Tuition: Out-of-state: Full year: Part-time: Per credit: $164.00 per quarter. Room and board: $4,500.00

Majors

• AGRICULTURE Business, Engineering, Horticultural, International Agriculture, Plant Science • ANIMAL SCIENCE Animal • AREA STUDIES American, American Indian, Asian, Black/Afro-American, Hispanic/American, Latin American, Urban, Women's Studies • ARTS Art History, Dance, Dramatic Arts, Music • BUSINESS Accounting, Agricultural, Business Administration, Business Management, Economics, Fashion Merchandising, Finance, Fruit Industries, Hotel & Restaurant Management, Human Resources Management, Industrial Operations, International Agriculture, International Business, Management, Marketing, Real Estate • COMMUNICATIONS Communication, English, Journalism, Public Relations, Speech • COMPUTER SCIENCE Computer Information Systems, Computer Science • EDUCATION Agricultural, Curriculum, Physical, Special • ENGINEERING Aerospace, Agricultural, Architectural, Civil, Electrical, Engineering Technology, Industrial, Manufacturing, Mechanical • HEALTH SCIENCES Environmental, Nutritional/Food • HUMANITIES Humanities, Liberal Arts , Philosophy • LANGUAGES English, Spanish • MATHEMATICS Mathematics • PREPROFESSIONAL Agriculture, Architecture, Engineering, Law, Recreation, Social Work, Urban Design • SCIENCES Agricultural, Agronomy, Animal, Anthropology, Behavioral, Biology, Biotechnology, Botany, Chemistry, Computer Science, Earth, Geography, Geology, Horticultural, Mathematics, Microbiology, Pest Management, Physics, Plant Science, Soil, Zoology • SOCIAL SCIENCES Anthropology, Corrections, Criminal Justice, Geography, History, Political Science, Psychology, Social Sciences, Sociology • SPECIAL EDUCATION Learning Disability • VISUAL AND PERFORMING ARTS Art, Art History, Dance, Music, Theater • VOCATIONAL Home Economics, Landscape Architecture, Landscaping Management

Sports/Activities

• SPORTS RELATED Baton Twirling, Cheerleading, Drill Team, Drum Major/Majorette, Marching Band, Pep Band, Team Managers • SPORTS-INTERCOLLEGIATE Baseball (M), Basketball (M), Cross Country, Football (M), Gymnastics (F), Soccer (M), Softball (F), Swimming, Tennis, Volleyball (F), Wrestling (M) • SPORTS-INTRAMURAL Crew, Racquetball, Rugby, Sailing, Softball, Volleyball, Water Polo (M) • STUDENT LIFE ACTIVITIES Academic Clubs, Choral, Concert Band, Dance, Drama Groups, Ethnic & Cultural Groups, Film, Fraternities, Jazz Band, Magazine, Newspaper, Radio/TV station, Sororities, Student Government

---

California State University: Bakersfield
9001 Stockdale Highway
Bakersfield, California 93311-1099
(805) 833-2172

School Enrollment: **5,226** Male: **2,000** Female: **3,226**
LD Enrollment: **125**

Admissions Contact: **Dr. Homer Montalvo, Admissions Officer**
LD Contact: **Jan Tharp, Director**
Name of Program: **Services/Disabled Students**
Telephone:**(805) 664-3360**

Admissions

Application Information:
Separate application:**Yes**
Application deadline: **Opens in November, closing date varies**

Secondary School Information
Most Important Criteria For Admissions (1-strongest)

1 SAT/ACT	**1** Application	**1** School transcript
Class rank	**1** Course selection	Personal statement
Interview	Extra activities	Psychoeducational
1 G.P.A.	Open admission	Recommendations

Test Requirements:
Diagnostic testing waived: **Yes**
Untimed SAT: **Yes** Untimed ACT: **Yes**
Range accepted: **90+**
Documentation of LD required: **Yes**
Tests recommended: **Woodcock-Johnson and/or WAIS-R**

Types of Disabilities Served
- Speech/Lang
- Study skills
- Written express
- Organizational
- Perceptual
- Reading
- Spelling
- Math
- Fine Motor
- ADD with LD
- ADD without LD
- ADHD with LD
- ADHD without LD

Admissions Process

Intake interview, review of prior diagnostic testing, diagnostic testing if necessary, determination of eligibility.

High School Course Requirements:
English: **4** Math: **3** Science: **1** Foreign Language: **2**

Learning Disability Program

Program: Reinforces course work: **Yes**
Students mainstreamed **100 %** of the day
Counseling: Individual: **Yes** Vocational Counseling: **Yes**

Faculty:
Faculty: **5** Including Director: **Yes** Full time: **5** M.A.: **2**
Meets with instructor: **As needed**

Diagnostic Testing

ADD	Personality •	Perceptual skills	•	Spelling
ADHD•	Organization	Fine motor skills	•	Reading
• I.Q.	Handwriting•	Spoken language	•	Study skills
• Math	Social skills•	Written language		

Tutoring:
Average size of group tutorials: **5**
Services rendered by:
•Graduates •Peers •Faculty •LD staff Teacher trainees

Tutorials

Grp.	Ind.	Tutorials	Grp.	Ind.	Tutorials
•	•	Math skills	•	•	Word processing
•	•	Study skills	•	•	Time management
•	•	Language arts	•	•	Learning strategies
•	•	Written express	•	•	Organizational skills

Academic Accommodations

Curriculum	Study Aids	Exams
Priority registration	Typist	• Oral
Math waiver	Reader	Untimed
Foreign lang. waiver •	• Notetaker	• Take home
Course substitution	• Proof reader	• With proctor
In Class	• Text on tape	• On computer
• Calculators	Early syllabus	• Extended time
• Tape recorder	Taped handouts	On tape
Word processor		Modified
Priority seating		Separate room

Graduation Requirements:
Course credits: **186 hours minimum** GPA: **2.0** Years to complete degree:
4 or more

Program Strengths
California State University, Bakersfield, offers a unique combination of benefits to the learning disabled college student: small size, California State University status, low student to faculty ratio, and a full range of support services.

General Information:
California State University: Bakersfield is a 4 year public university. Suburban campus of 375 acres is 112 miles from Los Angeles. Accessible by air, train or bus. Ski areas are 60 miles from campus. Beaches are 120 miles from campus. 2% of students are foreign. 5 residential halls on campus. Housing is guaranteed.Guaranteed through 4th year. 1 % of students remain on campus for the weekends. 2 % of students join fraternities/sororities.

Accreditation: WACS

SAT/ACT Scores:
Scores for incoming freshmen: **Verbal:**31%below 500. 15%between 500 and 599. 3%between 600 and 699. 1%above 700. **Math:**39% below 500. 22% between 500 and 599. 7% between 600 and 699. 1%above 700. 22% between 20 and 23. 68%between 24 and 251. 10%between 26 and 28.

Expenses:
Tuition: In-state: Full year: $872.00. Tuition: Out-of-state: Full year: $5,670.00 plus $875.00 for 95 units. Room and board: $3,269.00

Majors
• BUSINESS Accounting, Business Administration, Economics, Finance, Management, Marketing • COMMUNICATIONS Communication, English • EDUCATION Art, Child Development, Curriculum, Early Childhood, English, Mathematics, Physical, Special, Speech/Language, Theater Education • HEALTH SCIENCES Environmental, Health, Medical Technology, Nursing • HUMANITIES English, Philosophy, Religion • LAN-GUAGES Spanish • SCIENCES Biochemistry, Biology, Chemistry, Geology, Mathematics, Physics • SOCIAL SCIENCES Anthropology, Criminal Justice, Government/Political, History, International Studies, Psychology, Public Administration, Sociology • VISUAL AND PERFORMING ARTS Art, Art History, Music, Studio Art, Theater

Sports/Activities
OLLEGIATE Basketball, Cross Country, Soccer (M), Softball (F), Swimming, Tennis, Track and Field, Volleyball (F), Wrestling • SPORTS-INTRAMURAL Badminton, Basketball, Diving, Hand Ball, Judo, Martial Arts, Racquetball, Softball, Tennis, Volleyball • STUDENT LIFE ACTIVITIES Academic Clubs, Choral, Club for Disabled, Dance, Drama Groups, Ethnic & Cultural Groups, Fraternities, Jazz Band, Music Groups, Newspaper, Religious Organization, Sororities, Student Government, Yearbook

Selective **California Program**

California State University: Chico
Chico, California 95929
(916) 895-6321

School Enrollment: **14,000** Male: **7,000** Female: **7,000**
LD Enrollment: **230**

Admissions Contact: **Kenneth Edson, Director**
LD Contact: **Laura Ittelson, L.D. Specialist**
Name of Program: **Disabled Student Services**
Telephone: **(916) 898-5959**

Admissions

Application Information:
Enrolled: **230**
Separate application: **Yes**
Application deadline: **varies**

Secondary School Information
Most Important Criteria For Admissions (1-strongest)

1	SAT/ACT	Application	1 School transcript
	Class rank	Course selection	Personal statement
2	Interview	Extra activities	1 Psychoeducational
1	G.P.A.	Open admission	2 Recommendations

Test Requirements:
Diagnostic testing waived: **Yes**
Untimed SAT: **Yes** Untimed ACT: **Yes**
Documentation of LD required: **Yes**
Currency of diagnostic testing: **3 years**

Types of Disabilities Served
• Speech/Lang	• Reading	• ADD with LD
• Study skills	• Spelling	• ADD without LD
• Written express	• Math	• ADHD with LD
• Organizational	• Fine Motor	• ADHD without LD
• Perceptual		

High School Course Requirements:
English: **4** Math: **3** Science: **1** Foreign Language: **2**

Learning Disability Program

Program: Reinforces course work: **Yes**
Students mainstreamed **100** % of the day
Services only for LD students: **Yes**
Support groups are available:**Yes**

Faculty:
Faculty: **3** Full time: **1** Part time: **2**
LD faculty with: BS/BA: **3** M.A.: **3**
Faculty advocate: **Yes** Meets with instructor: **As needed**

Diagnostic Testing
ADD	Personality	Perceptual skills	Spelling
ADHD	Organization	Fine motor skills	Reading
I.Q.	Handwriting	Spoken language	Study skills
Math	Social skills	Written language	

Tutoring:
Services rendered by:
•Graduates •Peers Faculty •LD staff Teacher trainees

Tutorials
Grp.	Ind.	Tutorials	Grp.	Ind.	Tutorials
		Math skills	•	•	Word processing
•	•	Study skills	•	•	Time management
		Language arts	•	•	Learning strategies
	•	Written express	•	•	Organizational skills

Academic Accommodations
Curriculum	Study Aids	Exams
• Priority registration	Typist	Oral
Math waiver	Reader	Untimed
Foreign lang. waiver	• Notetaker	Take home
Course substitution	Proof reader	• With proctor
In Class	• Text on tape	• On computer
Calculators	Early syllabus	• Extended time
• Tape recorder	Taped handouts	• On tape
• Word processor		Modified
Priority seating		• Separate room

Graduation Requirements:
Other requirements: **Same as all students**

Program Strengths

Our goal is that all aspects of university life will be conducive to the physical, social, and intellectual growth of all students. Therefore, we work with the faculty and administration to promote accessibility of programs and facilities for students with disabilities, and we work with students to help them achieve their potential in this setting. We will accept students with deficits as long as they meet all other admission requirements.

General Information:

California State University: Chico is a 4 year public university. Rural campus of 133 acres is 100 miles from Sacramento. Accessible by air, train or bus. 5 residential halls on campus. Housing is not guaranteed.

Accreditation:Regional

Expenses:
Tuition: In-state: Full year: $548.00-6+ units per semester. Part-time: Per credit:0. Tuition: Out-of-state: Full year: $548.00 plus $205.00 per unit per semester. Room and board: $3,900.00

Majors

• AREA STUDIES American, Ethics, Latin American • BUSINESS Accounting, Agricultural, Banking, Business Administration, Economics, Finance, International Business, Marketing • COMMUNICATIONS Communication, English, Journalism, Speech, Television/Radio/Film • COMPUTER SCIENCE Computer Science, Computer Technology, Telecommunications • EDUCATION Child Development, Health, Industrial, Physical, Social Studies • ENGINEERING Agricultural, Chemical, Electrical, Mechanical • HEALTH SCIENCES Health, Nursing, Nutritional/Food, Speech/Audiology and Speech • HUMANITIES Liberal Arts, Philosophy, Religion • LANGUAGES French, German, Spanish • PREPROFESSIONAL Dentistry, Law, Medicine, Pharmacy, Social Work, Veterinarian • SCIENCES Biochemistry, Biology, Chemistry, Earth, Geography, Geology, Gerontology, Horticultural, Mathematics, Microbiology, Physical Chemistry, Physics, Statistics • SOCIAL SCIENCES Anthropology, Criminal Justice, History, International Studies, Political Science, Psychology, Public Relations, Sociology • VISUAL AND PERFORMING ARTS Art History, Dramatic Arts, Music • VOCATIONAL Home Economics, Industrial Equipment Maintenan, Medical Laboratory Technology, Park/Recreation, Textile and Clothing

Sports/Activities

• SPORTS RELATED Marching Band, Pep Band • SPORTS-INTERCOLLEGIATE Baseball (M), Basketball, Diving, Field Hockey (F), Football (M), Soccer, Softball (F), Tennis (F), Track and Field, Volleyball (F) • SPORTS-INTRAMURAL Badminton, Basketball, Cross Country, Gymnastics, Hand Ball, Racquetball, Rugby (M), Skiing - Snow, Soccer, Softball, Swimming, Tennis, Volleyball, Wrestling (M) • STUDENT LIFE ACTIVITIES Choral, Community Service, Concert Band, Dance, Drama Groups, Ethnic & Cultural Groups, Film, Fraternities, Jazz Band, Musical Ensembles, Newspaper, Political Groups, Radio/TV station, Sororities

---

Selective **California**
Program

California State University: Dominguez Hills
100 East Victoria Street
Carson, California 90749-9960
(213) 516-3969

School Enrollment: **5,200** Male: **2,100** Female: **3,100**
LD Enrollment: **49** Male: **25** Female: **24**

Admissions Contact: **Anita Gash, Director of Admissions**
LD Contact: **Ann Wells, Coordinator of DSS**
Name of Program: **Disabled Student Services**

Admissions

Application Information:
Application deadline: **June 1**
Applicant must apply **2.5** months in advance

Secondary School Information
Most Important Criteria For Admissions (1-strongest)
3 SAT/ACT	**2** Application	**4** School transcript
5 Class rank	**11** Course selection	**8** Personal statement
7 Interview	**10** Extra activities	**9** Psychoeducational
1 G.P.A.	Open admission	**6** Recommendations

Test Requirements:
Standardized tests waived: **Yes**
Currency of diagnostic testing: **3 years**

Types of Disabilities Served
- Speech/Lang
- Reading
- ADD with LD
- Study skills
- Spelling
- ADD without LD
- Written express
- Math
- ADHD with LD
- Organizational
- Fine Motor
- ADHD without LD
- Perceptual

Learning Disability Program
Program: Reinforces course work: **Yes**
Students mainstreamed **100** % of the day

Faculty:
Faculty: **4** Full time: **2** Part time: **2** M.A.: **2**

Diagnostic Testing
- ADD
- Personality
- Perceptual skills
- Spelling
- ADHD
- Organization
- Fine motor skills
- Reading
- I.Q.
- Handwriting
- Spoken language
- Study skills
- Math
- Social skills
- Written language

Tutoring:
Services rendered by:
- Graduates
- Peers
- Faculty
- LD staff
- Teacher trainees

Tutorials
Grp.	Ind.	Tutorials	Grp.	Ind.	Tutorials
	•	Math skills		•	Word processing
	•	Study skills		•	Time management
	•	Language arts		•	Learning strategies
	•	Written express		•	Organizational skills

Academic Accommodations
Curriculum	Study Aids	Exams
Priority registration	Typist	• Oral
• Math waiver	Reader	Untimed
• Foreign lang. waiver	• Notetaker	Take home
Course substitution	• Proof reader	With proctor
In Class	• Text on tape	On computer
• Calculators	Early syllabus	• Extended time
• Tape recorder	Taped handouts	On tape
Word processor		Modified
Priority seating		Separate room

Program Strengths
Programs and services are available to students once it is verified they are learning disabled. Testing is also provided through the Disabled Student Services office here on campus. Services are provided on an individual basis. Each student must request assistance personally before it is made available. A Support Group for students with learning disabilities is available.

General Information:
California State University: Dominguez Hills is a 4 year public university. Suburban campus of 350 acres is 10 miles from Los Angeles. Accessible by air, train, or bus. Ski areas are 100 miles from campus. Beaches are 10 miles from campus. Housing is not guaranteed.99 % of students remain on campus for the weekends. 2 % of students join fraternities/sororities.

Accreditation:WACS

Expenses:
Tuition: In-state: Full year: $831.00 (over 6 units); Part-time: $521.00 (6 units or less) . Tuition: Out-of-state: Full year: $5,488.00; Part-time: $1,655.00. Room and board: $5,820.00

Majors
- AREA STUDIES Asian, Black/Afro-American, Mexican/American
- BUSINESS Accounting, Banking, Business Administration, Business Management, Economics, Finance, Human Resources Management, Management, Marketing, Personnel, Real Estate • COMMUNICATIONS Advertising, Broadcasting, Communication, Creative Writing, English, Journalism, Linguistic, Literature, Television/Radio/Film • COMPUTER SCIENCE Computer Science, Data Processing, Programming, Systems Analysis • EDUCATION Curriculum, Elementary, Middle School, Physical, Recreation and Youth Leadershi, School Psychology, Secondary, Special, Vocational • HEALTH SCIENCES Health, Medical Technology, Nuclear Medicine, Nursing • HUMANITIES Humanities, Philosophy, Religion • LANGUAGES French, Japanese, Spanish • PREPROFESSIONAL Dentistry, Law, Medicine, Pharmacy, Recreation, Social Work • SCIENCES Biochemistry, Biology, Cell Biology, Earth, Geography, Geology, Mathematics, Microbiology, Physics • SOCIAL SCIENCES Anthropology, Criminal Justice, Geography, Government/Political, History, Human Service, Political Science, Psychology, Social Sciences, Sociology • VISUAL AND PERFORMING ARTS Art, Art History, Dance, Dramatic Arts, Music, Studio Art, Theater

Sports/Activities
- SPORTS-INTERCOLLEGIATE Baseball (M), Basketball, Golf (M), Soccer, Softball (F), Volleyball (F) • STUDENT LIFE ACTIVITIES Dance, Debate, Drama Groups, Ethnic & Cultural Groups, Film, Magazine, Music Ensembles, Newspaper, Religious Organization, Sororities, Student Government, Symphony Orchestra, Yearbook

---

Selective **California**
Services

California State University: Fullerton
Fullerton, California 92634
(714) 773-2370

School Enrollment: **20,905** Male: **9,400** Female: **11,500**

Admissions Contact: **William Gowler, Acting Admissions Officer**
LD Contact: **John Liverpool, Coordinator**
Name of Program: **Disabled Student Services**
Telephone:**(714) 773-3117**

Admissions

Application Information:
Application deadline: **November/August**
Rolling Admissions: **Yes**

Secondary School Information
Most Important Criteria For Admissions (1-strongest)

3 SAT/ACT	Application	School transcript
2 Class rank	Course selection	Personal statement
Interview	Extra activities	Psychoeducational
1 G.P.A.	Open admission	Recommendations

Test Requirements:
Standardized tests waived: **Yes**
Untimed SAT: **Yes** Untimed ACT: **Yes**
Currency of diagnostic testing: **3 years**

California

Types of Disabilities Served
- Speech/Lang
- Study skills
- Written express
- Organizational
- Perceptual
- Reading
- Spelling
- Math
- Fine Motor
- ADD with LD
- ADD without LD
- ADHD with LD
- ADHD without LD

Learning Disability Program
Counseling: Individual: **Yes**

Faculty:
Faculty: **1** Full time: **1**

Diagnostic Testing
ADD	Personality	Perceptual skills	Spelling
ADHD	Organization	Fine motor skills	Reading
I.Q.	Handwriting	Spoken language	Study skills
Math	Social skills	Written language	

Tutoring:
Services rendered by:
- Graduates
- Peers
- Faculty
- LD staff
- Teacher trainees

Tutorials
Grp.	Ind.	Tutorials	Grp.	Ind.	Tutorials
		Math skills			Word processing
		Study skills			Time management
		Language arts			Learning strategies
		Written express			Organizational skills

Academic Accommodations

Curriculum	Study Aids	Exams
Priority registration	Typist	• Oral
Math waiver	Reader	Untimed
Foreign lang. waiver	• Notetaker	• Take home
Course substitution	• Proof reader	With proctor
In Class	• Text on tape	On computer
• Calculators	Early syllabus	• Extended time
• Tape recorder	Taped handouts	On tape
Word processor		Modified
Priority seating		Separate room

Program Strengths
Students applying for special admission are expected to be well-motivated, grounded in basic skills, and have developed successful compensatory strategies. To be considered for special admission status, an applicant must apply and be denied admission through the normal application procedure. Our faculty is supportive of the reasonable accommodations needed for LD students. We accept students with deficits as long as they meet our admissions requirements. Our tutorial program is based on content areas.

General Information:
California State University: Fullerton is a 4 year public university. Suburban campus of 225 acres is 20 miles from Los Angeles. Accessible by bus. Beaches are 25 miles from campus. Housing is not guaranteed.

Accreditation: Regional and Specialized

Expenses:
Tuition: In-state: Full year: $880.00. Part-time: Per credit: $580.00. Tuition: Out-of-state: Full year: $880.00 plus $189.00 per unit. Part-time: Per credit: $580.00 plus $189.00 .

Majors
• AREA STUDIES Black/Afro-American • BUSINESS Accounting, Banking, Business Administration, Business Economics, Business Management, Economics, Finance • COMMUNICATIONS Advertising • COMPUTER SCIENCE Computer Science, Computer Technology • CRAFTS AND DESIGN Ceramics, Sculpture • EDUCATION Art, Child Development, Mathematics • ENGINEERING City Planning, Civil/Environmental • HEALTH SCIENCES Communication Disorders • HUMANITIES Liberal Arts • SCIENCES Biochemistry, Biophysics, Botany, Cell Biology, Chemistry, Ecology, Mathematics, Statistics • SOCIAL SCIENCES Anthropology, Criminal Justice • VISUAL AND PERFORMING ARTS Art History, Dance, Music, Theater

Sports/Activities
• SPORTS RELATED Cheerleading, Pep Band, Team Managers
• SPORTS-INTERCOLLEGIATE Basketball, Cross Country, dBaseball (M), Fencing (M), Football (M), Gymnastics, Soccer (M), Softball (F), Tennis (F), Track and Field, Wrestling (M) • STUDENT LIFE ACTIVITIES Dance, Debate, Drama Groups, Ethnic & Cultural Groups, Film, Fraternities, Music Groups, Newspaper, Radio/TV station, Religious Organization, Sororities, Student Government, Symphony Orchestra, Yearbook

---

Selective **California Program**

California State University: Northridge
18111 Nordhoff Street
Northridge, California 91330
(818) 885-3700

School Enrollment: **31,500** Male: **14,500** Female: **17,000**
LD Enrollment: **300**

Admissions Contact: **Lorraine Newlon, Director of Admissions**
LD Contact: **Dr. Marshall Raskind, Coordinator**
Name of Program: **Learning Disability Program**
Telephone: **(818) 885-2684**

Admissions

Application Information:
Enrolled: **300**
Application deadline: **Varies**
Applicant must apply **12** months in advance

Secondary School Information
Most Important Criteria For Admissions (1-strongest)

1 SAT/ACT	Application	School transcript
Class rank	Course selection	Personal statement
Interview	Extra activities	Psychoeducational
1 G.P.A.	Open admission	Recommendations

Test Requirements:
Diagnostic testing waived: **Yes**
Untimed SAT: **Yes** Untimed ACT: **Yes** Untimed ACH: **Yes**
Documentation of LD required: **Yes**
Currency of diagnostic testing: **3 years**
Tests recommended: **Comprehensive testing-full diagnostic battery**

Types of Disabilities Served
- Speech/Lang
- Study skills
- Written express
- Organizational
- Perceptual
- Reading
- Spelling
- Math
- Fine Motor
- ADD with LD
- ADD without LD
- ADHD with LD
- ADHD without LD

High School Course Requirements:

Learning Disability Program

Students mainstreamed **100 %** of the day
Recommended credits per semester:
Counseling: Individual: **Yes** Group Counseling: **Yes**

Faculty:

Faculty: **3** Including Director: **Yes** Full time: **2** Part time: **1** Ph.D.: **3**

Diagnostic Testing

- ADD Personality • Perceptual skills • Spelling
- ADHD• Organization• Fine motor skills • Reading
- I.Q. Handwriting• Spoken language Study skills
- Math • Social skills• Written language

Tutoring:

Services rendered by:
•Graduates Peers Faculty •LD staff Teacher trainees

Tutorials

Grp.	Ind.	Tutorials	Grp.	Ind.	Tutorials
		Math skills		•	Word processing
	•	Study skills		•	Time management
		Language arts		•	Learning strategies
	•	Written express		•	Organizational skills

Academic Accommodations

Curriculum	Study Aids	Exams
Priority registration	• Typist	• Oral
Math waiver	Reader	Untimed
Foreign lang. waiver	• Notetaker	Take home
Course substitution	• Proof reader	With proctor
In Class	• Text on tape	On computer
• Calculators	Early syllabus	• Extended time
• Tape recorder	Taped handouts	On tape
• Word processor		Modified
Priority seating		Separate room

Program Strengths

California State University has three Ph.D's on staff providing services.

General Information:

California State University: Northridge is a 4 year public college. Suburban campus. of 360 acres is 25 miles from Los Angeles. Housing is not guaranteed.

Accreditation:AACSB, ABET, ACEJMC, AHEA, APTA, CAHEA, NASM

Expenses:

Tuition: In-state: Full year: $375.00. Part-time: Per credit:$219.00 for 0-6 units. Tuition: Out-of-state: Full year: $375.00 plus $189.00 per unit.

Majors

• AREA STUDIES Black/Afro-American, Mexican/American, Urban • BUSINESS Accounting, Banking, Business Administration, Business Economics, Business Education, Business Management, Economics, Insurance, Investments and Securities, Marketing, Statistic • COMMUNICATIONS Creative Writing, English, Journalism, Speech, Television/Radio/ Film • COMPUTER SCIENCE Computer Science, Computer Technology, Hardware Engineer • CRAFTS AND DESIGN Ceramics, Glass, Graphic Design, Sculpture • ENGINEERING Chemical, Civil/Environmental, Electrical, Engineering Science, Environmental/Water Resources, Industrial, Materials, Mechanical, Nuclear, Ocean • HEALTH SCIENCES Medical

Technology, Physical Therapy • HUMANITIES Humanities, Liberal Arts, Philosophy • LANGUAGES French, German, Linguistic, Spanish • SCIENCES Bio-engineering, Biomedical, Cell Biology, Chemistry, Earth, Geography, Geology, Geophysics, Mathematics, Physical Science, Physics, Statistics • SOCIAL SCIENCES Anthropology, Government/Political, Human Service, Political Science, Psychology, Social Sciences, Sociology • VISUAL AND PERFORMING ARTS Art History, Fine Arts, Music, Music Performance, Theater • VOCATIONAL Food Service, Home Economics, Printing/Lithography, Textile and Clothing

Sports/Activities

• SPORTS RELATED Cheerleading, Chess, Drill Team, Marching Band, Pep Band, Team Managers • SPORTS-INTERCOLLEGIATE Baseball, Basketball, Cross Country, Cycling, Football (M), Golf (M), Hammer Throw, Judo, Karate, Sailing, Scuba, Skiing - Snow, Soccer, Softball, Swimming, Tennis (F), Track and Field, Volleyball, Water Polo, Weight Lifting, Wrestling • SPORTS-INTRAMURAL Badminton, Baseball, Cross Country, Diving, Football (M), Golf (M), Hand Ball, Ice Hockey (M), Rugby (M), Soccer, Softball, Swimming, Tennis (F), Volleyball • STUDENT LIFE ACTIVITIES Concert Band, Dance, Debate, Drama Groups, Ethnic & Cultural Groups, Film, Fraternities, Jazz Band, Music Ensembles, Music Groups, Newspaper, Radio/TV station, Sororities, Student Government

---

Selective   **California Program**

California State University: Sacramento

6000 J Street
Sacramento, California 95819
(916) 278-6111

School Enrollment: **20,000** Male: **9,000** Female: **11,000**

Admissions Contact: **Cretia Martinson, Director of Admissions**
LD Contact: **Susan Eiland Rickman, LD Specialist**
Name of Program: **Learning Disabilities Program**
Telephone:**(916) 278-6725**

Admissions

Application Information:

Application deadline: **March 1st**
Rolling Admissions: **Yes**

Secondary School Information

Most Important Criteria For Admissions (1-strongest)

1 SAT/ACT		Application	**1**	School transcript
	Class rank	**1** Course selection		Personal statement
	Interview	**2** Extra activities		Psychoeducational
	G.P.A.	Open admission	**2**	Recommendations

Test Requirements:

Standardized tests waived: **Yes**
Diagnostic testing waived: **Yes**
Untimed SAT: **Yes** Untimed ACT: **Yes**
Tests recommended: **No time constraint-testing can be done at college.**

Types of Disabilities Served

- Speech/Lang • Reading • ADD with LD
- Study skills • Spelling ADD without LD
- Written express • Math • ADHD with LD
- Organizational • Fine Motor • ADHD without LD
- Perceptual

California

Learning Disability Program

Program: Remedial: **Yes**
Program: Reinforces course work: **Yes**
Students mainstreamed **100** % of the day
Counseling: Individual: **Yes**

Faculty:
Faculty: **3** Full time: **2** Part time: **1** M.A.: **3**

Diagnostic Testing
ADD	Personality •	Perceptual skills	• Spelling
ADHD•	Organization•	Fine motor skills	• Reading
• I.Q.	• Handwriting•	Spoken language	• Study skills
• Math	Social skills	Written language	

Tutoring:
Services rendered by:
•Graduates •Peers Faculty •LD staff Teacher trainees

Tutorials
Grp.	Ind.	Tutorials	Grp.	Ind.	Tutorials
•	•	Math skills	•	•	Word processing
•	•	Study skills	•	•	Time management
•	•	Language arts	•	•	Learning strategies
•	•	Written express	•	•	Organizational skills

Academic Accommodations
Curriculum	Study Aids	Exams
Priority registration	Typist	• Oral
Math waiver	Reader	Untimed
Foreign lang. waiver	• Notetaker	Take home
Course substitution	• Proof reader	With proctor
In Class	• Text on tape	On computer
• Calculators	Early syllabus	• Extended time
• Tape recorder	Taped handouts	On tape
Word processor		Modified
Priority seating		Separate room

Program Strengths

California State University, Sacramento has one of the fullest arrays of services and is the oldest program among the state universities (11 years).

General Information:

California State University: Sacramento is a 4 year public university. Urban campus of 288 acres is 90 miles from San Francisco. 5 residential halls on campus. Housing is not guaranteed.

Accreditation: Regional

Expenses:
Tuition: In-state: Full year: $213.00 (under 6 units), $372.00 (more than 6 units). Tuition: Out-of-state: Full year: $1,043.00 (under 6 units).

Majors

• AREA STUDIES American/Indian, Asian, Black/Afro-American
• BUSINESS Accounting, Banking, Business Administration, Business Economics, Business Education, Business Management, Economics, Finance, Insurance, International Business, Marketing, Real Estate • COMMUNICATIONS Communication, English, Journalism • COMPUTER SCIENCE Computer Science, Computer Technology • EDUCATION Agricultural, Bilingual, Elementary, English, Health, Music, Physical, Recreation and Youth Leadershi, Secondary, Social Studies, Speech/Language • ENGINEERING Civil/Environmental, Electrical, Engineering Science, Mechanical • HEALTH SCIENCES Environmental, Medical Technology, Nursing • HUMANITIES Philosophy • LANGUAGES French, German, Spanish • PREPROFESSIONAL Social Work • SCIENCES Biology, Chemistry, Geography, Geology, Microbiology, Physical Science • SOCIAL SCIENCES Anthropology, History, Political Science, Psychology, Social Sciences • VISUAL AND PERFORMING ARTS Music, Theater • VOCATIONAL Home Economics, Interior Design

Sports/Activities

• SPORTS RELATED Marching Band, Pep Band • SPORTS-INTERCOLLEGIATE Baseball (M), Basketball, Cross Country, Football (M), Golf (M), Gymnastics (F), Soccer (M), Softball (F), Swimming, Tennis, Volleyball (F) • SPORTS-INTRAMURAL Badminton, Basketball, Bowling, Crew, Cross Country, Hand Ball, Ping-Pong, Racquetball, Soccer, Softball (F), Swimming, Tennis, Track and Field, Volleyball (F) • STUDENT LIFE ACTIVITIES Choral, Community Service, Concert Band, Dance, Debate, Drama Groups, Film, Fraternities, Jazz Band, Music Groups, Newspaper, Radio/TV station, Sororities, Student Government

---

Less Selective

California Program

California State University: San Bernardino
5500 University Parkway
San Bernardino, California 92407
(714) 887-7201

School Enrollment: **12,000**
LD Enrollment: **50** Male: **25** Female: **25**

Admissions Contact: **Cheryl Smith, Director of Admissions**
LD Contact: **Barbara Sovereign, MFCC L.D. Program Cor.**
Name of Program: **Learning Disabled Program**
Address: **University Hall, Room 235**
Telephone: **(714) 880-5239**

Admissions

Application Information:
Enrolled: **75**
Application deadline: **2 months prior to the quarter**
Applicant must apply **ASAP** months in advance

Secondary School Information
Most Important Criteria For Admissions (1-strongest)
4 SAT/ACT	**1** Application	**2** School transcript
Class rank	**7** Course selection	Personal statement
Interview	**6** Extra activities	**5** Psychoeducational
3 G.P.A.	Open admission	Recommendations

Test Requirements:
Diagnostic testing waived: **Yes**
WAIS-R required: **Yes**
Documentation of LD required: **Yes**
Tests recommended: **Bender-Gestalt, WRAT-R**

Types of Disabilities Served
• Speech/Lang	• Reading	• ADD with LD
• Study skills	• Spelling	ADD without LD
• Written express	• Math	• ADHD with LD
• Organizational	• Fine Motor	ADHD without LD
• Perceptual		

High School Course Requirements:
English: **4** Math: **3** Science: **1** Foreign Language: **2**

Learning Disability Program

Program: Reinforces course work: **Yes**
Program available through:**Daily**
Students mainstreamed **100** % of the day
Recommended credits per semester: **12**
Counseling: Individual: **Yes** Vocational Counseling: **Yes**

Faculty:

Faculty: **7** Including Director: **Yes** Full time: **3** Part time: **4**
LD faculty with: BS/BA: **2** M.A.: **5** Ph.D.: **1**
Faculty advocate: **Yes** Meets with instructor: **When necessary**

Diagnostic Testing

- ADD
- ADHD•
- I.Q.
- Math
- Personality
- Organization•
- Handwriting•
- Social skills•
- Perceptual skills
- Fine motor skills
- Spoken language
- Written language
- Spelling
- Reading
- Study skills

Tutoring:

Average size of group tutorials: **1**
Services rendered by:
  Graduates   Peers   Faculty   •LD staff   Teacher trainees

Tutorials

Grp.	Ind.	Tutorials	Grp.	Ind.	Tutorials
	•	Math skills		•	Word processing
	•	Study skills		•	Time management
	•	Language arts		•	Learning strategies
	•	Written express		•	Organizational skills

Academic Accommodations

Curriculum	Study Aids	Exams
• Priority registration	• Typist	• Oral
• Math waiver	• Reader	Untimed
Foreign lang. waiver	• Notetaker	• Take home
• Course substitution	• Proof reader	• With proctor
In Class	• Text on tape	• On computer
• Calculators	• Early syllabus	• Extended time
• Tape recorder	• Taped handouts	• On tape
• Word processor		Modified
Priority seating		• Separate room

Graduation Requirements:

Course credits: **186** GPA: **Depends on major** Years to complete degree:
As needed Language waiver: **Yes**
Other requirements: **As per the University**

Program Strengths

The LD Program is dedicated to assuring each student an opportunity to experience equity in education. After an assessment is obtained for each student, the staff works with each student to develop compensatory methods for handling assignments and classroom projects. Careful attention is paid to helping the student acquire learning skills and formulating and implementing specific strategies for notetaking and management of written materials. The emphasis is on aiding the LD student to find techniques to deal with his/her disability in the University setting and thereafter in the job market.

General Information:

California State University: San Bernardino is a 4 year public university. Suburban campus of 450 acres is 80 miles from Los Angeles. Accessible by air, train, or bus. 2% of students are foreign. 8 residential halls on campus. Housing is not guaranteed. 10 % of students join fraternities/sororities.

Accreditation: Regional

Expenses:

Tuition: In-state: Full year: $1,100.00. Tuition: Out-of-state: Full year: $7,100.00. Room and board: $4,077.00

Majors

- AREA STUDIES Ethnic/Cultural, Hispanic/American, Women's Studies
- ARTS Art History, Dramatic Arts, Graphic Arts, Music • BUSINESS Accounting, Business Administration, Business Management, Economics, Marketing • COMMUNICATIONS Communication, English • COMPUTER SCIENCE Computer Science • EDUCATION Art, Bilingual, Elementary, English, Health, Mathematics, Music, Physical, Science, Secondary, Vocational • HEALTH SCIENCES Environmental • HUMANITIES Humanities • LANGUAGES French, German, Spanish • MATHEMATICS Applied • PREPROFESSIONAL Medicine • SCIENCES Anthropology, Biology, Chemistry, Computer Science, Physics • SOCIAL SCIENCES Anthropology, Geography, Government/Political, History, Political Science, Psychology, Sociology • VISUAL AND PERFORMING ARTS Art History, Dramatic Arts, Music, Music Theatre

Sports/Activities

- SPORTS RELATED Cheerleading, Team Managers • SPORTS-INTERCOLLEGIATE Baseball (M), Basketball, Cross Country, Golf, Soccer (M), Softball (F), Swimming, Tennis, Volleyball (F), Water Polo (M) • SPORTS-INTRAMURAL Archery, Badminton, Basketball, Cross Country, Golf, Racquetball, Skiing - Snow, Soccer, Softball, Swimming, Tennis, Volleyball • STUDENT LIFE ACTIVITIES Academic Clubs, Community Service, Dance, Drama Groups, Ethnic & Cultural Groups, Fraternities, Music Groups, Musical Theater, Newspaper, Orchestra, Political Groups, Radio/TV station, Religious Organization, Sororities, Student Government

---

Less Selective　　　　　　　　　　　**California Program**

Canada College
4200 Farm Hill Boulevard
Redwood City, California 94061
(415) 364-1212

School Enrollment: **7,100** Male: **2,700** Female: **4,400**
LD Enrollment: **75**

Admissions Contact: **Scott Thomas, Registrar**
LD Contact: **Jane Hetrick, LD Specialist/Coordinator**
Name of Program: **Learning Disability Program**
Address: **4200 Farm Hill Blvd.**
Telephone:**(415) 306-3490**

Admissions

Application Information:

Enrolled:**75**
Separate application:**Yes**
Application deadline: **None**
Applicant must apply **2** months in advance
Rolling Admissions: **Yes**

Secondary School Information

Most Important Criteria For Admissions (1-strongest)

	SAT/ACT	**2**	Application	**3**	School transcript
	Class rank	**2**	Course selection		Personal statement
1	Interview		Extra activities		Psychoeducational
	G.P.A.	**1**	Open admission		Recommendations

California

Test Requirements:
Diagnostic testing waived: **Yes**
WAIS-R required: **Yes**
Documentation of LD required: **Yes**
Currency of diagnostic testing: **1-2 weeks**
Tests recommended: **Done at the community college by learning disability specialist, approximately 8 hours of testing.**

Types of Disabilities Served
• Speech/Lang	• Reading	ADD with LD
• Study skills	• Spelling	ADD without LD
• Written express	• Math	ADHD with LD
• Organizational	• Fine Motor	ADHD without LD
• Perceptual		

Learning Disability Program
Syllabus available during orientation: **Yes**
Program: Reinforces course work: **Yes**
Students mainstreamed **90** % of the day
Time required or recommended in learning center: **As needed**
Services available for all students: **Yes**
Counseling: Individual: **Yes**
Support groups are available: **DSKL 816-3 sections**

Faculty:
Faculty: **3** Including Director: **Yes** Full time: **1** Part time: **2** M.A.: **3**
Faculty advocate: **Yes** Meets with instructor: **As needed**

Diagnostic Testing
ADD	Personality	• Perceptual skills	• Spelling
ADHD	• Organization	Fine motor skills	• Reading
• I.Q.	Handwriting	Spoken language	Study skills
• Math	Social skills	• Written language	

Tutoring:
Average size of group tutorials: **2-7**
Services rendered by:
Graduates	Peers	•Faculty	•LD staff	Teacher trainees

Tutorials
Grp.	Ind.	Tutorials	Grp.	Ind.	Tutorials
•	•	Math skills	•	•	Word processing
•	•	Study skills	•	•	Time management
•	•	Language arts	•	•	Learning strategies
•	•	Written express	•	•	Organizational skills

Academic Accommodations
Curriculum	Study Aids	Exams
• Priority registration	Typist	• Oral
Math waiver	• Reader	• Untimed
Foreign lang. waiver	• Notetaker	Take home
Course substitution	• Proof reader	• With proctor
In Class	• Text on tape	On computer
Calculators	Early syllabus	• Extended time
• Tape recorder	Taped handouts	On tape
• Word processor		Modified
Priority seating		• Separate room

Graduation Requirements:
Course credits: **60** Years to complete degree: **2-3 years** Math waiver: **Yes**

Program Strengths
Canada College is a small community college where students receive attention needed to achieve their academic goals. The Learning Disabilities Program offers individual attention with the goal of providing the support which students need to be successful. Our goal for our students is to develop skills and strategies which will allow them to be successful students and independent learners. Canada College is one of 107 California Community Colleges. Standards of eligibility are statewide so that once a student is determined eligible he/she may receive services at any California Community College.

General Information:
Canada College is a 2 year public college. Suburban campus 20 miles from San Francisco. Accessible by train or bus. Ski areas are 4 hours from campus. Beaches are 1/2 hour from campus. 2% of students are foreign. Housing is not guaranteed.

Accreditation: WACS

Expenses:
Tuition: In-state: Full year: Part-time: Per credit: $5.00 per unit. Tuition: Out-of-state: Full year: $100.00 per unit.

Majors
• BUSINESS Accounting, Business Administration, Clerical, Economics, Travel/Tourism Management • COMMUNICATIONS Journalism, Speech • EDUCATION Child Development, Early Childhood, Physical • ENGINEERING Engineering Science, Mathematical • HEALTH SCIENCES Medical Technology, Nursing, Physical Therapy • HUMANITIES Philosophy • PREPROFESSIONAL Architecture, Dentistry, Industrial Design, Medicine, Optometry, Pharmacy, Veterinarian • SCIENCES Biology, Chemistry, Geography, Mathematics, Oceanography, Physical Science, Physics, Physiology • SOCIAL SCIENCES Anthropology, Political Science, Sociology • VISUAL AND PERFORMING ARTS Art, Dramatic Arts, Music, Theater • VOCATIONAL Fashion Merchandising, Home Economics, Industrial Design, Library Assistant, Paralegal, Park/Recreation, Radiological Technology, Secretarial

Sports/Activities
• SPORTS-INTERCOLLEGIATE Baseball (M), Basketball (M), Golf, Soccer (M), Softball (F), Tennis (M), Water Polo (F) • STUDENT LIFE ACTIVITIES Choral, Concert Band, Dance, Drama Groups, Music Ensemble, Symphony Orchestra

Less Selective   **California Program**

Cerritos Community College
1110 East Alondra Boulevard
Norwalk, California 90650
(310) 860-2451

School Enrollment: **23,000** Male: **9,200** Female: **13,800**
LD Enrollment: **125** Male: **75** Female: **50**

Admissions Contact: **Dr. Fran Newman, VP for Student Services**
LD Contact: **Al Spetrino, Program Specialist**
Name of Program: **Instructional Support Center**
Telephone: **(310) 860-2451 Ext. 358**

Admissions

Application Information:
LD Students Applying: **120** Accepted: **100** Enrolled: **98**
Rolling Admissions: **Yes**

Secondary School Information

Most Important Criteria For Admissions (1-strongest)

SAT/ACT	Application	School transcript
Class rank	Course selection	Personal statement
1 Interview	Extra activities	**1** Psychoeducational
G.P.A.	**1** Open admission	Recommendations

Test Requirements:

Standardized tests waived: **Yes**
Diagnostic testing waived: **Yes**
Untimed SAT: **Yes** Untimed ACT: **Yes**
Documentation of LD required: **Yes**
Currency of diagnostic testing: **3 years**
Tests recommended: **Woodcock-Johnson Psychoeducational Battery**

Types of Disabilities Served

- Speech/Lang
- Study skills
- Written express
- Organizational
- Perceptual
- Reading
- Spelling
- Math
- Fine Motor
- ADD with LD
- ADD without LD
- ADHD with LD
- ADHD without LD

Admissions Process

Open admissions

Learning Disability Program

Program: Reinforces course work: **Yes**
Services only for LD students: **Yes**
Counseling: Individual: **Yes**

Faculty:

Faculty: **15** Including Director: **Yes** Full time: **4** Part time: **11**
LD faculty with: BS/BA: **3** M.A.: **3**
Faculty advocate: **Yes** Meets with instructor: **When requested**

Diagnostic Testing

ADD	Personality	• Perceptual skills	• Spelling
ADHD	Organization	Fine motor skills	• Reading
I.Q.	Handwriting	Spoken language	• Study skills
• Math	Social skills	• Written language	

Tutoring:

Average size of group tutorials: **8-10**
Services rendered by:
  Graduates   Peers   •Faculty   •LD staff   •Teacher trainees

Tutorials

Grp.	Ind.	Tutorials	Grp.	Ind.	Tutorials
•	•	Math skills	•	•	Word processing
•	•	Study skills	•	•	Time management
•	•	Language arts	•	•	Learning strategies
•	•	Written express	•	•	Organizational skills

Academic Accommodations

Curriculum	Study Aids	Exams
Priority registration	• Typist	Oral
Math waiver	Reader	Untimed
Foreign lang. waiver	Notetaker	Take home
Course substitution	• Proof reader	With proctor
In Class	• Text on tape	On computer
• Calculators	Early syllabus	• Extended time
• Tape recorder	Taped handouts	On tape
• Word processor		Modified
Priority seating		Separate room

Graduation Requirements:

Course credits: **60** GPA: **2.0** Years to complete degree: **As needed** Math waiver: **Yes** Language waiver: **Yes**

Program Strengths

We have a full learning disability program but our hands are tied until the state test is taken. We recommend that students take the test as soon as possible. We are one of only three community colleges with a full summer session for LD students.

General Information:

Cerritos Community College is a 2 year public college. Suburban campus of 40+ acres is 15 miles from Los Angeles. Accessible by air, train, or bus. Housing is not guaranteed.

Accreditation: Regional

Expenses:

Tuition: In-state: Full year: $60.00 for 6 units or more per year. Tuition: Out-of-state: Full year: Part-time: Per Credit: $117.00 per unit. Part-time: Per credit:$117.00 per unit.

Majors

• AREA STUDIES Latin American • BUSINESS Accounting, Business Management, Economics, Finance, Marketing, Personnel, Real Estate • COMMUNICATIONS English, Journalism, Photography, Speech and Debate • COMPUTER SCIENCE Data Processing, Programming • EDUCATION Music • HEALTH SCIENCES Dental Assistant, Nursing, Physical Therapy • HUMANITIES Philosophy • LANGUAGES French, German, Spanish • PREPROFESSIONAL Agriculture, Architecture, Dentistry, Landscaping, Law Enforcement, Medicine, Pharmacy, Range Management, Veterinarian • SCIENCES Biology, Botany, Chemistry, Macrobiology, Mathematics, Physics, Zoology • VOCATIONAL Culinary Arts, Home Economics, Interior Design

Sports/Activities

• SPORTS RELATED Pep Band • SPORTS-INTRAMURAL Baseball (M), Basketball, Cross Country, Diving, Football (M), Golf (M), Soccer (M), Softball (F), Swimming, Tennis, Track and Field, Volleyball (F), Water Polo (M), Wrestling (M) • STUDENT LIFE ACTIVITIES Debate, Drama Groups, Ethnic & Cultural Groups, Fraternities, Magazine, Music Groups, Newspaper, Radio/TV station, Religious Organization, Sororities, Student Government, Symphony Orchestra

---

Less Selective	California Program

Chabot College
25555 Hesperian Boulevard
Haywood, California 94545
(415) 786-6714

School Enrollment: **20,686** Male: **9,507** Female: **11,179**
LD Enrollment: **350**

Admissions Contact: **Carlo Vecchiarelli, Director of Admissions**
LD Contact: **Jean Collins/Jerry Egusa**
Name of Program: **Learning Skills Program**
Telephone:**(415) 786-6812 - 6660**

Admissions

Application Information:

Application deadline: **ASAP**
Rolling Admissions: **Yes**

Secondary School Information

Most Important Criteria For Admissions (1-strongest)

SAT/ACT	Application	School transcript
Class rank	Course selection	Personal statement
Interview	Extra activities	Psychoeducational
G.P.A.	**1** Open admission	Recommendations

Test Requirements:

Tests recommended: **None - except on site.**

Types of Disabilities Served

- Speech/Lang
- Reading
- ADD with LD
- Study skills
- Spelling
- ADD without LD
- Written express
- Math
- ADHD with LD
- Organizational
- Fine Motor
- ADHD without LD
- Perceptual

Learning Disability Program

Students mainstreamed **varies** % of the day
Counseling: Individual: **Yes** Group Counseling: **Yes**

Faculty:

Faculty: **7** Full time: **4** Part time: **3**
LD faculty with: BS/BA: **5** M.A.: **1** Ph.D.: **1**
Faculty advocate: **Yes** Meets with instructor: **As needed**

Diagnostic Testing

ADD	Personality •	Perceptual skills	• Spelling
ADHD•	Organization•	Fine motor skills	• Reading
• I.Q.	• Handwriting•	Spoken language	• Study skills
• Math	Social skills •	Written language	

Tutoring:

Services rendered by:

Graduates	Peers	•Faculty	•LD staff	Teacher trainees

Tutorials

Grp.	Ind.	Tutorials	Grp.	Ind.	Tutorials
•	•	Math skills	•	•	Word processing
		Study skills	•	•	Time management
		Language arts	•	•	Learning strategies
•	•	Written express	•	•	Organizational skills

Academic Accommodations

Curriculum	Study Aids	Exams
Priority registration	Typist	• Oral
Math waiver	Reader	Untimed
Foreign lang. waiver	• Notetaker	Take home
Course substitution	Proof reader	With proctor
In Class	• Text on tape	On computer
• Calculators	Early syllabus	• Extended time
• Tape recorder	Taped handouts	On tape
• Word processor		Modified
Priority seating		Separate room

Program Strengths

The Learning Skills Program at Chabot has been in existence for over 15 years. Classes are actual college classes whereby students receive college credits for attendance and completion; they are not tutoring sessions. The Learning Skills Program meets the needs of students in ways that general remedial courses cannot due to the specialty and variety of the disability.

General Information:

Chabot College is a 2 year public college. Urban campus of 90-100 acres is 15 miles from Oakland. Accessible by train or bus. Ski areas are 3 hours from campus. Beaches are 1-1/2 hours from campus. 1% of students are foreign. Housing is not guaranteed.

Accreditation: WACS

Expenses:

Tuition: In-state: Full year: $100.00. Part-time: Per credit:$35.00. Tuition: Out-of-state: Full year: $2,304.00. Part-time: Per credit:$64.00. Room and board: $4,500.00-$5,500.00

Majors

• BUSINESS Accounting, Business Administration, Business Economics, Business Education, Business Management, Economics, Management, Marketing, Real Estate, Sports Management, Travel/Tourism Management • COMMUNICATIONS Advertising, Communication, English, Photography • COMPUTER SCIENCE Data Processing, Hardware Engineer, Programming, Software Engineer, Systems Analysis, Telecommunications • EDUCATION General • HEALTH SCIENCES Environmental, Health, Medical Technology, Nursing, Nutritional/Food, Occupational Therapy, Physical Therapy, Radiological Therapy, Speech Therapy, Speech/Audiology and Speech • HUMANITIES Humanities, Philosophy • LANGUAGES Spanish • PREPROFESSIONAL Agriculture, Architecture, Business, Dentistry, Engineering, Forestry, Law, Medicine, Natural Resources, Pharmacy, Recreation, Social Work • SCIENCES Astronomy, Biology, Botany, Chemistry, Ecology, Geography, Marine Biology, Microbiology, Physical Science, Physics, Physiology, Zoology • SOCIAL SCIENCES Anthropology, Criminal Justice, Geography, Government/Political, History, Psychology, Social Sciences, Sociology • VISUAL AND PERFORMING ARTS Art, Art History, Dance, Music, Theater

Sports/Activities

• SPORTS RELATED Cheerleading, Pep Band, Team Managers • SPORTS-INTERCOLLEGIATE Baseball (M), Basketball, Cross Country, Diving, Football (M), Golf, Soccer (M), Softball (F), Tennis, Track and Field, Volleyball (F), Wrestling (M) • SPORTS-INTRAMURAL Archery, Badminton, Basketball, Bowling, Gymnastics, Hammer Throw, Hand Ball, Judo, Karate, Ping-Pong, Racquetball, Soccer, Softball, Volleyball, Weight Lifting • STUDENT LIFE ACTIVITIES Debate, Debate, Ethnic & Cultural Groups, Jazz Band, Music Groups, Newspaper, Radio/TV station, Religious Organization, Student Government

---

Less Selective   **California Program**

Chaffey College

5885 Haven Avenue
Rancho Cucamonga, California 91701
(714) 987-1737

School Enrollment: **13,400** Male: **6,030** Female: **7,370**
LD Enrollment: **400** Male: **166** Female: **234**

Admissions Contact: **Jan Braustein, Dean of Students**
LD Contact: **Zenia K. Loggins, Director/LD Specialist**
Name of Program: **Learning Resource Program**
Telephone:**(714) 941-2332**

Admissions

Application Information:

LD Students Applying: **420** Accepted: **264** Enrolled:**235**
Separate application:**Yes**
Application deadline: **1st day of class**
Applicant must apply **1** months in advance
Rolling Admissions: **Yes**

Secondary School Information
Most Important Criteria For Admissions (1-strongest)

SAT/ACT	Application	School transcript
Class rank	Course selection	Personal statement
Interview	Extra activities	Psychoeducational
G.P.A.	**1** Open admission	Recommendations

Test Requirements:
Tests recommended: **Mandatory state testing for all community colleges**

Types of Disabilities Served
- Speech/Lang
- Study skills
- Written express
- Organizational
- Perceptual
- Reading
- Spelling
- Math
- Fine Motor
- ADD with LD
- ADD without LD
- ADHD with LD
- ADHD without LD

Learning Disability Program
Program: Reinforces course work: **Yes**
Counseling: Individual: **Yes**

Faculty:
Faculty: **16** Full time: **8** Part time: **8**
LD faculty with: BS/BA: **4** M.A.: **12**

Diagnostic Testing

ADD	Personality	• Perceptual skills	• Spelling
ADHD	Organization	Fine motor skills	• Reading
• I.Q.	Handwriting	Spoken language	• Study skills
• Math	Social skills	• Written language	

Tutoring:
Services rendered by:
Graduates •Peers •Faculty •LD staff Teacher trainees

Tutorials

Grp.	Ind.	Tutorials	Grp.	Ind.	Tutorials
•	•	Math skills		•	Word processing
•	•	Study skills	•	•	Time management
•	•	Language arts	•	•	Learning strategies
•	•	Written express	•	•	Organizational skills

Academic Accommodations

Curriculum	Study Aids	Exams
Priority registration	Typist	Oral
Math waiver	Reader	Untimed
Foreign lang. waiver	• Notetaker	Take home
Course substitution	Proof reader	With proctor
In Class	• Text on tape	On computer
Calculators	Early syllabus	• Extended time
• Tape recorder	Taped handouts	On tape
• Word processor		Modified
Priority seating		Separate room

Program Strengths
Chaffey College maintains a strong commitment to serving people with learning, physical, communicative, and developmental disabilities who desire post-secondary academic and vocational education.

General Information:
Chaffey College is a 2 year public college. Urban campus of 59 acres is 50 miles from Los Angeles. Accessible by air or bus. Ski areas are 25 miles from campus. Beaches are 50 miles from campus. 20% of students are foreign. Housing is not guaranteed.

Accreditation: WACS

Expenses:
Tuition: In-state: Full year: $3.50 per unit to 9 units, 10 or more $34.00. Tuition: Out-of-state: Full year: Part-time: Per credit:$68.50.

Majors
• BUSINESS Accounting, Banking, Business Administration, Economics, Finance, Hotel and Restaurant Managemen, Management, Real Estate • COMMUNICATIONS Broadcasting, Commercial Design, Communication, English, Photography, Speech • COMPUTER SCIENCE Computer Science, Data Processing • CRAFTS AND DESIGN Ceramics, Graphic Design • EDUCATION Child Development, Early Childhood • ENGINEERING Electrical • HEALTH SCIENCES Medical Secretary, Medical Technology, Nursing, Nutritional/Food • HUMANITIES Humanities, Liberal Arts, Philosophy, Religion • LANGUAGES French, German, Spanish • SCIENCES Biology, Chemistry, Earth, Geography, Geology, Gerontology, Mathematics, Physical Science, Physics, Radiology • SOCIAL SCIENCES Anthropology, Criminal Justice, Geography, Government/Political, Government/Political, Political Science, Psychology, Social Sciences, Sociology • VISUAL AND PERFORMING ARTS Art, Dance, Fine Arts, Music, Theater • VOCATIONAL Automobile Technology, Aviation Administration, Aviation Maintenance, Dental Assistant, Drafting, Fashion Design, Fashion Mechandizing, Food Service, Home Economics, Industrial Arts, Industrial Design, Legal Secretary, Secretarial, Textile and Clothing, Welding

Sports/Activities
• SPORTS RELATED Cheerleading, Flying Team • SPORTS-INTERCOLLEGIATE Baseball (M), Basketball (M), Cross Country, Diving, Football (M), Golf, Swimming, Tennis, Track and Field, Volleyball (F), Water Polo (M) • STUDENT LIFE ACTIVITIES Children's Theater, Concert Band, Dance, Debate, Drama Groups, Ethnic & Cultural Groups, Music Ensembles, Music Groups, Musical Theater, Newspaper, Religious Organization, Student Government

---

Less Selective

California Program

College of Alameda
555 Atlantic Avenue
Alameda, California 94501
(415) 522-7221

School Enrollment: **5,000** Male: **1,000** Female: **4,000**
LD Enrollment: **130**

Admissions Contact: **Becky Sanchez, Counselor, DSPS**
LD Contact: **Pat Kerr/Judy Merrell, L.D. Specialist**
Name of Program: **Learning Disabilities**
Telephone:**(510) 748-2388**

Admissions

Application Information:
Rolling Admissions: **Yes**

Secondary School Information
Most Important Criteria For Admissions (1-strongest)

SAT/ACT	Application	School transcript
Class rank	Course selection	Personal statement
Interview	Extra activities	Psychoeducational
G.P.A.	**1** Open admission	Recommendations

California

Test Requirements:
Diagnostic testing waived: **Yes**
WAIS-R required: **Yes**
Documentation of LD required: **Yes**
Currency of diagnostic testing: **3 years**
Tests recommended: **WAIS, Woodcock-Johnson, WRAT**

Types of Disabilities Served
- Speech/Lang
- Study skills
- Written express
- Organizational
- Perceptual
- Reading
- Spelling
- Math
- Fine Motor
- ADD with LD
  ADD without LD
- ADHD with LD
  ADHD without LD

Learning Disability Program
Program: Remedial: **Yes**
Program: Reinforces course work: **Yes**
Recommended credits per semester: **Varies**
Counseling: Individual: **Yes**

Faculty:
Faculty: **3** Including Director: **Yes** Full time: **1** Part time: **2**
LD faculty with: BS/BA: **3** M.A.: **3**
Faculty advocate: **Yes** Meets with instructor: **As necessary**

Diagnostic Testing
- ADD
  ADHD
- I.Q.
- Math
- Personality
- Organization
- Handwriting
- Social skills
- Perceptual skills
- Fine motor skills
- Spoken language
- Written language
- Spelling
- Reading
- Study skills

Tutoring:
Average size of group tutorials:
Services rendered by:
Graduates   Peers   Faculty   •LD staff   Teacher trainees

Tutorials
Grp.	Ind.	Tutorials	Grp.	Ind.	Tutorials
•		Math skills	•		Word processing
•		Study skills	•		Time management
•		Language arts	•		Learning strategies
•		Written express	•		Organizational skills

Academic Accommodations
Curriculum	Study Aids	Exams
Priority registration	• Typist	• Oral
Math waiver	Reader	Untimed
Foreign lang. waiver	• Notetaker	• Take home
Course substitution	• Proof reader	With proctor
In Class	• Text on tape	On computer
• Calculators	Early syllabus	• Extended time
• Tape recorder	Taped handouts	On tape
• Word processor		• Modified
Priority seating		Separate room

Program Strengths
Any student who is 18 may enroll; however, to be eligible for services as a learning disabled student in any California Community College, a student needs to go through a standard eligibility procedure.

General Information:
College of Alameda is a 2 year public college. Urban campus 1 miles from Oakland/Berkeley. Ski areas are 3 to 4 miles from campus. Beaches are less than 1 mile from campus. 15% of students are foreign. Housing is not guaranteed.

Accreditation: WACS

Expenses:
Tuition: In-state: Full year: $120.00. Tuition: Out-of-state: Full year: $69.00 per unit plus $120.00. Part-time: Per credit: $69.00 per unit plus $120.00.

Majors
- AREA STUDIES Black/Afro-American, Mexican/American • BUSINESS Accounting, Business Administration, Marketing, Small Business • EDUCATION Physical, Special Education Assistant, Teacher Aid • HEALTH SCIENCES Dental Assistant, Medical Assistant • HUMANITIES Humanities, Philosophy • LANGUAGES German, Spanish • SCIENCES Biology, Environmental Studies, Geography, Mathematics • SOCIAL SCIENCES Anthropology, History, Political Science, Psychology, Social Sciences • VISUAL AND PERFORMING ARTS Art, Dramatic Arts, Music • VOCATIONAL Aeronautical Technology, Auto Mechanics, Aviation Maintenance, Aviation Operations, Business and Office, Dental Assistant, Diesel Power Technology, Disability Service Provider, Fashion Merchandising, Graphic Arts Technology, Secretarial, Upholster

Sports/Activities
- SPORTS-INTERCOLLEGIATE Tennis, Track and Field • SPORTS-INTRAMURAL Tennis (M), Track and Field • STUDENT LIFE ACTIVITIES Academic Clubs, Choral, Community Service, Dance, Ethnic & Cultural Groups, Fraternities, Jazz Band, Magazine, Newspaper, Political Groups, Sororities, Student Government

Less Selective　　　　　　　　**California Program**

College of San Mateo
1700 West Hillside Boulevard
San Mateo, California 94402
(415) 574-6433

School Enrollment: **15,000**
LD Enrollment: **90** Male: **46** Female: **44**

Admissions Contact: **John Mullen, Dir. of Adm. and Records**
LD Contact: **Marie Paparelli, LD Specialist**
Name of Program: **LD Assessment Center**
Telephone: **(415) 574-6433**

Admissions

Application Information:
LD Students Applying: **100** Accepted: **86** Enrolled: **86**
Rolling Admissions: **Yes**

Secondary School Information
Most Important Criteria For Admissions (1-strongest)
5 SAT/ACT	2 Application	3	School transcript
4 Class rank	6 Course selection	10	Personal statement
8 Interview	7 Extra activities	11	Psychoeducational
1 G.P.A.	Open admission	9	Recommendations

Test Requirements:
Diagnostic testing waived: **Yes**
Untimed SAT: **Yes** Untimed ACT: **Yes** Achievement tests required: **One**
Documentation of LD required: **Yes**
Currency of diagnostic testing: **Within semester**
Tests recommended: **California Community College Standardized Eligibility Process.**

Types of Disabilities Served
- Speech/Lang
- Study skills
- Written express
- Organizational
- Perceptual
- Reading
- Spelling
- Math
- Fine Motor

ADD with LD
ADD without LD
ADHD with LD
ADHD without LD

Admissions Process

Open enrollment - over 18 years old. If under 18 high school diploma/GED required.

Learning Disability Program

Special orientation for LD students: **Yes**
Program: Reinforces course work: **Yes**
Students mainstreamed **100** % of the day
Recommended credits per semester: **9 units**
Services only for LD students: **Yes**
Counseling: Individual: **Yes** Group Counseling: **Yes**
Support groups are available: **Yes, AA/Drug Abuse, Peer Counseling**

Faculty:
Faculty: **2** Including Director: **Yes** Full time: **1** Part time: **1** M.A.: **1**
Faculty advocate: **Yes** Meets with instructor: **As necessary**

Diagnostic Testing
ADD	Personality •	Perceptual skills	• Spelling
ADHD	Organization•	Fine motor skills	• Reading
• I.Q.	Handwriting	Spoken language	• Study skills
• Math	Social skills•	Written language	

Tutoring:
Average size of group tutorials: **One on one**
Services rendered by:
Graduates   Peers   Faculty   LD staff   Teacher trainees

Tutorials
Grp.	Ind.	Tutorials	Grp.	Ind.	Tutorials
	•	Math skills			Word processing
		Study skills			Time management
		Language arts			Learning strategies
	•	Written express		•	Organizational skills

Academic Accommodations
Curriculum	Study Aids	Exams
Priority registration	Typist	• Oral
Math waiver	• Reader	• Untimed
Foreign lang. waiver	• Notetaker	• Take home
Course substitution	• Proof reader	• With proctor
In Class	• Text on tape	• On computer
• Calculators	• Early syllabus	• Extended time
• Tape recorder	• Taped handouts	• On tape
Word processor		• Modified
• Priority seating		• Separate room

Graduation Requirements:
Course credits: **60** GPA: **2.0** Years to complete degree: **3**

Program Strengths
Provides diagnostic assessment under state guidelines. I.E.P. supportive services for mainstreamed LD student, specialized tutoring and study skills class.

General Information:
College of San Mateo is a 2 year public college. Suburban campus of 153 acres is 25 miles from San Francisco. Accessible by air, train, or bus. Ski areas are 200 miles from campus. Beaches are 30 miles from campus. 1% of students are foreign. Housing is not guaranteed.

Accreditation: WACS, FRACHE

Expenses:
Tuition: In-state: Full year: $6.00/unit - maximum $50.00/semester. Tuition: Out-of-state: Full year: $102.00. Part-time: Per credit: $102.00.

Majors
• AGRICULTURE Business, Education, Horticultural, Journalism • AREA STUDIES Ethics • ARTS Commercial Art, Film & Video, Graphic Art, Interior Design, Music, Painting, Photography • BUSINESS Business Administration, Business Management, Fashion Merchandising, Management, Marketing, Real Estate • COMMUNICATIONS Broadcasting, Journalism • COMPUTER SCIENCE Business Data Programming, Computer Science, Data Processing • CRAFTS AND DESIGN Industrial Design • EDUCATION Mathematics, Speech/Language • ENGINEERING Aerospace, Aviation, Electrical • HEALTH SCIENCES Dental Assistant, Dental Hygiene, Nursing, Nutritional/Food, Public Health • HUMANITIES Humanities • PRE PROFESSIONAL Architecture, Business, Dentistry, Drafting, Engineering, Forestry, Industrial Design, Law, Optometry, Pharmacy, Recreation, Veterinarian, Wildlife • SCIENCES Anthropology, Archeology, Computer Science, Meteorology • SOCIAL SCIENCES • VISUAL AND PERFORMING ARTS Music • VOCATIONAL Aviation Maintenance, Aviation Pilot, Aviation Technology, Cosmetology, Dental Assistant, Dental Hygiene, Fire Science, Forestry, Industrial Arts, Medical Laboraotry Technology, Piloting, Plumbing, Veterinarian Assistant

Sports/Activities
• SPORTS-INTERCOLLEGIATE Baseball, Baseball (F), Baseball (M), Basketball, Basketball (F), Basketball (M), Football, Football (M), Tennis (F), Track and Field, Track and Field (F), Track and Field (M), Volleyball • SPORTS-INTRAMURAL Baseball, Basketball, Softball, Softball (F), Volleyball • STUDENT LIFE ACTIVITIES Academic Clubs, Ethnic & Cultural Groups, Political Groups, Radio/TV station, Religious Organization, Student Government

Less Selective — **California** / **Services**

College of the Canyons
26455 North Rockwell Canyon Road
Valencia, California 91355
(805) 259-7800

School Enrollment: **6,000**

Admissions Contact: **Dottie Duncan, Director of Admissions**
LD Contact: **Nina Ashur, Ed.D. Learning Specialist**

Admissions

Secondary School Information
Most Important Criteria For Admissions (1-strongest)
SAT/ACT	Application	School transcript
Class rank	Course selection	Personal statement
Interview	Extra activities	Psychoeducational
G.P.A.	Open admission	Recommendations

Test Requirements:
Diagnostic testing waived: **Yes**
Documentation of LD required: **Yes**
Tests recommended: **Assessment process requires use of the California Assessment System for Adults with Learning Disabili-**

California

Types of Disabilities Served

Speech/Lang	Reading	ADD with LD
Study skills	Spelling	ADD without LD
Written express	Math	ADHD with LD
Organizational	Fine Motor	ADHD without LD
Perceptual		

Admissions Process

A formal application, transcript or record from the high school of graduation or last attendance, must be filed with the Admissions and Records Office. Students working for an associate degree or a certificate should have transcripts sent from each college attended.

High School Course Requirements:

Learning Disability Program

Program: Reinforces course work: **Yes**
Recommended credits per semester: **12-15**
Services available for all students: **Yes**

Faculty:

Faculty: **3** Full time: **1** Part time: **2** M.A.: **1**

Diagnostic Testing

ADD	Personality	Perceptual skills	•	Spelling
ADHD	Organization	Fine motor skills	•	Reading
• I.Q.	Handwriting	Spoken language	•	Study skills
• Math	Social skills	Written language		

Tutoring:

Average size of group tutorials: **5-10**
Services rendered by:

Graduates	Peers	Faculty	•LD staff	Teacher trainees

Tutorials

Grp.	Ind.	Tutorials	Grp.	Ind.	Tutorials
•	•	Math skills	•	•	Word processing
		Study skills		•	Time management
	•	Language arts	•	•	Learning strategies
	•	Written express		•	Organizational skills

Academic Accommodations

Curriculum	Study Aids	Exams
• Priority registration	Typist	Oral
Math waiver	• Reader	• Untimed
Foreign lang. waiver	• Notetaker	Take home
• Course substitution	Proof reader	With proctor
In Class	• Text on tape	On computer
Calculators	Early syllabus	• Extended time
• Tape recorder	Taped handouts	• On tape
• Word processor		Modified
• Priority seating		• Separate room

General Information:

College of the Canyons is a 2 year public college. Suburban campus of 153 acres is Los Angeles. Accessible by plane, train or bus Housing is not guaranteed.

Accreditation: WACS

Expenses:

Tuition: In-state: Full year: $60.00. Part-time: Per credit:$6.00. Tuition: Out-of-state: Full year: $100.00.

Majors

• ARTS Dance, Drafting, Music, Photography • BUSINESS Accounting, Business Management, Economics, Hotel & Restaurant Management, Marketing • COMMUNICATIONS Journalism, Public Relations, Speech/Debate/Forensic, Television/Radio/Film • COMPUTER SCIENCE Computer Science • EDUCATION Early Childhood, English, Special • ENVIRONMENTAL CONTROL Water and Wastewater Technolog • HEALTH SCIENCES Nursing, Nursing Assistant • HUMANITIES English/Writing/Literature, Finance, Humanities, Liberal Arts , Philosophy • LANGUAGES French, German, Spanish • PRE PROFESSIONAL Drafting • SCIENCES Astronomy, Biology, Geography, Geology, Physics • SOCIAL SCIENCES Anthropology, Criminal Justice, Geography, History, Library Science, Polymer Science, Psychology, Sociology • VISUAL AND PERFORMING ARTS Art, Music, Theater

Sports/Activities

• SPORTS-INTERCOLLEGIATE Baseball (F), Baseball (M), Basketball (F), Basketball (M), Cross Country, Golf, Swimming, Track and Field, Volleyball

---

Less Selective

California Services

College of the Sequoias
915 South Mooney Boulevard
Visalia, California 93277
(209) 733-2050

School Enrollment: **8,913** Male: **3,500** Female: **5,413**

Admissions Contact: **Robert Heath, Registrar**
LD Contact: **Annie Silva, LD Specialist**
Name of Program: **Enabler's Program**
Telephone:**(209) 730-3805**

Admissions

Application Information:

LD Students Applying: **100** Accepted: **65** Enrolled:**60**

Secondary School Information

Most Important Criteria For Admissions (1-strongest)

SAT/ACT	Application	School transcript
Class rank	Course selection	Personal statement
Interview	Extra activities	Psychoeducational
G.P.A.	Open admission	Recommendations

Test Requirements:

Standardized tests waived: **Yes**
Diagnostic testing waived: **Yes**
Currency of diagnostic testing: **3 years**
Tests recommended: **WAIS-R or Woodcock Johnson (latter is preferred)**

Types of Disabilities Served

• Speech/Lang	• Reading	• ADD with LD
• Study skills	• Spelling	ADD without LD
• Written express	• Math	• ADHD with LD
• Organizational	• Fine Motor	ADHD without LD
• Perceptual		

Learning Disability Program

Program: Remedial: **Yes**
Program: Reinforces course work: **Yes**
Students mainstreamed **95** % of the day

Faculty:
Faculty: **1** Full time: **1** M.A.: **1**
Faculty advocate: **Yes** Meets with instructor: **Each semester**

Diagnostic Testing
- ADD
- ADHD
- I.Q.
- Math
- Personality
- Organization
- Handwriting
- Social skills
- Perceptual skills
- Fine motor skills
- Spoken language
- Written language
- Spelling
- Reading
- Study skills

Tutoring:
Average size of group tutorials: **3**
Services rendered by:
- Graduates
- Peers
- Faculty
- LD staff
- Teacher trainees

Tutorials

Grp.	Ind.	Tutorials	Grp.	Ind.	Tutorials
•	•	Math skills	•	•	Word processing
•	•	Study skills	•	•	Time management
•	•	Language arts	•	•	Learning strategies
•	•	Written express	•	•	Organizational skills

Academic Accommodations

Curriculum	Study Aids	Exams
Priority registration	• Typist	• Oral
Math waiver	• Reader	• Untimed
Foreign lang. waiver	• Notetaker	Take home
Course substitution	• Proof reader	• With proctor
In Class	• Text on tape	• On computer
• Calculators	Early syllabus	• Extended time
• Tape recorder	Taped handouts	• On tape
• Word processor		• Modified
• Priority seating		• Separate room

Program Strengths

We offer a wide range of supportive services in addition to having a remedial/tutorial program for the LD students. We also offer special academic counseling and registration assistance. We have a High Tech Center equipped with numerous computers and special adaptions for the physically and learning disabled.

General Information:

College of the Sequoias is a 2 year public college. Rural campus of 55+ acres is 45 miles from Fresno. Accessible by air, train or bus. Ski areas are 2 hours from campus. Beaches are 2.5 hours from campus. 7.1% of students are foreign. Housing is not guaranteed.

Accreditation: WACS

Expenses:
Tuition: In-state: Full year: $120.00. Tuition: Out-of-state: Full year: Partime: Per credit: $112.00.

Majors

• AREA STUDIES American, Black/Afro-American, Latin American • BUSINESS Accounting, Business Administration, Business Education, Business Management, Economics, Finance, Management, Marketing, Marketing Research, Personnel, Real Estate, Sports Management • COMMUNICATIONS Communication, English, Journalism, Photography, Sign Language, Television/Radio/Film • COMPUTER SCIENCE Data Processing, Hardware Engineer, Programming, Systems Analysis • EDUCATION Child Development, Early Childhood, Elementary, Industrial, Middle

School, Physical, Secondary, Teacher's Aid • ENGINEERING Air Conditioning Technology, Electrical, Engineering Science • HEALTH SCIENCES Nursing • HUMANITIES Classics, English/Writing/Literature, Liberal Arts, Philosophy • LANGUAGES French, German, Italian, Spanish • PRE-PROFESSIONAL Agriculture, Architecture, Drafting, Engineering, Recreation, Sports Medicine • SCIENCES Actuarial Technology, Astronomy, Biology, Botany, Chemistry, Earth, Ecology, Geography, Geology, Mathematics, Physical Chemistry, Physical Science, Physics, Zoology • SOCIAL SCIENCES Anthropology, Criminal Justice, Geography, History, Human Service, Law Enforcement, Police Academy, Psychology, Public Affairs, Social Sciences, Sociology • VISUAL AND PERFORMING ARTS Art, Art History, Dance, Fine Arts, Music, Studio Art, Theater • VOCATIONAL Air Conditioning/Heating/Refri, Automobile Technology, Automotive Service, Business and Office, Carpentry, Cosmetology, Drafting, Electronics Technology, Fire Science, Home Economics, Landscape Architecture, Machinist, Metal Technology, Military Science, Secretarial, Welding, Woodworking

Sports/Activities

• SPORTS RELATED Baton Twirling, Cheerleading, Drill Team, Drum Major/Majorette, Marching Band, Pep Band, Team Managers • SPORTS-INTERCOLLEGIATE Baseball, Basketball, Cross Country, Diving, Football (M), Golf, Softball (F), Swimming, Tennis, Track and Field, Volleyball (F), Water Polo (M), Wrestling • SPORTS-INTRAMURAL Badminton, Racquetball • STUDENT LIFE ACTIVITIES Choral, Concert Band, Dance, Drama Groups, Ethnic & Cultural Groups, Jazz Band, Music Ensembles, Music Groups, Musical Theater, Newspaper, Radio/TV station, Religious Organization, Student Government, Symphony Orchestra

---

Less Selective

California Services

College of the Siskiyous
800 College Avenue
Weed, California 96094
(916) 938-4462

School Enrollment: **2,728** Male: **1,091** Female: **1,637**
LD Enrollment: **24** Male: **14** Female: **10**

Admissions Contact: **James Arack, Ph.D. V.P. of Student Services**
LD Contact: **Charles Abel, LD Specialist**
Telephone: **(916) 938-4462**

Admissions

Secondary School Information
Most Important Criteria For Admissions (1-strongest)

SAT/ACT	Application	School transcript
Class rank	Course selection	Personal statement
Interview	Extra activities	Psychoeducational
G.P.A.	**1** Open admission	Recommendations

Types of Disabilities Served
- Speech/Lang
- Study skills
- Written express
- Organizational Perceptual
- Reading
- Spelling
- Math
- Fine Motor
- ADD with LD
- ADD without LD
- ADHD with LD
- ADHD without LD

Learning Disability Program
Counseling: Individual: **Yes**

California

Faculty:
Faculty: **2** Full time: **1** Part time: **1**
Faculty advocate: **Yes** Meets with instructor: **As needed**

Diagnostic Testing
ADD	Personality	Perceptual skills	Spelling
ADHD	Organization	Fine motor skills	Reading
I.Q.	Handwriting	Spoken language	Study skills
Math	Social skills	Written language	

Tutoring:
Services rendered by:
Graduates •Peers   Faculty   •LD staff   Teacher trainees

Tutorials
Grp.	Ind.	Tutorials	Grp.	Ind.	Tutorials
	•	Math skills		•	Word processing
	•	Study skills		•	Time management
	•	Language arts		•	Learning strategies
	•	Written express		•	Organizational skills

Academic Accommodations
Curriculum	Study Aids	Exams
Priority registration	• Typist	• Oral
Math waiver	Reader	Untimed
Foreign lang. waiver	• Notetaker	Take home
Course substitution	• Proof reader	With proctor
In Class	• Text on tape	On computer
• Calculators	Early syllabus	• Extended time
• Tape recorder	Taped handouts	On tape
• Word processor		• Modified
Priority seating		Separate room

Program Strengths
We are a small, rural environment that lends itself well to the individual needs of students. We also have a great student teacher ratio. All of our students take placement tests in math and English.

General Information:
College of the Siskiyous is a 2 year public college. Rural campus 75 miles from Redding. Accessible by train or bus. Ski areas are 25 minutes from campus. Beaches are 4 hours from campus. 2 residential halls on campus. Housing is not guaranteed.30 % of students remain on campus for the weekends.

Accreditation:WACS

Expenses:
Tuition: In-state: Full year: $50.00. Part-time: Per credit:$5.00. Tuition: Out-of-state: Full year: Part-time: Per credit: $94.00. Part-time: Per credit:$94.00.

Majors
• BUSINESS Accounting, Business Administration, Business Data Programming, Business Education, Economics, Family Consumer Management • COMMUNICATIONS Communication, Creative Writing, English, Photography, Television/Radio/Film • COMPUTER SCIENCE Programming • CRAFTS AND DESIGN Crafts • EDUCATION Art, Child Development, General • ENGINEERING Engineering Science • HEALTH SCIENCES Health, Nursing, Practical Nursing • HUMANITIES Humanities, Liberal Arts, Philosophy, Religion • LANGUAGES French, Spanish • PREPROFESSIONAL Agriculture, Dentistry, Engineering, Forestry, Law, Medicine, Pharmacy, Veterinarian • SCIENCES Animal, Astronomy, Biology, Chemistry, Earth, Ecology, Geography, Geology, Horticultural, Mathematics, Microbiology, Physical Chemistry, Physical Science, Physics, Physiology, Plant Science • SOCIAL SCIENCES Anthropology, Criminal Justice, Geography, Government/Political, History, Law Enforcement, Psychology, Social Sciences, Sociology • VISUAL AND PERFORMING ARTS Art, Art History, Dance, Fine Arts, Music • VOCATIONAL Automotive Service, Automotive Service, Business and Office, Fire Science, Home Economics, Precision Metal Work, Secretarial

Sports/Activities
• SPORTS RELATED Pep Band • SPORTS-INTERCOLLEGIATE Baseball (M), Basketball, Cross Country, Football (M), Softball (F), Track and Field • STUDENT LIFE ACTIVITIES Choral, Concert Band, Dance, Drama Groups, Jazz Band, Musical Ensembles, Musical Theater, Newspaper, Radio/TV station, Student Government, Symphony Orchestra, Yearbook

Less Selective   **California Program**

Columbia College
P.O. Box 1849
Columbia, California 95310
(209) 533-5106

School Enrollment: **3,500** Male: **1,750** Female: **1,750**
LD Enrollment: **60**

Admissions Contact: **Lenise Kimes, Admissions Clerk**
LD Contact: **Patricia Harrelson, LD Specialist**
Name of Program: **Learning Disabilities Programs**
Telephone:**(209) 533-5130**

Admissions

Application Information:
Enrolled:**60**
Separate application:**Yes**
Application deadline: **August 10th**
Applicant must apply **4-6 months** in advance
Notified when: **1 month**

Secondary School Information
Most Important Criteria For Admissions (1-strongest)
SAT/ACT	Application	School transcript
Class rank	Course selection	Personal statement
Interview	Extra activities	Psychoeducational
G.P.A. **1**	Open admission	Recommendations

Test Requirements:
Standardized tests waived: **Yes**
Diagnostic testing waived: **Yes**
WAIS-R required: **Yes** Range accepted: **CA Norms**
Currency of diagnostic testing: **3 years**
Tests recommended: **WAIS-R, Woodcock-Johnson**

Types of Disabilities Served
• Speech/Lang	• Reading	• ADD with LD
• Study skills	• Spelling	• ADD without LD
• Written express	• Math	• ADHD with LD
• Organizational	• Fine Motor	• ADHD without LD
• Perceptual		

Learning Disability Program
Program: Reinforces course work: **Yes**
Students mainstreamed **100** % of the day
Counseling: Individual: **Yes**

Faculty:
Faculty: **4** Full time: **4**
LD faculty with: BS/BA: **1** M.A.: **2**
Faculty advocate: **Yes** Meets with instructor: **As needed**

Diagnostic Testing
- ADD
- ADHD
- I.Q.
- Math

- Personality
- Organization
- Handwriting
- Social skills

- Perceptual skills
- Fine motor skills
- Spoken language
- Written language

- Spelling
- Reading
  Study skills

Tutoring:
Average size of group tutorials: **4-5**
Services rendered by:
Graduates •Peers Faculty •LD staff Teacher trainees

Tutorials

Grp.	Ind.	Tutorials	Grp.	Ind.	Tutorials
•	•	Math skills		•	Word processing
•	•	Study skills		•	Time management
•	•	Language arts		•	Learning strategies
•	•	Written express		•	Organizational skills

Academic Accommodations

Curriculum
- Priority registration
- Math waiver
- Foreign lang. waiver
- Course substitution

In Class
- Calculators
- Tape recorder
- Word processor
- Priority seating

Study Aids
- Typist
  Reader
- Notetaker
- Proof reader
- Text on tape
  Early syllabus
  Taped handouts

Exams
- Oral
  Untimed
- Take home
  With proctor
  On computer
- Extended time
  On tape
  Modified
  Separate room

Program Strengths
We serve students on a one-to-one basis.

General Information:
Columbia College is a 2 year public college. Rural campus of 200 acres is 125 miles from San Francisco. Accessible by air or bus. Ski areas are 25 miles from campus. Beaches are 125 miles from campus. 2% of students are foreign. 1 residential halls on campus. Housing is guaranteed.

Accreditation: Regional

Expenses:
Tuition: In-state: Full year: $100.00. Part-time: Per credit:$5.00. Tuition: Out-of-state: Full year: Part-time: Per credit: $94.00.

Majors
• BUSINESS Accounting, Business Administration, Business Economics, Business Education, Business Management, Food Management, Hotel and Restaurant Managemen, Marketing, Real Estate, Travel/Tourism Management • COMMUNICATIONS Creative Writing, English, Photography • COMPUTER SCIENCE Programming • EDUCATION Early Childhood • HEALTH SCIENCES Medical Technology, Nursing • HUMANITIES Humanities, Liberal Arts, Philosophy • LANGUAGES Spanish • PRE-PROFESSIONAL Forestry, Natural Resources • SCIENCES Astronomy, Biology, Chemistry, Earth, Mathematics, Physical Science • SOCIAL SCIENCES Anthropology, History, Psychology, Social Sciences, Sociology • VISUAL AND PERFORMING ARTS Art, Dance, Fine Arts, Music, Theater • VOCATIONAL Automobile Technology, Automotive Service, Business and Office, Fire Science, Secretarial, Welding

Sports/Activities
• SPORTS-INTERCOLLEGIATE Baseball (M) • SPORTS-INTRAMU-

RAL Fencing, Skiing - Cross Country, Skiing - Snow, Volleyball, Weight Lifting • STUDENT LIFE ACTIVITIES Choral, Dance, Drama Groups, Jazz Band, Music Groups, Musical Theater, Student Government, Symphony Orchestra

---

Less Selective

California Program

Crafton Hills College
11711 Sand Canyon Road
Yucaipa, California 92399
(714) 794-2161

School Enrollment: **4,420** Male: **1,820** Female: **2,600**

Admissions Contact: **Dr. Luis Gomez, Dean of Student Services**
LD Contact: **Kirsten Colvey, LD Specialist**
Name of Program: **Learning Disabilities Prog.**

Admissions

Application Information:
Separate application:**Yes**
Application deadline: **3rd Day of Classes**

Secondary School Information
Most Important Criteria For Admissions (1-strongest)

SAT/ACT	Application	School transcript
Class rank	Course selection	Personal statement
Interview	Extra activities	Psychoeducational
G.P.A.	**1** Open admission	Recommendations

Test Requirements:
Currency of diagnostic testing: **3 years**
Tests recommended: **WAIS-R, WRAT**

Types of Disabilities Served
- Speech/Lang
- Study skills
- Written express
- Organizational
  Perceptual

- Reading
- Spelling
- Math
- Fine Motor

- ADD with LD
- ADD without LD
- ADHD with LD
- ADHD without LD

Learning Disability Program
Program: Remedial: **Yes**
Program: Reinforces course work: **Yes**
Students mainstreamed **100** % of the day
Counseling: Individual: **Yes**

Faculty:
Faculty: **2** Including Director: **Yes** Full time: **2** M.A.: **2**
Faculty advocate: **Yes** Meets with instructor: **As needed**

Diagnostic Testing
- ADD
- ADHD
- I.Q.
- Math

- Personality
- Organization
- Handwriting
- Social skills

- Perceptual skills
- Fine motor skills
- Spoken language
- Written language

- Spelling
- Reading
  Study skills

Tutoring:
Services rendered by:
Graduates Peers •Faculty •LD staff Teacher trainees

California

Tutorials

Grp.	Ind.	Tutorials	Grp.	Ind.	Tutorials
	•	Math skills		•	Word processing
	•	Study skills		•	Time management
	•	Language arts		•	Learning strategies
	•	Written express		•	Organizational skills

Academic Accommodations

Curriculum	Study Aids	Exams
Priority registration	• Typist	• Oral
Math waiver	Reader	Untimed
Foreign lang. waiver	• Notetaker	• Take home
Course substitution	• Proof reader	With proctor
In Class	• Text on tape	On computer
• Calculators	Early syllabus	• Extended time
• Tape recorder	Taped handouts	On tape
• Word processor		Modified
Priority seating		Separate room

Program Strengths

The Learning Disability Program component of Disabled Student Services at Crafton Hills College primarily seeks to provide students who have the ability to profit from the instructional programs at the college with the appropriate support services, materials and equipment to enable those students to meet their educational or vocational training goals.

General Information:

Crafton Hills College is a 2 year public college. Rural campus of 500 acres is 10 miles from San Bernardino. Accessible by bus. Ski areas are 35 miles from campus. Beaches are 50 miles from campus. Housing is not guaranteed.

Accreditation: WACS

Expenses:

Tuition: In-state: Full year: $100.00. Part-time: Per credit:$5.00. Tuition: Out-of-state: Full year: Part-time: Per credit: $101.00.

Majors

• BUSINESS Accounting, Business Administration, Business Management, Economics, Marketing, Real Estate • COMMUNICATIONS Creative Writing, English, Speech • COMPUTER SCIENCE Data Processing, Programming • EDUCATION Early Childhood, Elementary, Secondary • HEALTH SCIENCES Medical Secretary • LANGUAGES French, German • PREPROFESSIONAL Engineering, Law, Medicine, Ministry • SCIENCES Astronomy, Biology, Chemistry, Geology, Mathematics, Microbiology, Physics • SOCIAL SCIENCES Government/Political, History, Law Enforcement, Political Science, Psychology, Social Sciences, Sociology • VISUAL AND PERFORMING ARTS Art, Art History, Music, Theater • VOCATIONAL Business and Office, Fire Science, Respiratory Therapy Technology, Secretarial

Sports/Activities

• SPORTS-INTRAMURAL Bowling, Golf, Tennis, Volleyball, Weight Lifting • STUDENT LIFE ACTIVITIES Choral, Dance, Drama Groups, Jazz Band, Music Ensembles, Music Groups, Musical Theate

Cuesta College
P.O. Box 8106
San Luis Obispo, California 93403-8106
(805) 546-3100

School Enrollment: **7,900** Male: **3,500** Female: **4,400**

Admissions Contact: **Frank Gonzales, Dean of Student Services**
LD Contact: **Dr. Lynn Frady, Director**
Name of Program: **Learning Disabilities Prog.**
Address: **P.O. Box 8106**
Telephone:**(805) 546-3148**

Admissions

Application Information:
Enrolled:**200**

Secondary School Information
Most Important Criteria For Admissions (1-strongest)

SAT/ACT	Application	School transcript
Class rank	Course selection	Personal statement
Interview	Extra activities	Psychoeducational
G.P.A.　**1**	Open admission	Recommendations

Test Requirements:
Documentation of LD required: **Yes**
Currency of diagnostic testing: **No more than 3 years**
Tests recommended: **California Community Colleges have a standardized process**

Types of Disabilities Served

• Speech/Lang	• Reading	• ADD with LD
• Study skills	• Spelling	ADD without LD
• Written express	• Math	• ADHD with LD
• Organizational	• Fine Motor	ADHD without LD
• Perceptual		

Admissions Process

Open admissions

Learning Disability Program

Program: Remedial: **Yes**
Program: Reinforces course work: **Yes**
Services only for LD students: **Yes**
Counseling: Individual: **Yes** Group Counseling: **Yes**
Support groups are available:**Academic support groups, others as requested**

Faculty:
Faculty: **3** Including Director: **Yes** Full time: **2** Part time: **1** M.A.: **2** Ph.D.: **1**
Faculty advocate: **Yes** Meets with instructor: **As needed**

Diagnostic Testing

ADD	Personality •	Perceptual skills	• Spelling
ADHD	Organization	Fine motor skills	• Reading
• I.Q.	Handwriting•	Spoken language	• Study skills
• Math	Social skills •	Written language	

Tutoring:
Average size of group tutorials: **6-10**
Services rendered by:
•Graduates •Peers •Faculty •LD staff •Teacher trainees

Tutorials

Grp.	Ind.	Tutorials	Grp.	Ind.	Tutorials
•	•	Math skills	•	•	Word processing
•	•	Study skills	•	•	Time management
•	•	Language arts	•	•	Learning strategies
•	•	Written express	•	•	Organizational skills

Academic Accommodations

Curriculum	Study Aids	Exams
• Priority registration	• Typist	• Oral
Math waiver	• Reader	• Untimed
Foreign lang. waiver	• Notetaker	• Take home
Course substitution	• Proof reader	• With proctor
In Class	• Text on tape	• On computer
• Calculators	• Early syllabus	• Extended time
• Tape recorder	• Taped handouts	• On tape
• Word processor		• Modified
• Priority seating		Separate room

Graduation Requirements: Math waiver: **Yes** Language waiver: **Yes**

Program Strengths
The Cuesta College LD Program provides special instruction and support services to eligible students.

General Information:
Cuesta College is a 2 year public college. Suburban campus of 72 acres is 100 miles from Santa Barbara. Accessible by air, train, or bus. Ski areas are 20 miles from campus. Beaches are 10 miles from campus. Housing is not guaranteed.

Accreditation: WACS

Expenses:
Tuition: In-state: Full year: $120.00. Tuition: Out-of-state: Full year: $102.00 per unit.

Majors
• BUSINESS Accounting, Business Administration, Marketing, Real Estate • COMMUNICATIONS Broadcasting, English • COMPUTER SCIENCE Data Processing • EDUCATION Art, Early Childhood • HEALTH SCIENCES Nursing • PREPROFESSIONAL Engineering • SCIENCES Biology, Chemistry, Geography, Mathematics, Physical Science • SOCIAL SCIENCES Criminal Justice, History • VISUAL AND PERFORMING ARTS Art

Sports/Activities
• SPORTS-INTRAMURAL Archery, Badminton, Baseball, Basketball, Cross Country, Cycling, Fencing, Golf, Softball, Swimming, Tennis, Track and Field (F), Volleyball, Water Polo, Weight Lifting, Wrestling • STUDENT LIFE ACTIVITIES Drama Groups, Jazz Band, Music Groups, Newspaper, Radio/TV station, Student Government

---

Less Selective — **California Program**

Cypress College
9200 Valley View
Cypress, California 90630
(714) 826-2220

School Enrollment: **13,878** Male: **5,821** Female: **8,057**
LD Enrollment: **75+**

Admissions Contact: **Dr. Alexander, McLeod Dean of Admissions**
LD Contact: **Robert Nadell, Director**
Name of Program: **Educational Services Center**
Telephone: **(714) 826-2220 Ext. 215**

Admissions

Application Information:
Enrolled: **75**
Separate application: **Yes**
Application deadline: **Beginning of semester**
Applicant must apply **2** months in advance

Secondary School Information
Most Important Criteria For Admissions (1-strongest)

SAT/ACT	Application	School transcript
Class rank	Course selection	Personal statement
Interview	Extra activities	Psychoeducational
G.P.A.	Open admission	Recommendations

Test Requirements:
Standardized tests waived: **Yes**
Tests recommended: **Testing will be administered after enrollment in college**

Types of Disabilities Served
• Speech/Lang	• Reading	• ADD with LD
• Study skills	• Spelling	ADD without LD
• Written express	• Math	• ADHD with LD
• Organizational	• Fine Motor	ADHD without LD
• Perceptual		

Learning Disability Program
Program: Reinforces course work: **Yes**
Students mainstreamed **100** % of the day
Counseling: Individual: **Yes**

Faculty:
Faculty: **5** Full time: **3** Part time: **2**
LD faculty with: BS/BA: **1** M.A.: **2**
Faculty advocate: **Yes** Meets with instructor: **As needed**

Diagnostic Testing
ADD	Personality	• Perceptual skills	• Spelling
ADHD	Organization	• Fine motor skills	• Reading
• I.Q.	• Handwriting	• Spoken language	Study skills
• Math	Social skills	• Written language	

Tutoring:
Services rendered by:
Graduates Peers Faculty •LD staff •Teacher trainees

California

Tutorials

Grp.	Ind.	Tutorials	Grp.	Ind.	Tutorials
	•	Math skills		•	Word processing
	•	Study skills		•	Time management
	•	Language arts		•	Learning strategies
	•	Written express		•	Organizational skills

Academic Accommodations

Curriculum	Study Aids	Exams
Priority registration	• Typist	Oral
Math waiver	Reader	Untimed
Foreign lang. waiver	• Notetaker	Take home
Course substitution	• Proof reader	With proctor
In Class	• Text on tape	On computer
• Calculators	Early syllabus	• Extended time
• Tape recorder	Taped handouts	On tape
Word processor		Modified
Priority seating		Separate room

Program Strengths

The primary goal of the Cypress College Educational Services Center is providing special academic, vocational, and social support to students with learning disabilities, enabling them to fulfill their college goals. The Center offers a wide range of services. Among recent developments is a high-technology computer component designed to serve the individual student's academic and vocational needs.

General Information:

Cypress College is a 2 year public college. Urban campus of 108 acres is Accessible by air, train, or bus. 12% of students are foreign. Housing is not guaranteed.

Accreditation: Regional

Expenses: Part-time: Per credit:$5.00. Tuition: Out-of-state: Full year: Part-time: Per credit: $103.00.

Majors

• AREA STUDIES Asian, Latin American • BUSINESS Accounting, Business Administration, Business Management, Economics, Food Management, Hotel and Restaurant Managemen, Management, Marketing, Travel/Tourism Management • COMMUNICATIONS Journalism • COMPUTER SCIENCE Computer Science, Data Processing • CRAFTS AND DESIGN Illustration Design • EDUCATION Elementary, General, Industrial, Physical, Secondary • ENGINEERING Engineering Science • HEALTH SCIENCES Dental Assistant, Dental Hygiene, Medical Assistant, Medical Records Technology, Mortuary Science, Nursing, Physical Therapy, Radiograph Medical Technology • LANGUAGES French, German, Spanish • PREPROFESSIONAL Dentistry, Forestry, Law, Medicine, Pharmacy, Veterinarian • SCIENCES Biology, Chemistry, Geography, Geology, Mathematics, Physics • SOCIAL SCIENCES Anthropology, Government/Political, History, Human Service, Psychology, Sociology • VISUAL AND PERFORMING ARTS Art, Dance, Fine Arts, Music • VOCATIONAL Aeronautical Technology, Air Condtioning/Heating/Refrig, Automobile Technology, Automotive Service, Aviation Management, Aviation Pilot, Court Reporting, Electronics Technology, Secretarial, Word Processing

Sports/Activities

• SPORTS RELATED Cheerleading • SPORTS-INTERCOLLEGIATE Baseball (M), Basketball, Cross Country, Golf (M), Soccer (M), Softball (F), Swimming, Tennis, Volleyball (F), Water Polo (M), Wrestling (M) • SPORTS-INTRAMURAL Archery, Badminton, Baseball (M), Basketball, Bowling, Diving, Football (M), Golf, Gymnastics, Hand Ball, Racquetball, Scuba, Skiing - Snow, Soccer, Softball, Track and Field, Trap and Skeet, Volleyball, Weight Lifting • STUDENT LIFE ACTIVITIES Concert Band, Dance, Debate, Drama Groups, Ethnic & Cultural Groups, Jazz Band, Magazine, Music Ensembles, Music Groups, Musical Theater,

Newspaper, Radio/TV station, Student Government, Student Government

Less Selective

De Anza College
21250 Stevens Creek Boulevard
Cupertino, California 95014
(408) 864-8419

School Enrollment: **28,000** Male: **12,500** Female: **15,500**
LD Enrollment: **250** Male: **137** Female: **113**

Admissions Contact: **Lewis Ham, Director of Admissions**
LD Contact: **Pauline Waathiq, Director**
Name of Program: **Educational Diagnostic Center**
Telephone:**(408) 864-8838 or 8839**

Admissions

Application Information:
Application deadline: **None**
Applicant must apply **3** months in advance
Rolling Admissions: **Yes**

Secondary School Information
Most Important Criteria For Admissions (1-strongest)

SAT/ACT	Application	School transcript
Class rank	Course selection	Personal statement
Interview	Extra activities	Psychoeducational
G.P.A.	Open admission	Recommendations

Test Requirements:
Standardized tests waived: **Yes**
Diagnostic testing waived: **Yes**
Currency of diagnostic testing: **2 years**
Tests recommended: **Woodcock-Johnson or WAIS-R**

Types of Disabilities Served

• Speech/Lang	• Reading	• ADD with LD
• Study skills	• Spelling	ADD without LD
• Written express	• Math	• ADHD with LD
• Organizational	• Fine Motor	ADHD without LD
• Perceptual		

Learning Disability Program
Program: Remedial: **Yes**
Program: Reinforces course work: **Yes**
Students mainstreamed **85** % of the day
Counseling: Individual: **Yes**

Faculty:
Faculty: **7** Including Director: **Yes** Full time: **7** M.A.: **6** Ph.D.: **1**
Faculty advocate: **Yes** Meets with instructor: **As needed**

Diagnostic Testing

ADD	Personality	Perceptual skills	• Spelling
ADHD	Organization	Fine motor skills	• Reading
I.Q.	Handwriting	Spoken language	Study skills
• Math	Social skills	• Written language	

Tutoring:
Average size of group tutorials: **5-8**
Services rendered by:

Graduates Peers •Faculty •LD staff •Teacher trainees

Tutorials

Grp.	Ind.	Tutorials	Grp.	Ind.	Tutorials
•	•	Math skills	•	•	Word processing
	•	Study skills	•	•	Time management
•	•	Language arts	•	•	Learning strategies
•	•	Written express	•	•	Organizational skills

Academic Accommodations

Curriculum
Priority registration
Math waiver
Foreign lang. waiver
Course substitution

In Class
• Calculators
• Tape recorder
• Word processor
  Priority seating

Study Aids
Typist
Reader
Notetaker
Proof reader
Text on tape
Early syllabus
Taped handouts

Exams
• Oral
  Untimed
  Take home
• With proctor
• On computer
• Extended time
  On tape
  Modified
  Separate room

Program Strengths

The Educational Diagnostic Center is a comprehensive LD support program. We offer a large array of precollegiate skills development classes, and frequent close contact with a large staff of LD specialists. California community colleges are excellent for the student in developing academic skills and exploring career options. The student body is diverse in its ethnic and cultural backgrounds.

General Information:

De Anza College is a 2 year public college. Suburban campus of 112 acres is 10 miles from San Jose. Accessible by air, train or bus. Ski areas are 200 miles from campus. Beaches are 40 miles from campus. Housing is not guaranteed.

Accreditation: WACS

Expenses: Part-time: Per credit: $4.00 . Tuition: Out-of-state: Full year: Part-time: Per credit: $71.00.

Majors

• AREA STUDIES • BUSINESS Accounting, Business Administration, Business Management, Business Writing, Economics, Purchasing, Real Estate, Taxation • COMMUNICATIONS Creative Writing, English, Photography, Technical Writing, Television/Radio/Film • COMPUTER SCIENCE Computer Science, Data Processing, Programming, Systems Analysis • EDUCATION Agricultural, Early Childhood • HEALTH SCIENCES Medical Assistant, Nursing, Physical Therapy • HUMANITIES Liberal Arts, Philosophy • LANGUAGES French, German, Japanese, Spanish • PREPROFESSIONAL Law, Legal Assistant • SCIENCES Biology, Chemistry, Geology, Mathematics, Physics • SOCIAL SCIENCES Anthropology, Criminal Justice, History, Law Enforcement, Political Science, Political Science, Sociology • VISUAL AND PERFORMING ARTS Dance, fine Arts, Music • VOCATIONAL Automobile Technology, Drafting, Electronics Technology, Industrial Arts, Machinist, Secretarial, Word Processing

Sports/Activities

• SPORTS-INTERCOLLEGIATE Baseball (M), Basketball, Cross Country, Diving, Football (M), Golf (M), Swimming, Tennis, Track and Field, Water Polo (M) • SPORTS-INTRAMURAL Fencing, Gymnastics, Volleyball • STUDENT LIFE ACTIVITIES Choral, Concert Band, Dance, Drama Groups, Jazz Band, Magazine, Music Ensembles, Music Groups, Newspaper, Student Government, Symphony Orchestra

Less Selective

East Los Angeles College
1301 Brooklyn Avenue
Monterey Park, California 91754
(213) 265-8712

School Enrollment: **14,000** Male: **6,000** Female: **8,000**
LD Enrollment: **75** Male: **37** Female: **38**

Admissions Contact: **Rudy Valles, Dean of Admissions**
LD Contact: **Mary Seneker/ Sheila Isomoto, LD Specialists**
Name of Program: **Learning Disabilities Program**
Telephone: **(213) 265-8630**

Admissions

Application Information:
Separate application: **Yes**

Secondary School Information
Most Important Criteria For Admissions (1-strongest)

SAT/ACT	Application	School transcript
Class rank	Course selection	Personal statement
Interview	Extra activities	Psychoeducational
G.P.A.	1 Open admission	Recommendations

Test Requirements:
Diagnostic testing waived: **Yes**
Documentation of LD required: **Yes**
Currency of diagnostic testing: **1 month**
Tests recommended: **Woodcock Johnson Part I and II, WAIS-R**

Types of Disabilities Served
• Speech/Lang • Reading • ADD with LD
• Study skills • Spelling • ADD without LD
• Written express • Math • ADHD with LD
• Organizational • Fine Motor • ADHD without LD
• Perceptual

Admissions Process

As per Community College guidelines, complete state elligibility process, and must meet state criteria.

Learning Disability Program

Program: Remedial: **Yes**
Program: Reinforces course work: **Yes**
Program available through: **September - June**
Recommended credits per semester: **9**
Services only for LD students: **Yes**
Counseling: Individual: **Yes** Vocational Counseling: **Yes**
Support groups are available: **Learning disability club and classes**

Faculty:
Faculty: **5** Full time: **4** Part time: **1** M.A.: **2**

Diagnostic Testing
• ADD Personality • Perceptual skills • Spelling
  ADHD Organization Fine motor skills • Reading
• I.Q. • Handwriting • Spoken language Study skills
• Math Social skills • Written language

79

California

Tutoring:
Average size of group tutorials: **2-3**
Services rendered by:
  Graduates •Peers Faculty •LD staff Teacher trainees

Tutorials

Grp.	Ind.	Tutorials	Grp.	Ind.	Tutorials
•	•	Math skills	•		Word processing
•	•	Study skills	•		Time management
•	•	Language arts	•	•	Learning strategies
•	•	Written express	•		Organizational skills

Academic Accommodations

Curriculum	Study Aids	Exams
• Priority registration	• Typist	• Oral
Math waiver	Reader	Untimed
Foreign lang. waiver	• Notetaker	• Take home
Course substitution	• Proof reader	With proctor
In Class	• Text on tape	On computer
• Calculators	Early syllabus	• Extended time
• Tape recorder	Taped handouts	On tape
• Word processor		Modified
Priority seating		• Separate room

Graduation Requirements:
Course credits: **60** GPA: **2.0** Years to complete degree: **2 years or more**

Program Strengths
We offer a package of services with a support group atmosphere, skill building, and mainstream support.

General Information:
East Los Angeles College is a 2 year public college. Urban campus of 87 acres is Accessible by bus. Ski areas are 37 miles from campus. Beaches are 25 miles from campus. Housing is not guaranteed.

Accreditation: WACS

Expenses: Part-time: Per credit:$6.00. Tuition: Out-of-state: Full year: Part-time: Per credit: $112.00.

Majors
• BUSINESS Accounting, Business Administration, Business Management, Marketing and Distribution, Real Estate • COMPUTER SCIENCE Data Processing • CRAFTS AND DESIGN Graphic Design • HEALTH SCIENCES Medical Assistant, Medical Technology, Nursing • PREPROFESSIONAL Recreation • SOCIAL SCIENCES Law Enforcement • VOCATIONAL Drafting, Fire Science, Respiratory Therapy Technology, Secretarial

Sports/Activities
• SPORTS-INTERCOLLEGIATE Baseball (M), Basketball, Cross Country, Football (M), Track and Field (F), Volleyball (F) • SPORTS-INTRAMURAL Basketball, Football, Flag, Softball, Volleyball • STUDENT LIFE ACTIVITIES Academic Clubs, Choral, Ethnic & Cultural Groups, Newspaper, Religious Organization

El Camino College
16007 Crenshaw Boulevard
Torrance, California 90506
(213) 715-3414

School Enrollment: **26,000** Male: **13,000** Female: **13,000**
LD Enrollment: **250** Male: **114** Female: **136**

Admissions Contact: **Bill Robinson, Director of Admissions**
LD Contact: **Bill Hoanzl, L.D. Specialist**
Name of Program: **Special Resource Center**
Telephone:**(213) 715-3276**

Admissions

Application Information:
LD Students Applying: **144** Accepted: **120** Enrolled:**120**
Separate application:**Yes**
Application deadline: **Beginning of Semester**
Applicant must apply **1-3** months in advance

Secondary School Information
Most Important Criteria For Admissions (1-strongest)

SAT/ACT **1**	Application **2**	School transcript
Class rank	Course selection	Personal statement
Interview	Extra activities	Psychoeducational
G.P.A.	Open admission	Recommendations

Test Requirements:
Standardized tests waived: **Yes**
Diagnostic testing waived: **Yes**
WAIS-R required: **Yes** Range accepted: **80**
Currency of diagnostic testing: **Open**
Tests recommended: **WRAT, WAIS-R, Woodcock, AAS**

Types of Disabilities Served

• Speech/Lang	• Reading	• ADD with LD
• Study skills	• Spelling	• ADD without LD
• Written express	• Math	• ADHD with LD
• Organizational	• Fine Motor	• ADHD without LD
• Perceptual		

Learning Disability Program
Program: Reinforces course work: **Yes**
Students mainstreamed **50+** % of the day
Counseling: Individual: **Yes**

Faculty:
Faculty: **20** Including Director: **Yes** Full time: **3** Part time: **17**
LD faculty with: BS/BA: **1** M.A.: **2**
Faculty advocate: **Yes** Meets with instructor: **Varies**

Diagnostic Testing

ADD	Personality	Perceptual skills	• Spelling
ADHD	Organization	Fine motor skills	• Reading
• I.Q.	Handwriting	Spoken language	Study skills
• Math	Social skills	Written language	

Tutoring:
Average size of group tutorials: **3**
Services rendered by:
Graduates •Peers •Faculty •LD staff Teacher trainees

Tutorials

Grp.	Ind.	Tutorials	Grp.	Ind.	Tutorials
	•	Math skills		•	Word processing
	•	Study skills		•	Time management
	•	Language arts		•	Learning strategies
	•	Written express		•	Organizational skills

Academic Accommodations

Curriculum	Study Aids	Exams
Priority registration	• Typist	• Oral
• Math waiver	Reader	Untimed
Foreign lang. waiver	• Notetaker	• Take home
Course substitution	• Proof reader	With proctor
In Class	• Text on tape	On computer
• Calculators	Early syllabus	• Extended time
• Tape recorder	Taped handouts	On tape
• Word processor		Modified
Priority seating		Separate room

Program Strengths
The Center is designed to help students make the most of their abilities in regular courses through a specialized staff and through special methods of instruction and materials.

General Information:
El Camino College is a 2 year public college. Urban campus. Accessible by air, train, or bus. Ski areas are 60 miles from campus. Beaches are 3 miles from campus. 5% of students are foreign. Housing is not guaranteed.

Accreditation: WACS

Expenses:
Tuition: In-state: Full year: Part-time: Per credit: $5.00. Tuition: Out-of-state: Full year: Part-time: Per credit: $102.00.

Majors
• AREA STUDIES Asian, Black/Afro-American, Ethics, Latin American • BUSINESS Accounting, Business Management, Economics, Finance, Marketing, Office Administration, Real Estate • COMMUNICATIONS Journalism • COMPUTER SCIENCE Computer Technology • EDUCATION Early Childhood, Physical, Speech/Language • HEALTH SCIENCES Nursing • HUMANITIES Philosophy • LANGUAGES French, German, Japanese, Russian, Spanish • PREPROFESSIONAL Architecture, Dentistry, Industrial Design, Legal Assistant • SCIENCES Biology, Chemistry, Geology, Gerontology, Horticultural, Mathematics, Physical Science, Physics • SOCIAL SCIENCES Anthropology, Political Science, Psychology, Sociology • VISUAL AND PERFORMING ARTS Art History, Music, Studio Art • VOCATIONAL Automobile Technology, Cosmetology, Diesel Power Technology, Fashion Design, Fashion Mechandizing, Fire Science, Food Service, Home Economics, Industrial Arts, Interior Design, Machinist, Office Administration, Piloting, Radiological Technology, Respiratory Therapy Technology, Secretarial, Word Processing

Sports/Activities
• SPORTS-INTERCOLLEGIATE Baseball (M), Basketball, Cross Country, Football (M), Soccer, Softball (F), Swimming, Tennis, Track and Field, Volleyball (F), Wrestling (M) • STUDENT LIFE ACTIVITIES Choral, Concert Band, Dance, Drama Groups, Jazz Band, Magazine, Music Ensembles, Music Groups, Musical Theater, Newspaper, Student Government, Symphony Orchestra

---

Less Selective

California Program

Evergreen Valley College
3095 Yerba Buena Road
San Jose, California 95135
(408) 274-7900

School Enrollment: **11,000**
LD Enrollment: **70** Male: **28** Female: **42**

Admissions Contact: **Robert L. Brown, Director of Admissions**
LD Contact: **Bonnie Clark, LD Specialist**
Name of Program: **Diagnostic Learning Program**
Telephone: **(408) 270-6447**

Admissions

Application Information:
LD Students Applying: **67** Accepted: **43**
Separate application: **Yes**
Application deadline: **None**
Applicant must apply **2** months in advance

Secondary School Information
Most Important Criteria For Admissions (1-strongest)

SAT/ACT	Application	School transcript
Class rank	Course selection	Personal statement
Interview	Extra activities	Psychoeducational
G.P.A. **1**	Open admission	Recommendations

Test Requirements:
Standardized tests waived: **Yes**
Diagnostic testing waived: **Yes**
Range accepted: **>81**
Documentation of LD required: **Yes**
Currency of diagnostic testing: **1 year**
Tests recommended: **Aptitude/cognitive processing, achievement**

Types of Disabilities Served
• Speech/Lang	• Reading	• ADD with LD
• Study skills	• Spelling	ADD without LD
• Written express	• Math	• ADHD with LD
• Organizational	Fine Motor	ADHD without LD
• Perceptual		

Admissions Process

If students have not been previously assessed at the community college, they must go through the assessment in the LD program. Special procedures required by the state are followed.

Learning Disability Program
Program: Reinforces course work: **Yes**
Students mainstreamed **Varies** % of the day
Services available for all students: **Yes**
Counseling: Individual: **Yes**

Faculty:
Faculty: **3** Full time: **1** Part time: **2**
Faculty advocate: **Yes**

California

Diagnostic Testing

ADD	Personality •	Perceptual skills	• Spelling
ADHD	Organization	Fine motor skills	• Reading
• I.Q.	Handwriting•	Spoken language	Study skills
• Math	Social skills •	Written language	

Tutoring:

Average size of group tutorials: **Maximum 11**
Services rendered by:
Graduates   Peers   Faculty   •LD staff   Teacher trainees

Tutorials

Grp.	Ind.	Tutorials	Grp.	Ind.	Tutorials
•		Math skills	•		Word processing
•		Study skills			Time management
•		Language arts	•		Learning strategies
•		Written express	•		Organizational skills

Academic Accommodations

Curriculum	Study Aids	Exams
• Priority registration	Typist	• Oral
• Math waiver	Reader	• Untimed
Foreign lang. waiver	• Notetaker	• Take home
Course substitution	• Proof reader	• With proctor
In Class	• Text on tape	On computer
• Calculators	Early syllabus	• Extended time
• Tape recorder	Taped handouts	On tape
• Word processor		• Modified
Priority seating		• Separate room

Graduation Requirements:

Course credits: **60** GPA: **2.0** Years to complete degree: **7**

Program Strengths

The program is designed to serve students enrolled in the college. We provide instruction to remediate deficits and to support mainstream classes. All students must be in mainstream classes. Students must be eligible for LD program according to the California Community College eligibility criteria for LD students.

General Information:

Evergreen Valley College is a 2 year public college. Suburban campus Accessible by air, train or bus. Ski areas are 4 miles from campus. Beaches are 1mile from campus. Housing is not guaranteed.

Accreditation:WACS

Expenses:

Tuition: In-state: Full year: $120.00. Part-time: Per credit:$6.00 . Tuition: Out-of-state: Full year: Part-time: Per credit: $107.00.

Majors

• BUSINESS Accounting, Business Administration, Real Estate • COMMUNICATIONS English, Television/Radio/Film • COMPUTER SCIENCE Data Processing • CRAFTS AND DESIGN Graphic Design • ENGINEERING Engineering Technology • HEALTH SCIENCES Nursing • SCIENCES Biology • SOCIAL SCIENCES Criminal Justice, History, Law Enforcement, Psychology, Social Sciences • VISUAL AND PERFORMING ARTS Art • VOCATIONAL Automobile Technology, Drafting, Fashion Merchandising, Paralegal, Secretarial

Sports/Activities

• SPORTS-INTRAMURAL Badminton, Baseball, Basketball (M), Golf, Racquetball, Tennis, Volleyball • STUDENT LIFE ACTIVITIES Black Student Union, Choral, Dance, Drama Groups, Newspaper, Student Government

---

Feather River College
P.O. Box 1110
Quincy, California 95971
(916) 283-0202

School Enrollment: **1,353** Male: **531** Female: **822**
LD Enrollment: **36** Male: **16** Female: **20**

Admissions Contact: **Tambra Armenta, Admissions Coordinator**
LD Contact: **Maureen McPhee, LD Specialist**
Name of Program: **L.D. Program**
Telephone:**(916) 283-0202 Ext. 284**

Admissions

Application Information:

LD Students Applying: **56** Accepted: **35** Enrolled:**35**
Separate application:**Yes**
Application deadline: **August/January**
Applicant must apply **1** months in advance

Secondary School Information

Most Important Criteria For Admissions (1-strongest)

3	SAT/ACT	**1**	Application	**5**	School transcript
11	Class rank	**7**	Course selection	**8**	Personal statement
2	Interview	**10**	Extra activities	**6**	Psychoeducational
4	G.P.A.		Open admission	**9**	Recommendations

Test Requirements:

Standardized tests waived: **Yes**
Diagnostic testing waived: **Yes**
Achievement tests required:**1**
WAIS-R required: **Yes** Range accepted: **80-90**
Currency of diagnostic testing: **N/A**
Tests recommended: **WAIS-R, Woodcock-Johnson**

Types of Disabilities Served

• Speech/Lang	• Reading	• ADD with LD
• Study skills	• Spelling	• ADD without LD
• Written express	• Math	• ADHD with LD
• Organizational	• Fine Motor	• ADHD without LD
• Perceptual		

Learning Disability Program

Program: Remedial: **Yes**
Program: Reinforces course work: **Yes**
Students mainstreamed **100** % of the day
Counseling: Individual: **Yes**

Faculty:

Faculty: **1** Part time: **1** M.A.: **1**
Faculty advocate: **Yes** Meets with instructor: **As needed**

Diagnostic Testing

• ADD	• Personality	• Perceptual skills	• Spelling
• ADHD	• Organization	• Fine motor skills	• Reading
• I.Q.	• Handwriting	• Spoken language	• Study skills
• Math	• Social skills •	Written language	

Tutoring:
Average size of group tutorials: **2-3**
Services rendered by:
Graduates •Peers Faculty •LD staff Teacher trainees

Tutorials

Grp.	Ind.	Tutorials	Grp.	Ind.	Tutorials
•	•	Math skills	•	•	Word processing
	•	Study skills		•	Time management
•	•	Language arts	•	•	Learning strategies
•	•	Written express		•	Organizational skills

Academic Accommodations

Curriculum	Study Aids	Exams
Priority registration	• Typist	• Oral
• Math waiver	Reader	Untimed
• Foreign lang. waiver	• Notetaker	Take home
Course substitution	• Proof reader	With proctor
In Class	• Text on tape	On computer
• Calculators	Early syllabus	• Extended time
• Tape recorder	Taped handouts	On tape
• Word processor		• Modified
Priority seating		Separate room

Program Strengths
We are a very small (2nd smallest in CA) community college which offers 1:15 ratio of faculty to students in most classes. In a small town, we know of our students as people, not just in an academic context. There is a very special support network between faculty, staff, current and former LD students.

General Information:
Feather River College is a 2 year public college. Rural campus 80 miles from Reno. Accessible by bus. Ski areas are 20 miles from campus. Housing is not guaranteed.

Accreditation: Regional

Expenses: Part-time: Per credit:$5.00. Tuition: Out-of-state: Full year: Part-time: Per credit: $98.00.

Majors
• BUSINESS Accounting, Business Administration, Business Management, Real Estate • COMMUNICATIONS English, Photography • EDUCATION Art, Early Childhood, General, Industrial, Physical, Recreation and Youth Leadershi, Vocational • HEALTH SCIENCES Nursing • HUMANITIES English/Writing/Literature, Humanities, Liberal Arts • LANGUAGES Spanish • PREPROFESSIONAL Forestry, Recreation • SCIENCES Biology, Chemistry, Equestrian Studies, Geology, Mathematics, Natural Resources, Physical Science, Physics • SOCIAL SCIENCES Administration of Justice, Government/Political, History, Law Enforcement, Psychology, Social Sciences • VISUAL AND PERFORMING ARTS Art, Fine Art • VOCATIONAL Fire Science, Office Administration, Pack Station and Stable Manage, Wildlife Management

Sports/Activities
• SPORTS-INTRAMURAL Basketball, Field Hockey, Golf, Horseback Riding, Skiing - Cross Country, Skiing - Snow, Softball, Volleyball, Weight Lifting • STUDENT LIFE ACTIVITIES Choral, Dance, Drama Groups, Musical Theater, Radio/TV station, Student Government

Less Selective — **California Program**

Foothill College
12345 El Monte Road
Los Altos Hills, California 94022-4599
(415) 949-7777

School Enrollment: **18,191** Male: **7,628** Female: **8,910**
LD Enrollment: **60** Male: **24** Female: **36**

Admissions Contact: **Eileen Paulson, Asst. Dir. of Admissions**
LD Contact: **Dr. Charlene Maltzman, LD Coordinator of "STEP"**
Name of Program: **STEP**
Telephone:**(415) 949-7377**

Admissions

Application Information:
LD Students Applying: **150** Accepted: **60** Enrolled:**60**
Separate application:**Yes**
Applicant must apply **3** months in advance
Rolling Admissions: **Yes**

Secondary School Information
Most Important Criteria For Admissions (1-strongest)

SAT/ACT	Application	School transcript
Class rank	Course selection	Personal statement
Interview	Extra activities	Psychoeducational
G.P.A.	**1** Open admission	Recommendations

Test Requirements:
Standardized tests waived: **Yes**
Documentation of LD required: **Yes**
Tests recommended:

Types of Disabilities Served

• Speech/Lang	• Reading	• ADD with LD
• Study skills	• Spelling	ADD without LD
• Written express	• Math	ADHD with LD
• Organizational	• Fine Motor	ADHD without LD
• Perceptual		

Learning Disability Program
Program: Reinforces course work: **Yes**
Program available through:**Fall, Winter, Spring**
Students mainstreamed **100** % of the day
Time required or recommended in learning center: **none**
Services only for LD students: **Yes**
Counseling: Individual: **Yes** Vocational Counseling: **Yes**

Faculty:
Faculty: **6** Including Director: **Yes** Full time: **1** Part time: **5**
LD faculty with: BS/BA: **1** M.A.: **4** Ph.D.: **2**
Faculty advocate: **Yes**

Diagnostic Testing

ADD	Personality	• Perceptual skills	• Spelling
ADHD	Organization	• Fine motor skills	• Reading
I.Q.	Handwriting	Spoken language	Study skills
• Math	Social skills	• Written language	

California

Tutoring:
Average size of group tutorials: **1-2**
Services rendered by:
Graduates   Peers   Faculty   •LD staff   Teacher trainees

Tutorials
Grp.	Ind.	Tutorials	Grp.	Ind.	Tutorials
	•	Math skills	•		Word processing
•		Study skills		•	Time management
	•	Language arts	•		Learning strategies
	•	Written express	•		Organizational skills

Academic Accommodations
Curriculum	Study Aids	Exams
• Priority registration	Typist	• Oral
Math waiver	Reader	Untimed
Foreign lang. waiver	• Notetaker	Take home
Course substitution	Proof reader	With proctor
In Class	• Text on tape	On computer
Calculators	Early syllabus	• Extended time
• Tape recorder	Taped handouts	On tape
• Word processor		Modified
Priority seating		Separate room

Program Strengths
A student receives services from our STEP program after they have been accepted and enrolled at Foothill and have had a diagnostic evaluation. All our students are mainstreamed and receive support services. Our special education counselor assists our students with academic schedules and individual counseling. We offer a half unit of credit for work in our center, and if the student has been assigned two periods a week, he or she will receive one full unit. A small computer lab is available to LD students.

General Information:
Foothill College is a 2 year public college. Urban campus of 122 acres is 20 miles from San Jose. Accessible by air, train, or bus. Housing is not guaranteed.

Accreditation: Regional

Expenses:
Tuition: In-state: Full year: $3.50 per unit. Tuition: Out-of-state: Full year: Part-time: Per credit: $66.00 per unit.

Majors
• AREA STUDIES American • BUSINESS Accounting, Business Administration, Economics, Finance, International Business, Real Estate, Travel/Tourism Management • COMMUNICATIONS Communication, Creative Writing, English, Journalism, Television/Radio/Film • COMPUTER SCIENCE Computer Science, Computer Technology • CRAFTS AND DESIGN Graphic Design • EDUCATION Physical • HUMANITIES Classics, Liberal Arts, Philosophy • LANGUAGES French, German, Japanese, Linguistic, Spanish • PREPROFESSIONAL Dentistry, Law, Medicine, Pharmacy, Veterinarian • SCIENCES Biology, Geography, Geology, Horticultural, Mathematics, Physics • SOCIAL SCIENCES Anthropology, Library Science, Political Science, Psychology, Social Sciences, Sociology • VISUAL AND PERFORMING ARTS Dramatic Arts, Fine Art • VOCATIONAL Business and Office, Dental Assistant, Dental Hygiene, Drafting, Fishery Studies, Library Assistant, Piloting, Respiratory Therapy Technology, Secretarial, Veteranian Assistant, Word Processing

Sports/Activities
• SPORTS-INTERCOLLEGIATE Baseball (M), Basketball, Cross Country, Football (M), Golf (M), Soccer, Softball (F), Tennis, Track and Field, Volleyball (F), Wrestling (M) • STUDENT LIFE ACTIVITIES Choral, Concert Band, Dance, Drama Groups, Film, Jazz Band, Music Ensembles, Musical Theater, Newspaper, Radio/TV station, Student Government, Symphony Orchestra

---

Less Selective

Fresno City College
1101 East University Avenue
Fresno, California 93741
(209) 442-8237

School Enrollment: **20,000**
LD Enrollment: **300**

Admissions Contact: **Mr. Joaquin, Jimenez Director of Admissions**
LD Contact: **Janice Emerzian, Director, Enabler Program**
Name of Program: **Enabler Program**
Address: **110 E. University**
Telephone: **(209) 442-8237**

Admissions

Application Information:
Application deadline: **Varies**
Applicant must apply **Advise 6** months in advance

Secondary School Information
Most Important Criteria For Admissions (1-strongest)

SAT/ACT	Application	School transcript
Class rank	Course selection	Personal statement
Interview	Extra activities	Psychoeducational
G.P.A.	1 Open admission	Recommendations

Test Requirements:
Standardized tests waived: **Yes**
Diagnostic testing waived: **Yes**
Untimed SAT: **Yes** Untimed ACT: **Yes**
WAIS-R required: **Yes**
Documentation of LD required: **Yes**
Tests recommended: **Woodcock-Johnson or WAIS-R**

Types of Disabilities Served
- Speech/Lang
- Study skills
- Written express
- Organizational
- Perceptual
- Reading
- Spelling
- Math
- Fine Motor
- ADD with LD
- ADD without LD
- ADHD with LD
- ADHD without LD

Admissions Process
Student must complete application. All individuals 18 or older are admitted.

Learning Disability Program
Syllabus available during orientation: **Yes**
Program available through: **Fall and Spring**
Recommended credits per semester: **4-6**
Time required or recommended in learning center: **Varies**
Services only for LD students: **Yes**
Counseling: Individual: **Yes** Vocational Counseling: **Yes**

Faculty:
Faculty: **15** Including Director: **Yes** Full time: **1** M.A.: **2**
Faculty advocate: **Yes** Meets with instructor: **As needed**

Diagnostic Testing

ADD	Personality	Perceptual skills	• Spelling
ADHD	Organization	Fine motor skills	• Reading
• I.Q.	Handwriting	Spoken language	Study skills
• Math	Social skills	Written language	

Tutoring:

Average size of group tutorials: **6**
Services rendered by:
•Graduates   Peers   Faculty   •LD staff   •Teacher trainees

Tutorials

Grp.	Ind.	Tutorials	Grp.	Ind.	Tutorials
•		Math skills	•		Word processing
		Study skills			Time management
•		Language arts	•		Learning strategies
•		Written express			Organizational skills

Academic Accommodations

Curriculum	Study Aids	Exams
• Priority registration	• Typist	• Oral
Math waiver	• Reader	• Untimed
Foreign lang. waiver	• Notetaker	• Take home
• Course substitution	• Proof reader	• With proctor
In Class	• Text on tape	• On computer
• Calculators	• Early syllabus	• Extended time
• Tape recorder	Taped handouts	On tape
• Word processor		• Modified
• Priority seating		• Separate room

Graduation Requirements:

Course credits: **60** GPA: **2.0** Years to complete degree: **2 +**

General Information:

Fresno City College is a 2 year public college. Suburban campus of 103 acres is 3 hours miles from Fresno. Accessible by air, train, or bus Ski areas are 65 miles from campus. Beaches are 130 miles from campus. Housing is not guaranteed.

Accreditation: Regional

Expenses:

Tuition: In-state: Full year: $120.00 . Part-time: Per credit:$5.00. Tuition: Out-of-state: Full year: Part-time: Per credit: $117.00.

Majors

• AGRICULTURE Business • AREA STUDIES American, Black/Afro-American, Mexican/American, Women's Studies • ARTS Dance, Drafting, Dramatic Arts, Music, Photography • BUSINESS Accounting, Agricultural, Business Administration, Clerical, Construction, Food Management, Insurance, Marketing, Real Estate, Retailing • COMMUNICATIONS Journalism, Photography, Television/Radio/Film • COMPUTER SCIENCE Computer Technology, Medical Records Technology, Telecommunications • ENGINEERING Air Pollution Control Technolo • HEALTH SCIENCES Dental Assistant, Dental Hygiene, Dietary Manager, Medical Records Administration, Nursing, Nutritional/Food, Radiological Therapy, Respiratory Therapy, Speech/Audiology and Speech • HUMANITIES English/Writing/Literature, Humanities • LANGUAGES French, German, Russian • SCIENCES Anthropology, Botany, Physical Science, Radiology • SOCIAL SCIENCES Anthropology, Criminology, Government/Political, History, Human Service, Law Enforcement, Political Science • VISUAL AND PERFORMING ARTS Art, Dance, Music, Theater

Sports/Activities

IATE Badminton (F), Baseball (M), Basketball (M), Cross Country (F), Cross Country (M), Football (M), Golf (M), Soccer (F), Soccer (M), Softball (F), Tennis (F), Track and Field (F), Track and Field (M), Volleyball (F), Wrestling (M) • SPORTS-INTRAMURAL Basketball (F), Football, Golf, Racquetball, Soccer, Softball, Tennis, Volleyball, Weight Lifting • STUDENT LIFE ACTIVITIES Academic Clubs, Choral, Concert Band, Dance, Drama Groups, Music Groups, Newspaper, Student Government

---

Less Selective **California**
Services

Fullerton College
321 East Chapman
Fullerton, California 92634
(714) 992-7568

School Enrollment: **19,236** Male: **9,351** Female: **9,885**
LD Enrollment: **236**

Admissions Contact: **Chris Burns, Registrar**
LD Contact: **Thomas Cantrell, LD Specialist**
Name of Program: **Learning Resource Services**

Admissions

Application Information:

LD Students Applying: **150** Accepted: **135** Enrolled:**135**
Application deadline: **August 22nd**
Applicant must apply **4-5** months in advance

Secondary School Information

Most Important Criteria For Admissions (1-strongest)

SAT/ACT	Application **1**	School transcript
Class rank	Course selection	Personal statement
Interview	Extra activities **1**	Psychoeducational
G.P.A.	Open admission	Recommendations

Test Requirements:

Diagnostic testing waived: **Yes**
Achievement tests required:**3**
WAIS-R required: **Yes**
Documentation of LD required: **Yes**
Tests recommended: **WAIS-R-, Wide Range Achievement, Woodcock-Johnson**

Types of Disabilities Served

• Speech/Lang	• Reading	• ADD with LD
• Study skills	• Spelling	• ADD without LD
• Written express	• Math	• ADHD with LD
• Organizational	• Fine Motor	• ADHD without LD
• Perceptual		

Learning Disability Program

Program: Reinforces course work: **Yes**
Counseling: Individual: **Yes**

Faculty:

Faculty: **1** Full time: **1** M.A.: **1**
Faculty advocate: **Yes** Meets with instructor: **As needed**

Diagnostic Testing

ADD	Personality •	Perceptual skills	• Spelling
ADHD	Organization	Fine motor skills	• Reading
• I.Q.	• Handwriting	Spoken language	• Study skills
• Math	• Social skills•	Written language	

California

Tutoring:
Services rendered by:
•Graduates •Peers •Faculty •LD staff Teacher trainees

Tutorials
Grp. Ind. Tutorials   Grp. Ind. Tutorials
• Math skills   • Word processing
• Study skills   • Time management
• Language arts   • Learning strategies
• Written express   • Organizational skills

Academic Accommodations

Curriculum   **Study Aids**   **Exams**
• Priority registration Typist   • Oral
  Math waiver   • Reader   Untimed
  Foreign lang. waiver • Notetaker   Take home
  Course substitution • Proof reader   With proctor
In Class   • Text on tape   On computer
• Calculators   Early syllabus   • Extended time
• Tape recorder   Taped handouts   • On tape
• Word processor   • Modified
  Priority seating   • Separate room

Program Strengths
Strictly mainstream support services program.

General Information:
Fullerton College is a 2 year public college. Suburban campus of 149 acres is Accessible by air, train or bus. Ski areas are 2 hours from campus. Beaches are 1 hour from campus. 11% of students are foreign. Housing is not guaranteed.1 % of students join fraternities/sororities.

Accreditation: Regional and National

Expenses:
Tuition: In-state: Full year: $6.00 per unit, $60.00 maximum. Tuition: Out-of-state: Full year: $106.00 per unit.

Majors
• AREA STUDIES African, American, Asian, Black/Afro-American, Jewish, Latin American, Urban • BUSINESS Accounting, Banking, Business Administration, Business Economics, Business Education, Business Management, Economics, Finance, Hotel and Restaurant Managemen, Insurance, Management, Marketing Research, Printing Manufacturing, Real Estate, Sports Management, Travel/Tourism Management • COMMUNICATION Advertising, Broadcasting, Communication, Creative Writing, English, Journalism, Photography, Television/Radio/Film • COMPUTER SCIENCE Data Processing, Engineering, Hardware Engineer, Programming, Software Engineer, Systems Analysis, Telecommunications
• CRAFTS AND DESIGN Graphic Design • EDUCATION Art, Early Childhood, Elementary, Health, Industrial, Music, Music Therapy, Physical, Recreation and Youth Leadershi, School Psychology, Secondary, Vocational • ENGINEERING Computer • FINE AND PERFORMING ARTS Art, Art History, Dance, Music, Studio Art, Theater • HEALTH SCIENCES Communication Disorders, Environmental, Health, Medical Technology, Nursing, Nutritional/Food, Occupational Therapy, Physical Therapy, Radiological Therapy, Speech Therapy, Speech/Audiology and Speech
• LANGUAGES Chinese, French, German, Italian, Russian, Spanish
• PHILOSOPHY Humanities, Philosophy, Religion • PREPROFESSIONAL Agriculture, Architecture, Dentistry, Engineering, Forestry, Law, Medicine, Ministry, Natural Resources, Pharmacy, Recreation, Social Work, Veterinarian • SCIENCES Astronomy, Astrophysics, Biochemistry, Biology, Botany, Chemistry, Earth Science, Ecology, Geography, Geology, Horticultural, Macrobiology, Marine Biology, Mathematics, Microbiology, Oceanography, Physical Chemistry, Physics, Physiology, Radiology, Zoology • SOCIAL SCIENCES Anthropology, Criminal Justice, Geography, Government/Political, History, Law Enforcement, Political Science, Psychology, Social Sciences, Sociology • VOCATIONAL Apparel Design, Automobile Mechanics, Automobile Technology, Construction, Drafting, Home Economics, Legal Secretary, Welding, Word Processing

Sports
• SPORTS INTERCOLLEGIATE Archery, Badminton, Baseball (M), Basketball, Bowling, Boxing, Cross Country, Cycling, Diving, Fencing, Field Hockey, Football (M), Golf, Gymnastics, Hammer Throw, Hand Ball, Racquetball, Scuba, Skiing - Cross Country, Skiing - Snow, Soccer (M), Softball (F), Swimming, Synchronized Swimming, Tennis, Track and Field, Volleyball, Water Polo, Weight Lifting • SPORTS RELATED Band, Cheerleading, Drill Team • STUDENT LIFE ACTIVITIES Debate, Drama Groups, Ethnic & Cultural Groups, Film Production, Fraternities, Jazz Band, Music Groups, Newspaper, Radio/TV station, Religious Organization, Sororities, Student Government, Symphony Orchestra, Yearbook

---

Selective   California
                                         Services

Golden Gate University
536 Mission Street
San Francisco, California 94105
(415) 442-7245

School Enrollment: **7,000** Male: **3,500** Female: **3,500**
LD Enrollment: **20** Male: **10** Female: **10**

Admissions Contact: **Archie Porter, Director of Admissions**
LD Contact: **Patrick F. O'Brien, Dean of Student Services**
Telephone: **(415) 442-7245**

Admissions

Application Information:
Applicant must apply **6** months in advance
Rolling Admissions: **Yes**

Secondary School Information
Most Important Criteria For Admissions (1-strongest)
SAT/ACT   Application   School transcript
Class rank   Course selection   Personal statement
Interview   Extra activities   Psychoeducational
G.P.A.   Open admission   Recommendations

Types of Disabilities Served
• Speech/Lang   • Reading   ADD with LD
  Study skills   • Spelling   ADD without LD
  Written express • Math   ADHD with LD
• Organizational • Fine Motor   ADHD without LD
• Perceptual

Admissions Process

Follow regular process, note disability and needs

Learning Disability Program
Services available for all students: **Yes**

Diagnostic Testing
ADD   Personality   Perceptual skills   Spelling
ADHD   Organization   Fine motor skills   Reading
I.Q.   Handwriting   Spoken language   Study skills
Math   Social skills Written language
Services rendered by:

Graduates   Peers   Faculty   LD staff   Teacher trainees

Tutorials

Grp.	Ind.	Tutorials	Grp.	Ind.	Tutorials
		Math skills			Word processing
		Study skills			Time management
		Language arts			Learning strategies
		Written express			Organizational skills

Academic Accommodations

Curriculum	Study Aids	Exams
Priority registration	Typist	• Oral
Math waiver	Reader	• Untimed
Foreign lang. waiver	Notetaker	• Take home
Course substitution	Proof reader	• With proctor
In Class	Text on tape	• On computer
• Calculators	Early syllabus	• Extended time
• Tape recorder	Taped handouts	• On tape
• Word processor		• Modified
• Priority seating		• Separate room

General Information:

Golden Gate University is a 4 year private university. Urban campus Accessible by air, train or bus. Ski areas are 200 miles from campus. 11% of students are foreign. Housing is not guaranteed.

Accreditation: WASC, ABA, AALS

Expenses:

Tuition: In-state: Full year: Part-time: Per credit: $176.00.

Majors

• BUSINESS Accounting, Aviation Management, Banking/Finance, Business Administration, Business Economics, Business Management, Data Processing, Economics, Hotel & Restaurant Management, Human Resources Management, Industrial Operations, Insurance, International Business, Investments and Securities, Management, Marketing, Marketing Research, Operations Research, Organizational Behavior, Personnel, Real Estate, Taxation, Travel/Tourism Management • COMMUNICATIONS Public Relations • COMPUTER SCIENCE Business Data Programming, Computer Science, Computer Technology, Data Processing, Systems Analysis, Telecommunications • MATHEMATICS Computer

Sports/Activities

• STUDENT LIFE ACTIVITIES Academic Clubs, Community Service, Ethnic & Cultural Groups, Magazine, Newspaper, Political Groups, Student Government

Less Selective   **California**
                                      Services

Golden West College

15744 Golden West Street
Huntington Beach, California 92647
(714) 895-8721

School Enrollment: **15,000**
LD Enrollment: **40**

Admissions Contact: **Paula Mucciaro, DSS Program Coordinator**
Name of Program: **Disabled Student Services**
Address: **15744 Golden West Street**
Telephone:**(714) 895-8721**

Admissions

Application Information:
LD Students Applying: **40** Accepted: **40** Enrolled:**40**
Application deadline: **Up to the day school starts**

Secondary School Information
Most Important Criteria For Admissions (1-strongest)

SAT/ACT	Application	School transcript
Class rank	Course selection	Personal statement
Interview	Extra activities	Psychoeducational
G.P.A.	Open admission	Recommendations

Test Requirements:
Diagnostic testing waived: **Yes**
WAIS-R required: **Yes**
Documentation of LD required: **Yes**
Tests recommended: **Special evaluation as prescribed by California State Chancellor's Office for Community Colleges**

Types of Disabilities Served
• Speech/Lang	• Reading	• ADD with LD
• Study skills	• Spelling	ADD without LD
• Written express	• Math	• ADHD with LD
• Organizational	• Fine Motor	ADHD without LD
• Perceptual		

Admissions Process

No special requirements for the college. For services from Disabled Students Services, LD evaluation is required.

Learning Disability Program

Special orientation for LD students: **Yes**
Syllabus available during orientation:**Yes**
Program: Reinforces course work: **Yes**
Program available through:**Upon request**
Students mainstreamed **100** % of the day
Recommended credits per semester: **9-12**
Services available for all students: **Yes**
Counseling: Individual: **Yes** Vocational Counseling: **Yes**

Faculty:
Faculty: **40** Including Director: **Yes** Full time: **5** Part time: **32**
Faculty advocate: **Yes** Meets with instructor: **When needed**

Diagnostic Testing
ADD	Personality	• Perceptual skills	• Spelling
ADHD	Organization	• Fine motor skills	• Reading
• I.Q.	Handwriting	• Spoken language	• Study skills
• Math	• Social skills	• Written language	

Tutoring:
Average size of group tutorials: **1:1**
Services rendered by:
•Graduates   •Peers   Faculty   LD staff   Teacher trainees

Tutorials

Grp.	Ind.	Tutorials	Grp.	Ind.	Tutorials
	•	Math skills			Word processing
	•	Study skills			Time management
	•	Language arts		•	Learning strategies
	•	Written express		•	Organizational skills

Academic Accommodations

Curriculum	Study Aids	Exams
• Priority registration	Typist	• Oral
Math waiver	• Reader	• Untimed
Foreign lang. waiver	• Notetaker	Take home
Course substitution	Proof reader	• With proctor
In Class	• Text on tape	On computer
Calculators	Early syllabus	Extended time
• Tape recorder	Taped handouts	On tape
Word processor		Modified
Priority seating		• Separate room

Graduation Requirements:
Course credits: **60** GPA: **2.0** Years to complete degree: **2-3**

General Information:

Golden West College is a 2 year public college. Suburban campus 40 miles from Los Angeles. Accessible by bus. Ski areas are 100 miles from campus. Beaches are 3 miles from campus. Housing is not guaranteed.

Accreditation:WACS, NLN, CBRN

Expenses:
Tuition: In-state: Full year: $60.00 over 10 units. Part-time: Per credit:$6.00 per unit up to 10 units. Tuition: Out-of-state: Full year: Part-time: Per credit: $103.00.

Majors

• ARTS Commercial Art, Design, Drafting, Film & Video, Graphic Arts, Music, Photography • BUSINESS Accounting, Bookkeeping, Business Administration, Business Management, Clerical, Data Processing, Management, Real Estate, Secretarial Science • COMMUNICATIONS Communication, English, Graphic Design, Journalism, Literature, Photography, Television/Radio/Film • COMPUTER SCIENCE Business Data Programming, Computer Science, Data Processing • CRAFTS AND DESIGN Ceramics, Graphic Design • EDUCATION Business, English, Foreign Language, General, Mathematics, Music, Psychology • ENGINEERING Architectural, Automotive, Drafting, Mathematical, Radio/Television • HEALTH SCIENCES Health, Nursing, Nursing Assistant • HUMANITIES English/Writing/Literature, Humanities • LANGUAGES English, French, German, Italian, Japanese, Russian, Spanish • MATHEMATICS Applied • SCIENCES Applied Mathematics, Chemistry, Computer Science, Mathematics • SOCIAL SCIENCES Anthropology, Criminal Justice, Geography, History, Political Science, Psychology, Social Sciences, Sociology • VISUAL AND PERFORMING ARTS Art, Dance, Dramatic Arts, Fine Arts, Music Performance, Theater • VOCATIONAL Auto Body, Automobile Technology, Automotive Service, Business and Office, Cosmetology, Diesel Power Technology, Drafting, Electronics Technology, Office Administration, Secretarial, Word Processing

Sports/Activities

• SPORTS RELATED Cheerleading, Pep Band • SPORTS-INTRAMURAL Baseball, Baseball (M), Basketball, Basketball (F), Basketball (M), Cross Country (F), Cross Country (M), Football (M), Softball (F), Swimming, Swimming (F), Swimming (M), Tennis, Track and Field, Track and Field (F), Track and Field (M), Volleyball, Volleyball (F), Volleyball (M), Water Polo (M), Wrestling, Wrestling (M) • STUDENT LIFE ACTIVITIES Academic Clubs, Choral, Concert Band, Dance, Music Groups, Newspaper, Orchestra, Religious Organization, Student Government

Hartnell College
156 Homestead Avenue
Salinas, California 93901
(408) 755-6700

School Enrollment: **10,000** Male: **4,700** Female: **5,300**
LD Enrollment: **150**

Admissions Contact: **Cheri Bishop, Director of Admissions**
LD Contact: **Deborah Shulman, LD Specialist**
Name of Program: **Enabler Program**
Telephone:**(408) 755-6760**

Admissions

Application Information:
LD Students Applying: **80** Accepted: **50** Enrolled:**50**
Application deadline: **August 20th**
Applicant must apply **6** months in advance
Rolling Admissions: **Yes**

Secondary School Information:
Most Important Criteria For Admissions (1-strongest)

SAT/ACT **1**	Application	School transcript
Class rank	Course selection	Personal statement
1 Interview	Extra activities **1**	Psychoeducational
G.P.A.	**1** Open admission	Recommendations

Test Requirements:
Diagnostic testing waived: **Yes**
WAIS-R required: **Yes** Range accepted: **80+**

Types of Disabilities Served

Speech/Lang	• Reading	ADD with LD
• Study skills	• Spelling	ADD without LD
• Written express	• Math	ADHD with LD
• Organizational	• Fine Motor	ADHD without LD
• Perceptual		

Admissions Process

Open admissions

Learning Disability Program

Students mainstreamed **100** % of the day
Recommended credits per semester: **varies**
Counseling: Individual: **Yes**

Faculty:
Faculty: **2** Full time: **1** Part time: **2** M.A.: **2**
Faculty advocate: **Yes** Meets with instructor: **As needed**

Diagnostic Testing

ADD	• Personality	• Perceptual skills	• Spelling
ADHD	• Organization	• Fine motor skills	• Reading
• I.Q.	Handwriting	Spoken language	• Study skills
• Math	Social skills	• Written language	

Tutoring:
Average size of group tutorials: **5-15**
Services rendered by:
Graduates   Peers   Faculty   •LD staff   Teacher trainees

Tutorials

Grp.	Ind.	Tutorials	Grp.	Ind.	Tutorials
	•	Math skills	•		Word processing
	•	Study skills	•		Time management
	•	Language arts	•		Learning strategies
	•	Written express	•		Organizational skills

Academic Accommodations

Curriculum	Study Aids	Exams
• Priority registration	• Typist	Oral
Math waiver	Reader	• Untimed
Foreign lang. waiver	• Notetaker	Take home
Course substitution	Proof reader	With proctor
In Class	• Text on tape	• On computer
• Calculators	Early syllabus	• Extended time
• Tape recorder	Taped handouts	On tape
• Word processor		Modified
Priority seating		• Separate room

Program Strengths

The LD program at Hartnell College serves the individual needs of the students. The Educational Skills Lab is available for students who need assistance with basic skills and/or assistance with other classes. Learning disabled students at Hartnell also have access to the college's learning skills program and tutorial services. LD students can be successful at Hartnell because of the varied services available for their individual needs.

General Information:

Hartnell College is a 2 year public college. Rural campus of 160 acres is Accessible by bus. Ski areas are 200 miles from campus. Beaches are 15 miles from campus. 2% of students are foreign. Housing is not guaranteed.

Accreditation: Regional

Expenses:

Tuition: In-state: Full year: $100.00 per year. Tuition: Out-of-state: Full year: $1,000.00 per year.

Majors

• BUSINESS Accounting, Business Administration, Economics, Real Estate • COMMUNICATIONS English, Photography • COMPUTER SCIENCE Data Processing, Programming, Symbolic Systems • EDUCATION Art, Early Childhood, Music • HEALTH SCIENCES Nursing • LANGUAGES French, Spanish • PREPROFESSIONAL Agriculture, Architecture, Dentistry, Engineering, Law, Medicine, Natural Resources, Pharmacy, Recreation, Social Work • SCIENCES Biology, Chemistry, Physics • VISUAL AND PERFORMING ARTS Art, Music, Studio Art, Theater

Sports/Activities

• STUDENT LIFE ACTIVITIES Student Government

Humboldt State University
Arcata, California 95521
(707) 826-4402

School Enrollment: **7,200** Male: **3,600** Female: **3,600**
LD Enrollment: **126** Male: **88** Female: **38**

Admissions Contact: **Margi Stevenson, Acting Director**
LD Contact: **Theresa Jordan, Coordinator**
Name of Program: **Disabled Student Services**
Telephone: **(707) 826-4678**

Admissions

Application Information:
Application deadline: **November/August**
Applicant must apply **10** months in advance
Rolling Admissions: **Yes**

Secondary School Information
Most Important Criteria For Admissions (1-strongest)

2 SAT/ACT	**1** Application	**1** School transcript
5 Class rank	**2** Course selection	**3** Personal statement
3 Interview	**6** Extra activities	Psychoeducational
1 G.P.A.	Open admission	**4** Recommendations

Test Requirements:
Diagnostic testing waived: **Yes**
Untimed SAT: **Yes** Untimed ACT: **Yes** Untimed ACH: **Yes**
WAIS-R required: **Yes** Range accepted: **90+**
Documentation of LD required: **Yes**
Currency of diagnostic testing: **No older than 36 months**
Tests recommended: **WAIS-R, Woodcock-Johnson, TONI, Detroit**

Types of Disabilities Served
• Speech/Lang	• Reading	• ADD with LD
• Study skills	• Spelling	• ADD without LD
• Written express	• Math	• ADHD with LD
• Organizational	• Fine Motor	• ADHD without LD
• Perceptual		

High School Course Requirements:
English: **4** Math: **3** Science: **1** Foreign Language: **2**
Waivers to standard high school courses
Foreign Language : **Yes** Math: **Yes**

Learning Disability Program

Program: Reinforces course work: **Yes**
Students mainstreamed **100** % of the day
Recommended credits per semester: **12**
Services only for LD students: **Yes**
Counseling: Individual: **Yes**

Faculty:
Faculty: **2** Full time: **1** Part time: **1** M.A.: **2**
Faculty advocate: **Yes** Meets with instructor: **As needed**

California

Diagnostic Testing

ADD   Personality • Perceptual skills • Spelling
ADHD• Organization• Fine motor skills • Reading
• I.Q.   Handwriting• Spoken language   Study skills
• Math   Social skills• Written language

Tutoring:

Average size of group tutorials: **1:1**
Services rendered by:
•Graduates   •Peers   •Faculty   LD staff   Teacher trainees

Tutorials

Grp.	Ind.	Tutorials	Grp.	Ind.	Tutorials
•	•	Math skills	•		Word processing
	•	Study skills		•	Time management
•	•	Language arts	•	•	Learning strategies
	•	Written express	•	•	Organizational skills

Academic Accommodations

Curriculum	Study Aids	Exams
• Priority registration	Typist	• Oral
Math waiver	• Reader	Untimed
Foreign lang. waiver	• Notetaker	Take home
Course substitution	• Proof reader	With proctor
In Class	• Text on tape	On computer
Calculators	Early syllabus	• Extended time
• Tape recorder	Taped handouts	On tape
• Word processor		Modified
Priority seating		• Separate room

Graduation Requirements:

Course credits: **124** GPA: **2.0** Years to complete degree: **4-7**

Program Strengths

We attempt to provide individualized services based on assessment. All services are optional and students must request them. We do advise them of appropriate services upon their enrollment in the program. Because our class enrollments are fairly small, individualized attention from faculty is easily available to students.

General Information:

Humboldt State University is a 4 year public university. Rural campus of 145 acres is 275 miles from San Francisco. Accessible by air or bus. Ski areas are 2-6 hours from campus. Beaches are 5 minutes from campus. 2% of students are foreign. Housing is not guaranteed.80 % of students remain on campus for the weekends. 2 % of students join fraternities/sororities.

Accreditation:WACS

SAT/ACT Scores:

Scores for incoming freshmen: **ACT:** 43% below 20. 25% between 20 and 23. 19%between 24 and 25l. 12%between 26 and 28. 1% above 28.

Expenses:

Tuition: In-state: Full year: $904.00. Tuition: Out-of-state: Full year: $452.00 plus $189.00 per unit. Part-time: Per credit:$293.00. Room and board: $3,795.00

Majors

• AREA STUDIES Native American • BUSINESS Accounting, Business Administration, Business Economics, Business Education, Business Management, Economics, Finance, Management, Marketing • COMMUNICATIONS English, Journalism, Television/Radio/Film • COMPUTER SCIENCE Computer Information Systems, Computer Science • EDUCATION Agricultural, Child Development, Early Childhood, Elementary, Industrial, Middle School, Music, Physical, Recreation and Youth Leadershi, School Psychology, Science, Speech/Language, Vocational • ENGINEER-ING Environmental/Water Resources • ENVIRONMENTAL CONTROL Air Pollution Control Technolo, Water and Wastewater Technolog • HEALTH SCIENCES Environmental, Medical Technology, Nursing, Speech Therapy, Speech/Audiology and Speech • HUMANITIES Philosophy, Religion • LANGUAGES French, German, Spanish • PREPROFESSIONAL Dentistry, Engineering, Fisheries, Forestry, Law, Medicine, Natural Resources, Range Management, Recreation, Social Work, Wildlife • SCIENCES Biochemistry, Biology, Botany, Chemistry, Ecology, Geography, Geology, Marine Biology, Mathematics, Molecular Biology, Oceanography, Physical Science, Physics, Zoology • SOCIAL SCIENCES Anthropology, Geography, Government/Political, History, Psychology, Social Sciences, Sociology • VISUAL AND PERFORMING ARTS Art, Art History, Dance, Music, Studio Art, Theater • VOCATIONAL Fishery Studies, Home Economics, Medical Laboratory Technology

Sports/Activities

• SPORTS RELATED Band, Cheerleading, Pep Band • SPORTS-INTERCOLLEGIATE Basketball, Cross Country, Football (M), Soccer (M), Swimming, Tennis, Track and Field, Volleyball (F), Weight Lifting • SPORTS-INTRAMURAL Archery, Badminton, Crew, Fencing, Field Hockey, Golf, Gymnastics, Hand Ball, Racquetball, Rugby, Sailing, Skiing - Snow, Soccer, Volleyball (M), Water Polo, Wrestling (M) • STUDENT LIFE ACTIVITIES Concert Band, Dance, Debate, Drama Groups, Ethnic & Cultural Groups, Film, Jazz Band, Music Ensembles, Music Groups, Musical Theater, Radio/TV station, Sororities, Student Government, Symphony Orchestra

---

Less Selective	**California**
	Program

Imperial Valley College
P.O. Box 158
Imperial, California 92251-015
(619) 352-8320

School Enrollment: **4,696** Male: **1,730** Female: **2,966**
LD Enrollment: **18**

Admissions Contact: **Sandra Standiford, Dean of Admissions**
LD Contact: **Norma Nava-Pinuelas, Instructional Specialist**
Name of Program: **Disabled Student Program & Service**

Admissions

Application Information:

LD Students Applying: **21** Accepted: **18** Enrolled:**18**
Separate application:**Yes**
Application deadline: **Open**

Secondary School Information

Most Important Criteria For Admissions (1-strongest)

SAT/ACT	Application	**2**	School transcript
Class rank	Course selection		Personal statement
Interview	Extra activities	**1**	Psychoeducational
G.P.A.	**1** Open admission		Recommendations

Test Requirements:

Diagnostic testing waived: **Yes**
Achievement tests required:**2**
Range accepted: **80 and up**
Documentation of LD required: **Yes**
Currency of diagnostic testing: **1 month**
Tests recommended: **WAIS-R or Woodcock-Johnson Part I & II, WRAT-R**

Types of Disabilities Served

- Speech/Lang
- Study skills
- Written express
- Organizational
- Perceptual
- Reading
- Spelling
- Math
- Fine Motor
- ADD with LD
- ADD without LD
- ADHD with LD
- ADHD without LD

Learning Disability Program

Program: Remedial: **Yes**
Program: Reinforces course work: **Yes**
Students mainstreamed **80** % of the day

Faculty:

Faculty: **2** Full time: **1** Part time: **1** Ph.D.: **2**
Faculty advocate: **Yes** Meets with instructor: **Weekly**

Diagnostic Testing

ADD	Personality •	Perceptual skills •	Spelling
ADHD	Organization•	Fine motor skills •	Reading
• I.Q.	• Handwriting	Spoken language •	Study skills
• Math	Social skills•	Written language	

Tutoring:

Average size of group tutorials: **4**
Services rendered by:

Graduates	•Peers	Faculty	•LD staff	Teacher trainees

Tutorials

Grp.	Ind.	Tutorials	Grp.	Ind.	Tutorials
•	•	Math skills	•	•	Word processing
•	•	Study skills	•	•	Time management
•	•	Language arts	•	•	Learning strategies
•	•	Written express	•	•	Organizational skills

Academic Accommodations

Curriculum	Study Aids	Exams
• Priority registration	• Typist	• Oral
Math waiver	• Reader	Untimed
Foreign lang. waiver	• Notetaker	• Take home
Course substitution	• Proof reader	• With proctor
In Class	• Text on tape	On computer
• Calculators	Early syllabus	• Extended time
• Tape recorder	Taped handouts	On tape
• Word processor		Modified
Priority seating		Separate room

Program Strengths

At Imperial Valley College the Learning Disability program provides both supportive services and courses to students with learning disabilities. Our program is a reflection of the state program which is a model program for the rest of the country. Each student is assigned to work with an instructional specialist or counselor who provides the student with academic counseling, tutorial services, financial assistance, enrollment in High Tech courses, and other supportive services deemed necessary to meet the student's needs. All of these services are available to students in one central location.

General Information:

Imperial Valley College is a 2 year public college. Rural campus of 225 acres is 215 miles from San Diego. Accessible by bus. Ski areas are 300 miles from campus. Beaches are 220 miles from campus. 5% of students are foreign. Housing is not guaranteed.

Accreditation: WACS

Class Rank:
About 2% of the present freshmen class were in the upper 20% of their high school class. 28% were in the top 40% of their class. 40% were in the top 60% of their class. 30% were in the top 80% of their class.

Expenses:
Tuition: In-state: Full year: $100.00. Part-time: Per credit: $6.00 per unit.
Tuition: Out-of-state: Full year: $1,178.00. Part-time: Per credit:$94.00 per unit.

Majors

• AGRICULTURE Mechanics, Science • BUSINESS Agri-business, Agricultural, Business Administration, Business Management, Finance • EDUCATION Early Childhood, Elementary • ENGINEERING Engineering • HEALTH SCIENCES Medical Records Administration, Medical Secretary, Nursing, Practical Nursing • HUMANITIES Fine Arts • SCIENCES Anthropology, Behavioral, Gerontology, Mathematics, Physical • SOCIAL SCIENCES Criminal Justice, Law Enforcement, Psychology, Social Science • VOCATIONAL Fire Control and Safety Techn, Industrial Equipment Maintenan, Legal Assistant, Legal Secretary, Precision Metal Works, Rehabilitation, Secretarial, Water and Wastewater Technolog, Welding Technology

Sports/Activities

• SPORTS-INTRAMURAL Baseball (M), Basketball (M), Soccer (M), Softball (F), Tennis, Volleyball (F) • STUDENT LIFE ACTIVITIES Debate, Ethnic & Cultural Groups, Jazz Band, Magazine, Music Ensembles, Music Groups, Newspaper, Student Government

Less Selective   **California**
                                        Program

Kings River Community College
995 North Reed
Reedley, California 93654
(209) 638-3641

School Enrollment: **4,000** Male: **1,600** Female: **2,400**
LD Enrollment: **90**

Admissions Contact: **Moire Charters, Assoc. Dean Admissions**
LD Contact: **Lynn Mancini, Enabler Director**
Name of Program: **Enabler Services**

Admissions

Application Information:
Enrolled:**90**
Application deadline: **July 1st**
Applicant must apply **4** months in advance
Rolling Admissions: **Yes**

Secondary School Information
Most Important Criteria For Admissions (1-strongest)

SAT/ACT	**1**	Application	**2**	School transcript
Class rank		Course selection		Personal statement
Interview		Extra activities		Psychoeducational
G.P.A.		Open admission		Recommendations

Test Requirements:
Tests recommended: **California Community College learning disability model**

California

Types of Disabilities Served
- Speech/Lang
- Study skills
- Written express
- Organizational
- Perceptual
- Reading
- Spelling
- Math
- Fine Motor
- ADD with LD
- ADD without LD
- ADHD with LD
- ADHD without LD

Learning Disability Program

Program: Remedial: **Yes**
Program: Reinforces course work: **Yes**
Students mainstreamed **100** % of the day
Counseling: Individual: **Yes** Group Counseling: **Yes**

Faculty:
Faculty: **2** Part time: **2** M.A.: **2**
Faculty advocate: **Yes** Meets with instructor: **As needed**

Diagnostic Testing
ADD	• Personality	• Perceptual skills	• Spelling
ADHD	Organization	• Fine motor skills	• Reading
• I.Q.	Handwriting	• Spoken language	Study skills
• Math	• Social skills	• Written language	

Tutoring:
Services rendered by:
Graduates •Peers •Faculty •LD staff Teacher trainees

Tutorials
Grp.	Ind.	Tutorials	Grp.	Ind.	Tutorials
•	•	Math skills		•	Word processing
•	•	Study skills			Time management
	•	Language arts	•	•	Learning strategies
	•	Written express		•	Organizational skills

Academic Accommodations
Curriculum	Study Aids	Exams
Priority registration	• Typist	• Oral
• Math waiver	Reader	Untimed
• Foreign lang. waiver	• Notetaker	• Take home
Course substitution	• Proof reader	With proctor
In Class	• Text on tape	On computer
• Calculators	Early syllabus	• Extended time
• Tape recorder	Taped handouts	On tape
• Word processor		• Modified
Priority seating		Separate room

Program Strengths
The LD program is distinctive due to our mainstream philosophy. We do not offer special classes for remediation of basic skills; that responsibility is assigned to the college's skills center. We do offer our LD students the opportunity to join evaluatory classes on learning strategies. We present strategies in the following areas: test taking, sentence wriitng, error monitoring, first letter mnemonics and self-advicacy. We have seen our LD students make splendid progress when utilizing these instructional services. We feel our program is comprehensive and meets the needs of our students.

General Information:
Kings River Community College is a 2 year public college. Rural campus of 300 acres is 22 miles from Fresno. Accessible by bus. Ski areas are 1.5 hours from campus. Beaches are 2.5 hours from campus. 1% of students are foreign. 1 residential halls on campus. Housing is not guaranteed.

Accreditation: WACS

Expenses:
Tuition: In-state: Full year: $115.00. Part-time: Per credit:$5.00. Tuition: Out-of-state: Full year: Part-time: Per credit: $94.00.

Majors
• BUSINESS Accounting, Business Administration, Business Management, Economics, Management, Marketing • COMMUNICATIONS Creative Writing, English, Journalism, Photography • COMPUTER SCIENCE Data Processing • EDUCATION Early Childhood, Elementary, Music • HEALTH SCIENCES Health, Nutritional/Food • HUMANITIES Humanities, Philosophy, Religion • LANGUAGES Spanish • PREPROFESSIONAL Agriculture, Engineering, Forestry • SCIENCES Biology, Botany, Geography, Geology, Mathematics, Physical Science, Physics, Physiology • SOCIAL SCIENCES Criminal Justice, Geography, History, Psychology, Social Sciences, Sociology • VISUAL AND PERFORMING ARTS Art, Art History, Theater

Sports/Activities
• SPORTS RELATED Cheerleading • SPORTS-INTRAMURAL Badminton, Baseball, Basketball, Football (M), Golf (M), Karate, Racquetball, Softball (F), Swimming, Tennis, Track and Field, Volleyball (F), Weight Lifting, Wrestling • STUDENT LIFE ACTIVITIES Drama Groups, Ethnic & Cultural Groups, Newspaper, Student Government

Less Selective   **California Program**

Laney College
900 Fallon Street
Oakland, California 94607
(510) 466-7200

School Enrollment: **11,250** Male: **3,000** Female: **8,250**
LD Enrollment: **50** Male: **25** Female: **25**

Admissions Contact: **Howard Perdue, Director of Admissions**
LD Contact: **Sondra Neiman, LD Specialist**
Name of Program: **Learning Skills Program**
Address: **900 Fallon St.**
Telephone:**(510) 464-3428**

Admissions

Application Information:
LD Students Applying: **30** Accepted: **15** Enrolled:**15**
Separate application:**Yes**
Application deadline: **August 30th**
Applicant must apply **1-6** months in advance

Secondary School Information
Most Important Criteria For Admissions (1-strongest)
SAT/ACT	Application	School transcript
Class rank	Course selection	Personal statement
Interview	Extra activities	1 Psychoeducational
G.P.A.	Open admission	Recommendations

Test Requirements:
Tests recommended: **Woodcock-Johnson Battery, AAS, WRAT-testing can be done on campus**

Types of Disabilities Served

- Speech/Lang
- Study skills
- Written express
- Organizational Perceptual

- Reading
- Spelling
- Math
- Fine Motor

ADD with LD
ADD without LD
ADHD with LD
ADHD without LD

Learning Disability Program

Syllabus available during orientation:**Yes**
Program: Remedial: **Yes**
Program: Reinforces course work: **Yes**
Students mainstreamed **80** % of the day
Counseling: Individual: **Yes** Vocational Counseling: **Yes**
Support groups are available:**Social Club**

Faculty:

Faculty: **11** Including Director: **Yes** Full time: **1** Part time: **10**
LD faculty with: BS/BA: **6** M.A.: **1** Ph.D.: **1**

Diagnostic Testing

ADD	Personality	• Perceptual skills	• Spelling
ADHD	Organization	Fine motor skills	• Reading
I.Q.	Handwriting	• Spoken language	Study skills
• Math	• Social skills	• Written language	

Tutoring:

Average size of group tutorials: **2-5**
Services rendered by:
Graduates • Peers • Faculty • LD staff Teacher trainees

Tutorials

Grp.	Ind.	Tutorials	Grp.	Ind.	Tutorials
	•	Math skills		•	Word processing
•		Study skills	•		Time management
•		Language arts	•		Learning strategies
•	•	Written express	•		Organizational skills

Academic Accommodations

Curriculum	Study Aids	Exams
Priority registration	• Typist	• Oral
Math waiver	Reader	Untimed
Foreign lang. waiver	• Notetaker	• Take home
Course substitution	• Proof reader	With proctor
In Class	• Text on tape	On computer
• Calculators	Early syllabus	• Extended time
• Tape recorder	Taped handouts	On tape
• Word processor		• Modified
Priority seating		Separate room

Program Strengths

The Learning Skills Program at Laney College is exceptional. The L.S.P. changes every semester according to the needs of the students. We have and welcome student input and have students who are also part of our paid teaching staff. We promote self-education regarding Learning Disabilities, a support group, and regularly scheduled social opportunities. We have many successes academically and socially.

General Information:

Laney College is a 2 year public college. Urban campus. San Francisco. Accessible by train or bus. Housing is not guaranteed.

Accreditation:Regional

Expenses:

Tuition: In-state: Full year: $104.00. Part-time: Per credit:$5.00. Tuition:

Out-of-state: Full year: Part-time: Per credit: $96.00 plus $2.000 fee per unit.

Majors

• AREA STUDIES African, Asian, Black/Afro-American, Urban • BUSINESS Accounting, Business Administration, Business Economics, Business Management, Economics, Finance, Marketing, Real Estate • COMMUNICATIONS Creative Writing, English, Journalism, Photography, Television/Radio/Film • COMPUTER SCIENCE Data Processing, Programming • EDUCATION Art, English As A Second Language (, Physical, Vocational • HUMANITIES • LANGUAGES Chinese, French • PRE-PROFESSIONAL Architecture • SCIENCES Biology, Chemistry, Geography, Geology, Physical Science, Physics • SOCIAL SCIENCES Anthropology, Geography, History, Psychology, Social Sciences, Sociology • VISUAL AND PERFORMING ARTS Art, Art History, Dance, Music, Studio Art, Theater • VOCATIONAL Air Conditioning/Heating/Refri, Carpentry, Cosmetology, Sheet Metal, Welding

Sports/Activities

• SPORTS-INTERCOLLEGIATE Baseball, Basketball, Diving, Football (M), Softball, Swimming, Tennis, Volleyball • SPORTS-INTRAMURAL Basketball • STUDENT LIFE ACTIVITIES Newspaper, Student Government

Less Selective

California
Services

Long Beach City College

4901 East Carson Street
Long Beach, California 90808
(213) 420-4206

School Enrollment: **30,000** Male: **14,048** Female: **15,970**
LD Enrollment: **50** Male: **20** Female: **30**

Admissions Contact: **Richard Dawdy, Dean of Admissions**
LD Contact: **Marvin Mastros, LD Specialist**
Name of Program: **Learning Disability Program**
Address: **1305 E. Pacific Coast Hgwy.**
Telephone:**(213) 599-7926**

Admissions

Application Information:

LD Students Applying: **75** Enrolled:**50**
Application deadline: **None**
Applicant must apply **3-6** months in advance
Rolling Admissions: **Yes**

Secondary School Information

Most Important Criteria For Admissions (1-strongest)

	SAT/ACT	**4** Application	School transcript
	Class rank	Course selection	Personal statement
1	Interview	Extra activities	**2** Psychoeducational
	G.P.A.	**1** Open admission	**3** Recommendations

Test Requirements:

Diagnostic testing waived: **Yes**
Achievement tests required:**1**
WAIS-R required: **Yes** Range accepted: **>80**
Documentation of LD required: **Yes**
Currency of diagnostic testing: **less than 3 years**
Tests recommended: **California Assessment System, Woodcock-Johnson Cognitive Achievement Test or WAIS-R**

California

Types of Disabilities Served
- Speech/Lang
- Study skills
- Written express
- Organizational
- Perceptual
- Reading
- Spelling
- Math
- Fine Motor
- ADD with LD
- ADD without LD
- ADHD with LD
- ADHD without LD

Admissions Process

LD intake interview required - LD assessment required if previous testing greater than 3 years old.

Learning Disability Program

Program: Reinforces course work: **Yes**
Services only for LD students: **Yes**
Counseling: Individual: **Yes**

Faculty:
Faculty: **3** Including Director: **Yes** Full time: **2** Part time: **1**
LD faculty with: BS/BA: **3** M.A.: **3**
Faculty advocate: **Yes** Meets with instructor: **As needed**

Diagnostic Testing
ADD	Personality	• Perceptual skills	• Spelling
ADHD	Organization	Fine motor skills	• Reading
• I.Q.	• Handwriting	• Spoken language	• Study skills
• Math	• Social skills	• Written language	

Tutoring:
Average size of group tutorials: **Individual**
Services rendered by:
Graduates   •Peers   •Faculty   •LD staff   Teacher trainees

Tutorials
Grp.	Ind.	Tutorials	Grp.	Ind.	Tutorials
	•	Math skills		•	Word processing
•	•	Study skills		•	Time management
	•	Language arts		•	Learning strategies
	•	Written express		•	Organizational skills

Academic Accommodations

Curriculum
- Priority registration
- Math waiver
- Foreign lang. waiver
- Course substitution

In Class
- Calculators
- Tape recorder
- Word processor
- Priority seating

Study Aids
- Typist
- Reader
- Notetaker
- Proof reader
- Text on tape
- Early syllabus
- Taped handouts

Exams
- Oral
- Untimed
- Take home
- With proctor
- On computer
- Extended time
- On tape
- Modified
- Separate room

Graduation Requirements:
Course credits: **60** GPA: **2.0** Years to complete degree: **2-3** Math waiver: **Yes**

Program Strengths
Each student is provided with a complete evaluation and report certifying his or her disability, strengths, and weaknesses and a list of recommended classroom accommodations. Students are mainstreamed with remediation available. We rely on flexibility to meet individual needs. Support services are provided on an individual basis.

General Information:
Long Beach City College is a 2 year public college. Urban campus of 5 acres is 15 miles from Los Angeles. Accessible by air, train, or bus. Ski areas are 30 miles from campus. Beaches are 3 miles from campus. 12% of students are foreign. Housing is not guaranteed.

Accreditation: State accredited

Expenses:
Tuition: In-state: Full year: $6.00 per unit. Part-time: Per course: $6.00 per unit. Tuition: Out-of-state: Full year: $102.00 per unit. Part-time: Per credit: $102.00.

Majors
• AGRICULTURE Horticultural • ARTS Art History, Commercial Art, Dance, Drafting, Dramatic Arts, Drawing, Fashion Design, Film & Video, Interior Design, Landscaping, Music, Music Performance, Painting, Photography, Sculpture, Theater Design • BUSINESS Accounting, Banking, Bookkeeping, Business Administration, Business Management, Clerical, Commercial Art, Construction, Data Processing, Fashion Merchandising, Food Management, Hotel and Restaurant Managemen, Insurance, International Business, Labor Relations, Marketing, Real Estate, Secretarial Science, Travel/Tourism Management • COMMUNICATIONS Broadcasting, English, Journalism, Photography, Speech/Debate/Forensic, Television/Radio/Film • COMPUTER SCIENCE Computer Science, Data Processing • CRAFTS AND DESIGN Apparel Design, Ceramics, Industrial Design, Jewelry, Sculpture • EDUCATION Adult, Outdoor, Special • HEALTH SCIENCES Dietary Manager, Medical Assistant, Nursing, Nutritional/Food, Practical Nursing, Radiological Therapy, Respiratory Therapy • HUMANITIES English/Writing/Literature, Fine Arts, Humanities, Liberal Arts, Philosophy • LANGUAGES Chinese, English, French, German, Italian, Japanese, Spanish • SCIENCES Anatomy, Anthropology, Astronomy, Biology, Botany, Chemistry, Computer Science, Earth, General, Geography, Geology, Horticultural, Marine Biology, Microbiology, Oceanography, Public Health, Radiology • SPECIAL EDUCATION Deaf/Hearing Impaired, Emotionally Disturbed, Gifted & Talented, Learning Disability, Mentally Retarded, Physically Handicapped, Visually Handicapped • VISUAL AND PERFORMING ARTS Art, Dance, Dramatic Arts, Fine Arts, Music, Music Performance, Theater • VOCATIONAL Air Conditioning/Heating/Refri, Auto Body, Automobile Technology, Automotive Service, Aviation Maintenance, Aviation Pilot, Building Construction, Business and Office, Carpentry, Chef Apprenticeship, Construction, Culinary Arts, Diesel Power Technology, Drafting, Electronics Technology, Fashion Design, Fashion Merchandising, Fire Science, Food Service, Home Economics, Interior Design, Jewelry-Metalsmithery, Legal Secretary, Machinist, Masonry, Secretarial, Welding, Woodworking, Word Processing

Sports/Activities
• SPORTS RELATED Cheerleading, Drill Team, Pep Band, Team Managers • SPORTS-INTERCOLLEGIATE Baseball (M), Cross Country, Diving, Football (M), Golf (M), Soccer, Softball (F), Swimming, Tennis, Track and Field, Volleyball, Water Polo (M) • SPORTS-INTRAMURAL Archery, Badminton (M), Basketball, Fencing, Gymnastics, Hand Ball, Judo, Ping-Pong, Racquetball, Sailing, Skiing - Water, Soccer, Softball, Swimming, Tennis, Track and Field, Volleyball, Water Polo, Weight Lifting, Wrestling • STUDENT LIFE ACTIVITIES Concert Band, Dance, Debate, Drama Groups, Film, Fraternities, Jazz Band, Music Groups, Newspaper, Radio/TV station, Religious Organization, Sororities, Student Government, Yearbook

Less Selective

Los Angeles City College

855 North Vermont Avenue
Los Angeles, California 90029
(213) 669-4385

School Enrollment: **14,000** Male: **7,000** Female: **7,000**
LD Enrollment: **150**

Admissions Contact: **Chad Woo, Jr. Assistant Dean**
LD Contact: **Susan Matranga, LD Specialist**
Name of Program: **Learning Disabilities Program**
Address: **855 N. Vermont Avenue**
Telephone:**(213) 669-5515**

Admissions

Application Information:
LD Students Applying: **200** Accepted: **70** Enrolled:**70**
Application deadline: **Open**
Rolling Admissions: **Yes**

Secondary School Information
Most Important Criteria For Admissions (1-strongest)

SAT/ACT	Application	School transcript
Class rank	Course selection	Personal statement
Interview	Extra activities	Psychoeducational
G.P.A.	**1** Open admission	Recommendations

Test Requirements:
Diagnostic testing waived: **Yes**
Documentation of LD required: **Yes**
Tests recommended: **We do testing established by CA Community Colleges**

Types of Disabilities Served
- Speech/Lang
- Study skills
- Written express
- Organizational
- Perceptual
- Reading
- Spelling
- Math
- Fine Motor
- ADD with LD
- ADD without LD
- ADHD with LD
- ADHD without LD

Learning Disability Program
Program: Reinforces course work: **Yes**
Students mainstreamed **90** % of the day
Recommended credits per semester: **12**
Services only for LD students: **Yes**
Counseling: Individual: **Yes** Group Counseling: **Yes** Vocational Counseling: **Yes**
Support groups are available:**Informal support groups**

Faculty:
Faculty: **2** Including Director: **Yes** Full time: **2** M.A.: **2**
Faculty advocate: **Yes** Meets with instructor: **Frequently**

Diagnostic Testing
- ADD
- ADHD
- I.Q.
- Math
- Personality
- Organization
- Handwriting
- Social skills
- Perceptual skills
- Fine motor skills
- Spoken language
- Written language
- Spelling
- Reading
- Study skills

Tutoring:
Average size of group tutorials: **1:1**
Services rendered by:
Graduates •Peers Faculty •LD staff Teacher trainees

Tutorials

Grp.	Ind.	Tutorials	Grp.	Ind.	Tutorials
	•	Math skills		•	Word processing
•		Study skills	•		Time management
	•	Language arts	•		Learning strategies
•	•	Written express	•		Organizational skills

Academic Accommodations

Curriculum	Study Aids	Exams
• Priority registration	Typist	• Oral
• Math waiver	• Reader	• Untimed
• Foreign lang. waiver	• Notetaker	• Take home
Course substitution	• Proof reader	• With proctor
In Class	• Text on tape	On computer
• Calculators	Early syllabus	• Extended time
• Tape recorder	Taped handouts	• On tape
• Word processor		• Modified
Priority seating		• Separate room

Graduation Requirements:
Course credits: **60-64 units** GPA: **2.0** Years to complete degree: **Open**
Math waiver: **Yes** Language waiver: **Yes**
Other requirements: **Competency requiremets: reading, writing, and math.**

Program Strengths
The LD Program at LACC provides a warm, caring environment within which students with learning disabilities can receive the support they need to reach their potential. LACC has a diverse, multi-cultural student body which is exciting and stimulating for all students and staff.

General Information:
Los Angeles City College is a 2 year public college. Urban campus of 40 acres is Accessible by air, train or bus. Ski areas are 50 miles from campus. Beaches are 15 miles from campus. 70% of students are foreign. Housing is not guaranteed.

Accreditation:WACS

Expenses:
Tuition: In-state: Full year: $6.00 per unit, $60.00 maximum. Part-time: Per credit: . Tuition: Out-of-state: Full year: Part-time: Per credit: $108.00.

Majors
• AREA STUDIES American, Asian, Black/Afro-American, Latin American, Mexican/American, Urban • BUSINESS Accounting, Business Administration, Business Economics, Business Education, Business Management, Economics, Finance, International Business, Marketing, Marketing Research, Real Estate, Travel/Tourism Management • COMMUNICATION Advertising, Broadcasting, Cinematography, Communication, Creative Writing, Journalism, Photography, Television/Radio/Film • COMPUTER SCIENCE Computer Maintenance, Computer Technology, Data Processing, Programming, Software Engineer, Systems Analysis, Telecommunications • EDUCATION Early Childhood, Elementary, Health, Music, Secondary • ENGINEERING Civil/Environmental • FINE AND PERFORMING ARTS Art, Art History, Dance, Music, Studio Art, Theater • HEALTH SCIENCES Dental Assistant, Dental Technician, Medical Technology, Nutritional/Food, Radiological Therapy • LANGUAGES Arabic, Chinese, French, German, Italian, Japanese, Korean, Latin, Russian, Spanish • PHILOSOPHY Humanities, Philosophy • PREPROFESSIONAL Architecture, Engineering, Legal Assistant, Social Work • SCIENCES Astronomy, Biology, Botany, Chemistry, Earth Science, Ecol-

ogy, Geography, Geology, Mathematics, Microbiology, Oceanography, Physical Chemistry, Physical Science, Physics, Physiology, Radiology, Zoology • SOCIAL SCIENCES Anthropology, Criminal Justice, Geography, Government/Political, History, Human Service, Law Enforcement, Psychology, Social Sciences, Sociology • VOCATIONAL Drafting, Food Service, Home Economics, Secretarial, Word Processing

Sports/Activities

, Cross Country, Football (M), Hand Ball, Judo, Karate, Martial Arts, Soccer (M), Track and Field (F), Volleyball (F), Weight Lifting, Wrestling • SPORTS INTRAMURAL Soccer (M), Softball, Swimming, Tennis, Volleyball (F) • SPORTS RELATED Band • STUDENT LIFE ACTIVITIES Concert Band, Dance, Debate, Drama Groups, Ethnic & Cultural Groups, Jazz Band, Music Ensembles, Music Groups, Musical Theater, Newspaper, Radio/TV station, Student Government, Yearbook

---

Less Selective **California Program**

Los Angeles Harbor College

1111 Figueroa Place
Wilmington, California 90744
(213) 518-1000

School Enrollment: **8,099** Male: **3,480** Female: **4,619**
LD Enrollment: **100** Male: **45** Female: **55**

Admissions Contact: **Luis Rosas, Assistant Dean of Admissions**
LD Contact: **Sally Fasteau, LD Specialist**
Name of Program: **Disabled Students' Program**
Telephone:**(213) 518-1000 Ext. 410**

Admissions

Application Information:
Enrolled:**125**
Application deadline: **None**
Applicant must apply **Open** months in advance
Rolling Admissions: **Yes**

Secondary School Information
Most Important Criteria For Admissions (1-strongest)

SAT/ACT	Application	School transcript
Class rank	Course selection	Personal statement
Interview	Extra activities	Psychoeducational
G.P.A.	Open admission	Recommendations

Test Requirements:
Untimed SAT: **Yes** Untimed ACT: **Yes** Untimed ACH: **Yes**
WAIS-R required: **Yes** Range accepted: **80+**
Documentation of LD required: **Yes**
Tests recommended: **Must meet the eligibility criteria for CA community colleges**

Types of Disabilities Served
- Speech/Lang
- Study skills
- Written express
- Organizational
- Perceptual
- Reading
- Spelling
- Math
- Fine Motor
- ADD with LD
- ADD without LD
- ADHD with LD
- ADHD without LD

Learning Disability Program

Program: Remedial: **Yes**
Program: Reinforces course work: **Yes**
Counseling: Individual: **Yes**

Faculty:
Faculty: **2** Full time: **1** Part time: **1** M.A.: **2**
Faculty advocate: **Yes** Meets with instructor: **As needed**

Diagnostic Testing
ADD	Personality	• Perceptual skills	• Spelling
ADHD	Organization	Fine motor skills	• Reading
• I.Q.	Handwriting	Spoken language	• Study skills
• Math	Social skills	• Written language	

Tutoring:
Average size of group tutorials: **3-5**
Services rendered by:
•Graduates   Peers   Faculty   •LD staff   Teacher trainees

Tutorials

Grp.	Ind.	Tutorials	Grp.	Ind.	Tutorials
•	•	Math skills	•	•	Word processing
•	•	Study skills	•	•	Time management
•	•	Language arts	•	•	Learning strategies
•	•	Written express	•	•	Organizational skills

Academic Accommodations

Curriculum	Study Aids	Exams
Priority registration	Typist	• Oral
Math waiver	Reader	Untimed
Foreign lang. waiver	• Notetaker	Take home
Course substitution	• Proof reader	With proctor
In Class	• Text on tape	On computer
• Calculators	Early syllabus	• Extended time
• Tape recorder	Taped handouts	On tape
• Word processor		• Modified
Priority seating		Separate room

General Information:

Los Angeles Harbor College is a 2 year public college. Suburban campus of 280 acres is Accessible by bus. Ski areas are 150 miles from campus. Beaches are 10 miles from campus. Housing is not guaranteed.

Accreditation: Regional

Expenses:
Tuition: In-state: Full year: $100.00. Tuition: Out-of-state: Full year: $2,448.00.

Majors

• AREA STUDIES Black/Afro-American, Mexican American • BUSINESS Accounting, Business Administration, Business Management, Office Administration, Real Estate • COMPUTER SCIENCE Computer Technology, Engineering • EDUCATION Early Childhood, Liberal Arts • ENGINEERING Electrical, Electronics • HEALTH SCIENCES Medical Assistant, Medical Secretary, Nursing • HUMANITIES Philosophy • PRE-PROFESSIONAL Architecture, Legal Assistant, Recreation • SCIENCES Science Technology • SOCIAL SCIENCES Administration of Justice, Law Enforcement • VOCATIONAL Automobile Technology, Drafting, Electronics Technology, Fire Science, Interior Design, Printing/Lithography, Word Processing

Sports/Activities

• SPORTS INTERCOLLEGIATE Baseball (M), Basketball, Cross Country, Football (M), Soccer, Tennis, Track and Field, Volleyball, Weight Lifting • SPORTS INTRAMURAL Golf, Softball • SPORTS RELATED

Cheerleading, Danc • STUDENT LIFE ACTIVITIES Alumni and Friends, Concert Band, Drama Groups, Ethnic & Cultural Groups, Honor Societies, Music Ensembles, Musical Theater, Radio/TV station, Student Government

---

Less Selective **California Program**

Los Angeles Mission College
13356 Eldridge Avenue
Sylmar, California 91342
(818) 364-7600

School Enrollment: **7,000** Male: **2,800** Female: **4,200**
LD Enrollment: **200** Male: **115** Female: **85**

Admissions Contact: **Carlos Nava, Dean of Support Services**
LD Contact: **Dr. Rick Scuderi, Learning Disabilities Specialist**
Name of Program: **Learning Disability Program**
Telephone:**(818) 364-7734**

Admissions

Application Information:
LD Students Applying: **160** Accepted: **90** Enrolled:**80**
Separate application:**Yes**
LD on admissions committee:**Yes**
Applicant must apply **2** months in advance
Rolling Admissions: **Yes**

Secondary School Information
Most Important Criteria For Admissions (1-strongest)
5 SAT/ACT	**2** Application	**4**	School transcript
7 Class rank	**5** Course selection	**5**	Personal statement
8 Interview	**10** Extra activities	**4**	Psychoeducational
7 G.P.A.	Open admission	**8**	Recommendations

Test Requirements:
Diagnostic testing waived: **Yes**
Untimed SAT: **Yes** Untimed ACT: **Yes**
WAIS-R required: **Yes** Range accepted: **Above 81**
Documentation of LD required: **Yes**
Currency of diagnostic testing: **Within 3 years**
Tests recommended: **WAIS-R or Woodcock Johnson I, WRAT, Woodcock Johnson II, in house testing.**

Types of Disabilities Served
- Speech/Lang
- Study skills
- Written express
- Organizational
- Perceptual
- Reading
- Spelling
- Math
- Fine Motor
- ADD with LD
- ADD without LD
- ADHD with LD
- ADHD without LD

Admissions Process

Testing through Disabled Program, then formal admission to college.

Learning Disability Program

Program: Reinforces course work: **Yes**
Time required or recommended in learning center: **varies**
Services available for all students: **Yes**
Counseling: Individual: **Yes** Group Counseling: **Yes** Vocational Counseling: **Yes**

Faculty:
Faculty: **6** Including Director: **Yes** Full time: **1** Part time: **5**
LD faculty with: BS/BA: **1** Ph.D.: **1**
Faculty advocate: **Yes** Meets with instructor: **Monthly**

Diagnostic Testing
- ADD
- ADHD
- I.Q.
- Math
- Personality
- Organization
- Handwriting
- Social skills
- Perceptual skills
- Fine motor skills
- Spoken language
- Written language
- Spelling
- Reading
- Study skills

Tutoring:
Average size of group tutorials: **2**
Services rendered by:
•Graduates   Peers   Faculty   •LD staff   Teacher trainees

Tutorials
Grp.	Ind.	Tutorials	Grp.	Ind.	Tutorials
	•	Math skills	•		Word processing
•		Study skills	•		Time management
	•	Language arts		•	Learning strategies
	•	Written express		•	Organizational skills

Academic Accommodations
Curriculum	Study Aids	Exams
• Priority registration	• Typist	• Oral
Math waiver	Reader	Untimed
Foreign lang. waiver	• Notetaker	• Take home
Course substitution	• Proof reader	With proctor
In Class	• Text on tape	On computer
• Calculators	Early syllabus	• Extended time
• Tape recorder	Taped handouts	On tape
• Word processor		• Modified
Priority seating		Separate room

Graduation Requirements:
Course credits: **60+** GPA: **2.0** Years to complete degree: **2** Language waiver: **Yes**

Program Strengths

One-to-one tutoring by university graduate students is core of the program. We also have personal counseling, vocational counseling, learning strategies classes, life management classes, and peer support classes.

General Information:

Los Angeles Mission College is a 2 year public College. Suburban campus of 23 acres is 35 miles from Los Angeles. Accessible by air, train, or bus. Ski areas are 20 miles from campus. Beaches are 20 miles from campus. 30% of students are foreign. Housing is not guaranteed.

Accreditation:CCC

Expenses:
Tuition: In-state: Full year: $60.00 maximum per semester. Part-time: Per credit:$6.00 per credit, $60.00 maximum. Tuition: Out-of-state: Full year: $112.00 plus $60.00. Cost of LD program:$6.00 - $12.00 per semester minimum

Majors

• AREA STUDIES American • BUSINESS Accounting, Banking/Finance, Business Administration, Business Management, Data Processing, Management • COMMUNICATIONS Journalism • COMPUTER SCIENCE Business Data Programming, Computer Science • HEALTH SCIENCES Speech/Audiology and Speech • HUMANITIES Humanities, Liberal Arts • LANGUAGES English, French, Spanish • PRE PROFESSIONAL Legal Assistant • SCIENCES Biology, Chemistry, Mathematics, Physical Science

California

• SOCIAL SCIENCES Family Counseling, History, Psychology, Social Sciences • VISUAL AND PERFORMING ARTS Dramatic Arts, Music • VOCATIONAL Business and Office, Electronics Technology, Home Economics, Paralegal, Textile and Clothing

Sports

• SPORTS-INTERCOLLEGIATE Baseball (M), Cross Country, Golf (M), Soccer (M)

Less Selective　　　　　　　　**California Program**

Los Angeles Valley College

5800 Fulton Avenue
Van Nuys, California 91401-4096
(818) 781-8542

School Enrollment: **16,959**
LD Enrollment: **125** Male: **63** Female: **62**

Admissions Contact: **Mary Spangler, Dean of Admissions**
LD Contact: **Robert T. Scott, Ph.D., Assistant Dean**
Name of Program: **Learning Disabled Program**
Telephone:**(818) 781-8542**

Admissions

Application Information:
LD Students Applying: **50** Accepted: **45** Enrolled:**45**
Application deadline: **2nd week in Feb./Aug.**
Applicant must apply **2-4** months in advance

Secondary School Information
Most Important Criteria For Admissions (1-strongest)
　6 SAT/ACT　**5** Application　　**3** School transcript
　9 Class rank　**8** Course selection **10** Personal statement
　1 Interview **11** Extra activities　**2** Psychoeducational
　7 G.P.A.　　　Open admission　**4** Recommendations

Test Requirements:
Standardized tests waived: **Yes**
Diagnostic testing waived: **Yes**
Documentation of LD required: **Yes**
Tests recommended: **Psychoeducational, Woodcock-Johnson**

Types of Disabilities Served
• Speech/Lang　• Reading　　• ADD with LD
• Study skills　• Spelling　　• ADD without LD
• Written express • Math　　　• ADHD with LD
• Organizational • Fine Motor　• ADHD without LD
• Perceptual

Learning Disability Program
Program: Remedial: **Yes**
Program: Reinforces course work: **Yes**
Students mainstreamed **85** % of the day
Services only for LD students: **Yes**
Counseling: Individual: **Yes** Group Counseling: **Yes** Vocational Counseling: **Yes**

Faculty:
Faculty: **5** Including Director: **Yes** Full time: **1** Part time: **4** M.A.: **3**
Faculty advocate: **Yes** Meets with instructor: **When necessary**

Diagnostic Testing
• ADD　• Personality　• Perceptual skills　• Spelling
• ADHD • Organization• Fine motor skills　• Reading
• I.Q.　• Handwriting• Spoken language　• Study skills
• Math　• Social skills• Written language

Tutoring:
Average size of group tutorials: **2**
Services rendered by:
•Graduates　•Peers　•Faculty　•LD staff　•Teacher trainees

Tutorials
Grp.	Ind.	Tutorials	Grp.	Ind.	Tutorials
	•	Math skills		•	Word processing
•	•	Study skills	•	•	Time management
•	•	Language arts	•	•	Learning strategies
•	•	Written express	•	•	Organizational skills

Academic Accommodations
Curriculum	Study Aids	Exams
• Priority registration	Typist	• Oral
Math waiver	Reader	Untimed
Foreign lang. waiver	Notetaker	• Take home
Course substitution	• Proof reader	• With proctor
In Class	• Text on tape	On computer
• Calculators	Early syllabus	• Extended time
• Tape recorder	Taped handouts	On tape
• Word processor		Modified
Priority seating		Separate room

Graduation Requirements:
Other requirements: **2 year AA degree; transfer to 4 year college**

Program Strengths
Los Angeles Valley College offers a comprehensive and supportive program for the learning disabled students. It is staffed with high quality, competent program assistants from nearby universities. The director is also a highly skilled learning specialist. Our unique program focuses on the following special services and activities: 1) a comprehensive orientation program for all new students: 2) individualized education plans and follow-up from semester to semester: 3) strong liaison with instructors and continuing in-service for faculty and staff.

General Information:
Los Angeles Valley College is a 2 year public college. Suburban campus 10 miles from Los Angeles. Accessible by bus. Ski areas are 79 miles from campus. Beaches are 15-20 miles from campus. Housing is not guaranteed.

Accreditation: WACS

Expenses:
Tuition: In-state: Full year: $5.00 per unit, $50.00 maximum per year. Tuition: Out-of-state: Full year: Part-time: Per credit: $102.00.

Majors
• AREA STUDIES American, Black/Afro-American, Jewish, Latin American • BUSINESS Accounting, Business Administration, Business Management, Economics, Finance, Management, Marketing, Real Estate, Recreation Marketing • COMMUNICATIONS Advertising, Broadcasting, Communication, Creative Writing, English, Journalism, Photography, Television/Radio/Film • COMPUTER SCIENCE Data Entry, Data Processing, Hardware Engineer, Software Engineer, Systems Analysis, Telecommunications • CRAFTS AND DESIGN Graphic Design • EDUCATION Art, Child Development, Early Childhood, Elementary, Health, Music, Physical, Recreation and Youth Leadershi, School Psychology, Special, Speech/Language, Vocational • ENGINEERING Engineering Science • HEALTH

SCIENCES Environmental, Health, Nursing, Nutritional/Food, Respiratory Therapy • HUMANITIES Liberal Arts, Philosophy, Religion • LANGUAGES French, German, Italian, Spanish • SCIENCES Astronomy, Biology, Botany, Chemistry, Earth, Ecology, Geography, Geology, Marine Biology, Mathematics, Microbiology, Oceanography, Physical Science, Physics, Physiology • SOCIAL SCIENCES Anthropology, Criminal Justice, Geography, Government/Political, History, Law Enforcement, Psychology, Social Sciences, Sociology • VISUAL AND PERFORMING ARTS Art, Art History, Dance, Fine Arts, Music, Theater • VOCATIONAL Business and Office, Electronics Technology, Fashion Merchandising, Fire Science, Home Economics, Park/Recreation, Respiratory Therapy Technology, Secretarial, Word Processing

Sports/Activities

INTERCOLLEGIATE Baseball (M), Basketball, Cross Country, Football (M), Softball (F), Swimming, Track and Field, Water Polo • SPORTS-INTRAMURAL Archery, Badminton, Diving, Fencing, Gymnastics, Judo, Ping-Pong, Skiing - Snow, Tennis, Volleyball, Weight Lifting, Wrestling • STUDENT LIFE ACTIVITIES Choral, Debate, Drama Groups, Ethnic & Cultural Groups, Film Production, Jazz Band, Music Groups, Newspaper, Radio/TV station, Religious Organization, Student Government, Symphony Orchestra, Yearbook

Less Selective	California Program

Merced College

3600 M Street
Merced, California 95348
(209) 384-6187

School Enrollment: **7,500** Male: **3,750** Female: **3,750**

Admissions Contact: **Stan Mattoon, Dean of Adm. and Records**
LD Contact: **Robert Lenz, Director Disabled Student Services**
Address: **3600 M Street**

Admissions

Secondary School Information
Most Important Criteria For Admissions (1-strongest)

SAT/ACT	Application	School transcript
Class rank	Course selection	Personal statement
Interview	Extra activities	Psychoeducational
G.P.A.	Open admission	Recommendations

Test Requirements:
Diagnostic testing waived: **Yes**
Documentation of LD required: **Yes**
Tests recommended: **Testing is completed at the college by the LD specialist if student doesn't have testing in conforming with that specified by the California Community College Chancellor's Office.**

Types of Disabilities Served

Speech/Lang	Reading	ADD with LD
Study skills	Spelling	ADD without LD
Written express	Math	ADHD with LD
Organizational	Fine Motor	ADHD without LD
Perceptual		

Admissions Process

This college is a California Community College. Admission is open to any student with a diploma from high school or 18 years of age or older.

Learning Disability Program
Program: Reinforces course work: **Yes**
Students mainstreamed **100** % of the day
Services available for all students: **Yes**
Counseling: Individual: **Yes** Vocational Counseling: **Yes**

Faculty:
Faculty: **7** Full time: **7**
LD faculty with: BS/BA: **1** M.A.: **3**
Faculty advocate: **Yes** Meets with instructor: **As needed**

Diagnostic Testing

ADD	Personality	Perceptual skills	• Spelling
ADHD	Organization	Fine motor skills	• Reading
• I.Q.	Handwriting	Spoken language	Study skills
• Math	Social skills	• Written language	

Services rendered by:

Graduates	Peers	Faculty	LD staff	Teacher trainees

Tutorials

Grp.	Ind. Tutorials	Grp.	Ind. Tutorials
	Math skills		Word processing
	Study skills		Time management
	Language arts		Learning strategies
	Written express		Organizational skills

Academic Accommodations

Curriculum	Study Aids	Exams
• Priority registration	Typist	• Oral
Math waiver	• Reader	• Untimed
Foreign lang. waiver	• Notetaker	Take home
Course substitution	Proof reader	• With proctor
In Class	• Text on tape	• On computer
Calculators	Early syllabus	• Extended time
• Tape recorder	Taped handouts	• On tape
• Word processor		Modified
Priority seating		• Separate room

Graduation Requirements:
Course credits: **varies** Years to complete degree: **No restrictions** Math waiver: **Yes**

Program Strengths
We have a lab with computers devoted specifically to hardware and software needed to allow disabled students to be competitive among their disabled peers. Tutoring is available to all students.

General Information:
Merced College is a 2 year public college. Suburban campus of 269 acres is 60 miles from Fresno. Accessible by bus. Ski areas are 1-1/2 hours from campus. Beaches are 2 hours from campus. Housing is not guaranteed.

Accreditation: WASC

Expenses:
Tuition: In-state: Full year: $50.00 - 10 or more units. Part-time: Per credit: Under 9 units $5.00. Tuition: Out-of-state: Full year: $102.00 .

Majors
• ARTS Landscaping • BUSINESS Accounting, Agricultural, Banking/Finance, Business Administration, Clerical, Small Business Management • COMMUNICATIONS English • COMPUTER SCIENCE Computer Science, Computer Technology • EDUCATION Early Childhood, Physical • ENGINEERING Engineering Science • HEALTH SCIENCES Dental

California

Assistant, Dental Technician, Health, Nursing, Radiological Technology, Speech/Audiology and Speech • HUMANITIES Humanities • LANGUAGES French, German, Spanish • SCIENCES Agricultural, Animal, Anthropology, Biology, Chemistry, Computer Science, Geology, Life Sciences, Mathematics, Physical Science, Physics • SOCIAL SCIENCES Anthropology, History, Human Service, Psychology, Social Sciences • VISUAL AND PERFORMING ARTS Dramatic Arts, Fine Arts, Music • VOCATIONAL Automotive Service, Building Construction, Carpentry, Cosmetology, Diesel Power Technology, Drafting, Electrician, Electronics Technology, Environmental Haxardous Materi, Fashion Merchandising, Fire Science, Food Service, Home Economics, Legal Secretary

Sports/Activities

• STUDENT LIFE ACTIVITIES Academic Clubs, Drama Groups, Ethnic & Cultural Groups, Music Groups, Newspaper, Political Groups, Student Government, Yearbook

---

Less Selective   **California**
                                                        Program

Merritt College
12500 Campus Drive
Oakland, California 94608
(510) 436-2429

School Enrollment: **6,000** Male: **3,000** Female: **3,000**
LD Enrollment: **120** Male: **60**

Admissions Contact: **George Herring, Dean of Student Services**
LD Contact: **Mary McGrath, Learning Specialist**
Name of Program: **Learning Arts Program**
Address: **12500 Campus Drive**
Telephone:**(415) 436-2579**

Admissions

Application Information:
LD Students Applying: **150** Accepted: **125** Enrolled:**125**
Application deadline: **None**

Secondary School Information
Most Important Criteria For Admissions (1-strongest)

SAT/ACT	Application	School transcript
Class rank	Course selection	Personal statement
Interview	Extra activities	Psychoeducational
G.P.A.	**1** Open admission	Recommendations

Test Requirements:
Standardized tests waived: **Yes**
Diagnostic testing waived: **Yes**
Documentation of LD required: **Yes**
Currency of diagnostic testing: **None**
Tests recommended: **None required; our college does the testing.**

Types of Disabilities Served
• Speech/Lang • Reading • ADD with LD
• Study skills • Spelling • ADD without LD
• Written express • Math • ADHD with LD
• Organizational • Fine Motor • ADHD without LD
• Perceptual

Admissions Process

Open admissions process to college; eligibility for LD program de-termined by LD specialist; interview with counselor required.

High School Course Requirements:
Waivers to standard high school courses
Course substitution: **Yes**

Learning Disability Program
Program: Remedial: **Yes**
Students mainstreamed **>50** % of the day
Recommended credits per semester: **9-12**
Services only for LD students: **Yes**
Counseling: Individual: **Yes** Group Counseling: **Yes** Vocational Counseling: **Yes**

Faculty:
Faculty: **7** Including Director: **Yes** Full time: **1** Part time: **6**
LD faculty with: BS/BA: **7** M.A.: **7**
Faculty advocate: **Yes** Meets with instructor: **As needed**

Diagnostic Testing
ADD	Personality	• Perceptual skills	• Spelling
ADHD	Organization	Fine motor skills	• Reading
• I.Q.	• Handwriting	Spoken language	• Study skills
• Math	• Social skills	• Written language	

Tutoring:
Average size of group tutorials: **8-10**
Services rendered by:
  Graduates   Peers   Faculty   •LD staff   •Teacher trainees

Tutorials
Grp.	Ind.	Tutorials	Grp.	Ind.	Tutorials
•	•	Math skills	•	•	Word processing
•	•	Study skills	•	•	Time management
•	•	Language arts	•	•	Learning strategies
•	•	Written express	•	•	Organizational skills

Academic Accommodations

Curriculum	**Study Aids**	**Exams**
Priority registration	Typist	• Oral
Math waiver	• Reader	Untimed
Foreign lang. waiver	• Notetaker	• Take home
• Course substitution	Proof reader	• With proctor
In Class	• Text on tape	• On computer
• Calculators	Early syllabus	• Extended time
• Tape recorder	Taped handouts	• On tape
• Word processor		• Modified
Priority seating		• Separate room

Graduation Requirements:
Course credits: **60** GPA: **2.0** Years to complete degree: **2+**

Program Strengths
Our LD Program is essentially a support service for students who are enrolled or who will enroll in the college. Strengths and weaknesses are evaluated and specifically addressed through the use of I.E.P.S. We assist the student in obtaining necessary accommodations for mainstream courses as well, which allows our program to be both comprehensive and thorough.

General Information:
Merritt College is a 2 year public college. Urban campus of 5 acres is Franci. Accessible by air, train or bus. Ski areas are 5 miles from campus. Beaches are 1/2 mile from campus. 14% of students are foreign. Housing is not guaranteed.

Accreditation: Full

Expenses: Part-time: Per credit:$6.00. Tuition: Out-of-state: Full year: Part time: Per credit: $104.00.

Majors

• AREA STUDIES African, American • BUSINESS Accounting, Business Administration, Economics • COMMUNICATIONS English • COMPUTER SCIENCE Computer Electronics, Data Processing • HEALTH SCIENCES Nursing • SCIENCES Horticultural • SOCIAL SCIENCES Criminal Justice • VOCATIONAL Landscape Architecture, Radiological Technology

---

Less Selective　　　　　　　**California Program**

Modesto Junior College
435 College Avenue
Modesto, California 95350
(209) 575-6181

School Enrollment: **11,000** Male: **5,000** Female: **6,000**

Admissions Contact: **Dr. Julius Manrique, Assc. Dean of Stud. Ser.**
LD Contact: **Alysa Pearson, LD Specialist**
Name of Program: **LD Program**
Telephone:**(209) 575-6181**

Admissions

Secondary School Information
Most Important Criteria For Admissions (1-strongest)

SAT/ACT	Application	School transcript
Class rank	Course selection	Personal statement
Interview	Extra activities	Psychoeducational
G.P.A.	**1** Open admission	Recommendations

Test Requirements:
Diagnostic testing waived: **Yes**
Currency of diagnostic testing: **3 years**
Tests recommended: **WAIS-R , Woodcock -Johnson I, Woodcock - Johnson II, or WRAT**

Types of Disabilities Served
- Speech/Lang
- Study skills
- Written express
- Organizational
- Perceptual
- Reading
- Spelling
- Math
- Fine Motor
- ADD with LD
- ADD without LD
- ADHD with LD
- ADHD without LD

Learning Disability Program
Program: Remedial: **Yes**
Program: Reinforces course work: **Yes**
Counseling: Individual: **Yes** Group Counseling: **Yes**

Faculty:
Faculty: **3** Full time: **1** Part time: **2**
LD faculty with: BS/BA: **2** M.A.: **1**
Faculty advocate: **Yes** Meets with instructor: **As needed**

Diagnostic Testing
• ADD	Personality	Perceptual skills	• Spelling
ADHD	Organization	Fine motor skills	• Reading
• I.Q.	Handwriting	Spoken language	Study skills
• Math	Social skills	Written language	

Tutoring:
Average size of group tutorials: **8**
Services rendered by:
Graduates　　Peers　　Faculty　　•LD staff　　Teacher trainees

Tutorials
Grp.	Ind.	Tutorials	Grp.	Ind.	Tutorials
•	•	Math skills	•		Word processing
•		Study skills			Time management
•		Language arts	•	•	Learning strategies
•	•	Written express	•		Organizational skills

Academic Accommodations

Curriculum	Study Aids	Exams
Priority registration	Typist	• Oral
Math waiver	Reader	Untimed
Foreign lang. waiver •	• Notetaker	Take home
Course substitution	• Proof reader	With proctor
In Class	• Text on tape	On computer
• Calculators	Early syllabus	• Extended time
• Tape recorder	Taped handouts	On tape
• Word processor		Modified
Priority seating		Separate room

Program Strengths
We emphasize compensatory strategies instruction, information related to learning disabilities, and assistance with transferring to 4 year colleges.

General Information:
Modesto Junior College is a 2 year public college. Suburban campus 90 miles from San Francisco. Ski areas are 80 miles from campus. Beaches are 100 miles from campus. Housing is not guaranteed.

Accreditation: Regional

Expenses:
Tuition: In-state: Full year: $100.00. Part-time: Per credit:$5.00. Tuition: Out-of-state: Full year: $2,256.00. Part-time: Per credit:$94.00.

Majors
• AREA STUDIES Urban • BUSINESS Accounting, Agricultural, Banking, Business Administration, Business Management, Economics, Finance, Marketing, Real Estate • COMMUNICATIONS Broadcasting, English, Journalism, Photography, Public Relations, Speech, Television/Radio/Film • COMPUTER SCIENCE Computer Science, Data Processing, Programming, Robotics • CRAFTS AND DESIGN Graphic Design • EDUCATION Child Development, Elementary, English As A Second Language (, General, Health, Industrial, Physical, Secondary • ENGINEERING Architectural, Engineering Science • ENVIRONMENTAL CONTROL Water and Wastewater Technolog • HEALTH SCIENCES Communication Disorders, Medical Assistant, Medical Technology, Nursing, Nutritional/Food, Radiological Therapy, Speech/Audiology and Speech • HUMANITIES Humanities, Liberal Arts, Philosophy • LANGUAGES French, German, Italian, Portuguese • PREPROFESSIONAL Architecture, Dentistry, Law, Medicine, Optometry, Pharmacy, Veterinarian • SCIENCES Animal, Astronomy, Bacteriology, Biology, Chemistry, Crop, Dairy, Earth, Geography, Geology, Gerontology, Mathematics, Microbiology, Physical Science, Physics, Physiology, Plant, Poultry, Zoology • SOCIAL SCIENCES Criminal Justice, History, Human Service, Law Enforcement, Political Science, Psychology, Social Sciences • VISUAL AND PERFORMING ARTS Art,

California

Music, Theater • VOCATIONAL Agricultural, Air Condtioning/Heating/ Refrig, Architectural, Automobile Technology, Automotive Service, Book-keeping, Building Inspection, Business and Office, Construction, Electron-ics Technology, Fashion Mechandizing, Food Processing, Forestry, Home Building, Home Economics, Industrial Design, Landscape Architecture, Machine Tool Technology, Nursery Production, Ornamental Horticulture, Park/Recreation, Printing/Lithography, Radiological Technology, Secre-tarial, Textile and Clothing, Welding

Sports/Activities

• SPORTS-INTERCOLLEGIATE Baseball (M), Basketball, Cross Coun-try, Diving, Football (M), Golf (M), Softball (F), Swimming, Tennis, Track and Field, Volleyball (F), Water Polo (M), Wrestling (M) • SPORTS-IN-TRAMURAL Ping-Pong, Softball, Tennis • STUDENT LIFE ACTIVI-TIES Choral, Concert Band, Dance, Ethnic & Cultural Groups, Film, Jazz Band, Music Groups, Newspaper, Opera, Radio/TV station, Student Gov-ernment

---

Less Selective   **California**
                                                        Program

Monterey Peninsula College
980 Fremont Street
Monterey, California 93940
(408) 646-4002

School Enrollment: **9,000** Male: **4,000** Female: **5,000**
LD Enrollment: **200** Male: **100** Female: **100**

Admissions Contact: **Debbie Carroll, Director of Admissions**
LD Contact: **Bill Jones, Coordinator**
Name of Program: **Learning Skills Program**
Telephone:**(408) 646-4070**

Admissions

Application Information:
LD Students Applying: **125** Accepted: **115**
Applicant must apply **2** months in advance

Secondary School Information
Most Important Criteria For Admissions (1-strongest)

11	SAT/ACT	3	Application	8	School transcript
10	Class rank	7	Course selection	4	Personal statement
1	Interview	5	Extra activities	2	Psychoeducational
9	G.P.A.		Open admission	6	Recommendations

Test Requirements:
Standardized tests waived: **Yes**
Diagnostic testing waived: **Yes**
WAIS-R required: **Yes**
Currency of diagnostic testing: **1 year**
Tests recommended: **The College uses the Woodcock-Johnson**

Types of Disabilities Served
• Speech/Lang   • Reading   • ADD with LD
• Study skills   • Spelling   • ADD without LD
• Written express • Math   • ADHD with LD
• Organizational • Fine Motor   • ADHD without LD
• Perceptual

Learning Disability Program
Program: Remedial: **Yes**
Program: Reinforces course work: **Yes**
Students mainstreamed **100** % of the day
Recommended credits per semester:
Counseling: Individual: **Yes** Group Counseling: **Yes**

Faculty:
Faculty: **2** Full time: **1** Part time: **2** M.A.: **2**
Faculty advocate: **Yes** Meets with instructor: **3-4 x a semester**

Diagnostic Testing
• ADD   • Personality • Perceptual skills   • Spelling
• ADHD   • Organization • Fine motor skills   • Reading
• I.Q.   • Handwriting • Spoken language   Study skills
• Math   • Social skills • Written language

Tutoring:
Average size of group tutorials: **3**
Services rendered by:
  Graduates   Peers   •Faculty   •LD staff   Teacher trainees

Tutorials

Grp.	Ind.	Tutorials	Grp.	Ind.	Tutorials
•	•	Math skills	•	•	Word processing
•	•	Study skills	•	•	Time management
•	•	Language arts	•	•	Learning strategies
•	•	Written express	•	•	Organizational skills

Academic Accommodations

Curriculum	Study Aids	Exams
Priority registration	• Typist	• Oral
• Math waiver	Reader	Untimed
• Foreign lang. waiver	• Notetaker	• Take home
Course substitution	• Proof reader	• With proctor
In Class	• Text on tape	On computer
• Calculators	Early syllabus	• Extended time
• Tape recorder	Taped handouts	On tape
• Word processor		• Modified
Priority seating		Separate room

Program Strengths
We were the pilot school for the California Community Colleges' "High Tech Centers." The Coordinator of the program is dyslexic and is a strong advocate for dyslexic students.

General Information:
Monterey Peninsula College is a 2 year public college. Urban campus of 150 acres is Accessible by air, train or bus. Ski areas are 4 hours from cam-pus. Beaches are 1 mile from campus. 20% of students are foreign. Housing is not guaranteed.

Accreditation: WACS

Expenses: Part-time: Per credit:$6.00. Tuition: Out-of-state: Full year: Part-time: Per credit: $104.00.

Majors

• AREA STUDIES African, American, Asian, Black/Afro-American • BUSINESS Accounting, Business Administration, Business Economics, Business Education, Business Management, Economics, Finance, Hotel and Restaurant Managemen, Insurance, Management, Marketing, Market-ing Research, Real Estate • COMMUNICATIONS Advertising, Broadcast-ing, Communication, Creative Writing, English, Journalism, Photography, Television/Radio/Film • COMPUTER SCIENCE Data Processing, Pro-gramming, Systems Analysis, Telecommunications • EDUCATION Art, Early Childhood, Health, Industrial, Music, Physical, School Psychology,

Special, Vocational • ENGINEERING Computer • HEALTH SCIENCES Communication Disorders, Environmental, Health, Medical Technology, Nursing, Nutritional/Food • HUMANITIES Humanities, Philosophy, Religion • LANGUAGES French, German, Japanese, Spanish • PREPROFESSIONAL Architecture, Forestry, Law, Medicine, Recreation, Social Work • SCIENCES Astronomy, Biology, Botany, Chemistry, Earth, Ecology, Geography, Geology, Marine Biology, Mathematics, Oceanography, Physical Chemistry, Physical Science, Physics, Radiology • SOCIAL SCIENCES Anthropology, Criminal Justice, Geography, Government/Political, History, Psychology, Social Sciences, Sociology • VISUAL AND PERFORMING ARTS Art, Art History, Dance, Music, Studio Art, Theater

Sports/Activities

• SPORTS RELATED Marching Band • SPORTS-INTERCOLLEGIATE Baseball (M), Basketball, Football (M), Golf, Sailing, Scuba, Softball, Swimming, Tennis, Track and Field, Volleyball, Weight Lifting • STUDENT LIFE ACTIVITIES Drama Groups, Film Production, Music Groups, Radio/TV station, Student Government

Less Selective　　　　　　　**California Program**

Mount San Jacinto College

1499 North State Street
San Jacinto, California 92583
(714) 654-8011

School Enrollment: **6,643** Male: **2,432** Female: **4,211**
LD Enrollment: **75** Male: **15**

Admissions Contact: **Elido Gonzales, Director of Admissions**
LD Contact: **Marcia Krull, Learning Disability Specialist**
Name of Program: **Learning Skills Program**
Telephone:**(714) 654-8011 Ext. 1524**

Admissions

Application Information:
Enrolled:**75**

Secondary School Information
Most Important Criteria For Admissions (1-strongest)

SAT/ACT	Application	School transcript
Class rank	Course selection	Personal statement
Interview	Extra activities	Psychoeducational
G.P.A.	**1** Open admission	Recommendations

Test Requirements:
Diagnostic testing waived: **Yes**
WAIS-R required: **Yes** Range accepted: **81+**
Documentation of LD required: **Yes**
Tests recommended: **WAIS-R, Woodcock-Johnson, others specific to California Community College**

Types of Disabilities Served
• Speech/Lang　• Reading　　• ADD with LD
• Study skills　• Spelling　　ADD without LD
• Written express • Math　　　• ADHD with LD
• Organizational • Fine Motor　ADHD without LD
• Perceptual

Admissions Process

Application, placement testing, orientation, advisement and sched-

ule planning.

Learning Disability Program
Syllabus available during orientation:**Yes**
Program: Remedial: **Yes**
Program: Reinforces course work: **Yes**
Services only for LD students: **Yes**
Counseling: Individual: **Yes** Vocational Counseling: **Yes**
Support groups are available:**Yes - campus "Survivors Club"**

Faculty:
Faculty: **4** Including Director: **Yes** Full time: **1** Part time: **3**
LD faculty with: BS/BA: **1** M.A.: **1**
Faculty advocate: **Yes** Meets with instructor: **As needed**

Diagnostic Testing
ADD	Personality	• Perceptual skills	• Spelling
ADHD	Organization	Fine motor skills	• Reading
• I.Q.	Handwriting	• Spoken language	Study skills
• Math	Social skills	• Written language	

Tutoring:
Average size of group tutorials:
Services rendered by:
Graduates　Peers　Faculty　•LD staff　Teacher trainees

Tutorials
Grp.	Ind.	Tutorials	Grp.	Ind.	Tutorials
•	•	Math skills		•	Word processing
•	•	Study skills	•		Time management
•	•	Language arts	•		Learning strategies
•	•	Written express	•		Organizational skills

Academic Accommodations

Curriculum	Study Aids	Exams
• Priority registration	Typist	• Oral
Math waiver	• Reader	Untimed
Foreign lang. waiver	• Notetaker	• Take home
Course substitution	Proof reader	• With proctor
In Class	• Text on tape	On computer
• Calculators	Early syllabus	• Extended time
• Tape recorder	Taped handouts	On tape
• Word processor		Modified
Priority seating		• Separate room

Graduation Requirements:
Course credits: **60** GPA: **2.0** Years to complete degree: **No limitations**
Other requirements: **Must meet general education requirements**

General Information:
Mount San Jacinto College is a 2 year public college. Rural campus of 180 acres is 30 miles from Riverside. Accessible by bus. Ski areas are 50 miles from campus. Beaches are 65 miles from campus. 4% of students are foreign. Housing is not guaranteed.

Accreditation:WACS

Expenses:
Tuition: In-state: Full year: $120.00. Part-time: Per credit:$6.00. Tuition: Out-of-state: Full year: $97.00. Part-time: Per credit:$97.00.

Majors
• BUSINESS Accounting, Business Administration, Business Management, Economics, Management, Marketing, Office Supervision and Managem, Real Estate • COMMUNICATIONS Communication, Creative Writing, English, Journalism, Photography • COMPUTER SCIENCE Data

California

Processing, Programming • EDUCATION Child Development, Early Childhood, General, Physical, Teacher's Aid • ENGINEERING Computer, Electrical, Engineering Science • HEALTH SCIENCES Environmental, Health, Nursing, Nutritional/Food, Practical Nursing • HUMANITIES Humanities, Liberal Arts, Philosophy, Religion • LANGUAGES French, Spanish • PREPROFESSIONAL Architecture • SCIENCES Astronomy, Biochemistry, Biology, Chemistry, Geography, Geography, Geology, Marine Biology, Physics • SOCIAL SCIENCES Anthropology, Criminal Justice, Criminology, Geography, Government/Political, History, Law Enforcement, Psychology, Social Sciences, Sociology • VISUAL AND PERFORMING ARTS Art, Art History, Dance, Dramatic Arts, Music, Studio Art, Theater • VOCATIONAL Auto Body, Automobile Technology, Automotive Service, Chemical Dependency, Electronics Technology, Fire Control and Safety Techno, Fire Science, Secretarial

Sports/Activities

LEGIATE Baseball (M), Basketball, Football (M), Golf (M), Tennis, Volleyball (M) • SPORTS-INTRAMURAL Volleyball • STUDENT LIFE ACTIVITIES Choral, Concert Band, Dance, Drama Groups, Jazz Band, Music Groups, Newspaper, Student Government

Less Selective   **California**
                                                   Services

Porterville College
900 South Main Street
Porterville, California 93257
(209) 781-3130

School Enrollment: **2,725** Male: **1,195** Female: **1,530**
LD Enrollment: **72**

Admissions Contact: **Charles N. Guerrero, Dean of Student Ser.**
LD Contact: **Carol Wilkins, LD Specialist**
Name of Program: **Learning Disabilities Program**
Address: **Academic Center 125**
Telephone:**(209) 781-3130 Ext. 324**

Admissions

Application Information:
LD Students Applying: **120** Accepted: **72** Enrolled:**72**
Application deadline: **Beginning of semester**
Rolling Admissions: **Yes**

Secondary School Information
Most Important Criteria For Admissions (1-strongest)

SAT/ACT	Application	School transcript
Class rank	Course selection	Personal statement
Interview	Extra activities **1**	Psychoeducational
G.P.A. **1**	Open admission	Recommendations

Test Requirements:
Standardized tests waived: **Yes**
Diagnostic testing waived: **Yes**
Untimed SAT: **Yes** Achievement tests required:**1**
WAIS-R required: **Yes** Range accepted: **80+**
Documentation of LD required: **Yes**
Currency of diagnostic testing: **No limit**
Tests recommended: **Ability-Achievement testing is done by our program.**

Types of Disabilities Served
- Speech/Lang
- Study skills
- Written express
- Organizational
- Perceptual
- Reading
- Spelling
- Math
- Fine Motor
- ADD with LD
- ADD without LD
- ADHD with LD
- ADHD without LD

Admissions Process

Application, placement or LD testing, orientation, advisor appointment and enrollment

Learning Disability Program
Students mainstreamed **100** % of the day
Services only for LD students: **Yes**
Counseling: Individual: **Yes**

Faculty:
Faculty: **2** Full time: **1** Part time: **1** M.A.: **1**
Faculty advocate: **Yes** Meets with instructor: **As needed**

Diagnostic Testing

ADD	Personality	• Perceptual skills	• Spelling
ADHD	Organization	• Fine motor skills	• Reading
• I.Q.	• Handwriting	Spoken language	• Study skills
• Math	Social skills	• Written language	

Tutoring:
Average size of group tutorials: **2-4**
Services rendered by:
Graduates •Peers •Faculty •LD staff Teacher trainees

Tutorials

Grp.	Ind.	Tutorials	Grp.	Ind.	Tutorials
•	•	Math skills	•	•	Word processing
•		Study skills	•		Time management
•	•	Language arts	•		Learning strategies
•		Written express		•	Organizational skills

Academic Accommodations

Curriculum	Study Aids	Exams
Priority registration	• Typist	• Oral
Math waiver	Reader	Untimed
Foreign lang. waiver	• Notetaker	• Take home
Course substitution	• Proof reader	• With proctor
In Class	• Text on tape	On computer
• Calculators	Early syllabus	• Extended time
• Tape recorder	Taped handouts	• On tape
• Word processor		Modified
• Priority seating		• Separate room

Graduation Requirements:
Course credits: **60** GPA: **2.0** Years to complete degree: **2-3**

Program Strengths
The Learning Disabilities Program at Porterville College is committed to the success of individual students, and because of our small campus and class size, students receive extra attention from instructors. Our faculty is knowledgeable and cooperative regarding students with learning disabilities and support services are excellent.

General Information:
Porterville College is a 2 year public college. Rural campus of 13 acres is 50 miles from Bakersfield. Accessible by bus. Ski areas are 45 miles from campus. Beaches are 3 miles from campus. 5% of students are foreign.

Housing is not guaranteed.

Accreditation: WACS

Class Rank:
About 10% of the present freshmen class were in the upper 20% of their high school class. 20% were in the top 40% of their class. 40% were in the top 60% of their class. 80% were in the top 80% of their class.

Expenses:
Tuition: In-state: Full year: $120.00. Part-time: Per credit:$6.00. Tuition: Out-of-state: Full year: $2,880.00. Part-time: Per credit:$96.00. Room and board: $3,500.00

Majors

• BUSINESS Aviation Management, Business Management, Finance, Real Estate • COMMUNICATIONS Communication • COMPUTER SCIENCE Computer Science, Data Processing • ENGINEERING Engineering Science • HEALTH SCIENCES Nursing • HUMANITIES Humanities, Liberal Arts • SCIENCES Earth, Mathematics, Physical Science, Physiology • SOCIAL SCIENCES Law Enforcement • VISUAL AND PERFORMING ARTS Fine Arts, Music • VOCATIONAL Automobile Technology, Carpentry, Drafting, Fire Science, Secretarial, Welding

Sports/Activities

ross Country, Football (M), Golf (M), Softball, Tennis, Track and Field (M) • STUDENT LIFE ACTIVITIES Choral, Drama Groups, Jazz Band, Music Ensembles, Music Groups, Musical Theater, Student Government

Less Selective   **California Program**

Rancho Santiago College
17th at Bristol
Santa Ana, California 92706
(714) 667-3000

School Enrollment: **43,000** Male: **23,220** Female: **19,780**
LD Enrollment: **315**

Admissions Contact: **Hal Bateman, Dean of Admissions**
LD Contact: **Cheryl Dunn, Coordinator**
Name of Program: **Learning Disabilities Program**
Telephone:**(714) 564-6260**

Admissions

Secondary School Information
Most Important Criteria For Admissions (1-strongest)

11 SAT/ACT	5 Application	3	School transcript
10 Class rank	6 Course selection	4	Personal statement
1 Interview	9 Extra activities	2	Psychoeducational
7 G.P.A.	Open admission	8	Recommendations

Test Requirements:
Standardized tests waived: **Yes**
Diagnostic testing waived: **Yes**
WAIS-R required: **Yes**
Documentation of LD required: **Yes**
Tests recommended: **California Community College Assessment for Learning Disabilities**

Types of Disabilities Served
• Speech/Lang • Reading • ADD with LD
• Study skills • Spelling   ADD without LD
• Written express • Math • ADHD with LD
• Organizational • Fine Motor   ADHD without LD
• Perceptual

Admissions Process

Intake, assessment, individual educational plan

High School Course Requirements:
Waivers to standard high school courses
Math: **Yes** Course substitution: **Yes**

Learning Disability Program
Program: Remedial: **Yes**
Program: Reinforces course work: **Yes**
Time required or recommended in learning center: **1-8 hours**
Counseling: Individual: **Yes** Group Counseling: **Yes** Vocational Counseling: **Yes**

Faculty:
Faculty: **18** Including Director: **Yes** Full time: **5** Part time: **13**
LD faculty with: BS/BA: **5** M.A.: **3** Ph.D.: **2**

Diagnostic Testing
ADD • Personality	• Perceptual skills	• Spelling
ADHD• Organization	• Fine motor skills	• Reading
• I.Q. • Handwriting	• Spoken language	• Study skills
• Math • Social skills	• Written language	

Tutoring:
Average size of group tutorials: **3**
Services rendered by:
•Graduates •Peers •Faculty •LD staff Teacher trainees

Tutorials
Grp.	Ind.	Tutorials	Grp.	Ind.	Tutorials
	•	Math skills		•	Word processing
	•	Study skills		•	Time management
	•	Language arts		•	Learning strategies
	•	Written express		•	Organizational skills

Academic Accommodations
Curriculum	Study Aids	Exams
• Priority registration	• Typist	• Oral
Math waiver	• Reader	• Untimed
Foreign lang. waiver	• Notetaker	• Take home
Course substitution	• Proof reader	• With proctor
In Class	• Text on tape	• On computer
• Calculators	Early syllabus	• Extended time
• Tape recorder	• Taped handouts	• On tape
• Word processor		• Modified
• Priority seating		• Separate room

Graduation Requirements: Math waiver: **Yes**

Program Strengths
Our program is designed to help students who have average or above average potential for learning and exhibit one or more disabilities, with the expected goal of enabling the student to participate in regular college courses leading to the accomplishment of realistic educational/vocational goals.

General Information:
Rancho Santiago College is a 2 year public college. Urban campus of 75

California

acres is Accessible by air, train or bus. Ski areas are 2 miles from campus. Beaches are 30 miles from campus. Housing is not guaranteed.

Accreditation: WACS

Expenses:

Tuition: In-state: Full year: $50.00. Part-time: Per credit:$5.00. Tuition: Out-of-state: Full year: Part-time: Per credit: $100.00. Part-time: Per credit:$100.00.

Majors

• AREA STUDIES Mexican/American, Women's Studies • BUSINESS Economics, Insurance, Real Estate, Travel/Tourism Management • COMMUNICATIONS Commercial Design, English, Television/Radio/Film • COMPUTER SCIENCE Telecommunications • EDUCATION Foreign Language • ENGINEERING Civil/Environmental, Electrical, Engineering Science, Environmental/Water Resources, Industrial, Mathematical, Mechanical • ENVIRONMENTAL CONTROL Water and Wastewater Technolog • HEALTH SCIENCES Medical Assistant, Nursing, Practical Nursing • HUMANITIES Philosophy • SCIENCES Bacteriology, Geography, Geology, Meteorology, Zoology • SOCIAL SCIENCES History, Political Science, Psychology, Social Sciences • VISUAL AND PERFORMING ARTS Dance, Dramatic Arts, Fine Art • VOCATIONAL Business and Office, Carpentry, Court Reporting, Diesel Power Technology, Drafting, Fashion Design, Fashion Merchandising, Fire Science, Home Economics, Interior Design, Legal Assistant, Legal Secretary, Secretarial, Surveying and Mapping, Welding, Word Processing

Sports/Activities

TERCOLLEGIATE Baseball (M), Basketball, Cross Country, Football (M), Golf, Soccer (F), Soccer (M), Softball (F), Tennis, Track and Field, Volleyball (F), Volleyball (M), Wrestling (M) • STUDENT LIFE ACTIVITIES Academic Clubs, Choral, Community Service, Concert Band, Dance, Debate, Drama Groups, Ethnic & Cultural Groups, Jazz Band, Music Groups, Musical Theater, Newspaper, Orchestra, Political Groups, Radio/TV station, Religious Organization, Student Government, Yearbook

Less Selective	California Program

Saddleback College
28000 Marguerite Parkway
Mission Viejo, California 92692
(714) 582-4571

School Enrollment: **15,800** Male: **6,320** Female: **9,480**
LD Enrollment: **150** Male: **90** Female: **60**

Admissions Contact: **M. David Hafiz, Acting Dean**
LD Contact: **Paula Jacobs, Coordinator**
Name of Program: **Special Services**
Telephone: **(714) 582-4612**

Admissions

Application Information:
LD Students Applying: **112** Accepted: **90** Enrolled: **90**
Applicant must apply **5** months in advance
Rolling Admissions: **Yes** Notified when: **November 1st**

Secondary School Information
Most Important Criteria For Admissions (1-strongest)

SAT/ACT	Application	School transcript
Class rank	Course selection	Personal statement
Interview	Extra activities	Psychoeducational
G.P.A.	**1** Open admission	Recommendations

Test Requirements:
Standardized tests waived: **Yes**
Diagnostic testing waived: **Yes**
WAIS-R required: **Yes**
Tests recommended: **English and math for 1st time/full time students**

Types of Disabilities Served
• Speech/Lang
• Study skills
• Written express
• Organizational
• Perceptual
• Reading
• Spelling
• Math
• Fine Motor
• ADD with LD
• ADD without LD
• ADHD with LD
• ADHD without LD

Learning Disability Program
Program: Remedial: **Yes**
Program: Reinforces course work: **Yes**
Students mainstreamed **100** % of the day
Counseling: Individual: **Yes** Group Counseling: **Yes**

Faculty:
Faculty: **3** Full time: **1** Part time: **2**
LD faculty with: BS/BA: **1** M.A.: **2**
Faculty advocate: **Yes** Meets with instructor: **As needed**

Diagnostic Testing
• ADD Personality • Perceptual skills • Spelling
  ADHD Organization • Fine motor skills • Reading
• I.Q. Handwriting Spoken language Study skills
• Math • Social skills • Written language

Tutoring:
Average size of group tutorials: **varies**
Services rendered by:
  Graduates •Peers •Faculty •LD staff Teacher trainees

Tutorials

Grp.	Ind.	Tutorials	Grp.	Ind.	Tutorials
		Math skills			Word processing
•	•	Study skills	•	•	Time management
		Language arts	•	•	Learning strategies
•	•	Written express	•	•	Organizational skills

Academic Accommodations

Curriculum	Study Aids	Exams
Priority registration	Typist	• Oral
Math waiver	Reader	Untimed
Foreign lang. waiver	• Notetaker	• Take home
Course substitution	Proof reader	With proctor
In Class	• Text on tape	On computer
• Calculators	Early syllabus	• Extended time
• Tape recorder	Taped handouts	On tape
• Word processor		• Modified
Priority seating		Separate room

Program Strengths
It is the philosophy of the Special Services Program that every student should have the opportunity to realize his or her greatest potential and achieve a richer and more productive life.

General Information:
Saddleback College is a 2 year public college. Suburban campus of 200 acres is 40 miles from San Diego. Accessible by air, train or bus. Ski areas are 250 miles from campus. Beaches are 15 miles from campus. 1% of students are foreign. Housing is not guaranteed.

Accreditation: WACS

Expenses:
Tuition: In-state: Full year: $50.00 (12 units or more). Part-time: Per credit:$5.00 (6 or less). Tuition: Out-of-state: Full year: Part-time: Per credit: $94.00. Part-time: Per credit:$94.0.

Majors

• AREA STUDIES American, Women's Studies • BUSINESS Accounting, Banking, Business Administration, Business Education, Business Management, Economics, Finance, Food Management, Management, Marketing, Real Estate, Retail Manufacturing, Small Business Ownership, Travel/Tourism Management • COMMUNICATIONS Advertising, Broadcasting, Commercial Design, Creative Writing, English, Journalism, Photography, Speech, Television/Radio/Film • COMPUTER SCIENCE Computer Science, Data Processing, Programming, Software Engineer, Systems Analysis • CRAFTS AND DESIGN Graphic Design, Illustration Design • EDUCATION Bilingual, Early Childhood, General, Special, Teacher's Aide • ENVIRONMENTAL CONTROL Solar Heating • HEALTH SCIENCES Environmental, Health, Medical Assistant, Medical Technology, Nursing, Nutritional/Food • HUMANITIES English/Writing/Literature, Humanities, Philosophy • LANGUAGES Chinese, French, German, Italian, Spanish • PREPROFESSIONAL Architecture, Engineering, Law, Recreation • SCIENCES Actuarial Technology, Anatomy, Astronomy, Astrophysics, Biology, Botany, Chemistry, Earth, Geography, Geology, Gerontology, Horticultural, Marine Biology, Mathematics, Oceanography, Physical Science, Physics, Physiology, Zoology • SOCIAL SCIENCES Anthropology, Criminal Justice, Geography, Government/Political, History, Human Service, Law Enforcement, Psychology, Public Affairs, Social Sciences, Sociology • VISUAL AND PERFORMING ARTS Art, Art History, Dance, Dramatic Arts, Fine Arts, Music, Studio Art, Theater • VOCATIONAL Automobile Technology, Automotive Service, Business and Office, Chemical Manufacturing Technol, Construction, Culinary Arts, Fashion Design, Fashion Mechandizing, Flight Attendant, Home Economics, Industrial Design, Library Assistant, Manufacturing Technology, Paralegal, Printing/Lithography, Printmaking, Secretarial, Surveying and Mapping, Textile and Clothing, Welding, Woodworking, Word Processing

Sports/Activities

• SPORTS RELATED Drill Team, Pep Band • SPORTS-INTERCOLLEGIATE Baseball (M), Basketball, Cross Country, Diving, Football (M), Golf, Soccer (M), Softball (F), Swimming, Tennis, Track and Field, Volleyball (F), Water Polo (M) • SPORTS-INTRAMURAL Archery, Badminton, Gymnastics, Judo, Karate, Martial Arts, Racquetball, Scuba, Weight Lifting, Wrestling • STUDENT LIFE ACTIVITIES Choral, Concert Band, Debate, Drama Groups, Ethnic & Cultural Groups, Film, Magazine, Music Groups, Newspaper, Political Groups, Radio/TV station, Religious Organization, Student Government, Symphony Orchestra

---

Less Selective   **California Program**

San Diego City College
1313 12th Street
San Diego, California 92101
(619) 230-2475

School Enrollment: **14,000** Male: **6,000** Female: **8,000**
LD Enrollment: **150**

Admissions Contact: **Frank Echevarria, Adm. Record Officer**
LD Contact: **Nancy Cary, LD Specialist**
Name of Program: **Learning Development Prog.**
Telephone:**(619) 230-2513**

Admissions

Application Information:
LD Students Applying: **350** Accepted: **300** Enrolled:**300**

Secondary School Information
Most Important Criteria For Admissions (1-strongest)

SAT/ACT	Application	School transcript
Class rank	Course selection	Personal statement
Interview	Extra activities	Psychoeducational
G.P.A. **1**	Open admission	Recommendations

Test Requirements:
Standardized tests waived: **Yes**
Diagnostic testing waived: **Yes**
Currency of diagnostic testing: **1**
Tests recommended: **Woodcock Johnson Psycho Ed. or WAIS-R**

Types of Disabilities Served
• Speech/Lang   • Reading   • ADD with LD
• Study skills   • Spelling   • ADD without LD
• Written express • Math   • ADHD with LD
• Organizational • Fine Motor   • ADHD without LD
• Perceptual

Learning Disability Program

Program: Remedial: **Yes**
Program: Reinforces course work: **Yes**
Students mainstreamed **100** % of the day
Counseling: Individual: **Yes**

Faculty:
Faculty: **5** Including Director: **Yes** Full time: **1** Part time: **4**
LD faculty with: BS/BA: **5** M.A.: **1**
Faculty advocate: **Yes** Meets with instructor: **Once a semester**

Diagnostic Testing

• ADD	Personality	• Perceptual skills	• Spelling
• ADHD	Organization	• Fine motor skills	• Reading
• I.Q.	Handwriting	• Spoken language	Study skills
• Math	Social skills	• Written language	

Tutoring:
Services rendered by:
Graduates • Peers   Faculty   • LD staff   Teacher trainees

Tutorials

Grp.	Ind.	Tutorials	Grp.	Ind.	Tutorials
	•	Math skills		•	Word processing
•		Study skills	•		Time management
•		Language arts	•		Learning strategies
•	•	Written express	•		Organizational skills

Academic Accommodations

Curriculum	Study Aids	Exams
Priority registration	Typist	• Oral
Math waiver	Reader	Untimed
• Foreign lang. waiver	• Notetaker	Take home
Course substitution	• Proof reader	With proctor
In Class	• Text on tape	On computer
• Calculators	Early syllabus	• Extended time
• Tape recorder	Taped handouts	On tape
• Word processor		• Modified
Priority seating		Separate room

California

Program Strengths

We offer small group classes with a strategies approach. Topics covered include spelling, sentence writing, math, keyboard introduction, and effective learning. Although we accept a larger number of students with learning disabilities, presently there are a smaller number who are actively involved in our program.

General Information:

San Diego City College is a 2 year public college. Urban campus 1 miles from San Diego. Accessible by bus. Beaches are 5 from campus. Housing is not guaranteed.

Accreditation: Regional

Expenses:

Tuition: In-state: Full year: $50.00. Part-time: Per credit:$5.00. Part-time: Per course: $15.00. Tuition: Out-of-state: Full year: Part-time: Per credit: $93.00.

Majors

• AREA STUDIES Black/Afro-American, Mexican/American, Russian/Slavic • BUSINESS Accounting, Banking, Business Administration, Business Management, Finance, Insurance, Marketing, Real Estate, Taxation • COMMUNICATIONS Commercial Design, English, Graphic Design, Journalism, Photography, Speech, Television/Radio/Film • COMPUTER SCIENCE Computer Science, Data Processing, Software Engineer, Telecommunications • CRAFTS AND DESIGN Graphic Design, Illustration Design • EDUCATION Bilingual, Child Development, Foreign Language, Physical, Special • ENGINEERING Air Conditioning Technology, Engineering Science, Materials • ENVIRONMENTAL CONTROL Environmental Control, Water and Wastewater Technolog • HEALTH SCIENCES Nursing, Nutritional/Food • HUMANITIES Liberal Arts, Philosophy • LANGUAGES French, German, Italian, Russian, Spanish • PREPROFESSIONAL Law, Social Work • SCIENCES Biology, Chemistry, Mathematics, Physical Science, Physics • SOCIAL SCIENCES Anthropology, History, Political Science, Psychology, Social Sciences, Sociology • VISUAL AND PERFORMING ARTS Art History, Dramatic Arts, Fine Arts, Music, Studio Art • VOCATIONAL Air Condtioning/Heating/Refrig, Automobile Technology, Business and Office, Carpentry, Commercial Art, Cosmetology, Drafting, Fashion Mechandizing, Legal Secretary, Secretarial, Textile and Clothing, Welding, Woodworking, Word Processing

Sports/Activities

• SPORTS-INTERCOLLEGIATE Badminton, Baseball (M), Basketball, Cross Country, Field Hockey (M), Football (M), Golf (M), Gymnastics, Soccer (M), Softball, Swimming, Tennis, Track and Field, Volleyball, Wrestling • SPORTS-INTRAMURAL Baseball, Bowling (M), Cross Country, Racquetball, Track and Field • STUDENT LIFE ACTIVITIES Choral, Community Service, Concert Band, Dance, Drama Groups, Ethnic & Cultural Groups, Music Ensembles, Musical Theater, Newspaper, Political Groups, Religious Organization, Student Government, Symphony Orchestra

---

Selective

California Program

San Diego Mesa College
7250 Mesa College Drive
San Diego, California 92111
(619) 627-2780

School Enrollment: **25,000** Male: **12,500** Female: **12,500**
LD Enrollment: **150**

Admissions Contact: **Admissions Office**
LD Contact: **Glenyth Turner, LD Assessment Specialist**
Name of Program: **DSPS**
Address: **Room H-201**
Telephone:**(619) 627-2780**

Admissions

Application Information:
Separate application:**Yes**
Application deadline: **None**
Applicant must apply **3-4** months in advance
Rolling Admissions: **Yes**

Secondary School Information
Most Important Criteria For Admissions (1-strongest)

SAT/ACT **1**	Application	**2**	School transcript
Class rank	Course selection		Personal statement
2 Interview	Extra activities	**1**	Psychoeducational
G.P.A.	**1** Open admission		Recommendations

Test Requirements:
Diagnostic testing waived: **Yes**
WAIS-R required: **Yes** Range accepted: **California norms**
Documentation of LD required: **Yes**
Currency of diagnostic testing: **3 years**
Tests recommended: **California Community College LD verification**

Types of Disabilities Served
- Speech/Lang
- Study skills
- Written express
- Organizational
- Perceptual
- Reading
- Spelling
- Math
- Fine Motor
- ADD with LD
- ADD without LD
- ADHD with LD
- ADHD without LD

Learning Disability Program
Program: Remedial: **Yes**
Program: Reinforces course work: **Yes**
Students mainstreamed **100** % of the day
Services only for LD students: **Yes**
Counseling: Individual: **Yes**

Faculty:
Faculty: **4** Including Director: **Yes** Full time: **2** Part time: **2** M.A.: **4** Ph.D.: **1**
Faculty advocate: **Yes**

Diagnostic Testing

ADD	Personality	Perceptual skills	• Spelling
ADHD	Organization	Fine motor skills	• Reading
• I.Q.	Handwriting	Spoken language	Study skills
• Math	Social skills	Written language	

Tutoring:
Services rendered by:
Graduates   Peers   Faculty   •LD staff   Teacher trainees

Tutorials

Grp.	Ind.	Tutorials	Grp.	Ind.	Tutorials
•	•	Math skills	•		Word processing
•	•	Study skills	•	•	Time management
•	•	Language arts	•		Learning strategies
•	•	Written express	•		Organizational skills

Academic Accommodations

Curriculum	Study Aids	Exams
• Priority registration	Typist	• Oral
Math waiver	• Reader	Untimed
Foreign lang. waiver	• Notetaker	Take home
Course substitution	Proof reader	• With proctor
In Class	• Text on tape	On computer
• Calculators	Early syllabus	• Extended time
• Tape recorder	Taped handouts	• On tape
• Word processor		• Modified
Priority seating		• Separate room

Program Strengths
We know students with learning disabilities can succeed and we are here to serve them. However, this is college, and they must do their part. Our goal is for students to become independent learners who no longer need assistance.

General Information:
San Diego Mesa College is a 2 year public college. Urban campus Accessible by air, train or bus. Ski areas are 25 miles from campus. Beaches are 3 miles from campus. Housing is not guaranteed.

Accreditation: Regional

Expenses:
Tuition: In-state: Full year: $60.00. Part-time: Per credit:$6.00. Part-time: Per credit:$102.00.

Majors
• AREA STUDIES African, American, Black/Afro-American, Latin American • BUSINESS Accounting, Business Administration, Business Data Processing, Business Economics, Business Education, Business Management, Economics, Food Management, Hotel and Restaurant Managemen, Marketing, Real Estate, Recreation Marketing • COMMUNICATION English, Journalism • COMPUTER SCIENCE Data Processing, Programming, Systems Analysis • EDUCATION Art, Child Development, Early Childhood, Education of Deaf and Hearing , Physical, Recreation and Youth Leadershi • FINE AND PERFORMING ARTS Art, Art History, Dance, Dramatic Arts, Fine Arts, Music, Studio Art, Theater • HEALTH SCIENCES Dental Assistant, Medical Assistant, Medical Recording Technology, Medical Records Administration, Physical Therapy, Radiological Therapy • HUMANITIES Liberal Arts, Philosophy • LANGUAGES French, German, Italian, Portuguese, Russian, Spanish • PREPROFESSIONAL Architecture, Engineering, Recreation, Veterinarian Assistant • SCIENCES Biology, Botany, Chemistry, Geography, Geology, Mathematics, Physical Science, Physics • SOCIAL SCIENCES Anthropology, Geography, Government/Political, History, Psychology, Sociology, Sociology • VOCATIONAL Air Traffic Control, Chemical Manufacturing Technol, Construction, Fashion Merchandising, Flight Attendants, Legal Secretary, Park/Recreation, Quality Assurance Technology, Radiological Technology, Secretarial

Sports/Activities
• SPORTS RELATED Dance, Fitness, Marching Band • SPORTS-INTERCOLLEGIATE Archery, Badminton (F), Badminton (M), Baseball, Baseball (F), Baseball (M), Basketball (F), Basketball (M), Canoeing, Cycling, Fencing, Field Hockey (F), Field Hockey (M), Football (M), Golf, Gymnastics, Hand Ball, Judo, Karate, Ping-Pong, Racquetball, Soccer (F), Soccer (M), Softball (F), Softball (M), Swimming, Synchronized Swimming, Tennis, Track and Field, Volleyball, Water Polo (M), Weight Lifting • SPORTS-INTRAMURAL Bowling, Diving, Fencing, Field Hockey, Golf, Hand Ball, Racquetball, Skiing - Snow, Soccer, Softball (F), Water Polo, Weight Lifting • STUDENT LIFE ACTIVITIES Academic Clubs, Choral, Community Service, Concert Band, Dance, Drama Groups, Ethnic & Cultural Groups, Newspaper, Religious Organization, Student Government

---

Selective   **California Program**

San Diego State University
5300 Campanile Drive
San Diego, California 92182
(619) 594-6871

School Enrollment: **35,500** Male: **16,500** Female: **19,000**
LD Enrollment: **500** Male: **250** Female: **250**

Admissions Contact: **Vicky Hokensen, Special Admissions Office**
LD Contact: **Dr. Frank Sighien, LD Specialist**
Name of Program: **Disabled Student Services**
Telephone: **(619) 594-6473**

Admissions

Application Information:
LD Students Applying: **300** Accepted: **300** Enrolled: **300**
Application deadline: **November 30/August 31**

Secondary School Information
Most Important Criteria For Admissions (1-strongest)

SAT/ACT	Application	School transcript
Class rank	Course selection	Personal statement
Interview	Extra activities	Psychoeducational
G.P.A.	1 Open admission	Recommendations

Test Requirements:
Diagnostic testing waived: **Yes**
Documentation of LD required: **Yes**
Currency of diagnostic testing: **3 years**
Tests recommended: **Appropriate for Learning Disabilities**

Types of Disabilities Served

• Speech/Lang	• Reading	• ADD with LD
• Study skills	• Spelling	• ADD without LD
• Written express	• Math	• ADHD with LD
• Organizational	• Fine Motor	• ADHD without LD
• Perceptual		

Learning Disability Program
Program: Reinforces course work: **Yes**
Students mainstreamed **100** % of the day

Faculty:
Faculty: **8** Including Director: **Yes** Full time: **8** M.A.: **1** Ph.D.: **1**
Faculty advocate: **Yes** Meets with instructor: **As needed**

California

Diagnostic Testing
ADD   Personality •   Perceptual skills   •   Spelling
ADHD   Organization   Fine motor skills   •   Reading
• I.Q.   •   Handwriting   Spoken language   Study skills
• Math   Social skills •   Written language

Tutoring:
Services rendered by:
•Graduates   •Peers   Faculty   •LD staff   Teacher trainees

Tutorials

Grp.	Ind.	Tutorials	Grp.	Ind.	Tutorials
•	•	Math skills	•	•	Word processing
		Study skills	•		Time management
		Language arts	•		Learning strategies
•	•	Written express	•		Organizational skills

Academic Accommodations

Curriculum	Study Aids	Exams
• Priority registration	Typist	Oral
Math waiver	• Reader	Untimed
Foreign lang. waiver	• Notetaker	Take home
Course substitution	• Proof reader	With proctor
In Class	• Text on tape	On computer
• Calculators	Early syllabus	• Extended time
• Tape recorder	Taped handouts	On tape
• Word processor		Modified
Priority seating		• Separate room

Program Strengths
Our program offers supportive services to students who are all in mainstream. All students with documented learning disabilities are eligible for full range of services. Counselors determine need and act as advisors and advocates. Assessment is done on campus if needed. Special admission process available through Disabled Students Office to applicants who self identify on university application.

General Information:
San Diego State University is a 4 year public university. Urban campus of 315 acres is 8 miles from San Diego. Accessible by air, train or bus. Ski areas are 3 hours from campus. Beaches are 15 miles from campus. 1% of students are foreign. 8 residential halls on campus. Housing is not guaranteed.25 % of students remain on campus for the weekends.

Accreditation: WACS

Expenses:
Tuition: In-state: Full year: $846.00. Tuition: Out-of-state: Full year: $846.00 pus $189.00 per unit . Room and board: $4,185.00

Majors
• AREA STUDIES American, Asian, Black/Afro-American, European, Latin American, Mexican/American, Russian/Slavic • BUSINESS Accounting, Banking, Business Administration, Business Management, Economics, Finance, Food Management, Insurance, Real Estate • COMMUNICATIONS English, Journalism, Literature, Television/Radio/Film • COMPUTER SCIENCE Computer Science • EDUCATION Music • ENGINEERING Aerospace, Civil/Environmental, Electrical, Engineering Science, Mechanical • HEALTH SCIENCES Nursing, Nutritional/Food, Speech Therapy, Speech/Audiology and Speech • HUMANITIES Classics, Philosophy, Religion • LANGUAGES French, German, Linguistic, Spanish • PREPROFESSIONAL Business, Social Work • SCIENCES Astronomy, Biology, Chemistry, Geography, Geology, Mathematics, Microbiology, Physical Chemistry, Physical Science, Physics, Zoology • SOCIAL SCIENCES Anthropology, Geography, History, Law Enforcement, Political Science, Psychology, Sociology • VISUAL AND PERFORMING ARTS Art History, Theater • VOCATIONAL Home Economics

Sports/Activities
• SPORTS RELATED Band, Cheerleading • SPORTS-INTERCOLLEGIATE Baseball (M), Basketball, Crew, Cross Country, Football (M), Golf, Gymnastics (F), Soccer (M), Softball (F), Squash, Tennis, Track and Field, Volleyball, Water Polo • SPORTS-INTRAMURAL Bowling, Fencing, Lacrosse, Racquetball, Sailing, Soccer (F), Water Polo, Wrestling (M) • STUDENT LIFE ACTIVITIES Concert Band, Dance, Debate, Drama Groups, Film, Fraternities, Jazz Band, Magazine, Music Groups, Radio/TV station, Religious Organization, Sororities, Student Government, Symphony Orchestra

---

Selective   **California Program**

San Francisco State University
1600 Holloway Avenue
San Francisco, California 94132
(415) 338-2411

School Enrollment: **30,000**
LD Enrollment: **250**

Admissions Contact: **Laura Ware, Admissions Officer**
LD Contact: **Molly Brodie, Director of DSS**
Name of Program: **Disabled Student Services**
Telephone:**(415) 338-2472**

Admissions

Application Information:
Enrolled:**250**
Application deadline: **November 30th**
Applicant must apply **10** months in advance

Secondary School Information
Most Important Criteria For Admissions (1-strongest)

1 SAT/ACT	Application	School transcript
Class rank	Course selection	Personal statement
Interview	Extra activities	Psychoeducational
1 G.P.A.	Open admission	Recommendations

Test Requirements:
Diagnostic testing waived: **Yes**
Untimed SAT: **Yes** Untimed ACT: **Yes**
Documentation of LD required: **Yes**
Tests recommended: **Only if special admission needed**

Types of Disabilities Served
• Speech/Lang   • Reading   • ADD with LD
• Study skills   • Spelling   • ADD without LD
• Written express   • Math   • ADHD with LD
• Organizational   • Fine Motor   • ADHD without LD
• Perceptual

High School Course Requirements:
Waivers to standard high school courses
Foreign Language : **Yes** Math: **Yes** Course substitution: **Yes**

Learning Disability Program
Program: Reinforces course work: **Yes**
Students mainstreamed **100** % of the day
Recommended credits per semester: **9-12**
Counseling: Individual: **Yes** Group Counseling: **Yes**

Faculty:
Faculty: **4** Including Director: **Yes** Full time: **3** Part time: **1** M.A.: **4**
Faculty advocate: **Yes** Meets with instructor: **As needed**

Diagnostic Testing
ADD Personality • Perceptual skills • Spelling
ADHD Organization• Fine motor skills • Reading
• I.Q. Handwriting• Spoken language Study skills
• Math • Social skills• Written language

Tutoring:
Average size of group tutorials: **2**
Services rendered by:
•Graduates •Peers Faculty •LD staff Teacher trainees

Tutorials
Grp.	Ind.	Tutorials	Grp.	Ind.	Tutorials
•	•	Math skills	•	•	Word processing
•	•	Study skills	•	•	Time management
•	•	Language arts	•	•	Learning strategies
•	•	Written express	•	•	Organizational skills

Academic Accommodations
Curriculum	Study Aids	Exams
• Priority registration	• Typist	• Oral
• Math waiver	• Reader	• Untimed
• Foreign lang. waiver	• Notetaker	• Take home
• Course substitution	• Proof reader	• With proctor
In Class	• Text on tape	• On computer
• Calculators	• Early syllabus	• Extended time
• Tape recorder	• Taped handouts	• On tape
• Word processor		• Modified
• Priority seating		• Separate room

Program Strengths
We are a comprehensive program. We offer counseling and full learning services, accommodations, etc. A team approach by staff treats the "whole student."

General Information:
San Francisco State University is a 4 year public university. Urban campus of 130 acres is San Francisco. Accessible by plane, train or bus 4 residential halls on campus. Housing is not guaranteed.

Accreditation: Regional

Expenses:
Tuition: In-state: Full year: $1,056.00.

Majors
• AREA STUDIES American, Black/Afro-American, Mexican/American, Women's Studies • BUSINESS Accounting, Banking, Business Administration, Economics, Finance, International Business, Marketing, Real Estate • COMMUNICATIONS Creative Writing, English, Journalism, Television/Radio/Film • COMPUTER SCIENCE Computer Science • CRAFTS AND DESIGN Graphic Design • EDUCATION Industrial, Speech/Language • ENGINEERING Electrical • HEALTH SCIENCES Nursing, Nutritional/Food, Speech/Audiology and Speech • HUMANITIES English/Writing/Literature, Humanities, Liberal Arts, Philosophy, Religion • LANGUAGES Chinese, French, German, Italian, Japanese, Russian, Spanish • SCIENCES Astronomy, Astrophysics, Biochemistry, Biology, Botany, Cell Biology, Chemistry, Ecology, Geography, Geology, Marine Biology, Mathematics, Meteorology, Microbiology, Molecular Biology, Physics, Statistics, Zoology • SOCIAL SCIENCES Anthropology, History, Political Science, Psychology, Social Sciences, Sociology • VISUAL AND PERFORMING ARTS Dance, Dramatic Arts, Music, Music Performance • VOCATIONAL Home Economics, Interior Design, Medical

Laboratory Technology, Park/Recreation

Sports
• SPORTS RELATED Cheerleading, Chess, Concert Band, Dance, Pep Band • SPORTS-INTERCOLLEGIATE Baseball (M), Cross Country, Football (M), Gymnastics (F), Soccer, Softball (F), Swimming, Tennis, Track and Field, Volleyball (F), Wrestling (M) • SPORTS-INTRAMURAL Badminton, Basketball, Golf, Gymnastics, Racquetball, Swimming, Tennis, Track and Field, Volleyball, Wrestling • STUDENT LIFE ACTIVITIES Dance, Debate, Drama Groups, Ethnic & Cultural Groups, Film, Fraternities, Jazz Band, Music Groups, Musical Theater, Newspaper, Opera, Sororities, Symphony Orchestra

---

Less Selective **California Program**

Santa Barbara City College
721 Cliff Drive
Santa Barbara, California 93109-2394
(805) 965-0581

School Enrollment: **11,500** Male: **5,500** Female: **6,000**
LD Enrollment: **350**

Admissions Contact: **Jane Craven, Assistant Dean**
LD Contact: **Mary Lawson, Learning Disability Specialist**
Name of Program: **Learning Disabilities Program**
Telephone:**(805) 965-0581 Ext. 2374**

Admissions

Application Information:
Separate application:**Yes**
Application deadline: **Week before semester begins**
Applicant must apply **4** months in advance

Secondary School Information
Most Important Criteria For Admissions (1-strongest)

SAT/ACT	Application	School transcript
Class rank	Course selection	Personal statement
Interview	Extra activities **1**	Psychoeducational
G.P.A. **1**	Open admission	Recommendations

Test Requirements:
Diagnostic testing waived: **Yes**
WAIS-R required: **Yes** Range accepted: **80+**
Documentation of LD required: **Yes**
Currency of diagnostic testing: **3 years**
Tests recommended: **Woodcock-Johnson PEB Parts 1 and 2, (or WAIS-R) and WRAT**

Types of Disabilities Served
• Speech/Lang • Reading • ADD with LD
• Study skills • Spelling ADD without LD
• Written express • Math • ADHD with LD
• Organizational • Fine Motor ADHD without LD
• Perceptual

Admissions Process

Submit SBCC application (only requirements are 18 years of age or high school diploma). Contact LD program for assistance with registration process (new students must take English and Math placement tests).

111

California

Learning Disability Program

Program: Reinforces course work: **Yes**
Students mainstreamed **100** % of the day
Recommended credits per semester: **9**
Services only for LD students: **Yes**
Counseling: Individual: **Yes** Vocational Counseling: **Yes**
Support groups are available:**Student-run LD support group**

Faculty:

Faculty: **4** Including Director: **Yes** Full time: **1** Part time: **3** M.A.: **4**
Faculty advocate: **Yes** Meets with instructor: **When requested**

Diagnostic Testing

ADD	Personality •	Perceptual skills	• Spelling
ADHD	Organization	Fine motor skills	• Reading
• I.Q.	Handwriting	Spoken language	Study skills
• Math	Social skills	Written language	

Tutoring:

Average size of group tutorials: **1:1**
Services rendered by:

Graduates	Peers	Faculty	•LD staff	Teacher trainees

Tutorials

Grp.	Ind.	Tutorials	Grp.	Ind.	Tutorials
•		Math skills	•		Word processing
•		Study skills	•		Time management
•		Language arts	•		Learning strategies
•		Written express	•		Organizational skills

Academic Accommodations

Curriculum	Study Aids	Exams
Priority registration	Typist	Oral
Math waiver	Reader	Untimed
Foreign lang. waiver	Notetaker	Take home
Course substitution	Proof reader	• With proctor
In Class	• Text on tape	• On computer
• Calculators	Early syllabus	• Extended time
• Tape recorder	Taped handouts	• On tape
• Word processor		Modified
Priority seating		• Separate room

Graduation Requirements: Years to complete degree: **2.5-3**

Program Strengths

In addition to the general support services offered by most California Community Colleges, SBCC offers the High Tech Center for developing computer and word processing skills.

General Information:

Santa Barbara City College is a 2 year public college. Urban campus 100 miles from Los Angeles. Beaches are 1 mile from campus. Housing is not guaranteed.

Accreditation: Regional

Expenses:

Tuition: In-state: Full year: $6.00 per unit to a maximum of $60.00. Part-time: Per credit:$6.00. Tuition: Out-of-state: Full year: Part-time: Per credit: $102.00.

Majors

• AREA STUDIES American, Black/Afro-American, Ethics, International Studies, Latin American, Mexican/American, Native American • BUSINESS Accounting, Banking, Business Administration, Business Economics, Business Education, Business Management, Economics, Escrow Management, Finance, Hotel and Restaurant Managemen, Insurance, Management, Marketing, Marketing Management, Real Estate • COMMUNICATIONS Advertising, Communication, Creative Writing, English, Journalism, Photography • COMPUTER SCIENCE Computer Technology, Data Processing, Programming, Systems Analysis • CRAFTS AND DESIGN Graphic Design • EDUCATION Child Care/Guidance, Child Development, Early Childhood, English As A Second Language (, Physical, Recreation and Youth Leadershi • ENGINEERING Electronic Technology • HEALTH SCIENCES Dental Assistant, EMT, Health, Nursing, Radiograph Medical Technology, Radiological Therapy • HUMANITIES English/Writing/Literature, Humanities, Philosophy, Religion • LANGUAGES Chinese, French, German, Italian, Japanese, Spanish • PREPROFESSIONAL Drafting, Engineering • SCIENCES Astronomy, Biology, Chemistry, Earth, Environmental Science, Geography, Geology, Marine Biology, Mathematics, Physical Science, Physics, Radiology, Zoology • SOCIAL SCIENCES Anthropology, Criminal Justice, Geography, Government/Political, History, International Studies, Law and Society, Psychology, Social Sciences, Sociology • VISUAL AND PERFORMING ARTS Art, Art Appreciation, Art History, Dramatic Arts, Music, Music Performance, Studio Art, Theater • VOCATIONAL Automobile Technology, Automotive Mechanics, Business and Office, Cosmetology, Drafting, Electronics Technology, Landscape Architecture, Machinist, Marine Diving, Park/Recreation, Printing/Lithography, Secretarial, Welding, Word Processing

Sports/Activities

ERCOLLEGIATE Baseball (M), Basketball, Cross Country, Football (M), Golf (M), Tennis, Track and Field, Volleyball • SPORTS-INTRAMURAL Archery, Badminton, Bowling, Fencing, Gymnastics, Hand Ball, Martial Arts, Racquetball, Soccer, Softball, Swimming, Weight Lifting • STUDENT LIFE ACTIVITIES Academic Clubs, Choral, Dance, Drama Groups, Ethnic & Cultural Groups, Jazz Band, Magazine, Music Groups, Newspaper, Orchestra, Political Groups, Radio/TV station, Religious Organization, Student Government

---

Less Selective   **California Program**

Santa Monica College
1900 Pico Boulevard
Santa Monica, California 90405
(213) 450-5150

School Enrollment: **20,011** Male: **9,004** Female: **11,007**
LD Enrollment: **150**

Admissions Contact: **Mary Jane, Weil Counselor**
LD Contact: **Dr. Ann Maddox, LD Specialist**
Name of Program: **Learning Disability Program**
Telephone:**(213) 452-9265**

Admissions

Application Information:

Enrolled:**150**
Separate application:**Yes**
Application deadline: **None**
Applicant must apply **3-4** months in advance

Secondary School Information

Most Important Criteria For Admissions (1-strongest)

SAT/ACT	Application	School transcript
Class rank	Course selection	Personal statement
Interview	Extra activities	Psychoeducational
G.P.A.	Open admission	Recommendations

Test Requirements:

Tests recommended: **All necesaary testing will be completed during first semester.**

Types of Disabilities Served

- Speech/Lang
- Study skills
- Written express
- Organizational
- Perceptual
- Reading
- Spelling
- Math
- Fine Motor
- ADD with LD
- ADD without LD
- ADHD with LD
- ADHD without LD

Learning Disability Program

Program: Reinforces course work: **Yes**
Students mainstreamed **100** % of the day
Counseling: Individual: **Yes**

Faculty:

Faculty: **4** Full time: **1** Part time: **3** M.A.: **4** Ph.D.: **2**

Diagnostic Testing

- ADD
- ADHD•
- I.Q.
- Math
- Personality
- Organization
- Handwriting•
- Social skills•
- Perceptual skills
- Fine motor skills
- Spoken language
- Written language
- Spelling
- Reading
- Study skills

Tutoring:

Average size of group tutorials: **4-5**
Services rendered by:
Graduates •Peers •Faculty •LD staff Teacher trainees

Tutorials

Grp.	Ind.	Tutorials	Grp.	Ind.	Tutorials
•	•	Math skills	•	•	Word processing
•	•	Study skills	•	•	Time management
•	•	Language arts	•	•	Learning strategies
•	•	Written express	•	•	Organizational skills

Academic Accommodations

Curriculum	Study Aids	Exams
Priority registration	Typist	• Oral
Math waiver	Reader	Untimed
Foreign lang. waiver	• Notetaker	Take home
Course substitution	• Proof reader	With proctor
In Class	• Text on tape	On computer
• Calculators	Early syllabus	• Extended time
• Tape recorder	Taped handouts	On tape
• Word processor		Modified
Priority seating		Separate room

Program Strengths

The Santa Monica College Learning Disability Program is geared to students who are enrolled in mainstream college courses. The main emphasis is on teaching students strategies that will help them be competitive, rather than on teaching remedial skills. Students receive a thorough assessment of learning strengths and weaknesses and are assisted in developing an appropriate educational plan. Specialized tutoring is available, as well as training in word processing and computer skills.

General Information:

Santa Monica College is a 2 year public college. Urban campus. Ski areas are 2-6 hours from campus. Beaches are 5 minutes from campus. Housing is not guaranteed.

Accreditation: WACS

Expenses:

Tuition: In-state: Full year: $57.50. Part-time: Per credit:$5.00. Tuition: Out-of-state: Full year: Part-time: Per credit: $110.00. Part-time: Per course:

Majors

• BUSINESS Accounting, Business Administration, Business Management, Finance, Management, Marketing, Merchandising, Printing Manufacturing, Real Estate • COMMUNICATIONS Broadcasting, Communication, English, Journalism, Photography • COMPUTER SCIENCE Data Processing, Programming • CRAFTS AND DESIGN Graphic Art Technology, Graphic Design, Graphic Production • EDUCATION Art, Early Childhood, Recreation and Youth Leadershi • ENGINEERING Communication, Electrical • HEALTH SCIENCES Nursing • HUMANITIES Liberal Arts, Philosophy • LANGUAGES French, German, Italian, Japanese, Russian, Spanish • PREPROFESSIONAL Architecture • SCIENCES Astronomy, Biology, Chemistry, Earth, Marine Biology, Mathematics, Physics, Zoology • SOCIAL SCIENCES Anthropology, Criminal Justice, Geography, Government/Political, History, Law Enforcement, Social Sciences, Sociology • VISUAL AND PERFORMING ARTS Art, Dance, Dramatic Arts, Music, Theater • VOCATIONAL Automobile Technology, Automotive Service, Construction, Drafting, Electronics Technology, Fire Science, Home Economics, Industrial Design, Metal Work, Office Administration, Park/Recreation, Respiratory Therapy Technology, Secretarial

Sports/Activities

• SPORTS RELATED Marching Band • SPORTS-INTERCOLLEGIATE Baseball (M), Basketball, Cross Country (M), Diving, Football (M), Soccer (M), Softball (F), Swimming, Tennis, Track and Field, Volleyball, Water Polo (M) • SPORTS-INTRAMURAL Badminton, Fencing, Weight Lifting • STUDENT LIFE ACTIVITIES Dance, Debate, Ethnic & Cultural Groups, Magazine, Music Groups, Musical Theater, Newspaper, Radio/TV station, Student Government, Symphony Orchestra

---

Less Selective   **California Program**

Santa Rosa Junior College

1501 Mendocino Avenue
Santa Rosa, California 95401
(707) 527-4685

School Enrollment: **19,200** Male: **9,200** Female: **10,000**
LD Enrollment: **250** Male: **125** Female: **125**

Admissions Contact: **Richard Navarrette, Dean of Admissions**
LD Contact: **Elizabeth Carlson, Department Chairperson**
Name of Program: **Disability Resources Department**
Address: **1501 Mendocino Ave.**
Telephone:**(707) 527-4278**

Admissions

Application Information:

Enrolled:**250**
Applicant must apply **6** months in advance
Rolling Admissions: **Yes**

Secondary School Information

Most Important Criteria For Admissions (1-strongest)

SAT/ACT	Application **1**	School transcript
Class rank	Course selection	Personal statement
Interview	Extra activities	Psychoeducational
G.P.A. **1**	Open admission	Recommendations

California

Test Requirements:
Diagnostic testing waived: **Yes**
Range accepted: **80+**
Documentation of LD required: **Yes**
Tests recommended: **Woodcock-Johnson Psycho-Educational, WAIS-R, WRAT**

Types of Disabilities Served
- Speech/Lang
- Study skills
- Written express
- Organizational
- Perceptual
- Reading
- Spelling
- Math
- Fine Motor
- ADD with LD
- ADD without LD
- ADHD with LD
- ADHD without LD

Admissions Process

The Disability Resources Department uses guidelines established by the California Community College's Chancellors Office for determining eligibility for LD services.

Learning Disability Program
Program: Remedial: **Yes**
Program: Reinforces course work: **Yes**
Program available through: **Day program**
Recommended credits per semester: **12-15**
Counseling: Individual: **Yes** Group Counseling: **Yes** Vocational Counseling: **Yes**
Support groups are available: **Some groups available to mainstream students might be of interest to LD students**

Faculty:
Faculty: **63** Including Director: **Yes** Full time: **3** Part time: **60** M.A.: **3**
Faculty advocate: **Yes** Meets with instructor: **As needed**

Diagnostic Testing
ADD	Personality •	Perceptual skills	• Spelling
ADHD	Organization	Fine motor skills	• Reading
I.Q.	Handwriting	Spoken language	• Study skills
• Math	• Social skills •	Written language	

Tutoring:
Average size of group tutorials: **10**
Services rendered by:
Graduates •Peers •Faculty •LD staff Teacher trainees

Tutorials
Grp.	Ind.	Tutorials	Grp.	Ind.	Tutorials
•	•	Math skills		•	Word processing
	•	Study skills		•	Time management
•	•	Language arts	•	•	Learning strategies
•	•	Written express		•	Organizational skills

Academic Accommodations
Curriculum	Study Aids	Exams
• Priority registration	Typist	• Oral
Math waiver	• Reader	• Untimed
Foreign lang. waiver	• Notetaker	Take home
Course substitution	• Proof reader	With proctor
In Class	• Text on tape	• On computer
• Calculators	Early syllabus	• Extended time
• Tape recorder	Taped handouts	On tape
• Word processor		Modified
Priority seating		Separate room

Graduation Requirements:
Course credits: **60 for A.A.** GPA: **2.0** Years to complete degree: **Usually**

2 years

Program Strengths
Hi Tech Center for Disabled, Acquired Brain Injury Program, staff of tutors who work with disabled students, special remedial classes for students with learning disabilities.

General Information:
Santa Rosa Junior College is a 2 year public college. Suburban campus of 93 acres is 60 miles from San Francisco. Accessible by air, train or bus. Ski areas are 200 miles from campus. Beaches are 30 miles from campus. 1 residential halls on campus. Housing is not guaranteed.

Accreditation: WACS

Expenses:
Tuition: In-state: Full year: $68.00. Part-time: Per credit: $6.00. Tuition: Out-of-state: Full year: $125.00 per unit.

Majors
• AREA STUDIES Ethics • BUSINESS Business Administration, Business Management, Economics, Human Resources Management, Insurance, Real Estate • COMMUNICATIONS Communication, English, Journalism • COMPUTER SCIENCE Computer Science • CRAFTS AND DESIGN Graphic Design • EDUCATION Child Development, Foreign Language, Industrial, Physical, Special, Speech/Language • ENGINEERING Aerospace, Agricultural, Chemical, Civil/Environmental, Electrical, Engineering Science, Environmental/Water Resources, Mechanical • HEALTH SCIENCES Medical Technology, Nursing, Nutritional/Food, Occupational Therapy • HUMANITIES Humanities, Liberal Arts, Philosophy • LANGUAGES French, German, Spanish • PREPROFESSIONAL Dentistry, Forestry, Industrial Design, Law, Medicine, Optometry, Pharmacy • SCIENCES Animal, Bio-medical, Biology, Geography, Geology, Horticultural, Oceanography, Physical Science • SOCIAL SCIENCES Anthropology, Criminal Justice, Law Enforcement, Library Science, Psychology, Social Sciences, Sociology • VISUAL AND PERFORMING ARTS Dance, Dramatic Arts, Music, Theater • VOCATIONAL Automobile Technology, Automotive Service, Business and Office, Dental Assistant, Dental Hygiene, Diesel Power Technology, Fashion Design, Fashion Merchandising, Fire Science, Fishery Studies, Food Service, Home Economics, Landscape Architecture, Legal Secretary, Machinist, Masonry, Plumbing, Respiratory Therapy Technology, Secretarial

Sports/Activities
• SPORTS-INTERCOLLEGIATE Baseball (M), Basketball, Cross Country, Diving, Football (M), Golf, Soccer (M), Softball (F), Swimming, Tennis, Track and Field, Volleyball (F), Water Polo (M), Wrestling (M)
• STUDENT LIFE ACTIVITIES Choral, Concert Band, Dance, Drama Groups, Film, Jazz Band, Music Ensembles, Music Groups, Musical Theater, Newspaper, Radio/TV station, Student Government, Symphony Orchestra

Less Selective　　　　　　　**California**
　　　　　　　　　　　　　　　　　Services

Sierra College
5000 Rocklin Road
Rocklin, California 95677
(916) 624-3333

School Enrollment: **12,859** Male: **5,575** Female: **7,284**
LD Enrollment: **400** Male: **200** Female: **200**

Admissions Contact: **Mandy Davies, Registrar**
LD Contact: **Denise Stone/K. Fields/N. Allsup, L.D Specialists**
Name of Program: **Learning Disabilities Program**
Telephone:**Ext. 2553**

Admissions

Application Information:
LD Students Applying: **300** Accepted: **180** Enrolled:**180**
Applicant must apply **2-9** months in advance

Secondary School Information
Most Important Criteria For Admissions (1-strongest)
SAT/ACT **1**	Application	School transcript
Class rank	Course selection	Personal statement
Interview	Extra activities	Psychoeducational
G.P.A.	Open admission	Recommendations

Test Requirements:
Standardized tests waived: **Yes**
Diagnostic testing waived: **Yes**
Achievement tests required:**1**
WAIS-R required: **Yes** Range accepted: **Varies**
Documentation of LD required: **Yes**
Currency of diagnostic testing: **3 years**
Tests recommended: **LD Assessment upon being admitted - Woodcock-Johnson Psycho. Educational Evaluation**

Types of Disabilities Served
- Speech/Lang
- Study skills
- Written express
- Organizational
- Perceptual
- Reading
- Spelling
- Math
- Fine Motor
- ADD with LD
- ADD without LD
- ADHD with LD
- ADHD without LD

Learning Disability Program
Program: Remedial: **Yes**
Program: Reinforces course work: **Yes**
Students mainstreamed **100** % of the day
Services available for all students: **Yes**
Counseling: Individual: **Yes**

Faculty:
Faculty: **8** Full time: **4** Part time: **4**
LD faculty with: BS/BA: **4** M.A.: **4**
Faculty advocate: **Yes** Meets with instructor: **As requested**

Diagnostic Testing
ADD	• Personality	• Perceptual skills	• Spelling
ADHD	Organization	Fine motor skills	• Reading
I.Q.	Handwriting	Spoken language	• Study skills
• Math	Social skills	• Written language	

Tutoring:
Average size of group tutorials: **1-6**
Services rendered by:
　Graduates　•Peers　•Faculty　•LD staff　•Teacher trainees

Tutorials
Grp.	Ind.	Tutorials	Grp.	Ind.	Tutorials
•	•	Math skills		•	Word processing
•	•	Study skills	•	•	Time management
•	•	Language arts	•	•	Learning strategies
•	•	Written express	•	•	Organizational skills

Academic Accommodations
Curriculum	Study Aids	Exams
• Priority registration	• Typist	• Oral
Math waiver	Reader	Untimed
Foreign lang. waiver	• Notetaker	• Take home
Course substitution	• Proof reader	• With proctor
In Class	• Text on tape	On computer
• Calculators	Early syllabus	• Extended time
• Tape recorder	Taped handouts	On tape
• Word processor		• Modified
Priority seating		• Separate room

Program Strengths
Sierra College offers a holistic learning disabilities program for identified students. Perceptual training classes offered include learning strategies, visual perception, and auditory development. The LD program offers ongoing support for the student with special learning needs including test taking facilitation and tutorial services.

General Information:
Sierra College is a 2 year public college. Rural campus of 310 acres is 18 miles from Sacramento. Accessible by bus. Ski areas are 2 hours from campus. Beaches are 2.5 hours from campus. 1% of students are foreign. 1 residential halls on campus. Housing is not guaranteed.1 % of students remain on campus for the weekends.

Accreditation:WACS

Expenses:
Tuition: In-state: Full year: $60.00 maximum. Part-time: Per credit:$6.00.
Part-time: Per credit:$99.00. Room and board: $3,244.00

Majors
• BUSINESS Accounting, Agricultural, Business Administration, Business Education, Business Management, Entrepreneur, Finance, Management, Marketing, Real Estate • COMMUNICATION Advertising, Communication, Creative Writing, English, Journalism, Television/Radio/Film • COMPUTER SCIENCE Data Processing, Hardware Engineer, Programming, Systems Analysis, Telecommunications • EDUCATION Art, Early Childhood, Elementary, Health, Industrial, Music, Physical, Speech/Language, Vocational • ENGINEERING Computer • FINE AND PERFORMING ARTS Art, Art History, Dance, Music, Studio Art, Theater • HEALTH SCIENCES Health, Medical Assistant, Nursing, Nutritional/Food • LANGUAGES French, German, Italian, Japanese, Russian, Spanish
• PHILOSOPHY Humanities, Philosophy • PREPROFESSIONAL Agriculture, Architecture, Dentistry, Engineering, Forestry, Legal Assistant
• SCIENCES Agricultural, Animal, Biology, Astronomy, Chemistry, Earth, Geography, Geology, Horticultural, Mathematics, Metal Technology, Physical Science, Physics, Physiology, Zoology • SOCIAL SCIENCES Anthropology, Criminal Justice, Geography, History, Law Enforcement, Psychology, Social Sciences, Sociology • VOCATIONAL Automobile Technology, Construction, Drafting, Electronics Technology, Fire Science, Home Economics, Landscape Architecture, Library Assistant, Office Administration, Secretarial, Surveying and Mapping, Word Processing

California

Sports/Activities

• SPORTS INTERCOLLEGIATE Baseball, Basketball, Cross Country, Diving, Football (M), Golf, Gymnastics, Skiing - Cross Country, Skiing - Snow, Swimming, Tennis, Track and Field, Volleyball (F), Water Polo (M), Weight Lifting, Wrestling (M) • SPORTS INTRAMURAL Archery, Badminton, Basketball, Bowling, Boxing, Karate, Racquetball, Soccer (M), Softball (F), Volleyball (F) • SPORTS RELATED Band • STUDENT LIFE ACTIVITIES Concert Band, Drama Groups, Jazz Band, Music Groups, Newspaper, Radio/TV station, Student Government, Symphony Orchestra

Selective   **California Services**

Sonoma State University

1801 E. Cotati Avenue
Rohnert Park, California 94928
(707) 664-2363

School Enrollment: **7,000** Male: **2,500** Female: **4,500**
LD Enrollment: **175**

Admissions Contact: **Marlene Ballaine, Admissions Spec.**
LD Contact: **Bill Clopton, Disability Advisor**
Name of Program: **Disability Resource Center**
Telephone:**(707) 664-2677**

Admissions

Application Information:
LD Students Applying: **175** Accepted: **175** Enrolled:**175**
Application deadline: **November for Fall, August for Spring**

Secondary School Information
Most Important Criteria For Admissions (1-strongest)

1 SAT/ACT	Application	**1**	School transcript
Class rank	Course selection		Personal statement
Interview	Extra activities		Psychoeducational
1 G.P.A.	Open admission		Recommendations

Test Requirements:
Untimed SAT: **Yes** Untimed ACT: **Yes**
Documentation of LD required: **Yes**
Currency of diagnostic testing: **3 years**

Types of Disabilities Served
• Speech/Lang   • Reading   ADD with LD
• Study skills   • Spelling   ADD without LD
• Written express • Math   ADHD with LD
• Organizational • Fine Motor   ADHD without LD
• Perceptual

Admissions Process

Apply for regular admissions, include letter saying you are LD. If denied, then contact our office for possible special admittance.

High School Course Requirements:
English: **4** Math: **3** Science: **1** Foreign Language: **2**
Waivers to standard high school courses
Foreign Language : **Yes**

Learning Disability Program

Program: Reinforces course work: **Yes**
Students mainstreamed **100** % of the day
Recommended credits per semester: **12**
Services only for LD students: **Yes**
Counseling: Individual: **Yes**

Faculty:
Faculty: **1** Full time: **1**
Faculty advocate: **Yes** Meets with instructor: **As requested**

Diagnostic Testing
ADD	Personality	Perceptual skills	Spelling
ADHD	Organization	Fine motor skills	Reading
I.Q.	Handwriting	Spoken language	Study skills
Math	Social skills	Written language	

Tutoring:
Services rendered by:
  Graduates   Peers   Faculty   •LD staff   Teacher trainees

Tutorials
Grp.	Ind.	Tutorials	Grp.	Ind.	Tutorials
	•	Math skills			Word processing
		Study skills			Time management
	•	Language arts			Learning strategies
		Written express		•	Organizational skills

Academic Accommodations
Curriculum	Study Aids	Exams
Priority registration	Typist	Oral
Math waiver	Reader	Untimed
Foreign lang. waiver	• Notetaker	Take home
Course substitution	• Proof reader	• With proctor
In Class	• Text on tape	On computer
• Calculators	Early syllabus	• Extended time
• Tape recorder	Taped handouts	On tape
Word processor		Modified
Priority seating		Separate room

Graduation Requirements:
Course credits: **124** GPA: **2.0** Years to complete degree: **Unlimited**
Other requirements: **Alternative math course**

Program Strengths

We do not have a "program", we only offer accommodations. We don't have LD classes or skills program. Tutoring is available through our Learning Skills Service (LSS) and is available for all students. Workshops are offered in study skills and management.

General Information:

Sonoma State University is a 4 year public university. Suburban campus of 65 acres is 10 miles from Santa Rosa. Accessible by bus. Ski areas are 150 miles from campus. Beaches are 25 miles from campus. Housing is not guaranteed.

Accreditation:NASAD, NASM, NLN

Expenses:
Tuition: In-state: Full year: $846.00. Part-time: Per credit:$546.00, 7 units or less. Tuition: Out-of-state: Full year: $846.00 plus $189.00 per unit. Part-time: Per credit:$540.00 plus $189.00 per unit.

Majors

• AREA STUDIES American, Black/Afro-American, Mexican/American, South Asia • BUSINESS Accounting, Business Administration, Economics • COMMUNICATIONS Communication, English, Journalism • COM-

PUTER SCIENCE Computer Science, Data Processing, Programming, Systems Analysis • EDUCATION Early Childhood, Elementary, Middle School, Secondary, Special • HEALTH SCIENCES Nursing • HUMANITIES Liberal Arts, Philosophy • LANGUAGES French, German, Spanish • SCIENCES Biology, Botany, Chemistry, Geography, Geology, Mathematics, Physics • SOCIAL SCIENCES Anthropology, Criminal Justice, Geography, Government/Political, History, Psychology, Sociology • VISUAL AND PERFORMING ARTS Art, Art History, Dramatic Arts, Music, Studio Art, Theater • VOCATIONAL City/Community/Regional Planni

Sports/Activities

• SPORTS RELATED Pep Band • SPORTS-INTERCOLLEGIATE Baseball (M), Basketball, Cross Country, Football (M), Soccer, Softball (F), Tennis, Track and Field, Volleyball (F) • SPORTS-INTRAMURAL Archery, Badminton, Basketball, Cross Country, Golf, Lacrosse, Racquetball, Scuba, Softball, Swimming, Tennis, Volleyball, Weight Lifting • STUDENT LIFE ACTIVITIES Academic Clubs, Dance, Drama Groups, Ethnic & Cultural Groups, Film, Fraternities, Jazz Band, Magazine, Music Groups, Newspaper, Radio/TV station, Sororities, Student Government, Symphony Orchestra

---

Most Selective **California Accommodations**

Stanford University

Old Union - Office of Undergraduate Admi Second Floor
Stanford, California 94305
(415) 723-2091

School Enrollment: **6,457** Male: **3,646** Female: **2,811**
LD Enrollment: **60**

Admissions Contact: **Jonathan Reider, Assoc. Dir. of Admissions**
LD Contact: **Molly Sandperl, Dir. Disability Resource Center**
Name of Program: **Disability Resource Center**
Address: **Meyer Library 123**
Telephone: **(415) 723-1066**

Admissions

Application Information:
Application deadline: **December 15th**
Notified when: **1st week of April**

Secondary School Information
Most Important Criteria For Admissions (1-strongest)

4 SAT/ACT		Application	**1** School transcript
5 Class rank	**2**	Course selection	**6** Personal statement
10 Interview	**6**	Extra activities	**9** Psychoeducational
2 G.P.A.		Open admission	**8** Recommendations

Test Requirements:
Untimed SAT: **Yes** Untimed ACT: **Yes** Untimed ACH: **Yes** Achievement tests required: **Not required**

Types of Disabilities Served
• Speech/Lang
• Study skills
• Written express
• Organizational
• Perceptual
• Reading
• Spelling
• Math
• Fine Motor
• ADD with LD
• ADD without LD
• ADHD with LD
• ADHD without LD

Admissions Process

Most selective (approximately 1 in 5 admitted). Strong academic

record in challenging program is very important, as are nonacademic activities and evidence of good character. Disability files are read with attention to their special circumstances.

Learning Disability Program

Program: Reinforces course work: **Yes**
Program available through: **Upon request**
Students mainstreamed **100** % of the day
Recommended credits per semester: **15**
Services available for all students: **Yes**
Counseling: Individual: **Yes**
Support groups are available: **LD students meet to discuss common concerns**

Faculty:
Faculty: **2** Full time: **1** Part time: **1**
LD faculty with: BS/BA: **2**
Faculty advocate: **Yes**

Diagnostic Testing
• ADD
• ADHD
• I.Q.
• Math
• Personality
• Organization
• Handwriting
• Social skills
• Perceptual skills
• Fine motor skills
• Spoken language
• Written language
• Spelling
• Reading
• Study skills

Tutoring:
Average size of group tutorials: **Individualized**
Services rendered by:
Graduates   •Peers   Faculty   •LD staff   Teacher trainees

Tutorials

Grp.	Ind.	Tutorials	Grp.	Ind.	Tutorials
	•	Math skills		•	Word processing
	•	Study skills		•	Time management
	•	Language arts		•	Learning strategies
	•	Written express		•	Organizational skills

Academic Accommodations

Curriculum	Study Aids	Exams
• Priority registration	• Typist	• Oral
Math waiver	• Reader	• Untimed
• Foreign lang. waiver	• Notetaker	• Take home
• Course substitution	• Proof reader	• With proctor
In Class	• Text on tape	• On computer
• Calculators	• Early syllabus	• Extended time
• Tape recorder	Taped handouts	• On tape
• Word processor		• Modified
• Priority seating		• Separate room

Graduation Requirements:
Course credits: **180** Years to complete degree: **4 or more** Language waiver: **Yes**
Other requirements: **2 quarters of Freshman English, l year Humanities, distribution requirements in Social Science, Math, And Science**

Program Strengths

Once applicants are admitted to Stanford, the Disability Resource Center can provide a number of services to help students adjust. These include note-taking, text recording and reading, specialized examination conditions, equipment loans, tutoring, and other forms of assistance where reasonable accommodation is possible.

General Information:

Stanford University is a 4 year private university. Suburban campus of 8,800 acres is 35/20 miles from San Francisco. Accessible by train, air or

California

bus. Ski areas are 5 hours from campus. Beaches are 1 hour from campus. 4% of students are foreign. Housing is guaranteed.Guaranteed through 4th year. 90 % of students remain on campus for the weekends. 10 % of students join fraternities/sororities.

Accreditation:WACS

SAT/ACT Scores:
Scores for incoming freshmen:**Verbal:**3%below 500. 21%between 500 and 599. 52%between 600 and 699. 22%above 700. **Math:**1% below 500. 8% between 500 and 599. 32% between 600 and 699. 59%above 700.

Class Rank:
About 95% of the present freshmen class were in the upper 20% of their high school class. 5% were in the top 40% of their class.

Expenses:
Tuition: In-state: Full year: $16,536.00. Room and board: $6,314.00

Majors
• AREA STUDIES African, African-American, American, Asian, Ethics, Feminist Studies, Jewish, Latin American, Urban • COMMUNICATIONS Communication, Creative Writing, English • COMPUTER SCIENCE Computer Science, Computer Technology • ENGINEERING Chemical, Civil/Environmental, Electrical, Engineering Science, Industrial, Materials, Mechanical • HUMANITIES Classics, English/Writing/Literature, Humanities, Philosophy, Religion • LANGUAGES Chinese, French, German, Greek, Italian, Japanese, Latin, Linguistic, Russian, Spanish • PREPROFESSIONAL Engineering • SCIENCES Biochemistry, Biology, Chemistry, Earth Systems, Geology, Mathematics, Microbiology, Physics, Statistics • SOCIAL SCIENCES Anthropology, Economics, Government/Political, History, International Relations, Political Science, Psychology, Sociology • VISUAL AND PERFORMING ARTS Art, Art History, Fine Arts, Music, Studio Art, Theater

Sports/Activities
• SPORTS RELATED Cheerleading, Marching Band, Team Managers • SPORTS-INTERCOLLEGIATE Baseball (M), Basketball, Crew, Cricket, Cross Country, Cycling, Field Hockey (F), Football (M), Golf, Gymnastics, Hammer Throw, Horseback Riding, Ice Hockey, Judo, Karate, Lacrosse, Martial Arts, Polo, Rugby, Sailing, Scuba, Skiing - Cross Country, Skiing - Snow, Soccer, Softball, Squash, Swimming, Synchronized Swimming, Tennis, Track and Field, Volleyball, Water Polo (M), Weight Lifting, Wrestling (M) • SPORTS-INTRAMURAL Badminton, Basketball, Cross Country, Diving, Fencing (F), Football (M), Golf, Gymnastics, Hand Ball, Ping-Pong, Racquetball, Soccer, Softball, Swimming, Tennis, Track and Field, Volleyball, Water Polo, Wrestling • STUDENT LIFE ACTIVITIES Academic Clubs, Debate, Drama Groups, Ethnic & Cultural Groups, Film, Fraternities, Jazz Band, Music Groups, Newspaper, Radio/TV station, Sororities, Student Government, Symphony Orchestra, Yearbook

---

Less Selective

California Program

Taft College
29 Emmons Park Drive
Taft, California 93268
(805) 763-4282

School Enrollment: **862** Male: **389** Female: **473**
LD Enrollment: **47** Male: **23** Female: **24**

Admissions Contact: **Juanita Perry, Admissions Officer**
LD Contact: **Jeff Ross, Coordinator, DSS**
Name of Program: **Learning Assistance Program**
Telephone:**Ext. 276**

Admissions

Application Information:
LD Students Applying: **40** Accepted: **37** Enrolled:**37**
Application deadline: **August 30th**
Applicant must apply **3** months in advance
Rolling Admissions: **Yes**

Secondary School Information
Most Important Criteria For Admissions (1-strongest)

SAT/ACT	Application	School transcript
Class rank	Course selection	Personal statement
Interview	Extra activities	Psychoeducational
G.P.A.	**1** Open admission	Recommendations

Test Requirements:
Untimed SAT: **Yes** Untimed ACT: **Yes** Untimed ACH: **Yes**
Documentation of LD required: **Yes**
Currency of diagnostic testing: **1 year**
Tests recommended: **Woodcock-Johnson or WAIS-R are required by state of California**

Types of Disabilities Served
• Speech/Lang	• Reading	• ADD with LD
• Study skills	• Spelling	• ADD without LD
• Written express	• Math	• ADHD with LD
• Organizational	• Fine Motor	• ADHD without LD
• Perceptual		

Learning Disability Program
Program: Remedial: **Yes**
Program: Reinforces course work: **Yes**
Students mainstreamed **90** % of the day
Services available for all students: **Yes**
Counseling: Individual: **Yes**

Faculty:
Faculty: **2** Including Director: **Yes** Full time: **2** M.A.: **1**
Faculty advocate: **Yes** Meets with instructor: **As needed**

Diagnostic Testing
ADD	• Personality	• Perceptual skills	• Spelling
ADHD	• Organization	• Fine motor skills	• Reading
• I.Q.	• Handwriting	• Spoken language	• Study skills
• Math	• Social skills	• Written language	

Tutoring:
Services rendered by:
•Graduates •Peers Faculty •LD staff Teacher trainees

Tutorials
Grp.	Ind.	Tutorials	Grp.	Ind.	Tutorials
	•	Math skills		•	Word processing
	•	Study skills		•	Time management
	•	Language arts		•	Learning strategies
	•	Written express		•	Organizational skills

Academic Accommodations

Curriculum	Study Aids	Exams
Priority registration	• Typist	• Oral
Math waiver	Reader	Untimed
Foreign lang. waiver	• Notetaker	Take home
Course substitution	• Proof reader	With proctor
In Class	• Text on tape	On computer
• Calculators	Early syllabus	• Extended time
• Tape recorder	Taped handouts	On tape
• Word processor		• Modified
Priority seating		Separate room

Graduation Requirements:
Course credits: **60** GPA: **2.0** Years to complete degree: **Unlimited**

Program Strengths
Taft College offers an individualized LD Program that can best serve its' students by mainstreaming and providing specialized services to ensure success.

General Information:
Taft College is a 2 year public college. Rural campus 100 miles from Los Angeles. Accessible by bus. Ski areas are 75 miles from campus. Beaches are 100 miles from campus. 28% of students are foreign. 2 residential halls on campus. Housing is not guaranteed.18 % of students remain on campus for the weekends.

Accreditation:Regional

Expenses:
Tuition: In-state: Full year: $100.00. Part-time: Per credit:0. Tuition: Out-of-state: Full year: $2,920.00. Part-time: Per credit:$99.00. Room and board: $1,550.00

Majors
• BUSINESS Accounting, Business Management, Economics, Finance • COMMUNICATIONS English, Journalism • COMPUTER SCIENCE Data Processing, Programming, Systems Analysis • EDUCATION Early Childhood, Physical • ENGINEERING Engineering Science • HEALTH SCIENCES Health, Nursing, Nursing Assistant • HUMANITIES Humanities, Liberal Arts, Philosophy, Religion • LANGUAGES German, Spanish • SCIENCES Biology, Chemistry, Earth, Ecology, Geography, Geology, Mathematics, Mining, Physical Science, Physics, Radiology, Zoology • SOCIAL SCIENCES Anthropology, Criminal Justice, Geography, Government/Political, History, Psychology, Social Sciences, Sociology • VISUAL AND PERFORMING ARTS Fine Art • VOCATIONAL Automobile Technology, Automotive Service, Business and Office, Drafting, Electronics Technology, Industrial Equipment Maintenan

Sports/Activities
• SPORTS-INTERCOLLEGIATE Baseball (M), Basketball (F), Cross Country, Football (M), Golf (M), Softball (F), Track and Field, Volleyball (F), Weight Lifting (M) • STUDENT LIFE ACTIVITIES Ethnic & Cultural Groups, Film Production, Fraternities, Magazine, Newspaper, Sororities, Student Government

---

Most Selective **California Program**

University of California: Berkeley
120 Sproul Hall
Berkeley, California 94720
(510) 642-0200

School Enrollment: **30,372** Male: **16,659** Female: **13,713**
LD Enrollment: **300**

Admissions Contact: **Robert Bailey, Director of Admissions**
LD Contact: **D. Semoff/K. Runyan/C. Summer, Co-Coordinators**
Name of Program: **Disabled Students' Program**
Address: **230 Golden Bear Center**
Telephone:**(510) 642-0518**

Admissions

Application Information:
LD Students Applying: **127** Accepted: **59** Enrolled:**50**
Application deadline: **November 30th for following Fall**

Secondary School Information
Most Important Criteria For Admissions (1-strongest)

1 SAT/ACT	**4** Application	**1** School transcript
12 Class rank	**2** Course selection	**2** Personal statement
Interview	**2** Extra activities	**3** Psychoeducational
1 G.P.A.	Open admission	**12** Recommendations

Test Requirements:
Untimed SAT: **Yes** Untimed ACT: **Yes** Untimed ACH: **Yes** Achievement tests required:**3**
WAIS-R required: **Yes**
Documentation of LD required: **Yes**
Currency of diagnostic testing: **3 years**

Types of Disabilities Served
• Speech/Lang • Reading • ADD with LD
• Study skills • Spelling • ADD without LD
• Written express • Math • ADHD with LD
• Organizational • Fine Motor • ADHD without LD
• Perceptual

High School Course Requirements:
English: **4** Math: **3** Science: **1** Foreign Language: **2**
Waivers to standard high school courses
Foreign Language : **Yes** Math: **Yes** Course substitution: **Yes**

Learning Disability Program
Special orientation for LD students:
Program: Reinforces course work: **Yes**
Students mainstreamed **100** % of the day
Services available for all students: **Yes**
Counseling: Individual: **Yes** Group Counseling: **Yes** Vocational Counseling: **Yes**
Support groups are available:**Yes**

Faculty:
Faculty: **4** Including Director: **Yes** Full time: **2** Part time: **2** M.A.: **3** Ph.D.: **1**
Faculty advocate: **Yes** Meets with instructor: **As needed**

California

Diagnostic Testing

ADD	Personality	Perceptual skills	Spelling
ADHD	Organization	Fine motor skills	Reading
I.Q.	Handwriting	Spoken language	Study skills
Math	Social skills	Written language	

Tutoring:

Average size of group tutorials: **10-15**

Services rendered by:

•Graduates •Peers Faculty LD staff •Teacher trainees

Tutorials

Grp.	Ind.	Tutorials	Grp.	Ind.	Tutorials
•	•	Math skills	•	•	Word processing
•	•	Study skills	•	•	Time management
•	•	Language arts	•	•	Learning strategies
•	•	Written express	•	•	Organizational skills

Academic Accommodations

Curriculum
- Priority registration
- Math waiver
- Foreign lang. waiver
  Course substitution

In Class
- Calculators
- Tape recorder
- Word processor
- Priority seating

Study Aids
- Typist
- Reader
- Notetaker
- Proof reader
- Text on tape
  Early syllabus
  Taped handouts

Exams
- Oral
  Untimed
  Take home
- With proctor
- On computer
- Extended time
- On tape
- Modified
- Separate room

Graduation Requirements:

Course credits: **120** GPA: **2.0** Years to complete degree: **4-5** Math waiver: **Yes** Language waiver: **Yes**
Other requirements: **Varies by college, school and major**

Program Strengths

Berkeley is a vigorous institution and for LD students, we allow them to take advantage of this. They gain a top-flight education.

General Information:

University of California: Berkeley is a 4 year public university. Urban campus of 1,232 acres is Berkeley. Accessible by subway or bus. Ski areas are 3 1/2 hours from campus. Beaches are 1 hour from campus. 3% of students are foreign. 6 residential halls on campus. Housing is not guaranteed.50 % of students remain on campus for the weekends. 15/13 % of students join fraternities/sororities.

Accreditation:NNAB, SAF, CSWE

SAT/ACT Scores:

Scores for incoming freshmen: **Verbal:** 26% below 500. 34% between 500 and 599. 32.5% between 600 and 699. 7.5% above 700. **Math:** 10.4% below 500. 17.6% between 500 and 599. 32.6% between 600 and 699. 39% above 700. 90% between 26 and 28.

Expenses:

Tuition: In-state: Full year: $3,200.00. Part-time: Per credit:0. Tuition: Out-of-state: Full year: $5,799.00. Room and board: $4,870.00

Majors

• AREA STUDIES American Indian, Asian, Black/Afro-American, Mexican/American, Middle Eastern, Russian/Slavic, Women's Studies • BUSINESS Agricultural, Business Management, Economics • COMMUNICATIONS Communication, Literature, Television/Radio/Film • COMPUTER SCIENCE Computer Science • EDUCATION English, Music • ENGINEERING Bioengineering, Biomedical, Chemical, Civil/Environmental, Electrical, Engineering Science, Environmental/Water Resources, Geological, Industrial, Mechanical, Metallurgical, Mining/Mineral, Naval Architecture, Nuclear, Petroleum • HEALTH SCIENCES Nursing Assistant • HUMANITIES Humanities, Philosophy, Religion • LANGUAGES Arabic, Chinese, Dutch, French, German, Greek, Hebrew, Italian, Japanese, Linguistic, Russian, Spanish • PREPROFESSIONAL Architecture, Forestry • SCIENCES Astronomy, Biochemistry, Biology, Biophysics, Earth, Ecology, Geology, Marine Biology, Mathematics, Microbiology, Molecular Biology, Physics, Soil, Zoology • SOCIAL SCIENCES Anthropology, Geography, Government/Political, History, Political Science, Psychology, Social Sciences, Sociology • VISUAL AND PERFORMING ARTS Art History, Dance, Theater

Sports/Activities

• SPORTS RELATED Concert Band, Team Managers • SPORTS-INTERCOLLEGIATE Baseball (M), Basketball, Crew, Cross Country, Field Hockey (F), Football (M), Golf (M), Gymnastics, Racquetball, Soccer, Softball (F), Swimming, Tennis, Track and Field, Volleyball (F), Volleyball (M), Water Polo (M), Wrestling (M) • SPORTS-INTRAMURAL Archery, Badminton, Baseball, Bowling, Cycling, Fencing, Hand Ball, Lacrosse, Rugby, Sailing, Soccer, Softball, Volleyball • STUDENT LIFE ACTIVITIES Drama Groups, Film Production, Fraternities, Jazz Band, Music Groups, Newspaper, Radio/TV station, Sororities, Student Government, Symphony Orchestra, Yearbook

---

Highly Selective

California Services

University of California: Davis
175 Mark Hall
Davis, California 95616
(916) 752-2971

School Enrollment: **18,400** Male: **9,581** Female: **8,909**
LD Enrollment: **350**

Admissions Contact: **Gary Tudor, Director of Admissions**
LD Contact: **Christine O'Dell, LD Coordinator**
Name of Program: **Disability Resource Center**
Address: **South Silo**
Telephone:**(916) 752-3184**

Admissions

Application Information:
Application deadline: **November 30th**
Applicant must apply **12** months in advance

Secondary School Information
Most Important Criteria For Admissions (1-strongest)

1	SAT/ACT	4	Application	6	School transcript
5	Class rank	10	Course selection	1	Personal statement
8	Interview	7	Extra activities	3	Psychoeducational
2	G.P.A.		Open admission	9	Recommendations

Test Requirements:
Diagnostic testing waived: **Yes**
Untimed SAT: **Yes** Untimed ACT: **Yes** Untimed ACH: **Yes**
Documentation of LD required: **Yes**
Currency of diagnostic testing: **3 years**
Tests recommended: **Learning Disability Evaluation (according to University of California guidelines)**

Types of Disabilities Served

- Speech/Lang
- Study skills
- Written express
- Organizational
- Perceptual
- Reading
- Spelling
- Math
- Fine Motor
- ADD with LD
- ADD without LD
- ADHD with LD
- ADHD without LD

Learning Disability Program

Program: Reinforces course work: **Yes**
Students mainstreamed **100** % of the day
Counseling: Individual: **Yes** Group Counseling: **Yes**
Support groups are available:**Yes**

Faculty:

Faculty: **2** Full time: **2** M.A.: **2**
Faculty advocate: **Yes** Meets with instructor: **As requested**

Diagnostic Testing

ADD	Personality	Perceptual skills	Spelling
ADHD	Organization	Fine motor skills	Reading
I.Q.	Handwriting	Spoken language	Study skills
Math	Social skills	Written language	

Tutoring:

Average size of group tutorials: **8-12**
Services rendered by:
•Graduates •Peers •Faculty •LD staff Teacher trainees

Tutorials

Grp.	Ind.	Tutorials	Grp.	Ind.	Tutorials
•	•	Math skills		•	Word processing
•	•	Study skills		•	Time management
•	•	Language arts	•	•	Learning strategies
•	•	Written express	•	•	Organizational skills

Academic Accommodations

Curriculum	Study Aids	Exams
• Priority registration	• Typist	• Oral
Math waiver	• Reader	Untimed
Foreign lang. waiver	• Notetaker	• Take home
Course substitution	• Proof reader	With proctor
In Class	• Text on tape	On computer
• Calculators	Early syllabus	• Extended time
• Tape recorder	Taped handouts	On tape
• Word processor		Modified
Priority seating		Separate room

Program Strengths

Students with learning disabilities apply and are admitted to the University of California, Davis (UCD), through the admission process followed by all UCD applicants. Counselors in the Disability Resource Center (DRC) will advise students with learning disabilities in the areas of academic course load and reasonable accommodation. A peer group program gives students an opportunity to share problems, concerns, and coping skills.

General Information:

University of California: Davis is a 4 year public university. Suburban campus of 3,600 acres is 13 miles from Sacramento. Accessible by air, train or bus. Ski areas are 60 miles from campus. Beaches are 110 miles from campus. Housing is not guaranteed.

Accreditation:WACS, AALS, AAMS

SAT/ACT Scores:
Scores for incoming freshmen:**Verbal:**16%below 500. 33%between 500 and 599. 38%between 600 and 699. 14%above 700. **Math:**18% below 500. 38% between 500 and 599. 35% between 600 and 699. 8%above 700.

Class Rank:
About 96% of the present freshmen class were in the upper 20% of their high school class.

Expenses:
Tuition: In-state: Full year: $1,299.00 per quarter. Part-time: Per credit:0.
Tuition: Out-of-state: Full year: $4,892.00 per quarter. Room and board: $4,757.00

Majors

• AREA STUDIES American, American/Indian Studies, Black/Afro-American, East Asian Studies, International Studies, Mexican/American, Women's Studies • BUSINESS Agricultural, Economics • COMMUNICATION Creative Writing, English, Linguistic, Speech/Debate/Forensic • COMPUTER SCIENCE Software Engineer • EDUCATION Agricultural • ENGINEERING Aerospace, Agricultural, Chemical, Civil/Environmental, Computer, Electrical, Electronics/Communications, Material • FINE AND PERFORMING ARTS Art, Art History, Dramatic Arts, Fine Arts, Music, Studio Art, Theater • HEALTH SCIENCES Environmental, Nutritional/Food • HUMANITIES Humanities, Philosophy, Religion • LANGUAGES French, German, Greek, Italian, Latin, Russian, Spanish • PREPROFESSIONAL Agriculture, Architecture, Dentistry, Engineering, Forestry, Landscaping, Law, Medicine, Pharmacy, Recreation, Social Work, Wildlife Management • SCIENCES Agricultural, Animal, Atmospheric, Bacteriology, Biochemistry, Biology, Botany, Chemistry, Entomology Geography, Geology, Mathematics, Physics, Physiology, Plant, Soil, Toxicology, Zoology • SOCIAL SCIENCES Anthropology, Geography, Government/Political, History, Psychology, Sociology • VOCATIONAL Aeronautical / Astronautical E

Sports/Activities

• SPORTS RELATED Cheerleading, Marching Band, Team Managers • SPORTS-INTERCOLLEGIATE Archery, Badminton, Baseball (M), Basketball, Bowling, Crew, Cross Country, Cycling, Field Hockey (F), Football (M), Golf, Gymnastics, Horseback Riding (F), Judo, Karate, Lacrosse, Ping-Pong, Polo, Racquetball, Riflery, Rodeo, Rugby, Sailing, Scuba, Skiing - Cross Country, Skiing - Snow, Soccer, Swimming, Tennis, Track and Field, Volleyball, Water Polo, Weight Lifting • SPORTS-INTRAMURAL Baseball, Basketball, Crew, Cross Country, Football (M), Golf, Gymnastics, Horseback Riding, Lacrosse, Racquetball, Rugby, Skiing - Snow (F), Soccer, Softball (F), Swimming, Tennis, Track and Field, Volleyball, Water Polo, Wrestling • STUDENT LIFE ACTIVITIES Choral, Community Service, Concert Band

---

Very Selective   California
                                                       Services

University of California: Riverside

1138 Administration Building
Riverside, California 92521
(714) 787-3411

School Enrollment: **8,890** Male: **4,199** Female: **4,691**
LD Enrollment: **15**

Admissions Contact: **Al Zamora, Outreach Counselor**
LD Contact: **M. Theise Schiffer, Director**
Name of Program: **Disabled Student Services**
Address: **1132 Library South**
Telephone:**(714) 787-4538**

California

Admissions

Application Information:
Application deadline: **Varies**

Secondary School Information
Most Important Criteria For Admissions (1-strongest)

1 SAT/ACT	**1** Application	School transcript
Class rank	Course selection	Personal statement
Interview	Extra activities	Psychoeducational
1 G.P.A.	Open admission	Recommendations

Test Requirements:
Diagnostic testing waived: **Yes**
Untimed SAT: **Yes** Untimed ACT: **Yes** Untimed ACH: **Yes** Achievement tests required:**3**
WAIS-R required: **Yes**
Documentation of LD required: **Yes**
Currency of diagnostic testing: **3 years**
Tests recommended: **Contact Disabled Student Services**

Types of Disabilities Served
- Speech/Lang
- Study skills
- Written express
- Organizational
- Perceptual
- Reading
- Spelling
- Math
- Fine Motor
- ADD with LD
- ADD without LD
- ADHD with LD
- ADHD without LD

High School Course Requirements:
English: **4** Math: **3** Science: **1** Foreign Language: **2**

Learning Disability Program
Program: Reinforces course work: **Yes**
Students mainstreamed **100** % of the day
Services available for all students: **Yes**
Counseling: Individual: **Yes**

Diagnostic Testing

ADD	Personality	Perceptual skills	Spelling
ADHD	Organization	Fine motor skills	Reading
I.Q.	Handwriting	Spoken language	Study skills
Math	Social skills	Written language	

Tutoring:
Services rendered by:
- Graduates • Peers   Faculty   • LD staff   Teacher trainees

Tutorials

Grp.	Ind.	Tutorials	Grp.	Ind.	Tutorials
•		Math skills			Word processing
	•	Study skills		•	Time management
		Language arts		•	Learning strategies
	•	Written express		•	Organizational skills

Academic Accommodations

Curriculum	Study Aids	Exams
• Priority registration	• Typist	• Oral
Math waiver	• Reader	Untimed
• Foreign lang. waiver	• Notetaker	• Take home
• Course substitution	• Proof reader	• With proctor
In Class	• Text on tape	• On computer
• Calculators	Early syllabus	• Extended time
• Tape recorder	• Taped handouts	• On tape
• Word processor		• Modified
Priority seating		• Separate room

Graduation Requirements:
Course credits: **180** GPA: **2.0**

Program Strengths
Our program is completely mainstreamed and is especially appropriate for students who are knowledgeable about their needs for service. All services are tailored to the needs of the individual student. There are no separate classes for students with Learning Disabilities.

General Information:
University of California: Riverside is a 4 year public university. Suburban campus of 1,200 acres is 60 miles from Los Angeles. Accessible by train, air, or bus. Ski areas are 1 hour from campus. Beaches are 1 mile from campus. 3% of students are foreign. 3 residential halls on campus. Housing is guaranteed.15 % of students join fraternities/sororities.

Accreditation:WACS

SAT/ACT Scores:
Scores for incoming freshmen:**Verbal:**67%below 500. 24%between 500 and 599. 8%between 600 and 699. 1%above 700. **Math:**30% below 500. 40% between 500 and 599. 25% between 600 and 699. 5%above 700.

Class Rank:
About 100% of the present freshmen class were in the upper 20% of their high school class.

Expenses:
Tuition: In-state: Full year: $2,900.00. Part-time: Per credit:0. Tuition: Out-of-state: Full year: $10,600.00. Room and board: $5,360.00

Majors
- AREA STUDIES Ethnic Studies, Latin American, Women's Studies
- BUSINESS Business Administration, Business Economics, Economics, Management • COMMUNICATIONS Creative Writing, English, Linguistic, Literature • COMPUTER SCIENCE Computer Science • EDUCATION Curriculum, Elementary, Middle School, Special • ENGINEERING Chemical, Electrical, Environmental • HEALTH SCIENCES Developmental Psychology, Environmental • HUMANITIES Classics, Humanities, Liberal Arts, Philosophy, Religion • LANGUAGES French, German, Russian, Spanish • PREPROFESSIONAL Medicine • SCIENCES Biochemistry, Biology, Biomedical, Botany, Chemistry, Earth, Geography, Geology, Geophysics, Mathematics, Physical Science, Physics, Soil, Statistics • SOCIAL SCIENCES Anthropology, Geography, Government/Political, History, Psychology, Social Sciences, Sociology • VISUAL AND PERFORMING ARTS Art, Dance, Dramatic Arts, Music, Studio Art, Theater

Sports/Activities
- SPORTS RELATED Cheerleading, Pep Band, Team Managers
- SPORTS-INTERCOLLEGIATE Baseball (M), Basketball, Cross Country, Karate, Softball (F), Swimming, Tennis, Volleyball (F), Water Polo (M)
- SPORTS-INTRAMURAL Basketball, Bowling, Golf, Racquetball, Rugby, Soccer, Softball, Volleyball (F), Water Polo • STUDENT LIFE ACTIVITIES Academic Clubs, Choral, Community Service, Concert Band, Dance, Drama Groups, Ethnic & Cultural Groups, Fraternities, Jazz Band, Magazine, Music Ensembles, Music Groups, Musical Theater, Newspaper, Political Groups, Radio, Religious Organization, Sororities, Student Government, Yearbook

Highly Selective

University of California: San Diego

Student Center
La Jolla, California 92093
(619) 534-4831

School Enrollment: **14,000** Male: **7,596** Female: **6,728**
LD Enrollment: **50** Male: **35** Female: **15**

Admissions Contact: **Ron Bowker, Director of Admissions**
LD Contact: **Roberta Gimblett, Dir., Disabled Student Services**
Name of Program: **Disabled Student Services**
Address: **9500 Gilman Drive 0019**
Telephone:**(619) 534-4382**

Admissions

Application Information:
LD Students Applying: **150** Accepted: **28** Enrolled:**28**
Application deadline: **November**
Applicant must apply **10** months in advance
Rolling Admissions: **Yes**

Secondary School Information
Most Important Criteria For Admissions (1-strongest)

SAT/ACT	Application	School transcript
Class rank	Course selection	Personal statement
Interview	Extra activities	Psychoeducational
G.P.A.	Open admission	Recommendations

Test Requirements:
Diagnostic testing waived: **Yes**
Untimed SAT: **Yes** Untimed ACT: **Yes** Untimed ACH: **Yes** Achievement tests required:**3**
WAIS-R required: **Yes**
Documentation of LD required: **Yes**
Currency of diagnostic testing: **Within 3 years**
Tests recommended: **WAIS-R and Woodcock-Johnson Psycho-Educational Battery-revised**

Types of Disabilities Served
- Speech/Lang
- Study skills
- Written express
- Organizational
- Perceptual
- Reading
- Spelling
- Math
- Fine Motor
- ADD with LD
- ADD without LD
- ADHD with LD
- ADHD without LD

Learning Disability Program
Students mainstreamed **99** % of the day
Recommended credits per semester: **12**
Services available for all students: **Yes**
Counseling: Individual: **Yes** Group Counseling: **Yes** Vocational Counseling: **Yes**
Support groups are available:**Peer Mentor Program (for new students), Disabled Student Union (student org.)**

Faculty:
Faculty: **9** Including Director: **Yes** Full time: **5** Part time: **4** M.A.: **1**
Faculty advocate: **Yes** Meets with instructor: **As needed**

Diagnostic Testing

ADD	Personality	Perceptual skills	Spelling
ADHD	Organization	Fine motor skills	Reading
I.Q.	Handwriting	Spoken language	Study skills
Math	Social skills	Written language	

Tutoring:
Average size of group tutorials: **5-10**
Services rendered by:
- •Graduates
- •Peers
- Faculty
- LD staff
- Teacher trainees

Tutorials

Grp.	Ind.	Tutorials	Grp.	Ind.	Tutorials
•		Math skills			Word processing
•		Study skills	•		Time management
	•	Language arts	•		Learning strategies
•		Written express	•		Organizational skills

Academic Accommodations

Curriculum	Study Aids	Exams
• Priority registration	• Typist	• Oral
Math waiver	• Reader	Untimed
Foreign lang. waiver	• Notetaker	• Take home
Course substitution	Proof reader	• With proctor
In Class	• Text on tape	• On computer
• Calculators	• Early syllabus	• Extended time
• Tape recorder	Taped handouts	On tape
Word processor		Modified
• Priority seating		• Separate room

General Information:
University of California: San Diego is a 4 year public university. Suburban campus of 1,200 acres is Accessible by air, bus, or train. Ski areas are 150 miles from campus. Beaches are 1 mile from campus. 1% of students are foreign. Housing is guaranteed.Guaranteed through 2nd year. 10 % of students join fraternities/sororities.

Accreditation:

Expenses:
Tuition: In-state: Full year: $3,036.00 per year. Tuition: Out-of-state: Full year: $11,000.00 per year. Room and board: $5,700.00

Majors
• AREA STUDIES African, Asian, European, Jewish/Judaism, Latin American • BUSINESS Economics • COMMUNICATIONS Communication, Linguistics, Literature • COMPUTER SCIENCE Computer Science • EDUCATION Elementary, English As A Second Language • ENGINEERING Aerospace, Bioengineering, Chemical, Computer, Electrical, Engineering Science, Mathematical, Mechanical, Ocean, Physics, Systems Analysis • HEALTH SCIENCES Pharmacology • HUMANITIES Humanities, Philosophy • LANGUAGES Chinese, Italian • MATHEMATICS Applied, Computer, Statistical • PRE PROFESSIONAL Medicine, Pharmacy • RELIGIOUS STUDIES Judaism & Jewish Studies, Religion & Theology • SCIENCES Anthropology, Biochemistry, Biology, Cell Biology, Chemistry, Cognitive, Computer Science, Earth, General, Microbiology, Molecular Biolog, Neuroscience, Physics, Physiology • SOCIAL SCIENCES Anthropology, History, International Studies, Political Science, Psychology, Sociology • VISUAL AND PERFORMING ARTS Art History, Music

Sports/Activities
• SPORTS RELATED Cheerleading, Pep Band, Skiing - Snow • SPORTS-INTERCOLLEGIATE Basketball, Basketball (F), Basketball (M), Crew, Crew (F), Crew (M), Cross Country, Cross Country (F), Cross Country (M), Diving, Diving (F), Diving (M), Fencing, Fencing (F), Fencing (M), Golf, Golf (F), Golf (M), Soccer, Soccer (F), Soccer (M), Softball, Softball (F), Softball (M), Swimming, Swimming (F), Swimming (M), Tennis, Tennis

(F), Tennis (M), Track and Field, Track and Field (F), Track and Field (M), Volleyball, Volleyball (F), Volleyball (M), Water Polo, Water Polo (F), Water Polo (M) • SPORTS-INTRAMURAL Badminton, Basketball, Basketball (F), Basketball (M), Bowling, Soccer, Softball, Softball (F), Softball (M), Volleyball, Volleyball (F), Volleyball (M), Water Polo • STUDENT LIFE ACTIVITIES Academic Clubs, Choral, Community Service, Dance, Drama Groups, Ethnic & Cultural Groups, Film, Fraternities, Magazine, Music Groups, Newspaper, Political Groups, Radio/TV station, Religious Organization, Sororities, Student Government, Yearbook

---

Very Selective

California Services

University of California: Santa Barbara
Santa Barbara, California 93106
(805) 961-2485

School Enrollment: **16,500** Male: **8,250** Female: **8,250**
LD Enrollment: **114** Male: **56** Female: **58**

Admissions Contact: **Admissions Office Information**
LD Contact: **Michele Bass, LD Specialist**
Name of Program: **Disabled Students Program**
Telephone:**(805) 893-8897**

Admissions

Application Information:
Enrolled:**114**
Application deadline: **November 30th for following Fall**

Secondary School Information
Most Important Criteria For Admissions (1-strongest)

2 SAT/ACT	**3** Application	**7**	School transcript
6 Class rank	**5** Course selection	**4**	Personal statement
11 Interview	**8** Extra activities	**9**	Psychoeducational
1 G.P.A.	Open admission	**10**	Recommendations

Test Requirements:
Diagnostic testing waived: **Yes**
Untimed SAT: **Yes**
WAIS-R required: **Yes**
Documentation of LD required: **Yes**
Currency of diagnostic testing: **3 years**
Tests recommended: **Documentation of learning disability**

Types of Disabilities Served
- Speech/Lang
- Study skills
- Written express
- Organizational
- Perceptual
- Reading
- Spelling
- Math
- Fine Motor
- ADD with LD
- ADD without LD
- ADHD with LD
- ADHD without LD

Admissions Process

Committee review of all students indicating any type of disability.

High School Course Requirements:
English: **4** Math: **3** Science: **2** Foreign Language: **2**

Learning Disability Program
Program: Reinforces course work: **Yes**
Students mainstreamed **100** % of the day
Services only for LD students: **Yes**

Faculty:
Faculty: **4** Full time: **4** Ph.D.: **1**
Faculty advocate: **Yes** Meets with instructor: **As needed**

Diagnostic Testing

ADD	Personality	Perceptual skills	Spelling
ADHD	Organization	Fine motor skills	Reading
I.Q.	Handwriting	Spoken language	Study skills
Math	Social skills	Written language	

Tutoring:
Average size of group tutorials:
Services rendered by:
•Graduates   Peers   Faculty   LD staff   Teacher trainees

Tutorials

Grp.	Ind.	Tutorials	Grp.	Ind.	Tutorials
•		Math skills			Word processing
•		Study skills	•		Time management
		Language arts	•		Learning strategies
•		Written express	•		Organizational skills

Academic Accommodations

Curriculum	Study Aids	Exams
• Priority registration	Typist	• Oral
Math waiver	• Reader	Untimed
Foreign lang. waiver	• Notetaker	• Take home
• Course substitution	• Proof reader	• With proctor
In Class	• Text on tape	On computer
• Calculators	Early syllabus	• Extended time
• Tape recorder	Taped handouts	On tape
• Word processor		Modified
Priority seating		• Separate room

Program Strengths
Accommodations and services are determined by the nature of the learning disability and are provided upon the recommendation of a learning disabilities specialist. Each academic accommodation should be determined on an individual basis and made available to the extent it does not compromise the academic integrity of the student's program. Documentation should be dated no more than 3 years prior to the request for services and include test results for intelligence, vocabulary, reading rate, reading comprehension, memory, and processing skills.

General Information:
University of California: Santa Barbara is a 4 year private university. Suburban campus 10 miles from Santa Barbara. Accessible by bus. 7 residential halls on campus. Housing is not guaranteed.

Accreditation: National

Expenses:
Tuition: In-state: Full year: $2,418. Part-time: Per credit:0. Tuition: Out-of-state: Full year: $10,116.00. Room and board: $4,961.00

Majors
• AREA STUDIES African, Asian, Black/Afro-American, Hispanic American, International Studies, Latin American • BUSINESS Business Economics • COMMUNICATIONS Communication, English, Linguistic, Speech • COMPUTER SCIENCE Computer Science, Engineering, Programming • EDUCATION Early Childhood, Elementary, Middle School, Secondary, Speech/Language • ENGINEERING Chemical, Electrical, Mechanical, Nuclear • HEALTH SCIENCES Speech/Audiology and Speech • HUMANITIES Classics, Comparative Literature, Philosophy, Religion • LANGUAGES Chinese, French, German, Italian, Japanese, Latin, Russian, Spanish • PREPROFESSIONAL Dentistry, Engineering, Human and

Animal Pharmacology, Law, Medicine, Natural Resources, Social Work • SCIENCES Archeology, Biochemistry, Biology, Botany, Cell Biology, Chemistry, Ecology, Environmental, Geography, Geology, Macrobiology, Marine Biology, Mathematics, Microbiology, Oceanography, Physical Science, Physics, Statistics, Zoology • SOCIAL SCIENCES Anthropology, Criminal Justice, History, Political Science, Psychology, Social Sciences, Sociology • VISUAL AND PERFORMING ARTS Art History and Appreciation, Dance, Dramatic Arts, Music, Studio Art

Sports/Activities

• SPORTS RELATED Cheerleading, Chess • SPORTS-INTERCOLLEGIATE Baseball, Basketball, Crew (M), Cross Country, Diving, Football (M), Golf (M), Gymnastics, Soccer, Softball, Swimming, Tennis, Track and Field, Volleyball, Water Polo • SPORTS-INTRAMURAL Badminton, Basketball, Bowling, Fencing, Fencing, Field Hockey, Lacrosse, Rugby, Sailing, Skiing - Snow, Soccer (M), Tennis, Volleyball, Water Polo • STUDENT LIFE ACTIVITIES Choral, Concert Band, Dance, Debate, Drama Groups, Ethnic & Cultural Groups, Film, Fraternities, Jazz Band, Magazine, Music Ensembles, Music Groups, Musical Theater, Newspaper

Very Selective	California
	Services

University of California: Santa Cruz

Cook House
Santa Cruz, California 95064
(408) 459-4008

School Enrollment: **8,883** Male: **3,996** Female: **4,887**
LD Enrollment: **75**

Admissions Contact: **Michael McCawley, Assocaite Director**
LD Contact: **Lea Van Meter, Director**
Name of Program: **Disabled Student Services**
Telephone:**(408) 459-2829**

Admissions

Application Information:
Application deadline: **November 30th**
Notified when: **Feb. 1st-Mar. 15th**

Secondary School Information
Most Important Criteria For Admissions (1-strongest)

1 SAT/ACT	**1** Application	**1** School transcript
Class rank	**1** Course selection	**1** Personal statement
Interview	**2** Extra activities	Psychoeducational
1 G.P.A.	Open admission	**2** Recommendations

Test Requirements:
Untimed SAT: **Yes** Untimed ACT: **Yes** Untimed ACH: **Yes**
Documentation of LD required: **Yes**

Types of Disabilities Served
• Speech/Lang	• Reading	• ADD with LD
• Study skills	• Spelling	• ADD without LD
• Written express	• Math	• ADHD with LD
• Organizational	• Fine Motor	• ADHD without LD
• Perceptual		

Learning Disability Program
Counseling: Individual: **Yes** Group Counseling: **Yes**

Faculty:
Faculty: **5** Full time: **4** Part time: **1**

Diagnostic Testing
ADD	Personality	Perceptual skills	Spelling
ADHD	Organization	Fine motor skills	Reading
I.Q.	Handwriting	Spoken language	Study skills
Math	Social skills	Written language	

Tutoring:
Services rendered by:
Graduates •Peers Faculty LD staff Teacher trainees

Tutorials
Grp.	Ind.	Tutorials	Grp.	Ind.	Tutorials
		Math skills			Word processing
		Study skills			Time management
		Language arts			Learning strategies
		Written express			Organizational skills

Academic Accommodations
Curriculum	Study Aids	Exams
Priority registration	• Typist	Oral
• Math waiver	• Reader	Untimed
• Foreign lang. waiver	• Notetaker	• Take home
• Course substitution	• Proof reader	With proctor
In Class	• Text on tape	On computer
• Calculators	Early syllabus	• Extended time
• Tape recorder	Taped handouts	On tape
Word processor		Modified
Priority seating		Separate room

Program Strengths
We provide (locate and fund) academic support services to approximately 75 students with learning disabilities. Our service is personal and relatively easy to obtain and utilize. Our campus is devoted to undergraduate education, historically with fewer than 10,000 students. Learning disabled students are responsible for arranging their own tutoring in subject area with peers who have participated in a tutoring orientation program.

General Information:
University of California: Santa Cruz is a 4 year public university. Urban campus 35 miles from San Jose. Accessible by bus. Ski areas are 4 hours from campus. Beaches are 2 minutes from campus. 1% of students are foreign. 8 residential halls on campus. Housing is guaranteed. Guaranteed through 2nd year.

Accreditation:WACS

Expenses:
Tuition: In-state: Full year: $1,732.00. Tuition: Out-of-state: Full year: $5,799.00. Room and board: $5,160.00

Majors
• AREA STUDIES American, Ethics, Latin American, Women's Studies • BUSINESS Economics • COMMUNICATIONS Linguistic, Literature • COMPUTER SCIENCE Computer Science, Computer Technology • ENGINEERING Computer • HUMANITIES Philosophy • PREPROFESSIONAL Law • SCIENCES Biochemistry, Biology, Chemistry, Earth, Geology, Marine Biology, Mathematics, Molecular Biology, Physics • SOCIAL SCIENCES Anthropology, History, Political Science, Psychology, Sociology • VISUAL AND PERFORMING ARTS Art, Art History, Dance, Music, Music Theatre

Sports
• SPORTS-INTERCOLLEGIATE Basketball, Cross Country, Fencing,

California

Sailing, Swimming, Tennis, Volleyball • SPORTS-INTRAMURAL Baseball, Basketball, Cross Country, Fencing, Gymnastics, Hand Ball, Racquetball, Rugby, Sailing, Soccer, Softball, Swimming, Tennis, Volleyball, Water Polo • STUDENT LIFE ACTIVITIES Choral, Dance, Drama Groups, Film, Jazz Band, Music Ensembles, Music Groups, Musical Theater, Newspaper, Opera, Radio/TV station, Student Government, Symphony Orchestra

---

Very Selective	California Services

University of Redlands
P.O. Box 3080
Redlands, California 92373-0999
(714) 793-2121

School Enrollment: **1,300** Male: **650** Female: **650**
LD Enrollment: **10** Male: **5** Female: **5**

Admissions Contact: **Paul Driscoll, Dean of Admission**
LD Contact: **Judy Strack, Director, Academic Support Services**
Name of Program: **Academic Support Services**
Telephone:**Ext. 2790**

Admissions

Application Information:
Application deadline: **Feb/Mar/April 1st**
Rolling Admissions: **Yes**

Secondary School Information
Most Important Criteria For Admissions (1-strongest)

2 SAT/ACT	Application	School transcript
Class rank	**1** Course selection	Personal statement
4 Interview	Extra activities	Psychoeducational
1 G.P.A.	Open admission	**3** Recommendations

Test Requirements:
Untimed SAT: **Yes** Untimed ACT: **Yes** Untimed ACH: **Yes**

Types of Disabilities Served

Speech/Lang	• Reading	ADD with LD
• Study skills	• Spelling	ADD without LD
• Written express	• Math	ADHD with LD
• Organizational	Fine Motor	ADHD without LD
Perceptual		

Learning Disability Program

Services available for all students: **Yes**
Counseling: Individual: **Yes**

Faculty:
Faculty: **1** Full time: **1** M.A.: **1**
Faculty advocate: **Yes** Meets with instructor: **As needed**

Diagnostic Testing

ADD	Personality	Perceptual skills	Spelling
ADHD	Organization	Fine motor skills	Reading
I.Q.	Handwriting	Spoken language	Study skills
Math	Social skills	Written language	

Tutoring:
Average size of group tutorials: **Individual**
Services rendered by:

Graduates	•Peers	Faculty	LD staff	Teacher trainees

Tutorials

Grp.	Ind.	Tutorials	Grp.	Ind.	Tutorials
•	•	Math skills		•	Word processing
•	•	Study skills	•	•	Time management
	•	Language arts		•	Learning strategies
	•	Written express		•	Organizational skills

Academic Accommodations

Curriculum	Study Aids	Exams
Priority registration	Typist	• Oral
Math waiver	• Reader	• Untimed
Foreign lang. waiver	Notetaker	Take home
Course substitution	• Proof reader	With proctor
In Class	• Text on tape	On computer
Calculators	Early syllabus	• Extended time
• Tape recorder	Taped handouts	On tape
Word processor		Modified
Priority seating		Separate room

Program Strengths
Learning disabilities are handled on an individual basis. If a student seeks help, arrangements may be made with professors for untimed or special testing, tutors may be assigned, or other special needs may be met on an individual basis.

General Information:
University of Redlands is a 4 year independent university. Suburban campus of 130 acres is 60 miles from Los Angeles. Accessible by bus. Ski areas are 45 miles from campus. Beaches are 60 miles from campus. 3% of students are foreign. 15 residential halls on campus. Housing is guaranteed.95 % of students remain on campus for the weekends. 17 % of students join fraternities/sororities.

Accreditation: WACS

Expenses:
Tuition: In-state: Full year: $13,930.00. Part-time: Per credit:$435.00.
Room and board: $5,370.00

Majors
• AREA STUDIES Asian, Ethics, Women's Studies • BUSINESS Accounting, Business Administration, Business Management, Economics • COMMUNICATIONS Creative Writing, English • COMPUTER SCIENCE Computer Science, Data Processing • EDUCATION Art, Elementary, English, Foreign Language, Mathematics, Middle School, Music, Science, Secondary • ENGINEERING Electrical, Engineering Science, Mechanical • HEALTH SCIENCES Communication Disorders, Speech/Audiology and Speech • HUMANITIES English/Writing/Literature, Humanities, Liberal Arts, Philosophy, Religion • LANGUAGES French, German, Spanish • SCIENCES Biology, Chemistry, Mathematics, Physics • SOCIAL SCIENCES Anthropology, Government/Political, History, International Relations, Sociology • VISUAL AND PERFORMING ARTS Art, Art History, Fine Arts, Music, Music History, Music Theory and Composition

Sports/Activities
• SPORTS RELATED Pep Band, Team Managers • SPORTS-INTERCOLLEGIATE Baseball (M), Basketball, Cross Country, Football (M), Golf, Soccer, Softball (F), Swimming, Tennis, Track and Field, Volleyball, Water Polo, Windsurfing • SPORTS-INTRAMURAL Archery, Badminton, Bowling, Cycling, Gymnastics, Karate, Racquetball, Softball, Swimming, Tennis, Volleyball • STUDENT LIFE ACTIVITIES Choral, Community Service, Debate, Drama Groups, Ethnic & Cultural Groups, Fraternities, Jazz Band, Music Groups, Newspaper, Orchestra, Radio/TV station, Religious Organization, Sororities, Student Government

---

Less Selective　　　　　　　**California Program**

Ventura College
4667 Telegraph Road
Ventura, California 93003
(805) 642-3211

School Enrollment: **12,000** Male: **4,000** Female: **8,000**
LD Enrollment: **460**

Admissions Contact: **Dr. Jeffrey Barsch, Director of Admissions**
LD Contact: **Arlene Bowers, Coordinator**
Name of Program: **Learning Skills**
Telephone:**(805) 654-6300**

Admissions

Application Information:
LD Students Applying: **350** Accepted: **300** Enrolled:**300**
Application deadline: **Every 6 weeks**
Applicant must apply **1.5** months in advance
Rolling Admissions: **Yes**

Secondary School Information
Most Important Criteria For Admissions (1-strongest)

SAT/ACT	Application	School transcript
Class rank	Course selection	Personal statement
1 Interview	Extra activities	**1** Psychoeducational
G.P.A.	**1** Open admission	Recommendations

Test Requirements:
Diagnostic testing waived: **Yes**
WAIS-R required: **Yes** Range accepted: **80+**
Documentation of LD required: **Yes**
Currency of diagnostic testing: **1 year**
Tests recommended: **Woodcock -Johnson (both sections)**

Types of Disabilities Served
- Speech/Lang
- Study skills
- Written express
- Organizational
- Perceptual
- Reading
- Spelling
- Math
- Fine Motor
- ADD with LD
- ADD without LD
- ADHD with LD
- ADHD without LD

Learning Disability Program
Program: Remedial: **Yes**
Program: Reinforces course work: **Yes**
Students mainstreamed **100 %** of the day
Recommended credits per semester: **12**
Services available for all students: **Yes**
Counseling: Individual: **Yes** Group Counseling: **Yes**
Support groups are available:**Personal Development Class**

Faculty:
Faculty: **6** Including Director: **Yes** Full time: **4** Part time: **2**
Faculty advocate: **Yes** Meets with instructor: **As needed**

Diagnostic Testing
- ADD
- ADHD
- I.Q.
- Math
- Personality
- Organization
- Handwriting
- Social skills
- Perceptual skills
- Fine motor skills
- Spoken language
- Written language
- Spelling
- Reading
- Study skills

Tutoring:
Average size of group tutorials:
Services rendered by:
　Graduates　•Peers　•Faculty　•LD staff　Teacher trainees

Tutorials

Grp.	Ind.	Tutorials	Grp.	Ind.	Tutorials
•	•	Math skills	•	•	Word processing
•	•	Study skills	•	•	Time management
•	•	Language arts	•	•	Learning strategies
•	•	Written express	•	•	Organizational skills

Academic Accommodations

Curriculum	Study Aids	Exams
Priority registration	• Typist	• Oral
Math waiver	Reader	Untimed
• Foreign lang. waiver	• Notetaker	• Take home
• Course substitution	• Proof reader	• With proctor
In Class	• Text on tape	On computer
• Calculators	Early syllabus	• Extended time
• Tape recorder	Taped handouts	On tape
• Word processor		• Modified
Priority seating		Separate room

Graduation Requirements:
Course credits: **60** GPA: **2.0** Years to complete degree: **3** Math waiver: **Yes**
Language waiver: **Yes**

Program Strengths
We specialize in serving dyslexic students. Both Dr. Ray Barsch and Dr. Jeffrey Barsch teach at Ventura College. Dr. Ray Barsch is one of the founders of the LD field and is most noted for his perceptual motor training. Up to 12 hours each week are offered to our students in the L.S. program, but each student may request extra time in the tutoring center.

General Information:
Ventura College is a 2 year public college. Suburban campus 50 miles from Los Angeles. Accessible by air, train or bus. Ski areas are 75 miles from campus. Beaches are 2 miles from campus. Housing is not guaranteed.

Accreditation: Regional

Expenses:
Tuition: In-state: Full year: $60.00 per 12 credits. Part-time: Per credit:$110.00.

Majors
• AREA STUDIES American, Mexican/American • BUSINESS Banking, Economics, Finance, Marketing, Real Estate • COMMUNICATIONS English, Journalism, Speech • COMPUTER SCIENCE Computer Science, Data Processing • CRAFTS AND DESIGN Graphic Design • EDUCATION Child Development • ENGINEERING Electrical, Engineering Science • ENVIRONMENTAL CONTROL Water and Wastewater Technolog • HEALTH SCIENCES Nursing • HUMANITIES Liberal Arts, Philosophy • LANGUAGES French, German, Spanish • PREPROFESSIONAL Dentistry, Law, Medicine, Pharmacy, Veterinarian • SCIENCES Botany, Geography, Geology, Horticultural, Mathematics, Physical Science, Physics, Soil • SOCIAL SCIENCES History, Human Service, Law Enforcement, Political Science, Psychology, Public Relations • VISUAL AND PERFORMING ARTS Dance, Fine Arts, Music • VOCATIONAL Automobile Technology, Building Construction, Drafting, Electronics Technology, Fashion Design, Fire Science, Food Service, Home Economics, Industrial Arts, Industrial Equipment Maintenan, Interior Design, Legal Secretary, Medical Laboratory Technology, Park/Recreation, Plumbing, Secretarial, Welding

Sports/Activities

SPORTS-INTERCOLLEGIATE Baseball, Basketball, Football, Golf, Softball, Swimming, Tennis, Track and Field, Volleyball, Water Polo • STUDENT LIFE ACTIVITIES Debate, Music Groups, Newspaper, Religious Organization, Student Government

Less Selective   **California Program**

Victor Valley College

18422 Bear Valley Road
Victorville, California 92392
(619) 245-4271

School Enrollment: **10,000** Male: **5,000** Female: **5,000**
LD Enrollment: **135** Male: **36** Female: **99**

Admissions Contact: **Laura White, Director of Admissions**
LD Contact: **Susan Tillman, LD Counselor**
Name of Program: **LD Center**
Telephone:**(619) 245-4271 - Ext. 433**

Admissions

Application Information:
Enrolled:**135**
Separate application:**Yes**
Application deadline: **Open**
Applicant must apply **0-4** months in advance

Secondary School Information
Most Important Criteria For Admissions (1-strongest)

SAT/ACT	Application	**2**	School transcript
Class rank	Course selection		Personal statement
Interview	Extra activities		Psychoeducational
G.P.A.	**1**	Open admission	Recommendations

Test Requirements:
Standardized tests waived: **Yes**
Diagnostic testing waived: **Yes**
WAIS-R required: **Yes**
Currency of diagnostic testing: **3 years**
Tests recommended: **Aptitude, achievement (offered at VVC)**

Types of Disabilities Served
- Speech/Lang
- Study skills
- Written express
- Organizational
- Perceptual
- Reading
- Spelling
- Math
- Fine Motor
- ADD with LD
- ADD without LD
- ADHD with LD
- ADHD without LD

Learning Disability Program

Program: Reinforces course work: **Yes**
Students mainstreamed **100** % of the day
Recommended credits per semester: **9-12**
Time required or recommended in learning center: **Varies**
Services only for LD students: **Yes**
Counseling: Individual: **Yes**

Faculty:
Faculty: **2** Full time: **2** Part time: **1** M.A.: **1** Ph.D.: **1**
Faculty advocate: **Yes** Meets with instructor: **As needed**

Diagnostic Testing

ADD	Personality	• Perceptual skills	• Spelling
ADHD	Organization	Fine motor skills	• Reading
• I.Q.	Handwriting	Spoken language	Study skills
• Math	Social skills	Written language	

Tutoring:
Services rendered by:
Graduates   Peers   •Faculty   •LD staff   Teacher trainees

Tutorials

Grp.	Ind.	Tutorials	Grp.	Ind.	Tutorials
		Math skills			Word processing
•		Study skills	•		Time management
		Language arts	•		Learning strategies
•		Written express	•		Organizational skills

Academic Accommodations

Curriculum	Study Aids	Exams
Priority registration	Typist	• Oral
Math waiver	Reader	Untimed
Foreign lang. waiver	Notetaker	Take home
Course substitution	Proof reader	With proctor
In Class	• Text on tape	On computer
Calculators	Early syllabus	• Extended time
• Tape recorder	Taped handouts	On tape
• Word processor		Modified
Priority seating		Separate room

Program Strengths

Victor Valley College's LD Program is a support-based program with very few "special" classes. We offer three classes to students defined as LD through California Community College Eligibility criteria: one is a support class emphasizing communication, self-awareness and self-advocacy, another uses intervention for remediation of basic skills, and one teaches strategies/techniques for learning.

General Information:

Victor Valley College is a 2 year public college. Rural campus 50 miles from San Bernardino. Ski areas are 30 miles from campus. Beaches are 100 miles from campus. Housing is not guaranteed.

Accreditation: Regional

Expenses:
Tuition: In-state: Full year: $6.00 - maximum $60.00 per semester. Part-time: Per credit:0. Tuition: Out-of-state: Full year: $97.00 per unit plus enrollment.

Majors

• BUSINESS Accounting, Banking, Business Administration, Business Management, Economics, Finance, Hotel and Restaurant Managemen, Management, Marketing, Real Estate • COMMUNICATIONS English, Journalism, Photography • COMPUTER SCIENCE Computer Science, Data Processing, Programming • EDUCATION Agricultural, Early Childhood, Music, Physical, Speech/Language, Teacher's Aid • HUMANITIES Humanities, Philosophy, Religion • LANGUAGES French, German, Spanish • PREPROFESSIONAL Agriculture • SCIENCES Astronomy, Biology, Botany, Chemistry, Ecology, Geography, Geology, Mathematics, Oceanography, Physical Science, Physics, Physiology • SOCIAL SCIENCES Anthropology, Criminal Justice, Geography, Government/Political, History, Law Enforcement, Social Sciences, Sociology • VISUAL AND PERFORMING ARTS Art, Art History, Music, Theater • VOCATIONAL Automobile Technology, Fire Science, Food Service, Respiratory Therapy Technology, Secretarial

Sports/Activities

- SPORTS-INTERCOLLEGIATE Basketball (M), Volleyball (F)
- SPORTS-INTRAMURAL Basketball (M), Bowling, Golf (M), Skiing - Snow, Soccer (M), Softball (M), Swimming, Table Tennis, Tennis, Volleyball • STUDENT LIFE ACTIVITIES Choral, Concert Band, Dance, Debate, Ethnic & Cultural Groups, Music Ensembles, Musical Theater, Newspaper, Religious Organization, Student Government, Symphony Orchestra

---

Less Selective　　　　　　**California Program**

West Hills College

300 Cherry Lane
Coalinga, California 93210
(209) 935-0801

School Enrollment: **2,452** Male: **1,067** Female: **1,385**
LD Enrollment: **63**

Admissions Contact: **Darlene Geogatos, Registrar**
LD Contact: **Diane L. Allen, Director of DSPS**
Name of Program: **Learning Skills Program**

Admissions

Application Information:
LD Students Applying: **63** Accepted: **63** Enrolled:**63**
Separate application:**Yes**
Application deadline: **None**
Rolling Admissions: **Yes**

Secondary School Information
Most Important Criteria For Admissions (1-strongest)

	SAT/ACT	Application		School transcript
	Class rank	Course selection		Personal statement
2	Interview	Extra activities	1	Psychoeducational
	G.P.A.	1 Open admission	3	Recommendations

Test Requirements:
Standardized tests waived: **Yes**
Diagnostic testing waived: **Yes**
Untimed SAT: **Yes** Untimed ACT: **Yes** Achievement tests required:**1**
Range accepted: **>81**
Documentation of LD required: **Yes**
Currency of diagnostic testing: **3 years**
Tests recommended: **WAIS-R, or Woodcock Johnson Psycho-Educational battery**

Types of Disabilities Served
- Speech/Lang
- Study skills
- Written express
- Organizational
- Perceptual
- Reading
- Spelling
- Math
- Fine Motor
- ADD with LD
- ADD without LD
- ADHD with LD
- ADHD without LD

Learning Disability Program

Program: Remedial: **Yes**
Program: Reinforces course work: **Yes**
Students mainstreamed **80+** % of the day
Counseling: Individual: **Yes** Vocational Counseling: **Yes**
Support groups are available:**On demand**

Faculty:
Faculty: **5** Including Director: **Yes** Full time: **2** Part time: **3** M.A.: **1**
Faculty advocate: **Yes** Meets with instructor: **As needed**

Diagnostic Testing
ADD	• Personality	• Perceptual skills	• Spelling
ADHD	Organization	Fine motor skills	• Reading
I.Q.	Handwriting	Spoken language	• Study skills
• Math	Social skills	• Written language	

Tutoring:
Services rendered by:
Graduates　Peers　•Faculty　•LD staff　Teacher trainees

Tutorials
Grp.	Ind.	Tutorials	Grp.	Ind.	Tutorials
•		Math skills	•		Word processing
•		Study skills	•		Time management
		Language arts		•	Learning strategies
		Written express			Organizational skills

Academic Accommodations

Curriculum	Study Aids	Exams
• Priority registration	• Typist	• Oral
• Math waiver	• Reader	Untimed
• Foreign lang. waiver	• Notetaker	Take home
Course substitution	• Proof reader	• With proctor
In Class	• Text on tape	• On computer
• Calculators	Early syllabus	• Extended time
• Tape recorder	Taped handouts	• On tape
• Word processor		• Modified
• Priority seating		• Separate room

Graduation Requirements:
Course credits: **60** GPA: **2.0** Math waiver: **Yes**

Program Strengths
We have a small LD Program that works closely with the students in the area of remediation and content area support. Although used for drills, computers are used mainly for word processing and spell checking. Because we are a small school and because we have a small program, we are able to work on a close personal level with our students. We are proud of their many successes.

General Information:
West Hills College is a 2 year public college. Rural campus 75 miles from Fresno. Accessible by bus. Ski areas are 2 hours from campus. Beaches are 1 hour from campus. Housing is not guaranteed.

Accreditation: Regional

Expenses:
Tuition: In-state: Full year: $120.00. Part-time: Per credit:$6.00. Part-time: Per course: $18.00. Part-time: Per credit:$82.00. Part-time: Per course:$94.00

Majors
• BUSINESS Accounting, Agricultural, Business Administration, Business Management, Economics, Management, Marketing, Marketing Research, Real Estate • COMMUNICATIONS Creative Writing, English, Journalism, Photography • COMPUTER SCIENCE Computer Science, Data Processing, Programming • EDUCATION Early Childhood, Industrial, Physical • ENGINEERING Engineering Science • HEALTH SCIENCES Medical Secretary • HUMANITIES Humanities, Liberal Arts, Philosophy, Religion • LANGUAGES French, Spanish • PREPROFESSIONAL Agriculture, Dentistry, Engineering, Medicine, Pharmacy • SCIENCES Agricultural, Biology, Botany, Chemistry, Geography, Geology, Mathematics, Organic

California

Chemistry, Physical Science, Physics, Soil • SOCIAL SCIENCES Criminal Justice, Criminology, Geography, Government/Political, History, Law Enforcement, Psychology, Social Sciences • VISUAL AND PERFORMING ARTS Art, Art, Music, Studio Art, Theater • VOCATIONAL Automobile Technology, Automotive Service, Business and Office, Diesel Power Technology, Secretarial, Welding, Word Processing

Sports/Activities

• SPORTS RELATED Cheerleading, Pep Band • SPORTS-INTERCOLLEGIATE Basketball (M), Softball (F), Volleyball • SPORTS-INTRAMURAL Badminton, Baseball, Fencing, Racquetball, Rodeo, Soccer, Swimming, Weight Lifting • STUDENT LIFE ACTIVITIES Choral, Dance, Drama Groups, Ethnic & Cultural Groups, Music Ensembles, Music Groups, Musical Theater, Newspaper, Religious Organization, Student Government

---

Less Selective **California Program**

West Valley College

14000 Fruitvale Avenue
Saratoga, California 95070
(408) 867-2200

School Enrollment: **13,000** Male: **6,000** Female: **7,000**
LD Enrollment: **125** Male: **62** Female: **63**

Admissions Contact: **Dr. Edward Myers, Dean of Student Services**
LD Contact: **R.J. Peck/Susan Bunch, LD Specialist**
Name of Program: **LEAP**
Telephone: **Ext. 2701**

Admissions

Application Information:
LD Students Applying: **100** Accepted: **80** Enrolled: **80**
Separate application: **Yes**
Application deadline: **Open**
Rolling Admissions: **Yes**

Secondary School Information
Most Important Criteria For Admissions (1-strongest)

SAT/ACT	Application	School transcript
Class rank	Course selection	Personal statement
Interview	Extra activities	Psychoeducational
G.P.A.	Open admission	Recommendations

Test Requirements:
Diagnostic testing waived: **Yes**
Documentation of LD required: **Yes**

Types of Disabilities Served
• Speech/Lang	• Reading	• ADD with LD
• Study skills	• Spelling	• ADD without LD
• Written express	• Math	• ADHD with LD
• Organizational	• Fine Motor	• ADHD without LD
• Perceptual		

High School Course Requirements:
Waivers to standard high school courses
Math: **Yes**

Learning Disability Program
Program: Remedial: **Yes**
Program: Reinforces course work: **Yes**
Counseling: Individual: **Yes** Group Counseling: **Yes**

Faculty:
Faculty: **3** Full time: **2** Part time: **2**
LD faculty with: BS/BA: **3** M.A.: **3**
Faculty advocate: **Yes** Meets with instructor: **student request**

Diagnostic Testing
• ADD	Personality	• Perceptual skills	• Spelling
ADHD	Organization	Fine motor skills	• Reading
I.Q.	Handwriting	Spoken language	Study skills
• Math	Social skills	• Written language	

Tutoring:
Average size of group tutorials: **3-5**
Services rendered by:
Graduates •Peers •Faculty •LD staff Teacher trainees

Tutorials
Grp.	Ind.	Tutorials	Grp.	Ind.	Tutorials
•	•	Math skills	•	•	Word processing
•	•	Study skills	•	•	Time management
•	•	Language arts	•	•	Learning strategies
•	•	Written express	•	•	Organizational skills

Academic Accommodations

Curriculum	Study Aids	Exams
Priority registration	Typist	• Oral
Math waiver	Reader	Untimed
Foreign lang. waiver	• Notetaker	Take home
Course substitution	• Proof reader	With proctor
In Class	• Text on tape	On computer
• Calculators	Early syllabus	• Extended time
• Tape recorder	Taped handouts	On tape
• Word processor		Modified
Priority seating		Separate room

Program Strengths

The LEAP program provides academic assistance to students with learning disabilities after they have completed a psychoeducational assessment. The learning disability specialist and students formulate an individual education plan (I.E.P.) designed to facilitate progress toward each student's academic and/or vocational goals.

General Information:

West Valley College is a 2 year public college. Suburban campus of 60 acres is 10 miles from San Jose. Ski areas are 4 hours from campus. Beaches are 30 miles from campus. Housing is not guaranteed.

Accreditation Regional

Expenses:
Tuition: In-state: Full year: $5.00 per credit maximum $50.00. Part-time: Per credit: $5.00. Tuition: Out-of-state: Full year: $98.00.

Majors

• AREA STUDIES Women's Studies • BUSINESS Accounting, Business Administration, Business Management, Management, Marketing, Real Estate • COMMUNICATIONS English, Speech • COMPUTER SCIENCE Computer Science, Programming • EDUCATION Child Development, Early Childhood, Music, Recreation and Youth Leadershi • ENGINEERING Electrical • HEALTH SCIENCES Medical Assistant • HUMANITIES English/Writing/Literature • LANGUAGES • PREPROFESSIONAL Architecture, Engineering • SCIENCES Chemistry, Geology, Mathematics,

Physics • SOCIAL SCIENCES Criminal Justice, History, Psychology, Social Sciences, Sociology • VISUAL AND PERFORMING ARTS Fine Arts, Music • VOCATIONAL Business and Office, Carpentry, Construction, Court Reporting, Drafting, Electronics Technology, Fashion Design, Industrial Design, Landscape Architecture, Park/Recreation, Secretarial, Word Processing

Sports/Activities

• SPORTS-INTERCOLLEGIATE Baseball (M), Basketball, Cross Country, Field Hockey (F), Football (M), Golf (M), Gymnastics, Soccer (M), Softball (F), Swimming, Tennis, Track and Field, Volleyball, Water Polo • SPORTS-INTRAMURAL Badminton, Basketball, Bowling, Swimming, Tennis, Volleyball • STUDENT LIFE ACTIVITIES Choral, Concert Band, Drama Groups, Ethnic & Cultural Groups, Jazz Band, Let's Do It Club, Magazine, Music Ensemble, Music Groups, Newspaper, Radio/TV station, Religious Organization, Student Government, Symphony Orchestra

Less Selective	Colorado Program

Arapahoe Community College

5900 So. Santa Fe Drive P.O. Box 9002
Littleton, Colorado 80160-9002
(303) 794-1550

School Enrollment: **7,415** Male: **2,967** Female: **4,448**
LD Enrollment: **120**

Admissions Contact: **Sharon Wink, Director of Admissions**
LD Contact: **Paula Pattschull, Ph.D., LD Specialist**
Name of Program: **Disability Services**
Telephone:**(303) 797-5655**

Admissions

Application Information:
LD Students Applying: **120** Accepted: **120** Enrolled:**120**

Secondary School Information
Most Important Criteria For Admissions (1-strongest)

SAT/ACT	Application	School transcript
Class rank	Course selection	Personal statement
Interview	Extra activities	Psychoeducational
G.P.A.	**1** Open admission	Recommendations

Test Requirements:
Standardized tests waived: **Yes**
Diagnostic testing waived: **Yes**
Documentation of LD required: **Yes**
Tests recommended: **WAIS-R or Woodcock-Johnson**

Types of Disabilities Served
• Speech/Lang	• Reading	• ADD with LD
• Study skills	• Spelling	• ADD without LD
• Written express	• Math	• ADHD with LD
• Organizational	• Fine Motor	• ADHD without LD
• Perceptual		

Learning Disability Program

Program: Remedial: **Yes**
Program: Reinforces course work: **Yes**
Students mainstreamed **100** % of the day
Counseling: Individual: **Yes**

Faculty:

Faculty: **4** Including Director: **Yes** Part time: **4**
LD faculty with: BS/BA: **1** M.A.: **1** Ph.D.: **1**
Faculty advocate: **Yes** Meets with instructor: **As needed**

Diagnostic Testing

ADD	Personality •	Perceptual skills	• Spelling
ADHD	Organization	Fine motor skills	• Reading
• I.Q.	Handwriting•	Spoken language	Study skills
• Math	Social skills •	Written language	

Tutoring:
Average size of group tutorials: **1:1**
Services rendered by:

Graduates	Peers	Faculty	•LD staff	Teacher trainees

Tutorials

Grp.	Ind.	Tutorials	Grp.	Ind.	Tutorials
•	•	Math skills	•		Word processing
•	•	Study skills		•	Time management
•	•	Language arts	•	•	Learning strategies
•	•	Written express	•	•	Organizational skills

Academic Accommodations

Curriculum	Study Aids	Exams
Priority registration	• Typist	• Oral
Math waiver	Reader	Untimed
• Foreign lang. waiver	• Notetaker	• Take home
Course substitution	• Proof reader	With proctor
In Class	• Text on tape	On computer
• Calculators	Early syllabus	• Extended time
• Tape recorder	Taped handouts	On tape
• Word processor		Modified
Priority seating		Separate room

Program Strengths

At this time we are in the process of developing a special program for learning disabilities that provides special classes (strategies, language skills, screening) beyond our already existing full continuum of tutorial and class modifications through Disability or Supplemental Services. Special classes for LD students are in the experimental stage and will vary from semester to semester.

General Information:

Arapahoe Community College is a 2 year public college. Suburban campus 5 miles from Denver. Accessible by bus. Ski areas are 1-2 hours from campus. Housing is not guaranteed.

Accreditation:Regional

Expenses:
Tuition: In-state: Full year: $537.60. Part-time: Per credit:$55.80. Tuition: Out-of-state: Full year: $1,950.60. Part-time: Per credit:$173.55.

Majors

• BUSINESS Accounting, Banking, Economics, Finance, Food Management, Marketing, Retailing, Travel/Tourism Management • COMPUTER SCIENCE Programming • ENGINEERING Mathematical • HEALTH SCIENCES Medical Assistant, Medical Technology, Nursing Assistant, Paramedics, Physical Therapy • HUMANITIES Humanities, Liberal Arts, Philosophy • LANGUAGES French, German, Spanish • PREPROFESSIONAL Architecture, Law • SCIENCES Astronomy, Biology, Chemistry, Geography, Geology, Mathematics, Physics • SOCIAL SCIENCES Anthropology, Criminal Justice, Geography, Government/Political, History, Law Enforcement, Psychology, Social Sciences, Sociology • VISUAL AND PERFORMING ARTS Art History, Music Appreciation, Theater • VOCATIONAL Air Conditioning/Heating/Refri, Auto Body, Automobile

Technology, Automotive Service, Business and Office, Construction, Electronics Technology, Fashion Merchandising, Interior Design, Landscape Architecture, Legal Assistant, Legal Secretary, Medical Laboratory Technology, Secretarial, Word Processing

Sports/Activities

• SPORTS-INTRAMURAL Basketball, Cross Country, Golf, Ping-Pong, Skiing - Snow, Soccer, Softball, Swimming, Tennis, Volleyball, Wrestling (M) • STUDENT LIFE ACTIVITIES Choral, Debate, Musical Theater, Newspaper, Radio/TV station, Student Government

---

Less Selective   **Colorado Services**

Colorado Northwestern Community College

500 Kennedy Drive
Rangely, Colorado 81648-9988
(303) 675-3220

School Enrollment: **1,386** Male: **606** Female: **780**
LD Enrollment: **8**

Admissions Contact: **Ms. Pat Kalahar, Director of Admissions**
LD Contact: **John D. Howe, Program Director**
Name of Program: **Special Population Programs**
Address: **CNCC Box 5**
Telephone:**(303) 675-3238**

Admissions

Application Information:
Application deadline: **None**
Rolling Admissions: **Yes**

Secondary School Information
Most Important Criteria For Admissions (1-strongest)

SAT/ACT	Application	School transcript
Class rank	Course selection	Personal statement
Interview	Extra activities	Psychoeducational
G.P.A.	**1** Open admission	Recommendations

Test Requirements:
Standardized tests waived: **Yes**

Types of Disabilities Served
- Speech/Lang
- Study skills
- Written express
- Organizational
- Perceptual
- Reading
- Spelling
- Math
- Fine Motor
- ADD with LD
- ADD without LD
- ADHD with LD
- ADHD without LD

Learning Disability Program
Counseling: Individual: **Yes**

Diagnostic Testing

ADD	Personality	Perceptual skills	Spelling
ADHD	Organization	Fine motor skills	Reading
I.Q.	Handwriting	Spoken language	Study skills
Math	Social skills	Written language	

Tutoring:
Average size of group tutorials: **1:1**
Services rendered by:
•Graduates •Peers   Faculty   LD staff   Teacher trainees

Tutorials

Grp.	Ind.	Tutorials	Grp.	Ind.	Tutorials
•		Math skills		•	Word processing
	•	Study skills	•		Time management
		Language arts	•		Learning strategies
•	•	Written express		•	Organizational skills

Academic Accommodations

Curriculum	Study Aids	Exams
Priority registration	Typist	Oral
Math waiver	Reader	Untimed
Foreign lang. waiver	Notetaker	Take home
Course substitution	Proof reader	With proctor
In Class	Text on tape	On computer
Calculators	Early syllabus	Extended time
• Tape recorder	Taped handouts	On tape
• Word processor		Modified
Priority seating		Separate room

Program Strengths
We serve the learning disabled student in the same fashion as we serve others. The Learning Assistance Center provides classroom assistance, tutorial help, and walk-in assistance.

General Information:
Colorado Northwestern Community College is a 2 year public college. Rural campus of 150 acres is 90 miles from Grand Junction. Ski areas are 100 miles from campus. 2% of students are foreign. Housing is guaranteed.50 % of students remain on campus for the weekends.

Accreditation:NCACS

Expenses:
Tuition: In-state: Full year: $700.00. Part-time: Per credit:$29.00. Tuition: Out-of-state: Full year: $2,590.00. Part-time: Per credit:$108.00. Room and board: $2,770.00

Majors

• BUSINESS Accounting, Agricultural, Business Administration, Business Management • COMPUTER SCIENCE Computer Science, Micros in Business • EDUCATION General, Physical • ENGINEERING Petroleum • HEALTH SCIENCES Dental Hygiene • HUMANITIES Liberal Arts • SCIENCES Biology, General, Physical Science • SOCIAL SCIENCES Criminal Justice • VOCATIONAL Aeronautical Technology, Aviation Maintenance, Aviation Pilot, Business and Office, Secretarial

Sports/Activities

• SPORTS RELATED Cheerleading • SPORTS-INTERCOLLEGIATE Baseball (M), Basketball, Softball (F), Volleyball (F), Wrestling (M) • SPORTS-INTRAMURAL Basketball, Golf, Ping-Pong, Soccer, Softball, Tennis, Volleyball • STUDENT LIFE ACTIVITIES Choral, Music Groups, Newsletter, Student Government

Very Selective   **Colorado
                                                       Program**

Colorado State University
Administration Annex
Fort Collins, Colorado 80523-0015
(303) 491-6909

School Enrollment: **20,000** Male: **10,000** Female: **10,000**
LD Enrollment: **235** Male: **132** Female: **103**

Admissions Contact: **John Heimbach, Admissions Counselor**
LD Contact: **Rosemary Kreston, Director**
Name of Program: **Resources for Disabled Students**
Address: **116 Student Services Building**
Telephone:**(303) 491-6385**

Admissions

Application Information:
Rolling Admissions: **Yes**

Secondary School Information
Most Important Criteria For Admissions (1-strongest)

1 SAT/ACT	1 Application	1 School transcript
1 Class rank	2 Course selection	2 Personal statement
3 Interview	3 Extra activities	2 Psychoeducational
1 G.P.A.	Open admission	3 Recommendations

Test Requirements:
Diagnostic testing waived: **Yes**
Untimed SAT: **Yes** Untimed ACT: **Yes**
Documentation of LD required: **Yes**
Tests recommended: **Diagnostic in nature**

Types of Disabilities Served
- Speech/Lang   • Reading   • ADD with LD
- Study skills   • Spelling   • ADD without LD
- Written express • Math   • ADHD with LD
- Organizational • Fine Motor   • ADHD without LD
- Perceptual

Admissions Process

Applicants must be secondary school graduates. The GED is accepted. Students should have completed 15 high school credits, including 4 yrs. of English, 3 yrs. of Math, 2 yrs. each of Science and Social Science plus 1 additional year of natural or social science. Either the ACT or SAT is required. Average SAT is 1014, average ACT is 24.

High School Course Requirements:
English: **4** Math: **3** Science: **5**

Learning Disability Program
Program: Reinforces course work: **Yes**
Program available through:**As needed**
Students mainstreamed **100** % of the day
Counseling: Individual: **Yes** Group Counseling: **Yes** Vocational Counseling: **Yes**
Support groups are available:**Limited, as available to all students**

Faculty:
Faculty: **11** Including Director: **Yes** Full time: **3** Part time: **8** M.A.: **11**
Faculty advocate: **Yes** Meets with instructor: **As needed**

Diagnostic Testing
- ADD   • Personality   Perceptual skills   • Spelling
- ADHD   • Organization   Fine motor skills   • Reading
- I.Q.   Handwriting•   Spoken language   • Study skills
- Math   • Social skills•   Written language

Tutoring:
Average size of group tutorials: **5**
Services rendered by:
•Graduates •Peers Faculty •LD staff Teacher trainees

Tutorials

Grp.	Ind.	Tutorials	Grp.	Ind.	Tutorials
•	•	Math skills		•	Word processing
•	•	Study skills	•	•	Time management
	•	Language arts	•	•	Learning strategies
•	•	Written express	•	•	Organizational skills

Academic Accommodations

Curriculum	Study Aids	Exams
• Priority registration	Typist	• Oral
• Math waiver	• Reader	Untimed
• Foreign lang. waiver	• Notetaker	Take home
Course substitution	• Proof reader	• With proctor
In Class	• Text on tape	• On computer
• Calculators	Early syllabus	• Extended time
• Tape recorder	Taped handouts	On tape
• Word processor		• Modified
Priority seating		• Separate room

Graduation Requirements:
Course credits: **128** GPA: **2.0** Years to complete degree: **10** Math waiver: **Yes**

Program Strengths
Our program is individually oriented, geared to self-motivated students willing to use assistance when needed. Our students must be geared towards a mainstreamed environment and demands.

General Information:
Colorado State University is a 4 year public university. Suburban campus of 833 acres is 65 miles from Denver. Accessible by air or bus. Ski areas are 2 hours from campus. Beaches are 2,000 miles from campus. 4% of students are foreign. 10 residential halls on campus. Housing is not guaranteed.Guaranteed through 1st year. 16 % of students join fraternities/sororities.

Accreditation:NCACS

SAT/ACT Scores:
Scores for incoming freshmen:**Verbal:**62%below 500. 30%between 500 and 599. 8%between 600 and 699. **Math:**32% below 500. 43% between 500 and 599. 22% between 600 and 699. 3%above 700. **ACT:** 14% below 20. 33% between 20 and 23. 31%between 24 and 25l. 13%between 26 and 28. 9% above 28.

Class Rank:
About 48% of the present freshmen class were in the upper 20% of their high school class. 84% were in the top 40% of their class.

Expenses:
Tuition: In-state: Full year: $2,356.00. Part-time: Per credit:$77.00. Tuition: Out-of-state: Full year: $7,059.00. Part-time: Per credit:$273.00.
Room and board: $3,624.00

Colorado

Majors

• AREA STUDIES Asian, Black/Afro-American, Latin American, Native American • BUSINESS Accounting, Agricultural, Agricultural Economics, Banking, Business Administration, Business Education, Business Management, Family/Consumer Management, Finance, Management, Marketing, Personnel, Range Management, Real Estate, Travel/Tourism Management • COMMUNICATIONS Advertising, Broadcasting, Communication, Creative Writing, English, Journalism, Photography, Television/Radio/Film • COMPUTER SCIENCE Computer Science, Programming, Systems Analysis • EDUCATION Agricultural, Art, Early Childhood, Elementary, English, Foreign Language, Industrial, Mathematics, Music, Music Therapy, Physical, Science, Social Studies, Speech/Language, Technical, Vocational • ENGINEERING Agricultural, Chemical, Civil/Environmental, Electrical, Engineering Science, Mechanical • HEALTH SCIENCES Communication Disorders, Environmental, Nutritional/Food, Occupational Therapy, Speech/Audiology and Speech • HUMANITIES Humanities, Philosophy • LANGUAGES French, German, Spanish • PREPROFESSIONAL Agriculture, Dentistry, Engineering, Forestry, Law, Medicine, Natural Resources, Pharmacy, Recreation, Social Work • SCIENCES Agricultural, Agronomy, Animal, Biochemistry, Biology, Botany, Chemistry, Ecology, Ecology, Entomology, Geology, Horticultural, Macrobiology, Mathematics, Microbiology, Physical Science, Physics, Watershed Science, Zoology • SOCIAL SCIENCES Anthropology, Government/Political, History, Political Science, Psychology, Social Sciences, Sociology • VISUAL AND PERFORMING ARTS Art, Art History, Dance, Dramatic Arts, Fine Arts, Music, Music Performance, Studio Art, Theater • VOCATIONAL Construction, Food Service, Home Economics, Industrial Equipment Maintenan, Interior Design, Landscape Architecture, Park/Recreation, Textile and Clothing

Sports/Activities

• SPORTS RELATED Baton Twirling, Cheerleading, Chess, Marching Band, Pep Band • SPORTS-INTERCOLLEGIATE Baseball (M), Basketball, Cross Country, Football (M), Golf, Softball (F), Swimming (F), Tennis, Track and Field, Volleyball (F) • SPORTS-INTRAMURAL Badminton, Basketball, Bowling, Cricket, Cross Country, Cycling, Diving, Fencing, Golf, Hammer Throw, Hand Ball, Horseback Riding, Ice Hockey (M), Judo, Karate, Lacrosse, Martial Arts, Polo, Racquetball, Rodeo, Rugby, Skiing - Cross Country, Skiing - Snow, Soccer, Softball, Squash, Swimming, Tennis, Volleyball, Water Polo • STUDENT LIFE ACTIVITIES Concert Band, Dance, Debate, Drama Groups, Ethnic & Cultural Groups, Fraternities, Jazz Band, Music Ensembles, Music Groups, Musical Theater, Newspaper, Radio/TV station, Sororities, Student Government

Less Selective	Colorado Program

Community College of Aurora

791 Chambers Road Suite 202
Aurora, Colorado 80011
(303) 360-4700

School Enrollment: **4,334** Male: **2,889** Female: **1,445**

Admissions Contact: **Joe Roth, Registrar**
LD Contact: **Theresa Campbell, Coordinator**
Name of Program: **Students with Disabilities**
Telephone:**(303) 360-4790 (V/TDD)**

Admissions

Application Information:
Application deadline: **None**

SAT/ACT	Application	School transcript
Class rank	Course selection	Personal statement
Interview	Extra activities	Psychoeducational
G.P.A.	**1** Open admission	Recommendations

Test Requirements:
Standardized tests waived: **Yes**

Types of Disabilities Served
• Speech/Lang	• Reading	• ADD with LD
• Study skills	• Spelling	• ADD without LD
• Written express	• Math	• ADHD with LD
• Organizational	• Fine Motor	• ADHD without LD
• Perceptual		

Learning Disability Program

Program: Remedial: **Yes**
Program: Reinforces course work: **Yes**
Students mainstreamed **100** % of the day

Faculty:
Faculty: **2** Including Director: **Yes** Full time: **1** Part time: **1** Ph.D.: **2**
Faculty advocate: **Yes** Meets with instructor: **As needed**

Diagnostic Testing
ADD	Personality	Perceptual skills	Spelling
ADHD	Organization	Fine motor skills	Reading
I.Q.	Handwriting	Spoken language	Study skills
Math	Social skills	Written language	

Tutoring:
Average size of group tutorials: **3-4**
Services rendered by:
•Graduates   •Peers   •Faculty   •LD staff   Teacher trainees

Tutorials
Grp.	Ind.	Tutorials	Grp.	Ind.	Tutorials
•	•	Math skills			Word processing
•	•	Study skills	•	•	Time management
•	•	Language arts	•	•	Learning strategies
•	•	Written express	•	•	Organizational skills

Academic Accommodations

Curriculum	Study Aids	Exams
Priority registration	• Typist	• Oral
• Math waiver	Reader	Untimed
Foreign lang. waiver	• Notetaker	• Take home
Course substitution	• Proof reader	With proctor
In Class	• Text on tape	On computer
• Calculators	Early syllabus	• Extended time
• Tape recorder	Taped handouts	On tape
• Word processor		Modified
Priority seating		Separate room

Program Strengths

The office of Resources for Students with Disabilities at the Community College of Aurora was established to insure that students with disabilities have the same potential for success as all other students. The office is committed to providing the services that are needed to achieve this goal.

General Information:

Community College of Aurora is a 2 year public college. Suburban campus

5 miles from Denver. Accessible by bus. Ski areas are 60 miles from campus. .004% of students are foreign. Housing is not guaranteed.

Accreditation: Regional

Expenses:
Tuition: In-state: Full year: $432.00 (12-18 credits). Part-time: Per credit:$36.00 (1-11 credits). Tuition: Out-of-state: Full year: $1,728.00 (12-18 credits). Part-time: Per credit:$144.00 (1-11 credits).

Majors
• BUSINESS Accounting, Business Management, Hotel and Restaurant Managemen, Marketing • COMMUNICATIONS Graphic Design • COMPUTER SCIENCE Computer Science, Computer Technology • EDUCATION Child Development • HEALTH SCIENCES Medical Secretary, Nursing, Radiological Therapy, Surgical Technology • HUMANITIES Liberal Arts • PREPROFESSIONAL Legal Assistant, Social Work • SOCIAL SCIENCES Social Sciences • VOCATIONAL Air Condtioning/Heating/Refrig, Air Traffic Control, Business and Office, Drafting, Legal Secretary, Medical Laboratory Technology, Paralegal, Radiological Technology, Respiratory Therapy Technology, Secretarial, Word Processing

Sports/Activities
• SPORTS-INTRAMURAL Archery, Badminton, Baseball, Basketball, Bowling, Cross Country, Diving, Fencing, Field Hockey, Golf, Hand Ball, Horseback Riding, Racquetball, Riflery, Rugby, Skiing - Snow, Soccer, Swimming, Tennis, Track and Field, Volleyball • STUDENT LIFE ACTIVITIES Amnesty International, Black Student Organization, Choral, Drama Groups, Mexican-American Organization, Newspaper, Student Government, Student Handbook

Less Selective   **Colorado**
Program

Community College of Denver
Campus Box 600 P.O. Box 173363
Denver, Colorado 80217-3363
(303) 556-3406

School Enrollment: **11,080**
LD Enrollment: **90**

Admissions Contact: **Michael Poindexter, Dir. of Reg. and Records**
LD Contact: **Gary Macdonald, Coordinator**
Name of Program: **Special Learning Support Program**
Address: **Campus Box 600**
Telephone:**(303) 556-3406**

Admissions

Application Information:
LD Students Applying: **264** Accepted: **100** Enrolled:**90**
Application deadline: **Open Enrollment**

Secondary School Information
Most Important Criteria For Admissions (1-strongest)
SAT/ACT   Application   School transcript
Class rank   Course selection   Personal statement
Interview   Extra activities   Psychoeducational
G.P.A.   **1** Open admission   Recommendations

Test Requirements:
Diagnostic testing waived: **Yes**
Documentation of LD required: **Yes**
Currency of diagnostic testing: **3 years**
Tests recommended: **WAIS-R/Woodcock-Johnson Psych-educa-**

tional battery plus achievement

Types of Disabilities Served
• Speech/Lang • Reading • ADD with LD
• Study skills • Spelling • ADD without LD
• Written express • Math • ADHD with LD
• Organizational • Fine Motor • ADHD without LD
• Perceptual

Admissions Process
Open enrollment - any student who would benefit from a college environment is welcome

High School Course Requirements:
Waivers to standard high school courses
Foreign Language : **Yes** Course substitution: **Yes**

Learning Disability Program
Program: Remedial: **Yes**
Program: Reinforces course work: **Yes**
Students mainstreamed **95** % of the day
Recommended credits per semester: **12**
Services available for all students: **Yes**
Counseling: Individual: **Yes** Vocational Counseling: **Yes**
Support groups are available:**LD support group**

Faculty:
Faculty: **7** Including Director: **Yes** Full time: **2** Part time: **5**
LD faculty with: BS/BA: **4** M.A.: **2** Ph.D.: **1**
Faculty advocate: **Yes** Meets with instructor: **As needed**

Diagnostic Testing
• ADD Personality • Perceptual skills • Spelling
• ADHD• Organization• Fine motor skills • Reading
• I.Q. Handwriting• Spoken language Study skills
• Math • Social skills• Written language

Tutoring:
Average size of group tutorials: **1-10**
Services rendered by:
Graduates Peers •Faculty •LD staff Teacher trainees

Tutorials
Grp. Ind. Tutorials   Grp. Ind. Tutorials
•   • Math skills   • Word processing
•   Study skills   • Time management
•   Language arts   • Learning strategies
•   • Written express   • Organizational skills

Academic Accommodations
Curriculum   **Study Aids**   **Exams**
Priority registration Typist   • Oral
Math waiver   Reader   • Untimed
• Foreign lang. waiver • Notetaker   Take home
Course substitution • Proof reader With proctor
In Class   • Text on tape   On computer
• Calculators   Early syllabus • Extended time
• Tape recorder   Taped handouts • On tape
• Word processor   Modified
Priority seating   • Separate room

Graduation Requirements:
Course credits: **varies** Years to complete degree: **2-6** Language waiver: **Yes**

Colorado

Program Strengths

The Special Learning Support Program is a learning disability program serving three post-secondary institutions on a single campus in the Denver Metropolitan area. Housed at the Community College of Denver, the program provides assessment, basic skill development, classroom support, and personal support, and counseling to individuals referred from community agencies, the Community College of Denver, Metropolitan State College, and the University of Colorado at Denver.

General Information:

Community College of Denver is a 2 and 4 year public college. Urban campus Accessible by air, train or bus. Ski areas are 100 miles from campus. Beaches are 1,000 miles from campus. Housing is not guaranteed.

Accreditation: Regional

Expenses:

Tuition: In-state: Full year: $950.00. Part-time: Per credit: $49.50. Tuition: Out-of-state: Full year: $3,900.00. Cost of LD program: $49.50 - $148.50

Majors

• BUSINESS Accounting, Business Management, Hotel and Restaurant Managemen, Marketing, Marketing Research • COMMUNICATIONS Photography • COMPUTER SCIENCE Computer Science, Data Processing, Programming • CRAFTS AND DESIGN Graphic Design • EDUCATION Child Development • ENGINEERING Nuclear • HEALTH SCIENCES Medical Secretary, Nursing, Practical Nursing • HUMANITIES Liberal Arts • PREPROFESSIONAL Social Work • SOCIAL SCIENCES Social Sciences • VOCATIONAL Air Conditioning/Heating/Refri, Aviation Maintenance, Business and Office, Drafting, Electronics Technology, Legal Assistant, Legal Secretary, Paralegal, Respiratory Therapy Technology, Secretarial, Word Processing

---

Less Selective   **Colorado Program**

Front Range Community College
3645 West 112 Avenue
Westminster, Colorado 80030
(303) 466-8811

School Enrollment: **5,000** Male: **2,000** Female: **3,000**
LD Enrollment: **120**

Admissions Contact: **Pat Lammers, Director of Admissions**
LD Contact: **Karol Janice Bennett, Educ. Assistant**
Name of Program: **Progressive Learning Program**
Telephone: **(303) 466-8811 - Ext. 243**

Admissions

Application Information:
Enrolled: **35**
Rolling Admissions: **Yes**

Secondary School Information
Most Important Criteria For Admissions (1-strongest)

SAT/ACT	Application	School transcript
Class rank	Course selection	Personal statement
Interview	Extra activities	Psychoeducational
G.P.A.	**1** Open admission	Recommendations

Test Requirements:
Diagnostic testing waived: **Yes**
Documentation of LD required: **Yes**
Tests recommended: **Own battery administered**

Types of Disabilities Served
- Speech/Lang
- Study skills
- Written express
- Organizational
- Perceptual
- Reading
- Spelling
- Math
- Fine Motor
- ADD with LD
- ADD without LD
- ADHD with LD
- ADHD without LD

Admissions Process

For remedial classes only, contact Progressive Learning directly; for college classes, follow school's procedures for admission, then contact Progressive Learning.

Learning Disability Program

Program: Remedial: **Yes**
Program: Reinforces course work: **Yes**
Services available for all students: **Yes**
Counseling: Individual: **Yes** Group Counseling: **Yes** Vocational Counseling: **Yes**
Support groups are available: **Club for students with learning disabilities**

Faculty:
Faculty: **3** Full time: **2** Part time: **1** M.A.: **2**
Faculty advocate: **Yes**

Diagnostic Testing

ADD	Personality •	Perceptual skills	• Spelling
ADHD	Organization•	Fine motor skills	• Reading
I.Q. •	Handwriting•	Spoken language	• Study skills
• Math	Social skills •	Written language	

Tutoring:
Average size of group tutorials: **4**
Services rendered by:
Graduates   Peers   Faculty   •LD staff   Teacher trainees

Tutorials

Grp.	Ind.	Tutorials	Grp.	Ind.	Tutorials
•	•	Math skills	•	•	Word processing
•	•	Study skills	•	•	Time management
•	•	Language arts	•	•	Learning strategies
•	•	Written express	•	•	Organizational skills

Academic Accommodations

Curriculum	Study Aids	Exams
Priority registration	Typist	• Oral
Math waiver	• Reader	• Untimed
Foreign lang. waiver	• Notetaker	Take home
Course substitution	• Proof reader	• With proctor
In Class	• Text on tape	On computer
• Calculators	Early syllabus	• Extended time
• Tape recorder	Taped handouts	On tape
• Word processor		• Modified
• Priority seating		• Separate room

Program Strengths

We do extensive remediation with adults with Learning Disabilities with very low reading, writing, and spelling skills. The purpose is to remediate to the point of college entry level. We also act as a support system to students enrolled in regular college classes who have been identified as having learning disabilities.

General Information:
Front Range Community College is a 2 year public college. Suburban campus of 12 acres is 15 miles from Denver. Ski areas are 30 miles from campus. Housing is not guaranteed.

Accreditation:

Expenses: Part-time: Per credit:$47.20. Part-time: Per credit:$164.95.

Majors
• BUSINESS Accounting, Business Administration, Marketing and Distribution, Marketing Management • COMPUTER SCIENCE Computer & Information Science, Programming • HEALTH SCIENCES Dietary Aide Assistant, Nursing, Practical Nursing, Respiratory Therapy, Respiratory Therapy Technology • SCIENCES Horticultural, Ornamental Horticulture • VOCATIONAL Electronics Technology, Interpreter for the Deaf, Precision Metal Works, Secretarial, Welding Technology, Word Processing

Sports/Activities
• SPORTS-INTRAMURAL Basketball, Softball, Volleyball • STUDENT LIFE ACTIVITIES Academic Clubs, Choral, Newspaper, Student Government

Less Selective **Colorado Program**

Northeastern Junior College
100 College Drive
Sterling, Colorado 80751
(303) 522-6600

School Enrollment: **950**
LD Enrollment: **26** Male: **18** Female: **8**

Admissions Contact: **Carnie Johnson, Dir. of Enrollment**
LD Contact: **Nancy Mann, Coordinator**
Name of Program: **Student Support Services**

Admissions

Application Information:
Rolling Admissions: **Yes**

Secondary School Information
Most Important Criteria For Admissions (1-strongest)

SAT/ACT	Application	School transcript
Class rank	Course selection	Personal statement
Interview	Extra activities	Psychoeducational
G.P.A.	**1** Open admission	Recommendations

Test Requirements:
Standardized tests waived: **Yes**
Diagnostic testing waived: **Yes**
Untimed ACT: **Yes**
Documentation of LD required: **Yes**
Currency of diagnostic testing:

Types of Disabilities Served
• Speech/Lang • Reading • ADD with LD
• Study skills • Spelling • ADD without LD
• Written express • Math • ADHD with LD
• Organizational • Fine Motor • ADHD without LD
• Perceptual

Admissions Process
Open enrollment. Student can be admitted with a high school diploma or GED. Required to take ASSET Exam for course placement.

Learning Disability Program
Program: Remedial: **Yes**
Program: Reinforces course work: **Yes**
Program available through:**throughout year**
Students mainstreamed **100** % of the day
Recommended credits per semester: **12-15**
Services available for all students: **Yes**
Counseling: Individual: **Yes** Vocational Counseling: **Yes**

Faculty:
Faculty: **6** Including Director: **Yes** Full time: **6**
LD faculty with: BS/BA: **6**
Faculty advocate: **Yes** Meets with instructor: **As needed**

Diagnostic Testing
ADD	Personality •	Perceptual skills	• Spelling
ADHD	Organization•	Fine motor skills	• Reading
• I.Q.	Handwriting•	Spoken language	• Study skills
• Math	Social skills •	Written language	

Tutoring:
Average size of group tutorials: **2-5**
Services rendered by:
Graduates •Peers •Faculty •LD staff Teacher trainees

Tutorials
Grp.	Ind.	Tutorials	Grp.	Ind.	Tutorials
•	•	Math skills	•	•	Word processing
•	•	Study skills	•	•	Time management
•	•	Language arts	•	•	Learning strategies
•	•	Written express	•	•	Organizational skills

Academic Accommodations
Curriculum	Study Aids	Exams
Priority registration	• Typist	• Oral
Math waiver	• Reader	Untimed
Foreign lang. waiver	• Notetaker	Take home
Course substitution	• Proof reader	With proctor
In Class	• Text on tape	On computer
• Calculators	Early syllabus	• Extended time
• Tape recorder	Taped handouts	On tape
• Word processor		Modified
• Priority seating		• Separate room

Graduation Requirements:
Course credits: **60** GPA: **2.0**

Program Strengths
The institution has an open enrollment meaning we take anyone who applies. We try to design a program of support services to meet the needs of individual students.

Colorado

General Information:

Northeastern Junior College is a 2 year public college. Rural campus 120 miles from Denver. Accessible by bus. Ski areas are 200 miles from campus. 5 residential halls on campus. Housing is guaranteed.Guaranteed through 2nd year. 10 % of students remain on campus for the weekends.

Accreditation:NCACS

SAT/ACT Scores:

Scores for incoming freshmen: 2% above 28.

Class Rank:

About 28% of the present freshmen class were in the upper 20% of their high school class.

Expenses:

Tuition: In-state: Full year: $1,324.00. Part-time: Per credit:$67.00. Tuition: Out-of-state: Full year: $3,066.00. Part-time: Per credit:$126.00. Room and board: $3,426.00

Majors

• BUSINESS Accounting, Business Administration, Business Economics, Business Education, Business Management, Economics, Finance, Management, Secretarial Science, Travel/Tourism Management • COMMUNICATIONS Advertising, Communication, English, Journalism • EDUCATION Art, Early Childhood, Elementary, Middle School, Music, Physical, Secondary, Special, Speech/Language, Vocational • HEALTH SCIENCES Nursing, Physical Therapy • PREPROFESSIONAL Agriculture, Dentistry, Engineering, Forestry, Law, Medicine, Pharmacy, Social Work, Veterinarian • SCIENCES Biochemistry, Biology, Botany, Chemistry, Geology, Mathematics, Physical Chemistry, Physical Science, Physics, Zoology • SOCIAL SCIENCES Anthropology, History, Psychology, Social Sciences, Sociology • VISUAL AND PERFORMING ARTS Art, Music, Studio Art, Theater • VOCATIONAL Auto Body, Automobile Technology, Cosmetology, Home Economics

Sports/Activities

• SPORTS RELATED Cheerleading, Pep Band, Team Managers • SPORTS-INTRAMURAL Archery, Basketball, Bowling, Canoeing, Cross Country, Cycling, Golf, Racquetball, Rodeo, Softball, Swimming, Tennis, Track and Field, Volleyball, Weight Lifting • STUDENT LIFE ACTIVITIES Drama Groups, Ethnic & Cultural Groups, Magazine, Newspaper, Religious Organization, Student Government

Less Selective

Colorado Services

Pikes Peak Community College

5675 South Academy Boulevard
Colorado Springs, Colorado 80906-5498
(303) 576-7711

School Enrollment: **5,000**

Admissions Contact: **Jim Tisdale, Director of Admissions**
LD Contact: **William B. Flynn, Coordinator**
Name of Program: **Program for the Disabled**
Telephone:**(719) 540-7128**

Admissions

Application Information:
Application deadline: **None**

Secondary School Information
Most Important Criteria For Admissions (1-strongest)

SAT/ACT	Application	School transcript
Class rank	Course selection	Personal statement
Interview	Extra activities	Psychoeducational
G.P.A.	Open admission	Recommendations

Test Requirements:
Tests recommended: **None**

Types of Disabilities Served

• Speech/Lang	• Reading	ADD with LD
• Study skills	• Spelling	ADD without LD
• Written express	• Math	ADHD with LD
• Organizational	• Fine Motor	ADHD without LD
• Perceptual		

Learning Disability Program
Counseling: Individual: **Yes**

Faculty:
Faculty: **1** Full time: **1**
LD faculty with: BS/BA: **1** M.A.: **1**
Faculty advocate: **Yes** Meets with instructor: **As needed**

Diagnostic Testing

ADD	Personality	Perceptual skills	Spelling
ADHD	Organization	Fine motor skills	Reading
I.Q.	Handwriting	Spoken language	Study skills
Math	Social skills	Written language	

Tutoring:
Services rendered by:
Graduates •Peers •Faculty •LD staff Teacher trainees

Tutorials

Grp.	Ind.	Tutorials	Grp.	Ind.	Tutorials
•				•	Word processing
•		Math skills			Time management
	•	Study skills		•	Learning strategies
	•	Language arts		•	Organizational skills
	•	Written express			

Academic Accommodations

Curriculum	Study Aids	Exams
Priority registration	• Typist	• Oral
• Math waiver	Reader	Untimed
• Foreign lang. waiver	• Notetaker	Take home
Course substitution	• Proof reader	With proctor
In Class	• Text on tape	On computer
• Calculators	Early syllabus	• Extended time
• Tape recorder	Taped handouts	On tape
• Word processor		Modified
Priority seating		Separate room

Program Strengths

Services to help disabled students with supplemental services inside and outside the classroom include tutoring, note-takers, readers and other special aids.

General Information:

Pikes Peak Community College is a 2 year public college. Urban campus of 212 acres is 70 miles from Denver. Ski areas are 1-2 hours from campus. Housing is not guaranteed.

Accreditation: Regional

Expenses:
Tuition: In-state: Full year: $816.00. Part-time: Per credit:$34.00. Tuition: Out-of-state: Full year: $3,264.00. Part-time: Per credit:$136.00.

Majors
• BUSINESS Accounting, Business Administration, Business Management, Finance, Food Management, Marketing • COMMUNICATIONS Broadcasting, Graphic Design • EDUCATION Early Childhood • HEALTH SCIENCES Nursing • PREPROFESSIONAL Architecture, Dentistry, Engineering, Fisheries, Law, Legal Assistant, Medicine, Natural Resources, Pharmacy, Recreation, Social Work • SOCIAL SCIENCES Criminal Justice • VOCATIONAL Air Condtioning/Heating/Refrig, Auto Body, Automobile Technology, Business and Office, Dental Assistant, Drafting, Machinist, Office Administration, Welding

Sports/Activities
• SPORTS-INTRAMURAL Basketball (M), Golf, Volleyball • STUDENT LIFE ACTIVITIES Drama Groups, Ethnic & Cultural Groups, Jazz Band, Magazine, Newspaper, Radio/TV station, Student Government

Less Selective

Colorado Program

Pueblo Community College
900 West Orman Avenue
Pueblo, Colorado 81004
(719)) 549-3311

School Enrollment: **2,800** Male: **1,120** Female: **1,680**
LD Enrollment: **120** Male: **42** Female: **78**

Admissions Contact: **Debbie Sagona, Director of Admissions**
LD Contact: **Chris Campos, Coordinator**
Name of Program: **Computer Access Center**
Telephone:**(719) 549-3228**

Admissions

Application Information:
Application deadline: **2 weeks prior to semester**
Applicant must apply **1-6** months in advance
Rolling Admissions: **Yes**

Secondary School Information
Most Important Criteria For Admissions (1-strongest)

SAT/ACT	**1** Application	**2**	School transcript
Class rank	Course selection	**3**	Personal statement
Interview	**4** Extra activities	**5**	Psychoeducational
G.P.A.	**1** Open admission		Recommendations

Test Requirements:
Standardized tests waived: **Yes**
Diagnostic testing waived: **Yes**
Documentation of LD required: **Yes**
Currency of diagnostic testing: **Prior to enrollment**
Tests recommended: **Students must take placement tests at the college**

Types of Disabilities Served
• Speech/Lang • Reading • ADD with LD
• Study skills • Spelling • ADD without LD
• Written express • Math • ADHD with LD
• Organizational • Fine Motor • ADHD without LD
• Perceptual

Admissions Process
Must have high school degree or GED, formal application, take Basic Skills Assessment, attend Orientation class, meet with advisor, pay tuition, obtain ID and parking permit.

Learning Disability Program
Program: Remedial: **Yes**
Program: Reinforces course work: **Yes**
Students mainstreamed **100** % of the day
Time required or recommended in learning center: **Varies**
Services available for all students: **Yes**
Counseling: Individual: **Yes** Vocational Counseling: **Yes**
Support groups are available:**Yes, C.H.A.T. (Creating Healthy Attitudes Together)**

Faculty:
Faculty: **12** Including Director: **Yes** Full time: **12** Part time: **12**
LD faculty with: BS/BA: **7** M.A.: **5**
Faculty advocate: **Yes** Meets with instructor: **Once a month**

Diagnostic Testing
ADD Personality Perceptual skills • Spelling
ADHD Organization• Fine motor skills • Reading
• I.Q. • Handwriting Spoken language • Study skills
• Math Social skills• Written language

Tutoring:
Average size of group tutorials: **3-5**
Services rendered by:
Graduates •Peers •Faculty •LD staff Teacher trainees

Tutorials

Grp.	Ind.	Tutorials	Grp.	Ind.	Tutorials
•	•	Math skills	•	•	Word processing
•	•	Study skills	•		Time management
•	•	Language arts	•	•	Learning strategies
•		Written express	•		Organizational skills

Academic Accommodations

Curriculum	Study Aids	Exams
Priority registration	• Typist	• Oral
Math waiver	• Reader	• Untimed
Foreign lang. waiver	• Notetaker	• Take home
Course substitution	• Proof reader	• With proctor
In Class	• Text on tape	• On computer
• Calculators	Early syllabus	• Extended time
• Tape recorder	Taped handouts	On tape
• Word processor		• Modified
• Priority seating		• Separate room

Graduation Requirements:
Course credits: **60** GPA: **2.0** Years to complete degree: **10**
Other requirements: **Certificate Programs- 30 semester hours, 2.0 GPA required**

Program Strengths
The faculty is now willing to allow modifications, and the students have formed a Student Handling Group on campus. Creating

Colorado

Healthy Attitudes Together (CHAT) provides peer support groups as well as a buddy system that assists new students. The following year, the students are then a buddy to another incoming student. This system helps new students learn about the facilities around the campus. They sponsor our annual "Disability Awareness Day".

General Information:

Pueblo Community College is a 2 year public college. Urban campus of 35 acres is 100 miles from Denver. Accessible by air or bus. Ski areas are 40 miles from campus. 5% of students are foreign. Housing is not guaranteed.

Accreditation: NCACS

Expenses:

Tuition: In-state: Full year: $1,216.70. Part-time: Per credit:Part-time: $55.60. Tuition: Out-of-state: Full year: $2,156.35. Part-time: Per credit:- Part-time: $184.60.

Majors

• BUSINESS Accounting, Business Management, Clerical, Data Processing, Entrepreneur, Food Management, Marketing, Secretarial Science, Travel/Tourism Management • COMPUTER SCIENCE Business Data Programming, Programming • EDUCATION Early Childhood • ENGINEERING Automotive, Computer, Drafting, Radio/Television, Welding • HEALTH SCIENCES Dental Hygiene, Nursing, Nutritional/Food, Occupational Therapy, Physical Therapy, Radiological Therapy, Respiratory Technology • PREPROFESSIONAL Agriculture, Business, Dentistry, Range Management • SCIENCES Agricultural, Computer Science • SOCIAL SCIENCES Criminal Justice • VOCATIONAL Business and Office, Carpentry, Construction, Diesel Power Technology, Drafting, Electronics Technology, Food Service, Machinist, Media Technician Program, Precision Metal Work, Radiological Technology, Secretarial, Travel/Tourism Management, Welding, Woodworking

Sports/Activities

• STUDENT LIFE ACTIVITIES Debate, Drama Groups, Student Government

---

Less Selective

Colorado

Red Rocks Community College

12600 West Sixth Avenue
Lakewood , Colorado 80401
(303) 988-6160

School Enrollment: **5,000**
LD Enrollment: **1,000** Male: **700** Female: **300**

Admissions Contact: **Robert Schantz, Director of Admissions**
LD Contact: **Sarah Dey, Director**
Name of Program: **Learning Development Center**
Address: **13300 W. 6th Avenue**
Telephone:**(303) 988-6160 - Ext. 395**

Admissions

Application Information:

Application deadline: **July 1st**
Rolling Admissions: **Yes**

Secondary School Information

Most Important Criteria For Admissions (1-strongest)

5 SAT/ACT	1 Application	2 School transcript
5 Class rank	3 Course selection	5 Personal statement
5 Interview	5 Extra activities	5 Psychoeducational
4 G.P.A.	1 Open admission	5 Recommendations

Test Requirements:

Diagnostic testing waived: **Yes**

Types of Disabilities Served

• Speech/Lang	• Reading	• ADD with LD
• Study skills	• Spelling	• ADD without LD
• Written express	• Math	• ADHD with LD
• Organizational	• Fine Motor	• ADHD without LD
• Perceptual		

Admissions Process

Student applies to admissions and is referred to appropriate testing.

Learning Disability Program

Services available for all students: **Yes**

Faculty:

Faculty: **3** Part time: **3**

Diagnostic Testing

ADD	Personality	Perceptual skills	Spelling
ADHD	Organization	Fine motor skills	Reading
I.Q.	Handwriting	Spoken language	Study skills
Math	Social skills	Written language	

Services rendered by:

Graduates	Peers	Faculty	LD staff	Teacher trainees

Tutorials

Grp.	Ind.	Tutorials	Grp.	Ind.	Tutorials
	•	Math skills		•	Word processing
	•	Study skills	•	•	Time management
	•	Language arts		•	Learning strategies
	•	Written express		•	Organizational skills

Academic Accommodations

Curriculum	Study Aids	Exams
Priority registration	• Typist	Oral
Math waiver	Reader	Untimed
Foreign lang. waiver	• Notetaker	• Take home
• Course substitution	• Proof reader	With proctor
In Class	• Text on tape	On computer
• Calculators	Early syllabus	• Extended time
• Tape recorder	Taped handouts	On tape
Word processor		Modified
Priority seating		Separate room

Program Strengths

We do not have an LD Program. We have a complete range of developmental courses which are offered for non-transferable credit. These courses are presented in a variety of learning modalities. We also offer free seminars in study skills and we have a computer management and computer assistance program. We now offer LD testing and accommodation strategies for testing and classes.

General Information:

Red Rocks Community College is a 2 year public college. Suburban campus 10 miles from Denver. Accessible by car or bus. Ski areas are 20-30 miles from campus. Housing is not guaranteed.

Accreditation:NCACS

Expenses:
Tuition: In-state: Full year: $990.00. Part-time: Per credit:0. Tuition: Out-of-state: Full year: $4,050.00.

Majors

• AREA STUDIES African, American, Latin American • BUSINESS Accounting, Business Administration, Business Economics, Business Education, Economics, Finance, Management, Real Estate • COMMUNICATIONS Creative Writing, English, Journalism, Photography • COMPUTER SCIENCE Computer Science, Data Processing, Programming, Systems Analysis, Telecommunications • EDUCATION Art, Early Childhood, Health, Speech/Language, Vocational • ENGINEERING Computer • ENVIRONMENTAL CONTROL Solar Heating, Water and Wastewater Technolog • HEALTH SCIENCES Medical Secretary, Nursing • HUMANITIES Humanities, Philosophy • LANGUAGES French, German, Spanish • PREPROFESSIONAL Engineering • SCIENCES Biology, Botany, Chemistry, Earth, Geography, Geology, Mathematics, Physical Chemistry, Physical Science, Physics, Physiology • SOCIAL SCIENCES Anthropology, Criminal Justice, Geography, Government/Political, History, Psychology, Public Relations, Social Sciences, Sociology • VISUAL AND PERFORMING ARTS Art, Art History, Theater • VOCATIONAL Automobile Technology, Diesel Power Technology, Drafting, Fire Science, Industrial Arts, Industrial Equipment Maintenan, Legal Secretary, Precision Metal Work, Secretarial, Word Processing

Sports/Activities

• SPORTS-INTRAMURAL Basketball (M), Softball, Volleyball • STUDENT LIFE ACTIVITIES Newspaper, Student Government

---

Selective **Colorado Program**

Regis College
3539 West 50th Avenue
Denver, Colorado 80221
(303) 458-4146

School Enrollment: **1,000** Male: **500** Female: **500**
LD Enrollment: **40**

Admissions Contact: **Robert Blust, Director of Admissions**
LD Contact: **Julie Ellgen, Dir. Freshman Commitment Prog.**
Name of Program: **Freshman Commitment Program**
Telephone:**(303) 458-4146**

Admissions

Application Information:
LD Students Applying: **200** Accepted: **100** Enrolled:**40**
LD on admissions committee:**Yes**
Rolling Admissions: **Yes**

Secondary School Information
Most Important Criteria For Admissions (1-strongest)
3	SAT/ACT	12	Application
7	Class rank	10	Course selection
9	Interview	5	Extra activities
1	G.P.A.		Open admission

4 School transcript
6 Personal statement
8 Psychoeducational
2 Recommendations

Test Requirements:
Untimed SAT: **Yes** Untimed ACT: **Yes**

Types of Disabilities Served
• Speech/Lang	• Reading	ADD with LD
• Study skills	• Spelling	ADD without LD
• Written express	• Math	ADHD with LD
• Organizational	• Fine Motor	ADHD without LD
• Perceptual		

Admissions Process

Files which seem to indicate that the student might benefit from the Commitment Program are referred to the director who considers numerous factors and makes the final decision.

Learning Disability Program

Program: Reinforces course work: **Yes**
Program available through:**Fall only**
Students mainstreamed **60-75** % of the day
Recommended credits per semester: **15**
Services available for all students: **Yes**
Counseling: Individual: **Yes** Group Counseling: **Yes** Vocational Counseling: **Yes**
Support groups are available:**Support classes, meetings, workshops, etc.**

Faculty:
Faculty: **3** Including Director: **Yes** Full time: **2** Part time: **1** M.A.: **3**
Faculty advocate: **Yes** Meets with instructor: **As needed**

Diagnostic Testing
ADD	Personality	Perceptual skills	Spelling
ADHD	Organization	Fine motor skills	• Reading
I.Q.	Handwriting	Spoken language	• Study skills
Math	Social skills	• Written language	

Tutoring:
Average size of group tutorials: **1-5**
Services rendered by:
Graduates •Peers   •Faculty   •LD staff   Teacher trainees

Tutorials
Grp.	Ind.	Tutorials	Grp.	Ind.	Tutorials
•		Math skills			Word processing
•		Study skills	•		Time management
		Language arts	•		Learning strategies
•		Written express	•		Organizational skills

Academic Accommodations
Curriculum	Study Aids	Exams
Priority registration	Typist	• Oral
Math waiver	Reader	• Untimed
• Foreign lang. waiver	• Notetaker	• Take home
• Course substitution	Proof reader	• With proctor
In Class	Text on tape	On computer
Calculators	Early syllabus	• Extended time
• Tape recorder	Taped handouts	On tape
Word processor		• Modified
Priority seating		• Separate room

Graduation Requirements:GPA: **2.0** Years to complete degree: **5** Language waiver: **Yes**

Program Strengths
We are a small school. Our classes are small and highly individualized. We do a lot of one-on-one work. Our faculty is supportive. We emphasize enablement through alternate learning strategies.

Colorado

General Information:

Regis College is a 4 year independent Roman Catholic university. Urban campus of 40 acres is Accessible by plane or bus Ski areas are 1 hour from campus. 3 residential halls on campus. Housing is guaranteed.Guaranteed through 1st year. 100 % of students remain on campus for the weekends.

Accreditation: Regional

Expenses:

Tuition: In-state: Full year: $5,170.00. Part-time: Per credit:$336.00. Tuition: Out-of-state: Full year: $5,170.00. Part-time: Per credit:$336.00. Room and board: $5,000.00 Cost of LD program:$1,000.00

Majors

• BUSINESS Accounting, Business Administration, Economics • COMMUNICATIONS Communication, English • HUMANITIES Philosophy • LANGUAGES French, Spanish • SCIENCES Biology, Chemistry, Mathematics • SOCIAL SCIENCES History, Political Science, Psychology, Sociology • VISUAL AND PERFORMING ARTS Theater

---

Very Selective   **Colorado**
                                                Program

University of Colorado at Boulder
Campus Box 107
Boulder, Colorado 80309-0107
(303) 492-6301

School Enrollment: **25,600** Male: **13,200** Female: **12,400**
LD Enrollment: **200**

Admissions Contact: **Pete List, Admissions/LD Liaison**
LD Contact: **Terri Bodhaine, LD Coordinator**
Name of Program: **Learning Disabilities Program**
Address: **Campus Box 107**
Telephone:**(303) 492-8671**

Admissions

Application Information:
LD Students Applying: **230** Accepted: **25** Enrolled:**20**
LD on admissions committee:**Yes**
Application deadline: **January 15th**
Rolling Admissions: **Yes**

Secondary School Information
Most Important Criteria For Admissions (1-strongest)

1 SAT/ACT	**1** Application	**1**	School transcript
Class rank	**1** Course selection		Personal statement
X Interview	Extra activities	**1**	Psychoeducational
1 G.P.A.	Open admission		Recommendations

Test Requirements:
Diagnostic testing waived: **Yes**
Untimed SAT: **Yes** Untimed ACT: **Yes** Untimed ACH: **Yes**
WAIS-R required: **Yes**
Documentation of LD required: **Yes**
Currency of diagnostic testing: **24 months**
Tests recommended: **WISC-R, or WAIS-R, Woodcock-Johnson. Required: IQ Test; recommended: measure of achievement in reading, math, written language**

Types of Disabilities Served

• Speech/Lang	• Reading	• ADD with LD
• Study skills	• Spelling	ADD without LD
• Written express	• Math	ADHD with LD
• Organizational	• Fine Motor	ADHD without LD
• Perceptual		

Admissions Process

LD students first complete the regular admissions process. If they do not meet this criteria, if requested, they will be considered for the LD department. An on-campus diagnostic interview affords us the opportunity to evaluate the student as well as the student to evaluate the university

High School Course Requirements:
English: **4** Math: **3** Science: **3** Foreign Language: **3**
Waivers to standard high school courses
Course substitution: **Yes**

Learning Disability Program

Special orientation for LD students: **Yes**
Program: Reinforces course work: **Yes**
Program available through:**while enrolled**
Students mainstreamed **100** % of the day
Recommended credits per semester: **12**
Time required or recommended in learning center: **2x week**
Services only for LD students: **Yes**
Counseling: Individual: **Yes** Group Counseling: **Yes**
Support groups are available:**Not at this time**

Faculty:
Faculty: **6** Including Director: **Yes** Full time: **1** Part time: **5** M.A.: **5** Ph.D.: **1**
Faculty advocate: **Yes** Meets with instructor: **When needed**

Diagnostic Testing

ADD	Personality	Perceptual skills	• Spelling
ADHD	Organization	Fine motor skills	• Reading
• I.Q.	Handwriting	Spoken language	• Study skills
• Math	Social skills	• Written language	

Tutoring:
Average size of group tutorials: **1:1 - 1:8**
Services rendered by:
•Graduates   Peers   Faculty   LD staff   Teacher trainees

Tutorials

Grp.	Ind.	Tutorials	Grp.	Ind.	Tutorials
		Math skills			Word processing
		Study skills			Time management
		Language arts			Learning strategies
		Written express			Organizational skills

Academic Accommodations

Curriculum	Study Aids	Exams
• Priority registration	Typist	• Oral
Math waiver	Reader	• Untimed
Foreign lang. waiver	Notetaker	Take home
Course substitution	• Proof reader	• With proctor
In Class	Text on tape	• On computer
• Calculators	Early syllabus	• Extended time
• Tape recorder	Taped handouts	On tape
• Word processor		• Modified
Priority seating		• Separate room

Graduation Requirements:
Course credits: **120 semester hours** GPA: **2.0** Years to complete degree: **4.5 usually**

Other requirements: **Skills Acquisition: Foreign Language, Quantitative Reasoning**

Program Strengths
Our students must attend a special LD orientation in August. All students must only take 12 hours the first two semesters and meet with the LD specialist twice a week. We evaluate a student's ability to use compensatory skills and we expect students to carry the information about their learning style to their instructors.

General Information:
University of Colorado at Boulder is a 4 year public university. Suburban campus of 600 acres is 30 miles from Denver. Accessible by air, train or bus. 11 residential halls on campus. Housing is not guaranteed.

Accreditation:

Expenses:
Tuition: In-state: Full year: $2,40.000. Part-time: Per credit:0. Tuition: Out-of-state: Full year: $10,500.00.

Majors
• AREA STUDIES American, Asian, Black/Afro-American, Eastern European, European, Latin American, Women's Studies • BUSINESS Accounting, Banking, Economics, Finance, International Business, Management, Organizational Behavior, Personnel, Real Estate, Small Business Management and , Transportation Management • COMMUNICATIONS Advertising, Communication, English, Linguistic, News/Editorial, Television/Radio/Film • COMPUTER SCIENCE Computer Science, Management Information Systems • EDUCATION Art, Music • ENGINEERING Aeronautical, Aerospace, Architectural, Chemical, Civil/Environmental, Communications, Computer, Electrical, Engineering Physics, Mechanical • ENVIRONMENTAL CONTROL Conservation and Control • HEALTH SCIENCES Speech/Audiology and Speech • HUMANITIES Classics, Humanities, Liberal Arts, Philosophy, Religion • LANGUAGES Chinese, French, German, Italian, Japanese, Russian, Spanish • PREPROFESSIONAL Pharmacy, Sports Medicine • SCIENCES Biology, Cell Biology, Mathematics, Molecular Biology, Physical Science, Physics • SOCIAL SCIENCES Anthropology, History, Human Resource Development, Political Science, Psychology, Public Relations, Social Sciences, Sociology • VISUAL AND PERFORMING ARTS Art History, Dance, Dramatic Arts, Music, Music History and Appreciation, Music Performance, Music Theory and Composition • VOCATIONAL Operations Research, Park/Recreation

Sports/Activities
• SPORTS-INTERCOLLEGIATE Basketball (F), Basketball (M), Football, Golf (M), Skiing - Snow (F), Skiing - Snow (M), Tennis (F), Tennis (M), Track and Field (F), Track and Field (M), Volleyball (F)

Selective
Colorado Program

University of Denver
Centennial Hall South #302
Denver, Colorado 80208-4540
(303) 871-2000

School Enrollment: **7,500** Male: **3,750** Female: **3,750**
LD Enrollment: **80** Male: **40** Female: **40**

Admissions Contact: **Susan Hunt, Director of Admissions**
LD Contact: **Lisa Switzer, Director, Learning Effectiveness**
Name of Program: **Learning Effectiveness Program**
Telephone:**(303) 871-2000**

Admissions

Application Information:
LD Students Applying: **265** Enrolled:**30**
LD on admissions committee:**Yes**
Application deadline: **None**
Rolling Admissions: **Yes**Notified when: **March**

Secondary School Information
Most Important Criteria For Admissions (1-strongest)

6 SAT/ACT	**5** Application	**3** School transcript
9 Class rank	**8** Course selection	**7** Personal statement
4 Interview	**10** Extra activities	**1** Psychoeducational
2 G.P.A.	Open admission	**5** Recommendations

Test Requirements:
Diagnostic testing waived: **Yes**
Untimed SAT: **Yes** Untimed ACT: **Yes** Untimed ACH: **Yes**
WAIS-R required: **Yes** Range accepted: **100+**
Documentation of LD required: **Yes**
Currency of diagnostic testing: **No older than 2 years**
Tests recommended: **WAIS-R, Woodcock-Johnson**

Types of Disabilities Served
• Speech/Lang
• Study skills
• Written express
• Organizational
• Perceptual
• Reading
• Spelling
• Math
• Fine Motor
• ADD with LD
ADD without LD
• ADHD with LD
ADHD without LD

Admissions Process

Students apply to the University and if they self-identify they must include diagnostics with application. Entire application is then sent to us. We highly recommend an interview. We make a recommendation and confer with admissions. We are involved in every LD student's decision.

High School Course Requirements:
English: **3** Math: **3** Science: **3** Foreign Language: **2**
Waivers to standard high school courses
Foreign Language : **Yes**

Learning Disability Program

Syllabus available during orientation:**Yes**
Program: Reinforces course work: **Yes**
Program available through:**Monday-Friday**
Students mainstreamed **100** % of the day
Recommended credits per semester: **13-16**
Time required or recommended in learning center: **1 hour**
Services only for LD students: **Yes**
Counseling: Individual: **Yes** Group Counseling: **Yes** Vocational Counseling: **Yes**
Support groups are available:**Yes, through the Counseling Center**

Faculty:

Faculty: **6** Full time: **3** Part time: **3**
LD faculty with: BS/BA: **2** M.A.: **4**

Diagnostic Testing

ADD	Personality	Perceptual skills	Spelling
ADHD	Organization	Fine motor skills	Reading
I.Q.	Handwriting	Spoken language	Study skills
Math	Social skills	Written language	

Tutoring:

Average size of group tutorials: **5-6**
Services rendered by:
•Graduates •Peers •Faculty •LD staff Teacher trainees

Tutorials

Grp.	Ind.	Tutorials	Grp.	Ind.	Tutorials
	•	Math skills			Word processing
	•	Study skills		•	Time management
	•	Language arts		•	Learning strategies
	•	Written express		•	Organizational skills

Academic Accommodations

Curriculum	Study Aids	Exams
• Priority registration	Typist	• Oral
Math waiver	• Reader	• Untimed
Foreign lang. waiver	• Notetaker	• Take home
Course substitution	Proof reader	• With proctor
In Class	• Text on tape	• On computer
• Calculators	Early syllabus	• Extended time
• Tape recorder	Taped handouts	• On tape
• Word processor		Modified
Priority seating		• Separate room

Graduation Requirements:

Course credits: **185** GPA: **2.0** Years to complete degree: **4-5** Language waiver: **Yes**

Program Strengths

Our program is structured so that each student has a primary counselor with whom the student meets at least once a week. That counselor provides academic/tutorial support as well as emotional support. We also have a student advisory board, a career counseling component and a full-time computer lab available to students.

General Information:

University of Denver is a 4 year independent university. Urban campus of 230 acres is Accessible by plane, bus or train Ski areas are 30 minutes from campus. 25% of students are foreign. 4 residential halls on campus. Housing is guaranteed.Guaranteed through the 4th year. 75 % of students remain on campus for the weekends. 75 % of students join fraternities/sororities.

Accreditation:AACSB, CSWE, NASAD, NASM, NCATE

Expenses:
Tuition: In-state: Full year: $12,852.00. Part-time: Per credit:$357.00. Room and board: $6,968.00 Cost of LD program:$2,000.00

Majors

• AREA STUDIES African, Black/Afro-American, Jewish/Judaism, Women's Studies • ARTS Art History, Design, Graphic Arts, Music, Music Performance • BUSINESS Accounting, Banking/Finance, Business Administration, Construction, Economics, Hotel & Restaurant Management, International Business, Management, Marketing, Real Estate, Travel/Tourism Management • COMMUNICATIONS Advertising, Communication, Creative Writing, English, Journalism, Literature, Public Relations, Speech/Debate/Forensic • COMPUTER SCIENCE Computer Science, Programming • CRAFTS AND DESIGN Graphic Design • EDUCATION Adult, Child Development, Early Childhood, Foreign Language • ENGINEERING Engineering Science • HUMANITIES English/Writing/Literature • LANGUAGES French, German, Hebrew, Italian, Japanese, Portuguese, Spanish • MATHEMATICS Applied, Computer, Statistical • PRE PROFESSIONAL Law • RELIGIOUS STUDIES Judaism & Jewish Studies, Philosophy, Religion & Theology

Sports/Activities

• SPORTS-INTERCOLLEGIATE Baseball (M), Baseball (M), Basketball (F), Cross Country (F), Cross Country (M), Diving (F), Diving (M), Field Hockey (F), Field Hockey (M), Figure Skating, Gymnastics (F), Gymnastics (M), Ice Hockey (F), Ice Hockey (M), Lacrosse (F), Lacrosse (M), Rugby (M), Skiing - Cross Country, Skiing - Snow (F), Skiing - Snow (M), Soccer (F), Soccer (M), Softball (F), Softball (M), Swimming (F), Swimming (M), Tennis (F), Tennis (M), Track and Field (F), Track and Field (M), Volleyball (F), Volleyball (M) • SPORTS-INTRAMURAL Basketball (F), Basketball (M), Field Hockey (F), Field Hockey (M), Skiing - Cross Country, Skiing - Snow (F), Skiing - Snow (M), Volleyball (F), Volleyball (M) • STUDENT LIFE ACTIVITIES Academic Clubs, Choral, Community Service, Drama Groups, Ethnic & Cultural Groups, Fraternities, Newspaper, Religious Organization, Sororities, Student Government, Yearbook

Selective   **Colorado**
Services

Western State College of Colorado

Gunnison, Colorado 81231
(303) 943-2119

School Enrollment: **2,231** Male: **1,339** Female: **892**
LD Enrollment: **40** Male: **26** Female: **14**

Admissions Contact: **Monica Bruning, Director of Admissions**
LD Contact: **Jane Martindell, Special Student Support Advisor**
Name of Program: **Special Student Support Services**
Address: **101 Quigley Hall**
Telephone:**(303) 943-2130**

Admissions

Application Information:
LD Students Applying: **75** Accepted: **45** Enrolled:**30**
LD on admissions committee:**Yes**
Application deadline: **Rolling**
Applicant must apply **9** months in advance
Rolling Admissions: **Yes**

Secondary School Information
Most Important Criteria For Admissions (1-strongest)

1 SAT/ACT	**2** Application	**1**	School transcript
5 Class rank	**2** Course selection	**3**	Personal statement
2 Interview	**4** Extra activities	**2**	Psychoeducational
1 G.P.A.	Open admission	**2**	Recommendations

Test Requirements:
Diagnostic testing waived: **Yes**
Untimed SAT: **Yes** Untimed ACT: **Yes**
Documentation of LD required: **Yes**
Tests recommended: **Woodcock-Johnson Psychoeducational Battery**

Types of Disabilities Served
- Speech/Lang
- Study skills
- Written express
- Organizational
- Perceptual
- Reading
- Spelling
- Math
- Fine Motor
- ADD with LD
- ADD without LD
- ADHD with LD
- ADHD without LD

Admissions Process

Student may check box on application form indicating interest in LD Program. Special committee reviews an LD application to determine if our services will meet the student's need.

High School Course Requirements:
English: **3-4** Math: **3-4** Science: **3-4** Foreign Language: **1**

Learning Disability Program
Program: Reinforces course work: **Yes**
Students mainstreamed **100** % of the day
Services only for LD students: **Yes**
Counseling: Individual: **Yes**

Faculty:
Faculty: **1** Including Director: **Yes** Full time: **1** M.A.: **1**
Faculty advocate: **Yes** Meets with instructor: **1 or 2x per semester**

Diagnostic Testing
- ADD
- ADHD
- I.Q.
- Math
- Personality
- Organization
- Handwriting
- Social skills
- Perceptual skills
- Fine motor skills
- Spoken language
- Written language
- Spelling
- Reading
- Study skills

Tutoring:
Services rendered by:
Graduates • Peers   Faculty   • LD staff   Teacher trainees

Tutorials

Grp.	Ind.	Tutorials	Grp.	Ind.	Tutorials
	•	Math skills		•	Word processing
•	•	Study skills		•	Time management
	•	Language arts		•	Learning strategies
	•	Written express	•	•	Organizational skills

Academic Accommodations

Curriculum	Study Aids	Exams
Priority registration	• Typist	• Oral
Math waiver	• Reader	Untimed
Foreign lang. waiver	• Notetaker	• Take home
Course substitution	• Proof reader	With proctor
In Class	• Text on tape	On computer
• Calculators	Early syllabus	• Extended time
• Tape recorder	Taped handouts	On tape
• Word processor		Modified
Priority seating		• Separate room

Program Strengths
Western State College offers study skills classes and individual consultation regarding academic concerns. Our services for learning disabled students include: tutoring, note-taking, readers, use of tape recorders - all available without charge to our students. Professors are notified of any students in their classes who are taking advantage of this program, and close communication is maintained throughout each semester between professors and the Advising Center.

General Information:
Western State College of Colorado is a 4 year public college. Rural campus of 228 acres is 210 miles from Denver. Accessible by air or bus. Ski areas are 30 minutes from campus. Beaches are 10 minutes from campus. 1% of students are foreign. 15 residential halls on campus. Housing is guaranteed. Guaranteed through 1st year. 60 % of students remain on campus for the weekends. 3 % of students join fraternities/sororities.

Accreditation: NACS, NASM

SAT/ACT Scores:
Scores for incoming freshmen: **Verbal: **86% below 500. 14% between 500 and 599. 6% between 600 and 699. **Math:** 69% below 500. 25% between 500 and 599. 6% between 600 and 699. **ACT:** 50% below 20. 28% between 20 and 23. 5% between 24 and 25l. 17% between 26 and 28.

Class Rank:
About 12% of the present freshmen class were in the upper 20% of their high school class. 44% were in the top 40% of their class. 44% were in the top 60% of their class.

Expenses:
Tuition: In-state: Full year: $1,206.00. Part-time: Per credit: $44.00. Tuition: Out-of-state: Full year: $4,596.00. Part-time: Per credit: $158.00. Room and board: $3,180.00

Majors
• BUSINESS Accounting, Business Administration, Business Management, Economics, Finance, Marketing • COMMUNICATIONS Broadcasting, Communication, English, Television/Radio/Film • EDUCATION Art, Curriculum, Elementary, Music, Physical, Recreation and Youth Leadershi, Secondary, Special • LANGUAGES French, Spanish • PREPROFESSIONAL Dentistry, Forestry, Law, Medicine, Recreation • SCIENCES Biology, Chemistry, Geology, Mathematics, Physics • SOCIAL SCIENCES Government/Political, History, Political Science, Psychology, Sociology • VISUAL AND PERFORMING ARTS Art, Dramatic Arts, Music, Theater • VOCATIONAL Park/Recreation

Sports/Activities
• SPORTS RELATED Cheerleading, Marching Band, Pep Band, Team Managers • SPORTS-INTERCOLLEGIATE Basketball, Cross Country, Football (M), Skiing - Snow, Track and Field, Volleyball (F), Wrestling (M) • SPORTS-INTRAMURAL Badminton, Basketball, Bowling, Boxing, Cross Country, Diving, Golf, Hand Ball, Ping-Pong, Racquetball, Racquetball, Skiing - Snow, Soccer, Softball, Tennis, Volleyball, Windsurfing, Wrestling (M) • STUDENT LIFE ACTIVITIES Choral, Debate, Drama

Connecticut

Groups, Film, Fraternities, Honors Programs, Jazz Band, Magazine, Newspaper, Political Groups, Radio/TV station, Religious Organization, Sororities, Student Government

Less Selective   **Connecticut Services**

Briarwood College
2279 Mount Vernon Road
Southington, Connecticut 06489
(203) 628-4751

School Enrollment: **277** Male: **24** Female: **253**
LD Enrollment: **18** Male: **3** Female: **15**

Admissions Contact: **Debra LaRoche, Director of Admissions**
LD Contact: **Barbara Mackay, Dean of Student Affairs**
Telephone:**(203) 628-4751**

Admissions

Application Information:
Enrolled:**18**
Application deadline: **None**
Applicant must apply **Prior to start of summer preferred** months in advance
Rolling Admissions: **Yes**

Secondary School Information
Most Important Criteria For Admissions (1-strongest)

SAT/ACT	Application	School transcript
Class rank	Course selection	Personal statement
Interview	Extra activities	Psychoeducational
G.P.A.	Open admission	Recommendations

Test Requirements:
Standardized tests waived: **Yes**
Diagnostic testing waived: **Yes**
Documentation of LD required: **Yes**
Currency of diagnostic testing: **Preferred 8th grade or later**

Types of Disabilities Served
- Speech/Lang
- Study skills
- Written express
- Organizational
- Perceptual
- Reading
- Spelling
- Math
- Fine Motor
- ADD with LD
- ADD without LD
- ADHD with LD
- ADHD without LD

Admissions Process

Rolling admissions

High School Course Requirements:
Waivers to standard high school courses
Foreign Language : **Yes** Math: **Yes** Course substitution: **Yes**

Learning Disability Program
Syllabus available during orientation:**Yes**
Program: Reinforces course work: **Yes**
Program available through:**On going**
Students mainstreamed **100** % of the day
Recommended credits per semester: **12-15**
Services available for all students: **Yes**
Counseling: Individual: **Yes** Vocational Counseling: **Yes**

Faculty:
Faculty: **1** Part time: **1** M.A.: **1**
Faculty advocate: **Yes** Meets with instructor: **As needed**

Diagnostic Testing
ADD	• Personality	• Perceptual skills	• Spelling
ADHD	• Organization	• Fine motor skills	• Reading
• I.Q.	• Handwriting	Spoken language	Study skills
• Math	• Social skills	Written language	

Tutoring:
Average size of group tutorials: **1:1**
Services rendered by:
Graduates   •Peers   •Faculty   LD staff   Teacher trainees

Tutorials
Grp.	Ind.	Tutorials	Grp.	Ind.	Tutorials
	•	Math skills		•	Word processing
	•	Study skills		•	Time management
	•	Language arts		•	Learning strategies
	•	Written express		•	Organizational skills

Academic Accommodations
Curriculum	Study Aids	Exams
Priority registration	• Typist	• Oral
• Math waiver	Reader	• Untimed
• Foreign lang. waiver	• Notetaker	• Take home
• Course substitution	• Proof reader	• With proctor
In Class	Text on tape	• On computer
• Calculators	• Early syllabus	• Extended time
• Tape recorder	Taped handouts	On tape
• Word processor		• Modified
• Priority seating		• Separate room

Graduation Requirements:GPA: **2.0** Years to complete degree: **3** Math waiver: **Yes** Language waiver: **Yes**

Program Strengths
Briarwood College does not have an LD program; however, we do serve LD students. Because of our intimate size and student/faculty ratio, we can usually assess a student's strengths and weaknesses and then help him or her to select an appropriate program. We also have our own test center. We can substitute courses and modify the program, particularly in non-degree programs.

General Information:
Briarwood College is a 2 year independent college. Suburban campus of 32 acres is 19 miles from Hartford. Ski areas are 2 miles from campus. Beaches are 35 miles from campus. 2 residential halls on campus. Housing is not guaranteed.15 % of students remain on campus for the weekends.

Accreditation:NEACS, CBHE, NAEYC, CAHEA

Expenses:
Tuition: In-state: Full year: $8,300.00. Part-time: Per credit:$125.00. Tuition: Out-of-state: Full year: $8,300.00. Part-time: Per credit:$125.00. Room and board: $2,296.00

Majors
• BUSINESS Accounting, Business Management, Hotel and Restaurant Managemen, Travel/Tourism Management • COMMUNICATIONS Broadcasting • EDUCATION Child Care • HEALTH SCIENCES Dental Assistant, Dietetics, Medical Assistant, Medical Records Technology, Medical Secretary • VOCATIONAL Business and Office, Fashion Merchandising, Legal Assistant, Legal Secretary, Legal Secretary, Medical Laboratory Technology, Paralegal, Secretarial, Word Processing

Sports/Activities

• SPORTS-INTRAMURAL Badminton, Badminton, Basketball, Basketball, Bowling, Bowling, Golf, Golf, Ping-Pong, Racquetball, Racquetball, Skiing - Snow, Softball, Softball, Swimming, Swimming, Tennis, Volleyball • STUDENT LIFE ACTIVITIES Choral, Fraternities, Sororities

Selective   **Connecticut Services**

Eastern Connecticut State University
Hurley Hall
Willimantic, Connecticut 06226
(203) 456-5286

School Enrollment: **2,638** Male: **1,199** Female: **1,439**

Admissions Contact: **Arthur Forst, Ph.D., Director of Admissions**
Name of Program: **Disabled Student Services**
Address: **Student Center**
Telephone: **(203) 456-5448**

Admissions

Secondary School Information
Most Important Criteria For Admissions (1-strongest)

3 SAT/ACT	Application	1	School transcript
1 Class rank	1 Course selection	5	Personal statement
3 Interview	5 Extra activities		Psychoeducational
1 G.P.A.	Open admission	3	Recommendations

Test Requirements:
Documentation of LD required: **Yes**

Types of Disabilities Served

Speech/Lang	Reading	ADD with LD
Study skills	Spelling	ADD without LD
Written express	Math	ADHD with LD
Organizational	Fine Motor	ADHD without LD
Perceptual		

High School Course Requirements:
English: **4** Math: **3** Science: **2** Foreign Language: **2**

Learning Disability Program
Services available for all students: **Yes**

Diagnostic Testing

ADD	Personality	Perceptual skills	Spelling
ADHD	Organization	Fine motor skills	Reading
I.Q.	Handwriting	Spoken language	Study skills
Math	Social skills	Written language	

Tutoring:
Average size of group tutorials: **1:1**
Services rendered by:
  Graduates   •Peers   Faculty   LD staff   Teacher trainees

Tutorials

Grp.	Ind.	Tutorials	Grp.	Ind.	Tutorials
•		Math skills	•		Word processing
•		Study skills	•		Time management
•		Language arts	•		Learning strategies
•		Written express	•		Organizational skills

Academic Accommodations

Curriculum	Study Aids	Exams
Priority registration	Typist	• Oral
Math waiver	Reader	• Untimed
Foreign lang. waiver	Notetaker	Take home
• Course substitution	• Proof reader	With proctor
In Class	• Text on tape	On computer
• Calculators	Early syllabus	Extended time
• Tape recorder	Taped handouts	On tape
Word processor		Modified
• Priority seating		Separate room

Graduation Requirements:
Course credits: **120** GPA: **2.0** Years to complete degree: **4-5**

General Information:
Eastern Connecticut State University is a 4 year public university. Suburban campus of 100 acres is 25 miles from Hartford. Accessible by air, bus, or train. Ski areas are 40 miles from campus. Beaches are 30 miles from campus. 2% of students are foreign. 4 residential halls on campus. Housing is guaranteed. Guaranteed through 4th year.

Accreditation: NEACS

SAT/ACT Scores:
Scores for incoming freshmen: **Verbal:** 83% below 500. 14% between 500 and 599. 2% between 600 and 699. 1% above 700. **Math:** 69% below 500. 25% between 500 and 599. 5% between 600 and 699. 1% above 700.

Expenses:
Tuition: In-state: Full year: $1,380.00. Part-time: Per credit: $95.00. Tuition: Out-of-state: Full year: $4,468.00. Part-time: Per credit: $95.00. Room and board: $3,464.00

Majors
• AREA STUDIES Women's Studies • ARTS Graphic Arts, Music • BUSINESS Accounting, Business Administration, Marketing • COMMUNICATIONS Communication, English, Television/Radio/Film • COMPUTER SCIENCE Computer Science • EDUCATION Early Childhood, Elementary, Middle School, Physical, Secondary • HUMANITIES English/Writing/Literature, Fine Arts, Liberal Arts • MATHEMATICS Theoretical • PHILOSOPHY Fine Arts • PRE PROFESSIONAL Dentistry, Law, Medicine, Optometry, Veterinarian • SCIENCES Biology, Earth, Mathematics • SOCIAL SCIENCES Criminal Justice, Government/Political, History, Human Service, Political Science, Psychology, Social Science, Sociology

Sports/Activities
• SPORTS RELATED Cheerleading, Team Managers • SPORTS-INTERCOLLEGIATE Baseball (M), Basketball (F), Basketball (M), Cross Country (F), Cross Country (M), Soccer (F), Soccer (M), Softball (F), Track and Field (F), Track and Field (M), Volleyball (F) • STUDENT LIFE ACTIVITIES Academic Clubs, Choral, Community Service, Dance, Debate, Drama Groups, Ethnic & Cultural Groups, Film, Magazine, Music Groups, Newspaper, Orchestra, Preprofessinal, Radio/TV station, Religious Organization, Student Government, Yearbook

Less Selective

Hartford College for Women

1265 Asylum Avenue
Hartford, Connecticut 06105
(203) 236-1215

School Enrollment: **126**

Admissions Contact: **Anne R. Baldwin, Director of Admissions**
LD Contact: **Patti Said, Director Student Support Services**
Name of Program: **Student Support Services**

Admissions

Application Information:
Application deadline: **March 1st**
Rolling Admissions: **Yes**

Secondary School Information
Most Important Criteria For Admissions (1-strongest)

2	SAT/ACT	8 Application	1 School transcript
3	Class rank	3 Course selection	5 Personal statement
4	Interview	9 Extra activities	7 Psychoeducational
1	G.P.A.	Open admission	6 Recommendations

Test Requirements:
Untimed SAT: **Yes** Untimed ACT: **Yes**
Documentation of LD required: **Yes**

Types of Disabilities Served
- Speech/Lang
- Reading
- ADD with LD
- Study skills
- Spelling
- ADD without LD
- Written express
- Math
- ADHD with LD
- Organizational
- Fine Motor
- ADHD without LD
- Perceptual

Learning Disability Program

Counseling: Individual: **Yes** Group Counseling: **Yes**

Diagnostic Testing

ADD	Personality	Perceptual skills	Spelling
ADHD	Organization	Fine motor skills	Reading
I.Q.	Handwriting	Spoken language	Study skills
Math	Social skills	Written language	

Tutoring:
Average size of group tutorials: **5**
Services rendered by:
Graduates •Peers •Faculty LD staff Teacher trainees

Tutorials

Grp.	Ind.	Tutorials	Grp.	Ind.	Tutorials
•	•	Math skills	•		Word processing
•	•	Study skills	•	•	Time management
		Language arts	•	•	Learning strategies
	•	Written express	•	•	Organizational skills

Academic Accommodations

Curriculum	Study Aids	Exams
Priority registration	Typist	Oral
Math waiver	Reader	Untimed
• Foreign lang. waiver	Notetaker	Take home
Course substitution	Proof reader	With proctor
In Class	Text on tape	On computer
• Calculators	Early syllabus	• Extended time
• Tape recorder	Taped handouts	On tape
• Word processor		Modified
• Priority seating		Separate room

Program Strengths

Because we are a small, liberal arts transfer college, well-known for our supportive environment, students with learning disabilities do very well without the need for special programs. They are, in effect, "mainstreamed." All of our students receive individualized attention.

General Information:

Hartford College for Women is a 2 year independent college. Urban campus of 13 acres is Hartford. Accessible by air, train, or bus. Ski areas are 1 hour from campus. Beaches are 1 hour from campus. 17% of students are foreign. 2 residential halls on campus. Housing is not guaranteed. 50 % of students remain on campus for the weekends.

Accreditation: Regional

SAT/ACT Scores:
Scores for incoming freshmen: **Verbal:** 82% below 500. 11% between 500 and 599. 5% between 600 and 699. **Math:** 85% below 500. 13% between 500 and 599. 2% between 600 and 699.

Class Rank:
About 24% of the present freshmen class were in the upper 20% of their high school class. 56% were in the top 40% of their class.

Expenses:
Tuition: In-state: Full year: $8,992.00. Part-time: Per credit: $200.00.
Room and board: $4,672.00

Majors

• BUSINESS Management • EDUCATION Education • HUMANITIES Liberal Arts • PREPROFESSIONAL Legal Assistant • SCIENCES Biology, Chemistry, Mathematics, Physical Science • SOCIAL SCIENCES Psychology, Social Sciences • VISUAL AND PERFORMING ARTS Fine Arts

Sports/Activities

• SPORTS-INTERCOLLEGIATE Basketball (F), Softball (F), Volleyball (F) • SPORTS-INTRAMURAL Basketball (F), Soccer (F), Softball (F) • STUDENT LIFE ACTIVITIES Choral, Dance, Drama Groups, Ethnic & Cultural Groups, Music Groups, Newspaper, Religious Organization, Student Government, Yearbook

Less Selective	Connecticut Services

Mattatuck Community College
750 Chase Parkway
Waterbury, Connecticut 06708
(203) 575-8013

School Enrollment: **4,000** Male: **1,600** Female: **2,400**
LD Enrollment: **105** Male: **50** Female: **55**

Admissions Contact: **Louise Summa**
LD Contact: **Carolyn Curtis, Coordinator, Academic Skills**
Name of Program: **Learning Disabilities Services**
Address: **750 Chase Parkway**
Telephone:**(203) 575-8161**

Admissions

Application Information:
Application deadline: **None**
Rolling Admissions: **Yes**

Secondary School Information
Most Important Criteria For Admissions (1-strongest)

SAT/ACT	Application	School transcript
Class rank	Course selection	Personal statement
Interview	Extra activities	Psychoeducational
G.P.A.	**1** Open admission	Recommendations

Test Requirements:
Untimed SAT: **Yes** Untimed ACT: **Yes**
Documentation of LD required: **Yes**

Types of Disabilities Served
- Speech/Lang
- Study skills
- Written express
- Organizational
- Perceptual
- Reading
- Spelling
- Math
- Fine Motor
- ADD with LD
- ADD without LD
- ADHD with LD
- ADHD without LD

Admissions Process

Student applies, a testing date is set, LD student may have untimed on the New Jersey. Scores place student in classes.

Learning Disability Program

Special orientation for LD students: **Yes**
Program: Reinforces course work: **Yes**
Students mainstreamed **100** % of the day
Services available for all students: **Yes**

Faculty:
Faculty: **2** Full time: **1** Part time: **1** M.A.: **2** Ph.D.: **1**
Faculty advocate: **Yes** Meets with instructor: **As needed**

Diagnostic Testing

ADD	Personality	Perceptual skills	Spelling
ADHD	Organization	Fine motor skills	Reading
I.Q.	Handwriting	Spoken language	Study skills
Math	Social skills	Written language	

Tutoring:
Average size of group tutorials: **1-4**
Services rendered by:
Graduates Peers Faculty •LD staff Teacher trainees

Tutorials

Grp.	Ind.	Tutorials	Grp.	Ind.	Tutorials
	•	Math skills			Word processing
•	•	Study skills	•		Time management
	•	Language arts		•	Learning strategies
•	•	Written express		•	Organizational skills

Academic Accommodations

Curriculum	Study Aids	Exams
• Priority registration	Typist	• Oral
Math waiver	Reader	• Untimed
Foreign lang. waiver	• Notetaker	Take home
Course substitution	Proof reader	• With proctor
In Class	• Text on tape	On computer
• Calculators	Early syllabus	• Extended time
• Tape recorder	Taped handouts	On tape
Word processor		Modified
• Priority seating		• Separate room

Program Strengths
We have the best LD services of all the community colleges in Connecticut. The services are grant related and therefore dependent. Students are more likely to self identify because of the exceptional quality of our services.

General Information:
Mattatuck Community College is a 2 year public college. Urban campus of 100 acres is 20 miles from Hartford. Accessible by bus. Housing is not guaranteed.

Accreditation:NEACS

Expenses:
Tuition: In-state: Full year: $467.00 per semester. Part-time: Per credit:$33.00. Tuition: Out-of-state: Full year: $1,358.00 per semester.

Majors
• BUSINESS Accounting, Business Administration, Business Management, Finance, Food Management, Hotel and Restaurant Managemen, Management, Marketing, Small Business Management • COMMUNICATIONS Creative Writing • COMPUTER SCIENCE Data Processing • EDUCATION Early Childhood, Special, Teacher's Aide • HEALTH SCIENCES Medical Secretary, Nursing, Radiological Therapy, Rehabilitation • HUMANITIES American Literature, Comparative Literature, Humanities, Liberal Arts • PREPROFESSIONAL Engineering, Law, Social Work • SCIENCES Earth, Gerontology, Horticultural, Mathematics • SOCIAL SCIENCES Criminal Justice, History, Human Service, International Relations, Law Enforcement, Social Sciences • VISUAL AND PERFORMING ARTS Fine Arts, Music • VOCATIONAL Automobile Technology, Automotive Service, EMT, Paralegal, Radiograph Medical Technology, Respiratory Therapy Technology, Secretarial

Sports/Activities
• SPORTS-INTERCOLLEGIATE Baseball (M), Basketball (M) • STUDENT LIFE ACTIVITIES Choral, Drama Groups, Ethnic & Cultural Groups, Magazine, Music Ensembles, Musical Theater, Newspaper, Religious Organization, Student Government

Connecticut

Mitchell College
437 Pequot Avenue
New London, Connecticut 06320
(203) 443-2811

School Enrollment: **1,200** Male: **650** Female: **550**
LD Enrollment: **50** Male: **34** Female: **16**

Admissions Contact: **Kathleen Crowley, Director of Admissions**
LD Contact: **Susan Duques, Ph.D., Director**
Name of Program: **Learning Resource Center**
Address: **437 Pequot Ave.**
Telephone:**(203) 443-2811 Ext. 277**

Admissions

Application Information:
LD Students Applying: **200** Accepted: **80** Enrolled:**36**
Separate application:**Yes**
Application deadline: **March 31st**
Applicant must apply **3-6** months in advance
Rolling Admissions: **Yes**Notified when: **May**

Secondary School Information
Most Important Criteria For Admissions (1-strongest)

1	SAT/ACT	6 Application	4 School transcript
10	Class rank	3 Course selection	8 Personal statement
7	Interview	9 Extra activities	2 Psychoeducational
5	G.P.A.	Open admission 11	Recommendations

Test Requirements:
Diagnostic testing waived: **Yes**
Untimed SAT: **Yes** Untimed ACT: **Yes** Achievement tests required:**3**
WAIS-R required: **Yes** Range accepted: **Average**
Documentation of LD required: **Yes**
Currency of diagnostic testing: **1-3 years**
Tests recommended: **Individualized, comprehensive reading, writing, math**

Types of Disabilities Served
- Speech/Lang
- Study skills
- Written express
- Organizational
- Perceptual
- Reading
- Spelling
- Math
- Fine Motor

- ADD with LD
- ADD without LD
- ADHD with LD
- ADHD without LD

Admissions Process

Submit LRC application packet to LRC, schedule LRC interview if requested to do so. Applications should be submitted in the preceeding fall.

High School Course Requirements:
English: **1-2** Math: **0-1** Science: **0-1**

Learning Disability Program
Program available through:**Fall, spring, summer**
Students mainstreamed **100** % of the day
Recommended credits per semester: **12**
Time required or recommended in learning center: **4-5 hours**
Services only for LD students: **Yes**
Counseling: Individual: **Yes** Vocational Counseling: **Yes**
Support groups are available:**At student's initiation**

Faculty:
Faculty: **12** Including Director: **Yes** Full time: **4** Part time: **8**
LD faculty with: BS/BA: **5** M.A.: **6** Ph.D.: **1**
Faculty advocate: **Yes** Meets with instructor: **As requested**

Diagnostic Testing
ADD	Personality	Perceptual skills	• Spelling
ADHD•	Organization	Fine motor skills	• Reading
I.Q.	Handwriting	Spoken language	• Study skills
• Math	Social skills•	Written language	

Tutoring:
Average size of group tutorials: **3**
Services rendered by:
Graduates   Peers   •Faculty   •LD staff   Teacher trainees

Tutorials
Grp.	Ind.	Tutorials	Grp.	Ind.	Tutorials
•	•	Math skills	•	•	Word processing
•	•	Study skills	•	•	Time management
•	•	Language arts	•	•	Learning strategies
•	•	Written express	•	•	Organizational skills

Academic Accommodations
Curriculum	Study Aids	Exams
Priority registration	Typist	• Oral
Math waiver	Reader	Untimed
Foreign lang. waiver	Notetaker	Take home
Course substitution	Proof reader	• With proctor
In Class	Text on tape	On computer
Calculators	Early syllabus	• Extended time
• Tape recorder	Taped handouts	On tape
• Word processor		Modified
Priority seating		• Separate room

Graduation Requirements:
Course credits: **60-62** GPA: **2.0** Years to complete degree: **2-3** Language waiver: **Yes**
Other requirements: **PE**

Program Strengths
The Learning Resource Center at Mitchell is a structured academic support program to help students develop college level skills and strategies for more independent functioning. Because Mitchell is a small, residential two- year college geared to low achievers, it is an ideal context for the student who is in need of transition between high school and a four year college.

General Information:
Mitchell College is a 2 year independent college. Urban campus 60-70 miles from Hartford. Accessible by air, train or bus. Ski areas are 2 hours from campus. Beaches are 1 mile from campus. 8 residential halls on campus. Housing is guaranteed.Guaranteed through 2nd year.

Accreditation:Regional

Expenses:
Tuition: In-state: Full year: $9,720.00 plus $600.00 fees. Part-time: Per

credit:Part-time: $95.00. Tuition: Out-of-state: Full year: $9,720.00 plus $600.00 fees. Room and board: $4,400.00 Cost of LD program:$1,600.00 per semester

Majors

• BUSINESS Accounting, Business Administration, Business Management • COMPUTER SCIENCE Computer Science, Data Processing • EDUCATION Early Childhood, Physical • HUMANITIES Liberal Arts • SCIENCES Biology, Gerontology, Marine Biology • SOCIAL SCIENCES Human Service, Law Enforcement, Political Science, Social Work • VOCATIONAL Athletic Training, Business and Office, Recreation

Sports/Activities

• SPORTS-INTERCOLLEGIATE Baseball (M), Basketball, Soccer, Softball (F) • SPORTS-INTRAMURAL Basketball, Sailing, Soccer (M), Softball, Tennis • STUDENT LIFE ACTIVITIES Choral, Dance, Drama Groups, Newspaper, Radio/TV station, Student Government, Yearbook

---

Less Selective   **Connecticut**
                                        Services

Northwestern Connecticut Community College

Park Place
Winsted, Connecticut 06098
(203) 738-6333

School Enrollment: **2,200**
LD Enrollment: **11** Male: **3** Female: **8**

Admissions Contact: **Richard Tracy, Director of Admissions**
LD Contact: **Beverly Chrzan**
Telephone:**Ext. 333**

Admissions

Application Information:
Application deadline: **None**
Rolling Admissions: **Yes**

Secondary School Information
Most Important Criteria For Admissions (1-strongest)

SAT/ACT	Application	School transcript
Class rank	Course selection	Personal statement
Interview	Extra activities	Psychoeducational
G.P.A.	**1** Open admission	Recommendations

Types of Disabilities Served
• Speech/Lang • Reading • ADD with LD
• Study skills • Spelling • ADD without LD
• Written express • Math • ADHD with LD
• Organizational • Fine Motor • ADHD without LD
• Perceptual

Faculty:
Faculty: **1** Full time: **1**

Diagnostic Testing

ADD	Personality	Perceptual skills	Spelling
ADHD	Organization	Fine motor skills	Reading
I.Q.	Handwriting	Spoken language	Study skills
Math	Social skills	Written language	

Tutoring:
Average size of group tutorials: **3-4**
Services rendered by:
Graduates •Peers Faculty LD staff Teacher trainees

Tutorials

Grp.	Ind.	Tutorials	Grp.	Ind.	Tutorials
		Math skills			Word processing
•		Study skills	•	•	Time management
		Language arts			Learning strategies
		Written express	•	•	Organizational skills

Academic Accommodations

Curriculum	Study Aids	Exams
Priority registration	Typist	Oral
Math waiver	Reader	Untimed
Foreign lang. waiver	Notetaker	Take home
• Course substitution	Proof reader	With proctor
In Class	• Text on tape	On computer
Calculators	Early syllabus	• Extended time
• Tape recorder	Taped handouts	On tape
Word processor		Modified
Priority seating		Separate room

Graduation Requirements:
Course credits: **60** Years to complete degree: **Open**

Program Strengths
Our services are described as "Sympathy and Support" by the Connecticut LD consortium. We are small enough to serve the uniqueness of each student while focusing on his strengths in working on his weaknesses.

General Information:
Northwestern Connecticut Community College is a 2 year public college. Suburban campus of 5 acres is 25 miles from Hartford. Ski areas are 5 miles from campus. Housing is not guaranteed.

Accreditation:Regional

Expenses:
Tuition: In-state: Full year: $565.00. Part-time: Per credit:0. Part-time: Per course: $151.00.

Majors
• BUSINESS Accounting, Business Administration, Business Management • COMMUNICATIONS English, Linguistic • COMPUTER SCIENCE Computer Science, Data Processing • CRAFTS AND DESIGN Graphic Design • EDUCATION Art, Special • HEALTH SCIENCES Medical Assistant, Medical Secretary • HUMANITIES Liberal Arts • SCIENCES Behavioral Biology, Mathematics • SOCIAL SCIENCES Criminal Justice, Law Enforcement • VISUAL AND PERFORMING ARTS Fine Arts • VOCATIONAL Business and Office, Legal Secretary, Park/Recreation

Sports/Activities
• SPORTS-INTERCOLLEGIATE Baseball (M), Softball (F), Tennis, Volleyball (F) • SPORTS-INTRAMURAL Basketball (M), Skiing - Snow, Tennis • STUDENT LIFE ACTIVITIES Academic Clubs, Choral, Drama Groups, Magazine, Radio/TV station, Student Government

Connecticut

Less Selective

**Connecticut
Services**

Norwalk Community College

188 Richards Avenue
Norwalk, Connecticut 06854-1655
(203) 857-7192

School Enrollment: **3,690** Male: **1,267** Female: **2,423**
LD Enrollment: **52**

Admissions Contact: **Barbara Drotman, Director Enrollment**
LD Contact: **Stephen A. Spillane, Ph.D., Coordinator**
Name of Program: **Program for Students with Disabilities**
Telephone:**(203) 857-7192**

Admissions

Application Information:
Enrolled:**52**

Secondary School Information
Most Important Criteria For Admissions (1-strongest)

11 SAT/ACT	Application	**4**	School transcript
11 Class rank	**2** Course selection	**8**	Personal statement
3 Interview	**7** Extra activities	**1**	Psychoeducational
5 G.P.A.	Open admission	**6**	Recommendations

Test Requirements:
Diagnostic testing waived: **Yes**
WAIS-R required: **Yes**
Documentation of LD required: **Yes**
Tests recommended: **WAIS, Woodcock-Johnson Part I, Diagnostic
& Achievement Tests**

Types of Disabilities Served
- Speech/Lang
- Reading
- ADD with LD
- Study skills
- Spelling
- ADD without LD
- Written express
- Math
- ADHD with LD
- Organizational
- Fine Motor
- ADHD without LD
- Perceptual

Learning Disability Program

Program: Reinforces course work: **Yes**
Counseling: Individual: **Yes**

Faculty:
Faculty: **1** Including Director: **Yes** Full time: **1** Ph.D.: **1**
Faculty advocate: **Yes** Meets with instructor: **As needed**

Diagnostic Testing

ADD	Personality	Perceptual skills	Spelling
ADHD	Organization	Fine motor skills	Reading
I.Q.	Handwriting	Spoken language	Study skills
Math	Social skills	Written language	

Tutoring:
Average size of group tutorials: **2-3**
Services rendered by:

Graduates	•Peers	Faculty	•LD staff	Teacher trainees

Tutorials

Grp.	Ind.	Tutorials	Grp.	Ind.	Tutorials
•	•	Math skills		•	Word processing
	•	Study skills		•	Time management
	•	Language arts		•	Learning strategies
	•	Written express		•	Organizational skills

Academic Accommodations

Curriculum	Study Aids	Exams
Priority registration	Typist	• Oral
Math waiver	Reader	Untimed
Foreign lang. waiver •	Notetaker	• Take home
Course substitution	Proof reader	With proctor
In Class	• Text on tape	On computer
• Calculators	Early syllabus	• Extended time
• Tape recorder	Taped handouts	On tape
• Word processor		• Modified
Priority seating		Separate room

Program Strengths

Norwalk Community College's Program for Students with Disabilities
encourages qualified students with learning disabilities to reach their
academic potential through learning strategies and related support
services.

General Information:

Norwalk Community College is a 2 year public college. Urban campus of
4 acres is 60 miles from New York. Accessible by train or bus. Housing is
not guaranteed.

Accreditation:NEACS

Expenses:
Tuition: In-state: Full year: $590.00 per semester. Part-time: Per credit:0.
Part-time: Per course: $118.00. Tuition: Out-of-state: Full year: $1,754.00
per semester.

Majors

• BUSINESS Accounting, Business Administration, Business Management, Economics, Finance, Hotel and Restaurant Managemen, Management, Marketing, Real Estate • COMMUNICATIONS Communication,
English, Journalism, Photography • COMPUTER SCIENCE Data Processing • EDUCATION Art, Early Childhood • HEALTH SCIENCES Nursing
• HUMANITIES Humanities, Liberal Arts • LANGUAGES French, Spanish • PREPROFESSIONAL Recreation, Social Work • SCIENCES Mathematics, Physical Chemistry, Physical Science, Physics • SOCIAL
SCIENCES Anthropology, Criminal Justice, Government/Political, History, Human Service, Law Enforcement, Psychology, Sociology • VOCA-
TIONAL Business and Office, Park/Recreation, Respiratory Therapy
Technology, Secretarial

Sports/Activities

• SPORTS-INTERCOLLEGIATE Baseball (M), Basketball, Golf, Softball
(F), Tennis, Volleyball (F) • SPORTS-INTRAMURAL Bowling, Ping-
Pong, Skiing - Snow, Tennis • STUDENT LIFE ACTIVITIES Debate,
Newspaper, Radio/TV station, Student Government

Academic Accommodations

Curriculum	Study Aids	Exams
Priority registration	Typist	Oral
Math waiver	Reader	Untimed
Foreign lang. waiver •	Notetaker	Take home
Course substitution	Proof reader	With proctor
In Class	• Text on tape	On computer
Calculators	Early syllabus	Extended time
• Tape recorder	Taped handouts	On tape
Word processor		Modified
Priority seating		Separate room

Program Strengths
We have no separate LD program. Alll students are mainstreamed at acceptance. Students are accommodated individually by request only. Diploma and Certificate Programs do not require SAT testing.

General Information:
Paier College of Art is a 2 and 4 year independent college. Urban campus of 3 acres is 1-1/2 miles from New Haven. Accessible by train or bus. Ski areas are 20 miles from campus. Beaches are 15 miles from campus. Housing is not guaranteed.

Accreditation: NATTS, CBHE

SAT/ACT Scores:
Scores for incoming freshmen: **Verbal:** 71% below 500. 24% between 500 and 599. 7% between 600 and 699. **Math:** 68% below 500. 28% between 500 and 599. 4% between 600 and 699.

Expenses:
Tuition: In-state: Full year: $8,250.00. Part-time: Per credit: $250.00. Room and board: $3,150.00

Majors
• COMMUNICATIONS Photography • CRAFTS AND DESIGN Graphic Design, Illustration Design • VISUAL AND PERFORMING ARTS Fine Arts • VOCATIONAL Industrial Design

Sports/Activities
• STUDENT LIFE ACTIVITIES Student Government, Yearbook

Less Selective — **Connecticut Services**

South Central Community College
60 Sargent Drive
New Haven, Connecticut 06511-5970
(203) 789-7043

School Enrollment: **3,500** Male: **1,050** Female: **2,450**
LD Enrollment: **26**

Admissions Contact: **Myrna E. Garcia, Director of Admissions**
LD Contact: **Tina McHugh, LD Coordinator**
Name of Program: **LD Student Services**
Telephone: **(203) 789-6928**

Admissions

Application Information:
Application deadline: **September 1st**
Rolling Admissions: **Yes**

Special — **Connecticut Services**

Paier College of Art
Six Prospect Court
Hamden, Connecticut 06517
(203) 777-7319

School Enrollment: **89**

Admissions Contact: **Debra D. Simone, Asst. to Academic Dean**
Telephone: **(203) 785-8264**

Admissions

Application Information:
Application deadline: **None**
Rolling Admissions: **Yes**

Secondary School Information
Most Important Criteria For Admissions (1-strongest)

1 SAT/ACT	2 Application	1 School transcript
8 Class rank	11 Course selection	2 Personal statement
2 Interview	10 Extra activities	9 Psychoeducational
3 G.P.A.	Open admission	2 Recommendations

Test Requirements:
Standardized tests waived: **Yes**
Untimed SAT: **Yes**

Types of Disabilities Served
• Speech/Lang	• Reading	ADD with LD
• Study skills	• Spelling	ADD without LD
• Written express	• Math	ADHD with LD
• Organizational	Fine Motor	ADHD without LD
Perceptual		

Learning Disability Program
Counseling: Individual: **Yes**

Faculty:
Faculty: **2** Full time: **1** Part time: **1**
Faculty advocate: **Yes** Meets with instructor: **As needed**

Diagnostic Testing
ADD	Personality	Perceptual skills	Spelling
ADHD	Organization	Fine motor skills	Reading
I.Q.	Handwriting	Spoken language	Study skills
Math	Social skills	Written language	

Tutoring:
Services rendered by:
Graduates • Peers • Faculty • LD staff Teacher trainees

Tutorials
Grp.	Ind.	Tutorials	Grp.	Ind.	Tutorials
		Math skills			Word processing
		Study skills			Time management
		Language arts			Learning strategies
		Written express			Organizational skills

Connecticut

Secondary School Information
Most Important Criteria For Admissions (1-strongest)

11 SAT/ACT	1 Application	2 School transcript
10 Class rank	6 Course selection	7 Personal statement
5 Interview	9 Extra activities	4 Psychoeducational
3 G.P.A.	Open admission	8 Recommendations

Test Requirements:
Standardized tests waived: **Yes**
Diagnostic testing waived: **Yes**
WAIS-R required: **Yes** Range accepted: **80+**
Currency of diagnostic testing: **Suggested/1 month**
Tests recommended: **Institutional Placement Test**

Types of Disabilities Served
- Speech/Lang
- Study skills
- Written express
- Organizational
- Perceptual
- Reading
- Spelling
- Math
- Fine Motor
- ADD with LD
- ADD without LD
- ADHD with LD
- ADHD without LD

Learning Disability Program
Counseling: Individual: **Yes** Group Counseling: **Yes**

Faculty:
Faculty: **1** Part time: **1** M.A.: **1**
Faculty advocate: **Yes** Meets with instructor: **As needed**

Diagnostic Testing

ADD	Personality	Perceptual skills	Spelling
ADHD	Organization	Fine motor skills	Reading
I.Q.	Handwriting	Spoken language	Study skills
Math	Social skills	Written language	

Tutoring:
Average size of group tutorials: **2**
Services rendered by:

Graduates   Peers   •Faculty   •LD staff   Teacher trainees

Tutorials

Grp.	Ind.	Tutorials	Grp.	Ind.	Tutorials
•	•	Math skills	•	•	Word processing
•	•	Study skills	•	•	Time management
•	•	Language arts	•	•	Learning strategies
•	•	Written express	•	•	Organizational skills

Academic Accommodations

Curriculum	Study Aids	Exams
Priority registration	Typist	• Oral
Math waiver	Reader	Untimed
• Foreign lang. waiver	• Notetaker	Take home
Course substitution	• Proof reader	With proctor
In Class	• Text on tape	On computer
Calculators	Early syllabus	• Extended time
• Tape recorder	Taped handouts	On tape
• Word processor		Modified
Priority seating		Separate room

Program Strengths
South Central Community College offers a support service for qualified students with specific learning disabilities through the Center for Educational Services. The philosophy is to assist students to become successful and independent learners within the regular curriculum of the college.

General Information:
South Central Community College is a 2 year public college. Urban campus. Accessible by bus. 1% of students are foreign. Housing is not guaranteed.

Accreditation: NEACS

Expenses:
Tuition: In-state: Full year: $396.00. Part-time: Per credit:$33.00. Part-time: Per course: $99.00. Tuition: Out-of-state: Full year: $1,287.00. Part-time: Per credit:$107.25. Part-time: Per course:$321.75

Majors
- BUSINESS Accounting, Business Education, Hotel and Restaurant Managemen, Insurance • COMPUTER SCIENCE Data Processing • EDUCATION Bilingual • HEALTH SCIENCES Medical Secretary • HUMANITIES Liberal Arts • VOCATIONAL Legal Secretary, Radiological Technology, Respiratory Therapy Technology, Secretarial, Word Processing

Sports/Activities
- SPORTS-INTERCOLLEGIATE Basketball (M) • SPORTS-INTRAMURAL Basketball, Hand Ball, Racquetball, Swimming, Tennis, Volleyball • STUDENT LIFE ACTIVITIES Choral, Dance, Drama Groups, Ethnic & Cultural Groups, Film, Magazine, Music Ensembles, Newspaper, Student Government, Yearbook

---

Less Selective

Connecticut Services

Thames Valley State Technical College
574 New London Turnpike
Norwich, Connecticut 06360
(203) 886-0177

School Enrollment: **1,133** Male: **952** Female: **181**
LD Enrollment: **5** Male: **2** Female: **3**

Admissions Contact: **Nancy Merritt, Enrollment Manager**
LD Contact: **Linda Jacobsen, Dean of Students**

Admissions

Application Information:
Application deadline: **None**
Rolling Admissions: **Yes** Notified when: **Rolling**

Secondary School Information
Most Important Criteria For Admissions (1-strongest)

7 SAT/ACT	8 Application	1 School transcript
4 Class rank	2 Course selection	10 Personal statement
5 Interview	9 Extra activities	11 Psychoeducational
3 G.P.A.	1 Open admission	6 Recommendations

Test Requirements:
Standardized tests waived: **Yes**
Diagnostic testing waived: **Yes**
Untimed SAT: **Yes** Untimed ACT: **Yes**
Documentation of LD required: **Yes**

Types of Disabilities Served
- Speech/Lang
- Study skills
- Written express
- Organizational
- Perceptual
- Reading
- Spelling
- Math
- Fine Motor

ADD with LD
ADD without LD
ADHD with LD
ADHD without LD

Admissions Process

Open admissions; $10.00 application fee; required placement testing in math and English; mandatory developmental course work.

Learning Disability Program

Program: Remedial: **Yes**
Program: Reinforces course work: **Yes**
Students mainstreamed **100** % of the day
Recommended credits per semester: **15**
Services only for LD students: **Yes**
Counseling: Individual: **Yes** Vocational Counseling: **Yes**

Faculty:
Faculty: **1** Part time: **1** Ph.D.: **1**

Diagnostic Testing
ADD	Personality	Perceptual skills	Spelling
ADHD	Organization	Fine motor skills	Reading
I.Q.	Handwriting	Spoken language	Study skills
Math	Social skills	Written language	

Tutoring:
Average size of group tutorials: **3-4**
Services rendered by:
•Graduates •Peers •Faculty LD staff Teacher trainees

Tutorials
Grp.	Ind.	Tutorials	Grp.	Ind.	Tutorials
•	•	Math skills	•	•	Word processing
•		Study skills	•		Time management
•	•	Language arts	•		Learning strategies
•	•	Written express	•		Organizational skills

Academic Accommodations

Curriculum	Study Aids	Exams
Priority registration	Typist	• Oral
Math waiver	• Reader	Untimed
• Foreign lang. waiver	• Notetaker	Take home
Course substitution	• Proof reader	With proctor
In Class	• Text on tape	On computer
• Calculators	Early syllabus	• Extended time
• Tape recorder	Taped handouts	On tape
• Word processor		Modified
Priority seating		• Separate room

Graduation Requirements:GPA: **2.0** Years to complete degree: **2 minimum**
Other requirements: **25% of courses in residence**

Program Strengths
As you will note from the responses, we do not have a formal LD Program. We offer limited LD services. We do not do any testing or diagnostic procedures. We offer the services recommended such as tutoring, oral testing, and untimed tests.

General Information:
Thames Valley State Technical College is a 2 year public college. Suburban campus of 40 acres is 40 miles from Hartford. Accessible by bus. Ski areas are 20 miles from campus. Beaches are 3 miles from campus. 1% of students are foreign. Housing is not guaranteed.

Accreditation:NEACS, ABET

Expenses:
Tuition: In-state: Full year: $1,320.00. Part-time: Per credit:$55.00. Tuition: Out-of-state: Full year: $4,290.00. Part-time: Per credit:$179.00.

Majors
• BUSINESS Marketing • COMPUTER SCIENCE Computer Science, Data Processing, Programming, Systems Analysis • ENGINEERING Aeronautical Technology, Chemical, Civil/Environmental, Electrical, Industrial, Manufacturing, Mechanical, Nuclear • PREPROFESSIONAL Architecture, Engineering • SOCIAL SCIENCES Public Relations • VOCATIONAL Chemical, Civil, Desktop Publishing, Drafting, Electrical Manufacturing, Fire ScienceASSOCIATE DEGREES:, Industrial Electronics, Mechanical, NuclearCERTIFICATES: Architect

Sports/Activities
• SPORTS-INTERCOLLEGIATE Basketball (M), Golf (F), Golf (M)
• SPORTS-INTRAMURAL Basketball, Skiing - Snow, Volleyball • STUDENT LIFE ACTIVITIES Newspaper, Student Government

---

Very Selective **Connecticut Program**

University of Connecticut
P. O. Box U88 28 No. Eagleville Rd.
Storrs, Connecticut 06268
(203) 486-3137

School Enrollment: **12,991** Male: **6,400** Female: **6,591**
LD Enrollment: **55-75**

Admissions Contact: **John Kolano, Assoc.Dir. of Admissions**
LD Contact: **Joan M. McGuire, Director**
Name of Program: **University Program for LD Students**
Telephone:**(203) 486-0178**

Admissions

Application Information:
LD Students Applying: **180** Accepted: **45** Enrolled:**20**
Application deadline: **March 1st**
Rolling Admissions: **Yes**

Secondary School Information
Most Important Criteria For Admissions (1-strongest)
5 SAT/ACT	Application	School transcript
4 Class rank	**2** Course selection	Personal statement
Interview	**6** Extra activities	**3** Psychoeducational
1 G.P.A.	Open admission	Recommendations

Test Requirements:
Untimed SAT: **Yes** Untimed ACT: **Yes**
Documentation of LD required: **Yes**
Currency of diagnostic testing: **3 years**
Tests recommended: **WAIS-R, Woodcock-Johnson, Stanford or California tests**

Connecticut

Types of Disabilities Served
- Speech/Lang
- Study skills
- Written express
- Organizational
- Perceptual
- Reading
- Spelling
- Math
- Fine Motor
- ADD with LD
- ADD without LD
- ADHD with LD
- ADHD without LD

High School Course Requirements:
English: **4** Math: **3** Science: **2** Foreign Language: **2**

Learning Disability Program
Students mainstreamed **100** % of the day
Recommended credits per semester: **Individual**
Services only for LD students: **Yes**
Counseling: Individual: **Yes** Group Counseling: **Yes**

Faculty:
Faculty: **5** Including Director: **Yes** Full time: **1** Part time: **4**
LD faculty with: BS/BA: **3** M.A.: **1** Ph.D.: **1**

Diagnostic Testing
ADD	Personality	Perceptual skills	• Spelling
ADHD	Organization	Fine motor skills	• Reading
• I.Q.	Handwriting	Spoken language	• Study skills
• Math	Social skills	• Written language	

Tutoring:
Average size of group tutorials:
Services rendered by:
•Graduates   Peers   Faculty   •LD staff   •Teacher trainees

Tutorials
Grp.	Ind.	Tutorials	Grp.	Ind.	Tutorials
	•	Math skills			Word processing
	•	Study skills		•	Time management
	•	Language arts		•	Learning strategies
	•	Written express		•	Organizational skills

Academic Accommodations
Curriculum	Study Aids	Exams
Priority registration	Typist	• Oral
• Math waiver	Reader	Untimed
• Foreign lang. waiver	Notetaker	Take home
Course substitution	• Proof reader	With proctor
In Class	• Text on tape	On computer
• Calculators	Early syllabus	• Extended time
• Tape recorder	Taped handouts	On tape
• Word processor		Modified
Priority seating		Separate room

Graduation Requirements:
Course credits: **120** GPA: **2.0**

Program Strengths
The University of Connecticut offers a support program for qualified students with specific learning disabilities through the Special Education Center. The philosophy is to assist students to become successful and independent learners within the regular curriculum of the University.

General Information:
University of Connecticut is a 4 year public university. Rural campus of 3,000 acres is 30 miles from Hartford. Housing is guaranteed. Guaranteed through 1st year. 10 % of students join fraternities/sororities.

Accreditation: Regional

Expenses:
Tuition: In-state: Full year:
$3,038.00. Part-time: Per credit:0. Tuition: Out-of-state: Full year:
$9,262.00. Room and board: $4,878.00

Majors
• AREA STUDIES Hispanic/American, Jewish, Latin American, Urban • BUSINESS Accounting, Agricultural, Banking, Business Administration, Business Management, Economics, Finance, Insurance, Labor Relations, Management, Marketing, Real Estate • COMMUNICATIONS Communication, English, Journalism, Linguistic, Photography, Speech • CRAFTS AND DESIGN Ceramics, Graphic Design, Painting, Printmaking, Sculpture • EDUCATION Curriculum, Early Childhood, Elementary, Music, Physical, School Psychology, Secondary, Special • ENGINEERING Agricultural, Chemical, Civil/Environmental, Electrical, Mechanical • HEALTH SCIENCES Communication Disorders, Health, Medical Technology, Nursing, Nutritional/Food, Physical Therapy, Speech Therapy, Speech/Audiology and Speech • HUMANITIES Classics, Liberal Arts, Philosophy • LANGUAGES French, German, Greek, Italian, Latin, Portuguese, Russian, Spanish • PREPROFESSIONAL Agriculture, Dentistry, Engineering, Landscaping, Natural Resources, Pharmacy, Recreation, Social Work • SCIENCES Agricultural, Animal, Biochemistry, Biology, Biophysics, Botany, Chemistry, Geography, Geology, Horticultural, Mathematics, Microbiology, Physical Chemistry, Physics, Physiology, Statistics, Zoology • SOCIAL SCIENCES Anthropology, Geography, Government/Political, History, Political Science, Psychology, Sociology • VISUAL AND PERFORMING ARTS Art, Art History, Dramatic Arts, Music, Music Appreciation, Studio Art, Theater • VOCATIONAL Home Economics, Medical Laboratory Technology, Textile and Clothing

Sports/Activities
• SPORTS RELATED Baton Twirling, Cheerleading, Drill Team, Drum Major/Majorette, Marching Band, Pep Band, Team Managers • SPORTS-INTERCOLLEGIATE Baseball (M), Basketball, Cricket (M), Diving, Field Hockey (F), Football (M), Golf (M), Gymnastics (F), Ice Hockey (M), Skiing - Snow, Soccer, Softball (F), Swimming, Tennis, Track and Field, Volleyball (F) • SPORTS-INTRAMURAL Baseball (M), Basketball, Cross Country (M), Football (M), Ice Hockey (M), Soccer, Softball • STUDENT LIFE ACTIVITIES Choral, Concert Band, Drama Groups, Ethnic & Cultural Groups, Film, Fraternities, Jazz Band, Magazine, Newspaper, Political Groups, Radio/TV station, Religious Organization, Sororities, Student Government

Less Selective   **Connecticut**
                                        Services

University of New Haven
300 Orange Avenue
West Haven, Connecticut 06516
(203) 932-7319

School Enrollment: **5,200** Male: **4,200** Female: **1,000**
LD Enrollment: **48** Male: **40** Female: **8**

Admissions Contact: **Dean Briggs, Dean of Admissions**
LD Contact: **David J. Kmetz, Dir. , Off. Students with Disabilities**
Name of Program: **Office for Students with Disabilities**
Address: **300 Orange Ave.**
Telephone: **(203) 932-7409**

Admissions

Application Information:
Rolling Admissions: **Yes**

Secondary School Information
Most Important Criteria For Admissions (1-strongest)

SAT/ACT	Application	School transcript
Class rank	Course selection	Personal statement
Interview	Extra activities	Psychoeducational
G.P.A.	Open admission	Recommendations

Test Requirements:
Diagnostic testing waived: **Yes**
Untimed SAT: **Yes** Untimed ACT: **Yes** Untimed ACH: **Yes** Achievement tests required:**3**
WAIS-R required: **Yes**
Documentation of LD required: **Yes**
Currency of diagnostic testing: **Maximum 36 months**
Tests recommended: **WAIS-R, Woodcock-Johnson Achievements**

Types of Disabilities Served
- Speech/Lang
- Study skills
- Written express
- Organizational
- Perceptual
- Reading
- Spelling
- Math
- Fine Motor
- ADD with LD
- ADD without LD
- ADHD with LD
- ADHD without LD

Admissions Process

Regular procedure

Learning Disability Program
Special orientation for LD students: **Yes**
Program: Remedial: **Yes**
Program available through:**Every semester**
Students mainstreamed **100** % of the day
Recommended credits per semester: **12**
Services available for all students: **Yes**
Counseling: Individual: **Yes** Vocational Counseling: **Yes**

Faculty:
Faculty: **1** Including Director: **Yes** Full time: **1** M.A.: **1**
Faculty advocate: **Yes** Meets with instructor: **As needed**

Diagnostic Testing

ADD	• Personality	• Perceptual skills	• Spelling
ADHD	• Organization	• Fine motor skills	• Reading
• I.Q.	Handwriting	Spoken language	• Study skills
• Math	• Social skills	• Written language	

Tutoring:
Average size of group tutorials: **4-6**
Services rendered by:
• Graduates   • Peers   • Faculty   LD staff   Teacher trainees

Tutorials

Grp.	Ind.	Tutorials	Grp.	Ind.	Tutorials
•	•	Math skills	•	•	Word processing
		Study skills	•	•	Time management
		Language arts	•	•	Learning strategies
•	•	Written express	•	•	Organizational skills

Academic Accommodations

Curriculum	Study Aids	Exams
Priority registration	Typist	Oral
Math waiver	• Reader	• Untimed
Foreign lang. waiver	• Notetaker	• Take home
• Course substitution	• Proof reader	• With proctor
In Class	• Text on tape	On computer
• Calculators	Early syllabus	• Extended time
• Tape recorder	Taped handouts	On tape
• Word processor		Modified
• Priority seating		• Separate room

Graduation Requirements:GPA: **2.0** Years to complete degree: **4 +**

General Information:
University of New Haven is a 4 year public university. Urban campus of 6 acres is 1 miles from New Haven. Accessible by air, train, or bus. Ski areas are 40 miles from campus. Beaches are 3 miles from campus. 10% of students are foreign. 4 residential halls on campus. Housing is guaranteed.Guaranteed through 4th year. 20 % of students remain on campus for the weekends. 3 % of students join fraternities/sororities.

Accreditation:NEACS, ACE, ACA

Expenses:
Tuition: In-state: Full year: $9,700.00. Part-time: Per credit:$314.00. Part-time: Per course: $940.00. Tuition: Out-of-state: Full year: $9,700.00. Room and board: $2,575.00

Majors
• ARTS Art History, Film & Video, Graphic Arts, Interior Design, Music History, Photography • BUSINESS Accounting, Aviation Management, Banking/Finance, Bookkeeping, Business Administration, Business Economics, Business Education, Business Management, Business Statistics, Commerce & Trade, Data Processing, Economics, Education, Entrepreneur, Food Management, Hotel & Restaurant Management, Human Resources Management, Industrial Operations, Insurance, International Business, Investments and Securities, Labor Relations, Management, Marketing, Marketing Research, Operations Research, Organizational Behavior, Personnel, Retail Manufacturing, Retailing, Sports Management, Taxation, Travel/Tourism Management, Vocational Studies • COMMUNICATIONS Advertising, Broadcasting, Communication, Creative Writing, English, Graphic Design, Journalism, Linguistics, Literature, Photography, Public Relations, Television/Radio/Film • COMPUTER SCIENCE Business Data Programming, Computer Maintenance, Computer Mathematics, Computer Science, Computer Technology, Data Processing, Programming, Software Engineer, Systems Analysis • CRAFTS AND DESIGN Graphic Design • ENGINEERING Architectural, Aviation, Chemical, Computer, Electrical, Engineering Science, Environmental/Water Resources, Industrial, Mechanical, Naval Architecture, Physics, Systems Analysis • HUMANITIES Humanities, Liberal Arts • MATHEMATICS Actuarial, Applied, Computer, Statistical • PRE PROFESSIONAL Business, Engineering, Law, Legal Assistant, Social Work • SCIENCES Applied Mathematics, Biology, Computer Science, Human Biology, Inorganic Chemistry, Mathematics • SOCIAL SCIENCES Criminal Justice, Criminology, Human Service, Psychology, Sociology • SPECIAL EDUCATION Mentally Retarded • VISUAL AND PERFORMING ARTS Music • VOCATIONAL Air Traffic Control, Aviation Management, Aviation Pilot, Chef Apprenticeship, Culinary Arts, Fire Science, Food Service, Paralegal, Piloting

Sports/Activities
• SPORTS-INTERCOLLEGIATE Baseball, Baseball (M), Basketball (F), Basketball (M), Football, Football (M), Golf, Lacrosse, Lacrosse (M), Racquetball, Soccer, Soccer (M), Softball, Softball (F), Tennis, Track and Field, Track and Field (F), Track and Field (M), Volleyball, Volleyball (F)
• SPORTS-INTRAMURAL Baseball, Basketball, Bowling, Crew, Golf, Racquetball, Soccer, Softball, Tennis, Volleyball, Volleyball (F), Volleyball (M) • STUDENT LIFE ACTIVITIES Academic Clubs, Community Ser-

vice, Drama Groups, Ethnic & Cultural Groups, Fraternities, Newspaper, Radio/TV station, Sororities, Student Government, Yearbook

Most Selective

Connecticut Services

Wesleyan University
High Street and Wyllis Avenue
Middletown, Connecticut 06457
(203) 344-7900

School Enrollment: 2,884

Admissions Contact: **Karl Furstenberg, Dean/Admissions**
LD Contact: **Denise Darrigrand, Dean of Student Life**
Telephone:**Ext. 2202**

Admissions

Application Information:
Application deadline: **January 15th**
Notified when: **April 15th**

Secondary School Information
Most Important Criteria For Admissions (1-strongest)

2 SAT/ACT	**3** Application	**1** School transcript
1 Class rank	**1** Course selection	Personal statement
4 Interview	**2** Extra activities	Psychoeducational
2 G.P.A.	Open admission	**2** Recommendations

Test Requirements:
Untimed SAT: **Yes** Untimed ACT: **Yes** Untimed ACH: **Yes**

Types of Disabilities Served
• Speech/Lang	Reading	ADD with LD
Study skills	Spelling	ADD without LD
Written express	Math	ADHD with LD
Organizational	Fine Motor	ADHD without LD
Perceptual		

Diagnostic Testing
ADD	Personality	Perceptual skills	Spelling
ADHD	Organization	Fine motor skills	Reading
I.Q.	Handwriting	Spoken language	Study skills
Math	Social skills	Written language	

Services rendered by:
Graduates   Peers   Faculty   LD staff   Teacher trainees

Tutorials
Grp.	Ind.	Tutorials	Grp.	Ind.	Tutorials
		Math skills			Word processing
		Study skills			Time management
		Language arts			Learning strategies
		Written express			Organizational skills

Academic Accommodations

Curriculum	Study Aids	Exams
Priority registration	Typist	Oral
Math waiver	Reader	Untimed
Foreign lang. waiver	Notetaker	Take home
Course substitution	Proof reader	With proctor
In Class	Text on tape	On computer
Calculators	Early syllabus	Extended time
Tape recorder	Taped handouts	On tape
Word processor		Modified
Priority seating		Separate room

Program Strengths
We do not have a formal learning disability program per se; however, through the good will of administrators and faculty members, various arrangements have been made for students with learning disabilities.

General Information:
Wesleyan University is a 4 year independent university. Suburban campus of 120 acres is 18 miles from Hartford. Accessible by train or bus. Ski areas are 30 minutes from campus. Beaches are 30 minutes from campus. 3% of students are foreign. 4 residential halls on campus. Housing is guaranteed.95 % of students remain on campus for the weekends. 13 % of students join fraternities/sororities.

Accreditation:NEACS

Class Rank:
About 90% of the present freshmen class were in the upper 20% of their high school class. 10% were in the top 40% of their class.

Expenses:
Tuition: In-state: Full year: $14,070.00. Room and board: $4,695.00

Majors
• AREA STUDIES African, American, Asian, Black/Afro-American, Jewish, Latin American, Urban • BUSINESS Economics • COMMUNICATIONS Creative Writing, English, Photography, Television/Radio/Film • COMPUTER SCIENCE Computer Science, Programming • EDUCATION Elementary, Middle School, Secondary • HUMANITIES Classics, English/Writing/Literature, Humanities, Liberal Arts, Philosophy, Religion • LANGUAGES Chinese, French, German, Greek, Hebrew, Italian, Japanese, Latin, Russian, Spanish • PREPROFESSIONAL Architecture, Landscaping, Medicine • SCIENCES Astronomy, Astrophysics, Behavioral Biology, Biochemistry, Biology, Cell Biology, Chemistry, Earth, Ecology, Mathematics, Microbiology, Physical Chemistry, Physical Science, Physics • SOCIAL SCIENCES Anthropology, Government/Political, History, Political Science, Social Sciences, Sociology • VISUAL AND PERFORMING ARTS Art, Art History, Dramatic Arts, Fine Arts, Music, Studio Art, Theater

Sports/Activities
• SPORTS RELATED Pep Band • SPORTS-INTERCOLLEGIATE Baseball (M), Basketball, Crew, Cross Country, Diving, Field Hockey (F), Football (M), Golf (M), Ice Hockey, Lacrosse, Rugby, Soccer, Softball (F), Squash, Swimming, Tennis, Track and Field, Volleyball (F), Water Polo, Wrestling (M) • SPORTS-INTRAMURAL Basketball, Cross Country, Fencing, Hammer Throw (M), Ice Hockey, Racquetball, Sailing, Skiing - Snow, Soccer, Softball, Squash, Swimming, Tennis, Volleyball • STUDENT LIFE ACTIVITIES Choral, Concert Band, Dance, Drama Groups, Ethnic & Cultural Groups, Film, Fraternities, Jazz Band, Musical Theater, Newspaper, Political Groups, Radio/TV station, Religious Organization, Sororities

Selective　　　　　　　　　**Connecticut Services**

Western Connecticut State University

181 White Street
Danbury, Connecticut 06810
(203) 797-4298

School Enrollment: **5,300** Male: **2,300** Female: **3,000**
LD Enrollment: **60** Male: **23** Female: **37**

Admissions Contact: **Carlton Lee, Assistant Director**
LD Contact: **H. Richard Dozier, Associate Dean, Student Affairs**
Address: **202 Old Main Building**
Telephone:**(203) 797-4392**

Admissions

Application Information:
Application deadline: **April 1st**
Rolling Admissions: **Yes** Notified when: **Starts mid-January**

Secondary School Information
Most Important Criteria For Admissions (1-strongest)

4 SAT/ACT	**1** Application	**2**	School transcript
3 Class rank	**6** Course selection	**8**	Personal statement
Interview	**7** Extra activities		Psychoeducational
5 G.P.A.	Open admission		Recommendations

Test Requirements:
Standardized tests waived: **Yes**
Untimed SAT: **Yes**
Documentation of LD required: **Yes**

Types of Disabilities Served
- Speech/Lang
- Study skills
- Written express
- Organizational
- Perceptual
- Reading
- Spelling
- Math
- Fine Motor
- ADD with LD
- ADD without LD
- ADHD with LD
- ADHD without LD

Admissions Process

No special admission process for LD. Student applies, if applicant meets the requirements he/she is admitted.

Learning Disability Program

Students mainstreamed **100** % of the day
Services available for all students: **Yes**
Counseling: Individual: **Yes**

Faculty:
Faculty: **1**
Faculty advocate: **Yes** Meets with instructor: **As needed**

Diagnostic Testing
ADD	Personality	Perceptual skills	Spelling
ADHD	Organization	Fine motor skills	Reading
I.Q.	Handwriting	Spoken language	Study skills
Math	Social skills	Written language	

Tutoring:
Services rendered by:

Graduates　•Peers　•Faculty　　LD staff　　Teacher trainees

Tutorials
Grp.	Ind.	Tutorials	Grp.	Ind.	Tutorials
	•	Math skills		•	Word processing
	•	Study skills		•	Time management
	•	Language arts		•	Learning strategies
	•	Written express		•	Organizational skills

Academic Accommodations

Curriculum	Study Aids	Exams
• Priority registration	Typist	• Oral
Math waiver	• Reader	• Untimed
• Foreign lang. waiver	• Notetaker	• Take home
• Course substitution	• Proof reader	• With proctor
In Class	• Text on tape	• On computer
• Calculators	Early syllabus	• Extended time
• Tape recorder	• Taped handouts	• On tape
• Word processor		• Modified
• Priority seating		• Separate room

Graduation Requirements:
Course credits: **120** GPA:　Years to complete degree: **4** Language waiver: **Yes**

Program Strengths
Services are provided on a one-to-one basis. As the Associate Dean of Student Affairs, I assist the students in course selection and notify their instructors of any potential problem areas.

General Information:
Western Connecticut State University is a 4 year public university. Suburban campus of 28 acres is 65 miles from New York City. Accessible by train or bus. Ski areas are 15 miles from campus. Beaches are 30 miles from campus. 1% of students are foreign. Housing is not guaranteed.50 % of students remain on campus for the weekends. 2 % of students join fraternities/sororities.

Accreditation:NEACS

SAT/ACT Scores:
Scores for incoming freshmen:**Verbal:**78%below 500. 15%between 500 and 599. 3%between 600 and 699. **Math:**67% below 500. 24% between 500 and 599. 6% between 600 and 699. 1%above 700.

Class Rank:
About 16% of the present freshmen class were in the upper 20% of their high school class. 32% were in the top 40% of their class. 38% were in the top 60% of their class. 6% were in the top 80% of their class.

Expenses:
Tuition: In-state: Full year: $1,380.00. Part-time: Per credit:0.　Tuition: Out-of-state: Full year: $4,468.00.　Part-time: Per credit:$105.00.　Room and board: $3,310.00.

Majors
• AREA STUDIES American • BUSINESS Accounting, Banking, Business Administration, Business Management, Economics, Finance, Marketing • COMMUNICATIONS Communication, Creative Writing, English, Journalism, Speech • COMPUTER SCIENCE Computer Science • CRAFTS AND DESIGN Graphic Design • EDUCATION Elementary, English, Foreign Language, Health, Mathematics, Music, Science, Secondary, Social Studies • ENGINEERING Bioengineering, Biomedical, Computer, Electrical, Mechanical • HEALTH SCIENCES Nursing, Speech/Audiology and Speech • HUMANITIES English/Writing/Literature, Humanities, Liberal Arts • LANGUAGES Spanish • PREPROFESSIONAL Social Work • SCIENCES Astronomy, Biochemistry, Biomedical, Botany, Chemistry, Earth, Physical Science • SOCIAL SCIENCES Anthropology,

Criminal Justice, Law Enforcement, Political Science, Psychology, Social Sciences, Sociology • VISUAL AND PERFORMING ARTS Music, Theater • VOCATIONAL Medical Laboratory Technology

Sports/Activities

• SPORTS RELATED Cheerleading, Marching Band, Pep Band
• SPORTS-INTERCOLLEGIATE Baseball (M), Basketball, Fencing, Fencing (F), Football (M), Golf (M), Soccer (M), Softball (F), Tennis, Volleyball (F) • SPORTS-INTRAMURAL Archery, Badminton, Baseball (M), Bowling, Cross Country, Lacrosse, Ping-Pong, Riflery, Skiing - Snow, Softball, Tennis, Volleyball • STUDENT LIFE ACTIVITIES Concert Band, Drama Groups, Ethnic & Cultural Groups, Fraternities, Jazz Band, Music Ensembles, Music Groups, Musical Theater, Newspaper, Radio/TV station, Religious Organization, Sororities, Student Government, Symphony Orchestra

Most Selective	Connecticut Services

Yale University

P.O. Box 1502A
New Haven, Connecticut 06520
(203) 432-1900

School Enrollment: **5,000** Male: **2,350** Female: **2,250**
LD Enrollment: **13**

Admissions Contact: **Margit Dahl, Director of Admissions**
LD Contact: **Fay Hanson, Director**
Name of Program: **Resource Office on Disabilities**
Address: **P.O. Box 2355, 80 Wall Street**
Telephone: **(203) 432-2324**

Admissions

Application Information:
Application deadline: **December 31st**

Secondary School Information
Most Important Criteria For Admissions (1-strongest)

3 SAT/ACT	Application	1 School transcript
1 Class rank	1 Course selection	4 Personal statement
5 Interview	4 Extra activities	Psychoeducational
1 G.P.A.	Open admission	2 Recommendations

Test Requirements:
Untimed SAT: **Yes** Untimed ACT: **Yes** Untimed ACH: **Yes** Achievement tests required: **3**
Documentation of LD required: **Yes**
Tests recommended: **For an application to be reviewed by Learning Disabilities Specialist documentation of disability is required.**

Types of Disabilities Served
• Speech/Lang • Reading • ADD with LD
• Study skills • Spelling ADD without LD
• Written express • Math • ADHD with LD
• Organizational • Fine Motor ADHD without LD
• Perceptual

Learning Disability Program

Students mainstreamed **100** % of the day
Services available for all students: **Yes**

Faculty:

Diagnostic Testing

ADD	Personality	Perceptual skills	Spelling
ADHD	Organization	Fine motor skills	Reading
I.Q.	Handwriting	Spoken language	Study skills
Math	Social skills	Written language	

Tutoring:
Average size of group tutorials: **1:1**
Services rendered by:
•Graduates •Peers •Faculty LD staff Teacher trainees

Tutorials

Grp.	Ind.	Tutorials	Grp.	Ind.	Tutorials
		Math skills			Word processing
		Study skills			Time management
		Language arts			Learning strategies
		Written express			Organizational skills

Academic Accommodations

Curriculum	Study Aids	Exams
Priority registration	• Typist	• Oral
Math waiver	Reader	• Untimed
• Foreign lang. waiver	• Notetaker	• Take home
Course substitution	• Proof reader	• With proctor
In Class	• Text on tape	On computer
Calculators	Early syllabus	• Extended time
• Tape recorder	Taped handouts	• On tape
• Word processor		• Modified
• Priority seating		• Separate room

Graduation Requirements:
Course credits: **36** Years to complete degree: **4 years** Language waiver: **Yes**

Program Strengths

Although Yale does not have an official "Learning Disability Program", a wide range of services are available for the learning disabled. For a specific list, students should write to the Resource Office on Disabilities. Tutoring is available in content areas.

General Information:

Yale University is a 4 year private university. Urban campus of 175 acres is 70 miles from New York City. Accessible by air, train or bus. Ski areas are 20 miles from campus. Beaches are a few miles from campus. 4% of students are foreign. 12 residential halls on campus. Housing is not guaranteed.

Accreditation: NEACS

SAT/ACT Scores:
Scores for incoming freshmen: **Verbal:** 3.3% below 500. 16.8% between 500 and 599. 44.4% between 600 and 699. 34.5% above 700. 6.8% between 500 and 599. 34.7% between 600 and 699. 57.1% above 700.

Expenses:
Tuition: In-state: Full year: $17,500.00. Part-time: Per course: $1,190.00. Room and board: $6,200.00.

Majors

• AREA STUDIES African, African-American, American, East Asian Studies, Jewish, Latin American, Women's Studies • BUSINESS Economics • COMMUNICATIONS English, Linguistics, Literature • COMPUTER SCIENCE Computer Mathematics, Computer Science • ENGINEERING Architectural, Chemical, Electrical, Engineering Science, Mechanical • HUMANITIES Classics, Humanities, Philosophy • LANGUAGES Chinese, French, German, Italian, Japanese, Russian, Spanish • MATHEMATICS Applied • RELIGIOUS STUDIES Religious Studies • SCIENCES Archeology, Astronomy, Biochemistry, Biology, Biophysics, Chemistry, Geology, Geophysics, Mathematics, Physics • SOCIAL SCIENCES History, Political Science, Psychology, Sociology • VISUAL AND PERFORMING ARTS Art, Art History, Film & Video, Music, Theater

Sports/Activities

• SPORTS RELATED Band, Cheerleading, Chess, Pep Band, Team Managers • SPORTS-INTERCOLLEGIATE Baseball (M), Basketball, Crew, Cross Country, Diving, Fencing, Field Hockey (F), Football (M), Golf, Gymnastics (F), Ice Hockey, Lacrosse, Soccer, Softball (F), Squash, Swimming, Tennis, Track and Field, Volleyball (F) • SPORTS-INTRAMURAL Baseball (M), Basketball, Bowling, Crew, Cross Country, Field Hockey, Football (M), Golf, Ice Hockey, Racquetball, Soccer, Softball, Squash, Swimming, Tennis, Volleyball, Water Polo, Wrestling (M) • STUDENT LIFE ACTIVITIES Debate, Drama Groups, Film Production, Fraternities, Jazz Band, Marching Band, Music Groups, Newspaper, Religious Organization, Sororities, Student Government, Symphony Orchestra, Yearbook

---

Selective **Delaware Services**

Goldey Beacom College

4701 Limestone Road
Wilmington, Delaware 19808
(302) 998-8814

School Enrollment: **1,724** Male: **645** Female: **1,179**

Admissions Contact: **Gail Lear, Director of Admissions**
LD Contact: **Roxine MacDonald, Associate Dean/Director**
Name of Program: **Learning Resource Center**
Telephone:**(302) 998-8814**

Admissions

Application Information:
Rolling Admissions: **Yes**

Secondary School Information
Most Important Criteria For Admissions (1-strongest)

3	SAT/ACT	11	Application	2	School transcript
5	Class rank	10	Course selection	8	Personal statement
6	Interview	7	Extra activities	9	Psychoeducational
1	G.P.A.		Open admission	4	Recommendations

Test Requirements:
Untimed SAT: **Yes**
Documentation of LD required: **Yes**

Types of Disabilities Served
Speech/Lang	Reading	ADD with LD
Study skills	Spelling	ADD without LD
Written express	Math	ADHD with LD
Organizational	Fine Motor	ADHD without LD
Perceptual		

Admissions Process

Student sends application and transcripts/scores. Interview is recommended but not required. Student is admitted based on criteria, grades/scores, recommendations, etc.

Learning Disability Program
Services available for all students: **Yes**

Diagnostic Testing
ADD	Personality	Perceptual skills	• Spelling
ADHD	Organization	Fine motor skills	• Reading
I.Q.	Handwriting	Spoken language	Study skills
• Math	Social skills	• Written language	

Tutoring:
Services rendered by:
Graduates   •Peers   •Faculty   •LD staff   Teacher trainees

Tutorials
Grp.	Ind.	Tutorials	Grp.	Ind.	Tutorials
	•	Math skills			Word processing
•	•	Study skills	•		Time management
	•	Language arts	•	•	Learning strategies
	•	Written express	•	•	Organizational skills

Academic Accommodations
Curriculum	Study Aids	Exams
Priority registration	Typist	• Oral
Math waiver	Reader	• Untimed
Foreign lang. waiver	Notetaker	Take home
• Course substitution	Proof reader	• With proctor
In Class	Text on tape	On computer
Calculators	• Early syllabus	• Extended time
• Tape recorder	Taped handouts	On tape
Word processor		Modified
Priority seating		• Separate room

Graduation Requirements:
Course credits: **66** GPA: **2.0**

General Information:
Goldey Beacom College is a 2 and 4 year private college. Suburban campus of 28 acres is Ski areas are 2 hours from campus. Beaches are 2 hours from campus. 9% of students are foreign. 4 residential halls on campus. Housing is not guaranteed.Guaranteed through 4th year.

Accreditation:MSCHE

Class Rank:
About 17% of the present freshmen class were in the upper 20% of their high school class. 35% were in the top 40% of their class. 78% were in the top 60% of their class. 92% were in the top 80% of their class.

Expenses:
Tuition: In-state: Full year: $5,250.00. Part-time: Per credit:$175.00. Part-time: Per course: $525.00-$700.00. Tuition: Out-of-state: Full year: $5,250.00. Part-time: Per credit:$175.00. Part-time: Per course:$525.00 - $700.00 Room and board: $2,589.00

Majors
• BUSINESS Accounting, Banking/Finance, Business Administration, Business Management, Clerical, Data Processing, International Business, Management, Marketing, Secretarial Science • COMMUNICATIONS Communication • COMPUTER SCIENCE Computer Science • VOCATIONAL Business and Office, Legal Secretary, Office Administration, Secretarial , Word Processing

Sports/Activities
• SPORTS RELATED Team Managers • SPORTS-INTERCOLLEGIATE Soccer (M), Softball (F) • SPORTS-INTRAMURAL Basketball, Bowling, Football, Golf, Racquetball, Soccer, Softball, Tennis, Volleyball • STUDENT LIFE ACTIVITIES Academic Clubs, Choral, Community Service,

Delaware

Ethnic & Cultural Groups, Fraternities, Newspaper, Religious Organization, Sororities, Student Government, Yearbook

Very Selective	**Delaware Services**

University of Delaware
116 Hullihen Hall
Newark, Delaware 19716
(320) 831-8123

School Enrollment: **15,000** Male: **6,600** Female: **8,400**

Admissions Contact: **Faye Duffy, Assistant Director of Admissions**
LD Contact: **David Johns**
Name of Program: **Academic Studies Assistance Programs**
Telephone:**(302) 831-1639**

Admissions

Application Information:
Application deadline: **March 1st**
Notified when: **April 15th**

Secondary School Information
Most Important Criteria For Admissions (1-strongest)

4 SAT/ACT	**6** Application	**1**	School transcript
3 Class rank	**2** Course selection	**6**	Personal statement
Interview	**5** Extra activities		Psychoeducational
1 G.P.A.	Open admission	**6**	Recommendations

Test Requirements:
Untimed SAT: **Yes** Untimed ACT: **Yes** Untimed ACH: **Yes**
WAIS-R required: **Yes**

Types of Disabilities Served
- Speech/Lang
- Reading
- ADD with LD
- Study skills
- Spelling
- ADD without LD
- Written express
- Math
- ADHD with LD
- Organizational
- Fine Motor
- ADHD without LD
- Perceptual

Learning Disability Program
Counseling: Individual: **Yes**

Faculty:
Faculty: **5** Full time: **3** Part time: **2**
Faculty advocate: **Yes** Meets with instructor: **As needed**

Diagnostic Testing
ADD	Personality	Perceptual skills	Spelling
ADHD	Organization	Fine motor skills	Reading
I.Q.	Handwriting	Spoken language	Study skills
Math	Social skills	Written language	

Tutoring:
Services rendered by:
Graduates   Peers   •Faculty   •LD staff   Teacher trainees

Tutorials
Grp.	Ind.	Tutorials	Grp.	Ind.	Tutorials
	•	Math skills		•	Word processing
	•	Study skills		•	Time management
	•	Language arts		•	Learning strategies
	•	Written express		•	Organizational skills

Academic Accommodations
Curriculum	Study Aids	Exams
Priority registration	Typist	• Oral
Math waiver	Reader	Untimed
Foreign lang. waiver	• Notetaker	• Take home
• Course substitution	• Proof reader	With proctor
In Class	• Text on tape	On computer
• Calculators	Early syllabus	• Extended time
• Tape recorder	Taped handouts	On tape
• Word processor		Modified
Priority seating		Separate room

Program Strengths
We offer a number of services for students with specific learning disabilities who qualify for regular admissions. Services are provided through the Academic Studies Assistance Program (ASAP). ASAP is able to deliver state of the art assistance as a part of the research and development mission of the program. Many ASAP services are available to all university students who seek to improve their learning. The special services for learning handicapped students are one part of the larger program. The ASAP staff works closely with learning handicapped students in conjunction with academic departments and other service units.

General Information:
University of Delaware is a 4 year public university. Suburban campus of 1,100 acres is 14 miles from Wilmington. Accessible by train or bus. Ski areas are 2 hours from campus. Beaches are 2 hours from campus. 1% of students are foreign. Housing is guaranteed.Guaranteed through 1st year. 90 % of students remain on campus for the weekends. 22 % of students join fraternities/sororities.

Accreditation:AACSB, ABET, ADA, APTA, NLN

Class Rank:
About 50% of the present freshmen class were in the upper 20% of their high school class. 88% were in the top 40% of their class.

Expenses:
Tuition: In-state: Full year: $2,700.00. Tuition: Out-of-state: Full year: $7,000.00. Room and board: $3,500.00

Majors

•AREA STUDIES American, Black/Afro-American, Latin American, Russsian/Slavic, Women's Studies • BUSINESS Accounting, Agricultural, Business Administration, Economics, Hotel and Restaurant Managemen • COMMUNICATIONS Communication, English, Literature, Television/Radio/Film • COMPUTER SCIENCE Computer Science • EDUCATION Agricultural, Early Childhood, Elementary, English, Music, Physical, Psychology, Recreation and Youth Leadership, Science • ENGINEERING Agricultural, Engineering Science • HEALTH SCIENCES Medical Technology, Nursing, Nutritional/Food • HUMANITIES Liberal Arts, Philosophy • LANGUAGES French, German, Italian, Russian, Spanish • SCIENCES Animal, Chemistry, Geology, Gerontology, Horticultural, Mathematics, Physics, Statistics • SOCIAL SCIENCES Anthropology,

Criminal Justice, History, International Studies, Political Science, Sociology • VISUAL AND PERFORMING ARTS Art, Art History, Fine Arts, Music • VOCATIONAL Food Service, Home Economics, Textile

Sports/Activities

• SPORTS-INTERCOLLEGIATE Baseball (M), Basketball, Cross Country, Field Hockey (F), Football (M), Golf (M), Lacrosse, Soccer (M), Softball (F), Swimming, Tennis, Track and Field, Volleyball (F), Wrestling (M)
• SPORTS-INTRAMURAL Badminton, Basketball, Bowling, Cross Country (M), Field Hockey (F), Gymnastics, Lacrosse (F), Ping-Pong, Racquetball, Soccer, Squash, Swimming, Tennis, Track and Field, Volleyball
• STUDENT LIFE ACTIVITIES Choral, Concert Band, Dance, Music Ensembles, Musical Theater

Highly Selective	District of Columbia Program

American University
4400 Massachusetts Avenue Northwest
Washington, District of Columbia 20016-8001
(202) 885-6000

School Enrollment: **11,676**
LD Enrollment: **130**

Admissions Contact: **Marquita Lightfoot, Assoc. Dir. of Admissions**
LD Contact: **Dr. Faith Leonard, Director**
Name of Program: **Learning Services Program**
Telephone:**(202) 885-3360**

Admissions

Application Information:
LD Students Applying: **150** Accepted: **30** Enrolled:**15**
Application deadline: **February 1st**
Notified when: **April 15th**

Secondary School Information
Most Important Criteria For Admissions (1-strongest)

1 SAT/ACT	Application	2	School transcript
4 Class rank	Course selection	4	Personal statement
11 Interview	6 Extra activities	2	Psychoeducational
1 G.P.A.	Open admission	5	Recommendations

Test Requirements:
Untimed SAT: **Yes** Untimed ACH: **Yes**
WAIS-R required: **Yes** Range accepted:
Currency of diagnostic testing: **3 years**

Types of Disabilities Served
• Speech/Lang
• Study skills
• Written express
• Organizational
• Perceptual
• Reading
• Spelling
• Math
• Fine Motor
• ADD with LD
• ADD without LD
• ADHD with LD
• ADHD without LD

Learning Disability Program
Program: Reinforces course work: **Yes**
Students mainstreamed **100** % of the day
Counseling: Individual: **Yes** Group Counseling: **Yes**

Faculty:
Faculty: **5** Including Director: **Yes** Full time: **2** Part time: **3**
LD faculty with: BS/BA: **5** M.A.: **4** Ph.D.: **1**
Faculty advocate: **Yes** Meets with instructor: **As needed**

Diagnostic Testing
ADD	Personality	Perceptual skills	Spelling
ADHD	Organization	Fine motor skills	Reading
I.Q.	Handwriting	Spoken language	Study skills
Math	Social skills	Written language	

Tutoring:
Average size of group tutorials: **3-4**
Services rendered by:
Graduates •Peers •Faculty •LD staff Teacher trainees

Tutorials
Grp.	Ind.	Tutorials	Grp.	Ind.	Tutorials
	•	Math skills		•	Word processing
	•	Study skills		•	Time management
	•	Language arts		•	Learning strategies
	•	Written express		•	Organizational skills

Academic Accommodations

Curriculum	Study Aids	Exams
Priority registration	Typist	Oral
Math waiver	Reader	Untimed
Foreign lang. waiver	Notetaker	• Take home
• Course substitution	Proof reader	With proctor
In Class	• Text on tape	On computer
Calculators	Early syllabus	• Extended time
• Tape recorder	Taped handouts	On tape
• Word processor		Modified
Priority seating		Separate room

Program Strengths
Respect for individual differences is the cornerstone of services for students with learning disabilities at the American University. Each student brings strengths and our goal is to facilitate the expression of those strengths by providing the support needed for achievement. American University is unique in that it is an intellectually rigorous, academically demanding institution and yet provides full support services for LD students.

General Information:
American University is a 4 year private university. Urban campus of 78 acres is Accessible by train or bus. Ski areas are 2-1/2 hours from campus. Beaches are 3 hours from campus. 15% of students are foreign. 8 residential halls on campus. Housing is guaranteed.Guaranteed through 1st year.

Accreditation:MSACS

SAT/ACT Scores:
Scores for incoming freshmen:**Verbal:**25%below 500. 25%between 500 and 599. **Math:**25% below 500. 25% between 500 and 599.

Expenses:
Tuition: In-state: Full year: $11,536.00. Part-time: Per credit:$379.00.
Room and board: $5,228.00

Majors
• AREA STUDIES American, Jewish, Latin American, Russian/Slavic
• BUSINESS Accounting, Business Management, Economics, Human Resources Management, International Business, Marketing, Real Estate
• COMMUNICATIONS Communication, Literature • COMPUTER SCIENCE Computer Science, Computer Technology • EDUCATION Elementary • HUMANITIES Philosophy, Religion • SCIENCES Biology,

District of Columbia

Chemistry, Mathematics, Physics, Statistics • SOCIAL SCIENCES Anthropology, History, Political Science, Psychology, Sociology • VISUAL AND PERFORMING ARTS Art History, Fine Arts, Music, Studio Art

Sports/Activities
• SPORTS RELATED Pep Band • SPORTS-INTERCOLLEGIATE Basketball, Cross Country, Diving, Field Hockey (F), Golf, Soccer (M), Swimming, Tennis, Volleyball (F), Wrestling (M) • SPORTS-INTRAMURAL Basketball, Golf, Racquetball, Soccer, Softball, Swimming, Tennis, Volleyball, Water Polo • STUDENT LIFE ACTIVITIES Choral, Dance, Jazz Band, Magazine, Music Groups, Musical Theater, Opera, Yearbook

---

Very Selective　　　　**District of Columbia**
　　　　　　　　　　　　　　　　　　　　Services

Catholic University of America
620 Michigan Avenue, Northeast
Washington, District of Columbia 20064
(202) 319-5618

School Enrollment: **6,000** Male: **2,520** Female: **3,480**
LD Enrollment: **40** Male: **20** Female: **20**

Admissions Contact: **Office of Admissions**
LD Contact: **Multicultural & Special Services**
Name of Program: **Multicultural & Special Services**
Address: **Room 251, University Center East**
Telephone:**(202) 319-5618**

Admissions

Application Information:
LD Students Applying: **15** Accepted: **6** Enrolled:**3**
LD on admissions committee:**Yes**
Notified when: **March 15th**

Secondary School Information
Most Important Criteria For Admissions (1-strongest)

SAT/ACT	Application	School transcript
Class rank	Course selection	Personal statement
Interview	Extra activities	Psychoeducational
G.P.A.	Open admission	Recommendations

Test Requirements:
Diagnostic testing waived: **Yes**
Untimed SAT: **Yes** Untimed ACT: **Yes**
WAIS-R required: **Yes**
Documentation of LD required: **Yes**
Currency of diagnostic testing: **Within a year**
Tests recommended: **WAIS-R, Achievement (W-J-R preferred) and written sample.**

Types of Disabilities Served
• Speech/Lang
• Study skills
• Written express
• Organizational
• Perceptual
• Reading
• Spelling
• Math
• Fine Motor
• ADD with LD
• ADD without LD
• ADHD with LD
• ADHD without LD

Admissions Process

Include Psycho-Educational Evaluation with regular admissions procedures.

High School Course Requirements:
Waivers to standard high school courses
Foreign Language : **Yes**

Learning Disability Program
Counseling: Individual: **Yes** Group Counseling: **Yes** Vocational Counseling: **Yes**

Faculty:
Faculty: **2** Part time: **2** M.A.: **1**
Faculty advocate: **Yes** Meets with instructor: **As needed**

Diagnostic Testing

ADD	Personality	Perceptual skills	Spelling
ADHD	Organization	Fine motor skills	• Reading
I.Q.	Handwriting	Spoken language	Study skills
Math	Social skills	Written language	

Tutoring:
Average size of group tutorials: **5-10**
Services rendered by:
•Graduates　•Peers　　Faculty　　•LD staff　　Teacher trainees

Tutorials

Grp.	Ind.	Tutorials	Grp.	Ind.	Tutorials
•	•	Math skills	•		Word processing
•	•	Study skills	•	•	Time management
		Language arts	•	•	Learning strategies
	•	Written express	•	•	Organizational skills

Academic Accommodations

Curriculum	Study Aids	Exams
• Priority registration	Typist	• Oral
Math waiver	• Reader	• Untimed
• Foreign lang. waiver	• Notetaker	• Take home
Course substitution	Proof reader	• With proctor
In Class	• Text on tape	• On computer
Calculators	• Early syllabus	• Extended time
• Tape recorder	• Taped handouts	• On tape
• Word processor		• Modified
• Priority seating		• Separate room

Graduation Requirements:
Course credits: **120** GPA: **Varies by department** Math waiver: **Yes**
Language waiver: **Yes**
Other requirements: **2 semesters foreign language, intermediate level**

General Information:
Catholic University of America is a 4 year independent Roman Catholic Church university. Urban campus Accessible by metro train or bus. Ski areas are 2 hours from campus. Beaches are 2 hours from campus. 10% of students are foreign. 10 residential halls on campus. Housing is guaranteed.Guaranteed through 4th year. 50 % of students remain on campus for the weekends.

Accreditation:MSACS

Expenses:
Tuition: In-state: Full year: $11,626.00 per year. Part-time: Per credit:$445.00 undergraduate-graduate, $560.00 law. Tuition: Out-of-state: Full year: $11,626.00 per year. Room and board: $5,600.00

Majors
• ARTS Art History, Dramatic Arts, Music, Music Performance, Painting,

Religious Music • BUSINESS Accounting, Economics, Education • COMMUNICATIONS English • COMPUTER SCIENCE Computer Science, Robotics • EDUCATION Early Childhood, Elementary, English, Foreign Language, General, Psychology, Religious • ENGINEERING Bio-medical, Civil/Environmental, Mechanical, Physics • HEALTH SCIENCES Medical Laboraotry Technology, Nursing • HUMANITIES Classics, English/Writing/Literature, Liberal Arts , Philosophy, Religion • LANGUAGES English, French, German, Italian, Latin, Spanish • PRE PROFESSIONAL Engineering, Law, Social Work, Urban Design • RELIGIOUS STUDIES Bible, Biblical Language, Ministry & Church Administrati, Philosophy, Religion & Theology, Religious Studies • SCIENCES Anthropology, Biomedical, Biology, Chemistry, Organic Chemistry, Physical Chemistry • SOCIAL SCIENCES • VISUAL AND PERFORMING ARTS Art, Dramatic Arts, Music, Music Performance, Music Theatre, Theater

Sports/Activities

• SPORTS-INTERCOLLEGIATE Baseball (F), Baseball (M), Basketball, Crew, Cross Country, Field Hockey (F), Football, Lacrosse, Ping-Pong, Racquetball, Soccer, Softball, Swimming, Tennis, Track and Field • SPORTS-INTRAMURAL

Special	District of Columbia Accommodations

Gallaudet University

800 Florida Avenue, N.E.
Washington, District of Columbia 20002
(202) 651-5338

School Enrollment: **1,800** Male: **600** Female: **1,200**
LD Enrollment: **55**

Admissions Contact: **Jamie Tucker, Director**
LD Contact: **Pam Rush, School Psychologist**
Name of Program: **Student Support Services**
Telephone:**(202) 651-5256**

Admissions

Application Information:
Application deadline: **April 15th**

Secondary School Information
Most Important Criteria For Admissions (1-strongest)

SAT/ACT	Application	School transcript
Class rank	Course selection	Personal statement
Interview	Extra activities	Psychoeducational
G.P.A.	Open admission	Recommendations

Test Requirements:
Documentation of LD required: **Yes**

Types of Disabilities Served

Speech/Lang	Reading	ADD with LD
Study skills	Spelling	ADD without LD
Written express	Math	ADHD with LD
Organizational	Fine Motor	ADHD without LD
Perceptual		

High School Course Requirements:
English: **2** Foreign Language: **2**
Waivers to standard high school courses
Foreign Language : **Yes** Math: **Yes** Course substitution: **Yes**

Learning Disability Program
Program: Remedial: **Yes**
Program: Reinforces course work: **Yes**
Students mainstreamed **100** % of the day
Services available for all students: **Yes**
Counseling: Individual: **Yes** Group Counseling: **Yes**
Support groups are available:**Academic Advocacy Group for Students with Learning Disabilities**

Faculty:
Faculty: **3** Full time: **2** Part time: **1**
LD faculty with: BS/BA: **1** M.A.: **2**
Meets with instructor:

Diagnostic Testing
• ADD	Personality • Perceptual skills	• Spelling
• ADHD•	Organization• Fine motor skills	• Reading
• I.Q.	• Handwriting Spoken language	Study skills
• Math	• Social skills• Written language	

Tutoring:
Average size of group tutorials: **1-3**
Services rendered by:
•Graduates •Peers •Faculty •LD staff Teacher trainees

Tutorials
Grp.	Ind.	Tutorials	Grp.	Ind.	Tutorials
•	•	Math skills			Word processing
	•	Study skills			Time management
•	•	Language arts		•	Learning strategies
	•	Written express		•	Organizational skills

Academic Accommodations

Curriculum	Study Aids	Exams
Priority registration	Typist	Oral
• Math waiver	Reader	• Untimed
• Foreign lang. waiver	Notetaker	Take home
Course substitution	Proof reader	With proctor
In Class	Text on tape	• On computer
• Calculators	Early syllabus	• Extended time
Tape recorder	Taped handouts	On tape
Word processor		Modified
Priority seating		Separate room

Graduation Requirements:
Course credits: **124** Math waiver: **Yes** Language waiver: **Yes**

Program Strengths
Unique tutoring, support groups, faculty/staff training and information dissemination. We are a university for hearing-impaired men and women.

General Information:
Gallaudet University is a 2 and 4 year independent university. of 108 acres is Accessible by car or bus Ski areas are 2 hours from campus. Beaches are 3 hours from campus. 8 residential halls on campus. Housing is guaranteed.Guaranteed through 4th year. 80 % of students remain on campus for the weekends. 10 % of students join fraternities/sororities.

Accreditation:MSACS

Expenses:
Tuition: In-state: Full year: $1,800.00. Part-time: Per credit:$180.00. Tuition: Out-of-state: Full year: $1,800.00. Part-time: Per credit:$180.00.
Room and board: $2,305.00

District of Columbia

Majors

• ARTS Art History, Film & Video, Theater Design • BUSINESS Accounting, Business Administration, Clerical, Data Processing, Economics, Education • COMMUNICATIONS Communication, Creative Writing, English, Linguistics, Television/Radio/Film • EDUCATIOn Business, Child Development, Early Childhood, Elementary, English, English As A Second Language, Foreign Language, General, Health, Home Economics, Mathematics, Middle School, Outdoor, Psychology, Reading, Rural Development, School Psychology, Science, Secondary, Social Studies • HEALTH SCIENCES Fitness, Health • HUMANITIES English/Writing/Literature, Liberal Arts , Philosophy • LANGUAGES English, French, Greek, Hebrew, Italian, Russian, Spanish • MATHEMATICS Applied, Computer • PRE PROFESSIONAL Business • SPECIAL EDUCATION Deaf/Hearing Impaired, Learning Disability • VISUAL AND PERFORMING ARTS Art

Sports/Activities

• SPORTS RELATED Cheerleading, Drill Team, Team Managers • SPORTS-INTERCOLLEGIATE Baseball (M), Basketball (F), Basketball (M), Bowling, Canoeing, Cross Country, Cycling, Diving, Football (M), Racquetball, Scuba, Soccer, Softball (F), Swimming, Tennis, Track and Field, Volleyball, Weight Lifting • SPORTS-INTRAMURAL Baseball, Bowling, Football, Ping-Pong, Soccer, Swimming, Tennis, Volleyball, Weight Lifting • STUDENT LIFE ACTIVITIES Community Service, Dance, Drama Groups, Ethnic & Cultural Groups, Film, Fraternities, Newspaper, Religious Organization, Sororities, Student Government, Yearbook

---

Very Selective

District of Columbia

George Washington University

2121 I Street Northwest
Washington, District of Columbia 20052
(202) 994-6710

School Enrollment: **6,400** Male: **3,000** Female: **3,400**
LD Enrollment: **91**

Admissions Contact: **William Perez, Associate Dir. of Admissions**
LD Contact: **Christy Willis, Coordinator**
Name of Program: **Disabled Student Services**
Telephone:**(202) 994-8250**

Admissions

Application Information:
Application deadline: **Febraury 1st**
Rolling Admissions: **Yes**Notified when: **April 15th**

Secondary School Information
Most Important Criteria For Admissions (1-strongest)

3 SAT/ACT	3 Application	1 School transcript
2 Class rank	2 Course selection	4 Personal statement
Interview	5 Extra activities	Psychoeducational
1 G.P.A.	Open admission	4 Recommendations

Test Requirements:
Untimed SAT: **Yes** Untimed ACT: **Yes**

Services

Types of Disabilities Served

Speech/Lang	• Reading	ADD with LD
• Study skills	• Spelling	ADD without LD
• Written express	• Math	ADHD with LD
• Organizational	Fine Motor	ADHD without LD
Perceptual		

Faculty:
Faculty: **2** Full time: **1** Part time: **1**

Diagnostic Testing

ADD	Personality	Perceptual skills	Spelling
ADHD	Organization	Fine motor skills	Reading
I.Q.	Handwriting	Spoken language	Study skills
Math	Social skills	Written language	

Tutoring:
Services rendered by:
•Graduates   •Peers   •Faculty   •LD staff   Teacher trainees

Tutorials

Grp.	Ind.	Tutorials	Grp.	Ind.	Tutorials
	•	Math skills	•	•	Word processing
•	•	Study skills		•	Time management
		Language arts		•	Learning strategies
	•	Written express		•	Organizational skills

Academic Accommodations

Curriculum	Study Aids	Exams
Priority registration	Typist	Oral
• Math waiver	Reader	Untimed
• Foreign lang. waiver	• Notetaker	Take home
Course substitution	Proof reader	With proctor
In Class	• Text on tape	On computer
• Calculators	Early syllabus	• Extended time
• Tape recorder	Taped handouts	On tape
• Word processor		Modified
Priority seating		Separate room

Program Strengths
LD students are serviced through the Office of Disabled Student Services. We offer ongoing housing and academic accommodations. We are not a structured LD Program.

General Information:
George Washington University is a 4 year private university. Urban campus of 36 acres is Accessible by air, train, or bus. Ski areas are 2 hours from campus. Beaches are 3 hours from campus. 13 residential halls on campus. Housing is guaranteed.Guaranteed through 1st year. 75 % of students remain on campus for the weekends. 25 % of students join fraternities/sororities.

Accreditation:MSACS

SAT/ACT Scores:
Scores for incoming freshmen:**Verbal:**28%below 500. 49%between 500 and 599. 21%between 600 and 699. 2%above 700. **Math:**11% below 500. 45% between 500 and 599. 35% between 600 and 699. 9%above 700. **ACT:** 3% below 20. 22% between 20 and 23. 19%between 24 and 25l. 37%between 26 and 28. 19% above 28.

Class Rank:
About 49% of the present freshmen class were in the upper 20% of their high school class. 33% were in the top 40% of their class. 15% were in the top 60% of their class. 3% were in the top 80% of their class.

Expenses:
Tuition: In-state: Full year: $13,560.00. Part-time: Per credit:$445.00. Tuition: Out-of-state: Full year: $13,560.00. Part-time: Per credit:$445.00. Room and board: $6,040.00

Majors

• AREA STUDIES American, International Studies, Jewish, Latin American, Middle Eastern • BUSINESS Accounting, Business Economics, Economics, Finance, Insurance, Marketing • COMMUNICATIONS English, Journalism, Television/Radio/Film • COMPUTER SCIENCE Computer Science, Data Processing • EDUCATION Early Childhood, Elementary, Physical, Special • ENGINEERING Civil/Environmental, Computer, Electrical, Mechanical, Nuclear • HEALTH SCIENCES Medical Technology, Radiological Therapy, Speech/Audiology and Speech • HUMANITIES Humanities, Liberal Arts, Philosophy, Religion • LANGUAGES Chinese, French, German, Russian • PREPROFESSIONAL Law, Medicine • SCIENCES Archeology, Biology, Botany, Chemistry, Geography, Geology, Mathematics, Physics, Statistics, Zoology • SOCIAL SCIENCES Anthropology, Criminal Justice, Human Service, Political Science, Psychology, Sociology • VISUAL AND PERFORMING ARTS Art History, Dance, Dance Education, Fine Arts, Music, Theater

Sports/Activities

• SPORTS-INTERCOLLEGIATE Badminton (F), Baseball (M), Basketball, Crew, Diving (F), Golf (M), Gymnastics (F), Soccer, Swimming, Tennis, Volleyball (F), Water Polo (M), Wrestling (M) • SPORTS-INTRAMURAL Badminton (F), Basketball, Bowling, Hand Ball, Ping-Pong, Racquetball, Soccer, Softball, Squash, Swimming, Tennis, Volleyball • STUDENT LIFE ACTIVITIES Choral, Community Service, Dance, Magazine, Music Ensembles, Musical Theater, Opera, Political Groups, Symphony Orchestra, Yearbook

---

Selective

District of Columbia Accommodations

Trinity College

125 Michigan Avenue, N.E.
Washington, District of Columbia 20017
(202) 939-5000

School Enrollment: **882** Female: **882**

Admissions Contact: **Maura Ambrosino, Director of Admissions**

Admissions

Secondary School Information
Most Important Criteria For Admissions (1-strongest)

5 SAT/ACT	**1** Application	**4**	School transcript
7 Class rank	**2** Course selection	**10**	Personal statement
8 Interview	**9** Extra activities	**11**	Psychoeducational
3 G.P.A.	Open admission	**6**	Recommendations

Types of Disabilities Served

Speech/Lang	Reading	ADD with LD
Study skills	Spelling	ADD without LD
Written express	Math	ADHD with LD
Organizational	Fine Motor	ADHD without LD
Perceptual		

High School Course Requirements:
English: **4** Math: **2-3** Science: **2-3** Foreign Language: **3-4**

Learning Disability Program

Services available for all students: **Yes**

Diagnostic Testing

ADD	Personality	Perceptual skills	Spelling
ADHD	Organization	Fine motor skills	Reading
I.Q.	Handwriting	Spoken language	Study skills
Math	Social skills	Written language	

Tutoring:
Services rendered by:

Graduates	Peers	•Faculty	LD staff	Teacher trainees

Tutorials

Grp.	Ind.	Tutorials	Grp.	Ind.	Tutorials
•	•	Math skills	•	•	Word processing
•	•	Study skills	•	•	Time management
•	•	Language arts			Learning strategies
•	•	Written express			Organizational skills

Academic Accommodations

Curriculum	Study Aids	Exams
Priority registration	Typist	• Oral
Math waiver	Reader	• Untimed
Foreign lang. waiver	Notetaker	• Take home
• Course substitution	Proof reader	With proctor
In Class	Text on tape	On computer
Calculators	Early syllabus	• Extended time
Tape recorder	Taped handouts	On tape
Word processor		Modified
• Priority seating		• Separate room

General Information:

Trinity College is a 4 year independent Roman Catholic college. Urban campus of 27 acres is Accessible by air, train, or bus. Ski areas are 1.5 hours from campus. Beaches are 1.5 hours from campus. 8% of students are foreign. 3 residential halls on campus. Housing is guaranteed.Guaranteed through 4th year. 95 % of students remain on campus for the weekends.

Accreditation:MSACS, NASDTEC

Expenses:
Tuition: In-state: Full year: $10,600.00. Part-time: Per credit:$347.00 (for 11 or fewer credits). Tuition: Out-of-state: Full year: $10,600.00. Room and board: $6,280.00

Majors

• AREA STUDIES American, Women's Studies • ARTS Art History, Music • BUSINESS Business Administration, Education, Human Resource Development • COMMUNICATIONS Communication • EDUCATION Early Childhood, Elementary, English, General, Leadership, Mathematics, Reading, Science, Secondary, Social Studies, Special • HUMANITIES English/Writing/Literature • MATHEMATICS Theoretical • PRE PROFESSIONAL Business • SCIENCES Biochemistry, Biology, Mathematics • SOCIAL SCIENCES International Studies, Political Science, Psychology, Sociology

Sports

• SPORTS RELATED Team Managers • SPORTS-INTERCOLLEGIATE Crew (F), Field Hockey (F), Lacrosse (F), Soccer (F), Tennis (F) • SPORTS-INTRAMURAL Canoeing, Golf, Horseback Riding, Ping-Pong, Skiing - Cross Country, Skiing - Snow, Softball, Swimming, Tennis, Volleyball, Weight Lifting • STUDENT LIFE ACTIVITIES Community Service, Drama Groups, Ethnic & Cultural Groups, Magazine, Music Groups, Newspaper, Political Groups, Student Government, Yearbook

Transitional
Florida Program

Beacon College
105 East Main Street
Leesburg, Florida 94748
(904) 787-7660

School Enrollment: **30** Male: **20** Female: **10**
LD Enrollment: **30** Male: **20** Female: **10**

Admissions Contact: **Debra Townley, Director of Admissions**
LD Contact: **D. Townley, Deborah Brodbeck, Dir. of Adms./Pres.**

Admissions

Application Information:
LD Students Applying: **50** Accepted: **30** Enrolled:**20**
Separate application:**Yes**
LD on admissions committee:**Yes**
Applicant must apply **2** months in advance
Rolling Admissions: **Yes**

Secondary School Information
Most Important Criteria For Admissions (1-strongest)

	SAT/ACT	**3**	Application	**6**	School transcript
	Class rank		Course selection	**5**	Personal statement
2	Interview	**7**	Extra activities	**1**	Psychoeducational
	G.P.A.		Open admission	**4**	Recommendations

Test Requirements:
Standardized tests waived: **Yes**
Diagnostic testing waived: **Yes**
WAIS-R required: **Yes** Range accepted: **80+**
Documentation of LD required: **Yes**
Currency of diagnostic testing: **24 months**
Tests recommended: **Projective**

Types of Disabilities Served
- Speech/Lang
- Study skills
- Written express
- Organizational
- Perceptual
- Reading
- Spelling
- Math
- Fine Motor
- ADD with LD
- ADD without LD
- ADHD with LD
- ADHD without LD

Admissions Process

Students submit recent psycho-educational testing to demonstrate potential and document LD diagnosis. Personal interview is required along with application, autobiographical statement and references.

High School Course Requirements:
English: **4** Math: **1** Science: **1**
Waivers to standard high school courses
Foreign Language : **Yes**

Learning Disability Program
Special orientation for LD students: **Yes**
Syllabus available during orientation:**Yes**
Program: Remedial: **Yes**
Program: Reinforces course work: **Yes**
Students mainstreamed **100** % of the day
Recommended credits per semester: **16**
Counseling: Individual: **Yes** Group Counseling: **Yes**
Support groups are available:**Freshman and residence group meetings**

Faculty:
Faculty: **14** Including Director: **Yes** Full time: **4** Part time: **10**
LD faculty with: BS/BA: **2** M.A.: **14** Ph.D.: **3**
Faculty advocate: **Yes** Meets with instructor: **Weekly**

Diagnostic Testing
- ADD
- ADHD
- I.Q.
- Math
- Personality
- Organization
- Handwriting
- Social skills
- Perceptual skills
- Fine motor skills
- Spoken language
- Written language
- Spelling
- Reading
- Study skills

Tutoring:
Average size of group tutorials: **3**
Services rendered by:
  Graduates   •Peers   •Faculty   •LD staff   Teacher trainees

Tutorials

Grp.	Ind.	Tutorials	Grp.	Ind.	Tutorials
•	•	Math skills		•	Word processing
•	•	Study skills	•	•	Time management
•	•	Language arts	•	•	Learning strategies
•	•	Written express	•	•	Organizational skills

Academic Accommodations

Curriculum	Study Aids	Exams
Priority registration	Typist	• Oral
Math waiver	Reader	• Untimed
• Foreign lang. waiver	Notetaker	• Take home
• Course substitution	• Proof reader	• With proctor
In Class	• Text on tape	On computer
• Calculators	• Early syllabus	• Extended time
• Tape recorder	Taped handouts	On tape
• Word processor		• Modified
• Priority seating		• Separate room

Graduation Requirements:
Course credits: **63** GPA: **2.0**

Program Strengths

We provide an interdisciplinary approach with intensive academic support services for the student with learning differences. Tutorials are provided across subject areas to ensure academic success. Field placements reinforce classroom instruction and provide work experience in related areas of interest. Residential life program provides counseling support.

General Information:

Beacon College is a 4 year private college. Urban campus 40 miles from Orlando. Accessible by air, train, or bus. Beaches are 45 minutes from campus. 6% of students are foreign. 2 residential halls on campus. Housing is guaranteed.95 % of students remain on campus for the weekends.

Accreditation:SACS pending

Expenses:
Tuition: In-state: Full year: $19,600.00. Part-time: Per credit:0. Tuition:

Out-of-state: Full year: $19,600.00. Room and board: Included

Majors

• SOCIAL SCIENCES Human Service

Sports/Activities

• SPORTS-INTRAMURAL Cycling, Ping-Pong, Skiing - Water, Swimming, Tennis, Weight Lifting • STUDENT LIFE ACTIVITIES Cultural/Social Activities, Newspaper, Yearbook

Less Selective   **Florida**
                                      Services

Brevard Community College

1519 Clearlake Road
Cocoa, Florida 32922
(407) 632-1111

School Enrollment: **13,524** Male: **7,493** Female: **6,031**
LD Enrollment: **150** Male: **75** Female: **75**

Admissions Contact: **Chris Macy, Director of Admissions**
LD Contact: **Brenda Fettrow, Director, Disabled Student Services**
Name of Program: **Disabled Student Services**
Telephone:**(407) 632-1111 Ext. 3606**

Admissions

Application Information:
LD Students Applying: **42** Accepted: **35** Enrolled:**35**
Application deadline: **None**
Applicant must apply **1** months in advance

Secondary School Information
Most Important Criteria For Admissions (1-strongest)

4 SAT/ACT	**9** Application	**5** School transcript
10 Class rank	**2** Course selection	**3** Personal statement
6 Interview	**11** Extra activities	**1** Psychoeducational
8 G.P.A.	Open admission	**7** Recommendations

Test Requirements:
Diagnostic testing waived: **Yes**
Untimed SAT: **Yes** Untimed ACT: **Yes** Untimed ACH: **Yes**
Documentation of LD required: **Yes**
Tests recommended: **WAIS-R or Woodcock-Johnson and Achievement (WRAT, BASIS, WJ, etc.)**

Types of Disabilities Served
• Speech/Lang   • Reading   • ADD with LD
• Study skills   • Spelling   • ADD without LD
• Written express • Math   • ADHD with LD
• Organizational • Fine Motor   • ADHD without LD
• Perceptual

Learning Disability Program

Program: Remedial: **Yes**
Program: Reinforces course work: **Yes**
Students mainstreamed **100** % of the day

Faculty:
Faculty: **12** Including Director: **Yes** Full time: **2** Part time: **10**
LD faculty with: BS/BA: **6** M.A.: **6**
Faculty advocate: **Yes** Meets with instructor: **As needed**

Diagnostic Testing

ADD	Personality •	Perceptual skills	• Spelling
ADHD	Organization	Fine motor skills	• Reading
• I.Q.	• Handwriting•	Spoken language	Study skills
• Math	Social skills •	Written language	

Tutoring:
Average size of group tutorials: **1-2**
Services rendered by:
  Graduates   Peers   •Faculty   •LD staff   Teacher trainees

Tutorials

Grp.	Ind.	Tutorials	Grp.	Ind.	Tutorials
•	•	Math skills		•	Word processing
•	•	Study skills	•		Time management
•	•	Language arts	•	•	Learning strategies
•	•	Written express	•		Organizational skills

Academic Accommodations

Curriculum	Study Aids	Exams
• Priority registration	• Typist	• Oral
• Math waiver	Reader	Untimed
• Foreign lang. waiver	• Notetaker	Take home
• Course substitution	• Proof reader	• With proctor
In Class	• Text on tape	On computer
• Calculators	Early syllabus	• Extended time
• Tape recorder	Taped handouts	On tape
• Word processor		• Modified
• Priority seating		• Separate room

Graduation Requirements:
Course credits: **64**

Program Strengths

The Disabled Student Services Office of Brevard Community College offers a number of services to their learning disabled students. These services include faculty notification of student needs, alternative test arrangements, priority registration, and the availability of various equipment (word processors, tape recorders). Other services include academic advisement, career advisement, and academic tutoring.

General Information:

Brevard Community College is a 2 year public college. of 140 acres is Accessible by air. Beaches are 10 miles from campus. Housing is not guaranteed.

Accreditation: Regional

Expenses: Part-time: Per credit:$30.00. Part-time: Per course: $90.00. Part-time: Per credit:$110.00. Part-time: Per course:$330.00

Majors

• BUSINESS Accounting, Banking, Business Administration, Business Economics, Business Management, Economics, Finance, Hotel and Restaurant Managemen, Insurance, Management, Marketing, Personnel, Real Estate • COMMUNICATIONS Advertising, Communication, English, Journalism, Photography, Television/Radio/Film • COMPUTER SCIENCE Computer Science, Computer Technology, Data Processing, Hardware Engineer, Programming • CRAFTS AND DESIGN Graphic Design • EDUCATION Elementary, Middle School, Music, Physical, Secondary • ENGINEERING Electrical, Engineering Science, Textile • HEALTH SCIENCES Health, Nursing, Occupational Therapy, Physical Therapy • HUMANITIES Liberal Arts • LANGUAGES French, German, Spanish • PREPROFESSIONAL Agriculture, Architecture, Engineering, Forestry, Pharmacy, Social Work • SCIENCES Biology, Biotechnology, Chemistry,

Mathematics, Physical Science, Physics, Radiology • SOCIAL SCIENCES Anthropology, Criminal Justice, History, Human Service, Law Enforcement, Library Science, Psychology, Public Relations, Social Sciences, Sociology • VISUAL AND PERFORMING ARTS Art, Art History, Dramatic Arts, Fine Arts, Music, Studio Art, Theater • VOCATIONAL Air Conditioning/Heating/Refri, Automobile Technology, Business and Office, Drafting, Electronics Technology, Fashion Merchandising, Fire Science, Home Economics, Industrial Equipment Maintenan, Medical Laboratory Technology, Park/Recreation, Respiratory Therapy Technology, Secretarial

Sports/Activities

• SPORTS-INTERCOLLEGIATE Baseball (M), Basketball, Cross Country, Diving, Golf (M), Softball (F), Swimming, Track and Field, Volleyball (F) • SPORTS-INTRAMURAL Archery, Bowling, Fencing, Racquetball, Sailing, Skiing - Water, Soccer, Tennis • STUDENT LIFE ACTIVITIES Choral, Concert Band, Ethnic & Cultural Groups, Magazine, Music Ensembles, Music Groups, Newspaper, Radio/TV station, Student Bulletin, Student Government

---

Less Selective   **Florida
                                                        Services**

Chipola Junior College
3094 Indian Circle
Marianna, Florida 32446
(904) 526-2761

School Enrollment: **2,040** Male: **1,020** Female: **1,020**
LD Enrollment: **15**

Admissions Contact: **Annette Widner, Registration Specialist**
LD Contact: **Wanda Haynie, Handicapped Service Counselor**
Name of Program: **Disabled Student Services**

Admissions

Application Information:
Application deadline: **August 1st**
Rolling Admissions: **Yes**

Secondary School Information
Most Important Criteria For Admissions (1-strongest)

SAT/ACT	Application	School transcript
Class rank	Course selection	Personal statement
Interview	Extra activities	Psychoeducational
G.P.A.	1 Open admission	Recommendations

Test Requirements:
Untimed SAT: **Yes** Untimed ACT: **Yes**
Range accepted:
Documentation of LD required: **Yes**

Types of Disabilities Served
- Speech/Lang
- Study skills
- Written express
- Organizational
- Perceptual
- Reading
- Spelling
- Math
- Fine Motor
- ADD with LD
- ADD without LD
- ADHD with LD
- ADHD without LD

Learning Disability Program
Program: Remedial: **Yes**
Students mainstreamed **100** % of the day
Services available for all students: **Yes**
Counseling: Individual: **Yes**
Support groups are available:**Tutors**

Faculty:
Faculty: **3** Full time: **2** Part time: **1**
Faculty advocate: **Yes** Meets with instructor: **Frequently**

Diagnostic Testing

ADD	Personality	Perceptual skills	Spelling
ADHD	Organization	Fine motor skills	Reading
I.Q.	Handwriting	Spoken language	Study skills
Math	Social skills	Written language	

Tutoring:
Services rendered by:
Graduates •Peers •Faculty •LD staff Teacher trainees

Tutorials

Grp.	Ind.	Tutorials	Grp.	Ind.	Tutorials
	•	Math skills		•	Word processing
	•	Study skills		•	Time management
	•	Language arts		•	Learning strategies
	•	Written express		•	Organizational skills

Academic Accommodations

Curriculum	Study Aids	Exams
Priority registration	• Typist	• Oral
Math waiver	Reader	Untimed
Foreign lang. waiver	• Notetaker	• Take home
• Course substitution	• Proof reader	• With proctor
In Class	• Text on tape	On computer
• Calculators	Early syllabus	• Extended time
• Tape recorder	Taped handouts	On tape
• Word processor		• Modified
Priority seating		Separate room

Graduation Requirements:
Course credits: **60** GPA: **1.5** Years to complete degree: **Indefinite** Math waiver: **Yes**

Program Strengths
Chipola Junior College is a very small school. We have been able to individualize our services, thus far, to meet our student's needs. What we lack in staff and material resources is balanced by an informal but very close interaction between faculty and students. Chipola is one of the few community colleges in Florida with a dormitory.

General Information:
Chipola Junior College is a 2 year public college. Rural campus of 105 acres is 65 miles from Tallahassee. Accessible by bus. Beaches are 65 miles from campus. 1% of students are foreign. 1 residential halls on campus. Housing is not guaranteed.1 % of students remain on campus for the weekends.

Accreditation:SACS

Expenses: Part-time: Per credit:$25.90. Part-time: Per credit:$99.10. Room and board: $500.00-$600.00

Majors
• BUSINESS Banking, Business Administration, Business Management, Finance • COMMUNICATIONS Communication • COMPUTER SCIENCE Computer Science, Computer Technology, Data Processing • EDU-

CATION General • HEALTH SCIENCES Nursing • HUMANITIES Liberal Arts • PREPROFESSIONAL Architecture, Dentistry, Engineering, Law, Medicine, Pharmacy, Social Work • SCIENCES Agricultural • SOCIAL SCIENCES Criminology, Law Enforcement • VISUAL AND PERFORMING ARTS Art • VOCATIONAL Business and Office, Secretarial

Sports/Activities

• SPORTS-INTERCOLLEGIATE Baseball (M), Basketball • SPORTS-INTRAMURAL Badminton, Basketball, Hand Ball, Ping-Pong, Racquetball, Volleyball • STUDENT LIFE ACTIVITIES Choral, Concert Band, Dance, Drama Groups, Music Ensembles, Newspaper, Religious Organization, Student Government

Less Selective   **Florida**
                                       Services

Edison Community College

8099 College Parkway, SW
Fort Myers, Florida 33906
(813) 489-9310

School Enrollment: **8,146** Male: **3,111** Female: **5,035**
LD Enrollment: **23** Male: **11** Female: **12**

Admissions Contact: **Sandra Fahey, Director of Admissions**
LD Contact: **Cathy Doyle, Director**
Name of Program: **Student Support Services**
Telephone:**(813) 489-9112**

Admissions

Application Information:
Application deadline: **None**
Rolling Admissions: **Yes**

Secondary School Information
Most Important Criteria For Admissions (1-strongest)

SAT/ACT	Application	School transcript
Class rank	Course selection	Personal statement
Interview	Extra activities	Psychoeducational
G.P.A.	**1** Open admission	Recommendations

Test Requirements:
Documentation of LD required: **Yes**

Types of Disabilities Served
- Speech/Lang
- Study skills
- Written express
- Organizational
- Perceptual
- Reading
- Spelling
- Math
- Fine Motor
- ADD with LD
- ADD without LD
- ADHD with LD
- ADHD without LD

Learning Disability Program
Counseling: Individual: **Yes**

Faculty:
Faculty: **3** Full time: **3**
Faculty advocate: **Yes** Meets with instructor: **As needed**

Diagnostic Testing

ADD	Personality	Perceptual skills	Spelling
ADHD	Organization	Fine motor skills	Reading
I.Q.	Handwriting	Spoken language	Study skills
Math	Social skills	Written language	

Tutoring:
Services rendered by:
Graduates • Peers   Faculty   LD staff   Teacher trainees

Tutorials

Grp.	Ind.	Tutorials	Grp.	Ind.	Tutorials
•	•	Math skills			Word processing
		Study skills			Time management
•	•	Language arts			Learning strategies
•	•	Written express			Organizational skills

Academic Accommodations

Curriculum	Study Aids	Exams
Priority registration	Typist	• Oral
Math waiver	Reader	Untimed
Foreign lang. waiver	• Notetaker	Take home
Course substitution	• Proof reader	With proctor
In Class	• Text on tape	On computer
Calculators	Early syllabus	• Extended time
• Tape recorder	Taped handouts	On tape
• Word processor		Modified
Priority seating		Separate room

Program Strengths
Our LD students are mainstreamed or referred to other institutions with LD Programs. We offer a college preparatory program, and many of these students start their college experience in this program.

General Information:
Edison Community College is a 2 year public college. Urban campus of 80 acres is Accessible by air or bus. Housing is not guaranteed.

Accreditation: Regional

Expenses: Part-time: Per credit:$30.33. Part-time: Per credit:$108.83.

Majors
• BUSINESS Accounting, Banking, Finance, Marketing, Real Estate
• COMPUTER SCIENCE Computer Technology, Data Processing, Programming • EDUCATION General, Teacher Aide • ENGINEERING Engineering Science • HEALTH SCIENCES EMT, Nursing • HUMANITIES Liberal Arts • SOCIAL SCIENCES Law Enforcement • VOCATIONAL Business and Office, Drafting, Fire Science, Respiratory Therapy Technology, Secretarial

Sports/Activities
• SPORTS-INTERCOLLEGIATE Baseball (M), Basketball, Golf (M), Softball (F), Volleyball (F) • STUDENT LIFE ACTIVITIES Choral, Concert Band, Drama Groups, Ethnic & Cultural Groups, Jazz Band, Music Ensembles, Newspaper, Political Groups, Radio/TV station, Radio/TV station, Student Government, Symphony Orchestra

Selective	Florida Services

Embry-Riddle Aeronautical University

600 S. Clyde Morris Boulevard
Daytona Beach, Florida 32114-3891
(904) 226-6000-(800) 226-3728

School Enrollment: **4,672** Male: **4,120** Female: **549**

Admissions Contact: **Darryl Neimeyer, Director of Admissions**
LD Contact: **Maureen Bridger, Coordinator**
Name of Program: **Disabled Student Services**
Telephone: **(904) 226-6036**

Admissions

Application Information:
Application deadline: **July 30th**
Rolling Admissions: **Yes**

Secondary School Information
Most Important Criteria For Admissions (1-strongest)

3 SAT/ACT	Application	1 School transcript
2 Class rank	Course selection	5 Personal statement
11 Interview	4 Extra activities	Psychoeducational
1 G.P.A.	Open admission	4 Recommendations

Test Requirements:
Diagnostic testing waived: **Yes**
Untimed SAT: **Yes** Untimed ACT: **Yes**
WAIS-R required: **Yes**
Documentation of LD required: **Yes**
Currency of diagnostic testing: **Within 3 years**
Tests recommended: **WAIS-R, Woodcock-Johnson Psycho Ed Battery, WRAT, Detroit**

Types of Disabilities Served
- Speech/Lang
- Study skills
- Written express
- Organizational
- Perceptual
- Reading
- Spelling
- Math
- Fine Motor
- ADD with LD
- ADD without LD
- ADHD with LD
- ADHD without LD

Learning Disability Program
Students mainstreamed **100** % of the day
Recommended credits per semester: **6-12**
Counseling: Individual: **Yes**
Support groups are available: **Campus has a career center**

Faculty:
Faculty: **1** Part time: **1**
Faculty advocate: **Yes** Meets with instructor: **As needed**

Diagnostic Testing

ADD	Personality	Perceptual skills	Spelling
ADHD	Organization	Fine motor skills	Reading
I.Q.	Handwriting	Spoken language	Study skills
Math	Social skills	Written language	

Tutoring:
Services rendered by:

Graduates	Peers	Faculty	•LD staff	Teacher trainees

Tutorials

Grp.	Ind.	Tutorials	Grp.	Ind.	Tutorials
•		Math skills		•	Word processing
•	•	Study skills	•	•	Time management
		Language arts	•	•	Learning strategies
	•	Written express	•	•	Organizational skills

Academic Accommodations

Curriculum	Study Aids	Exams
• Priority registration	Typist	• Oral
Math waiver	Reader	• Untimed
Foreign lang. waiver	Notetaker	• Take home
Course substitution	• Proof reader	• With proctor
In Class	Text on tape	On computer
• Calculators	Early syllabus	• Extended time
• Tape recorder	Taped handouts	On tape
• Word processor		Modified
• Priority seating		• Separate room

Graduation Requirements:
Course credits: **126-165** GPA: **2.0** Years to complete degree: **4-6**

Program Strengths
There is no formal program. The Director of Health Services acts as Coordinator for Handicapped/Disabled students. Numbers vary from time to time. Assistance is individualized but limited to resource referral assistance.

General Information:
Embry-Riddle Aeronautical University is a 4 year private university. Urban campus of 80 acres is 60 miles from Orlando. Beaches are 2 miles from campus. 8% of students are foreign. 4 residential halls on campus. Housing is not guaranteed.

Accreditation: SACS

SAT/ACT Scores:
Scores for incoming freshmen: **Verbal:** 70% below 500. 28% between 500 and 599. 5% between 600 and 699. 1% above 700. **Math:** 33% below 500. 42% between 500 and 599. 212% between 600 and 699. 3% above 700. **ACT:** 17% below 20. 29% between 20 and 23. 16% between 24 and 251. 25% between 26 and 28. 13% above 28.

Class Rank:
About 12% of the present freshmen class were in the upper 20% of their high school class. 23% were in the top 40% of their class. 31% were in the top 60% of their class. 34% were in the top 80% of their class.

Expenses:
Tuition: In-state: Full year: $3,100.00 per semester. Part-time: Per credit: $260.00. Room and board: $3,200.00

Majors
• BUSINESS Aviation Management, Business Administration • ENGINEERING Aerospace, Engineering Physics, Industrial Aviation • VOCATIONAL Aircraft Mechanics, Aviation Computer Technology, Aviation Maintenance, Aviation Pilot, Aviation Technology

Sports/Activities
• SPORTS RELATED Cheerleading, Drill Team, Flying Team, Pep Band • SPORTS-INTERCOLLEGIATE Baseball, Basketball, Golf, Soccer, Tennis • SPORTS-INTRAMURAL Basketball, Football, Golf, Ping-Pong, Racquetball, Soccer, Softball, Tennis, Volleyball, Water Polo • STUDENT LIFE ACTIVITIES Debate, Drama Groups, Ethnic & Cultural Groups, Film, Newspaper, Religious Organization, Sororities, Student Government, Yearbook

Selective   **Florida**
                                                  Program

Florida Agricultural and Mechanical University
Tallahassee, Florida 32307
(904) 599-3796

School Enrollment: **7,700** Male: **3,800** Female: **3,900**
LD Enrollment: **57**

Admissions Contact: **Daisy Young, Deputy Registrar**
LD Contact: **Dr. Sharon Wooten, Director**
Name of Program: **Learning Development Center**
Address: **205 University Commons Bldg.**
Telephone:**(904) 599-3180**

Admissions

Application Information:
LD Students Applying: **150** Accepted: **104** Enrolled:**94**
Separate application:**Yes**
Application deadline: **July/December**
Applicant must apply **6-12** months in advance
Rolling Admissions: **Yes**

Secondary School Information
Most Important Criteria For Admissions (1-strongest)

1	SAT/ACT	1	Application	1	School transcript
	Class rank		Course selection	1	Personal statement
1	Interview	1	Extra activities	1	Psychoeducational
1	G.P.A.		Open admission	1	Recommendations

Test Requirements:
Diagnostic testing waived: **Yes**
Untimed SAT: **Yes** Untimed ACT: **Yes** Untimed ACH: **Yes** Achievement
tests required:**Battery**
Tests recommended: **Psycoeducational Battery**

Types of Disabilities Served
- Speech/Lang
- Study skills
- Written express
- Organizational
- Perceptual
- Reading
- Spelling
- Math
- Fine Motor
- ADD with LD
- ADD without LD
- ADHD with LD
- ADHD without LD

Learning Disability Program
Program: Remedial: **Yes**
Program: Reinforces course work: **Yes**
Students mainstreamed **100** % of the day

Faculty:
Faculty: **13** Including Director: **Yes** Full time: **9** Part time: **4**
LD faculty with: BS/BA: **5** M.A.: **5** Ph.D.: **1**
Faculty advocate: **Yes** Meets with instructor: **As needed**

Diagnostic Testing
- ADD
- ADHD
- I.Q.
- Math
- Personality
- Organization
- Handwriting
- Social skills
- Perceptual skills
- Fine motor skills
- Spoken language
- Written language
- Spelling
- Reading
- Study skills

Tutoring:
Average size of group tutorials: **2-3**
Services rendered by:
- Graduates
- Peers
- Faculty
- LD staff
- Teacher trainees

Tutorials

Grp.	Ind.	Tutorials	Grp.	Ind.	Tutorials
•	•	Math skills	•	•	Word processing
		Study skills			Time management
		Language arts	•	•	Learning strategies
	•	Written express	•	•	Organizational skills

Academic Accommodations

Curriculum	Study Aids	Exams
Priority registration	• Typist	• Oral
• Math waiver	Reader	Untimed
• Foreign lang. waiver	• Notetaker	• Take home
• Course substitution	• Proof reader	With proctor
In Class	• Text on tape	On computer
• Calculators	Early syllabus	• Extended time
• Tape recorder	Taped handouts	On tape
• Word processor		• Modified
Priority seating		Separate room

Program Strengths
The accommodations and considerations that are made available to our learning disabled students are varied and individualized. We provide a comprehensive program with a special diagnostic and learning development center. By emphasizing career development and socialization, we are national and international leaders in the area of post-secondary education for learning disabled students.

General Information:
Florida Agricultural and Mechanical University is a 4 year public university. Urban campus of 396 acres is 250 miles from Orlando. Accessible by air or bus. Beaches are 100 miles from campus. 1.7% of students are foreign. 9 residential halls on campus. Housing is not guaranteed.90-100 % of students remain on campus for the weekends. 30 % of students join fraternities/sororities.

Accreditation:SACS

Expenses:
Tuition: In-state: Full year: $431.40. Part-time: Per credit:$39.90. Part-time: Per course: $107.85. Part-time: Per credit:$131.87. Room and board: $1,200.00

Majors
• AREA STUDIES African, American, Asian, Black/Afro-American, Jewish, Latin American, Urban • BUSINESS Accounting, Agricultural, Banking, Business Administration, Business Economics, Business Education, Business Management, Economics, Finance • COMMUNICATIONS Advertising, Broadcasting, Communication, Creative Writing, English, Journalism, Photography, Television/Radio/Film • COMPUTER SCIENCE Computer Science, Data Processing • CRAFTS AND DESIGN Graphic Design • EDUCATION Art, Early Childhood, Elementary, English, Health, Industrial, Music, Physical, Science, Social Studies, Vocational • ENGINEERING Chemical, Civil/Environmental, Electrical, Industrial, Mechanical • HEALTH SCIENCES Health, Medical Records Technology, Nursing, Physical Therapy • HUMANITIES Humanities, Philosophy, Religion • LANGUAGES French, Spanish • PREPROFESSIONAL Agriculture, Architecture, Dentistry, Engineering, Medicine, Pharmacy, Range Management, Social Work • SCIENCES Animal, Biology, Botany, Chemistry, Ecology, Geography, Horticultural, Macrobiology, Marine Biology, Mathematics, Microbiology, Physical Science, Physics, Zoology • SOCIAL SCIENCES Anthropology, Criminal Justice, Government/Political, History, Political Science, Psychology, Social Sciences, Sociology • VISUAL AND PERFORMING ARTS Art, Art History, Dance, Music, Theater • VO-

Florida

CATIONAL Electronics Technology, Landscape Architecture

Sports/Activities

• SPORTS RELATED Cheerleading, Marching Band, Pep Band
• SPORTS-INTERCOLLEGIATE Baseball (M), Basketball, Cross Country, Football (M), Golf, Softball (F), Swimming, Tennis, Track and Field, Volleyball (F) • SPORTS-INTRAMURAL Badminton, Basketball, Bowling, Diving, Football (M), Gymnastics, Hand Ball, Karate, Martial Arts, Ping-Pong, Racquetball, Soccer, Softball, Tennis, Track and Field, Volleyball, Weight Lifting • STUDENT LIFE ACTIVITIES Concert Band, Dance, Drama Groups, Ethnic & Cultural Groups, Film, Fraternities, Jazz Band, Music Ensembles, Music Groups, Newspaper, Radio/TV station, Religious Organization, Sororities, Student Government, Symphony Orchestra, Yearbook

Very Selective	Florida
	Services

Florida Atlantic University
500 Northwest 20th Street
Boca Raton, Florida 33431
(407) 367-3040

School Enrollment: **6,971** Male: **2,909** Female: **4,062**

Admissions Contact: **Dr. B. Levin-Stankevich, Dir. of Admissions**
LD Contact: **Dee Davis, Director**
Name of Program: **Disabled Student Services**
Telephone:**(407) 367-3880**

Admissions

Application Information:
Application deadline: **June 1st**
Rolling Admissions: **Yes**

Secondary School Information
Most Important Criteria For Admissions (1-strongest)

2 SAT/ACT	Application	**1**	School transcript
1 Class rank	**2** Course selection		Personal statement
Interview	Extra activities		Psychoeducational
1 G.P.A.	Open admission		Recommendations

Test Requirements:
Untimed SAT: **Yes** Untimed ACT: **Yes**

Types of Disabilities Served
• Speech/Lang
• Study skills
• Written express
• Organizational
• Perceptual
• Reading
• Spelling
• Math
• Fine Motor
• ADD with LD
• ADD without LD
• ADHD with LD
• ADHD without LD

Faculty:
Faculty: **1** Part time: **1**

Diagnostic Testing

ADD	Personality	Perceptual skills	Spelling
ADHD	Organization	Fine motor skills	Reading
I.Q.	Handwriting	Spoken language	Study skills
Math	Social skills	Written language	

Tutoring:
Services rendered by:

•Graduates •Peers •Faculty •LD staff Teacher trainees

Tutorials

Grp. Ind. Tutorials	Grp. Ind. Tutorials
• Math skills	• Word processing
• Study skills	• Time management
• Language arts	• Learning strategies
• Written express	• Organizational skills

Academic Accommodations

Curriculum	Study Aids	Exams
Priority registration	Typist	• Oral
Math waiver	Reader	Untimed
Foreign lang. waiver	• Notetaker	• Take home
Course substitution	• Proof reader	With proctor
In Class	• Text on tape	On computer
• Calculators	Early syllabus	• Extended time
• Tape recorder	Taped handouts	On tape
• Word processor		• Modified
Priority seating		Separate room

Program Strengths
We have no program per se, but we provide services to support the students in mainstream classes. There is no remedial instruction in Florida in the universities as that has been made the responsibility of the community colleges.

General Information:
Florida Atlantic University is a 4 year public university. Suburban campus of 900 acres is 15 miles from Fort Lauderdale. Accessible by air, train, or bus. Beaches are 1 mile from campus. 4% of students are foreign. 7 residential halls on campus. Housing is not guaranteed.10 % of students remain on campus for the weekends. 2 % of students join fraternities/sororities.

Accreditation:SACS, AACSB, ABET, NCATE, NASM, NLN, NAACLS

Expenses: Part-time: Per credit:$42.63. Part-time: Per credit:$134.60. Room and board: $3,345.00

Majors
• AREA STUDIES Urban • BUSINESS Accounting, Banking, Business Administration, Business Management, Economics, Entrepreneur, Finance, International Business, Management, Marketing, Personnel, Real Estate • COMMUNICATIONS Communication, English, Journalism, Linguistic, Literature, Television/Radio/Film • COMPUTER SCIENCE Computer Science • EDUCATION Art, Curriculum, Early Childhood, Elementary, English, Foreign Language, Music, Physical, School Psychology, Special • ENGINEERING Electrical, Mathematical, Ocean • HEALTH SCIENCES Health, Medical Technology, Nursing • HUMANITIES Humanities, Philosophy • LANGUAGES French, German, Spanish • PREPROFESSIONAL Dentistry, Engineering, Medicine, Pharmacy, Social Work, Veterinarian • SCIENCES Biology, Botany, Chemistry, Geography, Geology, Marine Biology, Mathematics, Microbiology, Physical Science, Physics, Zoology • SOCIAL SCIENCES Anthropology, Criminal Justice, Geography, Government/Political, History, Political Science, Psychology, Public Relations, Social Sciences, Sociology • VISUAL AND PERFORMING ARTS Art, Art History, Music, Theater • VOCATIONAL Medical Laboratory Technology

Sports/Activities
• SPORTS RELATED Band • SPORTS-INTERCOLLEGIATE Baseball (M), Basketball, Cross Country, Diving (F), Fencing, Golf, Swimming, Tennis, Track and Field • SPORTS-INTRAMURAL Archery, Basketball, Bowling, Cross Country, Fencing, Golf (M), Hand Ball, Racquetball, Soccer (M), Softball, Swimming, Tennis, Volleyball • STUDENT LIFE ACTIVITIES Choral, Drama Groups, Ethnic & Cultural Groups, Fraternities,

Jazz Band, Magazine, Music Ensembles, Music Groups, Musical Theater, Newspaper, Opera, Political Groups, Radio/TV station, Religious Organization, Sororities, Student Government, Symphony Orchestra, Yearbook

Less Selective

Florida Services

Florida Community College at Jacksonville

4501 Capper Road
Jacksonville, Florida 32218
(904) 632-3211

School Enrollment: **17,345** Male: **7,285** Female: **10,060**

Admissions Contact: **Sue Sumner, Admissions Officer**
LD Contact: **Jeffrey Oliver, Assistant Dean**
Name of Program: **Disabled Student Services**
Telephone:**(904) 766-6767**

Admissions

Application Information:
Rolling Admissions: **Yes**

Secondary School Information
Most Important Criteria For Admissions (1-strongest)

SAT/ACT	Application	School transcript
Class rank	Course selection	Personal statement
Interview	Extra activities	Psychoeducational
G.P.A.	**1** Open admission	Recommendations

Test Requirements:
Standardized tests waived: **Yes**
Documentation of LD required: **Yes**

Types of Disabilities Served
- Speech/Lang
- Study skills
- Written express
- Organizational
- Perceptual
- Reading
- Spelling
- Math
- Fine Motor
- ADD with LD
- ADD without LD
- ADHD with LD
- ADHD without LD

Admissions Process

Only additional step is to contact campus Disabled Student Specialist if special services are requested.

Learning Disability Program
Program: Reinforces course work: **Yes**
Program available through:**As needed**
Students mainstreamed **100** % of the day
Services available for all students: **Yes**
Counseling: Individual: **Yes**

Faculty:
Faculty: **2** Full time: **2**
Faculty advocate: **Yes** Meets with instructor: **As needed**

Diagnostic Testing
- ADD
- ADHD
- I.Q.
- Math
- Personality
- Organization
- Handwriting
- Social skills
- Perceptual skills
- Fine motor skills
- Spoken language
- Written language
- Spelling
- Reading
- Study skills

Tutoring:
Average size of group tutorials:
Services rendered by:
- •Graduates Peers •Faculty LD staff Teacher trainees

Tutorials

Grp.	Ind.	Tutorials	Grp.	Ind.	Tutorials
•		Math skills			Word processing
		Study skills			Time management
•		Language arts			Learning strategies
		Written express			Organizational skills

Academic Accommodations

Curriculum	Study Aids	Exams
Priority registration	Typist	• Oral
Math waiver	Reader	Untimed
Foreign lang. waiver	• Notetaker	Take home
• Course substitution	Proof reader	• With proctor
In Class	• Text on tape	On computer
• Calculators	Early syllabus	• Extended time
• Tape recorder	Taped handouts	On tape
• Word processor		• Modified
Priority seating		• Separate room

Program Strengths
If a student has a learning disability that has been documented and has requested services from our disability department, we do our best to service him or her.

General Information:
Florida Community College at Jacksonville is a 2 year public college. Suburban campus. Accessible by bus. Beaches are 15 miles from campus. Housing is not guaranteed.

Accreditation:SACS

Expenses: Part-time: Per credit:$30.00. Part-time: Per credit:$109.00.

Majors
• BUSINESS Accounting, Business Administration, Business Economics, Business Education, Business Management, Economics, Finance, Hotel and Restaurant Managemen, Insurance, Management, Marketing, Marketing Research, Personnel, Real Estate, Sports Management, Travel/Tourism Management • COMMUNICATIONS Communication, Creative Writing, English, Journalism, Television/Radio/Film • EDUCATION Art, Early Childhood, Elementary, Health, Music, Physical, Recreation and Youth Leadershi, Vocational • HEALTH SCIENCES Medical Technology, Nursing, Nutritional/Food, Radiological Therapy • HUMANITIES Humanities, Philosophy, Religion • LANGUAGES American Sign Language, French, German, Spanish • PREPROFESSIONAL Architecture, Dentistry, Medicine, Social Work • SCIENCES Biology, Chemistry, Earth, Mathematics, Microbiology • SOCIAL SCIENCES Criminal Justice, Geography, Government/Political, History, Political Science, Social Sciences • VISUAL AND PERFORMING ARTS Art, Art History, Music, Theater

Sports/Activities
• SPORTS RELATED Cheerleading • SPORTS-INTERCOLLEGIATE Baseball, Basketball, Cross Country, Golf, Softball, Tennis, Volleyball • SPORTS-INTRAMURAL Archery, Baseball, Basketball, Canoeing, Diving, Golf, Soccer • STUDENT LIFE ACTIVITIES Drama Groups, Ethnic & Cultural Groups, Film, Jazz Band, Magazine, Newspaper, Radio/TV station, Religious Organization, Student Government, Symphony Orchestra, Yearbook

Very Selective	Florida Services

Florida State University
216B WJB
Tallahassee, Florida 32306-1009
(904) 644-6200

School Enrollment: **19,700** Male: **9,300** Female: **10,400**

Admissions Contact: **Dr. Peter Metarko, Director of Admissions**
LD Contact: **Mr. Halie Nabi, Director**
Name of Program: **Disabled Student Services**
Telephone:**(904) 644-9569**

Admissions

Application Information:
Application deadline: **February 1st**

Secondary School Information
Most Important Criteria For Admissions (1-strongest)

SAT/ACT	Application	School transcript
Class rank	Course selection	Personal statement
Interview	Extra activities	Psychoeducational
G.P.A.	Open admission	Recommendations

Types of Disabilities Served
• Speech/Lang	• Reading	ADD with LD
• Study skills	• Spelling	ADD without LD
• Written express	• Math	ADHD with LD
• Organizational	• Fine Motor	ADHD without LD
• Perceptual		

Faculty:
Faculty advocate: **Yes** Meets with instructor: **As needed**

Diagnostic Testing
ADD	Personality	Perceptual skills	Spelling
ADHD	Organization	Fine motor skills	Reading
I.Q.	Handwriting	Spoken language	Study skills
Math	Social skills	Written language	

Tutoring:
Services rendered by:
•Graduates •Peers •Faculty LD staff •Teacher trainees

Tutorials
Grp.	Ind.	Tutorials	Grp.	Ind.	Tutorials
	•	Math skills		•	Word processing
		Study skills			Time management
	•	Language arts			Learning strategies
		Written express			Organizational skills

Academic Accommodations

Curriculum	Study Aids	Exams
Priority registration	• Typist	• Oral
• Math waiver	Reader	Untimed
• Foreign lang. waiver	• Notetaker	• Take home
• Course substitution	• Proof reader	With proctor
In Class	• Text on tape	On computer
• Calculators	Early syllabus	• Extended time
• Tape recorder	Taped handouts	On tape
• Word processor		• Modified
Priority seating		Separate room

Program Strengths
Services are provided at no cost to the disabled student; however, it is necessary for the student to provide documentation at the time of enrollment to confirm the presence of a learning disability. The learning disabled student is expected to meet the same requirements for admission and graduation as the traditional student.

General Information:
Florida State University is a 4 year public university. Urban campus. of 345 acres is Accessible by air or bus. 3% of students are foreign. Housing is not guaranteed.

Accreditation:AACSB, FIDER, NASM, NCATE, NLN

Expenses:
Tuition: In-state: Full year: $1,230.00. Part-time: Per credit:$41.00. Part-time: Per credit:$132.00. Room and board: $3,100.00

Majors
• AREA STUDIES American, Asian, Eastern European, Inter-American, Latin American • BUSINESS Accounting, Banking, Business Administration, Business Management, Economics, Finance, Hotel and Restaurant Managemen, Insurance, International Business, Management, Marketing, Purchasing and Materials, Real Estate • COMMUNICATIONS Communication, English, Political, Speech, Television/Radio/Film • COMPUTER SCIENCE Computer Science • EDUCATION Art, Early Childhood, Elementary, English, Health, Multicultural, Music, Music Therapy, Science, Secondary, Special, Specific Learning Disabilities • ENGINEERING Chemical, Civil/Environmental, Communications, Computer, Industrial, Mechanical • HEALTH SCIENCES Nursing, Nutritional/Food, Rehabilitation • HUMANITIES Classics, Humanities, Liberal Arts, Philosophy, Religion • LANGUAGES French, German, Greek, Italian, Latin, Russian, Spanish • PREPROFESSIONAL Social Work • SCIENCES Atmospheric, Biochemistry, Biology, Chemistry, Geography, Geology, Mathematics, Meteorology, Physics • SOCIAL SCIENCES Anthropology, Criminology, Government/Political, History, Human Resources Development, International Studies, Political Science, Psychology, Social Sciences, Sociology • VISUAL AND PERFORMING ARTS Art History, Dance, Dramatic Arts, Music, Music Composition and Theory, Music History, Studio Art • VOCATIONAL Home Economics, Interior Design, Medical Laboratory Technology

Sports/Activities
• SPORTS RELATED Marching Band • SPORTS-INTERCOLLEGIATE Baseball (M), Basketball, Cross Country, Diving, Football (M), Golf, Softball (F), Swimming, Tennis, Track and Field, Volleyball (F) • SPORTS-INTRAMURAL Badminton, Basketball, Bowling, Cross Country, Diving, Fencing, Golf, Hand Ball, Lacrosse, Ping-Pong, Racquetball, Rugby, Sailing, Scuba, Soccer, Softball (F), Swimming, Tennis, Track and Field, Volleyball, Water Polo, Wrestling • STUDENT LIFE ACTIVITIES Choral, Concert Band, Dance, Drama Groups, Film, Fraternities, Music Ensembles, Musical Theater, Newspaper, Radio/TV station, Religious Organization, Sororities, Student Government, Yearbook

Less Selective

Gulf Coast Community College
5230 West Highway 98
Panama City, Florida 32401
(904) 769-1551

School Enrollment: **6,135** Male: **2,579** Female: **3,556**
LD Enrollment: **61** Male: **34** Female: **27**

Admissions Contact: **Roy Smith, Director of Admissions**
LD Contact: **Linda Van Dalen, Coordinator**
Name of Program: **Disabled Student Services**
Address: **5230 West Highway 98**

Admissions

Application Information:
Application deadline: **Rolling**
Rolling Admissions: **Yes**

Secondary School Information
Most Important Criteria For Admissions (1-strongest)
SAT/ACT	Application	School transcript
Class rank	Course selection	Personal statement
Interview	Extra activities	Psychoeducational
G.P.A.	Open admission	Recommendations

Test Requirements:
Diagnostic testing waived: **Yes**
Documentation of LD required: **Yes**
Currency of diagnostic testing:
Tests recommended: **Documentation of learning disability - accept records and evaluations done while in K-12.**

Types of Disabilities Served
Speech/Lang	• Reading	• ADD with LD
• Study skills	• Spelling	• ADD without LD
• Written express	• Math	ADHD with LD
• Organizational	Fine Motor	ADHD without LD
Perceptual		

Admissions Process

All students must complete application to the college and an affidavit of residency. Applicant must take Gulf Coast placement test. A first-time in-college student must submit high school transcripts or copy of GED.

High School Course Requirements:
English:

Learning Disability Program

Program: Reinforces course work: **Yes**
Students mainstreamed **100** % of the day
Recommended credits per semester:
Time required or recommended in learning center: **Voluntary**
Counseling: Individual: **Yes**

Faculty:
Faculty: **3** Including Director: **Yes** Full time: **1** Part time: **2** M.A.: **2**
Faculty advocate: **Yes** Meets with instructor: **As needed**

Diagnostic Testing
ADD	Personality	Perceptual skills	Spelling
ADHD	Organization	Fine motor skills	Reading
I.Q.	Handwriting	Spoken language	Study skills
Math	Social skills	Written language	

Tutoring:
Average size of group tutorials: **2-4**
Services rendered by:
Graduates   Peers   Faculty   •LD staff   Teacher trainees

Tutorials
Grp.	Ind.	Tutorials	Grp.	Ind.	Tutorials
	•	Math skills			Word processing
		Study skills			Time management
	•	Language arts			Learning strategies
	•	Written express			Organizational skills

Academic Accommodations
Curriculum	Study Aids	Exams
• Priority registration	Typist	• Oral
Math waiver	• Reader	• Untimed
Foreign lang. waiver	• Notetaker	• Take home
• Course substitution	• Proof reader	• With proctor
In Class	• Text on tape	• On computer
• Calculators	• Early syllabus	• Extended time
• Tape recorder	Taped handouts	• On tape
• Word processor		• Modified
• Priority seating		• Separate room

Graduation Requirements:
Course credits: **65** GPA: **2.0**

Program Strengths
All students entering college credit programs are required to take the college placement tests before registration. The tests are required by the state and are given free of charge. These are not admissions tests but are used to place students in the proper courses. All first-time college students are required to take tests in English, reading, and mathematics. Test accommodations are available.

General Information:
Gulf Coast Community College is a 2 year public college. Suburban campus of 80 acres is 100 miles from Pensacola. Beaches are 6 miles from campus. Housing is not guaranteed.

Accreditation: SACS

Expenses: Part-time: Per credit:$28.00. Part-time: Per credit:$108.00.

Majors
• BUSINESS Accounting, Banking, Business Administration, Business Education, Finance, Food Management, Hotel and Restaurant Managemen, Management, Marketing, Real Estate • COMMUNICATIONS Advertising, Broadcasting, Communication, English, Journalism, Photography, Speech, Television/Radio/Film • COMPUTER SCIENCE Computer Science, Computer Technology, Data Processing, Programming, Systems Analysis • CRAFTS AND DESIGN Graphic Art Technology, Mechanical Design Technology • EDUCATION Elementary, General, Physical, Science, Secondary, Social Studies • ENGINEERING Computer, Engineering Science • HEALTH SCIENCES Dental Assistant, Medical Assistant, Medical Records Administration, Nursing, Physical Therapy, Radiological Therapy • HUMANITIES Humanities, Liberal Arts, Philosophy, Religion • LANGUAGES French, Spanish • PREPROFESSIONAL Architecture, Dentistry, Forestry, Law, Medicine, Pharmacy, Social Work, Veterinarian • SCIENCES Astronomy, Biology, Botany, Chemistry, Earth, Geography,

Florida

Geology, Marine Biology, Mathematics, Meteorology, Microbiology, Oceanography, Physical Chemistry, Physical Science, Physics, Physiology, Radiology, Zoology • SOCIAL SCIENCES Anthropology, Criminal Justice, Geography, Government/Political, History, Human Service, Law Enforcement, Library Science, Political Science, Psychology, Public Relations, Social Sciences, Sociology • VISUAL AND PERFORMING ARTS Fine Arts, Music, Music Performance • VOCATIONAL Aviation Administration, Business and Office, Drafting, Electronics Technology, Fashion Merchandising, Fire Science, Home Economics, Park/Recreation, Respiratory Therapy Technology, Robotics, Secretarial, Textile and Clothing

Sports/Activities

• SPORTS RELATED Cheerleading, Pep Band • SPORTS-INTERCOLLEGIATE Baseball (M), Basketball (M), Softball (F) • SPORTS-INTRA-MURAL Archery, Badminton, Basketball, Bowling, Golf, Karate, Martial Arts, Racquetball, Sailing, Softball, Tennis, Volleyball • STUDENT LIFE ACTIVITIES Choral, Community Service, Concert Band, Dance, Drama Groups, Ethnic & Cultural Groups, Fraternities, Jazz Band, Magazine, Music Ensembles, Music Groups, Musical Theater, Newspaper, Radio/TV station, Religious Organization, Sororities, Student Government, Symphony Orchestra

---

Less Selective　　　　　　　　**Florida**
Services

Lake City Community College
Route 3 Box 7
Lake City, Florida 32055
(904) 752-1822

School Enrollment: **2,520** Male: **1,210** Female: **1,310**

Admissions Contact: **Rayanne Giddis, Director of Admissions**
LD Contact: **Edna Hindson/Ron Johnsrud, Coordinator**
Name of Program: **Handicapped Services**
Telephone:**Ext. 315**

Admissions

Application Information:
Application deadline: **None**

Secondary School Information
Most Important Criteria For Admissions (1-strongest)

3 SAT/ACT	1 Application	2	School transcript
5 Class rank	4 Course selection	5	Personal statement
3 Interview	5 Extra activities	5	Psychoeducational
5 G.P.A.	Open admission	5	Recommendations

Test Requirements:
Documentation of LD required: **Yes**

Types of Disabilities Served
• Speech/Lang • Reading • ADD with LD
• Study skills • Spelling • ADD without LD
• Written express • Math • ADHD with LD
• Organizational • Fine Motor • ADHD without LD
• Perceptual

Learning Disability Program
Services available for all students: **Yes**
Counseling: Individual: **Yes**

Faculty:
Faculty: **2** Full time: **1** Part time: **1** M.A.: **2**
Faculty advocate: **Yes** Meets with instructor: **As needed**

Diagnostic Testing
ADD	Personality	Perceptual skills	Spelling
ADHD	Organization	Fine motor skills	Reading
I.Q.	Handwriting	Spoken language	Study skills
Math	Social skills	Written language	

Tutoring:
Services rendered by:
Graduates •Peers Faculty •LD staff Teacher trainees

Tutorials
Grp.	Ind.	Tutorials	Grp.	Ind.	Tutorials
	•	Math skills		•	Word processing
	•	Study skills		•	Time management
	•	Language arts		•	Learning strategies
	•	Written express		•	Organizational skills

Academic Accommodations

Curriculum	Study Aids	Exams
• Priority registration	• Typist	• Oral
• Math waiver	Reader	Untimed
Foreign lang. waiver	• Notetaker	• Take home
• Course substitution	• Proof reader	• With proctor
In Class	• Text on tape	On computer
• Calculators	Early syllabus	• Extended time
• Tape recorder	Taped handouts	On tape
• Word processor		• Modified
Priority seating		Separate room

Program Strengths
We do what we can in the light of the disability and available resources. We mainstream and students are very independent.

General Information:
Lake City Community College is a 2 year public college. Rural campus of 125 acres is 60 miles from Jacksonville. Accessible by bus. Ski areas are 400 miles from campus. Beaches are 80 miles from campus. 3% of students are foreign. 1 residential halls on campus. Housing is not guaranteed.

Accreditation:SACS

SAT/ACT Scores:
Scores for incoming freshmen: **ACT:** 73% below 20. 19% between 20 and 23. 5%between 24 and 25l. 3%between 26 and 28. .3% above 28.

Expenses: Part-time: Per credit:$26.25. Part-time: Per credit:$97.50. Room and board: $914.00

Majors
• BUSINESS Business Administration, Business Management, Management, Marketing, Real Estate • COMPUTER SCIENCE Programming, Symbolic Systems • EDUCATION Agricultural, Physical • ENGINEERING Electrical • HEALTH SCIENCES Health, Medical Technology, Nursing • HUMANITIES Liberal Arts • PREPROFESSIONAL Agriculture, Engineering, Forestry, Medicine, Recreation • SCIENCES Mathematics • SOCIAL SCIENCES Criminal Justice, Criminology, Law Enforcement • VOCATIONAL Business and Office, Carpentry, Golf Course Operations, Landscape Architecture, Masonry, Medical Laboratory Technology, Para-Medical, Secretarial, Welding

Sports/Activities
• SPORTS-INTERCOLLEGIATE Baseball (M), Basketball (M), Golf (M), Softball (F) • SPORTS-INTRAMURAL Basketball, Golf, Hand Ball, Ping-

Pong, Racquetball, Softball, Tennis, Volleyball • STUDENT LIFE ACTIVITIES Choral, Concert Band, Drama Groups, Jazz Band, Magazine, Music Ensembles, Music Groups, Newspaper, Radio/TV station, Religious Organization, Student Government

Less Selective	Florida Services

Miami-Dade Community College
11011 S.W. 104 Street
Miami, Florida 33176
(305) 237-2504

School Enrollment: **26,000** Male: **11,000** Female: **15,000**
LD Enrollment: **250** Male: **150** Female: **100**
LD Contact: **Elizabeth Smith, L.D. Specialist**
Name of Program: **Support Services**
Telephone:**(305) 237-2316**

Admissions

Application Information:
Enrolled:**250**
Rolling Admissions: **Yes**

Secondary School Information
Most Important Criteria For Admissions (1-strongest)

SAT/ACT	Application **1**	School transcript
Class rank	Course selection	Personal statement
Interview	Extra activities **2**	Psychoeducational
G.P.A. **1**	Open admission	Recommendations

Test Requirements:
Diagnostic testing waived: **Yes**
WAIS-R required: **Yes** Range accepted: **Average**
Documentation of LD required: **Yes**
Currency of diagnostic testing: **3 years**
Tests recommended: **Woodcock-Johnson Psychoeducational Battery**

Types of Disabilities Served
- Speech/Lang
- Reading
- ADD with LD
- Study skills
- Spelling
- ADD without LD
- Written express
- Math
- ADHD with LD
- Organizational
- Fine Motor
- ADHD without LD
- Perceptual

Admissions Process

Open admissions

High School Course Requirements:
Waivers to standard high school courses
 Math: **Yes**

Learning Disability Program

Program: Remedial: **Yes**
Program: Reinforces course work: **Yes**
Program available through:**Flexible scheduling**
Students mainstreamed **100** % of the day
Counseling: Individual: **Yes** Group Counseling: **Yes** Vocational Counseling: **Yes**

Support groups are available:**Student Pioneers Organization, Campus Support Group for Learning Disabled**

Faculty:
Faculty: **1** Including Director: **Yes** Part time: **1**
LD faculty with: BS/BA: **1** M.A.: **1**
Faculty advocate: **Yes** Meets with instructor: **As needed**

Diagnostic Testing
ADD	Personality	Perceptual skills	• Spelling
ADHD	Organization	Fine motor skills	• Reading
I.Q.	Handwriting	Spoken language	Study skills
• Math	Social skills•	Written language	

Tutoring:
Average size of group tutorials: **2**
Services rendered by:
 Graduates • Peers Faculty LD staff • Teacher trainees

Tutorials
Grp.	Ind.	Tutorials	Grp.	Ind.	Tutorials
•	•	Math skills	•	•	Word processing
•	•	Study skills	•	•	Time management
•	•	Language arts	•	•	Learning strategies
•	•	Written express	•	•	Organizational skills

Academic Accommodations
Curriculum	Study Aids	Exams
Priority registration	Typist	Oral
• Math waiver	Reader	Untimed
Foreign lang. waiver	Notetaker	Take home
• Course substitution	• Proof reader	With proctor
In Class	• Text on tape	On computer
Calculators	Early syllabus	• Extended time
• Tape recorder	Taped handouts	On tape
• Word processor		Modified
Priority seating		• Separate room

Graduation Requirements:
Course credits: **62** GPA: **2.0** Years to complete degree: **2** Math waiver: **Yes**
Other requirements: **C last exam**

Program Strengths
Support services are available for students with specific learning disabilities. A learning disability specialist is available on campus to work with individual students. In addition to working with the students, the specialist serves as a resource person on campus for our faculty members and recommends how to accommodate the student's disability.

General Information:
Miami-Dade Community College is a 2 year public college. Urban campus of 185 acres is Accessible by air, train or bus. Housing is not guaranteed.

Accreditation:FSDE

Expenses:
Tuition: In-state: Full year: $367.80 for 12 credit hours. Part-time: Per credit:$30.65. Tuition: Out-of-state: Full year: $1,309.80 for 12 credit hours. Part-time: Per credit:$109.15.

Majors
• AREA STUDIES American, Asian, Black/Afro-American, Latin American • BUSINESS Accounting, Aviation Management, Banking, Economics, Fashion Merchandising, Food Management, Hotel and Restaurant Managemen, Management, Marketing, Travel/Tourism Management • COMMUNICATIONS English, Journalism, Literature, Photography, Speech, Television/Radio/Film • COMPUTER SCIENCE Computer Science, Data Processing, Programming • CRAFTS AND DESIGN Commercial Art, Graphic Design • EDUCATION Elementary, Foreign Language,

Industrial, Physical, Secondary • ENGINEERING Aeronautical Technology, Chemical, Civil/Environmental, Electrical, Electrodiagnostic Communicatio, Electromechanical Technology, Industrial, Instrumentation Technology • HEALTH SCIENCES Dental Hygiene, Environmental, Medical Secretary, Medical Technology, Nursing, Nutritional/Food, Occupational Therapy, Physical Therapy • HUMANITIES English/Writing/ Literature, Liberal Arts, Philosophy, Religion • LANGUAGES French, Italian, Portuguese, Russian, Spanish • PREPROFESSIONAL Architecture, Chiropractic, Dentistry, Drafting, Fisheries, Law, Legal Assistant, Ophthalmic Services, Optometry, Pharmacy, Social Work, Veterinarian • SCIENCES Biology, Chemistry, Horticultural, Management, Mathematics, Meteorology, Physics • SOCIAL SCIENCES Anthropology, Court Reporting, Criminal Justice, International Studies, Political Science, Psychology, Public Relations, Sociology • VISUAL AND PERFORMING ARTS Cinematography/Film, Dance, Dramatic Arts, Fine Arts, Music • VOCATIONAL Air Conditioning/Heating/Refri, Aviation Pilot, Drafting, Electronics Technology, Fashion Design, Fire Science, Food Service, Home Economics, Industrial Arts, Interior Design, Landscape Architecture, Medical Laboratory Technology, Paralegal, Radiograph Medical Technology, Respiratory Therapy Technology, Secretarial, Surveying and Mapping

Sports/Activities

• SPORTS RELATED Band • SPORTS-INTERCOLLEGIATE Baseball (M), Basketball, Diving, Golf (M), Soccer (M), Softball (F), Swimming, Tennis, Volleyball • SPORTS-INTRAMURAL Basketball, Ping-Pong, Racquetball • STUDENT LIFE ACTIVITIES Choral, Concert Band, Dance, Debate, Drama Groups, Ethnic & Cultural Groups, Film, Fraternities, Jazz Band, Music Ensembles, Music Groups, Musical Theater, Radio/ TV station, Religious Organization, Sororities, Student Government, Yearbook

Less Selective	Florida
	Program

Okaloosa-Walton Junior College

100 College Boulevard
Niceville, Florida 32578
(904) 678-5111

School Enrollment: **9,138** Male: **3,926** Female: **5,212**
LD Enrollment: **17** Male: **7** Female: **10**

Admissions Contact: **Eugene Benvenutti, Registrar**
LD Contact: **Inez W. Bailey, Counselor**
Name of Program: **Special Needs**
Telephone:**Ext. 236**

Admissions

Application Information:
Application deadline: **None**

Secondary School Information
Most Important Criteria For Admissions (1-strongest)

SAT/ACT	Application	School transcript
Class rank	Course selection	Personal statement
Interview	Extra activities	Psychoeducational
G.P.A.	**1** Open admission	Recommendations

Test Requirements:
Diagnostic testing waived: **Yes**
Documentation of LD required: **Yes**

Types of Disabilities Served
• Speech/Lang	• Reading	• ADD with LD
• Study skills	• Spelling	• ADD without LD
• Written express	• Math	• ADHD with LD
• Organizational	• Fine Motor	• ADHD without LD
• Perceptual		

High School Course Requirements:
English: **4** Math: **3** Science: **3**

Learning Disability Program
Students mainstreamed **100** % of the day
Counseling: Individual: **Yes**

Faculty:
Faculty: **1**
Faculty advocate: **Yes** Meets with instructor: **When requested**

Diagnostic Testing
ADD	Personality	Perceptual skills	Spelling
ADHD	Organization	Fine motor skills	• Reading
I.Q.	Handwriting	Spoken language	Study skills
• Math	Social skills	• Written language	

Tutoring:
Services rendered by:
Graduates	•Peers	Faculty	LD staff	Teacher trainees

Tutorials
Grp.	Ind. Tutorials	Grp. Ind. Tutorials
	Math skills	Word processing
	Study skills	Time management
	Language arts	Learning strategies
	Written express	Organizational skills

Academic Accommodations
Curriculum	Study Aids	Exams
Priority registration	Typist	• Oral
Math waiver	• Reader	• Untimed
Foreign lang. waiver	• Notetaker	Take home
Course substitution	Proof reader	With proctor
In Class	Text on tape	On computer
• Calculators	Early syllabus	• Extended time
• Tape recorder	Taped handouts	On tape
Word processor		Modified
Priority seating		• Separate room

Graduation Requirements:
Course credits: **64** GPA: **2.0**

Program Strengths
We attempt to provide those services that will allow a student with a specific learning disability to succeed.

General Information:
Okaloosa-Walton Junior College is a 2 year public college. Rural campus of 264 acres is 20 miles from Ft. Walton. Beaches are 20 miles from campus. Housing is not guaranteed.

Accreditation:SACS, FSDE

Expenses: Part-time: Per credit:$24.15. Part-time: Per credit:$84.00.

Majors

• BUSINESS Accounting, Banking, Business Administration, Business Education, Business Management, Fashion Merchandising, Hotel and Restaurant Managemen, Management, Marketing, Real Estate
• COMMUNICATIONS Graphic Design • COMPUTER SCIENCE Computer Science, Data Processing, Programming • EDUCATION Art, Child Development, Elementary, Physical, Recreation and Youth Leadershi, Secondary • HEALTH SCIENCES Health, Nursing, Physical Therapy • HUMANITIES Humanities, Liberal Arts, Religion • LANGUAGES French, German, Spanish • PREPROFESSIONAL Dentistry, Engineering, Legal Assistant, Medicine, Pharmacy, Social Work, Veterinarian • SCIENCES Chemistry, Mathematics, Physical Science, Physics • SOCIAL SCIENCES Law Enforcement, Social Sciences • VOCATIONAL Air Conditioning/Heating/Refri, Automobile Technology, Aviation Maintenance, Business and Office, Construction, Drafting, Fashion Merchandising, Fire Science, Food Service, Home Economics, Industrial Arts, Interior Design, Medical Laboratory Technology, Paralegal, Secretarial, Welding, Word Processing

Sports/Activities

• SPORTS-INTERCOLLEGIATE Baseball (M), Basketball (F), Basketball (M), Softball (F) • SPORTS-INTRAMURAL Archery, Badminton, Basketball, Bowling, Cross Country, Football (M), Hand Ball, Ping-Pong, Sailing, Soccer • STUDENT LIFE ACTIVITIES Choral, Concert Band, Ethnic & Cultural Groups, Jazz Band, Magazine, Newspaper

Less Selective

**Florida
Services**

Polk Community College
999 Avenue H NE
Winter Haven, Florida 33881-4299
(813) 297-1001

School Enrollment: **2,384** Male: **952** Female: **1,432**

Admissions Contact: **Michelle Wampler, Dir. of Adm. and Records**
LD Contact: **Michelle R. Sams, Academic Program Planner**
Name of Program: **Handicapped Services**
Telephone:**(813) 297-1063**

Admissions

Secondary School Information
Most Important Criteria For Admissions (1-strongest)

SAT/ACT	**1** Application	**2**	School transcript
Class rank	Course selection		Personal statement
Interview	Extra activities		Psychoeducational
G.P.A.	**1** Open admission		Recommendations

Types of Disabilities Served

Speech/Lang	Reading	ADD with LD
• Study skills	Spelling	ADD without LD
Written express	• Math	ADHD with LD
• Organizational	Fine Motor	ADHD without LD
Perceptual		

Learning Disability Program
Counseling: Individual: **Yes**

Faculty:
Faculty: **6** Full time: **6**
Faculty advocate: **Yes** Meets with instructor: **As needed**

Diagnostic Testing

ADD	Personality	Perceptual skills	Spelling
ADHD	Organization	Fine motor skills	Reading
I.Q.	Handwriting	Spoken language	Study skills
Math	Social skills	Written language	

Tutoring:
Average size of group tutorials: **1:1**
Services rendered by:
Graduates   Peers   •Faculty   •LD staff   •Teacher trainees

Tutorials

Grp.	Ind.	Tutorials	Grp.	Ind.	Tutorials
•		Math skills			Word processing
•		Study skills	•		Time management
		Language arts			Learning strategies
		Written express			Organizational skills

Academic Accommodations

Curriculum	Study Aids	Exams
Priority registration	Typist	Oral
Math waiver	Reader	Untimed
Foreign lang. waiver	• Notetaker	Take home
Course substitution	• Proof reader	With proctor
In Class	• Text on tape	On computer
• Calculators	Early syllabus	• Extended time
• Tape recorder	Taped handouts	On tape
• Word processor		Modified
Priority seating		Separate room

Program Strengths
We service the students on a one to one basis and do everything we can to accommodate them on this campus.

General Information:
Polk Community College is a 2 year public college. Suburban campus of 100 acres is 50 miles from Orlando. Accessible by train or bus. Beaches are 49 miles from campus. 1% of students are foreign. Housing is not guaranteed.

Accreditation:Regional

Expenses:
Tuition: In-state: Full year: $992.00. Part-time: Per credit:$24.00. Part-time: Per course: $216.00. Tuition: Out-of-state: Full year: $1,244.00. Part-time: Per credit:$51.00. Part-time: Per course:$459.00

Majors

• BUSINESS Accounting, Agricultural, Banking, Business Administration, Business Education, Finance, Management, Real Estate • COMMUNICATIONS Communication, English, Journalism • COMPUTER SCIENCE Computer Science, Data Processing, Engineering • EDUCATION Art, Early Childhood, Elementary, Music, Physical, Recreation and Youth Leadershi, School Psychology, Secondary, Speech/Language
• ENVIRONMENTAL CONTROL Quality Control • HEALTH SCIENCES Dental Hygiene, Health, Nursing, Physical Therapy, Radiological Therapy • HUMANITIES Liberal Arts, Philosophy, Religion
• PREPROFESSIONAL Agriculture, Architecture, Engineering, Forestry, Law, Medicine, Recreation, Social Work • SCIENCES Agricultural, Biology, Botany, Chemistry, Horticultural, Mathematics, Physical Science, Physics, Radiology, Zoology • SOCIAL SCIENCES Anthropology, Criminal Justice, Government/Political, History, Law Enforcement, Psychology, Social Sciences, Sociology • VISUAL AND PERFORMING ARTS Art, Dramatic Arts, Music • VOCATIONAL Business and Office, Drafting, Electronics Technology, Home Economics, Instrumentation Technology, Park/Recreation, Radiological Technology

Sports/Activities

• SPORTS RELATED Band, Cheerleading • SPORTS-INTERCOLLE-GIATE Baseball (M), Basketball, Volleyball (F) • SPORTS-INTRAMU-RAL Archery, Badminton, Basketball, Bowling, Golf, Gymnastics, Hand Ball, Sailing, Softball, Swimming, Tennis, Volleyball (F) • STUDENT LIFE ACTIVITIES Choral, Concert Band, Dance, Drama Groups, Ethnic & Cultural Groups, Jazz Band, Magazine, Music Ensemble, SAB, Symphony Orchestra, Winning Society

Less Selective   **Florida**
                                                       Services

Saint Johns River Community College

5001 St. Johns Avenue
Palatka, Florida 32177
(904) 328-1571

School Enrollment: **2,937** Male: **1,116** Female: **1,821**

Admissions Contact: **O'Neal Williams, Dean of Student Services**
LD Contact: **Annette B. Jones, Counselor**
Name of Program: **Handicapped Student Services**

Admissions

Application Information:
Application deadline: **Open**
Rolling Admissions: **Yes**

Secondary School Information
Most Important Criteria For Admissions (1-strongest)

SAT/ACT	Application	School transcript
Class rank	Course selection	Personal statement
Interview	Extra activities	Psychoeducational
G.P.A.	1 Open admission	Recommendations

Test Requirements:
Documentation of LD required: **Yes**

Types of Disabilities Served
• Speech/Lang	• Reading	• ADD with LD
• Study skills	• Spelling	• ADD without LD
• Written express	• Math	• ADHD with LD
• Organizational	• Fine Motor	• ADHD without LD
• Perceptual		

Learning Disability Program
Recommended credits per semester: **12-15**
Counseling: Individual: **Yes**

Faculty:
Faculty: **1** Part time: **1**
Faculty advocate: **Yes** Meets with instructor: **As needed**

Diagnostic Testing
ADD	Personality	Perceptual skills	Spelling
ADHD	Organization	Fine motor skills	Reading
I.Q.	Handwriting	Spoken language	Study skills
Math	Social skills	Written language	

Tutoring:
Average size of group tutorials: **3**
Services rendered by:
Graduates   Peers   •Faculty   LD staff   Teacher trainees

Tutorials
Grp.	Ind.	Tutorials	Grp.	Ind.	Tutorials
•		Math skills	•		Word processing
•		Study skills			Time management
•		Language arts	•		Learning strategies
		Written express	•		Organizational skills

Academic Accommodations
Curriculum	Study Aids	Exams
Priority registration	Typist	• Oral
• Math waiver	Reader	Untimed
• Foreign lang. waiver	• Notetaker	Take home
• Course substitution	Proof reader	With proctor
In Class	Text on tape	On computer
Calculators	Early syllabus	• Extended time
• Tape recorder	Taped handouts	On tape
Word processor		• Modified
Priority seating		Separate room

Program Strengths
We do not have a program for LD students. All of our students are mainstreamed. Auxiliary assistance is provided to LD and other handicapped students based on their needs.

General Information:
Saint Johns River Community College is a 2 year public college. Rural campus of 105 acres is 50 miles from Jacksonville. Accessible by train or bus. Beaches are 35 miles from campus. 1% of students are foreign. Housing is not guaranteed.

Accreditation: SACS

Expenses:
Tuition: In-state: Full year: $750.00. Part-time: Per credit:$25.00. Tuition: Out-of-state: Full year: $3,000.00. Part-time: Per credit:$100.00.

Majors
• BUSINESS Business Management, Entrepreneur, Marketing • COMPUTER SCIENCE Data Processing • CRAFTS AND DESIGN Graphic Design • HEALTH SCIENCES Emergency Medical Technology • HUMANITIES Liberal Arts • VISUAL AND PERFORMING ARTS Art, Dance, Dramatic Arts, Fine Arts, Music, Music Theatre, Studio Art, Theater • VOCATIONAL Business and Office, Electronics Technology, Fire Science, Instrumentation Technology, Secretarial

Sports/Activities
• SPORTS-INTERCOLLEGIATE Baseball (M), Basketball (M) • SPORTS-INTRAMURAL Ping-Pong • STUDENT LIFE ACTIVITIES Academic Clubs, Choral, Dance, Drama Groups, Ethnic & Cultural Groups, Newspaper, Religious Organization, Student Government

Academic Accommodations

Curriculum	Study Aids	Exams
Priority registration	Typist	• Oral
• Math waiver	Reader	Untimed
• Foreign lang. waiver	• Notetaker	Take home
• Course substitution	• Proof reader	With proctor
In Class	• Text on tape	On computer
• Calculators	Early syllabus	• Extended time
• Tape recorder	Taped handouts	On tape
• Word processor		Modified
Priority seating		Separate room

Program Strengths

Our success rate is exceptionally high when the students really want to succeed and work hard to do so.

General Information:

Santa Fe Community College is a 2 year public college. Suburban campus of 125 acres is 70 miles from Jacksonville. Accessible by air or bus. Beaches are 50 from campus. 2% of students are foreign. Housing is not guaranteed.

Accreditation: SACS

Expenses: Part-time: Per credit: $22.00. Part-time: Per credit: $44.00.

Majors

• BUSINESS Accounting, Banking, Business Administration, Business Management, Entrepreneur, Finance, Food Management, Hotel and Restaurant Managemen, Management, Real Estate • COMPUTER SCIENCE Data Processing, Programming • CRAFTS AND DESIGN Apparel Design, Graphic Design • EDUCATION Early Childhood • ENGINEERING Nuclear • HEALTH SCIENCES Dental Assistant, Dental Hygiene, EMT, Environmental, Medical Assistant, Medical Secretary, Nursing, Radiological Therapy • HUMANITIES Liberal Arts • PREPROFESSIONAL Agriculture, Legal Assistant • SCIENCES Biological Park, Horticultural, Radiology, Zoology • SOCIAL SCIENCES Criminal Justice, Law Enforcement • VOCATIONAL Construction, Drafting, Paralegal, Park/Recreation, Respiratory Therapy Technology, Secretarial, Secretarial

Sports/Activities

• SPORTS-INTERCOLLEGIATE Baseball (M), Basketball, Cross Country, Golf (M), Softball (F), Track and Field • SPORTS-INTRAMURAL Bowling, Racquetball, Tennis, Volleyball • STUDENT LIFE ACTIVITIES Choral, Dance, Debate, Drama Groups, Jazz Band, Music Ensembles, Musical Theater, Religious Organization, Student Government

---

Less Selective   **Florida**
Services

Seminole Community College
100 Weldon Boulevard
Sanford, Florida 32733-6199
(407) 323-1450

School Enrollment: **6,549**
LD Enrollment: **120** Male: **75** Female: **45**

Admissions Contact: **Joseph Roof, Dean of Admissions**
LD Contact: **Dottie Paishon, Disabled Student Specialist**
Name of Program: **Disabled Student Services**
Address: **100 Weldon Blvd.**
Telephone: **(407) 323-1450 Ext. 674**

Less Selective   **Florida**
Services

Santa Fe Community College
P.O. Box 1530
Gainesville, Florida 32601
(904) 395-5443

School Enrollment: **10,000** Male: **4,900** Female: **5,100**

Admissions Contact: **Don Mott, Director of Admissions**
LD Contact: **Al Block**
Name of Program: **Student Support Services**
Telephone: **(904) 395-5068**

Admissions

Application Information:
Application deadline: **1st day of class**

Secondary School Information
Most Important Criteria For Admissions (1-strongest)

SAT/ACT	Application	School transcript
Class rank	Course selection	Personal statement
Interview	Extra activities	Psychoeducational
G.P.A.	1 Open admission	Recommendations

Types of Disabilities Served
- Speech/Lang
- Reading
- ADD with LD
- Study skills
- Spelling
- ADD without LD
- Written express
- Math
- ADHD with LD
- Organizational
- Fine Motor
- ADHD without LD
- Perceptual

Learning Disability Program

Counseling: Individual: **Yes** Group Counseling: **Yes**

Faculty:
Faculty: **5** Full time: **5**
Faculty advocate: **Yes** Meets with instructor: **As necessary**

Diagnostic Testing

ADD	Personality	Perceptual skills	Spelling
ADHD	Organization	Fine motor skills	Reading
I.Q.	Handwriting	Spoken language	Study skills
Math	Social skills	Written language	

Tutoring:
Average size of group tutorials: **1**
Services rendered by:
Graduates   •Peers   •Faculty   LD staff   Teacher trainees

Tutorials

Grp.	Ind.	Tutorials	Grp.	Ind.	Tutorials
	•	Math skills		•	Word processing
•	•	Study skills		•	Time management
		Language arts		•	Learning strategies
	•	Written express	•	•	Organizational skills

Florida

Admissions

Application Information:
LD Students Applying: **120** Accepted: **120** Enrolled:**120**
Application deadline: **None**

Secondary School Information
Most Important Criteria For Admissions (1-strongest)

2 SAT/ACT	Application	**3** School transcript
Class rank	Course selection	Personal statement
Interview	Extra activities	**1** Psychoeducational
G.P.A.	**1** Open admission	Recommendations

Test Requirements:
Standardized tests waived: **Yes**
Diagnostic testing waived: **Yes**
Untimed SAT: **Yes** Untimed ACT: **Yes** Untimed ACH: **Yes**
Documentation of LD required: **Yes**
Currency of diagnostic testing: **3 years**

Types of Disabilities Served
- Speech/Lang
- Reading
- ADD with LD
- Study skills
- Spelling
- ADD without LD
- Written express
- Math
- ADHD with LD
- Organizational
- Fine Motor
- ADHD without LD
- Perceptual

Admissions Process

We have an open admissions - all that is required is a standard high school diploma or GED.

High School Course Requirements:
Waivers to standard high school courses
Course substitution: **Yes**

Learning Disability Program

Program: Reinforces course work: **Yes**
Students mainstreamed **100** % of the day
Recommended credits per semester: **12**
Services only for LD students: **Yes**
Counseling: Individual: **Yes** Vocational Counseling: **Yes**
Support groups are available:**Disabled Student Support Group**

Faculty:
Faculty: **2** Full time: **2** Part time: **1**
LD faculty with: BS/BA: **1.5** Ph.D.: **1**
Faculty advocate: **Yes** Meets with instructor: **As needed**

Diagnostic Testing

ADD	• Personality • Perceptual skills	• Spelling
ADHD	Organization• Fine motor skills	• Reading
• I.Q.	Handwriting• Spoken language	• Study skills
• Math	Social skills• Written language	

Tutoring:
Average size of group tutorials: **1:1**
Services rendered by:

Graduates	•Peers	Faculty	•LD staff	Teacher trainees

Tutorials

Grp.	Ind.	Tutorials	Grp.	Ind.	Tutorials
•	•	Math skills			Word processing
	•	Study skills			Time management
	•	Language arts		•	Learning strategies
	•	Written express		•	Organizational skills

Academic Accommodations

Curriculum	Study Aids	Exams
Priority registration	Typist	• Oral
Math waiver	• Reader	Untimed
Foreign lang. waiver	• Notetaker	Take home
• Course substitution	• Proof reader	• With proctor
In Class	• Text on tape	On computer
Calculators	Early syllabus	• Extended time
• Tape recorder	Taped handouts	On tape
Word processor		• Modified
Priority seating		• Separate room

Graduation Requirements:
Course credits: **64** GPA: **2.0** Years to complete degree: **Open**

Program Strengths

All of our SLD students are mainstreamed. We, at this time, do not offer special classes or SLD teachers. We do offer academic support services to students based on the nature and severity of the learning disability.

General Information:

Seminole Community College is a 2 year public college. Suburban campus of 170 acres is 14 miles from Orlando. Accessible by bus. Beaches are 40 miles from campus. 9% of students are foreign. Housing is not guaranteed.

Accreditation:SACS

Expenses: Part-time: Per credit:$30.00. Part-time: Per credit:$107.75.

Majors

• BUSINESS Banking, Entrepreneur, Fashion Merchandising, Finance, Food Management, Marketing, Retailing • COMPUTER SCIENCE Computer Technology, Data Processing, Microcomputer Software • EDUCATION Child Development • HEALTH SCIENCES Nursing • PREPROFESSIONAL Architecture • SOCIAL SCIENCES Criminal Justice • VOCATIONAL Auto Body, Automobile Technology, Construction, Culinary Arts, Electronics Technology, Fire Science, Home Economics, Respiratory Therapy Technology, Secretarial, Word Processing

Sports/Activities

• SPORTS RELATED Cheerleading • SPORTS-INTERCOLLEGIATE Baseball (M), Basketball, Softball (F) • SPORTS-INTRAMURAL Basketball (M), Tennis • STUDENT LIFE ACTIVITIES Choral, Concert Band, Drama Groups, Ethnic & Cultural Groups, Jazz Band, Music Ensembles, Music Groups, Musical Theater, Religious Organization, Student Government, Symphony Orchestra

---

Less Selective

Florida Program

Tallahassee Community College
444 Appleyard Drive
Tallahassee, Florida 32304-2895
(904) 488-9200

School Enrollment: **9,886** Male: **4,633** Female: **5,283**

Admissions Contact: **Mike Bussell, Registrar**
LD Contact: **Gayle Dozier, Director of Counseling**
Name of Program: **Counseling/Disabled Student Services**
Telephone:**(904) 922-8128**

Admissions

Secondary School Information
Most Important Criteria For Admissions (1-strongest)

SAT/ACT	Application	School transcript
Class rank	Course selection	Personal statement
Interview	Extra activities	Psychoeducational
G.P.A.	Open admission	Recommendations

Test Requirements:
Standardized tests waived: **Yes**
Documentation of LD required: **Yes**

Types of Disabilities Served
- Speech/Lang
- Study skills
- Written express
- Organizational
- Perceptual
- Reading
- Spelling
- Math
- Fine Motor

ADD with LD
ADD without LD
ADHD with LD
ADHD without LD

Learning Disability Program
Services only for LD students: **Yes**
Counseling: Individual: **Yes**

Faculty:
Faculty: **4** Full time: **3** Part time: **1**
LD faculty with: BS/BA: **1** M.A.: **1**
Faculty advocate: **Yes** Meets with instructor: **When necessary**

Diagnostic Testing

ADD	Personality	Perceptual skills	Spelling
ADHD	Organization	Fine motor skills	Reading
I.Q.	Handwriting	Spoken language	Study skills
Math	Social skills	Written language	

Tutoring:
Average size of group tutorials: **10-15**
Services rendered by:
- Graduates
- Peers
- Faculty
- LD staff
- Teacher trainees

Tutorials

Grp.	Ind.	Tutorials	Grp.	Ind.	Tutorials
•	•	Math skills	•	•	Word processing
•	•	Study skills	•	•	Time management
•	•	Language arts	•	•	Learning strategies
•	•	Written express	•	•	Organizational skills

Academic Accommodations

Curriculum	Study Aids	Exams
• Priority registration	Typist	• Oral
• Math waiver	• Reader	• Untimed
• Foreign lang. waiver	• Notetaker	Take home
• Course substitution	• Proof reader	• With proctor
In Class	• Text on tape	• On computer
• Calculators	Early syllabus	• Extended time
• Tape recorder	Taped handouts	On tape
• Word processor		Modified
Priority seating		• Separate room

Program Strengths
Our LD Program is a support service program. All students are mainstreamed, and we individualize an assistance program for all students. When funding is available, we have full-time tutors on staff and also peer tutors. Support and advocacy are a strong component of the counseling program at Tallahassee Community College.

General Information:
Tallahassee Community College is a 2 year public college. Suburban campus of 64 acres is 4 miles from Tallahassee. Accessible by air or bus. Beaches are 85 miles from campus. Housing is not guaranteed.

Accreditation: SACS

Expenses:
Tuition: In-state: Full year: $780.00. Part-time: Per credit:$26.00. Part-time: Per course: $78.00. Tuition: Out-of-state: Full year: $2,940.00. Part-time: Per credit:$98.00.

Majors
• BUSINESS Accounting, Business Management, Economics, Finance, Management, Real Estate, Travel/Tourism Management • COMMUNICATIONS Communication, Creative Writing, English, Journalism, Photography, Television/Radio/Film • COMPUTER SCIENCE Programming • EDUCATION Art, Early Childhood, Health, Industrial, Physical, Speech/Language • ENGINEERING Civil/Environmental • HEALTH SCIENCES Dental Hygiene, EMT, Nursing, Nutritional/Food, Practical Nursing, Radiological Therapy • HUMANITIES Humanities, Liberal Arts, Philosophy, Religion • LANGUAGES French, German, Spanish • PREPROFESSIONAL Legal Assistant • SCIENCES Astronomy, Biochemistry, Biology, Botany, Chemistry, Earth, Ecology, Geography, Geology, Macrobiology, Mathematics, Microbiology, Oceanography, Physical Science, Radiology • SOCIAL SCIENCES Anthropology, Criminal Justice, Government/Political, History, Law Enforcement, Psychology, Social Sciences, Sociology • VISUAL AND PERFORMING ARTS Art, Art History, Dance, Music • VOCATIONAL Business and Office, Fire Science, Paralegal, Radiological Technology, Respiratory Therapy Technology, Secretarial

Sports/Activities
• SPORTS RELATED Community Band, Marching Band • SPORTS-INTRAMURAL Basketball, Golf, Racquetball, Softball, Swimming, Tennis, Volleyball, Water Polo • STUDENT LIFE ACTIVITIES Choral, Concert Band, Dance, Debate, Drama Groups, Ethnic & Cultural Groups, Film, Fraternities, Magazine, Newspaper, Religious Organization, Sororities, Student Government

---

Very Selective	Florida Accommodations

University of Tampa
401 W. Kennedy Blvd.
Tampa, Florida 33606
(813) 253-6228

School Enrollment: **2,527**
LD Enrollment: **5**

Admissions Contact: **Bob Cook, Associate Dean of Admissions**
LD Contact: **Jean Masquelier, Academic Counselor**
Name of Program: **Personal Career Development Ctr.**
Address: **401 W. Kennedy Blvd.**
Telephone:**(813) 253-6218**

Admissions

Application Information:
Application deadline: **Rolling**
Rolling Admissions: **Yes** Notified when: **Rolling**

Georgia

Secondary School Information
Most Important Criteria For Admissions (1-strongest)

2 SAT/ACT	**8** Application	**3**	School transcript
4 Class rank	**7** Course selection	**9**	Personal statement
Interview	**6** Extra activities	**10**	Psychoeducational
1 G.P.A.	Open admission	**5**	Recommendations

Test Requirements:
Untimed SAT: **Yes** Untimed ACT: **Yes**

Types of Disabilities Served

Speech/Lang	Reading	ADD with LD
Study skills	Spelling	ADD without LD
Written express	Math	ADHD with LD
Organizational	Fine Motor	ADHD without LD
Perceptual		

Admissions Process

Students submit high school transcript with at least 6 semesters, SAT or ACT test scores, a short essay, and two recommendations. The file is reviewed and presented to Admissions Committee for a decision. Notification is rolling - given immediately after decision.

High School Course Requirements:
English: **4** Math: **2** Science: **2**

Learning Disability Program
Special orientation for LD students: **Yes**
Services available for all students: **Yes**
Vocational Counseling: **Yes**

Diagnostic Testing

ADD	Personality	Perceptual skills	Spelling
ADHD	Organization	Fine motor skills	• Reading
I.Q.	Handwriting	Spoken language	• Study skills
• Math	Social skills	• Written language	

Tutoring:
Services rendered by:

Graduates	•Peers	Faculty	LD staff	Teacher trainees

Tutorials

Grp.	Ind.	Tutorials	Grp.	Ind.	Tutorials
•	•	Math skills			Word processing
•	•	Study skills	•	•	Time management
		Language arts		•	Learning strategies
	•	Written express	•	•	Organizational skills

Academic Accommodations

Curriculum	Study Aids	Exams
Priority registration	Typist	Oral
Math waiver	Reader	Untimed
Foreign lang. waiver	Notetaker	Take home
Course substitution	Proof reader	With proctor
In Class	Text on tape	On computer
Calculators	Early syllabus	Extended time
Tape recorder	Taped handouts	On tape
Word processor		Modified
Priority seating		Separate room

Graduation Requirements:
Course credits: **124** GPA: **2.0**

General Information:
University of Tampa is a 2 and 4 year private university. Urban campus of 69 acres is Accessible by air, train, or bus. 6% of students are foreign. 7 residential halls on campus. Housing is guaranteed.100 % of students remain on campus for the weekends. 15 % of students join fraternities/sororities.

Accreditation:SACS

Expenses:
Tuition: In-state: Full year: $11,685.00. Part-time: Per credit:0. Tuition: Out-of-state: Full year: $11,685.00. Room and board: $4,237.00

Majors
• ARTS Music • BUSINESS Accounting, Banking/Finance, Business Administration, Economics, International Business, Marketing • COMMUNICATIONS Communication, Creative Writing, English • COMPUTER SCIENCE Computer Science • EDUCATION Elementary, Physical • HEALTH SCIENCES Nursing • HUMANITIES Fine Arts, Philosophy • LANGUAGES English, French, Spanish • MATHEMATICS Applied, Computer • PRE PROFESSIONAL Dentistry, Engineering, Law, Medicine, Veterinarian • SCIENCES Biochemistry, Biology, Chemistry, Marine Biology, Mathematics • SOCIAL SCIENCES Criminology, History, International Studies, Political Science, Psychology, Social Science, Sociology • VISUAL AND PERFORMING ARTS Art, Music

Sports/Activities
• SPORTS RELATED Cheerleading • SPORTS-INTERCOLLEGIATE Baseball (M), Basketball (F), Basketball (M), Crew (F), Crew (M), Cross Country (F), Cross Country (M), Golf (M), Soccer (M), Softball (F), Swimming (F), Swimming (M), Tennis (F), Tennis (M), Volleyball (F) • SPORTS-INTRAMURAL Badminton, Baseball, Basketball, Bowling, Cross Country, Diving, Golf, Gymnastics, Ping-Pong, Soccer, Softball, Swimming, Tennis, Volleyball • STUDENT LIFE ACTIVITIES Academic Clubs, Choral, Community Service, Concert Band, Ethnic & Cultural Groups, Fraternities, Jazz Band, Magazine, Music Groups, Newspaper, Political Groups, Radio/TV station, Religious Organization, Sororities, Student Government, Symphony Orchestra, Yearbook

---

Less Selective **Georgia Program**

Brenau Women's College
One Centennial Circle
Gainesville, Georgia 30501-3697
(404) 534-6100

School Enrollment: **450** Female: **450**
LD Enrollment: **50** Female: **50**

Admissions Contact: **Dr. John Upchurch, Director of Admissions**
LD Contact: **Vince Yamilkoski, Ed.D., Director of Learning Center**
Name of Program: **Brenau College Learning Center**
Address: **One Centennial Circle**
Telephone:**(404) 534-6134**

Admissions

Application Information:
LD Students Applying: **25** Accepted: **15** Enrolled:**15**
Separate application:**Yes**
LD on admissions committee:**Yes**
Applicant must apply **1-9** months in advance
Rolling Admissions: **Yes**

Secondary School Information

Most Important Criteria For Admissions (1-strongest)

5 SAT/ACT Application School transcript
Class rank **6** Course selection Personal statement
3 Interview Extra activities **1** Psychoeducational
2 G.P.A. Open admission **4** Recommendations

Test Requirements:

Untimed SAT: **Yes** Untimed ACT: **Yes** Achievement tests required:**2**
WAIS-R required: **Yes** Range accepted: **90+**
Documentation of LD required: **Yes**
Currency of diagnostic testing: **1 year**
Tests recommended: **WAIS-R, Individual Achievement Testing in reading, math**

Types of Disabilities Served

- Speech/Lang
- Study skills
- Written express
- Organizational
- Perceptual
- Reading
- Spelling
- Math
- Fine Motor
- ADD with LD
- ADD without LD
- ADHD with LD
- ADHD without LD

Admissions Process

Student applies through Admissions. Learning disabled students applying for Learning Center Program must also include psychological and interview with Director.

High School Course Requirements:

English: **1** Math: **1/3-1** Science: **1** Foreign Language: **1/3-1**

Learning Disability Program

Special orientation for LD students: **Yes**
Program: Remedial: **Yes**
Program: Reinforces course work: **Yes**
Program available through:**All year**
Students mainstreamed **80** % of the day
Recommended credits per semester: **12-17**
Time required or recommended in learning center: **0-8 hours**
Services only for LD students: **Yes**
Counseling: Individual: **Yes** Vocational Counseling: **Yes**

Faculty:

Faculty: **22** Including Director: **Yes** Full time: **2** Part time: **20**
LD faculty with: BS/BA: **15** M.A.: **4** Ph.D.: **1**
Faculty advocate: **Yes** Meets with instructor: **When necessary**

Diagnostic Testing

ADD Personality Perceptual skills Spelling
ADHD Organization Fine motor skills • Reading
I.Q. Handwriting Spoken language Study skills
• Math Social skills• Written language

Tutoring:

Services rendered by:
Graduates Peers Faculty •LD staff Teacher trainees

Tutorials

Grp.	Ind.	Tutorials	Grp.	Ind.	Tutorials
	•	Math skills		•	Word processing
	•	Study skills		•	Time management
	•	Language arts		•	Learning strategies
	•	Written express		•	Organizational skills

Academic Accommodations

Curriculum	Study Aids	Exams
• Priority registration	Typist	• Oral
Math waiver	• Reader	• Untimed
Foreign lang. waiver	Notetaker	Take home
Course substitution	• Proof reader	• With proctor
In Class	• Text on tape	On computer
• Calculators	Early syllabus	• Extended time
• Tape recorder	Taped handouts	On tape
• Word processor		• Modified
Priority seating		• Separate room

Graduation Requirements:

Course credits: **200 quarter hours** GPA: **2.0**
Other requirements: **Some majors have higer GPA requirements**

Program Strengths

Brenau College offers personalized instruction to all its students, and the faculty supports the learning disability program. In that climate, the Learning Center student receives tutoring from adults with college degrees in the field being studied and tutoring in other areas such as: reading, math, writing or organizational skills. Students are also given frequent, careful advising, and plenty of attention from caring professionals.

General Information:

Brenau Women's College is a 4 year private college. Urban campus of 37 acres is 50 miles from Atlanta. Accessible by air, train, or bus. Ski areas are 2-3 hours from campus. Beaches are 5-1/2 hours from campus. 10% of students are foreign. Housing is not guaranteed.25 % of students remain on campus for the weekends. 80 % of students join fraternities/sororities.

Accreditation:SACS

Expenses:

Tuition: In-state: Full year: $12,900.00 includes room/board. Part-time: Per credit:0. Tuition: Out-of-state: Full year: $12,900.00. Cost of LD program:$1,300.00 per quarter-Level I Services

Majors

• BUSINESS Accounting, Business Administration, Business Management, Personnel • COMMUNICATIONS Broadcasting, Commercial Design, Communication, English, Journalism, Television/Radio/Film • EDUCATION Early Childhood, Elementary, Middle School, Music, Special • HEALTH SCIENCES Nursing • HUMANITIES Liberal Arts • PRE-PROFESSIONAL Law • SCIENCES Biology, Equestrian Studies • SOCIAL SCIENCES Criminal Justice, Government/Political, History, Human Resources Development, Political Science, Psychology, Social Sciences • VISUAL AND PERFORMING ARTS Art, Art History, Arts Management, Dance, Dramatic Arts, Fine Arts, Music, Music Performance, Studio Art, Theater • VOCATIONAL Medical Laboratory Technology, Public Administration

Sports/Activities

• SPORTS-INTERCOLLEGIATE Tennis (F) • STUDENT LIFE ACTIVITIES Dance, Drama Groups, Ethnic & Cultural Groups, Magazine, Music Groups, Musical Theater, Newspaper, Radio/TV station, Religious Organization, Sororities, Student Government, Yearbook

Georgia

Brunswick College
Atlanta Ave. at Fourth St.
Brunswick, Georgia 31523
(912) 264-7253

School Enrollment: **1,600** Male: **560** Female: **1,040**

Admissions Contact: **Dr. Harrison Fields, Director of Admissions**
LD Contact: **Dr. Morgan Stapleton, V.P. Academic Affairs**

Admissions

Application Information:
Rolling Admissions: **Yes**

Secondary School Information
Most Important Criteria For Admissions (1-strongest)

3 SAT/ACT	**1** Application	**4** School transcript
Class rank	**5** Course selection	Personal statement
Interview	Extra activities	Psychoeducational
2 G.P.A.	Open admission	Recommendations

Test Requirements:
Untimed SAT: **Yes** Untimed ACT: **Yes**
Documentation of LD required: **Yes**

Types of Disabilities Served

Speech/Lang	Reading	ADD with LD
Study skills	Spelling	ADD without LD
Written express	Math	ADHD with LD
Organizational	Fine Motor	ADHD without LD
Perceptual		

Admissions Process

Specific requests for accommodations must be made to the Regents System Committee on Learning Disabilities.

High School Course Requirements:
English: **4** Math: **3** Science: **3** Foreign Language: **2**

Learning Disability Program

Services available for all students: **Yes**

Diagnostic Testing

ADD	Personality	Perceptual skills	Spelling
ADHD	Organization	Fine motor skills	Reading
I.Q.	Handwriting	Spoken language	Study skills
Math	Social skills	Written language	

Tutoring:
Average size of group tutorials: **Individual**
Services rendered by:

Graduates	•Peers	•Faculty	LD staff	Teacher trainees

Tutorials

Grp.	Ind.	Tutorials	Grp.	Ind.	Tutorials
		Math skills			Word processing
		Study skills			Time management
		Language arts			Learning strategies
		Written express			Organizational skills

Academic Accommodations

Curriculum	Study Aids	Exams
Priority registration	Typist	• Oral
Math waiver	Reader	Untimed
Foreign lang. waiver	Notetaker	Take home
Course substitution	Proof reader	With proctor
In Class	• Text on tape	On computer
Calculators	Early syllabus	• Extended time
• Tape recorder	Taped handouts	On tape
Word processor		Modified
• Priority seating		• Separate room

Graduation Requirements: Language waiver: **Yes**

General Information:
Brunswick College is a 2 year public college. Urban campus of 200 acres is Brunswick. Accessible by car or taxi. Ski areas are 280 miles from campus. Beaches are 3 miles from campus. 1% of students are foreign. Housing is not guaranteed.

Accreditation: SACS

SAT/ACT Scores:
Scores for incoming freshmen: **Verbal:** 90% below 500. 10% between 500 and 599. **Math:** 81% below 500. 13% between 500 and 599. 5% between 600 and 699. 1% above 700.

Expenses:
Tuition: In-state: Full year: $326.00 per quarter. Part-time: Per credit: $27.00. Tuition: Out-of-state: Full year: $942.00 per quarter. Part-time: Per credit: $79.00.

Majors
• BUSINESS Accounting, Business Administration, Clerical, Data Processing, Economics, Education, Management, Marketing, Secretarial Science • COMPUTER SCIENCE • EDUCATION Early Childhood, General • HEALTH SCIENCES • HUMANITIES • LANGUAGES French, Spanish • PRE PROFESSIONAL Agriculture, Business, Dentistry, Forestry, Law, Medicine, Optometry, Pharmacy, Recreation, Social Work, Veterinarian • SCIENCES • SOCIAL SCIENCES Criminal Justice, History, Political Science, Psychology, Sociology • VOCATIONAL Business and Office, Drafting, Electronics Technology, Legal Secretary, Machinist, Medical Laboraotry Technology, Office Administration, Radiological Technology, Secretarial

Sports/Activities
• SPORTS RELATED Cheerleading • SPORTS-INTERCOLLEGIATE Basketball (M), Softball (F), Tennis (M) • SPORTS-INTRAMURAL Basketball (F), Volleyball • STUDENT LIFE ACTIVITIES Academic Clubs, Community Service, Ethnic & Cultural Groups, Magazine, Newspaper, Religious Organization, Student Government

Less Selective   **Georgia Services**

Clayton State College
P.O. Box 285
Morrow, Georgia 30260
(404) 961-3500

School Enrollment: **4,000**

Admissions Contact: **Tanya Hobson, Director of Admissions**
LD Contact: **Michelle Settle, Handicapped Specialist**
Name of Program: **Special Need Program**
Telephone:**(404) 961-3515**

Admissions

Application Information:
Rolling Admissions: **Yes**

Secondary School Information
Most Important Criteria For Admissions (1-strongest)

SAT/ACT	Application	School transcript
Class rank	Course selection **3**	Personal statement
2 Interview	Extra activities	**1** Psychoeducational
G.P.A.	Open admission	Recommendations

Test Requirements:
Untimed SAT: **Yes**
Documentation of LD required: **Yes**

Types of Disabilities Served
- Speech/Lang
- Reading
- ADD with LD
- Study skills
- Spelling
- ADD without LD
- Written express
- Math
- ADHD with LD
- Organizational
- Fine Motor
- ADHD without LD
- Perceptual

Learning Disability Program
Services available for all students: **Yes**

Faculty:
Faculty: **1** Full time: **1**
Faculty advocate: **Yes** Meets with instructor: **As needed**

Diagnostic Testing

ADD	Personality	Perceptual skills	Spelling
ADHD	Organization	Fine motor skills	Reading
I.Q.	Handwriting	Spoken language	Study skills
Math	Social skills	Written language	

Tutoring:
Average size of group tutorials: *
Services rendered by:
Graduates   Peers   Faculty   •LD staff   Teacher trainees

Tutorials

Grp.	Ind.	Tutorials	Grp.	Ind.	Tutorials
		Math skills			Word processing
		Study skills			Time management
		Language arts			Learning strategies
		Written express			Organizational skills

Academic Accommodations

Curriculum	Study Aids	Exams
Priority registration	Typist	• Oral
Math waiver	Reader	Untimed
Foreign lang. waiver	• Notetaker	• Take home
• Course substitution	Proof reader	• With proctor
In Class	• Text on tape	On computer
• Calculators	Early syllabus	• Extended time
• Tape recorder	Taped handouts	On tape
• Word processor		• Modified
Priority seating		Separate room

Program Strengths
Clayton State College has a support program for students with special needs including those with learning disabilities. Accommodations are provided in academic classes so that students may work toward their potential. There is one coordinator of special services for the entire program.
*Tutoring is offered to all students, not only those who have been identified as having a learning disability.

General Information:
Clayton State College is a 4 year public college. Suburban campus of 160 acres is 25 miles from Atlanta. Housing is not guaranteed.

Accreditation:ADA, NLN

Expenses: Part-time: Per credit:$33.00. Part-time: Per credit:$99.00.

Majors
• AREA STUDIES Urban • BUSINESS Accounting, Aviation Management, Banking, Business Administration, Business Management, Finance, Marketing • COMMUNICATIONS English, Journalism, Television/Radio/Film • COMPUTER SCIENCE Computer Science, Computer Technology, Data Processing • EDUCATION Art, General, Physical, Secondary • ENGINEERING Aeronautical, Agricultural, Engineering Science • HEALTH SCIENCES Dental Hygiene, Medical Records Administration, Nursing, Occupational Therapy, Physical Therapy • HUMANITIES Liberal Arts, Philosophy • LANGUAGES French, Spanish • PREPROFESSIONAL Dentistry, Forestry, Law, Medicine, Pharmacy, Veterinarian • SCIENCES Agricultural, Biology, Chemistry, Mathematics, Physics • SOCIAL SCIENCES Anthropology, Criminal Justice, Government/Political, History, Political Science, Psychology, Sociology • VISUAL AND PERFORMING ARTS Dramatic Arts, Music, Studio Art • VOCATIONAL Automated Manufacturing Techno, Business and Office, Drafting, Home Economics, Legal Secretary, Mechanical Design Technology, Medical Laboratory Technology, Radiograph Medical Technology, Secretarial

Sports/Activities
• SPORTS-INTRAMURAL Basketball, Cross Country, Golf, Ping-Pong, Softball, Tennis, Volleyball • STUDENT LIFE ACTIVITIES Choral, Concert Band, Drama Groups, Ethnic & Cultural Groups, Magazine, Music Ensembles, Musical Theater, Newspaper, Political Groups, Student Government, Symphony Orchestra

Less Selective	Georgia Services

DeKalb College
555 N. Indian Creek Drive
Clarkson, Georgia 30021
(404) 244-2246

School Enrollment: **15,000** Male: **7,500** Female: **7,500**
LD Enrollment: **70**

Admissions Contact: **Mr. Kim West, Director of Admissions**
LD Contact: **Louise B. Cebula, Ed.S., Counselor**
Name of Program: **Center for Special Academic Support Services**
Telephone:**(404) 299-4120**

Admissions

Application Information:
Enrolled:**70**
Application deadline: **1 month prior to quarter enrolled**
Applicant must apply **1** months in advance
Rolling Admissions: **Yes**

Secondary School Information
Most Important Criteria For Admissions (1-strongest)

1 SAT/ACT	**5** Application	**1**	School transcript
Class rank	Course selection		Personal statement
Interview	Extra activities		Psychoeducational
1 G.P.A.	Open admission		Recommendations

Test Requirements:
Untimed SAT: **Yes** Untimed ACT: **Yes** Untimed ACH: **Yes**
WAIS-R required: **Yes** Range accepted: **Over 90**
Documentation of LD required: **Yes**
Tests recommended: **Psychological evaluation including I.Q. measure, achievement measure, processing deficit measure.**

Types of Disabilities Served
- Speech/Lang
- Study skills
- Written express
- Organizational
- Perceptual
- Reading
- Spelling
- Math
- Fine Motor
- ADD with LD
- ADD without LD
- ADHD with LD
- ADHD without LD

Admissions Process

Students must meet admissions criteria of college. Application and all required documents must be submitted by deadline. Separate eligibility procedure for LD Support. Student must supply current psychological diagnosis to Center for Special Academic Support.

High School Course Requirements:
English: **4** Math: **3** Science: **3** Foreign Language: **2**
Waivers to standard high school courses
Foreign Language : **Yes**

Learning Disability Program
Program: Reinforces course work: **Yes**
Students mainstreamed **100** % of the day
Recommended credits per semester: **12-15**
Counseling: Individual: **Yes** Vocational Counseling: **Yes**

Faculty:
Faculty: **1** Full time: **1** Part time: **1**
LD faculty with: BS/BA: **1** M.A.: **1**
Faculty advocate: **Yes** Meets with instructor: **Every day**

Diagnostic Testing

ADD	Personality	Perceptual skills	Spelling
ADHD	Organization	Fine motor skills	Reading
I.Q.	Handwriting	Spoken language	Study skills
Math	Social skills	Written language	

Tutoring:
Average size of group tutorials: **3**
Services rendered by:
  Graduates   •Peers   •Faculty   •LD staff   Teacher trainees

Tutorials

Grp.	Ind.	Tutorials	Grp.	Ind.	Tutorials
•		Math skills			Word processing
•	•	Study skills			Time management
		Language arts		•	Learning strategies
•	•	Written express		•	Organizational skills

Academic Accommodations

Curriculum	Study Aids	Exams
• Priority registration	Typist	• Oral
Math waiver	• Reader	Untimed
• Foreign lang. waiver	• Notetaker	Take home
Course substitution	• Proof reader	• With proctor
In Class	• Text on tape	On computer
• Calculators	Early syllabus	• Extended time
• Tape recorder	Taped handouts	• On tape
• Word processor		Modified
• Priority seating		• Separate room

Graduation Requirements:
Course credits: **100** GPA: **2.0** Years to complete degree: **2-3** Language waiver: **Yes**
Other requirements: **Minimum 30 hours of last 45 credit hours taken at DeKalb.**

Program Strengths
The Center for Special Academic Support (CSAS) was created to accommodate the special needs of the Learning Disabled and other designated Handicapped Students. CSAS does all that it can to holistically serve these students and to make them as apt to succeed as possible. Each student is served individually, and all information is kept confidential. The entire faculty and staff at De Kalb College tries to make each student feel fortunate to have spent time here.

General Information:
DeKalb College is a 2 year public college. Suburban campus 10 miles from Atlanta. Accessible by air or bus. Ski areas are 300 miles from campus. Beaches are 240 miles from campus. 7% of students are foreign. Housing is not guaranteed.

Accreditation: Regional

Expenses: Part-time: Per credit:$22.00. Part-time: Per course: $22.00-$110.00. Part-time: Per credit:$57.00.

Majors
• BUSINESS Accounting, Business Administration, Business Education, Business Management, Marketing Management • COMMUNICATIONS English, Journalism, Journalism, Television/Radio/Film • COMPUTER SCIENCE Computer Science, Data Processing, Programming • EDUCATION General, Health, Interpreter for the Deaf, Physical, Secondary • EN-

GINEERING Agricultural, Engineering Science • HEALTH SCIENCES Dental Assistant, Dental Hygiene, Dental Hygiene, Dental Laboratory Technology, EMT, Medical Assistant, Nursing, Physical Therapy, Radiological Therapy, Respiratory Therapy Technology, Surgical Technology • HUMANITIES Humanities, Liberal Arts, Philosophy • PRE PROFESSIONAL Dentistry, Medicine, Pharmacy • SCIENCES Anthropology, Biology, Chemistry, Geology, Mathematics, Physical Science, Physics • SOCIAL SCIENCES History, Political Science, Psychology, Social Sciences, Sociology • VISUAL AND PERFORMING ARTS Art, Dramatic Arts, Music • VOCATIONAL Automated Manufacturing Techno, Drafting, Electronics Technology, Fashion Merchandising, Fire Science, Forestry, Home Economics, Industrial Management, Landscaping Management, Machine Tool Technology, Medical Laboratory Technology, Office Administration, Ornamental Horticulture, Respiratory Therapy Technology, Secretarial

Sports/Activities

• SPORTS-INTERCOLLEGIATE Baseball (M), Basketball (M), Tennis • SPORTS-INTRAMURAL Soccer (M), Softball, Volleyball • STUDENT LIFE ACTIVITIES Choral, Concert Band, Drama Groups, Jazz Band, Magazine, Music Ensemble, Musical Theater, Newspaper, Radio/TV station, Student Government, Symphony Orchestra

---

Less Selective

Georgia Services

East Georgia College

Thigpen Drive
Swainsboro, Georgia 30401-2699
(912) 237-7831

School Enrollment: 540 Male: 178 Female: 362

Admissions Contact: **Mark Taylor, Director of Admissions**
LD Contact: **Bennie Brinson, Director**
Name of Program: **Student Affairs**

Admissions

Secondary School Information

Most Important Criteria For Admissions (1-strongest)

1 SAT/ACT	**1** Application	**1** School transcript
Class rank	**1** Course selection	Personal statement
Interview	Extra activities	Psychoeducational
1 G.P.A.	Open admission	Recommendations

Test Requirements:

WAIS-R required: **Yes**

Types of Disabilities Served

• Speech/Lang	Reading	ADD with LD
Study skills	Spelling	ADD without LD
Written express	Math	ADHD with LD
Organizational	• Fine Motor	ADHD without LD
Perceptual		

Learning Disability Program

Counseling: Individual: **Yes**

Faculty:

Faculty advocate: **Yes** Meets with instructor: **As needed**

Diagnostic Testing

ADD	Personality	Perceptual skills	Spelling
ADHD	Organization	Fine motor skills	Reading
I.Q.	Handwriting	Spoken language	Study skills
Math	Social skills	Written language	

Services rendered by:

Graduates	Peers	Faculty	LD staff	Teacher trainees

Tutorials

Grp.	Ind.	Tutorials	Grp.	Ind.	Tutorials
		Math skills			Word processing
		Study skills			Time management
		Language arts			Learning strategies
		Written express			Organizational skills

Academic Accommodations

Curriculum	Study Aids	Exams
Priority registration	Typist	Oral
Math waiver	Reader	Untimed
Foreign lang. waiver	Notetaker	Take home
Course substitution	Proof reader	With proctor
In Class	Text on tape	On computer
Calculators	Early syllabus	• Extended time
• Tape recorder	Taped handouts	On tape
Word processor		Modified
Priority seating		Separate room

Program Strengths

We provide assistance for students with learning disabilities. *If tutoring is needed, it is discussed with specific instructor.

General Information:

East Georgia College is a 2 year public college. Rural campus of 200 acres is 88 miles from Savannah. Accessible by bus. Beaches are 95 miles from campus. Housing is not guaranteed.

Accreditation: SACS

SAT/ACT Scores:
Scores for incoming freshmen: **Verbal:** 60% below 500. **Math:** 60% below 500. **ACT:** 60% below 20.

Class Rank: 75% were in the top 60% of their class.

Expenses:
Tuition: In-state: Full year: $316.00. Part-time: Per credit: $25.00. Tuition: Out-of-state: Full year: $886.00. Part-time: Per credit: $70.00.

Majors

• BUSINESS Accounting, Business Administration, Business Economics, Business Education, Business Management • COMMUNICATIONS English, Journalism, Speech • COMPUTER SCIENCE Computer Science, Data Processing, Programming • EDUCATION Art, Early Childhood, Elementary, General, Middle School, Secondary • HEALTH SCIENCES Dental Assistant, Dental Hygiene, Health, Medical Technology, Nursing, Physical Therapy • HUMANITIES Liberal Arts • LANGUAGES French, Spanish • PREPROFESSIONAL Agriculture, Law, Social Work • SCIENCES Agricultural, Biology, Chemistry, Mathematics • SOCIAL SCIENCES Anthropology, Criminal Justice, Criminology, Government/Political, History, Law Enforcement, Psychology, Social Sciences, Sociology • VISUAL AND PERFORMING ARTS Art • VOCATIONAL Radiograph Medical Technology, Secretarial

Sports/Activities

• STUDENT LIFE ACTIVITIES Choral, Drama Groups, Ethnic & Cultural Groups, Fraternities, Magazine, Newspaper, Religious Organization, Student Government, Yearbook

Highly Selective

Emory University
P.O. Drawer VV
Atlanta, Georgia 30322
(404) 727-3300

School Enrollment: **9,398** Male: **4,559** Female: **4,839**
LD Enrollment: **17** Male: **10** Female: **7**

Admissions Contact: **Dan Walls, Dean of Admissions**
LD Contact: **Lelia Crawford, Director**
Name of Program: **Handicapped Student Services**
Address: **P.O. Drawer VV**
Telephone: **(404) 727-3300**

Admissions

Application Information:
Application deadline: **February 1st**
Notified when: **April 1st**

Secondary School Information
Most Important Criteria For Admissions (1-strongest)

SAT/ACT	Application	School transcript
Class rank	Course selection	Personal statement
Interview	Extra activities	Psychoeducational
G.P.A.	Open admission	Recommendations

Test Requirements:
Untimed SAT: **Yes** Untimed ACT: **Yes** Untimed ACH: **Yes**
Documentation of LD required: **Yes**
Currency of diagnostic testing: **1 year**

Types of Disabilities Served
- Speech/Lang
- Study skills
- Written express
- Organizational
- Perceptual
- Reading
- Spelling
- Math
- Fine Motor
- ADD with LD
- ADD without LD
- ADHD with LD
- ADHD without LD

Learning Disability Program
Counseling: Individual: **Yes**

Faculty: Part time: **1** M.A.: **1**
Faculty advocate: **Yes** Meets with instructor: **As needed**

Diagnostic Testing

ADD	Personality	Perceptual skills	Spelling
ADHD	Organization	Fine motor skills	Reading
I.Q.	Handwriting	Spoken language	Study skills
Math	Social skills	Written language	

Tutoring:
Services rendered by:
- Graduates
- Peers
- Faculty
- LD staff
- Teacher trainees

Tutorials

Grp.	Ind.	Tutorials	Grp.	Ind.	Tutorials
•		Math skills	•		Word processing
	•	Study skills		•	Time management
•		Language arts		•	Learning strategies
•		Written express		•	Organizational skills

Academic Accommodations

Curriculum	Study Aids	Exams
• Priority registration	• Typist	• Oral
Math waiver	• Reader	Untimed
Foreign lang. waiver	• Notetaker	• Take home
• Course substitution	• Proof reader	• With proctor
In Class	• Text on tape	On computer
• Calculators	Early syllabus	• Extended time
• Tape recorder	• Taped handouts	On tape
• Word processor		• Modified
• Priority seating		• Separate room

Graduation Requirements: GPA: **2.0**

Program Strengths
The goals of the services are: to remediate deficits, to provide equal access to programs, services, and activities; to reduce competitive disadvantage in academic work; to provide individual counseling and referral; to serve as an advocate for student needs; to provide a variety of support services; and to serve as a liaison between student, faculty, administrators, and community agencies.

General Information:
Emory University is a 4 year private United Methodist university. Suburban campus of 620 acres is 6 miles from Atlanta. Accessible by air, train or bus. 6% of students are foreign. 15 residential halls on campus. Housing is guaranteed through 1st year. Guaranteed through 1st year. 45 % of students join fraternities/sororities.

Accreditation: SACS

Expenses:
Tuition: In-state: Full year: $12,250.00. Part-time: Per credit: $510.00.
Room and board: $5,200.00

Majors
• AREA STUDIES African, American, Black/Afro-American, Caribbean, Eastern European, Jewish, Latin American, Medieval, Russian/Slavic • BUSINESS Accounting, Banking, Business Administration, Business Economics, Business Management, Economics, Finance, Management, Marketing • COMMUNICATIONS English • COMPUTER SCIENCE Computer Mathematics, Computer Science, Programming • EDUCATION Child Development, Early Childhood, Elementary, Middle School, Secondary • HEALTH SCIENCES Medical Assistant, Medical Radiation Dosimetry, Medical Records Administration, Nuclear Medical Technology, Nursing, Nutritional/Food, Physical Therapy • HUMANITIES Classics, Comparative Literature, English/Writing/Literature, Humanities, Liberal Arts, Philosophy, Religion • LANGUAGES Arabic, French, German, Greek, Italian, Latin, Russian, Spanish • PREPROFESSIONAL Dentistry, Engineering, Landscaping, Medicine, Ministry • SCIENCES Biochemistry, Biology, Chemistry, Mathematics, Microbiology, Physical Science, Physics, Physiology • SOCIAL SCIENCES Anthropology, Government/Political, History, International Studies, Political Science, Psychology, Social Sciences, Sociology • VISUAL AND PERFORMING ARTS Art History, Dramatic Arts, Music, Music History, Theater

Sports/Activities
• SPORTS-INTERCOLLEGIATE Basketball, Crew (M), Cross Country, Diving, Golf (M), Soccer, Swimming, Tennis, Track and Field, Volleyball (F) • SPORTS-INTRAMURAL Badminton, Basketball, Bowling, Crew (M), Cross Country, Diving, Fencing, Field Hockey (M), Golf, Hand Ball,

Ping-Pong, Racquetball, Soccer, Softball, Swimming, Tennis, Track and Field, Volleyball, Water Polo, Weight Lifting (M) • STUDENT LIFE AC-TIVITIES Academic Clubs, Choral, Community Service, Concert Band, Dance, Debate, Drama Groups, Ethnic & Cultural Groups, Fraternities, Jazz Band, Magazine, Music Ensembles, Music Groups, Musical Theater, Newspaper, Political Groups, Radio/TV station, Religious Organization, Sororities, Student Government, Symphony Orchestra, Yearbook

Less Selective	Georgia Services

Georgia College
Campus P. O. Box 023
Milledgeville, Georgia 31061
(912) 453-5004

School Enrollment: **3,573** Male: **1,381** Female: **2,192**
LD Enrollment: **12**

Admissions Contact: **Larry A. Peevy, Director of Admissions**
LD Contact: **Craig Smith, Ph.D., Chair, Dept. Spec. Ed. & Admin.**
Telephone:**(912) 453-4027**

Admissions

Application Information:
Separate application:**Yes**
Application deadline: **August 30th**
Rolling Admissions: **Yes**Notified when: **within 2 weeks**

Secondary School Information
Most Important Criteria For Admissions (1-strongest)

1	SAT/ACT	1	Application	1	School transcript
3	Class rank	2	Course selection	7	Personal statement
6	Interview	4	Extra activities	8	Psychoeducational
1	G.P.A.		Open admission	5	Recommendations

Test Requirements:
Diagnostic testing waived: **Yes**
Documentation of LD required: **Yes**
Tests recommended: **Criteria are University system requirement**

Types of Disabilities Served
- Speech/Lang
- Study skills
- Written express
- Organizational
- Perceptual
- Reading
- Spelling
- Math
- Fine Motor
- ADD with LD
- ADD without LD
- ADHD with LD
- ADHD without LD

High School Course Requirements:
English: **4** Math: **3** Science: **3** Foreign Language: **2**

Learning Disability Program
Services only for LD students: **Yes**

Faculty:
Faculty: **4** Part time: **4**
Faculty advocate: **Yes** Meets with instructor: **As needed**

Diagnostic Testing

ADD	Personality	Perceptual skills	Spelling
ADHD	Organization	Fine motor skills	Reading
I.Q.	Handwriting	Spoken language	Study skills
Math	Social skills	Written language	

Tutoring:
Services rendered by:
•Graduates •Peers •Faculty •LD staff Teacher trainees

Tutorials

Grp.	Ind.	Tutorials	Grp.	Ind.	Tutorials
		Math skills			Word processing
•	•	Study skills			Time management
		Language arts		•	Learning strategies
		Written express			Organizational skills

Academic Accommodations

Curriculum	Study Aids	Exams
Priority registration	Typist	• Oral
Math waiver	Reader	Untimed
Foreign lang. waiver	Notetaker	Take home
Course substitution	Proof reader	• With proctor
In Class	• Text on tape	On computer
• Calculators	Early syllabus	• Extended time
• Tape recorder	Taped handouts	On tape
Word processor		Modified
• Priority seating		Separate room

General Information:
Georgia College is a 4 year public college. Urban campus of 85 acres is 33 miles from Macon. Accessible by bus. Ski areas are 4 hours from campus. Beaches are 3 hours from campus. 3% of students are foreign. Housing is not guaranteed.65 % of students remain on campus for the weekends. 13 % of students join fraternities/sororities.

Accreditation:USG

SAT/ACT Scores:
Scores for incoming freshmen:**Verbal:**50%below 500. 45%between 500 and 599. 4%between 600 and 699. 1%above 700. **Math:**45% below 500. 45% between 500 and 599. 6% between 600 and 699. 4%above 700. **ACT:** 30% below 20. 48% between 20 and 23. 18%between 24 and 251. 3%between 26 and 28. 1% above 28.

Class Rank:
About 20% of the present freshmen class were in the upper 20% of their high school class. 50% were in the top 40% of their class. 75% were in the top 60% of their class. 95% were in the top 80% of their class.

Expenses:
Tuition: In-state: Full year: $1,632.00. Part-time: Per credit:$37.00. Part-time: Per course: $185.00. Tuition: Out-of-state: Full year: $4,314.00. Part-time: Per credit:$112.00. Part-time: Per course:$560.00 Room and board: $2,490.00

Majors
• BUSINESS Accounting, Business Administration, Business Economics, Business Education, Business Management, Economics, Management, Marketing • COMMUNICATIONS Communication, English, Journalism, Television/Radio/Film • COMPUTER SCIENCE Computer Technology, Data Processing, Programming • EDUCATION Art, Early Childhood, Elementary, English, General, Health, Mathematics, Middle School, Music, Music Therapy, Physical, Reading, Science, Social Science, Social Studies, Special • ENGINEERING Engineering Science • HEALTH SCIENCES Medical Technology, Nursing, Occupational Therapy, Physical Therapy • HUMANITIES Liberal Arts, Religion • LANGUAGES French, Spanish • PREPROFESSIONAL Dentistry, Engineering, Forestry, Law, Legal Assistant, Medicine, Ministry, Optometry, Pharmacy, Podiatry, Veterinarian • SCIENCES Biochemistry, Biology, Chemistry, Geology, Mathematics, Microbiology, Physical Chemistry, Physical Science, Physics • SOCIAL SCIENCES Criminal Justice, Government/Political, History, Library Science, Political Science, Psychology, Public Administration, Social Sciences, Sociology • VISUAL AND PERFORMING ARTS Art, Church Music,

Music, Music Performance, Music Theory, Studio Art, Theater, Voice • VOCATIONAL Business and Office, Home Economics, Paralegal, Secretarial

Sports/Activities

• SPORTS RELATED Cheerleading, Pep Band • SPORTS-INTERCOLLEGIATE Baseball (M), Basketball, Cross Country, Golf (M), Softball (F), Tennis • SPORTS-INTRAMURAL Badminton, Basketball, Golf (M), Ping-Pong, Soccer (M), Volleyball • STUDENT LIFE ACTIVITIES Concert Band, Dance, Debate, Drama Groups, Ethnic & Cultural Groups, Fraternities, Jazz Band, Magazine, Music Ensembles, Music Groups, Musical Theater, Newspaper, Radio/TV station, Religious Organization, Sororities, Student Government

Highly Selective　　　　　　　　　　　**Georgia Services**

Georgia Institute of Technology

353 Ferst Drive
Atlanta, Georgia 30332-0285
(404) 894-2564

School Enrollment: **12,814** Male: **9,789** Female: **3,025**
LD Enrollment: **13** Male: **10** Female: **3**

Admissions Contact: **Ms. Deborah Smith, Asst. Manager Admis.**
LD Contact: **Rose Mary Watkins, Asst. to VP/ Student Services**
Name of Program: **Disabled & Non-Traditional Program**
Address: **353 Ferst Dr., Student Service Bldg., Room 221**
Telephone: **(404) 894-2564**

Admissions

Application Information:
Application deadline: **February 1st**
Rolling Admissions: **Yes**

Secondary School Information
Most Important Criteria For Admissions (1-strongest)

3 SAT/ACT	**4** Application	**5** School transcript
Class rank	**2** Course selection	Personal statement
Interview	Extra activities	Psychoeducational
1 G.P.A.	Open admission	Recommendations

Test Requirements:
Untimed SAT: **Yes**
Documentation of LD required: **Yes**

Types of Disabilities Served
• Speech/Lang　• Reading　　• ADD with LD
• Study skills　• Spelling　　• ADD without LD
• Written express　• Math　　• ADHD with LD
• Organizational　• Fine Motor　• ADHD without LD
• Perceptual

Admissions Process

Freshmen and transfers may apply for any of the academic quarters. On-line application fees are waived. All applications on file by the deadline will be considered. Admissions is based on a combination of high school academic record, courses completed, and standardized test results.

High School Course Requirements:
English: **4** Math: **4** Science: **3** Foreign Language: **2**

Learning Disability Program

Special orientation for LD students: **None**
Students mainstreamed **100** % of the day
Recommended credits per semester: **12-15**
Counseling: Individual: **Yes** Group Counseling: **Yes** Vocational Counseling: **Yes**
Support groups are available: **Can be arranged, if needed**

Faculty:
Faculty: **1**

Diagnostic Testing
ADD	Personality	Perceptual skills	Spelling
ADHD	Organization	Fine motor skills	Reading
I.Q.	Handwriting	Spoken language	Study skills
Math	Social skills	Written language	

Tutoring:
Services rendered by:
•Graduates　•Peers　　Faculty　　LD staff　　Teacher trainees

Tutorials
Grp.	Ind.	Tutorials	Grp.	Ind.	Tutorials
		Math skills			Word processing
•	•	Study skills	•		Time management
		Language arts	•	•	Learning strategies
		Written express	•	•	Organizational skills

Academic Accommodations

Curriculum	Study Aids	Exams
• Priority registration	Typist	• Oral
Math waiver	• Reader	• Untimed
Foreign lang. waiver	• Notetaker	• Take home
Course substitution	• Proof reader	• With proctor
In Class	• Text on tape	On computer
• Calculators	• Early syllabus	• Extended time
• Tape recorder	• Taped handouts	• On tape
• Word processor		• Modified
• Priority seating		• Separate room

Graduation Requirements:
Course credits: **Varies** GPA: **2.0** Years to complete degree: **No minimum**

Program Strengths

We develop individualized plans for each student, based on their needs and desires. Letters are prepared and given to each student to give to faculty if they choose to. Our services are confidential, but students are encouraged to allow us to participate in their interactions with faculty.

General Information:

Georgia Institute of Technology is a 4 year public Institute. Urban campus of 300 acres is Accessible by air, bus, or train. 24 residential halls on campus. Housing is guaranteed. Guaranteed through 1st year.

Accreditation: SACS

SAT/ACT Scores:
Scores for incoming freshmen: **Verbal:** 30% below 500. 40% between 500 and 599. 20% between 600 and 699. 10% above 700. **Math:** 3% below 500. 15% between 500 and 599. 45% between 600 and 699. 37% above 700.

Class Rank:
About 89% of the present freshmen class were in the upper 20% of their high school class. 8% were in the top 40% of their class. 3% were in the top 60% of their class.

Expenses:
Tuition: In-state: Full year: $574.00 Matriculation fee per quarter. Part-time: Per credit:$48.00. Part-time: Per course: $144.00 . Tuition: Out-of-state: Full year: $1,387.00 plus $574.00 matriculation fee per quarter. Part-time: Per credit:$48.00. Part-time: Per course:$144.00 Room and board: $3,270.00

Majors

• AREA STUDIES International Studies • BUSINESS Economics, Management, Operations Research • CRAFTS AND DESIGN Industrial Design • CRAFTS AND DESIGN Computer Science • ENGINEERING Aerospace, Ceramic, Chemical, Civil/Environmental, Computer, Electrical, Engineering Science, Health Systems, Industrial, Materials, Mechanical, Nuclear, Physics, Health, Polymer & Textile Chemistry, Textile • MATHEMATICS Applied, Discrete Mathematics • PRE PROFESSIONAL Architecture, Building Construction • SCIENCES Biology, Chemistry, Physics • SOCIAL SCIENCES History of Science, Psychology, Sociology,Science, Tech & Cult

Sports/Activities

• SPORTS RELATED Baton Twirling, Cheerleading, Chess, Drill Team, Drum Major/Majorette, Marching Band, Pep Band, Team Managers • SPORTS-INTERCOLLEGIATE Baseball (M), Basketball, Cross Country, Diving, Football (M), Golf (M), Swimming, Tennis, Track and Field, Volleyball (F), Wrestling • SPORTS-INTRAMURAL Basketball, Bowling, Crew, Diving, Football (M), Gymnastics, Sailing, Skiing - Cross Country, Skiing - Snow, Soccer (M), Squash, Swimming (F), Tennis, Track and Field (M), Volleyball, Water Polo, Weight Lifting (M), Wrestling (M) • STUDENT LIFE ACTIVITIES Academic Clubs, Choral, Community Service, Concert Band, Dance, Drama Groups, Ethnic & Cultural Groups, Fraternities, Jazz Band, Magazine, Music Groups, Newspaper, Orchestra, Political Groups, Radio/TV station, Religious Organization, Sororities, Student Government, Yearbook

---

Less Selective	Georgia
	Services

Georgia Southern University

Landrum Box 8011
Statesboro, Georgia 30460-8011
(912) 681-5531

School Enrollment: **14,000** Male: **7,000** Female: **7,000**
LD Enrollment: **160**

Admissions Contact: **Mr. Dale Wasson Director of Admissions**
LD Contact: **Regina Blok Coordinator, Disability Services**
Name of Program: **Disability Services**
Address: **Landrum Box 8011**
Telephone:**(912) 681-5541**

Admissions

Application Information:
Rolling Admissions: **Yes**

Secondary School Information

Most Important Criteria For Admissions (1-strongest)

2 SAT/ACT	3 Application	1 School transcript
Class rank	4 Course selection	Personal statement
Interview	Extra activities	Psychoeducational
G.P.A.	Open admission	Recommendations

Test Requirements:
Diagnostic testing waived: **Yes**
Untimed SAT: **Yes** Untimed ACT: **Yes** Untimed ACH: **Yes**
WAIS-R required: **Yes**
Documentation of LD required: **Yes**
Currency of diagnostic testing: **3 years**
Tests recommended: **2 cognitive and achievement as outlined by Georgia Board of Regents.**

Types of Disabilities Served

• Speech/Lang	• Reading	• ADD with LD
Study skills	• Spelling	• ADD without LD
• Written express	• Math	ADHD with LD
• Organizational	• Fine Motor	ADHD without LD
• Perceptual		

High School Course Requirements:

Waivers to standard high school courses
Course substitution: **Yes**

Learning Disability Program

Counseling: Individual: **Yes**

Faculty:

Faculty: **1** Full time: **1** M.A.: **1** Ph.D.: **1**
Faculty advocate: **Yes** Meets with instructor: **As needed**

Diagnostic Testing

ADD	Personality	Perceptual skills	Spelling
ADHD	Organization	Fine motor skills	Reading
I.Q.	Handwriting	Spoken language	Study skills
Math	Social skills	Written language	

Tutoring:

Services rendered by:
•Graduates •Peers Faculty LD staff Teacher trainees

Tutorials

Grp.	Ind.	Tutorials	Grp.	Ind.	Tutorials
•	•	Math skills			Word processing
		Study skills			Time management
•	•	Language arts			Learning strategies
•	•	Written express			Organizational skills

Academic Accommodations

Curriculum	Study Aids	Exams
Priority registration	Typist	• Oral
Math waiver	• Reader	• Untimed
Foreign lang. waiver	• Notetaker	Take home
• Course substitution	Proof reader	• With proctor
In Class	• Text on tape	• On computer
• Calculators	Early syllabus	• Extended time
• Tape recorder	Taped handouts	On tape
• Word processor		Modified
Priority seating		Separate room

Graduation Requirements:

Course credits: **190** GPA: **2.0**

Georgia

Program Strengths

We do not have an LD program; we have LD services that are available to students once they are accepted into Georgia Southern University and voluntarily choose to disclose their disability.

General Information:

Georgia Southern University is a 4 year public college. Suburban campus of 457 acres is 40 miles from Savannah. Beaches are 45 miles from campus. 1.6% of students are foreign. 16 residential halls on campus. Housing is not guaranteed.20 % of students remain on campus for the weekends. 50 % of students join fraternities/sororities.

Accreditation:AACSB, ABET, ADA, AHEA, NASM, NCATE, NLN, NRPA

SAT/ACT Scores:

Scores for incoming freshmen:**Verbal:**74%below 500. 22%between 500 and 599. 4%between 600 and 699. 3%above 700.

Expenses:

Tuition: In-state: Full year: $413.00 per quarter. Part-time: Per credit:$34.00. Tuition: Out-of-state: Full year: $826.00 per quarter. Part-time: Per credit:$68.00. Room and board: $1,080.00-$1,640.00

Majors

• BUSINESS Accounting, Agricultural, Banking, Business Administration, Business Economics, Business Education, Business Management, Economics, Finance, Food Management, Hotel and Restaurant Managemen, Insurance, Management, Marketing, Public Accounting, Real Estate, Retailing, Trade & Industrial Management, Travel/Tourism Management • COMMUNICATIONS Advertising, Broadcasting, Communication, English, Journalism, Speech • COMPUTER SCIENCE Computer Science, Data Processing, Programming • CRAFTS AND DESIGN Mechanical Design Technology • EDUCATION Administration of Special Educ, Art, Child Development, Driver & Safety, Early Childhood, Elementary, English, General, Health, Industrial, Middle School, Music, Physical, Recreation and Youth Leadershi, School Psychology, Science, Secondary, Social Studies, Special, Vocational • ENGINEERING Civil/Environmental, Engineering Science • HEALTH SCIENCES Health, Nursing, Nutritional/ Food, Occupational Therapy, Physical Therapy, Practical Nursing • HUMANITIES Humanities, Liberal Arts, Philosophy • LANGUAGES French, German, Japanese, Spanish • PREPROFESSIONAL Architecture, Dentistry, Engineering, Forestry, Law, Medicine, Natural Resources, Recreation, Social Work, Veterinarian • SCIENCES Astronomy, Biochemistry, Biology, Botany, Chemistry, Earth, Geography, Geology, Macrobiology, Marine Biology, Mathematics, Microbiology, Oceanography, Physical Chemistry, Physical Science, Physics, Zoology • SOCIAL SCIENCES Anthropology, Criminal Justice, Criminology, Geography, Government/Political, History, Home and Family, Human Resources Development, Individual and Family Developm, Law Enforcement, Psychology, Public Relations, Social Sciences, Sociology • VISUAL AND PERFORMING ARTS Art, Art History, Dramatic Arts, Fine Arts, Music, Music History & Appreciation, Music Performance, Music Theory, Theater • VOCATIONAL Construction, Fashion Design, Fashion Merchandising, Home Economics, Industrial Arts, Interior Design, Manufacturing Technology, Medical Laboratory Technology, Park/Recreation, Secretarial, Textile and Clothing

Sports/Activities

• SPORTS RELATED Marching Band • SPORTS-INTERCOLLEGIATE Baseball (M), Basketball, Cross Country, Diving, Football (F), Golf (M), Soccer (M), Softball (F), Swimming, Tennis, Volleyball (F) • SPORTS-INTRAMURAL Badminton, Basketball, Bowling, Fencing, Golf, Racquetball, Riflery, Rugby, Soccer (M), Softball, Swimming, Tennis, Volleyball • STUDENT LIFE ACTIVITIES Choral, Concert Band, Drama Groups, Ethnic & Cultural Groups, Fraternities, Jazz Band, Magazine, Music Ensemble, Music Groups, Musical Theater, Newspaper, Opera, Radio/TV station, Religious Organization, Sororities, Student Government, Symphony Orchestra, Yearbook

---

Less Selective **Georgia Services**

Georgia State University
University Plaza
Atlanta, Georgia 30303
(404) 651-2365

School Enrollment: **12,300** Male: **5,300** Female: **7,000**

Admissions Contact: **Dr. Ernest W. Beals, Dean of Admission**
LD Contact: **Carole L. Pearson, Asst. Dean Handicapped Serv.**
Telephone:**(404) 651-4044**

Admissions

Application Information:
Application deadline: **August**
Rolling Admissions: **Yes**

Secondary School Information
Most Important Criteria For Admissions (1-strongest)

2 SAT/ACT	Application	School transcript
Class rank	**3** Course selection	**6** Personal statement
8 Interview	**5** Extra activities	**4** Psychoeducational
1 G.P.A.	Open admission	**7** Recommendations

Test Requirements:
Untimed SAT: **Yes** Untimed ACT: **Yes**

Types of Disabilities Served
- Speech/Lang
- Study skills
- Written express
- Organizational
- Perceptual
- Reading
- Spelling
- Math
- Fine Motor
- ADD with LD
- ADD without LD
- ADHD with LD
- ADHD without LD

Faculty:
Faculty advocate: **Yes** Meets with instructor: **As needed**

Diagnostic Testing

ADD	Personality	Perceptual skills	Spelling
ADHD	Organization	Fine motor skills	Reading
I.Q.	Handwriting	Spoken language	Study skills
Math	Social skills	Written language	

Tutoring:
Services rendered by:
•Graduates •Peers •Faculty LD staff •Teacher trainees

Tutorials

Grp.	Ind.	Tutorials	Grp.	Ind.	Tutorials
	•	Math skills		•	Word processing
•		Study skills	•		Time management
	•	Language arts		•	Learning strategies
•		Written express	•		Organizational skills

Academic Accommodations

Curriculum	Study Aids	Exams
Priority registration	Typist	• Oral
Math waiver	Reader	Untimed
Foreign lang. waiver	Notetaker	• Take home
• Course substitution	• Proof reader	With proctor
In Class	• Text on tape	On computer
• Calculators	Early syllabus	• Extended time
• Tape recorder	Taped handouts	On tape
• Word processor		• Modified
Priority seating		Separate room

Program Strengths

We do not have a formal LD Program. Our program for disabled students would best be described as supportive. All disabled students are encouraged to utilize the full array of services and programs offered by the university. Disabled Students are encouraged to register with the Services for the Handicapped Office as soon as they arrive on campus. A handbook describing the program and services will be provided on request.

General Information:

Georgia State University is a 4 year public university. Urban campus of 25 acres is Accessible by air, train, or bus. Ski areas are 100 miles from campus. Beaches are 200 miles from campus. Housing is not guaranteed.

Accreditation: SACS

SAT/ACT Scores:

Scores for incoming freshmen: **Verbal:** 78% below 500. 18% between 500 and 599. 3% between 600 and 699. 1% above 700. **Math:** 66% below 500. 26% between 500 and 599. 7% between 600 and 699. 1% above 700. **ACT:** 59% below 20. 24% between 20 and 23. 10% between 24 and 25l. 5% between 26 and 28. 2% above 28.

Expenses:

Tuition: In-state: Full year: $1,575.00. Part-time: Per credit: Part-time: $35.00. Tuition: Out-of-state: Full year: $5,400.00. Part-time: Per credit: Part-time: $120.00.

Majors

• AREA STUDIES Urban • BUSINESS Accounting, Banking, Business Administration, Business Economics, Business Education, Business Management, Economics, Finance, Hotel and Restaurant Managemen, Insurance, Management, Marketing, Marketing and Distribution, Personnel, Real Estate, Travel/Tourism Management • COMMUNICATIONS Advertising, Broadcasting, Commercial Design, English, Photography, Speech, Television/Radio/Film • COMPUTER SCIENCE Computer Information Systems, Data Processing, Programming, Systems Analysis • EDUCATION Art, Curriculum, Early Childhood, Education Administration, Elementary, Health, Industrial, Middle School, Music, Music Therapy, Physical, Recreation and Youth Leadershi, School Psychology, Secondary, Special, Speech/Language, Vocational • ENGINEERING • HEALTH SCIENCES Health, Medical Records Administration, Medical Technology, Nursing, Nutritional/Food, Physical Therapy • HUMANITIES Classics, Liberal Arts, Philosophy • LANGUAGES Arabic, French, German, Greek, Hebrew, Italian, Japanese, Latin, Russian, Spanish • PREPROFESSIONAL Law, Medicine, Social Work • SOCIAL SCIENCES Anthropology, Criminal Justice, Geography, Government/Political, History, Human Service, Political Science, Psychology, Sociology • VISUAL AND PERFORMING ARTS Art, Art History, Dance, Dramatic Arts, Fine Arts, Music, Studio Art, Theater • VOCATIONAL Business and Office, Park/Recreation, Radiological Technology, Secretarial

Sports/Activities

• SPORTS RELATED Cheerleading, Chess, Pep Band, Team Managers • SPORTS-INTERCOLLEGIATE Basketball, Cross Country, Diving, Golf (M), Soccer (M), Softball (F), Swimming, Tennis, Volleyball (F) • SPORTS-INTRAMURAL Badminton, Basketball, Bowling, Canoeing, Crew, Cross Country, Cycling, Diving, Fencing, Golf, Horseback Riding, Ice Hockey, Judo, Karate, Martial Arts, Ping-Pong, Racquetball, Rugby, Sailing, Scuba, Skiing - Snow, Soccer, Softball, Swimming, Tennis, Track and Field, Volleyball, Weight Lifting, Wrestling (M) • STUDENT LIFE ACTIVITIES Concert Band, Debate, Drama Groups, Ethnic & Cultural Groups, Film, Jazz Band, Music Ensembles, Music Groups, Musical Theater, Newspaper, Radio/TV station, Religious Organization, Sororities, Student Government, Symphony Orchestra, Yearbook

---

Selective — **Georgia** **Services**

Mercer University

1400 Coleman Avenue
Macon, Georgia 31207
(912) 752-2650

School Enrollment: **2,400** Male: **1,100** Female: **1,300**
LD Enrollment: **38**

Admissions Contact: **Tommy Eiland, Associate Director of Adm.**
LD Contact: **Linda Conrads**
Name of Program: **LD Services**

Admissions

Application Information:

Application deadline: **Rolling**
Rolling Admissions: **Yes**

Secondary School Information

Most Important Criteria For Admissions (1-strongest)

3 SAT/ACT	**6** Application	**1**	School transcript
5 Class rank	**1** Course selection	**8**	Personal statement
2 Interview	**6** Extra activities	**7**	Psychoeducational
1 G.P.A.	Open admission	**4**	Recommendations

Types of Disabilities Served

• Speech/Lang	• Reading	ADD with LD
• Study skills	• Spelling	ADD without LD
• Written express	• Math	ADHD with LD
• Organizational	• Fine Motor	ADHD without LD
• Perceptual		

Learning Disability Program

Counseling: Individual: **Yes**

Faculty:

Faculty: **1**
Faculty advocate: **Yes** Meets with instructor: **As needed**

Diagnostic Testing

ADD	Personality	Perceptual skills	Spelling
ADHD	Organization	Fine motor skills	Reading
I.Q.	Handwriting	Spoken language	Study skills
Math	Social skills	Written language	

Tutoring:

Average size of group tutorials: **7-8**
Services rendered by:
Graduates •Peers Faculty •LD staff Teacher trainees

Georgia

Tutorials

Grp.	Ind.	Tutorials	Grp.	Ind.	Tutorials
	•	Math skills		•	Word processing
•		Study skills		•	Time management
		Language arts		•	Learning strategies
	•	Written express			Organizational skills

Academic Accommodations

Curriculum	Study Aids	Exams
Priority registration	Typist	• Oral
Math waiver	Reader	Untimed
Foreign lang. waiver	Notetaker	• Take home
Course substitution	Proof reader	With proctor
In Class	Text on tape	On computer
Calculators	Early syllabus	• Extended time
Tape recorder	Taped handouts	On tape
Word processor		Modified
Priority seating		Separate room

Program Strengths

We provide services only! We have only one full-time person. Students must be very independent and very responsible. Tutoring is offered on a one-to-one basis, but we cannot guarantee this because it depends on the number of students in need.

General Information:

Mercer University is a 4 year private Southern Baptist Convention university. Urban campus of 133 acres is 70 miles from Atlanta. Accessible by air or bus. Ski areas are 3 hours from campus. Beaches are 3 hours from campus. 2% of students are foreign. 5 residential halls on campus. Housing is guaranteed.40 % of students remain on campus for the weekends. 35 % of students join fraternities/sororities.

Accreditation:NACAC, SACRAO, GACRAO

SAT/ACT Scores:

Scores for incoming freshmen:**Verbal:**45%below 500. 35%between 500 and 599. 15%between 600 and 699. 5%above 700. **Math:**45% below 500. 35% between 500 and 599. 15% between 600 and 699. 5%above 700. **ACT:** 45% below 20. 25% between 20 and 23. 15%between 24 and 25l. 10%between 26 and 28. 5% above 28.

Class Rank:

About 65% of the present freshmen class were in the upper 20% of their high school class. 25% were in the top 40% of their class. 5% were in the top 60% of their class. 5% were in the top 80% of their class.

Expenses:

Tuition: In-state: Full year: $7,800.00. Part-time: Per credit:$165.00. Part-time: Per course: $800.00. Tuition: Out-of-state: Full year: $7,800.00. Part-time: Per credit:Part-time: $165.00. Part-time: Per course:Part-time: $800.00

Majors

• AREA STUDIES African, Black/Afro-American • BUSINESS Accounting, Banking, Business Administration, Business Economics, Business Management, Economics, Finance, Management, Marketing • COMMUNICATIONS Advertising, Broadcasting, Communication, Creative Writing, English, Journalism, Photography, Television/Radio/Film • COMPUTER SCIENCE Computer Science, Programming, Systems Analysis, Telecommunications • EDUCATION Agricultural, Curriculum, Early Childhood, Elementary, Health, Middle School, Music, Music Therapy, Physical, Recreation and Youth Leadershi, School Psychology, Secondary, Special • ENGINEERING Aerospace, Bio-medical, Bioengineering, Communications, Electrical, Engineering Science, Mechanical • HEALTH SCIENCES Health, Medical Technology, Speech/Audiology and Speech • HUMANITIES Great Books, Humanities, Liberal Arts, Philosophy, Religion • LANGUAGES French, German, Greek, Italian, Latin, Spanish • PREPROFESSIONAL Engineering, Forestry, Law, Medicine, Pharmacy, Social Work • SCIENCES Biochemistry, Biology, Cognitive, Earth, Macrobiology, Mathematics, Microbiology, Physical Chemistry, Physical Science, Physics, Physiology • SOCIAL SCIENCES Geography, History, Human Service, Political Science, Psychology, Social Sciences, Sociology • VISUAL AND PERFORMING ARTS Art, Art History, Dramatic Arts, Music, Music History & Appreciation, Music Performance, Studio Art, Theater • VOCATIONAL Industrial Administration

Sports/Activities

• SPORTS RELATED Cheerleading, Pep Band, Team Managers
• SPORTS-INTERCOLLEGIATE Baseball (M), Basketball, Cross Country, Golf (M), Soccer, Softball (F), Squash, Tennis, Volleyball (F)
• SPORTS-INTRAMURAL Basketball, Golf (M), Hand Ball, Ping-Pong, Racquetball, Softball, Swimming, Tennis, Track and Field, Volleyball, Water Polo, Weight Lifting • STUDENT LIFE ACTIVITIES Choral, Community Service, Concert Band, Debate, Drama Groups, Ethnic & Cultural Groups, Fraternities, Jazz Band, Magazine, Music Ensembles, Music Groups, Musical Theater, Newspaper, Opera, Radio/TV station, Religious Organization, Sororities, Student Government, Symphony Orchestra, Yearbook

---

Less Selective	Georgia Program

Reinhardt College
Waleska, Georgia 30183
(404) 479-1454

School Enrollment: **650** Male: **300** Female: **350**
LD Enrollment: **48** Male: **30** Female: **18**

Admissions Contact: **Ray Tatum, Director of Admissions**
LD Contact: **Sylvia Robertson, Director, Academic Support**
Name of Program: **Academic Support Office**
Telephone:**(404) 479-1454**

Admissions

Application Information:
LD Students Applying: **40** Accepted: **20** Enrolled:**18**
LD on admissions committee:**Yes**
Application deadline: **Rolling**
Applicant must apply **8-10** months in advance
Rolling Admissions: **Yes**Notified when: **June 1st**

Secondary School Information
Most Important Criteria For Admissions (1-strongest)

5 SAT/ACT	6 Application	1 School transcript
12 Class rank	2 Course selection	Personal statement
7 Interview	8 Extra activities	4 Psychoeducational
3 G.P.A.	Open admission	9 Recommendations

Test Requirements:
Diagnostic testing waived: **Yes**
Untimed SAT: **Yes** Untimed ACT: **Yes**
WAIS-R required: **Yes**
Documentation of LD required: **Yes**
Currency of diagnostic testing: **Within 36 months**
Tests recommended: **WAIS-R or WISC-R, WRAT or Woodcock Johnson**

Types of Disabilities Served
- Speech/Lang
- Study skills
- Written express
- Organizational
- Perceptual
- Reading
- Spelling
- Math
- Fine Motor
- ADD with LD
- ADD without LD
- ADHD with LD
- ADHD without LD

Admissions Process

Students apply to school, provide transcripts, psych, IEP, 3 references and come to interview. Admissions decisions are made by LD faculty.

High School Course Requirements:
English: **4** Math: **1**

Learning Disability Program

Syllabus available during orientation:**Yes**
Program: Reinforces course work: **Yes**
Students mainstreamed **100** % of the day
Recommended credits per semester: **12-15**
Time required or recommended in learning center: **4-6 hours**
Services only for LD students: **Yes**
Counseling: Individual: **Yes** Group Counseling: **Yes** Vocational Counseling: **Yes**
Support groups are available:**LD, ACOA**

Faculty:
Faculty: **3** Including Director: **Yes** Full time: **3** M.A.: **3**
Meets with instructor: **Weekly**

Diagnostic Testing
ADD	Personality	Perceptual skills	Spelling
ADHD	Organization	Fine motor skills	Reading
I.Q.	Handwriting	Spoken language	Study skills
Math	Social skills	Written language	

Tutoring:
Average size of group tutorials: **1-4**
Services rendered by:
Graduates   Peers   •Faculty   LD staff   Teacher trainees

Tutorials
Grp.	Ind.	Tutorials	Grp.	Ind.	Tutorials
•	•	Math skills			Word processing
		Study skills			Time management
		Language arts			Learning strategies
•	•	Written express			Organizational skills

Academic Accommodations

Curriculum	Study Aids	Exams
• Priority registration	Typist	• Oral
Math waiver	Reader	Untimed
Foreign lang. waiver	• Notetaker	Take home
Course substitution	• Proof reader	• With proctor
In Class	• Text on tape	• On computer
• Calculators	Early syllabus	• Extended time
• Tape recorder	Taped handouts	On tape
Word processor		Modified
Priority seating		• Separate room

Graduation Requirements:
Course credits: **97** GPA: **2.0** Years to complete degree: **2.5 (7-8 quarters)**
Language waiver: **Yes**

Program Strengths
Academic Support is an integrated part of the Reinhardt program. Students are fully mainstreamed for course work but may test, write and use tutorials in ASO. Taped texts are coordinated, individual counseling is available. All tutorials are with faculty.

General Information:
Reinhardt College is a 2 year Methodist College. Rural campus of 15 acres is 40 miles from Atlanta. Accessible by car. Ski areas are 2 hours from campus. Beaches are 6 hours from campus. 5 residential halls on campus. Housing is guaranteed.10 % of students remain on campus for the weekends. 5 % of students join fraternities/sororities.

Accreditation:SACS

SAT/ACT Scores:
Scores for incoming freshmen:**Verbal:**50%below 500. 45%between 500 and 599. 5%between 600 and 699. **Math:**50% below 500. 45% between 500 and 599. 5% between 600 and 699. **ACT:** 10% below 20. 80% between 20 and 23. 5%between 24 and 25l. 5%between 26 and 28.

Expenses:
Tuition: In-state: Full year: $3,465.00. Part-time: Per credit:0. Room and board: $3,000.00 Cost of LD program:up to $3,465.00 additional

Majors
• AREA STUDIES American, European • ARTS Art History, Dramatic Arts, Music History • BUSINESS Accounting, Banking/Finance, Business Administration, Business Management, Data Processing, Management • COMMUNICATIONS Communication • COMPUTER SCIENCE Computer Science, Information Systems • HEALTH SCIENCES Health, Nursing, Physical Therapy • HUMANITIES Liberal Arts , Religion • LANGUAGES English • PRE PROFESSIONAL Dentistry, Forestry, Law, Medicine, Pharmacy, Veterinarian, Wildlife • SCIENCES Biology, Botany, Chemistry, Horticultural, Mathematics • SOCIAL SCIENCES Criminal Justice, History, Psychology, Social Science • VISUAL AND PERFORMING ARTS Fine Arts, Music • VOCATIONAL Ornamental Horticulture, Secretarial

Sports/Activities
• SPORTS RELATED Cheerleading • SPORTS-INTERCOLLEGIATE Baseball (M), Basketball (F), Basketball (M), Soccer (M), Softball (F), Tennis (F), Tennis (M) • SPORTS-INTRAMURAL Basketball (F), Basketball (M), Bowling, Football (F), Football (M), Volleyball (F), Volleyball (M) • STUDENT LIFE ACTIVITIES Academic Clubs, Choral, Community Service, Drama Groups, Fraternities, Newspaper, Religious Organization, Sororities, Student Government, Yearbook

---

Less Selective

**Georgia
Services**

South Georgia College
College Park Drive
Douglas, Georgia 31533
(912) 384-1100

School Enrollment: **1,000** Male: **400** Female: **600**
LD Enrollment: **10**

Admissions Contact: **John C. Wahl, Director of Admissions**
LD Contact: **Michael Vargo, Counselor**
Name of Program: **Student Support Services**
Telephone:**(912) 383-4276**

Georgia

Admissions

Application Information:
Application deadline: **Flexible**

Secondary School Information
Most Important Criteria For Admissions (1-strongest)

1 SAT/ACT	**1** Application	**1** School transcript
Class rank	**2** Course selection	Personal statement
Interview	Extra activities	Psychoeducational
1 G.P.A.	Open admission	Recommendations

Types of Disabilities Served
- Speech/Lang
- Study skills
- Written express
- Organizational
- Perceptual
- Reading
- Spelling
- Math
- Fine Motor
- ADD with LD
- ADD without LD
- ADHD with LD
- ADHD without LD

Learning Disability Program

Counseling: Individual: **Yes**

Faculty:
Faculty: **3** Full time: **3**
Faculty advocate: **Yes** Meets with instructor: **As needed**

Diagnostic Testing

ADD	Personality	Perceptual skills	Spelling
ADHD	Organization	Fine motor skills	Reading
I.Q.	Handwriting	Spoken language	Study skills
Math	Social skills	Written language	

Tutoring:
Average size of group tutorials: **1:1**
Services rendered by:

Graduates	•Peers	Faculty	LD staff	Teacher trainees

Tutorials

Grp.	Ind.	Tutorials	Grp.	Ind.	Tutorials
	•	Math skills			Word processing
•		Study skills	•		Time management
•		Language arts	•	•	Learning strategies
•	•	Written express	•	•	Organizational skills

Academic Accommodations

Curriculum	Study Aids	Exams
Priority registration	Typist	• Oral
Math waiver	Reader	Untimed
Foreign lang. waiver	Notetaker	Take home
Course substitution	• Proof reader	With proctor
In Class	Text on tape	On computer
Calculators	Early syllabus	• Extended time
• Tape recorder	Taped handouts	On tape
• Word processor		Modified
Priority seating		Separate room

Program Strengths

A student with a diagnosed learning disability is eligible for all services provided by Student Support Services. The support given by our program is found in the areas of academic tutoring, personal and academic counseling, cultural enrichment through periodic cultural trips, and various other areas of support. We offer a course called Coping for College Students which covers any deficits students may have. The Student Support Services Program at South Georgia College is not, however, designed specifically, and/or exclusively, for the learning disabled student.

General Information:
South Georgia College is a 2 year public college. Rural campus of 240 acres is 120 miles from Jacksonville. Accessible by bus. Ski areas are 6 hours from campus. Beaches are 100 miles from campus. 2% of students are foreign. 2 residential halls on campus. Housing is not guaranteed. 40 % of students remain on campus for the weekends.

Accreditation: Regional

Expenses:
Tuition: In-state: Full year: $867.00. Part-time: Per credit:$25.00. Part-time: Per course: $125.00. Tuition: Out-of-state: Full year: $2,508.00. Part-time: Per credit:$70.00. Part-time: Per course:$350.00 Room and board: $1,170.00.

Majors
• BUSINESS Accounting, Agricultural, Banking, Business Administration, Business Economics, Business Management, Economics, Finance, Management, Marketing • COMMUNICATIONS Communication, English, Journalism • COMPUTER SCIENCE Computer Science, Data Processing, Programming • EDUCATION Early Childhood, Elementary, General, Middle School, Secondary • ENGINEERING Agricultural, Engineering Science • HEALTH SCIENCES Medical Secretary, Nursing, Physical Therapy • HUMANITIES Liberal Arts, Philosophy • LANGUAGES French, Spanish • PREPROFESSIONAL Agriculture, Dentistry, Forestry, Law, Medicine, Pharmacy, Veterinarian • SCIENCES Agricultural, Biology, Chemistry, Earth, Mathematics, Physical Chemistry, Physical Science, Physics, Physiology • SOCIAL SCIENCES Criminal Justice, Government/Political, History, Law Enforcement, Psychology, Social Sciences, Sociology • VISUAL AND PERFORMING ARTS Art, Music, Theater • VOCATIONAL Business and Office, Legal Secretary, Park/Recreation, Secretarial

Sports/Activities
• SPORTS-INTERCOLLEGIATE Baseball (M), Basketball (M) • SPORTS-INTRAMURAL Basketball, Boxing, Golf, Ping-Pong, Softball, Tennis, Volleyball • STUDENT LIFE ACTIVITIES Drama Groups, Ethnic & Cultural Groups, Magazine, Music Groups, Newspaper, Religious Organization, Student Government, Yearbook

---

Less Selective

**Georgia
Services**

Southern College of Technology
South Marietta Parkway
Marietta, Georgia 30060
(404) 528-7281

School Enrollment: **2,843** Male: **2,343** Female: **500**

Admissions Contact: **Virginia A. Head Director of Admissions**
LD Contact: **Glenda Corwin Director of Counseling**

Admissions

Application Information:
Application deadline: **September 1st**
Rolling Admissions: **Yes**

Secondary School Information
Most Important Criteria For Admissions (1-strongest)

1 SAT/ACT	Application	School transcript
Class rank **2**	Course selection	Personal statement
Interview	Extra activities	Psychoeducational
G.P.A.	Open admission	Recommendations

Test Requirements:
Diagnostic testing waived: **Yes**
Untimed ACT: **Yes**
Documentation of LD required: **Yes**
Currency of diagnostic testing: **1 month**

Types of Disabilities Served

• Speech/Lang	• Reading	ADD with LD
Study skills	Spelling	ADD without LD
• Written express	• Math	ADHD with LD
Organizational	Fine Motor	ADHD without LD
Perceptual		

Faculty:
Faculty: **1** Full time: **1**

Diagnostic Testing

ADD	Personality	Perceptual skills	Spelling
ADHD	Organization	Fine motor skills	Reading
I.Q.	Handwriting	Spoken language	Study skills
Math	Social skills	Written language	

Tutoring:
Average size of group tutorials:
Services rendered by:

Graduates	Peers	Faculty	LD staff	Teacher trainees

Tutorials

Grp. Ind. Tutorials	Grp. Ind. Tutorials
Math skills	Word processing
Study skills	Time management
Language arts	Learning strategies
Written express	Organizational skills

Academic Accommodations

Curriculum	Study Aids	Exams
Priority registration	Typist	Oral
Math waiver	Reader	Untimed
Foreign lang. waiver	Notetaker	Take home
Course substitution	Proof reader	With proctor
In Class	Text on tape	On computer
Calculators	Early syllabus	• Extended time
• Tape recorder	Taped handouts	On tape
• Word processor		Modified
Priority seating		Separate room

General Information:
Southern College of Technology is a 4 year public college. Suburban campus of 200 acres is 15 miles from Atlanta. Accessible by bus. Ski areas are 150 miles from campus. Beaches are 200 miles from campus. 2.5% of students are foreign. 2 residential halls on campus. Housing is not guaranteed.10 % of students remain on campus for the weekends. 8 % of students join fraternities/sororities.

Accreditation:SACS

SAT/ACT Scores:
Scores for incoming freshmen:**Verbal:**88%below 500. 10%between 500 and 599. 2%between 600 and 699. **Math:**52% below 500. 39% between 500 and 599. 9% between 600 and 699.

Expenses:
Tuition: In-state: Full year: $1,450.00. Part-time: Per credit:$34.00. Tuition: Out-of-state: Full year: $3,900.00. Part-time: Per credit:$102.00. Room and board: $3,065.00

Majors
• COMPUTER SCIENCE Programming, Systems Analysis • ENGINEERING Apparel Engineering Technology, Civil/Environmental, Computer, Engineering Technology • VOCATIONAL Civil Technology, Construction, Electronics Technology, Industrial Technology, Mechanical Design Technology, Textile Technology

Sports/Activities
• SPORTS RELATED Chess • SPORTS-INTERCOLLEGIATE Baseball (M), Tennis (M) • SPORTS-INTRAMURAL Archery, Badminton, Baseball (M), Golf, Ping-Pong, Softball, Tennis, Volleyball • STUDENT LIFE ACTIVITIES Drama Groups, Ethnic & Cultural Groups, Fraternities, Jazz Band, Newspaper, Radio/TV station, Sororities, Student Government, Yearbook

---

Very Selective **Georgia Program**

University of Georgia
114 Academic Building
Athens, Georgia 30602
(404) 542-2112

School Enrollment: **25,000** Male: **12,500** Female: **12,500**
LD Enrollment: **100** Male: **50** Female: **50**

Admissions Contact: **John Albright, Assoc. Director of Admissions**
LD Contact: **Vicki Martin, Clinic Coordinator**
Name of Program: **Learning Disabilities Adult Clinic**
Telephone:**(404) 542-4589**

Admissions

Application Information:
LD Students Applying: **18** Accepted: **10** Enrolled:**8**
Separate application:**Yes**
Application deadline: **February 1st**
Rolling Admissions: **Yes**

Secondary School Information
Most Important Criteria For Admissions (1-strongest)

2 SAT/ACT	Application	School transcript
Class rank	Course selection	Personal statement
Interview	Extra activities	Psychoeducational
1 G.P.A.	Open admission	Recommendations

Test Requirements:
Diagnostic testing waived: **Yes**
Tests recommended: **2 day comprehensive evaluation by UGA LD Clinic**

Types of Disabilities Served

• Speech/Lang	• Reading	ADD with LD
• Study skills	• Spelling	ADD without LD
• Written express	• Math	ADHD with LD
• Organizational	• Fine Motor	ADHD without LD
• Perceptual		

Learning Disability Program

Program: Reinforces course work: **Yes**
Students mainstreamed **100** % of the day
Counseling: Individual: **Yes** Group Counseling: **Yes**

Faculty:

Faculty: **9** Including Director: **Yes** Full time: **4** Part time: **5**
LD faculty with: BS/BA: **9** M.A.: **5** Ph.D.: **3**
Faculty advocate: **Yes** Meets with instructor: **As needed**

Diagnostic Testing

ADD	• Personality	• Perceptual skills	• Spelling
ADHD	• Organization	• Fine motor skills	• Reading
• I.Q.	• Handwriting	• Spoken language	• Study skills
• Math	Social skills	• Written language	

Tutoring:

Services rendered by:
•Graduates   Peers   Faculty   •LD staff   Teacher trainees

Tutorials

Grp.	Ind.	Tutorials	Grp.	Ind.	Tutorials
	•	Math skills			Word processing
	•	Study skills			Time management
		Language arts		•	Learning strategies
	•	Written express		•	Organizational skills

Academic Accommodations

Curriculum	**Study Aids**	**Exams**
Priority registration	Typist	• Oral
Math waiver	Reader	Untimed
Foreign lang. waiver	• Notetaker	• Take home
Course substitution	• Proof reader	With proctor
In Class	• Text on tape	On computer
• Calculators	Early syllabus	• Extended time
• Tape recorder	Taped handouts	On tape
• Word processor		• Modified
Priority seating		Separate room

Program Strengths

The purpose of our clinic is to provide diagnostic assessment and direct services to students at the University of Georgia who demonstrate a specific learning disability. The assessment required of all students is used throughout the student's college career to obtain appropriate individual modifications. We encourage students to be independent and help them learn to be self-advocates, yet we are available at all times to help them. We have a good relationship with our faculty and make an effort to educate them about learning disabilities and assist them in working with our students.

General Information:

University of Georgia is a 4 year public university. Urban campus of 580 acres is 50 miles from Atlanta. Accessible by air or bus. Ski areas are 100 miles from campus. Beaches are 5 hours from campus. 5% of students are foreign. Housing is not guaranteed.50 % of students join fraternities/sororities.

Accreditation:SACS

Expenses:

Tuition: In-state: Full year: $667.00 per quarter. Tuition: Out-of-state: Full year: $1,171.00 per quarter. Room and board: $4,000.00

Majors

• AREA STUDIES African, American, Black/Afro-American, International Studies, Latin American, Medieval, Western European • BUSINESS Agricultural, Agronomy, Aviation Management, Business Administration, Business Economics, Business Education, Business Management, Consumer Economics, Economics, Finance, Food Management, Hotel and Restaurant Managemen, Insurance, International Business, Labor Relations, Management, Marketing, Marketing Research, Personnel, Real Estate, Sports Management, Wildlife Management • COMMUNICATIONS Advertising, Broadcasting, Communication, Creative Writing, Journalism, Photography, Speech, Television/Radio/Film • COMPUTER SCIENCE Computer Science, Data Processing, Programming, Systems Analysis, Telecommunications • CRAFTS AND DESIGN Graphic Design • EDUCATION Agricultural, Art, Child Development, Curriculum, Early Childhood, Elementary, English, Foreign Language, Health, Industrial, Mathematics, Middle School, Music, Physical, Reading, Recreation and Youth Leadershi, School Psychology, Special, Speech/Language, Vocational • ENGINEERING Agricultural • HEALTH SCIENCES Communication Disorders, Environmental, Health, Medical Technology, Nutritional/Food, Occupational Therapy, Physical Therapy, Recreation Therapy, Speech Therapy, Speech/Audiology and Speech • HUMANITIES Classics, Comparative Literature, English/Writing/Literature, Humanities, Liberal Arts, Philosophy, Religion • LANGUAGES Chinese, French, German, Greek, Italian, Japanese, Latin, Linguistic, Russian, Slavic, Spanish • PREPROFESSIONAL Agriculture, Architecture, Forestry, Law, Medicine, Natural Resources, Pharmacy, Recreation, Social Work • SCIENCES Agricultural, Animal, Biochemistry, Biology, Chemistry, Earth, Ecology, Entomology, Geography, Geology, Horticultural, Human & Animal Genetics, Mathematics, Microbiology, Physical Science, Physics, Plant Pathology, Plant Physiology, Zoology • SOCIAL SCIENCES Anthropology, Criminal Justice, Geography, Government/Political, History, Home Environment & Housing, Human Service, Individual & Family Developmen, Political Science, Psychology, Public Relations, Social Sciences, Sociology • VISUAL AND PERFORMING ARTS Art, Art History, Dance, Dramatic Arts, Music, Music History, Music Theory and Composition, Religious Music, Studio Art, Theater • VOCATIONAL Agricultural Mechanics, Fashion Mechandizing, Fire Science, Fishery Studies, Food Service, Home Economics, Interior Design, Landscape Architecture, Metal/Jewelry, Park/Recreation, Printmaking, Textile and Clothing

Sports/Activities

• SPORTS RELATED Cheerleading, Marching Band, Pep Band • SPORTS-INTERCOLLEGIATE Baseball (M), Basketball, Cross Country, Diving, Football (M), Golf, Gymnastics (F), Swimming, Tennis, Volleyball (F) • SPORTS-INTRAMURAL Archery, Badminton, Basketball, Bowling, Cross Country, Diving, Field Hockey (M), Golf, Horseback Riding, Lacrosse, Ping-Pong, Racquetball, Riflery, Rugby, Sailing, Soccer, Softball, Tennis, Track and Field, Volleyball, Water Polo (M) • STUDENT LIFE ACTIVITIES Choral, Community Service, Concert Band, Dance, Debate, Drama Groups, Ethnic & Cultural Groups, Film, Fraternities, Jazz Band, Music Ensembles, Music Groups, Musical Theater, Newspaper, Opera, Political Groups, Radio/TV station, Religious Organization, Sororities, Student Government, Symphony Orchestra, Yearbook

Selective   **Georgia**
Services

Valdosta State College

Valdosta, Georgia 31698
(912) 245-2498

School Enrollment: **7,436** Male: **2,987** Female: **4,449**
LD Enrollment: **55** Male: **40** Female: **15**

Admissions Contact: **Walter Peacock, Director of Admissions**
LD Contact: **Ms. Lee Day, Learning Assistance Coordinator**
Name of Program: **Special Services**
Telephone:**(912) 245-2498**

Admissions

Application Information:
Application deadline: **20 days prior to registration**
Rolling Admissions: **Yes**

Secondary School Information
Most Important Criteria For Admissions (1-strongest)

SAT/ACT	Application	School transcript
Class rank	Course selection	Personal statement
Interview	Extra activities	Psychoeducational
G.P.A.	Open admission	Recommendations

Test Requirements:
Untimed SAT: **Yes** Untimed ACT: **Yes** Untimed ACH: **Yes**
Range accepted: **Average +**
Documentation of LD required: **Yes**
Tests recommended: **A full psychoeducational battery of testing to indicate a learning disability is required, if not done prior, USC screens for disabilities. with diagnostic testing.**

Types of Disabilities Served
- Speech/Lang
- Study skills
- Written express
- Organizational
- Perceptual
- Reading
- Spelling
- Math
- Fine Motor
- ADD with LD
- ADD without LD
- ADHD with LD
- ADHD without LD

Admissions Process

LD director not included in process of admissions. Student identifies self by returning Student Data Sheet included in acceptance letter.

High School Course Requirements:
English: **4** Math: **3** Science: **3** Foreign Language: **2**
Waivers to standard high school courses
Course substitution: **Yes**

Learning Disability Program

Program: Reinforces course work: **Yes**
Program available through: **Year round**
Students mainstreamed **100** % of the day
Recommended credits per semester: **10-12**
Counseling: Individual: **Yes** Vocational Counseling: **Yes**

Faculty:
Faculty: **3** Including Director: **Yes** Full time: **1** Part time: **2**
LD faculty with: BS/BA: **2** M.A.: **1**
Faculty advocate: **Yes** Meets with instructor: **As needed**

Diagnostic Testing
- ADD
- ADHD
- I.Q.
- Math
- Personality
- Organization
- Handwriting
- Social skills
- Perceptual skills
- Fine motor skills
- Spoken language
- Written language
- Spelling
- Reading
- Study skills

Tutoring:
Average size of group tutorials: **One-on-one**
Services rendered by:
- Graduates
- Peers
- Faculty
- LD staff
- Teacher trainees

Tutorials

Grp.	Ind.	Tutorials	Grp.	Ind.	Tutorials
	•	Math skills		•	Word processing
	•	Study skills		•	Time management
	•	Language arts		•	Learning strategies
	•	Written express		•	Organizational skills

Academic Accommodations

Curriculum	Study Aids	Exams
• Priority registration	Typist	• Oral
Math waiver	• Reader	• Untimed
Foreign lang. waiver	• Notetaker	• Take home
Course substitution	• Proof reader	• With proctor
In Class	• Text on tape	• On computer
• Calculators	Early syllabus	• Extended time
• Tape recorder	Taped handouts	• On tape
• Word processor		Modified
• Priority seating		• Separate room

Graduation Requirements:
Course credits: **183** GPA: **2.0**
Other requirements: **Health 200, University system Regents' Test. Some degree programs require more than 183 credit hours, GA/US history and constitution.**

Program Strengths
We have a small program and strive to give each student personal attention. We have the support of the administration and a faculty willing to work with students who need modifications.

General Information:
Valdosta State College is a 4 year public college. Suburban campus of 168 acres is 125 miles from Jacksonville, FL. Accessible by plane or bus. Ski areas are 350 miles from campus. Beaches are 100 miles from campus. 1% of students are foreign. 9 residential halls on campus. Housing is not guaranteed. 30 % of students remain on campus for the weekends. 15 % of students join fraternities/sororities.

Accreditation: SACS, AACSB, NCATE, NLN

Expenses:
Tuition: In-state: Full year: $546.00 per quarter. Part-time: Per credit:$36.00. Part-time: Per course: $180.00. Tuition: Out-of-state: Full year: $1,406.00 per quarter. Part-time: Per credit:$72.00. Part-time: Per course:$360.00 Room and board: $920.00 per quarter

Majors

• BUSINESS Accounting, Banking/Finance, Business Administration, Business Economics, Marketing • COMMUNICATIONS Communication, English, Speech/Debate/Forensic, Telecommunications, Television/Radio/Film • EDUCATION Art, Business, Early Childhood, Elementary, Health, Middle School, Music, Science, Secondary • HEALTH SCIENCES Nursing • HUMANITIES Philosophy • LANGUAGES French, Spanish • PRE PROFESSIONAL Engineering, Law, Social Work • SCIENCES Astronomy, Biology, Chemistry, Computer Science, Mathematics, Physics • SOCIAL SCIENCES Anthropology, Criminal Justice, History, Political Science, Psychology, Public Relations, Social Science, Sociology • VISUAL AND PERFORMING ARTS Dramatic Arts, Fine Arts, Music

Less Selective

West Georgia College
Carrollton, Georgia 30118-0001
(404) 836-6428

School Enrollment: **7,000** Male: **3,400** Female: **3,600**
LD Enrollment: **30** Male: **16** Female: **14**

Admissions Contact: **Jennifer Payne, Director of Admissions**
LD Contact: **Dr. Ann Phillips, Coordinator**
Name of Program: **Disabled Student Services**
Address: **137 Mandeville Hall**
Telephone:**(404) 836-6428**

Admissions

Application Information:
Application deadline: **None**
Rolling Admissions: **Yes**

Secondary School Information
Most Important Criteria For Admissions (1-strongest)

1 SAT/ACT	Application	**1** School transcript
Class rank	Course selection	Personal statement
Interview	Extra activities	Psychoeducational
1 G.P.A.	Open admission	Recommendations

Test Requirements:
Diagnostic testing waived: **Yes**
Untimed SAT: **Yes** Untimed ACT: **Yes**
Documentation of LD required: **Yes**
Currency of diagnostic testing: **3 years**
Tests recommended: **Diagnostic testing and a document of deficit are required for services, not admissions.**

Types of Disabilities Served
- Speech/Lang
- Study skills
- Written express
- Organizational
- Perceptual
- Reading
- Spelling
- Math
- Fine Motor
- ADD with LD
- ADD without LD
- ADHD with LD
- ADHD without LD

Admissions Process

The same as for all students. There is no admissions process for the LD services/support.

High School Course Requirements:
English: **4** Math: **3** Science: **3** Foreign Language: **2**

Learning Disability Program

Program: Reinforces course work: **Yes**
Students mainstreamed **100** % of the day
Recommended credits per semester: **10-15**
Services available for all students: **Yes**
Counseling: Individual: **Yes** Vocational Counseling: **Yes**
Support groups are available:**Sometimes**

Faculty:
Faculty: **1** Part time: **1** Ph.D.: **1**
Faculty advocate: **Yes** Meets with instructor: **As necessary**

Diagnostic Testing
ADD •	Personality	Perceptual skills	Spelling
ADHD	Organization	Fine motor skills	Reading
I.Q.	Handwriting	Spoken language	Study skills
Math	Social skills	Written language	

Tutoring:
Average size of group tutorials:
Services rendered by:
•Graduates   Peers   •Faculty   LD staff   Teacher trainees

Tutorials
Grp.	Ind.	Tutorials	Grp.	Ind.	Tutorials
•		Math skills			Word processing
		Study skills			Time management
		Language arts		•	Learning strategies
•		Written express			Organizational skills

Academic Accommodations

Curriculum	Study Aids	Exams
• Priority registration	Typist	• Oral
Math waiver	• Reader	Untimed
Foreign lang. waiver	• Notetaker	Take home
• Course substitution	Proof reader	• With proctor
In Class	• Text on tape	On computer
• Calculators	• Early syllabus	• Extended time
• Tape recorder	Taped handouts	• On tape
• Word processor		• Modified
• Priority seating		• Separate room

Graduation Requirements:
Course credits: **196** GPA: **2.0**

Program Strengths

Learning disability services are aimed toward helping the student to be successful at the college. A student disability report is given to each LD student to take to teachers if he wishes. Content: the kind of learning disability, how it affects student in classroom, what accommodations are needed, strengths possessed by the student.

General Information:

West Georgia College is a 4 year public college. Rural campus 50 miles from Atlanta. Accessible by private car only. Ski areas are 2 miles from campus. Beaches are 6 miles from campus. 1% of students are foreign. 11 residential halls on campus. Housing is not guaranteed.10 % of students remain on campus for the weekends. 14 % of students join fraternities/sororities.

Accreditation:Regional

SAT/ACT Scores:
Scores for incoming freshmen:**Verbal:**87.8%below 500. 11.0%between 500 and 599. 1.1%between 600 and 699. .1%above 700. **Math:**77.1% below 500. 18.2% between 500 and 599. 4.6% between 600 and 699. .2%above 700. **ACT:** 25.4% below 20. 69.8% between 20 and 23. 4.7%between 24 and 25l.

Expenses:
Tuition: In-state: Full year: $430.00 per quarter. Part-time: Per credit:$36.00. Part-time: Per course: $180.00. Tuition: Out-of-state: Full year: $1,290.00. Part-time: Per credit:$108.00. Part-time: Per course:$540.00
Room and board: $912.00 per quarter

Majors

• BUSINESS Accounting, Banking, Business Administration, Business Economics, Business Education, Business Management, Economics, Finance, Management, Management Information Systems, Marketing

• COMMUNICATIONS Communication, English • COMPUTER SCIENCE Computer Science • EDUCATION Early Childhood, Elementary, Middle School, Music, Science, Secondary, Social Science, Special • HEALTH SCIENCES Nursing • HUMANITIES Philosophy • LANGUAGES French, Spanish • SCIENCES Biology, Chemistry, Earth, Geography, Geology, Gerontology, Mathematics, Physics • SOCIAL SCIENCES Anthropology, Criminal Justice, History, Political Science, Psychology, Sociology • VISUAL AND PERFORMING ARTS Dramatic Arts, Fine Arts, Music, Music Theater, Music Theory & Composition • VOCATIONAL Business and Office, Park/Recreation, Secretarial

Sports/Activities

• SPORTS RELATED Marching Band • SPORTS-INTERCOLLEGIATE Baseball (M), Basketball, Cross Country, Football (M), Golf (M), Softball (F), Tennis, Volleyball (F) • SPORTS-INTRAMURAL Badminton, Basketball, Bowling, Cross Country, Golf, Ping-Pong, Soccer, Softball, Swimming, Tennis, Volleyball, Water Polo, Wrestling • STUDENT LIFE ACTIVITIES Fraternities, Jazz Band, Magazine, Music Ensembles, Musical Theater, Newspaper, Opera, Political Groups, Radio/TV station, Religious Organization, Sororities, Student Government

Selective **Hawaii**
Services

Brigham Young University-Hawaii
BYU Box 1973
Laie, Hawaii 96762-1294
(808) 293-3738

School Enrollment: **2,000** Male: **1,200** Female: **800**

Admissions Contact: **David Settle, Director of Admissions**
LD Contact: **Midge Oler, Counselor**
Name of Program: **Special Needs**
Telephone:**(808) 293-3558**

Admissions

Application Information:
Application deadline: **February**
Rolling Admissions: **Yes**

Secondary School Information
Most Important Criteria For Admissions (1-strongest)

	SAT/ACT **2**	Application **3**	School transcript
6	Class rank **8**	Course selection **5**	Personal statement
4	Interview **7**	Extra activities	Psychoeducational
3	G.P.A.	Open admission	Recommendations

Types of Disabilities Served
• Speech/Lang • Reading • ADD with LD
• Study skills • Spelling ADD without LD
• Written express • Math • ADHD with LD
• Organizational • Fine Motor ADHD without LD
• Perceptual

Learning Disability Program
Counseling: Individual: **Yes**

Faculty:
Faculty: **1** Part time: **1**
Faculty advocate: **Yes** Meets with instructor: **As needed**

Diagnostic Testing
ADD	Personality	Perceptual skills	Spelling
ADHD	Organization	Fine motor skills	Reading
I.Q.	Handwriting	Spoken language	Study skills
Math	Social skills	Written language	

Tutoring:
Average size of group tutorials: **10**
Services rendered by:
Graduates Peers •Faculty LD staff Teacher trainees

Tutorials
Grp.	Ind.	Tutorials	Grp.	Ind.	Tutorials
•	•	Math skills	•		Word processing
•	•	Study skills	•		Time management
•	•	Language arts	•		Learning strategies
•	•	Written express	•		Organizational skills

Academic Accommodations
Curriculum	Study Aids	Exams
Priority registration	• Typist	• Oral
Math waiver	Reader	Untimed
Foreign lang. waiver	• Notetaker	• Take home
• Course substitution	• Proof reader	With proctor
In Class	• Text on tape	On computer
• Calculators	Early syllabus	• Extended time
• Tape recorder	Taped handouts	On tape
• Word processor		• Modified
Priority seating		Separate room

Program Strengths
We do not have a program as such. In our population we do have some students with learning disabilities and they are handled on an individual basis. Students have to meet the admission requirements. They also need to be members of the Church of Jesus Christ of Latter Day Saints and comply with our Code of Honors.

General Information:
Brigham Young University-Hawaii is a 4 year private Church of Latter Day Saints university. Rural campus 35 miles from Honolulu. Accessible by bus. Beaches are 5 miles from campus. 5 residential halls on campus. Housing is not guaranteed.

Accreditation:WASC

Expenses:
Tuition: In-state: Full year: $1,800.00. Room and board: $3,165.00

Majors
• BUSINESS Accounting, Business Administration, Business Education, Hotel & Restaurant Management, International Business, Travel/Tourism Management • COMMUNICATIONS Communication, English, Graphic Design • COMPUTER SCIENCE Computer Maintenance, Computer Science, Data Processing, Systems Analysis • EDUCATION Art, Child Development, Early Childhood, Elementary, English, Industrial, Middle School, Music, Physical, Recreation/Youth Leadership, Secondary • LANGUAGES Japanese, Spanish • PRE PROFESSIONAL Pre-Elementary Education, Social Work • SCIENCES Biology, Botany, Mathematics • SOCIAL SCIENCES Family Counseling, History, Human Service • VISUAL AND PERFORMING ARTS Art, Art History, Dramatic Arts, Music, Theater • VOCATIONAL Business and Office, Electronics Technology, Secretarial

Sports/Activities
• SPORTS RELATED Cheerleading, Marching Band, Pep Band • SPORTS-INTERCOLLEGIATE Basketball (M), Cross Country, Golf (M), Rugby (M), Tennis, Volleyball (F) • SPORTS-INTRAMURAL Basketball, Bowling, Ping-Pong, Racquetball, Rugby (M), Soccer (M), Soft-

ball, Swimming, Track and Field, Volleyball • STUDENT LIFE ACTIVITIES Drama Groups, Ethnic & Cultural Groups, Jazz Band, Music Groups, Newspaper, Radio/TV station, Religious Organization, Student Government, Yearbook

Less Selective	Hawaii
	Services

University of Hawaii: Kapiolani Community College
629 Pensacola Street
Honolulu, Hawaii 96814
(808) 734-9531

School Enrollment: **5,880** Male: **3,000** Female: **2,880**
LD Enrollment: **26**

Admissions Contact: **Cynthia Kimura, Cor. of Enrollment Serv.**
LD Contact: **Gloria Fiedler, Coordinator**
Name of Program: **Special Services**
Telephone:**(808) 734-9552**

Admissions

Application Information:
Application deadline: **July 1st, Dec. 1st**
Rolling Admissions: **Yes**

Secondary School Information
Most Important Criteria For Admissions (1-strongest)

SAT/ACT **1**	Application	School transcript
Class rank	Course selection	Personal statement
1 Interview	Extra activities	**1** Psychoeducational
G.P.A.	Open admission	Recommendations

Test Requirements:
Standardized tests waived: **Yes**

Types of Disabilities Served
- Speech/Lang
- Study skills
- Written express
- Organizational
- Perceptual
- Reading
- Spelling
- Math
- Fine Motor
- ADD with LD
- ADD without LD
- ADHD with LD
- ADHD without LD

High School Course Requirements:
Waivers to standard high school courses
 Course substitution: **Yes**

Faculty:
Faculty: **2** Full time: **2**
Faculty advocate: **Yes** Meets with instructor: **As necessary**

Diagnostic Testing

ADD	Personality	Perceptual skills	Spelling
ADHD	Organization	Fine motor skills	Reading
I.Q.	Handwriting	Spoken language	Study skills
Math	Social skills	Written language	

Tutoring:
Average size of group tutorials: **1:1**
Services rendered by:
•Graduates •Peers Faculty LD staff Teacher trainees

Tutorials

Grp.	Ind.	Tutorials	Grp.	Ind.	Tutorials
	•	Math skills		•	Word processing
	•	Study skills		•	Time management
	•	Language arts		•	Learning strategies
	•	Written express		•	Organizational skills

Academic Accommodations

Curriculum	Study Aids	Exams
Priority registration	Typist	• Oral
Math waiver	Reader	Untimed
Foreign lang. waiver	• Notetaker	• Take home
• Course substitution	• Proof reader	With proctor
In Class	• Text on tape	On computer
• Calculators	Early syllabus	• Extended time
• Tape recorder	Taped handouts	On tape
• Word processor		• Modified
Priority seating		Separate room

Program Strengths
Kapiolani provides support services, not a program, for LD students which consist of academic support in the classroom as well as counseling.

General Information:
University of Hawaii: Kapiolani Community College is a 2 year public university. Urban campus. Accessible by bus. Beaches are 10 from campus. Housing is not guaranteed.

Accreditation:WACS

Expenses:
Tuition: In-state: Full year: $207.50. Part-time: Per credit:$17.00. Tuition: Out-of-state: Full year: $1,237.50. Part-time: Per credit:$103.00.

Majors
• BUSINESS Accounting, Hotel and Restaurant Managemen, Retailing, Taxation • COMPUTER SCIENCE Data Processing • HEALTH SCIENCES Medical Assistant, Medical Technology, Nursing, Occupational Therapy, Physical Therapy, Radiological Therapy • HUMANITIES Liberal Arts • LANGUAGES French, Japanese, Russian • VOCATIONAL Food Service, Legal Secretary, Paralegal, Secretarial

Sports/Activities
• STUDENT LIFE ACTIVITIES Choral, Newspaper, Student Government

Less Selective	Hawaii
	Program

University of Hawaii: Leeward Community College
96-045 Ala Ike
Pearl City, Hawaii 96782
(808) 455-0217

School Enrollment: **6,000** Male: **2,500** Female: **3,500**
LD Enrollment: **150**

Admissions Contact: **Warren Mau, Registrar**
LD Contact: **C. Lynne Douglas, LD Specialist**
Name of Program: **Program for Adult Achievement**
Telephone:**(808) 455-0421 or 0412**

Admissions

Application Information:
Applicant must apply   months in advance

Secondary School Information
Most Important Criteria For Admissions (1-strongest)

SAT/ACT	Application	School transcript
Class rank	Course selection	Personal statement
Interview	Extra activities	Psychoeducational
G.P.A.	**1** Open admission	Recommendations

Test Requirements:
Diagnostic testing waived: **Yes**
Documentation of LD required: **Yes**

Types of Disabilities Served
- Speech/Lang
- Study skills
- Written express
- Organizational
- Perceptual
- Reading
- Spelling
- Math
- Fine Motor

ADD with LD
ADD without LD
ADHD with LD
ADHD without LD

Admissions Process

College enrollment is open door policy: high school graduate or age 18. LD program access is by registration. Students must have documentation of learning disability or receive diagnosis through the program. Registration is not complete until documentation is received.

Learning Disability Program

Program: Remedial: **Yes**
Program: Reinforces course work: **Yes**
Students mainstreamed **100** % of the day
Services only for LD students: **Yes**
Counseling: Individual: **Yes** Group Counseling: **Yes** Vocational Counseling: **Yes**
Support groups are available:**Student support groups available**

Faculty:
Faculty: **2** Including Director: **Yes** Full time: **1** Part time: **1** M.A.: **2**
Faculty advocate: **Yes** Meets with instructor: **As needed**

Diagnostic Testing
- ADD
- ADHD
- I.Q.
- Math

Personality
Organization
Handwriting
Social skills

- Perceptual skills
- Fine motor skills
- Spoken language
- Written language

- Spelling
- Reading
- Study skills

Tutoring:
Average size of group tutorials: **Individual**
Services rendered by:
Graduates •Peers   Faculty   LD staff   Teacher trainees

Tutorials

Grp.	Ind.	Tutorials	Grp.	Ind.	Tutorials
	•	Math skills		•	Word processing
	•	Study skills		•	Time management
	•	Language arts		•	Learning strategies
	•	Written express		•	Organizational skills

Academic Accommodations

Curriculum	Study Aids	Exams
• Priority registration	Typist	• Oral
Math waiver	• Reader	Untimed
Foreign lang. waiver	• Notetaker	• Take home
Course substitution	• Proof reader	• With proctor
In Class	• Text on tape	• On computer
• Calculators	Early syllabus	• Extended time
• Tape recorder	Taped handouts	• On tape
• Word processor		• Modified
Priority seating		• Separate room

Program Strengths

The Program for Adult Achievement at Leeward Community College has been re-established as of Fall, 1989. The program is staffed by a Learning Disabilities Specialist and a Counselor (60% time). We anticipate expansion of services, staff and resources over the next few years once the students are better identified and our program becomes established.

General Information:

University of Hawaii: Leeward Community College is a 2 year public university. Suburban campus 5 miles from Honolulu. Accessible by bus. Beaches are 5 miles from campus. Housing is not guaranteed.

Accreditation: Regional

Expenses:
Tuition: In-state: Full year: $440.00. Part-time: Per credit:$19.00. Tuition: Out-of-state: Full year: $2,680.00. Part-time: Per credit:$224.00.

Majors

• BUSINESS Accounting, Management, Marketing • COMMUNICATIONS Graphic Arts, Television/Radio/Film • COMPUTER SCIENCE Computer Science, Programming • HUMANITIES Liberal Arts • VOCATIONAL Automobile Technology, Drafting, Food Service, Office Administration

Sports/Activities

• STUDENT LIFE ACTIVITIES Choral, Concert Band, Drama Groups, Ethnic & Cultural Groups, Film, Jazz Band, Music Groups, Musical Theater, Newspaper, Radio/TV station, Student Government

Very Selective

Idaho
Services

Albertson College
2112 Cleveland Boulevard
Caldwell, Idaho 83605
(208) 459-5305

School Enrollment: **643** Male: **343** Female: **300**

Admissions Contact: **Carol Kriz, Director of Enrollment**
LD Contact: **Dorothy Gerber, Director of Study Skills**
Name of Program: **Study Skills**
Telephone:**(208) 459-5683**

Admissions

Application Information:
Application deadline: **March 15th**
Rolling Admissions: **Yes**Notified when: **within 2 weeks**

Idaho

Secondary School Information
Most Important Criteria For Admissions (1-strongest)

4 SAT/ACT	1 Application	3 School transcript
6 Class rank	5 Course selection	8 Personal statement
7 Interview	10 Extra activities	11 Psychoeducational
2 G.P.A.	Open admission	9 Recommendations

Test Requirements:
Diagnostic testing waived: **Yes**
Untimed SAT: **Yes** Untimed ACT: **Yes**
Documentation of LD required: **Yes**

Types of Disabilities Served
- Speech/Lang
- Study skills
- Written express
- Organizational
- Perceptual
- Reading
- Spelling
- Math
- Fine Motor

ADD with LD
ADD without LD
ADHD with LD
ADHD without LD

Admissions Process

$25.00 fee; application form, essay, recommendations, and test scores (ACT or SAT).

Learning Disability Program
Time required or recommended in learning center: **varies**
Services available for all students: **Yes**

Faculty:
Faculty: **1** Part time: **1**

Diagnostic Testing

ADD	Personality	Perceptual skills	Spelling
ADHD	Organization	Fine motor skills	Reading
I.Q.	Handwriting	Spoken language	Study skills
Math	Social skills	Written language	

Tutoring:
Average size of group tutorials: **15-25**
Services rendered by:

Graduates	Peers	Faculty	•LD staff	•Teacher trainees

Tutorials

Grp.	Ind.	Tutorials	Grp.	Ind.	Tutorials
		Math skills			Word processing
•	•	Study skills	•	•	Time management
•	•	Language arts	•	•	Learning strategies
•	•	Written express	•	•	Organizational skills

Academic Accommodations

Curriculum	Study Aids	Exams
Priority registration	Typist	• Oral
Math waiver	Reader	Untimed
Foreign lang. waiver	Notetaker	Take home
Course substitution	• Proof reader	With proctor
In Class	Text on tape	On computer
• Calculators	Early syllabus	• Extended time
• Tape recorder	Taped handouts	On tape
• Word processor		• Modified
Priority seating		Separate room

Graduation Requirements:
Course credits: **124** GPA: **2.0**

Program Strengths
The College of Idaho does not have a true LD program. It does offer assistance for minimal disabilities by allowing extended time for exam writing, tape recorders in class, etc. Arrangements can be made for tutoring. The Study Skills coordinator is available for assistance with general study assistance and tutoring. The college is not equipped for the physically handicapped. Because of the low faculty/ student ratio, faculty is available to give assistance.

General Information:
Albertson College is a 4 year private college. Rural campus of 40 acres is 35 miles from Boise. Accessible by bus. Ski areas are 50 miles from campus. 4.2% of students are foreign. 5 residential halls on campus. Housing is guaranteed.Guaranteed through 4th year. 80 % of students remain on campus for the weekends. 20 % of students join fraternities/sororities.

Accreditation:NWACS

SAT/ACT Scores:
Scores for incoming freshmen:**Verbal:**40%below 500. 31%between 500 and 599. 14%between 600 and 699. 5%above 700. **Math:**39% below 500. 27% between 500 and 599. 25% between 600 and 699. 9%above 700. **ACT:** 15% below 20. 30% between 20 and 23. 24%between 24 and 25l. 13%between 26 and 28. 19% above 28.

Class Rank:
About 45% of the present freshmen class were in the upper 20% of their high school class. 62% were in the top 40% of their class.

Expenses:
Tuition: In-state: Full year: $10,750.00. Part-time: Per credit:$304.00. Tuition: Out-of-state: Full year: $10,750.00. Part-time: Per credit:$304.00. Room and board: $2,850.00

Majors
• ARTS Art, Music, Music Performance • BUSINESS Accounting, Business Administration, Business Economics, Business Management, Economics, Management, Marketing, Sports Management • COMPUTER SCIENCE Information Systems, Management Information System • EDUCATION Elementary, English, Music, Physical, Secondary • HUMANITIES English/Writing/Literature, Philosophy, Religion • LANGUAGES French, German, Spanish • MATHEMATICS Applied, Computer, Theoretical • PREPROFESSIONAL Dentistry, Engineering, Law, Medicine, Pharmacy, Sports Medicine, Veterinarian • RELIGIOUS STUDIES Philosophy • SCIENCES Biology, Chemistry, Physics • SOCIAL SCIENCES Anthropology, History, Political Science, Psychology, Sociology • VISUAL AND PERFORMING ARTS Art, Music, Music Performance, Theater

Sports/Activities
• SPORTS-INTERCOLLEGIATE Baseball (M), Basketball (M), Skiing - Cross Country, Skiing - Snow, Soccer, Tennis (F), Volleyball (F)

Less Selective

Idaho Accommodations

Boise Bible College
8695 Marigold Street
Boise, Idaho 83714-1220
(208) 376-7731

School Enrollment: **90** Male: **61** Female: **29**

Admissions Contact: **Steve Crane, Director of Recruitment**
LD Contact: **Carl A. Anderson, Academic Dean**

Admissions

Application Information:
Application deadline: **September 1st**
Rolling Admissions: **Yes**

Secondary School Information
Most Important Criteria For Admissions (1-strongest)

8	SAT/ACT	1	Application	6	School transcript
5	Class rank		Course selection	3	Personal statement
7	Interview		Extra activities		Psychoeducational
4	G.P.A.		Open admission	2	Recommendations

Types of Disabilities Served

Speech/Lang	• Reading	ADD with LD
• Study skills	Spelling	ADD without LD
• Written express	Math	ADHD with LD
• Organizational	Fine Motor	ADHD without LD
Perceptual		

Diagnostic Testing

ADD	Personality	Perceptual skills	Spelling
ADHD	Organization	Fine motor skills	Reading
I.Q.	Handwriting	Spoken language	Study skills
Math	Social skills	Written language	

Tutoring:
Average size of group tutorials: **2-5**
Services rendered by:

Graduates	Peers	•Faculty	LD staff	Teacher trainees

Tutorials

Grp.	Ind.	Tutorials	Grp.	Ind.	Tutorials
		Math skills			Word processing
•		Study skills	•		Time management
•		Language arts	•		Learning strategies
•		Written express	•		Organizational skills

Academic Accommodations

Curriculum	Study Aids	Exams
Priority registration	Typist	Oral
Math waiver	Reader	Untimed
Foreign lang. waiver	Notetaker	Take home
Course substitution	Proof reader	With proctor
In Class	Text on tape	On computer
Calculators	Early syllabus	Extended time
Tape recorder	Taped handouts	On tape
Word processor		Modified
Priority seating		Separate room

Graduation Requirements:
Course credits: **128** GPA: **2.0** Years to complete degree: **4-5**

Program Strengths
We do not have a program as such, but if a student applies and has a slight deficit we will offer group tutoring. We do not require SAT or ACT tests but we have a diagnostic test that evaluates English and Bible knowledge.

General Information:
Boise Bible College is a 4 year private college. Suburban campus of 16 acres is 3 miles from Boise. Accessible by air, train or bus. 5% of students are foreign. Housing is not guaranteed. 50 % of students remain on campus for the weekends.

Accreditation: AABC

Expenses:
Tuition: In-state: Full year: $2,730.00. Part-time: Per credit: $116.00.
Room and board: $2,696.00

Majors
• AREA STUDIES Bible • EDUCATION Christian • HUMANITIES Religious Studies • VISUAL AND PERFORMING ARTS Religious Music

Sports
• SPORTS-INTRAMURAL Basketball, Ping-Pong, Soccer (M), Volleyball
• STUDENT LIFE ACTIVITIES Choral, Drama Groups, Student Government, Yearbook

---

Selective **Idaho**
Services

University of Idaho
Moscow, Idaho 83843
(208) 885-6326

School Enrollment: **9,804** Male: **5,764** Female: **4,040**
LD Enrollment: **50** Male: **25** Female: **25**

Admissions Contact: **Peter Brown, Director of Admissions**
LD Contact: **Meredith Goodwin, Dir., Student Support Services**
Name of Program: **Student Suport Services**
Address: **Phinney Hall 302, University of Idaho**
Telephone: **(208) 885-6746**

Admissions

Application Information:
LD on admissions committee: **Yes**
Applicant must apply **4-8** months in advance

Secondary School Information
Most Important Criteria For Admissions (1-strongest)

2	SAT/ACT	3	Application	6	School transcript
4	Class rank	5	Course selection		Personal statement
	Interview		Extra activities		Psychoeducational
1	G.P.A.		Open admission		Recommendations

Test Requirements:
Diagnostic testing waived: **Yes**
Untimed SAT: **Yes** Untimed ACT: **Yes**
WAIS-R required: **Yes**
Documentation of LD required: **Yes**
Currency of diagnostic testing: **no more than 3 years**
Tests recommended: **WAIS-R, Woodcock-Johnson**

Types of Disabilities Served

• Speech/Lang	• Reading	• ADD with LD
• Study skills	• Spelling	• ADD without LD
• Written express	• Math	• ADHD with LD
• Organizational	• Fine Motor	• ADHD without LD
• Perceptual		

High School Course Requirements:
English: **4** Math: **3** Science: **3**

Illinois

Learning Disability Program
Program: Reinforces course work: **Yes**
Students mainstreamed **100** % of the day
Services available for all students: **Yes**
Counseling: Individual: **Yes** Vocational Counseling: **Yes**
Support groups are available:**Yes, through SSS**

Faculty:
Faculty: **5** Including Director: **Yes** Full time: **2** Part time: **3**
LD faculty with: BS/BA: **5** M.A.: **5**
Faculty advocate: **Yes** Meets with instructor: **As needed**

Diagnostic Testing
ADD • Personality • Perceptual skills • Spelling
ADHD Organization Fine motor skills • Reading
• I.Q. Handwriting Spoken language • Study skills
• Math Social skills• Written language

Tutoring:
Average size of group tutorials: **2-6**
Services rendered by:
•Graduates •Peers Faculty •LD staff Teacher trainees

Tutorials
Grp.	Ind.	Tutorials	Grp.	Ind.	Tutorials
•	•	Math skills			Word processing
•	•	Study skills	•	•	Time management
		Language arts	•	•	Learning strategies
•	•	Written express	•	•	Organizational skills

Academic Accommodations
Curriculum	Study Aids	Exams
Priority registration	Typist	• Oral
Math waiver	Reader	• Untimed
Foreign lang. waiver	Notetaker	Take home
Course substitution	• Proof reader	• With proctor
In Class	• Text on tape	• On computer
• Calculators	Early syllabus	• Extended time
• Tape recorder	Taped handouts	On tape
Word processor		• Modified
Priority seating		• Separate room

Graduation Requirements:
Course credits: **128** GPA: **2.0** Years to complete degree: **7** Math waiver:
Yes Language waiver: **Yes**

Program Strengths
Individualized, comprehensive service.

General Information:
University of Idaho is a 4 year public university. rural campus of 7,924 acres is 90 miles from Spokane, Washington. Accessible by plane, bus or car. Ski areas are 30 minutes from campus. Beaches are 5 hours from campus. 5% of students are foreign. Housing is guaranteed.Guaranteed through 4th year. 30 % of students join fraternities/sororities.

Accreditation:ABET, ASLA, NAAB, NASM, NCATE, SAF

Class Rank: 85% were in the top 60% of their class. 98% were in the top 80% of their class.

Expenses:
Tuition: In-state: Full year: $648.00 per semester. Part-time: Per credit:$65.00. Tuition: Out-of-state: Full year: $2,098.00 per semester. Part-time: Per credit:$135.00. Room and board: $3,060.00

Majors
• AGRICULTURE Business, Education, Engineering, Horticultural, Journalism, Plant Science • ANIMAL SCIENCE Dairy, Poultry • AREA STUDIES American • ARTS Dance, Design, Interior Design, Landscaping, Music, Music History, Music Performance, Photography, Theater Design • COMMUNICATIONS Creative Writing, English, Journalism • ENGINEERING Agricultural, Chemical, Civil/Environmental, Computer, Electrical, Geological, Mechanical, Metallurgical, Mining/Mineral • HUMANITIES English/Writing/Literature, Liberal/General • LANGUAGES English, French, German, Spanish • SCIENCES Anatomy, Anthropology, Physics, Physiology • SOCIAL SCIENCES Anthropology, Family Counseling, Geography, Government/Political, History, International Studies, Library Science, Political Science, Psychology, Sociology

Sports/Activities
• SPORTS-INTERCOLLEGIATE Basketball, Basketball (F), Basketball (M), Cross Country, Cross Country (F), Cross Country (M), Football, Football (M), Golf, Golf (F), Golf (M), Rodeo, Tennis (F), Tennis (M), Track and Field (F), Track and Field (M), Volleyball (F)

Selective   **Illinois Program**

Barat College
700 East Westleigh Road
Lake Forest, Illinois 60045
(708) 234-3000

School Enrollment: **719** Male: **162** Female: **557**
LD Enrollment: **45**

Admissions Contact: **Loretta Brickman, Director of Admissions**
LD Contact: **Pamela Adelman, Director**
Name of Program: **Learning Opportunities Program**
Telephone:**(708) 234-3000**

Admissions

Application Information:
LD Students Applying: **60** Enrolled:**45**
Application deadline: **May 1st**
Applicant must apply **12** months in advance
Rolling Admissions: **Yes**

Secondary School Information
Most Important Criteria For Admissions (1-strongest)
	SAT/ACT		Application		School transcript
	Class rank	1	Course selection		Personal statement
1	Interview		Extra activities	1	Psychoeducational
	G.P.A.		Open admission	1	Recommendations

Test Requirements:
Diagnostic testing waived: **Yes**
Untimed SAT: **Yes** Untimed ACT: **Yes** Untimed ACH: **Yes**
WAIS-R required: **Yes**
Documentation of LD required: **Yes**
Tests recommended: **Psychoeducational**

Types of Disabilities Served
• Speech/Lang	• Reading	• ADD with LD
• Study skills	• Spelling	ADD without LD
• Written express	• Math	• ADHD with LD
• Organizational	• Fine Motor	ADHD without LD
• Perceptual		

Learning Disability Program

Program: Remedial: **Yes**
Program: Reinforces course work: **Yes**
Students mainstreamed **100** % of the day
Services only for LD students: **Yes**
Counseling: Individual: **Yes** Group Counseling: **Yes**

Faculty:
Faculty: **4** Full time: **4** M.A.: **3** Ph.D.: **1**
Faculty advocate: **Yes** Meets with instructor: **As needed**

Diagnostic Testing
ADD	Personality •	Perceptual skills	• Spelling
ADHD•	Organization•	Fine motor skills	• Reading
• I.Q.	• Handwriting•	Spoken language	• Study skills
• Math	• Social skills•	Written language	

Tutoring:
Average size of group tutorials: **2-5**
Services rendered by:
 Graduates Peers •Faculty LD staff Teacher trainees

Tutorials
Grp.	Ind. Tutorials	Grp.	Ind. Tutorials
•	• Math skills		• Word processing
	• Study skills		• Time management
	• Language arts		• Learning strategies
	• Written express		• Organizational skills

Academic Accommodations
Curriculum	Study Aids	Exams
Priority registration	• Typist	• Oral
Math waiver	Reader	Untimed
Foreign lang. waiver	• Notetaker	• Take home
Course substitution	• Proof reader	With proctor
In Class	• Text on tape	On computer
• Calculators	Early syllabus	• Extended time
• Tape recorder	Taped handouts	On tape
• Word processor		• Modified
• Priority seating		Separate room

Graduation Requirements:
Course credits: **120**

Program Strengths
The Learning Opportunities Program is a highly individualized, closely monitored program. Students work with professional LD specialists who provide support in course work and remediation of specific deficit areas.

General Information:
Barat College is a 4 year private Roman Catholic college. Suburban campus of 30 acres is 29 miles from Chicago. Accessible by train, air or bus. Ski areas are 60 miles from campus. Beaches are 2 miles from campus. 6% of students are foreign. 3 residential halls on campus. Housing is guaranteed.80 % of students remain on campus for the weekends.

Accreditation:NCACS

SAT/ACT Scores:
Scores for incoming freshmen:**Verbal:**80%below 500. 20%between 500 and 599. **Math:**75% below 500. 24% between 500 and 599. **ACT:** 24% below 20. 45% between 20 and 23. 19%between 24 and 25l. 12%between 26 and 28.

Class Rank:
About 22% of the present freshmen class were in the upper 20% of their

high school class. 41% were in the top 40% of their class. 57% were in the top 60% of their class. 85% were in the top 80% of their class.

Expenses:
Tuition: In-state: Full year: $8,640.00. Part-time: Per credit:$288.00. Tuition: Out-of-state: Full year: $8.640.00. Part-time: Per credit:$288.00. Room and board: $3,300.00

Majors
• AREA STUDIES Public Policy • BUSINESS Accounting, Banking, Business Administration, Business Economics, Business Management, Economics, Finance, International Business, Management, Marketing • COMMUNICATIONS Creative Writing, English, Photography • COMPUTER SCIENCE Computer Mathematics, Computer Science, Programming • EDUCATION Art Therapy, Elementary, Mathematics, Middle School, Secondary, Social Studies, Special • HEALTH SCIENCES Health, Medical Technology, Nursing, Physical Therapy • HUMANITIES Humanities, Philosophy, Religion • LANGUAGES French, Spanish • SCIENCES Chemistry, Mathematics • SOCIAL SCIENCES History, Human Resource Development, Political, Psychology, Social Sciences, Sociology • VISUAL AND PERFORMING ARTS Art, Art History, Dance, Dramatic Arts, Fine Arts, Studio Art, Theater

Sports/Activities
• SPORTS-INTRAMURAL Baseball, Basketball (M), Volleyball (F)
• STUDENT LIFE ACTIVITIES Choral, Community Service, Dance, Drama Groups, Ethnic & Cultural Groups, Magazine, Music Groups, Musical Theater, Newspaper, Political Groups, Religious Organization, Student Government, Yearbook

---

Selective **Illinois**
Accommodations

Bradley University
1501 West Bradley Avenue
Peoria, Illinois 61625
(309) 677-1000

School Enrollment: **4,800** Male: **2,400** Female: **2,400**
LD Enrollment: **15** Male: **8** Female: **7**

Admissions Contact: **Gary Bergman, Director of Admissions**
LD Contact: **Carolyn Griffith, Coordinator**
Name of Program: **Learning Assistance Program**
Address: **Cullom Davis Library 312**
Telephone:**(309) 677-2845**

Admissions

Application Information:
Application deadline: **June 1st**
Applicant must apply **4-12** months in advance
Rolling Admissions: **Yes**

Secondary School Information
Most Important Criteria For Admissions (1-strongest)
4 SAT/ACT		Application	**1**	School transcript
2 Class rank	**3**	Course selection	**5**	Personal statement
5 Interview	**7**	Extra activities	**2**	Psychoeducational
3 G.P.A.		Open admission	**6**	Recommendations

Test Requirements:
Diagnostic testing waived: **Yes**
Untimed SAT: **Yes** Untimed ACT: **Yes** Achievement tests required:**N/A**
Documentation of LD required: **Yes**
Tests recommended: **LD diagnosed and documented**

Illinois

Types of Disabilities Served

- Speech/Lang • Reading • ADD with LD
- Study skills • Spelling • ADD without LD
- Written express • Math   ADHD with LD
- Organizational   Fine Motor • ADHD without LD
- Perceptual

Learning Disability Program

Syllabus available during orientation:**Yes**
Students mainstreamed **100** % of the day
Services available for all students: **Yes**
Counseling: Individual: **Yes**

Faculty:

Faculty: **4** Full time: **2** Part time: **2**
LD faculty with: BS/BA: **4** M.A.: **4**
Meets with instructor: **As needed**

Diagnostic Testing

ADD	• Personality	• Perceptual skills	Spelling
ADHD	• Organization	Fine motor skills	• Reading
• I.Q.	Handwriting	Spoken language	• Study skills
• Math	Social skills	Written language	

Tutoring:

Average size of group tutorials: **varies**
Services rendered by:
•Graduates •Peers   Faculty •LD staff   Teacher trainees

Tutorials

Grp.	Ind.	Tutorials	Grp.	Ind.	Tutorials
	•	Math skills		•	Word processing
•	•	Study skills	•	•	Time management
		Language arts		•	Learning strategies
	•	Written express		•	Organizational skills

Academic Accommodations

Curriculum	Study Aids	Exams
Priority registration	• Typist	Oral
Math waiver	Reader	Untimed
• Foreign lang. waiver	Notetaker	• Take home
Course substitution	Proof reader	With proctor
In Class	Text on tape	On computer
• Calculators	Early syllabus	• Extended time
• Tape recorder	Taped handouts	On tape
• Word processor		Modified
Priority seating		Separate room

Graduation Requirements:

Course credits: **124 minimum** GPA: **2.0**

Program Strengths

We teach structured classes in speed reading and study skills, individualized and group, for full or part-time students. We offer mini talks on tapes like study skills and time management as the need arises. We also monitor extended time for tests for LD students as requested.

General Information:

Bradley University is a 4 year private university. Urban campus of 65 acres is 2 miles from Peoria. Accessible by air, train or bus. 3% of students are foreign. 10 residential halls on campus. Housing is guaranteed.Guaranteed through the 4th year. 80 % of students remain on campus for the weekends. 30 % of students join fraternities/sororities.

Accreditation:NCACS

Expenses:

Tuition: In-state: Full year: $8,500.00. Tuition: Out-of-state: Full year: $8,500.00. Room and board: $3,600.00

Majors

• AREA STUDIES Asian, Urban • BUSINESS Accounting, Banking, Business Administration, Business Economics, Business Education, Business Management, Economics, Finance, Food Management, International Business, Management, Marketing, Marketing Research • COMMUNICATIONS Advertising, Broadcasting, Communication, Creative Writing, English, Journalism, Speech, Television/Radio/Film • COMPUTER SCIENCE Computer Science, Systems Analysis • CRAFTS AND DESIGN Ceramics, Graphic Design, Mechanical Design Technology, Printmaking • EDUCATION Art, Early Childhood, Elementary, Home Economics, Middle School, Music, Nursing Education, Secondary, Special • ENGINEERING Civil/Environmental, Computer, Electrical, Engineering Science, Geological, Industrial, Manufacturing • HEALTH SCIENCES Medical Technology, Nursing, Physical Therapy, Speech/Audiology and Speech • HUMANITIES English/Writing/Literature, Humanities, Philosophy, Religion • LANGUAGES French, German, Spanish • PREPROFESSIONAL Dentistry, Law, Medicine, Social Work • SCIENCES Actuarial Technology, Biochemistry, Chemistry, Earth, Geography, Geology, Mathematics, Physical Science, Physics • SOCIAL SCIENCES Criminal Justice, Geography, Government/Political, History, Human Service, International Studies, Psychology, Public Relations, Social Sciences, Sociology • VISUAL AND PERFORMING ARTS Art, Art History, Dramatic Arts, Studio Art, Theater • VOCATIONAL Construction, Electronics Technology, Fashion Merchandising, Home Economics, Interior Design

Sports/Activities

• SPORTS RELATED Cheerleading, Chess, Marching Band, Pep Band, Team Managers • SPORTS-INTERCOLLEGIATE Baseball (M), Basketball, Bowling, Cross Country, Diving (M), Golf (F), Ice Hockey (M), Soccer (M), Swimming (M), Tennis, Track and Field, Volleyball (F) • SPORTS-INTRAMURAL Badminton, Basketball, Bowling, Boxing, Cross Country, Fencing, Golf, Hand Ball, Horseback Riding, Ice Hockey (M), Karate, Ping-Pong, Racquetball, Riflery, Rugby, Scuba, Soccer (M), Softball, Swimming, Tennis, Track and Field, Volleyball, Weight Lifting, Wrestling • STUDENT LIFE ACTIVITIES Academic Clubs, Choral, Community Service, Concert Band, Dance, Debate, Drama Groups, Ethnic & Cultural Groups, Fraternities, Jazz Band, Magazine, Music Ensemble, Music Groups, Musical Theater, Newspaper, Political Groups, Radio/TV station, Religious Organization, Sororities, Student Government, Symphony Orchestra, Yearbook

---

Less Selective   **Illinois**
                                                         Services

City Colleges of Chicago: Harold Washington College

30 E. Lake Street
Chicago, Illinois 60601
(312) 984-2760

School Enrollment: **7,528** Male: **2,687** Female: **4,841**
LD Enrollment: **12**

Admissions Contact: **Doranne Polcrack, Director**
LD Contact: **Deborah Miles, Special Needs Coordinator**
Name of Program: **Special Needs Center**
Address: **30 E. Lake St.**
Telephone:**(312) 984-2760**

Admissions

Application Information:
Application deadline: **None**
Rolling Admissions: **Yes**

Secondary School Information
Most Important Criteria For Admissions (1-strongest)

SAT/ACT	Application	School transcript
Class rank	Course selection	Personal statement
Interview	Extra activities	Psychoeducational
G.P.A.	Open admission	Recommendations

Test Requirements:
Diagnostic testing waived: **Yes**
Untimed SAT: **Yes** Untimed ACT: **Yes**
Documentation of LD required: **Yes**
Tests recommended: **Placement testing (as for non-LD) is required before registration.**

Types of Disabilities Served
- Speech/Lang
- Study skills
- Written express
- Organizational
- Perceptual
- Reading
- Spelling
- Math
- Fine Motor
- ADD with LD
- ADD without LD
- ADHD with LD
- ADHD without LD

Admissions Process

Have high school and ACT transcripts, GED test scores, or previous college transcripts mailed to Admissions Office. Fill out admissions application form. Receive permit to register and invitation to orientation. Attend orientation to learn about the registration process and the college in general.

Learning Disability Program

Special orientation for LD students: **Yes**

Faculty:
Faculty: **32** Full time: **2** Part time: **30**

Diagnostic Testing

ADD	Personality	Perceptual skills	Spelling
ADHD	Organization	Fine motor skills	Reading
I.Q.	Handwriting	Spoken language	Study skills
Math	Social skills	Written language	

Tutoring:
Average size of group tutorials: **5**
Services rendered by:
- Graduates
- Peers
Faculty LD staff Teacher trainees

Tutorials

Grp.	Ind.	Tutorials	Grp.	Ind.	Tutorials
		Math skills			Word processing
		Study skills			Time management
		Language arts			Learning strategies
		Written express			Organizational skills

Academic Accommodations

Curriculum	Study Aids	Exams
Priority registration	Typist	• Oral
Math waiver	• Reader	Untimed
Foreign lang. waiver	• Notetaker	Take home
Course substitution	Proof reader	• With proctor
In Class	Text on tape	On computer
Calculators	Early syllabus	• Extended time
• Tape recorder	Taped handouts	On tape
Word processor		Modified
• Priority seating		• Separate room

Program Strengths
The Special Needs Center has skilled, professional staff that work to provide accessibility while integrating the LD student into all areas of college life.

General Information:
City Colleges of Chicago: Harold Washington College is a 2 year public college. Urban campus Accessible by train or bus. Beaches are 3 miles from campus. Housing is not guaranteed.

Accreditation: NCACS

SAT/ACT Scores:
Scores for incoming freshmen: **ACT:** 90% below 20.

Class Rank: 80% were in the top 60% of their class.

Expenses: Part-time: Per credit:$31.50 (Chicago resid.), $92.91 (if not). Tuition: Out-of-state: Full year: Part-time: Per credit: $129.49 .

Majors
• ARTS Commercial Art, Drafting, Photography, Sculpture • BUSINESS Accounting, Banking/Finance, Business Administration, Business Management, Clerical, Commercial Art, Data Processing, International Business, Management, Marketing, Real Estate, Retailing, Secretarial Science • COMMUNICATIONS English, Journalism, Photography, Speech/Debate/Forensic • COMPUTER SCIENCE Computer Science, Data Processing • EDUCATION Child Development, Early Childhood, Elementary, Secondary • ENGINEERING Engineering Science, Physics • LANGUAGES English, French, German, Italian, Japanese, Russian, Spanish • MATHEMATICS Theoretical • PRE PROFESSIONAL Architecture, Business, Drafting, Engineering, Law, Medicine, Pharmacy, Social Work • SOCIAL SCIENCES Anthropology, Criminal Justice, Geography, History, Political Science, Psychology, Social Sciences, Sociology • VISUAL AND PERFORMING ARTS Art, Music, Music Performance, Studio Art, Theater

Less Selective

**Illinois
Services**

City Colleges of Chicago: Harry S. Truman College
1145 West Wilson Street
Chicago, Illinois 60640
(312) 989-6005

School Enrollment: **5,398** Male: **2,453** Female: **2,945**

Admissions Contact: **Yolanda Nieves, Director of Admissions**
LD Contact: **Linda Ford, Special Needs Advisor**
Telephone: **(312) 989-6018**

Admissions

Application Information:
Application deadline:
Rolling Admissions: **Yes**

Secondary School Information
Most Important Criteria For Admissions (1-strongest)

SAT/ACT **1**	Application	School transcript
Class rank	Course selection	Personal statement
Interview	Extra activities	Psychoeducational
G.P.A.	Open admission	Recommendations

Test Requirements:
Standardized tests waived: **Yes**
Documentation of LD required: **Yes**

Types of Disabilities Served
• Speech/Lang	• Reading	ADD with LD
• Study skills	• Spelling	ADD without LD
• Written express	• Math	ADHD with LD
• Organizational	• Fine Motor	ADHD without LD
• Perceptual		

Learning Disability Program
Services available for all students: **Yes**
Counseling: Individual: **Yes** Group Counseling: **Yes** Vocational Counseling: **Yes**
Support groups are available:**Yes T.O.U.C.H Club, Edgewater Threshold**

Faculty:
Faculty: **2** Full time: **1** Part time: **1**
Faculty advocate: **Yes** Meets with instructor: **1-2 times per semester**

Diagnostic Testing
ADD	Personality	Perceptual skills	Spelling
ADHD	Organization	Fine motor skills	Reading
I.Q.	Handwriting	Spoken language	Study skills
Math	Social skills	Written language	

Tutoring:
Average size of group tutorials: **3**
Services rendered by:
Graduates	Peers	•Faculty	LD staff	Teacher trainees

Tutorials
Grp.	Ind.	Tutorials	Grp.	Ind.	Tutorials
•	•	Math skills	•	•	Word processing
•	•	Study skills	•	•	Time management
•	•	Language arts	•	•	Learning strategies
•	•	Written express	•	•	Organizational skills

Academic Accommodations

Curriculum	Study Aids	Exams
• Priority registration	Typist	• Oral
• Math waiver	• Reader	Untimed
• Foreign lang. waiver	• Notetaker	• Take home
Course substitution	• Proof reader	With proctor
In Class	• Text on tape	On computer
• Calculators	Early syllabus	Extended time
• Tape recorder	Taped handouts	On tape
• Word processor		Modified
Priority seating		Separate room

Graduation Requirements:GPA: **C**

Program Strengths
Open admissions policy. School is open from 9:00 a.m. until 10:00 at night. Average age of student is 28 years.

General Information:
City Colleges of Chicago: Harry S. Truman College is a 2 year public college. Urban campus of 1 acres is Accessible by train or bus. Ski areas are 70 miles from campus. Beaches are 1/2 mile from campus. Housing is not guaranteed.1 % of students join fraternities/sororities.

Accreditation:ISB

Expenses: Part-time: Per credit:$31.50. Tuition: Out-of-state: Full year: $110.03 plus $31.50.

Majors
• BUSINESS Accounting, Business Administration, Commerce & Trade, Data Processing, Industrial Operations, Management, Marketing, Retailing • COMMUNICATIONS Journalism, Speech/Debate/Forensic • EDUCATION Child Development, Elementary, Modern Language, Physical • ENGINEERING Chemical • HEALTH SCIENCES Medical Laboratory Technology, Medical Secretary, Nursing • HUMANITIES Fine Arts, Liberal Arts • PREPROFESSIONAL Engineering, Law, Optometry, Pharmacy • SOCIAL SCIENCES Law Enforcement • VOCATIONAL Dentistry, Drafting, Office Administration, Secretarial

Sports/Activities
• SPORTS-INTERCOLLEGIATE Baseball (M), Basketball (F), Basketball (M), Softball (F), Softball (M), Tennis (F), Tennis (M), Wrestling (M) • SPORTS-INTRAMURAL Basketball, Diving, Swimming, Tennis, Volleyball

Selective   **Illinois Program**

DePaul University
2323 North Seminary #220
Chicago, Illinois 60614-3298
(312) 362-6897

School Enrollment: **16,414** Male: **7,824** Female: **8,590**
LD Enrollment: **48** Male: **25** Female: **23**

Admissions Contact: **Carmita McCoy, Assoc. Dir. of Admissions**
LD Contact: **Alisa Brickman, Director of Plus**
Name of Program: **Productive Learning Strategies**
Address: **2323 N. Seminary #220**
Telephone:**(312) 362-6897**

Admissions

Application Information:
LD Students Applying: **20** Accepted: **10** Enrolled:**10**
Separate application:**Yes**
Application deadline: **Mid August**
Applicant must apply **3-8** months in advance
Rolling Admissions: **Yes**

Secondary School Information

Most Important Criteria For Admissions (1-strongest)

1 SAT/ACT	2 Application	1	School transcript
1 Class rank	1 Course selection		Personal statement
3 Interview	4 Extra activities		Psychoeducational
1 G.P.A.	Open admission	3	Recommendations

Test Requirements:

Diagnostic testing waived: **Yes**
Untimed SAT: **Yes** Untimed ACT: **Yes**
WAIS-R required: **Yes** Range accepted: **Average +**
Documentation of LD required: **Yes**
Currency of diagnostic testing: **Within 3 years**
Tests recommended: **All areas of achievement and processing**

Types of Disabilities Served

- Speech/Lang
- Study skills
- Written express
- Organizational
- Perceptual
- Reading
- Spelling
- Math
- Fine Motor
- ADD with LD
- ADD without LD
- ADHD with LD
- ADHD without LD

Admissions Process

Eligibility for PLUS is contingent on the student's acceptance to DePaul University. For information regarding admissions contact Ms. Carmita McCoy (312) 362-8898. Questions regarding PLUS should be directed to Alisa Brickman.

High School Course Requirements:

English: **4** Math: **2** Science: **2** Foreign Language: **2**
Waivers to standard high school courses
Foreign Language : **Yes** Math: **Yes** Course substitution: **Yes**

Learning Disability Program

Program: Remedial: **Yes**
Program: Reinforces course work: **Yes**
Program available through: **Fall through Spring**
Students mainstreamed **100** % of the day
Recommended credits per semester: **8-12**
Time required or recommended in learning center: **1-2 hours**
Services only for LD students: **Yes**
Counseling: Individual: **Yes** Group Counseling: **Yes** Vocational Counseling: **Yes**

Faculty:

Faculty: **9** Including Director: **Yes** Full time: **1** Part time: **8** M.A.: **9**
Faculty advocate: **Yes** Meets with instructor: **As needed**

Diagnostic Testing

ADD	Personality	• Perceptual skills	• Spelling
ADHD	• Organization	• Fine motor skills	• Reading
• I.Q.	• Handwriting	• Spoken language	• Study skills
• Math	• Social skills	• Written language	

Tutoring:

Average size of group tutorials: **One-on-one**
Services rendered by:
• Graduates • Peers Faculty • LD staff Teacher trainees

Tutorials

Grp.	Ind.	Tutorials	Grp.	Ind.	Tutorials
	•	Math skills		•	Word processing
	•	Study skills		•	Time management
	•	Language arts			Learning strategies
	•	Written express		•	Organizational skills

Academic Accommodations

Curriculum	Study Aids	Exams
• Priority registration	Typist	• Oral
• Math waiver	• Reader	• Untimed
• Foreign lang. waiver	• Notetaker	Take home
• Course substitution	• Proof reader	• With proctor
In Class	• Text on tape	• On computer
• Calculators	• Early syllabus	• Extended time
• Tape recorder	Taped handouts	• On tape
• Word processor		• Modified
Priority seating		• Separate room

Graduation Requirements:

Course credits: **188 quarter hours** GPA: **2.0** Years to complete degree: **Individual basis** Math waiver: **Yes** Language waiver: **Yes**

Program Strengths

PLUS students participate in two hours per week of individual help for specific needs with a learning disabilities specialist. Members also may tape record class lectures and be provided with note takers. For students who require an alternative means of expression on exams, test proctoring is also available. Taped books are provided through Special Student Services. Students are carefully advised as to what courses are best to take in consideration of their various strengths and weaknesses.

General Information:

DePaul University is a 4 year private Roman Catholic university. Urban campus of 30 acres is Chicago. Accessible by air, train, or bus. Beaches are 1 mile from campus. 1.5% of students are foreign. 7 residential halls on campus. Housing is not guaranteed. 32.7 % of students remain on campus for the weekends.

Accreditation: Regional

Expenses: Part-time: Per credit:$194.00 per quarter hour. Room and board: $4,000.00 Cost of LD program:$400.00 per quarter for 2-one hour sessions - $200.00 per quarter once a week

Majors

• AREA STUDIES American, International Studies, Jewish, Latin American, Urban, Women's Studies • ARTS Art History, Commercial Art, Design • BUSINESS Accounting, Economics, Finance, Management, Marketing • COMMUNICATIONS Communication, Language & Culture, Television/Radio/Film • COMPUTER SCIENCE Computer Information Systems, Computer Science, Data Analysis • EDUCATION Chemistry, Computer Science, Early Childhood, Elementary, English, Geography, History, Mathematics, Modern Language, Physical, Physics, Science, Secondary, Social Science • ENGINEERING Biochemistry, Chemistry, Environmental, Microelectronics, Petroleum, Physics • HUMANITIES English/Writing/Literature, Fine Arts, Liberal Arts , Philosophy, Religion • RELIGIOUS STUDIES Bible, Christian, Ethics, Judaism & Jewish Studies, Religion • SCIENCES Biochemistry, Biology, Chemistry, Clinical Laboratory Science, Computer Science, Ecology, Environmental, Geography, Mathematics, Physics • SOCIAL SCIENCES Anthropology, Geography, History, Human Service, International Studies, Political Science, Psychology, Social Sciences, Sociology, Urban • VISUAL AND PERFORMING ARTS Art, Art History, Dramatic Arts, Music, Music Performance, Music Theatre, Studio Art, Theater

Sports/Activities

• SPORTS RELATED Pep Band • SPORTS-INTERCOLLEGIATE Basketball, Cross Country, Golf (M), Riflery, Soccer (M), Softball (F), Tennis, Track and Field, Volleyball (F) • SPORTS-INTRAMURAL Basketball, Racquetball, Softball, Weight Lifting • STUDENT LIFE ACTIVITIES Choral, Concert Band, Drama Groups, Ethnic & Cultural Groups, Fraternities, Jazz Band, Music Ensemble, Music Groups, Newspaper, Radio/TV station, Religious Organization, Sororities, Student Government, Symphony Orchestra, Yearbook

Less Selective

Elgin Community College

1700 Spartan Drive
Elgin, Illinois 60123
(708) 697-1000

School Enrollment: **10,000** Male: **3,500** Female: **6,500**
LD Enrollment: **50**

Admissions Contact: **Roberta Haskins, Director of Admissions**
LD Contact: **Annabelle Rhoades, Director, Learning Skills Center**
Telephone: **(708) 697-1000 Ext. 7220**

Admissions

Application Information:
Application deadline:

Secondary School Information
Most Important Criteria For Admissions (1-strongest)

SAT/ACT	Application	School transcript
Class rank	Course selection	Personal statement
Interview	Extra activities	Psychoeducational
G.P.A.	**1** Open admission	Recommendations

Test Requirements:
Untimed ACT: **Yes**
Documentation of LD required: **Yes**
Tests recommended: **None**

Types of Disabilities Served
- Speech/Lang
- Reading
- ADD with LD
- Study skills
- Spelling
- ADD without LD
- Written express
- Math
- ADHD with LD
- Organizational
- Fine Motor
- ADHD without LD
- Perceptual

Admissions Process

Open-door

Learning Disability Program

Services available for all students: **Yes**
Counseling: Individual: **Yes**
Support groups are available: **ADAPT club on campus**

Faculty:
Faculty: **1** Full time: **1** M.A.: **1**
Faculty advocate: **Yes** Meets with instructor: **As needed**

Diagnostic Testing

ADD	Personality	Perceptual skills	Spelling
ADHD	Organization	Fine motor skills	Reading
I.Q.	Handwriting	Spoken language	Study skills
Math	Social skills	Written language	

Tutoring:
Services rendered by:
Graduates   Peers   •Faculty   •LD staff   Teacher trainees

Tutorials

Grp.	Ind.	Tutorials	Grp.	Ind.	Tutorials
	•	Math skills			Word processing
•		Study skills		•	Time management
	•	Language arts			Learning strategies
	•	Written express			Organizational skills

Academic Accommodations

Curriculum	Study Aids	Exams
Priority registration	Typist	• Oral
• Math waiver	Reader	• Untimed
• Foreign lang. waiver	• Notetaker	Take home
Course substitution	Proof reader	• With proctor
In Class	• Text on tape	• On computer
• Calculators	Early syllabus	• Extended time
• Tape recorder	Taped handouts	• On tape
Word processor		• Modified
• Priority seating		• Separate room

Program Strengths

We provide services for students with learning disabilities. Students are mainstreamed in all cases. We have no classes exclusively for students with learning disabilities.

General Information:

Elgin Community College is a 2 year public college. Suburban campus 40 miles from Chicago. Accessible by train. Housing is not guaranteed.

Accreditation: NCA and others

Expenses:
Tuition: In-state: Full year: $1,000.00. Part-time: Per credit: $35.00 .

Majors

• BUSINESS Accounting, Agricultural, Banking, Business Management, Finance, Food Management, Hotel and Restaurant Managemen, Management, Marketing, Real Estate, Travel/Tourism Management • COMMUNICATIONS Advertising, Communication, Creative Writing, English, Journalism, Photography • COMPUTER SCIENCE Data Processing, Programming • CRAFTS AND DESIGN Graphic Design • EDUCATION Early Childhood, Elementary, Secondary • ENGINEERING Communication, Electrical, Engineering Science, Industrial • HEALTH SCIENCES Dental Assistant, Medical Secretary, Nursing, Surgical Technology • HUMANITIES Humanities, Liberal Arts, Philosophy, Religion • LANGUAGES Dutch, French, German, Greek, Italian, Japanese, Latin, Russian, Spanish • PREPROFESSIONAL Engineering • SCIENCES Agricultural, Astronomy, Botany, Chemistry, Earth, Ecology, Geography, Geology, Horticultural, Mathematics, Microbiology, Physical Science, Physics • SOCIAL SCIENCES Anthropology, Criminal Justice, Geography, History, Psychology, Social Sciences, Sociology • VISUAL AND PERFORMING ARTS Art, Art History, Music, Studio Art • VOCATIONAL Air Conditioning/Heating/Refri, Automobile Technology, Automotive Service, Business and Office, Chemical Manufacturing, Culinary Arts, Electronics Technology, Fire Science, Legal Secretary, Machinist, Paralegal, Piloting, Plastic Technology, Truck Driving, Welding

Sports/Activities

• SPORTS-INTERCOLLEGIATE Baseball (M), Basketball, Cross Country (M), Golf (M), Softball (F), Volleyball (F) • SPORTS-INTRAMURAL Bowling, Cross Country • STUDENT LIFE ACTIVITIES Choral, Concert Band, Dance, Drama Groups, Ethnic & Cultural Groups, Jazz Band, Magazine, Magazine, Musical Theater, Newspaper, Radio/TV station, Student Government, Symphony Orchestra

Less Selective

Illinois Services

Governors State University
University Parkway
University Park, Illinois 60466
(708) 534-5000

School Enrollment: **2,227**

Admissions Contact: **Richard S. Pride, Director of Admissions**
LD Contact: **Peggy Woodard, Outreach Counselor**
Name of Program: **Handicapped Student Services**

Admissions

Application Information:
Application deadline: **August 10th**
Rolling Admissions: **Yes**

Secondary School Information
Most Important Criteria For Admissions (1-strongest)

SAT/ACT **2**	Application **1**	School transcript
Class rank	Course selection	Personal statement
3 Interview	Extra activities	Psychoeducational
G.P.A.	Open admission	Recommendations

Test Requirements:
Documentation of LD required: **Yes**

Types of Disabilities Served
- Speech/Lang
- Study skills
- Written express
- Organizational
- Perceptual
- Reading
- Spelling
- Math
- Fine Motor
- ADD with LD
- ADD without LD
- ADHD with LD
- ADHD without LD

Learning Disability Program
Counseling: Individual: **Yes** Group Counseling: **Yes**

Faculty:
Faculty: **1** Part time: **1**

Diagnostic Testing

ADD	Personality	Perceptual skills	Spelling
ADHD	Organization	Fine motor skills	Reading
I.Q.	Handwriting	Spoken language	Study skills
Math	Social skills	Written language	

Tutoring:
Average size of group tutorials: **10**
Services rendered by:
•Graduates   Peers   •Faculty   LD staff   Teacher trainees

Tutorials

Grp.	Ind.	Tutorials	Grp.	Ind.	Tutorials
•	•	Math skills			Word processing
•	•	Study skills	•	•	Time management
		Language arts		•	Learning strategies
		Written express			Organizational skills

Academic Accommodations

Curriculum	Study Aids	Exams
Priority registration	Typist	• Oral
Math waiver	Reader	Untimed
Foreign lang. waiver	• Notetaker	Take home
Course substitution	Proof reader	With proctor
In Class	• Text on tape	On computer
Calculators	Early syllabus	• Extended time
• Tape recorder	Taped handouts	On tape
• Word processor		Modified
Priority seating		Separate room

Program Strengths
Governors State University does not have a specific LD Program. We provide support services and aids through the Office of Student Development Handicapped Services.

General Information:
Governors State University is a 2 year public university. Urban campus of 750 acres is 35 miles from Chicago. Accessible by train. 1% of students are foreign. Housing is not guaranteed.

Accreditation: NCACS

Expenses:
Tuition: In-state: Full year: $1,596.00. Part-time: Per credit:$66.50. Tuition: Out-of-state: Full year: $4,788.00. Part-time: Per credit:$199.50.

Majors
• BUSINESS Accounting, Banking, Business Administration, Business Management, Finance, Labor Relations, Management, Marketing • COMMUNICATIONS Communication, English, Media, Photography, Speech, Television/Radio/Film • COMPUTER SCIENCE Computer Science, Programming, Systems Analysis • EDUCATION Biology, Elementary, English, Music, School Psychology • HEALTH SCIENCES Communication Disorders, Health Administration, Medical Technology, Nursing • PRE-PROFESSIONAL Social Work • SCIENCES Alcohol & Drug Abuse, Biology, Chemistry • SOCIAL SCIENCES Criminal Justice, Psychology, Public Relations, Social Sciences • VISUAL AND PERFORMING ARTS Art, Art History, Music, Studio Art • VOCATIONAL Business and Office, Medical Laboratory Technology

Sports/Activities
• SPORTS-INTRAMURAL Basketball, Ping-Pong, Racquetball, Skiing - Snow, Softball, Volleyball • STUDENT LIFE ACTIVITIES Academic Clubs, Choral, Community Service, Concert Band, Ethnic & Cultural Groups, Film, Jazz Band, Magazine, Music Ensembles, Musical Theater, Radio/TV station, String Quartet, Student Government

Less Selective

Illinois Services

Highland Community College
Pearl City Road
Freeport, Illinois 61032-9341
(815) 235-6121

School Enrollment: **3,000** Male: **1,000** Female: **2,000**
LD Enrollment: **10** Male: **5** Female: **5**

Admissions Contact: **Karl Richards, Director of Admissions**
LD Contact: **Sue Wilson, Dir. Learning Assistance Services**
Name of Program: **Academic Assessment**
Telephone:**(815) 235-6121 - Ext. 236**

Illinois

Admissions

Application Information:
Application deadline: **Open admissions**

Secondary School Information
Most Important Criteria For Admissions (1-strongest)

SAT/ACT	Application	School transcript
Class rank	Course selection	Personal statement
Interview	Extra activities	Psychoeducational
G.P.A.	**1** Open admission	Recommendations

Test Requirements:
Diagnostic testing waived: **Yes**
WAIS-R required: **Yes** Range accepted: **Normal**
Documentation of LD required: **Yes**

Types of Disabilities Served
- Speech/Lang
- Study skills
- Written express
- Organizational
- Perceptual
- Reading
- Spelling
- Math
- Fine Motor
- ADD with LD
- ADD without LD
- ADHD with LD
- ADHD without LD

Learning Disability Program
Time required or recommended in learning center: **Varies**
Counseling: Individual: **Yes**

Faculty:
Faculty: **1** Full time: **1** M.A.: **1**
Faculty advocate: **Yes** Meets with instructor: **As needed**

Diagnostic Testing

ADD	Personality	Perceptual skills	Spelling
ADHD	Organization	Fine motor skills	Reading
I.Q.	Handwriting	Spoken language	Study skills
Math	Social skills	Written language	

Tutoring:
Services rendered by:
Graduates • Peers • Faculty • LD staff Teacher trainees

Tutorials

Grp.	Ind.	Tutorials	Grp.	Ind.	Tutorials
•	•	Math skills	•	•	Word processing
•	•	Study skills	•	•	Time management
•	•	Language arts	•	•	Learning strategies
•	•	Written express	•	•	Organizational skills

Academic Accommodations

Curriculum	Study Aids	Exams
Priority registration	• Typist	• Oral
Math waiver	• Reader	• Untimed
Foreign lang. waiver	• Notetaker	Take home
• Course substitution	• Proof reader	• With proctor
In Class	• Text on tape	• On computer
• Calculators	• Early syllabus	• Extended time
• Tape recorder	Taped handouts	• On tape
• Word processor		• Modified
• Priority seating		• Separate room

Program Strengths
For questions and concerns call the Learning Assistance Center at (815) 235-6121 Ext. 236. The services for students with disabilities at Highland Community College are increasing and improving as we strive to meet the diverse needs of our student population.

General Information:
Highland Community College is a 2 year public college. Rural campus 3 miles from Freeport. Ski areas are 60 miles from campus. Housing is not guaranteed.

Accreditation:

Expenses: Part-time: Per credit:$30.00 .

Majors
• BUSINESS Accounting, Agricultural, Business Administration, Business Economics, Business Education, Business Management, Economics, Fashion Merchandising, Food Management, Insurance, Management, Marketing, Real Estate • COMMUNICATIONS Communication, Creative Writing, English, Journalism, Photography, Television/Radio/Film • COMPUTER SCIENCE Computer Science, Data Processing, Programming, Telecommunications • EDUCATION Art, Child Development, Early Childhood, Elementary, Health, Music, Music Therapy, School Psychology, Special, Vocational • ENGINEERING Computer, Engineering Science • HEALTH SCIENCES Medical Technology, Nursing, Occupational Therapy • HUMANITIES Humanities, Liberal Arts, Philosophy • LANGUAGES French, German, Russian, Spanish • PREPROFESSIONAL Agriculture, Dentistry, Engineering, Medicine, Natural Resources, Pharmacy, Recreation, Veterinarian • SCIENCES Agricultural, Biochemistry, Biology, Botany, Chemistry, Earth, Ecology, Geography, Geology, Mathematics, Microbiology, Physical Science, Physics, Physiology, Radiology • SOCIAL SCIENCES Anthropology, Criminal Justice, Government/Political, History, Psychology, Social Sciences, Sociology • VISUAL AND PERFORMING ARTS Art, Art History, Dance, Fine Arts, Music, Studio Art, Theater • VOCATIONAL Automotive Service, Child Care, Electronics Technology, Secretarial, Welding

Sports/Activities
• SPORTS RELATED Cheerleading, Pep Band, Team Managers • SPORTS-INTERCOLLEGIATE Basketball, Golf, Volleyball (F) • SPORTS-INTRAMURAL Basketball (M), Canoeing, Cross Country, Cycling, Diving, Football, Martial Arts, Ping-Pong, Racquetball, Scuba, Skiing - Snow, Softball, Tennis, Volleyball • STUDENT LIFE ACTIVITIES Choral, Concert Band, Debate, Drama Groups, Ethnic & Cultural Groups, Film, Jazz Band, Music Ensembles, Music Groups, Musical Theater, Newspaper, Radio/TV station, Religious Organization, Sororities, Symphony Orchestra, Yearbook

---

Less Selective

**Illinois
Services**

Illinois Central College
East Peoria, Illinois 61635
(309) 694-5235

School Enrollment: **12,960** Male: **5,514** Female: **7,446**
LD Enrollment: **21** Male: **14** Female: **7**

Admissions Contact: **Dr. Lois J. Morais, Director of Admissions**
LD Contact: **Nancy Davidson, Coordinator**
Name of Program: **Students with Disabilities**
Telephone:**(309) 694-5131**

Admissions

Application Information:
Rolling Admissions: **Yes**

Secondary School Information
Most Important Criteria For Admissions (1-strongest)

SAT/ACT	**1**	Application **1**	School transcript
Class rank		Course selection	Personal statement
Interview		Extra activities	Psychoeducational
G.P.A.		Open admission	Recommendations

Types of Disabilities Served
- Speech/Lang
- Study skills
- Written express
- Organizational
- Perceptual
- Reading
- Spelling
- Math
- Fine Motor
- ADD with LD
- ADD without LD
- ADHD with LD
- ADHD without LD

Learning Disability Program
Counseling: Individual: **Yes** Group Counseling: **Yes**

Faculty:
Faculty: **1** Part time: **1**
Faculty advocate: **Yes** Meets with instructor: **As needed**

Diagnostic Testing

ADD	Personality	Perceptual skills	Spelling
ADHD	Organization	Fine motor skills	Reading
I.Q.	Handwriting	Spoken language	Study skills
Math	Social skills	Written language	

Tutoring:
Average size of group tutorials: **1:1**
Services rendered by:
Graduates   •Peers   Faculty   •LD staff   Teacher trainees

Tutorials

Grp.	Ind. Tutorials	Grp.	Ind. Tutorials
	• Math skills		• Word processing
	• Study skills		• Time management
	• Language arts		• Learning strategies
	• Written express		• Organizational skills

Academic Accommodations

Curriculum	Study Aids	Exams
Priority registration	• Typist	• Oral
Math waiver	Reader	Untimed
• Foreign lang. waiver	• Notetaker	Take home
• Course substitution	• Proof reader	With proctor
In Class	• Text on tape	On computer
• Calculators	Early syllabus	• Extended time
• Tape recorder	Taped handouts	On tape
• Word processor		• Modified
Priority seating		Separate room

Program Strengths
Illinois Central College maintains a strong support system to accommodate students with orthopedic, visual, learning and hearing impairments. Services include assistance in the following areas: identification, assessment of abilities, aptitudes, counseling and supplemental support services.

General Information:
Illinois Central College is a 2 year public college. Urban campus of 430 acres is 150 miles from Chicago. Accessible by air or bus. 1% of students are foreign. Housing is not guaranteed.

Accreditation:NCACS

Expenses:
Tuition: In-state: Full year: $896.00 (in district), $2,720.00 (out of district). Part-time: Per credit:$28.00 (in district). Tuition: Out-of-state: Full year: $4,000.00. Part-time: Per credit:$118.58.

Majors
• AREA STUDIES American • BUSINESS Accounting, Agricultural, Business Administration, Business Management, Economics, Finance, International Business, Investments and Securities, Management, Marketing, Real Estate • COMMUNICATIONS Advertising, Broadcasting, Commercial Design, English, Journalism, Television/Radio/Film • COMPUTER SCIENCE Data Processing, Robotics, Systems Analysis • CRAFTS AND DESIGN Graphic Design • EDUCATION Art, Child Development, Early Childhood, Elementary, Health, Industrial, Music, Physical, Secondary, Special, Teacher Aide, Vocational • ENGINEERING Computer, Engineering Science • HEALTH SCIENCES Dental Assistant, Environmental, Health, Medical Records, Medical Technology, Nursing, Nutritional/Food, Occupational Therapy, Physical Therapy, Radiograph Medical Technology, Radiological Therapy • HUMANITIES Humanities, Liberal Arts, Philosophy, Religion • LANGUAGES French, German, Japanese, Spanish • PRE-PROFESSIONAL Agriculture, Architecture, Dentistry, Engineering, Law, Medicine, Pharmacy, Social Work, Veterinarian • SCIENCES Astronomy, Biology, Chemistry, Geography, Geology, Horticultural, Mathematics, Physical Science, Physics, Statistics, Zoology • SOCIAL SCIENCES Anthropology, Criminal Justice, Geography, Government/Political, History, Law Enforcement, Psychology, Social Sciences, Sociology • VISUAL AND PERFORMING ARTS Art, Dance, Fine Arts, Music, Theater • VOCATIONAL Automobile Technology, Business and Office, Court Reporting, Diesel Power Technology, Electronics Technology, Fire Science, Home Economics, Industrial Equipment Maintenan, Interior Design, Library Assistant, Manufacturing Technology, Medical Laboratory Technology, Respiratory Therapy Technology, Secretarial

Sports/Activities
• SPORTS RELATED Cheerleading • SPORTS-INTERCOLLEGIATE Baseball, Basketball, Golf (M), Softball (F), Volleyball (F) • SPORTS-INTRAMURAL Basketball, Bowling, Golf, Tennis, Volleyball • STUDENT LIFE ACTIVITIES Choral, Concert Band, Dance, Debate, Drama Groups, Ethnic & Cultural Groups, Jazz Band, Music Groups, Newspaper, Religious Organization, Student Government, Symphony Orchestra

---

Selective   **Illinois**
Services

Illinois State University
Normal, Illinois 61761
(309) 438-2181

School Enrollment: **21,768** Male: **9,799** Female: **11,969**

Admissions Contact: **Larry Jobe, Director of Admissions**
LD Contact: **Heidi Bimrose, Asst. Director, Disability Concerns**
Name of Program: **Disability Concerns**
Address: **Disability Concerns 1290**
Telephone:**(309) 438-5853**

Admissions

Secondary School Information
Most Important Criteria For Admissions (1-strongest)

1	SAT/ACT	**4** Application	**5**	School transcript
2	Class rank	**7** Course selection	**9**	Personal statement
10	Interview	**8** Extra activities	**11**	Psychoeducational
3	G.P.A.	Open admission	**6**	Recommendations

Illinois

Test Requirements:
Untimed SAT: **Yes** Untimed ACT: **Yes**
Documentation of LD required: **Yes**

Types of Disabilities Served
- Speech/Lang
  Study skills
- Written express
  Organizational
- Perceptual
- Reading
- Spelling
- Math
- Fine Motor
- ADD with LD
- ADD without LD
- ADHD with LD
- ADHD without LD

Admissions Process

Students must meet the University's admission requirements.

High School Course Requirements:
English: **4** Math: **3** Science: **2** Foreign Language: **2**
Waivers to standard high school courses
Foreign Language : **Yes**

Learning Disability Program
Program available through:**Monday-Friday**
Students mainstreamed **100** % of the day
Recommended credits per semester: **12**
Counseling: Individual: **Yes** Vocational Counseling: **Yes**

Faculty:
Faculty: **12** Full time: **4** Part time: **8** M.A.: **2** Ph.D.: **1**

Diagnostic Testing
ADD	Personality	Perceptual skills	Spelling
ADHD	Organization	Fine motor skills	Reading
I.Q.	Handwriting	Spoken language	Study skills
Math	Social skills	Written language	

Services rendered by:
Graduates   Peers   Faculty   LD staff   Teacher trainees

Tutorials
Grp.	Ind.	Tutorials	Grp.	Ind.	Tutorials
		Math skills			Word processing
		Study skills			Time management
		Language arts			Learning strategies
		Written express			Organizational skills

Academic Accommodations
Curriculum	Study Aids	Exams
• Priority registration	• Typist	• Oral
Math waiver	• Reader	Untimed
Foreign lang. waiver	• Notetaker	Take home
Course substitution	• Proof reader	With proctor
In Class	• Text on tape	On computer
• Calculators	Early syllabus	• Extended time
• Tape recorder	Taped handouts	On tape
Word processor		Modified
Priority seating		• Separate room

Graduation Requirements:
Course credits: **120** GPA: **2.0** Language waiver: **Yes**
Other requirements: **Constitution test, University writing exam**

General Information:
Illinois State University is a 4 year public university. Suburban campus 50 miles from Peoria, Springfield,. Accessible by train or bus. 10.3% of students are foreign. 10 residential halls on campus. Housing is not guaranteed.

Accreditation:

Expenses:
Tuition: In-state: Full year: $2,430.00. Tuition: Out-of-state: Full year: $6,030.00. Room and board: $2,648.00

Majors
- AGRICULTURE Business, Education, Horticultural, Plant Science • ARTS Art History, Dance, Film & Video, Music, Music History • BUSINESS Accounting, Agricultural, Banking/Finance, Business Administration, Business Education, Economics, Education, Industrial Operations, International Business, Management, Marketing • COMMUNICATIONS Broadcasting, Communication, English, Journalism, Public Relations, Speech/Debate/Forensic • COMPUTER SCIENCE Computer Science, Computer Technology, Hardware Engineer, Programming, Telecommunications • CRAFTS AND DESIGN Apparel Design, Graphic Design, Sculpture • EDUCATION Early Childhood, Elementary, English, Health, Home Economics, Middle School, Music, Music Therapy, Physical, Recreation/Youth Leadership • HEALTH SCIENCES Dietary Manager, Environmental, Fitness, Health, Medical Laboratory Technology, Medical Records Administration, Nutritional/Food, Speech Therapy, Speech/Audiology and Speech • LANGUAGES English, French, German, Japanese, Latin, Russian, Spanish • SCIENCES Agricultural, Biology, Chemistry, Computer Science, Geography, Geology, Horticultural, Mathematics, Natural Science, Physics • SOCIAL SCIENCES Anthropology, Criminal Justice, Geography, Government/Political, History, Political Science, Psychology, Social Science, Sociology • SPECIAL EDUCATION Deaf/Hearing Impaired, Emotionally Disturbed, Learning Disability, Mentally Retarded, Physically Handicapped, Visually Handicapped • VISUAL AND PERFORMING ARTS Art, Art History, Dance, Fine Arts, Music, Music Performance, Theater

Sports/Activities
- SPORTS RELATED Cheerleading, Drill Team, Marching Band, Pep Band • SPORTS-INTERCOLLEGIATE Baseball (M), Basketball (F), Basketball (M), Bowling (F), Bowling (M), Cross Country (F), Cross Country (M), Diving (F), Diving (M), Football (M), Golf (F), Golf (M), Gymnastics (F), Gymnastics (M), Soccer (M), Softball (F), Swimming (F), Swimming (M), Tennis (F), Tennis (M), Track and Field (F), Track and Field (M), Volleyball (F), Wrestling (M) • SPORTS-INTRAMURAL Basketball (F), Basketball (M), Canoeing, Football (M), Hand Ball, Karate, Martial Arts, Racquetball (F), Racquetball (M), Skiing - Cross Country, Soccer (F), Soccer (M), Softball (F), Softball (M), Tennis (F), Tennis (M), Volleyball (F), Volleyball (M) • STUDENT LIFE ACTIVITIES Academic Clubs, Choral, Concert Band, Dance, Debate, Drama Groups, Ethnic & Cultural Groups, Fraternities, Jazz Band, Music Groups, Musical Theater, Newspaper, Political Groups, Radio/TV station, Religious Organization, Sororities, Student Government

---

Less Selective   **Illinois
                                                    Accommodations**

Kendall College
2408 Orrington Avenue
Evanston, Illinois 60201
(708) 866-1304

School Enrollment: **400** Male: **200** Female: **200**
LD Enrollment: **20** Male: **10** Female: **10**

Admissions Contact: **Peter Pauletti, Director of Admissions**
LD Contact: **Kathy McCarville, Reading/Writing Specialist**
Name of Program: **Freshman Year Program**
Telephone:**(708) 866-1350**

Admissions

Application Information:
Application deadline: **Rolling**
Rolling Admissions: **Yes**

Secondary School Information
Most Important Criteria For Admissions (1-strongest)

4 SAT/ACT	Application	3	School transcript
31 Class rank	7 Course selection	6	Personal statement
1 Interview	8 Extra activities	5	Psychoeducational
3 G.P.A.	Open admission	2	Recommendations

Test Requirements:
Untimed SAT: **Yes** Untimed ACT: **Yes**
Documentation of LD required: **Yes**

Types of Disabilities Served
Speech/Lang • Reading   ADD with LD
• Study skills • Spelling   ADD without LD
• Written express • Math   ADHD with LD
• Organizational • Fine Motor   ADHD without LD
• Perceptual

Learning Disability Program
Services available for all students: **Yes**
Counseling: Individual: **Yes**

Faculty:
Faculty: **2** Full time: **2**
Faculty advocate: **Yes** Meets with instructor: **As needed**

Diagnostic Testing
ADD	Personality	Perceptual skills	Spelling
ADHD	Organization	Fine motor skills	• Reading
I.Q.	Handwriting	Spoken language	Study skills
• Math	Social skills	• Written language	

Tutoring:
Services rendered by:
Graduates •Peers •Faculty •LD staff Teacher trainees

Tutorials
Grp.	Ind.	Tutorials	Grp.	Ind.	Tutorials
•	•	Math skills	•		Word processing
•	•	Study skills	•		Time management
•		Language arts	•	•	Learning strategies
•		Written express	•	•	Organizational skills

Academic Accommodations
Curriculum	Study Aids	Exams
Priority registration	• Typist	• Oral
Math waiver	Reader	Untimed
• Foreign lang. waiver	Notetaker	Take home
Course substitution	Proof reader	• With proctor
In Class	Text on tape	On computer
• Calculators	Early syllabus	Extended time
• Tape recorder	Taped handouts	On tape
• Word processor		Modified
Priority seating		Separate room

Graduation Requirements: GPA: **2.0** Math waiver: **Yes**
Other requirements: **Internship for all programs**

Program Strengths
Kendall in essence does not have a learning disability program. The "Freshman Year Program" is designed for high school grads who are not quite prepared for general education courses. Some of these students might have learning disabilities. After this term of reading, writing, and math fundamentals, the student's classes are completely mainstreamed. The main thing Kendall stresses is individual attention from faculty and staff. We have a high success rate for LD students.

General Information:
Kendall College is a 4 year private United Methodist college. Suburban campus 5 miles from Chicago. Accessible by air, train, or bus. Ski areas are 50 miles from campus. Beaches are 1/2 block from campus. 10% of students are foreign. 2 residential halls on campus. Housing is not guaranteed.20 % of students remain on campus for the weekends.

Accreditation: NCACS

SAT/ACT Scores:
Scores for incoming freshmen: **ACT:** 75% below 20.

Class Rank:
About 10% of the present freshmen class were in the upper 20% of their high school class. 15% were in the top 40% of their class. 50% were in the top 60% of their class. 25% were in the top 80% of their class.

Expenses:
Tuition: In-state: Full year: $6,954.00. Part-time: Per credit:$210.00. Part-time: Per course: $840.00. Tuition: Out-of-state: Full year: $6,954.00. Part-time: Per credit:$210.00. Part-time: Per course: $840.00 Room and board: $4,473.00

Majors
• AREA STUDIES American • BUSINESS Business Administration, Hotel and Restaurant Managemen • COMMUNICATIONS Communication • EDUCATION Early Childhood • SOCIAL SCIENCES Human Service • SPECIAL EDUCATION Deaf/Hearing Impaired • VOCATIONAL Business and Office, Culinary Arts

Sports/Activities
• SPORTS-INTRAMURAL Basketball (M) • STUDENT LIFE ACTIVITIES Ethnic & Cultural Groups, Newspaper, Religious Organization, Student Government, Yearbook

---

Less Selective **Illinois Services**

Lake Land College
Route 45, South
Mattoon, Illinois 61938
(217) 235-3131

School Enrollment: **2,889**
LD Enrollment: **25**

Admissions Contact: **Linda Von Behren, Director of Admissions**
LD Contact: **Lisa Hoekstra, Counselor**
Name of Program: **Special Needs Program**
Address: **5001 Lake Land Blvd.**
Telephone:**(217) 235-3131**

Illinois

Admissions

Application Information:
Application deadline: **First 5 days of school**
Applicant must apply **2** months in advance
Rolling Admissions: **Yes**

Secondary School Information
Most Important Criteria For Admissions (1-strongest)

SAT/ACT	Application	School transcript
Class rank	Course selection	Personal statement
Interview	Extra activities **1**	Psychoeducational
G.P.A. **1**	Open admission	Recommendations

Test Requirements:
Documentation of LD required: **Yes**
Tests recommended: **Placement testing done during the orientation process.**

Types of Disabilities Served
- Speech/Lang
- Reading
- ADD with LD
- Study skills
- Spelling
- ADD without LD
- Written express
- Math
- ADHD with LD
- Organizational
- Fine Motor
- ADHD without LD
- Perceptual

Admissions Process

We have an open-door policy and rolling admissions.

Learning Disability Program

Program: Reinforces course work: **Yes**

Faculty:
Faculty: **4** Including Director: **Yes** Full time: **1** Part time: **3**
LD faculty with: BS/BA: **1** M.A.: **1**
Faculty advocate: **Yes** Meets with instructor: **2 times per semester**

Diagnostic Testing

ADD	Personality	Perceptual skills	Spelling
ADHD	Organization	Fine motor skills	• Reading
I.Q.	Handwriting	Spoken language	Study skills
• Math	Social skills	• Written language	

Tutoring:
Services rendered by:
- Graduates
- Peers
- Faculty
- LD staff
- Teacher trainees

Tutorials

Grp.	Ind.	Tutorials	Grp.	Ind.	Tutorials
•	•	Math skills	•	•	Word processing
•	•	Study skills	•	•	Time management
•	•	Language arts	•	•	Learning strategies
•	•	Written express	•	•	Organizational skills

Academic Accommodations

Curriculum	Study Aids	Exams
Priority registration	• Typist	• Oral
• Math waiver	• Reader	• Untimed
Foreign lang. waiver	• Notetaker	Take home
Course substitution	• Proof reader	• With proctor
In Class	• Text on tape	On computer
• Calculators	• Early syllabus	• Extended time
• Tape recorder	Taped handouts	• On tape
• Word processor		Modified
• Priority seating		• Separate room

Program Strengths
We serve several students who have learning disabilities. The services provided include: tutoring, career and personal counseling, books on tape, teacher notifications, and the use of tape recorders and various devices.

General Information:
Lake Land College is a 2 year public college. Rural campus of 165 acres is 45 miles from Champaign. Accessible by air, train, or bus. Housing is not guaranteed.

Accreditation: NCACS

Expenses:
Tuition: In-state: Full year: $1,314.00. Part-time: Per credit:$37.00. Tuition: Out-of-state: Full year: $3,810.00. Part-time: Per credit:$127.33.

Majors
• BUSINESS Accounting, Agricultural, Banking, Business Administration, Business Economics, Business Education, Business Management, Economics, Finance, Hotel and Restaurant Managemen, Insurance, Management, Marketing, Personnel, Real Estate, Sports Management, Travel/Tourism Management • COMMUNICATIONS Advertising, Broadcasting, Communication, Creative Writing, English, Journalism, Photography, Television/Radio/Film • COMPUTER SCIENCE Data Processing, Programming, Systems Analysis, Telecommunications • CRAFTS AND DESIGN Design Technology • EDUCATION Art, Curriculum, Early Childhood, Elementary, Health, Industrial, Middle School, Music, Physical, Recreation and Youth Leadershi, School Psychology, Secondary, Speech/Language, Teacher Aide, Vocational • ENGINEERING Agricultural, Computer, Engineering Science • HEALTH SCIENCES Dental Assistant, Dental Hygiene, Environmental, Health, Medical Secretary, Medical Technology, Nursing, Nutritional/Food, Occupational Therapy, Physical Therapy, Practical Nursing, Radiological Therapy, Speech Therapy, Speech/Audiology and Speech • HUMANITIES Humanities, Liberal Arts, Philosophy • LANGUAGES French, Spanish • PREPROFESSIONAL Agriculture, Architecture, Dentistry, Engineering, Forestry, Law, Medicine, Natural Resources, Pharmacy, Range Management, Social Work • SCIENCES Agricultural, Biochemistry, Biology, Chemistry, Earth, Ecology, Geography, Geology, Macrobiology, Marine Biology, Mathematics, Microbiology, Physical Chemistry, Physical Science, Physics, Physiology, Radiology, Zoology • SOCIAL SCIENCES Anthropology, Criminal Justice, Geography, Government/Political, History, Law Enforcement, Psychology, Social Sciences, Sociology • VISUAL AND PERFORMING ARTS Art, Art History, Music • VOCATIONAL Automobile Technology, Automotive Service, Business and Office, Drafting, Electronics Technology, Fire Science, Legal Secretary, Secretarial

Sports/Activities
• SPORTS RELATED Band, Cheerleading, Team Managers • SPORTS-INTERCOLLEGIATE Baseball (M), Basketball, Tennis, Volleyball (F) • SPORTS-INTRAMURAL Archery, Baseball, Basketball, Bowling, Softball (F), Tennis, Volleyball (F) • STUDENT LIFE ACTIVITIES Choral, Ethnic & Cultural Groups, Jazz Band, Music Groups, Newspaper, Political Groups, Radio/TV station, Student Government, Yearbook

Less Selective

**Illinois
Services**

Lincoln College
300 Keokuk
Lincoln, Illinois 62656
(217) 732-3155

School Enrollment: **500** Male: **250** Female: **250**
LD Enrollment: **20**

Admissions Contact: **Michael W. Riley, Director of Admissions**

Admissions

Application Information:
Application deadline: **Open**
Rolling Admissions: **Yes**

Secondary School Information
Most Important Criteria For Admissions (1-strongest)

1 SAT/ACT	**9** Application	**3**	School transcript
2 Class rank	**5** Course selection		Personal statement
6 Interview	**8** Extra activities		Psychoeducational
4 G.P.A.	Open admission	**7**	Recommendations

Test Requirements:
Untimed SAT: **Yes** Untimed ACT: **Yes**

Types of Disabilities Served
Speech/Lang	• Reading	ADD with LD
• Study skills	• Spelling	ADD without LD
• Written express	• Math	ADHD with LD
• Organizational	Fine Motor	ADHD without LD
Perceptual		

Learning Disability Program
Counseling: Individual: **Yes**

Faculty:
Faculty advocate: **Yes** Meets with instructor: **As needed**

Diagnostic Testing
ADD	Personality	Perceptual skills	Spelling
ADHD	Organization	Fine motor skills	Reading
I.Q.	Handwriting	Spoken language	Study skills
Math	Social skills	Written language	

Tutoring:
Services rendered by:
Graduates •Peers •Faculty LD staff Teacher trainees

Tutorials
Grp.	Ind.	Tutorials	Grp.	Ind.	Tutorials
	•	Math skills		•	Word processing
	•	Study skills			Time management
	•	Language arts		•	Learning strategies
	•	Written express		•	Organizational skills

Academic Accommodations
Curriculum	Study Aids	Exams
Priority registration	Typist	Oral
Math waiver	Reader	Untimed
Foreign lang. waiver	Notetaker	Take home
Course substitution	Proof reader	With proctor
In Class	Text on tape	On computer
Calculators	Early syllabus	Extended time
Tape recorder	Taped handouts	On tape
Word processor		Modified
Priority seating		Separate room

Program Strengths
We do not offer a learning disability program. There is free tutoring and small classrooms. We are a small 2 year residential junior college and can supply a college atmosphere with special attention.

General Information:
Lincoln College is a 2 year private college. Rural campus of 38 acres is 45 miles from Peoria. Accessible by air, train, or bus. Ski areas are 4 hours from campus. .05% of students are foreign. 5 residential halls on campus. Housing is guaranteed.50 % of students remain on campus for the weekends.

Accreditation:NCACS

SAT/ACT Scores:
Scores for incoming freshmen: **ACT:** 80% below 20. 10% between 20 and 23. 5%between 24 and 25l. 4%between 26 and 28. 1% above 28.

Expenses:
Tuition: In-state: Full year: $6,485.00. Tuition: Out-of-state: Full year: $6,485.00. Room and board: $3,200.00

Majors
• AREA STUDIES American • BUSINESS Accounting, Agricultural, Business Administration, Economics • COMMUNICATIONS Creative Writing, English, Journalism, Photography, Television/Radio/Film • COMPUTER SCIENCE Computer Science, Data Processing • EDUCATION Art, Early Childhood, Elementary, Music • HEALTH SCIENCES Nursing • HUMANITIES English/Writing/Literature, Humanities, Philosophy, Religion • LANGUAGES Spanish • PREPROFESSIONAL Agriculture • SCIENCES Biology, Chemistry, Earth, Geography, Mathematics, Physical Science, Physics, Zoology • SOCIAL SCIENCES Criminal Justice, Geography, History, Law Enforcement, Political Science, Psychology, Social Sciences, Sociology • VISUAL AND PERFORMING ARTS Art, Art History, Dance, Dramatic Arts, Fine Arts, Music, Studio Art, Theater

Sports/Activities
• SPORTS RELATED Band, Cheerleading, Pep Band, Team Managers • SPORTS-INTERCOLLEGIATE Baseball (M), Basketball, Cross Country, Diving, Golf, Soccer (M), Softball (F), Swimming, Tennis, Volleyball (F), Wrestling (M) • SPORTS-INTRAMURAL Badminton, Baseball (M), Basketball, Softball, Tennis, Volleyball • STUDENT LIFE ACTIVITIES Academic Clubs, Children's Theater, Choral, Drama Groups, Jazz Band, Magazine, Music Ensembles, Music Groups, Musical Theater, Newspaper, Political Groups, Radio/TV station, Readers' Theater, Religious Organization, Student Government, Symphony Orchestra, Yearbook

Less Selective

Moraine Valley Community College
10900 South 88th Avenue
Palos Hills, Illinois 60465
(708) 974-2110

School Enrollment: **17,000** Male: **8,500** Female: **8,500**
LD Enrollment: **117** Male: **61** Female: **56**

Admissions Contact: **Mary Rita, Patricelli Registrar**
LD Contact: **Laura Von Borstel, Director**
Name of Program: **Learning Development Support System**
Address: **Room L-150**
Telephone:**(708) 974-5711**

Admissions

Application Information:
Enrolled:**117**
Separate application:**Yes**
Application deadline: **May 1st for fall; Nov. 1st for Spring**
Applicant must apply **3** months in advance

Secondary School Information
Most Important Criteria For Admissions (1-strongest)

SAT/ACT	Application	School transcript
Class rank	Course selection	Personal statement
Interview	Extra activities	Psychoeducational
G.P.A.	**1** Open admission	Recommendations

Test Requirements:
Standardized tests waived: **Yes**
Diagnostic testing waived: **Yes**
Untimed ACH: **Yes**
Documentation of LD required: **Yes**
Tests recommended: **Woodcock Johnson Battery**

Types of Disabilities Served
- Speech/Lang
- Study skills
- Written express
- Organizational
- Perceptual
- Reading
- Spelling
- Math
- Fine Motor
- ADD with LD
- ADD without LD
- ADHD with LD
- ADHD without LD

Learning Disability Program
Special orientation for LD students: **Yes**
Students mainstreamed **100** % of the day
Counseling: Individual: **Yes** Group Counseling: **Yes**

Faculty:
Faculty: **4** Including Director: **Yes** Full time: **3** Part time: **1** M.A.: **3** Ph.D.: **1**
Faculty advocate: **Yes** Meets with instructor: **As needed**

Diagnostic Testing
ADD	Personality •	Perceptual skills	• Spelling
ADHD	Organization	Fine motor skills	• Reading
• I.Q.	• Handwriting•	Spoken language	• Study skills
• Math	Social skills •	Written language	

Tutoring:
Average size of group tutorials: **3-4**
Services rendered by:
Graduates •Peers Faculty •LD staff •Teacher trainees

Tutorials
Grp.	Ind.	Tutorials	Grp.	Ind.	Tutorials
•	•	Math skills	•	•	Word processing
•	•	Study skills	•	•	Time management
•	•	Language arts	•	•	Learning strategies
•	•	Written express	•	•	Organizational skills

Academic Accommodations

Curriculum	Study Aids	Exams
Priority registration	• Typist	• Oral
Math waiver	Reader	Untimed
Foreign lang. waiver	• Notetaker	• Take home
Course substitution	• Proof reader	With proctor
In Class	• Text on tape	On computer
• Calculators	Early syllabus	• Extended time
• Tape recorder	Taped handouts	On tape
• Word processor		• Modified
Priority seating		Separate room

Program Strengths
The Learning Development Support System (LDSS) is designed to help the learning disabled student succeed at the college level. Success is fostered by creating a teaching and learning environment that uses a student's learning strengths and compensates for individual learning weaknesses.

General Information:
Moraine Valley Community College is a 2 year public college. Suburban campus. Accessible by bus. Ski areas are 3 miles from campus. Beaches are 1 mile from campus. Housing is not guaranteed.

Accreditation:

Expenses:
Tuition: In-state: Full year: $37.00. Part-time: Per credit:$37.00 plus $2.00 student activity fee.

Majors
• BUSINESS Agricultural, Banking, Business Administration, Business Management, Finance, Hotel and Restaurant Managemen, Marketing, Real Estate, Transportation, Travel/Tourism Management • COMPUTER SCIENCE Computer Science, Data Processing, Medical Records Administration, Programming, Telecommunications • EDUCATION Child Development • ENGINEERING Engineering Science, Metallurgical • HEALTH SCIENCES EMT, Nursing, Radiograph Medical Technology, Radiological Therapy • HUMANITIES Liberal Arts • PREPROFESSIONAL Recreation • SCIENCES Biology, Physical Science • SOCIAL SCIENCES Criminal Justice, Law Enforcement • VOCATIONAL Air Conditioning/Heating/Refri, Automotive Service, Business and Office, Drafting, Electronics Technology, Fire Science, Machinist, Medical Laboratory Technology, Respiratory Therapy Technology, Secretarial, Welding

Sports/Activities
• SPORTS-INTERCOLLEGIATE Baseball (M), Basketball, Cross Country, Football (M), Golf (M), Softball (F), Tennis, Volleyball (F) • SPORTS-INTRAMURAL Badminton, Bowling, Ping-Pong, Racquetball, Softball, Tennis, Volleyball • STUDENT LIFE ACTIVITIES Choral, Concert Band, Dance, Ethnic & Cultural Groups, Jazz Band, Music Groups, Newspaper, Student Government

Less Selective
Illinois Program

National-Louis University
2840 Sheridan Road
Evanston, Illinois 60201
(708) 256-6771

School Enrollment: **1,800** Male: **360** Female: **1,440**
LD Enrollment: **20**

Admissions Contact: **Gail Kligerman Straus, Dir. of Admissions**
LD Contact: **Carol Eckermann, Director, LAD**
Name of Program: **Center for Academic Development**
Telephone:**(708) 475-1100**

Admissions

Application Information:
Enrolled:**20**
Application deadline: **September 1st**
Rolling Admissions: **Yes** Notified when: **10 days of application**

Secondary School Information
Most Important Criteria For Admissions (1-strongest)

2 SAT/ACT	**1** Application	**1** School transcript
2 Class rank	**1** Course selection	**2** Personal statement
1 Interview	**2** Extra activities	**2** Psychoeducational
2 G.P.A.	Open admission	**1** Recommendations

Test Requirements:
Untimed SAT: **Yes** Untimed ACT: **Yes**
Documentation of LD required: **Yes**
Currency of diagnostic testing: **1 year**

Types of Disabilities Served
- Speech/Lang
- Study skills
- Written express
- Organizational
- Perceptual
- Reading
- Spelling
- Math
- Fine Motor

ADD with LD
ADD without LD
ADHD with LD
ADHD without LD

Admissions Process

Submission of admission credentials, LD documentation, review and interview with LD specialist, additional testing as needed, conference with LD specialist and admission director for recommendation.

Learning Disability Program

Special orientation for LD students: **Yes**
Program: Reinforces course work: **Yes**
Time required or recommended in learning center: **8 hours**
Services available for all students: **Yes**
Counseling: Individual: **Yes** Group Counseling: **Yes** Vocational Counseling: **Yes**

Faculty:
Faculty: **12** Full time: **2** Part time: **10**
Faculty advocate: **Yes** Meets with instructor: **As needed**

Diagnostic Testing
ADD	Personality	Perceptual skills	Spelling
ADHD	Organization	Fine motor skills	Reading
I.Q.	Handwriting	Spoken language	Study skills
Math	Social skills	Written language	

Tutoring:
Average size of group tutorials: **2-5**
Services rendered by:
Graduates •Peers •Faculty •LD staff Teacher trainees

Tutorials
Grp.	Ind.	Tutorials	Grp.	Ind.	Tutorials
•	•	Math skills		•	Word processing
•	•	Study skills		•	Time management
	•	Language arts	•	•	Learning strategies
•	•	Written express		•	Organizational skills

Academic Accommodations

Curriculum	Study Aids	Exams
• Priority registration	• Typist	• Oral
Math waiver	• Reader	• Untimed
Foreign lang. waiver	• Notetaker	• Take home
• Course substitution	• Proof reader	• With proctor
In Class	• Text on tape	• On computer
• Calculators	Early syllabus	• Extended time
• Tape recorder	• Taped handouts	• On tape
• Word processor		• Modified
• Priority seating		• Separate room

Graduation Requirements:
Course credits: **180** GPA: **2.0** Years to complete degree: **As needed** Language waiver: **Yes**

Program Strengths

Services for learning disabled students are provided in a supportive environment which focuses upon providing academic accommodations and the development of compensatory strategies. Students are carefully monitored while independence is fostered. Personal and career counseling are available. The success rate for LD students at NCES Evanston Campus is very high.

General Information:

National-Louis University is a 4 year private university. Suburban campus of 4 acres is 15 miles from Chicago. Accessible by train or bus. Ski areas are 40 miles from campus. Beaches are 3 blocks from campus. 2% of students are foreign. 1 residential halls on campus. Housing is guaranteed.Guaranteed through All. 75 % of students remain on campus for the weekends.

Accreditation:NCACS

SAT/ACT Scores:
Scores for incoming freshmen: **ACT:** 85% below 20. 15% between 20 and 23.

Expenses:
Tuition: In-state: Full year: $8,550.00. Part-time: Per credit:$190.00. Part-time: Per course: $190.00. Tuition: Out-of-state: Full year: $8,550.00. Part-time: Per credit:$190.00. Part-time: Per course:$190.00 Room and board: $4,489.00 Cost of LD program:$400.00

Majors

• BUSINESS Accounting, Business Administration, Business Management, International Business, Sports Management • COMMUNICATIONS English • COMPUTER SCIENCE Computer Science, Data Processing, Systems Analysis • EDUCATION Art, Early Childhood, Elementary, English, Mathematics, Middle School, Reading, School Psychology, Science, Special • HEALTH SCIENCES Geriatric Aide, Medical Technology, Radiograph Medical Technology, Radiological Therapy • HUMANITIES Humanities, Philosophy • SCIENCES General, Gerontology, Mathematics • SOCIAL SCIENCES Anthropology, History, Human Service, Psychology, Sociology • VISUAL AND PERFORMING ARTS Art, Dramatic Arts, Fine Arts, Theater • VOCATIONAL Respiratory Therapy

Sports/Activities

• SPORTS-INTERCOLLEGIATE Basketball (F), Soccer (M), Softball (F), Volleyball (F)

Less Selective

**Illinois
Services**

Northern Illinois University

Dekalb, Illinois 60115-2854
(815) 753-0446

School Enrollment: **25,000** Male: **12,500** Female: **12,500**
LD Enrollment: **10** Male: **5** Female: **5**

Admissions Contact: **Daniel S. Oborn, Director of Admissions**
LD Contact: **Sue Reinhardt & Linn Sorge, Coordinators**
Name of Program: **Services for Students with Disabilities**
Address: **Health Service 404**
Telephone:**(815) 753-1303**

Admissions

Application Information:

Application deadline: **July 15th**
Applicant must apply **8-10** months in advance

Secondary School Information

Most Important Criteria For Admissions (1-strongest)

1 SAT/ACT	Application	2	School transcript
1 Class rank	2 Course selection	4	Personal statement
4 Interview	Extra activities	3	Psychoeducational
1 G.P.A.	Open admission	4	Recommendations

Test Requirements:

Diagnostic testing waived: **Yes**
Untimed SAT: **Yes** Untimed ACT: **Yes**
Documentation of LD required: **Yes**
Currency of diagnostic testing: **3 years**
Tests recommended: **Verification by psychologist**

Types of Disabilities Served

• Speech/Lang   • Reading   • ADD with LD
• Study skills   • Spelling   • ADD without LD
• Written express   • Math   ADHD with LD
• Organizational   • Fine Motor   • ADHD without LD
• Perceptual

Admissions Process

Fill out regular application.

High School Course Requirements:

English: **4** Math: **3** Science: **2**
Waivers to standard high school courses
Foreign Language : **Yes**

Learning Disability Program

Students mainstreamed **100** % of the day
Recommended credits per semester: **12-15**
Services available for all students: **Yes**

Faculty:

Faculty: **2** Full time: **2** M.A.: **2**
Faculty advocate: **Yes** Meets with instructor: **Everyday**

Diagnostic Testing

ADD	Personality	Perceptual skills	Spelling
ADHD	Organization	Fine motor skills	Reading
I.Q.	Handwriting	Spoken language	Study skills
Math	Social skills	Written language	

Tutoring:

Services rendered by:
•Graduates   •Peers   •Faculty   LD staff   Teacher trainees

Tutorials

Grp.	Ind.	Tutorials	Grp.	Ind.	Tutorials
		Math skills			Word processing
		Study skills			Time management
		Language arts			Learning strategies
		Written express			Organizational skills

Academic Accommodations

Curriculum	Study Aids	Exams
• Priority registration	• Typist	• Oral
Math waiver	• Reader	Untimed
• Foreign lang. waiver	• Notetaker	• Take home
Course substitution	• Proof reader	• With proctor
In Class	• Text on tape	• On computer
• Calculators	Early syllabus	• Extended time
• Tape recorder	Taped handouts	• On tape
• Word processor		Modified
Priority seating		• Separate room

Graduation Requirements:

Course credits: **Depends on major** GPA: **Depends on major** Years to complete degree: **Depends on student** Math waiver: **Yes** Language waiver: **Yes**

Program Strengths

We do not offer a special program for any specific disabled population; however, we offer a variety of services from which self-directed mature students select those necessary to complete course requirements.

General Information:

Northern Illinois University is a 4 year public university. Suburban campus of 460 acres is 60 miles from Chicago. Accessible by bus. Ski areas are 100 miles from campus. 3% of students are foreign. 8 residential halls on campus. Housing is not guaranteed.50 % of students remain on campus for the weekends. 11 % of students join fraternities/sororities.

Accreditation:Regional

Expenses:

Tuition: In-state: Full year: $2,420.00. Part-time: Per credit:$71.50. Tuition: Out-of-state: Full year: $5,860.00. Part-time: Per credit:$214.50. Room and board: $2,600.00

Majors

• BUSINESS Accounting, Banking, Business Administration, Business Education, Business Management, Business Systems & Analysis, Economics, Finance, Management, Marketing • COMMUNICATIONS English, Journalism • COMPUTER SCIENCE Computer Science • EDUCATION Art, Education of Deaf & Hearing Im, Home Economics, Music, Physical, Social Studies, Special • ENGINEERING Communications, Electrical, Engineering Science, Industrial, Mathematical • HEALTH SCIENCES Community Health, Health, Nursing, Nutritional/Food, Physical Therapy, Speech/Audiology and Speech • HUMANITIES Liberal Arts, Philosophy • LANGUAGES French, German, Russian, Spanish • SCIENCES Atmospheric, Biology, Chemistry, Geography, Geology, Mathematics, Meteorology, Physics • SOCIAL SCIENCES Anthropology, Family & Community Services, Government/Political, History, Human Service, Political Science, Psychology, Social Sciences, Sociology • VISUAL AND PERFORMING ARTS Art History, Dance, Music, Studio Art • VOCATIONAL Business and Office, Fashion Merchandising, Food Service, Textile and Clothing

Sports/Activities

• SPORTS RELATED Marching Band, Pep Band • SPORTS-INTERCOLLEGIATE Basketball, Field Hockey (F), Football (M), Golf, Gymnastics, Soccer (M), Softball (F), Swimming, Tennis, Volleyball (F), Wrestling (M) • SPORTS-INTRAMURAL Badminton, Basketball, Golf, Racquetball, Soccer, Softball, Tennis, Volleyball, Wrestling • STUDENT LIFE ACTIVITIES Choral, Community Service, Concert Band, Dance, Drama Groups, Ethnic & Cultural Groups, Fraternities, Jazz Band, Magazine, Music Ensembles, Musical Theater, Newspaper, Opera, Radio/TV station, Religious Organization, Sororities, Student Government, Symphony Orchestra, Yearbook

---

Less Selective

Illinois Services

Oakton Community College

1600 East Golf Road
Des Plaines, Illinois 60016
(708) 635-1600

School Enrollment: **10,400** Male: **5,400** Female: **5,000**
LD Enrollment: **257** Male: **116** Female: **141**

Admissions Contact: **Dale Cohen, Admissions Specialist**
LD Contact: **Paula Griswold Wray, Special Needs Coordinator**
Name of Program: **ASSIST**
Telephone: **(708) 635-1759**

Admissions

Application Information:
Application deadline: **1st day of classes**

Secondary School Information
Most Important Criteria For Admissions (1-strongest)

SAT/ACT	**1**	Application	**2**	School transcript
3 Class rank		Course selection		Personal statement
Interview		Extra activities		Psychoeducational
G.P.A.	**1**	Open admission		Recommendations

Test Requirements:
Standardized tests waived: **Yes**
Untimed ACT: **Yes**
Documentation of LD required: **Yes**

Types of Disabilities Served
• Speech/Lang
• Study skills
• Written express
• Organizational
• Perceptual
• Reading
• Spelling
• Math
• Fine Motor
• ADD with LD
• ADD without LD
• ADHD with LD
• ADHD without LD

Admissions Process

Students must self-identify and request services. Accommodations are made according to documentation.

Learning Disability Program

Special orientation for LD students: **Yes**
Program: Reinforces course work: **Yes**
Students mainstreamed **100** % of the day
Recommended credits per semester: **less than 12 credits**
Services available for all students: **Yes**
Counseling: Individual: **Yes** Group Counseling: **Yes** Vocational Counseling: **Yes**

Faculty:
Faculty: **9** Full time: **1** Part time: **8**
LD faculty with: BS/BA: **9** M.A.: **9**
Faculty advocate: **Yes** Meets with instructor: **As needed**

Diagnostic Testing

ADD	Personality	Perceptual skills	Spelling
ADHD	Organization	Fine motor skills	Reading
I.Q.	Handwriting	Spoken language	Study skills
Math	Social skills	Written language	

Tutoring:
Average size of group tutorials: **2-3**
Services rendered by:

Graduates	Peers	Faculty	•LD staff	Teacher trainees

Tutorials

Grp.	Ind.	Tutorials	Grp.	Ind.	Tutorials
•	•	Math skills		•	Word processing
•	•	Study skills	•	•	Time management
•	•	Language arts	•	•	Learning strategies
•	•	Written express	•	•	Organizational skills

Academic Accommodations

Curriculum	Study Aids	Exams
Priority registration	Typist	• Oral
Math waiver	• Reader	• Untimed
Foreign lang. waiver	Notetaker	Take home
Course substitution	• Proof reader	With proctor
In Class	• Text on tape	• On computer
• Calculators	Early syllabus	• Extended time
• Tape recorder	Taped handouts	On tape
• Word processor		Modified
• Priority seating		• Separate room

Graduation Requirements:
Course credits: **60** GPA: **2.0** Language waiver: **Yes**

Program Strengths

ASSIST provides disabled students with the opportunity to participate in the mainstream college. Students are provided with the accommodations and tutorial support necessary to have an equal opportunity to meet with success at Oakton Community College.

General Information:

Oakton Community College is a 2 year public college. Suburban campus 10 miles from Chicago. Accessible by bus. Housing is not guaranteed.

Accreditation: NCACS

Expenses: Part-time: Per credit: In District: $25.00, Out of District (Part-time): $100.00. Tuition: Out-of-state: Full year: Part-time: Per credit: $150.00.

Majors

• BUSINESS Accounting, Banking, Business Administration, Business Economics, Business Management, Hotel and Restaurant Managemen, Insurance, Management, Marketing, Marketing Research, Real Estate, Retailing • COMPUTER SCIENCE Data Processing, Programming • EDUCATION Early Childhood, Teacher Aide • ENGINEERING Engineering Science • HEALTH SCIENCES Medical Records, Medical Technology, Medical Transcription, Nursing, Physical Therapy, Radiological Therapy • HUMANITIES Philosophy • PREPROFESSIONAL Architecture, Engineering • SCIENCES Bio-medical, General • SOCIAL SCIENCES Law Enforcement • VOCATIONAL Air Conditioning/Heating/Refri, Automobile Technology, Business and Office, Electronics Technology, Fire Science, Secretarial, Transportation Management

Sports/Activities

• SPORTS-INTERCOLLEGIATE Baseball (M), Basketball (M), Cross Country, Golf (M), Gymnastics (F), Softball (F), Tennis, Track and Field, Volleyball (F), Wrestling (M) • SPORTS-INTRAMURAL Badminton, Bowling, Ice Hockey (M), Soccer • STUDENT LIFE ACTIVITIES Choral, Drama Groups, Jazz Band, Music Groups, Newspaper, Student Government

---

Selective   **Illinois**
                                                  Program

Roosevelt University
420 South Michigan Avenue
Chicago, Illinois 60605
(312) 341-3515

School Enrollment: **4,300** Male: **2,000** Female: **2,300**
LD Enrollment: **25**

Admissions Contact: **Amy Price, Admissions Counselor**
LD Contact: **Dr. Margaret Policastro, Director**
Name of Program: **Learning Support Services Program**
Telephone:**(312) 341-3870**

Admissions

Application Information:
Separate application:**Yes**
LD on admissions committee:**Yes**
Application deadline: **July**
Applicant must apply **6** months in advance
Rolling Admissions: **Yes**

Secondary School Information
Most Important Criteria For Admissions (1-strongest)

	SAT/ACT	**1**	Application		School transcript
	Class rank		Course selection	**1**	Personal statement
1	Interview		Extra activities	**1**	Psychoeducational
	G.P.A.		Open admission	**1**	Recommendations

Test Requirements:
Standardized tests waived: **Yes**
Diagnostic testing waived: **Yes**
WAIS-R required: **Yes** Range accepted: **110+**
Documentation of LD required: **Yes**

Types of Disabilities Served
• Speech/Lang	• Reading	ADD with LD
• Study skills	• Spelling	ADD without LD
• Written express	• Math	ADHD with LD
• Organizational	• Fine Motor	ADHD without LD
• Perceptual		

Learning Disability Program
Special orientation for LD students: **Yes**
Syllabus available during orientation:**Yes**
Program: Reinforces course work: **Yes**
Students mainstreamed **100** % of the day
Recommended credits per semester: **Individual basis**
Time required or recommended in learning center: **3 sessions**
Services only for LD students: **Yes**
Counseling: Individual: **Yes**
Support groups are available:**Yes, Peer Counseling**

Faculty:
Faculty: **5** Including Director: **Yes** Full time: **4** Part time: **1**
LD faculty with: BS/BA: **1** M.A.: **3** Ph.D.: **1**
Faculty advocate: **Yes** Meets with instructor: **As needed**

Diagnostic Testing
ADD	Personality	Perceptual skills	Spelling
ADHD	Organization	Fine motor skills	Reading
I.Q.	Handwriting	Spoken language	Study skills
Math	Social skills	Written language	

Tutoring:
Services rendered by:
Graduates   Peers   Faculty   •LD staff   Teacher trainees

Tutorials
Grp.	Ind.	Tutorials	Grp.	Ind.	Tutorials
	•	Math skills		•	Word processing
	•	Study skills		•	Time management
	•	Language arts		•	Learning strategies
	•	Written express		•	Organizational skills

Academic Accommodations
Curriculum	Study Aids	Exams
Priority registration	Typist	• Oral
Math waiver	Reader	Untimed
Foreign lang. waiver	• Notetaker	• Take home
Course substitution	• Proof reader	With proctor
In Class	Text on tape	On computer
Calculators	Early syllabus	• Extended time
Tape recorder	Taped handouts	On tape
Word processor		• Modified
Priority seating		Separate room

Graduation Requirements:
Course credits: **120** GPA: **2.0** Language waiver: **Yes**

Program Strengths
Highly individualized and structured program which addresses the student's needs. We try to develop a relationship with students and educate faculty to their needs.

General Information:
Roosevelt University is a 4 year private university. Urban campus Chicago. Beaches are 1 mile from campus. 1 residential halls on campus. Housing is guaranteed.

Accreditation:

Expenses: Part-time: Per course: $758.00. Cost of LD program:$1,000.00 per semester

Majors

• AREA STUDIES African, American, Asian, Black/Afro-American, Jewish, Latin American, Urban, Women's Studies • BUSINESS Accounting, Banking, Business Administration, Business Economics, Business Education, Business Management, Economics, Finance, Hotel and Restaurant Managemen, International Business, Labor Relations, Management, Marketing, Marketing Research, Personnel, Real Estate • COMMUNICATIONS Advertising, Broadcasting, Communication, Creative Writing, English, Journalism, Photography, Speech, Television/Radio/Film • COMPUTER SCIENCE Computer Science, Data Processing, Programming, Systems Analysis, Telecommunications • EDUCATION Art, Early Childhood, Elementary, Middle School, Music, Pre-Education, Secondary, Special • ENGINEERING Computer • HEALTH SCIENCES Health, Nuclear Medical Technology, Radiological Therapy • HUMANITIES Humanities, Philosophy, Religion • LANGUAGES French, German, Russian, Spanish • PREPROFESSIONAL Dentistry, Law, Medicine, Pharmacy • SCIENCES Actuarial Technology, Astronomy, Biochemistry, Biology, Botany, Cell Biology, Chemistry, Earth, Ecology, Geology, Gerontology, Macrobiology, Marine Biology, Mathematics, Physical Science, Physics, Physiology, Zoology • SOCIAL SCIENCES Anthropology, Criminal Justice, Geography, History, International Studies, Political Science, Psychology, Public Relations, Social Sciences, Sociology • VISUAL AND PERFORMING ARTS Art, Art History, Dance, Dramatic Arts, Jazz, Music, Music Theatre, Theater • VOCATIONAL Electronics Technology, Interior Design, Medical Laboratory Technology

Sports/Activities

• SPORTS-INTRAMURAL Archery, Badminton, Ping-Pong, Soccer (M), Softball, Tennis • STUDENT LIFE ACTIVITIES Choral, Concert Band, Drama Groups, Ethnic & Cultural Groups, Fraternities, Jazz Band, Magazine, Music Groups, Musical Theater, Newspaper, Radio/TV station, Religious Organization, Sororities, Student Government, Symphony Orchestra

Special   **Illinois Services**

School of the Art Institute of Chicago

Columbus Drive at Jackson Boulevard
Chicago, Illinois 60603
(312) 899-5100

School Enrollment: **1,346** Male: **596** Female: **750**

Admissions Contact: **Timothy Robinson, Director of Admissions**
LD Contact: **Judith S. Watson, Director/Learning Center**
Name of Program: **Learning Center**

Admissions

Application Information:
Application deadline: **March 15th**
Rolling Admissions: **Yes**

Secondary School Information
Most Important Criteria For Admissions (1-strongest)

3 SAT/ACT	**2** Application	**2** School transcript
6 Class rank	**10** Course selection	**2** Personal statement
5 Interview	**11** Extra activities	**4** Psychoeducational
6 G.P.A.	Open admission	**2** Recommendations

Test Requirements:
Untimed SAT: **Yes** Untimed ACT: **Yes** Untimed ACH: **Yes**

Types of Disabilities Served
• Speech/Lang • Reading • ADD with LD
• Study skills • Spelling • ADD without LD
• Written express • Math • ADHD with LD
• Organizational • Fine Motor • ADHD without LD
• Perceptual

Learning Disability Program

Counseling: Individual: **Yes**

Faculty:
Faculty: **2** Full time: **2**
Faculty advocate: **Yes** Meets with instructor: **As necessary**

Diagnostic Testing

ADD	Personality	Perceptual skills	Spelling
ADHD	Organization	Fine motor skills	Reading
I.Q.	Handwriting	Spoken language	Study skills
Math	Social skills	Written language	

Tutoring:
Services rendered by:
Graduates   Peers   •Faculty   •LD staff   Teacher trainees

Tutorials

Grp.	Ind.	Tutorials	Grp.	Ind.	Tutorials
	•	Math skills		•	Word processing
	•	Study skills		•	Time management
	•	Language arts		•	Learning strategies
	•	Written express		•	Organizational skills

Academic Accommodations

Curriculum	Study Aids	Exams
Priority registration	Typist	• Oral
Math waiver	Reader	Untimed
Foreign lang. waiver	• Notetaker	Take home
• Course substitution	• Proof reader	With proctor
In Class	• Text on tape	On computer
• Calculators	Early syllabus	• Extended time
• Tape recorder	Taped handouts	On tape
Word processor		Modified
Priority seating		Separate room

Program Strengths

S.A.I.C. does not have an LD Program per se. We do have two trained and experienced LD specialists on staff to offer the support services listed to those students who identify themselves as LD and who actively seek help for themselves. We work in the context of a Learning Center which is available to our entire school population.

General Information:

School of the Art Institute of Chicago is a 4 year private college. Urban campus. Ski areas are 1 hour from campus. Beaches are 1/2 mile from campus. 6.2% of students are foreign. 1 residential halls on campus. Housing is not guaranteed.

Accreditation: Regional

SAT/ACT Scores:
Scores for incoming freshmen:**Verbal:**80%below 500. 45%between 500 and 599. 23%between 600 and 699.

Illinois

Expenses:
Tuition: In-state: Full year: $9,710.00. Part-time: Per credit:$310.00. Part-time: Per course: $930.00. Room and board: $4,360.00

Majors
• AREA STUDIES Black/Afro-American • BUSINESS Economics • COMMUNICATIONS Creative Writing, English, Journalism, Photography, Television/Radio/Film • COMPUTER SCIENCE Computer Graphics • CRAFTS AND DESIGN Ceramics, Drawing, Graphic Design, Sculpture • EDUCATION Art, Art Therapy • HUMANITIES Ethics, Humanities, Philosophy • SCIENCES Astronomy, Biology, Chemistry, Earth, Ecology, Geology, Mathematics, Oceanography, Physical Chemistry • SOCIAL SCIENCES Anthropology, Government/Political, History, Psychology, Social Science • VISUAL AND PERFORMING ARTS Art, Art History, Dance, Music, Music Performance, Studio Art • VOCATIONAL Fashion Design, Painting, Printing/Lithography, Textile and Clothing

Sports/Activities
• STUDENT LIFE ACTIVITIES Ethnic & Cultural Groups, Film, Gay & Lesbian Groups, Music Groups, Newspaper, Student Arts Journal, Student Government

---

Less Selective   **Illinois**

Accommodations

Shawnee College
Shawnee College Road
Ullin, Illinois 62992
(618) 634-2242

School Enrollment: **2,039**

Admissions Contact: **Dee Blakely, Director of Admissions**
LD Contact: **Annie Hubbard, Coordinator of Special Program**

Admissions

Secondary School Information
Most Important Criteria For Admissions (1-strongest)

SAT/ACT	Application	School transcript
Class rank	Course selection	Personal statement
Interview	Extra activities	Psychoeducational
G.P.A.	Open admission	Recommendations

Types of Disabilities Served

Speech/Lang	Reading	ADD with LD
Study skills	Spelling	ADD without LD
Written express	Math	ADHD with LD
Organizational	Fine Motor	ADHD without LD
Perceptual		

Admissions Process

High school transcript, application, and Asset scores.

High School Course Requirements:
English: **3** Math: **3** Science: **2**

Learning Disability Program
Services available for all students: **Yes**
Counseling: Individual: **Yes**
Support groups are available:**Tutorial services**

Diagnostic Testing

ADD	Personality	Perceptual skills	Spelling
ADHD	Organization	Fine motor skills	• Reading
I.Q.	Handwriting	Spoken language	Study skills
• Math	Social skills	• Written language	

Tutoring:
Average size of group tutorials: **6**
Services rendered by:

Graduates	•Peers	Faculty	LD staff	Teacher trainees

Tutorials

Grp.	Ind.	Tutorials	Grp.	Ind.	Tutorials
		Math skills			Word processing
		Study skills			Time management
		Language arts			Learning strategies
		Written express			Organizational skills

Academic Accommodations

Curriculum	Study Aids	Exams
Priority registration	Typist	• Oral
Math waiver	• Reader	• Untimed
Foreign lang. waiver	• Notetaker	Take home
Course substitution	• Proof reader	• With proctor
In Class	Text on tape	• On computer
• Calculators	• Early syllabus	• Extended time
• Tape recorder	Taped handouts	On tape
• Word processor		• Modified
• Priority seating		• Separate room

Graduation Requirements:
Course credits: **64** GPA: **2.0** Years to complete degree: **2**

General Information:
Shawnee College is a 2 year independent college. Rural campus 60 miles from Paducah, KY . Accessible by bus. Housing is not guaranteed.

Accreditation:NCACS

Expenses:
Tuition: In-state: Full year: $1,300 per year. Part-time: Per credit:$81.00, $23.00 (district residents). Tuition: Out-of-state: Full year: Part-time: Per credit: $117.00.

Majors
• AGRICULTURE Business • BUSINESS Accounting, Agricultural, Clerical, Data Processing, Management, Real Estate, Secretarial Science • COMPUTER SCIENCE Data Processing, Medical Records Technology, Programming • EDUCATION Early Childhood • HEALTH SCIENCES Dental Hygiene, Nursing, Nursing Assistant, Physical Therapy, Practical Nursing, Respiratory Therapy • SOCIAL SCIENCES Law Enforcement • VOCATIONAL Air Conditioning/Heating/Refri, Automobile Technology, Business and Office, Cosmetology, Dental Assistant, Dental Hygiene, Electronics Technology, Food Service, Legal Secretary, Radiological Technology, Respiratory Therapy Technology, Secretarial, Welding, Word Processing

Sports/Activities
• SPORTS RELATED Cheerleading • SPORTS-INTERCOLLEGIATE Baseball (M), Basketball (F), Basketball (M), Golf, Softball (F) • SPORTS-INTRAMURAL Basketball, Volleyball • STUDENT LIFE ACTIVITIES Academic Clubs, Choral, Community Service, Debate, Ethnic & Cultural Groups, Magazine, Music Groups, Newspaper, Student Government

Shimer College

P.O. Box A500
Waukegan, Illinois 60079-0500
(708) 623-8400

School Enrollment: **100** Male: **50** Female: **50**

Admissions Contact: **David B. Buchanan, Director of Admissions**

Admissions

Application Information:
LD Students Applying: **1** Accepted: **1** Enrolled:**1**
Application deadline: **Aug. 15th and Jan. 15th**
Applicant must apply **One** months in advance
Rolling Admissions: **Yes**Notified when: **3 weeks**

Secondary School Information
Most Important Criteria For Admissions (1-strongest)

8 SAT/ACT	**7** Application	**5**	School transcript
Class rank	Course selection	**2**	Personal statement
1 Interview	**6** Extra activities	**4**	Psychoeducational
G.P.A.	Open admission	**3**	Recommendations

Test Requirements:
Standardized tests waived: **Yes**

Types of Disabilities Served
- Speech/Lang
- Study skills
- Written express
- Organizational
- Perceptual
- Reading
- Spelling
- Math
- Fine Motor

ADD with LD
ADD without LD
ADHD with LD
ADHD without LD

Admissions Process

Shimer seeks reasons to accept students, not reject them. Any deficits in reading, speech, and writing must not be severe.

Learning Disability Program

Services available for all students: **Yes**

Diagnostic Testing
ADD	Personality	Perceptual skills	Spelling
ADHD	Organization	Fine motor skills	Reading
I.Q.	Handwriting	Spoken language	Study skills
Math	Social skills	Written language	

Tutoring:
Average size of group tutorials: **3**
Services rendered by:
Graduates   •Peers   •Faculty   LD staff   Teacher trainees

Tutorials
Grp.	Ind.	Tutorials	Grp.	Ind.	Tutorials
	•	Math skills		•	Word processing
•	•	Study skills	•	•	Time management
	•	Language arts	•	•	Learning strategies
•	•	Written express	•	•	Organizational skills

Academic Accommodations

Curriculum
Priority registration
Math waiver
Foreign lang. waiver
Course substitution

In Class
Calculators
Tape recorder
- Word processor
Priority seating

Study Aids
Typist
Reader
Notetaker
Proof reader
Text on tape
Early syllabus
Taped handouts

Exams
- Oral
- Untimed
- Take home
With proctor
On computer
- Extended time
On tape
Modified
- Separate room

Graduation Requirements:
Course credits: **125** GPA: **2.0** Years to complete degree: **4**

Program Strengths
All classes have twelve or less students, and are discussion based. All reading in original sources - no textbooks. Intense peer and staff support available. Intense student involvement in all aspects of the College.

General Information:
Shimer College is a 4 year private college. Urban campus 40 miles from Chicago. Accessible by train. Beaches are 1/2 mile from campus. 5% of students are foreign. 1 residential halls on campus. Housing is guaranteed.Guaranteed through 1st year. 95 % of students remain on campus for the weekends.

Accreditation:NCA, Consulting Member NAP, NSC

Expenses:
Tuition: In-state: Full year: $4,400.00 per semester. Room and board: $1,545.00

Majors

- AREA STUDIES Medieval Studies • BUSINESS Business Management • COMMUNICATIONS Creative Writing, English, Literature • EDUCATION Foreign Language • HUMANITIES English/Writing/Literature, Humanities, Liberal Arts , Philosophy • LANGUAGES French, German, Greek, Latin • PREPROFESSIONAL Law • SCIENCES Biology, Botany, Mathematics, Natural Science, Physical Science, Zoology • SOCIAL SCIENCES Government/Political, History, Political Science, Psychology, Social Sciences, Sociology • VISUAL AND PERFORMING ARTS Dramatic Arts, Folklore & Mythology

Sports/Activities

- SPORTS RELATED Chess • SPORTS-INTRAMURAL Basketball, Basketball (F), Basketball (M), Volleyball, Volleyball (F), Volleyball (M) • STUDENT LIFE ACTIVITIES Community Service, Drama Groups, Magazine, Newspaper, Student Government

Southeastern Illinois College

3575 College Drive
Harrisburg, Illinois 62946
(618) 252-6376

School Enrollment: **4,217**
LD Contact: **Dana Keating Special Populations Coordinator**

Illinois

Admissions

Secondary School Information
Most Important Criteria For Admissions (1-strongest)

SAT/ACT	Application	School transcript
Class rank	Course selection	Personal statement
Interview	Extra activities	Psychoeducational
G.P.A.	**1** Open admission	Recommendations

Types of Disabilities Served

Speech/Lang	Reading	ADD with LD
Study skills	Spelling	ADD without LD
Written express	Math	ADHD with LD
Organizational	Fine Motor	ADHD without LD
Perceptual		

Admissions Process

As a community college, we are an open door institution. Students complete an application for admission, take the ASSET test for course placement, and send a high school transcript or GED scores.

Learning Disability Program
Services available for all students: **Yes**

Diagnostic Testing

ADD	Personality	Perceptual skills	Spelling
ADHD	Organization	Fine motor skills	Reading
I.Q.	Handwriting	Spoken language	Study skills
Math	Social skills	Written language	

Tutoring:
Average size of group tutorials: **3**
Services rendered by:

Graduates	•Peers	Faculty	LD staff	Teacher trainees

Tutorials

Grp.	Ind.	Tutorials	Grp.	Ind.	Tutorials
		Math skills			Word processing
		Study skills			Time management
		Language arts			Learning strategies
		Written express			Organizational skills

Academic Accommodations

Curriculum	Study Aids	Exams
Priority registration	Typist	Oral
Math waiver	• Reader	Untimed
Foreign lang. waiver	• Notetaker	Take home
Course substitution	Proof reader	With proctor
In Class	• Text on tape	On computer
Calculators	Early syllabus	• Extended time
• Tape recorder	Taped handouts	On tape
Word processor		Modified
• Priority seating		Separate room

Graduation Requirements: GPA: **2.0**

Program Strengths
Individualized to students' needs.

General Information:
Southeastern Illinois College is a 2 year public college. Rural campus 60 miles from Housing is not guaranteed.

232

Accreditation: NCACS, recognized by ICCB

Expenses: Part-time: Per credit: $21.00 for in-district students. Tuition: Out-of-state: Full year: Part-time: Per credit: approximately $80.00.

Majors
• ARTS Art • BUSINESS Business Management, Real Estate • COMPUTER SCIENCE Data Processing • HEALTH SCIENCES Nursing, Nursing Assistant • SCIENCES Science • SOCIAL SCIENCES Law Enforcement • VOCATIONAL Agricultural Mechanics, Automobile Mechanics, Automobile Technology, Child Care, Clerical, Correctional Officer Training, Diesel Mechanics, Emergency Medical Technician, Food Service, Forestry, Industrial Electronics, Mining and Petroleum Technolog, Secretarial Science, Truck Driving, Welding Technology

Sports/Activities
• SPORTS-INTRAMURAL Baseball (M), Basketball (F), Basketball (M), Softball (F)

Selective　　　　　　　　　　　　　　**Illinois Program**

Southern Illinois University at Carbondale
Woody Hall
Carbondale, Illinois 62901
(618) 453-4381

School Enrollment: **21,789** Male: **12,609** Female: **9,180**
LD Enrollment: **150**

Admissions Contact: **Jerre C. Pfaff, Director of Admissions**
LD Contact: **Sally DeDecker, Associate Director**
Name of Program: **Project Achieve**
Address: **Clinical Center**
Telephone: **(618) 453-2595**

Admissions

Application Information:
LD Students Applying: **150** Accepted: **65** Enrolled: **65**
Separate application: **Yes**
Applicant must apply **12** months in advance
Rolling Admissions: **Yes**

Secondary School Information
Most Important Criteria For Admissions (1-strongest)

1 SAT/ACT	Application	School transcript
1 Class rank	Course selection	Personal statement
Interview	Extra activities	Psychoeducational
G.P.A.	Open admission	Recommendations

Test Requirements:
Diagnostic testing waived: **Yes**
Untimed SAT: **Yes** Untimed ACT: **Yes**
Range accepted: **Average +**
Documentation of LD required: **Yes**
Tests recommended: **Documentation of Learning Disability**

Types of Disabilities Served

• Speech/Lang	• Reading	• ADD with LD
• Study skills	• Spelling	ADD without LD
• Written express	• Math	• ADHD with LD
• Organizational	• Fine Motor	ADHD without LD
• Perceptual		

High School Course Requirements:

English: **4** Math: **3** Science: **3**
Waivers to standard high school courses
Foreign Language : **Yes**

Learning Disability Program

Special orientation for LD students: **Yes**
Program: Remedial: **Yes**
Program: Reinforces course work: **Yes**
Students mainstreamed **100** % of the day
Recommended credits per semester: **12**
Time required or recommended in learning center: **Flexible**
Services only for LD students: **Yes**
Counseling: Individual: **Yes** Group Counseling: **Yes** Vocational Counseling: **Yes**
Support groups are available:**Yes**

Faculty:

Faculty: **13** Including Director: **Yes** Full time: **3** Part time: **10**
LD faculty with: BS/BA: **9** M.A.: **3** Ph.D.: **1**

Diagnostic Testing

- ADD   Personality • Perceptual skills   • Spelling
  ADHD   Organization   Fine motor skills   • Reading
- I.Q.   Handwriting• Spoken language   Study skills
- Math   Social skills • Written language

Tutoring:

Average size of group tutorials: **One-on-one**
Services rendered by:
•Graduates •Peers   Faculty   •LD staff   Teacher trainees

Tutorials

Grp.	Ind.	Tutorials	Grp.	Ind.	Tutorials
	•	Math skills		•	Word processing
	•	Study skills		•	Time management
	•	Language arts		•	Learning strategies
•	•	Written express		•	Organizational skills

Academic Accommodations

Curriculum	Study Aids	Exams
Priority registration	Typist	• Oral
Math waiver	• Reader	Untimed
• Foreign lang. waiver	• Notetaker	Take home
Course substitution	• Proof reader	• With proctor
In Class	• Text on tape	On computer
Calculators	Early syllabus	• Extended time
Tape recorder	Taped handouts	On tape
• Word processor		Modified
Priority seating		• Separate room

Graduation Requirements:

Course credits: **120** Years to complete degree: **No limit** Language waiver: **Yes**

Program Strengths

Our program has been in service to the LD student for 12 years which means that we have established an atmosphere of support and understanding among the faculty and various departments. We also offer a developmental writing class to students in need.

General Information:

Southern Illinois University at Carbondale is a 4 year public university. Rural campus of 850 acres is 100 miles from St. Louis. Accessible by air or bus. 6% of students are foreign. 16 residential halls on campus. Housing is not guaranteed.90 % of students remain on campus for the weekends. 10 % of students join fraternities/sororities.

Accreditation:NCASC

SAT/ACT Scores:

Scores for incoming freshmen: **ACT:** 49% below 20. 24% between 20 and 23. 20%between 24 and 25l. 6%between 26 and 28. 1% above 28.

Class Rank:

About 21% of the present freshmen class were in the upper 20% of their high school class. 48% were in the top 40% of their class. 71% were in the top 60% of their class. 90% were in the top 80% of their class.

Expenses:

Tuition: In-state: Full year: $1,083.00 including fees. Part-time: Per credit:$185.25. Tuition: Out-of-state: Full year: $2,643.30 including fees. Part-time: Per credit:$315.25. Room and board: $2,636.00 Cost of LD program:$3,700.00

Majors

• AREA STUDIES Urban • BUSINESS Accounting, Agricultural, Banking, Business Administration, Business Economics, Business Education, Business Management, Economics, Finance, Management, Marketing • COMMUNICATIONS Advertising, Communication, Creative Writing, English, Journalism, Linguistic, Literature, Photography, Television/Radio/Film • COMPUTER SCIENCE Computer Science, Data Processing, Programming • CRAFTS AND DESIGN Ceramics, Graphic Design Technology, Sculpture • EDUCATION Agricultural, Art, Art Therapy, Child Development, Elementary, English, English As A Second Language, Foreign Language, Health, Industrial, Mathematics, Music, Physical, Pre-Education, Reading, Secondary, Social Science, Special, Technical • ENGINEERING Aerospace-Aeronautical Technol, Civil/Environmental, Electrical, Engineering Science, Materials, Mechanical, Mining/Mineral, Petroleum • HEALTH SCIENCES Dental Laboratory Technology, Environmental, Health, Medical Secretary, Nursing, Nutritional/Food, Physical Therapy, Speech Therapy, Speech/Audiology and Speech • HUMANITIES Classics, English/Writing/Literature, Liberal Arts, Philosophy, Religion, Religious Studies • LANGUAGES French, German, Russian, Spanish • PREPROFESSIONAL Agriculture, Architecture, Dentistry, Dentistry, Forestry, Legal Assistant, Medicine, Pharmacy, Veterinarian • SCIENCES Agronomy, Animal, Anthropology, Biology, Chemistry, Dairy, Equestrian Studies, Geography, Geology, Horticultural, Mathematics, Microbiology, Mining, Physics, Poultry, Zoology • SOCIAL SCIENCES Criminal Justice, Criminology, Family Counseling, Geography, History, International Studies, Law Enforcement, Political Science, Psychology, Public Relations, Sociology • VISUAL AND PERFORMING ARTS Art History, Dance, Dramatic Arts, Drawing, Jazz Performance, Music, Music Performance, Piano Pedagogy, Studio Art, Theater Design • VOCATIONAL Automobile Technology, Automotive Service, Aviation Maintenance, Aviation Technology, Business and Office, Civil Technology, Construction, Court Reporting, Diesel Power Technology, Drafting, Electronics Technology, Fashion Design, Fashion Merchandising, Fire Science, Food Service, Forestry, Funeral Service/Mortuary Scien, Home Economics, Industrial Design, Industrial Equipment Maintenan, Interior Design, Jewelry-Metalsmithery, Legal Secretary, Machinist, Painting, Park/Recreation, Piloting, Precision Metal Work, Printing/Lithography, Radiological Technology, Respiratory Therapy Technology, Secretarial, Textile and Clothing, Welding

Sports/Activities

• SPORTS RELATED Marching Band, Pep Band • SPORTS-INTERCOLLEGIATE Baseball (M), Basketball, Cross Country, Diving, Football (M), Golf, Softball (F), Swimming, Tennis, Track and Field, Volleyball (F) • SPORTS-INTRAMURAL Basketball, Cross Country, Fencing (F), Golf, Hammer Throw (M), Horseback Riding, Ping-Pong, Racquetball, Rugby, Soccer, Softball, Swimming, Tennis, Track and Field, Volleyball, Wrestling • STUDENT LIFE ACTIVITIES Choral, Concert Band, Dance, Drama Groups, Film, Fraternities, Jazz Band, Music Groups, Musical Theater, Newspaper, Opera, Radio/TV station, Sororities, Student Government, Symphony Orchestra, Yearbook

Less Selective

Southern Illinois University at Edwardsville
Box 1047
Edwardsville, Illinois 62026-1047
(618) 692-2720

School Enrollment: **8,574** Male: **3,761** Female: **4,813**
LD Enrollment: **60** Male: **35** Female: **25**

Admissions Contact: **Julious McNeese, Dir., Student Recruitment**
LD Contact: **Jane Dabbs, Disabled Student Advisor**
Name of Program: **Disabled Student Services**
Address: **Box 1640**
Telephone:**(618) 692-3701**

Admissions

Application Information:
Application deadline: **September**
Applicant must apply **6-9** months in advance
Rolling Admissions: **Yes**

Secondary School Information
Most Important Criteria For Admissions (1-strongest)

1 SAT/ACT	**1** Application	**4** School transcript
1 Class rank	**5** Course selection	**11** Personal statement
11 Interview	**7** Extra activities	**11** Psychoeducational
6 G.P.A.	Open admission	**8** Recommendations

Test Requirements:
Untimed SAT: **Yes** Untimed ACT: **Yes**
Range accepted: **50%**
Documentation of LD required: **Yes**
Currency of diagnostic testing: **1 month**
Tests recommended: **College Placement Test**

Types of Disabilities Served
- Speech/Lang
- Reading
- ADD with LD
- Study skills
- Spelling
- ADD without LD
- Written express
- Math
- ADHD with LD
- Organizational
- Fine Motor
- ADHD without LD
- Perceptual

Admissions Process

Untimed College Placement Test

High School Course Requirements:
English: **4** Math: **3** Science: **3** Foreign Language: **2**

Learning Disability Program
Program: Remedial: **Yes**
Students mainstreamed **100** % of the day
Services only for LD students: **Yes**
Services available for all students: **Yes**
Counseling: Individual: **Yes**
Support groups are available:**New Horizon - Disabled Student Organization**

Faculty:
Faculty: **5** Including Director: **Yes** Full time: **1** Part time: **4**
LD faculty with: BS/BA: **3** M.A.: **1**
Faculty advocate: **Yes** Meets with instructor: **On demand**

Diagnostic Testing
ADD	Personality	Perceptual skills	• Spelling
ADHD	Organization	Fine motor skills	• Reading
I.Q.	Handwriting	Spoken language	• Study skills
• Math	Social skills•	Written language	

Tutoring:
Average size of group tutorials: **1:1**
Services rendered by:
Graduates •Peers Faculty LD staff Teacher trainees

Tutorials
Grp.	Ind. Tutorials	Grp.	Ind. Tutorials
	• Math skills		• Word processing
	• Study skills		• Time management
	• Language arts		• Learning strategies
	• Written express		• Organizational skills

Academic Accommodations

Curriculum	Study Aids	Exams
• Priority registration	• Typist	• Oral
Math waiver	• Reader	• Untimed
Foreign lang. waiver	• Notetaker	Take home
Course substitution	• Proof reader	• With proctor
In Class	• Text on tape	• On computer
• Calculators	• Early syllabus	• Extended time
• Tape recorder	Taped handouts	• On tape
• Word processor		Modified
• Priority seating		• Separate room

Graduation Requirements:
Course credits: **192**

Program Strengths
We have the Kruzweil Personal Reader to aid students. This machine forms text into synthesized voice which goes on cassette tapes.

General Information:
Southern Illinois University at Edwardsville is a 4 year public university. Suburban campus of 2,600 acres is 18 miles from St. Louis. Accessible by bus. Ski areas are 50 miles from campus. 1% of students are foreign. Housing is not guaranteed.2 % of students join fraternities/sororities.

Accreditation:NCACS

SAT/ACT Scores:
Scores for incoming freshmen: **ACT:** 51% below 20. 29% between 20 and 23. 12%between 24 and 25l. 8%between 26 and 28. 1% above 28.

Class Rank:
About 34% of the present freshmen class were in the upper 20% of their high school class. 65% were in the top 40% of their class. 88% were in the top 60% of their class. 96% were in the top 80% of their class.

Expenses:
Tuition: In-state: Full year: $607.00. Part-time: Per course: $237.85. Tuition: Out-of-state: Full year: $1,581.25. Part-time: Per course:$561.85 Room and board: $3,095.00

Majors
• BUSINESS Accounting, Banking, Business Administration, Business

Economics, Economics, Finance, Labor Relations, Marketing, Music Business Management, Organizational Behavior, Personnel • COMMUNICATIONS Broadcasting, Communication, Creative Writing, English, Journalism, Literature, Speech/Debate/Forensics, Television/Radio/Film • COMPUTER SCIENCE Computer Science • EDUCATION Art, Child Development, Early Childhood, Elementary, English, Foreign Language, Health, Mathematics, Music, Physical, Pre-Education, Recreation and Youth Leadershi, Science, Secondary, Special • ENGINEERING Civil/Environmental, Industrial, Mechanical • HEALTH SCIENCES Nursing, Speech/Audiology and Speech • HUMANITIES Liberal Arts, Philosophy • LANGUAGES French, German, Spanish • PREPROFESSIONAL Dentistry, Engineering, Law, Social Work • SCIENCES Animal, Biology, Chemistry, Earth, Ecology, Geography, Human Biology, Mathematics, Physical Science, Physics, Statistics • SOCIAL SCIENCES Anthropology, Geography, Government/Political, History, Political Science, Psychology, Social Sciences, Sociology • VISUAL AND PERFORMING ARTS Art, Art History, Dramatic Arts, Music, Music Performance, Studio Art, Theater • VOCATIONAL Business and Office, Construction, Medical Laboratory Technology, Park/Recreation

Sports/Activities

• SPORTS RELATED Cheerleading, Chess, Pep Band, Team Managers
• SPORTS-INTERCOLLEGIATE Baseball (M), Basketball, Cross Country, Golf (M), Soccer, Softball (F), Tennis, Track and Field, Wrestling (M)
• SPORTS-INTRAMURAL Badminton, Basketball, Bowling, Cross Country, Diving, Fencing, Hand Ball, Racquetball, Sailing, Skiing - Snow, Soccer, Swimming, Tennis, Track and Field, Volleyball, Water Polo
• STUDENT LIFE ACTIVITIES Choral, Concert Band, Dance, Drama Groups, Ethnic & Cultural Groups, Film, Fraternities, Jazz Band, Magazine, Music Groups, Musical Theater, Newspaper, Radio/TV station, Religious Organization, Sororities, Student Government, Symphony Orchestra

Less Selective   **Illinois Program**

Triton College
2000 Fifth Avenue
River Grove, Illinois 60171
(708) 456-0300

School Enrollment: **13,000** Male: **6,500** Female: **6,500**

Admissions Contact: **Mary Rita Patricelli, Director of Admissions**
LD Contact: **Mary Mahoney, Coordinator - SNAP**
Name of Program: **Special Needs Assistance Program - SNAP**
Telephone:**(708) 456-0300 Ext. 854**

Admissions

Application Information:
Separate application:**Yes**
Application deadline: **Rolling**
Applicant must apply **3-6** months in advance
Rolling Admissions: **Yes**

Secondary School Information
Most Important Criteria For Admissions (1-strongest)

SAT/ACT	Application **1**	School transcript
Class rank	Course selection	Personal statement
1 Interview	Extra activities **1**	Psychoeducational
G.P.A.	Open admission	Recommendations

Test Requirements:
Documentation of LD required: **Yes**
Tests recommended: **Placement Test**

Types of Disabilities Served
• Speech/Lang   • Reading   • ADD with LD
• Study skills   • Spelling   ADD without LD
• Written express   • Math   ADHD with LD
  Organizational   • Fine Motor   ADHD without LD
• Perceptual

Learning Disability Program
Program: Reinforces course work: **Yes**
Students mainstreamed **100** % of the day
Counseling: Individual: **Yes**

Faculty:
Faculty: **2** Including Director: **Yes** Full time: **2** M.A.: **2**
Faculty advocate: **Yes** Meets with instructor: **As needed**

Diagnostic Testing

ADD	Personality	Perceptual skills	• Spelling
ADHD	Organization	Fine motor skills	• Reading
• I.Q.	• Handwriting	Spoken language	Study skills
• Math	Social skills•	Written language	

Tutoring:
Services rendered by:
  Graduates   Peers   •Faculty   •LD staff   Teacher trainees

Tutorials

Grp.	Ind.	Tutorials	Grp.	Ind.	Tutorials
	•	Math skills			Word processing
•		Study skills			Time management
	•	Language arts		•	Learning strategies
	•	Written express		•	Organizational skills

Academic Accommodations

Curriculum	Study Aids	Exams
Priority registration	Typist	• Oral
Math waiver	Reader	Untimed
Foreign lang. waiver	• Notetaker	Take home
Course substitution	• Proof reader	With proctor
In Class	• Text on tape	On computer
• Calculators	Early syllabus	• Extended time
• Tape recorder	Taped handouts	On tape
• Word processor		Modified
Priority seating		Separate room

Program Strengths
SNAP provides academic support, counseling, and advising services for learning disabled students. Unique aspects of the program are the one-on-one attention, degree of in-house taping, availability of notetakers and readers, and caring personnel.

General Information:
Triton College is a 2 year public college. Rural campus of 100 acres is 12 miles from Chicago. Accessible by air, train or bus. Housing is not guaranteed.

Accreditation:NCACS

Class Rank:

Expenses: Part-time: Per credit:$36.50 - out of district $113.62.
Tuition: Out-of-state: Full year: Part-time: Per credit: $163.29.

Majors
• BUSINESS Accounting, Banking, Business Administration, Business

Illinois

Management, Economics, Finance, Hotel and Restaurant Managemen, Management, Marketing, Personnel, Real Estate, Trade & Industrial Supervision • COMMUNICATIONS Advertising, Broadcasting, Communication, Creative Writing, English, Journalism, Photography, Television/Radio/Film • COMPUTER SCIENCE Computer Science, Data Processing, Programming, Systems Analysis, Telecommunications • CRAFTS AND DESIGN Graphic Arts Technology, Graphic Design • EDUCATION Early Childhood, Health, Industrial, Music, Recreation and Youth Leadershi • ENGINEERING Engineering Science, Nuclear • HEALTH SCIENCES Dental Technician, Health, Medical Technology, Nursing, Occupational Therapy, Ophthalmic Service, Physical Therapy, Radiological Therapy • HUMANITIES Humanities, Liberal Arts, Philosophy • LANGUAGES French, German, Italian, Spanish • PREPROFESSIONAL Agriculture, Architecture, Dentistry, Engineering, Law, Medicine, Pharmacy, Social Work • SCIENCES Astronomy, Biochemistry, Biology, Chemistry, Earth, Ecology, Geography, Geology, Horticultural, Macrobiology, Mathematics, Microbiology, Physical Chemistry, Physical Science, Physics, Physiology, Zoology • SOCIAL SCIENCES Anthropology, Criminal Justice, Criminology, Geography, Government/Political, History, Law Enforcement, Political Science, Social Sciences, Sociology • VISUAL AND PERFORMING ARTS Art, Art History, Dance, Music, Studio Art, Theater • VOCATIONAL Addiction Counseling, Air Condtioning/Heating/Refrig, Auto Body, Automobile Technology, Business and Office, Construction, Court Reporting, Dental Assistant, Electronics Technology, Fashion Mechandizing, Fire Science, Industrial Equipment Maintenan, Interior Design, Laser Electro-Optic Technology, Legal Secretary, Machinist, Manufacturing Technology, Park/Recreation, Plumbing, Precision Metal Work, Radiological Technology, Respiratory Therapy Technology, Secretarial, Transportation Management, Welding

Sports/Activities

• SPORTS-INTERCOLLEGIATE Baseball (F), Basketball, Cross Country, Diving, Football (M), Soccer (M), Softball (F), Swimming, Tennis, Track and Field, Volleyball (F), Wrestling (M) • SPORTS-INTRAMURAL Basketball, Bowling, Diving, Ice Hockey (M), Ping-Pong, Racquetball, Softball, Swimming, Tennis, Volleyball • STUDENT LIFE ACTIVITIES Choral, Concert Band, Dance, Drama Groups, Ethnic & Cultural Groups, Film, Jazz Band, Magazine, Music Groups, Newspaper, Radio/TV station, Religious Organization, Student Government

Less Selective	Illinois Program

Waubonsee Community College
Room 47
Sugar Grove, Illinois 60554
(708) 466-4811

School Enrollment: **7,000** Male: **4,200** Female: **2,800**
LD Enrollment: **90** Male: **48** Female: **42**

Admissions Contact: **Marcia Kolvitz-Fallert, Counselor**
LD Contact: **Iris Jorstad, Disabled Student Program Manager**
Name of Program: **LD Support Services Program**
Address: **Rte. 47 at Harter Road**
Telephone:**(708) 466-4811**

Admissions

Application Information:
LD Students Applying: **90** Accepted: **90** Enrolled:**90**
Separate application:**Yes**
LD on admissions committee:**Yes**
Application deadline: **June 1st**
Applicant must apply **2** months in advance

Secondary School Information
Most Important Criteria For Admissions (1-strongest)

5 SAT/ACT	1 Application	2	School transcript
4 Class rank	2 Course selection	2	Personal statement
1 Interview	3 Extra activities	1	Psychoeducational
2 G.P.A.	1 Open admission	2	Recommendations

Test Requirements:
Standardized tests waived: **Yes**
Diagnostic testing waived: **Yes**
Documentation of LD required: **Yes**
Currency of diagnostic testing: **3 years**
Tests recommended: **WISC-R, WAIS-R, Woodcock-Johnson**

Types of Disabilities Served
- Speech/Lang
- Study skills
- Written express
- Organizational
- Perceptual
- Reading
- Spelling
- Math
- Fine Motor
- ADD with LD
- ADD without LD
- ADHD with LD
- ADHD without LD

Learning Disability Program
Syllabus available during orientation:**Yes**
Program: Remedial: **Yes**
Program: Reinforces course work: **Yes**
Students mainstreamed **100** % of the day
Services available for all students: **Yes**
Counseling: Individual: **Yes** Group Counseling: **Yes**

Faculty:
Faculty: **4** Including Director: **Yes** Part time: **4** M.A.: **4**
Faculty advocate: **Yes** Meets with instructor: **As needed**

Diagnostic Testing
ADD	Personality	Perceptual skills	• Spelling
ADHD	Organization	Fine motor skills	• Reading
• I.Q.	• Handwriting•	Spoken language	Study skills
• Math	Social skills•	Written language	

Tutoring:
Average size of group tutorials: **2-5**
Services rendered by:
Graduates　　Peers　　•Faculty　　•LD staff　　Teacher trainees

Tutorials
Grp.	Ind.	Tutorials	Grp.	Ind.	Tutorials
•	•	Math skills	•	•	Word processing
•	•	Study skills	•	•	Time management
•	•	Language arts	•	•	Learning strategies
•	•	Written express	•	•	Organizational skills

Academic Accommodations

Curriculum	Study Aids	Exams
Priority registration	• Typist	• Oral
Math waiver	Reader	Untimed
Foreign lang. waiver	• Notetaker	Take home
Course substitution	• Proof reader	With proctor
In Class	• Text on tape	On computer
• Calculators	Early syllabus	• Extended time
• Tape recorder	Taped handouts	On tape
• Word processor		• Modified
Priority seating		Separate room

Program Strengths
Special Support Services are provided by a caring, flexible faculty and staff dedicated to fostering student success. The LD Program

also has an active student support group that meets regularly. We also have a Transition Network Committee composed of high school LD teachers and college staff that meets regularly to assist students in a smooth transition from high school to college.

General Information:

Waubonsee Community College is a 2 year public college. Rural campus of 183 acres is 40 miles from Chicago. Accessible by train or bus. Ski areas are 25 miles from campus. Beaches are 50 miles from campus. 1 residential halls on campus. Housing is not guaranteed.

Accreditation:NCACS

Class Rank:

About 9% of the present freshmen class were in the upper 20% of their high school class. 14% were in the top 40% of their class. 13% were in the top 60% of their class. 8% were in the top 80% of their class.

Expenses:

Tuition: In-state: Full year: $720.00. Part-time: Per credit:$33.00. Part-time: Per course: $99.00. Tuition: Out-of-state: Full year: $1,947.84. Part-time: Per credit:$144.41. Part-time: Per course:$433.23 Room and board: $2,600.00

Majors

• BUSINESS Accounting, Banking, Business Administration, Business Economics, Business Education, Business Management, Entrepreneur, Finance, Management, Marketing, Real Estate, Retailing, Travel/Tourism Management • COMMUNICATIONS Broadcasting, Communication, English, Journalism, Speech/Debate/Forensics, Television/Radio/Film • COMPUTER SCIENCE Data Processing, Programming, Robotics, Systems Analysis, Telecommunications • EDUCATION Art, Child Development, Early Childhood, Elementary, Industrial, Interpreter for Deaf, Music, Physical, Pre-Education • ENGINEERING Air Conditioning Technology, Engineering Science • ENVIRONMENTAL CONTROL Water and Wastewater Technolog • HEALTH SCIENCES Nursing • HUMANITIES Humanities • LANGUAGES Spanish • PREPROFESSIONAL Drafting • SCIENCES Astronomy, Biology, Chemistry, Earth, Mathematics, Physics • SOCIAL SCIENCES Criminal Justice, Family Counseling, Government/Political, History, Law Enforcement, Political Science, Psychology, Social Sciences, Sociology • VISUAL AND PERFORMING ARTS Art, Fine Arts, Music • VOCATIONAL Air Conditioning/Heating/Refri, Auto Body, Automobile Technology, Drafting, Electronics Technology, Fashion Merchandising, Industrial Equipment Maintenan, Manufacturing Technology, Secretarial, Word Processing

Sports/Activities

• SPORTS-INTERCOLLEGIATE Baseball (M), Basketball, Cross Country, Golf (M), Soccer (M), Softball (F), Tennis, Volleyball (F), Wrestling (M) • SPORTS-INTRAMURAL Badminton, Basketball, Ping-Pong, Softball, Tennis, Volleyball • STUDENT LIFE ACTIVITIES Choral, Drama Groups, Ethnic & Cultural Groups, Film, Jazz Band, Music Groups, Newspaper, Radio/TV station, Religious Organization, Steel Band, Student Government, Yearbook

---

Western Illinois University
900 West Adams Sherman Hall
Macomb, Illinois 61455
(309) 298-1891

School Enrollment: **10,000** Male: **5,100** Female: **4,900**

Admissions Contact: **Leroy Twilley, Dean of Admissions**
LD Contact: **Candace McLaughlin, Coordinator**
Name of Program: **Disabled Student Services**
Telephone:**(309) 298-1846**

Admissions

Application Information:
Application deadline: **None**
Rolling Admissions: **Yes**

Secondary School Information
Most Important Criteria For Admissions (1-strongest)

5 SAT/ACT	**9** Application	**1** School transcript
4 Class rank	**2** Course selection	**10** Personal statement
11 Interview	**8** Extra activities	**6** Psychoeducational
3 G.P.A.	Open admission	**7** Recommendations

Test Requirements:
Diagnostic testing waived: **Yes**
Untimed SAT: **Yes** Untimed ACT: **Yes** Untimed ACH: **Yes**
WAIS-R required: **Yes** Range accepted: **Average**
Documentation of LD required: **Yes**
Currency of diagnostic testing: **3 years**

Types of Disabilities Served
• Speech/Lang	• Reading	• ADD with LD
• Study skills	• Spelling	• ADD without LD
• Written express	• Math	• ADHD with LD
• Organizational	• Fine Motor	• ADHD without LD
• Perceptual		

Learning Disability Program
Counseling: Individual: **Yes**

Faculty:
Faculty: **2** Part time: **2**
Faculty advocate: **Yes** Meets with instructor: **As needed**

Diagnostic Testing
ADD	Personality	Perceptual skills	Spelling
ADHD	Organization	Fine motor skills	Reading
I.Q.	Handwriting	Spoken language	Study skills
Math	Social skills	Written language	

Tutoring:
Average size of group tutorials: **15**
Services rendered by:
•Graduates •Peers •Faculty LD staff Teacher trainees

Illinois

Tutorials

Grp.	Ind.	Tutorials	Grp.	Ind.	Tutorials
•	•	Math skills			Word processing
•	•	Study skills	•	•	Time management
	•	Language arts		•	Learning strategies
	•	Written express		•	Organizational skills

Academic Accommodations

Curriculum	Study Aids	Exams
Priority registration	Typist	• Oral
Math waiver	Reader	Untimed
Foreign lang. waiver	Notetaker	Take home
Course substitution	Proof reader	With proctor
In Class	Text on tape	On computer
Calculators	Early syllabus	• Extended time
• Tape recorder	Taped handouts	On tape
Word processor		Modified
Priority seating		Separate room

Program Strengths

We do not, as yet, have a structured program. Services are available through the Disabled Student Services Office located in the University Advising Center. Learning Disabled students applying to Western should have a strong background in college bound courses and need to be independently motivated in order to succeed. All students are mainstreamed.

General Information:

Western Illinois University is a 4 year public university. Rural campus of 1,050 acres is 80 miles from Springfield. Accessible by train or bus. Ski areas are 2-3 hours from campus. 3.3% of students are foreign. 12 residential halls on campus. Housing is guaranteed.8.3 % of students join fraternities/sororities.

Accreditation:NCACS

SAT/ACT Scores:

Scores for incoming freshmen: **ACT:** 44% below 20. 36% between 20 and 23. 10%between 24 and 25l. 9%between 26 and 28. 2% above 28.

Class Rank:

About 22% of the present freshmen class were in the upper 20% of their high school class. 29% were in the top 40% of their class. 27% were in the top 60% of their class. 23% were in the top 80% of their class.

Expenses:

Tuition: In-state: Full year: $1,600.00. Part-time: Per credit:$65.50. Tuition: Out-of-state: Full year: $4,716.00. Part-time: Per credit:$196.50. Room and board: $2,445.00

Majors

• AREA STUDIES Black/Afro-American • BUSINESS Accounting, Banking, Business Administration, Business Economics, Business Education, Business Management, Economics, Finance, Hotel and Restaurant Managemen, Management, Marketing, Personnel, Transportation Management, Travel/Tourism Management • COMMUNICATIONS Advertising, Broadcasting, Communication, English, Journalism, Television/Radio/Film • COMPUTER SCIENCE Computer Science, Programming • EDUCATION Agricultural, Art, Bilingual, Corrections, Early Childhood, Elementary, English, Foreign Language, Health, Industrial, Mathematics, Middle School, Music, Music Therapy, Physical, Secondary, Special, Speech/Language • ENGINEERING Industrial • HEALTH SCIENCES Health, Medical Secretary, Nutritional/Food, Speech Therapy, Speech/Audiology and Speech • HUMANITIES Philosophy • LANGUAGES French, German, Russian, Spanish • PREPROFESSIONAL Agriculture, Architecture, Dentistry, Engineering, Forestry, Law, Medicine, Pharmacy, Range Management, Social Work • SCIENCES Agricultural, Biology, Chemistry, Geography, Geology, Mathematics, Physical Chemistry, Physics • SO-CIAL SCIENCES Criminal Justice, Government/Political, History, Law Enforcement, Political Science, Psychology, Social Sciences, Sociology • VISUAL AND PERFORMING ARTS Art, Dramatic Arts, Music, Studio Art, Theater • VOCATIONAL Business and Office, Home Economics, Park/Recreation, Secretarial

Sports/Activities

• SPORTS RELATED Cheerleading, Marching Band, Pep Band • SPORTS-INTERCOLLEGIATE Baseball (M), Basketball, Cross Country (M), Diving, Football (M), Gymnastics, Soccer (M), Softball (F), Swimming, Tennis, Track and Field, Volleyball (F) • SPORTS-INTRAMURAL Badminton, Baseball (M), Basketball, Bowling, Cross Country (M), Diving, Field Hockey (F), Golf, Hand Ball, Ice Hockey, Lacrosse (F), Ping-Pong, Racquetball, Riflery, Rugby (M), Soccer (M), Softball, Swimming, Tennis, Track and Field, Volleyball, Water Polo, Wrestling (M) • STUDENT LIFE ACTIVITIES Choral, Concert Band, Debate, Drama Groups, Ethnic & Cultural Groups, Film, Fraternities, Jazz Band, Music Groups, Musical Theater, Newspaper, Radio/TV station, Sororities, Student Government, Symphony Orchestra, Yearbook

---

Less Selective   **Illinois**
                                        Program

William Rainey Harper College

1200 W. Algonquin Road
Palatine, Illinois 60067-7398
(708) 397-3000

School Enrollment: **28,000** Male: **13,000** Female: **15,000**
LD Enrollment: **225**

Admissions Contact: **Bruce Bohner, Director**
LD Contact: **Tom Thompson, Coordinator**
Name of Program: **Center for Students with Disabilities**
Telephone:**(708) 397-3000 Ext. 2266**

Admissions

Application Information:

Separate application:**Yes**
Application deadline: **August 1st**
Applicant must apply **3** months in advance

Secondary School Information

Most Important Criteria For Admissions (1-strongest)

9	SAT/ACT	**11**	Application	**3**	School transcript
8	Class rank	**5**	Course selection	**6**	Personal statement
1	Interview	**7**	Extra activities	**2**	Psychoeducational
4	G.P.A.	**1**	Open admission	**10**	Recommendations

Test Requirements:

Standardized tests waived: **Yes**
Diagnostic testing waived: **Yes**
Untimed ACT: **Yes**
Range accepted:
Documentation of LD required: **Yes**
Tests recommended: **Woodcock-Johnson Psychoeducational Battery**

Types of Disabilities Served

Speech/Lang	• Reading	• ADD with LD
• Study skills	• Spelling	• ADD without LD
• Written express	• Math	ADHD with LD
• Organizational	Fine Motor	ADHD without LD
• Perceptual		

Admissions Process

The college has an open admissions process. LD students need to apply for services, submit documentation and have a personal interview; students seen on first come, first served basis.

Learning Disability Program

Syllabus available during orientation:**Yes**
Program: Remedial: **Yes**
Program: Reinforces course work: **Yes**
Program available through:**Weekly**
Students mainstreamed **100** % of the day
Recommended credits per semester: **6-12**
Time required or recommended in learning center: **2-3 hours**
Services available for all students: **Yes**
Counseling: Individual: **Yes** Group Counseling: **Yes** Vocational Counseling: **Yes**
Support groups are available:**Yes**

Faculty:

Faculty: **5** Full time: **2** Part time: **3**
LD faculty with: BS/BA: **1** M.A.: **4**
Faculty advocate: **Yes** Meets with instructor: **As needed**

Diagnostic Testing

ADD	Personality •	Perceptual skills	• Spelling
ADHD	Organization	Fine motor skills	• Reading
• I.Q.	Handwriting•	Spoken language	• Study skills
Math	Social skills •	Written language	

Tutoring:

Average size of group tutorials: **2-4**
Services rendered by:

Graduates	Peers	Faculty	•LD staff	Teacher trainees

Tutorials

Grp.	Ind.	Tutorials	Grp.	Ind.	Tutorials
	•	Math skills		•	Word processing
•	•	Study skills	•		Time management
	•	Language arts		•	Learning strategies
	•	Written express		•	Organizational skills

Academic Accommodations

Curriculum	Study Aids	Exams
Priority registration	Typist	• Oral
Math waiver	• Reader	Untimed
Foreign lang. waiver	• Notetaker	Take home
• Course substitution	Proof reader	• With proctor
In Class	• Text on tape	On computer
• Calculators	Early syllabus	• Extended time
• Tape recorder	Taped handouts	On tape
• Word processor		• Modified
Priority seating		• Separate room

Graduation Requirements:

Course credits: **60** GPA: **2.0** Years to complete degree: **2-4**

Program Strengths

We do not have a program, however our services are comprehensive as noted. We individualize our support based upon a student's needs and motivation perhaps for direct services, advocacy, etc. as time permits. Our staff is very experienced, excellent with adults and younger students and faculty/staff are supportive of student needs. Our approach is somewhere between support and a program.

General Information:

William Rainey Harper College is a 2 year public college. Suburban campus of 200 acres is 5 miles from Palatine. Accessible by train, car or bus. Ski areas are 100-200 miles from campus. Beaches are 1,000 miles from campus. Housing is not guaranteed.

Accreditation:NVACS

Expenses:

Tuition: In-state: Full year: $720.00 - $900.00. Part-time: Per credit:$30.00.
Tuition: Out-of-state: Full year: $3,628.00 - $4,535.00. Part-time: Per credit:$151.16. Cost of LD program:$50.00 for diagnostic testing

Majors

• BUSINESS Accounting, Banking, Business Management, Finance, Food Management, International Business, Management, Marketing, Real Estate, Trade/Industrial Supervision • COMMUNICATIONS Communication, English, Journalism • COMPUTER SCIENCE Computer Science, Data Processing, Systems Analysis • EDUCATION Child Development, Early Childhood, Foreign Language, Health, Pre-Education • ENGINEERING Air Conditioning Technology, Engineering Science, Mechanical • HEALTH SCIENCES Dental Assistant, Dietary Manager Assistant, Medical Secretary, Nursing, Nutritional/Food, Practical Nursing • HUMANITIES Humanities, Liberal Arts • PREPROFESSIONAL Architecture, Dentistry, Engineering, Law, Legal Assistant, Medicine, Pharmacy, Veterinarian • SCIENCES Biology, Chemistry, Horticultural, Mathematics, Physical Chemistry, Physics • SOCIAL SCIENCES Criminal Justice, Law Enforcement, Psychology, Social Sciences • VISUAL AND PERFORMING ARTS Art, Dance, Fine Arts, Music • VOCATIONAL Air Conditioning/Heating/Refri, Business and Office, Culinary Arts, Electronics Technology, Fashion Design, Fashion Merchandising, Fire Science, Food Service, Interior Design, Legal Secretary, Paralegal, Park/Recreation, Secretarial, Welding

Sports/Activities

• SPORTS-INTERCOLLEGIATE Baseball, Basketball, Cross Country, Diving, Fencing (F), Football (M), Softball (F), Swimming, Tennis, Track and Field, Volleyball (F), Wrestling (M) • SPORTS-INTRAMURAL Badminton, Baseball, Basketball, Bowling (M), Diving, Hand Ball, Racquetball, Skiing - Cross Country, Softball, Swimming, Table Tennis, Tennis, Volleyball (F)

Selective   **Indiana Program**

Anderson University
1100 East Fifth
Anderson, Indiana 46012
(317) 641-4163

School Enrollment: **2,051** Male: **851** Female: **1,200**
LD Enrollment: **47**

Admissions Contact: **Phil Fair, Director of Admissions**
LD Contact: **Rinda Smith, Director, Special Educ. Programs**
Name of Program: **Program for Learning Disabilities**
Address: **Kissinger Learning Center**
Telephone:**(317) 641-4226**

Admissions

Application Information:

Enrolled:**13**
LD on admissions committee:**Yes**
Application deadline: **None**
Applicant must apply **9-10** months in advance

Indiana

Secondary School Information

Most Important Criteria For Admissions (1-strongest)

4	SAT/ACT	Application	**1**	School transcript
1	Class rank	Course selection	**6**	Personal statement
8	Interview	**4** Extra activities		Psychoeducational
1	G.P.A.	Open admission	**4**	Recommendations

Test Requirements:

Diagnostic testing waived: **Yes**
Untimed SAT: **Yes**
Documentation of LD required: **Yes**
Currency of diagnostic testing: **within 2 years**
Tests recommended: **Intelligence, achievement**

Types of Disabilities Served

Speech/Lang	Reading	ADD with LD
Study skills	Spelling	ADD without LD
Written express	Math	ADHD with LD
Organizational	Fine Motor	ADHD without LD
Perceptual		

Admissions Process

Students complete general admissions requirements. In addition they must supply verification of disability or complete an on campus interview; former teachers may be contacted.

High School Course Requirements:

English: **2** Math: **2**

Learning Disability Program

Special orientation for LD students: **Yes**
Syllabus available during orientation: **Yes**
Program: Remedial: **Yes**
Program: Reinforces course work: **Yes**
Students mainstreamed **100 %** of the day
Recommended credits per semester: **12-13**
Time required or recommended in learning center: **Varies**
Services only for LD students: **Yes**
Counseling: Individual: **Yes** Group Counseling: **Yes** Vocational Counseling: **Yes**

Faculty:

Faculty: **2** Full time: **1** Part time: **1**
LD faculty with: BS/BA: **1**

Diagnostic Testing

ADD	Personality	Perceptual skills	Spelling
ADHD	Organization	Fine motor skills	Reading
I.Q.	Handwriting	Spoken language	Study skills
Math	Social skills	Written language	

Tutoring:

Average size of group tutorials: **1-3**
Services rendered by:

Graduates　•Peers　Faculty　•LD staff　Teacher trainees

Tutorials

Grp.	Ind.	Tutorials	Grp.	Ind.	Tutorials
	•	Math skills		•	Word processing
•		Study skills		•	Time management
	•	Language arts	•		Learning strategies
	•	Written express	•		Organizational skills

Academic Accommodations

Curriculum	Study Aids	Exams
Priority registration	Typist	• Oral
Math waiver	• Reader	• Untimed
Foreign lang. waiver	• Notetaker	Take home
• Course substitution	• Proof reader	With proctor
In Class	• Text on tape	On computer
• Calculators	• Early syllabus	• Extended time
• Tape recorder	Taped handouts	On tape
• Word processor		Modified
• Priority seating		• Separate room

Graduation Requirements:

Course credits: **124** GPA: **2.0** Language waiver: **Yes**
Other requirements: **2.00 in major, attendance at chapel/convocation, meet residence requirements.**

General Information:

Anderson University is a 2 and 4 year independent university. Suburban campus of 100 acres is 35 miles from Indianapolis. Accessible by air or bus. 1% of students are foreign. 7 residential halls on campus. Housing is not guaranteed. 40 % of students remain on campus for the weekends.

Accreditation: NCACS, NCATE, NASM, CSWE

SAT/ACT Scores:

Scores for incoming freshmen: **Verbal:** 76.7% below 500. 17.3% between 500 and 599. 5.8% between 600 and 699. **Math:** 55.8% below 500. 28.2% between 500 and 599. 12.9% between 600 and 699. 2.9% above 700.

Class Rank:

About 36% of the present freshmen class were in the upper 20% of their high school class. 63% were in the top 40% of their class. 82% were in the top 60% of their class. 96% were in the top 80% of their class.

Expenses:

Tuition: In-state: Full year: $8,780.00. Part-time: Per credit: $366.00. Tuition: Out-of-state: Full year: $8,780.00. Part-time: Per credit: $366.00. Room and board: $3,120.00

Majors

• AREA STUDIES American • ARTS Dramatic Arts, Graphic Arts, Music Performance, Religious Music • BUSINESS Accounting, Business Administration, Business Management, Data Processing, Economics, Management, Marketing • COMMUNICATIONS Communication, Speech/Debate/Forensic • COMPUTER SCIENCE Business Data Programming, Computer Mathematics, Computer Science • EDUCATION Art, Early Childhood, Elementary, English, Foreign Language, General, Health, Mathematics, Middle School, Music, Physical, Reading, Religious, Science, Secondary, Social Studies, Speech/Language • ENGINEERING Electrical • HEALTH SCIENCES Nursing • HUMANITIES English/Writing/Literature, Fine Arts, Philosophy, Religion • LANGUAGES French, German, Spanish • MATHEMATICS Applied, Computer • PRE PROFESSIONAL Dentistry, Engineering, Law, Medicine • RELIGIOUS STUDIES Bible, Ministry & Church Administrati, Philosophy, Religion & Theology • SCIENCES Applied Mathematics, Biology, Chemistry, Computer Science, Physics • SOCIAL SCIENCES Criminal Justice, Government/Political, History, Political Science, Psychology, Social Sciences, Sociology • VISUAL AND PERFORMING ARTS Art, Dramatic Arts, Fine Arts, Music Performance, Studio Art

Sports/Activities

• SPORTS RELATED Cheerleading, Marching Band, Pep Band, Team Managers • SPORTS-INTERCOLLEGIATE Baseball (M), Basketball (F), Basketball (M), Cross Country (F), Cross Country (M), Football (M), Golf (M), Soccer (M), Softball (F), Tennis (F), Tennis (F), Track and Field (F), Track and Field (M), Volleyball (F) • SPORTS-INTRAMURAL Basketball (F), Basketball (M), Football (F), Football (M), Golf (F), Golf (M), Soccer (F), Softball (F), Softball (M), Tennis (F), Tennis (M), Track and Field (F),

Track and Field (M), Volleyball (F), Volleyball (M) • STUDENT LIFE ACTIVITIES Academic Clubs, Choral, Concert Band, Debate, Drama Groups, Ethnic & Cultural Groups, Jazz Band, Music Groups, Newspaper, Political Groups, Religious Organization, Student Government, Symphony Orchestra, Yearbook

Selective   Indiana
Accommodations

Indiana Institute of Technology
1600 East Washington Boulevard
Fort Wayne, Indiana 46803
(219) 422-5561

School Enrollment: **450** Male: **260** Female: **190**

Admissions Contact: **Donald St. Clair, V.P. of Marketing**
LD Contact: **Russell D. Baker, Director of SSS**
Name of Program: **Student Support Services**
Address: **Room 172, Anthony Building**
Telephone: **(219) 422-5561 Ext. 284**

Admissions

Application Information:
Application deadline: **Rolling**
Rolling Admissions: **Yes** Notified when: **August 1st**

Secondary School Information
Most Important Criteria For Admissions (1-strongest)

5	SAT/ACT	Application	**1**	School transcript
2	Class rank	**3** Course selection		Personal statement
8	Interview	**6** Extra activities		Psychoeducational
4	G.P.A.	Open admission	**7**	Recommendations

Test Requirements:
Standardized tests waived: **Yes**

Types of Disabilities Served
- Speech/Lang
- Study skills
- Written express
- Organizational
- Perceptual
- Reading
- Spelling
- Math
- Fine Motor

ADD with LD
ADD without LD
ADHD with LD
ADHD without LD

Learning Disability Program
Services available for all students: **Yes**
Counseling: Individual: **Yes** Group Counseling: **Yes**

Diagnostic Testing

ADD	Personality	Perceptual skills	Spelling
ADHD	Organization	Fine motor skills	Reading
I.Q.	Handwriting	Spoken language	Study skills
Math	Social skills	Written language	

Tutoring:
Average size of group tutorials: **10**
Services rendered by:
Graduates   •Peers   •Faculty   LD staff   Teacher trainees

Tutorials

Grp.	Ind.	Tutorials	Grp.	Ind.	Tutorials
•	•	Math skills	•	•	Word processing
•	•	Study skills	•	•	Time management
•	•	Language arts	•	•	Learning strategies
•	•	Written express	•	•	Organizational skills

Academic Accommodations

Curriculum	Study Aids	Exams
Priority registration	• Typist	• Oral
Math waiver	Reader	Untimed
Foreign lang. waiver	Notetaker	• Take home
Course substitution	• Proof reader	With proctor
In Class	Text on tape	On computer
• Calculators	Early syllabus	• Extended time
• Tape recorder	Taped handouts	On tape
• Word processor		Modified
Priority seating		Separate room

Program Strengths
Indiana Institute of Technology is a small college which specializes in providing individualized attention to meet the unique needs of each of our students. Although our size prohibits offering a comprehensive program for Learning Disabled Students, we are able to provide services for such students on an individually prescribed basis. Several campus buildings however pre-date governmentally prescribed access standards and are not accessible for the student with significant physical disability.

General Information:
Indiana Institute of Technology is a 2 and 4 year private college. Urban campus of 25 acres is Accessible by air, train or bus. Ski areas are 3 hours from campus. Beaches are 2 hours from campus. 15% of students are foreign. 1 residential halls on campus. Housing is guaranteed. 80 % of students remain on campus for the weekends. 30 % of students join fraternities/sororities.

Accreditation: NCACS

SAT/ACT Scores:
Scores for incoming freshmen: **Verbal:** 88% below 500. 10% between 500 and 599. 2% between 600 and 699. 1% above 700. **Math:** 59% below 500. 25% between 500 and 599. 12% between 600 and 699. 4% above 700. **ACT:** 49% below 20. 19% between 20 and 23. 15% between 24 and 25l. 14% between 26 and 28. 3% above 28.

Class Rank:
About 15% of the present freshmen class were in the upper 20% of their high school class. 48% were in the top 40% of their class. 80% were in the top 60% of their class. 93% were in the top 80% of their class.

Expenses:
Tuition: In-state: Full year: $7,350.00. Part-time: Per credit: $245.00. Room and board: $3,410.00

Majors
• BUSINESS Accounting, Business Administration, Business Management, Finance, Management • COMMUNICATIONS Communication • COMPUTER SCIENCE Programming, Systems Analysis • ENGINEERING Civil/Environmental, Computer, Electrical, Engineering Science, Mechanical • PREPROFESSIONAL Engineering, Recreation • VOCATIONAL Electronics Technology

Sports/Activities
• SPORTS-INTERCOLLEGIATE Baseball, Basketball, Soccer (M), Softball (F) • SPORTS-INTRAMURAL Badminton, Bowling, Field Hockey, Football (M), Ping-Pong, Racquetball, Softball, Swimming, Tennis, Volleyball, Weight Lifting

Indiana

Indiana University Bloomington
300 N. Jordan Avenue
Bloomington, Indiana 47405
(812) 855-0661

School Enrollment: **35,000** Male: **16,500** Female: **18,500**
LD Enrollment: **85**

Admissions Contact: **Joan Wright, Asst. Director of Admissions**
LD Contact: **Steve Morris, Director**
Name of Program: **Disabled Student Services & Veteran's Affairs**
Address: **Franklin Hall 096**
Telephone:**(812) 855-7578**

Admissions

Application Information:
Separate application:**Yes**
Application deadline: **February 15th**
Applicant must apply **2 months** in advance
Rolling Admissions: **Yes**

Secondary School Information
Most Important Criteria For Admissions (1-strongest)

6 SAT/ACT	Application	**2** School transcript
3 Class rank	**1** Course selection	Personal statement
Interview	**7** Extra activities	Psychoeducational
4 G.P.A.	Open admission	**8** Recommendations

Test Requirements:
Untimed SAT: **Yes** Untimed ACT: **Yes** Untimed ACH: **Yes**
Documentation of LD required: **Yes**
Currency of diagnostic testing: **3 years**

Types of Disabilities Served
- Speech/Lang
- Study skills
- Written express
- Organizational
- Perceptual
- Reading
- Spelling
- Math
- Fine Motor
- ADD with LD
- ADD without LD
- ADHD with LD
- ADHD without LD

Faculty:
Faculty: **2** Full time: **1** Part time: **1**
LD faculty with: BS/BA: **2** Ph.D.: **1**
Faculty advocate: **Yes** Meets with instructor: **As needed**

Diagnostic Testing

ADD	Personality	Perceptual skills	Spelling
ADHD	Organization	Fine motor skills	Reading
I.Q.	Handwriting	Spoken language	Study skills
Math	Social skills	Written language	

Tutoring:
Services rendered by:
- Graduates • Peers   Faculty   LD staff   Teacher trainees

Tutorials

Grp.	Ind.	Tutorials	Grp.	Ind.	Tutorials
	•	Math skills		•	Word processing
•	•	Study skills	•	•	Time management
	•	Language arts	•	•	Learning strategies
•	•	Written express	•	•	Organizational skills

Academic Accommodations

Curriculum	Study Aids	Exams
Priority registration	Typist	Oral
• Math waiver	Reader	Untimed
• Foreign lang. waiver	Notetaker	Take home
• Course substitution	• Proof reader	• With proctor
In Class	• Text on tape	On computer
Calculators	Early syllabus	• Extended time
• Tape recorder	Taped handouts	On tape
• Word processor		• Modified
Priority seating		Separate room

Program Strengths
We do not have an LD program, but we do offer certain services. We have a Basic Skills Center for all students.

General Information:
Indiana University Bloomington is a 4 year public university. Suburban campus of 120 acres is 50 miles from Indianapolis. Accessible by air, train or bus. 12% of students are foreign. 15 residential halls on campus. Housing is guaranteed.85 % of students remain on campus for the weekends. 20 % of students join fraternities/sororities.

Accreditation:Regional

SAT/ACT Scores:
Scores for incoming freshmen:**Verbal:**20%below 500. 50%between 500 and 599. 20%between 600 and 699. 10%above 700. **Math:**20% below 500. 50% between 500 and 599. 20% between 600 and 699. 10%above 700. **ACT:** 5% below 20. 25% between 20 and 23. 30%between 24 and 25l. 30%between 26 and 28. 10% above 28.

Class Rank:
About 35% of the present freshmen class were in the upper 20% of their high school class. 55% were in the top 40% of their class. 10% were in the top 60% of their class.

Expenses:
Tuition: In-state: Full year: $2,400.00. Part-time: Per credit:$74.55. Tuition: Out-of-state: Full year: $7,700.00. Part-time: Per credit:$240.00. Room and board: $3,400.00

Majors
• AREA STUDIES African, Black/Afro-American, East Asian, Jewish, Middle Eastern, Russian/Slavic, Urban, Women's Studies • BUSINESS Accounting, Banking, Business Administration, Business Economics, Business Education, Business Education, Business Management, Economics, Entrepreneur, Finance, Insurance, Labor Relations, Management, Marketing, Marketing Research, Personnel, Real Estate, Sports Management, Transportation • COMMUNICATIONS Advertising, Broadcasting, Communication, Creative Writing, English, Journalism, Literature, Media Services, Photography, Speech, Television/Radio/Film • COMPUTER SCIENCE Computer Science, Data Processing, Programming, Systems Analysis, Telecommunications • EDUCATION Art, Bilingual, Curriculum, Distribution Education, Early Childhood, Education of the deaf and hear, Elementary, English, Health, Mathematics, Middle School, Music, Physical, Pre-Education, Recreation and Youth Leadershi, School Psychology, Secondary, Special, Speech/Language • ENGINEERING Environmental/ Water Resources • HEALTH SCIENCES Environmental, Health, Medical Technology, Nursing, Nutritional/Food, Occupational Therapy, Physical Therapy, Radiological Therapy, Speech Therapy, Speech/Audiology and

Speech • HUMANITIES Classics, English/Writing/Literature, Humanities, Liberal Arts, Philosophy, Religion, Religious Studies • LANGUAGES Arabic, Chinese, Danish, Dutch, French, German, Greek, Italian, Japanese, Latin, Portuguese, Russian, Slavic, Spanish • PREPROFESSIONAL Dentistry, Law, Medicine, Ophathalmine Services, Optometry, Recreation, Social Work, Sports Medicine, Veterinarian • SCIENCES Actuarial Technology, Anthropology, Astronomy, Astrophysics, Biochemistry, Biology, Botany, Chemistry, Earth, Ecology, Geography, Geology, Macrobiology, Mathematics, Microbiology, Physical Chemistry, Physical Science, Physics, Physiology, Zoology • SOCIAL SCIENCES Anthropology, Criminal Justice, Criminology, Geography, History, Library Science, Political Science, Psychology, Public Relations, Social Sciences, Sociology • VISUAL AND PERFORMING ARTS Art, Art History, Dance, Dramatic Arts, Folklore/ Mythology, Music, Studio Art, Theater, Theater Design • VOCATIONAL Driver and Safety, Fashion Design, Fashion Merchandising, Food Service, Hazard Control, Home Economics, Interior Design, Jewelry-Metalsmithery, Painting, Park/Recreation, Printmaking, Textile and Clothing

Sports/Activities

• SPORTS RELATED Baton Twirling, Cheerleading, Chess, Drill Team, Drum Major/Majorette, Marching Band, Pep Band, Team Managers • SPORTS-INTERCOLLEGIATE Baseball (M), Basketball, Cross Country, Diving, Football (M), Golf, Soccer (M), Softball (F), Swimming, Tennis, Track and Field, Volleyball (F), Wrestling (M) • SPORTS-INTRAMURAL Badminton, Basketball, Cross Country, Fencing, Field Hockey (F), Gymnastics, Hand Ball, Horseback Riding, Ice Hockey (M), Lacrosse, Racquetball, Riflery, RowingRugby, Sailing, Scuba, Skiing - Snow, Soccer, Softball, Squash, Swimming, Tennis, Volleyball, Water Polo, Wrestling • STUDENT LIFE ACTIVITIES Dance, Debate, Ethnic & Cultural Groups, Film, Fraternities, Jazz Band, Music Groups, Newspaper, Opera, Radio/TV station, Religious Organization, Sororities, Student Government, Symphony Orchestra, Yearbook

Less Selective	Indiana Program

Indiana University East

2325 Chester Boulevard
Richmond, Indiana 47374
(317) 973-8200

School Enrollment: **2,197** Male: **659** Female: **1,538**
LD Enrollment: **52**

Admissions Contact: **Ken Christmon, Admissions Counselor**
LD Contact: **Sabrina Pennington, Director**
Name of Program: **Student Support Services**
Telephone:**(317) 973-8310**

Admissions

Secondary School Information
Most Important Criteria For Admissions (1-strongest)

SAT/ACT	Application	School transcript
Class rank	Course selection	Personal statement
Interview	Extra activities	Psychoeducational
G.P.A.	Open admission	Recommendations

Test Requirements:
Diagnostic testing waived: **Yes**
Documentation of LD required: **Yes**

Types of Disabilities Served

• Speech/Lang	• Reading	ADD with LD
• Study skills	• Spelling	ADD without LD
• Written express	• Math	ADHD with LD
• Organizational	Fine Motor	ADHD without LD
Perceptual		

Learning Disability Program

Program: Reinforces course work: **Yes**
Students mainstreamed **100** % of the day
Counseling: Individual: **Yes**

Faculty:
Faculty: **8** Full time: **5** Part time: **3**
LD faculty with: BS/BA: **3** M.A.: **5**

Diagnostic Testing

ADD	• Personality	Perceptual skills	Spelling
ADHD	Organization	Fine motor skills	• Reading
I.Q.	Handwriting	Spoken language	• Study skills
• Math	• Social skills	• Written language	

Tutoring:
Average size of group tutorials: **2-4**
Services rendered by:

Graduates • Peers Faculty • LD staff Teacher trainees

Tutorials

Grp.	Ind.	Tutorials	Grp.	Ind.	Tutorials
•	•	Math skills	•	•	Word processing
•	•	Study skills	•	•	Time management
•	•	Language arts	•	•	Learning strategies
•	•	Written express	•	•	Organizational skills

Academic Accommodations

Curriculum	Study Aids	Exams
Priority registration	• Typist	• Oral
Math waiver	• Reader	Untimed
Foreign lang. waiver	• Notetaker	Take home
• Course substitution	• Proof reader	• With proctor
In Class	• Text on tape	• On computer
• Calculators	Early syllabus	• Extended time
• Tape recorder	Taped handouts	On tape
• Word processor		Modified
Priority seating		• Separate room

Program Strengths

Assistance to learning disabled students is available through Student Support Services, a U.S. Dept. of Education Title IV program for disadvantaged and disabled students. Indiana University East, a small commuter campus of the IU System, offers disabled students the advantage of remaining in their home community while they make the major academic and social adjustment associated with the higher education experience. IU East's friendly atmosphere can provide disabled students with the personal service and attention they may require.

General Information:

Indiana University East is a 4 year public university. Rural campus of 16 acres is 65 miles from Indianapolis. Accessible by bus. Housing is not guaranteed.

Accreditation:NCACS

Expenses:
Tuition: In-state: Full year: $1,745.50. Part-time: Per credit:$63.75. Tu-

ition: Out-of-state: Full year: $4,235.50. Part-time: Per credit:$146.75.

Majors

• BUSINESS Accounting, Business Administration, Business Management, Labor Relations • COMMUNICATIONS English • COMPUTER SCIENCE Computer Science • EDUCATION Elementary, Middle School, Middle School, Pre-Elementary, Secondary • ENGINEERING Mechanical • HEALTH SCIENCES Nursing • PREPROFESSIONAL Social Work • SCIENCES Behavioral Biology, Mathematics, Natural • SOCIAL SCIENCES Criminal Justice

Sports/Activities

• STUDENT LIFE ACTIVITIES Newspaper, Student Government

Less Selective　　　　　　　　　**Indiana Services**

Indiana University Northwest

3400 Broadway
Gary, Indiana 46408
(219) 980-6821

School Enrollment: **3,966** Male: **1,166** Female: **2,800**

Admissions Contact: **William D. Lee, Director of Admissions**
LD Contact: **Ronald C. Thornton, Coordinator**
Name of Program: **Student Support Services**
Telephone:**(219) 980-6798**

Admissions

Application Information:
Application deadline: **July 15th**
Rolling Admissions: **Yes**

Secondary School Information
Most Important Criteria For Admissions (1-strongest)

1 SAT/ACT	**1** Application	**1**	School transcript
2 Class rank	**2** Course selection	**6**	Personal statement
3 Interview	**7** Extra activities	**5**	Psychoeducational
1 G.P.A.	Open admission	**4**	Recommendations

Types of Disabilities Served
• Speech/Lang　• Reading　　ADD with LD
• Study skills　• Spelling　　ADD without LD
• Written express • Math　　ADHD with LD
• Organizational • Fine Motor　ADHD without LD
Perceptual

Learning Disability Program
Counseling: Individual: **Yes** Group Counseling: **Yes**

Faculty:
Faculty: **1** Full time: **1**

Diagnostic Testing
ADD	Personality	Perceptual skills	Spelling
ADHD	Organization	Fine motor skills	Reading
I.Q.	Handwriting	Spoken language	Study skills
Math	Social skills	Written language	

Tutoring:
Average size of group tutorials: **6-8**
Services rendered by:
•Graduates　•Peers　•Faculty　•LD staff　　Teacher trainees

Tutorials
Grp.	Ind.	Tutorials	Grp.	Ind.	Tutorials
•	•	Math skills	•	•	Word processing
•	•	Study skills	•	•	Time management
•	•	Language arts	•	•	Learning strategies
•	•	Written express	•	•	Organizational skills

Academic Accommodations
Curriculum	Study Aids	Exams
Priority registration	• Typist	• Oral
• Math waiver	Reader	Untimed
• Foreign lang. waiver	• Notetaker	• Take home
• Course substitution	• Proof reader	With proctor
In Class	• Text on tape	On computer
• Calculators	Early syllabus	• Extended time
• Tape recorder	Taped handouts	On tape
• Word processor		• Modified
Priority seating		Separate room

Program Strengths
We look at the individual's needs and try to help each student with his/her special need. We work closely with each instructor and department head to make each student have an equal chance at a higher education.

General Information:
Indiana University Northwest is a 2 and 4 year public Urban campus of 27 acres is 30 miles from Chicago. Accessible by train or bus. Ski areas are 20 miles from campus. Housing is not guaranteed.

Accreditation:NCACS

Expenses:
Tuition: In-state: Full year: $1,836.00. Part-time: Per credit:$60.00. Tuition: Out-of-state: Full year: $4,177.00. Part-time: Per credit:$146.00.

Majors
• AREA STUDIES Black/Afro-American, Latin American, Miniority Studies • BUSINESS Accounting, Business Administration, Business Economics, Business Education, Business Management, Economics, Finance, Labor Relations, Marketing • COMMUNICATIONS Broadcasting, Communication, Creative Writing, English, Photography • COMPUTER SCIENCE Data Processing, Programming, Systems Analysis • EDUCATION Education, Elementary, Middle School, Secondary, Special • HEALTH SCIENCES Medical Records Technology, Medical Technology, Nursing, Physical Therapy, Practical Nursing • HUMANITIES Humanities, Philosophy • LANGUAGES French, German, Spanish • SCIENCES Actuarial Technology, Biology, Chemistry, Geography, Geology, Mathematics, Physical Chemistry, Physics • SOCIAL SCIENCES Criminal Justice, Government/Political, History, International Studies, Law Enforcement, Political Science, Psychology, Public Relations, Social Sciences, Sociology • VISUAL AND PERFORMING ARTS Art, Art History, Dramatic Arts, Fine Arts, Studio Art, Theater • VOCATIONAL Dental Hygiene, Medical Laboratory Technology, Respiratory Therapy Technology

Sports/Activities
• SPORTS RELATED Chess • SPORTS-INTRAMURAL Baseball (M), Basketball (M), Ping-Pong, Softball, Volleyball • STUDENT LIFE ACTIVITIES Debate, Drama Groups, Ethnic & Cultural Groups, Fraternities, Music Groups, Newspaper, Religious Organization, Sororities, Student Government

---

Selective   **Indiana Services**

Indiana UniversityPurdue Univeristy at Indianapolis

425 University Blvd. Cavanaugh Hall - Room 001C
Indianapolis, Indiana 46202
(317) 274-3241

School Enrollment: **28,000**
LD Enrollment: **200** Male: **80** Female: **120**

Admissions Contact: **Dr. Alan N. Crist, Director of Admissions**
LD Contact: **Pamela King, Dir., Adaptive Educational Services**
Name of Program: **Adaptive Educational Services**
Telephone:**(317) 274-3241**

Admissions

Application Information:
Application deadline: **June 15-Fall; October 15-Spring**
Rolling Admissions: **Yes**

Secondary School Information
Most Important Criteria For Admissions (1-strongest)

2 SAT/ACT	Application	School transcript
1 Class rank	**1** Course selection	Personal statement
Interview	Extra activities	Psychoeducational
G.P.A.	Open admission	**2** Recommendations

Test Requirements:
Untimed SAT: **Yes** Untimed ACT: **Yes**
Documentation of LD required: **Yes**

Types of Disabilities Served

Speech/Lang	Reading	ADD with LD
Study skills	Spelling	ADD without LD
Written express	Math	ADHD with LD
Organizational	Fine Motor	ADHD without LD
Perceptual		

Admissions Process

Admission for beginners is based on high school rank, curriculum and SAT/ACT scores. Admission for transfers is based on cumulative GPA.

High School Course Requirements:
English: **4** Math: **3** Science: **1** Foreign Language: **2**

Learning Disability Program

Time required or recommended in learning center: **3 hours**

Faculty:
Faculty: **3** Full time: **3** Part time: **6** M.A.: **1**
Faculty advocate: **Yes** Meets with instructor: **As needed**

Diagnostic Testing

ADD	Personality	Perceptual skills	• Spelling
ADHD	Organization	Fine motor skills	• Reading
I.Q.	Handwriting	Spoken language	• Study skills
Math	Social skills	Written language	

Tutoring:
Average size of group tutorials: **1:1**
Services rendered by:
•Graduates   •Peers   Faculty   LD staff   •Teacher trainees

Tutorials

Grp.	Ind.	Tutorials	Grp.	Ind.	Tutorials
	•	Math skills		•	Word processing
	•	Study skills		•	Time management
	•	Language arts		•	Learning strategies
	•	Written express		•	Organizational skills

Academic Accommodations

Curriculum	Study Aids	Exams
Priority registration	• Typist	• Oral
• Math waiver	• Reader	• Untimed
• Foreign lang. waiver	• Notetaker	• Take home
Course substitution	• Proof reader	• With proctor
In Class	• Text on tape	• On computer
• Calculators	Early syllabus	• Extended time
• Tape recorder	• Taped handouts	• On tape
• Word processor		• Modified
Priority seating		• Separate room

Graduation Requirements:
Course credits: **Varies by school**

General Information:
Indiana UniversityPurdue Univeristy at Indianapolis is a 4 year public university. of 410 acres is 113 miles from Indianapolis. Accessible by air, train or bus Ski areas are 75 miles from campus. 300 residential halls on campus. Housing is not guaranteed.

Accreditation: Regional

SAT/ACT Scores:
Scores for incoming freshmen: **Verbal:** 90% below 500. 9% between 500 and 599. 0.9% between 600 and 699. 0.1% above 700. **Math:** 77% below 500. 19% between 500 and 599. 4% between 600 and 699. 0.1% above 700. **ACT:** 59% below 20. 27% between 20 and 23. 9% between 24 and 25l. 4% between 26 and 28. 1% above 28.

Class Rank:
About 16%% of the present freshmen class were in the upper 20% of their high school class. 40 were in the top 40% of their class. 65% were in the top 60% of their class. 88% were in the top 80% of their class.

Expenses: Part-time: Per credit:$80.50. Part-time: Per credit:$242.60.

Majors
• BUSINESS Accounting, Banking/Finance, Business Management, Economics, Hotel & Restaurant Management, Human Resources Management, Labor Relations, Marketing, Organizational Behavior, Sports Management • COMMUNICATIONS Communication, English, Journalism, Speech/Debate/Forensic, Television/Radio/Film • COMPUTER SCIENCE Computer Science, Computer Technology, Medical Records Administration, Telecommunications • EDUCATION Art, Elementary, English, Foreign Language, Health, Mathematics, Middle School, Physical, Reading, Science, Secondary, Social Studies, Special, Speech/Language • ENGINEERING Biomedical, Civil/Environmental, Computer, Drafting, Electrical, Engineering Science, Industrial, Mechanical • HEALTH SCIENCES Dental Assistant, Dental Hygiene, Health, Medical Records Administration, Nuclear Medical Technology, Nursing, Occupational Therapy, Physical Therapy, Public Health, Radiological Therapy, Respiratory Therapy • HUMANITIES English/Writing/Literature, Fine Arts, Liberal Arts , Philosophy, Religion • LANGUAGES English, French, German, Spanish • PRE PROFESSIONAL Business, Dentistry, Law, Medicine, Pharmacy, Social

Work • SCIENCES Anthropology, Biology, Chemistry, Computer Science, Geography, Geology, Mathematics, Physics, Public Health • SOCIAL SCIENCES Anthropology, Criminal Justice, Geography, History, Political Science, Psychology, Sociology • SPECIAL EDUCATION Gifted & Talented, Learning Disability, Mentally Retarded, Physically Handicapped • VISUAL AND PERFORMING ARTS Art, Art History, Dance, Theater

Sports/Activities

• SPORTS-INTERCOLLEGIATE Baseball (F), Baseball (M), Basketball (F), Basketball (M), Golf, Soccer, Tennis (F), Tennis (M), Volleyball • SPORTS-INTRAMURAL Baseball, Basketball, Diving, Golf, Track and Field, Volleyball • STUDENT LIFE ACTIVITIES Academic Clubs, Dance, Debate, Drama Groups, Ethnic & Cultural Groups, Fraternities, Magazine, Music Groups, Sororities, Student Government, Yearbook

Less Selective **Indiana Program**

Indiana Vocational Technical College Central Indiana
P.O. Box 1763
Indianapolis, Indiana 46202
(317) 921-4800

School Enrollment: **4,018** Male: **1,805** Female: **2,213**
LD Enrollment: **70**

Admissions Contact: **Sonia Dickerson, Admissions/Counseling**
LD Contact: **Dianne Noe, Supervisor**
Name of Program: **Special Needs Program**
Telephone:**(317) 921-4983**

Admissions

Application Information:
Applicant must apply **3** months in advance
Rolling Admissions: **Yes**

Secondary School Information
Most Important Criteria For Admissions (1-strongest)

SAT/ACT	Application	School transcript
Class rank	Course selection	Personal statement
Interview	Extra activities	Psychoeducational
G.P.A.	**1** Open admission	Recommendations

Test Requirements:
Documentation of LD required: **Yes**
Tests recommended: **General admissions test**

Types of Disabilities Served
• Speech/Lang • Reading ADD with LD
• Study skills • Spelling ADD without LD
• Written express • Math ADHD with LD
• Organizational • Fine Motor ADHD without LD
• Perceptual

Learning Disability Program
Program: Remedial: **Yes**
Program: Reinforces course work: **Yes**
Program available through:**Monday-Friday**
Students mainstreamed **100** % of the day
Services available for all students: **Yes**
Counseling: Individual: **Yes**

Faculty:
Faculty: **3** Including Director: **Yes** Full time: **3** M.A.: **3**
Faculty advocate: **Yes** Meets with instructor: **As needed**

Diagnostic Testing

ADD	Personality	Perceptual skills	• Spelling
ADHD	Organization	Fine motor skills	• Reading
• I.Q.	Handwriting•	Spoken language	Study skills
• Math	Social skills•	Written language	

Tutoring:
Average size of group tutorials: **1:1**
Services rendered by:
Graduates   Peers   Faculty   •LD staff   Teacher trainees

Tutorials

Grp.	Ind.	Tutorials	Grp.	Ind.	Tutorials
	•	Math skills			Word processing
	•	Study skills			Time management
	•	Language arts		•	Learning strategies
	•	Written express			Organizational skills

Academic Accommodations

Curriculum	Study Aids	Exams
Priority registration	• Typist	Oral
Math waiver	Reader	Untimed
Foreign lang. waiver	Notetaker	Take home
Course substitution	Proof reader	With proctor
In Class	• Text on tape	On computer
• Calculators	Early syllabus	• Extended time
• Tape recorder	Taped handouts	On tape
• Word processor		Modified
Priority seating		Separate room

Graduation Requirements:
Course credits: **Varies 64-70** GPA: **2.0** Years to complete degree: **Unlimited** Math waiver: **Yes** Language waiver: **Yes**

Program Strengths
The Special Needs Program enables all students, regardless of their disability, to be successful within the college setting.

General Information:
Indiana Vocational Technical College Central Indiana is a 2 year public university. Urban campus. of 5-6 acres is Accessible by air or bus. Housing is not guaranteed.

Accreditation:Regional

Expenses: Part-time: Per credit:$50.30. Part-time: Per credit:$95.30.

Majors
• BUSINESS Accounting, Business Administration, Entrepreneur, Food Management, Hotel and Restaurant Managemen, Management, Trade and Industrial Supervisi • COMPUTER SCIENCE Computer Technology, Data Processing, Programming, Robotics • EDUCATION Child Development • ENGINEERING Electrical • ENVIRONMENTAL CONTROL Water and Wastewater Technolog • HEALTH SCIENCES Medical Assistant, Medical Technology, Nursing • PREPROFESSIONAL Architecture, Drafting • SCIENCES Process Quality Control, Statistics • VOCATIONAL Air Conditioning/Heating/Refri, Auto Body, Automobile Technology, Culinary Arts, Drafting, Electronics Technology, Fire Science, Industrial Equipment Maintenan, Machinist, Radiological Technology, Respiratory Therapy Technology, Secretarial

Sports/Activities

• STUDENT LIFE ACTIVITIES Student Government

Less Selective

**Indiana
Services**

Indiana Vocational Technical College: Eastcentral

4301 South Cowan Road
Muncie, Indiana 47302
(317) 289-2291

School Enrollment: **1,700** Male: **800** Female: **900**
LD Contact: **Gail Puckett, Director of Student Services**
Name of Program: **Instructional Support Services**

Admissions

Application Information:
Application deadline: **Open Admissions**
Rolling Admissions: **Yes**

Secondary School Information
Most Important Criteria For Admissions (1-strongest)

SAT/ACT	Application	School transcript
Class rank	Course selection	Personal statement
Interview	Extra activities	Psychoeducational
G.P.A.	**1** Open admission	Recommendations

Test Requirements:
Documentation of LD required: **Yes**

Types of Disabilities Served
• Speech/Lang	• Reading	ADD with LD
• Study skills	• Spelling	ADD without LD
• Written express	• Math	ADHD with LD
• Organizational	• Fine Motor	ADHD without LD
• Perceptual		

Learning Disability Program
Students mainstreamed **100** % of the day
Recommended credits per semester:
Counseling: Individual: **Yes** Group Counseling: **Yes** Vocational Counseling: **Yes**

Faculty:
Faculty: **2** Full time: **2**
Faculty advocate: **Yes** Meets with instructor: **As needed**

Diagnostic Testing
ADD	Personality	Perceptual skills	Spelling
ADHD	Organization	Fine motor skills	Reading
I.Q.	Handwriting	Spoken language	Study skills
Math	Social skills	Written language	

Tutoring:
Average size of group tutorials: **1-2**
Services rendered by:
Graduates •Peers Faculty •LD staff Teacher trainees

Tutorials
Grp.	Ind.	Tutorials	Grp.	Ind.	Tutorials
•	•	Math skills	•		Word processing
•	•	Study skills	•		Time management
•	•	Language arts	•		Learning strategies
•		Written express	•		Organizational skills

Academic Accommodations
Curriculum	Study Aids	Exams
• Priority registration	Typist	• Oral
Math waiver	Reader	• Untimed
Foreign lang. waiver	• Notetaker	• Take home
Course substitution	• Proof reader	• With proctor
In Class	• Text on tape	On computer
• Calculators	Early syllabus	• Extended time
• Tape recorder	Taped handouts	On tape
• Word processor		• Modified
• Priority seating		• Separate room

Program Strengths
The Instructional Support Services Program exists to provide assistance to all students who need additional services above and beyond what the average student entering our college needs.

General Information:
Indiana Vocational Technical College: Eastcentral is a 2 year public college. Suburban campus of 15 acres is 1 miles from Muncie. Accessible by bus. 1% of students are foreign. Housing is not guaranteed.

Accreditation: NCACS

Expenses:
Tuition: In-state: Full year: Part-time: Per credit: $55.00. Tuition: Out-of-state: Full year: Part-time: Per credit: $110.00.

Majors
• BUSINESS Accounting • COMPUTER SCIENCE Programming • HEALTH SCIENCES Medical Assistant, Mental Health/Human Services • VOCATIONAL Air Conditioning/Heating/Refri, Automotive Mechanics, Construction, Electrical/Electronics Equipme, Industrial Equipment Maintenan, Machinist, Office Administration, Secretarial, Small Business Management & Ow, Trade & Industrial Supervision

Sports/Activities
• STUDENT LIFE ACTIVITIES Student Government

Less Selective

**Indiana
Services**

Indiana Vocational Technical College: Northcentral

1534 West Sample Street
South Bend, Indiana 46619
(219) 289-7001

School Enrollment: **2,400** Male: **1,400** Female: **1,000**
LD Enrollment: **25**

Admissions Contact: **Larry Bartek, Director Student Services**
LD Contact: **Connie Johnston, Coordinator**
Name of Program: **Services for Handicapped Students**
Address: **Ivy Tech**
Telephone: **(219) 289-7001**

Indiana

Admissions

Application Information:
Separate application:**Yes**
Application deadline: **None**
Rolling Admissions: **Yes**

Secondary School Information
Most Important Criteria For Admissions (1-strongest)

SAT/ACT	Application **1**	School transcript
Class rank	Course selection	Personal statement
Interview	Extra activities	Psychoeducational
G.P.A.	Open admission	Recommendations

Test Requirements:
Standardized tests waived: **Yes**
Range accepted:
Documentation of LD required: **Yes**
Tests recommended: **Through Vocational Rehabilitation - psychological evaluation**

Types of Disabilities Served
- Speech/Lang
- Study skills
- Written express
- Organizational
- Perceptual
- Reading
- Spelling
- Math
- Fine Motor
- ADD with LD
- ADD without LD
- ADHD with LD
- ADHD without LD

Admissions Process

Take a Multiple Assessment and Placement Service (MAPS) test to assess skills in reading, writing, and math. Provide grade transcript or GED, complete form for admission and meet with Admissions Counselor, fill out financial aid form, go to orientation, and meet with Advisor.

Learning Disability Program

Program: Remedial: **Yes**
Program: Reinforces course work: **Yes**
Students mainstreamed **100** % of the day
Recommended credits per semester: **varies**
Services available for all students: **Yes**
Vocational Counseling: **Yes**

Faculty:
Faculty: **1** Part time: **1** M.A.: **1**

Diagnostic Testing

ADD	Personality	Perceptual skills	Spelling
ADHD	Organization	Fine motor skills	• Reading
I.Q.	Handwriting	Spoken language	Study skills
• Math	Social skills	• Written language	

Services rendered by:

Graduates	Peers	Faculty	LD staff	Teacher trainees

Tutorials

Grp.	Ind.	Tutorials	Grp.	Ind.	Tutorials
	•	Math skills		•	Word processing
•	•	Study skills	•		Time management
	•	Language arts			Learning strategies
	•	Written express		•	Organizational skills

Academic Accommodations

Curriculum	Study Aids	Exams
• Priority registration	• Typist	• Oral
Math waiver	Reader	Untimed
Foreign lang. waiver	• Notetaker	• Take home
• Course substitution	Proof reader	• With proctor
In Class	• Text on tape	• On computer
• Calculators	Early syllabus	• Extended time
• Tape recorder	Taped handouts	• On tape
• Word processor		• Modified
• Priority seating		• Separate room

Program Strengths
LD students are offered a variety of services geared to meet their individual needs.

General Information:
Indiana Vocational Technical College: Northcentral is a 2 year public college. Urban campus   Accessible by bus. Ski areas are 10 miles from campus. Beaches are 30 miles from campus. Housing is not guaranteed.

Accreditation:NCACS

Expenses:
Tuition: In-state: Full year: $1,200.00. Part-time: Per credit:$50.30. Part-time: Per course: $150.90. Tuition: Out-of-state: Full year: $2,200.00. Part-time: Per credit:$91.50. Part-time: Per course:$274.50

Majors
• BUSINESS Accounting, Business Management, Entrepreneur, Industrial Operations, Marketing • COMMUNICATIONS Commercial Design, Graphic Design, Photography, Television/Radio/Film • COMPUTER SCIENCE Business Data Programming, Systems Analysis • HEALTH SCIENCES Medical Assistant, Medical Laboraotry Technology, Nursing, Practical Nursing • VOCATIONAL Air Conditioning/Heating/Refri, Auto Body, Auto Manufacturing Technology, Automobile Technology, Automotive Service, Business and Office, Cosmetology, Diesel Power Technology, Drafting, Electronics Technology, Industrial Design, Industrial Equipment Maintenan, Interior Design, Machinist, Medical Laboratory Technology, Office Administration, Plastic Technology, Secretarial, Welding

Sports/Activities
• STUDENT LIFE ACTIVITIES Student Government

Less Selective   **Indiana**
                                                Accommodations

Indiana Vocational Technical College: Northeast
3800 North Anthony Boulevard
Fort Wayne, Indiana 46805
(219) 482-9171

School Enrollment: **4,100** Male: **2,210** Female: **1,890**
LD Enrollment: **20**

Admissions Contact: **Debra Clark, Admissions Coordinator**
LD Contact: **Rex Oechsle, Coordinator, Disabled Students**
Name of Program: **Basic Skills Advancement Services**
Telephone:**(219) 480-4207**

Admissions

Application Information:
Application deadline: **None**

Secondary School Information
Most Important Criteria For Admissions (1-strongest)

SAT/ACT	Application	School transcript
Class rank	Course selection	Personal statement
Interview	Extra activities	Psychoeducational
G.P.A.	**1** Open admission	Recommendations

Test Requirements:
Documentation of LD required: **Yes**

Types of Disabilities Served
- Speech/Lang
- Study skills
- Written express
- Organizational
- Perceptual
- Reading
- Spelling
- Math
- Fine Motor
- ADD with LD
- ADD without LD
- ADHD with LD
- ADHD without LD

Learning Disability Program
Students mainstreamed **100** % of the day
Recommended credits per semester: **6-9**
Counseling: Individual: **Yes** Vocational Counseling: **Yes**

Faculty:
Faculty: **4** Full time: **3** Part time: **1**
Faculty advocate: **Yes** Meets with instructor: **As needed**

Diagnostic Testing

ADD	Personality	Perceptual skills	Spelling
ADHD	Organization	Fine motor skills	Reading
I.Q.	Handwriting	Spoken language	Study skills
Math	Social skills	Written language	

Tutoring:
Average size of group tutorials:
Services rendered by:

Graduates	Peers	Faculty	•LD staff	Teacher trainees

Tutorials

Grp.	Ind.	Tutorials	Grp.	Ind.	Tutorials
	•	Math skills		•	Word processing
		Study skills			Time management
	•	Language arts			Learning strategies
	•	Written express			Organizational skills

Academic Accommodations

Curriculum	Study Aids	Exams
Priority registration	Typist	Oral
Math waiver	Reader	Untimed
Foreign lang. waiver •	Notetaker	Take home
Course substitution	Proof reader	• With proctor
In Class	Text on tape	On computer
• Calculators	Early syllabus	• Extended time
• Tape recorder	Taped handouts	On tape
Word processor		Modified
• Priority seating		• Separate room

Graduation Requirements:
Course credits: **60+** GPA: **2.0** Years to complete degree: **3-4**

Program Strengths
We do not have an LD Program. Support services and remedial courses are available but not required.

General Information:
Indiana Vocational Technical College: Northeast is a 2 year public college. Urban campus 120 miles from Chicago. Housing is not guaranteed.

Accreditation:NCACS

Expenses:
Tuition: In-state: Full year: $1,810.80. Part-time: Per credit:$50.30. Part-time: Per credit:$95.00.

Majors
• BUSINESS Accounting, Business Management, Marketing • COMPUTER SCIENCE Computer Maintenance, Computer Technology, Data Processing, Programming, Robotics • ENGINEERING Drafting • HEALTH SCIENCES Medical Assistant, Medical Secretary, Nursing, Respiratory Therapy • VOCATIONAL Air Condtioning/Heating/Refrig, Automated Manufacturing Techno, Automotive Service, Building Construction, Culinary Arts, Drafting, Electronics Technology, Fire Science, Machinist, Respiratory Therapy Technology, Secretarial, Welding, Word Processing

Sports/Activities
• STUDENT LIFE ACTIVITIES Accounting Club, Data Processing Management Ass, Student Government

---

Less Selective　　　　　　　　　　　**Indiana**
Services

Indiana Vocational Technical College: Southwest
3501 First Avenue
Evansville, Indiana 47710
(812) 426-2865

School Enrollment: **3,100** Male: **1,500** Female: **1,600**

Admissions Contact: **Phil Hesson, Enrollment Services Manager**
LD Contact: **Peggy Ehlen, Reading Specialist/Special Needs**
Name of Program: **Basic Skills Advancement Program**
Address: **3501 First Avenue**
Telephone:**(812) 429-1386**

Admissions

Application Information:
Application deadline: **Prior to 1st day of class**
Rolling Admissions: **Yes**

Secondary School Information
Most Important Criteria For Admissions (1-strongest)

SAT/ACT	Application	School transcript
Class rank	Course selection	Personal statement
Interview	Extra activities	**1** Psychoeducational
G.P.A.	**1** Open admission	Recommendations

Test Requirements:
Diagnostic testing waived: **Yes**
WAIS-R required: **Yes** Range accepted: **Normal**
Documentation of LD required: **Yes**
Tests recommended: **Woodcock-Johnson, MAPS Achievement**

Indiana

Types of Disabilities Served
- Speech/Lang
- Study skills
- Written express
- Organizational
- Perceptual
- Reading
- Spelling
- Math
- Fine Motor
- ADD with LD
- ADD without LD
- ADHD with LD
- ADHD without LD

Admissions Process

We have an open admissions policy.

High School Course Requirements:
Waivers to standard high school courses
Course substitution: **Yes**

Learning Disability Program

Program: Remedial: **Yes**
Program: Reinforces course work: **Yes**
Recommended credits per semester: **9**
Counseling: Individual: **Yes** Vocational Counseling: **Yes**

Faculty:
Faculty: **1** Full time: **1** M.A.: **1**
Faculty advocate: **Yes** Meets with instructor: **As needed**

Diagnostic Testing
ADD	Personality	Perceptual skills	• Spelling
ADHD	Organization	Fine motor skills	• Reading
I.Q.	Handwriting	Spoken language	• Study skills
• Math	Social skills	• Written language	

Tutoring:
Average size of group tutorials: **2**
Services rendered by:
Graduates	Peers	•Faculty	•LD staff	Teacher trainees

Tutorials
Grp.	Ind.	Tutorials	Grp.	Ind.	Tutorials
	•	Math skills	•	•	Word processing
•	•	Study skills	•	•	Time management
	•	Language arts	•	•	Learning strategies
	•	Written express	•	•	Organizational skills

Academic Accommodations
Curriculum	Study Aids	Exams
Priority registration	Typist	• Oral
Math waiver	Reader	• Untimed
Foreign lang. waiver	• Notetaker	Take home
Course substitution	• Proof reader	• With proctor
In Class	• Text on tape	• On computer
• Calculators	Early syllabus	• Extended time
• Tape recorder	• Taped handouts	• On tape
• Word processor		• Modified
• Priority seating		• Separate room

Graduation Requirements:
Course credits: **Varies by field** GPA: **2.0**

Program Strengths
We strive to help students make full use of their abilities while offering accommodations that are fair, feasible, and effective. When possible, we offer remediation in basic skills; primarily we concentrate on supporting the learning abilities of the qualified learning disabled.

General Information:
Indiana Vocational Technical College: Southwest is a 2 year public college. Urban campus Accessible by bus. 1% of students are foreign. Housing is not guaranteed.

Accreditation:NCACS, CAHEA

Expenses:
Tuition: In-state: Full year: $1,810.00. Part-time: Per credit:$50.30-$150.90. Tuition: Out-of-state: Full year: $3,396.00. Part-time: Per credit:$91.50-$274.50.

Majors
• BUSINESS Accounting, Business Administration, Entrepreneur, Food Management, Marketing • COMMUNICATIONS Art, Communication, Photography • COMPUTER SCIENCE Computer Maintenance, Data Processing, Programming • EDUCATION Child Development • HEALTH SCIENCES Medical Assistant, Nursing, Surgical Technology • SCIENCES Management Science • VOCATIONAL Air Conditioning/Heating/Refri, Automobile Technology, Automotive Service, Construction, Diesel Power Technology, Electronics Technology, Graphic Arts Technology, Industrial Equipment Maintenan, Interior Design, Secretarial, Welding

Sports/Activities
• SPORTS-INTRAMURAL Softball • STUDENT LIFE ACTIVITIES Student Government

---

Less Selective

**Indiana
Services**

Indiana Vocational Technical College: Whitewater
2325 Chester Boulevard
Richmond, Indiana 47374
(317) 966-2656

School Enrollment: **800** Male: **200** Female: **600**
LD Enrollment: **10**

Admissions Contact: **Linda Przybysz, Admissions Coordinator**
LD Contact: **Patricia M. Rush, Coordinator**
Name of Program: **Skills Advancement**
Telephone:**(317) 966-2656 Ext. 41**

Admissions

Application Information:
Application deadline: **Rolling**
Rolling Admissions: **Yes**

Secondary School Information
Most Important Criteria For Admissions (1-strongest)
SAT/ACT **7**	Application **4**	School transcript
Class rank **6**	Course selection	Personal statement
2 Interview	Extra activities	**1** Psychoeducational
5 G.P.A.	**1** Open admission	**3** Recommendations

Test Requirements:
Standardized tests waived: **Yes**

Types of Disabilities Served
- Speech/Lang
- Study skills
- Written express
- Organizational
- Perceptual
- Reading
- Spelling
- Math
- Fine Motor
- ADD with LD
- ADD without LD
- ADHD with LD
- ADHD without LD

Learning Disability Program
Counseling: Individual: **Yes** Group Counseling: **Yes**

Faculty:
Faculty: **6** Part time: **6**
Faculty advocate: **Yes** Meets with instructor: **As needed**

Diagnostic Testing

ADD	Personality	Perceptual skills	Spelling
ADHD	Organization	Fine motor skills	Reading
I.Q.	Handwriting	Spoken language	Study skills
Math	Social skills	Written language	

Tutoring:
Average size of group tutorials: **Varies**
Services rendered by:
Graduates   Peers   Faculty   •LD staff   Teacher trainees

Tutorials

Grp.	Ind.	Tutorials	Grp.	Ind.	Tutorials
•	•	Math skills	•	•	Word processing
•	•	Study skills	•	•	Time management
•	•	Language arts	•	•	Learning strategies
•	•	Written express	•	•	Organizational skills

Academic Accommodations

Curriculum	Study Aids	Exams
Priority registration	Typist	• Oral
• Math waiver	Reader	Untimed
Foreign lang. waiver	• Notetaker	• Take home
• Course substitution	• Proof reader	With proctor
In Class	Text on tape	On computer
Calculators	Early syllabus	• Extended time
• Tape recorder	Taped handouts	On tape
• Word processor		• Modified
Priority seating		Separate room

Program Strengths
The Skills Advancement Program provides classes and tutoring services for special needs students. The class and programs are mainstreamed with the general population. We do not have specific classes for students with learning disabilities, but we work with vocational rehabilitation to provide the best placement for students. In addition, we offer a support group for students with disabilities and work to provide services on an individual level.

General Information:
Indiana Vocational Technical College: Whitewater is a 2 year public college. Suburban campus 40 miles from Dayton. Accessible by train or bus. Housing is not guaranteed.

Accreditation: NCACS

Expenses: Part-time: Per credit: $30.00.

Majors
• BUSINESS Accounting, Business Management, Entrepreneur, Hotel Management • COMPUTER SCIENCE Information Data Management, Information Science and System, Programming • EDUCATION Early Childhood • HEALTH SCIENCES Nursing • SOCIAL SCIENCES Family Counseling • VOCATIONAL Automobile Technology, Automotive Service, Building Construction, Construction, Electronics Technology, Food Service, Industrial Equipment Maintenan, Machinist, Secretarial, Word Processing

Sports/Activities
• SPORTS-INTERCOLLEGIATE Softball • STUDENT LIFE ACTIVI- TIES Academic Clubs, Film, Student Government

---

Less Selective — **Indiana**

Indiana VocationalTechnical College Kokomo
1815 East Morgan Street
Kokomo, Indiana 46901
(317) 454-5103

School Enrollment: **1,700** Male: **962** Female: **736**

Admissions Contact: **Mary Bennett, Admissions Coordinator**
LD Contact: **M. Janice Chase, Coordinator**
Name of Program: **Basic Skills Advancement Project**
Telephone: **(317) 459-5103**

Admissions

Application Information:
Application deadline: **None**
Rolling Admissions: **Yes**

Secondary School Information
Most Important Criteria For Admissions (1-strongest)

SAT/ACT	**1** Application	**2**	School transcript
Class rank	**3** Course selection		Personal statement
4 Interview	Extra activities		Psychoeducational
G.P.A.	Open admission		Recommendations

Types of Disabilities Served

• Speech/Lang	• Reading	ADD with LD
• Study skills	• Spelling	ADD without LD
• Written express	• Math	ADHD with LD
• Organizational	• Fine Motor	ADHD without LD
• Perceptual		

Learning Disability Program
Counseling: Individual: **Yes**

Faculty:
Faculty: **13** Full time: **13**
Faculty advocate: **Yes** Meets with instructor: **Weekly**

Diagnostic Testing

ADD	Personality	Perceptual skills	Spelling
ADHD	Organization	Fine motor skills	Reading
I.Q.	Handwriting	Spoken language	Study skills
Math	Social skills	Written language	

Tutoring:
Average size of group tutorials: **Individual**
Services rendered by:
Graduates   Peers   •Faculty   •LD staff   •Teacher trainees

Tutorials

Grp.	Ind.	Tutorials	Grp.	Ind.	Tutorials
	•	Math skills		•	Word processing
	•	Study skills		•	Time management
	•	Language arts		•	Learning strategies
	•	Written express		•	Organizational skills

Indiana

Academic Accommodations

Curriculum	Study Aids	Exams
Priority registration	Typist	• Oral
Math waiver	Reader	Untimed
Foreign lang. waiver	• Notetaker	• Take home
Course substitution	Proof reader	With proctor
In Class	Text on tape	On computer
• Calculators	Early syllabus	• Extended time
• Tape recorder	Taped handouts	On tape
• Word processor		• Modified
Priority seating		Separate room

Program Strengths

Ivy Tech's Region 5 learning disabled students are served by the Basic Skills Advancement Project which assesses basic skills and places students in appropriate instructional settings. Computer assisted instruction, personal tutoring, and counseling are available. No additional expenses are incurred as all special needs services are free.

General Information:

Indiana VocationalTechnical College Kokomo is a 2 year public college. Urban campus of 20 acres is 2 miles from Kokomo. Ski areas are 100 miles from campus. Beaches are 60 miles from campus. Housing is not guaranteed.

Accreditation: Regional

Expenses:

Tuition: In-state: Full year: Part-time: Per credit: $30.35. Part-time: Per credit:$30.35.

Majors

• BUSINESS Accounting, Entrepreneur, Food Management, Hotel and Restaurant Managemen, Labor Relations, Marketing, Secretarial Science, Trade and Industrial Supervisi • COMPUTER SCIENCE Computer Technology, Programming, Robotics • ENGINEERING Industrial • ENVIRONMENTAL CONTROL Water and Wastewater Technolog • HEALTH SCIENCES Medical Assistant, Radiograph Medical Technology • PRE-PROFESSIONAL Architecture, Drafting • VOCATIONAL Air Condtioning/Heating/Refrig, Automobile Technology, Automotive Service, Carpentry, Construction, Drafting, Electronics Technology, Fire Science, Interior Design, Machinist, Radiological Technology, Respiratory Therapy Technology, Secretarial

Sports/Activities

• STUDENT LIFE ACTIVITIES Student Government

Less Selective

Indiana Services

Indiana Wesleyan University
4201 South Washington Street
Marion, Indiana 46953
(317) 674-6901

School Enrollment: **1,200** Male: **600** Female: **600**

Admissions Contact: **Chuck Mealy, Director of Admissions**
LD Contact: **Dr. Ruth Dixon, Director**
Name of Program: **Learning Center**
Telephone:**(317) 677-2192**

Admissions

Application Information:
Notified when: **May**

Secondary School Information
Most Important Criteria For Admissions (1-strongest)

1 SAT/ACT	6 Application	2 School transcript
3 Class rank	5 Course selection	4 Personal statement
10 Interview	7 Extra activities	9 Psychoeducational
1 G.P.A.	Open admission	8 Recommendations

Test Requirements:
Documentation of LD required: **Yes**

Types of Disabilities Served
- Speech/Lang
- Study skills
- Written express
- Organizational
- Perceptual
- Reading
- Spelling
- Math
- Fine Motor
- ADD with LD
- ADD without LD
- ADHD with LD
- ADHD without LD

Learning Disability Program
Counseling: Individual: **Yes**

Faculty:
Faculty: **2**
Faculty advocate: **Yes** Meets with instructor: **As needed**

Diagnostic Testing

ADD	Personality	Perceptual skills	Spelling
ADHD	Organization	Fine motor skills	Reading
I.Q.	Handwriting	Spoken language	Study skills
Math	Social skills	Written language	

Tutoring:
Average size of group tutorials: **15 maximum**
Services rendered by:

| Graduates | Peers | Faculty | LD staff | Teacher trainees |

Tutorials

Grp.	Ind.	Tutorials	Grp.	Ind.	Tutorials
	•	Math skills		•	Word processing
•	•	Study skills	•	•	Time management
•	•	Language arts	•	•	Learning strategies
•	•	Written express	•	•	Organizational skills

Academic Accommodations

Curriculum	Study Aids	Exams
Priority registration	Typist	Oral
Math waiver	Reader	Untimed
Foreign lang. waiver	Notetaker	Take home
Course substitution	Proof reader	With proctor
In Class	• Text on tape	On computer
• Calculators	Early syllabus	Extended time
• Tape recorder	Taped handouts	On tape
• Word processor		Modified
Priority seating		Separate room

Program Strengths

We have no LD Program as such, but our Learning Center strives to meet the needs of underprepared students in reading, writing and study skills. The counseling center offers individual tutoring for specific courses and counseling sessions as needed.

General Information:

Indiana Wesleyan University is a 4 year private Wesleyan Church university. Suburban campus of 60 acres is Accessible by air or bus. Beaches are 3 hours from campus. 2% of students are foreign. Housing is not guaranteed.50 % of students remain on campus for the weekends.

Accreditation:NCACS

Expenses:

Tuition: In-state: Full year: $7,000.00. Part-time: Per credit:$125.00. Tuition: Out-of-state: Full year: $7,000.00. Part-time: Per credit:$125.00. Room and board: $3,500.00

Majors

• AREA STUDIES Latin American • BUSINESS Business Administration, Business Data Processing, Business Economics, Business Education, Business Management, Economics, Music Business Management • COMMUNICATIONS Creative Writing, English • COMPUTER SCIENCE Data Processing, Programming, Systems Analysis • EDUCATION Art, Early Childhood, Elementary, English, Health, Leadership, Mathematics, Middle School, Music, Physical, Recreation and Youth Leadershi, Science, Secondary, Social Studies • HEALTH SCIENCES Health, Medical Assistant, Nursing • HUMANITIES Humanities, Philosophy, Religion, Religious Studies • LANGUAGES Spanish • PREPROFESSIONAL Dentistry, Law, Medicine, Ministry, Pharmacy, Recreation, Social Work, Veterinarian • SCIENCES Biology, Chemistry, Earth, Mathematics, Physics • SOCIAL SCIENCES Criminal Justice, Government/Political, History, Law Enforcement, Political Science, Psychology, Social Sciences, Sociology • VISUAL AND PERFORMING ARTS Art, Art History, Music, Music Performance, Religious Music, Studio Art • VOCATIONAL Business and Office, Medical Laboratory Technology, Park/Recreation

Sports/Activities

• SPORTS RELATED Band, Cheerleading, Pep Band, Team Managers • SPORTS-INTERCOLLEGIATE Baseball (M), Basketball, Cross Country (M), Field Hockey (F), Golf (M), Soccer (M), Tennis (M), Track and Field, Volleyball (F) • SPORTS-INTRAMURAL Badminton, Basketball, Bowling, Golf, Ping-Pong, Racquetball, Softball, Tennis, Volleyball • STUDENT LIFE ACTIVITIES Choral, Concert Band, Drama Groups, Ethnic & Cultural Groups, Jazz Band, Music Groups, Newspaper, Radio/TV station, Religious Organization, Student Government, Symphony Orchestra, Yearbook

Selective	Indiana
	Program

Manchester College

604 College Avenue
No. Manchester, Indiana 46962
(219) 982-5000

School Enrollment: **1,137** Male: **539** Female: **598**
LD Enrollment: **10**

Admissions Contact: **Denise Howe, Asst. Dir. of Admissions**
LD Contact: **Karen Doudt, Coordinator/Special Needs**
Name of Program: **Students with Special Needs**
Telephone:**(219) 982-5000**

Admissions

Application Information:

Application deadline: **August 1st**
Rolling Admissions: **Yes**

Secondary School Information

Most Important Criteria For Admissions (1-strongest)

8 SAT/ACT	**9** Application	**4** School transcript
3 Class rank	**3** Course selection **10**	Personal statement
6 Interview	**11** Extra activities	**5** Psychoeducational
1 G.P.A.	Open admission	Recommendations

Test Requirements:

Diagnostic testing waived: **Yes**
Untimed SAT: **Yes** Untimed ACT: **Yes**
WAIS-R required: **Yes**
Documentation of LD required: **Yes**
Currency of diagnostic testing: **3 years**

Types of Disabilities Served

• Speech/Lang	• Reading	ADD with LD
• Study skills	• Spelling	ADD without LD
• Written express	• Math	ADHD with LD
• Organizational	• Fine Motor	ADHD without LD
• Perceptual		

Admissions Process

Application, $20.00 application fee, high school transcript, high school counselor recommendation, psychological test results. If determined potential for success, interview with director of Special Needs who recommends to Admissions Committee who makes decision.

High School Course Requirements:

English: **4** Math: **2** Science: **2**
Waivers to standard high school courses
Course substitution: **Yes**

Learning Disability Program

Special orientation for LD students: **Yes**
Program available through:**All times**
Students mainstreamed **100** % of the day
Services only for LD students: **Yes**
Services available for all students: **Yes**
Counseling: Individual: **Yes** Group Counseling: **Yes** Vocational Counseling: **Yes**
Support groups are available:**Yes**

Faculty:

Faculty: **2** Including Director: **Yes**
Faculty advocate: **Yes** Meets with instructor: **As needed**

Diagnostic Testing

ADD	Personality	Perceptual skills	Spelling
ADHD	Organization	Fine motor skills	Reading
I.Q.	Handwriting	Spoken language	Study skills
Math	Social skills	Written language	

Tutoring:

Average size of group tutorials: **varies**
Services rendered by:
  Graduates •Peers •Faculty LD staff •Teacher trainees

Tutorials

Grp.	Ind.	Tutorials	Grp.	Ind.	Tutorials
•	•	Math skills			Word processing
•	•	Study skills	•	•	Time management
•	•	Language arts	•	•	Learning strategies
•	•	Written express	•	•	Organizational skills

Academic Accommodations

Curriculum	Study Aids	Exams
Priority registration	Typist	• Oral
Math waiver	• Reader	• Untimed
Foreign lang. waiver	• Notetaker	Take home
Course substitution	• Proof reader	• With proctor
In Class	• Text on tape	On computer
• Calculators	Early syllabus	• Extended time
• Tape recorder	Taped handouts	• On tape
Word processor		Modified
• Priority seating		Separate room

Graduation Requirements:
Course credits: **128** GPA: **2.0**

Program Strengths

Our program is limited to a small number of students. The students are mainstreamed full time. The unique feature of our program is the learning disability support group that meets one hour every two weeks. The group listens, supports, and provides training where necessary (assertiveness, study techniques, etc.)

General Information:

Manchester College is a 4 year private Church of the Brethren college. Rural campus of 120 acres is 35 miles from Fort Wayne. Accessible by air, train or bus. 3% of students are foreign. 6 residential halls on campus. Housing is guaranteed.Guaranteed through Unlimited. 75 % of students remain on campus for the weekends.

Accreditation:NCACS

SAT/ACT Scores:
Scores for incoming freshmen:**Verbal:**75%below 500. 22%between 500 and 599. 2%between 600 and 699. 3%above 700. **Math:**51% below 500. 35% between 500 and 599. 12% between 600 and 699. 3%above 700. **ACT:** 30% below 20. 45% between 20 and 23. 23%between 24 and 25l. 2% above 28.

Class Rank:
About 45% of the present freshmen class were in the upper 20% of their high school class. 79% were in the top 40% of their class. 97% were in the top 60% of their class. 100 were in the top 80% of their class.

Expenses:
Tuition: In-state: Full year: $8,690.00. Part-time: Per credit:$258.00. Tuition: Out-of-state: Full year: $8,690.00. Part-time: Per credit:$258.00. Room and board: $3,440.00

Majors

• BUSINESS Accounting, Business Administration, Business Education, Economics, Management, Marketing • COMMUNICATIONS Communication, English, Literature, Speech, Television/Radio/Film • COMPUTER SCIENCE Computer Science • EDUCATION Art, Early Childhood, Elementary, Foreign Language, Health, Music, Pre-Education, Science, Secondary, Social Studies • ENGINEERING Engineering Science, Environmental/Water Resources • HEALTH SCIENCES Health, Medical Technology, Nursing • HUMANITIES Philosophy, Religion • LANGUAGES French, German, Spanish • PREPROFESSIONAL Dentistry, Engineering, Law, Medicine, Social Work, Sports Medicine, Veterinarian • SCIENCES Biology, Chemistry, Mathematics • SOCIAL SCIENCES Anthropology, Criminal Justice, Criminology, Government/Political, History, Political Science, Psychology, Sociology • VISUAL AND PERFORMING ARTS Art, Dramatic Arts, Music, Religious Music, Theater

Sports/Activities

• SPORTS RELATED Cheerleading, Team Managers • SPORTS-INTERCOLLEGIATE Baseball (M), Basketball, Cross Country, Football (M), Golf (M), Soccer (M), Softball (F), Tennis, Track and Field, Volleyball (F), Wrestling (M) • SPORTS-INTRAMURAL Badminton, Basketball, Ping-Pong, Racquetball, Softball, Tennis, Volleyball • STUDENT LIFE ACTIVITIES Dance, Debate, Drama Groups, Ethnic & Cultural Groups, Jazz Band, Music Groups, Newspaper, Radio/TV station, Student Government, Symphony Orchestra, Yearbook

---

Very Selective **Indiana**
Services

Purdue University
Schleman Hall
West Lafayette, Indiana 47907
(317) 494-1247

School Enrollment: **34,000** Male: **19,568** Female: **14,389**
LD Enrollment: **225**

Admissions Contact: **Kristi A. Duebin Asst. Director of Admissions**
LD Contact: **Sarah Templin/Cathy Jones Program Specialists**
Name of Program: **Adaptive Programs**
Address: **Schleman Hall**
Telephone:**(317) 494-1144**

Admissions

Application Information:
Application deadline: **Rolling**
Rolling Admissions: **Yes**

Secondary School Information
Most Important Criteria For Admissions (1-strongest)

3 SAT/ACT	**7** Application	**1**	School transcript
2 Class rank	**4** Course selection	**8**	Personal statement
5 Interview	**9** Extra activities	**10**	Psychoeducational
2 G.P.A.	Open admission	**6**	Recommendations

Test Requirements:
Untimed SAT: **Yes** Untimed ACT: **Yes**
Range accepted:
Documentation of LD required: **Yes**

Types of Disabilities Served

• Speech/Lang	• Reading	ADD with LD
• Study skills	• Spelling	ADD without LD
• Written express	• Math	• ADHD with LD
• Organizational	• Fine Motor	• ADHD without LD
• Perceptual		

Learning Disability Program
Special orientation for LD students: **Yes**
Counseling: Individual: **Yes** Group Counseling: **Yes**

Faculty:
Faculty: **2** Part time: **2** M.A.: **2**
Faculty advocate: **Yes**

Diagnostic Testing

ADD	Personality	Perceptual skills	Spelling
ADHD	Organization	Fine motor skills	Reading
I.Q.	Handwriting	Spoken language	Study skills
Math	Social skills	Written language	

Tutoring:
Services rendered by:

•Graduates   Peers   Faculty   •LD staff   Teacher trainees

Tutorials

Grp.	Ind.	Tutorials	Grp.	Ind.	Tutorials
		Math skills			Word processing
•		Study skills		•	Time management
		Language arts		•	Learning strategies
•		Written express		•	Organizational skills

Academic Accommodations

Curriculum	Study Aids	Exams
Priority registration	• Typist	• Oral
Math waiver	Reader	Untimed
• Foreign lang. waiver	• Notetaker	• Take home
• Course substitution	• Proof reader	With proctor
In Class	• Text on tape	On computer
• Calculators	Early syllabus	• Extended time
• Tape recorder	Taped handouts	On tape
• Word processor		Modified
Priority seating		Separate room

Program Strengths

The Learning Disability Program at Purdue University is run in conjunction with the Dean of Students Office. The program is individualized to meet each eligible student's needs. We offer a wide variety of support services with an emphasis on student responsibility and control. We're proud that the percentage of Purdue University students who have received support services through our office and have gone on to graduate is extremely high.

General Information:

Purdue University is a 4 year public university. Urban campus of 1,565 acres is 65 miles from Indianapolis. Accessible by air, train or bus. 6.4% of students are foreign. 14 residential halls on campus. Housing is not guaranteed.20 % of students join fraternities/sororities.

Accreditation:NCACS

SAT/ACT Scores:

Scores for incoming freshmen:**Verbal:**45%below 500. 35%between 500 and 599. **Math:**17% below 500. 33% between 500 and 599. **ACT:** 4% below 20. 16% between 20 and 23.

Class Rank:

About 59% of the present freshmen class were in the upper 20% of their high school class. 89% were in the top 40% of their class.

Expenses:

Tuition: In-state: Full year: $2,280.00. Part-time: Per credit:$83.50. Tuition: Out-of-state: Full year: $7,310.00. Part-time: Per credit:$244.50. Room and board: $3,610.00

Majors

• AGRICULTURE Business, Education, Horticultural, Plant Science • AREA STUDIES American, Black/Afro-American • BUSINESS Accounting, Agricultural, Economics, Industrial Operations, Management • COMMUNICATIONS Advertising, Communication, English, Journalism, Linguistic, Photography, Public Relations, Television/Radio/Film • COMPUTER SCIENCE Computer Graphics, Computer Science, Computer Technology, Programming, Robotics, Systems Analysis, Systems Engineer, Telecommunications • CRAFTS AND DESIGN Apparel Design, Industrial Design • EDUCATION Agricultural, Child Development, Early Childhood, Elementary, English, Foreign Language, Health, Home Economics, Industrial, Mathematics, Physical, Social Studies, Special • ENGINEERING Aerospace, Agricultural, Chemical, Civil/Environmental, Computer, Electrical, Industrial, Materials, Mechanical, Nuclear • ENVIRONMENTAL CONTROL Environmental Control • HEALTH SCIENCES Environmental, Health, Medical Laboratory Technology, Nursing,

Nutritional/Food, Pharmacology • HUMANITIES English/Writing/Literature, Fine Arts, Philosophy, Religion • LANGUAGES English, French, German, Linguistics, Russian, Spanish • MATHEMATICS Applied, Computer, Statistical • PREPROFESSIONAL Agriculture, Dentistry, Forestry, Landscaping, Law, Medicine, Pharmacy, Veterinarian • SCIENCES Animal, Anthropology, Applied Mathematics, Biochemistry, Biology, Cell Biology, Chemistry, Computer Science, Ecology, Entomology, General, Genetics, Geology, Geophysics & Seismology, Mathematics, Meteorology, Microbiology, Molecular Biology, Paleontology, Physics, Statistics • SOCIAL SCIENCES Anthropology, History, Political Science, Psychology, Public Relations, Sociology • SPECIAL EDUCATION Deaf/Hearing Impaired, Emotionally Disturbed, Learning Disability, Mentally Retarded, Physically Handicapped, Visually Handicapped • VISUAL AND PERFORMING ARTS Art History, Fine Arts, Theater • VOCATIONAL Aviation Technology, Industrial Design, Interior Design

Sports/Activities

• SPORTS RELATED Baton Twirling, Cheerleading, Chess, Drum Major/Majorette, Marching Band, Pep Band, Team Managers • SPORTS-INTERCOLLEGIATE Baseball (M), Basketball (F), Basketball (M), Cross Country (F), Cross Country (M), Football (M), Golf (F), Golf (M), Swimming (F), Swimming (M), Tennis (F), Tennis (M), Track and Field (F), Track and Field (M), Volleyball (F), Wrestling (M) • SPORTS-INTRAMURAL Archery, Baseball, Basketball, Canoeing, Crew, Cricket, Fencing, Gymnastics, Lacrosse, Polo, Racquetball, Riflery, Rugby, Sailing, Soccer, Softball, Squash, Swimming, Trap and Skeet, Volleyball, Water Polo • STUDENT LIFE ACTIVITIES Academic Clubs, Choral, Community Service, Concert Band, Ethnic & Cultural Groups, Fraternities, Jazz Band, Music Groups, Orchestra, Religious Organization, Sororities, Student Government, Yearbook

---

Very Selective   **Indiana**
                         Services

University of Evansville

1800 Lincoln Avenue
Evansville, Indiana 47722
(800) 423-8633

School Enrollment: **2,326** Male: **1,024** Female: **1,302**
LD Enrollment: **1-2%**

Admissions Contact: **Office of Admissions**
LD Contact: **Dr. Richard Nicholas, Dean of Students**
Address: **Student Life Center**
Telephone:**(812) 479-2500**

Admissions

Application Information:

Application deadline: **May 1st**

Secondary School Information

Most Important Criteria For Admissions (1-strongest)

5	SAT/ACT	8	Application	3	School transcript
4	Class rank	1	Course selection	10	Personal statement
9	Interview	7	Extra activities	11	Psychoeducational
2	G.P.A.		Open admission	6	Recommendations

Test Requirements:

Untimed SAT: **Yes** Untimed ACT: **Yes** Untimed ACH: **Yes**
Documentation of LD required: **Yes**

Indiana

Types of Disabilities Served
- Speech/Lang
- Study skills
- Written express
- Organizational
- Perceptual
- Reading
- Spelling
- Math
- Fine Motor
- ADD with LD
- ADD without LD
- ADHD with LD
- ADHD without LD

Admissions Process

Application form, SAT or ACT, high school transcript required. Interview and campus visit recommended.

High School Course Requirements:
English: **4** Math: **3** Science: **2**

Learning Disability Program

Students mainstreamed **100 %** of the day
Recommended credits per semester: **12-16**
Services available for all students: **Yes**
Group Counseling: **Yes** Vocational Counseling: **Yes**
Support groups are available:**Yes, student formed support group, optional**

Diagnostic Testing
ADD	• Personality	Perceptual skills	• Spelling
ADHD	• Organization	Fine motor skills	• Reading
I.Q.	Handwriting	Spoken language	Study skills
• Math	Social skills	• Written language	

Tutoring:
Average size of group tutorials: **1:1**
Services rendered by:
 Graduates •Peers Faculty LD staff Teacher trainees

Tutorials
Grp.	Ind.	Tutorials	Grp.	Ind.	Tutorials
	•	Math skills			Word processing
		Study skills			Time management
		Language arts			Learning strategies
	•	Written express			Organizational skills

Academic Accommodations
Curriculum	Study Aids	Exams
Priority registration	Typist	• Oral
Math waiver	• Reader	• Untimed
Foreign lang. waiver	Notetaker	Take home
Course substitution	• Proof reader	• With proctor
In Class	• Text on tape	On computer
Calculators	Early syllabus	• Extended time
• Tape recorder	Taped handouts	On tape
• Word processor		Modified
• Priority seating		• Separate room

Graduation Requirements:
Course credits: **124 +** GPA: **2.0** Years to complete degree: **4**
Other requirements: **Complete general education requirement**

Program Strengths
Highly individualized

General Information:
University of Evansville is a 2 and 4 year private Methodist university. Suburban campus of 75 acres is 120 miles from St. Louis. Accessible by air, train or bus. 5% of students are foreign. 5 residential halls on campus. Housing is guaranteed.Guaranteed through 1st year. 90 % of students re-

main on campus for the weekends. 22 % of students join fraternities/sororities.

Accreditation:NCACS, NASM, NLN, NCATE, APTA, ABET, ABA, IDPI

Expenses:
Tuition: In-state: Full year: $10,500.00. Tuition: Out-of-state: Full year: $10,500.00. Room and board: $3,970.00

Majors
• ARTS Art History, Commercial Art, Music, Music Performance • BUSINESS Accounting, Banking/Finance, Business Administration, Economics, Human Resources Management, International Business, Marketing, Sports Management • EDUCATION Art, Elementary, Music, Physical, Secondary, Special • ENGINEERING Civil/Environmental, Electrical, Mechanical • HEALTH SCIENCES Health, Nursing, Physical Therapy • HUMANITIES English/Writing/Literature, Liberal Arts , Philosophy, Religion • LANGUAGES French, German, Spanish • PRE PROFESSIONAL Dentistry, Legal Assistant, Medicine, Optometry, Pharmacy, Social Work, Sports Medicine, Veterinarian • SCIENCES Biology, Chemistry, Physics • SOCIAL SCIENCES Anthropology, Criminal Justice, History, International Studies, Political Science, Psychology, Sociology • VISUAL AND PERFORMING ARTS Art, Art History, Music, Music Performance, Theater

Sports/Activities
• SPORTS-INTERCOLLEGIATE Baseball (M), Basketball, Bowling, Cross Country, Diving, Football (M), Golf (M), Soccer, Swimming, Tennis, Volleyball (F) • STUDENT LIFE ACTIVITIES Academic Clubs, Choral, Community Service, Concert Band, Dance, Drama Groups, Ethnic & Cultural Groups, Film, Fraternities, Jazz Band, Magazine, Music Groups, Newspaper, Orchestra, Political Groups, Radio/TV station, Religious Organization, Sororities, Student Government, Yearbook

---

Selective   **Indiana Program**

University of Indianapolis
1400 East Hanna Avenue
Indianapolis, Indiana 46227
(317) 788-3216

School Enrollment: **1,244** Male: **747** Female: **497**
LD Enrollment: **30** Male: **20** Female: **10**

Admissions Contact: **Mark Weigand, Director of Admissions**
LD Contact: **Patricia Cook, Director**
Name of Program: **B.U.I.L.D.**
Telephone:**(317) 788-3285**

Admissions

Application Information:
LD Students Applying: **40** Accepted: **20** Enrolled:**15**
Separate application:**Yes**
LD on admissions committee:**Yes**
Application deadline: **July 15th**
Applicant must apply **6** months in advance
Rolling Admissions: **Yes**

Secondary School Information

Most Important Criteria For Admissions (1-strongest)

2 SAT/ACT	7 Application	1 School transcript
3 Class rank	5 Course selection	11 Personal statement
6 Interview	10 Extra activities	9 Psychoeducational
4 G.P.A.	Open admission	8 Recommendations

Test Requirements:

Diagnostic testing waived: **Yes**
Untimed SAT: **Yes** Untimed ACT: **Yes** Achievement tests required:**2**
Reading, Math
WAIS-R required: **Yes**
Documentation of LD required: **Yes**
Currency of diagnostic testing: **3 years**
Tests recommended: **Wechsler- letters from teachers**

Types of Disabilities Served

Speech/Lang	• Reading	ADD with LD
Study skills	• Spelling	ADD without LD
Written express	• Math	ADHD with LD
Organizational	• Fine Motor	ADHD without LD
Perceptual		

High School Course Requirements:

English: **3** Math: **3** Science: **2**
Waivers to standard high school courses
Foreign Language : **Yes** Course substitution: **Yes**

Learning Disability Program

Program: Reinforces course work: **Yes**
Students mainstreamed **100** % of the day
Recommended credits per semester: **12**
Time required or recommended in learning center: **3 hours**
Services only for LD students: **Yes**
Counseling: Individual: **Yes** Group Counseling: **Yes** Vocational Counseling: **Yes**

Faculty:

Faculty: **3**
LD faculty with: BS/BA: **3** M.A.: **1** Ph.D.: **2**
Faculty advocate: **Yes** Meets with instructor: **As needed**

Diagnostic Testing

ADD	Personality •	Perceptual skills •	• Spelling
ADHD•	Organization•	Fine motor skills •	• Reading
• I.Q.	• Handwriting•	Spoken language •	• Study skills
• Math	• Social skills•	Written language	

Tutoring:

Average size of group tutorials: **4**
Services rendered by:
•Graduates •Peers •Faculty •LD staff •Teacher trainees

Tutorials

Grp.	Ind.	Tutorials	Grp.	Ind.	Tutorials
•	•	Math skills	•	•	Word processing
•	•	Study skills	•	•	Time management
•	•	Language arts	•	•	Learning strategies
•	•	Written express	•	•	Organizational skills

Academic Accommodations

Curriculum	Study Aids	Exams
• Priority registration	• Typist	• Oral
Math waiver	• Reader	• Untimed
• Foreign lang. waiver	• Notetaker	• Take home
• Course substitution	• Proof reader	• With proctor
In Class	• Text on tape	On computer
• Calculators	• Early syllabus	• Extended time
• Tape recorder	Taped handouts	On tape
• Word processor		• Modified
Priority seating		• Separate room

Graduation Requirements:

Course credits: **130** GPA: **Open** Years to complete degree: **4 - open** Language waiver: **Yes**

Program Strengths

B.U.I.L.D., Baccalaureate for University of Indianapolis Learning Disabled, is an intensive support system which will offer any assistance needed for individual progress.

General Information:

University of Indianapolis is a 4 year private United Methodist university. Urban campus of 60 acres is Accessible by bus. Ski areas are 50 miles from campus. Beaches are 160 miles from campus. % of students are foreign. 4 residential halls on campus. Housing is guaranteed.70 % of students remain on campus for the weekends.

Accreditation:NCATE, SDI

Expenses:

Tuition: In-state: Full year: $9,020.00. Part-time: Per credit:$376.00. Tuition: Out-of-state: Full year: $9,020.00. Part-time: Per credit:$376.00. Room and board: $3,470.00 Cost of LD program:$3,400.00

Majors

• BUSINESS Accounting, Banking, Business Administration, Business Communication, Business Economics, Business Education, Business Management, Economics, Finance, International Business, Management, Marketing, Sports Management • COMMUNICATIONS Communication, English, Journalism, Photography, Speech, Television/Radio/Film • COMPUTER SCIENCE Computer Science, Data Processing • EDUCATION Art, Early Childhood, Elementary, English, Foreign Language, Mathematics, Middle School, Music, Physical, Pre-Elementary, Recreation and Youth Leadershi, Science, Secondary, Social Studies, Special, Speech/Language • HEALTH SCIENCES Medical Technology, Nursing, Occupational Therapy, Physical Therapy • HUMANITIES Fine Arts, Philosophy, Religion • LANGUAGES French, German, Spanish • PREPROFESSIONAL Dentistry, Engineering, Forestry, Law, Medicine, Ministry, Social Work, Veterinarian • SCIENCES Behavioral Biology, Biology, Chemistry, Earth, Management, Mathematics, Physical Science, Physics • SOCIAL SCIENCES Criminal Justice, History, Law Enforcement, Political Science, Psychology, Sociology • VISUAL AND PERFORMING ARTS Art, Dramatic Arts, Fine Arts, Music, Music Performance, Theater • VOCATIONAL Business and Office, Driver Safety Education, Legal Secretary, Library Assistant, Medical Laboratory Technology, Paralegal

Sports/Activities

• SPORTS RELATED Cheerleading, Drill Team, Marching Band, Pep Band • SPORTS-INTERCOLLEGIATE Baseball (M), Basketball, Cross Country, Diving, Golf, Soccer (F), Soccer (M), Swimming, Tennis, Track and Field, Volleyball, Wrestling (M) • SPORTS-INTRAMURAL Badminton, Basketball, Racquetball, Softball, Tennis, Volleyball • STUDENT LIFE ACTIVITIES Debate, Drama Groups, Ethnic & Cultural Groups, Jazz Band, Music Groups, Newspaper, Radio/TV station, Student Government, Yearbook

---

Less Selective　　　　　　　　**Indiana**
Accommodations

University of Southern Indiana
8600 University Blvd.
Evansville, Indiana 47712
(812) 464-8600

School Enrollment: **7,021** Male: **2,625** Female: **4,140**
LD Enrollment: **20**

Admissions Contact: **Timothy Bucher, Director of Admissions**
LD Contact: **Leslie Morrow, Cnslr. Disabled Student Services**
Name of Program: **Disabled Student Services**
Address: **OC 1022, 8600 University Blvd.**
Telephone:**(812) 464-1867**

Admissions

Application Information:
Separate application:**Yes**

Secondary School Information
Most Important Criteria For Admissions (1-strongest)

	SAT/ACT	Application		School transcript
	Class rank	Course selection	**9**	Personal statement
10	Interview	**8** Extra activities	**11**	Psychoeducational
	G.P.A.	Open admission		Recommendations

Test Requirements:
Untimed SAT: **Yes** Untimed ACT: **Yes**
Documentation of LD required: **Yes**
Currency of diagnostic testing: **3 years**

Types of Disabilities Served
- Speech/Lang
- Study skills
- Written express
- Organizational
- Perceptual
- Reading
- Spelling
- Math
- Fine Motor
- ADD with LD
- ADD without LD
- ADHD with LD
- ADHD without LD

Admissions Process

Student must register in the Counseling Center 60 days prior to date services are needed.

High School Course Requirements:
English: **3** Math: **2** Science: **2** Foreign Language: **2**

Learning Disability Program

Students mainstreamed **100** % of the day
Recommended credits per semester: **9-12**
Time required or recommended in learning center: **Optional**
Services available for all students: **Yes**
Vocational Counseling: **Yes**
Support groups are available:**Encouraged**

Faculty:
Faculty: **2** Part time: **2** M.A.: **1**

Diagnostic Testing

ADD	Personality	Perceptual skills	Spelling
ADHD	Organization	Fine motor skills	Reading
I.Q.	Handwriting	Spoken language	Study skills
Math	Social skills	Written language	

Tutoring:
Average size of group tutorials: **1-10**
Services rendered by:
　Graduates　•Peers　　Faculty　　LD staff　　Teacher trainees

Tutorials

Grp.	Ind.	Tutorials	Grp.	Ind.	Tutorials
•		Math skills			Word processing
•		Study skills	•		Time management
		Language arts	•		Learning strategies
•		Written express	•		Organizational skills

Academic Accommodations

Curriculum	Study Aids	Exams
Priority registration	Typist	• Oral
Math waiver	• Reader	• Untimed
Foreign lang. waiver	• Notetaker	Take home
• Course substitution	Proof reader	• With proctor
In Class	• Text on tape	On computer
Calculators	Early syllabus	• Extended time
• Tape recorder	Taped handouts	• On tape
• Word processor		Modified
• Priority seating		• Separate room

Graduation Requirements:
Course credits: **124** GPA: **2.0** Years to complete degree: **4-5**
Other requirements: **Must complete minimum General Education Program. Incomplete grades removed 6 weeks prior to graduation, no financial obligation remaining, last 5 semester hours must be in residence.**

General Information:

University of Southern Indiana is a 2 and 4 year public university. Suburban campus of 300 acres is 120 miles from Louisville, KY. Accessible by air, train or bus. Ski areas are 2 hours from campus. Beaches are 6 hours from campus. .06% of students are foreign. Housing is guaranteed.Guaranteed through 1st year. 18 % of students remain on campus for the weekends. 10 % of students join fraternities/sororities.

Accreditation:NCACS

SAT/ACT Scores:
Scores for incoming freshmen:**Verbal:**90%below 500. 8%between 500 and 599. 1%between 600 and 699. **Math:**79% below 500. 15% between 500 and 599. 4% between 600 and 699. **ACT:** 85% below 20. 8% between 20 and 23. 4%between 24 and 25l. 1%between 26 and 28.

Class Rank:
About 11% of the present freshmen class were in the upper 20% of their high school class. 23% were in the top 40% of their class. 30% were in the top 60% of their class. 36% were in the top 80% of their class.

Expenses:
Tuition: In-state: Full year: $774.00 (12 credit hours). Part-time: Per credit:$64.50. Tuition: Out-of-state: Full year: $1,881.00 (12 credit hours). Part-time: Per credit:$156.75. Room and board: $791.00 per semester

Majors

• BUSINESS Accounting, Business Administration, Business Education, Economics • COMMUNICATIONS Communication, English • EDUCATION Early Childhood, Elementary, Physical, Secondary • ENGINEERING Civil/Environmental, Electrical, Mechanical • HEALTH SCIENCES

Dental Assistant, Dental Hygiene, Nursing, Occupational Therapy, Radiological Therapy, Respiratory Therapy • HUMANITIES Liberal Arts , Philosophy • LANGUAGES English, French, German, Spanish • MATHEMATICS Applied • PRE PROFESSIONAL Dentistry, Engineering, Law, Medicine, Optometry, Pharmacy, Social Work, Veterinarian • SCIENCES Biology, Biophysics, Chemistry, General, Geology • SOCIAL SCIENCES History, Political Science, Psychology, Sociology • VISUAL AND PERFORMING ARTS Art • VOCATIONAL Dental Assistant, Dental Hygiene, Radiological Technology, Respiratory Therapy Technology, Secretarial

Sports/Activities

• SPORTS RELATED Cheerleading, Chess, Drill Team, Pep Band • SPORTS-INTERCOLLEGIATE Baseball (M), Basketball, Basketball (F), Basketball (M), Cross Country, Cross Country (F), Cross Country (M), Golf (M), Rugby (M), Soccer (F), Soccer (M), Softball (F), Tennis, Tennis (F), Tennis (M), Track and Field, Volleyball (F) • SPORTS-INTRAMURAL Badminton, Basketball, Bowling, Cycling, Football, Golf, Soccer, Softball, Tennis, Volleyball • STUDENT LIFE ACTIVITIES Academic Clubs, Choral, Community Service, Dance, Drama Groups, Ethnic & Cultural Groups, Film, Fraternities, Magazine, Music Groups, Newspaper, Political Groups, Radio/TV station, Religious Organization, Sororities, Student Government

---

Less Selective   **Indiana Program**

Vincennes University
1002 First Street
Vincennes, Indiana 47591
(800) 742-9198

School Enrollment: **7,200** Male: **3,960** Female: **3,240**

Admissions Contact: **Steve Simonds, Director of Admissions**
LD Contact: **Jane Kavanaugh/Susie Laue, STEP Co-Directors**
Name of Program: **STEP-Student Transition into Educational Prg.**
Address: **1001 North 1st**
Telephone: **(812) 885-4209**

Admissions

Secondary School Information
Most Important Criteria For Admissions (1-strongest)

SAT/ACT	Application	School transcript
Class rank	Course selection	Personal statement
Interview	Extra activities	Psychoeducational
G.P.A.	Open admission	Recommendations

Test Requirements:
Documentation of LD required: **Yes**

Types of Disabilities Served

Speech/Lang	Reading	ADD with LD
Study skills	Spelling	ADD without LD
Written express	Math	ADHD with LD
Organizational	Fine Motor	ADHD without LD
Perceptual		

Learning Disability Program
Special orientation for LD students: **Yes**
Program available through: **Each semester**
Students mainstreamed **100** % of the day
Recommended credits per semester: **12-16**
Services only for LD students: **Yes**
Counseling: Individual: **Yes** Group Counseling: **Yes** Vocational Counseling: **Yes**
Support groups are available: **Yes, STEP student support groups and counseling support groups**

Faculty:
Faculty: **3** Part time: **3** M.A.: **3**
Faculty advocate: **Yes** Meets with instructor: **When needed**

Diagnostic Testing

ADD	Personality	Perceptual skills	Spelling
ADHD	Organization	Fine motor skills	• Reading
I.Q.	Handwriting	Spoken language	• Study skills
• Math	Social skills	• Written language	

Tutoring:
Average size of group tutorials: **varies**
Services rendered by:
Graduates •Peers •Faculty •LD staff Teacher trainees

Tutorials

Grp.	Ind.	Tutorials	Grp.	Ind.	Tutorials
	•	Math skills		•	Word processing
	•	Study skills			Time management
	•	Language arts			Learning strategies
		Written express			Organizational skills

Academic Accommodations

Curriculum	Study Aids	Exams
Priority registration	Typist	• Oral
Math waiver	Reader	• Untimed
Foreign lang. waiver	Notetaker	Take home
Course substitution	Proof reader	With proctor
In Class	Text on tape	• On computer
• Calculators	Early syllabus	• Extended time
• Tape recorder	Taped handouts	• On tape
• Word processor		• Modified
• Priority seating		• Separate room

Graduation Requirements:
Course credits: **62** GPA: **2.0** Years to complete degree: **No specified time**
Other requirements: **6 hours of Humanities, 6 hours of social science, 6 hours of science and math, PE, computer competency.**

Program Strengths
Moderately priced. Many of the skills are taught through classes which provides group reinforcement, support, and practice. STEP is designed to give LD students the opportunity to develop their own unique abilities and to achieve their highest academic potential. Students will develop a sense of self worth and the skills needed to function and learn independently in college.

General Information:
Vincennes University is a 2 year public university. Rural campus of 100 acres is 55 miles from Evansville and Terre. Accessible by car or bus. Ski areas are 40 miles from campus. 6 residential halls on campus. Housing is not guaranteed. 60% of students rema % of students remain on campus for the weekends.

Iowa

Accreditation:NCACS

SAT/ACT Scores:
Scores for incoming freshmen:**Verbal:**66%below 500. **Math:**66% below 500.

Class Rank:
About 6.4% of the present freshmen class were in the upper 20% of their high school class. 15% were in the top 40% of their class. 23% were in the top 60% of their class. 28.5% were in the top 80% of their class.

Expenses:
Tuition: In-state: Full year: Part-time: Per credit: $53.50. Tuition: Out-of-state: Full year: Part-time: Per credit: $146.00. Room and board: $1,470.00 Cost of LD program:$250.00 per semester

Majors

• AGRICULTURE Business, Engineering, Horticultural • ARTS Commercial Art, Graphic Design, Music Theatre, Theater Design • BUSINESS Accounting, Agri-business, Banking/Finance, Business Administration, Business Education, Business Management, Food Management, Hotel & Restaurant Management, Insurance, International Business Managem, Marketing Management, Secretarial Science, Small Busines • COMMUNICATIONS Broadcasting, English, Journalism, Public Relations • COMPUTER SCIENCE Automated Manufacturing Techno, Computer Science, Computer Technology, Information Science & Systems, Laser Electro-Optic Technology, Medical Records Technology, Programming, Robotics • EDUCATION Art, Early Childhood, Elementary, Middle School, Music, Physical, Secondary, Special, Speech • ENGINEERING Agricultural, Chemical, Civil, Electrical • HEALTH SCIENCES Dental Hygiene, Environmental Health, Medical Records Administration, Nuclear Medical Technology, Nursing, Occupational Therapy, Physical Therapy Assistant, Practical Nursing, Surgical Technology • HUMANITIES Fine Arts, General, Philosophy • MATHEMATICS Computer • PRE PROFESSIONAL Dentistry, Engineering, Law, Medicine, Nuclear Medical Technology, Occupational Therapy, Optometry, Pharmacy, Veterinarian • SCIENCES Anthropology, Biology, Chemistry, Earth, Geography, Geology, Gerontology, Horticultural, Mathematics, Natural Science, Physics • SOCIAL SCIENCES Anthropology, Consumer Economics, Economics, Geography, History, Law Enforcement, Political Science, Psychology, Public Administration, Social Work • SPECIAL EDUCATION Deaf/Hearing Impaired • VISUAL AND PERFORMING ARTS Fine Arts, Theater • VOCATIONAL Auto Body, Automobile Technology, Automotive Service, Aviation Maintenance, Aviation Technology, Bowling Equipment Technology, Child Care, Construction, Corrections, Cosmetology, Culinary Arts, Diesel Mechanics, Dietetics, Drafting and Design Technology, Electronics Technology, Fashion Merchandising, Forestry, Home Economics, Interior Design, Machine Tool Technology, Medical Laboraotry Technology, Paralegal, Park/Recreation, Printing Production, Respiratory Therapy, School Media Services, Secretarial, Surveying and Mapping, Tractor/Trailer Driving, Welding

Sports/Activities

• SPORTS RELATED Cheerleading, Pep Band, Team Managers • SPORTS-INTERCOLLEGIATE Baseball, Baseball (M), Basketball, Basketball (F), Basketball (M), Bowling, Bowling (F), Bowling (M), Cross Country, Cross Country (F), Cross Country (M), Diving, Diving (F), Diving (M), Golf, Golf (M), Hammer Throw, Hammer Throw (M), Swimming, Swimming (F), Swimming (M), Tennis, Tennis (M), Track and Field, Track and Field (F), Track and Field (M), Volleyball, Volleyball (F) • SPORTS-INTRAMURAL Archery, Archery (F), Archery (M), Badminton, Badminton (F), Badminton (M), Basketball, Basketball (F), Basketball (M), Bowling, Bowling (F), Bowling (M), Cross Country, Cross Country (F), Cross Country (M), Golf, Ping-Pong, Ping-Pong (F), Ping-Pong (M), Racquetball, Racquetball (F), Racquetball (M), Soccer, Soccer (M), Softball, Softball (F), Softball (M), Swimming, Swimming (F), Swimming (M), Tennis, Tennis (F), Tennis (M), Track and Field, Track and Field (F), Track and Field (M), Volleyball, Volleyball (F), Volleyball (M), Weight Lifting, Wrestling • STUDENT LIFE ACTIVITIES Academic Clubs, Choral, Community Service, Concert Band, Dance, Drama Groups, Ethnic & Cultural Groups, Film, Fraternities, Jazz Band, Magazine, Music Groups, Musical Theater, Newspaper, Political Groups, Radio/TV station, Religious Organization, Sororities, Student Government, Yearbook

Very Selective — **Iowa Services**

Coe College
1220 First Avenue, Northeast
Cedar Rapids, Iowa 52402
(319) 399-8500

School Enrollment: **1,220** Male: **600** Female: **620**
LD Enrollment: **10-15**

Admissions Contact: **Michael White, Director of Admissions**
LD Contact: **Lois Kabela, Director**
Name of Program: **Educational Support Program**
Address: **1220 First Avenue, NE**
Telephone:**(319) 399-8546**

Admissions

Application Information:
Application deadline: **Rolling**
Rolling Admissions: **Yes**Notified when: **May 1st**

Secondary School Information
Most Important Criteria For Admissions (1-strongest)

1 SAT/ACT	**1** Application	**1** School transcript
1 Class rank	**1** Course selection	Personal statement
2 Interview	**2** Extra activities	Psychoeducational
1 G.P.A.	Open admission	**2** Recommendations

Test Requirements:
Diagnostic testing waived: **Yes**
Untimed SAT: **Yes** Untimed ACT: **Yes**
Documentation of LD required: **Yes**
Tests recommended: **Standard LD testing methods.**

Types of Disabilities Served
• Speech/Lang   • Reading   ADD with LD
• Study skills   • Spelling   ADD without LD
• Written express   • Math   ADHD with LD
• Organizational   • Fine Motor   ADHD without LD
• Perceptual

Admissions Process

High school transcript, application and essay, high school rank, ACT/SAT scores, and counselor recommendation are all considerations for admittance. Marginal students will be referred to the committee for a decision.

High School Course Requirements:
English: **4** Math: **3** Science: **3** Foreign Language: **2**
Waivers to standard high school courses
Foreign Language : **Yes** Math: **Yes**

Learning Disability Program

Special orientation for LD students:
Program: Reinforces course work: **Yes**
Students mainstreamed **100** % of the day
Recommended credits per semester: **3-4**
Counseling: Individual: **Yes**
Support groups are available:**Yes**

Faculty:
Faculty: **3** Including Director: **Yes** Full time: **3** M.A.: **3**
Meets with instructor: **sporadic**

Diagnostic Testing
ADD	Personality	Perceptual skills	Spelling
ADHD	Organization	Fine motor skills	• Reading
I.Q.	Handwriting	Spoken language	• Study skills
Math	Social skills	Written language	

Tutoring:
Average size of group tutorials: **2-3**
Services rendered by:
Graduates •Peers •Faculty •LD staff Teacher trainees

Tutorials
Grp.	Ind.	Tutorials	Grp.	Ind.	Tutorials
	•	Math skills		•	Word processing
•	•	Study skills		•	Time management
	•	Language arts		•	Learning strategies
	•	Written express		•	Organizational skills

Academic Accommodations
Curriculum	Study Aids	Exams
• Priority registration	• Typist	• Oral
• Math waiver	• Reader	• Untimed
• Foreign lang. waiver	• Notetaker	Take home
• Course substitution	• Proof reader	• With proctor
In Class	• Text on tape	On computer
• Calculators	Early syllabus	• Extended time
• Tape recorder	Taped handouts	On tape
• Word processor		• Modified
• Priority seating		• Separate room

Graduation Requirements:
Course credits: **36** GPA: **2.0** Years to complete degree: **4-5 usually** Math waiver: **Yes** Language waiver: **Yes**

Program Strengths
We do not have an LD Program. However, we have an Educational Support Program which offers tutoring, note-takers, academic, career and personal counseling and study skills assistance. We also serve as a liaison between student and faculty and offer specific advice for individual students who possess learning disabilities.

General Information:
Coe College is a 4 year private college. Urban campus. of 1,000 acres is Accessible by air or bus. Ski areas are 60 miles from campus. 10% of students are foreign. 5 residential halls on campus. Housing is guaranteed.60-70 % of students remain on campus for the weekends. 30 % of students join fraternities/sororities.

Accreditation:NCACS

SAT/ACT Scores:
Scores for incoming freshmen:**Verbal:**54%below 500. 30%between 500 and 599. 13%between 600 and 699. 3%above 700. **Math:**21% below 500. 48% between 500 and 599. 28% between 600 and 699. 3%above 700. **ACT:** 16% below 20. 24% between 20 and 23. 27%between 24 and 25l. 18%between 26 and 28. 15% above 28.

Class Rank:
About 44% of the present freshmen class were in the upper 20% of their high school class. 80% were in the top 40% of their class. 97% were in the top 60% of their class. 98% were in the top 80% of their class.

Expenses:
Tuition: In-state: Full year: $11,440.00. Part-time: Per course: $680.00. Tuition: Out-of-state: Full year: $11,440.00. Room and board: $4,090.00

Majors
• AREA STUDIES African, American, Asian, Latin American • BUSINESS Accounting, Business Administration, Business Management, Economics • COMMUNICATIONS Creative Writing, English, Journalism • COMPUTER SCIENCE Computer Science, Programming •EDUCATION Art, Curriculum, Elementary, Music, Physical, Secondary • ENGINEERING Computer, Engineering Science • HEALTH SCIENCES Medical Technology, Nursing, Physical Therapy • HUMANITIES English/Writing/Literature, Liberal Arts, Philosophy, Religion • LANGUAGES French, German, Japanese, Latin, Spanish • PREPROFESSIONAL Agriculture, Architecture, Dentistry, Engineering, Law, Medicine • SCIENCES Biology, Chemistry, Mathematics, Physical Science, Physics • SOCIAL SCIENCES Government/Political, History, Political Science, Psychology, Social Sciences, Sociology • VISUAL AND PERFORMING ARTS Art, Art History, Dramatic Arts, Fine Arts, Music, Studio Art, Theater

Sports/Activities
• SPORTS RELATED Cheerleading, Pep Band, Team Managers • SPORTS-INTERCOLLEGIATE Baseball (M), Basketball, Cross Country, Football (M), Golf (M), Soccer, Softball (F), Swimming, Tennis, Volleyball (F), Wrestling (M) • SPORTS-INTRAMURAL Basketball, Football, Racquetball, Volleyball (F) • STUDENT LIFE ACTIVITIES Academic Clubs, Choral, Community Service, Concert Band, Drama Groups, Ethnic & Cultural Groups, Fraternities, Jazz Band, Magazine, Music Groups, Newspaper, Political Groups, Religious Organization, Sororities, Student Government, Yearbook

Very Selective **Iowa**
Services

Cornell College
600 First Street W.
Mt. Vernon, Iowa 52314-1098
(319) 895-4215

School Enrollment: **1,143** Male: **519** Female: **624**

Admissions Contact: **Peter Bryant, V.P./Enrollment**
LD Contact: **Connie Rosene, Dir. of Counseling**
Name of Program: **Student Support Services**
Telephone:**(319) 895-4292**

Admissions

Application Information:
Application deadline: **March 1st**
Notified when: **April 1st**

Secondary School Information
Most Important Criteria For Admissions (1-strongest)
2	SAT/ACT		Application	**1**	School transcript
1	Class rank	**2**	Course selection	**3**	Personal statement
3	Interview	**2**	Extra activities		Psychoeducational
1	G.P.A.		Open admission	**3**	Recommendations

Test Requirements:
Diagnostic testing waived: **Yes**
Untimed SAT: **Yes** Untimed ACT: **Yes** Achievement tests required:
WAIS-R required: **Yes** Range accepted: **90**
Documentation of LD required: **Yes**
Currency of diagnostic testing: **anytime**

Iowa

Types of Disabilities Served
- Speech/Lang
- Study skills
- Written express
- Organizational
- Perceptual
- Reading
- Spelling
- Math
- Fine Motor
- ADD with LD
- ADD without LD
- ADHD with LD
- ADHD without LD

Learning Disability Program
Counseling: Individual: **Yes**

Faculty:
Faculty: **1** Part time: **1**
Faculty advocate: **Yes** Meets with instructor: **As needed**

Diagnostic Testing
ADD	Personality	Perceptual skills	Spelling
ADHD	Organization	Fine motor skills	• Reading
I.Q.	Handwriting	Spoken language	• Study skills
Math	Social skills	Written language	

Tutoring:
Average size of group tutorials: **2-3**
Services rendered by:
Graduates •Peers •Faculty •LD staff Teacher trainees

Tutorials
Grp.	Ind.	Tutorials	Grp.	Ind.	Tutorials
		Math skills			Word processing
	•	Study skills		•	Time management
	•	Language arts		•	Learning strategies
	•	Written express		•	Organizational skills

Academic Accommodations

Curriculum	Study Aids	Exams
Priority registration	• Typist	• Oral
• Math waiver	• Reader	Untimed
• Foreign lang. waiver	• Notetaker	Take home
Course substitution	• Proof reader	• With proctor
In Class	• Text on tape	On computer
Calculators	Early syllabus	• Extended time
• Tape recorder	Taped handouts	On tape
Word processor		Modified
Priority seating		• Separate room

Graduation Requirements:
Course credits: **32** GPA: **2.0** Years to complete degree: **4**

Program Strengths
The services are personalized to meet the needs of each student based upon the recommendations of the professional who diagnosed the learning disability. In addition, each new student is assigned a Peer Advocate Group during orientation week. These groups are designed to assist students in making the ajustment to college life.

General Information:
Cornell College is a 4 year private college. Rural campus of 110 acres is 15 miles from Cedar Rapids. Ski areas are 20-25 miles from campus. Beaches are 50 miles from campus. 2% of students are foreign. Housing is guaranteed.85 % of students remain on campus for the weekends. 35 % of students join fraternities/sororities.

Accreditation:Regional

SAT/ACT Scores:
Scores for incoming freshmen: **ACT:** 8% below 20. 10% between 20 and 23. 20%between 24 and 25l. 34%between 26 and 28. 28% above 28.

Class Rank:
About 56% of the present freshmen class were in the upper 20% of their high school class. 80% were in the top 40% of their class. 89% were in the top 60% of their class. 100% were in the top 80% of their class.

Expenses:
Tuition: In-state: Full year: $11,310.00 . Room and board: $3,730.00

Majors
• AREA STUDIES Latin American, Russian/Slavic, Women's Studies • BUSINESS Business Administration, Business Economics, Business Education, Economics, International Business • COMMUNICATIONS Communication, English, Speech/Debate • COMPUTER SCIENCE Computer Science • EDUCATION Art, Elementary, English, Foreign Language, Health, Mathematics, Music, Physical, Science, Secondary, Social Studies • ENGINEERING Engineering Science • HEALTH SCIENCES Medical Technology • HUMANITIES Classics, Humanities, Liberal Arts, Philosophy, Religion • LANGUAGES French, German, Russian, Spanish • PRE-PROFESSIONAL Architecture, Dentistry, Engineering, Law, Medicine, Pharmacy, Social Work, Veterinarian • SCIENCES Anthropology, Biology, Chemistry, Earth, Ecology, Geology, Mathematics, Physical Science, Physics • SOCIAL SCIENCES Anthropology, Government/Political, History, International Studies, Political Science, Psychology, Social Sciences, Sociology • VISUAL AND PERFORMING ARTS Art, Dramatic Arts, Fine Arts, Music, Music Performance, Music Theatre, Theater • VOCATIONAL Medical Laboratory Technology

Sports/Activities
• SPORTS RELATED Pep Band • SPORTS-INTERCOLLEGIATE Baseball (M), Basketball, Cross Country, Field Hockey (F), Football (M), Golf, Ice Hockey (M), Soccer, Softball, Swimming, Tennis, Track and Field, Volleyball (F), Wrestling (M) • SPORTS-INTRAMURAL Badminton, Basketball, Bowling, Golf, Ice Hockey, Ping-Pong, Racquetball, Softball, Swimming, Tennis, Track and Field, Volleyball, Wrestling • STUDENT LIFE ACTIVITIES Choral, Concert Band, Dance, Drama Groups, Fraternities, Jazz Band, Magazine, Music Groups, Musical Theater, Newspaper, Radio/TV station, Sororities, Student Government, Symphony Orchestra, Yearbook

---

Selective   **Iowa**
                                                  Program

Graceland College
Lamoni, Iowa 50140
(515) 784-5196

School Enrollment: **898** Male: **499** Female: **499**
LD Enrollment: **54**

Admissions Contact: **Bonita A. Booth, Dean of Admissions**
LD Contact: **J. R. Smith, Director**
Name of Program: **CHANCE**
Address: **Box 151**
Telephone:**(515) 784-5226**

Admissions

Application Information:
LD Students Applying: **145** Accepted: **113** Enrolled:**54**
Application deadline: **August 15th**
Applicant must apply **1** months in advance
Rolling Admissions: **Yes**

Secondary School Information

Most Important Criteria For Admissions (1-strongest)

7 SAT/ACT	**8** Application	**9** School transcript
5 Class rank	**4** Course selection	**11** Personal statement
2 Interview	**12** Extra activities	**1** Psychoeducational
6 G.P.A.	Open admission	**3** Recommendations

Test Requirements:

Standardized tests waived: **Yes**
Diagnostic testing waived: **Yes**
Untimed SAT: **Yes** Untimed ACT: **Yes**
WAIS-R required: **Yes** Range accepted: **85+**
Documentation of LD required: **Yes**
Currency of diagnostic testing: **2-12 months**
Tests recommended: **vocabulary, decoding, encoding, comprehension**

Types of Disabilities Served

• Speech/Lang	Reading	ADD with LD
• Study skills	Spelling	ADD without LD
• Written express	• Math	ADHD with LD
• Organizational	• Fine Motor	ADHD without LD
• Perceptual		

Admissions Process

1) Diagnostic testing, (2) Recommended for acceptance, 3) Letter of acceptance sent by admissions.

Learning Disability Program

Syllabus available during orientation: **Yes**
Students mainstreamed **100** % of the day
Recommended credits per semester: **12-15**
Time required or recommended in learning center: **5**

Faculty:

Faculty: **6** Including Director: **Yes** Full time: **1** Part time: **5**
LD faculty with: BS/BA: **6**
Faculty advocate: **Yes** Meets with instructor: **As required**

Diagnostic Testing

ADD	Personality	Perceptual skills	• Spelling
ADHD	Organization	Fine motor skills	• Reading
• I.Q.	Handwriting	Spoken language	Study skills
Math	Social skills	Written language	

Tutoring:

Average size of group tutorials: ***2-3**
Services rendered by:

Graduates	•Peers	•Faculty	•LD staff	Teacher trainees

Tutorials

Grp.	Ind.	Tutorials	Grp.	Ind.	Tutorials
		Math skills			Word processing
		Study skills			Time management
		Language arts			Learning strategies
		Written express			Organizational skills

Academic Accommodations

Curriculum	Study Aids	Exams
Priority registration	• Typist	• Oral
Math waiver	Reader	Untimed
Foreign lang. waiver	Notetaker	Take home
Course substitution	• Proof reader	With proctor
In Class	• Text on tape	On computer
• Calculators	Early syllabus	• Extended time
• Tape recorder	Taped handouts	On tape
• Word processor		Modified
Priority seating		• Separate room

Graduation Requirements:

Course credits: **128** GPA: **2.0** Years to complete degree: **4-5**

Program Strengths

Our clinicians are trained in the Lindamood-Bell techniques to help LD students develop auditory conceptual abilities and concept imagery abilities. We provide daily one-on-one clinical sessions for the purpose of affecting some measure of correction of the student's learning disability. Our goal is to totally mainstream the LD student after he or she has participated three semesters in the CHANCE Program.
*Students meet with their instructors on a daily basis.

General Information:

Graceland College is a 4 year private Church of Latter Day Saints college. Rural campus of 183 acres is 80 miles from Des Moines. Accessible by bus. 16% of students are foreign. 4 residential halls on campus. Housing is guaranteed.50 % of students remain on campus for the weekends.

Accreditation: NCA, NCATE, NLN

SAT/ACT Scores:

Scores for incoming freshmen: **Verbal:** 68% below 500. 24% between 500 and 599. 6% between 600 and 699. 2% above 700. **Math:** 45% below 500. 36% between 500 and 599. 16% between 600 and 699. 3% above 700. **ACT:** 45% below 20. 11% between 24 and 25l. 13% between 26 and 28. 2% above 28.

Expenses:

Tuition: In-state: Full year: $7,765.00. Cost of LD program: $785.00 per semester

Majors

• BUSINESS Accounting, Business Administration, Business Economics, Business Education, Business Management, Economics, Finance, Marketing • COMMUNICATIONS Communication, Creative Writing, English, Graphic Design, Speech/Debate • COMPUTER SCIENCE Computer Science, Information Science System, Programming, Systems Analysis • EDUCATION Art, Early Childhood, Elementary, Health, Music, Physical, Recreation and Youth Leadershi, Secondary, Speech/Language • ENGINEERING Computer • HEALTH SCIENCES Health, Medical Technology, Nursing • HUMANITIES English/Writing/Literature, Humanities, Liberal Arts, Philosophy, Religion • LANGUAGES French, German, Japanese, Spanish • PREPROFESSIONAL Dentistry, Law, Medicine • SCIENCES Biochemistry, Biology, Chemistry, Mathematics, Physical Science • SOCIAL SCIENCES Government/Political, History, International Studies, Psychology, Social Sciences, Sociology • VISUAL AND PERFORMING ARTS Art, Art History, Dramatic Arts, Music, Theater • VOCATIONAL Park/Recreation

Sports/Activities

• SPORTS RELATED Cheerleading, Drill Team, Drum Major/Majorette, Marching Band, Pep Band, Team Managers • SPORTS-INTERCOLLEGIATE Baseball (M), Basketball, Cross Country, Football (M), Golf (M), Soccer, Softball (F), Tennis, Track and Field, Volleyball • SPORTS-INTRAMURAL Basketball, Football, Racquetball, Soccer, Softball • STU-

Iowa

DENT LIFE ACTIVITIES Choral, Concert Band, Drama Groups, Ethnic & Cultural Groups, Jazz Band, Music Groups, Musical Theater, Radio/TV station, Religious Organization, Student Government, Symphony Orchestra, Yearbook

Less Selective   **Iowa Program**

Grand View College
1200 Grandview Avenue
Des Moines, Iowa 50316
(515) 263-2800

School Enrollment: **1,407** Male: **590** Female: **817**
LD Enrollment: **5** Male: **3** Female: **2**

Admissions Contact: **Jerry Slater, Director of Admissions**
LD Contact: **A. Jane Molden, Dir. Academic Support Counseling**
Name of Program: **Learning Disability Program**
Telephone:**(515) 263-2884**

Admissions

Application Information:
Application deadline: **September 1st**

Secondary School Information
Most Important Criteria For Admissions (1-strongest)

2 SAT/ACT	Application	1	School transcript
3 Class rank	4 Course selection		Personal statement
5 Interview	7 Extra activities		Psychoeducational
1 G.P.A.	Open admission	6	Recommendations

Test Requirements:
Currency of diagnostic testing: **1 month**

Types of Disabilities Served
- Speech/Lang
- Study skills
- Written express
- Organizational
- Perceptual
- Reading
- Spelling
- Math
- Fine Motor
- ADD with LD
- ADD without LD
- ADHD with LD
- ADHD without LD

Learning Disability Program
Program: Remedial: **Yes**
Program: Reinforces course work: **Yes**
Students mainstreamed **90** % of the day
Counseling: Individual: **Yes**

Faculty:
Faculty: **2** Full time: **2** M.A.: **2**
Faculty advocate: **Yes** Meets with instructor: **As needed**

Diagnostic Testing
ADD	Personality	• Perceptual skills	• Spelling
• ADHD	Organization	• Fine motor skills	Reading
I.Q.	Handwriting	• Spoken language	• Study skills
• Math	• Social skills	• Written language	

Tutoring:
Average size of group tutorials: **1:1**
Services rendered by:
•Graduates •Peers •Faculty •LD staff Teacher trainees

Tutorials
Grp.	Ind.	Tutorials	Grp.	Ind.	Tutorials
	•	Math skills			Word processing
	•	Study skills		•	Time management
		Language arts		•	Learning strategies
	•	Written express			Organizational skills

Academic Accommodations

Curriculum
Priority registration
Math waiver
Foreign lang. waiver
Course substitution

In Class
- Calculators
- Tape recorder
- Word processor
Priority seating

Study Aids
- Typist
Reader
- Notetaker
- Proof reader
- Text on tape
Early syllabus
Taped handouts

Exams
- Oral
Untimed
Take home
With proctor
On computer
- Extended time
On tape
- Modified
Separate room

General Information:
Grand View College is a 4 year private Lutheran Church college. Urban campus of 25 acres is 300 miles from Minneapolis. Accessible by air, train, or bus. Ski areas are 80 miles from campus. Beaches are 25 miles from campus. 1% of students are foreign. 3 residential halls on campus. Housing is guaranteed.40 % of students remain on campus for the weekends.

Accreditation:NCACS

SAT/ACT Scores:
Scores for incoming freshmen: **ACT:** 12.5% below 20. 57% between 20 and 23. 12%between 24 and 25l. 14%between 26 and 28. 8% above 28.

Class Rank:
About 18% of the present freshmen class were in the upper 20% of their high school class. 25% were in the top 40% of their class. 24% were in the top 60% of their class. 18% were in the top 80% of their class.

Expenses:
Tuition: In-state: Full year: $6,690.00. Part-time: Per credit:Part-time: $280.00. Tuition: Out-of-state: Full year: $6,690.00. Part-time: Per credit:Part-time: $280.00.

Majors
• AREA STUDIES African • BUSINESS Accounting, Business Administration, Business Economics, Business Education, Business Management, Economics, Finance, Management, Marketing, Personnel, Real Estate • COMMUNICATIONS Advertising, Broadcasting, Communication, Creative Writing, English, Graphic Design, Journalism, Photography, Television/Radio/Film • COMPUTER SCIENCE Computer Science, Data Processing, Programming, Systems Analysis, Telecommunications • EDUCATION Art, Curriculum, Early Childhood, Elementary, English, Health, Mathematics, Middle School, Music, Physical, Recreation and Youth Leadershi, School Psychology, Science, Secondary, Social Studies, Special • HEALTH SCIENCES Communication Disorders, Environmental, Health, Medical Technology, Nursing, Nutritional/Food • HUMANITIES Liberal Arts, Philosophy, Religion, Religious Studies • LANGUAGES French, German, Spanish • PREPROFESSIONAL Law, Medicine, Social Work • SCIENCES Astronomy, Biochemistry, Biology, Chemistry, Earth, Geography, Geology, Human Biology, Macrobiology, Mathematics, Microbiology, Physical Chemistry, Physical Science, Physics, Physiology, Zoology • SOCIAL SCIENCES Anthropology, Criminal Justice, Geography, Government/Political, History, Psychology, Social Sciences, Sociology • VISUAL AND PERFORMING ARTS Art, Art History, Dramatic Arts, Fine Arts, Studio Art, Theater • VOCATIONAL Business and Office

Sports/Activities
• SPORTS-INTERCOLLEGIATE Baseball, Basketball, Cross Country, Golf, Soccer, Softball, Tennis, Track and Field, Volleyball • SPORTS-IN-

TRAMURAL Badminton, Basketball, Ping-Pong, Softball, Tennis, Volley-ball • STUDENT LIFE ACTIVITIES Choral, Dance, Drama Groups, Ethnic & Cultural Groups, Musical Theater, Newspaper, Radio/TV station, Religious Organization, Student Government

Less Selective　　　　　　　　　　　　　　　**Iowa**
　　　　　　　　　　　　　　　　　　　　　　　Program

Hawkeye Institute of Technology
P. O. 8015
Waterloo, Iowa 50704
(319) 296-2320

School Enrollment: **1,950**

Admissions Contact: **David Fish, Dir. Enrollment Services**
LD Contact: **Mary Manning, Evaluation Counselor**

Admissions

Application Information:
Application deadline: **A.S.A.P.**
Rolling Admissions: **Yes**

Secondary School Information
Most Important Criteria For Admissions (1-strongest)
5	SAT/ACT	**6** Application	**2** School transcript
1	Class rank	**4** Course selection	Personal statement
7	Interview	Extra activities	Psychoeducational
3	G.P.A.	Open admission	**8** Recommendations

Test Requirements:
Untimed ACH: **Yes**
Documentation of LD required: **Yes**

Types of Disabilities Served
• Speech/Lang	• Reading	ADD with LD
• Study skills	• Spelling	ADD without LD
• Written express	• Math	ADHD with LD
• Organizational	• Fine Motor	ADHD without LD
• Perceptual		

Learning Disability Program
Special orientation for LD students: **Yes**
Counseling: Individual: **Yes** Vocational Counseling: **Yes**

Diagnostic Testing
ADD	Personality	Perceptual skills	Spelling
ADHD	Organization	Fine motor skills	Reading
I.Q.	Handwriting	Spoken language	Study skills
Math	Social skills	Written language	

Tutoring:
Services rendered by:
Graduates　•Peers　•Faculty　•LD staff　Teacher trainees

Tutorials
Grp.	Ind.	Tutorials	Grp.	Ind.	Tutorials
•	•	Math skills		•	Word processing
	•	Study skills			Time management
•	•	Language arts	•	•	Learning strategies
•	•	Written express			Organizational skills

Academic Accommodations
Curriculum	Study Aids	Exams
Priority registration	Typist	• Oral
Math waiver	Reader	• Untimed
Foreign lang. waiver	• Notetaker	Take home
• Course substitution	Proof reader	With proctor
In Class	• Text on tape	On computer
• Calculators	Early syllabus	• Extended time
• Tape recorder	Taped handouts	On tape
Word processor		Modified
Priority seating		• Separate room

Program Strengths
Students who are LD take regular classes. They may have peer tutoring, teacher tutoring or computer tutoring. They are allowed to take tests untimed and have tape recorders in class, specialized schedules are developed, developmental classes are also available. Initial staffing is scheduled to ease transition from high school to post-secondary.

General Information:
Hawkeye Institute of Technology is a 2 year public college. Urban campus 3 miles from Waterloo. Accessible by air or bus. Ski areas are 60 miles from campus. Housing is not guaranteed.

Accreditation: NCACS, IDE

SAT/ACT Scores:
Scores for incoming freshmen: **ACT:** 25% below 20. 50% between 20 and 23. 40%between 24 and 25l. 10%between 26 and 28.

Class Rank:
About 10% of the present freshmen class were in the upper 20% of their high school class. 40% were in the top 40% of their class. 40% were in the top 60% of their class. 10% were in the top 80% of their class.

Expenses:
Tuition: In-state: Full year: $1,642.50. Part-time: Per credit:$54.75. Tuition: Out-of-state: Full year: $3,217.50. Part-time: Per credit:$107.25.

Majors
• BUSINESS Accounting, Agricultural, Management, Marketing • COMMUNICATIONS Commercial Design, Graphic Design, Photography • COMPUTER SCIENCE Data Processing, Robotics • ENGINEERING Civil/Environmental, Industrial, Mathematical • HEALTH SCIENCES Dental Assistant, Dental Hygiene, Medical Technology, Nursing • HUMANITIES Liberal Arts • SCIENCES Agricultural, Horticultural • SOCIAL SCIENCES Law Enforcement • VOCATIONAL Automated Manufacturing Techno, Automobile Technology, Automotive Service, Aviation Technology, Business and Office, Diesel Power Technology, Drafting, Electronics Technology, Farm Management, Fashion Merchandising, Home Economics, Interior Design, Machinist, Manufacturing Technology, Medical Laboratory Technology, Plastic Technology, Precision Metal Work, Respiratory Therapy Technology, Secretarial, Textile and Clothing

Sports/Activities
• SPORTS-INTRAMURAL Basketball, Bowling, Cross Country, Diving, Golf, Skiing - Snow, Softball, Swimming, Volleyball, Wrestling • STUDENT LIFE ACTIVITIES Student Government

Less Selective

Indian Hills Community College

525 Grandview
Ottumwa, Iowa 52501
(515) 683-5153

School Enrollment: **3,176** Male: **1,398** Female: **1,778**
LD Enrollment: **30** Male: **16** Female: **14**

Admissions Contact: **Jane Sapp, Admissions Officer**
LD Contact: **Judith K. Brickey, Coordinator**
Name of Program: **Transition Program**
Address: **525 Grandview**
Telephone:**(515) 683-5125**

Admissions

Application Information:
Accepted: **30** Enrolled:**30**
Application deadline: **None**
Rolling Admissions: **Yes**

Secondary School Information
Most Important Criteria For Admissions (1-strongest)

SAT/ACT	**2** Application	School transcript
Class rank	Course selection **3**	Personal statement
1 Interview	Extra activities	Psychoeducational
G.P.A.	Open admission	Recommendations

Test Requirements:
Standardized tests waived: **Yes**
Currency of diagnostic testing: **3 years**
Tests recommended: **Typical three year evaluation**

Types of Disabilities Served
- Speech/Lang
- Study skills
- Written express
- Organizational
- Perceptual
- Reading
- Spelling
- Math
- Fine Motor
- ADD with LD
- ADD without LD
- ADHD with LD
- ADHD without LD

Learning Disability Program
Program: Remedial: **Yes**
Program: Reinforces course work: **Yes**
Program available through:**Continuous**
Students mainstreamed **100** % of the day
Recommended credits per semester: **Individualized**
Time required or recommended in learning center: **varies**
Counseling: Individual: **Yes** Vocational Counseling: **Yes**

Faculty:
Faculty: **4** Including Director: **Yes** Full time: **1** Part time: **3**
LD faculty with: BS/BA: **3** M.A.: **1**
Faculty advocate: **Yes** Meets with instructor: **Every two weeks**

Diagnostic Testing

ADD	Personality	Perceptual skills	• Spelling
ADHD	Organization	Fine motor skills	• Reading
I.Q.	Handwriting	Spoken language	Study skills
Math	Social skills •	Written language	

Tutoring:
Average size of group tutorials: **4-6**
Services rendered by:
  Graduates •Peers •Faculty •LD staff Teacher trainees

Tutorials

Grp.	Ind.	Tutorials	Grp.	Ind.	Tutorials
	•	Math skills		•	Word processing
	•	Study skills		•	Time management
	•	Language arts		•	Learning strategies
	•	Written express		•	Organizational skills

Academic Accommodations

Curriculum	Study Aids	Exams
Priority registration	• Typist	• Oral
Math waiver	• Reader	• Untimed
Foreign lang. waiver	• Notetaker	Take home
Course substitution	• Proof reader	• With proctor
In Class	Text on tape	On computer
• Calculators	Early syllabus	• Extended time
• Tape recorder	Taped handouts	On tape
• Word processor		• Modified
• Priority seating		• Separate room

Graduation Requirements:GPA: **2.0** Years to complete degree:
2 Math waiver: **Yes**

Program Strengths
The program is an integrated program within the Indian Hills Community College. We offer a full- time program at the student's ability level with the possibility of mainstreaming into the college offerings at a pace appropriate for each individual student.

General Information:
Indian Hills Community College is a 2 year public college. Rural campus of 126 acres is 90 miles from Des Moines. Accessible by train or bus. Ski areas are 800 miles from campus. Beaches are 1,200 miles from campus. 3% of students are foreign. 4 residential halls on campus. Housing is not guaranteed.3 % of students remain on campus for the weekends.

Accreditation:NCACS

Expenses:
Tuition: In-state: Full year: $1,950.00. Part-time: Per credit:$40.00. Part-time: Per course: $130.00. Tuition: Out-of-state: Full year: $2,925.00. Part-time: Per credit:$60.00. Part-time: Per course:$195.00 Room and board: $1,989.00 Cost of LD program:$450.00

Majors
• BUSINESS Food Management • COMPUTER SCIENCE Computer Maintenance, Computer Technology, Programming, Robotics, Systems Analysis, Telecommunications • ENGINEERING Mechanical • HEALTH SCIENCES Health, Medical Secretary, Nursing, Physical Therapy, Radiological Therapy • HUMANITIES Liberal Arts • SCIENCES Agricultural • SOCIAL SCIENCES Criminal Justice • VOCATIONAL Automated Manufacturing Techno, Automotive Service, Aviation Maintenance, Aviation Technology, Diesel Power Technology, Electronics Technology, Food Service, Laser Electro Optic Technology, Machinist, Piloting

Sports/Activities
• SPORTS RELATED Cheerleading, Pep Band • SPORTS-INTERCOLLEGIATE Baseball (M), Basketball, Golf (M), Softball (F) • SPORTS-INTRAMURAL Basketball, Bowling, Fencing, Football (M), Racquetball, Softball, Tennis, Volleyball • STUDENT LIFE ACTIVITIES Choral, Dance, Debate, Drama Groups, Music Groups, Musical Theater, Student Government

Less Selective **Iowa**
Program

Iowa Central Community College

330 Avenue M
Fort Dodge, Iowa 50501
(515) 576-7201-(800) 362-2793

School Enrollment: **2,000** Male: **980** Female: **1,020**
LD Enrollment: **40** Male: **19** Female: **21**

Admissions Contact: **Dale Daggy, Director of Admissions**
LD Contact: **Barbara McClannahan, Coordinator**
Name of Program: **Individualized College Education**
Telephone: **Ext. 2501**

Admissions

Application Information:
Accepted: **50** Enrolled: **50**

Secondary School Information
Most Important Criteria For Admissions (1-strongest)

	SAT/ACT	Application	**1** School transcript
3	Class rank	Course selection	Personal statement
	Interview	Extra activities	**4** Psychoeducational
2	G.P.A.	Open admission	Recommendations

Test Requirements:
Diagnostic testing waived: **Yes**
Untimed ACT: **Yes**
Documentation of LD required: **Yes**
Tests recommended: **Documentation of disability**

Types of Disabilities Served
- Speech/Lang
- Study skills
- Written express
- Organizational
- Perceptual
- Reading
- Spelling
- Math
- Fine Motor
- ADD with LD
- ADD without LD
- ADHD with LD
- ADHD without LD

Learning Disability Program

Program: Reinforces course work: **Yes**
Students mainstreamed **90** % of the day
Counseling: Individual: **Yes** Vocational Counseling: **Yes**

Faculty:
Faculty: **11** Including Director: **Yes** Full time: **2** Part time: **9**
LD faculty with: BS/BA: **9** M.A.: **2**
Faculty advocate: **Yes** Meets with instructor: **As needed**

Diagnostic Testing

ADD	Personality	Perceptual skills	Spelling
ADHD	Organization	Fine motor skills	• Reading
I.Q.	Handwriting	Spoken language	Study skills
• Math	Social skills	• Written language	

Tutoring:
Average size of group tutorials: **2**
Services rendered by:

Graduates	Peers	Faculty	•LD staff	Teacher trainees

Tutorials

Grp.	Ind.	Tutorials	Grp.	Ind.	Tutorials
	•	Math skills		•	Word processing
	•	Study skills	•	•	Time management
	•	Language arts		•	Learning strategies
	•	Written express		•	Organizational skills

Academic Accommodations

Curriculum	Study Aids	Exams
Priority registration	Typist	• Oral
Math waiver	• Reader	Untimed
Foreign lang. waiver	• Notetaker	Take home
Course substitution	• Proof reader	With proctor
In Class	• Text on tape	On computer
• Calculators	Early syllabus	• Extended time
• Tape recorder	Taped handouts	On tape
• Word processor		Modified
Priority seating		• Separate room

Graduation Requirements:
Course credits: **60** GPA: **2.0**

Program Strengths

I.C.E. is a post-secondary program for the student who has a high school diploma, certificate of attendance, G.E.D. or whose peers have graduated from high school. It is a support service designed to assist those who are handicapped when enrolling in a traditional college program. Most students who enroll in I.C.E. would have been identified as disabled in previous educational or vocational programs.

General Information:

Iowa Central Community College is a 2 year public college. Rural campus 100 miles from Des Moines. Accessible by air. Ski areas are 125 miles from campus. 2 residential halls on campus. Housing is not guaranteed. 15 % of students remain on campus for the weekends.

Accreditation:

Expenses:
Tuition: In-state: Full year: $1,400.00. Part-time: Per credit: $57.00. Tuition: Out-of-state: Full year: $1,800.00. Part-time: Per credit: $75.00.
Room and board: $2,385.00

Majors

• AREA STUDIES Liberal/General • BUSINESS Accounting, Aviation Management, Business Administration, Marketing • COMPUTER SCIENCE Data Processing, Telecommunications • EDUCATION Child Develop & Family Service, Teacher Aide • HEALTH SCIENCES Medical Assistant, Nursing, Practical Nursing • SOCIAL SCIENCES Law Enforcement • VOCATIONAL Automotive Technology, Carpentry, Drafting, Electronics, Piloting, Protective Services, Radiograph Medical Technology, Secretarial

Sports/Activities

• SPORTS RELATED Pep Band • SPORTS-INTERCOLLEGIATE Baseball (M), Basketball (F), Basketball (M), Football (M), Golf, Softball (F), Volleyball (F), Wrestling (M) • SPORTS-INTRAMURAL Archery, Badminton, Bowling, Softball, Swimming, Tennis • STUDENT LIFE ACTIVITIES Choral, Community Service, Concert Band, Drama Groups, Film, Jazz Band, Music Groups, Newspaper, Radio/TV station, Student Government, Yearbook

Selective

Iowa State University of Science and Technology

Admissions Office Alumni Hall
Ames, Iowa 50011
(515) 294-5836

School Enrollment: **21,137** Male: **12,682** Female: **9,455**

Admissions Contact: **Vern Hawkins, Coordinator/Enrollment**
LD Contact: **James Copley, Coordinator**
Name of Program: **Student Counseling Services**
Telephone:**(515) 294-5056**

Admissions

Application Information:
Application deadline: **None**
Applicant must apply **6** months in advance
Rolling Admissions: **Yes**

Secondary School Information
Most Important Criteria For Admissions (1-strongest)

2 SAT/ACT	**4** Application	**5** School transcript
1 Class rank	**1** Course selection	**10** Personal statement
8 Interview	**9** Extra activities	**7** Psychoeducational
3 G.P.A.	Open admission	**6** Recommendations

Test Requirements:
Untimed SAT: **Yes** Untimed ACT: **Yes**

Types of Disabilities Served
- Speech/Lang
- Study skills
- Written express
- Organizational
- Perceptual
- Reading
- Spelling
- Math
- Fine Motor
- ADD with LD
- ADD without LD
- ADHD with LD
- ADHD without LD

Learning Disability Program
Counseling: Individual: **Yes** Group Counseling: **Yes**

Faculty:
Faculty: **4** Full time: **1** Part time: **3**
Faculty advocate: **Yes** Meets with instructor: **As needed**

Diagnostic Testing

ADD	Personality	Perceptual skills	Spelling
ADHD	Organization	Fine motor skills	Reading
I.Q.	Handwriting	Spoken language	Study skills
Math	Social skills	Written language	

Tutoring:
Average size of group tutorials: **3-4**
Services rendered by:
- Graduates • Peers • Faculty   LD staff   Teacher trainees

Tutorials

Grp.	Ind.	Tutorials	Grp.	Ind.	Tutorials
•	•	Math skills			Word processing
•	•	Study skills	•	•	Time management
•	•	Language arts	•	•	Learning strategies
•	•	Written express	•	•	Organizational skills

Academic Accommodations

Curriculum	Study Aids	Exams
Priority registration	Typist	• Oral
• Math waiver	Reader	Untimed
• Foreign lang. waiver	Notetaker	• Take home
• Course substitution	• Proof reader	With proctor
In Class	Text on tape	On computer
Calculators	Early syllabus	• Extended time
• Tape recorder	Taped handouts	On tape
• Word processor		• Modified
Priority seating		Separate room

Program Strengths
Although Iowa State does not have a formal program for learning disabled students, we do feel we can provide excellent services for them.

General Information:
Iowa State University of Science and Technology is a 4 year public university. Urban campus of 1,000 acres is 30 miles from Des Moines. Accessible by air or bus. 8% of students are foreign. 20 residential halls on campus. Housing is not guaranteed.17 % of students join fraternities/sororities.

Accreditation:NCACS

SAT/ACT Scores:
Scores for incoming freshmen:**Verbal:66%** 'below 500. 24%between 500 and 599. 9%between 600 and 699. 1%above 700. **Math:**41% below 500. 27% between 500 and 599. 23% between 600 and 699. 9%above 700. **ACT:** 21% below 20. 29% between 20 and 23. 18%between 24 and 25l. 23%between 26 and 28. 10% above 28.

Class Rank:
About 50% of the present freshmen class were in the upper 20% of their high school class. 84% were in the top 40% of their class. 97% were in the top 60% of their class. 99% were in the top 80% of their class.

Expenses:
Tuition: In-state: Full year: $1,880.00. Part-time: Per credit:$80.00. Tuition: Out-of-state: Full year: $6,160.00. Part-time: Per credit:$258.00. Room and board: $2,704.00

Majors
• AREA STUDIES African, American/Indian, Asian, Latin American, Urban, Women's Studies • BUSINESS Accounting, Agricultural, Business Administration, Economics, Finance, Food Management, Hotel and Restaurant Managemen, Management, Marketing • COMMUNICATIONS Advertising, Broadcasting, Communication, English, Graphic Design, Journalism, Linguistics, Speech, Television/Radio/Film • COMPUTER SCIENCE Computer Science, Programming, Telecommunications • CRAFTS AND DESIGN Apparel Design, Ceramics • EDUCATION Agricultural, Art, Child Development, Curriculum, Early Childhood, Health, Industrial, Middle School, Music, Physical, School Psychology, Secondary, Teacher Aide, Vocational • ENGINEERING Aerospace, Civil/Environmental, Computer, Electrical, Engineering Science, Industrial, Mechanical, Metallurgical, Nuclear • HEALTH SCIENCES Dietary Manager, Nutritional/Food, Veterinarian Assistant • HUMANITIES Humanities, Liberal Arts, Philosophy, Religion • LANGUAGES French, German, Greek, Italian, Russian, Spanish • PREPROFESSIONAL Agriculture, Architecture, Dentistry, Fisheries, Forestry, Law, Medicine, Ministry, Pharmacy, Wildlife • SCIENCES Actuarial Technology, Agronomy, Animal, Astronomy, As-

trophysics, Biochemistry, Biology, Biophysics, Botany, Chemistry, Dairy, Earth, Ecology, Entomology, Genetics, Geology, Gerontology, Marine Biology, Mathematics, Meteorology, Microbiology, Naval, Physical Chemistry, Physical Science, Physics, Plant Pathology, Statistics • SOCIAL SCIENCES Anthropology, Criminal Justice, Family Counseling, Geography, Government/Political, History, Political Science, Social Sciences, Sociology • VISUAL AND PERFORMING ARTS Art, Art History, Dance, Music, Theater • VOCATIONAL Construction, Fashion Design, Fashion Mechandizing, Fishery Studies, Food Service, Forestry, Home Economics, Interior Design, Park/Recreation, Textile and Clothing

Sports/Activities

• SPORTS RELATED Bagpipe Band, Cheerleading, Drum Major/Majorette, Marching Band, Pep Band, Team Managers • SPORTS-INTERCOLLEGIATE Baseball (M), Basketball, Cross Country, Diving, Golf (F), Gymnastics, Softball (F), Swimming, Tennis, Track and Field, Volleyball, Wrestling (M) • SPORTS-INTRAMURAL Badminton, Baseball, Basketball, Bowling, Cross Country, Diving, Fencing, Golf, Horseback Riding, Ice Hockey, Lacrosse, Ping-Pong, Racquetball, Riflery, Rugby (M), Sailing, Skiing - Snow, Soccer, Squash, Swimming, Tennis, Track and Field, Volleyball, Water Polo, Wrestling • STUDENT LIFE ACTIVITIES Academic Clubs, Community Service, Debate, Drama Groups, Ethnic & Cultural Groups, Fraternities, Music Groups, Newspaper, Radio/TV station, Religious Organization, Sororities, Student Government, Symphony Orchestra, Yearbook

Selective	Iowa
	Program

Loras College
1450 Alta Vista
Dubuque, Iowa 52004-0178
(319) 588-7236

School Enrollment: **1,700** Male: **884** Female: **816**
LD Enrollment: **65**

Admissions Contact: **Kelly Myers, Director of Admissions**
LD Contact: **Dianne Gibson, LD Specialist**
Name of Program: **Learning Disabilities Program**
Telephone:**(319) 588-7134**

Admissions

Application Information:
LD Students Applying: **60** Accepted: **16** Enrolled:**64**
Application deadline: **December**
Applicant must apply **12** months in advance
Rolling Admissions: **Yes**Notified when: **January**

Secondary School Information
Most Important Criteria For Admissions (1-strongest)
5 SAT/ACT	**9** Application	**4**	School transcript
7 Class rank	**1** Course selection	**10**	Personal statement
3 Interview	**11** Extra activities	**2**	Psychoeducational
6 G.P.A.	Open admission	**8**	Recommendations

Test Requirements:
Diagnostic testing waived: **Yes**
Untimed SAT: **Yes** Untimed ACT: **Yes**
WAIS-R required: **Yes** Range accepted: **95**
Documentation of LD required: **Yes**
Currency of diagnostic testing: **12 months or less**
Tests recommended: **Thorough educational battery ; Woodcock-Johnson, IRI**

Types of Disabilities Served
• Speech/Lang	• Reading	• ADD with LD
• Study skills	• Spelling	ADD without LD
• Written express	• Math	• ADHD with LD
• Organizational	• Fine Motor	ADHD without LD
• Perceptual		

Admissions Process

Applicants contact LD program staff and send documentation of their learning disability. After materials are received, LD staff contacts applicant to arrange visit. Applicant completes application after visit.

High School Course Requirements:
English: **3** Math: **2** Science: **2**
Waivers to standard high school courses
Foreign Language : **Yes** Course substitution: **Yes**

Learning Disability Program
Program: Remedial: **Yes**
Program: Reinforces course work: **Yes**
Program available through:**As long as needed**
Students mainstreamed **100** % of the day
Recommended credits per semester: **12-15**
Time required or recommended in learning center: **3 hours**
Services only for LD students: **Yes**
Counseling: Individual: **Yes** Vocational Counseling: **Yes**
Support groups are available:**Done as part of freshman class for students in program.**

Faculty:
Faculty: **2** Including Director: **Yes** Full time: **2**
LD faculty with: BS/BA: **1** M.A.: **1**
Faculty advocate: **Yes** Meets with instructor: **As needed**

Diagnostic Testing
ADD	• Personality	Perceptual skills	• Spelling
ADHD	Organization	Fine motor skills	• Reading
I.Q.	• Handwriting	Spoken language	• Study skills
• Math	Social skills	• Written language	

Tutoring:
Average size of group tutorials: **3-4**
Services rendered by:
Graduates	•Peers	Faculty	•LD staff	Teacher trainees

Tutorials
Grp.	Ind.	Tutorials	Grp.	Ind.	Tutorials
•	•	Math skills	•	•	Word processing
•	•	Study skills	•	•	Time management
•	•	Language arts	•	•	Learning strategies
•	•	Written express	•	•	Organizational skills

Academic Accommodations
Curriculum	Study Aids	Exams
Priority registration	• Typist	• Oral
Math waiver	Reader	Untimed
• Foreign lang. waiver	• Notetaker	Take home
Course substitution	• Proof reader	• With proctor
In Class	• Text on tape	On computer
• Calculators	Early syllabus	• Extended time
• Tape recorder	Taped handouts	On tape
• Word processor		Modified
Priority seating		• Separate room

269

Iowa

Graduation Requirements:
Course credits: **120** GPA: **2.0** Years to complete degree: **No limit**

Program Strengths
Freshmen attend a class called Learning Strategies both semesters (2 credits each semester- total 4 credit hours). College reading skills, written expression, current events, a unit on learning disabilities, career development and group-building projects form the content of this course. All students in the program meet with an LD staff member each week for individual instruction/counseling/guidance. LD staff members serve as advisors to students until they choose a major (they remain as secondary advisors after major is declared).

General Information:
Loras College is a 4 year private Roman Catholic college. Urban campus of 60 acres is 95 miles from Madison, Wisconsin. Accessible by air or bus. Ski areas are 2 miles from campus. Beaches are 850 miles from campus. 6 residential halls on campus. Housing is guaranteed.Guaranteed through 2nd year. 60-70 % of students remain on campus for the weekends.

Accreditation: NCACS, NCATE

Expenses:
Tuition: In-state: Full year: $9,900.00. Part-time: Per credit:$275.00.
Room and board: $3,470.00 Cost of LD program:$1,400.00-$1,800.00

Majors
• BUSINESS Accounting, Banking, Business Administration, Business Economics, Business Management, Economics, Finance, Insurance, Management, Marketing, Sports Management • COMMUNICATIONS Broadcasting, Communication, Creative Writing, English, Journalism, Speech, Television/Radio/Film • COMPUTER SCIENCE Computer Maintenance, Computer Technology, Programming • EDUCATION Art, Early Childhood, Elementary, English, Foreign Language, Mathematics, Middle School, Music, Physical, Science, Secondary, Special • HUMANITIES Classics, Liberal Arts, Philosophy, Religion • LANGUAGES French, German, Greek, Latin, Spanish • PREPROFESSIONAL Architecture, Dentistry, Engineering, Law, Medicine, Pharmacy, Recreation, Social Work, Sports Medicine, Veterinarian • SCIENCES Biology, Chemistry, Gerontology, Mathematics, Physical Science, Physics • SOCIAL SCIENCES Government/Political, History, Political Science, Social Sciences, Sociology • VISUAL AND PERFORMING ARTS Art, Art History, Music, Studio Art, Theater • VOCATIONAL Medical Laboratory Technology

Sports/Activities
• SPORTS-INTERCOLLEGIATE Baseball (M), Basketball, Cross Country, Diving, Football (M), Golf, Ice Hockey (M), Skiing - Cross Country, Soccer (M), Softball (F), Swimming, Tennis, Track and Field, Volleyball (F), Wrestling (M) • SPORTS-INTRAMURAL Badminton, Baseball (M), Basketball, Cross Country, Diving, Golf, Hand Ball, Racquetball, Softball, Swimming, Tennis, Track and Field, Volleyball

---

Less Selective   **Iowa**
                                                  Services

Scott Community College
500 Belmont Road
Bettendorf, Iowa 52722
(319) 359-7531

School Enrollment: **3,012**

Admissions Contact: **Steve Norton, Assoc. Dean Enrollment Serv.**
Name of Program: **Student Success Support Services**
Telephone:**(319) 359-7531**

Admissions

Secondary School Information
Most Important Criteria For Admissions (1-strongest)

SAT/ACT	Application	School transcript
Class rank	Course selection	Personal statement
Interview	Extra activities	Psychoeducational
G.P.A.	Open admission	Recommendations

Test Requirements:
Documentation of LD required: **Yes**
Tests recommended: **Testing is available through Vocational Rehabilitation and learning specialist.**

Types of Disabilities Served
• Speech/Lang • Reading • ADD with LD
• Study skills • Spelling • ADD without LD
• Written express • Math • ADHD with LD
• Organizational • Fine Motor • ADHD without LD
• Perceptual

Admissions Process

Fill out application and pay $20.00 application fee.

High School Course Requirements:
English: **4** Math: **2**

Learning Disability Program
Program: Remedial: **Yes**
Program: Reinforces course work: **Yes**
Students mainstreamed **100** % of the day
Recommended credits per semester: **9**
Services available for all students: **Yes**
Counseling: Individual: **Yes** Vocational Counseling: **Yes**
Support groups are available:**Yes**

Faculty:
Faculty: **5** Including Director: **Yes** Full time: **4** Part time: **1**
LD faculty with: BS/BA: **2** M.A.: **3**
Faculty advocate: **Yes** Meets with instructor: **As needed**

Diagnostic Testing
ADD	• Personality	Perceptual skills	• Spelling
ADHD	Organization	Fine motor skills	• Reading
• I.Q.	Handwriting	Spoken language	• Study skills
• Math	Social skills	• Written language	

Tutoring:
Average size of group tutorials: **3-4**
Services rendered by:
Graduates •Peers •Faculty •LD staff Teacher trainees

Tutorials
Grp.	Ind.	Tutorials	Grp.	Ind.	Tutorials
•	•	Math skills	•	•	Word processing
•		Study skills	•		Time management
	•	Language arts		•	Learning strategies
•	•	Written express		•	Organizational skills

Academic Accommodations

Curriculum	Study Aids	Exams
• Priority registration	Typist	• Oral
Math waiver	Reader	• Untimed
Foreign lang. waiver	Notetaker	Take home
• Course substitution	• Proof reader	• With proctor
In Class	• Text on tape	• On computer
• Calculators	• Early syllabus	• Extended time
• Tape recorder	Taped handouts	• On tape
• Word processor		• Modified
Priority seating		• Separate room

Graduation Requirements:
Course credits: **64** GPA: **2.0**

General Information:
Scott Community College is a 2 year public college. Rural campus of 3,600 acres is Accessible by bus. Housing is not guaranteed.

Accreditation:Regional

Expenses:
Tuition: In-state: Full year: Part-time: Per credit: $47.25. Part-time: Per course: Varies. Tuition: Out-of-state: Full year: Part-time: Per credit: $68.25. Part-time: Per course:Varies

Majors
• ARTS Interior Design • BUSINESS Accounting, Banking/Finance, Bookkeeping, Business Administration, Clerical, Data Processing, Fashion Merchandising, Hotel & Restaurant Management, Secretarial Science • COMMUNICATIONS Broadcasting, Communication • COMPUTER SCIENCE Business Data Programming, Computer Science • HEALTH SCIENCES Medical Laboratry Technology, Nursing, Practical Nursing, Radiological Technology, Respiratory Therapy • HUMANITIES Liberal Arts • PRE PROFESSIONAL Pharmacy, Social Work • SCIENCES Biology, Chemistry, General • SOCIAL SCIENCES Criminal Justice • VOCATIONAL Air Conditioning/Heating/Refri, Auto Body, Automated Manufacturing Techno, Automobile Technology, Business and Office, Chef Apprenticeship, Culinary Arts, Diesel Power Technology, Drafting, Fashion Merchandising, Interior Design, Legal Secretary, Medical Laboratry Technology, Office Administration, Radiological Technology, Respiratory Therapy Technology, Secretarial, Welding, Word Processing

Sports/Activities
• STUDENT LIFE ACTIVITIES Academic Clubs, Drama Groups, Ethnic & Cultural Groups, Film, Student Government

---

Less Selective

Iowa

Southeastern Community College: North Campus
Drawer F
West Burlington, Iowa 52655
(319) 752-2731

School Enrollment: **1,500**
LD Enrollment: **45**

Admissions Contact: **Dana Feinberg, Enrollment Representative**
LD Contact: **Dana Feinberg**
Name of Program: **Sec. Trans. Ed. Program**

Admissions

Application Information:
Application deadline: **August 30th**
Rolling Admissions: **Yes** Notified when: **July**

Secondary School Information
Most Important Criteria For Admissions (1-strongest)

SAT/ACT	**1**	Application	**2** School transcript
Class rank	**5**	Course selection	**4** Personal statement
Interview		Extra activities	Psychoeducational
G.P.A.		Open admission	Recommendations

Test Requirements:
Documentation of LD required: **Yes**

Types of Disabilities Served
• Speech/Lang	• Reading	• ADD with LD
• Study skills	• Spelling	• ADD without LD
• Written express	• Math	• ADHD with LD
• Organizational	• Fine Motor	• ADHD without LD
• Perceptual		

High School Course Requirements:
English: **3** Math: **2** Science: **2**
Waivers to standard high school courses
Course substitution: **Yes**

Learning Disability Program
Program: Remedial: **Yes**
Program: Reinforces course work: **Yes**
Program available through:**Mornings**
Services available for all students: **Yes**
Counseling: Individual: **Yes** Group Counseling: **Yes**

Faculty:
Faculty: **2** Full time: **2** M.A.: **2**
Faculty advocate: **Yes** Meets with instructor: **As needed**

Diagnostic Testing
ADD	• Personality	• Perceptual skills	• Spelling
ADHD	Organization	• Fine motor skills	• Reading
• I.Q.	Handwriting	Spoken language	• Study skills
• Math	• Social skills	Written language	

Tutoring:
Average size of group tutorials: **3-4**
Services rendered by:
Graduates •Peers •Faculty •LD staff •Teacher trainees

Tutorials
Grp.	Ind.	Tutorials	Grp.	Ind.	Tutorials
•	•	Math skills	•	•	Word processing
•	•	Study skills	•	•	Time management
•	•	Language arts	•	•	Learning strategies
•	•	Written express	•	•	Organizational skills

Iowa

Academic Accommodations

Curriculum	Study Aids	Exams
Priority registration	Typist	• Oral
Math waiver	Reader	• Untimed
Foreign lang. waiver	• Notetaker	Take home
• Course substitution	• Proof reader	With proctor
In Class	• Text on tape	On computer
Calculators	Early syllabus	• Extended time
• Tape recorder	Taped handouts	On tape
Word processor		Modified
Priority seating		Separate room

Graduation Requirements:
Course credits: **62** GPA: **2.0** Years to complete degree: **Indefinite**

Program Strengths
Started in 1983, we provide a lot of assistance. We do provide quite a bit of tutoring in a variety of areas. Also, we have a peer tutoring program. We do have a Learning Center and developmental programs.

General Information:
Southeastern Community College: North Campus is a 2 year public college. Rural campus of 160 acres acres is 60 miles from Davenport. Accessible by air, train or bus. 2 residential halls on campus. Housing is not guaranteed. 15 % of students remain on campus for the weekends.

Accreditation: NCA - 10 year approval

Expenses:
Tuition: In-state: Full year: $600.00. Part-time: Per credit:$40.00. Tuition: Out-of-state: Full year: $900.00. Part-time: Per credit:$60.00. Room and board: $2,400.00

Majors
• AGRICULTURE Business • BUSINESS Accounting, Clerical, Secretarial Science, Vocational Studies • COMPUTER SCIENCE Business Data Programming, Programming, Robotics, Software Engineer • EDUCATION Elementary • ENGINEERING Automotive, Drafting, Engineering Science • HEALTH SCIENCES Medical Assistant, Nursing • LANGUAGES French, Spanish

Sports/Activities
• SPORTS-INTERCOLLEGIATE Baseball (M), Basketball (M), Golf (M), Volleyball (F) • STUDENT LIFE ACTIVITIES Academic Clubs, Student Government

Less Selective   **Iowa**
Services

Southwestern Community College
1501 West Townline
Creston, Iowa 50801
(515) 782-7081

School Enrollment: **1,154** Male: **457** Female: **697**
LD Enrollment: **60** Male: **35** Female: **25**

Admissions Contact: **Bill Hitesman, Admissions Coordinator**
LD Contact: **Gary O'Daniels, Special Needs Coordinator**

Admissions

Application Information:
Application deadline: **None**
Rolling Admissions: **Yes**

Secondary School Information
Most Important Criteria For Admissions (1-strongest)

9 SAT/ACT	4 Application	1 School transcript
5 Class rank	4 Course selection	7 Personal statement
8 Interview	10 Extra activities	2 Psychoeducational
6 G.P.A.	Open admission	3 Recommendations

Test Requirements:
Standardized tests waived: **Yes**

Types of Disabilities Served
• Speech/Lang	• Reading	ADD with LD
• Study skills	• Spelling	ADD without LD
• Written express	• Math	ADHD with LD
• Organizational	• Fine Motor	ADHD without LD
• Perceptual		

Learning Disability Program
Services available for all students: **Yes**
Counseling: Individual: **Yes**

Faculty:
Faculty: **2** Full time: **2**
Faculty advocate: **Yes** Meets with instructor: **Frequently**

Diagnostic Testing
ADD	Personality	Perceptual skills	Spelling
ADHD	Organization	Fine motor skills	Reading
I.Q.	Handwriting	Spoken language	Study skills
Math	Social skills	Written language	

Tutoring:
Services rendered by:
Graduates   •Peers   Faculty   LD staff   Teacher trainees

Tutorials
Grp.	Ind.	Tutorials	Grp.	Ind.	Tutorials
•	•	Math skills	•	•	Word processing
•	•	Study skills	•	•	Time management
•	•	Language arts			Learning strategies
		Written express			Organizational skills

Academic Accommodations

Curriculum	Study Aids	Exams
Priority registration	Typist	• Oral
• Math waiver	Reader	Untimed
• Foreign lang. waiver	• Notetaker	Take home
• Course substitution	Proof reader	With proctor
In Class	Text on tape	On computer
Calculators	Early syllabus	• Extended time
• Tape recorder	Taped handouts	On tape
Word processor		Modified
Priority seating		Separate room

Program Strengths
SWCC's program for learning disabled students provides supplemental services in the form of counseling as well as course instruction in the Comprehensive Learning Center. Full-time faculty assist students on an individual basis. Students may receive credit for the

classes, if deserved, but classes do not count towards graduation.

General Information:

Southwestern Community College is a 2 year public college. Rural campus of 435 acres is 70 miles from Des Moines. Accessible by train. Ski areas are 3 hours from campus. 1% of students are foreign. 2 residential halls on campus. Housing is not guaranteed.2 % of students remain on campus for the weekends.

Accreditation:NCA, IDE

Expenses:

Tuition: In-state: Full year: Part-time: Per credit: $46.00. Tuition: Out-of-state: Full year: Part-time: Per credit: $65.50. Room and board: $2,232.00

Majors

• BUSINESS Accounting, Business Administration, Business Management, Marketing • COMPUTER SCIENCE Data Processing, Programming • HEALTH SCIENCES Nursing, Practical Nursing • HUMANITIES Liberal Arts • VOCATIONAL Auto Body, Automobile Technology, Business and Office, Carpentry, Cosmetology, Drafting, Electronics Technology, Industrial Equipment Maintenan, Secretarial, Welding

Sports/Activities

• SPORTS RELATED Pep Band • SPORTS-INTERCOLLEGIATE Baseball (M), Basketball, Golf (M), Volleyball • SPORTS-INTRAMURAL Basketball, Volleyball • STUDENT LIFE ACTIVITIES Choral, Concert Band, Jazz Band, Music Groups, Newspaper, Student Government

---

Very Selective   **Iowa**
                                                  Services

University of Iowa

3101 Burge Hall
Iowa City, Iowa 52242
(319) 335-3847

School Enrollment: **29,230** Male: **14,984** Female: **14,246**

Admissions Contact: **Michael Barron, Director of Admissions**
LD Contact: **Donna Chandler, Coordinator**
Name of Program: **Disabilities Services**
Address: **Services for Persons with Disabilities, 3101 Burge Hall**
Telephone:**(319) 335-1462**

Admissions

Application Information:

LD on admissions committee:**Yes**
Application deadline: **May 15th**
Applicant must apply **6** months in advance
Rolling Admissions: **Yes**

Secondary School Information

Most Important Criteria For Admissions (1-strongest)

2	SAT/ACT	10	Application	3	School transcript
1	Class rank	9	Course selection	8	Personal statement
7	Interview	6	Extra activities		Psychoeducational
4	G.P.A.		Open admission	5	Recommendations

Test Requirements:

Diagnostic testing waived: **Yes**
Untimed ACT: **Yes**
WAIS-R required: **Yes** Range accepted: **Average+**
Documentation of LD required: **Yes**
Currency of diagnostic testing: **3 years**
Tests recommended: **Woodcock-Johnson, WRAT**

Types of Disabilities Served

• Speech/Lang	• Reading	• ADD with LD
• Study skills	• Spelling	• ADD without LD
• Written express	• Math	• ADHD with LD
• Organizational	• Fine Motor	• ADHD without LD
• Perceptual		

High School Course Requirements:

English: **4** Math: **3** Science: **3** Foreign Language: **2**
Waivers to standard high school courses
Foreign Language : **Yes** Math: **Yes**

Learning Disability Program

Program: Reinforces course work: **Yes**
Students mainstreamed **100** % of the day
Recommended credits per semester: **varies**
Services available for all students: **Yes**
Counseling: Individual: **Yes** Group Counseling: **Yes**

Faculty:

Faculty: **4** Full time: **2** Part time: **2**
LD faculty with: BS/BA: **.5**
Faculty advocate: **Yes** Meets with instructor: **As needed**

Diagnostic Testing

• ADD	Personality	• Perceptual skills	• Spelling
• ADHD	Organization	Fine motor skills	• Reading
• I.Q.	• Handwriting	• Spoken language	• Study skills
• Math	Social skills	• Written language	

Tutoring:

Services rendered by:
•Graduates •Peers •Faculty •LD staff Teacher trainees

Tutorials

Grp.	Ind. Tutorials	Grp.	Ind. Tutorials
	• Math skills		• Word processing
•	Study skills		• Time management
	Language arts		• Learning strategies
	• Written express		• Organizational skills

Academic Accommodations

Curriculum	Study Aids	Exams
• Priority registration	• Typist	• Oral
• Math waiver	• Reader	Untimed
• Foreign lang. waiver	• Notetaker	• Take home
• Course substitution	• Proof reader	• With proctor
In Class	• Text on tape	• On computer
• Calculators	Early syllabus	• Extended time
• Tape recorder	Taped handouts	• On tape
• Word processor		• Modified
• Priority seating		• Separate room

Graduation Requirements:

Course credits: **124** GPA: **2.0** Years to complete degree: **Usually 5**

Program Strengths

We have a procedure to allow students to substitute foreign language and math with approved courses. We also have an LD specialist who does all of our LD assessment on our enrolled students. We have a procedure to help assist students through the admission process.

General Information:

University of Iowa is a 4 year public university. Urban campus of 900 acres is 300 miles from St. Louis. Accessible by air or bus. 9 residential halls on campus. Housing is guaranteed.

Accreditation: Regional

SAT/ACT Scores:

Scores for incoming freshmen: **ACT:** 8% below 20. 36% between 20 and 23. 20% between 24 and 25l. 22% between 26 and 28. 14% above 28.

Class Rank:

About 43% of the present freshmen class were in the upper 20% of their high school class. 76% were in the top 40% of their class. 96% were in the top 60% of their class. 99% were in the top 80% of their class.

Expenses:

Tuition: In-state: Full year: $853.00. Tuition: Out-of-state: Full year: $2,144.00.

Majors

• AREA STUDIES African, Eastern European • AREA STUDIES American, Asian, Urban • BUSINESS Accounting, Banking, Business Administration, Business Economics, Business Management, Economics, Finance, Labor Relations, Management, Marketing • COMMUNICATIONS Communication, English, Journalism, Linguistic, Television/Radio/Film • COMPUTER SCIENCE Computer Science • CRAFTS AND DESIGN Ceramics, Sculpture • EDUCATION Art, Elementary, English, Foreign Language, Health, Mathematics, Music, Physical, Science, Secondary, Social Studies, Speech/Language • ENGINEERING Bioengineering, Biomedical, Chemical, Civil/Environmental, Computer, Electrical, Engineering Science, Industrial, Mechanical • HEALTH SCIENCES Dental Hygiene, Environmental, Health, Medical Assistant, Medical Technology, Nursing, Physician's Assistant, Speech/Audiology and Speech • HUMANITIES Classics, Humanities, Liberal Arts, Philosophy, Religion • LANGUAGES French, German, Greek, Italian, Latin, Portuguese, Russian, Spanish • PREPROFESSIONAL Dentistry, Engineering, Law, Medicine, Pharmacy, Recreation, Social Work • SCIENCES Actuarial Technology, Anthropology, Astronomy, Biochemistry, Biology, Botany, Chemistry, Geography, Geology, Mathematics, Microbiology, Physics, Statistics • SOCIAL SCIENCES Anthropology, Family Counseling, Government/Political, History, Political Science, Psychology, Social Sciences, Sociology • VISUAL AND PERFORMING ARTS Art, Art History, Fine Arts, Music, Music Performance, Studio Art, Theater

Sports/Activities

• SPORTS RELATED Bagpipe Band, Baton Twirling, Cheerleading, Chess, Marching Band, Pep Band • SPORTS-INTERCOLLEGIATE Baseball (M), Basketball, Cross Country, Diving, Field Hockey (F), Football (M), Golf, Gymnastics, Softball (F), Swimming, Tennis, Track and Field, Volleyball (F), Wrestling (M) • SPORTS-INTRAMURAL Badminton, Basketball, Bowling, Crew, Diving, Golf, Ice Hockey, Lacrosse, Ping-Pong, Racquetball, Riflery, Sailing, Skiing - Snow, Soccer, Softball, Swimming, Tennis, Track and Field, Volleyball, Wrestling • STUDENT LIFE ACTIVITIES Academic Clubs, Choral, Community Service, Concert Band, Debate, Drama Groups, Ethnic & Cultural Groups, Fraternities, Jazz Band, Magazine, Music Groups, Musical Theater, Newspaper, Opera, Orchestra, Political Groups, Radio/TV station, Religious Organization, Sororities, Student Government, Symphony Orchestra, Yearbook

University of Northern Iowa
172 Gilchrsit Hall
Cedar Falls, Iowa 50614-0385
(319) 273-2676

School Enrollment: **10,517** Male: **4,519** Female: **5,998**
LD Enrollment: **16**

Admissions Contact: **Jack Wielenga, Director of Admissions**
Name of Program: **Disabled Student Services**
Address: **University of Northern Iowa, SSC 213**
Telephone: **(319) 273-2676**

Admissions

Secondary School Information
Most Important Criteria For Admissions (1-strongest)

1 SAT/ACT	**5** Application	**3**	School transcript
2 Class rank	**4** Course selection	**10**	Personal statement
7 Interview	**11** Extra activities	**9**	Psychoeducational
6 G.P.A.	Open admission	**8**	Recommendations

Test Requirements:
Documentation of LD required: **Yes**

Types of Disabilities Served

Speech/Lang	Reading	ADD with LD
Study skills	Spelling	ADD without LD
Written express	Math	ADHD with LD
Organizational	Fine Motor	ADHD without LD
Perceptual		

Admissions Process

No formal procedure. Contact DSS office.

High School Course Requirements:
English: **4** Math: **3** Science: **2**

Learning Disability Program
Services available for all students: **Yes**

Faculty: Part time: **1**

Diagnostic Testing

ADD	Personality	Perceptual skills	Spelling
ADHD	Organization	Fine motor skills	Reading
I.Q.	Handwriting	Spoken language	Study skills
Math	Social skills	Written language	

Services rendered by:

Graduates	Peers	Faculty	LD staff	Teacher trainees

Tutorials

Grp.	Ind.	Tutorials	Grp.	Ind.	Tutorials
		Math skills			Word processing
		Study skills			Time management
		Language arts			Learning strategies
		Written express			Organizational skills

Academic Accommodations

Curriculum	Study Aids	Exams
• Priority registration	Typist	• Oral
Math waiver	• Reader	• Untimed
Foreign lang. waiver	• Notetaker	Take home
Course substitution	Proof reader	• With proctor
In Class	• Text on tape	On computer
Calculators	Early syllabus	• Extended time
• Tape recorder	Taped handouts	On tape
Word processor		• Modified
Priority seating		• Separate room

Graduation Requirements:
Course credits: **Depends on major**

Program Strengths
Tutoring is offered by Student Support Services Office federally funded program. Some LD students qualify.

General Information:
University of Northern Iowa is a 4 year public university. Suburban campus of 13,000 acres is 90 miles from Cedar Rapids. Housing is not guaranteed.

Accreditation: AHEA, ASLA, NASM, NCATE, NRPA

SAT/ACT Scores:
Scores for incoming freshmen: 34% between 20 and 23. 20% between 24 and 251. 20% between 26 and 28. 5% above 28.

Class Rank:
About 41% of the present freshmen class were in the upper 20% of their high school class. 39% were in the top 40% of their class. 8% were in the top 60% of their class. 1% were in the top 80% of their class.

Expenses:
Tuition: In-state: Full year: $976.00 . Part-time: Per credit:$82.00 . Part-time: Per course: Approx. $246.00 . Tuition: Out-of-state: Full year: $2,491.00. Part-time: Per credit:$208.00 . Part-time: Per course:approx. $624.00 Room and board: $2,450.00-$2,900.00

Majors
• AREA STUDIES American, Asian, European, Latin American, Russian/Slavic • ARTS Theater Design • BUSINESS Accounting, Banking/Finance, Business Administration, Business Education, Business Management, Chemistry Marketing, Economics, Management, Marketing, Real Estate • COMMUNICATIONS Broadcasting, Communication, Graphic Design, Television/Radio/Film • COMPUTER SCIENCE Computer Science • EDUCATION Early Childhood, Elementary, English As A Second Language, Foreign Language, Health, Home Economics, Industrial Arts Education, Middle School, Music, Physical, Reading, Science, Social Science, Special, Trade and Industrial • ENGINEERING Architectural Design, Engineering Science, Industrial, Mechanical Design Technology • ENVIRONMENTAL CONTROL Energy Conservation • HEALTH SCIENCES Nutritional/Food, Speech/Audiology and Speech • HUMANITIES Humanities, Liberal Arts , Philosophy, Religion • LANGUAGES English, French, German, Spanish • PRE PROFESSIONAL Social Work, Urban Design • SCIENCES Anthropology, Biology, Biotechnology, Chemistry, Earth, Geography, Geology, Mathematics, Physical Science, Physics • SOCIAL SCIENCES Criminology, Government/Political, History, Political Science, Psychology, Public Relations, Social Sciencex, Sociology • VISUAL AND PERFORMING ARTS Dramatic Arts, Fine Arts, Music, Music Performance, Music Theatre • VOCATIONAL Construction, Drafting, Driver and Safety, Home Economics, Leisure Sservices, Manufacturing Technology, Park/Recreation, Recreational Therapy, Textile and Clothing, Youth Agency Administration

Sports/Activities
• SPORTS RELATED Drill Team, Marching Band, Pep Band • SPORTS-INTERCOLLEGIATE Baseball (M), Basketball, Cross Country, Diving, Football (M), Golf, Softball (F), Swimming, Tennis, Track and Field, Volleyball (F), Wrestling (M) • SPORTS-INTRAMURAL Badminton, Basketball, Bowling, Cross Country, Golf, Ping-Pong, Racquetball, Softball, Swimming, Tennis, Track and Field, Volleyball, Wrestling (M) • STUDENT LIFE ACTIVITIES Choral, Concert Band, Dance, Drama Groups, Fraternities, Jazz Band, Magazine, Musical Ensembles, Musical Theater, Newspaper, Opera, Political Groups, Radio, Religious Organization, Sororities, Student Government, Symphony Orchestra, Yearbook

---

Less Selective	Iowa Program

Waldorf College
106 South Sixth
Forest City, Iowa 50436
(515) 582-8207

School Enrollment: **600** Male: **312** Female: **288**
LD Enrollment: **17** Male: **9** Female: **8**

Admissions Contact: **Steve Lovik, Director of Admissions**
LD Contact: **Rebecca Hill, Learning Disabilities Program Dir.**
Name of Program: **Learning Disabilities Program**
Address: **106 S. 6th St.**
Telephone:**(515) 582-8207**

Admissions

Application Information:
LD Students Applying: **23** Accepted: **21** Enrolled:**17**
LD on admissions committee:**Yes**
Application deadline: **August 1st**
Rolling Admissions: **Yes**

Secondary School Information
Most Important Criteria For Admissions (1-strongest)

6 SAT/ACT	**1** Application	**3** School transcript
5 Class rank	**4** Course selection	**10** Personal statement
8 Interview	**11** Extra activities	**9** Psychoeducational
2 G.P.A.	Open admission	**7** Recommendations

Test Requirements:
Untimed SAT: **Yes** Untimed ACT: **Yes**
Documentation of LD required: **Yes**
Currency of diagnostic testing: **Within three years**
Tests recommended: **We would like some type of ability (I.Q.) testing and also achievement testing.**

Types of Disabilities Served
- Speech/Lang
- Study skills
- Written express
- Organizational
- Perceptual
- Reading
- Spelling
- Math
- Fine Motor
- ADD with LD
- ADD without LD
- ADHD with LD
- ADHD without LD

Admissions Process

Students must apply by sending in admissions application, high school transcripts, ACT or SAT scores, and academic recommendation form. A formal campus visit is also required. An admissions de-

Kansas

cision is then made.

High School Course Requirements:
English: **3** Math: **2** Science: **2**
Waivers to standard high school courses
 Math: **Yes** Course substitution: **Yes**

Learning Disability Program
Special orientation for LD students: **Yes**
Program: Remedial: **Yes**
Program: Reinforces course work: **Yes**
Students mainstreamed **100** % of the day
Recommended credits per semester: **12-16**
Time required or recommended in learning center: **Varies**
Services only for LD students: **Yes**
Services available for all students: **Yes**
Counseling: Individual: **Yes** Group Counseling: **Yes** Vocational Counseling: **Yes**
Support groups are available:**LD students meet with the director. These informal sessions meet periodically.**

Faculty:
Faculty: **5** Including Director: **Yes** Full time: **3** Part time: **2**
LD faculty with: BS/BA: **1** M.A.: **3**
Faculty advocate: **Yes** Meets with instructor: **As needed**

Diagnostic Testing
- ADD
- ADHD
- I.Q.
- Math
- Personality
- Organization
- Handwriting
- Social skills
- Perceptual skills
- Fine motor skills
- Spoken language
- Written language
- Spelling
- Reading
- Study skills

Tutoring:
Average size of group tutorials: **2-3**
Services rendered by:
 Graduates •Peers •Faculty •LD staff Teacher trainees

Tutorials
Grp.	Ind.	Tutorials	Grp.	Ind.	Tutorials
•	•	Math skills	•	•	Word processing
•	•	Study skills	•	•	Time management
•	•	Language arts	•	•	Learning strategies
•	•	Written express	•	•	Organizational skills

Academic Accommodations
Curriculum	Study Aids	Exams
Priority registration	• Typist	• Oral
Math waiver	Reader	• Untimed
Foreign lang. waiver	• Notetaker	Take home
• Course substitution	• Proof reader	• With proctor
In Class	• Text on tape	• On computer
• Calculators	Early syllabus	• Extended time
• Tape recorder	Taped handouts	• On tape
• Word processor		Modified
• Priority seating		• Separate room

Graduation Requirements:
Course credits: **64** GPA: **2.0** Years to complete degree: **No limit**

Program Strengths
Our LD Program is housed in our Academic Achievement Center which serves students of all ability levels, so there is no stigma attached to using our services. We also make much use of technology, including interactive videos, and a network computer system. We are in the main traffic area of campus so we are highly visible, accessible, accepted, and used.

General Information:
Waldorf College is a 2 year independent Lutheran college. Rural campus of 7 acres is 30 miles from Mason City. Accessible by air or bus. Ski areas are 70 miles from campus. Beaches are 24 miles from campus. 10% of students are foreign. 4 residential halls on campus. Housing is guaranteed.Guaranteed through 2nd year. 60 % of students remain on campus for the weekends.

Accreditation:NCACS

Class Rank:
About 12% of the present freshmen class were in the upper 20% of their high school class. 25% were in the top 40% of their class. 46% were in the top 60% of their class. 80% were in the top 80% of their class.

Expenses:
Tuition: In-state: Full year: $8,310.00. Part-time: Per credit:$105.00. Tuition: Out-of-state: Full year: $8,310.00. Part-time: Per credit:$105.00. Room and board: $3,050.00 Cost of LD program:$800.00 Freshman year, $600 Sophomore year

Majors
• AGRICULTURE Business • ARTS Commercial Art, Drawing, Music, Music Performance, Painting, Photography • BUSINESS Accounting, Agricultural, Business Administration, Business Education, Business Management, Commercial Art, Data Processing, Economics, Education • COMMUNICATIONS Broadcasting, Communication, Creative Writing, English, Journalism, Literature, Public Relations, Radio, Speech/Debate/Forensic • COMPUTER SCIENCE Business Data Programming, Computer Science, Data Processing • EDUCATION Child Development, Early Childhood, Elementary, General, Middle School, Secondary • ENGINEERING Drafting, Engineering Science • HEALTH SCIENCES Health, Nursing Pre, Occupational Therapy Pre, Physical Therapy Pre • HUMANITIES English/Writing/Literature, Liberal Arts , Philosophy, Religion • LANGUAGES German, Spanish • MATHEMATICS Applied • PRE PROFESSIONAL Agriculture, Business, Dentistry, Engineering, Fisheries, Forestry, Law, Legal Assistant, Medicine, Ministry, Natural Resources, Optometry, Pharmacy, Recreation, Social Work, Sports Medicine, Veterinarian, Wildlife • RELIGIOUS STUDIES Bible, Philosophy, Religion & Theology • SCIENCES Biology, Botany, Chemistry, Computer Science, General, Mathematics, Physical Science, Physics, Statistics, Zoology • SOCIAL SCIENCES Criminal Justice, Government/Political, History, Human Service, Law Enforcement, Political Science, Psychology, Public Relations, Social Science, Sociology • VISUAL AND PERFORMING ARTS Art, Dramatic Arts, Music, Music Performance, Theater, Video

Sports/Activities
• SPORTS RELATED Cheerleading, Team Managers • SPORTS-INTERCOLLEGIATE Baseball (M), Basketball (F), Basketball (M), Football (M), Golf (F), Golf (M), Softball (F), Volleyball (F), Wrestling (M) • SPORTS-INTRAMURAL Basketball (F), Basketball (M), Softball (F), Softball (M), Volleyball (F), Volleyball (M) • STUDENT LIFE ACTIVITIES Academic Clubs, Choral, Community Service, Concert Band, Drama Groups, Ethnic & Cultural Groups, Jazz Band, Magazine, Music Groups, Musical Theater, Newspaper, Political Groups, Radio/TV station, Religious Organization, Student Government, Yearbook

Less Selective | **Kansas Services**

Barton Community College
Route 3
Great Bend, Kansas 67530
(316) 792-2701

School Enrollment: **1,282** Male: **600** Female: **682**

Admissions Contact: **Dr. Mary Helen Misegadis, Dean Stud. Affairs**
LD Contact: **Dr. Mary Helen Misegadis, Dean of Student Affairs**
Telephone:**(316) 792-2701 Ext. 226**

Admissions

Application Information:
Rolling Admissions: **Yes**

Secondary School Information
Most Important Criteria For Admissions (1-strongest)

SAT/ACT	Application	School transcript
Class rank	Course selection	Personal statement
Interview	Extra activities	Psychoeducational
G.P.A.	1 Open admission	Recommendations

Test Requirements:
Standardized tests waived: **Yes**

Types of Disabilities Served
- Speech/Lang
- Study skills
- Written express
- Organizational
- Perceptual
- Reading
- Spelling
- Math
- Fine Motor
- ADD with LD
- ADD without LD
- ADHD with LD
- ADHD without LD

Diagnostic Testing

ADD	Personality	Perceptual skills	Spelling
ADHD	Organization	Fine motor skills	Reading
I.Q.	Handwriting	Spoken language	Study skills
Math	Social skills	Written language	

Tutoring:
Average size of group tutorials:
Services rendered by:
Graduates   •Peers   •Faculty   LD staff   Teacher trainees

Tutorials

Grp.	Ind.	Tutorials	Grp.	Ind.	Tutorials
•	•	Math skills			Word processing
•	•	Study skills			Time management
•	•	Language arts	•	•	Learning strategies
•	•	Written express			Organizational skills

Academic Accommodations

Curriculum	Study Aids	Exams
Priority registration	Typist	• Oral
Math waiver	Reader	Untimed
Foreign lang. waiver	Notetaker	Take home
Course substitution	Proof reader	With proctor
In Class	• Text on tape	On computer
• Calculators	Early syllabus	• Extended time
• Tape recorder	Taped handouts	On tape
• Word processor		Modified
Priority seating		Separate room

Program Strengths
Every student is provided with educational opportunities according to the results of his or her assesment test. Barton does offer a variety of programs that would benefit a learning disabled student.

General Information:
Barton Community College is a 2 year public college. Rural campus of 160 acres is 120 miles from Wichita. Accessible by air. 3% of students are foreign. Housing is not guaranteed. 10 % of students remain on campus for the weekends.

Accreditation:NCACS

Expenses:
Tuition: In-state: Full year: $736.00. Part-time: Per credit:$23.00. Tuition: Out-of-state: Full year: $975.00. Part-time: Per credit:$65.00. Room and board: $1,950.00

Majors
• BUSINESS Accounting, Economics, Management • COMMUNICATIONS English, Journalism • COMPUTER SCIENCE Computer Electronics, Information Systems • EDUCATION Early Childhood, Elementary, Music, Secondary • HEALTH SCIENCES Dental Assistant, Health, Medical Technology, Nursing, Nutritional/Food • HUMANITIES Philosophy, Religion • PREPROFESSIONAL Agriculture, Architecture, Dentistry, Engineering, Law, Pharmacy, Sports Medicine, Veterinarian • SCIENCES Biology, Chemistry, Geology, Mathematics • SOCIAL SCIENCES Anthropology, Criminal Justice, Government/Political, Psychology, Sociology • VISUAL AND PERFORMING ARTS Art, Music, Theater • VOCATIONAL Automobile Technology, Cosmetology

Sports/Activities
• SPORTS RELATED Cheerleading, Drill Team, Team Managers • STUDENT LIFE ACTIVITIES Drama Groups, Ethnic & Cultural Groups, Music Groups, Newspaper, Religious Organization, Student Government

Less Selective | **Kansas Services**

Cowley County Community College
125 South Second
Arkansas City, Kansas 67005
(316) 442-0430

School Enrollment: **2,700** Male: **1,150** Female: **1,550**

Admissions Contact: **Margaret Ann Picking, Dean of Students**
LD Contact: **Chris Vollweider, Director**
Name of Program: **Learning Skills Lab**
Address: **125 South Second**
Telephone:**(316) 442-0430 Ext. 258**

Kansas

Admissions

Application Information:
Application deadline: **Open**

Secondary School Information
Most Important Criteria For Admissions (1-strongest)

SAT/ACT	**1**	Application	**2**	School transcript
Class rank	**6**	Course selection		Personal statement
Interview		Extra activities		Psychoeducational
5 G.P.A.	**1**	Open admission		Recommendations

Test Requirements:
Standardized tests waived: **Yes**

Types of Disabilities Served
- Speech/Lang
- Study skills
- Written express
- Organizational
- Perceptual
- Reading
- Spelling
- Math
- Fine Motor
- ADD with LD
- ADD without LD
- ADHD with LD
- ADHD without LD

Learning Disability Program
Program: Remedial: **Yes**
Students mainstreamed **100** % of the day
Recommended credits per semester: **12-15**
Services available for all students: **Yes**
Counseling: Individual: **Yes**

Faculty:
Faculty: **2** Full time: **1** Part time: **1**
Faculty advocate: **Yes** Meets with instructor: **As needed**

Diagnostic Testing

ADD	Personality	Perceptual skills	Spelling
ADHD	Organization	Fine motor skills	Reading
I.Q.	Handwriting	Spoken language	Study skills
Math	Social skills	Written language	

Tutoring:
Average size of group tutorials: **5-6**
Services rendered by:

Graduates	•Peers	•Faculty	LD staff	Teacher trainees

Tutorials

Grp.	Ind.	Tutorials	Grp.	Ind.	Tutorials
•	•	Math skills			Word processing
•		Study skills			Time management
		Language arts		•	Learning strategies
		Written express		•	Organizational skills

Academic Accommodations

Curriculum	Study Aids	Exams
Priority registration	Typist	• Oral
Math waiver	Reader	Untimed
Foreign lang. waiver	• Notetaker	• Take home
Course substitution	Proof reader	With proctor
In Class	• Text on tape	On computer
• Calculators	Early syllabus	• Extended time
• Tape recorder	Taped handouts	On tape
• Word processor		Modified
Priority seating		Separate room

Program Strengths
We try to provide whatever assistance learning disabled students
need to be successful in their academics.

General Information:
Cowley County Community College is a 2 year public college. Rural campus of 19 acres is 50 miles from Wichita. Accessible by air or bus. Ski areas are 6 hours from campus. Beaches are 10-12 hours from campus. 1% of students are foreign. 2 residential halls on campus. Housing is guaranteed.100 % of students remain on campus for the weekends.

Accreditation:NCACS

Expenses:
Tuition: In-state: Full year: Part-time: Per credit $26.00. Room and board: $2,250.00

Majors
• BUSINESS Accounting, Business Administration, Business Economics, Business Education, Business Management, Economics, Hotel and Restaurant Managemen, Management, Marketing • COMMUNICATIONS Advertising, Broadcasting, Communication, English, Journalism, Photography • COMPUTER SCIENCE Data Processing, Programming • EDUCATION Art, Curriculum, Early Childhood, Elementary, Health, Industrial, Middle School, Music, Physical, Recreation and Youth Leadershi, Secondary, Speech/Language, Vocational • ENGINEERING Computer • HEALTH SCIENCES Health, Medical Technology, Nursing, Nutritional/Food, Occupational Therapy, Physical Therapy, Radiological Therapy, Speech Therapy, Speech/Audiology and Speech • HUMANITIES Humanities, Philosophy • LANGUAGES French, Spanish • SCIENCES Astronomy, Biology, Botany, Chemistry, Earth, Ecology, Geography, Geology, Macrobiology, Marine Biology, Mathematics, Microbiology, Physical Chemistry, Physical Science, Physics • SOCIAL SCIENCES Anthropology, Criminal Justice, Government/Political, History, Psychology, Social Sciences, Sociology • VISUAL AND PERFORMING ARTS Art, Art History, Music, Studio Art, Theater • VOCATIONAL Automobile Technology, Carpentry, Cosmetology, Drafting, Electronics Technology, Machinist, Welding

Sports/Activities
• SPORTS RELATED Band, Cheerleading, Drill Team, Pep Band • SPORTS-INTERCOLLEGIATE Baseball, Basketball, Softball, Tennis, Volleyball • SPORTS-INTRAMURAL Baseball, Basketball, Softball, Tennis, Volleyball • STUDENT LIFE ACTIVITIES Drama Groups, Jazz Band, Music Groups, Newspaper, Religious Organization, Student Government, Yearbook

---

Less Selective

**Kansas
Accommodations**

Emporia State University
1200 Commercial
Emporia, Kansas 66801
(316) 343-1200

School Enrollment: **6,000** Male: **3,000** Female: **3,000**
LD Enrollment: **40**

Admissions Contact: **Dr. Barb Hilgendorf, Director of Admissions**
LD Contact: **Dr. Keith Frank, Coordinator**
Name of Program: **Disabled Student Services**

Admissions

Application Information:
Application deadline: **Before classes begin**
Rolling Admissions: **Yes**

Secondary School Information
Most Important Criteria For Admissions (1-strongest)

SAT/ACT	Application	School transcript
Class rank	Course selection	Personal statement
Interview	Extra activities	Psychoeducational
G.P.A.	**1** Open admission	Recommendations

Test Requirements:
Untimed SAT: **Yes** Untimed ACT: **Yes** Untimed ACH: **Yes**
Documentation of LD required: **Yes**
Currency of diagnostic testing: **3 years**

Types of Disabilities Served
- Speech/Lang
- Reading
- ADD with LD
- Study skills
- Spelling
- ADD without LD
- Written express
- Math
- ADHD with LD
- Organizational
- Fine Motor
- ADHD without LD
- Perceptual

Admissions Process

Open door policy

Learning Disability Program
Services only for LD students: **Yes**
Counseling: Individual: **Yes** Group Counseling: **Yes**

Faculty:
Faculty: **1** Part time: **1**
Faculty advocate: **Yes** Meets with instructor: **As needed**

Diagnostic Testing

ADD	Personality	Perceptual skills	Spelling
ADHD	Organization	Fine motor skills	Reading
I.Q.	Handwriting	Spoken language	Study skills
Math	Social skills	Written language	

Tutoring:
Average size of group tutorials: *
Services rendered by:

Graduates	Peers	Faculty	LD staff	Teacher trainees

Tutorials

Grp.	Ind.	Tutorials	Grp.	Ind.	Tutorials
		Math skills			Word processing
		Study skills			Time management
		Language arts			Learning strategies
		Written express			Organizational skills

Academic Accommodations

Curriculum	Study Aids	Exams
Priority registration	Typist	• Oral
Math waiver	Reader	• Untimed
• Foreign lang. waiver	• Notetaker	Take home
Course substitution	Proof reader	• With proctor
In Class	• Text on tape	On computer
• Calculators	Early syllabus	• Extended time
• Tape recorder	Taped handouts	On tape
• Word processor		Modified
• Priority seating		Separate room

Graduation Requirements: GPA: 2.0

Program Strengths
Our services are mainstreaming with accommodations.
*Tutoring for all students, not just LD, in math, reading and writing labs.

General Information:
Emporia State University is a 4 year public university. Urban campus 55 miles from Topeka. Accessible by bus. 2 residential halls on campus. Housing is guaranteed.

Accreditation: Regional

Expenses:
Tuition: In-state: Full year: $1,300.00. Part-time: Per credit:$47.35. Tuition: Out-of-state: Full year: $3,200.00. Part-time: Per credit:$110.35. Room and board: $2,400.00

Majors
• BUSINESS Accounting, Banking, Business Administration, Business Economics, Business Education, Business Management, Economics, Finance, Management, Marketing • COMMUNICATIONS Communication, English, Journalism, Speech • COMPUTER SCIENCE Computer Science, Programming, Systems Analysis • EDUCATION Art, Curriculum, Early Childhood, Elementary, English, Foreign Language, Health, Mathematics, Middle School, Music, Physical, Recreation and Youth Leadershi, School Psychology, Secondary, Social Science, Special, Speech/Language • HEALTH SCIENCES Medical Technology, Nursing • HUMANITIES Liberal Arts • LANGUAGES French, German, Russian, Spanish • PRE-PROFESSIONAL Architecture, Dentistry, Engineering, Law, Medicine, Pharmacy • SCIENCES Biology, Botany, Chemistry, Earth, Geography, Geology, Mathematics, Microbiology, Physical Science, Physics, Zoology • SOCIAL SCIENCES Family Counseling, Government/Political, History, Political Science, Psychology, Social Sciences, Sociology • VISUAL AND PERFORMING ARTS Art, Dramatic Arts, Music, Theater • VOCATIONAL Business and Office, Home Economics, Office Administration, Painting, Park/Recreation, Secretarial

Sports/Activities
• SPORTS RELATED Cheerleading, Drill Team, Marching Band, Pep Band, Team Managers • SPORTS-INTERCOLLEGIATE Baseball (M), Basketball, Cross Country, Football (M), Golf, Softball (F), Tennis, Track and Field, Volleyball (F) • SPORTS-INTRAMURAL Badminton, Basketball, Bowling, Golf, Hand Ball, Racquetball, Rugby, Soccer, Softball, Swimming, Tennis, Track and Field, Volleyball, Wrestling (M) • STUDENT LIFE ACTIVITIES Choral, Concert Band, Dance, Debate, Drama Groups, Ethnic & Cultural Groups, Fraternities, Jazz Band, Magazine, Music Groups, Musical Theater, Newspaper, Political Groups, Radio/TV station, Religious Organization, Sororities, Student Government, Symphony Orchestra, Yearbook

Less Selective

Kansas Services

Hutchinson Community College
1300 North Plum
Hutchinson, Kansas 67501
(316) 665-3500

School Enrollment: **5,000** Male: **2,000** Female: **3,000**
LD Enrollment: **40**

Admissions Contact: **Duane Halpain, Director of Admissions**
LD Contact: **Mary Coplen, Director**
Name of Program: **Student Support Services**
Address: **1300 North Plum**
Telephone:**(316) 665-3563**

Admissions

Application Information:
LD Students Applying: **40** Accepted: **40** Enrolled:**40**
Rolling Admissions: **Yes**

Secondary School Information
Most Important Criteria For Admissions (1-strongest)

SAT/ACT	Application	School transcript
Class rank	Course selection	Personal statement
Interview	Extra activities	Psychoeducational
G.P.A.	**1** Open admission	Recommendations

Test Requirements:
Diagnostic testing waived: **Yes**
WAIS-R required: **Yes**
Documentation of LD required: **Yes**

Types of Disabilities Served
- Speech/Lang
- Study skills
- Written express
- Organizational
- Perceptual
- Reading
- Spelling
- Math
- Fine Motor
- ADD with LD
- ADD without LD
- ADHD with LD
- ADHD without LD

Admissions Process

Open access for all in-state high school graduates.

Learning Disability Program

Special orientation for LD students: **Yes**
Program available through:**August-May**
Students mainstreamed **100** % of the day
Recommended credits per semester: **12**
Services available for all students: **Yes**
Counseling: Individual: **Yes** Group Counseling: **Yes**
Support groups are available:**Yes, upon demand and need**

Faculty:
Faculty: **26** Full time: **6** Part time: **20**
LD faculty with: BS/BA: **1** M.A.: **4**
Faculty advocate: **Yes** Meets with instructor: **As needed**

Diagnostic Testing

ADD •	Personality	Perceptual skills	Spelling
ADHD•	Organization	Fine motor skills	• Reading
I.Q.	Handwriting	Spoken language	• Study skills
Math	Social skills	Written language	

Tutoring:
Average size of group tutorials: **5**
Services rendered by:
  Graduates •Peers •Faculty •LD staff Teacher trainees

Tutorials

Grp.	Ind.	Tutorials	Grp.	Ind.	Tutorials
•	•	Math skills	•	•	Word processing
•	•	Study skills	•	•	Time management
•	•	Language arts	•	•	Learning strategies
•	•	Written express	•	•	Organizational skills

Academic Accommodations

Curriculum	Study Aids	Exams
Priority registration	• Typist	• Oral
Math waiver	• Reader	Untimed
Foreign lang. waiver	• Notetaker	Take home
• Course substitution	Proof reader	• With proctor
In Class	• Text on tape	On computer
Calculators	Early syllabus	• Extended time
• Tape recorder	Taped handouts	On tape
• Word processor		Modified
• Priority seating		• Separate room

Graduation Requirements:
Course credits: **64** GPA: **2.0** Years to complete degree: **2.5-3 years**
Other requirements: **General Education Disabilities requirements**

General Information:
Hutchinson Community College is a 2 year public college. Rural campus 60 miles from Wichita. Accessible by bus. Ski areas are 500 miles from campus. .05% of students are foreign. 2 residential halls on campus. Housing is not guaranteed.

Accreditation:NCACS

Expenses:
Tuition: In-state: Full year: Part-time: Per credit $26.00. Tuition: Out-of-state: Full year: Part-time: Per credit: $70.00. Room and board: $2,100.00

Majors
• BUSINESS Accounting, Agricultural, Banking, Business Administration, Business Management, Economics, Entrepreneur, Hotel and Restaurant Managemen, Insurance, Marketing, Real Estate, Retailing, Travel/Tourism Management • COMMUNICATIONS Commercial Design, English, Graphic Design, Journalism, Photography, Speech, Television/Radio/Film • COMPUTER SCIENCE Computer Maintenance, Computer Science, Data Processing, Programming • EDUCATION Art, Child Development, Curriculum, Early Childhood, Elementary, Health, Industrial, Middle School, Music, Physical, Recreation and Youth Leadershi, School Psychology, Secondary, Speech/Language • ENGINEERING Computer, Electrical, Engineering Science, Industrial, Mechanical, Mining/Mineral, Petroleum • HEALTH SCIENCES Chiropractic, Dental Assistant, Dental Hygiene, EMT, Health, Medical Technology, Nursing, Nutritional/Food, Occupational Therapy, Physical Therapy, Radiological Therapy • HUMANITIES Humanities, Liberal Arts, Philosophy, Religion • LANGUAGES German, Spanish • PREPROFESSIONAL Agriculture, Architecture, Dentistry, Engineering, Forestry, Law, Legal Assistant, Medicine, Optometry, Pharmacy, Recreation, Social Work, Sports Medicine, Veterinarian • SCIENCES Agricultural, Astronomy, Biology, Cell Biology, Chemistry, Earth, Geography, Geology, Mathematics, Microbiology, Physical Science, Physics, Physiology, Radiology, Science Technology, Zoology • SOCIAL SCIENCES

Criminal Justice, Government/Political, History, Law Enforcement, Library Science, Political Science, Psychology, Public Relations, Social Sciences, Sociology • VISUAL AND PERFORMING ARTS Art, Art History, Dance, Dramatic Arts, Fine Arts, Music, Studio Art, Theater • VOCATIONAL Automated Manufacturing Techno, Automobile Technology, Business and Office, Construction, Diesel Power Technology, Drafting, Electronics Technology, Fashion Merchandising, Fire Science, Forestry, Funeral Services/Mortuary, Home Economics, Legal Secretary, Office Administration, Paralegal, Park/Recreation, Radiological Technology, Secretarial

Sports/Activities

• SPORTS RELATED Cheerleading, Drill Team, Pep Band, Team Managers • SPORTS-INTERCOLLEGIATE Baseball (M), Basketball, Cross Country, Football (M), Golf (M), Tennis, Track and Field, Volleyball (F) • SPORTS-INTRAMURAL Badminton, Basketball, Bowling, Ping-Pong, Racquetball, Soccer, Softball, Tennis, Track and Field, Volleyball • STUDENT LIFE ACTIVITIES Choral, Concert Band, Drama Groups, Ethnic & Cultural Groups, Jazz Band, Magazine, Music Groups, Newspaper, Radio/TV station, Student Government, Symphony Orchestra, Yearbook

Less Selective	Kansas Services

Kansas City Kansas Community College

7250 State Avenue
Kansas City, Kansas 66112
(913) 334-1100

School Enrollment: **5,466** Male: **1,886** Female: **3,354**
LD Enrollment: **40** Male: **25** Female: **15**

Admissions Contact: **Don Stump, Director of Admissions**
LD Contact: **Linda Wildgen, Supervisor**
Name of Program: **Disabled Student Services**
Telephone:**(913) 334-1100 Ext. 170**

Admissions

Application Information:
Rolling Admissions: **Yes**

Secondary School Information
Most Important Criteria For Admissions (1-strongest)

SAT/ACT	Application	School transcript
Class rank	Course selection	Personal statement
Interview	Extra activities	Psychoeducational
G.P.A.	**1** Open admission	Recommendations

Test Requirements:
Documentation of LD required: **Yes**
Tests recommended: **WAIS-R, Woodscock-Johnson**

Types of Disabilities Served
• Speech/Lang • Reading • ADD with LD
• Study skills • Spelling • ADD without LD
• Written express • Math • ADHD with LD
• Organizational • Fine Motor • ADHD without LD
• Perceptual

Admissions Process

The student needs to contact the Services for Students with Disabilities Office after they have applied to the college.

Learning Disability Program
Program: Remedial: **Yes**
Program: Reinforces course work: **Yes**
Students mainstreamed **100** % of the day

Faculty:
Faculty advocate: **Yes** Meets with instructor: **As needed**

Diagnostic Testing
ADD	Personality	Perceptual skills	• Spelling
ADHD	Organization	Fine motor skills	• Reading
I.Q.	Handwriting	Spoken language	• Study skills
Math	Social skills	Written language	

Tutoring:
Services rendered by:
Graduates •Peers Faculty LD staff Teacher trainees

Tutorials
Grp.	Ind.	Tutorials	Grp.	Ind.	Tutorials
	•	Math skills			Word processing
		Study skills			Time management
	•	Language arts			Learning strategies
	•	Written express			Organizational skills

Academic Accommodations

Curriculum	Study Aids	Exams
Priority registration	Typist	• Oral
Math waiver	Reader	Untimed
• Foreign lang. waiver	• Notetaker	• Take home
• Course substitution	Proof reader	• With proctor
In Class	• Text on tape	On computer
• Calculators	Early syllabus	• Extended time
• Tape recorder	Taped handouts	On tape
• Word processor		• Modified
Priority seating		Separate room

Graduation Requirements:
Course credits: **60** GPA: **2.0**

Program Strengths

We do not have a Learning Disabilities Program. We offer support services to learning disabled students. Faculty members conduct courses in Organizational Skills, Learning Strategies, Time Management, and Study Skills in the Learning Center. These can be one day seminars.

General Information:

Kansas City Kansas Community College is a 2 year public college. Urban campus of 148 acres is Housing is not guaranteed.

Accreditation:NCACS

Expenses:
Tuition: In-state: Full year: Part-time: Per credit: $25.00. Part-time: Per credit:. Tuition: Out-of-state: Full year: Part-time: Per credit: $68.00. Part-time: Per credit:$68.00.

Majors

• AREA STUDIES African, American • BUSINESS Accounting, Business Administration, Business Economics, Business Management, Economics, Management, Marketing, Real Estate, Travel/Tourism Management • COMMUNICATIONS Advertising, Commercial Design, Creative Writing, English, Graphic Design, Journalism • COMPUTER SCIENCE Computer Maintenance, Computer Science, Computer Technology, Data Processing, Programming • EDUCATION Art, Early Childhood, Elementary, Middle School, Music, Physical, Secondary • ENGINEERING Air

Kansas

Conditioning Technology, Computer, Engineering Science • HEALTH SCIENCES Health, Medical Assistant, Nursing, Physical Therapy • HUMANITIES Humanities, Philosophy • LANGUAGES French, German, Spanish • PREPROFESSIONAL Architecture, Dentistry, Law, Medicine, Pharmacy, Recreation, Social Work • SCIENCES Agricultural, Biochemistry, Chemistry, Earth, Geography, Mathematics, Microbiology, Physical Chemistry, Physics, Physiology, Science Technology • SOCIAL SCIENCES Anthropology, Criminal Justice, Government/Political, History, Law Enforcement, Psychology, Social Sciences, Sociology • VISUAL AND PERFORMING ARTS Art, Art History, Fine Arts, Music, Studio Art, Theater • VOCATIONAL Air Conditioning/Heating/Refri, Automobile Technology, Automotive Service, Business and Office, Carpentry, Drafting, Electronics Technology, Fire Science, Funeral/Mortuary, Home Economics, Industrial Equipment Maintenan, Park/Recreation, Precision Metal Work, Printing/Lithography, Respiratory Therapy Technology, Secretarial

Sports/Activities

• SPORTS RELATED Band, Cheerleading • SPORTS-INTERCOLLEGIATE Baseball (M), Basketball, Cross Country, Golf, Softball (F), Tennis, Track and Field, Volleyball (F) • SPORTS-INTRAMURAL Baseball, Basketball, Bowling, Soccer • STUDENT LIFE ACTIVITIES Choral, Concert Band, Drama Groups, Jazz Band, Music Groups, Newspaper, Religious Organization, Student Government

Less Selective   **Kansas Program**

Kansas State University
Anderson Hall Room 118
Manhattan, Kansas 66506
(913) 532-6250

School Enrollment: **20,352** Male: **11,077** Female: **9,635**
LD Enrollment: **75**

Admissions Contact: **Richard N. Elkins, Director of Admissions**
LD Contact: **Gretchen Holden, Director**
Name of Program: **Students with Physcial Limitations**
Telephone:**(913) 532-6441**

Admissions

Application Information:
LD Students Applying: **95** Accepted: **75** Enrolled:**75**
Application deadline: **1st day of class**
Applicant must apply **3** months in advance

Secondary School Information
Most Important Criteria For Admissions (1-strongest)

3 SAT/ACT	Application	1	School transcript
2 Class rank	5 Course selection	6	Personal statement
6 Interview	6 Extra activities	6	Psychoeducational
4 G.P.A.	Open admission	6	Recommendations

Test Requirements:
Diagnostic testing waived: **Yes**
Currency of diagnostic testing: **Variable**
Tests recommended: **Documentation of testing and learning disability**

Types of Disabilities Served
- Speech/Lang
- Study skills
- Written express
- Organizational
- Perceptual
- Reading
- Spelling
- Math
- Fine Motor
- ADD with LD
- ADD without LD
- ADHD with LD
- ADHD without LD

Learning Disability Program
Program: Reinforces course work: **Yes**
Students mainstreamed **100** % of the day
Counseling: Individual: **Yes**

Faculty:
Faculty: **2** Including Director: **Yes** Full time: **1** Part time: **1** M.A.: **2**
Faculty advocate: **Yes** Meets with instructor: **As needed**

Diagnostic Testing
ADD	• Personality	Perceptual skills	Spelling
ADHD	Organization	Fine motor skills	Reading
I.Q.	Handwriting	Spoken language	Study skills
• Math	Social skills	Written language	

Tutoring:
Average size of group tutorials: **1-3**
Services rendered by:
•Graduates   •Peers   •Faculty   •LD staff   Teacher trainees

Tutorials
Grp.	Ind.	Tutorials	Grp.	Ind.	Tutorials
•		Math skills	•		Word processing
•		Study skills	•		Time management
•		Language arts			Learning strategies
•	•	Written express	•		Organizational skills

Academic Accommodations

Curriculum	Study Aids	Exams
Priority registration	• Typist	• Oral
Math waiver	Reader	Untimed
Foreign lang. waiver	• Notetaker	• Take home
Course substitution	• Proof reader	With proctor
In Class	• Text on tape	On computer
• Calculators	Early syllabus	• Extended time
• Tape recorder	Taped handouts	On tape
• Word processor		• Modified
Priority seating		Separate room

Program Strengths
Learning disabled students constitute the fastest growing group of disabled students on the Kansas State University campus. K-State provides a broad range of supportive services to learning disabled students through Services for Students with Physical Limitations as well as through numerous other university departments. Faculty and staff at K-State are sensitive to the special needs of learning disabled students and will work with them in their pursuit of educational goals.

General Information:
Kansas State University is a 4 year public university. Rural campus of 4,000 acres is 70 miles from Topeka. Accessible by plane or bus. Ski areas are 550 miles from campus. 5% of students are foreign. 9 residential halls on campus. Housing is not guaranteed.95 % of students remain on campus for the weekends. 12 % of students join fraternities/sororities.

Accreditation:NCAC

SAT/ACT Scores:
Scores for incoming freshmen: **ACT:** 44% below 20. 25% between 20 and 23. 11%between 24 and 25l. 14%between 26 and 28. 6% above 28.

Expenses:
Tuition: In-state: Full year: $1,760.00. Tuition: Out-of-state: Full year: $5,934.00. Room and board: $3,200.00.

Majors

• AREA STUDIES African, American, Asian, Urban • BUSINESS Accounting, Agricultural, Banking, Business Administration, Business Economics, Business Education, Business Management, Economics, Hotel and Restaurant Managemen, Management, Marketing • COMMUNICATIONS Advertising, Broadcasting, Communication, Creative Writing, English, Journalism, Speech, Television/Radio/Film • COMPUTER SCIENCE Computer Science, Computer Technology, Programming, Systems Analysis, Telecommunications • EDUCATION Art, Curriculum, Early Childhood, Elementary, English, Foreign Language, Health, Mathematics, Middle School, Music, Physical, Pre-Education, School Psychology, Science, Secondary, Social Studies, Special, Speech/Language • ENGINEERING Agricultural, Architectural, Chemical, Civil/Environmental, Computer, Electrical, Industrial, Mechanical, Nuclear • ENVIRONMENTAL CONTROL Water and Wastewater Technolog • HEALTH SCIENCES Health, Medical Technology, Nursing, Nutritional/Food, Occupational Therapy, Physical Therapy, Speech Therapy, Speech/Audiology and Speech • HUMANITIES Humanities, Philosophy • LANGUAGES French, German, Japanese, Russian, Spanish • PREPROFESSIONAL Agriculture, Architecture, Dentistry, Engineering, Fisheries, Forestry, Law, Medicine, Natural Resources, Optometry, Range Management, Recreation, Social Work, Veterinarian, Wildlife • SCIENCES Agronomy, Animal, Biochemistry, Biology, Botany, Chemistry, Dairy, Earth, Equestrian Studies, Geography, Geology, Geophysics & Seismology, Horticultural, Human Biology, Mathematics, Microbiology, Physical Chemistry, Physical Science, Physics, Plant Protection, Plant Science, Poultry, Soil, Statistics, Zoology • SOCIAL SCIENCES Anthropology, Criminal Justice, Family Counseling, Government/Political, History, Political Science, Psychology, Public Relations, Social Sciences, Sociology • VISUAL AND PERFORMING ARTS Art, Art History, Dance, Dramatic Arts, Fine Arts, Music, Studio Art, Theater • VOCATIONAL Dental Assistant, Electronics Technology, Fashion Design, Fishery Studies, Food Service, Forestry, Home Economics, Interior Design, Landscape Architecture, Park/Recreation, Textile and Clothing

Sports/Activities

• SPORTS RELATED Baton Twirling, Cheerleading, Drill Team, Drum Major/Majorette, Marching Band • SPORTS-INTERCOLLEGIATE Baseball (M), Basketball, Crew, Cross Country, Football (M), Golf, Riflery, Rugby, Soccer, Softball (F), Tennis (F), Track and Field, Volleyball (F) • SPORTS-INTRAMURAL Badminton, Bowling, Cross Country, Golf, Hand Ball, Racquetball, Soccer, Softball, Swimming, Tennis, Track and Field, Volleyball, Water Polo, Wrestling • STUDENT LIFE ACTIVITIES Choral, Community Service, Concert Band, Dance, Debate, Drama Groups, Ethnic & Cultural Groups, Film, Fraternities, Jazz Band, Magazine, Music Groups, Newspaper, Opera, Political Groups, Radio/TV station, Religious Organization, Sororities, Student Government, Symphony Orchestra, Yearbook

---

Less Selective	Kansas Program

Pittsburg State University
1701 South Broadway
Pittsburg, Kansas 66762
(316) 231-7000

School Enrollment: **5,500** Male: **2,250** Female: **2,250**
LD Enrollment: **32** Male: **19** Female: **13**
LD Contact: **Nick A. Henry, Coordinator**
Name of Program: **Learning Disabilities Assistance Team**
Telephone:**(316) 231-8464**

Admissions

Application Information:
LD Students Applying: **26** Accepted: **26** Enrolled:**26**
Application deadline: **August 21st**
Applicant must apply **6** months in advance

Secondary School Information
Most Important Criteria For Admissions (1-strongest)

SAT/ACT	Application	School transcript
Class rank	Course selection	Personal statement
Interview	Extra activities	Psychoeducational
G.P.A.	**1** Open admission	Recommendations

Test Requirements:
Documentation of LD required: **Yes**
Tests recommended: **Documentation of Learning Disability**

Types of Disabilities Served
• Speech/Lang • Reading • ADD with LD
• Study skills • Spelling • ADD without LD
• Written express • Math • ADHD with LD
• Organizational • Fine Motor • ADHD without LD
• Perceptual

Learning Disability Program

Program: Reinforces course work: **Yes**
Students mainstreamed **100** % of the day
Counseling: Individual: **Yes** Group Counseling: **Yes**

Faculty:
Faculty: **1** Part time: **2** Ph.D.: **1**
Faculty advocate: **Yes** Meets with instructor: **As needed**

Diagnostic Testing

ADD	Personality	Perceptual skills	• Spelling
ADHD	Organization	Fine motor skills	• Reading
I.Q.	• Handwriting	• Spoken language	Study skills
• Math	Social skills	• Written language	

Tutoring:
Services rendered by:
Graduates Peers •Faculty •LD staff Teacher trainees

Kansas

Tutorials

Grp.	Ind.	Tutorials	Grp.	Ind.	Tutorials
		Math skills			Word processing
		Study skills		•	Time management
		Language arts			Learning strategies
		Written express		•	Organizational skills

Academic Accommodations

Curriculum	Study Aids	Exams
Priority registration	• Typist	• Oral
Math waiver	Reader	Untimed
Foreign lang. waiver	Notetaker	Take home
Course substitution	• Proof reader	With proctor
In Class	Text on tape	On computer
Calculators	Early syllabus	• Extended time
• Tape recorder	Taped handouts	On tape
Word processor		Modified
• Priority seating		Separate room

Graduation Requirements:
Course credits: **124** GPA: **2.0**

Program Strengths

Our program is unique because it is totally individualized - based solely on the specific individual needs of each student.

General Information:

Pittsburg State University is a 4 year public university. Urban campus of 125 acres is 100 miles from Kansas City. Accessible by bus. 9% of students are foreign. 6 residential halls on campus. Housing is guaranteed. 40 % of students remain on campus for the weekends. 20 % of students join fraternities/sororities.

Accreditation: NCATE

Expenses:
Tuition: In-state: Full year: $679.00. Part-time: Per credit:$43.25. Tuition: Out-of-state: Full year: $1,740.00. Part-time: Per credit:$114.00. Room and board: $2,562.00

Majors

• BUSINESS Accounting, Banking, Business Administration, Business Economics, Business Management, Economics, Fashion Merchandising, Finance, Management, Printing Manufacturing, Retailing • COMMUNICATIONS Advertising, Broadcasting, Communication, English, Graphic Design, Journalism, Photography, Speech, Television/Radio/Film • COMPUTER SCIENCE Computer Science, Programming • EDUCATION Art, Art Therapy, Curriculum, Early Childhood, Elementary, English, Health, Industrial, Mathematics, Music, Music Therapy, Physical, Recreation and Youth Leadershi, School Psychology, Science, Secondary, Social Science Education, Special, Vocational • ENGINEERING Chemical, Electrical, Industrial, Mechanical • HEALTH SCIENCES Health, Medical Technology, Nursing, Nutritional/Food • HUMANITIES Liberal Arts, Philosophy • LANGUAGES French, Spanish • PREPROFESSIONAL Architecture, Dentistry, Engineering, Law, Medicine, Optometry, Pharmacy, Recreation, Social Work • SCIENCES Astronomy, Biochemistry, Biology, Botany, Chemistry, Geography, Geology, Mathematics, Microbiology, Physical Science, Physics, Zoology • SOCIAL SCIENCES Government/Political, History, Political Science, Psychology, Social Sciences, Sociology • VISUAL AND PERFORMING ARTS Art, Fine Arts, Music, Music Performance, Studio Art, Theater • VOCATIONAL Automobile Technology, Construction, Drafting, Electronics Technology, Home Economics, Interior Design, Printing/Lithography, Textile and Clothing, Woodworking

Sports/Activities

• SPORTS RELATED Cheerleading, Drill Team, Drum Major/Majorette, Marching Band, Pep Band, Team Managers • SPORTS-INTERCOLLEGIATE Basketball, Cross Country (M), Football (M), Golf (F), Softball (F), Track and Field (M), Volleyball (F) • SPORTS-INTRAMURAL Archery, Badminton, Baseball (M), Basketball, Cross Country, Diving, Racquetball, Rugby, Softball, Swimming, Tennis, Track and Field, Volleyball, Water Polo • STUDENT LIFE ACTIVITIES Choral, Concert Band, Debate, Drama Groups, Ethnic & Cultural Groups, Fraternities, Jazz Band, Magazine, Music Groups, Newspaper, Opera, Political Groups, Radio/TV station, Religious Organization, Sororities, Student Government, Yearbook

---

Less Selective   **Kansas Services**

University of Kansas
126 Strong Hall
Lawrence, Kansas 66045-0215
(913) 864-3911

School Enrollment: **19,900** Male: **10,500** Female: **9,400**
LD Enrollment: **140**

Admissions Contact: **Bruce A. Lindvall, Director of Admissions**
LD Contact: **Michael Shuttic, Assistant Director**
Name of Program: **Student Assistance Center**
Address: **133 Strong Hall**
Telephone: **(913) 864-4064**

Admissions

Application Information:
Application deadline: **April in state/Feb. out of state**
Rolling Admissions: **Yes**

Secondary School Information
Most Important Criteria For Admissions (1-strongest)

1 SAT/ACT	Application	School transcript
Class rank	Course selection	Personal statement
Interview	Extra activities	Psychoeducational
1 G.P.A.	**1** Open admission	Recommendations

Test Requirements:
Untimed SAT: **Yes** Untimed ACT: **Yes**
Documentation of LD required: **Yes**
Currency of diagnostic testing: **3 years**
Tests recommended: **WAIS-R and Woodcock-Johnson Revised**

Types of Disabilities Served
- Speech/Lang
- Study skills
- Written express
- Organizational
- Perceptual
- Reading
- Spelling
- Math
- Fine Motor
- ADD with LD
- ADD without LD
- ADHD with LD
- ADHD without LD

Admissions Process

Open door policy to in-state residents

Learning Disability Program

Counseling: Individual: **Yes**
Support groups are available: **Yes, student group meets twice a month**

Faculty:
Faculty: **1** Full time: **1**
Faculty advocate: **Yes** Meets with instructor: **As needed**

Diagnostic Testing

ADD	Personality	Perceptual skills	Spelling
ADHD	Organization	Fine motor skills	Reading
I.Q.	Handwriting	Spoken language	Study skills
Math	Social skills	Written language	

Tutoring:
Services rendered by:
Graduates   Peers   •Faculty   •LD staff   Teacher trainees

Tutorials

Grp.	Ind.	Tutorials	Grp.	Ind.	Tutorials
	•	Math skills			Word processing
•		Study skills		•	Time management
		Language arts		•	Learning strategies
•		Written express		•	Organizational skills

Academic Accommodations

Curriculum	Study Aids	Exams
Priority registration	• Typist	• Oral
Math waiver	• Reader	Untimed
Foreign lang. waiver	• Notetaker	Take home
Course substitution	Proof reader	• With proctor
In Class	• Text on tape	On computer
Calculators	Early syllabus	• Extended time
• Tape recorder	Taped handouts	On tape
• Word processor		• Modified
Priority seating		Separate room

Graduation Requirements: GPA: **2.0**

Program Strengths

The Student Assistance Center works with students with disabilities to ensure classroom and course content access. K.U.'s philosophy is one of mainstreaming students with disabilities, including learning disabilities.
* Tutoring services for all students for many subjects are available through Supportive Educational Services.

General Information:

University of Kansas is a 4 year public university. Urban campus 40 miles from Kansas City. 6.9% of students are foreign. 9 residential halls on campus. Housing is not guaranteed. 20 % of students join fraternities/sororities.

Accreditation: NCACS

Expenses:

Tuition: In-state: Full year: $1,798.00. Part-time: Per credit:$74.00. Tuition: Out-of-state: Full year: $5,.970.00. Part-time: Per course:$213.00
Room and board: #3,080.00

Majors

• AREA STUDIES African, American, Asian, Black/Afro-American, Latin American, Russian/Slavic, Women's Studies • BUSINESS Accounting, Business Administration, Business Management, Personnel, Printing Manufacturing • COMMUNICATIONS Advertising, Broadcasting, Communication, English, Journalism, Linguistic, Literature, Photography, Television/Radio/Film • COMPUTER SCIENCE Computer Science • CRAFTS AND DESIGN Ceramics, Sculpture • EDUCATION Art, Curriculum, Early Childhood, English, Health, Mathematics, Middle School, Music, Music Therapy, Physical, Recreation and Youth Leadershi, Science, Secondary, Social Studies, Speech/Language • ENGINEERING Aerospace, Architectural, Chemical, Civil/Environmental, Computer, Mechanical, Petroleum • HEALTH SCIENCES Communication Disorders, Health, Nursing, Occupational Therapy, Physical Therapy, Speech Therapy, Speech/Audiology and Speech • HUMANITIES Classics, English/Writing/Literature, Humanities, Liberal Arts, Philosophy, Religion • LANGUAG-

ES French, German, Greek, Italian, Japanese, Latin, Russian, Slavic, Spanish • PREPROFESSIONAL Architecture, Dentistry, Engineering, Law, Medicine, Pharmacy, Recreation, Social Work • SCIENCES Archeology, Astronomy, Biochemistry, Biology, Cell Biology, Chemistry, Ecology, Geography, Geology, Mathematics, Meteorology, Microbiology, Physical Science, Physics • SOCIAL SCIENCES Anthropology, Government/Political, History, Political Science, Psychology, Public Relations, Social Sciences, Sociology • VISUAL AND PERFORMING ARTS Art History, Dance, Dramatic Arts, Fine Arts, Music, Music Performance, Theater • VOCATIONAL Industrial Design, Interior Design, Jewelry-Metalsmithery, Painting, Printing/Lithography, Textile and Clothing

Sports/Activities

• SPORTS RELATED Bagpipe Band, Cheerleading, Chess, Drill Team, Drum Major/Majorette, Marching Band, Team Managers • SPORTS-INTERCOLLEGIATE Baseball (M), Basketball, Cross Country, Diving, Golf, Softball (F), Swimming, Tennis, Track and Field, Volleyball (F) • SPORTS-INTRAMURAL Badminton, Basketball, Crew, Cross Country, Field Hockey (F), Lacrosse (M), Racquetball, Sailing, Soccer, Softball, Tennis, Volleyball, Water Polo, Wrestling (M) • STUDENT LIFE ACTIVITIES Choral, Concert Band, Dance, Debate, Drama Groups, Ethnic & Cultural Groups, Fraternities, Jazz Band, Music Groups, Musical Theater, Newspaper, Radio/TV station, Religious Organization, Sororities, Student Government, Symphony Orchestra, Yearbook

Less Selective	Kansas
	Services

Wichita State University
111 Jardine Hall
Wichita , Kansas 67208-1595
(316) 689-3085

School Enrollment: **17,500** Male: **8,250** Female: **8,250**
LD Enrollment: **12**

Admissions Contact: **Glenn Lygrisse, Director of Admissions**
LD Contact: **Grady Landrum, Director**
Name of Program: **Handicapped Services**
Address: **Campus Box 132, Grace Wilke Hall, East**
Telephone:**(316) 689-3309**

Admissions

Application Information:
Application deadline:
Rolling Admissions: **Yes**

Secondary School Information
Most Important Criteria For Admissions (1-strongest)

4 SAT/ACT	**1** Application	**2** School transcript	
Class rank	Course selection	Personal statement	
Interview	Extra activities	Psychoeducational	
3 G.P.A.	**1** Open admission	Recommendations	

Test Requirements:
Diagnostic testing waived: **Yes**
Untimed SAT: **Yes** Untimed ACT: **Yes**
Documentation of LD required: **Yes**

Types of Disabilities Served

• Speech/Lang	• Reading	• ADD with LD
• Study skills	• Spelling	• ADD without LD
• Written express	• Math	• ADHD with LD
• Organizational	• Fine Motor	• ADHD without LD
• Perceptual		

285

Kentucky

Admissions Process

Open admission, high school diploma or G.E.D. only requirement.

Learning Disability Program

Program: Remedial: **Yes**
Program: Reinforces course work: **Yes**
Students mainstreamed **100** % of the day
Counseling: Individual: **Yes** Group Counseling: **Yes** Vocational Counseling: **Yes**

Faculty:
Faculty: **3** Full time: **3**
Faculty advocate: **Yes** Meets with instructor: **As needed**

Diagnostic Testing
ADD	Personality	Perceptual skills	Spelling
ADHD	Organization	Fine motor skills	Reading
I.Q.	Handwriting	Spoken language	Study skills
Math	Social skills	Written language	

Tutoring:
Services rendered by:
•Graduates •Peers •Faculty •LD staff •Teacher trainees

Tutorials
Grp.	Ind.	Tutorials	Grp.	Ind.	Tutorials
•	•	Math skills	•	•	Word processing
•	•	Study skills	•	•	Time management
•	•	Language arts	•	•	Learning strategies
•	•	Written express	•	•	Organizational skills

Academic Accommodations
Curriculum	Study Aids	Exams
Priority registration	• Typist	• Oral
• Math waiver	Reader	Untimed
• Foreign lang. waiver	• Notetaker	Take home
Course substitution	Proof reader	With proctor
In Class	• Text on tape	On computer
• Calculators	Early syllabus	• Extended time
• Tape recorder	Taped handouts	On tape
• Word processor		Modified
Priority seating		Separate room

Graduation Requirements:
Course credits: **124** GPA: **2.0**

Program Strengths
The University has a Handicapped Services Program. There are 17,500 students enrolled at WSU; 206 are enrolled at Handicapped Services and 12 of them are LD.

General Information:
Wichita State University is a 4 year public university. Urban campus of 320 acres is Wichita. Ski areas are 10 hours from campus. Beaches are 10 hours from campus. 2 residential halls on campus. Housing is guaranteed.

Accreditation:Regional

SAT/ACT Scores:
Scores for incoming freshmen: **ACT:** 22.5% below 20. 50.4% between 20 and 23. 26.4%between 24 and 25l.

Expenses:
Tuition: In-state: Full year: Part-time: Per credit: $58.00. Tuition: Out-of-state: Full year: Part-time: Per credit: $180.60. Room and board: $1,380.00

Majors
• AREA STUDIES American, Black/Afro-American, Women's Studies • BUSINESS Accounting, Aviation Management, Banking, Business Administration, Business Economics, Business Management, Economics, Finance, International Business, Management, Marketing, Personnel, Real Estate • COMMUNICATIONS English, Journalism, Speech, Television/Radio/Film • COMPUTER SCIENCE Computer Science • EDUCATION Art, Elementary, Industrial, Music, Physical, Psychology • ENGINEERING Engineering Science, Industrial, Mechanical • HEALTH SCIENCES Dental Hygiene, Health, Medical Assistant, Medical Technology, Nursing, Physical Therapy, Speech/Audiology and Speech • HUMANITIES Humanities, Liberal Arts, Philosophy • LANGUAGES French, German, Latin, Spanish • PREPROFESSIONAL Legal Assistant • SCIENCES Anthropology, Biology, Chemistry, Gerontology, Mathematics, Physical Science • SOCIAL SCIENCES Criminal Justice, Government/Political, History, Political Science, Social Sciences, Sociology • VISUAL AND PERFORMING ARTS Art History, Dance, Dramatic Arts, Fine Arts, Music, Music Performance, Studio Art • VOCATIONAL Electronics Technology, Legal Secretary, Painting, Paralegal, Respiratory Therapy Technology, Secretarial

Sports/Activities
• SPORTS RELATED Pep Band • SPORTS-INTERCOLLEGIATE Baseball (M), Basketball, Crew, Golf, Softball (F), Tennis, Track and Field, Volleyball (F) • SPORTS-INTRAMURAL Badminton, Basketball, Bowling, Fencing, Gymnastics, Hand Ball, Ping-Pong, Racquetball, Riflery, Soccer, Softball, Swimming, Track and Field, Volleyball, Water Polo, Wrestling (M) • STUDENT LIFE ACTIVITIES Choral, Community Service, Concert Band, Dance, Drama Groups, Ethnic & Cultural Groups, Fraternities, Jazz Band, Magazine, Music Groups, Musical Theater, Newspaper, Political Groups, Radio/TV station, Religious Organization, Sororities, Student Government

---

Selective | Kentucky

Services

Cumberland College
Williamsburg, Kentucky 40769
(606) 549-2200

School Enrollment: **1,820** Male: **870** Female: **950**

Admissions Contact: **Danny E. Hall, Acting Dean, Admissions**
LD Contact: **Dr. John Nelson**
Name of Program: **Learning Skills Center**
Telephone:**(606) 549-2200 Ext. 4312**

Admissions

Application Information:
Application deadline: **Rolling**
Rolling Admissions: **Yes**

Secondary School Information
Most Important Criteria For Admissions (1-strongest)
1	SAT/ACT	1	Application	1	School transcript
3	Class rank		Course selection	1	Personal statement
6	Interview	4	Extra activities	7	Psychoeducational
2	G.P.A.		Open admission	5	Recommendations

Types of Disabilities Served

- Speech/Lang
- Study skills
- Written express
- Organizational
- Perceptual

- Reading
- Spelling
- Math
- Fine Motor

- ADD with LD
- ADD without LD
- ADHD with LD
- ADHD without LD

Learning Disability Program

Counseling: Individual: **Yes** Group Counseling: **Yes**

Faculty:

Faculty: **5**
Faculty advocate: **Yes** Meets with instructor: **As needed**

Diagnostic Testing

ADD	Personality	Perceptual skills	Spelling
ADHD	Organization	Fine motor skills	Reading
I.Q.	Handwriting	Spoken language	Study skills
Math	Social skills	Written language	

Tutoring:

Average size of group tutorials: **5**
Services rendered by:
Graduates • Peers Faculty LD staff Teacher trainees

Tutorials

Grp.	Ind.	Tutorials	Grp.	Ind.	Tutorials
•	•	Math skills			Word processing
		Study skills			Time management
		Language arts			Learning strategies
•	•	Written express			Organizational skills

Academic Accommodations

Curriculum	Study Aids	Exams
Priority registration	Typist	• Oral
• Math waiver	Reader	Untimed
• Foreign lang. waiver	Notetaker	Take home
Course substitution	Proof reader	With proctor
In Class	Text on tape	On computer
Calculators	Early syllabus	Extended time
Tape recorder	Taped handouts	On tape
Word processor		Modified
Priority seating		Separate room

Program Strengths

We do not have a learning disability program. We do have a Learning Skills Center which provides remedial help for students who score low on the ACT and SAT. Students must test out after one year. It is possible to test out after a semester. Credits earned count as electives toward graduation, but do not fulfill the basic Math and English requirements.

General Information:

Cumberland College is a 4 year private Southern Baptist Convention college. Rural campus of 30 acres is 75 miles from Knoxville. Accessible by air or bus. 6% of students are foreign. 10 residential halls on campus. Housing is guaranteed.

Accreditation:NASM

SAT/ACT Scores:

Scores for incoming freshmen: **Verbal:** 74% below 500. 20% between 500 and 599. 5% between 600 and 699. 1% above 700. **Math:** 67% below 500. 24% between 500 and 599. 7% between 600 and 699. 1% above 700. **ACT:** 60% below 20. 18% between 20 and 23. 9% between 24 and 25l. 9% between 26 and 28. 4% above 28.

Class Rank:

About 45% of the present freshmen class were in the upper 20% of their high school class. 79% were in the top 40% of their class. 94% were in the top 60% of their class. 100% were in the top 80% of their class.

Expenses:

Tuition: In-state: Full year: $3,980.00. Tuition: Out-of-state: Full year: $3,980.00. Room and board: $2,456.00

Majors

• BUSINESS Accounting, Business Administration, Business Education, Business Management • COMMUNICATIONS Creative Writing, English, Journalism, Photography, Speech, Television/Radio/Film • COMPUTER SCIENCE Data Processing, Programming • EDUCATION Art, Early Childhood, Elementary, English, Health, Middle School, Music, Physical, Pre-Education, Secondary, Special, Speech/Language • HEALTH SCIENCES Health, Medical Technology • HUMANITIES Philosophy, Religion • LANGUAGES French, Greek, Hebrew, Spanish • PREPROFESSIONAL Dentistry, Engineering, Law, Medicine, Nursing, Optometry, Pharmacy, Veterinarian • SCIENCES Biology, Chemistry, Geography, Geology, Mathematics, Physics • SOCIAL SCIENCES Criminal Justice, Government/Political, History, Political Science, Psychology, Public Relations, Sociology • VISUAL AND PERFORMING ARTS Art, Dramatic Arts, Fine Arts, Music, Music Performance, Religious Music, Studio Art, Theater • VOCATIONAL Secretarial

Sports/Activities

• SPORTS-INTERCOLLEGIATE Baseball (M), Basketball, Fencing, Football (M), Golf (M), Judo, Softball (F), Tennis • SPORTS-INTRAMURAL Archery, Badminton, Bowling, Ping-Pong, Soccer, Swimming, Tennis, Volleyball, Weight Lifting

Less Selective   **Kentucky Services**

Eastern Kentucky University
Coates Building Box 2A
Richmond, Kentucky 40475
(606) 622-2106

School Enrollment: **13,275** Male: **6,650** Female: **6,625**
LD Enrollment: **30**

Admissions Contact: **James Grigsby, Director of Admissions**
LD Contact: **Norma Reynolds, Senior Clerk**
Name of Program: **Student Special Services**
Telephone:**(606) 622-1500**

Admissions

Application Information:

Application deadline: **None**
Rolling Admissions: **Yes**

Secondary School Information

Most Important Criteria For Admissions (1-strongest)

SAT/ACT	Application	School transcript
Class rank	Course selection	Personal statement
Interview	Extra activities	Psychoeducational
G.P.A.	1 Open admission	Recommendations

Kentucky

Types of Disabilities Served
- Speech/Lang
- Study skills
- Written express
- Organizational
- Perceptual
- Reading
- Spelling
- Math
- Fine Motor
- ADD with LD
- ADD without LD
- ADHD with LD
- ADHD without LD

Faculty:
Faculty: **1** Full time: **1**
Faculty advocate: **Yes** Meets with instructor: **As needed**

Diagnostic Testing

ADD	Personality	Perceptual skills	Spelling
ADHD	Organization	Fine motor skills	Reading
I.Q.	Handwriting	Spoken language	Study skills
Math	Social skills	Written language	

Services rendered by:

Graduates	Peers	Faculty	LD staff	Teacher trainees

Tutorials

Grp.	Ind.	Tutorials	Grp.	Ind.	Tutorials
		Math skills			Word processing
		Study skills			Time management
		Language arts			Learning strategies
		Written express			Organizational skills

Academic Accommodations

Curriculum	Study Aids	Exams
Priority registration	Typist	• Oral
Math waiver	Reader	Untimed
Foreign lang. waiver	• Notetaker	Take home
Course substitution	Proof reader	With proctor
In Class	• Text on tape	On computer
Calculators	Early syllabus	• Extended time
• Tape recorder	Taped handouts	On tape
Word processor		Modified
Priority seating		Separate room

Program Strengths
The Office of Student Special Services must have copies of testing showing the student is LD before services can be provided. No one else would see this report unless student signed a permission form.

General Information:
Eastern Kentucky University is a 4 year public university. Urban campus of 350 acres is 25 miles from Lexington. Ski areas are 2 hours from campus. Beaches are 8 hours from campus. 1% of students are foreign. 17 residential halls on campus. Housing is guaranteed.Guaranteed through 4th year.

Accreditation:SACS

Expenses:
Tuition: In-state: Full year: $1,300.00. Part-time: Per credit:$55.00. Tuition: Out-of-state: Full year: $3,660.00. Part-time: Per credit:$153.00. Room and board: $543.00

Majors
• AREA STUDIES Latin American, Urban • BUSINESS Accounting, Agricultural, Banking, Business Administration, Business Economics, Business Management, Economics, Finance, Food Management, Insurance, Marketing, Personnel, Real Estate • COMMUNICATIONS Advertising, English, Graphic Design, Journalism, Speech, Television/Radio/Film • COMPUTER SCIENCE Computer Science, Robotics • EDUCATION Early Childhood, Elementary, Foreign Language, Pre-Education, Special • ENGINEERING Computer • HEALTH SCIENCES Medical Assistant, Medical Secretary, Medical Technology, Nursing, Nutritional/Food, Occu-

pational Therapy, Speech Therapy, Speech/Audiology and Speech • HUMANITIES Philosophy, Religion • LANGUAGES French, German, Russian, Spanish • PREPROFESSIONAL Fisheries, Natural Resources, Social Work, Wildlife • SCIENCES Agricultural, Animal, Anthropology, Biology, Chemistry, Earth, Ecology, Geography, Geology, Horticultural, Mathematics, Microbiology, Physics, Statistics • SOCIAL SCIENCES Anthropology, Family Counseling, Government/Political, History, Law Enforcement, Political Science, Psychology, Public Relations, Sociology • VISUAL AND PERFORMING ARTS Dance, Dramatic Arts • VOCATIONAL Business and Office, Drafting, Electronics Technology, Fire Science, Food Service, Industrial Equipment Maintenan, Interior Design, Landscape Architecture, Legal Secretary, Office Administration, Park/Recreation, Printing/Lithography, Secretarial, Textile and Clothing

Sports/Activities
• SPORTS RELATED Marching Band, Pep Band • SPORTS-INTERCOLLEGIATE Baseball (M), Basketball, Cross Country, Diving, Field Hockey, Football (M), Golf (M), Tennis, Track and Field, Volleyball (F) • SPORTS-INTRAMURAL Badminton, Basketball, Hand Ball, Racquetball, Rugby, Soccer, Softball, Tennis, Volleyball • STUDENT LIFE ACTIVITIES Choral, Concert Band, Dance, Drama Groups, Ethnic & Cultural Groups, Film, Fraternities, Jazz Band, Magazine, Music Groups, Musical Theater, Newspaper, Political Groups, Radio/TV station, Religious Organization, Sororities, Student Government, Symphony Orchestra, Yearbook

---

Less Selective   **Kentucky**
Accommodations

Elizabethtown Community College
600 College Street Rd.
Elizabethtown, Kentucky 42701
(502) 769-2371

School Enrollment: **3,988** Male: **2,592** Female: **1,396**

Admissions Contact: **Ronald Thomas, Dean of Student Affairs**

Admissions

Application Information:
Application deadline: **None**

Secondary School Information
Most Important Criteria For Admissions (1-strongest)

SAT/ACT	Application	School transcript
Class rank	Course selection	Personal statement
Interview	Extra activities	Psychoeducational
G.P.A.	**1** Open admission	Recommendations

Types of Disabilities Served
- Speech/Lang
- Study skills
- Written express
- Organizational
- Perceptual
- Reading
- Spelling
- Math
- Fine Motor
- ADD with LD
- ADD without LD
- ADHD with LD
- ADHD without LD

Learning Disability Program
Counseling: Individual: **Yes**

Faculty:
Faculty: **4** Full time: **4**
Faculty advocate: **Yes** Meets with instructor: **As needed**

Diagnostic Testing

ADD	Personality	Perceptual skills	Spelling
ADHD	Organization	Fine motor skills	Reading
I.Q.	Handwriting	Spoken language	Study skills
Math	Social skills	Written language	

Tutoring:

Services rendered by:
Graduates • Peers • Faculty • LD staff Teacher trainees

Tutorials

Grp.	Ind.	Tutorials	Grp.	Ind.	Tutorials
	•	Math skills		•	Word processing
	•	Study skills		•	Time management
	•	Language arts		•	Learning strategies
	•	Written express		•	Organizational skills

Academic Accommodations

Curriculum	Study Aids	Exams
Priority registration	Typist	• Oral
Math waiver	Reader	Untimed
Foreign lang. waiver	Notetaker	• Take home
Course substitution	Proof reader	With proctor
In Class	• Text on tape	On computer
Calculators	Early syllabus	• Extended time
• Tape recorder	Taped handouts	On tape
Word processor		Modified
Priority seating		Separate room

Program Strengths

We are a two year "open door" institution. Anyone with a high school diploma, G.E.D., or eligible to take G.E.D. can be admitted. We have no LD program as such. We offer tutoring, study skills, and individualized academic counseling as necessary through our Learning Resources Center.

General Information:

Elizabethtown Community College is a 2 year public college. Rural campus 45 miles from Louisville. 1% of students are foreign. Housing is not guaranteed.

Accreditation:SACS

Expenses:

Tuition: In-state: Full year: $340.00. Part-time: Per credit:$29.00. Tuition: Out-of-state: Full year: $1,020.00. Part-time: Per credit:$87.00.

Majors

• BUSINESS Banking, Business Management, Real Estate • COMPUTER SCIENCE Computer Information Systems • HEALTH SCIENCES Nursing • HUMANITIES Liberal Arts • VOCATIONAL Business and Office, Secretarial

Sports

• SPORTS-INTRAMURAL Basketball, Soccer, Volleyball • STUDENT LIFE ACTIVITIES Choral, Newspaper, Student Government

Lexington Community College

203 Oswald Building
Lexington, Kentucky 40506
(606) 257-6068

School Enrollment: **5,000** Male: **3,500** Female: **1,500**
LD Enrollment: **200** Male: **135** Female: **65**

Admissions Contact: **Toni Bishop, Director of Admissions**
LD Contact: **Marlene Huff, MSW Coordinator**
Name of Program: **Disability Support Services**
Address: **102F Oswald Bldg.**
Telephone:**(606) 257-6068**

Admissions

Application Information:

LD Students Applying: **150** Accepted: **150** Enrolled:**150**
Application deadline: **1 week before start of class**
Applicant must apply **1** months in advance

Secondary School Information

Most Important Criteria For Admissions (1-strongest)

4	SAT/ACT	3	Application	1	School transcript
9	Class rank	6	Course selection	11	Personal statement
7	Interview	10	Extra activities	2	Psychoeducational
5	G.P.A.		Open admission	8	Recommendations

Test Requirements:

Diagnostic testing waived: **Yes**
Untimed ACT: **Yes**
Documentation of LD required: **Yes**
Currency of diagnostic testing: **3 years**
Tests recommended: **WAIS-R, Woodcock-Johnson Achievement Test**

Types of Disabilities Served

• Speech/Lang	• Reading	• ADD with LD
• Study skills	• Spelling	• ADD without LD
• Written express	• Math	• ADHD with LD
• Organizational	• Fine Motor	• ADHD without LD
• Perceptual		

High School Course Requirements:

English: **4** Math: **2** Science: **2**
Waivers to standard high school courses
Course substitution: **Yes**

Learning Disability Program

Special orientation for LD students: **Yes**
Syllabus available during orientation:**Yes**
Program: Reinforces course work: **Yes**
Students mainstreamed **100** % of the day
Recommended credits per semester: **12**
Time required or recommended in learning center: **Individual basis**
Services only for LD students: **Yes**
Counseling: Individual: **Yes** Group Counseling: **Yes** Vocational Counseling: **Yes**
Support groups are available:**Group meetings that focus on academic issues.**

Kentucky

Faculty:
Faculty: **2** Including Director: **Yes** Full time: **2**
LD faculty with: BS/BA: **1** M.A.: **1**
Faculty advocate: **Yes** Meets with instructor: **As needed**

Diagnostic Testing
- ADD
- Personality
- Perceptual skills
- Spelling
- ADHD
- Organization
- Fine motor skills
- Reading
- I.Q.
- Handwriting
- Spoken language
- Study skills
- Math
- Social skills
- Written language

Tutoring:
Average size of group tutorials: **5**
Services rendered by:
- Graduates
- Peers
- Faculty
- LD staff
- Teacher trainees

Tutorials

Grp.	Ind.	Tutorials	Grp.	Ind.	Tutorials
•	•	Math skills		•	Word processing
•	•	Study skills		•	Time management
•	•	Language arts	•	•	Learning strategies
•	•	Written express		•	Organizational skills

Academic Accommodations

Curriculum	Study Aids	Exams
Priority registration	Typist	• Oral
• Math waiver	• Reader	• Untimed
• Foreign lang. waiver	• Notetaker	Take home
• Course substitution	• Proof reader	• With proctor
In Class	• Text on tape	On computer
• Calculators	• Early syllabus	• Extended time
• Tape recorder	• Taped handouts	On tape
• Word processor		Modified
• Priority seating		• Separate room

Graduation Requirements:
Course credits: **60-120** GPA: **2.0** Years to complete degree: **Unlimited**
Math waiver: **Yes** Language waiver: **Yes**

General Information:
Lexington Community College is a 2 year public college. Urban campus 70-100 miles from Louisville. Accessible by plane or bus. Ski areas are 300 miles from campus. Beaches are 8 hours from campus. 5% of students are foreign. 10 residential halls on campus. Housing is not guaranteed. 3 % of students join fraternities/sororities.

Accreditation: SACRA

SAT/ACT Scores:
Scores for incoming freshmen: **ACT:** 75% below 20. 25%. between 20 and 23.

Expenses:
Tuition: In-state: Full year: $1,844.00 per year. Part-time: Per credit:$70.00 . Part-time: Per course: $210.00. Tuition: Out-of-state: Full year: $5,084.00 per year. Part-time: Per credit:$205.00. Part-time: Per course:$615.00 Room and board: $1,300.00

Majors
• ARTS Drafting • BUSINESS Accounting, Clerical, Management, Secretarial Science • COMPUTER SCIENCE Computer Technology • ENGINEERING Architectural, Drafting, Electrical, Mechanical • HEALTH SCIENCES Dental Hygiene, Nuclear Medical Technology, Nursing • PRE PROFESSIONAL Business, Drafting, Engineering • VOCATIONAL Business and Office, Dental Hygiene, Drafting, Office Administration, Radiological Technology, Respiratory Therapy Technology, Secretarial

Sports/Activities
• SPORTS-INTERCOLLEGIATE Baseball, Baseball (M), Basketball, Basketball (F), Basketball (M), Cross Country (F), Cross Country (M), Golf (F), Golf (M), Gymnastics (F), Swimming (F), Swimming (M), Tennis (F), Tennis (M), Track and Field (F), Track and Field (M) • SPORTS-INTRAMURAL Basketball (F), Basketball (M) • STUDENT LIFE ACTIVITIES Fraternities, Newspaper, Religious Organization, Sororities, Student Government, Yearbook

---

Less Selective **Kentucky**
Accommodations

Lindsey Wilson College
210 Lindsey Wilson Street
Columbia, Kentucky 42728
(502) 384-2126

School Enrollment: **729** Male: **400** Female: **329**

Admissions Contact: **Kevin Thompson, Director of Admissions**
LD Contact: **Barbara Peterson, Director, Developmental Studies**
Name of Program: **Developmental Services**
Telephone:**(502) 384-8031**

Admissions

Application Information:
Application deadline: **Beginning of semester**
Rolling Admissions: **Yes**

Secondary School Information
Most Important Criteria For Admissions (1-strongest)

SAT/ACT	Application	School transcript
Class rank	Course selection	Personal statement
Interview	Extra activities	Psychoeducational
G.P.A.	**1** Open admission	Recommendations

Test Requirements:
Untimed SAT: **Yes** Untimed ACT: **Yes** Untimed ACH: **Yes**

Types of Disabilities Served
- Speech/Lang
- Reading
- ADD with LD
- Study skills
- Spelling
- ADD without LD
- Written express
- Math
- ADHD with LD
- Organizational
- Fine Motor
- ADHD without LD
- Perceptual

Admissions Process

We are open admissions.

Learning Disability Program
Program: Reinforces course work: **Yes**
Students mainstreamed **100** % of the day
Recommended credits per semester: **12-17**
Services available for all students: **Yes**
Counseling: Individual: **Yes** Group Counseling: **Yes** Vocational Counseling: **Yes**

Faculty:
Faculty: **4** Full time: **4**

290

Diagnostic Testing

ADD	Personality	Perceptual skills	Spelling
ADHD	Organization	Fine motor skills	Reading
I.Q.	Handwriting	Spoken language	Study skills
Math	Social skills	Written language	

Tutoring:

Average size of group tutorials: **5-11**
Services rendered by:
Graduates •Peers Faculty LD staff Teacher trainees

Tutorials

Grp.	Ind.	Tutorials	Grp.	Ind.	Tutorials
•		Math skills	•		Word processing
•		Study skills	•		Time management
•		Language arts	•		Learning strategies
•		Written express	•		Organizational skills

Academic Accommodations

Curriculum	Study Aids	Exams
Priority registration	Typist	• Oral
Math waiver	Reader	Untimed
Foreign lang. waiver	Notetaker	Take home
• Course substitution	Proof reader	With proctor
In Class	Text on tape	On computer
• Calculators	Early syllabus	• Extended time
• Tape recorder	Taped handouts	On tape
• Word processor		• Modified
Priority seating		Separate room

Graduation Requirements:

Course credits: **128** GPA: **2.0** Years to complete degree: **2 and 4 years**

Program Strengths

We have a Reading and Developmental Program which are basic skills courses. A Student Success Course maybe required for all freshmen. LD students have been successful at Lindsey.

General Information:

Lindsey Wilson College is a 4 year private United Methodist college. Rural campus of 70 acres is 100 miles from Louisville. 2% of students are foreign. 6 residential halls on campus. Housing is guaranteed.10 % of students remain on campus for the weekends.

Accreditation: SACS

SAT/ACT Scores:

Scores for incoming freshmen: **ACT:** 80% below 20. 15% between 20 and 23. 4%between 24 and 25l. 1%between 26 and 28.

Class Rank:

About 15% of the present freshmen class were in the upper 20% of their high school class. 35% were in the top 40% of their class. 65% were in the top 60% of their class. 85% were in the top 80% of their class.

Expenses:

Tuition: In-state: Full year: $5,888.00. Part-time: Per credit:$212.00. Room and board: $3,280.00

Majors

• BUSINESS Accounting, Agri-business, Business Administration, Business Management • COMMUNICATIONS English • COMPUTER SCIENCE Computer Information Systems • EDUCATION Elementary, Middle School • HUMANITIES Liberal Arts • SCIENCES Biology, Chemistry, Mathematics • SOCIAL SCIENCES History, Human Services, Social Sciences • VISUAL AND PERFORMING ARTS Studio Art • VOCATIONAL Secretarial

Sports/Activities

• SPORTS RELATED Cheerleading, Team Managers • SPORTS-INTER-COLLEGIATE Baseball (M), Basketball (F), Basketball (M), Soccer (F), Soccer (M), Softball (F) • SPORTS-INTRAMURAL Basketball, Ping-Pong, Softball, Tennis, Volleyball • STUDENT LIFE ACTIVITIES Choral, Drama Groups, Music Groups, Political Groups, Religious Organization, Student Government, Yearbook

---

Less Selective

Kentucky Services

Murray State University
Murray, Kentucky 42071
(502) 762-3163

School Enrollment: **8,398** Male: **3,729** Female: **4,599**
LD Enrollment: **50** Male: **31** Female: **19**

Admissions Contact: **Phil Bryan, Dean of Admissions**
LD Contact: **Ann Narewski, Coordinator, Services for LD**
Name of Program: **Services for Students with LD**
Address: **The Learning Center**
Telephone:**(502) 762-3163**

Admissions

Application Information:
Application deadline: **None**
Rolling Admissions: **Yes**

Secondary School Information
Most Important Criteria For Admissions (1-strongest)

2 SAT/ACT	Application	School transcript
3 Class rank	**1** Course selection	Personal statement
Interview	Extra activities	Psychoeducational
G.P.A.	Open admission	Recommendations

Test Requirements:
Diagnostic testing waived: **Yes**
Untimed SAT: **Yes** Untimed ACT: **Yes** Achievement tests required:**None**
Documentation of LD required: **Yes**

Types of Disabilities Served

Speech/Lang	• Reading	• ADD with LD
Study skills	• Spelling	• ADD without LD
• Written express	• Math	• ADHD with LD
Organizational	Fine Motor	• ADHD without LD
• Perceptual		

Admissions Process

Student must apply with Admissions Office, then if accepted provide documentation which has been done within the last three years to the Coordinator of Services for LD students.

High School Course Requirements:
English: **4** Math: **3** Science: **3**

Kentucky

Learning Disability Program

Special orientation for LD students: **Yes**
Program: Reinforces course work: **Yes**
Program available through:**Fall & spring semester**
Students mainstreamed **100** % of the day
Recommended credits per semester: **12**
Services only for LD students: **Yes**
Counseling: Individual: **Yes** Group Counseling: **Yes** Vocational Counseling: **Yes**
Support groups are available:**Yes, group meets once a week**

Faculty:

Faculty: **1** Full time: **1** M.A.: **1**
Faculty advocate: **Yes** Meets with instructor: **As needed**

Diagnostic Testing

ADD	Personality	Perceptual skills	Spelling
ADHD	Organization	Fine motor skills	Reading
I.Q.	Handwriting	Spoken language	Study skills
Math	Social skills	Written language	

Tutoring:

Services rendered by:
Graduates •Peers Faculty LD staff Teacher trainees

Tutorials

Grp.	Ind.	Tutorials	Grp.	Ind.	Tutorials
	•	Math skills			Word processing
•		Study skills		•	Time management
		Language arts			Learning strategies
	•	Written express		•	Organizational skills

Academic Accommodations

Curriculum	Study Aids	Exams
• Priority registration	Typist	Oral
Math waiver	• Reader	• Untimed
Foreign lang. waiver	Notetaker	Take home
Course substitution	• Proof reader	• With proctor
In Class	• Text on tape	• On computer
Calculators	Early syllabus	• Extended time
• Tape recorder	Taped handouts	• On tape
• Word processor		Modified
• Priority seating		• Separate room

Graduation Requirements:

Course credits: **128** GPA: **2.0**
Other requirements: **32 hours in residence**

General Information:

Murray State University is a 2 and 4 year public university. Rural campus of 232 acres is 150 miles from Nashville, TN. Accessible by car. Ski areas are 5 hours from campus. Beaches are 12 hours from campus. 2% of students are foreign. 10 residential halls on campus. Housing is guaranteed.Guaranteed through 4th year. 50 % of students remain on campus for the weekends. 15.4 % of students join fraternities/sororities.

Accreditation:SACS, NCATE, AACSB

SAT/ACT Scores:

Scores for incoming freshmen:**ACT:** 39% below 20. 36% between 20 and 23. 8%between 24 and 251. 10%between 26 and 28. 5% above 28.

Expenses:

Tuition: In-state: Full year: $705.00 per semester. Part-time: Per credit:$59.00. Tuition: Out-of-state: Full year: $2,005.00. Part-time: Per credit:$168.00. Room and board: $525.00-$790.00

Majors

• AGRICULTURE Business, Economics, Education, Horticultural, Mechanization, Plant Science • ARTS Drafting, Music, Music Performance • BUSINESS Accounting, Agricultural, Business Administration, Business Education, Economics, Education, Fashion Merchandising, Food Management, Management, Marketing, Printing Manufacturing, Vocational Studies • COMPUTER SCIENCE Computer Science, Data Processing • CRAFTS AND DESIGN Graphic Design, Interior Design • EDUCATION Agricultural, Art, Business, Child Development, Elementary, English, Health, Industrial, Middle School, Music, Physical, Recreation, Secondary, Vocational • ENGINEERING Civil/Environmental, Computer, Electrical, Environmental, Mechanical, Mining/Mineral, Physics • HEALTH SCIENCES Medical Technology, Nursing, Rehabilitation • HUMANITIES English/Writing/Literature, Philosophy • LANGUAGES English, French, German, Spanish • MATHEMATICS Applied • PHILOSOPHY Advertising, Creative Writing, English, Journalism, Public Relations, Television/Radio/Film • PRE PROFESSIONAL Agriculture, Dentistry, Forestry, Law, Medicine, Optometry, Pharmacy, Social Work, Veterinarian, Wildlife, Biology • SCIENCES Agricultural, Animal, Applied Mathematics, Bio-medical, Biochemistry, Biology, Chemistry, Earth, Geography, Geology, Horticultural, Mathematics, Molecular Biology, Physics • SOCIAL SCIENCES Criminal Justice, History, Law Enforcement, Library Science, Political Science, Psychology, Social Sciences, Sociology • SPECIAL EDUCATION Learning Disability, Mentally Retarded • VISUAL AND PERFORMING ARTS Art, Music, Music Performance, Music Theatre, Theater • VOCATIONAL Drafting, Fashion Merchandising, Fishery Studies, Food Service, Forestry, Home Economics, Interior Design, Legal Assistant, Medical Technology, Veterinarian Assistant

Sports/Activities

• SPORTS RELATED Baton Twirling, Cheerleading, Chess, Drill Team, Drum Major/Majorette, Marching Band • SPORTS-INTERCOLLEGIATE Baseball, Basketball, Cross Country, Football, Golf, Riflery, Rodeo, Tennis, Track and Field, Volleyball • SPORTS-INTRAMURAL Baseball, Baseball (F), Baseball (M), Basketball, Basketball (F), Basketball (M), Bowling, Cross Country, Football, Golf, Golf (F), Golf (M), Racquetball, Soccer, Soccer (F), Soccer (M), Softball, Softball (F), Softball (M), Swimming, Tennis, Track and Field, Volleyball, Volleyball (F), Volleyball (M), Water Polo • STUDENT LIFE ACTIVITIES Academic Clubs, Choral, Dance, Film, Fraternities, Musical Theater, Newspaper, Political Groups, Radio/TV station, Religious Organization, Sororities, Student Government, Yearbook

---

Less Selective   **Kentucky**
                                       Services

Prestonsburg Community College

1 Bert T. Combs Dr.
Prestonsburg, Kentucky 41653
(606) 886-3863

School Enrollment: **3,000** Male: **892** Female: **1,971**

Admissions Contact: **G. Hall, Director of Admissions**
LD Contact: **D. Lee Beard, Counselor**
Name of Program: **Handicapped Student Services**
Telephone:**(606) 886-3863**

Admissions

Application Information:

Rolling Admissions: **Yes**

Secondary School Information
Most Important Criteria For Admissions (1-strongest)

SAT/ACT	Application	School transcript
Class rank	Course selection	Personal statement
Interview	Extra activities	Psychoeducational
G.P.A.	Open admission	Recommendations

Test Requirements:
Diagnostic testing waived: **Yes**
Untimed ACT: **Yes**
Documentation of LD required: **Yes**

Types of Disabilities Served
- Speech/Lang
- Study skills
- Written express
- Organizational
- Perceptual
- Reading
- Spelling
- Math
- Fine Motor
- ADD with LD
- ADD without LD
- ADHD with LD
- ADHD without LD

Faculty:
Faculty: **2** Including Director: **Yes** Full time: **2** M.A.: **1**
Faculty advocate: **Yes** Meets with instructor: **Frequently**

Diagnostic Testing
ADD	Personality	Perceptual skills	• Spelling
ADHD	Organization	Fine motor skills	• Reading
I.Q.	Handwriting	Spoken language	Study skills
• Math	Social skills	• Written language	

Tutoring:
Average size of group tutorials: **2**
Services rendered by:
Graduates •Peers Faculty LD staff Teacher trainees

Tutorials
Grp.	Ind.	Tutorials	Grp.	Ind.	Tutorials
		Math skills			Word processing
•	•	Study skills	•	•	Time management
		Language arts	•	•	Learning strategies
		Written express		•	Organizational skills

Academic Accommodations
Curriculum
Priority registration
Math waiver
Foreign lang. waiver
Course substitution
In Class
- Calculators
- Tape recorder
Word processor
Priority seating

Study Aids
Typist
- Reader
- Notetaker
- Proof reader
- Text on tape
Early syllabus
Taped handouts

Exams
- Oral
- Untimed
- Take home
- With proctor
On computer
- Extended time
On tape
- Modified
- Separate room

Graduation Requirements:
Course credits: **60** GPA: **2.0** Years to complete degree: **2**

General Information:
Prestonsburg Community College is a 2 and 4 year public college. Rural campus 75 miles from Huntington, W. VA. Accessible by private transportation. Ski areas are 150 miles from campus. Beaches are 500 miles from campus. 1% of students are foreign. Housing is not guaranteed. 1 % of students join fraternities/sororities.

Accreditation: SACS

Expenses:
Tuition: In-state: Full year: $340.00 per semester. Part-time: Per credit: $29.00. Tuition: Out-of-state: Full year: $1,020.00. Part-time: Per credit: $85.00.

Majors
• BUSINESS Accounting, Management, Real Estate • HEALTH SCIENCES Nursing

Sports/Activities
• SPORTS-INTRAMURAL Archery, Badminton, Basketball, Bowling, Football, Ping-Pong, Softball, Tennis, Volleyball • STUDENT LIFE ACTIVITIES Choral, Concert Band, Dance, Drama Groups, Newspaper, Political Groups, Religious Organization, Student Government

Selective   **Kentucky**
Services

Thomas More College
333 Thomas More Parkway
Crestview Hills, Kentucky 41017
(606) 341-5800

School Enrollment: **1,300** Male: **702** Female: **598**
LD Enrollment: **50** Male: **35** Female: **15**

Admissions Contact: **Victoria Thompson, Director of Admissions**
LD Contact: **Barb Davis, Director, Student Support Services**
Name of Program: **Student Support Services**
Address: **Thomas More Parkway**
Telephone: **(606) 344-3521**

Admissions

Application Information:
Application deadline: **August 15th**
Rolling Admissions: **Yes**

Secondary School Information
Most Important Criteria For Admissions (1-strongest)

2 SAT/ACT	Application	**1** School transcript
2 Class rank	**1** Course selection	**3** Personal statement
Interview	**3** Extra activities	**1** Psychoeducational
1 G.P.A.	Open admission	Recommendations

Test Requirements:
Untimed SAT: **Yes** Untimed ACT: **Yes** Untimed ACH: **Yes**
Documentation of LD required: **Yes**
Tests recommended: **It depends on the LD. Usually reading should be diagnosed.**

Types of Disabilities Served
- Speech/Lang
- Study skills
- Written express
- Organizational
- Perceptual
- Reading
- Spelling
- Math
- Fine Motor
- ADD with LD
- ADD without LD
- ADHD with LD
- ADHD without LD

Admissions Process

Steps of the admissions process are listed: 1) Application, 2) High school transcript, 3) ACT or SAT, 4) Information on LD submitted,

5) Admissions Committee, 6) Name submitted to Student Support Services.

High School Course Requirements:
English: **4** Math: **2** Science: **2** Foreign Language: **2**
Waivers to standard high school courses
Foreign Language : **Yes**

Learning Disability Program
Syllabus available during orientation:**Yes**
Program: Remedial: **Yes**
Program: Reinforces course work: **Yes**
Program available through:**Academic year**
Students mainstreamed **100** % of the day
Recommended credits per semester: **13-15**
Counseling: Individual: **Yes** Group Counseling: **Yes** Vocational Counseling: **Yes**
Support groups are available:**To cope with college life, personal problems, academics**

Faculty:
Faculty: **5** Full time: **3** Part time: **2** M.A.: **3**
Faculty advocate: **Yes** Meets with instructor: **As needed**

Diagnostic Testing
ADD	Personality	Perceptual skills	Spelling
ADHD	Organization	Fine motor skills	• Reading
I.Q.	Handwriting	Spoken language	• Study skills
Math	Social skills	Written language	

Tutoring:
Average size of group tutorials: **2-3**
Services rendered by:
  Graduates   •Peers   •Faculty   •LD staff   Teacher trainees

Tutorials
Grp.	Ind.	Tutorials	Grp.	Ind.	Tutorials
•	•	Math skills		•	Word processing
•	•	Study skills	•	•	Time management
•	•	Language arts	•	•	Learning strategies
•	•	Written express	•	•	Organizational skills

Academic Accommodations
Curriculum	Study Aids	Exams
• Priority registration	• Typist	• Oral
Math waiver	• Reader	• Untimed
• Foreign lang. waiver	• Notetaker	Take home
• Course substitution	• Proof reader	• With proctor
In Class	• Text on tape	• On computer
• Calculators	• Early syllabus	• Extended time
• Tape recorder	• Taped handouts	• On tape
• Word processor		Modified
• Priority seating		• Separate room

Graduation Requirements:
Course credits: **128** GPA: **2.0** Years to complete degree: **4+** Language waiver: **Yes**
Other requirements: **Core courses, requirements of major**

Program Strengths
TMC's program is federally funded, and it is a middle-of-the-road one. We do little diagnosing, but we require documentation of the LD. We work with students individually and in groups. We teach Basic Comprehension, Reading, and Study Skills courses. Study Skills is paired with the World History course (a core course) to help students successfully complete the first semester in that history course.

General Information:
Thomas More College is a 2 and 4 year independent Roman Catholic college. Suburban campus of 120 acres is 5 miles from Cincinnati, Ohio. Accessible by air, car or bus Ski areas are 40 miles from campus. Beaches are 300+ miles from campus. 2% of students are foreign. 3 residential halls on campus. Housing is guaranteed.Guaranteed through 4th year. 20 % of students remain on campus for the weekends. 4 % of students join fraternities/sororities.

Accreditation:SACS, KBE, NLN

SAT/ACT Scores:
Scores for incoming freshmen:**Verbal:**15%below 500. 85%between 500 and 599. 85%between 600 and 699. 85%above 700. **Math:**15% below 500. 85% between 500 and 599. 85% between 600 and 699. 85%above 700. **ACT:** 15% below 20. 85% between 20 and 23.

Class Rank: 50% were in the top 40% of their class. 50% were in the top 60% of their class.

Expenses:
Tuition: In-state: Full year: $8,400.00. Part-time: Per credit:$226.00. Tuition: Out-of-state: Full year: $8,400.00. Part-time: Per credit:$226.00. Room and board: $3,600.00

Majors
• ARTS Dramatic Arts, Music • BUSINESS Accounting, Business Administration, Business Management, Economics • COMMUNICATIONS English, Speech • COMPUTER SCIENCE Computer Information Systems, Computer Science • EDUCATION Elementary, Middle School, Secondary • HEALTH SCIENCES Exercise, Medical Technology, Nursing • HUMANITIES Philosophy • PRE PROFESSIONAL Law • RELIGIOUS STUDIES Religion & Theology • SCIENCES Biology, Chemistry, Gerontology, Mathematics, Physics • SOCIAL SCIENCES History, International Studies, Political Science, Psychology, Social Work, Sociology • VISUAL AND PERFORMING ARTS Fine Arts

Sports/Activities
• SPORTS RELATED Cheerleading, Pep Band, Team Managers • SPORTS-INTERCOLLEGIATE Baseball, Baseball (M), Basketball, Basketball (F), Basketball (M), Football, Football (M), Soccer, Soccer (F), Soccer (M), Softball, Softball (F), Tennis, Tennis (F), Tennis (M), Volleyball, Volleyball (F) • SPORTS-INTRAMURAL Basketball, Basketball (F), Basketball (M), Football, Football (F), Football (M), Softball, Softball (F), Softball (M), Tennis, Tennis (F), Tennis (M), Volleyball, Volleyball (F), Volleyball (M) • STUDENT LIFE ACTIVITIES Academic Clubs, Choral, Debate, Drama Groups, Ethnic & Cultural Groups, Film, Fraternities, Magazine, Newspaper, Sororities, Student Government, Yearbook

Very Selective   **Kentucky**
                                      Services

University of Kentucky
100 Funkhouser Building
Lexington, Kentucky 40506-0054
(606) 257-7148

School Enrollment: **16,052** Male: **7,762** Female: **8,290**
LD Enrollment: **25**

Admissions Contact: **Randy Mills, Assoc. Dir., Admissions**
LD Contact: **Jacob Karnes, Asst. Dean of Students**
Name of Program: **Handicapped Student Services**
Address: **Rm.2, Alumni Gym**
Telephone:**(606) 257-2754**

Admissions

Application Information:
Application deadline: **June 1st**
Rolling Admissions: **Yes**

Secondary School Information
Most Important Criteria For Admissions (1-strongest)

1	SAT/ACT	7	Application	7	School transcript
7	Class rank	7	Course selection	11	Personal statement
11	Interview	7	Extra activities	11	Psychoeducational
1	G.P.A.		Open admission	11	Recommendations

Test Requirements:
Diagnostic testing waived: **Yes**
Untimed SAT: **Yes** Untimed ACT: **Yes**
Documentation of LD required: **Yes**
Currency of diagnostic testing: **3 years**
Tests recommended: **Diagnostic testing is required for services/accommodations.**

Types of Disabilities Served
- Speech/Lang
- Study skills
- Written express
- Organizational
- Perceptual
- Reading
- Spelling
- Math
- Fine Motor
- ADD with LD
- ADD without LD
- ADHD with LD
- ADHD without LD

Admissions Process

We accept all of the above if they can meet our admissions criteria.

Learning Disability Program

Services available for all students: **Yes**
Counseling: Individual: **Yes** Group Counseling: **Yes**

Faculty:
Faculty: **3** Part time: **3**
Faculty advocate: **Yes** Meets with instructor: **As needed**

Diagnostic Testing
- ADD
- ADHD
- I.Q.
- Math
- Personality
- Organization
- Handwriting
- Social skills
- Perceptual skills
- Fine motor skills
- Spoken language
- Written language
- Spelling
- Reading
- Study skills

Tutoring:
Services rendered by:

Graduates	Peers	•Faculty	•LD staff	Teacher trainees

Tutorials

Grp.	Ind.	Tutorials	Grp.	Ind.	Tutorials
•	•	Math skills			Word processing
•	•	Study skills	•	•	Time management
		Language arts			Learning strategies
•	•	Written express	•	•	Organizational skills

Academic Accommodations

Curriculum	Study Aids	Exams
• Priority registration	Typist	• Oral
Math waiver	Reader	• Untimed
Foreign lang. waiver	Notetaker	• Take home
• Course substitution	Proof reader	• With proctor
In Class	• Text on tape	• On computer
• Calculators	Early syllabus	• Extended time
Tape recorder	Taped handouts	• On tape
• Word processor		• Modified
• Priority seating		• Separate room

Program Strengths

We do not have a comprehensive program for students with learning disabilities. We do, however, make reasonable efforts to accommodate this important group of students. For special consideration in admissions and to verify the need for support services, a psychoeducational report less than three years old along with other supportive documentation is required.

General Information:

University of Kentucky is a 4 year public university. Urban campus of 714 acres is 80 miles from Cincinnati. Accessible by air or bus . Ski areas are 80 miles from campus. 5% of students are foreign. 18 residential halls on campus. Housing is not guaranteed.60 % of students remain on campus for the weekends. 16 % of students join fraternities/sororities.

Accreditation: SACS

SAT/ACT Scores:
Scores for incoming freshmen: **Verbal:** 63% below 500. 29% between 500 and 599. 8% between 600 and 699. 1% above 700. **Math:** 40% below 500. 35% between 500 and 599. 20% between 600 and 699. 5% above 700. **ACT:** 24% below 20. 37% between 20 and 23. 15% between 24 and 25l. 17% between 26 and 28. 7% above 28.

Expenses:
Tuition: In-state: Full year: $1,560.00. Part-time: Per credit:$60.00. Tuition: Out-of-state: Full year: $4,320.00. Part-time: Per credit:$175.00. Room and board: $2,500.00

Majors

• AREA STUDIES East European, Latin American, Middle Eastern, Russian/Slavic • BUSINESS Accounting, Agricultural, Banking, Business Administration, Business Economics, Business Education, Business Management, Economics, Finance, Hotel and Restaurant Managemen, Labor Relations, Management, Marketing, Personnel • COMMUNICATIONS Advertising, Broadcasting, Communication, Creative Writing, English, Journalism, Linguistic, Speech, Television/Radio/Film • COMPUTER SCIENCE Computer Science, Systems Analysis, Telecommunications • EDUCATION Art, Early Childhood, Elementary, English, Foreign Language, Health, Industrial, Middle School, Music, Physical, Pre-Education, Recreation and Youth Leadershi, School Psychology, Science, Secondary, Social Studies, Special, Speech/Language, Vocational • ENGINEERING Agricultural, Chemical, Civil/Environmental, Computer, Electrical, Mechanical, Mining/Mineral • HEALTH SCIENCES Health, Medical Assistant, Medical Technology, Nursing, Nutritional/Food, Physical Therapy, Radiological Therapy, Speech Therapy, Speech/Audiology and Speech • HUMANITIES Classics, English/Writing/Literature, Liberal Arts, Philosophy • LANGUAGES German, Greek, Italian, Latin, Russian, Spanish • PREPROFESSIONAL Architecture, Dentistry, Engineering, Fisheries, Law, Medicine, Natural Resources, Pharmacy, Social Work, Veterinarian • SCIENCES Agricultural, Animal, Anthropology, Astronomy, Biology, Biotechnology, Botany, Chemistry, Earth, Geography, Geology, Mathematics, Microbiology, Physics, Plant Pathology, Zoology • SOCIAL SCIENCES Anthropology, Government/Political, History, Political Science, Psychology, Sociology • VISUAL AND PERFORMING ARTS Art, Art History, Dramatic Arts, Music, Music Performance, Studio Art, Theater • VOCATIONAL Food Service, Forestry, Interior Design, Landscape Architecture, Textile and Clothing

Sports/Activities

• SPORTS RELATED Cheerleading, Chess, Drum Major/Majorette, Marching Band, Pep Band, Team Managers • SPORTS-INTERCOLLE-GIATE Baseball, Basketball, Cross Country, Diving, Football (M), Golf, Gymnastics (F), Ice Hockey (M), Riflery, Swimming, Tennis, Track and Field, Volleyball • SPORTS-INTRAMURAL Field Hockey (F), Golf, Hand Ball, Ice Hockey (M), Lacrosse, Ping-Pong, Racquetball, Rugby, Skiing - Snow, Softball, Squash, Swimming, Tennis, Track and Field, Volleyball, Wrestling (M) • STUDENT LIFE ACTIVITIES Choral, Community Service, Dance, Debate, Drama Groups, Ethnic & Cultural Groups, Film, Fraternities, Jazz Band, Magazine, Music Groups, Musical Theater, Newspaper, Radio/TV station, Religious Organization, Sororities, Student Government, Yearbook

Selective	Louisiana Program

Louisiana College
P.O. Box 545
Pineville, Louisiana 71359
(318) 487-7303

School Enrollment: **1,204** Male: **393** Female: **811**

Admissions Contact: **Byron McGee, Director of Admissions**
LD Contact: **Thomas W. Kelly, Chair, Dept. of Education**
Name of Program: **Program to Assist Student Success**
Address: **Box 545**
Telephone:**(318) 487-7303**

Admissions

Application Information:
Accepted: **10** Enrolled:**10**
Separate application:**Yes**
LD on admissions committee:**Yes**
Application deadline: **March 1st (Fall) - Oct. 1st (Spring)**
Applicant must apply **6** months in advance
Notified when: **May 31st**

Secondary School Information
Most Important Criteria For Admissions (1-strongest)
2 SAT/ACT	**11** Application	**8** School transcript
10 Class rank	**6** Course selection	**3** Personal statement
7 Interview	**4** Extra activities	**1** Psychoeducational
9 G.P.A.	Open admission	**5** Recommendations

Test Requirements:
Diagnostic testing waived: **Yes**
Untimed SAT: **Yes** Untimed ACT: **Yes** Untimed ACH: **Yes**
Documentation of LD required: **Yes**
Currency of diagnostic testing: **Open**
Tests recommended: **Diagnosis by qualified professional.**

Types of Disabilities Served
• Speech/Lang	• Reading	• ADD with LD
• Study skills	• Spelling	• ADD without LD
• Written express	• Math	ADHD with LD
• Organizational	• Fine Motor	ADHD without LD
• Perceptual		

Admissions Process

All applicants must meet L.C. admissions requirements. In addition appropriate documentation of disorder must be provided. A screening committee reviews applications, and student writes a 750 word essay which is used to select our students. In some cases a personal interview is required.

High School Course Requirements:
English: **4** Math: **2** Science: **2** Foreign Language: **1**

Learning Disability Program
Program: Remedial: **Yes**
Program: Reinforces course work: **Yes**
Program available through:**Daily**
Students mainstreamed **100** % of the day
Recommended credits per semester: **12**
Time required or recommended in learning center: **6 hours**
Services available for all students: **Yes**
Counseling: Individual: **Yes** Group Counseling: **Yes** Vocational Counseling: **Yes**

Faculty:
Faculty: **2** Including Director: **Yes** Full time: **2** Part time: **1**
LD faculty with: BS/BA: **1** M.A.: **3**
Faculty advocate: **Yes** Meets with instructor: **Weekly**

Diagnostic Testing
ADD	• Personality	• Perceptual skills	• Spelling
ADHD	• Organization	• Fine motor skills	• Reading
I.Q.	Handwriting	• Spoken language	• Study skills
• Math	• Social skills	• Written language	

Tutoring:
Average size of group tutorials: **5**
Services rendered by:
Graduates •Peers •Faculty •LD staff •Teacher trainees

Tutorials
Grp.	Ind.	Tutorials	Grp.	Ind.	Tutorials
•	•	Math skills			Word processing
•	•	Study skills	•	•	Time management
•	•	Language arts	•	•	Learning strategies
•	•	Written express	•	•	Organizational skills

Academic Accommodations
Curriculum	Study Aids	Exams
Priority registration	Typist	• Oral
Math waiver	• Reader	• Untimed
Foreign lang. waiver	• Notetaker	Take home
Course substitution	• Proof reader	• With proctor
In Class	• Text on tape	On computer
• Calculators	• Early syllabus	• Extended time
• Tape recorder	Taped handouts	• On tape
Word processor		Modified
Priority seating		• Separate room

Graduation Requirements:
Course credits: **127** GPA: **2.0** Years to complete degree: **4+**

Program Strengths

PASS is designed for students with a diagnosed physical or learning disability who have average-to-superior intellectual potential. This highly individualized, limited enrollment program provides support services and personal attention to students who may need special counseling, tutoring, or classroom assistance.

General Information:

Louisiana College is a 4 year independent Baptist college. Suburban campus of 81 acres is 3 miles from Alexandria. Accessible by air or bus. 5% of students are foreign. 4 residential halls on campus. Housing is guaranteed.Guaranteed through 4th year. 30 % of students remain on campus for the weekends.

Accreditation:SACS, LDE, NLN

SAT/ACT Scores:

Scores for incoming freshmen: **ACT:** 15% below 20. 50% between 20 and 23. 30%between 24 and 25l. 5%between 26 and 28.

Class Rank:

About 10% of the present freshmen class were in the upper 20% of their high school class. 30% were in the top 40% of their class. 55% were in the top 60% of their class. 5% were in the top 80% of their class.

Expenses:

Tuition: In-state: Full year: Part-time: Per credit: $139.00 plus fees. Tuition: Out-of-state: Full year: Part-time: Per credit: $139.00 plus fees. Part-time: Per credit:$139.00 plus fees. Room and board: $1,787.00 semester Cost of LD program:$850.00-1st year, $435.00-2nd year, $200.00-3rd & 4th years.

Majors

• ARTS Design, Drawing, Graphic Arts, Music, Music Performance, Painting, Religious Music • BUSINESS Accounting, Business Administration, Business Economics, Business Education, Business Management, Clerical, Economics, Education, Management, Marketing, Secretarial Science • COMMUNICATIONS Communication, English, Graphic Design, Journalism, Literature, Speech/Debate/Forensic • COMPUTER SCIENCE Computer Mathematics, Computer Science • CRAFTS AND DESIGN Ceramics, Graphic Design, Printmaking, Sculpture • EDUCATION Art, Business, Early Childhood, Elementary, English, Foreign Language, Health, Mathematics, Middle School, Music, Physical, Psychology, Religious, Science, Secondary, Social Studies, Special • HEALTH SCIENCES Dental Assistant, Dental Hygiene, Dental Technician, Fitness, Health, Nursing • HUMANITIES English/Writing/Literature, Fine Arts, Philosophy, Religion. • LANGUAGES English, French, Greek, Hebrew, Russian, Spanish • MATHEMATICS Applied • PRE PROFESSIONAL Business, Dentistry, Engineering, Forestry, Law, Medicine, Ministry, Pharmacy, Social Work, Veterinarian • RELIGIOUS STUDIES Bible, Ministry and Church Administra, Philosophy, Religious Music • SCIENCES Biology, Chemistry, Computer Science, General, Inorganic Chemistry, Mathematics, Organic Chemistry, Physical Science, Physics • SOCIAL SCIENCES Criminal Justice, Family Counseling, Government/Political, History, Law Enforcement, Political Science, Psychology, Social Sciences, Sociology • VISUAL AND PERFORMING ARTS Art, Dramatic Arts, Music, Music Performance, Studio Art, Theater

Sports/Activities

• SPORTS RELATED Cheerleading, Team Managers • SPORTS-INTERCOLLEGIATE Baseball (M), Basketball (F), Basketball (M), Cross Country, Golf, Tennis • SPORTS-INTRAMURAL Archery, Badminton, Baseball, Basketball, Football, Golf, Ping-Pong, Scuba, Soccer, Soccer, Swimming, Tennis, Volleyball • STUDENT LIFE ACTIVITIES Academic Clubs, Choral, Community Service, Debate, Drama Groups, Magazine, Music Groups, Musical Theater, Newspaper, Religious Organization, Student Government, Symphony Orchestra, Yearbook

Less Selective	Louisiana Services

Louisiana State University Agricultural and Mechanical College

117 David Boyd Hall
Baton Rouge, Louisiana 70803-2750
(504) 388-1175

School Enrollment: **21,657** Male: **10,128** Female: **10,829**
LD Enrollment: **52**

Admissions Contact: **Theresa Hay, Asst. Dir. of Admissions**
LD Contact: **Tina Schultz, Coordinator**
Name of Program: **Services for Students w/Disabilities**
Address: **114 David Boyd Hall**
Telephone:**(504) 388-4423**

Admissions

Secondary School Information
Most Important Criteria For Admissions (1-strongest)

2 SAT/ACT	Application	**1** School transcript
Class rank	Course selection	Personal statement
Interview	Extra activities	**3** Psychoeducational
4 G.P.A.	Open admission	Recommendations

Test Requirements:
Diagnostic testing waived: **Yes**
Untimed ACT: **Yes**
Documentation of LD required: **Yes**
Currency of diagnostic testing: **No more than 3 years**

Types of Disabilities Served
- Speech/Lang
- Study skills
- Written express
- Organizational
- Perceptual
- Reading
- Spelling
- Math
- Fine Motor
- ADD with LD
- ADD without LD
- ADHD with LD
- ADHD without LD

High School Course Requirements:
Waivers to standard high school courses
Course substitution: **Yes**

Learning Disability Program
Services available for all students: **Yes**

Faculty:
Faculty: **2** Full time: **2**
Faculty advocate: **Yes** Meets with instructor: **As needed**

Diagnostic Testing

ADD	Personality	Perceptual skills	Spelling
ADHD	Organization	Fine motor skills	Reading
I.Q.	Handwriting	Spoken language	Study skills
Math	Social skills	Written language	

Tutoring:
Services rendered by:
•Graduates •Peers •Faculty •LD staff Teacher trainees

Louisiana

Tutorials

Grp.	Ind.	Tutorials	Grp.	Ind.	Tutorials
•	•	Math skills			Word processing
•		Study skills		•	Time management
•	•	Language arts		•	Learning strategies
•		Written express		•	Organizational skills

Academic Accommodations

Curriculum	Study Aids	Exams
• Priority registration	• Typist	• Oral
Math waiver	• Reader	Untimed
Foreign lang. waiver	• Notetaker	• Take home
• Course substitution	Proof reader	• With proctor
In Class	• Text on tape	• On computer
• Calculators	Early syllabus	• Extended time
• Tape recorder	Taped handouts	• On tape
• Word processor		• Modified
• Priority seating		• Separate room

Program Strengths

The office of Services for Students With Disabilities assists learning disabled students in acquiring appropriate academic accommodations based on documentation and recommendations and in accordance with LSU policy. The Dean of the respective college in which the student is enrolled retains final responsibility for ensuring that accommodations are implemented.

General Information:

Louisiana State University Agricultural and Mechanical College is a 2 and 4 year public university. Urban campus of 1,944 acres is Baton Rouge. Accessible by air or bus Beaches are 4 hours from campus. 15-20% of students are foreign. 21 residential halls on campus. Housing is guaranteed.17 % of students join fraternities/sororities.

Accreditation:SACS

SAT/ACT Scores:

Scores for incoming freshmen: **ACT:** 34% below 20. 30% between 20 and 23. 14%between 24 and 25l. 17%between 26 and 28. 6% above 28.

Expenses:

Tuition: In-state: Full year: $2,040.00. Part-time: Per credit:$205.00. Tuition: Out-of-state: Full year: $5,240.00. Part-time: Per credit:$350.00. Room and board: $2,766.00

Majors

• AREA STUDIES American, Asian, Black/Afro-American, Jewish, Latin American, Russian/Slavic, Urban • BUSINESS Accounting, Agricultural, Banking, Business Administration, Business Economics, Business Education, Business Management, Finance, Insurance, International Business, Management, Marketing, Marketing Research, Real Estate • COMMUNICATIONS Advertising, Communication, Creative Writing, English, Graphic Design, Journalism, Photography, Speech, Television/Radio/Film • COMPUTER SCIENCE Computer Science, Data Processing, Programming, Systems Analysis • CRAFTS AND DESIGN Ceramics, Graphic Design • EDUCATION Agricultural, Art, Curriculum, Early Childhood, Elementary, English, Foreign Language, Health, Industrial, Mathematics, Music, Physical, Secondary, Special, Speech/Language, Vocational • ENGINEERING Agricultural, Chemical, Civil/Environmental, Computer, Engineering Science, Industrial, Mechanical, Petroleum • HEALTH SCIENCES Communication Disorders, Environmental, Health, Medical Technology, Nursing, Nutritional/Food, Occupational Therapy, Physical Therapy, Radiological Therapy, Speech Therapy, Speech/Audiology and Speech • HUMANITIES Humanities, Liberal Arts , Philosophy, Religion • LANGUAGES Chinese, French, German, Greek, Italian, Russian, Spanish • PRE PROFESSIONAL Architecture, Dentistry, Engineering, Forestry, Law, Medicine, Ministry, Pharmacy, Recreation, Social Work, Veterinarian, Wildlife • SCIENCES Agronomy, Animal, Astronomy, Astro-physics, Biochemistry, Biology, Botany, Chemistry, Earth, Ecology, Entomology, Geography, Geology, Horticultural, Mathematics, Microbiology, Physical Chemistry, Physical Science, Physics, Physiology, Zoology • SOCIAL SCIENCES Anthropology, Criminal Justice, Family Counseling, Geography, Government/Political, History, Political Science, Psychology, Social Science, Sociology • VISUAL AND PERFORMING ARTS Art, Art History, Dance, Music, Music Performance, Studio Art, Theater • VOCATIONAL Business and Office, Fashion Merchandising, Food Service, Forestry, Home Economics, Industrial Design, Landscape Architecture, Painting, Printing/Lithography, Textile and Clothing

Sports/Activities

• SPORTS RELATED Cheerleading, Chess, Drill Team, Drum Major/Majorette, Marching Band, Pep Band, Team Managers • SPORTS-INTERCOLLEGIATE Baseball (M), Basketball, Cross Country, Diving, Football (M), Golf, Gymnastics (F), Softball (F), Swimming, Tennis, Track and Field, Volleyball (F) • SPORTS-INTRAMURAL Badminton, Bowling (F), Football (M), Golf, Lacrosse (M), Ping-Pong, Racquetball, Rugby (M), Sailing, Soccer, Softball, Swimming, Tennis, Track and Field, Volleyball, Wrestling (M) • STUDENT LIFE ACTIVITIES Choral, Dance, Debate, Drama Groups, Ethnic & Cultural Groups, Film, Fraternities, Jazz Band, Music Groups, Opera, Radio/TV station, Religious Organization, Sororities, Student Government, Symphony Orchestra, Yearbook

---

Less Selective　　　　　　　　**Louisiana**
Services

Louisiana State University at Alexandria
Alexandria, Louisiana 71302-9633
(318) 473-6416

School Enrollment: **2,213** Male: **659** Female: **1,550**

Admissions Contact: **Richard Averitt, Dir. of Adm. and Records**
LD Contact: **Mrs. Vickie Kelly, Coordinator**
Name of Program: **Learning Center**

Admissions

Secondary School Information

Most Important Criteria For Admissions (1-strongest)

1 SAT/ACT	Application	1	School transcript
1 Class rank	Course selection		Personal statement
1 Interview	1 Extra activities		Psychoeducational
1 G.P.A.	1 Open admission	1	Recommendations

Types of Disabilities Served

Speech/Lang	• Reading	ADD with LD
• Study skills	Spelling	ADD without LD
• Written express	• Math	ADHD with LD
Organizational	Fine Motor	ADHD without LD
Perceptual		

Faculty:
Faculty: **5**

Diagnostic Testing

ADD	Personality	Perceptual skills	Spelling
ADHD	Organization	Fine motor skills	Reading
I.Q.	Handwriting	Spoken language	Study skills
Math	Social skills	Written language	

Tutoring:
Services rendered by:

Graduates	•Peers	•Faculty	LD staff	Teacher trainees

Tutorials

Grp.	Ind.	Tutorials	Grp.	Ind.	Tutorials
		Math skills			Word processing
		Study skills			Time management
		Language arts			Learning strategies
		Written express			Organizational skills

Academic Accommodations

Curriculum	Study Aids	Exams
Priority registration	Typist	Oral
Math waiver	Reader	Untimed
Foreign lang. waiver	Notetaker	Take home
Course substitution	Proof reader	With proctor
In Class	Text on tape	On computer
Calculators	Early syllabus	Extended time
Tape recorder	Taped handouts	On tape
• Word processor		Modified
Priority seating		Separate room

Program Strengths

We believe students will have as fair a chance of succeeding at LSU-A as at any other two or four year college or university because of the superb faculty in the Learning Center.

General Information:

Louisiana State University at Alexandria is a 2 year public university. Rural campus 6 miles from Baton Rouge. Accessible by air or bus. 4% of students are foreign. Housing is not guaranteed.

Accreditation: SACS

Expenses:

Tuition: In-state: Full year: $370.00 (12 credit hours). Part-time: Per credit:$117.00. Tuition: Out-of-state: Full year: $922.00 (12 credit hours). Part-time: Per credit:$163.00.

Majors

• BUSINESS Accounting, Business Administration, Business Data Processing, Business Management • COMPUTER SCIENCE Data Processing, Programming • EDUCATION Elementary, Teacher Aide • HEALTH SCIENCES Nursing • HUMANITIES Liberal Arts • LANGUAGES Spanish • PREPROFESSIONAL Agriculture, Engineering, Forestry • SCIENCES Astronomy, Biology, Chemistry, Mathematics, Science Technology, Zoology • SOCIAL SCIENCES History, Psychology, Social Sciences • VOCATIONAL Secretarial

Sports/Activities

• SPORTS-INTRAMURAL Badminton, Basketball, Golf, Ping-Pong, Soccer, Softball, Swimming, Tennis, Volleyball • STUDENT LIFE ACTIVITIES Choral, Drama Groups, Newspaper, Student Government, Yearbook

---

University of Southwestern Louisiana
P. O. Box 41650
Lafayette, Louisiana 70504
(318) 231-5282

School Enrollment: **16,000**

Admissions Contact: **Leroy Broussard, Dir. of Admissions**
LD Contact: **Jackie Ortego, Counselor**
Name of Program: **Handicapped Student Services**
Telephone:**(318) 231-5252**

Admissions

Application Information:
Rolling Admissions: **Yes**

Secondary School Information
Most Important Criteria For Admissions (1-strongest)

3 SAT/ACT	4 Application	5 School transcript
2 Class rank	6 Course selection	10 Personal statement
8 Interview	11 Extra activities	7 Psychoeducational
1 G.P.A.	Open admission	9 Recommendations

Test Requirements:
Untimed ACT: **Yes**
Currency of diagnostic testing: **3 months**

Types of Disabilities Served

Speech/Lang	• Reading	• ADD with LD
Study skills	• Spelling	ADD without LD
• Written express	• Math	• ADHD with LD
Organizational	Fine Motor	ADHD without LD
Perceptual		

Learning Disability Program

Counseling: Individual: **Yes**

Faculty:
Faculty: **1** Full time: **1**
Faculty advocate: **Yes** Meets with instructor: **As needed**

Diagnostic Testing

ADD	Personality	Perceptual skills	Spelling
ADHD	Organization	Fine motor skills	Reading
I.Q.	Handwriting	Spoken language	Study skills
Math	Social skills	Written language	

Tutoring:
Average size of group tutorials: **12-15**
Services rendered by:

•Graduates	•Peers	•Faculty	LD staff	Teacher trainees

Tutorials

Grp.	Ind.	Tutorials	Grp.	Ind.	Tutorials
•	•	Math skills			Word processing
•		Study skills	•		Time management
	•	Language arts		•	Learning strategies
	•	Written express		•	Organizational skills

299

Maine

Academic Accommodations

Curriculum	Study Aids	Exams
Priority registration	Typist	• Oral
• Math waiver	Reader	Untimed
• Foreign lang. waiver	• Notetaker	Take home
Course substitution	Proof reader	With proctor
In Class	• Text on tape	On computer
Calculators	Early syllabus	• Extended time
• Tape recorder	Taped handouts	On tape
• Word processor		Modified
Priority seating		Separate room

General Information:

University of Southwestern Louisiana is a 4 year public university. Urban campus of 1,436 acres is 50 miles from Baton Rouge. Accessible by air, train or bus. Beaches are 4 hours from campus. Housing is guaranteed.25 % of students remain on campus for the weekends. 10-15 % of students join fraternities/sororities.

Accreditation: SACS

Expenses:

Tuition: In-state: Full year: $1,800.00. Part-time: Per credit:$214.25. Tuition: Out-of-state: Full year: $3,870.00. Room and board: $2,960.00.

Majors

• AREA STUDIES Black/Afro-American, French Area Studies, Latin American, Urban • BUSINESS Accounting, Agricultural, Banking, Business Administration, Business Education, Business Management, Economics, Fashion Merchandising, Hotel and Restaurant Managemen, Management, Marketing, Personnel • COMMUNICATIONS Advertising, Broadcasting, Communication, English, Journalism, Photography, Speech, Television/Radio/Film • COMPUTER SCIENCE Programming, Systems Analysis • CRAFTS AND DESIGN Graphic Design Technology • EDUCATION Agricultural, Art, Elementary, English, Foreign Language, Health, Industrial, Mathematics, Music, Physical, Science, Secondary, Social Studies, Speech/Language • ENGINEERING Agricultural, Chemical, Civil/Environmental, Electrical, Electro-mechanical Engineering, Mechanical, Petroleum • HEALTH SCIENCES Communication Disorders, Medical Technology, Nursing, Nutritional/Food, Physical Therapy, Speech Therapy • HUMANITIES Liberal Arts, Philosophy • LANGUAGES French, German, Latin, Russian, Spanish • PREPROFESSIONAL Agriculture, Architecture, Dentistry, Engineering, Forestry, Law, Medicine, Optometry, Pharmacy, Social Work, Veterinarian, Wildlife • SCIENCES Agronomy, Animal, Biology, Botany, Chemistry, Geography, Geology, Horticultural, Marine Biology, Mathematics, Microbiology, Physical Chemistry, Physical Science, Physics, Statistics, Zoology • SOCIAL SCIENCES Anthropology, Criminal Justice, Family Counseling, Geography, Government/Political, History, Law Enforcement, Political Science, Psychology, Social Sciences, Sociology • VISUAL AND PERFORMING ARTS Art, Dance, Fine Arts, Music, Theater, Theater Design • VOCATIONAL Automobile Technology, Fashion Design, Food Service, Interior Design, Medical Laboratory Technology, Park/Recreation, Precision Metal Work, Secretarial

Sports/Activities

• SPORTS RELATED Baton Twirling, Cheerleading, Drill Team, Drum Major/Majorette, Marching Band, Team Managers • SPORTS-INTERCOLLEGIATE Baseball (M), Basketball, Cross Country, Football (M), Golf (M), Softball (F), Tennis, Track and Field, Volleyball (F) • SPORTS-INTRAMURAL Basketball, Cross Country, Golf, Horseback Riding, Ping-Pong, Racquetball, Rugby (M), Sailing, Scuba, Soccer, Softball, Synchronized Swimming, Tennis, Track and Field, Volleyball, Water Polo, Wrestling (M) • STUDENT LIFE ACTIVITIES Academic Clubs, Choral, Concert Band, Dance, Debate, Drama Groups, Ethnic & Cultural Groups, Fraternities, Music Groups, Musical Theater, Newspaper, Radio/TV station, Religious Organization, Sororities, Student Government, Symphony Orchestra, Yearbook

Bowdoin College
Brunswick, Maine 04011
(207) 725-3100

School Enrollment: **1,380** Male: **738** Female: **642**
LD Enrollment: **5**

Admissions Contact: **William R. Mason, Director of Admissions**
LD Contact: **Beverly Gelwick, Counselor**
Telephone:**(207) 725-3224**

Admissions

Application Information:
Application deadline: **January 15th**
Notified when: **April 15th**

Secondary School Information
Most Important Criteria For Admissions (1-strongest)

SAT/ACT	**6**	Application	**2** School transcript
2 Class rank	**1**	Course selection	**8** Personal statement
11 Interview	**7**	Extra activities	**3** Psychoeducational
3 G.P.A.		Open admission	**5** Recommendations

Test Requirements:
Standardized tests waived: **Yes**

Types of Disabilities Served

• Speech/Lang	Reading	• ADD with LD
Study skills	Spelling	• ADD without LD
Written express	Math	• ADHD with LD
Organizational	Fine Motor	• ADHD without LD
Perceptual		

Learning Disability Program
Counseling: Individual: **Yes**

Faculty:
Faculty: **3** Full time: **3**
Faculty advocate: **Yes** Meets with instructor: **As needed**

Diagnostic Testing

ADD	Personality	Perceptual skills	Spelling
ADHD	Organization	Fine motor skills	Reading
I.Q.	Handwriting	Spoken language	Study skills
Math	Social skills	Written language	

Tutoring:
Services rendered by:

Graduates	•Peers	•Faculty	LD staff	Teacher trainees

Tutorials

Grp.	Ind.	Tutorials	Grp.	Ind.	Tutorials
	•	Math skills		•	Word processing
	•	Study skills		•	Time management
	•	Language arts		•	Learning strategies
	•	Written express		•	Organizational skills

Academic Accommodations

Curriculum	Study Aids	Exams
Priority registration	Typist	Oral
• Math waiver	Reader	Untimed
Foreign lang. waiver	• Notetaker	• Take home
• Course substitution	Proof reader	With proctor
In Class	• Text on tape	On computer
Calculators	Early syllabus	• Extended time
• Tape recorder	Taped handouts	On tape
• Word processor		• Modified
Priority seating		Separate room

Program Strengths

Bowdoin College will provide appropriate accommodations for hand-icapped students on an individual basis. Bowdoin is committed to supporting our students in any way that is appropriate and possible. The counseling service is the designated place to seek assistance.

General Information:

Bowdoin College is a 4 year private college. Suburban campus of 40 acres is 30 miles from Portland. Accessible by bus. Ski areas are 1 hour from campus. Beaches are 30 minutes from campus. 10% of students are foreign. 10 residential halls on campus. Housing is guaranteed. Guaranteed through 1st year. 80 % of students remain on campus for the weekends. 35 % of students join fraternities/sororities.

Accreditation: Regional

Class Rank:

About 90% of the present freshmen class were in the upper 20% of their high school class. 100% were in the top 40% of their class.

Expenses:

Tuition: In-state: Full year: $13,930.00. Room and board: $4,500.00

Majors

• AREA STUDIES American, Black/Afro-American, Latin American, Russian/Slavic, Women's Studies • BUSINESS Economics • COMMUNI-CATIONS English • EDUCATION Agricultural, Foreign Language • HEALTH SCIENCES Environmental • HUMANITIES Classics, Philosophy, Religion • LANGUAGES French, German, Greek, Italian, Japanese, Latin, Russian, Spanish • PREPROFESSIONAL Engineering • SCIENCES Archeology, Astronomy, Astrophysics, Biochemistry, Biology, Chemistry, Geology, Marine Biology, Mathematics, Nuerosciences, Physical Chemistry, Physical Science, Physics • SOCIAL SCIENCES Anthropology, Government/Political, History, Political Science, Psychology, Sociology

Sports/Activities

• SPORTS RELATED Marching Band, Pep Band • SPORTS-INTERCOL-LEGIATE Baseball (M), Basketball, Cross Country, Diving, Field Hockey (F), Golf, Ice Hockey, Lacrosse, Sailing, Skiing - Snow, Soccer, Softball (F), Squash, Swimming, Tennis, Track and Field, Volleyball (F), Wrestling (M) • SPORTS-INTRAMURAL Basketball, Cross Country, Football (M), Ice Hockey, Soccer, Softball, Volleyball • STUDENT LIFE ACTIVITIES Choral, Community Service, Dance, Drama Groups, Ethnic & Cultural Groups, Fraternities, Jazz Band, Magazine, Music Groups, Musical Theater, Newspaper, Opera, Radio/TV station, Religious Organization, Sororities, Student Government, Symphony Orchestra, Yearbook

---

Most Selective

Colby College
Waterville, Maine 04901
(207) 872-3000

School Enrollment: **1,719** Male: **882** Female: **837**

Admissions Contact: **Ronald G. Whittle, Assoc. Dean of Admis.**
LD Contact: **Mark Serdjenian, Associate Dean of Students**

Admissions

Application Information:
Application deadline: **January 15th**
Notified when: **Mid April**

Secondary School Information
Most Important Criteria For Admissions (1-strongest)

7 SAT/ACT	**8** Application	**11** School transcript
10 Class rank	**11** Course selection	Personal statement
Interview	**7** Extra activities	Psychoeducational
11 G.P.A.	Open admission	**8** Recommendations

Test Requirements:
Diagnostic testing waived: **Yes**
Untimed SAT: **Yes** Untimed ACT: **Yes** Untimed ACH: **Yes**

Types of Disabilities Served

Speech/Lang	• Reading	ADD with LD
Study skills	Spelling	ADD without LD
• Written express	• Math	ADHD with LD
• Organizational	Fine Motor	ADHD without LD
Perceptual		

Learning Disability Program

Counseling: Individual: **Yes**

Faculty:
Faculty advocate: **Yes** Meets with instructor: **As needed**

Diagnostic Testing

ADD	Personality	Perceptual skills	Spelling
ADHD	Organization	Fine motor skills	Reading
I.Q.	Handwriting	Spoken language	Study skills
Math	Social skills	Written language	

Tutoring:
Services rendered by:

Graduates	•Peers	•Faculty	LD staff	Teacher trainees

Tutorials

Grp.	Ind.	Tutorials	Grp.	Ind.	Tutorials
		Math skills	•	•	Word processing
	•	Study skills		•	Time management
		Language arts		•	Learning strategies
	•	Written express			Organizational skills

Academic Accommodations

Curriculum	Study Aids	Exams
Priority registration	Typist	• Oral
Math waiver	Reader	Untimed
Foreign lang. waiver	Notetaker	• Take home
Course substitution	Proof reader	With proctor
In Class	Text on tape	On computer
Calculators	Early syllabus	• Extended time
• Tape recorder	Taped handouts	On tape
• Word processor		• Modified
Priority seating		Separate room

Program Strengths

Colby has no formal program for learning disabled students and does not treat such student differently than other students in the admissions process. It is the policy of Colby College to provide academic support for all students.

General Information:

Colby College is a 4 year private college. Urban campus of 600 acres is 75 miles from Portland. Accessible by bus. Ski areas are 40 miles from campus. Beaches are 40 miles from campus. 2% of students are foreign. 22 residential halls on campus. Housing is guaranteed.

Accreditation: Regional, ACS

SAT/ACT Scores:

Scores for incoming freshmen: **Verbal:** 12% below 500. 50% between 500 and 599. 37% between 600 and 699. 1% above 700. **Math:** 6% below 500. 33% between 500 and 599. 52% between 600 and 699. 9% above 700. **ACT:** 2% below 20. 20% between 24 and 25l. 67% between 26 and 28. 11% above 28.

Class Rank:

About 80% of the present freshmen class were in the upper 20% of their high school class. 97% were in the top 40% of their class.

Expenses:

Tuition: In-state: Full year: $13,470.00. Room and board: $4,860.00

Majors

• AREA STUDIES American, East Asian, Russian/Slavic • BUSINESS Business Administration, Economics • COMMUNICATIONS English • COMPUTER SCIENCE Computer Science • EDUCATION Middle School, Secondary • HUMANITIES Classics, Philosophy, Religion • LANGUAGES French, German, Japanese, Russian, Spanish • SCIENCES Administrative Science, Biochemistry, Biology, Chemistry, Geology, Mathematics, Physics • SOCIAL SCIENCES Government/Political, History, Political Science, Psychology, Sociology

Sports/Activities

• SPORTS RELATED Pep Band, Team Managers • SPORTS-INTERCOLLEGIATE Baseball (M), Basketball, Crew, Cross Country, Diving, Field Hockey (F), Football (M), Golf, Ice Hockey, Lacrosse, Rugby, Sailing, Skiing - Snow, Soccer, Softball (F), Squash, Swimming, Tennis, Track and Field, Volleyball, Water Polo • SPORTS-INTRAMURAL Badminton, Basketball, Fencing, Golf, Horseback Riding, Ice Hockey, Lacrosse, Ping-Pong, Racquetball, Sailing, Scuba, Skiing - Snow, Soccer, Softball, Swimming, Tennis, Volleyball, Water Polo • STUDENT LIFE ACTIVITIES Academic Clubs, Choral, Community Service, Concert Band, Dance, Debate, Drama Groups, Ethnic & Cultural Groups, Jazz Band, Magazine, Music Groups, Musical Theater, Newspaper, Political Groups, Radio/TV station, Religious Organization, Student Government, Symphony Orchestra, Yearbook

---

Less Selective

Southern Maine Technical College

Fort Road
South Portland, Maine 04106
(207) 767-9536

School Enrollment: **1,000** Male: **600** Female: **400**
LD Enrollment: **40** Male: **20** Female: **20**

Admissions Contact: **Robert Weimont, Director of Admissions**
LD Contact: **Gail Christiansen, Learning Center Director**
Name of Program: **Learning Assistance Center**
Address: **Fort Rd.**
Telephone: **(207) 767-9536**

Admissions

Application Information:

LD on admissions committee: **Yes**
Application deadline: **Early Spring/late Winter**
Rolling Admissions: **Yes**

Secondary School Information

Most Important Criteria For Admissions (1-strongest)

7	SAT/ACT	6	Application	2	School transcript
4	Class rank	1	Course selection	8	Personal statement
11	Interview	10	Extra activities	9	Psychoeducational
3	G.P.A.		Open admission	5	Recommendations

Test Requirements:

Untimed SAT: **Yes** Untimed ACT: **Yes** Untimed ACH: **Yes**
Documentation of LD required: **Yes**
Currency of diagnostic testing: **36 preferred**
Tests recommended: **SAT's (untimed) for degree candidates. Basic Skills ETS for diploma candidates (tested on site).**

Types of Disabilities Served

Speech/Lang	Reading	ADD with LD
Study skills	Spelling	ADD without LD
Written express	Math	ADHD with LD
Organizational	Fine Motor	ADHD without LD
Perceptual		

Admissions Process

Apply for admissions, campus tour and testing, interview, review of file, acceptance and/or recommendations for summer courses (conditional acceptance).

High School Course Requirements:

English: **4** Math: **2-3** Science: **1-2**
Waivers to standard high school courses
Course substitution: **Yes**

Learning Disability Program

Special orientation for LD students: **Yes**
Syllabus available during orientation:**Yes**
Program: Reinforces course work: **Yes**
Program available through:**Monday-Friday**
Students mainstreamed **100** % of the day
Recommended credits per semester: **12**
Services available for all students: **Yes**
Counseling: Individual: **Yes** Vocational Counseling: **Yes**

Faculty:
Faculty: **4** Including Director: **Yes** Full time: **2** Part time: **2** M.A.: **1**
Faculty advocate: **Yes** Meets with instructor: **As needed**

Diagnostic Testing
ADD	Personality	Perceptual skills	Spelling
ADHD	Organization	Fine motor skills	Reading
I.Q.	Handwriting	Spoken language	Study skills
Math	Social skills	Written language	

Tutoring:
Average size of group tutorials: **2-3**
Services rendered by:
Graduates •Peers •Faculty •LD staff Teacher trainees

Tutorials
Grp.	Ind.	Tutorials	Grp.	Ind.	Tutorials
	•	Math skills		•	Word processing
	•	Study skills		•	Time management
	•	Language arts		•	Learning strategies
	•	Written express		•	Organizational skills

Academic Accommodations

Curriculum
Priority registration
Math waiver
Foreign lang. waiver
• Course substitution
In Class
• Calculators
• Tape recorder
• Word processor
• Priority seating

Study Aids
Typist
Reader
• Notetaker
Proof reader
• Text on tape
• Early syllabus
Taped handouts

Exams
• Oral
• Untimed
Take home
With proctor
On computer
• Extended time
On tape
Modified
• Separate room

Graduation Requirements:
Course credits: **60+ varies with prog** GPA: **2.0**

Program Strengths
We are connected to Nova NET, a national network of tutorials in all subject areas at all levels of difficulty. Very successful with many people with a history of learning problems or specific disabilities.

General Information:
Southern Maine Technical College is a 2 year public college. Suburban campus of 50 acres is 90 miles from Boston. Accessible by plane or bus. Ski areas are 1 hour from campus. Beaches are 5 mins. from campus. 3 residential halls on campus. Housing is not guaranteed.

Accreditation:Regional

SAT/ACT Scores:
Scores for incoming freshmen:**Verbal:**65below 500. 25between 500 and 599. 10between 600 and 699. **Math:**50 below 500. 35 between 500 and 599. 15 between 600 and 699.

Expenses:
Tuition: In-state: Full year: $1,910.00 including fees. Part-time: Per cred-

it:$48.00. Part-time: Per course: $144.00. Tuition: Out-of-state: Full year: $4,140.00 including fees. Part-time: Per credit:$110.00. Part-time: Per course:$330.00 Room and board: $2,800.00

Majors
• AGRICULTURE Horticultural • ARTS Drafting, Landscaping • BUSINESS Clerical, Construction, Food Management, Hotel & Restaurant Management, Management, Office, Secretarial Science • COMPUTER SCIENCE Computer Technology • ENGINEERING Air Conditioning Technology, Automotive, Drafting, Electrical, Environmental/Water Resources, Marine , Mechanical, Ocean • ENVIRONMENTAL CONTROL Sanitation Technology, Water and Wastewater Technolog • HEALTH SCIENCES Dietary Manager, Environmental, Nursing, Nursing Assistant, Nutritional/Food, Practical Nursing, Respiratory Therapy • PRE PROFESSIONAL Drafting, Engineering • SCIENCES Horticultural, Marine Biology, Metal Technology, Radiology • SOCIAL SCIENCES Criminal Justice, Law Enforcement • VOCATIONAL Air Conditioning/Heating/Refri, Automobile Technology, Automotive Service, Building Construction, Business and Office, Carpentry, Chef Apprenticeship, Construction, Culinary Arts, Drafting, Electronics Technology, Fire Science, Food Service, Landscape Architecture, Machinist, Office Administration, Plumbing, Radiological Technology, Respiratory Therapy Technology, Secretarial

Sports/Activities
• SPORTS RELATED • SPORTS-INTERCOLLEGIATE Baseball, Baseball (F), Baseball (M), Basketball, Basketball (M), Golf, Soccer, Softball, Softball (F), Volleyball • SPORTS-INTRAMURAL Baseball, Basketball, Diving, Golf, Ping-Pong, Sailing, Scuba, Skiing - Cross Country, Skiing - Snow, Soccer, Softball, Volleyball, Weight Lifting • STUDENT LIFE ACTIVITIES Student Government

Less Selective   **Maine**
Accommodations

St. Joseph's College
Windham, Maine 04062-1198
(207) 892-6766

School Enrollment: **651** Male: **273** Female: **378**

Admissions Contact: **Fredric V. Stone, Director of Admissions**
LD Contact: **Fredric V. Stone**

Admissions

Application Information:
Application deadline: **None**
Rolling Admissions: **Yes**Notified when: **3-4 weeks**

Secondary School Information
Most Important Criteria For Admissions (1-strongest)
5 SAT/ACT	11 Application	1 School transcript
4 Class rank	2 Course selection	8 Personal statement
10 Interview	9 Extra activities	7 Psychoeducational
3 G.P.A.	Open admission	6 Recommendations

Test Requirements:
Diagnostic testing waived: **Yes**
Untimed SAT: **Yes** Untimed ACT: **Yes** Untimed ACH: **Yes**
Documentation of LD required: **Yes**
Currency of diagnostic testing: **12**
Tests recommended: **Non specific**

Maine

Types of Disabilities Served

Speech/Lang	Reading	ADD with LD
Study skills	Spelling	ADD without LD
Written express	Math	ADHD with LD
Organizational	Fine Motor	ADHD without LD
Perceptual		

Admissions Process

Can the student do our work with no special services for LD students?

High School Course Requirements:

English: **4** Math: **3** Science: **2** Foreign Language: **2**
Waivers to standard high school courses
Foreign Language : **Yes**

Learning Disability Program

Services available for all students: **Yes**
Counseling: Individual: **Yes** Group Counseling: **Yes**

Diagnostic Testing

ADD	Personality	Perceptual skills	Spelling
ADHD	Organization	Fine motor skills	Reading
I.Q.	Handwriting	Spoken language	Study skills
Math	Social skills	Written language	

Tutoring:

Services rendered by:
Graduates • Peers • Faculty LD staff Teacher trainees

Tutorials

Grp.	Ind.	Tutorials	Grp.	Ind.	Tutorials
		Math skills			Word processing
•		Study skills			Time management
		Language arts			Learning strategies
		Written express			Organizational skills

Academic Accommodations

Curriculum	Study Aids	Exams
Priority registration	Typist	Oral
Math waiver	Reader	Untimed
Foreign lang. waiver	Notetaker	Take home
Course substitution	Proof reader	With proctor
In Class	Text on tape	On computer
Calculators	Early syllabus	Extended time
Tape recorder	Taped handouts	On tape
Word processor		Modified
Priority seating		Separate room

Graduation Requirements:

Course credits: **128** GPA: **2.0** Years to complete degree: **No Limit** Language waiver: **Yes**

Program Strengths

Academic assistance programs are available to all students at the College. Students choose or are assigned a faculty member who serves as an advisor. Students are strongly encouraged to take advantage of these opportunities that are provided at convenient times and at no extra cost to assist them in achieving the best possible college education.

General Information:

St. Joseph's College is a 4 year private Roman Catholic college. Rural campus of 285 acres is 18 miles from Portland. Ski areas are 20 miles from campus. Beaches are 18 miles from campus. 1% of students are foreign. 12

residential halls on campus. Housing is guaranteed.Guaranteed through 4th year. 70 % of students remain on campus for the weekends.

Accreditation:NEACS

SAT/ACT Scores:

Scores for incoming freshmen:**Verbal:89%**below 500. 9%between 500 and 599. 2%between 600 and 699. **Math:78%** below 500. 14% between 500 and 599. 7% between 600 and 699. 1%above 700.

Class Rank:

About 29% of the present freshmen class were in the upper 20% of their high school class. 54% were in the top 40% of their class. 77% were in the top 60% of their class. 93% were in the top 80% of their class.

Expenses:

Tuition: In-state: Full year: $8,250.00. Part-time: Per credit:$180.00. Tuition: Out-of-state: Full year: $8,250.00. Part-time: Per credit:$180.00. Room and board: $4,300.00

Majors

• AGRICULTURE • BUSINESS Accounting, Business Administration, International Business, Management, Marketing • COMMUNICATIONS Broadcasting, Communication, English, Journalism, Literature, Television/Radio/Film • COMPUTER SCIENCE Computer Science • EDUCATION Early Childhood, Elementary, English, General, Mathematics, Middle School, Physical, Reading, Science, Secondary, Social Studies • HEALTH SCIENCES Nursing, Radiological Technology • HUMANITIES English/Writing/Literature, Liberal Arts , Philosophy, Religion • MATHEMATICS Applied, Computer • PRE PROFESSIONAL Business, Dentistry, Law, Medicine, Pharmacy, Social Work, Veterinarian • SCIENCES Applied Mathematics, Biology, Natural , Radiology • SOCIAL SCIENCES History, Human Service, International Studies, Political Science, Psychology, Social Sciences, Sociology

Sports/Activities

• SPORTS RELATED Cheerleading, Chess, Team Managers • SPORTS-INTERCOLLEGIATE Baseball, Basketball (F), Basketball (M), Cross Country (F), Cross Country (M), Golf (M), Soccer (F), Soccer (M), Softball (F), Volleyball (F) • SPORTS-INTRAMURAL Baseball (M), Basketball (F), Basketball (M), Bowling, Cross Country, Football, Golf, Ice Hockey, Karate, Ping-Pong, Racquetball, Skiing - Cross Country, Skiing - Snow, Soccer, Softball, Swimming, Tennis, Volleyball, Weight Lifting • STUDENT LIFE ACTIVITIES Academic Clubs, Choral, Community Service, Drama Groups, Film, Magazine, Newspaper, Political Groups, Radio/TV station, Religious Organization, Student Government, Yearbook

---

Less Selective

Maine Services

Unity College
P.O. Box 532
Unity, Maine 04988
(207) 948-3131

School Enrollment: **450** Male: **325** Female: **125**
LD Enrollment: **50**

Admissions Contact: **John M. B. Craig, Ed.D., Director of Adm.**
LD Contact: **Ann Dailey, LD Specialist**

Admissions

Application Information:
Application deadline: **None**
Rolling Admissions: **Yes**

Secondary School Information
Most Important Criteria For Admissions (1-strongest)

SAT/ACT	Application	**3**	School transcript
Class rank	**4** Course selection		Personal statement
1 Interview	**5** Extra activities		Psychoeducational
G.P.A.	Open admission	**2**	Recommendations

Test Requirements:
Diagnostic testing waived: **Yes**
WAIS-R required: **Yes**
Documentation of LD required: **Yes**
Currency of diagnostic testing: **no more than 12 months**
Tests recommended: **WAIS, documentation of L.D.**

Types of Disabilities Served
- Speech/Lang   Reading   ADD with LD
- Study skills   Spelling   ADD without LD
- Written express   Math   ADHD with LD
- Organizational   Fine Motor   ADHD without LD
- Perceptual

High School Course Requirements:
English: **Y**

Learning Disability Program
Program: Reinforces course work: **Yes**
Students mainstreamed **100** % of the day
Counseling: Individual: **Yes** Group Counseling: **Yes**

Faculty:
Faculty: **6** Including Director: **Yes** Full time: **6** M.A.: **6**
Faculty advocate: **Yes** Meets with instructor: **As needed**

Diagnostic Testing

ADD	Personality	Perceptual skills	Spelling
ADHD	Organization	Fine motor skills	Reading
I.Q.	Handwriting	Spoken language	Study skills
Math	Social skills	Written language	

Tutoring:
Average size of group tutorials: **2-3**
Services rendered by:
  Graduates   •Peers   •Faculty   •LD staff   Teacher trainees

Tutorials

Grp.	Ind. Tutorials	Grp.	Ind. Tutorials
	• Math skills		• Word processing
	• Study skills		• Time management
	• Language arts		• Learning strategies
	• Written express		• Organizational skills

Academic Accommodations

Curriculum	Study Aids	Exams
Priority registration	Typist	Oral
• Math waiver	Reader	Untimed
Foreign lang. waiver	• Notetaker	• Take home
Course substitution	• Proof reader	With proctor
In Class	• Text on tape	On computer
• Calculators	Early syllabus	• Extended time
• Tape recorder	Taped handouts	On tape
• Word processor		Modified
Priority seating		Separate room

Program Strengths
Our program provides students with individual instruction, consults with college faculty concerning specific student needs and appropri-

ate accommodations. We work with individual students on organization, course selection, study skills, and academic courses.

General Information:
Unity College is a 2 and 4 year private college. Rural campus of 180 acres is 18 miles from Waterville. Ski areas are 45 minutes from campus. Beaches are 40 minutes from campus. 2% of students are foreign. 3 residential halls on campus. Housing is not guaranteed.

Accreditation: NEACS

Expenses:
Tuition: In-state: Full year: $6,050.00. Part-time: Per credit:0. Tuition: Out-of-state: Full year: $7,350.00. Room and board: $4,100.00

Majors
• EDUCATION Environmental • ENVIRONMENTAL CONTROL Conservation & Regulation, Environmental Policy • PRE PROFESSIONAL Forestry, Natural Resources, Recreation • SCIENCES Ecology • VOCATIONAL Aquaculture, City Planning, Fisheries, Park/Recreation Management, Wildlife

Sports/Activities
• SPORTS-INTRAMURAL Basketball, Cross Country, Lacrosse, Soccer, Volleyball • STUDENT LIFE ACTIVITIES Drama Groups, Magazine, Newspaper, Radio/TV station, Student Government, Yearbook

---

Selective   **Maine**
                                                              Services

University of Maine
Chadbourne Hall
Orono, Maine 04469-0113
(207) 581-1561

School Enrollment: **11,190** Male: **5,595** Female: **5,595**
LD Contact: **Ann Smith, Coordinator**
Name of Program: **Disabilities Services**
Address: **Onward Building**
Telephone: **(207) 581-2319**

Admissions

Application Information:
Application deadline: **February 15th**

Secondary School Information
Most Important Criteria For Admissions (1-strongest)

8 SAT/ACT	**8** Application	**10**	School transcript
10 Class rank	**10** Course selection	**8**	Personal statement
10 Interview	**8** Extra activities	**10**	Psychoeducational
10 G.P.A.	Open admission	**8**	Recommendations

Test Requirements:
Diagnostic testing waived: **Yes**
Untimed SAT: **Yes**
WAIS-R required: **Yes**
Documentation of LD required: **Yes**
Currency of diagnostic testing: **3 years**
Tests recommended: **I.Q. and Achievement**

Maine

Types of Disabilities Served
- Speech/Lang
- Study skills
- Written express
- Organizational
- Perceptual
- Reading
- Spelling
- Math
- Fine Motor
- ADD with LD
- ADD without LD
- ADHD with LD
- ADHD without LD

Learning Disability Program
Counseling: Individual: **Yes** Group Counseling: **Yes**

Faculty:
Faculty: **1** Full time: **1**

Diagnostic Testing
ADD	Personality	Perceptual skills	Spelling
ADHD	Organization	Fine motor skills	Reading
I.Q.	Handwriting	Spoken language	Study skills
Math	Social skills	Written language	

Tutoring:
Average size of group tutorials: **3-5**
Services rendered by:
Graduates   •Peers   Faculty   LD staff   Teacher trainees

Tutorials
Grp.	Ind.	Tutorials	Grp.	Ind.	Tutorials
•	•	Math skills			Word processing
•		Study skills			Time management
		Language arts			Learning strategies
		Written express			Organizational skills

Academic Accommodations
Curriculum	Study Aids	Exams
Priority registration	Typist	• Oral
• Math waiver	Reader	Untimed
• Foreign lang. waiver	• Notetaker	Take home
Course substitution	Proof reader	• With proctor
In Class	• Text on tape	• On computer
• Calculators	Early syllabus	• Extended time
• Tape recorder	Taped handouts	• On tape
• Word processor		• Modified
Priority seating		Separate room

Program Strengths
No program presently exists. The coordinator of Services for Students with Disabilities provides a vast range of services.

General Information:
University of Maine is a 4 year public university. Rural campus of 3,300 acres is 120 miles from Bangor. Accessible by air or bus. Ski areas are 2-1/2 hours from campus. Beaches are 1 hour from campus. 3% of students are foreign. 23 residential halls on campus. Housing is not guaranteed. 70 % of students remain on campus for the weekends.

Accreditation: NEACS

Class Rank:
About 60% of the present freshmen class were in the upper 20% of their high school class. 90% were in the top 40% of their class. 100% were in the top 60% of their class.

Expenses: Part-time: Per credit: $89.00. Part-time: Per credit: $252.00. Room and board: $4,241.00

Majors
• AREA STUDIES Women's Studies • BUSINESS Accounting, Agricultural, Banking, Business Administration, Business Economics, Business Management, Economics, Fashion Merchandising, Finance, Management, Marketing, Personnel • COMMUNICATIONS Broadcasting, Communication, Creative Writing, English, Journalism, Speech, Television/Radio/Film • COMPUTER SCIENCE Data Processing, Medical Records Technology, Programming, Systems Analysis • EDUCATION Art, Child Development, Early Childhood, Elementary, Foreign Language, Home Economics Education, Music, Physical, Recreation and Youth Leadershi, Secondary, Special • ENGINEERING Agricultural, Chemical, Civil/Environmental, Computer, Engineering Physics, Engineering Science, Mechanical • HEALTH SCIENCES Communication Disorders, Dental Hygiene, Medical Technology, Nursing, Nutritional/Food, Speech/Audiology and Speech • HUMANITIES English/Writing/Literature, Humanities, Liberal Arts, Philosophy, Religion • LANGUAGES French, German, Latin, Russian, Spanish • PRE-PROFESSIONAL Agriculture, Engineering, Forestry, Law, Natural Resources, Range Management, Social Work, Wildlife • SCIENCES Agricultural, Animal, Anthropology, Astronomy, Biochemistry, Biology, Botany, Cell Biology, Chemistry, Earth, Entomology, Geology, Horticultural, Marine Biology, Mathematics, Microbiology, Molecular Biology, Oceanography, Physical Chemistry, Physical Science, Physics, Soil, Zoology • SOCIAL SCIENCES Anthropology, Government/Political, History, Human Service, International Studies, Law Enforcement, Political Science, Psychology, Public Relations, Social Sciences, Sociology • VISUAL AND PERFORMING ARTS Art, Art History, Dance, Dramatic Arts, Fine Arts, Music, Music Performance, Studio Art, Theater • VOCATIONAL Dental Assistant, Electronics Technology, Food Service, Forestry, Home Economics, Medical Laboratory Technology, Park/Recreation, Surveying and Mapping

Sports/Activities
• SPORTS RELATED Cheerleading, Chess, Marching Band, Team Managers • SPORTS-INTERCOLLEGIATE Baseball (M), Basketball, Cross Country, Diving, Field Hockey (F), Football (M), Golf (M), Ice Hockey (M), Soccer (M), Softball (F), Swimming, Tennis, Track and Field • SPORTS-INTRAMURAL Badminton, Basketball, Bowling, Cross Country, Field Hockey (F), Golf, Racquetball, Skiing - Snow, Softball, Squash, Swimming, Tennis, Track and Field, Volleyball, Water Polo • STUDENT LIFE ACTIVITIES Drama Groups, Ethnic & Cultural Groups, Fraternities, Jazz Band, Music Groups, Newspaper, Opera, Radio/TV station, Religious Organization, Sororities, Student Government, Symphony Orchestra, Yearbook

---

Selective | **Maine**
Accommodations

University of Maine at Machias
O'Brien Avenue
Machias, Maine 04654
(207) 255-3313

School Enrollment: **966** Male: **322** Female: **644**

Admissions Contact: **David P. Baldwin, Director of Admissions**

Admissions

Application Information:
Application deadline: **Rolling**
Rolling Admissions: **Yes**

Secondary School Information

Most Important Criteria For Admissions (1-strongest)

5 SAT/ACT	**5** Application	**1** School transcript
4 Class rank	**3** Course selection	Personal statement
7 Interview	**8** Extra activities	Psychoeducational
2 G.P.A.	Open admission	**6** Recommendations

Types of Disabilities Served

- Speech/Lang
- Study skills
- Written express
- Organizational
- Perceptual

- Reading
- Spelling
- Math
- Fine Motor

ADD with LD
ADD without LD
ADHD with LD
ADHD without LD

Diagnostic Testing

ADD	Personality	Perceptual skills	Spelling
ADHD	Organization	Fine motor skills	Reading
I.Q.	Handwriting	Spoken language	Study skills
Math	Social skills	Written language	

Tutoring:

Average size of group tutorials: **10**
Services rendered by:

Graduates •Peers •Faculty LD staff •Teacher trainees

Tutorials

Grp.	Ind.	Tutorials	Grp.	Ind.	Tutorials
•	•	Math skills		•	Word processing
•	•	Study skills	•	•	Time management
	•	Language arts	•	•	Learning strategies
•	•	Written express	•	•	Organizational skills

Academic Accommodations

Curriculum	Study Aids	Exams
Priority registration	Typist	• Oral
Math waiver	Reader	Untimed
Foreign lang. waiver	• Notetaker	Take home
Course substitution	Proof reader	With proctor
In Class	Text on tape	On computer
Calculators	Early syllabus	• Extended time
• Tape recorder	Taped handouts	On tape
• Word processor		Modified
Priority seating		Separate room

Program Strengths

The University has no LD Program but it does have a Learning Center with tutors in every subject area.

General Information:

University of Maine at Machias is a 2 and 4 year public university. Rural campus of 42 acres is 85 miles from Bangor. Accessible by bus. Ski areas are 85 miles from campus. Beaches are 8 miles from campus. 3% of students are foreign. 2 residential halls on campus. Housing is not guaranteed. 90 % of students remain on campus for the weekends. 5 % of students join fraternities/sororities.

Accreditation: NEACS

Expenses:

Tuition: In-state: Full year: $2,460.00. Part-time: Per credit: $82.00. Tuition: Out-of-state: Full year: $6,000.00. Part-time: Per credit: $200.00.
Room and board: $3,230.00

Majors

- BUSINESS Accounting, Business Administration, Business Education, Business Information Systems, Business Management, Entrepreneur, Management, Marketing, Real Estate, Travel/Tourism Management • COMMUNICATIONS English • COMPUTER SCIENCE Computer Maintenance, Computer Science, Data Processing, Programming, Systems Analysis • EDUCATION Early Childhood, Elementary, Middle School, Secondary • HEALTH SCIENCES Environmental, Health • HUMANITIES Humanities, Liberal Arts • PREPROFESSIONAL Recreation, Social Work • SCIENCES Behavioral Biology, Biology, Ecology, Marine Biology • SOCIAL SCIENCES History, Psychology, Social Sciences • VOCATIONAL Business and Office, Office Administration, Park/Recreation, Secretarial

Sports/Activities

- SPORTS RELATED Cheerleading, Pep Band • SPORTS-INTERCOLLEGIATE Basketball (F), Basketball (M), Soccer (M), Volleyball (F) • SPORTS-INTRAMURAL Archery, Basketball, Cross Country, Hand Ball, Ice Hockey (M), Ping-Pong (M), Racquetball, Sailing, Soccer (F), Tennis, Volleyball, Wrestling (M) • STUDENT LIFE ACTIVITIES Choral, Drama Groups, Ethnic & Cultural Groups, Fraternities, Music Groups, Musical Theater, Newspaper, Religious Organization, Sororities, Student Government, Yearbook

---

Selective

Maine
Program

University of New England

11 Hills Beach Road
Biddeford, Maine 04005
(207) 283-0171

School Enrollment: **650** Male: **130** Female: **520**
LD Enrollment: **35**

Admissions Contact: **Ann Rousselle, Assistant Dir. of Admissions**
LD Contact: **Dr. Robert Manganello, Coordinator**
Name of Program: **Individual Learning Program**
Telephone: **(207) 283-0171**

Admissions

Application Information:

LD Students Applying: **75** Accepted: **30** Enrolled: **17**
Application deadline: **Rolling**
Rolling Admissions: **Yes**

Secondary School Information

Most Important Criteria For Admissions (1-strongest)

11 SAT/ACT	**10** Application	**3** School transcript
6 Class rank	**5** Course selection	**8** Personal statement
2 Interview	**9** Extra activities	**1** Psychoeducational
4 G.P.A.	Open admission	**7** Recommendations

Test Requirements:

Standardized tests waived: **Yes**
Diagnostic testing waived: **Yes**
Untimed SAT: **Yes** Achievement tests required: **3**
WAIS-R required: **Yes** Range accepted: **High Average**
Documentation of LD required: **Yes**
Currency of diagnostic testing: **12 months**

Types of Disabilities Served

- Speech/Lang
- Study skills
- Written express
- Organizational
- Perceptual

- Reading
- Spelling
- Math
- Fine Motor

- ADD with LD
ADD without LD
- ADHD with LD
ADHD without LD

Maine

Admissions Process

The same as for other applicants except for the required interview with a faculty member of the individual learning program; decision is made cooperatively between the ILP and the Admissions Office.

High School Course Requirements:
English: **4** Math: **3** Science: **2**

Learning Disability Program

Special orientation for LD students: **Yes**
Program: Remedial: **Yes**
Program: Reinforces course work: **Yes**
Program available through:**Fall and Spring**
Students mainstreamed **100** % of the day
Recommended credits per semester: **varies**
Time required or recommended in learning center: **1-4 hours**
Services only for LD students: **Yes**
Counseling: Individual: **Yes** Group Counseling: **Yes** Vocational Counseling: **Yes**
Support groups are available:**Yes, for incoming freshmen and transfer sudents.**

Faculty:
Faculty: **5** Including Director: **Yes** Full time: **2** Part time: **3** M.A.: **3** Ph.D.: **2**
Faculty advocate: **Yes** Meets with instructor: **As needed**

Diagnostic Testing
- ADD
- ADHD
- I.Q.
- Math
- Personality
- Organization
- Handwriting
- Social skills
- Perceptual skills
- Fine motor skills
- Spoken language
- Written language
- Spelling
- Reading
- Study skills

Tutoring:
Average size of group tutorials: **5-7**
Services rendered by:
- Graduates
- Peers
- Faculty
- LD staff
- Teacher trainees

Tutorials

Grp.	Ind.	Tutorials	Grp.	Ind.	Tutorials
•	•	Math skills		•	Word processing
•	•	Study skills	•	•	Time management
		Language arts	•	•	Learning strategies
	•	Written express	•	•	Organizational skills

Academic Accommodations

Curriculum	Study Aids	Exams
Priority registration	Typist	• Oral
Math waiver	• Reader	• Untimed
Foreign lang. waiver	Notetaker	• Take home
Course substitution	• Proof reader	• With proctor
In Class	• Text on tape	• On computer
• Calculators	Early syllabus	• Extended time
• Tape recorder	Taped handouts	• On tape
• Word processor		• Modified
• Priority seating		• Separate room

Graduation Requirements:
Course credits: **129** GPA: **2.0** Years to complete degree: **Varies**
Other requirements: **3 Winter term courses**

Program Strengths

The primary goal of the ILP is to promote and enhance learning disabled students' independent and successful academic functioning as quickly as possible. The time that is achieved varies and depends upon the nature and severity of a student's learning disability, as well as the student's level of maturity.

General Information:

University of New England is a 2 and 4 year private university. Rural campus of 125 acres is 20-30 miles from Portland. Accessible by air or bus. Ski areas are 2 miles from campus. Beaches are campus from campus. 5 residential halls on campus. Housing is guaranteed.75 % of students remain on campus for the weekends.

Accreditation:NEACS

Expenses:
Tuition: In-state: Full year: $9,300.00. Part-time: Per credit:$310.00. Tuition: Out-of-state: Full year: $9,300.00. Part-time: Per credit:$310.00.
Room and board: $4,550.00 Cost of LD program:$1,250.00-$3,100.00

Majors

• BUSINESS Business Administration, Human Resources Management, Management • EDUCATION Elementary, Science, Secondary, Special • HEALTH SCIENCES Environmental, Health, Medical Technology, Nursing, Occupational Therapy, Physical Therapy • HUMANITIES Liberal Arts • PREPROFESSIONAL Dentistry, Medicine, Pharmacy, Social Work • SCIENCES Biology, Marine Biology, Physical Science • SOCIAL SCIENCES Psychology • VOCATIONAL Medical Laboratory Technology

Sports/Activities

• SPORTS-INTERCOLLEGIATE Basketball, Lacrosse (M), Soccer, Softball (F), Volleyball (F) • SPORTS-INTRAMURAL Basketball, Bowling, Ice Hockey (M), Tennis, Volleyball, Water Polo • STUDENT LIFE ACTIVITIES Academic Clubs, Drama Groups, Magazine, Music Groups, Musical Theater, Newspaper, Student Government, Yearbook

---

Selective   **Maine**
Services

University of Southern Maine
Corthell Hall
Gorham, Maine 04038
(207) 780-5215

School Enrollment: **1,600** Male: **960** Female: **640**
LD Contact: **Margo W. Druschel, Coordinator**
Name of Program: **Academic Support Services**
Telephone:**(207) 780-4706**

Admissions

Application Information:
Application deadline: **Rolling**
Rolling Admissions: **Yes**

Secondary School Information
Most Important Criteria For Admissions (1-strongest)

3 SAT/ACT	1 Application	1 School transcript
2 Class rank	1 Course selection	1 Personal statement
2 Interview	4 Extra activities	1 Psychoeducational
G.P.A.	Open admission	2 Recommendations

Test Requirements:
Diagnostic testing waived: **Yes**
Untimed SAT: **Yes** Untimed ACT: **Yes**
WAIS-R required: **Yes** Range accepted: **Varies**
Currency of diagnostic testing: **3 years**

Types of Disabilities Served
- Speech/Lang
- Study skills
- Written express
- Organizational
- Perceptual
- Reading
- Spelling
- Math
- Fine Motor

ADD with LD
ADD without LD
ADHD with LD
ADHD without LD

Learning Disability Program
Counseling: Individual: **Yes** Group Counseling: **Yes**

Faculty:
Faculty: **1** Full time: **1**
Faculty advocate: **Yes** Meets with instructor: **As needed**

Diagnostic Testing
ADD	Personality	Perceptual skills	Spelling
ADHD	Organization	Fine motor skills	Reading
I.Q.	Handwriting	Spoken language	Study skills
Math	Social skills	Written language	

Tutoring:
Services rendered by:
Graduates •Peers   Faculty   LD staff   •Teacher trainees

Tutorials
Grp.	Ind.	Tutorials	Grp.	Ind.	Tutorials
	•	Math skills		•	Word processing
•		Study skills		•	Time management
	•	Language arts		•	Learning strategies
	•	Written express		•	Organizational skills

Academic Accommodations
Curriculum	Study Aids	Exams
Priority registration	• Typist	• Oral
Math waiver	Reader	Untimed
Foreign lang. waiver	• Notetaker	Take home
• Course substitution	• Proof reader	With proctor
In Class	• Text on tape	On computer
• Calculators	Early syllabus	• Extended time
• Tape recorder	Taped handouts	On tape
• Word processor		Modified
Priority seating		Separate room

Program Strengths
The University of Southern Maine provides support services to all students with disabilities, including LD students.

General Information:
University of Southern Maine is a 2 and 4 year public university. Rural campus of 300 acres is 10 miles from Portland. Accessible by air, train or bus. Ski areas are 45 minutes from campus. Beaches are 10 miles from campus. 8 residential halls on campus. Housing is guaranteed. 50 % of students remain on campus for the weekends. 5 % of students join fraternities/sororities.

Accreditation: Regional

Expenses:
Tuition: In-state: Full year: $1,830.00. Part-time: Per credit: $61.00. Tuition: Out-of-state: Full year: $5,160.00. Part-time: Per credit: $180.00. Room and board: $3,490.00.

Majors
• AREA STUDIES Women's Studies • BUSINESS Accounting, Business Administration, Business Management, Economics, Hotel and Restaurant Managemen • COMMUNICATIONS Communication, English • COM-PUTER SCIENCE Computer Science • EDUCATION Art, Elementary, Industrial, Mathematics, Secondary • ENGINEERING Electrical • HEALTH SCIENCES Nursing • HUMANITIES Classics, Humanities, Liberal Arts, Philosophy • LANGUAGES French • PREPROFESSIONAL Social Work • SCIENCES Biology, Biotechnology, Chemistry, Geography, Geology, Mathematics, Physical Science • SOCIAL SCIENCES Anthropology, Criminal Justice, Criminology, Government/Political, History, Political Science, Psychology, Social Sciences, Sociology • VISUAL AND PERFORMING ARTS Dramatic Arts, Fine Arts, Music Performance • VOCATIONAL Park/Recreation

Sports/Activities
• SPORTS-INTERCOLLEGIATE Baseball (M), Basketball, Cross Country, Field Hockey (F), Golf, Ice Hockey (M), Soccer, Softball (F), Tennis • SPORTS-INTRAMURAL Basketball, Racquetball, Soccer, Softball, Volleyball • STUDENT LIFE ACTIVITIES Choral, Concert Band, Dance, Drama Groups, Ethnic & Cultural Groups, Fraternities, Jazz Band, Magazine, Music Groups, Newspaper, Radio/TV station, Religious Organization, Sororities, Student Government, Symphony Orchestra

---

Less Selective   **Maryland Services**

Charles County Community College
P.O. Box 910 Mitchell Road
La Plata, Maryland 20646
(301) 934-2251

School Enrollment: **5,817** Male: **2,036** Female: **3,781**

Admissions Contact: **Charlotte Hill, Director of Admissions**
LD Contact: **M. Penelope Appel, Director, LAC**
Name of Program: **Learning Assistance Center**
Address: **Box 910**
Telephone: **(301) 934-2251 Ext. 611,614**

Admissions

Secondary School Information
Most Important Criteria For Admissions (1-strongest)

SAT/ACT	Application **1**	School transcript
Class rank **1**	Course selection	Personal statement
Interview **1**	Extra activities	Psychoeducational
1 G.P.A.	**1** Open admission	Recommendations

Test Requirements:
Documentation of LD required: **Yes**

Types of Disabilities Served
- Speech/Lang
- Study skills
- Written express
- Organizational
- Perceptual
- Reading
- Spelling
- Math
- Fine Motor

ADD with LD
ADD without LD
ADHD with LD
ADHD without LD

Learning Disability Program
Services available for all students: **Yes**
Counseling: Individual: **Yes** Group Counseling: **Yes**

Faculty:
Faculty: **2** Full time: **1** Part time: **1**
Faculty advocate: **Yes** Meets with instructor: **As needed**

Maryland

Diagnostic Testing
ADD	Personality •	Perceptual skills	• Spelling
ADHD•	Organization	Fine motor skills	• Reading
• I.Q.	Handwriting	Spoken language	• Study skills
• Math	Social skills•	Written language	

Tutoring:
Average size of group tutorials: **3-5**
Services rendered by:
Graduates •Peers Faculty •LD staff Teacher trainees

Tutorials
Grp.	Ind.	Tutorials	Grp.	Ind.	Tutorials
•		Math skills	•		Word processing
•		Study skills	•		Time management
		Language arts	•		Learning strategies
	•	Written express	•		Organizational skills

Academic Accommodations
Curriculum	Study Aids	Exams
Priority registration	Typist	• Oral
Math waiver	Reader	• Untimed
Foreign lang. waiver	• Notetaker	Take home
• Course substitution	• Proof reader	• With proctor
In Class	• Text on tape	• On computer
• Calculators	Early syllabus	• Extended time
• Tape recorder	Taped handouts	• On tape
• Word processor		• Modified
Priority seating		• Separate room

Program Strengths
We provide services on an as needed basis. All LD students are part of the regular college program. We provide developmental studies courses. All incoming students are required to take placements tests.

General Information:
Charles County Community College is a 2 year public college. Rural campus of 100 acres is 45 miles from Washington. Accessible by bus. Housing is not guaranteed.

Accreditation:MSACS

Expenses: Part-time: Per credit:$50.00. Part-time: Per credit:$150.00.

Majors
• BUSINESS Accounting, Agricultural, Business Administration, Business Management, Real Estate • COMPUTER SCIENCE Computer Science, Computer Technology, Data Processing • EDUCATION Child Development, Early Childhood, Elementary, Music, Secondary, Teacher Aide • ENGINEERING Engineering Science • HEALTH SCIENCES Nursing • HUMANITIES Liberal Arts • SCIENCES Agricultural, Biology, Mathematics • SOCIAL SCIENCES Law Enforcement • VISUAL AND PERFORMING ARTS Fine Arts • VOCATIONAL Automobile Technology, Automotive Service, Drafting, Electronics Technology, Food Service, Office Administration, Radiological Technology

Sports/Activities
• SPORTS-INTERCOLLEGIATE Baseball (M) • STUDENT LIFE ACTIVITIES Drama Groups, Jazz Band, Newspaper, Student Government

---

Chesapeake College
P.O. Box 8
Wye Mills, Maryland 21679
(410) 822-5400

School Enrollment: **2,042** Male: **510** Female: **1,532**
LD Enrollment: **80**

Admissions Contact: **Tim Albert, Director of Admissions**
LD Contact: **Rick McLennan, Student Support**
Name of Program: **Developmental Studies**

Admissions

Application Information:
Rolling Admissions: **Yes**

Secondary School Information
Most Important Criteria For Admissions (1-strongest)
SAT/ACT	Application	School transcript
Class rank	Course selection	Personal statement
Interview	Extra activities	Psychoeducational
G.P.A.	Open admission	Recommendations

Test Requirements:
Diagnostic testing waived: **Yes**
Achievement tests required:

Types of Disabilities Served
• Speech/Lang	• Reading	ADD with LD
• Study skills	• Spelling	ADD without LD
• Written express	• Math	ADHD with LD
• Organizational	Fine Motor	ADHD without LD
Perceptual		

Admissions Process

Open admissions with placement and diagnostic testing required before course registration

Learning Disability Program
Program: Remedial: **Yes**
Program: Reinforces course work: **Yes**
Recommended credits per semester: **individualized**
Services available for all students: **Yes**
Counseling: Individual: **Yes** Vocational Counseling: **Yes**

Diagnostic Testing
ADD	Personality	Perceptual skills	• Spelling
ADHD	Organization	Fine motor skills	• Reading
I.Q.	Handwriting	Spoken language	• Study skills
Math	Social skills•	Written language	

Services rendered by:
Graduates Peers Faculty LD staff Teacher trainees

Tutorials

Grp.	Ind.	Tutorials	Grp.	Ind.	Tutorials
•	•	Math skills			Word processing
•	•	Study skills			Time management
		Language arts	•	•	Learning strategies
•	•	Written express	•	•	Organizational skills

Academic Accommodations

Curriculum	Study Aids	Exams
Priority registration	Typist	Oral
Math waiver	Reader	Untimed
Foreign lang. waiver	Notetaker	Take home
Course substitution	Proof reader	• With proctor
In Class	Text on tape	On computer
Calculators	Early syllabus	Extended time
Tape recorder	Taped handouts	On tape
Word processor		Modified
Priority seating		Separate room

Graduation Requirements:
Course credits: **60** Years to complete degree: **2-3**

General Information:
Chesapeake College is a 2 year public college. Rural campus 25 miles from Annapolis. Beaches are 80 miles from campus. Housing is not guaranteed.

Accreditation: MSACS

Expenses: Part-time: Per credit:$45.00. Part-time: Per credit:$189.00.

Majors
• ARTS Music • BUSINESS Accounting, Data Processing • COMMUNICATIONS English • COMPUTER SCIENCE Business Data Programming, Computer Technology, Programming • EDUCATION Early Childhood, Elementary, Secondary • ENGINEERING Air Conditioning Technology • HEALTH SCIENCES Surgical Technology • PRE PROFESSIONAL Engineering • VOCATIONAL Air Conditioning/Heating/Refri, Aviation Maintenance, Electronics Technology, Legal Secretary, Office Administration, Radiological Technology, Secretarial, Word Processing

Sports/Activities
• SPORTS-INTERCOLLEGIATE Baseball (M), Basketball, Lacrosse, Soccer (M), Tennis • SPORTS-INTRAMURAL Basketball, Volleyball • STUDENT LIFE ACTIVITIES Academic Clubs, Community Service, Music Groups, Student Government

---

Selective   **Maryland Services**

Frostburg State University
Frostburg, Maryland 21532-1099
(301) 689-4201

School Enrollment: **4,525** Male: **2,082** Female: **2,443**
LD Enrollment: **173** Male: **64** Female: **109**

Admissions Contact: **Dave Sanford, Dean of Admissions**
LD Contact: **Beth Hoffman, Director, Student Support Services**
Name of Program: **Disabled Student Services**
Telephone:**(301) 689-4481**

Admissions

Application Information:
Rolling Admissions: **Yes** Notified when: **Mid-May**

Secondary School Information
Most Important Criteria For Admissions (1-strongest)

2 SAT/ACT	5 Application	3 School transcript
4 Class rank	7 Course selection	8 Personal statement
7 Interview	9 Extra activities	10 Psychoeducational
1 G.P.A.	Open admission	6 Recommendations

Test Requirements:
Diagnostic testing waived: **Yes**
Untimed SAT: **Yes** Untimed ACT: **Yes**
Documentation of LD required: **Yes**
Currency of diagnostic testing: **3 years**

Types of Disabilities Served
- Speech/Lang
- Study skills
- Written express
- Organizational
- Perceptual
- Reading
- Spelling
- Math
- Fine Motor
- ADD with LD
- ADD without LD
- ADHD with LD
- ADHD without LD

High School Course Requirements:
English: **4** Math: **3** Science: **2**
Waivers to standard high school courses
Foreign Language : **Yes** Course substitution: **Yes**

Learning Disability Program
Time required or recommended in learning center: **Varies**
Counseling: Individual: **Yes** Group Counseling: **Yes**

Faculty:
Faculty: **4** Full time: **3** Part time: **1** M.A.: **1**
Faculty advocate: **Yes** Meets with instructor: **As needed**

Diagnostic Testing
ADD	• Personality	• Perceptual skills	• Spelling
ADHD	• Organization	• Fine motor skills	• Reading
• I.Q.	Handwriting	• Spoken language	• Study skills
• Math	Social skills	• Written language	

Tutoring:
Average size of group tutorials: **4**
Services rendered by:
•Graduates •Peers •Faculty •LD staff Teacher trainees

Tutorials

Grp.	Ind.	Tutorials	Grp.	Ind.	Tutorials
	•	Math skills		•	Word processing
•	•	Study skills		•	Time management
	•	Language arts	•	•	Learning strategies
	•	Written express	•	•	Organizational skills

Academic Accommodations

Curriculum	Study Aids	Exams
Priority registration	• Typist	• Oral
Math waiver	Reader	Untimed
• Foreign lang. waiver	• Notetaker	Take home
• Course substitution	• Proof reader	• With proctor
In Class	• Text on tape	On computer
• Calculators	Early syllabus	• Extended time
• Tape recorder	Taped handouts	On tape
• Word processor		• Modified
Priority seating		Separate room

Maryland

Graduation Requirements:
Course credits: **120** GPA: **2.0** Years to complete degree: **4-5** Math waiver: **Yes** Language waiver: **Yes**

Program Strengths
Services are based on the needs of an individual student, not program requirements. Independent students can be fully mainstreamed yet when help is needed, they know where to come.

General Information:
Frostburg State University is a 4 year public university. Rural campus 150 miles from Baltimore/Pittsburgh. Accessible by air, train or bus. Ski areas are 30 miles from campus. Beaches are 190 miles from campus. 20% of students are foreign. 9 residential halls on campus. Housing is guaranteed.Guaranteed through 4th year. 30 % of students join fraternities/ sororities.

Accreditation:MSACS

Expenses:
Tuition: In-state: Full year: $1,198.00 per semester. Part-time: Per credit:$78.00. Tuition: Out-of-state: Full year: $2,279.00 per semester. Room and board: $4,290.00

Majors
• AREA STUDIES African, American, Black/Afro-American, Latin American, Urban • BUSINESS Accounting, Business Administration, Business Education, Economics, Finance, Management, Marketing • COMMUNICATIONS Advertising, Broadcasting, Communication, Creative Writing, English, Journalism, Photography, Speech, Television/Radio/Film • COMPUTER SCIENCE Computer Science, Computer Technology, Data Processing, Systems Analysis • CRAFTS AND DESIGN Graphic Design • EDUCATION Art, Early Childhood, Elementary, Health, Middle School, Music, Physical, Recreation and Youth Leadershi, Secondary • HUMANITIES Humanities, Philosophy • LANGUAGES French, German, Latin, Russian, Spanish • PREPROFESSIONAL Dentistry, Engineering, Law, Medicine, Natural Resources, Pharmacy, Recreation, Social Work, Veterinarian • SCIENCES Biology, Botany, Chemistry, Earth, Geography, Geology, Mathematics, Physical Science, Physics • SOCIAL SCIENCES Criminal Justice, Government/Political, History, International Studies, Psychology, Social Sciences, Sociology • VISUAL AND PERFORMING ARTS Art, Art History, Dance, Dramatic Arts, Music, Studio Art, Theater

Sports/Activities
• SPORTS RELATED Marching Band, Pep Band • SPORTS-INTERCOLLEGIATE Baseball (M), Basketball, Cross Country, Diving, Field Hockey (F), Football (M), Lacrosse (F), Soccer, Swimming, Tennis, Track and Field • SPORTS-INTRAMURAL Badminton, Bowling, Field Hockey (F), Lacrosse (F), Racquetball, Rugby, Soccer, Softball, Squash, Tennis, Volleyball • STUDENT LIFE ACTIVITIES Choral, Concert Band, Fraternities, Magazine, Music Groups, Musical Theater, Newspaper, Radio/TV station, Religious Organization, Sororities, Student Government, Yearbook

Less Selective   **Maryland**
                                                Services

Hagerstown Junior College
751 Robinwood Drive
Hagerstown, Maryland 21740-6590
(301) 790-2800

School Enrollment: **2,589** Male: **960** Female: **1,629**

Admissions Contact: **Max E. Creager, Director of Admissions**
LD Contact: **Lynn Schlossberg, Coordinator**
Name of Program: **Handicapped Student Services**

Admissions

Application Information:
Application deadline: **September 1st**

Secondary School Information
Most Important Criteria For Admissions (1-strongest)

SAT/ACT	Application	School transcript
Class rank	Course selection	Personal statement
Interview	Extra activities	Psychoeducational
G.P.A.	**1** Open admission	Recommendations

Test Requirements:
Standardized tests waived: **Yes**

Types of Disabilities Served
• Speech/Lang	• Reading	ADD with LD
• Study skills	• Spelling	ADD without LD
• Written express	• Math	ADHD with LD
• Organizational	Fine Motor	ADHD without LD
• Perceptual		

Learning Disability Program
Counseling: Individual: **Yes** Group Counseling: **Yes**

Faculty:
Faculty: **1** Part time: **1**
Faculty advocate: **Yes** Meets with instructor: **As needed**

Diagnostic Testing
ADD	Personality	Perceptual skills	Spelling
ADHD	Organization	Fine motor skills	Reading
I.Q.	Handwriting	Spoken language	Study skills
Math	Social skills	Written language	

Tutoring:
Services rendered by:
•Graduates   •Peers   •Faculty   •LD staff   Teacher trainees

Tutorials
Grp.	Ind.	Tutorials	Grp.	Ind.	Tutorials
•	•	Math skills		•	Word processing
		Study skills			Time management
	•	Language arts			Learning strategies
		Written express			Organizational skills

Academic Accommodations
Curriculum	Study Aids	Exams
Priority registration	• Typist	• Oral
Math waiver	Reader	Untimed
Foreign lang. waiver	• Notetaker	• Take home
• Course substitution	Proof reader	With proctor
In Class	• Text on tape	On computer
• Calculators	Early syllabus	• Extended time
• Tape recorder	Taped handouts	On tape
• Word processor		• Modified
Priority seating		Separate room

Program Strengths
Hagerstown Junior College is a small community college unique in its ability to provide individual attention to its students. We provide numerous support services to our students who are learning disabled. Each LD student meets with our Handicapped Program Coordinator to assess his or her individual needs. Every student is encouraged to learn the skills necessary to become his or her own

advocate.

General Information:

Hagerstown Junior College is a 2 year public college. Suburban campus of 187 acres is 70 miles from Washington, D.C. Accessible by bus. Ski areas are 30 miles from campus. Beaches are 150 miles from campus. Housing is not guaranteed.

Accreditation: MSACS

Expenses:

Tuition: In-state: Full year: $1,952.00. Part-time: Per credit:$61.00. Tuition: Out-of-state: Full year: $2,752.00. Part-time: Per credit:$86.00.

Majors

• BUSINESS Accounting, Business Administration, Business Education, Hotel and Restaurant Managemen, Management • COMMUNICATIONS Television/Radio/Film • ENGINEERING Engineering Science • HEALTH SCIENCES Nursing, Radiological Therapy • HUMANITIES Liberal Arts • PREPROFESSIONAL Engineering • SCIENCES Biology, Chemistry, Mathematics, Physics • SOCIAL SCIENCES Criminal Justice, Law Enforcement • VOCATIONAL Electronics Technology, Secretarial

Sports/Activities

• SPORTS-INTERCOLLEGIATE Basketball, Basketball (M), Cross Country, Soccer, Tennis, Track and Field, Volleyball (F) • SPORTS-INTRAMURAL Bowling, Ping-Pong, Racquetball, Softball • STUDENT LIFE ACTIVITIES Choral, Drama Groups, Jazz Band, Newspaper, Student Government

---

Less Selective   **Maryland**
                                   Services

Howard Community College

Little Patuxent Parkway
Columbia, Maryland 21044
(301) 992-4856

School Enrollment: **4,278** Male: **1,703** Female: **2,575**
LD Enrollment: **78** Male: **47** Female: **31**

Admissions Contact: **Barbara Greenfield, Director of Admissions**
LD Contact: **Janice Marks, Director**
Name of Program: **Student Support Services**
Telephone:**(301) 992-4822**

Admissions

Application Information:

LD Students Applying: **78** Accepted: **78** Enrolled:**78**
Separate application:**Yes**
Rolling Admissions: **Yes**

Secondary School Information

Most Important Criteria For Admissions (1-strongest)

SAT/ACT	Application	School transcript
Class rank	Course selection	Personal statement
Interview	Extra activities	Psychoeducational
G.P.A.	**1** Open admission	Recommendations

Test Requirements:

Standardized tests waived: **Yes**
Diagnostic testing waived: **Yes**
Untimed SAT: **Yes** Untimed ACT: **Yes** Untimed ACH: **Yes**
WAIS-R required: **Yes**
Documentation of LD required: **Yes**
Tests recommended: **Woodcock-Johnson**

Types of Disabilities Served

• Speech/Lang	• Reading	• ADD with LD
• Study skills	• Spelling	• ADD without LD
• Written express	• Math	• ADHD with LD
• Organizational	• Fine Motor	• ADHD without LD
• Perceptual		

Admissions Process

We are an open enrollment institution.

Learning Disability Program

Program: Remedial: **Yes**
Program: Reinforces course work: **Yes**
Students mainstreamed 100 % of the day
Recommended credits per semester: **6-12**
Services available for all students: **Yes**
Counseling: Individual: **Yes** Vocational Counseling: **Yes**

Faculty:

Faculty: **11** Including Director: **Yes** Full time: **5** Part time: **6**
Faculty advocate: **Yes** Meets with instructor: **2x per semester**

Diagnostic Testing

ADD	Personality	Perceptual skills	Spelling
ADHD	Organization	Fine motor skills	Reading
I.Q.	Handwriting	Spoken language	• Study skills
Math	Social skills	Written language	

Tutoring:

Average size of group tutorials: **2-3**
Services rendered by:
•Graduates   Peers   •Faculty   •LD staff   Teacher trainees

Tutorials

Grp.	Ind.	Tutorials	Grp.	Ind.	Tutorials
•	•	Math skills	•	•	Word processing
•	•	Study skills	•	•	Time management
•	•	Language arts	•	•	Learning strategies
•	•	Written express	•	•	Organizational skills

Academic Accommodations

Curriculum	Study Aids	Exams
Priority registration	Typist	• Oral
• Math waiver	• Reader	Untimed
Foreign lang. waiver	• Notetaker	• Take home
• Course substitution	• Proof reader	• With proctor
In Class	• Text on tape	On computer
• Calculators	• Early syllabus	• Extended time
• Tape recorder	Taped handouts	On tape
• Word processor		• Modified
Priority seating		• Separate room

Graduation Requirements:

Course credits: **64** GPA: **2.0** Years to complete degree: **10** Math waiver: **Yes**

Maryland

Program Strengths

Student Support Services is a federally funded program to serve low income, first generation, and disabled students. Students must document their eligibility for the program. Our success rate is approximately 70% for LD students each semester. After looking at students succeeding, the most important characteristic is motivation, not high test scores for academic success.

General Information:

Howard Community College is a 2 year public college. Suburban campus 20 miles from Baltimore. Accessible by air, train or bus. Ski areas are 2 hours from campus. Beaches are 2 hours from campus. .5% of students are foreign. Housing is not guaranteed.

Accreditation: Regional

Expenses:

Tuition: In-state: Full year: In county $795.00 - out of county $1,230.00. Part-time: Per credit: In county $53.00 - out of county $82.00. Part-time: Per credit: $140.00.

Majors

• BUSINESS Accounting, Business Administration, Business Education, Business Management, Economics, Finance, International Business, Management, Marketing, Real Estate, Retailing • COMMUNICATIONS Communication, Creative Writing, Photography • COMPUTER SCIENCE Computer Science, Computer Technology, Data Processing, Hardware Engineer, Programming, Systems Analysis, Telecommunications • CRAFTS AND DESIGN Ceramics, Crafts, Sculpture • EDUCATION Art, Early Childhood, Elementary, Secondary • ENGINEERING Aerospace, Agricultural, Chemical, Civil/Environmental, Electrical, Engineering Science, Environmental/Water Resources, Industrial, Mechanical, Mining/Mineral, Nuclear • HEALTH SCIENCES Health, Medical Secretary, Medical Technology, Nursing • PREPROFESSIONAL Architecture, Dentistry, Medicine, Optometry, Pharmacy, Veterinarian • SCIENCES Astronomy, Bacteriology, Biochemistry, Biomedical, Botany, Chemistry, Human Biology, Meteorology, Microbiology, Physical Science, Physics • SOCIAL SCIENCES Criminal Justice, Government/Political, Political Science, Psychology, Social Sciences, Sociology • VISUAL AND PERFORMING ARTS Art, Art History, Dramatic Arts, Fine Arts, Music, Music Performance, Studio Art, Theater • VOCATIONAL Business and Office, Carpentry, Painting, Textile and Clothing

Sports/Activities

• SPORTS-INTERCOLLEGIATE Baseball (M), Cross Country, Diving, Golf, Soccer (M), Swimming, Tennis, Track and Field • SPORTS-INTRAMURAL Badminton, Basketball, Cross Country, Diving, Ping-Pong, Soccer, Swimming, Track and Field, Volleyball • STUDENT LIFE ACTIVITIES Film, Musical Theater, Newspaper, Student Government

---

Most Selective **Maryland**

Johns Hopkins University

140 Garland Hall, 34th and Charles Streets
Baltimore, Maryland 21218
(410) 516-8171

School Enrollment: **3,125** Male: **1,875** Female: **1,250**
LD Enrollment: **28**

Admissions Contact: **Richard M. Fuller Director of Admissions**
LD Contact: **Martha Roseman Dean, Academic Advising**

Admissions

Application Information:
Application deadline: **January 1st**

Secondary School Information
Most Important Criteria For Admissions (1-strongest)

2 SAT/ACT	**3** Application	**1** School transcript
1 Class rank	**1** Course selection	**3** Personal statement
6 Interview	**4** Extra activities	**1** Psychoeducational
1 G.P.A.	Open admission	**5** Recommendations

Test Requirements:
Diagnostic testing waived: **Yes**
Untimed SAT: **Yes** Untimed ACT: **Yes** Untimed ACH: **Yes**
Documentation of LD required: **Yes**

Types of Disabilities Served
• Speech/Lang • Reading • ADD with LD
• Study skills • Spelling • ADD without LD
• Written express • Math • ADHD with LD
• Organizational • Fine Motor • ADHD without LD
• Perceptual

Admissions Process

If a student cannot read at a high level, they cannot succeed here.

Learning Disability Program

Students mainstreamed **100** % of the day
Recommended credits per semester: **12-15**
Counseling: Individual: **Yes** Group Counseling: **Yes**

Faculty:
Faculty advocate: **Yes** Meets with instructor: **As needed**

Diagnostic Testing

ADD	Personality	Perceptual skills	Spelling
ADHD	Organization	Fine motor skills	Reading
I.Q.	Handwriting	Spoken language	Study skills
Math	Social skills	Written language	

Tutoring:
Services rendered by:
•Graduates •Peers Faculty LD staff Teacher trainees

Tutorials

Grp.	Ind. Tutorials	Grp.	Ind. Tutorials
	• Math skills		• Word processing
	• Study skills		• Time management
	• Language arts		• Learning strategies
	• Written express		• Organizational skills

Academic Accommodations

Curriculum	Study Aids	Exams
Priority registration	• Typist	• Oral
Math waiver	Reader	• Untimed
Foreign lang. waiver	• Notetaker	• Take home
• Course substitution	• Proof reader	• With proctor
In Class	• Text on tape	On computer
• Calculators	Early syllabus	• Extended time
• Tape recorder	Taped handouts	On tape
• Word processor		Modified
• Priority seating		• Separate room

Graduation Requirements:
Course credits: **120** GPA: **2.0** Years to complete degree: **4-5 years**
Other requirements: **Math and a foreign language are not required for all majors.**

Program Strengths
We do not have a specific LD Program. Counseling is provided by the staff of the Office of Academic Counseling.

General Information:
Johns Hopkins University is a 4 year private university. Urban campus of 140 acres is Baltimore. Accessible by air, train or bus. Ski areas are 1 hour from campus. Beaches are 3 hours from campus. 3% of students are foreign. 4 residential halls on campus. Housing is guaranteed. Guaranteed through 1st year. 30 % of students join fraternities/sororities.

Accreditation: MSACS

SAT/ACT Scores:
Scores for incoming freshmen: **Verbal:** 5%below 500. 33%between 500 and 599. 55%between 600 and 699. 7%above 700. **Math:** 2% below 500. 11% between 500 and 599. 46% between 600 and 699. 41%above 700. 5% between 20 and 23. 6%between 24 and 25l. 28%between 26 and 28. 61% above 28.

Class Rank:
About 88% of the present freshmen class were in the upper 20% of their high school class. 97% were in the top 40% of their class.

Expenses:
Tuition: In-state: Full year: $17,000.00. Part-time: Per credit: $500.00. Part-time: Per course: $1,500.00. Room and board: $6,300.00

Majors
• AREA STUDIES Latin American, Middle Eastern • BUSINESS Economics • COMMUNICATIONS Creative Writing, English • ENGINEERING Bioengineering, Chemical, Civil/Environmental, Computer, Electrical, Geological, Materials, Mathematical, Mechanical • HUMANITIES Classics, Humanities, Philosophy • LANGUAGES Chinese, French, German, Italian, Russian, Spanish • SCIENCES Astronomy, Behavioral Biology, Biology, Biophysics, Chemistry, Geology, Mathematics, Meteorology, Oceanography, Physics • SOCIAL SCIENCES Anthropology, History, International Studies, Political Science, Psychology, Sociology • VISUAL AND PERFORMING ARTS Art History, Music

Sports/Activities
• SPORTS RELATED Cheerleading, Chess, Pep Band, Team Managers • SPORTS-INTERCOLLEGIATE Baseball (M), Basketball, Crew, Cross Country, Diving, Fencing, Field Hockey (F), Football (M), Golf, Lacrosse, Riflery, Soccer, Squash, Tennis, Track and Field, Volleyball, Water Polo, Wrestling • SPORTS-INTRAMURAL Basketball, Cross Country, Football (M), Golf, Ice Hockey (M), Lacrosse, Racquetball, Rugby, Sailing, Skiing - Snow, Softball, Squash, Swimming, Tennis, Track and Field, Wrestling (M) • STUDENT LIFE ACTIVITIES Choral, Concert Band, Dance, Debate, Drama Groups, Ethnic & Cultural Groups, Fraternities, Music Groups, Newspaper, Political Groups, Religious Organization, Sororities, Student Government, Symphony Orchestra, Yearbook

---

Less Selective **Maryland Program**

Montgomery Community College: Rockville Campus
51 Mannakee Street
Rockville, Maryland 20850
(301) 279-5038

School Enrollment: **21,571** Male: **9,350** Female: **12,221**
LD Enrollment: **250**

Admissions Contact: **Mr. James E. Darr, Dir. of Admissions**
LD Contact: **Janet Merrick, Coordinator**
Name of Program: **Learning Center Program**
Address: **Office of Disability Support Services**
Telephone: **(301) 279-5058**

Admissions

Application Information:
LD Students Applying: **50** Accepted: **50** Enrolled: **45**
Separate application: **Yes**
Application deadline: **None**
Applicant must apply **7** months in advance
Rolling Admissions: **Yes**

Secondary School Information
Most Important Criteria For Admissions (1-strongest)

SAT/ACT	Application	School transcript
Class rank	Course selection	Personal statement
Interview	Extra activities 1	Psychoeducational
G.P.A. 1	Open admission	Recommendations

Test Requirements:
Diagnostic testing waived: **Yes**
WAIS-R required: **Yes** Range accepted: **90+**
Documentation of LD required: **Yes**
Currency of diagnostic testing: **3 years**
Tests recommended: **WAIS, Woodcock-Johnson**

Types of Disabilities Served
Speech/Lang	• Reading	• ADD with LD
• Study skills	• Spelling	ADD without LD
• Written express	• Math	ADHD with LD
• Organizational	Fine Motor	ADHD without LD
• Perceptual		

Learning Disability Program
Program: Remedial: **Yes**
Program: Reinforces course work: **Yes**
Recommended credits per semester: **Varies**
Time required or recommended in learning center: **2 hours**
Counseling: Individual: **Yes**

Faculty:
Faculty: **7** Full time: **4** Part time: **3**
LD faculty with: BS/BA: **2** M.A.: **5**
Faculty advocate: **Yes** Meets with instructor: **As needed**

Maryland

Diagnostic Testing

ADD	Personality •	Perceptual skills	•	Spelling
ADHD•	Organization	Fine motor skills	•	Reading
• I.Q.	Handwriting	Spoken language	•	Study skills
• Math	Social skills•	Written language		

Tutoring:
Average size of group tutorials:
Services rendered by:
  Graduates •Peers •Faculty •LD staff Teacher trainees

Tutorials

Grp.	Ind.	Tutorials	Grp.	Ind.	Tutorials
	•	Math skills	•	•	Word processing
•		Study skills	•		Time management
•	•	Language arts	•		Learning strategies
•	•	Written express	•	•	Organizational skills

Academic Accommodations

Curriculum	Study Aids	Exams
Priority registration	• Typist	• Oral
Math waiver	Reader	Untimed
Foreign lang. waiver	• Notetaker	• Take home
Course substitution	Proof reader	• With proctor
In Class	• Text on tape	• On computer
• Calculators	Early syllabus	• Extended time
• Tape recorder	Taped handouts	On tape
• Word processor		• Modified
Priority seating		• Separate room

Graduation Requirements:
Course credits: **varies**

Program Strengths
The Learning Center Program at Montgomery College was established in 1978 to serve those students with specific learning disabilities who have the motivation and potential for success in regular college classes, but who require special support services because of deficits in basic skills, particularly language skills. The program is designed to assist learning disabled students in the development of effective oral and written communication skills so that they are better prepared to participate in the total college program.

General Information:
Montgomery Community College: Rockville Campus is a 2 year public college. Suburban campus 25 miles from Washington, D.C.. Accessible by air or bus . Housing is not guaranteed.

Accreditation:NAJCC (Community College)

Expenses:
Tuition: In-state: Full year: $52.00 per credit hour-maximum $780.00. Part-time: Per credit:$52.00. Tuition: Out-of-state: Full year: $138.00 per credit hour-maximum $2,070.00. Part-time: Per credit:$138.00.

Majors
• ARTS Advertising Art, Art History, Design, Illustration Design, Music • BUSINESS Accounting, Banking/Finance, Business Administration, Hotel Management, International Business, Marketing, Merchandising • COMMUNICATIONS Advertising, Broadcasting, Communication, Photography, Radio/Television, Telecommunications • COMPUTER SCIENCE Computer Applications, Computer Information Systems, Computer Science, Computer Technology, Programming • EDUCATION Art, Business, Child Care, Early Childhood, Elementary, Physical, Secondary, Secretarial • ENGINEERING Architectural Technology, Civil, Drafting, Electrical, Electromechanical Technology, Engineering Science, Engineering Technology, Mechanical • HEALTH SCIENCES Dental Assistant, Di-

etary Manager, Medical Laboratory Technology, Medical Records Technology, Medical Secretary, Nursing, Physician's Assistant • HUMANITIES Liberal Arts • MATHEMATICS Mathematics • PRE PROFESSIONAL City Planning, Dentistry, Interior Design, Medical Technology, Medicine, Optometry, Pharmacy • SCIENCES Cartography, Geography, Gerontology, Mathematics • SOCIAL SCIENCES Corrections, Geography, International Studies, Law Enforcement, Sociology • VISUAL AND PERFORMING ARTS Art, Art History, Dance, Music, Studio Art, Theater • VOCATIONAL Automobile Technology, Construction, Electronics Technology, Fire Science, Food Service, Landscape Technology, Legal Secretary, Library Assistant, Office Administration, Paralegal, Radiological Technology, Technical Writing, Word Processing

Sports/Activities
• SPORTS-INTERCOLLEGIATE Baseball (M), Soccer (M), Swimming (M), Tennis, Volleyball (F) • SPORTS-INTRAMURAL Baseball (M), Ping-Pong, Racquetball, Tennis, Volleyball • STUDENT LIFE ACTIVITIES Choral, Concert Band, Dance, Drama Groups, Magazine, Musical Theater, Newspaper, Political Groups, Radio/TV station, Religious Organization, Student Government

---

Very Selective   **Maryland Services**

Towson State University
Administration Building President's Office
Towson, Maryland 21204-7097
(410) 830-2112-(800) 225-5878

School Enrollment: **15,403** Male: **13,757** Female: **8,120**
LD Enrollment: **130**

Admissions Contact: **Ms. Linda Collins, Director of Admissions**
LD Contact: **Margaret Warrington, Coordinator**
Name of Program: **Handicapped Student Services**
Address: **Dowell Hall, 2L**
Telephone:**(410) 830-2638**

Admissions

Application Information:
Enrolled:**130**
Application deadline: **March 1st**
Rolling Admissions: **Yes**

Secondary School Information
Most Important Criteria For Admissions (1-strongest)

3 SAT/ACT	4 Application	1 School transcript
Class rank	Course selection	6 Personal statement
8 Interview	5 Extra activities	9 Psychoeducational
2 G.P.A.	Open admission	7 Recommendations

Test Requirements:
Diagnostic testing waived: **Yes**
Untimed SAT: **Yes** Untimed ACT: **Yes**
WAIS-R required: **Yes**
Documentation of LD required: **Yes**
Currency of diagnostic testing: **Within the past 3 years**

Types of Disabilities Served

• Speech/Lang	• Reading	• ADD with LD
• Study skills	• Spelling	• ADD without LD
• Written express	• Math	• ADHD with LD
• Organizational	• Fine Motor	• ADHD without LD
• Perceptual		

High School Course Requirements:
English: **4** Math: **3** Science: **2** Foreign Language: **2**

Learning Disability Program

Students mainstreamed **100** % of the day
Recommended credits per semester: **Varies**
Services only for LD students: **Yes**
Counseling: Individual: **Yes** Vocational Counseling: **Yes**

Faculty:

Faculty: **2** Full time: **2**
LD faculty with: BS/BA: **1**
Faculty advocate: **Yes** Meets with instructor: **As needed**

Diagnostic Testing

ADD	Personality	Perceptual skills	Spelling
ADHD	Organization	Fine motor skills	Reading
I.Q.	Handwriting	Spoken language	Study skills
Math	Social skills	Written language	

Tutoring:

Services rendered by:
Graduates •Peers •Faculty LD staff Teacher trainees

Tutorials

Grp.	Ind.	Tutorials	Grp.	Ind.	Tutorials
	•	Math skills			Word processing
	•	Study skills			Time management
	•	Language arts		•	Learning strategies
	•	Written express			Organizational skills

Academic Accommodations

Curriculum	Study Aids	Exams
Priority registration	• Typist	• Oral
Math waiver	• Reader	Untimed
Foreign lang. waiver	• Notetaker	Take home
Course substitution	Proof reader	• With proctor
In Class	• Text on tape	On computer
Calculators	Early syllabus	• Extended time
• Tape recorder	Taped handouts	On tape
• Word processor		Modified
• Priority seating		• Separate room

Graduation Requirements:
Course credits: **120** GPA: **2.0** Years to complete degree: **7-10** Language
waiver: **Yes**

Program Strengths

Although Towson State does not have a learning disability program, we do offer support services through our Handicapped Student Services Office. These services include note-taking, tutoring, remedial assistance in reading, writing and math, extra time on exams and assignments, tape recorded textbooks through Recordings for the Blind, a Learning Center, interpreters, counseling, oral exams, and a Writing Lab. Also, special consideration is given in admission when documented proof of disability is provided by school psychologist.

General Information:

Towson State University is a 4 year public university. Suburban campus of 306 acres is 1.5 miles from Baltimore. Accessible by air, train or bus. Ski areas are 75 miles from campus. Beaches are 180 miles from campus. 1.6% of students are foreign. 12 residential halls on campus. Housing is not guaranteed. 35 % of students remain on campus for the weekends. 10 % of students join fraternities/sororities.

Accreditation: MSACS

SAT/ACT Scores:
Scores for incoming freshmen: **Verbal:** 66% below 500. 27% between 500 and 599. 4% between 600 and 699. 1% above 700. **Math:** 42% below 500. 46% between 500 and 599. 11% between 600 and 699. 1% above 700.

Expenses:
Tuition: In-state: Full year: $1,848.00. Part-time: Per credit: Part-time: $86.00. Tuition: Out-of-state: Full year: $4,058.00. Part-time: Per credit: $86.00. Room and board: $4,290.00

Majors

• BUSINESS Accounting, Business Administration, Economics • COMMUNICATIONS Communication • COMPUTER SCIENCE Computer Science • EDUCATION Art, Early Childhood, Elementary, General, Music, Secondary • HEALTH SCIENCES Health, Medical Laboratory Technology, Nursing, Occupational Therapy, Speech/Audiology and Speech • HUMANITIES English/Writing/Literature, Philosophy • LANGUAGES French, German, Spanish • SCIENCES Biology, Chemistry, Computer Science, Mathematics, Natural Science, Physics • SOCIAL SCIENCES Anthropology, Geography, History, Psychology, Social Science, Sociology • SPECIAL EDUCATION Occupational Therapy • VISUAL AND PERFORMING ARTS Art, Dance, Dance Education, Music, Theater

Sports/Activities

• SPORTS RELATED Cheerleading, Chess, Marching Band, Pep Band, Team Managers • SPORTS-INTERCOLLEGIATE Baseball (M), Basketball, Cross Country, Diving, Field Hockey (F), Football (M), Golf (M), Gymnastics (F), Lacrosse, Soccer, Softball (F), Swimming, Tennis, Track and Field, Volleyball (F) • SPORTS-INTRAMURAL Basketball, Bowling, Cycling, Ping-Pong, Racquetball, Soccer, Softball, Tennis, Volleyball, Weight Lifting, Wrestling (M) • STUDENT LIFE ACTIVITIES Academic Clubs, Choral, Community Service, Concert Band, Dance, Debate, Drama Groups, Ethnic & Cultural Groups, Film, Fraternities, Jazz Band, Magazine, Music Groups, Musical Theater, Newspaper, Orchestra, Political Groups, Radio/TV station, Religious Organization, Sororities, Student Government, Symphony Orchestra, Yearbook

Less Selective	Maryland
	Services

University of Maryland: Eastern Shore
Princess Anne, Maryland 21853-1299
(301) 651-2200

School Enrollment: **1,700** Male: **680** Female: **1,020**

Admissions Contact: **Mr. Rochell Peoples, Director of Admissions**
LD Contact: **Dr. Diann Showell, Director**
Name of Program: **Student Special Services**
Telephone: **(301) 651-2200 Ext. 259**

Admissions

Application Information:
Application deadline: **June 20th**
Rolling Admissions: **Yes**

Secondary School Information
Most Important Criteria For Admissions (1-strongest)

4 SAT/ACT	**5** Application	**2**	School transcript
3 Class rank	**6** Course selection	**11**	Personal statement
7 Interview	**9** Extra activities	**10**	Psychoeducational
1 G.P.A.	Open admission	**8**	Recommendations

Maryland

Types of Disabilities Served

- Speech/Lang
- Study skills
- Written express
- Organizational
- Perceptual
- Reading
- Spelling
- Math
- Fine Motor

ADD with LD
ADD without LD
ADHD with LD
ADHD without LD

Learning Disability Program

Counseling: Individual: **Yes** Group Counseling: **Yes**

Faculty:
Faculty: **6** Full time: **6**
Faculty advocate: **Yes** Meets with instructor: **As needed**

Diagnostic Testing

ADD	Personality	Perceptual skills	Spelling
ADHD	Organization	Fine motor skills	Reading
I.Q.	Handwriting	Spoken language	Study skills
Math	Social skills	Written language	

Tutoring:
Average size of group tutorials: **3-5**
Services rendered by:
Graduates •Peers •Faculty LD staff Teacher trainees

Tutorials

Grp.	Ind.	Tutorials	Grp.	Ind.	Tutorials
	•	Math skills		•	Word processing
•		Study skills		•	Time management
		Language arts		•	Learning strategies
•		Written express	•		Organizational skills

Academic Accommodations

Curriculum	Study Aids	Exams
Priority registration	Typist	• Oral
• Math waiver	Reader	Untimed
• Foreign lang. waiver	• Notetaker	• Take home
• Course substitution	• Proof reader	With proctor
In Class	Text on tape	On computer
• Calculators	Early syllabus	• Extended time
• Tape recorder	Taped handouts	On tape
• Word processor		• Modified
Priority seating		Separate room

Program Strengths

Our LD students are mainstreamed, yet they receive special attention as needed. Most of our support efforts are directed toward the individual student.

General Information:

University of Maryland: Eastern Shore is a 4 year public university. Rural campus of 540 acres is 15 miles from Salisbury. Accessible by air or bus. Ski areas are 250 miles from campus. Beaches are 35 miles from campus. 4% of students are foreign. 11 residential halls on campus. Housing is not guaranteed.35 % of students remain on campus for the weekends. 25 % of students join fraternities/sororities.

Accreditation: MSACS

SAT/ACT Scores:
Scores for incoming freshmen: **Verbal:**95%below 500. 5%between 500 and 599. **Math:**91% below 500. 6% between 500 and 599. 3% between 600 and 699.

Expenses:
Tuition: In-state: Full year: $2,102.000. Part-time: Per credit:$104.00. Tuition: Out-of-state: Full year: $5,752.00. Room and board: $3,532.00

Majors

• BUSINESS Accounting, Business Administration, Business Education, Business Management, Hotel and Restaurant Managemen • COMMUNICATIONS Communication, English • COMPUTER SCIENCE Computer Science, Data Processing • EDUCATION Agricultural, Art, Elementary, English, Health, Industrial, Mathematics, Music, Physical, Social Studies, Special • ENGINEERING Aerospace, Electrical, Engineering Science, Environmental/Water Resources • HEALTH SCIENCES Medical Technology, Occupational Therapy, Physical Therapy • HUMANITIES Liberal Arts • PREPROFESSIONAL Law, Medicine, Pharmacy • SCIENCES Agricultural, Biology, Chemistry, Mathematics • SOCIAL SCIENCES Criminology, Family Counseling, History, Social Sciences, Sociology • VISUAL AND PERFORMING ARTS Music • VOCATIONAL Construction, Electronics Technology, Fashion Design, Fashion Mechandizing, Food Service, Home Economics

Sports/Activities

• SPORTS-INTERCOLLEGIATE Baseball (M), Basketball, Boxing (M), Cross Country, Golf, Softball (F), Tennis, Track and Field, Volleyball (F), Wrestling (M) • SPORTS-INTRAMURAL Bowling, Softball (F), Swimming • STUDENT LIFE ACTIVITIES Choral, Concert Band, Drama Groups, Fraternities, Jazz Band, Music Groups, Newspaper, Political Groups, Radio/TV station, Sororities, Student Government, Yearbook

---

Selective
Maryland
Services

Western Maryland College
Westminster, Maryland 21157-4390
(410) 857-2504

School Enrollment: **1,200** Male: **520** Female: **680**
LD Enrollment: **45** Male: **35** Female: **10**

Admissions Contact: **Martha O'Connell, Director of Admissions**
LD Contact: **Tom Gibbon, Coordinator, 504 Services**
Name of Program: **Academic Skills Center**
Telephone:**(410) 857-2504**

Admissions

Application Information:
Enrolled:**45**
Application deadline: **March 15th**
Rolling Admissions: **Yes**

Secondary School Information
Most Important Criteria For Admissions (1-strongest)

9 SAT/ACT	Application	2	School transcript
5 Class rank	4 Course selection	7	Personal statement
8 Interview	10 Extra activities	1	Psychoeducational
3 G.P.A.	Open admission	6	Recommendations

Test Requirements:
Diagnostic testing waived: **Yes**
Untimed SAT: **Yes** Untimed ACT: **Yes**
Range accepted: **90+**
Documentation of LD required: **Yes**
Currency of diagnostic testing: **3 years**
Tests recommended: **WAIS-R, Woodcock Johnson Achievement or similar.**

Types of Disabilities Served
- Speech/Lang
- Study skills
- Written express
- Organizational
- Perceptual
- Reading
- Spelling
- Math
- Fine Motor
- ADD with LD
- ADD without LD
- ADHD with LD
- ADHD without LD

Admissions Process

Application form, official transcripts, official scores from SAT or ACT, $25.00 non-refundable fee. Visit/interview strongly recommended.

High School Course Requirements:
English: **4** Math: **3** Science: **2** Foreign Language: **2**
Waivers to standard high school courses
Foreign Language : **Yes** Course substitution: **Yes**

Learning Disability Program
Special orientation for LD students: **Yes**
Program: Reinforces course work: **Yes**
Program available through:**All year**
Students mainstreamed **100** % of the day
Recommended credits per semester: **12-15**
Time required or recommended in learning center: **1-2 hours**
Services available for all students: **Yes**
Counseling: Individual: **Yes** Group Counseling: **Yes** Vocational Counseling: **Yes**
Support groups are available:**Monthly support group meetings.**

Faculty:
Faculty: **3** Including Director: **Yes** Full time: **1** Part time: **2** M.A.: **2** Ph.D.: **1**
Faculty advocate: **Yes** Meets with instructor: **As needed**

Diagnostic Testing
ADD	Personality	Perceptual skills	Spelling
ADHD	Organization	Fine motor skills	Reading
I.Q.	Handwriting	Spoken language	Study skills
Math	Social skills	Written language	

Tutoring:
Average size of group tutorials: **5**
Services rendered by:
- Graduates
- Peers
Faculty
- LD staff
Teacher trainees

Tutorials
Grp.	Ind.	Tutorials	Grp.	Ind.	Tutorials
•	•	Math skills	•	•	Word processing
•	•	Study skills	•	•	Time management
	•	Language arts	•	•	Learning strategies
	•	Written express	•	•	Organizational skills

Academic Accommodations
Curriculum	Study Aids	Exams
• Priority registration	Typist	• Oral
Math waiver	• Reader	• Untimed
• Foreign lang. waiver	• Notetaker	• Take home
• Course substitution	• Proof reader	• With proctor
In Class	• Text on tape	• On computer
• Calculators	• Early syllabus	• Extended time
• Tape recorder	Taped handouts	• On tape
Word processor		• Modified
• Priority seating		• Separate room

Graduation Requirements:
Course credits: **120** GPA: **2.0** Years to complete degree: **5** Language waiver: **Yes**

Program Strengths
The small size of the college makes an ideal environment for students with learning disabilities. The faculty and administration are committed to meeting individual needs. Students are fully mainstreamed and benefit from total involvement in a liberal arts college.

General Information:
Western Maryland College is a 4 year independent college. Suburban campus of 160 acres is 35 miles from Baltimore. Accessible by bus. Ski areas are 25 miles from campus. Beaches are 150 miles from campus. 10% of students are foreign. 7 residential halls on campus. Housing is guaranteed.70-90 % of students remain on campus for the weekends. 33 % of students join fraternities/sororities.

Accreditation:MSACS, MSDE

SAT/ACT Scores:
Scores for incoming freshmen:**Verbal:**35%below 500. 35%between 500 and 599. 20%between 600 and 699. 10%above 700. **Math:**35% below 500. 35% between 500 and 599. 20% between 600 and 699. 10%above 700.

Class Rank:
About 30% of the present freshmen class were in the upper 20% of their high school class. 50% were in the top 40% of their class. 75% were in the top 60% of their class. 100% were in the top 80% of their class.

Expenses:
Tuition: In-state: Full year: $11,590.00. Room and board: $4,390.00 Cost of LD program:Under consideration

Majors
• AREA STUDIES American • ART Art History, Dramatic Arts, Graphic Art • BUSINESS Business Economics, Economics • COMMUNICATIONS Communication, English • EDUCATION Elementary, Physical, Secondary • LANGUAGES English, French, German, Spanish • PRE PROFESSIONAL Social Work • RELIGIOUS STUDIES Philosophy, Religion & Theology • SCIENCES Biology, Chemistry, Mathematics, Physics, Psychobiology • SOCIAL SCIENCES History, Political Science, Psychology, Sociology • VISUAL AND PERFORMING ARTS Art, Music, Theater

Sports/Activities
• SPORTS RELATED Cheerleading, Team Managers • SPORTS-INTERCOLLEGIATE Baseball (M), Basketball (F), Basketball (M), Cross Country (F), Cross Country (M), Field Hockey (F), Football (M), Golf (F), Golf (M), Lacrosse (F), Lacrosse (M), Soccer (F), Soccer (M), Softball (F), Swimming (F), Swimming (M), Tennis (F), Tennis (M), Track and Field (F), Track and Field (M), Volleyball (F), Wrestling (M) • SPORTS-INTRAMURAL Badminton (F), Badminton (M), Basketball (F), Basketball (M), Football (F), Football (M), Golf (F), Golf (M), Ice Hockey (M), Softball (F), Softball (M), Volleyball (F), Volleyball (M) • STUDENT LIFE ACTIVITIES Academic Clubs, Choral, Community Service, Concert Band, Drama Groups, Ethnic & Cultural Groups, Film, Fraternities, Jazz Band, Magazine, Music Groups, Musical Theater, Newspaper, Orchestra, Political Groups, Radio/TV station, Religious Organization, Sororities, Student Government, Yearbook

Less Selective

Maryland
Services

Wor-Wic Tech Community College
1409 Wesley Drive
Salisbury, Maryland 21801
(410) 749-8181

School Enrollment: **1,200**
LD Enrollment: **3**

Admissions Contact: **Holly Smith, Director of Admissions**
LD Contact: **Karen Ann Goyer, Director of Counseling**
Name of Program: **Handicapped Student Services**
Address: **1409 Wesley Dr.**
Telephone:**(410) 749-8181**

Admissions

Application Information:
LD Students Applying: **3** Accepted: **3** Enrolled:**3**

Secondary School Information
Most Important Criteria For Admissions (1-strongest)

SAT/ACT	Application	School transcript
Class rank	Course selection	Personal statement
Interview	Extra activities	Psychoeducational
G.P.A.	**1** Open admission	Recommendations

Test Requirements:
Diagnostic testing waived: **Yes**
Untimed SAT: **Yes** Untimed ACT: **Yes**

Types of Disabilities Served
- Speech/Lang
- Study skills
- Written express
- Organizational
- Perceptual
- Reading
- Spelling
- Math
- Fine Motor
- ADD with LD
- ADD without LD
- ADHD with LD
- ADHD without LD

Admissions Process

Fill out application, send high school transcript or GED copy, take diagnostic tests, and register.

Learning Disability Program
Special orientation for LD students: **Yes**
Program: Reinforces course work: **Yes**
Students mainstreamed **100** % of the day
Recommended credits per semester: **9-12**
Counseling: Individual: **Yes** Vocational Counseling: **Yes**

Diagnostic Testing

ADD	• Personality	Perceptual skills	Spelling
ADHD	Organization	Fine motor skills	• Reading
I.Q.	Handwriting	Spoken language	• Study skills
• Math	Social skills	• Written language	

Tutoring:
Average size of group tutorials: **1**
Services rendered by:
Graduates •Peers •Faculty •LD staff Teacher trainees

Tutorials

Grp.	Ind.	Tutorials	Grp.	Ind.	Tutorials
		Math skills			Word processing
		Study skills			Time management
		Language arts			Learning strategies
		Written express			Organizational skills

Academic Accommodations

Curriculum	Study Aids	Exams
Priority registration	Typist	• Oral
Math waiver	• Reader	• Untimed
Foreign lang. waiver	• Notetaker	Take home
Course substitution	Proof reader	• With proctor
In Class	• Text on tape	On computer
• Calculators	Early syllabus	• Extended time
• Tape recorder	Taped handouts	On tape
• Word processor		• Modified
• Priority seating		• Separate room

Graduation Requirements:
Course credits: **varies** Years to complete degree: **2 minimum** Math waiver: **Yes**
Other requirements: **Diagnostic testing, completion of any develomental course work required.**

General Information:
Wor-Wic Tech Community College is a 2 year public college. Rural campus of 1,700 acres is 150 miles from Baltimore or D.C.. Accessible by air or car. Housing is not guaranteed.

Accreditation:

Expenses:
Tuition: In-state: Full year: In county $44.00 per credit hour. Part-time: Per credit:$102.00. Part-time: Per course: $306.00. Part-time: Per credit:$145.00. Part-time: Per course:$435.00

Majors
• BUSINESS Accounting, Banking/Finance, Business Administration, Business Management, Clerical, Data Processing, Hotel & Restaurant Management, Secretarial Science • COMPUTER SCIENCE Computer Science, Data Processing • HEALTH SCIENCES Nursing, Radiological Technology • SOCIAL SCIENCES Human Service, Law Enforcement • VOCATIONAL Legal Secretary, Office Administration, Radiological Technology, Secretarial, Word Processing

Sports/Activities
• SPORTS-INTERCOLLEGIATE • SPORTS-INTRAMURAL Soccer, Volleyball • STUDENT LIFE ACTIVITIES Academic Clubs, Community Service, Newspaper, Student Government

Less Selective   **Massachusetts Program**

American International College
1000 State Street
Springfield, Massachusetts 01109-9989
(413) 737-7000

School Enrollment: **1,400** Male: **742** Female: **658**
LD Enrollment: **102**

Admissions Contact: **Peter Miller, Dean of Admissions**
LD Contact: **Mary Saltus, Coordinator**
Name of Program: **Supportive Learning Services**
Address: **1000 State Street**
Telephone:**(413) 737-7000 Ext. 426**

Admissions

Application Information:
Application deadline: **May**
Rolling Admissions: **Yes**

Secondary School Information
Most Important Criteria For Admissions (1-strongest)

8	SAT/ACT	6	Application	1	School transcript
7	Class rank	2	Course selection		Personal statement
4	Interview	9	Extra activities	3	Psychoeducational
1	G.P.A.		Open admission	5	Recommendations

Test Requirements:
Diagnostic testing waived: **Yes**
Untimed SAT: **Yes** Untimed ACT: **Yes**
WAIS-R required: **Yes**
Documentation of LD required: **Yes**
Currency of diagnostic testing: **after 16.5 years of age**
Tests recommended: **Standardized achievement tests: math, reading, spelling, written expression.**

Types of Disabilities Served
- Speech/Lang
- Study skills
- Written express
- Organizational
- Perceptual
- Reading
- Spelling
- Math
- Fine Motor
- ADD with LD
- ADD without LD
- ADHD with LD
- ADHD without LD

Admissions Process

Submit application, letter or recommendation, SAT, transcript, WAIS-R subtest scores and accompanying report. Interview required.

High School Course Requirements:
English: **4** Math: **2** Science: **2**

Learning Disability Program
Students mainstreamed **100** % of the day
Recommended credits per semester: **4 courses**
Time required or recommended in learning center: **2 hours**
Services only for LD students: **Yes**
Counseling: Individual: **Yes** Group Counseling: **Yes** Vocational Counseling: **Yes**
Support groups are available:**Yes**

Faculty:
Faculty: **20** Full time: **10** Part time: **10**
LD faculty with: BS/BA: **15** M.A.: **5**
Faculty advocate: **Yes** Meets with instructor: **As needed**

Diagnostic Testing
ADD	Personality	Perceptual skills	Spelling
ADHD	Organization	Fine motor skills	Reading
I.Q.	Handwriting	Spoken language	Study skills
Math	Social skills	Written language	

Tutoring:
Average size of group tutorials: **1:1**
Services rendered by:
Graduates   Peers   Faculty   •LD staff   Teacher trainees

Tutorials
Grp.	Ind.	Tutorials	Grp.	Ind.	Tutorials
•	•	Math skills		•	Word processing
•	•	Study skills	•	•	Time management
		Language arts	•	•	Learning strategies
	•	Written express	•	•	Organizational skills

Academic Accommodations

Curriculum	Study Aids	Exams
Priority registration	Typist	• Oral
Math waiver	Reader	Untimed
• Foreign lang. waiver	Notetaker	• Take home
Course substitution	• Proof reader	With proctor
In Class	• Text on tape	On computer
• Calculators	Early syllabus	• Extended time
• Tape recorder	Taped handouts	On tape
• Word processor		• Modified
Priority seating		Separate room

Graduation Requirements:
Course credits: **120** GPA: **2.0**

Program Strengths

The program is housed in its own facility and is staffed by a full-time coordinator and assistant, clerical staff and a professional teaching staff called Instructional Supervisors. At the heart of services provided is a minimum of two hours of regularly scheduled direct, one-to-one assistance provided by an Instructional Supervisor who is a learning disabilities specialist. In conjunction with the student, the specialist develops an individually tailored support program determined by the student's needs. A priority is given to practical assistance designed to help the student negotiate the ongoing demands of the undergraduate curriculum.

General Information:

American International College is a 4 year private university. Urban campus of 53 acres is 30 miles from Hartford. Accessible by air, train or bus. Ski areas are 15 miles from campus. Beaches are 65 miles from campus. 7% of students are foreign. 5 residential halls on campus. Housing is guaranteed.Guaranteed through 4th year. 70 % of students remain on campus for the weekends.

Accreditation:NEACS

SAT/ACT Scores:
Scores for incoming freshmen:**Verbal:**81%below 500. 17%between 500 and 599. 3%between 600 and 699. **Math:**83% below 500. 14% between 500 and 599. 3% between 600 and 699.

Class Rank:
About 18% of the present freshmen class were in the upper 20% of their high school class. 43% were in the top 40% of their class. 81% were in the

top 60% of their class. 97% were in the top 80% of their class.

Expenses:
Tuition: In-state: Full year: $8,352.00. Part-time: Per credit:$261.00.
Room and board: $4,132.00 Cost of LD program:$2,800.00

Majors
• BUSINESS Accounting, Banking, Business Administration, Business Education, Business Management, Economics, Finance, Insurance, International Business Managem, Management, Marketing, Personnel, Public Administration • COMMUNICATIONS English • COMPUTER SCIENCE Computer Science, Data Processing • EDUCATION Early Childhood, Elementary, Middle School, School Psychology, Secondary, Special • HEALTH SCIENCES Medical Technology, Nursing • HUMANITIES Liberal Arts, Philosophy • LANGUAGES Spanish • PREPROFESSIONAL Dentistry, Law, Medicine, Veterinarian • SCIENCES Biochemistry, Biology, Chemistry, Mathematics • SOCIAL SCIENCES Criminal Justice, Government/Political, History, Psychology, Sociology

Sports/Activities
• SPORTS-INTERCOLLEGIATE Baseball, Baseball (F), Baseball (M), Basketball, Basketball (F), Basketball (M), Football (M), Golf (F), Golf (M), Horseback Riding, Horseback Riding (F), Horseback Riding (M), Ice Hockey (M), Lacrosse, Lacrosse (M), Soccer, Soccer (F), Soccer (M), Softball, Softball (F), Softball (M), Tennis, Tennis (F), Tennis (M), Volleyball (F), Wrestling (M) • SPORTS-INTRAMURAL Basketball, Horseback Riding, Skiing - Snow, Soccer, Swimming, Volleyball • STUDENT LIFE ACTIVITIES Choral, Fraternities, Musical Theater, Newspaper, Radio/TV station, Religious Organization, Sororities, Student Government, Yearbook

---

Selective   **Massachusetts**

Anna Maria College for Men & Women
Sunset Lane
Paxton, Massachusetts 01612
(508) 757-4586

School Enrollment: **681** Male: **172** Female: **509**

Admissions Contact: **Christopher Lydon, Dir. Enroll. Management**
LD Contact: **Olivia Tarleton, Director**
Name of Program: **Learning Assistance Center**
Telephone:**(508) 757-4586 Ext. 229**

Admissions

Application Information:
Application deadline: **June 1st**
Rolling Admissions: **Yes**

Secondary School Information
Most Important Criteria For Admissions (1-strongest)

8 SAT/ACT	**5** Application	**1** School transcript
3 Class rank	**4** Course selection	**7** Personal statement
10 Interview	**6** Extra activities	**11** Psychoeducational
2 G.P.A.	Open admission	**9** Recommendations

Test Requirements:
Untimed SAT: **Yes** Untimed ACT: **Yes** Untimed ACH: **Yes**
Documentation of LD required: **Yes**

Types of Disabilities Served
• Speech/Lang	• Reading	ADD with LD
• Study skills	• Spelling	ADD without LD
• Written express	• Math	ADHD with LD
• Organizational	• Fine Motor	ADHD without LD
• Perceptual		

High School Course Requirements:
English: **4** Math: **3** Science: **2** Foreign Language: **2**

Learning Disability Program
Program: Reinforces course work: **Yes**
Services available for all students: **Yes**
Counseling: Individual: **Yes**

Faculty:
Faculty: **3** Full time: **1** Part time: **2**
Faculty advocate: **Yes** Meets with instructor: **As needed**

Diagnostic Testing
ADD	Personality	Perceptual skills	Spelling
ADHD	Organization	Fine motor skills	Reading
I.Q.	Handwriting	Spoken language	Study skills
Math	Social skills	Written language	

Tutoring:
Services rendered by:
Graduates   •Peers   •Faculty   •LD staff   Teacher trainees

Tutorials
Grp.	Ind.	Tutorials	Grp.	Ind.	Tutorials
	•	Math skills		•	Word processing
	•	Study skills		•	Time management
		Language arts		•	Learning strategies
	•	Written express		•	Organizational skills

Academic Accommodations
Curriculum	Study Aids	Exams
Priority registration	Typist	• Oral
Math waiver	Reader	• Untimed
• Foreign lang. waiver	• Notetaker	Take home
Course substitution	Proof reader	With proctor
In Class	• Text on tape	On computer
Calculators	Early syllabus	• Extended time
• Tape recorder	Taped handouts	On tape
• Word processor		Modified
Priority seating		• Separate room

Program Strengths
The Learning Assistance Center creates an Individualized Education Plan to assist the student with the adjustment to college. Communication is established with the faculty to ensure help is available. With an undergraduate population of 600, individual attention is the cornerstone of the program.

General Information:
Anna Maria College for Men & Women is a 4 year private Roman Catholic college. Suburban campus of 180 acres is 8 miles from Worcester. Accessible by air, train or bus. Ski areas are 20 miles from campus. Beaches are 90 miles from campus. 6% of students are foreign. 1 residential halls on campus. Housing is guaranteed.Guaranteed through 4th year. 50 % of students remain on campus for the weekends.

Accreditation:NEACS

SAT/ACT Scores:
Scores for incoming freshmen:**Verbal:**87%below 500. 11%between 500 and 599. 1%between 600 and 699. 1%above 700. **Math:**77% below 500. 21% between 500 and 599. 2% between 600 and 699.

Class Rank:
About 26% of the present freshmen class were in the upper 20% of their high school class. 51% were in the top 40% of their class. 79% were in the top 60% of their class. 90% were in the top 80% of their class.

Expenses:
Tuition: In-state: Full year: $9,980.00. Room and board: $4,650.00

Majors

• ARTS Art Therapy, Commercial Art, Music, Music Performance, Music Therapy • BUSINESS Accounting, Banking/Finance, Business Administration, Business Management, Management, Marketing • COMMUNICATIONS English, Literature • EDUCATION Art, Art Therapy, Early Childhood, Elementary, Music, Music Therapy • HEALTH SCIENCES Medical Laboratory Technology • HUMANITIES English/Writing/Literature, Liberal Arts • LANGUAGES Spanish • PREPROFESSIONAL Dentistry, Law, Social Work • SCIENCES Biology • SOCIAL SCIENCES Criminal Justice, Government/Political, History, Political Science, Psychology • VISUAL AND PERFORMING ARTS Art, Music • VOCATIONAL Paralegal

Sports/Activities

• SPORTS RELATED Cheerleading • SPORTS-INTERCOLLEGIATE Baseball (M), Basketball (F), Basketball (M), Field Hockey (F), Golf (M), Soccer (F), Soccer (M), Softball (F), Volleyball (F) • SPORTS-INTRAMURAL Basketball (F), Basketball (M), Field Hockey (F), Soccer, Soccer (F), Softball, Tennis (F), Tennis (M) • STUDENT LIFE ACTIVITIES Academic Clubs, Choral, Community Service, Drama Groups, Ethnic & Cultural Groups, Music Groups, Religious Organization, Student Government, Yearbook

Less Selective

Massachusetts Accommodations

Aquinas College at Newton
15 Walnut Park
Newton, Massachusetts 02158
(617) 969-4400

School Enrollment: **150** Female: **150**

Admissions Contact: **Georgia Hall, Director of Admissions**
LD Contact: **Sister Eleanor K. Shea, Director**
Name of Program: **Academic Skills Center**

Admissions

Application Information:
Application deadline: **August 31st**
Rolling Admissions: **Yes**

Secondary School Information
Most Important Criteria For Admissions (1-strongest)

SAT/ACT	1	Application	1 School transcript
2 Class rank		Course selection	3 Personal statement
2 Interview	3	Extra activities	2 Psychoeducational
1 G.P.A.		Open admission	1 Recommendations

Test Requirements:
Standardized tests waived: **Yes**

Types of Disabilities Served
• Speech/Lang • Reading • ADD with LD
• Study skills • Spelling • ADD without LD
• Written express • Math • ADHD with LD
• Organizational • Fine Motor • ADHD without LD
• Perceptual

Learning Disability Program
Syllabus available during orientation:**Yes**
Program: Remedial: **Yes**
Program: Reinforces course work: **Yes**
Recommended credits per semester: **Varies**
Services available for all students: **Yes**
Counseling: Individual: **Yes**

Faculty:
Faculty: **1**
Faculty advocate: **Yes** Meets with instructor: **As needed**

Diagnostic Testing
ADD	Personality	Perceptual skills	Spelling
ADHD	Organization	Fine motor skills	• Reading
• I.Q.	Handwriting	Spoken language	Study skills
Math	Social skills	Written language	

Tutoring:
Services rendered by:
Graduates •Peers •Faculty LD staff Teacher trainees

Tutorials
Grp.	Ind.	Tutorials	Grp.	Ind.	Tutorials
•	•	Math skills	•	•	Word processing
•	•	Study skills	•	•	Time management
		Language arts	•	•	Learning strategies
•	•	Written express	•	•	Organizational skills

Academic Accommodations
Curriculum	Study Aids	Exams
Priority registration	Typist	• Oral
Math waiver	Reader	• Untimed
Foreign lang. waiver	• Notetaker	• Take home
• Course substitution	• Proof reader	• With proctor
In Class	Text on tape	On computer
• Calculators	Early syllabus	• Extended time
• Tape recorder	Taped handouts	On tape
• Word processor		• Modified
• Priority seating		• Separate room

Graduation Requirements:
Course credits: **60**

Program Strengths
Small college with small classes. Individualized learning. Learning Skills Center.

General Information:
Aquinas College at Newton is a 2 year private Roman Catholic college. Suburban campus of 14 acres is 5 miles from Boston. Accessible by bus. Ski areas are 1-1/2 hours from campus. Beaches are 1-1/2 hours from campus. 10% of students are foreign. Housing is not guaranteed.

Massachusetts

Accreditation: NEACS

Expenses:
Tuition: In-state: Full year: $6,700.00.

Majors

• BUSINESS Accounting, Business Administration, Business Management, Marketing • COMPUTER SCIENCE Data Processing • EDUCATION Early Childhood • HUMANITIES Liberal Arts • SOCIAL SCIENCES Human Service, Social Sciences • VOCATIONAL Business and Office

Sports/Activities

• SPORTS-INTRAMURAL Softball, Volleyball

Selective   **Massachusetts**
                                      Services

Bentley College
175 Forest Street
Waltham, Massachusetts 02154-4705
(617) 891-2244

School Enrollment: **5,506** Male: **2,787** Female: **2,719**

Admissions Contact: **Ed Gillis, Director of Admissions**
LD Contact: **Dr. Roger Danchise, Director**
Name of Program: **Counseling & Student Development**
Telephone:**(617) 891-2274**

Admissions

Application Information:
Application deadline: **March 10th**
Notified when: **April 1st**

Secondary School Information
Most Important Criteria For Admissions (1-strongest)

2	SAT/ACT	3	Application	1	School transcript
1	Class rank	2	Course selection		Personal statement
3	Interview	3	Extra activities		Psychoeducational
1	G.P.A.		Open admission	3	Recommendations

Test Requirements:
Untimed SAT: **Yes**
Documentation of LD required: **Yes**

Types of Disabilities Served

Speech/Lang	Reading	ADD with LD
Study skills	Spelling	ADD without LD
Written express	Math	ADHD with LD
Organizational	Fine Motor	ADHD without LD
Perceptual		

Admissions Process

Application with standardized scores required. No special procedures for students with learning disabilities. They may or may not self-identify.

Learning Disability Program

Services available for all students: **Yes**
Counseling: Individual: **Yes** Group Counseling: **Yes**

Diagnostic Testing

ADD	Personality	Perceptual skills	Spelling
ADHD	Organization	Fine motor skills	Reading
I.Q.	Handwriting	Spoken language	Study skills
Math	Social skills	Written language	

Tutoring:
Average size of group tutorials:
Services rendered by:

Graduates	•Peers	•Faculty	LD staff	Teacher trainees

Tutorials

Grp.	Ind.	Tutorials	Grp.	Ind.	Tutorials
•	•	Math skills	•	•	Word processing
•	•	Study skills	•	•	Time management
•	•	Language arts	•	•	Learning strategies
•	•	Written express	•	•	Organizational skills

Academic Accommodations

Curriculum	Study Aids	Exams
• Priority registration	Typist	• Oral
Math waiver	Reader	Untimed
Foreign lang. waiver	• Notetaker	• Take home
• Course substitution	Proof reader	• With proctor
In Class	• Text on tape	On computer
• Calculators	Early syllabus	• Extended time
• Tape recorder	Taped handouts	On tape
• Word processor		• Modified
• Priority seating		Separate room

Graduation Requirements:
Course credits: **120** GPA: **2.0** Years to complete degree: **Variable**

Program Strengths

The Office of Counseling and Student Development at Bentley College provides counseling for all students with learning disabilities. Counseling and advocacy are the key roles assumed by the office. In addition to services in this office, the staff will work with each student to insure that he or she receives every accommodation needed.

General Information:

Bentley College is a 4 year private college. Suburban campus of 110 acres is 9 miles from Boston. Accessible by air, train or bus. 5% of students are foreign. Housing is not guaranteed.

Accreditation: NEACS, AACSB

SAT/ACT Scores:
Scores for incoming freshmen: **Verbal:** 72% below 500. 25% between 500 and 599. 4% between 600 and 699. **Math:** 26% below 500. 51% between 500 and 599. 22% between 600 and 699. 2% above 700.

Class Rank:
About 43% of the present freshmen class were in the upper 20% of their high school class. 79% were in the top 40% of their class. 97% were in the top 60% of their class. 99% were in the top 80% of their class.

Expenses:
Tuition: In-state: Full year: $10,760.00. Room and board: $4,520.00

Majors

• BUSINESS Accounting, Banking, Business Administration, Business Communication, Business Economics, Business Management, Economics, Finance, Management, Marketing • COMMUNICATIONS English • COMPUTER SCIENCE Information Science & Systems • HUMANITIES Philosophy • PREPROFESSIONAL Legal Assistant • VOCATIONAL Paralegal

Sports/Activities

• SPORTS RELATED Pep Band • SPORTS-INTERCOLLEGIATE Baseball (M), Basketball, Cross Country, Field Hockey, Football (M), Golf (M), Ice Hockey (M), Lacrosse (M), Soccer (M), Softball (F), Swimming, Tennis, Track and Field, Volleyball (F) • SPORTS-INTRAMURAL Baseball (M), Basketball, Ice Hockey (M), Soccer (F), Softball, Volleyball • STUDENT LIFE ACTIVITIES Choral, Dance, Drama Groups, Ethnic & Cultural Groups, Fraternities, Jazz Band, Magazine, Newspaper, Radio/TV station, Religious Organization, Sororities, Student Government, Yearbook

Most Selective

Massachusetts Services

Boston College
Lyons Hall
Chestnut Hill, Massachusetts 02167
(617) 552-3100

School Enrollment: **8,806** Male: **3,997** Female: **4,809**
LD Enrollment: **182**

Admissions Contact: **John L. Mahoney, Director of Admissions**
LD Contact: **David Smith, Ph.D., ,Associate Director-Counseling**
Name of Program: **Committee on Learning Disorders**
Telephone:**(617) 552-3310**

Admissions

Application Information:
LD Students Applying: **150** Accepted: **40** Enrolled:**28**
Application deadline: **February 1st**
Applicant must apply **3-6** months in advance
Notified when: **April 1st**

Secondary School Information
Most Important Criteria For Admissions (1-strongest)

9 SAT/ACT	**7** Application	**1**	School transcript
8 Class rank	**3** Course selection	**6**	Personal statement
10 Interview	**11** Extra activities	**2**	Psychoeducational
4 G.P.A.	Open admission	**5**	Recommendations

Test Requirements:
Diagnostic testing waived: **Yes**
Untimed SAT: **Yes** Untimed ACT: **Yes** Untimed ACH: **Yes**
Documentation of LD required: **Yes**
Currency of diagnostic testing: **No specific number**
Tests recommended: **Woodcock-Johnson Psychoeducational Battery**

Types of Disabilities Served
- Speech/Lang
- Study skills
- Written express
- Organizational
- Perceptual
- Reading
- Spelling
- Math
- Fine Motor
- ADD with LD
- ADD without LD
- ADHD with LD
- ADHD without LD

Admissions Process

Consultation between Admissions Office and Committee on Learning Disabilities.

High School Course Requirements:
English: **4** Math: **4** Science: **3** Foreign Language: **4**
Waivers to standard high school courses
Foreign Language : **Yes**

Learning Disability Program
Services available for all students: **Yes**
Counseling: Individual: **Yes** Group Counseling: **Yes**

Faculty:
Faculty: **10** Part time: **10**
LD faculty with: BS/BA: **10** M.A.: **10** Ph.D.: **9**
Faculty advocate: **Yes** Meets with instructor: **Occasionally**

Diagnostic Testing
ADD	Personality	Perceptual skills	Spelling
ADHD	Organization	Fine motor skills	Reading
I.Q.	Handwriting	Spoken language	Study skills
Math	Social skills	Written language	

Tutoring:
Average size of group tutorials: **2-4**
Services rendered by:
•Graduates •Peers Faculty LD staff •Teacher trainees

Tutorials
Grp.	Ind.	Tutorials	Grp.	Ind.	Tutorials
•		Math skills	•		Word processing
•		Study skills	•		Time management
•		Language arts	•		Learning strategies
•		Written express	•		Organizational skills

Academic Accommodations

Curriculum	Study Aids	Exams
Priority registration	• Typist	• Oral
Math waiver	Reader	Untimed
• Foreign lang. waiver	Notetaker	• Take home
Course substitution	• Proof reader	• With proctor
In Class	• Text on tape	• On computer
• Calculators	Early syllabus	• Extended time
• Tape recorder	Taped handouts	• On tape
• Word processor		• Modified
• Priority seating		• Separate room

Graduation Requirements:GPA: **2.0** Years to complete degree: **4** Language waiver: **Yes**
Other requirements: **Consult catalog for core and major requirements in each division/school**

Program Strengths
Boston College provides support services for talented and motivated students with learning disorders. Remedial services are not available. The Academic Development Center provides tutoring for all students in specific courses and provides learning strategies assistance for LD students.

General Information:
Boston College is a 4 year private Roman Catholic university. Suburban campus of 240 acres is 5 miles from Boston. Accessible by air, train or bus. Ski areas are 50 miles from campus. Beaches are 25 miles from campus. 3% of students are foreign. 30 residential halls on campus. Housing is not guaranteed.80 % of students remain on campus for the weekends.

Accreditation:NEACS

SAT/ACT Scores:
Scores for incoming freshmen:**Verbal:**19%below 500. 48%between 500 and 599. 30%between 600 and 699. 3%above 700. **Math:**3% below 500. 26% between 500 and 599. 53% between 600 and 699. 18%above 700.

Class Rank:
About 95% of the present freshmen class were in the upper 20% of their

high school class. 100% were in the top 40% of their class. 100% were in the top 60% of their class. 100% were in the top 80% of their class.

Expenses:
Tuition: In-state: Full year: $14,580.00. Tuition: Out-of-state: Full year: $14,580.00. Room and board: $6,470.00

Majors
• AREA STUDIES Russian/Slavic • BUSINESS Accounting, Business Administration, Business Management, Economics, Finance, Management, Marketing • COMMUNICATIONS Communication, English • COMPUTER SCIENCE Computer Science • EDUCATION Early Childhood, Elementary, Middle School, Secondary, Special • HEALTH SCIENCES Nursing • HUMANITIES Classics, Philosophy, Religious Studies • LANGUAGES French, German, Greek, Italian, Latin, Linguistic, Russian, Spanish • SCIENCES Biochemistry, Biology, Chemistry, Ecology, Geology, Geophysics, Geoscience, Mathematics, Physics • SOCIAL SCIENCES Government/Political, History, Human Service, Psychology, Sociology • VISUAL AND PERFORMING ARTS Art History, Dramatic Arts, Music, Studio Art, Theater

Sports/Activities
• SPORTS RELATED Marching Band, Pep Band • SPORTS-INTERCOLLEGIATE Baseball (M), Basketball, Crew, Cross Country, Diving, Fencing (F), Field Hockey (F), Football (M), Golf, Ice Hockey (M), Lacrosse, Sailing, Skiing - Snow, Soccer, Softball (F), Swimming, Tennis, Track and Field, Volleyball (F), Water Polo (M), Wrestling (M) • SPORTS-INTRAMURAL Basketball, Crew, Cross Country, Football (M), Hand Ball, Ice Hockey (M), Racquetball, Rugby (M), Sailing, Soccer, Squash, Swimming, Tennis, Volleyball, Water Polo (M) • STUDENT LIFE ACTIVITIES Magazine, Musical Theater, Newspaper, Political Groups, Radio/TV station, Religious Organization, Student Government, Yearbook

---

Highly Selective **Massachusetts Program**

Boston University
19 Deerfield Street
Boston, Massachusetts 02215
(617) 353-2300

School Enrollment: **26,000** Male: **13,000** Female: **13,000**
LD Enrollment: **150** Male: **85** Female: **65**

Admissions Contact: **Steve Inzer, Assistant Director of Admissions**
LD Contact: **Dr. Loring Brinckerhoff, Director**
Name of Program: **Learning Disabilities Support Services**
Address: **19 Deerfield Street, Second Floor**
Telephone:**(617) 353-6880**

Admissions

Application Information:
Application deadline: **Before April**

Secondary School Information
Most Important Criteria For Admissions (1-strongest)

2	SAT/ACT	1	Application	1	School transcript
1	Class rank	1	Course selection	3	Personal statement
5	Interview	4	Extra activities	3	Psychoeducational
1	G.P.A.		Open admission	3	Recommendations

Test Requirements:
WAIS-R required: **Yes**
Documentation of LD required: **Yes**
Currency of diagnostic testing: **48 months**

Types of Disabilities Served
• Speech/Lang • Reading • ADD with LD
• Study skills • Spelling • ADD without LD
• Written express • Math • ADHD with LD
• Organizational • Fine Motor • ADHD without LD
• Perceptual

High School Course Requirements:
Waivers to standard high school courses
Foreign Language : **Yes**

Learning Disability Program
Syllabus available during orientation:**Yes**
Program: Reinforces course work: **Yes**
Program available through:**on-going**
Students mainstreamed **100** % of the day
Services only for LD students: **Yes**
Counseling: Individual: **Yes** Group Counseling: **Yes**
Support groups are available:**There are three support groups available.**

Faculty:
Faculty: **9** Full time: **3** Part time: **6**
LD faculty with: BS/BA: **2** M.A.: **6** Ph.D.: **1**
Faculty advocate: **Yes** Meets with instructor: **As needed**

Diagnostic Testing
ADD	Personality	Perceptual skills	Spelling
ADHD	Organization	Fine motor skills	Reading
I.Q.	Handwriting	Spoken language	Study skills
Math	Social skills	Written language	

Tutoring:
Services rendered by:
Graduates   Peers   Faculty   •LD staff   Teacher trainees

Tutorials
Grp.	Ind.	Tutorials	Grp.	Ind.	Tutorials
	•	Math skills		•	Word processing
	•	Study skills		•	Time management
	•	Language arts		•	Learning strategies
	•	Written express		•	Organizational skills

Academic Accommodations
Curriculum	Study Aids	Exams
Priority registration	• Typist	• Oral
Math waiver	• Reader	Untimed
Foreign lang. waiver	• Notetaker	• Take home
• Course substitution	Proof reader	• With proctor
In Class	• Text on tape	• On computer
• Calculators	Early syllabus	• Extended time
• Tape recorder	Taped handouts	• On tape
• Word processor		• Modified
Priority seating		• Separate room

Program Strengths
We are expanding our LD services to include the LDSS office. It will be professionally staffed. We are offering a summer transition program for LD students through the LDSS office. We offer a full range of LD support services in a competitive university setting.

General Information:
Boston University is a 4 year private university. Urban campus of 100 acres is Boston. Accessible by air, train or bus. Ski areas are 1 hour from campus. Beaches are 1/2 hour from campus. 10% of students are foreign. 130 residential halls on campus. Housing is guaranteed.

Accreditation:NEACS

SAT/ACT Scores:
Scores for incoming freshmen: Meanbetween 500 and 599.

Expenses:
Tuition: In-state: Full year: $14,950.00. Part-time: Per credit:$467.00. Part-time: Per course: $1,868.00. Tuition: Out-of-state: Full year: $14,950.00. Part-time: Per credit:$467.00. Part-time: Per course:41,868.00 Room and board: $5,960.00 Cost of LD program:$1,200.00 per semester

Majors

• AREA STUDIES African, American, Asian, Black/Afro-American, International Studies, Latin American, Russian/Slavic, Urban • BUSINESS Accounting, Banking, Business Administration, Business Economics, Business Education, Business Management, Economics, Finance, Hotel and Restaurant Managemen, International Business, Management • COMMUNICATIONS Advertising, Broadcasting, Communication, Creative Writing, English, Journalism, Photography, Television/Radio/Film • COMPUTER SCIENCE Computer Science, Computer Technology, Data Processing • CRAFTS AND DESIGN Sculpture • EDUCATION Art, Curriculum, Early Childhood, Elementary, English, English As A Second Language (, Foreign Language, Health, Middle School, Music, Psychology, Recreation and Youth Leadershi, School Psychology, Science, Secondary, Special, Speech/Language, Vocational • ENGINEERING Bio-medical, Bioengineering, Engineering Science, Industrial • HEALTH SCIENCES Communication Disorders, Health, Medical Technology, Nutritional/Food, Occupational Therapy, Speech Therapy, Speech/Audiology and Speech • HUMANITIES Classics, English/Writing/Literature, Humanities, Liberal Arts, Philosophy, Religion • LANGUAGES Arabic, Chinese, French, German, Hebrew, Japanese, Latin, Linguistic, Russian, Spanish • PREPROFESSIONAL Architecture, Dentistry, Education, Engineering, Law, Medicine, Ministry, Recreation, Social Work • SCIENCES Anthropology, Archeology, Astronomy, Astrophysics, Bacteriology, Biology, Chemistry, Earth, Geography, Geology, Macrobiology, Marine Biology, Mathematics, Microbiology, Oceanography, Physical Chemistry, Physical Science, Physics, Physiology • SOCIAL SCIENCES Anthropology, Criminal Justice, Government/Political, History, Human Service, International Studies, Law Enforcement, Political Science, Public Relations, Social Sciences, Sociology • VISUAL AND PERFORMING ARTS Art, Art History, Dance, Dramatic Arts, Fine Arts, Music, Studio Art, Theater • VOCATIONAL Business and Office, Food Service, Painting

Sports/Activities

• SPORTS RELATED Marching Band, Pep Band • SPORTS-INTERCOLLEGIATE Baseball (M), Basketball, Crew, Cross Country, Diving, Field Hockey (F), Football (M), Horseback Riding, Ice Hockey (M), Lacrosse (F), Sailing, Sailing, Skiing - Snow, Tennis, Track and Field, Volleyball, Wrestling (M) • SPORTS-INTRAMURAL Badminton, Basketball, Diving, Field Hockey (F), Football (M), Horseback Riding, Ice Hockey, Lacrosse (M), Rugby (M), Sailing, Skiing - Snow, Swimming, Tennis, Volleyball • STUDENT LIFE ACTIVITIES Choral, Concert Band, Drama Groups, Ethnic & Cultural Groups, Fraternities, Jazz Band, Magazine, Music Groups, Musical Theater, Newspaper, Political Groups, Radio/TV station, Sororities, Student Government, Symphony Orchestra, Yearbook

Selective	Massachusetts Program

Bradford College
320 South Main Street
Bradford, Massachusetts 01835
(508) 372-7161

School Enrollment: **450** Male: **270** Female: **180**
LD Enrollment: **30** Male: **18** Female: **12**

Admissions Contact: **William Dunfey, Dean of Admissions**
LD Contact: **Diane Waldron**
Name of Program: **College Learning Program**
Telephone:**(508) 372-7161 Ext. 319**

Admissions

Application Information:
LD Students Applying: **153** Accepted: **50** Enrolled:**15**
LD on admissions committee:**Yes**
Application deadline: **Open**
Rolling Admissions: **Yes**

Secondary School Information
Most Important Criteria For Admissions (1-strongest)

11 SAT/ACT	**9** Application	**2** School transcript
6 Class rank	**3** Course selection	**7** Personal statement
4 Interview	**10** Extra activities	**1** Psychoeducational
8 G.P.A.	Open admission	**5** Recommendations

Test Requirements:
Standardized tests waived: **Yes**
Diagnostic testing waived: **Yes**
Untimed SAT: **Yes**
WAIS-R required: **Yes** Range accepted: **95+**
Documentation of LD required: **Yes**
Tests recommended: **Reading diagnostic testing**

Types of Disabilities Served

Speech/Lang	• Reading	• ADD with LD
• Study skills	• Spelling	ADD without LD
• Written express	• Math	• ADHD with LD
• Organizational	• Fine Motor	ADHD without LD
• Perceptual		

High School Course Requirements:
English: **4** Math: **2-3** Science: **2** Foreign Language: **2**
Waivers to standard high school courses
Foreign Language : **Yes**

Learning Disability Program

Program: Reinforces course work: **Yes**
Students mainstreamed **100** % of the day
Counseling: Individual: **Yes** Group Counseling: **Yes**

Faculty:
Faculty: **4** Including Director: **Yes** Full time: **2** Part time: **2** M.A.: **4**
Faculty advocate: **Yes** Meets with instructor: **2-3x per semester**

Massachusetts

Diagnostic Testing

ADD	Personality	Perceptual skills	Spelling
ADHD	Organization	Fine motor skills	Reading
I.Q.	Handwriting	Spoken language	Study skills
Math	Social skills	Written language	

Tutoring:
Average size of group tutorials: **2-5**
Services rendered by:
  Graduates   Peers   Faculty   •LD staff   Teacher trainees

Tutorials

Grp.	Ind.	Tutorials	Grp.	Ind.	Tutorials
•	•	Math skills		•	Word processing
•	•	Study skills	•	•	Time management
•	•	Language arts	•	•	Learning strategies
•	•	Written express		•	Organizational skills

Academic Accommodations

Curriculum	Study Aids	Exams
Priority registration	Typist	Oral
Math waiver	Reader	Untimed
Foreign lang. waiver	• Notetaker	Take home
Course substitution	Proof reader	With proctor
In Class	• Text on tape	On computer
• Calculators	Early syllabus	• Extended time
• Tape recorder	Taped handouts	On tape
• Word processor		• Modified
Priority seating		Separate room

Graduation Requirements:
Course credits: **121** GPA: **2.0** Language waiver: **Yes**

Program Strengths
Bradford is a college with a long tradition of liberal arts education of high quality and a commitment to an individual approach to learning. Within this context, the College Learning Program is designed to meet the educational needs of students with mild-to-moderate learning disabilities. The goal of the program is to help students become successful learners, capable of earning a college degree.

General Information:
Bradford College is a 4 year private college. Urban campus of 75 acres is 35 miles from Boston. Accessible by train or bus. Ski areas are 2 miles from campus. Beaches are 1 hour from campus. 10% of students are foreign. 4 residential halls on campus. Housing is guaranteed. Guaranteed through 4th year.

Accreditation: NEACS

Expenses:
Tuition: In-state: Full year: $11,600.00. Room and board: $5,875.00 Cost of LD program: $3,500.00

Majors
• BUSINESS Accounting, Business Administration, Finance, Management • COMMUNICATIONS Communication, English • COMPUTER SCIENCE Computer Science • EDUCATION Physical, Social Studies • HUMANITIES English/Writing/Literature, Humanities, Liberal Arts, Philosophy • SCIENCES Chemistry, Geoscience, Mathematics, Physics • SOCIAL SCIENCES Government/Political, History, Human Service, Psychology, Sociology • VISUAL AND PERFORMING ARTS Creative Arts, Dance, Music, Theater

---

Brandeis University
415 South Street
Waltham, Massachusetts 02254
(617) 736-3500-(800) 622-0622

School Enrollment: **2,898** Male: **1,372** Female: **1,526**
LD Enrollment: **95** Male: **50** Female: **45**

Admissions Contact: **Betty B. Lloyd, Asst. Dir. of Admissions**
LD Contact: **Walter Anthony, Associate Dean**
Name of Program: **Office of Academic Affairs**
Telephone:**(617) 736-3460**

Admissions

Application Information:
Application deadline: **February 1st**
Notified when: **April 1st**

Secondary School Information
Most Important Criteria For Admissions (1-strongest)

4	SAT/ACT	Application	**1**	School transcript
5	Class rank	**1** Course selection	**5**	Personal statement
5	Interview	**2** Extra activities		Psychoeducational
6	G.P.A.	Open admission	**3**	Recommendations

Test Requirements:
Diagnostic testing waived: **Yes**
Untimed SAT: **Yes** Untimed ACT: **Yes** Untimed ACH: **Yes** Achievement tests required:**3**
Documentation of LD required: **Yes**
Currency of diagnostic testing: **2 years**
Tests recommended: **Woodcock-Johnson P.E.B., Boston Naming Test, Boston Diagnostic Aphasia Exam, Parts of ITPA and DTLA, PPVT-R**

Types of Disabilities Served
• Speech/Lang	• Reading	• ADD with LD
• Study skills	• Spelling	• ADD without LD
• Written express	• Math	• ADHD with LD
• Organizational	• Fine Motor	• ADHD without LD
• Perceptual		

High School Course Requirements:
English: **4** Math: **3** Science: **1** Foreign Language: **3**
Waivers to standard high school courses
Foreign Language : **Yes** Math: **Yes** Course substitution: **Yes**

Learning Disability Program
Special orientation for LD students:
Syllabus available during orientation:**Yes**
Students mainstreamed **100** % of the day
Recommended credits per semester: **16**
Counseling: Individual: **Yes** Vocational Counseling: **Yes**
Support groups are available:**Yes, student organization**

Faculty:
Faculty: **1**
Faculty advocate: **Yes** Meets with instructor: **As needed**

Diagnostic Testing
- ADD
- Personality
- Perceptual skills
- Spelling
- ADHD
- Organization
- Fine motor skills
- Reading
- I.Q.
- Handwriting
- Spoken language
- Study skills
- Math
- Social skills
- Written language

Tutoring:
Services rendered by:
Graduates   Peers   •Faculty   LD staff   Teacher trainees

Tutorials

Grp.	Ind.	Tutorials	Grp.	Ind.	Tutorials
•	•	Math skills	•	•	Word processing
•	•	Study skills	•	•	Time management
•	•	Language arts	•	•	Learning strategies
•	•	Written express	•	•	Organizational skills

Academic Accommodations

Curriculum	Study Aids	Exams
Priority registration	Typist	• Oral
• Math waiver	Reader	• Untimed
• Foreign lang. waiver	Notetaker	• Take home
• Course substitution	Proof reader	With proctor
In Class	• Text on tape	On computer
• Calculators	Early syllabus	• Extended time
• Tape recorder	Taped handouts	On tape
• Word processor		• Modified
Priority seating		• Separate room

Graduation Requirements:
Course credits: **128** Math waiver: **Yes** Language waiver: **Yes**

Program Strengths
Brandeis University encourages students with learning disabilities who have achieved strong secondary school records to apply for admission. All services for learning disabled students are coordinated through the Office of Academic Affairs under the supervision of an assistant dean. Each student is advised on an individual basis in terms of course selection and any special services he or she may require, such as books or tape recorders in class, or waivers of certain academic requirements.

General Information:
Brandeis University is a 4 year private university. Suburban campus of 235 acres is 10 miles from Boston. Accessible by air, train or bus. Ski areas are 1 hour from campus. Beaches are 1/2 hour from campus. 5% of students are foreign. 40 residential halls on campus. Housing is guaranteed. Guaranteed through 2nd year. 95 % of students remain on campus for the weekends.

Accreditation: NEACS

SAT/ACT Scores:
Scores for incoming freshmen: **Verbal:** 12% below 500. 42% between 500 and 599. 39% between 600 and 699. 7% above 700. **Math:** 5% below 500. 24% between 500 and 599. 46% between 600 and 699. 25% above 700.

Class Rank:
About 75% of the present freshmen class were in the upper 20% of their high school class. 95% were in the top 40% of their class. 100% were in the top 60% of their class.

Expenses:
Tuition: In-state: Full year: $17,320.00. Room and board: $6,505.00

Majors
• AREA STUDIES American, Black/Afro-American, European, Jewish, Latin American, Middle Eastern, Russian/Slavic, Women's Studies • BUSI-

NESS Economics • COMMUNICATIONS English • COMPUTER SCIENCE Computer Science, Programming • HUMANITIES Classics, English/Writing/Literature, Philosophy • LANGUAGES French, German, Linguistics, Russian, Spanish • SCIENCES Biochemistry, Biology, Chemistry, General, Mathematics, Nuerosciences, Physics • SOCIAL SCIENCES Anthropology, Government/Political, History, Linguistics, Psychology, Sociology • VISUAL AND PERFORMING ARTS Art, Art History, Dramatic Arts, Fine Arts, Music, Theater

Sports/Activities
• SPORTS RELATED Pep Band • SPORTS-INTERCOLLEGIATE Baseball (M), Basketball, Crew, Cross Country, Diving, Fencing, Golf (M), Ice Hockey (M), Sailing, Soccer, Softball (F), Swimming, Tennis, Track and Field, Volleyball (F) • SPORTS-INTRAMURAL Basketball, Cross Country, Football, Golf, Lacrosse, Rugby, Skiing - Snow, Soccer, Softball, Squash, Tennis, Volleyball, Water Polo (M), Wrestling • STUDENT LIFE ACTIVITIES Academic Clubs, Choral, Community Service, Concert Band, Dance, Debate, Drama Groups, Ethnic & Cultural Groups, Jazz Band, Magazine, Music Groups, Musical Theater, Newspaper, Orchestra, Political Groups, Radio/TV station, Religious Organization, Student Government, Symphony Orchestra, Yearbook

---

Selective   **Massachusetts**
                                 Services

Bridgewater State College
Tilinghast Hall
Bridgewater, Massachusetts 02324
(617) 697-1237

School Enrollment: **4,759** Male: **1,814** Female: **2,945**
LD Enrollment: **37** Male: **13** Female: **24**

Admissions Contact: **James F. Plotner, Jr., Director of Admissions**
LD Contact: **William Drapeau, Assistant Director**
Name of Program: **Student Services**
Telephone: **(508) 697-1208**

Admissions

Application Information:
Application deadline: **March 1st**
Notified when: **April 15th**

Secondary School Information
Most Important Criteria For Admissions (1-strongest)

11	SAT/ACT	10 Application	1 School transcript
5	Class rank	2 Course selection	8 Personal statement
9	Interview	7 Extra activities	3 Psychoeducational
4	G.P.A.	Open admission	6 Recommendations

Test Requirements:
Standardized tests waived: **Yes**

Types of Disabilities Served
- Speech/Lang
- Reading
- ADD with LD
- Study skills
- Spelling
- ADD without LD
- Written express
- Math
- ADHD with LD
- Organizational
- Fine Motor
- ADHD without LD
- Perceptual

Learning Disability Program
Services available for all students: **Yes**
Counseling: Individual: **Yes** Group Counseling: **Yes**

Massachusetts

Faculty:
Faculty: **4** Part time: **4**

Diagnostic Testing
ADD	Personality	Perceptual skills	Spelling
ADHD	Organization	Fine motor skills	Reading
I.Q.	Handwriting	Spoken language	Study skills
Math	Social skills	Written language	

Tutoring:
Average size of group tutorials: **15**
Services rendered by:
•Graduates •Peers •Faculty •LD staff Teacher trainees

Tutorials
Grp.	Ind.	Tutorials	Grp.	Ind.	Tutorials
	•	Math skills			Word processing
	•	Study skills		•	Time management
	•	Language arts		•	Learning strategies
	•	Written express		•	Organizational skills

Academic Accommodations
Curriculum	Study Aids	Exams
Priority registration	• Typist	• Oral
• Math waiver	Reader	Untimed
• Foreign lang. waiver	• Notetaker	• Take home
• Course substitution	• Proof reader	With proctor
In Class	• Text on tape	On computer
• Calculators	Early syllabus	• Extended time
• Tape recorder	Taped handouts	On tape
• Word processor		• Modified
Priority seating		Separate room

Program Strengths
We do not have a formal program for learning disabled students but rather a series of support services available to all students.

General Information:
Bridgewater State College is a 4 year public college. Suburban campus of 170 acres is 28 miles from Boston. Accessible by bus. Ski areas are 100 miles from campus. Beaches are 20 miles from campus. 1% of students are foreign. 8 residential halls on campus. Housing is not guaranteed.80 % of students remain on campus for the weekends. 7 % of students join fraternities/sororities.

Accreditation:NACS, NCATE, ACS, ICC, FAA

Expenses:
Tuition: In-state: Full year: $2,112.00. Part-time: Per credit:$52.08. Tuition: Out-of-state: Full year: $4,325.00. Part-time: Per credit:$180.20. Room and board: $3,714.00

Majors
• BUSINESS Accounting, Banking, Business Management, Finance, Management, Marketing • COMMUNICATIONS Communication, English • COMPUTER SCIENCE Computer Science, Data Processing, Programming • CRAFTS AND DESIGN Ceramics, Graphic Design • EDUCATION Early Childhood, Elementary, Health, Mathematics, Middle School, Physical, Secondary, Special, Speech/Language • ENVIRONMENTAL CONTROL Energy Conservation • HEALTH SCIENCES Communication Disorders, Speech Therapy, Speech/Audiology and Speech • HUMANITIES Philosophy • LANGUAGES French, Spanish • PREPROFESSIONAL Architecture, Dentistry, Elementary, Law, Medicine, Social Work • SCIENCES Archeology, Biochemistry, Biology, Chemistry, Earth, Geochemistry, Geography, Geology, Mathematics, Oceanography, Physical Chemistry, Physics • SOCIAL SCIENCES Anthropology, Criminology, Government/Political, History, International Studies, Psychology, Sociolo-gy • VISUAL AND PERFORMING ARTS Art, Art History, Dramatic Arts, Fine Arts, Studio Art, Theater

Sports
• SPORTS RELATED Pep Band • SPORTS-INTERCOLLEGIATE Baseball (M), Basketball, Cross Country, Diving, Field Hockey (F), Football (M), Gymnastics (F), Lacrosse, Soccer, Softball (F), Swimming, Tennis, Track and Field, Volleyball (F), Wrestling (M) • SPORTS-INTRAMURAL Basketball, Cross Country, Diving, Lacrosse (M), Soccer, Softball, Swimming, Volleyball, Water Polo (M) • STUDENT LIFE ACTIVITIES Choral, Ethnic & Cultural Groups, Fraternities, Magazine, Musical Theater, Newspaper, Radio/TV station, Religious Organization, Sororities, Student Government

---

Less Selective **Massachusetts Services**

Bristol Community College
777 Elsbree Street
Fall River, Massachusetts 02720
(508) 678-2811

School Enrollment: **2,800** Male: **1,680** Female: **1,120**
LD Enrollment: **124**

Admissions Contact: **Frank Noble, Director of Admissions**
LD Contact: **Susan Boissoneault, Learning Specialist**
Name of Program: **Center for Developmental Education**
Telephone:**(508) 678-2811 Ext.**

Admissions

Application Information:
LD on admissions committee:**Yes**
Application deadline: **None**
Rolling Admissions: **Yes**

Secondary School Information
Most Important Criteria For Admissions (1-strongest)
SAT/ACT	Application	School transcript
Class rank	Course selection	Personal statement
Interview	Extra activities	Psychoeducational
G.P.A.	**1** Open admission	Recommendations

Test Requirements:
Diagnostic testing waived: **Yes**
WAIS-R required: **Yes** Range accepted: **85-115**
Documentation of LD required: **Yes**
Currency of diagnostic testing: **3 years**
Tests recommended: **Current testing to substantiate learning disability and cognitive ability**

Types of Disabilities Served
• Speech/Lang	• Reading	• ADD with LD
• Study skills	• Spelling	• ADD without LD
• Written express	• Math	• ADHD with LD
• Organizational	• Fine Motor	• ADHD without LD
• Perceptual		

Admissions Process
Open admissions; students who present a high school diploma are admitted but admission to specific academic programs is selective.

Learning Disability Program

Program: Reinforces course work: **Yes**
Students mainstreamed **100** % of the day
Recommended credits per semester: **12-15**
Services available for all students: **Yes**
Counseling: Individual: **Yes** Group Counseling: **Yes**

Faculty:
Faculty: **7** Including Director: **Yes** Full time: **6** Part time: **1**
LD faculty with: BS/BA: **3** M.A.: **4**
Faculty advocate: **Yes** Meets with instructor: **1-3x per semester**

Diagnostic Testing
ADD	Personality •	Perceptual skills	• Spelling
ADHD•	Organization	Fine motor skills	• Reading
• I.Q.	• Handwriting•	Spoken language	• Study skills
• Math	Social skills •	Written language	

Tutoring:
Average size of group tutorials: **12**
Services rendered by:
Graduates •Peers Faculty •LD staff •Teacher trainees

Tutorials
Grp.	Ind.	Tutorials	Grp.	Ind.	Tutorials
	•	Math skills		•	Word processing
•	•	Study skills	•	•	Time management
	•	Language arts	•	•	Learning strategies
•	•	Written express	•	•	Organizational skills

Academic Accommodations
Curriculum	Study Aids	Exams
Priority registration	Typist	• Oral
Math waiver	Reader	Untimed
Foreign lang. waiver	• Notetaker	• Take home
Course substitution	• Proof reader	With proctor
In Class	• Text on tape	On computer
Calculators	Early syllabus	• Extended time
• Tape recorder	Taped handouts	On tape
• Word processor		• Modified
Priority seating		Separate room

Graduation Requirements:
Course credits: **60-76** GPA: **2.0** Years to complete degree: **2-3**

Program Strengths

The Center for Developmental Education serves all non-traditional students via: Quest Project, which is comprised of Learning Labs in reading, math, and writing; a Tutoring and Academic Support Center, TASC; ESL Program, study skills courses, advisement (academic, personal, and career); an LD support group and student advocate. Our LD students are served within one or more of these components as well as students with disabilities, bilingual students, students in transition, and underprepared students.

General Information:

Bristol Community College is a 2 year public college. Urban campus of 105 acres is 20 miles from Providence, RI. Ski areas are 65 miles from campus. Beaches are 12 miles from campus. 1% of students are foreign. Housing is not guaranteed.

Accreditation:

Expenses:
Tuition: In-state: Full year: $1,474.00. Part-time: Per credit:$34.50. Part-time: Per course: $223.50. Tuition: Out-of-state: Full year: $3,666.00. Part-time: Per credit:$125.50. Part-time: Per course:$498.50

Majors

• BUSINESS Accounting, Business Administration, Business Economics, Business Education, Business Management, Management, Marketing, Real Estate • COMMUNICATIONS Communication • COMPUTER SCIENCE Programming • EDUCATION Child Development, Early Childhood, Elementary • ENGINEERING Civil/Environmental, Electrical, Engineering Science, Mechanical • HEALTH SCIENCES Dental Assistant, Medical Technology, Nursing • HUMANITIES Liberal Arts • PREPROFESSIONAL Dentistry, Engineering • SCIENCES Mathematics • SOCIAL SCIENCES Criminal Justice, Library Science, Social Sciences • VISUAL AND PERFORMING ARTS Art, Fine Arts • VOCATIONAL Culinary Arts, Fire Science, Legal Secretary

Sports/Activities

• STUDENT LIFE ACTIVITIES Choral, Drama Groups, Ethnic & Cultural Groups, Magazine, Newspaper, Radio/TV station, Student Government

---

Less Selective   **Massachusetts**
                                        Program

Cape Cod Community College
Route 132
West Barnstable, Massachusetts 02668
(508) 362-2131

School Enrollment: **2,026** Male: **778** Female: **1,248**
LD Enrollment: **145**

Admissions Contact: **Susan Kline-Symington, Acting Dir. of Ad.**
LD Contact: **Richard H. Sommers, Ph.D., Learning Specialist**
Name of Program: **LD Support Services Program**

Admissions

Application Information:
Application deadline: **August 1st**
Rolling Admissions: **Yes**

Secondary School Information
Most Important Criteria For Admissions (1-strongest)
SAT/ACT	Application	School transcript
Class rank	Course selection	Personal statement
Interview	Extra activities	Psychoeducational
G.P.A.	**1** Open admission	Recommendations

Test Requirements:
Diagnostic testing waived: **Yes**
Untimed SAT: **Yes**
Documentation of LD required: **Yes**

Types of Disabilities Served
• Speech/Lang	• Reading	• ADD with LD
• Study skills	• Spelling	• ADD without LD
• Written express	• Math	• ADHD with LD
• Organizational	• Fine Motor	• ADHD without LD
• Perceptual		

Admissions Process

We are an open admission college. Require high school graduation or equivalent.

Massachusetts

Learning Disability Program

Program: Reinforces course work: **Yes**
Students mainstreamed **100** % of the day
Counseling: Individual: **Yes** Vocational Counseling: **Yes**
Support groups are available:

Faculty:
Faculty: **5** Including Director: **Yes** Part time: **5** Ph.D.: **1**
Faculty advocate: **Yes** Meets with instructor: **As needed**

Diagnostic Testing

ADD	Personality	Perceptual skills	• Spelling
ADHD	Organization	Fine motor skills	• Reading
I.Q.	Handwriting	Spoken language	Study skills
• Math	Social skills	• Written language	

Tutoring:
Services rendered by:
  Graduates   •Peers   •Faculty   •LD staff   Teacher trainees

Tutorials

Grp.	Ind.	Tutorials	Grp.	Ind.	Tutorials
•	•	Math skills	•	•	Word processing
•		Study skills		•	Time management
		Language arts		•	Learning strategies
	•	Written express		•	Organizational skills

Academic Accommodations

Curriculum	Study Aids	Exams
Priority registration	Typist	• Oral
Math waiver	Reader	Untimed
Foreign lang. waiver	Notetaker	Take home
Course substitution	Proof reader	With proctor
In Class	Text on tape	On computer
• Calculators	Early syllabus	• Extended time
• Tape recorder	Taped handouts	• On tape
• Word processor		• Modified
Priority seating		Separate room

Graduation Requirements:
Course credits: **60** GPA: **2.0** Years to complete degree: **No time limit**

Program Strengths

This is a data based learning disability support services program. Students are required to submit documentation of specific LD problems to be included in the program. An individual educational plan is developed for each student and shared with his or her instructors and tutors, if requested. Emphasis is on developing learning strategies.

General Information:

Cape Cod Community College is a 2 year public college. Rural campus of 120 acres is 75 miles from Boston. Accessible by air, train or bus. Ski areas are 2 hours from campus. Beaches are 20 miles from campus. 1% of students are foreign. Housing is not guaranteed.

Accreditation: NEACS

Expenses:
Tuition: In-state: Full year: $1,008.00 plus fees. Part-time: Per credit:$42.00. Tuition: Out-of-state: Full year: $4,680.00. Part-time: Per credit:$195.00.

Majors

• BUSINESS Accounting, Business Administration, Hotel and Restaurant Managemen, Management, Retailing, Secretarial Science • COMPUTER SCIENCE Business Data Programming, Computer Science • EDUCA-TION Early Childhood • ENGINEERING Engineering Science • HEALTH SCIENCES Dental Hygiene, Nursing • PRE PROFESSIONAL Business, Engineering • SOCIAL SCIENCES Criminal Justice • VOCATIONAL Construction, Fire Science, Legal Secretary, Medical Secretary, Office Administration, Secretarial

Sports/Activities

• SPORTS-INTRAMURAL Basketball (M), Crew, Karate, Ping-Pong, Racquetball, Skiing - Snow, Softball, Tennis, Volleyball • STUDENT LIFE ACTIVITIES Academic Clubs, Choral, Community Service, Dance, Drama Groups, Ethnic & Cultural Groups, Magazine, Newspaper, Political Groups, Radio/TV station, Student Government

---

Very Selective   **Massachusetts Program**

Clark University
950 Main Street
Worcester, Massachusetts 01610
(508) 793-7431

School Enrollment: **2,300** Male: **1,219** Female: **1,081**
LD Enrollment: **100** Male: **50** Female: **50**

Admissions Contact: **Everett Goodwin, Assoc. Dir. Admissions**
LD Contact: **Martin Patwell, Associate Dir., Academic Advising**
Name of Program: **Special Services for Disabled Students**
Address: **22 Downing Street**
Telephone:**(508) 793-7468**

Admissions

Application Information:
LD Students Applying: **120** Accepted: **40** Enrolled:**36**
Application deadline: **February 15th**

Secondary School Information
Most Important Criteria For Admissions (1-strongest)

7 SAT/ACT	10 Application	2	School transcript
5 Class rank	3 Course selection	9	Personal statement
8 Interview	11 Extra activities	4	Psychoeducational
1 G.P.A.	Open admission	6	Recommendations

Test Requirements:
Diagnostic testing waived: **Yes**
Untimed SAT: **Yes** Untimed ACT: **Yes** Untimed ACH: **Yes** Achievement tests required:**1-English**
WAIS-R required: **Yes** Range accepted: **None**
Documentation of LD required: **Yes**
Currency of diagnostic testing: **1 year**
Tests recommended: **WAIS-R, Woodcock-Johnson**

Types of Disabilities Served
• Speech/Lang	• Reading	• ADD with LD
• Study skills	• Spelling	• ADD without LD
• Written express	• Math	• ADHD with LD
• Organizational	• Fine Motor	• ADHD without LD
• Perceptual		

Admissions Process

LD specialist is consultant to committee. Specialist views all LD files and meets with all applicants.

High School Course Requirements:
Waivers to standard high school courses
Foreign Language : **Yes**

Learning Disability Program
Syllabus available during orientation:**Yes**
Program: Reinforces course work: **Yes**
Program available through:**As necessary**
Students mainstreamed **100** % of the day
Recommended credits per semester: **12-16**
Services only for LD students: **Yes**
Counseling: Individual: **Yes** Group Counseling: **Yes**
Support groups are available:**LD students peer support group**

Faculty:
Faculty: **1** Including Director: **Yes** Full time: **1** Part time: **1** Ph.D.: **1**
Faculty advocate: **Yes** Meets with instructor: **As needed**

Diagnostic Testing
ADD	Personality	Perceptual skills	• Spelling
ADHD•	Organization	Fine motor skills	• Reading
• I.Q.	Handwriting	Spoken language	• Study skills
• Math	Social skills•	Written language	

Tutoring:
Average size of group tutorials: **5**
Services rendered by:
•Graduates •Peers Faculty •LD staff Teacher trainees

Tutorials
Grp.	Ind.	Tutorials	Grp.	Ind.	Tutorials
•		Math skills		•	Word processing
•	•	Study skills	•	•	Time management
		Language arts		•	Learning strategies
	•	Written express		•	Organizational skills

Academic Accommodations
Curriculum	Study Aids	Exams
• Priority registration	Typist	• Oral
Math waiver	• Reader	Untimed
Foreign lang. waiver	• Notetaker	• Take home
• Course substitution	• Proof reader	• With proctor
In Class	• Text on tape	On computer
Calculators	Early syllabus	• Extended time
• Tape recorder	Taped handouts	On tape
• Word processor		• Modified
• Priority seating		• Separate room

Graduation Requirements:
Course credits: **128** GPA: **2.3** Years to complete degree: **4-5** Language waiver: **Yes**
Other requirements: **Individual major - 6 liberal arts courses required.**

Program Strengths
The Learning Disabilities program at Clark University, based within the Academic Advising Center, was developed in 1983 to advocate and support the needs of the learning disabled student in a college environment. LD support services at the Academic Advising Center are coordinated with services offered by the University's Writing Center, the Math Clinic, Computer Lab, and the Dean of Students.

General Information:
Clark University is a 4 year private university. Urban campus of 2,800 acres is Worcester. Accessible by air, train or bus. Ski areas are 7 miles from campus. Beaches are 50 miles from campus. 10% of students are foreign. 18 residential halls on campus. Housing is guaranteed.Guaranteed through 4th year. 1 % of students join fraternities/sororities.

Accreditation:

Class Rank:
About 40% of the present freshmen class were in the upper 20% of their high school class. 50% were in the top 40% of their class. 10% were in the top 60% of their class.

Expenses:
Tuition: In-state: Full year: $20,000.00. Room and board: $4,500.00

Majors
• AREA STUDIES African, American, Asian, Jewish, Latin American, Women's Studies • BUSINESS Business Economics, Business Management, Economics, Management • COMMUNICATIONS Communication, English • COMPUTER SCIENCE Programming • HUMANITIES Classics, Philosophy • LANGUAGES French, German, Italian, Japanese, Russian, Spanish • PREPROFESSIONAL Dentistry, Law • SCIENCES Biochemistry, Biology, Chemistry, Ecology, Geography, Geology, Mathematics, Molecular Biology, Physical Chemistry, Physical Science, Physics • SOCIAL SCIENCES Government/Political, History, International Studies, Psychology, Sociology • VISUAL AND PERFORMING ARTS Art, Art History, Music, Studio Art, Theater

Sports/Activities
• SPORTS-INTERCOLLEGIATE Baseball (M), Basketball, Crew, Cross Country, Field Hockey (F), Golf (M), Soccer, Softball (F), Swimming, Tennis, Track and Field, Volleyball (F) • SPORTS-INTRAMURAL Basketball, Bowling, Horseback Riding, Ice Hockey (M), Lacrosse (M), Racquetball, Sailing, Skiing - Snow, Squash, Tennis, Volleyball, Water Polo • STUDENT LIFE ACTIVITIES Choral, Concert Band, Dance, Drama Groups, Ethnic & Cultural Groups, Film, Jazz Band, Magazine, Music Groups, Musical Theater, Newspaper, Political Groups, Radio/TV station, Student Government, Symphony Orchestra, Videotape, Yearbook

Less Selective	Massachusetts Program

Curry College
1071 Blue Hill Avenue
Milton, Massachusetts 02186-9984
(617) 333-0500

School Enrollment: **871** Male: **465** Female: **406**
LD Enrollment: **150**

Admissions Contact: **Dana K. Denault, Director of Admissions**
LD Contact: **Donna Cataldo, Coordinator of P.A.L.**
Name of Program: **Advancement of Learning**
Telephone:**(617) 335-0500 Ext. 2250**

Admissions

Application Information:
LD Students Applying: **510** Accepted: **283** Enrolled:**115**
Application deadline: **April 1st**
Applicant must apply **6-12** months in advance
Rolling Admissions: **Yes**

Massachusetts

Secondary School Information
Most Important Criteria For Admissions (1-strongest)

SAT/ACT	**1**	Application	**1**	School transcript
5 Class rank	**2**	Course selection	**3**	Personal statement
4 Interview	**4**	Extra activities	**1**	Psychoeducational
2 G.P.A.		Open admission	**3**	Recommendations

Test Requirements:
Standardized tests waived: **Yes**
Diagnostic testing waived: **Yes**
WAIS-R required: **Yes**

Types of Disabilities Served

Speech/Lang	Reading	ADD with LD
Study skills	Spelling	ADD without LD
Written express	Math	ADHD with LD
Organizational	Fine Motor	ADHD without LD
Perceptual		

Admissions Process

Joint Admissions and PAL committee evaluates LD testing and academic credentials to determine appropriateness.

Learning Disability Program
Program: Remedial: **Yes**
Program: Reinforces course work: **Yes**
Students mainstreamed **100** % of the day
Recommended credits per semester: **12-15**
Services only for LD students: **Yes**
Counseling: Individual: **Yes** Group Counseling: **Yes**
Support groups are available: **Yes**

Faculty:
Faculty: **17** Full time: **11** Part time: **6** M.A.: **17**
Faculty advocate: **Yes** Meets with instructor: **As requested**

Diagnostic Testing

ADD	Personality	Perceptual skills	Spelling
ADHD	Organization	Fine motor skills	Reading
I.Q.	Handwriting	Spoken language	Study skills
Math	Social skills	Written language	

Tutoring:
Average size of group tutorials: **3**
Services rendered by:

Graduates	Peers	Faculty	•LD staff	Teacher trainees

Tutorials

Grp.	Ind.	Tutorials	Grp.	Ind.	Tutorials
		Math skills	•		Word processing
•		Study skills	•		Time management
		Language arts	•		Learning strategies
•		Written express	•		Organizational skills

Academic Accommodations

Curriculum	Study Aids	Exams
Priority registration	Typist	Oral
Math waiver	Reader	Untimed
• Foreign lang. waiver	Notetaker	Take home
Course substitution	• Proof reader	With proctor
In Class	• Text on tape	On computer
• Calculators	Early syllabus	• Extended time
• Tape recorder	Taped handouts	On tape
• Word processor		Modified
Priority seating		Separate room

334

Graduation Requirements:
Course credits: **120** GPA: **2.0** Years to complete degree: **Normally 4** Math waiver: **Yes** Language waiver: **Yes**

Program Strengths
Curry's Program for Advancement of Learning is distinguished by the depth and richness that our 20 year history provides. Our meta-cognitive approach, which values students' thinking ability as well as focuses on student strengths, enables us to facilitate our students' move toward independence.

General Information:
Curry College is a 4 year private college. Suburban campus of 120 acres is 7 miles from Boston. Accessible by air, train or bus. Ski areas are 1 hour from campus. Beaches are 1 hour from campus. 2% of students are foreign. 12 residential halls on campus. Housing is guaranteed.

Accreditation: NEACS

SAT/ACT Scores:
Scores for incoming freshmen: **Verbal:** 92% below 500. 7% between 500 and 599. 1% between 600 and 699. **Math:** 86% below 500. 11% between 500 and 599. 3% between 600 and 699.

Expenses:
Tuition: In-state: Full year: $12,495.00. Part-time: Per credit: $345.00. Room and board: $5,280.00 Cost of LD program: $3,000.00

Majors
• AREA STUDIES Ethnic, Women's Studies • BUSINESS Business Management, Economics, Entrepreneur, Finance, Marketing, Organizational Behavior • COMMUNICATIONS Communication, English, Journalism, Photography, Public Relations, Television/Radio/Film • COMPUTER SCIENCE Computer Science • CRAFTS AND DESIGN Graphic Design • EDUCATION Early Childhood, Elementary, Special • HEALTH SCIENCES Nursing • HUMANITIES Philosophy, Religion • LANGUAGES Spanish • SCIENCES Biochemistry, Biology, Chemistry, Ecology • SOCIAL SCIENCES Government/Political, Psychology, Sociology • VISUAL AND PERFORMING ARTS Dance, Music, Theater • VOCATIONAL Painting

Sports/Activities
• SPORTS-INTERCOLLEGIATE Baseball (M), Basketball, Football (M), Ice Hockey (M), Lacrosse (M), Rugby (M), Softball (F), Tennis (F), Wrestling (M) • SPORTS-INTRAMURAL Basketball, Field Hockey (F), Softball, Tennis, Volleyball • STUDENT LIFE ACTIVITIES Choral, Dance, Drama Groups, International Club, Literary Club, Music Groups, Musical Theater, Newspaper, Nursing Association, Radio/TV station, Student Activities Board, Student Government, Yearbook

Less Selective **Massachusetts Program**

Dean Junior College
99 Main Street
Franklin, Massachusetts 02038
(508) 528-9100

School Enrollment: **1,100** Male: **555** Female: **545**
LD Enrollment: **60**

Admissions Contact: **Steven Kesman, Assoc. Dir. of Admissions**
LD Contact: **Laura Choiniere, Coordinator, Academic Support**
Name of Program: **Academic Support Program**

Admissions

Application Information:
Enrolled: **60**
Separate application: **Yes**
Application deadline: **Rolling**
Rolling Admissions: **Yes**

Secondary School Information
Most Important Criteria For Admissions (1-strongest)

	SAT/ACT		Application	**4**	School transcript
	Class rank	**5**	Course selection		Personal statement
	Interview	**6**	Extra activities	**2**	Psychoeducational
4	G.P.A.		Open admission	**4**	Recommendations

Test Requirements:
Diagnostic testing waived: **Yes**
WAIS-R required: **Yes** Range accepted: **100 full scale**
Documentation of LD required: **Yes**
Currency of diagnostic testing: **3 years**
Tests recommended: **Full neuropsychological battery focusing on cognitive characteristics and language testing.**

Types of Disabilities Served
- Speech/Lang
- Study skills
- Written express
- Organizational
- Perceptual
- Reading
- Spelling
- Math
- Fine Motor
- ADD with LD
- ADD without LD
- ADHD with LD
- ADHD without LD

Learning Disability Program
Students mainstreamed **100** % of the day
Time required or recommended in learning center: **1 hour**

Faculty:
Faculty: **5** Including Director: **Yes** Full time: **2** Part time: **3** M.A.: **5**
Faculty advocate: **Yes** Meets with instructor: **As needed**

Diagnostic Testing
ADD	Personality •	Perceptual skills	• Spelling
ADHD•	Organization	Fine motor skills	• Reading
I.Q. •	Handwriting•	Spoken language	• Study skills
• Math	Social skills •	Written language	

Tutoring:
Average size of group tutorials: **Individual**
Services rendered by:
Graduates   Peers   Faculty   •LD staff   Teacher trainees

Tutorials
Grp.	Ind.	Tutorials	Grp.	Ind.	Tutorials
	•	Math skills		•	Word processing
	•	Study skills		•	Time management
	•	Language arts		•	Learning strategies
	•	Written express		•	Organizational skills

Academic Accommodations

Curriculum	Study Aids	Exams
Priority registration	• Typist	• Oral
Math waiver	Reader	Untimed
Foreign lang. waiver	• Notetaker	• Take home
• Course substitution	• Proof reader	With proctor
In Class	• Text on tape	On computer
• Calculators	Early syllabus	• Extended time
• Tape recorder	Taped handouts	On tape
• Word processor		Modified
Priority seating		Separate room

Program Strengths
Students receive individual strategy tutoring matched to their cognitive profile, determined by formal testing results submitted during the Admissions process, and informal testing once students arrive on campus. Focus on accountability, developing independence and lifetime skills for transfer to other colleges and the workplace.

General Information:
Dean Junior College is a 2 year private college. Suburban campus of 100 acres is 30 miles from Boston. Accessible by train or bus. Ski areas are 45 mins. from campus. Beaches are 45 mins. from campus. 3% of students are foreign. 15 residential halls on campus. Housing is guaranteed.

Accreditation: NEACS

Expenses:
Tuition: In-state: Full year: $8,500.00. Part-time: Per credit:$270.00. Part-time: Per course: $90.00. Room and board: $5,800.00

Majors
• BUSINESS Business Administration, Business Management, Entrepreneur, Fashion Merchandising, Secretarial Science, Sports Management
• COMMUNICATIONS Broadcasting, Communication, Journalism, Photography, Speech, Television/Radio/Film • COMPUTER SCIENCE Computer Science • EDUCATION Early Childhood, Elementary, English As A Second Language, Mathematics, Music, Physical, Recreation/Youth Leadership, Science • HEALTH SCIENCES Medical Secretary • SOCIAL SCIENCES Criminal Justice, Human Service, Law Enforcement, Social Science • VISUAL AND PERFORMING ARTS Art, Dance, Dramatic Arts, Music, Music Performance, Music Theatre, Studio Art, Theater • VOCATIONAL Fashion Merchandising, Office Administration, Park/Recreation, Secretarial

Sports/Activities
• SPORTS RELATED Cheerleading • SPORTS-INTRAMURAL Archery (F), Archery (M), Badminton (F), Badminton (M), Basketball (F), Basketball (M), Bowling (F), Bowling (M), Field Hockey (F), Football (M), Golf (F), Golf (M), Gymnastics (F), Gymnastics (M), Lacrosse (M), Swimming (F), Swimming (M), Tennis (F), Tennis (M), Volleyball (F), Volleyball (M), Water Polo (F), Water Polo (M), Weight Lifting • STUDENT LIFE ACTIVITIES Academic Clubs, Choral, Dance, Drama Groups, Jazz Band, Magazine, Music Groups, Musical Theater, Newspaper, Radio/TV station, Religious Organization, Student Government, Yearbook

Endicott College
376 Hale Street
Beverly, Massachusetts 01915-9985
(617) 927-0585

School Enrollment: **800** Female: **800**

Admissions Contact: **Elizabeth Macomber, Director of Admissions**
LD Contact: **Jane Lang, SSP Coordinator**
Name of Program: **Academic Support Center**
Address: **376 Hale St.**
Telephone:**(508) 927-0585 - Ext. 2290**

Admissions

Application Information:
Application deadline: **Rolling**
Rolling Admissions: **Yes**

Secondary School Information
Most Important Criteria For Admissions (1-strongest)

SAT/ACT	Application **1**	School transcript
Class rank	Course selection	Personal statement
Interview	Extra activities	Psychoeducational
G.P.A.	Open admission	Recommendations

Test Requirements:
Standardized tests waived: **Yes**
Untimed SAT: **Yes**
WAIS-R required: **Yes**
Documentation of LD required: **Yes**

Types of Disabilities Served
- Speech/Lang
- Study skills
- Written express
- Organizational
- Perceptual
- Reading
- Spelling
- Math
- Fine Motor

ADD with LD
ADD without LD
ADHD with LD
ADHD without LD

Admissions Process

Admission is a rolling process. Upon receipt of high school transcript, application, reference, application fee and any other related materials, application is reviewed by Admissions Committee. Notification is generally within two weeks.

High School Course Requirements:
English: **4** Math: **1** Science: **1**

Learning Disability Program
Students mainstreamed **100** % of the day
Recommended credits per semester: **12-15**
Counseling: Individual: **Yes**
Support groups are available:**Yes**

Faculty: Full time: **5** Part time: **15**

Diagnostic Testing

ADD	Personality	Perceptual skills	Spelling
ADHD	Organization	Fine motor skills	Reading
I.Q.	Handwriting	Spoken language	Study skills
Math	Social skills	Written language	

Tutoring:
Services rendered by:
Graduates   •Peers   Faculty   •LD staff   Teacher trainees

Tutorials

Grp.	Ind.	Tutorials	Grp.	Ind.	Tutorials
•	•	Math skills			Word processing
•	•	Study skills	•	•	Time management
•	•	Language arts	•	•	Learning strategies
•	•	Written express	•	•	Organizational skills

Academic Accommodations

Curriculum	Study Aids	Exams
Priority registration	Typist	• Oral
Math waiver	Reader	• Untimed
Foreign lang. waiver	Notetaker	Take home
Course substitution	Proof reader	With proctor
In Class	Text on tape	On computer
• Calculators	Early syllabus	• Extended time
• Tape recorder	Taped handouts	On tape
Word processor		Modified
• Priority seating		Separate room

Graduation Requirements:
Course credits: **67** GPA: **1.8**

Program Strengths
LD students may be required or recommended to be part of the Student Support Program which deals with high risk students. The student works with a professional tutor on a one-to-one basis, usually two times a week. Some students are seen four times a week.

General Information:
Endicott College is a 2 and 4 year private college. Suburban campus of 160 acres is 22 miles from Boston. Accessible by train. Ski areas are 1/2 hour from campus. Beaches are the campus from campus. 9% of students are foreign. 11 residential halls on campus. Housing is guaranteed.75 % of students remain on campus for the weekends.

Accreditation:NEACS

Expenses:
Tuition: In-state: Full year: $10,310.00. Part-time: Per credit:$315.00. Part-time: Per course: $945.00. Tuition: Out-of-state: Full year: $10,310.00. Part-time: Per credit:$315.00. Part-time: Per course:$945.00 Room and board: $5,610.00 Cost of LD program:varies

Majors
• BUSINESS Accounting, Business Administration, Business Management, Hotel and Restaurant Managemen, Retailing, Travel/Tourism Management • COMMUNICATIONS Advertising, Broadcasting, Commercial Design, Communication, Photography, Television/Radio/Film • CRAFTS AND DESIGN Graphic Design • EDUCATION Child Development, Elementary, Physical, Teacher Aide • HEALTH SCIENCES Health, Nursing, Occupational Therapy • HUMANITIES Humanities, Liberal Arts • PRE-PROFESSIONAL Occupational Therapy, Pre-Elementary • SCIENCES Gerontology • SOCIAL SCIENCES Human Service, Psychology, Social Sciences • VISUAL AND PERFORMING ARTS Art • VOCATIONAL Athletic Training, Fashion Design, Fashion Merchandising, Interior De-

sign, Paralegal

Sports/Activities

• SPORTS-INTERCOLLEGIATE Basketball, Field Hockey (F), Soccer (F), Softball (F), Tennis (F), Volleyball (F) • SPORTS-INTRAMURAL Basketball (F), Field Hockey (F), Sailing (F), Soccer (F), Softball (F), Tennis (F), Volleyball (F) • STUDENT LIFE ACTIVITIES Choral, Dance, Drama Groups, Music Groups, Newspaper, Student Government, Yearbook

---

Selective   **Massachusetts**

Gordon College

255 Grapevine Road
Wenham, Massachusetts 01984
(508) 927-2300

School Enrollment: **1,200** Male: **540** Female: **660**

Admissions Contact: **Pamela Bradstreet, Director of Admissions**
LD Contact: **Eleanor Vandevort, Education Specialist**
Name of Program: **Academic Support Center**
Telephone: **(508) 927-2300**

Admissions

Application Information:
LD on admissions committee: **CAN**
Application deadline: **Rolling**
Rolling Admissions: **Yes**

Secondary School Information
Most Important Criteria For Admissions (1-strongest)

4 SAT/ACT	**11** Application	**1**	School transcript
3 Class rank	**7** Course selection		Personal statement
5 Interview	**9** Extra activities	**10**	Psychoeducational
8 G.P.A.	Open admission	**6**	Recommendations

Test Requirements:
Diagnostic testing waived: **Yes**
Untimed SAT: **Yes** Untimed ACT: **Yes**
Documentation of LD required: **Yes**

Types of Disabilities Served
• Speech/Lang • Reading • ADD with LD
• Study skills • Spelling • ADD without LD
• Written express • Math • ADHD with LD
• Organizational • Fine Motor • ADHD without LD
• Perceptual

Admissions Process

All deficits are accepted if student meets other requirements.

High School Course Requirements:
English: **4** Math: **2** Science: **2** Foreign Language: **3**

Learning Disability Program

Program: Reinforces course work: **Yes**
Students mainstreamed **100** % of the day
Services available for all students: **Yes**
Vocational Counseling: **Yes**
Support groups are available: **Supplemental instruction groups for**

specified courses.

Diagnostic Testing

ADD	Personality	Perceptual skills	Spelling
ADHD	Organization	Fine motor skills	Reading
I.Q.	Handwriting	Spoken language	Study skills
Math	Social skills	Written language	

Tutoring:
Average size of group tutorials: **Walk in services**
Services rendered by:
  Graduates •Peers Faculty LD staff Teacher trainees

Tutorials

Grp.	Ind.	Tutorials	Grp.	Ind.	Tutorials
		Math skills			Word processing
		Study skills			Time management
		Language arts			Learning strategies
		Written express			Organizational skills

Academic Accommodations

Curriculum	Study Aids	Exams
• Priority registration	• Typist	• Oral
Math waiver	• Reader	• Untimed
• Foreign lang. waiver	• Notetaker	• Take home
Course substitution	• Proof reader	• With proctor
In Class	• Text on tape	• On computer
• Calculators	• Early syllabus	• Extended time
• Tape recorder	Taped handouts	• On tape
• Word processor		• Modified
• Priority seating		• Separate room

Graduation Requirements:
Course credits: **127** GPA: **2.0** Language waiver: **Yes**

General Information:

Gordon College is a 4 year independent college. Suburban campus of 700 acres is 27 miles from Boston. Accessible by car, plane or bus Beaches are 3 miles from campus. 12 residential halls on campus. Housing is guaranteed. Guaranteed through 4th year.

Accreditation: NEACS, DEM, MBHE, NAM

Expenses:
Tuition: In-state: Full year: $10,940.00. Part-time: Per credit: $780.00. Part-time: Per course: $1,480.00. Tuition: Out-of-state: Full year: $10,940.00. Part-time: Per credit: $780.00. Part-time: Per course: $1,480.00 Room and board: $3,630.00

Majors

• BUSINESS Accounting, Business Administration, Economics • COMMUNICATIONS English • COMPUTER SCIENCE Computer Science • EDUCATION Early Childhood, Elementary, Middle School, Music, Recreation and Youth Leadershi, Secondary, Special • HUMANITIES English/Writing/Literature, Philosophy, Religion • LANGUAGES English, French, Spanish • PRE PROFESSIONAL Law, Medicine, Recreation, Social Work, Sports Medicine • RELIGIOUS STUDIES Bible, Philosophy • SCIENCES Applied Mathematics, Biology, Chemistry, Computer Science, Physics • SOCIAL SCIENCES History, Human Service, Political Science, Psychology, Sociology • SPECIAL EDUCATION Deaf/Hearing Impaired, Emotionally Disturbed, Mentally Retarded • VISUAL AND PERFORMING ARTS Music, Music Performance

Sports/Activities

• SPORTS RELATED Cheerleading • SPORTS-INTERCOLLEGIATE Baseball, Baseball (M), Basketball, Basketball (F), Basketball (M), Cross Country, Cross Country (F), Cross Country (M), Field Hockey (F), Soccer (M), Softball (F), Tennis, Tennis (F), Tennis (M), Volleyball • SPORTS-IN-

Massachusetts

TRAMURAL Basketball, Basketball (F), Basketball (M), Football, Flag, Ice Hockey (M), Ping-Pong, Soccer (M), Softball, Tennis, Volleyball, Volleyball (F) • STUDENT LIFE ACTIVITIES Academic Clubs, Choral, Community Service, Concert Band, Dance, Drama Groups, Ethnic & Cultural Groups, Film, Jazz Band, Magazine, Music Groups, Musical Theater, Newspaper, Orchestra, Political Groups, Religious Organization, Student Government, Yearbook

Most Selective

Massachusetts Services

Harvard University
837 Holyoke Center
Cambridge, Massachusetts 02138
(617) 495-1551

School Enrollment: **6,592** Male: **3,857** Female: **2,735**

Admissions Contact: **Marilyn McGrath, Lewis Dir. of Admissions**
LD Contact: **Louise Russell, Coordinator**
Name of Program: **Disability Resources**
Telephone:**(617) 496-8707**

Admissions

Application Information:
Application deadline: **Jan. 1st**
Applicant must apply **9** months in advance
Notified when: **Mid-April**

Secondary School Information
Most Important Criteria For Admissions (1-strongest)

2 SAT/ACT	**2** Application	**2** School transcript
2 Class rank	**2** Course selection	Personal statement
2 Interview	**2** Extra activities	Psychoeducational
1 G.P.A.	Open admission	**2** Recommendations

Test Requirements:
Untimed SAT: **Yes** Untimed ACT: **Yes**
Documentation of LD required: **Yes**

Types of Disabilities Served
- Speech/Lang
- Study skills
- Written express
- Organizational
- Perceptual
- Reading
- Spelling
- Math
- Fine Motor
- ADD with LD
- ADD without LD
- ADHD with LD
- ADHD without LD

Learning Disability Program
Students mainstreamed **100** % of the day
Recommended credits per semester: **4 courses**
Services available for all students: **Yes**
Counseling: Individual: **Yes** Group Counseling: **Yes**
Support groups are available:**Peer and group counseling**

Faculty:
Faculty: **11** Including Director: **Yes** Full time: **1** Part time: **10**

Diagnostic Testing

ADD	Personality	Perceptual skills	Spelling
ADHD	Organization	Fine motor skills	Reading
I.Q.	Handwriting	Spoken language	Study skills
Math	Social skills	Written language	

Tutoring:
Average size of group tutorials: **1:1**
Services rendered by:
Graduates •Peers Faculty LD staff Teacher trainees

Tutorials

Grp.	Ind.	Tutorials	Grp.	Ind.	Tutorials
		Math skills			Word processing
		Study skills			Time management
		Language arts			Learning strategies
		Written express			Organizational skills

Academic Accommodations

Curriculum	Study Aids	Exams
Priority registration	Typist	• Oral
Math waiver	Reader	Untimed
• Foreign lang. waiver	• Notetaker	Take home
• Course substitution	Proof reader	With proctor
In Class	• Text on tape	On computer
Calculators	Early syllabus	• Extended time
• Tape recorder	Taped handouts	On tape
• Word processor		• Modified
Priority seating		Separate room

Graduation Requirements:
Course credits: **32 courses** Years to complete degree: **4**

Program Strengths
We do not have a program, only support services for students with disabilities. Each student has a faculty coordinator of services for students with disabilities. Services are decentralized. Individualized programs.
* Tutoring is for all students.

General Information:
Harvard University is a 4 year private university. Urban campus Boston. Accessible by air, train or bus. Beaches are 30 miles from campus. 6% of students are foreign. 20 residential halls on campus. Housing is guaranteed.Guaranteed through 4th year.

Accreditation:

SAT/ACT Scores:
Scores for incoming freshmen: 50%between 600 and 699. 50% between 600 and 699.

Expenses:
Tuition: In-state: Full year: $15,410.00. Room and board: $6,670.00

Majors
• AREA STUDIES African, American, Asian, Black/Afro-American, European, Jewish, Latin American, Middle Eastern, Russian/Slavic, Women's Studies • BUSINESS Economics • COMMUNICATIONS Creative Writing, English • COMPUTER SCIENCE Computer Science, Computer Technology • ENGINEERING Bioengineering, Biomedical, Computer, Electrical, Environmental/Water Resources, Geophysical, Materials, Mechanical, Physics • HUMANITIES Classics, English/Writing/Literature, Humanities, Philosophy, Religion • LANGUAGES Chinese, French, German, Greek, Hebrew, Japanese, Latin, Linguistic, Russian, Spanish • SCIENCES Archeology, Astronomy, Biochemistry, Biology, Chemistry, Geology, Geophysics & Seismology, Mathematics, Physical Science, Physics, Statistics • SOCIAL SCIENCES Anthropology, Government/Political, History, Psychology, Social Sciences, Sociology • VISUAL AND PERFORMING ARTS Art History, Music

Sports/Activities
• SPORTS RELATED Marching Band • SPORTS-INTERCOLLEGIATE Baseball (M), Basketball, Crew, Cross Country, Diving, Fencing, Field

Hockey (F), Football (M), Golf (M), Ice Hockey, Lacrosse, Sailing, Skiing - Snow, Soccer, Softball (F), Squash, Swimming, Tennis, Track and Field, Volleyball, Water Polo, Weight Lifting (M) • SPORTS-INTRAMURAL Badminton, Basketball, Crew, Fencing, Field Hockey (F), Football (M), Gymnastics (F), Ice Hockey, Ping-Pong, Rugby (M), Sailing, Skiing - Snow, Soccer, Softball, Squash, Swimming, Tennis, Track and Field, Volleyball, Weight Lifting (M) • STUDENT LIFE ACTIVITIES Choral, Concert Band, Dance, Drama Groups, Ethnic & Cultural Groups, Jazz Band, Magazine, Music Groups, Musical Theater, Political Groups, Radio/TV station, Religious Organization, Student Government, Symphony Orchestra, Yearbook

---

Transitional   Massachusetts Program

Lesley College-Threshold
29 Everett Street
Cambridge, Massachusetts 02138-2790
(617) 491-3739
LD Enrollment: 48 Male: 12 Female: 36

Admissions Contact: **Jim Wilbur, Director of Admissions**
LD Contact: **Jim Wilbur, Admissions Coordinator**
Name of Program: **Threshold**

Admissions

Application Information:
Accepted: 24 Enrolled:24
Separate application:**Yes**
Application deadline: **March 1st**
Notified when: **May 1st**

Secondary School Information
Most Important Criteria For Admissions (1-strongest)

SAT/ACT	Application	School transcript
Class rank	Course selection	Personal statement
Interview	Extra activities	Psychoeducational
G.P.A.	Open admission	Recommendations

Test Requirements:
Diagnostic testing waived: **Yes**
WAIS-R required: **Yes** Range accepted: **75-95**
Documentation of LD required: **Yes**
Currency of diagnostic testing: **within one year**
Tests recommended: **PIAT-R, TAT/Rorschach**

Types of Disabilities Served
- Speech/Lang
- Study skills
- Written express
- Organizational
- Perceptual
- Reading
- Spelling
- Math
- Fine Motor
- ADD with LD
- ADD without LD
- ADHD with LD
- ADHD without LD

Admissions Process

Applicant submits application, test results and recommendations. Director of Admissions screens for appropriate candidates who are then invited for an interview. Applicants notified by May 1st.

Faculty:
Faculty: **20** Including Director: **Yes** Full time: **5** Part time: **15** M.A.: **18** Ph.D.: **2**

Diagnostic Testing

ADD	Personality	Perceptual skills	Spelling
ADHD•	Organization	Fine motor skills	Reading
I.Q.	Handwriting	Spoken language	• Study skills
Math	Social skills	Written language	

Services rendered by:
Graduates   Peers   Faculty   LD staff   Teacher trainees

Tutorials

Grp.	Ind.	Tutorials	Grp.	Ind.	Tutorials
•	•	Math skills			Word processing
•	•	Study skills	•	•	Time management
•	•	Language arts	•	•	Learning strategies
•	•	Written express	•	•	Organizational skills

Academic Accommodations

Curriculum	Study Aids	Exams
Priority registration	Typist	• Oral
Math waiver	Reader	Untimed
Foreign lang. waiver	Notetaker	Take home
Course substitution	Proof reader	With proctor
In Class	• Text on tape	On computer
• Calculators	Early syllabus	• Extended time
• Tape recorder	Taped handouts	On tape
• Word processor		• Modified
• Priority seating		Separate room

Graduation Requirements: Math waiver: **Yes** Language waiver: **Yes**

Program Strengths

Our program is for students who are motivated to continue their education after high school but who would have difficulty succeeding in a traditional college program. Through practical courses and field practicum, students develop a variety of skills essential for independent adulthood. Upon graduation, students receive a certificate of completion and six college credits for the vocational component of the program. The twelve month outreach program after graduation offers additional support as graduates put to full-time practical use the vocational and independent living skills learned in their course work.

General Information:

Lesley College-Threshold is a 2 year private college. Urban campus 8 miles from Boston. Accessible by air, train, or bus. Ski areas are 1 hour from campus. Beaches are 1 hour from campus. 3 residential halls on campus. Housing is guaranteed.Guaranteed through 2nd year.

Accreditation: Regional

Expenses:
Tuition: In-state: Full year: $13,200.00. Room and board: $5,730.00

Majors
• EDUCATION Adult, Early Childhood • SOCIAL SCIENCES Human Service

Massachusetts

Massachusetts Bay Community College

50 Oakland Street
Wellesley Hills, Massachusetts 02181
(617) 237-0165

School Enrollment: **4,674** Male: **1,722** Female: **2,952**
LD Enrollment: **130** Male: **56** Female: **74**

Admissions Contact: **Jim Regan, Director of Admissions**
LD Contact: **Gail Hammond/Joan Stone, Learning Specialist**
Telephone:**(617) 237-1100 Ext.**

Admissions

Application Information:
LD Students Applying: **53** Accepted: **53**
Application deadline: **Open**
Rolling Admissions: **Yes**

Secondary School Information
Most Important Criteria For Admissions (1-strongest)

SAT/ACT	Application	School transcript
Class rank	Course selection	Personal statement
Interview	Extra activities	Psychoeducational
G.P.A.	Open admission	Recommendations

Test Requirements:
Untimed SAT: **Yes** Untimed ACT: **Yes** Untimed ACH: **Yes**
Documentation of LD required: **Yes**
Currency of diagnostic testing: **2 years**
Tests recommended: **Recommended: WAIS-R**

Types of Disabilities Served
- Speech/Lang
- Reading
- ADD with LD
- Study skills
- Spelling
- ADD without LD
- Written express
- Math
- ADHD with LD
- Organizational
- Fine Motor
- ADHD without LD
- Perceptual

Learning Disability Program

Special orientation for LD students: **Yes**
Program: Reinforces course work: **Yes**
Students mainstreamed **100** % of the day
Time required or recommended in learning center: **no limit**
Services only for LD students: **Yes**

Faculty:
Faculty: **2** Including Director: **Yes** Full time: **1** Part time: **2** M.A.: **2**
Faculty advocate: **Yes** Meets with instructor: **As needed**

Diagnostic Testing

ADD	Personality	Perceptual skills	Spelling
ADHD	Organization	Fine motor skills	Reading
I.Q.	Handwriting	Spoken language	Study skills
Math	Social skills •	Written language	

Tutoring:
Services rendered by:
Graduates • Peers   Faculty   • LD staff   Teacher trainees

Tutorials

Grp.	Ind.	Tutorials	Grp.	Ind.	Tutorials
•	•	Math skills	•	•	Word processing
•		Study skills	•	•	Time management
•	•	Language arts	•	•	Learning strategies
•	•	Written express	•	•	Organizational skills

Academic Accommodations

Curriculum	Study Aids	Exams
Priority registration	Typist	• Oral
Math waiver	Reader	Untimed
Foreign lang. waiver	Notetaker	Take home
Course substitution	Proof reader	• With proctor
In Class	• Text on tape	On computer
• Calculators	Early syllabus	• Extended time
• Tape recorder	Taped handouts	On tape
• Word processor		• Modified
Priority seating		• Separate room

Program Strengths
It stresses self-advocacy and mainstreaming of students into the college. Student advocacy groups meet weekly. Mentor tutors are used to foster independent learning behavior.

General Information:
Massachusetts Bay Community College is a 2 year public college. Suburban campus of 86 acres is 8 miles from Boston. Accessible by train or bus. Ski areas are 25 miles from campus. Beaches are 15 miles from campus. 5% of students are foreign. Housing is not guaranteed.

Accreditation:

Expenses:
Tuition: In-state: Full year: $1,008.00. Part-time: Per credit:$42.00. Tuition: Out-of-state: Full year: $4,680.00. Part-time: Per credit:$195.00.

Majors
• BUSINESS Accounting, Banking, Business Management, Finance, Hotel and Restaurant Managemen, Management, Marketing, Real Estate, Travel/ Tourism Management • COMMUNICATIONS Communication • COMPUTER SCIENCE Computer Science, Computer Technology, Data Processing, Programming • EDUCATION Child Development, Early Childhood, Teacher Aide • ENGINEERING Electrical • HEALTH SCIENCES Medical Secretary, Medical Technology, Nursing, Occupational Therapy • HUMANITIES Liberal Arts • PREPROFESSIONAL Dentistry, Medicine, Pharmacy, Veterinarian • SCIENCES Horticultural, Radiology • SOCIAL SCIENCES International Studies, Law Enforcement • VISUAL AND PERFORMING ARTS Theater • VOCATIONAL Automobile Technology, Automotive Service, Business and Office, Electronics Technology, Fire Science, Food Service, Paralegal, Radiological Technology, Secretarial

Sports/Activities
• SPORTS-INTERCOLLEGIATE Baseball (M), Basketball, Soccer (M), Softball (F) • SPORTS-INTRAMURAL Basketball, Field Hockey, Golf, Ice Hockey, Racquetball, Soccer, Softball, Tennis, Track and Field • STUDENT LIFE ACTIVITIES Choral, Community Service, Drama Groups, Musical Theater, Newspaper, Student Government, Yearbook

Special

Massachusetts Accommodations

Massachusetts College of Art

621 Huntington Avenue
Boston, Massachusetts 02115
(617) 232-1555

School Enrollment: **1,085** Male: **421** Female: **659**

Admissions Contact: **Kay Ransdell, Assoc. Dean Admissions**

Admissions

Application Information:
Application deadline: **May 1st**
Rolling Admissions: **Yes**

Secondary School Information
Most Important Criteria For Admissions (1-strongest)

2 SAT/ACT	Application	**1**	School transcript
1 Class rank	**2** Course selection	**2**	Personal statement
3 Interview	**4** Extra activities	**2**	Psychoeducational
1 G.P.A.	Open admission	**3**	Recommendations

Test Requirements:
Untimed SAT: **Yes**
Documentation of LD required: **Yes**

Types of Disabilities Served
- Speech/Lang
- Study skills
- Written express
- Organizational
- Perceptual
- Reading
- Spelling
- Math
- Fine Motor
- ADD with LD
- ADD without LD
- ADHD with LD
- ADHD without LD

High School Course Requirements:
English: **4** Math: **3** Science: **2** Foreign Language: **2**
Waivers to standard high school courses
Foreign Language : **Yes**

Diagnostic Testing
ADD	Personality	Perceptual skills	Spelling
ADHD	Organization	Fine motor skills	Reading
I.Q.	Handwriting	Spoken language	Study skills
Math	Social skills	Written language	

Tutoring:
Average size of group tutorials: **Individualized**
Services rendered by:

Graduates	Peers	Faculty	LD staff	Teacher trainees

Tutorials
Grp.	Ind.	Tutorials	Grp.	Ind.	Tutorials
		Math skills			Word processing
		Study skills			Time management
		Language arts			Learning strategies
		Written express			Organizational skills

Academic Accommodations

Curriculum	Study Aids	Exams
Priority registration	Typist	• Oral
Math waiver	Reader	Untimed
Foreign lang. waiver	Notetaker	• Take home
Course substitution	Proof reader	With proctor
In Class	• Text on tape	On computer
• Calculators	Early syllabus	• Extended time
• Tape recorder	Taped handouts	On tape
• Word processor		• Modified
Priority seating		Separate room

Graduation Requirements:
Course credits: **132**

Program Strengths
The college can coordinate a student program of accommodations based on a recent diagnosis of learning disabilities, but we have no special LD services or programs. Therefore, we encourage applications for LD students who have well-developed compensatory skills which have enabled them to be successful in traditional academic curricula.

General Information:
Massachusetts College of Art is a 4 year public college. Urban campus Accessible by air, train or bus. Ski areas are 100 miles from campus. Beaches are 30 miles from campus. 5% of students are foreign. 1 residential halls on campus. Housing is not guaranteed.

Accreditation:NEACS, NASAD

SAT/ACT Scores:
Scores for incoming freshmen:**Verbal:**54%below 500. 29%between 500 and 599. 7%between 600 and 699. 2%above 700. **Math:**54% below 500. 31% between 500 and 599. 13% between 600 and 699. 1%above 700.

Class Rank:
About 29% of the present freshmen class were in the upper 20% of their high school class. 63% were in the top 40% of their class. 95% were in the top 60% of their class. 98% were in the top 80% of their class.

Expenses:
Tuition: In-state: Full year: $3,734.00. Part-time: Per course: $774.25. Tuition: Out-of-state: Full year: $8,294.00. Part-time: Per course:$1,344.25 Room and board: $5,247.00

Majors
• COMMUNICATIONS Photography, Television/Radio/Film • CRAFTS AND DESIGN Ceramics, Glass, Graphic Design, Illustration Design, Sculpture • EDUCATION Art • VISUAL AND PERFORMING ARTS Art, Art History, Fine Arts, Studio Art • VOCATIONAL Fashion Design, Industrial Design, Jewelry-Metalsmithery, Painting

Sports/Activities
• SPORTS-INTERCOLLEGIATE Basketball (F) • SPORTS-INTRAMURAL Basketball, Ping-Pong, Racquetball • STUDENT LIFE ACTIVITIES Dance, Drama Groups, Newspaper, Radio/TV station, Student Government, Yearbook

Massachusetts

Most Selective **Massachusetts Accommodations**

Massachusetts Institute of Technology
77 Massachusetts Ave.
Cambridge, Massachusetts 02139
(617) 253-4791

School Enrollment: **4,389** Male: **2,941** Female: **1,448**

Admissions Contact: **Bette Johnson, Assoc. Dir. Admissions**
LD Contact: **Arnold Henderson, Asst. Dean of Student Affairs**

Admissions

Application Information:
Application deadline: **January 1st**
Notified when: **April 1st**

Secondary School Information
Most Important Criteria For Admissions (1-strongest)

2 SAT/ACT	**3** Application	**1** School transcript	
1 Class rank	**3** Course selection	Personal statement	
4 Interview	**4** Extra activities	Psychoeducational	
1 G.P.A.	Open admission	**4** Recommendations	

Test Requirements:
Untimed SAT: **Yes** Untimed ACT: **Yes** Untimed ACH: **Yes** Achievement tests required:**3**

Types of Disabilities Served

Speech/Lang	Reading	ADD with LD
Study skills	Spelling	ADD without LD
Written express	Math	ADHD with LD
Organizational	Fine Motor	ADHD without LD
Perceptual		

Learning Disability Program
Program: Reinforces course work: **Yes**
Students mainstreamed **100** % of the day

Faculty:
Faculty advocate: **Yes**

Diagnostic Testing

ADD	Personality	Perceptual skills	Spelling
ADHD	Organization	Fine motor skills	Reading
I.Q.	Handwriting	Spoken language	Study skills
Math	Social skills	Written language	

Tutoring:
Average size of group tutorials:
Services rendered by:
•Graduates　Peers　Faculty　LD staff　Teacher trainees

Tutorials

Grp.	Ind.	Tutorials	Grp.	Ind.	Tutorials
	•	Math skills			Word processing
		Study skills		•	Time management
	•	Language arts			Learning strategies
	•	Written express		•	Organizational skills

Academic Accommodations

Curriculum	Study Aids	Exams
Priority registration	• Typist	• Oral
Math waiver	Reader	Untimed
Foreign lang. waiver	• Notetaker	• Take home
Course substitution	• Proof reader	With proctor
In Class	• Text on tape	On computer
• Calculators	Early syllabus	• Extended time
• Tape recorder	Taped handouts	On tape
• Word processor		• Modified
Priority seating		Separate room

Program Strengths
We don't have a program per se. We will provide individual assistance as needed to accommodate our students.

General Information:
Massachusetts Institute of Technology is a 4 year private university. Urban campus of 147 acres is Boston. Accessible by air, train or bus. Ski areas are 1 hour from campus. Beaches are 1 hour from campus. 8% of students are foreign. 15 residential halls on campus. Housing is guaranteed.100 % of students remain on campus for the weekends. 33 % of students join fraternities/sororities.

Accreditation:NEACS

SAT/ACT Scores:
Scores for incoming freshmen:**Verbal:**9%below 500. 23%between 500 and 599. 49%between 600 and 699. 17%above 700. 1% between 500 and 599. 18% between 600 and 699. 80%above 700.

Class Rank:
About 99% of the present freshmen class were in the upper 20% of their high school class.

Expenses:
Tuition: In-state: Full year: $18,000.00. Room and board: $5,565.00

Majors
• AREA STUDIES American, Latin American, Russian/Slavic, Urban, Women's Studies • BUSINESS Business Management, Economics, Management • COMMUNICATIONS Communication, Creative Writing, Television/Radio/Film • COMPUTER SCIENCE Computer Science, Programming, Robotics • ENGINEERING Aerospace, Bio-medical, Bioengineering, Civil/Environmental, Electrical, Engineering Science, Environmental/Water Resources, Geological, Geophysical, Materials, Mathematical, Metallurgical, Mining/Mineral, Naval Architecture, Nuclear, Ocean, Physics • HEALTH SCIENCES Nutritional/Food • HUMANITIES English/Writing/Literature, Liberal Arts, Philosophy • LANGUAGES French, German, Linguistics, Russian, Spanish • PRE-PROFESSIONAL Architecture, Engineering • SCIENCES Astronomy, Astrophysics, Bacteriology, Biochemistry, Biology, Cell Biology, Chemistry, Earth, Geochemistry, Geology, Geophysics & Seismology, Inorganic Chemistry, Mathematics, Microbiology, Mining, Oceanography, Organic Chemistry, Physical Chemistry, Physics • SOCIAL SCIENCES Anthropology, Government/Political, Psychology • VISUAL AND PERFORMING ARTS Music • VOCATIONAL Urban Design

Sports/Activities
• SPORTS RELATED Cheerleading, Chess, Marching Band, Team Managers • SPORTS-INTERCOLLEGIATE Baseball, Baseball (M), Basketball, Basketball (F), Basketball (M), Bowling, Crew, Crew (F), Crew (M), Cross Country, Cross Country (F), Cross Country (M), Cycling, Fencing, Fencing (F), Field Hockey, Field Hockey (F), Football, Football (M), Gymnastics, Gymnastics (F), Gymnastics (M), Ice Hockey, Ice Hockey (M), Lacrosse, Lacrosse (F), Lacrosse (M), Ping-Pong, Ping-Pong (F), Ping-Pong (M), Riflery, Riflery (F), Riflery (M), Rugby, Rugby (F), Rugby (M), Sailing, Sailing (F), Sailing (M), Skiing - Snow, Skiing - Snow (F), Skiing - Snow (M),

Soccer, Soccer (F), Soccer (M), Softball, Softball (F), Squash, Squash (F), Squash (M), Swimming, Swimming (F), Swimming (M), Tennis, Tennis (F), Tennis (M), Track and Field, Track and Field (F), Track and Field (M), Volleyball, Volleyball (F), Volleyball (M), Water Polo, Water Polo (F), Water Polo (M) • SPORTS-INTRAMURAL Archery, Archery (F), Archery (M), Badminton, Badminton (F), Badminton (M), Basketball, Basketball (F), Basketball (M), Bowling, Bowling (F), Bowling (M), Cycling, Fencing, Fencing (F), Fencing (M), Figure Skating, Football, Football (F), Football (M), Golf, Golf (F), Golf (M), Ice Hockey, Ice Hockey (F), Ice Hockey (M), Judo, Karate, Martial Arts, Ping-Pong, Ping-Pong (F), Ping-Pong (M), Racquetball, Racquetball (F), Racquetball (M), Riflery, Riflery (F), Riflery (M), Scuba, Soccer, Soccer (F), Soccer (M), Softball, Softball (F), Softball (M), Swimming, Swimming (F), Swimming (M), Tennis, Tennis (F), Tennis (M), Volleyball, Volleyball (F), Volleyball (M) • STUDENT LIFE ACTIVITIES Academic Clubs, Choral, Community Service, Concert Band, Dance, Debate, Drama Groups, Fraternities, Jazz Band, Music Groups, Musical Theater, Newspaper, Orchestra, Political Groups, Radio/TV station, Religious Organization, Sororities, Student Government, Symphony Orchestra, Yearbook

Less Selective — Massachusetts Services

Massasoit Community College
1 Massasoit Boulevard
Brockton, Massachusetts 02402
(508) 588-9100

School Enrollment: **4,000** Male: **2,000** Female: **2,000**
LD Enrollment: **100** Male: **35** Female: **65**

Admissions Contact: **Roberta Noodell, Director of Admissions**
LD Contact: **Peter Johnston, Dir. Academic Resource Center**

Admissions

Application Information:
Application deadline: **None**
Rolling Admissions: **Yes**

Secondary School Information
Most Important Criteria For Admissions (1-strongest)
SAT/ACT, Application, School transcript, Class rank, Course selection, Personal statement, Interview, Extra activities, Psychoeducational, G.P.A., **1** Open admission, Recommendations

Types of Disabilities Served
• Speech/Lang • Reading • ADD with LD
• Study skills • Spelling • ADD without LD
• Written express • Math • ADHD with LD
• Organizational • Fine Motor • ADHD without LD
• Perceptual

Learning Disability Program
Counseling: Individual: **Yes** Group Counseling: **Yes**

Faculty:
Faculty: **5** Full time: **1** Part time: **4**
Faculty advocate: **Yes** Meets with instructor: **As needed**

Massachusetts

Diagnostic Testing
ADD, Personality, Perceptual skills, Spelling
ADHD, Organization, Fine motor skills, Reading
I.Q., Handwriting, Spoken language, Study skills
Math, Social skills, Written language

Tutoring:
Services rendered by:
Graduates, Peers, Faculty, •LD staff, Teacher trainees

Tutorials
Grp. Ind. Tutorials / Grp. Ind. Tutorials
• Math skills • Word processing
• Study skills • Time management
• Language arts • Learning strategies
• Written express • Organizational skills

Academic Accommodations
Curriculum / **Study Aids** / **Exams**
Priority registration / Typist / • Oral
Math waiver / Reader / Untimed
Foreign lang. waiver / • Notetaker / Take home
Course substitution / Proof reader / With proctor
In Class / • Text on tape / On computer
Calculators / Early syllabus / • Extended time
• Tape recorder / Taped handouts / On tape
• Word processor / / Modified
Priority seating / / Separate room

Program Strengths
Massasoit does not offer a learning disabilities program. We do, however, offer tutoring and some diagnostic testing for LD students.

General Information:
Massasoit Community College is a 2 year public college. Suburban campus of 100 acres is 30 miles from Boston. Housing is not guaranteed.

Accreditation: Regional

Expenses: Part-time: Per credit:$61.00. Part-time: Per credit:$149.50.

Majors
• BUSINESS Business Administration, Business Management, Hotel and Restaurant Managemen, Marketing, Travel/Tourism Management • COMMUNICATIONS Commercial Design, Communication, Television/Radio/Film • COMPUTER SCIENCE Computer Science, Data Processing, Programming • EDUCATION Early Childhood • ENGINEERING Civil/Environmental, Electrical, Engineering Science • HEALTH SCIENCES Medical Secretary, Medical Technology, Nursing, Radiological Therapy • HUMANITIES Philosophy • PREPROFESSIONAL Architecture • SOCIAL SCIENCES Criminal Justice, Human Service, Law Enforcement • VISUAL AND PERFORMING ARTS Advertising Art • VOCATIONAL Air Condtioning/Heating/Refrig, Business and Office, Dental Assistant, Diesel Power Technology, Electronics Technology, Fire Science, Food Service, Legal Secretary, Respiratory Therapy Technology, Secretarial

Sports/Activities
• SPORTS-INTERCOLLEGIATE Baseball (M), Basketball, Soccer, Softball (F), Volleyball (F) • STUDENT LIFE ACTIVITIES Drama Groups, Jazz Band, Magazine, Newspaper, Student Government, Yearbook

343

Massachusetts

Massachusetts Accommodations

Merrimack College
Turnpike Street
No. Andover, Massachusetts 01845
(508) 837-5000

School Enrollment: 2,200 Male: **1,100** Female: **1,100**

Admissions Contact: **Dennis P. Farrell, Dean of Admin. & Fin. Aid**
Telephone: **(508) 837-5100**

Admissions

Application Information:
Application deadline: **March 1st**
Rolling Admissions: **Yes**

Secondary School Information
Most Important Criteria For Admissions (1-strongest)

4 SAT/ACT	**6** Application	**1** School transcript
2 Class rank	**5** Course selection	**10** Personal statement
9 Interview	**8** Extra activities	**11** Psychoeducational
3 G.P.A.	Open admission	**7** Recommendations

Test Requirements:
Untimed SAT: **Yes** Untimed ACT: **Yes**

Types of Disabilities Served

Speech/Lang	Reading	ADD with LD
Study skills	Spelling	ADD without LD
Written express	Math	ADHD with LD
Organizational	Fine Motor	ADHD without LD
Perceptual		

Admissions Process

Moderately selective. Documented LD taken into consideration. Untimed testing allowed.

Learning Disability Program
Students mainstreamed **100** % of the day
Services available for all students: **Yes**

Diagnostic Testing

ADD	Personality	Perceptual skills	Spelling
ADHD	Organization	Fine motor skills	Reading
I.Q.	Handwriting	Spoken language	Study skills
Math	Social skills	Written language	

Tutoring:
Services rendered by:
Graduates   •Peers   •Faculty   LD staff   Teacher trainees

Tutorials

Grp.	Ind.	Tutorials	Grp.	Ind.	Tutorials
•	•	Math skills			Word processing
		Study skills			Time management
		Language arts			Learning strategies
•	•	Written express			Organizational skills

Academic Accommodations

Curriculum	Study Aids	Exams
Priority registration	Typist	Oral
Math waiver	Reader	• Untimed
Foreign lang. waiver	• Notetaker	Take home
Course substitution	Proof reader	With proctor
In Class	Text on tape	On computer
Calculators	Early syllabus	• Extended time
• Tape recorder	Taped handouts	On tape
Word processor		Modified
Priority seating		Separate room

Graduation Requirements:
Course credits: **122-124** GPA: **2.0** Years to complete degree: **5**
Other requirements: **40 courses**

Program Strengths
Although we have no specific LD program, students who have learning disabilities can arrange with professors for untimed tests, tape recorders in class, tutoring services, etc.

General Information:
Merrimack College is a 4 year independent Roman Catholic college. Suburban campus of 220 acres is 25 miles from Boston. Accessible by air, train or bus. Ski areas are 1/2 hour from campus. Beaches are 1/2 hour from campus. 3% of students are foreign. 11 residential halls on campus. Housing is guaranteed.Guaranteed through 4th year. 50 % of students remain on campus for the weekends. 21 % of students join fraternities/sororities.

Accreditation: NEACS, EAC, ACS

SAT/ACT Scores:
Scores for incoming freshmen: **Verbal:** 78% below 500. 18% between 500 and 599. 3% between 600 and 699. **Math:** 49% below 500. 39% between 500 and 599. 10% between 600 and 699. 1% above 700.

Class Rank:
About 44% of the present freshmen class were in the upper 20% of their high school class. 78% were in the top 40% of their class. 91% were in the top 60% of their class. 99% were in the top 80% of their class.

Expenses:
Tuition: In-state: Full year: $11,000.00. Part-time: Per credit: $330.00.
Room and board: $6,000.00

Majors
• BUSINESS Accounting, Banking, Business Administration, Business Economics, Economics, Finance, International Business, Management, Marketing • COMMUNICATIONS English • COMPUTER SCIENCE Computer Science, Computer Technology, Data Processing • EDUCATION Elementary, Secondary • ENGINEERING Civil/Environmental, Computer, Industrial • HEALTH SCIENCES Medical Technology • HUMANITIES Philosophy, Religion • SCIENCES Biology, Cell Biology, Chemistry, Mathematics, Physics • SOCIAL SCIENCES Government/Political, International Studies, Political Science, Psychology, Sociology • VISUAL AND PERFORMING ARTS Art History, Fine Arts, Studio Art

Sports/Activities
• SPORTS-INTERCOLLEGIATE Baseball (M), Basketball, Cross Country, Golf, Ice Hockey (M), Lacrosse (M), Soccer, Softball (F), Tennis, Volleyball (F) • SPORTS-INTRAMURAL Badminton, Basketball, Football (F), Ice Hockey (M), Lacrosse (F), Ping-Pong, Racquetball, Skiing - Snow, Squash, Swimming, Tennis, Volleyball • STUDENT LIFE ACTIVITIES Choral, Drama Groups, Fraternities, Musical Theater, Newspaper, Radio/TV station, Sororities, Student Government, Yearbook

Less Selective   **Massachusetts Program**

Middlesex Community College
Springs Road
Bedford, Massachusetts 01730
(617) 275-8910

School Enrollment: **3,600** Male: **1,512** Female: **2,088**
LD Enrollment: **315**

Admissions Contact: **Nina K. Anton, Director of Admissions**
LD Contact: **Karen Muncaster, Dir. of Programs for the LD**
Name of Program: **Program for the Learning Disabled**
Telephone:**(617) 272-7342 Ext.3038**

Admissions

Application Information:
LD Students Applying: **50** Accepted: **22** Enrolled:**21**
Separate application:**Yes**
Application deadline: **None**
Rolling Admissions: **Yes**

Secondary School Information
Most Important Criteria For Admissions (1-strongest)

SAT/ACT	Application	**4**	School transcript
Class rank	Course selection		Personal statement
3 Interview	Extra activities	**1**	Psychoeducational
G.P.A.	**1** Open admission	**2**	Recommendations

Test Requirements:
Standardized tests waived: **Yes**
Diagnostic testing waived: **Yes**
WAIS-R required: **Yes** Range accepted: **70-80**
Documentation of LD required: **Yes**
Currency of diagnostic testing: **less than 3 years**
Tests recommended: **WAIS, reading and math achievements, diagnostic interview**

Types of Disabilities Served
- Speech/Lang
- Study skills
- Written express
- Organizational
- Perceptual
- Reading
- Spelling
- Math
- Fine Motor
- ADD with LD
- ADD without LD
- ADHD with LD
- ADHD without LD

Admissions Process

Program: applicant submits packet containing test results, applications, references and IEP. If the material indicates an appropriate candidate, she/he is invited in for an interview.

Learning Disability Program

Program: Reinforces course work: **Yes**
Students mainstreamed **100** % of the day
Recommended credits per semester: **12**
Services only for LD students: **Yes**
Counseling: Individual: **Yes**
Support groups are available:**Peer support groups**

Faculty:
Faculty: **6** Full time: **1** Part time: **5** M.A.: **6**
Faculty advocate: **Yes** Meets with instructor: **As needed**

Diagnostic Testing

ADD	Personality	Perceptual skills	Spelling
ADHD	Organization	Fine motor skills	Reading
I.Q.	Handwriting	Spoken language	Study skills
Math	Social skills	Written language	

Tutoring:
Services rendered by:
Graduates   Peers   Faculty   •LD staff   Teacher trainees

Tutorials

Grp.	Ind. Tutorials	Grp.	Ind. Tutorials
	• Math skills		• Word processing
	• Study skills		• Time management
	• Language arts		• Learning strategies
	• Written express		• Organizational skills

Academic Accommodations

Curriculum	Study Aids	Exams
Priority registration	Typist	• Oral
Math waiver	• Reader	• Untimed
Foreign lang. waiver	• Notetaker	• Take home
• Course substitution	• Proof reader	• With proctor
In Class	• Text on tape	• On computer
• Calculators	Early syllabus	• Extended time
• Tape recorder	Taped handouts	On tape
• Word processor		• Modified
Priority seating		• Separate room

Graduation Requirements:
Course credits: **60** GPA: **2.0** Years to complete degree: **2-4**

Program Strengths

Middlesex offers two options for LD students. One consists of support services for students enrolled in traditional college programs. The goal of these academic and emotional support services is to assist students in becoming independent learners who achieve to their maximum potential. The second option is the transition program, a unique certificate program for lower-functioning LD students. This substantially separate program trains students in the areas of clerical/business support, independent living and personal social skills while placing them on job co-ops.

General Information:

Middlesex Community College is a 2 year public college. Suburban campus 15 miles from Boston. Accessible by bus. 2% of students are foreign. Housing is not guaranteed.

Accreditation: Regional

Expenses:
Tuition: In-state: Full year: $1,024.00. Part-time: Per credit:$93.00. Part-time: Per credit:$195.00 plus fees.

Majors

• BUSINESS Accounting, Business Administration, Business Management, Hotel and Restaurant Managemen, Management, Marketing, Travel/ Tourism Management • COMMUNICATIONS Communication • COMPUTER SCIENCE Computer Science, Programming • HEALTH SCIENCES Dental Assistant, Dental Hygiene, Dental Technician, Medical Technology, Radiological Therapy • SOCIAL SCIENCES Human Service • VISUAL AND PERFORMING ARTS Art, Dance, Theater

Sports/Activities
- SPORTS-INTRAMURAL Basketball, Golf, Softball, Tennis, Volleyball
- STUDENT LIFE ACTIVITIES Drama Groups, Newspaper, Student Government, Yearbook

Highly Selective **Massachusetts**
Services

Mount Holyoke College
College Street
South Hadley, Massachusetts 01075
(413) 538-2023

School Enrollment: **1,860**
LD Enrollment: **35**

Admissions Contact: **Jennifer Blake, Assistant Director of Admis.**
LD Contact: **Barry Wadsworth, Prof., Psychology and Educator**
Name of Program: **Student Learning Center**
Address: **Psychology & Education Dept.**
Telephone:**(413) 538-2504**

Admissions

Application Information:
Application deadline: **February 1st**
Notified when: **April 15th**

Secondary School Information
Most Important Criteria For Admissions (1-strongest)

3 SAT/ACT	**7** Application	**1** School transcript
2 Class rank	**1** Course selection	**4** Personal statement
8 Interview	**5** Extra activities	Psychoeducational
1 G.P.A.	Open admission	**6** Recommendations

Test Requirements:
Untimed SAT: **Yes** Untimed ACT: **Yes** Untimed ACH: **Yes** Achievement tests required:**3**
Documentation of LD required: **Yes**

Types of Disabilities Served
- Speech/Lang
- Study skills
- Written express
- Organizational
- Perceptual
- Reading
- Spelling
- Math
- Fine Motor
- ADD with LD
- ADD without LD
- ADHD with LD
- ADHD without LD

Admissions Process

All applications are read by two readers. If there are questions they go to the Admissions Committee. LD applications are reviewed by LD specialist and then sent to committee.

High School Course Requirements:
Waivers to standard high school courses
Foreign Language : **Yes** Math: **Yes** Course substitution: **Yes**

Learning Disability Program
Special orientation for LD students: **Yes**
Program: Remedial: **Yes**
Program: Reinforces course work: **Yes**
Program available through:**Daily**
Students mainstreamed **100** % of the day
Recommended credits per semester: **12-16**
Services available for all students: **Yes**
Counseling: Individual: **Yes** Vocational Counseling: **Yes**
Support groups are available:**Weekly meeting of scheduled support group with professional staff.**

Faculty:
Faculty: **2** Full time: **1** Part time: **1** M.A.: **1** Ph.D.: **1**
Faculty advocate: **Yes** Meets with instructor: **As needed**

Diagnostic Testing
- ADD
- ADHD
- I.Q.
- Math
- Personality
- Organization
- Handwriting
- Social skills
- Perceptual skills
- Fine motor skills
- Spoken language
- Written language
- Spelling
- Reading
- Study skills

Tutoring:
Average size of group tutorials: **12**
Services rendered by:
  Graduates •Peers Faculty •LD staff •Teacher trainees

Tutorials

Grp.	Ind.	Tutorials	Grp.	Ind.	Tutorials
	•	Math skills		•	Word processing
•	•	Study skills	•	•	Time management
•	•	Language arts	•	•	Learning strategies
•	•	Written express	•	•	Organizational skills

Academic Accommodations

Curriculum	Study Aids	Exams
Priority registration	Typist	• Oral
Math waiver	• Reader	• Untimed
• Foreign lang. waiver	• Notetaker	• Take home
• Course substitution	• Proof reader	• With proctor
In Class	• Text on tape	On computer
• Calculators	• Early syllabus	• Extended time
• Tape recorder	Taped handouts	On tape
• Word processor		• Modified
• Priority seating		Separate room

Graduation Requirements:
Course credits: **128** Years to complete degree: **Usually 4** Math waiver: **Yes** Language waiver: **Yes**

Program Strengths
Highly individualized in service to LD students. We are active in identifying undiagnosed LD students.

General Information:
Mount Holyoke College is a 4 year independent college. Suburban campus of 800 acres is 22 miles from Springfield. Accessible by air, train or bus. Ski areas are 6 miles from campus. Beaches are 2 hours from campus. 13% of students are foreign. 18 residential halls on campus. Housing is guaranteed.Guaranteed through 4th year. 85 % of students remain on campus for the weekends.

Accreditation:NEACS

Expenses:
Tuition: In-state: Full year: $15,590.00. Tuition: Out-of-state: Full year: $15,590.00. Room and board: $4,900.00

Majors

• AGRICULTURE • AREA STUDIES African, American, Asian, Black/Afro-American, European, International Studies, Latin American, Russian/Slavic, Women's Studies • ARTS Art History, Dance, Music, Music History, Photography • BUSINESS Economics • EDUCATION Bilingual, Early Childhood, Elementary, Middle School, Secondary, Special • HUMANITIES Classics, English/Writing/Literature, Liberal Arts , Philosophy • LANGUAGES • MATHEMATICS Statistical, Theoretical • PRE PROFESSIONAL Architecture, Business, Engineering, Law, Medicine • RELIGIOUS STUDIES Religion & Theology • SCIENCES Applied Mathematics, Astronomy, Biology, Sciences, Biomedical, Chemistry, Geography, Geology, Mathematics, Psychology • SOCIAL SCIENCES Geography, History, International Studies, Political Science, Psychology, Sociology • VISUAL AND PERFORMING ARTS Art, Art History, Dance, Music

Sports/Activities

• SPORTS-INTERCOLLEGIATE Basketball, Crew, Cross Country, Diving, Field Hockey, Golf, Soccer, Softball, Squash, Swimming, Tennis, Track and Field, Volleyball • STUDENT LIFE ACTIVITIES Academic Clubs, Choral, Community Band, Debate, Drama Groups, Ethnic & Cultural Groups, Film, Magazine, Music Groups, Musical Theater, Newspaper, Orchestra, Political Groups, Radio/TV station, Religious Organization, Student Government, Symphony Orchestra, Yearbook

Less Selective   **Massachusetts**
                                        Program

Mount Ida College
777 Dedham Street
Newton Centre, Massachusetts 02159
(617) 969-7000

School Enrollment: **1,600** Male: **600** Female: **1,000**
LD Enrollment: **77** Male: **41** Female: **36**

Admissions Contact: **Harold Duvall, III, Asst. to Dean of Admis.**
LD Contact: **Jill Mehler, Director, Learning Opportunities**
Name of Program: **Learning Opportunities Program**
Telephone:**(617) 969-7000 Ext. 248**

Admissions

Application Information:
LD Students Applying: **245** Accepted: **145** Enrolled:**45**
LD on admissions committee:**Yes**
Application deadline: **None**
Rolling Admissions: **Yes**

Secondary School Information
Most Important Criteria For Admissions (1-strongest)
10 SAT/ACT **9** Application **4** School transcript
11 Class rank **5** Course selection **7** Personal statement
2 Interview **8** Extra activities **1** Psychoeducational
G.P.A. Open admission **5** Recommendations

Test Requirements:
Standardized tests waived: **Yes**
Diagnostic testing waived: **Yes**
WAIS-R required: **Yes** Range accepted: **90+**
Documentation of LD required: **Yes**
Currency of diagnostic testing: **Within 2 years**
Tests recommended: **WAIS-R, Woodcock-Johnson, Detroit Apt., Peabody**

Types of Disabilities Served

• Speech/Lang • Reading • ADD with LD
• Study skills • Spelling • ADD without LD
• Written express • Math • ADHD with LD
• Organizational • Fine Motor • ADHD without LD
• Perceptual

Admissions Process

Rolling admissions. We request a WAIS-R and other documentation, high school transcript and recommendations. Personal interviews are strongly recommended. Decisions are made as soon as all materials are in.

High School Course Requirements:
Waivers to standard high school courses
 Math: **Yes**

Learning Disability Program

Program: Reinforces course work: **Yes**
Students mainstreamed **95-98** % of the day
Time required or recommended in learning center: **2 hours**
Services only for LD students: **Yes**
Counseling: Individual: **Yes** Group Counseling: **Yes**
Support groups are available:**Student groups**

Faculty:
Faculty: **9** Including Director: **Yes** Full time: **1** Part time: **8**
LD faculty with: BS/BA: **2** M.A.: **7**
Faculty advocate: **Yes** Meets with instructor: **As needed**

Diagnostic Testing
• ADD • Personality Perceptual skills • Spelling
• ADHD • Organization Fine motor skills • Reading
• I.Q. Handwriting Spoken language • Study skills
• Math • Social skills • Written language

Tutoring:
Services rendered by:
 Graduates Peers Faculty •LD staff Teacher trainees

Tutorials
Grp. Ind. Tutorials Grp. Ind. Tutorials
 • Math skills • Word processing
• • Study skills • Time management
 • Language arts • • Learning strategies
 • Written express • • Organizational skills

Academic Accommodations

Curriculum	Study Aids	Exams
• Priority registration	• Typist	• Oral
• Math waiver	Reader	Untimed
• Foreign lang. waiver	• Notetaker	• Take home
Course substitution	• Proof reader	• With proctor
In Class	• Text on tape	On computer
• Calculators	Early syllabus	• Extended time
• Tape recorder	Taped handouts	On tape
• Word processor		• Modified
• Priority seating		• Separate room

Graduation Requirements:
Course credits: **130** Language waiver: **Yes**

Program Strengths

We best serve students by providing them with one-to-one strategy-based tutoring up to 2.5 hours per week by professional educators who all have competence working with students with learning dis-

Massachusetts

abilities. Mount Ida's philosophy is that of a supportive environment which provides opportunity, and the LOP is a natural extension of this philosophy.

General Information:

Mount Ida College is a 2 and 4 year independent college. Suburban campus of 85 acres is 10 miles from Boston. Accessible by train or bus. Ski areas are 10 miles from campus. Beaches are 10 miles from campus. 10% of students are foreign. Housing is guaranteed.Guaranteed through 1st year. 50 % of students remain on campus for the weekends.

Accreditation:NEACS

Expenses:

Tuition: In-state: Full year: $9,305.00. Part-time: Per course: $650.00.
Room and board: $6,540.00 Cost of LD program:$2,310.00

Majors

• ANIMAL SCIENCE Equestrian Studies • ARTS Fashion Design, Graphic Arts, Interior Design • BUSINESS Accounting, Banking/Finance, Business Administration, Fashion Merchandising, Hotel and Restaurant Managemen, Management, Marketing, Sports Management, Travel/Tourism Management • COMMUNICATIONS Broadcasting, Communication, Graphic Design, Journalism, Television/Radio/Film • COMPUTER SCIENCE Computer Science • CRAFTS AND DESIGN Apparel Design, Graphic Design, Illustration Design • EDUCATION Child Development, Early Childhood • HEALTH SCIENCES Dental Technician, Fitness, Health, Occupational Therapy, Physical Therapy, Veterinary Assistant • HUMANITIES Liberal Arts • PREPROFESSIONAL Business, Engineering, Law, Legal Assistant, Social Work, Sports Medicine, Veterinarian • SCIENCES Anatomy, Biology, Chemistry, Computer Science, Equestrian Studies, General Science • SOCIAL SCIENCES Criminal Justice, Human Service • SPECIAL EDUCATION Occupational Therapy • VOCATIONAL Dental Assistant, Electronics Technology, Fashion Design, Fashion Merchandising, Funeral Services/Mortuary, Paralegal, Veterinarian Assistant

Sports/Activities

• SPORTS-INTERCOLLEGIATE Basketball (M), Lacrosse (M), Soccer, Soccer (F), Soccer (M), Softball (F), Volleyball (F) • SPORTS-INTRAMURAL Badminton, Badminton (F), Badminton (M), Basketball, Football, Horseback Riding, Skiing - Snow, Soccer, Softball, Tennis, Volleyball, Weight Lifting • STUDENT LIFE ACTIVITIES Academic Clubs, Choral, Community Service, Drama Groups, Ethnic & Cultural Groups, Film, Fraternities, Newspaper, Radio/TV station, Sororities, Student Government, Yearbook

---

Less Selective

Massachusetts
Services

Mount Wachusett Community College
444 Green Street
Gardner, Massachusetts 01440
(508) 632-6600

School Enrollment: **2,067** Male: **855** Female: **1,212**
LD Enrollment: **80**

Admissions Contact: **Sidney Goldfader, Director of Admissions**
LD Contact: **Francine Meigs, Learning Disabilities Specialist**

Admissions

Application Information:
Application deadline: **Rolling**
Rolling Admissions: **Yes**

Secondary School Information
Most Important Criteria For Admissions (1-strongest)

10 SAT/ACT	**7** Application	**1**	School transcript
8 Class rank	**2** Course selection	**11**	Personal statement
4 Interview	**6** Extra activities	**5**	Psychoeducational
3 G.P.A.	Open admission	**9**	Recommendations

Test Requirements:
Standardized tests waived: **Yes**
Diagnostic testing waived: **Yes**
Documentation of LD required: **Yes**
Currency of diagnostic testing: **3 years**
Tests recommended: **Psycho-educational evaluation.**

Types of Disabilities Served
- Speech/Lang
- Reading
- ADD with LD
- Study skills
- Spelling
- ADD without LD
- Written express
- Math
- ADHD with LD
- Organizational
- Fine Motor
- ADHD without LD
- Perceptual

Learning Disability Program

Program: Reinforces course work: **Yes**
Students mainstreamed **100** % of the day
Recommended credits per semester: **varies**
Services available for all students: **Yes**
Counseling: Individual: **Yes** Vocational Counseling: **Yes**
Support groups are available:**Yes**

Faculty:
Faculty: **4** Full time: **1** Part time: **3**
LD faculty with: BS/BA: **2** M.A.: **2**
Faculty advocate: **Yes** Meets with instructor: **As needed**

Diagnostic Testing
ADD	Personality	Perceptual skills	Spelling
ADHD	Organization	Fine motor skills	Reading
I.Q.	Handwriting	Spoken language	Study skills
Math	Social skills	Written language	

Tutoring:
Average size of group tutorials: **2**
Services rendered by:
  Graduates •Peers •Faculty •LD staff Teacher trainees

Tutorials
Grp.	Ind.	Tutorials	Grp.	Ind.	Tutorials
•	•	Math skills	•	•	Word processing
•	•	Study skills	•	•	Time management
•	•	Language arts	•	•	Learning strategies
•	•	Written express	•	•	Organizational skills

Academic Accommodations
Curriculum	Study Aids	Exams
Priority registration	Typist	• Oral
Math waiver	Reader	Untimed
Foreign lang. waiver	• Notetaker	• Take home
• Course substitution	• Proof reader	• With proctor
In Class	• Text on tape	• On computer
• Calculators	Early syllabus	• Extended time
• Tape recorder	Taped handouts	On tape
• Word processor		Modified
• Priority seating		• Separate room

Graduation Requirements: Language waiver: **Yes**

Program Strengths

LD students receive individual attention and individualized goals and plans to assist them in accomplishing their future objectives. LD students have many college services available as well as the individual LD services. College services include: writing lab, math lab, academic support center, counseling and computer labs.

General Information:

Mount Wachusett Community College is a 2 year public college. Rural campus of 270 acres is 75 miles from Boston. Ski areas are 10 miles from campus. 1% of students are foreign. Housing is not guaranteed.

Accreditation: Regional

Expenses:

Tuition: In-state: Full year: $1,050.00. Part-time: Per credit:$44.00. Part-time: Per course: $132.00. Tuition: Out-of-state: Full year: $5,075.00. Part-time: Per credit:$203.00. Part-time: Per course:$609.00

Majors

• BUSINESS Accounting, Business Administration, Business Management, Management • COMMUNICATIONS Broadcasting, Television/Radio/Film • COMPUTER SCIENCE Computer Technology, Data Processing, Programming • EDUCATION Child Study, Early Childhood, English As A Second Language • HEALTH SCIENCES Medical Laboratory Technology, Nursing • HUMANITIES Liberal Arts • SOCIAL SCIENCES Criminal Justice, Human Service • VISUAL AND PERFORMING ARTS Art • VOCATIONAL Automobile Technology, Corrections, Electronics Technology, Fire Science, Legal Secretary, Medical Laboratory Technology, Office Administration, Secretarial, Word Processing

Sports/Activities

• SPORTS-INTERCOLLEGIATE Baseball (M), Basketball, Softball (F), Tennis • SPORTS-INTRAMURAL Baseball (M), Basketball, Cross Country, Golf, Racquetball, Skiing - Snow, Soccer, Softball, Squash, Swimming, Tennis, Volleyball • STUDENT LIFE ACTIVITIES Choral, Drama Groups, Film, Musical Theater, Newman Club, Newspaper, Radio/TV station, Student Government, Yearbook

---

Selective **Massachusetts**

Services

North Adams State College

Learning Center Church Street
North Adams, Massachusetts 01247
(413) 664-4511

School Enrollment: **2,000** Male: **1,000** Female: **1,000**
LD Enrollment: **50** Male: **25** Female: **25**

Admissions Contact: **Kris Callen Director of Admissions**
LD Contact: **Terry Miller Asst. Director Learning Center**
Name of Program: **Learning Center**
Address: **North Adams State College**
Telephone: **(413) 664-4511**

Admissions

Application Information:
LD Students Applying: **80** Accepted: **35** Enrolled: **10**
LD on admissions committee: **Yes**
Application deadline: **Feb./Mar for Sept.; Nov. for Feb.**
Applicant must apply **6** months in advance
Rolling Admissions: **Yes** Notified when: **March-May for September**

Secondary School Information
Most Important Criteria For Admissions (1-strongest)

SAT/ACT	Application	**1**	School transcript
4 Class rank	**3** Course selection	**7**	Personal statement
Interview	**5** Extra activities	**2**	Psychoeducational
1 G.P.A.	Open admission	**6**	Recommendations

Test Requirements:
Standardized tests waived: **Yes**
Diagnostic testing waived: **Yes**
Untimed SAT: **Yes** Achievement tests required: **WJPEB preferred**
WAIS-R required: **Yes**
Currency of diagnostic testing: **3 years**
Tests recommended: **WAIS, WJPEB**

Types of Disabilities Served

• Speech/Lang	• Reading	ADD with LD
• Study skills	• Spelling	ADD without LD
• Written express	• Math	ADHD with LD
• Organizational	• Fine Motor	ADHD without LD
• Perceptual		

Admissions Process

Students apply through Admissions Office, providing individualized testing as alternative to SAT scores. Learning Center LD counselor acts as consultant with Admissions Office on these applications. Decision is one of Admissions.

High School Course Requirements:
English: **4** Math: **3** Science: **2**
Waivers to standard high school courses
Foreign Language : **Yes**

Learning Disability Program

Program available through: **Fall/Spring term**
Students mainstreamed **100** % of the day
Recommended credits per semester: **12-15**
Counseling: Individual: **Yes**

Faculty:
Faculty: **2** Full time: **1** Part time: **1** M.A.: **2**
Faculty advocate: **Yes** Meets with instructor: **As needed**

Diagnostic Testing

ADD	Personality	Perceptual skills	Spelling
ADHD	Organization	Fine motor skills	Reading
• I.Q.	Handwriting	Spoken language	Study skills
Math	Social skills	Written language	

Tutoring:
Average size of group tutorials: **6**
Services rendered by:

Graduates	•Peers	Faculty	LD staff	Teacher trainees

Tutorials

Grp.	Ind.	Tutorials	Grp.	Ind.	Tutorials
		Math skills			Word processing
		Study skills			Time management
		Language arts			Learning strategies
		Written express			Organizational skills

Academic Accommodations

Curriculum	Study Aids	Exams
• Priority registration	Typist	• Oral
Math waiver	• Reader	Untimed
Foreign lang. waiver	• Notetaker	• Take home
Course substitution	Proof reader	• With proctor
In Class	Text on tape	• On computer
• Calculators	Early syllabus	• Extended time
• Tape recorder	Taped handouts	On tape
• Word processor		• Modified
• Priority seating		• Separate room

Graduation Requirements:

Course credits: **120** GPA: **2.0** Years to complete degree: **4-5**

Program Strengths

Small college and classes (approximately 30 students) allow for more individual follow up. Tutoring is available in all subjects.

General Information:

North Adams State College is a 4 year public college. Rural campus of 2,100 acres is 30 miles from Northampton. Accessible by bus Ski areas are 10 miles from campus. Beaches are 2 miles from campus. 2% of students are foreign. 3 residential halls on campus. Housing is guaranteed.Guaranteed through 1st year. 80 % of students remain on campus for the weekends. 10 % of students join fraternities/sororities.

Accreditation:NEACS

SAT/ACT Scores:

Scores for incoming freshmen:**Verbal:**60%below 500. 35%between 500 and 599. 5%between 600 and 699. **Math:**60% below 500. 35% between 500 and 599. 5% between 600 and 699.

Class Rank: 40% were in the top 40% of their class. 60% were in the top 60% of their class.

Expenses:

Tuition: In-state: Full year: $1,326.00. Part-time: Per credit:$55.25. Part-time: Per course: $165.75. Tuition: Out-of-state: Full year: $5,040.00. Part-time: Per credit:$210.00. Part-time: Per course:$630.00 Room and board: $2,050.00

Majors

• BUSINESS Accounting • COMMUNICATIONS Communication • COMPUTER SCIENCE Computer Science • EDUCATION Early Childhood, Elementary, Middle School, Secondary • HEALTH SCIENCES Medical Technology • HUMANITIES English/Writing/Literature, Philosophy • MATHEMATICS Mathematics • SCIENCES Biology, Chemistry, Physics • SOCIAL SCIENCES Anthropology, History, Psychology, Sociology

Sports/Activities

• SPORTS-INTERCOLLEGIATE Baseball, Basketball (F), Basketball (M), Cross Country, Ice Hockey, Rugby, Soccer (F), Soccer (M) • SPORTS-INTRAMURAL Field Hockey, Ice Hockey, Racquetball, Soccer, Softball, Squash, Tennis, Volleyball • STUDENT LIFE ACTIVITIES Academic Clubs, Choral, Community Service, Concert Band, Dance, Drama Groups, Ethnic & Cultural Groups, Fraternities, Jazz Band, Magazine, Music Groups, Newspaper, Political Groups, Radio/TV station, Religious Organization, Sororities, Yearbook

---

Very Selective **Massachusetts Program**

Northeastern University

360 Huntington Avenue
Boston, Massachusetts 02115-9959
(617) 437-2211

School Enrollment: **28,882** Male: **15,574** Female: **13,308**
LD Enrollment: **275**

Admissions Contact: **Michael Clifford, Admission Counselor**
LD Contact: **Dean Ruth Bork, Director**
Name of Program: **Disability Resource Center**
Address: **380 Huntington Avenue**
Telephone:**(617) 437-2675**

Admissions

Application Information:

Accepted: **35** Enrolled:**250**
Separate application:**Yes**
Application deadline: **March 1st preferred**
Applicant must apply **Varies** months in advance
Rolling Admissions: **Yes**Notified when: **April 15th**

Secondary School Information

Most Important Criteria For Admissions (1-strongest)

2 SAT/ACT	Application	**1** School transcript
Class rank	Course selection	Personal statement
Interview	Extra activities	Psychoeducational
G.P.A.	Open admission	**3** Recommendations

Test Requirements:

Standardized tests waived: **Yes**
Diagnostic testing waived: **Yes**
Untimed SAT: **Yes** Untimed ACT: **Yes** Untimed ACH: **Yes** Achievement tests required:**None**
WAIS-R required: **Yes**
Documentation of LD required: **Yes**
Currency of diagnostic testing: **within 3 years**

Types of Disabilities Served

• Speech/Lang	• Reading	• ADD with LD
• Study skills	• Spelling	• ADD without LD
• Written express	• Math	• ADHD with LD
• Organizational	• Fine Motor	• ADHD without LD
• Perceptual		

High School Course Requirements:

English: **4** Math: **4** Science: **3** Foreign Language: **3**

Learning Disability Program

Special orientation for LD students: **Yes**
Program available through:**Any time**
Students mainstreamed **100** % of the day
Recommended credits per semester: **varies**
Vocational Counseling: **Yes**
Support groups are available:**Yes**

Faculty:

Faculty: **20** Including Director: **Yes** Full time: **8** Part time: **12**
LD faculty with: BS/BA: **2** M.A.: **5** Ph.D.: **1**
Faculty advocate: **Yes** Meets with instructor: **As needed**

Diagnostic Testing

ADD	• Personality	• Perceptual skills	Spelling
ADHD	Organization	Fine motor skills	• Reading
I.Q.	Handwriting	Spoken language	• Study skills
• Math	• Social skills	• Written language	

Tutoring:

Services rendered by:
•Graduates •Peers •Faculty •LD staff Teacher trainees

Tutorials

Grp.	Ind.	Tutorials	Grp.	Ind.	Tutorials
•	•	Math skills			Word processing
	•	Study skills		•	Time management
		Language arts		•	Learning strategies
		Written express		•	Organizational skills

Academic Accommodations

Curriculum	Study Aids	Exams
Priority registration	Typist	• Oral
• Math waiver	• Reader	• Untimed
• Foreign lang. waiver	• Notetaker	• Take home
• Course substitution	• Proof reader	• With proctor
In Class	• Text on tape	• On computer
• Calculators	Early syllabus	• Extended time
• Tape recorder	• Taped handouts	• On tape
• Word processor		• Modified
• Priority seating		• Separate room

Graduation Requirements:

Course credits: **172 - 210** GPA: **2.0** Years to complete degree: **4-5** Math waiver: **Yes**

Program Strengths

The Disability Resource Center has been an advocate for people with disabilities who seek the right to an equal education. OSH was established in an effort to eliminate the disadvantages which confront persons with disabilities. Two options are available at Northeastern: Support Services and Accommodations (for no charge) and a small Learning Disability Program of a maximum of 35 students (for $1,200.00 per quarter).

General Information:

Northeastern University is a 4 & 5 year private university. Urban campus of 55 acres is Boston. Ski areas are 15 miles from campus. Beaches are 6 miles from campus. 6% of students are foreign. 20 residential halls on campus. Housing is not guaranteed.3 % of students join fraternities/sororities.

Accreditation:NEACS

SAT/ACT Scores:

Scores for incoming freshmen:**Verbal:**70%below 500. 24%between 500 and 599. 5%between 600 and 699. 1%above 700. **Math:**41% below 500. 40% between 500 and 599. 16% between 600 and 699. 3%above 700. **ACT:** 22% below 20. 40% between 20 and 23. 13%between 24 and 25l. 18%between 26 and 28. 7% above 28.

Class Rank:

About 31% of the present freshmen class were in the upper 20% of their high school class. 60% were in the top 40% of their class. 82% were in the top 60% of their class. 95% were in the top 80% of their class.

Expenses:

Tuition: In-state: Full year: $11,489.00. Part-time: Per credit:$131.00 - $270.00. Room and board: $6,780.00

Majors

• AGRICULTURE Business, Education, Engineering, Journalism • AREA STUDIES Black/Afro-American • BUSINESS Accounting, Banking/Finance, Business Administration, Business Management, Entrepreneur, Human Resources Management, Insurance, International Business, Management, Management Information System, Marketing • COMMUNICATIONS Advertising, English, Journalism, Media, Public Relations, Radio/Television • COMPUTER SCIENCE Computer Science, Programming, Systems Analysis • EDUCATION Early Childhood, Elementary, Health, Human Service, Physical, Recreation/Youth Leadership • ENGINEERING Chemical, Civil/Environmental, Computer, Electrical, Engineering Science, General, Industrial, Mechanical • HEALTH SCIENCES Medical Laboratory Technology, Medical Records Administration, Nursing, Pharmacology, Physical Therapy, Radiological Therapy, Respiratory Therapy, Toxicology • HUMANITIES Philosophy, Religion • LANGUAGES French, German, Italian, Linguistic, Russian, Spanish • PREPROFESSIONAL Architecture, Elementary, Engineering, Law, Pharmacy, Recreation, Social Work • SCIENCES Biochemistry, Biology, Chemistry, Geology, Mathematics, Physical Science, Physics, Radiology, Toxicology • SOCIAL SCIENCES Anthropology, Criminal Justice, Government/Political, History, Human Service, Law Enforcement, Political Science, Psychology, Public Relations, Social Sciences, Sociology • VISUAL AND PERFORMING ARTS Art, Art History, Fine Arts, Music, Studio Art, Theater • VOCATIONAL Park/Recreation, Respiratory Therapy Technology

Sports/Activities

• SPORTS RELATED Cheerleading, Chess, Flying Team, Marching Band, Pep Band • SPORTS-INTERCOLLEGIATE Baseball (M), Basketball (F), Basketball (M), Crew (F), Crew (M), Cross Country (F), Cross Country (M), Diving (F), Diving (M), Field Hockey (F), Football (M), Golf (M), Gymnastics (F), Ice Hockey (F), Ice Hockey (M), Soccer (M), Swimming (F), Swimming (M), Tennis (M), Track and Field (F), Track and Field (M), Volleyball (F) • SPORTS-INTRAMURAL Basketball, Fitness, Football, Flag, Ice Hockey, Racquetball, Soccer, Softball, Tennis, Volleyball • STUDENT LIFE ACTIVITIES Academic Clubs, Choral, Concert Band, Dance, Drama Groups, Ethnic & Cultural Groups, Fraternities, Musical Theater, Newspaper, Orchestra, Political Groups, Radio, Religious Organization, Sororities, Student Government, Symphony Orchestra, Yearbook

---

Less Selective   **Massachusetts**
                                          Services

Pine Manor College
400 Heath Street
Chestnut Hill, Massachusetts 02167
(617) 731-7104

School Enrollment: **500** Female: **500**

Admissions Contact: **Gillian Lloyd, Director of Admissions**
LD Contact: **Mary Walsh, Director**
Name of Program: **Learning Resource Center**
Telephone:**(617) 731-7181**

Admissions

Application Information:

Application deadline: **Rolling**
Rolling Admissions: **Yes**

Massachusetts

Secondary School Information
Most Important Criteria For Admissions (1-strongest)

3 SAT/ACT	2 Application	1	School transcript
3 Class rank	2 Course selection	3	Personal statement
4 Interview	4 Extra activities		Psychoeducational
2 G.P.A.	Open admission	2	Recommendations

Test Requirements:
Untimed SAT: **Yes** Untimed ACT: **Yes**

Types of Disabilities Served
- Speech/Lang
- Reading
- ADD with LD
- Study skills
- Spelling
- ADD without LD
- Written express
- Math
- ADHD with LD
- Organizational
- Fine Motor
- ADHD without LD
- Perceptual

Admissions Process

Emphasis placed on transcript (especially Jr./Sr. years) and recommendations. Director of LRC is available to consult with applicants.

High School Course Requirements:
English: **4**

Learning Disability Program

Special orientation for LD students: **Yes**
Students mainstreamed **100** % of the day
Recommended credits per semester: **12-16**
Services available for all students: **Yes**
Counseling: Individual: **Yes**
Support groups are available:**Yes**

Faculty:
Faculty: **4** Including Director: **Yes** Full time: **4**
LD faculty with: BS/BA: **1** M.A.: **3**
Faculty advocate: **Yes**

Diagnostic Testing

ADD	Personality	Perceptual skills	• Spelling
ADHD	Organization	Fine motor skills	• Reading
I.Q.	Handwriting	Spoken language	• Study skills
Math	Social skills	• Written language	

Tutoring:
Average size of group tutorials: **15**
Services rendered by:

Graduates	•Peers	Faculty	•LD staff	Teacher trainees

Tutorials

Grp.	Ind.	Tutorials	Grp.	Ind.	Tutorials
	•	Math skills		•	Word processing
•	•	Study skills	•	•	Time management
	•	Language arts		•	Learning strategies
	•	Written express		•	Organizational skills

Academic Accommodations

Curriculum	Study Aids	Exams
Priority registration	Typist	Oral
Math waiver	Reader	Untimed
Foreign lang. waiver	Notetaker	Take home
Course substitution	Proof reader	With proctor
In Class	• Text on tape	On computer
• Calculators	Early syllabus	• Extended time
• Tape recorder	Taped handouts	On tape
• Word processor		Modified
Priority seating		• Separate room

Graduation Requirements:
Course credits: **132** GPA: **2.0**
Other requirements: **Freshman Comp., broad disribution req.**

Program Strengths
The Learning Resource Center has a staff of four full-time professional tutors, including the director. Two are trained to assist learning disabled students. A math tutor and a writing tutor are also available. We service all students, not just learning disabled students, on an individual basis. Students refer themselves and are also referred by the faculty and the Dean's office. When students identify themselves as LD, we work with them, often on a weekly basis. We help them to develop the skills and strategies they need to make the transition to college. We do not have a program specifically for LD students but offer tutoring and support to these students and coordinate the accommodations.

General Information:
Pine Manor College is a 2 and 4 year independent college. Suburban campus of 79 acres is 5 miles from Boston. Accessible by subway or van. Ski areas are 2 hours from campus. Beaches are 1 hour from campus. 20% of students are foreign. 17 residential halls on campus. Housing is guaranteed.90 % of students remain on campus for the weekends.

Accreditation:NEACS

Expenses:
Tuition: In-state: Full year: $14,100.00. Room and board: $6,050.00

Majors

• AREA STUDIES American, Women's Studies • BUSINESS Accounting, Economics, International Business, Management, Marketing • COMMUNICATIONS Communication, English • COMPUTER SCIENCE Computer Science • EDUCATION English As A Second Language (
• HUMANITIES Philosophy, Religion • LANGUAGES French, Italian, Spanish • SCIENCES Biology, Chemistry, Marine Biology, Mathematics • SOCIAL SCIENCES Anthropology, Political Science, Psychology • VISUAL AND PERFORMING ARTS Art History, Dance, Dramatic Arts, Interior Design

Sports/Activities

• SPORTS-INTERCOLLEGIATE Basketball, Cross Country, Field Hockey, Lacrosse, Soccer, Tennis • SPORTS-INTRAMURAL Badminton, Basketball, Soccer, Softball, Tennis, Volleyball • STUDENT LIFE ACTIVITIES Drama Groups, Ethnic & Cultural Groups, Music Groups, Newspaper, Political Groups, Radio/TV station, Student Government, Yearbook

Selective   **Massachusetts**
Services

Simmons College
300 The Fenway
Boston, Massachusetts 02115
(617) 738-2107

School Enrollment: **1,583** Female: **1,583**
LD Enrollment: **50+**

Admissions Contact: **Tara Dowling, Ass. Director of Admissions**
LD Contact: **Carolyn Holland, Associate Dean**

Admissions

Application Information:
Application deadline: **February 1st**

Secondary School Information
Most Important Criteria For Admissions (1-strongest)

SAT/ACT	Application	**1**	School transcript
Class rank	**2** Course selection	**5**	Personal statement
Interview	**6** Extra activities		Psychoeducational
G.P.A.	Open admission	**4**	Recommendations

Test Requirements:
Untimed SAT: **Yes**
Documentation of LD required: **Yes**

Types of Disabilities Served
- Speech/Lang   • Reading   • ADD with LD
  Study skills   Spelling   • ADD without LD
  Written express   Math   • ADHD with LD
  Organizational   Fine Motor   • ADHD without LD
  Perceptual

High School Course Requirements:
English: **4** Math: **3** Science: **2-3** Foreign Language: **2**
Waivers to standard high school courses
Foreign Language : **Yes** Math: **Yes**

Learning Disability Program
Services available for all students: **Yes**
Counseling: Individual: **Yes** Group Counseling: **Yes**

Faculty:
Faculty: **1**
Faculty advocate: **Yes**

Diagnostic Testing

ADD	Personality	Perceptual skills	Spelling
ADHD	Organization	Fine motor skills	Reading
I.Q.	Handwriting	Spoken language	Study skills
Math	Social skills	Written language	

Tutoring:
Services rendered by:
Graduates   •Peers   Faculty   LD staff   Teacher trainees

Tutorials

Grp.	Ind.	Tutorials	Grp.	Ind.	Tutorials
•	•	Math skills			Word processing
•	•	Study skills	•	•	Time management
		Language arts			Learning strategies
•	•	Written express	•	•	Organizational skills

Academic Accommodations

Curriculum	Study Aids	Exams
Priority registration	Typist	• Oral
Math waiver	Reader	Untimed
• Foreign lang. waiver	• Notetaker	Take home
Course substitution	Proof reader	With proctor
In Class	• Text on tape	On computer
• Calculators	Early syllabus	• Extended time
• Tape recorder	Taped handouts	On tape
• Word processor		Modified
• Priority seating		Separate room

Graduation Requirements:
Course credits: **128** GPA: **1.67** Years to complete degree: **4-5** Language waiver: **Yes**
Other requirements: **Designated writing course, 2 semesters of freshman writing, 1 year of physical education**

Program Strengths
We do not have a formal LD program. Occasionally, we will admit a student with a learning disability who is mainstreamed who meets the regular admission criteria - and may only have need for occasional help. Our Supportive Instructional Service (SIS) offers tutoring, workshops in study skills and counseling to the general population of students.

General Information:
Simmons College is a 4 year independent college. Urban campus of 12 acres is Boston. Ski areas are 2.5 hours from campus. Beaches are 1 hour from campus. 4% of students are foreign. Housing is guaranteed. Guaranteed through 4th year. 75 % of students remain on campus for the weekends. 0 % of students join fraternities/sororities.

Accreditation: NEACS, APTA, CSWE, ACS, ALA, NLN, ICC

Expenses:
Tuition: In-state: Full year: $13,632.00. Room and board: $6,000.00

Majors
• AREA STUDIES African, Black/Afro-American, Women's Studies
• BUSINESS Accounting, Economics, Finance, International Business, Management, Retailing • COMMUNICATIONS Advertising, Communication, English, Journalism • COMPUTER SCIENCE Computer Science, Data Processing • EDUCATION Early Childhood, Elementary, Middle School, Secondary, Special • HEALTH SCIENCES Nursing, Nutritional/Food, Physical Therapy • HUMANITIES English/Writing/Literature, Humanities, Liberal Arts, Philosophy • LANGUAGES French, Spanish
• PREPROFESSIONAL Law, Medicine, Pharmacy, Social Work • SCIENCES Biochemistry, Biology, Chemistry, Mathematics, Physics • SOCIAL SCIENCES Government/Political, International Studies, Psychology, Social Sciences, Sociology • VISUAL AND PERFORMING ARTS Art, Art History, Music, Studio Art

Sports/Activities
• SPORTS-INTERCOLLEGIATE Crew (F), Cross Country (F), Diving (F), Field Hockey (F), Sailing (F), Soccer (F), Swimming (F), Tennis (F)
• STUDENT LIFE ACTIVITIES Choral, Dance, Magazine, Newspaper, Student Government, Yearbook

Highly Selective

Massachusetts Services

Smith College
Northampton, Massachusetts 01063
(413) 584-0515

School Enrollment: **2,607** Female: **2,607**
LD Enrollment: **40**

Admissions Contact: **Juliet Brigham, Director of Admissions**
LD Contact: **Mary Jane Maccardini, Coordinator**
Name of Program: **Special Needs Services**
Telephone:**(413) 585-2071, 2072**

Admissions

Application Information:
Application deadline: **January 15th**
Notified when: **April 1st**

Secondary School Information
Most Important Criteria For Admissions (1-strongest)

3 SAT/ACT	Application	1	School transcript
2 Class rank	1 Course selection	3	Personal statement
5 Interview	4 Extra activities		Psychoeducational
1 G.P.A.	Open admission	4	Recommendations

Test Requirements:
Untimed SAT: **Yes** Untimed ACT: **Yes** Untimed ACH: **Yes** Achievement tests required:**3**
Documentation of LD required: **Yes**
Tests recommended: **Diagnostic testing is not required as part of the admissions process. It is required once a student has enrolled, in order to receive supportive services.**

Types of Disabilities Served
- Speech/Lang
- Reading
- ADD with LD
- Study skills
- Spelling
- ADD without LD
- Written express
- Math
- ADHD with LD
- Organizational
- Fine Motor
- ADHD without LD
- Perceptual

High School Course Requirements:
English: **4** Math: **3** Science: **2** Foreign Language: **3**

Learning Disability Program
Services only for LD students: **Yes**
Services available for all students: **Yes**

Diagnostic Testing

ADD	Personality	Perceptual skills	Spelling
ADHD	Organization	Fine motor skills	Reading
I.Q.	Handwriting	Spoken language	Study skills
Math	Social skills	Written language	

Services rendered by:

Graduates	Peers	Faculty	LD staff	Teacher trainees

Tutorials

Grp.	Ind.	Tutorials	Grp.	Ind.	Tutorials
	•	Math skills		•	Word processing
	•	Study skills		•	Time management
	•	Language arts		•	Learning strategies
	•	Written express		•	Organizational skills

Academic Accommodations

Curriculum	Study Aids	Exams
• Priority registration	Typist	• Oral
Math waiver	• Reader	• Untimed
Foreign lang. waiver	• Notetaker	Take home
Course substitution	• Proof reader	With proctor
In Class	• Text on tape	• On computer
• Calculators	• Early syllabus	• Extended time
• Tape recorder	Taped handouts	• On tape
• Word processor		Modified
• Priority seating		• Separate room

Program Strengths
Academic assistance is offered to all students at Smith College through our center for Academic Development. We have two writing assistance counselors as well as peer tutors for academic areas.

General Information:
Smith College is a 4 year independent college. Rural campus of 125 acres is 90 miles from Boston. Accessible by bus. Ski areas are 1/2 hour from campus. Beaches are 2 hours from campus. 5% of students are foreign. 42 residential halls on campus. Housing is guaranteed.Guaranteed through 4th year. 85 % of students remain on campus for the weekends.

Accreditation: Regional

SAT/ACT Scores:
Scores for incoming freshmen:**Verbal:15%**below 500. 44%between 500 and 599. 36%between 600 and 699. 5%above 700. **Math:**10% below 500. 41% between 500 and 599. 41% between 600 and 699. 8%above 700.

Class Rank:
About 80% of the present freshmen class were in the upper 20% of their high school class. 97% were in the top 40% of their class. 99% were in the top 60% of their class. 100% were in the top 80% of their class.

Expenses:
Tuition: In-state: Full year: $16,850.00. Tuition: Out-of-state: Full year: $16,850.00. Room and board: $6,100.00

Majors
• AREA STUDIES American, Black/Afro-American, Jewish, Latin American, Third World Studies, Urban, Women's Studies • ARTS Art History, Graphic Art • BUSINESS Economics • COMMUNICATIONS English • COMPUTER SCIENCE Computer Science, Mathematical, Systems Analysis • EDUCATION Child Development • ENGINEERING Engineering Science • HEALTH SCIENCES Fitness • HUMANITIES Classics, English/Writing/Literature, Philosophy, Religious Studies • LANGUAGES Arabic, East Asian, English, French, German, Greek, Italian, Japanese, Latin, Portuguese, Russian, Spanish • RELIGIOUS STUDIES Bible, Religion • SCIENCES Anthropology, Archeology, Astronomy, Biochemistry, Biology, Chemistry, Geology, Marine Biology, Mathematics, Nuerosciences, Physics • SOCIAL SCIENCES Anthropology, Archeology, Ethics, Government/Political, History, International Relations, International Studies, Medieval, Psychology, Public Policy, Sociology • VISUAL AND PERFORMING ARTS Art, Dance, Film & Video, Music, Studio Art, Theater

Sports/Activities
• SPORTS-INTERCOLLEGIATE Basketball, Crew, Cross Country, Diving, Field Hockey, Horseback Riding, Lacrosse, Skiing - Snow, Soccer,

Softball, Squash, Swimming, Tennis, Track and Field, Volleyball • SPORTS-INTRAMURAL Badminton, Baseball, Basketball, Crew, Cross Country, Field Hockey, Ping-Pong, Skiing - Snow, Soccer, Softball, Squash, Swimming, Tennis, Track and Field, Volleyball • STUDENT LIFE ACTIVITIES Choral, Dance, Magazine, Music Groups, Musical Theater, Political Groups, Radio, Student Government, Symphony Orchestra, Yearbook

Less Selective	Massachusetts Services

Springfield Technical Community College

1 Armory Square
Springfield, Massachusetts 01105
(413) 781-7822

School Enrollment: **3,400** Male: **1,500** Female: **1,900**
LD Enrollment: **45** Male: **30** Female: **15**

Admissions Contact: **Christina Tigue, Admissions Counselor**
LD Contact: **Deena Shriver, Counselor for Students with LD**
Address: **Counseling Center, 1 Armory Square**
Telephone:**(413) 781-7822 - Ext. 3884**

Admissions

Application Information:
Application deadline: **None**
Rolling Admissions: **Yes**

Secondary School Information
Most Important Criteria For Admissions (1-strongest)

SAT/ACT	Application	School transcript
Class rank	Course selection	Personal statement
Interview	Extra activities	Psychoeducational
G.P.A.	**1** Open admission	Recommendations

Test Requirements:
Documentation of LD required: **Yes**

Types of Disabilities Served

Speech/Lang	Reading	ADD with LD
Study skills	Spelling	ADD without LD
Written express	Math	ADHD with LD
Organizational	Fine Motor	ADHD without LD
Perceptual		

Admissions Process

Open admission as in all Massachusetts Community Colleges.

Learning Disability Program

Program: Remedial: **Yes**
Program: Reinforces course work: **Yes**
Program available through:**Days, Sept.-May**
Students mainstreamed **100** % of the day
Recommended credits per semester: **9**
Services available for all students: **Yes**
Counseling: Individual: **Yes** Group Counseling: **Yes** Vocational Counseling: **Yes**
Support groups are available:**Once a week. Topic - centered academic support group**

Faculty:
Faculty: **1** Part time: **1** M.A.: **1**
Meets with instructor: **As needed**

Diagnostic Testing

ADD	• Personality	Perceptual skills	Spelling
ADHD	Organization	Fine motor skills	Reading
I.Q.	Handwriting	Spoken language	• Study skills
Math	Social skills	Written language	

Tutoring:
Services rendered by:

Graduates	•Peers	•Faculty	LD staff	Teacher trainees

Tutorials

Grp.	Ind.	Tutorials	Grp.	Ind.	Tutorials
	•	Math skills		•	Word processing
•		Study skills		•	Time management
	•	Language arts		•	Learning strategies
	•	Written express		•	Organizational skills

Academic Accommodations

Curriculum	Study Aids	Exams
Priority registration	Typist	• Oral
Math waiver	Reader	• Untimed
Foreign lang. waiver	Notetaker	• Take home
Course substitution	Proof reader	• With proctor
In Class	• Text on tape	• On computer
• Calculators	Early syllabus	• Extended time
• Tape recorder	Taped handouts	• On tape
Word processor		Modified
Priority seating		• Separate room

Graduation Requirements:
Course credits: **varies**

Program Strengths

No formalized program available - support services only.

General Information:

Springfield Technical Community College is a 2 year public college. Urban campus of 34 acres is Accessible by bus. Ski areas are 20 miles from campus. Beaches are 3 hours from campus. 5% of students are foreign. Housing is not guaranteed.

Accreditation:NEACS

Expenses:
Tuition: In-state: Full year: $504.00 per semester. Part-time: Per credit:$42.00. Tuition: Out-of-state: Full year: $2,340.00 per semester. Part-time: Per credit:$195.00.

Majors

• ARTS Drafting, Graphic Arts, Landscaping • BUSINESS Accounting, Business Administration, Business Management, Data Processing, Management, Marketing • COMMUNICATIONS Television/Radio/Film • COMPUTER SCIENCE Computer Maintenance, Computer Science, Data Processing, Robotics • EDUCATION Early Childhood • ENGINEERING Electrical • ENVIRONMENTAL CONTROL Water and Wastewater Technolog • HEALTH SCIENCES Dental Assistant, Dental Hygiene, Medical Assistant, Medical Laboratry Technology, Medical Secretary, Nuclear Medical Technology, Nursing, Radiological Technology, Respiratory Therapy, Surgical Technology • HUMANITIES Liberal Arts • SCIENCES Radiology • SOCIAL SCIENCES Criminal Justice • VOCATIONAL Air Conditioning/Heating/Refri, Automobile Technology, Court Reporting, Dental Hygiene, Drafting, Electronics Technology, Legal Secretary, Radiological Technology, Secretarial

Sports/Activities

• SPORTS-INTERCOLLEGIATE Basketball (M), Softball (F), Softball (M)

Very Selective	Massachusetts Services

Stonehill College
320 Washington Street
North Easton, Massachusetts 02357
(617) 238-1081

School Enrollment: **1,900** Male: **855** Female: **1,145**
LD Enrollment: **20** Male: **14** Female: **6**

Admissions Contact: **Brian Murphy, Dean of Ad. and Enrollment**
LD Contact: **Richard Grant, Assistant Dean of Academic Services**
Name of Program: **Office of Academic Services**
Telephone:**(508) 230-1306**

Admissions

Application Information:
Application deadline: **February 15th**
Notified when: **April 15th**

Secondary School Information
Most Important Criteria For Admissions (1-strongest)

3 SAT/ACT	7 Application	1	School transcript
2 Class rank	5 Course selection	8	Personal statement
7 Interview	6 Extra activities	4	Psychoeducational
2 G.P.A.	Open admission	4	Recommendations

Test Requirements:
Untimed SAT: **Yes**
Currency of diagnostic testing: **No limit-one year is recommended**

Types of Disabilities Served
• Speech/Lang
• Study skills
• Written express
• Organizational
• Perceptual
• Reading
• Spelling
• Math
• Fine Motor
• ADD with LD
• ADD without LD
• ADHD with LD
• ADHD without LD

Learning Disability Program
Counseling: Individual: **Yes** Group Counseling: **Yes**

Faculty:
Faculty: **2** Part time: **2**
Faculty advocate: **Yes**

Diagnostic Testing
ADD	Personality	Perceptual skills	Spelling
ADHD	Organization	Fine motor skills	Reading
I.Q.	Handwriting	Spoken language	Study skills
Math	Social skills	Written language	

Tutoring:
Services rendered by:
Graduates •Peers Faculty •LD staff Teacher trainees

Tutorials

Grp.	Ind.	Tutorials	Grp.	Ind.	Tutorials
	•	Math skills		•	Word processing
	•	Study skills		•	Time management
	•	Language arts		•	Learning strategies
	•	Written express		•	Organizational skills

Academic Accommodations

Curriculum	Study Aids	Exams
Priority registration	Typist	• Oral
Math waiver	Reader	Untimed
• Foreign lang. waiver	• Notetaker	Take home
Course substitution	Proof reader	With proctor
In Class	• Text on tape	On computer
• Calculators	Early syllabus	• Extended time
• Tape recorder	Taped handouts	On tape
• Word processor		Modified
Priority seating		Separate room

Program Strengths

The services are primarily provided by the Assistant Dean of Academic Services, with the assistance of numerous professors who are consulted as appropriate. The Learning Center provides tutoring and the Writing Center assists with writing problems. Our small dedicated faculty helps considerably. Our Learning Center serves all students and is staffed by peers. We also have a three credit study skills course.

General Information:

Stonehill College is a 4 year independent Roman Catholic college. Suburban campus of 650 acres is 25 miles from Boston. Accessible by bus. Ski areas are 15 miles from campus. Beaches are 20 miles from campus. 1-2% of students are foreign. Housing is not guaranteed.70 % of students remain on campus for the weekends.

Accreditation: Regional

Expenses:
Tuition: In-state: Full year: $9,400.00. Part-time: Per credit:$300.00. Part-time: Per course: $900.00. Room and board: $5,000.00

Majors

• AREA STUDIES American, Asian, International Studies • BUSINESS Accounting, Banking, Business Administration, Business Management, Economics, Finance, Management, Marketing • COMMUNICATIONS Communication, English, Journalism • COMPUTER SCIENCE Computer Science • EDUCATION Early Childhood, Elementary • ENGINEERING Aerospace, Chemical, Civil/Environmental, Computer, Electrical, Environmental/Water Resources, Mechanical, Metallurgical, Nuclear • HEALTH SCIENCES Health, Medical Technology • HUMANITIES English/Writing/Literature, Philosophy, Religion • LANGUAGES French, German, Italian, Latin, Russian, Spanish • PREPROFESSIONAL Dentistry, Engineering, Law • SCIENCES Biology, Chemistry, Mathematics • SOCIAL SCIENCES Criminal Justice, Government/Political, History, International Studies, Political Science • VISUAL AND PERFORMING ARTS Theater

Sports/Activities

• SPORTS-INTERCOLLEGIATE Baseball (M), Basketball, Cross Country, Football (M), Golf (M), Horseback Riding, Ice Hockey (M), Sailing, Soccer, Softball (F), Tennis, Track and Field, Volleyball (F) • SPORTS-INTRAMURAL Basketball, Football (M), Racquetball, Soccer, Softball, Squash, Tennis, Volleyball • STUDENT LIFE ACTIVITIES Choral, Community Service, Drama Groups, Magazine, Musical Theater, Newspaper, Radio/TV station, Student Government, Symphony Orchestra, Yearbook

Highly Selective

**Massachusetts
Services**

Tufts University
72 Professors Row
Medford, Massachusetts 02155
(617) 381-3170

School Enrollment: **4,500** Male: **2,250** Female: **2,250**
LD Enrollment: **24** Male: **12** Female: **12**

Admissions Contact: **R.M. Uhrig, Director of Admissions**
LD Contact: **Jean Herbert, Director**
Name of Program: **Academic Resource Center**
Telephone:**(617) 627-3724**

Admissions

Application Information:
Application deadline: **January 1st**
Notified when: **April 1st**

Secondary School Information
Most Important Criteria For Admissions (1-strongest)

1 SAT/ACT	**3** Application	**1** School transcript
1 Class rank	**4** Course selection	**8** Personal statement
6 Interview	**5** Extra activities	**7** Psychoeducational
1 G.P.A.	Open admission	**2** Recommendations

Test Requirements:
Untimed SAT: **Yes** Untimed ACT: **Yes**
Documentation of LD required: **Yes**

Types of Disabilities Served
- Speech/Lang
- Study skills
- Written express
- Organizational
- Perceptual
- Reading
- Spelling
- Math
- Fine Motor
- ADD with LD
- ADD without LD
- ADHD with LD
- ADHD without LD

Admissions Process

LD students must satisfy same criteria for admission as all other students - good grades, good SAT scores (untimed).

High School Course Requirements:
English: **1** Math: **1** Science: **1** Foreign Language: **2**
Waivers to standard high school courses
Foreign Language : **Yes** Math: **Yes** Course substitution: **Yes**

Learning Disability Program
Special orientation for LD students:
Services available for all students: **Yes**
Counseling: Individual: **Yes** Group Counseling: **Yes**

Faculty:
Faculty: **1** Part time: **1**
Meets with instructor: **seldom**

Diagnostic Testing
ADD	Personality	Perceptual skills	Spelling
ADHD	Organization	Fine motor skills	Reading
I.Q.	Handwriting	Spoken language	Study skills
Math	Social skills	Written language	

Tutoring:
Average size of group tutorials: **4-10**
Services rendered by:
Graduates •Peers Faculty •LD staff Teacher trainees

Tutorials
Grp.	Ind.	Tutorials	Grp.	Ind.	Tutorials
•	•	Math skills			Word processing
•	•	Study skills	•	•	Time management
•	•	Language arts	•	•	Learning strategies
•	•	Written express	•	•	Organizational skills

Academic Accommodations
Curriculum	Study Aids	Exams
Priority registration	• Typist	• Oral
• Math waiver	Reader	Untimed
• Foreign lang. waiver	• Notetaker	• Take home
• Course substitution	• Proof reader	• With proctor
In Class	• Text on tape	On computer
Calculators	Early syllabus	• Extended time
• Tape recorder	Taped handouts	On tape
• Word processor		Modified
Priority seating		Separate room

Program Strengths
We offer support services for LD students who have been admitted under the same criteria as the other students. Extended exam time, alternative tutoring and tape recorders are allowed with the permission of the professor.
*Students are accepted with any of the identified deficits as long as these students have compensatory techniques and can be their own advocates.

General Information:
Tufts University is a 4 year independent university. Suburban campus 8 miles from Boston. Accessible by air, train, or bus. Ski areas are 2 hours from campus. Beaches are 30 mils from campus. 17 residential halls on campus. Housing is guaranteed.Guaranteed through 1st year. 95 % of students remain on campus for the weekends.

Accreditation: Regional

SAT/ACT Scores:
Scores for incoming freshmen:**Verbal:**14%below 500. 25%between 500 and 599. 48%between 600 and 699. 73%above 700.

Class Rank:
About 30% of the present freshmen class were in the upper 20% of their high school class. 15% were in the top 40% of their class. 15% were in the top 60% of their class. 15% were in the top 80% of their class.

Expenses:
Tuition: In-state: Full year: $15,917.00. Room and board: $5,170.00

Majors
• AREA STUDIES African, American, Asian, Black/Afro-American, European, Jewish, Middle Eastern, Russian/Slavic • BUSINESS Economics • COMMUNICATIONS English • COMPUTER SCIENCE Computer Science, Programming, Systems Analysis • EDUCATION Art, Curriculum, Early Childhood, Elementary, English, Mathematics, Middle School, Physical, Science, Secondary, Special • ENGINEERING Civil/Environmental, Engineering Science, Geophysical, Mechanical, Physics • HEALTH SCIENCES Health • HUMANITIES Classics, English/Writing/Literature, Humanities, Liberal Arts, Philosophy, Religion • LANGUAGES Chinese, French, German, Italian, Japanese, Latin, Russian, Spanish • PREPROFESSIONAL Dentistry, Engineering, Law, Medicine • SCIENCES Archeology, Astronomy, Biology, Chemistry, Ecology, Geography, Geology, Mathematics, Physics, Statistics • SOCIAL SCIENCES Anthropology, Government/Political, History, International Studies, Psychology, Social Sciences • VI-

Massachusetts

SUAL AND PERFORMING ARTS Art History, Dance, Fine Arts, Music, Theater

Sports/Activities
• SPORTS-INTERCOLLEGIATE Baseball (M), Basketball, Crew, Cross Country, Diving, Field Hockey (F), Football (M), Golf (M), Horseback Riding, Ice Hockey (M), Lacrosse, Rugby, Sailing, Soccer, Softball (F), Squash, Swimming, Tennis, Track and Field, Volleyball (F), Wrestling (M)
• SPORTS-INTRAMURAL Basketball, Cross Country, Diving, Fencing, Racquetball, Skiing - Snow, Softball, Squash, Swimming, Tennis, Track and Field, Volleyball (F) • STUDENT LIFE ACTIVITIES Choral, Concert Band, Drama Groups, Film, Fraternities, Jazz Band, Magazine, Music Groups, Musical Theater, Newspaper, Opera, Radio/TV station, Sororities, Student Government

---

Selective   **Massachusetts Services**

University of Massachusetts - Dartmouth
Old Westport Road
North Dartmouth, Massachusetts 02747-2300
(508) 999-8605

School Enrollment: **5,680** Male: **2,801** Female: **2,879**
LD Enrollment: **26** Male: **13** Female: **13**

Admissions Contact: **Barrie Phelps, Director of Admissions**
LD Contact: **Carole Johnson, Director**
Name of Program: **Disabled Students Services**
Address: **Old Westport Road**
Telephone:**(508) 999-8711**

Admissions

Application Information:
Application deadline: **None**
Rolling Admissions: **Yes**

Secondary School Information
Most Important Criteria For Admissions (1-strongest)

4 SAT/ACT	Application	**1**	School transcript
1 Class rank	**3** Course selection	**7**	Personal statement
Interview	**6** Extra activities		Psychoeducational
2 G.P.A.	Open admission	**5**	Recommendations

Test Requirements:
Standardized tests waived: **Yes**
Untimed SAT: **Yes**
WAIS-R required: **Yes** Range accepted: **No Range**
Currency of diagnostic testing: **No Requirements**

Types of Disabilities Served
• Speech/Lang   • Reading   • ADD with LD
• Study skills   • Spelling   • ADD without LD
• Written express   • Math   • ADHD with LD
• Organizational   • Fine Motor   • ADHD without LD
• Perceptual

Admissions Process

We admit LD students who show a record of good performance in their previous schooling as indicated principally by class rank standing and by grades. These expectations are essentially the same as those of non-LD applicants, although allowances are made from evidence on the IAP forms from the secondary schools.

High School Course Requirements:
English: **4** Math: **3** Science: **2** Foreign Language: **2**

Learning Disability Program
Program: Reinforces course work: **Yes**
Students mainstreamed **100** % of the day
Recommended credits per semester: **9-12**
Services available for all students: **Yes**
Counseling: Individual: **Yes** Group Counseling: **Yes** Vocational Counseling: **Yes**
Support groups are available:**Yes, special interest groups**

Faculty:
Faculty: **1** Full time: **1**
Meets with instructor: **As needed**

Diagnostic Testing
ADD	Personality	Perceptual skills	Spelling
ADHD	Organization	Fine motor skills	Reading
I.Q.	Handwriting	Spoken language	Study skills
Math	Social skills	Written language	

Tutoring:
Average size of group tutorials: **3-7**
Services rendered by:
•Graduates   •Peers   Faculty   •LD staff   Teacher trainees

Tutorials
Grp.	Ind.	Tutorials	Grp.	Ind.	Tutorials
•	•	Math skills	•	•	Word processing
•	•	Study skills	•	•	Time management
•	•	Language arts	•	•	Learning strategies
•	•	Written express	•	•	Organizational skills

Academic Accommodations

Curriculum	Study Aids	Exams
• Priority registration	• Typist	• Oral
Math waiver	• Reader	• Untimed
• Foreign lang. waiver	• Notetaker	Take home
Course substitution	• Proof reader	• With proctor
In Class	• Text on tape	• On computer
Calculators	• Early syllabus	• Extended time
• Tape recorder	Taped handouts	• On tape
• Word processor		• Modified
• Priority seating		• Separate room

Graduation Requirements:
Course credits: **120** GPA: **2.0** Years to complete degree: **4** Language waiver: **Yes**

Program Strengths
We provide any service within reason that is required to help the LD student succeed in college.

General Information:
University of Massachusetts - Dartmouth is a 4 year public university. Suburban campus of 710 acres is 50 miles from Boston. Accessible by bus. Ski areas are 98 miles from campus. Beaches are 13 miles from campus. 2% of students are foreign. Housing is guaranteed.50 % of students remain on campus for the weekends.

Accreditation: Regional

SAT/ACT Scores:
Scores for incoming freshmen: **Verbal:** 85% below 500. 14% between 500 and 599. 2% between 600 and 699. **Math:** 56% below 500. 33% between 500 and 599. 9% between 600 and 699. 1% above 700.

Class Rank:
About 29% of the present freshmen class were in the upper 20% of their high school class. 41% were in the top 40% of their class. 20% were in the top 60% of their class. 9% were in the top 80% of their class.

Expenses:
Tuition: In-state: Full year: $1,698.00 plus fees. Part-time: Per credit:$70.75 plus fees. Tuition: Out-of-state: Full year: $6,396.00 plus fees. Part-time: Per credit:$195.75 plus fees. Room and board: $4,200.00

Majors
• ARTS Art History, Design, Graphic Arts, Music, Music Performance, Painting, Photography, Sculpture • BUSINESS Accounting, Business Information Systems, Economics, Finance, Human Resources Management, Management, Marketing • COMMUNICATIONS English, Literature • COMPUTER SCIENCE Computer Science • CRAFTS AND DESIGN Ceramics, Illustration Design, Jewelry-Metalsmithery, Printmaking, Sculpture, Textile/Weaving, Woodworking • EDUCATION Art • ENGINEERING Civil, Computer, Electrical, Mechanical, Mechanical Engineering Technol • HEALTH SCIENCES Medical Laboratory Technology, Nursing • HUMANITIES English/Writing/Literature, Fine Arts, Humanities, Liberal Arts , Philosophy • LANGUAGES English, French, German, Portuguese, Spanish • MATHEMATICS Applied • RELIGIOUS STUDIES Philosophy • SCIENCES Applied Mathematics, Biochemistry, Biology, Chemistry, Marine Biology, Mathematics, Physics • SOCIAL SCIENCES Anthropology, Criminal Justice, History, Psychology, Sociology • VISUAL AND PERFORMING ARTS Art, Art History, Fine Arts, Music, Music Performance, Studio Art

Sports/Activities
• SPORTS RELATED Cheerleading • SPORTS-INTERCOLLEGIATE Baseball (M), Basketball (F), Basketball (M), Diving (F), Diving (M), Field Hockey (F), Football (M), Golf (M), Horseback Riding (F), Ice Hockey (M), Lacrosse (M), Soccer (F), Soccer (M), Softball (F), Swimming (F), Swimming (M), Tennis (F), Tennis (M), Track and Field (F), Track and Field (M), Volleyball (F) • SPORTS-INTRAMURAL Basketball (F), Basketball (M), Softball (F), Softball (M), Tennis (F), Tennis (M), Volleyball (F), Volleyball (M), Water Polo (F), Water Polo (M) • STUDENT LIFE ACTIVITIES Academic Clubs, Choral, Concert Band, Drama Groups, Ethnic & Cultural Groups, Music Groups, Musical Theater, Newspaper, Orchestra, Radio, Religious Organization, Student Government, Symphony Orchestra, Yearbook

---

Very Selective

Massachusetts Services

University of Massachusetts at Amherst
University Admissions Center
Amherst, Massachusetts 01003
(413) 545-0222

School Enrollment: **20,000** Male: **10,000** Female: **10,000**
LD Enrollment: **310** Male: **186** Female: **124**

Admissions Contact: **Dr. Juan P. Caban, Assis. Dir. of Admissions**
LD Contact: **Dr. Patricia Gillespie-Silver, Director**
Name of Program: **Learning Disabled Student Services**
Address: **Berkshire House**
Telephone: **(413) 545-4602**

Admissions

Application Information:
LD Students Applying: **160** Accepted: **40** Enrolled: **22**
Application deadline: **February 15th**
Rolling Admissions: **Yes** Notified when: **April 15th**

Secondary School Information
Most Important Criteria For Admissions (1-strongest)

SAT/ACT	Application	**3**	School transcript
Class rank	**1**	Course selection	**6** Personal statement
Interview		Extra activities	**4** Psychoeducational
2 G.P.A.		Open admission	**5** Recommendations

Test Requirements:
Standardized tests waived: **Yes**
Diagnostic testing waived: **Yes**
Untimed SAT: **Yes**
WAIS-R required: **Yes**

Types of Disabilities Served
• Speech/Lang • Reading • ADD with LD
• Study skills • Spelling • ADD without LD
• Written express • Math • ADHD with LD
• Organizational • Fine Motor • ADHD without LD
• Perceptual

High School Course Requirements:
English: **4** Math: **3** Science: **2** Foreign Language: **2**

Learning Disability Program
Program: Reinforces course work: **Yes**
Students mainstreamed **100** % of the day

Faculty:
Faculty: **14** Full time: **1** Part time: **13**
LD faculty with: BS/BA: **14** M.A.: **4** Ph.D.: **6**
Faculty advocate: **Yes** Meets with instructor: **Twice a semester**

Diagnostic Testing
• ADD • Personality • Perceptual skills • Spelling
• ADHD • Organization • Fine motor skills • Reading
• I.Q. • Handwriting • Spoken language • Study skills
• Math • Social skills • Written language

Tutoring:
Services rendered by:
• Graduates • Peers • Faculty • LD staff • Teacher trainees

Tutorials

Grp.	Ind.	Tutorials	Grp.	Ind.	Tutorials
•	•	Math skills		•	Word processing
•	•	Study skills		•	Time management
	•	Language arts		•	Learning strategies
	•	Written express		•	Organizational skills

Academic Accommodations

Curriculum	Study Aids	Exams
Priority registration	Typist	• Oral
• Math waiver	Reader	Untimed
• Foreign lang. waiver	• Notetaker	• Take home
Course substitution	• Proof reader	With proctor
In Class	• Text on tape	On computer
• Calculators	Early syllabus	• Extended time
• Tape recorder	Taped handouts	On tape
• Word processor		Modified
Priority seating		Separate room

Graduation Requirements:

Course credits: **120** GPA: **2.0** Years to complete degree: **5** Language waiver: **Yes**

Program Strengths

We are a well-funded, research-based program. We offer a full range of services by qualified staff and faculty.

General Information:

University of Massachusetts at Amherst is a 4 year public university. Suburban campus of 1,200 acres is 30 miles from Springfield. Accessible by air, train or bus. Ski areas are 20 miles from campus. Beaches are 100 miles from campus. 2% of students are foreign. 54 residential halls on campus. Housing is guaranteed.85 % of students remain on campus for the weekends. 5 % of students join fraternities/sororities.

Accreditation: Full, Regional

Class Rank: 36 were in the top 40% of their class.

Expenses:

Tuition: In-state: Full year: $2,134.00 plus fees $2,928.00. Part-time: Per credit:$89.00. Part-time: Per course: $267.00. Tuition: Out-of-state: Full year: $8,236.00 plus fees $2,928.00. Part-time: Per credit:$343.25. Part-time: Per course:$1,026.75 Room and board: $3,693.00

Majors

• AREA STUDIES American, Asian, Black/Afro-American, Jewish, Latin American, Urban • BUSINESS Accounting, Business Administration, Economics, Finance, Hotel and Restaurant Managemen, Management, Marketing, Sports Management, Travel/Tourism Management
• COMMUNICATIONS Broadcasting, Communication, English, Journalism • COMPUTER SCIENCE Computer Science, Hardware Engineer, Software Engineer, Systems Analysis • EDUCATION Art, Child Development, Early Childhood, Elementary, Industrial, Music, Physical, Secondary, Special • ENGINEERING Chemical, Civil/Environmental, Computer, Electrical, Industrial, Mathematical • HEALTH SCIENCES Communication Disorders, Environmental, Fitness, Nursing, Nutritional/Food • HUMANITIES Classics, English/Writing/Literature, Humanities, Philosophy
• LANGUAGES Arabic, Chinese, Danish, French, German, Greek, Italian, Japanese, Latin, Linguistics, Russian, Spanish • PREPROFESSIONAL Agriculture, Architecture, Dentistry, Engineering, Forestry, Law, Medicine, Ministry, Natural Resources, Pharmacy, Recreation, Social Work, Sports Medicine, Veterinarian • SCIENCES Agricultural, Astronomy, Astrophysics, Biochemistry, Biology, Chemistry, Ecology, Entomology, Equestrian Studies, Geography, Geology, Macrobiology, Physical Chemistry, Physical Science, Physics, Physiology, Statistics, Zoology • SOCIAL SCIENCES Anthropology, Government/Political, History, Human Service, Political Science, Psychology, Social Sciences, Sociology • VISUAL AND PERFORMING ARTS Art, Art History, Dance, Music, Studio Art, Theater
• VOCATIONAL Forestry, Home Economics, Landscape Architecture

Sports/Activities

• SPORTS RELATED Marching Band • SPORTS-INTERCOLLEGIATE Baseball (M), Basketball, Cross Country, Diving, Field Hockey (F), Football (M), Gymnastics, Lacrosse, Skiing - Snow, Soccer, Softball (F), Squash, Swimming, Tennis, Track and Field, Volleyball (F), Water Polo (M) • SPORTS-INTRAMURAL Badminton, Basketball, Cross Country, Diving, Fencing, Field Hockey (F), Football (M), Gymnastics, Hand Ball, Ice Hockey (M), Lacrosse, Racquetball, Rugby (F), Soccer, Softball, Squash, Swimming, Tennis, Track and Field, Volleyball, Wrestling • STUDENT LIFE ACTIVITIES Choral, Concert Band, Drama Groups, Ethnic & Cultural Groups, Film, Fraternities, Jazz Band, Magazine, Music Groups, Musical Theater, Newspaper, Political Groups, Radio/TV station, Religious Organization, Sororities, Student Government, Symphony Orchestra, Yearbook

---

Selective

Massachusetts Services

University of Massachusetts at Boston
020-3/435
Boston, Massachusetts 02125
(617) 929-7870

School Enrollment: **12,000**

Admissions Contact: **Zoe Anponte-Gonzalez, Assis. Dir. of Adms.**
LD Contact: **Carol Desouza, Director**
Name of Program: **ACCESS**
Telephone:**(617) 287-5820**

Admissions

Application Information:
Application deadline: **June 15th**
Applicant must apply **1-9** months in advance
Rolling Admissions: **Yes**

Secondary School Information
Most Important Criteria For Admissions (1-strongest)

5 SAT/ACT	**1** Application	**2** School transcript
5 Class rank	**1** Course selection	**3** Personal statement
4 Interview	**6** Extra activities	**1** Psychoeducational
2 G.P.A.	Open admission	**3** Recommendations

Test Requirements:
Documentation of LD required: **Yes**

Types of Disabilities Served
• Speech/Lang	• Reading	• ADD with LD
• Study skills	• Spelling	• ADD without LD
• Written express	• Math	• ADHD with LD
• Organizational	• Fine Motor	• ADHD without LD
• Perceptual		

Learning Disability Program
Counseling: Individual: **Yes** Group Counseling: **Yes**

Faculty:
Faculty: **2** Full time: **2**
Faculty advocate: **Yes**

Diagnostic Testing
ADD	Personality	Perceptual skills	Spelling
ADHD	Organization	Fine motor skills	Reading
I.Q.	Handwriting	Spoken language	Study skills
Math	Social skills	Written language	

Tutoring:
Services rendered by:
•Graduates •Peers   Faculty   •LD staff   Teacher trainees

Tutorials

Grp.	Ind.	Tutorials	Grp.	Ind.	Tutorials
•	•	Math skills	•	•	Word processing
•	•	Study skills	•	•	Time management
•	•	Language arts	•	•	Learning strategies
•	•	Written express	•	•	Organizational skills

Academic Accommodations

Curriculum	Study Aids	Exams
Priority registration	• Typist	• Oral
• Math waiver	Reader	Untimed
• Foreign lang. waiver	• Notetaker	• Take home
Course substitution	• Proof reader	With proctor
In Class	• Text on tape	On computer
• Calculators	Early syllabus	• Extended time
• Tape recorder	Taped handouts	On tape
• Word processor		Modified
Priority seating		Separate room

Program Strengths

The university has no formal LD program. We provide services to students who request assistance.

General Information:

University of Massachusetts at Boston is a 4 year public university. Urban campus. of 177 acres is Accessible by train or bus. Ski areas are 1 from campus. 2% of students are foreign. Housing is not guaranteed.

Accreditation: NEASC

Expenses:

Tuition: In-state: Full year: $1,512.00. Part-time: Per credit:$63.00. Part-time: Per course: $189.00. Tuition: Out-of-state: Full year: $6,388.00. Part-time: Per credit:$266.00. Part-time: Per course:$698.00

Majors

• AREA STUDIES Black/Afro-American, Latin American • BUSINESS Accounting, Business Management, Economics, Finance, Management, Marketing • COMMUNICATIONS Communication, Creative Writing, English • COMPUTER SCIENCE Computer Science, Computer Technology, Systems Analysis • EDUCATION Art, Early Childhood, Elementary, Physical, Recreation and Youth Leadershi, Secondary • HEALTH SCIENCES Medical Technology • LANGUAGES French, German, Greek, Latin, Russian, Spanish • PREPROFESSIONAL Dentistry, Engineering, Law, Medicine • SCIENCES Biology, Botany, Chemistry, Geography, Mathematics, Physics • SOCIAL SCIENCES Anthropology, Criminal Justice, Government/Political, History, Human Service, Psychology, Social Sciences, Sociology • VISUAL AND PERFORMING ARTS Art, Dramatic Arts, Fine Arts, Music, Theater

Sports/Activities

• SPORTS-INTERCOLLEGIATE Baseball (M), Basketball, Cross Country, Diving, Football (M), Ice Hockey (M), Lacrosse (M), Soccer (M), Softball (M), Tennis (M), Track and Field, Volleyball (F), Weight Lifting, Wrestling (M) • SPORTS-INTRAMURAL Basketball, Cross Country, Ice Hockey (M), Ping-Pong, Sailing, Softball, Squash, Swimming, Tennis, Volleyball (F) • STUDENT LIFE ACTIVITIES Debate, Drama Groups, Ethnic & Cultural Groups, Film, Jazz Band, Music Groups, Newspaper, Radio/TV station, Religious Organization, Student Government, Yearbook

---

Most Selective

Massachusetts Services

Wellesley College
Wellesley, Massachusetts 02182
(617) 235-0320

School Enrollment: **2,200** Female: **2,200**
LD Enrollment: **20**

Admissions Contact: **Janet Lavin, Director of Admissions**
LD Contact: **Barbara Boger, Coor., Learning & Teaching Cen.**
Telephone:**(617) 283-2641**

Admissions

Application Information:
Application deadline: **February 1st**

Secondary School Information
Most Important Criteria For Admissions (1-strongest)

2 SAT/ACT	**5** Application	**1** School transcript
4 Class rank	**1** Course selection	Personal statement
6 Interview	**5** Extra activities	Psychoeducational
1 G.P.A.	Open admission	**3** Recommendations

Test Requirements:
Untimed SAT: **Yes** Untimed ACH: **Yes**
Documentation of LD required: **Yes**
Tests recommended: **Woodcock-Johnson**

Types of Disabilities Served
- Speech/Lang
- Study skills
- Written express
- Organizational
- Perceptual
- Reading
- Spelling
- Math
- Fine Motor
- ADD with LD
- ADD without LD
- ADHD with LD
- ADHD without LD

Learning Disability Program

Program: Reinforces course work: **Yes**
Program available through:**4th year**
Students mainstreamed **100** % of the day
Services available for all students: **Yes**
Group Counseling: **Yes**
Support groups are available:**Yes**

Faculty:
Faculty: **1** Full time: **1**

Diagnostic Testing

ADD	Personality	Perceptual skills	Spelling
ADHD	Organization	Fine motor skills	Reading
I.Q.	Handwriting	Spoken language	Study skills
Math	Social skills	Written language	

Tutoring:
Average size of group tutorials: **varies**
Services rendered by:
Graduates •Peers   Faculty   LD staff   Teacher trainees

Massachusetts

Tutorials

Grp.	Ind.	Tutorials	Grp.	Ind.	Tutorials
•	•	Math skills	•	•	Word processing
•	•	Study skills	•	•	Time management
		Language arts	•	•	Learning strategies
•	•	Written express	•	•	Organizational skills

Academic Accommodations

Curriculum	Study Aids	Exams
Priority registration	Typist	Oral
Math waiver	Reader	Untimed
Foreign lang. waiver	• Notetaker	Take home
Course substitution	• Proof reader	With proctor
In Class	Text on tape	On computer
Calculators	Early syllabus	• Extended time
• Tape recorder	Taped handouts	On tape
Word processor		Modified
• Priority seating		• Separate room

Program Strengths

Wellesley College is committed to assisting all enrolled students on an individual basis. Students with learning disabilities are expected to perform academically at the same level as all other enrolled students. However, assistance is available for any student who feels she needs help.

General Information:

Wellesley College is a 4 year independent college. Suburban campus of 500 acres is 12 miles from Boston. Accessible by train. 5.7% of students are foreign. Housing is guaranteed.

Accreditation: NEACS

SAT/ACT Scores:

Scores for incoming freshmen: **Verbal:** 8% below 500. 35% between 500 and 599. 48% between 600 and 699. 9% above 700. **Math:** 8% below 500. 26% between 500 and 599. 47% between 600 and 699. 19% above 700.

Class Rank:

About 92% of the present freshmen class were in the upper 20% of their high school class. 99% were in the top 40% of their class. 100% were in the top 60% of their class.

Expenses:

Tuition: In-state: Full year: $14,840.00. Room and board: $5,310.00

Majors

• AREA STUDIES American, Black/Afro-American, Jewish, Women's Studies • BUSINESS Economics • COMMUNICATIONS English • COMPUTER SCIENCE Computer Science • HUMANITIES Classics, English/Writing/Literature, Humanities, Philosophy, Religion • LANGUAGES Chinese, French, German, Greek, Italian, Japanese, Latin, Russian, Spanish • SCIENCES Astronomy, Biochemistry, Biology, Chemistry, Geology, Mathematics, Physics • SOCIAL SCIENCES Anthropology, Government/Political, History, Psychology, Sociology • VISUAL AND PERFORMING ARTS Art History, Music, Studio Art

Sports/Activities

• SPORTS-INTERCOLLEGIATE Basketball (F), Crew (F), Cross Country (F), Diving (F), Fencing (M), Field Hockey (F), Lacrosse (F), Soccer (F), Squash (F), Swimming (F), Tennis (F), Volleyball (F) • SPORTS-INTRAMURAL Badminton (F), Baseball (F), Crew (F), Cross Country (F), Golf (F), Ping-Pong (F), Racquetball (F), Sailing (F), Soccer (F), Squash (F), Swimming (F), Tennis (F), Volleyball (F) • STUDENT LIFE ACTIVITIES Choral, Magazine, Newspaper, Radio/TV station, Student Government, Yearbook

---

Very Selective　　　　　**Massachusetts Services**

Wheaton College
Norton, Massachusetts 02766
(617) 285-7722

School Enrollment: **1,302** Male: **392** Female: **910**
LD Enrollment: **63** Male: **30** Female: **33**

Admissions Contact: **Gail Berson Executive, Dir. of Admissions**
LD Contact: **Susan Dearing, Assistant Dean for College Skills**
Name of Program: **Advising Center**
Address: **Advising Center**
Telephone: **(508) 285-7722 Ext.**

Admissions

Application Information:
LD on admissions committee: **Yes**
Application deadline: **Feb.1**
Notified when: **April 1st**

Secondary School Information
Most Important Criteria For Admissions (1-strongest)

6 SAT/ACT	**1** Application	**3** School transcript
5 Class rank	**2** Course selection	**7** Personal statement
10 Interview	**9** Extra activities	**11** Psychoeducational
4 G.P.A.	Open admission	**8** Recommendations

Test Requirements:
Untimed SAT: **Yes** Untimed ACT: **Yes** Untimed ACH: **Yes**
Documentation of LD required: **Yes**

Types of Disabilities Served
• Speech/Lang	• Reading	• ADD with LD
• Study skills	• Spelling	• ADD without LD
• Written express	• Math	• ADHD with LD
• Organizational	Fine Motor	• ADHD without LD
• Perceptual		

High School Course Requirements:
English: **4** Math: **3-4** Science: **2-3** Foreign Language: **3-4**

Learning Disability Program
Special orientation for LD students: **Yes**
Program: Reinforces course work: **Yes**
Students mainstreamed **100** % of the day
Recommended credits per semester: **3-4 courses**
Services available for all students: **Yes**
Counseling: Individual: **Yes** Vocational Counseling: **Yes**
Support groups are available: **Yes, student run, meets to discuss issues; concerns to participants**

Faculty:
Faculty: **1** Part time: **1** M.A.: **1**
Faculty advocate: **Yes**

Diagnostic Testing
ADD	Personality	Perceptual skills	Spelling
ADHD	Organization	Fine motor skills	Reading
I.Q.	Handwriting	Spoken language	Study skills
Math	Social skills	Written language	

Tutoring:
Services rendered by:
Graduates •Peers •Faculty •LD staff Teacher trainees

Tutorials

Grp.	Ind.	Tutorials	Grp.	Ind.	Tutorials
•	•	Math skills	•	•	Word processing
	•	Study skills		•	Time management
		Language arts		•	Learning strategies
	•	Written express		•	Organizational skills

Academic Accommodations

Curriculum	Study Aids	Exams
Priority registration	Typist	Oral
Math waiver	Reader	Untimed
Foreign lang. waiver	• Notetaker	Take home
Course substitution	Proof reader	• With proctor
In Class	Text on tape	On computer
• Calculators	Early syllabus	• Extended time
• Tape recorder	Taped handouts	On tape
• Word processor		Modified
Priority seating		• Separate room

Graduation Requirements:
Course credits: **32** GPA: **1.67** Years to complete degree: **4**

Program Strengths

Services for learning disabled students are coordinated by the Assistant Dean for College Skills who is a part time member of the advising office staff. Students consult with the Assistant Dean in order to arrange tutoring, request accommodations, and/or develop appropriate strategies for academic success.

General Information:

Wheaton College is a 4 year independent college. Suburban campus of 376 acres is 15 miles from Providence. Accessible by air, train or bus. Ski areas are 30 miles from campus. Beaches are 1 mile from campus. 5% of students are foreign. 13 residential halls on campus. Housing is guaranteed.75 % of students remain on campus for the weekends.

Accreditation: NEACS

SAT/ACT Scores:
Scores for incoming freshmen: **Verbal:** 56% below 500. 37% between 500 and 599. 6% between 600 and 699. 1% above 700. **Math:** 38% below 500. 49% between 500 and 599. 12% between 600 and 699. 1% above 700. **ACT:** 14% below 20. 45% between 20 and 23. 17% between 24 and 25l. 24% between 26 and 28.

Class Rank:
About 42% of the present freshmen class were in the upper 20% of their high school class. 74% were in the top 40% of their class. 91% were in the top 60% of their class. 100% were in the top 80% of their class.

Expenses:
Tuition: In-state: Full year: $15,650.00. Part-time: Per course: Part-time: $1,955.00. Room and board: $5,470.00

Majors

• AREA STUDIES American, Asian, Italian, Russian • BUSINESS Economics • COMMUNICATIONS Creative Writing, English • COMPUTER SCIENCE Computer Science • HUMANITIES Classics, English/Writing/Literature, Liberal Arts, Philosophy, Religion • LANGUAGES English, French, German, Italian, Russian, Spanish • MATHEMATICS Computer • SCIENCES Anthropology, Astronomy, Biochemistry, Biology, Chemistry, Mathematics, Physics, Psychobiology • SOCIAL SCIENCES Anthropology, History, International Studies, Psychology, Social Psychology, Sociology • VISUAL AND PERFORMING ARTS Art History, Music, Studio Art, Theater

Sports/Activities

• SPORTS RELATED Chess • SPORTS-INTERCOLLEGIATE Baseball (F), Baseball (M), Cross Country (F), Cross Country (M), Field Hockey (F), Lacrosse (F), Lacrosse (M), Soccer (F), Soccer (M), Softball (F), Swimming (F), Swimming (M), Synchronized Swimming, Tennis (F), Tennis (M), Track and Field (F), Track and Field (M), Volleyball (F)
• SPORTS-INTRAMURAL Badminton (F), Badminton (M), Basketball (F), Basketball (M), Cross Country (F), Cross Country (M), Cycling, Fencing (F), Fencing (M), Football, Flag, Golf (F), Golf (M), Horseback Riding (F), Horseback Riding (M), Ping-Pong (F), Ping-Pong (M), Sailing (F), Sailing (M), Soccer (F), Soccer (M), Softball (F), Softball (M), Swimming (F), Swimming (M), Tennis (F), Tennis (M), Track and Field (F), Track and Field (M), Volleyball (F), Volleyball (M), Water Polo (F), Water Polo (M)
• STUDENT LIFE ACTIVITIES Academic Clubs, Choir, Choral, Dance, Drama Groups, Ethnic & Cultural Groups, Film, Music Groups, Newspaper, Political Groups, Radio, Religious Organization, Student Government, Yearbook

---

Selective

Massachusetts Services

Wheelock College

200 The Riverway
Boston, Massachusetts 02215
(617) 734-5200

School Enrollment: **771** Male: **14** Female: **757**

Admissions Contact: **Joan F. Wexler, Dean of Ad. &Financial Aid**
LD Contact: **Susan Graham, Director of Academic Advising**
Name of Program: **Academic Advising & Assistance**
Address: **Wheelock College, Riverway Faculty Office, 45 Pilgrim Road, Boston, MA 02215**
Telephone: **(617) 734-5200**

Admissions

Application Information:
Application deadline: **February 15th**
Rolling Admissions: **Yes** Notified when: **within one month**

Secondary School Information
Most Important Criteria For Admissions (1-strongest)

7 SAT/ACT	Application	**1**	School transcript
8 Class rank	**1** Course selection		Personal statement
6 Interview	**3** Extra activities		Psychoeducational
2 G.P.A.	Open admission	**5**	Recommendations

Test Requirements:
Standardized tests waived: **Yes**
Untimed SAT: **Yes** Untimed ACT: **Yes**

Types of Disabilities Served

Speech/Lang	Reading	ADD with LD
Study skills	Spelling	ADD without LD
Written express	Math	ADHD with LD
Organizational	Fine Motor	ADHD without LD
Perceptual		

Admissions Process

Students are evaluated on their depth of experience working with children, their GPA and level of high school classes, their writing ability, two recommendations, an interview and SAT/ACT scores (unless the student has a documented LD).

High School Course Requirements:
English: **4** Math: **3** Science: **1**

Learning Disability Program

Program: Remedial: **Yes**
Program: Reinforces course work: **Yes**
Program available through:**hours vary**
Students mainstreamed **100** % of the day
Recommended credits per semester: **12-16**
Services available for all students: **Yes**
Counseling: Individual: **Yes** Group Counseling: **Yes**

Faculty:
Faculty: **2** Full time: **1** Part time: **1** M.A.: **1**
Meets with instructor: **As needed**

Diagnostic Testing
ADD	Personality	Perceptual skills	Spelling
ADHD	Organization	Fine motor skills	Reading
I.Q.	Handwriting	Spoken language	Study skills
Math	Social skills	Written language	

Tutoring:
Average size of group tutorials: **Mostly individual**
Services rendered by:
  Graduates •Peers Faculty •LD staff Teacher trainees

Tutorials
Grp.	Ind. Tutorials	Grp.	Ind. Tutorials
	• Math skills		Word processing
	Study skills	•	Time management
	• Language arts	•	Learning strategies
	• Written express		Organizational skills

Academic Accommodations

Curriculum	Study Aids	Exams
• Priority registration	Typist	Oral
Math waiver	Reader	• Untimed
Foreign lang. waiver	Notetaker	• Take home
Course substitution	Proof reader	• With proctor
In Class	• Text on tape	On computer
• Calculators	Early syllabus	• Extended time
• Tape recorder	Taped handouts	On tape
Word processor		Modified
• Priority seating		• Separate room

Graduation Requirements:
Course credits: **132-140** GPA: **2.0** Years to complete degree: **No limit**

General Information:
Wheelock College is a 4 year independent college. Urban campus of 5 acres is Accessible by air, bus or train. Ski areas are 2 hours from campus. Beaches are 30 minutes from campus. 2% of students are foreign. 5 residential halls on campus. Housing is not guaranteed.Guaranteed through 4th year.

Accreditation:NEACS, CSWE, NCATE

SAT/ACT Scores:
Scores for incoming freshmen:**Verbal:**71%below 500. 16%between 500 and 599. 3%between 600 and 699. **Math:**75% below 500. 22% between 500 and 599. 3% between 600 and 699.

Expenses:
Tuition: In-state: Full year: $11,776.00. Part-time: Per credit:$368.00. Part-time: Per course: $1,472.00. Tuition: Out-of-state: Full year: $11,776.00. Part-time: Per credit:$368.00. Part-time: Per course:$1,472.00 Room and board: $5,224.00

Majors
• EDUCATION Child Development, Early Childhood, Elementary, Special
• SOCIAL SCIENCES Social Work

Sports/Activities
• SPORTS-INTERCOLLEGIATE Field Hockey (F) • SPORTS-INTRA-MURAL Badminton, Basketball, Horseback Riding, Volleyball • STUDENT LIFE ACTIVITIES Academic Clubs, Choral, Community Service, Drama Groups, Ethnic & Cultural Groups, Religious Organization, Student Government, Yearbook

---

Highly Selective   **Massachusetts Services**

Worcester Polytechnic Institute
100 Institute Road
Worcester, Massachusetts 01609
(508) 831-5286

School Enrollment: **2,600**
LD Enrollment: **7**

Admissions Contact: **Kay K. Dietrich, Director of Admissions**
LD Contact: **Ann Garvin, Director of Academic Advising**
Telephone:**(508) 831-5381**

Admissions

Application Information:
Application deadline: **February 15th**

Secondary School Information
Most Important Criteria For Admissions (1-strongest)
SAT/ACT	Application	**1**	School transcript
Class rank	Course selection		Personal statement
Interview	Extra activities		Psychoeducational
G.P.A.	Open admission		Recommendations

Test Requirements:
Untimed SAT: **Yes** Untimed ACT: **Yes** Untimed ACH: **Yes**
Documentation of LD required: **Yes**

Types of Disabilities Served
Speech/Lang	• Reading	ADD with LD
Study skills	• Spelling	ADD without LD
• Written express	Math	ADHD with LD
Organizational	Fine Motor	ADHD without LD
Perceptual		

Faculty:
Faculty advocate: **Yes**

Diagnostic Testing
ADD	Personality	Perceptual skills	Spelling
ADHD	Organization	Fine motor skills	Reading
I.Q.	Handwriting	Spoken language	Study skills
Math	Social skills	Written language	

Tutoring:

Services rendered by:

Graduates   Peers   •Faculty   LD staff   Teacher trainees

Tutorials

Grp.	Ind.	Tutorials	Grp.	Ind.	Tutorials
	•	Math skills			Word processing
		Study skills			Time management
		Language arts			Learning strategies
		Written express			Organizational skills

Academic Accommodations

Curriculum	Study Aids	Exams
Priority registration	Typist	Oral
Math waiver	Reader	Untimed
Foreign lang. waiver	Notetaker	Take home
• Course substitution	Proof reader	• With proctor
In Class	Text on tape	On computer
Calculators	Early syllabus	• Extended time
Tape recorder	Taped handouts	On tape
Word processor		• Modified
Priority seating		Separate room

Program Strengths

WPI does not have a specific program for learning disabled students. Being a small school, we do not actually have many LD applicants. We have, however, adopted a policy to accommodate learning disabled students (with untimed tests, reduced course loads, etc.) specific to their disabilities. LD students may work out these special circumstances with the Director of Academic Advising, on a case by case basis.

*Tutoring is available for all students.

General Information:

Worcester Polytechnic Institute is a 4 year independent university. Urban campus of 62 acres is 2 miles from Worcester. Accessible by air, train, or bus. Ski areas are 30 miles from campus. Beaches are 60 miles from campus. 6% of students are foreign. 7 residential halls on campus. Housing is guaranteed.Guaranteed through 1st year. 40 % of students join fraternities/sororities.

Accreditation: Regional

SAT/ACT Scores:

Scores for incoming freshmen:**Verbal:**32%below 500. 46%between 500 and 599. 20%between 600 and 699. 2%above 700. **Math:**1% below 500. 17% between 500 and 599. 55% between 600 and 699. 27%above 700. 2% between 20 and 23. 10%between 24 and 25l. 22%between 26 and 28. 66% above 28.

Class Rank:

About 81% of the present freshmen class were in the upper 20% of their high school class. 96% were in the top 40% of their class. 100% were in the top 60% of their class.

Expenses:

Tuition: In-state: Full year: $14,125.00. Part-time: Per course: Part-time: $999.00. Room and board: $4,600.00

Majors

• AREA STUDIES Urban • BUSINESS Business Administration, Business Management, Economics, Management • COMPUTER SCIENCE Computer Science, Computer Technology, Programming, Systems Analysis • ENGINEERING Aerospace, Bioengineering, Chemical, Civil/Environmental, Computer, Electrical, Environmental/Water Resources, Industrial, Mechanical, Nuclear, Ocean • HUMANITIES Humanities • PREPROFESSIONAL Dentistry, Engineering, Law, Medicine, Pharmacy, Veterinarian • SCIENCES Actuarial Technology, Biochemistry, Biology, Biomedical,

Cell Biology, Chemistry, Ecology, Mathematics, Microbiology, Molecular Biology, Nuclear Physics, Oceanography, Organic Chemistry, Physical Chemistry, Physical Science, Physics, Statistics, Urban Design

Sports/Activities

• SPORTS RELATED Pep Band • SPORTS-INTERCOLLEGIATE Baseball (M), Basketball, Crew, Cross Country, Fencing, Field Hockey (F), Football (M), Golf, Ice Hockey (M), Lacrosse, Riflery, Rugby, Sailing, Skiing - Snow, Soccer, Softball (F), Tennis, Track and Field, Volleyball, Water Polo (M), Weight Lifting (M) • SPORTS-INTRAMURAL Basketball, Bowling, Cross Country, Golf, Ice Hockey (M), Ping-Pong, Soccer, Softball, Swimming, Track and Field, Volleyball, Wrestling (M) • STUDENT LIFE ACTIVITIES Choral, Concert Band, Dance, Drama Groups, Fraternities, Jazz Band, Magazine, Music Groups, Musical Theater, Newspaper, Religious Organization, Sororities, Student Government, Symphony Orchestra, Yearbook

---

Selective **Michigan Services**

Adrian College

110 South Madison Street
Adrian, Michigan 49221-2575
(517) 265-5161-(800) 877-2246

School Enrollment: **1,194** Male: **540** Female: **654**

Admissions Contact: **George Wolf, Director of Admissions**
LD Contact: **Mary Ann Stibbe, Director**
Name of Program: **Learning Development's Excel**

Admissions

Application Information:

Enrolled:**30**
Application deadline: **August 15th**
Rolling Admissions: **Yes**Notified when: **Rolling**

Secondary School Information

Most Important Criteria For Admissions (1-strongest)

4	SAT/ACT	Application	**3**	School transcript
5	Class rank	**2** Course selection	**2**	Personal statement
6	Interview	**8** Extra activities	**1**	Psychoeducational
1	G.P.A.	Open admission	**7**	Recommendations

Test Requirements:

Diagnostic testing waived: **Yes**
Untimed SAT: **Yes** Untimed ACT: **Yes** Untimed ACH: **Yes**
WAIS-R required: **Yes**
Documentation of LD required: **Yes**
Currency of diagnostic testing: **No more than 2 years**
Tests recommended: **Appropriate battery to diagnose disability and to prescribe academic accommodations**

Types of Disabilities Served

• Speech/Lang	• Reading	• ADD with LD
• Study skills	• Spelling	• ADD without LD
• Written express	• Math	• ADHD with LD
• Organizational	• Fine Motor	• ADHD without LD
• Perceptual		

High School Course Requirements:

English: **4** Math: **3** Science: **3**

Michigan

Learning Disability Program

Program: Remedial: **Yes**
Program: Reinforces course work: **Yes**
Students mainstreamed **100** % of the day
Recommended credits per semester: **12-13**
Counseling: Individual: **Yes**
Support groups are available:**Through the Counseling Center**

Faculty:

Faculty: **3** Full time: **2** Part time: **1** M.A.: **2** Ph.D.: **1**
Faculty advocate: **Yes** Meets with instructor: **As needed**

Diagnostic Testing

ADD	Personality	Perceptual skills	Spelling
ADHD	Organization	Fine motor skills	Reading
I.Q.	Handwriting	Spoken language	Study skills
Math	Social skills	Written language	

Tutoring:

Average size of group tutorials: **Individual only**
Services rendered by:

Graduates	•Peers	Faculty	LD staff	Teacher trainees

Tutorials

Grp.	Ind.	Tutorials	Grp.	Ind.	Tutorials
•	•	Math skills	•	•	Word processing
•	•	Study skills	•	•	Time management
•	•	Language arts	•	•	Learning strategies
•	•	Written express	•	•	Organizational skills

Academic Accommodations

Curriculum	Study Aids	Exams
Priority registration	• Typist	• Oral
Math waiver	• Reader	• Untimed
Foreign lang. waiver	• Notetaker	Take home
Course substitution	• Proof reader	• With proctor
In Class	• Text on tape	On computer
Calculators	Early syllabus	• Extended time
• Tape recorder	Taped handouts	• On tape
• Word processor		• Modified
Priority seating		• Separate room

Program Strengths

The learning disabilities program at Adrian College develops an individualized educational plan with each student based on admissions data, standardized tests, the psychological report, campus placement testing, and career interest and personality inventories. Following development of the plan, students meet with counselors regularly and/or as needed to assess academic progress and implementation of personal goals.

General Information:

Adrian College is a 4 year private United Methodist college. Suburban campus of 100 acres is 35 miles from Toledo, Ohio. Accessible by car. Ski areas are 70 miles from campus. Beaches are 25 miles from campus. 2% of students are foreign. 10 residential halls on campus. Housing is guaranteed.65 % of students remain on campus for the weekends. 30 % of students join fraternities/sororities.

Accreditation:NCACS

SAT/ACT Scores:

Scores for incoming freshmen:**Verbal:**77%below 500. 20%between 500 and 599. 3%between 600 and 699. **Math:**37% below 500. 45% between 500 and 599. 18% between 600 and 699. **ACT:** 17% below 20. 47% between 20 and 23. 14%between 24 and 25l. 19%between 26 and 28. 3% above 28.

Class Rank:

About 47% of the present freshmen class were in the upper 20% of their high school class. 80% were in the top 40% of their class. 91% were in the top 60% of their class. 100% were in the top 80% of their class.

Expenses:

Tuition: In-state: Full year: $9,340.00. Part-time: Per credit:$220.00.

Majors

• AREA STUDIES International Studies • ARTS Art History, Art Therapy, Design, Fashion Design, Interior Design, Music, Music History, Music Performance, Painting, Sculpture • BUSINESS Accounting, Business Administration, Business Economics, Business Education, Business Management, Economics, Education, Marketing, Sports Management • COMMUNICATIONS Advertising, Broadcasting, Communication, Creative Writing, English, Journalism, Literature, Public Relations, Speech/Debate/Forensic, Television/Radio/Film • COMPUTER SCIENCE Computer Mathematics, Computer Science, Programming • EDUCATION Art, Business, Elementary, English, English As A Second Language, Foreign Language, General, Home Economics, Mathematics, Music, Physical, Psychology, Religious, School Psychology, Science, Secondary, Social Studies, Speech/Language • HEALTH SCIENCES Environmental, Fitness, Health, Physical Therapy • HUMANITIES English/Writing/Literature, Fine Arts, Humanities, Liberal Arts , Philosophy, Religion • LANGUAGES English, French, German • MATHEMATICS Applied, Computer, Statistical • PREPROFESSIONAL Law, Medicine, Optometry, Pharmacy, Sports Medicine • RELIGIOUS STUDIES Ministry, Philosophy, Religion and Theology • SCIENCES Biology, Chemistry, Earth, Physical Science, Physics • SOCIAL SCIENCES Criminal Justice, Government/Political, History, Human Service, International Studies, Political Science, Psychology, Public Relations, Social Science, Sociology • VISUAL AND PERFORMING ARTS Art, Art History, Fine Arts, Music, Music Performance, Music Theatre, Theater, Video

Sports/Activities

• SPORTS RELATED Cheerleading, Marching Band, Pep Band, Team Managers • SPORTS-INTERCOLLEGIATE Baseball (M), Basketball (F), Basketball (M), Cross Country (F), Cross Country (M), Football (M), Golf (F), Golf (M), Soccer (F), Soccer (M), Softball (F), Swimming (F), Swimming (M), Tennis (F), Tennis (M), Track and Field (F), Track and Field (M), Volleyball (F) • SPORTS-INTRAMURAL Basketball, Bowling, Football, Hand Ball, Ice Hockey (M), Racquetball, Soccer, Softball, Swimming, Volleyball • STUDENT LIFE ACTIVITIES Academic Clubs, Choral, Community Service, Concert Band, Debate, Drama Groups, Ethnic & Cultural Groups, Fraternities, Jazz Band, Magazine, Music Groups, Musical Theater, Newspaper, Orchestra, Political Groups, Radio/TV station, Religious Organization, Sororities, Student Government, Symphony Orchestra, Yearbook

---

Very Selective

Michigan Services

Albion College
Albion, Michigan 49224
(517) 629-1000

School Enrollment: **1,700** Male: **860** Female: **840**

Admissions Contact: **Frank Bonta, Dean of Admissions**

Admissions

Application Information:

Application deadline: **Open**
Rolling Admissions: **Yes**

Secondary School Information

Most Important Criteria For Admissions (1-strongest)

2	SAT/ACT	Application	1 School transcript
3	Class rank	1 Course selection	Personal statement
	Interview	Extra activities	Psychoeducational
3	G.P.A.	Open admission	4 Recommendations

Test Requirements:
Untimed SAT: **Yes** Untimed ACT: **Yes**

Types of Disabilities Served
- Speech/Lang
- Study skills
- Written express
- Organizational
  Perceptual
- Reading
  Spelling
- Math
  Fine Motor

ADD with LD
ADD without LD
ADHD with LD
ADHD without LD

Learning Disability Program
Counseling: Individual: **Yes**

Faculty:
Faculty: **1**
Faculty advocate: **Yes** Meets with instructor: **As needed**

Diagnostic Testing

ADD	Personality	Perceptual skills	Spelling
ADHD	Organization	Fine motor skills	Reading
I.Q.	Handwriting	Spoken language	Study skills
Math	Social skills	Written language	

Tutoring:
Services rendered by:
Graduates •Peers •Faculty •LD staff Teacher trainees

Tutorials

Grp.	Ind.	Tutorials	Grp.	Ind.	Tutorials
•	•	Math skills		•	Word processing
	•	Study skills		•	Time management
	•	Language arts		•	Learning strategies
	•	Written express		•	Organizational skills

Academic Accommodations

Curriculum	Study Aids	Exams
Priority registration	Typist	• Oral
Math waiver	Reader	Untimed
• Foreign lang. waiver	• Notetaker	• Take home
Course substitution	Proof reader	With proctor
In Class	• Text on tape	On computer
Calculators	Early syllabus	• Extended time
• Tape recorder	Taped handouts	On tape
Word processor		Modified
Priority seating		Separate room

Program Strengths
Although Albion College is not equipped to render every possible service to the disabled, the college welcomes academically qualified students with varying disabilities and will work toward meeting their needs. These disabilities include those students with impaired vision, hearing, or mobility and those with learning disabilities, such as dyslexia, dyscalculia, and dysgraphia.

General Information:
Albion College is a 4 year private United Methodist college. Rural campus of 225 acres is 90 miles from Detroit. Ski areas are 1 hour from campus. Beaches are 2 hours from campus. 1% of students are foreign. 3 residential halls on campus. Housing is guaranteed.Guaranteed through 4th year. 80-85 % of students remain on campus for the weekends. 50 % of students join fraternities/sororities.

Accreditation:Regional

Expenses:
Tuition: In-state: Full year: $9,222.00. Part-time: Per credit:$364.00.
Room and board: $3,682.00

Majors
• AREA STUDIES American • BUSINESS Business Administration, Business Management, Economics, Management • COMMUNICATIONS Communication, English • EDUCATION Music • LANGUAGES Spanish • SCIENCES Biology, Chemistry, Geology, Mathematics, Physics • SOCIAL SCIENCES Anthropology, Government/Political, History, Psychology, Social Sciences, Sociology • VISUAL AND PERFORMING ARTS Fine Arts, Music

Sports/Activities
• SPORTS RELATED Marching Band, Pep Band • SPORTS-INTERCOLLEGIATE Baseball (M), Cross Country, Field Hockey (F), Football (M), Golf (M) • SPORTS-INTRAMURAL Basketball, Bowling, Diving (M), Golf (M), Gymnastics, Ping-Pong, Soccer, Softball, Swimming, Tennis, Track and Field • STUDENT LIFE ACTIVITIES Choral, Concert Band, Drama Groups, Fraternities, Jazz Band, Music Groups, Musical Theater, Newspaper, Radio/TV station, Sororities, Student Government, Symphony Orchestra, Yearbook

Very Selective	Michigan Services

Alma College
Alma, Michigan 48801-1599
(517) 463-7139-(800) 321-ALMA

School Enrollment: **1,186** Male: **528** Female: **658**

Admissions Contact: **John Seveland, VP Enrollment & Stud. Affairs**
LD Contact: **Dr. Robert Perkins, Director**
Name of Program: **Center for Student Development**
Telephone:**(517) 463-7225**

Admissions

Application Information:
LD on admissions committee:**Yes**
Application deadline: **Rolling**
Rolling Admissions: **Yes**Notified when: **May 1st**

Secondary School Information
Most Important Criteria For Admissions (1-strongest)

1 SAT/ACT	9 Application	5 School transcript
3 Class rank	8 Course selection	12 Personal statement
4 Interview	11 Extra activities	10 Psychoeducational
1 G.P.A.	Open admission	6 Recommendations

Test Requirements:
Untimed SAT: **Yes** Untimed ACT: **Yes** Untimed ACH: **Yes**
Range accepted:
Documentation of LD required: **Yes**
Tests recommended: **Testing verifying specific deficit.**

Michigan

Types of Disabilities Served

Speech/Lang	Reading	ADD with LD
• Study skills	Spelling	ADD without LD
• Written express	Math	ADHD with LD
• Organizational	Fine Motor	ADHD without LD
Perceptual		

High School Course Requirements:
English: **3** Math: **2** Science: **2** Foreign Language: **2**

Learning Disability Program

Program: Reinforces course work: **Yes**
Program available through:**As needed**
Students mainstreamed **100** % of the day
Recommended credits per semester: **13-15**
Services available for all students: **Yes**
Counseling: Individual: **Yes** Group Counseling: **Yes** Vocational Counseling: **Yes**
Support groups are available:**Yes (if requested in sufficient numbers)**

Faculty:
Faculty: **3** Including Director: **Yes** Full time: **3** Part time: **1** M.A.: **3** Ph.D.: **1**

Diagnostic Testing

ADD	• Personality	Perceptual skills	Spelling
ADHD	Organization	Fine motor skills	Reading
I.Q.	Handwriting	Spoken language	• Study skills
Math	• Social skills	Written language	

Tutoring:
Average size of group tutorials: **1:1**
Services rendered by:
•Graduates   Peers   Faculty   •LD staff   Teacher trainees

Tutorials

Grp.	Ind.	Tutorials	Grp.	Ind.	Tutorials
•	•	Math skills	•	•	Word processing
•	•	Study skills	•	•	Time management
		Language arts	•	•	Learning strategies
•	•	Written express	•	•	Organizational skills

Academic Accommodations

Curriculum	Study Aids	Exams
Priority registration	Typist	• Oral
Math waiver	Reader	Untimed
• Foreign lang. waiver	• Notetaker	• Take home
Course substitution	• Proof reader	• With proctor
In Class	• Text on tape	On computer
• Calculators	Early syllabus	• Extended time
• Tape recorder	Taped handouts	On tape
• Word processor		• Modified
Priority seating		Separate room

General Information:
Alma College is a 4 year private Presbyterian Church college. Rural campus of 85 acres is 40 miles from Saginaw. Accessible by air or train. Ski areas are 2 hours from campus. Beaches are 2 hours from campus. 1.3% of students are foreign. 8 residential halls on campus. Housing is guaranteed.Guaranteed through 4th year. 60 % of students remain on campus for the weekends. 40 % of students join fraternities/sororities.

Accreditation:NCACS, MDE, ACS, NASM

SAT/ACT Scores:
Scores for incoming freshmen:**Verbal:**43%below 500. 34%between 500 and 599. 21%between 600 and 699. 2%above 700. **Math:**25% below 500. 39% between 500 and 599. 23% between 600 and 699. 13%above 700. **ACT:** 10% below 20. 30% between 20 and 23. 18%between 24 and 251. 29%between 26 and 28. 13% above 28.

Class Rank:
About 63% of the present freshmen class were in the upper 20% of their high school class. 90% were in the top 40% of their class. 99% were in the top 60% of their class. 100% were in the top 80% of their class.

Expenses:
Tuition: In-state: Full year: $11,232.00. Room and board: $4,108.00

Majors
• ARTS Dance, Design, Dramatic Arts, Drawing, Graphic Arts, Music, Music Performance, Painting, Sculpture • BUSINESS Business Administration, Economics, International Business • COMMUNICATIONS Communication, English • COMPUTER SCIENCE Computer Science, Systems Analysis • CRAFTS AND DESIGN Graphic Design, Sculpture • EDUCATION Elementary, Middle School, Secondary • HEALTH SCIENCES Health Science, Occupational Therapy, Physical Therapy • HUMANITIES English/Writing/Literature, Liberal Arts, Philosophy, Religion • LANGUAGES French, German, Spanish • MATHEMATICS Applied, Computer • PREPROFESSIONAL Dentistry, Engineering, Law, Medicine, Ministry, Occupational Therapy, Physical Therapy, Veterinarian • RELIGIOUS STUDIES Philosophy, Religion and Theology • SCIENCES Biochemistry, Biology, Chemistry, Mathematics, Physics • SOCIAL SCIENCES History, Political Science, Psychology, Sociology • VISUAL AND PERFORMING ARTS Art, Dance, Music, Music Performance, Theater

Sports/Activities
• SPORTS RELATED Cheerleading, Marching Band, Pep Band • SPORTS-INTERCOLLEGIATE Baseball (M), Basketball, Cross Country, Football (M), Golf, Soccer, Softball (F), Swimming, Tennis, Track and Field, Volleyball (F) • SPORTS-INTRAMURAL Basketball (F), Basketball (M), Football, Flag, Racquetball, Softball, Volleyball, Water Polo • STUDENT LIFE ACTIVITIES Academic Clubs, Choral, Community Service, Concert Band, Dance, Drama Groups, Ethnic & Cultural Groups, Fraternities, Jazz Band, Magazine, Music Groups, Newspaper, Radio, Religious Organization, Sororities, Student Government, Symphony Orchestra, Yearbook

---

Selective   **Michigan**
                                                 Services

Aquinas College
1607 Robinson Road, Southeast
Grand Rapids, Michigan 49506
(616) 459-8281

School Enrollment: **1,947** Male: **697** Female: **1,250**

Admissions Contact: **John C. Baird, Director of Admissions**
LD Contact: **Jane McCloskey, Specialist**
Name of Program: **Academic Achievement Center**
Telephone:**(616) 459-8281**

Admissions

Application Information:
Application deadline: **Rolling**
Rolling Admissions: **Yes** Notified when: **2 weeks later**

Secondary School Information
Most Important Criteria For Admissions (1-strongest)

2 SAT/ACT	Application	School transcript
3 Class rank	**4** Course selection	Personal statement
6 Interview	**5** Extra activities	Psychoeducational
1 G.P.A.	Open admission	**7** Recommendations

Test Requirements:
WAIS-R required: **Yes**

Types of Disabilities Served
Speech/Lang	• Reading	• ADD with LD
• Study skills	• Spelling	ADD without LD
• Written express	• Math	• ADHD with LD
• Organizational	• Fine Motor	ADHD without LD
• Perceptual		

High School Course Requirements:
English: **4** Math: **3** Science: **3**

Learning Disability Program
Counseling: Individual: **Yes**
Support groups are available: **Yes, also mentorship program**

Faculty:
Faculty: **4** Part time: **4**
LD faculty with: BS/BA: **1** M.A.: **2** Ph.D.: **1**
Meets with instructor: **As needed**

Diagnostic Testing
ADD	Personality	Perceptual skills	Spelling
ADHD	Organization	Fine motor skills	• Reading
I.Q.	Handwriting	Spoken language	• Study skills
Math	Social skills	Written language	

Tutoring:
Services rendered by:
Graduates • Peers • Faculty • LD staff Teacher trainees

Tutorials
Grp.	Ind.	Tutorials	Grp.	Ind.	Tutorials
	•	Math skills			Word processing
	•	Study skills		•	Time management
	•	Language arts		•	Learning strategies
	•	Written express		•	Organizational skills

Academic Accommodations
Curriculum	Study Aids	Exams
Priority registration	Typist	• Oral
Math waiver	Reader	• Untimed
Foreign lang. waiver	Notetaker	Take home
Course substitution	• Proof reader	• With proctor
In Class	Text on tape	On computer
Calculators	Early syllabus	• Extended time
Tape recorder	Taped handouts	• On tape
Word processor		Modified
Priority seating		• Separate room

Program Strengths
Our efforts to assist learning disabled students are housed in the Academic Achievement Center, which has been in existence at Aquinas for nearly ten years. Its role has been to assist students on a one-to-one basis, whatever the need. For the last several years the center has been assuming a more active role in identifying and assisting students with learning disabilities.

General Information:
Aquinas College is a 4 year private Roman Catholic college. Suburban campus of 101 acres is 150 miles from Detroit. Accessible by air, train, or bus. Ski areas are 10 miles from campus. Beaches are 25 miles from campus. 8 residential halls on campus. Housing is not guaranteed.

Accreditation: NCACS

SAT/ACT Scores:
Scores for incoming freshmen: **ACT:** 38% below 20. 34% between 20 and 23. 18% between 24 and 25l. 5% between 26 and 28. 5% above 28.

Class Rank:
About 30 of the present freshmen class were in the upper 20% of their high school class. 51 were in the top 40% of their class. 66 were in the top 60% of their class. 72 were in the top 80% of their class.

Expenses:
Tuition: In-state: Full year: $8,960.00. Part-time: Per credit: Part-time: $177.00. Tuition: Out-of-state: Full year: $8,960.00. Room and board: $3,950.00

Majors
• AREA STUDIES Women's Studies • BUSINESS Accounting, Banking/Finance, Business Economics, Business Education, Business Management, Education, Human Resources Management, International Business, Management, Marketing, Personnel • COMMUNICATIONS Communication, English, Photography • COMPUTER SCIENCE Business Data Programming, Systems Analysis • EDUCATION Art, Bilingual, Business, Elementary, English, Foreign Language, General, Mathematics, Middle School, Music, Psychology, Reading, Recreation and Youth Leadershi, Religious, Science, Secondary, Social Studies • HEALTH SCIENCES Environmental, Health, Pharmacology • HUMANITIES English/Writing/Literature, Fine Arts, Humanities, Liberal Arts, Philosophy, Religion • LANGUAGES French, German, Spanish • PREPROFESSIONAL Dentistry, Engineering, Law, Medicine, Optometry, Pharmacy • RELIGIOUS STUDIES Philosophy, Religion and Theology • SCIENCES Biology, Chemistry, Geography, Mathematics • SOCIAL SCIENCES Geography, History, International Studies, Political Science, Psychology, Sociology • VISUAL AND PERFORMING ARTS Art, Art History, Fine Arts, Music, Music Performance, Studio Art

Sports/Activities
• SPORTS RELATED Cheerleading • SPORTS-INTERCOLLEGIATE Baseball (M), Basketball (F), Basketball (M), Cross Country (F), Cross Country (M), Golf (M), Soccer (F), Soccer (M), Softball (F), Tennis (F), Tennis (M), Track and Field (F), Track and Field (M), Volleyball (F), Volleyball (M) • SPORTS-INTRAMURAL Basketball • STUDENT LIFE ACTIVITIES Academic Clubs, Choral, Community Service, Concert Band, Drama Groups, Ethnic & Cultural Groups, Jazz Band, Music Groups, Newspaper, Political Groups, Religious Organization, Student Government

Very Selective

Central Michigan University
105 Warriner Hall
Mount Pleasant, Michigan 48859
(517) 774-3076

School Enrollment: **16,000**
LD Enrollment: **60**

Admissions Contact: **Betty Wagner, Associate Director**
LD Contact: **Carol L. Wojcik, Coordinator**
Name of Program: **Handicapped Student Services**
Address: **148 Foust Hall**
Telephone:**(517) 774-3465**

Admissions

Application Information:
Application deadline: **Early Spring**
Rolling Admissions: **Yes**

Secondary School Information
Most Important Criteria For Admissions (1-strongest)

	SAT/ACT		Application	4	School transcript
2	Class rank	1	Course selection		Personal statement
7	Interview	6	Extra activities		Psychoeducational
2	G.P.A.		Open admission	5	Recommendations

Test Requirements:
Documentation of LD required: **Yes**

Types of Disabilities Served
Speech/Lang	Reading	ADD with LD
Study skills	Spelling	ADD without LD
Written express	Math	ADHD with LD
Organizational	Fine Motor	ADHD without LD
Perceptual		

High School Course Requirements:
English: **4** Math: **3** Science: **4**

Faculty:
Faculty: **1** Part time: **1**
Faculty advocate: **Yes** Meets with instructor: **As needed**

Diagnostic Testing
- ADD
- ADHD
- I.Q.
- Math
- Personality
- Organization
- Handwriting
- Social skills
- Perceptual skills
- Fine motor skills
- Spoken language
- Written language
- Spelling
- Reading
- Study skills

Tutoring:
Services rendered by:
Graduates •Peers   Faculty   LD staff   Teacher trainees

Tutorials
Grp.	Ind.	Tutorials	Grp.	Ind.	Tutorials
	•	Math skills			Word processing
	•	Study skills			Time management
	•	Language arts		•	Learning strategies
	•	Written express		•	Organizational skills

Academic Accommodations
Curriculum	Study Aids	Exams
Priority registration	Typist	• Oral
Math waiver	Reader	Untimed
Foreign lang. waiver	• Notetaker	Take home
Course substitution	Proof reader	• With proctor
In Class	• Text on tape	On computer
• Calculators	Early syllabus	• Extended time
• Tape recorder	Taped handouts	On tape
Word processor		Modified
Priority seating		Separate room

Graduation Requirements:
Course credits: **120+** GPA: **2.0** Years to complete degree: **Indefinite** Language waiver: **Yes**

Program Strengths
There is not a specific program for learning disabled students at CMU. LD students are encouraged to self-identify and be their own advocates. There are classes offered in reading and study skills for the learning disabled students. Central's tutoring system is very effective, and LD students may use a tutor for up to two classes for any semester. There are no special admissions procedure for LD students at Central.

General Information:
Central Michigan University is a 4 year public university. Suburban campus of 900 acres is 66 miles from Lansing. Accessible by air, train or bus. Ski areas are 2 hours from campus. Beaches are 1/2 mile from campus. 2% of students are foreign. 19 residential halls on campus. Housing is not guaranteed.75 % of students remain on campus for the weekends. 10 % of students join fraternities/sororities.

Accreditation:NCACS

Expenses: Part-time: Per credit:$70.50. Part-time: Per credit:$181.00. Room and board: $3,582.00

Majors
• AREA STUDIES American • BUSINESS Accounting, Banking, Business Administration, Business Economics, Business Education, Business Management, Economics, Fashion Merchandising, Hotel and Restaurant Managemen, Management, Marketing, Marketing Research, Travel/Tourism Management • COMMUNICATIONS Advertising, Broadcasting, Communication, English, Journalism, Photography, Television/Radio/Film • COMPUTER SCIENCE Computer Science, Computer Technology, Data Processing, Programming • CRAFTS AND DESIGN Ceramics, Graphic Design, Sculpture • EDUCATION Art, Bilingual, Child Development, Early Childhood, Elementary, Health, Industrial, Mathematics, Music, Physical, Recreation and Youth Leadershi, School Psychology, Secondary, Special, Speech/Language • HEALTH SCIENCES Communication Disorders, Health, Medical Secretary, Medical Technology, Nutritional/Food, Speech Therapy, Speech/Audiology and Speech • HUMANITIES Liberal Arts, Philosophy, Religion • LANGUAGES French, German, Japanese, Linguistic, Spanish • PREPROFESSIONAL Dentistry, Engineering, Forestry, Law, Medicine, Pharmacy, Recreation • SCIENCES Biology, Chemistry, Earth, Geography, Geology, Mathematics, Microbiology, Physical Science, Physics, Statistics • SOCIAL SCIENCES Anthropology, Criminal Justice, Geography, Government/Political, History, Human Service, Psychology, Social Sciences, Sociology • VOCATIONAL Automobile Technology, Drafting, Food Service, Home Economics, Industrial Arts, Industrial Design, Legal Secretary, Printing/Lithography, Secretarial, Textile and Clothing

Sports/Activities
• SPORTS RELATED Marching Band, Pep Band • SPORTS-INTERCOLLEGIATE Baseball (M), Basketball, Cross Country, Field Hockey (F), Football (M), Gymnastics (F), Soccer (M), Softball (F), Track and Field,

Volleyball (F), Wrestling (M) • SPORTS-INTRAMURAL Archery, Badminton, Basketball, Bowling, Cross Country, Golf, Ping-Pong, Racquetball, Skiing - Snow, Soccer, Softball, Swimming, Tennis, Track and Field, Volleyball, Water Polo, Wrestling (M) • STUDENT LIFE ACTIVITIES Choral, Concert Band, Dance, Debate, Drama Groups, Ethnic & Cultural Groups, Fraternities, Jazz Band, Music Groups, Newspaper, Radio/TV station, Religious Organization, Sororities, Student Government, Symphony Orchestra, Yearbook

Less Selective	Michigan Services

Charles Stewart Mott Community College

1401 East Court Street
Flint, Michigan 48502
(313) 762-0940

School Enrollment: **10,858** Male: **4,293** Female: **6,565**
LD Enrollment: **80-90**
LD Contact: **Delores Williams**
Name of Program: **Handicapped Student Services**
Telephone:**(313) 762-0399**

Admissions

Application Information:
Application deadline: **August 27th**
Rolling Admissions: **Yes**

Secondary School Information
Most Important Criteria For Admissions (1-strongest)

SAT/ACT	Application	School transcript
Class rank	Course selection	Personal statement
Interview	Extra activities	Psychoeducational
G.P.A.	Open admission	Recommendations

Test Requirements:
Documentation of LD required: **Yes**
Currency of diagnostic testing: **2 years**

Types of Disabilities Served
- Speech/Lang
- Study skills
- Written express
- Organizational
- Perceptual
- Reading
- Spelling
- Math
- Fine Motor
- ADD with LD
- ADD without LD
- ADHD with LD
- ADHD without LD

Faculty:
Faculty advocate: **Yes** Meets with instructor: **As needed**

Diagnostic Testing

ADD	Personality	Perceptual skills	Spelling
ADHD	Organization	Fine motor skills	Reading
I.Q.	Handwriting	Spoken language	Study skills
Math	Social skills	Written language	

Tutoring:
Services rendered by:

Graduates	•Peers	Faculty	LD staff	Teacher trainees

Tutorials

Grp.	Ind.	Tutorials	Grp.	Ind.	Tutorials
	•	Math skills			Word processing
		Study skills			Time management
	•	Language arts			Learning strategies
	•	Written express			Organizational skills

Academic Accommodations

Curriculum	Study Aids	Exams
Priority registration	Typist	• Oral
Math waiver	• Reader	Untimed
Foreign lang. waiver	• Notetaker	Take home
• Course substitution	Proof reader	• With proctor
In Class	• Text on tape	On computer
Calculators	Early syllabus	• Extended time
• Tape recorder	Taped handouts	• On tape
Word processor		• Modified
Priority seating		• Separate room

Graduation Requirements:
Course credits: **30-62** GPA: **2.0**

Program Strengths

Handicapped Student Services does not have a learning disability program. We do offer services to students to accommodate some of the disability related difficulties typically encountered. These services are provided at no charge to the students.

General Information:

Charles Stewart Mott Community College is a 2 year public college. Urban campus of 20 acres is 65 miles from Detroit. Accessible by train or bus. 1% of students are foreign. Housing is not guaranteed.

Accreditation:

Expenses: Part-time: Per credit:$42.00. Part-time: Per credit:$79.00.

Majors

• BUSINESS Accounting, Banking, Business Administration, Business Education, Business Management, Finance, Management, Marketing • COMPUTER SCIENCE Computer Science, Computer Technology, Data Processing, Hardware Engineer, Programming • EDUCATION Child Development, Special • ENGINEERING Aerospace, Air Conditioning Technology, Engineering Science • HEALTH SCIENCES Nursing, Practical Nursing • HUMANITIES Liberal Arts • PREPROFESSIONAL Agriculture, Architecture, Legal Assistant, Recreation, Social Work • SCIENCES Biochemistry, Biology, Chemistry, Gerontology, Physical Science • SOCIAL SCIENCES Criminal Justice, Social Sciences • VISUAL AND PERFORMING ARTS Fine Arts, Music • VOCATIONAL Automobile Technology, Dental Assistant, Dental Hygiene, Drafting, Fire Science, Industrial Design, Paralegal, Respiratory Therapy Technology, Secretarial

Sports/Activities

• SPORTS-INTERCOLLEGIATE Baseball (M), Basketball, Golf (M), Softball (F), Volleyball (F) • SPORTS-INTRAMURAL Basketball, Golf (M), Ping-Pong, Racquetball, Softball, Swimming, Tennis, Volleyball • STUDENT LIFE ACTIVITIES Choral, Drama Groups, Jazz Band, Music Groups, Newspaper, Radio/TV station, Student Government

Less Selective

Delta College
University Center, Michigan 48710
(517) 696-9094

School Enrollment: **11,000** Male: **6,600** Female: **4,400**
LD Enrollment: **12** Male: **7** Female: **5**

Admissions Contact: **Margaret Mosqueda, Director of Admissions**
LD Contact: **Caroline Wirtz, Director**
Name of Program: **Dyslexia Program**
Telephone:**(517) 686-9556**

Admissions

Application Information:
Enrolled:**30**
Application deadline: **Open**
Applicant must apply **1** months in advance
Rolling Admissions: **Yes**

Secondary School Information
Most Important Criteria For Admissions (1-strongest)

SAT/ACT	Application	School transcript
Class rank	Course selection	Personal statement
Interview	Extra activities	Psychoeducational
G.P.A.	Open admission	Recommendations

Test Requirements:
Diagnostic testing waived: **Yes**
Untimed SAT: **Yes** Untimed ACT: **Yes** Untimed ACH: **Yes**
Documentation of LD required: **Yes**
Currency of diagnostic testing: **3 months**
Tests recommended: **Woodcock-Johnson**

Types of Disabilities Served
- Speech/Lang
- Study skills
- Written express
- Organizational
- Perceptual
- Reading
- Spelling
- Math
- Fine Motor
- ADD with LD
- ADD without LD
- ADHD with LD
- ADHD without LD

Admissions Process

Delta is an all inclusive college.

Learning Disability Program

Syllabus available during orientation:**Yes**
Program: Remedial: **Yes**
Program: Reinforces course work: **Yes**
Time required or recommended in learning center: **5 hours**
Services only for LD students: **Yes**
Counseling: Individual: **Yes** Group Counseling: **Yes**

Faculty:
Faculty: **2** Including Director: **Yes** Part time: **2**
LD faculty with: BS/BA: **1** M.A.: **1**

Diagnostic Testing

ADD	Personality	Perceptual skills	• Spelling
ADHD	Organization	Fine motor skills	• Reading
• I.Q.	Handwriting	Spoken language	Study skills
• Math	Social skills	Written language	

Tutoring:
Average size of group tutorials: **4-5**
Services rendered by:
Graduates •Peers •Faculty •LD staff Teacher trainees

Tutorials

Grp.	Ind.	Tutorials	Grp.	Ind.	Tutorials
	•	Math skills	•		Word processing
•		Study skills	•		Time management
	•	Language arts	•		Learning strategies
		Written express	•		Organizational skills

Academic Accommodations

Curriculum	Study Aids	Exams
Priority registration	Typist	• Oral
Math waiver	Reader	Untimed
Foreign lang. waiver	• Notetaker	Take home
Course substitution	• Proof reader	• With proctor
In Class	• Text on tape	On computer
• Calculators	Early syllabus	• Extended time
• Tape recorder	Taped handouts	On tape
• Word processor		Modified
Priority seating		Separate room

General Information:

Delta College is a 2 year public college. Rural campus of 640 acres is 5 miles from Bay City. Accessible by bus. Ski areas are 15 miles from campus. Beaches are 10 hours from campus. 9.7% of students are foreign. 2 residential halls on campus. Housing is not guaranteed.1 % of students remain on campus for the weekends.

Accreditation:NCACS

Expenses: Part-time: Per credit:$59.00. Part-time: Per credit:$88.00. Room and board: $2,886.00

Majors

• BUSINESS Accounting, Banking, Business Administration, Business Education, Business Management, Finance, Management, Marketing, Real Estate • COMMUNICATIONS Broadcasting, English, Television/Radio/Film • COMPUTER SCIENCE Computer Science, Hardware Engineer, Programming • EDUCATION Art, Elementary, Secondary, Teacher Aide • ENGINEERING Engineering Science • HEALTH SCIENCES Medical Assistant, Medical Secretary, Nursing, Physical Therapy, Radiological Therapy • HUMANITIES Liberal Arts • LANGUAGES Spanish • PRE-PROFESSIONAL Agriculture, Architecture, Engineering • SCIENCES Biology, Chemistry • SOCIAL SCIENCES Criminal Justice, Law Enforcement • VOCATIONAL Automobile Technology, Fashion Merchandising, Fashion Merchandising, Legal Secretary, Respiratory Therapy Technology, Secretarial, Word Processing

Sports/Activities

• SPORTS RELATED Cheerleading • SPORTS-INTERCOLLEGIATE Basketball, Golf, Racquetball, Soccer, Tennis (M) • SPORTS-INTRAMURAL Badminton, Basketball, Golf, Racquetball, Sailing, Softball (F), Swimming, Tennis, Volleyball, Water Polo • STUDENT LIFE ACTIVITIES Drama Groups, Newspaper, Radio/TV station, Student Government

Less Selective

Detroit College of Business

27500 Dequindre
Warren, Michigan 48092
(313) 558-8700

School Enrollment: **827** Male: **209** Female: **618**

Admissions Contact: **Amy Thelen, Director of Admissions**
LD Contact: **Mary Cross, Associate Dean**

Admissions

Application Information:
Application deadline: **None**
Rolling Admissions: **Yes**

Secondary School Information
Most Important Criteria For Admissions (1-strongest)

SAT/ACT **2**	Application **1**	School transcript
Class rank	Course selection	Personal statement
Interview	Extra activities	Psychoeducational
G.P.A.	Open admission	Recommendations

Test Requirements:
Standardized tests waived: **Yes**

Types of Disabilities Served
- Speech/Lang
- Study skills
- Written express
- Organizational
- Perceptual
- Reading
- Spelling
- Math
- Fine Motor
- ADD with LD
- ADD without LD
- ADHD with LD
- ADHD without LD

Learning Disability Program

Counseling: Individual: **Yes**

Faculty:
Faculty: **4** Full time: **1** Part time: **3**
Faculty advocate: **Yes** Meets with instructor: **As needed**

Diagnostic Testing

ADD	Personality	Perceptual skills	Spelling
ADHD	Organization	Fine motor skills	Reading
I.Q.	Handwriting	Spoken language	Study skills
Math	Social skills	Written language	

Tutoring:
Services rendered by:
Graduates •Peers •Faculty LD staff Teacher trainees

Tutorials

Grp.	Ind.	Tutorials	Grp.	Ind.	Tutorials
•	•	Math skills	•		Word processing
•		Study skills	•		Time management
•		Language arts	•		Learning strategies
•		Written express	•		Organizational skills

Academic Accommodations

Curriculum	Study Aids	Exams
Priority registration	Typist	• Oral
Math waiver	Reader	Untimed
Foreign lang. waiver	Notetaker	• Take home
• Course substitution	Proof reader	With proctor
In Class	Text on tape	On computer
• Calculators	Early syllabus	• Extended time
• Tape recorder	Taped handouts	On tape
• Word processor		• Modified
Priority seating		Separate room

General Information:
Detroit College of Business is a 2 and 4 year private college. Suburban campus of 3.5 acres is 3 miles from Detroit. Accessible by bus. Housing is not guaranteed.

Accreditation:NCACS

Expenses:
Tuition: In-state: Full year: $5,232.00. Part-time: Per credit:$109.00. Part-time: Per course: $436.00. Tuition: Out-of-state: Full year: $5,232.00. Part-time: Per credit:$109.00. Part-time: Per course:$436.00

Majors

• BUSINESS Accounting, Banking, Business Administration, Business Management, Finance, Management, Marketing, Travel/Tourism Management • COMPUTER SCIENCE Data Processing, Programming, Systems Analysis • HEALTH SCIENCES Medical Assistant, Medical Secretary • HUMANITIES Liberal Arts • VOCATIONAL Business and Office, Legal Secretary, Office Administration, Secretarial

Sports/Activities

• SPORTS-INTERCOLLEGIATE Golf (M) • SPORTS-INTRAMURAL Bowling, Soccer (M), Softball • STUDENT LIFE ACTIVITIES Drama Groups, Fraternities, Newspaper, Sororities, Student Government

Less Selective

Glen Oaks Community College

62249 Shimmel Road
Centreville, Michigan 49032
(616) 467-9945

School Enrollment: **1,200** Male: **240** Female: **960**
LD Enrollment: **10**

Admissions Contact: **Jill Peck, Director of Admissions**
LD Contact: **Luella Briggs, Coordinator**
Name of Program: **Special Needs Program**

Admissions

Application Information:
Application deadline: **Open**
Applicant must apply **Open** months in advance
Rolling Admissions: **Yes**

Michigan

Secondary School Information
Most Important Criteria For Admissions (1-strongest)

SAT/ACT	Application	School transcript
Class rank	Course selection	Personal statement
Interview	Extra activities	Psychoeducational
G.P.A.	**1** Open admission	Recommendations

Types of Disabilities Served
- Speech/Lang
- Study skills
- Written express
- Organizational
- Perceptual
- Reading
- Spelling
- Math
- Fine Motor

ADD with LD
ADD without LD
ADHD with LD
ADHD without LD

Learning Disability Program
Program: Remedial: **Yes**
Program: Reinforces course work: **Yes**
Students mainstreamed **100** % of the day

Faculty:
Faculty: **1** Part time: **1** M.A.: **1**
Faculty advocate: **Yes** Meets with instructor: **Regularly**

Diagnostic Testing

ADD	Personality	Perceptual skills	Spelling
ADHD	Organization	Fine motor skills	Reading
I.Q.	Handwriting	Spoken language	Study skills
Math	Social skills	Written language	

Tutoring:
Services rendered by:
Graduates   Peers   •Faculty   •LD staff   •Teacher trainees

Tutorials

Grp.	Ind.	Tutorials	Grp.	Ind.	Tutorials
•	•	Math skills	•	•	Word processing
•	•	Study skills	•	•	Time management
•	•	Language arts	•	•	Learning strategies
•	•	Written express	•	•	Organizational skills

Academic Accommodations

Curriculum	Study Aids	Exams
Priority registration	• Typist	• Oral
Math waiver	Reader	Untimed
Foreign lang. waiver	• Notetaker	Take home
Course substitution	• Proof reader	With proctor
In Class	• Text on tape	On computer
• Calculators	Early syllabus	• Extended time
• Tape recorder	Taped handouts	On tape
• Word processor		• Modified
Priority seating		Separate room

Program Strengths
Each student is unique with a unique program designed to the student's special need. The student is served in a one on one tutoring atmosphere with success gained and built upon each small improvement. We believe success builds success.

General Information:
Glen Oaks Community College is a 2 year public college. Rural campus of 300 acres is 35 miles from Kalamazoo. Ski areas are 20 miles from campus. .08% of students are foreign. Housing is not guaranteed.

Accreditation:NCACS

Expenses:
Tuition: In-state: Full year: $1,080.00. Part-time: Per credit:$36.00. Tuition: Out-of-state: Full year: $1,380.00. Part-time: Per credit:.$46.00.

Majors
• BUSINESS Accounting, Management, Marketing • COMMUNICATIONS Communication • COMPUTER SCIENCE Data Processing • EDUCATION Vocational • HEALTH SCIENCES Nursing, Practical Nursing • HUMANITIES Humanities • SOCIAL SCIENCES Criminal Justice, Social Sciences • VOCATIONAL Automobile Technology, Drafting, Machinist, Welding

Sports/Activities
• SPORTS-INTERCOLLEGIATE Badminton, Baseball, Basketball, Bowling, Golf, Weight Lifting • STUDENT LIFE ACTIVITIES Concert Band, Music Groups, Newspaper, Student Government, Symphony Orchestra

---

Selective

Michigan
Services

Grand Valley State University
1 Campus Drive
Allendale, Michigan 49401
(616) 895-6611-(800) 748-0246

School Enrollment: **12,565** Male: **5,228** Female: **7,337**
LD Enrollment: **35**

Admissions Contact: **Jo Ann Foerster, Director of Admissions**
LD Contact: **Kelley Conrad, Director**
Name of Program: **Special Services Program**
Address: **132 Commons**
Telephone:**(616) 895-3401**

Admissions

Application Information:
Application deadline: **60 Days/Prior Registration**
Applicant must apply **12** months in advance
Rolling Admissions: **Yes**Notified when: **3 weeks**

Secondary School Information
Most Important Criteria For Admissions (1-strongest)

1 SAT/ACT	**1** Application	**1** School transcript
Class rank	**1** Course selection	Personal statement
Interview	Extra activities	Psychoeducational
1 G.P.A.	Open admission	Recommendations

Test Requirements:
Diagnostic testing waived: **Yes**
Untimed ACT: **Yes**
Documentation of LD required: **Yes**
Currency of diagnostic testing: **1-2 Years**
Tests recommended: **Woodcock-Johnson, Wechsler**

Types of Disabilities Served
- Speech/Lang
- Study skills
- Written express
- Organizational
- Perceptual
- Reading
- Spelling
- Math
- Fine Motor
- ADD with LD
- ADD without LD
- ADHD with LD
- ADHD without LD

High School Course Requirements:
English: **4** Math: **3** Science: **3**
Waivers to standard high school courses
Foreign Language : **Yes** Math: **Yes** Course substitution: **Yes**

Learning Disability Program
Program: Reinforces course work: **Yes**
Students mainstreamed **100** % of the day
Services only for LD students: **Yes**
Services available for all students: **Yes**
Counseling: Individual: **Yes**

Faculty:
Faculty: **4** Including Director: **Yes** Full time: **2** Part time: **2** M.A.: **3**
Faculty advocate: **Yes** Meets with instructor: **As necessary**

Diagnostic Testing
ADD	• Personality	Perceptual skills	• Spelling
ADHD	Organization	Fine motor skills	• Reading
• I.Q.	Handwriting	Spoken language	• Study skills
• Math	Social skills	• Written language	

Tutoring:
Average size of group tutorials: **4**
Services rendered by:
Graduates •Peers Faculty •LD staff Teacher trainees

Tutorials
Grp.	Ind.	Tutorials	Grp.	Ind.	Tutorials
	•	Math skills		•	Word processing
	•	Study skills		•	Time management
•	•	Language arts		•	Learning strategies
•	•	Written express		•	Organizational skills

Academic Accommodations
Curriculum	Study Aids	Exams
Priority registration	• Typist	• Oral
Math waiver	Reader	Untimed
Foreign lang. waiver	• Notetaker	• Take home
Course substitution	• Proof reader	With proctor
In Class	• Text on tape	On computer
• Calculators	Early syllabus	• Extended time
• Tape recorder	Taped handouts	On tape
• Word processor		• Modified
Priority seating		Separate room

Graduation Requirements:
Course credits: **120** GPA: **2.0** Years to complete degree: **Unlimited**
Other requirements: **English requirement**

Program Strengths
Our program for learning disabled students is part of a larger program for a group of students who are at risk of leaving college without a degree. We provide advocacy, support, and accommodations.

General Information:
Grand Valley State University is a 4 year public university. Rural campus of 900 acres is 15 miles from Grand Rapids. Accessible by bus. Beaches are 15 miles from campus. .05% of students are foreign. 9 residential halls on campus. Housing is not guaranteed.15 % of students remain on campus for the weekends. 4 % of students join fraternities/sororities.

Accreditation: NCACS

Class Rank:
About 17% of the present freshmen class were in the upper 20% of their high school class. 45% were in the top 40% of their class. 83% were in the top 60% of their class.

Expenses:
Tuition: In-state: Full year: $2,186.00. Part-time: Per credit:$96.00. Tuition: Out-of-state: Full year: $4,840.00. Part-time: Per credit:$220.00.
Room and board: $3,590.00

Majors
• BUSINESS Accounting, Business Administration, Business Economics, Business Management, Economics, Finance, Hotel and Restaurant Managemen, Management, Marketing, Travel/Tourism Management • COMMUNICATIONS Advertising, Broadcasting, Communication, Creative Writing, English, Journalism, Photography, Television/Radio/Film • COMPUTER SCIENCE Computer Science, Hardware Engineer, Programming • EDUCATION Art, Elementary, Middle School, Music, Physical, Recreation and Youth Leadershi, Secondary, Special, Speech/Language • HEALTH SCIENCES Medical Technology, Nursing, Occupational Therapy, Physical Therapy • HUMANITIES Philosophy • LANGUAGES French, German, Russian, Spanish • PREPROFESSIONAL Dentistry, Engineering, Law, Medicine, Natural Resources, Recreation, Social Work • SCIENCES Biochemistry, Biology, Chemistry, Earth, Geology, Mathematics, Physics • SOCIAL SCIENCES Anthropology, Criminal Justice, History, Psychology, Social Sciences, Sociology • VISUAL AND PERFORMING ARTS Art, Music, Studio Art, Theater

Sports/Activities
• SPORTS RELATED Cheerleading, Drum Major/Majorette, Marching Band, Pep Band, Team Managers • SPORTS-INTERCOLLEGIATE Baseball (M), Basketball, Cross Country, Football (M), Softball, Swimming, Tennis, Track and Field, Volleyball (F), Wrestling (M) • SPORTS-INTRAMURAL Baseball (M), Basketball, Bowling, Crew, Golf, Ice Hockey (M), Ping-Pong, Racquetball, Soccer, Softball, Tennis, Wrestling (M) • STUDENT LIFE ACTIVITIES Drama Groups, Ethnic & Cultural Groups, Fraternities, Jazz Band, Music Groups, Newspaper, Radio/TV station, Religious Organization, Sororities, Student Government, Symphony Orchestra, Yearbook

---

Less Selective

**Michigan
Services**

Henry Ford Community College
5101 Evergreen Road
Dearborn, Michigan 48128
(313) 845-9613

School Enrollment: **16,000** Male: **8,192** Female: **7,808**
LD Enrollment: **25**

Admissions Contact: **Dorothy Murphy, Admissions Coordinator**
LD Contact: **Ted Hunt, Director**
Name of Program: **Special Needs**
Telephone:**(313) 845-9617**

Admissions

Application Information:
Applicant must apply **1** months in advance
Rolling Admissions: **Yes**

Secondary School Information
Most Important Criteria For Admissions (1-strongest)
7 SAT/ACT	**1** Application	**5**	School transcript
9 Class rank	**4** Course selection	**6**	Personal statement
3 Interview	**10** Extra activities	**1**	Psychoeducational
8 G.P.A.	Open admission	**2**	Recommendations

Michigan

Test Requirements:
Standardized tests waived: **Yes**
Untimed ACT: **Yes**
Documentation of LD required: **Yes**

Types of Disabilities Served
- Speech/Lang
- Study skills
- Written express
- Organizational
- Perceptual
- Reading
- Spelling
- Math
- Fine Motor
- ADD with LD
- ADD without LD
- ADHD with LD
- ADHD without LD

High School Course Requirements:
English: **2**
Waivers to standard high school courses
  Course substitution: **Yes**

Learning Disability Program

Special orientation for LD students: **Yes**
Students mainstreamed **100** % of the day
Recommended credits per semester: **6-9**
Time required or recommended in learning center: **No requirement**
Services available for all students: **Yes**
Counseling: Individual: **Yes** Group Counseling: **Yes** Vocational Counseling: **Yes**
Support groups are available:**Yes**

Faculty:
Faculty: **6** Including Director: **1** Full time: **5** Part time: **1**
Faculty advocate: **Yes** Meets with instructor: **As needed**

Diagnostic Testing
ADD	• Personality	Perceptual skills	• Spelling
ADHD	• Organization	Fine motor skills	• Reading
I.Q.	Handwriting	Spoken language	• Study skills
Math	• Social skills	• Written language	

Tutoring:
Average size of group tutorials: **4**
Services rendered by:
•Graduates •Peers •Faculty •LD staff Teacher trainees

Tutorials
Grp.	Ind.	Tutorials	Grp.	Ind.	Tutorials
•	•	Math skills	•	•	Word processing
•	•	Study skills	•	•	Time management
•	•	Language arts	•	•	Learning strategies
•	•	Written express	•	•	Organizational skills

Academic Accommodations
Curriculum	Study Aids	Exams
• Priority registration	• Typist	• Oral
Math waiver	• Reader	• Untimed
Foreign lang. waiver	• Notetaker	• Take home
• Course substitution	• Proof reader	• With proctor
In Class	• Text on tape	• On computer
• Calculators	• Early syllabus	• Extended time
• Tape recorder	Taped handouts	• On tape
• Word processor		• Modified
• Priority seating		• Separate room

Graduation Requirements:GPA: **2.0** Years to complete degree:
2 years Math waiver: **Yes** Language waiver: **Yes**

General Information:
Henry Ford Community College is a 2 year public college. Suburban campus of 20 acres is 12 miles from Detroit. Accessible by bus. Ski areas are 30 miles from campus. Beaches are 15 miles from campus. .20% of students are foreign. Housing is not guaranteed.

Accreditation: Regional

Expenses: Part-time: Per credit:$58.00. Part-time: Per credit:$58.00.

Majors
• BUSINESS Accounting, Business Administration, Business Management, Economics, Hotel and Restaurant Managemen, Management, Marketing, Personnel, Retailing • COMMUNICATIONS Broadcasting, Communication, English, Journalism, Speech, Television/Radio/Film • COMPUTER SCIENCE Computer Science, Data Processing, Programming, Telecommunications • CRAFTS AND DESIGN Graphic Design • EDUCATION Elementary • ENGINEERING Air Conditioning Technology • HEALTH SCIENCES Health, Medical Technology, Nursing, Occupational Therapy • HUMANITIES Liberal Arts • LANGUAGES French, Spanish • PREPROFESSIONAL Architecture, Engineering, Law, Legal Assistant, Pharmacy • SCIENCES Biology, Chemistry, Geography, Mathematics, Physics, Physiology • SOCIAL SCIENCES Criminal Justice, Geography, Government/Political, History, Psychology, Social Sciences, Sociology • VISUAL AND PERFORMING ARTS Art, Art History, Dance, Dramatic Arts, Music, Theater • VOCATIONAL Automobile Technology, Electronics Technology, Fire Science, Food Service, Industrial Design, Interior Design, Legal Secretary, Paralegal, Respiratory Therapy Technology, Secretarial, Word Processing

Sports/Activities
• SPORTS RELATED Cheerleading • SPORTS-INTERCOLLEGIATE Baseball (M), Basketball, Golf (M), Softball (F), Tennis, Volleyball (F) • SPORTS-INTRAMURAL Basketball, Bowling, Ping-Pong, Sailing • STUDENT LIFE ACTIVITIES Choral, Concert Band, Debate, Ethnic & Cultural Groups, Fraternities, Jazz Band, Music Groups, Newspaper, Radio/TV station, Religious Organization, Sororities, Student Government

---

Less Selective   **Michigan**
                                         Services

Jackson Community College
2111 Emmons Road
Jackson, Michigan 49201
(517) 787-0800

School Enrollment: **7,000**

Admissions Contact: **Gordon Glair, Director of Admissions**
LD Contact: **Chris Kane, Department Chair**
Name of Program: **Developmental Educational Office**
Telephone:**(517) 787-0800**

Admissions

Application Information:
Application deadline: **Open**
Rolling Admissions: **Yes**

Secondary School Information
Most Important Criteria For Admissions (1-strongest)
SAT/ACT	Application	School transcript
Class rank	Course selection	Personal statement
Interview	Extra activities	Psychoeducational
G.P.A.	**1** Open admission	Recommendations

Test Requirements:
Untimed SAT: **Yes** Untimed ACT: **Yes** Untimed ACH: **Yes**

Types of Disabilities Served
- Speech/Lang
- Reading
- ADD with LD
- Study skills
- Spelling
- ADD without LD
- Written express
- Math
- ADHD with LD
- Organizational
- Fine Motor
- ADHD without LD
- Perceptual

Learning Disability Program

Program: Reinforces course work: **Yes**
Students mainstreamed **100** % of the day
Services available for all students: **Yes**
Counseling: Individual: **Yes**

Faculty:
Faculty advocate: **Yes** Meets with instructor: **As needed**

Diagnostic Testing
ADD	Personality	Perceptual skills	Spelling
ADHD	Organization	Fine motor skills	Reading
I.Q.	Handwriting	Spoken language	Study skills
Math	Social skills	Written language	

Tutoring:
Average size of group tutorials: *
Services rendered by:
Graduates •Peers •Faculty LD staff Teacher trainees

Tutorials
Grp.	Ind.	Tutorials	Grp.	Ind.	Tutorials
	•	Math skills		•	Word processing
•	•	Study skills			Time management
		Language arts		•	Learning strategies
	•	Written express		•	Organizational skills

Academic Accommodations

Curriculum	Study Aids	Exams
Priority registration	• Typist	• Oral
Math waiver	• Reader	Untimed
Foreign lang. waiver	• Notetaker	Take home
Course substitution	• Proof reader	• With proctor
In Class	• Text on tape	• On computer
• Calculators	Early syllabus	• Extended time
• Tape recorder	Taped handouts	On tape
• Word processor		Modified
• Priority seating		Separate room

Graduation Requirements:
Course credits: **63** GPA: **2.0** Language waiver: **Yes**

Program Strengths

The college tries to meet the needs of all students by being flexible and making a commitment to help all students to be a success in college.
*Tutoring for all students in all areas.

General Information:

Jackson Community College is a 2 year public college. Rural campus of 500 acres is 5 miles from Jackson. Accessible by bus. Housing is not guaranteed.

Accreditation:NCACS

Expenses:
Tuition: In-state: Full year: Approximately $1,300.00, $1,600.00 (out-of-district). Part-time: Per credit:$51.00 (in state), $41.00 (in county). Tuition: Out-of-state: Full year: Approximately $1,800.00. Part-time: Per credit:$59.00.

Majors

• BUSINESS Accounting, Banking, Business Management, Finance, Management, Marketing, Real Estate • COMPUTER SCIENCE Data Processing • ENGINEERING Engineering Science, Industrial • HEALTH SCIENCES Medical Assistant, Medical Secretary, Nursing, Practical Nursing • HUMANITIES Liberal Arts • PREPROFESSIONAL Agriculture, Architecture, Business, Dentistry, Drafting, Engineering, Fisheries, Forestry, Law, Medicine, Ministry, Optometry, Pharmacy, Recreation, Social Work, Veterinarian • SCIENCES Radiology • SOCIAL SCIENCES Law Enforcement • VISUAL AND PERFORMING ARTS Music, Theater • VOCATIONAL Air Conditioning/Heating/Refri, Automobile Technology, Aviation Technology, Business and Office, Drafting, Fire Science, Legal Secretary, Radiological Technology, Secretarial, Welding, Word Processing

Sports/Activities

• SPORTS-INTRAMURAL Baseball, Basketball, Golf (M), Ping-Pong, Racquetball, Soccer, Tennis, Wrestling (M) • STUDENT LIFE ACTIVITIES Choral, Concert Band, Debate, Drama Groups, Jazz Band, Magazine, Music Groups, Musical Theater, Newspaper, Student Government

---

Very Selective   **Michigan Accommodations**

Kalamazoo College
1200 Academy Street
Kalamazoo, Michigan 49006-3295
(616) 383-8492

School Enrollment: **1,271** Male: **572** Female: **699**

Admissions Contact: **Teresa M. Lahti, Dean of Admissions**
LD Contact: **Marilyn J. La Plante, Dean of Students**

Admissions

Application Information:
Rolling Admissions: **Yes**

Secondary School Information
Most Important Criteria For Admissions (1-strongest)

4 SAT/ACT	Application		School transcript
3 Class rank	**1** Course selection		Personal statement
Interview	**5** Extra activities		Psychoeducational
2 G.P.A.	Open admission	**6**	Recommendations

Test Requirements:
Documentation of LD required: **Yes**

Types of Disabilities Served
Speech/Lang	Reading	ADD with LD
Study skills	Spelling	ADD without LD
Written express	Math	ADHD with LD
Organizational	Fine Motor	ADHD without LD
Perceptual		

High School Course Requirements:
English: **4** Math: **2** Science: **2** Foreign Language: **2**

Learning Disability Program

Services available for all students: **Yes**

Michigan

Diagnostic Testing

ADD	Personality	Perceptual skills	Spelling
ADHD	Organization	Fine motor skills	Reading
I.Q.	Handwriting	Spoken language	Study skills
Math	Social skills	Written language	

Tutoring:

Services rendered by:

Graduates   Peers   •Faculty   LD staff   Teacher trainees

Tutorials

Grp.	Ind.	Tutorials	Grp.	Ind.	Tutorials
		Math skills			Word processing
		Study skills			Time management
		Language arts			Learning strategies
		Written express			Organizational skills

Academic Accommodations

Curriculum	Study Aids	Exams
Priority registration	Typist	Oral
Math waiver	Reader	Untimed
Foreign lang. waiver	Notetaker	Take home
• Course substitution	Proof reader	With proctor
In Class	• Text on tape	On computer
• Calculators	Early syllabus	• Extended time
• Tape recorder	Taped handouts	On tape
Word processor		Modified
• Priority seating		• Separate room

General Information:

Kalamazoo College is a 4 year independent college. Suburban campus of 60 acres is 140 miles from Detroit or Chicago. Accessible by air, train or bus. Ski areas are 12 miles from campus. Beaches are 35 miles from campus. 4% of students are foreign. 6 residential halls on campus. Housing is guaranteed.Guaranteed through 4th year. 85 % of students remain on campus for the weekends.

Accreditation:NCACS

SAT/ACT Scores:

Scores for incoming freshmen: 47%between 500 and 599. 16%between 600 and 699. 4%above 700. 38% between 500 and 599. 35% between 600 and 699. 11%above 700. 42%between 24 and 25l. 54% above 28.

Class Rank:

About 78% of the present freshmen class were in the upper 20% of their high school class. 96% were in the top 40% of their class.

Expenses:

Tuition: In-state: Full year: $12,669.00. Part-time: Per credit:0. Tuition: Out-of-state: Full year: $12,669.00. Room and board: $4,053.00.

Majors

• AGRICULTURE • AREA STUDIES African, American, Asian, Black/Afro-American, European, International Studies, Latin American, Women's Studies • BUSINESS Economics • COMMUNICATIONS English • COMPUTER SCIENCE Computer Science • HEALTH SCIENCES Pre-Med • HUMANITIES Classics, English/Writing/Literature, Fine Arts, Philosophy • LANGUAGES Chinese, French, German, Greek, Japanese, Latin, Russian, Spanish • MATHEMATICS Theoretical • PRE PROFESSIONAL Architecture, Dentistry, Law, Medicine • SCIENCES Biochemistry, Biology, Chemistry, Physics • SOCIAL SCIENCES Anthropology, History, International Studies, Political Science, Psychology, Sociology • VISUAL AND PERFORMING ARTS Art, Art History, Music, Theater

Sports/Activities

• SPORTS RELATED Cheerleading • SPORTS-INTERCOLLEGIATE Baseball (M), Basketball (F), Basketball (M), Cross Country (F), Cross Country (M), Football (M), Golf (F), Golf (M), Soccer (F), Soccer (M), Softball (F), Swimming (F), Swimming (M), Tennis (F), Tennis (M), Volleyball (F) • SPORTS-INTRAMURAL Baseball (M), Basketball, Cycling, Football, Racquetball, Softball, Tennis, Volleyball • STUDENT LIFE ACTIVITIES Academic Clubs, Choral, Community Service, Concert Band, Dance, Drama Groups, Ethnic & Cultural Groups, Jazz Band, Music Groups, Newspaper, Orchestra, Political Groups, Radio/TV station, Religious Organization, Student Government, Yearbook

Less Selective	Michigan Services

Kellogg Community College

450 North Avenue
Battle Creek, Michigan 49016-3397
(616) 965-3931

School Enrollment: **8,137** Male: **3,255** Female: **4,882**
LD Enrollment: **35**

Admissions Contact: **Connie Speers, Director of Admissions**
LD Contact: **Joyce Bishop, Counselor**
Name of Program: **Support Services**
Address: **Kellogg Community College**
Telephone:**(616) 965-4150**

Admissions

Application Information:

Application deadline: **30 days prior to semester**
Rolling Admissions: **Yes**

Secondary School Information

Most Important Criteria For Admissions (1-strongest)

SAT/ACT	Application	School transcript
Class rank	Course selection	Personal statement
Interview	Extra activities	1 Psychoeducational
G.P.A.	1 Open admission	Recommendations

Test Requirements:

Diagnostic testing waived: **Yes**
Documentation of LD required: **Yes**
Tests recommended: **Asset Test and External Diagnosis for Accommodations**

Types of Disabilities Served

• Speech/Lang	• Reading	• ADD with LD
• Study skills	• Spelling	• ADD without LD
• Written express	• Math	• ADHD with LD
• Organizational	• Fine Motor	• ADHD without LD
• Perceptual		

Admissions Process

KCC will admit any of the following individuals who have the ability to benefit from the education and training: high school graduate, 18 years or older, completion of G.E.D. test. An application must be completed.

High School Course Requirements:
English: **4** Math: **3** Science: **3** Foreign Language: **2**
Waivers to standard high school courses
Math: **Yes**

Learning Disability Program
Special orientation for LD students: **Yes**
Program: Remedial: **Yes**
Program: Reinforces course work: **Yes**
Students mainstreamed **100** % of the day
Time required or recommended in learning center: **varies**
Counseling: Individual: **Yes** Group Counseling: **Yes**

Faculty:
Faculty: **12** Including Director: **Yes** Full time: **4** Part time: **8**
LD faculty with: BS/BA: **8** M.A.: **4**
Faculty advocate: **Yes** Meets with instructor: **As needed**

Diagnostic Testing
ADD	Personality	Perceptual skills	• Spelling
ADHD	Organization	Fine motor skills	• Reading
I.Q.	Handwriting	Spoken language	• Study skills
• Math	Social skills	• Written language	

Tutoring:
Services rendered by:
•Graduates •Peers •Faculty •LD staff Teacher trainees

Tutorials
Grp.	Ind.	Tutorials	Grp.	Ind.	Tutorials
•	•	Math skills	•	•	Word processing
•	•	Study skills	•	•	Time management
•	•	Language arts	•	•	Learning strategies
•	•	Written express	•	•	Organizational skills

Academic Accommodations
Curriculum	Study Aids	Exams
Priority registration	• Typist	• Oral
Math waiver	• Reader	Untimed
Foreign lang. waiver	• Notetaker	• Take home
• Course substitution	• Proof reader	• With proctor
In Class	• Text on tape	On computer
• Calculators	Early syllabus	• Extended time
• Tape recorder	Taped handouts	• On tape
• Word processor		• Modified
Priority seating		Separate room

Graduation Requirements:
Course credits: **62** GPA: **2.0** Years to complete degree: **Unlimited** Math waiver: **Yes**
Other requirements: **Political Science**

Program Strengths
Support Services is an integrated department within Student Services. Program participants are: Handicapped/Disabled, Academically Disadvantaged, Economically Disadvantaged, and First Generation College Students.

General Information:
Kellogg Community College is a 2 year public college. Urban campus of 15 acres is 30 miles from Kalamazoo. Accessible by air, train, or bus. Ski areas are 2 hours from campus. Beaches are 1 hour from campus. 5% of students are foreign. Housing is not guaranteed.

Accreditation:NCACS

Expenses: Part-time: Per credit:$32.00 plus activity fees. Part-time: Per credit:$53.85 plus activity fees.

Majors
• BUSINESS Accounting, Business Administration, Business Management, Economics, Management • COMMUNICATIONS Broadcasting, Communication, Journalism, Photography, Television/Radio/Film • COMPUTER SCIENCE Computer Science, Data Processing, Hardware Engineer, Systems Analysis • EDUCATION Art, Early Childhood, Elementary, Music, Physical, School Psychology, Secondary, Social Studies, Special, Speech/Language • ENGINEERING Chemical • ENVIRONMENTAL CONTROL Water and Wastewater Technolog • HEALTH SCIENCES Environmental, Health, Medical Technology, Nursing, Physical Therapy, Practical Nursing, Radiological Therapy • HUMANITIES Humanities, Philosophy • LANGUAGES French, German, Japanese, Spanish • PRE-PROFESSIONAL Dentistry, Engineering, Law, Medicine, Pharmacy, Social Work, Veterinarian • SCIENCES Biochemistry, Biology, Botany, Chemistry, Earth, Ecology, Geography, Histology, Mathematics, Microbiology, Physical Science, Physics, Radiology, Zoology • SOCIAL SCIENCES Anthropology, Criminal Justice, Geography, Government/Political, History, Law Enforcement, Psychology, Social Sciences, Sociology • VISUAL AND PERFORMING ARTS Art, Art History, Fine Arts, Music, Studio Art, Theater • VOCATIONAL Automobile Technology, Automotive Service, Business and Office, Dental Hygiene, Drafting, Fire Science, Food Service, Hazardous Materials Technology, Legal Secretary, Medical Laboratory Technology, Paralegal, Word Processing

Sports/Activities
• SPORTS-INTERCOLLEGIATE Baseball (M), Basketball, Softball (F), Swimming, Volleyball • SPORTS-INTRAMURAL Basketball, Hand Ball, Racquetball, Softball, Volleyball • STUDENT LIFE ACTIVITIES Drama Groups, Ethnic & Cultural Groups, Jazz Band, Music Groups, Newspaper, Religious Organization, Student Government

Less Selective **Michigan Services**

Lake Michigan College
2755 East Napier
Benton Harbor, Michigan 49022-1899
(616) 927-3571

School Enrollment: **3,304** Male: **1,413** Female: **1,927**
LD Enrollment: **6**
LD Contact: **Sherry Hoadley Pries, Counselor**
Name of Program: **Special Needs**

Admissions

Application Information:
Application deadline: **None**
Rolling Admissions: **Yes**

Secondary School Information
Most Important Criteria For Admissions (1-strongest)
10 SAT/ACT	**1** Application	**2**	School transcript
9 Class rank	Course selection	**11**	Personal statement
7 Interview	Extra activities		Psychoeducational
G.P.A.	Open admission	**8**	Recommendations

Types of Disabilities Served

- Speech/Lang
- Study skills
- Written express
- Organizational
- Perceptual
- Reading
- Spelling
- Math
- Fine Motor
- ADD with LD
- ADD without LD
- ADHD with LD
- ADHD without LD

Learning Disability Program

Counseling: Individual: **Yes** Group Counseling: **Yes**

Faculty:

Faculty: **2** Full time: **2**
Faculty advocate: **Yes** Meets with instructor: **As needed**

Diagnostic Testing

ADD	Personality	Perceptual skills	Spelling
ADHD	Organization	Fine motor skills	Reading
I.Q.	Handwriting	Spoken language	Study skills
Math	Social skills	Written language	

Tutoring:

Services rendered by:
Graduates •Peers •Faculty LD staff •Teacher trainees

Tutorials

Grp.	Ind.	Tutorials	Grp.	Ind.	Tutorials
•	•	Math skills	•	•	Word processing
	•	Study skills	•	•	Time management
•	•	Language arts	•	•	Learning strategies
•		Written express	•	•	Organizational skills

Academic Accommodations

Curriculum	Study Aids	Exams
Priority registration	• Typist	• Oral
Math waiver	Reader	Untimed
Foreign lang. waiver	• Notetaker	• Take home
Course substitution	• Proof reader	With proctor
In Class	• Text on tape	On computer
Calculators	Early syllabus	• Extended time
• Tape recorder	Taped handouts	On tape
• Word processor		• Modified
Priority seating		Separate room

Program Strengths

We do not have a program targeted at LD students. We offer notetaking, readers, taped text books, group and individual tutoring, tape recorders, and much more. We have remedial labs which allow students to develop special skills. Students have an advocate to help them chose instructors and courses.

General Information:

Lake Michigan College is a 2 year public college. Rural campus 40 miles from Kalamazoo. Accessible by bus. Ski areas are 5-40 miles from campus. Beaches are 5 miles from campus. 5% of students are foreign. Housing is not guaranteed.

Accreditation:NCACS, NCCA

Expenses:

Tuition: In-state: Full year: $528.00. Part-time: Per credit:$44.00. Tuition: Out-of-state: Full year: $648.00. Part-time: Per credit:$54.00.

Majors

• BUSINESS Accounting, Banking, Business Administration, Business Economics, Business Education, Business Management, Finance, Food Management, Hotel and Restaurant Managemen, Management, Marketing, Retailing • COMMUNICATIONS English • COMPUTER SCIENCE Computer Science, Data Processing, Programming, Systems Analysis • EDUCATION Art, Elementary, Foreign Language, Industrial, Physical, Secondary, Speech/Language • ENGINEERING Electromechanical, Engineering Science, Industrial, Mechanical Design • ENVIRONMENTAL CONTROL Water and Wastewater Technolog • HEALTH SCIENCES Dental Assistant, Dental Hygiene, Dietary Manager Assistant, Medical Assistant, Medical Secretary, Medical Technology, Nursing, Nutritional/Food, Occupational Therapy, Practical Nursing, Radiological Therapy • HUMANITIES Humanities, Liberal Arts, Philosophy • LANGUAGES French, German, Spanish • PREPROFESSIONAL Dentistry, Engineering, Law, Medicine, Pharmacy, Veterinarian • SCIENCES Biology, Chemistry, Geography, Geology, Mathematics, Mortuary Science, Physical Science, Physics • SOCIAL SCIENCES Geography, Government/Political, History, Law Enforcement, Political Science, Psychology, Social Sciences, Sociology • VISUAL AND PERFORMING ARTS Fine Arts, Music, Theater • VOCATIONAL Drafting, Electronics Technology, Food Service, Legal Secretary, Medical Laboratory Technology, Office Administration, Radiological Technology, Respiratory Therapy Technology, Secretarial, Word Processing

Sports/Activities

• SPORTS RELATED Cheerleading, Pep Band • SPORTS-INTERCOLLEGIATE Baseball (M), Basketball, Softball (F), Volleyball (F) • SPORTS-INTRAMURAL Badminton, Baseball (M), Basketball, Bowling, Ping-Pong, Softball, Tennis, Volleyball • STUDENT LIFE ACTIVITIES Choral, Concert Band, Drama Groups, Ethnic & Cultural Groups, Fraternities, Jazz Band, Music Groups, Newspaper, Sororities, Student Government

---

Selective   **Michigan**
                                                 Services

Lake Superior State University

Sault St. Marie, Michigan 49783
(906) 635-2231

School Enrollment: **3,400** Male: **1,900** Female: **1,500**

Admissions Contact: **Bruce Johnson, Dean of Admissions**
LD Contact: **Dave Castner, Director**
Name of Program: **Counseling and Testing**
Telephone:**(906) 635-2453**

Admissions

Application Information:

Application deadline: **None**
Rolling Admissions: **Yes**

Secondary School Information

Most Important Criteria For Admissions (1-strongest)

2	SAT/ACT	**10**	Application	**1**	School transcript
3	Class rank	**4**	Course selection		Personal statement
	Interview	**8**	Extra activities	**9**	Psychoeducational
1	G.P.A.		Open admission	**6**	Recommendations

Types of Disabilities Served

- Speech/Lang
- Study skills
- Written express
- Organizational
- Perceptual
- Reading
- Spelling
- Math
- Fine Motor
- ADD with LD
- ADD without LD
- ADHD with LD
- ADHD without LD

Learning Disability Program

Counseling: Individual: **Yes** Group Counseling: **Yes**

Faculty:
Faculty: **4** Full time: **3** Part time: **1**
Faculty advocate: **Yes** Meets with instructor: **As needed**

Diagnostic Testing
ADD	Personality	Perceptual skills	Spelling
ADHD	Organization	Fine motor skills	Reading
I.Q.	Handwriting	Spoken language	Study skills
Math	Social skills	Written language	

Tutoring:
Services rendered by:

Graduates • Peers Faculty LD staff Teacher trainees

Tutorials
Grp.	Ind.	Tutorials	Grp.	Ind.	Tutorials
	•	Math skills			Word processing
•		Study skills	•		Time management
		Language arts	•		Learning strategies
	•	Written express	•		Organizational skills

Academic Accommodations

Curriculum	Study Aids	Exams
Priority registration	Typist	• Oral
Math waiver	Reader	Untimed
Foreign lang. waiver	• Notetaker	Take home
Course substitution	Proof reader	With proctor
In Class	Text on tape	On computer
Calculators	Early syllabus	• Extended time
• Tape recorder	Taped handouts	On tape
Word processor		Modified
Priority seating		Separate room

Program Strengths
We do not have any experts trained in the LD field but realize that the services we offer all students are the accommodations for our LD students. Our University is small and we can offer a personal touch.

General Information:
Lake Superior State University is a 4 year public university. Suburban campus of 121 acres is 3 miles from Lansing. Accessible by air or bus. Ski areas are 1 mile from campus. Beaches are 3 miles from campus. 20% of students are foreign. 7 residential halls on campus. Housing is not guaranteed.60 % of students remain on campus for the weekends. 5 % of students join fraternities/sororities.

Accreditation:ABET, NLN

Expenses:
Tuition: In-state: Full year: $1,851.00. Part-time: Per credit:$50.50. Tuition: Out-of-state: Full year: $3,507.00. Part-time: Per credit:$96.50. Room and board: $2,986.00

Majors
• BUSINESS Accounting, Banking, Business Administration, Business Economics, Business Management, Economics, Management, Marketing, Sports Management • COMMUNICATIONS English, Journalism, Literature, Speech • COMPUTER SCIENCE Computer Science, Data Processing, Robotics • EDUCATION Child Development • ENGINEERING Electrical, Mechanical • ENVIRONMENTAL CONTROL Energy Conservation, Water and Wastewater Technolog • HEALTH SCIENCES Environmental, Medical Secretary, Medical Technology, Nursing • LANGUAGES Latin • PREPROFESSIONAL Dentistry, Engineering, Forestry, Law, Legal Assistant, Medicine, Natural Resources, Pharmacy, Recreation, Social

Work, Veterinarian, Wildlife • SCIENCES Biology, Geology, Mathematics • SOCIAL SCIENCES Criminal Justice, Government/Political, History, Human Service, Law Enforcement, Political Science, Psychology, Social Sciences, Sociology • VOCATIONAL Business and Office, Drafting, Electronics Technology, Fire Science, Fishery Studies, Legal Secretary, Medical Laboratory Technology, Office Administration, Paralegal, Park/Recreation, Secretarial

Sports/Activities
• SPORTS RELATED Cheerleading, Pep Band • SPORTS-INTERCOLLEGIATE Basketball, Cross Country, Golf (M), Ice Hockey (M), Softball (F), Tennis, Volleyball (F), Wrestling (M) • SPORTS-INTRAMURAL Badminton, Basketball, Bowling, Ice Hockey (M), Racquetball, Riflery, Softball, Tennis, Track and Field, Volleyball, Water Polo, Wrestling (M) • STUDENT LIFE ACTIVITIES Choral, Concert Band, Debate, Drama Groups, Ethnic & Cultural Groups, Fraternities, Jazz Band, Music Groups, Musical Theater, Newspaper, Political Groups, Radio/TV station, Religious Organization, Sororities, Student Government, Symphony Orchestra, Yearbook

---

Less Selective	Michigan
	Services

Lansing Community College
430 North Capitol
Lansing, Michigan 48901
(517) 483-1252

School Enrollment: **21,716** Male: **9,716** Female: **11,962**
LD Enrollment: **46** Male: **30** Female: **16**
LD Contact: **Marcia Campbell, Counselor**
Name of Program: **Handicapped Student Services**
Telephone:**(517) 483-1207**

Admissions

Application Information:
Rolling Admissions: **Yes**

Secondary School Information
Most Important Criteria For Admissions (1-strongest)

SAT/ACT	**1** Application		School transcript
Class rank	Course selection		Personal statement
2 Interview	Extra activities		Psychoeducational
G.P.A.	Open admission	**2**	Recommendations

Test Requirements:
Standardized tests waived: **Yes**
Documentation of LD required: **Yes**

Types of Disabilities Served
• Speech/Lang	• Reading	• ADD with LD
• Study skills	• Spelling	• ADD without LD
• Written express	• Math	• ADHD with LD
• Organizational	• Fine Motor	• ADHD without LD
• Perceptual		

Learning Disability Program

Counseling: Individual: **Yes**

Faculty:
Faculty: **21** Full time: **1** Part time: **20**
Faculty advocate: **Yes** Meets with instructor: **As needed**

Michigan

Diagnostic Testing

ADD	Personality	Perceptual skills	Spelling
ADHD	Organization	Fine motor skills	Reading
I.Q.	Handwriting	Spoken language	Study skills
Math	Social skills	Written language	

Tutoring:

Average size of group tutorials: **4-8**
Services rendered by:

Graduates •Peers Faculty LD staff Teacher trainees

Tutorials

Grp.	Ind.	Tutorials	Grp.	Ind.	Tutorials
	•	Math skills		•	Word processing
•	•	Study skills	•	•	Time management
•	•	Language arts	•	•	Learning strategies
•	•	Written express	•	•	Organizational skills

Academic Accommodations

Curriculum	Study Aids	Exams
Priority registration	Typist	• Oral
Math waiver	Reader	Untimed
Foreign lang. waiver	• Notetaker	Take home
• Course substitution	Proof reader	With proctor
In Class	• Text on tape	On computer
Calculators	Early syllabus	• Extended time
• Tape recorder	Taped handouts	On tape
Word processor		Modified
Priority seating		Separate room

Program Strengths

Our program serves LD, TBI, EI, VI, PI, and HI students. We provide advising for class, supportive counseling, career counseling, registration for classes, and coordinate with the registrar's and financial aid offices and department instructors on campus.

General Information:

Lansing Community College is a 2 year public college. Urban campus of 28 acres is Accessible by bus. Ski areas are 60 miles from campus. Beaches are 100 miles from campus. 1% of students are foreign. Housing is not guaranteed.

Accreditation: NCACS

Expenses:

Tuition: In-state: Full year: Part-time: Per credti: $22.00. Tuition: Out-of-state: Full year: Part-time: Per credit: $43.00.

Majors

• AREA STUDIES Black/Afro-American • BUSINESS Accounting, Banking, Business Administration, Business Management, Economics, Finance, Food Management, Hotel and Restaurant Managemen, Insurance, International Business, Management, Marketing, Personnel, Real Estate • COMMUNICATIONS Advertising, Broadcasting, Commercial Design, Communication, Creative Writing, English, Graphic Design, Journalism, Photography, Television/Radio/Film • COMPUTER SCIENCE Computer Maintenance, Computer Science, Computer Technology, Data Processing, Medical Records Administration, Programming, Robotics, Software Engineer, Systems Analysis, Telecommunications • CRAFTS AND DESIGN Illustration Design • EDUCATION Art, Child Development, Early Childhood, English, Foreign Language, Health, Mathematics, Music, Physical, Social Studies, Special • ENGINEERING Aerospace, Air Conditioning Technology, Bio-medical, Civil/Environmental, Electrical, Engineering Science, Industrial, Mechanical • ENVIRONMENTAL CONTROL Energy Conservation, Solar Heating • HEALTH SCIENCES Dental Assistant, Dental Hygiene, Emeregency Medcial Technician, Medical Assistant, Medical Secretary, Nursing, Occupational Therapy, Physical Therapy, Practical Nursing, Speech/Audiology and Speech • HUMANITIES Humanities, Liberal Arts, Philosophy, Religion • LANGUAGES German, Japanese, Spanish • PREPROFESSIONAL Architecture, Dentistry, Law, Legal Assistant, Medicine, Natural Resources, Optometry, Pharmacy, Recreation, Social Work, Sports Medicine, Veterinarian • SCIENCES Biology, Chemistry, Earth, Geography, Gerontology, Horticultural, Mathematics, Oceanography, Physical Science, Physics • SOCIAL SCIENCES Anthropology, Criminal Justice, Government/Political, History, Human Service, Law Enforcement, Political Science, Psychology, Public Relations, Social Sciences, Sociology • VISUAL AND PERFORMING ARTS Art, Art History, Dance, Dramatic Arts, Drawing, Fine Arts, Music, Music Performance, Music Theatre, Studio Art, Theater • VOCATIONAL Air Condtioning/Heating/Refrig, Automobile Technology, Aviation Maintenance, Aviation Technology, Business and Office, Carpentry, Construction, Court Reporting, Diesel Power Technology, Drafting, Electronics Technology, Fashion Mechandizing, Fire Science, Food Service, Home Economics, Industrial Equipment Maintenan, Interior Design, Legal Secretary, Machinist, Masonry, Office Administration, Painting, Park/Recreation, Piloting, Plumbing, Printing/Lithography, Radiological Technology, Respiratory Therapy Technology, Secretarial, Surveying and Mapping, Welding

Sports/Activities

• SPORTS-INTERCOLLEGIATE Basketball, Cross Country, Golf, Softball (F), Track and Field, Volleyball (F) • SPORTS-INTRAMURAL Baseball (M), Bowling • STUDENT LIFE ACTIVITIES Choral, Concert Band, Dance, Drama Groups, Ethnic & Cultural Groups, Film, Jazz Band, Music Groups, Musical Theater, Newspaper, Radio/TV station, Religious Organization, Student Government, Symphony Orchestra

---

Selective **Michigan**
Services

Mercy College of Detroit

8200 W. Outer Drive
Detroit, Michigan 48219
(313) 592-6030

School Enrollment: **2,300**

Admissions Contact: **Lisa Kujawa, Director of Admissions**
LD Contact: **Jay Thomson, V.P./Student Affairs**

Admissions

Application Information:

Application deadline: **August 15th**
Rolling Admissions: **Yes** Notified when: **2-4 weeks later**

Secondary School Information

Most Important Criteria For Admissions (1-strongest)

SAT/ACT	Application	School transcript
Class rank	Course selection	Personal statement
Interview	Extra activities	Psychoeducational
G.P.A.	Open admission	Recommendations

Types of Disabilities Served

• Speech/Lang	• Reading	ADD with LD
• Study skills	• Spelling	ADD without LD
• Written express	• Math	ADHD with LD
• Organizational	Fine Motor	ADHD without LD
• Perceptual		

Learning Disability Program

Counseling: Individual: **Yes** Group Counseling: **Yes**

Faculty:
Faculty: **1** Full time: **1**
Faculty advocate: **Yes** Meets with instructor: **As needed**

Diagnostic Testing
ADD	Personality	Perceptual skills	Spelling
ADHD	Organization	Fine motor skills	Reading
I.Q.	Handwriting	Spoken language	Study skills
Math	Social skills	Written language	

Tutoring:
Services rendered by:
•Graduates •Peers •Faculty LD staff Teacher trainees

Tutorials
Grp.	Ind.	Tutorials	Grp.	Ind.	Tutorials
•	•	Math skills			Word processing
•	•	Study skills	•	•	Time management
•	•	Language arts	•	•	Learning strategies
•	•	Written express	•	•	Organizational skills

Academic Accommodations
Curriculum	Study Aids	Exams
Priority registration	• Typist	Oral
Math waiver	Reader	Untimed
• Foreign lang. waiver	• Notetaker	• Take home
• Course substitution	• Proof reader	With proctor
In Class	Text on tape	On computer
• Calculators	Early syllabus	• Extended time
• Tape recorder	Taped handouts	On tape
Word processor		Modified
Priority seating		Separate room

Program Strengths
We do not offer an LD Program. We have a Developmental Services Program.

General Information:
Mercy College of Detroit is a 4 year private Roman Catholic college. Urban campus of 40 acres is 1 residential halls on campus. Housing is guaranteed.Guaranteed through 4th year. 5 % of students remain on campus for the weekends. 5 % of students join fraternities/sororities.

Accreditation: Regional

Expenses:
Tuition: In-state: Full year: $6,138.00. Part-time: Per course: Part-time: $198.00. Tuition: Out-of-state: Full year: $6,138.00. Part-time: Per course:Part-time: $198.00 Room and board: $1,800.00

Majors
• BUSINESS Accounting, Business Administration, Business Management, Hotel and Restaurant Managemen, Management, Marketing • COMMUNICATIONS English • COMPUTER SCIENCE Computer Science, Medical Records Technology • EDUCATION Child Development, English, Secondary • HEALTH SCIENCES Dietary Manager Assistant, Health, Health Care Administration, Medical Assistant, Medical Technology, Nursing • HUMANITIES Humanities • PREPROFESSIONAL Law, Legal Assistant, Medicine, Social Work • SCIENCES Biology, Chemistry, Physical Science • SOCIAL SCIENCES Government/Political, History, Political Science, Psychology, Public Relations, Social Sciences, Sociology • VOCATIONAL Paralegal, Respiratory Therapy Technology

Sports/Activities
• SPORTS-INTERCOLLEGIATE Baseball (M), Basketball, Golf, Softball (F), Volleyball (F) • SPORTS-INTRAMURAL Basketball, Racquetball, Soccer, Tennis, Volleyball (F) • STUDENT LIFE ACTIVITIES Choral, Community Service, Dance, Drama Groups, Fraternities, Newspaper, Religious Organization, Sororities, Student Government

Highly Selective

Michigan Technological University
1400 Townsend Drive
Houghton, Michigan 49931
(906) 487-2335

School Enrollment: **6,921** Male: **5,246** Female: **1,675**
LD Enrollment: **12** Male: **9** Female: **3**

Admissions Contact: **James Turnquist, Assoc. Dir. of Admissions**
LD Contact: **Richard Drenovsky, Associate Dean of Studies**
Telephone:**(906) 487-2212**

Admissions

Application Information:
Application deadline: **August 1st**
Rolling Admissions: **Yes**

Secondary School Information
Most Important Criteria For Admissions (1-strongest)
5	SAT/ACT		Application	**2**	School transcript
1	Class rank	**4**	Course selection	**7**	Personal statement
9	Interview	**6**	Extra activities	**10**	Psychoeducational
3	G.P.A.		Open admission	**8**	Recommendations

Test Requirements:
Untimed SAT: **Yes** Untimed ACT: **Yes**
Documentation of LD required: **Yes**
Tests recommended: **The Michigan Department of Rehabilitation Services inform us who should receive services.**

Types of Disabilities Served
• Speech/Lang	• Reading	• ADD with LD
• Study skills	• Spelling	• ADD without LD
• Written express	• Math	ADHD with LD
• Organizational	Fine Motor	ADHD without LD
Perceptual		

High School Course Requirements:
English: **3** Math: **2**

Learning Disability Program
Students mainstreamed **100** % of the day

Faculty:
Faculty: **1** Part time: **1**

Diagnostic Testing
ADD	• Personality	Perceptual skills	Spelling
ADHD	Organization	Fine motor skills	Reading
I.Q.	Handwriting	Spoken language	Study skills
Math	Social skills	Written language	

Tutoring:
Average size of group tutorials: **Individual**
Services rendered by:
Graduates •Peers •Faculty LD staff Teacher trainees

Michigan

Tutorials

Grp.	Ind.	Tutorials	Grp.	Ind.	Tutorials
•	•	Math skills	•	•	Word processing
•	•	Study skills	•	•	Time management
•	•	Language arts	•	•	Learning strategies
•	•	Written express	•	•	Organizational skills

Academic Accommodations

Curriculum	Study Aids	Exams
• Priority registration	• Typist	Oral
Math waiver	Reader	• Untimed
Foreign lang. waiver	• Notetaker	• Take home
• Course substitution	Proof reader	With proctor
In Class	• Text on tape	On computer
• Calculators	Early syllabus	• Extended time
• Tape recorder	Taped handouts	On tape
Word processor		• Modified
• Priority seating		• Separate room

Program Strengths

Michigan Technological University does not have a special program for handicapper students, however, the University does everything in their power to accommodate all students with learning disabilities or any other deficits. These deficits must be verified by the Vocational Rehabilitation Center in order for the program to receive funding.

General Information:

Michigan Technological University is a 2 and 4 year public university. Rural campus of 240 acres is 380 miles from Milwaukee. Accessible by air or bus. Ski areas are 2 miles from campus. Beaches are 2 miles from campus. 3% of students are foreign. 3 residential halls on campus. Housing is guaranteed.Guaranteed through 1st year. 85 % of students remain on campus for the weekends. 17 % of students join fraternities/sororities.

Accreditation:NCACS

SAT/ACT Scores:

Scores for incoming freshmen:**Verbal:**52%below 500. 35%between 500 and 599. 12%between 600 and 699. 1%above 700. **Math:**10% below 500. 32% between 500 and 599. 28% between 600 and 699. 20%above 700. **ACT:** 7% below 20. 24% between 20 and 23. 20%between 24 and 25l. 34%between 26 and 28. 15% above 28.

Class Rank:

About 63% of the present freshmen class were in the upper 20% of their high school class. 88% were in the top 40% of their class. 96% were in the top 60% of their class. 100% were in the top 80% of their class.

Expenses:

Tuition: In-state: Full year: $2,841.00. Part-time: Per credit:$75.00. Tuition: Out-of-state: Full year: $6,480.00. Part-time: Per credit:$180.00. Room and board: $3,390.00

Majors

• BUSINESS Accounting, Business Administration, Business Economics, Business Management, Economics, Entrepreneur, Labor Relations, Management, Marketing, Personnel • COMMUNICATIONS Communication, English • COMPUTER SCIENCE Computer Science, Programming • EDUCATION Secondary • ENGINEERING Bioengineering, Biomedical, Chemical, Civil/Environmental, Computer, Electrical, Engineering Science, Forestry, Geological, Mechanical, Metallurgical, Mining/Mineral, Physics • HEALTH SCIENCES Environmental, Medical Technology • HUMANITIES Humanities, Liberal Arts • PREPROFESSIONAL Dentistry, Law, Medicine, Veterinarian • SCIENCES Biochemistry, Biology, Chemistry, Earth, Ecology, Geology, Geophysics, Inorganic Chemistry, Mathematics, Microbiology, Organic Chemistry, Physics, Statistics • SOCIAL SCIENCES History, Social Sciences • VOCATIONAL Forestry, Medical Laboratory Technology, Surveying and Mapping, Woodworking

Sports/Activities

• SPORTS RELATED Cheerleading, Chess, Pep Band, Team Managers • SPORTS-INTERCOLLEGIATE Basketball, Cross Country, Diving, Football (M), Ice Hockey (M), Swimming (M), Tennis, Track and Field, Volleyball (F) • SPORTS-INTRAMURAL Basketball, Bowling, Cross Country, Football, Golf, Hand Ball, Ice Hockey, Ping-Pong, Racquetball, Soccer, Softball, Squash, Swimming, Tennis, Track and Field, Volleyball, Water Polo, Wrestling • STUDENT LIFE ACTIVITIES Choral, Concert Band, Debate, Drama Groups, Ethnic & Cultural Groups, Film, Fraternities, Jazz Band, Music Groups, Musical Theater, Newspaper, Political Groups, Radio/TV station, Religious Organization, Sororities, Student Government, Symphony Orchestra, Yearbook

---

Less Selective   **Michigan Services**

Mid Michigan Community College

1375 South Clare Avenue
Harrison, Michigan 48625
(517) 386-7792

School Enrollment: **2,100** Male: **840** Female: **1,260**

Admissions Contact: **Jerry Hand, Admissions Coordinator**
LD Contact: **Susan Cobb, Director**
Name of Program: **Student Support Center**
Telephone:**(517) 386-7792 Ext. 286**

Admissions

Application Information:
Application deadline: **Open**
Rolling Admissions: **Yes**

Secondary School Information
Most Important Criteria For Admissions (1-strongest)

SAT/ACT	Application	School transcript
Class rank	Course selection	Personal statement
Interview	Extra activities	Psychoeducational
G.P.A.	1 Open admission	Recommendations

Test Requirements:
Standardized tests waived: **Yes**
WAIS-R required: **Yes**
Documentation of LD required: **Yes**

Types of Disabilities Served

• Speech/Lang	• Reading	• ADD with LD
• Study skills	• Spelling	• ADD without LD
• Written express	• Math	• ADHD with LD
• Organizational	• Fine Motor	• ADHD without LD
• Perceptual		

Learning Disability Program

Services available for all students: **Yes**
Counseling: Individual: **Yes**

Faculty:
Faculty: **5** Full time: **2** Part time: **3** M.A.: **3**
Faculty advocate: **Yes** Meets with instructor: **Monthly**

Diagnostic Testing

ADD	• Personality	Perceptual skills	• Spelling
ADHD	Organization	Fine motor skills	• Reading
I.Q.	Handwriting	Spoken language	Study skills
• Math	Social skills	• Written language	

Tutoring:
Average size of group tutorials: **10**
Services rendered by:
Graduates   •Peers   •Faculty   •LD staff   Teacher trainees

Tutorials

Grp.	Ind.	Tutorials	Grp.	Ind.	Tutorials
•	•	Math skills	•	•	Word processing
•	•	Study skills	•		Time management
•	•	Language arts	•	•	Learning strategies
•	•	Written express	•	•	Organizational skills

Academic Accommodations

Curriculum	Study Aids	Exams
Priority registration	• Typist	• Oral
Math waiver	Reader	• Untimed
Foreign lang. waiver	• Notetaker	• Take home
• Course substitution	• Proof reader	• With proctor
In Class	• Text on tape	On computer
Calculators	Early syllabus	• Extended time
• Tape recorder	Taped handouts	On tape
• Word processor		• Modified
Priority seating		• Separate room

Program Strengths

The institution is large enough to offer a support program but small enough to provide individualized services to the students.

General Information:

Mid Michigan Community College is a 2 year public college. Rural campus of 560 acres is 10 miles from Clare. Accessible by bus. Ski areas are 1 mile from campus. Beaches are 5 miles from campus. 1% of students are foreign. Housing is not guaranteed.

Accreditation: NCACS

Expenses:

Tuition: In-state: Full year: $1,500.00. Part-time: Per credit:$39.00. Part-time: Per credit:$70.00.

Majors

• BUSINESS Accounting, Banking, Business Administration, Business Management, Entrepreneur, Finance, Management, Marketing • COMPUTER SCIENCE Computer Science, Data Processing, Programming • EDUCATION Art, Elementary, Middle School, School Psychology, Secondary, Special • ENGINEERING Air Conditioning Technology, Engineering Science, Industrial, Mechanical • HEALTH SCIENCES Nursing, Practical Nursing, Radiological Therapy • HUMANITIES Humanities, Liberal Arts • PREPROFESSIONAL Engineering, Forestry, Law, Pharmacy • SCIENCES Biochemistry, Biology, Chemistry, Mathematics, Physical Science • SOCIAL SCIENCES Criminal Justice, Law Enforcement, Psychology, Social Sciences, Sociology • VISUAL AND PERFORMING ARTS Theater • VOCATIONAL Air Conditioning/Heating/Refri, Automobile Technology, Automotive Service, Business and Office, Diesel Power Technology, Drafting, Fire Science, Machinist, Office Information Systems, Radiological Technology, Secretarial, Welding, Word Processing

Sports/Activities

• SPORTS-INTRAMURAL Bowling, Cross Country, Golf, Karate, Skiing - Snow, Tennis, Weight Lifting • STUDENT LIFE ACTIVITIES Choral, Drama Groups, Musical Theater, Student Government

Montcalm Community College
2800 College Drive
Sidney, Michigan 48885-9746
(517) 328-2111

School Enrollment: **1,900** Male: **700** Female: **1,200**

Admissions Contact: **Carol Krumbach, Director of Admissions**
LD Contact: **Dan Snook, Lab Supervisor**
Name of Program: **Skill Development Lab**
Address: **2800 College Drive**
Telephone:**(517) 328-2111 Ext. 282**

Admissions

Application Information:
Application deadline: **None**
Rolling Admissions: **Yes**

Secondary School Information
Most Important Criteria For Admissions (1-strongest)

SAT/ACT	Application	School transcript
Class rank	Course selection	Personal statement
Interview	Extra activities	Psychoeducational
G.P.A.	**1** Open admission	Recommendations

Test Requirements:
Standardized tests waived: **Yes**

Types of Disabilities Served
• Speech/Lang	• Reading	• ADD with LD
• Study skills	• Spelling	• ADD without LD
• Written express	• Math	• ADHD with LD
• Organizational	• Fine Motor	• ADHD without LD
• Perceptual		

Learning Disability Program
Recommended credits per semester: **1-6**
Time required or recommended in learning center: **2 hours**
Services available for all students: **Yes**
Counseling: Individual: **Yes** Vocational Counseling: **Yes**

Faculty:
Faculty: **4** Including Director: **Yes** Full time: **2** Part time: **2**
LD faculty with: BS/BA: **2** M.A.: **2**

Diagnostic Testing

ADD	Personality	Perceptual skills	Spelling
ADHD	Organization	Fine motor skills	• Reading
I.Q.	Handwriting	Spoken language	• Study skills
Math	Social skills	• Written language	

Tutoring:
Services rendered by:
Graduates   •Peers   Faculty   LD staff   Teacher trainees

Michigan

Tutorials

Grp.	Ind.	Tutorials	Grp.	Ind.	Tutorials
	•	Math skills		•	Word processing
	•	Study skills			Time management
	•	Language arts		•	Learning strategies
	•	Written express		•	Organizational skills

Academic Accommodations

Curriculum
Priority registration
• Math waiver
• Foreign lang. waiver
Course substitution

In Class
• Calculators
• Tape recorder
Word processor
• Priority seating

Study Aids
• Typist
• Reader
• Notetaker
• Proof reader
• Text on tape
Early syllabus
Taped handouts

Exams
• Oral
• Untimed
Take home
• With proctor
On computer
• Extended time
On tape
• Modified
• Separate room

Graduation Requirements:
Course credits: **60** GPA: **2.0** Years to complete degree: **2 or more**
Other requirements: **Generally 1 year English and 1 year Social Science (specific requirements vary for each program of study)**

Program Strengths

The primary support services for Special Needs students consist of providing tutors for vocational/non-vocational, academically disadvantaged students. An additional support component involves support assessment followed by assigning services or recommending other support services on campus or within the community. Scheduled courses are offered in skill development, i.e. reading, writing, math, and study skills.

General Information:

Montcalm Community College is a 2 year public college. Rural campus 45 miles from Grand Rapids. Accessible by auto. Ski areas are 45 miles from campus. Beaches are 60 miles from campus. 1% of students are foreign. Housing is not guaranteed.

Accreditation: NCACS

Expenses: Part-time: Per credit:$36.00 (in-district), $54.00 (in Michigan). Part-time: Per credit:$66.00.

Majors

• BUSINESS Business Administration, Food Management, Secretarial Science • COMPUTER SCIENCE Business Data Programming • EDUCATION Child Development • HEALTH SCIENCES Medical Assistant, Medical Secretary, Nursing, Practical Nursing, Radiological Technology • HUMANITIES Liberal Arts • PRE PROFESSIONAL Legal Assistant • SCIENCES Physical Science • SOCIAL SCIENCES Criminal Justice, Social Sciences • VISUAL AND PERFORMING ARTS Art • VOCATIONAL Automobile Technology, Automotive Service, Business and Office, Cosmetology, Drafting, Electronics Technology, Food Service, Industrial Arts, Industrial Technology, Legal Secretary, Machinist, Paralegal, Radiological Technology, Secretarial, Welding, Word Processing

Sports/Activities

• SPORTS-INTRAMURAL Basketball, Ping-Pong, Skiing - Snow, Softball, Tennis, Volleyball • STUDENT LIFE ACTIVITIES Choral, Drama Groups, Jazz Band, Music Groups, Newspaper, Student Government

Northern Michigan University
405 Cohodas Administrative Center Presque Isle Boulevard
Marquette, Michigan 49855
(906) 227-2650

School Enrollment: **8,722** Male: **3,994** Female: **4,728**
LD Enrollment: **400** Male: **180** Female: **220**

Admissions Contact: **Nancy Rehling, Director of Admissions**
LD Contact: **Dr. Masud A. Mufti, Director**
Name of Program: **Student Supportive Services**
Telephone:**(906) 227-1550**

Admissions

Application Information:
Application deadline: **February 1st**
Applicant must apply **No requirement** months in advance
Rolling Admissions: **Yes** Notified when: **ASAP**

Secondary School Information
Most Important Criteria For Admissions (1-strongest)

1 SAT/ACT	**5** Application	**4** School transcript
2 Class rank	**1** Course selection	**5** Personal statement
3 Interview	**5** Extra activities	**4** Psychoeducational
1 G.P.A.	Open admission	**3** Recommendations

Test Requirements:
Diagnostic testing waived: **Yes**
Untimed SAT: **Yes** Untimed ACT: **Yes**
Documentation of LD required: **Yes**
Currency of diagnostic testing: **Within past 3 years**
Tests recommended: **WAIS-R, Woodcock-Johnson Tests of Achievement, others as needed to test deficit areas.**

Types of Disabilities Served
• Speech/Lang
• Study skills
• Written express
• Organizational
• Perceptual
• Reading
• Spelling
• Math
• Fine Motor
• ADD with LD
• ADD without LD
• ADHD with LD
• ADHD without LD

Admissions Process

Documentation of a disability is reviewed by Student Supportive Services staff member.

Learning Disability Program

Program: Remedial: **Yes**
Program: Reinforces course work: **Yes**
Students mainstreamed **100** % of the day
Services available for all students: **Yes**
Counseling: Individual: **Yes**
Support groups are available:**Yes, through Student Supportive Services**

Faculty: M.A.: **1**
Faculty advocate: **Yes** Meets with instructor: **As needed**

Diagnostic Testing

ADD	Personality	Perceptual skills	Spelling
ADHD	Organization	Fine motor skills	Reading
I.Q.	Handwriting	Spoken language	Study skills
Math	Social skills	Written language	

Tutoring:

Average size of group tutorials: **2-3**
Services rendered by:
•Graduates •Peers •Faculty •LD staff Teacher trainees

Tutorials

Grp.	Ind.	Tutorials	Grp.	Ind.	Tutorials
	•	Math skills		•	Word processing
	•	Study skills		•	Time management
•	•	Language arts		•	Learning strategies
	•	Written express		•	Organizational skills

Academic Accommodations

Curriculum	Study Aids	Exams
Priority registration	• Typist	• Oral
Math waiver	• Reader	• Untimed
Foreign lang. waiver	• Notetaker	Take home
Course substitution	• Proof reader	• With proctor
In Class	• Text on tape	On computer
• Calculators	• Early syllabus	• Extended time
• Tape recorder	Taped handouts	On tape
• Word processor		• Modified
• Priority seating		• Separate room

Graduation Requirements:

Course credits: **124** GPA: **2.0**

Program Strengths

We do not have a Learning Disabilities Program. We provide free tutoring, basic skills workshops, study skills workshops, personal development workshops, academic advisement, career counseling and limited personal counseling. The University provides free counseling in the counseling center. Handicapper aides are available, but students must assume the cost.

General Information:

Northern Michigan University is a 4 year public college. Urban campus of 320 acres is 180 miles from Green Bay, WI. Accessible by air or bus. Ski areas are 3 miles from campus. Beaches are 1mile from campus. 1% of students are foreign. 10 residential halls on campus. Housing is not guaranteed.80 % of students remain on campus for the weekends. 1 % of students join fraternities/sororities.

Accreditation: NCACS

SAT/ACT Scores:

Scores for incoming freshmen: **ACT:** 41% below 20. 40% between 20 and 23. 14% between 24 and 25l. 4% between 26 and 28. 1% above 28.

Expenses:

Tuition: In-state: Full year: $1,528.00. Part-time: Per credit:$64.00. Part-time: Per course: $255.00. Tuition: Out-of-state: Full year: $2,968.00. Part-time: Per credit:$124.00. Part-time: Per course:$495.00 Room and board: $3,473.00.

Majors

• AREA STUDIES Urban • BUSINESS Accounting, Banking, Business Administration, Business Education, Business Management, Economics, Finance, Food Management, Hotel and Restaurant Managemen, Management, Marketing • COMMUNICATIONS Broadcasting, Communication, English, Graphic Design Technology, Journalism, Photography, Speech, Television/Radio/Film • COMPUTER SCIENCE Computer Maintenance, Computer Science, Computer Technology, Data Processing, Programming, Systems Analysis • CRAFTS AND DESIGN Ceramics, Crafts, Graphic Design, Illustration Design, Sculpture • EDUCATION Art, Child Development, Early Childhood, Elementary, English, Foreign Language, Health, Home Economics, Mathematics, Middle School, Music, Physical, Pre-Education, Science, Secondary, Social Science, Social Studies, Special • ENGINEERING Air Conditioning Technology, Bio-medical, Electrical, Industrial • ENVIRONMENTAL CONTROL Energy Conservation, Water and Wastewater Technolog • HEALTH SCIENCES Communication Disorders, Environmental, Health, Medical Secretary, Medical Technology, Nursing, Nutritional/Food, Speech Therapy, Speech/Audiology and Speech • HUMANITIES English/Writing/Literature, Humanities, Liberal Arts, Philosophy • LANGUAGES French, German, Spanish • PREPROFESSIONAL Architecture, Dentistry, Engineering, Law, Medicine, Pharmacy, Social Work, Sports Medicine • SCIENCES Animal, Biochemistry, Biology, Botany, Cell Biology, Chemistry, Earth, Ecology, Geography, Gerontology, Marine Biology, Mathematics, Microbiology, Physical Science, Physics, Physiology, Water Science, Zoology • SOCIAL SCIENCES Criminal Justice, Geography, Government/Political, History, Law Enforcement, Political Science, Psychology, Public Relations, Social Sciences, Sociology • VISUAL AND PERFORMING ARTS Art, Dramatic Arts, Music, Theater • VOCATIONAL Air Conditioning/Heating/Refri, Automobile Technology, Automotive Service, Business and Office, Construction, Diesel Power Technology, Drafting, Electronics Technology, Fashion Merchandising, Food Service, Home Economics, Industrial Design, Interior Design, Jewelry-Metalsmithery, Legal Secretary, Medical Laboratory Technology, Office Administration, Painting, Park/Recreation, Printing/Lithography, Secretarial, Textile and Clothing, Woodworking

Sports/Activities

• SPORTS RELATED Cheerleading, Drill Team, Marching Band, Pep Band, Team Managers • SPORTS-INTERCOLLEGIATE Basketball, Cross Country, Diving (F), Field Hockey (F), Football (M), Ice Hockey (M), Skiing - Snow, Swimming (F), Track and Field, Volleyball (F) • SPORTS-INTRAMURAL Badminton, Basketball, Bowling, Hand Ball, Ice Hockey, Ping-Pong, Racquetball, Skiing - Snow, Soccer, Softball, Squash, Tennis, Volleyball • STUDENT LIFE ACTIVITIES Choral, Concert Band, Dance, Drama Groups, Ethnic & Cultural Groups, Film, Fraternities, Jazz Band, Magazine, Music Groups, Musical Theater, Newspaper, Opera, Radio/TV station, Religious Organization, Sororities, Student Government, Symphony Orchestra, Yearbook

---

Less Selective **Michigan Program**

Oakland Community College
2480 Opdyke Road Box 182
Bloomfield Hills, Michigan 48013
(313) 540-1549

School Enrollment: **28,000**
LD Enrollment: **128**

Admissions Contact: **Dr. Maurice McCall, Dir. of Enrollment Serv.**
LD Contact: **Paula Green-Smith, Assoc. Dean of Students**
Name of Program: **Programs for Academic Support**
Address: **2900 Featherstone Rd., Auburn Hills,MI 48326**
Telephone:**(313) 340-6730**

Admissions

Application Information:
Enrolled:**128**

Michigan

Secondary School Information
Most Important Criteria For Admissions (1-strongest)

SAT/ACT	Application	**2**	School transcript
Class rank	Course selection		Personal statement
Interview	Extra activities	**3**	Psychoeducational
1 G.P.A.	**1** Open admission		Recommendations

Test Requirements:
WAIS-R required: **Yes** Range accepted: **All**
Documentation of LD required: **Yes**
Currency of diagnostic testing: **No more than 3 years**

Types of Disabilities Served
- Speech/Lang
- Study skills
- Written express
- Organizational
- Perceptual
- Reading
- Spelling
- Math
- Fine Motor
- ADD with LD
- ADD without LD
- ADHD with LD
- ADHD without LD

Learning Disability Program
Students mainstreamed **100** % of the day
Recommended credits per semester: **Varies**
Services available for all students: **Yes**
Counseling: Individual: **Yes** Group Counseling: **Yes** Vocational Counseling: **Yes**
Support groups are available:**Yes**

Faculty:
Faculty: **7**
LD faculty with: BS/BA: **2** M.A.: **5**

Diagnostic Testing

ADD	Personality	Perceptual skills	Spelling
ADHD	Organization	Fine motor skills	Reading
I.Q.	Handwriting	Spoken language	Study skills
Math	Social skills	Written language	

Tutoring:
Average size of group tutorials: **15**
Services rendered by:

Graduates	Peers	Faculty	LD staff	Teacher trainees

Tutorials

Grp.	Ind.	Tutorials	Grp.	Ind.	Tutorials
•	•	Math skills		•	Word processing
•	•	Study skills	•	•	Time management
	•	Language arts		•	Learning strategies
	•	Written express		•	Organizational skills

Academic Accommodations

Curriculum	Study Aids	Exams
Priority registration	• Typist	• Oral
Math waiver	• Reader	• Untimed
Foreign lang. waiver	• Notetaker	Take home
Course substitution	• Proof reader	• With proctor
In Class	• Text on tape	On computer
• Calculators	Early syllabus	• Extended time
• Tape recorder	• Taped handouts	On tape
• Word processor		Modified
Priority seating		• Separate room

General Information:
Oakland Community College is a 2 year Community College Suburban campus of 5 acres is 30 miles from Detroit. Accessible by car or bus. Ski areas are 15 miles from campus. Beaches are 10-15 miles from campus. Housing is not guaranteed.

388

Accreditation:CINCACS

Expenses:
Tuition: In-state: Full year: $663.00 (17 credits) plus registration fee. Part-time: Per credit:$39.00. Part-time: Per course: Varies. Tuition: Out-of-state: Full year: $1,564.00 (17 credits). Part-time: Per credit:$92.00 plus registration fee. Part-time: Per course:Varies

Majors
• ARTS Drafting, Graphic Arts • BUSINESS Accounting, Business Administration, Business Data Processing, Business Data Programming, Business Management, Fashion Merchandising, Finance, Hotel & Restaurant Management, International Business, Marketing • COMMUNICATIONS Broadcasting, Printing, Radio/Television • COMPUTER SCIENCE Data Processing, Programming, Robotics, Systems Analysis • CRAFTS AND DESIGN Ceramics • EDUCATION Child Development • ENGINEERING Engineering Science • HEALTH SCIENCES Dental Hygiene, Health, Health Care Administration, Medical Laboratory Technology, Nursing, Physician's Assistant, Respiratory Therapy Technology, Ultrasound Technology • HUMANITIES Liberal/General • SCIENCES Clinical Laboratory Science • SOCIAL SCIENCES Corrections, Criminal Justice, Human Service, Law Enforcement • VISUAL AND PERFORMING ARTS Fine Arts • VOCATIONAL Air Conditioning/Heating/Refri, Automobile Technology, Aviation Management, Business and Office, Child Care/Guidance, Court Reporting, Drafting and Design Technology, Electromechanical Technology, Electronics Technology, Emergency Medical Technology, Food Management, Food Service, Industrial Technology, Landscape Architecture, Legal Secretary, Library Assistant, Mechanical Design Technology, Mechanics, Paralegal, Precision Metal Works, Printing, Quality Control Technology, Radiological Technology, Respiratory Therapy Technology, Secretarial, Solar Heating, Welding

Sports/Activities
• SPORTS RELATED Pep Band • SPORTS-INTERCOLLEGIATE Baseball (M), Basketball, Football (M), Golf (M), Softball (F), Tennis, Volleyball (F) • SPORTS-INTRAMURAL Basketball, Bowling, Ice Hockey (M), Rugby (M), Skiing - Snow, Soccer (M), Softball, Swimming, Volleyball • STUDENT LIFE ACTIVITIES Academic Clubs, Drama Groups, Ethnic & Cultural Groups, Fraternities, Jazz Band, Newspaper, Radio, Religious Organization, Sororities, Student Government, Yearbook

Less Selective **Michigan Services**

Schoolcraft College
18600 Haggerty Road
Livonia, Michigan 48152-9990
(313) 462-4400

School Enrollment: **2,500**
LD Enrollment: **80**

Admissions Contact: **Admissions Office**
LD Contact: **Dr. Sirkka Gudan, Director**
Name of Program: **Learning Assistance Center**
Address: **18600 Haggerty Rd.**
Telephone:**(313) 462-4436**

Admissions

Application Information:
Application deadline: **Open**
Rolling Admissions: **Yes**

Secondary School Information

Most Important Criteria For Admissions (1-strongest)

SAT/ACT	Application	School transcript
Class rank	Course selection	Personal statement
Interview	Extra activities	Psychoeducational
G.P.A.	1 Open admission	Recommendations

Test Requirements:

Standardized tests waived: **Yes**
Diagnostic testing waived: **Yes**
Untimed SAT: **Yes** Untimed ACT: **Yes**
Documentation of LD required: **Yes**
Currency of diagnostic testing: **Within 3 year period**
Tests recommended: **Psychological Reports**

Types of Disabilities Served

- Speech/Lang
- Study skills
- Written express
- Organizational
- Perceptual
- Reading
- Spelling
- Math
- Fine Motor
- ADD with LD
- ADD without LD
- ADHD with LD
- ADHD without LD

Admissions Process

Open, all students admitted, high school graduate or G.E.D.

Learning Disability Program

Special orientation for LD students: **Yes**
Program: Reinforces course work: **Yes**
Program available through:**All times**
Students mainstreamed **100** % of the day
Counseling: Individual: **Yes** Vocational Counseling: **Yes**

Faculty:

Faculty: **7** Including Director: **Yes** Full time: **3** Part time: **4** M.A.: **6** Ph.D.: **1**
Faculty advocate: **Yes** Meets with instructor: **As needed**

Diagnostic Testing

ADD	Personality	Perceptual skills	Spelling
ADHD	Organization	Fine motor skills	• Reading
I.Q.	Handwriting	Spoken language	• Study skills
• Math	Social skills	• Written language	

Tutoring:

Average size of group tutorials: **1-7**
Services rendered by:
Graduates •Peers •Faculty LD staff •Teacher trainees

Tutorials

Grp.	Ind.	Tutorials	Grp.	Ind.	Tutorials
•	•	Math skills	•	•	Word processing
•	•	Study skills		•	Time management
•	•	Language arts	•	•	Learning strategies
•	•	Written express	•	•	Organizational skills

Academic Accommodations

Curriculum	Study Aids	Exams
Priority registration	Typist	• Oral
Math waiver	• Reader	• Untimed
Foreign lang. waiver	• Notetaker	• Take home
Course substitution	Proof reader	• With proctor
In Class	• Text on tape	• On computer
• Calculators	Early syllabus	• Extended time
• Tape recorder	• Taped handouts	• On tape
• Word processor		• Modified
• Priority seating		• Separate room

Graduation Requirements:GPA: **2.0**

Program Strengths

Dyslexics and other learning disabled students may enroll in any of the regular courses offered and may receive individualized tutoring. Other services include: test taking adaptatives, liaison with faculty, textbook recording, and notetaking assistance.

General Information:

Schoolcraft College is a 2 year public college. Suburban campus of 183 acres is 20 miles from Detroit. Accessible by auto. Housing is not guaranteed.

Accreditation:NCACS

Expenses: Part-time: Per credit:$33.50. Part-time: Per credit:$47.00.

Majors

• BUSINESS Accounting, Business Administration, Business Management, Entrepreneur, Food Management, Hotel and Restaurant Managemen, Labor Relations, Management, Marketing • COMMUNICATIONS Broadcasting, Creative Writing, English • COMPUTER SCIENCE Computer Technology, Data Processing, Medical Records Technology, Programming, Robotics, Telecommunications • EDUCATION Child Development, Early Childhood, Elementary • ENGINEERING Bioengineering, Biomedical, Engineering Science, Mechanical, Metallurgical • HEALTH SCIENCES Health, Medical Assistant, Medical Technology, Nursing, Occupational Therapy Assistant, Practical Nursing • HUMANITIES Humanities, Liberal Arts, Philosophy • LANGUAGES French, German, Spanish • PREPROFESSIONAL Architecture, Dentistry, Engineering, Law, Medicine, Pharmacy, Recreation, Social Work • SCIENCES Astronomy, Biology, Chemistry, Geography, Geology, Mathematics, Microbiology, Physical Science, Physics, Physiology • SOCIAL SCIENCES Anthropology, Criminal Justice, Geography, Government/Political, History, Law Enforcement, Psychology, Social Sciences, Sociology • VISUAL AND PERFORMING ARTS Art, Music, Theater • VOCATIONAL Business and Office, Construction, Cosmetology, Culinary Arts, Drafting, Electronics Technology, Food Service, Medical Laboratory Technology, Office Administration, Secretarial, Welding

Sports/Activities

• SPORTS-INTERCOLLEGIATE Basketball, Cross Country (F), Golf (M), Soccer, Volleyball (F) • SPORTS-INTRAMURAL Badminton, Basketball, Cross Country, Golf, Racquetball, Tennis, Volleyball • STUDENT LIFE ACTIVITIES Choral, Drama Groups, Fraternities, Jazz Band, Music Groups, Newspaper, Radio/TV station, Student Government, Symphony Orchestra

Selective   **Michigan Services**

Spring Arbor College
106 East Main
Spring Arbor, Michigan 49283
(517) 750-1200

School Enrollment: **878** Male: **373** Female: **505**
LD Enrollment: **12** Male: **4** Female: **8**

Admissions Contact: **Steve Schippers, Director of Admissions**
LD Contact: **Carolee Hamilton, Director**
Name of Program: **Learning Center**
Telephone:**(517) 750-1200 Ext. 235**

Admissions

Application Information:
Applicant must apply **6** months in advance
Rolling Admissions: **Yes**

Secondary School Information
Most Important Criteria For Admissions (1-strongest)

2 SAT/ACT	Application	**1**	School transcript
3 Class rank	Course selection		Personal statement
4 Interview	**4** Extra activities		Psychoeducational
1 G.P.A.	Open admission	**4**	Recommendations

Test Requirements:
Untimed SAT: **Yes** Untimed ACT: **Yes**
Tests recommended: **General Application including transcripts, recommendations**

Types of Disabilities Served
- Speech/Lang
- Study skills
- Written express
- Organizational
- Perceptual
- Reading
- Spelling
- Math
- Fine Motor

ADD with LD
ADD without LD
ADHD with LD
ADHD without LD

Learning Disability Program
Program: Remedial: **Yes**
Program: Reinforces course work: **Yes**
Services available for all students: **Yes**
Counseling: Individual: **Yes** Group Counseling: **Yes** Vocational Counseling: **Yes**

Faculty:
Faculty: **2** Full time: **1** Part time: **1** M.A.: **2**
Faculty advocate: **Yes** Meets with instructor: **As needed**

Diagnostic Testing

ADD	Personality	Perceptual skills	Spelling
ADHD	Organization	Fine motor skills	• Reading
I.Q.	Handwriting	Spoken language	Study skills
Math	Social skills	• Written language	

Tutoring:
Average size of group tutorials: **4**
Services rendered by:
Graduates   •Peers   •Faculty   •LD staff   Teacher trainees

Tutorials

Grp.	Ind.	Tutorials	Grp.	Ind.	Tutorials
•	•	Math skills	•	•	Word processing
•	•	Study skills	•	•	Time management
•	•	Language arts	•	•	Learning strategies
•	•	Written express	•	•	Organizational skills

Academic Accommodations

Curriculum	Study Aids	Exams
Priority registration	Typist	• Oral
Math waiver	Reader	Untimed
Foreign lang. waiver	• Notetaker	Take home
Course substitution	• Proof reader	• With proctor
In Class	• Text on tape	On computer
Calculators	Early syllabus	• Extended time
Tape recorder	Taped handouts	On tape
Word processor		• Modified
Priority seating		Separate room

Graduation Requirements:
Course credits: **124** GPA: **2.0** Years to complete degree: **4-5** Math waiver: **Yes** Language waiver: **Yes**

Program Strengths
Our Learning Skills program is three years old and growing. We service handicapped, LD, and students with no known disabilities. Foreign students who are learning English, deaf, blind, and physically handicapped students all have requested services. Many students receive individual assistance with coursework, from library research to proofreading. Remedial classes and in-services are offered in math, reading, writing, study skills, and learning strategies. Most of the assistance is given by faculty.

General Information:
Spring Arbor College is a 4 year private Free Methodist Church of North college. Rural campus of 70 acres is 8 miles from Jackson. Accessible by air, train, or bus. Ski areas are 1 hour from campus. 2% of students are foreign. 6 residential halls on campus. Housing is guaranteed.65-70 % of students remain on campus for the weekends.

Accreditation:NCACS

Expenses:
Tuition: In-state: Full year: $7,900.00. Part-time: Per credit:$160.00. Tuition: Out-of-state: Full year: $7,900.00. Part-time: Per credit:$160.00. Room and board: $3,400.00

Majors
• BUSINESS Business Administration, Business Economics, Business Management, Management • COMMUNICATIONS Communication, English • COMPUTER SCIENCE Computer Science • EDUCATION Early Childhood, Elementary, Physical, Pre-Education, Secondary, Speech/Language • HUMANITIES Liberal Arts, Philosophy, Religion • LANGUAGES Spanish • PREPROFESSIONAL Ministry, Social Work • SCIENCES Biology, Chemistry, Mathematics, Physics • SOCIAL SCIENCES History, Psychology, Social Sciences, Sociology

Sports/Activities
• SPORTS-INTERCOLLEGIATE Baseball (M), Basketball, Cross Country, Soccer (M), Softball (F), Tennis, Track and Field, Volleyball (F)
• SPORTS-INTRAMURAL Basketball, Soccer, Softball, Volleyball
• STUDENT LIFE ACTIVITIES Choral, Community Service, Concert Band, Drama Groups, Jazz Band, Music Groups, Musical Theater, Newspaper, Radio/TV station, Religious Organization, Student Government, Yearbook

Selective   **Michigan**
                                                   Accommodations

St. Mary's College
Commerce & Orchard Lake Road
Orchard Lake, Michigan 48324-1601
(313) 683-0507

School Enrollment: **400**

Admissions Contact: **Darrell Brockway, Dean, Enrollment Services**
Name of Program: **Teaching-Learning Lab**
Telephone:**(313) 683-0709**

Admissions

Application Information:
Application deadline: **Rolling**
Rolling Admissions: **Yes**

Secondary School Information
Most Important Criteria For Admissions (1-strongest)

2 SAT/ACT	Application	School transcript
Class rank	Course selection	Personal statement
3 Interview	Extra activities	Psychoeducational
1 G.P.A.	Open admission	Recommendations

Test Requirements:
Diagnostic testing waived: **Yes**
Untimed SAT: **Yes** Untimed ACT: **Yes** Achievement tests required:**1**
Currency of diagnostic testing: **1 month**

Types of Disabilities Served
- Speech/Lang
- Study skills
- Written express
- Organizational
- Perceptual
- Reading
- Spelling
- Math
- Fine Motor

ADD with LD
ADD without LD
ADHD with LD
ADHD without LD

Admissions Process

Rolling admission basis. To be admitted student need a high school diploma and a grade point average of 2.5 and an ACT composite of 19. Provisional status for those with a GPA of 2.0 - 2.4 and ACT of 13 - 18.

High School Course Requirements:
English: **4** Math: **2-3** Science: **2** Foreign Language: **2**

Learning Disability Program
Time required or recommended in learning center: **Varies**
Services available for all students: **Yes**

Diagnostic Testing

ADD	Personality	Perceptual skills	Spelling
ADHD	Organization	Fine motor skills	Reading
I.Q.	Handwriting	Spoken language	Study skills
Math	Social skills	Written language	

Services rendered by:

Graduates	Peers	Faculty	LD staff	Teacher trainees

Tutorials

Grp.	Ind.	Tutorials	Grp.	Ind.	Tutorials
		Math skills			Word processing
		Study skills			Time management
		Language arts			Learning strategies
		Written express			Organizational skills

Academic Accommodations

Curriculum	Study Aids	Exams
Priority registration	Typist	• Oral
Math waiver	Reader	• Untimed
Foreign lang. waiver	Notetaker	Take home
Course substitution	Proof reader	With proctor
In Class	Text on tape	On computer
Calculators	Early syllabus	Extended time
• Tape recorder	Taped handouts	On tape
Word processor		Modified
• Priority seating		• Separate room

Graduation Requirements:
Course credits: **120** GPA: **2.0** Years to complete degree: **4-10** Language waiver: **Yes**

General Information:
St. Mary's College is a 4 year independent Roman Catholic college. Suburban campus 18 miles from Detroit. Accessible by air. Ski areas are 2 hours from campus. Beaches are 10 minutes from campus. 5% of students are foreign. 2 residential halls on campus. Housing is not guaranteed.10 % of students remain on campus for the weekends.

Accreditation:NCACS

SAT/ACT Scores:
Scores for incoming freshmen:**Verbal:**5%below 500. 60%between 500 and 599. 35%between 600 and 699. **Math:**5% below 500. 65% between 500 and 599. 20% between 600 and 699. **ACT:** 20% below 20. 30% between 20 and 23. 30%between 24 and 251. 15%between 26 and 28. 5% above 28.

Class Rank:
About 10% of the present freshmen class were in the upper 20% of their high school class. 70% were in the top 40% of their class. 15% were in the top 60% of their class. 5% were in the top 80% of their class.

Expenses: Part-time: Per credit:$159.00. Room and board: $1,525.00

Majors
• AREA STUDIES European • BUSINESS Business Administration • COMMUNICATIONS Communication, English • EDUCATION English, Mathematics, Psychology, Social Studies • HUMANITIES Humanities, Liberal Arts , Philosophy, Religion • LANGUAGES French, Polish, Spanish • MATHEMATICS Theoretical • PRE PROFESSIONAL Dentistry, Law, Medicine, Pharmacy • RELIGIOUS STUDIES Philosophy, Religion & Theology • SCIENCES Biochemistry, Biology, Chemistry, Mathematics • SOCIAL SCIENCES History, Human Service, Psychology, Social Sciences, Sociology

Sports/Activities
• SPORTS RELATED Cheerleading • SPORTS-INTERCOLLEGIATE Basketball (M), Swimming, Volleyball • SPORTS-INTRAMURAL Basketball (F), Basketball (M), Swimming • STUDENT LIFE ACTIVITIES Choral, Ethnic & Cultural Groups, Newspaper, Religious Organization

Less Selective	Michigan Program

Suomi College
Quincy Street
Hancock, Michigan 49930
(906) 487-7258

School Enrollment: **482** Male: **147** Female: **335**
LD Enrollment: **12** Male: **8** Female: **4**

Admissions Contact: **Sue Forbes, Director of Admissions**
LD Contact: **Carol Bates, Learning Disabilities Coordinator**
Address: **Wargelin Hall 201A**
Telephone:**(906) 487-7258**

Admissions

Application Information:
LD Students Applying: **15** Accepted: **12** Enrolled:**12**
LD on admissions committee:**Yes**
Applicant must apply **4** months in advance

Secondary School Information
Most Important Criteria For Admissions (1-strongest)

8	SAT/ACT	**11**	Application	**6**	School transcript
12	Class rank	**5**	Course selection	**3**	Personal statement
4	Interview	**7**	Extra activities	**2**	Psychoeducational
9	G.P.A.		Open admission	**1**	Recommendations

Test Requirements:
Diagnostic testing waived: **Yes**
Untimed SAT: **Yes** Untimed ACT: **Yes** Achievement tests required:-
Woodcock-Johnson
Documentation of LD required: **Yes**
Currency of diagnostic testing: **Less than 3 years**
Tests recommended: **WAIS-R or WISC-R, Woodcock-Johnson Psycho-Educational Battery Cognitive and Achievement Tests Revised.**

Types of Disabilities Served

Speech/Lang	Reading	• ADD with LD
• Study skills	• Spelling	• ADD without LD
Written express	Math	• ADHD with LD
• Organizational	Fine Motor	• ADHD without LD
Perceptual		

Admissions Process

Once a week the Admissions Committee meets including the LD Director to look at applications. We accept, reject or ask for other kinds of information. We may also request an interview or visit.

Learning Disability Program

Special orientation for LD students: **Yes**
Program: Reinforces course work: **Yes**
Students mainstreamed **100** % of the day
Recommended credits per semester: **12**
Time required or recommended in learning center: **1+ hours**
Counseling: Individual: **Yes**

Faculty:
Faculty: **1** Including Director: **Yes** Full time: **1** M.A.: **1**
Meets with instructor: **As needed**

Diagnostic Testing

ADD	Personality	Perceptual skills	• Spelling
ADHD	Organization	Fine motor skills	• Reading
I.Q.	Handwriting	Spoken language	• Study skills
Math	Social skills	• Written language	

Tutoring:
Average size of group tutorials: **1-5**
Services rendered by:
•Graduates   Peers   Faculty   LD staff   Teacher trainees

Tutorials

Grp.	Ind.	Tutorials	Grp.	Ind.	Tutorials
•	•	Math skills			Word processing
•	•	Study skills	•	•	Time management
		Language arts	•	•	Learning strategies
		Written express	•	•	Organizational skills

Academic Accommodations

Curriculum	Study Aids	Exams
• Priority registration	Typist	• Oral
Math waiver	• Reader	• Untimed
Foreign lang. waiver	• Notetaker	• Take home
Course substitution	• Proof reader	• With proctor
In Class	• Text on tape	• On computer
• Calculators	• Early syllabus	• Extended time
• Tape recorder	• Taped handouts	• On tape
• Word processor		• Modified
• Priority seating		• Separate room

Graduation Requirements:
Course credits: **60** GPA: **2.0** Years to complete degree: **2-3**

Program Strengths

I worked with LD students in public schools before coming here and so I have experience and endorsement. I am able to spend the necessary time with each person to establish a relationship. As their advisor and support person, I oversee and coordinate each individual's program.

General Information:

Suomi College is a 2 year private Lutheran college. Rural campus 100 miles from Marquette. Accessible by air or bus. Ski areas are 1 mile from campus. Beaches are 1 mile from campus. 10% of students are foreign. 3 residential halls on campus. Housing is guaranteed.90 % of students remain on campus for the weekends.

Accreditation:NCACS, MCCA, MDPI

Expenses:
Tuition: In-state: Full year: $7,400.00. Part-time: Per credit:$240.00 .
Room and board: $2,078.00

Majors

• ARTS Dramatic Arts, Music, Photography, Theater Design • BUSINESS Accounting, Banking/Finance, Bookkeeping, Business Administration, Business Education, Business Management, Clerical, Data Processing, Education, Food Management, Hotel & Restaurant Management, Human Resources Management, Secretarial Science, Small Business Management, Sports Management, Travel/Tourism Management • COMMUNICATIONS English • COMPUTER SCIENCE Business Data Programming, Computer Information Systems, Computer Technology, Data Processing, Programming • CRAFTS AND DESIGN Textile/Weaving • EDUCATION

Elementary, Pre Ed, English, English As A Second Language, Foreign Language, General, Secondary, Pre Ed • HEALTH SCIENCES Nursing • HUMANITIES English/Writing/Literature, Fine Arts, Humanities, Liberal Arts , Philosophy, Religion • LANGUAGES Finnish • PRE PROFESSIONAL Health Science, Law, Pre-technology, Sports Medicine • RELIGIOUS STUDIES Philosophy, Religion & Theology • SOCIAL SCIENCES Anthropology, Criminal Justice, Geography, History, Human Service, Law Enforcement, Psychology, Public Relations, Social Sciences, Sociology • VISUAL AND PERFORMING ARTS Fine Arts, Theater

Sports/Activities

• SPORTS-INTRAMURAL Badminton, Basketball, Canoeing, Cycling, Figure Skating, Golf, Horseback Riding, Ice Hockey, Martial Arts, Ping-Pong, Racquetball, Skiing - Cross Country, Skiing - Snow, Swimming, Tennis, Volleyball, Weight Lifting • STUDENT LIFE ACTIVITIES Community Service, Ethnic & Cultural Groups, Magazine, Student Government

Most Selective   **Michigan Program**

University of Michigan
1220 Student Activities Building
Ann Arbor, Michigan 48109-1316
(313) 764-7433

School Enrollment: **23,156** Male: **12,191** Female: **10,965**
LD Enrollment: **65** Male: **40** Female: **25**

Admissions Contact: **Rhonda Gilmore, Admissions Counselor**
LD Contact: **John W. Hagen, Ph.D., Director**
Name of Program: **LD Program**
Telephone:**(313) 998-7195**

Admissions

Application Information:
Application deadline: **Feruary 1st**
Applicant must apply **3-4** months in advance
Rolling Admissions: **Yes**

Secondary School Information
Most Important Criteria For Admissions (1-strongest)

4	SAT/ACT	6	Application	3	School transcript
5	Class rank	2	Course selection	8	Personal statement
11	Interview	9	Extra activities	7	Psychoeducational
1	G.P.A.		Open admission	10	Recommendations

Test Requirements:
Diagnostic testing waived: **Yes**
Untimed SAT: **Yes** Untimed ACT: **Yes**
Documentation of LD required: **Yes**
Currency of diagnostic testing: **Current**
Tests recommended: **Appropriate for individual**

Types of Disabilities Served
• Speech/Lang   • Reading   ADD with LD
• Study skills   • Spelling   ADD without LD
• Written express   • Math   ADHD with LD
• Organizational   Fine Motor   ADHD without LD
• Perceptual

High School Course Requirements:
English: **4** Math: **3** Science: **2-3** Foreign Language: **2-3**
Waivers to standard high school courses
Foreign Language : **Yes**

Learning Disability Program
Program: Remedial: **Yes**
Program: Reinforces course work: **Yes**
Students mainstreamed **100** % of the day
Counseling: Individual: **Yes**

Faculty:
Faculty: **3** Full time: **3**
Faculty advocate: **Yes** Meets with instructor: **As needed**

Diagnostic Testing
ADD	•	Personality		Perceptual skills	•	Spelling
ADHD	•	Organization	•	Fine motor skills	•	Reading
• I.Q.		Handwriting	•	Spoken language	•	Study skills
• Math		Social skills	•	Written language		

Tutoring:
Services rendered by:
Graduates   Peers   Faculty   •LD staff   Teacher trainees

Tutorials
Grp.	Ind.	Tutorials	Grp.	Ind.	Tutorials
•	•	Math skills	•	•	Word processing
•	•	Study skills	•	•	Time management
•	•	Language arts	•	•	Learning strategies
•	•	Written express	•	•	Organizational skills

Academic Accommodations
Curriculum	Study Aids	Exams
Priority registration	Typist	• Oral
Math waiver	Reader	Untimed
• Foreign lang. waiver	Notetaker	Take home
Course substitution	Proof reader	With proctor
In Class	• Text on tape	On computer
Calculators	Early syllabus	• Extended time
• Tape recorder	Taped handouts	On tape
• Word processor		Modified
Priority seating		Separate room

Graduation Requirements:
Course credits: **120** GPA: **2.0** Years to complete degree: **Indefinite** Math waiver: **Yes** Language waiver: **Yes**

Program Strengths
The program is based on a cognitive developmental model and includes a coordinator and learning specialists who work closely with students especially in the freshman year. The emphasis is on skill development with special attention paid to reading and study skills, writing, and time management. The learning specialists are trained to administer exams to the students with appropriate modifications in time and format.

General Information:
University of Michigan is a 4 year public university. Urban campus of 2540 acres is 39 miles from Detroit. Accessible by bus. Ski areas are 2 miles from campus. Beaches are 1 miles from campus. 1.6% of students are foreign. 22 residential halls on campus. Housing is not guaranteed.66 % of students remain on campus for the weekends.

Accreditation:NCACS

SAT/ACT Scores:
Scores for incoming freshmen:

Class Rank:
About 88% of the present freshmen class were in the upper 20% of their high school class. 12% were in the top 40% of their class.

Michigan

Expenses:
Tuition: In-state: Full year: $1,683.00. Tuition: Out-of-state: Full year: $5,937.00.

Majors
• AREA STUDIES African, American, Asian, Black/Afro-American, Ethics, Latin American, Middle Eastern, Russian/Slavic, Women's Studies • BUSINESS Accounting, Banking, Business Administration, Business Management, Economics, Finance, International Business, Labor Relations, Management, Marketing, Marketing Research, Personnel, Real Estate, Sports Management • COMMUNICATIONS Advertising, Broadcasting, Communication, Creative Writing, English, Graphic Design, Journalism, Photography, Television/Radio/Film • COMPUTER SCIENCE Computer Science, Data Processing • CRAFTS AND DESIGN Ceramics • EDUCATION Art, Curriculum, Early Childhood, Elementary, English, Health, Middle School, Music, Physical, Psychology, School Psychology, Science, Secondary, Special, Speech/Language • ENGINEERING Aerospace, Chemical, Civil/Environmental, Computer, Engineering Science, Industrial, Mechanical, Metallurgical, Naval Architecture, Nuclear, Ocean • HEALTH SCIENCES Dental Hygiene, Environmental, Health, Nursing, Physical Therapy, Radiological Therapy • HUMANITIES Philosophy, Religion • LANGUAGES Arabic, Chinese, French, German, Greek, Hebrew, Italian, Japanese, Latin, Russian, Spanish • PREPROFESSIONAL Architecture, Dentistry, Engineering, Forestry, Law, Medicine, Natural Resources, Pharmacy, Social Work • SCIENCES Astronomy, Biochemistry, Biology, Biophysics, Botany, Cell Biology, Chemistry, Ecology, Geology, Inorganic Chemistry, Marine Biology, Mathematics, Meteorology, Microbiology, Molecular Biology, Oceanography, Organic Chemistry, Physical Science, Physics, Physiology, Zoology • SOCIAL SCIENCES Anthropology, Geography, Government/Political, History, Political Science, Psychology, Social Sciences, Sociology • VISUAL AND PERFORMING ARTS Art, Art History, Dance, Music, Studio Art, Theater • VOCATIONAL Interior Design, Jewelry-Metalsmithery, Landscape Architecture, Printing/Lithography

Sports/Activities
• SPORTS RELATED Marching Band, Pep Band • SPORTS-INTERCOLLEGIATE Baseball (M), Basketball, Cross Country, Diving, Field Hockey (M), Football (M), Golf, Gymnastics, Ice Hockey (M), Softball (F), Swimming, Tennis, Track and Field, Volleyball (F), Wrestling (M) • SPORTS-INTRAMURAL Archery, Badminton, Baseball (M), Basketball, Crew, Golf, Hand Ball, Ice Hockey (M), Lacrosse (M), Ping-Pong, Racquetball, Rugby (M), Sailing (M), Skiing - Snow (M), Soccer (M), Softball, Squash, Swimming, Tennis, Track and Field, Volleyball, Water Polo • STUDENT LIFE ACTIVITIES Choral, Concert Band, Dance, Drama Groups, Film, Fraternities, Jazz Band, Magazine, Music Groups, Musical Theater, Newspaper, Opera, Radio/TV station, Sororities, Student Government, Symphony Orchestra, Yearbook

Very Selective	Michigan Accommodations

University of Michigan: Flint
Flint, Michigan 48502
(313) 762-3450

School Enrollment: **6,400**

Admissions Contact: **David James, Director of Admissions**

Admissions

Application Information:
Application deadline: **Late August or late Dec.**
Rolling Admissions: **Yes**

Secondary School Information
Most Important Criteria For Admissions (1-strongest)

4 SAT/ACT	**11** Application	**2**	School transcript
6 Class rank	**3** Course selection	**9**	Personal statement
7 Interview	**8** Extra activities	**10**	Psychoeducational
1 G.P.A.	Open admission	**5**	Recommendations

Test Requirements:
Untimed SAT: **Yes** Untimed ACT: **Yes**

Types of Disabilities Served
• Speech/Lang	• Reading	• ADD with LD
• Study skills	• Spelling	• ADD without LD
• Written express	• Math	• ADHD with LD
• Organizational	• Fine Motor	• ADHD without LD
• Perceptual		

Admissions Process
Academic computed G.P.A. must be 2.7 or greater with 20 academic courses over 3 years of high school.

High School Course Requirements:
English: **4** Math: **3** Science: **3** Foreign Language: **2**

Diagnostic Testing
ADD	Personality	Perceptual skills	Spelling
ADHD	Organization	Fine motor skills	Reading
I.Q.	Handwriting	Spoken language	Study skills
Math	Social skills	Written language	

Tutoring:
Average size of group tutorials: **1:1 mostly**
Services rendered by:
Graduates •Peers Faculty LD staff Teacher trainees

Tutorials
Grp.	Ind.	Tutorials	Grp.	Ind.	Tutorials
		Math skills			Word processing
	•	Study skills		•	Time management
		Language arts			Learning strategies
		Written express			Organizational skills

Academic Accommodations

Curriculum	Study Aids	Exams
Priority registration	Typist	Oral
Math waiver	• Reader	• Untimed
Foreign lang. waiver	• Notetaker	Take home
Course substitution	Proof reader	With proctor
In Class	• Text on tape	On computer
• Calculators	Early syllabus	• Extended time
• Tape recorder	Taped handouts	On tape
Word processor		Modified
Priority seating		Separate room

Graduation Requirements:
Course credits: **Varies** GPA: **2.0**

Program Strengths
We work with students within our school program and try to accommodate the best we can.

General Information:
University of Michigan: Flint is a 4 year public university. Urban campus Flint. Accessible by air, train or bus. Ski areas are 25 miles from campus.

Beaches are 6 miles from campus. 1% of students are foreign. Housing is not guaranteed.25 % of students join fraternities/sororities.

Accreditation:NCACS

SAT/ACT Scores:
Scores for incoming freshmen: **ACT:** 5% below 20. 30% between 20 and 23. 30%between 24 and 251. 30%between 26 and 28. 5% above 28.

Class Rank:
About 30% of the present freshmen class were in the upper 20% of their high school class. 30% were in the top 40% of their class. 10% were in the top 60% of their class. 20% were in the top 80% of their class.

Expenses:
Tuition: In-state: Full year: $1,264.00 per semester. Part-time: Per credit:$102.00 plus $40.00 registration fee. Tuition: Out-of-state: Full year: $3,800.00. Part-time: Per credit:$319.00.

Majors

• ARTS Music • BUSINESS Accounting, Banking/Finance, Business Administration, Business Management, Economics, Marketing • HEALTH SCIENCES Nursing, Physical Therapy • LANGUAGES English, French, German, Spanish • PRE PROFESSIONAL Dentistry, Law, Medicine, Pharmacy • SCIENCES Biology, Chemistry, Computer Science, Geography, Physical Science, Physics • SOCIAL SCIENCES Anthropology, Criminal Justice, History, Political Science, Psychology, Social Sciences, Sociology • VISUAL AND PERFORMING ARTS Fine Arts, Music, Theater

Sports/Activities

• SPORTS-INTRAMURAL Basketball (M)

Less Selective

Michigan Services

Washtenaw Community College
P.O. Box D-1
Ann Arbor, Michigan 48106-0978
(313) 973-3542

School Enrollment: **10,121** Male: **4,655** Female: **5,465**

Admissions Contact: **Bradley D. Hoth, Admissions Representative**
LD Contact: **Marjorie Cash, Coordinator**
Name of Program: **Special Needs Office**
Telephone:**(313) 973-3342**

Admissions

Application Information:
Application deadline: **Rolling**
Rolling Admissions: **Yes**

Secondary School Information
Most Important Criteria For Admissions (1-strongest)

SAT/ACT	Application	School transcript
Class rank	Course selection	Personal statement
Interview	Extra activities	Psychoeducational
G.P.A.	**1** Open admission	Recommendations

Test Requirements:
Standardized tests waived: **Yes**

Types of Disabilities Served
• Speech/Lang	• Reading	• ADD with LD
• Study skills	• Spelling	• ADD without LD
• Written express	• Math	• ADHD with LD
• Organizational	• Fine Motor	• ADHD without LD
• Perceptual		

Learning Disability Program
Counseling: Individual: **Yes**

Faculty:
Faculty: **5** Full time: **2** Part time: **3**
Faculty advocate: **Yes** Meets with instructor: **As needed**

Diagnostic Testing
ADD	Personality	Perceptual skills	Spelling
ADHD	Organization	Fine motor skills	Reading
I.Q.	Handwriting	Spoken language	Study skills
Math	Social skills	Written language	

Tutoring:
Average size of group tutorials: **2-3**
Services rendered by:

Graduates	•Peers	Faculty	•LD staff	Teacher trainees

Tutorials
Grp.	Ind. Tutorials	Grp.	Ind. Tutorials
	• Math skills		• Word processing
	• Study skills		• Time management
	• Language arts		• Learning strategies
	• Written express		• Organizational skills

Academic Accommodations

Curriculum	Study Aids	Exams
Priority registration	Typist	• Oral
Math waiver	Reader	Untimed
Foreign lang. waiver	• Notetaker	Take home
Course substitution	Proof reader	With proctor
In Class	• Text on tape	On computer
Calculators	Early syllabus	• Extended time
• Tape recorder	Taped handouts	On tape
Word processor		Modified
Priority seating		Separate room

Program Strengths
We serve approximately 30 LD students every semester as part of our special needs program. The LD component is not separate nor is it a special program. We have three part-time professional LD tutors who work with the students who enroll in regular classes/programs here at WCC. There is no cost to the student for support services.

General Information:
Washtenaw Community College is a 2 year public college. Suburban campus of 126 acres is 3 miles from Ann Arbor. Accessible by bus. Ski areas are 1 hour from campus. Beaches are 1 hour from campus. 2% of students are foreign. Housing is not guaranteed.

Accreditation:NCACS

Expenses:
Tuition: In-state: Full year: $1,020.00. Part-time: Per credit:$34.00. Tuition: Out-of-state: Full year: $1,560.00. Part-time: Per credit:$52.00.

Majors
• AREA STUDIES Black/Afro-American • BUSINESS Accounting, Busi-

Michigan

ness Administration, Business Management, Food Management, Hotel and Restaurant Managemen, Management, Marketing • COMMUNICATIONS Creative Writing, English, Graphic Design Technology, Photography • COMPUTER SCIENCE Computer Science, Data Processing, Programming, Robotics, Telecommunications • EDUCATION Child Development • ENGINEERING Air Conditioning Technology, Engineering Science, Mechanical • HEALTH SCIENCES Dental Assistant, Medical Assistant, Nursing, Nursing Assistant, Practical Nursing, Radiological Therapy, Ultrasound Technology • HUMANITIES Humanities, Liberal Arts, Philosophy • LANGUAGES French, German, Italian, Russian, Spanish • PREPROFESSIONAL Architecture, Engineering • SCIENCES Astronomy, Biology, Chemistry, Earth, Geography, Geology, Mathematics, Physical Chemistry, Physical Science, Physics • SOCIAL SCIENCES Anthropology, Criminal Justice, Government/Political, History, Law Enforcement, Psychology, Public Relations, Social Sciences, Sociology • VISUAL AND PERFORMING ARTS Art, Music, Studio Art, Theater • VOCATIONAL Air Condtioning/Heating/Refrig, Automated Manufacturing Techno, Automobile Technology, Business and Office, Dental Assistant, Drafting, Fire Science, Food Service, Radiological Technology, Respiratory Therapy Technology, Secretarial, Welding, Word Processing

Sports/Activities

• STUDENT LIFE ACTIVITIES Dance, Drama Groups, Jazz Band, Newspaper, Student Government

---

Less Selective   **Michigan**

Wayne State University
583 Student Center Building
Detroit, Michigan 48202
(313) 577-3398

School Enrollment: **34,000** Male: **15,565** Female: **18,435**

Admissions Contact: **Ronald Hughes, Director of Admissions**
LD Contact: **Marge Chmielewski ,Coordinator, ERSD**
Name of Program: **Ed. Resources for Students with Disabilities**
Address: **583 Student Center Building**
Telephone:**(313) 577-3398**

Admissions

Application Information:
Rolling Admissions: **Yes**

Secondary School Information
Most Important Criteria For Admissions (1-strongest)

2 SAT/ACT	**3** Application	**4** School transcript
Class rank	Course selection	Personal statement
Interview	Extra activities	Psychoeducational
1 G.P.A.	Open admission	Recommendations

Test Requirements:
Untimed SAT: **Yes** Untimed ACT: **Yes**
Documentation of LD required: **Yes**
Tests recommended: **Disability must be certified by M.D. or other professional licensed to diagnose and treat**

Types of Disabilities Served
• Speech/Lang	• Reading	• ADD with LD
• Study skills	• Spelling	• ADD without LD
• Written express	• Math	• ADHD with LD
• Organizational	• Fine Motor	• ADHD without LD
• Perceptual		

Admissions Process

Students follow same admissions process as all other students. They must register with ERSR Office 6 weeks prior to starting classes.

High School Course Requirements:
English: **4** Math: **4** Science: **3** Foreign Language: **2**
Waivers to standard high school courses
Foreign Language : **Yes** Math: **Yes** Course substitution: **Yes**

Learning Disability Program
Time required or recommended in learning center: **varies**
Services available for all students: **Yes**

Faculty:
Faculty: **1** Including Director: **Yes** Part time: **6** M.A.: **1**
Faculty advocate: **Yes** Meets with instructor: **As needed**

Diagnostic Testing
ADD	• Personality	Perceptual skills	Spelling
ADHD	Organization	Fine motor skills	• Reading
• I.Q.	Handwriting	Spoken language	• Study skills
Math	Social skills	Written language	

Tutoring:
Average size of group tutorials: **10**
Services rendered by:
•Graduates •Peers •Faculty   LD staff   Teacher trainees

Tutorials
Grp.	Ind.	Tutorials	Grp.	Ind.	Tutorials
•	•	Math skills		•	Word processing
•	•	Study skills	•	•	Time management
		Language arts	•	•	Learning strategies
•	•	Written express	•	•	Organizational skills

Academic Accommodations
Curriculum	Study Aids	Exams
• Priority registration	• Typist	• Oral
• Math waiver	• Reader	Untimed
• Foreign lang. waiver	• Notetaker	Take home
Course substitution	Proof reader	With proctor
In Class	• Text on tape	On computer
Calculators	Early syllabus	• Extended time
• Tape recorder	Taped handouts	• On tape
Word processor		Modified
Priority seating		• Separate room

Graduation Requirements:
Course credits: **120** GPA: **2.0** Years to complete degree: **Varies** Math waiver: **Yes** Language waiver: **Yes**

General Information:
Wayne State University is a 4 year public university. Urban campus of 185 acres is Detroit. Accessible by car or bus Ski areas are 5-100 miles from campus. Beaches are 5-100 miles from campus. 6% of students are foreign. Housing is not guaranteed.

Accreditation:NCACS

Expenses:
Tuition: In-state: Full year: $1,481.00. Part-time: Per credit:$119.00. Tuition: Out-of-state: Full year: $3,152.00. Part-time: Per credit:$258.00.

Majors
• AREA STUDIES American, Black/Afro-American • BUSINESS Accounting, Business Administration, Business Economics, Management,

Management Information System, Marketing • COMPUTER SCIENCE Computer Science • EDUCATION Adult, Art, Bilingual, Counseling, Curriculum, Elementary, English, Foreign Language, General, Health, Industrial, Leadership, Mathematics, Music, Physical, Psychology, Reading, Recreation and Park Services, School Psychology, Science, Secondary, Social Studies, Special, Speech/Language, Vocational • ENGINEERING Chemical, Civil/Environment, Computer, Electrical, Environmental/Water Resources, Industrial, Materials, Mechanical • HEALTH SCIENCES Occupational Therapy, Pharmacology, Physical Therapy, Radiological Therapy • HUMANITIES Classics, English/Writing/Literature, Fine Arts, Humanities, Liberal Arts , Philosophy • LANGUAGES English, French, German, Greek, Hebrew, Italian, Latin, Linguistic, Polish, Russian • MATHEMATICS Applied, Statistical • PRE PROFESSIONAL Social Work • SCIENCES Anatomy, Anthropology, Applied Mathematics, Biochemistry, Biology, Biophysics, Cell Biology, Chemical, Computer Science, Geography, Geology, Inorganic Chemistry, Mathematics, Molecular Biology, Organic Chemistry • SOCIAL SCIENCES Anthropology, Criminal Justice, Family Counseling, Geography, History, Library Science, Political Science, Psychology, Public Relations, Sociology • SPECIAL EDUCATION Audiology, Deaf/Hearing Impaired, Occupational Therapy • VISUAL AND PERFORMING ARTS Art, Art History, Dance, Dance Education, Film , Museum Practice, Music, Music Performance, Music Theatre, Radio &Television , Theater

Sports/Activities

• SPORTS RELATED Baton Twirling, Cheerleading, Chess, Drum Major/ Majorette, Marching Band, Pep Band, Team Managers • SPORTS-INTERCOLLEGIATE Baaeball (M), Cross Country (M), Fencing (F), Fencing (M), Football (M), Golf (M), Swimming • SPORTS-INTRAMURAL Basketball (F), Basketball (M), Football, Touch, Ping-Pong, Racquetball, Soccer, Softball (F), Tennis, Volleyball, Wallyball • STUDENT LIFE ACTIVITIES Academic Club, Choral, Community Service, Concert Band, Dance, Debate, Drama Groups, Ethnic & Cultural Groups, Film, Fraternities, Jazz Band, Magazine, Music Groups, Musical Theater, Newspaper, Orchestra, Political Groups, Radio/TV station, Religious Organization, Sororities, Student Government, Symphony Orchestra, Yearbook

Selective	Michigan Program

Western Michigan University
Kalamazoo, Michigan 49008
(616) 387-2000

School Enrollment: **19,927** Male: **9,473** Female: **10,454**
LD Enrollment: **89** Male: **50** Female: **39**

Admissions Contact: **Stanley Henderson, Director of Admissions**
LD Contact: **Kate Welser, LD Coordinator**
Name of Program: **Special Services Program**
Address: **1044 Moore Hall**
Telephone: **(616) 387-4440**

Admissions

Application Information:
Enrolled: **81**
Application deadline: **None**
Rolling Admissions: **Yes**

Secondary School Information
Most Important Criteria For Admissions (1-strongest)

1 SAT/ACT	Application	School transcript
Class rank	Course selection	Personal statement
Interview	Extra activities	Psychoeducational
2 G.P.A.	Open admission	Recommendations

Test Requirements:
Untimed ACT: **Yes** Untimed ACH: **Yes**
Documentation of LD required: **Yes**
Tests recommended: **LD Documentation**

Types of Disabilities Served
• Speech/Lang	• Reading	• ADD with LD
• Study skills	• Spelling	• ADD without LD
• Written express	• Math	ADHD with LD
• Organizational	• Fine Motor	ADHD without LD
• Perceptual		

Learning Disability Program

Program: Reinforces course work: **Yes**
Students mainstreamed **100** % of the day
Counseling: Individual: **Yes**

Faculty:
Faculty: **3** Full time: **1** Part time: **2**
LD faculty with: BS/BA: **1.5** M.A.: **1**
Faculty advocate: **Yes** Meets with instructor: **As needed**

Diagnostic Testing
ADD	Personality	Perceptual skills	Spelling
ADHD	Organization	Fine motor skills	Reading
I.Q.	Handwriting	Spoken language	• Study skills
Math	Social skills	Written language	

Tutoring:
Services rendered by:
•Graduates •Peers Faculty •LD staff Teacher trainees

Tutorials
Grp.	Ind.	Tutorials	Grp.	Ind.	Tutorials
	•	Math skills		•	Word processing
•		Study skills	•		Time management
	•	Language arts		•	Learning strategies
	•	Written express	•		Organizational skills

Academic Accommodations

Curriculum	Study Aids	Exams
• Priority registration	Typist	Oral
Math waiver	• Reader	Untimed
Foreign lang. waiver	• Notetaker	Take home
Course substitution	• Proof reader	With proctor
In Class	• Text on tape	On computer
• Calculators	Early syllabus	• Extended time
• Tape recorder	Taped handouts	On tape
Word processor		Modified
Priority seating		• Separate room

Graduation Requirements:
Course credits: **122** GPA: **2.0**

Program Strengths

The Special Services Program is a federally funded TRIO project that seeks to assist physically handicapped, learning disabled, low-income, and first generation college students in ways that contribute to graduation from the University. It provides academic support and offers guidance toward achieving a balance among academic, social, financial, and career concerns.

General Information:

Western Michigan University is a 4 year public university. Urban campus. Accessible by air, train, or bus. Ski areas are 10 miles from campus. Beaches are 35 miles from campus. 22 residential halls on campus. Housing is not

Minnesota

guaranteed.

Accreditation:NCACS

Expenses:
Tuition: In-state: Full year: $2,130.00. Room and board: $3,060.00

Majors

• AREA STUDIES African, American, Asian, European, Latin American, Urban • BUSINESS Accounting, Agricultural, Banking, Business Administration, Business Communications, Business Economics, Business Education, Business Management, Economics, Finance, Food Management, Insurance, International Business, Management, Marketing, Real Estate, Retailing, Travel/Tourism Management • COMMUNICATIONS Advertising, English, Linguistics, Speech • COMPUTER SCIENCE Computer Science • EDUCATION Agricultural, Art, Elementary, English, Foreign Language, Health, Industrial, Marketing and Distributive Education, Mathematics, Middle School, Music, Music Therapy, Physical, Science, Secondary, Social Studies, Special, Technical • ENGINEERING Aerospace, Computer, Industrial, Mechanical, Metallurgical, Paper • HEALTH SCIENCES Environmental, Health, Medical Assistant, Nutritional/Food, Occupational Therapy, Speech Therapy, Speech/Audiology and Speech • HUMANITIES Humanities, Liberal Arts, Philosophy, Religion • LANGUAGES French, German, Latin, Spanish • PREPROFESSIONAL Dentistry, Law, Medicine, Social Work • SCIENCES Agricultural, Biology, Biomedical, Chemistry, Earth, Geography, Geology, Geophysics and Seismology, Mathematics, Physical Science, Physics, Statistics • SOCIAL SCIENCES Anthropology, Criminal Justice, Government/Political, History, Political Science, Psychology, Public Relations, Social Sciences, Sociology • VISUAL AND PERFORMING ARTS Dance, Dramatic Arts, Fine Arts, Jazz, Music, Music Performance, Music Theatre • VOCATIONAL Automobile Technology, Automotive Service, Drafting, Fashion Merchandising, Home Economics, Interior Design, Park/Recreation, Piloting, Precision Metal Work, Printing/Lithography, Textile and Clothing, Woodworking

Sports/Activities

SPORTS RELATED Marching Band, Pep Band • SPORTS-INTERCOLLEGIATE Baseball (M), Basketball, Cross Country, Football (M), Gymnastics, Ice Hockey (M), Soccer (M), Softball (F), Tennis, Track and Field, Volleyball (F) • SPORTS-INTRAMURAL Badminton, Basketball, Bowling, Golf, Ice Hockey (M), Lacrosse, Ping-Pong, Racquetball, Riflery, Sailing, Skiing - Snow, Soccer, Softball, Swimming, Tennis, Track and Field, Volleyball, Water Polo, Wrestling (M) • STUDENT LIFE ACTIVITIES Choral, Concert Band, Dance, Drama Groups, Ethnic & Cultural Groups, Film, Fraternities, Jazz Band, Magazine, Music Groups, Musical Theater, Newspaper, Opera, Political Groups, Radio/TV station, Religious Organization, Sororities, Student Government, Symphony Orchestra, Yearbook

Augsburg College
731 21st Avenue
Minneapolis, Minnesota 55454
(612) 330-1001

School Enrollment: **1,672** Male: **737** Female: **935**
LD Enrollment: **102** Male: **64** Female: **38**

Admissions Contact: **Sally Daniels, Director of Admissions**
LD Contact: **Sue Carlson, Coordinator**
Name of Program: **C.L.A.S.S.**
Address: **731-21st Avenue S.**
Telephone:**(612) 330-1053**

Admissions

Application Information:
Application deadline: **August 1st**
Applicant must apply **2** months in advance
Rolling Admissions: **Yes**Notified when: **Rolling**

Secondary School Information
Most Important Criteria For Admissions (1-strongest)

SAT/ACT		Application	**1** School transcript
Class rank	**1**	Course selection	**2** Personal statement
Interview		Extra activities	**2** Psychoeducational
1 G.P.A.		Open admission	Recommendations

Test Requirements:
Diagnostic testing waived: **Yes**
Untimed SAT: **Yes** Untimed ACT: **Yes**
WAIS-R required: **Yes**
Documentation of LD required: **Yes**
Currency of diagnostic testing: **within last 3 years**
Tests recommended: **Ability, Achievement and I.Q.**

Types of Disabilities Served
• Speech/Lang • Reading • ADD with LD
• Study skills • Spelling ADD without LD
• Written express • Math • ADHD with LD
• Organizational • Fine Motor ADHD without LD
• Perceptual

High School Course Requirements:
Waivers to standard high school courses
Foreign Language : **Yes** Course substitution: **Yes**

Learning Disability Program
Special orientation for LD students: **Yes**
Syllabus available during orientation:**Yes**
Program: Remedial: **Yes**
Program: Reinforces course work: **Yes**
Students mainstreamed **100** % of the day
Time required or recommended in learning center: **1 hour**
Counseling: Individual: **Yes** Group Counseling: **Yes** Vocational Counseling: **Yes**
Support groups are available:**Resource Group meets weekly Fall and Spring semesters**

Faculty:
Faculty: **4** Including Director: **Yes** Full time: **4** M.A.: **4**
Faculty advocate: **Yes** Meets with instructor: **As needed**

Diagnostic Testing
ADD	Personality	Perceptual skills	Spelling
ADHD	Organization	Fine motor skills	Reading
I.Q.	Handwriting	Spoken language	Study skills
Math	Social skills	Written language	

Tutoring:
Average size of group tutorials: **3-5**
Services rendered by:
 Graduates •Peers Faculty •LD staff Teacher trainees

Tutorials
Grp.	Ind.	Tutorials	Grp.	Ind.	Tutorials
•	•	Math skills	•	•	Word processing
•	•	Study skills	•	•	Time management
•	•	Language arts	•	•	Learning strategies
•	•	Written express	•	•	Organizational skills

Academic Accommodations

Curriculum	Study Aids	Exams
Priority registration	• Typist	• Oral
• Math waiver	• Reader	Untimed
• Foreign lang. waiver	• Notetaker	• Take home
Course substitution	• Proof reader	• With proctor
In Class	• Text on tape	On computer
• Calculators	Early syllabus	• Extended time
• Tape recorder	Taped handouts	On tape
• Word processor		• Modified
Priority seating		Separate room

Graduation Requirements: GPA: 2.5 Math waiver: **Yes** Language waiver: **Yes**

Program Strengths
We strive for maximum student-advisor contact. We pride ourselves on being the only private-four year liberal arts college in Minnesota with a specific program for the support of learning disabled students. Our commitment to diversity has been ahead of its time. We began our program in 1982-83 and have continued to grow. We now have over 100 learning disabled students on campus with a high graduation rate among our students. We are a caring, supportive program that encourages self-advocacy and independence.

General Information:
Augsburg College is a 4 year private Evangelical Lutheran Church in college. Urban campus of 28 acres is Minneapolis. Accessible by air, train, or bus. Ski areas are 30 miles from campus. 4% of students are foreign. 2 residential halls on campus. Housing is not guaranteed.

Accreditation: NCACS

Class Rank:
About 30% of the present freshmen class were in the upper 20% of their high school class. 53% were in the top 40% of their class. 75% were in the top 60% of their class. 100% were in the top 80% of their class.

Expenses:
Tuition: In-state: Full year: $10,148.00. Part-time: Per course: $768.00.
Room and board: $3,832.00

Majors
• AREA STUDIES East Asian, Russian/Slavic, Scandinavian, Urban
• BUSINESS Accounting, Banking, Business Administration, Business Economics, Business Management, Economics, Finance, International Business, Management, Marketing • COMMUNICATIONS Communication, English, Speech • COMPUTER SCIENCE Computer Science • EDUCATION Art, Elementary, Health, Music, Music Therapy, Physical, Secondary • HEALTH SCIENCES Nursing, Occupational Therapy • HUMANITIES Humanities, Philosophy, Religion • LANGUAGES French, German, Japanese, Norwegian, Russian, Spanish • PREPROFESSIONAL Dentistry, Engineering, Law, Medicine, Ministry, Pharmacy, Social Work • SCIENCES Biology, Chemistry, Mathematics, Physical Science, Physics, Space Physics • SOCIAL SCIENCES Government/Political, History, International Studies, Political Science, Psychology, Social Sciences, Sociology • VISUAL AND PERFORMING ARTS Art, Art History, Dramatic Arts, Music, Music Performance, Studio Art, Theater

Sports/Activities
• SPORTS RELATED Cheerleading • SPORTS-INTERCOLLEGIATE Baseball (M), Basketball, Football (M), Ice Hockey (M), Track and Field, Wrestling (M) • SPORTS-INTRAMURAL Basketball, Racquetball, Softball, Tennis (M), Volleyball • STUDENT LIFE ACTIVITIES Choral, Community Service, Concert Band, Debate, Drama Groups, Ethnic & Cultural Groups, Jazz Band, Magazine, Music Groups, Newspaper, Radio/TV station, Religious Organization, Student Government, Symphony Orchestra, Yearbook

---

Selective — **Minnesota Services**

College of St. Catherine: St. Catherine Campus
2004 Randolph Avenue
St. Paul, Minnesota 55105
(612) 690-6505

School Enrollment: **1,606**

Admissions Contact: **Cindy Kalahar, Admission Counselor**
LD Contact: **Elaine McDonough**
Name of Program: **Learning Disability Service**
Telephone: **(612) 609-6563**

Admissions

Application Information:
Application deadline: **None**
Rolling Admissions: **Yes** Notified when: **within 2 weeks**

Secondary School Information
Most Important Criteria For Admissions (1-strongest)
2 SAT/ACT	2 Application	1 School transcript
2 Class rank	1 Course selection	3 Personal statement
3 Interview	3 Extra activities	3 Psychoeducational
1 G.P.A.	Open admission	3 Recommendations

Test Requirements:
Diagnostic testing waived: **Yes**
Untimed SAT: **Yes** Untimed ACT: **Yes**
WAIS-R required: **Yes**
Currency of diagnostic testing: **2 years**

Minnesota

Types of Disabilities Served
- Speech/Lang
- Study skills
- Written express
- Organizational
- Perceptual
- Reading
- Spelling
- Math
- Fine Motor
- ADD with LD
- ADD without LD
- ADHD with LD
- ADHD without LD

Learning Disability Program
Counseling: Individual: **Yes**

Faculty:
Faculty: **1** Full time: **1**
Faculty advocate: **Yes** Meets with instructor: **As needed**

Diagnostic Testing
ADD	Personality	Perceptual skills	Spelling
ADHD	Organization	Fine motor skills	Reading
I.Q.	Handwriting	Spoken language	Study skills
Math	Social skills	Written language	

Tutoring:
Average size of group tutorials: **3-5**
Services rendered by:
Graduates •Peers Faculty •LD staff Teacher trainees

Tutorials
Grp.	Ind.	Tutorials	Grp.	Ind.	Tutorials
	•	Math skills		•	Word processing
•	•	Study skills	•	•	Time management
	•	Language arts	•	•	Learning strategies
•	•	Written express	•	•	Organizational skills

Academic Accommodations
Curriculum	Study Aids	Exams
Priority registration	Typist	• Oral
• Math waiver	Reader	Untimed
• Foreign lang. waiver	Notetaker	• Take home
Course substitution	Proof reader	With proctor
In Class	Text on tape	On computer
• Calculators	Early syllabus	• Extended time
• Tape recorder	Taped handouts	On tape
• Word processor		• Modified
Priority seating		Separate room

Program Strengths
We do not have a formal program for students with learning disabilities. Applicants with learning disabilities apply via the Admissions Office and are invited to meet with the Coordinator of Learning Programs in the Learning Centers. The Learning Centers offer support services to all students and particular support services to students with learning disabilities.

General Information:
College of St. Catherine: St. Catherine Campus is a 4 year private Roman Catholic college. Suburban campus of 110 acres is Accessible by bus. Ski areas are 15 miles from campus. 3% of students are foreign. Housing is guaranteed.

Accreditation:NCACS

SAT/ACT Scores:
Scores for incoming freshmen: **Verbal:** 58% below 500. 32% between 500 and 599. 10% between 600 and 699. **Math:** 65% below 500. 18% between 500 and 599. 13% between 600 and 699. 3% above 700. **ACT:** 32% below 20. 35% between 20 and 23. 13% between 24 and 251. 18% between 26 and 28. 3% above 28.

Class Rank:
About 48% of the present freshmen class were in the upper 20% of their high school class. 79% were in the top 40% of their class. 96% were in the top 60% of their class. 99% were in the top 80% of their class.

Expenses:
Tuition: In-state: Full year: $8,544.00. Part-time: Per credit:$272.00. Room and board: $3,140.00

Majors
- AREA STUDIES Asian, Russian/Slavic, Urban, Women's Studies
- BUSINESS Accounting, Banking, Business Administration, Business Education, Business Management, Economics, Fashion Merchandising, Finance, International Business, Management, Marketing
- COMMUNICATIONS Communication, English, Journalism, Speech
- COMPUTER SCIENCE Telecommunications • EDUCATION Art, Early Childhood, Elementary, English, Foreign Language, Home Economics Education, Mathematics, Middle School, Music, Physical, Secondary, Speech/Language • HEALTH SCIENCES Medical Technology, Nursing, Nutritional/Food, Occupational Therapy, Physical Therapy • HUMANITIES Philosophy, Religion • LANGUAGES French, German, Latin, Russian, Spanish • PREPROFESSIONAL Dentistry, Engineering, Forestry, Law, Medicine, Optometry, Pharmacy, Social Work, Veterinarian • SCIENCES Biochemistry, Biology, Chemistry, Geography, Mathematics, Physics • SOCIAL SCIENCES Government/Political, History, International Studies, Political Science, Psychology, Social Sciences, Sociology • VISUAL AND PERFORMING ARTS Art, Art History, Dramatic Arts, Music, Music Performance, Music Theatre, Studio Art • VOCATIONAL Fashion Mechandizing, Food Service, Home Economics, Medical Laboratory Technology, Textile and Clothing

Sports/Activities
- SPORTS-INTERCOLLEGIATE Basketball, Cross Country, Softball (F)
- SPORTS-INTRAMURAL Basketball (F), Golf (F), Soccer (F), Softball (F), Tennis (F), Volleyball (F) • STUDENT LIFE ACTIVITIES Academic Clubs, Choral, Concert Band, Dance, Drama Groups, Ethnic & Cultural Groups, Jazz Band, Magazine, Music Groups, Musical Theater, Newspaper, Opera, Political Groups, Radio/TV station, Student Government, Symphony Orchestra, Yearbook

---

Less Selective

Minnesota
Accommodations

Concordia College: St. Paul
Hamline & Marshall Aves.
St. Paul, Minnesota 55104
(612) 641-8278

School Enrollment: **1,162** Male: **475** Female: **687**

Admissions Contact: **Tim Utter, Director of Admissions**
LD Contact: **Dr. Eunice Streufert Dir., Student Academic Affairs**
Name of Program: **Study Skills Area**
Address: **275 N. Syndicate**
Telephone:**(612) 641-8278**

Admissions

Application Information:
Rolling Admissions: **Yes**

Secondary School Information

Most Important Criteria For Admissions (1-strongest)

1 SAT/ACT	Application	**5** School transcript
2 Class rank	Course selection	Personal statement
6 Interview	**7** Extra activities	Psychoeducational
3 G.P.A.	Open admission	**4** Recommendations

Test Requirements:

Untimed ACT: **Yes**

Documentation of LD required: **Yes**

Tests recommended: **So far no extra testing is required unless they are not verified as LD by a legitimate testing agency.**

Types of Disabilities Served

Speech/Lang	Reading	ADD with LD
Study skills	Spelling	ADD without LD
Written express	Math	ADHD with LD
Organizational	Fine Motor	ADHD without LD
Perceptual		

Admissions Process

We do not turn down students because of a handicapping condition. We serve their needs if they are accepted according to our admission policies and with recommendation of the committee.

High School Course Requirements:

English: **2** Math: **2** Science: **2**

Learning Disability Program

Program: Reinforces course work: **Yes**

Students mainstreamed **100** % of the day

Recommended credits per semester: **12-18**

Services available for all students: **Yes**

Counseling: Individual: **Yes**

Support groups are available: In **Study Skills Area**

Faculty:

Diagnostic Testing

ADD	Personality	Perceptual skills	Spelling
ADHD	Organization	Fine motor skills	Reading
I.Q.	Handwriting	Spoken language	Study skills
Math	Social skills	Written language	

Tutoring:

Services rendered by:

Graduates	•Peers	Faculty	LD staff	Teacher trainees

Tutorials

Grp.	Ind.	Tutorials	Grp.	Ind.	Tutorials
		Math skills			Word processing
•		Study skills		•	Time management
		Language arts			Learning strategies
	•	Written express			Organizational skills

Academic Accommodations

Curriculum	Study Aids	Exams
Priority registration	Typist	Oral
Math waiver	Reader	• Untimed
Foreign lang. waiver	• Notetaker	Take home
Course substitution	Proof reader	With proctor
In Class	Text on tape	On computer
• Calculators	Early syllabus	• Extended time
• Tape recorder	Taped handouts	On tape
Word processor		Modified
• Priority seating		• Separate room

Graduation Requirements:

Course credits: **198** GPA: **2.0** Years to complete degree: **4**

Program Strengths

We confer, as a team of professionals with the student, to ascertain needs and then write an ICP which the students have professors sign. In this respect they advocate for themselves.

General Information:

Concordia College: St. Paul is a 4 year private Lutheran college. Urban campus of 26 acres is Accessible by air, train or bus. Ski areas are 6 miles from campus. Beaches are 2 miles from campus. 1% of students are foreign. Housing is guaranteed.30 % of students remain on campus for the weekends.

Accreditation:NCACS, NCATE

Expenses:

Tuition: In-state: Full year: $9,000.00. Part-time: Per credit:$250.00. Room and board: $3,180.00

Majors

• ARTS Art, Dramatic Arts, Multicultural, Religious Music • BUSINESS Banking/Finance, Management • COMMUNICATIONS Communication, Literature • EDUCATION Art, Early Childhood, Elementary, English, General, Health, Mathematics, Middle School, Music, Physical, Psychology, Religious, Science, Secondary, Social Studies • HUMANITIES English/Writing/Literature, Liberal Arts , Religion • LANGUAGES Greek, Hebrew • PRE PROFESSIONAL Dentistry, Forestry, Law, Medicine, Social Work, Veterinarian • RELIGIOUS STUDIES Bible, Ministry & Church Administration, Religious Music • SCIENCES Biology, Chemistry, Earth, General, Mathematics, Natural, Physics • SOCIAL SCIENCES Government/Political, History, Psychology, Social Science, Sociology • VISUAL AND PERFORMING ARTS Art, Dramatic Arts, Music

Sports/Activities

• SPORTS RELATED Cheerleading, Drill Team, Pep Band, Team Managers • SPORTS-INTERCOLLEGIATE Baseball (M), Basketball (F), Basketball (M), Cross Country (F), Cross Country (M), Football (M), Soccer (M), Softball (F), Tennis (F), Tennis (M), Volleyball (F) • SPORTS-INTRAMURAL Badminton, Basketball (F), Basketball (M), Bowling, Football (M), Golf, Ice Hockey (M), Ping-Pong, Skiing - Cross Country, Softball, Tennis, Volleyball • STUDENT LIFE ACTIVITIES Academic Clubs, Choral, Concert Band, Drama Groups, Ethnic & Cultural Groups, Jazz Band, Music Groups, Newspaper, Orchestra, Religious Organization, Student Government, Yearbook

Very Selective	Minnesota Services

Hamline University
1536 Hewitt Avenue
St. Paul, Minnesota 55104
(612) 641-2207

School Enrollment: **1,382** Male: **613** Female: **769**

Admissions Contact: **Scott Friedhoff Dean, Undergraduate Ad.**
LD Contact: **Barbara Simmons Director, Study Resource Center**
Name of Program: **Study Resource Center**
Telephone:**(612) 641-2417**

Admissions

Application Information:
Rolling Admissions: **Yes** Notified when:

Secondary School Information
Most Important Criteria For Admissions (1-strongest)

4 SAT/ACT	Application	**1**	School transcript
3 Class rank	**2** Course selection		Personal statement
Interview	**5** Extra activities		Psychoeducational
1 G.P.A.	Open admission	**4**	Recommendations

Test Requirements:
Untimed SAT: **Yes** Untimed ACT: **Yes**

Types of Disabilities Served
- Speech/Lang
- Study skills
- Written express
- Organizational
- Perceptual
- Reading
- Spelling
- Math
- Fine Motor
- ADD with LD
- ADD without LD
- ADHD with LD
- ADHD without LD

Admissions Process

Applications are reviewed individually with emphasis placed on academic program, grades, class rank, recommendations and testing. Student's personal statement and interview provide additional information that is reviewed carefully.

High School Course Requirements:
English: **4** Math: **3** Science: **3** Foreign Language: **3**

Learning Disability Program
Services available for all students: **Yes**
Counseling: Individual: **Yes** Group Counseling: **Yes**

Faculty:
Faculty: **5** Including Director: Full time: **1** Part time: **4**
Faculty advocate: **Yes** Meets with instructor: **As needed**

Diagnostic Testing

ADD	Personality	Perceptual skills	Spelling
ADHD	Organization	Fine motor skills	Reading
I.Q.	Handwriting	Spoken language	Study skills
Math	Social skills	Written language	

Tutoring:
Average size of group tutorials: **Very small**
Services rendered by:
Graduates •Peers Faculty •LD staff Teacher trainees

Tutorials

Grp.	Ind.	Tutorials	Grp.	Ind.	Tutorials
•		Math skills	•		Word processing
•		Study skills	•		Time management
•		Language arts	•		Learning strategies
•		Written express	•		Organizational skills

Academic Accommodations

Curriculum	Study Aids	Exams
Priority registration	• Typist	• Oral
Math waiver	Reader	Untimed
Foreign lang. waiver	• Notetaker	• Take home
Course substitution	• Proof reader	With proctor
In Class	Text on tape	On computer
Calculators	Early syllabus	• Extended time
• Tape recorder	Taped handouts	On tape
Word processor		• Modified
Priority seating		Separate room

Graduation Requirements:
Course credits: **32**

Program Strengths
We handle students one-on-one on a personal needs basis as needs arise. Please contact the undergraduate admission officer if you have any questions.

General Information:
Hamline University is a 4 year private United Methodist Church university. Urban campus of 35 acres is 4 miles from Minneapolis. Accessible by air, train or bus. Ski areas are 25 miles from campus. Beaches are 15 miles from campus. 5% of students are foreign. 6 residential halls on campus. Housing is guaranteed. Guaranteed through 4th year. 65 % of students remain on campus for the weekends. 7 % of students join fraternities/sororities.

Accreditation: NCACS, NCATE, ACS, MNSDE

Expenses:
Tuition: In-state: Full year: $12,190.00. Tuition: Out-of-state: Full year: $12,190.00. Room and board: $3,895.00

Majors
• AREA STUDIES American, Asian, International Studies, Latin American, Russian/Slavic, Urban, Women's Studies • BUSINESS Business Management, Economics, International Business • COMMUNICATIONS Communication • EDUCATION Elementary, English, Health, Mathematics, Music, Physical, Science, Secondary, Social Science • HEALTH SCIENCES Environmental, Medical Laboratory Technology, Occupational Therapy • HUMANITIES English/Writing/Literature, Philosophy, Religion • LANGUAGES Chinese, French, German, Spanish • MATHEMATICS Theoretical • PREPROFESSIONAL Dentistry, Engineering, Law, Legal Assistant, Medicine, Veterinarian • SCIENCES Biology, Chemistry, Physics • SOCIAL SCIENCES Anthropology, History, Political Science, Psychology, Sociology • VISUAL AND PERFORMING ARTS Art, Art History, Music, Music Performance, Theater • VOCATIONAL Paralegal

Sports/Activities
• SPORTS-INTERCOLLEGIATE Baseball (M), Basketball, Cross Country, Football (M), Golf (M), Gymnastics (F), Ice Hockey (M), Soccer (F), Soccer (M), Softball (F), Swimming, Tennis (F), Tennis (M), Track and Field (F), Track and Field (M), Volleyball (F) • SPORTS-INTRAMURAL Aerobics, Basketball, Bicycling, Bowling, Cross-Country Skiing, Dance, Fencing, Flag Football, Karate, Racquetball, Softball, Tennis, Volleyball

• STUDENT LIFE ACTIVITIES Academic Clubs, Choral, Concert Band, Dance, Drama Groups, Ethnic & Cultural Groups, Fraternities, Jazz Band, Magazine, Music Groups, Newspaper, Orchestra, Political Groups, Sororities, Student Government, Yearbook

Less Selective

Minnesota Services

Hibbing Community College
1515 East 25th Street
Hibbing, Minnesota 55746
(218) 262-6700

School Enrollment: **1,100** Male: **495** Female: **605**
LD Enrollment: **10**

Admissions Contact: **Teri McKusky, Student Services Director**
LD Contact: **Barbara Anderson, EASE Director**
Name of Program: **EASE**
Address: **1515 E. 25th Street**
Telephone:**(218) 262-6775**

Admissions

Application Information:
Application deadline: **None**
Rolling Admissions: **Yes**

Secondary School Information
Most Important Criteria For Admissions (1-strongest)

SAT/ACT **1**	Application **1**	School transcript
Class rank	Course selection	Personal statement
Interview	Extra activities	Psychoeducational
G.P.A. **1**	Open admission	Recommendations

Test Requirements:
Untimed SAT: **Yes** Untimed ACT: **Yes** Untimed ACH: **Yes**
Documentation of LD required: **Yes**
Tests recommended: **All students: DTLS, Reading, Conventions of Written English, Math (Arithmetic, El. Algebra, Int. Algebra Function and Graph)**

Types of Disabilities Served
- Speech/Lang
- Study skills
- Written express
- Organizational
- Perceptual
- Reading
- Spelling
- Math
- Fine Motor
- ADD with LD
- ADD without LD
- ADHD with LD
- ADHD without LD

Admissions Process

Open Admissions. Students apply, submit high school transcript or GED and are accepted. If they don't have a high school diploma or GED, student must take DTLS and achieve a certain score to attend and receive financial aid.

Learning Disability Program

Program: Reinforces course work: **Yes**
Students mainstreamed **100** % of the day
Recommended credits per semester: **Individual choice**
Counseling: Individual: **Yes** Vocational Counseling: **Yes**
Support groups are available: Peer **tutoring, group tutoring, Student Support Services, non-traditional student**

Faculty:
Faculty: **1** Including Director: **Yes** Part time: **1**
LD faculty with: BS/BA: **1**

Diagnostic Testing
ADD	Personality	Perceptual skills	Spelling
ADHD	Organization	Fine motor skills	Reading
I.Q.	Handwriting	Spoken language	Study skills
Math	Social skills	Written language	

Tutoring:
Services rendered by:
Graduates •Peers •Faculty •LD staff Teacher trainees

Tutorials
Grp.	Ind.	Tutorials	Grp.	Ind.	Tutorials
	•	Math skills			Word processing
•	•	Study skills	•	•	Time management
•	•	Language arts	•	•	Learning strategies
•	•	Written express	•	•	Organizational skills

Academic Accommodations

Curriculum	Study Aids	Exams
Priority registration	• Typist	• Oral
Math waiver	• Reader	Untimed
Foreign lang. waiver	• Notetaker	• Take home
• Course substitution	• Proof reader	• With proctor
In Class	• Text on tape	On computer
• Calculators	• Early syllabus	• Extended time
• Tape recorder	Taped handouts	On tape
Word processor		• Modified
• Priority seating		• Separate room

Graduation Requirements:
Course credits: **96** GPA: **2.0** Years to complete degree: **No limit**
Other requirements: **Meet subject area requirements in Communications, Math/Science, Social/Behavioral Science, Humanities and P.E.**

Program Strengths

LD students on campus are encouraged to use the Learning Assistance Center to its maximum. The center is equipped with computers and word processors. The staff works one-on-one and in small classes in selected areas of study. Peer tutoring is also an advantage at Hibbing Community College. Very basic skills courses are available in math, English and reading.

General Information:

Hibbing Community College is a 2 year public college. Rural campus 75 miles from Duluth. Accessible by air or bus. Ski areas are 40 miles from campus. Beaches are 2 miles from campus. Housing is not guaranteed.

Accreditation:NCACS

Expenses:
Tuition: In-state: Full year: $1,700.00. Part-time: Per credit:$35.50. Tuition: Out-of-state: Full year: $3,400.00. Part-time: Per credit:$71.50.

Majors
• AREA STUDIES American • BUSINESS Accounting, Banking, Business Administration, Business Education, Business Management, Finance, Hotel and Restaurant Management, Management, Marketing, Real Estate • COMMUNICATIONS Communication, English, Journalism • COMPUTER SCIENCE Computer Science, Data Processing, Programming • EDUCATION Art, Early Childhood, Elementary, Middle School, Music, Music Therapy, Pre-Education, Secondary, Special • ENGINEERING Aerospace, Chemical, Civil/Environmental, Computer, Engineering Sci-

ence, Mechanical, Mining/Mineral • HEALTH SCIENCES Medical Secretary, Medical Technology, Nursing, Occupational Therapy, Physical Therapy, Radiological Therapy, Respiratory Therapy • HUMANITIES Humanities, Liberal Arts • LANGUAGES Spanish • PREPROFESSIONAL Architecture, Dentistry, Drafting, Law, Medicine, Pharmacy, Social Work, Veterinarian • SCIENCES Biology, Chemistry, Mathematics, Physical Chemistry, Physical Science, Physics • SOCIAL SCIENCES Anthropology, Criminal Justice, Government/Political, History, Law Enforcement, Psychology, Social Sciences, Sociology • VISUAL AND PERFORMING ARTS Art, Fine Arts, Music, Theater • VOCATIONAL Business and Office, Drafting, Legal Secretary, Medical Laboratory Technology, Radiological Technology, Secretarial

Sports/Activities

• SPORTS-INTERCOLLEGIATE Baseball (M), Basketball, Football (M), Ice Hockey (M), Softball (F), Tennis, Volleyball (F) • SPORTS-INTRAMURAL Archery, Badminton, Bowling, Cross Country, Hand Ball, Ping-Pong, Racquetball, Skiing - Snow, Soccer, Swimming, Volleyball • STUDENT LIFE ACTIVITIES Choral, Concert Band, Drama Groups, Film, Jazz Band, Music Groups, Musical Theater, Radio/TV station, Student Government

Less Selective	Minnesota Services

Itasca Community College: Arrowhead
1851 Highway 169 East
Grand Rapids, Minnesota 55744
(218) 327-4210

School Enrollment: **1,240** Male: **447** Female: **793**
LD Enrollment: **10-15**

Admissions Contact: **Candace Perry, Enrollment Manager**
LD Contact: **Sally Velzen, Coordinator of Disability Services**
Name of Program: **Office for Students with Disabilities**
Address: **1851 Highway 169 East**
Telephone:**(218) 327-4210**

Admissions

Application Information:
Application deadline: **Open admission**
Applicant must apply **None** months in advance
Rolling Admissions: **Yes**

Secondary School Information
Most Important Criteria For Admissions (1-strongest)

SAT/ACT	Application	School transcript
Class rank	Course selection	Personal statement
Interview	Extra activities	Psychoeducational
G.P.A.	**1** Open admission	Recommendations

Test Requirements:
Diagnostic testing waived: **Yes**
Documentation of LD required: **Yes**
Tests recommended: **WAIS-R and WJ-R**

Types of Disabilities Served

Speech/Lang	Reading	ADD with LD
Study skills	Spelling	ADD without LD
Written express	Math	ADHD with LD
Organizational	Fine Motor	ADHD without LD
Perceptual		

Admissions Process

We are an open admissions college requiring a high school diploma or G.E.D. An application form for admission must be completed. LD students must register with the Office for Students With Disabilities to receive services.

Learning Disability Program

Special orientation for LD students: **Yes**
Program: Remedial: **Yes**
Program: Reinforces course work: **Yes**
Students mainstreamed **100** % of the day
Recommended credits per semester: **12-15**
Time required or recommended in learning center: **As needed**
Services only for LD students: **Yes**
Services available for all students: **Yes**
Counseling: Individual: **Yes** Vocational Counseling: **Yes**

Faculty:
Faculty: **2** Including Director: **Yes** Part time: **2** M.A.: **1**
Faculty advocate: **Yes** Meets with instructor: **As needed**

Diagnostic Testing

ADD	Personality	Perceptual skills	Spelling
ADHD	Organization	Fine motor skills	Reading
I.Q.	Handwriting	Spoken language	Study skills
Math	Social skills	Written language	

Tutoring:
Average size of group tutorials: **2-4**
Services rendered by:
Graduates •Peers Faculty •LD staff Teacher trainees

Tutorials

Grp.	Ind.	Tutorials	Grp.	Ind.	Tutorials
•	•	Math skills	•	•	Word processing
	•	Study skills	•	•	Time management
	•	Language arts	•	•	Learning strategies
•	•	Written express	•	•	Organizational skills

Academic Accommodations

Curriculum	Study Aids	Exams
• Priority registration	• Typist	• Oral
Math waiver	• Reader	Untimed
Foreign lang. waiver	• Notetaker	Take home
• Course substitution	• Proof reader	• With proctor
In Class	• Text on tape	• On computer
• Calculators	• Early syllabus	• Extended time
• Tape recorder	Taped handouts	• On tape
Word processor		• Modified
• Priority seating		• Separate room

Graduation Requirements:
Course credits: **Varies** GPA: **2.0** Years to complete degree: **Varies**

Program Strengths
We are a small school that offers a lot of individual attention and support.

General Information:
Itasca Community College: Arrowhead is a 2 year public college. Rural campus of 4.5 acres is 80 miles from Duluth. Accessible by plane or bus. Ski areas are 20 miles from campus. .4% of students are foreign. 1 residential halls on campus. Housing is not guaranteed.

Accreditation: NCACS

Expenses:
Tuition: In-state: Full year: $1,704.00. Part-time: Per credit:$35.50. Tuition: Out-of-state: Full year: $3,408.00. Part-time: Per credit:$71.00. Room and board: $1,900.00 -$3,000.00

Majors

• HEALTH SCIENCES Medical Secretary, Practical Nursing • VOCATIONAL Business and Office, Forestry, Legal Secretary, Secretarial

Sports/Activities

• SPORTS-INTERCOLLEGIATE Baseball (M), Basketball (F), Football (M), Ice Hockey (M), Softball (F), Volleyball (F) • SPORTS-INTRAMURAL Basketball, Volleyball • STUDENT LIFE ACTIVITIES Academic Clubs, Community Service, Drama Groups, Ethnic & Cultural Groups, Newspaper, Student Government

Less Selective　　　　　　　　　**Minnesota**
Program

Lakewood Community College

3401 Century Avenue
White Bear Lake, Minnesota 55110
(612) 779-3300

School Enrollment: **6,500** Male: **2,500** Female: **4,000**
LD Enrollment: **32**

Admissions Contact: **Ken Hoff, Director of Admissions**
LD Contact: **Dr. Peggi Hunt, Disabilities Coordinator**
Name of Program: **Disability Services**

Admissions

Application Information:
LD Students Applying: **85** Accepted: **85** Enrolled:**85**
Separate application:**Yes**
Application deadline: **None**

Secondary School Information
Most Important Criteria For Admissions (1-strongest)

11 SAT/ACT	1 Application	4	School transcript
10 Class rank	6 Course selection	5	Personal statement
3 Interview	8 Extra activities	2	Psychoeducational
7 G.P.A.	Open admission	9	Recommendations

Test Requirements:
Diagnostic testing waived: **Yes**
Untimed ACH: **Yes** Achievement tests required:**3**
WAIS-R required: **Yes**
Documentation of LD required: **Yes**
Tests recommended: **Intelligence Test and Academic Achievement**

Types of Disabilities Served
• Speech/Lang　• Reading　　• ADD with LD
• Study skills　• Spelling　　• ADD without LD
• Written express　• Math　　• ADHD with LD
• Organizational　• Fine Motor　• ADHD without LD
• Perceptual

Learning Disability Program
Program: Remedial: **Yes**
Program: Reinforces course work: **Yes**
Students mainstreamed **100** % of the day
Counseling: Individual: **Yes** Group Counseling: **Yes**

Faculty:
Faculty: **2** Including Director: **Yes** Full time: **1** Part time: **1**
LD faculty with: BS/BA: **1** Ph.D.: **1**
Faculty advocate: **Yes** Meets with instructor: **As needed**

Diagnostic Testing
　ADD　• Personality　• Perceptual skills　• Spelling
　ADHD　Organization• Fine motor skills　• Reading
• I.Q.　• Handwriting• Spoken language　• Study skills
• Math　• Social skills• Written language

Tutoring:
Average size of group tutorials: **5-10**
Services rendered by:
　Graduates　•Peers　•Faculty　•LD staff　Teacher trainees

Tutorials

Grp.	Ind.	Tutorials	Grp.	Ind.	Tutorials
•	•	Math skills	•	•	Word processing
•	•	Study skills	•	•	Time management
•	•	Language arts	•	•	Learning strategies
•	•	Written express	•	•	Organizational skills

Academic Accommodations

Curriculum	Study Aids	Exams
Priority registration	Typist	• Oral
• Math waiver	Reader	Untimed
Foreign lang. waiver	• Notetaker	• Take home
• Course substitution	Proof reader	With proctor
In Class	• Text on tape	On computer
• Calculators	Early syllabus	• Extended time
• Tape recorder	Taped handouts	On tape
• Word processor		• Modified
Priority seating		Separate room

Program Strengths
Students enrolled in this program receive individualized assistance which begins at the submission of application through graduation. We have an open door policy and provide educational plans. We work closely with community organizations and agencies. Students are encouraged to participate in extracurricular activities and support groups (LD Club/Able Club). Transfer assistance is available to 4 year colleges.

General Information:
Lakewood Community College is a 2 year public college. 12 miles from St. Paul. Ski areas are 10 miles from campus. Beaches are 4 miles from campus. 2% of students are foreign. Housing is not guaranteed.

Accreditation: National

Expenses:
Tuition: In-state: Full year: $1,372.00. Part-time: Per credit:$30.50. Tuition: Out-of-state: Full year: $2,059.00. Part-time: Per credit:$45.50.

Majors

• BUSINESS Accounting, Business Management, Management, Marketing • COMMUNICATIONS Graphic Design, Printing Production • COMPUTER SCIENCE Data Processing • EDUCATION Child Development • HEALTH SCIENCES Dietary Aide Assistant, Nursing • HUMANITIES Liberal Arts • PREPROFESSIONAL Social Work • SOCIAL SCIENCES

Minnesota

Human Service, Law Enforcement • VOCATIONAL Bio-medical Equipment Technology, Electronics Technology, Emergency Medical Technician, Industrial Equipment Maintenance, Radiological Technology, Secretarial, Textile and Clothing

Sports/Activities

• SPORTS-INTERCOLLEGIATE Basketball (M), Bowling, Golf (M), Ice Hockey (M), Ping-Pong, Skiing - Snow, Soccer, Softball, Swimming, Tennis, Volleyball • SPORTS-INTRAMURAL Cross Country • STUDENT LIFE ACTIVITIES Choral, Community Service, Concert Band, Dance, Drama Groups, Ethnic & Cultural Groups, Jazz Band, Music Groups, Musical Theater, Newspaper, Political Groups, Student Government, Symphony Orchestra

Selective   **Minnesota**
                                                  Accommodations

Moorhead State University
P.O. Box 12
Moorhead, Minnesota 56563
(218) 236-2161

School Enrollment: **9,000** Male: **4,000** Female: **5,000**
LD Enrollment: **50** Male: **35** Female: **15**

Admissions Contact: **Floyd Brown, Director of Admissions**
LD Contact: **Paula Ahles, Coordinator**
Name of Program: **Services to Students w/Disabilities**
Address: **P.O. Box 12**
Telephone:**(218) 299-5859**

Admissions

Application Information:
Application deadline: **Fall quarter - August 15th**
Applicant must apply **6** months in advance

Secondary School Information
Most Important Criteria For Admissions (1-strongest)

2 SAT/ACT	**9** Application	**3** School transcript
1 Class rank	**4** Course selection	**6** Personal statement
10 Interview	**11** Extra activities	**7** Psychoeducational
8 G.P.A.	Open admission	**5** Recommendations

Test Requirements:
Diagnostic testing waived: **Yes**
Untimed SAT: **Yes** Untimed ACT: **Yes** Untimed ACH: **Yes**
Documentation of LD required: **Yes**
Currency of diagnostic testing: **Varies**
Tests recommended: **Any I.Q., Aptitude, Achievement Tests that can verify disability.**

Types of Disabilities Served
• Speech/Lang
• Study skills
• Written express
• Organizational
• Perceptual
• Reading
• Spelling
• Math
• Fine Motor
• ADD with LD
• ADD without LD
• ADHD with LD
• ADHD without LD

Admissions Process

Complete application, send high school transcript and copies of standardized testing to Office of Admissions.

High School Course Requirements:
English: **4** Math: **3** Science: **3**
Waivers to standard high school courses
Course substitution: **Yes**

Learning Disability Program
Syllabus available during orientation:**Yes**
Program: Reinforces course work: **Yes**
Program available through:**Daily**
Students mainstreamed **100** % of the day
Recommended credits per semester: **15**
Counseling: Individual: **Yes** Vocational Counseling: **Yes**

Faculty:
Faculty: **1** Including Director: **Yes** Full time: **1**
Faculty advocate: **Yes** Meets with instructor: **As necessary**

Diagnostic Testing
ADD	Personality	Perceptual skills	• Spelling
ADHD	Organization	Fine motor skills	• Reading
• I.Q.	Handwriting•	Spoken language	Study skills
• Math	Social skills•	Written language	

Services rendered by:
Graduates   Peers   Faculty   LD staff   Teacher trainees

Tutorials
Grp.	Ind.	Tutorials	Grp.	Ind.	Tutorials
		Math skills			Word processing
		Study skills			Time management
		Language arts			Learning strategies
		Written express			Organizational skills

Academic Accommodations
Curriculum	Study Aids	Exams
• Priority registration	Typist	• Oral
• Math waiver	• Reader	• Untimed
• Foreign lang. waiver	• Notetaker	• Take home
• Course substitution	Proof reader	• With proctor
In Class	• Text on tape	On computer
• Calculators	Early syllabus	• Extended time
• Tape recorder	Taped handouts	• On tape
• Word processor		Modified
• Priority seating		• Separate room

Graduation Requirements:
Course credits: **192** GPA: **2.0** Years to complete degree: **varies**
Other requirements: **Specific requirements of departments**

General Information:
Moorhead State University is a 4 year public university. Suburban campus of 104 acres is 240 miles from Minneapolis. Accessible by air, train or bus. Ski areas are 50 miles from campus. Beaches are 50 miles from campus. 7 residential halls on campus. Housing is not guaranteed.

Accreditation:NCA, NCATE, ACS, CSWE, NASAD, NASM, NLN, ASLHA

Class Rank: 90% were in the top 60% of their class.

Expenses:
Tuition: In-state: Full year: $2,193.60. Part-time: Per credit:$39.20. Tuition: Out-of-state: Full year: $3,832.80. Part-time: Per credit:$73.35.
Room and board: $2,529.00

Majors

• AGRICULTURE • ARTS Art, Music • BUSINESS Accounting, Banking/Finance, Business Administration, Business Economics, Business Education, Business Management, Economics, Education, Hotel & Restaurant Management, Industrial Operations, International Business, Management, Marketing • COMMUNICATIONS Communication, English • COMPUTER SCIENCE Computer Science, Programming • EDUCATION Art, Business, Early Childhood, Elementary, English, Foreign Language, Health, Industrial, Mathematics, Music, Physical, Reading, School Psychology, Science, Social Studies, Special, Speech/Language • ENGINEERING Physics • HEALTH SCIENCES Nursing, Physical Therapy, Speech/Audiology and Speech • HUMANITIES English/Writing/Literature • LANGUAGES French, German • MATHEMATICS Statistical, Theoretical • PRE PROFESSIONAL Agriculture, Architecture, Dentistry, Engineering, Forestry, Law, Legal Assistant, Medicine, Ministry, Pharmacy, Veterinarian, Wildlife • RELIGIOUS STUDIES Philosophy • SCIENCES Biology, Chemistry, Computer Science, Mathematics, Physics • SOCIAL SCIENCES Anthropology, Criminal Justice, History, Political Science, Sociology • SPECIAL EDUCATION Deaf/Hearing Impaired, Emotionally Disturbed, Learning Disability, Mentally Retarded • VISUAL AND PERFORMING ARTS Art, Music

Sports/Activities

• SPORTS RELATED Cheerleading, Pep Band, Team Managers • SPORTS-INTERCOLLEGIATE Basketball (F), Basketball (M), Cross Country (F), Cross Country (M), Football (M), Golf (F), Golf (M), Softball (F), Tennis (F), Tennis (M), Track and Field (F), Track and Field (M), Volleyball (F), Wrestling (M) • SPORTS-INTRAMURAL Basketball, Golf, Ice Hockey, Racquetball, Softball, Swimming, Tennis, Track and Field, Volleyball, Wrestling • STUDENT LIFE ACTIVITIES Academic Clubs, Choral, Community Service, Concert Band, Dance, Debate, Drama Groups, Ethnic & Cultural Groups, Film, Fraternities, Jazz Band, Music Groups, Newspaper, Orchestra, Political Groups, Radio/TV station, Religious Organization, Sororities, Student Government

Less Selective   **Minnesota**
                                       Services

Rochester Community College
Highway 14 East
Rochester, Minnesota 55904-4999
(507) 285-7265

School Enrollment: **3,987** Male: **1,480** Female: **2,507**
LD Enrollment: **70**

Admissions Contact: **Mrs. Barbara Schultz, Admissions Officer**
LD Contact: **Bonnie Parent, LD Specialist**
Name of Program: **Student Academic Support Center**
Telephone:**(507) 285-7230**

Admissions

Application Information:
Enrolled:**70**
Application deadline: **None**
Rolling Admissions: **Yes**

Secondary School Information
Most Important Criteria For Admissions (1-strongest)

	SAT/ACT	Application	School transcript
0	Class rank	**3** Course selection	Personal statement
2	Interview	Extra activities	**1** Psychoeducational
4	G.P.A.	**1** Open admission	Recommendations

Test Requirements:
Diagnostic testing waived: **Yes**
Documentation of LD required: **Yes**
Tests recommended: **Verified LD, usually high school records**

Types of Disabilities Served
• Speech/Lang   • Reading   • ADD with LD
• Study skills   • Spelling   • ADD without LD
• Written express • Math   • ADHD with LD
• Organizational   • Fine Motor   • ADHD without LD
• Perceptual

Admissions Process

Open door policy, students need a high school diploma or GED. The college does placement testing for courses.

Learning Disability Program
Program: Remedial: **Yes**
Program: Reinforces course work: **Yes**
Students mainstreamed **100** % of the day
Recommended credits per semester: **0**
Counseling: Individual: **Yes**

Faculty:
Faculty: **7** Including Director: **Yes** Full time: **7** M.A.: **7**
Faculty advocate: **Yes** Meets with instructor: **As needed**

Diagnostic Testing
ADD	Personality	Perceptual skills	•	Spelling
ADHD	Organization	Fine motor skills	•	Reading
I.Q.	Handwriting•	Spoken language		Study skills
• Math	Social skills•	Written language		

Tutoring:
Average size of group tutorials: **1:1**
Services rendered by:
   Graduates   •Peers   •Faculty   •LD staff   Teacher trainees

Tutorials
Grp.	Ind.	Tutorials	Grp.	Ind.	Tutorials
	•	Math skills		•	Word processing
•	•	Study skills	•	•	Time management
	•	Language arts		•	Learning strategies
	•	Written express	•	•	Organizational skills

Academic Accommodations

Curriculum	Study Aids	Exams
• Priority registration	• Typist	• Oral
Math waiver	• Reader	Untimed
Foreign lang. waiver	• Notetaker	Take home
Course substitution	• Proof reader	• With proctor
In Class	• Text on tape	• On computer
• Calculators	Early syllabus	• Extended time
• Tape recorder	Taped handouts	On tape
• Word processor		• Modified
Priority seating		• Separate room

Graduation Requirements:
Course credits: **varies** GPA: **2.0** Years to complete degree: **2-3**

Program Strengths

Rochester Community College has an Academic Support Center. The Center provides small group and personalized instruction in basic math, reading, algebra, study skills, and English composition. Student peer tutors are available in most classes. An advisor can as-

Minnesota

sist with class selection and financial aid.

General Information:

Rochester Community College is a 2 year public college. Urban campus of 160 acres is 80 miles from Minneapolis. Accessible by air or bus. Housing is not guaranteed.

Accreditation: NCACS

Expenses:

Tuition: In-state: Full year: $1,704.00. Part-time: Per credit:$36.00. Tuition: Out-of-state: Full year: $3,408.00. Part-time: Per credit:$71.00.

Majors

• BUSINESS Accounting, Business Administration, Economics, Fashion Merchandising, Management, Marketing • COMMUNICATIONS Journalism • COMPUTER SCIENCE Computer Science, Data Processing • EDUCATION Elementary, Secondary • ENGINEERING Civil/Environmental, Engineering Science, Mechanical • HEALTH SCIENCES Medical Secretary, Medical Technology, Nursing, Occupational Therapy, Physical Therapy, Radiological Therapy • HUMANITIES Liberal Arts
• PREPROFESSIONAL Agriculture, Dentistry, Engineering, Forestry, Law, Medicine, Pharmacy, Veterinarian • SCIENCES Agricultural, Biology, Chemistry, Mathematics, Physics • SOCIAL SCIENCES Law Enforcement, Psychology, Social Sciences • VISUAL AND PERFORMING ARTS Music, Studio Art, Visual and Performing Arts • VOCATIONAL Auto Manufacturing Technology, Business and Office, Electronics Technology, Fashion Merchandising, Home Economics, Legal Secretary, Park/Recreation, Radiological Technology, Respiratory Therapy Technology, Secretarial

Sports/Activities

• SPORTS RELATED Cheerleading, Pep Band • SPORTS-INTERCOLLEGIATE Baseball (M), Basketball, Football (M), Golf, Softball (F), Tennis, Volleyball (F), Wrestling (M) • SPORTS-INTRAMURAL Badminton, Field Hockey (F), Golf, Softball, Volleyball • STUDENT LIFE ACTIVITIES Choral, Concert Band, Drama Groups, Jazz Band, Music Groups, Musical Theater, Newspaper, Radio/TV station, Student Government

Selective	Minnesota
	Services

Saint Cloud State University

Saint Cloud, Minnesota 56301
(612) 255-4047

School Enrollment: **16,300** Male: **7,335** Female: **8,965**
LD Enrollment: **67**

Admissions Contact: **Sherwood Reid, Director of Admissions**
LD Contact: **Patricia Borgert, Acting Director**
Name of Program: **Handicapped Services**
Telephone:**(612) 255-4080**

Admissions

Application Information:
Application deadline: **None**
Rolling Admissions: **Yes**

Secondary School Information
Most Important Criteria For Admissions (1-strongest)

SAT/ACT	Application	School transcript
Class rank	Course selection	Personal statement
Interview	Extra activities	Psychoeducational
G.P.A.	Open admission	Recommendations

Test Requirements:
Diagnostic testing waived: **Yes**
Untimed SAT: **Yes** Untimed ACT: **Yes**
WAIS-R required: **Yes** Range accepted: **None**
Documentation of LD required: **Yes**
Currency of diagnostic testing: **3 years**

Types of Disabilities Served
• Speech/Lang
• Study skills
• Written express
• Organizational
• Perceptual
• Reading
• Spelling
• Math
• Fine Motor
• ADD with LD
• ADD without LD
• ADHD with LD
• ADHD without LD

Admissions Process

Student completes freshman application, returns with non-refundable $15.00 fee. Official transcript directly from high school to Office of Records and Registration. Applications reviewed weekly, acceptance letter sent to student.

Faculty:
Faculty advocate: **Yes**

Diagnostic Testing

ADD	Personality	Perceptual skills	Spelling
ADHD	Organization	Fine motor skills	Reading
I.Q.	Handwriting	Spoken language	Study skills
Math	Social skills	Written language	

Tutoring:
Services rendered by:
•Graduates •Peers •Faculty LD staff Teacher trainees

Tutorials

Grp.	Ind.	Tutorials	Grp.	Ind.	Tutorials
	•	Math skills			Word processing
		Study skills			Time management
	•	Language arts			Learning strategies
		Written express			Organizational skills

Academic Accommodations

Curriculum	Study Aids	Exams
• Priority registration	Typist	• Oral
Math waiver	Reader	• Untimed
Foreign lang. waiver	• Notetaker	Take home
Course substitution	• Proof reader	• With proctor
In Class	Text on tape	On computer
Calculators	Early syllabus	• Extended time
• Tape recorder	Taped handouts	On tape
• Word processor		Modified
• Priority seating		• Separate room

Graduation Requirements:
Course credits: **192**

Program Strengths
Services are aimed at equal opportunity education for all students.

General Information:
Saint Cloud State University is a 4 year public college. Urban campus of 82 acres is 70 miles from Minneapolis. Accessible by plane or bus. 1% of students are foreign. 9 residential halls on campus. Housing is not guaranteed.4 % of students join fraternities/sororities.

Accreditation: Regional

Expenses:
Tuition: In-state: Full year: $2,019.21. Part-time: Per credit:$39.20. Tuition: Out-of-state: Full year: $3,765.60. Part-time: Per credit:$80.10. Room and board: $2,625.00.

Majors

• AREA STUDIES American, Eastern Asian, Latin American, Urban • BUSINESS Accounting, Banking, Business Administration, Business Education, Business Management, Economics, Finance, Insurance, International Business, Marketing, Real Estate • COMMUNICATIONS Advertising, Communication, English, Journalism, Photography, Speech, Television/Radio/Film • COMPUTER SCIENCE Computer Science, Data Processing • CRAFTS AND DESIGN Ceramics • EDUCATION Art, Curriculum, Early Childhood, Elementary, English, Foreign Language, Health, Industrial, Mathematics, Middle School, Music, Psychology, Reading, Science, Secondary, Social Studies, Special, Speech/Language • ENGINEERING Engineering Science, Industrial • HEALTH SCIENCES Medical Secretary, Physical Therapy • HUMANITIES Liberal Arts, Philosophy • LANGUAGES French, German, Spanish • PREPROFESSIONAL Dentistry, Medicine, Social Work, Veterinarian • SCIENCES Anthropology, Bio-medical, Biology, Chemistry, Earth, Ecology, Macrobiology, Mathematics, Oceanography, Physical Science, Zoology • SOCIAL SCIENCES Criminal Justice, Family Counseling, Government/Political, History, Psychology, Public Relations, Sociology • VISUAL AND PERFORMING ARTS Art History, Dance, Music, Studio Art • VOCATIONAL Aviation Maintenance, Nuclear Medical Technology, Secretarial

Sports/Activities

• SPORTS RELATED Marching Band, Pep Band • SPORTS-INTERCOLLEGIATE Baseball (M), Basketball (F), Basketball (M), Cross Country (F), Cross Country (M), Diving (F), Diving (M), Football (M), Golf (F), Golf (M), Ice Hockey (M), Softball (F), Swimming (F), Swimming (M), Tennis (F), Tennis (M), Track and Field (F), Track and Field (M), Volleyball (F), Wrestling (M) • SPORTS-INTRAMURAL Badminton (F), Badminton (M), Baseball, Baseball (F), Basketball (F), Basketball (M), Bowling, Bowling (F), Bowling (M), Canoeing (F) , Cross Country, Diving, Fencing, Field Hockey (F), Golf, Gymnastics, Hand Ball, Ping-Pong, Racquetball, Riflery, Rugby, Skiing - Snow, Soccer, Softball, Swimming, Tennis, Track and Field, Volleyball, Water Polo, Wrestling (M) • STUDENT LIFE ACTIVITIES Choral, Concert Band, Dance, Drama Groups, Fraternities, Jazz Band, Magazine, Music Groups, Musical Theater, Newspaper, Opera, Radio/TV station, Sororities, Student Government, Symphony Orchestra

Selective	Minnesota

Southwest State University

Marshall, Minnesota 56258
(800) 642-0684

School Enrollment: **2,900** Male: **1,500** Female: **1,400**
LD Enrollment: **55** Male: **40** Female: **15**

Admissions Contact: **Phil Coltart, Director of Admissions**
LD Contact: **Marilyn Leach, Director Learning Resources**
Name of Program: **Learning Resources**
Address: **Bellows Academic Services 246**
Telephone:**(507) 537-6169**

Admissions

Application Information:
Separate application:**Yes**
Application deadline: **None**
Applicant must apply **3** months in advance
Rolling Admissions: **Yes**

Secondary School Information
Most Important Criteria For Admissions (1-strongest)

4 SAT/ACT	7 Application	2 School transcript
1 Class rank	3 Course selection	6 Personal statement
4 Interview	10 Extra activities	5 Psychoeducational
9 G.P.A.	Open admission	8 Recommendations

Test Requirements:
Diagnostic testing waived: **Yes**
Untimed SAT: **Yes** Untimed ACT: **Yes**
WAIS-R required: **Yes** Range accepted: **100 verbal**
Documentation of LD required: **Yes**
Currency of diagnostic testing: **24**
Tests recommended: **WAIS-R, Woodcock-Johnson Revised Cognitive and Achievement Batteries**

Types of Disabilities Served
• Speech/Lang • Reading • ADD with LD
• Study skills • Spelling • ADD without LD
• Written express • Math • ADHD with LD
• Organizational • Fine Motor • ADHD without LD
• Perceptual

Admissions Process

We have an Affirmative Action admissions process. If student indicates a disability and does not meet admission requirements, student may submit documentation/testing to Learning Resources for review and recommendations.

Learning Disability Program

Special orientation for LD students: **Yes**
Program: Remedial: **Yes**
Program: Reinforces course work: **Yes**
Students mainstreamed **100** % of the day
Recommended credits per semester: **12-16**
Services available for all students: **Yes**
Counseling: Individual: **Yes** Group Counseling: **Yes** Vocational Counseling: **Yes**
Support groups are available: Students **with Alternative Learning Styles - (organized club)**

Faculty:
Faculty: **6** Full time: **3** Part time: **3**
LD faculty with: BS/BA: **1** M.A.: **5**
Faculty advocate: **Yes** Meets with instructor: **As needed**

Diagnostic Testing
ADD • Personality • Perceptual skills • Spelling
ADHD • Organization Fine motor skills • Reading
• I.Q. Handwriting • Spoken language • Study skills
• Math Social skills • Written language

Tutoring:
Average size of group tutorials: **2-3**
Services rendered by:
Graduates •Peers Faculty •LD staff Teacher trainees

Minnesota

Tutorials

Grp.	Ind.	Tutorials	Grp.	Ind.	Tutorials
•	•	Math skills	•	•	Word processing
•	•	Study skills	•	•	Time management
•	•	Language arts	•	•	Learning strategies
•	•	Written express	•	•	Organizational skills

Academic Accommodations

Curriculum	Study Aids	Exams
• Priority registration	• Typist	• Oral
• Math waiver	• Reader	• Untimed
• Foreign lang. waiver	• Notetaker	Take home
• Course substitution	• Proof reader	• With proctor
In Class	• Text on tape	• On computer
• Calculators	Early syllabus	• Extended time
• Tape recorder	• Taped handouts	• On tape
• Word processor		Modified
• Priority seating		• Separate room

Graduation Requirements:
Course credits: **192** GPA: **varies** Years to complete degree: **Average 5**

Program Strengths

Integrated with all academic support services - lessens stigma.

General Information:

Southwest State University is a 4 year public university. Rural campus of 216 acres is 90 miles from Sioux Falls, SD. Accessible by bus. Ski areas are 100 miles from campus. Beaches are 1,500 miles from campus. 2% of students are foreign. 26 residential halls on campus. Housing is guaranteed.Guaranteed through 1st year.

Accreditation:NCACS

Expenses: Part-time: Per credit:$42.35. Part-time: Per credit:$83.80. Room and board: $2,600.00

Majors

• AGRICULTURE Business • ARTS Music, Music Performance, Painting, Sculpture, Theater Design • BUSINESS Accounting, Banking/Finance, Business Administration, Business Management, Hotel & Restaurant Management, Human Resources Management, International Business, Management, Marketing • COMMUNICATIONS Creative Writing, English, Literature, Speech/Debate/Forensic, Television/Radio/Film • COMPUTER SCIENCE Computer Science • EDUCATION Art, Early Childhood, Elementary, English, Health, Mathematics, Middle School, Music, Physical, Science, Secondary, Social Studies, Speech/Language • HEALTH SCIENCES Medical Laboratory Technology • HUMANITIES English/Writing/Literature • MATHEMATICS Applied, Statistical, Theoretical • PRE PROFESSIONAL Agriculture, Business, Dentistry, Engineering, Fisheries, Forestry, Law, Medicine, Ministry, Optometry, Pharmacy, Social Work, Sports Medicine • SCIENCES Biology, Chemistry, Computer Science, Earth, Inorganic Chemistry, Mathematics, Organic Chemistry, Physical Chemistry, Physical Science • SOCIAL SCIENCES Government/Political, History, Political Science, Psychology, Sociology • VISUAL AND PERFORMING ARTS Music, Music Performance, Studio Art, Theater

Sports/Activities

• SPORTS-INTERCOLLEGIATE Baseball (M), Basketball, Football (M), Softball (F), Tennis (F), Volleyball (F), Wrestling (M) • SPORTS-INTRAMURAL Badminton, Basketball, Ice Hockey (M), Rugby, Sailing, Softball, Tennis, Track and Field, Volleyball, Wrestling (M)

St. Cloud State University
720 4th Avenue South
St. Cloud, Minnesota 56301
(800) 369-4260

School Enrollment: **16,300** Male: **7,335** Female: **8,965**
LD Enrollment: **67**

Admissions Contact: **Sherwood Reid Admissions Director**
LD Contact: **Patricia Borgert Acting Director**
Name of Program: **Handicapped Student Services**
Telephone:**(612) 255-3004**

Admissions

Application Information:
Application deadline: **None**
Rolling Admissions: **Yes**

Secondary School Information
Most Important Criteria For Admissions (1-strongest)

2 SAT/ACT	Application	School transcript
1 Class rank	Course selection	Personal statement
Interview	Extra activities	Psychoeducational
3 G.P.A.	Open admission	Recommendations

Test Requirements:
Untimed SAT: **Yes** Untimed ACT: **Yes**
WAIS-R required: **Yes**
Documentation of LD required: **Yes**
Currency of diagnostic testing: **3 years**

Types of Disabilities Served
• Speech/Lang	• Reading	• ADD with LD
• Study skills	• Spelling	• ADD without LD
• Written express	• Math	• ADHD with LD
• Organizational	• Fine Motor	• ADHD without LD
• Perceptual		

Admissions Process

Student completes freshman application, returns with non-refundable $15 fee. Official transcript directly from high school to Office of Records and Registration. Applications reviewed weekly, acceptance letter sent to student.

Learning Disability Program

Services available for all students: **Yes**

Faculty:
Faculty advocate: **Yes**

Diagnostic Testing
• ADD	• Personality	• Perceptual skills	• Spelling
• ADHD	• Organization	• Fine motor skills	• Reading
• I.Q.	• Handwriting	• Spoken language	• Study skills
• Math	• Social skills	• Written language	

410

Tutoring:
Services rendered by:
•Graduates •Peers •Faculty LD staff Teacher trainees

Tutorials
Grp. Ind. Tutorials
- • Math skills
  Study skills
- • Language arts
  Written express

Grp. Ind. Tutorials
Word processing
Time management
Learning strategies
Organizational skills

Academic Accommodations
Curriculum
- • Priority registration
  Math waiver
  Foreign lang. waiver
  Course substitution

In Class
  Calculators
- • Tape recorder
- • Word processor
- • Priority seating

Study Aids
  Typist
  Reader
- • Notetaker
- • Proof reader
  Text on tape
  Early syllabus
  Taped handouts

Exams
- • Oral
- • Untimed
  Take home
- • With proctor
  On computer
- • Extended time
  On tape
  Modified
  Separate room

Graduation Requirements:
Course credits: **192**

General Information:
St. Cloud State University is a Urban Campus of 82 acres is 70 miles from Minneapolis. Accessible by plane, bus 1% of students are foreign. 9 residential halls on campus. Housing is not guaranteed.4 % of students join fraternities/sororities.

Accreditation: Regional

Expenses:
Tuition: In-state: Full year: $2,019.00. Part-time: Per credit:$39.00. Tuition: Out-of-state: Full year: $3,766.00. Part-time: Per credit:$80.00. Room and board: $2,625.00

Majors
• BUSINESS Accounting, BCIS, Business Education, Finance, General Business, Insurance, International Business, Management, Marketing, Office Administration, Real Estate, Records & Office Management • EDUCATION Elementary, Health, Human Relations, Physical, Reading Instruction, Recreation, Secondary, Special • FINE ARTS/HUMANITIES Art, Art History, Communication Disorders, English, French, German, Mass Communication, Music, Philosophy, Spanish, Speech - Interdepartmental, Speech Communication, Theater • SCIENCES Applied Computer Science, Aviation, Biological Park, Biomedical, Biotechnology, Chemistry,. Biology, Comp. Earth Science, Comp. General Science, Computer Science, Earth Science, Electrical Engineering, Engineering Technology, Gen. Physical Science, Industrial Studies, Manufacturing Engineering, Mathematics, Medical Technology, Meteorology, Nuclear Medicine Technology, Photo Engineering Technology, Photo Science & Instrumentation, Physics, Statistics, Vocational Tech. Education • SOCIAL SCIENCES American Studies, Anthropology, Criminal Justice, Economics, Geography, History, International Relations, Latin American Studies, Local & Urban Studies, Political Science, Psychology, Public Administration, Social Science, Social Studies, Social Work, Sociology

Sports/Activities
• SPORTS INTRAMURAL Badminton (F), Badminton (M), Baseball (M), Basketball (F), Basketball (M), Bowling (F), Bowling (M), Canoeing (F), Canoeing (M), Crew (F), Crew (M), Cricket (F), Cricket (M), Cross Country (F), Cross Country (M), Cycling (F), Cycling (M), Fencing (F), Fencing (M), Football Flag (F), Golf (F), Golf (M), Gymnastics, Hand Ball (F), Hand Ball (M), Ice Hockey (F), Ice Hockey (M), Judo (F), Judo (M), Karate (F), Karate (M), Lacrosse (F), Lacrosse (M), Martial Arts (F), Martial Arts

(M), Racquetball (F), Racquetball (M), Rugby (F), Rugby (M), Skiing - Cross Country (F), Skiing - Cross Country (M), Soccer (F), Soccer (M), Softball (F), Softball (M), Swimming (F), Swimming (M), Tennis (F), Tennis (M), Track and Field (F), Track and Field (M), Volleyball (F), Volleyball (M), Weight Lifting (M), Wrestling (M) • SPORTS RELATED Cheerleading, Chess, Team Managers • SPORTS-INTERCOLLEGIATE Baseball (M), Basketball (F), Basketball (M), Cross Country (F), Cross Country (M), Diving (F), Diving (M), Golf, Golf (F), Golf (M), Ice Hockey (M), Softball (F), Swimming (F), Swimming (M), Tennis (F), Tennis (M), Track and Field (F), Track and Field (M), Volleyball (F), Wrestling (M) • STUDENT LIFE ACTIVITIES Academic Clubs, Choral, Community Service, Concert Band, Dance, Debate, Drama Groups, Ethnic & Cultural Groups, Film, Fraternities, Jazz Band, Magazine, Music Groups, Musical Theater, Newspaper, Orchestra, Political Groups, Radio/TV station, Religious Organization, Sororities, Student Government, Symphony Orchestra

Very Selective   **Minnesota**
                                       Services

St. John's University
Collegeville, Minnesota 56321
(612) 363-2196

School Enrollment: **1,920** Male: **1,920**
LD Enrollment: **16** Male: **16**

Admissions Contact: **Ms. Mary Milbert, Director of Admissions**
LD Contact: **Fr. Antony Hellenberg, Director**
Name of Program: **Academic Advising**
Telephone:**(612) 363-2248**

Admissions

Application Information:
Application deadline: **Rolling**
Rolling Admissions: **Yes**

Secondary School Information
Most Important Criteria For Admissions (1-strongest)

5 SAT/ACT	Application	1 School transcript
2 Class rank	Course selection	4 Personal statement
Interview	6 Extra activities	Psychoeducational
1 G.P.A.	Open admission	3 Recommendations

Test Requirements:
Untimed SAT: **Yes** Untimed ACT: **Yes**
Documentation of LD required: **Yes**

Types of Disabilities Served
- • Speech/Lang
- • Study skills
- • Written express
- • Organizational
- • Perceptual
- • Reading
- • Spelling
- • Math
- • Fine Motor
- • ADD with LD
- • ADD without LD
- • ADHD with LD
- • ADHD without LD

Admissions Process

Complete application form, submit high school transcripts for review.

High School Course Requirements:
English: **4** Math: **3** Science: **2**

Minnesota

Learning Disability Program
Students mainstreamed **100** % of the day
Recommended credits per semester: **15+**
Services available for all students: **Yes**
Counseling: Individual: **Yes**

Faculty:
Faculty: **2** Including Director: **Yes** Full time: **2** M.A.: **2**
Faculty advocate: **Yes** Meets with instructor: **As needed**

Diagnostic Testing
ADD	Personality	Perceptual skills	Spelling
ADHD	Organization	Fine motor skills	Reading
I.Q.	Handwriting	Spoken language	Study skills
Math	Social skills	Written language	

Tutoring:
Average size of group tutorials: **2**
Services rendered by:
  Graduates •Peers Faculty •LD staff Teacher trainees

Tutorials
Grp.	Ind.	Tutorials	Grp.	Ind.	Tutorials
	•	Math skills	•		Word processing
•	•	Study skills		•	Time management
	•	Language arts	•	•	Learning strategies
•	•	Written express		•	Organizational skills

Academic Accommodations
Curriculum	Study Aids	Exams
• Priority registration	Typist	• Oral
• Math waiver	Reader	• Untimed
• Foreign lang. waiver	Notetaker	• Take home
• Course substitution	Proof reader	• With proctor
In Class	• Text on tape	• On computer
• Calculators	Early syllabus	• Extended time
• Tape recorder	Taped handouts	On tape
• Word processor		• Modified
Priority seating		Separate room

Graduation Requirements:
Course credits: **124** GPA: **2.0** Years to complete degree: **No limit** Math waiver: **Yes** Language waiver: **Yes**

Program Strengths
At St. Johns and our coordinate institution, the College of St. Benedict, the Academic Advising Office is responsible for providing the kind of assistance that will improve opportunities for our LD students. Generally only those with a moderate LD apply to a college like ours. The programs at our schools do not provide remedial services but only essential accommodations, as required by federal regulations.

General Information:
St. John's University is a 4 year private Roman Catholic college. Rural campus of 2,400 acres is 80 miles from Minneapolis/St. Paul. Accessible by air, train or bus. Ski areas are 20 miles from campus. Beaches are campus from campus. 2% of students are foreign. Housing is guaranteed.Guaranteed through 1st year. 85 % of students remain on campus for the weekends.

Accreditation:NCACS

SAT/ACT Scores:
Scores for incoming freshmen:**Verbal:**60%below 500. 32%between 500 and 599. 7%between 600 and 699. 1%above 700. **Math:**36% below 500. 37% between 500 and 599. 20% between 600 and 699. 6%above 700. **ACT:** 16% below 20. 38% between 20 and 23. 17%between 24 and 25l. 21%between 26 and 28. 8% above 28.

Class Rank:
About 41% of the present freshmen class were in the upper 20% of their high school class. 70% were in the top 40% of their class. 90% were in the top 60% of their class. 99% were in the top 80% of their class.

Expenses:
Tuition: In-state: Full year: $10,498.00. Part-time: Per credit:$435.00.
Room and board: $4,450.00

Majors
• AREA STUDIES Medieval, Peace Studies • BUSINESS Business Administration, Economics, Management • COMMUNICATIONS Communication, English • COMPUTER SCIENCE Computer Science, Data Processing, Programming • EDUCATION Art, Early Childhood, Elementary, Music, Pre-education, Secondary • HEALTH SCIENCES Medical Technology, Nursing, Nursing Assistant, Nutritional/Food, Occupational Therapy, Physical Therapy • HUMANITIES Classics, Humanities, Philosophy, Religion Studies • LANGUAGES French, German, Greek, Latin, Spanish • PREPROFESSIONAL Dentistry, Engineering, Law, Medicine, Ministry, Pharmacy, Social Work, Veterinarian • SCIENCES Biology, Chemistry, Mathematics, Physical Science, Physics • SOCIAL SCIENCES Government/Political, History, Political Science, Psychology, Social Sciences, Sociology • VOCATIONAL Food Service

Sports/Activities
• SPORTS RELATED Drill Team, Pep Band, Team Managers • SPORTS-INTERCOLLEGIATE Baseball , Basketball, Crew, Cross Country, Cycling, Diving, Football, Golf, Ice Hockey, Lacrosse, Rugby, Skiing - Cross Country, Soccer, Swimming, Tennis, Track and Field, Volleyball, Wrestling • SPORTS-INTRAMURAL Basketball (F), Basketball (M), Bowling (F), Bowling (M), Crew (F), Crew (M), Cross Country (M), Football, Hand Ball , Ice Hockey, Karate, Lacrosse , Martial Arts, Racquetball, Rugby , Skiing - Cross Country, Softball, Tennis, Trap and Skeet, Volleyball (M), Weight Lifting • STUDENT LIFE ACTIVITIES Academic Clubs, Choral, Community Service, Concert Band, Debate, Drama Groups, Ethnic & Cultural Groups, Film, Fraternities, Jazz Band, Magazine, Music Groups, Musical Theater, Newspaper, Orchestra, Political Groups, Radio/TV station, Religious Organization, Student Government, Symphony Orchestra, Yearbook

---

Less Selective   **Minnesota**
                                                       Services

St. Mary's Campus of the College of St. Catherine
2500 South Sixth Street
Minneapolis, Minnesota 55454
(612) 690-7848

School Enrollment: **943** Male: **160** Female: **783**
LD Enrollment: **20** Male: **5** Female: **15**

Admissions Contact: **Pamela Johnson, Director of Admissions**
LD Contact: **Debra Evon/Rose Mary Johnson, Coor. /LD Spec.**
Name of Program: **Learning Center**
Telephone:**(612) 690-7832**

Admissions

Application Information:
Application deadline: **None**
Rolling Admissions: **Yes**

Secondary School Information

Most Important Criteria For Admissions (1-strongest)

	SAT/ACT	**3** Application	**1**	School transcript
6	Class rank	**2** Course selection	**4**	Personal statement
	Interview	Extra activities		Psychoeducational
5	G.P.A.	Open admission	**1**	Recommendations

Test Requirements:

Standardized tests waived: **Yes**
Diagnostic testing waived: **Yes**
Documentation of LD required: **Yes**
Currency of diagnostic testing: **any number**

Types of Disabilities Served

- Speech/Lang
- Study skills
- Written express
- Organizational
  Perceptual

- Reading
- Spelling
- Math
  Fine Motor

ADD with LD
ADD without LD
ADHD with LD
ADHD without LD

Admissions Process

Candidates must complete an application for admission; must have graduated from an accredited secondary school, or have completed the GED; and must provide evidence of ability to succeed in an academic program (e.g. rank in class, post-secondary grades, test results, letters of recommendation).

High School Course Requirements:

Learning Disability Program

Students mainstreamed **100** % of the day
Services available for all students: **Yes**
Counseling: Individual: **Yes** Group Counseling: **Yes** Vocational Counseling: **Yes**
Support groups are available:**Upon request**

Faculty:

Faculty: **1** Part time: **1** M.A.: **1**
Faculty advocate: **Yes** Meets with instructor: **As needed**

Diagnostic Testing

ADD	Personality	Perceptual skills	• Spelling
ADHD	Organization	Fine motor skills	• Reading
I.Q.	Handwriting	Spoken language	• Study skills
• Math	Social skills	• Written language	

Tutoring:

Average size of group tutorials: **3-5**
Services rendered by:

Graduates	•Peers	Faculty	•LD staff	Teacher trainees

Tutorials

Grp.	Ind.	Tutorials	Grp.	Ind.	Tutorials
•	•	Math skills		•	Word processing
•	•	Study skills	•	•	Time management
•	•	Language arts	•	•	Learning strategies
•	•	Written express	•	•	Organizational skills

Academic Accommodations

Curriculum	Study Aids	Exams
Priority registration	Typist	• Oral
Math waiver	Reader	Untimed
Foreign lang. waiver	• Notetaker	• Take home
Course substitution	Proof reader	• With proctor
In Class	Text on tape	• On computer
Calculators	Early syllabus	• Extended time
• Tape recorder	Taped handouts	• On tape
Word processor		Modified
Priority seating		• Separate room

Graduation Requirements: Years to complete degree: **2-3**

Program Strengths

At this time, St. Mary's Campus of the College of St. Catherine does not have a program for students with learning disabilities. However, these students may utilize established learning assistance services along with their mainstream peers, plus a few services for which they alone qualify, such as notetakers, tests on tape, and advising.

General Information:

St. Mary's Campus of the College of St. Catherine is a 2 year private Roman Catholic college. Urban campus. Minneapolis. Accessible by air, train or bus. Ski areas are 20 miles from campus. Beaches are 5 miles from campus. 1 residential halls on campus. Housing is not guaranteed.

Accreditation:NCACS

Expenses:

Tuition: In-state: Full year: $7.552.00. Part-time: Per credit:$250.00. Room and board: $1,200.00

Majors

• COMPUTER SCIENCE Medical Records Administration • EDUCATION Early Childhood • HEALTH SCIENCES Health & Wellness Counseling, Health Care Interpreter, Holistic Therapies, Medical Transcription Special, Nursing, Occupational Therapy Assistant, Phlebotomy, Physical Therapy Assistant • SOCIAL SCIENCES Family Counseling • VOCATIONAL Business and Office, Respiratory Therapy Technology

Sports/Activities

• STUDENT LIFE ACTIVITIES Newspaper, Religious Organization, Student Government

Highly Selective   **Minnesota Accommodations**

St. Olaf College

1520 St. Olaf Avenue
Northfield, Minnesota 55057-1098
(507) 663-3025

School Enrollment: **3,000** Male: **1,400** Female: **1,600**
LD Enrollment: **10** Male: **6** Female: **4**

Admissions Contact: **John P. Ruohoniemi, Director of Admissions**
LD Contact: **Linda Hunter, Director**
Name of Program: **Academic Support Center**
Telephone:**(507) 663-3288**

Minnesota

Admissions

Application Information:
Application deadline: **February 15th**
Rolling Admissions: **Yes**

Secondary School Information
Most Important Criteria For Admissions (1-strongest)

4 SAT/ACT	6 Application	1 School transcript
8 Class rank	2 Course selection	10 Personal statement
9 Interview	3 Extra activities	11 Psychoeducational
7 G.P.A.	Open admission	5 Recommendations

Test Requirements:
Documentation of LD required: **Yes**

Types of Disabilities Served

Speech/Lang	• Reading	ADD with LD
• Study skills	• Spelling	ADD without LD
• Written express	• Math	ADHD with LD
Organizational	Fine Motor	ADHD without LD
Perceptual		

Learning Disability Program

Services available for all students: **Yes**

Faculty:
Faculty: **2** Full time: **1** Part time: **1**
Faculty advocate: **Yes** Meets with instructor: **When necessary**

Diagnostic Testing

ADD	Personality	Perceptual skills	Spelling
ADHD	Organization	Fine motor skills	Reading
I.Q.	Handwriting	Spoken language	Study skills
Math	Social skills	Written language	

Tutoring:
Average size of group tutorials: **4**
Services rendered by:
Graduates •Peers Faculty •LD staff Teacher trainees

Tutorials

Grp.	Ind.	Tutorials	Grp.	Ind.	Tutorials
	•	Math skills	•		Word processing
•	•	Study skills	•	•	Time management
	•	Language arts			Learning strategies
	•	Written express			Organizational skills

Academic Accommodations

Curriculum	Study Aids	Exams
Priority registration	Typist	• Oral
Math waiver	Reader	Untimed
Foreign lang. waiver	• Notetaker	• Take home
Course substitution	• Proof reader	• With proctor
In Class	• Text on tape	On computer
• Calculators	Early syllabus	• Extended time
• Tape recorder	Taped handouts	On tape
• Word processor		• Modified
Priority seating		Separate room

Program Strengths

St. Olaf does not have a learning disability program. It tries to meet the needs of all its students on an individual basis.

General Information:
St. Olaf College is a 4 year private Evangelical Lutheran Church college. Rural campus of 350 acres is 40 miles from Minneapolis/St. Paul. Accessible by air, train, bus. Ski areas are 25 from campus. 11 residential halls on campus. Housing is guaranteed.

Accreditation: NCACS

SAT/ACT Scores:
Scores for incoming freshmen: **Verbal:** 34% below 500. 40% between 500 and 599. 23% between 600 and 699. 34% above 700. **Math:** 19% below 500. 32% between 500 and 599. 37% between 600 and 699. 12% above 700. **ACT:** 6% below 20. 21% between 20 and 23. 18% between 24 and 25l. 37% between 26 and 28. 19% above 28.

Class Rank:
About 74% of the present freshmen class were in the upper 20% of their high school class. 94% were in the top 40% of their class. 100% were in the top 60% of their class. 100% were in the top 80% of their class.

Expenses:
Tuition: In-state: Full year: $12,750.00. Room and board: $3,900.00

Majors

• AREA STUDIES American, Asian, Women's Studies • ARTS Art History, Dance, Dramatic Arts, Music, Music Performance • BUSINESS Economics • COMMUNICATIONS English, Speech/Debate/Forensics • EDUCATION Art, English, Foreign Language, Mathematics, Music, Physical, Science, Social Studies, Speech/Language • HUMANITIES Classics, English/Writing/Literature, Fine Arts, Philosophy, Religion • LANGUAGES Chinese, English, French, German, Japanese, Russian, Scandinavian, Spanish • MATHEMATICS Applied • PREPROFESSIONAL Social Work • SCIENCES Biology, Chemistry, Mathematics, Physics • SOCIAL SCIENCES History, Political Science, Psychology, Sociology • VISUAL AND PERFORMING ARTS Art, Art History, Dance, Dramatic Arts, Fine Arts, Music, Music Performance, Theater • VOCATIONAL Food Service, Home Economics

Sports/Activities

• SPORTS RELATED Cheerleading, Chess, Pep Band, Team Managers • SPORTS-INTERCOLLEGIATE Baseball, Cross Country (F), Cross Country (M), Football (M), Golf (F), Golf (M), Ice Hockey (M), Skiing - Cross Country, Skiing - Snow (F), Skiing - Snow (M), Soccer (F), Soccer (M), Softball (F), Swimming (F), Swimming (M), Tennis (F), Tennis (M), Track and Field (F), Track and Field (M), Volleyball (F), Wrestling (M) • SPORTS-INTRAMURAL Basketball, Football, Hand Ball, Ice Hockey, Soccer, Softball, Tennis, Volleyball • STUDENT LIFE ACTIVITIES Choral, Community Service, Concert Band, Dance, Ethnic & Cultural Groups, Ethnic & Cultural Groups, Music Groups, Musical Theater, Newspaper, Orchestra, Political Groups, Radio/TV station, Religious Organization, Student Government, Yearbook

Very Selective   **Minnesota Program**

University of Minnesota: Duluth
10 University Circle
Duluth, Minnesota 55812
(218) 726-7171

School Enrollment: **7,800** Male: **3,900** Female: **3,900**
LD Enrollment: **100**

Admissions Contact: **Gerald R. Allen, Director of Admissions**
LD Contact: **Penny Cragun or Judy Bromen, Director/Coor.**
Name of Program: **Learning Disabilities Program**
Address: **Access Center, Cina 104**
Telephone:**(218) 726-8727**

Admissions

Application Information:
Enrolled:**100**
Application deadline: **February 1st**

Secondary School Information
Most Important Criteria For Admissions (1-strongest)

2 SAT/ACT	Application	**1**	School transcript
1 Class rank	**3** Course selection		Personal statement
Interview	Extra activities	**4**	Psychoeducational
G.P.A.	Open admission	**5**	Recommendations

Test Requirements:
Diagnostic testing waived: **Yes**
Untimed ACT: **Yes** Achievement tests required:**3**
WAIS-R required: **Yes** Range accepted: **Average +**
Documentation of LD required: **Yes**
Currency of diagnostic testing: **3 years**
Tests recommended: **Woodcock Johnson Psychoeducational Battery and/or WAIS-R**

Types of Disabilities Served
- Speech/Lang
- Study skills
- Written express
- Organizational
- Perceptual
- Reading
- Spelling
- Math
- Fine Motor
- ADD with LD
- ADD without LD
- ADHD with LD
- ADHD without LD

Admissions Process

Admission to the University and acceptance for support services through the Access Center are separate processes.

High School Course Requirements:
English: **4** Math: **3** Science: **3** Foreign Language: **2**
Waivers to standard high school courses
Foreign Language : **Yes** Math: **Yes** Course substitution: **Yes**

Learning Disability Program
Program: Reinforces course work: **Yes**
Program available through: While **enrolled**
Students mainstreamed **100** % of the day
Recommended credits per semester: **12-16**
Services only for LD students: **Yes**
Counseling: Individual: **Yes** Vocational Counseling: **Yes**
Support groups are available: Informal **discussion group**

Faculty:
Faculty: **2** Including Director: **Yes** Full time: **2** M.A.: **2**
Faculty advocate: **Yes**

Diagnostic Testing
ADD	Personality	Perceptual skills	• Spelling
ADHD	Organization	Fine motor skills	• Reading
• I.Q.	Handwriting	Spoken language	Study skills
• Math	Social skills	• Written language	

Tutoring:
Services rendered by:
Graduates   •Peers   Faculty   LD staff   Teacher trainees

Tutorials
Grp.	Ind.	Tutorials	Grp.	Ind.	Tutorials
	•	Math skills		•	Word processing
•		Study skills	•	•	Time management
		Language arts	•	•	Learning strategies
	•	Written express	•	•	Organizational skills

Academic Accommodations
Curriculum	Study Aids	Exams
Priority registration	• Typist	• Oral
Math waiver	Reader	Untimed
• Foreign lang. waiver	• Notetaker	• Take home
• Course substitution	• Proof reader	• With proctor
In Class	• Text on tape	On computer
• Calculators	Early syllabus	• Extended time
• Tape recorder	Taped handouts	On tape
• Word processor		• Modified
Priority seating		Separate room

Graduation Requirements:
Course credits: **180** GPA: **2.0** Math waiver: **Yes** Language waiver: **Yes**

Program Strengths
The Learning Disabilities Program at University of Minnesota, Duluth, provides guidance, advocacy and assistance to students with learning disabilities, so that each can achieve his or her fullest potential.

General Information:
University of Minnesota: Duluth is a 4 year public university. Urban campus Accessible by air or bus. Ski areas are 5 miles from campus. Beaches are 3 miles from campus. Housing is not guaranteed.

Accreditation:NCACS

SAT/ACT Scores:
Scores for incoming freshmen: **ACT:** 18% below 20. 49% between 20 and 23. 24%between 26 and 28. 2% above 28.

Class Rank:
About 37% of the present freshmen class were in the upper 20% of their high school class. 36% were in the top 40% of their class. 14% were in the top 60% of their class. 11% were in the top 80% of their class.

Expenses:
Tuition: In-state: Full year: $2,437.00. Part-time: Per credit:$59.00. Tuition: Out-of-state: Full year: $3,120.00. Part-time: Per credit:$76.00.
Room and board: $3,000.00

Majors
• AREA STUDIES American Indian, Urban • BUSINESS Accounting, Banking, Business Administration, Business Economics, Business Management, Economics, Finance, Labor Relations, Management, Marketing,

Minnesota

Personnel • COMMUNICATIONS Advertising, Communication, English, Linguistic, Literature, Speech, Television/Radio/Film • COMPUTER SCIENCE Computer Science, Data Processing, Programming, Robotics, Systems Analysis • EDUCATION Art, Child Development, Early Childhood, Elementary, English, English As A Second Language (, Foreign Language, Home Economics Education, Industrial, Mathematics, Middle School, Music, Physical, Pre-education, Science, Secondary, Social Science, Social Studies, Special, Speech/Language, Technical • ENGINEERING Chemical, Electrical, Engineering Science, Geological, Industrial, Materials, Mechanical, Mining/Mineral, Petroleum • HEALTH SCIENCES Dental Hygiene, Health, Nutritional/Food, Speech Therapy, Speech/Audiology and Speech • HUMANITIES English/Writing/Literature, Humanities, Liberal Arts, Philosophy • LANGUAGES French, German, Spanish • PRE-PROFESSIONAL Architecture, Engineering, Forestry, Law, Medicine, Social Work, Sports Medicine, Veterinarian • SCIENCES Biology, Chemistry, Geography, Geology, Inorganic Chemistry, Mathematics, Oceanography, Physical Chemistry, Physical Science, Physics, Statistics • SOCIAL SCIENCES Anthropology, Criminal Justice, Criminology, Family Counseling, Geography, Government/Political, History, International Studies, Law Enforcement, Political Science, Psychology, Social Sciences, Sociology • VISUAL AND PERFORMING ARTS Art, Art History, Dance, Dramatic Arts, Drawing, Music, Music Performance, Studio Art, Theater • VOCATIONAL Auto Manufacturing Technology, Electronics Technology, Food Service, Home Economics, Industrial Equipment Maintenance, Painting, Park/Recreation, Textile and Clothing

Sports/Activities

• SPORTS RELATED Marching Band, Pep Band • SPORTS-INTERCOLLEGIATE Baseball (M), Basketball, Cross Country, Football (M), Golf, Ice Hockey (M), Softball (F), Tennis, Track and Field, Volleyball (F), Wrestling (M) • SPORTS-INTRAMURAL Archery, Basketball, Bowling, Crew (M), Crew (M), Cross Country, Field Hockey, Golf, Gymnastics, Hand Ball, Ice Hockey, Racquetball, Rugby, Sailing, Skiing - Snow, Soccer (M), Softball, Swimming, Tennis, Track and Field, Volleyball • STUDENT LIFE ACTIVITIES Choral, Community Service, Concert Band, Dance, Debate, Drama Groups, Ethnic & Cultural Groups, Fraternities, Jazz Band, Music Groups, Musical Theater, Newspaper, Opera, Political Groups, Radio/TV station, Religious Organization, Sororities, Student Government, Symphony Orchestra

---

Highly Selective	Minnesota
	Services

University of Minnesota: Morris
Behmler Hall
Morris, Minnesota 56267
(612) 589-2211-(800) 992-8863

School Enrollment: **2,041** Male: **878** Female: **1,073**

Admissions Contact: **Robert Vikander, Director of Admissions**
LD Contact: **Ferolyn Angell, Coordinator**
Name of Program: **Academic Assistance**
Address: **Briggs Library, Room 362**
Telephone:**(612) 589-6178**

Admissions

Application Information:
Application deadline: **March 15th**
Notified when: **April 1st**

Secondary School Information
Most Important Criteria For Admissions (1-strongest)

1 SAT/ACT	Application	School transcript
1 Class rank	Course selection	Personal statement
Interview	Extra activities	Psychoeducational
G.P.A.	Open admission	Recommendations

Test Requirements:
Diagnostic testing waived: **Yes**
Untimed SAT: **Yes** Untimed ACT: **Yes**
Documentation of LD required: **Yes**

Types of Disabilities Served
• Speech/Lang	• Reading	• ADD with LD
• Study skills	• Spelling	• ADD without LD
• Written express	• Math	• ADHD with LD
• Organizational	• Fine Motor	• ADHD without LD
• Perceptual		

Admissions Process

Applications obtained by writing to Office of Admissions & Financial Aid, University of Minnesota, Morris, MN 56267

High School Course Requirements:
English: **4** Math: **3** Science: **3** Foreign Language: **2**

Learning Disability Program
Program: Reinforces course work: **Yes**
Students mainstreamed **100** % of the day
Services available for all students: **Yes**
Counseling: Individual: **Yes** Vocational Counseling: **Yes**
Support groups are available: Can **be arranged**

Faculty:
Faculty: **1** Including Director: **Yes** Part time: **1**
Faculty advocate: **Yes** Meets with instructor: **As needed**

Diagnostic Testing
ADD	• Personality	Perceptual skills	• Spelling
ADHD	Organization	Fine motor skills	• Reading
• I.Q.	Handwriting	Spoken language	Study skills
• Math	Social skills	Written language	

Tutoring:
Average size of group tutorials: **2-4**
Services rendered by:
Graduates •Peers Faculty •LD staff Teacher trainees

Tutorials
Grp.	Ind.	Tutorials	Grp.	Ind.	Tutorials
•	•	Math skills			Word processing
•	•	Study skills	•	•	Time management
•	•	Language arts	•	•	Learning strategies
•	•	Written express	•	•	Organizational skills

Academic Accommodations

Curriculum	Study Aids	Exams
Priority registration	• Typist	• Oral
Math waiver	• Reader	Untimed
Foreign lang. waiver	• Notetaker	• Take home
• Course substitution	• Proof reader	• With proctor
In Class	• Text on tape	On computer
• Calculators	Early syllabus	• Extended time
• Tape recorder	Taped handouts	On tape
• Word processor		• Modified
Priority seating		• Separate room

Graduation Requirements:
Course credits: **180** GPA: **2.0**
Other requirements: **90 credits of General Education Major**

Program Strengths

Small, residential liberal arts college. We can make accommodations on an individualized basis.

General Information:

University of Minnesota: Morris is a 4 year public university. Rural campus of 165 acres is 150 miles from Minneapolis. Accessible by bus. Ski areas are 30 miles from campus. 5% of students are foreign. 5 residential halls on campus. Housing is guaranteed.70 % of students remain on campus for the weekends. 5 % of students join fraternities/sororities.

Accreditation:NCACS

SAT/ACT Scores:
Scores for incoming freshmen: **ACT:** 15% below 20. 24% between 20 and 23. 20%between 24 and 25l. 30%between 26 and 28. 11% above 28.

Class Rank:
About 82% of the present freshmen class were in the upper 20% of their high school class. 96% were in the top 40% of their class. 100% were in the top 60% of their class.

Expenses:
Tuition: In-state: Full year: $2,237.00. Part-time: Per credit:$58.00. Tuition: Out-of-state: Full year: $5,592.00. Part-time: Per credit:$144.00. Room and board: $2,835.00

Majors

• AREA STUDIES European, Latin American • BUSINESS Business Economics, Economics • COMMUNICATIONS Communication, English, Speech • COMPUTER SCIENCE Computer Science • EDUCATION Elementary, Health, Middle School, Secondary • HUMANITIES English/ Writing/Literature, Philosophy • LANGUAGES Hebrew • PREPROFESSIONAL Law • SCIENCES Biology, Chemistry, Geology, Mathematics, Physics • SOCIAL SCIENCES Government/Political, History, Political Science, Psychology, Social Sciences, Sociology • VISUAL AND PERFORMING ARTS Art, Art History, Dramatic Arts, Music, Studio Art, Theater

Sports/Activities

• SPORTS RELATED Cheerleading, Pep Band, Team Managers
• SPORTS-INTERCOLLEGIATE Baseball (M), Basketball, Football (M), Golf, Softball (F), Tennis, Track and Field, Volleyball (F), Wrestling (M)
• SPORTS-INTRAMURAL Basketball, Field Hockey, Hand Ball, Ping-Pong, Racquetball, Soccer, Softball, Swimming, Volleyball, Water Polo, Wrestling (M) • STUDENT LIFE ACTIVITIES Choral, Concert Band, Debate, Drama Groups, Ethnic & Cultural Groups, Fraternities, Jazz Band, Magazine, Music Groups, Musical Theater, Newspaper, Radio/TV station, Religious Organization, Sororities, Student Government, Symphony Orchestra, Yearbook

---

Less Selective — **Minnesota Services**

University of Minnesota: Crookston
Crookston, Minnesota 56716
(218) 281-6510

School Enrollment: **1,200** Male: **600** Female: **600**
LD Enrollment: **20** Male: **15** Female: **5**

Admissions Contact: **John Bywater, Director of Admissions**
LD Contact: **Laurie Wilson, Coordinator**
Name of Program: **Students with Disabilities**
Address: **Bede Student Center**
Telephone:**(218) 281-6510 Ext. 379**

Admissions

Application Information:
Application deadline: **Quarterly**
Applicant must apply **6** months in advance
Rolling Admissions: **Yes**

Secondary School Information
Most Important Criteria For Admissions (1-strongest)

SAT/ACT **1**	Application **2**	School transcript
3 Class rank	Course selection	Personal statement
Interview	Extra activities	Psychoeducational
G.P.A.	**1** Open admission	Recommendations

Test Requirements:
Standardized tests waived: **Yes**
Untimed ACT: **Yes**
Documentation of LD required: **Yes**
Currency of diagnostic testing: **within three years**

Types of Disabilities Served
• Speech/Lang • Reading ADD with LD
• Study skills • Spelling ADD without LD
• Written express • Math ADHD with LD
• Organizational • Fine Motor ADHD without LD
• Perceptual

Admissions Process

Apply to Office of Admissions and Enrollment Management, Hill Hall, UMC, Crookston, MN 56716

High School Course Requirements:
English: **4** Math: **3** Science: **3** Foreign Language: **2**

Learning Disability Program

Time required or recommended in learning center: **Varies**
Services available for all students: **Yes**
Counseling: Individual: **Yes**

Faculty:
Faculty: **1** Full time: **1** M.A.: **1**
Faculty advocate: **Yes**

Minnesota

Diagnostic Testing

ADD	Personality	Perceptual skills	Spelling
ADHD	Organization	Fine motor skills	Reading
I.Q.	Handwriting	Spoken language	Study skills
Math	Social skills	Written language	

Tutoring:
Services rendered by:
Graduates •Peers •Faculty LD staff Teacher trainees

Tutorials

Grp.	Ind.	Tutorials	Grp.	Ind.	Tutorials
•	•	Math skills			Word processing
•	•	Study skills	•		Time management
		Language arts	•	•	Learning strategies
•	•	Written express	•	•	Organizational skills

Academic Accommodations

Curriculum
- Priority registration
- Math waiver
- Foreign lang. waiver
- Course substitution

In Class
- Calculators
- Tape recorder
- Word processor
- Priority seating

Study Aids
- Typist
- Reader
- Notetaker
- Proof reader
- Text on tape
- Early syllabus
- Taped handouts

Exams
- Oral
- Untimed
- Take home
- With proctor
- On computer
- Extended time
- On tape
- Modified
- Separate room

Graduation Requirements:
Course credits: **96** GPA: **2.0** Years to complete degree: **Variable**

Program Strengths
University of Minnesota, Crookston, does not have a special learning disability program, but we do work closely with students to accommodate their needs as identified on their educational assessments. Faculty are generally very responsive to accommodating those requests as well as providing one-to-one assistance.

General Information:
University of Minnesota: Crookston is a 2 year public university. Rural campus of 92 acres is 1 miles from Crookston. Accessible by air or bus Ski areas are 90 miles from campus. Beaches are 25 miles from campus. 5% of students are foreign. 4 residential halls on campus. Housing is guaranteed.25 % of students remain on campus for the weekends.

Accreditation:NCACS

Expenses: Part-time: Per credit:$59.00. Part-time: Per credit:$174.00. Room and board: $3,080.00

Majors
• BUSINESS Accounting, Agricultural, Banking, Business Management, Fashion Merchandising, Finance, Hotel and Restaurant Management, Marketing, Real Estate • COMPUTER SCIENCE Data Processing, Programming, Systems Analysis • EDUCATION Early Childhood • HEALTH SCIENCES Medical Secretary, Nutritional/Food • HUMANITIES Liberal Arts • PREPROFESSIONAL Agriculture, Farm Management, Forestry, Natural Resources • SCIENCES Agricultural, Agronomy, Animal, Biology, Dairy, Equestrian Studies, Gerontology, Horticultural, Mechanical Agriculture • SOCIAL SCIENCES Social Sciences • VOCATIONAL Business and Office, Court Reporting, Forestry, Legal Secretary, Park/Recreation, Secretarial

Sports/Activities
• SPORTS RELATED Cheerleading, Fitness Center • SPORTS-INTERCOLLEGIATE Baseball (M), Basketball (F), Basketball (M), Football (M), Ice Hockey (M), Softball (F), Volleyball (F) • SPORTS-INTRAMURAL Basketball, Hockey, Racquetball, Tennis, Volleyball • STUDENT LIFE ACTIVITIES Choral, Concert Band, Drama Groups, Ethnic & Cultural Groups, Music Groups, Newspaper, Religious Organization, Student Government, Yearbook

---

Less Selective **Minnesota Services**

Wilmar Community College
P. O. Box 797
Wilmar, Minnesota 56201
(612) 231-5115

School Enrollment: **1,300** Male: **520** Female: **780**
LD Enrollment: **30** Male: **18** Female: **12**

Admissions Contact: **Arlen Sjerven, Director of Admissions**
LD Contact: **Bernice Grabber-Tintes, Director**
Name of Program: **DEEDS**
Telephone:**(612) 231-5176**

Admissions

Application Information:
LD Students Applying: **25** Accepted: **25** Enrolled:**23**
Separate application:**Yes**
Application deadline: **September 1st**
Applicant must apply **1** months in advance
Rolling Admissions: **Yes**

Secondary School Information
Most Important Criteria For Admissions (1-strongest)

11 SAT/ACT	1 Application	3	School transcript
11 Class rank	11 Course selection	5	Personal statement
4 Interview	11 Extra activities	2	Psychoeducational
6 G.P.A.	1 Open admission	7	Recommendations

Test Requirements:
Standardized tests waived: **Yes**
Diagnostic testing waived: **Yes**
Documentation of LD required: **Yes**
Tests recommended: **We need verified documentation of learning disability from qualified personnel**

Types of Disabilities Served
- Speech/Lang
- Study skills
- Written express
- Organizational
- Perceptual
- Reading
- Spelling
- Math
- Fine Motor
- ADD with LD
- ADD without LD
- ADHD with LD
- ADHD without LD

Admissions Process

1) Apply to college, 2) take placement test- may be extended if LD verified, 3) apply to DEEDS Program.

High School Course Requirements:
Waivers to standard high school courses
Course substitution: **Yes**

Learning Disability Program

Program: Reinforces course work: **Yes**
Program available through: Each **quarter**
Students mainstreamed **100** % of the day
Recommended credits per semester: **9-15**
Counseling: Individual: **Yes** Group Counseling: **Yes** Vocational Counseling: **Yes**
Support groups are available:**Yes**

Faculty:
Faculty: **2** Including Director: **Yes** Part time: **2**
LD faculty with: BS/BA: **1** M.A.: **1**
Faculty advocate: **Yes** Meets with instructor: **As needed**

Diagnostic Testing

ADD •	Personality	Perceptual skills	Spelling
ADHD	Organization	Fine motor skills •	Reading
I.Q.	Handwriting	Spoken language	Study skills
• Math	Social skills •	Written language	

Tutoring:
Services rendered by:
Graduates •Peers •Faculty •LD staff Teacher trainees

Tutorials

Grp.	Ind.	Tutorials	Grp.	Ind.	Tutorials
•	•	Math skills			Word processing
•	•	Study skills	•	•	Time management
•	•	Language arts	•	•	Learning strategies
•	•	Written express	•	•	Organizational skills

Academic Accommodations

Curriculum	Study Aids	Exams
• Priority registration	• Typist	• Oral
Math waiver	Reader	Untimed
Foreign lang. waiver	• Notetaker	Take home
Course substitution	Proof reader	• With proctor
In Class	• Text on tape	On computer
• Calculators	Early syllabus	• Extended time
• Tape recorder	Taped handouts	• On tape
Word processor		• Modified
Priority seating		• Separate room

Graduation Requirements:
Course credits: **96** GPA: **2.0**

Program Strengths

Our program is in its formative stages. We have a trained notetaker who provides, in addition to notetaking, training and support to volunteer notetakers. We have monthly support group meetings for members of our DEEDS (Designing Educational Experience for Disabled Students) Program and have services available for the blind student as well as signers for the hearing impaired.

General Information:

Wilmar Community College is a 2 year public college. Rural campus of 30 acres is 100 miles from Minneapolis. Accessible by air or bus. Ski areas are 35 miles from campus. Beaches are town from campus. 1% of students are foreign. Housing is not guaranteed.1 % of students join fraternities/sororities.

Accreditation:NCACS

SAT/ACT Scores:
Scores for incoming freshmen: **ACT:** 50% below 20. 30% between 20 and 23. 10%between 24 and 25l. 5%between 26 and 28. 5% above 28.

Class Rank:
About 5% of the present freshmen class were in the upper 20% of their high school class. 20% were in the top 40% of their class. 55% were in the top 60% of their class. 85% were in the top 80% of their class.

Expenses: Part-time: Per credit:$35.50.

Majors

• AREA STUDIES Women's Studies • BUSINESS Accounting, Agricultural, Business Administration, Business Economics, Business Education, Business Management, Economics, Entrepreneur, Finance, Hotel and Restaurant Management, Insurance, Management, Marketing, Marketing Research, Personnel, Travel/Tourism Management • COMMUNICATIONS Advertising, Broadcasting, Communication, English, Journalism, Literature, Photography, Speech • COMPUTER SCIENCE Computer Science, Computer Technology, Data Processing, Programming, Systems Analysis • EDUCATION Agricultural, Art, Child Development, Early Childhood, Elementary, Foreign Language, Health, Home Economics Education, Mathematics, Middle School, Music, Music Therapy, Nursing Education, Physical, Pre-Education, Reading Education, Science, Secondary, Social Science Education, Social Studies, Special, Speech/Language, Teacher Aide • ENGINEERING Chemical, Civil/Environmental, Computer, Electrical, Engineering Science, Mechanical • HEALTH SCIENCES Chiropractic, Communication Disorders, Environmental, Health, Medical Secretary, Medical Technology, Nursing, Nutritional/Food, Occupational Therapy, Physical Therapy, Radiological Therapy, Speech Therapy, Speech/Audiology and Speech • HUMANITIES English/Writing/Literature, Humanities, Liberal Arts, Philosophy, Religion • LANGUAGES German, Spanish • MATHEMATICS Actuarial, Applied, Computer • PREPROFESSIONAL Agriculture, Architectural, Business, Dentistry, Engineering, Fisheries, Forestry, Landscaping, Law, Legal Assistant, Medicine, Ministry, Natural Resources, Optometry, Pharmacy, Range Management, Recreation, Social Work, Sports Medicine, Urban Design, Veterinarian, Wildlife • SCIENCES Agricultural, Animal, Anthropology, Biology, Botany, Chemistry, Computer Science, General, Geography, Geology, Horticultural, Marine Biology, Meteorology, Oceanography, Physical Science, Zoology • SOCIAL SCIENCES Anthropology, Criminal Justice, Criminology, Family Counseling, Geography, Government/Political, History, Human Service, International Studies, Law Enforcement, Library Science, Political Science, Psychology, Public Relations, Social Sciences, Sociology • SPECIAL EDUCATION Occupational Therapy • VISUAL AND PERFORMING ARTS Art, Dramatic Arts, Fine Arts, Music, Music Performance, Theater • VOCATIONAL Aviation Administration, Business and Office, Park/Recreation, Radiological Technology, Secretarial

Sports/Activities

• SPORTS-INTERCOLLEGIATE Baseball (M), Basketball (F), Basketball (M), Football (M), Softball (F), Tennis (F), Tennis (M), Wrestling (M) • SPORTS-INTRAMURAL Basketball, Football, Softball • STUDENT LIFE ACTIVITIES Academic Clubs, Choral, Community Service, Music Groups, Musical Theater, Newspaper, Orchestra, Student Government

---

Less Selective

Minnesota Services

Worthington Community College

1450 College Way
Worthington, Minnesota 56187
(507) 372-2107

School Enrollment: **875** Male: **350** Female: **525**

Admissions Contact: **Cheryl Avenel-Navara, Counselor**
LD Contact: **Don Fleming, Dean of Students**
Address: **1450 College Way**
Telephone:**(507) 372-2107**

Admissions

Application Information:
Rolling Admissions: **Yes**

Secondary School Information
Most Important Criteria For Admissions (1-strongest)

SAT/ACT	Application	School transcript
Class rank	Course selection	Personal statement
Interview	Extra activities	Psychoeducational
G.P.A.	**1** Open admission	Recommendations

Test Requirements:
Documentation of LD required: **Yes**

Types of Disabilities Served
- Speech/Lang
- Study skills
- Written express
- Organizational
- Perceptual
- Reading
- Spelling
- Math
- Fine Motor
- ADD with LD
- ADD without LD
- ADHD with LD
- ADHD without LD

Admissions Process

Open admissions - high school graduate or G.E.D.

Learning Disability Program

Program: Remedial: **Yes**
Program: Reinforces course work: **Yes**
Program available through: Each **quarter**
Students mainstreamed **100** % of the day
Recommended credits per semester: **12 per quarter**
Services available for all students: **Yes**
Counseling: Individual: **Yes**

Faculty:
Faculty: **1** Part time: **1**
LD faculty with: BS/BA: **1**
Meets with instructor: **As needed**

Diagnostic Testing

ADD	Personality	Perceptual skills	Spelling
ADHD	Organization	Fine motor skills	Reading
I.Q.	Handwriting	Spoken language	Study skills
Math	Social skills	Written language	

Tutoring:
Average size of group tutorials: **1:1**
Services rendered by:
Graduates •Peers •Faculty LD staff Teacher trainees

Tutorials

Grp.	Ind.	Tutorials	Grp.	Ind.	Tutorials
	•	Math skills		•	Word processing
•		Study skills		•	Time management
	•	Language arts		•	Learning strategies
	•	Written express		•	Organizational skills

Academic Accommodations

Curriculum	Study Aids	Exams
Priority registration	Typist	• Oral
Math waiver	• Reader	• Untimed
Foreign lang. waiver	• Notetaker	• Take home
• Course substitution	• Proof reader	• With proctor
In Class	• Text on tape	On computer
Calculators	Early syllabus	• Extended time
• Tape recorder	• Taped handouts	• On tape
Word processor		• Modified
Priority seating		• Separate room

Graduation Requirements:
Course credits: **96** GPA: **2.0** Years to complete degree: **Indefinite** Math waiver: **Yes**
Other requirements: **Meet general degree requirements**

General Information:
Worthington Community College is a 2 year public college. Rural campus Accessible by air or bus. Ski areas are 200 miles from campus. Beaches are 2,500 miles from campus. Housing is not guaranteed.

Accreditation:NCACS

Expenses:
Tuition: In-state: Full year: $1,872.00. Part-time: Per credit:$39.00. Part-time: Per course: Varies. Tuition: Out-of-state: Full year: $3,744.00. Part-time: Per credit:$78.00. Part-time: Per course: Varies

Majors
• AGRICULTURE Business, Education, Engineering, Journalism • BUSINESS Business Administration, Business Management • HEALTH SCIENCES Nursing, Practical Nursing • HUMANITIES Liberal Arts • PRE PROFESSIONAL Agriculture, Architecture, Business, Dentistry, Engineering, Fisheries, Forestry, Law, Medicine, Ministry, Optometry, Pharmacy, Social Work, Veterinarian • SOCIAL SCIENCES Human Service

Sports/Activities
• SPORTS-INTERCOLLEGIATE Basketball, Basketball (F), Basketball (M), Football (M), Volleyball (F), Wrestling (M)

Less Selective   **Mississippi**
                                      Services

Hinds Community College
Raymond, Mississippi 39154-9799
(601) 857-5261

School Enrollment: **10,000** Male: **5,000** Female: **5,000**
LD Enrollment: **30** Male: **15** Female: **15**

Admissions Contact: **Billy Irby, Director of Admissions**
LD Contact: **Ginger Manchester, Director**
Name of Program: **Student Support Services**
Address: **Box 1290**
Telephone:**(601) 857-3386**

Admissions

Application Information:
LD Students Applying: **49** Accepted: **49** Enrolled:**49**
Separate application:**Yes**
Application deadline: **Open**
Applicant must apply **6** months in advance
Rolling Admissions: **Yes**

Secondary School Information
Most Important Criteria For Admissions (1-strongest)

SAT/ACT	Application	**3**	School transcript
Class rank	**4** Course selection		Personal statement
2 Interview	Extra activities		Psychoeducational
G.P.A.	**1** Open admission	**5**	Recommendations

Test Requirements:
Diagnostic testing waived: **Yes**
Untimed SAT: **Yes** Untimed ACT: **Yes**
WAIS-R required: **Yes**
Documentation of LD required: **Yes**
Currency of diagnostic testing: **within last 3 years**
Tests recommended: **Documentation of Learning Disability**

Types of Disabilities Served
- Speech/Lang
- Study skills
- Written express
- Organizational
- Perceptual
- Reading
- Spelling
- Math
- Fine Motor
- ADD with LD
- ADD without LD
- ADHD with LD
- ADHD without LD

Admissions Process

Apply to college, acceptance to college; apply to Student Support Services and send appropriate documentation of learning disability.

Learning Disability Program

Program: Reinforces course work: **Yes**
Students mainstreamed **100** % of the day
Services available for all students: **Yes**

Faculty:
Faculty: **15** Including Director: **Yes** Full time: **3** Part time: **12**
LD faculty with: BS/BA: **4** M.A.: **9**
Faculty advocate: **Yes** Meets with instructor: **As needed**

Diagnostic Testing

ADD	Personality	Perceptual skills	Spelling
ADHD	Organization	Fine motor skills	Reading
I.Q.	Handwriting	Spoken language	Study skills
• Math	Social skills	• Written language	

Tutoring:
Average size of group tutorials: **3**
Services rendered by:
   Graduates   Peers   Faculty   •LD staff   Teacher trainees

Tutorials

Grp.	Ind.	Tutorials	Grp.	Ind.	Tutorials
	•	Math skills		•	Word processing
	•	Study skills		•	Time management
	•	Language arts		•	Learning strategies
	•	Written express		•	Organizational skills

Academic Accommodations

Curriculum	Study Aids	Exams
• Priority registration	Typist	• Oral
Math waiver	Reader	Untimed
Foreign lang. waiver	• Notetaker	Take home
Course substitution	• Proof reader	With proctor
In Class	• Text on tape	On computer
• Calculators	Early syllabus	• Extended time
• Tape recorder	Taped handouts	On tape
• Word processor		• Modified
Priority seating		Separate room

Graduation Requirements: Math waiver: **Yes** Language waiver: **Yes**

General Information:

Hinds Community College is a 2 year public college. Rural campus of 5800 acres is 10 miles from Jackson. Accessible by air or car. Beaches are 25 miles from campus. .05% of students are foreign. 8 residential halls on campus. Housing is not guaranteed.5 % of students remain on campus for the weekends.

Accreditation: Regional

Expenses:
Tuition: In-state: Full year: $720.00. Tuition: Out-of-state: Full year: $2,200.00.

Majors

• BUSINESS Accounting, Agricultural, Banking, Business Administration, Business Education, Business Management, Economics, Fashion Merchandising, Hotel and Restaurant Management, Marketing, Real Estate • COMMUNICATIONS Commercial Design, English, Graphic Design Technology • COMPUTER SCIENCE Data Processing, Programming • EDUCATION Art, Child Development, Curriculum, Early Childhood, Elementary, Middle School, Music, Physical, Secondary, Special, Speech/Language • ENGINEERING Aerospace, Agricultural, Computer, Engineering Science, Mechanical, Nuclear • HEALTH SCIENCES Dental Assistant, Medical Technology, Nursing, Occupational Therapy, Physical Therapy, Surgical Technology, Veterinarian Assistant • HUMANITIES Liberal Arts, Philosophy • LANGUAGES French, Spanish • PREPROFESSIONAL Agriculture, Architecture, Engineering, Law, Medicine, Ministry, Pharmacy, Social Work • SCIENCES Biology, Chemistry, Geography, Geology, Physics • SOCIAL SCIENCES Criminal Justice, Human Service, Law Enforcement, Psychology, Sociology • VISUAL AND PERFORMING ARTS Art, Music • VOCATIONAL Automated Manufacturing Technology, Business and Office, Diesel Power Technology, Drafting, Electronics Technology, Landscaping Management, Medical Laboratory Technology, Park/Recreation, Precision Metal Work, Printing/Lithography, Respiratory Therapy Technology, Secretarial

Mississippi

Sports/Activities

• SPORTS RELATED Cheerleading, Drill Team, Drum Major/Majorette, Marching Band, Pep Band • SPORTS-INTERCOLLEGIATE Baseball (M), Basketball, Football (M), Golf (M), Softball (F), Tennis, Track and Field (M) • SPORTS-INTRAMURAL Basketball, Golf, Soccer, Softball, Tennis, Track and Field (F), Volleyball • STUDENT LIFE ACTIVITIES Academic Clubs, Choral, Concert Band, Drama Groups, Ethnic & Cultural Groups, Jazz Band, Music Groups, Musical Theater, Newspaper, Religious Organization, Student Government, Yearbook

Selective   **Mississippi Program**

University of Mississippi

Room 300, Lyceum
University, Mississippi 38677
(601) 232-726

School Enrollment: **11,033** Male: **5,610** Female: **5,423**
LD Enrollment: **87**

Admissions Contact: **Beckett Howorth, Director of Admissions**
LD Contact: **Ardessa Minor, Assoc. Dir/Student Development**
Name of Program: **Office of Special Services**
Address: **Suite 11-A, J.D. Williams Library**
Telephone:**(601) 232-7128**

Admissions

Application Information:
Enrolled:**87**
Separate application:**Yes**
Applicant must apply **6** months in advance

Secondary School Information
Most Important Criteria For Admissions (1-strongest)

1 SAT/ACT	**1** Application	**1** School transcript
Class rank	Course selection	Personal statement
1 Interview	Extra activities	Psychoeducational
G.P.A.	Open admission	Recommendations

Test Requirements:
Diagnostic testing waived: **Yes**
Untimed SAT: **Yes** Untimed ACT: **Yes**
Documentation of LD required: **Yes**
Currency of diagnostic testing: **3 years**
Tests recommended: **WAIS-R and Woodcock-Johnson**

Types of Disabilities Served
• Speech/Lang   • Reading   • ADD with LD
• Study skills   • Spelling   • ADD without LD
• Written express • Math   • ADHD with LD
• Organizational   • Fine Motor   • ADHD without LD
• Perceptual

Admissions Process

Initial contact (phone call or interview). Applicant is admitted to UM. Applicant applies and admitted to LD Program (with documentation).

Learning Disability Program

Syllabus available during orientation:**Yes**
Program: Reinforces course work: **Yes**
Students mainstreamed **100** % of the day
Time required or recommended in learning center: **3-4 hours**
Services only for LD students: **Yes**
Services available for all students: **Yes**
Counseling: Individual: **Yes**
Support groups are available:**Yes**

Faculty:
Faculty: **3** Including Director: **Yes** Full time: **1** Part time: **1**
LD faculty with: BS/BA: **1** Ph.D.: **1**
Faculty advocate: **Yes** Meets with instructor: **When necessary**

Diagnostic Testing
ADD	• Personality	Perceptual skills	Spelling
ADHD	Organization	Fine motor skills	Reading
I.Q.	Handwriting	Spoken language	• Study skills
Math	Social skills	Written language	

Tutoring:
Average size of group tutorials: **5+**
Services rendered by:
•Graduates   •Peers   •Faculty   LD staff   Teacher trainees

Tutorials
Grp.	Ind. Tutorials	Grp.	Ind. Tutorials
	• Math skills		Word processing
	• Study skills	•	Time management
	Language arts	•	Learning strategies
	• Written express	• •	Organizational skills

Academic Accommodations

Curriculum	Study Aids	Exams
• Priority registration	Typist	• Oral
Math waiver	• Reader	• Untimed
Foreign lang. waiver	• Notetaker	Take home
Course substitution	• Proof reader	• With proctor
In Class	• Text on tape	• On computer
• Calculators	Early syllabus	• Extended time
• Tape recorder	Taped handouts	On tape
• Word processor		• Modified
• Priority seating		Separate room

General Information:

University of Mississippi is a 4 year public university. rural campus 95 miles from Memphis. Accessible by air, train or bus. 14 residential halls on campus. Housing is not guaranteed.40 % of students remain on campus for the weekends. 70 % of students join fraternities/sororities.

Accreditation:

Expenses:
Tuition: In-state: Full year: $1,010.50. Part-time: Per credit:$74.00. Tuition: Out-of-state: Full year: $1,841.50. Part-time: Per credit:$90.00.
Room and board: $680.00 Cost of LD program:$500.00

Majors

• AREA STUDIES Black/Afro-American, Latin American • ARTS Art History, Drawing, Interior Design, Music, Music History, Painting, Sculpture • BUSINESS Accounting, Business Administration, Economics, Education, Fashion Merchandising, Hotel & Restaurant Management, International Business, Management, Marketing, Real Estate • COMMUNICATIONS Advertising, Broadcasting, English, Journalism, Linguistics, Speech/Debate/Forensics, Television/Radio/Film • COMPUTER SCIENCE Computer Mathematics, Medical Records Technology, Telecommunications • CRAFTS AND DESIGN Ceramics, Jewelry, Printmaking, Sculpture • EDUCATION Art, Curriculum, Early Childhood, Elementary, Leadership, Music, Psychology, Reading, Secondary, Special • ENGINEERING Chemical, Civil/Environmental, Electrical, Geological, Mechanical • HEALTH SCIENCES Communication Disorders, Dental Assistant, Dental Hygiene, Dental Technician, Pharmacology, Physical Therapy, Radiological Therapy • HUMANITIES Classics • LANGUAGES Arabic, Chinese, French, German, Italian, Japanese, Portuguese, Russian, Spanish • MATHEMATICS Theoretical • PREPROFESSIONAL Dentistry, Law, Pharmacy, Veterinarian • RELIGIOUS STUDIES Philosophy • SCIENCES Astronomy, Biology, Botany, Chemistry, Microbiology, Physics • SOCIAL SCIENCES Anthropology, Criminal Justice, Law Enforcement, Political Science, Sociology • VISUAL AND PERFORMING ARTS Art, Art History, Theater

Sports/Activities

• SPORTS-INTERCOLLEGIATE Baseball (M), Basketball (F), Basketball (M), Football (M), Golf, Riflery, Tennis (F), Tennis (M), Track and Field (F), Track and Field (M), Volleyball (F), Volleyball (M) • SPORTS-INTRAMURAL Archery, Bowling, Canoeing, Golf, Horseback Riding, Racquetball, Riflery, Sailing, Soccer, Swimming, Tennis, Volleyball, Weight Lifting • STUDENT LIFE ACTIVITIES Academic Clubs, Community Service, Concert Band, Drama Groups, Ethnic & Cultural Groups, Fraternities, Music Groups, Musical Theater, Newspaper, Radio/TV station, Religious Organization, Sororities, Student Government, Yearbook

---

Less Selective

Missouri Services

Central Missouri State University

Union 215
Warrensburg, Missouri 64093
(816) 429-4673

School Enrollment: **11,209** Male: **5,500** Female: **5,709**

Admissions Contact: **Delores Hudson, Director of Admissions**
LD Contact: **Mary Alice Lyon, Dir. Project Advance**
Name of Program: **Project Advance**

Admissions

Secondary School Information
Most Important Criteria For Admissions (1-strongest)

2 SAT/ACT	Application	1	School transcript
2 Class rank	Course selection		Personal statement
Interview	Extra activities		Psychoeducational
3 G.P.A.	Open admission		Recommendations

Test Requirements:
Untimed ACT: **Yes**

Types of Disabilities Served
- Speech/Lang
- Study skills
- Written express
- Organizational Perceptual
- Reading
- Spelling
- Math
- Fine Motor

ADD with LD
ADD without LD
ADHD with LD
ADHD without LD

Diagnostic Testing

ADD	Personality	Perceptual skills	Spelling
ADHD	Organization	Fine motor skills	Reading
I.Q.	Handwriting	Spoken language	Study skills
Math	Social skills	Written language	

Tutoring:
Services rendered by:
•Graduates •Peers •Faculty LD staff Teacher trainees

Tutorials

Grp.	Ind.	Tutorials	Grp.	Ind.	Tutorials
•		Math skills	•		Word processing
•		Study skills	•		Time management
•		Language arts	•		Learning strategies
•		Written express	•		Organizational skills

Academic Accommodations

Curriculum	Study Aids	Exams
Priority registration	Typist	• Oral
Math waiver	Reader	Untimed
• Foreign lang. waiver	Notetaker	• Take home
Course substitution	• Proof reader	With proctor
In Class	• Text on tape	On computer
• Calculators	Early syllabus	• Extended time
• Tape recorder	Taped handouts	On tape
• Word processor		Modified
Priority seating		Separate room

Program Strengths
Central Missouri State University tries to accommodate students with learning disabilities according to their needs. There is no program just for LD students.

General Information:
Central Missouri State University is a 4 year public university. of 1,038 acres is 60 miles from Kansas City. Accessible by train or bus. 4% of students are foreign. Housing is not guaranteed.

Accreditation: Regional

Expenses: Part-time: Per credit:$56.00. Part-time: Per credit:$100.00. Room and board: $1,338.00

Majors

• BUSINESS Accounting, Agricultural, Banking, Business Administration, Business Economics, Business Education, Business Management, Economics, Finance, Hotel and Restaurant Management, Insurance, Management, Marketing, Personnel, Real Estate, Travel/Tourism Management • COMMUNICATIONS Advertising, Broadcasting, Commercial Design, Communication, English, Journalism, Photography, Speech, Television/Radio/Film • COMPUTER SCIENCE Computer Science, Data Processing, Programming, Systems Analysis, Telecommunications • CRAFTS AND DESIGN Apparel Design Marketing • EDUCATION Agricultural, Art, Child Development, Curriculum, Early Childhood, Elementary, English, Foreign Language, Health, Industrial, Mathematics, Middle School, Music, Music Therapy, Physical, Pre-Education, Recreation and Youth Leadership, School Psychology, Science, Secondary, Social Studies, Special, Speech/Language, Vocational • HEALTH SCIENCES Communication Disorders, Dietary Manager, Environmental, Health, Medical Technology, Nursing, Nutritional/Food, Speech Therapy, Speech/Audiology and Speech • HUMANITIES Humanities, Philosophy • LANGUAGES French, German, Spanish • PREPROFESSIONAL Agriculture, Recreation, Social Work • SCIENCES Actuarial Technology, Agricultural, Astronomy, Biochemistry, Biology, Chemistry, Earth, Ecology, Geography, Geology, Mathematics, Oceanography, Physical Chemistry, Physical Science, Physics • SOCIAL SCIENCES Criminal Justice, Government/Political, History, Law Enforcement, Political Science, Psychology, Public Relations, Sociology • VISUAL AND PERFORMING ARTS Art, Art History, Dance, Music, Music Performance, Studio Art, Theater • VOCATIONAL Air Conditioning/Heating/Refrig, Automobile Technology, Drafting, Electronics Technology, Food Service, Home Economics, Interior Design, Office Administration, Printing/Lithography, Secretarial, Textile and Clothing

Sports/Activities

• SPORTS RELATED Marching Band, Pep Band • SPORTS-INTERCOLLEGIATE Baseball (M), Basketball, Bowling, Cross Country, Football (M), Golf (M), Softball (F), Tennis, Track and Field, Volleyball (F), Wrestling (M) • SPORTS-INTRAMURAL Badminton, Basketball, Bowling, Cross Country, Golf (M), Gymnastics (F), Hand Ball, Ping-Pong, Racquetball, Rugby, Soccer, Swimming, Tennis, Track and Field, Volleyball, Water Polo, Wrestling (M) • STUDENT LIFE ACTIVITIES Choral, Concert Band, Dance, Debate, Drama Groups, Ethnic & Cultural Groups, Film, Fraternities, Jazz Band, Music Groups, Musical Theater, Newspaper, Opera, Radio/TV station, Religious Organization, Sororities, Student Government, Symphony Orchestra, Yearbook

---

Selective   **Missouri Program**

Evangel College
Box 574
Springfield, Missouri 65802
(417) 865-2811

School Enrollment: **1,411** Male: **637** Female: **764**
LD Enrollment: **50** Male: **35** Female: **15**

Admissions Contact: **David Schoolfield, Director of Enrollment**
LD Contact: **Eleanor G. Syler, Coordinator**
Name of Program: **Learning Skills Center**
Telephone:**(417) 865-2811- Ext. 7232**

Admissions

Application Information:
Enrolled:**50**
Application deadline: **August**
Applicant must apply **3 months in advance**
Notified when: **September 1st**

Secondary School Information
Most Important Criteria For Admissions (1-strongest)

2 SAT/ACT	**6** Application	**5** School transcript
4 Class rank	**7** Course selection	**11** Personal statement
10 Interview	**8** Extra activities	**9** Psychoeducational
3 G.P.A.	Open admission	**1** Recommendations

Test Requirements:
Diagnostic testing waived: **Yes**
Tests recommended: **Only English and math placement**

Types of Disabilities Served
• Speech/Lang • Reading   ADD with LD
• Study skills • Spelling   ADD without LD
• Written express • Math   ADHD with LD
• Organizational • Fine Motor   ADHD without LD
• Perceptual

Learning Disability Program

Program: Remedial: **Yes**
Program: Reinforces course work: **Yes**
Students mainstreamed **90** % of the day
Time required or recommended in learning center: **3 hours**
Services available for all students: **Yes**
Counseling: Individual: **Yes** Group Counseling: **Yes**

Faculty:

Faculty: **2** Full time: **2** M.A.: **1** Ph.D.: **1**
Faculty advocate: **Yes** Meets with instructor: **When needed**

Diagnostic Testing
ADD	• Personality	Perceptual skills	• Spelling
ADHD	• Organization	Fine motor skills	• Reading
• I.Q.	Handwriting	Spoken language	• Study skills
• Math	Social skills	• Written language	

Tutoring:
Services rendered by:
Graduates •Peers •Faculty •LD staff Teacher trainees

Tutorials
Grp.	Ind. Tutorials	Grp.	Ind. Tutorials
	• Math skills		• Word processing
	• Study skills		• Time management
	• Language arts		• Learning strategies
	• Written express		• Organizational skills

Academic Accommodations

Curriculum	Study Aids	Exams
Priority registration	Typist	• Oral
Math waiver	Reader	Untimed
• Foreign lang. waiver	Notetaker	Take home
Course substitution	• Proof reader	• With proctor
In Class	• Text on tape	On computer
Calculators	Early syllabus	Extended time
Tape recorder	Taped handouts	On tape
Word processor		Modified
Priority seating		Separate room

Graduation Requirements:
Course credits: **124** GPA: **2.0** Years to complete degree: **4**

Program Strengths

Our program is unique in so far as we emphasize study skills rather than working on primary LD problems. We also give individual attention. Time is also spent in CAI labs. Tutors are available. Small classes allow for close interaction socially and academically.

General Information:

Evangel College is a 4 year private Assemblies of God college. Urban campus of 80 acres is 150 miles from Kansas City. Accessible by air or bus. 6 residential halls on campus. Housing is not guaranteed.100 % of students remain on campus for the weekends.

Accreditation: NCATE, NCACSS, MSDE, DEGCAG

Expenses:

Tuition: In-state: Full year: $4,970.00. Part-time: Per credit:$193.00. Room and board: $1,330.00

Majors

• BUSINESS Accounting, Business Administration, Business Education, Business Management, Economics, Management, Marketing • COMMUNICATIONS Advertising, Broadcasting, Creative Writing, English, Graphic Design, Journalism, Photography, Speech, Television/Radio/Film • COMPUTER SCIENCE Computer Science, Data Processing, Programming, Systems Analysis • EDUCATION Art, Curriculum, Early Childhood, Elementary, English, Foreign Language, Health, Mathematics, Middle School, Music, Physical, Pre-Education, Recreation and Youth Leadership, Science, Secondary, Social Studies, Special, Speech/Language • HEALTH SCIENCES Health, Nursing • HUMANITIES Philosophy, Religion • LANGUAGES French, Spanish • PREPROFESSIONAL Law, Ministry, Recreation, Social Work, Veterinarian • SCIENCES Biology, Botany,

Chemistry, Earth, Geography, Geology, Macrobiology, Physical Science, Physics • SOCIAL SCIENCES Anthropology, Criminal Justice, Government/Political, History, Political Science, Psychology, Public Relations, Social Sciences, Sociology • VISUAL AND PERFORMING ARTS Art, Dramatic Arts, Music, Music Performance, Studio Art, Theater • VOCATIONAL Business and Office, Secretarial

Sports/Activities

• SPORTS RELATED Pep Band • SPORTS-INTERCOLLEGIATE Baseball (M), Basketball, Football (M), Tennis (F), Volleyball (F) • SPORTS-INTRAMURAL Basketball, Soccer (M), Softball, Volleyball (F) • STUDENT LIFE ACTIVITIES Academic Clubs, Choral, Concert Band, Debate, Drama Groups, Ethnic & Cultural Groups, Music Groups, Newspaper, Radio/TV station, Religious Organization, Student Government, Symphony Orchestra, Yearbook

---

Less Selective　　　　　　　　　**Missouri Services**

Jefferson College

1000 Viking Drive
Hillsboro, Missouri 63050
(314) 789-3951

School Enrollment: **3,800** Male: **1,786** Female: **2,014**

Admissions Contact: **Peter Ross, Director of Admissions**
LD Contact: **Beth Ferguson, Assessment Counselor**
Name of Program: **Learning Center**

Admissions

Secondary School Information
Most Important Criteria For Admissions (1-strongest)

SAT/ACT	**2** Application	School transcript
1 Class rank	**3** Course selection	**8** Personal statement
5 Interview	**7** Extra activities	**9** Psychoeducational
1 G.P.A.	Open admission	**6** Recommendations

Types of Disabilities Served
- Speech/Lang
- Study skills
- Written express
- Organizational
- Perceptual
- Reading
- Spelling
- Math
- Fine Motor
- ADD with LD
- ADD without LD
- ADHD with LD
- ADHD without LD

Learning Disability Program
Services available for all students: **Yes**
Counseling: Individual: **Yes** Group Counseling: **Yes**

Faculty:
Faculty: **1** Part time: **1**
Faculty advocate: **Yes**

Diagnostic Testing
ADD	Personality	Perceptual skills	Spelling
ADHD	Organization	Fine motor skills	Reading
I.Q.	Handwriting	Spoken language	Study skills
Math	Social skills	Written language	

Tutoring:
Average size of group tutorials: **2-3**
Services rendered by:
Graduates　•Peers　•Faculty　LD staff　Teacher trainees

Tutorials

Grp.	Ind.	Tutorials	Grp.	Ind.	Tutorials
•	•	Math skills	•	•	Word processing
•	•	Study skills	•	•	Time management
•	•	Language arts		•	Learning strategies
	•	Written express		•	Organizational skills

Academic Accommodations

Curriculum	Study Aids	Exams
Priority registration	• Typist	• Oral
• Math waiver	• Reader	• Untimed
• Foreign lang. waiver	• Notetaker	• Take home
• Course substitution	• Proof reader	• With proctor
In Class	• Text on tape	• On computer
• Calculators	Early syllabus	• Extended time
• Tape recorder	• Taped handouts	• On tape
• Word processor		• Modified
• Priority seating		• Separate room

Program Strengths
At the present time we offer a few services to LD students. Our long range plans include many more additions and modifications.

General Information:
Jefferson College is a 2 year public college. Rural campus of 480 acres is 30 miles from St. Louis. Accessible by car. Ski areas are 40 miles from campus. 3% of students are foreign. Housing is not guaranteed.

Accreditation: NCACS

Expenses: Part-time: Per credit:$32.00 in district, $45.00 out of district. Part-time: Per credit:$56.00.

Majors
• AREA STUDIES American • BUSINESS Accounting, Hotel and Restaurant Management, Retailing • COMMUNICATIONS Communication, English • COMPUTER SCIENCE Computer Technology, Data Processing, Programming, Robotics, Telecommunications • EDUCATION English, Secondary • ENGINEERING Civil/Environmental, Mathematical • HEALTH SCIENCES Medical Secretary, Nursing, Practical Nursing • HUMANITIES Liberal Arts • LANGUAGES French, Spanish • PRE-PROFESSIONAL Architecture, Law, Medicine, Veterinarian • SCIENCES Biology, Emergency Science, Mathematics, Physical Science • SOCIAL SCIENCES Government/Political, History, Law Enforcement, Political Science, Psychology, Social Sciences, Sociology • VISUAL AND PERFORMING ARTS Art History, Fine Arts, Music, Music Performance • VOCATIONAL Air Conditioning/Heating/Refri, Automobile Technology, Drafting, Electronics Technology, Fire Science, Legal Secretary, Machinist, Precision Metal Work, Secretarial, Veterinarian Assistant

Sports/Activities
• SPORTS-INTERCOLLEGIATE Baseball (M), Basketball (F), Tennis (M) • SPORTS-INTRAMURAL Basketball, Softball, Tennis, Volleyball • STUDENT LIFE ACTIVITIES Academic Clubs, Choral, Concert Band, Drama Groups, Jazz Band, Music Groups, Musical Theater, Newspaper, Radio/TV station, Student Government, Yearbook

Kansas City Art Institute
4415 Warwick Boulevard
Kansas City, Missouri 64111
(816) 561-4852

School Enrollment: **560**

Admissions Contact: **Dr. Jan Norman, Director of Admissions**
LD Contact: **Kimberly Tyson, Director**
Name of Program: **Academic Resource Center**
Telephone:**(816) 561-4852 Ext. 264**

Admissions

Application Information:
Application deadline: **February 15th**
Rolling Admissions: **Yes**

Secondary School Information
Most Important Criteria For Admissions (1-strongest)

SAT/ACT	Application	School transcript
Class rank	Course selection	Personal statement
Interview	Extra activities	Psychoeducational
G.P.A.	Open admission	Recommendations

Types of Disabilities Served

Speech/Lang	• Reading	ADD with LD
• Study skills	• Spelling	ADD without LD
• Written express	• Math	ADHD with LD
• Organizational	Fine Motor	ADHD without LD
Perceptual		

Learning Disability Program
Program: Reinforces course work: **Yes**
Students mainstreamed **100** % of the day
Counseling: Individual: **Yes**

Faculty:
Faculty: **3** Including Director: **Yes** Full time: **2** Part time: **1** M.A.: **3**

Diagnostic Testing

ADD	Personality	• Perceptual skills	• Spelling
ADHD	Organization	Fine motor skills	• Reading
I.Q.	Handwriting	• Spoken language	• Study skills
• Math	Social skills	• Written language	

Tutoring:
Average size of group tutorials: **2**
Services rendered by:

Graduates	Peers	Faculty	•LD staff	Teacher trainees

Tutorials

Grp.	Ind.	Tutorials	Grp.	Ind.	Tutorials
		Math skills		•	Word processing
•	•	Study skills	•	•	Time management
	•	Language arts	•	•	Learning strategies
	•	Written express	•	•	Organizational skills

Academic Accommodations

Curriculum	Study Aids	Exams
Priority registration	• Typist	• Oral
Math waiver	Reader	Untimed
Foreign lang. waiver	Notetaker	Take home
Course substitution	Proof reader	With proctor
In Class	• Text on tape	On computer
Calculators	Early syllabus	• Extended time
• Tape recorder	Taped handouts	On tape
• Word processor		Modified
Priority seating		Separate room

Program Strengths
The key to our program is "individuality". We have a small number of LD students, therefore, we are able to meet each student's needs. We offer individual sessions as often as needed, texts on tape, study groups, word processing, untimed tests and encourage students to tape record lectures. Since the Academic Resource Center is located in the same building as the Liberal Arts professors and classrooms, the center is convenient for students to drop in and out. The staff at the ARC has a good relationship with the faculty in helping them meet individual needs of students.

General Information:
Kansas City Art Institute is a 4 year independent college. Urban campus of 20 acres is Accessible by air, train, or bus. 1 residential halls on campus. Housing is not guaranteed.

Accreditation:NCACS

Expenses:
Tuition: In-state: Full year: $5,105.00. Part-time: Per credit:$400.00. Room and board: $3,400.00-$4,200.00

Majors
• COMMUNICATIONS Graphic Design, Photography • CRAFTS AND DESIGN Ceramics, Crafts, Drawing, Film Arts, Illustration Design, Sculpture • VISUAL AND PERFORMING ARTS Art, Fine Arts, Studio Art, Video • VOCATIONAL Painting, Printing/Lithography, Textile and Clothing

Sports/Activities
• STUDENT LIFE ACTIVITIES Ethnic & Cultural Groups, Music Groups, Newspaper, Student Film Series, Student Operated Gallery, Visiting Arts Program

Longview Community College
500 Longview Road
Lee's Summit, Missouri 64063
(816) 763-7777

School Enrollment: **9,536** Male: **3,910** Female: **5,626**
LD Enrollment: **47** Male: **32** Female: **15**

Admissions Contact: **Julie Royal-Ferris College Relations Coor.**
LD Contact: **Mary Ellen Jenison Project ABLE Coordinator**
Name of Program: **Project ABLE**
Address: **Longview Campus, 500 SW Longview Rd.**
Telephone:**(816) 763-7777**

Admissions

Application Information:
LD Students Applying: **70** Accepted: **61** Enrolled: **47**
Separate application: **Yes**
Application deadline: **April 1st, June 1st, November 1st**
Applicant must apply **2** months in advance
Rolling Admissions: **Yes**

Secondary School Information
Most Important Criteria For Admissions (1-strongest)

SAT/ACT	Application	School transcript
Class rank	Course selection	Personal statement
Interview	Extra activities	Psychoeducational
G.P.A.	**1** Open admission	Recommendations

Test Requirements:
Diagnostic testing waived: **Yes**
Untimed SAT: **Yes** Untimed ACT: **Yes** Untimed ACH: **Yes** Achievement tests required: **3**
WAIS-R required: **Yes** Range accepted: **80+**
Documentation of LD required: **Yes**
Currency of diagnostic testing: **No more than 36 months**
Tests recommended: **Global Intelligence, Standardized Achievement (WRAT-R or Woodcock-Johnson), ASSET Placement or ACT (untimed), WRMT-R Word Attack. Lindamood Auditory Conceptualizing Test.**

Types of Disabilities Served
- Speech/Lang
- Study skills
- Written express
- Organizational
- Perceptual
- Reading
- Spelling
- Math
- Fine Motor
- ADD with LD
- ADD without LD
- ADHD with LD
- ADHD without LD

Admissions Process

Potential students take untimed placement tests and any diagnostic testing needed. An interview, consisting of questions regarding background history and reading and study skills, is scheduled with the Coordinator. Acceptance is contingent upon receipt of validating documentation.

Learning Disability Program

Special orientation for LD students: **Yes**
Syllabus available during orientation: **Yes**
Program: Remedial: **Yes**
Program: Reinforces course work: **Yes**
Program available through: Each **semester**
Students mainstreamed **0-75** % of the day
Recommended credits per semester: **varies**
Time required or recommended in learning center: **Individual basis**
Services available for all students: **Yes**
Counseling: Individual: **Yes** Group Counseling: **Yes** Vocational Counseling: **Yes**
Support groups are available: **Project ABLE students are scheduled into support groups on a weekly basis.**

Faculty:
Faculty: **18** Including Director: **Yes** Full time: **1** Part time: **17**
LD faculty with: BS/BA: **2**
Faculty advocate: **Yes** Meets with instructor: **Weekly**

Diagnostic Testing
ADD	• Personality	• Perceptual skills	• Spelling
ADHD	Organization	Fine motor skills	• Reading
• I.Q.	Handwriting	Spoken language	Study skills
Math	Social skills	• Written language	

Tutoring:
Average size of group tutorials: **3**
Services rendered by:
Graduates •Peers •Faculty •LD staff Teacher trainees

Tutorials
Grp.	Ind.	Tutorials	Grp.	Ind.	Tutorials
•	•	Math skills	•	•	Word processing
•	•	Study skills	•	•	Time management
		Language arts	•	•	Learning strategies
•	•	Written express	•	•	Organizational skills

Academic Accommodations

Curriculum	Study Aids	Exams
• Priority registration	Typist	• Oral
Math waiver	• Reader	• Untimed
Foreign lang. waiver	• Notetaker	Take home
• Course substitution	• Proof reader	• With proctor
In Class	• Text on tape	• On computer
• Calculators	Early syllabus	• Extended time
• Tape recorder	• Taped handouts	• On tape
• Word processor		Modified
• Priority seating		• Separate room

Graduation Requirements:
Course credits: **Vary by degree** GPA: **2.0** Years to complete degree: **Not restricted**

Program Strengths

Project ABLE is a structured program of courses and services that interface with the regular college program. ABLE students are taught essential skills and receive needed services, yet are familiarized with general college services and activities from the beginning. Specialized ABLE classes are limited in size to no more than 12 students each. All ABLE students are scheduled into weekly support group sessions, which are separated according to disability (learning disability or traumatic brain injury). The object of the program is the successful transition to a regular college curriculum or the workplace.

General Information:
Longview Community College is a 2 year public college. Suburban campus of 146 acres is 15 miles from Kansas City. Accessible by car. Housing is not guaranteed.

Accreditation: NCACS

Expenses:
Tuition: In-state: Full year: Charged per credit hour. Part-time: Per credit: $37.00 in district, $60.00 out of district. Tuition: Out-of-state: Full year: Charged per credit hour. Part-time: Per credit: $87.00. Cost of LD program: $75.00 per credit hour (in-state), $116.00 per credit hour (out of state)

Majors
• BUSINESS Accounting, Business Administration, Business Management, Data Processing, Management, Marketing • COMPUTER SCIENCE Business Data Programming, Programming • HEALTH SCIENCES Medical Secretary • HUMANITIES Liberal Arts • SCIENCES ChemiSTRY • SOCIAL SCIENCES Criminal Justice, Human Service, Law Enforcement • VOCATIONAL Automobile Technology, Business and Office, Diesel Power Technology, Drafting, Electronics Technology, Legal Secretary, Quality Control Technology, Secretarial, Word Processing

Less Selective

Maple Woods Community College

2601 Northeast Barry Road
Kansas City, Missouri 64156
(816) 436-6500

School Enrollment: **4,880** Male: **2,158** Female: **2,722**
LD Enrollment: **75+**

Admissions Contact: **Barbara Reinwald, Registrar**
LD Contact: **Kathy Acosta, Learning Specialist**

Admissions

Secondary School Information
Most Important Criteria For Admissions (1-strongest)

SAT/ACT	Application	School transcript
Class rank	Course selection	Personal statement
Interview	Extra activities	Psychoeducational
G.P.A.	Open admission	Recommendations

Test Requirements:
Diagnostic testing waived: **Yes**
Untimed SAT: **Yes** Untimed ACT: **Yes**
Documentation of LD required: **Yes**
Tests recommended: **We accept testing performed by school psychometrist, private psychologist, or vocational rehabilitation psychologist.**

Types of Disabilities Served
- Speech/Lang
- Study skills
- Written express
- Organizational
- Perceptual
- Reading
- Spelling
- Math
- Fine Motor
- ADD with LD
- ADD without LD
- ADHD with LD
- ADHD without LD

Admissions Process

As a community college, we are an "open-door" institution. To be admitted a student completes an application. The ASSET is administered to most students and is used for placement purposes.

Learning Disability Program

Program: Remedial: **Yes**
Program: Reinforces course work: **Yes**
Students mainstreamed **100** % of the day
Recommended credits per semester: **6-9**
Counseling: Individual: **Yes** Vocational Counseling: **Yes**
Support groups are available: Not **every semester**

Faculty:
Faculty: **1** Part time: **1** M.A.: **1**

Diagnostic Testing

ADD	Personality	Perceptual skills	Spelling
ADHD	Organization	Fine motor skills	• Reading
I.Q.	Handwriting	Spoken language	Study skills
• Math	Social skills	• Written language	

Tutoring:
Services rendered by:
Graduates • Peers • Faculty • LD staff Teacher trainees

Tutorials

Grp.	Ind.	Tutorials	Grp.	Ind.	Tutorials
•		Math skills			Word processing
	•	Study skills		•	Time management
	•	Language arts		•	Learning strategies
	•	Written express		•	Organizational skills

Academic Accommodations

Curriculum	Study Aids	Exams
Priority registration	Typist	• Oral
Math waiver	• Reader	• Untimed
Foreign lang. waiver	Notetaker	Take home
Course substitution	Proof reader	• With proctor
In Class	Text on tape	On computer
• Calculators	Early syllabus	• Extended time
• Tape recorder	Taped handouts	On tape
Word processor		Modified
• Priority seating		• Separate room

Graduation Requirements:
Course credits: **30** GPA: **2.0** Years to complete degree: **No limit**

Program Strengths
We work with LD students on an individual basis in the Learning Center.

General Information:
Maple Woods Community College is a 2 year public college. Suburban campus of 200 acres is Kansas City. Ski areas are 500 miles from campus. 2% of students are foreign. Housing is not guaranteed.

Accreditation: NCACS

Expenses:
Tuition: In-state: Full year: $444.00 (12 hours). Part-time: Per credit:$37.00. Part-time: Per course: $111.00. Tuition: Out-of-state: Full year: $720.00. Part-time: Per credit:$60.00. Part-time: Per course:$180.00

Majors
• BUSINESS Accounting, Data Processing, Travel/Tourism • ENGINEERING Engineering Science • PHILOSOPHY Aviation Maintenance, Aviation Technology, Business and Office, Electronics Technology, Legal Secretary, Machinist, Office Administration, Secretarial, Veterinarian Assistant, Word Processing • SCIENCES Biology, Chemistry, Computer Science • SOCIAL SCIENCES Criminal Justice

Sports/Activities
• SPORTS-INTERCOLLEGIATE Baseball (M) • STUDENT LIFE ACTIVITIES Academic Clubs, Choral, Drama Groups, Newspaper, Religious Organization, Student Government

Selective   **Missouri Services**

Rockhurst College
1100 Rockhurst Road
Kansas City, Missouri 64110
(816) 926-4100

School Enrollment: **2,758** Male: **1,259** Female: **1,499**
LD Enrollment: **5**

Admissions Contact: **Jack Reichmeie, Assoc. Dir. Admissions**
LD Contact: **Deborah Spickelmier, Learning Center Instructor**
Name of Program: **Learning Center**
Telephone: **(816) 926-4815**

Admissions

Application Information:
Application deadline: **June 30th**
Rolling Admissions: **Yes** Notified when: **Mid-July**

Secondary School Information
Most Important Criteria For Admissions (1-strongest)

1 SAT/ACT	1 Application	1	School transcript
1 Class rank	1 Course selection	3	Personal statement
2 Interview	2 Extra activities	4	Psychoeducational
1 G.P.A.	Open admission	1	Recommendations

Test Requirements:
Untimed SAT: **Yes** Untimed ACT: **Yes**
WAIS-R required: **Yes** Range accepted: **88 and up**
Documentation of LD required: **Yes**

Types of Disabilities Served
- Speech/Lang
- Study skills
- Written express
- Organizational
- Perceptual
- Reading
- Spelling
- Math
- Fine Motor
- ADD with LD
- ADD without LD
- ADHD with LD
- ADHD without LD

Admissions Process

ACT - English-20, Math-20, Composite-20, or SAT - English 4-, Math 400; Rank - top 60%

High School Course Requirements:
English: **4** Math: **2** Science: **2** Foreign Language: **2**

Learning Disability Program

Services available for all students: **Yes**

Faculty:
Faculty: **1** Full time: **1** M.A.: **1**
Faculty advocate: **Yes** Meets with instructor: **As needed**

Diagnostic Testing
ADD	Personality	Perceptual skills	Spelling
ADHD	Organization	Fine motor skills	Reading
I.Q.	Handwriting	Spoken language	Study skills
Math	Social skills	Written language	

Tutoring:
Average size of group tutorials: **3**
Services rendered by:
Graduates   •Peers   •Faculty   •LD staff   Teacher trainees

Tutorials
Grp.	Ind.	Tutorials	Grp.	Ind.	Tutorials
•	•	Math skills	•	•	Word processing
•	•	Study skills	•	•	Time management
	•	Language arts	•	•	Learning strategies
	•	Written express	•	•	Organizational skills

Academic Accommodations

Curriculum	Study Aids	Exams
Priority registration	Typist	Oral
Math waiver	Reader	Untimed
Foreign lang. waiver	Notetaker	Take home
Course substitution	• Proof reader	With proctor
In Class	Text on tape	On computer
Calculators	Early syllabus	Extended time
Tape recorder	Taped handouts	On tape
Word processor		Modified
Priority seating		Separate room

Program Strengths

We seek to provide services that meet the needs of LD students holistically. First, in addressing academic needs, students can receive the services of a learning disabilities specialist, a peer-tutor, and a writing lab instructor. Academic advising and advocacy are also provided. Second, in addressing the social and emotional needs, students are encouraged to take advantage of the career counseling, and campus ministry services when appropriate. Finally, the LD student is directed toward campus activities, such as school clubs, social events, and community service projects. Thus the student is supported in a multi-dimensional fashion, with an integration of services.

General Information:

Rockhurst College is a 4 year independent Roman Catholic college. Urban campus of 25 acres is 1% of students are foreign. 3 residential halls on campus. Housing is not guaranteed. 40 % of students remain on campus for the weekends. 20 % of students join fraternities/sororities.

Accreditation: NCACS

SAT/ACT Scores:
Scores for incoming freshmen: **Verbal:** 52% below 500. 37% between 500 and 599. 11% between 600 and 699. **Math:** 32% below 500. 42% between 500 and 599. 22% between 600 and 699. 4% above 700. **ACT:** 18% below 20. 35% between 20 and 23. 16% between 24 and 25l. 18% between 26 and 28. 13% above 28.

Class Rank:
About 47% of the present freshmen class were in the upper 20% of their high school class. 73% were in the top 40% of their class. 87% were in the top 60% of their class. 98% were in the top 80% of their class.

Expenses:
Tuition: In-state: Full year: $8,610.00. Part-time: Per credit: $294.00. Part-time: Per course: $519.00. Tuition: Out-of-state: Full year: $8,610.00. Part-time: Per credit: $294.00. Room and board: $3,700.00

Majors

• BUSINES Accounting, Business Administration, Business Economics, Business Management, Economics, Finance, Human Resources Management, Labor Relations, Management, Marketing, Personnel • COMMUNICATIONS Communication, English • COMPUTER SCIENCE Computer & Information Science, Computer Science • EDUCATION Art, Elementa-

Missouri

ry, Middle School, Secondary • HEALTH SCIENCES Nursing, Occupational Therapy, Physical Therapy • HUMANITIES Humanities, Philosophy, Religion • LANGUAGES French, Spanish • PREPROFESSIONAL Dentistry, Engineering, Law, Medicine, Pharmacy, Social Work • SCIENCES Biology, Chemistry, Mathematics, Physics • SOCIAL SCIENCES History, International Studies, Political Science, Psychology, Social Sciences, Sociology

Sports/Activities

• SPORTS-INTERCOLLEGIATE Basketball, Basketball (F), Cross Country, Cross Country (F), Soccer, Soccer (M), Volleyball (F) • SPORTS-INTRAMURAL Badminton, Basketball, Field Hockey (M), Football, Flag (M), Golf, Hand Ball, Ping-Pong, Racquetball, Soccer, Softball, Tennis, Volleyball • STUDENT LIFE ACTIVITIES Choral, Concert Band, Drama Groups, Ethnic & Cultural Groups, Fraternities, Magazine, Music Groups, Musical Theater, Political Groups, Radio/TV station, Religious Organization, Student Government, Yearbook

---

Less Selective **Missouri Services**

Southwest Baptist University

1601 South Springfield
Bolivar, Missouri 65613-2496
(417) 326-5281

School Enrollment: **1,650** Male: **825** Female: **825**
LD Enrollment: **170**

Admissions Contact: **Claude Pressnell, Director of Admissions**
LD Contact: **Joanne Vaughan**
Name of Program: **University Learning Center**
Telephone:**(417) 326-1615**

Admissions

Application Information:
Rolling Admissions: **Yes**

Secondary School Information
Most Important Criteria For Admissions (1-strongest)

1 SAT/ACT	**6** Application	**4**	School transcript
3 Class rank	**5** Course selection		Personal statement
Interview	**7** Extra activities	**11**	Psychoeducational
2 G.P.A.	Open admission	**9**	Recommendations

Types of Disabilities Served
• Speech/Lang • Reading • ADD with LD
• Study skills • Spelling ADD without LD
• Written express • Math ADHD with LD
• Organizational Fine Motor ADHD without LD
• Perceptual

Learning Disability Program

Counseling: Individual: **Yes** Group Counseling: **Yes**

Faculty:
Faculty: **3** Full time: **1** Part time: **2**
Faculty advocate: **Yes** Meets with instructor: **As needed**

Diagnostic Testing

ADD	Personality	Perceptual skills	Spelling
ADHD	Organization	Fine motor skills	Reading
I.Q.	Handwriting	Spoken language	Study skills
Math	Social skills	Written language	

Tutoring:
Services rendered by:
Graduates Peers Faculty •LD staff •Teacher trainees

Tutorials

Grp.	Ind.	Tutorials	Grp.	Ind.	Tutorials
•	•	Math skills			Word processing
•	•	Study skills	•	•	Time management
•	•	Language arts	•	•	Learning strategies
•	•	Written express	•	•	Organizational skills

Academic Accommodations

Curriculum	**Study Aids**	**Exams**
Priority registration	• Typist	• Oral
• Math waiver	Reader	Untimed
• Foreign lang. waiver	Notetaker	• Take home
Course substitution	Proof reader	With proctor
In Class	Text on tape	On computer
• Calculators	Early syllabus	• Extended time
• Tape recorder	Taped handouts	On tape
• Word processor		Modified
Priority seating		Separate room

Program Strengths
We service LD students on an individual needs basis.

General Information:
Southwest Baptist University is a 4 year independent Baptist university. Rural campus of 120 acres is 28 miles from Springfield. Accessible by bus. 8 residential halls on campus. Housing is not guaranteed. 70 % of students remain on campus for the weekends.

Accreditation: NCACS

Expenses:
Tuition: In-state: Full year: $5,785.00. Part-time: Per credit: $241.00. Room and board: $2,210.00

Majors
• BUSINESS Accounting, Business Administration, Business Economics, Business Education, Business Management, Economics, Finance, Management, Marketing, Sports Management • COMMUNICATIONS Communication, English, Photography, Speech, Television/Radio/Film • COMPUTER SCIENCE Computer Science, Data Processing, Programming, Software Engineer, Telecommunications • EDUCATION Art, Child Development, Curriculum, Early Childhood, Elementary, English, Foreign Language, Health, Mathematics, Middle School, Music, Music Therapy, Physical, Recreation/Youth Leadership, Science, Secondary, Social Studies, Special, Speech/Language • HEALTH SCIENCES Dietary Manager, Medical Technology, Nursing, Nutritional/Food, Physical Therapy • LANGUAGES Spanish • PRE PROFESSIONAL Dentistry, Engineering, Law, Medicine, Ministry, Pharmacy, Recreation, Social Work • SCIENCES Astronomy, Biochemistry, Biology, Botany, Chemistry, Early Childhood, Geology, Macrobiology, Mathematics, Microbiology, Physical Chemistry, Physical Science, Physics, Zoology • SOCIAL SCIENCES Government/Political, History, Political Science, Psychology, Public Relations, Social Science, Sociology • VISUAL AND PERFORMING ARTS Art, Art History, Dramatic Arts, Music, Music Performance, Studio Art, Theater • VOCATIONAL Fashion Design, Fashion Merchandising, Food Service, Home Economics, Park/Recreation, Secretarial

Sports/Activities

• SPORTS RELATED Marching Band, Pep Band • SPORTS-INTERCOL-LEGIATE Baseball (M), Basketball, Cross Country, Football (M), Golf (M), Softball (F), Tennis, Track and Field, Volleyball (F) • SPORTS-IN-TRAMURAL Baseball (M), Basketball, Bowling, Golf (M), Ping-Pong, Soccer (M), Softball (F), Volleyball • STUDENT LIFE ACTIVITIES Choral, Concert Band, Debate, Drama Groups, Ethnic & Cultural Groups, Jazz Band, Music Groups, Musical Theater, Newspaper, Opera, Political Groups, Religious Organization, Student Government, Symphony Orchestra, Yearbook

---

Less Selective **Missouri Services**

St. Louis Community College at Florissant

3400 Pershall Road
St. Louis, Missouri 63135
(314) 595-4244

School Enrollment: **10,000**
LD Enrollment: **61**

Admissions Contact: **Milt Woody, Director of Admissions**
LD Contact: **Suelaine Matthews, Coordinator**
Name of Program: **Project Ability**
Telephone:**(314) 595-4549**

Admissions

Application Information:
LD Students Applying: **61** Accepted: **61** Enrolled:**61**
Applicant must apply **6 months in advance**

Secondary School Information
Most Important Criteria For Admissions (1-strongest)

SAT/ACT **1**	Application **1**	School transcript
Class rank	Course selection	Personal statement
Interview	Extra activities	Psychoeducational
G.P.A. **1**	Open admission	Recommendations

Test Requirements:
Standardized tests waived: **Yes**
Diagnostic testing waived: **Yes**
Documentation of LD required: **Yes**
Tests recommended: **Diagnosis of learning disability**

Types of Disabilities Served

• Speech/Lang	• Reading	• ADD with LD
• Study skills	• Spelling	• ADD without LD
• Written express	• Math	• ADHD with LD
• Organizational	• Fine Motor	• ADHD without LD
• Perceptual		

Admissions Process

High school diploma or GED. Application

Learning Disability Program

Program: Reinforces course work: **Yes**
Students mainstreamed **98** % of the day
Services only for LD students: **Yes**
Counseling: Individual: **Yes** Group Counseling: **Yes** Vocational Counseling: **Yes**

Faculty:
Faculty: **2** Including Director: **Yes** Full time: **2**
LD faculty with: BS/BA: **1** M.A.: **1**
Meets with instructor: **Daily**

Diagnostic Testing

ADD	• Personality	Perceptual skills	• Spelling
ADHD	• Organization	Fine motor skills	• Reading
I.Q.	Handwriting	Spoken language	• Study skills
• Math	Social skills	• Written language	

Tutoring:
Average size of group tutorials: **2**
Services rendered by:

Graduates	•Peers	•Faculty	LD staff	Teacher trainees

Tutorials

Grp.	Ind.	Tutorials	Grp.	Ind.	Tutorials
•	•	Math skills		•	Word processing
	•	Study skills		•	Time management
	•	Language arts			Learning strategies
•	•	Written express		•	Organizational skills

Academic Accommodations

Curriculum	Study Aids	Exams
Priority registration	• Typist	• Oral
Math waiver	• Reader	Untimed
Foreign lang. waiver	• Notetaker	• Take home
Course substitution	• Proof reader	• With proctor
In Class	• Text on tape	• On computer
• Calculators	• Early syllabus	• Extended time
• Tape recorder	Taped handouts	• On tape
• Word processor		• Modified
• Priority seating		• Separate room

Graduation Requirements:
Course credits: **64** GPA: **2.0**

General Information:

St. Louis Community College at Florissant is a 2 year public college. Suburban campus. Accessible by air, train or bus. Housing is not guaranteed.

Accreditation:NCACS

Expenses: Part-time: Per credit:$37.00. Tuition: Out-of-state: Full year: Part-time: Per credit: $47.00.

Majors

• BUSINESS Accounting, Banking, Business Administration, Business Management, Fashion Merchandising, Marketing • COMMUNICATIONS Advertising, Communication, Creative Writing, Journalism, Speech, Television/Radio/Film • COMPUTER SCIENCE Computer Science, Computer Technology, Data Processing, Programming • CRAFTS AND DESIGN Graphic Design • EDUCATION Child Development, Teacher Aide • ENGINEERING Civil/Environmental, Engineering Science • HEALTH SCIENCES Nursing, Speech/Audiology and Speech • HUMANITIES Liberal Arts • SCIENCES Biology, Mathematics, Physics • SOCIAL SCIENCES Law Enforcement, Psychology, Social Sciences • VISUAL AND PERFORMING ARTS Dramatic Arts, Fine Arts, Music • VOCATIONAL Business and Office, Drafting, Electronics Technology, Fashion Mechandizing, Food Service, Home Economics, Mechanical Design, Secretarial, Word Processing

Sports/Activities

• SPORTS-INTERCOLLEGIATE Baseball (M), Basketball, Bowling, Cross Country, Soccer, Softball (F), Swimming, Tennis, Track and Field, Volleyball (F) • STUDENT LIFE ACTIVITIES Concert Band, Drama

Groups, Ethnic & Cultural Groups, Musical Theater, Newspaper, Radio/TV station, Student Government

Less Selective	Missouri Services

St. Louis Community College at Forest Park
5600 Oakland
St. Louis, Missouri 63110
(314) 644-9127

School Enrollment: **10,000** Male: **4,000** Female: **6,000**
LD Enrollment: **55**

Admissions Contact: **Bart Devoti, Director of Admissions**
LD Contact: **Monica L. Hebert, Coordinator**
Name of Program: **Services for Students with Disabilities**
Telephone:**(314) 644-9243, 9259**

Admissions

Application Information:
LD Students Applying: **55** Accepted: **55** Enrolled:**55**
Separate application:**Yes**
Application deadline: **2 weeks before semester**
Applicant must apply **3** months in advance
Rolling Admissions: **Yes**

Secondary School Information
Most Important Criteria For Admissions (1-strongest)

7 SAT/ACT	**11** Application	**5** School transcript
6 Class rank	**8** Course selection	**9** Personal statement
2 Interview	**10** Extra activities	**1** Psychoeducational
4 G.P.A.	**1** Open admission	**3** Recommendations

Test Requirements:
Diagnostic testing waived: **Yes**
Range accepted:
Documentation of LD required: **Yes**
Currency of diagnostic testing: **Within 5 years**
Tests recommended: **IQ - Achievement, indicating strengths and weaknesses, and recommended accommodations**

Types of Disabilities Served
- Speech/Lang
- Study skills
- Written express
- Organizational
- Perceptual
- Reading
- Spelling
- Math
- Fine Motor
- ADD with LD
- ADD without LD
- ADHD with LD
- ADHD without LD

Admissions Process

Open Door Policy for institution. Students must request accommodations in writing after submitting documentation of disability.

Learning Disability Program

Program: Reinforces course work: **Yes**
Students mainstreamed **100** % of the day
Recommended credits per semester: **9-14**
Counseling: Individual: **Yes** Vocational Counseling: **Yes**
Support groups are available:**Offered**

Faculty:
Faculty: **1** Full time: **1** M.A.: **1**
Faculty advocate: **Yes** Meets with instructor: **As needed**

Diagnostic Testing
ADD	Personality	Perceptual skills	Spelling
ADHD	Organization	Fine motor skills	Reading
I.Q.	Handwriting	Spoken language	Study skills
Math	Social skills	Written language	

Tutoring:
Services rendered by:
Graduates •Peers •Faculty •LD staff Teacher trainees

Tutorials
Grp.	Ind. Tutorials	Grp.	Ind. Tutorials
	• Math skills		• Word processing
	• Study skills		• Time management
	Language arts		Learning strategies
	Written express		Organizational skills

Academic Accommodations

Curriculum
- Priority registration
- Math waiver
- Foreign lang. waiver
- Course substitution

In Class
- Calculators
- Tape recorder
- Word processor
- Priority seating

Study Aids
- Typist
- Reader
- Notetaker
- Proof reader
- Text on tape
- Early syllabus
- Taped handouts

Exams
- Oral
- Untimed
- Take home
- With proctor
- On computer
- Extended time
- On tape
- Modified
- Separate room

Graduation Requirements:GPA: **2.0**

Program Strengths
The VRE program at Forest Park emphasizes self-awareness and self-advocacy. We assist students in reaching their potential through the philosophy of Student Development and a counseling mode.

General Information:
St. Louis Community College at Forest Park is a 2 year Community College Urban campus   Accessible by air, train or bus. Housing is not guaranteed.

Accreditation:NCACS

Expenses: Part-time: Per credit:$37.00. Tuition: Out-of-state: Full year: Part-time: Per credit: $57.00.

Majors
• ARTS Commercial Art, Drafting, Dramatic Arts, Graphic Arts, Music, Photography • BUSINESS Accounting, Business Administration, Clerical, Data Processing, Food Management, Hotel and Restaurant Management, International Business, Secretarial Science, Travel/Tourism Management • COMMUNICATIONS Broadcasting, Communication, Journalism, Photography, Television/Radio/Film • COMPUTER SCIENCE Computer Science, Data Processing, Programming, Robotics, Systems Analysis • CRAFTS AND DESIGN Graphic Design • EDUCATION Early Childhood, Elementary, Secondary • ENGINEERING Automotive, Biomedical, Drafting, Electrical • HEALTH SCIENCES Dental Assistant, Dental Hygiene, Medical Laboratory Technology, Nursing, Radiological Therapy, Respiratory Therapy, Surgical Technology • HUMANITIES Fine Arts, Liberal Arts • LANGUAGES French • PRE PROFESSIONAL Business, Drafting, Engineering • SCIENCES Applied Mathematics, Computer Science, General, Mathematics • SOCIAL SCIENCES Criminal Justice, Human Service • VISUAL AND PERFORMING ARTS Art, Fine Arts, Music, Theater • VOCATIONAL Automobile Technology, Business and Office,

Chef Apprenticeship, Culinary Arts, Dental Hygiene, Drafting, Electronics Technology, Medical Laboratory Technology, Office Administration, Radiological Technology, Respiratory Therapy Technology, Secretarial, Word Processing

Sports/Activities

- SPORTS-INTRAMURAL Badminton, Basketball, Soccer, Wrestling
- STUDENT LIFE ACTIVITIES Ethnic & Cultural Groups, Newspaper, Religious Organization, Student Government

Selective

Missouri Services

St. Louis University

221 No. Grand Boulevard
St. Louis, Missouri 63103
(314) 658-2930

School Enrollment: **6,958** Male: **3,803** Female: **3,155**
LD Enrollment: **16**

Admissions Contact: **Kent Hopkins, Director of Admissions**
LD Contact: **Kay Balthazor, Disabilities Coordinator**
Name of Program: **Student Educational Services**
Address: **221 N. Grand**
Telephone:**(314) 658-2930**

Admissions

Application Information:
Rolling Admissions: **Yes**

Secondary School Information
Most Important Criteria For Admissions (1-strongest)

5 SAT/ACT	Application	**3**	School transcript
4 Class rank	**2** Course selection		Personal statement
Interview	Extra activities		Psychoeducational
1 G.P.A.	Open admission		Recommendations

Test Requirements:
Untimed SAT: **Yes** Untimed ACT: **Yes**
Documentation of LD required: **Yes**
Tests recommended: **Psychoeducational**

Types of Disabilities Served
- Speech/Lang
- Reading
- ADD with LD
- Study skills
- Spelling
- ADD without LD
- Written express
- Math
- ADHD with LD
- Organizational
- Fine Motor
- ADHD without LD
- Perceptual

Admissions Process

In general, Committee examines secondary grades, activities and other indications of applicant's character, maturity and ability.

High School Course Requirements:
English: **4** Math: **3** Science: **2** Foreign Language: **2**

Learning Disability Program

Special orientation for LD students: **Yes**

Faculty:
Faculty: **1** Full time: **1** M.A.: **1**

Diagnostic Testing

ADD	Personality	Perceptual skills	Spelling
ADHD	Organization	Fine motor skills	Reading
I.Q.	Handwriting	Spoken language	Study skills
Math	Social skills	Written language	

Tutoring:
Services rendered by:
Graduates •Peers Faculty LD staff Teacher trainees

Tutorials

Grp.	Ind.	Tutorials	Grp.	Ind.	Tutorials
•	•	Math skills			Word processing
•		Study skills	•		Time management
		Language arts	•		Learning strategies
	•	Written express	•		Organizational skills

Academic Accommodations

Curriculum	Study Aids	Exams
Priority registration	• Typist	• Oral
Math waiver	Reader	Untimed
Foreign lang. waiver	• Notetaker	Take home
Course substitution	Proof reader	• With proctor
In Class	• Text on tape	On computer
• Calculators	Early syllabus	• Extended time
• Tape recorder	• Taped handouts	On tape
Word processor		Modified
• Priority seating		• Separate room

Graduation Requirements:
Course credits: **120 hours** GPA: **2.0**
Other requirements: **Specific to respective schools**

Program Strengths

We take each student's individual needs and try to accommodate them accordingly. We try to help with academic advising and steer student to specific faculty to help with individual needs.

General Information:

St. Louis University is a 4 year independent Roman Catholic university. Urban campus Accessible by air, train or bus. 7 residential halls on campus. Housing is not guaranteed.

Accreditation:NCASC, AMACAHEA

SAT/ACT Scores:
Scores for incoming freshmen: **ACT:** 9.3% below 20. 24.5% between 20 and 23. 24.8%between 24 and 251. 14.4%between 26 and 28. 19.4% above 28.

Class Rank:
About 47.9% of the present freshmen class were in the upper 20% of their high school class. 72.9% were in the top 40% of their class. 87.7% were in the top 60% of their class. 96.7% were in the top 80% of their class.

Expenses:
Tuition: In-state: Full year: $4,850.00. Part-time: Per credit:$279.00 - $335.00 dependent on division. Room and board: $2,000.00 per term

Majors

- AREA STUDIES Black/Afro-American, Russian/Eastern European, Urban, Women's Studies • ARTS Art History • BUSINESS Accounting, Aviation Management, Business Administration, Economics, International Business, Marketing, Personnel, Travel/Tourism Management • COMMUNICATIONS Communication, Creative Writing, Political Journalism • COMPUTER SCIENCE Computer Science • EDUCATION Early Childhood, Elementary, General, Middle School, Secondary, Special • ENGI-

Missouri

NEERING Aerospace, Aviation, Electrical, Mathematical, Physics
• HEALTH SCIENCES Communication Disorders, Medical Laboratory Technology, Medical Records Administration, Nuclear Medical Technology, Nursing, Occupational Therapy, Pharmacology, Physical Therapy, Physician's Assistant • HUMANITIES Humanities, Philosophy
• LANGUAGES English, French, German, Greek, Latin, Russian, Spanish
• MATHEMATICS Applied, Computer, Theoretical • PRE PROFESSIONAL Catholic Priesthood Studies, Law, Medicine, Philosophy and Letters, Social Work • RELIGIOUS STUDIES Jesuit Program, Philosophy, Religion & Theology • SCIENCES Biochemistry, Biology, Chemistry, Geology, Geophysics/Seismology, Meteorology, Microbiology, Neuroscience, Physics, Physiology • SOCIAL SCIENCES Criminal Justice, History, Political Science, Psychology, Public Relations, Sociology • SPECIAL EDUCATION Emotionally Disturbed, Learning Disability, Mentally Retarded
• VISUAL AND PERFORMING ARTS Art, Art History, Music, Theater

Sports/Activities

• SPORTS-INTERCOLLEGIATE Basketball (F), Basketball (M), Field Hockey (F), Soccer (M) • SPORTS-INTRAMURAL Basketball (F), Basketball (M), Racquetball (F), Racquetball (M), Softball, Softball (F), Softball (M), Volleyball, Water Polo • STUDENT LIFE ACTIVITIES Academic Clubs, Community Service, Ethnic & Cultural Groups, Fraternities, Newspaper, Religious Organization, Sororities, Student Government, Yearbook

---

Very Selective   **Missouri Services**

University of Missouri: Columbia

407 General Classroom Building
Columbia, Missouri 65211
(314) 882-7651

School Enrollment: **16,800** Male: **8,400** Female: **8,400**

Admissions Contact: **Gary L. Smith, Provost**
LD Contact: **Drew Love, Learning Resource Coordinator**
Name of Program: **Access Office**
Telephone: **(314) 882-4696**

Admissions

Application Information:
Rolling Admissions: **Yes**

Secondary School Information
Most Important Criteria For Admissions (1-strongest)

1 SAT/ACT	Application	School transcript
1 Class rank	Course selection	Personal statement
Interview	Extra activities	**1** Psychoeducational
G.P.A.	Open admission	Recommendations

Test Requirements:
Untimed ACT: **Yes**

Types of Disabilities Served
• Speech/Lang	• Reading	ADD with LD
Study skills	• Spelling	ADD without LD
• Written express	• Math	ADHD with LD
Organizational	Fine Motor	ADHD without LD
Perceptual		

Learning Disability Program
Counseling: Individual: **Yes**

434

Faculty:
Faculty: **1** Full time: **1**
Faculty advocate: **Yes** Meets with instructor: **As needed**

Diagnostic Testing
ADD	Personality	Perceptual skills	Spelling
ADHD	Organization	Fine motor skills	Reading
I.Q.	Handwriting	Spoken language	Study skills
Math	Social skills	Written language	

Tutoring:
Services rendered by:
•Graduates   Peers   Faculty   •LD staff   Teacher trainees

Tutorials
Grp.	Ind.	Tutorials	Grp.	Ind.	Tutorials
•	•	Math skills		•	Word processing
	•	Study skills		•	Time management
•	•	Language arts		•	Learning strategies
	•	Written express		•	Organizational skills

Academic Accommodations
Curriculum	Study Aids	Exams
Priority registration	• Typist	Oral
Math waiver	Reader	Untimed
Foreign lang. waiver	• Notetaker	Take home
Course substitution	• Proof reader	With proctor
In Class	• Text on tape	On computer
• Calculators	Early syllabus	• Extended time
• Tape recorder	Taped handouts	On tape
• Word processor		Modified
Priority seating		Separate room

Program Strengths
Students must be regularly admissible to the University. Services are then provided to support the LD student. All services are free.

General Information:
University of Missouri: Columbia is a 4 year public university. 110 miles from St. Louis. Accessible by air or bus. Housing is not guaranteed.

Accreditation: Fully accredited, Big Eight

Expenses:
Tuition: In-state: Full year: $1,800.00. Part-time: Per credit: $56.30-$62.30. Part-time: Per credit: $165.20-$186.50. Room and board: $2,663.00

Majors
• AREA STUDIES African, Asian, Black/Afro-American, Latin American, Russian/Slavic, Urban • BUSINESS Accounting, Banking, Business Administration, Business Economics, Business Education, Business Management, Economics, Finance, Hotel and Restaurant Management, Insurance, Labor Relations, Management, Marketing, Personnel, Real Estate, Travel/Tourism Management • COMMUNICATIONS Advertising, Broadcasting, Communication, English, Linguistics, Photography, Television/Radio/Film • COMPUTER SCIENCE Computer Science, Data Processing, Hardware Engineer, Systems Analysis, Telecommunications • EDUCATION Agricultural, Art, Curriculum, Early Childhood, Elementary, Foreign Language, Health, Industrial, Middle School, Music, Music Therapy, Physical, Pre-Education, Recreation and Youth Leadership, School Psychology, Secondary, Social Studies, Special, Speech/Language, Vocational • ENGINEERING Aerospace, Agricultural, Chemical, Civil/Environmental, Computer, Electrical, Industrial, Mechanical, Nuclear • HEALTH SCIENCES Communication Disorders, Environmental, Health, Medical Technology, Nursing, Nutritional/Food, Occupational Therapy, Physical Therapy, Radiological Therapy, Speech Therapy, Speech/Audiology and Speech
• HUMANITIES Classics, Humanities, Liberal Arts, Philosophy, Religion

• LANGUAGES French, German, Greek, Latin, Russian, Spanish • PRE-PROFESSIONAL Agriculture, Dentistry, Engineering, Forestry, Law, Medicine, Ministry, Natural Resources, Pharmacy, Range Management, Social Work, Wildlife • SCIENCES Agricultural, Agronomy, Animal, Archeology, Astronomy, Biochemistry, Biology, Chemistry, Dairy, Earth, Ecology, Geography, Geology, Horticultural, Macrobiology, Marine Biology, Mathematics, Meteorology, Microbiology, Physical Chemistry, Physical Science, Physics, Physiology, Poultry, Radiology, Statistics, Zoology • SOCIAL SCIENCES Anthropology, Criminal Justice, Family Counseling, Government/Political, History, Political Science, Psychology, Public Relations, Social Sciences, Sociology • VISUAL AND PERFORMING ARTS Art, Art History, Dance, Dramatic Arts, Fine Arts, Music, Studio Art, Theater • VOCATIONAL Fishery Studies, Food Service, Forestry, Home Economics, Interior Design, Park/Recreation, Radiological Technology, Respiratory Therapy Technology, Textile and Clothing

Sports/Activities

• SPORTS RELATED Marching Band, Pep Band • SPORTS-INTERCOL-LEGIATE Baseball (M), Basketball, Cross Country, Diving, Football (M), Golf, Gymnastics (F), Softball (F), Swimming, Tennis, Track and Field, Volleyball (F), Wrestling (M) • SPORTS-INTRAMURAL Badminton, Basketball, Bowling, Cross Country, Diving, Golf, Gymnastics (F), Hand Ball, Ping-Pong, Racquetball, Soccer, Softball, Swimming, Tennis, Track and Field, Volleyball, Wrestling (M) • STUDENT LIFE ACTIVITIES Choral, Community Service, Concert Band, Dance, Drama Groups, Ethnic & Cultural Groups, Film, Fraternities, Jazz Band, Magazine, Music Groups, Musical Theater, Newspaper, Political Groups, Radio/TV station, Religious Organization, Sororities, Student Government, Symphony Orchestra, Yearbook

Less Selective	**Missouri**
	Accommodations

University of Missouri: Rolla

102 Parker Hall
Rolla, Missouri 65401
(314) 341-4164

School Enrollment: **4,304**

Admissions Contact: **Robert Lewis, Director of Admissions**
LD Contact: **George Schowengerdt, Associate Vice Chancellor**

Admissions

Application Information:
Application deadline: **July 1st**
Rolling Admissions: **Yes**

Secondary School Information
Most Important Criteria For Admissions (1-strongest)

1	SAT/ACT	Application	1	School transcript
1	Class rank	Course selection		Personal statement
	Interview	Extra activities		Psychoeducational
	G.P.A.	Open admission		Recommendations

Test Requirements:
Documentation of LD required: **Yes**

Types of Disabilities Served

• Speech/Lang	• Reading	• ADD with LD
• Study skills	• Spelling	• ADD without LD
• Written express	• Math	• ADHD with LD
• Organizational	• Fine Motor	• ADHD without LD
• Perceptual		

Learning Disability Program

Students mainstreamed **100** % of the day
Services available for all students: **Yes**
Counseling: Individual: **Yes** Group Counseling: **Yes** Vocational Counseling: **Yes**

Faculty:

Diagnostic Testing

ADD	• Personality	Perceptual skills	Spelling
ADHD	Organization	Fine motor skills	• Reading
• I.Q.	Handwriting	Spoken language	• Study skills
• Math	Social skills	Written language	

Tutoring:
Services rendered by:

Graduates	•Peers	Faculty	LD staff	Teacher trainees

Tutorials

Grp.	Ind.	Tutorials	Grp.	Ind.	Tutorials
	•	Math skills			Word processing
•		Study skills	•		Time management
		Language arts			Learning strategies
		Written express			Organizational skills

Academic Accommodations

Curriculum	Study Aids	Exams
Priority registration	Typist	• Oral
Math waiver	Reader	Untimed
Foreign lang. waiver	• Notetaker	Take home
• Course substitution	Proof reader	With proctor
In Class	• Text on tape	On computer
• Calculators	Early syllabus	• Extended time
• Tape recorder	Taped handouts	On tape
Word processor		• Modified
• Priority seating		• Separate room

Graduation Requirements:
Course credits: **Varies with major**

General Information:

University of Missouri: Rolla is a 4 year public university. Rural campus of 260 acres is 100 miles from St. Louis. Accessible by bus. Ski areas are 763 miles from campus. Beaches are 698 miles from campus. 8% of students are foreign. 5 residential halls on campus. Housing is not guaranteed. 25 % of students join fraternities/sororities.

Accreditation: NCACS

SAT/ACT Scores:
Scores for incoming freshmen: **Verbal:** 43% below 500. 38% between 500 and 599. 17% between 600 and 699. 2% above 700. **Math:** 14% below 500. 29% between 500 and 599. 42% between 600 and 699. 15% above 700. **ACT:** 9% below 20. 17% between 20 and 23. 16% between 24 and 251. 18% between 26 and 28. 40% above 28.

Class Rank:
About 63% of the present freshmen class were in the upper 20% of their high school class. 88% were in the top 40% of their class. 97% were in the

top 60% of their class. 99% were in the top 80% of their class.

Expenses:
Tuition: In-state: Full year: $1,800.00. Part-time: Per credit:$60.00. Tuition: Out-of-state: Full year: $5,391.00. Part-time: Per credit:$180.00. Room and board: $3,080.00

Majors
• BUSINESS Economics • COMMUNICATIONS English • COMPUTER SCIENCE Computer Science, Data Processing • ENGINEERING Aerospace, Chemical, Civil/Environmental, Electrical, Engineering Mechanics, Engineering Science, Geological, Industrial, Mechanical, Metallurgical, Mining/Mineral, Naval Architecture, Petroleum • HUMANITIES Philosophy • SCIENCES Biology, Cognitive, Geology, Mathematics, Physics • SOCIAL SCIENCES History, Psychology

Sports/Activities
INTERCOLLEGIATE Baseball (M), Basketball, Cross Country, Diving, Football (M), Golf (M), Riflery (M), Soccer, Softball (F), Swimming (M), Tennis (M), Track and Field • SPORTS-INTRAMURAL Badminton, Basketball, Bowling, Cross Country (F), Diving (M), Golf (M), Hand Ball (M), Racquetball, Rugby (M), Soccer, Softball, Swimming, Tennis, Track and Field, Volleyball • STUDENT LIFE ACTIVITIES Choral, Concert Band, Drama Groups, Fraternities, Jazz Band, Magazine, Music Groups, Newspaper, Radio/TV station, Sororities, Student Government, Symphony Orchestra, Yearbook

Highly Selective	Missouri
	Accommodations

Washington University
Campus Box 1134
St. Louis, Missouri 63130
(800) 638-0700

School Enrollment: **5,000** Male: **2,500** Female: **2,500**
LD Enrollment: **48** Male: **24** Female: **24**

Admissions Contact: **Julie M. Shimabukuro Director of Admissions**
LD Contact: **Donald A. Strano Assistant Dean of Students**
Name of Program: **Disabled Student Services**
Address: **Box 1136, One Brookings Dr.**
Telephone:**(314) 935-4062**

Admissions

Application Information:
LD on admissions committee:**Yes**
Application deadline: **February 1st**
Notified when: **April 1st**

Secondary School Information
Most Important Criteria For Admissions (1-strongest)

5	SAT/ACT	6	Application	1	School transcript
4	Class rank	2	Course selection	9	Personal statement
	Interview	8	Extra activities	10	Psychoeducational
3	G.P.A.		Open admission	7	Recommendations

Test Requirements:
Diagnostic testing waived: **Yes**
Untimed SAT: **Yes** Untimed ACT: **Yes** Untimed ACH: **Yes**
Documentation of LD required: **Yes**

Types of Disabilities Served

Speech/Lang	Reading	ADD with LD
Study skills	Spelling	ADD without LD
Written express	Math	ADHD with LD
Organizational	Fine Motor	ADHD without LD
Perceptual		

Admissions Process
Files are read first regionally by an admission officer familiar with the territory. Files are then reviewed by another officer - if there is a disagreement the case is discussed or sent on for committee discussion. LD cases are reviewed with dean from Disabled Student Services on a case by case basis.

High School Course Requirements:
English: **4** Math: **3-4** Science: **3-4** Foreign Language: **2**

Learning Disability Program
Special orientation for LD students: **Yes**
Students mainstreamed **100** % of the day
Recommended credits per semester: **12-15**
Counseling: Individual: **Yes** Group Counseling: **Yes** Vocational Counseling: **Yes**

Faculty:
Faculty: **15** Full time: **1** Part time: **1** Ph.D.: **1**
Faculty advocate: **Yes** Meets with instructor: **As needed**

Diagnostic Testing

ADD	Personality	Perceptual skills	Spelling
ADHD	Organization	Fine motor skills	Reading
I.Q.	Handwriting	Spoken language	Study skills
Math	Social skills	Written language	

Tutoring:
Average size of group tutorials: **5-15**
Services rendered by:

Graduates	Peers	Faculty	•LD staff	Teacher trainees

Tutorials

Grp.	Ind.	Tutorials	Grp.	Ind.	Tutorials
		Math skills			Word processing
•	•	Study skills	•	•	Time management
		Language arts	•	•	Learning strategies
•	•	Written express	•	•	Organizational skills

Academic Accommodations

Curriculum	Study Aids	Exams
Priority registration	Typist	• Oral
Math waiver	• Reader	Untimed
Foreign lang. waiver	• Notetaker	• Take home
Course substitution	• Proof reader	• With proctor
In Class	• Text on tape	On computer
• Calculators	Early syllabus	• Extended time
• Tape recorder	Taped handouts	On tape
• Word processor		• Modified
• Priority seating		• Separate room

Graduation Requirements:
Course credits: **120** Years to complete degree: **4 years**

Program Strengths
Although we don't have a specific program, any reasonable accommodation will be provided on an individual basis.

General Information:

Washington University is a 4 year independent university. Suburban campus of 169 acres is 300 miles from Chicago. Accessible by air or bus. 4% of students are foreign. 16 residential halls on campus. Housing is guaranteed.Guaranteed through 1st year. 90 % of students remain on campus for the weekends. 35 % of students join fraternities/sororities.

Accreditation:

SAT/ACT Scores:

Scores for incoming freshmen: 50%between 500 and 599. 50% between 600 and 699.

Class Rank:

About 80% of the present freshmen class were in the upper 20% of their high school class.

Expenses:

Tuition: In-state: Full year: $16,750.00. Tuition: Out-of-state: Full year: $16,750.00. Room and board: $5,394.00 Cost of LD program: Varies

Majors

• AGRICULTURE • AREA STUDIES African, American, Asian, Black/ Afro-American, Caribbean, Ethics, Ethnic/Cultural, European, Hispanic/ American, International Studies, Islamic, Jewish/Judaism, Latin American, Mexican/American, Middle Eastern, Russian/Slavic, Scandinavian, Urban, Women's Studies • ARTS Art History, Art Therapy, Commercial Art, Dance, Design, Dramatic Arts, Drawing, Fashion Design, Graphic Arts, Music, Music History, Music Performance, Painting, Photography, Sculpture, Theater Design • BUSINESS Accounting, Banking/Finance, Business Administration, Business Economics, Economics, International Business, Investments and Securities, Labor Relations, Management, Marketing, Marketing Research, Operations Research, Organizational Behavior, Personnel, Taxation • COMPUTER SCIENCE Computer Science, Computer Technology • CRAFTS AND DESIGN Ceramics, Glass, Graphic Design, Illustration Design, Printmaking, Sculpture, Textile/Weaving • ENGINEERING Bio-medical, Chemical, Civil/Environmental, Computer, Electrical, Environmental/Water Resources, Mechanical, Physics, Systems Analysis • HEALTH SCIENCES Occupational Therapy, Physical Therapy, Speech/Audiology and Speech • HUMANITIES Classics, English/Writing/ Literature, Fine Arts, Humanities, Liberal Arts , Philosophy, Religion • LANGUAGES Arabic, Chinese, Danish, Dutch, English, French, German, Greek, Hebrew, Italian, Japanese, Latin, Linguistic, Portuguese, Russian, Scandinavian, Spanish • MATHEMATICS Applied, Theoretical • PHILOSOPHY Art, Early Childhood, Elementary, Secondary • PRE PROFESSIONAL Architecture, Business, Engineering, Medicine, Social Work • RELIGIOUS STUDIES Hebrew, Judaism & Jewish Studies, Philosophy • SCIENCES Anthropology, Applied Mathematics, Archeology, Astronomy, Astrophysics, Biochemistry, Biology, Chemistry, Geology, Mathematics, Physics • SOCIAL SCIENCES Anthropology, History, International Studies, Political Science, Psychology • SPECIAL EDUCATION Occupational Therapy • VISUAL AND PERFORMING ARTS Art, Art History, Dance, Dramatic Arts, Fine Arts, Music, Music Performance, Studio Art, Theater

Sports/Activities

• SPORTS RELATED Cheerleading, Chess, Pep Band, Team Managers • SPORTS-INTERCOLLEGIATE Baseball (F), Baseball (M), Basketball, Basketball (F), Basketball (M), Cross Country, Cross Country (F), Cross Country (M), Diving, Diving (F), Diving (M), Football, Football (M), Golf, Golf (M), Soccer, Soccer (F), Soccer (M), Swimming, Swimming (F), Swimming (M), Tennis, Tennis (F), Tennis (M), Track and Field, Track and Field (F), Track and Field (M), Volleyball, Volleyball (F) • SPORTS-INTRAMURAL Badminton (F), Badminton (M), Baseball, Baseball (M), Basketball, Basketball (F), Basketball (M), Bowling, Bowling (F), Bowling (M), Crew, Crew (F), Crew (M), Cross Country, Cross Country (F), Cross Country (M), Cycling, Diving, Diving (F), Diving (M), Fencing, Fencing (F), Fencing (M), Field Hockey, Field Hockey (F), Football, Football (M), Golf, Golf (M), Ice Hockey, Ice Hockey (M), Judo, Ping-Pong, Ping-Pong (F), Ping-Pong (M), Racquetball, Racquetball (F), Racquetball (M), Rugby,

Rugby (M), Soccer, Soccer (F), Soccer (M), Softball, Softball (F), Softball (M), Swimming, Swimming (F), Swimming (M), Tennis, Tennis (F), Tennis (M), Track and Field, Track and Field (F), Track and Field (M), Volleyball, Volleyball (F), Volleyball (M) • STUDENT LIFE ACTIVITIES Academic Clubs, Choral, Community Service, Dance, Drama Groups, Ethnic & Cultural Groups, Film, Fraternities, Jazz Band, Magazine, Music Groups, Newspaper, Orchestra, Political Groups, Radio/TV station, Religious Organization, Sororities, Student Government, Symphony Orchestra, Yearbook

---

Very Selective　　　　　　　　　　　　　**Missouri Program**

Westminster College
Seventh and Westminster Avenues
Fulton, Missouri 65251
(314) 642-3361

School Enrollment: **704**
LD Enrollment: **15**

Admissions Contact: **Gary R. Forney, Dean of Admissions**
LD Contact: **Henry Ottinger, Director**
Name of Program: **Learning Disability Program**

Admissions

Application Information:
LD Students Applying: **50** Accepted: **17** Enrolled:**15**
Separate application:**Yes**
Application deadline: **February 1st**
Rolling Admissions: **Yes**

Secondary School Information
Most Important Criteria For Admissions (1-strongest)

4	SAT/ACT	10	Application	11	School transcript
9	Class rank	2	Course selection	8	Personal statement
5	Interview	7	Extra activities	3	Psychoeducational
1	G.P.A.		Open admission	6	Recommendations

Test Requirements:
Diagnostic testing waived: **Yes**
Untimed SAT: **Yes** Untimed ACT: **Yes**
WAIS-R required: **Yes**
Documentation of LD required: **Yes**
Currency of diagnostic testing: **6-12 months**

Types of Disabilities Served
• Speech/Lang　　• Reading　　　• ADD with LD
• Study skills　　• Spelling　　　ADD without LD
• Written express　• Math　　　　• ADHD with LD
• Organizational　• Fine Motor　ADHD without LD
• Perceptual

Learning Disability Program
Program: Reinforces course work: **Yes**
Students mainstreamed **100** % of the day
Counseling: Individual: **Yes** Group Counseling: **Yes**

Faculty:
Faculty: **3** Including Director: **Yes** Full time: **3** M.A.: **1** Ph.D.: **2**
Faculty advocate: **Yes** Meets with instructor: **As necessary**

Montana

Diagnostic Testing

ADD	Personality	Perceptual skills	Spelling
ADHD	Organization	Fine motor skills	• Reading
• I.Q.	Handwriting	Spoken language	• Study skills
• Math	Social skills	Written language	

Tutoring:
Services rendered by:
Graduates •Peers Faculty •LD staff Teacher trainees

Tutorials

Grp.	Ind.	Tutorials	Grp.	Ind.	Tutorials
•	•	Math skills	•	•	Word processing
•	•	Study skills	•		Time management
	•	Language arts	•		Learning strategies
•		Written express		•	Organizational skills

Academic Accommodations

Curriculum	Study Aids	Exams
Priority registration	Typist	• Oral
Math waiver	Reader	Untimed
Foreign lang. waiver	• Notetaker	Take home
Course substitution	• Proof reader	With proctor
In Class	• Text on tape	On computer
• Calculators	Early syllabus	• Extended time
• Tape recorder	Taped handouts	On tape
• Word processor		• Modified
Priority seating		Separate room

General Information:
Westminster College is a 4 year private Presbyterian college. Rural campus of 250 acres is 100 miles from St. Louis. 1% of students are foreign. 8 residential halls on campus. Housing is guaranteed.95 % of students remain on campus for the weekends. 60 % of students join fraternities/sororities.

Accreditation:NCACS

SAT/ACT Scores:
Scores for incoming freshmen: **ACT:** 7% below 20. 25% between 20 and 23. 35%between 24 and 25l. 23%between 26 and 28. 10% above 28.

Class Rank:
About 40% of the present freshmen class were in the upper 20% of their high school class. 70% were in the top 40% of their class. 88% were in the top 60% of their class. 99% were in the top 80% of their class.

Expenses:
Tuition: In-state: Full year: $6,850.00. Room and board: $3,100.00 Cost of LD program:$1,800.00

Majors
• BUSINESS Accounting, Business Administration, Business Economics, Business Management, Economics, International Business, Management • COMMUNICATIONS Creative Writing, English • EDUCATION Art, Early Childhood, Elementary, English, Foreign Language, Mathematics, Physical, Science, Secondary, Social Studies, Special • HUMANITIES Philosophy, Religion • LANGUAGES German, Spanish • PREPROFESSIONAL Dentistry, Engineering, Law, Medicine, Ministry, Veterinarian • SCIENCES Biology, Chemistry, Mathematics, Physics • SOCIAL SCIENCES Anthropology, History, International Studies, Political Science, Psychology, Sociology • VISUAL AND PERFORMING ARTS Dance, Fine Arts, Music, Studio Art, Theater

Sports/Activities
• SPORTS-INTERCOLLEGIATE Baseball (M), Basketball (M), Cross Country, Golf (M), Riflery, Soccer, Softball (F), Tennis, Track and Field, Volleyball (F) • SPORTS-INTRAMURAL Badminton, Basketball, Bowl-ing, Golf (M), Ping-Pong, Racquetball, Softball, Swimming, Tennis, Track and Field (M), Volleyball, Wrestling (M) • STUDENT LIFE ACTIVITIES Choral, Dance, Drama Groups, Ethnic & Cultural Groups, Fraternities, Jazz Band, Magazine, Music Groups, Musical Theater, Newspaper, Political Groups, Religious Organization, Sororities, Student Government, Yearbook

---

Less Selective   **Montana Services**

Flathead Valley Community College
777 Grandview Drive
Kalispell, Montana 59901
(406) 755-5222

School Enrollment: **1,762** Male: **617** Female: **1,145**

Admissions Contact: **Loraine Bundrock, Registrar**
LD Contact: **Brian Bechtold, Advocate**
Name of Program: **Students with Disabilities**

Admissions

Application Information:
Application deadline: **Quarterly**
Applicant must apply **1** months in advance
Rolling Admissions: **Yes**

Secondary School Information
Most Important Criteria For Admissions (1-strongest)

SAT/ACT	Application	School transcript
Class rank	Course selection	Personal statement
Interview	Extra activities	Psychoeducational
G.P.A.	**1** Open admission	Recommendations

Test Requirements:
Standardized tests waived: **Yes**
Documentation of LD required: **Yes**

Types of Disabilities Served

• Speech/Lang	• Reading	• ADD with LD
• Study skills	• Spelling	• ADD without LD
• Written express	• Math	• ADHD with LD
• Organizational	• Fine Motor	• ADHD without LD
• Perceptual		

Learning Disability Program
Program: Remedial: **Yes**
Program: Reinforces course work: **Yes**
Students mainstreamed **100** % of the day
Services available for all students: **Yes**
Counseling: Individual: **Yes** Group Counseling: **Yes**

Faculty:
Faculty: **2** Including Director: **Yes** Part time: **2** M.A.: **1** Ph.D.: **1**
Faculty advocate: **Yes** Meets with instructor: **As needed**

Diagnostic Testing

ADD	• Personality	• Perceptual skills	• Spelling
ADHD	• Organization	Fine motor skills	• Reading
• I.Q.	Handwriting	Spoken language	Study skills
• Math	Social skills	• Written language	

Tutoring:
Services rendered by:
  Graduates •Peers •Faculty •LD staff Teacher trainees

Tutorials

Grp.	Ind.	Tutorials	Grp.	Ind.	Tutorials
•	•	Math skills			Word processing
•	•	Study skills	•	•	Time management
•	•	Language arts	•	•	Learning strategies
•	•	Written express	•	•	Organizational skills

Academic Accommodations

Curriculum	Study Aids	Exams
Priority registration	Typist	• Oral
Math waiver	Reader	Untimed
Foreign lang. waiver	• Notetaker	• Take home
Course substitution	• Proof reader	With proctor
In Class	• Text on tape	On computer
• Calculators	Early syllabus	• Extended time
• Tape recorder	Taped handouts	On tape
Word processor		• Modified
Priority seating		Separate room

Program Strengths

Flathead Valley Community College's program for students with a learning disability is an extension of the Learning Center. Professionals in the Learning Center provide a variety of services to LD students. The Academic Reinforcement Center, a component of the Learning Center, provides individual and small group remedial classes. The community college atmosphere enables the students to participate in small classes with more individualized attention. The Advocate for Students with Disabilities meets with students on an individual basis to explore their individual learning programs.

General Information:

Flathead Valley Community College is a 2 year public college. Suburban campus of 40 acres is 120 miles from Missoula. Accessible by air, train, or bus Ski areas are 15 miles from campus. Beaches are 7 miles from campus. 2% of students are foreign. Housing is not guaranteed.

Accreditation: NWACS

Expenses:
Tuition: In-state: Full year: $981.00 in district, $1,224.00 out of district. Part-time: Per credit:$27.25 in district,$34.00 out of district. Tuition: Out-of-state: Full year: $1,719.00. Part-time: Per credit:$47.75.

Majors

• BUSINESS Accounting, Business Education, Business Management, Hotel and Restaurant Management, Marketing, Travel/Tourism Management • COMMUNICATIONS English • HEALTH SCIENCES Health, Nursing • HUMANITIES Liberal Arts • PREPROFESSIONAL Forestry • SCIENCES Biology, Botany • SOCIAL SCIENCES Human Service, Law Enforcement • VOCATIONAL Business and Office, Park/Recreation, Secretarial, Surveying and Mapping

Sports/Activities

ball (M), Ping-Pong, Softball, Tennis, Volleyball • STUDENT LIFE ACTIVITIES Academic Clubs, Ethnic & Cultural Groups, Newspaper, Religious Organization, Student Government

---

Selective   **Montana Services**

Montana College of Mineral Science
West Park Street
Butte, Montana 59701
(800) 445-8324

School Enrollment: **1,881** Male: **1,129** Female: **752**
LD Enrollment: **7** Male: **5** Female: **2**

Admissions Contact: **Chris Van Nulano, Admissions Counselor**
LD Contact: **Paul Beatty, Student Life Director**
Telephone:**(406) 496-4198**

Admissions

Application Information:
Application deadline: **July 1st**
Applicant must apply **3** months in advance
Rolling Admissions: **Yes** Notified when: **2 weeks after applying**

Secondary School Information
Most Important Criteria For Admissions (1-strongest)

1 SAT/ACT	**7** Application	**5** School transcript
4 Class rank	**2** Course selection	**10** Personal statement
9 Interview	**8** Extra activities	**11** Psychoeducational
3 G.P.A.	Open admission	**6** Recommendations

Types of Disabilities Served

Speech/Lang	Reading	ADD with LD
Study skills	Spelling	ADD without LD
Written express	Math	ADHD with LD
Organizational	Fine Motor	ADHD without LD
Perceptual		

Admissions Process

We accept LD students on a review basis after meeting with the student and considering the program they intend to study.

High School Course Requirements:
English: **4** Math: **3** Science: **2** Foreign Language: **2**
Waivers to standard high school courses
Foreign Language : **Yes**

Learning Disability Program

Syllabus available during orientation:**Yes**
Program: Remedial: **Yes**
Recommended credits per semester: **varies**
Services available for all students: **Yes**
Counseling: Individual: **Yes**

Faculty:
Faculty: **2** Full time: **2** M.A.: **1**

Diagnostic Testing

ADD	Personality	Perceptual skills	Spelling
ADHD	Organization	Fine motor skills	Reading
I.Q.	Handwriting	Spoken language	Study skills
Math	Social skills	Written language	

Services rendered by:
  Graduates Peers Faculty LD staff Teacher trainees

Montana

Tutorials

Grp.	Ind.	Tutorials	Grp.	Ind.	Tutorials
		Math skills			Word processing
		Study skills			Time management
		Language arts			Learning strategies
		Written express			Organizational skills

Academic Accommodations

Curriculum	Study Aids	Exams
Priority registration	• Typist	Oral
Math waiver	• Reader	Untimed
Foreign lang. waiver	Notetaker	Take home
Course substitution	Proof reader	With proctor
In Class	• Text on tape	On computer
• Calculators	Early syllabus	Extended time
• Tape recorder	Taped handouts	On tape
• Word processor		Modified
• Priority seating		Separate room

Graduation Requirements:
Course credits: **varies** GPA: **2.0** Years to complete degree: **4-5**

Program Strengths

We really have no formal program. Our strength lies in the commitment to accommodate any student who needs special help. We make these arrangements possible through our Counseling Center.

General Information:

Montana College of Mineral Science is a 4 year public college. Rural campus of 100,000 acres is 2.5 miles from Missoula. Accessible by air, bus or car. Ski areas are 45 minutes from campus. 5% of students are foreign. 1 residential halls on campus. Housing is not guaranteed.27 % of students remain on campus for the weekends.

Accreditation:NACS, ABET, ACS

SAT/ACT Scores:
Scores for incoming freshmen: **ACT:** 5% below 20. 60% between 20 and 23. 20%between 24 and 25l. 10%between 26 and 28. 5% above 28.

Expenses:
Tuition: In-state: Full year: $1,697.00. Part-time: Per credit:$80.00. Tuition: Out-of-state: Full year: $2,425.00 for Western Undergraduate States; $5,421.00 all others. Room and board: $3,250.00

Majors

• BUSINESS Accounting, Management, Marketing • COMMUNICATIONS Communication • COMPUTER SCIENCE Aerospace, Computer Mathematics, Computer Science, Programming • ENGINEERING Aerospace, Computer, Engineering Science, Environmental/Water Resources, Geological, Metallurgical, Mining/Mineral, Petroleum, Systems Analysis • HUMANITIES Liberal Arts • MATHEMATICS Actuarial, Applied, Computer • PHILOSOPHY Engineering • SCIENCES Applied Mathematics, Chemistry, Computer Science, Mathematics, Mining

Sports/Activities

• SPORTS RELATED Cheerleading, Pep Band • SPORTS-INTERCOLLEGIATE Basketball, Basketball (F), Basketball (M), Football (M), Volleyball (F), Wrestling (M) • SPORTS-INTRAMURAL Basketball (F), Basketball (M), Cross Country (F), Cross Country (M), Field Hockey (M), Golf (F), Golf (M), Hand Ball, Hand Ball (M), Ice Hockey (M), Skiing - Cross Country, Skiing - Snow (F), Skiing - Snow (M), Soccer (M) • STUDENT LIFE ACTIVITIES Academic Clubs, Ethnic & Cultural Groups, Newspaper, Radio, Religious Organization, Student Government, Yearbook

Northern Montana College
Havre, Montana 59501
(406) 265-9376

School Enrollment: **2,000** Male: **900** Female: **1,100**
LD Enrollment: **20** Male: **15** Female: **5**

Admissions Contact: **Kelly Palmer, Director of Admissions**
LD Contact: **Linda Hoines, Learning Specialist**
Name of Program: **Student Support Service**
Address: **213 Cown Hall**
Telephone:**(406) 265-3783**

Admissions

Application Information:
Application deadline: **Same for all students**

Secondary School Information
Most Important Criteria For Admissions (1-strongest)

3 SAT/ACT	Application	School transcript
4 Class rank	1 Course selection	Personal statement
Interview	Extra activities	Psychoeducational
2 G.P.A.	1 Open admission	Recommendations

Test Requirements:
Untimed SAT: **Yes** Untimed ACT: **Yes** Untimed ACH: **Yes**
Documentation of LD required: **Yes**
Tests recommended: **Verification of disability for accommodations**

Types of Disabilities Served

Speech/Lang	Reading	ADD with LD
Study skills	Spelling	ADD without LD
Written express	Math	ADHD with LD
Organizational	Fine Motor	ADHD without LD
Perceptual		

Admissions Process

If out of school less than 3 years, must meet Montana admission standards. However, there is a 5% exemption rate and students (LD and those not meeting criteria) may enroll on a part-time basis.

High School Course Requirements:
English: **4** Math: **3** Science: **2**

Learning Disability Program

Time required or recommended in learning center:

Faculty:
Faculty: **1** Part time: **1** M.A.: **1**
Meets with instructor: **As needed**

Diagnostic Testing

ADD	Personality	Perceptual skills	• Spelling
ADHD	Organization	Fine motor skills	• Reading
I.Q.	Handwriting	Spoken language	• Study skills
• Math	Social skills	Written language	

440

Tutoring:
Average size of group tutorials: **1-5**
Services rendered by:
Graduates •Peers Faculty LD staff Teacher trainees

Tutorials
Grp.	Ind.	Tutorials	Grp.	Ind.	Tutorials
•	•	Math skills	•	•	Word processing
•	•	Study skills	•	•	Time management
		Language arts			Learning strategies
		Written express			Organizational skills

Academic Accommodations
Curriculum	Study Aids	Exams
Priority registration	Typist	• Oral
Math waiver	Reader	Untimed
Foreign lang. waiver	• Notetaker	Take home
Course substitution	• Proof reader	• With proctor
In Class	• Text on tape	On computer
• Calculators	Early syllabus	• Extended time
• Tape recorder	Taped handouts	On tape
Word processor		Modified
• Priority seating		Separate room

Graduation Requirements:
Course credits: **64-128** GPA: **2.0** Years to complete degree: **Unlimited**
Language waiver: **Yes**
Other requirements: **4 year-40 credits at 300-400 level**

General Information:
Northern Montana College is a 2 and 4 year public college. Urban campus of 105 acres is 100 miles from Great Falls. Accessible by air, train or bus. Ski areas are 120 miles from campus. 3 residential halls on campus. Housing is guaranteed.Guaranteed through 1st year. 25 % of students remain on campus for the weekends.

Accreditation:NWACS

Expenses:
Tuition: In-state: Full year: $1,732.00. Tuition: Out-of-state: Full year: $5,036.00. Room and board: $3,400.00

Majors
• AGRICULTURE Technology • COMMUNICATIONS Communication, English • COMPUTER SCIENCE Computer Technology • EDUCATION Business, Elementary, English, Mathematics, Physical, Science, Secondary, Social Studies, Technical, Vocational • ENVIRONMENTAL CONTROL Water and Wastewater Technology • HEALTH SCIENCES Nursing • HUMANITIES Liberal Arts • LANGUAGES French • PHILOSOPHY Business Administration, Business Economics, Construction, Economics, Secretarial Science • PRE PROFESSIONAL Agricultural, Business, Drafting, Engineering • SCIENCES Biology, Chemical, Ecology, Mathematics • SOCIAL SCIENCES History, Social Science • VISUAL AND PERFORMING ARTS Art, Dramatic Arts • VOCATIONAL Auto Body, Automotive Technology, Construction, Drafting, Electronics Technology, Secretarial, Welding

Sports/Activities
• SPORTS ACTIVITIES Archery, Badminton, Basketball, Bowling, Canoeing, Cycling, Field Hockey, Football, Golf, Gymnastics, Hand Ball, Ice Hockey, Ping-Pong, Racquetball, Rugby, Skiing - Cross Country, Skiing - Snow, Skiing - Water, Soccer, Softball, Swimming, Tennis, Track and Field, Volleyball, Water Polo, Weight Lifting • SPORTS LIFE ACTIVITIES Academic Clubs, Community Service, Dance, Drama Groups, Ethnic & Cultural Groups, Newspaper, Religious Organization, Student Government, Yearbook • SPORTS RELATED Cheerleading, Team Managers • SPORTS-INTERCOLLEGIATE Basketball (F), Basketball (M), Volleyball (F), Wrestling (M)

Selective   **Montana Services**

Rocky Mountain College
1511 Poly Drive
Billings, Montana 59102
(406) 657-1070

School Enrollment: **766** Male: **361** Female: **405**
LD Enrollment: **20** Male: **10** Female: **10**

Admissions Contact: **Dave Heringer, Director of Admissions**
LD Contact: **Dr. Jane Van Dyk, Director, Academic Success**
Name of Program: **Services for Academic Success**
Address: **Fortin 132**
Telephone:**(406) 657-1070**

Admissions

Application Information:
Rolling Admissions: **Yes**

Secondary School Information
Most Important Criteria For Admissions (1-strongest)

2 SAT/ACT	Application	School transcript
3 Class rank	Course selection	Personal statement
Interview	Extra activities	Psychoeducational
1 G.P.A.	Open admission **4**	Recommendations

Test Requirements:
Standardized tests waived: **Yes**
Untimed SAT: **Yes** Untimed ACT: **Yes**
Documentation of LD required: **Yes**

Types of Disabilities Served
• Speech/Lang	• Reading	• ADD with LD
• Study skills	• Spelling	• ADD without LD
• Written express	• Math	• ADHD with LD
• Organizational	• Fine Motor	• ADHD without LD
• Perceptual		

Admissions Process

Students fill out an official application form, send two recommendations, high school transcript, $15.00, results of ACT, SAT, or PSAT scores, and immunization record. Each applicant is considered on the basis of potential success.

High School Course Requirements:
English: **4** Math: **3** Science: **2** Foreign Language: **2**
Waivers to standard high school courses
Foreign Language : **Yes** Math: **Yes** Course substitution: **Yes**

Learning Disability Program
Special orientation for LD students: **Yes**
Program: Reinforces course work: **Yes**
Students mainstreamed **100** % of the day
Recommended credits per semester: **9**
Counseling: Individual: **Yes** Group Counseling: **Yes** Vocational Counseling: **Yes**
Support groups are available:**Varies**

Montana

Faculty:
Faculty: **4** Full time: **4**
LD faculty with: BS/BA: **3** Ph.D.: **1**

Diagnostic Testing

ADD	Personality	Perceptual skills	Spelling
ADHD	Organization	Fine motor skills	• Reading
I.Q.	Handwriting	Spoken language	• Study skills
Math	Social skills	Written language	

Tutoring:
Average size of group tutorials: **3-4**
Services rendered by:
•Graduates   Peers   Faculty   •LD staff   Teacher trainees

Tutorials

Grp.	Ind.	Tutorials	Grp.	Ind.	Tutorials
•	•	Math skills	•		Word processing
•	•	Study skills	•	•	Time management
•		Language arts	•	•	Learning strategies
•	•	Written express	•	•	Organizational skills

Academic Accommodations

Curriculum	Study Aids	Exams
Priority registration	• Typist	• Oral
• Math waiver	• Reader	• Untimed
• Foreign lang. waiver	• Notetaker	• Take home
Course substitution	• Proof reader	• With proctor
In Class	• Text on tape	• On computer
• Calculators	Early syllabus	• Extended time
• Tape recorder	Taped handouts	On tape
Word processor		Modified
• Priority seating		• Separate room

Graduation Requirements:
Course credits: **124 semester hours** GPA: **2.0 - 2.25 in major** Math waiver: **Yes** Language waiver: **Yes**

Program Strengths
Personalized attention given to every student. Also RMC is a small college, with a friendly environment.

General Information:
Rocky Mountain College is a 2 year independent U.C.C., Methodist, Presbyterian college. Urban campus 500 miles from Denver. Accessible by air, train or bus. Ski areas are 60 miles from campus. 3% of students are foreign. 3 residential halls on campus. Housing is guaranteed.Guaranteed through 2nd year.

Accreditation:NACS, OPI, USUMC

Expenses:
Tuition: In-state: Full year: $3,556.00 per semester. Part-time: Per credit:$296.00. Room and board: $1,664.00

Majors
• BUSINESS Business Administration • EDUCATION Elementary, Health, Physical • HUMANITIES English/Writing/Literature • MATHEMATICS Applied • RELIGIOUS STUDIES Philosophy • SCIENCES Biology, Chemistry, Geology • SOCIAL SCIENCES Anthropology, History, Political Science, Psychology • VISUAL AND PERFORMING ARTS Art, Music, Theater • VOCATIONAL Aviation Administration, Aviation Maintenance, Aviation Pilot, Equestrian Studies

Sports/Activities
• SPORTS-INTERCOLLEGIATE Basketball (F), Basketball (M), Football (M), Skiing - Snow (F), Skiing - Snow (M), Volleyball (F), Volleyball (M)

• STUDENT LIFE ACTIVITIES Academic Clubs, Choral, Community Service, Concert Band, Debate, Drama Groups, Ethnic & Cultural Groups, Film, Religious Organization, Student Government

Less Selective   **Montana Program**

Western Montana College University of Montana
Dillon, Montana 59725
(406) 683-7331

School Enrollment: **1,100** Male: **5,050** Female: **5,050**
LD Enrollment: **24**

Admissions Contact: **Robert G. Cashell, Admissions Counselor**
LD Contact: **Clarence Kostelecky, Coordinator/Director**
Name of Program: **Learning Center**
Telephone:**(406) 683-7330**

Admissions

Application Information:
LD Students Applying: **2** Accepted: **2** Enrolled:**2**
Application deadline: **September 1st**
Applicant must apply **2** months in advance

Secondary School Information
Most Important Criteria For Admissions (1-strongest)

2 SAT/ACT	**1** Application	**4** School transcript
5 Class rank	**11** Course selection	**10** Personal statement
6 Interview	**8** Extra activities	**9** Psychoeducational
3 G.P.A.	Open admission	**7** Recommendations

Test Requirements:
Untimed ACT: **Yes**

Types of Disabilities Served

• Speech/Lang	• Reading	ADD with LD
• Study skills	• Spelling	ADD without LD
• Written express	• Math	ADHD with LD
• Organizational	• Fine Motor	ADHD without LD
• Perceptual		

High School Course Requirements:
English: **4** Math: **3** Science: **3**

Learning Disability Program
Program: Remedial: **Yes**
Program: Reinforces course work: **Yes**
Students mainstreamed **100** % of the day
Recommended credits per semester: **12**
Services available for all students: **Yes**
Counseling: Individual: **Yes**

Faculty:
Faculty: **2** Including Director: **Yes** Full time: **2** Part time: **1**
LD faculty with: BS/BA: **1** M.A.: **1**
Faculty advocate: **Yes** Meets with instructor: **Almost daily**

Diagnostic Testing

ADD	Personality	Perceptual skills	• Spelling
ADHD	Organization	Fine motor skills	• Reading
I.Q.	Handwriting	Spoken language	• Study skills
Math	Social skills	• Written language	

Tutoring:

Services rendered by:
   Graduates •Peers •Faculty •LD staff •Teacher trainees

Tutorials

Grp.	Ind.	Tutorials	Grp.	Ind.	Tutorials
•	•	Math skills	•	•	Word processing
•	•	Study skills	•	•	Time management
•	•	Language arts	•	•	Learning strategies
•	•	Written express	•	•	Organizational skills

Academic Accommodations

Curriculum	Study Aids	Exams
Priority registration	• Typist	• Oral
Math waiver	• Reader	• Untimed
Foreign lang. waiver	• Notetaker	Take home
Course substitution	• Proof reader	• With proctor
In Class	• Text on tape	On computer
• Calculators	Early syllabus	• Extended time
• Tape recorder	Taped handouts	On tape
• Word processor		• Modified
• Priority seating		• Separate room

Graduation Requirements:

Course credits: **144** GPA: **2.0**

Program Strengths

This program is unique because it is completely individualized for LD students. One advisor works with each student. The developmental program is comprehensive and small so that the students receive as much individual help as needed. All services are free to the student, including tutoring, testing, and computer-use. We are a small institution so we can give the extra assistance students need.

General Information:

Western Montana College University of Montana is a 4 year public college. Rural campus of 20 acres is 60 miles from Butte. Accessible by bus. Ski areas are 15 miles from campus. 1% of students are foreign. 4 residential halls on campus. Housing is not guaranteed.5 % of students remain on campus for the weekends.

Accreditation:NWACS

SAT/ACT Scores:

Scores for incoming freshmen: **ACT:** 45% below 20. 25% between 20 and 23. 20%between 24 and 25l. 5%between 26 and 28. 5% above 28.

Class Rank:

About 5% of the present freshmen class were in the upper 20% of their high school class. 25% were in the top 40% of their class. 50% were in the top 60% of their class. 20% were in the top 80% of their class.

Expenses:

Tuition: In-state: Full year: $1,274.00. Part-time: Per credit:$78.50. Tuition: Out-of-state: Full year: $2,945.00. Part-time: Per credit:$143.00. Room and board: $3,000.00

Majors

• BUSINESS Business Education, Business Management, Human Resources Management, Sports Management, Travel/Tourism Management • COMMUNICATIONS English, Journalism • COMPUTER SCIENCE

Computer Science, Data Processing, Programming, Systems Analysis • EDUCATION Art, Early Childhood, Elementary, English, Industrial, Mathematics, Middle School, Music, Physical, Science, Secondary, Social Science • HEALTH SCIENCES Medical Secretary • PREPROFESSIONAL Sports Medicine • SCIENCES Biology, Chemistry, Earth, Mathematics, Physical Chemistry, Physical Science, Physics • SOCIAL SCIENCES Government/Political, History, Psychology, Social Sciences, Sociology • VISUAL AND PERFORMING ARTS Art, Theater • VOCATIONAL Business and Office, Legal Secretary, Office Administration, Secretarial

Sports/Activities

• SPORTS RELATED Band, Cheerleading, Drill Team, Pep Band • SPORTS-INTERCOLLEGIATE Basketball, Football (M), Volleyball (F), Wrestling (M) • SPORTS-INTRAMURAL Badminton, Basketball, Golf, Hand Ball, Ping-Pong, Racquetball, Skiing - Snow, Softball, Tennis, Volleyball • STUDENT LIFE ACTIVITIES Choral, Concert Band, Dance, Drama Groups, Ethnic & Cultural Groups, Jazz Band, Music Groups, Musical Theater, Newspaper, Religious Organization, Student Government, Symphony Orchestra, Yearbook

Selective **Nebraska**
Services

Dana College

2848 College Drive
Blair, Nebraska 68008-1099
(402) 426-7222

School Enrollment: **501** Male: **220** Female: **281**

Admissions Contact: **John Schueth, Director of Admissions**
LD Contact: **Prof. Liesa Montag-Siegel, Dir. of Learning Resources**

Admissions

Application Information:

Application deadline: **Rolling**
Rolling Admissions: **Yes**

Secondary School Information

Most Important Criteria For Admissions (1-strongest)

3 SAT/ACT	**11** Application	**10** School transcript
2 Class rank	**4** Course selection	**9** Personal statement
5 Interview	**7** Extra activities	**8** Psychoeducational
1 G.P.A.	Open admission	**6** Recommendations

Test Requirements:

Diagnostic testing waived: **Yes**
Untimed SAT: **Yes** Untimed ACT: **Yes** Untimed ACH: **Yes** Achievement tests required:**None**
Currency of diagnostic testing: **No preference**

Types of Disabilities Served

Speech/Lang	• Reading	ADD with LD
• Study skills	• Spelling	ADD without LD
• Written express	• Math	ADHD with LD
• Organizational	• Fine Motor	ADHD without LD
Perceptual		

Admissions Process

Submit application high school, and college transcripts, and inter-

443

view with special admissions committee.

High School Course Requirements:
English: **4** Math: **3** Science: **2** Foreign Language: **2**

Learning Disability Program

Program: Reinforces course work: **Yes**
Students mainstreamed **100** % of the day
Recommended credits per semester: **12-16**
Services available for all students: **Yes**
Counseling: Individual: **Yes** Vocational Counseling: **Yes**
Support groups are available: Mentoring **team for freshman level (10 new students plus 2 returning students and**

Faculty:
Faculty: **1** Including Director: **Yes** M.A.: **1**

Diagnostic Testing

ADD	Personality	Perceptual skills	Spelling
ADHD	Organization	Fine motor skills	Reading
I.Q.	Handwriting	Spoken language	Study skills
Math	Social skills	Written language	

Tutoring:
Average size of group tutorials: **Individualized**
Services rendered by:

Graduates	•Peers	•Faculty	LD staff	Teacher trainees

Tutorials

Grp.	Ind.	Tutorials	Grp.	Ind.	Tutorials
	•	Math skills		•	Word processing
	•	Study skills		•	Time management
	•	Language arts		•	Learning strategies
	•	Written express		•	Organizational skills

Academic Accommodations

Curriculum	Study Aids	Exams
• Priority registration	• Typist	• Oral
• Math waiver	• Reader	Untimed
• Foreign lang. waiver	• Notetaker	Take home
Course substitution	• Proof reader	• With proctor
In Class	• Text on tape	On computer
Calculators	• Early syllabus	• Extended time
• Tape recorder	Taped handouts	On tape
Word processor		Modified
• Priority seating		• Separate room

Graduation Requirements:
Course credits: **128** GPA: **2.0** Years to complete degree: **4** Math waiver: **Yes** Language waiver: **Yes**

Program Strengths
We can offer a small school environment with lots of personal attention with agency assistance financially. We will offer what is needed in most cases to ensure academic success.

General Information:
Dana College is a 4 year private Lutheran college. Rural campus of 150 acres is 17 miles from Omaha. Accessible by air, train or bus. Ski areas are 10 miles from campus. 6% of students are foreign. 4 residential halls on campus. Housing is guaranteed. Guaranteed through 4th year. 50 % of students remain on campus for the weekends.

Accreditation: NCACS, NCSWE, NCATE

SAT/ACT Scores:
Scores for incoming freshmen: **ACT:** 42% below 20. 35% between 20 and 23. 9%between 24 and 25l. 12%between 26 and 28. 2% above 28.

Class Rank:
About 23% of the present freshmen class were in the upper 20% of their high school class. 50% were in the top 40% of their class. 71% were in the top 60% of their class. 93% were in the top 80% of their class.

Expenses:
Tuition: In-state: Full year: $7,600.00. Part-time: Per credit:$255.00. Part-time: Per course: $765.00. Tuition: Out-of-state: Full year: $7,600.00. Part-time: Per credit:$255.00. Part-time: Per course:$765.00 Room and board: $2,930.00

Majors

• ARTS Commercial Art, Graphic Arts, Music, Music Performance, Painting, Photography • BUSINESS Accounting, Banking/Finance, Business Education, Economics, Management, Marketing, Organizational Behavior • COMMUNICATIONS Broadcasting, English, Journalism, Painting, Photography, Speech/Debate/Forensics, Television/Radio/Film • COMPUTER SCIENCE Computer Science • EDUCATION Art, Business, Elementary, English, Foreign Language, Mathematics, Middle School, Music, Science, Secondary, Social Studies, Special, Speech/Language • HEALTH SCIENCES Environmental • HUMANITIES Humanities, Liberal Arts , Religion • LANGUAGES Dance, French, German, Spanish • PREPROFESSIONAL Dentistry, Engineering, Law, Medicine, Ministry, Optometry, Pharmacy, Sports Medicine • RELIGIOUS STUDIES Ministry & Church Administration, Religion & Theology • SCIENCES Biology, Chemistry, Computer Science, General, Mathematics, Natural • SOCIAL SCIENCES History, Human Service, International Studies, Psychology, Social Sciences, Sociology • VISUAL AND PERFORMING ARTS Art, Dramatic Arts, Music, Theater

Sports/Activities

• SPORTS RELATED Cheerleading, Pep Band • SPORTS-INTERCOLLEGIATE Baseball (M), Basketball, Football (M), Golf, Softball (F), Tennis, Track and Field, Volleyball (F), Wrestling (M) • SPORTS-INTRAMURAL Basketball, Football, Golf, Hand Ball, Ping-Pong, Racquetball, Soccer, Softball, Swimming, Tennis, Track and Field, Volleyball • STUDENT LIFE ACTIVITIES Campus Ministry, Choral, Community Service, Concert Band, Departmental Clubs, Drama Groups, Ethnic & Cultural Groups, Honorories, Jazz Band, Literary Magazine, Music Groups, Newspaper, Opera, Radio/TV station, Religious Organization, Student Government, Symphony Orchestra, Theater, Yearbook

Less Selective

Nebraska Services

Southeast Community College: Beatrice Campus
Route 2 Box 35A
Beatrice, Nebraska 68310
(402) 228-3468

School Enrollment: **628** Male: **228** Female: **400**
LD Enrollment: **5** Male: **2** Female: **3**

Admissions Contact: **Sharon Wittler**
LD Contact: **Jim Rakers Director Rural Career Dev. Ctr.**
Name of Program: **MAP**

Admissions

Application Information:
Application deadline: **Prior to start of classes**
Rolling Admissions: **Yes**

Secondary School Information
Most Important Criteria For Admissions (1-strongest)

1 SAT/ACT	Application	**1**	School transcript
1 Class rank	Course selection		Personal statement
Interview	Extra activities		Psychoeducational
1 G.P.A.	Open admission	**1**	Recommendations

Test Requirements:
Standardized tests waived: **Yes**
Diagnostic testing waived: **Yes**
Achievement tests required:**2**
WAIS-R required: **Yes** Range accepted: **85+**
Documentation of LD required: **Yes**
Tests recommended: **WAIS, Woodcock-Johnson ,TOWL**

Types of Disabilities Served
- Speech/Lang
- Study skills
- Written express
- Organizational
- Perceptual

- Reading
- Spelling
- Math
- Fine Motor

- ADD with LD
- ADD without LD
- ADHD with LD
- ADHD without LD

Learning Disability Program

Program: Reinforces course work: **Yes**
Students mainstreamed **100 %** of the day
Services only for LD students: **Yes**

Faculty:
Faculty: **1** Including Director: **Yes** Part time: **1** M.A.: **1**
Faculty advocate: **Yes** Meets with instructor: **As needed**

Diagnostic Testing

ADD	• Personality	• Perceptual skills	• Spelling
ADHD	Organization	Fine motor skills	• Reading
• I.Q.	Handwriting	• Spoken language	• Study skills
• Math	Social skills	• Written language	

Tutoring:
Services rendered by:
Graduates •Peers •Faculty •LD staff Teacher trainees

Tutorials

Grp.	Ind. Tutorials	Grp.	Ind. Tutorials
	• Math skills		• Word processing
	• Study skills		• Time management
	• Language arts		• Learning strategies
	• Written express		• Organizational skills

Academic Accommodations

Curriculum	Study Aids	Exams
Priority registration	Typist	• Oral
Math waiver	Reader	Untimed
Foreign lang. waiver	Notetaker	• Take home
Course substitution	Proof reader	• With proctor
In Class	Text on tape	On computer
Calculators	Early syllabus	• Extended time
• Tape recorder	Taped handouts	On tape
• Word processor		• Modified
Priority seating		Separate room

General Information:
Southeast Community College: Beatrice Campus is a 2 year public college. Rural campus of 640 acres is 40 miles from Lincoln. Ski areas are 600 miles from campus. Beaches are 1800 miles from campus. .016% of students are foreign. 2 residential halls on campus. Housing is not guaranteed.10 % of students remain on campus for the weekends.

Accreditation:NCACS

Expenses:
Tuition: In-state: Full year: $968.00. Part-time: Per credit:$32.00. Tuition: Out-of-state: Full year: $1,282.00. Part-time: Per credit:$43.00. Room and board: $1,040.00

Majors

• BUSINESS Accounting, Agricultural, Banking, Business Management, Finance, Management, Marketing • COMMUNICATIONS Advertising, Broadcasting, Communication, English, Journalism, Photography, Television/Radio/Film • COMPUTER SCIENCE Computer Science, Computer Technology, Data Processing, Programming • EDUCATION Art, Elementary, Music, Physical, Secondary • ENGINEERING Agricultural • HEALTH SCIENCES Medical Secretary, Medical Technology, Nursing, Physical Therapy, Practical Nursing, Radiological Therapy • HUMANITIES Humanities, Liberal Arts, Philosophy • LANGUAGES French, German, Spanish • PREPROFESSIONAL Architecture, Engineering, Law, Medicine, Social Work • SCIENCES Agricultural, Animal, Biology, Botany, Chemistry, Geography, Geology, Mathematics, Physical Science • SOCIAL SCIENCES Anthropology, Government/Political, History, Political Science, Psychology, Public Relations, Social Sciences, Sociology • VISUAL AND PERFORMING ARTS Art, Fine Arts, Music • VOCATIONAL Business and Office, Legal Secretary, Secretarial

Sports/Activities

• SPORTS-INTERCOLLEGIATE Basketball, Golf (M), Volleyball (F)
• STUDENT LIFE ACTIVITIES Academic Clubs, Choral, Drama Groups, Music Groups, Musical Theater, Newspaper, Radio/TV station, Religious Organization, Student Government

Less Selective   **Nebraska**
                                       Services

Southeast Community College: Lincoln Campus
8800 O Street
Lincoln, Nebraska 68520
(402) 471-3333

School Enrollment: **1,791** Male: **733** Female: **1,958**

Admissions Contact: **Gerald Gruber, Dean of Student Services**
LD Contact: **Darlene Williams, Counselor**

Admissions

Application Information:
Application deadline: **Until program is filled**

Secondary School Information
Most Important Criteria For Admissions (1-strongest)

SAT/ACT	**1** Application	**2**	School transcript
Class rank	**3** Course selection		Personal statement
Interview	Extra activities		Psychoeducational
4 G.P.A.	**1** Open admission		Recommendations

Nebraska

Test Requirements:
Documentation of LD required: **Yes**

Types of Disabilities Served
• Speech/Lang	Reading	ADD with LD
• Study skills	• Spelling	ADD without LD
• Written express	Math	ADHD with LD
• Organizational	• Fine Motor	ADHD without LD
• Perceptual		

Faculty:
Faculty advocate: **Yes** Meets with instructor: **As needed**

Diagnostic Testing
ADD	Personality	Perceptual skills	Spelling
ADHD	Organization	Fine motor skills	Reading
I.Q.	Handwriting	Spoken language	Study skills
Math	Social skills	Written language	

Tutoring:
Services rendered by:
Graduates   Peers   •Faculty   LD staff   Teacher trainees

Tutorials
Grp.	Ind.	Tutorials	Grp.	Ind.	Tutorials
•	•	Math skills			Word processing
•	•	Study skills	•	•	Time management
•	•	Language arts	•	•	Learning strategies
•	•	Written express	•	•	Organizational skills

Academic Accommodations
Curriculum	Study Aids	Exams
Priority registration	Typist	• Oral
• Math waiver	• Reader	• Untimed
Foreign lang. waiver	• Notetaker	Take home
• Course substitution	Proof reader	• With proctor
In Class	Text on tape	• On computer
• Calculators	• Early syllabus	• Extended time
• Tape recorder	Taped handouts	• On tape
Word processor		• Modified
• Priority seating		• Separate room

Program Strengths
Our Beatrice Campus is working with the University of Nebraska on a special project designed to identify and refer LD students. The Lincoln Campus of Southeast Community College is one campus in a three campus system.

General Information:
Southeast Community College: Lincoln Campus is a 2 year public college. Suburban campus of 110 acres is 50 miles from Lincoln. Accessible by air, train or bus. 1% of students are foreign. Housing is not guaranteed.

Accreditation:NCACS

Expenses:
Tuition: In-state: Full year: $1,290.00. Part-time: Per credit:$21.50. Tuition: Out-of-state: Full year: $1,710.00. Part-time: Per credit:$28.50.

Majors
• ARTS Drafting • BUSINESS Accounting, Banking/Finance, Bookkeeping, Business Administration, Business Management, Clerical, Data Processing, Fashion Merchandising, Food Management, Marketing, Real Estate, Secretarial Science • EDUCATION Child Development, Early Childhood • ENVIRONMENTAL CONTROL Water and Wastewater Technology • HEALTH SCIENCES Dental Assistant, Dietary Manager, Environmental, Medical Assistant, Medical Laboratory/Technology, Medical Secretary, Nursing, Practical Nursing • SOCIAL SCIENCES Human Service • VOCATIONAL Automobile Technology, Automotive Service, Business and Office, Chef Apprenticeship, Culinary Arts, Dental Assistant, Drafting, Electronics Technology, Fashion Merchandising, Fire Science, Legal Secretary, Machinist, Medical Laboratory Technology, Printing/Lithography, Radiological Technology, Respiratory Therapy Technology, Secretarial, Welding, Word Processing

Sports/Activities
• SPORTS-INTRAMURAL Basketball, Ping-Pong, Softball, Volleyball
• STUDENT LIFE ACTIVITIES Academic Clubs, Ethnic & Cultural Groups, Student Government

---

Less Selective   **Nebraska**
                                                      Services

Southeast Community College: Milford
Milford, Nebraska 68405
(402) 761-2131

School Enrollment: **1,000** Male: **950** Female: **50**
LD Enrollment: **25** Male: **25**

Admissions Contact: **Larry Meyer, Dean of Students**
LD Contact: **Joan Sterns, LD Coordinator**
Name of Program: **Maximum Achievement**
Address: **RR 2, Box D**
Telephone:**(402) 761-2131 Ext. 202**

Admissions

Application Information:
LD on admissions committee:**Yes**
Application deadline: **Open admission**

Secondary School Information
Most Important Criteria For Admissions (1-strongest)
SAT/ACT	Application	School transcript
Class rank	Course selection	Personal statement
Interview	Extra activities	Psychoeducational
G.P.A.	Open admission	Recommendations

Test Requirements:
Standardized tests waived: **Yes**
Diagnostic testing waived: **Yes**
Untimed SAT: **Yes** Untimed ACT: **Yes**
WAIS-R required: **Yes** Range accepted: **85+**
Documentation of LD required: **Yes**
Currency of diagnostic testing: **within 3 years**
Tests recommended: **WAIS-R, Woodcock Johnson**

Types of Disabilities Served
• Speech/Lang	• Reading	ADD with LD
• Study skills	• Spelling	ADD without LD
• Written express	• Math	ADHD with LD
• Organizational	• Fine Motor	ADHD without LD
• Perceptual		

Admissions Process

We have open admission.

Learning Disability Program

Special orientation for LD students: **Yes**
Program: Reinforces course work: **Yes**
Program available through:**all times**
Students mainstreamed **100** % of the day
Services only for LD students: **Yes**
Counseling: Individual: **Yes** Vocational Counseling: **Yes**
Support groups are available:**The LD Group-for each other. Student Services staff**

Faculty:

Faculty: **1** Full time: **1** M.A.: **1**
Meets with instructor: **As needed**

Diagnostic Testing

ADD	Personality	Perceptual skills	Spelling
ADHD	Organization	Fine motor skills	• Reading
• I.Q.	Handwriting•	Spoken language	• Study skills
• Math	Social skills•	Written language	

Tutoring:

Services rendered by:
Graduates • Peers • Faculty • LD staff Teacher trainees

Tutorials

Grp.	Ind.	Tutorials	Grp.	Ind.	Tutorials
•				•	Word processing
	•	Math skills		•	Time management
	•	Study skills		•	Learning strategies
	•	Language arts		•	Organizational skills
	•	Written express			

Academic Accommodations

Curriculum	Study Aids	Exams
Priority registration	Typist	• Oral
Math waiver	Reader	• Untimed
Foreign lang. waiver	• Notetaker	Take home
Course substitution	Proof reader	• With proctor
In Class	• Text on tape	On computer
• Calculators	Early syllabus	• Extended time
• Tape recorder	Taped handouts	• On tape
• Word processor		Modified
• Priority seating		• Separate room

Graduation Requirements:GPA: **2.0**

General Information:

Southeast Community College: Milford is a 2 year public college. Rural campus 25 miles from Lincoln. Accessible by car. Ski areas are 500 miles from campus. 4 residential halls on campus. Housing is not guaranteed.5 % of students remain on campus for the weekends.

Accreditation:NCACS

Expenses:

Tuition: In-state: Full year: $322.50 per quarter. Part-time: Per credit:$21.50. Part-time: Per course: Varies. Tuition: Out-of-state: Full year: $427.50. Part-time: Per credit:$28.50. Part-time: Per course:Varies Room and board: $351.50-$645.00/qtr.

Majors

• ARTS Commercial Art, Drafting • BUSINESS Commercial Art, Data Processing • COMPUTER SCIENCE Computer Maintenance, Data Processing, Programming, Robotics • EDUCATION Technical, Vocational • VOCATIONAL Air Conditioning/Heating/Refri, Auto Body, Automotive Service, Building Construction, Diesel Power Technology, Drafting, Electronics Technology, Machinist, Surveying and Mapping, Welding

Sports/Activities

• SPORTS-INTRAMURAL Baseball, Basketball, Football, Golf, Ping-Pong, Racquetball, Softball, Tennis, Volleyball, Weight Lifting, Wrestling

Less Selective

Nebraska Program

Union College

3800 South 48th Street
Lincoln, Nebraska 68506
(402) 486-2506-(800) 228-4600

School Enrollment: **609** Male: **274** Female: **335**
LD Enrollment: **25**

Admissions Contact: **Mrs. Leona Murray, Director of Admissions**
LD Contact: **Joan C. Stoner, Ed. D. Director, Learning Center**
Name of Program: **People of Promise**
Telephone:**(402) 486-2506**

Admissions

Application Information:

LD Students Applying: **10** Accepted: **5** Enrolled:**25**
Separate application:**Yes**
Application deadline: **June 1st**
Applicant must apply **3-6** months in advance
Rolling Admissions: **Yes**Notified when: **August 1st**

Secondary School Information

Most Important Criteria For Admissions (1-strongest)

3 SAT/ACT	Application	**2**	School transcript
Class rank	**5** Course selection	**8**	Personal statement
6 Interview	Extra activities	**1**	Psychoeducational
4 G.P.A.	Open admission	**7**	Recommendations

Test Requirements:

Diagnostic testing waived: **Yes**
Untimed ACT: **Yes**
WAIS-R required: **Yes**
Documentation of LD required: **Yes**
Currency of diagnostic testing: **3 months**
Tests recommended: **WAIS-R, Woodcock-Johnson Psychoeducational Battery**

Types of Disabilities Served

• Speech/Lang	• Reading	ADD with LD
• Study skills	• Spelling	ADD without LD
• Written express	• Math	ADHD with LD
• Organizational	• Fine Motor	ADHD without LD
• Perceptual		

Learning Disability Program

Program: Remedial: **Yes**
Program: Reinforces course work: **Yes**
Students mainstreamed **100** % of the day
Counseling: Individual: **Yes**

Faculty:

Faculty: **3** Full time: **2** Part time: **1**
LD faculty with: BS/BA: **1** M.A.: **1** Ph.D.: **1**
Faculty advocate: **Yes** Meets with instructor: **As needed**

Nebraska

Diagnostic Testing

ADD	Personality	Perceptual skills	• Spelling
ADHD	Organization	Fine motor skills	• Reading
I.Q.	Handwriting	Spoken language	Study skills
• Math	Social skills	• Written language	

Tutoring:
Services rendered by:
Graduates •Peers •Faculty •LD staff •Teacher trainees

Tutorials

Grp.	Ind.	Tutorials	Grp.	Ind.	Tutorials
•	•	Math skills	•	•	Word processing
•	•	Study skills	•	•	Time management
•	•	Language arts	•	•	Learning strategies
•	•	Written express	•	•	Organizational skills

Academic Accommodations

Curriculum	Study Aids	Exams
Priority registration	• Typist	• Oral
Math waiver	Reader	Untimed
Foreign lang. waiver	• Notetaker	• Take home
• Course substitution	• Proof reader	With proctor
In Class	• Text on tape	On computer
• Calculators	Early syllabus	• Extended time
• Tape recorder	Taped handouts	On tape
• Word processor		• Modified
Priority seating		Separate room

Program Strengths
Union College is the only Seventh Day Adventist College offering a program to remediate and accommodate learning disabled students.

General Information:
Union College is a 4 year private Seventh Day Adventist college. Urban campus. Accessible by air, train or bus. Ski areas are 35 miles from campus. 6% of students are foreign. 3 residential halls on campus. Housing is guaranteed.

Accreditation:NCACS

SAT/ACT Scores:
Scores for incoming freshmen: **ACT:** 61% below 20. 19% between 20 and 23. 8%between 24 and 25l. 10%between 26 and 28. 2% above 28.

Expenses:
Tuition: In-state: Full year: $7,200.00. Part-time: Per credit:$300.00. Room and board: $2,250.00 Cost of LD program:$500.00

Majors
• BUSINESS Accounting, Business Administration, Business Education, Marketing Management • COMMUNICATIONS English, Journalism • EDUCATION Art, English, Mathematics, Music, Physical, Science, Secondary, Social Science • HEALTH SCIENCES Nursing, Physician's Assistant • LANGUAGES Spanish • RELIGIOUS STUDIES Religion, Religious Education, Religious Music, Theological Studies • SCIENCES Behavioral biology Chemistry, Management Science, Mathematics, Physics • SOCIAL SCIENCES History, Psychology, Public Relations, Social Science, Social Work • VISUAL AND PERFORMING ARTS Music, Music Performance, Studio Art • VOCATIONAL Office Supervision and Management, Sports Management

Sports/Activities
• SPORTS-INTERCOLLEGIATE Basketball • SPORTS-INTRAMURAL Badminton, Baseball, Basketball, Soccer, Softball, Tennis, Volleyball

---

Western Nebraska Community College: Scottsbluff
1601 East 27th Street
Scottsbluff, Nebraska 69361-1899
(308) 635-3606

School Enrollment: **790** Male: **316** Female: **474**
LD Enrollment: **12** Male: **4** Female: **8**

Admissions Contact: **Roger Horey, Dir. of Enrollment Management**
LD Contact: **Vanessa Harrison, Director of Counseling**
Name of Program: **LD Talents**
Telephone:**(308) 635-6010**

Admissions

Application Information:
Application deadline: **None**
Rolling Admissions: **Yes**

Secondary School Information
Most Important Criteria For Admissions (1-strongest)

SAT/ACT	Application	School transcript
Class rank	Course selection	Personal statement
Interview	Extra activities	Psychoeducational
G.P.A.	**1** Open admission	Recommendations

Test Requirements:
Diagnostic testing waived: **Yes**
WAIS-R required: **Yes** Range accepted: **85+**
Documentation of LD required: **Yes**
Tests recommended: **WAIS-R, Woodcock-Johnson**

Types of Disabilities Served

• Speech/Lang	• Reading	ADD with LD
• Study skills	• Spelling	ADD without LD
• Written express	• Math	ADHD with LD
• Organizational	• Fine Motor	ADHD without LD
• Perceptual		

Admissions Process

Complete admission data forms-submit high school transcripts, as well as those from other colleges attended-meet with counselor to discuss special needs.

High School Course Requirements:
Waivers to standard high school courses
Course substitution: **Yes**

Learning Disability Program
Program: Reinforces course work: **Yes**
Students mainstreamed **70** % of the day
Recommended credits per semester: **Varies**
Services available for all students: **Yes**
Counseling: Individual: **Yes** Group Counseling: **Yes**
Support groups are available:**As needed**

Faculty:
Faculty: **3** Including Director: **Yes** Full time: **1** Part time: **2**
LD faculty with: BS/BA: **2** M.A.: **2**
Faculty advocate: **Yes** Meets with instructor: **Monthly**

Diagnostic Testing

ADD	Personality	Perceptual skills	Spelling
ADHD•	Organization	Fine motor skills	• Reading
• I.Q.	Handwriting•	Spoken language	Study skills
• Math	Social skills•	Written language	

Tutoring:
Services rendered by:
  Graduates •Peers •Faculty •LD staff Teacher trainees

Tutorials

Grp.	Ind.	Tutorials	Grp.	Ind.	Tutorials
	•	Math skills		•	Word processing
	•	Study skills		•	Time management
	•	Language arts		•	Learning strategies
	•	Written express		•	Organizational skills

Academic Accommodations

Curriculum	Study Aids	Exams
Priority registration	Typist	• Oral
Math waiver	Reader	Untimed
Foreign lang. waiver	• Notetaker	Take home
• Course substitution	• Proof reader	• With proctor
In Class	• Text on tape	On computer
• Calculators	Early syllabus	• Extended time
• Tape recorder	Taped handouts	On tape
• Word processor		• Modified
Priority seating		Separate room

Graduation Requirements:
Course credits: **60** Years to complete degree: **No limit**

Program Strengths

The program at Western Nebraska Community College exists to (1) identify LD or potentially verifiable LD college students, (2) complete verification by having the students take a battery of tests designed to highlight the presence of specific learning disabilities, and (3) interpret and explain the results to the students.

General Information:

Western Nebraska Community College: Scottsbluff is a 2 year public college. Rural campus of 4 acres is 100 miles from Cheyenne. Accessible by air, train or bus Ski areas are 120 miles from campus. .02% of students are foreign. 1 residential halls on campus. Housing is not guaranteed.

Accreditation: Regional

Expenses:
Tuition: In-state: Full year: $852.00. Part-time: Per credit:$36.00. Part-time: Per course: $178.00. Tuition: Out-of-state: Full year: $876.00. Part-time: Per credit:$36.00. Part-time: Per course:$178.00 Room and board: $2,250.00

Majors

• BUSINESS Accounting, Agricultural, Business Administration, Business Economics, Business Education, Business Management, Economics, Management, Marketing, Real Estate • COMMUNICATIONS Advertising, Communication, English, Journalism, Photography, Television/Radio/Film • EDUCATION Art, Early Childhood, Elementary, Middle School, Music, Physical, Pre-Education, Secondary • ENGINEERING Engineering Science • HEALTH SCIENCES Health, Nursing, Practical Nursing, Radiological Therapy • HUMANITIES Humanities, Liberal Arts • LANGUAGES

German, Spanish • PREPROFESSIONAL Agriculture, Architecture, Dentistry, Engineering, Forestry, Law, Medicine, Ministry, Pharmacy, Recreation, Social Work, Wildlife • SCIENCES Agricultural, Biochemistry, Biology, Chemistry, Earth, Geography, Mathematics, Physical Science, Physics • SOCIAL SCIENCES Anthropology, Criminal Justice, History, Psychology, Social Sciences • VISUAL AND PERFORMING ARTS Art, Art History, Music, Theater • VOCATIONAL Automobile Technology, Automotive Service, Business and Office, Home Economics, Precision Metal Work, Secretarial, Welding

Sports/Activities

Basketball, Golf, Volleyball (F) • SPORTS-INTRAMURAL Basketball, Hand Ball, Racquetball, Softball, Tennis, Volleyball • STUDENT LIFE ACTIVITIES Choral, Drama Groups, Jazz Band, Music Groups, Musical Theater, Newspaper, Student Government

---

Less Selective **Nevada**
Services

Truckee Meadows Community College
7000 Dandini Boulevard
Reno, Nevada 89512
(702) 673-7000

School Enrollment: **9,600** Male: **4,100** Female: **5,500**
LD Enrollment: **50**

Admissions Contact: **Bob Losser, Director Enrollment Outreach**
LD Contact: **Tom Tooke, Counselor**
Name of Program: **Student Support Services**
Telephone:**(702) 673-7060**

Admissions

Secondary School Information
Most Important Criteria For Admissions (1-strongest)

SAT/ACT	Application	School transcript
Class rank	Course selection	Personal statement
Interview	Extra activities	Psychoeducational
G.P.A.	Open admission	Recommendations

Test Requirements:
Documentation of LD required: **Yes**

Types of Disabilities Served

• Speech/Lang	• Reading	• ADD with LD
• Study skills	• Spelling	• ADD without LD
• Written express	• Math	• ADHD with LD
• Organizational	• Fine Motor	• ADHD without LD
• Perceptual		

Learning Disability Program
Counseling: Individual: **Yes**

Faculty:
Faculty: **3** Full time: **2** Part time: **1**
Faculty advocate: **Yes** Meets with instructor: **As needed**

Diagnostic Testing

ADD	Personality	Perceptual skills	Spelling
ADHD	Organization	Fine motor skills	Reading
I.Q.	Handwriting	Spoken language	Study skills
Math	Social skills	Written language	

Tutoring:
Average size of group tutorials: **3**
Services rendered by:
  Graduates •Peers Faculty LD staff Teacher trainees

Tutorials

Grp.	Ind.	Tutorials	Grp.	Ind.	Tutorials
•	•	Math skills			Word processing
•	•	Study skills			Time management
		Language arts		•	Learning strategies
•		Written express		•	Organizational skills

Academic Accommodations

Curriculum	Study Aids	Exams
Priority registration	Typist	Oral
Math waiver	Reader	Untimed
Foreign lang. waiver	• Notetaker	Take home
Course substitution	Proof reader	With proctor
In Class	• Text on tape	On computer
Calculators	Early syllabus	• Extended time
• Tape recorder	Taped handouts	On tape
Word processor		Modified
Priority seating		Separate room

Graduation Requirements:
Course credits: **60** GPA: **2.0** Years to complete degree: **No limit**

Program Strengths

We offer an individualized approach to serving disabled students depending on need. We are expanding our Supplemental Instruction Program. We offer: tutors, enablers, notetakers, interpreters, books on tapes, etc.

General Information:

Truckee Meadows Community College is a 2 year public college. Urban campus of 310 acres is 2 miles from Reno. Accessible by air, train or bus. Ski areas are 30 minutes from campus. Beaches are 1 hour from campus. Housing is not guaranteed.

Accreditation: Regional

Expenses:
Tuition: In-state: Full year: $780.00. Part-time: Per credit:$26.00. Tuition: Out-of-state: Full year: $780.00. Part-time: Per credit:$26.00 plus $1,500.00 per semester.

Majors

• BUSINESS Accounting, Banking, Business Administration, Business Management, Entrepreneur, Finance, Legal Assistant, Management, Marketing, Real Estate • COMPUTER SCIENCE Computer Science, Data Processing, Programming, Software Engineer • ENGINEERING Air Conditioning Technology, Engineering Science • ENVIRONMENTAL CONTROL Sanitation Technology • HEALTH SCIENCES Dental Assistant, Medical Secretary, Nursing, Practical Nursing, Radiological Therapy • HUMANITIES Liberal Arts • PREPROFESSIONAL Architecture • SOCIAL SCIENCES Criminal Justice, Law Enforcement • VOCATIONAL Automated Manufacturing Technology, Automobile Technology, Automotive Service, Business and Office, Diesel Power Technology, Drafting, Electronics Technology, Fire Science, Food Service, Landscape Architecture, Legal Secretary, Masonry, Painting, Plumbing, Precision Metal Work, Radiological Technology, Secretarial, Welding

Sports/Activities

• STUDENT LIFE ACTIVITIES Ethnic & Cultural Groups, Magazine, Newspaper, Student Government

University of Nevada: Las Vegas
4505 Maryland Parkway
Las Vegas, Nevada 89154
(702) 739-3443

School Enrollment: **19,500** Male: **9,555** Female: **9,945**
LD Enrollment: **41** Male: **22** Female: **19**

Admissions Contact: **Carl Cook, Admissions Counselor**
LD Contact: **Jan Hurtubise, Director**
Name of Program: **Learning Abilities Program**
Address: **4505 Maryland Parkway**
Telephone:**(702) 739-3781**

Admissions

Application Information:
Enrolled:**41**
Applicant must apply **4-5** months in advance
Rolling Admissions: **Yes**

Secondary School Information
Most Important Criteria For Admissions (1-strongest)

2 SAT/ACT	**1** Application	**1** School transcript
3 Class rank	**4** Course selection	**6** Personal statement
Interview	**5** Extra activities	**7** Psychoeducational
1 G.P.A.	Open admission	Recommendations

Test Requirements:
Standardized tests waived: **Yes**
Diagnostic testing waived: **Yes**
Untimed SAT: **Yes** Untimed ACT: **Yes**
Documentation of LD required: **Yes**
Tests recommended: **Testing done on UNLV campus through the Learning Abilities Program.**

Types of Disabilities Served

• Speech/Lang	• Reading	• ADD with LD
• Study skills	• Spelling	ADD without LD
• Written express	• Math	• ADHD with LD
• Organizational	• Fine Motor	ADHD without LD
• Perceptual		

Learning Disability Program

Program: Reinforces course work: **Yes**
Students mainstreamed **100** % of the day
Recommended credits per semester: **12-15**
Time required or recommended in learning center: **1 hour**
Services only for LD students: **Yes**
Counseling: Individual: **Yes**

Faculty:
Faculty: **6** Including Director: **Yes** Full time: **1** Part time: **5**
LD faculty with: BS/BA: **5** M.A.: **1**
Faculty advocate: **Yes** Meets with instructor: **As needed**

Diagnostic Testing

ADD	Personality •	Perceptual skills	• Spelling
ADHD	Organization	Fine motor skills	• Reading
• I.Q.	• Handwriting	Spoken language	Study skills
• Math	Social skills•	Written language	

Tutoring:

Services rendered by:
•Graduates   Peers   •Faculty   •LD staff   Teacher trainees

Tutorials

Grp.	Ind.	Tutorials	Grp.	Ind.	Tutorials
		Math skills		•	Word processing
	•	Study skills		•	Time management
		Language arts			Learning strategies
	•	Written express		•	Organizational skills

Academic Accommodations

Curriculum
- Priority registration
  Math waiver
  Foreign lang. waiver
  Course substitution

In Class
- Calculators
- Tape recorder
- Word processor
  Priority seating

Study Aids
  Typist
- Reader
- Notetaker
- Proof reader
- Text on tape
  Early syllabus
  Taped handouts

Exams
- Oral
  Untimed
  Take home
- With proctor
  On computer
- Extended time
  On tape
- Modified
  Separate room

Graduation Requirements: Math waiver: **Yes** Language waiver: **Yes**

Program Strengths

The Learning Abilities Program emphasizes strengths of the student and helps the student to utilize his/her strengths to achieve success. The students are assisted individually by the staff of the Learning Abilities Program. There are several computers available for the Learning Abilities Program students' use to help with writing term papers, etc.

General Information:

University of Nevada: Las Vegas is a 4 year public university. Urban campus of 335 acres is Accessible by air, train or bus. Ski areas are 28 miles from campus. Beaches are 280 miles from campus. 1% of students are foreign. 8 residential halls on campus. Housing is not guaranteed.5 % of students join fraternities/sororities.

Accreditation: NWACS

Expenses:

Tuition: In-state: Full year: Part-time: Per credit: $55.50. Tuition: Out-of-state: Full year: $2,025.00. Part-time: Per credit:$55.50. Room and board: $4,086.00

Majors

• AREA STUDIES African, American, Asian, Black/Afro-American, Latin American • BUSINESS Accounting, Banking, Business Administration, Business Economics, Business Management, Economics, Finance, Hotel and Restaurant Management, Management, Marketing, Marketing Research • COMMUNICATIONS Advertising, Broadcasting, Communication, Creative Writing, English, Journalism, Photography, Television/Radio/Film • COMPUTER SCIENCE Computer Science, Computer Technology, Data Processing, Programming, Telecommunications • EDUCATION Curriculum, Early Childhood, Elementary, Foreign Language, Health, Industrial, Middle School, Physical, Recreation and Youth Leadership, School Psychology, Secondary, Special, Vocational • ENGINEERING Civil/Environmental, Computer, Electrical, Mechanical, Naval

Architecture • HEALTH SCIENCES Health, Medical Technology, Nursing, Nutritional/Food, Physical Therapy, Radiological Therapy • HUMANITIES Humanities, Liberal Arts, Philosophy • LANGUAGES French, German, Italian, Japanese, Russian, Spanish • PREPROFESSIONAL Architecture, Engineering, Law, Medicine, Recreation, Social Work • SCIENCES Biology, Botany, Chemistry, Earth, Geology, Marine Biology, Mathematics, Microbiology, Physical Chemistry, Physical Science, Physics, Radiology • SOCIAL SCIENCES Anthropology, Criminal Justice, Government/Political, History, Political Science, Psychology, Social Sciences, Sociology • VISUAL AND PERFORMING ARTS Art, Dance, Dramatic Arts, Fine Arts, Music, Studio Art, Theater

Sports/Activities

• SPORTS RELATED Marching Band, Pep Band • SPORTS-INTERCOLLEGIATE Baseball (M), Basketball, Diving, Football (M), Golf (M), Soccer (M), Softball (F), Swimming, Tennis, Track and Field • SPORTS-INTRAMURAL Bowling, Softball • STUDENT LIFE ACTIVITIES Choral, Concert Band, Dance, Debate, Drama Groups, Film, Fraternities, Jazz Band, Magazine, Music Groups, Musical Theater, Newspaper, Opera, Political Groups, Radio/TV station, Religious Organization, Sororities, Student Government, Symphony Orchestra

---

Selective   **Nevada**
                                                   Program

University of Nevada: Reno

Reno, Nevada 89557-0002
(702) 784-6865

School Enrollment: **8,246** Male: **4,123** Female: **4,123**
LD Enrollment: **50**

Admissions Contact: **Dr. Barry Davidson, Asoc. Dir. of Admissions**
LD Contact: **Hazel Ralston, Counselor**
Name of Program: **Special Services**
Telephone:**(702) 784-6801**

Admissions

Application Information:

LD Students Applying: **60** Accepted: **50** Enrolled:**40**
Application deadline: **July 1st**
Applicant must apply **3** months in advance
Rolling Admissions: **Yes**

Secondary School Information

Most Important Criteria For Admissions (1-strongest)

3 SAT/ACT	**6** Application	**4** School transcript
5 Class rank	**2** Course selection	**9** Personal statement
10 Interview	**7** Extra activities	**8** Psychoeducational
1 G.P.A.	Open admission	**11** Recommendations

Types of Disabilities Served

- Speech/Lang
- Study skills
- Written express
- Organizational
- Perceptual

- Reading
- Spelling
- Math
- Fine Motor

- ADD with LD
- ADD without LD
- ADHD with LD
- ADHD without LD

Learning Disability Program

Program: Reinforces course work: **Yes**
Students mainstreamed **100** % of the day
Counseling: Individual: **Yes** Group Counseling: **Yes**

Faculty:

Faculty: **45** Full time: **35** Part time: **10**
LD faculty with: BS/BA: **27** M.A.: **9** Ph.D.: **9**
Faculty advocate: **Yes** Meets with instructor: **Each semester**

Diagnostic Testing

ADD	Personality •	Perceptual skills	• Spelling
ADHD	Organization•	Fine motor skills	• Reading
• I.Q.	• Handwriting	Spoken language	• Study skills
Math	• Social skills•	Written language	

Tutoring:

Average size of group tutorials: **5**
Services rendered by:
•Graduates •Peers •Faculty •LD staff Teacher trainees

Tutorials

Grp.	Ind.	Tutorials	Grp.	Ind.	Tutorials
	•	Math skills			Word processing
•	•	Study skills			Time management
		Language arts	•	•	Learning strategies
•	•	Written express	•	•	Organizational skills

Academic Accommodations

Curriculum	Study Aids	Exams
Priority registration	Typist	• Oral
Math waiver	Reader	Untimed
Foreign lang. waiver	• Notetaker	• Take home
Course substitution	• Proof reader	With proctor
In Class	• Text on tape	On computer
• Calculators	Early syllabus	• Extended time
• Tape recorder	Taped handouts	On tape
Word processor		• Modified
Priority seating		Separate room

Program Strengths

We offer one-on-one tutoring and counseling, and have separate accessible facilities for LD students. Faculty and staff are available, and we place special emphasis on individual independence.

General Information:

University of Nevada: Reno is a 4 year public university. Urban campus of 200 acres is 250 miles from San Francisco. Accessible by air, train or bus. Ski areas are 30 miles from campus. Beaches are 250 miles from campus. 4% of students are foreign. 5 residential halls on campus. Housing is not guaranteed.15 % of students remain on campus for the weekends. 3 % of students join fraternities/sororities.

Accreditation: AACSB, ABET, ACEJML, AHEA, CSWE, NASM, NCATE, NLN

SAT/ACT Scores:

Scores for incoming freshmen: **Verbal:**28%below 500. 60%between 500 and 599. 6%between 600 and 699. 2%above 700. **Math:**22% below 500. 60% between 500 and 599. 10% between 600 and 699. 8%above 700. **ACT:** 38% below 20. 40% between 20 and 23. 10%between 24 and 25l. 8%between 26 and 28. 4% above 28.

Class Rank:

About 35% of the present freshmen class were in the upper 20% of their high school class. 60% were in the top 40% of their class. 75% were in the top 60% of their class. 90% were in the top 80% of their class.

Expenses:

Tuition: In-state: Full year: $1,280.00. Part-time: Per credit:$26.00. Tuition: Out-of-state: Full year: $4,280.00. Part-time: Per credit:$40.00.
Room and board: $3,500.00

Majors

• AREA STUDIES Urban • BUSINESS Accounting, Agricultural, Banking, Business Administration, Business Economics, Business Management, Economics, Finance, Management, Marketing • COMMUNICATIONS English, Journalism, Speech • COMPUTER SCIENCE Computer Science • EDUCATION Agricultural, Child Development, Elementary, Music, Pre-Education, Secondary, Special • ENGINEERING Chemical, Civil/Environmental, Electrical, Engineering Science, Geological, Mechanical, Metallurgical, Mining/Mineral • HEALTH SCIENCES Medical Technology, Nursing, Nutritional/Food, Speech/Audiology and Speech • HUMANITIES Philosophy • LANGUAGES Spanish • PREPROFESSIONAL Dentistry, Law, Medicine, Natural Resources, Pharmacy, Range Management, Recreation, Social Work, Veterinarian • SCIENCES Agricultural, Animal, Biochemistry, Biology, Botany, Chemistry, Earth, Geography, Geology, Geophysics, Mathematics, Physics, Plant Science, Zoology • SOCIAL SCIENCES Anthropology, Criminal Justice, Family Counseling, Government/Political, History, Law Enforcement, Political Science, Psychology, Sociology • VISUAL AND PERFORMING ARTS Art, Fine Arts, Music, Music Performance, Theater • VOCATIONAL Fashion Mechandizing, Food Service, Textile and Clothing

Sports/Activities

• SPORTS RELATED Marching Band, Pep Band • SPORTS-INTERCOLLEGIATE Baseball (M), Basketball, Cross Country, Diving, Football (M), Golf (M), Skiing - Snow, Softball (F), Swimming (F), Tennis, Track and Field (M), Volleyball (F) • SPORTS-INTRAMURAL Basketball, Cross Country, Football (M), Hand Ball (M), Ping-Pong, Racquetball, Soccer (M), Swimming, Track and Field, Volleyball, Water Polo, Wrestling (M) • STUDENT LIFE ACTIVITIES Choral, Concert Band, Dance, Drama Groups, Ethnic & Cultural Groups, Fraternities, Jazz Band, Magazine, Music Groups, Musical Theater, Newspaper, Opera, Political Groups, Radio/TV station, Religious Organization, Sororities, Student Government, Symphony Orchestra, Yearbook

Most Selective **New Hampshire Services**

Dartmouth College
Hanover, New Hampshire 03755
(603) 646-2875

School Enrollment: **4,210** Male: **2,278** Female: **1,932**

Admissions Contact: **Steve Silver**
LD Contact: **Nancy Pompian, Coordinator**
Name of Program: **Student Disabilities**
Address: **6173 College Hall**
Telephone:**(603) 646-2014**

Admissions

Application Information:
Application deadline: **January 1st**
Notified when: **April 15th**

Secondary School Information
Most Important Criteria For Admissions (1-strongest)

1 SAT/ACT	1 Application	1 School transcript
1 Class rank	1 Course selection	1 Personal statement
1 Interview	1 Extra activities	Psychoeducational
1 G.P.A.	Open admission	1 Recommendations

Test Requirements:
Diagnostic testing waived: **Yes**
Untimed SAT: **Yes** Untimed ACT: **Yes** Untimed ACH: **Yes** Achievement

tests required:**3**
Documentation of LD required: **Yes**

Types of Disabilities Served
- Speech/Lang
- Study skills
- Written express
- Organizational
- Perceptual
- Reading
- Spelling
- Math
- Fine Motor
- ADD with LD
- ADD without LD
- ADHD with LD
- ADHD without LD

Admissions Process

Dartmouth seeks students who have a record of high achievement in a challenging academic curriculum. Careful attention is given to extracurricular involvement, intellectual curiosity, passion for ideas, etc.

Learning Disability Program

Program: Reinforces course work: **Yes**
Students mainstreamed **100** % of the day
Recommended credits per semester: **3**
Counseling: Individual: **Yes** Group Counseling: **Yes** Vocational Counseling: **Yes**
Support groups are available:**Yes**

Faculty:
Faculty: **1** Part time: **1** M.A.: **1**
Faculty advocate: **Yes** Meets with instructor: **As requested**

Diagnostic Testing
- ADD
- ADHD
- I.Q.
- Math
- Personality
- Organization
- Handwriting
- Social skills
- Perceptual skills
- Fine motor skills
- Spoken language
- Written language
- Spelling
- Reading
- Study skills

Services rendered by:
Graduates   Peers   Faculty   LD staff   Teacher trainees

Tutorials

Grp.	Ind.	Tutorials	Grp.	Ind.	Tutorials
		Math skills			Word processing
		Study skills			Time management
		Language arts			Learning strategies
		Written express			Organizational skills

Academic Accommodations

Curriculum	Study Aids	Exams
Priority registration	Typist	Oral
Math waiver	Reader	Untimed
• Foreign lang. waiver	• Notetaker	Take home
Course substitution	Proof reader	With proctor
In Class	Text on tape	On computer
• Calculators	Early syllabus	• Extended time
• Tape recorder	Taped handouts	On tape
• Word processor		Modified
Priority seating		Separate room

Graduation Requirements:
Course credits: **35** Years to complete degree: **4** Language waiver: **Yes**

Program Strengths

Dartmouth does not have a formal program for learning disabled students. That is, the College does not have a learning disabilities remedial specialist or tutor, nor does it have special classes or programs for learning disabled students. A learning disabled student at Dartmouth takes the normal load of courses, although a reduced course load is possible at no tuition reduction. In general, learning

disabled high school students are admitted to Dartmouth with the understanding that they are and will be able to perform well academically at the College without special conditions.

General Information:
Dartmouth College is a 4 year private college. Rural campus of 216 acres is 130 miles from Boston. Accessible by air, bus, train or interstate highway. Ski areas are 10 miles from campus. Beaches are 1.5 hours from campus. 6% of students are foreign. 5 residential halls on campus. Housing is guaranteed.Guaranteed through 2nd year. 95 % of students remain on campus for the weekends. 45 % of students join fraternities/sororities.

Accreditation:Regional

SAT/ACT Scores:
Scores for incoming freshmen:**Verbal:**6%below 500. 27%between 500 and 599. 50%between 600 and 699. 17%above 700. **Math:**2% below 500. 11% between 500 and 599. 37% between 600 and 699. 50%above 700.

Class Rank:
About 96% of the present freshmen class were in the upper 20% of their high school class. 4% were in the top 40% of their class.

Expenses:
Tuition: In-state: Full year: $17,354.00. Tuition: Out-of-state: Full year: $17,354.00. Room and board: $6,086.00.

Majors
• AREA STUDIES African, American Indian, Asian, Black/Afro-American, Russian/Slavic • BUSINESS Economics • COMMUNICATIONS English, Linguistics, Television/Radio/Film • COMPUTER SCIENCE Computer Science • EDUCATION Foreign Language • ENGINEERING Engineering Science • HUMANITIES Classics, English/Writing/Literature, Philosophy, Religion • LANGUAGES Arabic, Chinese, French, German, Greek, Italian, Portuguese, Russian, Spanish • SCIENCES Astronomy, Biochemistry, Biology, Chemistry, Earth, Geography, Mathematics, Physics • SOCIAL SCIENCES Anthropology, Government/Political, History, Political Science, Psychology, Sociology • VISUAL AND PERFORMING ARTS Art History, Dance, Dramatic Arts, Fine Arts, Music, Studio Art, Theater

Sports/Activities
• SPORTS-INTERCOLLEGIATE Baseball (M), Basketball, Crew, Cross Country, Diving, Fencing, Field Hockey (F), Football (M), Golf, Gymnastics (M), Horseback Riding, Ice Hockey, Lacrosse, Rugby, Skiing - Snow, Soccer, Softball (F), Squash, Swimming, Tennis, Track and Field, Volleyball, Water Polo, Wrestling (M) • SPORTS-INTRAMURAL Basketball, Bowling, Cross Country, Diving, Golf, Hammer Throw, Ice Hockey, Lacrosse, Racquetball, Riflery, Rugby, Skiing - Snow, Soccer, Softball, Squash, Swimming, Tennis, Track and Field, Volleyball, Water Polo, Wrestling (M) • STUDENT LIFE ACTIVITIES Choral, Concert Band, Dance, Debate, Drama Groups, Ethnic & Cultural Groups, Film, Fraternities, Jazz Band, Magazine, Music Groups, Musical Theater, Newspaper, Opera, Political Groups, Radio/TV station, Religious Organization, Sororities, Student Government, Symphony Orchestra, Yearbook

Selective   New Hampshire Accommodations

Keene State College

Elliot Hall 229 Main Street
Keene, New Hampshire 03431
(603) 352-1909

School Enrollment: **3,000** Male: **1,200** Female: **1,800**

Admissions Contact: **Kathryn Dodge, Director of Admissions**
LD Contact: **Deborah Merchant, Special Needs Coordinator**
Name of Program: **Student Academic Support Services**

Admissions

Application Information:
Application deadline: **April 1st**
Rolling Admissions: **Yes**

Secondary School Information
Most Important Criteria For Admissions (1-strongest)

5 SAT/ACT	**11** Application	**1**	School transcript
3 Class rank	**2** Course selection	**8**	Personal statement
6 Interview	**10** Extra activities	**7**	Psychoeducational
4 G.P.A.	Open admission	**9**	Recommendations

Test Requirements:
Diagnostic testing waived: **Yes**
Untimed SAT: **Yes**
Documentation of LD required: **Yes**

Types of Disabilities Served
- Speech/Lang
- Study skills
- Written express
- Organizational
- Perceptual
- Reading
- Spelling
- Math
- Fine Motor
- ADD with LD
- ADD without LD
- ADHD with LD
- ADHD without LD

Admissions Process

Students must be enrolled in a college prep program with 3 years of math, 2 years of science, 4 years of English, and an even distribution of social sciences.

High School Course Requirements:
English: **4** Math: **3** Science: **2**

Faculty:
Faculty: **1** Full time: **1** M.A.: **1**
Meets with instructor: **As necessary**

Diagnostic Testing

ADD	Personality	Perceptual skills	Spelling
ADHD	Organization	Fine motor skills	Reading
I.Q.	Handwriting	Spoken language	Study skills
Math	Social skills	Written language	

Tutoring:
Services rendered by:

Graduates	Peers	Faculty	•LD staff	Teacher trainees

Tutorials

Grp.	Ind.	Tutorials	Grp.	Ind.	Tutorials
	•	Math skills		•	Word processing
	•	Study skills		•	Time management
	•	Language arts		•	Learning strategies
	•	Written express		•	Organizational skills

Academic Accommodations

Curriculum	Study Aids	Exams
• Priority registration	Typist	• Oral
Math waiver	Reader	Untimed
Foreign lang. waiver	• Notetaker	Take home
Course substitution	• Proof reader	• With proctor
In Class	• Text on tape	• On computer
• Calculators	Early syllabus	• Extended time
• Tape recorder	Taped handouts	On tape
• Word processor		• Modified
Priority seating		• Separate room

Program Strengths

We do not have a formal program for learning disabled students. We do have services which are available to students with documentation.

General Information:

Keene State College is a 4 year public college. Urban campus of 160 acres is 90 miles from Boston. Accessible by air or bus. Ski areas are 40 miles from campus. Beaches are 2 hours from campus. 2% of students are foreign. 20 residential halls on campus. Housing is not guaranteed.65 % of students remain on campus for the weekends. 20 % of students join fraternities/sororities.

Accreditation: NEACS

SAT/ACT Scores:
Scores for incoming freshmen: **Verbal:** 81% below 500. 16% between 500 and 599. 3% between 600 and 699. **Math:** 66% below 500. 28% between 500 and 599. 5% between 600 and 699.

Class Rank:
About 16% of the present freshmen class were in the upper 20% of their high school class. 54% were in the top 40% of their class. 86% were in the top 60% of their class. 99% were in the top 80% of their class.

Expenses:
Tuition: In-state: Full year: $2,150.00. Part-time: Per credit:$108.00. Part-time: Per course: $324.00. Tuition: Out-of-state: Full year: $6,310.00. Part-time: Per credit:$315.00. Part-time: Per course:$945.00 Room and board: $3,600.00

Majors

• AREA STUDIES American • ARTS Dance, Drafting, Dramatic Arts, Drawing, Film & Video, Graphic Arts, Music, Music Performance, Painting, Sculpture • BUSINESS Business Economics, Business Management • COMMUNICATIONS Broadcasting, English, Graphic Design, Journalism, Speech/Debate/Forensic, Television/Radio/Film • COMPUTER SCIENCE Computer Mathematics, Computer Science • EDUCATION Child Development, Early Childhood, Elementary, English, Foreign Language, Home Economics, Mathematics, Middle School, Music, Physical, Science, Secondary, Social Studies, Special, Vocational • HEALTH SCIENCES Nutritional/Food, Physical Therapy • HUMANITIES English/Writing/Literature, Fine Arts, Philosophy • MATHEMATICS Applied, Computer • PREPROFESSIONAL Drafting, Sports Medicine • SCIENCES Biology, Chemistry, Computer Science, Geography, Geology, Mathematics, Physical Science • SOCIAL SCIENCES Geography, Government/Political, History, Human Service, Political Science, Psychology, Social Sciences, Sociology • VISUAL AND PERFORMING ARTS Art, Dance, Dramatic Arts, Fine Arts, Music, Music Performance, Studio Art, Theater • VOCA-

TIONAL Home Economics

Sports/Activities

• SPORTS RELATED Cheerleading • SPORTS-INTERCOLLEGIATE Basketball, Football, Hand Ball, Judo, Lacrosse, Racquetball, Rugby, Soccer, Softball (F), Tennis, Volleyball (F) • SPORTS-INTRAMURAL Badminton, Basketball, Hammer Throw, Ice Hockey (M), Lacrosse, Racquetball, Rugby, Soccer, Softball, Squash, Swimming, Tennis, Volleyball, Water Polo • STUDENT LIFE ACTIVITIES Academic Clubs, Choral, Community Service, Concert Band, Dance, Ethnic & Cultural Groups, Film, Fraternities, Jazz Band, Music Groups, Musical Theater, Newspaper, Radio/TV station, Religious Organization, Sororities, Student Government, Yearbook

Less Selective   **New Hampshire Services**

New England College
Henniker, New Hampshire 03242
(603) 428-2223

School Enrollment: **900** Male: **540** Female: **360**
LD Enrollment: **216**

Admissions Contact: **John Spaulding, Director**
LD Contact: **Dr. Joanne MacEachran, Director**
Name of Program: **College Skills Center**
Telephone:**(603) 428-2218**

Admissions

Application Information:
LD on admissions committee:**Yes**
Application deadline: **None**
Notified when: **May**

Secondary School Information
Most Important Criteria For Admissions (1-strongest)

	SAT/ACT		Application	**2**	School transcript
	Class rank	**4**	Course selection		Personal statement
1	Interview		Extra activities	**5**	Psychoeducational
	G.P.A.		Open admission	**3**	Recommendations

Test Requirements:
Diagnostic testing waived: **Yes**
Untimed SAT: **Yes** Untimed ACT: **Yes** Untimed ACH: **Yes**
WAIS-R required: **Yes** Range accepted: **95+**
Documentation of LD required: **Yes**
Currency of diagnostic testing: **2 years**
Tests recommended: **WAIS-R, Reading, Math**

Types of Disabilities Served
• Speech/Lang   • Reading   ADD with LD
• Study skills   • Spelling   ADD without LD
• Written express • Math   ADHD with LD
• Organizational • Fine Motor   ADHD without LD
• Perceptual

Learning Disability Program
Program: Reinforces course work: **Yes**
Students mainstreamed **100** % of the day
Services available for all students: **Yes**

Faculty:
Faculty: **12** Including Director: **Yes** Full time: **7** Part time: **5**
LD faculty with: BS/BA: **6** M.A.: **6** Ph.D.: **1**
Faculty advocate: **Yes** Meets with instructor: **As needed**

Diagnostic Testing
ADD	Personality	Perceptual skills	Spelling
ADHD	Organization	Fine motor skills	Reading
I.Q.	Handwriting	Spoken language	Study skills
Math	Social skills	Written language	

Tutoring:
Average size of group tutorials: **2-3**
Services rendered by:
  Graduates   Peers   •Faculty   •LD staff   Teacher trainees

Tutorials
Grp.	Ind.	Tutorials	Grp.	Ind.	Tutorials
	•	Math skills	•	•	Word processing
	•	Study skills	•	•	Time management
	•	Language arts	•	•	Learning strategies
	•	Written express	•	•	Organizational skills

Academic Accommodations

Curriculum	Study Aids	Exams
Priority registration	Typist	• Oral
• Math waiver	• Reader	Untimed
• Foreign lang. waiver	• Notetaker	• Take home
• Course substitution	• Proof reader	• With proctor
In Class	• Text on tape	On computer
• Calculators	Early syllabus	• Extended time
• Tape recorder	Taped handouts	On tape
• Word processor		• Modified
Priority seating		Separate room

Graduation Requirements:
Course credits: **120** GPA: **2.0** Years to complete degree: **4-10** Math waiver: **Yes**

Program Strengths
We offer support services for all students. These services are individualized and based on student needs.

General Information:
New England College is a 4 year private College. Rural campus 40 miles from Manchester. Accessible by bus. Ski areas are 2 miles from campus. Beaches are 50 miles from campus. 10% of students are foreign. 6 residential halls on campus. Housing is guaranteed.Guaranteed through 4th year. 75 % of students remain on campus for the weekends. 2 % of students join fraternities/sororities.

Accreditation:NEACS

Expenses:
Tuition: In-state: Full year: $10,000.00. Room and board: $4,500.00

Majors
• ARTS Art History, Commercial Art, Design, Dramatic Arts, Drawing, Film & Video, Graphic & Printing Production, Painting, Photography, Theater Design • BUSINESS Accounting, Banking/Finance, Business Administration, Business Management, International Business, Management, Marketing, Marketing Research, Organizational Behavior, Sports Management • COMMUNICATIONS Broadcasting, Communication, Creative Writing, English, Journalism, Photography, Public Relations, Speech/Debate/Forensic, Television/Radio/Film • CRAFTS AND DESIGN Ceramics, Printmaking • EDUCATION Child Development, Early Childhood, Elementary, English, Mathematics, Reading, Science, Secondary, Social Stud-

ies • ENGINEERING Civil/Environmental • HUMANITIES English/ Writing/Literature, Humanities, Liberal Arts, Philosophy • LANGUAGES Chinese, English, French, Japanese, Spanish • MATHEMATICS Applied, Statistical • SCIENCES Biology, Natural • SOCIAL SCIENCES Human Service, Psychology, Sociology • VISUAL AND PERFORMING ARTS Art History, Dramatic Arts, Fine Arts, Studio Art, Video

Sports/Activities

• SPORTS-INTERCOLLEGIATE Baseball (M), Basketball, Field Hockey (F), Golf, Horseback Riding, Ice Hockey (M), Lacrosse, Rugby (M), Skiing - Snow, Skiing - Snow, Skiing-Cross Country, Soccer, Softball (F), Tennis, Track and Field • SPORTS-INTRAMURAL Badminton, Baseball , Bowling, Cycling, Field Hockey , Football, Rugby, Skiing - Snow, Skiing - Snow, Soccer, Softball, Tennis, Track and Field, Volleyball • STUDENT LIFE ACTIVITIES Academic Clubs, Community Service, Debate, Drama Groups, Ethnic & Cultural Groups, Film, Fraternities, Music Groups, Newspaper, Political Groups, Radio/TV station, Religious Organization, Sororities, Student Government, Yearbook

Selective   **New Hampshire Services**

New Hampshire College

2500 North River Road
Manchester, New Hampshire 03104
(603) 645-9611

School Enrollment: **1,565** Male: **800** Female: **765**

Admissions Contact: **Mike Deblasi, Director**
LD Contact: **Dr. Francis Doucette, Director, The Learning Center**
Name of Program: **The Learning Center**
Telephone:**(603) 645-9606**

Admissions

Application Information:
LD on admissions committee:**Yes**
Application deadline: **Rolling**
Rolling Admissions: **Yes**

Secondary School Information
Most Important Criteria For Admissions (1-strongest)

3	SAT/ACT	2	Application	1	School transcript
4	Class rank	2	Course selection	5	Personal statement
3	Interview	4	Extra activities		Psychoeducational
2	G.P.A.		Open admission	3	Recommendations

Test Requirements:
Untimed SAT: **Yes** Untimed ACT: **Yes**
Documentation of LD required: **Yes**

Types of Disabilities Served
• Speech/Lang   • Reading   ADD with LD
• Study skills   • Spelling   ADD without LD
• Written express   • Math   ADHD with LD
• Organizational   Fine Motor   ADHD without LD
  Perceptual

Learning Disability Program

Services available for all students: **Yes**
Counseling: Individual: **Yes** Group Counseling: **Yes**

Diagnostic Testing

ADD	Personality	Perceptual skills	Spelling
ADHD	Organization	Fine motor skills	Reading
I.Q.	Handwriting	Spoken language	Study skills
Math	Social skills	Written language	

Tutoring:
Average size of group tutorials: **6-10**
Services rendered by:
•Graduates   •Peers   •Faculty   LD staff   Teacher trainees

Tutorials

Grp.	Ind.	Tutorials	Grp.	Ind.	Tutorials
•	•	Math skills	•	•	Word processing
•	•	Study skills	•	•	Time management
•	•	Language arts	•	•	Learning strategies
•	•	Written express	•	•	Organizational skills

Academic Accommodations

Curriculum	Study Aids	Exams
Priority registration	Typist	• Oral
Math waiver	Reader	• Untimed
• Foreign lang. waiver	Notetaker	Take home
Course substitution	Proof reader	• With proctor
In Class	Text on tape	On computer
• Calculators	Early syllabus	• Extended time
• Tape recorder	Taped handouts	On tape
• Word processor		• Modified
Priority seating		Separate room

Graduation Requirements:
Course credits: **120** GPA: **2.0** Years to complete degree: **As long as needed** Language waiver: **Yes**

Program Strengths

We do not have an LD program. Our Learning Center offers a wide array of support services that often are useful for LD students. We do not maintain any data specifically focused on the performance of LD students. The Learning Center is staffed by a full-time staff of 6 professionals (Masters or Doctorate) and approximately 60 peer tutors. Learning Center services are available to all undergraduates at no extra cost.

General Information:

New Hampshire College is a 4 year private college. Suburban campus of 700 acres is 2-1/2 miles from Manchester. Accessible by air or bus. Ski areas are 30 minutes from campus. Beaches are 45 minutes from campus. 10% of students are foreign. 15 residential halls on campus. Housing is not guaranteed.75 % of students remain on campus for the weekends. 10 % of students join fraternities/sororities.

Accreditation:NEACS

Expenses:
Tuition: In-state: Full year: $9,408.00. Room and board: $4,500.00

Majors

• COMPUTER SCIENCE Computer Science, Data Processing, Programming, Systems Analysis • VOCATIONAL Business and Office, Culinary Arts, Fashion Merchandising, Liberal Arts , Word Processing

Sports/Activities

• SPORTS RELATED Cheerleading, Pep Band • SPORTS-INTERCOLLEGIATE Baseball (M), Basketball, Crew, Ice Hockey (M), Lacrosse (M), Soccer, Softball (F), Tennis, Volleyball (F) • SPORTS-INTRAMURAL Basketball, Ice Hockey (M), Racquetball, Softball, Swimming, Tennis, Volleyball, Water Polo • STUDENT LIFE ACTIVITIES Choral, Dance, Drama Groups, Ethnic & Cultural Groups, Fraternities, Music Groups, Newspaper, Radio/TV station, Religious Organization, Sororities, Student Government, Yearbook

Less Selective	New Hampshire Services

New Hampshire Technical College

505 Amherst Street
Nashua, New Hampshire 03061-2052
(603) 882-6923

School Enrollment: **275**

Admissions Contact: **John Fischer, Dean of Students**

Admissions

Application Information:
Rolling Admissions: **Yes** Notified when: **Within 30 days**

Secondary School Information
Most Important Criteria For Admissions (1-strongest)

SAT/ACT	Application	**2**	School transcript
Class rank	Course selection		Personal statement
1 Interview	Extra activities	**4**	Psychoeducational
G.P.A.	Open admission	**3**	Recommendations

Test Requirements:
Diagnostic testing waived: **Yes**
WAIS-R required: **Yes**

Types of Disabilities Served

Speech/Lang	Reading	ADD with LD
Study skills	Spelling	ADD without LD
Written express	Math	ADHD with LD
Organizational	Fine Motor	ADHD without LD
Perceptual		

Admissions Process

Personal interview, review of IEP, consultation with LD professor.

High School Course Requirements:
English: **4** Math: **2**
Waivers to standard high school courses
Course substitution: **Yes**

Learning Disability Program

Services available for all students: **Yes**
Counseling: Individual: **Yes** Vocational Counseling: **Yes**
Support groups are available: **Tutoring**

Faculty:
Faculty: **1** Part time: **1** M.A.: **1**
Meets with instructor: **As needed**

Diagnostic Testing

ADD	Personality	Perceptual skills	Spelling
ADHD	Organization	Fine motor skills	Reading
I.Q.	Handwriting	Spoken language	Study skills
Math	Social skills	Written language	

Tutoring:
Average size of group tutorials: **1-5**
Services rendered by:
Graduates •Peers •Faculty •LD staff Teacher trainees

Tutorials

Grp.	Ind.	Tutorials	Grp.	Ind.	Tutorials
		Math skills			Word processing
		Study skills			Time management
		Language arts			Learning strategies
		Written express			Organizational skills

Academic Accommodations

Curriculum	Study Aids	Exams
• Priority registration	• Typist	• Oral
Math waiver	• Reader	• Untimed
Foreign lang. waiver	• Notetaker	Take home
• Course substitution	• Proof reader	With proctor
In Class	• Text on tape	• On computer
• Calculators	• Early syllabus	• Extended time
• Tape recorder	• Taped handouts	On tape
• Word processor		• Modified
• Priority seating		• Separate room

Graduation Requirements:
Course credits: **Varies by program** Years to complete degree: **Varies**

General Information:

New Hampshire Technical College is a 2 year public college. Suburban campus Accessible by bus or car. Ski areas are 60 miles from campus. Beaches are 60 miles from campus. 1% of students are foreign. Housing is not guaranteed.

Accreditation: NEACS

Expenses:
Tuition: In-state: Full year: $1,960.00. Part-time: Per credit: $82.00. Part-time: Per course: Varies. Tuition: Out-of-state: Full year: $4,650.00; $2,940.00 (New England Region).

Majors

• BUSINESS Accounting, Business Computer Applications, Business Management, Marketing, Paralegal Studies • COMPUTER SCIENCE Computer Maintenance, Computer Technology, Robotics, Telecommunications • ENGINEERING Computer, Drafting • VOCATIONAL Automobile Technology, Aviation Technology, Collision Repair, Machine Tool Technology

Sports/Activities

• SPORTS-INTERCOLLEGIATE Baseball, Basketball, Ice Hockey, Soccer • STUDENT LIFE ACTIVITIES Academic Clubs, Newspaper, Student Government, Yearbook

---

Less Selective

New Hampshire Vocational-Technical

277 RR Portsmouth Avenue
Stratham, New Hampshire 03885
(603) 772-1195

School Enrollment: **467** Male: **218** Female: **249**
LD Enrollment: **5** Male: **2** Female: **3**

Admissions Contact: **Karen Blanchard, College Counselor**

Admissions

Application Information:
Application deadline: **None**
Rolling Admissions: **Yes**

Secondary School Information
Most Important Criteria For Admissions (1-strongest)

5 SAT/ACT	**10** Application	**1**	School transcript
3 Class rank	**2** Course selection	**8**	Personal statement
11 Interview	**7** Extra activities	**9**	Psychoeducational
4 G.P.A.	Open admission	**6**	Recommendations

Test Requirements:
Diagnostic testing waived: **Yes**
Untimed SAT: **Yes** Untimed ACT: **Yes** Untimed ACH: **Yes**
Currency of diagnostic testing: **Within one year**
Tests recommended: **No specific document**

Types of Disabilities Served

Speech/Lang	Reading	ADD with LD
Study skills	Spelling	ADD without LD
Written express	Math	ADHD with LD
Organizational	Fine Motor	ADHD without LD
Perceptual		

Admissions Process

All students file application and supporting documents. LD students required to have additional academic testing and documents on file. All students take part in college testing program. LD students have untimed tests.

High School Course Requirements:
English: **4** Math: **2** Science: **2**

Diagnostic Testing

ADD	Personality	Perceptual skills	Spelling
ADHD	Organization	Fine motor skills	Reading
I.Q.	Handwriting	Spoken language	Study skills
Math	Social skills	Written language	

Tutoring:
Average size of group tutorials: **5**
Services rendered by:
•Graduates •Peers Faculty LD staff Teacher trainees

Tutorials

Grp.	Ind.	Tutorials	Grp.	Ind.	Tutorials
•	•	Math skills			Word processing
•	•	Study skills	•	•	Time management
		Language arts	•	•	Learning strategies
•	•	Written express	•	•	Organizational skills

Academic Accommodations

Curriculum	Study Aids	Exams
Priority registration	Typist	• Oral
Math waiver	Reader	• Untimed
Foreign lang. waiver	Notetaker	• Take home
Course substitution	Proof reader	With proctor
In Class	Text on tape	On computer
• Calculators	Early syllabus	• Extended time
• Tape recorder	Taped handouts	On tape
• Word processor		• Modified
• Priority seating		• Separate room

Graduation Requirements:
Course credits: **72** GPA: **2.0** Years to complete degree: **5 years**

General Information:

New Hampshire Vocational-Technical is a 2 year public college. Rural campus of 90 acres is 50 miles from Boston. Accessible by bus or car. Ski areas are 40 miles from campus. Beaches are 5 miles from campus. Housing is not guaranteed.

Accreditation: NEACS

Class Rank:
About 10% of the present freshmen class were in the upper 20% of their high school class. 40% were in the top 40% of their class. 50% were in the top 60% of their class.

Expenses:
Tuition: In-state: Full year: $2,075.00. Part-time: Per credit:$87.00. Part-time: Per course: $261.00. Tuition: Out-of-state: Full year: $4,923.00. Part-time: Per credit:$130.00. Part-time: Per course:$390.00

Majors

• BUSINESS Accounting, Human Resources Management, Secretarial Science • COMPUTER SCIENCE Computer Science, Computer Technology • ENGINEERING Drafting • HEALTH SCIENCES Nursing, Surgical Technology, Veterinarian Assistant • PHILOSOPHY Automobile Technology, Aviation Maintenance, Drafting, Electronics Technology, Machinist, Secretarial, Veterinarian Assistant

Sports/Activities

• SPORTS-INTERCOLLEGIATE Baseball (F), Baseball (M), Basketball (F), Basketball (M), Golf (F), Golf (M), Skiing - Cross Country, Soccer (M), Volleyball • SPORTS-INTRAMURAL Basketball (F), Basketball (M), Golf (F), Golf (M), Skiing - Snow (F), Skiing - Snow (M), Soccer (F), Soccer (M), Volleyball (F), Volleyball (M) • STUDENT LIFE ACTIVITIES Academic Clubs, Newspaper, Student Government

Less Selective — **New Hampshire Services**

New Hampshire Vocational-Technical College: Laconia
Route 106 Prescott Hill
Laconia, New Hampshire 03246
(603) 524-3207

School Enrollment: **305** Male: **198** Female: **107**
LD Enrollment: **23** Male: **14** Female: **9**

Admissions Contact: **Donald E. Morrissey, Director of Admissions**
LD Contact: **Neal Steiger, Learning Services Coordinator**
Name of Program: **LD Services**
Address: **Prescott Hill**
Telephone:**(603) 524-3207**

Admissions

Application Information:
LD on admissions committee:**Yes**
Application deadline: **August 1st**
Applicant must apply **6** months in advance
Rolling Admissions: **Yes**

Secondary School Information
Most Important Criteria For Admissions (1-strongest)

7 SAT/ACT	**10** Application	**3**	School transcript
11 Class rank	**5** Course selection	**9**	Personal statement
4 Interview	**6** Extra activities	**1**	Psychoeducational
8 G.P.A.	Open admission	**2**	Recommendations

Test Requirements:
Standardized tests waived: **Yes**
Untimed SAT: **Yes**
WAIS-R required: **Yes**
Documentation of LD required: **Yes**
Currency of diagnostic testing: **Within 2 years**

Types of Disabilities Served
- Speech/Lang
- Study skills
- Written express
- Organizational
- Perceptual
- Reading
- Spelling
- Math
- Fine Motor
- ADD with LD
- ADD without LD
- ADHD with LD
- ADHD without LD

High School Course Requirements:
English: **4** Math: **3** Science: **3**
Waivers to standard high school courses
Course substitution: **Yes**

Learning Disability Program
Students mainstreamed **100** % of the day
Counseling: Individual: **Yes** Group Counseling: **Yes** Vocational Counseling: **Yes**

Faculty:
Faculty: **2** Full time: **1** Part time: **1** M.A.: **2**
Faculty advocate: **Yes** Meets with instructor: **As needed**

Diagnostic Testing
- ADD
- ADHD
- I.Q.
- Math
- Personality
- Organization
- Handwriting
- Social skills
- Perceptual skills
- Fine motor skills
- Spoken language
- Written language
- Spelling
- Reading
- Study skills

Tutoring:
Average size of group tutorials: **Individual**
Services rendered by:
Graduates • Peers • Faculty • LD staff   Teacher trainees

Tutorials
Grp.	Ind.	Tutorials	Grp.	Ind.	Tutorials
	•	Math skills		•	Word processing
	•	Study skills		•	Time management
	•	Language arts			Learning strategies
	•	Written express		•	Organizational skills

Academic Accommodations

Curriculum	Study Aids	Exams
Priority registration	Typist	• Oral
Math waiver	• Reader	• Untimed
Foreign lang. waiver	• Notetaker	Take home
• Course substitution	• Proof reader	• With proctor
In Class	• Text on tape	On computer
• Calculators	Early syllabus	• Extended time
• Tape recorder	Taped handouts	On tape
• Word processor		• Modified
• Priority seating		• Separate room

Graduation Requirements:
Course credits: **64** GPA: **2.0**
Other requirements: **Competency tests (pending)**

Program Strengths
NHTC Laconia was the first of the seven system colleges to provide services specifically for LD students. We have no separate program for LD students, rather, all our students receive a quality education, regardless of disability. The small size of our college helps provide an active, informal system. We are all here for each other.

General Information:
New Hampshire Vocational-Technical College: Laconia is a 2 year public college. Suburban campus of 42 acres is 50 miles from Manchester. Accessible by air or bus. Ski areas are 8 miles from campus. Beaches are 4 miles from campus. Housing is not guaranteed.

Accreditation:NEACS

Class Rank:
About 5% of the present freshmen class were in the upper 20% of their high school class. 45% were in the top 40% of their class. 70% were in the top 60% of their class. 95% were in the top 80% of their class.

Expenses:
Tuition: In-state: Full year: $2,088.00. Part-time: Per credit:$87.00. Part-time: Per course: $261.00. Tuition: Out-of-state: Full year: $4,920.00-$3,120.00 for qualified New England residents. Part-time: Per credit:$87.00. Part-time: Per course:$261.00

Majors
• BUSINESS Accounting, Business Management, Computer Applications, Hospitality Management • COMMUNICATIONS Graphic Arts • ENGINEERING Industrial Electricity • VOCATIONAL Administration Support/Informal, Automobile Technology, Electrical Construction, Fire Protection, Fire Science

New Hampshire

Sports/Activities
• SPORTS RELATED Cheerleading • SPORTS-INTERCOLLEGIATE Baseball (M), Golf, Skiing - Snow, Soccer (M), Softball (F), Volleyball (F), Volleyball (M) • STUDENT LIFE ACTIVITIES Honor Societies, Student Government, Tutors, Yearbook

Very Selective **New Hampshire Services**

University of New Hampshire
Grant House
Durham, New Hampshire 03824
(603) 862-1360

School Enrollment: **11,131** Male: **4,181** Female: **5,129**
LD Contact: **Donna Sorrentino, Cord. Affirmative Action Office**
Name of Program: **ACCESS**
Telephone:**(603) 862-2607**

Admissions

Secondary School Information
Most Important Criteria For Admissions (1-strongest)

SAT/ACT	Application	School transcript
Class rank	Course selection	Personal statement
Interview	Extra activities	Psychoeducational
G.P.A.	Open admission	Recommendations

Test Requirements:
Diagnostic testing waived: **Yes**
WAIS-R required: **Yes**
Documentation of LD required: **Yes**
Currency of diagnostic testing: **3 Years**

Types of Disabilities Served
• Speech/Lang • Reading • ADD with LD
• Study skills • Spelling • ADD without LD
• Written express • Math • ADHD with LD
• Organizational • Fine Motor • ADHD without LD
• Perceptual

Diagnostic Testing

ADD	Personality	Perceptual skills	Spelling
ADHD	Organization	Fine motor skills	Reading
I.Q.	Handwriting	Spoken language	Study skills
Math	Social skills	Written language	

Tutoring:
Services rendered by:
•Graduates •Peers •Faculty LD staff •Teacher trainees

Tutorials

Grp.	Ind.	Tutorials	Grp.	Ind.	Tutorials
		Math skills	•		Word processing
•	•	Study skills	•	•	Time management
•	•	Language arts	•	•	Learning strategies
•	•	Written express	•	•	Organizational skills

Academic Accommodations

Curriculum	Study Aids	Exams
Priority registration	Typist	• Oral
Math waiver	Reader	Untimed
Foreign lang. waiver	• Notetaker	• Take home
• Course substitution	Proof reader	With proctor
In Class	• Text on tape	On computer
• Calculators	Early syllabus	• Extended time
• Tape recorder	Taped handouts	On tape
• Word processor		• Modified
Priority seating		Separate room

Program Strengths
We work with all types of disabilities. If a student self-discloses his disability, an individual program is designed to help the student with his/her needs. UNH has 2 support services: TASK and ACCESS. TASK assists students with study skills, reading, and written expression. ACCESS is concerned with faculty awareness and classroom modifications for students. We set up whatever is most reasonable to insure our students' success.

General Information:
University of New Hampshire is a 2 and 4 year public university. Rural campus of 188 acres is 65 miles from Boston. Accessible by bus. Housing is not guaranteed.45 % of students remain on campus for the weekends.

Accreditation:NEACS

SAT/ACT Scores:
Scores for incoming freshmen:**Verbal:**43%below 500. 43%between 500 and 599. 13%between 600 and 699. 1%above 700. **Math:**17% below 500. 39% between 500 and 599. 36% between 600 and 699. 8%above 700.

Expenses:
Tuition: In-state: Full year: $2,900.00. Tuition: Out-of-state: Full year: $7,500.00. Room and board: $3,400.00

Majors
• AREA STUDIES Urban • BUSINESS Business Administration, Business Management, Economics, Hotel and Restaurant Management, Management, Marketing • COMMUNICATIONS Communication, English, Journalism, Linguistics • COMPUTER SCIENCE Computer Science • EDUCATION Elementary, Physical • ENGINEERING Chemical, Civil/Environmental, Electrical, Mechanical • HEALTH SCIENCES Environmental, Health, Medical Technology, Nursing, Nutritional/Food, Occupational Therapy, Speech/Audiology and Speech • HUMANITIES Classics, Humanities, Liberal Arts, Philosophy • LANGUAGES French, German, Greek, Latin, Russian, Spanish • PREPROFESSIONAL Forestry, Natural Resources, Social Work, Veterinarian • SCIENCES Agricultural, Animal, Anthropology, Biochemistry, Biology, Botany, Chemistry, Entomology, Geography, Geology, Mathematics, Microbiology, Physics, Physiology, Zoology • SOCIAL SCIENCES Family Counseling, Government/Political, History, Political Science, Psychology, Social Sciences, Sociology • VISUAL AND PERFORMING ARTS Art History, Dramatic Arts, Fine Arts, Music, Music Performance, Studio Art • VOCATIONAL Food Service, Forestry, Park/Recreation, Wildlife

Sports/Activities
• SPORTS RELATED Marching Band, Pep Band • SPORTS-INTERCOLLEGIATE Baseball (M), Basketball, Cross Country, Diving, Field Hockey (F), Football (M), Golf (M), Gymnastics (F), Ice Hockey, Lacrosse, Skiing - Snow, Soccer, Swimming, Tennis, Track and Field, Wrestling (M) • SPORTS-INTRAMURAL Basketball, Bowling, Crew, Cross Country, Ice Hockey (M), Sailing, Soccer, Softball, Squash, Swimming, Tennis, Track and Field, Volleyball, Water Polo • STUDENT LIFE ACTIVITIES Choral, Concert Band, Dance, Drama Groups, Fraternities, Jazz Band, Magazine, Music Groups, Musical Theater, Newspaper, Radio/TV station, Sororities, Student Government, Symphony Orchestra, Yearbook

---

Less Selective   **New Jersey**
Services

Caldwell College
Ryerson Avenue
Caldwell, New Jersey 07006
(201) 228-4424

School Enrollment: **507** Male: **107** Female: **400**

Admissions Contact: **Raymond Sheenan, Director of Admissions**
LD Contact: **Harriet Schenk, Director**
Name of Program: **Learning Center**

Admissions

Application Information:
Application deadline: **March 15th**
Rolling Admissions: **Yes**

Secondary School Information
Most Important Criteria For Admissions (1-strongest)

2 SAT/ACT	Application	School transcript
1 Class rank	**3** Course selection	Personal statement
4 Interview	**5** Extra activities	Psychoeducational
1 G.P.A.	Open admission	**3** Recommendations

Test Requirements:
Untimed SAT: **Yes**

Types of Disabilities Served

Speech/Lang	• Reading	ADD with LD
• Study skills	• Spelling	ADD without LD
Written express	• Math	ADHD with LD
• Organizational	Fine Motor	ADHD without LD
Perceptual		

Learning Disability Program
Counseling: Individual: **Yes**

Faculty:
Faculty advocate: **Yes** Meets with instructor: **1x semester**

Diagnostic Testing

ADD	Personality	Perceptual skills	Spelling
ADHD	Organization	Fine motor skills	Reading
I.Q.	Handwriting	Spoken language	Study skills
Math	Social skills	Written language	

Tutoring:
Average size of group tutorials: **3-5**
Services rendered by:
Graduates   •Peers   •Faculty   LD staff   Teacher trainees

Tutorials

Grp.	Ind.	Tutorials	Grp.	Ind.	Tutorials
•	•	Math skills			Word processing
•		Study skills	•	•	Time management
•	•	Language arts	•		Learning strategies
		Written express		•	Organizational skills

Academic Accommodations

Curriculum	Study Aids	Exams
Priority registration	Typist	• Oral
Math waiver	Reader	Untimed
Foreign lang. waiver	• Notetaker	Take home
Course substitution	• Proof reader	With proctor
In Class	Text on tape	On computer
• Calculators	Early syllabus	• Extended time
• Tape recorder	Taped handouts	On tape
Word processor		• Modified
Priority seating		Separate room

Program Strengths
Caldwell College does not have a learning disability program. The Learning Center facilities can be utilized by students to obtain tutoring in most academic areas. The director can intercede on behalf of students to provide accommodations such as extended testing time, use of tape recorders in class, and copies of class notes. Workshops are provided on time management, study skills, and test-taking.

General Information:
Caldwell College is a 4 year private Roman Catholic college. Suburban campus of 110 acres is 20 miles from New York City. Accessible by air, train, or bus. Ski areas are 1 hour from campus. Beaches are 1 hour from campus. 5% of students are foreign. 1 residential halls on campus. Housing is guaranteed.Guaranteed through 4th year. 40 % of students remain on campus for the weekends. 10 % of students join fraternities/sororities.

Accreditation: Regional - MSACS

SAT/ACT Scores:
Scores for incoming freshmen:**Verbal:**77%below 500. 22%between 500 and 599. 1%between 600 and 699. **Math:**69% below 500. 23% between 500 and 599. 8% between 600 and 699. 1%above 700.

Class Rank:
About 13% of the present freshmen class were in the upper 20% of their high school class. 36% were in the top 40% of their class. 56% were in the top 60% of their class. 79% were in the top 80% of their class.

Expenses:
Tuition: In-state: Full year: $6,800.00. Part-time: Per credit:$179.00. Room and board: $3,000.00.

Majors
• BUSINESS Banking, Business Administration, Business Management, Finance, Management, Marketing • COMMUNICATIONS English • COMPUTER SCIENCE Computer Science • EDUCATION Art, Elementary, English, Foreign Language, Mathematics, Music, Science, Secondary, Social Studies • HEALTH SCIENCES Medical Technology • HUMANITIES Religion • LANGUAGES French, Spanish • SCIENCES Biology, Chemistry, Mathematics • SOCIAL SCIENCES Criminal Justice, History, Psychology, Social Sciences, Sociology • VISUAL AND PERFORMING ARTS Art, Fine Arts, Music • VOCATIONAL Painting

Sports/Activities
• SPORTS RELATED Cheerleading • SPORTS-INTERCOLLEGIATE Basketball, Horseback Riding, Softball (F), Volleyball (F) • SPORTS-INTRAMURAL Basketball, Horseback Riding, Soccer, Softball, Tennis, Volleyball • STUDENT LIFE ACTIVITIES Drama Groups, Ethnic & Cultural Groups, Fraternities, Music Groups, Newspaper, Radio/TV station, Religious Organization, Sororities, Student Government, Yearbook

---

Less Selective

County College of Morris
Route 10 and Center Grove Road
Randolph, New Jersey 07889
(201) 361-5000

School Enrollment: **9,994** Male: **4,997** Female: **4,997**
LD Enrollment: **225**

Admissions Contact: **Kenneth W. Albiston, Asst. Dir. of Admissions**
LD Contact: **Audrey Lebar, LD Coordinator**
Name of Program: **Horizons**
Address: **LRC 214**
Telephone:**(201) 328-5284**

Admissions

Application Information:
LD Students Applying: **230** Accepted: **225** Enrolled:**225**
Separate application:**Yes**
Application deadline: **Open**
Applicant must apply **6** months in advance
Rolling Admissions: **Yes**

Secondary School Information
Most Important Criteria For Admissions (1-strongest)

	SAT/ACT	Application	**3**	School transcript
	Class rank	**2** Course selection		Personal statement
6	Interview	Extra activities	**1**	Psychoeducational
5	G.P.A.	Open admission	**4**	Recommendations

Test Requirements:
Standardized tests waived: **Yes**
Diagnostic testing waived: **Yes**
Range accepted: **Average+**
Documentation of LD required: **Yes**
Tests recommended: **Psychoeducational evaluation**

Types of Disabilities Served
- Speech/Lang
- Study skills
- Written express
- Organizational
- Perceptual
- Reading
- Spelling
- Math
- Fine Motor
- ADD with LD
- ADD without LD
- ADHD with LD
- ADHD without LD

Admissions Process

1) Information meeting, 2) Submission of documentation, 3) Diagnostic testing, 4) Clinical interview

Learning Disability Program

Program: Reinforces course work: **Yes**
Students mainstreamed **100** % of the day
Counseling: Individual: **Yes** Group Counseling: **Yes**

Faculty:
Faculty: **16** Including Director: **Yes** Full time: **3** Part time: **13**
LD faculty with: BS/BA: **2** M.A.: **14**
Faculty advocate: **Yes** Meets with instructor: **As needed**

Diagnostic Testing
- ADD
- ADHD
- I.Q.
- Math
- Personality
- Organization
- Handwriting
- Social skills
- Perceptual skills
- Fine motor skills
- Spoken language
- Written language
- Spelling
- Reading
- Study skills

Tutoring:
Average size of group tutorials: **3**
Services rendered by:
Graduates   Peers   •Faculty   •LD staff   Teacher trainees

Tutorials

Grp.	Ind.	Tutorials	Grp.	Ind.	Tutorials
•	•	Math skills	•	•	Word processing
•	•	Study skills	•	•	Time management
•	•	Language arts	•	•	Learning strategies
•	•	Written express	•	•	Organizational skills

Academic Accommodations

Curriculum	Study Aids	Exams
• Priority registration	Typist	• Oral
Math waiver	• Reader	• Untimed
Foreign lang. waiver	• Notetaker	Take home
Course substitution	• Proof reader	• With proctor
In Class	• Text on tape	• On computer
• Calculators	Early syllabus	• Extended time
• Tape recorder	Taped handouts	• On tape
• Word processor		• Modified
• Priority seating		• Separate room

Graduation Requirements:
Course credits: **64-66** GPA: **2.0**

Program Strengths
Our goal is to help students develop the skills needed to be independent, effective, and efficient learners. To this end, we focus on self-advocacy (with our support), learning strategies, and accommodations which leave the responsibility with the student (e.g. taped lecture rather than notetaker if possible).

General Information:
County College of Morris is a 2 year public college. Suburban campus of 218 acres is 50 miles from New York City. Accessible by train or bus. Ski areas are 20 miles from campus. Beaches are 65 miles from campus. 7% of students are foreign. Housing is not guaranteed.

Accreditation:MSACS

Expenses:
Tuition: In-state: Full year: $1,090.00 per semester. Part-time: Per credit:$90.00. Tuition: Out-of-state: Full year: $1,477.00 per semester. Part-time: Per credit:$98.00.

Majors
• BUSINESS Accounting, Banking, Business Administration, Finance, Hotel and Restaurant Management, Marketing, Retailing • COMMUNICATIONS Broadcasting, Communication, Graphic Design, Journalism, Photography • COMPUTER SCIENCE Computer Science, Programming, Telecommunications • EDUCATION Music, Recreation and Youth Leadership • ENGINEERING Biomedical, Electrical, Engineering Science, Mechanical • HEALTH SCIENCES Dental Assistant, Medical Technology, Nursing • HUMANITIES Humanities, Liberal Arts • PREPROFESSIONAL Agriculture, Engineering • SCIENCES Biology, Chemistry, Mathematics • SOCIAL SCIENCES Criminal Justice, Law Enforcement, Public Relations, Social Sciences • VISUAL AND PERFORMING ARTS Dance, Music • VOCATIONAL Automobile Technology, Electronics Technology, Park/Recreation, Secretarial, Surveying and Mapping

Sports/Activities

• STUDENT LIFE ACTIVITIES Choral, Concert Band, Debate, Drama Groups, Ethnic & Cultural Groups, Fraternities, Jazz Band, Magazine, Music Groups, Newspaper, Radio/TV station, Religious Organization, Sororities, Student Government, Symphony Orchestra, Yearbook

Selective   **New Jersey Program**

Fairleigh Dickinson University
Teaneck-Hackensack Campus
Teaneck, New Jersey 07666
(201) 692-2087

School Enrollment: **4,092** Male: **2,030** Female: **2,062**
LD Enrollment: **91**

Admissions Contact: **Felicia Salvacion, Director of Admissions**
LD Contact: **Carolyn Angelosante, Learning Specialist**
Name of Program: **Regional Center for College Students**
Address: **1000 River Road**
Telephone:**(201) 692-2087**

Admissions

Application Information:
LD Students Applying: **320** Accepted: **100** Enrolled:**35**
Separate application:**Yes**
LD on admissions committee:**Yes**
Rolling Admissions: **Yes**

Secondary School Information
Most Important Criteria For Admissions (1-strongest)

2 SAT/ACT	**7** Application	**1** School transcript
4 Class rank	**5** Course selection	Personal statement
Interview	**9** Extra activities	**11** Psychoeducational
3 G.P.A.	Open admission	**6** Recommendations

Test Requirements:
Diagnostic testing waived: **Yes**
Untimed SAT: **Yes** Untimed ACT: **Yes**
WAIS-R required: **Yes**
Documentation of LD required: **Yes**
Currency of diagnostic testing: **24 months**

Types of Disabilities Served
• Speech/Lang • Reading • ADD with LD
• Study skills Spelling ADD without LD
• Written express • Math • ADHD with LD
• Organizational • Fine Motor ADHD without LD
• Perceptual

Admissions Process

Students fill out both University and Regional Center applications. When documentation is complete, decisions will be made and student notified. Interview for LD program not required.

High School Course Requirements:
English: **4** Math: **2** Science: **1** Foreign Language: **1-3**

Learning Disability Program

Program: Reinforces course work: **Yes**
Program available through:**All four years**
Students mainstreamed **100** % of the day
Recommended credits per semester: **12-15**
Time required or recommended in learning center: **1-6 hours**
Services only for LD students: **Yes**
Counseling: Individual: **Yes** Group Counseling: **Yes** Vocational Counseling: **Yes**

Faculty:
Faculty: **12** Including Director: **Yes** Full time: **9** Part time: **3**
LD faculty with: BS/BA: **4** M.A.: **6** Ph.D.: **1**
Meets with instructor: **As needed**

Diagnostic Testing
ADD Personality • Perceptual skills • Spelling
ADHD• Organization• Fine motor skills • Reading
• I.Q. • Handwriting• Spoken language • Study skills
• Math Social skills• Written language

Tutoring:
Average size of group tutorials: **1-3**
Services rendered by:
Graduates Peers Faculty •LD staff Teacher trainees

Tutorials

Grp.	Ind.	Tutorials	Grp.	Ind.	Tutorials
•	•	Math skills	•	•	Word processing
•	•	Study skills	•	•	Time management
•	•	Language arts	•	•	Learning strategies
•	•	Written express	•	•	Organizational skills

Academic Accommodations

Curriculum	Study Aids	Exams
• Priority registration	Typist	Oral
Math waiver	Reader	• Untimed
Foreign lang. waiver	Notetaker	Take home
Course substitution	Proof reader	• With proctor
In Class	• Text on tape	• On computer
• Calculators	Early syllabus	• Extended time
Tape recorder	Taped handouts	On tape
• Word processor		Modified
• Priority seating		• Separate room

Graduation Requirements:
Course credits: **128** GPA: **2.0** Math waiver: **Yes** Language waiver: **Yes**

Program Strengths

Student/teacher ratio (1 professional educator for each 15 students). Nature and amount of support (e.g. freshmen receive 4 content-specific support sessions per week). Career and academic counseling available. Student progress systematically monitored.

General Information:

Fairleigh Dickinson University is a 2 and 4 year independent university. suburban campus of 125 acres is 6 miles from New York City. Accessible by train, automobile or bus. Ski areas are 35 miles from campus. Beaches are 70 miles from campus. Housing is guaranteed.Guaranteed through freshman. 12 % of students join fraternities/sororities.

Accreditation:MSACS

SAT/ACT Scores:
Scores for incoming freshmen:**Verbal:**86%below 500. 10%between 500 and 599. 4%between 600 and 699. **Math:**55% below 500. 31% between 500 and 599. 14% between 600 and 699.

Expenses:
Tuition: In-state: Full year: $9,240.00. Part-time: Per credit:$308.00. Part-time: Per course: $924.00. Tuition: Out-of-state: Full year: $9,240.00. Part-time: Per credit:$308.00. Part-time: Per course:$924.00 Room and board: $5,540.00

Majors

• AREA STUDIES Black/Afro-American, European, Latin American • ARTS Art History, Drawing, Graphic Art, Painting, Photography, Theater Design • BUSINESS Accounting, Business Administration, Business Economics, Business Management, Economics, Entrepreneur, Food Management, Hotel & Restaurant Management, International Business, Marketing, Real Estate • COMMUNICATIONS Advertising, Broadcasting, Journalism, Public Relations, Television/Radio/Film • COMPUTER SCIENCE Data Processing, Programming, Robotics • EDUCATION Elementary, English, English As A Second Language • ENGINEERING Electrical • HEALTH SCIENCES Environmental, Nursing, Radiological Technology, Respiratory Therapy • HUMANITIES Classics, English/Writing/Literature, Fine Arts, Liberal Arts , Philosophy • LANGUAGES English, French, German, Italian, Latin, Spanish • MATHEMATICS Computer, Theoretical • PRE PROFESSIONAL Dentistry, Law, Medicine, Pharmacy • SCIENCES Biochemistry, Biology, Chemistry, Computer Science, Marine Biology, Mathematics • SOCIAL SCIENCES Criminal Justice, History, Political Science, Psychology, Social Science, Sociology • SPECIAL EDUCATION Learning Disability • VISUAL AND PERFORMING ARTS Art History, Theater

Sports/Activities

• SPORTS-INTERCOLLEGIATE Baseball (M), Basketball (F), Basketball (M), Cross Country (F), Cross Country (M), Fencing (F), Field Hockey (F), Football (M), Golf, Lacrosse (M), Soccer (M), Softball (F), Tennis (F), Tennis (M), Track and Field (M), Volleyball (F) • SPORTS-INTRAMURAL Archery (M), Badminton (M), Basketball (F), Basketball (M), Bowling (F), Bowling (M), Cross Country, Field Hockey (F), Golf, Ping-Pong (F), Ping-Pong (M), Soccer (M), Softball (F), Softball (M), Swimming, Tennis (F), Tennis (M), Track and Field, Volleyball (F), Volleyball (M), Weight Lifting, Wrestling (M) • STUDENT LIFE ACTIVITIES Drama Groups, Ethnic & Cultural Groups, Film, Fraternities, Radio/TV station, Sororities, Student Government

Selective   **New Jersey Program**

Georgian Court College
900 Lakewood Avenue
Lakewood, New Jersey 08701
(908) 364-2200

School Enrollment: **1,044** Female: **1,044**
LD Enrollment: **8** Female: **8**

Admissions Contact: **John P. Burke, Director of Admissions**
LD Contact: **Genevieve Van Pelt, M.A., Director**
Name of Program: **The Learning Center**
Telephone:**(908) 364-2200**

Admissions

Application Information:
LD Students Applying: **4** Accepted: **3** Enrolled:**3**
LD on admissions committee:**Yes**
Application deadline: **August 1st**
Rolling Admissions: **Yes**

Secondary School Information
Most Important Criteria For Admissions (1-strongest)

3 SAT/ACT	Application	**1**	School transcript
2 Class rank	**1** Course selection	**5**	Personal statement
7 Interview	**5** Extra activities	**6**	Psychoeducational
2 G.P.A.	Open admission	**4**	Recommendations

Test Requirements:
Standardized tests waived: **Yes**
Diagnostic testing waived: **Yes**
Untimed SAT: **Yes**
WAIS-R required: **Yes** Range accepted: **Average**
Documentation of LD required: **Yes**
Currency of diagnostic testing: **30 months**
Tests recommended: **Verification of learning problem**

Types of Disabilities Served
• Speech/Lang   • Reading   • ADD with LD
• Study skills   • Spelling   • ADD without LD
• Written express   • Math   • ADHD with LD
• Organizational   • Fine Motor   ADHD without LD
• Perceptual

Admissions Process

Upon receipt of admission application, high school transcripts and learning disability documentation, the applicant is reviewed by the Admission Committee and the LRC Director and notified of the decision.

High School Course Requirements:
English: **4** Math: **2** Science: **2** Foreign Language: **2**

Learning Disability Program
Program: Remedial: **Yes**
Program: Reinforces course work: **Yes**
Students mainstreamed **100 %** of the day
Recommended credits per semester: **12**
Time required or recommended in learning center: **2 hours**
Services only for LD students: **Yes**
Counseling: Individual: **Yes**

Faculty:
Faculty: **1** Full time: **1** M.A.: **1**
Faculty advocate: **Yes** Meets with instructor: **Ongoing**

Diagnostic Testing
• ADD   • Personality • Perceptual skills   • Spelling
• ADHD • Organization• Fine motor skills   • Reading
• I.Q.   • Handwriting• Spoken language   • Study skills
• Math   • Social skills• Written language

Tutoring:
Services rendered by:
Graduates   Peers   •Faculty   •LD staff   •Teacher trainees

Tutorials

Grp.	Ind.	Tutorials	Grp.	Ind.	Tutorials
	•	Math skills		•	Word processing
	•	Study skills		•	Time management
	•	Language arts		•	Learning strategies
	•	Written express		•	Organizational skills

Academic Accommodations

Curriculum	Study Aids	Exams
• Priority registration	Typist	• Oral
Math waiver	Reader	• Untimed
Foreign lang. waiver	• Notetaker	• Take home
• Course substitution	• Proof reader	• With proctor
In Class	• Text on tape	• On computer
• Calculators	Early syllabus	• Extended time
• Tape recorder	• Taped handouts	• On tape
Word processor		• Modified
• Priority seating		• Separate room

Graduation Requirements:
Course credits: **132** GPA: **2.5**

Program Strengths

The Learning Center at Georgian Court College is an assistance program designed to provide an environment for students with mild to moderate learning disabilities who desire a college education. The program provides individual attention to meet the specific needs of each student within a small, caring setting.

General Information:

Georgian Court College is a 4 year private Roman Catholic college. Suburban campus of 150 acres is 65 miles from New York City. Accessible by bus. Ski areas are 70 miles from campus. Beaches are 10 miles from campus. 1% of students are foreign. 2 residential halls on campus. Housing is guaranteed.20 % of students remain on campus for the weekends. % of students join fraternities/sororities.

Accreditation:MSACS, NJDE, NASDTEC

SAT/ACT Scores:
Scores for incoming freshmen:**Verbal:**86%below 500. 12%between 500 and 599. 2%between 600 and 699. **Math:**74% below 500. 18% between 500 and 599. 7% between 600 and 699.

Class Rank:
About 36% of the present freshmen class were in the upper 20% of their high school class. 70% were in the top 40% of their class. 91% were in the top 60% of their class. 99% were in the top 80% of their class.

Expenses:
Tuition: In-state: Full year: $7,750.00. Part-time: Per credit:$215.00. Room and board: $3,750.00 Cost of LD program:$1,750.00

Majors

• BUSINESS Accounting, Business Administration • COMMUNICATIONS English • EDUCATION Elementary, Secondary, Special • HUMANITIES Humanities, Religion • LANGUAGES French, Spanish • PREPROFESSIONAL Dentistry, Engineering, Law, Medicine, Social Work • SCIENCES Biochemistry, Biology, Chemistry, Mathematics, Physics • SOCIAL SCIENCES History, Psychology, Sociology • VISUAL AND PERFORMING ARTS Art, Art History, Music, Music Performance, Studio Art

Sports/Activities

• SPORTS RELATED Team Managers • SPORTS-INTERCOLLEGIATE Basketball (F), Cross Country (F), Soccer (F), Softball (F) • SPORTS-INTRAMURAL Volleyball (F) • STUDENT LIFE ACTIVITIES Choral, Concert Band, Drama Groups, Ethnic & Cultural Groups, Magazine, Music Groups, Newspaper, Religious Organization, Student Government, Yearbook

---

Gloucester County College
Tanyard Road Deptford Township
Sewell Post Office, New Jersey 08080
(609) 468-5000

School Enrollment: **4,115** Male: **1,523** Female: **2,592**
LD Enrollment: **170** Male: **92** Female: **78**
LD Contact: **Edward J. Hudak, Coordinator**
Name of Program: **Special Needs**
Telephone:**Ext. 361**

Admissions

Application Information:
Application deadline: **3 Months Prior**

Secondary School Information
Most Important Criteria For Admissions (1-strongest)

9 SAT/ACT	**1** Application	**3** School transcript
8 Class rank	**6** Course selection	**5** Personal statement
2 Interview	**11** Extra activities	**4** Psychoeducational
7 G.P.A.	Open admission **10**	Recommendations

Test Requirements:
Standardized tests waived: **Yes**
Documentation of LD required: **Yes**

Types of Disabilities Served

• Speech/Lang	• Reading	ADD with LD
• Study skills	• Spelling	ADD without LD
• Written express	• Math	ADHD with LD
• Organizational	• Fine Motor	ADHD without LD
• Perceptual		

Learning Disability Program

Counseling: Individual: **Yes**

Faculty:
Faculty: **3** Full time: **3**
Faculty advocate: **Yes** Meets with instructor: **As needed**

Diagnostic Testing

ADD	Personality	Perceptual skills	Spelling
ADHD	Organization	Fine motor skills	Reading
I.Q.	Handwriting	Spoken language	Study skills
Math	Social skills	Written language	

Tutoring:
Services rendered by:
  Graduates   •Peers   •Faculty   LD staff   •Teacher trainees

Tutorials

Grp.	Ind.	Tutorials	Grp.	Ind.	Tutorials
•	•	Math skills	•		Word processing
•	•	Study skills	•		Time management
•	•	Language arts	•	•	Learning strategies
•	•	Written express	•	•	Organizational skills

Academic Accommodations

Curriculum	Study Aids	Exams
Priority registration	• Typist	• Oral
Math waiver	Reader	Untimed
Foreign lang. waiver	• Notetaker	Take home
• Course substitution	• Proof reader	• With proctor
In Class	• Text on tape	On computer
• Calculators	Early syllabus	• Extended time
• Tape recorder	Taped handouts	On tape
• Word processor		• Modified
Priority seating		Separate room

General Information:

Gloucester County College is a 2 year public college. Rural campus of 27 acres is 19 miles from Camden. Accessible by bus. Ski areas are 100 miles from campus. Beaches are 40 miles from campus. 7% of students are foreign. Housing is not guaranteed.

Accreditation: NSACS

Expenses:

Tuition: In-state: Full year: Part-time: Per credit: $38.00. Tuition: Out-of-state: Full year: Part-time: Per credit: $39.00. Part-time: Per credit:$39.00.

Majors

• BUSINESS Accounting, Banking, Business Administration, Business Management, Entrepreneur, Finance, Management, Retailing • COMPUTER SCIENCE Data Processing • EDUCATION Child Development, Physical, Special • ENGINEERING Chemical, Civil/Environmental • HEALTH SCIENCES Medical Secretary, Nuclear Medical Technology, Nursing • HUMANITIES Liberal Arts • SCIENCES Biology, Chemistry, Physical Science • SOCIAL SCIENCES Law Enforcement • VOCATIONAL Drafting, Legal Secretary, Park/Recreation, Respiratory Therapy Technology, Secretarial

Sports/Activities

• SPORTS-INTERCOLLEGIATE Baseball (F), Basketball, Cross Country, Golf (M), Soccer (M), Tennis, Track and Field, Volleyball (F), Wrestling (M) • SPORTS-INTRAMURAL Softball (F) • STUDENT LIFE ACTIVITIES Choral, Concert Band, Newspaper, Radio/TV station, Student Government

Selective **New Jersey**

Services

Jersey City State College

2039 Kennedy Boulevard
Jersey City, New Jersey 07305
(201) 200-3234

School Enrollment: **5,615** Male: **2,509** Female: **3,106**
LD Enrollment: **50**

Admissions Contact: **Samuel T. McGhee, Director of Admissions**
LD Contact: **Dr. Myrna Ehrlich, Director**
Name of Program: **Project Mentor**
Telephone:**(201) 200-3120**

Admissions

Application Information:
LD Students Applying: **60** Accepted: **20** Enrolled:**20**
LD on admissions committee:**Yes**
Application deadline: **June 1st**
Applicant must apply **2-3** months in advance
Rolling Admissions: **Yes**

Secondary School Information
Most Important Criteria For Admissions (1-strongest)

8 SAT/ACT	**9** Application	**4**	School transcript
7 Class rank	**5** Course selection	**11**	Personal statement
2 Interview	**10** Extra activities	**1**	Psychoeducational
6 G.P.A.	Open admission	**3**	Recommendations

Test Requirements:
Diagnostic testing waived: **Yes**
Untimed SAT: **Yes**
WAIS-R required: **Yes** Range accepted: **Normal**
Documentation of LD required: **Yes**
Currency of diagnostic testing: **within last 2 years**
Tests recommended: **Psychoeducational diagnosis**

Types of Disabilities Served
• Speech/Lang	• Reading	• ADD with LD
• Study skills	• Spelling	ADD without LD
• Written express	• Math	• ADHD with LD
• Organizational	• Fine Motor	ADHD without LD
• Perceptual		

Admissions Process

An individual interview is part of the admissions process for LD students. Contact is also made with high school personnel. LD students complete a regular application and add a notation regarding their disability.

High School Course Requirements:
English: **4** Math: **3** Science: **2** Foreign Language: **2**
Waivers to standard high school courses
Foreign Language : **Yes**

Learning Disability Program
Syllabus available during orientation:**Yes**
Program: Reinforces course work: **Yes**
Program available through:**Daily**
Students mainstreamed **100** % of the day
Recommended credits per semester: **13**
Counseling: Individual: **Yes** Vocational Counseling: **Yes**
Support groups are available:**Informal study groups**

Faculty:
Faculty: **10** Including Director: **Yes** Part time: **10** M.A.: **5** Ph.D.: **5**
Faculty advocate: **Yes** Meets with instructor: **2 times per semester**

Diagnostic Testing
ADD	Personality	Perceptual skills	Spelling
ADHD	Organization	Fine motor skills	Reading
I.Q.	Handwriting	Spoken language	Study skills
Math	Social skills	Written language	

Tutoring:
Average size of group tutorials: **1-3 or 1:1**
Services rendered by:

Graduates	Peers	•Faculty	•LD staff	Teacher trainees

Tutorials

Grp.	Ind.	Tutorials	Grp.	Ind.	Tutorials
	•	Math skills		•	Word processing
	•	Study skills	•	•	Time management
	•	Language arts	•	•	Learning strategies
•	•	Written express	•	•	Organizational skills

Academic Accommodations

Curriculum	Study Aids	Exams
Priority registration	Typist	• Oral
Math waiver	Reader	Untimed
Foreign lang. waiver	Notetaker	Take home
Course substitution	• Proof reader	With proctor
In Class	Text on tape	On computer
• Calculators	Early syllabus	• Extended time
• Tape recorder	Taped handouts	On tape
• Word processor		• Modified
Priority seating		Separate room

Graduation Requirements:
Course credits: **128** GPA: **2.0** Years to complete degree: **Minimum 4**

Program Strengths

The admissions process involves: 1) reviewing child study team reports to determine potential as well as achievement, 2) interviewing each applicant; having each perform reading, writing, and mathematical tasks, and 3) consulting with a high school counselor and/or teacher. Accepted students attend a pre-college summer orientation program that provides an intensive orientation to the college, personalized instruction in reading, writing, and math, and instruction in a variety of study strategies necessary for college success, as well as advising and registration.

General Information:

Jersey City State College is a 4 year public college. Urban campus of 17 acres is 15 miles from New York City. Accessible by air, train or bus. Ski areas are 1 hour from campus. Beaches are 1.5 hours from campus. 4% of students are foreign. 3 residential halls on campus. Housing is not guaranteed.60 % of students remain on campus for the weekends. 2 % of students join fraternities/sororities.

Accreditation:MSACS

SAT/ACT Scores:
Scores for incoming freshmen:**Verbal:**89%below 500. 10%between 500 and 599. 1%between 600 and 699. **Math:**72% below 500. 24% between 500 and 599. 4% between 600 and 699.

Class Rank:
About 24% of the present freshmen class were in the upper 20% of their high school class. 83% were in the top 40% of their class. 93% were in the top 60% of their class. 100% were in the top 80% of their class.

Expenses:
Tuition: In-state: Full year: $2,422.00. Part-time: Per credit:$65.00. Tuition: Out-of-state: Full year: $3,182.00. Part-time: Per credit:$91.00. Room and board: $4,650.00

Majors

• AREA STUDIES Black/Afro-American, Latin American, Women's Studies • BUSINESS Accounting, Banking, Business Administration, Business Economics, Business Management, Economics, Finance, Marketing, Personnel • COMMUNICATIONS Broadcasting, Creative Writing, English, Graphic Design, Photography, Television/Radio/Film • COMPUTER SCIENCE Computer Science • CRAFTS AND DESIGN Crafts • EDUCATION Art, Art Therapy, Early Childhood, Elementary, English, Foreign Language, Health, Mathematics, Music, Science, Secondary, Social Studies • HEALTH SCIENCES Health, Medical Technology, Nuclear Medical

Technology, Nursing • HUMANITIES English/Writing/Literature, Philosophy • LANGUAGES Spanish • PREPROFESSIONAL Dentistry, Engineering, Law, Medicine, Pharmacy, Veterinarian • SCIENCES Biology, Geography, Geology, Mathematics • SOCIAL SCIENCES Criminal Justice, Government/Political, History, Political Science, Psychology, Sociology • VISUAL AND PERFORMING ARTS Art, Art History, Jazz, Music, Studio Art • VOCATIONAL Fashion Merchandising, Fire Science, Sports Management

Sports/Activities

• SPORTS-INTERCOLLEGIATE Baseball (M), Basketball (F), Basketball (M), Cross Country (F), Football (M), Soccer (M), Softball (F), Tennis, Volleyball (F), Volleyball (F), Volleyball (M) • SPORTS-INTRAMURAL Basketball, Bowling, Golf, Ping-Pong, Softball, Volleyball • STUDENT LIFE ACTIVITIES Choral, Concert Band, Dance, Drama Groups, Ethnic & Cultural Groups, Fraternities, Jazz Band, Magazine, Music Groups, Musical Theater, Newspaper, Radio/TV station, Religious Organization, Sororities, Student Government, Symphony Orchestra, Yearbook

---

Less Selective **New Jersey Program**

Middlesex County College
Edison, New Jersey 08818
(201) 549-8000

School Enrollment: **3,312** Male: **1,656** Female: **1,656**
LD Enrollment: **150**

Admissions Contact: **Marjorie Cooke, Director of Admissions**
LD Contact: **Joan Ikle, Director**
Name of Program: **Project Connections**
Telephone:**(201) 906-2546**

Admissions

Application Information:
LD Students Applying: **150** Accepted: **150** Enrolled:**150**
Application deadline: **Rolling**
Rolling Admissions: **Yes**Notified when:

Secondary School Information
Most Important Criteria For Admissions (1-strongest)

SAT/ACT	**1** Application	**2**	School transcript
Class rank	**3** Course selection	**7**	Personal statement
1 Interview	**6** Extra activities	**2**	Psychoeducational
G.P.A.	Open admission	**1**	Recommendations

Test Requirements:
Standardized tests waived: **Yes**
Diagnostic testing waived: **Yes**
Documentation of LD required: **Yes**
Tests recommended: **Battery of tests from high school**

Types of Disabilities Served
- Speech/Lang
- Study skills
- Written express
- Organizational
- Perceptual
- Reading
- Spelling
- Math
- Fine Motor
- ADD with LD
- ADD without LD
- ADHD with LD
- ADHD without LD

467

Learning Disability Program

Program: Reinforces course work: **Yes**
Students mainstreamed **100** % of the day
Counseling: Individual: **Yes** Group Counseling: **Yes**

Faculty:

Faculty: **9** Including Director: **Yes** Full time: **4** Part time: **5** M.A.: **9**
Faculty advocate: **Yes** Meets with instructor: **As needed**

Diagnostic Testing

ADD •	Personality •	Perceptual skills •	Spelling
ADHD•	Organization•	Fine motor skills •	Reading
• I.Q. •	Handwriting•	Spoken language •	Study skills
• Math •	Social skills•	Written language	

Tutoring:

Average size of group tutorials: **4**
Services rendered by:
Graduates   Peers   •Faculty   •LD staff   Teacher trainees

Tutorials

Grp.	Ind.	Tutorials	Grp.	Ind.	Tutorials
•	•	Math skills	•	•	Word processing
•	•	Study skills	•	•	Time management
•	•	Language arts	•	•	Learning strategies
•	•	Written express	•	•	Organizational skills

Academic Accommodations

Curriculum	Study Aids	Exams
Priority registration	Typist	• Oral
Math waiver	Reader	Untimed
Foreign lang. waiver	Notetaker	Take home
Course substitution	• Proof reader	With proctor
In Class	• Text on tape	On computer
• Calculators	Early syllabus	• Extended time
• Tape recorder	Taped handouts	On tape
• Word processor		• Modified
Priority seating		Separate room

Program Strengths

Our staff is made up of specialists in learning disabilities with years of experience serving college-level LD students, primarily in one-to-one sessions. Both academic and counseling needs are met by a team of providers with certification beyond the Master's level. A diagnostic center is housed at our site. The staff also provides awareness programs for faculty each year.

General Information:

Middlesex County College is a 2 year public college. Suburban campus of 200 acres is 5 miles from New Brunswick. Accessible by bus. Ski areas are 75 miles from campus. Beaches are 25 miles from campus. 2% of students are foreign. Housing is not guaranteed.

Accreditation: MSACS

Expenses:

Tuition: In-state: Full year: $1,000.00. Part-time: Per credit:$58.00. Tuition: Out-of-state: Full year: $2,200.00. Part-time: Per credit:$116.00.

Majors

• BUSINESS Accounting, Business Administration, Business Management, Economics, Hotel and Restaurant Management, Management, Marketing • COMMUNICATIONS Advertising, English, Journalism, Photography • COMPUTER SCIENCE Data Processing, Programming, Robotics, Systems Analysis • EDUCATION Early Childhood, Physical, Special • ENGINEERING Computer, Engineering Science • HEALTH SCIENCES Medical Technology, Nursing, Nutritional/Food, Radiological Therapy • LANGUAGES French, German, Italian, Spanish • PREPROFESSIONAL Dentistry, Engineering, Law, Social Work • SCIENCES Biology, Chemistry, Mathematics, Physical Science, Physics, Radiology • SOCIAL SCIENCES Criminal Justice, Government/Political, History, Psychology, Social Sciences, Sociology • VISUAL AND PERFORMING ARTS Art, Art History, Music, Studio Art, Theater • VOCATIONAL Automobile Technology, Culinary Arts, Fire Science, Legal Assistant, Secretarial

Sports/Activities

• SPORTS RELATED Cheerleading, Team Managers • SPORTS-INTERCOLLEGIATE Baseball (M), Basketball, Cross Country, Field Hockey, Golf, Gymnastics, Racquetball, Skiing - Snow, Soccer, Softball, Tennis, Track and Field, Volleyball, Wrestling (M) • STUDENT LIFE ACTIVITIES Choral, Dance, Drama Groups, Ethnic & Cultural Groups, Fraternities, Jazz Band, Magazine, Music Groups, Musical Theater, Newspaper, Radio/TV station, Religious Organization, Sororities, Student Government, Yearbook

---

Very Selective   **New Jersey**
                              Accommodations

New Jersey Institute of Technology

323 Martin Luther King Blvd.
Newark, New Jersey 07102
(201) 596-3000

School Enrollment: **7,397** Male: **6,142** Female: **1,255**

Admissions Contact: **Kathy Kelly, Director of Admissions**
LD Contact: **Dr. Edith Frank, Director, Counseling Center**
Name of Program: **Counseling Center**
Telephone:**(201) 596-3416**

Admissions

Application Information:

Application deadline: **March 1st-architecture, April 1st all others**
Rolling Admissions: **Yes**

Secondary School Information

Most Important Criteria For Admissions (1-strongest)

4 SAT/ACT	**8** Application	**3** School transcript
2 Class rank	**5** Course selection	Personal statement
Interview	**6** Extra activities	Psychoeducational
1 G.P.A.	Open admission	**7** Recommendations

Types of Disabilities Served

Speech/Lang	Reading	ADD with LD
Study skills	Spelling	ADD without LD
Written express	Math	ADHD with LD
Organizational	Fine Motor	ADHD without LD
Perceptual		

Admissions Process

NJIT judges each applicant on the basis of his/her overall individual merits. "Deficits" are of no importance to NJIT as long as the student can work effectively with the NJIT resources available.

Learning Disability Program

Students mainstreamed **100** % of the day
Services available for all students: **Yes**
Counseling: Individual: **Yes** Vocational Counseling: **Yes**

Diagnostic Testing

ADD	Personality	Perceptual skills	Spelling
ADHD	Organization	Fine motor skills	Reading
I.Q.	Handwriting	Spoken language	Study skills
Math	Social skills	Written language	

Tutoring:

Services rendered by:
Graduates •Peers •Faculty LD staff Teacher trainees

Tutorials

Grp.	Ind.	Tutorials	Grp.	Ind.	Tutorials
		Math skills			Word processing
		Study skills			Time management
		Language arts			Learning strategies
		Written express			Organizational skills

Academic Accommodations

Curriculum	Study Aids	Exams
Priority registration	Typist	Oral
Math waiver	Reader	Untimed
Foreign lang. waiver	Notetaker	Take home
Course substitution	Proof reader	With proctor
In Class	Text on tape	On computer
Calculators	Early syllabus	Extended time
Tape recorder	Taped handouts	On tape
Word processor		Modified
Priority seating		Separate room

Graduation Requirements:

Course credits: **125** GPA: **2.0** Years to complete degree: **Can be done in 4**

Other requirements: **Individual program requirements in addition to general University requirements.**

Program Strengths

The above academic adjustments may be arranged on a case by case basis.

General Information:

New Jersey Institute of Technology is a 4 year public university. Urban campus of 40 acres is 10 miles from New York. Accessible by air, train or bus. Ski areas are 50 miles from campus. Beaches are 50 miles from campus. 15% of students are foreign. 3 residential halls on campus. Housing is not guaranteed.80 % of students remain on campus for the weekends. 18 % of students join fraternities/sororities.

Accreditation:MSACS, NAAB, CSAB, EAC/ABET, TAC/ABET

SAT/ACT Scores:

Scores for incoming freshmen:**Verbal:**67%below 500. 27%between 500 and 599. 5%between 600 and 699. 1%above 700. **Math:**4% below 500. 50% between 500 and 599. 35% between 600 and 699. 11%above 700.

Class Rank:

About 43% of the present freshmen class were in the upper 20% of their high school class. 78% were in the top 40% of their class. 95% were in the top 60% of their class. 100% were in the top 80% of their class.

Expenses:

Tuition: In-state: Full year: $4,288.00. Part-time: Per credit:$135.00. Tuition: Out-of-state: Full year: $8,228.00 plus fees . Part-time: Per credit:$281.00. Room and board: $4,772.00

Majors

• BUSINESS Business Administration, Management • COMPUTER SCI-ENCE Computer Science, Systems Analysis • ENGINEERING Chemical, Civil/Environmental, Computer, Electrical, Engineering Science, Environmental/Water Resources, Mechanical • SCIENCES Chemistry, Mechanical, Physics

Sports/Activities

• SPORTS RELATED Cheerleading • SPORTS-INTERCOLLEGIATE Baseball (M), Basketball (F), Basketball (M), Bowling, Cross Country, Skiing - Snow (F), Skiing - Snow (M), Soccer (M), Softball (F), Tennis (F), Tennis (M), Volleyball (F), Volleyball (M) • SPORTS-INTRAMURAL Baseball (M), Basketball, Bowling, Cross Country, Fencing, Golf, Judo, Racquetball, Squash, Tennis, Volleyball • STUDENT LIFE ACTIVITIES Academic Clubs, Community Service, Ethnic & Cultural Groups, Fraternities, Newspaper, Radio/TV station, Sororities, Student Government, Yearbook

---

Less Selective   **New Jersey Program**

Ocean County College
College Drive P.O. Box 2001
Toms River, New Jersey 08753-2001
(201) 255-0400

School Enrollment: **8,117** Male: **3,332** Female: **4,785**
LD Enrollment: **176** Male: **84** Female: **92**

Admissions Contact: **Carey R. Trevisan, Jr., Director of Admissions**
LD Contact: **Maureen Reustle, Director, P.A.S.S.**
Name of Program: **Project Academic Skills Support**
Telephone:**(201) 255-0456**

Admissions

Application Information:
Application deadline: **Open admission policy**
Rolling Admissions: **Yes**

Secondary School Information
Most Important Criteria For Admissions (1-strongest)

SAT/ACT	Application	School transcript
Class rank	Course selection	Personal statement
Interview	Extra activities	Psychoeducational
G.P.A.	**1** Open admission	Recommendations

Test Requirements:
Standardized tests waived: **Yes**
Documentation of LD required: **Yes**
Tests recommended: **Current Child Study Team Evaluations, Woodcock-Johnson, and WAIS-III**

Types of Disabilities Served
• Speech/Lang	• Reading	• ADD with LD
• Study skills	• Spelling	• ADD without LD
• Written express	• Math	• ADHD with LD
• Organizational	• Fine Motor	• ADHD without LD
• Perceptual		

Learning Disability Program

Program: Reinforces course work: **Yes**
Students mainstreamed **100 %** of the day
Services only for LD students: **Yes**
Counseling: Individual: **Yes** Group Counseling: **Yes** Vocational Counseling: **Yes**

Faculty:

Faculty: **5** Including Director: **Yes** Full time: **4** Part time: **1** M.A.: **5**
Faculty advocate: **Yes** Meets with instructor: **As needed**

Diagnostic Testing

ADD	Personality •	Perceptual skills •	Spelling
ADHD•	Organization•	Fine motor skills	Reading
• I.Q.	• Handwriting•	Spoken language	• Study skills
• Math	Social skills•	Written language	

Tutoring:

Average size of group tutorials: **10**
Services rendered by:

| Graduates | Peers | Faculty | •LD staff | Teacher trainees |

Tutorials

Grp.	Ind.	Tutorials	Grp.	Ind.	Tutorials
	•	Math skills		•	Word processing
•		Study skills	•		Time management
•	•	Language arts	•		Learning strategies
•	•	Written express	•		Organizational skills

Academic Accommodations

Curriculum	Study Aids	Exams
Priority registration	Typist	• Oral
Math waiver	Reader	Untimed
• Foreign lang. waiver	• Notetaker	Take home
Course substitution	• Proof reader	• With proctor
In Class	• Text on tape	On computer
• Calculators	Early syllabus	• Extended time
• Tape recorder	Taped handouts	On tape
• Word processor		• Modified
Priority seating		Separate room

Graduation Requirements:

Course credits: **64** Years to complete degree: **No limit** Math waiver: **Yes**
Language waiver: **Yes**

Program Strengths

We provide services in all important areas - academic, interpersonal, and career. We believe our students need to understand how their learning disabilities impact in all these areas of functioning and how they can work best to compensate. Our goal is to help our students become independent - as learners and as human beings.

General Information:

Ocean County College is a 2 year public college. Suburban campus 50 miles from Atlantic City. Beaches are 5 miles from campus. Housing is not guaranteed.

Accreditation: Regional

Expenses:

Tuition: In-state: Full year: Part-time: Per credit: $50.00. Tuition: Out-of-state: Full year: Part-time: Per credit: $60.00.

Majors

• BUSINESS Accounting, Banking, Business Administration, Business Management, Finance, Management, Marketing • COMMUNICATIONS English, Graphic Design, Journalism, Photography, Speech, Television/Radio/Film • COMPUTER SCIENCE Computer Science, Programming • EDUCATION Elementary, Music, Social Studies • ENGINEERING Civil/Environmental, Engineering Science • HEALTH SCIENCES Medical Technology, Nursing • HUMANITIES Liberal Arts • PREPROFESSIONAL Engineering • SCIENCES Biology, Chemistry, Mathematics, Physical Chemistry, Physics • SOCIAL SCIENCES Criminal Justice, Government/Political, History, Law Enforcement, Political Science, Social Sciences, Sociology • VISUAL AND PERFORMING ARTS Dramatic Arts, Fine Arts • VOCATIONAL Building Construction, Business and Office, Construction, Electronics Technology, Fire Science, Secretarial

Sports/Activities

• SPORTS-INTERCOLLEGIATE Baseball (M), Basketball, Cross Country, Diving, Field Hockey (F), Golf, Ice Hockey (M), Soccer (M), Softball (F), Swimming, Tennis, Volleyball (F) • SPORTS-INTRAMURAL Badminton, Basketball, Bowling, Cross Country, Swimming, Tennis, Track and Field, Volleyball • STUDENT LIFE activities Choral, Community Service, Concert Band, Dance, Drama Groups, Ethnic & Cultural Groups, Magazine, Musical Theater, Newspaper, Radio/TV station, Student Government, Yearbook

Selective	New Jersey
	Services

William Paterson College of New Jersey

300 Pompton Road
Wayne, New Jersey 07470
(201) 595-2125

School Enrollment: **9,500** Male: **4,500** Female: **5,000**
LD Contact: **Barbara D. Milne**
Telephone: **(201) 595-2491**

Admissions

Application Information:

Application deadline: **June 30th/November 15th**
Rolling Admissions: **Yes**

Secondary School Information

Most Important Criteria For Admissions (1-strongest)

1 SAT/ACT	Application	School transcript
1 Class rank	Course selection	Personal statement
Interview	Extra activities	Psychoeducational
G.P.A.	Open admission	Recommendations

Test Requirements:

Untimed SAT: **Yes** Untimed ACT: **Yes**

Types of Disabilities Served

• Speech/Lang	• Reading	ADD with LD
• Study skills	• Spelling	ADD without LD
• Written express	• Math	ADHD with LD
• Organizational	Fine Motor	ADHD without LD
Perceptual		

Faculty:

Faculty: **1** Part time: **1**
Faculty advocate: **Yes** Meets with instructor: **As needed**

Diagnostic Testing

ADD	Personality	Perceptual skills	Spelling
ADHD	Organization	Fine motor skills	Reading
I.Q.	Handwriting	Spoken language	Study skills
Math	Social skills	Written language	

Tutoring:

Average size of group tutorials: **5-10**
Services rendered by:

| •Graduates | •Peers | Faculty | LD staff | Teacher trainees |

Tutorials

Grp.	Ind.	Tutorials	Grp.	Ind.	Tutorials
•		Math skills	•		Word processing
•		Study skills	•		Time management
•		Language arts	•		Learning strategies
•		Written express	•		Organizational skills

Academic Accommodations

Curriculum	Study Aids	Exams
Priority registration	Typist	• Oral
Math waiver	Reader	Untimed
• Foreign lang. waiver	• Notetaker	• Take home
• Course substitution	Proof reader	With proctor
In Class	• Text on tape	On computer
Calculators	Early syllabus	• Extended time
• Tape recorder	Taped handouts	On tape
• Word processor		• Modified
Priority seating		Separate room

General Information:

William Paterson College of New Jersey is a 4 year public college. Suburban campus of 250 acres is 5 miles from Paterson. Accessible by bus. Ski areas are 25 miles from campus. Beaches are 60 miles from campus. Housing is not guaranteed.

Accreditation: MSACS

Expenses:

Tuition: In-state: Full year: Part-time: Per credit: $75.00. Tuition: Out-of-state: Full year: Part-time: Per credit: $95.00. Room and board: $1,200.00

Majors

• AREA STUDIES African, American, Black/Afro-American • BUSINESS Accounting, Business Administration, Business Economics, Business Management, Economics, Finance, Management, Marketing • COMMUNICATIONS Broadcasting, Communication, English, Graphic Design, Television/Radio/Film • COMPUTER SCIENCE Computer Science, Data Processing, Programming • EDUCATION Art, Early Childhood, Elementary, Health, Middle School, Music, Physical, Pre-Education, Secondary, Special, Speech/Language • HEALTH SCIENCES Communication Disorders, Environmental, Nursing, Speech Therapy, Speech/Audiology and Speech • HUMANITIES English/Writing/Literature, Philosophy • LANGUAGES French, German, Italian, Japanese, Spanish • SCIENCES Biology, Chemistry, Ecology, Geology, Mathematics, Physical Science, Physics • SOCIAL SCIENCES Anthropology, Criminology, Government/Political, History, Psychology, Public Relations, Social Science, Sociology • VISUAL AND PERFORMING ARTS Art, Art History, Dramatic Arts, Music, Music Performance, Studio Art, Theater

Sports/Activities

• SPORTS RELATED Cheerleading • SPORTS-INTERCOLLEGIATE Baseball (M), Basketball, Bowling, Cross Country, Diving, Fencing, Field Hockey (F), Football (M), Golf (M), Horseback Riding, Ice Hockey (M), Skiing - Snow, Soccer (M), Softball (F), Swimming, Tennis, Track and Field, Volleyball (F) • SPORTS-INTRAMURAL Baseball, Basketball, Bowling, Cross Country, Diving, Fencing, Field Hockey (F), Golf, Ping-Pong, Racquetball, Soccer, Softball, Swimming, Tennis, Track and Field, Volleyball • STUDENT LIFE ACTIVITIES Choral, Concert Band, Drama Groups, Ethnic & Cultural Groups, Film, Fraternities, Jazz Band, Magazine, Music Groups, Musical Theater, Newspaper, Orchestra, Radio/TV station, Religious Organization, Sororities, Student Government, Yearbook

---

Less Selective	New Mexico Program

Albuquerque Technical-Vocational Institute
525 Buena Vista Southeast
Albuquerque, New Mexico 87106
(505) 848-1540

School Enrollment: **8,496** Male: **4,200** Female: **4,248**
LD Enrollment: **73**

Admissions Contact: **Orin Lundberg, Assoc. Dean of Counseling**
LD Contact: **Gladys Bennett, Director**
Name of Program: **Special Services**
Telephone: **(505) 243-1741**

Admissions

Application Information:
Enrolled: **73**
Separate application: **Yes**
Applicant must apply **4** months in advance

Secondary School Information
Most Important Criteria For Admissions (1-strongest)

11 SAT/ACT	9 Application	4 School transcript
10 Class rank	3 Course selection	7 Personal statement
8 Interview	6 Extra activities	1 Psychoeducational
5 G.P.A.	Open admission	2 Recommendations

Test Requirements:
Diagnostic testing waived: **Yes**
Untimed ACT: **Yes** Untimed ACH: **Yes**
Tests recommended: **Intelligence, Achievement, Process**

Types of Disabilities Served
- Speech/Lang
- Study skills
- Written express
- Organizational
- Perceptual
- Reading
- Spelling
- Math
- Fine Motor
- ADD with LD
- ADD without LD
- ADHD with LD
- ADHD without LD

Learning Disability Program
Program: Remedial: **Yes**
Program: Reinforces course work: **Yes**
Students mainstreamed **100** % of the day
Counseling: Individual: **Yes**

Faculty:
Faculty: **35** Including Director: **Yes** Full time: **14** Part time: **21**
Faculty advocate: **Yes** Meets with instructor: **As needed**

Diagnostic Testing

ADD	• Personality	• Perceptual skills	• Spelling
ADHD	Organization	• Fine motor skills	• Reading
• I.Q.	• Handwriting	Spoken language	Study skills
• Math	Social skills	• Written language	

Tutoring:
Services rendered by:
Graduates •Peers •Faculty   LD staff   Teacher trainees

New Mexico

Tutorials

Grp.	Ind.	Tutorials	Grp.	Ind.	Tutorials
	•	Math skills		•	Word processing
	•	Study skills		•	Time management
	•	Language arts		•	Learning strategies
	•	Written express		•	Organizational skills

Academic Accommodations

Curriculum	Study Aids	Exams
Priority registration	Typist	• Oral
• Math waiver	Reader	Untimed
Foreign lang. waiver	• Notetaker	• Take home
• Course substitution	Proof reader	With proctor
In Class	• Text on tape	On computer
• Calculators	Early syllabus	• Extended time
• Tape recorder	Taped handouts	On tape
• Word processor		• Modified
Priority seating		Separate room

Program Strengths

Albuquerque Technical-Vocational Institute Special Services provides instructional and support services necessary to facilitate learning disabled students' completion of training objectives and transition to employment. Services provided include diagnostic assessment, guidance and personal counseling, remedial instruction, curriculum accommodation and modification, tutorial assistance, notetakers, auxiliary equipment (i.e. spell checkers, etc.) and job placement.

General Information:

Albuquerque Technical-Vocational Institute is a 2 year public college. Urban campus 90 miles from Santa Fe. Accessible by van shuttle. Ski areas are 15 miles from campus. Housing is not guaranteed.

Accreditation: NCACS

Expenses:
Tuition: In-state: Full year: $290.00. Tuition: Out-of-state: Full year: $696.00.

Majors

• BUSINESS Accounting, Business Administration • COMPUTER SCIENCE Data Processing • HEALTH SCIENCES Nursing • LANGUAGES Spanish

Sports/Activities

• STUDENT LIFE ACTIVITIES Student Government

Selective

New Mexico

Services

College of Santa Fe
Saint Michael's Drive
Santa Fe, New Mexico 87501-5634
(505) 473-6131

School Enrollment: **1,470** Male: **700** Female: **770**

Admissions Contact: **Monica Martinez, Director of Admissions**
LD Contact: **Beth Gudbrandsen, Director**
Name of Program: **Center for Academic Development**
Address: **Building T-44**
Telephone: **(505) 473-6112**

Admissions

Application Information:
LD Students Applying: **21** Accepted: **20** Enrolled: **18**
LD on admissions committee: **Yes**
Rolling Admissions: **Yes** Notified when: **3 weeks after file is complete**

Secondary School Information
Most Important Criteria For Admissions (1-strongest)

2 SAT/ACT	**3** Application	**5** School transcript
Class rank	**8** Course selection	Personal statement
Interview	**10** Extra activities	**7** Psychoeducational
1 G.P.A.	Open admission	**4** Recommendations

Test Requirements:
Diagnostic testing waived: **Yes**
Untimed SAT: **Yes** Untimed ACT: **Yes** Untimed ACH: **Yes**
Range accepted: **Normal**
Documentation of LD required: **Yes**
Currency of diagnostic testing: **9 months**

Types of Disabilities Served
• Speech/Lang	• Reading	• ADD with LD
• Study skills	• Spelling	• ADD without LD
• Written express	• Math	• ADHD with LD
• Organizational	• Fine Motor	• ADHD without LD
• Perceptual		

Admissions Process

Students testing/file is reviewed by Director of Admissions and Director of Center for Academic Development.

High School Course Requirements:
English: **4** Math: **2** Science: **2**

Learning Disability Program

Program: Remedial: **Yes**
Program: Reinforces course work: **Yes**
Students mainstreamed **100** % of the day
Recommended credits per semester: **12**
Services available for all students: **Yes**
Counseling: Individual: **Yes** Group Counseling: **Yes** Vocational Counseling: **Yes**
Support groups are available: **Disabled Students Advisory Board promotes understanding of learning disabilities**

Faculty:
Faculty: **5** Including Director: **Yes** Full time: **1** Part time: **4** M.A.: **4** Ph.D.: **1**
Faculty advocate: **Yes** Meets with instructor: **On demand**

Diagnostic Testing
ADD	Personality	Perceptual skills	Spelling
ADHD	Organization	Fine motor skills	Reading
I.Q.	Handwriting	Spoken language	Study skills
Math	Social skills	Written language	

Tutoring:
Average size of group tutorials: **2-8**
Services rendered by:
| Graduates | •Peers | Faculty | •LD staff | Teacher trainees |

Tutorials

Grp.	Ind.	Tutorials	Grp.	Ind.	Tutorials
•	•	Math skills	•	•	Word processing
•	•	Study skills	•	•	Time management
•	•	Language arts	•	•	Learning strategies
•	•	Written express	•	•	Organizational skills

Academic Accommodations

Curriculum	Study Aids	Exams
• Priority registration	• Typist	• Oral
• Math waiver	Reader	• Untimed
Foreign lang. waiver	• Notetaker	Take home
• Course substitution	• Proof reader	With proctor
In Class	• Text on tape	On computer
• Calculators	Early syllabus	• Extended time
• Tape recorder	Taped handouts	On tape
• Word processor		• Modified
• Priority seating		• Separate room

Graduation Requirements:
Course credits: **128** GPA: **2.0** Years to complete degree: **varies** Math waiver: **Yes**

Program Strengths
Student and support advisor set up a semesters support program based on student needs and curriculum. Student's progress is monitored on a bi-monthly basis and follow-up is provided by the peer counselor.

General Information:
College of Santa Fe is a 4 year private Roman Catholic college. Urban campus of 98 acres is 45 miles from Albuquerque. Ski areas are 20 miles from campus. 2% of students are foreign. 3 residential halls on campus. Housing is guaranteed.90 % of students remain on campus for the weekends.

Accreditation:NCACS

SAT/ACT Scores:
Scores for incoming freshmen:**Verbal:**10%below 500. 60%between 500 and 599. 30%between 600 and 699. **Math:**25% below 500. 40% between 500 and 599. 35% between 600 and 699. **ACT:** 20% below 20. 30% between 20 and 23. 25%between 24 and 25l. 15%between 26 and 28. 10% above 28.

Class Rank:
About 15% of the present freshmen class were in the upper 20% of their high school class. 80% were in the top 40% of their class. 90% were in the top 60% of their class. 100% were in the top 80% of their class.

Expenses:
Tuition: In-state: Full year: $8,778.00 per year. Part-time: Per credit:$292.00. Tuition: Out-of-state: Full year: $8,778.00. Room and board: $4,500.00

Majors
• BUSINESS Accounting, Business Administration, Business Management, Management, Marketing • COMMUNICATIONS Creative Writing, English, Journalism, Photography, Television/Radio/Film • COMPUTER SCIENCE Computer Science, Programming • EDUCATION Art, Elementary, Secondary • HUMANITIES English/Writing/Literature, Humanities, Liberal Arts, Religion • PREPROFESSIONAL Dentistry, Engineering, Law • SCIENCES Biology, Cognitive, Mathematics, Physical Science • SOCIAL SCIENCES Government/Political, History, Political Science, Psychology, Public Relations, Social Sciences • VISUAL AND PERFORMING ARTS Dramatic Arts, Fine Arts, Music Performance, Studio Art • VOCATIONAL Business and Office, Secretarial

Sports/Activities
• SPORTS-INTRAMURAL Baseball, Basketball, Bowling, Ping-Pong, Racquetball, Skiing - Snow, Soccer, Softball, Swimming, Tennis, Volleyball • STUDENT LIFE ACTIVITIES Choral, Dance, Drama Groups, Ethnic & Cultural Groups, Magazine, Music Groups, Musical Theater, Newspaper, Radio/TV station, Religious Organization, Sororities, Student Government, Yearbook

Selective **New Mexico**
Services

Eastern New Mexico University: Roswell
P.O. Box 6000
Roswell, New Mexico 88201
(505) 624-7145-(800) 243-6687

School Enrollment: **2,072** Male: **751** Female: **1,321**

Admissions Contact: **Baeta Howse, Registrar**
LD Contact: **Linda Green, Special Services**
Name of Program: **Special Services**
Telephone:**(505) 624-7286**

Admissions

Secondary School Information
Most Important Criteria For Admissions (1-strongest)

SAT/ACT	Application	School transcript
Class rank	Course selection	Personal statement
Interview	Extra activities	Psychoeducational
G.P.A.	Open admission	Recommendations

Test Requirements:
Documentation of LD required: **Yes**

Types of Disabilities Served
• Speech/Lang	• Reading	• ADD with LD
• Study skills	• Spelling	• ADD without LD
• Written express	• Math	• ADHD with LD
• Organizational	• Fine Motor	• ADHD without LD
• Perceptual		

Learning Disability Program
Program: Remedial: **Yes**
Program: Reinforces course work: **Yes**
Students mainstreamed **100 %** of the day
Recommended credits per semester: **varies**
Services only for LD students: **Yes**
Counseling: Individual: **Yes** Group Counseling: **Yes** Vocational Counseling: **Yes**

Diagnostic Testing
ADD	Personality	Perceptual skills	Spelling
ADHD	Organization	Fine motor skills	Reading
I.Q.	Handwriting	Spoken language	Study skills
Math	Social skills	Written language	

Tutoring:
Average size of group tutorials: **1-5**
Services rendered by:
Graduates •Peers   •Faculty   LD staff   Teacher trainees

New Mexico

Tutorials

Grp.	Ind.	Tutorials	Grp.	Ind.	Tutorials
•	•	Math skills			Word processing
		Study skills			Time management
•	•	Language arts			Learning strategies
•	•	Written express			Organizational skills

Academic Accommodations

Curriculum	Study Aids	Exams
Priority registration	Typist	• Oral
Math waiver	Reader	• Untimed
Foreign lang. waiver	Notetaker	Take home
Course substitution	Proof reader	With proctor
In Class	Text on tape	On computer
Calculators	Early syllabus	Extended time
Tape recorder	Taped handouts	On tape
Word processor		Modified
Priority seating		• Separate room

Graduation Requirements:
Course credits: **varies**

Program Strengths

Our program is unique in that our students are referred through D.V.R. for training in special areas of study. The areas of study are determined by vocational testing and O.J.T. skills.

General Information:

Eastern New Mexico University: Roswell is a 2 year public university. Urban campus 202 miles from Albuquerque. Accessible by air or bus. Ski areas are 70 miles from campus. Beaches are 900 miles from campus. 2 residential halls on campus. Housing is not guaranteed.1 % of students remain on campus for the weekends.

Accreditation:NCACS

Expenses:
Tuition: In-state: Full year: $276.00. Part-time: Per credit:$24.00. Tuition: Out-of-state: Full year: $780.00. Part-time: Per credit:$63.00. Room and board: $920.00 - $1,215.00.

Majors

• BUSINESS Accounting, Banking/Finance, Bookkeeping, Business Administration, Retailing, Vocational Studies • EDUCATION Child Development • HEALTH SCIENCES Nursing, Nursing Assistant, Practical Nursing • SOCIAL SCIENCES Criminal Justice • VOCATIONAL Automotive Service, Aviation Maintenance, Medical Laboratory Technology, Welding

Sports/Activities

• SPORTS-INTRAMURAL Baseball (M), Basketball (M), Racquetball, Softball (F), Tennis, Volleyball

Institute of American Indian Arts
Santa Fe, New Mexico 87501
(505) 988-6432

School Enrollment: **227** Male: **118** Female: **109**

Admissions Contact: **Ramos Suina, Recruiter**
LD Contact: **Karen Roberts, Strong LRC, Director**
Name of Program: **Learning Resource Center**
Address: **P.O. Box 20007**
Telephone:**(505) 988-6432**

Admissions

Application Information:
Application deadline: **April 15th**
Rolling Admissions: **Yes**

Secondary School Information
Most Important Criteria For Admissions (1-strongest)

12 SAT/ACT	6 Application	2 School transcript
7 Class rank	8 Course selection	4 Personal statement
9 Interview	10 Extra activities	11 Psychoeducational
1 G.P.A.	Open admission	5 Recommendations

Test Requirements:
Untimed SAT: **Yes** Untimed ACT: **Yes** Untimed ACH: **Yes**
Tests recommended: **ACT, Asset, Pre Test B**

Types of Disabilities Served

Speech/Lang	• Reading	ADD with LD
• Study skills	• Spelling	ADD without LD
• Written express	• Math	ADHD with LD
Organizational	Fine Motor	ADHD without LD
Perceptual		

Admissions Process

1. Application; 2. High School transcript; 3. Three reference letters; 4. Portfolio; 5. Personal essay

Learning Disability Program

Students mainstreamed **100** % of the day
Recommended credits per semester: **12-15**
Time required or recommended in learning center: **4 hours**
Services available for all students: **Yes**
Counseling: Individual: **Yes** Group Counseling: **Yes**
Support groups are available:**Art Therapy - Talking Circle**

Faculty:
Faculty: **5** Including Director: **Yes** Part time: **1** M.A.: **1**
Meets with instructor: **Daily**

Diagnostic Testing

ADD	Personality	Perceptual skills	• Spelling
ADHD	Organization	Fine motor skills	• Reading
I.Q.	Handwriting	Spoken language	• Study skills
• Math	Social skills	• Written language	

Tutoring:
Average size of group tutorials: **1:1**
Services rendered by:
Graduates •Peers   Faculty   LD staff   Teacher trainees

Tutorials

Grp.	Ind.	Tutorials	Grp.	Ind.	Tutorials
•		Math skills	•		Word processing
•		Study skills	•		Time management
	•	Language arts		•	Learning strategies
	•	Written express		•	Organizational skills

Academic Accommodations

Curriculum	Study Aids	Exams
Priority registration	Typist	Oral
Math waiver	Reader	Untimed
Foreign lang. waiver	Notetaker	Take home
Course substitution	Proof reader	With proctor
In Class	Text on tape	On computer
Calculators	Early syllabus	Extended time
Tape recorder	Taped handouts	On tape
Word processor		Modified
Priority seating		Separate room

Graduation Requirements:
Course credits: **64** Years to complete degree: **2**

Program Strengths
Whole language approach. Discourse analysis theory. Thematic systems structure.

General Information:
Institute of American Indian Arts is a 2 year independent Urban campus Accessible by air, train or bus. Ski areas are 18 miles from campus. 4% of students are foreign. 2 residential halls on campus. Housing is not guaranteed.100 % of students remain on campus for the weekends.

Accreditation:NASAD, NCACS

Expenses:
Tuition: In-state: Full year: $1,800.00. Part-time: Per credit:$75.00. Part-time: Per course: $225.00. Tuition: Out-of-state: Full year: $1,800.00. Part-time: Per credit:$75.00. Part-time: Per course:$225.00 Room and board: $3,166.00

Majors
• ARTS Creative Writing, Museum Preservation, Painting, Sculpture • COMMUNICATIONS Creative Writing • CRAFTS AND DESIGN Ceramics, Jewelry, Printmaking, Sculpture, Textile/Weaving

Sports/Activities
• SPORTS-INTRAMURAL Archery, Baseball, Basketball, Bowling, Diving, Football, Skiing - Cross Country, Skiing - Snow, Softball, Swimming, Table tennis, Track and Field, Volleyball

---

Less Selective	New Mexico Accommodations

San Juan College
4601 College Boulevard
Farmington, New Mexico 87401
(505) 326-3311

School Enrollment: **4,000**

Admissions Contact: **Jim Ratliff, Director of Admissions**
LD Contact: **Nancy Wray, Director, Disabled on Campus**

Admissions

Application Information:
LD Students Applying: **15** Accepted: **15**
Separate application:**Yes**

Secondary School Information
Most Important Criteria For Admissions (1-strongest)

SAT/ACT	Application	School transcript
Class rank	Course selection	Personal statement
Interview	Extra activities	Psychoeducational
G.P.A.	Open admission	Recommendations

Test Requirements:
Diagnostic testing waived: **Yes**
Documentation of LD required: **Yes**
Currency of diagnostic testing: **No specification**

Types of Disabilities Served
• Speech/Lang	• Reading	• ADD with LD
• Study skills	• Spelling	• ADD without LD
• Written express	• Math	• ADHD with LD
• Organizational	• Fine Motor	• ADHD without LD
• Perceptual		

Admissions Process

Open admissions - completed application form is all that is needed.

High School Course Requirements:
Waivers to standard high school courses
Course substitution: **Yes**

Learning Disability Program
Services available for all students: **Yes**

Diagnostic Testing
ADD	Personality	Perceptual skills	Spelling
ADHD	Organization	Fine motor skills	Reading
I.Q.	Handwriting	Spoken language	Study skills
Math	Social skills	Written language	

Tutoring:
Services rendered by:
Graduates •Peers   Faculty   LD staff   Teacher trainees

Tutorials

Grp.	Ind.	Tutorials	Grp.	Ind.	Tutorials
		Math skills			Word processing
		Study skills			Time management
		Language arts			Learning strategies
		Written express			Organizational skills

Academic Accommodations

Curriculum	Study Aids	Exams
• Priority registration	Typist	• Oral
Math waiver	Reader	• Untimed
Foreign lang. waiver	Notetaker	Take home
Course substitution	Proof reader	• With proctor
In Class	• Text on tape	On computer
Calculators	Early syllabus	• Extended time
• Tape recorder	Taped handouts	On tape
Word processor		Modified
Priority seating		• Separate room

General Information:

San Juan College is a 2 year college. Suburban campus 250 miles from Albuquerque. Ski areas are 60 miles from campus. Beaches are 900 miles from campus. Housing is not guaranteed.

Accreditation:

Expenses:

Tuition: In-state: Full year: $180.00 per semester. Part-time: Per credit:$15.00. Part-time: Per course: $45.00. Tuition: Out-of-state: Full year: $300.00. Part-time: Per credit:$25.00. Part-time: Per course:$75.00

Majors

• BUSINESS Accounting, Banking/Finance, Business Administration, Clerical, Data Processing, Secretarial Science • COMMUNICATIONS Television/Radio/Film • COMPUTER SCIENCE Business Data Programming, Data Processing • HEALTH SCIENCES Nursing, Physical Therapy • SCIENCES Biology, Chemistry, Computer Science, Geology, Mathematics, Physics • VOCATIONAL Auto Body, Automobile Technology, Aviation Pilot, Carpentry, Diesel Power Technology, Drafting, Machinist, Paralegal, Secretarial, Welding, Word Processing

Sports/Activities

• STUDENT LIFE ACTIVITIES Academic Clubs, Concert Band, Radio/TV station, Student Government

---

Less Selective

Santa Fe Community College

P.O. Box 4187
Santa Fe, New Mexico 87502-4187
(505) 471-8200 Ext. 331

School Enrollment: **3,000**
LD Enrollment: **19**

Admissions Contact: **Anita Shields, Director of Admissions**
LD Contact: **Jill Douglass, Coordinator, Special Services**
Name of Program: **Special Student Services**
Telephone:**(505) 438-1331**

Admissions

Application Information:
Rolling Admissions: **Yes**

Secondary School Information
Most Important Criteria For Admissions (1-strongest)

SAT/ACT	Application	School transcript
Class rank	Course selection	Personal statement
Interview	Extra activities	Psychoeducational
G.P.A.	**1** Open admission	Recommendations

Test Requirements:
Documentation of LD required: **Yes**

Types of Disabilities Served
• Speech/Lang	• Reading	• ADD with LD
• Study skills	• Spelling	• ADD without LD
• Written express	• Math	• ADHD with LD
• Organizational	• Fine Motor	• ADHD without LD
• Perceptual		

Learning Disability Program

Counseling: Individual: **Yes**

Faculty:
Faculty: **1** Full time: **1**
Faculty advocate: **Yes**

Diagnostic Testing
ADD	Personality	Perceptual skills	Spelling
ADHD	Organization	Fine motor skills	Reading
I.Q.	Handwriting	Spoken language	Study skills
Math	Social skills	Written language	

Tutoring:
Services rendered by:
Graduates •Peers •Faculty LD staff Teacher trainees

Tutorials

Grp.	Ind.	Tutorials	Grp.	Ind.	Tutorials
•	•	Math skills	•	•	Word processing
•	•	Study skills			Time management
•	•	Language arts	•	•	Learning strategies
•	•	Written express			Organizational skills

Academic Accommodations

Curriculum	Study Aids	Exams
Priority registration	Typist	• Oral
Math waiver	• Reader	Untimed
Foreign lang. waiver	• Notetaker	Take home
Course substitution	Proof reader	• With proctor
In Class	Text on tape	On computer
• Calculators	Early syllabus	• Extended time
• Tape recorder	Taped handouts	On tape
• Word processor		Modified
• Priority seating		• Separate room

Program Strengths

We do not have a program but do attempt to meet the special needs of someone with a learning disability through our Guidance Department Office of Special Student Services and developmental studies division. We offer classes in Organizational Skills, Learning Strategies, Written Expression, and Study Skills.

General Information:

Santa Fe Community College is a 2 year public college. Urban campus. 60 miles from Albuquerque. Ski areas are 20 miles from campus. Housing is not guaranteed.

Accreditation: Regional

Expenses:

Tuition: In-state: Full year: Approximately $480.00. Tuition: Out-of-state: Full year: Approximately $1,100.00.

Majors

• AREA STUDIES Southwest Studies • BUSINESS Accounting, Banking, Business Administration, Business Management, Entrepreneur, Finance, Food Management, Hotel and Restaurant Management, Management, Real Estate • COMPUTER SCIENCE Computer Science, Telecommunications • EDUCATION Early Childhood • ENGINEERING Engineering Science • HEALTH SCIENCES Nursing • HUMANITIES Humanities, Liberal Arts • PREPROFESSIONAL Legal Assistant • SCIENCES Biology, Mathematics, Physical Science • SOCIAL SCIENCES Criminal Justice • VOCATIONAL Business and Office, Culinary Arts, Drafting, Electronics Technology, Paralegal, Secretarial, Surveying and Mapping, Word Processing

Sports/Activities

• STUDENT LIFE ACTIVITIES Choral, Music Groups, Newsletter, Newspaper, Radio/TV station, Student Government

Less Selective

New Mexico Services

University of New Mexico

Albuquerque, New Mexico 87131-2101
(505) 277-3506

LD Enrollment: **55**

Admissions Contact: **Cynthia Stuart, Director of Admissions**
LD Contact: **Juan Candelaria, Dir., Disabled Student Services**
Name of Program: **Disabled Student Services**
Telephone:**(505) 277-3506**

Admissions

Application Information:

LD Students Applying: **45** Accepted: **45** Enrolled:**45**
Application deadline: **December, May, July**
Applicant must apply **1** months in advance
Rolling Admissions: **Yes**

Secondary School Information

Most Important Criteria For Admissions (1-strongest)

2	SAT/ACT	**1**	Application	**2**	School transcript
2	Class rank	**7**	Course selection	**5**	Personal statement
	Interview	**8**	Extra activities	**5**	Psychoeducational
2	G.P.A.		Open admission	**6**	Recommendations

Test Requirements:

Diagnostic testing waived: **Yes**
Untimed SAT: **Yes** Untimed ACT: **Yes** Achievement tests required:**1**
Documentation of LD required: **Yes**

Types of Disabilities Served

- Speech/Lang
- Study skills
- Written express
- Organizational
- Perceptual
- Reading
- Spelling
- Math
- Fine Motor
- ADD with LD
- ADD without LD
- ADHD with LD
- ADHD without LD

Admissions Process

1) Application and $15.00 application fee 2) High school transcripts 3) ACT or SAT

High School Course Requirements:

English: **4** Math: **3** Science: **2** Foreign Language: **2**
Waivers to standard high school courses
Foreign Language : **Yes** Course substitution: **Yes**

Learning Disability Program

Program available through:**Upon request**
Counseling: Individual: **Yes**

Faculty:

Faculty: **9** Including Director: **Yes** Full time: **8** Part time: **1**
LD faculty with: BS/BA: **5** Ph.D.: **1**

Diagnostic Testing

- ADD
- ADHD
- I.Q.
- Math
- Personality
- Organization
- Handwriting
- Social skills
- Perceptual skills
- Fine motor skills
- Spoken language
- Written language
- Spelling
- Reading
- Study skills

Tutoring:

Average size of group tutorials: **1:1**
Services rendered by:
•Graduates •Peers Faculty LD staff Teacher trainees

Tutorials

Grp.	Ind.	Tutorials	Grp.	Ind.	Tutorials
	•	Math skills			Word processing
		Study skills			Time management
		Language arts			Learning strategies
	•	Written express			Organizational skills

Academic Accommodations

Curriculum	Study Aids	Exams
Priority registration	• Typist	Oral
Math waiver	• Reader	• Untimed
Foreign lang. waiver	• Notetaker	Take home
Course substitution	Proof reader	• With proctor
In Class	• Text on tape	• On computer
Calculators	Early syllabus	• Extended time
• Tape recorder	Taped handouts	On tape
Word processor		Modified
Priority seating		• Separate room

Graduation Requirements:

Course credits: **128** GPA: **2.0** Math waiver: **Yes**
Other requirements: **English 102 (C grade or better).**

Program Strengths

We provide academic support services such as the following: counseling, tutoring, proctoring, notetakers, writers, and reading.

General Information:

University of New Mexico is a 2 and 4 year public university. Urban campus Accessible by bus, car or bicycle. Ski areas are 30 miles from campus.

New York

Beaches are 500 miles from campus. 2% of students are foreign. Housing is not guaranteed.4 % of students join fraternities/sororities.

Accreditation: Regional

Expenses:

Tuition: In-state: Full year: $777.00. Part-time: Per credit:$64.75. Part-time: Per course: $194.25. Tuition: Out-of-state: Full year: $2,760.00. Part-time: Per credit:$64.75. Part-time: Per course:$194.25

Majors

• AREA STUDIES American, Latin American, Russian/Slavic • ARTS Art History, Dance, Music, Music History • BUSINESS Accounting, Economics, Education, Human Resource Development, International Business, Management, Marketing, Travel/Tourism Management • COMMUNICA-TIONS Communication, Creative Writing, English, Journalism, Linguistic, Speech/Debate/Forensic • COMPUTER SCIENCE Business Data Programming, Computer Science, Computer Technology, Medical Records Technology • CRAFTS AND DESIGN Graphic Design, Printmaking • EDUCATION English As A Second Language, General, Special • ENGINEERING Chemical, Civil/Environmental, Computer, Electrical, Environmental/Water Resources, Mechanical, Nuclear • HEALTH SCIENCES Communication Disorders, Dental Hygiene, Medical Laboratory Technology, Nursing, Pharmacology, Physical Therapy • HUMANITIES English/Writing/Literature, Philosophy • LANGUAGES French, German, Linguistic, Russian, Spanish • PRE PROFESSIONAL Architectural, Business, Engineering, Law, Medicine, Pharmacy • SCIENCES Anthropology, Archeology, Astronomy, Astrophysics, Biochemistry, Biology, Chemical, Computer Science, Geography, Geology, Mathematics, Physics • SOCIAL SCIENCES Anthropology, Criminal Justice, Family Counseling, Geography, Government/Political, History, Political Science, Psychology, Sociology • VISUAL AND PERFORMING ARTS Art, Art History, Dance, Music, Theater • VOCATIONAL Dental Hygiene

Sports/Activities

• SPORTS RELATED Cheerleading, Drill Team, Drum Major/Majorette, Marching Band, Pep Band, Team Managers • SPORTS-INTERCOLLE-GIATE Baseball (M), Basketball (F), Basketball (M), Cross Country (F), Diving (F), Diving (M), Football (M), Golf (F), Golf (M), Gymnastics (F), Gymnastics (M), Music Ensemble, Skiing - Cross Country, Skiing - Snow (F), Skiing - Snow (M), Soccer (M), Softball (F), Swimming (M), Tennis (F), Tennis (M), Track and Field (F), Track and Field (M), Volleyball (F), Winning Society, Wrestling (M) • SPORTS-INTRAMURAL Archery, Badminton (F), Badminton (M), Basketball (F), Basketball (M), Cross Country, Football (F), Football (M), Football, Flag, Golf (F), Golf (M), Judo, Karate, Ping-Pong (F), Ping-Pong (M), Racquetball (F), Racquetball (M), Skiing - Cross Country, Skiing - Snow (F), Skiing - Snow (M), Soccer (F), Soccer (M), Softball (F), Softball (M), Squash (F), Squash (M), Swimming (F), Swimming (M), Tennis (F), Tennis (M), Track and Field (F), Track and Field (M), Volleyball (F), Volleyball (M), Water Polo (F), Water Polo (M), Weight Lifting (F), Weight Lifting (M), Wrestling (M) • STUDENT LIFE ACTIVITIES Academic Clubs, Choral, Community Service, Concert Band, Dance, Debate, Drama Groups, Fashion Club, Film, Fraternities, Jazz Band, Magazine, Music Groups, Musical Theater, Newspaper, Orchestra, Political Groups, Radio/TV station, Religious Organization, Sororities, Student Government, Symphony Orchestra, Yearbook

---

Adelphi University
Box 701 Eddy Hall
Garden City, New York 11530
(516) 663-1100

School Enrollment: **8,535** Male: **2,667** Female: **5,868**
LD Enrollment: **141** Male: **96** Female: **45**

Admissions Contact: **Esther Goodcuff, Ass. Director**
LD Contact: **Sandra Holzinger, Director LD Program**
Name of Program: **Learning Disabled College Students**
Telephone:**(516) 877-4710**

Admissions

Application Information:
LD Students Applying: **225** Accepted: **101** Enrolled:**45**
Application deadline: **March 1st**
Applicant must apply **12** months in advance
Rolling Admissions: **Yes**

Secondary School Information
Most Important Criteria For Admissions (1-strongest)

12 SAT/ACT	**12** Application	**1** School transcript
10 Class rank	**2** Course selection	Personal statement
Interview	**12** Extra activities	**3** Psychoeducational
11 G.P.A.	Open admission	**7** Recommendations

Test Requirements:
Diagnostic testing waived: **Yes**
Untimed SAT: **Yes** Untimed ACT: **Yes**
WAIS-R required: **Yes** Range accepted: **Average+**
Documentation of LD required: **Yes**
Currency of diagnostic testing: **1 year**
Tests recommended: **Woodcock-Johnson Psychoeducational Battery-R or other comprehensive testing.**

Types of Disabilities Served
• Speech/Lang	• Reading	• ADD with LD
• Study skills	• Spelling	• ADD without LD
• Written express	• Math	• ADHD with LD
• Organizational	• Fine Motor	• ADHD without LD
• Perceptual		

Admissions Process

Application and documentation are sent to admissions. File is sent to LD program for review, interview, and decision. Admissions director informs LD applicant of acceptance decision.

High School Course Requirements:
English: **4** Math: **3** Science: **3** Foreign Language: **2-3**

Learning Disability Program

Special orientation for LD students:
Syllabus available during orientation:**Yes**
Program: Reinforces course work: **Yes**
Students mainstreamed **100** % of the day
Recommended credits per semester: **12-15**
Time required or recommended in learning center: **3 hours per week**
Services only for LD students: **Yes**
Counseling: Individual: **Yes** Group Counseling: **Yes** Vocational Counseling: **Yes**

Faculty:

Faculty: **41** Including Director: **Yes** Full time: **17** Part time: **24** M.A.: **41**
Faculty advocate: **Yes** Meets with instructor: **As needed**

Diagnostic Testing

- ADD
- ADHD
- I.Q.
- Math
- Personality
- Organization
- Handwriting
- Social skills
- Perceptual skills
- Fine motor skills
- Spoken language
- Written language
- Spelling
- Reading
- Study skills

Tutoring:

Average size of group tutorials: **3-5**
Services rendered by:
Graduates   Peers   Faculty   •LD staff   Teacher trainees

Tutorials

Grp.	Ind.	Tutorials	Grp.	Ind.	Tutorials
	•	Math skills	•	•	Word processing
•	•	Study skills	•	Time management
	•	Language arts	•	Learning strategies
	•	Written express	•	Organizational skills

Academic Accommodations

Curriculum	Study Aids	Exams
• Priority registration	• Typist	• Oral
Math waiver	• Reader	Untimed
Foreign lang. waiver	• Notetaker	Take home
• Course substitution	• Proof reader	• With proctor
In Class	• Text on tape	On computer
• Calculators	Early syllabus	• Extended time
• Tape recorder	Taped handouts	On tape
• Word processor		• Modified
Priority seating		• Separate room

Graduation Requirements:

Course credits: **120** GPA: **2.0** Years to complete degree: **4**

Program Strengths

Adelphi has made a strong commitment to the expansion of educational opportunities for students with learning problems. The nationally praised program stresses extensive support services including tutorials, assignments, strong counseling, and untimed tests. According to the evaluation scan of Middle States, the Learning Disabled Program is a unique and effective one involving joint efforts of faculty from social work and education.

General Information:

Adelphi University is a 4 year private university. Suburban Campus of 75 acres is 20 miles from New York City. Accessible by air, train or bus. Ski areas are 90 miles from campus. Beaches are 10 miles from campus. 3% of students are foreign. 5 residential halls on campus. Housing is guaranteed.Guaranteed through first year. 30 % of students remain on campus for the weekends. 29 % of students join fraternities/sororities.

Accreditation:MSACS

SAT/ACT Scores:
Scores for incoming freshmen:**Verbal:**60%below 500. 32%between 500 and 599. 7%between 600 and 699. 1%above 700. **Math:**25% below 500. 52% between 500 and 599. 21% between 600 and 699. 2%above 700.

Class Rank:
About 51% of the present freshmen class were in the upper 20% of their high school class. 81% were in the top 40% of their class. 95% were in the top 60% of their class. 100% were in the top 80% of their class.

Expenses:
Tuition: In-state: Full year: $10,420.00 for district . Part-time: Per credit:$310.00. Tuition: Out-of-state: Full year: $10,420.00. Part-time: Per credit:$310.00. Room and board: $5,530.00 Cost of LD program:$3,500.00

Majors

• AREA STUDIES Latin American • ARTS Art History, Art Therapy, Dance, Design, Dramatic Arts, Music, Music Performance, Theater Design • BUSINESS Accounting, Banking/Finance, Business Administration, Business Management, Data Processing, Economics, Management, Marketing, Sports Medicine • COMMUNICATIONS Communication, English • COMPUTER SCIENCE Computer Science • EDUCATION Art, Bilingual, Early Childhood, Elementary, English, English As A Second Language, Foreign Language, Health, Mathematics, Music, Physical, Reading, Science, Secondary, Social Studies, Special, Speech/Language • HEALTH SCIENCE Communication Disorders, Health, Nursing, Speech Therapy, Speech/Audiology and Speech • HUMANITIES English/Writing/Literature, Philosophy • LANGUAGES French, German, Spanish • PRE PROFESSIONAL Business, Dentistry, Engineering, Law, Medicine, Optometry, Social Work, Veterinarian • SCIENCES Anthropology, Biochemistry, Biology, Chemistry, Computer Science, Earth, Mathematics, Physics • SOCIAL SCIENCES Anthropology, History, Political Science, Psychology, Sociology • SPECIAL EDUCATION Deaf/Hearing Impaired • VISUAL AND PERFORMING ARTS Art, Art History, Dance, Theater

Sports/Activities

• SPORTS-INTERCOLLEGIATE Baseball (M), Basketball (M), Cross Country (F), Cross Country (M), Fencing (F), Fencing (M), Golf (F), Golf (M), Lacrosse, Soccer (F), Soccer (M), Tennis (F), Tennis (M) • STUDENT LIFE ACTIVITIES Academic Clubs, Community Service, Dance, Ethnic & Cultural Groups, Film, Fraternities, Magazine, Newspaper, Radio/TV station, Religious Organization, Sororities, Student Government, Yearbook

Less Selective   **New York**
                                          Services

Broome Community College
P.O. Box 1017
Binghamton, New York 13902
(607) 771-5001

School Enrollment: **4,500**
LD Enrollment: **50**

Admissions Contact: **Anthony Fiorelli, Director of Admissions**
LD Contact: **Bruce E. Pomeroy, Director**
Name of Program: **Student Support Services**
Telephone:**(607) 771-5234**

New York

Admissions

Application Information:
LD on admissions committee:**Yes**
Application deadline: **None**
Applicant must apply **1** months in advance
Rolling Admissions: **Yes**

Secondary School Information
Most Important Criteria For Admissions (1-strongest)

SAT/ACT	Application	School transcript
Class rank	Course selection	Personal statement
Interview	Extra activities	Psychoeducational
G.P.A.	**1** Open admission	Recommendations

Test Requirements:
WAIS-R required: **Yes**
Documentation of LD required: **Yes**
Currency of diagnostic testing: **3 years**

Types of Disabilities Served
- Speech/Lang
- Study skills
- Written express
- Organizational
- Perceptual
- Reading
- Spelling
- Math
- Fine Motor

ADD with LD
ADD without LD
ADHD with LD
ADHD without LD

Admissions Process

Apply, if completed high school then accepted, possible pre-requirements requested based on academic background.

High School Course Requirements:
Waivers to standard high school courses
Foreign Language : **Yes** Math: **Yes** Course substitution: **Yes**

Learning Disability Program

Special orientation for LD students: **Yes**
Students mainstreamed **100** % of the day
Recommended credits per semester: **12-15**
Counseling: Individual: **Yes** Group Counseling: **Yes** Vocational Counseling: **Yes**
Support groups are available:**Yes, LD Academic Support Group**

Faculty:
Faculty: **2** Full time: **2** M.A.: **1**
Meets with instructor: **As needed**

Diagnostic Testing

ADD	Personality	Perceptual skills	Spelling
ADHD	Organization	Fine motor skills	Reading
I.Q.	Handwriting	Spoken language	Study skills
Math	Social skills	Written language	

Tutoring:
Average size of group tutorials: **3**
Services rendered by:
- Graduates
- Peers
- Faculty
- LD staff
- Teacher trainees

Tutorials

Grp.	Ind.	Tutorials	Grp.	Ind.	Tutorials
•	•	Math skills	•	•	Word processing
•	•	Study skills	•	•	Time management
•	•	Language arts	•	•	Learning strategies
•	•	Written express	•	•	Organizational skills

Academic Accommodations

Curriculum	Study Aids	Exams
• Priority registration	• Typist	• Oral
• Math waiver	• Reader	• Untimed
• Foreign lang. waiver	• Notetaker	• Take home
• Course substitution	• Proof reader	• With proctor
In Class	• Text on tape	• On computer
• Calculators	Early syllabus	• Extended time
• Tape recorder	Taped handouts	• On tape
• Word processor		• Modified
Priority seating		• Separate room

Graduation Requirements:
Course credits: **Varies** GPA: **2.0** Years to complete degree: **Varies** Math waiver: **Yes** Language waiver: **Yes**

Program Strengths
We do not have an LD program. We offer supportive services to LD students in order to meet the objectives of their courses.

General Information:
Broome Community College is a 2 year public college. Urban campus of 40 acres is 2 miles from Binghamton. Accessible by air or bus. Ski areas are 20 miles from campus. Housing is not guaranteed.10 % of students join fraternities/sororities.

Accreditation:MSACS

Expenses:
Tuition: In-state: Full year: $1,500.00. Part-time: Per credit:$54.00. Tuition: Out-of-state: Full year: $1,500.00. Part-time: Per credit:$108.00.

Majors
• BUSINESS Accounting, Business Administration, Business Economics, Business Management, Economics, Hotel and Restaurant Management, Management, Marketing, Real Estate, Travel/Tourism Management
• COMMUNICATIONS Advertising, Broadcasting, Communication, Creative Writing, English, Journalism, Photography, Television/Radio/Film
• COMPUTER SCIENCE Computer Science, Data Processing, Programming, Systems Analysis • EDUCATION Child Development, Early Childhood, Music • ENGINEERING Chemical, Civil/Environmental, Computer, Electrical, Engineering Science, Industrial, Manufacturing, Mechanical • HEALTH SCIENCES Dental Hygiene, Medical Assistant, Medical Records Technology, Medical Technology, Nursing, Occupational Therapy, Physical Therapy, Radiological Therapy • HUMANITIES Liberal Arts, Philosophy • PREPROFESSIONAL Forestry, Social Work • SOCIAL SCIENCES Criminal Justice • VOCATIONAL Electronics Technology, Fire Science, Radiological Technology, Secretarial, Tool & Die Making

Sports/Activities
• SPORTS RELATED Cheerleading, Chess, Flying Team, Team Managers • SPORTS-INTERCOLLEGIATE Baseball (M), Basketball, Cross Country, Golf, Ice Hockey (M), Soccer (M), Softball (F), Tennis, Volleyball (F), Wrestling (M) • SPORTS-INTRAMURAL Basketball, Cross Country, Volleyball • STUDENT LIFE ACTIVITIES Choral, Concert Band, Dance, Debate, Drama Groups, Ethnic & Cultural Groups, Film, Jazz Band, Music Groups, Musical Theater, Newspaper, Radio/TV station, Sororities, Student Government, Yearbook

Cazenovia College
Learning Center
Cazenovia, New York 13035
(315) 655-9446

School Enrollment: **1,000** Male: **100** Female: **900**
LD Enrollment: **60** Male: **10** Female: **50**

Admissions Contact: **Dr. James Parker, VP of Enrollment Mngt.**
LD Contact: **Faith M. Cobb, Ph.D., Coordinator Special Services**
Telephone:**(315) 655-9446 Ext. 176**

Admissions

Application Information:
Application deadline: **Priority given prior to March 1st**
Applicant must apply **No limit** months in advance
Rolling Admissions: **Yes**

Secondary School Information
Most Important Criteria For Admissions (1-strongest)

SAT/ACT	Application **1**	School transcript
Class rank	Course selection	Personal statement
Interview	Extra activities	Psychoeducational
G.P.A.	Open admission	Recommendations

Test Requirements:
Standardized tests waived: **Yes**
Untimed SAT: **Yes** Untimed ACT: **Yes** Untimed ACH: **Yes**
WAIS-R required: **Yes**
Documentation of LD required: **Yes**
Currency of diagnostic testing: **30 months**
Tests recommended: **Intellectual and educational diagnosis by certified psychologist.**

Types of Disabilities Served
- Speech/Lang
- Study skills
- Written express
- Organizational
- Perceptual
- Reading
- Spelling
- Math
- Fine Motor
- ADD with LD
- ADD without LD
- ADHD with LD
- ADHD without LD

Admissions Process

File application, forward transcript, arrange campus visit with appointment with Coordinator of Special Services, bring documenting data, acceptance/approval contingent upon meeting/review by Admissions Committee.

High School Course Requirements:
Waivers to standard high school courses
Foreign Language : **Yes** Course substitution: **Yes**

Learning Disability Program
Program: Reinforces course work: **Yes**
Program available through:**As long as needed**
Services only for LD students: **Yes**
Services available for all students: **Yes**
Counseling: Individual: **Yes** Vocational Counseling: **Yes**

Faculty:
Faculty: **2** Full time: **1** Part time: **1** M.A.: **1** Ph.D.: **1**
Faculty advocate: **Yes** Meets with instructor: **As needed**

Diagnostic Testing

ADD	Personality	Perceptual skills	Spelling
ADHD	Organization	Fine motor skills	Reading
I.Q.	Handwriting	Spoken language	Study skills
Math	Social skills	Written language	

Tutoring:
Average size of group tutorials: **1 on 1**
Services rendered by:
Graduates •Peers •Faculty •LD staff Teacher trainees

Tutorials

Grp.	Ind. Tutorials	Grp.	Ind. Tutorials
•	Math skills	•	Word processing
	Study skills	•	Time management
	Language arts	•	Learning strategies
	Written express	•	Organizational skills

Academic Accommodations

Curriculum	Study Aids	Exams
Priority registration	Typist	• Oral
Math waiver	Reader	• Untimed
Foreign lang. waiver	• Notetaker	Take home
Course substitution	• Proof reader	• With proctor
In Class	• Text on tape	On computer
• Calculators	Early syllabus	• Extended time
• Tape recorder	Taped handouts	On tape
• Word processor		Modified
• Priority seating		• Separate room

Graduation Requirements:
Course credits: **2 years-60 - 4 years 127** GPA: **2.0** Years to complete degree: **2-1/2 or 5** Language waiver: **Yes**
Other requirements: **Student must complete successful courses in composition, effective speaking and math/science and have proper distribution for their major.**

General Information:
Cazenovia College is a 2 and 4 year independent college. Suburban campus 10 miles from Syracuse. Accessible by air, train or bus. Ski areas are 8 miles from campus. Beaches are 10 miles from campus. 5% of students are foreign. 4 residential halls on campus. Housing is not guaranteed.25 % of students remain on campus for the weekends.

Accreditation:NYSED, MSACS

Expenses:
Tuition: In-state: Full year: $8,030.00. Part-time: Per credit:$175.00. Part-time: Per course: $525.00. Tuition: Out-of-state: Full year: $8,030.00. Part-time: Per credit:$175.00. Part-time: Per course:$525.00 Room and board: $4,100.00

Majors
• ARTS Commercial Art, Fashion Design, Interior Design • BUSINESS Accounting, Business Management, Fashion Merchandising • EDUCATION Child Development, Early Childhood • HUMANITIES Liberal Arts • SCIENCES Equestrian Studies • SOCIAL SCIENCES Human Service • VISUAL AND PERFORMING ARTS Studio Art • VOCATIONAL Office Administration, Secretarial

Sports/Activities
• SPORTS RELATED Cheerleading, Team Managers • SPORTS-INTERCOLLEGIATE Basketball (F), Basketball (M), Golf (M), Horseback

Riding, Soccer (F), Soccer (M), Softball (F), Tennis (F), Tennis (M), Volleyball (F) • SPORTS-INTRAMURAL Basketball (M), Football, Flag, Softball (M), Volleyball • STUDENT LIFE ACTIVITIES Choral, Drama Groups, Ethnic & Cultural Groups, Radio/TV station, Student Government, Yearbook

---

Selective **New York**
Accommodations

City University New York: Brooklyn College

1602 William James Hall
Brooklyn, New York 11210
(718) 780-5001

School Enrollment: **11,326** Male: **4,680** Female: **6,646**
LD Enrollment: **42**

Admissions Contact: **M. Booufall Tynan, Assoc. Dir. Recruitment**
LD Contact: **Barbara Sirois, Coordinator**
Name of Program: **Disabilities Services**
Telephone:**(718) 780-5001**

Admissions

Application Information:
Application deadline: **None**
Rolling Admissions: **Yes** Notified when: **Rolling**

Secondary School Information
Most Important Criteria For Admissions (1-strongest)

1 SAT/ACT	**4** Application	School transcript
1 Class rank	**2** Course selection	**11** Personal statement
11 Interview	**10** Extra activities	Psychoeducational
1 G.P.A.	Open admission	**3** Recommendations

Types of Disabilities Served
- Speech/Lang
- Study skills
- Written express
- Organizational
- Perceptual
- Reading
- Spelling
- Math
- Fine Motor
- ADD with LD
- ADD without LD
- ADHD with LD
- ADHD without LD

Learning Disability Program
Students mainstreamed **100** % of the day
Support groups are available:**Yes**

Faculty:
Faculty: **1** Including Director: **Yes** Full time: **1** M.A.: **1**
Faculty advocate: **Yes** Meets with instructor: **As necessary**

Diagnostic Testing

ADD	Personality	Perceptual skills	Spelling
ADHD	Organization	Fine motor skills	Reading
• I.Q.	Handwriting	Spoken language	Study skills
Math	Social skills	Written language	

Tutoring:
Services rendered by:

Graduates	Peers	Faculty	•LD staff	Teacher trainees

Tutorials

Grp.	Ind.	Tutorials	Grp.	Ind.	Tutorials
		Math skills			Word processing
		Study skills			Time management
		Language arts	•	•	Learning strategies
•	•	Written express	•	•	Organizational skills

Academic Accommodations

Curriculum	Study Aids	Exams
• Priority registration	• Typist	• Oral
Math waiver	• Reader	Untimed
• Foreign lang. waiver	• Notetaker	Take home
• Course substitution	• Proof reader	• With proctor
In Class	• Text on tape	• On computer
• Calculators	• Early syllabus	• Extended time
• Tape recorder	Taped handouts	On tape
• Word processor		• Modified
• Priority seating		• Separate room

Graduation Requirements: Language waiver: **Yes**

Program Strengths
We supply reasonable accommodations for the motivated LD student.

General Information:
City University New York: Brooklyn College is a 4 year public college. Urban campus of 26 acres is Accessible by train or bus. Ski areas are 3 hours from campus. Beaches are 40 minutes from campus. 4% of students are foreign. Housing is not guaranteed.4 % of students join fraternities/sororities.

Accreditation:MSACS

Expenses:
Tuition: In-state: Full year: $1,850.00. Part-time: Per credit:$77.00. Tuition: Out-of-state: Full year: $4,450.00. Part-time: Per credit:$187.00.

Majors
• AREA STUDIES African, American, Asian, Black/Afro-American, Caribbean, Hispanic/American, Jewish, Latin American, Middle Eastern • ARTS Art History, Dance • BUSINESS Accounting, Business Management • COMMUNICATIONS Broadcasting, Creative Writing, Journalism • COMPUTER SCIENCE Computer Mathematics, Computer Science • EDUCATION Bilingual, Early Childhood, Elementary, English, English As A Second Language , Foreign Language, Health, Mathematics, Music, Physical, Secondary, Speech/Language • HEALTH SCIENCES Health, Speech/Audiology and Speech • HUMANITIES Classics, English/Writing/Literature, Philosophy • LANGUAGES Arabic, Chinese, English, French, German, Greek, Hebrew, Italian, Linguistic, Russian, Spanish • MATHEMATICS Actuarial, Applied • PREPROFESSIONAL Dentistry, Engineering, Law, Medicine • RELIGIOUS STUDIES Judaism & Jewish Studies • SCIENCES Archeology, Biology, Chemistry, Geology, Physical Chemistry • SOCIAL SCIENCES Anthropology, History, Political Science, Psychology, Sociology • SPECIAL EDUCATION Emotionally Disturbed, Mentally Retarded, Physically Handicapped • VISUAL AND PERFORMING ARTS Art, Art History, Dance, Music, Music Performance, Theater • VOCATIONAL Food Service, Home Economics

Sports/Activities
GIATE Archery, Baseball (M), Basketball, Cross Country, Fencing, Soccer (M), Softball (F), Swimming, Tennis, Track and Field, Volleyball (F) • SPORTS-INTRAMURAL Badminton (F), Basketball, Fencing (F), Racquetball, Soccer (M), Softball (F), Tennis, Track and Field (F), Volleyball (F), Volleyball (M), Water Polo • STUDENT LIFE ACTIVITIES Academic Clubs, Choral, Dance, Debate, Drama Groups, Ethnic & Cultural Groups, Fraternities, Music Groups, Musical Theater, Newspaper, Religious Organization, Sororities, Student Government, Yearbook

Selective

City University of New York: College of Staten Island
715 Ocean Terrace
Staten Island, New York 10301
(718) 390-7557

School Enrollment: **9,000** Male: **4,000** Female: **5,000**
LD Enrollment: **61**

Admissions Contact: **Raymond Hulsey, Director of Admissions**
LD Contact: **Dr. Audrey Glynn, Director**
Name of Program: **Special Student Services**
Telephone:**(718) 390-7626**

Admissions

Application Information:
Rolling Admissions: **Yes**

Secondary School Information
Most Important Criteria For Admissions (1-strongest)

SAT/ACT	Application	School transcript
Class rank	Course selection	Personal statement
Interview	Extra activities	Psychoeducational
G.P.A.	Open admission	Recommendations

Test Requirements:
Documentation of LD required: **Yes**

Types of Disabilities Served
- Speech/Lang
- Study skills
- Written express
- Organizational
- Perceptual
- Reading
- Spelling
- Math
- Fine Motor
- ADD with LD
- ADD without LD
- ADHD with LD
- ADHD without LD

Learning Disability Program

Program: Remedial: **Yes**
Program: Reinforces course work: **Yes**
Students mainstreamed **100** % of the day
Recommended credits per semester: **8-9**
Counseling: Individual: **Yes** Group Counseling: **Yes** Vocational Counseling: **Yes**

Faculty:
Faculty advocate: **Yes** Meets with instructor: **As needed**

Diagnostic Testing

ADD	Personality	Perceptual skills	Spelling
ADHD	Organization	Fine motor skills	Reading
I.Q.	Handwriting	Spoken language	Study skills
Math	Social skills	Written language	

Tutoring:
Services rendered by:
Graduates   Peers   •Faculty   •LD staff   Teacher trainees

Tutorials

Grp.	Ind.	Tutorials	Grp.	Ind.	Tutorials
	•	Math skills		•	Word processing
	•	Study skills		•	Time management
	•	Language arts		•	Learning strategies
	•	Written express		•	Organizational skills

Academic Accommodations

Curriculum	Study Aids	Exams
Priority registration	• Typist	• Oral
Math waiver	Reader	Untimed
Foreign lang. waiver	• Notetaker	Take home
• Course substitution	• Proof reader	• With proctor
In Class	• Text on tape	On computer
• Calculators	Early syllabus	• Extended time
• Tape recorder	Taped handouts	On tape
• Word processor		• Modified
Priority seating		Separate room

Graduation Requirements:
Course credits: **128** GPA: **2.0** Years to complete degree: **6** Math waiver: **Yes** Language waiver: **Yes**

Program Strengths
Once identified, students who are learning disabled receive orientation, counseling and advisement. Once requested, students receive tutoring and other support services. The office will also serve as Advocate with the faculty to determine reasonable accommodations.

General Information:
City University of New York: College of Staten Island is a 2 and 4 year public University. Urban campus Accessible by air, train, bus or ferry. Ski areas are 100 miles from campus. Beaches are 2-10 miles from campus. 4% of students are foreign. Housing is not guaranteed.

Accreditation:MSACS

Expenses:
Tuition: In-state: Full year: $1,950.00. Part-time: Per credit:$77.00. Tuition: Out-of-state: Full year: $4,450.00. Part-time: Per credit:$187.00.

Majors
• AREA STUDIES American, International Studies • ARTS Film & Video, Neuroscience • BUSINESS Accounting, Economics, Management, Marketing, Secretarial Science • COMMUNICATIONS Communication, Creative Writing, English, Literature • COMPUTER SCIENCE Computer Maintenance, Computer Science • EDUCATION Early Childhood, Elementary, English, Foreign Language, Mathematics, Secondary, Social Studies, Special • ENGINEERING Engineering Science • HEALTH SCIENCES Medical Assistant, Medical Laboratory Technology, Nursing, Physical Therapy • HUMANITIES English/Writing/Literature, Liberal Arts • LANGUAGES French, Italian, Spanish • MATHEMATICS Theoretical • PREPROFESSIONAL Business, Engineering • SCIENCES Biochemistry, Biology, Chemistry, Computer Science, Physics • SOCIAL SCIENCES Anthropology, Government/Political, History, International Studies, Political Science, Psychology, Sociology • VISUAL AND PERFORMING ARTS Art, Art History, Dramatic Arts • VOCATIONAL Business and Office, Park/Recreation, Secretarial

Sports/Activities
• SPORTS-INTERCOLLEGIATE Baseball (M), Basketball, Fencing (F), Soccer (M), Softball (F), Tennis, Volleyball (F) • SPORTS-INTRAMURAL Badminton, Baseball (M), Basketball, Bowling, Fencing, Golf, Ping-Pong, Racquetball, Skiing - Snow, Soccer (M), Softball (F), Swimming, Track and Field • STUDENT LIFE ACTIVITIES Choral, Drama Groups, Ethnic & Cultural Groups, Film, Magazine, Music Groups, Newspaper, Radio/TV station, Religious Organization, Student Government, Yearbook

Highly Selective

City University of New York: City College
Convent Avenue at 138th Street
New York, New York 10031
(212) 650-6977

School Enrollment: **10,918** Male: **6,257** Female: **4,661**
LD Enrollment: **36**

Admissions Contact: **Alan Sabal, Director of Admissions**
LD Contact: **Frances Geteles, Professor**
Name of Program: **Disabled Student Services**
Telephone:**(212) 650-4264**

Admissions

Application Information:
Application deadline: **March lst/November 1st**
Rolling Admissions: **Yes**

Secondary School Information
Most Important Criteria For Admissions (1-strongest)

	SAT/ACT	Application	**1** School transcript
3	Class rank	Course selection	Personal statement
4	Interview	Extra activities	Psychoeducational
2	G.P.A.	Open admission	Recommendations

Types of Disabilities Served
- Speech/Lang
- Study skills
- Written express
- Organizational
  Perceptual
- Reading
- Spelling
- Math
  Fine Motor

ADD with LD
ADD without LD
ADHD with LD
ADHD without LD

Learning Disability Program
Counseling: Individual: **Yes**

Faculty:
Faculty: **4** Part time: **4**
Faculty advocate: **Yes** Meets with instructor: **As needed**

Diagnostic Testing

ADD	Personality	Perceptual skills	Spelling
ADHD	Organization	Fine motor skills	Reading
I.Q.	Handwriting	Spoken language	Study skills
Math	Social skills	Written language	

Tutoring:
Services rendered by:
•Graduates •Peers Faculty LD staff Teacher trainees

Tutorials

Grp.	Ind.	Tutorials	Grp.	Ind.	Tutorials
	•	Math skills		•	Word processing
	•	Study skills		•	Time management
	•	Language arts		•	Learning strategies
	•	Written express		•	Organizational skills

Academic Accommodations

Curriculum	Study Aids	Exams
Priority registration	Typist	• Oral
• Math waiver	Reader	Untimed
• Foreign lang. waiver	• Notetaker	Take home
Course substitution	Proof reader	With proctor
In Class	• Text on tape	On computer
Calculators	Early syllabus	• Extended time
• Tape recorder	Taped handouts	On tape
• Word processor		Modified
Priority seating		Separate room

Program Strengths
The three aspects of the Disabled Student Services are referrals, tutoring and supportive counseling.

General Information:
City University of New York: City College is a 4 year public college. Urban campus. of 34 acres is Accessible by air, train, or bus. Ski areas are 100 miles from campus. Beaches are 25 miles from campus. 10% of students are foreign. Housing is not guaranteed.

Accreditation:MSACS

SAT/ACT Scores:
Scores for incoming freshmen:**Verbal:**below 500.

Expenses:
Tuition: In-state: Full year: $1,250.00. Part-time: Per credit:$47.00. Tuition: Out-of-state: Full year: $4,050.00. Part-time: Per credit:$82.00.

Majors
• AREA STUDIES African, Asian, Black/Afro-American, Caribbean, European, Jewish, Latin American, Mexican/American, Puerto Rican Studies, Russian/Slavic • BUSINESS Business Management, Economics, Management • COMMUNICATIONS Advertising, Broadcasting, Communication, Creative Writing, English, Journalism, Linguistic, Literature, Photography, Speech, Television/Radio/Film • COMPUTER SCIENCE Computer Science • EDUCATION Bilingual, Elementary, Foreign Language, Industrial, Mathematics, Physical, Science, Secondary, Social Studies, Special, Speech/Language • ENGINEERING Aerospace, Chemical, Civil/Environmental, Computer, Electrical, Mechanical • HEALTH SCIENCES Health, Medical Assistant, Nursing, Speech Therapy, Speech/Audiology and Speech • HUMANITIES Classics, English/Writing/Literature, Philosophy • LANGUAGES Arabic, French, German, Greek, Hebrew, Italian, Latin, Russian, Spanish • PREPROFESSIONAL Architecture, Dentistry, Engineering, Law, Medicine, Veterinarian • SCIENCES Astronomy, Biochemistry, Biology, Chemistry, Earth, Geography, Geology, Marine Biology, Mathematics, Meteorology, Oceanography, Physical Science, Physics • SOCIAL SCIENCES Anthropology, Government/Political, History, International Studies, Political Science, Psychology, Social Sciences, Sociology • VISUAL AND PERFORMING ARTS Art History, Dance, Dramatic Arts, Music, Studio Art, Video • VOCATIONAL Industrial Design, Landscape Architecture

Sports/Activities
• SPORTS RELATED Marching Band • SPORTS-INTERCOLLEGIATE Baseball (M), Basketball, Cross Country, Diving, Fencing, Gymnastics, Lacrosse (M), Soccer (M), Softball (F), Swimming, Tennis, Track and Field, Volleyball (F), Wrestling (M) • SPORTS-INTRAMURAL Badminton, Baseball, Basketball, Bowling, Fencing, Gymnastics, Hand Ball, Ping-Pong, Soccer (M), Softball, Swimming, Tennis, Track and Field, Volleyball • STUDENT LIFE ACTIVITIES Choral, Dance, Debate, Drama Groups, Ethnic & Cultural Groups, Film, Fraternities, Jazz Band, Music Groups, Musical Theater, Newspaper, Political Groups, Radio/TV station, Religious Organization, Student Government, Symphony Orchestra, Yearbook

Less Selective

City University of New York: Borough of Manhattan Community College
199 Chambers Street
New York, New York 10007
(212) 618-1228

School Enrollment: **14,500** Male: **5,800** Female: **8,700**

Admissions Contact: **Dennis Bonner, Director of Admissions**
LD Contact: **Prof. John Little, Counselor**
Name of Program: **Student Life Department**

Admissions

Application Information:
Application deadline: **None**
Rolling Admissions: **Yes**

Secondary School Information
Most Important Criteria For Admissions (1-strongest)

SAT/ACT	**2** Application	**1**	School transcript
Class rank	Course selection		Personal statement
Interview	Extra activities		Psychoeducational
G.P.A.	**1** Open admission		Recommendations

Test Requirements:
Standardized tests waived: **Yes**

Types of Disabilities Served
- Speech/Lang
- Study skills
- Written express
- Organizational
- Perceptual
- Reading
- Spelling
- Math
- Fine Motor
- ADD with LD
- ADD without LD
- ADHD with LD
- ADHD without LD

Learning Disability Program
Counseling: Individual: **Yes** Group Counseling: **Yes**

Diagnostic Testing

ADD	Personality	Perceptual skills	Spelling
ADHD	Organization	Fine motor skills	Reading
I.Q.	Handwriting	Spoken language	Study skills
Math	Social skills	Written language	

Tutoring:
Average size of group tutorials: **6-8**
Services rendered by:
- Graduates •Peers •Faculty •LD staff Teacher trainees

Tutorials

Grp.	Ind.	Tutorials	Grp.	Ind.	Tutorials
•	•	Math skills	•	•	Word processing
•	•	Study skills	•	•	Time management
•	•	Language arts	•	•	Learning strategies
•	•	Written express	•	•	Organizational skills

Academic Accommodations

Curriculum	Study Aids	Exams
Priority registration	Typist	Oral
Math waiver	Reader	Untimed
Foreign lang. waiver	Notetaker	Take home
Course substitution	Proof reader	With proctor
In Class	Text on tape	On computer
Calculators	Early syllabus	Extended time
Tape recorder	Taped handouts	On tape
Word processor		Modified
Priority seating		Separate room

Program Strengths
We do not have a formal LD admissions; however, once admitted the student is advised by Prof. Little of the Student Life Department. We also have a Learning Resource Center under the direction of Mr. James Tynes.

General Information:
City University of New York: Borough of Manhattan Community College is a 2 year public college. Urban campus. of 26 acres is Accessible by air, train or bus. Housing is not guaranteed.

Accreditation:MSACS

Expenses:
Tuition: In-state: Full year: $612.50. Part-time: Per credit:$40.00. Tuition: Out-of-state: Full year: $1,012.50. Part-time: Per credit:$76.00. Part-time: Per course: Room and board: Cost of LD program:

Majors
• BUSINESS Accounting, Business Administration, Management, Marketing, Real Estate, Travel/Tourism Management • COMPUTER SCIENCE Data Processing, Telecommunications • EDUCATION Early Childhood, Pre-Education • HEALTH SCIENCES Emergency Medical Technician, Medical Records Technology • HUMANITIES Liberal Arts • SOCIAL SCIENCES Human Service, Public Relations • VOCATIONAL Business and Office, Legal Secretary, Park/Recreation, Respiratory Therapy Technology

Sports/Activities
• SPORTS-INTERCOLLEGIATE Baseball (M), Basketball, Bowling, Diving, Fencing, Golf (M), Soccer (M), Softball (M), Swimming, Tennis, Track and Field, Volleyball, Water Polo (M), Wrestling (M) • SPORTS-INTRAMURAL Gymnastics, Skiing - Snow • STUDENT LIFE ACTIVITIES Choral, Dance, Drama Groups, Ethnic & Cultural Groups, Fraternities, Jazz Band, Magazine, Music Groups, Newspaper, Political Groups, Radio/TV station, Religious Organization, Sororities, Student Government, Yearbook

---

City University of New York: John Jay-Criminal Justice

445 West 59th Street
New York, New York 10019
(212) 237-8122

School Enrollment: **8,522** Male: **4,330** Female: **4,192**
LD Enrollment: **35**

Admissions Contact: **Frank Marouser, Dean**
LD Contact: **Farris Forsythe, Dir. Serv. for Stud. with Disabilities**
Name of Program: **Services for Students with Disabilities**
Address: **445 West 59th Street**
Telephone:**(212) 237-8122**

Admissions

Application Information:
Enrolled:**35**
Rolling Admissions: **Yes**Notified when: **March 1st**

Secondary School Information
Most Important Criteria For Admissions (1-strongest)

5 SAT/ACT	1 Application	2 School transcript
4 Class rank	12 Course selection	12 Personal statement
12 Interview	12 Extra activities	12 Psychoeducational
3 G.P.A.	Open admission	12 Recommendations

Test Requirements:
Diagnostic testing waived: **Yes**
Documentation of LD required: **Yes**
Currency of diagnostic testing: **12 months**

Types of Disabilities Served
- Speech/Lang
- Study skills
- Written express
- Organizational
- Perceptual
- Reading
- Spelling
- Math
- Fine Motor
- ADD with LD
- ADD without LD
- ADHD with LD
- ADHD without LD

High School Course Requirements:
English: **4** Math: **3** Science: **2** Foreign Language: **1**
Waivers to standard high school courses
Foreign Language : **Yes** Math: **Yes** Course substitution: **Yes**

Learning Disability Program

Special orientation for LD students: **No**
Program: Reinforces course work: **Yes**
Students mainstreamed **100** % of the day
Recommended credits per semester: **9-12**
Counseling: Individual: **Yes** Group Counseling: **Yes** Vocational Counseling: **Yes**
Support groups are available:**Yes**

Faculty:
Faculty: **4** Full time: **1** Part time: **3**
LD faculty with: BS/BA: **2** M.A.: **1** Ph.D.: **1**
Faculty advocate: **Yes** Meets with instructor: **2-3x per semester**

Diagnostic Testing
- ADD
- ADHD
- I.Q.
- Math
- Personality
- Organization
- Handwriting
- Social skills
- Perceptual skills
- Fine motor skills
- Spoken language
- Written language
- Spelling
- Reading
- Study skills

Tutoring:
Average size of group tutorials: **2**
Services rendered by:
- Graduates
- Peers
- Faculty
- LD staff
- Teacher trainees

Tutorials

Grp.	Ind.	Tutorials	Grp.	Ind.	Tutorials
	•	Math skills		•	Word processing
	•	Study skills		•	Time management
		Language arts		•	Learning strategies
•	•	Written express		•	Organizational skills

Academic Accommodations

Curriculum
- Priority registration
- Math waiver
- Foreign lang. waiver
- Course substitution

In Class
- Calculators
- Tape recorder
- Word processor
- Priority seating

Study Aids
- Typist
- Reader
- Notetaker
- Proof reader
- Text on tape
- Early syllabus
- Taped handouts

Exams
- Oral
- Untimed
- Take home
- With proctor
- On computer
- Extended time
- On tape
- Modified
- Separate room

Graduation Requirements:
Course credits: **128** GPA: **2.0**

Program Strengths
Diagnostic testing is available for students/faculty who suspect a student has a learning disability. All services are tailored to the individual needs of each student. Students are fully mainstreamed with support services available and as recommended by the learning specialist.

General Information:
City University of New York: John Jay-Criminal Justice is a 2 and 4 year public college. Urban campus of 5 acres is Accessible by air, train or bus. Ski areas are 40 miles from campus. Beaches are 6 miles from campus. .4% of students are foreign. Housing is not guaranteed.

Accreditation:MSACS

Expenses:
Tuition: In-state: Full year: $925.00 per semester. Part-time: Per credit:$77.00. Part-time: Per course: $231.00. Tuition: Out-of-state: Full year: $2,225.00 per semester. Part-time: Per credit:$187.00. Part-time: Per course:$561.00

Majors
• COMPUTER SCIENCE Computer Mathematics, Computer Science, Programming, Systems Analysis • PRE PROFESSIONAL Law • SOCIAL SCIENCES Criminal Justice, Criminology, Government/Political, Law Enforcement, Psychology, Sociology • VOCATIONAL Fire Science

Sports/Activities
• SPORTS RELATED Cheerleading, Team Managers • SPORTS-INTERCOLLEGIATE Baseball (M), Basketball, Basketball (F), Basketball (M), Cross Country, Cross Country (F), Cross Country (M), Judo, Karate, Marching Band, Riflery, Riflery (F), Riflery (M), Soccer, Soccer (M), Softball, Softball (F), Swimming, Swimming (F), Swimming (M), Tennis, Tennis (F), Tennis (M), Volleyball, Volleyball (F), Wrestling, Wrestling (M)

• SPORTS-INTRAMURAL Baseball (M), Basketball, Basketball (F), Basketball (M), Football, Football (F), Football (M), Hand Ball, Hand Ball (M), Judo, Karate, Martial Arts, Racquetball, Racquetball (F), Racquetball (M), Riflery, Riflery (F), Riflery (M), Scuba, Soccer, Soccer (F), Soccer (M), Softball, Softball (F), Softball (M), Swimming, Swimming (F), Swimming (M), Volleyball, Volleyball (F), Volleyball (M), Weight Lifting, Weight Lifting (M) • STUDENT LIFE ACTIVITIES Academic Clubs, Choral, Community Service, Dance, Debate, Drama Groups, Ethnic & Cultural Groups, Film, Newspaper, Political Groups, Radio/TV station, Religious Organization, Student Government, Yearbook

Less Selective	New York Program

City University of New York: La Guardia Community College
31-10 Thomson Avenue
Long Island City, New York 11101
(718) 482-7206

School Enrollment: **9,231** Male: **2,309** Female: **6,922**
LD Enrollment: **810**

Admissions Contact: **Linda Tobash, Director of Admissions**
Name of Program: **Learning Project**
Telephone:**(718) 482-5288**

Admissions

Application Information:
Application deadline: **Rolling**
Rolling Admissions: **Yes**

Secondary School Information
Most Important Criteria For Admissions (1-strongest)

SAT/ACT	Application	School transcript
Class rank	Course selection	Personal statement
Interview	Extra activities	Psychoeducational
G.P.A.	**1** Open admission	Recommendations

Test Requirements:
Diagnostic testing waived: **Yes**
Tests recommended: **City University of New York Freshman Skills Assessment Placement**

Types of Disabilities Served
- Speech/Lang
- Study skills
- Written express
- Organizational
- Perceptual
- Reading
- Spelling
- Math
- Fine Motor
- ADD with LD
- ADD without LD
- ADHD with LD
- ADHD without LD

Learning Disability Program
Program: Remedial: **Yes**
Program: Reinforces course work: **Yes**
Students mainstreamed **100** % of the day
Counseling: Individual: **Yes** Group Counseling: **Yes**

Faculty:
Faculty: **3** Full time: **1** Part time: **2** M.A.: **2** Ph.D.: **1**
Faculty advocate: **Yes** Meets with instructor: **Often**

Diagnostic Testing
ADD • Personality	• Perceptual skills	• Spelling
ADHD• Organization	• Fine motor skills	• Reading
• I.Q. • Handwriting	• Spoken language	• Study skills
• Math • Social skills	• Written language	

Tutoring:
Average size of group tutorials: **3**
Services rendered by:
•Graduates •Peers •Faculty •LD staff Teacher trainees

Tutorials
Grp.	Ind.	Tutorials	Grp.	Ind.	Tutorials
•	•	Math skills		•	Word processing
•	•	Study skills	•	•	Time management
•	•	Language arts	•	•	Learning strategies
•	•	Written express	•	•	Organizational skills

Academic Accommodations
Curriculum	Study Aids	Exams
Priority registration	• Typist	• Oral
Math waiver	Reader	Untimed
Foreign lang. waiver	• Notetaker	• Take home
Course substitution	• Proof reader	With proctor
In Class	• Text on tape	On computer
• Calculators	Early syllabus	• Extended time
• Tape recorder	Taped handouts	On tape
• Word processor		• Modified
Priority seating		Separate room

General Information:
City University of New York: La Guardia Community College is a 2 year public college. Urban campus. New York City. Accessible by air, train or bus. 8% of students are foreign. Housing is not guaranteed.

Accreditation:MSACS

Expenses:
Tuition: In-state: Full year: $1,225.00. Part-time: Per credit:$40.00. Tuition: Out-of-state: Full year: $2,025.00. Part-time: Per credit:$76.00.

Majors
• BUSINESS Accounting, Business Administration, Business Management, Food Management, Management, Secretarial Science, Travel/Tourism Management • COMMUNICATIONS Journalism, Photography • COMPUTER SCIENCE Computer Maintenance, Computer Science, Computer Technology, Data Processing, Programming, Telecommunications • EDUCATION Bilingual, Child Development, Early Childhood, Teacher Aide • HEALTH SCIENCES EMT, Nursing, Nutritional/Food, Occupational Therapy Assistant, Physical Therapy Assistant • HUMANITIES Liberal Arts • PREPROFESSIONAL Recreation, Veterinarian • SCIENCES Animal, Gerontology • SOCIAL SCIENCES Human Service • VOCATIONAL Business and Office, Court Reporting, Funeral/Mortuary, Legal Secretary, Secretarial

Sports/Activities
• SPORTS-INTRAMURAL Badminton, Basketball, Bowling, Hand Ball, Ping-Pong, Soccer, Softball, Swimming, Volleyball • STUDENT LIFE ACTIVITIES Choral, Concert Band, Dance, Drama Groups, Ethnic & Cultural Groups, Jazz Band, Music Groups, Newspaper, Radio/TV station, Student Government, Yearbook

Clinton Community College

Plattsburgh, New York 12901-4297
(518) 561-6650

School Enrollment: **2,020** Male: **800** Female: **1,120**
LD Enrollment: **26** Male: **14** Female: **12**

Admissions Contact: **Nora Germain, Dean Enrollment Management**
LD Contact: **Robert C. Wood, Counselor**

Admissions

Application Information:
Application deadline: **Rolling**
Rolling Admissions: **Yes**

Secondary School Information
Most Important Criteria For Admissions (1-strongest)

SAT/ACT	**1**	Application	**4** School transcript
Class rank	**7**	Course selection	**5** Personal statement
2 Interview	**8**	Extra activities	**3** Psychoeducational
6 G.P.A.		Open admission	**9** Recommendations

Test Requirements:
Standardized tests waived: **Yes**
Diagnostic testing waived: **Yes**
Range accepted: **90+**
Documentation of LD required: **Yes**
Tests recommended: **Full Psychological or Psychoeducational Evaluation recommended**

Types of Disabilities Served
- Speech/Lang
- Study skills
- Written express
- Organizational
- Perceptual
- Reading
- Spelling
- Math
- Fine Motor
- ADD with LD
- ADD without LD
- ADHD with LD
- ADHD without LD

Admissions Process

Open admissions for all programs except Nursing and Medical Laboratory Technology.

High School Course Requirements:

Learning Disability Program

Program: Reinforces course work: **Yes**
Students mainstreamed **100** % of the day
Time required or recommended in learning center:
Services only for LD students: **Yes**
Counseling: Individual: **Yes** Group Counseling: **Yes**
Support groups are available:**Learning Challenge Club**

Diagnostic Testing

ADD	Personality	Perceptual skills	• Spelling
ADHD	Organization	Fine motor skills	• Reading
I.Q.	Handwriting	Spoken language	• Study skills
• Math	Social skills	• Written language	

Tutoring:
Average size of group tutorials: **3**
Services rendered by:
•Graduates •Peers •Faculty •LD staff Teacher trainees

Tutorials

Grp.	Ind.	Tutorials	Grp.	Ind.	Tutorials
•	•	Math skills	•	•	Word processing
•	•	Study skills	•	•	Time management
•	•	Language arts	•	•	Learning strategies
•	•	Written express	•		Organizational skills

Academic Accommodations

Curriculum	Study Aids	Exams
• Priority registration	• Typist	• Oral
Math waiver	• Reader	• Untimed
• Foreign lang. waiver	• Notetaker	• Take home
• Course substitution	• Proof reader	• With proctor
In Class	• Text on tape	On computer
• Calculators	Early syllabus	• Extended time
• Tape recorder	Taped handouts	On tape
• Word processor		• Modified
• Priority seating		Separate room

Graduation Requirements:
Course credits: **64** GPA: **2.0**

Program Strengths
LD services are coordinated by the Counseling and Advisement Office. Services are individualized, the college's tutoring center provides assistance to support learning and accommodation needs.

General Information:
Clinton Community College is a 2 year public college. Rural campus of 100 acres is 60 miles from Montreal. Accessible by air, train or bus. Ski areas are 50 miles from campus. Beaches are 10 miles from campus. Housing is not guaranteed.

Accreditation:MSACS

Expenses:
Tuition: In-state: Full year: $1,400.00. Part-time: Per credit:$55.00. Part-time: Per course: $169.50. Tuition: Out-of-state: Full year: $2,800.00. Part-time: Per credit:$110.00.

Majors
• BUSINESS Accounting, Business Administration, Business Management, Hotel and Restaurant Management, Management • EDUCATION Physical • HEALTH SCIENCES Medical Technology, Nursing • HUMANITIES Humanities, Liberal Arts • SCIENCES Mathematics • SOCIAL SCIENCES Criminal Justice, Law Enforcement, Social Sciences • VOCATIONAL Business and Office, Office Administration, Secretarial

Sports/Activities
• SPORTS RELATED Chess • SPORTS-INTERCOLLEGIATE Baseball (M), Basketball, Ice Hockey (M), Soccer, Softball (F), Volleyball (F) • SPORTS-INTRAMURAL Bowling, Racquetball, Skiing - Snow, Tennis, Weight Lifting • STUDENT LIFE ACTIVITIES Academic Clubs, Choral, Drama Groups, Ethnic & Cultural Groups, Sororities, Student Government

Less Selective

Community College of the Finger Lakes
Lincoln Hill
Canandaigua, New York 14424-8399
(716) 394-3500

School Enrollment: **3,800**
LD Enrollment: **60**

Admissions Contact: **John M. Meuser, Director of Admissions**
LD Contact: **Peggy Smith, LD Coordinator**
Name of Program: **Services for LD Students**

Admissions

Application Information:
Application deadline: **August 1st**
Rolling Admissions: **Yes**Notified when: **3-4 weeks**

Secondary School Information
Most Important Criteria For Admissions (1-strongest)

SAT/ACT	Application	School transcript
Class rank	1 Course selection	Personal statement
Interview	Extra activities	Psychoeducational
1 G.P.A.	1 Open admission	Recommendations

Types of Disabilities Served
- Speech/Lang
- Study skills
- Written express
- Organizational
- Perceptual
- Reading
- Spelling
- Math
- Fine Motor
- ADD with LD
- ADD without LD
- ADHD with LD
- ADHD without LD

Faculty:
Faculty: **1** Part time: **1**
Faculty advocate: **Yes** Meets with instructor: **As needed**

Diagnostic Testing

ADD	Personality	Perceptual skills	Spelling
ADHD	Organization	Fine motor skills	Reading
I.Q.	Handwriting	Spoken language	Study skills
Math	Social skills	Written language	

Tutoring:
Services rendered by:
Graduates •Peers Faculty •LD staff Teacher trainees

Tutorials

Grp.	Ind.	Tutorials	Grp.	Ind.	Tutorials
•		Math skills	•		Word processing
•		Study skills	•	•	Time management
•		Language arts		•	Learning strategies
	•	Written express	•		Organizational skills

Academic Accommodations

Curriculum	Study Aids	Exams
Priority registration	Typist	Oral
Math waiver	Reader	Untimed
Foreign lang. waiver	• Notetaker	Take home
• Course substitution	• Proof reader	With proctor
In Class	• Text on tape	On computer
• Calculators	Early syllabus	• Extended time
• Tape recorder	Taped handouts	On tape
• Word processor		• Modified
Priority seating		Separate room

Program Strengths
CCFL does not offer a program for LD students. A combination of services is designed for each individual. Self-advocacy skills, strategies instruction, 12 hour course load and careful course selection are emphasized. The Developmental Studies Division and Learning Center play a central role in building up reading, writing, and study skills to college level.

General Information:
Community College of the Finger Lakes is a 2 year public college. Rural campus of 250 acres is 30 miles from Rochester. Accessible by bus. Ski areas are 20 miles from campus. Beaches are 1/4 mile from campus. 1% of students are foreign. 6 residential halls on campus. Housing is not guaranteed.30 % of students remain on campus for the weekends. 3 % of students join fraternities/sororities.

Accreditation:MSACS

Expenses:
Tuition: In-state: Full year: $1,375.00. Part-time: Per credit:$56.00. Tuition: Out-of-state: Full year: $2,700.00. Part-time: Per credit:$112.00. Room and board: $3,400.00

Majors
• BUSINESS Banking, Business Administration, Business Management, Hotel and Restaurant Management, Management, Marketing, Real Estate, Retailing, Secretarial Science, Travel/Tourism Management • COMMUNICATIONS Advertising, Broadcasting, Communication, Graphic Design Technology, Television/Radio/Film • COMPUTER SCIENCE Computer Maintenance, Data Processing, Programming • EDUCATION Early Childhood • ENGINEERING Electrical, Engineering Science, Mechanical • HEALTH SCIENCES Medical Secretary, Nursing • HUMANITIES Humanities, Liberal Arts • PREPROFESSIONAL Athletic Training, Forestry, Natural Resources, Wildlife • SCIENCES Biology, Chemistry, Horticultural, Mathematics, Physics • SOCIAL SCIENCES Criminal Justice, History, Law Enforcement, Psychology, Social Sciences • VISUAL AND PERFORMING ARTS Art, Dramatic Arts, Fine Arts, Music, Studio Art, Theater • VOCATIONAL Business and Office, Drafting, Landscape Architecture, Legal Secretary, Office Administration, Secretarial, Word Processing

Sports/Activities
• SPORTS-INTERCOLLEGIATE Baseball (M), Basketball, Cross Country, Soccer, Softball (F) • SPORTS-INTRAMURAL Basketball (M), Volleyball • STUDENT LIFE ACTIVITIES Academic Clubs, Choral, Drama Groups, Ethnic & Cultural Groups, Film, Fraternities, Music Groups, Musical Theater, Newspaper, Radio/TV station, Religious Organization, Sororities, Student Government

Most Selective

Cornell University
410 Thurston Avenue
Ithaca, New York 14850
(607) 255-5241

School Enrollment: **12,585** Male: **6,918** Female: **5,667**
LD Enrollment: **65**

Admissions Contact: **Nancy Meislahn, Director of Admissions**
LD Contact: **Joan B. Fisher, Coordinator**
Name of Program: **Disability Services**
Address: **234 Day Hall**
Telephone:**(607) 255-3976**

Admissions

Application Information:
Application deadline: **January 1st**
Notified when: **April 1st**

Secondary School Information
Most Important Criteria For Admissions (1-strongest)

2 SAT/ACT	**1** Application	**1** School transcript
1 Class rank	**1** Course selection	Personal statement
Interview	**2** Extra activities	Psychoeducational
2 G.P.A.	Open admission	**1** Recommendations

Test Requirements:
Standardized tests waived: **Yes**
Untimed SAT: **Yes**
Documentation of LD required: **Yes**
Currency of diagnostic testing: **3 years**

Types of Disabilities Served
- Speech/Lang
- Reading
- ADD with LD
- Study skills
- Spelling
- ADD without LD
- Written express
- Math
- ADHD with LD
- Organizational
- Fine Motor
- ADHD without LD
- Perceptual

Admissions Process

Same as admissions process for all students.

Learning Disability Program
Counseling: Individual: **Yes**

Faculty:
Faculty: **1** Full time: **1** M.A.: **1**
Faculty advocate: **Yes**

Diagnostic Testing

ADD	Personality	Perceptual skills	Spelling
ADHD	Organization	Fine motor skills	Reading
I.Q.	Handwriting	Spoken language	Study skills
Math	Social skills	Written language	

Tutoring:
Services rendered by:
- Graduates
- Peers
- Faculty
- LD staff
- Teacher trainees

Tutorials

Grp.	Ind.	Tutorials	Grp.	Ind.	Tutorials
•	•	Math skills	•	•	Word processing
•		Study skills	•		Time management
•	•	Language arts	•		Learning strategies
•		Written express	•		Organizational skills

Academic Accommodations

Curriculum	Study Aids	Exams
• Priority registration	• Typist	• Oral
Math waiver	• Reader	Untimed
• Foreign lang. waiver	• Notetaker	Take home
Course substitution	• Proof reader	• With proctor
In Class	• Text on tape	On computer
• Calculators	Early syllabus	• Extended time
• Tape recorder	Taped handouts	On tape
• Word processor		• Modified
• Priority seating		• Separate room

Graduation Requirements:
Course credits: **Varies** Language waiver: **Yes**
Other requirements: **Varies**

Program Strengths
All students applying to Cornell apply equally, they do not apply to an LD program. However, accepted students are provided with services based on the remediation suggestions outlined in their psycho-educational testing. There is also a peer support group which meets on a monthly basis.

General Information:
Cornell University is a 4 year private university. Rural Campus of 3,500 acres is 45 miles from Syracuse. Accessible by air or bus. Ski areas are 1/2 hour from campus. Beaches are 2 miles from campus. 11% of students are foreign. 44 residential halls on campus. Housing is guaranteed.Guaranteed through 1st year. 100 % of students remain on campus for the weekends. 35 % of students join fraternities/sororities.

Accreditation:MSACS

SAT/ACT Scores:
Scores for incoming freshmen:**Verbal:**12%below 500. 37%between 500 and 599. 42%between 600 and 699. 9%above 700. **Math:**1% below 500. 13% between 500 and 599. 41% between 600 and 699. 45%above 700. **ACT:** 21% below 20. 5% between 20 and 23. 8%between 24 and 25l. 29%between 26 and 28. 57% above 28.

Class Rank:
About 96% of the present freshmen class were in the upper 20% of their high school class. 99% were in the top 40% of their class. 100% were in the top 60% of their class. 100% were in the top 80% of their class.

Expenses:
Tuition: In-state: Full year: $17,276.00. Room and board: $5,676.00

Majors

• AGRICULTURE Business, Engineering, Plant Science • ANIMAL SCIENCE Poultry • AREA STUDIES African, Asian, Ethnic/Cultural, Hispanic/American, Islamic, Jewish/Judaism, Latin American, Russian/Slavic, Urban, Women's Studies • ARTS Dance, Design, Drawing, Fashion Design, Interior Design, Landscaping, Music, Photography, Sculpture • BUSINESS Accounting, Agricultural, Banking/Finance, Business Administration, Business Economics, Business Management, Business Statistics, Economics, Education, Fashion Merchandising, Food Management, Hotel & Restaurant Management, International Business, Labor Relations, Management, Marketing, Marketing Research, Organizational Behavior, Personnel, Real Estate, Sports Management, Travel/Tourism Management • COMMUNICATIONS Communication, English • COM-

PUTER SCIENCE Computer Science, Programming • CRAFTS AND DE-SIGN Apparel Design, Sculpture • EDUCATION Child Development, Early Childhood, Elementary • HEALTH SCIENCES Environmental, Nutritional/Food • HUMANITIES Classics, English/Writing/Literature, Fine Arts, Humanities, Liberal Arts, Philosophy, Religion • LANGUAGES English, French, German, Greek, Hebrew, Italian, Latin, Spanish • MATHEMATICS Applied, Computer, Statistical • PREPROFESSIONAL Architecture, Business, Engineering, Landscaping, Law, Medicine, Natural Resources, Social Work, Urban Design, Veterinarian • RELIGIOUS STUDIES Islamic, Judaism & Jewish Studies, Philosophy • SCIENCES Agricultural, Animal, Anthropology, Applied Mathematics, Astronomy, Biology, Botany, Cell Biology, Chemistry, Computer Science, Entomology, Genetics, Geology, Geophysical and Seismology, Gerontology, horticultural Human Biology, Inorganic Chemistry, Marine Biology, Mathematics, Microbiology, Molecular Biology, Nuclear Physics, Organic Chemistry, Physics, Plant Pathology, Poultry • VISUAL AND PERFORMING ARTS Art, Art History, Dance, Fine Arts, Music

Sports/Activities

• SPORTS RELATED Cheerleading, Marching Band, Pep Band, Team Managers • SPORTS-INTERCOLLEGIATE Baseball (M), Basketball, Crew, Cross Country, Diving, Field Hockey (F), Football (M), Golf (M), Hammer Throw, Ice Hockey, Lacrosse, Polo, Soccer, Squash (M), Swimming, Tennis, Track and Field, Volleyball (F), Wrestling (M) • SPORTS-INTRAMURAL Badminton, Basketball, Bowling, Cross Country, Fencing, Football, Golf, Ice Hockey, Lacrosse, Ping-Pong, Polo, Sailing, Skiing - Cross Country, Skiing - Snow, Soccer, Softball, Squash, Swimming, Tennis, Track and Field, Volleyball, Water Polo, Wrestling (M) • STUDENT LIFE ACTIVITIES Academic Clubs, Choral, Community Service, Concert Band, Dance, Debate, Drama Groups, Ethnic & Cultural Groups, Film, Fraternities, Jazz Band, Magazine, Music Groups, Musical Theater, Newspaper, Orchestra, Political Groups, Radio/TV station, Religious Organization, Sororities, Student Government, Symphony Orchestra, Yearbook

Selective	**New York**

New York Accommodations

D'Youville College

320 Porter Avenue
Buffalo, New York 14201
(716) 881-7600

School Enrollment: **1,581** Male: **309** Female: **1,272**
LD Enrollment: **6** Male: **2** Female: **4**

Admissions Contact: **Ronald Dannecker, Director of Admissions**
LD Contact: **Diane Stoelting, Counselor, Learning Center**
Name of Program: **Student Support Services**
Address: **320 Porter Avenue**
Telephone: **(716) 881-7690**

Admissions

Application Information:
Application deadline: **July 1st - December 1st**
Applicant must apply **1** months in advance
Rolling Admissions: **Yes** Notified when: **Within 30 days**

Secondary School Information
Most Important Criteria For Admissions (1-strongest)

2 SAT/ACT	**8** Application	**1** School transcript
2 Class rank	**3** Course selection	**7** Personal statement
4 Interview	**5** Extra activities	Psychoeducational
2 G.P.A.	Open admission	**6** Recommendations

Test Requirements:
Diagnostic testing waived: **Yes**
Untimed SAT: **Yes** Untimed ACT: **Yes**
Documentation of LD required: **Yes**
Currency of diagnostic testing: **No longer than 3 years old**

Types of Disabilities Served
- Speech/Lang
- Study skills
- Written express
- Organizational
- Perceptual
- Reading
- Spelling
- Math
- Fine Motor
- ADD with LD
- ADD without LD
- ADHD with LD
- ADHD without LD

Admissions Process

The admission decision is based on high school grade point average, rank in class, and scores on the SAT or ACT. Students who have difficulty meeting normal admission standards may be admitted with a reduced academic load.

High School Course Requirements:
English: **3** Math: **3** Science: **2** Foreign Language: **2**

Learning Disability Program

Program: Remedial: **Yes**
Program: Reinforces course work: **Yes**
Students mainstreamed **100** % of the day
Recommended credits per semester: **12-15**
Services available for all students: **Yes**
Counseling: Individual: **Yes** Group Counseling: **Yes** Vocational Counseling: **Yes**

Faculty:
Faculty: **1** Full time: **1**
Faculty advocate: **Yes** Meets with instructor: **As needed**

Diagnostic Testing
ADD	Personality	Perceptual skills	• Spelling
ADHD	Organization	Fine motor skills	• Reading
I.Q.	Handwriting	Spoken language	Study skills
• Math	Social skills	• Written language	

Tutoring:
Average size of group tutorials: **3**
Services rendered by:
Graduates •Peers •Faculty LD staff Teacher trainees

Tutorials
Grp.	Ind.	Tutorials	Grp.	Ind.	Tutorials
•	•	Math skills			Word processing
•	•	Study skills			Time management
		Language arts			Learning strategies
•	•	Written express			Organizational skills

Academic Accommodations

Curriculum	Study Aids	Exams
Priority registration	Typist	• Oral
Math waiver	• Reader	Untimed
Foreign lang. waiver	• Notetaker	Take home
Course substitution	• Proof reader	With proctor
In Class	• Text on tape	On computer
• Calculators	Early syllabus	• Extended time
• Tape recorder	Taped handouts	On tape
• Word processor		• Modified
Priority seating		• Separate room

491

New York

Graduation Requirements:
Course credits: **120** GPA: **2.0** Language waiver: **Yes**
Other requirements: **30 credit hours must be completed at D'Youville (minimum).**

General Information:
D'Youville College is a 4 year private College. Urban campus of 2 acres is Accessible by air, train or bus. Ski areas are 35 miles from campus. Beaches are 5 miles from campus. 15% of students are foreign. 1 residential halls on campus. Housing is guaranteed.Guaranteed through 4th year. 60 % of students remain on campus for the weekends.

Accreditation:

SAT/ACT Scores:
Scores for incoming freshmen:**Verbal:**83%below 500. 17%between 500 and 599. **Math:**52% below 500. 48% between 500 and 599. **ACT:** 35% below 20. 51% between 20 and 23. 11%between 26 and 28.

Class Rank:
About 8% of the present freshmen class were in the upper 20% of their high school class. 17% were in the top 40% of their class. 38% were in the top 60% of their class. 35% were in the top 80% of their class.

Expenses:
Tuition: In-state: Full year: $4,070.00. Part-time: Per credit:$222.00-$243.00. Room and board: $3,940.00

Majors
• BUSINESS Accounting, Business Administration, Business Education, Business Management, Human Resources Management, Marketing • EDUCATION Bilingual, Business, Elementary, English, Mathematics, Science, Secondary, Social Studies, Special • HEALTH SCIENCES Nursing, Nutritional/Food, Occupational Therapy, Physical Therapy, Physician's Assistant • HUMANITIES English/Writing/Literature, Philosophy • PRE-PROFESSIONAL Dentistry, Law, Medicine, Social Work, Veterinarian • SCIENCES Biology • SOCIAL SCIENCES Sociology • SPECIAL EDUCATION Visually Handicapped

Sports/Activities
• SPORTS-INTERCOLLEGIATE Basketball, Volleyball (F) • SPORTS-INTRAMURAL Basketball, Skiing - Snow, Volleyball • STUDENT LIFE ACTIVITIES Academic Clubs, Community Service, Drama Groups, Ethnic & Cultural Groups, Newspaper, Religious Organization, Student Government, Yearbook

Selective   **New York**
                                 Program

Dowling College
Idle Hour Boulevard
Oakdale, New York 11769
(516) 244-3000

School Enrollment: **4,695** Male: **1,831** Female: **2,864**

Admissions Contact: **Stephen Dougherty, Asst. Provost Enrol. Ser**
LD Contact: **Dorothy A. Stracher, Dir., Prog. for LD College Stu.**
Name of Program: **Program for LD College Students**
Address: **Dowling College**
Telephone:**(516) 244-3306**

Admissions

Application Information:
Separate application:**Yes**
Application deadline: **Open**
Rolling Admissions: **Yes**

Secondary School Information
Most Important Criteria For Admissions (1-strongest)

SAT/ACT	Application	School transcript
Class rank	Course selection	Personal statement
Interview	Extra activities	Psychoeducational
G.P.A.	Open admission	Recommendations

Test Requirements:
Untimed SAT: **Yes** Untimed ACT: **Yes**
Documentation of LD required: **Yes**

Types of Disabilities Served

Speech/Lang	Reading	ADD with LD
Study skills	Spelling	ADD without LD
Written express	Math	ADHD with LD
Organizational	Fine Motor	ADHD without LD
Perceptual		

Admissions Process

Students first apply to admissions and once accepted can then apply to the LD Program.

Learning Disability Program
Program: Reinforces course work: **Yes**
Students mainstreamed **100** % of the day
Recommended credits per semester: **12**
Services only for LD students: **Yes**
Vocational Counseling: **Yes**
Support groups are available:**Rap sessions - meeting with a qualified counselor for an hour a week.**

Faculty:

Diagnostic Testing

ADD	Personality	Perceptual skills	Spelling
ADHD	Organization	Fine motor skills	Reading
I.Q.	Handwriting	Spoken language	Study skills
Math	Social skills	Written language	

Tutoring:
Average size of group tutorials:
Services rendered by:

Graduates	Peers	Faculty	LD staff	Teacher trainees

Tutorials

Grp.	Ind.	Tutorials	Grp.	Ind.	Tutorials
		Math skills			Word processing
		Study skills			Time management
		Language arts			Learning strategies
		Written express			Organizational skills

Academic Accommodations

Curriculum	Study Aids	Exams
Priority registration	Typist	Oral
Math waiver	Reader	Untimed
Foreign lang. waiver	Notetaker	Take home
Course substitution	Proof reader	With proctor
In Class	Text on tape	On computer
Calculators	Early syllabus	Extended time
Tape recorder	Taped handouts	On tape
Word processor		Modified
Priority seating		Separate room

Program Strengths

Each LD student has an individual tutor who is a graduate student in the Education Dept. and who has had at least two courses in working with LD students. In addition, the two hourly tutoring sessions are supervised by the Director and an assistant. The program is a laboratory setting so that all faculty are immediately notified of the LD students in their classes and share their syllabi with the tutors. The faculty is again contacted during mid-semester to check student progress. The Director and the tutors hold a weekly two hour seminar to discuss each LD student's progress.

General Information:

Dowling College is a 4 year private college. Suburban campus of 46 acres is 50 miles from New York City. Accessible by car, air, train, or bus. Housing is not guaranteed.

Accreditation: Regional

Expenses: Part-time: Per credit:$249.00. Cost of LD program:$1,500.00 per semester

Majors

• AGRICULTURE Education • ARTS Music • BUSINESS Accounting, Aviation Management, Banking/Finance, Economics, Education, Management, Marketing • COMMUNICATIONS English • COMPUTER SCIENCE Computer Science • EDUCATION Elementary, English, Foreign Language, Mathematics, Music, Secondary, Social Studies, Special • HUMANITIES English/Writing/Literature • LANGUAGES English, French, Italian, Spanish • MATHEMATICS Applied • PRE PROFESSIONAL Law • SCIENCES Aerospace, Anthropology, Biology, Physics • SOCIAL SCIENCES Anthropology, Government/Political, History, Psychology, Social Science, Sociology • VISUAL AND PERFORMING ARTS Art, Dramatic Arts, Music • Vocational Air Traffic Control, Aviation Administration, Piloting

Sports/Activities

• SPORTS RELATED Cheerleading • SPORTS-INTERCOLLEGIATE Baseball, Basketball, Golf, Lacrosse, Soccer, Tennis, Volleyball • STUDENT LIFE ACTIVITIES Academic Clubs, Choral, Community Service, Concert Band, Drama Groups, Fraternities, Music Groups, Newspaper, Political Groups, Radio/TV station, Religious Organization, Sororities, Student Government, Yearbook

Less Selective

Dutchess Community College
Hudson Hall 209
Poughkeepsie, New York 12601-1595
(914) 471-4500

School Enrollment: **5,943** Male: **2,577** Female: **3,366**

Admissions Contact: **Al Cutonilli Director of Admissions**
LD Contact: **Mary Staskel Coordinator**
Name of Program: **Disabled Student Services**
Telephone: **Ext. 1806**

Admissions

Application Information:
Application deadline: **None**

Secondary School Information
Most Important Criteria For Admissions (1-strongest)

SAT/ACT	Application	School transcript
Class rank	Course selection	Personal statement
Interview	Extra activities	Psychoeducational
G.P.A.	1 Open admission	Recommendations

Types of Disabilities Served
- Speech/Lang
- Study skills
- Written express
- Organizational
- Perceptual
- Reading
- Spelling
- Math
- Fine Motor
- ADD with LD
- ADD without LD
- ADHD with LD
- ADHD without LD

Faculty:
Faculty: **1** Part time: **1**

Diagnostic Testing

ADD	Personality	Perceptual skills	Spelling
ADHD	Organization	Fine motor skills	Reading
I.Q.	Handwriting	Spoken language	Study skills
Math	Social skills	Written language	

Tutoring:
Services rendered by:
Graduates   •Peers   Faculty   •LD staff   Teacher trainees

Tutorials

Grp.	Ind.	Tutorials	Grp.	Ind.	Tutorials
	•	Math skills			Word processing
	•	Study skills		•	Time management
	•	Language arts		•	Learning strategies
	•	Written express		•	Organizational skills

Academic Accommodations

Curriculum	Study Aids	Exams
Priority registration	Typist	• Oral
• Math waiver	Reader	Untimed
• Foreign lang. waiver	• Notetaker	Take home
Course substitution	Proof reader	With proctor
In Class	• Text on tape	On computer
• Calculators	Early syllabus	• Extended time
• Tape recorder	Taped handouts	On tape
• Word processor		Modified
Priority seating		Separate room

Program Strengths

There is no specific program, but support services are available to diagnosed LD students.

General Information:

Dutchess Community College is a 2 year public college. Urban campus of 10 acres is 60 miles from New York City. Accessible by train or bus. Ski areas are 5 miles from campus. Beaches are 50 miles from campus. Housing is not guaranteed.

Accreditation: MSACS

Expenses: Part-time: Per credit: $56.00.

Majors

• BUSINESS Accounting, Business Administration, Business Management, Food Management, Management, Retailing • COMMUNICATIONS Broadcasting, Communication, Creative Writing, English, Graphic Design Technology, Journalism, Photography, Television/Radio/Film • COMPUTER SCIENCE Computer Science, Data Processing, Programming, Systems Analysis, Telecommunications • EDUCATION Early Childhood, Music, Pre-Education, Recreation and Youth Leadership • ENGINEERING Agricultural, Electrical, Engineering Science, Mechanical • HEALTH SCIENCES Medical Technology, Nursing, Nutritional/Food • HUMANITIES Humanities • PREPROFESSIONAL Architecture, Natural Resources • SCIENCES Biology, Earth, Mathematics, Physical Science • SOCIAL SCIENCES Criminal Justice, Criminology, History, Law Enforcement, Psychology, Social Sciences • VISUAL AND PERFORMING ARTS Dance, Music • VOCATIONAL Drafting, Park/Recreation, Secretarial

Sports/Activities

• SPORTS-INTERCOLLEGIATE Baseball (M), Basketball, Cross Country, Golf, Soccer, Softball, Tennis, Volleyball (F) • SPORTS-INTRAMURAL Archery, Basketball, Bowling, Fencing, Racquetball, Softball, Tennis, Volleyball • STUDENT LIFE ACTIVITIES Choral, Dance, Drama Groups, Ethnic & Cultural Groups, Film, Jazz Band, Magazine, Newspaper, Radio/TV station, Student Government, Yearbook

Eugene Lang College

65 West 11th Street
New York, New York 10011
(212) 229-5665

School Enrollment: **350** Male: **135** Female: **215**
LD Enrollment: **17**

Admissions Contact: **Laura A. Bruno, Director of Admissions**

Admissions

Application Information:
Application deadline: **February 1st**
Notified when: **April 1st**

Secondary School Information
Most Important Criteria For Admissions (1-strongest)

4	SAT/ACT	6	Application	1 School transcript
6	Class rank	2	Course selection	Personal statement
2	Interview	7	Extra activities	Psychoeducational
3	G.P.A.		Open admission	5 Recommendations

Test Requirements:
Untimed SAT: **Yes** Untimed ACT: **Yes** Untimed ACH: **Yes**

Types of Disabilities Served

Speech/Lang	Reading	ADD with LD
Study skills	Spelling	ADD without LD
Written express	Math	ADHD with LD
Organizational	Fine Motor	ADHD without LD
Perceptual		

Admissions Process

Each folder is read by 3 staff members and a cumulative rank is calculated. Borderline applicants may be read by faculty committee and/or Dean.

Diagnostic Testing

ADD	Personality	Perceptual skills	Spelling
ADHD	Organization	Fine motor skills	Reading
I.Q.	Handwriting	Spoken language	Study skills
Math	Social skills	Written language	

Services rendered by:

Graduates	Peers	Faculty	LD staff	Teacher trainees

Tutorials

Grp.	Ind.	Tutorials	Grp.	Ind.	Tutorials
		Math skills			Word processing
		Study skills			Time management
		Language arts			Learning strategies
		Written express			Organizational skills

Academic Accommodations

Curriculum	Study Aids	Exams
Priority registration	Typist	Oral
Math waiver	Reader	Untimed
Foreign lang. waiver	Notetaker	Take home
Course substitution	Proof reader	With proctor
In Class	Text on tape	On computer
Calculators	Early syllabus	Extended time
Tape recorder	Taped handouts	On tape
Word processor		Modified
Priority seating		Separate room

Graduation Requirements:
Course credits: **120** GPA: **2.5** Years to complete degree: **4**

General Information:
Eugene Lang College is a 4 year independent college. Urban campus Accessible by air, train or bus. 5% of students are foreign. 3 residential halls on campus. Housing is guaranteed.Guaranteed through 1st year. 100 % of students remain on campus for the weekends.

Accreditation:MSACS

SAT/ACT Scores:
Scores for incoming freshmen:**Verbal:**20%below 500. 41%between 500 and 599. 28%between 600 and 699. 4%above 700. **Math:**25% below 500. 44% between 500 and 599. 20% between 600 and 699. 4%above 700.

Class Rank:
About 29% of the present freshmen class were in the upper 20% of their high school class. 68% were in the top 40% of their class. 85% were in the top 60% of their class.

Expenses:
Tuition: In-state: Full year: $11,794.00. Tuition: Out-of-state: Full year: $11,794.00. Room and board: $7,500.00

Majors
• AREA STUDIES Urban, Women's Studies • COMMUNICATIONS Creative Writing, English, Literature • EDUCATION Early Childhood, Elementary • HUMANITIES English/Writing/Literature, Humanities, Liberal Arts , Philosophy • PHILOSOPHY Law • SOCIAL SCIENCES Government/Political, History, International Studies, Political Science, Psychology, Social Science, Sociology • VISUAL AND PERFORMING ARTS Dramatic Arts, Theater

Sports/Activities
• SPORTS-INTRAMURAL Basketball, Bowling, Fencing, Golf, Racquetball, Skiing - Cross Country, Softball, Table Tennis, Tennis, Volleyball

Special　　　　　　　　　　　**New York Services**

Fashion Institute of Technology
227 West 27th Street
New York, New York 10001
(212) 760-7994

School Enrollment: **12,007**
LD Enrollment: **70**

Admissions Contact: **James Pidgeon, Director of Admissions**
LD Contact: **Dr. Irene Buchman, Chairman, Education/Skill Dept.**

Admissions

Secondary School Information
Most Important Criteria For Admissions (1-strongest)

SAT/ACT	Application	School transcript
Class rank	Course selection	Personal statement
Interview	Extra activities	Psychoeducational
G.P.A.	Open admission	Recommendations

Test Requirements:
Untimed SAT: **Yes**

Types of Disabilities Served
Speech/Lang	Reading	ADD with LD
Study skills	Spelling	ADD without LD
Written express	Math	ADHD with LD
Organizational	Fine Motor	ADHD without LD
Perceptual		

Learning Disability Program
Program: Reinforces course work: **Yes**
Students mainstreamed **100** % of the day
Recommended credits per semester: **12-15**
Counseling: Individual: **Yes** Vocational Counseling: **Yes**

Faculty:
Faculty: **2** Full time: **1** Part time: **1** M.A.: **1** Ph.D.: **1**
Faculty advocate: **Yes**

Diagnostic Testing
ADD	Personality	Perceptual skills	Spelling
ADHD	Organization	Fine motor skills	Reading
I.Q.	Handwriting	Spoken language	Study skills
Math	Social skills	Written language	

Tutoring:
Average size of group tutorials: **1:1**
Services rendered by:
•Graduates　　Peers　　•Faculty　　•LD staff　　Teacher trainees

Tutorials
Grp.	Ind.	Tutorials	Grp.	Ind.	Tutorials
	•	Math skills		•	Word processing
	•	Study skills		•	Time management
	•	Language arts		•	Learning strategies
	•	Written express		•	Organizational skills

Academic Accommodations

Curriculum	Study Aids	Exams
Priority registration	Typist	• Oral
Math waiver	• Reader	• Untimed
Foreign lang. waiver	• Notetaker	Take home
Course substitution	• Proof reader	With proctor
In Class	• Text on tape	On computer
• Calculators	Early syllabus	• Extended time
• Tape recorder	Taped handouts	On tape
Word processor		• Modified
• Priority seating		• Separate room

Graduation Requirements:Years to complete degree: **3-5**

General Information:
Fashion Institute of Technology is a 2 year public university (SUNY). urban campus Accessible by air, train or bus. 3 residential halls on campus. Housing is not guaranteed.

New York

Accreditation: MSACS, NASAD

Majors

• ARTS Drafting, Drawing, Fashion Design, Graphic Arts, Interior Design, Painting • BUSINESS Fashion Merchandising, Marketing, Retailing • COMMUNICATIONS Advertising, Broadcasting, Commercial Design, Communication, Graphic Design, Journalism, Photography, Public Relations • CRAFTS AND DESIGN Apparel Design, Graphic Design, Illustration Design, Jewelry, Textile/Weaving • VOCATIONAL Fashion Design, Fashion Merchandising, Interior Design, Jewelry-Metalsmithery, Painting, Textile and Clothing

Sports/Activities

• SPORTS-INTERCOLLEGIATE Basketball (M), Tennis, Volleyball (F)
• SPORTS-INTRAMURAL Basketball, Tennis, Volleyball

Highly Selective

New York Services

Fordham University

East Fordham Road
Bronx, New York 10458
(212) 579-2000

School Enrollment: **13,158** Male: **5,878** Female: **7,280**

Admissions Contact: **Christopher Howley, Admissions Counselor**
LD Contact: **Greg Pappas, Dean of Student Services**
Name of Program: **Student Services**
Address: **McGinley Center, Room 224**
Telephone: **(212) 364-4191**

Admissions

Application Information:
Application deadline: **February 1st**
Notified when: **April 1st**

Secondary School Information
Most Important Criteria For Admissions (1-strongest)

4	SAT/ACT	7	Application	2	School transcript
6	Class rank	1	Course selection	9	Personal statement
10	Interview	8	Extra activities	11	Psychoeducational
3	G.P.A.		Open admission	5	Recommendations

Test Requirements:
Untimed SAT: **Yes** Untimed ACT: **Yes**

Types of Disabilities Served

Speech/Lang	Reading	ADD with LD
Study skills	Spelling	ADD without LD
Written express	Math	ADHD with LD
Organizational	Fine Motor	ADHD without LD
Perceptual		

Admissions Process

Students are required to submit high school transcript, recommendation from guidance counselor, results of SAT/ACT. Interview is optional but recommended.

High School Course Requirements:
English: **4** Math: **3-4** Science: **1-2** Foreign Language: **2**
Waivers to standard high school courses
Foreign Language : **Yes** Math: **Yes** Course substitution: **Yes**

Learning Disability Program

Special orientation for LD students: **Yes**
Program: Reinforces course work: **Yes**
Students mainstreamed **100** % of the day
Recommended credits per semester: **15**
Services available for all students: **Yes**
Counseling: Individual: **Yes** Vocational Counseling: **Yes**

Faculty:
Faculty: **11** Including Director: **Yes** Full time: **11**
LD faculty with: BS/BA: **11**
Faculty advocate: **Yes** Meets with instructor: **As necessary**

Diagnostic Testing

ADD	Personality	Perceptual skills	Spelling
ADHD	Organization	Fine motor skills	Reading
I.Q.	Handwriting	Spoken language	Study skills
Math	Social skills	Written language	

Tutoring:
Average size of group tutorials: **2**
Services rendered by:

•Graduates	•Peers	Faculty	LD staff	Teacher trainees

Tutorials

Grp.	Ind.	Tutorials	Grp.	Ind.	Tutorials
•		Math skills	•		Word processing
•		Study skills	•		Time management
•		Language arts	•		Learning strategies
•		Written express	•		Organizational skills

Academic Accommodations

Curriculum	Study Aids	Exams
Priority registration	• Typist	Oral
Math waiver	Reader	Untimed
• Foreign lang. waiver	Notetaker	Take home
• Course substitution	• Proof reader	• With proctor
In Class	Text on tape	On computer
• Calculators	Early syllabus	• Extended time
• Tape recorder	Taped handouts	On tape
• Word processor		Modified
• Priority seating		Separate room

Graduation Requirements:
Course credits: **120-124** GPA: **2.0** Years to complete degree: **Generally 4** Language waiver: **Yes**

General Information:

Fordham University is a 4 year independent Roman Catholic university. Urban campus of 85 acres is 12 miles from New York City. Accessible by plane, train or bus. Ski areas are 60 miles from campus. Beaches are 5 miles from campus. 2.5% of students are foreign. 9 residential halls on campus. Housing is guaranteed. Guaranteed through 4th year. 70 % of students remain on campus for the weekends.

Accreditation: MSACS, BRSNY, AACSB

SAT/ACT Scores:
Scores for incoming freshmen: **Verbal:** 49.5% below 500. 54% between 500 and 599. 14% between 600 and 699. 2.5% above 700. **Math:** 26% below 500. 51% between 500 and 599. 19% between 600 and 699. 3% above 700.

Class Rank:
About 45% of the present freshmen class were in the upper 20% of their high school class. 78% were in the top 40% of their class.

Expenses:
Tuition: In-state: Full year: $10,950.00. Tuition: Out-of-state: Full year: $10,950.00. Room and board: $6,800.00 Cost of LD program: No charge if qualify; otherwise $6.00 per hour for tutor.

Majors

• AREA STUDIES Asian, Black/Afro-American, Hispanic/American, International Studies, Jewish/Judaism, Latin American, Middle Eastern, Russian/Slavic, Women's Studies • ARTS Art History, Film & Video, Graphic Arts, Music History, Painting, Photography, Theater Design • BUSINESS Accounting, Banking/Finance, Business Administration, Business Economics, Business Management, Economics, Human Resources Management, International Business, Investments and Securities, Labor Relations, Management, Marketing, Marketing Research, Operations Research, Organizational Behavior • COMMUNICATIONS Broadcasting, Communication, Creative Writing, English, Journalism, Literature, Public Relations, Speech/Debate/Forensic, Television/Radio/Film • COMPUTER SCIENCE Computer Science, Programming • EDUCATION Elementary, English, English As A Second Language, Secondary • HUMANITIES Classics, English/Writing/Literature, Fine Arts, Humanities, Liberal Arts , Philosophy, Religion • LANGUAGES Arabic, English, French, German, Greek, Hebrew, Italian, Latin, Russian, Spanish • MATHEMATICS Applied, Computer, Statistical • PHILOSOPHY Architecture, Business, Dentistry, Engineering, Law, Medicine, Pharmacy, Veterinarian • RELIGIOUS STUDIES Bible, Hebrew, Philosophy, Religion & Theology • SCIENCES Biology, Chemistry, Computer Science, General • SOCIAL SCIENCES Anthropology, Criminal Justice, Government/Political, History, International Studies, Political Science, Psychology, Public Relations, Social Science, Sociology • VISUAL AND PERFORMING ARTS Art, Art History, Fine Arts, Studio Art, Theater

Sports/Activities

• SPORTS RELATED Cheerleading, Marching Band, Team Managers • SPORTS-INTERCOLLEGIATE Baseball (M), Basketball, Basketball (F), Basketball (M), Crew, Crew (F), Crew (M), Cross Country, Cross Country (F), Cross Country (M), Diving, Diving (F), Diving (M), Field Hockey (F), Football (M), Golf (M), Horseback Riding, Horseback Riding (F), Horseback Riding (M), Ice Hockey (M), Lacrosse, Lacrosse (F), Lacrosse (M), Rugby (M), Soccer, Soccer (F), Soccer (M), Softball (F), Squash, Squash (F), Squash (M), Swimming, Swimming (F), Swimming (M), Tennis, Tennis (F), Tennis (M), Track and Field, Track and Field (F), Track and Field (M), Volleyball, Volleyball (F), Volleyball (M), Water Polo (M), Wrestling (M) • SPORTS-INTRAMURAL Karate, Martial Arts, Racquetball, Racquetball (F), Racquetball (M), Riflery, Riflery (F), Riflery (M), Squash, Squash (F), Squash (M), Weight Lifting, Weight Lifting (M) • STUDENT LIFE ACTIVITIES Academic Clubs, Choral, Community Service, Concert Band, Dance, Debate, Drama Groups, Ethnic & Cultural Groups, Film, Magazine, Music Groups, Musical Theater, Newspaper, Orchestra, Political Groups, Radio/TV station, Student Government, Yearbook

---

Less Selective　　　　　　　**New York Services**

Fulton-Montgomery Community College
Route 67
Johnstown, New York 12095
(518) 762-4651

School Enrollment: **1,500**
LD Enrollment: **72**

Admissions Contact: **Caroline Baker, Director of Admissions**
LD Contact: **Harold R. Morrell, Director**
Name of Program: **Academic Support Services**
Address: **FMCC, Route 67**
Telephone:**(518) 762-4651 Ext. 273**

Admissions

Application Information:
LD Students Applying: **72** Accepted: **72** Enrolled:**72**
Application deadline: **Open admissions**
Applicant must apply **6** months in advance

Secondary School Information
Most Important Criteria For Admissions (1-strongest)
　2 SAT/ACT **10** Application　　**10** School transcript
　5 Class rank　**7** Course selection　**1** Personal statement
　9 Interview　**1** Extra activities　**9** Psychoeducational
　5 G.P.A.　　Open admission　**8** Recommendations

Test Requirements:
Standardized tests waived: **Yes**
Untimed SAT: **Yes** Untimed ACT: **Yes**
Documentation of LD required: **Yes**
Tests recommended: **Intelligence, Achievement, Diagnostic Tools**

Types of Disabilities Served
• Speech/Lang　• Reading　　• ADD with LD
• Study skills　• Spelling　　• ADD without LD
• Written express　• Math　　• ADHD with LD
• Organizational　• Fine Motor　• ADHD without LD
• Perceptual

High School Course Requirements:
Waivers to standard high school courses
Foreign Language : **Yes** Math: **Yes** Course substitution: **Yes**

Learning Disability Program

Program: Remedial: **Yes**
Program: Reinforces course work: **Yes**
Program available through:**Every semester**
Students mainstreamed **100** % of the day
Recommended credits per semester: **12**
Time required or recommended in learning center: **As needed**
Services available for all students: **Yes**
Counseling: Individual: **Yes** Group Counseling: **Yes** Vocational Counseling: **Yes**
Support groups are available:**Yes**

Faculty:
Faculty: **3** Including Director: **Yes** Full time: **1** Part time: **3**
LD faculty with: BS/BA: **1** M.A.: **2**
Faculty advocate: **Yes** Meets with instructor: **As needed**

Diagnostic Testing

ADD	Personality	• Perceptual skills	• Spelling
ADHD	Organization	• Fine motor skills	• Reading
• I.Q.	• Handwriting	• Spoken language	• Study skills
• Math	Social skills	• Written language	

Tutoring:

Average size of group tutorials: **2**
Services rendered by:
Graduates •Peers •Faculty •LD staff •Teacher trainees

Tutorials

Grp.	Ind.	Tutorials	Grp.	Ind.	Tutorials
•	•	Math skills	•	•	Word processing
•	•	Study skills	•	•	Time management
•	•	Language arts	•	•	Learning strategies
•	•	Written express	•	•	Organizational skills

Academic Accommodations

Curriculum	Study Aids	Exams
• Priority registration	• Typist	• Oral
• Math waiver	• Reader	• Untimed
• Foreign lang. waiver	• Notetaker	• Take home
• Course substitution	• Proof reader	• With proctor
In Class	• Text on tape	On computer
• Calculators	• Early syllabus	• Extended time
• Tape recorder	Taped handouts	On tape
• Word processor		• Modified
• Priority seating		• Separate room

Graduation Requirements:

Course credits: **62** GPA: **2.0** Years to complete degree: **Open** Math waiver: **Yes** Language waiver: **Yes**

Program Strengths

The Learning Disability Program at FMCC is designed to meet the individual needs of the student and to maintain confidentiality. Every attempt is made to help the student make the transition from the high school to the community college.

General Information:

Fulton-Montgomery Community College is a 2 year public college. Rural campus of 268 acres is 6 miles from Johnstown. Accessible by bus. Ski areas are 15 miles from campus. Beaches are 20 miles from campus. 3% of students are foreign. 2 residential halls on campus. Housing is guaranteed.15 % of students remain on campus for the weekends.

Accreditation:MSACS

Expenses:

Tuition: In-state: Full year: $1,750.00. Part-time: Per credit:$73.00. Tuition: Out-of-state: Full year: $3,500.00. Part-time: Per credit:$146.00. Room and board: $2,875.00

Majors

• BUSINESS Accounting, Banking, Business Administration, Business Management, Entrepreneur, Finance, Food Management, Management • COMMUNICATIONS Communication, Graphic Design Technology • COMPUTER SCIENCE Computer Science, Computer Technology, Data Processing, Medical Records Technology, Programming • CRAFTS AND DESIGN Crafts Management • EDUCATION Early Childhood, Elementary, Health, Physical • ENGINEERING Electrical, Engineering Science, Industrial • HEALTH SCIENCES Medical Secretary, Medical Technology, Nursing • HUMANITIES Humanities, Liberal Arts • LANGUAGES French, German, Italian • PREPROFESSIONAL Engineering, Forestry, Medicine, Natural Resources, Social Work • SCIENCES Biology, Botany, Mathematics, Microbiology, Physical Science, Physics • SOCIAL SCI-

ENCES Criminal Justice, Government/Political, History, Law Enforcement, Political Science, Psychology, Social Sciences, Sociology • VISUAL AND PERFORMING ARTS Art, Fine Arts, Theater • VOCATIONAL Automobile Technology, Automotive Service, Business and Office, Construction, Food Service, Forestry, Funeral/Mortuary, Leather Technology, Legal Secretary, Medical Laboratory Technology, Piloting, Printing/Lithography, Secretarial, Textile and Clothing, Word Processing

Sports/Activities

• SPORTS-INTERCOLLEGIATE Baseball (M), Basketball (M), Bowling, Cross Country, Golf, Soccer (M), Softball (F), Track and Field, Volleyball (F), Wrestling (M) • SPORTS-INTRAMURAL Basketball (M), Racquetball, Volleyball • STUDENT LIFE ACTIVITIES Drama Groups, Ethnic & Cultural Groups, Magazine, Musical Theater, Newspaper, Radio/TV station, Student Government, Yearbook

Less Selective	New York Services

Herkimer County Community College

Reservoir Road
Herkimer, New York 13350
(315) 866-0300

School Enrollment: **1,670** Male: **668** Female: **1,002**
LD Enrollment: **60** Male: **35** Female: **25**

Admissions Contact: **Janet Tamburrino, Director of Admissions**
LD Contact: **Mrs. Michele Weaver, LD Specialist**
Name of Program: **College Learning Center**
Telephone:**(315) 866-0300 Ext. 331**

Admissions

Application Information:

Enrolled:**85**
Application deadline: **August 1st**
Applicant must apply **2** months in advance
Rolling Admissions: **Yes**Notified when: **As soon as possible**

Secondary School Information

Most Important Criteria For Admissions (1-strongest)

6	SAT/ACT	1	Application	2	School transcript
5	Class rank	9	Course selection	11	Personal statement
7	Interview	10	Extra activities	4	Psychoeducational
3	G.P.A.	1	Open admission	8	Recommendations

Test Requirements:

Documentation of LD required: **Yes**

Types of Disabilities Served

• Speech/Lang	• Reading	• ADD with LD
• Study skills	• Spelling	• ADD without LD
• Written express	• Math	• ADHD with LD
• Organizational	• Fine Motor	• ADHD without LD
• Perceptual		

Admissions Process

Open admissions

Learning Disability Program

Program: Remedial: **Yes**
Program: Reinforces course work: **Yes**
Program available through:**Monday-Friday**
Students mainstreamed **100** % of the day
Recommended credits per semester: **12**
Services available for all students: **Yes**
Counseling: Individual: **Yes** Group Counseling: **Yes** Vocational Counseling: **Yes**
Support groups are available:**Yes, Higher Education to Learning Potential (HELP)**

Faculty:

Faculty: **2** Full time: **1** Part time: **1**
LD faculty with: BS/BA: **1** M.A.: **1**
Faculty advocate: **Yes** Meets with instructor: **As needed**

Diagnostic Testing

ADD	Personality	Perceptual skills	Spelling
ADHD	Organization	Fine motor skills	Reading
I.Q.	Handwriting	Spoken language	Study skills
Math	Social skills	Written language	

Tutoring:

Average size of group tutorials: **1-10**
Services rendered by:
  Graduates   •Peers   •Faculty   •LD staff   Teacher trainees

Tutorials

Grp.	Ind.	Tutorials	Grp.	Ind.	Tutorials
•	•	Math skills	•	•	Word processing
•	•	Study skills	•	•	Time management
•	•	Language arts	•	•	Learning strategies
•	•	Written express	•	•	Organizational skills

Academic Accommodations

Curriculum	**Study Aids**	**Exams**
• Priority registration	• Typist	• Oral
• Math waiver	Reader	• Untimed
Foreign lang. waiver	• Notetaker	• Take home
• Course substitution	• Proof reader	• With proctor
In Class	Text on tape	• On computer
• Calculators	Early syllabus	• Extended time
• Tape recorder	Taped handouts	• On tape
• Word processor		• Modified
• Priority seating		• Separate room

Graduation Requirements:

Course credits: **64-67** GPA: **2.0**

Program Strengths

HCCC offers services appropriate for each learning disabled student rather than programming. Students are served by a full-time LD specialist who is a member of the College Learning Center staff. Opportunity for the student to access all of the special features of the Learning Center is encouraged by this arrangement. Student self-advocacy and independence skills are a high priority. Also stressed is faculty awareness of LD issues, and the LD specialist maintains rapport with the college faculty and staff to facilitate increased awareness and understanding.

General Information:

Herkimer County Community College is a 2 year public college. Suburban campus of 500 acres is 12 miles from Utica. Accessible by bus. Ski areas are 8 miles from campus. Beaches are 20 miles from campus. 1% of students are foreign. Housing is not guaranteed.

Accreditation:MSACS

Expenses:
Tuition: In-state: Full year: $1,650.00. Part-time: Per credit:$50.00. Tuition: Out-of-state: Full year: $2,700.00. Part-time: Per credit:$90.00.
Room and board: $3,200.00

Majors

• BUSINESS Accounting, Banking, Business Administration, Business Management, Entrepreneur, Finance, Food Management, Insurance, Management, Marketing, Marketing Research, Personnel, Sports Management, Travel/Tourism Management • COMMUNICATIONS Broadcasting, Journalism, Photography, Television/Radio/Film • COMPUTER SCIENCE Computer Science, Data Processing, Programming, Robotics, Telecommunications • EDUCATION Early Childhood, Physical, Pre-Education, Special • ENGINEERING Chemical, Engineering Science, Industrial • HEALTH SCIENCES Health, Medical Assistant, Medical Secretary, Medical Technology, Occupational Therapy Assistant, Physical Therapy • HUMANITIES Humanities, Liberal Arts • PREPROFESSIONAL Architecture, Engineering, Forestry, Legal Assistant, Pharmacy, Recreation, Social Work, Sports Medicine • SCIENCES Biology, Chemistry, Gerontology, Mathematics, Physical Science, Physics • SOCIAL SCIENCES Criminal Justice, Human Service, Law Enforcement, Psychology, Social Sciences, Sociology • VISUAL AND PERFORMING ARTS Fine Arts • VOCATIONAL Business and Office, Construction, Drafting, Flight Attendants, Food Service, Forestry, Funeral/Mortuary, Landscape Architecture, Legal Secretary, Medical Laboratory Technology, Paralegal, Park/Recreation, Secretarial, Word Processing

Sports/Activities

• SPORTS-INTERCOLLEGIATE Baseball (M), Basketball, Bowling, Field Hockey (F), Lacrosse (M), Soccer, Softball (F), Tennis (F), Track and Field, Volleyball (F) • SPORTS-INTRAMURAL Basketball, Bowling, Lacrosse (M), Skiing - Snow, Soccer, Softball, Tennis (M), Volleyball (F) • STUDENT LIFE ACTIVITIES Dance, Drama Groups, Fraternities, Magazine, Musical Theater, Newspaper, Radio/TV station, Sororities, Student Government

Very Selective   **New York Program**

Hofstra University

107 Barnard Hall
Hempstead, New York 11550
(516) 560-6700

School Enrollment: **7,000** Male: **3,500** Female: **3,500**

Admissions Contact: **Robert Pertusati, Admissions Counselor**
LD Contact: **I. Gotz, Director**
Name of Program: **Program for Academic Learning**
Telephone:**(516) 560-5840**

Admissions

Application Information:
LD Students Applying: **350** Accepted: **40** Enrolled:**18**
Separate application:**Yes**
Application deadline: **None**
Applicant must apply **10** months in advance
Rolling Admissions: **Yes** Notified when: **Rolling**

New York

Secondary School Information
Most Important Criteria For Admissions (1-strongest)

3 SAT/ACT	**3** Application	**8** School transcript
5 Class rank	**3** Course selection	**11** Personal statement
11 Interview	**1** Extra activities	**11** Psychoeducational
5 G.P.A.	Open admission	**11** Recommendations

Test Requirements:
Standardized tests waived: **Yes**
Diagnostic testing waived: **Yes**
WAIS-R required: **Yes** Range accepted: **110 FS**
Currency of diagnostic testing: **12 months**

Types of Disabilities Served
- Speech/Lang
- Study skills
- Written express
- Organizational
- Perceptual
- Reading
- Spelling
- Math
- Fine Motor
- ADD with LD
- ADD without LD
- ADHD with LD
- ADHD without LD

Learning Disability Program
Students mainstreamed **100** % of the day

Faculty:
Faculty: **6** Full time: **2** Part time: **4** M.A.: **5** Ph.D.: **1**
Faculty advocate: **Yes** Meets with instructor: **As needed**

Diagnostic Testing
- ADD
- ADHD
- I.Q.
- Math
- Personality
- Organization
- Handwriting
- Social skills
- Perceptual skills
- Fine motor skills
- Spoken language
- Written language
- Spelling
- Reading
- Study skills

Tutoring:
Services rendered by:
- Graduates
- Peers
- Faculty
- LD staff
- Teacher trainees

Tutorials

Grp.	Ind.	Tutorials	Grp.	Ind.	Tutorials
	•	Math skills		•	Word processing
	•	Study skills		•	Time management
	•	Language arts		•	Learning strategies
	•	Written express		•	Organizational skills

Academic Accommodations

Curriculum	Study Aids	Exams
Priority registration	• Typist	• Oral
• Math waiver	Reader	Untimed
Foreign lang. waiver	• Notetaker	• Take home
Course substitution	• Proof reader	With proctor
In Class	• Text on tape	On computer
• Calculators	Early syllabus	• Extended time
• Tape recorder	Taped handouts	On tape
• Word processor		• Modified
Priority seating		Separate room

General Information:
Hofstra University is a 4 year private university. of 238 acres is 30 miles from New York City. Accessible by air, train, or bus. Beaches are 20 miles from campus. Housing is not guaranteed.

Accreditation: MSACS

Expenses:
Tuition: In-state: Full year: $9,600.00. Part-time: Per credit:$240.00. Tuition: Out-of-state: Full year: $9,600.00. Part-time: Per credit:$240.00.

Room and board: $4,000.00 Cost of LD program:$3,000.00 - Freshman year only

Majors
- AREA STUDIES African, American, Asian, Jewish, Latin American
- BUSINESS Accounting, Banking, Business Administration, Business Economics, Business Education, Business Management, Economics, Finance, International Business, Management, Marketing, Marketing Research, Personnel • COMMUNICATIONS Advertising, Broadcasting, Communication, Creative Writing, English, Journalism, Linguistics, Literature, Photography, Speech, Television/Radio/Film • COMPUTER SCIENCE Computer Science, Data Processing, Programming, Systems Analysis, Telecommunications • CRAFTS AND DESIGN Ceramics, Sculpture • EDUCATION Art, Elementary, English, Foreign Language, Health, Mathematics, Music, Physical, Science, Secondary, Social Studies • ENGINEERING Electrical, Engineering Science, Industrial, Mechanical • HEALTH SCIENCES Environmental, Health, Nutritional/Food, Occupational Therapy, Physical Therapy, Speech Therapy, Speech/Audiology and Speech • HUMANITIES Classics, English/Writing/Literature, Humanities, Liberal Arts, Philosophy • LANGUAGES Chinese, French, German, Greek, Hebrew, Italian, Latin, Russian, Spanish • PREPROFESSIONAL Engineering, Law, Social Work • SCIENCES Astronomy, Biochemistry, Biology, Chemistry, Earth, Ecology, Geography, Geology, Marine Biology, Mathematics, Oceanography, Physical Chemistry, Physical Science, Physics, Zoology • SOCIAL SCIENCES Anthropology, Government/Political, History, Human Service, Political Science, Psychology, Social Sciences, Sociology • VISUAL AND PERFORMING ARTS Art History, Dance, Dramatic Arts, Music, Studio Art, Theater • VOCATIONAL Jewelry-Metalsmithery, Painting, Secretarial

Sports/Activities
- SPORTS RELATED Pep Band • SPORTS-INTERCOLLEGIATE Baseball (M), Basketball, Cross Country, Field Hockey (F), Football (M), Golf (M), Gymnastics (F), Lacrosse, Soccer (M), Softball (F), Tennis, Volleyball (F), Wrestling (M) • SPORTS-INTRAMURAL Badminton, Basketball, Bowling, Football (M), Golf, Horseback Riding, Ice Hockey (M), Rugby (M), Soccer (M), Softball (F), Swimming, Track and Field, Volleyball, Water Polo (M), Wrestling (M) • STUDENT LIFE ACTIVITIES Academic Clubs, Choral, Community Service, Concert Band, Dance, Drama Groups, Ethnic & Cultural Groups, Film, Fraternities, Jazz Band, Magazine, Music Groups, Musical Theater, Newspaper, Opera, Political Groups, Radio/TV station, Religious Organization, Sororities, Student Government, Symphony Orchestra, Yearbook

Very Selective   **New York Services**

Houghton College
Houghton, New York 14744
(716) 567-9200

School Enrollment: **1,153** Male: **458** Female: **695**
LD Enrollment: **12** Male: **9** Female: **3**

Admissions Contact: **Tim Fulle, Director of Admissions**
LD Contact: **Mary Jayne Allen, Coordinator, LD Student Services**
Name of Program: **Academic Support Services**
Telephone:**(716) 567-9622**

Admissions

Application Information:
LD Students Applying: **6** Accepted: **4** Enrolled:**3**
Application deadline: **Rolling**
Rolling Admissions: **Yes**

Secondary School Information
Most Important Criteria For Admissions (1-strongest)

6 SAT/ACT	**5** Application	**1** School transcript
4 Class rank	**2** Course selection	**1** Personal statement
9 Interview	**10** Extra activities	**8** Psychoeducational
3 G.P.A.	Open admission	**7** Recommendations

Test Requirements:
Untimed SAT: **Yes** Untimed ACT: **Yes**
Documentation of LD required: **Yes**
Tests recommended: **Psycho-educational evaluation**

Types of Disabilities Served
- Speech/Lang
- Study skills
- Written express
- Organizational
- Perceptual
- Reading
- Spelling
- Math
- Fine Motor
- ADD with LD
- ADD without LD
- ADHD with LD
- ADHD without LD

Admissions Process

Students are encouraged to disclose the fact that they have a learning disability. Admissions decisions are made on the basis of transcript, GPA, etc. However, disclosure allows student and Coordinator of LD Student Services to discuss support services offered and whether they are well matched with the student's needs.

High School Course Requirements:
English: **4** Math: **2** Science: **2** Foreign Language: **2**

Learning Disability Program
Students mainstreamed **100** % of the day
Counseling: Individual: **Yes**

Faculty:
Faculty: **1** Part time: **1** M.A.: **1**
Faculty advocate: **Yes** Meets with instructor: **1-2X semester**

Diagnostic Testing

ADD	Personality	Perceptual skills	Spelling
ADHD	Organization	Fine motor skills	Reading
I.Q.	Handwriting	Spoken language	Study skills
Math	Social skills	Written language	

Tutoring:
Average size of group tutorials: **1-2**
Services rendered by:
Graduates •Peers •Faculty •LD staff Teacher trainees

Tutorials

Grp.	Ind.	Tutorials	Grp.	Ind.	Tutorials
•	•	Math skills			Word processing
		Study skills	•	•	Time management
		Language arts		•	Learning strategies
•	•	Written express	•	•	Organizational skills

Academic Accommodations

Curriculum	Study Aids	Exams
Priority registration	Typist	• Oral
• Math waiver	Reader	Untimed
• Foreign lang. waiver	Notetaker	• Take home
Course substitution	• Proof reader	• With proctor
In Class	• Text on tape	• On computer
• Calculators	Early syllabus	• Extended time
• Tape recorder	Taped handouts	On tape
• Word processor		• Modified
Priority seating		• Separate room

Graduation Requirements:
Course credits: **125** GPA: **2.0** Years to complete degree: **4** Math waiver: **Yes** Language waiver: **Yes**

Program Strengths
At the moment we have no formal program with a special curriculum for LD students. We do, however, offer special services to students with a learning disability. We ask that these individuals be thoroughly tested and the results sent to the school indicating the interventions suggested for these students to help them academically while at Houghton College. We work with faculty to provide necessary accommodations.

General Information:
Houghton College is a 4 year private Wesleyan Church college. Rural campus of 1300 acres is 60 miles from Buffalo. Accessible by bus. Ski areas are 20 miles from campus. 5% of students are foreign. 4 residential halls on campus. Housing is guaranteed.Guaranteed through 2nd year. 80 % of students remain on campus for the weekends.

Accreditation:MSACS

SAT/ACT Scores:
Scores for incoming freshmen: **Verbal:** 43% below 500. 37% between 500 and 599. 19% between 600 and 699. 1% above 700. **Math:** 28% below 500. 41% between 500 and 599. 28% between 600 and 699. 3% above 700. **ACT:** 26% below 20. 24% between 20 and 23. 15% between 24 and 25l. 26% between 26 and 28. 8% above 28.

Class Rank:
About 58% of the present freshmen class were in the upper 20% of their high school class. 86% were in the top 40% of their class. 94% were in the top 60% of their class. 97% were in the top 80% of their class.

Expenses:
Tuition: In-state: Full year: $8,870.00. Tuition: Out-of-state: Full year: $8,870.00. Room and board: $3,260.00

Majors
• BUSINESS Accounting, Business Administration • COMMUNICATIONS Communication, Creative Writing, Literature • EDUCATION Art, Elementary, English, Music, Physical, Religious, Secondary • HEALTH SCIENCES Medical Technology • HUMANITIES Humanities, Liberal Arts, Philosophy, Religion, Religion Studies • LANGUAGES French, Spanish • PREPROFESSIONAL Dentistry, Engineering, Law, Medicine, Ministry, Recreation • SCIENCES Biology, Chemistry, General, Mathematics, Physical Science, Physics • SOCIAL SCIENCES History, International Studies, Political Science, Psychology, Social Sciences, Sociology • VISUAL AND PERFORMING ARTS Art, Fine Arts, Music, Music Performance • VOCATIONAL Medical Laboratory Technology, Park/Recreation

Sports/Activities
• SPORTS-INTERCOLLEGIATE Basketball, Cross Country, Field Hockey (F), Soccer, Track and Field, Volleyball (F) • SPORTS-INTRAMURAL Basketball, Horseback Riding, Racquetball, Soccer, Softball, Swimming,

Tennis, Volleyball • STUDENT LIFE ACTIVITIES Choral, Concert Band, Drama Groups, Jazz Band, Magazine, Music Groups, Newspaper, Opera, Radio/TV station, Religious Organization, Student Government, Symphony Orchestra, Yearbook

Less Selective

New York Services

Hudson Valley Community College

80 Vandenburgh Avenue
Troy, New York 12180
(518) 283-1100

School Enrollment: **9,329**

Admissions Contact: **Linda Sweetman, Director**
LD Contact: **Mary Archibee Blake, LD Specialist**
Telephone:**(518) 270-7230**

Admissions

Application Information:
Application deadline: **August 29th**
Rolling Admissions: **Yes**

Secondary School Information
Most Important Criteria For Admissions (1-strongest)

SAT/ACT	Application	School transcript
Class rank	Course selection	Personal statement
Interview	Extra activities	Psychoeducational
G.P.A.	**1** Open admission	Recommendations

Types of Disabilities Served
- Speech/Lang
- Study skills
- Written express
- Organizational
- Perceptual
- Reading
- Spelling
- Math
- Fine Motor
- ADD with LD
- ADD without LD
- ADHD with LD
- ADHD without LD

Faculty:
Faculty: **1** Part time: **1**
Faculty advocate: **Yes** Meets with instructor: **As needed**

Diagnostic Testing

ADD	Personality	Perceptual skills	Spelling
ADHD	Organization	Fine motor skills	Reading
I.Q.	Handwriting	Spoken language	Study skills
Math	Social skills	Written language	

Tutoring:
Services rendered by:
Graduates •Peers •Faculty LD staff Teacher trainees

Tutorials

Grp.	Ind.	Tutorials	Grp.	Ind.	Tutorials
•	•	Math skills		•	Word processing
		Study skills			Time management
		Language arts			Learning strategies
		Written express			Organizational skills

Academic Accommodations

Curriculum	Study Aids	Exams
Priority registration	• Typist	• Oral
Math waiver	Reader	Untimed
Foreign lang. waiver	• Notetaker	• Take home
Course substitution	• Proof reader	With proctor
In Class	• Text on tape	On computer
• Calculators	Early syllabus	• Extended time
• Tape recorder	Taped handouts	On tape
• Word processor		• Modified
Priority seating		Separate room

Program Strengths
We do not advertise our services as a Learning Disability Program because, although we do offer a number of support services, we do not provide diagnostic testing such as the WAIS-R. We work closely with our Learning Assistance Center staff, the Coordinator for Tutorial Services and faculty to provide our LD students with quality support.

General Information:
Hudson Valley Community College is a 2 year public college. Urban campus 8 miles from Albany. Accessible by bus. Housing is not guaranteed.

Accreditation:MACS

Expenses:
Tuition: In-state: Full year: $1,180.00. Part-time: Per credit:$50.00. Tuition: Out-of-state: Full year: $2,560.00. Part-time: Per credit:$110.00.

Majors
• AREA STUDIES Black/Afro-American • BUSINESS Accounting, Banking, Business Administration, Business Management, Economics, Finance, Insurance, International Business, Management, Marketing, Real Estate • COMMUNICATIONS Communication, Creative Writing, English, Journalism, Photography • COMPUTER SCIENCE Computer Science, Data Processing, Programming, Telecommunications • EDUCATION Child Development, Early Childhood, Physical • ENGINEERING Air Conditioning Technology, Chemical, Civil/Environmental, Electrical, Engineering Science, Industrial, Mechanical • HEALTH SCIENCES Dental Hygiene, Environmental, Medical Assistant, Medical Secretary, Medical Technology, Nursing • HUMANITIES Humanities, Liberal Arts • LANGUAGES Chinese, French, German, Italian, Japanese, Russian, Spanish • PREPROFESSIONAL Engineering, Forestry, Recreation, Social Work • SCIENCES Biology, Chemistry, Mathematics, Physical Science • SOCIAL SCIENCES Criminal Justice • VISUAL AND PERFORMING ARTS Art, Studio Art, Theater • VOCATIONAL Air Conditioning/Heating/Refrig, Automobile Technology, Automotive Service, Business and Office, Carpentry, Construction, Drafting, Forestry, Funeral/Mortuary, Medical Laboratory Technology, Park/Recreation, Radiological Technology, Respiratory Therapy Technology, Secretarial

Sports/Activities
• SPORTS-INTERCOLLEGIATE Baseball (M), Basketball, Bowling (F), Cross Country, Football (M), Golf (M), Lacrosse (M), Soccer (M), Softball (F), Tennis, Track and Field, Volleyball (F), Wrestling (M) • SPORTS-INTRAMURAL Baseball, Basketball, Bowling, Cross Country, Field Hockey, Golf, Ice Hockey, Lacrosse, Ping-Pong, Racquetball, Skiing - Snow, Softball, Tennis, Track and Field, Volleyball, Wrestling (M) • STUDENT LIFE ACTIVITIES Concert Band, Drama Groups, Jazz Band, Musical Theater, Newspaper, Radio/TV station, Student Government, Yearbook

Very Selective   **New York**
Services

Hunter College
695 Park Avenue
New York, New York 10021
(212) 772-4857

School Enrollment: **9,350** Male: **2,650** Female: **6,700**

Admissions Contact: **Bill Zlata, Director of Admissions**
LD Contact: **Sandy LaPorta, Coordinator, Disabled Students**
Name of Program: **Office of Students with Disabilities**
Telephone:**(212) 772-4857**

Admissions

Application Information:
Applicant must apply **5** months in advance

Secondary School Information
Most Important Criteria For Admissions (1-strongest)

SAT/ACT	Application **1**	School transcript
Class rank	Course selection	Personal statement
Interview	Extra activities	Psychoeducational
1 G.P.A.	Open admission	Recommendations

Test Requirements:
Diagnostic testing waived: **Yes**
Achievement tests required:**None**
Documentation of LD required: **Yes**
Currency of diagnostic testing: **any history of diagnosis accepted**

Types of Disabilities Served
- Speech/Lang
- Study skills
- Written express
- Organizational
- Perceptual
- Reading
- Spelling
- Math
- Fine Motor
- ADD with LD
- ADD without LD
- ADHD with LD
- ADHD without LD

Admissions Process

All students apply through CUNY Admissions Services. Special admissions possible under special circumstances.

Learning Disability Program

Program: Reinforces course work: **Yes**
Program available through:**All year**
Students mainstreamed **100** % of the day
Recommended credits per semester: **6-12**
Services available for all students: **Yes**
Counseling: Individual: **Yes** Group Counseling: **Yes**
Support groups are available:**Voluntary support groups**

Faculty:
Faculty: **8** Full time: **5** Part time: **3**
Faculty advocate: **Yes** Meets with instructor: **As needed**

Diagnostic Testing

ADD	Personality	Perceptual skills	Spelling
ADHD	Organization	Fine motor skills	Reading
I.Q.	Handwriting	Spoken language	Study skills
Math	Social skills	Written language	

Tutoring:
Services rendered by:
- Graduates
- Peers
- Faculty
- LD staff
- Teacher trainees

Tutorials

Grp.	Ind.	Tutorials	Grp.	Ind.	Tutorials
		Math skills		•	Word processing
		Study skills			Time management
		Language arts			Learning strategies
		Written express			Organizational skills

Academic Accommodations

Curriculum	Study Aids	Exams
• Priority registration	Typist	• Oral
• Math waiver	• Reader	• Untimed
Foreign lang. waiver	• Notetaker	Take home
• Course substitution	• Proof reader	• With proctor
In Class	Text on tape	• On computer
• Calculators	Early syllabus	• Extended time
• Tape recorder	Taped handouts	• On tape
• Word processor		• Modified
• Priority seating		Separate room

Graduation Requirements:
Course credits: **125** GPA: **2.0**
Other requirements: **Distribution requirements, major/minor**

Program Strengths

Individual and group tutoring offered in content and skills area and geared toward LD student and his/her needs.

General Information:

Hunter College is a 4 year public college. Urban campus New York City. Accessible by train or bus. Ski areas are 2 hours from campus. Beaches are 1 hour from campus. 1 residential halls on campus. Housing is not guaranteed.

Accreditation:

Expenses:
Tuition: In-state: Full year: $1,450.00. Part-time: Per credit:$125.00. Part-time: Per course: $375.00. Tuition: Out-of-state: Full year: $4,050.00. Part-time: Per credit:$210.00. Part-time: Per course:$630.00 Room and board: $2,600.00

Majors

• AREA STUDIES African, Black/Afro-American, Caribbean, Hispanic/American, Jewish/Judaism, Latin American, Urban, Women's Studies • ARTS Art History, Dance, Film & Video, Music, Painting • BUSINESS Accounting, Economics • COMMUNICATIONS Communication, English, Literature • COMPUTER SCIENCE Computer Science, Programming • CRAFTS AND DESIGN Sculpture • EDUCATION Art Therapy, Elementary, English, English As A Second Language, Foreign Language, General, Mathematics, Middle School, Music, Physical, Secondary, Social Studies, Special, Speech/Language • HEALTH SCIENCES Nursing, Rehabilitation • HUMANITIES Classics, English/Writing/Literature, Fine Arts, Humanities, Liberal Arts , Philosophy, Religion • LANGUAGES Chinese, English, French, German, Hebrew, Italian, Japanese, Russian, Spanish • MATHEMATICS Applied, Computer, Statistical • PRE PROFESSIONAL Social Work • RELIGIOUS STUDIES Hebrew, Judaism & Jewish Studies • SCIENCES Anthropology, Archeology, Astronomy, Biology, Chemistry, Computer Science, Geography, Geology, Physics • SOCIAL SCIENCES Anthropology, Geography, History, Political Science, Psychology, Sociology • VISUAL AND PERFORMING ARTS Art, Art History, Dance, Music, Studio Art, Theater

Sports/Activities

• SPORTS RELATED Cheerleading, Team Managers • SPORTS-INTER-

New York

COLLEGIATE Baseball (F), Baseball (M), Basketball (F), Basketball (M), Cross Country (F), Cross Country (M), Fencing (F), Fencing (M), Soccer (F), Soccer (M), Softball (F), Swimming (F), Tennis (F), Tennis (M), Track and Field (F), Track and Field (M), Volleyball (F), Volleyball (M), Wrestling (M) • SPORTS-INTRAMURAL Basketball (F), Basketball (M), Field Hockey (F), Field Hockey (M), Football, Flag, Ping-Pong (F), Ping-Pong (M), Soccer (F), Soccer (M), Swimming (F), Swimming (M), Volleyball (F), Volleyball (M) • STUDENT LIFE ACTIVITIES Academic Clubs, Choral, Community Service, Debate, Drama Groups, Ethnic & Cultural Groups, Film, Fraternities, Magazine, Music Groups, Musical Theater, Newspaper, Orchestra, Political Groups, Radio/TV station, Religious Organization, Sororities, Student Government, Symphony Orchestra, Yearbook

Less Selective — New York Program

Iona College - Seton School
1061 North Broadway
Yonkers, New York 10701
(914) 633-2000

School Enrollment: **700** Male: **350** Female: **350**
LD Enrollment: **40** Male: **20** Female: **20**

Admissions Contact: **Laurie Austin, Director of Admissions**
LD Contact: **Elsa De Vita, Director**
Name of Program: **College Assistance Program**
Address: **1061 North Broadway**
Telephone: **(914) 378-8014**

Admissions

Application Information:
LD Students Applying: **60** Accepted: **35** Enrolled: **20**
LD on admissions committee: **Yes**
Application deadline: **April 30th**
Rolling Admissions: **Yes**

Secondary School Information
Most Important Criteria For Admissions (1-strongest)
10 SAT/ACT **8** Application **5** School transcript
9 Class rank **4** Course selection **11** Personal statement
1 Interview **12** Extra activities **2** Psychoeducational
7 G.P.A. Open admission **6** Recommendations

Test Requirements:
Standardized tests waived: **Yes**
Diagnostic testing waived: **Yes**
Untimed SAT: **Yes**
WAIS-R required: **Yes** Range accepted: **Average +**
Documentation of LD required: **Yes**
Currency of diagnostic testing: **Less than 2 years**
Tests recommended: **WAIS-R (subject scores and evaluation), Achievement Test.**

Types of Disabilities Served
Speech/Lang • Reading • ADD with LD
• Study skills • Spelling ADD without LD
• Written express • Math • ADHD with LD
• Organizational • Fine Motor ADHD without LD
• Perceptual

Admissions Process

Send application, transcript, IEP, psychological testing and letters of recommendation to Admission. Student is then required to arrange for personal interview with parent/guardian.

High School Course Requirements:
English: **4** Math: **2** Science: **2**
Waivers to standard high school courses
Foreign Language : **Yes** Math: **Yes** Course substitution: **Yes**

Learning Disability Program
Special orientation for LD students: **Yes**
Syllabus available during orientation: **Yes**
Program: Reinforces course work: **Yes**
Program available through: **As needed**
Students mainstreamed **100** % of the day
Recommended credits per semester: **12**
Time required or recommended in learning center: **2 hours**
Services only for LD students: **Yes**
Counseling: Individual: **Yes** Group Counseling: **Yes** Vocational Counseling: **Yes**
Support groups are available: **Yes, rap session with professional counselor - meets weekly during 1st semester.**

Faculty:
Faculty: **7** Including Director: **Yes** Full time: **2** Part time: **5** M.A.: **7**
Faculty advocate: **Yes** Meets with instructor: **As needed**

Diagnostic Testing
ADD Personality • Perceptual skills • Spelling
ADHD • Organization • Fine motor skills • Reading
I.Q. • Handwriting • Spoken language • Study skills
• Math • Social skills • Written language

Tutoring:
Average size of group tutorials: **1**
Services rendered by:
Graduates Peers Faculty • LD staff Teacher trainees

Tutorials
Grp. Ind. Tutorials Grp. Ind. Tutorials
• Math skills • Word processing
• Study skills • Time management
• Language arts • Learning strategies
• Written express • Organizational skills

Academic Accommodations
Curriculum **Study Aids** **Exams**
• Priority registration • Typist • Oral
• Math waiver • Reader • Untimed
• Foreign lang. waiver • Notetaker • Take home
• Course substitution • Proof reader • With proctor
In Class • Text on tape On computer
• Calculators • Early syllabus • Extended time
• Tape recorder • Taped handouts On tape
• Word processor Modified
• Priority seating • Separate room

Graduation Requirements:
Course credits: **60 +** GPA: **2.0** Years to complete degree: **2-1/2** Math waiver: **Yes** Language waiver: **Yes**

Program Strengths
The program provides a warm supportive environment for students who need comprehensive support for success in college. In addition it also provides the professional varied strengths and experiences.

General Information:
Iona College - Seton School is a 2 year independent Roman Catholic col-

lege. Suburban campus of 21 acres is 10 miles from New York City. Accessible by air, bus, or train. Ski areas are 2 hours from campus. Beaches are 1 hour from campus. 5% of students are foreign. 1 residential halls on campus. Housing is guaranteed.Guaranteed through 2nd year. 25 % of students remain on campus for the weekends.

Accreditation:MSACS

Expenses:
Tuition: In-state: Full year: $7,590.00. Part-time: Per credit:$250.00. Part-time: Per course: $750.00. Tuition: Out-of-state: Full year: $7,590.00. Part-time: Per credit:$250.00. Part-time: Per course:$750.00 Room and board: $4,670.00 Cost of LD program:$660.00 summer session 1st year, $950 per semester

Majors
• AREA STUDIES American, Urban • BUSINESS Accounting, Business Administration, Business Economics, Business Education, Business Management, Data Processing, Economics, International Business, Marketing, Retailing • COMMUNICATIONS Advertising, Broadcasting, Communication, English, Journalism, Literature, Television/Radio/Film • COMPUTER SCIENCE Computer Science • CRAFTS AND DESIGN Illustration Design • EDUCATION Business, Early Childhood, Elementary, English, Foreign Language, Mathematics, Middle School, Science, Secondary, Social Studies, Special, Speech/Language • HEALTH SCIENCES Health, Medical Laboratory Technology, Nursing, Practical Nursing, Speech Therapy, Speech/Audiology and Speech • HUMANITIES Classics, Fine Arts, Humanities, Liberal Arts , Philosophy, Religion • PRE PROFESSIONAL Dentistry, Law, Legal Assistant, Medicine, Social Work • SCIENCES Behavioral Biology, Biochemistry, Biology, Chemistry, Ecology, Mathematics, Physical Science, Physics • SOCIAL SCIENCES Criminal Justice, Criminology, Government/Political, Law Enforcement, Political Science, Psychology, Public Relations, Social Science, Sociology • VISUAL AND PERFORMING ARTS Dramatic Arts, Fine Arts, Theater • VOCATIONAL Business and Office, Paralegal

Sports/Activities
• SPORTS-INTRAMURAL Basketball, Football (M), Volleyball (F), Volleyball (M) • STUDENT LIFE ACTIVITIES Academic Clubs, Community Service, Dance, Drama Groups, Magazine, Newspaper, Radio/TV station, Religious Organization, Student Government, Yearbook

Less Selective   **New York**
                                      Services

Jefferson Community College
Watertown, New York 13601
(315) 782-5250

School Enrollment: **3,000** Male: **1,200** Female: **1,800**

Admissions Contact: **Rosanne N. Weir, Director of Admissions**
LD Contact: **Ted Hogancamp, Director, Learning Skills Center**
Name of Program: **Learning Skills Center**
Telephone:**(315) 786-2288**

Admissions

Application Information:
Application deadline: **Rolling**
Rolling Admissions: **Yes**

Secondary School Information
Most Important Criteria For Admissions (1-strongest)

SAT/ACT	Application	School transcript
Class rank	Course selection	Personal statement
Interview	Extra activities	Psychoeducational
G.P.A.	**1** Open admission	Recommendations

Test Requirements:
Standardized tests waived: **Yes**
Documentation of LD required: **Yes**

Types of Disabilities Served
• Speech/Lang • Reading • ADD with LD
• Study skills • Spelling • ADD without LD
• Written express • Math • ADHD with LD
• Organizational • Fine Motor • ADHD without LD
• Perceptual

Admissions Process

Open door for Jefferson City, non-competitive.

Learning Disability Program
Program: Remedial: **Yes**
Program: Reinforces course work: **Yes**
Recommended credits per semester:
Services available for all students: **Yes**
Counseling: Individual: **Yes** Group Counseling: **Yes** Vocational Counseling: **Yes**
Support groups are available:**Yes, student groups**

Diagnostic Testing

ADD	Personality	Perceptual skills	Spelling
ADHD	Organization	Fine motor skills	Reading
I.Q.	Handwriting	Spoken language	Study skills
Math	Social skills	Written language	

Tutoring:
Average size of group tutorials: **2-10**
Services rendered by:
Graduates •Peers •Faculty LD staff Teacher trainees

Tutorials

Grp.	Ind.	Tutorials	Grp.	Ind.	Tutorials
•	•	Math skills	•	•	Word processing
•	•	Study skills	•	•	Time management
•	•	Language arts	•	•	Learning strategies
•	•	Written express	•	•	Organizational skills

Academic Accommodations

Curriculum	Study Aids	Exams
Priority registration	• Typist	• Oral
Math waiver	Reader	Untimed
Foreign lang. waiver	• Notetaker	• Take home
• Course substitution	• Proof reader	• With proctor
In Class	• Text on tape	On computer
• Calculators	Early syllabus	• Extended time
• Tape recorder	Taped handouts	On tape
• Word processor		• Modified
Priority seating		Separate room

Program Strengths
We do not have a specific program but do offer services through our Learning Skills Center.

General Information:

Jefferson Community College is a 2 year public college. Urban campus 1 miles from Watertown. Accessible by bus. Ski areas are 10 miles from campus. Beaches are 20 miles from campus. Housing is not guaranteed.

Accreditation:MSACS

Expenses:

Tuition: In-state: Full year: $1,350.00. Part-time: Per credit:$56.00. Tuition: Out-of-state: Full year: $2,700.00. Part-time: Per credit:$112.00.

Majors

• BUSINESS Accounting, Banking, Business Administration, Business Management, Finance, Food Management, Hotel and Restaurant Management, Management, Retailing, Travel/Tourism Management • COMMUNICATIONS Journalism, Television/Radio/Film • COMPUTER SCIENCE Computer Science, Data Processing, Programming • ENGINEERING Engineering Science, Industrial • HEALTH SCIENCES Medical Secretary, Medical Technology, Nursing • HUMANITIES Humanities, Liberal Arts • PREPROFESSIONAL Recreation • SCIENCES Behavioral Biology, Biology, Chemistry, Geology, Mathematics, Physical Science, Physics • SOCIAL SCIENCES Criminal Justice, Family Counseling, Law Enforcement, Public Relations, Social Sciences • VOCATIONAL Business and Office, Fashion Design, Fashion Merchandising, Forestry, Secretarial

Sports/Activities

• SPORTS-INTERCOLLEGIATE Baseball (M), Basketball, Golf, Soccer (M), Softball (F), Volleyball (F) • SPORTS-INTRAMURAL Badminton, Baseball (M), Basketball, Bowling, Field Hockey (F), Ping-Pong, Softball, Tennis, Volleyball • STUDENT LIFE ACTIVITIES Academic Clubs, Choral, Drama Groups, Magazine, Newspaper, Religious Organization, Student Government, Yearbook

Most Selective	New York
	Accommodations

Julliard School

60 Lincoln Center Plaza
New York, New York 10023-6590
(212) 799-5000 Ext. 223

School Enrollment: **849** Male: **376** Female: **473**

Admissions Contact: **Carole Everett, Director of Admissions**

Admissions

Application Information:

Application deadline: **Jan. 8th and March 15th**
Notified when: **1 month after audition**

Secondary School Information

Most Important Criteria For Admissions (1-strongest)

SAT/ACT **2**	Application	**3** School transcript
Class rank	Course selection	**4** Personal statement
Interview	Extra activities	Psychoeducational
G.P.A.	Open admission	Recommendations

Types of Disabilities Served

Speech/Lang	Reading	ADD with LD
Study skills	Spelling	ADD without LD
Written express	Math	ADHD with LD
Organizational	Fine Motor	ADHD without LD
Perceptual		

Admissions Process

Admission to Julliard is based primarily on the quality of the personal audition. All applicants must prepare required repertoire and audition in person for the faculty.

Diagnostic Testing

ADD	Personality	Perceptual skills	Spelling
ADHD	Organization	Fine motor skills	Reading
I.Q.	Handwriting	Spoken language	Study skills
Math	Social skills	Written language	

Tutoring:

Average size of group tutorials: **One-to-one**
Services rendered by:
•Graduates   Peers   Faculty   LD staff   Teacher trainees

Tutorials

Grp.	Ind.	Tutorials	Grp.	Ind.	Tutorials
		Math skills			Word processing
		Study skills			Time management
		Language arts			Learning strategies
		Written express			Organizational skills

Academic Accommodations

Curriculum	Study Aids	Exams
Priority registration	Typist	Oral
Math waiver	Reader	Untimed
Foreign lang. waiver	Notetaker	Take home
Course substitution	Proof reader	With proctor
In Class	Text on tape	On computer
Calculators	Early syllabus	Extended time
Tape recorder	Taped handouts	On tape
Word processor		Modified
Priority seating		Separate room

General Information:

Julliard School is a 4 year independent Conservatory. Urban campus   Accessible by plane, train, or bus. Ski areas are 2 hours from campus. Beaches are 1 hour from campus. 33% of students are foreign. 1 residential halls on campus. Housing is guaranteed.Guaranteed through 1st year. 90 % of students remain on campus for the weekends.

Accreditation:MSACS

Expenses:

Tuition: In-state: Full year: $9,800.00. Tuition: Out-of-state: Full year: $9,800.00. Room and board: $6,300.00

Majors

• ARTS Dance, Dramatic Arts, Music • VISUAL AND PERFORMING ARTS Dance, Dramatic Arts, Music, Music Performance

Sports/Activities

• SPORTS-INTERCOLLEGIATE Ice Hockey, Tennis • SPORTS-INTRAMURAL Ice Hockey, Tennis • STUDENT LIFE ACTIVITIES Ethnic & Cultural Groups, Film, Newspaper, Orchestra, Student Government, Symphony Orchestra, Yearbook

Selective	New York Program

Keuka College
Keuka Park, New York 14478
(315) 536-4411

School Enrollment: **600** Male: **200** Female: **400**

Admissions Contact: **Robert J. Iannuzzo, Dean of Admissions**
LD Contact: **Dr. David Shinn, Academic Skills Counselor**

Admissions

Application Information:
Application deadline: **May 1st**
Applicant must apply **6** months in advance
Rolling Admissions: **Yes** Notified when: **3 weeks**

Secondary School Information
Most Important Criteria For Admissions (1-strongest)

3 SAT/ACT	**11** Application	**1**	School transcript
5 Class rank	**4** Course selection	**6**	Personal statement
8 Interview	**9** Extra activities	**10**	Psychoeducational
2 G.P.A.	Open admission	**7**	Recommendations

Test Requirements:
Untimed SAT: **Yes** Untimed ACT: **Yes**

Types of Disabilities Served
Speech/Lang	• Reading	ADD with LD
• Study skills	Spelling	ADD without LD
• Written express	Math	ADHD with LD
• Organizational	Fine Motor	ADHD without LD
Perceptual		

Learning Disability Program
Program: Reinforces course work: **Yes**

Faculty:
Faculty: **1**

Diagnostic Testing
ADD	Personality	Perceptual skills	Spelling
ADHD	Organization	Fine motor skills	Reading
I.Q.	Handwriting	Spoken language	Study skills
Math	Social skills	Written language	

Tutoring:
Average size of group tutorials: **5-6**
Services rendered by:
• Graduates • Peers • Faculty • LD staff Teacher trainees

Tutorials
Grp.	Ind.	Tutorials	Grp.	Ind.	Tutorials
•	•	Math skills	•	•	Word processing
•	•	Study skills	•	•	Time management
•	•	Language arts	•	•	Learning strategies
•	•	Written express	•	•	Organizational skills

Academic Accommodations
Curriculum	Study Aids	Exams
Priority registration	Typist	• Oral
Math waiver	Reader	Untimed
Foreign lang. waiver	Notetaker	• Take home
Course substitution	Proof reader	With proctor
In Class	Text on tape	On computer
• Calculators	Early syllabus	• Extended time
Tape recorder	Taped handouts	On tape
• Word processor		• Modified
Priority seating		Separate room

Program Strengths
The program provides a mentor who works with 5-8 students who have moderate learning disabilities. Diagnostic testing will be done, remediation support services will be provided and class monitoring and advocacy will be part of the program. At this point our program is too new to determine scope of services. We will purposely be limiting enrollment to 5-8 students.

General Information:
Keuka College is a 4 year private college. Rural campus of 173 acres is 50 miles from Rochester. Accessible by air or bus. Ski areas are 45 minutes from campus. Beaches are on campus from campus. 2% of students are foreign. 4 residential halls on campus. Housing is guaranteed. Guaranteed through 4th year. 55 % of students remain on campus for the weekends.

Accreditation: MSACS

SAT/ACT Scores:
Scores for incoming freshmen: **Verbal:** 56% below 500. 10% between 500 and 599. 5% between 600 and 699. 1% above 700. **Math:** 48% below 500. 14% between 500 and 599. 7% between 600 and 699. 1% above 700.

Class Rank:
About 43% of the present freshmen class were in the upper 20% of their high school class. 67% were in the top 40% of their class. 88% were in the top 60% of their class. 95% were in the top 80% of their class.

Expenses:
Tuition: In-state: Full year: $7,400.00. Part-time: Per credit: $200.00. Tuition: Out-of-state: Full year: $7,400.00. Part-time: Per credit: $200.00. Room and board: $3,400.00.

Majors
• AREA STUDIES American • BUSINESS Accounting, Business Administration, Business Management, Finance, Hotel and Restaurant Management, Management, Marketing • COMMUNICATIONS English • EDUCATION Elementary, English, English As A Second Language (, Foreign Language, Mathematics, Science, Secondary, Social Studies, Special • HEALTH SCIENCES Medical Technology, Nursing, Occupational Therapy • PREPROFESSIONAL Dentistry, Engineering, Law, Medicine, Social Work • SCIENCES Biochemistry, Biology, Mathematics • SOCIAL SCIENCES Government/Political, History, Political Science, Psychology, Public Relations, Sociology

Sports/Activities
• SPORTS-INTERCOLLEGIATE Basketball, Lacrosse (M), Soccer (F), Softball (M), Volleyball (F) • STUDENT LIFE ACTIVITIES Choral, Community Service, Dance, Drama Groups, Ethnic & Cultural Groups, Magazine, Music Groups, Newspaper, Political Groups, Radio/TV station, Religious Organization, Student Government, Yearbook

Long Island University: C.W. Post Campus
Northern Boulevard
Brookville, New York 11548
(516) 299-2413

School Enrollment: **5,000** Male: **2,250** Female: **2,750**
LD Enrollment: **80**

Admissions Contact: **Christine Natali, Director of Admissions**
LD Contact: **Carol Rundlett/M. Traina Power, Assistant Dir./Dir.**
Name of Program: **Academic Resource Center**
Address: **Student Service Building**
Telephone:**(516) 299-2937**

Admissions

Application Information:
Accepted: **20** Enrolled:**80**
Separate application:**Yes**
Application deadline: **Rolling**
Rolling Admissions: **Yes**

Secondary School Information
Most Important Criteria For Admissions (1-strongest)

2	SAT/ACT	10	Application	4	School transcript
3	Class rank	6	Course selection	8	Personal statement
9	Interview	7	Extra activities	5	Psychoeducational
1	G.P.A.		Open admission	11	Recommendations

Test Requirements:
Diagnostic testing waived: **Yes**
Untimed SAT: **Yes** Untimed ACT: **Yes** Achievement tests required:**3**
WAIS-R required: **Yes**
Documentation of LD required: **Yes**
Currency of diagnostic testing: **1 year**
Tests recommended: **WAIS-R plus at least one test showing strengths and needs**

Types of Disabilities Served
- Speech/Lang
- Reading
- ADD with LD
- Study skills
- Spelling
- ADD without LD
- Written express
- Math
- ADHD with LD
- Organizational
- Fine Motor
- ADHD without LD
- Perceptual

Admissions Process

Student must be accepted to the University prior to application to the Academic Resource Center.

Learning Disability Program

Special orientation for LD students: **Yes**
Program: Reinforces course work: **Yes**
Students mainstreamed **100** % of the day
Recommended credits per semester: **12**
Time required or recommended in learning center: **2 hours**
Services only for LD students: **Yes**
Counseling: Individual: **Yes** Vocational Counseling: **Yes**
Support groups are available:**Yes, peer groups, ARC**

Faculty:
Faculty: **18** Full time: **2** Part time: **16**
LD faculty with: BS/BA: **18** M.A.: **7** Ph.D.: **1**
Faculty advocate: **Yes** Meets with instructor: **As needed**

Diagnostic Testing
- ADD
- Personality
- Perceptual skills
- Spelling
- ADHD
- Organization
- Fine motor skills
- Reading
- I.Q.
- Handwriting
- Spoken language
- Study skills
- Math
- Social skills
- Written language

Tutoring:
Average size of group tutorials: **5**
Services rendered by:
- Graduates
- Peers
- Faculty
- LD staff
- Teacher trainees

Tutorials

Grp.	Ind.	Tutorials	Grp.	Ind.	Tutorials
•	•	Math skills		•	Word processing
•	•	Study skills	•	•	Time management
•	•	Language arts	•	•	Learning strategies
•	•	Written express	•	•	Organizational skills

Academic Accommodations

Curriculum	Study Aids	Exams
Priority registration	Typist	Oral
• Math waiver	• Reader	• Untimed
• Foreign lang. waiver	• Notetaker	• Take home
Course substitution	• Proof reader	• With proctor
In Class	• Text on tape	• On computer
• Calculators	Early syllabus	• Extended time
• Tape recorder	Taped handouts	On tape
• Word processor		• Modified
Priority seating		• Separate room

Graduation Requirements:GPA: **2.0** Years to complete degree: **4-5** Math waiver: **Yes** Language waiver: **Yes**

Program Strengths

We are a supportive program which encourages independence, social skills, and self-confidence. Students are given individual attention, and sessions are planned according to their academic needs.

General Information:

Long Island University: C.W. Post Campus is a 4 year private university. Suburban campus of 450 acres is 24 miles from New York. Accessible by air, train or bus. Beaches are 15 miles from campus. 5% of students are foreign. 11 residential halls on campus. Housing is not guaranteed.50 % of students remain on campus for the weekends. 15 % of students join fraternities/sororities.

Accreditation:MSACS

SAT/ACT Scores:
Scores for incoming freshmen:**Verbal:**55% below 500. 43% between 500 and 599. 1% between 600 and 699. 1% above 700. **Math:**51% below 500. 47% between 500 and 599. 1% between 600 and 699. 1% above 700.

Expenses:
Tuition: In-state: Full year: $4,025.00. Part-time: Per credit:$350.00. Room and board: $4,350.00 Cost of LD program:$3,000.00

Majors

• AREA STUDIES American, European, Jewish, Russian/Slavic • BUSINESS Accounting, Banking, Business Administration, Business Education, Business Management, Economics, Finance, Management, Marketing • COMMUNICATIONS Broadcasting, Communication, English, Journalism, Photography, Speech, Television/Radio/Film • COMPUTER SCIENCE Computer Science, Programming • EDUCATION Art, Art Therapy, Bilingual, Curriculum, Early Childhood, Elementary, English, English As A Second Language (, Foreign Language, Health, Mathematics, Music, Music Therapy, Physical, Science, Secondary, Social Studies, Special • ENGINEERING Nuclear Medical Technology • HEALTH SCIENCES Environmental, Health, Medical Records Technology, Medical Technology, Nursing, Nutritional/Food, Radiological Therapy, Speech Therapy • HUMANITIES Philosophy • LANGUAGES French, German, Hebrew, Italian, Spanish • PREPROFESSIONAL Dentistry, Engineering, Law, Medicine, Pharmacy, Veterinarian • SCIENCES Biology, Chemistry, Earth, Geography, Geology, Mathematics, Medical Biology, Physics • SOCIAL SCIENCES Criminal Justice, Government/Political, History, Law Enforcement, Political Science, Psychology, Public Relations, Sociology • VISUAL AND PERFORMING ARTS Art, Art History, Dramatic Arts, Fine Arts, Music, Music Theatre, Studio Art, Theater • VOCATIONAL Radiological Technology

Sports/Activities

• SPORTS RELATED Pep Band • SPORTS-INTERCOLLEGIATE Baseball (M), Basketball, Cross Country, Field Hockey (F), Football (M), Golf (M), Lacrosse (M), Soccer (M), Softball (F), Tennis, Track and Field, Volleyball (F), Wrestling (M) • SPORTS-INTRAMURAL Basketball, Bowling, Field Hockey (F), Golf (M), Horseback Riding, Lacrosse (M), Racquetball, Soccer, Softball, Tennis, Track and Field, Volleyball • STUDENT LIFE ACTIVITIES Choral, Concert Band, Dance, Ethnic & Cultural Groups, Film, Fraternities, Jazz Band, Magazine, Music Groups, Musical Theater, Newspaper, Orchestra, Political Groups, Radio/TV station, Religious Organization, Sororities, Student Government, Yearbook

Selective	New York

Long Island University: Southampton Campus

Montauk Highway
Southampton, New York 11968
(516) 283-4000

School Enrollment: **1,300** Male: **570** Female: **730**

Admissions Contact: **Carol Gilbert, Director of Admissions**
LD Contact: **Pamela Topping, Director, Study Center**
Address: **Study Center, 239 Montauk Hwy.**
Telephone:**(516) 283-4000**

Admissions

Application Information:
Application deadline: **None**
Rolling Admissions: **Yes**

Secondary School Information
Most Important Criteria For Admissions (1-strongest)

4 SAT/ACT	Application	**2** School transcript
9 Class rank	**1** Course selection	**7** Personal statement
6 Interview	**8** Extra activities	**10** Psychoeducational
3 G.P.A.	Open admission	**5** Recommendations

Test Requirements:
Untimed SAT: **Yes** Untimed ACT: **Yes** Untimed ACH: **Yes**

Types of Disabilities Served

Speech/Lang	Reading	ADD with LD
Study skills	Spelling	ADD without LD
Written express	Math	ADHD with LD
Organizational	Fine Motor	ADHD without LD
Perceptual		

Admissions Process

Mandatory on campus interview and placement testing for all LD students.

High School Course Requirements:
English: **4** Math: **2** Science: **2**

Learning Disability Program

Time required or recommended in learning center: **1 hour per course**
Services available for all students: **Yes**

Faculty:
Faculty: **4** Full time: **3** Part time: **1** M.A.: **4**

Diagnostic Testing

ADD	Personality	Perceptual skills	Spelling
ADHD	Organization	Fine motor skills	Reading
I.Q.	Handwriting	Spoken language	Study skills
Math	Social skills	Written language	

Tutoring:
Average size of group tutorials: **3**
Services rendered by:

Graduates	•Peers	•Faculty	LD staff	Teacher trainees

Tutorials

Grp.	Ind.	Tutorials	Grp.	Ind.	Tutorials
•	•	Math skills	•	•	Word processing
	•	Study skills		•	Time management
	•	Language arts		•	Learning strategies
•	•	Written express		•	Organizational skills

Academic Accommodations

Curriculum	Study Aids	Exams
Priority registration	Typist	Oral
Math waiver	Reader	Untimed
Foreign lang. waiver	Notetaker	Take home
Course substitution	Proof reader	With proctor
In Class	Text on tape	On computer
Calculators	Early syllabus	• Extended time
Tape recorder	Taped handouts	On tape
Word processor		Modified
Priority seating		Separate room

Graduation Requirements:
Course credits: **128** GPA: **2.0 (2.25 in major)** Years to complete degree: **No limit**

Program Strengths

Ours is a program both of developmental courses in reading, writing, and math, and of tutorial support in almost all academic areas - required in developmental courses - elective (and POPULAR) in "mainstream" academic courses.

General Information:

Long Island University: Southampton Campus is a 4 year independent college. Rural campus of 110 acres is 90 miles from New York City. Accessible by plane, train or bus. Ski areas are 3 hours from campus. Beaches are 2 miles from campus. 2% of students are foreign. 11 residential halls on campus. Housing is guaranteed.Guaranteed through the 4th year. 50 % of students remain on campus for the weekends.

Accreditation:MSACS

Expenses:
Tuition: In-state: Full year: $10,050.00. Part-time: Per credit:$296.00. Part-time: Per course: $888.00. Tuition: Out-of-state: Full year: 10,050.00. Part-time: Per credit:$296.00. Part-time: Per course:$888.00 Room and board: $5,000.00

Majors

• ARTS Drawing, Graphic Arts • BUSINESS Accounting, Business Administration, Business Management, Management, Marketing • COMMUNICATIONS Communication, English • EDUCATION Art, Elementary, English, Science, Social Studies • HUMANITIES English/Writing/Literature, Fine Arts, Liberal Arts • PRE PROFESSIONAL Dentistry, Medicine, Veterinarian • SCIENCES Biology, Chemistry, Ecology, Geology, Gerontology, Marine Biology, Oceanography • SOCIAL SCIENCES History, Psychology, Sociology • VISUAL AND PERFORMING ARTS Art, Fine Arts, Studio Art

Sports/Activities

• SPORTS-INTERCOLLEGIATE Basketball (F), Basketball (M), Lacrosse (M), Soccer (F), Soccer (M), Softball (F), Volleyball (F), Volleyball (M) • SPORTS-INTRAMURAL Basketball, Basketball (F), Basketball (M), Lacrosse (M), Sailing, Soccer, Soccer (F), Soccer (M), Softball, Softball (F), Softball (M), Volleyball, Volleyball (F), Volleyball (M) • STUDENT LIFE ACTIVITIES Academic Clubs, Community Service, Drama Groups, Ethnic & Cultural Groups, Film, Music Groups, Newspaper, Radio/TV station, Student Government, Yearbook

Special   **New York**
                                    Accommodations

Manhattan School of Music

120 Clarement Avenue
New York, New York 10027
(212) 749-2802

School Enrollment: **422** Male: **223** Female: **199**
LD Enrollment: **2-3**

Admissions Contact: **James Gandre, Director of Admissions**
LD Contact: **Dana Fili/Kenneth Fuchs, Dir. Residential Life**

Admissions

Application Information:
Application deadline: **July 1st**

Secondary School Information
Most Important Criteria For Admissions (1-strongest)

4 SAT/ACT	9 Application	2 School transcript
10 Class rank	8 Course selection	7 Personal statement
Interview	6 Extra activities	Psychoeducational
3 G.P.A.	Open admission	5 Recommendations

Types of Disabilities Served
• Speech/Lang	• Reading	ADD with LD
• Study skills	• Spelling	ADD without LD
• Written express	Math	ADHD with LD
Organizational	Fine Motor	ADHD without LD
Perceptual		

Learning Disability Program
Services available for all students: **Yes**

Faculty:
Faculty: **2** M.A.: **1**

Diagnostic Testing
ADD	Personality	Perceptual skills	Spelling
ADHD	Organization	Fine motor skills	Reading
I.Q.	Handwriting	Spoken language	Study skills
Math	Social skills	Written language	

Tutoring:
Services rendered by:
•Graduates   •Peers   •Faculty   LD staff   Teacher trainees

Tutorials

Grp.	Ind.	Tutorials	Grp.	Ind.	Tutorials
		Math skills			Word processing
	•	Study skills		•	Time management
	•	Language arts		•	Learning strategies
	•	Written express		•	Organizational skills

Academic Accommodations

Curriculum	Study Aids	Exams
Priority registration	Typist	• Oral
Math waiver	Reader	Untimed
Foreign lang. waiver	Notetaker	Take home
Course substitution	Proof reader	With proctor
In Class	• Text on tape	On computer
Calculators	Early syllabus	• Extended time
• Tape recorder	Taped handouts	On tape
Word processor		• Modified
Priority seating		Separate room

Graduation Requirements:
Course credits: **122** GPA: **2.0** Years to complete degree: **7**

Program Strengths
We are a small institution but we will do our best to try to accommodate any student who needs extra help.

General Information:
Manhattan School of Music is a 4 year private college. Urban campus of 1 acres is Accessible by air, train or bus. Ski areas are 100 miles from campus. Beaches are 100 miles from campus. 1% of students are foreign. 1 residential halls on campus. Housing is not guaranteed.

Accreditation:MSACS

Expenses:
Tuition: In-state: Full year: $10,700.00. Part-time: Per credit:$330.00. Tuition: Out-of-state: Full year: $10,700.00. Room and board: $4,000.00-$7,000.00

Majors
• VISUAL AND PERFORMING ARTS Jazz, Music Performance

Sports/Activities

• STUDENT LIFE ACTIVITIES Choral, Concert Band, Jazz Band, Music Groups, Opera, Student Government, Symphony Orchestra

Selective   **New York Program**

Marist College
290 North Road
Poughkeepsie, New York 12601
(914) 575-3274

School Enrollment: **3,000** Male: **1,500** Female: **1,500**
LD Enrollment: **40** Male: **32** Female: **8**

Admissions Contact: **Cathy Quakenbush, Director of Admissions**
LD Contact: **Dr. Diane Perreira, Director of Special Services**
Name of Program: **Special Services Program**
Telephone:**(914) 575-3274**

Admissions

Application Information:
LD Students Applying: **200** Accepted: **40** Enrolled:**25**
Separate application:**Yes**
Application deadline: **March 1st**
Notified when: **March 15th**

Secondary School Information
Most Important Criteria For Admissions (1-strongest)

11 SAT/ACT **10** Application   **3** School transcript
6 Class rank **8** Course selection **9** Personal statement
2 Interview **7** Extra activities **1** Psychoeducational
5 G.P.A.   Open admission **4** Recommendations

Test Requirements:
Standardized tests waived: **Yes**
WAIS-R required: **Yes** Range accepted: **100+**
Documentation of LD required: **Yes**
Currency of diagnostic testing: **3 years**
Tests recommended: **Woodcock-Johnson**

Types of Disabilities Served
• Speech/Lang   • Reading   • ADD with LD
• Study skills   • Spelling   • ADD without LD
• Written express • Math   • ADHD with LD
• Organizational • Fine Motor • ADHD without LD
• Perceptual

High School Course Requirements:
English: Math: **3** Science: **2**
Waivers to standard high school courses
Foreign Language : **Yes**

Learning Disability Program

Program: Reinforces course work: **Yes**
Students mainstreamed **100** % of the day
Services only for LD students: **Yes**
Counseling: Individual: **Yes** Vocational Counseling: **Yes**
Support groups are available:**Peer support**

Faculty:
Faculty: **8** Including Director: **Yes** Full time: **4** Part time: **3** M.A.: **5** Ph.D.: **1**
Faculty advocate: **Yes** Meets with instructor: **As needed**

Diagnostic Testing
ADD   Personality   Perceptual skills   Spelling
ADHD• Organization   Fine motor skills   Reading
I.Q.   Handwriting   Spoken language   • Study skills
Math   Social skills• Written language

Tutoring:
Services rendered by:
Graduates •Peers   Faculty   •LD staff   Teacher trainees

Tutorials
Grp. Ind. Tutorials   Grp. Ind. Tutorials
   • Math skills   • Word processing
   • Study skills   • Time management
   • Language arts   • Learning strategies
   • Written express   • Organizational skills

Academic Accommodations

Curriculum	Study Aids	Exams
Priority registration	Typist	Oral
Math waiver	• Reader	Untimed
Foreign lang. waiver	• Notetaker	Take home
Course substitution	• Proof reader	With proctor
In Class	• Text on tape	On computer
• Calculators	Early syllabus	• Extended time
• Tape recorder	Taped handouts	On tape
• Word processor		• Modified
Priority seating		Separate room

Program Strengths

Marist College offers a comprehensive support service program for students with learning disabilities. We seek highly motivated, bright students who are completing a college preparatory course of study. Participating students receive support services on an individualized basis while enrolled in a completely mainstreamed environment.

General Information:

Marist College is a 4 year private college. Suburban campus of 1,200 acres is 75 miles from New York. Accessible by air, train or bus. Ski areas are 1 hour from campus. Beaches are 2 hours from campus. 9 residential halls on campus. Housing is guaranteed.Guaranteed through 2nd year. 70 % of students remain on campus for the weekends. 10 % of students join fraternities/sororities.

Accreditation:NSACS

Expenses:
Tuition: In-state: Full year: $8,970.00. Part-time: Per credit:$256.00. Room and board: $5,200.00 Cost of LD program:$1,800.00

Majors

• AREA STUDIES American • BUSINES Accounting, Economics, Finance, Management, Marketing, Personnel • COMMUNICATIONS Advertising, Broadcasting, Communication, Creative Writing, English, Journalism, Public Address, Public Relations, Television/Radio/Film • COMPUTER SCIENCE Computer Mathematics, Computer Science • EDUCATION Middle School, Secondary, Special • HEALTH SCIENCES Environmental, Medical Technology • HUMANITIES Philosophy, Religion • LANGUAGES French, Russian, Spanish • PREPROFESSIONAL Engineering, Law, Social Work • SCIENCES Biology, Chemistry, Mathematics, Physics • SOCIAL SCIENCES Criminal Justice, Government/Political, History, Political Science, Psychology • VISUAL AND PERFORMING ARTS Art, Fine Arts • VOCATIONAL Fashion Design

Sports/Activities

• SPORTS RELATED Pep Band • SPORTS-INTERCOLLEGIATE Basketball, Crew, Cross Country, Diving, Football (M), Ice Hockey (M), La-

511

New York

crosse (M), Rugby (M), Skiing - Snow, Soccer (F), Soccer (M), Swimming, Tennis, Track and Field, Volleyball (F) • SPORTS-INTRAMURAL Archery, Badminton, Basketball (M), Bowling, Golf, Hand Ball, Ping-Pong, Racquetball, Sailing, Skiing - Snow, Soccer, Softball, Tennis, Volleyball, Wrestling (M) • STUDENT LIFE ACTIVITIES Choral, Debate, Drama Groups, Ethnic & Cultural Groups, Film, Fraternities, Magazine, Musical Theater, Newspaper, Religious Organization, Student Government, Yearbook

---

Selective   **New York Services**

Medaille College
18 Agassiz Circle
Buffalo, New York 14214
(716) 884-3281

School Enrollment: **1,500**

Admissions Contact: **Jacqueline Mathery, Director of Admissions**
LD Contact: **Dr. Frances Kinsley, Director, Learning Services Ctr.**

Admissions

Secondary School Information
Most Important Criteria For Admissions (1-strongest)

SAT/ACT **1**	Application **1**	School transcript
Class rank	Course selection	Personal statement
1 Interview	Extra activities	Psychoeducational
G.P.A.	Open admission **1**	Recommendations

Test Requirements:
Untimed SAT: **Yes** Untimed ACT: **Yes**
Documentation of LD required: **Yes**

Types of Disabilities Served
Speech/Lang	• Reading	ADD with LD
• Study skills	• Spelling	ADD without LD
• Written express	• Math	ADHD with LD
• Organizational	• Fine Motor	ADHD without LD
• Perceptual		

Admissions Process

Student is interviewed by admissions counselor. Must submit documentation of disability.

Learning Disability Program
Program: Reinforces course work: **Yes**
Students mainstreamed **100** % of the day
Recommended credits per semester: **12**
Services available for all students: **Yes**

Faculty:
Faculty: **5** Full time: **3** Part time: **2** M.A.: **4** Ph.D.: **1**
Faculty advocate: **Yes** Meets with instructor: **As needed**

Diagnostic Testing
ADD	Personality	Perceptual skills	Spelling
ADHD	Organization	Fine motor skills	Reading
I.Q.	Handwriting	Spoken language	Study skills
Math	Social skills	Written language	

Tutoring:
Average size of group tutorials: **1:1**
Services rendered by:
Graduates •Peers •Faculty •LD staff Teacher trainees

Tutorials
Grp.	Ind. Tutorials	Grp.	Ind. Tutorials
	• Math skills		• Word processing
	• Study skills		• Time management
	• Language arts		• Learning strategies
	• Written express		• Organizational skills

Academic Accommodations
Curriculum	Study Aids	Exams
Priority registration	• Typist	• Oral
Math waiver	• Reader	• Untimed
Foreign lang. waiver	• Notetaker	• Take home
Course substitution	• Proof reader	• With proctor
In Class	Text on tape	• On computer
• Calculators	Early syllabus	• Extended time
• Tape recorder	Taped handouts	On tape
• Word processor		Modified
• Priority seating		• Separate room

Graduation Requirements:
Course credits: **120** GPA: **2.0**

Program Strengths
Individual attention, small personal atmosphere of the institution. Well qualified and experienced staff.

General Information:
Medaille College is a 2 and 4 year independent college. Urban campus Housing is not guaranteed.

Accreditation: MSACS, BRUSNY

Expenses:
Tuition: In-state: Full year: $3,540.00 per semester. Part-time: Per credit:$236.00.

Majors
• BUSINESS Business Administration • COMMUNICATIONS Media • COMPUTER SCIENCE Computer Information Systems • EDUCATION K-6 • HUMANITIES Humanities, Liberal Arts • SOCIAL SCIENCES Child & Youth Services, Human Services, Social Science

Sports/Activities
• STUDENT LIFE ACTIVITIES Newspaper, Radio/TV station, Yearbook

512

Selective   **New York Program**

Mercy College
555 Broadway
Dobbs Ferry, New York 10522
(914) 693-7600

School Enrollment: **4,864** Male: **1,862** Female: **3,002**
LD Enrollment: **45**

Admissions Contact: **Kathleen O'Brien, Admissions Counselor**
LD Contact: **Catherine Leon, Coordinator**
Name of Program: **Program for LD College Students**
Telephone:**(914) 693-4500**

Admissions

Application Information:
Application deadline: **July 1st**
Notified when: **1 month after application**

Secondary School Information
Most Important Criteria For Admissions (1-strongest)

4 SAT/ACT	**4** Application	**2** School transcript
4 Class rank	**4** Course selection	**5** Personal statement
3 Interview	**5** Extra activities	**1** Psychoeducational
2 G.P.A.	Open admission	**3** Recommendations

Test Requirements:
Diagnostic testing waived: **Yes**
Untimed SAT: **Yes** Achievement tests required:**3**
WAIS-R required: **Yes** Range accepted: **85+**
Documentation of LD required: **Yes**
Tests recommended: **Achievement, I.Q., other**

Types of Disabilities Served
- Speech/Lang
- Study skills
- Written express
- Organizational
- Perceptual
- Reading
- Spelling
- Math
- Fine Motor
- ADD with LD
- ADD without LD
- ADHD with LD
- ADHD without LD

Learning Disability Program
Special orientation for LD students: **Yes**
Program: Remedial: **Yes**
Program: Reinforces course work: **Yes**
Students mainstreamed **100** % of the day
Recommended credits per semester: **9-12**
Counseling: Individual: **Yes** Vocational Counseling: **Yes**

Faculty:
Faculty: **9** Including Director: **Yes** Full time: **9** M.A.: **8** Ph.D.: **1**
Faculty advocate: **Yes** Meets with instructor: **3-4 times per semester**

Diagnostic Testing

ADD	Personality	Perceptual skills	Spelling
ADHD	Organization	Fine motor skills	• Reading
I.Q.	Handwriting	Spoken language	Study skills
• Math	Social skills	• Written language	

Tutoring:
Average size of group tutorials: **Individual**
Services rendered by:
- Graduates •Peers •Faculty •LD staff •Teacher trainees

Tutorials

Grp.	Ind.	Tutorials	Grp.	Ind.	Tutorials
	•	Math skills		•	Word processing
	•	Study skills		•	Time management
	•	Language arts		•	Learning strategies
	•	Written express		•	Organizational skills

Academic Accommodations

Curriculum	Study Aids	Exams
Priority registration	Typist	• Oral
Math waiver	Reader	Untimed
Foreign lang. waiver	• Notetaker	Take home
Course substitution	• Proof reader	With proctor
In Class	• Text on tape	On computer
• Calculators	Early syllabus	• Extended time
• Tape recorder	Taped handouts	On tape
• Word processor		• Modified
Priority seating		• Separate room

Graduation Requirements:
Course credits: **120** GPA: **2.0** Years to complete degree: **4-6**

Program Strengths
The Mercy College Program for LD College Students offers students strong support during their years at the college. The college personnel are professionals and they monitor progress throughout the year. Mentors work to make students successful, and we have a supportive faculty. Mercy's classes are kept small to promote individualized attention.

General Information:
Mercy College is a 2 and 4 year private college. Suburban campus of 77 acres is 15 miles from New York. Accessible by train or bus. Ski areas are 45 miles from campus. Beaches are 30 miles from campus. 10% of students are foreign. Housing is not guaranteed.

Accreditation:MSACS

Expenses:
Tuition: In-state: Full year: $6,990.00. Part-time: Per credit:$233.00.

Majors
• ARTS Music • BUSINESS Accounting, Banking/Finance, Business Administration, Business Management, Human Resources Management, Labor Relations, Management, Marketing • COMMUNICATIONS Broadcasting, English, Film & Video, Journalism, Speech/Debate/Forensic • COMPUTER SCIENCE Computer Science, Programming • EDUCATION Adult, Early Childhood, Elementary, English, English As A Second Language, Mathematics, Middle School, Music, Reading, Science, Secondary, Social Studies, Special, Speech/Language • HEALTH SCIENCES Medical Laboratory Technology, Speech Therapy, Speech/Audiology and Speech, Veterinarian Assistant • HUMANITIES English/Writing/Literature, Humanities, Liberal Arts • LANGUAGES French, Italian, Spanish • MATHEMATICS Applied • PREPROFESSIONAL Dentistry, Law, Optometry, Pharmacy, Social Work, Veterinarian • SCIENCES Biology, Computer Science, Gerontology, Mathematics • SOCIAL SCIENCES Criminal Justice, Government/Political, History, Human Service, Psychology, Social Sciences, Sociology • SPECIAL EDUCATION Deaf/Hearing Impaired, Emotionally Disturbed, Learning Disability, Mentally Retarded • VISUAL AND PERFORMING ARTS Music • VOCATIONAL Veterinarian Assistant

Sports/Activities

• SPORTS-INTERCOLLEGIATE Baseball (M), Basketball (F), Basketball (M), Cross Country, Golf, Horseback Riding, Soccer (M), Softball (F), Tennis, Volleyball (F) • SPORTS-INTRAMURAL Basketball (M), Ping-Pong • STUDENT LIFE ACTIVITIES Choral, Dance, Drama Groups, Ethnic & Cultural Groups, Film, Jazz Band, Magazine, Music Groups, Musical Theater, Newspaper, Radio/TV station, Sororities, Student Government, Symphony Orchestra, Yearbook

---

Less Selective

New York
Services

Mohawk Valley Community College

1101 Sherman Drive
Utica, New York 13501-5394
(315) 792-5354

School Enrollment: **8,000**
LD Enrollment: **71** Male: **51** Female: **20**

Admissions Contact: **Ian Lindsey, Director of Admissions**
LD Contact: **Lynn Igoe Holland, Coordinator**
Name of Program: **Services to Students with Disabilities**
Telephone:**(315) 792-5413**

Admissions

Application Information:

Application deadline: **Rolling**

Secondary School Information

Most Important Criteria For Admissions (1-strongest)

SAT/ACT	Application	School transcript
Class rank	Course selection	Personal statement
Interview	Extra activities	Psychoeducational
G.P.A.	**1** Open admission	Recommendations

Test Requirements:

Diagnostic testing waived: **Yes**
Documentation of LD required: **Yes**
Currency of diagnostic testing: **No cut off date**

Types of Disabilities Served

• Speech/Lang	• Reading	• ADD with LD
• Study skills	• Spelling	• ADD without LD
• Written express	• Math	• ADHD with LD
• Organizational	• Fine Motor	• ADHD without LD
• Perceptual		

Learning Disability Program

Students mainstreamed **100** % of the day
Recommended credits per semester: **12-13**
Counseling: Individual: **Yes** Vocational Counseling: **Yes**

Faculty:

Faculty: **1** Full time: **1**
LD faculty with: BS/BA: **1**
Faculty advocate: **Yes** Meets with instructor: **As needed**

Diagnostic Testing

ADD	Personality	Perceptual skills	Spelling
ADHD	Organization	Fine motor skills	Reading
I.Q.	Handwriting	Spoken language	Study skills
Math	Social skills	Written language	

Tutoring:

Average size of group tutorials: **8**
Services rendered by:

Graduates	Peers	•Faculty	LD staff	Teacher trainees

Tutorials

Grp.	Ind.	Tutorials	Grp.	Ind.	Tutorials
•	•	Math skills	•	•	Word processing
•	•	Study skills	•	•	Time management
•	•	Language arts	•	•	Learning strategies
•	•	Written express	•	•	Organizational skills

Academic Accommodations

Curriculum	Study Aids	Exams
• Priority registration	• Typist	• Oral
• Math waiver	• Reader	• Untimed
• Foreign lang. waiver	• Notetaker	• Take home
• Course substitution	• Proof reader	• With proctor
In Class	• Text on tape	• On computer
• Calculators	Early syllabus	• Extended time
• Tape recorder	• Taped handouts	• On tape
• Word processor		• Modified
• Priority seating		• Separate room

Graduation Requirements:

Course credits: **Varies** GPA: **2.0** Years to complete degree: **Varies** Math waiver: **Yes** Language waiver: **Yes**

Program Strengths

Services for learning disabled students are provided through the Office for Services to Students with Disabilities. We do not have a separate LD program at this time. The Office is working to improve the quantity and quality of available services and hopes to establish an LD program in the future.

General Information:

Mohawk Valley Community College is a 2 year public College. Suburban campus of 80 acres is Accessible by air, train or bus. Ski areas are 1 mile from campus. Beaches are 20 miles from campus. 1% of students are foreign. 4 residential halls on campus. Housing is not guaranteed.20 % of students remain on campus for the weekends.

Accreditation:MSACS

Expenses:

Tuition: In-state: Full year: $1,350.00. Part-time: Per credit:$50.00. Tuition: Out-of-state: Full year: $2,700.00. Part-time: Per credit:$100.00. Room and board: $3,000.00

Majors

• ARTS Graphic Arts, Photography • BUSINESS Accounting, Banking/Finance, Business Administration, Business Management, Hotel & Restaurant Management • COMMUNICATIONS Advertising, Graphic Design • HEALTH SCIENCES Nursing, Respiratory Therapy • HUMANITIES Fine Arts, Liberal Arts • PREPROFESSIONAL Drafting, Engineering, Forestry, Pharmacy, Recreation, Social Work • SCIENCES Biology, Chemistry, Computer Science, General, Mathematics, Physics • SOCIAL SCIENCES Criminal Justice, Human Service • VOCATIONAL Air Conditioning/Heating/Refri, Aviation Maintenance, Carpentry, Drafting, Electronics Technology, Food Service, Legal Secretary, Radiological Technology, Respiratory Therapy Technology, Secretarial, Surveying and Mapping, Welding, Word Processing

Sports/Activities

• SPORTS RELATED Cheerleading • SPORTS-INTERCOLLEGIATE Baseball (M), Basketball (F), Basketball (M), Bowling (F), Bowling (M), Cross Country (F), Cross Country (M), Golf (M), Ice Hockey (M), Lacrosse (M), Soccer (F), Soccer (M), Softball (F), Tennis (F), Tennis (M), Track and

Field (F), Track and Field (M), Volleyball (F), Wrestling (M) • SPORTS-INTRAMURAL Badminton, Basketball, Canoeing, Football, Touch, Judo, Ping-Pong, Racquetball, Soccer, Softball, Volleyball • STUDENT LIFE ACTIVITIES Academic Clubs, Community Service, Concert Band, Dance, Drama Groups, Ethnic & Cultural Groups, Film, Magazine, Newspaper, Radio/TV station, Religious Organization, Student Government, Yearbook

---

Selective   **New York Program**

Molloy College
1000 Hempstead Avenue
Rockville Centre, New York 11570
(516) 678-5000

School Enrollment: **2,481**
LD Enrollment: **20**

Admissions Contact: **Wayne James, Director of Admissions**
LD Contact: **Sister Therese Forker, Liaison**
Name of Program: **STEEP**
Telephone:**(516) 678-5000 Ext. 381**

Admissions

Application Information:
LD Students Applying: **20** Accepted: **8** Enrolled:**8**
Application deadline: **Rolling**
Rolling Admissions: **Yes**

Secondary School Information
Most Important Criteria For Admissions (1-strongest)

1 SAT/ACT	**3** Application	**2**	School transcript
4 Class rank	**8** Course selection	**7**	Personal statement
5 Interview	**9** Extra activities	**10**	Psychoeducational
1 G.P.A.	Open admission	**6**	Recommendations

Test Requirements:
Untimed SAT: **Yes** Untimed ACT: **Yes**
WAIS-R required: **Yes** Range accepted: **Varies**
Documentation of LD required: **Yes**
Currency of diagnostic testing: **12 months**
Tests recommended: **WAIS-R, a recommendation from Special Educator**

Types of Disabilities Served
- Speech/Lang
- Study skills
- Written express
- Organizational
- Perceptual
- Reading
- Spelling
- Math
- Fine Motor

ADD with LD
ADD without LD
ADHD with LD
ADHD without LD

High School Course Requirements:
English: **4** Math: **4** Science: **2** Foreign Language: **2**
Waivers to standard high school courses
Foreign Language : **Yes** Math: **Yes** Course substitution: **Yes**

Learning Disability Program
Special orientation for LD students: **Yes**
Students mainstreamed **100** % of the day
Recommended credits per semester: **Varies**
Time required or recommended in learning center: **1 hour**
Services available for all students: **Yes**
Counseling: Individual: **Yes** Vocational Counseling: **Yes**

Faculty:
Faculty: **1** Including Director: **Yes** Full time: **1** M.A.: **1**
Faculty advocate: **Yes** Meets with instructor: **As needed**

Diagnostic Testing
ADD	Personality	Perceptual skills	Spelling
ADHD	Organization	Fine motor skills	• Reading
I.Q.	Handwriting	Spoken language	Study skills
Math	Social skills	Written language	

Tutoring:
Average size of group tutorials: **5-10**
Services rendered by:
Graduates •Peers •Faculty •LD staff Teacher trainees

Tutorials

Grp.	Ind.	Tutorials	Grp.	Ind.	Tutorials
	•	Math skills		•	Word processing
	•	Study skills		•	Time management
	•	Language arts		•	Learning strategies
	•	Written express		•	Organizational skills

Academic Accommodations

Curriculum	Study Aids	Exams
Priority registration	• Typist	• Oral
• Math waiver	• Reader	• Untimed
• Foreign lang. waiver	• Notetaker	Take home
Course substitution	• Proof reader	With proctor
In Class	Text on tape	On computer
• Calculators	Early syllabus	• Extended time
• Tape recorder	Taped handouts	• On tape
• Word processor		Modified
Priority seating		• Separate room

Graduation Requirements:
Course credits: **128** GPA: **2.0** Years to complete degree: **Varies** Math waiver: **Yes** Language waiver: **Yes**

Program Strengths
Our formal program, STEEP (Success Through Expanded Education Program), provides individualized training in areas of difficulty, e.g, note taking, studying techniques, reading, etc. Our goal is to develop independence through a recognition of one's specific disability and the accompanying compensations/modifications necessary for success.

General Information:
Molloy College is a 4 year independent college. Suburban campus of 25 acres is 17 miles from New York City. Accessible by train and bus. Beaches are 5 miles from campus. 3% of students are foreign. Housing is not guaranteed.

Accreditation:MSACS

SAT/ACT Scores:
Scores for incoming freshmen:**Verbal:**80%below 500. 18%between 500 and 599. 5%between 600 and 699. **Math:**76% below 500. 22% between 500 and 599. 2% between 600 and 699.

Expenses:
Tuition: In-state: Full year: $7,800.00. Part-time: Per credit:$260.00. Cost of LD program:$600.00

Majors
• ARTS Art History, Art Therapy, Design, Music, Photography • BUSINESS Accounting, Management • COMMUNICATIONS Communication, English • COMPUTER SCIENCE Computer Science • EDUCATION En-

glish , Music Therapy, Special • HEALTH SCIENCES Nursing, Respiratory Therapy, Speech/Audiology and Speech • HUMANITIES Philosophy • LANGUAGES French, Spanish • PREPROFESSIONAL Dentistry, Law, Medicine, Veterinarian • RELIGIOUS STUDIES Philosophy, Religion ¶ Theology • SCIENCES Biology, Gerontology, Mathematics • SOCIAL SCIENCES History, International Studies, Political Science, Psychology, Sociology • VISUAL AND PERFORMING ARTS Art, Music

Sports/Activities

• SPORTS-INTERCOLLEGIATE Baseball (F), Basketball (F), Basketball (M), Golf (F), Golf (M), Softball, Tennis (F), Volleyball (F) • SPORTS-INTRAMURAL Golf, Softball, Volleyball, Weight Lifting • STUDENT LIFE ACTIVITIES Academic Clubs, Choral, Community Service, Concert Band, Dance, Debate, Drama Groups, Ethnic & Cultural Groups, Music Groups, Musical Theater, Newspaper, Religious Organization, Student Government, Yearbook

---

Less Selective　　　　　　　**New York Program**

Nassau Community College

Garden City, New York 11530
(516) 222-7345

School Enrollment: **20,677**
LD Enrollment: **300** Male: **180** Female: **120**

Admissions Contact: **Bernard Iatasca, Director of Admissions**
LD Contact: **Dr. Victor Margolis, Director**
Name of Program: **Disabled Student Services**
Telephone:**(516) 222-7138**

Admissions

Application Information:
Application deadline: **August 1st**
Rolling Admissions: **Yes**

Secondary School Information
Most Important Criteria For Admissions (1-strongest)

6 SAT/ACT	**2** Application	**4**	School transcript
1 Class rank	**3** Course selection		Personal statement
9 Interview	**8** Extra activities		Psychoeducational
5 G.P.A.	Open admission	**7**	Recommendations

Test Requirements:
Standardized tests waived: **Yes**
Diagnostic testing waived: **Yes**

Types of Disabilities Served
• Speech/Lang	• Reading	ADD with LD
• Study skills	• Spelling	ADD without LD
• Written express	• Math	ADHD with LD
• Organizational	• Fine Motor	ADHD without LD
• Perceptual		

Learning Disability Program
Program: Remedial: **Yes**
Program: Reinforces course work: **Yes**
Students mainstreamed **100** % of the day

Faculty:
Faculty: **5** Full time: **3** Part time: **2** M.A.: **4** Ph.D.: **1**
Faculty advocate: **Yes** Meets with instructor: **As needed**

Diagnostic Testing
ADD	Personality	Perceptual skills	Spelling
ADHD	Organization	Fine motor skills	Reading
I.Q.	Handwriting	Spoken language	Study skills
Math	Social skills	Written language	

Tutoring:
Services rendered by:
•Graduates　•Peers　•Faculty　•LD staff　Teacher trainees

Tutorials
Grp.	Ind.	Tutorials	Grp.	Ind.	Tutorials
	•	Math skills		•	Word processing
	•	Study skills		•	Time management
	•	Language arts		•	Learning strategies
	•	Written express		•	Organizational skills

Academic Accommodations
Curriculum	Study Aids	Exams
Priority registration	Typist	• Oral
• Math waiver	Reader	Untimed
Foreign lang. waiver	• Notetaker	• Take home
Course substitution	• Proof reader	With proctor
In Class	• Text on tape	On computer
• Calculators	Early syllabus	• Extended time
• Tape recorder	Taped handouts	On tape
• Word processor		• Modified
Priority seating		Separate room

Program Strengths
Ours is a support service program. Each student is assigned an advocate who will assist the student in obtaining the resources he or she needs to be successful.

General Information:
Nassau Community College is a 2 year public college. Suburban campus of 225 acres is 20 miles from New York. Accessible by train or bus. 1% of students are foreign. Housing is not guaranteed.

Accreditation:MSACS

Class Rank:
About 10% of the present freshmen class were in the upper 20% of their high school class. 30% were in the top 40% of their class. 48% were in the top 60% of their class. 85% were in the top 80% of their class.

Expenses:
Tuition: In-state: Full year: $1,350.00. Part-time: Per credit:$49.00. Tuition: Out-of-state: Full year: $2,700.00. Part-time: Per credit:$98.00.

Majors
• AREA STUDIES African, Black/Afro-American • BUSINESS Accounting, Banking, Business Administration, Business Management, Economics, Finance, Food Management, Hotel and Restaurant Management, Insurance, Management, Marketing, Real Estate, Retailing • COMMUNICATIONS Advertising, American Sign Language, Communication, English, Photography • COMPUTER SCIENCE Computer Science, Data Processing • EDUCATION Child Development, Early Childhood, Physical, Teacher Aide • ENGINEERING Civil/Environmental, Engineering Science, Industrial • HEALTH SCIENCES Medical Secretary, Medical Technology, Nursing, Physical Therapy, Surgical Technology • HUMANITIES Humanities, Liberal Arts, Philosophy • LANGUAGES French, German, Italian, Japanese, Latin, Russian, Spanish • SCIENCES Biology, Botany, Chemistry, Earth, Geography, Geology, Mathematics, Physical Science, Physics • SOCIAL SCIENCES Law Enforcement, Social Sciences • VISUAL AND PERFORMING ARTS Fine Arts, Music Performance • VOCATIONAL Fashion Mechandizing, Legal Secretary, Paralegal, Ra-

diological Technology, Respiratory Therapy Technology, Secretarial

Sports/Activities

• SPORTS RELATED Marching Band, Pep Band • SPORTS-INTERCOL-LEGIATE Baseball (M), Basketball, Bowling (M), Cross Country, Diving (F), Football (M), Golf (M), Gymnastics (F), Ice Hockey (M), Lacrosse (M), Soccer, Softball (F), Tennis, Track and Field, Volleyball (F), Wrestling (M) • SPORTS-INTRAMURAL Badminton (F), Baseball (M), Basketball, Bowling, Cross Country, Diving (F), Field Hockey (F), Lacrosse (M), Racquetball, Soccer, Softball (F), Swimming (M), Tennis, Volleyball, Wrestling (M) • STUDENT LIFE ACTIVITIES Choral, Concert Band, Dance, Drama Groups, Fraternities, Jazz Band, Magazine, Music Groups, Musical Theater, Newspaper, Radio/TV station, Sororities, Student Government, Symphony Orchestra, Yearbook

---

Less Selective   **New York Program**

New York Institute of Technology

Gold Program French Chateau
Old Westbury, New York 11568
(516) 686-7655

School Enrollment: **11,000** Male: **8,250** Female: **2,750**
LD Enrollment: **50**

Admissions Contact: **Dr. Glenn Berman, Director of Admissions**
LD Contact: **Dr. Judith Amster, Director, Gold Program**
Name of Program: **Gold Program**
Telephone:**(516) 686-7655**

Admissions

Application Information:
LD Students Applying: **40** Accepted: **37** Enrolled:**37**
Separate application:**Yes**
Rolling Admissions: **Yes**

Secondary School Information
Most Important Criteria For Admissions (1-strongest)

2 SAT/ACT	Application	School transcript
Class rank	Course selection	Personal statement
Interview	**4** Extra activities	Psychoeducational
1 G.P.A.	**1** Open admission	**3** Recommendations

Test Requirements:
Standardized tests waived: **Yes**
Diagnostic testing waived: **Yes**
Untimed SAT: **Yes** Untimed ACT: **Yes**
WAIS-R required: **Yes** Range accepted: **85+**
Documentation of LD required: **Yes**
Tests recommended: **WAIS-R, full reading evaluation, psychoeducational battery and achievement.**

Types of Disabilities Served
• Speech/Lang   • Reading   • ADD with LD
• Study skills   • Spelling   ADD without LD
• Written express   • Math   ADHD with LD
• Organizational   • Fine Motor   ADHD without LD
• Perceptual

Admissions Process

Comprehensive admissions forms given to parent at the time of interview or prior to formal interview. Decision made on basis of all relevant diagnosis, records, interview, and discussion with counselor. Letter of acceptance sent out.

High School Course Requirements:
Waivers to standard high school courses
Foreign Language : **Yes** Math: **Yes** Course substitution: **Yes**

Learning Disability Program

Special orientation for LD students: **Yes**
Program: Remedial: **Yes**
Program: Reinforces course work: **Yes**
Program available through:**Daily**
Students mainstreamed **100** % of the day
Recommended credits per semester: **12-13**
Time required or recommended in learning center: **10 hours**
Services only for LD students: **Yes**
Counseling: Individual: **Yes** Group Counseling: **Yes** Vocational Counseling: **Yes**
Support groups are available:**Yes, counseling, under the direction of program psychologist**

Faculty:
Faculty: **21** Including Director: **Yes** Full time: **1** Part time: **20** M.A.: **19**
Ph.D.: **2**
Faculty advocate: **Yes** Meets with instructor: **As needed**

Diagnostic Testing

ADD	Personality	• Perceptual skills	• Spelling
ADHD	• Organization	• Fine motor skills	• Reading
• I.Q.	• Handwriting	• Spoken language	• Study skills
• Math	• Social skills	• Written language	

Tutoring:
Average size of group tutorials: **1:1**
Services rendered by:
   Graduates   Peers   •Faculty   LD staff   Teacher trainees

Tutorials

Grp.	Ind.	Tutorials	Grp.	Ind.	Tutorials
•	•	Math skills	•	•	Word processing
	•	Study skills	•	•	Time management
•	•	Language arts	•	•	Learning strategies
	•	Written express	•	•	Organizational skills

Academic Accommodations

Curriculum	Study Aids	Exams
• Priority registration	Typist	• Oral
• Math waiver	• Reader	• Untimed
• Foreign lang. waiver	• Notetaker	• Take home
• Course substitution	• Proof reader	• With proctor
In Class	• Text on tape	• On computer
• Calculators	Early syllabus	• Extended time
• Tape recorder	Taped handouts	• On tape
• Word processor		• Modified
• Priority seating		Separate room

Graduation Requirements:
Course credits: **120+** GPA: **2.0** Math waiver: **Yes** Language waiver: **Yes**
Other requirements: **Certain schools have other requirements**

Program Strengths

The intensity of services with students receiving 10+ hours per week of individual and additional small group remediation/tutoring is unique. The advanced level of all staff who hold graduate degrees in this area of expertise is a major success factor. Close monitoring of each student is an integral facet of our program.

General Information:

New York Institute of Technology is a 4 year public college. Urban campus 1 miles from New York City. Accessible by air, train or bus. Ski areas are 2 hours from campus. 20% of students are foreign. 7 residential halls on campus. Housing is guaranteed.Guaranteed through 4th year.

Accreditation:Regional

Expenses:

Tuition: In-state: Full year: $6,740.00. Part-time: Per credit:$225.00. Room and board: $2,426.00 Cost of LD program:$4,000.00

Majors

• ARTS Design, Drafting, Graphic Arts, Interior Design, Painting, Sculpture • BUSINESS Accounting, Business Administration, Business Education, Business Management, Commercial Art, Food Management, Hotel & Restaurant Management, Management, Marketing, Secretarial Science, Travel/Tourism Management, Vocational • COMMUNICATIONS Advertising, Broadcasting, Commercial Design, Communication, Graphic Design • COMPUTER SCIENCE Computer Science, Computer Technology, Robotics, Telecommunications • CRAFTS AND DESIGN Graphic Design • EDUCATION Adult , Art, Business, Mathematical, Science, Secondary, Technical, Vocational • ENGINEERING Aerospace, Architectural, Automotive, Aviation, Bioengineering, Biomedical, Chemical, Computer, Drafting, Electrical, Engineering Science, Environmental/Water Resources, Industrial, Mechanical, Radio/Television • ENVIRONMENTAL CONTROL Energy Conservation • HUMANITIES Fine Arts, Liberal Arts • PRE PROFESSIONAL Engineering, Legal Assistant • SCIENCES Biomedical, Computer Science, Life Sciences, Mathematics, Physics • SOCIAL SCIENCES Criminal Justice, Family Counseling, Human Service, Law Enforcement, Political Science, Psychology, Social Science • VISUAL AND PERFORMING ARTS Art, Art History, Fine Arts, Studio Art, Video • VOCATIONAL Business and Office, Culinary Arts, Electronics Technology, Paralegal

Sports/Activities

• SPORTS-INTERCOLLEGIATE Baseball (M), Basketball (M), Cross Country (F), Cross Country (M), Hammer Throw (M), Lacrosse (M), Soccer (F), Soccer (M), Softball (F), Track and Field (F), Track and Field (M), Volleyball (F)

Highly Selective

New York Program

New York University
22 Washington Square North
New York, New York 10011
(212) 998-4500

School Enrollment: **12,153** Male: **5,387** Female: **6,766**
LD Enrollment: **120**

Admissions Contact: **Rob Erwin, Assistant Director**
LD Contact: **Georgeann du Chossois, Cord./Learning Serv Prog.**
Name of Program: **Access to Learning**
Address: **566 LaGuardia Pl., Room 701**
Telephone:**(212) 998-4980**

Admissions

Application Information:
LD Students Applying: **80** Accepted: **30** Enrolled:**25**
Application deadline: **February 1st**

Secondary School Information
Most Important Criteria For Admissions (1-strongest)

3 SAT/ACT	Application	**1**	School transcript
12 Class rank	**4** Course selection		Personal statement
12 Interview	**6** Extra activities	**2**	Psychoeducational
1 G.P.A.	Open admission	**5**	Recommendations

Test Requirements:
Diagnostic testing waived: **Yes**
Untimed SAT: **Yes** Untimed ACT: **Yes** Untimed ACH: **Yes**
WAIS-R required: **Yes**
Documentation of LD required: **Yes**
Currency of diagnostic testing: **Within 3 years**
Tests recommended: **WAIS-Reading, math, writing, study skills**

Types of Disabilities Served
• Speech/Lang   • Reading   • ADD with LD
• Study skills   • Spelling   • ADD without LD
• Written express • Math   • ADHD with LD
• Organizational • Fine Motor   • ADHD without LD
• Perceptual

Admissions Process

Admission is based on several factors: academic records, test scores, extracurricular activities, essay and recommendations. An interview may be required. An interview is required for LD applicants. Audition or creative review required for certain majors.

High School Course Requirements:
English: **4** Math: **4** Science: **3-4** Foreign Language: **2-3**

Learning Disability Program
Program: Reinforces course work: **Yes**
Program available through:**On going**
Students mainstreamed **100** % of the day
Recommended credits per semester: **12-16**
Time required or recommended in learning center: **1-2 hours**
Services only for LD students: **Yes**
Counseling: Individual: **Yes** Vocational Counseling: **Yes**
Support groups are available:**Yes, students meet once a week, one hour, with trained facilitator.**

Faculty:
Faculty: **5** Including Director: **Yes** Full time: **2** Part time: **3**
LD faculty with: BS/BA: **5** M.A.: **3**
Faculty advocate: **Yes** Meets with instructor: **As needed**

Diagnostic Testing
ADD	Personality	Perceptual skills	Spelling
ADHD	Organization	Fine motor skills	Reading
I.Q.	Handwriting	Spoken language	Study skills
Math	Social skills	Written language	

Tutoring:
Average size of group tutorials: **1:1**
Services rendered by:
•Graduates   Peers   Faculty   •LD staff   Teacher trainees

Tutorials
Grp.	Ind.	Tutorials	Grp.	Ind.	Tutorials
	•	Math skills		•	Word processing
	•	Study skills		•	Time management
	•	Language arts		•	Learning strategies
	•	Written express		•	Organizational skills

Academic Accommodations

Curriculum	Study Aids	Exams
Priority registration	Typist	Oral
• Math waiver	Reader	Untimed
• Foreign lang. waiver	• Notetaker	Take home
Course substitution	Proof reader	• With proctor
In Class	• Text on tape	• On computer
• Calculators	Early syllabus	• Extended time
• Tape recorder	Taped handouts	• On tape
• Word processor		Modified
• Priority seating		• Separate room

Graduation Requirements:
Course credits: **120** GPA: **2.0** Math waiver: **Yes** Language waiver: **Yes**

Program Strengths

There are few programs with full time qualified coordinators at colleges which are as academically challenging as NYU. We work best with students who are looking for a stimulating environment such as New York City and an LD program which encourages the highest possible level of academic independence.

General Information:

New York University is a 4 year private university. Urban campus of 29 acres is Accessible by all forms of transportation. Ski areas are 4 hours from campus. Beaches are 2 hours from campus. 5% of students are foreign. 12 residential halls on campus. Housing is guaranteed. Guaranteed through 4th year. 95 % of students remain on campus for the weekends. 5 % of students join fraternities/sororities.

Accreditation: Regional, State, National by Programs

Expenses:
Tuition: In-state: Full year: $15,620.00. Tuition: Out-of-state: Full year: $15,620.00. Room and board: $6,775.00.

Majors

• AREA STUDIES African, East Asian, Jewish, Latin American, Medieval Studies, Middle Eastern, Russian/Slavic, Urban • BUSINESS Accounting, Actuarial, Economics, Finance, General, Information Systems, International Business, Management, Marketing, Organizational Behavior, Statistics • COMMUNICATIONS Communication, English, Journalism, Literature • COMPUTER SCIENCE Computer Mathematics, Computer Science • EDUCATION Early Childhood, Elementary, English, Foreign Language, Mathematics, Science, Secondary, Social Studies, Special • ENGINEERING Chemical, Civil/Environmental, Computer, Electrical, Mechanical, Physics • HEALTH SCIENCES Food Service, Hotel & Restaurant Management, Nursing, Occupational Therapy, Physical Therapy, Rehabilitation, Speech/Audiology and Speech • HUMANITIES Classics, Philosophy • LANGUAGES Arabic, Chinese, French, German, Greek, Hebrew, Italian, Latin, Portuguese, Russian, Spanish • PREPROFESSIONAL Dentistry, Law, Medicine, Optometry, Podiatry • SCIENCES Anthropology, Archeology, Biochemistry, Biology, Chemistry, Geology, Mathematics, Physics, Psychobiology • SOCIAL SCIENCES History, Psychology, Social Work, Sociology • VISUAL AND PERFORMING ARTS Art, Art History, Dance, Dramatic Arts, Fine Arts, Music, Photography, Television/Radio/Film • VOCATIONAL Business and Office, Food Service, Home Economics, Printing/Lithography, Urban Design

Sports/Activities

• SPORTS RELATED Bagpipe Band, Cheerleading, Pep Band • SPORTS-INTERCOLLEGIATE Basketball (F), Basketball (M), Cross Country (F), Cross Country (M), Fencing (F), Fencing (M), Golf (M), Soccer (M), Swimming (F), Swimming (M), Tennis (F), Tennis (M), Track and Field (F), Track and Field (M), Volleyball (F), Volleyball (M), Wrestling (M) • SPORTS-INTRAMURAL Badminton (M), Baseball (M), Basketball (F), Basketball (M), Crew (F), Crew (M), Cross Country (F), Cross Country (M), Fencing (F), Fencing (M), Golf (M), Horseback Riding (F), Horseback Riding (M), Ice Hockey (M), Lacrosse (M), Racquetball (F), Racquetball (M), Softball (F), Softball (M), Squash (F), Squash (M), Swimming (F), Swimming (M), Tennis (F), Tennis (M), Track and Field (F), Track and Field (M), Volleyball (F), Volleyball (M), Water Polo (F), Water Polo (M)

Selective

Niagara University
Room 104 Saint Vincent's Hall
Niagara Falls, New York 14109
(716) 285-1212

School Enrollment: **2,552** Male: **1,088** Female: **1,464**

Admissions Contact: **Mr. Peter Lindsay, Associate Director**
LD Contact: **Linda H. McGrath, Coordinator**
Name of Program: **Support Services**
Telephone: **Ext. 580**

Admissions

Application Information:
Application deadline: **August 1st**
Rolling Admissions: **Yes**

Secondary School Information
Most Important Criteria For Admissions (1-strongest)

3 SAT/ACT	Application	**1**	School transcript
2 Class rank	Course selection		Personal statement
Interview	Extra activities		Psychoeducational
G.P.A.	Open admission	**4**	Recommendations

Test Requirements:
Untimed SAT: **Yes** Untimed ACT: **Yes**

Types of Disabilities Served

Speech/Lang	• Reading	ADD with LD
Study skills	• Spelling	ADD without LD
• Written express	• Math	ADHD with LD
Organizational	Fine Motor	ADHD without LD
Perceptual		

Diagnostic Testing

ADD	Personality	Perceptual skills	Spelling
ADHD	Organization	Fine motor skills	Reading
I.Q.	Handwriting	Spoken language	Study skills
Math	Social skills	Written language	

Tutoring:
Average size of group tutorials: **1-4 ***
Services rendered by:

Graduates	Peers	Faculty	LD staff	Teacher trainees

Tutorials

Grp.	Ind.	Tutorials	Grp.	Ind.	Tutorials
		Math skills			Word processing
		Study skills			Time management
		Language arts			Learning strategies
		Written express			Organizational skills

Academic Accommodations

Curriculum	Study Aids	Exams
Priority registration	Typist	Oral
Math waiver	Reader	Untimed
Foreign lang. waiver	Notetaker	Take home
Course substitution	• Proof reader	With proctor
In Class	Text on tape	On computer
• Calculators	Early syllabus	• Extended time
• Tape recorder	Taped handouts	On tape
• Word processor		Modified
Priority seating		Separate room

Program Strengths

At the present time, Niagara University does not have a program for learning disabled students. We do, however, have a number of learning disabled students who receive support through our learning center and appropriate accommodations in classes and test taking are provided.

* Tutoring is available for all students not only those who have been identified as having a learning disability.

General Information:

Niagara University is a 4 year private college. Suburban campus of 160 acres is 25 miles from Buffalo. Housing is not guaranteed.

Accreditation: Regional

Expenses:

Tuition: In-state: Full year: $8,400.00. Part-time: Per credit:$654.00. Tuition: Out-of-state: Full year: $8,400.00. Part-time: Per credit:$654.00. Room and board: $1,926.00.

Majors

• BUSINESS Accounting, Business Administration, Business Economics, Business Education, Business Management, Hotel and Restaurant Management, International Business, Management, Marketing, Travel/Tourism Management • COMMUNICATIONS Communication, English • COMPUTER SCIENCE Computer Science • EDUCATION Early Childhood, Elementary, Foreign Language, Mathematics, Middle School, Science, Secondary, Social Studies • ENGINEERING Engineering Science • HEALTH SCIENCES Nursing • HUMANITIES Liberal Arts, Philosophy, Religion • LANGUAGES French, Spanish • PREPROFESSIONAL Dentistry, Law, Medicine, Social Work, Veterinarian • SCIENCES Biochemistry, Biology, Chemistry, Mathematics • SOCIAL SCIENCES Criminal Justice, Criminology, Government/Political, History, International Studies, Political Science, Psychology, Social Sciences, Sociology • VISUAL AND PERFORMING ARTS Dramatic Arts

Sports/Activities

• SPORTS RELATED Pep Band • SPORTS-INTERCOLLEGIATE Baseball (M), Basketball, Cross Country, Diving, Golf (M), Soccer, Softball (F), Swimming, Track and Field, Volleyball (F) • SPORTS-INTRAMURAL Baseball (M), Basketball, Ice Hockey (M), Lacrosse (M), Ping-Pong, Racquetball (M), Rugby, Skiing - Snow, Softball, Volleyball • STUDENT LIFE ACTIVITIES Academic Clubs, Choral, Community Service, Dance, Drama Groups, Ethnic & Cultural Groups, Musical Theater, Newspaper, Political Groups, Radio/TV station, Student Government, Yearbook

Onondaga Community College

Onondaga Road
Syracuse, New York 13215
(315) 469-7741

School Enrollment: **8,178** Male: **3,693** Female: **4,485**
LD Enrollment: **213**

Admissions Contact: **Joseph R. Insel, Director of Admissions**
LD Contact: **Deborah F. Knight, Coordinator**
Name of Program: **LD Assistance Program**
Telephone:**(315) 469-2245**

Admissions

Application Information:
Accepted: **130** Enrolled:**128**
Application deadline: **August 10th**
Rolling Admissions: **Yes**

Secondary School Information
Most Important Criteria For Admissions (1-strongest)

5 SAT/ACT	Application	**1** School transcript
4 Class rank	**3** Course selection	Personal statement
6 Interview	Extra activities	Psychoeducational
2 G.P.A.	**1** Open admission	**7** Recommendations

Test Requirements:
Untimed SAT: **Yes**
Documentation of LD required: **Yes**

Types of Disabilities Served
- Speech/Lang
- Study skills
- Written express
- Organizational
- Perceptual
- Reading
- Spelling
- Math
- Fine Motor
- ADD with LD
- ADD without LD
- ADHD with LD
- ADHD without LD

Admissions Process

A Placement test is required for classes once a student has been admitted.

Learning Disability Program

Program: Reinforces course work: **Yes**
Students mainstreamed **100** % of the day
Services only for LD students: **Yes**
Counseling: Individual: **Yes** Group Counseling: **Yes**

Faculty:
Faculty: **6** Including Director: **Yes** Full time: **2** Part time: **4**
LD faculty with: BS/BA: **5** M.A.: **1**
Faculty advocate: **Yes** Meets with instructor: **As needed**

Diagnostic Testing

ADD	Personality •	Perceptual skills	• Spelling
ADHD•	Organization	Fine motor skills	• Reading
I.Q.	Handwriting•	Spoken language	• Study skills
• Math	Social skills •	Written language	

Tutoring:

Average size of group tutorials:
Services rendered by:
Graduates   Peers   •Faculty   •LD staff   Teacher trainees

Tutorials

Grp.	Ind.	Tutorials	Grp.	Ind.	Tutorials
	•	Math skills		•	Word processing
	•	Study skills		•	Time management
	•	Language arts		•	Learning strategies
	•	Written express		•	Organizational skills

Academic Accommodations

Curriculum	Study Aids	Exams
Priority registration	Typist	• Oral
Math waiver	Reader	Untimed
Foreign lang. waiver	• Notetaker	Take home
Course substitution	• Proof reader	• With proctor
In Class	• Text on tape	• On computer
• Calculators	Early syllabus	• Extended time
• Tape recorder	Taped handouts	• On tape
• Word processor		• Modified
Priority seating		Separate room

Graduation Requirements:

Course credits: **60** GPA: **2.0** Years to complete degree: **3** Math waiver: **Yes**
Language waiver: **Yes**

Program Strengths

The Learning Disabilities Assistance Program (LDAP) offers LD students on campus a variety of services to make it possible for them to participate in all of the curricula on campus.

General Information:

Onondaga Community College is a 2 year public college. Rural campus of 180 acres is 2 miles from Syracuse. Accessible by bus. Ski areas are 20 miles from campus. Housing is not guaranteed.

Accreditation: MSACS

Expenses:

Tuition: In-state: Full year: $1,628.00. Part-time: Per credit:$65.00. Tuition: Out-of-state: Full year: $4,078.00. Part-time: Per credit:$195.00.

Majors

• AREA STUDIES Black/Afro-American, Women's Studies • BUSINESS Accounting, Banking, Business Administration, Business Management, Finance, Food Management, Hotel and Restaurant Management, Labor Relations, Management • COMMUNICATIONS Advertising, Broadcasting, Commercial Design, Communication, English, Graphic Design, Journalism, Photography, Television/Radio/Film • COMPUTER SCIENCE Computer Maintenance, Computer Science, Computer Technology, Data Processing, Software Engineer, Systems Analysis, Telecommunications • EDUCATION Early Childhood, Music Therapy, Recreation and Youth Leadership, Special • ENGINEERING Bioengineering, Chemical, Electrical, Engineering Science, Mechanical • HEALTH SCIENCES Dental Assistant, Environmental, Health, Medical Records Technology, Medical Technology, Nursing, Physical Therapy, Surgical Technology • HUMANITIES Humanities, Liberal Arts • LANGUAGES French, German, Spanish • PREPROFESSIONAL Architecture, Dentistry, Engineering, Forestry, Range Management, Social Work • SCIENCES Biology, Botany, Chemistry, Earth, Geology, Mathematics, Microbiology, Physical Science • SOCIAL SCIENCES Criminal Justice, Law Enforcement, Social Sciences • VISUAL AND PERFORMING ARTS Art, Art History, Dance, Fine Arts, Music, Music Performance, Studio Art • VOCATIONAL Business and Office, Electronics Technology, Fire Science, Food Service, Interior Design, Legal Secretary, Printing/Lithography, Respiratory Therapy Technology, Secretarial

Sports

• SPORTS-INTERCOLLEGIATE Baseball (M), Basketball, Lacrosse (M), Softball (F), Tennis, Volleyball (F) • SPORTS-INTRAMURAL Badminton, Basketball, Bowling, Fencing, Golf, Horseback Riding, Lacrosse (M), Racquetball, Skiing - Snow, Softball (F), Swimming, Tennis, Volleyball • STUDENT LIFE ACTIVITIES Choral, Concert Band, Dance, Ethnic & Cultural Groups, Film, Jazz Band, Music Groups, Musical Theater, Newspaper, Radio/TV station, Religious Organization, Student Government, Yearbook

---

Selective   **New York**
Accommodations

Pace University: College of White Plain

78 North Broadway
White Plains, New York 10603
(914) 422-4070

School Enrollment: **1,313** Male: **500** Female: **813**

Admissions Contact: **Christine Richard, Assoc. Dir. of Admissions**

Admissions

Application Information:
Application deadline: **August 15th**
Rolling Admissions: **Yes**

Secondary School Information
Most Important Criteria For Admissions (1-strongest)

2 SAT/ACT	Application	**5**	School transcript
3 Class rank	Course selection	**6**	Personal statement
7 Interview	**8** Extra activities	**9**	Psychoeducational
1 G.P.A.	Open admission	**4**	Recommendations

Types of Disabilities Served

Speech/Lang	Reading	ADD with LD
Study skills	Spelling	ADD without LD
Written express	Math	ADHD with LD
Organizational	Fine Motor	ADHD without LD
Perceptual		

Admissions Process

We do not have a formal Learning Disability Program. It is suggested that a learning disabled student visit the campus to meet with an admissions counselor to discuss their particular needs, and availability of services.

High School Course Requirements:
English: **4** Math: **3-4** Science: **2-4** Foreign Language: **2-3**

Learning Disability Program
Services available for all students: **Yes**

Diagnostic Testing

ADD	Personality	Perceptual skills	Spelling
ADHD	Organization	Fine motor skills	Reading
I.Q.	Handwriting	Spoken language	Study skills
Math	Social skills	Written language	

Services rendered by:
Graduates   Peers   Faculty   LD staff   Teacher trainees

521

Tutorials

Grp.	Ind.	Tutorials	Grp.	Ind.	Tutorials
		Math skills			Word processing
		Study skills			Time management
		Language arts			Learning strategies
		Written express			Organizational skills

Academic Accommodations

Curriculum	Study Aids	Exams
Priority registration	Typist	Oral
Math waiver	Reader	Untimed
Foreign lang. waiver	Notetaker	Take home
Course substitution	Proof reader	With proctor
In Class	Text on tape	On computer
Calculators	Early syllabus	Extended time
Tape recorder	Taped handouts	On tape
Word processor		Modified
Priority seating		Separate room

Program Strengths

Although we have no formal program we feel it is necessary for students to contact us and discuss how we can help service the student.

General Information:

Pace University: College of White Plain is a 4 year private university. 28 miles from New York City. Accessible by air, train, or bus. Ski areas are 1 hour from campus. Beaches are 10-45 minutes from campus. 40% of students are foreign. 2 residential halls on campus. Housing is not guaranteed.40-50 % of students remain on campus for the weekends. 5 % of students join fraternities/sororities.

Accreditation:MCACS

SAT/ACT Scores:

Scores for incoming freshmen:**Verbal:**83%below 500. 13%between 500 and 599. 3%between 600 and 699. 1%above 700. **Math:**57% below 500. 32% between 500 and 599. 10% between 600 and 699. 1%above 700.

Class Rank:

About 30% of the present freshmen class were in the upper 20% of their high school class. 28% were in the top 40% of their class. 18% were in the top 60% of their class. 11% were in the top 80% of their class.

Expenses:

Tuition: In-state: Full year: $9,494.00. Part-time: Per credit:$192.00. Tuition: Out-of-state: Full year: $9,494.00. Part-time: Per credit:$291.00. Room and board: $4,480.00

Majors

• BUSINESS Accounting, Banking/Finance, Business Education, Economics, Education, Management, Marketing • COMMUNICATIONS English, Journalism • COMPUTER SCIENCE Computer Science • EDUCATION Business, Elementary, Secondary • ENGINEERING Biomedical, Chemical, Civil/Environmental, Computer, Electrical, Environmental/Water Resources, Industrial, Materials, Nuclear • LANGUAGES French, Spanish • MATHEMATICS Applied, Computer • PRE PROFESSIONAL Dentistry, Medicine, Veterinarian • SCIENCES Anthropology, Biology, Chemistry, Equestrian Studies, General, Physics • SOCIAL SCIENCES Anthropology, Criminal Justice, History, Human Service, Political Science, Psychology, Sociology • VOCATIONAL Office Administration, Word Processing

Sports/Activities

• SPORTS-INTERCOLLEGIATE Baseball (M), Basketball (F), Basketball (M), Cross Country (F), Cross Country (M), Golf (F), Golf (M), Gymnastics (M), Lacrosse (M), Softball (F), Tennis (F), Tennis (M), Track and Field (F), Track and Field (M), Volleyball • SPORTS-INTRAMURAL Badminton (F), Baseball (F), Football (M), Softball (F), Softball (M), Tennis (F), Tennis (M), Volleyball (F), Volleyball (M) • STUDENT LIFE ACTIVI-

TIES Ethnic & Cultural Groups, Magazine, Newspaper, Radio/TV station, Yearbook

Transitional **New York Program**

Para-Educator Center for Young Adults

One Washington Place
New York, New York 10003
(212) 998-5800

School Enrollment: **50** Male: **5** Female: **45**
LD Enrollment: **50** Male: **5** Female: **45**

Admissions Contact: **Ms. Sharon Morando, Admissions**
LD Contact: **Dr. Jane E. Herzog, Director**
Name of Program: **Para-Educator Center**
Address: **One Washington Place, New York, NY 10003**
Telephone:**(212) 998-5800**

Admissions

Application Information:

LD Students Applying: **125** Accepted: **35** Enrolled:**25**
Separate application:**Yes**
LD on admissions committee:**Yes**
Application deadline: **May 31st**
Applicant must apply **4-12** months in advance
Rolling Admissions: **Yes**

Secondary School Information

Most Important Criteria For Admissions (1-strongest)

SAT/ACT	**6**	Application	**8**	School transcript
Class rank	**9**	Course selection		Personal statement
Interview	**7**	Extra activities	**2**	Psychoeducational
G.P.A.		Open admission	**4**	Recommendations

Test Requirements:

Standardized tests waived: **Yes**
Diagnostic testing waived: **Yes**
WAIS-R required: **Yes** Range accepted: **70-95**
Documentation of LD required: **Yes**
Currency of diagnostic testing: **within year applying**
Tests recommended: **WAIS-R, Bender-Gestalt, Draw-A-Person, Rorschach, Thematic Apperception Test**

Types of Disabilities Served

• Speech/Lang	• Reading	• ADD with LD
• Study skills	• Spelling	ADD without LD
• Written express	• Math	• ADHD with LD
• Organizational	• Fine Motor	ADHD without LD
• Perceptual		

High School Course Requirements:

Waivers to standard high school courses
Course substitution: **Yes**

Learning Disability Program

Special orientation for LD students: **Yes**
Syllabus available during orientation:**Yes**
Program: Remedial: **Yes**
Program available through:**September-May**
Students mainstreamed **50** % of the day
Time required or recommended in learning center: **12-15**
Services only for LD students: **Yes**
Counseling: Individual: **Yes** Vocational Counseling: **Yes**
Support groups are available:**Yes, Understanding Learning Disabilities**

Faculty:

Faculty: **20** Including Director: **Yes** Full time: **5** Part time: **15**
LD faculty with: BS/BA: **12** M.A.: **7**
Faculty advocate: **Yes** Meets with instructor: **As needed**

Diagnostic Testing

ADD •	Personality •	Perceptual skills •	Spelling
ADHD	Organization•	Fine motor skills	Reading
I.Q.	Handwriting•	Spoken language	Study skills
Math •	Social skills	Written language	

Tutoring:

Average size of group tutorials: **1:1**
Services rendered by:
•Graduates   Peers   •Faculty   •LD staff   •Teacher trainees

Tutorials

Grp.	Ind.	Tutorials	Grp.	Ind.	Tutorials
	•	Math skills	•	•	Word processing
•	•	Study skills	•	•	Time management
•	•	Language arts	•	•	Learning strategies
	•	Written express	•	•	Organizational skills

Academic Accommodations

Curriculum	Study Aids	Exams
Priority registration	Typist	Oral
Math waiver	Reader	Untimed
Foreign lang. waiver	Notetaker	Take home
Course substitution	Proof reader	With proctor
In Class	Text on tape	On computer
Calculators	Early syllabus	Extended time
Tape recorder	Taped handouts	On tape
Word processor		Modified
Priority seating		Separate room

Graduation Requirements:

Course credits: **6** Years to complete degree: **2 (Certificate Program)**
Other requirements: **Field work performance**

Program Strengths

The Para-Educator Center was founded over 25 years ago and is the first program of its kind. The program's goals are to help students develop professional skills needed in the workplace and guide the student's personal growth so that they become mature, independent and employable individuals. We train young adults with LD to work in nursery schools, day care or geriatric centers as aides.

General Information:

Para-Educator Center for Young Adults is a 2 year independent university. Urban campus in New York City. Accessible by air, train or bus. Ski areas are 1 hour from campus. Beaches are 30 minutes from campus. Housing is guaranteed.Guaranteed through 2nd year. 75 % of students remain on campus for the weekends.

Accreditation:SCE

Expenses:
Tuition: In-state: Full year: $13,780.00. Tuition: Out-of-state: Full year: $13,780.00. Room and board: $5,000.00-$6,000.00 Cost of LD program:Included in tuition

Majors

• HEALTH SCIENCES Geriatric Aide • VOCATIONAL Child Care

Less Selective

New York Services

Paul Smith's College

Paul Smiths, New York 12970
(518) 327-6227

School Enrollment: **637** Male: **433** Female: **204**
LD Enrollment: **45**

Admissions Contact: **Jamie Mowst, Asst. Dir. Admissions**
LD Contact: **Carol McKillip, LD Specialist**
Name of Program: **Academic Support Services**
Telephone:**(518) 327-6307**

Admissions

Application Information:

Application deadline: **Rolling**
Rolling Admissions: **Yes**Notified when: **3-4 weeks**

Secondary School Information

Most Important Criteria For Admissions (1-strongest)

SAT/ACT	Application	School transcript
Class rank	Course selection	Personal statement
Interview	Extra activities	Psychoeducational
G.P.A.	Open admission	Recommendations

Test Requirements:

WAIS-R required: **Yes**
Documentation of LD required: **Yes**
Currency of diagnostic testing: **Recent**

Types of Disabilities Served

• Speech/Lang	• Reading	• ADD with LD
• Study skills	• Spelling	• ADD without LD
• Written express	• Math	• ADHD with LD
• Organizational	• Fine Motor	• ADHD without LD
• Perceptual		

Learning Disability Program

Counseling: Individual: **Yes** Group Counseling: **Yes**

Faculty:

Faculty: **1** Full time: **1**
Faculty advocate: **Yes** Meets with instructor: **As needed**

Diagnostic Testing

ADD	Personality	Perceptual skills	Spelling
ADHD	Organization	Fine motor skills	Reading
I.Q.	Handwriting	Spoken language	Study skills
Math	Social skills	Written language	

New York

Tutoring:
Average size of group tutorials: **5**
Services rendered by:
Graduates •Peers •Faculty •LD staff Teacher trainees

Tutorials

Grp.	Ind.	Tutorials	Grp.	Ind.	Tutorials
•	•	Math skills	•	•	Word processing
•	•	Study skills	•	•	Time management
•	•	Language arts	•	•	Learning strategies
•	•	Written express	•	•	Organizational skills

Academic Accommodations

Curriculum	Study Aids	Exams
Priority registration	• Typist	• Oral
Math waiver	Reader	Untimed
Foreign lang. waiver	• Notetaker	• Take home
• Course substitution	• Proof reader	With proctor
In Class	• Text on tape	On computer
• Calculators	Early syllabus	• Extended time
• Tape recorder	Taped handouts	On tape
• Word processor		• Modified
Priority seating		Separate room

Program Strengths

Our program is small and meets the individual needs of each student. Hands-on experience and concerned faculty aid student success. PSC aims to develop all areas for skills for each LD student - academic, interpersonal, career, etc. Students should contact Learning Specialist for information specific to their needs and visit the college if possible.

General Information:

Paul Smith's College is a 2 year private college. Rural campus of 15,000 acres is 45 miles from Plattsburgh. Accessible by air or bus. Ski areas are 15 minutes from campus. Beaches are 1-1/2 hours from campus. 10% of students are foreign. 11 residential halls on campus. Housing is guaranteed.95 % of students remain on campus for the weekends.

Accreditation:MSACS

Expenses:

Tuition: In-state: Full year: $7,150.00. Tuition: Out-of-state: Full year: $7,150.00. Room and board: $2,670.00

Majors

• AREA STUDIES American • BUSINESS Business Administration, Business Management, Food Management, Hotel and Restaurant Management, Management, Travel/Tourism Management • COMMUNICATIONS Communication • COMPUTER SCIENCE Telecommunications • HEALTH SCIENCES Environmental, Nutritional/Food • HUMANITIES Liberal Arts • PREPROFESSIONAL Forestry • SCIENCES Biology, Ecology, Mathematics, Physical Science • VOCATIONAL Chef Apprenticeship, Drafting, Food Service, Forestry, Park/Recreation, Surveying and Mapping, Urban Tree Management

Sports/Activities

• SPORTS-INTERCOLLEGIATE Basketball, Skiing - Snow, Soccer, Volleyball (F) • SPORTS-INTRAMURAL Basketball, Bowling, Golf, Judo, Skiing - Snow, Swimming, Volleyball, Wrestling (M) • STUDENT LIFE ACTIVITIES Drama Groups, Newspaper, Radio/TV station, Religious Organization, Student Government, Yearbook

---

Rochester Institute of Technology
1 Lomb Memorial Drive
Rochester, New York 14623-0887
(716) 475-6631

School Enrollment: **8,500**
LD Enrollment: **81**

Admissions Contact: **Diane Ellison, Asst. Dir. of Admissions**
LD Contact: **Jacqueline Czamanske, LD Specialist**
Name of Program: **Office of Special Services**
Telephone:**(716) 475-2832**

Admissions

Application Information:
Application deadline: **Rolling**
Applicant must apply **3** months in advance
Rolling Admissions: **Yes**Notified when: **4-6 weeks**

Secondary School Information
Most Important Criteria For Admissions (1-strongest)

3 SAT/ACT	**8** Application	**1** School transcript
2 Class rank	**1** Course selection	**6** Personal statement
5 Interview	**9** Extra activities	**4** Psychoeducational
1 G.P.A.	Open admission	**7** Recommendations

Test Requirements:
Diagnostic testing waived: **Yes**
Untimed SAT: **Yes** Untimed ACT: **Yes**
WAIS-R required: **Yes** Range accepted: **Varies**
Documentation of LD required: **Yes**
Currency of diagnostic testing: **3 years**
Tests recommended: **Include Academic Modification Requirements**

Types of Disabilities Served
- Speech/Lang
- Study skills
- Written express
- Organizational
- Perceptual
- Reading
- Spelling
- Math
- Fine Motor
- ADD with LD
- ADD without LD
- ADHD with LD
- ADHD without LD

Learning Disability Program
Program: Reinforces course work: **Yes**
Students mainstreamed **100 %** of the day
Counseling: Individual: **Yes** Group Counseling: **Yes**

Faculty:
Faculty: **5** Including Director: **Yes** Full time: **1** Part time: **4** M.A.: **5**
Faculty advocate: **Yes** Meets with instructor: **Student's request**

Diagnostic Testing
ADD	• Personality	Perceptual skills	• Spelling
ADHD	• Organization	Fine motor skills	• Reading
I.Q.	• Handwriting	• Spoken language	• Study skills
• Math	Social skills	• Written language	

Tutoring:
Services rendered by:
•Graduates •Peers •Faculty •LD staff Teacher trainees

Tutorials

Grp.	Ind.	Tutorials	Grp.	Ind.	Tutorials
•	•	Math skills	•	•	Word processing
•	•	Study skills	•	•	Time management
•	•	Language arts	•	•	Learning strategies
•	•	Written express	•	•	Organizational skills

Academic Accommodations

Curriculum
Priority registration
Math waiver
Foreign lang. waiver
Course substitution

In Class
• Calculators
• Tape recorder
• Word processor
Priority seating

Study Aids
Typist
• Reader
• Notetaker
• Proof reader
• Text on tape
Early syllabus
Taped handouts

Exams
• Oral
Untimed
• Take home
With proctor
On computer
• Extended time
On tape
• Modified
Separate room

Program Strengths

RIT offers over 200 academic program options to choose from. The majority of these programs are of a scientific, engineering, or technology type, and many are very unique within American higher education. Due to the nature of these programs, a "hands on" or applied approach to education is taken and quantitative skills are often more important than verbal skills in academic success at RIT. These factors (and others) make RIT very attractive to students with learning disabilities.

General Information:

Rochester Institute of Technology is a 4 year private university. Suburban campus of 1,300 acres is 5 miles from Rochester. Accessible by air, train, or bus. Ski areas are 60 miles from campus. Beaches are 15 miles from campus. 2% of students are foreign. 10 residential halls on campus. Housing is guaranteed.90 % of students remain on campus for the weekends. 13 % of students join fraternities/sororities.

Accreditation:MSACS

SAT/ACT Scores:

Scores for incoming freshmen:**Verbal:**54%below 500. 36%between 500 and 599. 8%between 600 and 699. 2%above 700. **Math:**26% below 500. 36% between 500 and 599. 32% between 600 and 699. 6%above 700. **ACT:** 45% below 20. 20% between 20 and 23. 9%between 24 and 25l. 13%between 26 and 28. 13% above 28.

Class Rank:

About 56% of the present freshmen class were in the upper 20% of their high school class. 83% were in the top 40% of their class. 96% were in the top 60% of their class. 99% were in the top 80% of their class.

Expenses:

Tuition: In-state: Full year: $10,959.00. Part-time: Per credit:$260.00. Room and board: $4,701.00

Majors

• BUSINESS Accounting, Banking, Business Administration, Business Management, Economics, Entrepreneur, Finance, Food Management, Hotel and Restaurant Management, Human Resources Management, International Business, Management, Marketing, Personnel, Retailing, Travel/Tourism Management • COMMUNICATIONS Advertising, Communication, Graphic Design Technology, Photography, Television/Radio/Film • COMPUTER SCIENCE Computer Science, Computer Technology, Programming, Systems Analysis • CRAFTS AND DESIGN Ceramics, Glass, Graphic Design, Illustration Design • EDUCATION Special • ENGINEERING Bio-medical, Civil/Environmental, Computer, Electrical, Industrial, Mechanical, Nuclear Medical • HEALTH SCIENCES Health, Medical Technology, Nutritional/Food • PREPROFESSIONAL Dentistry,

Engineering, Law, Medicine, Pharmacy, Recreation, Social Work • SCIENCES Bio-medical, Biochemistry, Biology, Chemistry, Mathematics, Physical Chemistry, Physical Science, Physics, Statistics • SOCIAL SCIENCES Criminal Justice, Criminology, Law Enforcement • VISUAL AND PERFORMING ARTS Art, Video • VOCATIONAL Electronics Technology, Fashion Mechandizing, Food Service, Industrial Design, Interior Design, Jewelry-Metalsmithery, Medical Laboratory Technology, Painting, Printing/Lithography, Textile and Clothing, Woodworking

Sports/Activities

• SPORTS RELATED Pep Band • SPORTS-INTERCOLLEGIATE Baseball (M), Basketball, Cross Country, Diving, Ice Hockey, Lacrosse (M), Soccer, Softball (F), Swimming, Tennis, Track and Field, Volleyball (F), Wrestling (M) • SPORTS-INTRAMURAL Basketball, Bowling, Cross Country, Diving, Football (M), Golf, Gymnastics, Ice Hockey, Lacrosse (M), Rugby (M), Skiing - Snow, Soccer, Softball, Swimming, Tennis, Track and Field, Volleyball, Water Polo • STUDENT LIFE ACTIVITIES Academic Clubs, Choral, Drama Groups, Ethnic & Cultural Groups, Film, Fraternities, Jazz Band, Magazine, Music Groups, Newspaper, Radio/TV station, Religious Organization, Sororities, Student Government, Yearbook

Less Selective

New York Services

Rockland Community College

145 College Road
Suffern, New York 10901
(914) 356-4650

School Enrollment: 8,271 Male: 3,501 Female: 4,770
LD Enrollment: **250**

Admissions Contact: **Mr. Larry Guiney, Director of Admissions**
LD Contact: **Ms. Marge Zemek, L.D. Specialist**
Name of Program: **Disabilities Services**
Telephone:**Ext. 316**

Admissions

Application Information:
Enrolled:**250**
Application deadline: **None**
Rolling Admissions: **Yes**

Secondary School Information
Most Important Criteria For Admissions (1-strongest)

SAT/ACT	**1**	Application	School transcript
Class rank		Course selection	Personal statement
Interview		Extra activities	**2** Psychoeducational
G.P.A.	**1**	Open admission	Recommendations

Test Requirements:
Standardized tests waived: **Yes**
Diagnostic testing waived: **Yes**
WAIS-R required: **Yes**
Documentation of LD required: **Yes**
Tests recommended: **Psychoeducational evaluation, Phase I I.E.P.**

Types of Disabilities Served
• Speech/Lang   • Reading   • ADD with LD
• Study skills   • Spelling   • ADD without LD
• Written express   • Math   • ADHD with LD
• Organizational   • Fine Motor   • ADHD without LD
• Perceptual

Learning Disability Program

Program: Reinforces course work: **Yes**
Students mainstreamed **100** % of the day
Recommended credits per semester: **12**
Services only for LD students: **Yes**
Counseling: Individual: **Yes**

Faculty:

Faculty: **2** Including Director: **Yes** Full time: **2** M.A.: **2**
Faculty advocate: **Yes** Meets with instructor: **As needed**

Diagnostic Testing

ADD	Personality	Perceptual skills	Spelling
ADHD	Organization	Fine motor skills	Reading
I.Q.	Handwriting	Spoken language	Study skills
Math	Social skills	Written language	

Tutoring:

Services rendered by:
Graduates   Peers   •Faculty   •LD staff   Teacher trainees

Tutorials

Grp.	Ind.	Tutorials	Grp.	Ind.	Tutorials
	•	Math skills		•	Word processing
	•	Study skills		•	Time management
	•	Language arts		•	Learning strategies
	•	Written express		•	Organizational skills

Academic Accommodations

Curriculum	Study Aids	Exams
Priority registration	• Typist	• Oral
• Math waiver	Reader	Untimed
Foreign lang. waiver	• Notetaker	Take home
• Course substitution	• Proof reader	• With proctor
In Class	• Text on tape	On computer
• Calculators	Early syllabus	• Extended time
• Tape recorder	Taped handouts	On tape
• Word processor		• Modified
Priority seating		Separate room

Graduation Requirements:

Course credits: **60** GPA: **2.0** Years to complete degree: **Unlimited**

Program Strengths

We work to have the student become his/her own advocate. All course work is mainstream with support for course and instructor selection, on-going supportive counseling, and help with course organization, test taking and accommodations. Students elect to use support services if they wish.

General Information:

Rockland Community College is a 2 year public college. Suburban campus of 30 acres is 3 miles from Suffern. Accessible by bus. Ski areas are 30 from campus. Beaches are 100 miles from campus. Housing is not guaranteed.

Accreditation:MSACS

Expenses:

Tuition: In-state: Full year: $875.00. Part-time: Per credit:$73.00. Tuition: Out-of-state: Full year: $1,750.00. Part-time: Per credit:$146.00.

Majors

• BUSINESS Accounting, Banking, Business Administration, Business Management, Finance, Food Management, Insurance, Management, Marketing, Real Estate, Travel/Tourism Management • COMMUNICATIONS Commercial Design, Communication, Graphic Design Technology • COMPUTER SCIENCE Data Processing, Medical Records Technology • CRAFTS AND DESIGN Graphic Design • ENGINEERING Electrical, Engineering Science, Mechanical • HEALTH SCIENCES Medical Assistant, Medical Technology, Nursing, Occupational Therapy Assistant • HUMANITIES Humanities, Liberal Arts • SCIENCES Biology, Mathematics, Physical Science • SOCIAL SCIENCES Criminal Justice, Law Enforcement, Social Sciences • VISUAL AND PERFORMING ARTS Art, Music, Performing Art • VOCATIONAL Automobile Technology, Business and Office, Electronics Technology, Fire Science, Food Service, Medical Laboratory Technology, Respiratory Therapy Technology, Secretarial

Sports/Activities

• SPORTS-INTERCOLLEGIATE Baseball (M), Basketball, Golf (M), Lacrosse (M), Soccer, Softball (F), Tennis, Volleyball • SPORTS-INTRAMURAL Baseball (M), Basketball, Bowling, Cross Country, Diving, Field Hockey, Gymnastics, Hand Ball, Ice Hockey, Lacrosse (M), Skiing - Snow, Soccer, Softball, Swimming, Tennis, Track and Field • STUDENT LIFE ACTIVITIES Choral, Dance, Drama Groups, Jazz Band, Magazine, Musical Theater, Newspaper, Radio/TV station, Student Government, Symphony Orchestra

Less Selective   **New York**
                                                    Services

Schenectady County Community College

78 Washington Avenue
Schenectady, New York 12305
(518) 346-6211

School Enrollment: **2,962** Male: **1,271** Female: **1,691**
LD Enrollment: **40** Male: **28** Female: **12**

Admissions Contact: **Robert Dinello, Director of Admissions**
LD Contact: **Gail V. Williams, Coordinator**
Name of Program: **Disabled Student Services**
Telephone:**Ext. 145**

Admissions

Application Information:

Application deadline: **Rolling**
Rolling Admissions: **Yes**

Secondary School Information

Most Important Criteria For Admissions (1-strongest)

SAT/ACT	Application	School transcript
Class rank	Course selection	Personal statement
Interview	Extra activities	Psychoeducational
G.P.A.	**1** Open admission	Recommendations

Test Requirements:

Standardized tests waived: **Yes**

Types of Disabilities Served

• Speech/Lang	• Reading	• ADD with LD
• Study skills	• Spelling	• ADD without LD
• Written express	• Math	• ADHD with LD
• Organizational	• Fine Motor	• ADHD without LD
• Perceptual		

Learning Disability Program

Counseling: Individual: **Yes**

Faculty:

Faculty: **1**
Faculty advocate: **Yes** Meets with instructor: **As needed**

Diagnostic Testing

ADD	Personality	Perceptual skills	Spelling
ADHD	Organization	Fine motor skills	Reading
I.Q.	Handwriting	Spoken language	Study skills
Math	Social skills	Written language	

Tutoring:

Average size of group tutorials: **6-8**
Services rendered by:
  Graduates •Peers •Faculty LD staff •Teacher trainees

Tutorials

Grp.	Ind.	Tutorials	Grp.	Ind.	Tutorials
•		Math skills	•	•	Word processing
•		Study skills	•	•	Time management
•		Language arts		•	Learning strategies
•		Written express		•	Organizational skills

Academic Accommodations

Curriculum	Study Aids	Exams
Priority registration	Typist	Oral
Math waiver	Reader	Untimed
Foreign lang. waiver	• Notetaker	Take home
Course substitution	Proof reader	With proctor
In Class	• Text on tape	On computer
• Calculators	Early syllabus	• Extended time
• Tape recorder	Taped handouts	On tape
Word processor		• Modified
Priority seating		Separate room

Program Strengths

We do not have a learning disability program in place. Our office consists of the coordinator. We are trying to bring in a part-time LD specialist. Also, we're implementing an Orientation Program for LD students during the summer. There is a part-time advisor who will be assisting students with disabilities with their schedules and helping with exams.

General Information:

Schenectady County Community College is a 2 year public college. Urban campus 10 miles from Albany. Accessible by bus. Ski areas are 1 hour from campus. Beaches are 4 hours from campus. Housing is not guaranteed.

Accreditation:MSACS

Expenses:

Tuition: In-state: Full year: $1,350.00. Part-time: Per credit:$54.00. Tuition: Out-of-state: Full year: $2,700.00.

Majors

• BUSINESS Accounting, Business Administration, Hotel and Restaurant Management, Travel/Tourism Management • COMMUNICATIONS English • COMPUTER SCIENCE Data Processing, Programming, Telecommunications • EDUCATION General • HUMANITIES Humanities • LANGUAGES French, German, Spanish • PREPROFESSIONAL Engineering • SCIENCES Mathematics • SOCIAL SCIENCES Criminal Justice • VISUAL AND PERFORMING ARTS Music, Theater • VOCATIONAL Culinary Arts

Sports/Activities

• SPORTS RELATED Team Managers • SPORTS-INTRAMURAL Baseball, Basketball, Bowling • STUDENT LIFE ACTIVITIES Drama Groups, Ethnic & Cultural Groups, Jazz Band, Music Groups, Student Government

---

Special	New York
	Accommodations

School of Visual Arts

209 East 23rd Street
New York, New York 10010
(212) 679-7350

School Enrollment: **2,530** Male: **1,423** Female: **1,107**

Admissions Contact: **Martha Schindler, Director of Admissions**

Admissions

Application Information:
Application deadline: **Rolling**
Rolling Admissions: **Yes**

Secondary School Information
Most Important Criteria For Admissions (1-strongest)

7 SAT/ACT	**5** Application	**3** School transcript	
Class rank	Course selection	**4** Personal statement	
2 Interview	Extra activities	Psychoeducational	
6 G.P.A.	Open admission	Recommendations	

Test Requirements:
Untimed SAT: **Yes** Untimed ACT: **Yes**

Types of Disabilities Served

Speech/Lang	Reading	ADD with LD
Study skills	Spelling	ADD without LD
Written express	Math	ADHD with LD
Organizational	Fine Motor	ADHD without LD
Perceptual		

Admissions Process

Application, $25.00 fee, transcripts, ACT/SAT, interview and portfolio review.

Diagnostic Testing

ADD	Personality	Perceptual skills	Spelling
ADHD	Organization	Fine motor skills	Reading
I.Q.	Handwriting	Spoken language	Study skills
Math	Social skills	Written language	

Services rendered by:
  Graduates Peers Faculty LD staff Teacher trainees

Tutorials

Grp.	Ind.	Tutorials	Grp.	Ind.	Tutorials
		Math skills			Word processing
		Study skills			Time management
		Language arts			Learning strategies
		Written express			Organizational skills

New York

Academic Accommodations

Curriculum	Study Aids	Exams
Priority registration	Typist	Oral
Math waiver	Reader	Untimed
Foreign lang. waiver	Notetaker	Take home
Course substitution	Proof reader	With proctor
In Class	Text on tape	On computer
Calculators	Early syllabus	Extended time
Tape recorder	Taped handouts	On tape
Word processor		Modified
Priority seating		Separate room

Graduation Requirements:
Course credits: **128** Years to complete degree: **4** Math waiver: **Yes** Language waiver: **Yes**

Program Strengths
BFA degrees in animation, advertising, art education, art therapy, cartooning, film/video, graphic design, illustration, interior design, photography, fine arts. Over 700 working professionals and exhibiting artists who work and exhibit in New York City, teach at SVA. MFA degrees in computer art, fine arts, illustration, photography. We have a Learning Center which is aware of the learning disabled.

General Information:
School of Visual Arts is a 4 year independent college. Urban campus   Accessible by air, train or bus. 9% of students are foreign. Housing is not guaranteed.

Accreditation: MSACS, NASAD

Expenses:
Tuition: In-state: Full year: $10,500.00. Tuition: Out-of-state: Full year: $10,500.00. Room and board: $6,000.00

Majors
• ARTS Art Therapy, Drawing, Film & Video, Graphic Arts, Interior Design, Painting, Photography, Sculpture • COMMUNICATIONS Advertising, Graphic Design, Photography, Television/Radio/Film • CRAFTS AND DESIGN Graphic Design, Illustration Design, Printmaking, Sculpture • VISUAL AND PERFORMING ARTS Art, Fine Arts, Studio Art, Video+

Sports/Activities
• STUDENT LIFE ACTIVITIES Magazine, Newspaper, Radio/TV station, Student Government, Yearbook

Secondary School Information
Most Important Criteria For Admissions (1-strongest)

5 SAT/ACT	**7** Application	**1** School transcript
10 Class rank	**2** Course selection	**8** Personal statement
9 Interview	**6** Extra activities	**11** Psychoeducational
3 G.P.A.	Open admission	**4** Recommendations

Test Requirements:
Achievement tests required: **None**

Types of Disabilities Served
- Speech/Lang
- Study skills
- Written express
- Organizational
- Perceptual
- Reading
- Spelling
- Math
- Fine Motor
- ADD with LD
- ADD without LD
- ADHD with LD
- ADHD without LD

Admissions Process

Candidates who present documentation of LD with application may request consideration for substitution of foreign language requirement. Evaluations and decisions are given by April 1st along with admission's decision. Otherwise, no special accommodations are made in the admissions process.

High School Course Requirements:
English: **4** Math: **3** Science: **2** Foreign Language: **3**

Learning Disability Program
Recommended credits per semester: **15**
Services available for all students: **Yes**
Counseling: Individual: **Yes**

Diagnostic Testing

ADD	Personality	Perceptual skills	Spelling
ADHD	Organization	Fine motor skills	Reading
I.Q.	Handwriting	Spoken language	Study skills
Math	Social skills	Written language	

Tutoring:
Average size of group tutorials:
Services rendered by:
Graduates   •Peers   Faculty   LD staff   Teacher trainees

Tutorials

Grp.	Ind.	Tutorials	Grp.	Ind.	Tutorials
	•	Math skills			Word processing
		Study skills			Time management
		Language arts			Learning strategies
	•	Written express			Organizational skills

Academic Accommodations

Curriculum	Study Aids	Exams
Priority registration	• Typist	Oral
Math waiver	• Reader	Untimed
Foreign lang. waiver	• Notetaker	• Take home
Course substitution	Proof reader	With proctor
In Class	• Text on tape	• On computer
• Calculators	Early syllabus	• Extended time
• Tape recorder	Taped handouts	On tape
• Word processor		• Modified
• Priority seating		Separate room

Highly Selective   **New York**
                              Accommodations

Skidmore College
Saratoga Springs, New York 12866
(518) 587-7569

School Enrollment: **2,174** Male: **913** Female: **1,261**

Admissions Contact: **Mary Lou W. Bates, Director of Admissions**
LD Contact: **Jon Ramsey, Associate Dean Academic Affairs**

Admissions

Application Information:
Application deadline: **February 1st**
Notified when: **April 1st**

Graduation Requirements:
Course credits: **120** GPA: **2.0** Years to complete degree: **4**
Other requirements: **Math, foreign language, writing, non-western culture**

Program Strengths
Skidmore does not offer a formal program for learning disabled students. Applicants who identify a learning disability during the admissions process are considered for admission on the same competitive basis as other applicants. If it is clear that a candidate's record of achievement and potential for success in a rigorous liberal arts curriculum compare favorably to the very keen competition for admission, that student will be admitted without regard to his or her handicap. Candidates who present documentation of a LD by application deadline may request consideration for substitution of foreign language requirement and decisions will be made by April 1st.

General Information:
Skidmore College is a 4 year private college. Suburban campus of 800 acres is 35 miles from Albany. Accessible by air, train or bus. Ski areas are 15 miles from campus. Beaches are 3.5 miles from campus. 2% of students are foreign. 9 residential halls on campus. Housing is guaranteed.90 % of students remain on campus for the weekends.

Accreditation:MSACS

SAT/ACT Scores:
Scores for incoming freshmen:**Verbal:**38%below 500. 46%between 500 and 599. 15%between 600 and 699. 1%above 700. **Math:**20% below 500. 52% between 500 and 599. 25% between 600 and 699. 3%above 700. 26% between 20 and 23. 37%between 24 and 25l. 26%between 26 and 28. 11% above 28.

Expenses:
Tuition: In-state: Full year: $16,650.00. Part-time: Per credit:$482.00. Tuition: Out-of-state: Full year: $16,580.00. Room and board: $5,270.00

Majors
• AREA STUDIES Asian, Women's Studies • BUSINESS Business Management, Economics • COMMUNICATIONS Creative Writing, English • COMPUTER SCIENCE Computer Science • EDUCATION Art, Elementary • HUMANITIES Classics, English/Writing/Literature, Fine Arts, Philosophy • LANGUAGES English, French, German, Spanish • MATHEMATICS Theoretical • PREPROFESSIONAL Business, Dentistry, Law, Medicine, Social Work, Veterinarian • RELIGIOUS STUDIES Philosophy • SCIENCES Biology, Chemistry, Computer Science, Geology, Mathematics, Physics • SOCIAL SCIENCES Anthropology, Government/Political, History, Political Science, Psychology, Sociology • VISUAL AND PERFORMING ARTS Art History, Dance, Dramatic Arts, Music, Studio Art, Theater

Sports/Activities
• SPORTS-INTERCOLLEGIATE Baseball (M), Basketball (F), Basketball (M), Crew (F), Crew (M), Diving (F), Field Hockey (F), Golf (M), Horseback Riding (F), Horseback Riding (M), Ice Hockey (M), Lacrosse (F), Lacrosse (M), Soccer (F), Soccer (M), Softball (F), Swimming (F), Tennis (F), Tennis (M), Volleyball (F) • SPORTS-INTRAMURAL Basketball, Cross Country, Cycling, Football, Golf, Racquetball, Skiing - Snow, Soccer, Softball, Squash, Swimming, Tennis, Volleyball, Weight Lifting, Wrestling • STUDENT LIFE ACTIVITIES Academic Clubs, Choral, Community Service, Dance, Debate, Drama Groups, Ethnic and Cultural Groups, Film, Jazz Band, Magazine, Music Groups, Musical Theater, Newspaper, Orchestra, Political Groups, Radio/TV station, Religious Organization, Student Government, Symphony Orchestra, Yearbook

---

Selective   **New York Program**

St. Bonaventure University
St. Bonaventure, New York 14778
(716) 375-2066

School Enrollment: **2,300** Male: **1,148** Female: **1,111**
LD Enrollment: **30** Male: **16** Female: **14**

Admissions Contact: **June Salan, Director of Admissions**
LD Contact: **Cora Dzubak, Coordinator, Disabled Student Serv.**
Name of Program: **Disabled Student Services**
Address: **26 Doyle Hall**
Telephone:**(716) 375-2066**

Admissions

Application Information:
LD Students Applying: **19** Accepted: **13** Enrolled:**5**
Application deadline: **April 15th**
Rolling Admissions: **Yes**

Secondary School Information
Most Important Criteria For Admissions (1-strongest)

4 SAT/ACT	**7** Application	**2** School transcript
6 Class rank	**1** Course selection	**9** Personal statement
Interview	**10** Extra activities	**5** Psychoeducational
3 G.P.A.	Open admission	**8** Recommendations

Test Requirements:
Diagnostic testing waived: **Yes**
Untimed SAT: **Yes** Untimed ACT: **Yes**
WAIS-R required: **Yes**
Documentation of LD required: **Yes**
Currency of diagnostic testing: **within 3 years**
Tests recommended: **Psychological (WISC-R, WAIS-R), Achievement (Woodcock Johnson)**

Types of Disabilities Served
• Speech/Lang	• Reading	• ADD with LD
• Study skills	• Spelling	• ADD without LD
• Written express	• Math	• ADHD with LD
• Organizational	• Fine Motor	• ADHD without LD
• Perceptual		

Admissions Process

All applications are reviewed by the Admission's Committee. All LD applications are then reviewed by the LD Screening Committee and they make their recommendations.

High School Course Requirements:
English: **4** Math: **3** Science: **3** Foreign Language: **2**
Waivers to standard high school courses
Foreign Language : **Yes**

New York

Learning Disability Program

Program: Reinforces course work: **Yes**
Program available through:**Monday - Friday**
Students mainstreamed **100** % of the day
Recommended credits per semester: **12-18**
Services available for all students: **Yes**
Counseling: Individual: **Yes** Vocational Counseling: **Yes**
Support groups are available:**No, organized as need arises. An LD support group can be started.**

Faculty:
Faculty: **1** Including Director: **Yes** Full time: **1** M.A.: **1**
Meets with instructor: **As needed**

Diagnostic Testing
- ADD
- ADHD
- I.Q.
- Math
- Personality
- Organization
- Handwriting
- Social skills
- Perceptual skills
- Fine motor skills
- Spoken language
- Written language
- Spelling
- Reading
- Study skills

Tutoring:
Average size of group tutorials: **Individual**
Services rendered by:
- Graduates • Peers • Faculty • LD staff   Teacher trainees

Tutorials

Grp.	Ind.	Tutorials	Grp.	Ind.	Tutorials
	•	Math skills		•	Word processing
	•	Study skills		•	Time management
		Language arts		•	Learning strategies
	•	Written express		•	Organizational skills

Academic Accommodations

Curriculum	Study Aids	Exams
Priority registration	Typist	• Oral
Math waiver	• Reader	• Untimed
• Foreign lang. waiver	Notetaker	Take home
Course substitution	• Proof reader	• With proctor
In Class	• Text on tape	• On computer
• Calculators	Early syllabus	• Extended time
• Tape recorder	Taped handouts	On tape
• Word processor		• Modified
• Priority seating		• Separate room

Graduation Requirements:
Course credits: **129** GPA: **2.0** Years to complete degree: **Individualized**
Language waiver: **Yes**
Other requirements: **Residency, last 36 hours on campus; one half of credits in major completed on campus.**

Program Strengths
Individual tutoring is offered twice weekly for each course. Taped tests and individual tape players are provided. The LD coordinator meets weekly with all new students. Faculty consultations scheduled as often as requested.

General Information:
St. Bonaventure University is a 4 year independent Franciscan university. Rural campus of 600 acres is Accessible by bus. Ski areas are 30 miles from campus. Beaches are 8 hours from campus. 1% of students are foreign. 6 residential halls on campus. Housing is guaranteed.Guaranteed through 4th year. 80 % of students remain on campus for the weekends.

Accreditation:MSACS

SAT/ACT Scores:
Scores for incoming freshmen:**Verbal:**72%below 500. 23%between 500 and 599. 4%between 600 and 699. 1%above 700. **Math:**43% below 500. 39% between 500 and 599. 15% between 600 and 699. 2%above 700. **ACT:** 17% below 20. 40% between 20 and 23. 20%between 24 and 25l. 16%between 26 and 28. 7% above 28.

Class Rank:
About 25% of the present freshmen class were in the upper 20% of their high school class. 48% were in the top 40% of their class. 65% were in the top 60% of their class. 81% were in the top 80% of their class.

Expenses:
Tuition: In-state: Full year: $8,842.00. Part-time: Per credit:$275.00. Tuition: Out-of-state: Full year: $8,842.00. Part-time: Per credit:$275.00.
Room and board: $4,594.00

Majors
• AGRICULTURE • BUSINESS Accounting, Economics, Management, Marketing • COMMUNICATIONS Communication • EDUCATION Elementary, English, Physical, Psychology • HEALTH SCIENCES Medical Laboratory Technology • HUMANITIES Philosophy • LANGUAGES Classics, English • SCIENCES Biology, Chemistry, Computer Science, Mathematics, Medical Technology, Physics • SOCIAL SCIENCES History, Political Science, Psychology, Social Science, Sociology

Sports/Activities
• SPORTS-INTERCOLLEGIATE Baseball, Basketball (F), Basketball (M), Cross Country, Golf, Ice Hockey, Lacrosse, Soccer (F), Soccer (M), Swimming (F), Swimming (M), Tennis (F), Tennis (M) • SPORTS-INTRAMURAL Badminton, Basketball (F), Basketball (M), Bowling, Cross Country, Football, Ping-Pong, Softball (F), Swimming, Tennis (F), Tennis (M), Track and Field, Volleyball, Water Polo, Weight Lifting, Wrestling • STUDENT LIFE ACTIVITIES Academic Clubs, Choral, Concert Band, Fraternities, Jazz Band, Music Groups, Newspaper, Sororities, Student Government

Very Selective   **New York**
                                      Services

St. Lawrence University
Canton, New York 13617
(315) 379-5261

School Enrollment: **1,853** Male: **1,104** Female: **749**
LD Enrollment: **101** Male: **51** Female: **50**

Admissions Contact: **Peter K. Richardson, Director of Admissions**
LD Contact: **Jim Cohn, Director**
Name of Program: **Students with Special Needs**
Telephone:**(315) 379-5104**

Admissions

Application Information:
Application deadline: **February 1st**

Secondary School Information
Most Important Criteria For Admissions (1-strongest)

3 SAT/ACT	3 Application	2 School transcript
2 Class rank	1 Course selection	3 Personal statement
3 Interview	3 Extra activities	Psychoeducational
2 G.P.A.	Open admission	2 Recommendations

Test Requirements:
Standardized tests waived: **Yes**
Diagnostic testing waived: **Yes**
Untimed SAT: **Yes** Untimed ACT: **Yes** Untimed ACH: **Yes**
Documentation of LD required: **Yes**
Currency of diagnostic testing: **4 years**
Tests recommended: **Psychoeducational evaluation, I.Q. Achievement administered by licensed psychologist.**

Types of Disabilities Served
- Speech/Lang
- Study skills
- Written express
- Organizational
- Perceptual
- Reading
- Spelling
- Math
- Fine Motor
- ADD with LD
- ADD without LD
- ADHD with LD
- ADHD without LD

High School Course Requirements:
English: **4**

Learning Disability Program
Program: Reinforces course work: **Yes**
Program available through:**As needed**
Students mainstreamed **100** % of the day
Recommended credits per semester: **3-4**
Counseling: Individual: **Yes** Group Counseling: **Yes** Vocational Counseling: **Yes**

Faculty:
Faculty: **1** Part time: **1** M.A.: **1**
Faculty advocate: **Yes** Meets with instructor: **As needed**

Diagnostic Testing
ADD	Personality	Perceptual skills	Spelling
ADHD	Organization	Fine motor skills	Reading
I.Q.	Handwriting	Spoken language	Study skills
Math	Social skills	Written language	

Tutoring:
Average size of group tutorials: **1:1**
Services rendered by:
Graduates •Peers •Faculty •LD staff Teacher trainees

Tutorials
Grp.	Ind.	Tutorials	Grp.	Ind.	Tutorials
	•	Math skills		•	Word processing
•	•	Study skills	•	•	Time management
	•	Language arts	•	•	Learning strategies
	•	Written express	•	•	Organizational skills

Academic Accommodations
Curriculum	Study Aids	Exams
• Priority registration	Typist	• Oral
Math waiver	• Reader	Untimed
Foreign lang. waiver	• Notetaker	• Take home
• Course substitution	Proof reader	• With proctor
In Class	• Text on tape	• On computer
• Calculators	Early syllabus	• Extended time
• Tape recorder	Taped handouts	• On tape
• Word processor		• Modified
• Priority seating		• Separate room

Graduation Requirements:
Course credits: **33.5** GPA: **2.0**

Program Strengths
St. Lawrence University is committed to providing accommodation services to students with learning challenges. We have a clear, strong policy for disabled students. The director works with faculty to bring about cooperative and collaborative behaviors when dealing with stduents' needs. Students are encouraged to self-identify, and self-advocacy is the goal of services rendered. The Director facilitates communication between faculty and students which enhances the education process. Our rural location, and small student-teacher ratio is ideal for students with learning challenges.

General Information:
St. Lawrence University is a 4 year private university. Rural campus of 1,000 acres is 70 miles from Ottawa. Ski areas are 53 miles from campus. 3.7% of students are foreign. 10 residential halls on campus. Housing is guaranteed.70 % of students remain on campus for the weekends. 45 % of students join fraternities/sororities.

Accreditation:Regional, NYSBR

SAT/ACT Scores:
Scores for incoming freshmen:**Verbal:**38%below 500. 48%between 500 and 599. 13%between 600 and 699. 1%above 700. **Math:**7% below 500. 48% between 500 and 599. 35% between 600 and 699. 5%above 700.

Class Rank:
About 47% of the present freshmen class were in the upper 20% of their high school class. 82% were in the top 40% of their class. 97% were in the top 60% of their class. 99% were in the top 80% of their class.

Expenses:
Tuition: In-state: Full year: $14,000.00. Room and board: $4,500.00

Majors
• AREA STUDIES Asian • BUSINESS • COMMUNICATIONS Creative Writing • COMPUTER SCIENCE Computer Science • EDUCATION Foreign Language, Physical • HEALTH SCIENCES Environmental • HUMANITIES Fine Arts • LANGUAGES Russian • SCIENCES Biology, Biophysics, Chemistry, Geology, Geophysics, Mathematics, Physics • SOCIAL SCIENCES Anthropology, Government/Political, History, Political Science, Psychology, Sociology • VISUAL AND PERFORMING ARTS Dramatic Arts, Fine Arts, Music

Sports/Activities
• SPORTS RELATED Pep Band • SPORTS-INTERCOLLEGIATE Baseball (M), Basketball, Cross Country, Diving, Fencing, Field Hockey (F), Football (M), Ice Hockey, Lacrosse, Skiing - Snow, Soccer, Swimming, Tennis, Track and Field (M), Volleyball (F), Wrestling (M) • SPORTS-INTRAMURAL Badminton, Basketball, Bowling, Crew (M), Fencing, Golf, Gymnastics, Hand Ball, Horseback Riding, Ice Hockey (M), Riflery, Rugby, Sailing, Soccer, Squash, Water Polo • STUDENT LIFE ACTIVITIES Choral, Concert Band, Dance, Drama Groups, Fraternities, Magazine, Music Groups, Musical Theater, Newspaper, Radio/TV station, Religious Organization, Sororities, Student Government, Yearbook

St. Thomas Aquinas College
Route 340
Sparkill, New York 10976
(914) 359-9500

School Enrollment: **1,983** Male: **839** Female: **1,144**
LD Enrollment: **80** Male: **48** Female: **32**

Admissions Contact: **Andrea Kraeft, Director of Admissions**
LD Contact: **Dr. Mary Janet Doonan, Director, The STAC Exch.**
Name of Program: **The STAC Exchange**

Admissions

Application Information:
LD Students Applying: **147** Accepted: **25** Enrolled:**24**
Application deadline: **Rolling**
Applicant must apply **10** months in advance
Rolling Admissions: **Yes**

Secondary School Information
Most Important Criteria For Admissions (1-strongest)
10	SAT/ACT		Application	**6**	School transcript
	Class rank	**1**	Course selection	**5**	Personal statement
4	Interview	**3**	Extra activities	**2**	Psychoeducational
9	G.P.A.		Open admission	**7**	Recommendations

Test Requirements:
Diagnostic testing waived: **Yes**
Untimed SAT: **Yes**
WAIS-R required: **Yes** Range accepted: **Average**
Documentation of LD required: **Yes**
Currency of diagnostic testing: **1 year**
Tests recommended: **Documentation of LD by certified professionals**

Types of Disabilities Served
- Speech/Lang
- Study skills
- Written express
- Organizational
- Perceptual
- Reading
- Spelling
- Math
- Fine Motor
- ADD with LD
- ADD without LD
- ADHD with LD
- ADHD without LD

Admissions Process

All materials are sent to Admissions. Once folder is complete, it is reviewed and forwarded to the Program Office. Reviewed again. Committee meeting. If candidate seems appropriate, only then will they be interviewed.

High School Course Requirements:
English: **4** Math: **3** Science: **3** Foreign Language: **2**
Waivers to standard high school courses
Math: **Yes**

Learning Disability Program
Special orientation for LD students: **Yes**
Students mainstreamed **100** % of the day
Recommended credits per semester: **12-15**
Time required or recommended in learning center: **4**
Services only for LD students: **Yes**
Counseling: Individual: **Yes** Group Counseling: **Yes** Vocational Counseling: **Yes**
Support groups are available:**Yes, Services in Study Strategies, et.**

Faculty:
Faculty: **12** Including Director: **Yes** Full time: **6** Part time: **6**
LD faculty with: BS/BA: **12** M.A.: **12** Ph.D.: **1**
Faculty advocate: **Yes** Meets with instructor: **As needed**

Diagnostic Testing
ADD	• Personality	• Perceptual skills	Spelling
ADHD	• Organization	Fine motor skills	Reading
• I.Q.	Handwriting	• Spoken language	• Study skills
• Math	• Social skills	• Written language	

Tutoring:
Services rendered by:
Graduates	Peers	Faculty	•LD staff	Teacher trainees

Tutorials
Grp.	Ind.	Tutorials	Grp.	Ind.	Tutorials
		Math skills	•	•	Word processing
•	•	Study skills		•	Time management
		Language arts	•	•	Learning strategies
	•	Written express	•	•	Organizational skills

Academic Accommodations
Curriculum	Study Aids	Exams
• Priority registration	Typist	• Oral
Math waiver	• Reader	• Untimed
Foreign lang. waiver	• Notetaker	Take home
Course substitution	• Proof reader	• With proctor
In Class	• Text on tape	• On computer
• Calculators	Early syllabus	• Extended time
• Tape recorder	Taped handouts	• On tape
• Word processor		Modified
Priority seating		• Separate room

Graduation Requirements:
Course credits: **120** GPA: **2.0** Years to complete degree: **4-6**

Program Strengths
The STAC EXCHANGE is a program designed for high school graduates who have the potential to earn a college degree but who need a specially designed program to compensate for their learning process dysfunction. Strength based; teaches compensatory strategies; very individualized.

General Information:
St. Thomas Aquinas College is a 4 year private college. Suburban campus of 42 acres is 15 miles from New York. Accessible by bus. Ski areas are 2 miles from campus. Beaches are 2 miles from campus. 6% of students are foreign. Housing is not guaranteed.80 % of students remain on campus for the weekends.

Accreditation:MSACS

SAT/ACT Scores:
Scores for incoming freshmen:**Verbal:**20%below 500. 58%between 500 and 599. 16%between 600 and 699. 6%above 700. **Math:**19% below 500. 56% between 500 and 599. 19% between 600 and 699. 6%above 700.

Class Rank:
About 19% of the present freshmen class were in the upper 20% of their high school class. 39% were in the top 40% of their class. 82% were in the top 60% of their class. 100% were in the top 80% of their class.

Expenses:
Tuition: In-state: Full year: $6,600.00. Part-time: Per credit:$220.00. Tuition: Out-of-state: Full year: $6,600.00. Part-time: Per credit:$220.00. Room and board: $4,250.00 Cost of LD program:$2,300.00

Majors
• BUSINESS Accounting, Banking, Business Administration, Business Management, Finance, Management, Marketing, Personnel, Real Estate • COMMUNICATIONS Advertising, Art Therapy, Broadcasting, Commercial Design, Communication, Creative Writing, English, Journalism, Television/Radio/Film • EDUCATION Art, Early Childhood, Elementary, English, Foreign Language, Mathematics, Middle School, Secondary, Social Studies, Special • ENGINEERING Engineering Science • HEALTH SCIENCES Medical Laboratory Technology, Medical Technology • HUMANITIES English/Writing/Literature, Liberal Arts, Philosophy, Religion • LANGUAGES French, Italian, Spanish • PREPROFESSIONAL Dentistry, Engineering, Law, Medicine, Recreation • SCIENCES Gerontology, Mathematics, Natural • SOCIAL SCIENCES Criminal Justice, History, Psychology, Recreational Therapy, Social Sciences • VISUAL AND PERFORMING ARTS Art, Studio Art

Sports/Activities
• SPORTS-INTERCOLLEGIATE Baseball (M), Basketball, Cross Country, Golf, Softball (F), Volleyball (F) • SPORTS-INTRAMURAL Basketball, Softball, Tennis • STUDENT LIFE ACTIVITIES Choral, Community Service, Drama Groups, Magazine, Musical Theater, Newspaper, Political Groups, Radio/TV station, Student Government, Yearbook

Highly Selective　　　　　**New York Services**

State University of New York at Albany
1400 Washington Avenue Campus Center 137
Albany, New York 12222
(518) 442-5435

School Enrollment: **10,000** Male: **5,000** Female: **5,000**
LD Enrollment: **52** Male: **26** Female: **26**

Admissions Contact: **Thomas Flemming, Admissions Counselor**
LD Contact: **Nancy Belowich-Negron, Director**
Name of Program: **Disabled Student Services**
Telephone:**(518) 442-5490**

Admissions

Application Information:
LD on admissions committee:**Yes**
Application deadline: **February 15th**
Rolling Admissions: **Yes**Notified when: **April 15th**

Secondary School Information
Most Important Criteria For Admissions (1-strongest)

2	SAT/ACT	Application	1 School transcript
3	Class rank	1 Course selection	Personal statement
	Interview	Extra activities	Psychoeducational
1	G.P.A.	Open admission	Recommendations

Test Requirements:
Untimed SAT: **Yes**
Documentation of LD required: **Yes**

Types of Disabilities Served
• Speech/Lang	• Reading	• ADD with LD
• Study skills	• Spelling	• ADD without LD
• Written express	• Math	• ADHD with LD
• Organizational	• Fine Motor	• ADHD without LD
• Perceptual		

Learning Disability Program
Counseling: Individual: **Yes**

Faculty:
Faculty: **3** Full time: **1** Part time: **2** M.A.: **1**
Faculty advocate: **Yes** Meets with instructor: **Regularly**

Diagnostic Testing
• ADD	• Personality	Perceptual skills	Spelling
• ADHD	• Organization	Fine motor skills	Reading
• I.Q.	• Handwriting	Spoken language	Study skills
Math	• Social skills	Written language	

Tutoring:
Average size of group tutorials: **8**
Services rendered by:
•Graduates　•Peers　Faculty　•LD staff　Teacher trainees

Tutorials
Grp.	Ind.	Tutorials	Grp.	Ind.	Tutorials
		Math skills		•	Word processing
•		Study skills		•	Time management
		Language arts		•	Learning strategies
		Written express		•	Organizational skills

Academic Accommodations
Curriculum	Study Aids	Exams
• Priority registration	• Typist	• Oral
Math waiver	• Reader	Untimed
Foreign lang. waiver	• Notetaker	Take home
Course substitution	• Proof reader	• With proctor
In Class	• Text on tape	• On computer
• Calculators	• Early syllabus	• Extended time
• Tape recorder	Taped handouts	• On tape
• Word processor		• Modified
Priority seating		• Separate room

Program Strengths
Our program tries to be as flexible to individual students' needs as possible. While we encourage independence, we are absolutely there to provide support services as needed. Fully integrated campus services including a Writing Center, Academic Support Services, Center for Computing and Disability and Disabled Student Services.

General Information:
State University of New York at Albany is a 4 year public university. Urban campus of 500 acres is 4 miles from Albany. Ski areas are 45-60 mins. from campus. Beaches are 60-90 minutes from campus. 4 residential halls on campus. Housing is guaranteed.Guaranteed through 1st year. 80 % of students remain on campus for the weekends. 20 % of students join fraternities/sororities.

Accreditation:Regional

Class Rank:
About 70% of the present freshmen class were in the upper 20% of their high school class.

Expenses:
Tuition: In-state: Full year: $2,650.00. Part-time: Per credit:$45.00. Tuition: Out-of-state: Full year: $4,700.00. Part-time: Per credit:$90.00. Room and board: $3,000.00

Majors
• AREA STUDIES Asian, Black/Afro-American, Latin American, Women's Studies • ARTS Art History, Art Therapy, Commercial Art, Crafts, Design, Fashion Design, Film & Video, Graphic Arts, Interior Design, Music, Music History, Music Performance, Painting, Photography, Sculpture • BUSINESS Accounting, Banking/Finance, Business Administration, Business Economics, Business Management, Economics, Fashion Merchandising, Management, Marketing • COMMUNICATIONS Advertising, Creative Writing, English, Literature, Photography, Television/Radio/Film • COMPUTER SCIENCE Computer Science, Computer Technology, Data Processing • CRAFTS AND DESIGN Crafts • EDUCATION Art, Art Therapy, Bilingual, Early Childhood, Elementary, English, English As A Second Language, Mathematics, Music, Secondary, Social Studies, Special, Vocational • HEALTH SCIENCES Medical Laboratory Technology, Nuclear Medical Technology • HUMANITIES English/Writing/Literature • LANGUAGES Spanish • PREPROFESSIONAL Dentistry, Engineering, Law, Medicine, Optometry, Pharmacy • SCIENCES Astronomy, Biology, Chemistry, Geography, Geology, Geoscience • SOCIAL SCIENCES Criminal Justice, Geography, Government/Political, History, Law Enforcement, Political Science, Psychology, Sociology • SPECIAL EDUCATION Emotionally Disturbed, Learning Disability, Mentally Retarded, Physically Handicapped • VISUAL AND PERFORMING ARTS Art, Art History, Fine Arts, Music, Music Performance, Music Theatre, Studio Art, Theater, Video • VOCATIONAL Painting

Sports/Activities
• SPORTS RELATED Pep Band • SPORTS-INTERCOLLEGIATE Baseball (M), Basketball, Crew, Cross Country, Diving, Football, Lacrosse (M), Rugby (M), Soccer, Softball (F), Swimming, Tennis, Track and Field, Volleyball (F), Wrestling (M) • SPORTS-INTRAMURAL Baseball, Basketball, Bowling, Field Hockey, Hand Ball, Racquetball, Soccer, Softball, Squash, Tennis, Track and Field, Volleyball, Water Polo, Wrestling (M) • STUDENT LIFE ACTIVITIES Choral, Concert Band, Dance, Drama Groups, Fraternities, Jazz Band, Magazine, Music Groups, Newspaper, Radio/TV station, Sororities, Student Government, Symphony Orchestra, Yearbook

Highly Selective	New York Services

State University of New York at Binghamton
Vestal Parkway East
Binghamton, New York 13901
(607) 777-2171

School Enrollment: **11,883** Male: **5,689** Female: **6,194**
LD Enrollment: **22** Male: **13** Female: **9**

Admissions Contact: **Geoffrey Gould, Director of Admissions**
LD Contact: **B. Jean Fairbairn, Coordinator**
Name of Program: **Services for Students with Disabilities**
Address: **Box 6000**
Telephone:**(607) 777-2686 (Voice/TTY)**

Admissions

Application Information:
Application deadline: **Mid February**
Notified when: **March-May**

Secondary School Information
Most Important Criteria For Admissions (1-strongest)

3 SAT/ACT	1 Application	1 School transcript
1 Class rank	1 Course selection	2 Personal statement
2 Interview	2 Extra activities	1 Psychoeducational
2 G.P.A.	Open admission	2 Recommendations

Test Requirements:
Diagnostic testing waived: **Yes**
Untimed SAT: **Yes** Untimed ACT: **Yes**
Documentation of LD required: **Yes**

Types of Disabilities Served
• Speech/Lang	• Reading	• ADD with LD
• Study skills	• Spelling	• ADD without LD
• Written express	• Math	• ADHD with LD
• Organizational	• Fine Motor	• ADHD without LD
• Perceptual		

Admissions Process

University admissions criteria include grade average, class rank, courses taken, extracurricular activities and results of standardized tests. There is no special admission process for students with learning disabilities but each student's application is considered individually.

High School Course Requirements:
English: **4** Math: **2.5** Science: **2** Foreign Language: **2-3**
Waivers to standard high school courses
Foreign Language : **Yes**

Learning Disability Program
Program: Reinforces course work: **Yes**
Program available through:**Fall and on going as necessary**
Students mainstreamed **100** % of the day
Recommended credits per semester: **12-16**
Counseling: Individual: **Yes** Group Counseling: **Yes** Vocational Counseling: **Yes**
Support groups are available:**Students for a Barrier-Free Campus**

Faculty:
Faculty: **2** Full time: **1** Part time: **1**
LD faculty with: BS/BA: **1** M.A.: **1**
Faculty advocate: **Yes** Meets with instructor: **As needed**

Diagnostic Testing
ADD	Personality	Perceptual skills	Spelling
ADHD	Organization	Fine motor skills	Reading
I.Q.	Handwriting	Spoken language	Study skills
Math	Social skills	Written language	

Tutoring:
Services rendered by:
•Graduates •Peers Faculty LD staff Teacher trainees

Tutorials
Grp.	Ind.	Tutorials	Grp.	Ind.	Tutorials
		Math skills		•	Word processing
		Study skills			Time management
		Language arts			Learning strategies
		Written express			Organizational skills

Academic Accommodations

Curriculum	Study Aids	Exams
Priority registration	• Typist	• Oral
Math waiver	• Reader	Untimed
• Foreign lang. waiver	• Notetaker	• Take home
Course substitution	• Proof reader	• With proctor
In Class	• Text on tape	• On computer
• Calculators	• Early syllabus	• Extended time
• Tape recorder	Taped handouts	• On tape
• Word processor		• Modified
Priority seating		• Separate room

Graduation Requirements: Years to complete degree: **Varies**
Language waiver: **Yes**

Program Strengths

Students who are most successful are those who have an understanding of their abilities, limitations, and accommodations needed and are willing to discuss these issues with faculty and support staff. Services handbook available upon request.

General Information:

State University of New York at Binghamton is a 4 year public university. Suburban campus of 606 acres is 70 miles from Syracuse. Accessible by plane or bus Ski areas are 1 hour from campus. .04% of students are foreign. 32 residential halls on campus. Housing is guaranteed.Guaranteed through 4th year. 90 % of students remain on campus for the weekends. 18 % of students join fraternities/sororities.

Accreditation:MSACS, ABET, NLN

SAT/ACT Scores:

Scores for incoming freshmen:**Verbal:**30%below 500. 48%between 500 and 599. 20%between 600 and 699. 2%above 700. **Math:**7% below 500. 35% between 500 and 599. 45% between 600 and 699. 13%above 700.

Class Rank:

About 94% of the present freshmen class were in the upper 20% of their high school class. 100% were in the top 40% of their class.

Expenses:

Tuition: In-state: Full year: $2,650.00. Tuition: Out-of-state: Full year: $6,550.00 . Room and board: $4,760.00

Majors

• AREA STUDIES American, Black/Afro-American, Caribbean, Jewish, Latin American, Medieval • BUSINESS Accounting, Economics, Management • COMMUNICATIONS English, Linguistics, Television/Radio/Film • COMPUTER SCIENCE Computer Science • EDUCATION Elementary, Reading, Special • ENGINEERING Electrical, Industrial, Mechanical • HEALTH SCIENCES Environmental, Nursing • HUMANITIES Classics, English/Writing/Literature, Liberal Arts, Philosophy • LANGUAGES Arabic, French, German, Hebrew, Italian, Spanish • SCIENCES Biochemistry, Biology, Chemistry, Geography, Geology, Mathematics, Physics • SOCIAL SCIENCES Anthropology, Government/Political, History, Law Enforcement, Political Science, Psychology, Social Sciences, Sociology • VISUAL AND PERFORMING ARTS Art, Art History, Music, Theater • VOCATIONAL Electronics Technology

Sports/Activities

• SPORTS-INTERCOLLEGIATE Baseball (M), Basketball, Cross Country, Diving, Golf (M), Ice Hockey (M), Soccer, Softball (F), Swimming, Tennis, Track and Field, Volleyball (F), Wrestling (M) • SPORTS-INTRAMURAL Badminton, Basketball, Bowling, Cross Country, Golf, Horseback Riding, Lacrosse (M), Racquetball, Rugby (M), Skiing - Snow, Soccer, Softball, Squash, Tennis, Track and Field, Volleyball, Wrestling (M) • STUDENT LIFE ACTIVITIES Choral, Community Service, Concert Band, Drama Groups, Ethnic & Cultural Groups, Film, Fraternities, Jazz

Band, Magazine, Music Groups, Musical Theater, Newspaper, Opera, Radio/TV station, Religious Organization, Sororities, Student Government, Symphony Orchestra, Yearbook

Highly Selective

New York Services

State University of New York at Buffalo
272 Capen Hall
Buffalo, New York 14260
(716) 831-2111

School Enrollment: **26,015** Male: **14,258** Female: **11,757**
LD Enrollment: **44** Male: **29** Female: **15**

Admissions Contact: **David Cook, Assistant Director**
LD Contact: **Toby Bloom Schoellkopf, Director**
Name of Program: **Disability Services**
Telephone:**(716) 636-2608**

Admissions

Application Information:
Application deadline: **January 5th**

Secondary School Information
Most Important Criteria For Admissions (1-strongest)

1 SAT/ACT	Application	School transcript
1 Class rank	Course selection	Personal statement
Interview	Extra activities	Psychoeducational
1 G.P.A.	Open admission	Recommendations

Test Requirements:
Diagnostic testing waived: **Yes**
Untimed SAT: **Yes**
Documentation of LD required: **Yes**

Types of Disabilities Served

• Speech/Lang	Reading	ADD with LD
• Study skills	Spelling	ADD without LD
Written express	Math	ADHD with LD
• Organizational	Fine Motor	ADHD without LD
Perceptual		

Admissions Process

File a standard SUNY application indicating you are learning disabled.

High School Course Requirements:
English: **4** Math: **3** Science: **3** Foreign Language: **3**

Learning Disability Program

Services available for all students: **Yes**

Faculty:
Faculty: **4** Including Director: **Yes** Full time: **3** Part time: **1**
LD faculty with: BS/BA: **2**

Diagnostic Testing

ADD	Personality	Perceptual skills	Spelling
ADHD	Organization	Fine motor skills	Reading
I.Q.	Handwriting	Spoken language	Study skills
Math	Social skills	Written language	

535

Tutoring:

Average size of group tutorials: **Varies**
Services rendered by:
•Graduates   Peers   Faculty   •LD staff   Teacher trainees

Tutorials

Grp.	Ind.	Tutorials	Grp.	Ind.	Tutorials
		Math skills			Word processing
•		Study skills	•		Time management
		Language arts	•		Learning strategies
		Written express			Organizational skills

Academic Accommodations

Curriculum	Study Aids	Exams
• Priority registration	Typist	Oral
Math waiver	• Reader	• Untimed
Foreign lang. waiver	• Notetaker	Take home
Course substitution	Proof reader	• With proctor
In Class	Text on tape	On computer
Calculators	Early syllabus	• Extended time
• Tape recorder	Taped handouts	• On tape
Word processor		Modified
Priority seating		• Separate room

Graduation Requirements:

Course credits: **128** GPA: **2.0** Years to complete degree: **usually 4**

General Information:

State University of New York at Buffalo is a 4 year public university. Urban campus of 1,350 acres is 3 miles from Buffalo. Accessible by plane, train or bus Ski areas are 25 miles from campus. Beaches are 10 miles from campus. 7% of students are foreign. 7 residential halls on campus. Housing is guaranteed.Guaranteed through Graduate School. 7 % of students join fraternities/sororities.

Accreditation:MSACS0

SAT/ACT Scores:

Scores for incoming freshmen:**Verbal:**45%below 500. 42%between 500 and 599. 11%between 600 and 699. 2%above 700. **Math:**7% below 500. 41% between 500 and 599. 40% between 600 and 699. 12%above 700.

Class Rank:

About 81% of the present freshmen class were in the upper 20% of their high school class. 100% were in the top 40% of their class.

Expenses:

Tuition: In-state: Full year: $1,259.76 (12 or more credit hours). Part-time: Per credit:$90.00 (less than 12). Tuition: Out-of-state: Full year: plus fees $3,059.75. Part-time: Per credit:$240.00. Room and board: $2,188.00

Majors

• ARTS Art History, Music • BUSINESS Business Administration • EDUCATION Art • ENGINEERING Aerospace, Chemical, Civil, Electrical, Industrial, Mechanical • HEALTH SCIENCES Medical Technology, Nuclear Medical Technology, Nursing, Occupational Therapy, Physical Therapy • PRE PROFESSIONAL Pharmacy • SOCIAL SCIENCES Library Science • VISUAL AND PERFORMING ARTS Fine Arts, Music, Studio Art

Sports/Activities

• SPORTS RELATED Pep Band • SPORTS-INTERCOLLEGIATE Basketball, Cross Country, Diving, Football (M), Soccer, Swimming, Tennis, Track and Field, Volleyball (F), Wrestling (M) • SPORTS-INTRAMURAL Archery, Badminton, Basketball, Bowling, Crew, Cross Country, Fencing, Football (M), Golf (M), Gymnastics, Hand Ball, Ice Hockey (M), Lacrosse, Ping-Pong, Racquetball, Rugby, Skiing - Snow, Soccer, Squash, Tennis, Volleyball, Water Polo • STUDENT LIFE ACTIVITIES Choral, Dance, Drama Groups, Ethnic & Cultural Groups, Film, Fraternities, Jazz Band,

Magazine, Music Ensemble, Musical Theater, Newspaper, Opera, Radio, Religious Organization, Sororities, Student Government, Symphony Orchestra, Yearbook

---

Very Selective

State University of New York at Stony Brook

Room 133 Humanities Building
Stony Brook, New York 11794
(516) 632-6868

School Enrollment: **10,675** Male: **5,551** Female: **5,124**
LD Enrollment: **85** Male: **60** Female: **25**

Admissions Contact: **Ms. Gigi Lamens, Asst. Dean Admissions**
LD Contact: **Carol Dworkin, LD Specialist**
Name of Program: **Support Services**
Telephone:**(516) 632-6748**

Admissions

Application Information:

Rolling Admissions: **Yes**

Secondary School Information

Most Important Criteria For Admissions (1-strongest)

SAT/ACT	Application	School transcript
Class rank	Course selection	Personal statement
Interview	Extra activities	Psychoeducational
G.P.A.	Open admission	Recommendations

Test Requirements:

Diagnostic testing waived: **Yes**
Untimed SAT: **Yes** Untimed ACT: **Yes**
Documentation of LD required: **Yes**
Currency of diagnostic testing: **3 years**

Types of Disabilities Served

Speech/Lang	Reading	ADD with LD
Study skills	Spelling	ADD without LD
Written express	Math	ADHD with LD
Organizational	Fine Motor	ADHD without LD
Perceptual		

Admissions Process

No special admissions, same for all applicants

Learning Disability Program

Services only for LD students: **Yes**

Faculty:

Faculty: **1** Full time: **1** M.A.: **1**

Diagnostic Testing

ADD	Personality	Perceptual skills	Spelling
ADHD	Organization	Fine motor skills	Reading
I.Q.	Handwriting	Spoken language	Study skills
Math	Social skills	Written language	

Tutoring:

Services rendered by:
Graduates   •Peers   Faculty   •LD staff   Teacher trainees

Tutorials

Grp.	Ind.	Tutorials	Grp.	Ind.	Tutorials
	•	Math skills		•	Word processing
	•	Study skills		•	Time management
	•	Language arts		•	Learning strategies
	•	Written express		•	Organizational skills

Academic Accommodations

Curriculum
Priority registration
- Math waiver
- Foreign lang. waiver
Course substitution

In Class
- Calculators
- Tape recorder
- Word processor
Priority seating

Study Aids
- Typist
Reader
- Notetaker
- Proof reader
- Text on tape
Early syllabus
Taped handouts

Exams
- Oral
Untimed
Take home
- With proctor
On computer
- Extended time
On tape
- Modified
Separate room

Graduation Requirements:
Course credits: **120** GPA: **2.0** Math waiver: **Yes** Language waiver: **Yes**

Program Strengths

A Learning Disabilities Specialist acts as a student advocate and facilitates an array of support services. There is not a remedial or tutorial component. Students must have initiative and independence and at least some compensating skills.

General Information:

State University of New York at Stony Brook is a 4 year public university. Suburban campus of 1100 acres is 60 miles from New York City. Accessible by train. 25 residential halls on campus. Housing is guaranteed. Guaranteed through 4th year. 55 % of students remain on campus for the weekends.

Accreditation: ABET, APTA, CAHEA, CSWE, NLN

Expenses:

Tuition: In-state: Full year: $1,650.00. Part-time: Per credit:0. Tuition: Out-of-state: Full year: $5,000.00. Room and board: $2,070.00

Majors

• AREA STUDIES African • BUSINESS Economics • COMMUNICATIONS English • COMPUTER SCIENCE Computer Technology • EDUCATION Music • HEALTH SCIENCES Cardiopulmonary Technology, Medical Assistant, Medical Technology, Nursing, Physical Therapy • HUMANITIES Humanities, Religion • LANGUAGES French, German, Italian, Linguistic, Russian, Spanish • PREPROFESSIONAL Engineering, Social Work • SCIENCES Astronomy, Biochemistry, Biology, Chemistry, Geology, Mathematics, Meteorology, Physics • SOCIAL SCIENCES Anthropology, Government/Political, History, Psychology, Social Sciences • VISUAL AND PERFORMING ARTS Art History, Studio Art • VOCATIONAL Respiratory Therapy Technology

Sports/Activities

• SPORTS-INTERCOLLEGIATE Badminton, Baseball (M), Basketball, Cross Country, Diving, Football (M), Horseback Riding, Lacrosse (M), Soccer, Softball (M), Swimming, Tennis, Track and Field, Volleyball (F) • SPORTS-INTRAMURAL Badminton, Basketball, Cross Country, Hand Ball (M), Lacrosse, Soccer, Softball, Squash (M), Tennis, Volleyball • STUDENT LIFE ACTIVITIES Choral, Concert Band, Drama Groups, Film, Fraternities, Magazine, Music Groups, Musical Theater, Newspaper, Radio/TV station, Sororities, Student Government, Symphony Orchestra, Yearbook

Selective **New York**
Services

State University of New York College at Oneonta

Alumni Hall P.O. Box 4016
Oneonta, New York 13820
(607) 431-2524

School Enrollment: **5,200**
LD Enrollment: **40** Male: **20** Female: **20**

Admissions Contact: **Richard H. Burr, Director of Admissions**
LD Contact: **Joan Marshall, Director**
Name of Program: **Learning Support Services**
Telephone: **(607) 431-3010**

Admissions

Application Information:
Application deadline: **Rolling**
Rolling Admissions: **Yes** Notified when: **April 15th**

Secondary School Information
Most Important Criteria For Admissions (1-strongest)

3	SAT/ACT	Application	1	School transcript
2	Class rank	1 Course selection	4	Personal statement
	Interview	4 Extra activities		Psychoeducational
1	G.P.A.	Open admission	4	Recommendations

Test Requirements:
Diagnostic testing waived: **Yes**
Untimed SAT: **Yes** Untimed ACT: **Yes**
Documentation of LD required: **Yes**
Currency of diagnostic testing: **3 years**

Types of Disabilities Served
- Speech/Lang
- Study skills
- Written express
- Organizational
- Perceptual
- Reading
- Spelling
- Math
- Fine Motor
- ADD with LD
- ADD without LD
- ADHD with LD
- ADHD without LD

Learning Disability Program

Counseling: Individual: **Yes** Group Counseling: **Yes**

Diagnostic Testing

ADD	Personality	Perceptual skills	Spelling
ADHD	Organization	Fine motor skills	Reading
I.Q.	Handwriting	Spoken language	Study skills
Math	Social skills	Written language	

Tutoring:
Services rendered by:

Graduates	Peers	•Faculty	LD staff	Teacher trainees

Tutorials

Grp.	Ind.	Tutorials	Grp.	Ind.	Tutorials
•	•	Math skills	•	•	Word processing
•	•	Study skills	•	•	Time management
•	•	Language arts	•	•	Learning strategies
•	•	Written express	•	•	Organizational skills

Academic Accommodations

Curriculum	Study Aids	Exams
Priority registration	• Typist	• Oral
• Math waiver	Reader	Untimed
• Foreign lang. waiver	• Notetaker	• Take home
• Course substitution	• Proof reader	With proctor
In Class	• Text on tape	On computer
• Calculators	Early syllabus	• Extended time
• Tape recorder	Taped handouts	On tape
• Word processor		• Modified
Priority seating		Separate room

Program Strengths

Please be certain to note our Learning Support Services Center provides services for disabled students (both LD and physically disabled). It is not a center with a formalized program.

General Information:

State University of New York College at Oneonta is a 4 year public university. Rural campus of 200 acres is 90 miles from Albany. Accessible by bus. 1% of students are foreign. 14 residential halls on campus. Housing is guaranteed.Guaranteed through 4th year.

Accreditation:MSACS

Expenses:

Tuition: In-state: Full year:
$1,350.00. Tuition: Out-of-state: Full year: $4,700.00. Room and board: $3,500.00

Majors

• AREA STUDIES Urban • BUSINESS Accounting, Business Administration, Business Education, Economics • COMMUNICATIONS Communication, Speech • COMPUTER SCIENCE Computer Science, Computer Technology • EDUCATION Art, Early Childhood, Elementary, English, Foreign Language, Home Economics, Mathematics, Middle School, Pre-Education, Science, Secondary, Social Science, Social Studies • HEALTH SCIENCES Medical Technology, Nutritional/Food, Physical Therapy • HUMANITIES English/Writing/Literature, Liberal Arts , Philosophy • LANGUAGES French, German, Spanish • PRE PROFESSIONAL Dentistry, Law, Medicine, Social Work • SCIENCES Biology, Chemistry, Earth, Geography, Geology, Mathematics, Physics • SOCIAL SCIENCES Anthropology, Family Counseling, Government/Political, History, Political Science, Psychology, Sociology • VISUAL AND PERFORMING ARTS Art, Art History, Dramatic Arts, Music, Studio Art, Theater • VOCATIONAL Home Economics, Textile and Clothing

Sports/Activities

• SPORTS RELATED Pep Band • SPORTS-INTERCOLLEGIATE Baseball (M), Basketball, Cross Country, Field Hockey (F), Lacrosse, Rugby, Soccer, Softball (F), Swimming (F), Tennis, Volleyball (F), Wrestling (M) • SPORTS-INTRAMURAL Band, Crew, Hand Ball, Ice Hockey, Skiing - Snow, Soccer, Softball, Swimming, Tennis, Volleyball • STUDENT LIFE ACTIVITIES Choral, Community Service, Concert Band, Drama Groups, Film, Fraternities, Jazz Band, Magazine, Music Groups, Musical Theater, Newspaper, Opera, Radio/TV station, Religious Organization, Sororities, Student Government, Symphony Orchestra, Yearbook

---

Very Selective

State University of New York College at Plattsburg
Angell Center 110
Plattsburgh, New York 12901
(518) 564-2040

School Enrollment: **5,500** Male: **2,365** Female: **3,135**
LD Enrollment: **104** Male: **69** Female: **35**

Admissions Contact: **Jeannine Abballe, Admissions Counselor**
LD Contact: **Michele Little, Director, Special Services Project**
Name of Program: **Special Services Project**
Address: **Angell Center, 110 SUNY**
Telephone:**(518) 564-2810**

Admissions

Application Information:
Accepted: **47** Enrolled:**32**
LD on admissions committee:**Yes**
Application deadline: **October of preceding year**
Rolling Admissions: **Yes**

Secondary School Information
Most Important Criteria For Admissions (1-strongest)

11 SAT/ACT	**7** Application	**10**	School transcript
9 Class rank	**4** Course selection	**2**	Personal statement
1 Interview	**5** Extra activities	**6**	Psychoeducational
8 G.P.A.	Open admission	**3**	Recommendations

Test Requirements:
Diagnostic testing waived: **Yes**
Untimed SAT: **Yes** Untimed ACT: **Yes** Untimed ACH: **Yes**
WAIS-R required: **Yes** Range accepted: **90+**
Documentation of LD required: **Yes**
Currency of diagnostic testing: **within 3 years**
Tests recommended: **WAIS-R, Woodcock-Johnson**

Types of Disabilities Served
• Speech/Lang	• Reading	• ADD with LD
• Study skills	• Spelling	• ADD without LD
• Written express	• Math	• ADHD with LD
• Organizational	• Fine Motor	• ADHD without LD
• Perceptual		

Admissions Process

Standard admissions - flagged for counselor trained in LD issues - reviewed by LD services staff - offered either regular or committee admissions (contracted) entrance to University.

High School Course Requirements:
English: **1** Math: **1** Science: **2**
Waivers to standard high school courses
Course substitution: **Yes**

Learning Disability Program

Program: Remedial: **Yes**
Program: Reinforces course work: **Yes**
Students mainstreamed **100** % of the day
Recommended credits per semester: **12-15**
Counseling: Individual: **Yes** Group Counseling: **Yes** Vocational Counseling: **Yes**
Support groups are available:**Yes, Renascence-group which handles issues regarding students with disabilities**

Faculty:

Faculty: **10** Full time: **5** Part time: **5**
LD faculty with: BS/BA: **1** M.A.: **8**
Faculty advocate: **Yes** Meets with instructor: **Continual**

Diagnostic Testing

- ADD
- ADHD
- I.Q.
- Math
- Personality
- Organization
- Handwriting
- Social skills
- Perceptual skills
- Fine motor skills
- Spoken language
- Written language
- Spelling
- Reading
- Study skills

Tutoring:

Average size of group tutorials: **4-5**
Services rendered by:
- Graduates •Peers •Faculty •LD staff Teacher trainees

Tutorials

Grp.	Ind.	Tutorials	Grp.	Ind.	Tutorials
•	•	Math skills	•	•	Word processing
•	•	Study skills	•	•	Time management
		Language arts	•	•	Learning strategies
•	•	Written express	•	•	Organizational skills

Academic Accommodations

Curriculum	Study Aids	Exams
• Priority registration	• Typist	• Oral
• Math waiver	• Reader	• Untimed
Foreign lang. waiver	• Notetaker	• Take home
• Course substitution	• Proof reader	• With proctor
In Class	• Text on tape	On computer
• Calculators	Early syllabus	• Extended time
• Tape recorder	Taped handouts	• On tape
Word processor		• Modified
• Priority seating		• Separate room

Graduation Requirements:

Course credits: **125** GPA: **2.0** Years to complete degree: **No limit** Math waiver: **Yes**
Other requirements: **General Education Sequence**

Program Strengths

What makes SUNY at Plattsburgh such a unique place for the LD student is that the staff here believe that each and every student has strengths which allow him/her to find an area of real success. We are honest with our students about their abilities and help them through the difficult challenges of college with humor and caring. We do a good job with LD students because we value them, as individuals and as contributors to our college family.

General Information:

State University of New York College at Plattsburg is a 4 year public college. Rural campus of 6,000 acres is 60 miles from Montreal, Canada. Accessible by air, train or bus Ski areas are 30 miles from campus. Beaches are town from campus. 2% of students are foreign. Housing is guaranteed.Guaranteed through 4th year. 95 % of students remain on campus for the weekends.

Accreditation:MSACS

Expenses:
Tuition: In-state: Full year: $1,325.00. Part-time: Per credit:$105.00. Part-time: Per course: $315.00. Tuition: Out-of-state: Full year: $3,275.00. Part-time: Per credit:$274.00. Part-time: Per course:$822.00 Room and board: $1,846.00 per semester

Majors

• ARTS Art History, Music • BUSINESS Accounting, Business Administration, Business Economics, Business Management, Economics, Education, Fashion Merchandising, Food Management, Hotel & Restaurant Management, Human Resources Management, International Business, Management, Marketing • COMMUNICATIONS Broadcasting, Communication, English, Journalism • COMPUTER SCIENCE Computer Science • EDUCATION Child Development, Early Childhood, Elementary, English, Foreign Language, Mathematics, Music, Reading, School Psychology, Science, Secondary, Social Studies • HEALTH SCIENCES Medical Assistant, Medical Laboratory Technology, Nursing, Nutritional/Food, Speech/Audiology and Speech • HUMANITIES Philosophy • LANGUAGES French, German, Spanish • MATHEMATICS Applied • PRE PROFESSIONAL Engineering, Recreation, Social Work • SCIENCES Anthropology, Biochemistry, Biology, Biomedical, Biophysics, Chemistry, Computer Science, Earth, Ecology, Geography, Geology, Mathematics, Microbiology, Physics • SOCIAL SCIENCES Anthropology, Criminal Justice, Criminology, Family Counseling, Geography, Government/Political, History, Human Service, International Studies, Political Science, Psychology, Social Science, Sociology • SPECIAL EDUCATION Deaf/Hearing Impaired, Emotionally Disturbed, Gifted & Talented, Learning Disability, Mentally Retarded, Physically Handicapped, Visually Handicapped • VISUAL AND PERFORMING ARTS Art, Art History, Dramatic Arts, Music, Studio Art, Theater

Sports/Activities

• SPORTS-INTERCOLLEGIATE Basketball, Basketball (F), Basketball (M), Cross Country, Cross Country (F), Cross Country (M), Diving, Diving (F), Diving (M), Ice Hockey, Ice Hockey (M), Soccer, Soccer (F), Soccer (M), Swimming, Swimming (F), Swimming (M), Tennis, Tennis (F), Tennis (M), Track and Field, Track and Field (F), Track and Field (M) • SPORTS-INTRAMURAL Archery, Archery (F), Archery (M), Basketball, Basketball (F), Basketball (M), Bowling, Bowling (F), Bowling (M), Cross Country, Cross Country (F), Cross Country (M), Diving, Diving (F), Diving (M), Fencing, Fencing (F), Fencing (M), Golf, Golf (F), Golf (M), Hand Ball, Ice Hockey, Ice Hockey (F), Ice Hockey (M), Karate, Lacrosse, Lacrosse (F), Lacrosse (M), Racquetball, Racquetball (F), Racquetball (M), Soccer, Soccer (F), Soccer (M), Swimming, Swimming (F), Swimming (M), Tennis, Tennis (F), Tennis (M), Track and Field, Track and Field (F), Track and Field (M), Volleyball, Volleyball (F), Volleyball (M), Weight Lifting • STUDENT LIFE ACTIVITIES Academic Clubs, Choral, Community Service, Concert Band, Dance, Debate, Drama Groups, Ethnic & Cultural Groups, Fraternities, Jazz Band, Newspaper, Political Groups, Radio/TV station, Religious Organization, Sororities, Student Government, Yearbook

Highly Selective　　　　　　　　**New York Services**

State University of New York College of Environmental Science

106 Bray Hall
Syracuse, New York 13210-9974
(315) 470-6600

School Enrollment: **1,190** Male: **810** Female: **380**
LD Enrollment: **19** Male: **14** Female: **5**

Admissions Contact: **Dennis Stratton, Director of Admissions**
LD Contact: **Thomas O. Slocum, Director of Counseling**
Name of Program: **Academic Support Program**
Telephone:**(315) 470-6660**

Admissions

Application Information:
Rolling Admissions: **Yes**

Secondary School Information
Most Important Criteria For Admissions (1-strongest)

4 SAT/ACT	Application	**2**	School transcript
Class rank	**1** Course selection		Personal statement
10 Interview	**11** Extra activities		Psychoeducational
3 G.P.A.	Open admission		Recommendations

Test Requirements:
Diagnostic testing waived: **Yes**
Untimed SAT: **Yes** Untimed ACT: **Yes**
WAIS-R required: **Yes**
Documentation of LD required: **Yes**
Currency of diagnostic testing: **5 years**

Types of Disabilities Served
- Speech/Lang
- Study skills
- Written express
- Organizational
- Perceptual
- Reading
- Spelling
- Math
- Fine Motor
- ADD with LD
- ADD without LD
- ADHD with LD
- ADHD without LD

High School Course Requirements:Math: **4** Science: **4**

Learning Disability Program
Counseling: Individual: **Yes** Group Counseling: **Yes**

Faculty:
Faculty: **5** Full time: **3** Part time: **2**
Faculty advocate: **Yes** Meets with instructor: **1x semester**

Diagnostic Testing

ADD	Personality	Perceptual skills	Spelling
ADHD	Organization	Fine motor skills	Reading
I.Q.	Handwriting	Spoken language	Study skills
Math	Social skills	Written language	

Tutoring:
Average size of group tutorials: **3-5**
Services rendered by:
- Graduates
- Peers
- Faculty
- LD staff
- Teacher trainees

Tutorials

Grp.	Ind.	Tutorials	Grp.	Ind.	Tutorials
	•	Math skills		•	Word processing
•	•	Study skills	•		Time management
	•	Language arts	•	•	Learning strategies
•	•	Written express	•	•	Organizational skills

Academic Accommodations

Curriculum	Study Aids	Exams
Priority registration	Typist	• Oral
Math waiver	Reader	Untimed
Foreign lang. waiver	• Notetaker	Take home
Course substitution	• Proof reader	• With proctor
In Class	• Text on tape	On computer
• Calculators	Early syllabus	• Extended time
• Tape recorder	Taped handouts	On tape
• Word processor		• Modified
Priority seating		Separate room

Program Strengths
Our services are run through Syracuse University and are directly related to their graduate program of study in special education. All testing, support services, and modifications are run through Syracuse. An advocate and counseling support are available on the ESF campus to deal with special cases and circumstances unique to this college's programs of study.

General Information:
State University of New York College of Environmental Science is a 4 year public university. Urban campus of 12 acres is 1 miles from Syracuse. Accessible by plane, train or bus. 1% of students are foreign. 25 residential halls on campus. Housing is guaranteed.Guaranteed through 1st year. 90 % of students remain on campus for the weekends.

Accreditation:MSACS,SAF, ABET, ASLA

SAT/ACT Scores:
Scores for incoming freshmen: 50%between 24 and 25l.

Expenses:
Tuition: In-state: Full year: $2,650.00. Part-time: Per credit:$90.00. Tuition: Out-of-state: Full year: $6,250.00. Part-time: Per credit:$150.00.
Room and board: $5,845.00

Majors
• SCIENCES Chemistry, Environmental & Forest Biology, Environmental Studies, Paper Science and Engineering • VOCATIONAL Forest Engineering, Landscape Architecture, Wood Products and Engineering

Sports/Activities
• SPORTS-INTRAMURAL Baseball (M), Basketball, Fencing, Football (M), Golf, Ice Hockey, Lacrosse, Racquetball, Riflery (M), Rugby, Sailing, Skiing - Snow, Soccer, Softball (M), Swimming, Tennis, Track and Field, Volleyball, Wrestling (M) • STUDENT LIFE ACTIVITIES Fraternities, Newspaper, Sororities, Student Government, Yearbook

Less Selective   **New York**
                                       Services

State University of New York College of Technology at Delhi
Main Street
Delhi, New York 13753-1190
(607) 746-4246

School Enrollment: **2,415**

Admissions Contact: **Carolyn Hamilton, Asst. Dir. Admissions**
LD Contact: **Ellen D'Acguisto, Coordinator**
Name of Program: **Services for LD Students**
Telephone:**(607) 746-4364**

Admissions

Application Information:
Application deadline: **Rolling**
Rolling Admissions: **Yes**

Secondary School Information
Most Important Criteria For Admissions (1-strongest)

3 SAT/ACT	5 Application	1 School transcript
5 Class rank	2 Course selection	5 Personal statement
3 Interview	5 Extra activities	5 Psychoeducational
2 G.P.A.	Open admission	4 Recommendations

Test Requirements:
Standardized tests waived: **Yes**
Documentation of LD required: **Yes**
Currency of diagnostic testing: **3 years**

Types of Disabilities Served

Speech/Lang	Reading	ADD with LD
• Study skills	Spelling	ADD without LD
• Written express	• Math	ADHD with LD
• Organizational	Fine Motor	ADHD without LD
Perceptual		

Learning Disability Program
Counseling: Individual: **Yes** Group Counseling: **Yes**

Faculty:
Faculty: **1** Full time: **1**
Faculty advocate: **Yes** Meets with instructor: **As requested**

Diagnostic Testing

ADD	Personality	Perceptual skills	Spelling
ADHD	Organization	Fine motor skills	Reading
I.Q.	Handwriting	Spoken language	Study skills
Math	Social skills	Written language	

Tutoring:
Average size of group tutorials: **3**
Services rendered by:
Graduates •Peers •Faculty   LD staff   Teacher trainees

Tutorials

Grp.	Ind.	Tutorials	Grp.	Ind.	Tutorials
•	•	Math skills	•		Word processing
•	•	Study skills	•	•	Time management
		Language arts	•	•	Learning strategies
•	•	Written express	•	•	Organizational skills

Academic Accommodations

Curriculum	Study Aids	Exams
Priority registration	Typist	• Oral
Math waiver	Reader	Untimed
Foreign lang. waiver	• Notetaker	Take home
Course substitution	• Proof reader	• With proctor
In Class	• Text on tape	On computer
• Calculators	Early syllabus	• Extended time
• Tape recorder	Taped handouts	On tape
• Word processor		• Modified
Priority seating		Separate room

Program Strengths
After admission, to be eligible for Learning Disabled Student Services, students must request services and submit documentation of their learning disability in the form of a psychoeducational report not more than three years old. The documentation serves two purposes. It justifies to the institution the need for accommodations and serves as a guide to optimal services for the individual student.

General Information:
State University of New York College of Technology at Delhi is a 2 year public University. Rural campus of 1,100 acres is 70 miles from Binghamton. Accessible by bus. Ski areas are 35 miles from campus. 1% of students are foreign. 5 residential halls on campus. Housing is not guaranteed.

Accreditation:MSACS

Expenses:
Tuition: In-state: Full year: $1,350.00. Part-time: Per credit:$45.00. Tuition: Out-of-state: Full year: $4,700.00. Part-time: Per credit:$157.85. Room and board: $3,310.00 Cost of LD program:

Majors
• BUSINESS Accounting, Business Administration, Business Management, Food Management, Hotel & Restaurant Management, Management, Marketing, Travel/Tourism Management • COMPUTER SCIENCE Computer Science, Data Processing, Programming • EDUCATION Physical • ENGINEERING Air Conditioning Technology, Civil/Environmental, Electrical, Engineering Science • ENVIRONMENTAL CONTROL Water and Wastewater Technology • HEALTH SCIENCES Nursing, Practical Nursing • HUMANITIES Humanities, Liberal Arts • PRE PROFESSIONAL Architecture, Engineering, Forestry, Range Management, Veterinarian • SCIENCES Bio-Technology, Biology, Chemistry, Horticultural, Mathematics, Physics, Physiology • SOCIAL SCIENCES History, Psychology, Social Science, Sociology • VOCATIONAL Air Conditioning/Heating/Refri, Automobile Technology, Automotive Service, Business and Office, Carpentry, Drafting, Food Service, Forestry, Legal Secretary, Masonry, Office Administration, Park/Recreation, Plumbing, Secretarial, Welding, Word Processing

Sports/Activities
• SPORTS-INTERCOLLEGIATE Baseball (M), Basketball, Cross Country, Field Hockey (F), Golf (M), Soccer, Softball (F), Tennis (M), Track and Field, Wrestling (M) • SPORTS-INTRAMURAL Badminton, Baseball (M), Basketball, Bowling, Cross Country, Golf, Hand Ball, Ping-Pong, Racquetball, Skiing - Snow, Soccer, Softball, Swimming, Tennis, Volleyball, Wrestling (M) • STUDENT LIFE ACTIVITIES Choral, Concert Band, Drama Groups, Ethnic & Cultural Groups, Jazz Band, Magazine, Musical Theater, Newspaper, Radio/TV station, Religious Organization, Student Government, Yearbook

Less Selective

State University of New York College of Technology at Canton
Cornell Drive
Canton, New York 13617
(315) 386-7123

School Enrollment: **2,357**
LD Enrollment: **61** Male: **41**

Admissions Contact: **Enrico Miller, Director of Admissions**
LD Contact: **Debora Camp, Coordinator**
Name of Program: **Accommodative Services**

Admissions

Application Information:
Application deadline: **July 15th**
Rolling Admissions: **Yes**

Secondary School Information
Most Important Criteria For Admissions (1-strongest)

10 SAT/ACT	1 Application	3	School transcript
11 Class rank	7 Course selection	5	Personal statement
2 Interview	8 Extra activities	4	Psychoeducational
9 G.P.A.	Open admission	6	Recommendations

Test Requirements:
Standardized tests waived: **Yes**
Diagnostic testing waived: **Yes**
WAIS-R required: **Yes**
Documentation of LD required: **Yes**

Types of Disabilities Served
- Speech/Lang
- Reading
- ADD with LD
- Study skills
- Spelling
- ADD without LD
- Written express
- Math
- ADHD with LD
- Organizational
- Fine Motor
- ADHD without LD
- Perceptual

Learning Disability Program
Counseling: Individual: **Yes** Group Counseling: **Yes**

Faculty:
Faculty: **5** Full time: **5** Part time: **1**
Faculty advocate: **Yes** Meets with instructor: **1x per semester**

Diagnostic Testing

ADD	Personality	Perceptual skills	Spelling
ADHD	Organization	Fine motor skills	Reading
I.Q.	Handwriting	Spoken language	Study skills
Math	Social skills	Written language	

Tutoring:
Average size of group tutorials: **5**
Services rendered by:
- Graduates
- Peers
- Faculty
- LD staff
- Teacher trainees

Tutorials

Grp.	Ind.	Tutorials	Grp.	Ind.	Tutorials
•	•	Math skills	•	•	Word processing
•	•	Study skills	•	•	Time management
•	•	Language arts	•	•	Learning strategies
•	•	Written express	•	•	Organizational skills

Academic Accommodations

Curriculum	Study Aids	Exams
Priority registration	• Typist	• Oral
Math waiver	Reader	Untimed
Foreign lang. waiver	• Notetaker	Take home
• Course substitution	• Proof reader	With proctor
In Class	• Text on tape	On computer
• Calculators	Early syllabus	• Extended time
• Tape recorder	Taped handouts	On tape
• Word processor		• Modified
Priority seating		Separate room

Program Strengths
Students with documented disabilities may request a variety of accommodations to enhance classroom instruction. It is the student's responsibility to identify himself/herself and request appropriate accommodations which can be implemented through the cooperative efforts of the Coordinator of Accommodative Services, Deans Office, Faculty Member and/or Academic Advisor.

General Information:
State University of New York College of Technology at Canton is a 2 year public college. 75 miles from Ottawa, Canada. Accessible by air or bus. Ski areas are 1 from campus. Beaches are 1 from campus. 4 residential halls on campus. Housing is not guaranteed.44 % of students remain on campus for the weekends. 7 % of students join fraternities/sororities.

Accreditation: MSACS

Class Rank:
About 7% of the present freshmen class were in the upper 20% of their high school class. 22% were in the top 40% of their class.

Expenses:
Tuition: In-state: Full year: $1,350.00. Part-time: Per credit:$49.35. Tuition: Out-of-state: Full year: $4,700.00. Room and board: $3,694.00

Majors
• BUSINESS Accounting, Banking, Business Administration, Business Management, Finance, Hotel and Restaurant Management, Insurance, Management, Real Estate, Retailing • COMPUTER SCIENCE Computer Science • ENGINEERING Air Conditioning Technology, Civil/Environmental, Electrical, Engineering Science, Industrial, Mechanical • HEALTH SCIENCES Medical Technology, Nursing • HUMANITIES Humanities, Liberal Arts • SCIENCES Biology, Physical Science • SOCIAL SCIENCES Criminal Justice, Social Sciences • VOCATIONAL Automobile Technology, Business and Office, Electronics Technology, Forestry, Funeral/Mortuary, Medical Laboratory Technology, Secretarial, Veterinarian Assistant

Sports/Activities
• SPORTS RELATED Pep Band • SPORTS-INTERCOLLEGIATE Basketball, Horseback Riding, Ice Hockey (M), Lacrosse (M), Skiing - Snow, Soccer, Softball (F) • SPORTS-INTRAMURAL Badminton, Basketball, Golf, Ping-Pong, Skiing - Snow, Soccer, Softball, Swimming, Tennis, Volleyball • STUDENT LIFE ACTIVITIES Dance, Drama Groups, Ethnic & Cultural Groups, Fraternities, Newspaper, Radio/TV station, Sororities, Student Government, Yearbook

Less Selective　　　　　　　　　**New York Services**

State University of New York College of Technology at Farmington
Roosevelt Hall
Farmingdale, New York 11735
(516) 420-2200

School Enrollment: **11,336** Male: **5,827** Female: **5,509**
LD Enrollment: **170** Male: **85** Female: **85**

Admissions Contact: **Janet Snyder, Director of Admissions**
LD Contact: **Malka Edelman, Coordinator**
Name of Program: **Support Services**
Telephone:**(516) 420-2411**

Admissions

Application Information:
Application deadline: **None**
Rolling Admissions: **Yes**

Secondary School Information
Most Important Criteria For Admissions (1-strongest)

SAT/ACT	**1**	Application	**2** School transcript
Class rank	**4**	Course selection	Personal statement
Interview		Extra activities	Psychoeducational
3 G.P.A.		Open admission	Recommendations

Test Requirements:
Standardized tests waived: **Yes**
Diagnostic testing waived: **Yes**
WAIS-R required: **Yes**
Documentation of LD required: **Yes**
Currency of diagnostic testing: **3 years**

Types of Disabilities Served
- Speech/Lang
- Study skills
- Written express
- Organizational
- Perceptual
- Reading
- Spelling
- Math
- Fine Motor
- ADD with LD
- ADD without LD
- ADHD with LD
- ADHD without LD

Admissions Process

Student applies through regular admissions, gets accepted and identifies him/herself as needing support services.

Learning Disability Program
Recommended credits per semester: **12**
Counseling: Individual: **Yes**

Faculty:
Faculty: **2** Full time: **2**
Faculty advocate: **Yes** Meets with instructor: **As needed**

Diagnostic Testing

ADD	Personality	Perceptual skills	Spelling
ADHD	Organization	Fine motor skills	Reading
I.Q.	Handwriting	Spoken language	Study skills
Math	Social skills	Written language	

Tutoring:
Average size of group tutorials: **3-6**
Services rendered by:
　Graduates　•Peers　•Faculty　•LD staff　Teacher trainees

Tutorials

Grp.	Ind.	Tutorials	Grp.	Ind.	Tutorials
•	•	Math skills	•	•	Word processing
•	•	Study skills		•	Time management
	•	Language arts	•	•	Learning strategies
	•	Written express	•	•	Organizational skills

Academic Accommodations

Curriculum	Study Aids	Exams
Priority registration	Typist	• Oral
Math waiver	Reader	• Untimed
Foreign lang. waiver	• Notetaker	• Take home
• Course substitution	• Proof reader	• With proctor
In Class	• Text on tape	On computer
• Calculators	Early syllabus	• Extended time
• Tape recorder	Taped handouts	On tape
• Word processor		• Modified
Priority seating		• Separate room

Graduation Requirements:
Course credits: **60** GPA: **2.0**

Program Strengths
SUNY Farmingdale does not have an LD program. We offer support services at no additional fee. Primarily, academic support is through staff of learning center. Academic advisement, advocacy training, and personal counseling is through counselor for Support Services.

General Information:
State University of New York College of Technology at Farmington is a 2 and 4 year public university. Suburban campus 30 miles from New York City. Accessible by air, train or bus. Beaches are 1/2 hour from campus. Housing is not guaranteed.40 % of students remain on campus for the weekends.

Accreditation: Regional

Expenses:
Tuition: In-state: Full year: $1,075.00. Part-time: Per credit:$90.00. Tuition: Out-of-state: Full year: $2,875.00. Part-time: Per credit:$157.00. Room and board: $2,070.00

Majors
• BUSINESS Accounting, Business Administration, Business Management, Food Management, Management, Marketing • COMMUNICATIONS Graphic Design Technology • COMPUTER SCIENCE Computer Science, Data Processing, Programming • CRAFTS AND DESIGN Graphic Design • EDUCATION Teacher Aide • ENGINEERING Aerospace, Air Conditioning Technology, Bio-medical, Electrical, Engineering Science, Mechanical • HEALTH SCIENCES Dental Hygiene, Medical Secretary, Medical Technology, Nursing • HUMANITIES Liberal Arts • PREPROFESSIONAL Architecture • SCIENCES Bio-medical, Horticultural • SOCIAL SCIENCES Criminal Justice, Law Enforcement • VOCATIONAL Automobile Technology, Business and Office, Drafting, Food Service, Legal Secretary, Medical Laboratory Technology, Office Administration, Printing/Lithography, Secretarial, Veterinarian Assistant

Sports/Activities
• SPORTS-INTERCOLLEGIATE Baseball (M), Basketball, Bowling, Cross Country, Golf (M), Lacrosse (M), Soccer (F), Soccer (M), Softball (F), Tennis, Wrestling (M) • STUDENT LIFE ACTIVITIES Academic Clubs, Choral, Community Service, Drama Groups, Ethnic & Cultural Groups, Magazine, Music Groups, Musical Theater, Newspaper, Radio/TV

station, Religious Organization, Student Government, Yearbook

Highly Selective	**New York Services**

Syracuse University
Syracuse, New York 13244-1120
(315) 443-3611

School Enrollment: **12,200** Male: **6,000** Female: **6,200**
LD Enrollment: **230** Male: **138** Female: **92**

Admissions Contact: **Dean David Smith, Dean of Admissions**
LD Contact: **Bethany Heaton, Coordinator**
Name of Program: **LD Services**
Address: **804 University Avenue**
Telephone:**(315) 443-4498**

Admissions

Application Information:
LD on admissions committee:**Yes**
Application deadline: **December**
Notified when: **March 15th**

Secondary School Information
Most Important Criteria For Admissions (1-strongest)

1 SAT/ACT	1 Application	1 School transcript
1 Class rank	1 Course selection	1 Personal statement
Interview	1 Extra activities	1 Psychoeducational
1 G.P.A.	Open admission	1 Recommendations

Test Requirements:
Diagnostic testing waived: **Yes**
Untimed SAT: **Yes** Untimed ACT: **Yes** Untimed ACH: **Yes**
WAIS-R required: **Yes**
Documentation of LD required: **Yes**
Currency of diagnostic testing: **5 years**
Tests recommended: **Full psycho-educational battery**

Types of Disabilities Served
- Speech/Lang
- Study skills
- Written express
- Organizational
- Perceptual
- Reading
- Spelling
- Math
- Fine Motor
- ADD with LD
- ADD without LD
- ADHD with LD
- ADHD without LD

Admissions Process

Students are accepted under regular admission criteria

Learning Disability Program
Services only for LD students: **Yes**
Counseling: Individual: **Yes** Group Counseling: **Yes**

Faculty:
Faculty: **4** Full time: **2** Part time: **2**
Faculty advocate: **Yes** Meets with instructor: **As needed**

Diagnostic Testing

ADD	Personality	Perceptual skills	Spelling
ADHD	Organization	Fine motor skills	Reading
I.Q.	Handwriting	Spoken language	Study skills
Math	Social skills	Written language	

Tutoring:
Average size of group tutorials: **5**
Services rendered by:
- Graduates
- Peers
- Faculty
- LD staff
- Teacher trainees

Tutorials

Grp.	Ind.	Tutorials	Grp.	Ind.	Tutorials
•	•	Math skills	•	•	Word processing
•	•	Study skills	•	•	Time management
•	•	Language arts	•	•	Learning strategies
•	•	Written express	•	•	Organizational skills

Academic Accommodations

Curriculum	Study Aids	Exams
Priority registration	• Typist	• Oral
• Math waiver	Reader	Untimed
• Foreign lang. waiver	• Notetaker	• Take home
• Course substitution	• Proof reader	• With proctor
In Class	• Text on tape	On computer
• Calculators	Early syllabus	• Extended time
• Tape recorder	Taped handouts	On tape
• Word processor		• Modified
Priority seating		Separate room

Graduation Requirements:
Course credits: **120** GPA: **2.0** Years to complete degree: **4.5** Math waiver: **Yes** Language waiver: **Yes**

Program Strengths
Our program provides an integrated network of academic support and counseling services to meet the needs of an increasing number of students who identify themselves as learning disabled. These services are provided by a professional staff who sincerely care about the needs of every student.

General Information:
Syracuse University is a 4 year private university. Urban campus of 600 acres is 3% of students are foreign. 26 residential halls on campus. Housing is guaranteed.Guaranteed through 1st year. 90 % of students remain on campus for the weekends. 28 % of students join fraternities/sororities.

Accreditation:Regional

Class Rank:
About 82% of the present freshmen class were in the upper 20% of their high school class.

Expenses:
Tuition: In-state: Full year: $12,630.00. Part-time: Per credit:$390.00.
Room and board: $5,920.00

Majors

• AREA STUDIES African, American, Asian, Black/Afro-American, Jewish, Latin American, Russian/Slavic, Urban • BUSINESS Accounting, Banking, Business Administration, Business Management, Business Statistics, Economics, Finance, Food Management, Labor Relations, Management, Personnel, Retailing, Transportation Management
• COMMUNICATIONS Advertising, Broadcasting, Communication, Creative Writing, English, Journalism, Linguistics, Photography, Speech, Television/Radio/Film • COMPUTER SCIENCE Computer Science, Data Processing, Programming, Telecommunications • CRAFTS AND DESIGN Ceramics, Illustration Design, Sculpture • EDUCATION Agricultural, Curriculum, Early Childhood, Elementary, English, Foreign Language, Health, Industrial, Marketing Education, Mathematics, Middle School, Music, Music Therapy, Physical, Pre-Education, Recreation and Youth Leadership, School Psychology, Science, Secondary, Social Studies, Special, Speech/Language • ENGINEERING Aerospace, Bioengineering, Biomedical, Chemical, Civil/Environmental, Computer, Electrical, Mathematical

- HEALTH SCIENCES Communication Disorders, Environmental, Nursing, Nutritional/Food, Speech Therapy, Speech/Audiology and Speech
- HUMANITIES Classics, English/Writing/Literature, Humanities, Liberal Arts, Philosophy, Religion • LANGUAGES French, German, Italian, Japanese, Russian, Spanish • PREPROFESSIONAL Architecture, Dentistry, Engineering, Forestry, Law, Medicine, Social Work • SCIENCES Biology, Chemistry, Geology, Gerontology, Mathematics, Physical Science, Physics
- SOCIAL SCIENCES Anthropology, Family Counseling, Government/Political, History, International Studies, Library Science, Political Science, Psychology, Public Relations, Sociology • VISUAL AND PERFORMING ARTS Art, Art History, Dance, Fine Arts, Music, Music Performance, Theater • VOCATIONAL Fashion Design, Food Service, Home Economics, Industrial Design, Interior Design, Jewelry-Metalsmithery, Painting, Printing/Lithography, Textile and Clothing

Sports/Activities

- SPORTS RELATED Marching Band, Pep Band • SPORTS-INTERCOLLEGIATE Basketball, Crew, Cross Country, Diving, Field Hockey (F), Football (M), Gymnastics (M), Lacrosse (M), Skiing - Snow (M), Soccer (M), Swimming, Tennis (F), Track and Field, Volleyball (F), Wrestling (M)
- SPORTS-INTRAMURAL Badminton, Baseball (M), Basketball, Bowling, Cross Country, Diving, Fencing, Football, Golf, Gymnastics (F), Hand Ball (M), Horseback Riding, Ice Hockey (M), Lacrosse, Ping-Pong, Racquetball, Riflery, Rugby, Skiing - Snow, Soccer, Squash, Swimming, Tennis, Track and Field, Volleyball, Water Polo (M), Wrestling (M)
- STUDENT LIFE ACTIVITIES Choral, Concert Band, Debate, Ethnic & Cultural Groups, Film, Fraternities, Jazz Band, Magazine, Music Groups, Musical Theater, Newspaper, Opera, Political Groups, Radio/TV station, Religious Organization, Sororities, Student Government, Symphony Orchestra, Yearbook

Less Selective **New York Services**

Ulster County Community College
George Clinton Administration Building Cottekill Road
Stone Ridge, New York 12484
(914) 687-5022-(800) 724-0833

School Enrollment: **3,000**

Admissions Contact: **Thomas Maiello, Director of Admissions**
LD Contact: **James Quirk, Dean for Student Development**
Name of Program: **Student Development**
Telephone:**(914) 687-5041**

Admissions

Application Information:
Application deadline: **Rolling**
Applicant must apply **3** months in advance
Rolling Admissions: **Yes**

Secondary School Information
Most Important Criteria For Admissions (1-strongest)

SAT/ACT **4**	Application **1**	School transcript
5 Class rank	**3** Course selection	Personal statement
Interview	Extra activities	Psychoeducational
2 G.P.A.	Open admission	Recommendations

Test Requirements:
Standardized tests waived: **Yes**
Tests recommended: **Any documentation of specific disability would be helpful; this would assist the college in providing accommodation services.**

Types of Disabilities Served
- Speech/Lang
- Study skills
- Written express
- Organizational
- Perceptual
- Reading
- Spelling
- Math
- Fine Motor
- ADD with LD
- ADD without LD
- ADHD with LD
- ADHD without LD

Admissions Process
High school diploma or GED required for admission; applicant submits SUNY Common Application and official copies of all academic documents. All applicants are required to take Assessment Test.

High School Course Requirements:
English: **4** Math: **3** Science: **2** Foreign Language: **1**

Learning Disability Program
Time required or recommended in learning center: **As needed**
Services available for all students: **Yes**
Counseling: Individual: **Yes** Vocational Counseling: **Yes**
Support groups are available:**Tutorials, Counseling, College Skills**

Faculty:
Faculty advocate: **Yes** Meets with instructor: **As needed**

Diagnostic Testing
ADD	Personality	Perceptual skills	Spelling
ADHD	Organization	Fine motor skills	Reading
I.Q.	Handwriting	Spoken language	Study skills
Math	Social skills	Written language	

Tutoring:
Average size of group tutorials: **2-5**
Services rendered by:
Graduates •Peers •Faculty LD staff Teacher trainees

Tutorials
Grp.	Ind.	Tutorials	Grp.	Ind.	Tutorials
•	•	Math skills	•	•	Word processing
•	•	Study skills	•	•	Time management
•	•	Language arts	•	•	Learning strategies
•	•	Written express	•	•	Organizational skills

Academic Accommodations
Curriculum	Study Aids	Exams
Priority registration	• Typist	• Oral
Math waiver	• Reader	Untimed
Foreign lang. waiver	• Notetaker	Take home
• Course substitution	Proof reader	With proctor
In Class	• Text on tape	On computer
• Calculators	Early syllabus	• Extended time
• Tape recorder	Taped handouts	On tape
• Word processor		• Modified
• Priority seating		• Separate room

Graduation Requirements:
Course credits: **62** GPA: **2.0**
Other requirements: **Not all programs require math and a foreign language**

Program Strengths
Ulster works to meet the needs of the LD student on an individual basis. Similarly, Ulster will not accept a student it cannot service. Student Development Director works with students on an individual basis to assess what accommodations are needed; faculty and staff are actively involved in making realistic accommodations for stu-

dents with special needs.

General Information:

Ulster County Community College is a 2 year public college. Rural campus of 150 acres is 60 miles from Albany. Accessible by air, train or bus. Ski areas are 20 minutes from campus. Beaches are 1 hour from campus. 8% of students are foreign. Housing is not guaranteed.

Accreditation: MSACS

Expenses:

Tuition: In-state: Full year: $1,650.00. Part-time: Per credit:$60.00. Tuition: Out-of-state: Full year: $3,300.00. Part-time: Per credit:$120.00.

Majors

• BUSINESS Accounting, Business Administration, Business Management, Management, Retailing • COMMUNICATIONS Advertising, Broadcasting, Communication, English, Graphic Design, Journalism, Television/Radio/Film • COMPUTER SCIENCE Computer Science, Data Processing, Programming • ENGINEERING Engineering Science • ENVIRONMENTAL CONTROL Water and Wastewater Technology • HEALTH SCIENCES Environmental, Nursing • HUMANITIES Humanities, Liberal Arts, Philosophy, Religion • LANGUAGES French, German • PREPROFESSIONAL Engineering, Natural Resources, Recreation • SCIENCES Biology, Chemistry, Earth, Mathematics, Physical Science, Physics • SOCIAL SCIENCES Criminal Justice, Government/Political, History, Law Enforcement, Social Sciences • VISUAL AND PERFORMING ARTS Art, Studio Art • VOCATIONAL Business and Office, Drafting, Secretarial

Sports/Activities

• SPORTS-INTERCOLLEGIATE Baseball (M), Basketball, Soccer (M), Softball (F), Volleyball (F) • SPORTS-INTRAMURAL Badminton, Basketball (M), Ping-Pong, Skiing - Snow, Soccer (M), Tennis, Volleyball • STUDENT LIFE ACTIVITIES Choral, Concert Band, Drama Groups, Magazine, Music Groups, Musical Theater, Newspaper, Radio/TV station, Student Government

---

Selective   **New York**
                                                 Services

Utica College of Syracuse University

Burrstone Road
Utica, New York 13502
(315) 792-3006

School Enrollment: **1,800** Male: **828** Female: **972**
LD Enrollment: **25** Male: **10** Female: **15**

Admissions Contact: **Thomas Delahunt, Admissions Counselor**
LD Contact: **Stephen Pattarini, Director**
Name of Program: **Student Development**
Telephone:**(315) 792-3032**

Admissions

Application Information:
Application deadline: **Rolling**
Rolling Admissions: **Yes**

Secondary School Information
Most Important Criteria For Admissions (1-strongest)

4 SAT/ACT	3 Application	1 School transcript
1 Class rank	2 Course selection	4 Personal statement
3 Interview	2 Extra activities	6 Psychoeducational
2 G.P.A.	Open admission	5 Recommendations

Test Requirements:
Standardized tests waived: **Yes**
Diagnostic testing waived: **Yes**
Untimed SAT: **Yes**
WAIS-R required: **Yes**
Documentation of LD required: **Yes**
Currency of diagnostic testing: **24 or less**

Types of Disabilities Served
• Speech/Lang	• Reading	• ADD with LD
• Study skills	• Spelling	• ADD without LD
• Written express	• Math	• ADHD with LD
• Organizational	• Fine Motor	• ADHD without LD
• Perceptual		

Learning Disability Program
Students mainstreamed **100** % of the day
Recommended credits per semester: **12**
Services available for all students: **Yes**
Counseling: Individual: **Yes** Vocational Counseling: **Yes**

Faculty:
Faculty: **1** Full time: **1** M.A.: **1**
Faculty advocate: **Yes** Meets with instructor: **As needed**

Diagnostic Testing
ADD	Personality	Perceptual skills	Spelling
ADHD	Organization	Fine motor skills	Reading
I.Q.	Handwriting	Spoken language	Study skills
Math	Social skills	Written language	

Tutoring:
Average size of group tutorials: **3**
Services rendered by:
Graduates •Peers •Faculty •LD staff Teacher trainees

Tutorials
Grp.	Ind.	Tutorials	Grp.	Ind.	Tutorials
	•	Math skills			Word processing
•	•	Study skills		•	Time management
	•	Language arts		•	Learning strategies
•	•	Written express		•	Organizational skills

Academic Accommodations
Curriculum	Study Aids	Exams
Priority registration	• Typist	• Oral
Math waiver	Reader	Untimed
Foreign lang. waiver	Notetaker	Take home
Course substitution	• Proof reader	• With proctor
In Class	• Text on tape	On computer
• Calculators	Early syllabus	• Extended time
• Tape recorder	Taped handouts	On tape
• Word processor		• Modified
Priority seating		Separate room

Program Strengths
The college is committed to providing tutorial support and other basic academic services such as alternative testing environments, the use of taped lectures, and extended time periods for certified LD students. Additionally, the counseling staff is prepared to provide the personal support that is often necessary to help students effectively deal with the frustration associated with being learning disabled.

General Information:
Utica College of Syracuse University is a 4 year private college. Suburban campus of 100 acres is 49 miles from Syracuse. Accessible by air, train or

bus. 4 residential halls on campus. Housing is guaranteed.Guaranteed through 1st year. 75 % of students remain on campus for the weekends. 10 % of students join fraternities/sororities.

Accreditation: Regional

SAT/ACT Scores:
Scores for incoming freshmen:**Verbal:**59%below 500. 32%between 500 and 599. 8%between 600 and 699. 1%above 700. **Math:**59% below 500. 28% between 500 and 599. 9% between 600 and 699. 3%above 700. **ACT:** 9% below 20. 4% between 20 and 23. 3%between 24 and 25l. 2%between 26 and 28. 2% above 28.

Class Rank:
About 30% of the present freshmen class were in the upper 20% of their high school class. 27% were in the top 40% of their class. 23% were in the top 60% of their class. 22% were in the top 80% of their class.

Expenses:
Tuition: In-state: Full year: $10,446.00. Part-time: Per credit:$435.00. Room and board: $4,460.00

Majors

• BUSINESS Accounting, Business Administration, Business Economics, Business Education, Economics • COMMUNICATIONS English, Journalism, Speech • COMPUTER SCIENCE Computer Science • EDUCATION Child Development, English, Mathematics, Secondary, Social Studies • HEALTH SCIENCES Medical Technology, Nursing, Occupational Therapy • HUMANITIES Humanities, Philosophy • LANGUAGES Chinese, Italian, Russian, Spanish • PREPROFESSIONAL Dentistry, Engineering, Law, Medicine, Recreation • SCIENCES Actuarial Technology, Biology, Chemistry, Mathematics, Physics • SOCIAL SCIENCES Anthropology, Criminal Justice, Government/Political, History, International Studies, Political Science, Psychology, Public Relations, Social Sciences, Sociology • VISUAL AND PERFORMING ARTS Dramatic Arts, Fine Arts • VOCATIONAL Construction

Sports/Activities

• SPORTS-INTERCOLLEGIATE Baseball (M), Basketball, Cross Country, Diving, Golf (M), Soccer, Softball (F), Swimming, Tennis • SPORTS-INTRAMURAL Badminton, Basketball, Bowling, Fencing, Golf, Lacrosse (M), Ping-Pong, Racquetball, Soccer, Softball (F), Swimming, Tennis, Volleyball, Water Polo • STUDENT LIFE ACTIVITIES Choral, Dance, Drama Groups, Ethnic & Cultural Groups, Film, Fraternities, Magazine, Music Groups, Musical Theater, Newspaper, Political Groups, Radio/TV station, Religious Organization, Sororities, Student Government, Yearbook

Less Selective   **New York Program**

Westchester Community College
75 Grasslands Road
Valhalla, New York 10595-1698
(914) 285-6735

School Enrollment: **7,300** Male: **4,000** Female: **3,300**

Admissions Contact: **Donald Whitely, Admissions Counselor**
LD Contact: **Susan Putnam, LD Coordinator**
Address: **Library Building**
Telephone:**(914) 285-6626**

Admissions

Application Information:
Application deadline: **None**
Applicant must apply **3** months in advance
Rolling Admissions: **Yes**

Secondary School Information
Most Important Criteria For Admissions (1-strongest)

11 SAT/ACT	**1** Application	**1** School transcript
12 Class rank	**12** Course selection	**12** Personal statement
1 Interview	**12** Extra activities	**1** Psychoeducational
12 G.P.A.	**1** Open admission	**12** Recommendations

Test Requirements:
Diagnostic testing waived: **Yes**
Documentation of LD required: **Yes**
Tests recommended: **Psychoeducational Evaluation**

Types of Disabilities Served
• Speech/Lang   • Reading   • ADD with LD
• Study skills   • Spelling   • ADD without LD
• Written express   • Math   • ADHD with LD
• Organizational   • Fine Motor   • ADHD without LD
• Perceptual

Admissions Process

Open admissions

Learning Disability Program

Syllabus available during orientation:**Yes**
Program: Remedial: **Yes**
Program: Reinforces course work: **Yes**
Program available through:**Throughout year**
Students mainstreamed **90** % of the day
Recommended credits per semester: **12**
Time required or recommended in learning center: **Varies**
Services available for all students: **Yes**
Counseling: Individual: **Yes** Vocational Counseling: **Yes**
Support groups are available:**Yes, academic support center**

Faculty:
Faculty: **1** Full time: **1** M.A.: **1**
Faculty advocate: **Yes** Meets with instructor: **As needed**

Diagnostic Testing

ADD	Personality	Perceptual skills	Spelling
ADHD	Organization	Fine motor skills	• Reading
I.Q.	Handwriting	Spoken language	Study skills
• Math	Social skills	Written language	

Tutoring:
Services rendered by:
Graduates   Peers   •Faculty   •LD staff   Teacher trainees

Tutorials

Grp.	Ind.	Tutorials	Grp.	Ind.	Tutorials
	•	Math skills			Word processing
		Study skills			Time management
		Language arts		•	Learning strategies
	•	Written express	•		Organizational skills

North Carolina

Academic Accommodations

Curriculum	Study Aids	Exams
Priority registration	Typist	Oral
Math waiver	Reader	• Untimed
Foreign lang. waiver	Notetaker	Take home
Course substitution	Proof reader	With proctor
In Class	Text on tape	On computer
Calculators	Early syllabus	Extended time
Tape recorder	Taped handouts	On tape
Word processor		Modified
Priority seating		Separate room

Graduation Requirements:
Course credits: **64 minimum** GPA: **2.0**

Program Strengths

Westchester Community College does not have a Learning Disability Program. We are a community college open to anyone able to benefit from attending college. This means that we provide a host of services to assist all Westchester Community College students, including an Academic Support Center for tutoring in reading, writing, and mathematics, remedial courses for academically underprepared students, and counselors to provide personal, academic, and career counseling.

General Information:

Westchester Community College is a 2 year public college. Suburban campus 30 miles from New York City. Accessible by public transportation. Housing is not guaranteed.

Accreditation: Regional

Expenses:
Tuition: In-state: Full year: $875.00 per semester. Part-time: Per credit: $73.00. Tuition: Out-of-state: Full year: $2,187.00 per semester. Part-time: Per credit: $182.00.

Majors

• AREA STUDIES American, Black/Afro-American • ARTS Dance, Music • BUSINESS Accounting, Business Administration, Data Processing, Food Management, Hotel & Restaurant Management, Marketing, Real Estate, Retailing, Secretarial Science, Travel/Tourism Management • COMMUNICATIONS Communication • COMPUTER SCIENCE Computer Science, Data Processing • ENGINEERING Civil/Environmental, Electrical, Engineering Science, Mechanical • ENVIRONMENTAL CONTROL Air Pollution Control Technology • HEALTH SCIENCES Medical Laboratory Technology, Nursing, Nutritional/Food, Practical Nursing, Radiological Therapy, Respiratory Therapy • HUMANITIES English/Writing/Literature, Fine Arts, Humanities, Liberal Arts • LANGUAGES English, Italian, Spanish • MATHEMATICS Applied • SCIENCES Biology, Chemistry, Mathematics, Physical Science, Radiology • SOCIAL SCIENCES Criminology, Human Service • VISUAL AND PERFORMING ARTS Art, Dance, Fine Arts, Music, Theater • VOCATIONAL Drafting, Machinist, Paralegal, Secretarial, Word Processing

Sports/Activities

• SPORTS-INTERCOLLEGIATE Baseball (M), Basketball, Golf (M), Lacrosse (M), Soccer (M), Softball (F), Tennis (F), Volleyball (F) • SPORTS-INTRAMURAL Basketball, Bowling, Boxing, Football, Skiing - Snow, Volleyball • STUDENT LIFE ACTIVITIES Academic Clubs, Choral, Community Service, Dance, Drama Groups, Ethnic & Cultural Groups, Film, Musical Theater, Newspaper, Radio/TV station, Religious Organization, Student Government

---

Very Selective

Appalachian State University
Boone, North Carolina 28608
(704) 262-2291

School Enrollment: **11,795** Male: **5,674** Female: **6,121**
LD Enrollment: **101** Male: **84** Female: **17**

Admissions Contact: **Joe Watts, Director of Admissions**
LD Contact: **Arlene Lundquist, Coordinator, LD Program**
Name of Program: **Learning Disability Program**
Address: **200 Dougherty Library**
Telephone: **(704) 262-2291**

Admissions

Application Information:
Applicant must apply **12** months in advance
Rolling Admissions: **Yes**

Secondary School Information
Most Important Criteria For Admissions (1-strongest)

1 SAT/ACT	Application	**1** School transcript
1 Class rank	**1** Course selection	Personal statement
Interview	**1** Extra activities	Psychoeducational
1 G.P.A.	Open admission	**1** Recommendations

Test Requirements:
Diagnostic testing waived: **Yes**
Untimed SAT: **Yes**
Documentation of LD required: **Yes**
Currency of diagnostic testing: **within 3 years**
Tests recommended: **Psychoeducational documentation requested after admission, WAIS-R, Woodcock-Johnson, etc.**

Types of Disabilities Served

Speech/Lang	Reading	ADD with LD
Study skills	Spelling	ADD without LD
Written express	Math	ADHD with LD
Organizational	Fine Motor	ADHD without LD
Perceptual		

Admissions Process

If student meets admission requirements they are admitted regardless of disability.

High School Course Requirements:
English: **4** Math: **3** Science: **3**
Waivers to standard high school courses
Foreign Language : **Yes** Course substitution: **Yes**

Learning Disability Program

Program: Reinforces course work: **Yes**
Students mainstreamed **100** % of the day
Recommended credits per semester: **12-15**
Counseling: Individual: **Yes** Vocational Counseling: **Yes**

Faculty:
Faculty: **2** Full time: **1** Part time: **2** M.A.: **1**
Faculty advocate: **Yes** Meets with instructor: **As needed**

Diagnostic Testing

ADD	Personality	Perceptual skills	Spelling
ADHD	Organization	Fine motor skills	Reading
I.Q.	Handwriting	Spoken language	Study skills
Math	Social skills	Written language	

Tutoring:

Average size of group tutorials: **1:1**
Services rendered by:
•Graduates •Peers Faculty LD staff •Teacher trainees

Tutorials

Grp.	Ind.	Tutorials	Grp.	Ind.	Tutorials
		Math skills			Word processing
		Study skills			Time management
		Language arts			Learning strategies
		Written express			Organizational skills

Academic Accommodations

Curriculum	Study Aids	Exams
• Priority registration	Typist	• Oral
Math waiver	Reader	Untimed
Foreign lang. waiver	• Notetaker	Take home
Course substitution	Proof reader	With proctor
In Class	• Text on tape	On computer
• Calculators	Early syllabus	• Extended time
• Tape recorder	Taped handouts	On tape
Word processor		Modified
Priority seating		• Separate room

Graduation Requirements:

Course credits: **122** GPA: **2.0**

Program Strengths

In spite of what the answers on this form may indicate, our program has a 75% success rate, it is highly individualized, students are guided and encouraged to be independent and self-sufficient. University resources already in place are utilized. We do not have everything separate for LD students. They are 100% mainstreamed. We have been in operation for 13 years and have an excellent reputation.

General Information:

Appalachian State University is a 4 year public university. Rural campus of 255 acres is 100 miles from Charlotte. Accessible by air or bus. Ski areas are 15 miles from campus. Beaches are 300 miles from campus. 17 residential halls on campus. Housing is guaranteed.Guaranteed through 1st year.

Accreditation: Regional

Expenses:

Tuition: In-state: Full year: $1,464.50. Tuition: Out-of-state: Full year: $6,314.50. Room and board: $2,300.00

Majors

• AREA STUDIES Women's Studies • ARTS Commercial Art, Dance, Drafting, Dramatic Arts, Drawing, Film & Video, Graphic Arts, Interior Design, Music, Music History, Music Performance • BUSINESS Accounting, Banking/Finance, Business Administration, Business Economics, Business Education, Business Management, Economics, Education, Fashion Merchandising, Hotel & Restaurant Management, Industrial Operations, International Business, Management, Marketing, Printing Manufacturing, Real Estate, Travel/Tourism Management • COMMUNICATIONS Advertising, Broadcasting, Journalism, Public Relations • COMPUTER SCIENCE Computer Science, Programming • EDUCATION Adult, Art, Business, Child Development, Curriculum, Early Childhood, Elementary, English, Foreign Language, Health, Home Economics, Industrial, Leadership, Mathematics, Middle School, Music, Physical, Psy-

chology, Reading, Recreation/Youth Leadership, School Psychology, Science, Secondary, Social Studies, Special, Speech/Language • HEALTH SCIENCES Speech Therapy, Speech/Audiology and Speech • HUMANITIES English/Writing/Literature, Fine Arts, Philosophy, Religion • LANGUAGES Chinese, English, French, German, Latin, Spanish • MATHEMATICS Applied, Computer, Statistical • PRE PROFESSIONAL Dentistry, Drafting, Engineering, Forestry, Industrial Design, Medicine, Recreation, Social Work, Sports Medicine, Veterinarian, Wildlife • RELIGIOUS STUDIES Bible, Philosophy, Religion and Theology • SCIENCES Biology, Chemistry, Geography, Geology, Physics • SOCIAL SCIENCES Anthropology, Geography, Government/Political, History, Library Science, Political Science, Psychology, Sociology • SPECIAL EDUCATION Emotionally Disturbed, Gifted & Talented, Learning Disability, Mentally Retarded • VISUAL AND PERFORMING ARTS Art, Dance, Dramatic Arts, Music, Theater

Sports/Activities

• SPORTS RELATED Cheerleading, Drill Team, Drum Major/Majorette, Marching Band, Pep Band, Team Managers • SPORTS-INTERCOLLEGIATE Baseball, Basketball, Cross Country, Field Hockey, Football, Golf, Skiing - Snow, Soccer, Tennis, Track and Field, Volleyball, Wrestling • SPORTS-INTRAMURAL Badminton, Basketball, Bowling, Cross Country, Fencing, Golf, Gymnastics, Hand Ball, Ping-Pong, Racquetball, Skiing - Snow, Soccer, Softball, Squash, Swimming, Tennis, Track and Field, Volleyball, Water Polo, Wrestling • STUDENT LIFE ACTIVITIES Academic Clubs, Choral, Community Service, Concert Band, Dance, Debate, Drama Groups, Ethnic & Cultural Groups, Film, Fraternities, Jazz Band, Magazine, Music Groups, Musical Theater, Newspaper, Orchestra, Political Groups, Radio/TV station, Religious Organization, Sororities, Student Government, Symphony Orchestra, Yearbook

---

Less Selective **North Carolina Services**

Blue Ridge Community College

Route 2
Flat Rock, North Carolina 28731
(704) 692-3572

Admissions Contact: **Donald Shoemaker, Dean of Admissions**
LD Contact: **Victoria E. McKee, Dir, Special Populations Office**
Name of Program: **Special Populations Office**
Telephone:**(704) 692-3572, Ext. 290**

Admissions

Application Information:

LD Students Applying: **15** Accepted: **15** Enrolled:**15**
Separate application:**Yes**
Application deadline: **Open**
Rolling Admissions: **Yes**

Secondary School Information

Most Important Criteria For Admissions (1-strongest)

SAT/ACT	Application	School transcript
Class rank	Course selection	Personal statement
Interview	Extra activities	Psychoeducational
G.P.A.	**1** Open admission	Recommendations

Test Requirements:

Diagnostic testing waived: **Yes**
Documentation of LD required: **Yes**
Currency of diagnostic testing: **12**

North Carolina

Types of Disabilities Served
- Speech/Lang
- Study skills
- Written express
- Organizational
- Perceptual
- Reading
- Spelling
- Math
- Fine Motor
- ADD with LD
- ADD without LD
- ADHD with LD
- ADHD without LD

Admissions Process

Open door - high school graduation or equivalent recommended for all programs and required before entry into any degree-granting program. Must demonstrate ability to benefit from the training provided.

Learning Disability Program

Program: Reinforces course work: **Yes**
Students mainstreamed **100** % of the day
Counseling: Individual: **Yes** Vocational Counseling: **Yes**
Support groups are available:**Yes**

Faculty:
Faculty: **2** Including Director: **1** Full time: **1** Part time: **1**
LD faculty with: BS/BA: **1** M.A.: **1**
Faculty advocate: **Yes** Meets with instructor: **Daily**

Diagnostic Testing
ADD	Personality •	Perceptual skills	• Spelling
ADHD•	Organization	Fine motor skills	• Reading
• I.Q.	• Handwriting•	Spoken language	• Study skills
• Math	Social skills•	Written language	

Tutoring:
Average size of group tutorials: **3**
Services rendered by:
Graduates •Peers Faculty •LD staff Teacher trainees

Tutorials
Grp.	Ind.	Tutorials	Grp.	Ind.	Tutorials
•	•	Math skills		•	Word processing
	•	Study skills		•	Time management
	•	Language arts		•	Learning strategies
	•	Written express		•	Organizational skills

Academic Accommodations
Curriculum	Study Aids	Exams
Priority registration	Typist	• Oral
Math waiver	• Reader	• Untimed
Foreign lang. waiver	• Notetaker	Take home
Course substitution	Proof reader	• With proctor
In Class	• Text on tape	On computer
• Calculators	Early syllabus	• Extended time
• Tape recorder	Taped handouts	On tape
• Word processor		• Modified
• Priority seating		• Separate room

Graduation Requirements:
Course credits: **Varies** Years to complete degree: **2+**

General Information:
Blue Ridge Community College is a 2 year public college. Rural campus 45 miles from Asheville. Accessible by air or bus. Ski areas are 2 hours from campus. Beaches are 4 hours from campus. Housing is not guaranteed.

Accreditation:SACS

Expenses:
Tuition: In-state: Full year: $105.00. Part-time: Per credit:$8.75. Tuition: Out-of-state: Full year: $981.00. Part-time: Per credit:$81.75.

Majors
• BUSINESS Business Administration, Data Processing, Secretarial Science, Travel/Tourism Management, Vocational Studies • COMPUTER SCIENCE Business Data Programming, Computer Science, Computer Technology, Data Processing, Medical Records Technology, Programming, Robotics • EDUCATION Technical, Vocational • ENGINEERING Air Conditioning Technology, Automotive, Drafting, Electrical, Mechanical • HUMANITIES Fine Arts, Liberal Arts • SCIENCES Horticultural • VOCATIONAL Air Conditioning/Heating/Refri, Auto Body, Automated Manufacturing Technology, Automotive Service, Building Construction, Business and Office, Carpentry, Cosmetology, Drafting, Electronics Technology, Machinist, Masonry, Office Administration, Plumbing, Secretarial, Welding

---

Less Selective — **North Carolina Services**

Caldwell Community College and Technical Institute
1000 Hickory Boulevard
Hudson, North Carolina 28638
(704) 728-4323

School Enrollment: **2,600**
LD Enrollment: **20**

Admissions Contact: **Elaine Setzee, Counselor**
LD Contact: **Teena McKary, Director Academic Support**
Name of Program: **Developmental Studies**
Telephone:**(704) 726-2238**

Admissions

Application Information:
Application deadline: **None**

Secondary School Information
Most Important Criteria For Admissions (1-strongest)
SAT/ACT	Application	School transcript
Class rank	Course selection	Personal statement
Interview	Extra activities	Psychoeducational
G.P.A. **1**	Open admission	Recommendations

Test Requirements:
Standardized tests waived: **Yes**
Documentation of LD required: **Yes**

Types of Disabilities Served
- Speech/Lang
- Study skills
- Written express
- Organizational
- Perceptual
- Reading
- Spelling
- Math
- Fine Motor
- ADD with LD
- ADD without LD
- ADHD with LD
- ADHD without LD

Admissions Process

Must take placement test, may request untimed tests.

Learning Disability Program

Counseling: Individual: **Yes**

Faculty:

Faculty advocate: **Yes** Meets with instructor: **As needed**

Diagnostic Testing

ADD	Personality	Perceptual skills	Spelling
ADHD	Organization	Fine motor skills	Reading
I.Q.	Handwriting	Spoken language	Study skills
Math	Social skills	Written language	

Tutoring:

Average size of group tutorials: **1:1**
Services rendered by:
  Graduates   •Peers   Faculty   •LD staff   Teacher trainees

Tutorials

Grp.	Ind.	Tutorials	Grp.	Ind.	Tutorials
	•	Math skills			Word processing
	•	Study skills			Time management
	•	Language arts			Learning strategies
		Written express			Organizational skills

Academic Accommodations

Curriculum	Study Aids	Exams
Priority registration	• Typist	• Oral
Math waiver	• Reader	Untimed
Foreign lang. waiver	• Notetaker	Take home
Course substitution	• Proof reader	• With proctor
In Class	• Text on tape	On computer
• Calculators	Early syllabus	• Extended time
• Tape recorder	Taped handouts	• On tape
• Word processor		• Modified
Priority seating		Separate room

Graduation Requirements:

Course credits: **Varies** GPA: **2.0**

Program Strengths

We do not have a separate program for LD students but we serve them through our developmental program. We only have a few LD students and we work with them on an individual basis.

General Information:

Caldwell Community College and Technical Institute is a 2 year public college. Rural campus 70 miles from Charlotte. Accessible by bus. Ski areas are 30 miles from campus. Beaches are 300 miles from campus. 1% of students are foreign. Housing is not guaranteed.

Accreditation: SACS

Expenses:

Tuition: In-state: Full year: $498.00. Part-time: Per credit:$11.50. Tuition: Out-of-state: Full year: $4,650.00. Part-time: Per credit:$107.50.

Majors

• BUSINESS Accounting, Business Administration, Business Management, Management • COMPUTER SCIENCE Data Processing, Programming • EDUCATION Early Childhood • ENGINEERING Biomedical, Engineering Science • HEALTH SCIENCES Medical Secretary, Nursing, Occupational Therapy, Physical Therapy, Radiological Therapy • HU-

MANITIES Liberal Arts • VISUAL AND PERFORMING ARTS Music • VOCATIONAL Drafting, Electronics Technology, Industrial Equipment Maintenance, Legal Assistant, Paralegal, Secretarial

Sports/Activities

• SPORTS-INTRAMURAL Basketball (M), Ping-Pong, Tennis, Volleyball • STUDENT LIFE ACTIVITIES Academic Clubs, Choral, Concert Band, Drama Groups, Jazz Band, Magazine, Music Groups, Religious Organization, Student Government

---

Selective

Catawba Valley Community College

Route 3 Box 283
Hickory, North Carolina 28602
(704) 327-9124

School Enrollment: **2,520** Male: **1,020** Female: **1,500**

Admissions Contact: **Louise Garrison, Director of Admissions**
LD Contact: **Dr. Dan R. Gwaltney, Director**
Name of Program: **Career Resource Center**
Telephone:**(704) 327-7000**

Admissions

Application Information:

Rolling Admissions: **Yes**

Secondary School Information

Most Important Criteria For Admissions (1-strongest)

SAT/ACT	Application	School transcript
Class rank	Course selection	Personal statement
Interview	Extra activities	Psychoeducational
G.P.A.	**1** Open admission	Recommendations

Test Requirements:

Standardized tests waived: **Yes**
Diagnostic testing waived: **Yes**
Documentation of LD required: **Yes**
Currency of diagnostic testing: **early as possible**
Tests recommended: **Placement testing (English, Math, Algebra, Reading)**

Types of Disabilities Served

• Speech/Lang	• Reading	ADD with LD
• Study skills	• Spelling	ADD without LD
• Written express	• Math	ADHD with LD
• Organizational	• Fine Motor	ADHD without LD
• Perceptual		

High School Course Requirements:

English: **4** Math: **2** Science: **2** Foreign Language: **2**
Waivers to standard high school courses
  Course substitution: **Yes**

Learning Disability Program

Program: Remedial: **Yes**
Program: Reinforces course work: **Yes**
Students mainstreamed **50** % of the day
Recommended credits per semester: **12**
Services available for all students: **Yes**
Counseling: Individual: **Yes** Group Counseling: **Yes** Vocational Counsel-

North Carolina

ing: **Yes**
Support groups are available:**Self esteem workshops**

Faculty:
Faculty: **1** Part time: **6**
Faculty advocate: **Yes** Meets with instructor: **As necessary**

Diagnostic Testing
ADD	Personality	Perceptual skills	Spelling
ADHD	Organization	Fine motor skills	Reading
I.Q.	Handwriting	Spoken language	Study skills
Math	Social skills	Written language	

Tutoring:
Average size of group tutorials: **1:1**
Services rendered by:
  Graduates •Peers •Faculty LD staff Teacher trainees

Tutorials
Grp.	Ind.	Tutorials	Grp.	Ind.	Tutorials
	•	Math skills			Word processing
•	•	Study skills	•	•	Time management
	•	Language arts	•	•	Learning strategies
	•	Written express	•	•	Organizational skills

Academic Accommodations
Curriculum	Study Aids	Exams
Priority registration	• Typist	• Oral
Math waiver	• Reader	• Untimed
Foreign lang. waiver	• Notetaker	• Take home
Course substitution	• Proof reader	• With proctor
In Class	Text on tape	• On computer
• Calculators	Early syllabus	• Extended time
• Tape recorder	Taped handouts	• On tape
• Word processor		• Modified
• Priority seating		• Separate room

Program Strengths
Our LD program is limited to assistance in the classroom, tutorial services, and study skills development.

General Information:
Catawba Valley Community College is a 2 year public college. Suburban campus 60 miles from Charlotte. Accessible by air or bus. Ski areas are 60 miles from campus. Beaches are 250 miles from campus. Housing is not guaranteed.

Accreditation:SACS

Expenses:
Tuition: In-state: Full year: $288.00. Part-time: Per credit:$8.00. Tuition: Out-of-state: Full year: $2,538.00. Part-time: Per credit:$70.00.

Majors
• BUSINESS Accounting, Banking, Business Education, Business Management, Finance, Food Management, Management, Marketing, Real Estate • COMMUNICATIONS Graphic Design • COMPUTER SCIENCE Business Data Programming, Computer Maintenance, Data Processing, Medical Records Technology, Programming • EDUCATION Adult, Business, Early Childhood, English, English As A Second Language, Foreign Language, Psychology • ENGINEERING Agricultural, Air Conditioning Technology, Architectural, Drafting, Electrical, Mechanical • HEALTH SCIENCES Medical Records Administration, Nursing • HUMANITIES Liberal Arts • LANGUAGES Spanish • MATHEMATICS Applied • PRE-PROFESSIONAL Agricultural, Architecture, Business, Drafting, Engineering, Landscaping, Range Management • RELIGIOUS STUDIES Bible • SCIENCES Agricultural, Anatomy, Anthropology, Bacteriology, Chemistry, Horticultural, Microbiology, Soil • SOCIAL SCIENCES Anthropolo-gy, History, Political Science, Psychology, Social Science, Sociology • VISUAL AND PERFORMING ARTS Music Performance • VOCATIONAL Air Conditioning/Heating/Refri, Automated Manufacturing Technology, Automobile Technology, Automotive Service, Drafting, Electronics Technology, Landscape Architecture, Machinist, Park/Recreation, Respiratory Therapy Technology, Secretarial, Word Processing

Sports/Activities
• SPORTS-INTERCOLLEGIATE Golf, Golf (F), Golf (M), Tennis, Tennis (F), Tennis (M) • STUDENT LIFE ACTIVITIES Academic Clubs, Community Service, Ethnic & Cultural Groups, Music Groups, Student Government, Yearbook

---

Less Selective

North Carolina Program

Central Piedmont Community College
P.O. Box 35009
Charlotte , North Carolina 28235
(704) 342-6687

School Enrollment: **16,000** Male: **7,000** Female: **9,000**
LD Enrollment: **125** Male: **52** Female: **73**
LD Contact: **Norma-Jean Arey, Learning Disability Specialist**
Name of Program: **Department of Special Services**
Address: **Box 35009**

Admissions

Application Information:
Enrolled:**125**
LD on admissions committee:**Yes**
Application deadline: **None**
Applicant must apply **1** months in advance
Rolling Admissions: **Yes**

Secondary School Information
Most Important Criteria For Admissions (1-strongest)
SAT/ACT	Application	School transcript
Class rank	Course selection	Personal statement
Interview	Extra activities	Psychoeducational
G.P.A.	**1** Open admission	Recommendations

Test Requirements:
Standardized tests waived: **Yes**
Diagnostic testing waived: **Yes**
Untimed SAT: **Yes** Untimed ACT: **Yes** Achievement tests required:**None**
Documentation of LD required: **Yes**
Tests recommended: **College Placement Test**

Types of Disabilities Served
• Speech/Lang	• Reading	• ADD with LD
• Study skills	• Spelling	• ADD without LD
• Written express	• Math	• ADHD with LD
• Organizational	• Fine Motor	• ADHD without LD
• Perceptual		

Learning Disability Program
Special orientation for LD students: **Yes**
Syllabus available during orientation:**Yes**
Program: Remedial: **Yes**
Students mainstreamed **100** % of the day
Recommended credits per semester: **12-15**
Counseling: Individual: **Yes** Vocational Counseling: **Yes**
Support groups are available:**SOLD, Student Organization for Learn-**

ing Disability Awareness

Faculty:
Faculty: **8** Full time: **1** Part time: **7**
LD faculty with: BS/BA: **7** M.A.: **1**

Diagnostic Testing

ADD	Personality	Perceptual skills	Spelling
ADHD	Organization	Fine motor skills	• Reading
I.Q.	Handwriting	Spoken language	• Study skills
• Math	Social skills	• Written language	

Tutoring:
Services rendered by:
Graduates •Peers   Faculty   •LD staff   Teacher trainees

Tutorials

Grp.	Ind.	Tutorials	Grp.	Ind.	Tutorials
	•	Math skills		•	Word processing
	•	Study skills		•	Time management
	•	Language arts		•	Learning strategies
	•	Written express		•	Organizational skills

Academic Accommodations

Curriculum
- Priority registration
- Math waiver
- Foreign lang. waiver
- Course substitution

In Class
- Calculators
- Tape recorder
- Word processor
- Priority seating

Study Aids
- Typist
- Reader
- Notetaker
- Proof reader
- Text on tape
- Early syllabus
- Taped handouts

Exams
- Oral
- Untimed
- Take home
- With proctor
- On computer
- Extended time
- On tape
- Modified
- Separate room

Graduation Requirements:
Course-credits: **96** GPA: **2.0** Years to complete degree: **2** Math waiver: **Yes**

Program Strengths

The support services program for learning disabled students was established at CPCC in 1981 under a federal grant. The program is designed to provide students with the necessary educational assistance to complete a college program designed around their individual needs and career interests.

General Information:

Central Piedmont Community College is a 2 year Community College college. Urban campus   Accessible by bus. Ski areas are 85 miles from campus. Beaches are 130 miles from campus. Housing is not guaranteed.

Accreditation:SACS

Expenses:
Tuition: In-state: Full year: $161.00. Part-time: Per credit:$11.50. Tuition: Out-of-state: Full year: $1,505.00. Part-time: Per credit:$107.50.

Majors

• ARTS Commercial Art, Drafting, Dramatic Arts, Fashion Design, Graphic Arts, Interior Design, Landscaping • BUSINESS Accounting, Banking/Finance, Bookkeeping, Business Administration, Business Management, Clerical, Commercial Art, Construction, Data Processing, Food Management, Hotel and Restaurant Management, Human Resources Management, Insurance, Marketing, Real Estate, Retailing, Secretarial Science, Travel/Tourism Management • COMPUTER SCIENCE Business Data Programming • ENGINEERING Air Conditioning Technology, Architectural, Automotive, Civil/Environmental, Drafting, Electrical • HEALTH SCIENCES Dental Hygiene, Dental Technician, Physical Therapy • LANGUAGES French • SCIENCES Horticultural • SOCIAL SCIENCES Law Enforcement • VOCATIONAL Air Conditioning/Heating/Refri, Auto Body, Automobile Technology, Automotive Service, Carpentry, Chef Apprenticeship, Construction, Culinary Arts, Dental Assistant, Dental Hygiene, Diesel Power Technology, Drafting, Electronics Technology, Fashion Design, Fashion Merchandising, Fire Science, Food Service, Industrial Design, Legal Secretary, Secretarial, Welding, Woodworking, Word Processing

Sports/Activities

• SPORTS-INTERCOLLEGIATE Basketball (M), Football (M), Judo, Soccer (M) • SPORTS-INTRAMURAL Basketball (M), Football (M), Judo • STUDENT LIFE ACTIVITIES Academic Clubs

---

Less Selective

Craven Community College
P.O. Box 885
New Bern, North Carolina 28563
(919) 638-4131

School Enrollment: **2,200**

Admissions Contact: **Matlynn Bryant, Dean of Students**
LD Contact: **Catherine Hewlette, Dean of Developmental Studies**
Name of Program: **Developmental Studies**
Address: **P.O. Box 885**
Telephone:**(919) 638-7284**

Admissions

Application Information:
Application deadline: **During Registration**

Secondary School Information
Most Important Criteria For Admissions (1-strongest)

SAT/ACT	Application	School transcript
Class rank	Course selection	Personal statement
Interview	Extra activities	Psychoeducational
G.P.A.	**1** Open admission	Recommendations

Test Requirements:
Documentation of LD required: **Yes**
Currency of diagnostic testing: **within 3 years of application**

Types of Disabilities Served
- Speech/Lang
- Study skills
- Written express
- Organizational
- Perceptual
- Reading
- Spelling
- Math
- Fine Motor
- ADD with LD
- ADD without LD
- ADHD with LD
- ADHD without LD

Admissions Process

Open door admission policy

Learning Disability Program

Counseling: Individual: **Yes**

Diagnostic Testing

ADD	Personality	Perceptual skills	• Spelling
ADHD	Organization	Fine motor skills	• Reading
I.Q.	Handwriting	Spoken language	Study skills
• Math	Social skills	• Written language	

Tutoring:
Average size of group tutorials: **2-3**
Services rendered by:
Graduates •Peers •Faculty LD staff Teacher trainees

Tutorials

Grp.	Ind.	Tutorials	Grp.	Ind.	Tutorials
	•	Math skills			Word processing
•		Study skills	•		Time management
		Language arts			Learning strategies
		Written express			Organizational skills

Academic Accommodations

Curriculum	Study Aids	Exams
Priority registration	Typist	• Oral
Math waiver	Reader	Untimed
Foreign lang. waiver	• Notetaker	Take home
Course substitution	Proof reader	With proctor
In Class	• Text on tape	On computer
Calculators	Early syllabus	• Extended time
• Tape recorder	Taped handouts	• On tape
• Word processor		Modified
• Priority seating		• Separate room

Graduation Requirements:
Course credits: **Varies** GPA: **2.0** Years to complete degree: **As long as necessary**

Program Strengths
We offer specific services such as notetaking on a needs basis only. We do not have a comprehensive program for the learning disabled.

General Information:
Craven Community College is a 2 year public college. Rural campus of 100 acres is 150 miles from Raleigh. Accessible by air or bus. Ski areas are 2-1/2 hours from campus. Beaches are 30 miles from campus. 1% of students are foreign. Housing is not guaranteed.

Accreditation: SACS

Expenses:
Tuition: In-state: Full year: $510.00. Part-time: Per credit: $11.50. Tuition: Out-of-state: Full year: $4,542.00. Part-time: Per credit: $107.50.

Majors
• COMPUTER SCIENCE Business Data Programming • EDUCATION Early Childhood • HEALTH SCIENCES Medical Secretary, Nursing, Nursing Assistant, Practical Nursing • VOCATIONAL Air Conditioning/ Heating/Refri, Auto Body, Automobile Technology, Automotive Service, Cosmetology, Drafting, Industrial Equipment Maintenance, Legal Secretary, Machinist, Office Administration, Secretarial, Welding

Sports/Activities
• SPORTS-INTERCOLLEGIATE Basketball (M), Golf, Tennis • STUDENT LIFE ACTIVITIES Academic Clubs, Drama Groups, Music Groups, Radio/TV station, Student Government

Davidson College
P.O. Box 1737
Davidson, North Carolina 28036
(704) 892-2225

School Enrollment: **1,543** Male: **855** Female: **688**

Admissions Contact: **Dr. Nancy Cable Wells, Dean of Admissions**
LD Contact: **Leslie Marsicano, Assistant Dean of Students**
Address: **Office of Dean of Students, P.O. Box 1719**
Telephone: **(704) 892-2225**

Admissions

Application Information:
Application deadline: **February**

Secondary School Information
Most Important Criteria For Admissions (1-strongest)

5 SAT/ACT	6 Application	1 School transcript
4 Class rank	1 Course selection	6 Personal statement
Interview	7 Extra activities	Psychoeducational
2 G.P.A.	Open admission	3 Recommendations

Test Requirements:
Untimed SAT: **Yes** Untimed ACT: **Yes** Untimed ACH: **Yes**
Documentation of LD required: **Yes**
Tests recommended: **Testing by college specialist after matriculation.**

Types of Disabilities Served
• Speech/Lang • Reading • ADD with LD
• Study skills • Spelling • ADD without LD
• Written express • Math • ADHD with LD
• Organizational • Fine Motor • ADHD without LD
• Perceptual

Admissions Process

LD students follow same admissions process as other students. Encouraged to visit campus and/or speak with LD service provider.

High School Course Requirements:
English: **4** Math: **3** Science: **2-4** Foreign Language: **2**
Waivers to standard high school courses
Course substitution: **Yes**

Learning Disability Program
Special orientation for LD students: **Yes**
Program: Reinforces course work: **Yes**
Students mainstreamed **100** % of the day
Services only for LD students: **Yes**
Services available for all students: **Yes**
Counseling: Individual: **Yes** Group Counseling: **Yes** Vocational Counseling: **Yes**
Support groups are available: **As needed**

Faculty:
Faculty: **1** M.A.: **1**
Meets with instructor: **As needed**

Diagnostic Testing
- ADD • Personality • Perceptual skills • Spelling
- ADHD• Organization• Fine motor skills • Reading
- I.Q. • Handwriting• Spoken language • Study skills
- Math • Social skills• Written language

Tutoring:
Average size of group tutorials: **1:1**
Services rendered by:
Graduates •Peers •Faculty LD staff Teacher trainees

Tutorials
Grp. Ind. Tutorials   Grp. Ind. Tutorials
     Math skills   Word processing
     Study skills   Time management
     Language arts   Learning strategies
     Written express   Organizational skills

Academic Accommodations

Curriculum	Study Aids	Exams
Priority registration	Typist	• Oral
• Math waiver	• Reader	Untimed
• Foreign lang. waiver	• Notetaker	• Take home
• Course substitution	• Proof reader	With proctor
In Class	• Text on tape	• On computer
• Calculators	• Early syllabus	• Extended time
• Tape recorder	• Taped handouts	• On tape
Word processor		• Modified
• Priority seating		• Separate room

Graduation Requirements:
Course credits: **34** Years to complete degree: **No limit** Math waiver: **Yes**
Language waiver: **Yes**
Other requirements: **Must meet standards of progress.**

Program Strengths
Davidson College has a philosophy and tradition of individual attention. Services to LD students are entirely mainstreamed within this tradition.

General Information:
Davidson College is a 4 year independent Presbyterian college. Rural campus of 450 acres is 20 miles from Charlotte. Accessible by air, train, or bus to Charlotte. 4% of students are foreign. 14 residential halls on campus. Housing is guaranteed.Guaranteed through 1st year. 95 % of students remain on campus for the weekends. 65 % of students join fraternities/sororities.

Accreditation:SACS, NCDPI

Expenses:
Tuition: In-state: Full year: $13,680.00 plus fees. Room and board: $4,160.00

Majors
• ARTS Art History, Graphic Arts, Music • BUSINESS Economics • EDUCATION Secondary • HUMANITIES Classics, English/Writing/Literature, Philosophy, Religion • LANGUAGES English, French, German, Spanish • PRE PROFESSIONAL Law, Medicine, Ministry • RELIGIOUS STUDIES Reading & Theology • SCIENCES Anthropology, Biology, Chemistry, Mathematics, Physics • SOCIAL SCIENCES Anthropology, Economics, History, International Studies, Political Science, Psychology, Sociology • VISUAL AND PERFORMING ARTS Art, Art History, Dramatic Arts, Music, Theater

Sports
• SPORTS RELATED Cheerleading, Pep Band • SPORTS-INTERCOL-LEGIATE Baseball, Basketball, Basketball (F), Basketball (M), Cross Country, Cross Country (F), Cross Country (M), Field Hockey (F), Football (M), Golf, Golf (F), Golf (M), Soccer, Soccer (F), Soccer (M), Swimming, Swimming (F), Swimming (M), Tennis, Tennis (F), Tennis (M), Track and Field, Track and Field (F), Track and Field (M), Volleyball (F) • SPORTS-INTRAMURAL Basketball, Basketball (F), Basketball (M), Bowling, Bowling (F), Bowling (M), Canoeing, Crew, Crew (F), Crew (M), Golf, Golf (F), Golf (M), Lacrosse, Lacrosse (M), Racquetball, Racquetball (F), Racquetball (M), Sailing, Sailing (F), Sailing (M), Skiing - Water, Squash, Squash (F), Swimming, Swimming (F), Swimming (M), Tennis, Tennis (F), Tennis (M), Volleyball, Volleyball (F), Volleyball (M), Weight Lifting, Weight Lifting (M), Wrestling, Wrestling (M) • STUDENT LIFE ACTIVITIES Academic Clubs, Choral, Community Service, Concert Band, Debate, Drama Groups, Ethnic & Cultural Groups, Film, Fraternities, Jazz Band, Magazine, Music Groups, Musical Theater, Newspaper, Orchestra, Political Groups, Radio/TV station, Religious Organization, Student Government, Yearbook

---

Less Selective   **North Carolina Services**

Davidson County Community College
P.O. Box 1287
Lexington, North Carolina 27293-1287
(704) 249-8186

School Enrollment: **2,400** Male: **1,080** Female: **1,320**

Admissions Contact: **Judith Cottrell, Director of Admissions**
LD Contact: **Dr. Ed. Morse, Vice President**

Admissions

Application Information:
Application deadline: **None**

Secondary School Information
Most Important Criteria For Admissions (1-strongest)

SAT/ACT	Application	**1**	School transcript
Class rank	Course selection		Personal statement
Interview	Extra activities		Psychoeducational
G.P.A.	Open admission		Recommendations

Test Requirements:
Standardized tests waived: **Yes**

Types of Disabilities Served
- Speech/Lang • Reading • ADD with LD
- Study skills • Spelling • ADD without LD
- Written express • Math • ADHD with LD
- Organizational • Fine Motor • ADHD without LD
- Perceptual

Learning Disability Program
Counseling: Individual: **Yes**

Diagnostic Testing
ADD	Personality	Perceptual skills	Spelling
ADHD	Organization	Fine motor skills	Reading
I.Q.	Handwriting	Spoken language	Study skills
Math	Social skills	Written language	

Tutoring:
Services rendered by:

Graduates •Peers •Faculty LD staff Teacher trainees

Tutorials

Grp.	Ind.	Tutorials	Grp.	Ind.	Tutorials
•	•	Math skills	•	•	Word processing
•	•	Study skills	•		Time management
•	•	Language arts	•		Learning strategies
	•	Written express	•		Organizational skills

Academic Accommodations

Curriculum	Study Aids	Exams
Priority registration	Typist	Oral
• Math waiver	• Reader	Untimed
• Foreign lang. waiver	• Notetaker	Take home
Course substitution	Proof reader	With proctor
In Class	• Text on tape	On computer
• Calculators	Early syllabus	Extended time
• Tape recorder	Taped handouts	On tape
Word processor		Modified
Priority seating		Separate room

Graduation Requirements:
Course credits: **Varies** GPA: **2.0**

General Information:

Davidson County Community College is a 2 year public college. Rural campus of 100 acres is 25 miles from Greensboro. 1% of students are foreign. Housing is not guaranteed.

Accreditation: SACS

Expenses:
Tuition: In-state: Full year: $483.00. Part-time: Per credit: $11.50. Tuition: Out-of-state: Full year: $1,505.00. Part-time: Per credit: $107.50.

Majors

• BUSINESS Accounting, Business Administration, Data Processing, Management, Personnel, Secretarial Science • COMMUNICATIONS Broadcasting, Radio/Television • COMPUTER SCIENCE Business Data Programming, Computer Technology, Data Processing, Medical Records Technology • EDUCATION Early Childhood, Teacher's Aide • HEALTH SCIENCES Medical Records Administration, Nursing, Nursing Assistant • HUMANITIES Liberal/General • PREPROFESSIONAL Legal Assistant • SOCIAL SCIENCES Law Enforcement • VISUAL AND PERFORMING ARTS Art, Music • VOCATIONAL Air Conditioning/Heating/Refri, Auto Body, Automotive Service, Child Care, Child Development, Cosmetology, Drafting, Electronics Technology, Fashion Merchandising, Machinist, Paralegal, Secretarial, Welding, Word Processing

Sports/Activities

• SPORTS-INTRAMURAL Basketball (M), Softball (F), Softball (M), Volleyball • STUDENT LIFE ACTIVITIES Academic Clubs, Religious Organization, Student Government

---

Selective

East Carolina University

106 Whichard Building
Greenville, North Carolina 27858-4353
(919) 757-6640

School Enrollment: **2,637**
LD Enrollment: **60**

Admissions Contact: **Dr. Thomas Powell, Director of Admissions**
LD Contact: **C.C. Rowe, Coordinator**
Name of Program: **Handicapped Student Services**
Telephone: **(919) 757-6799**

Admissions

Application Information:
Enrolled: **60**
Separate application: **Yes**
Application deadline: **February 15th**
Applicant must apply **6** months in advance
Rolling Admissions: **Yes**

Secondary School Information
Most Important Criteria For Admissions (1-strongest)

5 SAT/ACT	**1** Application	**2** School transcript
3 Class rank	**4** Course selection	Personal statement
Interview	Extra activities	Psychoeducational
3 G.P.A.	Open admission	Recommendations

Test Requirements:
Diagnostic testing waived: **Yes**
Untimed SAT: **Yes** Untimed ACT: **Yes**
WAIS-R required: **Yes** Range accepted: **15 point discrepancy**
Currency of diagnostic testing: **3 years**
Tests recommended: **WISC, Woodcock-Johnson, SBIS or equivalent**

Types of Disabilities Served

• Speech/Lang	• Reading	• ADD with LD
• Study skills	• Spelling	• ADD without LD
• Written express	• Math	• ADHD with LD
• Organizational	• Fine Motor	• ADHD without LD
• Perceptual		

Learning Disability Program

Program: Reinforces course work: **Yes**

Faculty:
Faculty: **1** Including Director: **Yes** Full time: **1** M.A.: **1**
Faculty advocate: **Yes** Meets with instructor: **As needed**

Diagnostic Testing

ADD	Personality	Perceptual skills	• Spelling
ADHD	Organization	Fine motor skills	• Reading
• I.Q.	Handwriting	• Spoken language	Study skills
• Math	Social skills	• Written language	

Tutoring:
Services rendered by:
•Graduates •Peers •Faculty LD staff Teacher trainees

Tutorials

Grp.	Ind.	Tutorials	Grp.	Ind.	Tutorials
•		Math skills		•	Word processing
•		Study skills	•		Time management
		Language arts		•	Learning strategies
	•	Written express		•	Organizational skills

Academic Accommodations

Curriculum	Study Aids	Exams
Priority registration	Typist	• Oral
Math waiver	Reader	Untimed
• Foreign lang. waiver	• Notetaker	• Take home
• Course substitution	• Proof reader	With proctor
In Class	• Text on tape	On computer
• Calculators	Early syllabus	• Extended time
• Tape recorder	Taped handouts	On tape
• Word processor		• Modified
Priority seating		Separate room

General Information:

East Carolina University is a 4 year public university. Urban campus of 420 acres is 90 miles from Raleigh. Accessible by air, train, or bus. Ski areas are 300 miles from campus. Beaches are 85 miles from campus. 15 residential halls on campus. Housing is guaranteed.Guaranteed through 1st year. 85 % of students remain on campus for the weekends. 12 % of students join fraternities/sororities.

Accreditation:SACS

SAT/ACT Scores:

Scores for incoming freshmen:**Verbal:**86%below 500. 12%between 500 and 599. 2%between 600 and 699. 1%above 700. **Math:**70% below 500. 26% between 500 and 599. 4% between 600 and 699. 1%above 700.

Class Rank: 17% were in the top 40% of their class. 83% were in the top 80% of their class.

Expenses:

Tuition: In-state: Full year: Approximately $980.00. Tuition: Out-of-state: Full year: Approximately $5,300.00. Room and board: Approx. $2,600.00

Majors

• AREA STUDIES African, Asian, Urban • BUSINESS Accounting, Banking, Business Administration, Business Economics, Business Education, Business Management, Economics, Finance, Management, Marketing, Real Estate, Sports Management • COMMUNICATIONS Advertising, Broadcasting, Communication, Creative Writing, English, Graphic Design, Journalism, Photography, Television/Radio/Film • COMPUTER SCIENCE Computer Science, Medical Records Administration, Programming • CRAFTS AND DESIGN Ceramics, Sculpture • EDUCATION Art, Child Development, Curriculum, Early Childhood, English, Foreign Language, Health, Industrial, Mathematics, Middle School, Music, Music Therapy, Physical, Recreation and Youth Leadership, School Psychology, Science, Secondary, Special, Speech/Language, Technical, Vocational • ENGINEERING Industrial • HEALTH SCIENCES Communication Disorders, Environmental, Health, Medical Technology, Nursing, Nutritional/Food, Occupational Therapy, Physical Therapy, Speech/Audiology and Speech • HUMANITIES Humanities, Philosophy, Religion • LANGUAGES French, German, Italian, Latin, Russian, Spanish • PREPROFESSIONAL Dentistry, Law, Medicine, Pharmacy, Recreation, Social Work • SCIENCES Biochemistry, Biology, Botany, Chemistry, Earth, Ecology, Geography, Geology, Macrobiology, Marine Biology, Mathematics, Microbiology, Oceanography, Physical Chemistry, Physical Science, Physics, Physiology, Zoology • SOCIAL SCIENCES Anthropology, Criminal Justice, Family Counseling, Government/Political, History, Law Enforcement, Library Science, Political Science, Psychology, Social Sciences, Sociology • VISUAL AND PERFORMING ARTS Art, Art History, Dance, Dramatic Arts, Drawing, Music, Music Performance, Studio Art, Theater • VOCATIONAL

Food Service, Home Economics, Interior Design, Painting, Park/Recreation, Printing/Lithography, Secretarial, Textile and Clothing, Urban Design

Sports/Activities

• SPORTS RELATED Marching Band, Pep Band • SPORTS-INTERCOLLEGIATE Baseball (M), Basketball, Cross Country, Diving, Golf (M), Soccer (M), Softball (F), Swimming, Tennis, Track and Field, Volleyball (F) • SPORTS-INTRAMURAL Archery, Badminton, Baseball, Crew, Cross Country, Golf, Horseback Riding, Ice Hockey, Lacrosse, Racquetball, Rugby, Sailing, Skiing - Snow, Soccer, Softball, Swimming, Tennis, Track and Field, Volleyball, Water Polo, Wrestling (M) • STUDENT LIFE ACTIVITIES Choral, Concert Band, Dance, Drama Groups, Ethnic & Cultural Groups, Fraternities, Jazz Band, Magazine, Music Groups, Musical Theater, Newspaper, Opera, Radio/TV station, Religious Organization, Sororities, Student Government, Symphony Orchestra, Yearbook

Less Selective	North Carolina Services

Guilford Technical Community College

P.O. Box 309
Jamestown, North Carolina 27282
(919) 292-1101-454-1126

School Enrollment: **6,000** Male: **3,000** Female: **3,000**
LD Contact: **James K. Gripper, Ph.D., Director**
Name of Program: **Special Services**

Admissions

Application Information:
Application deadline: **Early**
Rolling Admissions: **Yes**

Secondary School Information
Most Important Criteria For Admissions (1-strongest)

SAT/ACT	Application	School transcript
Class rank	Course selection	Personal statement
Interview	Extra activities	Psychoeducational
G.P.A.	1 Open admission	Recommendations

Test Requirements:
Untimed SAT: **Yes** Untimed ACT: **Yes**
Documentation of LD required: **Yes**

Types of Disabilities Served
- Speech/Lang
- Study skills
- Written express
- Organizational
- Perceptual
- Reading
- Spelling
- Math
- Fine Motor
- ADD with LD
- ADD without LD
- ADHD with LD
- ADHD without LD

Faculty:
Faculty: **1** Full time: **1**
Faculty advocate: **Yes**

Diagnostic Testing

ADD	Personality	Perceptual skills	Spelling
ADHD	Organization	Fine motor skills	Reading
I.Q.	Handwriting	Spoken language	Study skills
Math	Social skills	Written language	

Tutoring:
Services rendered by:

North Carolina

Graduates   •Peers   Faculty   LD staff   Teacher trainees

Tutorials

Grp.	Ind.	Tutorials	Grp.	Ind.	Tutorials
	•	Math skills		•	Word processing
		Study skills			Time management
	•	Language arts		•	Learning strategies
	•	Written express			Organizational skills

Academic Accommodations

Curriculum	Study Aids	Exams
Priority registration	Typist	Oral
Math waiver	Reader	Untimed
Foreign lang. waiver	Notetaker	Take home
Course substitution	Proof reader	With proctor
In Class	Text on tape	On computer
• Calculators	Early syllabus	• Extended time
• Tape recorder	Taped handouts	On tape
Word processor		Modified
Priority seating		Separate room

Program Strengths

We have no special program, per se, for students with learning disabilities. GTCC places no different or additional requirements for admission on students with learning disabilities. We do, however, request that any prospective student who has a learning disability which requires special accommodations disclose that information at the time of application.

General Information:

Guilford Technical Community College is a 2 year public college. Suburban campus 11 miles from Greensboro. Housing is not guaranteed.

Accreditation: Regional

Expenses:

Tuition: In-state: Full year: Approximately $300.00. Tuition: Out-of-state: Full year: Approximately $2,500.00.

Majors

• AREA STUDIES Peace • BUSINESS Accounting, Business Administration, Business Management, Economics • COMMUNICATIONS English • EDUCATION Elementary, Physical, Secondary, Special • HEALTH SCIENCES Sports Medicine • HUMANITIES Humanities, Philosophy, Religion • LANGUAGES French, German, Spanish • PREPROFESSIONAL Law, Medicine, Pharmacy, Veterinarian • SCIENCES Anthropology, Biology, Chemistry, Geology, Mathematics, Physics • SOCIAL SCIENCES Criminal Justice, Government/Political, History, Psychology, Sociology • VISUAL AND PERFORMING ARTS Dramatic Arts, Fine Arts, Music

Sports/Activities

• SPORTS-INTERCOLLEGIATE Baseball (M), Basketball, Football (M), Golf (M), Lacrosse, Soccer, Softball, Tennis, Volleyball (F) • SPORTS-INTRAMURAL Basketball, Racquetball, Rugby (M), Soccer, Softball, Swimming, Tennis, Volleyball, Water Polo, Weight Lifting (M) • STUDENT LIFE ACTIVITIES Choral, Drama Groups, Magazine, Musical Theater, Newspaper, Radio/TV station, Student Government, Yearbook

---

Less Selective

Halifax Community College

P.O. Drawer 809
Weldon, North Carolina 27890
(919) 536-2551

School Enrollment: **1,200** Male: **504** Female: **696**
LD Enrollment: **20** Male: **12** Female: **8**

Admissions Contact: **Scottie Dickens, Admission Officer**
LD Contact: **Jan Cooper, Counselor**
Name of Program: **Student Support Services**

Admissions

Secondary School Information
Most Important Criteria For Admissions (1-strongest)

SAT/ACT	Application	School transcript
Class rank	Course selection	Personal statement
Interview	Extra activities	Psychoeducational
G.P.A.	**1** Open admission	Recommendations

Test Requirements:
Tests recommended: **Open door policy admissions. Placement test only requirement. Time and a half allowed for LD students on tests.**

Types of Disabilities Served

• Speech/Lang	• Reading	• ADD with LD
• Study skills	• Spelling	• ADD without LD
• Written express	• Math	• ADHD with LD
• Organizational	• Fine Motor	• ADHD without LD
• Perceptual		

Admissions Process

Halifax Community College has an open door policy. We accept all students who wish to attend who have a high school diploma or G.E.D. Classes initially taken are based upon placement test results.

Learning Disability Program

Students mainstreamed **100** % of the day
Services available for all students: **Yes**
Counseling: Individual: **Yes**
Support groups are available: **School provides accommodations only.**

Diagnostic Testing

ADD	Personality	Perceptual skills	Spelling
ADHD	Organization	Fine motor skills	Reading
I.Q.	Handwriting	Spoken language	Study skills
Math	Social skills	Written language	

Tutoring:
Average size of group tutorials: **2-3**
Services rendered by:

Graduates   •Peers   Faculty   LD staff   Teacher trainees

Tutorials

Grp.	Ind.	Tutorials	Grp.	Ind.	Tutorials
•	•	Math skills			Word processing
•	•	Study skills	•	•	Time management
•	•	Language arts		•	Learning strategies
•	•	Written express	•	•	Organizational skills

Academic Accommodations

Curriculum

Priority registration
- Math waiver
Foreign lang. waiver
Course substitution

In Class
- Calculators
- Tape recorder
Word processor
- Priority seating

Study Aids

Typist
- Reader
- Notetaker
Proof reader
- Text on tape
Early syllabus
Taped handouts

Exams

- Oral
Untimed
Take home
- With proctor
On computer
- Extended time
- On tape
- Modified
- Separate room

Graduation Requirements:

Course credits: **Varies** GPA: **2.0** Math waiver: **Yes**

General Information:

Halifax Community College is a 2 year public college. Suburban campus of 109 acres is 80 miles from Raleigh. Accessible by bus only. Ski areas are 250 miles from campus. Beaches are 200 miles from campus. Housing is not guaranteed.

Accreditation: SASC

Expenses:

Tuition: In-state: Full year: $168.00 per quarter - includes activity fee and insurance. Part-time: Per credit:$11.50. Part-time: Per course: $34.50 - $57.50 (3, 5 hours). Tuition: Out-of-state: Full year: $1,505.00 (14 credits), $1,290.00 (12 credits) . Part-time: Per credit:$107.50. Part-time: Per course:$322.50 - $537.50

Majors

• AGRICULTURE Business, Engineering • ARTS Commercial Art, Interior Design • BUSINESS Accounting, Business Administration, Clerical, Commercial Art, Data Processing, Education, Secretarial Science • COMPUTER SCIENCE Business Data Programming, Computer Technology, Medical Records Technology • EDUCATION Child Development, Early Childhood, Elementary, Middle School • ENGINEERING Electrical, Engineering Science • HEALTH SCIENCES Medical Laboratory Technology, Medical Secretary, Nursing • HUMANITIES Liberal Arts • SOCIAL SCIENCES Criminal Justice • VOCATIONAL Automobile Technology, Electronics Technology, Industrial Equipment Maintenance, Interior Design, Medical Laboratory Technology

Sports/Activities

• STUDENT LIFE ACTIVITIES Academic Clubs, Student Government

Less Selective

Isothermal Community College

P.O. Box 804
Spindale, North Carolina 28160
(704) 286-3636

School Enrollment: **1,600**
LD Enrollment: **15**

Admissions Contact: **Tammy Hollifield, Admission Counselor**
LD Contact: **Ruth Boehning, Coordinator**
Name of Program: **Learning Support Program**
Telephone:**(704) 286-3636 Ext. 268**

Admissions

Application Information:

LD Students Applying: **15** Accepted: **15** Enrolled:**15**
Application deadline: **None**
Rolling Admissions: **Yes**

Secondary School Information

Most Important Criteria For Admissions (1-strongest)

SAT/ACT	Application	School transcript
Class rank	Course selection	Personal statement
Interview	Extra activities	Psychoeducational
G.P.A.	**1** Open admission	Recommendations

Test Requirements:

Standardized tests waived: **Yes**
Diagnostic testing waived: **Yes**
Range accepted: **80+**
Documentation of LD required: **Yes**
Currency of diagnostic testing: **2 years**
Tests recommended: **Public school evaluations, WAIS-R, Bender, etc., vocational rehabilitation, Woodcock -Johnson Psychoeducational Battery, TOWL 2, etc.**

Types of Disabilities Served

- Speech/Lang
- Study skills
- Written express
- Organizational
- Perceptual
- Reading
- Spelling
- Math
- Fine Motor
- ADD with LD
- ADD without LD
ADHD with LD
ADHD without LD

Learning Disability Program

Program: Reinforces course work: **Yes**
Program available through:**As needed**
Recommended credits per semester: **12**
Counseling: Individual: **Yes** Vocational Counseling: **Yes**
Support groups are available:**planned**

Faculty:

Faculty: **1** Part time: **1**
Faculty advocate: **Yes** Meets with instructor: **As needed**

Diagnostic Testing

ADD	Personality	Perceptual skills	Spelling
ADHD	Organization	Fine motor skills	Reading
I.Q.	Handwriting	Spoken language	Study skills
Math	Social skills	Written language	

Tutoring:
Services rendered by:
Graduates •Peers •Faculty •LD staff Teacher trainees

Tutorials

Grp.	Ind.	Tutorials	Grp.	Ind.	Tutorials
	•	Math skills		•	Word processing
	•	Study skills		•	Time management
	•	Language arts		•	Learning strategies
	•	Written express		•	Organizational skills

Academic Accommodations

Curriculum	Study Aids	Exams
Priority registration	• Typist	• Oral
Math waiver	• Reader	Untimed
Foreign lang. waiver	• Notetaker	Take home
Course substitution	• Proof reader	• With proctor
In Class	• Text on tape	On computer
• Calculators	• Early syllabus	• Extended time
Tape recorder	Taped handouts	On tape
• Word processor		• Modified
• Priority seating		• Separate room

Program Strengths

The services for learning disabled students at Isothermal Community College are rather unique for a two year college in western No. Carolina. Much of the funds and all personnel are provided through a US Dept. of Education grant for Student Support Services. Serving LD students is one of our goals. Our developmental education instructor and counselors double in services to LD students. We are able to assist LD students from initial inquiry.

General Information:

Isothermal Community College is a 2 year public college. Rural campus of 120 acres is 37 miles from Spartanburg, SC. Ski areas are 60 miles from campus. Beaches are 200 miles from campus. Housing is not guaranteed.

Accreditation: SACS

Expenses:
Tuition: In-state: Full year: $414.00. Part-time: Per credit:$11.50. Tuition: Out-of-state: Full year: $3,870.00. Part-time: Per credit:$107.50.

Majors

• BUSINESS Banking, Business Administration, Business Education, Business Management, Finance, Food Management, Management, Marketing, Real Estate • COMMUNICATIONS Broadcasting, Creative Writing, English, Journalism, Photography, Television/Radio/Film • COMPUTER SCIENCE Programming, Telecommunications • EDUCATION Art, Early Childhood, Elementary, Middle School, Music, Pre-Education, School Psychology, Secondary, Special, Teacher Aide • ENGINEERING Electrical, Engineering Science, Mechanical • HEALTH SCIENCES Health, Practical Nursing • HUMANITIES Liberal Arts, Religion • LANGUAGES Spanish • PREPROFESSIONAL Engineering, Law, Medicine, Optometry, Pharmacy, Recreation, Veterinarian • SOCIAL SCIENCES Criminal Justice, Law Enforcement, Social Sciences, Sociology • VISUAL AND PERFORMING ARTS Art, Fine Arts, Music • VOCATIONAL Auto Body, Automated Manufacturing Technology, Automobile Technology, Business and Office, Cosmetology, Drafting, Electronics Technology, Industrial Management, Machinist, Mechanical Engineering Technology, Park/Recreation, Printing/Lithography, Secretarial, Textile and Clothing, Welding

Sports/Activities

• SPORTS-INTRAMURAL Badminton, Basketball, Ping-Pong, Soccer (M), Volleyball • STUDENT LIFE ACTIVITIES Academic Clubs, Choral, Drama Groups, Newspaper, Radio/TV station, Student Government, Yearbook

---

Less Selective

Johnston Community College
P.O. Box 2350
Smithfield, North Carolina 27577
(919) 934-3051

School Enrollment: **2,500**
LD Enrollment: **50**

Admissions Contact: **Jimmy O'Neal, Director of Admissions**
LD Contact: **Bessie Locus, Counselor**
Name of Program: **Handicapped Student Services**
Address: **P.O. Box 2350**
Telephone:**(919) 934-3051**

Admissions

Application Information:
Application deadline: **None**
Rolling Admissions: **Yes**

Secondary School Information
Most Important Criteria For Admissions (1-strongest)

SAT/ACT	Application	School transcript
Class rank	Course selection	Personal statement
Interview	Extra activities	Psychoeducational
G.P.A.	1 Open admission	Recommendations

Test Requirements:
Documentation of LD required: **Yes**
Tests recommended: **We have an open door policy. A placement test is administered after the student applies.**

Types of Disabilities Served

• Speech/Lang	• Reading	ADD with LD
• Study skills	• Spelling	ADD without LD
• Written express	• Math	ADHD with LD
• Organizational	• Fine Motor	ADHD without LD
• Perceptual		

Admissions Process

The Community Colleges in North Carolina have an open door policy. Anyone can apply to a community college. Normally a student is accepted after all credentials are received.

Learning Disability Program

Program: Reinforces course work: **Yes**
Services available for all students: **Yes**
Counseling: Individual: **Yes** Vocational Counseling: **Yes**

Faculty:
Faculty: **1**

Diagnostic Testing

ADD	Personality	Perceptual skills	Spelling
ADHD	Organization	Fine motor skills	Reading
I.Q.	Handwriting	Spoken language	Study skills
Math	Social skills	Written language	

Services rendered by:

Graduates   Peers   Faculty   LD staff   Teacher trainees

Tutorials
Grp. Ind. Tutorials   Grp. Ind. Tutorials
- Math skills   Word processing
- Study skills   Time management
  Language arts   • Learning strategies
- Written express   • Organizational skills

Academic Accommodations
Curriculum   **Study Aids**   **Exams**
Priority registration   Typist   Oral
Math waiver   Reader   Untimed
Foreign lang. waiver   Notetaker   Take home
Course substitution   Proof reader • With proctor
In Class   • Text on tape   On computer
Calculators   Early syllabus Extended time
Tape recorder   Taped handouts On tape
Word processor   Modified
Priority seating   Separate room

Graduation Requirements:
Course credits: **124 quarter hours** GPA: **2.0** Years to complete degree: **2**

Program Strengths

General Information:
Johnston Community College is a 2 year public college. Rural campus 30 miles from Raleigh. Ski areas are 5 hours from campus. Beaches are 2 hours from campus. Housing is not guaranteed.

Accreditation: SACS

Expenses:
Tuition: In-state: Full year: $168.00 per quarter. Part-time: Per credit:$11.50. Tuition: Out-of-state: Full year: $1,512.00 per quarter. Part-time: Per credit:$107.50. Cost of LD program:$3,000.00 per year

Majors
• BUSINESS Accounting, Business Administration, Clerical, Data Processing, Secretarial Science • COMPUTER SCIENCE Business Data Programming • EDUCATION Early Childhood • VOCATIONAL Air Conditioning/Heating/Refri, Auto Body, Automotive Service, Carpentry, Cosmetology, Electronics Technology, Machinist, Paralegal, Radiological Technology, Secretarial, Welding

Sports/Activities
• SPORTS RELATED Chess • STUDENT LIFE ACTIVITIES Community Service, Student Government

McDowell Technical Community College
Route 1 Box 170
Marion, North Carolina 28752
(704) 652-6021

School Enrollment: **700**
LD Enrollment: **11**

Admissions Contact: **Jim Biddix, Dean of Students**
LD Contact: **Dr. James R. Robinson, Director Career Center**
Name of Program: **MTCC LD Project**

Admissions

Application Information:
LD Students Applying: **14** Accepted: **14**
Applicant must apply **1-2** months in advance

Secondary School Information
Most Important Criteria For Admissions (1-strongest)
SAT/ACT   Application   School transcript
Class rank Course selection Personal statement
Interview   Extra activities Psychoeducational
G.P.A.   **1** Open admission Recommendations

Test Requirements:
Diagnostic testing waived: **Yes**
Untimed ACH: **Yes** Achievement tests required:**1**
WAIS-R required: **Yes** Range accepted: **Low Average +**
Documentation of LD required: **Yes**
Tests recommended: **Psychoeducational Assessment (WAIS-R, Woodcock-Johnson, Achievement)**

Types of Disabilities Served
- Speech/Lang   • Reading   • ADD with LD
- Study skills   • Spelling   • ADD without LD
- Written express • Math   • ADHD with LD
- Organizational • Fine Motor • ADHD without LD
- Perceptual

Learning Disability Program
Program: Remedial: **Yes**
Program: Reinforces course work: **Yes**
Students mainstreamed **100** % of the day
Counseling: Individual: **Yes** Group Counseling: **Yes**

Faculty:
Faculty: **7** Including Director: **Yes** Full time: **7**
LD faculty with: BS/BA: **2** M.A.: **3** Ph.D.: **1**
Faculty advocate: **Yes** Meets with instructor: **quarterly**

Diagnostic Testing
ADD   • Personality • Perceptual skills • Spelling
ADHD   Organization• Fine motor skills • Reading
• I.Q.   Handwriting   Spoken language • Study skills
• Math   Social skills• Written language

Tutoring:
Services rendered by:
Graduates •Peers •Faculty •LD staff Teacher trainees

Tutorials

Grp.	Ind.	Tutorials	Grp.	Ind.	Tutorials
•	•	Math skills	•	•	Word processing
•	•	Study skills	•		Time management
•	•	Language arts	•		Learning strategies
	•	Written express	•		Organizational skills

Academic Accommodations

Curriculum	Study Aids	Exams
Priority registration	• Typist	• Oral
Math waiver	Reader	Untimed
Foreign lang. waiver	• Notetaker	• Take home
Course substitution	• Proof reader	• With proctor
In Class	• Text on tape	On computer
• Calculators	Early syllabus	• Extended time
• Tape recorder	Taped handouts	On tape
• Word processor		• Modified
Priority seating		Separate room

Program Strengths

MTCC is an open admission institution. We provide individualized educational planning to meet the specific needs of the student through use of an array of auxiliary aids and services. Our entire faculty and staff are in-serviced in the area of LD and services. Being a community college, we are committed to career training and mainstreaming the student into jobs of their choice but offer intense counseling to assist in setting realistic goals which provide the student with a real sense of accomplishment and ultimate satisfaction.

General Information:

McDowell Technical Community College is a 2 year public college. Rural campus of 10 acres is 25 miles from Ashville. Accessible by auto. Ski areas are 1 hour from campus. Beaches are 5 miles from campus. Housing is not guaranteed.

Accreditation: SACS

Expenses:

Tuition: In-state: Full year: $400.00. Part-time: Per credit:$11.50. Tuition: Out-of-state: Full year: $800.00.

Majors

• BUSINESS Accounting, Business Administration, Business Management, Labor Relations, Management, Marketing, Real Estate • COMMUNICATIONS Graphic Design • COMPUTER SCIENCE Computer Maintenance, Data Processing, Programming • EDUCATION Early Childhood, Elementary • ENGINEERING Industrial • HUMANITIES Liberal Arts • SOCIAL SCIENCES Law Enforcement • VOCATIONAL Auto Body, Automobile Technology, Business and Office, Cosmetology, Electronics Technology, Printing/Lithography, Secretarial

Sports/Activities

• SPORTS-INTERCOLLEGIATE Tennis • SPORTS-INTRAMURAL Basketball, Golf, Tennis, Volleyball • STUDENT LIFE ACTIVITIES Newspaper, Student Government, Yearbook

---

Highly Selective **North Carolina Services**

North Carolina State University
P.O. Box 7103
Raleigh, North Carolina 27695-7103
(919) 515-2434

School Enrollment: **19,000** Male: **11,400** Female: **7,600**
LD Enrollment: **132**

Admissions Contact: **Melinda Bissett, Assistant Director**
LD Contact: **Lelia Brettmann, Coordinator**
Name of Program: **Handicapped Student Services**
Telephone:**(919) 515-7653**

Admissions

Application Information:
Application deadline: **Feb.1st-Jan.1st for School of Design**
Rolling Admissions: **Yes** Notified when: **April 1st**

Secondary School Information
Most Important Criteria For Admissions (1-strongest)

4 SAT/ACT	Application	School transcript
3 Class rank	**2** Course selection	**6** Personal statement
Interview	**5** Extra activities	Psychoeducational
1 G.P.A.	Open admission	**7** Recommendations

Test Requirements:
Untimed SAT: **Yes** Untimed ACT: **Yes**
Documentation of LD required: **Yes**
Tests recommended: **To receive LD services a current psychoeducational evaluation including WAIS-R and academic testing is required.**

Types of Disabilities Served
- Speech/Lang
- Study skills
- Written express
- Organizational
- Perceptual
- Reading
- Spelling
- Math
- Fine Motor
- ADD with LD
- ADD without LD
- ADHD with LD
- ADHD without LD

Admissions Process

Admission to the University is based on academic achievement with no preadmission inquiry regarding disability. After admission, LD documentation is submitted to the LD Coordinator.

High School Course Requirements:
English: **4** Math: **3** Science: **3**

Learning Disability Program

Program: Reinforces course work: **Yes**
Students mainstreamed **100** % of the day
Recommended credits per semester: **12-15**
Counseling: Individual: **Yes** Vocational Counseling: **Yes**
Support groups are available:**Yes, SODA, Student Organization for the Differently Abled**

Faculty:
Faculty: **1** Including Director: **Yes** Full time: **1** M.A.: **1**
Faculty advocate: **Yes** Meets with instructor: **As needed**

Diagnostic Testing

ADD	Personality	Perceptual skills	Spelling
ADHD	Organization	Fine motor skills	Reading
I.Q.	Handwriting	Spoken language	Study skills
Math	Social skills	Written language	

Tutoring:

Average size of group tutorials: **One-on-one**
Services rendered by:
•Graduates •Peers   Faculty   LD staff   Teacher trainees

Tutorials

Grp.	Ind.	Tutorials	Grp.	Ind.	Tutorials
		Math skills			Word processing
		Study skills			Time management
		Language arts			Learning strategies
		Written express			Organizational skills

Academic Accommodations

Curriculum	Study Aids	Exams
• Priority registration	Typist	Oral
Math waiver	• Reader	Untimed
Foreign lang. waiver	• Notetaker	Take home
Course substitution	• Proof reader	• With proctor
In Class	• Text on tape	On computer
• Calculators	Early syllabus	• Extended time
• Tape recorder	Taped handouts	On tape
• Word processor		Modified
• Priority seating		• Separate room

Graduation Requirements:

Course credits: **Varies** GPA: **2.0** Years to complete degree: **Unlimited**
Language waiver: **Yes**

Program Strengths

The LD Program at NCSU is purely support for those students who meet regular admission requirements. Students are fully mainstreamed and learn to use their strengths and advocate for themselves.

General Information:

North Carolina State University is a 4 year public university. Urban campus of 623 acres is Accessible by air, train, or bus. Ski areas are 3-4 miles from campus. Beaches are 3 miles from campus. 4.5% of students are foreign. 19 residential halls on campus. Housing is guaranteed.Guaranteed through 1st year. 10 % of students join fraternities/sororities.

Accreditation:SACS

SAT/ACT Scores:

Scores for incoming freshmen:**Verbal:**56%below 500. 34%between 500 and 599. 9%between 600 and 699. 1%above 700. **Math:**21% below 500. 43% between 500 and 599. 30% between 600 and 699. 6%above 700.

Class Rank:

About 73% of the present freshmen class were in the upper 20% of their high school class. 97% were in the top 40% of their class.

Expenses:

Tuition: In-state: Full year: $1,254.00. Tuition: Out-of-state: Full year: $7,122.00. Room and board: $3,150.00

Majors

• BUSINESS Accounting, Agricultural, Business Administration, Business Economics, Business Management, Economics, Human Resources Management, International Business, Management, Marketing • COMMUNICATIONS Communication, Creative Writing, English, Graphic Design, Journalism, Linguistic, Speech • COMPUTER SCIENCE Computer Science, Computer Technology, Programming, Telecommunications • EDUCATION Agricultural, Elementary, Foreign Language, Health, Industrial, Middle School, Science, Secondary, Social Studies, Technical • ENGINEERING Aerospace, Chemical, Civil/Environmental, Computer, Electrical, Industrial, Mechanical, Nuclear, Textile • HEALTH SCIENCES Environmental, Medical Technology, Nutritional/Food • HUMANITIES English/Writing/Literature, Humanities, Liberal Arts, Philosophy • LANGUAGES French, Spanish • PREPROFESSIONAL Agriculture, Architecture, Dentistry, Engineering, Forestry, Law, Medicine, Natural Resources, Recreation, Veterinarian, Wildlife • SCIENCES Agricultural, Agronomy, Animal, Biochemistry, Biology, Earth, Entomology, Geology, Horticultural, Mathematics, Meteorology, Physics, Plant Protection, Poultry, Soil, Statistics • SOCIAL SCIENCES Anthropology, Criminal Justice, Government/Political, History, Political Science, Psychology, Social Sciences, Sociology

Sports/Activities

• SPORTS RELATED Marching Band • SPORTS-INTERCOLLEGIATE Baseball (F), Basketball, Cross Country, Diving, Fencing, Football (M), Golf, Gymnastics, Riflery, Soccer, Swimming, Tennis, Track and Field, Volleyball (F), Wrestling (M) • SPORTS-INTRAMURAL Archery, Badminton, Basketball, Bowling, Cross Country, Fencing, Field Hockey (F), Golf, Gymnastics, Hand Ball, Ice Hockey (M), Lacrosse (M), Ping-Pong, Racquetball, Sailing, Skiing - Snow, Soccer, Softball, Squash, Swimming, Tennis, Track and Field, Volleyball, Wrestling (M) • STUDENT LIFE ACTIVITIES Choral, Concert Band, Drama Groups, Fraternities, Jazz Band, Magazine, Music Groups, Musical Theater, Newspaper, Political Groups, Radio/TV station, Religious Organization, Sororities, Student Government, Symphony Orchestra, Yearbook

---

Less Selective　　　　　　　　　**North Carolina Accommodations**

Richmond Community College

P. O. Box 1189
Hamlet, North Carolina 28345
(919) 582-7000

School Enrollment: **1,100** Male: **400** Female: **700**
LD Enrollment: **2** Male: **2**

Admissions Contact: **Teri Jacobs, Director of Admissions**
LD Contact: **Dr. Bill Moss, Counselor**

Admissions

Secondary School Information

Most Important Criteria For Admissions (1-strongest)

SAT/ACT	Application	School transcript
Class rank	Course selection	Personal statement
Interview	Extra activities	Psychoeducational
G.P.A.	Open admission	Recommendations

Types of Disabilities Served

Speech/Lang	Reading	ADD with LD
Study skills	Spelling	ADD without LD
Written express	Math	ADHD with LD
Organizational	Fine Motor	ADHD without LD
Perceptual		

Admissions Process

Open door admissions

Learning Disability Program

Special orientation for LD students: **Yes**
Students mainstreamed **100 %** of the day
Services available for all students: **Yes**
Counseling: Individual: **Yes** Vocational Counseling: **Yes**

Diagnostic Testing

ADD	Personality	Perceptual skills	Spelling
ADHD	Organization	Fine motor skills	Reading
I.Q.	Handwriting	Spoken language	Study skills
Math	Social skills	Written language	

Tutoring:

Average size of group tutorials: **Usually 1 on 1**
Services rendered by:
　Graduates　•Peers　•Faculty　　LD staff　•Teacher trainees

Tutorials

Grp.	Ind.	Tutorials	Grp.	Ind.	Tutorials
•	•	Math skills			Word processing
•	•	Study skills	•	•	Time management
		Language arts	•	•	Learning strategies
		Written express	•	•	Organizational skills

Academic Accommodations

Curriculum	Study Aids	Exams
Priority registration	Typist	Oral
Math waiver	• Reader	• Untimed
Foreign lang. waiver	• Notetaker	Take home
Course substitution	Proof reader	With proctor
In Class	Text on tape	• On computer
• Calculators	Early syllabus	• Extended time
• Tape recorder	Taped handouts	• On tape
• Word processor		Modified
• Priority seating		Separate room

Graduation Requirements:

Course credits: **Varied per program**

Program Strengths

Individualized attention to student needs. Students totally mainstreamed. Adaptations to student needs.

General Information:

Richmond Community College is a 2 year public college. Rural campus of 160 acres is 75 miles from Charlotte. Accessible by bus or train. Ski areas are 300 miles from campus. Beaches are 125 miles from campus. Housing is not guaranteed.

Accreditation: SACS

Expenses:

Tuition: In-state: Full year: $170.00. Part-time: Per credit: $11.50. Part-time: Per course: 3 hours - $34.50, 5 hours - $57.50. Tuition: Out-of-state: Full year: $1,505.00. Part-time: Per credit: $107.50. Part-time: Per course: 3 hours - $322.50

Majors

• BUSINESS Accounting, Clerical • COMPUTER SCIENCE Business Data Programming • ENGINEERING Electrical, Mechanical • HEALTH SCIENCES Nursing • VOCATIONAL Business and Office, Electronics Technology, Industrial Equipment Maintenance, Machinist, Office Administration, Secretarial, Welding

Sports/Activities

• SPORTS-INTRAMURAL Volleyball • STUDENT LIFE ACTIVITIES Academic Clubs, Community Service, Ethnic & Cultural Groups, Student

Government

Surry Community College

P.O. Box 304
Dobson, North Carolina 27017
(919) 386-8121

School Enrollment: **3,000** Male: **1,400** Female: **1,600**

Admissions Contact: **Michael McHone, Dean of Student Services**
LD Contact: **Larry Earl Rooks, Counselor**
Address: **P.O. Box 304**
Telephone: **(919) 386- 8121**

Admissions

Application Information:

Application deadline: **August 1st**
Rolling Admissions: **Yes**

Secondary School Information

Most Important Criteria For Admissions (1-strongest)

SAT/ACT	Application	School transcript
Class rank	Course selection	Personal statement
Interview	Extra activities	Psychoeducational
G.P.A.	Open admission	Recommendations

Types of Disabilities Served

Speech/Lang.	Reading	ADD with LD
Study skills	Spelling	ADD without LD
Written express	Math	ADHD with LD
Organizational	Fine Motor	ADHD without LD
Perceptual		

Admissions Process

Open admissions to high school graduates, except nursing programs.

Learning Disability Program

Services available for all students: **Yes**

Faculty: Part time: **1**

LD faculty with: BS/BA: **1**

Diagnostic Testing

ADD	Personality	Perceptual skills	Spelling
ADHD	Organization	Fine motor skills	Reading
I.Q.	Handwriting	Spoken language	Study skills
Math	Social skills	Written language	

Tutoring:

Average size of group tutorials: **Individual**
Services rendered by:
　Graduates　•Peers　　Faculty　　LD staff　　Teacher trainees

Tutorials

Grp.	Ind.	Tutorials	Grp.	Ind.	Tutorials
	•	Math skills			Word processing
		Study skills			Time management
•	•	Language arts			Learning strategies
		Written express			Organizational skills

Academic Accommodations

Curriculum	Study Aids	Exams
Priority registration	Typist	Oral
Math waiver	Reader	Untimed
Foreign lang. waiver	Notetaker	Take home
Course substitution	Proof reader	With proctor
In Class	Text on tape	On computer
Calculators	Early syllabus	Extended time
Tape recorder	Taped handouts	On tape
Word processor		Modified
Priority seating		Separate room

Graduation Requirements:
Course credits: **96 quarter hours for college transfers** GPA: **2.0**

General Information:
Surry Community College is a 2 year public college. Rural campus of 15 acres is 45 miles from Winston-Salem. Accessible by car. Ski areas are 90 miles from campus. Beaches are 200 miles from campus. Housing is not guaranteed.

Accreditation: SASC, SNC

Expenses:
Tuition: In-state: Full year: $161.00 per quarter. Part-time: Per credit:$11.50. Tuition: Out-of-state: Full year: $1,505.00 per quarter. Part-time: Per credit:$107.50.

Majors

• AGRICULTURE Business, Horticultural • BUSINESS Accounting, Agricultural, Business Administration, Clerical, Data Processing, Marketing, Real Estate, Retailing, Secretarial Science • COMPUTER SCIENCE Business Data Programming • ENGINEERING Automotive, Drafting, Electrical • HEALTH SCIENCES Medical Secretary, Nursing, Practical Nursing • HUMANITIES Liberal Arts • VOCATIONAL Auto Body, Automobile Technology, Construction, Cosmetology, Drafting, Industrial Equipment Maintenance, Machinist, Secretarial, Welding

Sports/Activities

• SPORTS-INTERCOLLEGIATE Golf, Tennis • SPORTS-INTRAMURAL Basketball, Softball, Volleyball • STUDENT LIFE ACTIVITIES Academic Clubs, Community Service, Newspaper, Student Government, Yearbook

---

Very Selective	North Carolina Services

University of North Carolina: Greensboro
157 Elliot University Center
Greensboro, North Carolina 27412-5001
(919) 334-5243

School Enrollment: **11,000** Male: **7,370** Female: **3,630**
LD Enrollment: **136** Male: **87** Female: **49**

Admissions Contact: **Charles Rickard, Director of Admissions**
LD Contact: **Patricia Bailey, Program Coordinator**
Name of Program: **Disabled Student Services**
Address: **157 Elliot University Center**
Telephone:**(919) 334-5440**

Admissions

Application Information:
Enrolled:**130**
Application deadline: **August 1st**
Rolling Admissions: **Yes**

Secondary School Information
Most Important Criteria For Admissions (1-strongest)

2 SAT/ACT	Application	**1**	School transcript
1 Class rank	**3** Course selection		Personal statement
4 Interview	Extra activities		Psychoeducational
2 G.P.A.	Open admission		Recommendations

Test Requirements:
Diagnostic testing waived: **Yes**
Untimed SAT: **Yes** Untimed ACT: **Yes** Untimed ACH: **Yes**
Documentation of LD required: **Yes**
Currency of diagnostic testing: **3 years**
Tests recommended: **Aptitude and achievement**

Types of Disabilities Served
- Speech/Lang
- Study skills
- Written express
- Organizational
- Perceptual
- Reading
- Spelling
- Math
- Fine Motor
- ADD with LD
- ADD without LD
- ADHD with LD
- ADHD without LD

Admissions Process

Best to write cover letter describing disability and its affect on standardized tests, if any.

High School Course Requirements:
English: **4** Math: **3** Science: **3** Foreign Language: **23**
Waivers to standard high school courses
Course substitution: **Yes**

Learning Disability Program
Special orientation for LD students: **Yes**
Counseling: Individual: **Yes** Group Counseling: **Yes** Vocational Counseling: **Yes**
Support groups are available:**Yes, drop-in**

Faculty:
Faculty: **3** Including Director: **Yes** Full time: **1** Part time: **1** M.A.: **2** Ph.D.:

1
Faculty advocate: **Yes** Meets with instructor: **As needed**

Diagnostic Testing
ADD	Personality	Perceptual skills	• Spelling
ADHD	Organization	Fine motor skills	• Reading
• I.Q.	Handwriting•	Spoken language	Study skills
• Math	Social skills•	Written language	

Tutoring:
Services rendered by:
•Graduates •Peers •Faculty •LD staff Teacher trainees

Tutorials
Grp.	Ind.	Tutorials	Grp.	Ind.	Tutorials
•	•	Math skills	•	•	Word processing
•	•	Study skills	•	•	Time management
•	•	Language arts	•	•	Learning strategies
•	•	Written express	•	•	Organizational skills

Academic Accommodations

Curriculum	Study Aids	Exams
Priority registration	Typist	Oral
Math waiver	Reader	Untimed
Foreign lang. waiver	• Notetaker	Take home
• Course substitution	• Proof reader	• With proctor
In Class	• Text on tape	On computer
• Calculators	Early syllabus	• Extended time
• Tape recorder	Taped handouts	On tape
• Word processor		• Modified
Priority seating		Separate room

Graduation Requirements:
Course credits: **122** GPA: **2.0** Years to complete degree: **7** Math waiver: **Yes** Language waiver: **Yes**

Program Strengths
Our learning disabled students are completely mainstreamed. There are no separate courses. Each student is treated as an individual, and accommodations are based on educational needs in their documentation. Priority registration, alternative testing, academic adjustment, counseling, workshops, and career exploration are all part of the services.

General Information:
University of North Carolina: Greensboro is a 4 year public university. Urban campus 70 miles from Raleigh, NC. Accessible by air, train or bus. Ski areas are 200 miles from campus. Beaches are 250 miles from campus. 2% of students are foreign. Housing is not guaranteed.15 % of students join fraternities/sororities.

Accreditation: SACS

Expenses:
Tuition: In-state: Full year: $634.00 per semester. Part-time: Per credit:$76.00. Part-time: Per course: $136.50. Tuition: Out-of-state: Full year: $2,885 per semester. Part-time: Per credit:$638.00. Part-time: Per course:$698.50 Room and board: $1,490.00 - $2,295.0

Majors
• AREA STUDIES African, Ethnic, Latin American, Russian/Slavic, Urban • BUSINESS Accounting, Banking, Business Administration, Business Economics, Business Education, Business Management, Economics, Finance, Food Management, Management, Marketing, Personnel • COMMUNICATIONS English, Linguistic, Speech, Television/Radio/Film • COMPUTER SCIENCE Data Processing • CRAFTS AND DESIGN Sculpture • EDUCATION Art, Early Childhood, Elementary, English, Foreign Language, Health, Mathematics, Middle School, Music, Physical, Pre- Education, Science, Secondary, Special • HEALTH SCIENCES Medical Technology, Nursing, Nutritional/Food, Speech Therapy, Speech/Audiology and Speech • HUMANITIES Classics, Humanities, Liberal Arts, Philosophy, Religion • LANGUAGES French, German, Greek, Latin, Spanish • PREPROFESSIONAL Dentistry, Law, Medicine, Pharmacy, Recreation, Social Work, Veterinarian • SCIENCES Biology, Chemistry, Earth, Gerontology, Macrobiology, Physics, Statistics • SOCIAL SCIENCES Anthropology, Family Counseling, Government/Political, History, Political Science, Psychology, Public Relations, Social Sciences, Sociology • VISUAL AND PERFORMING ARTS Art History, Dance, Dramatic Arts, Music, Music Performance, Studio Art • VOCATIONAL Fashion Design, Food Service, Home Economics, Interior Design, Office Administration, Painting, Park/Recreation, Secretarial, Textile and Clothing, Urban Design

Sports/Activities
• SPORTS-INTERCOLLEGIATE Basketball, Golf, Soccer, Softball (F), Tennis, Volleyball (F) • SPORTS-INTRAMURAL Badminton, Basketball, Bowling, Golf, Ping-Pong, Racquetball, Soccer, Softball, Swimming, Tennis, Track and Field, Volleyball • STUDENT LIFE ACTIVITIES Choral, Concert Band, Dance, Drama Groups, Film, Fraternities, Jazz Band, Magazine, Music Groups, Musical Theater, Newspaper, Opera, Radio/TV station, Sororities, Student Government, Symphony Orchestra, Yearbook

---

Selective **North Carolina Services**

University of North Carolina:Wilmington
601 South College Road
Wilmington, North Carolina 28403-3297
(919) 395-3243

School Enrollment: **7,800**
LD Enrollment: **68** Male: **38** Female: **30**

Admissions Contact: **Douglas L. Johnson, Assoc. Dir. Admissions**
LD Contact: **Phillip Sharp, Coordinator**
Name of Program: **Disabled Student Services**
Telephone:**(919) 395-3746**

Admissions

Secondary School Information
Most Important Criteria For Admissions (1-strongest)

2	SAT/ACT	1	Application	1	School transcript
11	Class rank	1	Course selection	11	Personal statement
11	Interview	11	Extra activities	11	Psychoeducational
1	G.P.A.		Open admission	11	Recommendations

Test Requirements:
Untimed SAT: **Yes** Untimed ACT: **Yes**
Documentation of LD required: **Yes**
Currency of diagnostic testing: **3 years**

Types of Disabilities Served
• Speech/Lang	• Reading	• ADD with LD
• Study skills	• Spelling	• ADD without LD
• Written express	• Math	• ADHD with LD
• Organizational	• Fine Motor	• ADHD without LD
• Perceptual		

Learning Disability Program
Program: Reinforces course work: **Yes**
Students mainstreamed **100** % of the day
Counseling: Individual: **Yes** Group Counseling: **Yes**

Faculty:
Faculty: **2** Full time: **1** Part time: **1**
Faculty advocate: **Yes** Meets with instructor: **As needed**

Diagnostic Testing

ADD	Personality	Perceptual skills	Spelling
ADHD	Organization	Fine motor skills	Reading
I.Q.	Handwriting	Spoken language	Study skills
Math	Social skills	Written language	

Tutoring:
Services rendered by:
•Graduates •Peers •Faculty •LD staff Teacher trainees

Tutorials

Grp.	Ind.	Tutorials	Grp.	Ind.	Tutorials
	•	Math skills		•	Word processing
•	•	Study skills	•	•	Time management
	•	Language arts	•	•	Learning strategies
	•	Written express		•	Organizational skills

Academic Accommodations

Curriculum	Study Aids	Exams
Priority registration	• Typist	• Oral
Math waiver	Reader	Untimed
• Foreign lang. waiver	• Notetaker	Take home
Course substitution	• Proof reader	• With proctor
In Class	• Text on tape	On computer
• Calculators	Early syllabus	• Extended time
• Tape recorder	Taped handouts	On tape
• Word processor		• Modified
Priority seating		Separate room

Graduation Requirements:
Course credits: **124** GPA: **2.0** Years to complete degree: **5** Language waiver: **Yes**

Program Strengths

Services are provided based on individual need as assessed through recent diagnostic information and a personal interview. As new needs are identified, services may be modified or developed to accommodate them.

General Information:

University of North Carolina:Wilmington is a 4 year public university. Urban campus of 650 acres is 123 miles from Raleigh. Accessible by air or bus. Ski areas are 4 hours from campus. Beaches are 5 miles from campus. 9 residential halls on campus. Housing is not guaranteed.40 % of students remain on campus for the weekends. 33 % of students join fraternities/sororities.

Accreditation:SACS

Expenses:

Tuition: In-state: Full year: $595.00 per semester. Part-time: Per credit:$135.00 (1-5 credits). Tuition: Out-of-state: Full year: $2,900.00 per semester . Part-time: Per credit:$700.00 (1-5 credits). Room and board: $1,600.00-$1,900.00 Cost of LD program:

Majors

• BUSINESS Accounting, Banking, Business Administration, Business Economics, Business Management, Finance, Management, Marketing • COMMUNICATIONS English, Speech • COMPUTER SCIENCE Computer Science • EDUCATION Elementary, Middle School, Physical, Special • HEALTH SCIENCES Environmental, Medical Technology, Nursing • HUMANITIES Philosophy, Religion • LANGUAGES French, Spanish • SCIENCES Biology, Chemistry, Geography, Geology, Marine Biology, Mathematics, Physics • SOCIAL SCIENCES Anthropology, Government/Political, History, Political Science, Psychology, Social Sciences, Sociology • VISUAL AND PERFORMING ARTS Fine Arts • VOCATIONAL Park/Recreation

Sports/Activities

• SPORTS RELATED Pep Band • SPORTS-INTERCOLLEGIATE Baseball (M), Basketball, Cross Country, Golf, Soccer (M), Softball (M), Swimming, Tennis, Volleyball (F) • SPORTS-INTRAMURAL Archery, Badminton, Baseball (M), Bowling, Cross Country, Golf, Ping-Pong, Soccer, Softball, Swimming, Tennis, Volleyball • STUDENT LIFE ACTIVITIES Academic Clubs, Choral, Concert Band, Dance, Drama Groups, Ethnic & Cultural Groups, Jazz Band, Magazine, Music Groups, Musical Theater, Newspaper, Political Groups, Radio/TV station, Religious Organization, Student Government, Symphony Orchestra, Yearbook

---

Most Selective	**North Carolina Program**

Wake Forest University
P.O. Box 7305
Winston-Salem, North Carolina 27109
(919) 759-5201

School Enrollment: **3,329** Male: **1,862** Female: **1,467**
LD Enrollment: **6** Male: **4** Female: **2**

Admissions Contact: **Mr. Rob Jackson, Asst. Dir. of Admissions**
LD Contact: **Sandra Chadwick, Director**
Name of Program: **Learning Assistance Program**
Address: **P.O. Box 7283**
Telephone:**(919) 759-5929**

Admissions

Application Information:
LD Students Applying: **10** Accepted: **4** Enrolled:**3**
Application deadline: **January 15th**
Applicant must apply **12** months in advance
Notified when: **April 1st**

Secondary School Information
Most Important Criteria For Admissions (1-strongest)

2 SAT/ACT	**3** Application	**1** School transcript
1 Class rank	**1** Course selection	**3** Personal statement
Interview	**3** Extra activities	**4** Psychoeducational
1 G.P.A.	Open admission	**5** Recommendations

Test Requirements:
Diagnostic testing waived: **Yes**
Untimed SAT: **Yes**
WAIS-R required: **Yes** Range accepted: **Normal +**
Documentation of LD required: **Yes**
Currency of diagnostic testing: **1 year**
Tests recommended: **Reading and Psychological tests to identify specific LD**

Types of Disabilities Served

• Speech/Lang	• Reading	• ADD with LD
• Study skills	• Spelling	• ADD without LD
• Written express	• Math	• ADHD with LD
• Organizational	• Fine Motor	• ADHD without LD
• Perceptual		

Learning Disability Program

Program: Reinforces course work: **Yes**
Students mainstreamed **100** % of the day
Time required or recommended in learning center: **Varies**
Services available for all students: **Yes**
Counseling: Individual: **Yes** Group Counseling: **Yes**

Faculty:
Faculty: **1** Including Director: **Yes** Full time: **1** M.A.: **1**
Faculty advocate: **Yes** Meets with instructor: **As necessary**

Diagnostic Testing
- ADD • Personality • Perceptual skills • Spelling
- ADHD • Organization • Fine motor skills • Reading
- I.Q. • Handwriting • Spoken language • Study skills
- Math • Social skills • Written language

Tutoring:
Average size of group tutorials: **3-4**
Services rendered by:
• Graduates   Peers   Faculty   • LD staff   Teacher trainees

Tutorials

Grp.	Ind.	Tutorials	Grp.	Ind.	Tutorials
	•	Math skills			Word processing
•	•	Study skills	•	•	Time management
	•	Language arts	•	•	Learning strategies
•	•	Written express	•	•	Organizational skills

Academic Accommodations

Curriculum	Study Aids	Exams
Priority registration	Typist	• Oral
Math waiver	Reader	Untimed
Foreign lang. waiver	• Notetaker	• Take home
Course substitution	• Proof reader	• With proctor
In Class	• Text on tape	On computer
• Calculators	Early syllabus	• Extended time
• Tape recorder	Taped handouts	On tape
• Word processor		• Modified
Priority seating		Separate room

Program Strengths

All students at Wake Forest may receive free services at the Learning Assistance Program including individual academic counseling in study skills, individual or group tutoring, and computer assisted instruction. Learning disabled students who are appropriately identified receive skill building support and assistance in arranging for course accommodations.

General Information:

Wake Forest University is a 4 year private Baptist university. Urban campus of 5,600 acres is 4 miles from Winston-Salem. Accessible by air or bus. Ski areas are 2 hours from campus. Beaches are 4 hours from campus. 2% of students are foreign. 12 residential halls on campus. Housing is guaranteed. 40 % of students join fraternities/sororities.

Accreditation: SACS

Expenses:
Tuition: In-state: Full year: $12,000.00.

Majors

• BUSINESS Accounting, Business Administration, Business Management, Economics, Management • COMMUNICATIONS Communication, English, Journalism, Speech • COMPUTER SCIENCE Computer Science • EDUCATION Art, Elementary, Middle School, Music, Secondary, Speech/Language • HEALTH SCIENCES Health, Medical Assistant, Med-ical Technology, Speech Therapy, Speech/Audiology and Speech • HUMANITIES Classics, Humanities, Philosophy, Religion • LANGUAGES French, German, Greek, Italian, Japanese, Latin, Russian, Spanish • SCIENCES Biology, Chemistry, Mathematics, Microbiology, Physics • SOCIAL SCIENCES Anthropology, Government/Political, History, Political Science, Psychology, Sociology • VISUAL AND PERFORMING ARTS Art, Art History, Dance, Dramatic Arts, Music, Studio Art

Sports/Activities

• SPORTS RELATED Marching Band, Pep Band • SPORTS-INTERCOLLEGIATE Baseball (M), Basketball, Cross Country, Field Hockey (F), Football (M), Golf, Soccer (M), Tennis, Track and Field • SPORTS-INTRAMURAL Basketball, Bowling, Cross Country, Diving, Golf, Hand Ball, Lacrosse (M), Ping-Pong, Racquetball, Rugby, Softball, Swimming, Tennis, Track and Field, Volleyball, Water Polo, Wrestling (M) • STUDENT LIFE ACTIVITIES Choral, Concert Band, Drama Groups, Ethnic & Cultural Groups, Film, Fraternities, Jazz Band, Magazine, Music Groups, Musical Theater, Newspaper, Political Groups, Radio/TV station, Religious Organization, Sororities, Student Government, Symphony Orchestra, Yearbook

---

Less Selective   **North Carolina**
Services

Wilkes Community College
P.O. Box 120
Wilkesboro, North Carolina 28697-0120
(919) 651-8642

School Enrollment: **1,950** Male: **758** Female: **1,192**
LD Enrollment: **25**

Admissions Contact: **Mac Warren, Director of Admissions**
LD Contact: **Barbara Holt, Ed.D., Director**
Name of Program: **Student Support Services**
Telephone: **(919) 651-8753**

Admissions

Application Information:
Application deadline: **None**
Rolling Admissions: **Yes**

Secondary School Information
Most Important Criteria For Admissions (1-strongest)

SAT/ACT	Application	School transcript
Class rank	Course selection	Personal statement
Interview	Extra activities	Psychoeducational
G.P.A.	**1** Open admission	Recommendations

Test Requirements:
Standardized tests waived: **Yes**
Diagnostic testing waived: **Yes**

Types of Disabilities Served
- Speech/Lang • Reading • ADD with LD
- Study skills • Spelling • ADD without LD
- Written express • Math • ADHD with LD
- Organizational • Fine Motor • ADHD without LD
- Perceptual

Learning Disability Program

Program: Remedial: **Yes**
Program: Reinforces course work: **Yes**
Students mainstreamed **100** % of the day
Counseling: Individual: **Yes** Vocational Counseling: **Yes**

Faculty:
Faculty: **2** Including Director: **Yes** Full time: **2** Part time: **12** M.A.: **1**
Ph.D.: **1**
Faculty advocate: **Yes** Meets with instructor: **As needed**

Diagnostic Testing
ADD • Personality • Perceptual skills • Spelling
ADHD• Organization• Fine motor skills • Reading
• I.Q. • Handwriting• Spoken language • Study skills
• Math • Social skills• Written language

Tutoring:
Average size of group tutorials: **3**
Services rendered by:
 Graduates •Peers •Faculty •LD staff Teacher trainees

Tutorials

Grp.	Ind.	Tutorials	Grp.	Ind.	Tutorials
•	•	Math skills	•	•	Word processing
•	•	Study skills	•	•	Time management
•	•	Language arts	•	•	Learning strategies
•	•	Written express	•	•	Organizational skills

Academic Accommodations

Curriculum	Study Aids	Exams
Priority registration	Typist	• Oral
Math waiver	• Reader	• Untimed
Foreign lang. waiver	• Notetaker	Take home
Course substitution	• Proof reader	• With proctor
In Class	• Text on tape	On computer
• Calculators	Early syllabus	• Extended time
• Tape recorder	Taped handouts	On tape
Word processor		• Modified
• Priority seating		• Separate room

Program Strengths

Our program is designed to be supportive for LD students, providing personal counseling, tutoring and advocacy with staff, faculty, and administration. We encourage our LD students to become self-advocates and help them develop skills necessary to do this.

General Information:

Wilkes Community College is a 2 year public college. Rural campus of 90 acres is 60 miles from Winston Salem. Accessible by air or bus. Ski areas are 1 hour from campus. Beaches are 6 miles from campus. 1% of students are foreign. Housing is not guaranteed.

Accreditation:SACS

Expenses:
Tuition: In-state: Full year: $270.00. Part-time: Per credit:$7.50 . Tuition: Out-of-state: Full year: $2,520.00. Part-time: Per credit:$70.00. Room and board: $3,600.00

Majors

• BUSINESS Accounting, Business Administration, Business Management, Food Management, Hotel and Restaurant Management, Management • COMMUNICATIONS Broadcasting, Television/Radio/Film • COMPUTER SCIENCE Programming • EDUCATION Art, Early Childhood • ENGINEERING Electromechanical Technology • HEALTH SCIENCES Nursing • HUMANITIES Liberal Arts • LANGUAGES • PREPROFES-SIONAL Social Work • SCIENCES Horticultural, Mathematics • SOCIAL SCIENCES Criminal Justice • VISUAL AND PERFORMING ARTS Art, Dramatic Arts, Fine Arts, Music, Theater • VOCATIONAL Business and Office, Construction, Culinary Arts, Diesel Power Technology, Electronics Technology, Secretarial

Sports/Activities

• SPORTS-INTERCOLLEGIATE Wrestling (M) • SPORTS-INTRAMURAL Archery, Badminton, Basketball, Ping-Pong, Softball, Tennis, Volleyball • STUDENT LIFE ACTIVITIES Choral, Concert Band, Drama Groups, Ethnic & Cultural Groups, Jazz Band, Magazine, Music Groups, Musical Theater, Newspaper, Religious Organization, Student Government, Symphony Orchestra, Yearbook

---

Less Selective　　　　　　　　**North Carolina Program**

Wingate College
Wingate, North Carolina 28174
(704) 233-8201-(800) 755-5550

School Enrollment: **1,364**
LD Enrollment: **35**

Admissions Contact: **Patricia LeDonne, Director of Admissions**
LD Contact: **Lucie Karnes, Ph.D.**
Name of Program: **Dyslexia/Specific LDs**

Admissions

Application Information:
LD Students Applying: **65** Accepted: **25** Enrolled:**18**
Application deadline: **March 15th**
Rolling Admissions: **Yes**

Secondary School Information
Most Important Criteria For Admissions (1-strongest)

3 SAT/ACT	1 Application	1 School transcript
4 Class rank	1 Course selection	6 Personal statement
5 Interview	7 Extra activities	2 Psychoeducational
4 G.P.A.	Open admission	5 Recommendations

Test Requirements:
Diagnostic testing waived: **Yes**
Untimed SAT: **Yes** Untimed ACT: **Yes**
WAIS-R required: **Yes** Range accepted: **100+**
Documentation of LD required: **Yes**
Tests recommended: **Psychological, WAIS, WRAT, SAT**

Types of Disabilities Served

Speech/Lang	Reading	ADD with LD
• Study skills	Spelling	ADD without LD
• Written express	Math	ADHD with LD
• Organizational	Fine Motor	ADHD without LD
Perceptual		

High School Course Requirements:
English: **4** Math: **2** Science: **2**

Learning Disability Program

Special orientation for LD students: **Yes**
Program: Reinforces course work: **Yes**
Students mainstreamed **100** % of the day
Services only for LD students: **Yes**
Counseling: Individual: **Yes**

Faculty:

Faculty: **3** Including Director: **Yes** Full time: **2** Part time: **1** Ph.D.: **1**
Faculty advocate: **Yes** Meets with instructor: **As needed**

Diagnostic Testing

ADD	Personality	Perceptual skills	•	Spelling
ADHD	Organization	Fine motor skills	•	Reading
• I.Q.	Handwriting	Spoken language		Study skills
• Math	Social skills	• Written language		

Tutoring:

Services rendered by:
•Graduates •Peers •Faculty •LD staff Teacher trainees

Tutorials

Grp.	Ind.	Tutorials	Grp.	Ind.	Tutorials
		Math skills	•	•	Word processing
•		Study skills	•		Time management
		Language arts			Learning strategies
•		Written express	•		Organizational skills

Academic Accommodations

Curriculum	Study Aids	Exams
Priority registration	Typist	• Oral
Math waiver	Reader	Untimed
• Foreign lang. waiver	Notetaker	Take home
Course substitution	Proof reader	• With proctor
In Class	Text on tape	On computer
Calculators	Early syllabus	• Extended time
• Tape recorder	Taped handouts	On tape
• Word processor		Modified
Priority seating		Separate room

Program Strengths

Small individualized support program. Careful admission policy. Regular program with modified schedules with excellent professor understanding.

General Information:

Wingate College is a 4 year private Southern Baptist Convention college. Suburban campus of 350 acres is 25 miles from Charlotte. Accessible by air, train, or bus. Ski areas are 2 hours from campus. Beaches are 2-1/2 hours from campus. 1% of students are foreign. 10 residential halls on campus. Housing is guaranteed.60 % of students remain on campus for the weekends.

Accreditation: SACS

SAT/ACT Scores:

Scores for incoming freshmen: **Verbal:** 65% below 500. 25% between 500 and 599. 10% between 600 and 699. **Math:** 60% below 500. 30% between 500 and 599. 10% between 600 and 699.

Class Rank:

About 23% of the present freshmen class were in the upper 20% of their high school class. 50% were in the top 40% of their class. 80% were in the top 60% of their class. 90% were in the top 80% of their class.

Expenses:

Tuition: In-state: Full year: $6,740.00 tuition and fees. Part-time: Per credit:0. Room and board: $3,050.00 Cost of LD program:$1,000.00 first year - $500.00 each year after first

Majors

• AREA STUDIES American • BUSINESS Accounting, Business Administration, Business Economics, Business Management, Economics, Entrepreneur, Management • COMMUNICATIONS Broadcasting, English, Journalism, Speech, Television/Radio/Film • COMPUTER SCIENCE Computer Science, Data Processing, Programming, Systems Analysis, Telecommunications • CRAFTS AND DESIGN Drawing • EDUCATION Art, Early Childhood, Elementary, English, Mathematics, Middle School, Music, Pre-Education, Reading, Science, Secondary, Social Science, Social Studies • HEALTH SCIENCES Health, Medical Assistant, Sports Medicine • HUMANITIES Humanities, Liberal Arts, Religion • LANGUAGES French, German, Spanish • PREPROFESSIONAL Law, Medicine, Pharmacy, Veterinarian • SCIENCES Biology, Chemistry, Mathematics • SOCIAL SCIENCES History, Human Service, Psychology, Social Sciences, Sociology • VOCATIONAL Business and Office, Painting, Park/Recreation

Sports/Activities

• SPORTS RELATED Marching Band, Pep Band • SPORTS-INTERCOLLEGIATE Baseball (M), Basketball, Football (M), Golf, Soccer (F), Soccer (M), Softball (F), Tennis, Volleyball (F) • SPORTS-INTRAMURAL Basketball, Bowling, Diving, Football, Ping-Pong, Racquetball, Softball (F), Swimming, Tennis, Volleyball, Water Polo • STUDENT LIFE ACTIVITIES Choral, Concert Band, Dance, Ethnic & Cultural Groups, Film, Jazz Band, Magazine, Music Groups, Newspaper, Political Groups, Radio/TV station, Religious Organization, Student Government, Yearbook

---

Less Selective **North Dakota**
Accommodations

Dickinson State University

Dickinson, North Dakota 58601
(701) 227-2175

School Enrollment: **1,440** Male: **599** Female: **841**

Admissions Contact: **Kevin Thompson, Admissions Counselor**
LD Contact: **Joyce White, Director of Counseling**
Telephone:**(701) 227-2686**

Admissions

Application Information:

Rolling Admissions: **Yes**

Secondary School Information

Most Important Criteria For Admissions (1-strongest)

SAT/ACT	Application	School transcript
Class rank	Course selection	Personal statement
Interview	Extra activities	Psychoeducational
G.P.A.	Open admission	Recommendations

Test Requirements:

Untimed SAT: **Yes** Untimed ACT: **Yes**
Documentation of LD required: **Yes**

Types of Disabilities Served

Speech/Lang	Reading	ADD with LD
Study skills	Spelling	ADD without LD
Written express	Math	ADHD with LD
Organizational	Fine Motor	ADHD without LD
Perceptual		

Admissions Process

Complete application form, pay $20.00 application fee, send in all previous transcripts, complete health record, and submit SAT or ACT test results.

Learning Disability Program

Program: Reinforces course work: **Yes**
Students mainstreamed **100** % of the day
Recommended credits per semester: **12**
Counseling: Individual: **Yes** Vocational Counseling: **Yes**
Support groups are available:**On request**

Diagnostic Testing

ADD	Personality	Perceptual skills	Spelling
ADHD	Organization	Fine motor skills	Reading
I.Q.	Handwriting	Spoken language	Study skills
Math	Social skills	Written language	

Tutoring:
Services rendered by:
Graduates •Peers Faculty LD staff Teacher trainees

Tutorials

Grp.	Ind.	Tutorials	Grp.	Ind.	Tutorials
		Math skills			Word processing
		Study skills			Time management
		Language arts			Learning strategies
		Written express			Organizational skills

Academic Accommodations

Curriculum	Study Aids	Exams
• Priority registration	Typist	• Oral
Math waiver	• Reader	Untimed
Foreign lang. waiver	• Notetaker	Take home
Course substitution	Proof reader	• With proctor
In Class	• Text on tape	• On computer
Calculators	• Early syllabus	• Extended time
• Tape recorder	Taped handouts	On tape
Word processor		Modified
Priority seating		• Separate room

General Information:

Dickinson State University is a 2 and 4 year University. Rural campus of 100 acres is 100 miles from Bismarck, ND. Accessible by bus. Ski areas are 220 miles from campus. Beaches are 1 mile from campus. 1% of students are foreign. 3 residential halls on campus. Housing is not guaranteed.1 % of students join fraternities/sororities.

Accreditation:NCACS

Expenses:

Tuition: In-state: Full year: $1,706.00 per year. Part-time: Per credit:$71.08. Tuition: Out-of-state: Full year: $4,256.00 per year. Part-time: Per credit:$177.33. Room and board: $1,850.00 per year

Majors

• AGRICULTURE Business • BUSINESS Accounting, Agricultural, Business Administration, Business Education, Business Management, Management • COMMUNICATIONS Communication, Speech • COMPUTER SCIENCE Computer Information Systems • EDUCATION Art, Business, Communication, Elementary, Foreign Language, Mathematics, Middle School, Music, Physical, Science, Secondary, Social Science, Speech, Theater • HEALTH SCIENCES Medical Secretary, Nursing • HUMANITIES Liberal/General • LANGUAGES Spanish • MATHEMATICS Mathematics • SCIENCES Behavioral, Biology, Chemistry, Earth, Environmental

Science, Physical Science • SOCIAL SCIENCES Government/Political, History, Political Science, Social Science • VISUAL AND PERFORMING ARTS Dramatic Arts, Music, Visual and Performing Arts • VOCATIONAL Business and Office, Legal Secretary, Office Administration, Secretarial

Sports/Activities

• SPORTS-INTERCOLLEGIATE Baseball (M), Basketball (F), Basketball (M), Cross Country (F), Cross Country (M), Football (M), Golf (M), Rodeo, Tennis (M), Track and Field (F), Track and Field (M), Volleyball (F), Wrestling (M) • STUDENT LIFE ACTIVITIES Academic Clubs, Choral, Community Service, Concert Band, Debate, Drama Groups, Ethnic & Cultural Groups, Film, Jazz Band, Magazine, Music Groups, Musical Theater, Newspaper, Political Groups, Religious Organization, Student Government, Yearbook

---

Less Selective   **North Dakota
                                    Accommodations**

Mayville State University

330 Third Street, Northeast
Mayville, North Dakota 58257
(701) 786-4873

School Enrollment: **785**

Admissions Contact: **Ron Brown, Director of Admissions**
LD Contact: **Deb Glennen, Coordinator**
Name of Program: **Learning Services**

Admissions

Secondary School Information

Most Important Criteria For Admissions (1-strongest)

SAT/ACT	Application	School transcript
Class rank	Course selection	Personal statement
Interview	Extra activities	Psychoeducational
G.P.A.	**1** Open admission	Recommendations

Test Requirements:
Untimed SAT: **Yes** Untimed ACT: **Yes** Untimed ACH: **Yes**

Types of Disabilities Served
• Speech/Lang.   • Reading   • ADD with LD
• Study skills   • Spelling   • ADD without LD
• Written express   • Math   • ADHD with LD
• Organizational   • Fine Motor   • ADHD without LD
• Perceptual

Learning Disability Program

Services available for all students: **Yes**

Faculty:
Faculty: **1** Full time: **1**

Diagnostic Testing

ADD	Personality	Perceptual skills	Spelling
ADHD	Organization	Fine motor skills	Reading
I.Q.	Handwriting	Spoken language	Study skills
Math	Social skills	Written language	

Tutoring:
Average size of group tutorials: **4**
Services rendered by:
Graduates •Peers •Faculty •LD staff Teacher trainees

North Dakota

Tutorials

Grp.	Ind.	Tutorials	Grp.	Ind.	Tutorials
•	•	Math skills	•	•	Word processing
•	•	Study skills	•	•	Time management
•	•	Language arts	•	•	Learning strategies
•	•	Written express	•	•	Organizational skills

Academic Accommodations

Curriculum	Study Aids	Exams
Priority registration	Typist	• Oral
Math waiver	Reader	Untimed
Foreign lang. waiver	• Notetaker	Take home
Course substitution	• Proof reader	• With proctor
In Class	Text on tape	On computer
• Calculators	Early syllabus	• Extended time
• Tape recorder	Taped handouts	On tape
• Word processor		Modified
Priority seating		Separate room

Program Strengths

Mayville State does not have a learning disabilities program but does have services that may assist a learning disabled student to successfully participate in higher education. These services include: advocacy, tutoring, learning lab with computer assisted instruction, and access to instructors due to the small instructor/student ratios.

General Information:

Mayville State University is a 4 year public university. Rural campus 38 miles from Grand Forks. Ski areas are 2 miles from campus. Beaches are 25 miles from campus. 3 residential halls on campus. Housing is not guaranteed. 30 % of students remain on campus for the weekends.

Accreditation: NCATE, NCC

Expenses:

Tuition: In-state: Full year: $1,530.00. Part-time: Per credit: $63.75. Tuition: Out-of-state: Full year: $4,080.00. Part-time: Per credit: $170.00. Room and board: $2,196.00.

Majors

• BUSINESS Accounting, Business Administration, Business Economics, Business Management, Economics, Management • COMMUNICATIONS Communication, English • COMPUTER SCIENCE Computer Science, Data Processing, Programming • EDUCATION Early Childhood, Elementary, English, Health, Mathematics, Music, Physical, Science, Secondary, Social Studies • LANGUAGES Spanish • PREPROFESSIONAL Law, Medicine • SCIENCES Biology, Chemistry, Mathematics, Physical Science

Sports/Activities

• SPORTS RELATED Pep Band • SPORTS-INTERCOLLEGIATE Baseball (M), Basketball, Football (M), Golf (M), Gymnastics (F), Softball (F), Track and Field, Volleyball (F), Wrestling (M) • SPORTS-INTRAMURAL Badminton, Basketball, Racquetball, Softball, Tennis, Volleyball • STUDENT LIFE ACTIVITIES Choral, Concert Band, Debate, Jazz Band, Music Groups, Musical Theater, Newspaper, Religious Organization, Student Government, Yearbook

---

Less Selective

North Dakota Services

North Dakota State College of Science
Wahpeton, North Dakota 58075
(701) 671-2201

School Enrollment: **2,360** Male: **1,560** Female: **800**
LD Enrollment: **78** Male: **64** Female: **14**

Admissions Contact: **Keath Borchert, Director of Admissions**
LD Contact: **Georgia Vosberg, Coordinator**
Name of Program: **Resource Program Handicapped**
Address: **Old Main**
Telephone: **(701) 671-2327**

Admissions

Application Information:
Enrolled: **78**
Application deadline: **None**
Rolling Admissions: **Yes**

Secondary School Information
Most Important Criteria For Admissions (1-strongest)

5 SAT/ACT	1 Application	3 School transcript
7 Class rank	2 Course selection	11 Personal statement
6 Interview	9 Extra activities	8 Psychoeducational
4 G.P.A.	Open admission	10 Recommendations

Test Requirements:
Standardized tests waived: **Yes**
Untimed SAT: **Yes** Untimed ACT: **Yes**
Range accepted:
Documentation of LD required: **Yes**
Currency of diagnostic testing: **As recent as possible**
Tests recommended: **Ability, Achievement, Diagnostic**

Types of Disabilities Served

• Speech/Lang	• Reading	• ADD with LD
• Study skills	• Spelling	• ADD without LD
• Written express	• Math	• ADHD with LD
• Organizational	• Fine Motor	• ADHD without LD
• Perceptual		

Admissions Process

$20.00 application fee and application form required. All programs are open enrollment except: Nursing, OTA, Dental Hygiene, Dental Assisting, Medical Records, John Deere Ag. Tech., Melroe Bobcat.

Learning Disability Program

Program: Remedial: **Yes**
Program: Reinforces course work: **Yes**
Students mainstreamed **100** % of the day
Recommended credits per semester: **varies**
Services available for all students: **Yes**
Counseling: Individual: **Yes** Group Counseling: **Yes** Vocational Counseling: **Yes**
Support groups are available: **Yes, A.A. Older than Average**

Faculty:

Faculty: **10** Including Director: **Yes** Full time: **5** Part time: **5**
LD faculty with: BS/BA: **7** M.A.: **1**
Faculty advocate: **Yes** Meets with instructor: **Upon request**

Diagnostic Testing

	ADD	• Personality •	Perceptual skills	• Spelling
	ADHD•	Organization	Fine motor skills	• Reading
•	I.Q.	Handwriting	Spoken language	• Study skills
•	Math	• Social skills•	Written language	

Tutoring:

Average size of group tutorials: **1:3**
Services rendered by:
  Graduates •Peers •Faculty •LD staff Teacher trainees

Tutorials

Grp.	Ind.	Tutorials	Grp.	Ind.	Tutorials
•	•	Math skills	•	•	Word processing
•	•	Study skills	•	•	Time management
•	•	Language arts	•	•	Learning strategies
•	•	Written express	•	•	Organizational skills

Academic Accommodations

Curriculum	Study Aids	Exams
Priority registration	• Typist	• Oral
Math waiver	• Reader	Untimed
Foreign lang. waiver	• Notetaker	Take home
• Course substitution	• Proof reader	• With proctor
In Class	• Text on tape	On computer
• Calculators	Early syllabus	Extended time
• Tape recorder	Taped handouts	• On tape
• Word processor		Modified
• Priority seating		• Separate room

Graduation Requirements:

Course credits: **96** GPA: **2.0** Years to complete degree: **Unlimited**
Other requirements: **Some programs require general education requirements**

Program Strengths

Students are interviewed by the Resource Program coordinator who assists the students with vocational plans, class schedule and modifications. Students report, as needed, for follow-up throughout each quarter. Students are referred to the Learning Skills Center for academic support: classes in reading, spelling, writing; tutorial help in content courses, summarized chapters, study guides, and support for content course study; study skills, organizational, learning strategies, and help for related individual needs; individual help in writing and math labs.

General Information:

North Dakota State College of Science is a 2 year public college. Rural campus of 125 acres is 45 miles from Fargo. Accessible by bus. Ski areas are 120 miles from campus. Beaches are 30 miles from campus. .01% of students are foreign. 9 residential halls on campus. Housing is not guaranteed.50 % of students remain on campus for the weekends.

Accreditation:NCACS

Expenses:

Tuition: In-state: Full year: $1,563.00. Tuition: Out-of-state: Full year: $3,987.00. Room and board: $2,130.00

Majors

• BUSINESS Accounting, Agricultural, Banking, Business Administration, Business Education, Business Management, Human Resources Manage-
ment, Insurance, Marketing, Real Estate, Secretarial Science • COMMUNICATIONS Communication • COMPUTER SCIENCE Computer Information Systems, Computer Science, Robotics • EDUCATION Pre-Education • ENGINEERING Architectural, Civil/Environmental, Drafting, Electrical, Mechanical Design • HEALTH SCIENCES Dental Assistant, Dental Hygiene, Health, Medical Secretary, Medical Secretary, nursing Nutritional/Food, Occupational Therapy Assistant, Practical Nursing • HUMANITIES Humanities, Liberal Arts • PREPROFESSIONAL Agriculture, Architecture, Chiropractic, Dentistry, Education, engineering Health, Industrial Arts, Law, Law Enforcement, Medical Technology, Medicine, Nursing, Optometry, Pharmacy, Range Management, recreation Wildlife Management • SCIENCES Computer Science, Natural Science, Pharmacy, Physical Science, Public Health, Wildlife Management • VISUAL AND PERFORMING ARTS Music • VOCATIONAL Air Conditioning/Heating/Refri, Auto Body, Automotive Technology, Chef Apprenticeship, Construction, Dental Assistant, Dental Hygiene, Diesel Power Technology, Drafting, Electronics Technology, Machine Tool Technology, Medical Records Technology, Plumbing, Secretarial, Sheet Metal, Surveying and Mapping, Welding

Sports/Activities

• SPORTS RELATED Marching Band • SPORTS-INTERCOLLEGIATE Basketball, Cross Country, Football (M), Volleyball, Wrestling • SPORTS-INTRAMURAL Badminton, Basketball, Bowling, Football, Flag, Golf, Ping-Pong, Racquetball, Softball, Volleyball, Weight Lifting • STUDENT LIFE ACTIVITIES Academic Clubs, Choir, Concert Band, Drama Groups, Newspaper, Religious Organization, Student Government, Yearbook

---

Selective **North Dakota Services**

North Dakota State University

Ceres Hall 212
Fargo, North Dakota 58105
(701) 237-8643-(800) 362-3145

School Enrollment: **8,842** Male: **5,372** Female: **3,470**
LD Enrollment: **59**

Admissions Contact: **Rich Shearer, Assoc. Dir. Admissions**
LD Contact: **Liz Sepe, LD Specialist**
Name of Program: **Learning Disabilities Program**
Address: **201 Old Main, Counseling Center**
Telephone:**(701) 237-7671**

Admissions

Application Information:

Enrolled:**59**
Application deadline: **None**
Rolling Admissions: **Yes**

Secondary School Information

Most Important Criteria For Admissions (1-strongest)

SAT/ACT	Application	1	School transcript
Class rank	1 Course selection		Personal statement
Interview	Extra activities		Psychoeducational
G.P.A.	Open admission		Recommendations

Test Requirements:

Diagnostic testing waived: **Yes**
Untimed SAT: **Yes** Untimed ACT: **Yes**
WAIS-R required: **Yes** Range accepted: **No specific**
Documentation of LD required: **Yes**
Currency of diagnostic testing: **No specific time**
Tests recommended: **WAIS-R, Woodcock-Johnson, any other LD**

North Dakota

testing

Types of Disabilities Served
- Speech/Lang
- Study skills
- Written express
- Organizational
- Perceptual
- Reading
- Spelling
- Math
- Fine Motor
- ADD with LD
- ADD without LD
- ADHD with LD
- ADHD without LD

High School Course Requirements:
English: **4** Math: **3** Science: **3**

Learning Disability Program
Special orientation for LD students: **Yes**
Program: Reinforces course work: **Yes**
Students mainstreamed **100** % of the day
Counseling: Individual: **Yes** Group Counseling: **Yes**

Faculty:
Faculty: **3** Including Director: **Yes** Full time: **1** Part time: **2**
LD faculty with: BS/BA: **1** M.A.: **2**
Faculty advocate: **Yes** Meets with instructor: **As needed**

Diagnostic Testing
ADD	Personality	• Perceptual skills	• Spelling
ADHD	Organization	Fine motor skills	• Reading
I.Q.	Handwriting	• Spoken language	• Study skills
• Math	Social skills	• Written language	

Tutoring:
Services rendered by:
Graduates •Peers •Faculty •LD staff Teacher trainees

Tutorials
Grp.	Ind.	Tutorials	Grp.	Ind.	Tutorials
	•	Math skills		•	Word processing
•		Study skills	•	•	Time management
	•	Language arts	•	•	Learning strategies
	•	Written express	•	•	Organizational skills

Academic Accommodations
Curriculum	Study Aids	Exams
Priority registration	• Typist	• Oral
Math waiver	Reader	Untimed
Foreign lang. waiver	• Notetaker	• Take home
Course substitution	• Proof reader	• With proctor
In Class	• Text on tape	On computer
• Calculators	Early syllabus	• Extended time
• Tape recorder	Taped handouts	On tape
• Word processor		• Modified
Priority seating		• Separate room

Program Strengths
We offer strong one-on-one sessions in learning strategies with certified LD instructors. We are located within a counseling center so in addition to courses on reading, study skills and career planning, we also offer courses in self-esteem, interpersonal relationships, assertiveness, etc.

General Information:
North Dakota State University is a 4 year public university. Suburban campus of 2,100 acres is 230 miles from Minneapolis/St. Paul. Accessible by air, train, or bus. Ski areas are 150 miles from campus. Beaches are 40 miles from campus. 4% of students are foreign. 12 residential halls on campus. Housing is guaranteed.Guaranteed through 1st year. 75 % of students remain on campus for the weekends. 5 % of students join fraternities/sorori-ties.

Accreditation:NCACS

SAT/ACT Scores:
Scores for incoming freshmen: **ACT:** 41% below 20. 25% between 20 and 23. 14%between 24 and 25l. 16%between 26 and 28. 5% above 28.

Expenses:
Tuition: In-state: Full year: $1,946.00. Part-time: Per credit:$64.89. Tuition: Out-of-state: Full year: $5,197.50. Part-time: Per credit:$173.25.
Room and board: $2,394.00

Majors
• BUSINESS Accounting, Agricultural, Business Administration, Business Management, Economics, Hotel and Restaurant Management, Human Resources Management • COMMUNICATIONS Communication, English, Speech • COMPUTER SCIENCE Computer Science, Programming, Software Engineer, Systems Analysis • EDUCATION Agricultural, Art, Early Childhood, English, Foreign Language, Home Economics Education, Mathematics, Music, Physical, Science, Speech/Language • ENGINEERING Agricultural, Civil/Environmental, Electrical, Mathematical, Petroleum, Physics • HEALTH SCIENCES Health, Medical Technology, Nursing, Nutritional/Food • HUMANITIES Humanities, Liberal Arts • LANGUAGES French, German, Spanish • PREPROFESSIONAL Agriculture, Architecture, Dentistry, Engineering, Law, Medicine, Pharmacy, Recreation • SCIENCES Agricultural, Agronomy, Animal, Bacteriology, Biochemistry, Biology, Biotechnology, Botany, Chemistry, Earth, Horticultural, Mathematics, Microbiology, Physics, Plant Pathology, Soil, Zoology • SOCIAL SCIENCES Government/Political, History, Human Service, Psychology, Social Sciences • VISUAL AND PERFORMING ARTS Art, Dramatic Arts, Fine Arts, Music • VOCATIONAL Fashion Merchandising, Food Service, Home Economics, Interior Design, Landscape Architecture, Respiratory Therapy Technology, Textile and Clothing, Veterinarian Assistant

Sports/Activities
• SPORTS RELATED Marching Band • SPORTS-INTERCOLLEGIATE Baseball (M), Basketball, Cross Country, Diving, Football (M), Golf, Riflery, Softball (F), Swimming, Tennis • SPORTS-INTRAMURAL Archery, Badminton, Basketball, Cross Country, Golf, Ice Hockey (M), Racquetball, Soccer, Swimming, Tennis, Track and Field, Water Polo, Wrestling (M) • STUDENT LIFE ACTIVITIES chorale Concert Band, Drama Groups, Film, Jazz Band, Music Groups, Newspaper, Opera, Political Groups, Radio/TV station, Religious Organization, Sororities, Student Government

---

Selective　　　　　　　　　　**North Dakota**
　　　　　　　　　　　　　　　　　　Program

North Dakota State University: Bottineau
Bottineau, North Dakota 58318
(701) 228-2277

School Enrollment: **470** Male: **250** Female: **220**

Admissions Contact: **Dr. Ken Grosz, Registrar**
LD Contact: **Faye Bernstein, Cord. Student Support Services**
Name of Program: **Special Services**
Address: **Student Opportunity Office**
Telephone:**Ext. 279**

Admissions

Application Information:
Application deadline: **Start of school**

Secondary School Information
Most Important Criteria For Admissions (1-strongest)
3	SAT/ACT	1 Application	4 School transcript
6	Class rank	2 Course selection	9 Personal statement
10	Interview	7 Extra activities	8 Psychoeducational
5	G.P.A.	Open admission	11 Recommendations

Test Requirements:
Standardized tests waived: **Yes**

Types of Disabilities Served
Speech/Lang	Reading	ADD with LD
Study skills	Spelling	ADD without LD
Written express	Math	ADHD with LD
Organizational	Fine Motor	ADHD without LD
Perceptual		

Faculty:

Diagnostic Testing
ADD	Personality	Perceptual skills	Spelling
ADHD	Organization	Fine motor skills	• Reading
I.Q.	Handwriting	Spoken language	Study skills
• Math	Social skills	• Written language	

Tutoring:
Average size of group tutorials: **3**
Services rendered by:
Graduates •Peers Faculty •LD staff Teacher trainees

Tutorials
Grp.	Ind.	Tutorials	Grp.	Ind.	Tutorials
	•	Math skills		•	Word processing
•	•	Study skills	•	•	Time management
•	•	Language arts	•	•	Learning strategies
	•	Written express	•	•	Organizational skills

Academic Accommodations
Curriculum	Study Aids	Exams
Priority registration	• Typist	• Oral
Math waiver	• Reader	Untimed
Foreign lang. waiver	• Notetaker	Take home
Course substitution	• Proof reader	With proctor
In Class	• Text on tape	On computer
• Calculators	Early syllabus	• Extended time
• Tape recorder	Taped handouts	On tape
• Word processor		Modified
Priority seating		Separate room

Program Strengths
Three instructors with bachelor's degree are available to tutor students in math, science, English and reading, Student tutors are available to tutor other subjects such as accounting. Our program offers two one-credit courses which help students adjust to their regular class: reading improvement and study skills. The college also offers a developmental English class, and basic writing skills. Additional staff: Learning Disabilities Instruction, Computer Instructor, Orientation Counselor.

General Information:
North Dakota State University: Bottineau is a 2 year public university. Rural campus 80 miles from Minot. Accessible by air, train or bus. Ski areas are 12 miles from campus. Housing is not guaranteed.

Accreditation: NCACS

Expenses:
Tuition: In-state: Full year: $1,500.00. Tuition: Out-of-state: Full year: $3,100.00.

Majors
• ARTS Drafting, Drawing, Landscaping, Music, Painting • BUSINESS Accounting, Agricultural, Bookkeeping, Business Administration, Business Management, Clerical, Data Processing, Education, Entrepreneur, Fashion Merchandising, Management, Marketing, Secretarial, Travel/Tourism Management, Vocational • COMMUNICATIONS English, Literature • COMPUTER SCIENCE Business Data Programming, Data Processing, Programming • EDUCATION Adult, Agricultural, Business, Elementary, English, Mathematics, Music, Physical, Science, Secondary, Social Studies, Vocational • HEALTH SCIENCES Environmental, Medical Laboratory Technology, Pharmacology • HUMANITIES English As A Second Language, Humanities, Liberal Arts • MATHEMATICS Applied, Statistical • PREPROFESSIONAL Agriculture, Fisheries, Forestry, Law, Legal Assistant, Pharmacy, Range Management, Wildlife • SCIENCES Agricultural, Anatomy, Animal, Applied Mathematics, Biochemistry, Biology, Botany, Cell Biology, Chemistry, Ecology, Entomology, General, Genetics, Geography, Horticultural, Inorganic Chemistry, Macrobiology, Mathematics, Microbiology, Organic Chemistry, Physics, Physiology, Plant Pathology, Soil, Zoology • SOCIAL SCIENCES Geography, Government/Political, History, Psychology, Social Sciences, Sociology • SPECIAL EDUCATION Learning Disability • VISUAL AND PERFORMING ARTS Dramatic Arts, Music, Music Performance, Theater • VOCATIONAL Business and Office, Fashion Merchandising, Fishery Studies, Forestry, Medical Laboratory Technology, Office Administration, Park/Recreation, Secretarial, Word Processing

Sports/Activities
• SPORTS RELATED Pep Band • SPORTS-INTERCOLLEGIATE Baseball (M), Basketball, Ice Hockey (M), Volleyball (F) • SPORTS-INTRAMURAL Archery, Basketball, Bowling, Football, Ice Hockey (M), Skiing - Cross Country, Skiing - Snow, Soccer, Softball, Volleyball • STUDENT LIFE ACTIVITIES Choral, Concert Band, Drama Groups, Musical Theater, Student Government

Selective — **Ohio Services**

Bowling Green State University
705 Administration Building
Bowling Green, Ohio 43403
(419) 372-8495

School Enrollment: **12,700** Male: **5,500** Female: **7,200**
LD Enrollment: **66**
LD Contact: **Rob Cunningham, Director Handicapped Services**
Name of Program: **Handicapped Services**
Address: **705 Administration Building**
Telephone: **(419) 372-8495**

Admissions

Application Information:
Application deadline: **February**

Secondary School Information
Most Important Criteria For Admissions (1-strongest)
1	SAT/ACT	5 Application	3 School transcript
4	Class rank	7 Course selection	8 Personal statement
10	Interview	6 Extra activities	Psychoeducational
2	G.P.A.	Open admission	9 Recommendations

Ohio

Test Requirements:
Untimed SAT: **Yes** Untimed ACT: **Yes** Untimed ACH: **Yes**
Documentation of LD required: **Yes**

Types of Disabilities Served
- Speech/Lang
- Study skills
- Written express
- Organizational
- Perceptual
- Reading
- Spelling
- Math
- Fine Motor
- ADD with LD
- ADD without LD
- ADHD with LD
- ADHD without LD

High School Course Requirements:
English: **4** Math: **3** Science: **3** Foreign Language: **2**

Learning Disability Program
Students mainstreamed **100** % of the day
Recommended credits per semester: **12-14**
Services available for all students: **Yes**
Counseling: Individual: **Yes** Group Counseling: **Yes** Vocational Counseling: **Yes**

Faculty:
Faculty: **1** Full time: **1** M.A.: **1**
Meets with instructor: **As needed**

Diagnostic Testing
ADD	Personality	Perceptual skills	Spelling
ADHD	Organization	Fine motor skills	Reading
I.Q.	Handwriting	Spoken language	Study skills
Math	Social skills	Written language	

Tutoring:
Average size of group tutorials: **5-10**
Services rendered by:
Graduates   Peers   •Faculty   LD staff   Teacher trainees

Tutorials
Grp.	Ind.	Tutorials	Grp.	Ind.	Tutorials
•	•	Math skills	•	•	Word processing
•	•	Study skills	•	•	Time management
•	•	Language arts	•	•	Learning strategies
•	•	Written express	•	•	Organizational skills

Academic Accommodations
Curriculum	Study Aids	Exams
• Priority registration	Typist	• Oral
Math waiver	• Reader	Untimed
Foreign lang. waiver	Notetaker	Take home
Course substitution	Proof reader	• With proctor
In Class	• Text on tape	On computer
• Calculators	Early syllabus	• Extended time
• Tape recorder	Taped handouts	On tape
• Word processor		• Modified
Priority seating		• Separate room

Graduation Requirements:
Course credits: **122** GPA: **2.0**

Program Strengths
LD students are provided with basic, reasonable accommodations as required by law.

General Information:
Bowling Green State University is a 4 year public university. Suburban campus 20 miles from Toledo. Accessible by bus. Ski areas are 50 miles from campus. 5% of students are foreign. 10 residential halls on campus.

Housing is guaranteed.70 % of students remain on campus for the weekends. 35 % of students join fraternities/sororities.

Accreditation: Regional

Expenses:
Tuition: In-state: Full year: $2,900.00. Tuition: Out-of-state: Full year: $6,200.00. Room and board: $2,500.00

Majors
• AREA STUDIES American, Asian, Black/Afro-American, Ethnic, Latin American, Russian/Slavic, Women's Studies • BUSINESS Accounting, Banking, Business Administration, Business Economics, Business Education, Business Management, Economics, Finance, Hotel and Restaurant Management, Human Resources Management, Insurance, Labor Relations, Management, Manufacturing Technology, Marketing, Marketing Research, Sports Management, Statistics • COMMUNICATIONS Advertising, Communication, Creative Writing, English, Journalism, Television/Radio/Film • COMPUTER SCIENCE Computer Science, Data Processing, Medical Records Technology, Systems Analysis, Telecommunications • CRAFTS AND DESIGN Ceramics, Glass, Graphic Design, Illustration Design, Sculpture • EDUCATION Art, Child Development, Curriculum, Early Childhood, Elementary, English, Foreign Language, Health, Home Economics, Industrial, Mathematics, Middle School, Music, Psychology, Recreation and Youth Leadership, Science, Secondary, Special, Speech/Language • ENGINEERING Aerospace, Civil/Environmental, Environmental/Water Resources • HEALTH SCIENCES Communication Disorders, Environmental, Health, Medical Technology, Nursing, Nutritional/Food, Physical Therapy, Speech/Audiology and Speech • HUMANITIES Classics, English/Writing/Literature, Humanities, Liberal Arts, Philosophy • LANGUAGES Chinese, French, German, Japanese, Latin, Russian, Spanish • PREPROFESSIONAL Architecture, Dentistry, Engineering, Law, Medicine, Pharmacy, Range Management, Social Work, Veterinarian • SCIENCES Astronomy, Bacteriology, Biology, Botany, Chemistry, Earth, Entomology, Geochemistry, Geography, Geology, Geophysics, Gerontology, Health, Mathematics, Microbiology, Paleontology, Parasitology, Physical Chemistry, Physical Science, Physics, Physiology, Statistics • SOCIAL SCIENCES Criminal Justice, Family Counseling, Government/Political, History, Law Enforcement, Political Science, Psychology, Public Relations, Social Sciences, Sociology • VISUAL AND PERFORMING ARTS Art, Art History, Dance, Fine Arts, Jazz, Music, Music Performance, Religious Music, Theater • VOCATIONAL Business and Office, Drafting, Electromechanical Technology, Electronics Technology, Fashion Design, Fashion Merchandising, Food Service, Home Economics, Industrial Technology, Jewelry-Metalsmithery, Painting, Park/Recreation, Secretarial, Textile and Clothing

Sports/Activities
• SPORTS RELATED Marching Band, Pep Band • SPORTS-INTERCOLLEGIATE Baseball (M), Basketball, Cross Country, Football (M), Golf, Gymnastics (F), Ice Hockey (M), Soccer (M), Softball (F), Swimming, Tennis, Track and Field, Volleyball (F) • SPORTS-INTRAMURAL Basketball, Bowling, Golf (M), Racquetball, Soccer, Softball, Swimming (M), Tennis, Track and Field, Volleyball, Water Polo (F), Wrestling (M) • STUDENT LIFE ACTIVITIES Choral, Community Service, Concert Band, Dance, Drama Groups, Jazz Band, Music Groups, Musical Theater, Newspaper, Opera, Radio/TV station, Sororities, Student Government, Symphony Orchestra, Yearbook

Highly Selective   **Ohio**
      Services

Case Western Reserve University
10900 Euclid Avenue
Cleveland, Ohio 44106
(216) 368-4450

School Enrollment: **4,869** Male: **1,900** Female: **2,969**

Admissions Contact: **William T. Conley, Dean of Admissions**
LD Contact: **Mayo Bulloch, Director**
Name of Program: **Educational Support Services**
Address: **4 Yost Hall**
Telephone:**(216) 368-5230**

Admissions

Application Information:
Application deadline: **March 1st**
Notified when: **April 1st**

Secondary School Information
Most Important Criteria For Admissions (1-strongest)

6 SAT/ACT	**7** Application	**4**	School transcript
3 Class rank	**1** Course selection	**8**	Personal statement
Interview	Extra activities		Psychoeducational
5 G.P.A.	Open admission	**2**	Recommendations

Test Requirements:
Untimed SAT: **Yes** Untimed ACT: **Yes** Untimed ACH: **Yes**
Documentation of LD required: **Yes**

Types of Disabilities Served
- Speech/Lang
- Study skills
- Written express
- Organizational
- Perceptual
- Reading
- Spelling
- Math
- Fine Motor

ADD with LD
ADD without LD
ADHD with LD
ADHD without LD

Admissions Process

LD students must meet criteria for admission though grade deficits and standardized test scores are given wider latitude

High School Course Requirements:
English: **4** Math: **3** Science: **3** Foreign Language: **2**
Waivers to standard high school courses
Foreign Language : **Yes** Course substitution: **Yes**

Learning Disability Program
Services available for all students: **Yes**
Counseling: Individual: **Yes**

Faculty:
Faculty: **4** Full time: **4** M.A.: **4**
Faculty advocate: **Yes** Meets with instructor: **As needed**

Diagnostic Testing

ADD	Personality	Perceptual skills	Spelling
ADHD	Organization	Fine motor skills	• Reading
I.Q.	Handwriting	Spoken language	• Study skills
• Math	Social skills	• Written language	

Tutoring:
Average size of group tutorials: **6**
Services rendered by:
•Graduates   •Peers   Faculty   •LD staff   Teacher trainees

Tutorials

Grp.	Ind.	Tutorials	Grp.	Ind.	Tutorials
•	•	Math skills			Word processing
•	•	Study skills	•	•	Time management
		Language arts	•		Learning strategies
•		Written express	•		Organizational skills

Academic Accommodations

Curriculum	Study Aids	Exams
Priority registration	Typist	• Oral
Math waiver	Reader	• Untimed
• Foreign lang. waiver	• Notetaker	• Take home
• Course substitution	Proof reader	With proctor
In Class	• Text on tape	• On computer
• Calculators	Early syllabus	• Extended time
• Tape recorder	Taped handouts	On tape
• Word processor		• Modified
Priority seating		• Separate room

Graduation Requirements:
Course credits: **120** GPA: **2.0** Math waiver: **Yes** Language waiver: **Yes**

Program Strengths

Educational Support Services is a department that provides academic support (i.e. tutoring, reading and study skills improvement, advising, and special services) to all students. LD students are seen individually, and their needs are assessed to make appropriate accommodations.

General Information:

Case Western Reserve University is a 4 year private university. Urban campus of 128 acres is 4 miles from Cleveland. Accessible by air, train or bus. 11% of students are foreign. 18 residential halls on campus. Housing is guaranteed.85 % of students remain on campus for the weekends. 30 % of students join fraternities/sororities.

Accreditation:NCACS

SAT/ACT Scores:
Scores for incoming freshmen:**Verbal:**32%below 500. 40%between 500 and 599. 24%between 600 and 699. 4%above 700. **Math:**5% below 500. 25% between 500 and 599. 44% between 600 and 699. 26%above 700. 19% between 20 and 23. 12%between 24 and 25l. 69%between 26 and 28.

Class Rank:
About 88% of the present freshmen class were in the upper 20% of their high school class. 98% were in the top 40% of their class. 99% were in the top 60% of their class. 100% were in the top 80% of their class.

Expenses:
Tuition: In-state: Full year: $13,600.00. Part-time: Per credit:$567.00. Room and board: $4,620.00

Majors
• AREA STUDIES American, Asian • BUSINESS Accounting, Business Administration, Business Management, Economics, Finance, Management • COMMUNICATIONS Communication, English, Literature • COMPUTER SCIENCE Computer Science, Hardware Engineer • EDUCATION Art, Foreign Language, Mathematics, Music, Music Therapy, Secondary, Social Studies • ENGINEERING Aerospace, Bio-medical, Bioengineering, Chemical, Civil/Environmental, Computer, Electrical, Engineering Science, Industrial, Materials, Mechanical, Metallurgical • HEALTH SCIENCES Communication Disorders, Medical Technology, Nursing,

Nutritional/Food, Speech/Audiology and Speech • HUMANITIES Classics, English/Writing/Literature, Humanities, Philosophy, Religion • LANGUAGES French • PREPROFESSIONAL Architecture, Social Work • SCIENCES Astronomy, Bio-medical, Biochemistry, Biology, Chemistry, Earth, Geology, Gerontology, Mathematics, Physical Science, Physics, Polymer Science, Statistics • SOCIAL SCIENCES Anthropology, Government/Political, History, Political Science, Psychology, Public Relations, Social Sciences, Sociology • VOCATIONAL Medical Laboratory Technology

Sports/Activities

• SPORTS RELATED Marching Band, Pep Band • SPORTS-INTERCOLLEGIATE Archery, Baseball (M), Basketball, Cross Country, Diving, Fencing, Football (M), Golf (M), Ice Hockey (M), Lacrosse (M), Soccer, Swimming, Tennis, Track and Field, Volleyball (F), Water Polo (M), Wrestling (M) • SPORTS-INTRAMURAL Badminton, Basketball, Bowling, Cross Country, Golf, Ping-Pong, Racquetball, Riflery, Skiing - Snow, Soccer, Softball, Squash, Swimming, Tennis, Track and Field, Volleyball, Water Polo, Wrestling (M) • STUDENT LIFE ACTIVITIES Choral, Community Service, Concert Band, Dance, Drama Groups, Ethnic & Cultural Groups, Film, Fraternities, Jazz Band, Magazine, Music Groups, Newspaper, Political Groups, Radio/TV station, Religious Organization, Sororities, Student Government, Symphony Orchestra, Yearbook

Very Selective	Ohio
	Accommodations

Cedarville College
P.O. Box 601
Cedarville, Ohio 45314-0601
(513) 766-2211

School Enrollment: **2,046** Male: **888** Female: **1,158**

Admissions Contact: **Roscoe Smith, Assoc. Director Admissions**
LD Contact: **Dr. Pamela Diehl, Coordinator, Academic Programs**
Name of Program: **Academic Development Program**

Admissions

Application Information:
LD on admissions committee:**Yes**
Application deadline: **Rolling**
Applicant must apply **6-12** months in advance
Rolling Admissions: **Yes**Notified when: **Rolling**

Secondary School Information
Most Important Criteria For Admissions (1-strongest)

5 SAT/ACT	**2** Application	**4** School transcript
6 Class rank	**8** Course selection	**1** Personal statement
9 Interview	**11** Extra activities	**10** Psychoeducational
3 G.P.A.	Open admission	**7** Recommendations

Test Requirements:
Untimed SAT: **Yes** Untimed ACT: **Yes**
WAIS-R required: **Yes**

Types of Disabilities Served

Speech/Lang	Reading	ADD with LD
Study skills	Spelling	ADD without LD
Written express	Math	ADHD with LD
Organizational	Fine Motor	ADHD without LD
Perceptual		

High School Course Requirements:
English: **4** Math: **3** Science: **3** Foreign Language: **2**
Waivers to standard high school courses
Foreign Language : **Yes** Math: **Yes**

Learning Disability Program
Students mainstreamed **100** % of the day
Services available for all students: **Yes**

Diagnostic Testing

ADD	Personality	Perceptual skills	Spelling
ADHD	Organization	Fine motor skills	Reading
I.Q.	Handwriting	Spoken language	Study skills
Math	Social skills	Written language	

Services rendered by:

Graduates	Peers	Faculty	LD staff	Teacher trainees

Tutorials

Grp.	Ind.	Tutorials	Grp.	Ind.	Tutorials
		Math skills			Word processing
		Study skills			Time management
		Language arts			Learning strategies
		Written express			Organizational skills

Academic Accommodations

Curriculum	Study Aids	Exams
Priority registration	Typist	Oral
Math waiver	Reader	Untimed
Foreign lang. waiver	Notetaker	Take home
Course substitution	Proof reader	With proctor
In Class	Text on tape	On computer
Calculators	Early syllabus	Extended time
Tape recorder	Taped handouts	On tape
Word processor		Modified
Priority seating		Separate room

Graduation Requirements:
Course credits: **192** GPA: **2.0**

Program Strengths
We do not offer a formal program. We do evaluate LD applicants on an individual basis to determine if we can meet their needs. We do provide academic advising, testing, limited tutoring, and study skills development.

General Information:
Cedarville College is a 4 year private Baptist college. Rural campus of 100 acres is 20 miles from Dayton. Accessible by air or bus. Ski areas are 1 hour from campus. 1% of students are foreign. 13 residential halls on campus. Housing is guaranteed.Guaranteed through 4th year. 80 % of students remain on campus for the weekends.

Accreditation:NCACS

SAT/ACT Scores:
Scores for incoming freshmen:**Verbal:**55%below 500. 33%between 500 and 599. 10%between 600 and 699. 2%above 700. **Math:**41% below 500. 35% between 500 and 599. 20% between 600 and 699. 4%above 700. **ACT:** 17% below 20. 34% between 20 and 23. 16%between 24 and 251. 19%between 26 and 28. 14% above 28.

Class Rank:
About 45% of the present freshmen class were in the upper 20% of their high school class. 71% were in the top 40% of their class. 88% were in the top 60% of their class. 97% were in the top 80% of their class.

Expenses:
Tuition: In-state: Full year: $5,712.00. Part-time: Per credit:$119.00. Tuition: Out-of-state: Full year: $5,712.00. Part-time: Per credit:$119.00.
Room and board: $3,579.00

Majors

• AREA STUDIES American • BUSINESS Accounting, Banking/Finance, Business Education, International Business, Management, Marketing, Secretarial Science • COMMUNICATIONS Broadcasting, Communication, English, Speech/Debate/Forensic, Television/Radio/Film • COMPUTER SCIENCE Computer Information Systems • EDUCATION Business, Early Childhood, Elementary, English, English As A Second Language, Foreign Language, Mathematics, Music, Physical, Science, Secondary, Social Studies, Speech/Language • ENGINEERING Electrical, Mechanical • HEALTH SCIENCES Medical Laboratory Technology, Nursing • HUMANITIES English/Writing/Literature, Religion • MATHEMATICS Theoretical • PREPROFESSIONAL Agriculture, Engineering, Law, Medicine, Ministry, Optometry, Pharmacy • RELIGIOUS STUDIES Bible, Religious Music • SCIENCES Biology, Chemistry, Mathematics • SOCIAL SCIENCES Criminal Justice, History, International Studies, Political Science, Psychology, Social Sciences, Sociology • VISUAL AND PERFORMING ARTS Music, Music Performance • VOCATIONAL Medical Laboratory Technology, Office Administration, Secretarial

Sports/Activities

• SPORTS RELATED Pep Band, Team Managers • SPORTS-INTERCOLLEGIATE Baseball (M), Basketball, Cross Country, Golf (M), Soccer (M), Softball (F), Tennis, Track and Field, Volleyball (F) • SPORTS-INTRAMURAL Badminton, Basketball, Bowling, Cycling, Football, Flag Football, Golf, Ping-Pong, Racquetball, Skiing - Snow, Soccer, Softball, Tennis, Volleyball • STUDENT LIFE ACTIVITIES Academic Clubs, Choral, Community Service, Concert Band, Debate, Drama Groups, Ethnic & Cultural Groups, Music Groups, Newspaper, Orchestra, Political Groups, Radio/TV station, Religious Organization, Student Government, Symphony Orchestra, Yearbook

---

Less Selective **Ohio**
Program

Central Ohio Technical College
University Drive
Newark, Ohio 43055
(614) 366-9222

School Enrollment: **2,400** Male: **880** Female: **1,600**
LD Enrollment: **25**

Admissions Contact: **John Merrin, Admissions Coordinator**
LD Contact: **Lisa Williams, LD Specialist**
Name of Program: **Developmental Education**
Telephone:**(614) 366-9246**

Admissions

Application Information:
Applicant must apply **1** months in advance
Rolling Admissions: **Yes**

Secondary School Information
Most Important Criteria For Admissions (1-strongest)

SAT/ACT	Application	School transcript
Class rank	Course selection	Personal statement
Interview	Extra activities **1**	Psychoeducational
G.P.A.	Open admission	Recommendations

Test Requirements:
Standardized tests waived: **Yes**
Diagnostic testing waived: **Yes**
Untimed SAT: **Yes** Untimed ACT: **Yes**
WAIS-R required: **Yes** Range accepted: **90+**
Documentation of LD required: **Yes**
Tests recommended: **Woodcock -Johnson**

Types of Disabilities Served
• Speech/Lang	• Reading	• ADD with LD
• Study skills	• Spelling	• ADD without LD
• Written express	• Math	ADHD with LD
• Organizational	• Fine Motor	ADHD without LD
• Perceptual		

Learning Disability Program
Program: Reinforces course work: **Yes**
Students mainstreamed **100** % of the day
Recommended credits per semester: **varies**
Counseling: Individual: **Yes**

Faculty:
Faculty: **3** Including Director: **Yes** Full time: **1** Part time: **2** M.A.: **2** Ph.D.: **1**

Diagnostic Testing
ADD	Personality •	Perceptual skills	• Spelling
ADHD	Organization•	Fine motor skills	• Reading
• I.Q.	• Handwriting	Spoken language	• Study skills
• Math	Social skills •	Written language	

Tutoring:
Average size of group tutorials: **2-3**
Services rendered by:
Graduates •Peers •Faculty •LD staff Teacher trainees

Tutorials
Grp.	Ind. Tutorials	Grp.	Ind. Tutorials
•	• Math skills		• Word processing
	• Study skills		• Time management
	• Language arts		• Learning strategies
	• Written express		• Organizational skills

Academic Accommodations

Curriculum	Study Aids	Exams
Priority registration	• Typist	• Oral
Math waiver	• Reader	Untimed
Foreign lang. waiver	• Notetaker	Take home
• Course substitution	• Proof reader	• With proctor
In Class	• Text on tape	On computer
• Calculators	Early syllabus	• Extended time
• Tape recorder	Taped handouts	On tape
• Word processor		• Modified
• Priority seating		Separate room

Program Strengths
Our role is to provide advocacy and accommodations. All students receive support services as needed, thus LD students are not isolated.

General Information:
Central Ohio Technical College is a 2 year public college. Rural campus of 10 acres is 40 miles from Columbus. 1% of students are foreign. 1 residential halls on campus. Housing is not guaranteed.39 % of students remain on campus for the weekends.

Ohio

Accreditation: NCACS

Expenses:
Tuition: In-state: Full year: $1,600.00. Part-time: Per credit:$43.00. Tuition: Out-of-state: Full year: $2,200.00. Part-time: Per credit:$62.00.

Majors

• BUSINESS Accounting, Business Administration, Business Management, Management, Real Estate • COMPUTER SCIENCE Data Processing, Programming • ENGINEERING Electrical, Industrial, Mechanical • HEALTH SCIENCES Nursing, Physical Therapy Assistant, Radiological Therapy, Ultrasound Technology • SOCIAL SCIENCES Criminal Justice, Law Enforcement • VOCATIONAL Drafting, Electronics Technology, Radiological Technology, Secretarial

Sports/Activities

• SPORTS-INTERCOLLEGIATE Baseball (M), Basketball, Golf, Soccer (M), Tennis • SPORTS-INTRAMURAL Basketball, Bowling, Golf, Ping-Pong, Racquetball, Skiing - Snow, Softball, Tennis, Volleyball • STUDENT LIFE ACTIVITIES Choral, Drama Groups, Newspaper, Student Government

---

Less Selective   **Ohio**
                                                       Services

Cleveland State University

Room 205A - Corlett Building 1935 Euclid Avenue
Cleveland, Ohio 44115
(216) 687-3755

School Enrollment: **18,000** Male: **9,000** Female: **9,000**
LD Enrollment: **40** Male: **23** Female: **17**

Admissions Contact: **Linda Frank, Asst. Dir. Admissions**
LD Contact: **Michael Zuccaro, Coordinator**
Name of Program: **Handicapped Services**
Telephone:**(216) 687-2015**

Admissions

Application Information:
Application deadline: **April 1st**
Rolling Admissions: **Yes** Notified when: **June 1st**

Secondary School Information
Most Important Criteria For Admissions (1-strongest)

2 SAT/ACT	Application	**1**	School transcript
Class rank	Course selection		Personal statement
Interview	Extra activities		Psychoeducational
G.P.A.	Open admission		Recommendations

Test Requirements:
Diagnostic testing waived: **Yes**
Untimed SAT: **Yes** Untimed ACT: **Yes**
Currency of diagnostic testing: **6 months**

Types of Disabilities Served
• Speech/Lang • Reading • ADD with LD
• Study skills • Spelling • ADD without LD
• Written express • Math • ADHD with LD
• Organizational • Fine Motor • ADHD without LD
• Perceptual

High School Course Requirements:
Waivers to standard high school courses
Foreign Language : **Yes** Math: **Yes** Course substitution: **Yes**

Learning Disability Program
Counseling: Individual: **Yes** Group Counseling: **Yes**

Faculty:
Faculty: **5** Full time: **2** Part time: **3**
Faculty advocate: **Yes** Meets with instructor: **As needed**

Diagnostic Testing
ADD	Personality	Perceptual skills	Spelling
ADHD	Organization	Fine motor skills	Reading
I.Q.	Handwriting	Spoken language	Study skills
Math	Social skills	Written language	

Tutoring:
Services rendered by:
•Graduates •Peers •Faculty LD staff •Teacher trainees

Tutorials
Grp.	Ind.	Tutorials	Grp.	Ind.	Tutorials
•	•	Math skills			Word processing
	•	Study skills	•		Time management
•	•	Language arts			Learning strategies
•	•	Written express	•	•	Organizational skills

Academic Accommodations

Curriculum	Study Aids	Exams
Priority registration	• Typist	• Oral
• Math waiver	Reader	Untimed
• Foreign lang. waiver	• Notetaker	Take home
Course substitution	• Proof reader	With proctor
In Class	• Text on tape	On computer
• Calculators	Early syllabus	• Extended time
• Tape recorder	Taped handouts	On tape
• Word processor		• Modified
Priority seating		Separate room

Program Strengths
We attempt to mainstream LD students into the university. I feel we work best with self-motivated students and most with social/behavioral problems. Our emphasis is academic.

General Information:
Cleveland State University is a 4 year public college. Urban campus of 10 acres is Accessible by air, train, or bus. Ski areas are 10 miles from campus. Beaches are 5 miles from campus. 10% of students are foreign. Housing is not guaranteed.2 % of students remain on campus for the weekends. 1 % of students join fraternities/sororities.

Accreditation: NCACS

Expenses:
Tuition: In-state: Full year: $2,550.00. Part-time: Per credit:$71.00. Tuition: Out-of-state: Full year: $4,100.00. Part-time: Per credit:$142.00. Room and board: $3,300.00

Majors

• AREA STUDIES Black/Afro-American, Urban • BUSINESS Accounting, Banking, Business Administration, Business Economics, Business Education, Business Management, Economics, Finance, Labor Relations, Management, Marketing, Personnel • COMMUNICATIONS Advertising, Broadcasting, Communication, English, Linguistic, Television/Radio/Film • COMPUTER SCIENCE Computer Science, Systems Analysis • EDUCATION Art, Curriculum, Early Childhood, Elementary, Health, Music,

Music Therapy, Physical, Pre -Education, Secondary, Special, Speech/Language, Vocational • ENGINEERING Chemical, Civil/Environmental, Electrical, Industrial, Mechanical • HEALTH SCIENCES Medical Technology, Nursing, Occupational Therapy, Physical Therapy, Speech Therapy, Speech/Audiology and Speech • HUMANITIES Classics, Humanities, Philosophy, Religion • LANGUAGES French, German, Italian, Latin, Spanish • PREPROFESSIONAL Dentistry, Law, Medicine, Recreation, Social Work • SCIENCES Biochemistry, Biology, Chemistry, Geology, Mathematics, Microbiology, Physics, Physiology • SOCIAL SCIENCES Anthropology, Criminal Justice, Government/Political, History, Law Enforcement, Political Science, Psychology, Social Sciences, Sociology • VISUAL AND PERFORMING ARTS Art, Art History, Dance, Dramatic Arts, Music, Music Theatre, Studio Art, Theater • VOCATIONAL Electronics Technology, Medical Laboratory Technology

Sports/Activities

• SPORTS RELATED Pep Band • SPORTS-INTERCOLLEGIATE Baseball (M), Basketball, Cross Country, Diving, Fencing, Golf (M), Soccer (M), Softball (F), Swimming, Tennis, Track and Field, Volleyball (F), Wrestling (M) • SPORTS-INTRAMURAL Badminton, Basketball, Bowling, Cross Country, Fencing, Field Hockey, Golf, Hammer Throw, Ping-Pong, Racquetball, Soccer, Softball, Swimming, Tennis, Track and Field, Volleyball, Water Polo, Wrestling (M) • STUDENT LIFE ACTIVITIES Choral, Drama Groups, Ethnic & Cultural Groups, Fraternities, Jazz Band, Magazine, Music Groups, Newspaper, opera, Radio/TV station, Religious Organization, Sororities, Student Government, Symphony Orchestra

Selective   **Ohio Program**

College of Mount St. Joseph
5701 Delhi Road
Cincinnati, Ohio 45233-1670
(513) 244-4531

School Enrollment: **237**

Admissions Contact: **Edward C. Eckel, Director of Admissions**
LD Contact: **Dollie Kelly, Director**
Name of Program: **Project EXCEL**
Telephone:**(513) 244-4623**

Admissions

Application Information:
Accepted: **50**
Separate application:**Yes**
Application deadline: **Rolling**
Applicant must apply **12** months in advance
Rolling Admissions: **Yes**

Secondary School Information
Most Important Criteria For Admissions (1-strongest)
3 SAT/ACT **8** Application **5** School transcript
4 Class rank **1** Course selection **10** Personal statement
6 Interview **9** Extra activities **11** Psychoeducational
2 G.P.A.   Open admission **7** Recommendations

Test Requirements:
Diagnostic testing waived: **Yes**
Untimed SAT: **Yes** Untimed ACT: **Yes**
WAIS-R required: **Yes**
Documentation of LD required: **Yes**
Tests recommended: **On campus testing by EXCEL staff**

Types of Disabilities Served
• Speech/Lang • Reading • ADD with LD
• Study skills • Spelling ADD without LD
• Written express • Math • ADHD with LD
• Organizational Fine Motor ADHD without LD
Perceptual

Admissions Process

Special admissions process which includes review of psycho-educational evaluation and other pertinent data by placement committee.

High School Course Requirements:
English: **4** Math: **2** Science: **1**

Learning Disability Program
Program: Remedial: **Yes**
Program: Reinforces course work: **Yes**
Students mainstreamed **100** % of the day
Time required or recommended in learning center: **10 hours**
Services only for LD students: **Yes**
Counseling: Individual: **Yes** Group Counseling: **Yes**
Support groups are available:**Student Support Groups**

Faculty:
Faculty: **9** Including Director: **Yes** Full time: **3** Part time: **6**
LD faculty with: BS/BA: **4** M.A.: **4**
Faculty advocate: **Yes** Meets with instructor: **When necessary**

Diagnostic Testing
ADD • Personality • Perceptual skills • Spelling
ADHD Organization• Fine motor skills • Reading
• I.Q. • Handwriting• Spoken language Study skills
• Math Social skills • Written language

Tutoring:
Average size of group tutorials: **3-5**
Services rendered by:
Graduates Peers Faculty •LD staff Teacher trainees

Tutorials

Grp.	Ind.	Tutorials	Grp.	Ind.	Tutorials
•	•	Math skills		•	Word processing
•	•	Study skills	•	•	Time management
		Language arts	•	•	Learning strategies
	•	Written express	•		Organizational skills

Academic Accommodations

Curriculum	Study Aids	Exams
Priority registration	• Typist	• Oral
Math waiver	Reader	• Untimed
• Foreign lang. waiver	• Notetaker	Take home
Course substitution	• Proof reader	• With proctor
In Class	• Text on tape	• On computer
• Calculators	Early syllabus	• Extended time
• Tape recorder	Taped handouts	On tape
• Word processor		• Modified
Priority seating		• Separate room

Graduation Requirements: Math waiver: **Yes** Language waiver: **Yes**

Program Strengths
Project EXCEL is a highly structured support program which provides services for LD students enrolled in a regular academic pro-

gram. Support services available include the following: a learning lab; instruction in study skills and written expression; tutorial assistance; accommodated testing; taped texts; and a student support group. In addition, the program director acts as a full-time advisor and counselor, coordinating services to meet the needs of each student.

General Information:
College of Mount St. Joseph is a 4 year private Roman Catholic college. Suburban campus of 72 acres is 5 miles from Cincinnati. Ski areas are 30 miles from campus. 3% of students are foreign. 1 residential halls on campus. Housing is guaranteed.

Accreditation:NCACS

SAT/ACT Scores:
Scores for incoming freshmen:**Verbal:**80%below 500. 18%between 500 and 599. 2%between 600 and 699. **Math:**62% below 500. 31% between 500 and 599. 7% between 600 and 699. **ACT:** 61% below 20. 26% between 20 and 23. 12%between 24 and 25l. 1%between 26 and 28.

Class Rank:
About 36% of the present freshmen class were in the upper 20% of their high school class. 69% were in the top 40% of their class. 83% were in the top 60% of their class. 89% were in the top 80% of their class.

Expenses:
Tuition: In-state: Full year: $8,170.00. Part-time: Per credit:$213.00. Room and board: $3,810.00 Cost of LD program:$900.00 per semester

Majors
• BUSINESS Accounting, Business Administration, Business Management, Food Management, Management • COMMUNICATIONS Communication, English, Graphic Design • COMPUTER SCIENCE Computer Science • EDUCATION Art, Early Childhood, Elementary, Health, Music, Music Therapy, Physical, Pre-Education, Religion, Secondary, Special • HEALTH SCIENCES Medical Technology, Nursing, Nutritional/Food • HUMANITIES Humanities, Liberal Arts, Religion, Religious Studies • PREPROFESSIONAL Dentistry, Law, Legal Assistant, Medicine, Optometry, Pharmacy, Podiatry, Social Work • SCIENCES Biology, Chemistry, Gerontology, Natural • SOCIAL SCIENCES History, Human Service, Sociology • VISUAL AND PERFORMING ARTS Fine Arts, Music • VOCATIONAL Interior Design, Medical Laboratory Technology, Paralegal

Sports/Activities
• SPORTS-INTERCOLLEGIATE Baseball (F), Football (M), Softball (F), Volleyball (F) • SPORTS-INTRAMURAL Badminton, Basketball, Ping-Pong, Soccer, Softball, Swimming, Tennis, Volleyball • STUDENT LIFE ACTIVITIES Choral, Community Service, Concert Band, Ethnic & Cultural Groups, Jazz Band, Music Groups, Newspaper, Student Government, Yearbook

Columbus State Community College
550 East Spring Street
Columbus, Ohio 43215
(614) 227-2459

School Enrollment: **15,209** Male: **6,506** Female: **8,703**
LD Enrollment: **211** Male: **123** Female: **88**

Admissions Contact: **Mary Jo Deerwester, Director of Admissions**
LD Contact: **Linda Wetters, Director**
Name of Program: **Handicapped Student Services**
Telephone:**(614) 227-2570**

Admissions

Application Information:
Application deadline: **Open Admissions**

Secondary School Information
Most Important Criteria For Admissions (1-strongest)

SAT/ACT	Application	School transcript
Class rank	Course selection	Personal statement
Interview	Extra activities	Psychoeducational
G.P.A.	**1** Open admission	Recommendations

Test Requirements:
Documentation of LD required: **Yes**

Types of Disabilities Served
• Speech/Lang	• Reading	• ADD with LD
• Study skills	• Spelling	• ADD without LD
• Written express	• Math	• ADHD with LD
• Organizational	• Fine Motor	• ADHD without LD
• Perceptual		

Admissions Process

Open admission

Learning Disability Program
Special orientation for LD students: **Yes**
Program: Remedial: **Yes**
Program: Reinforces course work: **Yes**
Program available through:**As requested**
Students mainstreamed **100** % of the day
Recommended credits per semester: **varies**
Counseling: Individual: **Yes** Vocational Counseling: **Yes**
Support groups are available:**LD Support Group-student managed support group**

Faculty:
Faculty: **5** Including Director: **Yes** Full time: **4** Part time: **1**
LD faculty with: BS/BA: **4** M.A.: **1**
Faculty advocate: **Yes** Meets with instructor: **As needed**

Diagnostic Testing
ADD	Personality	Perceptual skills	Spelling
ADHD	Organization	Fine motor skills	• Reading
• I.Q.	Handwriting	Spoken language	Study skills
• Math	Social skills	• Written language	

Tutoring:
Services rendered by:
  Graduates •Peers •Faculty •LD staff Teacher trainees

Tutorials
Grp.	Ind.	Tutorials	Grp.	Ind.	Tutorials
	•	Math skills		•	Word processing
	•	Study skills		•	Time management
	•	Language arts		•	Learning strategies
	•	Written express		•	Organizational skills

Academic Accommodations

Curriculum	Study Aids	Exams
• Priority registration	• Typist	• Oral
Math waiver	• Reader	Untimed
Foreign lang. waiver	• Notetaker	• Take home
• Course substitution	• Proof reader	• With proctor
In Class	• Text on tape	• On computer
• Calculators	Early syllabus	• Extended time
• Tape recorder	Taped handouts	• On tape
• Word processor		• Modified
Priority seating		• Separate room

Graduation Requirements:
Course credits: **Varies by program** GPA: **2.0** Years to complete degree: **2 or more** Math waiver: **Yes** Language waiver: **Yes**

Program Strengths
A wide variety of services are available through Handicapped Student Services for students with documented disabilities. Specific services are recommended for each student with a disability based upon the individualized assessment results. LD services include: academic counseling, private testing room, access to tutors, access to test readers, access to scribes, and access to tape recorded textbooks through a national organization.

General Information:
Columbus State Community College is a 2 year public college. Urban campus of 50 acres is Accessible by air or bus. Ski areas are 100 from campus. Beaches are 600 from campus. .3% of students are foreign. Housing is not guaranteed.

Accreditation:NCACS

SAT/ACT Scores:
Scores for incoming freshmen: **ACT**: 76% below 20. 18% between 20 and 23. 3%between 24 and 251. 2%between 26 and 28.

Class Rank:
About 12% of the present freshmen class were in the upper 20% of their high school class. 33% were in the top 40% of their class. 58% were in the top 60% of their class. 82% were in the top 80% of their class.

Expenses:
Tuition: In-state: Full year: $2,208.00. Part-time: Per credit:$49.00. Tuition: Out-of-state: Full year: $4,800.00. Part-time: Per credit:$100.00.

Majors
• BUSINESS Accounting, Banking, Business Administration, Business Management, Finance, Hotel and Restaurant Management, Manufacturing Technology, Marketing, Marketing Research, Personnel, Real Estate, Retailing, Secretarial Science, Travel/Tourism Management • COMMUNICATIONS Graphic Design • COMPUTER SCIENCE Computer Science, Computer Technology, Data Processing, Programming • CRAFTS AND DESIGN Glass • EDUCATION Child Development, Early Childhood • ENGINEERING Bio-medical, Civil/Environmental, Electrical, Engineering Science, Mechanical • HEALTH SCIENCES Dental Technician, Dietary Manager, Medical Secretary, Medical Technology, Mental Health,

Nursing • PREPROFESSIONAL Architecture, Optometry, Social Work, Veterinarian • SCIENCES Animal, Bio-medical, Gerontology • SOCIAL SCIENCES Criminal Justice, Family Counseling, Law Enforcement • VOCATIONAL Air Conditioning/Heating/Refri, Automated Manufacturing Technology, Automobile Technology, Aviation Maintenance, Business and Office, Chef Apprenticeship, Construction, Dental Lab Technology, Drafting, Electronics Technology, Fashion Design, Fashion Merchandising, Fire Science, Food Service, Legal Secretary, Mechanical Design Technology, Paralegal, Printing/Lithography, Respiratory Therapy Technology, Secretarial

Sports/Activities
• SPORTS-INTERCOLLEGIATE Baseball (M), Basketball (M)
• SPORTS-INTRAMURAL Basketball, Bowling, Golf, Ping-Pong, Softball, Tennis, Volleyball • STUDENT LIFE ACTIVITIES Ethnic & Cultural Groups, Jazz Band, Newspaper, Student Government

---

Less Selective　　　　　　　　　**Ohio**
Accommodations

Cuyahoga Community College
Western Campus 11000 Pleasant Valley Road
Parma, Ohio 44130
(216) 842-7773

Admissions Contact: **Dr. Sharon Akridge, Director of Admissions**
Name of Program: **Student Support Services**
Address: **11000 Pleasant Valley Road**
Telephone:**(216) 987-5078**

Admissions

Application Information:
Applicant must apply **2** months in advance
Rolling Admissions: **Yes**

Secondary School Information
Most Important Criteria For Admissions (1-strongest)
SAT/ACT	Application	School transcript
Class rank	Course selection	Personal statement
Interview	Extra activities	Psychoeducational
G.P.A.	Open admission	Recommendations

Test Requirements:
Diagnostic testing waived: **Yes**
Documentation of LD required: **Yes**

Types of Disabilities Served
Speech/Lang	Reading	ADD with LD
Study skills	Spelling	ADD without LD
Written express	Math	ADHD with LD
Organizational	Fine Motor	ADHD without LD
Perceptual		

Learning Disability Program
Program: Reinforces course work: **Yes**
Students mainstreamed **100** % of the day
Recommended credits per semester: **varies**
Counseling: Individual: **Yes** Vocational Counseling: **Yes**
Support groups are available:**at one campus (West)**

Faculty:
Faculty: **8** Full time: **8**
LD faculty with: BS/BA: **1** M.A.: **5**

583

Ohio

Diagnostic Testing

ADD	Personality	Perceptual skills	Spelling
ADHD	Organization	Fine motor skills	Reading
I.Q.	Handwriting	Spoken language	Study skills
Math	Social skills	Written language	

Services rendered by:
Graduates   Peers   Faculty   LD staff   Teacher trainees

Tutorials

Grp.	Ind.	Tutorials	Grp.	Ind.	Tutorials
	•	Math skills		•	Word processing
	•	Study skills		•	Time management
	•	Language arts		•	Learning strategies
	•	Written express		•	Organizational skills

Academic Accommodations

Curriculum	Study Aids	Exams
Priority registration	Typist	Oral
Math waiver	• Reader	Untimed
Foreign lang. waiver	• Notetaker	• Take home
• Course substitution	Proof reader	• With proctor
In Class	• Text on tape	• On computer
• Calculators	Early syllabus	• Extended time
• Tape recorder	• Taped handouts	• On tape
Word processor		• Modified
• Priority seating		• Separate room

Graduation Requirements: Math waiver: **Yes** Language waiver: **Yes**

General Information:

Cuyahoga Community College is a 2 year public college. Housing is not guaranteed.

Accreditation: Regional

Expenses:

Tuition: In-state: Full year: In county $450.00 - out of county $596.25. Part-time: Per credit: In county $30.00 - out of county $39.75. Tuition: Out-of-state: Full year: $1,192.50. Part-time: Per credit: $79.50.

Majors

• BUSINESS Accounting, Finance, Marketing and Distribution, Real Estate, Small Business Management, Small Business Ownership • COMPUTER SCIENCE Computer & Information Science • EDUCATION Early Childhood • HEALTH SCIENCES Nursing, Physician's Assistant, Respiratory Therapy Technology, Surgical Technology, Ultrasound Technology • SOCIAL SCIENCES Court Reporting, Law Enforcement • VOCATIONAL Automotive Technology, Graphic & Printing Production, Legal Assistant, Office Supervision and Management, Radiograph Medical Technology, Secretarial, Veterinarian Assistant, Word Processing

Sports/Activities

• SPORTS-INTERCOLLEGIATE Baseball (M), Basketball, Bowling, Golf, Wrestling (M)

Defiance College
701 North Clinton Street
Defiance, Ohio 43512-1695
(419) 784-4010

School Enrollment: **1,001** Male: **445** Female: **556**
LD Enrollment: **3** Male: **1** Female: **2**

Admissions Contact: **Penny D. Bell, Director of Admissions**
LD Contact: **Penny D. Bell, Dean of Enrollment Management**

Admissions

Application Information:
Application deadline: **August 1st**
Rolling Admissions: **Yes**

Secondary School Information
Most Important Criteria For Admissions (1-strongest)

4	SAT/ACT	6	Application	1	School transcript
5	Class rank	3	Course selection		Personal statement
8	Interview	7	Extra activities		Psychoeducational
2	G.P.A.		Open admission	9	Recommendations

Test Requirements:
Untimed SAT: **Yes** Untimed ACT: **Yes**

Types of Disabilities Served

• Speech/Lang	• Reading	ADD with LD
• Study skills	• Spelling	ADD without LD
• Written express	• Math	ADHD with LD
• Organizational	• Fine Motor	ADHD without LD
• Perceptual		

Admissions Process

Transcript and student history is evaluated by Admission Committee plus faculty member who directs The Learning Center. We have virtually no LD support services, however a limited number of students have succeeded here due to personal attention and self-motivation.

Learning Disability Program

Time required or recommended in learning center: **5 hours**
Services available for all students: **Yes**
Counseling: Individual: **Yes**

Faculty:
Faculty: **2** Full time: **1** Part time: **1**
Faculty advocate: **Yes** Meets with instructor: **As needed**

Diagnostic Testing

ADD	Personality	Perceptual skills	Spelling
ADHD	Organization	Fine motor skills	• Reading
I.Q.	Handwriting	Spoken language	• Study skills
Math	Social skills	Written language	

Tutoring:
Services rendered by:

Graduates •Peers •Faculty LD staff Teacher trainees

Tutorials

Grp.	Ind.	Tutorials		Grp.	Ind.	Tutorials
•	•	Math skills				Word processing
•	•	Study skills			•	Time management
		Language arts			•	Learning strategies
	•	Written express			•	Organizational skills

Academic Accommodations

Curriculum	Study Aids	Exams
Priority registration	Typist	Oral
Math waiver	Reader	Untimed
Foreign lang. waiver	Notetaker	Take home
Course substitution	Proof reader	With proctor
In Class	Text on tape	On computer
Calculators	Early syllabus	Extended time
• Tape recorder	Taped handouts	On tape
Word processor		Modified
Priority seating		Separate room

Graduation Requirements:
Course credits: **120** GPA: **2.0**

Program Strengths
We do not offer an LD program, but we do work with LD students if admitted.

General Information:
Defiance College is a 4 year private United Church of Christ college. Rural campus of 150 acres is 55 miles from Toledo. Accessible by air, train, or bus. 2% of students are foreign. 2 residential halls on campus. Housing is guaranteed. 40 % of students remain on campus for the weekends. 15 % of students join fraternities/sororities.

Accreditation: NCACS, CSWE

SAT/ACT Scores:
Scores for incoming freshmen: **Verbal:** 83% below 500. 14% between 500 and 599. **Math:** 75% below 500. 19% between 500 and 599. 6% between 600 and 699. **ACT:** 48% below 20. 35% between 20 and 23. 7% between 24 and 25l. 8% between 26 and 28. 2% above 28.

Class Rank:
About 19% of the present freshmen class were in the upper 20% of their high school class. 31% were in the top 40% of their class. 21% were in the top 60% of their class. 21% were in the top 80% of their class.

Expenses:
Tuition: In-state: Full year: $9,385.00. Part-time: Per credit: $170.00. Tuition: Out-of-state: Full year: $9,385.00. Part-time: Per credit: $170.00. Room and board: $3,425.00.

Majors
• BUSINESS Accounting, Business Administration, Business Education, Business Management, Finance, Marketing, Marketing Research, Sports Management • COMMUNICATIONS Advertising, Broadcasting, English, Journalism • COMPUTER SCIENCE Computer Science • EDUCATION Art, Elementary, English, Health, Mathematics, Middle School, Music, Physical, Reading, Recreation and Youth Leadership, Religious Education, Science, Secondary, Social Studies, Special, Speech/Language, Technical • HEALTH SCIENCES Fitness, Medical Technology • HUMANITIES English/Writing/Literature, Humanities, Liberal Arts, Philosophy, Religion • PREPROFESSIONAL Dentistry, Engineering, Law, Medicine, Ministry, Social Work, Veterinarian • SCIENCES Biology, Chemistry, Earth, Ecology, Environmental Science, Mathematics, Physical Science, Physics • SOCIAL SCIENCES Criminal Justice, History, International Studies, Psychology, Public Relations, Social Sciences • VISUAL AND PER-

FORMING ARTS Art, Fine Arts, Music

Sports/Activities
• SPORTS-INTERCOLLEGIATE Baseball (M), Basketball, Cross Country, Football (M), Golf (M), Soccer (M), Softball (F), Track and Field, Volleyball (F) • SPORTS-INTRAMURAL Badminton, Basketball, Bowling, Cross Country, Ping-Pong, Racquetball, Softball, Tennis, Volleyball • STUDENT LIFE ACTIVITIES Choral, Drama Groups, Fraternities, Magazine, Musical Theater, Newspaper, Religious Organization, Sororities, Student Government, Yearbook

---

Less Selective   **Ohio**
                                                Services

Edison State Community College
1973 Edison Drive
Piqua, Ohio 45356
(513) 778-8600

School Enrollment: **3,600** Male: **1,200** Female: **2,400**
LD Enrollment: **8** Male: **4** Female: **4**

Admissions Contact: **Dr. Dotty Muir, Asoc. Dean Stu. Development**
LD Contact: **Linda Verceles, Coordinator**
Name of Program: **Special Needs**

Admissions

Application Information:
Application deadline: **Saturday before classes begin**

Secondary School Information
Most Important Criteria For Admissions (1-strongest)

SAT/ACT	Application	School transcript
Class rank	Course selection	Personal statement
Interview	Extra activities	Psychoeducational
G.P.A.	**1** Open admission	Recommendations

Test Requirements:
Documentation of LD required: **Yes**
Tests recommended: **Asset Test**

Types of Disabilities Served
• Speech/Lang	• Reading	• ADD with LD
• Study skills	• Spelling	• ADD without LD
• Written express	• Math	• ADHD with LD
• Organizational	• Fine Motor	• ADHD without LD
• Perceptual		

Learning Disability Program
Students mainstreamed **100 %** of the day
Recommended credits per semester: **12**
Counseling: Individual: **Yes**

Faculty:
Faculty: **1** Full time: **1**

Diagnostic Testing
ADD	Personality	Perceptual skills	Spelling
ADHD	Organization	Fine motor skills	Reading
I.Q.	Handwriting	Spoken language	Study skills
Math	Social skills	Written language	

Ohio

Tutoring:
Average size of group tutorials: **2-10**
Services rendered by:
  Graduates •Peers   •Faculty   •LD staff   Teacher trainees

Tutorials

Grp.	Ind.	Tutorials	Grp.	Ind.	Tutorials
•	•	Math skills	•	•	Word processing
•	•	Study skills	•	•	Time management
•	•	Language arts	•	•	Learning strategies
•	•	Written express	•	•	Organizational skills

Academic Accommodations

Curriculum	Study Aids	Exams
Priority registration	Typist	• Oral
Math waiver	• Reader	• Untimed
Foreign lang. waiver	• Notetaker	Take home
Course substitution	• Proof reader	• With proctor
In Class	• Text on tape	On computer
• Calculators	Early syllabus	• Extended time
• Tape recorder	Taped handouts	• On tape
• Word processor		Modified
• Priority seating		• Separate room

Graduation Requirements:
Course credits: **90**

Program Strengths
We are a small college, and students get individual attention.

General Information:
Edison State Community College is a 2 year public college. Rural campus 2 miles from Piqua. 1% of students are foreign. Housing is not guaranteed.

Accreditation: NCACS

Expenses:
Tuition: In-state: Full year: $561.00 - 16 hours. Part-time: Per credit:$37.40. Tuition: Out-of-state: Full year: $1,091.00 - 16 hours. Part-time: Per credit:$69.40 .

Majors
• BUSINESS Accounting, Banking, Business Management, Finance, Marketing, Real Estate • COMMUNICATIONS English • COMPUTER SCIENCE Computer Technology, Data Processing • CRAFTS AND DESIGN Graphic Design • EDUCATION Early Childhood Development, Education • ENGINEERING Civil/Environmental, Engineering Science • HEALTH SCIENCES Nursing • HUMANITIES Humanities, Liberal Arts • PRE-PROFESSIONAL Architecture, Engineering, Legal Assistant • SCIENCES Agricultural, Biology, Mathematics, Physical Science • SOCIAL SCIENCES Criminal Justice, Law Enforcement, Psychology, Social Sciences • VISUAL AND PERFORMING ARTS Fine Arts • VOCATIONAL Business and Office, Drafting, Electronics Technology, Industrial Technology, Legal Secretary

Sports/Activities
• SPORTS-INTERCOLLEGIATE Baseball (M), Basketball (M), Golf, Softball (F)

Franklin University
201 South Grant Avenue
Columbus, Ohio 43215-5399
(614) 224-6237

School Enrollment: **4,000** Male: **1,920** Female: **2,080**
LD Enrollment: **25** Male: **15** Female: **10**

Admissions Contact: **Linda Steele, Director**
LD Contact: **Linda Turley, Assistant Director**
Name of Program: **Disability Services**
Telephone:**(614) 341-6415**

Admissions

Application Information:
Application deadline: **None**

Secondary School Information
Most Important Criteria For Admissions (1-strongest)

SAT/ACT	Application	School transcript
Class rank	Course selection	Personal statement
Interview	Extra activities	Psychoeducational
G.P.A.	**1** Open admission	Recommendations

Types of Disabilities Served
• Speech/Lang	• Reading	• ADD with LD
• Study skills	• Spelling	• ADD without LD
• Written express	• Math	• ADHD with LD
• Organizational	• Fine Motor	• ADHD without LD
• Perceptual		

Learning Disability Program
Counseling: Individual: **Yes**

Faculty:
Faculty: **1** Full time: **1**
Faculty advocate: **Yes** Meets with instructor: **As needed**

Diagnostic Testing
ADD	Personality	Perceptual skills	Spelling
ADHD	Organization	Fine motor skills	Reading
I.Q.	Handwriting	Spoken language	Study skills
Math	Social skills	Written language	

Tutoring:
Services rendered by:
  Graduates •Peers   •Faculty   LD staff   Teacher trainees

Tutorials

Grp.	Ind.	Tutorials	Grp.	Ind.	Tutorials
•		Math skills			Word processing
		Study skills			Time management
•	•	Language arts			Learning strategies
		Written express			Organizational skills

Academic Accommodations

Curriculum	Study Aids	Exams
Priority registration	Typist	• Oral
Math waiver	Reader	Untimed
Foreign lang. waiver	• Notetaker	Take home
• Course substitution	• Proof reader	With proctor
In Class	• Text on tape	On computer
• Calculators	Early syllabus	• Extended time
• Tape recorder	Taped handouts	On tape
• Word processor		• Modified
Priority seating		Separate room

Program Strengths

We have no program. Our services are designed individually for all students with disabilities.

General Information:

Franklin University is a 4 year private university. Urban campus of 13 acres is 1.5% of students are foreign. Housing is not guaranteed.

Accreditation: NCACS

Expenses:

Tuition: In-state: Full year: $3,450.00. Part-time: Per credit:$115.00. Part-time: Per course: $460.00. Tuition: Out-of-state: Full year: $3,450.00. Part-time: Per credit:$115.00. Part-time: Per course:$460.00

Majors

• BUSINESS Accounting, Banking, Business Administration, Business Management, Finance, Human Resources Management, Marketing, Marketing Research, Real Estate • COMMUNICATIONS Communication • COMPUTER SCIENCE Computer Science • HEALTH SCIENCES Nursing • VOCATIONAL Electronics Technology Management, Employment Assistance Counseling, Mechanical Design

Sports/Activities

• SPORTS-INTERCOLLEGIATE Soccer (M) • SPORTS-INTRAMURAL Basketball (M), Soccer (M), Softball (F), Volleyball • STUDENT LIFE ACTIVITIES Ethnic & Cultural Groups, Newspaper, Student Government

Less Selective

Hocking Technical College

Route 1
Nelsonville, Ohio 45764
(614) 753-3591

School Enrollment: **3,240** Male: **1,760** Female: **1,480**

Admissions Contact: **Candy Vancko, Director of Admissions**
LD Contact: **Kim Forbes Shaner**
Name of Program: **Center for Alternative Ed.**
Telephone:**Ext. 223**

Admissions

Application Information:

Application deadline: **None**
Rolling Admissions: **Yes**

Secondary School Information

Most Important Criteria For Admissions (1-strongest)

SAT/ACT	Application	School transcript
Class rank	Course selection	Personal statement
Interview	Extra activities	Psychoeducational
G.P.A.	**1** Open admission	Recommendations

Test Requirements:

Standardized tests waived: **Yes**
Documentation of LD required: **Yes**

Types of Disabilities Served

• Speech/Lang	• Reading	• ADD with LD
• Study skills	• Spelling	• ADD without LD
• Written express	• Math	• ADHD with LD
• Organizational	• Fine Motor	• ADHD without LD
• Perceptual		

Learning Disability Program

Counseling: Individual: **Yes**

Faculty:

Faculty: **1** Part time: **1**
Faculty advocate: **Yes** Meets with instructor: **As needed**

Diagnostic Testing

ADD	Personality	Perceptual skills	Spelling
ADHD	Organization	Fine motor skills	Reading
I.Q.	Handwriting	Spoken language	Study skills
Math	Social skills	Written language	

Tutoring:

Services rendered by:
Graduates •Peers •Faculty •LD staff Teacher trainees

Tutorials

Grp.	Ind. Tutorials	Grp.	Ind. Tutorials
	• Math skills		Word processing
•	• Study skills		Time management
	• Language arts	•	• Learning strategies
	• Written express	•	• Organizational skills

Academic Accommodations

Curriculum	Study Aids	Exams
Priority registration	Typist	• Oral
• Math waiver	Reader	Untimed
• Foreign lang. waiver	• Notetaker	Take home
Course substitution	• Proof reader	With proctor
In Class	• Text on tape	On computer
• Calculators	Early syllabus	• Extended time
• Tape recorder	Taped handouts	On tape
Word processor		• Modified
Priority seating		Separate room

General Information:

Hocking Technical College is a 2 year public college. Rural campus of 250 acres is 60 miles from Columbus. Accessible by air, train, or bus. Ski areas are 15 miles from campus. Beaches are 20 miles from campus. 1 residential halls on campus. Housing is not guaranteed.9 % of students remain on campus for the weekends.

Accreditation: Regional

Expenses:

Tuition: In-state: Full year: $1,473.00 - 3 quarters. Part-time: Per credit:$43.00. Tuition: Out-of-state: Full year: $2,946.00 - 3 quarters. Part-time:

Ohio

Per credit:$86.00. Room and board: $3,600.00

Majors

• BUSINESS Accounting, Business Management, Finance, Hotel and Restaurant Management, Travel/Tourism Management • COMPUTER SCIENCE Data Processing, Programming, Systems Analysis, Telecommunications • CRAFTS AND DESIGN Ceramics • HEALTH SCIENCES Fitness, Medical Technology, Nursing, Nutritional/Food • VOCATIONAL Automotive Service, Fire Science, Sawmill, Timber Harvesting

---

Less Selective	Ohio
	Accommodations

Jefferson Technical College

4000 Sunset Boulevard
Steubenville, Ohio 43952
(614) 264-5591

School Enrollment: **1,300** Male: **500** Female: **800**

Admissions Contact: **Chuck Mascellino, Director of Admissions**
LD Contact: **Kathy Caleodis, Director**
Name of Program: **Learning Skills Lab**
Address: **400 Sunset Blvd.**
Telephone:**(614) 264-5591 Ext.**

Admissions

Application Information:
Application deadline: **Open**
Rolling Admissions: **Yes** Notified when: **Immediately**

Secondary School Information
Most Important Criteria For Admissions (1-strongest)

SAT/ACT	Application	**1**	School transcript
Class rank	Course selection		Personal statement
Interview	Extra activities		Psychoeducational
G.P.A.	Open admission		Recommendations

Test Requirements:
Standardized tests waived: **Yes**

Types of Disabilities Served

Speech/Lang	• Reading	ADD with LD
• Study skills	• Spelling	ADD without LD
Written express	• Math	ADHD with LD
Organizational	Fine Motor	ADHD without LD
Perceptual		

Learning Disability Program

Program: Remedial: **Yes**
Program: Reinforces course work: **Yes**
Students mainstreamed **Vary** % of the day
Services available for all students: **Yes**

Faculty:
Faculty: **6** Including Director: **Yes** Part time: **6**
LD faculty with: BS/BA: **5**

Diagnostic Testing

ADD	Personality	Perceptual skills	• Spelling
ADHD	Organization	Fine motor skills	• Reading
I.Q.	Handwriting	Spoken language	Study skills
• Math	Social skills	• Written language	

Tutoring:
Services rendered by:
Graduates   •Peers   •Faculty   •LD staff   Teacher trainees

Tutorials

Grp.	Ind.	Tutorials	Grp.	Ind.	Tutorials
	•	Math skills		•	Word processing
	•	Study skills			Time management
	•	Language arts			Learning strategies
		Written express			Organizational skills

Academic Accommodations

Curriculum	Study Aids	Exams
Priority registration	Typist	Oral
• Math waiver	Reader	Untimed
Foreign lang. waiver	Notetaker	Take home
Course substitution	Proof reader	With proctor
In Class	Text on tape	On computer
Calculators	Early syllabus	Extended time
Tape recorder	Taped handouts	On tape
Word processor		Modified
Priority seating		Separate room

Program Strengths

Our Learning Skills Lab is for remediation of basic skills and is open to Jefferson Technical College students and the community at large. Only a small percentage of Lab participants are diagnosed as Learning Disabled. We do not do any diagnosis of learning disabilities. Each student's program is developed on an individual basis according to his or her needs.

General Information:

Jefferson Technical College is a 2 year public college. Urban campus of 80 acres is 35 miles from Pittsburgh. Accessible by bus. Housing is not guaranteed.

Accreditation:NCACS

Expenses:
Tuition: In-state: Full year: $1,080.00. Part-time: Per credit:$30.00 (in county), $33.00 (out of county). Tuition: Out-of-state: Full year: $1,500.00. Part-time: Per credit:$45.00.

Majors

• BUSINESS Accounting, Banking/Finance, Business Management, Data Processing, Real Estate, Retailing, Secretarial Science • COMPUTER SCIENCE Computer Technology, Data Processing • ENGINEERING Drafting, Electrical, Mechanical • HEALTH SCIENCES Dental Assistant, Medical Laboratory Technology, Medical Secretary, Respiratory Therapy • SOCIAL SCIENCES Law Enforcement • VOCATIONAL Dental Assistant, Food Service, Legal Secretary, Radiological Technology, Respiratory Therapy Technology, Secretarial

Sports/Activities

• SPORTS-INTERCOLLEGIATE Baseball (M) • SPORTS-INTRAMURAL Baseball, Basketball, Bowling, Ping-Pong, Softball, Volleyball • STUDENT LIFE ACTIVITIES Newspaper, Student Government

Academic Accommodations

Curriculum	Study Aids	Exams
Priority registration	Typist	• Oral
• Math waiver	Reader	Untimed
Foreign lang. waiver	• Notetaker	Take home
Course substitution	Proof reader	With proctor
In Class	Text on tape	On computer
• Calculators	Early syllabus	• Extended time
• Tape recorder	Taped handouts	On tape
• Word processor		Modified
Priority seating		Separate room

Program Strengths

This is a regional campus and the diagnostic and true LD services are provided through this institution by the Basic Education Department. A more comprehensive program exists at the Kent campus.

General Information:

Kent State University: Ashtabula Regional Campus is a 2 year public college. Rural campus of 60 acres is 50 miles from Cleveland. Ski areas are 30 miles from campus. Beaches are 1 mile from campus. Housing is not guaranteed.

Accreditation: NCACS

Expenses:

Tuition: In-state: Full year: $2,850.00. Part-time: Per credit: $118.75. Tuition: Out-of-state: Full year: $6,384.00. Part-time: Per credit: $266.00.

Majors

• BUSINESS Accounting, Business Administration, Business Management, Management, Real Estate • COMMUNICATIONS English • COMPUTER SCIENCE Computer Science, Computer Technology, Data Processing, Programming • EDUCATION Early Childhood, Elementary, Secondary • HEALTH SCIENCES Nursing • HUMANITIES Liberal Arts, Philosophy • SCIENCES Biology, Chemistry • SOCIAL SCIENCES Anthropology, Criminal Justice, Government/Political, History, Law Enforcement, Psychology, Sociology • VOCATIONAL Industrial Technology, Mechanical Design, Secretarial

Sports/Activities

• SPORTS-INTERCOLLEGIATE Baseball (M), Basketball, Cross Country, Golf, Softball, Tennis, Volleyball • STUDENT LIFE ACTIVITIES Academic Clubs, Drama Groups, Ethnic & Cultural Groups, Newspaper, Radio, Student Government

---

Less Selective — **Ohio**
Accommodations

Kent State University: Salem Regional

2491 State Route 45 South
Salem, Ohio 44460
(216) 332-0361

School Enrollment: **929** Male: **310** Female: **619**

Admissions Contact: **Marilyn Ward, Director of Admissions**

Admissions

Application Information:
Application deadline: **None**
Rolling Admissions: **Yes**

Less Selective — **Ohio**
Services

Kent State University: Ashtabula Regional Campus

3325 West 13th Street
Ashtabula, Ohio 44004
(216) 964-3322

School Enrollment: **990**

Admissions Contact: **Christopher Dalheim, Dir. Student Services**
LD Contact: **Roxana Christopher, Director/Developmental Ed.**

Admissions

Application Information:
Application deadline: **August 15th**
Rolling Admissions: **Yes**

Secondary School Information

Most Important Criteria For Admissions (1-strongest)

2 SAT/ACT	**3** Application	**6** School transcript
5 Class rank	**4** Course selection	**11** Personal statement
9 Interview	**7** Extra activities	**8** Psychoeducational
1 G.P.A.	Open admission	**10** Recommendations

Test Requirements:

Standardized tests waived: **Yes**
Documentation of LD required: **Yes**

Types of Disabilities Served

- Speech/Lang
- Reading
- ADD with LD
- Study skills
- Spelling
- ADD without LD
- Written express
- Math
- ADHD with LD
- Organizational
- Fine Motor
- ADHD without LD
- Perceptual

Faculty:

Diagnostic Testing

ADD	Personality	Perceptual skills	Spelling
ADHD	Organization	Fine motor skills	Reading
I.Q.	Handwriting	Spoken language	Study skills
Math	Social skills	Written language	

Tutoring:

Services rendered by:
Graduates • Peers • Faculty LD staff Teacher trainees

Tutorials

Grp.	Ind.	Tutorials	Grp.	Ind.	Tutorials
	•	Math skills			Word processing
	•	Study skills			Time management
	•	Language arts		•	Learning strategies
	•	Written express		•	Organizational skills

Ohio

Secondary School Information
Most Important Criteria For Admissions (1-strongest)

SAT/ACT	**1** Application	School transcript
Class rank	Course selection	Personal statement
Interview	Extra activities	Psychoeducational
G.P.A.	**1** Open admission	Recommendations

Test Requirements:
Standardized tests waived: **Yes**
Tests recommended: **Basic skills assessment required for all students.**

Types of Disabilities Served

Speech/Lang	Reading	ADD with LD
Study skills	Spelling	ADD without LD
Written express	Math	ADHD with LD
Organizational	Fine Motor	ADHD without LD
Perceptual		

Admissions Process

The campus has an open admission policy. All students are recommended or required to fulfill BSAT prescription. LD students are counseled carefully and advised of support services, but no special program is available.

High School Course Requirements:
English: **4** Math: **3** Science: **3** Foreign Language: **3/2**

Learning Disability Program
Students mainstreamed **100** % of the day
Services available for all students: **Yes**
Counseling: Individual: **Yes** Vocational Counseling: **Yes**

Diagnostic Testing

ADD	Personality	Perceptual skills	Spelling
ADHD	Organization	Fine motor skills	• Reading
I.Q.	Handwriting	Spoken language	Study skills
• Math	Social skills	Written language	

Tutoring:
Services rendered by:

Graduates	•Peers	•Faculty	LD staff	Teacher trainees

Tutorials

Grp.	Ind.	Tutorials	Grp.	Ind.	Tutorials
•	•	Math skills	•	•	Word processing
•		Study skills			Time management
	•	Language arts	•	•	Learning strategies
	•	Written express			Organizational skills

Academic Accommodations

Curriculum	Study Aids	Exams
Priority registration	Typist	Oral
Math waiver	Reader	Untimed
Foreign lang. waiver	Notetaker	Take home
Course substitution	Proof reader	With proctor
In Class	Text on tape	On computer
Calculators	Early syllabus	Extended time
Tape recorder	Taped handouts	On tape
Word processor		Modified
Priority seating		Separate room

Graduation Requirements:
Course credits: **65** GPA: **2.0**

General Information:
Kent State University: Salem Regional is a 2 year public university. Rural campus of 98 acres is 40 miles from Youngstown. Accessible by air, train, or bus. Ski areas are 1 hour from campus. Housing is not guaranteed.

Accreditation: NCASC

Expenses:
Tuition: In-state: Full year: $2,663.00. Part-time: Per credit:$111.00. Tuition: Out-of-state: Full year: $5,933.00. Part-time: Per credit:$247.00.

Majors
• AGRICULTURE Horticultural • BUSINESS Accounting, Business Management, Clerical, Secretarial Science • COMPUTER SCIENCE Computer Technology • ENGINEERING Mechanical • HEALTH SCIENCES Radiological Technology • MATHEMATICS Applied • SOCIAL SCIENCES Human Service

Sports/Activities
• SPORTS-INTRAMURAL Basketball, Basketball (F), Basketball (M), Football, Ping-Pong, Racquetball, Racquetball (F), Racquetball (M), Skiing - Snow, Tennis, Volleyball, Weight Lifting • STUDENT LIFE ACTIVITIES Academic Clubs, Drama Groups, Student Government

Highly Selective   **Ohio**
                                        Services

Kenyon College
Gambier, Ohio 43022-9623
(614) 427-2244-(800) 848-2468

School Enrollment: **1,443**

Admissions Contact: **John Anderson, Dean of Admissions**

Admissions

Application Information:
Application deadline: **February 15th**
Notified when: **April 1st**

Secondary School Information
Most Important Criteria For Admissions (1-strongest)

5 SAT/ACT	**9** Application	**1** School transcript
3 Class rank	**2** Course selection	**6** Personal statement
10 Interview	**8** Extra activities	**11** Psychoeducational
4 G.P.A.	Open admission	**7** Recommendations

Test Requirements:
Untimed SAT: **Yes** Untimed ACT: **Yes**

Types of Disabilities Served

Speech/Lang	Reading	ADD with LD
Study skills	Spelling	ADD without LD
Written express	Math	ADHD with LD
Organizational	Fine Motor	ADHD without LD
Perceptual		

Diagnostic Testing

ADD	Personality	Perceptual skills	Spelling
ADHD	Organization	Fine motor skills	Reading
I.Q.	Handwriting	Spoken language	Study skills
Math	Social skills	Written language	

Services rendered by:

Graduates   Peers   Faculty   LD staff   Teacher trainees

Tutorials

Grp.	Ind. Tutorials	Grp.	Ind. Tutorials
	Math skills		Word processing
	Study skills		Time management
	Language arts		Learning strategies
	Written express		Organizational skills

Academic Accommodations

Curriculum	Study Aids	Exams
Priority registration	• Typist	Oral
Math waiver	Reader	Untimed
Foreign lang. waiver	Notetaker	• Take home
Course substitution	• Proof reader	With proctor
In Class	• Text on tape	On computer
• Calculators	Early syllabus	• Extended time
• Tape recorder	Taped handouts	On tape
• Word processor		Modified
Priority seating		Separate room

Program Strengths

Kenyon does not have an organized LD program. The LD students must have the same qualifications and evidence of readiness as other applicants.

General Information:

Kenyon College is a 4 year independent college. Rural campus of 800 acres is 50 miles from Columbus . Ski areas are 45 miles from campus. Beaches are 1,000 miles from campus. 2% of students are foreign. 18 residential halls on campus. Housing is guaranteed.Guaranteed through 4th year. 95 % of students remain on campus for the weekends. 20 % of students join fraternities/sororities.

Accreditation:NCACS

Expenses:

Tuition: In-state: Full year: $14,350.00. Room and board: $3,260.00

Majors

• AREA STUDIES American, Asian, European, International Studies, Latin American, Middle Eastern, Russian/Slavic • BUSINESS Economics • COMMUNICATIONS English • HUMANITIES Classics, English/Writing/Literature, Philosophy, Religion • LANGUAGES Chinese, French, German, Greek, Italian, Japanese, Russian, Spanish • PREPROFESSIONAL Dentistry, Engineering, Law, Medicine • SCIENCES Archeology, Biology, Biotechnology, Chemistry, Mathematics, Physical Science, Physics, Zoology • SOCIAL SCIENCES Anthropology, Government/Political, History, International Studies, Psychology, Sociology • VISUAL AND PERFORMING ARTS Art, Art History, Dance, Dramatic Arts, Music, Studio Art, Theater

Sports/Activities

• SPORTS RELATED Pep Band • SPORTS-INTERCOLLEGIATE Baseball (M), Basketball, Cross Country, Diving, Field Hockey (F), Football (M), Golf, Lacrosse, Soccer, Swimming, Tennis, Track and Field, Volleyball (F) • SPORTS-INTRAMURAL Basketball, Bowling, Cross Country, Fencing, Golf, Horseback Riding, Ice Hockey (M), Racquetball, Rugby, Sailing, Skiing - Snow, Soccer, Softball, Squash, Swimming, Tennis, Track and Field, Volleyball, Water Polo (M) • STUDENT LIFE ACTIVITIES Choral, Dance, Drama Groups, Ethnic & Cultural Groups, Film, Fraternities, Jazz Band, Music Groups, Musical Theater, Newspaper, Opera, Orchestra, Radio/TV station, Sororities, Student Government, Symphony Orchestra, Yearbook

---

Very Selective	Ohio
	Accommodations

Malone College

515 25th Street, Northwest
Canton, Ohio 44709
(216) 489-0800

School Enrollment: **1,695** Male: **571** Female: **1,124**
LD Enrollment: **9** Male: **9**

Admissions Contact: **Lee Sommers, Dean of Admissions**
LD Contact: **Patricia Long, Ed.D., Professor of Education**
Name of Program: **Services for Students with Special Needs**
Address: **515 25th St., N.W., Canton**
Telephone:**(216) 471-8222**

Admissions

Application Information:
LD on admissions committee:**Yes**
Application deadline: **September 1st**
Rolling Admissions: **Yes**Notified when: **Rolling**

Secondary School Information
Most Important Criteria For Admissions (1-strongest)

5	SAT/ACT	4	Application	1	School transcript
6	Class rank	2	Course selection	8	Personal statement
7	Interview	9	Extra activities	11	Psychoeducational
3	G.P.A.		Open admission	10	Recommendations

Test Requirements:
Diagnostic testing waived: **Yes**
Untimed SAT: **Yes** Untimed ACT: **Yes**
WAIS-R required: **Yes** Range accepted: **Varies**
Documentation of LD required: **Yes**
Currency of diagnostic testing: **within last 3 years**
Tests recommended: **Assessment of Aptitude and Academic Achievement**

Types of Disabilities Served
• Speech/Lang   • Reading   • ADD with LD
• Study skills   • Spelling   • ADD without LD
• Written express   • Math   • ADHD with LD
• Organizational   • Fine Motor   • ADHD without LD
• Perceptual

Admissions Process

Apply in the Fall, $20.00 application fee, official high school transcript and ACT required, other testing or recommendations may be requested.

High School Course Requirements:
English: **4** Math: **3** Science: **3** Foreign Language: **2**
Waivers to standard high school courses
Foreign Language : **Yes**

Learning Disability Program

Program: Reinforces course work: **Yes**
Program available through:**throughout semester**
Recommended credits per semester: **12**
Services only for LD students: **Yes**
Services available for all students: **Yes**
Counseling: Individual: **Yes** Vocational Counseling: **Yes**

Faculty:

Faculty: **1** Part time: **1** Ph.D.: **1**
Faculty advocate: **Yes** Meets with instructor: **As needed**

Diagnostic Testing

ADD	Personality	Perceptual skills	Spelling
ADHD	Organization	Fine motor skills	Reading
I.Q.	Handwriting	Spoken language	Study skills
Math	Social skills	Written language	

Tutoring:

Services rendered by:
  Graduates •Peers •Faculty •LD staff   Teacher trainees

Tutorials

Grp.	Ind.	Tutorials	Grp.	Ind.	Tutorials
•	•	Math skills			Word processing
•	•	Study skills	•	•	Time management
		Language arts	•	•	Learning strategies
	•	Written express	•	•	Organizational skills

Academic Accommodations

Curriculum	Study Aids	Exams
• Priority registration	• Typist	• Oral
Math waiver	• Reader	• Untimed
Foreign lang. waiver	• Notetaker	Take home
• Course substitution	• Proof reader	• With proctor
In Class	• Text on tape	• On computer
• Calculators	• Early syllabus	• Extended time
• Tape recorder	Taped handouts	• On tape
• Word processor		• Modified
• Priority seating		• Separate room

Graduation Requirements:

Course credits: **124** GPA: **2.0**

General Information:

Malone College is a 2 and 4 year independent Evangelical Friends Church college. Urban campus of 78 acres is 56 miles from Cleveland. Accessible by air, train, or bus. Ski areas are 45 miles from campus. 1% of students are foreign. 9 residential halls on campus. Housing is guaranteed.Guaranteed through 1st year.

Accreditation:NCACS

SAT/ACT Scores:

Scores for incoming freshmen:**Verbal:**66%below 500. 20%between 500 and 599. 13%between 600 and 699. **Math:**36% below 500. 53% between 500 and 599. 6% between 600 and 699. 3%above 700. **ACT:** 44% below 20. 36% between 20 and 23. 9%between 24 and 25l. 8%between 26 and 28. 3% above 28.

Class Rank:

About 53% of the present freshmen class were in the upper 20% of their high school class. 78% were in the top 40% of their class. 93% were in the top 60% of their class. 98% were in the top 80% of their class.

Expenses: Part-time: Per credit:$250.00. Part-time: Per cred-

it:$250.00. Room and board: $3,000.00

Majors

• BUSINESS Accounting, Business Administration, Business Education, Business Management, Education, Management, Real Estate, Sports Science • COMMUNICATIONS Broadcasting, Communication, English, Journalism, Television/Radio/Film • COMPUTER SCIENCE Computer Science • EDUCATION Early Childhood, Elementary, English, General, Health, Mathematics, Middle School, Music, Physical, Religious Education, Science, Secondary, Social Studies, Special • HEALTH SCIENCES Allied Health, Health, Medical Laboratory Technology, Nursing • HUMANITIES English/Writing/Literature, Liberal Arts, Philosophy, Religion • PREPROFESSIONAL Dentistry, Engineering, Law, Medicine, Pharmacy, Social Work, Veterinarian • RELIGIOUS STUDIES Ministry, Religion and Theology, Religious Music • SCIENCES Biology, Chemistry, Computer Science, General, Mathematics, Radiology • SOCIAL SCIENCES History, Psychology, Social Sciences • VISUAL AND PERFORMING ARTS Music, Music Performance

Sports/Activities

• SPORTS RELATED Cheerleading, Pep Band • SPORTS-INTERCOLLEGIATE Baseball (M), Basketball, Cross Country, Golf (M), Soccer (M), Softball (F), Tennis, Track and Field, Volleyball (F) • SPORTS-INTRAMURAL Basketball (F), Basketball (M), Bowling, Football (M), Softball (M), Volleyball • STUDENT LIFE ACTIVITIES Academic Clubs, Choral, Community Service, Drama Groups, Ethnic & Cultural Groups, Film, Jazz Band, Magazine, Music Groups, Musical Theater, Newspaper, Radio/TV station, Religious Organization, Student Government, Yearbook

Selective   **Ohio**
                                              Program

Muskingum College

219 Montgomery Hall
New Concord, Ohio 43762
(614) 826-8137

School Enrollment: **1,077** Male: **567** Female: **510**
LD Enrollment: **111**

Admissions Contact: **Matt Smucker, Admissions**
LD Contact: **Dr. Paul Naour, Director**
Name of Program: **PLUS Program**
Address: **Center for the Advancement of Learning**
Telephone:**(614) 826-8280**

Admissions

Application Information:

LD Students Applying: **160** Accepted: **40** Enrolled:**29**
Application deadline: **March 1st**
Applicant must apply **12** months in advance
Rolling Admissions: **Yes**

Secondary School Information

Most Important Criteria For Admissions (1-strongest)

2	SAT/ACT	3	Application	1	School transcript
3	Class rank	1	Course selection	3	Personal statement
1	Interview	3	Extra activities	1	Psychoeducational
2	G.P.A.		Open admission	2	Recommendations

Ohio

Test Requirements:
Diagnostic testing waived: **Yes**
Untimed SAT: **Yes** Untimed ACT: **Yes**
WAIS-R required: **Yes**
Documentation of LD required: **Yes**
Currency of diagnostic testing: **3 years**
Tests recommended: **WAIS-R/Achievement**

Types of Disabilities Served
- Speech/Lang
- Study skills
- Written express
- Organizational
- Perceptual
- Reading
- Spelling
- Math
- Fine Motor
- ADD with LD
- ADD without LD
- ADHD with LD
- ADHD without LD

Admissions Process
Regular admissions material and WAIS submitted . Invitation for interview

High School Course Requirements:
English: **4** Math: **2** Science: **2**

Learning Disability Program
Program: Reinforces course work: **Yes**
Students mainstreamed **100** % of the day
Recommended credits per semester: **13-15**
Time required or recommended in learning center: **6-8 hours**
Services available for all students: **Yes**

Faculty:
Faculty: **22** Including Director: **Yes** Full time: **10** Part time: **12**
LD faculty with: BS/BA: **22** M.A.: **7** Ph.D.: **1**

Diagnostic Testing
ADD	Personality	Perceptual skills	Spelling
ADHD	Organization	Fine motor skills	Reading
I.Q.	Handwriting	Spoken language	Study skills
Math	Social skills	Written language	

Tutoring:
Average size of group tutorials: **3-4**
Services rendered by:
Graduates Peers Faculty •LD staff Teacher trainees

Tutorials
Grp.	Ind.	Tutorials	Grp.	Ind.	Tutorials
•	•	Math skills	•	•	Word processing
•	•	Study skills	•	•	Time management
•	•	Language arts	•	•	Learning strategies
•	•	Written express	•	•	Organizational skills

Academic Accommodations
Curriculum	Study Aids	Exams
Priority registration	Typist	• Oral
Math waiver	• Reader	• Untimed
Foreign lang. waiver	Notetaker	Take home
Course substitution	• Proof reader	• With proctor
In Class	• Text on tape	• On computer
• Calculators	Early syllabus	• Extended time
• Tape recorder	Taped handouts	• On tape
• Word processor		Modified
Priority seating		• Separate room

Graduation Requirements:
Course credits: **124** GPA: **2.0** Years to complete degree: **4.5-5**

Program Strengths
Muskingum College's pervasive philosophy holds that each student is unique, with the potential to succeed in the academic world. This philosophy is best reflected in our PLUS Program for learning disabled college students. Our intent is to provide all students with every opportunity to achieve according to his or her academic potential and to encourage students to take responsibility for their own learning.

General Information:
Muskingum College is a 4 year private Presbyterian college. Rural campus of 215 acres is 70 miles from Columbus. 3% of students are foreign. 6 residential halls on campus. Housing is guaranteed.50 % of students join fraternities/sororities.

Accreditation:NCACS

SAT/ACT Scores:
Scores for incoming freshmen:**Verbal**:73%below 500. 23%between 500 and 599. 4%between 600 and 699. **Math:**57% below 500. 24% between 500 and 599. 17% between 600 and 699. 2%above 700. **ACT:** 57% below 20. 21% between 20 and 23. 14%between 24 and 25l. 8%between 26 and 28.

Class Rank:
About 39% of the present freshmen class were in the upper 20% of their high school class. 61% were in the top 40% of their class. 87% were in the top 60% of their class. 98% were in the top 80% of their class.

Expenses:
Tuition: In-state: Full year: $10,980.00. Room and board: $3,300.00 Cost of LD program:$3,000.00/$1,500.00

Majors
• ARTS Art History, Art Therapy, Drawing, Music, Music Performance, Painting, Sculpture • BUSINESS Accounting, Business Administration, Business Economics, Economics • COMMUNICATIONS Communication, Speech/Debate/Forensic • COMPUTER SCIENCE Computer Science • EDUCATION Art, Business, Child Development, Early Childhood, Elementary, Middle School, Secondary • HUMANITIES English/Writing/Literature, Humanities, Liberal Arts , Philosophy, Religion • LANGUAGES English, French, Spanish • MATHEMATICS Applied • RELIGIOUS STUDIES Philosophy, Religion & Theology • SCIENCES Biology, Chemistry, Computer Science, Geology, Human Biology, Mathematics, Neuroscience, Physical Chemistry • SOCIAL SCIENCES Political Science, Psychology, Social Sciences, Sociology • SPECIAL EDUCATION Learning Disability • VISUAL AND PERFORMING ARTS Art, Music, Theater

Sports/Activities
• SPORTS RELATED Cheerleading, Marching Band, Pep Band • SPORTS-INTERCOLLEGIATE Baseball (M), Basketball, Cross Country, Football (M), Golf (M), Soccer, Softball (F), Tennis, Track and Field, Volleyball (F), Wrestling (M) • SPORTS-INTRAMURAL Archery, Badminton, Baseball, Basketball, Bowling, Cross Country, Field Hockey, Football, Racquetball, Soccer, Swimming, Tennis, Volleyball, Weight Lifting, Wrestling • STUDENT LIFE ACTIVITIES Drama Groups, Ethnic & Cultural Groups, Fraternities, Jazz Band, Music Groups, Newspaper, Radio/TV station, Religious Organization, Sororities, Student Government, Symphony Orchestra, Yearbook

Highly Selective

Ohio Program

Oberlin College

Room 6 - Peters Hall
Oberlin, Ohio 44074
(216) 775-8467

School Enrollment: **2,909** Male: **1,346** Female: **1,563**
LD Enrollment: **45**

Admissions Contact: **H. Scroto Campbell, Assis. Dir. Admissions**
LD Contact: **Dr. Dean Kelly, Coordinator**
Name of Program: **Student Support Services**
Address: **110 Peters Hall**
Telephone:**(216) 775-8467**

Admissions

Application Information:
Application deadline: **January 15th**
Notified when: **April 1st**

Secondary School Information
Most Important Criteria For Admissions (1-strongest)

1 SAT/ACT	**8** Application	**2** School transcript
1 Class rank	**2** Course selection	**5** Personal statement
6 Interview	**3** Extra activities	**7** Psychoeducational
1 G.P.A.	Open admission	**4** Recommendations

Test Requirements:
Diagnostic testing waived: **Yes**
Untimed SAT: **Yes** Untimed ACT: **Yes**
Documentation of LD required: **Yes**
Currency of diagnostic testing: **18 months**

Types of Disabilities Served
- Speech/Lang
- Reading
- ADD with LD
- Study skills
- Spelling
- ADD without LD
- Written express
- Math
- ADHD with LD
- Organizational
- Fine Motor
- ADHD without LD
- Perceptual

Learning Disability Program

Program: Reinforces course work: **Yes**
Students mainstreamed **100** % of the day
Services only for LD students: **Yes**
Counseling: Individual: **Yes**

Faculty:
Faculty: **3** Including Director: **Yes** Full time: **3**
LD faculty with: BS/BA: **1** M.A.: **1** Ph.D.: **1**
Faculty advocate: **Yes** Meets with instructor: **1x per semester**

Diagnostic Testing
- ADD
- Personality
- Perceptual skills
- Spelling
- ADHD
- Organization
- Fine motor skills
- Reading
- I.Q.
- Handwriting
- Spoken language
- Study skills
- Math
- Social skills
- Written language

Tutoring:
Average size of group tutorials: **2-3**
Services rendered by:

- Graduates • Peers • Faculty • LD staff   Teacher trainees

Tutorials

Grp.	Ind.	Tutorials	Grp.	Ind.	Tutorials
•	•	Math skills		•	Word processing
•	•	Study skills	•	•	Time management
	•	Language arts		•	Learning strategies
	•	Written express	•	•	Organizational skills

Academic Accommodations

Curriculum	Study Aids	Exams
Priority registration	• Typist	• Oral
Math waiver	Reader	Untimed
Foreign lang. waiver	• Notetaker	• Take home
• Course substitution	• Proof reader	• With proctor
In Class	• Text on tape	On computer
Calculators	Early syllabus	• Extended time
• Tape recorder	Taped handouts	On tape
• Word processor		• Modified
Priority seating		Separate room

Program Strengths
The LD Program is individualized. Each student's accommodations relate directly to his or her needs. The LD Program also includes a strong student support component.

General Information:
Oberlin College is a 4 year private college. Rural campus of 440 acres is 35 miles from Cleveland. Accessible by air or train. Ski areas are 25 miles from campus. Beaches are 7 miles from campus. 3% of students are foreign. Housing is guaranteed.

Accreditation:NCACS, NASAD, NASM

SAT/ACT Scores:
Scores for incoming freshmen:**Verbal:**9%below 500. 33%between 500 and 599. 45%between 600 and 699. 12%above 700. **Math:**7% below 500. 27% between 500 and 599. 46% between 600 and 699. 20%above 700.

Expenses:
Tuition: In-state: Full year: $17,600.00. Room and board: $5,320.00

Majors
• AREA STUDIES American, Asian, Black/Afro-American, Jewish, Latin American, Middle Eastern, Russian/Slavic, Third World Studies, Urban, Women's Studies • BUSINESS Economics • COMMUNICATIONS Creative Writing, English • COMPUTER SCIENCE Computer Science • EDUCATION Music • HUMANITIES Classics, Comparative Literature, Philosophy, Religion • LANGUAGES Chinese, French, German, Greek, Japanese, Latin, Russian, Spanish • PREPROFESSIONAL Architecture, Engineering, Law, Medicine • SCIENCES Astronomy, Biochemistry, Biology, Biopsychology, Chemistry, Ecology, Geology, Mathematics, Neuroscience, Physics, Psychobiology • SOCIAL SCIENCES Anthropology, Government/Political, History, Psychology, Sociology

Sports/Activities
• SPORTS-INTERCOLLEGIATE Baseball (M), Basketball, Cross Country, Diving, Field Hockey (F), Football (M), Lacrosse, Soccer, Swimming, Tennis, Track and Field, Volleyball (F) • SPORTS-INTRAMURAL Baseball (M), Basketball, Bowling, Hand Ball, Ping-Pong, Racquetball, Rugby (M), Soccer, Softball, Squash, Tennis, Volleyball • STUDENT LIFE ACTIVITIES Choral, Concert Band, Dance, Drama Groups, Ethnic & Cultural Groups, Jazz Band, Magazine, Music Groups, Musical Theater, Newspaper, Opera, Radio, Religious Organization, Student Government, Symphony Orchestra, Yearbook

Less Selective

**Ohio
Program**

Ohio State University
Agricultural Technical Institute

1328 Dover Road
Wooster, Ohio 44691
(216) 264-3911

School Enrollment: **700** Male: **525** Female: **175**

Admissions Contact: **Mark R. Thompson, Admissions Counselor**
LD Contact: **Denise Porter, LD Specialist**
Name of Program: **Project Build**

Admissions

Application Information:
Application deadline: **August 15th**
Applicant must apply **6-9** months in advance
Rolling Admissions: **Yes** Notified when: **4-6 weeks**

Secondary School Information
Most Important Criteria For Admissions (1-strongest)

	SAT/ACT	**1** Application	**1** School transcript
	Class rank	Course selection	Personal statement
1	Interview	Extra activities	Psychoeducational
	G.P.A.	Open admission	Recommendations

Test Requirements:
Diagnostic testing waived: **Yes**
WAIS-R required: **Yes** Range accepted: **Average+**
Documentation of LD required: **Yes**
Currency of diagnostic testing: **3 years**
Tests recommended: **Woodcock-Johnson**

Types of Disabilities Served
- Speech/Lang
- Study skills
- Written express
- Organizational
- Perceptual
- Reading
- Spelling
- Math
- Fine Motor
- ADD with LD
- ADD without LD
- ADHD with LD
- ADHD without LD

Learning Disability Program
Program: Reinforces course work: **Yes**
Students mainstreamed **100** % of the day
Counseling: Individual: **Yes** Group Counseling: **Yes**

Faculty:
Faculty: **4** Full time: **1** Part time: **3**
LD faculty with: BS/BA: **1** M.A.: **3**
Faculty advocate: **Yes** Meets with instructor: **As needed**

Diagnostic Testing
ADD	Personality •	Perceptual skills	• Spelling
ADHD•	Organization•	Fine motor skills	• Reading
• I.Q.	• Handwriting•	Spoken language	• Study skills
• Math	• Social skills•	Written language	

Tutoring:
Average size of group tutorials: **5**
Services rendered by:

Graduates •Peers •Faculty •LD staff Teacher trainees

Tutorials
Grp.	Ind.	Tutorials	Grp.	Ind.	Tutorials
•	•	Math skills	•	•	Word processing
•	•	Study skills	•	•	Time management
•	•	Language arts	•	•	Learning strategies
•	•	Written express	•	•	Organizational skills

Academic Accommodations
Curriculum	Study Aids	Exams
Priority registration	• Typist	• Oral
Math waiver	Reader	Untimed
• Foreign lang. waiver	• Notetaker	Take home
• Course substitution	• Proof reader	With proctor
In Class	• Text on tape	On computer
• Calculators	Early syllabus	• Extended time
• Tape recorder	Taped handouts	On tape
• Word processor		• Modified
Priority seating		Separate room

Program Strengths
The Learning Disability Program provides and coordinates academic support services to all learning disabled students. The ultimate goal of the program is to assist individuals to increase their independence, develop self-advocacy skills and to maximize their potential.

General Information:
Ohio State University Agricultural Technical Institute is a 2 year public college. Rural campus of 1,800 acres is 65 miles from Cleveland. Accessible by bus. Ski areas are 1 hour from campus. Beaches are 2 hours from campus. 1% of students are foreign. 1 residential halls on campus. Housing is not guaranteed.15 % of students remain on campus for the weekends.

Accreditation: NCACS

Expenses:
Tuition: In-state: Full year: $702.00. Part-time: Per credit:$56.00. Tuition: Out-of-state: Full year: $2,106.00. Part-time: Per credit:$113.00. Room and board: $1,740.00 Cost of LD program:$390.00

Majors
• BUSINESS Agricultural, Business Management, Food Management, Management • ENVIRONMENTAL CONTROL Fluid Power, Forest Products Processing Con • PREPROFESSIONAL Agriculture • SCIENCES Agronomy, Animal, Dairy, Equestrian Studies, Horticultural, Science Technologies, Soil • VOCATIONAL Agricultural Industrial Power , Biology Laboratory Technology, Business and Office, Food Service, Industrial Equipment Maintenance

Sports/Activities
• SPORTS-INTERCOLLEGIATE Basketball (M), Golf • SPORTS-INTRAMURAL Basketball, Bowling, Golf, Racquetball, Skiing - Snow, Soccer, Softball, Tennis, Volleyball

Ohio

Ohio State University: Columbus Campus

1800 Cannon Drive
Columbus, Ohio 43210-1230
(614) 292-3980

School Enrollment: **38,090**
LD Enrollment: **500**

Admissions Contact: **Lillian Zarzar, Admissions Counselor**
LD Contact: **Lois Burke, Counselor**
Name of Program: **Office for Disability Services**
Telephone:**(614) 292-3307**

Admissions

Application Information:
Application deadline: **February 15th**
Applicant must apply **6-12** months in advance
Rolling Admissions: **Yes** Notified when: **March 21st**

Secondary School Information
Most Important Criteria For Admissions (1-strongest)

2 SAT/ACT	Application	School transcript
1 Class rank	**1** Course selection	**3** Personal statement
Interview	**2** Extra activities	Psychoeducational
G.P.A.	Open admission	**2** Recommendations

Test Requirements:
Standardized tests waived: **Yes**
Documentation of LD required: **Yes**
Tests recommended: **Documentation of learning disability**

Types of Disabilities Served
- Speech/Lang
- Study skills
- Written express
- Organizational
- Perceptual
- Reading
- Spelling
- Math
- Fine Motor
- ADD with LD
- ADD without LD
- ADHD with LD
- ADHD without LD

Learning Disability Program
Special orientation for LD students: **Yes**
Students mainstreamed **100** % of the day
Recommended credits per semester: **12-15**
Services only for LD students: **Yes**
Counseling: Individual: **Yes** Group Counseling: **Yes**
Support groups are available:**Yes**

Faculty:
Faculty: **5** Full time: **2** Part time: **3** M.A.: **4** Ph.D.: **1**
Faculty advocate: **Yes** Meets with instructor: **As needed**

Diagnostic Testing

ADD	Personality	• Perceptual skills	• Spelling
ADHD	Organization	• Fine motor skills	• Reading
• I.Q.	• Handwriting	• Spoken language	Study skills
• Math	• Social skills	• Written language	

Tutoring:
Average size of group tutorials: **3-4**
Services rendered by:

Graduates	•Peers	Faculty	LD staff	Teacher trainees

Tutorials

Grp.	Ind.	Tutorials	Grp.	Ind.	Tutorials
•		Math skills		•	Word processing
•	•	Study skills	•	•	Time management
		Language arts	•	•	Learning strategies
		Written express			Organizational skills

Academic Accommodations

Curriculum	Study Aids	Exams
Priority registration	Typist	• Oral
Math waiver	Reader	Untimed
Foreign lang. waiver	Notetaker	• Take home
• Course substitution	• Proof reader	• With proctor
In Class	• Text on tape	On computer
• Calculators	Early syllabus	• Extended time
• Tape recorder	Taped handouts	On tape
• Word processor		• Modified
Priority seating		Separate room

Graduation Requirements:
Course credits: **Varies** GPA: **2.0** Years to complete degree: **5**

Program Strengths
The Office for Disability Services, in addition to having counselors who work directly with students with learning disabilities, also has a multi-disciplinary team that consists of a psychologist and diagnostician/speech and hearing specialist. Many of the support services available to our students are in one facility. We have a computer lab and individual test studios for exam administration. There are no special courses or admission requirements for our students. They are expected to be as competitive as their peers with the use of appropriate and available accommodations. Academic adjustments such as a foreign language substitution are done on a case by case basis. Currently, there are no waivers of the foreign language requirement.

General Information:
Ohio State University: Columbus Campus is a 4 year public university. Urban campus of 2,737 acres is 3 miles from Columbus. Accessible by air, train, or bus. Ski areas are 90 miles from campus. 1.3% of students are foreign. Housing is not guaranteed.10 % of students join fraternities/sororities.

Accreditation:NCACS

SAT/ACT Scores:
Scores for incoming freshmen:**Verbal:**63%below 500. 23%between 500 and 599. 6%between 600 and 699. 1%above 700. **Math:**39% below 500. 30% between 500 and 599. 18% between 600 and 699. 1%above 700.

Class Rank:
About 47% of the present freshmen class were in the upper 20% of their high school class. 80% were in the top 40% of their class. 95% were in the top 60% of their class. 99% were in the top 80% of their class.

Expenses:
Tuition: In-state: Full year: $2,343.00. Tuition: Out-of-state: Full year: $6,942.00. Room and board: $3,636.00

Majors
• AREA STUDIES Black/Afro-American, European, Islamic, Jewish, Russian/Slavic, Urban, Women's Studies • BUSINESS Accounting, Banking, Business Administration, Business Economics, Business Education, Business Management, Economics, Finance, Hotel and Restaurant Management, Human Resources Management, Insurance, International Business, Labor Relations, Management, Marketing, Marketing Research, Personnel, Printing Manufacturing, Real Estate, Sports Management, Transportation

Management • COMMUNICATIONS Advertising, Broadcasting, Communication, Creative Writing, English, Journalism, Photography, Television/Radio/Film • COMPUTER SCIENCE Computer Science, Medical Records Administration, Programming, Systems Analysis, Telecommunications • CRAFTS AND DESIGN Ceramics, Drawing, Glass, Sculpture • EDUCATION Agricultural, Art, Bilingual, Early Childhood, Elementary, English, Foreign Language, Health, Home Economics, Industrial, Marketing & Distributive, Mathematics, Middle School, Physical, Recreation and Youth Leadership, Science, Secondary, Social Studies, Special, Speech/Language, Vocational • ENGINEERING Aerospace, Agricultural, Chemical, Civil/Environmental, Computer, Electrical, Industrial, Mechanical, Metallurgical, Mining/Mineral, Physics • HEALTH SCIENCES Communication Disorders, Environmental, Health, Medical Technology, Nursing, Nutritional/Food, Occupational Therapy, Physical Therapy, Radiological Therapy, Speech Therapy, Speech/Audiology and Speech • HUMANITIES Classics, Humanities, Liberal Arts, Philosophy, Religion • LANGUAGES Arabic, Chinese, French, German, Greek, Hebrew, Italian, Japanese, Linguistics, Russian, Spanish • PREPROFESSIONAL Agriculture, Architecture, Dentistry, Engineering, Forestry, Law, Medicine, Natural Resources, Optometry, Pharmacy, Recreation, Social Work • SCIENCES Actuarial Technology, Agronomy, Animal, Astronomy, Biochemistry, Biology, Botany, Chemistry, Earth, Ecology, Entomology, Geography, Geology, Horticultural, Macrobiology, Mathematics, Microbiology, Physical Chemistry, Physical Science, Physics, Plant Pathology, Zoology • SOCIAL SCIENCES Anthropology, Criminal Justice, Criminology, Government/Political, History, International Studies, Political Science, Social Sciences, Sociology • VISUAL AND PERFORMING ARTS Art, Art History, Dance, Dramatic Arts, Fine Arts, Jazz, Music, Music Performance, Musical Theory, Theater • VOCATIONAL Dairy, Dental Hygiene, Fishery Studies, Forestry, Home Economics, Industrial Design, Landscape Architecture, Painting, Park/Recreation, Poultry, Respiratory Therapy Technology, Secretarial, Textile and Clothing, Welding, Wildlife Management

Sports/Activities

• SPORTS RELATED Marching Band, Pep Band • SPORTS-INTERCOLLEGIATE Baseball (M), Basketball, Cross Country, Diving, Fencing, Field Hockey (F), Football (M), Golf, Gymnastics, Ice Hockey (M), Lacrosse (M), Riflery, Soccer (M), Softball (F), Swimming, Tennis, Track and Field, Volleyball, Wrestling (M) • SPORTS-INTRAMURAL Archery, Badminton, Basketball, Bowling, Crew, Cross Country, Diving, Fencing, Golf, Hand Ball, Ice Hockey (M), Ping-Pong, Racquetball, Rugby (M), Sailing, Skiing - Snow, Softball, Squash, Swimming, Tennis, Track and Field, Volleyball, Wrestling • STUDENT LIFE ACTIVITIES Choral, Concert Band, Dance, Drama Groups, Ethnic & Cultural Groups, Film, Fraternities, Jazz Band, Magazine, Music Groups, Musical Theater, Newspaper, Opera, Radio/TV station, Sororities, Student Government, Symphony Orchestra, Yearbook

Less Selective	Ohio
	Program

Ohio State University: Marion Campus

1465 Mount Vernon Avenue
Marion, Ohio 43302
(614) 389-2361

School Enrollment: **1,132**
LD Enrollment: **9**

Admissions Contact: **Peg Hendricks**
LD Contact: **Cheri Brent, LD Specialist**
Name of Program: **Learning Disability Program**

Admissions

Application Information:
Enrolled:**9**
Application deadline: **July 15th**
Applicant must apply **2** months in advance

Secondary School Information
Most Important Criteria For Admissions (1-strongest)

SAT/ACT	Application	School transcript
Class rank	Course selection	Personal statement
Interview	Extra activities	Psychoeducational
G.P.A.	**1** Open admission	Recommendations

Test Requirements:
Diagnostic testing waived: **Yes**
Untimed ACT: **Yes**
WAIS-R required: **Yes**
Documentation of LD required: **Yes**
Currency of diagnostic testing: **3 years**
Tests recommended: **I.Q. and Achievement**

Types of Disabilities Served
- Speech/Lang
- Study skills
- Written express
- Organizational
- Perceptual
- Reading
- Spelling
- Math
- Fine Motor
- ADD with LD
- ADD without LD
- ADHD with LD
- ADHD without LD

Learning Disability Program
Program: Remedial: **Yes**
Program: Reinforces course work: **Yes**
Students mainstreamed **100 %** of the day

Faculty:
Faculty: **1** Part time: **1** M.A.: **1**

Diagnostic Testing
- ADD
- ADHD
- I.Q.
- Math
- Personality
- Organization
- Handwriting
- Social skills
- Perceptual skills
- Fine motor skills
- Spoken language
- Written language
- Spelling
- Reading
- Study skills

Tutoring:
Average size of group tutorials: **3**
Services rendered by:
Graduates •Peers •Faculty •LD staff   Teacher trainees

Tutorials

Grp.	Ind.	Tutorials	Grp.	Ind.	Tutorials
•	•	Math skills	•	•	Word processing
•	•	Study skills	•		Time management
•		Language arts	•	•	Learning strategies
	•	Written express	•		Organizational skills

Academic Accommodations

Curriculum	Study Aids	Exams
Priority registration	Typist	• Oral
Math waiver	Reader	Untimed
Foreign lang. waiver	• Notetaker	Take home
Course substitution	Proof reader	With proctor
In Class	• Text on tape	On computer
Calculators	Early syllabus	• Extended time
• Tape recorder	Taped handouts	On tape
• Word processor		• Modified
Priority seating		Separate room

Ohio

Program Strengths

This is a small campus with faculty and staff who are concerned about students with special needs and are willing to be of assistance. It is a good place to get started before transferring to the main campus.

General Information:

Ohio State University: Marion Campus is a 2 and 4 year public university. Suburban campus of 160 acres is 45 miles from Columbus. Ski areas are 35 miles from campus. Beaches are 25 miles from campus. Housing is not guaranteed.

Accreditation:NCACS

Expenses:

Tuition: In-state: Full year: $702.00 per quarter. Tuition: Out-of-state: Full year: $2,065.00 per quarter.

Majors

• AREA STUDIES African, American, Asian, Black/Afro-American, Jewish, Latin American, Urban • BUSINESS Accounting, Business Administration, Business Economics, Business Education, Business Management, Economics, Finance, Hotel and Restaurant Management, Insurance, Management, Marketing, Marketing Research, Personnel, Real Estate, Sports Management, Travel/Tourism Management • COMMUNICATIONS Advertising, Broadcasting, Communication, Creative Writing, English, Journalism, Photography, Television/Radio/Film • EDUCATION Art, Curriculum, Early Childhood, Elementary, Health, Industrial, Middle School, Music, Music Therapy, Physical, Recreation and Youth Leadership, School Psychology, Special, Speech/Language • HEALTH SCIENCES Communication Disorders, Environmental, Health, Medical Technology, Nursing, Nutritional/Food, Occupational Therapy, Physical Therapy, Radiological Therapy, Speech Therapy, Speech/Audiology and Speech • HUMANITIES Humanities, Liberal Arts, Philosophy, Religion • LANGUAGES Arabic, Chinese, Danish, French, German, Greek, Italian, Japanese, Russian, Spanish • PREPROFESSIONAL Agriculture, Architecture, Dentistry, Engineering, Forestry, Law, Medicine, Ministry, Natural Resources, Pharmacy, Recreation, Social Work • SCIENCES Astronomy, Astrophysics, Biochemistry, Biology, Botany, Chemistry, Earth, Ecology, Geography, Geology, Macrobiology, Marine Biology, Mathematics, Microbiology, Physical Chemistry, Physical Science, Physics, Physiology, Radiology • SOCIAL SCIENCES Anthropology, Criminal Justice, Geography, Government/Political, History, Psychology, Social Sciences, Sociology • VISUAL AND PERFORMING ARTS Art, Art History, Dance, Music, Studio Art, Theater

Sports/Activities

• SPORTS-INTERCOLLEGIATE Baseball (M), Basketball, Golf, Soccer (M), Tennis, Volleyball (F) • SPORTS-INTRAMURAL Badminton, Basketball, Bowling, Golf, Ping-Pong, Racquetball, Skiing - Snow, Soccer, Softball, Tennis, Volleyball • STUDENT LIFE ACTIVITIES Choral, Drama Groups, Student Government

Ohio State University: Newark Campus
University Drive
Newark, Ohio 43055
(614) 366-9333

School Enrollment: **1,656** Male: **656** Female: **1,000**
LD Enrollment: **20** Male: **15** Female: **5**

Admissions Contact: **Ann Donahue, Admissions Coordinator**
LD Contact: **Lisa Williams, LD Specialist**
Name of Program: **Developmental Education**
Telephone:**(614) 366-9246**

Admissions

Application Information:
Application deadline: **July 1st**
Rolling Admissions: **Yes**Notified when: **4-6 weeks**

Secondary School Information
Most Important Criteria For Admissions (1-strongest)

SAT/ACT	Application	School transcript
2 Class rank	**1** Course selection	Personal statement
Interview	Extra activities	Psychoeducational
G.P.A.	**1** Open admission	Recommendations

Test Requirements:
Untimed SAT: **Yes** Untimed ACT: **Yes**
WAIS-R required: **Yes**
Documentation of LD required: **Yes**
Currency of diagnostic testing: **3 years**

Types of Disabilities Served
• Speech/Lang • Reading • ADD with LD
• Study skills • Spelling • ADD without LD
• Written express • Math • ADHD with LD
• Organizational • Fine Motor • ADHD without LD
• Perceptual

Admissions Process

Open admissions for Ohio resident freshmen. Competitive admissions for non-residents and transfer students.

High School Course Requirements:
English: **4** Math: **3** Science: **2** Foreign Language: **2**

Learning Disability Program
Services only for LD students: **Yes**
Counseling: Individual: **Yes**

Faculty:
Faculty: **1** Part time: **1**
Faculty advocate: **Yes** Meets with instructor: **Occasionally**

Diagnostic Testing

ADD	Personality	Perceptual skills	Spelling
ADHD	Organization	Fine motor skills	Reading
I.Q.	Handwriting	Spoken language	Study skills
Math	Social skills	Written language	

598

Tutoring:
Average size of group tutorials: **3**
Services rendered by:
 Graduates •Peers •Faculty •LD staff Teacher trainees

Tutorials

Grp.	Ind.	Tutorials	Grp.	Ind.	Tutorials
•	•	Math skills	•	•	Word processing
•	•	Study skills	•	•	Time management
•	•	Language arts	•	•	Learning strategies
•	•	Written express	•	•	Organizational skills

Academic Accommodations

Curriculum	Study Aids	Exams
• Priority registration	• Typist	• Oral
Math waiver	• Reader	Untimed
• Foreign lang. waiver	• Notetaker	Take home
Course substitution	• Proof reader	With proctor
In Class	• Text on tape	On computer
• Calculators	Early syllabus	• Extended time
• Tape recorder	Taped handouts	• On tape
• Word processor		• Modified
Priority seating		• Separate room

Graduation Requirements: GPA: **2.0** Years to complete degree: **Minimum 2 years** Language waiver: **Yes**

Program Strengths
Services are available on an individual basis. OSU-Newark is a 2 year school, except for elementary majors, and is a good environment in which to get started on a 4 year degree. Class size is smaller and professors are more available to students when compared to a larger campus. Professors are aware of learning disabilities and make every effort to meet individual student needs.

General Information:
Ohio State University: Newark Campus is a 2 and 4 year public university. Urban campus of 150 acres is 35 miles from Columbus. Accessible by air. Housing is not guaranteed.

Accreditation: NCACS

Expenses:
Tuition: In-state: Full year: $2,478.00. Part-time: Per credit: Sliding scale. Tuition: Out-of-state: Full year: $7,518.00. Part-time: Per credit: Sliding scale. Room and board: $850.00 quarter (room)

Majors
• AREA STUDIES Black/Afro-American, European, Islamic, Jewish, Russian/Slavic, Urban, Women's Studies • BUSINESS Accounting, Banking, Business Administration, Business Economics, Business Management, Economics, Finance, Hotel and Restaurant Management, Human Resources Management, Insurance, International Business, Labor Relations, Management, Marketing, Personnel, Printing Manufacturing, Real Estate, Sports Management • COMMUNICATIONS Advertising, Broadcasting, Communication, Creative Writing, English, Journalism, Photography, Television/Radio/Film • COMPUTER SCIENCE Computer Science, Medical Records Administration, Programming, Systems Analysis, Telecommunications • CRAFTS AND DESIGN Ceramics, Drawing, Glass, Sculpture • EDUCATION Agricultural, Art, Bilingual, Early Childhood, Elementary, English, Foreign Language, Health, Industrial, Mathematics, Middle School, Music, Physical, Recreation and Youth Leadership, Science, Secondary, Social Studies, Special, Speech/Language, Vocational • ENGINEERING Aerospace, Agricultural, Chemical, Civil/Environmental, Computer, Electrical, Industrial, Mechanical, Metallurgical, Mining/Mineral, Physics • HEALTH SCIENCES Communication Disorders, Environmental, Health, Medical Technology, Nursing, Nutritional/Food, Occupational Therapy, Physical Therapy, Radiological Therapy, Speech

Therapy, Speech/Audiology and Speech • HUMANITIES Classics, Humanities, Liberal Arts, Philosophy, Religion • LANGUAGES Arabic, Chinese, French, German, Hebrew, Italian, Japanese, Linguistic, Russian, Spanish • PREPROFESSIONAL Agriculture, Architecture, Dentistry, Engineering, Forestry, Law, Medicine, Natural Resources, Optometry, Pharmacy, Range Management, Social Work • SCIENCES Actuarial Technology, Agronomy, Animal, Astronomy, Biochemistry, Biology, Botany, Chemistry, Earth, Ecology, Geography, Geology, Horticultural, Mathematics, Microbiology, Physical Chemistry, Physical Science, Physics, Physiology, Plant Pathology, Zoology • SOCIAL SCIENCES Anthropology, Criminal Justice, Criminology, Family Counseling, Human Service, International Studies, Psychology, Social Sciences, Sociology • VISUAL AND PERFORMING ARTS Art, Art History, Dance, Dramatic Arts, Fine Arts, Music, Music Performance, Theater • VOCATIONAL Dental Hygiene, Fishery Studies, Forestry, Home Economics, Industrial Design, Landscape Architecture, Painting, Park/Recreation, Poultry, Respiratory Therapy Technology, Surveying and Mapping, Textile and Clothing, Welding, Wildlife Management

Sports/Activities
• SPORTS-INTERCOLLEGIATE Baseball (M), Basketball, Golf, Soccer (M), Tennis, Volleyball (F) • SPORTS-INTRAMURAL Badminton, Bowling, Golf, Ping-Pong, Racquetball, Softball, Tennis, Volleyball • STUDENT LIFE ACTIVITIES Choral, Newspaper, Student Government

---

Very Selective **Ohio**
Services

Ohio University
101 Chubb Hall
Athens, Ohio 45701
(614) 593-4100

School Enrollment: **12,500**
LD Enrollment: **100**

Admissions Contact: **James C. Walters, Director of Admissions**
LD Contact: **Susan Wagner, Asst. Dir. Affirmative Action**
Telephone: **(614) 593-2620**

Admissions

Application Information:
Application deadline: **March 1st**
Rolling Admissions: **Yes**

Secondary School Information
Most Important Criteria For Admissions (1-strongest)

2 SAT/ACT	Application	**1**	School transcript
1 Class rank	**1** Course selection		Personal statement
Interview	Extra activities		Psychoeducational
3 G.P.A.	Open admission	**4**	Recommendations

Test Requirements:
Diagnostic testing waived: **Yes**
Untimed ACT: **Yes**
Documentation of LD required: **Yes**
Currency of diagnostic testing: **3 years**

Ohio

Types of Disabilities Served
- Speech/Lang
- Study skills
- Written express
- Organizational
- Perceptual
- Reading
- Spelling
- Math
- Fine Motor

ADD with LD
ADD without LD
ADHD with LD
ADHD without LD

Faculty:
Faculty: **2** Full time: **1** Part time: **1**

Diagnostic Testing
ADD	Personality	Perceptual skills	Spelling
ADHD	Organization	Fine motor skills	Reading
I.Q.	Handwriting	Spoken language	Study skills
Math	Social skills	Written language	

Tutoring:
Services rendered by:
- Graduates
- Peers
- Faculty
- LD staff
- Teacher trainees

Tutorials
Grp.	Ind.	Tutorials	Grp.	Ind.	Tutorials
•	•	Math skills	•	•	Word processing
•	•	Study skills	•	•	Time management
•	•	Language arts	•	•	Learning strategies
•	•	Written express	•	•	Organizational skills

Academic Accommodations

Curriculum	Study Aids	Exams
Priority registration	Typist	• Oral
Math waiver	Reader	Untimed
Foreign lang. waiver	Notetaker	Take home
Course substitution	Proof reader	With proctor
In Class	• Text on tape	On computer
• Calculators	Early syllabus	• Extended time
• Tape recorder	Taped handouts	On tape
• Word processor		• Modified
Priority seating		Separate room

Program Strengths
If a student is admitted to the University, he/she qualifies (if verification of LD can be provided) for support services (free tutoring, contact with faculty re: accommodations needed, CAP program, priority scheduling, textbooks on tape if required through R.F.B.). This is not a structured program.

General Information:
Ohio University is a 4 year public university. Rural campus of 700 acres is 70 miles from Columbus. Accessible by bus. Ski areas are 200 miles from campus. Beaches are 400 miles from campus. 9% of students are foreign. 39 residential halls on campus. Housing is guaranteed.Guaranteed through 4th year. 90 % of students remain on campus for the weekends. 20 % of students join fraternities/sororities.

Accreditation:NCACS

SAT/ACT Scores:
Scores for incoming freshmen:**Verbal:**65%below 500. 28%between 500 and 599. 6%between 600 and 699. 1%above 700. **Math:**40% below 500. 35% between 500 and 599. 22% between 600 and 699. 3%above 700. **ACT:** 16% below 20. 50% between 20 and 23. 12%between 24 and 25l. 28%between 26 and 28. 4% above 28.

Class Rank:
About 40% of the present freshmen class were in the upper 20% of their high school class. 75% were in the top 40% of their class. 95% were in the top 60% of their class. 100% were in the top 80% of their class.

Expenses:
Tuition: In-state: Full year: $2,721.00. Part-time: Per credit:$89.00. Tuition: Out-of-state: Full year: $5,805.00. Part-time: Per credit:$191.00. Room and board: $3,474.00

Majors
• AREA STUDIES African, Asian, Black/Afro-American, European, Latin American • BUSINESS Accounting, Agricultural, Banking, Business Administration, Business Administration, Business Education, Business Management, Economics, Finance, Human Resources Management, International Business, Labor Relations, Management, Marketing, Marketing Research, Personnel • COMMUNICATIONS Advertising, Broadcasting, Communication, Creative Writing, English, Graphic Design, Journalism, Photography, Television/Radio/Film • COMPUTER SCIENCE Computer Science, Systems Analysis, Telecommunications • CRAFTS AND DESIGN Ceramics, Drawing • EDUCATION Art, Child Development, Early Childhood, Elementary, English, Foreign Language, Health, Industrial, Mathematics, Middle School, Music, Music Therapy, Physical, Recreation and Youth Leadership, Secondary, Special • ENGINEERING Aerospace, Chemical, Civil, Computer, Electrical, Industrial, Mechanical, Mining/Mineral, Physics • HEALTH SCIENCES Communication Disorders, Environmental, Health, Medical Technology, Nursing, Nutritional/Food, Physical Therapy, Speech Therapy, Speech/Audiology and Speech • HUMANITIES English/Writing/Literature, Humanities, Liberal Arts, Philosophy • LANGUAGES French, German, Greek, Italian, Japanese, Russian, Spanish • PREPROFESSIONAL Dentistry, Forestry, Law, Medicine, Natural Resources, Recreation, Social Work • SCIENCES Biomedical, Biochemistry, Botany, Chemistry, Earth, Ecology, Geography, Geology, Marine Biology, Mathematics, Microbiology, Physical Chemistry, Physical Science, Physics, Physiology, Zoology • SOCIAL SCIENCES Anthropology, Criminal Justice, Criminology, Family Counseling, Geography, Government/Political, History, International Studies, Psychology, Sociology • VISUAL AND PERFORMING ARTS Art, Art History, Dance, Dramatic Arts, Music, Studio Art, Theater • VOCATIONAL Aviation Technology, Fashion Mechandizing, Food Service, Home Economics, Interior Design, Painting, Park/Recreation, Piloting, Textile and Clothing

Sports/Activities
• SPORTS RELATED Marching Band, Pep Band • SPORTS-INTERCOLLEGIATE Baseball (M), Basketball, Bowling, Boxing (M), Cross Country, Diving, Field Hockey (F), Golf (M), Ice Hockey (M), Lacrosse, Riflery, Rugby, Sailing, Skiing - Snow, Soccer (M), Softball (F), Swimming, Tennis, Track and Field, Volleyball, Wrestling (M) • SPORTS-INTRAMURAL Archery, Badminton, Baseball (M), Basketball, Bowling, Boxing (M), Cross Country, Diving, Fencing, Golf, Gymnastics, Hand Ball, Horseback Riding, Lacrosse, Racquetball, Soccer, Softball, Squash, Swimming, Tennis, Track and Field, Volleyball, Water Polo, Wrestling (M) • STUDENT LIFE ACTIVITIES Choral, Community Service, Concert Band, Dance, Drama Groups, Ethnic & Cultural Groups, Film, Fraternities, Jazz Band, Magazine, Music Groups, Musical Theater, Newspaper, Opera, Political Groups, Radio/TV station, Religious Organization, Sororities, Student Government, Symphony Orchestra, Yearbook

Selective

Accommodations Ohio

Otterbein College
West College Avenue and Grove Street
Westerville, Ohio 43081
(614) 890-0004

School Enrollment: **2,490** Male: **890** Female: **1,600**

Admissions Contact: **Dr. William Stahler, V.P. of Admissions**
LD Contact: **Ellen E. Kasulis, Director, Learning Assistance Ctr.**
Name of Program: **Academic Support Services**
Address: **Learning Assistance Center, Towers 106**
Telephone:**(614) 898-1413**

Admissions

Application Information:
LD on admissions committee:**Yes**
Application deadline: **April 20th**
Rolling Admissions: **Yes**

Secondary School Information
Most Important Criteria For Admissions (1-strongest)

2 SAT/ACT	4 Application	1 School transcript
3 Class rank	2 Course selection	5 Personal statement
5 Interview	5 Extra activities	4 Psychoeducational
1 G.P.A.	Open admission	5 Recommendations

Test Requirements:
Untimed SAT: **Yes** Untimed ACT: **Yes**
Documentation of LD required: **Yes**
Tests recommended: **In order for students to receive substitutions or to have special testing accommodations they must have a psycho educational evaluation with both ability and achievement scores and a report of prior history of accommodations.**

Types of Disabilities Served
- Speech/Lang
- Study skills
- Written express
- Organizational Perceptual
- Reading
- Spelling
- Math
- Fine Motor
- ADD with LD
- ADD without LD
- ADHD with LD
- ADHD without LD

High School Course Requirements:
English: **4** Math: **3** Science: **2** Foreign Language: **2-3**

Learning Disability Program
Services available for all students: **Yes**

Faculty:
Faculty: **1** Full time: **1**

Diagnostic Testing

ADD	Personality	Perceptual skills	Spelling
ADHD	Organization	Fine motor skills	Reading
I.Q.	Handwriting	Spoken language	Study skills
Math	Social skills	Written language	

Tutoring:
Services rendered by:
Graduates •Peers •Faculty LD staff Teacher trainees

Tutorials

Grp.	Ind.	Tutorials	Grp.	Ind.	Tutorials
	•	Math skills		•	Word processing
•	•	Study skills	•	•	Time management
	•	Language arts	•	•	Learning strategies
	•	Written express	•	•	Organizational skills

Academic Accommodations

Curriculum	Study Aids	Exams
Priority registration	Typist	Oral
Math waiver	Reader	Untimed
Foreign lang. waiver	Notetaker	Take home
Course substitution	Proof reader	• With proctor
In Class	• Text on tape	On computer
• Calculators	Early syllabus	• Extended time
• Tape recorder	Taped handouts	On tape
Word processor		Modified
Priority seating		Separate room

Graduation Requirements:
Course credits: **180 - B.A.** GPA: **2.0** Years to complete degree: **4**

Program Strengths
While we have no LD program, academic support services are offered to all students through the Writing Center, academic departments (some tutorials), and The Learning Assistance Center (individualized help in study skills and time management, peer tutoring in some areas, a developmental, not remedial, reading/study skills course. Some academic adjustments, special services and special aides are possible, but no LD diagnostic testing is available.

General Information:
Otterbein College is a 4 year private United Methodist college. Suburban campus of 70 acres is 12 miles from Columbus. Accessible by air or bus. Ski areas are 60 miles from campus. 5% of students are foreign. 9 residential halls on campus. Housing is guaranteed.40 % of students remain on campus for the weekends. 50 % of students join fraternities/sororities.

Accreditation:NCACS

SAT/ACT Scores:
Scores for incoming freshmen:**Verbal:**71%below 500. 25%between 500 and 599. 4%between 600 and 699. **Math:**56% below 500. 28% between 500 and 599. 16% between 600 and 699. 5%above 700. **ACT:** 39% below 20. 26% between 20 and 23. 18%between 24 and 251. 15%between 26 and 28. 3% above 28.

Class Rank:
About 62% of the present freshmen class were in the upper 20% of their high school class. 85% were in the top 40% of their class. 100% were in the top 60% of their class. 100% were in the top 80% of their class.

Expenses:
Tuition: In-state: Full year: $11,502.00. Part-time: Per credit:$152.00. Tuition: Out-of-state: Full year: $11,502.00. Part-time: Per credit:$152.00. Room and board: $4,107.00

Majors
• BUSINESS Accounting, Banking, Business Administration, Business Economics, Business Management, Economics, Finance, Food Management, Management, Marketing • COMMUNICATIONS Broadcasting, Communication, English, Journalism, Television/Radio/Film • COMPUTER SCIENCE Computer Science • EDUCATION Art, Early Childhood, Elementary, Health, Middle School, Music, Physical, Pre-Education, Secondary • HEALTH SCIENCES Environmental, Nursing • HUMANITIES Philosophy, Religion • LANGUAGES French, Spanish • PREPROFESSIONAL Dentistry, Engineering, Law, Medicine, Natural Resources, Optometry, Pharmacy, Sports Medicine, Veterinarian • SCIENCES Astron-

Ohio

omy, Biology, Chemistry, Equestrian Studies, Mathematics, Physics • SOCIAL SCIENCES Government/Political, History, International Studies, Political Science, Psychology, Public Relations, Sociology • VISUAL AND PERFORMING ARTS Dance, Dramatic Arts, Fine Arts, Music, Music Performance, Music Theatre, Studio Art, Theater • VOCATIONAL Fashion Merchandising, Home Economics, Industrial Equipment Maintenance

Sports/Activities

• SPORTS RELATED Marching Band, Pep Band • SPORTS-INTERCOLLEGIATE Baseball (M), Basketball, Cross Country, Football (M), Golf (M), Horseback Riding, Soccer, Softball (F), Tennis, Track and Field, Volleyball • SPORTS-INTRAMURAL Archery, Badminton, Basketball, Bowling, Cross Country (M), Football (M), Golf, Ping-Pong, Racquetball, Softball, Tennis, Track and Field (M), Volleyball • STUDENT LIFE ACTIVITIES Choral, Concert Band, Drama Groups, Ethnic & Cultural Groups, Fraternities, Jazz Band, Music Groups, Musical Theater, Newspaper, Opera, Radio/TV station, Religious Organization, Sororities, Student Government, Symphony Orchestra, Yearbook

Less Selective	Ohio
	Services

Owens Technical College

Caller Number 10,000 Oregon Road
Toledo, Ohio 43699
(419) 666-3282

School Enrollment: **5,900** Male: **3,200** Female: **2,700**

Admissions Contact: **William Iuoska, Director of Admissions**
LD Contact: **Carol Russel,I Coordinator**
Name of Program: **Handicapped Services**

Admissions

Secondary School Information
Most Important Criteria For Admissions (1-strongest)

SAT/ACT	Application	School transcript
Class rank	Course selection	Personal statement
Interview	Extra activities	Psychoeducational
G.P.A.	1 Open admission	Recommendations

Test Requirements:
Diagnostic testing waived: **Yes**
Documentation of LD required: **Yes**
Currency of diagnostic testing: **3 years**

Types of Disabilities Served

Speech/Lang	• Reading	ADD with LD
Study skills	• Spelling	ADD without LD
Written express	• Math	ADHD with LD
Organizational	• Fine Motor	ADHD without LD
Perceptual		

Diagnostic Testing

ADD	Personality	Perceptual skills	Spelling
ADHD	Organization	Fine motor skills	Reading
I.Q.	Handwriting	Spoken language	Study skills
Math	Social skills	Written language	

Services rendered by:

Graduates	Peers	Faculty	LD staff	Teacher trainees

Tutorials

Grp.	Ind.	Tutorials	Grp.	Ind.	Tutorials
		Math skills			Word processing
		Study skills			Time management
		Language arts			Learning strategies
		Written express			Organizational skills

Academic Accommodations

Curriculum	Study Aids	Exams
Priority registration	Typist	• Oral
Math waiver	Reader	Untimed
Foreign lang. waiver	• Notetaker	• Take home
• Course substitution	• Proof reader	With proctor
In Class	• Text on tape	On computer
• Calculators	Early syllabus	• Extended time
• Tape recorder	Taped handouts	On tape
• Word processor		• Modified
Priority seating		Separate room

Program Strengths
We really do not have an LD Program. Instead, we provide services for LD students which include notetaking, untimed tests, and oral exams.

General Information:
Owens Technical College is a 2 year public college. Urban campus 4 miles from Toledo. Ski areas are 2 hours from campus. 1% of students are foreign. Housing is not guaranteed.

Accreditation:NCACS

Expenses:
Tuition: In-state: Full year: $1,440.00. Part-time: Per credit:$60.00. Tuition: Out-of-state: Full year: $2,880.00.

Majors
• BUSINESS Accounting, Agricultural, Banking, Business Administration, Business Management, Finance, Food Management, Hotel and Restaurant Management, Management, Marketing • COMPUTER SCIENCE Computer Technology, Data Processing, Programming, Software Engineer, Telecommunications • EDUCATION Child Development, Early Childhood, Pre-Education • ENGINEERING Air Conditioning Technology, Civil/Environmental, Electrical, Engineering Science, Industrial, Mechanical, Nuclear Medical Technology • HEALTH SCIENCES Dental Hygiene, Nursing, Nutritional/Food, Surgical Technology, Ultrasound Technology • PREPROFESSIONAL Architecture, Optometry • SCIENCES Bio-medical • SOCIAL SCIENCES Law Enforcement • VOCATIONAL Air Conditioning/Heating/Refrig, Automobile Technology, Automotive Service, Diesel Power Technology, Drafting, Electronics Technology, Fashion Mechandizing, Quality Control Technology, Radiological Technology, Secretarial, Word Processing

Sports/Activities
• SPORTS-INTERCOLLEGIATE Basketball (M) • SPORTS-INTRAMURAL Basketball, Skiing - Snow, Softball, Tennis, Volleyball • STUDENT LIFE ACTIVITIES Special Interest Clubs, Student Government

Less Selective   **Ohio Program**

Sinclair Community College
444 West Third Street
Dayton, Ohio 45402
(513) 226-2963

School Enrollment: **6,200**

Admissions Contact: **Sara P. Smith, Director of Admissions**
LD Contact: **Diane McConnell, LD Specialist**
Name of Program: **Handicapped Student Services**
Telephone:**(513) 226-2752**

Admissions

Application Information:
Application deadline: **Open**
Rolling Admissions: **Yes**

Secondary School Information
Most Important Criteria For Admissions (1-strongest)

SAT/ACT **1**	Application	School transcript
Class rank	Course selection	Personal statement
Interview	Extra activities	Psychoeducational
G.P.A.	Open admission	Recommendations

Test Requirements:
Diagnostic testing waived: **Yes**
WAIS-R required: **Yes** Range accepted: **Normal**
Currency of diagnostic testing: **3 years**
Tests recommended: **Woodcock-Johnson**

Types of Disabilities Served
- Speech/Lang
- Study skills
- Written express
- Organizational
- Perceptual
- Reading
- Spelling
- Math
- Fine Motor
- ADD with LD
- ADD without LD
- ADHD with LD
- ADHD without LD

Learning Disability Program
Program: Remedial: **Yes**
Program: Reinforces course work: **Yes**
Students mainstreamed **100** % of the day
Counseling: Individual: **Yes** Group Counseling: **Yes**

Faculty:
Faculty: **1** Including Director: **Yes** Part time: **1** M.A.: **1**
Faculty advocate: **Yes** Meets with instructor: **When necessary**

Diagnostic Testing

ADD •	Personality	Perceptual skills	Spelling
ADHD	Organization	Fine motor skills	• Reading
I.Q.	Handwriting	Spoken language	• Study skills
• Math	Social skills •	Written language	

Tutoring:
Services rendered by:
Graduates   •Peers   Faculty   LD staff   Teacher trainees

Tutorials

Grp.	Ind.	Tutorials	Grp.	Ind.	Tutorials
	•	Math skills		•	Word processing
•	•	Study skills	•	•	Time management
	•	Language arts	•	•	Learning strategies
	•	Written express	•	•	Organizational skills

Academic Accommodations

Curriculum	Study Aids	Exams
Priority registration	Typist	• Oral
Math waiver	Reader	Untimed
Foreign lang. waiver	• Notetaker	• Take home
Course substitution	• Proof reader	With proctor
In Class	• Text on tape	On computer
Calculators	Early syllabus	• Extended time
• Tape recorder	Taped handouts	On tape
• Word processor		• Modified
Priority seating		Separate room

Program Strengths
The LD student at Sinclair is expected to be his/her own advocate. The student arranges with professors and tutorial services any accommodations he/she will need. The LD Specialist acts as a coach, intervening with professors only when necessary. The specialist also plans with the student a strategy for successful learning at Sinclair

General Information:
Sinclair Community College is a 2 year public college. Urban campus of 44 acres is Accessible by air or bus. .5% of students are foreign. Housing is not guaranteed.

Accreditation:NCACS

Expenses: Part-time: Per credit:$39.00 State - $29.00 County. Tuition: Out-of-state: Full year: Part-time: Per credit: $59.00. Part-time: Per credit:$59.00.

Majors
• BUSINESS Accounting, Aviation Management, Banking, Business Administration, Business Management, Finance, Labor Relations, Management, Marketing, Real Estate, Retailing, Travel/Tourism Management • COMMUNICATIONS Communication, Graphic Design • COMPUTER SCIENCE Data Processing, Medical Records Administration, Robotics • CRAFTS AND DESIGN Illustration Design • EDUCATION Child Development, Early Childhood, Elementary, Physical, Secondary, Special • ENGINEERING Air Conditioning Technology, Civil/Environmental, Electrical, Engineering Science, Mechanical • HEALTH SCIENCES Dental Assistant, Medical Secretary, Nursing, Nutritional/Food, Physical Therapy, Surgical Technology • HUMANITIES Humanities, Philosophy • LANGUAGES French, German, Spanish • PREPROFESSIONAL Architecture, Legal Assistant, Social Work • SCIENCES Biology, Chemistry, Geography, Geology, Gerontology, Physics • SOCIAL SCIENCES History, Human Service, Law Enforcement, Political Science, Psychology, Public Relations, Social Sciences, Sociology • VISUAL AND PERFORMING ARTS Dance, Dramatic Arts, Fine Arts, Music, Theater • VOCATIONAL Air Conditioning/Heating/Refrig, Automobile Technology, Aviation Maintenance, Business and Office, Diesel Power Technology, Drafting, Electronics Technology, Fire Science, Food Service, Interior Design, Legal Secretary, Park/Recreation, Radiological Technology, Respiratory Therapy Technology, Secretarial, Word Processing

Sports/Activities
• SPORTS-INTERCOLLEGIATE Baseball (M), Basketball, Golf (M), Softball (M), Tennis, Volleyball (F) • SPORTS-INTRAMURAL Archery, Badminton, Basketball, Gymnastics, Hand Ball (M), Ping-Pong, Racquetball, Softball (M), Swimming, Volleyball, Wrestling (M) • STUDENT LIFE ACTIVITIES Choral, Concert Band, Dance, Drama Groups, Jazz Band, Music Groups, Musical Theater, Newspaper, Opera, Student Gov-

Less Selective

The University of Akron - Wayne College

10470 Smucker Road
Orrville, Ohio 44667
(216) 683-2010

School Enrollment: **1,492** Male: **530** Female: **962**
LD Enrollment: **4** Male: **2** Female: **2**

Admissions Contact: **Peggy J. Shallenberger, Cord. of Admissions**
LD Contact: **Julia Beyeler, Director, Learning Support Services**
Name of Program: **Learning Support Services**
Address: **10470 Smucker Road**
Telephone:**(216) 682-1671**

Admissions

Application Information:
Application deadline: **May 1st**
Rolling Admissions: **Yes**

Secondary School Information
Most Important Criteria For Admissions (1-strongest)

4 SAT/ACT	**1** Application	School transcript
3 Class rank	Course selection	Personal statement
Interview	Extra activities	Psychoeducational
2 G.P.A.	Open admission	Recommendations

Test Requirements:
Diagnostic testing waived: **Yes**
Untimed SAT: **Yes** Untimed ACT: **Yes**
Documentation of LD required: **Yes**
Currency of diagnostic testing: **12-18**

Types of Disabilities Served
- Speech/Lang
- Study skills
- Written express
- Organizational
- Perceptual
- Reading
- Spelling
- Math
- Fine Motor
- ADD with LD
- ADD without LD
- ADHD with LD
- ADHD without LD

Admissions Process

File application with $25.00 fee. Provide high school transcripts and ACT scores. Take Placement Tests in mathematics and English writing and reading.

High School Course Requirements:
English: **4** Math: **4** Science: **4** Foreign Language: **3**
Waivers to standard high school courses
Math: **Yes** Course substitution: **Yes**

Learning Disability Program

Special orientation for LD students:
Program: Reinforces course work: **Yes**
Program available through:**at student request**
Students mainstreamed **100** % of the day
Services available for all students: **Yes**
Counseling: Individual: **Yes**

Faculty:
Faculty: **7** Including Director: **Yes** Part time: **6**
LD faculty with: BS/BA: **1** M.A.: **5**

Diagnostic Testing
ADD	Personality	Perceptual skills	Spelling
ADHD	Organization	Fine motor skills	• Reading
• I.Q.	Handwriting•	Spoken language	• Study skills
• Math	Social skills•	• Written language	

Tutoring:
Average size of group tutorials: **1:1**
Services rendered by:
Graduates •Peers •Faculty •LD staff •Teacher trainees

Tutorials
Grp.	Ind.	Tutorials	Grp.	Ind.	Tutorials
•	•	Math skills	•	•	Word processing
•	•	Study skills	•	•	Time management
		Language arts	•	•	Learning strategies
•	•	Written express	•	•	Organizational skills

Academic Accommodations

Curriculum	Study Aids	Exams
Priority registration	Typist	• Oral
• Math waiver	• Reader	• Untimed
Foreign lang. waiver	• Notetaker	Take home
Course substitution	Proof reader	• With proctor
In Class	• Text on tape	On computer
Calculators	Early syllabus	• Extended time
• Tape recorder	Taped handouts	On tape
Word processor		Modified
• Priority seating		• Separate room

Graduation Requirements:
Course credits: **66** Years to complete degree: **No limit** Math waiver: **Yes**

General Information:
The University of Akron - Wayne College is a 2 year public college. Rural campus of 158 acres is Accessible by car. Housing is not guaranteed.

Accreditation:NCAC

SAT/ACT Scores:
Scores for incoming freshmen: **ACT:** 90% below 20.

Expenses:
Tuition: In-state: Full year: $2,600.00. Part-time: Per credit:$97.92. Tuition: Out-of-state: Full year: $6,200.00. Part-time: Per credit:$241.12.

Majors

• BUSINESS Accounting, Banking/Finance, Bookkeeping, Business Administration, Business Economics, Business Education, Business Management, Clerical, Data Processing, Education, Marketing, Secretarial Science • COMPUTER SCIENCE Business Data Programming, Computer Maintenance, Computer Science, Data Processing, Medical Records Administration, Medical Records Technology, Programming • EDUCATION Elementary, Secondary • HEALTH SCIENCES Medical Assistant, Medical Records Administration, Medical Secretary • HUMANITIES English/Writing/Literature, Humanities • LANGUAGES German, Spanish • PRE PROFESSIONAL Business, Legal Assistant, Social Work

Sports/Activities

• SPORTS-INTERCOLLEGIATE Basketball (F), Basketball (M), Volleyball (F)

University of Cincinnati: Raymond Walters College

9555 Plainfield Road
Cincinnati, Ohio 45236
(513) 745-5600

School Enrollment: **4,194** Male: **1,498** Female: **2,696**
LD Enrollment: **80**

Admissions Contact: **Tom Minter**
LD Contact: **Carol Robinson, Director**
Name of Program: **College Study Skills**
Address: **9555 Plainfield Rd.**
Telephone:**(513) 745-5730**

Admissions

Application Information:
Application deadline: **Open**
Applicant must apply **Open** months in advance
Rolling Admissions: **Yes** Notified when: **4 weeks later**

Secondary School Information
Most Important Criteria For Admissions (1-strongest)

SAT/ACT	**1** Application	**2** School transcript
3 Class rank	**5** Course selection	Personal statement
Interview	Extra activities	Psychoeducational
4 G.P.A.	**1** Open admission	Recommendations

Test Requirements:
Standardized tests waived: **Yes**
Currency of diagnostic testing: **Open**
Tests recommended: **Asset Placement**

Types of Disabilities Served
- Speech/Lang
- Study skills
- Written express
- Organizational
- Perceptual
- Reading
- Spelling
- Math
- Fine Motor
- ADD with LD
- ADD without LD
- ADHD with LD
- ADHD without LD

Admissions Process

Open admissions - $30.00 application fee - student must be high school graduate or have GED - transcripts must be sent - fill out forms and take Asset Placement Test - see advisor.

Learning Disability Program

Students mainstreamed **100** % of the day
Recommended credits per semester: **12**
Time required or recommended in learning center: **3.5 hours**
Services available for all students: **Yes**
Counseling: Individual: **Yes** Vocational Counseling: **Yes**

Diagnostic Testing

ADD	Personality	Perceptual skills	• Spelling
ADHD	Organization	Fine motor skills	• Reading
I.Q.	Handwriting	Spoken language	• Study skills
• Math	Social skills	• Written language	

Tutoring:
Services rendered by:
Graduates •Peers •Faculty LD staff Teacher trainees

Tutorials

Grp.	Ind.	Tutorials	Grp.	Ind.	Tutorials
	•	Math skills			Word processing
•	•	Study skills	•	•	Time management
	•	Language arts		•	Learning strategies
	•	Written express		•	Organizational skills

Academic Accommodations

Curriculum	Study Aids	Exams
• Priority registration	Typist	• Oral
Math waiver	• Reader	Untimed
Foreign lang. waiver	• Notetaker	Take home
Course substitution	• Proof reader	• With proctor
In Class	• Text on tape	• On computer
• Calculators	Early syllabus	• Extended time
• Tape recorder	Taped handouts	On tape
• Word processor		• Modified
Priority seating		• Separate room

Graduation Requirements:
Course credits: **90-100 hours** GPA: **2.0** Years to complete degree: **As many as needed**
Other requirements: **Residency hours-at least half of hours at RWC**

Program Strengths

We are an open door, state-supported, two-year college associated with the University of Cincinnati. We have developmental classes in math, chemistry, English, reading, and study skills. These classes are open to all students, but we give additional help to LD students in the form of extra time, counseling, and tutoring.

General Information:

University of Cincinnati: Raymond Walters College is a 2 year public college. Suburban campus of 150 acres is 10 miles from Cincinnati. Housing is not guaranteed.

Accreditation: NCACS

Expenses:
Tuition: In-state: Full year: $2,850.00. Part-time: Per credit:$79.00. Tuition: Out-of-state: Full year: $7,020.00. Part-time: Per credit:$195.00.

Majors

• AREA STUDIES Black/Afro-American, Ethnic, Jewish, Latin American, Urban • BUSINESS Accounting, Banking, Business Administration, Business Management, Economics, Finance, Insurance, Investments and Securities, Management, Marketing, Personnel, Real Estate, Retailing, Travel/Tourism Management • COMMUNICATIONS Commercial Design, Communication, English, Graphic Design, Linguistics, Literature • COMPUTER SCIENCE Computer Science, Data Processing, Programming, Systems Analysis • EDUCATION Child Development, Early Childhood, Elementary, Health, Middle School, Pre-Education Secondary, Special • ENGINEERING Aerospace, Air Conditioning Technology, Chemical, Civil/Environmental, Computer, Electrical, Engineering Science, Industrial, Mechanical, Metallurgical, Nuclear • ENVIRONMENTAL CONTROL Energy Conservation • HEALTH SCIENCES Dental Hygiene, Emergency Medical Technology, Environmental, Health, Medical Secretary, Nuclear Medical Technology, Nursing, Nutritional/Food, Radiological Therapy, Surgical Technology • HUMANITIES Classics, English/Writing/Literature, Humanities, Liberal Arts, Philosophy • LANGUAGES French, German, Japanese, Spanish • PREPROFESSIONAL Agriculture, Dentistry, Engineering, Law, Legal Assistant, Medicine, Pharmacy, Recreation, Social Work, Veterinarian • SCIENCES Animal, Biochemistry, Biology, Chemistry, Earth, Geography, Geology, Mathematics, Meteorology, Nuclear Medical Technology, Physics • SOCIAL SCIENCES Anthropology, Criminal Justice, Government/Political, History, Human Service, International Studies, Library Science, Political Science, Psychology, Public Relations, Sociology • VISUAL AND PERFORMING ARTS Dance, Dramatic Arts, Fine Arts, Jazz, Music, Music Performance, Music Theatre, Theater • VOCATIONAL Air Conditioning/Heating/Refri, Automotive Technology, Business and Office, Dental Hygiene, Electronics Technology, Fashion Design, Fire Science, Industrial Design, Interior Design, Legal Secretary, Office Administration, Radiological Technology, Secretarial, Urban Design, Word Processing

Sports/Activities

• SPORTS RELATED Marching Band, Pep Band • SPORTS-INTERCOLLEGIATE Baseball (M), Basketball, Cross Country, Diving, Football (M), Golf (M), Soccer, Swimming, Tennis, Track and Field, Volleyball (F), Wrestling (M) • SPORTS-INTRAMURAL Archery, Badminton, Baseball (M), Basketball, Bowling, Diving, Golf, Hand Ball, Ping-Pong, Racquetball, Soccer, Softball, Squash, Swimming, Tennis, Track and Field, Volleyball • STUDENT LIFE ACTIVITIES Choral, Concert Band, Dance, Drama Groups, Film, Fraternities, Jazz Band, Magazine, Music Groups, Musical Theater, Newspaper, Radio/TV station, Sororities, Student Government, Symphony Orchestra, Yearbook

Selective	Ohio
	Services

University of Dayton

300 College Park
Dayton, Ohio 45469
(513) 229-4411-(800) 837-7433

School Enrollment: **6,245** Male: **3,208** Female: **3,037**

Admissions Contact: **Myron Achbach, Director of Admissions**
LD Contact: **L.B. Fred, Director**
Name of Program: **Special Programs**
Address: **123 Grosiger Hall**
Telephone:**(513) 229-2229**

Admissions

Application Information:

Application deadline: **Rolling-None**
Rolling Admissions: **Yes**Notified when: **3-4 weeks**

Secondary School Information

Most Important Criteria For Admissions (1-strongest)

5 SAT/ACT	**10** Application	**1** School transcript
4 Class rank	**3** Course selection	**8** Personal statement
9 Interview	**7** Extra activities	**11** Psychoeducational
2 G.P.A.	Open admission	**6** Recommendations

Test Requirements:

Documentation of LD required: **Yes**

Types of Disabilities Served

• Speech/Lang	• Reading	• ADD with LD
• Study skills	• Spelling	• ADD without LD
• Written express	• Math	• ADHD with LD
• Organizational	• Fine Motor	• ADHD without LD
• Perceptual		

Admissions Process

Upon receipt of application for admission, high school transcripts,

ACT or SAT, personal statement, counselor recommendation, a selection committee reviews each application individually.

High School Course Requirements:

English: **4** Math: **3** Science: **3** Foreign Language: **2**

Learning Disability Program

Program: Reinforces course work: **Yes**
Services only for LD students: **Yes**
Counseling: Individual: **Yes**

Faculty:

Faculty: **1** Part time: **1** M.A.: **1**

Diagnostic Testing

ADD	Personality	Perceptual skills	Spelling
ADHD	Organization	Fine motor skills	Reading
I.Q.	Handwriting	Spoken language	Study skills
Math	Social skills	Written language	

Tutoring:

Average size of group tutorials: **8-10**
Services rendered by:

Graduates	•Peers	Faculty	LD staff	Teacher trainees

Tutorials

Grp.	Ind.	Tutorials	Grp.	Ind.	Tutorials
•	•	Math skills			Word processing
•	•	Study skills	•	•	Time management
•	•	Language arts			Learning strategies
•	•	Written express	•	•	Organizational skills

Academic Accommodations

Curriculum	Study Aids	Exams
Priority registration	Typist	Oral
Math waiver	Reader	Untimed
Foreign lang. waiver	Notetaker	Take home
Course substitution	Proof reader	• With proctor
In Class	Text on tape	On computer
Calculators	Early syllabus	• Extended time
• Tape recorder	Taped handouts	On tape
Word processor		Modified
Priority seating		Separate room

Graduation Requirements:

Course credits: **Varies** GPA: **2.0** Years to complete degree: **Varies**
Other requirements: **One year (30 semester hours) of residence (residence meaning taking courses at the University of Dayton).**

Program Strengths

We provide services on an individual basis based on the student's needs.

General Information:

University of Dayton is a 4 year private Roman Catholic university. Suburban campus of 102 acres is 2 miles from Dayton. Accessible by air, train, or bus. Ski areas are 1.5 hours from campus. Beaches are 10 hours from campus. 1.1% of students are foreign. 4 residential halls on campus. Housing is guaranteed.Guaranteed through 4th year. 95 % of students remain on campus for the weekends. 21 % of students join fraternities/sororities.

Accreditation:NCACS

SAT/ACT Scores:

Scores for incoming freshmen:**Verbal:**54%below 500. 35%between 500 and 599. 10%between 600 and 699. 1%above 700. **Math:**23% below 500.

45% between 500 and 599. 24% between 600 and 699. 8% above 700. **ACT:** 9.0% below 20. 34% between 20 and 23. 18% between 24 and 25l. 22% between 26 and 28. 17% above 28.

Class Rank:
About 40% of the present freshmen class were in the upper 20% of their high school class. 66% were in the top 40% of their class. 88% were in the top 60% of their class. 98% were in the top 80% of their class.

Expenses:
Tuition: In-state: Full year: $9,790.00. Part-time: Per credit:$287.90. Part-time: Per course: $863.70 (3 credit hour course). Tuition: Out-of-state: Full year: $9,790.00. Part-time: Per credit:$287.90. Part-time: Per course:$863.70-3 credits Room and board: $3,930.00

Majors

• AREA STUDIES American, International Studies • ARTS Design, Dramatic Arts, Drawing, Interior Design, Music, Music Performance, Painting, Photography • BUSINESS Accounting, Banking/Finance, Business Administration, Business Economics, Business Education, Business Management, Economics, Management, Marketing • COMMUNICATIONS Broadcasting, Communication, Journalism, Public Relations, Television/Radio/Film • COMPUTER SCIENCE Computer Science, Systems Analysis • CRAFTS AND DESIGN Graphic Design, Illustration Design, Jewelry, Printmaking, Sculpture, Textile/Weaving • EDUCATION Art, Early Childhood, Elementary, Health, Music, Physical, Secondary • ENGINEERING Chemical, Civil, Electrical, Mechanical • HEALTH SCIENCES Medical Laboratory Technology, Nuclear Medical Technology • HUMANITIES Classics, English/Writing/Literature, Fine Arts, Humanities, Liberal Arts, Philosophy, Religion • LANGUAGES French, German, Spanish • PRE-PROFESSIONAL Dentistry, Law, Medicine • RELIGIOUS STUDIES Philosophy, Religion and Theology • SCIENCES Biochemistry, Biology, Chemistry, Computer Science, Ecology, Geology, Mathematics, Physical Science, Physics • SOCIAL SCIENCES Anthropology, Criminal Justice, History, International Studies, Political Science, Psychology, Sociology • SPECIAL EDUCATION Emotionally Disturbed, Gifted & Talented, Learning Disability, Mentally Retarded, Physically Handicapped, Visually Handicapped • VISUAL AND PERFORMING ARTS Art, Dramatic Arts, Fine Arts, Music, Music Performance, Studio Art, Theater

Sports/Activities

• SPORTS RELATED Baton Twirling, Cheerleading, Chess, Drill Team, Marching Band, Pep Band, Team Managers • SPORTS-INTERCOLLEGIATE Baseball (M), Basketball, Cross Country, Cross Country (F), Cross Country (M), Football (M), Golf (M), Soccer, Soccer (F), Soccer (M), Softball (F), Tennis, Tennis (F), Tennis (M), Volleyball (F), Water Polo (M), Wrestling (M) • SPORTS-INTRAMURAL Badminton, Baseball (M), Basketball, Basketball (F), Basketball (M), Bowling, Bowling (F), Bowling (M), Field Hockey (F), Football, Football (F), Football (M), Ice Hockey (M), Lacrosse (M), Martial Arts, Ping-Pong, Racquetball, Racquetball (F), Racquetball (M), Rugby (M), Soccer, Soccer (F), Soccer (M), Softball, Softball (F), Softball (M), Volleyball, Volleyball (F), Volleyball (M), Weight Lifting, Wrestling • STUDENT LIFE ACTIVITIES Academic Clubs, Choral, Community Service, Concert Band, Dance, Debate, Drama Groups, Ethnic & Cultural Groups, Fraternities, Jazz Band, Magazine, Music Groups, Musical Theater, Newspaper, Orchestra, Political Groups, Radio/TV station, Religious Organization, Sororities, Student Government, Yearbook

University of Toledo
2801 West Bancroft Street
Toledo, Ohio 43606
(419) 537-2696

School Enrollment: **20,688** Male: **10,101** Female: **10,587**
LD Enrollment: **275**

Admissions Contact: **Richard Eastop, Dean**
LD Contact: **Carl Earwood, Director**
Name of Program: **Physically and Mentally Challenged**
Address: **2801 West Bancroft**
Telephone:**(419) 537-2624**

Admissions

Application Information:
Applicant must apply **1** months in advance
Rolling Admissions: **Yes**

Secondary School Information
Most Important Criteria For Admissions (1-strongest)

4 SAT/ACT	**6** Application	**1**	School transcript
5 Class rank	**3** Course selection	**8**	Personal statement
10 Interview	**7** Extra activities	**11**	Psychoeducational
2 G.P.A.	Open admission	**9**	Recommendations

Test Requirements:
Diagnostic testing waived: **Yes**
Untimed SAT: **Yes** Untimed ACT: **Yes**
WAIS-R required: **Yes** Range accepted: **Flexible**
Documentation of LD required: **Yes**
Currency of diagnostic testing: **5 years**

Types of Disabilities Served
• Speech/Lang	• Reading	ADD with LD
• Study skills	• Spelling	ADD without LD
• Written express	• Math	ADHD with LD
• Organizational	• Fine Motor	ADHD without LD
• Perceptual		

High School Course Requirements:
English: **1** Math: **1** Science: **2**
Waivers to standard high school courses
Foreign Language : **Yes** Course substitution: **Yes**

Learning Disability Program
Program: Remedial: **Yes**
Program: Reinforces course work: **Yes**
Program available through:**Year round**
Students mainstreamed **100** % of the day
Recommended credits per semester: **12-16**
Services available for all students: **Yes**
Counseling: Individual: **Yes** Group Counseling: **Yes**

Faculty:
Faculty: **3** Including Director: **Yes** Full time: **2** Part time: **1**
LD faculty with: BS/BA: **1** M.A.: **3** Ph.D.: **1**
Faculty advocate: **Yes** Meets with instructor: **As needed**

Ohio

Diagnostic Testing

ADD	Personality	Perceptual skills	Spelling
ADHD	Organization	Fine motor skills	Reading
• I.Q.	Handwriting	Spoken language	Study skills
Math	Social skills	Written language	

Tutoring:

Average size of group tutorials: **5**

Services rendered by:

•Graduates •Peers •Faculty •LD staff •Teacher trainees

Tutorials

Grp.	Ind.	Tutorials	Grp.	Ind.	Tutorials
•	•	Math skills	•	•	Word processing
•	•	Study skills	•	•	Time management
•	•	Language arts	•	•	Learning strategies
•	•	Written express	•	•	Organizational skills

Academic Accommodations

Curriculum	Study Aids	Exams
• Priority registration	Typist	• Oral
Math waiver	• Reader	• Untimed
• Foreign lang. waiver	• Notetaker	• Take home
• Course substitution	• Proof reader	• With proctor
In Class	• Text on tape	On computer
Calculators	Early syllabus	• Extended time
• Tape recorder	• Taped handouts	• On tape
• Word processor		• Modified
Priority seating		• Separate room

Graduation Requirements:

Course credits: **Varies** GPA: **2.0** Language waiver: **Yes**

Program Strengths

Our program is unique due to full mainstreaming and providing full assistance when needed. Each student's needs are reviewed and managed individually.

General Information:

University of Toledo is a 2 and 4 year public university. Suburban campus of 400 acres is 6 miles from Toledo. Accessible by air, train or bus. Ski areas are 1 hour from campus. Beaches are 1 hour from campus. 8% of students are foreign. 7 residential halls on campus. Housing is not guaranteed. 11% of students join fraternities/sororities.

Accreditation: NCACS

SAT/ACT Scores:

Scores for incoming freshmen: **Verbal:** 76% below 500. 18% between 500 and 599. 5% between 600 and 699. 1% above 700. **Math:** 58% below 500. 25% between 500 and 599. 13% between 600 and 699. 4% above 700. **ACT:** 54% below 20. 25% between 20 and 23. 9% between 24 and 25l. 8% between 26 and 28. 4% above 28.

Expenses:

Tuition: In-state: Full year: $2,232.00. Part-time: Per credit: $62.25. Tuition: Out-of-state: Full year: $5,085.00. Part-time: Per credit: $79.50. Room and board: $2,625.00.

Majors

• AREA STUDIES American, Asian, European, Latin American, Medieval, Middle Eastern, Urban, Women's Studies • BUSINESS Accounting, Banking, Business Administration, Business Economics, Business Education, Business Management, Business Statistics, Economics, Finance, Food Management, Hotel and Restaurant Management, Human Resources Management, Insurance, International Business, Labor Relations, Management, Marketing, Marketing Research, Personnel, Real Estate, Retailing, Travel/ Tourism Management • COMMUNICATIONS Advertising, Broadcasting, Communication, English, Journalism, Linguistics, Literature, Speech, Television/Radio/Film • COMPUTER SCIENCE Computer Science, Data Processing, Medical Records Administration, Medical Records Technology, Programming, Systems Analysis, Telecommunications • CRAFTS AND DESIGN Glass, Sculpture • EDUCATION Adult and Continuing Education, Art, Early Childhood, Elementary, English, Foreign Language, Health, Industrial, Marketing and Distribution Education, Mathematics, Middle School, Music, Physical, Pre-Education, Reading, Science, Secondary, Social Studies, Special, Speech/Language, Technical, Vocational • ENGINEERING Air Conditioning Technology, Chemical, Civil/Environmental, Computer, Engineering Science, Environmental/Water Resources, Industrial, Mechanical, Physics • ENVIRONMENTAL CONTROL Air Pollution Control Technology, Water and Wastewater Technology • HEALTH SCIENCES Communication Disorders, Environmental, Health, Medical Assistant, Medical Secretary, Medical Technology, Nursing, Physical Therapy, Speech Therapy, Speech/Audiology and Speech • HUMANITIES Classics, English/Writing/Literature, Humanities, Liberal Arts, Philosophy • LANGUAGES French, German, Greek, Latin, Spanish • PREPROFESSIONAL Architecture, Dentistry, Drafting, Engineering, Law, Legal Assistant, Medicine, Pharmacy, Recreation, Social Work, Sports Medicine • SCIENCES Astronomy, Biology, Chemistry, General, Geography, Geology, Gerontology, Mathematics, Physical Science, Physics, Statistics • SOCIAL SCIENCES Anthropology, Criminal Justice, Government/Political, History, Human Service, International Studies, Law Enforcement, Political Science, Psychology, Public Relations, Social Sciences, Sociology • VISUAL AND PERFORMING ARTS Art, Art History, Dance, Dramatic Arts, Fine Arts, Music, Visual and Performing Arts • VOCATIONAL Air Conditioning/Heating/Refri, Business and Office, Drafting, Electronics Technology, Food Service, Home Economics, Legal Secretary, Medical Laboratory Technology, Painting, Paralegal, Park/Recreation, Printing/Lithography, Respiratory Therapy Technology, Secretarial, Word Processing

Sports/Activities

• SPORTS RELATED Marching Band, Pep Band • SPORTS-INTERCOLLEGIATE Baseball (M), Basketball, Cross Country, Diving (M), Field Hockey (F), Football (M), Golf (M), Softball (F), Swimming (M), Tennis, Track and Field, Volleyball (F), Wrestling (M) • SPORTS-INTRAMURAL Badminton, Basketball, Bowling, Crew, Cross Country, Fencing, Golf, Hand Ball, Ice Hockey (M), Lacrosse, Racquetball, Rugby, Sailing, Skiing - Snow, Soccer, Softball, Swimming, Tennis, Track and Field, Volleyball, Wrestling • STUDENT LIFE ACTIVITIES Choral, Community Service, Concert Band, Dance, Drama Groups, Ethnic & Cultural Groups, Film, Fraternities, Jazz Band, Music Groups, Musical Theater, Newspaper, Opera, Political Groups, Radio/TV station, Religious Organization, Sororities, Student Government, Yearbook

---

Selective   **Ohio**
                                                              Services

Walsh College

2020 Easton Street, Northwest
Canton, Ohio 44720
(216) 499-7090

School Enrollment: **1,420**
LD Enrollment: **15**

Admissions Contact: **Jim Abbuhl, Director of Admissions**
LD Contact: **James S. Korcuska, Director**

Admissions

Application Information:

Rolling Admissions: **Yes**

Secondary School Information

Most Important Criteria For Admissions (1-strongest)

2 SAT/ACT	**11** Application	**4**	School transcript
3 Class rank	**5** Course selection	**7**	Personal statement
6 Interview	**10** Extra activities	**8**	Psychoeducational
1 G.P.A.	Open admission	**9**	Recommendations

Test Requirements:

Standardized tests waived: **Yes**
Diagnostic testing waived: **Yes**
Untimed SAT: **Yes** Untimed ACT: **Yes**
Documentation of LD required: **Yes**

Types of Disabilities Served

- Speech/Lang
- Study skills
- Written express
- Organizational
- Perceptual
- Reading
- Spelling
- Math
- Fine Motor
- ADD with LD
- ADD without LD
- ADHD with LD
- ADHD without LD

Learning Disability Program

Counseling: Individual: **Yes**

Faculty:

Faculty: **1**
Faculty advocate: **Yes** Meets with instructor: **As needed**

Diagnostic Testing

ADD	Personality	Perceptual skills	Spelling
ADHD	Organization	Fine motor skills	Reading
I.Q.	Handwriting	Spoken language	Study skills
Math	Social skills	Written language	

Tutoring:

Average size of group tutorials: **1-5**
Services rendered by:
- Graduates
- Peers
- Faculty
- LD staff
- Teacher trainees

Tutorials

Grp.	Ind.	Tutorials	Grp.	Ind.	Tutorials
•	•	Math skills	•	•	Word processing
•	•	Study skills	•	•	Time management
•	•	Language arts	•	•	Learning strategies
•	•	Written express	•	•	Organizational skills

Academic Accommodations

Curriculum	Study Aids	Exams
Priority registration	Typist	• Oral
Math waiver	Reader	Untimed
Foreign lang. waiver	Notetaker	Take home
Course substitution	Proof reader	With proctor
In Class	• Text on tape	On computer
• Calculators	Early syllabus	• Extended time
• Tape recorder	Taped handouts	On tape
• Word processor		Modified
Priority seating		Separate room

Program Strengths

Walsh College offers services to LD students. We have been most successful with students who can function with tutoring and counseling, i.e., moderately learning disabled. Our small classes, caring faculty and our summer program can make a difference in a student's academic life.

General Information:

Walsh College is a 4 year independent Roman Catholic college. Suburban campus of 52 acres is 5 miles from Canton. Accessible by air or bus. Ski areas are 15 miles from campus. Beaches are 50 miles from campus. 5% of students are foreign. 2 residential halls on campus. Housing is guaranteed.

Accreditation: NCACS

Expenses:

Tuition: In-state: Full year: $6,016.00. Part-time: Per credit:$188.00. Room and board: $1,550.00 Cost of LD program:$1,040.00 summer program

Majors

- BUSINESS Accounting, Banking, Business Administration, Business Education, Business Management, Fashion Merchandising, Management
- COMMUNICATIONS Communication, English • COMPUTER SCIENCE Programming • EDUCATION Early Childhood, Elementary, English, Foreign Language, Mathematics, Middle School, Music, Physical, Pre-Education, Reading, Religious Education, Science, Secondary, Social Science, Social Studies, Special, Speech/Language • HEALTH SCIENCES Medical Technology, Nursing • HUMANITIES Humanities, Liberal Arts, Philosophy, Religion, Religious Studies • LANGUAGES French, German, Italian, Spanish • PREPROFESSIONAL Dentistry, Law, Medicine, Ministry, Natural Resources, Pharmacy, Social Work, Veterinarian • SCIENCES Biology, Chemistry, Mathematics, Physical Science • SOCIAL SCIENCES Government/Political, History, International Studies, Political Science, Psychology, Social Sciences, Sociology • VOCATIONAL Forestry, Medical Laboratory Technology

Sports/Activities

- SPORTS RELATED Pep Band • SPORTS-INTERCOLLEGIATE Baseball (M), Basketball, Cross Country, Golf (M), Soccer (M), Softball (F), Tennis, Track and Field, Volleyball (F) • SPORTS-INTRAMURAL Baseball, Basketball, Bowling, Ping-Pong, Racquetball, Skiing - Snow, Softball, Swimming, Tennis, Volleyball • STUDENT LIFE ACTIVITIES Choral, Community Service, Dance, Drama Groups, Ethnic & Cultural Groups, Magazine, Newspaper, Student Government, Yearbook

Less Selective   **Ohio**
Program

Wilmington College
319 College Street
Wilmington, Ohio 45177
(513) 382-6661

School Enrollment: **820** Male: **420** Female: **400**
LD Enrollment: **30**

Admissions Contact: **Julie L. Curtis, Admissions Counselor**
LD Contact: **Laurel Eckels, Director**
Name of Program: **Skills Center**
Telephone:**(513) 382-6661 Ext. 430**

Admissions

Application Information:

Accepted: **10** Enrolled:**30**
Separate application:**Yes**
Applicant must apply **12** months in advance
Rolling Admissions: **Yes**

Oklahoma

Secondary School Information
Most Important Criteria For Admissions (1-strongest)

SAT/ACT	Application **1**	School transcript
1 Class rank	**1** Course selection **1**	Personal statement
1 Interview	Extra activities **1**	Psychoeducational
1 G.P.A.	Open admission	Recommendations

Test Requirements:
Diagnostic testing waived: **Yes**
Achievement tests required: **2**
WAIS-R required: **Yes** Range accepted: **Average+**
Documentation of LD required: **Yes**
Tests recommended: **Writing samples and Standardized reading**

Types of Disabilities Served

Speech/Lang	• Reading	ADD with LD
• Study skills	Spelling	ADD without LD
• Written express	• Math	ADHD with LD
Organizational	Fine Motor	ADHD without LD
Perceptual		

Learning Disability Program
Program: Reinforces course work: **Yes**
Students mainstreamed **100** % of the day
Counseling: Individual: **Yes**

Faculty:
Faculty: **2** Including Director: **Yes** Full time: **2** M.A.: **2**
Faculty advocate: **Yes** Meets with instructor: **As needed**

Diagnostic Testing

ADD	Personality	Perceptual skills	Spelling
ADHD	Organization	Fine motor skills	Reading
I.Q.	Handwriting	Spoken language	Study skills
Math	Social skills	Written language	

Tutoring:
Average size of group tutorials: **5-10**
Services rendered by:
Graduates •Peers •Faculty •LD staff Teacher trainees

Tutorials

Grp.	Ind.	Tutorials	Grp.	Ind.	Tutorials
•	•	Math skills		•	Word processing
•	•	Study skills	•	•	Time management
		Language arts	•	•	Learning strategies
•	•	Written express	•		Organizational skills

Academic Accommodations

Curriculum	Study Aids	Exams
Priority registration	Typist	Oral
Math waiver	Reader	Untimed
Foreign lang. waiver	Notetaker	Take home
Course substitution	• Proof reader	With proctor
In Class	Text on tape	On computer
Calculators	Early syllabus	• Extended time
Tape recorder	Taped handouts	On tape
Word processor		Modified
Priority seating		Separate room

Program Strengths
There are several options available to assist the learning disabled students at Wilmington. They are: untimed testing, textbooks on tape, notetakers, and professional, peer and group tutoring. In addition, there are drop-in help counselors in both writing and math.

General Information:
Wilmington College is a 4 year independent Religious Society of Friends college. Rural campus of 65 acres is 45 miles from Cincinnati. Beaches are 20 miles from campus. 5% of students are foreign. 6 residential halls on campus. Housing is guaranteed.Guaranteed through 1st year. 50 % of students join fraternities/sororities.

Accreditation:NCACS

Expenses:
Tuition: In-state: Full year: $7,900.00. Room and board: $3,000.00

Majors
• BUSINESS Accounting, Banking, Business Administration, Business Management, Economics, Finance, Management, Marketing • COMMUNICATIONS Communication, English, Journalism • COMPUTER SCIENCE Computer Science • EDUCATION Art, Elementary, Health, Middle School, Music, Physical, Secondary • ENGINEERING Industrial • HEALTH SCIENCES Medical Technology • HUMANITIES Liberal Arts, Philosophy, Religion • LANGUAGES French, Spanish • PREPROFESSIONAL Agriculture, Dentistry, Law, Medicine, Sports Medicine, Veterinarian • SCIENCES Agricultural, Biology, Chemistry, Mathematics, Physics • SOCIAL SCIENCES Criminal Justice, History, Psychology, Sociology • VISUAL AND PERFORMING ARTS Theater

Sports/Activities
• SPORTS-INTERCOLLEGIATE Baseball (M), Basketball, Cross Country, Football (M), Golf (M), Soccer, Softball (F), Tennis, Track and Field, Volleyball (F), Wrestling (M) • SPORTS-INTRAMURAL Basketball, Hand Ball, Racquetball, Softball, Squash, Tennis, Volleyball • STUDENT LIFE ACTIVITIES choral Community Service, Concert Band, Drama Groups, Ethnic & Cultural Groups, Fraternities, Jazz Band, Magazine, Music Groups, Musical Theater, Newspaper, Religious Organization, Sororities, Student Government, Yearbook

---

Less Selective   **Oklahoma
                                                      Services**

Carl Albert Junior College
1507 South McKenna
Poteau, Oklahoma 74953
(918) 647-8660

School Enrollment: **1,674**

Admissions Contact: **Lynda Hicks, Registrar**
LD Contact: **Michael Logan**
Telephone:**(918) 647-8660 Ext. 274**

Admissions

Application Information:
Application deadline: **2 weeks after start of classes**

Secondary School Information
Most Important Criteria For Admissions (1-strongest)

SAT/ACT	Application	School transcript
Class rank	Course selection	Personal statement
Interview	Extra activities	Psychoeducational
G.P.A.	**1** Open admission	Recommendations

Test Requirements:
WAIS-R required: **Yes**

Types of Disabilities Served
- Speech/Lang
- Study skills
- Written express
- Organizational
- Perceptual
- Reading
- Spelling
- Math
- Fine Motor
- ADD with LD
- ADD without LD
- ADHD with LD
- ADHD without LD

Learning Disability Program
Counseling: Individual: **Yes**

Faculty:

Diagnostic Testing
ADD	Personality	Perceptual skills	Spelling
ADHD	Organization	Fine motor skills	Reading
I.Q.	Handwriting	Spoken language	Study skills
Math	Social skills	Written language	

Tutoring:
Average size of group tutorials: **3**
Services rendered by:
- Graduates
- Peers
- Faculty
- LD staff
- Teacher trainees

Tutorials
Grp.	Ind.	Tutorials	Grp.	Ind.	Tutorials
•	•	Math skills	•	•	Word processing
	•	Study skills			Time management
•	•	Language arts			Learning strategies
		Written express			Organizational skills

Academic Accommodations
Curriculum	Study Aids	Exams
Priority registration	• Typist	Oral
Math waiver	Reader	Untimed
Foreign lang. waiver	• Notetaker	Take home
Course substitution	Proof reader	With proctor
In Class	• Text on tape	On computer
Calculators	Early syllabus	Extended time
• Tape recorder	Taped handouts	On tape
Word processor		Modified
Priority seating		Separate room

Program Strengths
The contact person on learning disabilities at our institution is Michael Logan.

General Information:
Carl Albert Junior College is a 2 year public college. Rural campus of 32 acres is 35 miles from Fort Smith, Arkansas. Accessible by bus. 2 residential halls on campus. Housing is not guaranteed.2 % of students remain on campus for the weekends. 1 % of students join fraternities/sororities.

Accreditation:NCACS

SAT/ACT Scores:
Scores for incoming freshmen: **ACT:** 28% below 20. 14% between 20 and 23. 19%between 24 and 25l. 15%between 26 and 28.

Expenses:
Tuition: In-state: Full year: $765.00. Part-time: Per credit:$25.50. Tuition: Out-of-state: Full year: $2,640.00. Room and board: $2,050.00

Majors
• BUSINESS Accounting, Business Administration, Business Education, Business Management, Hotel and Restaurant Management • COMMUNICATIONS English, Journalism • COMPUTER SCIENCE Data Processing • EDUCATION Art, Early Childhood, Elementary, Physical, Secondary • HEALTH SCIENCES Nursing • PREPROFESSIONAL Pharmacy • SCIENCES Zoology • SOCIAL SCIENCES Government/Political, History, Psychology, Sociology

Sports/Activities
• SPORTS-INTRAMURAL Baseball, Basketball • STUDENT LIFE ACTIVITIES Fraternities, Music Groups, Newspaper, Religious Organization, Student Government

Oklahoma

Selective

Oklahoma Services

East Central University
Ada, Oklahoma 74820-6899
(405) 332-8000

School Enrollment: **3,585** Male: **1,470** Female: **2,115**

Admissions Contact: **Pamela Armstrong, Registrar**
LD Contact: **Dwain West**
Name of Program: **Student Support Services**
Telephone:**(405) 332-8000 - Ext. 300**

Admissions

Application Information:
Application deadline: **None**

Secondary School Information
Most Important Criteria For Admissions (1-strongest)
1 SAT/ACT	Application	3	School transcript
2 Class rank	4 Course selection	1	Personal statement
Interview	Extra activities		Psychoeducational
2 G.P.A.	Open admission		Recommendations

Test Requirements:
Untimed ACT: **Yes**
Documentation of LD required: **Yes**

Types of Disabilities Served
- Speech/Lang
- Study skills
- Written express
- Organizational
- Perceptual
- Reading
- Spelling
- Math
- Fine Motor
- ADD with LD
- ADD without LD
- ADHD with LD
- ADHD without LD

High School Course Requirements:
English: **4** Math: **3** Science: **2**

Learning Disability Program
Special orientation for LD students: **Yes**
Students mainstreamed **100** % of the day
Services available for all students: **Yes**
Counseling: Individual: **Yes**

Diagnostic Testing
ADD	Personality	Perceptual skills	Spelling
ADHD	Organization	Fine motor skills	Reading
I.Q.	Handwriting	Spoken language	Study skills
Math	Social skills	Written language	

Services rendered by:
Graduates	Peers	Faculty	LD staff	Teacher trainees

611

Oklahoma

Tutorials

Grp.	Ind.	Tutorials	Grp.	Ind.	Tutorials
•	•	Math skills	•	•	Word processing
•	•	Study skills	•	•	Time management
		Language arts	•	•	Learning strategies
		Written express	•	•	Organizational skills

Academic Accommodations

Curriculum
- Priority registration
- Math waiver
- Foreign lang. waiver
- Course substitution

In Class
- Calculators
- Tape recorder
- Word processor
- Priority seating

Study Aids
- Typist
- Reader
- Notetaker
- Proof reader
- Text on tape
- Early syllabus
- Taped handouts

Exams
- Oral
- Untimed
- Take home
- With proctor
- On computer
- Extended time
- On tape
- Modified
- Separate room

Program Strengths

Appropriate support services provided best describes our program. We are not a full LD program in and of itself.

General Information:

East Central University is a 4 year public university. Urban campus of 160 acres is 90 miles from Oklahoma City. 1% of students are foreign. 3 residential halls on campus. Housing is not guaranteed. 40 % of students remain on campus for the weekends.

Accreditation: NCACS

Expenses:

Tuition: In-state: Full year: $1,200.00. Tuition: Out-of-state: Full year: $4,200.00. Room and board: $1,988.00

Majors

• BUSINESS Accounting, Banking, Business Administration, Business Education, Business Management, Finance, Management, Marketing • COMMUNICATIONS Communication, English, Journalism, Speech, Television/Radio/Film • COMPUTER SCIENCE Computer Science, Programming • EDUCATION Art, Early Childhood, Elementary, English, Industrial, Mathematics, Music, Physical, Secondary, Special, Speech/Language, Vocational • HEALTH SCIENCES Environmental, Medical Records, Medical Technology, Nursing • PREPROFESSIONAL Dentistry, Engineering, Law, Medicine, Pharmacy, Social Work • SCIENCES Biology, Chemistry, Ecology, Mathematics, Physical Chemistry, Physics • SOCIAL SCIENCES Criminal Justice, Criminology, Government/Political, History, Law Enforcement, Psychology, Sociology • VISUAL AND PERFORMING ARTS Art, Dramatic Arts, Fine Arts, Music, Theater • VOCATIONAL Business and Office, Construction, Fashion Merchandising, Home Economics, Industrial Design, Industrial Equipment Maintenance

Sports/Activities

• SPORTS RELATED Marching Band, Pep Band • SPORTS-INTERCOLLEGIATE Baseball (M), Basketball, Bowling, Football (M), Golf (M), Tennis (M), Track and Field (M) • SPORTS-INTRAMURAL Basketball, Softball, Tennis (M), Volleyball • STUDENT LIFE ACTIVITIES Choral, Dance, Drama Groups, Fraternities, Jazz Band, Music Ensembles, Musical Theater, Newspaper, Sororities, Student Government, Yearbook

---

Oklahoma State University
310 Student Union
Stillwater, Oklahoma 74078
(405) 744-5000

School Enrollment: **18,516** Male: **10,047** Female: **8,469**
LD Enrollment: **21**

Admissions Contact: **Robin Lacey, Director of Admissions**
LD Contact: **Maureen McCarthy, Coordinator**
Name of Program: **Disabled Student Services**
Telephone: **(405) 744-7116**

Admissions

Secondary School Information
Most Important Criteria For Admissions (1-strongest)

2 SAT/ACT	**1** Application	**3** School transcript
4 Class rank	Course selection	Personal statement
7 Interview	Extra activities	**6** Psychoeducational
5 G.P.A.	Open admission	Recommendations

Test Requirements:
Untimed SAT: **Yes** Untimed ACT: **Yes** Untimed ACH: **Yes**
Documentation of LD required: **Yes**
Currency of diagnostic testing: **3 years**

Types of Disabilities Served

Speech/Lang	Reading	ADD with LD
Study skills	Spelling	ADD without LD
Written express	Math	ADHD with LD
Organizational	Fine Motor	ADHD without LD
Perceptual		

Admissions Process

Standard admission process

Learning Disability Program

Services only for LD students: **Yes**
Counseling: Individual: **Yes** Group Counseling: **Yes**

Faculty:
Faculty: **1** Full time: **1**
Faculty advocate: **Yes** Meets with instructor: **As needed**

Diagnostic Testing

ADD	Personality	Perceptual skills	Spelling
ADHD	Organization	Fine motor skills	Reading
I.Q.	Handwriting	Spoken language	Study skills
Math	Social skills	Written language	

Tutoring:
Services rendered by:

Graduates	•Peers	Faculty	LD staff	Teacher trainees

Tutorials

Grp.	Ind.	Tutorials	Grp.	Ind.	Tutorials
•		Math skills	•		Word processing
•		Study skills	•		Time management
•		Language arts	•		Learning strategies
•		Written express	•		Organizational skills

Academic Accommodations

Curriculum	Study Aids	Exams
• Priority registration	Typist	• Oral
• Math waiver	Reader	Untimed
• Foreign lang. waiver	• Notetaker	Take home
• Course substitution	• Proof reader	• With proctor
In Class	• Text on tape	• On computer
Calculators	Early syllabus	• Extended time
• Tape recorder	Taped handouts	On tape
Word processor		Modified
• Priority seating		• Separate room

Program Strengths

Services are offered to students on an individual basis.

General Information:

Oklahoma State University is a 4 year public university. Urban campus 60 miles from Tulsa. Housing is not guaranteed.

Accreditation: NCACS

Expenses:

Tuition: In-state: Full year: $1,568.00. Tuition: Out-of-state: Full year: $4,525.00. Room and board: $2,876.00.

Majors

• BUSINESS Accounting, Agricultural, Banking, Business Administration, Business Economics, Business Education, Business Management, Economics, Finance, Hotel and Restaurant Management, Insurance, Management, Marketing • COMMUNICATIONS Advertising, Broadcasting, Communication, English, Journalism, Television/Radio/Film • COMPUTER SCIENCE Data Processing, Programming • CRAFTS AND DESIGN Graphic Design • EDUCATION Agricultural, Art, Early Childhood, Elementary, Foreign Language, Health, Industrial, Mathematics, Middle School, Music, Physical, School Psychology, Science, Secondary, Social Studies, Special, Speech/Language • ENGINEERING Aerospace, Agricultural, Architectural, Chemical, Civil/Environmental, Engineering Science, Environmental/Water Resources, Industrial, Mechanical, Petroleum • HEALTH SCIENCES Dietary Manager, Health, Medical Technology, Nutritional/Food, Speech/Audiology and Speech • HUMANITIES Humanities, Philosophy, Religion • LANGUAGES French, German, Russian, Spanish • PREPROFESSIONAL Agriculture, Architecture, Engineering, Forestry, Medicine • SCIENCES Agricultural, Agronomy, Animal, Anthropology, Biochemistry, Biology, Botany, Chemistry, Entomology, Geography, Geology, Horticultural, Mathematics, Microbiology, Mining, Physical Chemistry, Physical Science, Physics, Zoology • SOCIAL SCIENCES Criminal Justice, Family Counseling, Government/Political, History, Library Science, Psychology, Social Sciences, Sociology • VISUAL AND PERFORMING ARTS Fine Arts, Music, Studio Art, Theater • VOCATIONAL Electronics Technology, Fire Science, Forestry, Industrial Design, Park/Recreation, Textile and Clothing

Sports/Activities

• SPORTS RELATED Marching Band, Pep Band • SPORTS-INTERCOLLEGIATE Baseball (M), Basketball, Cross Country, Diving, Football (M), Golf, Softball (F), Tennis, Track and Field, Wrestling (M) • SPORTS-INTRAMURAL Archery, Badminton, Basketball, Bowling, Cross Country, Diving, Fencing, Golf, Hand Ball, Ping-Pong, Racquetball, Soccer, Softball, Squash, Swimming, Track and Field, Volleyball, Water Polo, Wrestling (M) • STUDENT LIFE ACTIVITIES Choral, Concert Band, Dance, Drama Groups, Fraternities, Jazz Band, Magazine, Music Groups, Musical Theater, Orchestra, Radio/TV station, Religious Organization, Sororities, Student Government, Yearbook

---

Less Selective

Rose State College

6420 Southeast 15th
Midwest City, Oklahoma 73110
(405) 733-7308

School Enrollment: **10,000**
LD Enrollment: **10**

Admissions Contact: **Evelyn Dutchings, Registrar**
LD Contact: **Linda Jansen, Director**
Name of Program: **Student Support Services**
Telephone: **(405) 733-7407**

Admissions

Application Information:

Application deadline: **Open**
Rolling Admissions: **Yes**

Secondary School Information

Most Important Criteria For Admissions (1-strongest)

SAT/ACT	Application	School transcript
Class rank	Course selection	Personal statement
Interview	Extra activities	Psychoeducational
G.P.A.	1 Open admission	Recommendations

Test Requirements:

Untimed ACT: **Yes**

Types of Disabilities Served

• Speech/Lang	• Reading	• ADD with LD
• Study skills	• Spelling	• ADD without LD
• Written express	• Math	• ADHD with LD
• Organizational	• Fine Motor	• ADHD without LD
• Perceptual		

Learning Disability Program

Counseling: Individual: **Yes**

Diagnostic Testing

ADD	Personality	Perceptual skills	Spelling
ADHD	Organization	Fine motor skills	Reading
I.Q.	Handwriting	Spoken language	Study skills
Math	Social skills	Written language	

Tutoring:

Average size of group tutorials: **1-5**
Services rendered by:

Graduates	Peers	Faculty	LD staff	Teacher trainees

Tutorials

Grp.	Ind.	Tutorials	Grp.	Ind.	Tutorials
•	•	Math skills			Word processing
•	•	Study skills	•	•	Time management
	•	Language arts	•		Learning strategies
	•	Written express	•		Organizational skills

Oklahoma

Academic Accommodations

Curriculum	Study Aids	Exams
Priority registration	Typist	• Oral
Math waiver	Reader	Untimed
Foreign lang. waiver	• Notetaker	Take home
Course substitution	• Proof reader	With proctor
In Class	• Text on tape	On computer
Calculators	Early syllabus	• Extended time
• Tape recorder	Taped handouts	On tape
Word processor		Modified
Priority seating		Separate room

Program Strengths

The Student Support Services Program is designed to assist low income, first-generation, and disabled students to be successful in college and transfer to a four year university. We provide study skills, career planning, financial aid information, and special assistance to meet the needs of disabled students.

General Information:

Rose State College is a 4 year public college. Urban campus of 90 acres is 4 miles from Oklahoma City. Accessible by air, train or bus. .005% of students are foreign. Housing is not guaranteed.

Accreditation:NCACS, OSRHE, ABA, AMA, OBNR

Expenses:

Tuition: In-state: Full year: $560.00. Part-time: Per credit:$23.30. Tuition: Out-of-state: Full year: $1,740.00. Part-time: Per credit:$72.50.

Majors

• BUSINESS Accounting, Business Administration, Business Management, Economics, Finance, Insurance, Management, Marketing • COMMUNICATIONS Broadcasting, English, Journalism • COMPUTER SCIENCE Data Processing • EDUCATION Elementary, Health, Physical, Secondary • PREPROFESSIONAL Education, Engineering, Law, Medicine • SCIENCES Astronomy, Biology, Botany, Chemistry, Geography, Geology, Mathematics, Physical Science, Zoology • SOCIAL SCIENCES Criminal Justice, Government/Political, History, Psychology, Sociology • VISUAL AND PERFORMING ARTS Art, Music

Sports/Activities

• SPORTS RELATED Pep Band • SPORTS-INTRAMURAL Basketball, Ping-Pong, Soccer • STUDENT LIFE ACTIVITIES Choral, Concert Band, Country Western Band, Drama Groups, Ethnic & Cultural Groups, Music Ensembles, Musical Theater, Newspaper, Radio/TV station, Student Government, Yearbook

---

Less Selective

Oklahoma Services

Tulsa Junior College

909 S. Boston Avenue Room 331B
Tulsa, Oklahoma 74119
(918) 587-6561 Ext. 427

School Enrollment: **23,400**
LD Enrollment: **40**

Admissions Contact: **Leanne Brewer, Director of Admissions**
LD Contact: **Yolanda Williams, Counselor**
Name of Program: **Diagnostic & Prescriptive L.C.**
Telephone:**(918) 587-6561**

Admissions

Application Information:
Application deadline: **Prior to beginning of class**
Rolling Admissions: **Yes**

Secondary School Information
Most Important Criteria For Admissions (1-strongest)

SAT/ACT	Application	School transcript
Class rank	Course selection	Personal statement
Interview	Extra activities	Psychoeducational
G.P.A.	Open admission	Recommendations

Test Requirements:
Untimed ACT: **Yes**
Range accepted:
Documentation of LD required: **Yes**
Tests recommended: **Diagnostic or educational evaluation is recommended**

Types of Disabilities Served
- Speech/Lang
- Reading
- ADD with LD
- Study skills
- Spelling
- ADD without LD
- Written express
- Math
- ADHD with LD
- Organizational
- Fine Motor
- ADHD without LD
- Perceptual

Learning Disability Program

Recommended credits per semester: **6-9**
Counseling: Individual: **Yes**
Support groups are available:**Yes, Disabled Student Support Group (New Horizons)**

Faculty:
Faculty: **8** Full time: **4** Part time: **4**
LD faculty with: BS/BA: **1**
Faculty advocate: **Yes** Meets with instructor: **As needed**

Diagnostic Testing

ADD	Personality	Perceptual skills	Spelling
ADHD	Organization	Fine motor skills	Reading
I.Q.	Handwriting	Spoken language	Study skills
Math	Social skills	Written language	

Tutoring:
Average size of group tutorials: *
Services rendered by:

Graduates	•Peers	•Faculty	•LD staff	Teacher trainees

Tutorials

Grp.	Ind.	Tutorials	Grp.	Ind.	Tutorials
		Math skills			Word processing
		Study skills			Time management
		Language arts			Learning strategies
		Written express			Organizational skills

Academic Accommodations

Curriculum	Study Aids	Exams
Priority registration	Typist	• Oral
Math waiver	Reader	Untimed
Foreign lang. waiver	• Notetaker	Take home
Course substitution	Proof reader	• With proctor
In Class	• Text on tape	• On computer
• Calculators	Early syllabus	• Extended time
• Tape recorder	Taped handouts	• On tape
• Word processor		• Modified
• Priority seating		• Separate room

Program Strengths

Tulsa Junior College provides comprehensive services for the disabled student through the Diagnostic and Prescriptive Learning Center located on the Metro Campus. Disabled students are strongly encouraged to contact the Diagnostic Center for help with special needs. In addition to meeting the needs of students, the Diagnostic Center staff acts as a resource for faculty, staff, and various community and state agencies.

*Students take name from a posted list of tutors and make their own arrangements.

General Information:

Tulsa Junior College is a 2 year public college. Urban campus. Housing is not guaranteed.

Accreditation: Regional

Expenses:

Tuition: In-state: Full year: $605.00. Part-time: Per credit: $31.00. Tuition: Out-of-state: Full year: $1,241.00. Part-time: Per credit: $84.00.

Majors

• BUSINESS Accounting, Banking, Finance, Insurance, Real Estate • COMPUTER SCIENCE Data Processing • ENGINEERING Engineering Science • HEALTH SCIENCES Medical Assistant, Medical Technology, Nursing, Radiological Therapy • HUMANITIES Liberal Arts • SOCIAL SCIENCES Law Enforcement • VOCATIONAL Automobile Technology, Drafting, Electronics Technology, Fire Science, Food Service, Industrial Technology, Mechanical Design, Precision Metal Work, Respiratory Therapy Technology, Secretarial

Sports/Activities

• SPORTS-INTRAMURAL Basketball, Soccer, Softball, Table Tennis, Tennis, Volleyball

---

Very Selective

Oklahoma Services

University of Oklahoma

407 West Boyd
Norman, Oklahoma 73069
(403) 325-2151

School Enrollment: **19,650** Male: **10,791** Female: **8,859**
LD Enrollment: **24**

Admissions Contact: **Marc Borish, Director**
LD Contact: **Suzette Dyer, Coordinator**
Name of Program: **Disabled Student Services**
Telephone: **(405) 325-1459**

Admissions

Application Information:
Application deadline: **None**
Applicant must apply **2** months in advance

Secondary School Information
Most Important Criteria For Admissions (1-strongest)

1 SAT/ACT	Application	2	School transcript
1 Class rank	3 Course selection		Personal statement
2 Interview	4 Extra activities	2	Psychoeducational
1 G.P.A.	Open admission	2	Recommendations

Test Requirements:
Diagnostic testing waived: **Yes**
Untimed SAT: **Yes** Untimed ACT: **Yes**
WAIS-R required: **Yes**
Documentation of LD required: **Yes**
Currency of diagnostic testing: **3 years**

Types of Disabilities Served
- Speech/Lang • Reading • ADD with LD
- Study skills • Spelling • ADD without LD
- Written express • Math • ADHD with LD
- Organizational • Fine Motor • ADHD without LD
- Perceptual

High School Course Requirements:
English: **4** Math: **3** Science: **2**

Learning Disability Program

Special orientation for LD students: **Yes**
Program: Reinforces course work: **Yes**
Students mainstreamed **100** % of the day
Services available for all students: **Yes**
Counseling: Individual: **Yes** Vocational Counseling: **Yes**
Support groups are available: **Yes**

Faculty:
Faculty: **1** Full time: **1**
Faculty advocate: **Yes** Meets with instructor: **Varies**

Diagnostic Testing

ADD	Personality	Perceptual skills	• Spelling
ADHD	Organization	Fine motor skills	• Reading
• I.Q.	Handwriting•	Spoken language	• Study skills
• Math	Social skills•	Written language	

Tutoring:
Services rendered by:
•Graduates •Peers Faculty •LD staff Teacher trainees

Tutorials

Grp.	Ind.	Tutorials	Grp.	Ind.	Tutorials
		Math skills		•	Word processing
	•	Study skills		•	Time management
	•	Language arts		•	Learning strategies
	•	Written express		•	Organizational skills

Academic Accommodations

Curriculum	Study Aids	Exams
• Priority registration	Typist	• Oral
Math waiver	• Reader	Untimed
Foreign lang. waiver	• Notetaker	Take home
Course substitution	• Proof reader	• With proctor
In Class	• Text on tape	• On computer
• Calculators	Early syllabus	• Extended time
• Tape recorder	Taped handouts	• On tape
• Word processor		• Modified
Priority seating		• Separate room

Program Strengths

We provide individual assistance to students with a wide variety of learning disabilities and needs. Accommodations vary but may include counseling, special classroom testing, recorded books, and communication with professors.

General Information:

University of Oklahoma is a 4 year public university. Urban campus of 900 acres is 25 miles from Oklahoma City. 7% of students are foreign. Housing is not guaranteed.

Accreditation: NCACS

SAT/ACT Scores:

Scores for incoming freshmen: **ACT:** 15.8% below 20. 38.6% between 20 and 23. 14.1% between 24 and 25l. 18.2% between 26 and 28. 13.3% above 28.

Class Rank:

About 52.4% of the present freshmen class were in the upper 20% of their high school class. 81.4% were in the top 40% of their class.

Expenses:

Tuition: In-state: Full year: $1,750.00. Part-time: Per credit:$45.00-$48.00. Tuition: Out-of-state: Full year: $4,941.00. Part-time: Per credit:$145.00-$161.00. Room and board: $3,358.00

Majors

• AREA STUDIES Asian, European, Latin American, Russian/Slavic • BUSINESS Accounting, Banking/Finance, Business Administration, Management, Marketing, Real Estate • COMMUNICATIONS Advertising, Broadcasting, Communication, Creative Writing, Journalism, Public Relations • COMPUTER SCIENCE Computer Science • EDUCATION Adult, Early Childhood, Elementary, Foreign Language, Health, Mathematics, Music, Physical, Psychology, Reading, Science, Secondary, Social Studies, Special, Speech/Language • ENGINEERING Aerospace, Chemical, Civil, Environmental, Electrical, Environmental/Water Resources, Geological, Industrial, Mechanical, Metallurgical, Petroleum, Physics • HEALTH SCIENCES Biometrics, Biostatistics, Communication Disorders, Dental Hygiene, Environmental, Nuclear Medical Technology, Nursing, Occupational Therapy, Pharmaceutical Chemistry, Pharmacology, Physical Therapy, Physician's Assistant, Radiological Therapy • HUMANITIES Classics, English/Writing/Literature, Philosophy • LANGUAGES French, German, Linguistics, Russian, Spanish • MATHEMATICS Computer, Theoretical • PREPROFESSIONAL Dentistry, Medicine, Optometry, Pharmacy, Social Work, Veterinarian • SCIENCES Astronomy, Astrophysics, Biochemistry, Botany, Chemistry, Geology, Geophysics and Seismology, Geoscience, Meteorology, Microbiology, Natural Science, Physics, Zoology • SOCIAL SCIENCES Anthropology, Geography, History, Law Enforcement, Library Science, Political Science, Psychology, Social Sciences, Sociology • SPECIAL EDUCATION Learning Disability, Mentally Retarded • VISUAL AND PERFORMING ARTS Art, Art History, Dance, Dramatic Arts, Fine Arts, Music, Music Performance, Music Theatre, Studio Art, Theater, Video

Sports/Activities

• SPORTS RELATED Cheerleading, Chess, Marching Band • SPORTS-INTERCOLLEGIATE Baseball (M), Basketball (F), Basketball (M), Cross Country (F), Cross Country (M), Football (M), Golf (F), Golf (M), Gymnastics (F), Gymnastics (M), Softball (F), Tennis (F), Tennis (M), Track and Field (F), Track and Field (M), Volleyball (F), Wrestling (M) • SPORTS-INTRAMURAL Badminton, Basketball, Bowling, Cross Country, Diving, Fencing, Football, Golf, Ping-Pong, Racquetball, Rugby, Soccer, Softball, Squash, Swimming, Tennis, Track and Field, Volleyball, Water Polo, Weight Lifting • STUDENT LIFE ACTIVITIES Academic Clubs, Choral, Debate, Ethnic & Cultural Groups, Film, Fraternities, Newspaper, Political Groups, Radio/TV station, Religious Organization, Sororities, Student Government

---

Less Selective   **Oregon**
Accommodations

Central Oregon Community College
2600 Northwest College Way
Bend, Oregon 97701-5998
(503) 382-6112

School Enrollment: **3,118**

Admissions Contact: **Donna L. Beck, Admissions Advisor**

Admissions

Application Information:
Application deadline: **Rolling**
Rolling Admissions: **Yes**

Secondary School Information
Most Important Criteria For Admissions (1-strongest)

SAT/ACT	Application	School transcript
Class rank	Course selection	Personal statement
Interview	Extra activities	Psychoeducational
G.P.A.	**1** Open admission	Recommendations

Test Requirements:
Standardized tests waived: **Yes**

Types of Disabilities Served
• Speech/Lang	• Reading	• ADD with LD
• Study skills	• Spelling	• ADD without LD
• Written express	• Math	• ADHD with LD
• Organizational	• Fine Motor	• ADHD without LD
• Perceptual		

Admissions Process

As a Community College we have an open admission policy. We do not have a specific LD program. We ask all students to take our placement test in reading, writing, and math.

Learning Disability Program

Program: Reinforces course work: **Yes**
Students mainstreamed **100 %** of the day
Counseling: Individual: **Yes** Group Counseling: **Yes**

Faculty:
Faculty advocate: **Yes** Meets with instructor: **As appropriate**

Diagnostic Testing

ADD	Personality	Perceptual skills	Spelling
ADHD	Organization	Fine motor skills	Reading
I.Q.	Handwriting	Spoken language	Study skills
Math	Social skills	Written language	

Tutoring:

Services rendered by:
Graduates •Peers •Faculty LD staff Teacher trainees

Tutorials

Grp.	Ind.	Tutorials	Grp.	Ind.	Tutorials
•	•	Math skills	•	•	Word processing
•	•	Study skills	•	•	Time management
•	•	Language arts	•	•	Learning strategies
•	•	Written express	•	•	Organizational skills

Academic Accommodations

Curriculum	Study Aids	Exams
Priority registration	Typist	Oral
Math waiver	Reader	Untimed
Foreign lang. waiver	Notetaker	Take home
Course substitution	Proof reader	With proctor
In Class	Text on tape	On computer
Calculators	Early syllabus	Extended time
Tape recorder	Taped handouts	On tape
Word processor		Modified
Priority seating		Separate room

Graduation Requirements:

Course credits: **93** GPA: **2.0**
Other requirements: **Complete at least 65% of all work attempted**

Program Strengths

We do not have an LD specialist or staff. We offer support services for all students. Usually, a student with mild learning disabilities will be successful here and find support through our faculty, peer tutoring, and reading/writing labs. The faculty member is the one who decides which aid/services he/she is willing to render or allow.

General Information:

Central Oregon Community College is a 2 year public college. Urban campus of 193 acres is 170 miles from Portland. Accessible by air or bus. Ski areas are 30 miles from campus. Beaches are 4 hours from campus. 1% of students are foreign. 1 residential halls on campus. Housing is not guaranteed.3.6 % of students remain on campus for the weekends.

Accreditation:NACS

Expenses:

Tuition: In-state: Full year: $870.00. Part-time: Per credit:Part-time: 31.00.
Tuition: Out-of-state: Full year: $1,625.00. Part-time: Per credit:$31.00.
Room and board: $3,066.00

Majors

• BUSINESS Accounting, Business Administration, Clerical, Data Processing, Hotel and Restaurant Management, Management, Marketing, Secretarial Science • COMMUNICATIONS Communication, English, Journalism, Literature • COMPUTER SCIENCE Computer Science, Computer Technology, Data Processing, Medical Records Technology, Programming • CRAFTS AND DESIGN Ceramics, Crafts, Graphic Design, Sculpture • EDUCATION Early Childhood, General • ENGINEERING Drafting • HEALTH SCIENCES Medical Secretary, Nursing, Nursing Assistant, Practical Nursing • HUMANITIES English/Writing/Literature, Fine Arts, Humanities, Liberal Arts • LANGUAGES English, French, Spanish • MATHEMATICS Applied • PREPROFESSIONAL Architecture, Business, Dentistry, Drafting, Engineering, Fisheries, Forestry, Law, Med-

icine, Pharmacy, Range Management, Veterinarian • SCIENCES Anthropology, Biology, Botany, Chemistry, Computer Science, General, Geography, Geology, Mathematics, Physical Science, Physics, Zoology • SOCIAL SCIENCES Anthropology, Criminal Justice, Geography, History, Political Science, Psychology, Social Sciences, Sociology • VISUAL AND PERFORMING ARTS Art, Art History, Dance, Fine Arts, Music, Music Performance, Music Theatre, Studio Art, Theater • VOCATIONAL Automated Manufacturing Technology, Automobile Technology, Business and Office, Drafting, Electronics Technology, Fire Science, Forestry, Legal Secretary, Machinist, Office Administration, Secretarial, Welding, Word Processing

Sports/Activities

• SPORTS-INTERCOLLEGIATE Archery (F), Archery (M), Cross Country (F), Cross Country (M), Golf (F), Golf (M), Racquetball (F), Racquetball (M), Skiing - Snow (F), Skiing - Snow (M), Soccer (F), Soccer (M), Softball (F), Softball (M), Tennis (F), Tennis (M), Track and Field (F), Track and Field (M), Volleyball (F) • SPORTS-INTRAMURAL Archery (F), Archery (M), Badminton (F), Badminton (M), Baseball, Basketball (F), Basketball (M), Bowling (F), Bowling (M), Cross Country (F), Cross Country (M), Football (M), Golf (F), Golf (M), Racquetball (F), Racquetball (M), Skiing - Cross Country, Skiing - Snow (F), Skiing - Snow (M), Soccer (F), Soccer (M), Softball (F), Softball (M), Tennis (F), Tennis (M), Track and Field (F), Track and Field (M), Volleyball (M) • STUDENT LIFE ACTIVITIES Academic Clubs, Choral, Community Service, Dance, Drama Groups, Ethnic & Cultural Groups, Jazz Band, Newspaper, Orchestra, Student Government, Symphony Orchestra

---

Less Selective **Oregon Program**

Clackamas Community College

19600 South Molalla Avenue
Oregon City, Oregon 97045
(503) 657-6958

School Enrollment: **5,990** Male: **2,662** Female: **3,328**
LD Enrollment: **35**

Admissions Contact: **Susan Manzella, Assistant to the Registrar**
LD Contact: **David H. Campbell, Counselor/Coordinator**
Name of Program: **Disabled Student Services**
Address: **19600 South Molalla Avenue**
Telephone:**(503) 657-6958 Ext. 2600**

Admissions

Application Information:

LD Students Applying: **50** Accepted: **45** Enrolled:**35**
Applicant must apply **2** months in advance
Rolling Admissions: **Yes**

Secondary School Information

Most Important Criteria For Admissions (1-strongest)

SAT/ACT	Application	**4**	School transcript
Class rank	**3** Course selection	**1**	Personal statement
1 Interview	**5** Extra activities	**2**	Psychoeducational
G.P.A.	Open admission		Recommendations

Test Requirements:

Diagnostic testing waived: **Yes**
Tests recommended: **WAIS, Woodcock-Johnson, WRAT, CTBS, etc.**

Oregon

Types of Disabilities Served
- Speech/Lang
- Study skills
- Written express
- Organizational
- Perceptual
- Reading
- Spelling
- Math
- Fine Motor
- ADD with LD
- ADD without LD
- ADHD with LD
- ADHD without LD

Learning Disability Program

Program: Remedial: **Yes**
Program: Reinforces course work: **Yes**
Students mainstreamed **90** % of the day
Counseling: Individual: **Yes** Group Counseling: **Yes**

Faculty:
Faculty: **4** Including Director: **Yes** Part time: **4**
LD faculty with: BS/BA: **2** M.A.: **2**
Faculty advocate: **Yes** Meets with instructor: **As necessary**

Diagnostic Testing
- ADD
- ADHD
- I.Q.
- Math
- Personality
- Organization
- Handwriting
- Social skills
- Perceptual skills
- Fine motor skills
- Spoken language
- Written language
- Spelling
- Reading
- Study skills

Tutoring:
Average size of group tutorials: **3-4**
Services rendered by:
- Graduates
- Peers
- Faculty
- LD staff
- Teacher trainees

Tutorials

Grp.	Ind.	Tutorials	Grp.	Ind.	Tutorials
•	•	Math skills		•	Word processing
•	•	Study skills	•	•	Time management
•	•	Language arts	•	•	Learning strategies
•	•	Written express	•	•	Organizational skills

Academic Accommodations

Curriculum	Study Aids	Exams
Priority registration	• Typist	• Oral
Math waiver	Reader	Untimed
Foreign lang. waiver	• Notetaker	• Take home
• Course substitution	• Proof reader	• With proctor
In Class	• Text on tape	On computer
• Calculators	Early syllabus	• Extended time
• Tape recorder	Taped handouts	On tape
• Word processor		Modified
Priority seating		Separate room

Program Strengths

Program emphasizes self-advocacy; support services as necessary; advocacy and education staff; high tech center for cognitive/word processing training. Our goal is to assist each individual to maximize his or her potential and to help the student become as competitive as possible. Our hopes are that the students will utilize the support services to a lesser degree as college success skills improve.

General Information:

Clackamas Community College is a 2 year public college. Suburban campus 15 miles from Portland. Accessible by air, train or bus. Ski areas are 60 miles from campus. Beaches are 80 miles from campus. Housing is not guaranteed.

Accreditation: NWACS

Expenses:
Tuition: In-state: Full year: $705.00. Part-time: Per credit: $27.00. Tuition: Out-of-state: Full year: $2,550.00. Part-time: Per course: $85.00

Majors

• BUSINESS Accounting, Business Administration, Business Education, Business Management, Real Estate • CRAFTS AND DESIGN Graphic Design • ENVIRONMENTAL CONTROL Water and Wastewater Technology • HEALTH SCIENCES Medical Assistant, Medical Technology, Nursing • HUMANITIES Humanities, Liberal Arts • SCIENCES Biology, Horticultural, Physical Science • SOCIAL SCIENCES Criminal Justice, Law Enforcement, Social Sciences • VOCATIONAL Auto Body, Automated Manufacturing Technology, Automobile Technology, Business and Office, Drafting, Fire Science, Industrial Design, Industrial Equipment Maintenance, Manufacturing Technology, Precision Metal Work, Secretarial

Sports/Activities

• SPORTS RELATED Band • SPORTS-INTRAMURAL Archery, Badminton, Baseball, Basketball, Cross Country, Golf, Karate, Skiing - Cross Country, Skiing - Snow, Soccer, Softball, Swimming, Tennis, Track and Field, Volleyball, Weight Lifting, Wrestling • STUDENT LIFE ACTIVITIES Drama Groups, Ethnic & Cultural Groups, Music Groups, Newspaper, Religious Organization, Student Government

Selective | **Oregon Services**

Eastern Oregon State College
1410 L Avenue Inlow Hall
LaGrande, Oregon 97850
(503) 963-2171

School Enrollment: **1,658**
LD Enrollment: **6**

Admissions Contact: **Terral Schut, Director of Admissions**
LD Contact: **Alan Davis, Director Student Development**
Name of Program: **Student Support Services**
Telephone: **(503) 962-3393**

Admissions

Application Information:
Application deadline: **August 1st**
Applicant must apply **3 months in advance**
Rolling Admissions: **Yes** Notified when: **2 weeks**

Secondary School Information
Most Important Criteria For Admissions (1-strongest)

4 SAT/ACT	**7** Application	**2** School transcript
6 Class rank	**3** Course selection	**8** Personal statement
Interview	**9** Extra activities	**10** Psychoeducational
1 G.P.A.	Open admission	**5** Recommendations

Test Requirements:
Diagnostic testing waived: **Yes**
Tests recommended: **Math, placement test if no documentation of learning disability.**

Types of Disabilities Served
- Speech/Lang
- Study skills
- Written express
- Organizational
- Perceptual
- Reading
- Spelling
- Math
- Fine Motor
- ADD with LD
- ADD without LD
- ADHD with LD
- ADHD without LD

Learning Disability Program

Program: Reinforces course work: **Yes**
Students mainstreamed **100** % of the day
Counseling: Individual: **Yes**

Faculty:

Faculty: **3** Including Director: **Yes** Full time: **3** M.A.: **2** Ph.D.: **1**
Faculty advocate: **Yes** Meets with instructor: **When needed**

Diagnostic Testing

ADD	Personality	Perceptual skills	Spelling
ADHD	Organization	Fine motor skills	Reading
I.Q.	Handwriting	Spoken language	• Study skills
• Math	Social skills	Written language	

Tutoring:

Average size of group tutorials: **7**
Services rendered by:
Graduates   •Peers   •Faculty   •LD staff   Teacher trainees

Tutorials

Grp.	Ind.	Tutorials		Grp.	Ind.	Tutorials
•	•	Math skills			•	Word processing
•	•	Study skills		•	•	Time management
•	•	Language arts		•	•	Learning strategies
•	•	Written express		•	•	Organizational skills

Academic Accommodations

Curriculum	Study Aids	Exams
Priority registration	Typist	Oral
Math waiver	Reader	Untimed
Foreign lang. waiver	• Notetaker	Take home
Course substitution	• Proof reader	• With proctor
In Class	• Text on tape	On computer
• Calculators	Early syllabus	• Extended time
• Tape recorder	Taped handouts	On tape
• Word processor		Modified
Priority seating		Separate room

Program Strengths

Our program involves a combination of peer tutoring and peer counseling and focuses on the twin goals of academic and social integration of the student within the campus community.

General Information:

Eastern Oregon State College is a 4 year public college. Ski areas are 25 miles from campus. Beaches are 7 hours from campus. 2 residential halls on campus. Housing is guaranteed.

Accreditation:

Expenses:

Tuition: In-state: Full year: $2,361.00. Room and board: $3,160.00

Majors

• BUSINESS Accounting, Agricultural, Bookkeeping, Business Economics, Business Management, Economics, Finance • COMMUNICATIONS Creative Writing, English, Journalism • COMPUTER SCIENCE Computer Technology, Data Processing, Programming • EDUCATION Art, Elementary, Health, Middle School, Music, Secondary • HEALTH SCIENCES Health, Nursing, Nutritional/Food • HUMANITIES Liberal Arts, Philosophy • LANGUAGES French, German, Japanese, Spanish • PREPROFESSIONAL Agriculture, Engineering, Veterinarian • SCIENCES Biology, Botany, Chemistry, Earth, Geography, Mathematics, Physics • SOCIAL SCIENCES Anthropology, Government/Political, History, Psychology, Sociology • VISUAL AND PERFORMING ARTS Art, Fine Arts, Music, Theater • VOCATIONAL Fire Science

Sports/Activities

• SPORTS RELATED Pep Band • SPORTS-INTERCOLLEGIATE Baseball (M), Basketball, Cross Country, Football (M), Skiing - Cross Country, Track and Field, Volleyball (F) • SPORTS-INTRAMURAL Badminton, Basketball, Bowling, Racquetball, Soccer, Softball, Swimming, Tennis, Volleyball • STUDENT LIFE ACTIVITIES Choral, Concert Band, Jazz Band, Magazine, Music Groups, Musical Theater, Newspaper, Radio/TV station, Student Government, Symphony Orchestra

---

Less Selective   **Oregon Services**

Lane Community College

4000 East 30th Avenue
Eugene, Oregon 97405
(503) 747-4501

School Enrollment: **8,143**
LD Enrollment: **24**

Admissions Contact: **Sharon K. Moore, Director of Admissions**
LD Contact: **Dolores May, Coordinator**
Name of Program: **Disabled Student Services**
Telephone:**(503) 747-4501**

Admissions

Application Information:

Application deadline: **Open**
Rolling Admissions: **Yes**

Secondary School Information

Most Important Criteria For Admissions (1-strongest)

SAT/ACT	Application	School transcript
Class rank	Course selection	Personal statement
Interview	Extra activities	Psychoeducational
G.P.A.	**1** Open admission	Recommendations

Test Requirements:

Diagnostic testing waived: **Yes**
Documentation of LD required: **Yes**
Currency of diagnostic testing: **3 years**

Types of Disabilities Served

• Speech/Lang	• Reading	• ADD with LD
• Study skills	• Spelling	• ADD without LD
• Written express	• Math	• ADHD with LD
• Organizational	• Fine Motor	• ADHD without LD
• Perceptual		

Diagnostic Testing

ADD	Personality	Perceptual skills	Spelling
ADHD	Organization	Fine motor skills	Reading
I.Q.	Handwriting	Spoken language	Study skills
Math	Social skills	Written language	

Tutoring:

Services rendered by:
Graduates   •Peers   •Faculty   •LD staff   Teacher trainees

Oregon

Tutorials

Grp.	Ind.	Tutorials	Grp.	Ind.	Tutorials
•	•	Math skills			Word processing
•	•	Study skills			Time management
		Language arts	•	•	Learning strategies
•		Written express	•	•	Organizational skills

Academic Accommodations

Curriculum
- Priority registration
- Math waiver
- Foreign lang. waiver
- Course substitution

In Class
- Calculators
- • Tape recorder
- Word processor
- Priority seating

Study Aids
- Typist
- Reader
- • Notetaker
- Proof reader
- • Text on tape
- Early syllabus
- Taped handouts

Exams
- • Oral
- Untimed
- Take home
- With proctor
- On computer
- • Extended time
- On tape
- Modified
- Separate room

Program Strengths

We offer basic support services that all colleges offer.

General Information:

Lane Community College is a 2 year public college. Suburban campus. Accessible by bus. Ski areas are 3 hours from campus. Beaches are 2 hours from campus. Housing is not guaranteed.

Accreditation: Regional

Expenses:

Tuition: In-state: Full year: $849.00. Part-time: Per credit:$23.00. Tuition: Out-of-state: Full year: $1,125.00. Part-time: Per credit:$92.00. Room and board: $3,870.00

Majors

• AREA STUDIES Russian/Slavic, Women's Studies • BUSINESS Accounting, Agricultural, Banking, Business Administration, Business Economics, Business Education, Business Management, Economics, Fashion Merchandising, Hotel and Restaurant Management, Management, Marketing, Real Estate • COMMUNICATIONS Broadcasting, English, Graphic Design, Journalism, Photography, Television/Radio/Film • COMPUTER SCIENCE Computer Science, Data Processing, Programming, Software Engineer • CRAFTS AND DESIGN Ceramics, Sculpture • EDUCATION Art, Early Childhood, Elementary, Health, Physical, Secondary • ENGINEERING Engineering Science, Mathematical • HEALTH SCIENCES Medical Assistant, Nursing • HUMANITIES English/Writing/Literature, Humanities, Liberal Arts, Philosophy, Religion • LANGUAGES French, Spanish • PREPROFESSIONAL Agriculture, Architecture, Dentistry, Engineering, Forestry, Law, Medicine, Pharmacy, Recreation, Veterinarian • SCIENCES Anthropology, Biology, Botany, Chemistry, Ecology, Geology, Gerontology, Mathematics, Physics, Zoology • SOCIAL SCIENCES Anthropology, Criminal Justice, Government/Political, History, Law Enforcement, Psychology, Public Relations, Social Sciences, Sociology • VISUAL AND PERFORMING ARTS Art History, Dance, Fine Arts, Music, Music Performance • VOCATIONAL Automobile Technology, Automotive Service, Aviation Maintenance, Business and Office, Construction, Culinary Arts, Dental Assistant, Dental Hygiene, Drafting, Electronics Technology, Fire Science, Food Service, Forestry, Industrial Design, Jewelry-Metalsmithery, Landscape Architecture, Legal Secretary, Mechanical Design, Painting, Paralegal, Precision Metal Work, Secretarial, Textile and Clothing, Welding

Sports/Activities

• SPORTS RELATED Pep Band • SPORTS-INTERCOLLEGIATE Baseball (M), Basketball, Cross Country, Track and Field, Volleyball (F) • SPORTS-INTRAMURAL Basketball, Field Hockey (F) • STUDENT LIFE ACTIVITIES Choral, Concert Band, Dance, Drama Groups, Jazz Band, Music Groups, Musical Theater, Newspaper, Student Government

---

Less Selective

Oregon Program

Linn-Benton Community College

6500 Southwest Pacific Boulevard
Albany, Oregon 97321-3774
(503) 967-6105

School Enrollment: **2,364** Male: **1,174** Female: **1,190**
LD Enrollment: **31** Male: **23** Female: **8**

Admissions Contact: **Blaine Nisson, Director of Admissions**
LD Contact: **Paula Grigsby, Coordinator**
Name of Program: **Disabled Student Services**

Admissions

Application Information:
Separate application: **Yes**
Application deadline: **None**

Secondary School Information
Most Important Criteria For Admissions (1-strongest)

SAT/ACT	Application	1	School transcript
Class rank	Course selection		Personal statement
Interview	Extra activities		Psychoeducational
G.P.A.	Open admission		Recommendations

Test Requirements:
Standardized tests waived: **Yes**
Diagnostic testing waived: **Yes**
WAIS-R required: **Yes** Range accepted: **80+**
Documentation of LD required: **Yes**
Tests recommended: **Woodcock-Johnson Psychoeducational Battery, WAIS-R**

Types of Disabilities Served
- • Speech/Lang
- • Study skills
- • Written express
- • Organizational
- • Perceptual
- • Reading
- • Spelling
- • Math
- • Fine Motor
- • ADD with LD
- • ADD without LD
- • ADHD with LD
- • ADHD without LD

Learning Disability Program

Program: Reinforces course work: **Yes**
Students mainstreamed **88** % of the day
Counseling: Individual: **Yes**

Faculty:
Faculty: **4** Including Director: **Yes** Full time: **2** Part time: **2**
LD faculty with: BS/BA: **2** M.A.: **2**
Faculty advocate: **Yes** Meets with instructor: **As needed**

Diagnostic Testing

ADD	Personality	• Perceptual skills	• Spelling
ADHD	Organization	Fine motor skills	• Reading
• I.Q.	• Handwriting	Spoken language	Study skills
• Math	Social skills	• Written language	

Tutoring:
Average size of group tutorials: **12-15**
Services rendered by:

Graduates	Peers	Faculty	•LD staff	Teacher trainees

Tutorials

Grp.	Ind.	Tutorials	Grp.	Ind.	Tutorials
	•	Math skills		•	Word processing
	•	Study skills		•	Time management
	•	Language arts		•	Learning strategies
	•	Written express		•	Organizational skills

Academic Accommodations

Curriculum	Study Aids	Exams
Priority registration	• Typist	• Oral
Math waiver	Reader	Untimed
Foreign lang. waiver	• Notetaker	• Take home
• Course substitution	• Proof reader	With proctor
In Class	• Text on tape	On computer
• Calculators	Early syllabus	• Extended time
• Tape recorder	Taped handouts	On tape
• Word processor		• Modified
Priority seating		Separate room

Program Strengths

Our program provides services and aids to LD students attending LBCC. Services and aids are assigned on an individual basis. Every effort is made to meet the needs of the student.

General Information:

Linn-Benton Community College is a 2 year public college. Rural campus of 10 acres is 80 miles from Portland. Accessible by bus. Ski areas are 80 miles from campus. Beaches are 50 miles from campus. 1% of students are foreign. Housing is not guaranteed.

Accreditation: NWACS

Expenses:

Tuition: In-state: Full year: $828.00. Part-time: Per credit:$23.00. Tuition: Out-of-state: Full year: $3,420.00. Part-time: Per credit:$95.00.

Majors

• BUSINESS Accounting, Business Administration, Business Management, Finance, Hotel and Restaurant Management, Marketing • COMMUNICATIONS Advertising, Journalism, Photography • COMPUTER SCIENCE Data Processing • EDUCATION Early Childhood, Elementary • ENGINEERING Engineering Science, Metallurgical • HEALTH SCIENCES Dental Assistant, Health, Medical Secretary, Medical Technology, Nursing, Nutritional/Food • HUMANITIES Humanities, Liberal Arts • PREPROFESSIONAL Agriculture, Engineering • SCIENCES Animal, Astronomy, Biochemistry, Biology, Botany, Chemistry, Earth, Equestrian Studies, Geography, Horticultural, Marine Biology, Mathematics, Microbiology, Oceanography, Physical Chemistry, Physical Science, Physics • SOCIAL SCIENCES Criminal Justice, History, Law Enforcement, Political Science, Social Sciences, Sociology • VISUAL AND PERFORMING ARTS Art, Dance, Fine Arts, Music, Theater • VOCATIONAL Air Conditioning/Heating/Refrig, Auto Body, Culinary Arts, Diesel Power Technology, Drafting, Legal Secretary, Manufacturing Technology, Precision Metal Work, Printing/Lithography, Secretarial, Welding

Sports/Activities

• SPORTS-INTERCOLLEGIATE Baseball (M), Basketball, Cross Country, Track and Field, Volleyball (F) • SPORTS-INTRAMURAL Basketball, Bowling, Cross Country, Football (M), Ping-Pong, Softball, Tennis, Volleyball

---

Mount Hood Community College
26000 Southeast Stark Street
Gresham, Oregon 97030
(503) 667-7391

School Enrollment: **13,647** Male: **6,157** Female: **7,490**
LD Enrollment: **80**

Admissions Contact: **Marilyn J. Kennedy, Director of Admissions**
LD Contact: **Debbie Derr, Coordinator**
Name of Program: **Special Services Office**
Telephone:**(503) 667-7650 Voice**

Admissions

Application Information:
Enrolled:**80**
Application deadline: **None**
Applicant must apply **2** months in advance
Rolling Admissions: **Yes**

Secondary School Information
Most Important Criteria For Admissions (1-strongest)

SAT/ACT	**1**	Application	School transcript
Class rank		Course selection	Personal statement
Interview		Extra activities	Psychoeducational
G.P.A.		Open admission	Recommendations

Test Requirements:
Diagnostic testing waived: **Yes**
Untimed ACH: **Yes** Achievement tests required:**3**
Documentation of LD required: **Yes**
Tests recommended: **WAIS-R, Woodcock-Johnson, Psychoeducational Battery Revised**

Types of Disabilities Served

• Speech/Lang	• Reading	• ADD with LD
• Study skills	• Spelling	• ADD without LD
• Written express	• Math	• ADHD with LD
• Organizational	• Fine Motor	• ADHD without LD
• Perceptual		

Learning Disability Program

Special orientation for LD students: **Yes**
Syllabus available during orientation:**Yes**
Program: Remedial: **Yes**
Program: Reinforces course work: **Yes**
Students mainstreamed **100** % of the day
Recommended credits per semester: **Varies**
Counseling: Individual: **Yes** Vocational Counseling: **Yes**
Support groups are available:**Yes**

Faculty:
Faculty: **2** Including Director: **Yes** Full time: **1** Part time: **1** M.A.: **2**
Faculty advocate: **Yes** Meets with instructor: **As needed**

Oregon

Diagnostic Testing
- ADD • Personality • Perceptual skills • Spelling
- ADHD• Organization• Fine motor skills • Reading
- • I.Q. • Handwriting• Spoken language • Study skills
- • Math • Social skills• Written language

Tutoring:
Average size of group tutorials: **5**
Services rendered by:
Graduates •Peers •Faculty •LD staff Teacher trainees

Tutorials

Grp.	Ind.	Tutorials	Grp.	Ind.	Tutorials
•	•	Math skills	•		Word processing
•	•	Study skills	•	•	Time management
•		Language arts	•	•	Learning strategies
•		Written express	•	•	Organizational skills

Academic Accommodations

Curriculum	Study Aids	Exams
• Priority registration	• Typist	• Oral
Math waiver	• Reader	Untimed
Foreign lang. waiver	• Notetaker	Take home
• Course substitution	• Proof reader	• With proctor
In Class	• Text on tape	On computer
• Calculators	Early syllabus	• Extended time
• Tape recorder	Taped handouts	• On tape
• Word processor		• Modified
• Priority seating		• Separate room

Graduation Requirements:
Course credits: **90** GPA: **2.0**

Program Strengths
Our program provides services to all students with disabilities, the largest group being the learning disabled. The Special Services Office works closely with Developmental Education and the Tutorial Center.

General Information:
Mount Hood Community College is a 2 year public college. Suburban campus 15 miles from Portland. Accessible by air, train, or bus. Ski areas are 50 miles from campus. Beaches are 90 miles from campus. Housing is not guaranteed.

Accreditation: NACS

Expenses:
Tuition: In-state: Full year: $260.00 per quarter. Part-time: Per credit:$29.00. Tuition: Out-of-state: Full year: Part-time: Per credit:$82.00.

Majors
• AGRICULTURE Horticultural • ARTS Art History, Commercial Art, Drafting, Dramatic Arts, Drawing, Film & Video, Graphic Art, Landscaping, Music, Music History, Music Performance, Painting • BUSINESS Accounting, Aviation Management, Bookkeeping, Business Administration, Business Management, Clerical, Hotel & Restaurant Management, Management, Real Estate, Retailing, Secretarial Science, Travel/Tourism Management • COMMUNICATIONS Broadcasting, Graphic Design, Journalism, Printing, Television/Radio/Film • COMPUTER SCIENCE Computer Maintenance, Computer Technology, Data Processing, Medical Recording Technology, Medical Records Administration, Robotics, Systems Analysis • CRAFTS AND DESIGN Ceramics, Graphic Design, Industrial Design • EDUCATION Early Childhood • ENGINEERING Architectural, Automotive, Civil/Environmental, Computer, Drafting, Electrical, Mechanical, Radio/Television • HEALTH SCIENCES Dental Hygiene, Medical Assistant, Medical Records Administration, Medical Secretary, Nursing, Nursing Assistant, Occupational Therapy, Physical Therapy, Respiratory Therapy, Surgical Technology • PRE PROFESSIONAL Agriculture, Architecture, Business, Dentistry, Drafting, Engineering, Fisheries, Forestry, Industrial Design, Landscaping, Law, Legal Assistant, Medicine, Ministry, Natural Resources, Optometry, Pharmacy, Range Management, Recreation, Social Work, Sports Medicine, Urban Design, Veterinarian, Wildlife • SCIENCES Anthropology, Applied Mathematics, Astronomy, Biology, Botany, Chemistry, Computer Science, Ecology, Geography, Geology, Human Biology, Mathematics, Microbiology, Natural Science, Organic Chemistry, Physical Chemistry, Physical Science, Physics • SOCIAL SCIENCES Anthropology, Criminal Justice, Geography, Government/Political, History, Human Service, Political Science, Psychology, Social Science, Sociology • SPECIAL EDUCATION Occupational Therapy • VISUAL AND PERFORMING ARTS Art, Art History, Dramatic Arts, Music, Music Performance, Theater

Sports/Activities
• SPORTS RELATED Cheerleading • SPORTS-INTERCOLLEGIATE Baseball (M), Basketball (M), Track and Field (F), Track and Field (M), Volleyball (F) • SPORTS-INTRAMURAL Bowling, Football, Golf, Hand Ball, Karate, Racquetball, Skiing - Cross Country, Skiing - Snow, Softball, Swimming, Tennis, Weight Lifting • STUDENT LIFE ACTIVITIES Academic Clubs, Choral, Concert Band, Dance, Debate, Drama Groups, Ethnic & Cultural Groups, Jazz Band, Magazine, Music Groups, Musical Theater, Newspaper, Orchestra, Radio/TV station, Religious Organization, Student Government, Symphony Orchestra, Yearbook

---

Selective   **Oregon**
                                                                 Services

Oregon State University
A200 Administration Building
Corvallis, Oregon 97331-2130
(503) 737-3661

School Enrollment: **14,915** Male: **8,595** Female: **6,320**
LD Enrollment: **40**

Admissions Contact: **Kay Conrad, Director of Admissions**
LD Contact: **Tracy Bentley, Director, Disabled Student Services**
Name of Program: **Special Services Project**

Admissions

Application Information:
Accepted: **15** Enrolled:**14**
Application deadline: **May 1st**
Applicant must apply **4** months in advance
Rolling Admissions: **Yes** Notified when: **Within 30 days**

Secondary School Information
Most Important Criteria For Admissions (1-strongest)

4 SAT/ACT	**1** Application	**3** School transcript
Class rank	**3** Course selection	Personal statement
Interview	Extra activities	Psychoeducational
2 G.P.A.	Open admission	Recommendations

Test Requirements:
Diagnostic testing waived: **Yes**
Documentation of LD required: **Yes**
Currency of diagnostic testing: **3 years**
Tests recommended: **One cognitive, one achievement and at least one if not more processing tests.**

Types of Disabilities Served
- Speech/Lang
- Study skills
- Written express
- Organizational
- Perceptual
- Reading
- Spelling
- Math
- Fine Motor
- ADD with LD
- ADD without LD
- ADHD with LD
- ADHD without LD

Admissions Process

If students do not meet standard admission, they may be admitted through the Education Opportunities Program. Before an application is denied, the application will be forwarded to the appropriate personnel.

Learning Disability Program

Program: Reinforces course work: **Yes**
Counseling: Individual: **Yes** Group Counseling: **Yes**

Faculty:
Faculty: **3** Including Director: **Yes** Full time: **3** M.A.: **3**
Faculty advocate: **Yes** Meets with instructor: **When needed**

Diagnostic Testing

ADD	Personality	Perceptual skills	Spelling
ADHD	Organization	Fine motor skills	Reading
I.Q.	Handwriting	Spoken language	Study skills
Math	Social skills	Written language	

Tutoring:
Average size of group tutorials: **4-6**
Services rendered by:
- Graduates
- Peers
- Faculty
- LD staff
- Teacher trainees

Tutorials

Grp.	Ind.	Tutorials	Grp.	Ind.	Tutorials
•	•	Math skills	•	•	Word processing
•	•	Study skills	•		Time management
•	•	Language arts	•		Learning strategies
•	•	Written express	•	•	Organizational skills

Academic Accommodations

Curriculum	Study Aids	Exams
• Priority registration	Typist	• Oral
• Math waiver	• Reader	Untimed
• Foreign lang. waiver	• Notetaker	Take home
• Course substitution	Proof reader	• With proctor
In Class	• Text on tape	• On computer
• Calculators	Early syllabus	• Extended time
• Tape recorder	Taped handouts	• On tape
• Word processor		• Modified
• Priority seating		• Separate room

Program Strengths

The Special Services Project at Oregon State University serves approximately 40 LD students. Services provided are: counseling/advising; tutoring; access to development classes in writing, math, study skills, and personal adjustment; access to a computer laboratory with word processing capability; and a comprehensive alternative testing program. However, not all students with a disability are accepted into this program.

General Information:

Oregon State University is a 4 year public university. Urban campus of 530 acres is 85 miles from Portland. Accessible by train or bus. Ski areas are 90 miles from campus. Beaches are 50 miles from campus. 10.3% of students are foreign. 20 residential halls on campus. Housing is guaranteed.Guaranteed through 1st year. 22.8 % of students join fraternities/sororities.

Accreditation:NACS and 17 Professional Accreditations

SAT/ACT Scores:
Scores for incoming freshmen:**Verbal:**71%below 500. 23%between 500 and 599. 5%between 600 and 699. 2%above 700. **Math:**46% below 500. 33% between 500 and 599. 19% between 600 and 699. 3%above 700. **ACT:** 42% below 20. 34% between 20 and 23. 9%between 24 and 25l. 11%between 26 and 28. 4% above 28.

Expenses:
Tuition: In-state: Full year: $866.00 per term. Tuition: Out-of-state: Full year: $2,206.00 per term. Room and board: $3,225.00

Majors

• AREA STUDIES American, Latin American, Russian/Slavic, Women's Studies • BUSINESS Accounting, Agricultural, Banking, Business Administration, Business Education, Business Management, Economics, Finance, Hotel and Restaurant Management, International Business, Management, Marketing, Personnel, Travel/Tourism Management • COMMUNICATIONS Broadcasting, Communication, Graphic Design, Journalism, Television/Radio/Film • COMPUTER SCIENCE Computer Maintenance, Computer Science, Computer Technology, Programming, Software Engineer, Systems Analysis • EDUCATION Agricultural, Child Development, Elementary, English, Health, Industrial, Mathematics, Middle School, Physical, Science, Secondary, Social Studies, Vocational • ENGINEERING Agricultural, Chemical, Mechanical, Metallurgical, Mining/Mineral, Nuclear, Physics • HEALTH SCIENCES Environmental, Health, Medical Technology, Nursing, Nutritional/Food, Occupational Therapy, Physical Therapy, Speech/Audiology and Speech • HUMANITIES Liberal Arts, Philosophy, Religion • LANGUAGES French, German, Spanish • PRE-PROFESSIONAL Agriculture, Dentistry, Engineering, Forestry, Medicine, Natural Resources, Pharmacy, Range Management, Recreation, Veterinarian • SCIENCES Agricultural, Agronomy, Animal, Anthropology, Biochemistry, Biology, Biotechnology, Botany, Chemistry, Earth, Ecology, Entomology, Genetics, Geography, Geophysics, Gerontology, Horticultural, Macrobiology, Marine Biology, Mathematics, Meteorology, Microbiology, Oceanography, Physical Chemistry, Physical Science, Physics, Physiology, Soil, Toxicology, Zoology • SOCIAL SCIENCES Anthropology, Government/Political, History, Human Service, Psychology, Social Sciences, Sociology • VISUAL AND PERFORMING ARTS Art, Art History, Fine Arts, Music Performance, Studio Art, Theater • VOCATIONAL Fishery Studies, Food Service, Home Economics, Interior Design, Landscape Architecture, Medical Records, Park/Recreation, Textile and Clothing, Welding

Sports/Activities

• SPORTS RELATED Bagpipe Band, Cheerleading, Chess, Drill Team, Drum Major/Majorette, Marching Band, Pep Band, Team Managers • SPORTS-INTERCOLLEGIATE Baseball (M), Basketball, Crew, Diving, Football (M), Golf, Gymnastics (F), Soccer, Softball (F), Swimming (F), Volleyball (F), Wrestling (M) • SPORTS-INTRAMURAL Archery, Badminton, Basketball, Football (M), Racquetball, Soccer, Softball, Swimming, Tennis, Volleyball • STUDENT LIFE ACTIVITIES Choral, Dance, Debate, Drama Groups, Ethnic & Cultural Groups, Film, Fraternities, Jazz Band, Music Groups, Newspaper, Radio/TV station, Religious Organization, Sororities, Student Government, Symphony Orchestra, Yearbook

Selective	Oregon Program

Pacific University
2043 College Way
Forest Grove, Oregon 97116-1797
(503) 359-6151

School Enrollment: **810** Male: **400** Female: **410**

Admissions Contact: **Barbara Mergen, Director of Admissions**
LD Contact: **George Hill, Ph.D.**
Telephone:**(503) 359-2218**

Admissions

Application Information:
Application deadline: **June 1st**
Applicant must apply **3** months in advance

Secondary School Information
Most Important Criteria For Admissions (1-strongest)

4 SAT/ACT	**5** Application	**1** School transcript
10 Class rank	**3** Course selection	**8** Personal statement
6 Interview	**9** Extra activities	**11** Psychoeducational
2 G.P.A.	Open admission	**7** Recommendations

Test Requirements:
Diagnostic testing waived: **Yes**
Untimed SAT: **Yes** Untimed ACT: **Yes**
Documentation of LD required: **Yes**

Types of Disabilities Served

Speech/Lang	• Reading	ADD with LD
• Study skills	• Spelling	ADD without LD
• Written express	• Math	ADHD with LD
• Organizational	Fine Motor	ADHD without LD
Perceptual		

Learning Disability Program
Program: Reinforces course work: **Yes**
Students mainstreamed **100** % of the day
Counseling: Individual: **Yes**

Faculty:
Faculty: **2** Part time: **2** Ph.D.: **2**
Faculty advocate: **Yes** Meets with instructor: **As needed**

Diagnostic Testing

ADD	Personality	Perceptual skills	Spelling
ADHD	Organization	Fine motor skills	Reading
I.Q.	Handwriting	Spoken language	Study skills
Math	Social skills	Written language	

Tutoring:
Services rendered by:
Graduates •Peers •Faculty •LD staff Teacher trainees

Tutorials

Grp.	Ind.	Tutorials	Grp.	Ind.	Tutorials
	•	Math skills			Word processing
	•	Study skills			Time management
	•	Language arts		•	Learning strategies
	•	Written express		•	Organizational skills

Academic Accommodations

Curriculum	Study Aids	Exams
Priority registration	Typist	• Oral
Math waiver	Reader	Untimed
Foreign lang. waiver	Notetaker	Take home
• Course substitution	Proof reader	With proctor
In Class	Text on tape	On computer
Calculators	Early syllabus	• Extended time
• Tape recorder	Taped handouts	On tape
Word processor		• Modified
Priority seating		Separate room

Program Strengths
The "program" at this point is barely beginning - it mostly involves identification of problems, suggestions for learning or test-taking, and slight modifications in the classroom. Much more education of college faculty and administration and additional resources are needed before we really have a program for LD students. We've only had a few identified LD students.

General Information:
Pacific University is a 4 year private university. Suburban campus of 57 acres is 25 miles from Portland. Accessible by bus. Ski areas are 70 miles from campus. Beaches are 50 miles from campus. 5% of students are foreign. 3 residential halls on campus. Housing is guaranteed.Guaranteed through 1st year. 75 % of students remain on campus for the weekends. 32 % of students join fraternities/sororities.

Accreditation:NACS

SAT/ACT Scores:
Scores for incoming freshmen:**Verbal:**48%below 500. 20%between 500 and 599. 8%between 600 and 699. 1%above 700. **Math:**40% below 500. 24% between 500 and 599. 12% between 600 and 699. 1%above 700. 4% between 20 and 23. 10%between 24 and 251. 6%between 26 and 28. 3% above 28.

Class Rank:
About 65% of the present freshmen class were in the upper 20% of their high school class. 20% were in the top 40% of their class. 15% were in the top 60% of their class.

Expenses:
Tuition: In-state: Full year: $10,200.00. Tuition: Out-of-state: Full year: $10,200.00. Room and board: $3,175.00

Majors
• AREA STUDIES Asian, International Studies, Latin American • BUSINESS Accounting, Business Administration, Business Management, Economics, Finance, Marketing, Marketing Research • COMMUNICATIONS Communication, Creative Writing, English, Journalism, Television/Radio/Film • COMPUTER SCIENCE Computer Science • EDUCATION Elementary, Foreign Language, Music, Physical • HEALTH SCIENCES Medical Technology, Occupational Therapy, Physical Therapy • HUMANITIES Humanities, Philosophy, Religion • LANGUAGES Chinese, French, German, Italian, Japanese, Spanish • PREPROFESSIONAL Dentistry, Law, Medicine, Pharmacy, Social Work • SCIENCES Biology, Chemistry, Mathematics, Physical Science, Physics • SOCIAL SCIENCES Anthropology, Government/Political, History, International Studies, Psychology, Social Sciences, Sociology • VISUAL AND PERFORMING ARTS Dance, Fine Arts, Music

Sports/Activities

• SPORTS-INTERCOLLEGIATE Baseball (M), Basketball, Cross Country, Football (M), Golf, Hand Ball, Soccer, Softball, Swimming, Tennis, Volleyball (F), Wrestling (M) • SPORTS-INTRAMURAL Basketball (M), Hand Ball, Racquetball, Soccer, Volleyball • STUDENT LIFE ACTIVITIES Choral, Concert Band, Dance, Drama Groups, Ethnic & Cultural Groups, Fraternities, Jazz Band, Magazine, Music Groups, Musical Theater, Newspaper, Radio/TV station, Religious Organization, Sororities, Student Government, Symphony Orchestra, Yearbook

---

Less Selective　　　　　　　　　　**Oregon**
　　　　　　　　　　　　　　　　　　　Services

Portland Community College
P.O. Box 19000
Portland, Oregon 97068
(503) 244-6111

School Enrollment: **47,600** Male: **23,324** Female: **24,276**
LD Enrollment: **275** Male: **150** Female: **125**
LD Contact: **Carolee Schmeer, LD Specialist**
Name of Program: **Office for Students with Disabilities**
Telephone:**(503) 244-6111 Ext. 4840**

Admissions

Application Information:
Application deadline: **None**

Secondary School Information
Most Important Criteria For Admissions (1-strongest)

SAT/ACT	Application	School transcript
Class rank	Course selection	Personal statement
Interview	Extra activities	Psychoeducational
G.P.A.	1 Open admission	Recommendations

Test Requirements:
Documentation of LD required: **Yes**
Tests recommended: **We accept evaluations that verify LD that contains a psychological test, a standardized achievement, and a processing test suggested. We also do LD evaluations for students taking 6 or more credits if they feel they may be LD.**

Types of Disabilities Served
• Speech/Lang　• Reading　　• ADD with LD
• Study skills　• Spelling　　• ADD without LD
• Written express　• Math　　• ADHD with LD
• Organizational　• Fine Motor　• ADHD without LD
• Perceptual

Admissions Process

Fill out form, take a placement test in reading, writing and math once admissions is complete.

Learning Disability Program

Students mainstreamed **100** % of the day
Counseling: Individual: **Yes** Vocational Counseling: **Yes**

Faculty:
Faculty: **5** Full time: **1** Part time: **4**
Faculty advocate: **Yes** Meets with instructor: **As needed**

Diagnostic Testing

ADD	Personality	• Perceptual skills	• Spelling
ADHD	Organization	• Fine motor skills	• Reading
• I.Q.	Handwriting	• Spoken language	• Study skills
• Math	Social skills	• Written language	

Tutoring:
Services rendered by:
•Graduates　•Peers　　Faculty　　•LD staff　　Teacher trainees

Tutorials

Grp.	Ind.	Tutorials	Grp.	Ind.	Tutorials
	•	Math skills		•	Word processing
	•	Study skills		•	Time management
	•	Language arts		•	Learning strategies
	•	Written express		•	Organizational skills

Academic Accommodations

Curriculum	Study Aids	Exams
• Priority registration	Typist	• Oral
• Math waiver	• Reader	• Untimed
• Foreign lang. waiver	• Notetaker	• Take home
• Course substitution	• Proof reader	• With proctor
In Class	• Text on tape	• On computer
• Calculators	Early syllabus	• Extended time
• Tape recorder	Taped handouts	• On tape
• Word processor		• Modified
• Priority seating		• Separate room

Graduation Requirements:
Course credits: **90** Math waiver: **Yes** Language waiver: **Yes**

Program Strengths

We are able to provide most support services that are seen as reasonable. We are able to provide evaluation to those who have not yet been identified.

General Information:
Portland Community College is a 2 year public college. Urban campus 5 miles from Portland. Accessible by air, train or bus. Ski areas are 1 hour from campus. Beaches are 2 hours from campus. Housing is not guaranteed.

Accreditation: Regional

Expenses:
Tuition: In-state: Full year: $235.00. Part-time: Per credit:$23.50. Part-time: Per credit:$75.00.

Majors

• BUSINESS Accounting, Agricultural, Banking, Business Administration, Business Management, Economics, Finance, Hotel and Restaurant Management, Real Estate • COMMUNICATIONS Commercial Design, Communication, English, Journalism, Speech • COMPUTER SCIENCE Computer Science, Data Processing, Programming, Software Engineer • CRAFTS AND DESIGN Glass, Illustration Design, Sculpture • EDUCATION Child Development, Elementary, Foreign Language, Industrial, Secondary, Special • ENGINEERING Civil/Environmental, Computer, Electrical, Mechanical • HEALTH SCIENCES Dental Assistant, Dental Hygiene, Medical Records, Medical Technology, Nursing, Nutritional/Food • HUMANITIES Humanities, Liberal Arts, Philosophy • LANGUAGES German, Spanish • PREPROFESSIONAL Architecture, Dentistry, Legal Assistant, Medicine, Pharmacy, Social Work, Veterinarian • SCIENCES Anthropology, Biology, Chemistry, Geography, Geology, Mathematics, Meteorology, Physics • SOCIAL SCIENCES Criminal Justice, Government/Political, History, International Studies, Law Enforcement, Psychology, Social Sciences, Sociology • VISUAL AND

Oregon

PERFORMING ARTS Art, Dance, Fine Arts, Music, Music Performance • VOCATIONAL Automobile Technology, Automotive Service, Aviation Maintenance, Business and Office, Carpentry, Diesel Power Technology, Drafting, Electronics Technology, Fire Science, Food Service, Home Economics, Industrial Arts, Jewelry-Metalsmithery, Landscape Architecture, Machinist, Mechanical Design, Park/Recreation, Precision Metal Work, Printing/Lithography, Radiography, Secretarial

---

Less Selective   **Oregon Services**

Umpqua Community College
P. O. Box 967
Roseburg, Oregon 97470
(503) 440-4600

School Enrollment: **3,992**
LD Enrollment: **34**

Admissions Contact: **Dr. Larry Shipley, Director of Admissions**
LD Contact: **Mary Sharp, Coordinator**
Name of Program: **Disabled Student Services**
Address: **P.O. Box 967**
Telephone:**(503) 440-4600**

Admissions

Application Information:
Application deadline: **None**

Secondary School Information
Most Important Criteria For Admissions (1-strongest)

10 SAT/ACT	**8** Application	**4**	School transcript
11 Class rank	**6** Course selection	**3**	Personal statement
2 Interview	**9** Extra activities	**1**	Psychoeducational
7 G.P.A.	**1** Open admission	**5**	Recommendations

Test Requirements:
Diagnostic testing waived: **Yes**
Untimed SAT: **Yes** Untimed ACT: **Yes** Untimed ACH: **Yes**
Range accepted: **85+**
Documentation of LD required: **Yes**
Tests recommended:

Types of Disabilities Served
- Speech/Lang
- Study skills
- Written express
- Organizational
- Perceptual
- Reading
- Spelling
- Math
- Fine Motor
- ADD with LD
- ADD without LD
- ADHD with LD
- ADHD without LD

Admissions Process

Students take mandatory placement tests and are placed in appropriate classes. Tests can be waived with LD documentation.

High School Course Requirements:
English: **1** Math: **1** Science: **1**

Learning Disability Program
Program: Reinforces course work: **Yes**
Students mainstreamed **100** % of the day
Recommended credits per semester: **6-9**
Services only for LD students: **Yes**
Services available for all students: **Yes**
Counseling: Individual: **Yes** Vocational Counseling: **Yes**

Faculty:
Faculty: **3** Full time: **1** Part time: **3**
Faculty advocate: **Yes** Meets with instructor: **As needed**

Diagnostic Testing
ADD	Personality	Perceptual skills	• Spelling
ADHD	Organization	Fine motor skills	• Reading
• I.Q.	Handwriting	Spoken language	Study skills
• Math	Social skills	• Written language	

Tutoring:
Average size of group tutorials: **3-5**
Services rendered by:
Graduates   •Peers   Faculty   •LD staff   Teacher trainees

Tutorials
Grp.	Ind.	Tutorials	Grp.	Ind.	Tutorials
	•	Math skills		•	Word processing
•		Study skills		•	Time management
	•	Language arts		•	Learning strategies
	•	Written express	•		Organizational skills

Academic Accommodations
Curriculum	Study Aids	Exams
Priority registration	• Typist	• Oral
Math waiver	• Reader	• Untimed
Foreign lang. waiver	• Notetaker	Take home
Course substitution	• Proof reader	• With proctor
In Class	• Text on tape	On computer
• Calculators	Early syllabus	• Extended time
• Tape recorder	Taped handouts	• On tape
• Word processor		• Modified
• Priority seating		• Separate room

Graduation Requirements:
Course credits: **96-108** GPA: **2.0** Years to complete degree: **As needed**

Program Strengths
Umpqua Community College provides support services to learning disabled students in order to insure success in career goals and programs. Our services include assessment, evaluation and diagnosis, readers, notetakers, alternative testing arrangements, and individual academic and career counseling.

General Information:
Umpqua Community College is a 2 year public college. Rural campus of 100 acres is 70 miles from Eugene. Accessible by bus. Ski areas are 100 miles from campus. Beaches are 100 miles from campus. 1% of students are foreign. Housing is not guaranteed.

Accreditation:NACS

Expenses:
Tuition: In-state: Full year: $975.00. Part-time: Per credit:$25.00. Tuition: Out-of-state: Full year: $3,888.00. Part-time: Per credit:$108.00.

Majors
• BUSINESS Accounting, Business Administration, Business Management, Marketing • COMPUTER SCIENCE Data Processing, Program-

ming, Software Engineer • EDUCATION Child Development, Physical • ENGINEERING Civil/Environmental, Engineering Science • HEALTH SCIENCES Medical Secretary, Nursing • HUMANITIES Humanities, Liberal Arts • PREPROFESSIONAL Engineering • SCIENCES Physical Science • SOCIAL SCIENCES Social Sciences • VISUAL AND PERFORMING ARTS Art, Music, Theater • VOCATIONAL Automobile Technology, Automotive Service, Cosmetology, Fire Science, Forestry, Legal Secretary, Secretarial, Welding

Sports/Activities

• SPORTS RELATED Pep Band • SPORTS-INTERCOLLEGIATE Basketball, Cross Country, Track and Field • STUDENT LIFE ACTIVITIES Choral, Concert Band, Drama Groups, Jazz Band, Music Groups, Musical Theater, Newspaper, Student Government

---

Selective　　　　　　　　　　　　　　　**Oregon**
　　　　　　　　　　　　　　　　　　　　　Services

University of Oregon

164 Oregon Hall
Eugene, Oregon 97403-1217
(503) 346-3201

School Enrollment: **13,169**
LD Enrollment: **75**

Admissions Contact: **Martha Pitts, Associate Admissions Director**

Admissions

Application Information:
Application deadline: **March 1st**
Rolling Admissions: **Yes** Notified when: **April 15th**

Secondary School Information
Most Important Criteria For Admissions (1-strongest)

1 SAT/ACT	**6** Application	**3**	School transcript
9 Class rank	**4** Course selection	**7**	Personal statement
Interview	**10** Extra activities	**2**	Psychoeducational
5 G.P.A.	Open admission	**8**	Recommendations

Test Requirements:
Diagnostic testing waived: **Yes**
Untimed SAT: **Yes**

Types of Disabilities Served
• Speech/Lang	• Reading	• ADD with LD
• Study skills	• Spelling	• ADD without LD
• Written express	• Math	• ADHD with LD
• Organizational	• Fine Motor	• ADHD without LD
• Perceptual		

Learning Disability Program
Services only for LD students: **Yes**
Counseling: Individual: **Yes** Group Counseling: **Yes**

Diagnostic Testing
ADD	Personality	Perceptual skills	Spelling
ADHD	Organization	Fine motor skills	Reading
I.Q.	Handwriting	Spoken language	Study skills
Math	Social skills	Written language	

Tutoring:
Average size of group tutorials: **6-8**
Services rendered by:
　Graduates　•Peers　•Faculty　　LD staff　　Teacher trainees

Tutorials
Grp.	Ind.	Tutorials	Grp.	Ind.	Tutorials
•	•	Math skills			Word processing
•	•	Study skills			Time management
•	•	Language arts	•	•	Learning strategies
•	•	Written express			Organizational skills

Academic Accommodations

Curriculum	Study Aids	Exams
Priority registration	• Typist	• Oral
Math waiver	Reader	Untimed
Foreign lang. waiver	• Notetaker	• Take home
Course substitution	• Proof reader	With proctor
In Class	Text on tape	On computer
• Calculators	Early syllabus	• Extended time
• Tape recorder	Taped handouts	On tape
• Word processor		• Modified
Priority seating		Separate room

Program Strengths
We have no formalized LD program. Services are provided through 2 offices, Disabled Student Services and Academic Learning Services. Because the program is not "structured", most LD students who come here need to be self-directed and not require much supervision.

General Information:
University of Oregon is a 4 year public university. Urban campus Accessible by air, train or bus. Ski areas are 1 from campus. Beaches are 1 from campus. Housing is not guaranteed.85 % of students remain on campus for the weekends. 18 % of students join fraternities/sororities.

Accreditation: Regional

Expenses:
Tuition: In-state: Full year: $1,936.75. Tuition: Out-of-state: Full year: $5,610.00.

Majors
• AREA STUDIES American, Asian, Latin American • BUSINESS Accounting, Banking, Business Administration, Business Management, Economics, Finance, Management, Marketing, Sports Management, Travel/Tourism Management • COMMUNICATIONS Advertising, Broadcasting, Communication, Creative Writing, English, Photography, Television/Radio/Film • COMPUTER SCIENCE Programming, Systems Analysis • EDUCATION Art, Curriculum, Early Childhood, Elementary, Foreign Language, Health, Music, Physical, Recreation and Youth Leadership, School Psychology, Special, Speech/Language • HUMANITIES Humanities, Philosophy, Religion • LANGUAGES Dutch, French, German, Greek, Italian, Japanese, Latin, Russian, Spanish • PREPROFESSIONAL Architecture, Engineering, Law, Medicine, Natural Resources, Recreation, Social Work • SCIENCES Astronomy, Biochemistry, Biology, Botany, Chemistry, Earth, Ecology, Geography, Geology, Macrobiology, Marine Biology, Mathematics, Microbiology, Physical Science, Physics, Zoology • SOCIAL SCIENCES Anthropology, Government/Political, History, Psychology, Social Sciences, Sociology • VISUAL AND PERFORMING ARTS Art, Art History, Dance, Fine Arts • VOCATIONAL Painting, Park/Recreation, Printing/Lithography

Sports/Activities
• SPORTS RELATED Marching Band, Pep Band • SPORTS-INTERCOLLEGIATE Basketball, Cross Country, Football (M), Golf, Softball (F), Tennis, Track and Field, Volleyball (F), Wrestling (M) • SPORTS-

627

Oregon

INTRAMURAL Archery, Badminton, Baseball (M), Bowling, Crew, Cross Country, Fencing, Field Hockey (F), Golf, Hand Ball, Horseback Riding, Ice Hockey, Lacrosse, Ping-Pong, Racquetball, Sailing, Soccer, Softball (F), Squash, Swimming, Tennis, Track and Field, Volleyball, Wrestling (M) • STUDENT LIFE ACTIVITIES Choral, Concert Band, Dance, Drama Groups, Fraternities, Jazz Band, Music Groups, Musical Theater, Newspaper, Opera, Radio/TV station, Religious Organization, Sororities, Student Government, Symphony Orchestra, Yearbook

Selective	Oregon Services

Western Oregon State College

345 North Monmouth Avenue
Monmouth, Oregon 97361
(503) 838-8211

School Enrollment: **3,857** Male: **1,562** Female: **2,295**

Admissions Contact: **Craig Kohns, Director of Admissions**
LD Contact: **Martha Smith, Dir., Serv. for Students w/Disabiliites**
Name of Program: **Services for Students with Disabilities**
Address: **Werner College Center**
Telephone:**(503) 838-8250 V/TDD**

Admissions

Application Information:
LD on admissions committee:**Yes**
Application deadline: **April 15th**
Rolling Admissions: **Yes**

Secondary School Information
Most Important Criteria For Admissions (1-strongest)

2	SAT/ACT	**1**	Application	**1**	School transcript
	Class rank	**1**	Course selection		Personal statement
	Interview	**12**	Extra activities	**10**	Psychoeducational
1	G.P.A.		Open admission	**5**	Recommendations

Test Requirements:
Untimed SAT: **Yes** Untimed ACT: **Yes** Untimed ACH: **Yes** Achievement tests required:**Yes**
Documentation of LD required: **Yes**

Types of Disabilities Served
- Speech/Lang
- Study skills
- Written express
- Organizational
- Perceptual
- Reading
- Spelling
- Math
- Fine Motor
- ADD with LD
- ADD without LD
- ADHD with LD
- ADHD without LD

Admissions Process

Students must have an overall 2.75 GPA, completed 14 units of college prep coursework, and take an ACT/SAT. Stduents below a 2.75 must have an SAT of 890, ACT 21 to be considered for admission.

High School Course Requirements:
English: **4** Math: **3** Science: **2** Foreign Language: **2**

Learning Disability Program

Services available for all students: **Yes**

Faculty:
Faculty: **4** Including Director: **Yes** Full time: **2** Part time: **2** M.A.: **1**
Meets with instructor: **As needed**

Diagnostic Testing
ADD	Personality	Perceptual skills	Spelling
ADHD	Organization	Fine motor skills	Reading
I.Q.	Handwriting	Spoken language	Study skills
Math	Social skills	Written language	

Tutoring:
Services rendered by:
Graduates •Peers Faculty LD staff Teacher trainees

Tutorials
Grp.	Ind.	Tutorials	Grp.	Ind.	Tutorials
		Math skills			Word processing
		Study skills			Time management
		Language arts			Learning strategies
		Written express			Organizational skills

Academic Accommodations

Curriculum	Study Aids	Exams
Priority registration	Typist	• Oral
• Math waiver	• Reader	• Untimed
• Foreign lang. waiver	• Notetaker	• Take home
• Course substitution	Proof reader	• With proctor
In Class	• Text on tape	• On computer
• Calculators	Early syllabus	• Extended time
• Tape recorder	• Taped handouts	• On tape
Word processor		• Modified
• Priority seating		• Separate room

Graduation Requirements:
Course credits: **192** GPA: **2.0** Years to complete degree: **varies** Math waiver: **Yes** Language waiver: **Yes**

Program Strengths
We are a small college that deals with students on an individual basis. There is a great deal of support for students on this campus based on its size. We encourage students to advocate for themselves, and their rights while taking on the responsibilities of these rights. If students have the willingness to learn, we will work with them individually to provide support towards their success here at Western.

General Information:
Western Oregon State College is a 4 year public college. Rural campus of 135 acres is 22 miles from Salem, OR. Accessible by car. Ski areas are 2 hours from campus. Beaches are 1 hour from campus. 4% of students are foreign. 6 residential halls on campus. Housing is guaranteed.Guaranteed through 1st year.

Accreditation:AACTE, CACREP, NASM, NWASE

Expenses:
Tuition: In-state: Full year: $827.00. Part-time: Per credit:$57.00. Tuition: Out-of-state: Full year: $1,994.00. Part-time: Per credit:$154.00. Room and board: $3,166.00

Majors
• ARTS Commercial Art, Design, Dramatic Arts, Graphic Arts, Music, Theater Design • BUSINESS Business Administration • COMMUNICATIONS Communication • COMPUTER SCIENCE Computer Science • EDUCATION Bilingual, Child Development, Curriculum, Early Childhood, Elementary, English, English As A Second Language, Foreign Language, Health, Leadership, Mathematics, Middle School, Music,

Psychology, Reading, Science, Secondary, Social Studies, Special • HU-MANITIES English/Writing/Literature, Humanities, Philosophy, Religion • LANGUAGES French, German, Spanish • MATHEMATICS Applied, Theoretical • PRE PROFESSIONAL Dentistry, Engineering, Forestry, Law, Medicine, Optometry, Pharmacy, Veterinarian • SCIENCES Biology, Chemistry, Mathematics, Physical Science • SOCIAL SCIENCES Criminal Justice, Geography, History, International Studies, Law Enforcement, Library Science, Political Science, Psychology, Social Science, Sociology • SPECIAL EDUCATION Deaf/Hearing Impaired, Gifted & Talented, Learning Disability, Mentally Retarded • VISUAL AND PERFORMING ARTS Art, Dramatic Arts, Music, Music Performance, Music Theatre, Studio Art, Theater

Sports/Activities

• SPORTS RELATED Cheerleading, Chess, Marching Band, Pep Band • SPORTS-INTERCOLLEGIATE Baseball (M), Basketball (F), Basketball (M), Cross Country, Cross Country (F), Cross Country (M), Football (M), Softball (F), Track and Field, Track and Field (F), Track and Field (M), Volleyball (F) • SPORTS-INTRAMURAL Archery, Baseball, Bowling, Football, Golf, Judo, Karate, Martial Arts, Ping-Pong, Racquetball, Soccer, Softball, Swimming, Track and Field, Volleyball, Water Polo, Weight Lifting, Wrestling • STUDENT LIFE ACTIVITIES Academic Clubs, Choral, Community Service, Concert Band, Dance, Debate, Drama Groups, Ethnic & Cultural Groups, Jazz Band, Magazine, Music Groups, Musical Theater, Newspaper, Orchestra, Political Groups, Radio/TV station, Religious Organization, Student Government, Yearbook

Highly Selective	Pennsylvania
	Services

Albright College
P.O. Box 15234
Reading, Pennsylvania 19612-5234
(215) 921-2381

School Enrollment: **1,538** Male: **769** Female: **769**
LD Enrollment: **16** Male: **10** Female: **6**

Admissions Contact: **Brian Niles, Admissions Counselor**
LD Contact: **R. Jane Williams, Director of Counseling**
Name of Program: **LD Support Services**
Address: **P.O. Box 15234**
Telephone:**(215) 921-2381**

Admissions

Application Information:
Enrolled:**16**
Application deadline: **February 1st**
Notified when: **March 27th**

Secondary School Information
Most Important Criteria For Admissions (1-strongest)

5	SAT/ACT	**6** Application	**1** School transcript
4	Class rank	**2** Course selection	**9** Personal statement
10	Interview	**8** Extra activities	Psychoeducational
3	G.P.A.	Open admission	**7** Recommendations

Test Requirements:
Diagnostic testing waived: **Yes**
Untimed SAT: **Yes** Untimed ACT: **Yes** Untimed ACH: **Yes**
WAIS-R required: **Yes**
Documentation of LD required: **Yes**
Currency of diagnostic testing: **Within 3 years**
Tests recommended: **WAIS-R, Woodcock-Johnson**

Types of Disabilities Served
• Speech/Lang • Reading • ADD with LD
Study skills • Spelling ADD without LD
• Written express • Math • ADHD with LD
• Organizational • Fine Motor ADHD without LD
• Perceptual

Admissions Process

Coordination between the admissions office and the Director of the Counseling Center in respect to those indicating a learning disability in order to determine possible needs.

High School Course Requirements:
English: **4** Math: **2** Science: **2** Foreign Language: **2**
Waivers to standard high school courses
Foreign Language : **Yes** Course substitution: **Yes**

Learning Disability Program
Program: Reinforces course work: **Yes**
Program available through: **Monday-Friday**
Students mainstreamed **100** % of the day
Recommended credits per semester: **1/2 full time**
Services only for LD students: **Yes**
Counseling: Individual: **Yes** Vocational Counseling: **Yes**
Support groups are available:**for mentoring, socializing, problem solving**

Faculty:
Faculty advocate: **Yes** Meets with instructor: **As needed**

Diagnostic Testing
• ADD • Personality • Perceptual skills • Spelling
• ADHD Organization• Fine motor skills • Reading
• I.Q. Handwriting• Spoken language • Study skills
• Math Social skills• Written language

Tutoring:
Services rendered by:
Graduates •Peers Faculty LD staff Teacher trainees

Tutorials

Grp.	Ind.	Tutorials	Grp.	Ind.	Tutorials
	•	Math skills	•	•	Word processing
•	•	Study skills	•	•	Time management
	•	Language arts			Learning strategies
	•	Written express		•	Organizational skills

Academic Accommodations

Curriculum	Study Aids	Exams
• Priority registration	Typist	• Oral
• Math waiver	• Reader	• Untimed
• Foreign lang. waiver	• Notetaker	Take home
• Course substitution	• Proof reader	With proctor
In Class	• Text on tape	• On computer
• Calculators	• Early syllabus	• Extended time
• Tape recorder	Taped handouts	• On tape
• Word processor		• Modified
• Priority seating		• Separate room

Graduation Requirements:
Course credits: **32** GPA: **2.0** Years to complete degree: **4** Math waiver: **Yes**
Language waiver: **Yes**

Program Strengths
Albright is known for its individualized attention to its students. This most certainly carries over to its LD program. Albright also offers a

Pennsylvania

unique program called "Alpha" for those students undecided about a major and/or career options.

General Information:

Albright College is a 4 year private United Methodist college. of 110 acres is 45 miles from Philadelphia. Accessible by air or bus. Ski areas are 75 miles from campus. Beaches are 125 miles from campus. 6% of students are foreign. 7 residential halls on campus. Housing is guaranteed.Guaranteed through 4th year. 27 % of students join fraternities/sororities.

Accreditation:MSACS

SAT/ACT Scores:

Scores for incoming freshmen:**Verbal:**46%below 500. 40%between 500 and 599. 13%between 600 and 699. 1%above 700. **Math:**16% below 500. 46% between 500 and 599. 32% between 600 and 699. 6%above 700.

Class Rank:

About 50.9% of the present freshmen class were in the upper 20% of their high school class. 79.8% were in the top 40% of their class. 94.7% were in the top 60% of their class. 100% were in the top 80% of their class.

Expenses:

Tuition: In-state: Full year: $13,400.00. Tuition: Out-of-state: Full year: $13,400.00. Room and board: $4,015.00

Majors

• AREA STUDIES American • BUSINESS Accounting, Banking/Finance, Business Administration, Business Economics, Business Management, Economics, International Business, Management, Psychology/Business • COMMUNICATIONS Communication • COMPUTER SCIENCE Computer Science, Systems Analysis • EDUCATION Early Childhood, Elementary, English, Foreign Language, Home Economics, Mathematics, Religious, Science, Secondary, Social Studies • HEALTH SCIENCES Nutritional/Food • HUMANITIES Fine Arts, Philosophy, Religion • LANGUAGES English, French, German, Spanish • PRE PROFESSIONAL Dentistry, Law, Medicine, Pharmacy, Social Work, Veterinarian • SCIENCES Biochemistry, Biology, Chemistry, Environmental, Mathematics, Physics, Psychology • SOCIAL SCIENCES Government/Political, History, Political Science, Psychology, Public Relations, Sociology, Theological Studies • VOCATIONAL Fashion Merchandising, Home Economics, Textile and Clothing

Sports/Activities

• SPORTS RELATED Cheerleading, Pep Band, Team Managers • SPORTS-INTERCOLLEGIATE Badminton (F), Baseball (M), Basketball (F), Basketball (M), Cross Country (F), Cross Country (M), Field Hockey (F), Football (M), Golf (M), Soccer (M), Softball (F), Swimming (F), Swimming (M), Tennis (F), Tennis (M), Track and Field (F), Track and Field (M), Volleyball (F), Wrestling (M) • SPORTS-INTRAMURAL Basketball (M), Bowling, Football (M), Lacrosse, Racquetball, Softball (M), Volleyball • STUDENT LIFE ACTIVITIES Academic Clubs, Choral, Community Service, Concert Band, Debate, Drama Groups, Ethnic & Cultural Groups, Fraternities, Jazz Band, Magazine, Music Groups, Musical Theater, Newspaper, Political Groups, Radio, Religious Organization, Sororities, Student Government, Yearbook

---

Bloomsburg University of Pennsylvania
Room 10 Ben Franklin Building
Bloomsburg, Pennsylvania 17815
(717) 389-4316

School Enrollment: **7,099** Male: **2,578** Female: **4,521**

Admissions Contact: **James Christy, Director of Admissions**
LD Contact: **Peter Walters, Director**
Name of Program: **504 Services**
Telephone:**(717) 389-4491**

Admissions

Application Information:
Application deadline: **Rolling**
Rolling Admissions: **Yes**

Secondary School Information
Most Important Criteria For Admissions (1-strongest)

1 SAT/ACT	Application	**1**	School transcript
1 Class rank	Course selection		Personal statement
Interview	Extra activities		Psychoeducational
1 G.P.A.	Open admission	**2**	Recommendations

Test Requirements:
Diagnostic testing waived: **Yes**
Untimed SAT: **Yes**
Currency of diagnostic testing: **3 years**

Types of Disabilities Served
Speech/Lang	Reading	ADD with LD
Study skills	Spelling	ADD without LD
Written express	Math	ADHD with LD
Organizational	Fine Motor	ADHD without LD
Perceptual		

Faculty:
Faculty advocate: **Yes** Meets with instructor: **As necessary**

Diagnostic Testing
ADD	Personality	Perceptual skills	Spelling
ADHD	Organization	Fine motor skills	Reading
I.Q.	Handwriting	Spoken language	Study skills
Math	Social skills	Written language	

Tutoring:
Services rendered by:
Graduates	Peers	•Faculty	LD staff	Teacher trainees

Tutorials
Grp.	Ind.	Tutorials	Grp.	Ind.	Tutorials
•	•	Math skills	•	•	Word processing
•	•	Study skills	•	•	Time management
•	•	Language arts		•	Learning strategies
	•	Written express		•	Organizational skills

Academic Accommodations

Curriculum	Study Aids	Exams
Priority registration	• Typist	• Oral
Math waiver	Reader	Untimed
Foreign lang. waiver	• Notetaker	Take home
Course substitution	• Proof reader	With proctor
In Class	• Text on tape	On computer
• Calculators	Early syllabus	• Extended time
• Tape recorder	Taped handouts	On tape
• Word processor		• Modified
Priority seating		Separate room

Program Strengths

Bloomsburg University does not have a formal learning disability program.

General Information:

Bloomsburg University of Pennsylvania is a 4 year public university. Rural campus of 167 acres is 50 miles from Wilkes-Barre. Accessible by air. Ski areas are 1 hour from campus. Beaches are 3.5 hours from campus. 7 residential halls on campus. Housing is guaranteed.Guaranteed through 1st year.

Accreditation:CSWE, NCATE, NLN

Expenses:

Tuition: In-state: Full year: $2,026.00. Part-time: Per credit:$91.00. Tuition: Out-of-state: Full year: $3,552.00. Part-time: Per credit:$148.00. Room and board: $2,064.00

Majors

• BUSINESS Accounting, Banking, Business Administration, Business Economics, Business Education, Business Management, Economics, Finance, Management, Marketing • COMMUNICATIONS Advertising, Broadcasting, Communication, English, Journalism, Speech, Television/Radio/Film • COMPUTER SCIENCE Computer Science, Data Processing, Programming • EDUCATION Early Childhood, Elementary, Middle School, Pre-Education, Science, Secondary, Social Studies, Special • HEALTH SCIENCES Communication Disorders, Dental Hygiene, Health, Medical Technology, Nursing, Occupational Therapy, Physical Therapy, Radiological Therapy, Speech Therapy, Speech/Audiology and Speech • HUMANITIES Humanities, Liberal Arts, Philosophy • LANGUAGES Chinese, French, German, Italian, Japanese, Latin, Polish, Russian, Spanish • PREPROFESSIONAL Dentistry, Engineering, Law, Medicine, Social Work • SCIENCES Biology, Chemistry, Geography, Geology, Marine Biology, Mathematics, Physical Science, Physics, Physics • SOCIAL SCIENCES Anthropology, Criminal Justice, Geography, Government/Political, History, Political Science, Psychology, Social Sciences, Sociology • VISUAL AND PERFORMING ARTS Art, Art History, Dramatic Arts, Fine Arts, Music, Studio Art, Theater • VOCATIONAL Medical Laboratory Technology, Office Administration, Radiological Technology

Sports/Activities

• SPORTS RELATED Baton Twirling, Cheerleading, Drill Team, Drum Major/Majorette, Marching Band, Pep Band, Team Managers • SPORTS-INTERCOLLEGIATE Baseball (M), Basketball, Cross Country, Field Hockey (F), Football (M), Golf (M), Lacrosse (F), Soccer (M), Softball (F), Swimming, Tennis, Track and Field, Wrestling (M) • SPORTS-INTRAMURAL Archery (M), Badminton, Basketball, Bowling (F), Cross Country (M), Golf, Gymnastics (F), Ping-Pong, Racquetball, Soccer (M), Softball, Tennis, Volleyball, Water Polo (M), Wrestling (M) • STUDENT LIFE ACTIVITIES Choral, Concert Band, Debate, Drama Groups, Ethnic & Cultural Groups, Fraternities, Jazz Band, Magazine, Music Groups, Musical Theater, Newspaper, Political Groups, Radio/TV station, Religious Organization, Sororities, Student Government, Symphony Orchestra, Yearbook

---

Most Selective	Pennsylvania Services

Bryn Mawr College

Bryn Mawr, Pennsylvania 19010
(215) 645-5152

School Enrollment: **1,195** Female: **1,195**

Admissions Contact: **Elizabeth Vermey, Director of Admissions**
LD Contact: **Jo Ellen Parker, Assistant Dean**

Admissions

Application Information:
Application deadline: **January 15th**
Notified when: **April 15th**

Secondary School Information
Most Important Criteria For Admissions (1-strongest)

3	SAT/ACT	3	Application	1	School transcript
2	Class rank	1	Course selection		Personal statement
4	Interview	4	Extra activities		Psychoeducational
2	G.P.A.		Open admission	3	Recommendations

Test Requirements:
Untimed SAT: **Yes** Untimed ACH: **Yes**

Types of Disabilities Served
• Speech/Lang	• Reading	• ADD with LD
• Study skills	• Spelling	• ADD without LD
• Written express	• Math	• ADHD with LD
• Organizational	• Fine Motor	• ADHD without LD
• Perceptual		

Learning Disability Program

Counseling: Individual: **Yes**

Diagnostic Testing
ADD	Personality	Perceptual skills	Spelling
ADHD	Organization	Fine motor skills	Reading
I.Q.	Handwriting	Spoken language	Study skills
Math	Social skills	Written language	

Tutoring:
Services rendered by:

Graduates	•Peers	•Faculty	LD staff	Teacher trainees

Tutorials
Grp.	Ind.	Tutorials	Grp.	Ind.	Tutorials
•	•	Math skills	•	•	Word processing
•	•	Study skills	•	•	Time management
•	•	Language arts	•	•	Learning strategies
•	•	Written express	•	•	Organizational skills

Academic Accommodations

Curriculum	Study Aids	Exams
Priority registration	• Typist	• Oral
Math waiver	Reader	Untimed
Foreign lang. waiver	• Notetaker	• Take home
• Course substitution	• Proof reader	With proctor
In Class	• Text on tape	On computer
• Calculators	Early syllabus	• Extended time
• Tape recorder	Taped handouts	On tape
• Word processor		• Modified
Priority seating		Separate room

Program Strengths

For LD students who want to have the experience of education in a liberal arts program, we provide a wealth of supportive services in an individualized way.

General Information:

Bryn Mawr College is a 4 year private college. Suburban campus of 135 acres is 10 miles from Philadelphia. Accessible by air, train, or bus. Ski areas are 50 miles from campus. Beaches are 60 miles from campus. 9% of students are foreign. 11 residential halls on campus. Housing is guaranteed.Guaranteed through 4th year. 90 % of students remain on campus for the weekends.

Accreditation:MSACS

SAT/ACT Scores:

Scores for incoming freshmen: 50%between 600 and 699. 50% between 600 and 699.

Class Rank:

About 90% of the present freshmen class were in the upper 20% of their high school class.

Expenses:

Tuition: In-state: Full year: $13,200.00. Tuition: Out-of-state: Full year: $13,200.00. Room and board: $5,100.00

Majors

• AREA STUDIES African, American, Asian, Black/Afro-American, Jewish, Latin American, Peace Studies, Russian/Slavic, Urban, Women's Studies • BUSINESS Economics • COMMUNICATIONS Creative Writing, English, Photography • EDUCATION Early Childhood, Music, Secondary • HUMANITIES Classics, English/Writing/Literature, Humanities, Philosophy, Religion • LANGUAGES Chinese Foreign Language, French, German, Greek, Italian, Latin, Russian, Spanish • PREPROFESSIONAL Law • SCIENCES Archeology, Astronomy, Biochemistry, Biology, Chemistry, Earth, Geology, Mathematics, Microbiology, Molecular Biology, Neuroscience, Physical Chemistry, Physics, Physiology • SOCIAL SCIENCES Anthropology, Government/Political, History, International Studies, Political Science, Psychology, Sociology • VISUAL AND PERFORMING ARTS Art, Art History, Dance, Fine Arts, Music, Studio Art, Theater • VOCATIONAL Urban Design

Sports/Activities

• SPORTS RELATED Chess, Team Managers • SPORTS-INTERCOLLEGIATE Badminton (F), Basketball (F), Cross Country (F), Diving (F), Lacrosse (F), Soccer (F), Swimming (F), Tennis (F), Volleyball (F) • SPORTS-INTRAMURAL Archery (F), Basketball (F), Cross Country (F), Fencing (F), Golf (F), Gymnastics (F), Horseback Riding (F), Ice Hockey (F), Rugby (F), Sailing (F), Softball (F), Squash (F), Track and Field (F), Volleyball (F) • STUDENT LIFE ACTIVITIES Choral, Community Service, Dance, Drama Groups, Ethnic & Cultural Groups, Jazz Band, Magazine, Music Groups, Musical Theater, Newspaper, Political Groups, Radio/TV station, Religious Organization, Sororities, Student Government, Symphony Orchestra, Yearbook

---

Selective   **Pennsylvania Program**

California University of Pennsylvania

Keystone Education Building Box 66 - Room 112
California, Pennsylvania 15419
(412) 938-5781

School Enrollment: **5,996** Male: **2,817** Female: **3,186**
LD Enrollment: **38** Male: **29** Female: **9**

Admissions Contact: **Norman G. Hasbrouck, Dir. of Admissions**
LD Contact: **Cheryl Bilitski, Director, College CARE Program**
Name of Program: **CARE (Specialized Support Service Program)**
Telephone:**(412) 938-5781**

Admissions

Application Information:

Accepted: **40** Enrolled:**33**
Separate application:**Yes**
Application deadline: **None**
Rolling Admissions: **Yes**

Secondary School Information

Most Important Criteria For Admissions (1-strongest)

6 SAT/ACT	**1** Application	**2** School transcript
4 Class rank	**5** Course selection	**8** Personal statement
10 Interview	**9** Extra activities	Psychoeducational
3 G.P.A.	Open admission	**7** Recommendations

Test Requirements:

Diagnostic testing waived: **Yes**
Untimed SAT: **Yes** Untimed ACT: **Yes**
Documentation of LD required: **Yes**
Currency of diagnostic testing: **Most recent as possible**
Tests recommended: **Complete recent psychological evaluation including assessment of intellectual status, achievement levels, personal-social indicators and other testing deemed necessary by the psychologist.**

Types of Disabilities Served

• Speech/Lang	• Reading	• ADD with LD
• Study skills	• Spelling	ADD without LD
• Written express	• Math	• ADHD with LD
• Organizational	• Fine Motor	ADHD without LD
• Perceptual		

Admissions Process

LD documentation is requested by CARE, not the Admissions Office; students should apply directly to the Admissions Office for a University application and have an official transcript forwarded; recommendations and interviews not required but highly recommended.

High School Course Requirements:

English: **4** Math: **2** Science: **2** Foreign Language: **2**
Waivers to standard high school courses
Course substitution: **Yes**

Learning Disability Program

Program: Reinforces course work: **Yes**
Students mainstreamed **100** % of the day
Recommended credits per semester: **12-15**
Time required or recommended in learning center: **8 hours**
Services only for LD students: **Yes**
Counseling: Individual: **Yes** Group Counseling: **Yes** Vocational Counseling: **Yes**
Support groups are available:**Program operates as intensive academic support system**

Faculty:

Faculty: **16** Including Director: **Yes** Full time: **1** Part time: **15**
LD faculty with: BS/BA: **7** M.A.: **1** Ph.D.: **2**
Faculty advocate: **Yes** Meets with instructor: **As needed**

Diagnostic Testing

- ADD
- ADHD
- I.Q.
- Math
- Personality
- Organization
- Handwriting
- Social skills
- Perceptual skills
- Fine motor skills
- Spoken language
- Written language
- Spelling
- Reading
- Study skills

Tutoring:

Average size of group tutorials: **1-6**
Services rendered by:
- Graduates
- Peers
- Faculty
- LD staff
- Teacher trainees

Tutorials

Grp.	Ind.	Tutorials	Grp.	Ind.	Tutorials
	•	Math skills	•	•	Word processing
•	•	Study skills	•	•	Time management
	•	Language arts	•	•	Learning strategies
	•	Written express	•	•	Organizational skills

Academic Accommodations

Curriculum	Study Aids	Exams
Priority registration	Typist	• Oral
Math waiver	• Reader	• Untimed
Foreign lang. waiver	• Notetaker	Take home
Course substitution	• Proof reader	• With proctor
In Class	• Text on tape	• On computer
• Calculators	• Early syllabus	• Extended time
• Tape recorder	Taped handouts	• On tape
• Word processor		• Modified
• Priority seating		• Separate room

Graduation Requirements:

Course credits: **64-128** GPA: **2.0** Years to complete degree: **Usually five**
Other requirements: **College of Liberal Arts and College of Science and Technology-2.0 overall, 2.3 in major. College of Education-2.5 overall, 2.5 in major**

Program Strengths

The Specialized Support Service Program, (SSSP), of the CARE Project is an intensive fee-for-service, support program. Students work four days per week with a staff monitor during Structured Academic Management Seminars. The seminars are the foundation of the Program focusing on daily evaluation and management of student academic performance. Individual intervention strategies/recommendations are based on staff evaluation of a student's academic needs. NOTE: The University also has a non-fee basic service program available to students with a documented learning disability.

General Information:

California University of Pennsylvania is a 2 and 4 year public college. Rural campus of 48 acres is 35 miles from Pittsburgh. Accessible by bus. Ski areas are 75 miles from campus. Beaches are 400 miles from campus. 1% of students are foreign. 6 residential halls on campus. Housing is not guaranteed.50 % of students remain on campus for the weekends. 10 % of students join fraternities/sororities.

Accreditation:MSACS, NCATE, CSWE, NATA, NLN

Expenses:
Tuition: In-state: Full year: $1,314.00 per semester. Part-time: Per credit:$110.00. Tuition: Out-of-state: Full year: $2,446.00 per semester. Part-time: Per credit:$204.00. Room and board: $1,200.00-$1,600.00 Cost of LD program:$1,285.00-$1,950.00 per semester

Majors

• AREA STUDIES Russian, Urban • ARTS Music • BUSINESS Accounting, Economics, Finance, Management, Marketing • COMMUNICATIONS Communication, English, Graphic Communications Technology, Literature • COMPUTER SCIENCE Computer Science • EDUCATION Athletic Training Education, Early Childhood, Elementary, Health, Physical, Secondary, Special, Technology Education • ENGINEERING Electrical, Petroleum • HEALTH SCIENCES Nursing, Speech/Audiology and Speech • HUMANITIES Philosophy • LANGUAGES French, German, Russian, Spanish • MATHEMATICS Mathematics • SCIENCES Anthropology, Biology, Chemistry, Earth, Environmental Science, Geography, Geology, Gerontology, Mathematics, Physical Science, Physics • SOCIAL SCIENCES Anthropology, History, Political Science, Psychology, Social Science, Social Work, Sociology • VISUAL AND PERFORMING ARTS Art, Music, Theater • VOCATIONAL Driver Safety Education, Industrial Arts, Industrial Technology, Manufacturing Technology

Sports/Activities

• SPORTS RELATED Marching Band, Pep Band • SPORTS-INTERCOLLEGIATE Baseball (M), Basketball (F), Basketball (M), Cross Country (F), Cross Country (M), Soccer (F), Soccer (M), Softball (F), Tennis (F), Track and Field (F), Track and Field (M), Volleyball (F), Wrestling (M) • SPORTS-INTRAMURAL Badminton (F), Basketball, Hand Ball, Ping-Pong, Racquetball, Skiing - Snow, Soccer, Softball, Swimming, Tennis, Track and Field, Volleyball, Wrestling (M) • STUDENT LIFE ACTIVITIES Choir, Choral, Concert Band, Drama Groups, Film, Fraternities, Jazz Band, Magazine, Music Ensemble, Musical Theater, Newspaper, Pep Band, Radio/TV station, Sororities, Student Government, Symphony Orchestra

Highly Selective **Pennsylvania Accommodations**

Carnegie Mellon University

5000 Forbes Avenue
Pittsburgh, Pennsylvania 15213-3890
(412) 268-2082

School Enrollment: **4,286** Male: **3,003** Female: **1,283**
LD Enrollment: **32** Male: **20** Female: **12**

Admissions Contact: **Michael Steidel, Director of Admissions**
LD Contact: **Marcia Wratcher, Director Instructional Development**
Address: **5000 Forbes Avenue**
Telephone:**(412) 268-6878**

Admissions

Application Information:
Application deadline: **February 1st**
Notified when: **April 15th**

Pennsylvania

Secondary School Information
Most Important Criteria For Admissions (1-strongest)

5 SAT/ACT	10 Application	1 School transcript
2 Class rank	4 Course selection	9 Personal statement
8 Interview	7 Extra activities	11 Psychoeducational
3 G.P.A.	Open admission	6 Recommendations

Test Requirements:
Untimed SAT: **Yes** Untimed ACT: **Yes** Untimed ACH: **Yes** Achievement tests required:**3**
Documentation of LD required: **Yes**
Currency of diagnostic testing: **2 years**
Tests recommended: **Testing is required by a medical doctor or psychologist who specializes in learning disabilities**

Types of Disabilities Served
- Speech/Lang
- Study skills
- Written express
- Organizational
- Perceptual
- Reading
- Spelling
- Math
- Fine Motor
- ADD with LD
- ADD without LD
- ADHD with LD
- ADHD without LD

Admissions Process

High school performance, standardized testing, extracurricular participation, essay, recommendations, other supporting materials.

High School Course Requirements:
English: 4

Learning Disability Program
Special orientation for LD students: **Yes**
Students mainstreamed **100** % of the day
Recommended credits per semester: **12-15**
Services only for LD students: **Yes**
Support groups are available:**Informal networking - according to majors/colleges**

Faculty:
Faculty advocate: **Yes** Meets with instructor: **Once per term**

Diagnostic Testing

ADD	Personality	Perceptual skills	Spelling
ADHD	Organization	Fine motor skills	Reading
I.Q.	Handwriting	Spoken language	• Study skills
Math	Social skills	Written language	

Tutoring:
Services rendered by:

Graduates	•Peers	Faculty	LD staff	Teacher trainees

Tutorials

Grp.	Ind.	Tutorials	Grp.	Ind.	Tutorials
		Math skills			Word processing
	•	Study skills		•	Time management
		Language arts		•	Learning strategies
	•	Written express		•	Organizational skills

Academic Accommodations

Curriculum	Study Aids	Exams
Priority registration	• Typist	• Oral
Math waiver	Reader	• Untimed
Foreign lang. waiver	• Notetaker	Take home
• Course substitution	• Proof reader	• With proctor
In Class	• Text on tape	On computer
• Calculators	Early syllabus	• Extended time
• Tape recorder	Taped handouts	On tape
• Word processor		• Modified
• Priority seating		• Separate room

Graduation Requirements:
Course credits: **Varies**

Program Strengths
While we have no formal program, we do work closely with students on an individual basis, providing advocacy for them. Letters of introduction are provided to faculty members. A handbook for disabled students is also available.

General Information:
Carnegie Mellon University is a 4 year private university. Urban campus of 103 acres is 5 miles from Pittsburgh. Accessible by air, train, or bus. Ski areas are 30 miles from campus. Beaches are 9 miles from campus. 5% of students are foreign. 12 residential halls on campus. Housing is guaranteed.80 % of students remain on campus for the weekends. 30 % of students join fraternities/sororities.

Accreditation:MSACS

SAT/ACT Scores:
Scores for incoming freshmen:**Verbal:**25%below 500. 43%between 500 and 599. 28%between 600 and 699. 4%above 700. **Math:**9% below 500. 19% between 500 and 599. 41% between 600 and 699. 31%above 700.

Class Rank:
About 78% of the present freshmen class were in the upper 20% of their high school class. 94% were in the top 40% of their class. 98% were in the top 60% of their class. 99% were in the top 80% of their class.

Expenses:
Tuition: In-state: Full year: $16,000.00. Tuition: Out-of-state: Full year: $16,000.00. Room and board: $5,450.00

Majors
• AREA STUDIES European, Urban • BUSINESS Business Administration, Business Economics, Business Management, Economics, Management, Operating Research • COMMUNICATIONS Communication, Creative Writing, English, Graphic Design, Journalism, Linguistic, Literature • COMPUTER SCIENCE Computer Mathematics, Computer Science, Programming, Robotics, Systems Analysis • CRAFTS AND DESIGN Ceramics, Crafts, Enameling, Glass, Graphic Design, Illustration Design, Sculpture • EDUCATION Art, Early Childhood, Music, Pre-Education • ENGINEERING Bioengineering, Biomedical, Chemical, Civil/Environmental, Computer, Electrical, Engineering Science, Environmental/Water Resources, Materials, Mechanical, Metallurgical • HUMANITIES English/Writing/Literature, Humanities, Philosophy • LANGUAGES French, German, Spanish • PREPROFESSIONAL Architecture • SCIENCES Animal, Biochemistry, Biology, Cell Biology, Chemistry, Human Biology, Inorganic Chemistry, Mathematics, Molecular Biology, Organic Chemistry, Physical Chemistry, Physical Science, Physics, Statistics • SOCIAL SCIENCES Government/Political, History, Political Science, Psychology, Social Sciences, Sociology • VISUAL AND PERFORMING ARTS Dramatic Arts, Music, Music Performance, Theater • VOCATIONAL Industrial Design, Jewelry-Metalsmithery, Painting, Printing/Lithography, Textile and Clothing

Sports/Activities

• SPORTS RELATED Bagpipe Band, Cheerleading, Chess, Marching Band, Pep Band • SPORTS-INTERCOLLEGIATE Baseball (M), Basketball, Crew, Cross Country, Diving, Fencing, Field Hockey (F), Football (M), Golf (M), Ice Hockey (M), Lacrosse (M), Rugby (M), Soccer (M), Swimming, Tennis, Track and Field, Volleyball (F) • SPORTS-INTRAMURAL Badminton, Basketball, Bowling, Crew, Cross Country, Diving, Fencing, Golf, Gymnastics, Hand Ball, Lacrosse (M), Ping-Pong, Racquetball, Riflery, Rugby (M), Sailing, Skiing - Snow, Soccer, Softball, Squash, Swimming, Tennis, Track and Field, Volleyball, Water Polo, Wrestling (M) • STUDENT LIFE ACTIVITIES Choral, Concert Band, Drama Groups, Ethnic & Cultural Groups, Fraternities, Jazz Band, Magazine, Music Ensembles, Musical Theater, Newspaper, Opera, Radio, Religious Organization, Sororities, Student Government, Symphony Orchestra, Yearbook

---

Less Selective	Pennsylvania
	Services

Churchman Business School

355 Spring Garden Street
Easton, Pennsylvania 18042
(215) 258-5345

School Enrollment: **250** Male: **125** Female: **125**
LD Enrollment: **4** Male: **1** Female: **3**

Admissions Contact: **Vickey Churchman, Admissions Counselor**

Admissions

Application Information:
Application deadline: **July 1st**

Secondary School Information
Most Important Criteria For Admissions (1-strongest)

10 SAT/ACT	11 Application	4	School transcript
9 Class rank	1 Course selection	8	Personal statement
3 Interview	6 Extra activities	5	Psychoeducational
1 G.P.A.	Open admission	7	Recommendations

Test Requirements:
Standardized tests waived: **Yes**

Types of Disabilities Served
• Speech/Lang   • Reading   • ADD with LD
• Study skills   • Spelling   • ADD without LD
• Written express   • Math   • ADHD with LD
• Organizational   • Fine Motor   • ADHD without LD
• Perceptual

Diagnostic Testing

ADD	Personality	Perceptual skills	Spelling
ADHD	Organization	Fine motor skills	Reading
I.Q.	Handwriting	Spoken language	Study skills
Math	Social skills	Written language	

Tutoring:
Services rendered by:
Graduates   Peers   •Faculty   LD staff   Teacher trainees

Tutorials

Grp.	Ind.	Tutorials	Grp.	Ind.	Tutorials
	•	Math skills			Word processing
	•	Study skills		•	Time management
		Language arts		•	Learning strategies
	•	Written express		•	Organizational skills

Academic Accommodations

Curriculum	Study Aids	Exams
Priority registration	Typist	Oral
Math waiver	Reader	Untimed
Foreign lang. waiver	Notetaker	Take home
Course substitution	Proof reader	• With proctor
In Class	Text on tape	On computer
Calculators	Early syllabus	Extended time
Tape recorder	Taped handouts	On tape
Word processor		Modified
Priority seating		Separate room

Program Strengths

We do not offer an LD program. However we are a small college (250 students) and therefore can offer personal attention. Students must be able to handle college level work.

General Information:

Churchman Business School is a 2 year private college. Urban campus of 2 acres is 60 miles from Philadelphia. Accessible by bus. Ski areas are 1/2 hour from campus. Beaches are 3 hours from campus. 2% of students are foreign. Housing is not guaranteed.

Accreditation: AICS

Expenses:
Tuition: In-state: Full year: $3,585.00. Part-time: Per credit:$66.00.

Majors

• BUSINESS Accounting, Business Administration, Business Management, Finance, Management, Secretarial Science • HEALTH SCIENCES Medical Secretary • VOCATIONAL Business and Office, Legal Secretary, Secretarial, Word Processing

Sports/Activities

• SPORTS-INTRAMURAL Baseball, Bowling, Golf, Ping-Pong, Skiing - Snow, Softball, Volleyball • STUDENT LIFE ACTIVITIES Student Government, Yearbook

---

Less Selective	Pennsylvania
	Program

College Misericordia

Lake Street
Dallas, Pennsylvania 18612
(717) 675-4449

School Enrollment: **1,595** Male: **383** Female: **1,212**
LD Enrollment: **50** Male: **25** Female: **25**

Admissions Contact: **Michael Joseph, Director of Admissions**
LD Contact: **Dr. Joseph Rogan, Director**
Name of Program: **Alternative Learners Project**
Telephone:**(717) 674-6347**

Pennsylvania

Admissions

Application Information:
LD Students Applying: **152** Accepted: **18** Enrolled:**15**
Application deadline: **None**
Applicant must apply **10** months in advance
Rolling Admissions: **Yes**Notified when: **10 Days**

Secondary School Information
Most Important Criteria For Admissions (1-strongest)

6 SAT/ACT	**7** Application	**1** School transcript
5 Class rank	**1** Course selection	**8** Personal statement
3 Interview	**9** Extra activities	**4** Psychoeducational
1 G.P.A.	Open admission	**2** Recommendations

Test Requirements:
Diagnostic testing waived: **Yes**
Untimed SAT: **Yes** Untimed ACT: **Yes**
WAIS-R required: **Yes** Range accepted: **100+**
Documentation of LD required: **Yes**
Tests recommended: **Full psychological report (WAIS +)**

Types of Disabilities Served

Speech/Lang	• Reading	• ADD with LD
• Study skills	• Spelling	• ADD without LD
• Written express	• Math	• ADHD with LD
• Organizational	• Fine Motor	• ADHD without LD
• Perceptual		

Admissions Process

Applicants send cover letter, application, psychological report, high school transcript, SAT scores, and letters of recommendation. Files are reviewed. Students who look good on paper are invited to interview.

Learning Disability Program

Special orientation for LD students: **Yes**
Syllabus available during orientation:**Yes**
Students mainstreamed **100** % of the day

Faculty:
Faculty: **5** Including Director: **Yes** Full time: **5** M.A.: **5** Ph.D.: **1**
Faculty advocate: **Yes** Meets with instructor: **Very frequently**

Diagnostic Testing

ADD	Personality	Perceptual skills	Spelling
ADHD	Organization	Fine motor skills	Reading
I.Q.	Handwriting	Spoken language	Study skills
Math	Social skills	Written language	

Tutoring:
Average size of group tutorials: **1:1 and group**
Services rendered by:
•Graduates •Peers •Faculty •LD staff Teacher trainees

Tutorials

Grp.	Ind.	Tutorials	Grp.	Ind.	Tutorials
•	•	Math skills	•	•	Word processing
•	•	Study skills	•	•	Time management
		Language arts	•	•	Learning strategies
•	•	Written express	•	•	Organizational skills

Academic Accommodations

Curriculum	Study Aids	Exams
• Priority registration	• Typist	• Oral
Math waiver	• Reader	• Untimed
Foreign lang. waiver	• Notetaker	Take home
• Course substitution	• Proof reader	• With proctor
In Class	• Text on tape	• On computer
• Calculators	• Early syllabus	• Extended time
• Tape recorder	Taped handouts	On tape
• Word processor		• Modified
• Priority seating		• Separate room

Graduation Requirements:
Course credits: **120+** GPA: **2.0** Years to complete degree: **4+**

Program Strengths
All students who participate in the Alternative Learners Project participate in regular college classes. In most cases, they take a carefully selected, reduced credit load each semester. Because of the reduced credit load, it is likely that participants in ALP will spend more than the standard eight semesters earning a degree. Only full-time students are eligible for ALP.

General Information:
College Misericordia is a 4 year private college. Suburban campus of 100 acres is 10 miles from Wilkes-Barre. Accessible by air or bus. Ski areas are 12 miles from campus. Beaches are 5 miles from campus. 2% of students are foreign. 4 residential halls on campus. Housing is guaranteed.Guaranteed through 4th year. 50 % of students remain on campus for the weekends. 10 % of students join fraternities/sororities.

Accreditation:MSACS

SAT/ACT Scores:
Scores for incoming freshmen:**Verbal:**60%below 500. 32%between 500 and 599. 7%between 600 and 699. 1%above 700. **Math:**50% below 500. 39% between 500 and 599. 10% between 600 and 699. 1%above 700.

Class Rank:
About 30% of the present freshmen class were in the upper 20% of their high school class. 90% were in the top 40% of their class. 100% were in the top 60% of their class.

Expenses:
Tuition: In-state: Full year: $8,250.00. Part-time: Per credit:$205.00. Room and board: $4,446.00 Cost of LD program:Summer Pre College Experience $1,500.00

Majors
• BUSINESS Accounting, Business Administration, Business Management, Management, Marketing, Personnel • COMMUNICATIONS English • COMPUTER SCIENCE Computer Science, Data Processing, Programming, Systems Analysis • EDUCATION Curriculum, Early Childhood, Elementary, Pre-Education, Secondary, Special • HEALTH SCIENCES Medical Technology, Nursing, Occupational Therapy, Physical Therapy, Radiological Therapy • HUMANITIES Humanities, Liberal Arts, Philosophy • PREPROFESSIONAL Dentistry, Law, Medical Social Work, Medicine, Sports Medicine, Veterinarian • SCIENCES Biology, Chemistry, Mathematics, Radiology • SOCIAL SCIENCES History, Psychology • VOCATIONAL Medical Laboratory Technology, Radiological Technology

Sports/Activities
• SPORTS RELATED Cheerleading, Team Managers • SPORTS-INTERCOLLEGIATE Baseball (M), Basketball (F), Basketball (M), Field Hockey (F), Field Hockey (M), Soccer (F), Soccer (M), Softball (F), Volleyball (F) • SPORTS-INTRAMURAL Baseball (M), Basketball, Cross Country, Football, Golf, Racquetball, Skiing - Snow, Softball, Tennis, Track and

Field, Volleyball • STUDENT LIFE ACTIVITIES Choral, Concert Band, Dance, Drama Groups, Ethnic & Cultural Groups, Fraternities, Jazz Band, Magazine, Music Groups, Newspaper, Orchestra, Political Groups, Religious Organization, Student Government, Symphony Orchestra, Yearbook

Less Selective — **Pennsylvania Services**

Community College of Allegheny College
8701 Perry Highway
Pittsburgh, Pennsylvania 15237
(412) 369-3686

School Enrollment: **4,400** Male: **1,900** Female: **2,500**
LD Enrollment: **40**

Admissions Contact: **Ray Oyler, Director of Admissions**
LD Contact: **Kathleen White, Director**
Name of Program: **Special Services**
Telephone:**(412) 369-3686**

Admissions

Application Information:
Application deadline: **Day before class begins**
Rolling Admissions: **Yes**

Secondary School Information
Most Important Criteria For Admissions (1-strongest)

SAT/ACT	Application	School transcript
Class rank	Course selection	Personal statement
Interview	Extra activities	Psychoeducational
G.P.A.	1 Open admission	Recommendations

Test Requirements:
Documentation of LD required: **Yes**
Tests recommended: **Psychological, neurological. If unavailable, high school placement in special classes (documentation of).**

Types of Disabilities Served
- Speech/Lang
- Study skills
- Written express
- Organizational
- Perceptual
- Reading
- Spelling
- Math
- Fine Motor
- ADD with LD
- ADD without LD
- ADHD with LD
- ADHD without LD

Admissions Process

Fill out application, send high school transcript, and make appointment for placement test.

Learning Disability Program

Special orientation for LD students: **Yes**
Program: Reinforces course work: **Yes**
Program available through:**Ongoing - daytime hours**
Students mainstreamed **100** % of the day
Services available for all students: **Yes**
Counseling: Individual: **Yes** Vocational Counseling: **Yes**

Faculty:
Faculty: **2** Including Director: **Yes**
LD faculty with: BS/BA: **1** M.A.: **1**
Faculty advocate: **Yes** Meets with instructor: **As needed**

Diagnostic Testing

ADD	Personality	Perceptual skills	Spelling
ADHD	Organization	Fine motor skills	Reading
I.Q.	Handwriting	Spoken language	Study skills
Math	Social skills	Written language	

Tutoring:
Average size of group tutorials:
Services rendered by:
 Graduates   Peers   •Faculty   •LD staff   Teacher trainees

Tutorials

Grp.	Ind.	Tutorials	Grp.	Ind.	Tutorials
	•	Math skills			Word processing
	•	Study skills		•	Time management
	•	Language arts		•	Learning strategies
	•	Written express		•	Organizational skills

Academic Accommodations

Curriculum	Study Aids	Exams
Priority registration	Typist	• Oral
Math waiver	• Reader	Untimed
Foreign lang. waiver	• Notetaker	Take home
Course substitution	Proof reader	• With proctor
In Class	Text on tape	On computer
Calculators	Early syllabus	• Extended time
• Tape recorder	Taped handouts	On tape
Word processor		Modified
Priority seating		Separate room

Graduation Requirements:
Course credits: **60** GPA: **2.0** Years to complete degree: **2**

Program Strengths
We provide services for learning disabled students based on their individual needs.

General Information:
Community College of Allegheny College is a 2 year public college. Suburban campus 1 miles from Pittsburgh. Accessible by bus. Ski areas are 80 miles from campus. Beaches are 400 miles from campus. Housing is not guaranteed.

Accreditation:

Expenses:
Tuition: In-state: Full year: $1,344.00 plus fees. Part-time: Per credit:$56.00. Tuition: Out-of-state: Full year: $1,850.00. Part-time: Per credit:$168.00.

Majors
• BUSINESS Accounting, Appraisal Science, Banking/Finance, Business Management, Data Processing, Economics, Financial Planning Assistance, Hotel and Restaurant Management, Management, Marketing, Personnel, Real Estate, Secretarial Science, Travel/Tourism Management • COMMUNICATIONS Communication, English, Speech • COMPUTER SCIENCE Computer Information Systems, Computer Science, Computer Technology, Data Processing, Programming • ENGINEERING Engineering Science • ENGINEERING Drafting • HEALTH SCIENCES Fitness, Health, Medical Secretary, Medical Transcription, Nursing • HUMANITIES Humanities • PRE PROFESSIONAL Health • SCIENCES Biology, Chemistry, Computer Science, Mathematics, Physics • SOCIAL SCIENCES Anthropology, Human Service, Social Science, Sociology • VISUAL AND PERFORMING ARTS Art, Fine Arts, Theater • VOCATIONAL Air Conditioning/Heating/Refri, Automobile Technology, Building Construction, Child Care, Drafting, Legal Secretary, Office Administration, Quality Control, Secretarial, Welding, Word Processing

Sports/Activities

• STUDENT LIFE ACTIVITIES Fraternities, Newspaper, Student Government

Less Selective

Pennsylvania Services

Community College of Philadelphia

1700 Spring Garden Street
Philadelphia, Pennsylvania 19130
(215) 751-8010

School Enrollment: **44,000**
LD Enrollment: **130**
LD Contact: **Jay L. Segal, Coordinator**
Name of Program: **LD Project**
Telephone:**(215) 751-8050**

Admissions

Application Information:
Application deadline: **None**
Rolling Admissions: **Yes**

Secondary School Information
Most Important Criteria For Admissions (1-strongest)

SAT/ACT	**1** Application	**1**	School transcript
Class rank	Course selection		Personal statement
Interview	Extra activities	**1**	Psychoeducational
G.P.A.	**1** Open admission		Recommendations

Test Requirements:
Standardized tests waived: **Yes**
Diagnostic testing waived: **Yes**
WAIS-R required: **Yes** Range accepted: **85**
Documentation of LD required: **Yes**
Tests recommended: **WAIS-R, WRAT-R**

Types of Disabilities Served
• Speech/Lang • Reading • ADD with LD
• Study skills • Spelling • ADD without LD
• Written express • Math ADHD with LD
• Organizational • Fine Motor ADHD without LD
• Perceptual

Admissions Process

Student provides documentation to LD Project Director to initiate process. Student receives accommodations beginning with placement test which is required prior to registration.

Learning Disability Program

Program: Reinforces course work: **Yes**
Students mainstreamed **100** % of the day
Services only for LD students: **Yes**
Counseling: Individual: **Yes**

Faculty:
Faculty: **2** Including Director: **Yes** Full time: **2** M.A.: **2**
Faculty advocate: **Yes** Meets with instructor: **As needed**

Diagnostic Testing
• ADD Personality • Perceptual skills • Spelling
• ADHD• Organization Fine motor skills • Reading
• I.Q. Handwriting Spoken language Study skills
• Math • Social skills• Written language

Tutoring:
Average size of group tutorials: **4-5**
Services rendered by:
Graduates •Peers •Faculty •LD staff Teacher trainees

Tutorials

Grp.	Ind.	Tutorials	Grp.	Ind.	Tutorials
	•	Math skills		•	Word processing
•	•	Study skills	•	•	Time management
	•	Language arts	•	•	Learning strategies
	•	Written express	•	•	Organizational skills

Academic Accommodations

Curriculum	Study Aids	Exams
Priority registration	Typist	• Oral
Math waiver	• Reader	Untimed
Foreign lang. waiver	• Notetaker	Take home
Course substitution	Proof reader	• With proctor
In Class	• Text on tape	On computer
• Calculators	Early syllabus	• Extended time
• Tape recorder	Taped handouts	On tape
• Word processor		• Modified
Priority seating		Separate room

Program Strengths

There are comprehensive services, including diagnostic testing, tutoring by LD specialist, word processing training, and individualized accommodations.

General Information:

Community College of Philadelphia is a 2 year public college. Urban campus Housing is not guaranteed.

Accreditation:MSACS

Expenses:
Tuition: In-state: Full year: Approximately $1,800.00 per semester. Tuition: Out-of-state: Full year: Approximately $3,600.00 per semester.

Majors

• BUSINESS Accounting, Business Education, Business Management, Finance, Food Management, Hotel and Restaurant Management, International Business, Management, Marketing, Real Estate, Retailing
• COMMUNICATIONS Photography • COMPUTER SCIENCE Computer Science, Computer Technology, Data Processing, Medical Records Administration, Medical Records Technology, Programming • EDUCATION Child Development, Early Childhood, Pre-Education, Special • ENGINEERING Biomedical, Chemical, Engineering Science • HEALTH SCIENCES Dental Assistant, Dental Hygiene, Dietary Manager Assistant, Medical Technology, Nursing • HUMANITIES Liberal Arts • PREPROFESSIONAL Architecture, Recreation • SOCIAL SCIENCES Criminal Justice, Human Service, Law Enforcement, Library Science, Public Relations • VISUAL AND PERFORMING ARTS Music, Studio Art • VOCATIONAL Automobile Technology, Automotive Service, Business and Office, Construction, Electronics Technology, Fashion Merchandising, Fire Science, Food Service, Medical Laboratory Technology, Radiological Technology, Respiratory Therapy Technology, Secretarial, Word Processing

Sports/Activities

• SPORTS-INTERCOLLEGIATE Baseball (M), Basketball, Cross Coun-

try, Soccer (M), Softball (F), Tennis, Track and Field, Volleyball (F)
• SPORTS-INTRAMURAL Basketball, Soccer, Softball, Volleyball
• STUDENT LIFE ACTIVITIES Academic Clubs, Choral, Dance, Drama Groups, Ethnic & Cultural Groups, Jazz Band, Music Groups, Political Groups, Radio/TV station, Religious Organization, Student Government

---

Less Selective

Pennsylvania Program

Delaware County Community College
Route 252 and Media Line Road
Media, Pennsylvania 19063
(215) 359-5000

School Enrollment: **7,900** Male: **3,400** Female: **4,500**

Admissions Contact: **Joseph Piorkowski, Director of Admissions**
LD Contact: **Stuart J. Dix, Counselor**
Name of Program: **Special Services**

Admissions

Application Information:
Enrolled:**85**
Application deadline: **Rolling**
Rolling Admissions: **Yes**

Secondary School Information
Most Important Criteria For Admissions (1-strongest)

SAT/ACT	**1** Application	School transcript
Class rank	Course selection	Personal statement
Interview	Extra activities	Psychoeducational
G.P.A.	**1** Open admission	Recommendations

Test Requirements:
Standardized tests waived: **Yes**
Untimed SAT: **Yes** Untimed ACT: **Yes**
Tests recommended: **Latest diagnostic evaluation or other proof of LD**

Types of Disabilities Served
- Speech/Lang
- Study skills
- Written express
- Organizational
- Perceptual
- Reading
- Spelling
- Math
- Fine Motor
- ADD with LD
- ADD without LD
- ADHD with LD
- ADHD without LD

Learning Disability Program
Students mainstreamed **100** % of the day
Counseling: Individual: **Yes**

Faculty:
Faculty: **2** Including Director: **Yes** Full time: **1** Part time: **1**
Faculty advocate: **Yes** Meets with instructor: **As needed**

Diagnostic Testing

ADD	Personality	Perceptual skills	Spelling
ADHD	Organization	Fine motor skills	Reading
I.Q.	Handwriting	Spoken language	Study skills
Math	Social skills	Written language	

Tutoring:
Average size of group tutorials: **Varies**
Services rendered by:

Graduates •Peers •Faculty LD staff Teacher trainees

Tutorials

Grp.	Ind.	Tutorials	Grp.	Ind.	Tutorials
•	•	Math skills	•	•	Word processing
•	•	Study skills	•	•	Time management
•	•	Language arts	•	•	Learning strategies
•	•	Written express	•	•	Organizational skills

Academic Accommodations

Curriculum	Study Aids	Exams
Priority registration	• Typist	• Oral
• Math waiver	Reader	Untimed
Foreign lang. waiver	• Notetaker	• Take home
Course substitution	• Proof reader	With proctor
In Class	• Text on tape	On computer
• Calculators	Early syllabus	• Extended time
• Tape recorder	Taped handouts	On tape
• Word processor		• Modified
Priority seating		Separate room

General Information:
Delaware County Community College is a 2 year public college. Suburban campus of 125 acres is 15 miles from Philadelphia. Accessible by bus. Ski areas are 1.5 hours from campus. Beaches are 1.5 hours from campus. 1% of students are foreign. Housing is not guaranteed.

Accreditation:MSACS

Expenses:
Tuition: In-state: Full year: $1,120.00. Part-time: Per credit:$46.00. Tuition: Out-of-state: Full year: $2,320.00. Part-time: Per credit:$97.00.

Majors
• BUSINESS Accounting, Banking, Business Administration, Business Management, Finance, Hotel and Restaurant Management, Insurance, Management, Retailing • COMMUNICATIONS Commercial Design • COMPUTER SCIENCE Computer Science, Computer Technology, Data Processing, Programming, Robotics, Telecommunications • EDUCATION Early Childhood, Pre-Education • ENGINEERING Bio-medical, Computer, Engineering Science, Instrumentation Technology, Manufacturing Technology • ENVIRONMENTAL CONTROL Energy Conservation • HEALTH SCIENCES Medical Assistant, Medical Secretary, Nursing, Surgical Technology • HUMANITIES Liberal Arts • PREPROFESSIONAL Architecture • SCIENCES Biology, Physical Science • SOCIAL SCIENCES Criminal Justice • VISUAL AND PERFORMING ARTS Art • VOCATIONAL Air Conditioning/Heating/Refrig, Business and Office, Drafting, Electronics Technology, Fire Science, Legal Secretary, Respiratory Therapy Technology, Secretarial, Welding

Sports/Activities
• SPORTS RELATED Cheerleading • SPORTS-INTERCOLLEGIATE Baseball (M), Basketball, Soccer (M), Softball (F), Tennis, Volleyball (F) • SPORTS-INTRAMURAL Basketball, Bowling, Ice Hockey (M), Softball, Volleyball • STUDENT LIFE ACTIVITIES Choral, Concert Band, Drama Groups, Ethnic & Cultural Groups, Magazine, Music Groups, Newspaper, Radio/TV station, Religious Organization, Student Government, Symphony Orchestra

Selective   **Pennsylvania Services**

Delaware Valley College
Doylestown, Pennsylvania 18901
(215) 345-1500

School Enrollment: **1,133**
LD Enrollment: **9**

Admissions Contact: **Stephen W. Zenko, Director of Admissions**
LD Contact: **Joseph Fulcoly, Associate Dean**
Name of Program: **Choices**

Admissions

Application Information:
Application deadline: **Rolling**
Rolling Admissions: **Yes**

Secondary School Information
Most Important Criteria For Admissions (1-strongest)

2 SAT/ACT	6 Application	1 School transcript
2 Class rank	5 Course selection	6 Personal statement
8 Interview	6 Extra activities	6 Psychoeducational
2 G.P.A.	Open admission	7 Recommendations

Test Requirements:
Untimed SAT: **Yes**
Currency of diagnostic testing: **3**

Types of Disabilities Served
- Speech/Lang
- Reading
- ADD with LD
- Study skills
- Spelling
- ADD without LD
- Written express
- Math
- ADHD with LD
- Organizational
- Fine Motor
- ADHD without LD
- Perceptual

Learning Disability Program
Counseling: Individual: **Yes** Group Counseling: **Yes**

Diagnostic Testing

ADD	Personality	Perceptual skills	Spelling
ADHD	Organization	Fine motor skills	Reading
I.Q.	Handwriting	Spoken language	Study skills
Math	Social skills	Written language	

Tutoring:
Average size of group tutorials: **5**
Services rendered by:

Graduates	•Peers	Faculty	•LD staff	Teacher trainees

Tutorials

Grp.	Ind.	Tutorials	Grp.	Ind.	Tutorials
•	•	Math skills	•	•	Word processing
•	•	Study skills	•	•	Time management
		Language arts	•	•	Learning strategies
•	•	Written express	•	•	Organizational skills

Academic Accommodations

Curriculum	Study Aids	Exams
Priority registration	Typist	• Oral
Math waiver	Reader	Untimed
Foreign lang. waiver	Notetaker	Take home
Course substitution	Proof reader	With proctor
In Class	Text on tape	On computer
• Calculators	Early syllabus	• Extended time
• Tape recorder	Taped handouts	On tape
• Word processor		• Modified
Priority seating		Separate room

Program Strengths
We do not have an LD program as such but do offer special help to all students including LD students through our Counseling Center.

General Information:
Delaware Valley College is a 4 year private college. Suburban campus of 750 acres is 20 miles from Philadelphia. Accessible by train or bus. Ski areas are 40 miles from campus. Beaches are 65 miles from campus. 1% of students are foreign. Housing is guaranteed.50 % of students remain on campus for the weekends.

Accreditation: MSACS

SAT/ACT Scores:
Scores for incoming freshmen: **Verbal:** 43% below 500. 51% between 500 and 599. 4% between 600 and 699. 2% above 700. **Math:** 41% below 500. 53% between 500 and 599. 3% between 600 and 699. 3% above 700.

Class Rank:
About 24% of the present freshmen class were in the upper 20% of their high school class. 59% were in the top 40% of their class. 92% were in the top 60% of their class. 100% were in the top 80% of their class.

Expenses:
Tuition: In-state: Full year: $8,125.00. Part-time: Per credit:$190.00. Tuition: Out-of-state: Full year: $8,125.00. Part-time: Per credit:$190.00. Room and board: $3,615.00

Majors
• BUSINESS Accounting, Agricultural, Business Administration, Business Management, Management, Marketing • COMMUNICATIONS English • COMPUTER SCIENCE Systems Analysis • EDUCATION Science • HEALTH SCIENCES Nutritional/Food • PREPROFESSIONAL Agriculture, Medicine • SCIENCES Agronomy, Animal, Biochemistry, Biology, Chemistry, Dairy, Equestrian Studies, Horticultural, Physical Chemistry

Sports/Activities
• SPORTS RELATED Cheerleading, Chess, Pep Band • SPORTS-INTERCOLLEGIATE Baseball (M), Basketball, Cross Country, Field Hockey (F), Football (M), Golf, Horseback Riding, Soccer (M), Softball (F), Track and Field, Wrestling (M) • SPORTS-INTRAMURAL Basketball (M), Golf (M), Horseback Riding, Lacrosse (M), Softball, Tennis, Volleyball • STUDENT LIFE ACTIVITIES Academic Clubs, Choral, Concert Band, Drama Groups, Ethnic & Cultural Groups, Magazine, Music Groups, Newspaper, Political Groups, Radio/TV station, Religious Organization, Student Government, Yearbook

Selective

Pennsylvania Services

Duquesne University
600 Forbes Avenue
Pittsburgh, Pennsylvania 115282
(412) 434-6220

School Enrollment: **4,200**
LD Enrollment: **12**

Admissions Contact: **Dr. Fredrick Lorenses, Dir. of Admissions**
LD Contact: **Pat Bagle, Director of Student Development**
Name of Program: **Accommodations for Special Needs**

Admissions

Application Information:
Application deadline: **July 1st**
Rolling Admissions: **Yes** Notified when: **4-6 weeks**

Secondary School Information
Most Important Criteria For Admissions (1-strongest)

2 SAT/ACT	1 Application	1 School transcript
1 Class rank	1 Course selection	3 Personal statement
3 Interview	3 Extra activities	Psychoeducational
1 G.P.A.	Open admission	3 Recommendations

Types of Disabilities Served
- Speech/Lang
- Study skills
- Written express
- Organizational Perceptual
- Reading
- Spelling
- Math
- Fine Motor
- ADD with LD
- ADD without LD
- ADHD with LD
- ADHD without LD

Faculty:
Faculty advocate: **Yes** Meets with instructor: **As needed**

Diagnostic Testing

ADD	Personality	Perceptual skills	Spelling
ADHD	Organization	Fine motor skills	Reading
I.Q.	Handwriting	Spoken language	Study skills
Math	Social skills	Written language	

Services rendered by:

Graduates	Peers	Faculty	LD staff	Teacher trainees

Tutorials

Grp.	Ind.	Tutorials	Grp.	Ind.	Tutorials
	•	Math skills			Word processing
•		Study skills		•	Time management
	•	Language arts		•	Learning strategies
	•	Written express		•	Organizational skills

Academic Accommodations

Curriculum	Study Aids	Exams
Priority registration	Typist	• Oral
Math waiver	Reader	Untimed
• Foreign lang. waiver	Notetaker	Take home
Course substitution	Proof reader	With proctor
In Class	• Text on tape	On computer
• Calculators	Early syllabus	• Extended time
• Tape recorder	Taped handouts	On tape
• Word processor		• Modified
Priority seating		Separate room

Program Strengths
Duquesne University does not have a formal program for learning disabled students. We do however, offer services that could be of help to learning disabled students.

General Information:
Duquesne University is a 4 year private Roman Catholic university. Urban campus of 40 acres is Accessible by air, train, or bus. Ski areas are 1 hour from campus. Beaches are 15 minutes from campus. 3.1% of students are foreign. 4 residential halls on campus. Housing is guaranteed. Guaranteed through 4th year. 14 % of students join fraternities/sororities.

Accreditation: CHE, MSACS, SBEPDE

Class Rank:
About 50% of the present freshmen class were in the upper 20% of their high school class. 76% were in the top 40% of their class. 94% were in the top 60% of their class. 100% were in the top 80% of their class.

Expenses:
Tuition: In-state: Full year: $8,340.00. Tuition: Out-of-state: Full year: $8,340.00. Room and board: $4,268.00

Majors
• BUSINESS Accounting, Banking/Finance, Business Administration, Business Economics, Business Management, Economics, Human Resources Management, Insurance, International Business Management, Management, Marketing, Personnel, Real Estate • COMMUNICATIONS Advertising, Broadcasting, Communication, English, Journalism, Linguistics, Media Arts, Speech, Television/Radio/Film • COMPUTER SCIENCE Computer Science, Programming, Systems Analysis • EDUCATION Early Childhood, Elementary, Middle School, Music, Music Therapy, School Psychology, Secondary, Special • ENGINEERING Computer • HEALTH SCIENCES Nursing, Occupational Therapy, Physical Therapy • HUMANITIES Classics, English/Writing/Literature, Philosophy, Religion, Religious Studies • LANGUAGES French, German, Greek, Latin, Spanish • PRE PROFESSIONAL Dentistry, Law, Medicine, Pharmacy, Social Work, Veterinarian • SCIENCES Animal, Biochemistry, Biology, Chemistry, Human Biology, Mathematics, Physics • SOCIAL SCIENCES Criminal Justice, Criminology, Government/Political, History, Political Science, Psychology, Public Relations, Sociology • VISUAL AND PERFORMING ARTS Music, Music Performance

Sports/Activities
• SPORTS RELATED Cheerleading, Pep Band • SPORTS-INTERCOLLEGIATE Baseball (M), Basketball, Bowling, Crew, Cross Country, Diving, Football (M), Golf, Ice Hockey (M), Riflery, Swimming, Tennis, Track and Field, Volleyball (F) • SPORTS-INTRAMURAL Basketball, Bowling, Ping-Pong, Soccer, Softball, Tennis, Volleyball, Water Polo (M) • STUDENT LIFE ACTIVITIES Choral, Concert Band, Dance, Debate, Drama Groups, Ethnic & Cultural Groups, Fraternities, Magazine, Music Groups, Newspaper, Radio/TV station, Religious Organization, Sororities, Student Government, Symphony Orchestra, Yearbook

Selective **Pennsylvania Program**

Edinboro University of Pennsylvania
Shafer Hall
Edinboro, Pennsylvania 16444
(814) 732-2761

School Enrollment: **8,165** Male: **3,366** Female: **4,799**
LD Enrollment: **132** Male: **83** Female: **49**

Admissions Contact: **Terrence Carlin, Asst. V.P. Admissions**
LD Contact: **Kathleen Strosser, Assistant to Director, ODSS**
Name of Program: **Disabled to Student Services**
Address: **ODSS, Shafer Hall**
Telephone:**(814) 732-2462/2272**

Admissions

Application Information:
Application deadline: **Rolling**
Rolling Admissions: **Yes**

Secondary School Information
Most Important Criteria For Admissions (1-strongest)

SAT/ACT	Application	School transcript
Class rank	Course selection	Personal statement
Interview	Extra activities	Psychoeducational
G.P.A.	Open admission	Recommendations

Test Requirements:
Diagnostic testing waived: **Yes**
Untimed SAT: **Yes** Untimed ACT: **Yes** Achievement tests required:**1**
WAIS-R required: **Yes**
Documentation of LD required: **Yes**
Currency of diagnostic testing: **2 years**

Types of Disabilities Served
- Speech/Lang
- Study skills
- Written express
- Organizational
- Perceptual
- Reading
- Spelling
- Math
- Fine Motor
- ADD with LD
- ADD without LD
- ADHD with LD
- ADHD without LD

Learning Disability Program
Program: Reinforces course work: **Yes**
Students mainstreamed **100** % of the day
Recommended credits per semester: **12-15**
Services available for all students: **Yes**
Counseling: Individual: **Yes** Group Counseling: **Yes**
Support groups are available:**Academic Support Services - Career Counseling**

Faculty:
Faculty: **5** Full time: **5**
LD faculty with: BS/BA: **1** M.A.: **3** Ph.D.: **1**
Faculty advocate: **Yes** Meets with instructor: **As needed**

Diagnostic Testing

ADD	Personality	Perceptual skills	Spelling
ADHD	Organization	Fine motor skills	Reading
I.Q.	Handwriting	Spoken language	Study skills
Math	Social skills	Written language	

Tutoring:
Services rendered by:
•Graduates •Peers Faculty •LD staff Teacher trainees

Tutorials

Grp.	Ind.	Tutorials	Grp.	Ind.	Tutorials
	•	Math skills	•	•	Word processing
•	•	Study skills	•	•	Time management
•	•	Language arts	•	•	Learning strategies
•	•	Written express	•	•	Organizational skills

Academic Accommodations

Curriculum	Study Aids	Exams
• Priority registration	Typist	• Oral
Math waiver	• Reader	Untimed
Foreign lang. waiver	Notetaker	Take home
Course substitution	• Proof reader	• With proctor
In Class	• Text on tape	On computer
• Calculators	Early syllabus	• Extended time
• Tape recorder	Taped handouts	On tape
• Word processor		• Modified
Priority seating		• Separate room

Graduation Requirements:
Course credits: **128** GPA: **2.0** Years to complete degree: **No deadline**
Other requirements: **Must complete the last 32 credits in courses scheduled by the University.**

Program Strengths
We provide comprehensive support services to participating learning disabled students. Peer tutoring for study skills support is available on a one-to-one basis for up to twelve hours per week.

General Information:
Edinboro University of Pennsylvania is a 4 year public university. Rural campus of 585 acres is 20 miles from Erie. Accessible by air, train or bus. Ski areas are 6 miles from campus. Beaches are 1 mile from campus. 2% of students are foreign. 8 residential halls on campus. Housing is guaranteed.10 % of students join fraternities/sororities.

Accreditation:MSACS

Expenses:
Tuition: In-state: Full year: $2,628.00. Part-time: Per credit:$110.00. Tuition: Out-of-state: Full year: $4,892.00. Part-time: Per credit:$204.00.
Room and board: $3,090.00 Cost of LD program:$800.00 per semester

Majors
• ARTS Art History, Drawing, Film & Video, Graphic Arts, Painting, Photography • BUSINESS Accounting, Business Administration, Business Management, Economics, Industrial Operations • COMMUNICATIONS Communication, Creative Writing, English, Literature • COMPUTER SCIENCE Computer Science, Computer Technology • CRAFTS AND DESIGN Ceramics, Jewelry, Printmaking, Sculpture, Textile/Weaving • EDUCATION Art, Early Childhood, Elementary, English, Foreign Language, Health, Mathematics, Music, Physical, Science, Secondary, Social Studies, Special • ENGINEERING Biomedical • HEALTH SCIENCES Environmental, Medical Laboratory Technology, Nuclear Medical Technology, Nursing, Nutritional/Food, Speech/Audiology and Speech • HUMANITIES English/Writing/Literature, Humanities, Liberal Arts, Philosophy • LANGUAGES French, German, Russian, Spanish • MATHEMATICS Applied • PREPROFESSIONAL Dentistry, Engineering, Law, Medicine, Pharmacy, Veterinarian • SCIENCES Anthropology, Chemistry, Computer Science, Earth • SOCIAL SCIENCES Criminal Justice, Geography, History, Human Service, Political Science, Psychology, Social Sciences, Sociology • VISUAL AND PERFORMING ARTS Art, Art History, Dramatic Arts, Fine Arts, Music

Sports/Activities

• SPORTS RELATED Cheerleading, Chess, Marching Band • SPORTS-INTERCOLLEGIATE Baseball (M), Basketball (F), Basketball (M), Cross Country (F), Cross Country (M), Diving (F), Diving (M), Football (M), Golf (M), Softball (F), Swimming (F), Swimming (M), Tennis (F), Tennis (M), Track and Field (F), Track and Field (M), Volleyball (F), Wrestling (M) • SPORTS-INTRAMURAL Baseball (F), Baseball (M), Bowling (F), Bowling (M), Cross Country, Cross Country (F), Golf (F), Golf (M), Volleyball, Volleyball (F), Water Polo, Water Polo (F), Wrestling (M) • STUDENT LIFE ACTIVITIES Academic Clubs, Choral, Community Service, Dance, Drama Groups, Ethnic & Cultural Groups, Fraternities, Jazz Band, Music Groups, Newspaper, Orchestra, Political Groups, Radio/TV station, Religious Organization, Sororities, Student Government, Symphony Orchestra, Yearbook

---

Selective

Pennsylvania Program

Harcum Junior College

Morris and Montgomery Avenues
Bryn Mawr, Pennsylvania 19010
(215) 525-4100

School Enrollment: **579** Male: **34** Female: **545**
LD Enrollment: **40**

Admissions Contact: **Mary M. Pontius, Dean of Admissions**
LD Contact: **Dr. Tania Bailey, Director of Talent Development**
Name of Program: **Talent Development**
Address: **Academic Center, 2nd Floor, Room 201**
Telephone:**(215) 526-6034**

Admissions

Application Information:
LD Students Applying: **67** Accepted: **47** Enrolled:**36**
Separate application:**Yes**
Application deadline: **Rolling**
Applicant must apply **6** months in advance
Rolling Admissions: **Yes** Notified when: **2-4 Weeks**

Secondary School Information
Most Important Criteria For Admissions (1-strongest)

SAT/ACT **3**	Application **1**	School transcript
6 Class rank	**1** Course selection	Personal statement
4 Interview	**5** Extra activities	**3** Psychoeducational
1 G.P.A.	Open admission	**2** Recommendations

Test Requirements:
Diagnostic testing waived: **Yes**
Untimed SAT: **Yes**
Documentation of LD required: **Yes**
Tests recommended: **Any documentation of LD, WAIS-R**

Types of Disabilities Served
• Speech/Lang
• Study skills
• Written express
• Organizational
• Perceptual
• Reading
• Spelling
• Math
• Fine Motor
• ADD with LD
• ADD without LD
• ADHD with LD
• ADHD without LD

Admissions Process

Students applying to the program need a psychoeducational evaluation within the last two years or less, have average intelligence, no

major emotional problems, high motivation to attend college, documented learning disability and an interview.

High School Course Requirements:
Waivers to standard high school courses
Foreign Language : **Yes** Math: **Yes**

Learning Disability Program
Program: Remedial: **Yes**
Program: Reinforces course work: **Yes**
Students mainstreamed **100** % of the day
Counseling: Individual: **Yes**

Faculty:
Faculty: **10** Including Director: **Yes** Full time: **4** Part time: **6**
LD faculty with: BS/BA: **3** M.A.: **5** Ph.D.: **2**
Faculty advocate: **Yes** Meets with instructor: **As needed**

Diagnostic Testing
ADD • Personality	Perceptual skills	• Spelling
ADHD• Organization	Fine motor skills	• Reading
I.Q. Handwriting•	Spoken language	• Study skills
• Math Social skills •	Written language	

Tutoring:
Average size of group tutorials: **3**
Services rendered by:
•Graduates •Peers •Faculty •LD staff Teacher trainees

Tutorials
Grp.	Ind.	Tutorials	Grp.	Ind.	Tutorials
•	•	Math skills	•	•	Word processing
•	•	Study skills	•	•	Time management
•	•	Language arts	•	•	Learning strategies
•	•	Written express	•	•	Organizational skills

Academic Accommodations

Curriculum	Study Aids	Exams
Priority registration	• Typist	• Oral
Math waiver	Reader	Untimed
• Foreign lang. waiver	• Notetaker	• Take home
• Course substitution	• Proof reader	• With proctor
In Class	• Text on tape	On computer
• Calculators	Early syllabus	• Extended time
• Tape recorder	Taped handouts	On tape
• Word processor		• Modified
Priority seating		Separate room

Program Strengths

Harcum Junior College is proud of its support services for both the learning disabled student and the student who is academically underprepared. The college is committed to providing them with counseling and remedial services.

General Information:

Harcum Junior College is a 2 year private college. Suburban campus of 12 acres is 12 miles from Philadelphia. Accessible by train. Ski areas are 1 hour from campus. Beaches are 1.5 hour from campus. 8% of students are foreign. 2 residential halls on campus. Housing is guaranteed.50 % of students remain on campus for the weekends.

Accreditation:MSACS

Class Rank: 59% were in the top 60% of their class.

Expenses:
Tuition: In-state: Full year: $6,124.00. Part-time: Per credit:$205.00. Room

Pennsylvania

and board: $4,096.00 Cost of LD program:$1,200.00 per semester, $500.00 Summer session

Majors

• ANIMAL SCIENCE Equestrian Studies • ARTS Fashion Design, Graphic Art, Interior Design • BUSINESS Business Administration, Fashion Merchandising, Retailing, Secretarial Science, Travel/Tourism Management • COMMUNICATIONS Advertising, Communication • COMPUTER SCIENCE Computer Technology • EDUCATION Early Childhood • HEALTH SCIENCES Dental Assistant, Dental Hygiene, Medical Laboratory Technology, Occupational Therapy, Physical Therapy, Veterinarian Assistant • PREPROFESSIONAL Legal Assistant, Social Work, Veterinarian • SCIENCES Equestrian Studies • VISUAL AND PERFORMING ARTS Art • VOCATIONAL Legal Secretary, Office Administration, Secretarial

Sports/Activities

• SPORTS-INTERCOLLEGIATE Badminton (F), Field Hockey (F), Softball (F), Tennis (F), Volleyball (F) • SPORTS-INTRAMURAL Lacrosse (F) • STUDENT LIFE ACTIVITIES Academic Clubs, Choral, Dance, Musical Theater, Newspaper, Religious Organization, Student Government, Yearbook

---

Selective   **Pennsylvania**

Kutztown University of Pennsylvania
College Hill
Kutztown, Pennsylvania 19530
(215) 683-4060

School Enrollment: **8,000**
LD Enrollment: **74**

Admissions Contact: **George McKinley, Director of Admissions**
LD Contact: **Barbara N. Peters, Cord, Program Human Diversity**
Telephone:**(215) 683-4108**

Admissions

Application Information:
Applicant must apply **12** months in advance
Rolling Admissions: **Yes**

Secondary School Information
Most Important Criteria For Admissions (1-strongest)

3 SAT/ACT	4 Application	5 School transcript
1 Class rank	Course selection	Personal statement
Interview	Extra activities	Psychoeducational
2 G.P.A.	Open admission	Recommendations

Test Requirements:
Diagnostic testing waived: **Yes**
Untimed SAT: **Yes** Untimed ACT: **Yes**
Documentation of LD required: **Yes**
Currency of diagnostic testing: **within 3 years**

Types of Disabilities Served
• Speech/Lang • Reading   ADD with LD
• Study skills • Spelling   ADD without LD
• Written express • Math   ADHD with LD
• Organizational • Fine Motor   ADHD without LD
• Perceptual

Admissions Process

Rolling admission is granted competitively to academically qualified students, conditional upon their graduation from secondary school or receiving the GED equivalent.

High School Course Requirements:
Waivers to standard high school courses
Foreign Language : **Yes** Math: **Yes** Course substitution: **Yes**

Learning Disability Program

Special orientation for LD students:
Program: Remedial: **Yes**
Program: Reinforces course work: **Yes**
Program available through:**during enrollment**
Students mainstreamed **100** % of the day
Recommended credits per semester: **12**
Counseling: Individual: **Yes** Vocational Counseling: **Yes**
Support groups are available:**Attempting to put into place**

Faculty:
Faculty: **2** Part time: **2**

Diagnostic Testing

ADD	Personality	Perceptual skills	Spelling
ADHD	Organization	Fine motor skills	Reading
I.Q.	Handwriting	Spoken language	Study skills
Math	Social skills	Written language	

Tutoring:
Services rendered by:
•Graduates •Peers •Faculty LD staff Teacher trainees

Tutorials

Grp.	Ind.	Tutorials	Grp.	Ind.	Tutorials
•	•	Math skills	•	•	Word processing
•	•	Study skills	•	•	Time management
•	•	Language arts	•	•	Learning strategies
•	•	Written express	•	•	Organizational skills

Academic Accommodations

Curriculum	Study Aids	Exams
• Priority registration	Typist	• Oral
• Math waiver	• Reader	• Untimed
• Foreign lang. waiver	• Notetaker	Take home
Course substitution	Proof reader	With proctor
In Class	• Text on tape	On computer
• Calculators	Early syllabus	• Extended time
• Tape recorder	Taped handouts	On tape
• Word processor		• Modified
Priority seating		• Separate room

Graduation Requirements:
Course credits: **128** GPA: **Varies** Math waiver: **Yes** Language waiver: **Yes**

Program Strengths
Hands on approach. LD students are achieving academic success.

General Information:
Kutztown University of Pennsylvania is a 4 year public university. Rural campus 15 miles from Allentown or Reading. Accessible by air or bus. Ski areas are 14 miles from campus. Beaches are 2 hours from campus. 10 residential halls on campus. Housing is not guaranteed.Guaranteed through 1st year. 30 % of students remain on campus for the weekends.

Accreditation: MSACS, NCATE

Expenses:

Tuition: In-state: Full year: $1,314.00. Part-time: Per credit:$110.00. Part-time: Per course: $330.00. Tuition: Out-of-state: Full year: $2,466.00. Part-time: Per credit:$204.00. Part-time: Per course:$612.00 Room and board: $1,340.00

Majors

• AREA STUDIES American, Russian/Slavic • ARTS Dramatic Arts, Music • BUSINESS Accounting, Business Administration, Business Economics, Business Management, Economics, International Business, Management, Marketing • COMMUNICATIONS Broadcasting, Commercial Design, English, Speech, Television/Radio/Film • COMPUTER SCIENCE Computer & Information Science • CRAFTS AND DESIGN Crafts • EDUCATION Art, Elementary, Secondary, Special, Speech/Language • ENGINEERING Physics • HEALTH SCIENCES Medical Laboratory Technology, Nursing • HUMANITIES Fine Arts, Liberal Arts , Philosophy • LANGUAGES French, German, Russian, Spanish • PRE PROFESSIONAL Social Work • SCIENCES Anthropology, Biology, Chemistry, Earth, Environmental Science, Geography, Geology, Marine Biology, Mathematics, Physical Science, Physics • SOCIAL SCIENCES Anthropology, Criminal Justice, Government/Political, History, Library Science, Political Science, Psychology, Public Administration, Social Welfare, Sociology • SPECIAL EDUCATION Visually Handicapped • VISUAL AND PERFORMING ARTS Dramatic Arts, Fine Arts, Music, Studio Art

Sports/Activities

• SPORTS RELATED Marching Band, Pep Band • SPORTS-INTERCOLLEGIATE Baseball (M), Basketball, Cross Country, Diving, Field Hockey, Football (M), Soccer, Softball (F), Swimming, Tennis, Track and Field, Volleyball (F), Wrestling (M) • SPORTS-INTRAMURAL Baseball (M), Basketball, Racquetball, Softball (F), Tennis, Volleyball • STUDENT LIFE ACTIVITIES Choral, Concert Band, Dance, Drama Groups, Ethnic & Cultural Groups, Film, Fraternities, Jazz Band, Magazine, Music Ensemble, Musical Theater, Newspaper, Opera, Radio/TV station, Religious Organization, Sororities, Student Government, Symphony Orchestra, Yearbook

---

Less Selective

Pennsylvania Services

Lehigh County Community College

2370 Main Street
Schnecksville, Pennsylvania 18078
(215) 799-1117

School Enrollment: **4,200** Male: **1,596** Female: **2,704**
LD Enrollment: **50**

Admissions Contact: **David Moyer, Director of Admissions**
LD Contact: **Karen Goode-Ferguson, Dir. Learning Assistance**

Admissions

Application Information:

Application deadline: **None**

Secondary School Information

Most Important Criteria For Admissions (1-strongest)

SAT/ACT	Application	School transcript
Class rank	Course selection	Personal statement
Interview	Extra activities	Psychoeducational
G.P.A.	**1** Open admission	Recommendations

Test Requirements:

Documentation of LD required: **Yes**

Types of Disabilities Served

• Speech/Lang	• Reading	• ADD with LD
• Study skills	• Spelling	• ADD without LD
• Written express	• Math	• ADHD with LD
• Organizational	• Fine Motor	• ADHD without LD
• Perceptual		

Admissions Process

A completed application, appropriate transcripts, and institution placement test.

Learning Disability Program

Services available for all students: **Yes**

Faculty:

Faculty: **1** Full time: **1**

Diagnostic Testing

ADD	Personality	Perceptual skills	Spelling
ADHD	Organization	Fine motor skills	Reading
I.Q.	Handwriting	Spoken language	Study skills
Math	Social skills	Written language	

Tutoring:

Average size of group tutorials: **4**
Services rendered by:

Graduates	Peers	Faculty	•LD staff	Teacher trainees

Tutorials

Grp.	Ind.	Tutorials	Grp.	Ind.	Tutorials
	•	Math skills		•	Word processing
	•	Study skills		•	Time management
	•	Language arts		•	Learning strategies
	•	Written express		•	Organizational skills

Academic Accommodations

Curriculum	Study Aids	Exams
Priority registration	Typist	• Oral
Math waiver	• Reader	• Untimed
Foreign lang. waiver	• Notetaker	Take home
• Course substitution	• Proof reader	With proctor
In Class	• Text on tape	On computer
• Calculators	Early syllabus	• Extended time
• Tape recorder	Taped handouts	On tape
• Word processor		• Modified
• Priority seating		• Separate room

Graduation Requirements:

Course credits: **60** GPA: **2.0**

Program Strengths

We offer services to LD students but do not have an LD program. Counseling, tutoring (peer and professional), special testing, academic accommodations, and referral services are offered to LD students.

General Information:

Lehigh County Community College is a 2 year public college. Suburban campus 8 miles from Allentown. Accessible by bus. Housing is not guaranteed.

Pennsylvania

Accreditation: MSACS

Expenses:
Tuition: In-state: Full year: Part-time: Per credit: $47.00. Tuition: Out-of-state: Full year: Part-time: Per credit: $149.00.

Majors

• BUSINESS Accounting, Business Administration, Business Management, Hotel and Restaurant Management, Management, Marketing, Real Estate, Travel/Tourism Management • COMMUNICATIONS English • COMPUTER SCIENCE Computer Science, Data Processing, Medical Records Administration, Medical Records Technology, Programming • CRAFTS AND DESIGN Mechanical Design Technology • EDUCATION Early Childhood, General • ENGINEERING Air Conditioning Technology, Electrical • HEALTH SCIENCES Medical Assistant, Medical Secretary, Nursing, Occupational Therapy, Physical Therapy • HUMANITIES Humanities, Philosophy, Religion • LANGUAGES German, Spanish • PRE-PROFESSIONAL Engineering • SCIENCES Biology, Mathematics, Physical Science • SOCIAL SCIENCES Criminal Justice, Law Enforcement, Public Relations, Social Sciences • VOCATIONAL Air Conditioning/Heating/Refri, Automobile Technology, Automotive Service, Business and Office, Drafting, Electronics Technology, Legal Secretary, Respiratory Therapy Technology, Secretarial, Word Processing

Sports/Activities

• SPORTS-INTERCOLLEGIATE Basketball (M), Golf, Tennis, Volleyball (F) • SPORTS-INTRAMURAL Baseball (M), Basketball, Field Hockey (F), Ping-Pong, Racquetball, Soccer (M), Softball, Tennis, Volleyball • STUDENT LIFE ACTIVITIES Drama Groups, Newspaper, Radio/TV station, Student Government, Yearbook

---

Highly Selective

Pennsylvania Services

Lehigh University
Alumni Memorial Building 27
Bethlehem, Pennsylvania 18015
(215) 758-3100

School Enrollment: **4,500** Male: **2,925** Female: **1,575**

Admissions Contact: **Patricia Boig, Director of Admissions**
LD Contact: **Susan Hanks, Assistant Director**

Admissions

Application Information:
Application deadline: **February 15th**
Notified when: **April 1st**

Secondary School Information
Most Important Criteria For Admissions (1-strongest)

5 SAT/ACT	11 Application	1 School transcript
4 Class rank	2 Course selection	7 Personal statement
10 Interview	6 Extra activities	8 Psychoeducational
3 G.P.A.	Open admission	9 Recommendations

Test Requirements:
Untimed SAT: **Yes** Untimed ACH: **Yes**

Types of Disabilities Served
• Speech/Lang • Reading • ADD with LD
• Study skills • Spelling • ADD without LD
• Written express • Math • ADHD with LD
• Organizational • Fine Motor • ADHD without LD
• Perceptual

Diagnostic Testing

ADD	Personality	Perceptual skills	Spelling
ADHD	Organization	Fine motor skills	Reading
I.Q.	Handwriting	Spoken language	Study skills
Math	Social skills	Written language	

Services rendered by:
Graduates   Peers   Faculty   LD staff   Teacher trainees

Tutorials

Grp.	Ind.	Tutorials	Grp.	Ind.	Tutorials
		Math skills			Word processing
		Study skills			Time management
		Language arts			Learning strategies
		Written express			Organizational skills

Academic Accommodations

Curriculum	Study Aids	Exams
Priority registration	Typist	Oral
Math waiver	Reader	Untimed
Foreign lang. waiver	Notetaker	Take home
Course substitution	Proof reader	With proctor
In Class	Text on tape	On computer
Calculators	Early syllabus	Extended time
Tape recorder	Taped handouts	On tape
Word processor		Modified
Priority seating		Separate room

Program Strengths

Our learning disabled program is done on an individual basis. For students who will need additional facilities/programs, it is important for them to notify the admissions office upon submitting the application. We will then work with them to meet their needs, providing they are qualified for admission.

General Information:

Lehigh University is a 4 year private university. Urban campus of 160 acres is 60 miles from Philadelphia. Accessible by air or bus. Ski areas are 1 hour from campus. Beaches are 2 hours from campus. 2% of students are foreign. 17 residential halls on campus. Housing is guaranteed. Guaranteed through 1st year. 99 % of students remain on campus for the weekends. 50 % of students join fraternities/sororities.

Accreditation: MSACS

Class Rank:
About 80% of the present freshmen class were in the upper 20% of their high school class. 99% were in the top 40% of their class. 100% were in the top 60% of their class.

Expenses:
Tuition: In-state: Full year: $14,600.00. Tuition: Out-of-state: Full year: $14,600.00. Room and board: $4,530.00.

Majors

• AREA STUDIES American, Russian/Slavic, Urban • BUSINESS Accounting, Banking, Business Administration, Business Economics, Business Education, Business Management, Business Statistics, Economics, Fashion Merchandising, Management, Marketing • COMMUNICATIONS English, Journalism • COMPUTER SCIENCE Computer Science, Programming • ENGINEERING Chemical, Civil/Environmental, Computer, Electrical, Environmental/Water Resources, Geological, Industrial, Materials, Mathematical, Physics • HEALTH SCIENCES Environmental • HUMANITIES Classics, Humanities, Liberal Arts, Philosophy, Religion • LANGUAGES French, German, Spanish • PREPROFESSIONAL Architecture, Dentistry, Engineering, Landscaping, Medicine, Natural Resources, Social Work, Veterinarian • SCIENCES Biochemistry, Biology, Biophysics, Cell Biology, Chemistry, Geology, Geophysics & Seismology, Mathematics, Molecular Biology, Neuroscience, Physical Science, Physics, Statistics • SOCIAL SCIENCES Anthropology, Government/Political, History, International Studies, Political Science, Psychology, Social Sciences, Sociology • VISUAL AND PERFORMING ARTS Art, Dramatic Arts, Music, Studio Art, Theater

Sports/Activities

• SPORTS RELATED Marching Band • SPORTS-INTERCOLLEGIATE Baseball (M), Basketball, Cross Country, Diving, Field Hockey (F), Football (M), Golf (M), Lacrosse, Riflery, Soccer (M), Softball (F), Tennis, Track and Field, Volleyball (F), Wrestling (M) • SPORTS-INTRAMURAL Badminton, Baseball (M), Basketball, Bowling, Boxing (M), Crew (M), Fencing, Golf, Horseback Riding, Ice Hockey (M), Ping-Pong, Rugby (M), Sailing, Skiing - Snow, Soccer, Softball (F), Squash, Swimming, Tennis, Track and Field, Volleyball, Water Polo (M), Wrestling (M) • STUDENT LIFE ACTIVITIES Choral, Concert Band, Dance, Debate, Film, Fraternities, Jazz Band, Magazine, Music Groups, Musical Theater, Newspaper, Radio/TV station, Sororities, Student Government, Symphony Orchestra, Yearbook

---

Less Selective

Pennsylvania

Luzerne County Community College

1333 Prospect Street
Nanticoke, Pennsylvania 18634
(717) 735-8300

School Enrollment: **6,881** Male: **2,728** Female: **4,153**

Admissions Contact: **Thomas P. Leary ,Dean of Admissions**
LD Contact: **Thomas P. Leary, Dean of Admissions**

Admissions

Application Information:
Application deadline: **Rolling**
Rolling Admissions: **Yes**

Secondary School Information
Most Important Criteria For Admissions (1-strongest)

SAT/ACT	Application	School transcript
Class rank	Course selection	Personal statement
Interview	Extra activities	Psychoeducational
G.P.A.	**1** Open admission	Recommendations

Test Requirements:
Documentation of LD required: **Yes**
Tests recommended: **In house Assessment Test after acceptance for placement purposes**

Types of Disabilities Served
• Speech/Lang	• Reading	• ADD with LD
• Study skills	• Spelling	• ADD without LD
• Written express	• Math	• ADHD with LD
• Organizational	• Fine Motor	• ADHD without LD
• Perceptual		

Admissions Process

Open Admissions

Learning Disability Program
Services available for all students: **Yes**

Diagnostic Testing
ADD	Personality	Perceptual skills	Spelling
ADHD	Organization	Fine motor skills	Reading
I.Q.	Handwriting	Spoken language	Study skills
Math	Social skills	Written language	

Tutoring:
Services rendered by:
Graduates   •Peers   •Faculty   LD staff   Teacher trainees

Tutorials
Grp.	Ind.	Tutorials	Grp.	Ind.	Tutorials
•	•	Math skills	•	•	Word processing
•	•	Study skills	•	•	Time management
•	•	Language arts	•	•	Learning strategies
•	•	Written express	•	•	Organizational skills

Academic Accommodations
Curriculum	Study Aids	Exams
Priority registration	Typist	• Oral
Math waiver	Reader	Untimed
Foreign lang. waiver	• Notetaker	Take home
Course substitution	Proof reader	With proctor
In Class	• Text on tape	On computer
• Calculators	Early syllabus	• Extended time
• Tape recorder	Taped handouts	On tape
• Word processor		Modified
Priority seating		Separate room

Graduation Requirements:
Course credits: **60+** GPA: **2.0** Years to complete degree: **2**

Program Strengths
Luzerne County Community College has no learning disabilities program. Support services are provided in the form of tutoring, counseling, and study skills seminars. A developmental studies program is available to all enrolled students.

General Information:
Luzerne County Community College is a 2 year public college. Suburban campus of 122 acres is 10 miles from Wilkes-Barre. Accessible by bus. Ski areas are 25 miles from campus. Housing is not guaranteed.

Accreditation:MSACS

Expenses: Part-time: Per credit:$48.00 in county - $96.00 out of county. Tuition: Out-of-state: Full year: Part-time: Per credit: $144.00.

Majors
• ARTS Commercial Art, Graphic Arts, Painting, Photography • BUSINESS Accounting, Banking, Business Administration, Business Management, Commercial Art, Food Management, Hotel & Restaurant Management, Management, Real Estate, Secretarial Science, Travel/Tourism Management • COMMUNICATIONS Broadcasting, Graphic Design, Journalism, Photography • COMPUTER SCIENCE Business Data Programming, Computer Maintenance, Computer Science, Computer Technology, Robotics • EDUCATION Child Development, Early Childhood, General • ENGINEERING Architectural, Drafting • HEALTH SCIENCES

Pennsylvania

Dental Assistant, Dental Hygiene, Medical Secretary, Nursing, Respiratory Therapy, Surgical Technology • HUMANITIES Humanities • MATHEMATICS Theoretical • PREPROFESSIONAL Optometry, Pharmacy • SCIENCES General • SOCIAL SCIENCES Criminal Justice, Human Service, Social Sciences • VOCATIONAL Air Conditioning/Heating/Refri, Automated Manufacturing Technology, Automobile Technology, Aviation Pilot, Aviation Technology, Building Construction, Business and Office, Culinary Arts, Dental Assistant, Dental Hygiene, Drafting, Electronics Technology, Emergency Medical Technician, Fire Science, Laser Electro-Optic Technology, Legal Assistant, Nuclear Technology, Plumbing, Respiratory Therapy Technology, Secretarial, Word Processing

Sports/Activities

• SPORTS RELATED Cheerleading • SPORTS-INTERCOLLEGIATE Baseball (M), Basketball (F), Basketball (M), Cross Country, Golf, Softball (F), Volleyball (F) • SPORTS-INTRAMURAL Badminton, Basketball, Boxing, Softball, Tennis, Volleyball • STUDENT LIFE ACTIVITIES Academic Clubs, Community Service, Concert Band, Debate, Ethnic & Cultural Groups, Newspaper, Radio/TV station, Religious Organization, Student Government

---

Selective

Pennsylvania
Services

Mansfield University of Pennsylvania

202 South Hall
Mansfield, Pennsylvania 16933
(717) 662-4243

School Enrollment: **2,965** Male: **1,232** Female: **1,733**
LD Enrollment: **20** Male: **13** Female: **7**

Admissions Contact: **John Abplanalp, Director of Enrollment**
LD Contact: **Dr. Celeste Sexauer, Assoc. Professor**
Name of Program: **Learning Resource Center**
Address: **111 Retan Center**

Admissions

Application Information:
LD on admissions committee:**Yes**
Application deadline: **March 1st**
Rolling Admissions: **Yes**

Secondary School Information
Most Important Criteria For Admissions (1-strongest)

3 SAT/ACT	4 Application	1 School transcript
2 Class rank	1 Course selection	6 Personal statement
5 Interview	7 Extra activities	5 Psychoeducational
1 G.P.A.	Open admission	6 Recommendations

Test Requirements:
Untimed SAT: **Yes** Untimed ACT: **Yes**
Documentation of LD required: **Yes**

Types of Disabilities Served
- Speech/Lang
- Reading
- ADD with LD
- Study skills
- Spelling
- ADD without LD
- Written express
- Math
- ADHD with LD
- Organizational
- Fine Motor
- ADHD without LD
- Perceptual

Admissions Process

Applicants who identify themselves as LD are screened by a special committee and may be required to participate in an interview.

Learning Disability Program
Program: Reinforces course work: **Yes**
Students mainstreamed **100** % of the day
Services only for LD students: **Yes**
Services available for all students: **Yes**
Counseling: Individual: **Yes** Group Counseling: **Yes**

Faculty:
Faculty: **1** Full time: **1**
Faculty advocate: **Yes** Meets with instructor: **As needed**

Diagnostic Testing
ADD	Personality	Perceptual skills	Spelling
ADHD	Organization	Fine motor skills	• Reading
• I.Q.	Handwriting	Spoken language	Study skills
• Math	Social skills	• Written language	

Tutoring:
Average size of group tutorials: **3-4**
Services rendered by:
•Graduates •Peers •Faculty •LD staff Teacher trainees

Tutorials

Grp.	Ind.	Tutorials	Grp.	Ind.	Tutorials
•	•	Math skills	•	•	Word processing
•	•	Study skills	•	•	Time management
•	•	Language arts	•	•	Learning strategies
•	•	Written express	•	•	Organizational skills

Academic Accommodations

Curriculum	Study Aids	Exams
• Priority registration	Typist	• Oral
• Math waiver	• Reader	• Untimed
Foreign lang. waiver	• Notetaker	Take home
Course substitution	• Proof reader	• With proctor
In Class	• Text on tape	On computer
• Calculators	Early syllabus	• Extended time
• Tape recorder	Taped handouts	On tape
• Word processor		• Modified
• Priority seating		• Separate room

Graduation Requirements:
Course credits: **128** GPA: **2.0** Math waiver: **Yes**

Program Strengths
We do not have a learning disabled program but offer services to students for their individual needs. If students have specific needs, we work one-on-one with them to give them the best learning environment possible.

General Information:
Mansfield University of Pennsylvania is a 4 year public university. Rural campus of 174 acres is 50 miles from Williamsport. Accessible by air or bus. Ski areas are 60 miles from campus. 1.3% of students are foreign. 5 residential halls on campus. Housing is guaranteed.

Accreditation:MSACS, NCATE

Expenses:
Tuition: In-state: Full year: $2,628.00. Part-time: Per credit:Part-time: $110.00. Tuition: Out-of-state: Full year: $4,892.00. Part-time: Per credit:-Part-time: $204.00. Room and board: $2,638.00

Majors

- ARTS Art History, Music, Music History, Music Performance, Painting
- BUSINESS Business Administration, Fashion Merchandising, Travel/Tourism Management • COMMUNICATIONS Broadcasting, English, Journalism, Literature, Public Relations, Speech/Debate/Forensic, Television/Radio/Film • COMPUTER SCIENCE Computer Science • EDUCATION Art, Early Childhood, Elementary, English, Foreign Language, Mathematics, Music, Psychology, Reading, Science, Secondary, Social Studies, Special • HEALTH SCIENCES Nursing, Nutritional/Food, Radiological Therapy, Respiratory Therapy • HUMANITIES English/Writing/Literature, Liberal Arts , Philosophy • HUMANITIES English/Writing/Literature, Humanities, Liberal Arts, Philosophy • LANGUAGES French, German, Spanish • PREPROFESSIONAL Law, Medicine • SCIENCES Biology, Chemistry, Geography, Geology, Physics • SOCIAL SCIENCES Anthropology, Geography, History, International Studies, Law Enforcement, Political Science, Psychology • SPECIAL EDUCATION Emotionally Disturbed, Gifted & Talented, Learning Disability, Mentally Retarded, Physically Handicapped, Visually Handicapped • VISUAL AND PERFORMING ARTS Art, Music, Music Performance, Studio Art

Sports/Activities

- SPORTS RELATED Cheerleading • SPORTS-INTERCOLLEGIATE Baseball (M), Basketball (F), Basketball (M), Cross Country (F), Cross Country (M), Field Hockey (F), Football (M), Softball (F), Swimming (F), Swimming (M), Tennis (F), Tennis (M), Track and Field (F), Track and Field (M), Wrestling (M) • SPORTS-INTRAMURAL Badminton (F), Badminton (M), Skiing - Snow, Soccer (M), Softball (F), Volleyball (F), Volleyball (M) • STUDENT LIFE ACTIVITIES Choral, Community Service, Concert Band, Debate, Drama Groups, Ethnic & Cultural Groups, Fraternities, Music Groups, Musical Theater, Newspaper, Orchestra, Radio/TV station, Religious Organization, Sororities, Student Government, Symphony Orchestra, Yearbook

Selective	Pennsylvania Program

Mercyhurst College

Glenwood Hills
Erie, Pennsylvania 16546
(814) 825-0200

School Enrollment: **2,120**
LD Enrollment: **35**

Admissions Contact: **Andrew Roth, Dean of Enrollment**
LD Contact: **Dr. Barbara Weigert, Director**
Name of Program: **Program For LD Students**
Telephone:**(814) 824-2239**

Admissions

Application Information:
LD Students Applying: **75** Accepted: **35** Enrolled:**19**
Separate application:**Yes**
LD on admissions committee:**Yes**
Application deadline: **February 20th**
Applicant must apply **7** months in advance
Rolling Admissions: **Yes** Notified when: **March 15th**

Secondary School Information
Most Important Criteria For Admissions (1-strongest)

9 SAT/ACT	**10** Application	**1**	School transcript
8 Class rank	**2** Course selection	**11**	Personal statement
6 Interview	**7** Extra activities	**4**	Psychoeducational
5 G.P.A.	Open admission	**3**	Recommendations

Test Requirements:
Untimed SAT: **Yes** Untimed ACT: **Yes**
WAIS-R required: **Yes**
Documentation of LD required: **Yes**
Currency of diagnostic testing: **1 year**

Types of Disabilities Served

Speech/Lang	• Reading	• ADD with LD
• Study skills	• Spelling	ADD without LD
• Written express	• Math	ADHD with LD
• Organizational	• Fine Motor	ADHD without LD
Perceptual		

High School Course Requirements:
English: **4** Math: **3** Science: **2** Foreign Language: **1**
Waivers to standard high school courses
Foreign Language : **Yes** Math: **Yes** Course substitution: **Yes**

Learning Disability Program

Special orientation for LD students: **Yes**
Syllabus available during orientation:**Yes**
Program: Reinforces course work: **Yes**
Students mainstreamed **100** % of the day
Time required or recommended in learning center: **6**
Services only for LD students: **Yes**
Counseling: Individual: **Yes**

Faculty:
Faculty: **3** Including Director: **Yes** Part time: **3** M.A.: **2** Ph.D.: **1**
Faculty advocate: **Yes** Meets with instructor: **At least 1x term**

Diagnostic Testing

ADD	Personality	Perceptual skills	• Spelling
ADHD	Organization	Fine motor skills	• Reading
I.Q.	Handwriting	Spoken language	Study skills
• Math	Social skills	Written language	

Tutoring:
Average size of group tutorials: **2-3**
Services rendered by:

Graduates	•Peers	Faculty	•LD staff	•Teacher trainees

Tutorials

Grp.	Ind.	Tutorials	Grp.	Ind.	Tutorials
•	•	Math skills	•	•	Word processing
	•	Study skills	•	•	Time management
	•	Language arts		•	Learning strategies
•	•	Written express	•	•	Organizational skills

Academic Accommodations

Curriculum	Study Aids	Exams
• Priority registration	Typist	• Oral
Math waiver	Reader	Untimed
Foreign lang. waiver	Notetaker	Take home
Course substitution	• Proof reader	• With proctor
In Class	Text on tape	On computer
Calculators	Early syllabus	• Extended time
• Tape recorder	Taped handouts	On tape
• Word processor		Modified
Priority seating		• Separate room

Graduation Requirements:
Course credits: **120** GPA: **2.0** Language waiver: **Yes**

Program Strengths

The Mercyhurst Program for students with learning differences is based on the needs of the individual. The close relationship of the

Pennsylvania

student with his/her advisor is a key ingredient of the program.

General Information:

Mercyhurst College is a 4 year private college. Suburban campus of 86 acres is 100 miles from Buffalo. Accessible by air, train, or bus. Ski areas are 25 miles from campus. Beaches are 15 miles from campus. 5% of students are foreign. 14 residential halls on campus. Housing is guaranteed.Guaranteed through 4th year. 85 % of students remain on campus for the weekends.

Accreditation:MSACS

SAT/ACT Scores:

Scores for incoming freshmen:**Verbal:**71%below 500. 27%between 500 and 599. 3%between 600 and 699. **Math:**66% below 500. 30% between 500 and 599. 4% between 600 and 699. **ACT:** 3% below 20. 72% between 20 and 23. 14%between 24 and 25l. 8%between 26 and 28. 3% above 28.

Class Rank:

About 12% of the present freshmen class were in the upper 20% of their high school class. 90% were in the top 40% of their class. 100% were in the top 60% of their class.

Expenses:

Tuition: In-state: Full year: $8,790.00. Part-time: Per credit:$879.00. Room and board: $3,543.00 Cost of LD program:$700.00

Majors

• ARTS Commercial Art, Dance, Graphic Art, Interior Design, Music, Music Performance, Painting, Photography, Sculpture • BUSINESS Accounting, Banking/Finance, Business Administration, Business Education, Business Management, Fashion Merchandising, Food Management, Hotel and Restaurant Management, Management, Marketing, Sports Management • COMMUNICATIONS Communication, English, Journalism, Literature, Public Relations, Television/Radio/Film • COMPUTER SCIENCE Data Processing, Systems Analysis • CRAFTS AND DESIGN Ceramics • EDUCATION Adult, Art, Art Therapy, Business, Child Development, Early Childhood, Elementary, English, Mathematics, Music, Secondary, Special • ENGINEERING Engineering Science • HEALTH SCIENCES Environmental, Medical Laboratory Technology, Nursing, Nutritional/Food, Physical Therapy • HUMANITIES English/Writing/Literature, Liberal Arts , Philosophy • MATHEMATICS Computer, Theoretical • PRE-PROFESSIONAL Dentistry, Law, Medicine, Optometry, Pharmacy, Sports Medicine • RELIGIOUS STUDIES Ministry • SCIENCES Anthropology, Archeology, Biology, Chemistry, Computer Science, General, Geology, Human Biology, Mathematics, Physics • SOCIAL SCIENCES Anthropology, Criminal Justice, Criminology, History, Law Enforcement, Political Science, Psychology, Social Sciences, Sociology • SPECIAL EDUCATION Learning Disability, Mentally Retarded • VISUAL AND PERFORMING ARTS Art, Art History, Dance, Dance Education, Music, Music Performance, Studio Art

Sports/Activities

• SPORTS RELATED Cheerleading, Pep Band, Team Managers
• SPORTS-INTERCOLLEGIATE Baseball (M), Basketball (F), Basketball (M), Crew (F), Crew (M), Cross Country (F), Cross Country (M), Cycling, Football (M), Golf (F), Golf (M), Ice Hockey (M), Soccer (F), Soccer (M), Softball (F), Tennis (F), Tennis (M), Volleyball (F) • SPORTS-INTRAMURAL Badminton (F), Bowling, Ice Hockey (M), Ping-Pong, Skiing - Snow
• STUDENT LIFE ACTIVITIES Choral, Dance, Drama Groups, Ethnic & Cultural Groups, Film, Jazz Band, Magazine, Music Groups, Musical Theater, Newspaper, Opera, Radio/TV station, Religious Organization, Student Government, Yearbook

Peirce Junior College
1420 Pine Street
Philadelphia, Pennsylvania 19102
(215) 545-6400

School Enrollment: **700**
LD Enrollment: **10**

Admissions Contact: **David Schleicker, Director of Admissions**
LD Contact: **Robert Naseef, Director Special Programs**
Name of Program: **Student Support Services**

Admissions

Application Information:
Application deadline: **July 31st**
Rolling Admissions: **Yes**

Secondary School Information
Most Important Criteria For Admissions (1-strongest)

5 SAT/ACT	**8** Application	**4** School transcript
3 Class rank	**2** Course selection	**9** Personal statement
6 Interview	**11** Extra activities	**10** Psychoeducational
1 G.P.A.	Open admission	**7** Recommendations

Test Requirements:
Untimed SAT: **Yes**
Documentation of LD required: **Yes**

Types of Disabilities Served
• Speech/Lang	• Reading	• ADD with LD
• Study skills	• Spelling	• ADD without LD
• Written express	• Math	• ADHD with LD
• Organizational	• Fine Motor	• ADHD without LD
• Perceptual		

Learning Disability Program
Counseling: Individual: **Yes** Group Counseling: **Yes**

Faculty:
Faculty: **4** Full time: **2** Part time: **2**
Faculty advocate: **Yes**

Diagnostic Testing
ADD	Personality	Perceptual skills	Spelling
ADHD	Organization	Fine motor skills	Reading
I.Q.	Handwriting	Spoken language	Study skills
Math	Social skills	Written language	

Services rendered by:
Graduates　　Peers　　Faculty　　LD staff　　Teacher trainees

Tutorials
Grp.	Ind.	Tutorials	Grp.	Ind.	Tutorials
	•	Math skills		•	Word processing
•	•	Study skills	•	•	Time management
	•	Language arts		•	Learning strategies
	•	Written express		•	Organizational skills

650

Academic Accommodations

Curriculum	Study Aids	Exams
Priority registration	Typist	• Oral
Math waiver	Reader	Untimed
Foreign lang. waiver	Notetaker	• Take home
• Course substitution	• Proof reader	With proctor
In Class	Text on tape	On computer
• Calculators	Early syllabus	• Extended time
• Tape recorder	Taped handouts	On tape
• Word processor		• Modified
Priority seating		Separate room

General Information:

Peirce Junior College is a 2 year private college. Urban campus of .5 acres is Ski areas are 100 miles from campus. Beaches are 60 miles from campus. 3% of students are foreign. 2 residential halls on campus. Housing is not guaranteed.5 % of students remain on campus for the weekends. 10 % of students join fraternities/sororities.

Accreditation:MSACS

SAT/ACT Scores:

Scores for incoming freshmen:**Verbal:**95%below 500. 5%between 500 and 599. **Math:**94% below 500. 5% between 500 and 599. 1% between 600 and 699.

Expenses:

Tuition: In-state: Full year: $5,000.00. Part-time: Per credit:$120.00. Room and board: $2,400.00

Majors

• BUSINESS Accounting, Banking, Business Administration, Business Management, Finance, Hotel and Restaurant Management, Insurance, Management, Marketing • COMPUTER SCIENCE Computer Science, Programming, Telecommunications • HEALTH SCIENCES Medical Secretary • HUMANITIES Liberal Arts • PREPROFESSIONAL Legal Assistant, Recreation • VOCATIONAL Business and Office, Court Reporting, Fashion Mechandizing, Legal Secretary, Office Administration, Paralegal, Secretarial

Sports/Activities

• STUDENT LIFE ACTIVITIES Ethnic & Cultural Groups, Fraternities, Newspaper, Sororities, Student Government, Yearbook

Less Selective   **Pennsylvania Services**

Penn State Fayette Campus
P. O. Box 519
Uniontown, Pennsylvania 15401
(412) 430-4130

School Enrollment: **900**
LD Enrollment: **10** Male: **3** Female: **7**

Admissions Contact: **Louis E. Ridgley ,Asst. Dir. Student Programs**
LD Contact: **Dr. Ellen Laun, DUS Program Coordinator**
Name of Program: **Student Services**

Admissions

Application Information:
Application deadline: **up until registration**
Rolling Admissions: **Yes** Notified when: **2 weeks**

Secondary School Information
Most Important Criteria For Admissions (1-strongest)

9 SAT/ACT	**1** Application	**4** School transcript
10 Class rank	**3** Course selection	**6** Personal statement
5 Interview	**11** Extra activities	**7** Psychoeducational
8 G.P.A.	Open admission	**2** Recommendations

Test Requirements:
Untimed ACT: **Yes**

Types of Disabilities Served

• Speech/Lang	• Reading	ADD with LD
• Study skills	Spelling	ADD without LD
• Written express	• Math	ADHD with LD
Organizational	• Fine Motor	ADHD without LD
Perceptual		

Learning Disability Program
Counseling: Individual: **Yes**

Faculty:
Faculty: **5** Full time: **5**
Faculty advocate: **Yes** Meets with instructor: **As needed**

Diagnostic Testing

ADD	Personality	Perceptual skills	Spelling
ADHD	Organization	Fine motor skills	Reading
I.Q.	Handwriting	Spoken language	Study skills
Math	Social skills	Written language	

Tutoring:
Services rendered by:
•Graduates   Peers   Faculty   •LD staff   Teacher trainees

Tutorials

Grp.	Ind.	Tutorials	Grp.	Ind.	Tutorials
•	•	Math skills	•	•	Word processing
•	•	Study skills	•	•	Time management
•	•	Language arts	•	•	Learning strategies
•	•	Written express	•	•	Organizational skills

Academic Accommodations

Curriculum	Study Aids	Exams
Priority registration	Typist	• Oral
Math waiver	Reader	Untimed
Foreign lang. waiver	• Notetaker	Take home
Course substitution	Proof reader	With proctor
In Class	• Text on tape	On computer
Calculators	Early syllabus	• Extended time
Tape recorder	Taped handouts	On tape
Word processor		Modified
Priority seating		Separate room

Program Strengths

We're a small campus with small classrooms. The faculty and staff get to know each student personally and take an interest in their individual needs.

General Information:

Penn State Fayette Campus is a 2 year public college. Rural campus 2.5 miles from Uniontown. Accessible by bus. Ski areas are 25 miles from campus. Beaches are 6 hours from campus. 1% of students are foreign. Housing is not guaranteed.

Pennsylvania

Accreditation: Regional

Class Rank:
About 30% of the present freshmen class were in the upper 20% of their high school class. 40% were in the top 40% of their class.

Expenses:
Tuition: In-state: Full year: $1,817.00. Part-time: Per credit:$146.00. Tuition: Out-of-state: Full year: $3,634.00. Part-time: Per credit:$290.00.

Majors

• AREA STUDIES Asian, Medieval • BUSINESS Accounting, Agricultural, Business Administration, Business Economics, Economics, Finance, Hotel and Restaurant Management, Human Resources Management, Insurance, International Business, Labor Relations, Management, Marketing • COMMUNICATIONS Advertising, Broadcasting, Journalism, Speech • COMPUTER SCIENCE Computer Science, Computer Technology, Telecommunications • CRAFTS AND DESIGN Ceramics • EDUCATION Agricultural, Art, Elementary, Health, Secondary, Special • ENGINEERING Aerospace, Agricultural, Architectural, Bio-medical, Chemical, Civil/Environmental, Electrical, Engineering Science, Environmental/Water Resources, Nuclear, Petroleum • HEALTH SCIENCES Communication Disorders, Fitness, Nursing, Nutritional/Food, Physical Therapy, Radiological Therapy • HUMANITIES Classics, English/Writing/Literature, Humanities, Liberal Arts • LANGUAGES French, Greek, Italian, Linguistic, Russian, Spanish • PREPROFESSIONAL Architecture, Law, Medicine • SCIENCES Agricultural, Agronomy, Animal, Anthropology, Behavioral, Biochemistry, Biology, Dairy, Earth, Entomology, Geography, Horticultural, Metal Technology, Microbiology, Mining, Molecular Biology • SOCIAL SCIENCES Criminal Justice, Family Counseling, History, Law Enforcement, Political Science, Psychology, Public Relations, Sociology • VISUAL AND PERFORMING ARTS Art, Art History, Music, Studio Art • VOCATIONAL Forestry, Landscape Architecture, Park/Recreation, Poultry Technology, Wildlife

Sports/Activities

• STUDENT LIFE ACTIVITIES Ethnic & Cultural Groups, Music Groups, Newspaper, Student Government

Less Selective

Pennsylvania Services

Penn State Mont Alto Campus
Campus Drive
Mont Alto, Pennsylvania 17237
(717) 749-3111

School Enrollment: **870** Male: **500** Female: **370**

Admissions Contact: **Jennifer Garver, Admissions Officer**
LD Contact: **Norene Moskalski, Director of Learning Center**
Name of Program: **Learning Center**
Address: **301 General Studies Building**
Telephone:**(717) 749-3111**

Admissions

Application Information:
Application deadline: **Open**
Rolling Admissions: **Yes**Notified when: **6-8 Weeks**

Secondary School Information
Most Important Criteria For Admissions (1-strongest)

3 SAT/ACT	**5** Application	**2** School transcript
4 Class rank	Course selection	Personal statement
Interview	Extra activities	Psychoeducational
1 G.P.A.	Open admission	Recommendations

Test Requirements:
Diagnostic testing waived: **Yes**
Untimed SAT: **Yes** Untimed ACT: **Yes**
Documentation of LD required: **Yes**
Currency of diagnostic testing: **within 3 years**
Tests recommended: **Psychoeducational report stating student has a learning disability**

Types of Disabilities Served
• Speech/Lang • Reading • ADD with LD
• Study skills • Spelling • ADD without LD
• Written express • Math • ADHD with LD
• Organizational • Fine Motor • ADHD without LD
• Perceptual

Learning Disability Program

Students mainstreamed **100** % of the day
Recommended credits per semester: **12**
Time required or recommended in learning center: **As needed**
Services available for all students: **Yes**
Counseling: Individual: **Yes** Group Counseling: **Yes**
Support groups are available:**Supplemental instruction, study groups, professional and peer tutoring**

Faculty:
Faculty: **4** Full time: **1** Part time: **3** M.A.: **1**
Faculty advocate: **Yes** Meets with instructor: **As appropriate**

Diagnostic Testing
ADD Personality • Perceptual skills • Spelling
ADHD Organization• Fine motor skills • Reading
• I.Q. Handwriting• Spoken language • Study skills
• Math Social skills • Written language

Tutoring:
Average size of group tutorials: **6-8**
Services rendered by:
Graduates •Peers •Faculty •LD staff Teacher trainees

Tutorials

Grp.	Ind.	Tutorials	Grp.	Ind.	Tutorials
•	•	Math skills		•	Word processing
•	•	Study skills	•	•	Time management
•	•	Language arts	•	•	Learning strategies
•	•	Written express	•	•	Organizational skills

Academic Accommodations

Curriculum	Study Aids	Exams
Priority registration	• Typist	• Oral
Math waiver	Reader	• Untimed
• Foreign lang. waiver	• Notetaker	Take home
Course substitution	Proof reader	• With proctor
In Class	• Text on tape	On computer
• Calculators	Early syllabus	• Extended time
• Tape recorder	Taped handouts	On tape
• Word processor		• Modified
Priority seating		• Separate room

Program Strengths

Our Learning Disability Services basically are a component of our Learning Center which offers assistance to all students referred to the center or who request services from the center. Once LD test results are available, our Learning Center, within the limits of its services, works with LD students. LD students need to be responsible for their learning.

General Information:

Penn State Mont Alto Campus is a 2 year public university. Rural campus of 54 acres is 6 miles from Waynesboro. Ski areas are 18 miles from campus. 3 residential halls on campus. Housing is not guaranteed.60 % of students remain on campus for the weekends.

Accreditation:MSACS

Expenses:

Tuition: In-state: Full year: $3,634.00. Part-time: Per credit:$146.00. Tuition: Out-of-state: Full year: $7,900.00. Part-time: Per credit:$330.00. Room and board: $3,300.00

Majors

• AREA STUDIES Asian, Medieval • BUSINESS Accounting, Agricultural, Business Administration, Business Economics, Economics, Finance, Hotel and Restaurant Management, Human Resources Management, Insurance, International Business, Labor Relations, Management, Marketing, Real Estate • COMMUNICATIONS Advertising, Broadcasting, Journalism, Speech • COMPUTER SCIENCE Computer Science, Computer Technology, Telecommunications • CRAFTS AND DESIGN Ceramics • EDUCATION Agricultural, Art, Elementary, Health, Secondary, Special • ENGINEERING Aerospace, Agricultural, Architectural, Bio-medical, Chemical, Civil/Environmental, Electrical, Engineering Science, Environmental/Water Resources, Nuclear, Petroleum • HEALTH SCIENCES Communication Disorders, Fitness, Nursing, Nutritional/Food, Radiological Therapy • HUMANITIES Classics, English/Writing/Literature, Humanities, Liberal Arts, Religion • LANGUAGES French, German, Italian, Linguistic, Russian, Spanish • PREPROFESSIONAL Architecture, Law, Medicine • SCIENCES Agricultural, Agronomy, Animal, Anthropology, Behavioral, Biochemistry, Biology, Dairy, Earth, Entomology, Geography, Horticultural, Metal Technology, Microbiology, Mining, Molecular Biology • SOCIAL SCIENCES Criminal Justice, Family Counseling, History, Law Enforcement, Political Science, Psychology, Public Relations, Sociology • VISUAL AND PERFORMING ARTS Art, Art History, Music, Studio Art • VOCATIONAL Forestry, Landscape Architecture, Park/Recreation, Poultry Technology, Wildlife

Sports/Activities

• SPORTS RELATED Cheerleading, Team Managers • SPORTS-INTRAMURAL Baseball, Basketball, Soccer, Softball, Tennis, Volleyball • STUDENT LIFE ACTIVITIES Drama Groups, Ethnic & Cultural Groups, Newspaper, Religious Organization, Student Government, Yearbook

---

Highly Selective

Pennsylvania Services

Penn State University Park Campus

105 Boucke Building
University Park, Pennsylvania 16802
(814) 865-5471

School Enrollment: **38,911** Male: **21,807** Female: **17,104**
LD Enrollment: **160**

Admissions Contact: **Scott F. Healy, Director**
LD Contact: **Marianne Karwacki, Learning Disability Specialist**
Name of Program: **Support Services**
Address: **105 Boucke Building**
Telephone:**(814) 863-1807**

Admissions

Application Information:
Rolling Admissions: **Yes**

Secondary School Information
Most Important Criteria For Admissions (1-strongest)

2 SAT/ACT	Application	School transcript
Class rank	Course selection	Personal statement
Interview	Extra activities	Psychoeducational
1 G.P.A.	Open admission	Recommendations

Test Requirements:
Untimed SAT: **Yes**
Documentation of LD required: **Yes**

Types of Disabilities Served
• Speech/Lang • Reading • ADD with LD
• Study skills • Spelling • ADD without LD
• Written express • Math • ADHD with LD
• Organizational • Fine Motor • ADHD without LD
• Perceptual

Admissions Process

Applicants for freshman admission submit secondary school records and standardized test scores.

High School Course Requirements:
English: **4** Math: **3** Science: **3** Foreign Language: **2**

Learning Disability Program

Program: Reinforces course work: **Yes**
Students mainstreamed **100** % of the day
Recommended credits per semester: **12-15**
Services only for LD students: **Yes**
Counseling: Individual: **Yes** Vocational Counseling: **Yes**
Support groups are available:**Yes**

Faculty:
Faculty: **3** Including Director: **Yes** Full time: **2** Part time: **1** M.A.: **3** Ph.D.: **1**
Faculty advocate: **Yes** Meets with instructor: **As needed**

Pennsylvania

Diagnostic Testing

ADD	Personality	Perceptual skills	Spelling
ADHD	Organization	Fine motor skills	Reading
I.Q.	Handwriting	Spoken language	Study skills
Math	Social skills	Written language	

Tutoring:
Services rendered by:
•Graduates •Peers •Faculty •LD staff •Teacher trainees

Tutorials

Grp.	Ind.	Tutorials	Grp.	Ind.	Tutorials
	•	Math skills		•	Word processing
	•	Study skills		•	Time management
	•	Language arts		•	Learning strategies
	•	Written express		•	Organizational skills

Academic Accommodations

Curriculum	Study Aids	Exams
• Priority registration	Typist	• Oral
Math waiver	• Reader	Untimed
Foreign lang. waiver	Notetaker	Take home
• Course substitution	• Proof reader	• With proctor
In Class	• Text on tape	• On computer
• Calculators	Early syllabus	• Extended time
• Tape recorder	Taped handouts	On tape
• Word processor		• Modified
• Priority seating		• Separate room

Graduation Requirements:
Course credits: **Varies according to** GPA: **2.0** Years to complete degree: **Flexible** Math waiver: **Yes** Language waiver: **Yes**

Program Strengths
An individualized and University mainstreamed program.

General Information:
Penn State University Park Campus is a 2 and 4 year public university. Suburban campus of 5,162 acres is 110 miles from Harrisburg. Accessible by air, train or bus. Ski areas are 3 miles from campus. Beaches are 16 miles from campus. 5% of students are foreign. 43 residential halls on campus. Housing is guaranteed.Guaranteed through 1st year. 15 % of students join fraternities/sororities.

Accreditation:MSACS

Class Rank:
About 50% of the present freshmen class were in the upper 20% of their high school class.

Expenses:
Tuition: In-state: Full year: $2,116.00. Part-time: Per credit:$179.00. Tuition: Out-of-state: Full year: $4,559.00. Part-time: Per credit:$381.00. Room and board: $3,900.00.

Majors
• AGRICULTURE Agricultural Mechanics, Business, Horticultural, Plant Science • ANIMAL SCIENCE Dairy, Poultry • AREA STUDIES American, Asian, Latin American, Medieval • BUSINESS Accounting, Actuarial, Agricultural, Business Administration, Business Economics, Business Management, Economics, Finance, Hotel and Restaurant Management, Industrial Operations, Insurance, International Business, Labor Relations, Management, Management Information System, Marketing, Quantitative Business Analysis, Real Estate • COMMUNICATIONS Advertising, Broadcasting, Communication, English, Journalism, Linguistics, Literature, Speech, Television/Radio/Film • COMPUTER SCIENCE Computer & Information Science • CRAFTS AND DESIGN Ceramics • EDUCA-

TION Agricultural, Art, Elementary, Health, Home Economics, Industrial, Music, Rehabilitation, Secondary, Special, Vocational • ENGINEERING Aerospace, Agricultural, Architectural, Ceramic, Chemical, Civil, Computer, Electrical, Engineering Science, Industrial, Mechanical, Metallurgical, Mining/Mineral, Nuclear, Petroleum • ENVIRONMENTAL CONTROL Solar Heating • HEALTH SCIENCES Communication Disorders, Fitness, Health, Health Administration, Nursing, Nutritional/Food • HUMANITIES Classics, English/Writing/Literature, Liberal Arts, Philosophy • LANGUAGES Chinese, English, French, German, Italian, Linguistics, Russian, Spanish • PREPROFESSIONAL Agriculture, Architecture, Engineering, Fisheries, Forestry, Law, Medicine, Social Work, Wildlife • SCIENCES Agricultural, Agronomy, Animal, Anthropology, Astronomy, Astrophysics, Biochemistry, Biology, Botany, Cell Biology, Ceramic, Chemistry, Computer Science, Earth, Entomology, Environmental Resource Management, Food Science, Forest Products, Fuel Science, Geography, Geology, Geoscience, Horticultural, Mathematics, Metal Technology, Meteorology, Microbiology, Mining/Mineral, Molecular Biology, Physics, Polymer Science, Poultry, Soil • SOCIAL SCIENCES Administration of Justice, Anthropology, History, Human Development & Family Stu, International Studies, Political Science, Psychology, Public Service, Rural Sociology, Sociology • VISUAL AND PERFORMING ARTS Art, Art History, Film Arts, Music, Theater • VOCATIONAL Landscape Architecture, Landscaping Management, Park/Recreation

Sports/Activities
• SPORTS RELATED Marching Band, Pep Band • SPORTS-INTERCOLLEGIATE Baseball (M), Basketball, Cross Country, Diving, Fencing, Field Hockey (F), Football (M), Golf, Gymnastics, Lacrosse, Soccer (M), Softball (F), Swimming, Tennis, Track and Field, Volleyball, Wrestling (M) • SPORTS-INTRAMURAL Badminton, Basketball, Bowling (M), Cross Country, Field Hockey (F), Football (M), Golf, Hand Ball (M), Racquetball, Soccer, Softball, Squash, Swimming, Tennis, Track and Field, Volleyball, Wrestling • STUDENT LIFE ACTIVITIES Choral, Concert Band, Dance, Drama Groups, Film, Fraternities, Jazz Band, Magazine, Music Groups, Musical Theater, Newspaper, Radio/TV station, Sororities, Student Government, Symphony Orchestra, Yearbook

---

Less Selective	Pennsylvania Accommodations

Penn State Worthington Scranton Campus
120 Ridge View Road
Dunmore, Pennsylvania 18512
(717) 961-4757

School Enrollment: **1,154** Male: **685** Female: **469**

Admissions Contact: **Dr. Ralph Mastriani, Registrar/Admissions**
LD Contact: **Michele Steele, Coordinator**
Name of Program: **Learning Assistance Center**
Telephone:**(717) 963-4128**

Admissions

Application Information:
Application deadline: **None**

Secondary School Information
Most Important Criteria For Admissions (1-strongest)

SAT/ACT	Application	School transcript
Class rank	Course selection	Personal statement
Interview	Extra activities	Psychoeducational
G.P.A.	Open admission	Recommendations

Test Requirements:
Untimed SAT: **Yes**
Documentation of LD required: **Yes**

Types of Disabilities Served

Speech/Lang	Reading	ADD with LD
Study skills	Spelling	ADD without LD
Written express	Math	ADHD with LD
Organizational	Fine Motor	ADHD without LD
Perceptual		

Admissions Process

File an application. If offered provisional status, an interview is required.

High School Course Requirements:
Waivers to standard high school courses
Foreign Language : **Yes** Math: **Yes**

Learning Disability Program
Students mainstreamed **100** % of the day
Recommended credits per semester: **12-13**
Services available for all students: **Yes**
Counseling: Individual: **Yes**

Faculty:
Faculty: **1** Full time: **1**
Faculty advocate: **Yes** Meets with instructor: **When necessary**

Diagnostic Testing

ADD	Personality	Perceptual skills	Spelling
ADHD	Organization	Fine motor skills	Reading
I.Q.	Handwriting	Spoken language	Study skills
Math	Social skills	Written language	

Tutoring:
Average size of group tutorials: **4-5**
Services rendered by:
Graduates •Peers •Faculty LD staff Teacher trainees

Tutorials

Grp.	Ind.	Tutorials	Grp.	Ind.	Tutorials
•	•	Math skills	•	•	Word processing
•	•	Study skills	•	•	Time management
		Language arts	•	•	Learning strategies
	•	Written express			Organizational skills

Academic Accommodations

Curriculum	Study Aids	Exams
Priority registration	Typist	• Oral
Math waiver	Reader	Untimed
• Foreign lang. waiver	• Notetaker	Take home
Course substitution	Proof reader	• With proctor
In Class	Text on tape	On computer
Calculators	Early syllabus	• Extended time
• Tape recorder	Taped handouts	On tape
• Word processor		Modified
Priority seating		Separate room

Graduation Requirements:
Course credits: **varies**

Program Strengths
LD services are administered on an individual basis.

General Information:
Penn State Worthington Scranton Campus is a 2 and 4 year public university. Urban campus of 45 acres is 3 miles from Scranton. Accessible by air or bus. Ski areas are 10 miles from campus. Housing is not guaranteed.

Accreditation:

Expenses:
Tuition: In-state: Full year: $4,332.00. Part-time: Per credit:$167.00. Tuition: Out-of-state: Full year: $9,118.00. Part-time: Per credit:$381.00.

Majors
• AREA STUDIES African, American, Asian, Black/Afro-American, Latin American, Medieval, Russian/Slavic • BUSINESS Accounting, Agricultural Economics, Economics, Farm Management, Finance, Insurance, International Business, Labor Relations, Management, Real Estate, Resource Economics, Rural Development • COMMUNICATIONS Advertising, Broadcasting, Creative Writing, English, Journalism, Literature, Television/Radio/Film • COMPUTER SCIENCE Computer Science, Telecommunications • CRAFTS AND DESIGN Ceramics • EDUCATION Agricultural, Art, Elementary, English, Foreign Language, Health, Home Economics, Mathematics, Music, Physical, Science, Secondary, Social Studies, Special, Vocational • ENGINEERING Aerospace, Agricultural, Architectural, Bio-medical, Chemical, Civil/Environmental, Computer, Construction Engineering, Electrical, Engineering Science, Environmental/Water Resources, Industrial, Mechanical, Metallurgical, Mining/Mineral, Nuclear, Petroleum, Polymer Science • HEALTH SCIENCES Communication Disorders, Environmental, Fitness, Health, Nursing, Nutritional/Food, Rehabilitation, Speech/Audiology and Speech • HUMANITIES Classics, English/Writing/Literature, Liberal Arts, Philosophy, Religious Studies • LANGUAGES Chinese, French, German, Italian, Japanese, Russian, Spanish • PREPROFESSIONAL Agriculture, Architecture, Law, Medicine, Social Work • SCIENCES Actuarial Technology, Agricultural, Agronomy, Astronomy, Biochemistry, Biology, Botany, Cell Biology, Dairy, Earth, Ecology, Entomology, Geography, Geoscience, Gerontology, Horticultural, Marine Biology, Mathematics, Meteorology, Microbiology, Molecular Biology, Physics, Poultry, Soil • SOCIAL SCIENCES Anthropology, Criminal Justice, Family Counseling, Government/Political, History, Law Enforcement, Political Science, Psychology, Public Relations, Sociology • VISUAL AND PERFORMING ARTS Art, Art History, Fine Arts, Music, Theater, Video • VOCATIONAL Fishery Studies, Food Science, Forestry, Landscape Architecture, Landscape Contracting, Park/Recreation, Wildlife

Sports/Activities
• SPORTS RELATED Cheerleading • SPORTS-INTERCOLLEGIATE Baseball (M), Basketball (M), Cross Country, Volleyball (F) • SPORTS-INTRAMURAL Band, Volleyball • STUDENT LIFE ACTIVITIES Academic Clubs, Ethnic & Cultural Groups, Newspaper, Student Government

Less Selective

Pinebrook Junior College
600 South Main Street
Coopersburg, Pennsylvania 18036
(215) 282-4000

School Enrollment: **142** Male: **57** Female: **85**

Admissions Contact: **Dr. Rodney Long, Director of Admissions**

Admissions

Application Information:
Application deadline: **Flexible**
Rolling Admissions: **Yes**

Secondary School Information
Most Important Criteria For Admissions (1-strongest)

SAT/ACT	Application	School transcript
Class rank	Course selection	Personal statement
Interview	Extra activities	Psychoeducational
G.P.A. 1	Open admission 1	Recommendations

Types of Disabilities Served
- Speech/Lang
- Study skills
- Written express
- Organizational
- Perceptual
- Reading
- Spelling
- Math
- Fine Motor

ADD with LD
ADD without LD
ADHD with LD
ADHD without LD

Diagnostic Testing

ADD	Personality	Perceptual skills	Spelling
ADHD	Organization	Fine motor skills	Reading
I.Q.	Handwriting	Spoken language	Study skills
Math	Social skills	Written language	

Tutoring:
Average size of group tutorials:
Services rendered by:

Graduates	Peers	Faculty	LD staff	Teacher trainees

Tutorials

Grp.	Ind.	Tutorials	Grp.	Ind.	Tutorials
		Math skills			Word processing
		Study skills			Time management
		Language arts			Learning strategies
		Written express			Organizational skills

Academic Accommodations

Curriculum	Study Aids	Exams
Priority registration	• Typist	• Oral
Math waiver	Reader	Untimed
Foreign lang. waiver	Notetaker	• Take home
Course substitution	Proof reader	With proctor
In Class	Text on tape	On computer
Calculators	Early syllabus	• Extended time
Tape recorder	Taped handouts	On tape
Word processor		Modified
Priority seating		Separate room

Program Strengths
*Tutoring is for all students.

General Information:
Pinebrook Junior College is a 2 year private college. Suburban campus of 26 acres is 8 miles from Allentown. Accessible by air or bus. Ski areas are 25 miles from campus. Beaches are 10 miles from campus. 13% of students are foreign. 7 residential halls on campus. Housing is guaranteed. 75% of students remain on campus for the weekends.

Accreditation: AABC

Expenses:
Tuition: In-state: Full year: $2,495.00. Part-time: Per credit: $140.00. Room and board: $2,960.00

Majors
• BUSINESS Business Administration • COMMUNICATIONS English • COMPUTER SCIENCE Data Processing • HEALTH SCIENCES Medical Secretary, Surgical Technology • HUMANITIES Humanities, Religion, Religious Studies • LANGUAGES German • PREPROFESSIONAL Ministry, Social Work • SCIENCES Earth, Mathematics • SOCIAL SCIENCES History, Psychology, Sociology • VISUAL AND PERFORMING ARTS Art • VOCATIONAL Legal Secretary, Secretarial

Sports/Activities
• SPORTS RELATED Cheerleading, Team Managers • SPORTS-INTER-COLLEGIATE Basketball, Soccer (M), Softball (F), Volleyball (F) • SPORTS-INTRAMURAL Baseball, Basketball, Ping-Pong, Soccer, Softball, Volleyball • STUDENT LIFE ACTIVITIES Choral, Drama Groups, Ethnic & Cultural Groups, Magazine, Music Groups, Newspaper, Religious Organization, Student Government, Yearbook

Selective

Point Park College
201 Wood Street
Pittsburgh, Pennsylvania 15222
(412) 392-3840

School Enrollment: **1,240** Male: **570** Female: **670**

Admissions Contact: **Terrance Kizina, Director**
LD Contact: **Office of Student Development**
Name of Program: **Office of Student Development**
Address: **Point Park College, 201 Wood St.**
Telephone: **(412) 392-3840**

Admissions

Application Information:
Rolling Admissions: **Yes**

Secondary School Information
Most Important Criteria For Admissions (1-strongest)

5 SAT/ACT	12 Application	1 School transcript
3 Class rank	4 Course selection	9 Personal statement
6 Interview	8 Extra activities	10 Psychoeducational
2 G.P.A.	Open admission	7 Recommendations

Test Requirements:
Untimed SAT: **Yes** Untimed ACT: **Yes**
Documentation of LD required: **Yes**

Types of Disabilities Served
- Speech/Lang
- Study skills
- Written express
- Organizational
- Perceptual
- Reading
- Spelling
- Math

Fine Motor

ADD with LD
ADD without LD
ADHD with LD
ADHD without LD

Admissions Process

Our admissions process is individualized, personal and humanistic. Each student is viewed in terms of his/her personal and academic record.

High School Course Requirements:
English: **4** Math: **2** Science: **2**
Waivers to standard high school courses
Foreign Language : **Yes** Math: **Yes** Course substitution: **Yes**

Learning Disability Program
Services available for all students: **Yes**

Faculty:
Faculty advocate: **Yes** Meets with instructor: **Varies**

Diagnostic Testing
ADD	Personality	Perceptual skills	Spelling
ADHD	Organization	Fine motor skills	• Reading
I.Q.	Handwriting	Spoken language	Study skills
• Math	Social skills	Written language	

Tutoring:
Average size of group tutorials: **1**
Services rendered by:
Graduates •Peers Faculty LD staff Teacher trainees

Tutorials
Grp.	Ind.	Tutorials	Grp.	Ind.	Tutorials
	•	Math skills			Word processing
		Study skills		•	Time management
		Language arts		•	Learning strategies
	•	Written express		•	Organizational skills

Academic Accommodations
Curriculum	Study Aids	Exams
Priority registration	Typist	• Oral
Math waiver	Reader	Untimed
Foreign lang. waiver	• Notetaker	Take home
Course substitution	Proof reader	With proctor
In Class	Text on tape	On computer
Calculators	Early syllabus	• Extended time
• Tape recorder	Taped handouts	On tape
Word processor		Modified
Priority seating		Separate room

General Information:

Point Park College is a 2 and 4 year independent college. Urban campus Accessible by air, train, or bus. Ski areas are 80 miles from campus. Housing is not guaranteed.

Accreditation:MSACS, TACABET

SAT/ACT Scores:
Scores for incoming freshmen:**Verbal:**88%below 500. 10%between 500 and 599. 2%between 600 and 699. **Math:**78% below 500. 17% between 500 and 599. 5% between 600 and 699.

Class Rank:
About 22% of the present freshmen class were in the upper 20% of their high school class. 33% were in the top 40% of their class. 31% were in the top 60% of their class. 13% were in the top 80% of their class.

Expenses:
Tuition: In-state: Full year: $8,622.00 tuition and fees. Part-time: Per credit:$225.00. Part-time: Per course: $675.00. Tuition: Out-of-state: Full year: $8,622.00. Part-time: Per credit:$225.00. Part-time: Per course:$675.00
Room and board: $4,390.00

Majors
• ARTS Dance, Film & Video, Photography • BUSINESS Accounting, Banking/Finance, Business Management, Fashion Merchandising, Hotel & Restaurant Management • COMMUNICATIONS Communication, Journalism • COMPUTER SCIENCE Computer Science • EDUCATION Early Childhood, Elementary, Secondary • ENGINEERING Civil/Environmental, Electrical, Environmental/Water Resources, Mechanical • HUMANITIES English/Writing/Literature • PRE PROFESSIONAL Law • SCIENCES Biology, General • SOCIAL SCIENCES Government/Political, History, Political Science, Psychology • VISUAL AND PERFORMING ARTS Dance, Theater

Sports/Activities
• SPORTS RELATED Cheerleading • SPORTS-INTERCOLLEGIATE Baseball (M), Basketball (F), Basketball (M), Soccer (M), Softball (F), Volleyball (F) • SPORTS-INTRAMURAL Basketball (F), Basketball (M), Football, Football (M), Volleyball, Volleyball (F), Volleyball (M) • STUDENT LIFE ACTIVITIES Academic Clubs, Choral, Community Service, Dance, Ethnic & Cultural Groups, Fraternities, Magazine, Musical Theater, Newspaper, Political Groups, Radio/TV station, Religious Organization, Sororities, Student Government, Yearbook

---

Less Selective

**Pennsylvania
Services**

Reading Area Community College
P. O. Box 1706 10 South Second Street
Reading, Pennsylvania 19603
(215) 372-4721

School Enrollment: **2,075** Male: **682** Female: **1,393**
LD Enrollment: **25** Male: **13** Female: **12**

Admissions Contact: **Bridgette, Admissions Coordinator**
LD Contact: **Cathy V. Hunsicker, Tutorial Coordinator**
Name of Program: **Learning Skills Project (LSP)**
Address: **P.O. Box 1706, 10 S. Second Street**
Telephone:**(215) 372-4721 - Ext. 250**

Admissions

Application Information:
LD Students Applying: **30**
Applicant must apply **3** months in advance
Rolling Admissions: **Yes**

Secondary School Information
Most Important Criteria For Admissions (1-strongest)
SAT/ACT	Application	School transcript
Class rank	Course selection	Personal statement
Interview	Extra activities	Psychoeducational
G.P.A.	**1** Open admission	Recommendations

Pennsylvania

Test Requirements:
Standardized tests waived: **Yes**
Documentation of LD required: **Yes**
Tests recommended: **Placement testing**

Types of Disabilities Served
- Speech/Lang
- Study skills
- Written express
- Organizational
- Perceptual
- Reading
- Spelling
- Math
- Fine Motor
- ADD with LD
- ADD without LD
- ADHD with LD
- ADHD without LD

Admissions Process

1) - Admissions package sent; 2) - Appointment with Admissions; 3) - Appointment with LD specialist; 4) - Placement tests; 5) - Registration.

High School Course Requirements:
Waivers to standard high school courses
 Course substitution: **Yes**

Learning Disability Program
Program: Remedial: **Yes**
Program: Reinforces course work: **Yes**
Students mainstreamed **100** % of the day
Recommended credits per semester: **6**
Services available for all students: **Yes**
Counseling: Individual: **Yes**

Faculty:
Faculty: **1** Full time: **1** M.A.: **1**
Faculty advocate: **Yes** Meets with instructor: **2x in ten weeks**

Diagnostic Testing
ADD	• Personality	• Perceptual skills	• Spelling
ADHD	• Organization	• Fine motor skills	• Reading
I.Q.	• Handwriting	• Spoken language	• Study skills
• Math	Social skills	• Written language	

Tutoring:
Average size of group tutorials: **3**
Services rendered by:
•Graduates •Peers •Faculty •LD staff Teacher trainees

Tutorials
Grp.	Ind.	Tutorials	Grp.	Ind.	Tutorials
•	•	Math skills	•	•	Word processing
•	•	Study skills	•	•	Time management
•	•	Language arts	•	•	Learning strategies
•	•	Written express		•	Organizational skills

Academic Accommodations
Curriculum	Study Aids	Exams
Priority registration	Typist	• Oral
Math waiver	• Reader	• Untimed
Foreign lang. waiver	• Notetaker	• Take home
• Course substitution	• Proof reader	• With proctor
In Class	• Text on tape	On computer
• Calculators	• Early syllabus	• Extended time
• Tape recorder	Taped handouts	• On tape
• Word processor		• Modified
• Priority seating		• Separate room

Program Strengths
LSP works as part of the Center for Counseling and Academic Development. As such the students have access to two LD specialists, 12 counselors, and tutors (both peer and professional). Our school is small, and we are able to provide LD students with the individual attention they need to be mainstreamed successfully.

General Information:
Reading Area Community College is a 2 year public college. Urban campus 60 miles from Philadelphia. Accessible by air or bus. Housing is not guaranteed.

Accreditation: MSACS

Expenses: Part-time: Per credit:$50.00 in county - $100.00 in state. Part-time: Per course: $156.00 - $312.00. Tuition: Out-of-state: Full year: Part-time: Per credit: $150.00. Part-time: Per course:$460.00

Majors
• BUSINESS Accounting, Business Administration, Business Education, Business Management, Finance, Management, Travel/Tourism Management • COMPUTER SCIENCE Data Processing, Telecommunications • EDUCATION Early Childhood, Elementary, Pre-Education, Teacher Aide • ENGINEERING Computer, Electrical, Industrial, Mechanical • HEALTH SCIENCES Medical Secretary, Medical Technology, Nursing, Radiological Therapy • HUMANITIES Humanities, Liberal Arts • PRE-PROFESSIONAL Dentistry, Engineering, Law, Medicine, Pharmacy, Social Work • SCIENCES Biology, Chemistry, Gerontology • SOCIAL SCIENCES Human Service, Psychology, Public Relations, Social Sciences, Sociology • VOCATIONAL Automobile Technology, Electronics Technology, Legal Secretary, Machine Tool Technology, Medical Laboratory Technology, Office Administration, Secretarial, Word Processing

Sports/Activities
• SPORTS RELATED Cheerleading • SPORTS-INTERCOLLEGIATE Basketball (M), Cross Country, Volleyball (F) • SPORTS-INTRAMURAL Basketball (M), Cross Country, Softball, Volleyball (F) • STUDENT LIFE ACTIVITIES Ethnic & Cultural Groups, Honor Societies, Newspaper, Radio/TV station, Student Government

---

Selective   **Pennsylvania**
Program

Spring Garden College
7500 Germantown Avenue
Philadelphia, Pennsylvania 19119
(215) 248-7904

School Enrollment: **650**
LD Enrollment: **3** Male: **2** Female: **1**

Admissions Contact: **Ronald C. Mickey, Director of Admissions**
LD Contact: **Peter Rondinaro, Director, Student Development**
Telephone:**(215) 248-7910**

Admissions

Application Information:
LD Students Applying: **6** Accepted: **5** Enrolled:**4**
Application deadline: **July 1st & December 15th**
Applicant must apply **3** months in advance
Rolling Admissions: **Yes**

Secondary School Information
Most Important Criteria For Admissions (1-strongest)

7 SAT/ACT	10 Application	5	School transcript
8 Class rank	6 Course selection	11	Personal statement
1 Interview	9 Extra activities	2	Psychoeducational
4 G.P.A.	Open admission	3	Recommendations

Test Requirements:
Untimed SAT: **Yes** Untimed ACT: **Yes**
Documentation of LD required: **Yes**
Currency of diagnostic testing: **3 years**
Tests recommended: **Psycheducational evaluation**

Types of Disabilities Served
- Speech/Lang
- Study skills
- Written express
- Organizational
- Perceptual
- Reading
- Spelling
- Math
- Fine Motor
- ADD with LD
- ADD without LD
- ADHD with LD
- ADHD without LD

Learning Disability Program
Program: Reinforces course work: **Yes**
Students mainstreamed **100** % of the day
Counseling: Individual: **Yes** Group Counseling: **Yes**

Faculty:
Faculty: **1** Including Director: **Yes** Full time: **1** M.A.: **1**

Diagnostic Testing
ADD	Personality	Perceptual skills	Spelling
ADHD	Organization	Fine motor skills	Reading
I.Q.	Handwriting	Spoken language	Study skills
Math	Social skills	Written language	

Tutoring:
Average size of group tutorials: **2-5**
Services rendered by:
Graduates • Peers Faculty • LD staff Teacher trainees

Tutorials
Grp.	Ind.	Tutorials	Grp.	Ind.	Tutorials
•	•	Math skills	•	•	Word processing
•	•	Study skills	•	•	Time management
	•	Language arts	•	•	Learning strategies
	•	Written express	•	•	Organizational skills

Academic Accommodations
Curriculum	Study Aids	Exams
Priority registration	Typist	• Oral
Math waiver	Reader	Untimed
Foreign lang. waiver	Notetaker	Take home
Course substitution	• Proof reader	With proctor
In Class	Text on tape	On computer
• Calculators	Early syllabus	• Extended time
• Tape recorder	Taped handouts	On tape
• Word processor		• Modified
Priority seating		Separate room

Program Strengths
Spring Garden College is very capable of assisting students with mild learning disabilities. Several have enrolled and, with special aid, worked hard and received degrees. This institution is not equipped to service students with severe disabilities. A personal interview with the Director of Student Development and Counseling is required.

General Information:
Spring Garden College is a 4 year private college. Urban campus of 33 acres is Accessible by air, train or bus. Ski areas are 1 hour from campus. Beaches are 1.5 hours from campus. 1 residential halls on campus. Housing is not guaranteed.

Accreditation:MSACS

Expenses:
Tuition: In-state: Full year: $7,600.00. Part-time: Per credit:$175.00. Room and board: $4,000.00

Majors
• BUSINESS Accounting, Business Administration, Business Management, Management, Technical and Business Writing • COMPUTER SCIENCE Computer Science, Computer Technology, Programming, Software Engineer, Systems Analysis • ENGINEERING Civil/Environmental, Computer, Electrical, Industrial, Mechanical • HEALTH SCIENCES Medical Technology • PREPROFESSIONAL Architecture • SCIENCES Biochemistry, Biophysics, Management Science, Mathematics • SOCIAL SCIENCES Social Sciences • VOCATIONAL Construction, Electronics Technology, Interior Design, Manufacturing Technology, Medical Laboratory Technology, Surveying and Mapping

Sports/Activities
• SPORTS-INTERCOLLEGIATE Baseball (M), Basketball, Cross Country, Golf (M), Soccer (M), Softball (F), Volleyball (F) • SPORTS-INTRAMURAL Basketball, Cross Country, Golf, Ping-Pong, Soccer, Softball, Tennis, Volleyball • STUDENT LIFE ACTIVITIES Dance, Ethnic & Cultural Groups, Fraternities, Magazine, Radio/TV station, Sororities, Student Government, Yearbook

Selective **Pennsylvania Accommodations**

University of Pittsburgh at Bradford
300 Campus Drive
Bradford, Pennsylvania 16701-2898
(814) 362-7555-(800) 872-1787

School Enrollment: **1,300** Male: **660** Female: **640**
LD Enrollment: **6**

Admissions Contact: **Stephen Edison, Director of Admissions**
LD Contact: **Joanne Cree Burgert, Director**
Name of Program: **Academic Development Center**
Telephone:**(814) 362-7533**

Admissions

Application Information:
LD Students Applying: **6** Accepted: **6** Enrolled:**6**
Application deadline: **July 1st**
Applicant must apply **2** months in advance
Rolling Admissions: **Yes** Notified when: **2 weeks after application**

Secondary School Information
Most Important Criteria For Admissions (1-strongest)

4 SAT/ACT	Application	1	School transcript
2 Class rank	6 Course selection	4	Personal statement
5 Interview	6 Extra activities	6	Psychoeducational
2 G.P.A.	Open admission	6	Recommendations

Pennsylvania

Test Requirements:
Standardized tests waived: **Yes**
Untimed SAT: **Yes** Untimed ACT: **Yes**
Documentation of LD required: **Yes**

Types of Disabilities Served
- Speech/Lang
- Study skills
- Written express
- Organizational
- Perceptual
- Reading
- Spelling
- Math
- Fine Motor

ADD with LD
ADD without LD
ADHD with LD
ADHD without LD

High School Course Requirements:
English: **4** Math: **3** Science: **4** Foreign Language: **3**

Learning Disability Program
Services available for all students: **Yes**
Counseling: Individual: **Yes** Group Counseling: **Yes**

Faculty:
Faculty: **2** Full time: **2**
Faculty advocate: **Yes**

Diagnostic Testing

ADD	Personality	Perceptual skills	Spelling
ADHD	Organization	Fine motor skills	Reading
I.Q.	Handwriting	Spoken language	Study skills
Math	Social skills	Written language	

Tutoring:
Services rendered by:
Graduates •Peers Faculty LD staff Teacher trainees

Tutorials

Grp.	Ind.	Tutorials	Grp.	Ind.	Tutorials
•	•	Math skills			Word processing
•	•	Study skills			Time management
•	•	Language arts			Learning strategies
•	•	Written express			Organizational skills

Academic Accommodations

Curriculum
Priority registration
Math waiver
Foreign lang. waiver
Course substitution

In Class
- Calculators
- Tape recorder
- Word processor
Priority seating

Study Aids
- Typist
Reader
- Notetaker
- Proof reader
- Text on tape
Early syllabus
Taped handouts

Exams
- Oral
Untimed
- Take home
- With proctor
On computer
- Extended time
On tape
- Modified
Separate room

Graduation Requirements:
Course credits: **120** GPA: **2.0** Language waiver: **Yes**

Program Strengths
Students who self-disclose a disability may work through the Academic Development Center. We provide tutoring, editors, readers, etc. We also help students secure testing if we suspect a disability.

General Information:
University of Pittsburgh at Bradford is a 4 year public university. Rural campus 100 miles from Buffalo, NY. Accessible by air or bus. Ski areas are 25 miles from campus. 8 residential halls on campus. Housing is guaranteed.

Accreditation: MSACS, NLN

SAT/ACT Scores:
Scores for incoming freshmen: **Verbal:** 30% below 500. 67% between 500 and 599. 3% between 600 and 699. **Math:** 35% below 500. 60% between 500 and 599. 5% between 600 and 699. 1% above 700. **ACT:** 5% below 20. 40% between 20 and 23. 40% between 24 and 251. 10% between 26 and 28. 5% above 28.

Class Rank:
About 30% of the present freshmen class were in the upper 20% of their high school class. 70% were in the top 40% of their class. 98% were in the top 60% of their class. 100% were in the top 80% of their class.

Expenses:
Tuition: In-state: Full year: $4,290.00. Part-time: Per credit: $150.00. Tuition: Out-of-state: Full year: $9,140.00. Part-time: Per credit: $300.00. Room and board: $3,610.00

Majors
• AREA STUDIES American • BUSINESS Business Management, Economics • COMMUNICATIONS Communication, Creative Writing, English, Journalism, Literature, Technical & Business Writing, Television/Radio/Film • COMPUTER SCIENCE Computer Science, Medical Records Administration, Programming • EDUCATION Child Development, Early Childhood, Elementary, English, Health, Mathematics, Science, Secondary, Social Science, Social Studies • ENGINEERING Chemical, Civil/Environmental, Computer, Industrial, Materials, Mechanical, Metallurgical, Mining/Mineral • HEALTH SCIENCES Health, Medical Technology, Nursing, Occupational Therapy, Physical Therapy, Speech/Audiology and Speech • HUMANITIES English/Writing/Literature, Liberal Arts • LANGUAGES Chinese, French, German, Italian, Japanese, Linguistics, Russian, Spanish • PREPROFESSIONAL Dentistry, Law, Medicine, Pharmacy, Social Work, Veterinarian • SCIENCES Anthropology, Biochemistry, Biology, Chemistry, Earth, Geology, Gerontology, Mathematics, Physical Science, Physics, Statistics • SOCIAL SCIENCES Government/Political, History, International Studies, Law Enforcement, Library Science, Political Science, Psychology, Public Relations, Social Sciences, Sociology • VOCATIONAL Medical Laboratory Technology

Sports/Activities
• SPORTS RELATED Pep Band • SPORTS-INTERCOLLEGIATE Baseball (M), Basketball, Cross Country, Soccer (M), Volleyball (F) • SPORTS-INTRAMURAL Badminton, Baseball (M), Basketball, Bowling, Cross Country, Ping-Pong, Tennis, Volleyball • STUDENT LIFE ACTIVITIES Choral, Community Service, Drama Groups, Ethnic & Cultural Groups, Fraternities, Jazz Band, Magazine, Newspaper, Radio/TV station, Religious Organization, Student Government, Yearbook

Very Selective

Pennsylvania Services

University of Pittsburgh: Pittsburgh Campus
Office of Admissions and Financial Aid Second Floor, Bruce Hall
Pittsburgh, Pennsylvania 15260
(414) 624-PITT

School Enrollment: **18,250** Male: **9,207** Female: **9,043**
LD Enrollment: **60** Male: **30** Female: **30**

Admissions Contact: **Dr. Betsy Porter, Dir. Admissions/Financial**

Aid

LD Contact: **Sabina Bilder Student Services Specialist**
Name of Program: **Disabled Student Services**
Address: **216 William Pitt Union**
Telephone: **(414) 648-7890**

Admissions

Application Information:

Enrolled: **60**
Application deadline: **Rolling**
Rolling Admissions: **Yes** Notified when: **May 1st**

Secondary School Information

Most Important Criteria For Admissions (1-strongest)

3 SAT/ACT	Application	**1** School transcript
2 Class rank	Course selection	**5** Personal statement
Interview	Extra activities	Psychoeducational
G.P.A.	Open admission	**4** Recommendations

Test Requirements:

Standardized tests waived: **Yes**
Untimed SAT: **Yes** Untimed ACT: **Yes**
Documentation of LD required: **Yes**
Currency of diagnostic testing: **3 years**
Tests recommended: **WAIS-R, WISC-R, Lurea-Nebraska, Peabody, MMPT, etc.**

Types of Disabilities Served

- Speech/Lang
- Study skills
- Written express
- Organizational
- Perceptual
- Reading
- Spelling
- Math
- Fine Motor
- ADD with LD
- ADD without LD
- ADHD with LD
- ADHD without LD

Admissions Process

Students must submit high school transcript, either SAT or ACT scores, and completed University of Pittsburgh application. Requirements vary by school and/or program.

High School Course Requirements:

English: **4** Math: **3** Science: **3**

Learning Disability Program

Students mainstreamed **100** % of the day
Recommended credits per semester: **12-15**
Services only for LD students: **Yes**

Faculty:

Faculty: **1** Full time: **1** M.A.: **1**
Faculty advocate: **Yes** Meets with instructor: **When requested**

Diagnostic Testing

ADD	Personality	Perceptual skills	Spelling
ADHD•	Organization	Fine motor skills	• Reading
I.Q.	Handwriting	Spoken language	• Study skills
Math	Social skills	Written language	

Tutoring:

Services rendered by:
- Graduates
- Peers
- Faculty
- LD staff
- Teacher trainees

Tutorials

Grp.	Ind.	Tutorials	Grp.	Ind.	Tutorials
		Math skills			Word processing
•	•	Study skills	•	•	Time management
		Language arts	•	•	Learning strategies
		Written express	•	•	Organizational skills

Academic Accommodations

Curriculum	Study Aids	Exams
Priority registration	Typist	• Oral
• Math waiver	• Reader	Untimed
• Foreign lang. waiver	• Notetaker	• Take home
Course substitution	Proof reader	• With proctor
In Class	• Text on tape	• On computer
• Calculators	Early syllabus	• Extended time
• Tape recorder	Taped handouts	• On tape
• Word processor		• Modified
Priority seating		• Separate room

Graduation Requirements:

Course credits: **120** GPA: **2.0** Years to complete degree: **Varies** Math waiver: **Yes** Language waiver: **Yes**
Other requirements: **For the College of Arts and Sciences, students must satisfy skills requirements in writing quantitative, formal reasoning and foreign language. Students must also satisfy general education requirements.**

General Information:

University of Pittsburgh: Pittsburgh Campus is a 4 year public university. Urban campus of 132 acres is 3 miles from Pittsburgh. Accessible by air, train, or bus. Ski areas are 5 miles from campus. Beaches are from campus. 1% of students are foreign. 10 residential halls on campus. Housing is guaranteed. Guaranteed through 1st year. 10 % of students join fraternities/sororities.

Accreditation: MSACS

Expenses:

Tuition: In-state: Full year: $4,290.00. Part-time: Per credit: $150.00. Tuition: Out-of-state: Full year: $9,140.00. Part-time: Per credit: $313.00.
Room and board: $3,790.00

Majors

• AREA STUDIES Asian, Black/Afro-American • BUSINESS Accounting, Business Management, Human Resources Management, Management Information System, Marketing, Real Estate • COMMUNICATIONS Communication, Speech/Debate/Forensic, Telecommunications • COMPUTER SCIENCE Computer Science • EDUCATION English As A Second Language, General, Health, Physical, Psychology, Recreation/Youth Leadership, Vocational • ENGINEERING Bioengineering, Chemical, Civil/Environmental, Electrical, Energy Conservation and Regula, Industrial, Manufacturing Technology, Materials, Mechanical, Metallurgical, Mining/Mineral, Petroleum, Physics • HEALTH SCIENCES Biometrics, Biostatistics, Dental Hygiene, Medical Laboratory Technology, Medical Records Administration, Nursing, Occupational Therapy, Pharmacology, Physical Therapy, Public Health, Speech Therapy, Speech/Audiology and Speech • HUMANITIES Classics, English/Writing/Literature, Fine Arts, Humanities, Liberal Arts, Philosophy, Religion • LANGUAGES Chinese, English, French, German, Italian, Japanese, Russian, Spanish • MATHEMATICS Applied, Computer, Statistical • RELIGIOUS STUDIES Religious Studies • SCIENCES Anatomy, Anthropology, Applied Mathematics, Astronomy, Biology, Biostatistics, Chemistry, Computer Science, Geology, Mathematics, Microbiology, Neurosciences, Physics, Public Health, Statistics • SOCIAL SCIENCES Anthropology, Criminal Justice, Family Counseling, Government/Political, History, International Studies, Library Science, Political Science, Psychology, Social Sciences, Sociology • SPECIAL EDUCATION Deaf/Hearing Impaired, Gifted & Talented, Learning Disability, Occupational Therapy, Physically Handicapped, Visually Handicapped • VISUAL AND PERFORMING ARTS Fine Arts, Music, Studio Art, Theater

Sports/Activities

• SPORTS RELATED Cheerleading, Chess, Drum Major/Majorette, Marching Band • SPORTS-INTERCOLLEGIATE Baseball (M), Basketball (F), Basketball (M), Cross Country (F), Cross Country (M), Diving (F), Diving (M), Football (M), Gymnastics (F), Gymnastics (M), Soccer (M), Swimming (F), Swimming (M), Tennis (F), Tennis (M), Track and Field (F), Track and Field (M), Volleyball (F), Wrestling (M) • SPORTS-INTRAMURAL Basketball (F), Basketball (M), Football (F), Football (M), Hand Ball (M), Racquetball (F), Racquetball (M), Soccer (F), Soccer (M), Softball (F), Softball (M), Squash (F), Squash (M), Swimming (F), Swimming (M), Volleyball (F), Volleyball (M), Wrestling (M) • STUDENT LIFE ACTIVITIES Academic Clubs, Choral, Community Service, Dance, Drama Groups, Ethnic & Cultural Groups, Film, Fraternities, Jazz Band, Music Groups, Newspaper, Political Groups, Radio/TV station, Religious Organization, Sororities, Student Government, Yearbook

Less Selective	**Pennsylvania**
	Services

Waynesburg College

51 West College Street
Waynesburg, Pennsylvania 15370
(412) 627-8191

School Enrollment: **788**

Admissions Contact: **Robin L. Moore, Director of Admissions**
LD Contact: **Chuck Berter, Chairman, Academ. Support Services**
Name of Program: **Act 101**
Telephone:**(412) 852-3248**

Admissions

Application Information:
Application deadline: **None**
Rolling Admissions: **Yes**

Secondary School Information
Most Important Criteria For Admissions (1-strongest)

5	SAT/ACT	6 Application	1 School transcript
4	Class rank	3 Course selection	10 Personal statement
8	Interview	7 Extra activities	Psychoeducational
2	G.P.A.	Open admission	9 Recommendations

Types of Disabilities Served
• Speech/Lang   • Reading   • ADD with LD
• Study skills   • Spelling   • ADD without LD
• Written express • Math   ADHD with LD
• Organizational • Fine Motor   ADHD without LD
• Perceptual

Learning Disability Program

Counseling: Individual: **Yes**

Faculty:
Faculty advocate: **Yes** Meets with instructor: **Upon request**

Diagnostic Testing

ADD	Personality	Perceptual skills	Spelling
ADHD	Organization	Fine motor skills	Reading
I.Q.	Handwriting	Spoken language	Study skills
Math	Social skills	Written language	

Tutoring:
Services rendered by:
  Graduates   •Peers   •Faculty   LD staff   Teacher trainees

Tutorials

Grp.	Ind.	Tutorials	Grp.	Ind.	Tutorials
•		Math skills	•		Word processing
•	•	Study skills	•		Time management
•	•	Language arts	•	•	Learning strategies
•	•	Written express	•	•	Organizational skills

Academic Accommodations

Curriculum	Study Aids	Exams
Priority registration	Typist	• Oral
Math waiver	Reader	Untimed
• Foreign lang. waiver	• Notetaker	Take home
Course substitution	• Proof reader	With proctor
In Class	Text on tape	On computer
• Calculators	Early syllabus	• Extended time
• Tape recorder	Taped handouts	On tape
• Word processor		• Modified
Priority seating		Separate room

Program Strengths

Waynesburg college offers support services for students with needs. The program consists of a study skills class that meets one hour a week and tutoring is available.

General Information:

Waynesburg College is a 4 year private college. of 30 acres is 50 miles from Pittsburgh. Accessible by air or bus. Ski areas are 1 hour from campus. Beaches are 7 hours from campus. 1% of students are foreign. 4 residential halls on campus. Housing is guaranteed.60 % of students remain on campus for the weekends. 25 % of students join fraternities/sororities.

Accreditation:MSACS

Class Rank:
About 41% of the present freshmen class were in the upper 20% of their high school class. 73% were in the top 40% of their class. 97% were in the top 60% of their class. 100% were in the top 80% of their class.

Expenses:
Tuition: In-state: Full year: $7,030.00. Part-time: Per credit:$295.00. Room and board: $2.900.00

Majors

• BUSINESS Accounting, Banking, Business Administration, Business Education, Business Management, Economics, Entrepreneur, Finance, Management, Marketing • COMMUNICATIONS Communication, English, Journalism, Photography, Television/Radio/Film • COMPUTER SCIENCE Data Processing • EDUCATION Early Childhood, Elementary, Mathematics, Science, Secondary, Social Studies • ENVIRONMENTAL CONTROL Water and Wastewater Technology • HEALTH SCIENCES Environmental, Medical Secretary, Medical Technology, Nursing • PRE-PROFESSIONAL Dentistry, Engineering, Law, Medicine, Sports Medicine • SCIENCES Biology, Chemistry, Mathematics • SOCIAL SCIENCES Criminal Justice, Government/Political, History, Human Service, Law Enforcement, Political Science, Psychology, Public Relations, Sociology • VISUAL AND PERFORMING ARTS Visual and Performing Arts • VOCATIONAL Business and Office, Legal Secretary, Medical Laboratory Technology, Secretarial

Sports/Activities

• SPORTS RELATED Marching Band, Pep Band • SPORTS-INTERCOLLEGIATE Baseball (M), Basketball, Football (M), Softball (F), Volleyball, Wrestling (M) • SPORTS-INTRAMURAL Archery, Baseball, Bowling, Golf, Ping-Pong, Racquetball, Soccer, Softball, Tennis, Volleyball (F),

Wrestling (M) • STUDENT LIFE ACTIVITIES Choral, Concert Band, Drama Groups, Ethnic & Cultural Groups, Fraternities, Jazz Band, Magazine, Music Groups, Musical Theater, Newspaper, Radio/TV station, Religious Organization, Sororities, Student Government, Yearbook

---

Less Selective	Pennsylvania
	Services

Westmoreland County Community College
Armburst Road College Station
Youngwood, Pennsylvania 15697
(412) 925-4062

School Enrollment: **6,395** Male: **2,425** Female: **3,990**
LD Enrollment: **15**

Admissions Contact: **Rick Sparks, Director of Admissions**
LD Contact: **Mary Ellen Beres, Counselor**
Name of Program: **Student Support Services**
Telephone:**(412) 925-4189**

Admissions

Application Information:
Rolling Admissions: **Yes**

Secondary School Information
Most Important Criteria For Admissions (1-strongest)

SAT/ACT	Application	School transcript
Class rank	Course selection	Personal statement
Interview	Extra activities	Psychoeducational
G.P.A.	**1** Open admission	Recommendations

Test Requirements:
Standardized tests waived: **Yes**
Documentation of LD required: **Yes**

Types of Disabilities Served
• Speech/Lang	• Reading	• ADD with LD
• Study skills	• Spelling	• ADD without LD
• Written express	• Math	• ADHD with LD
• Organizational	• Fine Motor	• ADHD without LD
• Perceptual		

Learning Disability Program
Recommended credits per semester: **Varies**
Services available for all students: **Yes**
Counseling: Individual: **Yes** Vocational Counseling: **Yes**

Faculty:
Faculty: **3** Full time: **1** Part time: **2**

Diagnostic Testing
ADD	Personality	Perceptual skills	Spelling
ADHD	Organization	Fine motor skills	Reading
I.Q.	Handwriting	Spoken language	Study skills
Math	Social skills	Written language	

Tutoring:
Average size of group tutorials: **2-3**
Services rendered by:
Graduates   •Peers   Faculty   •LD staff   Teacher trainees

Tutorials
Grp.	Ind.	Tutorials	Grp.	Ind.	Tutorials
•		Math skills	•	•	Word processing
	•	Study skills		•	Time management
	•	Language arts		•	Learning strategies
•	•	Written express		•	Organizational skills

Academic Accommodations
Curriculum	Study Aids	Exams
Priority registration	• Typist	• Oral
Math waiver	• Reader	Untimed
Foreign lang. waiver	• Notetaker	Take home
Course substitution	• Proof reader	• With proctor
In Class	• Text on tape	On computer
Calculators	Early syllabus	• Extended time
• Tape recorder	Taped handouts	On tape
• Word processor		• Modified
• Priority seating		• Separate room

Program Strengths
The program at WCCC for the LD student provides a variety of support services. After receiving the assessment of student needs, an individualized program is instituted to provide for basic study or compensatory needs. Students are monitored on an ongoing basis to assess achievements or to redefine goals.

General Information:
Westmoreland County Community College is a 2 year public college. Suburban campus 5 miles from Greensburg. Accessible by bus. Housing is not guaranteed.

Accreditation:MSACS

Expenses:
Tuition: In-state: Full year: $585.00 (Full time 15 credits). Part-time: Per credit:$83.00. Tuition: Out-of-state: Full year: $1,245.00 (Full time 15 credits).

Majors
• AGRICULTURE Horticultural • ARTS Commercial Art, Film & Video, Graphic Arts, Landscaping • BUSINESS Accounting, Banking/Finance, Business Administration, Business Management, Fashion Merchandising, Food Management, Hotel and Restaurant Management, Real Estate, Retailing • COMMUNICATIONS Graphic Design • COMPUTER SCIENCE Business Data Programming, Computer Science • CRAFTS AND DESIGN Graphic Design • HEALTH SCIENCES Dental Assistant, Dental Hygiene, Dietary Manager, Medical Laboratory Technology, Medical Secretary, Nursing, Nursing Assistant • HUMANITIES Liberal Arts • PREPROFESSIONAL Business, Law • SOCIAL SCIENCES Human Service, Psychology • VOCATIONAL Air Conditioning/Heating/Refri, Air Traffic Control, Chef Apprenticeship, Culinary Arts, Dental Assistant, Dental Hygiene, Drafting, Electronics Technology, Fashion Merchandising, Fire Science, Food Service, Legal Secretary, Medical Laboratory Technology, Paralegal, Secretarial, Word Processing

Sports/Activities
• SPORTS-INTERCOLLEGIATE Baseball (M), Basketball (M), Golf (M), Racquetball (F), Racquetball (M), Softball (F), Tennis (F), Tennis (M), Volleyball (F) • SPORTS-INTRAMURAL Baseball (M), Basketball (M), Football (M), Ping-Pong (F), Ping-Pong (M), Racquetball, Softball • STUDENT LIFE ACTIVITIES Academic Clubs, Choral, Debate, Newspaper, Radio, Student Government

Pennsylvania

Very Selective

Pennsylvania Services

Widener University
Webb Hall
Chester, Pennsylvania 19013-5792
(215) 499-4000

School Enrollment: **2,500** Male: **1,300** Female: **1,200**

Admissions Contact: **Daniel Bowers, Associate Director**
LD Contact: **Linda Baum, Learning Specialist**
Name of Program: **ENABLE**
Telephone:**(215) 499-4000**

Admissions

Application Information:
Rolling Admissions: **Yes**

Secondary School Information
Most Important Criteria For Admissions (1-strongest)

5 SAT/ACT	**1** Application	**2**	School transcript
6 Class rank	**3** Course selection	**11**	Personal statement
8 Interview	**7** Extra activities	**9**	Psychoeducational
4 G.P.A.	Open admission	**10**	Recommendations

Test Requirements:
Diagnostic testing waived: **Yes**
Untimed SAT: **Yes** Untimed ACT: **Yes** Untimed ACH: **Yes**
WAIS-R required: **Yes**
Documentation of LD required: **Yes**
Currency of diagnostic testing: **24**
Tests recommended: **WAIS-R, Bender, Achievement Testing, Reading, Math and Written English, Process Testing.**

Types of Disabilities Served
- Speech/Lang
- Reading
- ADD with LD
- Study skills
- Spelling
- ADD without LD
- Written express
- Math
- ADHD with LD
- Organizational
- Fine Motor
- ADHD without LD
- Perceptual

Admissions Process

Above deficits accepted if they are mild or controlled by medication. Formal application and official school records and other data supplied are reviewed by the admissions officer. Notification to applicant is usually within three weeks.

High School Course Requirements:
English: **4** Math: **3** Science: **2** Foreign Language: **2**

Learning Disability Program

Students mainstreamed **100** % of the day
Recommended credits per semester: **12**
Time required or recommended in learning center: **varies**
Services only for LD students: **Yes**
Counseling: Individual: **Yes** Vocational Counseling: **Yes**
Support groups are available:**Informal as need arises**

Faculty:
Faculty: **2** Full time: **1** Part time: **1**
Faculty advocate: **Yes** Meets with instructor: **As needed**

Diagnostic Testing
- ADD
- Personality
- Perceptual skills
- Spelling
- ADHD
- Organization
- Fine motor skills
- Reading
- I.Q.
- Handwriting
- Spoken language
- Study skills
- Math
- Social skills
- Written language

Tutoring:
Average size of group tutorials: **1-4**
Services rendered by:
Graduates •Peers •Faculty •LD staff Teacher trainees

Tutorials

Grp.	Ind.	Tutorials	Grp.	Ind.	Tutorials
•	•	Math skills	•		Word processing
•	•	Study skills	•	•	Time management
•	•	Language arts	•	•	Learning strategies
•	•	Written express	•	•	Organizational skills

Academic Accommodations

Curriculum	Study Aids	Exams
• Priority registration	Typist	• Oral
Math waiver	• Reader	• Untimed
• Foreign lang. waiver	• Notetaker	Take home
Course substitution	• Proof reader	• With proctor
In Class	• Text on tape	• On computer
• Calculators	• Early syllabus	• Extended time
• Tape recorder	Taped handouts	• On tape
• Word processor		Modified
• Priority seating		• Separate room

Graduation Requirements:
Course credits: **121** GPA: **2.0** Language waiver: **Yes**

Program Strengths

The students are tracked from entrance to exit and carefully monitored by the Learning Specialist. Individual attention provided according to need.

General Information:

Widener University is a 4 year independent university. Urban campus of 100 acres is 12 miles from Philadelphia. Accessible by air, train, or bus. Ski areas are 2 hours from campus. Beaches are 2 hours from campus. 6% of students are foreign. 16 residential halls on campus. Housing is guaranteed.Guaranteed through 4th year. 50 % of students remain on campus for the weekends. 30 % of students join fraternities/sororities.

Accreditation:MSASC

Expenses:
Tuition: In-state: Full year: $10,500.00. Tuition: Out-of-state: Full year: $10,500.00. Room and board: $4,560.00

Majors

• BUSINESS Accounting, Banking/Finance, Business Administration, Business Economics, Business Management, Economics, Hotel & Restaurant Management, Human Resources Management, Management, Marketing • COMPUTER SCIENCE Computer Science, Data Processing • EDUCATION Early Childhood, Elementary, English, Foreign Language, Mathematics, Science, Secondary, Social Studies • ENGINEERING Chemical, Civil/Environmental, Electrical, Mechanical • HEALTH SCIENCES Nursing, Physical Therapy • HUMANITIES English/Writing/Literature, Humanities, Liberal Arts , Philosophy • LANGUAGES French, German, Italian, Spanish • MATHEMATICS Actuarial • PRE PROFES-

SIONAL Dentistry, Law, Medicine, Optometry, Social Work, Veterinarian • RELIGIOUS STUDIES Philosophy • SCIENCES Biology, Chemistry, Computer Science, General, Physics3 • SOCIAL SCIENCES Government/ Political, Human Service, Psychology, Social Science, Sociology

Sports/Activities

• SPORTS RELATED Cheerleading, Chess, Team Managers • SPORTS-INTERCOLLEGIATE Baseball (M), Basketball (F), Basketball (M), Cross Country (F), Cross Country (M), Field Hockey (F), Football, Golf (M), La-crosse (F), Lacrosse (M), Soccer (M), Softball (F), Squash, Swimming (F), Swimming (M), Tennis (F), Tennis (M), Track and Field (F), Track and Field (M), Volleyball (F) • SPORTS-INTRAMURAL Badminton (F), Bad-minton (M), Basketball (F), Basketball (M), Football (F), Football (M), Hand Ball, Ping-Pong (F), Ping-Pong (M), Racquetball (F), Racquetball (M), Riflery, Soccer, Softball, Swimming, Tennis, Volleyball, Weight Lift-ing • STUDENT LIFE ACTIVITIES Academic Clubs, Community Ser-vice, Drama Groups, Ethnic & Cultural Groups, Film, Fraternities, Jazz Band, Magazine, Newspaper, Political Groups, Radio/TV station, Reli-gious Organization, Sororities, Student Government, Yearbook

Less Selective	Puerto Rico
	Services

American University of Puerto Rico

P.O. Box 2037
Bayamon, Puerto Rico 00960-2037
(809) 798-2040

School Enrollment: **1,330**

Admissions Contact: **Margarita Cruz, Director of Admissions**
LD Contact: **Adela Costa, Coordinator**
Name of Program: **Special Education**

Admissions

Application Information:
Application deadline: **July 1st**

Secondary School Information
Most Important Criteria For Admissions (1-strongest)

SAT/ACT **1**	Application **1**	School transcript
Class rank	Course selection	Personal statement
Interview	Extra activities	Psychoeducational
1 G.P.A.	Open admission	Recommendations

Types of Disabilities Served
- Speech/Lang
- Study skills
- Written express
- Organizational
- Perceptual
- Reading
- Spelling
- Math
- Fine Motor
- ADD with LD
- ADD without LD
- ADHD with LD
- ADHD without LD

Admissions Process

LD students undergo all the same processes as anyone else. This way assures them the chance of doing college work on their own.

Learning Disability Program
Counseling: Individual: **Yes**

Faculty:
Faculty: **2** Full time: **2**
Faculty advocate: **Yes** Meets with instructor: **As necessary**

Diagnostic Testing

ADD	Personality	Perceptual skills	Spelling
ADHD	Organization	Fine motor skills	Reading
I.Q.	Handwriting	Spoken language	Study skills
Math	Social skills	Written language	

Services rendered by:

Graduates	Peers	Faculty	LD staff	Teacher trainees

Tutorials

Grp.	Ind.	Tutorials	Grp.	Ind.	Tutorials
		Math skills			Word processing
		Study skills			Time management
		Language arts			Learning strategies
		Written express			Organizational skills

Academic Accommodations

Curriculum	Study Aids	Exams
Priority registration	• Typist	• Oral
• Math waiver	Reader	Untimed
Foreign lang. waiver	• Notetaker	• Take home
Course substitution	• Proof reader	• With proctor
In Class	Text on tape	On computer
• Calculators	Early syllabus	• Extended time
• Tape recorder	Taped handouts	On tape
• Word processor		• Modified
Priority seating		Separate room

Program Strengths
We provide services because we understand it is our responsibility to employ our own resources. Should we get funds, it would be unique.

General Information:
American University of Puerto Rico is a 2 and 4 year private university. Suburban campus of 20 acres is 12 miles from Bayamon. Beaches are 5 miles from campus. Housing is not guaranteed.

Accreditation:MSACS, HEC, AACS

Expenses:
Tuition: In-state: Full year: $2,300.00. Part-time: Per course: $288.00.

Majors
• BUSINESS Accounting, Business Administration, Business Manage-ment, retailing Secretarial Science • EDUCATION Elementary, English, English As A Second Language, Physical, Special • HEALTH SCIENCES Communication Disorders

Sports/Activities
• SPORTS RELATED Cheerleading • SPORTS-INTERCOLLEGIATE Basketball (F), Basketball (M), Cross Country (F), Cross Country (M), Hammer Throw, Track and Field (F), Track and Field (M) • STUDENT LIFE ACTIVITIES Academic Clubs, Community Service, Dance, Drama Groups, Student Government

Less Selective

Puerto Rico
Services

Inter American University of Puerto Rico
Call Box 5100
San German, Puerto Rico 00753
(809) 892-3090

School Enrollment: **5,964** Male: **2,384** Female: **3,580**
LD Enrollment: **1** Female: **1**

Admissions Contact: **Mrs. Mildred Camacho, Dir. of Admissions**
LD Contact: **Mrs. Ramonita Pabon, Dir. Vocational Rehab. Office**
Name of Program: **Vocational Rehabilitation Office**
Address: **Box 5100**
Telephone: **(809) 892-4150**

Admissions

Application Information:
Application deadline: **April, November**
Applicant must apply **3** months in advance

Secondary School Information
Most Important Criteria For Admissions (1-strongest)

SAT/ACT **1**	Application **1**	School transcript
Class rank	Course selection	Personal statement
Interview	Extra activities	Psychoeducational
1 G.P.A.	Open admission	Recommendations

Test Requirements:
Untimed SAT: **Yes**
Documentation of LD required: **Yes**

Types of Disabilities Served

Speech/Lang	Reading	ADD with LD
Study skills	Spelling	ADD without LD
Written express	Math	ADHD with LD
Organizational	Fine Motor	ADHD without LD
Perceptual		

Admissions Process

LD students undergo all the same processes as anyone else. This way assures them the chance of doing college work on their own.

High School Course Requirements:
English: **2** Math: **1** Science: **2** Foreign Language: **2**

Learning Disability Program
Services available for all students: **Yes**

Diagnostic Testing

• ADD	Personality	Perceptual skills	Spelling
ADHD	Organization	Fine motor skills	Reading
I.Q.	Handwriting	Spoken language	Study skills
Math	Social skills	Written language	

Tutoring:
Services rendered by:
•Graduates •Peers Faculty LD staff Teacher trainees

Tutorials

Grp.	Ind.	Tutorials	Grp.	Ind.	Tutorials
		Math skills			Word processing
		Study skills			Time management
		Language arts			Learning strategies
		Written express			Organizational skills

Academic Accommodations

Curriculum	Study Aids	Exams
Priority registration	Typist	Oral
Math waiver	Reader	Untimed
Foreign lang. waiver	Notetaker	Take home
Course substitution	Proof reader	With proctor
In Class	Text on tape	On computer
Calculators	Early syllabus	Extended time
Tape recorder	Taped handouts	On tape
Word processor		Modified
Priority seating		Separate room

Graduation Requirements:
Course credits: **132 minimum** GPA: **2.25** Years to complete degree: **4-5**

General Information:
Inter American University of Puerto Rico is a 4 year independent university. Urban campus 15 miles from Mayaguez. Accessible by public car transportation. Beaches are 30 miles from campus. Housing is guaranteed. 10 % of students join fraternities/sororities.

Accreditation: MSACS

Expenses:
Tuition: In-state: Full year: $1,125.00 per semester $90.00 fees. Part-time: Per credit: $75.00. Tuition: Out-of-state: Full year: $1,125.00 per semester $90.00 fees. Part-time: Per credit: $75.00. Room and board: $1,030.00/semester

Majors
• ARTS Graphic Art, Music, Music Performance • BUSINESS Accounting, Business Administration, Personnel, Secretarial Science • COMPUTER SCIENCE Computer Science, Management Information System • EDUCATION Art, Early Childhood, Elementary, English, English As A Second Language, Health, Mathematics, Music, Physical, Special • HEALTH SCIENCES Medical Laboratory Technology, Medical Records Administration, Nursing, Radiological Technology • LANGUAGES English, Spanish • SCIENCES Biology, Chemistry, Mathematics • SOCIAL SCIENCES History, Library Science, Political Science, Psychology, Sociology • VISUAL AND PERFORMING ARTS Art

Sports/Activities
• SPORTS-INTRAMURAL Baseball (M), Basketball (F), Basketball (M), Hammer Throw, Ping-Pong (F), Ping-Pong (M), Tennis (F), Tennis (M), Track and Field (F), Track and Field (M), Volleyball (F), Volleyball (M), Weight Lifting (M), Wrestling (M) • STUDENT LIFE ACTIVITIES Academic Clubs, Choral, Community Service, Concert Band, Dance, Drama Groups, Ethnic & Cultural Groups, Fraternities, Jazz Band, Music Groups, Musical Theater, Religious Organization, Sororities, Student Government

Most Selective

Brown University
P. O. Box 1876
Providence, Rhode Island 02912
(401) 863-2378

School Enrollment: **5,400** Male: **2,700** Female: **2,700**
LD Enrollment: **80**

Admissions Contact: **Michael Goldberger**
LD Contact: **Dean Robert Shaw**
Name of Program: **Students with Alternate Learning Styles**
Telephone:**(401) 863-2315**

Admissions

Application Information:
Application deadline: **January 1st**

Secondary School Information
Most Important Criteria For Admissions (1-strongest)

4 SAT/ACT	Application	**1**	School transcript
1 Class rank	**1** Course selection	**2**	Personal statement
5 Interview	**3** Extra activities		Psychoeducational
1 G.P.A.	Open admission	**2**	Recommendations

Test Requirements:
Untimed SAT: **Yes** Untimed ACH: **Yes** Achievement tests required:**3**
Documentation of LD required: **Yes**
Currency of diagnostic testing: **None**

Types of Disabilities Served
- Speech/Lang
- Reading
- ADD with LD
- Study skills
- Spelling
- ADD without LD
- Written express
- Math
- ADHD with LD
- Organizational
- Fine Motor
- ADHD without LD
- Perceptual

Admissions Process

Highly competitive

High School Course Requirements:
English: **4** Math: **3** Science: **3** Foreign Language: **3**
Waivers to standard high school courses
Foreign Language : **Yes** Math: **Yes** Course substitution: **Yes**

Learning Disability Program
Program: Reinforces course work: **Yes**
Students mainstreamed **100** % of the day
Services only for LD students: **Yes**
Services available for all students: **Yes**

Faculty:
Faculty: **1** Full time: **1** Ph.D.: **1**
Meets with instructor: **As needed**

Diagnostic Testing
- ADD
- Personality
- Perceptual skills
- Spelling
- ADHD
- Organization
- Fine motor skills
- Reading
- I.Q.
- Handwriting
- Spoken language
- Study skills
- Math
- Social skills
- Written language

Tutoring:
Average size of group tutorials:
Services rendered by:
Graduates •Peers Faculty LD staff Teacher trainees

Tutorials
Grp.	Ind.	Tutorials	Grp.	Ind.	Tutorials
		Math skills			Word processing
		Study skills			Time management
		Language arts			Learning strategies
		Written express			Organizational skills

Academic Accommodations

Curriculum	Study Aids	Exams
Priority registration	Typist	• Oral
• Math waiver	Reader	Untimed
• Foreign lang. waiver	• Notetaker	• Take home
• Course substitution	Proof reader	• With proctor
In Class	• Text on tape	On computer
• Calculators	Early syllabus	• Extended time
• Tape recorder	Taped handouts	On tape
• Word processor		• Modified
• Priority seating		• Separate room

Graduation Requirements: Language waiver: **Yes**

Program Strengths
The program is designed to help qualified dyslexic students succeed at Brown through providing minimal accommodations to the normal academic routine. A measure of the success of the program is that the dyslexic students at Brown are virtually indistinguishable from other students in terms of choice of major, academic record, and post-graduate activities.

General Information:
Brown University is a 4 year private university. Urban campus of 146 acres is Accessible by air, train, or bus. Ski areas are 3 hours from campus. Beaches are 1/2 hour from campus. 14 residential halls on campus. Housing is guaranteed.Guaranteed through 1st year.

Accreditation:NEACS

SAT/ACT Scores:
Scores for incoming freshmen:**Verbal:**9%below 500. 27%between 500 and 599. 48%between 600 and 699. 9%above 700. **Math:**2% below 500. 16% between 500 and 599. 39% between 600 and 699. 43%above 700.

Class Rank:
About 92% of the present freshmen class were in the upper 20% of their high school class. 99% were in the top 40% of their class. 100% were in the top 60% of their class.

Expenses:
Tuition: In-state: Full year: $17,384.00. Room and board: $5,969.00

Majors
• AREA STUDIES American, Asian, Black/Afro-American, European, Jewish, Latin American, Russian/Slavic, Urban • BUSINESS Business Economics, Economics • COMMUNICATIONS Creative Writing, English, Linguistic, Literature, Modern Culture and Media • COMPUTER SCIENCE Computer Science, Programming, Systems Analysis • EDUCATION Elementary • ENGINEERING Bio-medical, Bioengineering, Chemical, Civil/Environmental, Computer, Electrical, Engineering Science, Environmental/Water Resources, Materials, Mechanical, Nuclear • HEALTH SCIENCES Environmental • HUMANITIES Classics, English/Writing/Literature, Liberal Arts, Philosophy, Religion • LANGUAGES French, German, Greek, Hebrew, Italian, Japanese, Latin, Russian, Slavic, Spanish • PREPROFESSIONAL Landscaping • SCIENCES Archeology,

Astronomy, Astrophysics, Biochemistry, Biology, Biophysics, Botany, Cell Biology, Chemistry, Earth, Ecology, Geochemistry, Geology, Geophysics and Seismology, Inorganic Chemistry, Macrobiology, Marine Biology, Mathematics, Microbiology, Nuclear Physics, Oceanography, Organic Chemistry, Physical Chemistry, Physical Science, Physics, Physiology, Statistics, Zoology • SOCIAL SCIENCES Anthropology, Government/Political, History, International Studies, Political Science, Social Sciences, Sociology

Sports/Activities

• SPORTS RELATED Cheerleading, Chess, Marching Band, Pep Band, Team Managers • SPORTS-INTERCOLLEGIATE Baseball (M), Basketball, Crew, Cross Country, Diving, Fencing, Field Hockey (F), Football (M), Ice Hockey, Lacrosse, Ping-Pong, Rugby (M), Sailing, Skiing - Snow, Soccer, Softball (F), Squash, Swimming, Tennis, Track and Field, Wrestling (M) • SPORTS-INTRAMURAL Archery, Badminton, Basketball, Field Hockey, Ice Hockey, Soccer, Softball, Squash, Swimming, Tennis, Volleyball, Water Polo • STUDENT LIFE ACTIVITIES Choral, Community Service, Concert Band, Dance, Debate, Drama Groups, Ethnic & Cultural Groups, Fraternities, Jazz Band, Magazine, Music Groups, Musical Theater, Newspaper, Political Groups, Radio/TV station, Religious Organization, Sororities, Student Government, Symphony Orchestra, Yearbook

Very Selective

Rhode Island Services

Bryant College
1150 Douglas Pike
Smithfield, Rhode Island 02917-1285
(401) 232-6100

School Enrollment: **2,933** Male: **1,659** Female: **1,274**
LD Enrollment: **6** Male: **5** Female: **1**

Admissions Contact: **Roy A. Nelson, Dean of Admissions**
LD Contact: **William Phillips, Director of Counseling**
Telephone:**(401) 232-6046**

Admissions

Application Information:
Application deadline: **Rolling**
Rolling Admissions: **Yes**

Secondary School Information
Most Important Criteria For Admissions (1-strongest)

3 SAT/ACT	5 Application	1 School transcript
4 Class rank	2 Course selection	8 Personal statement
Interview	7 Extra activities	Psychoeducational
G.P.A.	Open admission	6 Recommendations

Test Requirements:
Untimed SAT: **Yes** Untimed ACT: **Yes**
Documentation of LD required: **Yes**

Types of Disabilities Served

Speech/Lang	Reading	• ADD with LD
• Study skills	Spelling	• ADD without LD
Written express	Math	• ADHD with LD
• Organizational	• Fine Motor	• ADHD without LD
• Perceptual		

Admissions Process

Application, high school transcript, mid-year grades from senior year, SATS or ACTS, essay on the application, recommendations.

High School Course Requirements:
English: **4** Math: **3** Science: **1**

Learning Disability Program
Students mainstreamed **100** % of the day
Services available for all students: **Yes**
Counseling: Individual: **Yes**

Faculty:
Faculty: **1** Full time: **1**
Faculty advocate: **Yes**

Diagnostic Testing

ADD	Personality	Perceptual skills	Spelling
ADHD	Organization	Fine motor skills	Reading
I.Q.	Handwriting	Spoken language	Study skills
Math	Social skills	Written language	

Tutoring:
Average size of group tutorials:
Services rendered by:

Graduates	•Peers	Faculty	LD staff	Teacher trainees

Tutorials

Grp.	Ind.	Tutorials	Grp.	Ind.	Tutorials
•	•	Math skills	•		Word processing
•	•	Study skills	•	•	Time management
		Language arts	•	•	Learning strategies
		Written express			Organizational skills

Academic Accommodations

Curriculum	Study Aids	Exams
Priority registration	Typist	• Oral
Math waiver	Reader	• Untimed
Foreign lang. waiver	• Notetaker	• Take home
Course substitution	Proof reader	• With proctor
In Class	• Text on tape	• On computer
Calculators	Early syllabus	• Extended time
• Tape recorder	Taped handouts	• On tape
• Word processor		• Modified
Priority seating		• Separate room

Graduation Requirements:
Course credits: **120** GPA: **2.0** Years to complete degree: **4 on average**

Program Strengths
Bryant College does not have a program for LD students. "Support Services" would be a more appropriate description.

General Information:
Bryant College is a 4 year private college. Suburban campus of 287 acres is 12 miles from Providence. Accessible by air, train or bus. Ski areas are 30 miles from campus. Beaches are 50 miles from campus. 1.2% of students are foreign. 16 residential halls on campus. Housing is guaranteed.72-75 % of students remain on campus for the weekends. 20 % of students join fraternities/sororities.

Accreditation:NEACS

SAT/ACT Scores:
Scores for incoming freshmen:**Verbal:76.3%**below 500. 21.4%between 500 and 599. 2.0%between 600 and 699. 0.3%above 700. **Math:23.5%** below 500. 51.0% between 500 and 599. 21.7% between 600 and 699. 3.8%above 700.

Class Rank:
About 39.4% of the present freshmen class were in the upper 20% of their high school class. 77.2% were in the top 40% of their class. 95.5% were in the top 60% of their class. 99.8% were in the top 80% of their class.

Expenses:
Tuition: In-state: Full year: $11,653.00. Part-time: Per credit:$125.00-$486.00. Part-time: Per course: $375.00-$1,457.00. Tuition: Out-of-state: Full year: $11,653.00. Part-time: Per credit:$125.00-$486.00. Part-time: Per course:$375.00-$1,457.00 Room and board: $6,079.00

Majors
• BUSINESS Accounting, Business Administration, Business Management, Economics, Finance, Management, Marketing, Marketing Research • COMMUNICATIONS Advertising, Business Communication, Communication • COMPUTER SCIENCE Computer Science, Systems Analysis • SCIENCES Actuarial Technology Mathematical • SOCIAL SCIENCES History, International Studies

Sports/Activities
• SPORTS RELATED Cheerleading, Team Managers • SPORTS-INTERCOLLEGIATE Baseball (M), Basketball, Bowling, Cross Country, Golf, Soccer, Softball (F), Tennis, Track and Field, Volleyball (F) • SPORTS-INTRAMURAL Basketball, Racquetball, Soccer, Softball, Tennis, Volleyball • STUDENT LIFE ACTIVITIES Academic Clubs, Dance, Debate, Drama Groups, Ethnic & Cultural Groups, Fraternities, Music Groups, Musical Theater, Newspaper, Radio, Sororities, Student Government, Yearbook

Less Selective   **Rhode Island**
                                            Services

Community College of Rhode Island
400 East Avenue
Warwick, Rhode Island 02886-1805
(401) 825-2285

School Enrollment: **12,400**
LD Enrollment: **52**

Admissions Contact: **Joseph DiMaria**
LD Contact: **Julie White**
Name of Program: **Access to Opportunity**
Telephone:**(401) 825-2305**

Admissions

Application Information:
Rolling Admissions: **Yes**

Secondary School Information
Most Important Criteria For Admissions (1-strongest)

SAT/ACT	Application	School transcript
Class rank	Course selection **1**	Personal statement
Interview	Extra activities	Psychoeducational
G.P.A. **1**	Open admission	Recommendations

Test Requirements:
Documentation of LD required: **Yes**

Types of Disabilities Served
• Speech/Lang	• Reading	• ADD with LD
• Study skills	• Spelling	• ADD without LD
• Written express	• Math	• ADHD with LD
• Organizational	• Fine Motor	• ADHD without LD
• Perceptual		

Admissions Process
Open admission institution

Learning Disability Program
Program: Remedial: **Yes**
Students mainstreamed **100** % of the day
Recommended credits per semester: **9-12**
Services only for LD students: **Yes**
Counseling: Individual: **Yes** Group Counseling: **Yes** Vocational Counseling: **Yes**
Support groups are available:**Yes**

Faculty:
Faculty: **2** Full time: **1**
Faculty advocate: **Yes** Meets with instructor: **1x per semester**

Diagnostic Testing
ADD	Personality	Perceptual skills	Spelling
ADHD	Organization	Fine motor skills	Reading
I.Q.	Handwriting	Spoken language	Study skills
Math	Social skills	Written language	

Tutoring:
Services rendered by:
•Graduates   •Peers   •Faculty   •LD staff   Teacher trainees

Tutorials
Grp.	Ind.	Tutorials	Grp.	Ind.	Tutorials
•	•	Math skills	•	•	Word processing
•	•	Study skills	•		Time management
		Language arts		•	Learning strategies
•	•	Written express		•	Organizational skills

Academic Accommodations
Curriculum	Study Aids	Exams
Priority registration	Typist	• Oral
• Math waiver	Reader	Untimed
• Foreign lang. waiver	• Notetaker	• Take home
Course substitution	• Proof reader	• With proctor
In Class	• Text on tape	On computer
• Calculators	Early syllabus	• Extended time
• Tape recorder	Taped handouts	• On tape
• Word processor		• Modified
Priority seating		• Separate room

Graduation Requirements:
Course credits: **60**

General Information:
Community College of Rhode Island is a 2 year public college. Suburban campus 9 miles from Providence. Accessible by bus. Housing is not guaranteed.

Accreditation:Regional

Expenses:
Tuition: In-state: Full year: $1,298.00. Part-time: Per credit:$60.00. Tuition: Out-of-state: Full year: $2,780.00. Part-time: Per credit:$130.00.

Majors
• BUSINESS Accounting, Business Administration, Data Processing, Fashion Merchandising, Management, Real Estate, Retail Manufacturing, Secretarial Science • COMPUTER SCIENCE Computer Science, Data Processing • EDUCATION Child Development, Early Childhood • ENGINEERING Engineering Science, Mechanical • HEALTH SCIENCES Den-

tal Assistant, Dental Hygiene, Medical Laboratory Technology, Medical Secretary, Nursing, Radiological Therapy, Respiratory Therapy • HUMANITIES Liberal Arts • SOCIAL SCIENCES Human Service, Law Enforcement • SPECIAL EDUCATION General • VISUAL AND PERFORMING ARTS Fine Arts, Music, Music Performance, Studio Art, Theater • VOCATIONAL Electronics Technology, Fire Science, Legal Secretary, Medical Laboratory Technology, Respiratory Therapy Technology, Secretarial, Word Processing

Sports/Activities

• SPORTS-INTERCOLLEGIATE Baseball (M), Basketball (F), Basketball (M), Cross Country, Golf, Ice Hockey (M), Soccer (M), Softball (F), Tennis, Volleyball (F) • SPORTS-INTRAMURAL Badminton, Basketball, Golf, Soccer, Swimming, Tennis, Track and Field, Volleyball, Water Polo • STUDENT LIFE ACTIVITIES Choral, Concert Band, Drama Groups, Ethnic & Cultural Groups, Newspaper, Radio/TV station, Student Government, Yearbook

Less Selective	Rhode Island
	Services

Johnson and Wales University

8 Abbott Park Place
Providence, Rhode Island 02903
(401) 456-1000

School Enrollment: **5,579**

Admissions Contact: **Mark Burke, Director, Enrollment**
LD Contact: **Angela Renaud, Ed.D., Dean, Student Success**
Name of Program: **Special Needs Services**
Telephone: **(401) 456-4660**

Admissions

Application Information:
Application deadline: **Rolling**
Rolling Admissions: **Yes**

Secondary School Information
Most Important Criteria For Admissions (1-strongest)

SAT/ACT **3**	Application	School transcript
Class rank	Course selection	Personal statement
1 Interview	Extra activities	Psychoeducational
2 G.P.A.	Open admission	Recommendations

Test Requirements:
Untimed SAT: **Yes** Untimed ACT: **Yes** Untimed ACH: **Yes**
WAIS-R required: **Yes**
Currency of diagnostic testing: **3 years**

Types of Disabilities Served
• Speech/Lang • Reading • ADD with LD
• Study skills • Spelling • ADD without LD
• Written express • Math ADHD with LD
• Organizational • Fine Motor ADHD without LD
• Perceptual

Learning Disability Program

Special orientation for LD students: **Yes**
Program: Reinforces course work: **Yes**
Counseling: Individual: **Yes** Group Counseling: **Yes** Vocational Counseling: **Yes**
Support groups are available: **Yes**

Faculty:
Faculty: **10** Full time: **3** Part time: **7**
Faculty advocate: **Yes** Meets with instructor: **As needed**

Diagnostic Testing
ADD	Personality	Perceptual skills	Spelling
ADHD	Organization	Fine motor skills	Reading
I.Q.	Handwriting	Spoken language	Study skills
Math	Social skills	Written language	

Tutoring:
Average size of group tutorials: **2**
Services rendered by:
•Graduates •Peers •Faculty •LD staff Teacher trainees

Tutorials
Grp.	Ind.	Tutorials	Grp.	Ind.	Tutorials
•	•	Math skills	•	•	Word processing
•	•	Study skills	•	•	Time management
•	•	Language arts	•	•	Learning strategies
•	•	Written express	•	•	Organizational skills

Academic Accommodations

Curriculum	Study Aids	Exams
Priority registration	Typist	• Oral
Math waiver	Reader	• Untimed
• Foreign lang. waiver	• Notetaker	• Take home
• Course substitution	• Proof reader	• With proctor
In Class	• Text on tape	On computer
• Calculators	Early syllabus	• Extended time
• Tape recorder	Taped handouts	On tape
• Word processor		• Modified
• Priority seating		• Separate room

Graduation Requirements: GPA: **2.0** Language waiver: **Yes**

Program Strengths

Johnson and Wales University is dedicated to providing reasonable accommodation to allow learning disabled and other handicapped students to succeed in academic pursuits. While maintaining the highest academic integrity, the University strives to balance scholarship with support services which will assist special needs students to function in the post-secondary learning process.

General Information:

Johnson and Wales University is a 2 and 4 year private university. Urban campus . Housing is guaranteed. Guaranteed through 4th year.

Accreditation:

Expenses:
Tuition: In-state: Full year: $8,646.00. Room and board: $4,182.00

Majors

• BUSINESS Accounting, Banking, Business Administration, Business Education, Business Management, Entrepreneur, Finance, Food Management, Hotel and Restaurant Management, Investments and Securities, Management, Marketing, Retailing, Small Business Management, Travel/Tourism Management • COMMUNICATIONS Advertising, Public Relations • COMPUTER SCIENCE Computer Science, Data Processing, Programming • EDUCATION Industrial, Marketing and Distributive Education • ENGINEERING Electrical, Engineering Science • HEALTH SCIENCES Dental Assistant, Medical Assistant, Medical Secretary, Nursing Assistant • PREPROFESSIONAL Legal Assistant, Range Management • SCIENCES Equestrian Studies • SOCIAL SCIENCES Public Relations • VOCATIONAL Baking and Pastry Arts, Business and Office, Court Reporting, Culinary Arts, Dental Assistant, Drafting, Electronics Technology, Fashion

Merchandising, Food Service, Legal Secretary, Office Administration, Paralegal, Park/Recreation, Secretarial, Word Processing

Sports/Activities

• SPORTS-INTERCOLLEGIATE Horseback Riding, Ice Hockey, Soccer
• SPORTS-INTRAMURAL Basketball, Bowling, Ice Hockey, Ping-Pong, Racquetball, Skiing - Snow, Soccer, Softball, Swimming, Tennis, Volleyball • STUDENT LIFE ACTIVITIES Choral, Dance, Drama Groups, Fraternities, Newspaper, Preprofessional, Sororities, Student Government, Yearbook

Special	Rhode Island Services

Rhode Island School of Design

2 College Street
Providence, Rhode Island 02903
(401) 331-3511

School Enrollment: **1,800**
LD Enrollment: **30** Male: **15** Female: **15**

Admissions Contact: **Kevin Jankowski, Admissions Officer**
LD Contact: **Roberta McMann, V.P. for Student Affairs**
Telephone:**(401) 331-3511 x 274**

Admissions

Application Information:
Application deadline: **February 15th**
Notified when: **April 1st**

Secondary School Information
Most Important Criteria For Admissions (1-strongest)

3 SAT/ACT	**3** Application	**1** School transcript	
Class rank	**3** Course selection	Personal statement	
Interview	**4** Extra activities	Psychoeducational	
2 G.P.A.	Open admission	**4** Recommendations	

Types of Disabilities Served

Speech/Lang	Reading	ADD with LD
Study skills	Spelling	ADD without LD
Written express	Math	ADHD with LD
Organizational	Fine Motor	ADHD without LD
Perceptual		

Learning Disability Program
Counseling: Individual: **Yes**

Faculty:
Faculty: **1**

Diagnostic Testing

ADD	Personality	Perceptual skills	Spelling
ADHD	Organization	Fine motor skills	Reading
I.Q.	Handwriting	Spoken language	Study skills
Math	Social skills	Written language	

Tutoring:
Services rendered by:

Graduates	•Peers	Faculty	LD staff	Teacher trainees

Tutorials

Grp.	Ind.	Tutorials	Grp.	Ind.	Tutorials
		Math skills			Word processing
		Study skills			Time management
		Language arts			Learning strategies
		Written express			Organizational skills

Academic Accommodations

Curriculum	Study Aids	Exams
Priority registration	Typist	• Oral
Math waiver	Reader	Untimed
Foreign lang. waiver	• Notetaker	• Take home
• Course substitution	Proof reader	With proctor
In Class	• Text on tape	On computer
Calculators	Early syllabus	• Extended time
• Tape recorder	Taped handouts	On tape
Word processor		• Modified
Priority seating		Separate room

Program Strengths
Where such disability exists, it is important that educators at RISD develop a variety of evaluation procedures for students who are learning disabled or physically handicapped. Tutoring is available in subject areas.

General Information:
Rhode Island School of Design is a 4 year private college. Urban campus. Accessible by train or bus. 12% of students are foreign. Housing is guaranteed.

Accreditation: Regional

Expenses:
Tuition: In-state: Full year: $12,210.00. Room and board: $5,200.00

Majors
• COMMUNICATIONS Cinematography and Film, Photography
• CRAFTS AND DESIGN Ceramics, Glass, Graphic Design, Illustration Design, Industrial Design, Sculpture • PREPROFESSIONAL Architecture
• VOCATIONAL Fashion Design, Interior Design, Jewelry-Metalsmithery, Landscape Architecture, Painting, Printing/Lithography, Textile and Clothing

Sports/Activities
• SPORTS-INTERCOLLEGIATE Ice Hockey • SPORTS-INTRAMURAL Badminton, Baseball, Basketball, Sailing, Skiing - Snow, Swimming, Tennis, Volleyball • STUDENT LIFE ACTIVITIES Dance, Drama Groups, Film, Newspaper, Religious Organization, Student Government, Yearbook

Selective	Rhode Island SUPPORT

Roger Williams College

Ferry Road
Bristol, Rhode Island 02809
(401) 253-1967

School Enrollment: **2,170** Male: **1,193** Female: **977**

Admissions Contact: **Brian E. Davis, Asoc. Dir. Admissions Cord.**
Name of Program: **Academic Resources Center**
Telephone:**(401) 254-3219**

South Carolina

Admissions

Application Information:
Application deadline: **Rolling**

Secondary School Information
Most Important Criteria For Admissions (1-strongest)

4 SAT/ACT	Application	**1**	School transcript
3 Class rank	**3** Course selection		Personal statement
6 Interview	Extra activities		Psychoeducational
2 G.P.A.	Open admission	**5**	Recommendations

Test Requirements:
Untimed SAT: **Yes** Untimed ACT: **Yes**
Documentation of LD required: **Yes**

Types of Disabilities Served

Speech/Lang	Reading	ADD with LD
Study skills	Spelling	ADD without LD
Written express	Math	ADHD with LD
Organizational	Fine Motor	ADHD without LD
Perceptual		

High School Course Requirements:
English: **4** Math: **3** Science: **2**

Learning Disability Program
Services only for LD students: **Yes**

Faculty: Full time: **1**
LD faculty with: BS/BA: **1**
Faculty advocate: **Yes** Meets with instructor: **As needed**

Diagnostic Testing

ADD	Personality	Perceptual skills	Spelling
ADHD	Organization	Fine motor skills	Reading
I.Q.	Handwriting	Spoken language	Study skills
Math	Social skills	Written language	

Tutoring:
Services rendered by:

Graduates	•Peers	•Faculty	LD staff	Teacher trainees

Tutorials

Grp.	Ind.	Tutorials	Grp.	Ind.	Tutorials
		Math skills			Word processing
		Study skills			Time management
		Language arts			Learning strategies
		Written express			Organizational skills

Academic Accommodations

Curriculum	Study Aids	Exams
Priority registration	Typist	• Oral
Math waiver	• Reader	• Untimed
Foreign lang. waiver	• Notetaker	Take home
Course substitution	Proof reader	With proctor
In Class	• Text on tape	• On computer
• Calculators	Early syllabus	• Extended time
• Tape recorder	Taped handouts	On tape
• Word processor		• Modified
Priority seating		• Separate room

Program Strengths
We do not have an LD specialist and tutoring is free to all students.

General Information:
Roger Williams College is a 4 year private college. Rural campus of 80 acres is 12 miles from Providence. Accessible by air, train or bus. Ski areas are 3 hours from campus. Beaches are 1 minute from campus. 6% of students are foreign. 5 residential halls on campus. Housing is guaranteed. 60% of students remain on campus for the weekends.

Accreditation: NEACS

SAT/ACT Scores:
Scores for incoming freshmen: **Verbal:** 90% below 500. 5% between 500 and 599. 5% between 600 and 699. **Math:** 90% below 500. 5% between 500 and 599. 5% between 600 and 699.

Class Rank:
About 10% of the present freshmen class were in the upper 20% of their high school class. 40% were in the top 40% of their class. 80% were in the top 60% of their class. 90% were in the top 80% of their class.

Expenses:
Tuition: In-state: Full year: $8,800.00. Room and board: $4,400.00

Majors
• BUSINESS Accounting, Business Administration, Business Management, Finance, Management, Marketing • COMMUNICATIONS Communication, Creative Writing, English, Journalism • COMPUTER SCIENCE Computer Science, Programming • ENGINEERING Aerospace, Civil/Environmental, Electrical, Mechanical • HUMANITIES English/Writing/Literature, Humanities, Philosophy • PREPROFESSIONAL Architecture, Dentistry, Engineering, Law, Legal Assistant, Medicine, Veterinarian • SCIENCES Biology, Chemistry, Marine Biology, Mathematics • SOCIAL SCIENCES Criminal Justice, Government/Political, History, Law Enforcement, Political Science, Psychology, Public Relations, Social Sciences • VISUAL AND PERFORMING ARTS Art, Dance, Studio Art, Theater • VOCATIONAL Construction, Historic Preservation, Paralegal

Sports/Activities
• SPORTS RELATED Cheerleading • SPORTS-INTERCOLLEGIATE Baseball (M), Basketball, Golf, Horseback Riding, Ice Hockey (M), Lacrosse (M), Sailing, Soccer (M), Softball (F), Tennis, Volleyball • STUDENT LIFE ACTIVITIES Choral, Dance, Drama Groups, Ethnic & Cultural Groups, Magazine, Music Groups, Musical Theater, Newspaper, Radio/TV station, Religious Organization, Student Government, Yearbook

---

Less Selective   **South Carolina**
                                        Services

Central Wesleyan College
Central, South Carolina 29630-1020
(803)639-2453

School Enrollment: **415** Male: **195** Female: **220**

Admissions Contact: **Tim Wilkerson, Dean of Enrollment Mang.**
LD Contact: **Prof. Winnie Williams, Prof. of Special Education**
Name of Program: **LD Services**
Telephone: **(803)639-2453**

Admissions

Application Information:
Application deadline: **August 20th**
Rolling Admissions: **Yes**

672

Secondary School Information

Most Important Criteria For Admissions (1-strongest)

3 SAT/ACT	**6** Application	**5**	School transcript
2 Class rank	**11** Course selection	**7**	Personal statement
10 Interview	**8** Extra activities	**9**	Psychoeducational
1 G.P.A.	Open admission	**4**	Recommendations

Test Requirements:

Untimed SAT: **Yes** Untimed ACT: **Yes**
Range accepted: **Varies**
Documentation of LD required: **Yes**
Currency of diagnostic testing: **No deadline**

Types of Disabilities Served

- Speech/Lang
- Study skills
- Written express
- Organizational
- Perceptual
- Reading
- Spelling
- Math
- Fine Motor
- ADD with LD
- ADD without LD
- ADHD with LD
- ADHD without LD

Admissions Process

Admissions Committee reviews rank, SAT/ACT, academic, and GPA.

High School Course Requirements:

English: **4** Math: **2** Science: **2**

Learning Disability Program

Program: Remedial: **Yes**
Program: Reinforces course work: **Yes**
Students mainstreamed **100** % of the day
Recommended credits per semester: **12-14**
Counseling: Individual: **Yes** Group Counseling: **Yes** Vocational Counseling: **Yes**
Support groups are available:**Yes, through Freshman Seminar and groups gathered by coordinator of LD program**

Faculty:

Faculty: **1**
Faculty advocate: **Yes** Meets with instructor: **As needed**

Diagnostic Testing

ADD	• Personality	Perceptual skills	Spelling
ADHD	Organization	Fine motor skills	• Reading
• I.Q.	Handwriting	Spoken language	Study skills
• Math	Social skills	• Written language	

Tutoring:

Average size of group tutorials: **Individual**
Services rendered by:
Graduates •Peers •Faculty •LD staff •Teacher trainees

Tutorials

Grp. Ind. Tutorials	Grp. Ind. Tutorials
Math skills	Word processing
Study skills	Time management
Language arts	Learning strategies
Written express	Organizational skills

Academic Accommodations

Curriculum	Study Aids	Exams
Priority registration	Typist	• Oral
Math waiver	Reader	• Untimed
Foreign lang. waiver	Notetaker	Take home
Course substitution	Proof reader	With proctor
In Class	Text on tape	On computer
Calculators	Early syllabus	• Extended time
• Tape recorder	Taped handouts	On tape
Word processor		Modified
• Priority seating		Separate room

Graduation Requirements:

Course credits: **128** GPA: **2.0**
Other requirements: **Competency in English, math and reading**

Program Strengths

Christian college that gives a Christian perspective.

General Information:

Central Wesleyan College is a 4 year independent college. Rural campus of 140 acres is 25 miles from Greenville. Accessible by air, car, train or bus. Ski areas are 2.5 hours from campus. Beaches are 250 miles from campus. 3 residential halls on campus. Housing is not guaranteed.Guaranteed through 4th year.

Accreditation:SACS

SAT/ACT Scores:

Scores for incoming freshmen:**Verbal:**85.6%below 500. 10.1%between 500 and 599. 4.3%between 600 and 699. **Math:**75.5% below 500. 17.3% between 500 and 599. 7.2% between 600 and 699.

Expenses:

Tuition: In-state: Full year: $7,500.00. Part-time: Per credit:$250.00. Part-time: Per course: Varies. Tuition: Out-of-state: Full year: $7,500.00. Part-time: Per credit:$250.00. Part-time: Per course:Varies Room and board: $3,080.00 Cost of LD program:No charge except for tutoring

Majors

• ARTS Music, Religious Music • BUSINESS Accounting, Business Administration • EDUCATION Early Childhood, Elementary, English, Mathematics, Music, Physical, Recreation/Youth Leadership, Religious, Social Studies, Special • HEALTH SCIENCES Medical Laboratory Technology • HUMANITIES English/Writing/Literature, Religion • RELIGIOUS STUDIES Bible, Biblical Language, Ministry and Church Administrator, Religion & Theology, Religious Music • SCIENCES Biology, Chemistry • SOCIAL SCIENCES History, Psychology, Social Science • SPECIAL EDUCATION Learning Disability, Mentally Retarded • VISUAL AND PERFORMING ARTS Music

Sports/Activities

• SPORTS RELATED Cheerleading • SPORTS-INTERCOLLEGIATE Baseball (M), Baseball (M), Basketball (F), Golf (M), Soccer (F), Soccer (M), Volleyball (F) • SPORTS-INTRAMURAL Basketball (F), Basketball (M), Ping-Pong (F), Ping-Pong (M), Tennis (F), Tennis (M), Volleyball (F), Volleyball (M) • STUDENT LIFE ACTIVITIES Academic Clubs, Choral, Community Service, Drama Groups, Ethnic & Cultural Groups, Music Groups, Musical Theater, Political Groups, Religious Organization, Student Government, Yearbook

Less Selective

Services

Francis Marion College
P.O. Box F-7500
Florence, South Carolina 29501
(803) 661-1231

School Enrollment: **3,883**

Admissions Contact: **Marvin W. Lynch, Director of Admissions**
LD Contact: **Kenneth R. Dye, Dir. Guidance & Placement**
Name of Program: **Special Services**
Telephone:**(803) 661-1290**

Admissions

Application Information:
Application deadline: **August 10th**

Secondary School Information
Most Important Criteria For Admissions (1-strongest)

5 SAT/ACT	1 Application	2 School transcript
4 Class rank	3 Course selection	9 Personal statement
10 Interview	8 Extra activities	6 Psychoeducational
7 G.P.A.	Open admission	11 Recommendations

Test Requirements:
Untimed SAT: **Yes** Untimed ACT: **Yes**

Types of Disabilities Served
- Speech/Lang
- Study skills
- Written express
- Organizational
- Perceptual
- Reading
- Spelling
- Math
- Fine Motor
- ADD with LD
- ADD without LD
- ADHD with LD
- ADHD without LD

Faculty:
Faculty advocate: **Yes** Meets with instructor: **Each semester**

Diagnostic Testing

ADD	Personality	Perceptual skills	Spelling
ADHD	Organization	Fine motor skills	Reading
I.Q.	Handwriting	Spoken language	Study skills
Math	Social skills	Written language	

Services rendered by:

Graduates	Peers	Faculty	LD staff	Teacher trainees

Tutorials

Grp.	Ind.	Tutorials	Grp.	Ind.	Tutorials
		Math skills			Word processing
		Study skills			Time management
		Language arts			Learning strategies
		Written express			Organizational skills

Academic Accommodations

Curriculum	Study Aids	Exams
Priority registration	Typist	• Oral
Math waiver	Reader	Untimed
Foreign lang. waiver	• Notetaker	• Take home
Course substitution	Proof reader	With proctor
In Class		On computer
Calculators	• Text on tape	• Extended time
• Tape recorder	Early syllabus	On tape
• Word processor	Taped handouts	Modified
Priority seating		Separate room

Program Strengths
Our college offers special services, not a program. Each applicant with special needs should apply, and each situation is considered on an individual basis.

General Information:
Francis Marion College is a 4 year public college. Rural campus of 350 acres is 8 miles from Florence. Accessible by air, train, or bus. Ski areas are 5 hours from campus. Beaches are 1 hour from campus. 1% of students are foreign. 3 residential halls on campus. Housing is not guaranteed.20 % of students remain on campus for the weekends. 10 % of students join fraternities/sororities.

Accreditation:SACS

Expenses:
Tuition: In-state: Full year: Approximately $1,800.00. Tuition: Out-of-state: Full year: Approximately $3,600.00. Room and board: $1,335.00-$2,270.00

Majors
• BUSINESS Banking, Business Administration, Business Economics, Business Management, Economics, Finance, Management, Marketing • COMMUNICATIONS Communication, English • COMPUTER SCIENCE Computer Science, Programming, Systems Analysis • EDUCATION Early Childhood, Elementary, Pre-Education, Secondary • ENGINEERING Civil/Environmental • HEALTH SCIENCES Medical Technology • HUMANITIES Liberal Arts, Philosophy, Religion • LANGUAGES French, Spanish • PREPROFESSIONAL Dentistry, Engineering, Forestry, Law, Medicine, Pharmacy • SCIENCES Biology, Chemistry, Geography, Health Physics, Mathematics, Physics • SOCIAL SCIENCES Government/Political, History, Political Science, Psychology, Sociology • VISUAL AND PERFORMING ARTS Art, Dance, Fine Arts, Theater • VOCATIONAL Electronics Technology, Forestry

Sports/Activities
• SPORTS RELATED Cheerleading, Team Managers • SPORTS-INTERCOLLEGIATE Baseball (M), Basketball, Cross Country (M), Golf (M), Soccer (M), Softball (F), Tennis, Track and Field (M), Volleyball (F) • SPORTS-INTRAMURAL Basketball, Bowling, Diving, Ping-Pong, Racquetball, Softball, Swimming, Tennis, Track and Field, Volleyball • STUDENT LIFE ACTIVITIES Choral, Drama Groups, Ethnic & Cultural Groups, Fraternities, Music Groups, Newspaper, Political Groups, Religious Organization, Sororities, Student Government, Yearbook

Less Selective   **South Carolina Program**

Midlands Technical College
P. O. Box 2408
Columbia, South Carolina 29202
(803) 738-1400

School Enrollment: **6,848**
LD Enrollment: **8**

Admissions Contact: **Richard Tinneny, Director of Admissions**
LD Contact: **Dr. Willie Long, Counselor**
Name of Program: **Disabled Services**
Telephone:**(803) 738-7678**

Admissions

Application Information:
Application deadline: **September 1st**
Applicant must apply **1** months in advance
Rolling Admissions: **Yes**

Secondary School Information
Most Important Criteria For Admissions (1-strongest)

1	SAT/ACT	**1**	Application	**1**	School transcript
	Class rank	**1**	Course selection		Personal statement
1	Interview		Extra activities		Psychoeducational
	G.P.A.	**1**	Open admission	**1**	Recommendations

Test Requirements:
Documentation of LD required: **Yes**

Types of Disabilities Served
- Speech/Lang
- Study skills
- Written express
- Organizational
- Perceptual
- Reading
- Spelling
- Math
- Fine Motor

ADD with LD
ADD without LD
ADHD with LD
ADHD without LD

Learning Disability Program

Program: Reinforces course work: **Yes**
Students mainstreamed **100** % of the day

Faculty:
Faculty: **3** Including Director: **Yes** Full time: **3**

Diagnostic Testing

	ADD	Personality	Perceptual skills
	ADHD	Organization	Fine motor skills
•	I.Q.	Handwriting	Spoken language
•	Math	Social skills	Written language

- Spelling
- Reading
- Study skills

Tutoring:
Average size of group tutorials: **1 on 1**
Services rendered by:
Graduates   •Peers   •Faculty   LD staff   Teacher trainees

Tutorials

Grp.	Ind.	Tutorials	Grp.	Ind.	Tutorials
•	•	Math skills	•	•	Word processing
•	•	Study skills	•	•	Time management
•	•	Language arts	•	•	Learning strategies
•	•	Written express	•	•	Organizational skills

Academic Accommodations

Curriculum	Study Aids	Exams
• Priority registration	• Typist	• Oral
• Math waiver	• Reader	• Untimed
• Foreign lang. waiver	• Notetaker	• Take home
• Course substitution	• Proof reader	• With proctor
In Class	• Text on tape	• On computer
• Calculators	• Early syllabus	• Extended time
• Tape recorder	• Taped handouts	• On tape
• Word processor		• Modified
Priority seating		• Separate room

Graduation Requirements: GPA: **2.0** Years to complete degree: **Indefinite**

Program Strengths
Tutoring is offered according to student's needs.

General Information:
Midlands Technical College is a 2 year public college. Urban campus of 114 acres is Accessible by air or bus. Beaches are 2.5 from campus. Housing is not guaranteed.

Accreditation: SACS

Expenses:
Tuition: In-state: Full year: $1,238.00. Part-time: Per credit:$52.00. Tuition: Out-of-state: Full year: $1,980.00. Part-time: Per credit:$83.00.

Majors
• BUSINESS Accounting, Business Administration, Business Management, Management, Marketing • COMPUTER SCIENCE Computer Graphics, Data Processing, Medical Records Technology, Telecommunications • HEALTH SCIENCES Dental Hygiene, Health, Medical Secretary, Nuclear Medicine, Nursing, Radiological Therapy, Surgical Technology • HUMANITIES Liberal Arts • PREPROFESSIONAL Engineering, Law, Pharmacy, Social Work • SCIENCES Radiology • SOCIAL SCIENCES Criminal Justice • VOCATIONAL Automotive Service, Diesel Power Technology, Electronics Technology, Machinist, Respiratory Therapy Technology, Secretarial

Sports/Activities
• SPORTS-INTERCOLLEGIATE Football, Softball, Volleyball • STUDENT LIFE ACTIVITIES Ethnic & Cultural Groups, Newspaper, Student Government

Selective

South Carolina Services

University of South Carolina
1625 College Street
Columbia, South Carolina 29208
(803) 777-7700

School Enrollment: **26,133** Male: **11,723** Female: **14,410**
LD Enrollment: **55** Male: **38** Female: **17**

Admissions Contact: **Rosvelt Martain, Assistant Dean**
LD Contact: **Debbie Haynes, Dir., Academic Support Services**
Name of Program: **Learning Disability Program**
Address: **1625 College St., Columbia, SC 29208**
Telephone:**(803) 777-6142/0742**

Admissions

Application Information:
Enrolled:**55**
Application deadline: **Nov. 1st & May 1st**
Applicant must apply **3** months in advance
Rolling Admissions: **Yes**

Secondary School Information
Most Important Criteria For Admissions (1-strongest)

2	SAT/ACT	Application	**1** School transcript
1	Class rank	**4** Course selection	Personal statement
	Interview	Extra activities	Psychoeducational
3	G.P.A.	Open admission	Recommendations

Test Requirements:
Diagnostic testing waived: **Yes**
Untimed SAT: **Yes** Untimed ACT: **Yes**
Documentation of LD required: **Yes**
Tests recommended: **None specified**

Types of Disabilities Served
- Speech/Lang
- Study skills
- Written express
- Organizational
- Perceptual
- Reading
- Spelling
- Math
- Fine Motor
- ADD with LD
- ADD without LD
- ADHD with LD
- ADHD without LD

High School Course Requirements:
English: **4** Math: **3** Science: **2** Foreign Language: **2**
Waivers to standard high school courses
Foreign Language : **Yes** Math: **Yes** Course substitution: **Yes**

Learning Disability Program
Program: Reinforces course work: **Yes**
Students mainstreamed **100** % of the day
Recommended credits per semester: **Varies**
Services available for all students: **Yes**
Counseling: Individual: **Yes**
Support groups are available:**Yes**

Faculty:
Faculty: **11** Including Director: **Yes** Full time: **5** Part time: **6**
LD faculty with: BS/BA: **11** M.A.: **4** Ph.D.: **1**
Faculty advocate: **Yes** Meets with instructor: **As needed**

Diagnostic Testing
- ADD
- ADHD
- I.Q.
- Math
- Personality
- Organization
- Handwriting
- Social skills
- Perceptual skills
- Fine motor skills
- Spoken language
- Written language
- Spelling
- Reading
- Study skills

Tutoring:
Services rendered by:
- Graduates   Peers   Faculty   •LD staff   Teacher trainees

Tutorials

Grp.	Ind.	Tutorials	Grp.	Ind.	Tutorials
	•	Math skills			Word processing
	•	Study skills		•	Time management
	•	Language arts			Learning strategies
	•	Written express		•	Organizational skills

Academic Accommodations

Curriculum	Study Aids	Exams
• Priority registration	Typist	• Oral
• Math waiver	• Reader	• Untimed
• Foreign lang. waiver	• Notetaker	Take home
Course substitution	Proof reader	• With proctor
In Class	• Text on tape	On computer
Calculators	Early syllabus	• Extended time
• Tape recorder	Taped handouts	On tape
Word processor		• Modified
• Priority seating		• Separate room

Graduation Requirements:
Course credits: **120+** GPA: **2.0** Years to complete degree: **4+** Math waiver: **Yes** Language waiver: **Yes**

General Information:
University of South Carolina is a 4 year public university. Urban campus of 120 acres is 300 miles from Atlanta. Accessible by air, bus, or train. Ski areas are 3-4 hours from campus. Beaches are 3-4 hours from campus. 5% of students are foreign. 23 residential halls on campus. Housing is not guaranteed.

Accreditation:SACS

SAT/ACT Scores:
Scores for incoming freshmen:**Verbal:**72%below 500. 22%between 500 and 599. 5%between 600 and 699. 1%above 700. **Math:**47% below 500. 36% between 500 and 599. 14% between 600 and 699. 2%above 700.

Class Rank:
About 46% of the present freshmen class were in the upper 20% of their high school class. 79% were in the top 40% of their class. 95% were in the top 60% of their class. 100% were in the top 80% of their class.

Expenses:
Tuition: In-state: Full year: $2,686.00. Part-time: Per credit:$120.00. Tuition: Out-of-state: Full year: $6,716.00. Part-time: Per credit:$291.00.
Room and board: $3,066.00

Majors
• AREA STUDIES Black/Afro-American, International Studies, Latin American, Women's Studies • ARTS Art History, Dance, Dramatic Arts, Drawing, Film & Video, Interior Design, Music, Music History, Music Performance, Painting, Photography, Sculpture • BUSINESS Accounting, Banking/Finance, Business Administration, Business Economics, Business Education, Business Management, Economics, Hotel & Restaurant Management, Insurance, Investments and Securities, Management, Marketing, Personnel, Real Estate, Retailing, Secretarial Science, Sports Management, Taxation, Travel/Tourism Management • COMMUNICATIONS Advertising, Broadcasting, English, Journalism, Literature, Public Relations, Tele-

vision/Radio/Film • COMPUTER SCIENCE Computer Science • EDUCATION Art, Business, Child Development, Early Childhood, Elementary, English, Foreign Language, Health, Mathematics, Middle School, Music, Physical, Psychology, School Psychology, Science, Secondary, Social Studies • ENGINEERING Chemical, Civil/Environmental, Electrical, Mechanical • HEALTH SCIENCES Health, Nursing, Pharmacology • HUMANITIES Classics, English/Writing/Literature, Fine Arts • LANGUAGES English, French, German, Italian, Latin, Spanish • SCIENCES Anthropology, Applied Mathematics, Astronomy, Biology, Chemistry, Computer Science, Geography, Geology, Marine Biology, Mathematics, Physics, Statistics • SOCIAL SCIENCES Anthropology, Criminal Justice, Geography, Government/Political, History, International Studies, Political Science, Psychology, Sociology • VISUAL AND PERFORMING ARTS Art, Art History, Dance, Dramatic Arts, Music, Music Performance, Studio Art, Theater

Sports/Activities

• SPORTS RELATED Cheerleading, Drill Team, Drum Major/Majorette, Marching Band, Pep Band, Team Managers • SPORTS-INTERCOLLEGIATE Baseball (M), Basketball (F), Basketball (M), Cross Country (F), Cross Country (M), Diving (F), Diving (M), Football (M), Golf (F), Golf (M), Soccer (M), Softball (F), Swimming (F), Swimming (M), Tennis (F), Tennis (M), Track and Field (F), Track and Field (M), Volleyball (F) • SPORTS-INTRAMURAL Badminton, Badminton (F), Badminton (M), Baseball (M), Basketball, Basketball (F), Basketball (M), Bowling, Bowling (F), Bowling (M), Fencing, Football, Flag, Golf (F), Golf (M), Martial Arts, Ping-Pong, Ping-Pong (F), Ping-Pong (M), Racquetball (F), Racquetball (M), Rugby, Scuba, Soccer, Soccer (F), Soccer (M), Softball, Softball (F), Softball (M), Swimming (F), Swimming (M), Tennis (F), Tennis (M), Track and Field, Track and Field (F), Track and Field (M), Volleyball, Volleyball (F), Volleyball (M), Wrestling (M) • STUDENT LIFE ACTIVITIES Academic Clubs, Choral, Community Service, Concert Band, Dance, Debate, Drama Groups, Ethnic & Cultural Groups, Fraternities, Jazz Band, Magazine, Music Groups, Newspaper, Political Groups, Radio/TV station, Religious Organization, Sororities, Student Government, Symphony Orchestra, Yearbook

Less Selective	South Dakota Program

Black Hills State College
Room J110 Jonas Hall
Spearfish, South Dakota 57799
(800) 255-2478

School Enrollment: **2,412** Male: **950** Female: **1,462**
LD Enrollment: **10**

Admissions Contact: **Diana Bercier Koch, Dir. of Admissions**
LD Contact: **Betty Marie Anderson, Director**
Name of Program: **Academic Skill Center**
Telephone:**(605) 642-6259**

Admissions

Application Information:
Application deadline: **September**
Rolling Admissions: **Yes** Notified when: **2 weeks**

Secondary School Information
Most Important Criteria For Admissions (1-strongest)

1 SAT/ACT	**5** Application	**4** School transcript
2 Class rank	**6** Course selection	**11** Personal statement
8 Interview	**9** Extra activities	**10** Psychoeducational
3 G.P.A.	Open admission	**7** Recommendations

Types of Disabilities Served
- Speech/Lang
- Reading
- ADD with LD
- Study skills
- Spelling
- ADD without LD
- Written express
- Math
- ADHD with LD
- Organizational
- Fine Motor
- ADHD without LD
- Perceptual

Learning Disability Program
Program: Reinforces course work: **Yes**
Students mainstreamed **100** % of the day

Faculty:
Faculty: **23** Including Director: **Yes** Full time: **1** Part time: **22**

Diagnostic Testing
ADD	Personality	Perceptual skills	Spelling
ADHD	Organization	Fine motor skills	Reading
I.Q.	Handwriting	Spoken language	Study skills
Math	Social skills	Written language	

Tutoring:
Services rendered by:
Graduates   •Peers   Faculty   •LD staff   Teacher trainees

Tutorials
Grp.	Ind.	Tutorials	Grp.	Ind.	Tutorials
•	•	Math skills		•	Word processing
•	•	Study skills	•	•	Time management
•	•	Language arts	•	•	Learning strategies
•	•	Written express	•	•	Organizational skills

Academic Accommodations
Curriculum	Study Aids	Exams
Priority registration	Typist	• Oral
Math waiver	Reader	Untimed
Foreign lang. waiver	• Notetaker	Take home
Course substitution	• Proof reader	With proctor
In Class	Text on tape	On computer
Calculators	Early syllabus	• Extended time
• Tape recorder	Taped handouts	On tape
Word processor		• Modified
Priority seating		Separate room

Program Strengths
We work with and support all students. We have about 10 LD students now, however our students' grades range from 3.2 - 1.00. We work with all students to meet their academic goals. We are locally funded (students' fees). We welcome LD students, but they must take the same courses as others. Our service is supportive, our faculty cooperative, but we have no special technical aids. We assist students on an individual basis.

General Information:
Black Hills State College is a 4 year public university. Rural campus of 123 acres is 45 miles from Rapid City. Accessible by bus. Ski areas are 30 miles from campus. 2% of students are foreign. 5 residential halls on campus. Housing is not guaranteed.25 % of students remain on campus for the weekends. 5 % of students join fraternities/sororities.

Accreditation:NCACS, NCATE

SAT/ACT Scores:
Scores for incoming freshmen: **ACT:** 30% below 20. 25% between 20 and 23. 20%between 24 and 25l. 15%between 26 and 28. 10% above 28.

South Dakota

Class Rank:
About 10% of the present freshmen class were in the upper 20% of their high school class. 35% were in the top 40% of their class. 75% were in the top 60% of their class. 100% were in the top 80% of their class.

Expenses:
Tuition: In-state: Full year: $600.00. Part-time: Per credit:$38.05. Tuition: Out-of-state: Full year: $1,280.00. Part-time: Per credit:$80.05. Room and board: $1,030.00

Majors

• AREA STUDIES American • BUSINESS Accounting, Business Administration, Business Education, Business Management, Economics, Hotel and Restaurant Management, Management, Sports Management, Travel/Tourism Management • COMMUNICATIONS Communication, English, Graphic Design, Journalism, Photography, Speech, Television/Radio/Film • COMPUTER SCIENCE Data Processing, Programming • EDUCATION Art, Curriculum, Early Childhood, Elementary, English, Industrial, Mathematics, Middle School, Music, Physical, Pre-Education, Recreation and Youth Leadership, Remedial, Science, Secondary, Social Science, Social Studies, Speech/Language, Teacher Aide • ENGINEERING Electrical • HEALTH SCIENCES Dental Hygiene, Health, Medical Assistant, Medical Secretary, Medical Technology, Physical Therapy, Practical Nursing • HUMANITIES English/Writing/Literature, Humanities, Liberal Arts • PREPROFESSIONAL Architecture, Dentistry, Forestry, Law, Medicine, Pharmacy, Recreation, Social Work, Veterinarian • SCIENCES Biology, Botany, Chemistry, Earth, Geography, Gerontology, Mathematics, Physical Science, Physics, Zoology • SOCIAL SCIENCES Criminal Justice, Government/Political, History, Human Service, Law Enforcement, Library Science, Political Science, Psychology, Social Sciences, Sociology • VISUAL AND PERFORMING ARTS Art, Dramatic Arts, Music, Studio Art, Theater, Theater Design • VOCATIONAL Business and Office, Construction, Drafting, Legal Secretary, Painting, Park/Recreation, Radiological Technology, Secretarial, Woodworking

Sports/Activities

• SPORTS RELATED Cheerleading, Pep Band • SPORTS-INTERCOLLEGIATE Basketball, Cross Country, Football (M), Track and Field, Volleyball (F), Wrestling (M) • SPORTS-INTRAMURAL Archery, Badminton, Basketball, Bowling, Golf, Gymnastics, Ping-Pong, Racquetball, Skiing - Snow, Soccer, Softball, Swimming, Tennis, Volleyball, Wrestling (M) • STUDENT LIFE ACTIVITIES Choral, Concert Band, Dance, Debate, Drama Groups, Ethnic & Cultural Groups, Fraternities, Jazz Band, Magazine, Music Groups, Musical Theater, Newspaper, Political Groups, Radio/TV station, Religious Organization, Sororities, Student Government, Yearbook

Less Selective

South Dakota

Huron University
333 9th Street Southwest
Huron, South Dakota 57350
(605) 352-8721

School Enrollment: **510**

Admissions Contact: **Monica Wepking, Director of Admissions**
LD Contact: **Gretchen Rich, Director**
Name of Program: **Learning Center**

Admissions

Application Information:
Application deadline: **Open**

Secondary School Information
Most Important Criteria For Admissions (1-strongest)

10 SAT/ACT	**11** Application	**1**	School transcript
9 Class rank	**3** Course selection	**7**	Personal statement
5 Interview	**4** Extra activities	**6**	Psychoeducational
2 G.P.A.	Open admission	**8**	Recommendations

Test Requirements:
Documentation of LD required: **Yes**

Types of Disabilities Served
• Speech/Lang	• Reading	ADD with LD
• Study skills	• Spelling	ADD without LD
• Written express	• Math	ADHD with LD
• Organizational	Fine Motor	ADHD without LD
• Perceptual		

Learning Disability Program
Counseling: Individual: **Yes**

Faculty:
Faculty: **1** Full time: **1**

Diagnostic Testing
ADD	Personality	Perceptual skills	Spelling
ADHD	Organization	Fine motor skills	Reading
I.Q.	Handwriting	Spoken language	Study skills
Math	Social skills	Written language	

Tutoring:
Average size of group tutorials: **2-5**
Services rendered by:
Graduates •Peers •Faculty LD staff Teacher trainees

Tutorials
Grp.	Ind.	Tutorials	Grp.	Ind.	Tutorials
•	•	Math skills	•	•	Word processing
•		Study skills			Time management
•	•	Language arts	•	•	Learning strategies
•	•	Written express	•	•	Organizational skills

Academic Accommodations

Curriculum	Study Aids	Exams
Priority registration	• Typist	• Oral
Math waiver	Reader	Untimed
• Foreign lang. waiver	• Notetaker	• Take home
• Course substitution	• Proof reader	With proctor
In Class	Text on tape	On computer
• Calculators	Early syllabus	• Extended time
• Tape recorder	Taped handouts	On tape
• Word processor		• Modified
Priority seating		Separate room

Program Strengths
Our program is best described as developmental learning. We use peer tutors to aid those who need it and we work on a referral basis with the other instructors.

General Information:
Huron University is a 2 and 4 year private university. Rural campus of 1 acres is 150 miles from Sioux Falls. Accessible by air or bus. Ski areas are 400 miles from campus. Beaches are 20 miles from campus. 1% of students are foreign. 2 residential halls on campus. Housing is guaranteed.Guaranteed through 4th year. 30 % of students remain on campus for the weekends.

Accreditation:NCACS

SAT/ACT Scores:

Scores for incoming freshmen: **ACT:** 30% below 20. 20% between 20 and 23. 10%between 24 and 25l. 10%between 26 and 28.

Class Rank:

About 10% of the present freshmen class were in the upper 20% of their high school class. 30% were in the top 40% of their class. 50% were in the top 60% of their class. 80% were in the top 80% of their class.

Expenses:

Tuition: In-state: Full year: $5,775.00. Part-time: Per credit:$160.00. Tuition: Out-of-state: Full year: $5,775.00. Part-time: Per credit:$160.00. Room and board: $2,816.00.

Majors

• BUSINESS Accounting, Business Administration, Business Economics, Business Education, Business Management, Economics, Hotel and Restaurant Management, Management, Marketing, Travel/Tourism Management • COMMUNICATIONS Communication, Creative Writing, English, Journalism • COMPUTER SCIENCE Data Processing, Programming • EDUCATION Elementary, Health, Middle School, Physical, Secondary, Social Science • HEALTH SCIENCES Health, Medical Technology, Nursing, Nutritional/Food • HUMANITIES Liberal Arts • LANGUAGES Spanish • PREPROFESSIONAL Dentistry, Engineering, Law, Medicine, Pharmacy, Social Work • SCIENCES Biology, Chemistry, Earth • SOCIAL SCIENCES Criminal Justice, History, Human Service, Law Enforcement, Public Relations, Social Sciences • VOCATIONAL Business and Office, Secretarial, Word Processing

Sports/Activities

• SPORTS RELATED Cheerleading • SPORTS-INTERCOLLEGIATE Basketball, Football (M), Golf, Tennis, Track and Field, Volleyball (F), Wrestling (M) • SPORTS-INTRAMURAL Basketball, Ping-Pong, Softball, Swimming • STUDENT LIFE ACTIVITIES Drama Groups, Ethnic & Cultural Groups, Music Groups, Newspaper, Religious Organization, Student Government, Symphony Orchestra

---

Less Selective   **South Dakota**
                                             Program

Northern State University

Aberdeen, South Dakota 57401
(605) 622-2544

School Enrollment: **3,100** Male: **1,800** Female: **1,300**

Admissions Contact: **Barry Samsula, Director of Admissions**
LD Contact: **Ellen Engelhart, Coordinator**
Name of Program: **Learning Disabilities**
Telephone:**(605) 662-7717**

Admissions

Application Information:
Application deadline: **August 15th**
Rolling Admissions: **Yes**

Secondary School Information
Most Important Criteria For Admissions (1-strongest)

SAT/ACT **1**	Application **2**	School transcript
4 Class rank	Course selection	Personal statement
Interview	Extra activities	Psychoeducational
3 G.P.A.	Open admission	Recommendations

Types of Disabilities Served

Speech/Lang	Reading	ADD with LD
Study skills	Spelling	ADD without LD
Written express	Math	ADHD with LD
Organizational	Fine Motor	ADHD without LD
Perceptual		

Learning Disability Program

Program: Remedial: **Yes**
Program: Reinforces course work: **Yes**
Students mainstreamed **100** % of the day
Counseling: Individual: **Yes**

Faculty:
Faculty: **2** Full time: **1** Part time: **1** M.A.: **2**
Faculty advocate: **Yes** Meets with instructor: **As needed**

Diagnostic Testing

ADD •	Personality •	Perceptual skills •	Spelling
ADHD	Organization•	Fine motor skills •	Reading
• I.Q.	• Handwriting•	Spoken language	• Study skills
• Math	• Social skills•	Written language	

Tutoring:
Average size of group tutorials: **2-5**
Services rendered by:
•Graduates   Peers   •Faculty   •LD staff   Teacher trainees

Tutorials

Grp.	Ind.	Tutorials	Grp.	Ind.	Tutorials
	•	Math skills			Word processing
		Study skills			Time management
	•	Language arts		•	Learning strategies
	•	Written express		•	Organizational skills

Academic Accommodations

Curriculum	Study Aids	Exams
Priority registration	Typist	• Oral
Math waiver	Reader	Untimed
Foreign lang. waiver	• Notetaker	• Take home
• Course substitution	• Proof reader	With proctor
In Class	• Text on tape	On computer
• Calculators	Early syllabus	• Extended time
• Tape recorder	Taped handouts	On tape
• Word processor		• Modified
Priority seating		Separate room

Program Strengths

Our program at Northern State University is trying to refine a program for identifying such students. The faculty has been very helpful in the referral process. Services that have been incorporated are: tutoring, counseling, individual conferences with instructors, talking books, use of Reading Lab and Writing Lab, and instructional and test taking modifications. This is our first year and we are happy that the college will see the benefit of the program and include funding for next year.

General Information:

Northern State University is a 4 year public university. Urban campus of 52 acres is Accessible by air or bus. Ski areas are 170 miles from campus. Beaches are 1/2 mile from campus. 1% of students are foreign. 6 residential halls on campus. Housing is guaranteed.Guaranteed through 4th year. 50 % of students remain on campus for the weekends. 10 % of students join fraternities/sororities.

South Dakota

Accreditation: AACSB, NASM, NCATE

SAT/ACT Scores:
Scores for incoming freshmen: **ACT:** 58% below 20. 15% between 20 and 23. 9% between 24 and 25l. 6% between 26 and 28. 2% above 28.

Expenses:
Tuition: In-state: Full year: $1,088.00. Tuition: Out-of-state: Full year: $2,300.00. Room and board: $1,780.00

Majors

• BUSINESS Accounting, Banking, Business Administration, Business Economics, Business Education, Business Management, Economics, Finance, Management, Marketing • COMMUNICATIONS English, Journalism • COMPUTER SCIENCE Data Processing • EDUCATION Art, Early Childhood, Elementary, English, Foreign Language, Health, Industrial, Mathematics, Middle School, Music, Physical, Science, Secondary, Social Science, Social Studies, Special, Speech/Language • ENGINEERING Industrial • HEALTH SCIENCES Communication Disorders, Environmental, Health, Medical Technology, Nursing, Occupational Therapy, Physical Therapy, Speech Therapy, Speech/Audiology and Speech • HUMANITIES Humanities, Liberal Arts, Philosophy • LANGUAGES French, German, Spanish • PREPROFESSIONAL Architecture, Dentistry, Engineering, Law, Medicine, Recreation, Social Work • SCIENCES Biology, Chemistry, Mathematics, Physical Science, Physics • SOCIAL SCIENCES Community Service, Criminal Justice, Government/Political, History, Library Science, Political Science, Psychology, Public Relations, Social Sciences, Sociology • VISUAL AND PERFORMING ARTS Art, Dance, Fine Arts, Music • VOCATIONAL Drafting, Secretarial

Sports/Activities

• SPORTS RELATED Cheerleading, Marching Band, Pep Band, Team Managers • SPORTS-INTERCOLLEGIATE Baseball (M), Basketball, Cross Country, Football (M), Golf, Softball (F), Tennis, Track and Field, Volleyball (F), Wrestling (M) • SPORTS-INTRAMURAL Badminton, Baseball (M), Bowling, Racquetball, Softball (F), Tennis, Volleyball • STUDENT LIFE ACTIVITIES Choral, Concert Band, Debate, Drama Groups, Ethnic & Cultural Groups, Jazz Band, Music Groups, Musical Theater, Newspaper, Political Groups, Radio/TV station, Religious Organization, Student Government, Symphony Orchestra, Yearbook

---

Selective   **South Dakota Program**

South Dakota State University
Administration 200
Brookings, South Dakota 57007
(605) 688-4121

School Enrollment: **6,283** Male: **3,141** Female: **3,142**
LD Enrollment: **17** Male: **10** Female: **7**

Admissions Contact: **Lori Cook, Admissions Counselor**
LD Contact: **James Carlson, Coordinator**
Name of Program: **Disabled Student Services**
Address: **Administration Building #318**
Telephone: **(605) 688-4496**

Admissions

Application Information:
Application deadline: **August 1, December 1**
Applicant must apply **6** months in advance
Rolling Admissions: **Yes** Notified when: **Within 2 weeks**

Secondary School Information
Most Important Criteria For Admissions (1-strongest)

SAT/ACT **3**	Application **1**	School transcript
2 Class rank	Course selection **5**	Personal statement
6 Interview	**4** Extra activities	Psychoeducational
1 G.P.A.	Open admission **7**	Recommendations

Test Requirements:
Documentation of LD required: **Yes**

Types of Disabilities Served
- Speech/Lang
- Study skills
- Written express
- Organizational
- Perceptual
- Reading
- Spelling
- Math
- Fine Motor
- ADD with LD
- ADD without LD
- ADHD with LD
- ADHD without LD

Learning Disability Program
Program: Reinforces course work: **Yes**
Students mainstreamed **100** % of the day
Services available for all students: **Yes**
Counseling: Individual: **Yes** Group Counseling: **Yes**
Support groups are available: **Yes**

Faculty:
Faculty: **2** Full time: **1** Part time: **1**
LD faculty with: BS/BA: **2**
Faculty advocate: **Yes** Meets with instructor: **As needed**

Diagnostic Testing
ADD	Personality	Perceptual skills	Spelling
ADHD	Organization	Fine motor skills	Reading
I.Q.	Handwriting	Spoken language	Study skills
Math	Social skills	Written language	

Tutoring:
Services rendered by:
• Graduates   • Peers   • Faculty   LD staff   • Teacher trainees

Tutorials
Grp.	Ind.	Tutorials	Grp.	Ind.	Tutorials
	•	Math skills		•	Word processing
	•	Study skills		•	Time management
	•	Language arts		•	Learning strategies
	•	Written express		•	Organizational skills

Academic Accommodations

Curriculum	Study Aids	Exams
• Priority registration	• Typist	• Oral
• Math waiver	• Reader	• Untimed
• Foreign lang. waiver	• Notetaker	• Take home
• Course substitution	• Proof reader	• With proctor
In Class	• Text on tape	• On computer
• Calculators	• Early syllabus	• Extended time
• Tape recorder	• Taped handouts	• On tape
• Word processor		• Modified
• Priority seating		• Separate room

Graduation Requirements:
Course credits: **128** GPA: **2.0**

Program Strengths

The uniqueness of the program is that it is brand new and that we are trying to develop the curriculum. Presently we are on a limited budget and hopefully, with hard work and the receiving of grant money, our program will expand substantially to better accommodate persons with learning disabilities as well as all disabilities. Persons with learning disabilities are one of our primary concerns as they make up the largest percentage of disabled students on campus.

General Information:

South Dakota State University is a 4 year public university. Rural campus of 220 acres is 50 miles from Sioux Falls. Accessible by bus. Ski areas are 350 miles from campus. 3% of students are foreign. 8 residential halls on campus. Housing is guaranteed.5 % of students join fraternities/sororities.

Accreditation:NCACS

SAT/ACT Scores:
Scores for incoming freshmen: **ACT:** 36% below 20. 30% between 20 and 23. 15%between 24 and 251. 14%between 26 and 28. 4% above 28.

Class Rank:
About 35% of the present freshmen class were in the upper 20% of their high school class. 65% were in the top 40% of their class. 90% were in the top 60% of their class. 100% were in the top 80% of their class.

Expenses:
Tuition: In-state: Full year: $1,200.00. Part-time: Per credit:$60.15. Tuition: Out-of-state: Full year: $2,700.00. Part-time: Per credit:$108.00. Room and board: $1,700.00

Majors

• BUSINESS Agricultural, Business Economics, Economics, Hotel and Restaurant Management • COMMUNICATIONS Advertising, Communication, English, Graphic Design, Journalism, Speech, Television/Radio/Film • COMPUTER SCIENCE Computer Science • EDUCATION Art, Child Development, Early Childhood, Elementary, English, Foreign Language, Health, Mathematics, Middle School, Music, Physical, Pre-Education, Secondary, Social Science, Social Studies, Speech/Language, Technical • ENGINEERING Agricultural, Civil/Environmental, Electrical, Engineering Science, Mechanical, Physics • HEALTH SCIENCES Environmental, Medical Technology, Nursing, Nutritional/Food, Speech Therapy, Speech/Audiology and Speech • HUMANITIES Liberal Arts • LANGUAGES French, German, Spanish • PREPROFESSIONAL Architecture, Dentistry, Law, Medicine, Ministry, Natural Resources, Pharmacy, Range Management, Sports Medicine, Veterinarian, Wildlife • SCIENCES Agricultural, Agronomy, Animal, Biology, Botany, Chemistry, Dairy, Ecology, Geography, Horticultural, Mathematics, Microbiology, Physics, Plant Sciences, Soil, Zoology • SOCIAL SCIENCES Family Counseling, Geography, History, Political Science, Psychology, Social Sciences, Sociology • VISUAL AND PERFORMING ARTS Art, Music, Music Performance, Theater • VOCATIONAL Electronics Technology, Fashion Design, Fishery Studies, Home Economics, Interior Design, Landscape Architecture, Park/Recreation, Textile and Clothing

Sports/Activities

• SPORTS RELATED Cheerleading, Chess, Drum Major/Majorette, Marching Band, Pep Band, Team Managers • SPORTS-INTERCOLLEGIATE Baseball (M), Basketball, Cross Country, Football (F), Golf (F), Softball (F), Swimming, Track and Field, Volleyball (F), Wrestling (M) • SPORTS-INTRAMURAL Badminton, Basketball, Cross Country, Diving, Golf, Racquetball, Soccer, Softball, Swimming, Tennis, Track and Field, Volleyball, Water Polo, Wrestling (M) • STUDENT LIFE ACTIVITIES Choral, Concert Band, Dance, Debate, Drama Groups, Ethnic & Cultural Groups, Fraternities, Music Groups, Musical Theater, Newspaper, Radio/TV station, Religious Organization, Sororities, Student Government, Symphony Orchestra, Yearbook

---

Selective	Tennessee Services

Austin Peay State University
P. O. Box 4476
Clarksville, Tennessee 37044
(615) 648-7661

School Enrollment: **6,000**
LD Enrollment: **30**

Admissions Contact: **Charles McCorkle, Director of Admissions**
LD Contact: **Charlotte Hardin, Director**
Name of Program: **Student Support Program**
Telephone:**(615) 648-7612**

Admissions

Application Information:
Application deadline: **August 1st**

Secondary School Information
Most Important Criteria For Admissions (1-strongest)

1 SAT/ACT	Application	**4** School transcript
5 Class rank	**3** Course selection	Personal statement
Interview	Extra activities	Psychoeducational
2 G.P.A.	Open admission	Recommendations

Test Requirements:
Untimed SAT: **Yes** Untimed ACT: **Yes**
Documentation of LD required: **Yes**

Types of Disabilities Served
• Speech/Lang	• Reading	• ADD with LD
• Study skills	• Spelling	• ADD without LD
• Written express	• Math	ADHD with LD
• Organizational	• Fine Motor	ADHD without LD
• Perceptual		

High School Course Requirements:
English: **4** Math: **3** Science: **2** Foreign Language: **2**

Learning Disability Program
Counseling: Individual: **Yes**

Faculty:
Faculty: **3**
Faculty advocate: **Yes** Meets with instructor: **As needed**

Diagnostic Testing
ADD	Personality	Perceptual skills	Spelling
ADHD	Organization	Fine motor skills	• Reading
I.Q.	Handwriting	Spoken language	Study skills
• Math	Social skills	• Written language	

Tutoring:
Services rendered by:
Graduates   •Peers   •Faculty   •LD staff   Teacher trainees

Tennessee

Tutorials

Grp.	Ind.	Tutorials	Grp.	Ind.	Tutorials
	•	Math skills			Word processing
	•	Study skills		•	Time management
	•	Language arts		•	Learning strategies
	•	Written express		•	Organizational skills

Academic Accommodations

Curriculum
- Priority registration
- Math waiver
- Foreign lang. waiver
- Course substitution

In Class
- Calculators
- Tape recorder
- Word processor
- Priority seating

Study Aids
- Typist
- Reader
- Notetaker
- Proof reader
- Text on tape
- Early syllabus
- Taped handouts

Exams
- Oral
- Untimed
- Take home
- With proctor
- On computer
- Extended time
- On tape
- Modified
- Separate room

Graduation Requirements:
Course credits: **128** GPA: **2.0**

Program Strengths
We try to help learning disabled students become part of the main-stream of college life.

General Information:
Austin Peay State University is a 4 year public university. Urban campus 50 miles from Nashville. Housing is not guaranteed. 20 % of students remain on campus for the weekends. 10 % of students join fraternities/sororities.

Accreditation: NASM, NCATE, NLN

Expenses:
Tuition: In-state: Full year: $606.00 per semester. Part-time: Per credit:$55.00. Tuition: Out-of-state: Full year: $1,477.00. Part-time: Per credit:$129.00. Room and board: $1,000.00

Majors
• AREA STUDIES Urban • BUSINESS Accounting, Agricultural, Banking, Business Administration, Business Economics, Business Management, Economics, Finance, Marketing • COMMUNICATIONS Advertising, Broadcasting, Communication, English, Graphic Design Technology, Journalism, Literature, Photography, Speech, Television/Radio/Film • COMPUTER SCIENCE Computer Science, Data Processing, Programming • EDUCATION Curriculum, Early Childhood, Elementary, Health, Music, Pre-Education, School Psychology, Secondary, Special • ENGINEERING Engineering Science • HEALTH SCIENCES Dental Hygiene, Environmental, Health, Medical Technology, Nuclear Medical Technology, Nursing, Occupational Therapy, Physical Therapy, Radiological Therapy • HUMANITIES English/Writing/Literature, Liberal Arts, Philosophy • LANGUAGES Foreign Languages, French, Spanish • PREPROFESSIONAL Agriculture, Dentistry, Law, Pharmacy, Social Work • SCIENCES Agricultural, Animal, Biology, Chemistry, Geography, Geology, Horticultural, Physics, Soil • SOCIAL SCIENCES Geography, Government/Political, History, Law Enforcement, Political Science, Psychology, Public Relations, Sociology • VISUAL AND PERFORMING ARTS Art, Dramatic Arts, Fine Arts, Music, Studio Art, Theater, Visual and Performing Arts • VOCATIONAL Auto Body, Business and Office, Construction, Culinary Arts, Electronics Technology, Medical Laboratory Technology, Radiological Technology, Secretarial

Sports/Activities
• SPORTS RELATED Marching Band, Pep Band • SPORTS-INTERCOLLEGIATE Baseball (M), Basketball, Cross Country, Football (M), Golf, Softball (F), Tennis, Track and Field, Volleyball (F) • SPORTS-INTRAMURAL Badminton, Basketball, Bowling, Gymnastics, Hand Ball, Ping-Pong, Racquetball, Riflery, Soccer, Softball, Swimming, Tennis, Volley-ball, Wrestling (M) • STUDENT LIFE ACTIVITIES Choral, Concert Band, Dance, Drama Groups, Fraternities, Jazz Band, Music Groups, Musical Theater, Newspaper, Radio/TV station, Sororities, Student Government, Symphony Orchestra, Yearbook

---

Very Selective

Freed-Hardeman University
158 East Main Street
Henderson, Tennessee 38340
(901) 989-6651-(800) 342-7837

School Enrollment: **1,164**
LD Enrollment: **6** Male: **4** Female: **2**

Admissions Contact: **Paul E. Pinckley, Director of Admissions**
Name of Program: **Center for Personal Development**

Admissions

Application Information:
Application deadline: **June 1st**
Applicant must apply **3** months in advance
Rolling Admissions: **Yes**

Secondary School Information
Most Important Criteria For Admissions (1-strongest)

3 SAT/ACT	**4** Application	**1** School transcript
Class rank	**5** Course selection	Personal statement
8 Interview	**7** Extra activities	Psychoeducational
2 G.P.A.	Open admission	**6** Recommendations

Test Requirements:
Untimed SAT: **Yes** Untimed ACT: **Yes**

Types of Disabilities Served
- Speech/Lang
- Study skills
- Written express
- Organizational
- Perceptual
- Reading
- Spelling
- Math
- Fine Motor
- ADD with LD
- ADD without LD
- ADHD with LD
- ADHD without LD

High School Course Requirements:
English: **4** Math: **2** Science: **2**

Learning Disability Program
Counseling: Individual: **Yes**

Faculty:
Faculty: **4** Full time: **4**
Faculty advocate: **Yes** Meets with instructor: **As needed**

Diagnostic Testing
ADD	• Personality	Perceptual skills	Spelling
ADHD	Organization	Fine motor skills	• Reading
I.Q.	Handwriting	Spoken language	• Study skills
• Math	Social skills	Written language	

Tutoring:
Services rendered by:
Graduates   •Peers   •Faculty   LD staff   Teacher trainees

682

Tutorials

Grp.	Ind.	Tutorials	Grp.	Ind.	Tutorials
	•	Math skills		•	Word processing
	•	Study skills			Time management
	•	Language arts		•	Learning strategies
	•	Written express		•	Organizational skills

Academic Accommodations

Curriculum	Study Aids	Exams
Priority registration	Typist	Oral
Math waiver	Reader	Untimed
Foreign lang. waiver	Notetaker	Take home
Course substitution	Proof reader	With proctor
In Class	Text on tape	On computer
• Calculators	Early syllabus	Extended time
• Tape recorder	Taped handouts	On tape
Word processor		Modified
• Priority seating		Separate room

Graduation Requirements:
Course credits: **132** GPA: **2.0**

Program Strengths

While F-H does not have a formalized program for LD students, we do endeavor to provide a liberal arts education in a Christian setting for students who are willing and interested.

General Information:

Freed-Hardeman University is a 4 year private Church of Christ university. Rural campus of 95 acres is 85 miles from Memphis. Accessible by air, train or bus. 9 residential halls on campus. Housing is not guaranteed.

Accreditation: SACS

Class Rank:
About 10% of the present freshmen class were in the upper 20% of their high school class. 50% were in the top 40% of their class.

Expenses:
Tuition: In-state: Full year: $4,960.00. Part-time: Per credit: $190.00. Room and board: $2,910.00

Majors

• AGRICULTURE Business • AREA STUDIES American, International Studies • ARTS Graphic Arts, Interior Design, Music • BUSINESS Accounting, Agricultural, Banking, Education, Fashion Merchandising, Management, Marketing • COMMUNICATIONS Broadcasting, Communication, English, Public Relations, Speech/Debate/Forensic, Television/Radio/Film • COMPUTER SCIENCE Computer Science • EDUCATION Art, Business, Early Childhood, Elementary, English, General, Mathematics, Music, Physical, Science, Social Studies, Speech/Language • HUMANITIES Fine Arts, Humanities, Religion • MATHEMATICS Applied • PREPROFESSIONAL Dentistry, Engineering, Law, Medicine, Optometry, Pharmacy, Social Work, Veterinarian • RELIGIOUS STUDIES Bible • SCIENCES Biology, Chemistry, General • SOCIAL SCIENCES International Studies, Psychology, Public Relations • VISUAL AND PERFORMING ARTS Art, Music, Theater • VOCATIONAL Fashion Design, Home Economics, Medical Laboratory Technology, Office Administration

Sports/Activities

• SPORTS RELATED Cheerleading • SPORTS-INTERCOLLEGIATE Baseball (M), Basketball, Golf (M), Softball (F), Tennis • SPORTS-INTRAMURAL Badminton, Basketball, Football, Ping-Pong, Softball, Swimming, Tennis, Volleyball • STUDENT LIFE ACTIVITIES Academic Clubs, Choral, Community Service, Concert Band, Drama Groups, Jazz Band, Music Groups, Musical Theater, Newspaper, Political Groups, Radio/TV station, Religious Organization, Student Government, Yearbook

Selective

Lee College
North Ocoee Street
Cleveland, Tennessee 37311
(615) 472-2111

School Enrollment: **1,827** Male: **895** Female: **932**
LD Enrollment: **12** Male: **7**

Admissions Contact: **Gary T. Ray, Director of Admissions**
LD Contact: **Bill Winters, Director, Student Support Services**
Name of Program: **Student Support Services**
Telephone: **800-LEE-9930**

Admissions

Application Information:
LD Students Applying: **12** Accepted: **12** Enrolled: **12**
LD on admissions committee: **Yes**
Application deadline: **Rolling**
Applicant must apply **6** months in advance
Rolling Admissions: **Yes**

Secondary School Information
Most Important Criteria For Admissions (1-strongest)

3 SAT/ACT	**1** Application	**2**	School transcript
5 Class rank	**6** Course selection	**8**	Personal statement
10 Interview	**7** Extra activities	**11**	Psychoeducational
4 G.P.A.	Open admission	**9**	Recommendations

Test Requirements:
Untimed SAT: **Yes** Untimed ACT: **Yes**
Documentation of LD required: **Yes**

Types of Disabilities Served
- Speech/Lang • Reading • ADD with LD
- Study skills • Spelling • ADD without LD
- Written express • Math ADHD with LD
- Organizational • Fine Motor ADHD without LD
- Perceptual

High School Course Requirements:
English: **2** Math: **1-2** Science: **1**

Learning Disability Program

Program: Reinforces course work: **Yes**
Students mainstreamed **85** % of the day
Recommended credits per semester: **12-14**
Time required or recommended in learning center: **No requirement**
Services available for all students: **Yes**
Counseling: Individual: **Yes** Vocational Counseling: **Yes**

Faculty:
Faculty: **5** Including Director: **Yes** Full time: **5**
LD faculty with: BS/BA: **2** M.A.: **3**
Meets with instructor: **Bi-semester**

Tennessee

Diagnostic Testing

ADD	Personality	Perceptual skills	Spelling
ADHD	Organization	Fine motor skills	• Reading
• I.Q.	Handwriting	Spoken language	Study skills
• Math	Social skills	Written language	

Tutoring:

Average size of group tutorials: **1-3**
Services rendered by:

Graduates •Peers Faculty •LD staff Teacher trainees

Tutorials

Grp.	Ind.	Tutorials	Grp.	Ind.	Tutorials
	•	Math skills		•	Word processing
	•	Study skills		•	Time management
	•	Language arts	•	•	Learning strategies
•	•	Written express			Organizational skills

Academic Accommodations

Curriculum	Study Aids	Exams
Priority registration	Typist	• Oral
Math waiver	• Reader	• Untimed
Foreign lang. waiver	• Notetaker	Take home
• Course substitution	Proof reader	• With proctor
In Class	Text on tape	On computer
Calculators	Early syllabus	• Extended time
• Tape recorder	Taped handouts	On tape
Word processor		Modified
• Priority seating		Separate room

Graduation Requirements:

Course credits: **130 semester hours** GPA: **2.0** Years to complete degree:
5 years average

Program Strengths

The Student Support Services Program assists the individual needs of each student. Should the student have educational impairment, we will strive to support with tutors, remedial math and reading, and counseling.

General Information:

Lee College is a 4 year private Church of God college. Rural campus of 40 acres is 25 miles from Chattanooga. Accessible by air or bus. Ski areas are 85 miles from campus. Beaches are 300-400 miles from campus. 9% of students are foreign. 11 residential halls on campus. Housing is guaranteed.Guaranteed through 4th year. 65 % of students remain on campus for the weekends. 12 % of students join fraternities/sororities.

Accreditation: Regional

SAT/ACT Scores:

Scores for incoming freshmen: **Verbal:** 80% below 500. 15% between 500 and 599. 3% between 600 and 699. 2% above 700. **Math:** 70% below 500. 21% between 500 and 599. 8% between 600 and 699. 1% above 700. **ACT:** 54% below 20. 23% between 20 and 23. 12% between 24 and 251. 8% between 26 and 28. 3% above 28.

Expenses:

Tuition: In-state: Full year: $4,128.00. Part-time: Per credit:$172.00. Tuition: Out-of-state: Full year: $4,128.00. Part-time: Per credit:$172.00. Room and board: $3,000.00

Majors

• AREA STUDIES American, Latin American, Missionary Studies • BUSINESS Accounting, Business Administration, Business Economics, Business Education, Business Management, Economics, Finance, Management, Marketing • COMMUNICATIONS Advertising, Broadcasting, Communi-cation, Creative Writing, English, Journalism • COMPUTER SCIENCE Data Processing, Programming, Systems Analysis • EDUCATION Art, Curriculum, Early Childhood, Elementary, Health, Middle School, Music, Physical, Pre-Education, Recreation and Youth Leadership, Religious Education, School Psychology, Secondary, Special, Speech/Language • HEALTH SCIENCES Health, Medical Technology • HUMANITIES Humanities, Philosophy, Religion, Religious Studies • LANGUAGES Foreign Languages, French, German, Greek, Spanish • PREPROFESSIONAL Law, Legal Assistant, Medicine, Pharmacy • SCIENCES Biochemistry, Biology, Botany, Chemistry, Earth, Geology, Mathematics, Physical Chemistry, Physical Science, Physics, Physiology, Zoology • SOCIAL SCIENCES Anthropology, Criminal Justice, Government/Political, History, Psychology, Social Sciences, Sociology • VISUAL AND PERFORMING ARTS Art, Art History, Music, Music Performance, Theater • VOCATIONAL Medical Laboratory Technology

Sports/Activities

• SPORTS RELATED Cheerleading, Team Managers • SPORTS-INTERCOLLEGIATE Academic Clubs, Basketball, Golf (M), Soccer (M), Tennis (M), Volleyball (F) • SPORTS-INTRAMURAL Basketball, Racquetball, Softball, Volleyball • STUDENT LIFE ACTIVITIES Academic Clubs, Choral, Concert Band, Drama Groups, Ethnic & Cultural Groups, Fraternities, Jazz Band, Magazine, Musical Theatre, Newspaper, Religious Organization, Sororities, Student Government, Yearbook

Less Selective	Tennessee Services

Martin Methodist College

433 West Madison
Pulaski, Tennessee 38478
(615) 363-7456

School Enrollment: **375**
LD Enrollment: **10**

Admissions Contact: **Bill Rutherford, Dean of Admissions**
Telephone: **(615) 363-9807**

Admissions

Application Information:

Application deadline: **September 1st**

Secondary School Information

Most Important Criteria For Admissions (1-strongest)

	SAT/ACT		Application	**1** School transcript
	Class rank	**1**	Course selection	Personal statement
	Interview	**1**	Extra activities	Psychoeducational
1	G.P.A.		Open admission	Recommendations

Types of Disabilities Served

Speech/Lang	Reading	ADD with LD
Study skills	Spelling	ADD without LD
Written express	Math	ADHD with LD
Organizational	Fine Motor	ADHD without LD
Perceptual		

Diagnostic Testing

ADD	Personality	Perceptual skills	Spelling
ADHD	Organization	Fine motor skills	Reading
I.Q.	Handwriting	Spoken language	Study skills
Math	Social skills	Written language	

Services rendered by:

Graduates   Peers   Faculty   LD staff   Teacher trainees

Tutorials

Grp.	Ind.	Tutorials	Grp.	Ind.	Tutorials
		Math skills			Word processing
•		Study skills			Time management
		Language arts			Learning strategies
		Written express			Organizational skills

Academic Accommodations

Curriculum	Study Aids	Exams
Priority registration	Typist	• Oral
Math waiver	Reader	Untimed
• Foreign lang. waiver	Notetaker	Take home
Course substitution	Proof reader	With proctor
In Class	• Text on tape	On computer
• Calculators	Early syllabus	• Extended time
• Tape recorder	Taped handouts	On tape
Word processor		Modified
Priority seating		Separate room

Program Strengths

In essence we do not have a formal LD program, but in reality we do a lot of the same things: small student body; a genuinely caring faculty and staff; a new computerized (20 computers) learning lab with two full-time staff persons; a credit class on how to study and survive in college; and individualized tutoring.

General Information:

Martin Methodist College is a 2 year private United Methodist college. Rural campus of 6 acres is 70 miles from Nashville. Accessible by bus. Ski areas are 4 hours from campus. Beaches are 6.5 hours from campus. 7% of students are foreign. 2 residential halls on campus. Housing is guaranteed.

Accreditation: Regional

Expenses:

Tuition: In-state: Full year: $4,000.00. Part-time: Per credit:$170.00. Tuition: Out-of-state: Full year: $4,000.00. Part-time: Per credit:$170.00.

Majors

• AREA STUDIES American • BUSINESS Accounting, Agricultural, Business Administration, Business Economics, Business Education, Business Management, Economics, Finance, Hotel and Restaurant Management, Insurance, Labor Relations, Management, Real Estate, Transportation Management • COMMUNICATIONS Advertising, Broadcasting, Communication, English, Journalism • COMPUTER SCIENCE Data Processing, Programming • EDUCATION Art, Early Childhood, Elementary, Health, Physical, Pre-Education • ENGINEERING Computer, Industrial • HEALTH SCIENCES Radiological Therapy • HUMANITIES Humanities, Liberal Arts, Philosophy, Religion • LANGUAGES French, Spanish • PREPROFESSIONAL Agriculture, Architecture, Dentistry, Engineering, Forestry, Law, Medical Record Administration, Medical Technology, Medicine, Ministry, Nursing, Optometry, Pharmacy, Physical Therapy, Radiological Therapy, Recreation, Social Work • SCIENCES Biology, Botany, Chemistry, Mathematics, Physical Science • SOCIAL SCIENCES Criminal Justice, Government/Political, History, Library Science, Psychology, Social Sciences, Sociology • VISUAL AND PERFORMING ARTS Art, Music, Studio Art, Theater • VOCATIONAL Business and Office, Dental Hygiene, Forestry, Park/Recreation, Secretarial, Wildlife

Sports/Activities

• SPORTS RELATED Cheerleading, Pep Band • SPORTS-INTERCOLLEGIATE Baseball (M), Basketball, Golf (M), Soccer, Softball (F), Tennis • SPORTS-INTRAMURAL Badminton, Baseball (M), Basketball, Ping-Pong, Racquetball, Soccer, Softball, Swimming, Volleyball • STUDENT LIFE ACTIVITIES Choral, Drama Groups, Ethnic & Cultural Groups, Music Groups, Newspaper, Religious Organization, Student Government,

Yearbook

Special

Tennessee Services

Memphis College of Art
Overton Park
Memphis, Tennessee 38112
(901) 726-4085

School Enrollment: **250** Male: **150** Female: **100**

Admissions Contact: **Susan S. Miller, Director of Admissions**

Admissions

Application Information:
Application deadline: **Rolling**
Notified when: **3 weeks**

Secondary School Information
Most Important Criteria For Admissions (1-strongest)

6 SAT/ACT	**2** Application	**5** School transcript		
9 Class rank	Course selection	**7** Personal statement		
3 Interview	**10** Extra activities	Psychoeducational		
8 G.P.A.	Open admission	**4** Recommendations		

Test Requirements:
Untimed SAT: **Yes** Untimed ACT: **Yes** Untimed ACH: **Yes**

Types of Disabilities Served
• Speech/Lang	• Reading	ADD with LD
• Study skills	• Spelling	ADD without LD
• Written express	• Math	ADHD with LD
• Organizational	• Fine Motor	ADHD without LD
• Perceptual		

Admissions Process

Students are reviewed by a committee based on art skills shown in a portfolio requirement. Test scores and transcripts are also considered.

Learning Disability Program

Students mainstreamed **100** % of the day
Counseling: Individual: **Yes** Group Counseling: **Yes** Vocational Counseling: **Yes**

Faculty:
Faculty advocate: **Yes** Meets with instructor: **As needed**

Diagnostic Testing
ADD	Personality	Perceptual skills	Spelling
ADHD	Organization	Fine motor skills	Reading
I.Q.	Handwriting	Spoken language	Study skills
Math	Social skills	Written language	

Tutoring:
Services rendered by:
•Graduates   •Peers   •Faculty   LD staff   Teacher trainees

Tennessee

Tutorials

Grp.	Ind.	Tutorials	Grp.	Ind.	Tutorials
	•	Math skills		•	Word processing
	•	Study skills		•	Time management
	•	Language arts		•	Learning strategies
	•	Written express		•	Organizational skills

Academic Accommodations

Curriculum	Study Aids	Exams
Priority registration	Typist	Oral
Math waiver	Reader	Untimed
Foreign lang. waiver	Notetaker	Take home
Course substitution	Proof reader	With proctor
In Class	Text on tape	On computer
Calculators	Early syllabus	Extended time
Tape recorder	Taped handouts	On tape
Word processor		Modified
Priority seating		Separate room

Graduation Requirements:
Course credits: **129** GPA: **2.0** Years to complete degree: **4** Math waiver: **Yes** Language waiver: **Yes**

Program Strengths

Liberal studies requirements are mostly electives. Memphis College of Art is a visual arts school, most classes are studio. Most students are visually oriented.

General Information:

Memphis College of Art is a 4 year private college. Urban campus of 200 acres is Memphis. Accessible by air, train, or bus. 15% of students are foreign. 1 residential halls on campus. Housing is not guaranteed.80 % of students remain on campus for the weekends.

Accreditation: SACS, NASRD

Expenses:
Tuition: In-state: Full year: $8,550.00. Part-time: Per credit:$360.00. Part-time: Per course: $1,080.00. Tuition: Out-of-state: Full year: $8,550.00. Part-time: Per credit:$360.00. Part-time: Per course:$1,080.00 Room and board: $4,000.00

Majors

• COMMUNICATIONS Advertising, Photography • CRAFTS AND DESIGN Ceramics, Crafts, Graphic Design, Illustration Design, Sculpture • VISUAL ARTS Art, Drawing, Fine Arts, Studio Art • VOCATIONAL Jewelry-Metalsmithery, Painting, Printing/Lithography, Textile and Clothing

Sports/Activities

• SPORTS-INTRAMURAL Volleyball • STUDENT LIFE ACTIVITIES Film, Newspaper, Student Government

---

Middle Tennessee State University
Murfreesboro, Tennessee 37132
(615) 898-2111

School Enrollment: **12,461**
LD Enrollment: **80**

Admissions Contact: **Roger Sims, Director of Admissions**
LD Contact: **John Harris, Director**
Name of Program: **Disabled Student Services**
Address: **Box 7**
Telephone:**(615) 898-2783**

Admissions

Application Information:
LD on admissions committee:**Yes**
Application deadline: **July 1st**
Notified when: **July 21st**

Secondary School Information
Most Important Criteria For Admissions (1-strongest)

1 SAT/ACT	2 Application	1 School transcript
7 Class rank	9 Course selection	6 Personal statement
5 Interview	4 Extra activities	8 Psychoeducational
1 G.P.A.	Open admission	3 Recommendations

Test Requirements:
Documentation of LD required: **Yes**

Types of Disabilities Served
- Speech/Lang
- Study skills
- Written express
- Organizational
- Perceptual
- Reading
- Spelling
- Math
- Fine Motor
- ADD with LD
- ADD without LD
- ADHD with LD
- ADHD without LD

Learning Disability Program
Services available for all students: **Yes**
Counseling: Individual: **Yes** Group Counseling: **Yes**

Faculty:
Faculty: **2** Full time: **1** Part time: **1**
Faculty advocate: **Yes** Meets with instructor: **As needed**

Diagnostic Testing

ADD	Personality	Perceptual skills	Spelling
ADHD	Organization	Fine motor skills	Reading
I.Q.	Handwriting	Spoken language	Study skills
Math	Social skills	Written language	

Tutoring:
Average size of group tutorials: **5**
Services rendered by:
•Graduates •Peers •Faculty •LD staff •Teacher trainees

Tutorials

Grp.	Ind.	Tutorials	Grp.	Ind.	Tutorials
	•	Math skills	•	•	Word processing
	•	Study skills	•	•	Time management
	•	Language arts	•	•	Learning strategies
	•	Written express	•	•	Organizational skills

Academic Accommodations

Curriculum	Study Aids	Exams
Priority registration	• Typist	• Oral
• Math waiver	Reader	Untimed
• Foreign lang. waiver	• Notetaker	• Take home
• Course substitution	• Proof reader	• With proctor
In Class	• Text on tape	On computer
• Calculators	Early syllabus	• Extended time
• Tape recorder	Taped handouts	On tape
• Word processor		• Modified
Priority seating		Separate room

Program Strengths

The needs of MTSU students with learning disabilities are served by the concerted efforts of both the Office of Handicapped Student Services and the Office of Developmental Studies. These coordinating bodies distribute information concerning services available to students with disabilities as well as academic deficiencies. These offices also act as advocates for such students at the University, surveying the needs of these students and developing programs to meet those needs.

General Information:

Middle Tennessee State University is a 4 year public university. 32 miles from Nashville. Accessible by air or bus. Ski areas are 175 from campus. 21 residential halls on campus. Housing is guaranteed.15 % of students remain on campus for the weekends. 1 % of students join fraternities/sororities.

Accreditation: SACS

Expenses:

Tuition: In-state: Full year: $1,232.00. Part-time: Per credit:$56.00. Tuition: Out-of-state: Full year: $4,186.00. Part-time: Per credit:$185.00. Room and board: $1,682.00

Majors

• AREA STUDIES Urban • BUSINESS Accounting, Agricultural, Banking, Business Administration, Business Economics, Business Education, Business Management, Economics, Finance, Insurance, Management, Marketing, Marketing Research • COMMUNICATIONS Advertising, Broadcasting, Communication, Creative Writing, English, Journalism, Photography, Television/Radio/Film • COMPUTER SCIENCE Computer Science, Computer Technology, Data Processing, Programming, Systems Analysis, Telecommunications • EDUCATION Art, Curriculum, Early Childhood, Elementary, English, Health, Home Economics Education, Mathematics, Middle School, Music, Physical, Pre-Education, Recreation and Youth Leadership, School Psychology, Secondary, Special, Speech/Language • ENGINEERING Aerospace, Electrical, Industrial • HEALTH SCIENCES Environmental, Health, Medical Technology, Nursing, Nutritional/Food, Physical Therapy, Speech Therapy, Speech/Audiology and Speech • HUMANITIES Humanities, Philosophy • LANGUAGES Foreign Languages, French, German, Spanish • PREPROFESSIONAL Agriculture, Dentistry, Forestry, Law, Medicine, Pharmacy, Recreation, Social Work, Veterinarian • SCIENCES Actuarial Technology, Aerospace, Animal, Biology, Chemistry, Earth, Geography, Geology, Mathematics, Military Science, Physical Science, Physics, Plant Science, Soil • SOCIAL SCIENCES Anthropology, Criminal Justice, Geography, Government/Political, Historical Preservation, Human Service, International Studies, Law Enforcement, Political Science, Political Science, Psychology, Public Relations, Social Sciences, Sociology • VISUAL AND PERFORMING ARTS

Art, Art History, Dance, Dramatic Arts, Music, Studio Art, Theater • VOCATIONAL Business and Office, Court Reporting, Fashion Merchandising, Home Economics, Manufacturing Technology, Medical Laboratory Technology, Office Administration, Secretarial

Sports/Activities

• SPORTS RELATED Cheerleading, Chess, Drill Team, Drum Major/Majorette, Flying Team, Marching Band, Pep Band, Team Managers • SPORTS-INTERCOLLEGIATE Baseball (M), Basketball, Cross Country, Football (M), Golf (M), Horseback Riding, Riflery, Tennis, Volleyball (F) • SPORTS-INTRAMURAL Basketball (M), Boxing (M), Rugby (M), Soccer, Softball, Swimming, Volleyball • STUDENT LIFE ACTIVITIES Choral, Concert Band, Dance, Debate, Drama Groups, Ethnic & Cultural Groups, Film, Fraternities, Jazz Band, Magazine, Music Groups, Musical Theater, Newspaper, Opera, Radio/TV station, Religious Organization, Sororities, Student Government, Symphony Orchestra, Yearbook

---

Less Selective

Tennessee Services

Pellissippi State Technical Community College
P.O. Box 22990
Knoxville, Tennessee 37933
(615) 694-6453

School Enrollment: **7,200** Male: **3,240** Female: **3,960**
LD Enrollment: **50**

Admissions Contact: **Joan C. Newman, Dir. Acad. Support Services**
LD Contact: **Joan C. Newman**
Address: **Pellissippi State**
Telephone:**(615) 694-6453**

Admissions

Application Information:
Enrolled:**50**
Application deadline: **Through late registration**

Secondary School Information
Most Important Criteria For Admissions (1-strongest)

2 SAT/ACT	Application	**1**	School transcript
Class rank	**3** Course selection		Personal statement
Interview	Extra activities	**4**	Psychoeducational
G.P.A.	Open admission		Recommendations

Test Requirements:
Untimed SAT: **Yes** Untimed ACT: **Yes**
Documentation of LD required: **Yes**
Currency of diagnostic testing: **Within 3 years**
Tests recommended: **ACT/SAT, AAPP (mandated by TN Board of Regents), AAPP depends on ACT/SAT results and is required for all first time freshmen.**

Types of Disabilities Served
- Speech/Lang • Reading • ADD with LD
- Study skills • Spelling • ADD without LD
- Written express • Math • ADHD with LD
- Organizational • Fine Motor • ADHD without LD
- Perceptual

Admissions Process

1) Applicant fills out application and submits with $5.00 application

fee. 2) Applicant submits high school transcripts/GED scores and transfer credits if applicable. 3) Applicant participates in TBR mandated testing - ACT/SAT and possibly AAPP.

High School Course Requirements:
English: **4** Math: **2** Science: **2** Foreign Language: **2**

Learning Disability Program

Special orientation for LD students: **Yes**
Students mainstreamed **100** % of the day
Recommended credits per semester: **varies**
Services only for LD students: **Yes**
Counseling: Individual: **Yes** Group Counseling: **Yes** Vocational Counseling: **Yes**

Faculty:
Faculty: **3** Full time: **1** Part time: **2**
Faculty advocate: **Yes** Meets with instructor: **As needed**

Diagnostic Testing

ADD	Personality	Perceptual skills	Spelling
ADHD	Organization	Fine motor skills	Reading
I.Q.	Handwriting	Spoken language	Study skills
Math	Social skills	Written language	

Tutoring:
Average size of group tutorials: **Individual**
Services rendered by:
  Graduates •Peers •Faculty   LD staff   Teacher trainees

Tutorials

Grp.	Ind.	Tutorials	Grp.	Ind.	Tutorials
	•	Math skills		•	Word processing
	•	Study skills			Time management
	•	Language arts			Learning strategies
	•	Written express			Organizational skills

Academic Accommodations

Curriculum	Study Aids	Exams
• Priority registration	Typist	• Oral
Math waiver	• Reader	• Untimed
Foreign lang. waiver	• Notetaker	• Take home
• Course substitution	Proof reader	• With proctor
In Class	• Text on tape	• On computer
• Calculators	Early syllabus	• Extended time
• Tape recorder	Taped handouts	• On tape
• Word processor		• Modified
• Priority seating		• Separate room

Graduation Requirements:
Course credits: **66** GPA: **2.0** Years to complete degree: **None set**

Program Strengths

Programs include remedial/development courses in reading, English, math and study skills. Self-contained class for hearing impaired. Learning Center with tutorials and one-on-one tutoring in variety of areas. Make up testing center for alternate testing arrangements.

General Information:

Pellissippi State Technical Community College is a 2 year public college. Rural campus of 350 acres is 3-5 miles from Knoxville. Accessible by car or bus. Ski areas are 45 miles from campus. Housing is not guaranteed.

Accreditation: SASC

SAT/ACT Scores:
Scores for incoming freshmen: **ACT:** 60% below 20. 40% between 20 and 23.

Expenses:
Tuition: In-state: Full year: $420.00 per semester. Part-time: Per credit:$38.00. Tuition: Out-of-state: Full year: $1,215.00 per semester. Part-time: Per credit:$107.00.

Majors

• BUSINESS Accounting, Banking/Finance, Business Administration, Business Management, Data Processing, Management, Marketing • COMPUTER SCIENCE Business Data Programming, Computer Graphics, Computer Mathematics, Computer Science, Computer Servicing, Computer Technology, Programming • ENGINEERING Civil/Environmental, Electrical, Mechanical, Radio/Television • HEALTH SCIENCES Medical Secretary • PRE PROFESSIONAL Law, Legal Assistant • VOCATIONAL Automobile Technology, Drafting, Electrical Technology, Industrial Technology, Legal Secretary, Paralegal, Quality Control Technology, Secretarial, Word Processing

Sports/Activities

• SPORTS-INTRAMURAL Basketball • STUDENT LIFE ACTIVITIES Academic Clubs, Choral, Drama Groups, Ethnic & Cultural Groups, Newspaper, Radio/TV station, Religious Organization, Student Government

---

Selective   **Tennessee**
                                                  Services

Tennessee Technological University
P.O. Box 5006
Cookeville, Tennessee 38505
(615) 372-388 - (800) 255-8881

School Enrollment: **8,160** Male: **4,369** Female: **3,791**

Admissions Contact: **James C. Perry, Director of Admissions**
LD Contact: **Dr. John N. Flanders, Director**
Name of Program: **Counseling Center**
Address: **Box 5094**
Telephone:**(615) 372-3331**

Admissions

Application Information:
Application deadline: **None**

Secondary School Information
Most Important Criteria For Admissions (1-strongest)

1	SAT/ACT	Application	School transcript
	Class rank	Course selection	Personal statement
	Interview	Extra activities	Psychoeducational
2	G.P.A.	Open admission	Recommendations

Test Requirements:
Documentation of LD required: **Yes**
Tests recommended: **Personal interview, psychological report.**

Types of Disabilities Served

Speech/Lang	Reading	ADD with LD
Study skills	Spelling	ADD without LD
Written express •	Math	ADHD with LD
Organizational	Fine Motor	ADHD without LD
Perceptual		

Admissions Process

Same as rest of students, ACT 19, graduate of high school

High School Course Requirements:
English: **4** Math: **3** Science: **2** Foreign Language: **2**

Learning Disability Program

Syllabus available during orientation:**Yes**
Program: Reinforces course work: **Yes**
Students mainstreamed **100** % of the day
Recommended credits per semester: **12**
Services available for all students: **Yes**
Counseling: Individual: **Yes** Group Counseling: **Yes** Vocational Counseling: **Yes**

Faculty:
Faculty advocate: **Yes** Meets with instructor: **As Needed**

Diagnostic Testing

ADD •	Personality	Perceptual skills	• Spelling
ADHD	Organization	Fine motor skills	• Reading
• I.Q.	Handwriting	Spoken language	Study skills
• Math	Social skills	Written language	

Tutoring:
Average size of group tutorials: **Individual**
Services rendered by:
•Graduates   Peers   •Faculty   LD staff   Teacher trainees

Tutorials

Grp.	Ind.	Tutorials	Grp.	Ind.	Tutorials
•	•	Math skills	•	•	Word processing
•	•	Study skills			Time management
•	•	Language arts	•	•	Learning strategies
•	•	Written express			Organizational skills

Academic Accommodations

Curriculum	Study Aids	Exams
Priority registration	Typist	• Oral
Math waiver	• Reader	• Untimed
• Foreign lang. waiver	• Notetaker	• Take home
• Course substitution	• Proof reader	• With proctor
In Class	Text on tape	On computer
• Calculators	• Early syllabus	• Extended time
• Tape recorder	Taped handouts	On tape
• Word processor		• Modified
• Priority seating		• Separate room

Graduation Requirements:GPA: **2.0** Years to complete degree: **Regular** Language waiver: **Yes**

General Information:

Tennessee Technological University is a 4 year public university. Urban campus of 235 acres is 80 miles from Nashville. Accessible by bus. 3% of students are foreign. 25 residential halls on campus. Housing is guaranteed.29 % of students join fraternities/sororities.

Accreditation:SACS, BS, ES

SAT/ACT Scores:
Scores for incoming freshmen: **ACT:** 79% below 20. 18% between 20 and 23. 2%between 24 and 25l. 4%between 26 and 28.

Expenses:
Tuition: In-state: Full year: $768.00 per semester. Part-time: Per credit:$67.00. Part-time: Per course: Depends on hours. Tuition: Out-of-state: Full year: $1,682.00 per semester. Part-time: Per credit:$67.00. Part-time: Per course:Depends on hours Room and board: $1,425.00/semester

Majors

• AGRICULTURE Business, Education • ANIMAL SCIENCE Husbandry • BUSINESS Accounting, Banking/Finance, Business Administration, Business Economics, Business Management, Data Processing, Economics, Marketing, Personnel • COMMUNICATIONS English, Journalism • COMPUTER SCIENCE Business Data Programming, Computer Science • EDUCATION Agricultural, Art, Child Development, Early Childhood, Elementary, Health, Home Economics, Music Therapy, Physical, Psychology, School Psychology, Secondary, Special • ENGINEERING Chemical, Civil/Environmental, Electrical, Environmental/Water Resources, Industrial, Mechanical, Physics • HEALTH SCIENCES Dental Assistant, Dental Hygiene, Dental Technician, Dietary Manager, Health, Education, Medical Records Administration, Nursing, Nursing Assistant, Nutritional/Food, Physical Therapy, Practical Nursing • HUMANITIES English/Writing/Literature, Fine Arts • LANGUAGES English, French, German • PRE PROFESSIONAL Dentistry, Law, Medicine • SCIENCES Agricultural, Animal, Biochemistry, Biology, Chemistry, Computer Science, Geology, Horticultural, Physics • SOCIAL SCIENCES Criminal Justice, Family Counseling, Government/Political, History, Library Science, Political Science, Psychology, Social Science, Sociology • VISUAL AND PERFORMING ARTS Art, Art History, Fine Arts, Music • VOCATIONAL Dental Assistant, Dental Hygiene, Fashion Design, Fashion Merchandising, Food Service, Forestry, Home Economics, Medical Laboratory Technology, Office Administration

Sports/Activities

• SPORTS RELATED Baton Twirling, Cheerleading, Drum Major/Majorette, Marching Band, Pep Band, Team Managers • SPORTS-INTERCOLLEGIATE Baseball (M), Basketball (F), Basketball (M), Cross Country (M), Football (M), Golf (F), Golf (M), Riflery (F), Riflery (M), Softball (F), Tennis (F), Tennis (M), Volleyball (F) • SPORTS-INTRAMURAL Basketball (F), Basketball (M), Cross Country (M), Racquetball (F), Racquetball (M), Riflery (F), Riflery (M), Soccer (F), Soccer (M), Softball (F), Softball (M), Volleyball (F), Volleyball (M) • STUDENT LIFE ACTIVITIES Academic Clubs, Choral, Community Service, Concert Band, Dance, Debate, Drama Groups, Ethnic & Cultural Groups, Fraternities, Jazz Band, Magazine, Music Groups, Newspaper, Orchestra, Political Groups, Radio/TV station, Religious Organization, Sororities, Student Government, Symphony Orchestra, Yearbook

Tennessee

Selective   **Tennessee**
                                                  Program

University of Tennessee
615 McCallie Avenue
Chattanooga, Tennessee 37403
(615) 755-4111

School Enrollment: **7,888** Male: **3,677** Female: **4,211**
LD Enrollment: **130**

Admissions Contact: **Patsy Reynolds, Director of Admissions**
LD Contact: **Pollyanna Campbell, Sec., College Access Program**
Name of Program: **College Access Program**
Telephone:**(615) 755-4006**

Admissions

Application Information:
Accepted: **30** Enrolled:**130**
Separate application:**Yes**
Application deadline: **August 1st, December 1st**
Applicant must apply **12** months in advance
Rolling Admissions: **Yes**

Secondary School Information
Most Important Criteria For Admissions (1-strongest)

4 SAT/ACT	**6** Application	**1**	School transcript
7 Class rank	**3** Course selection	**5**	Personal statement
8 Interview	**11** Extra activities	**10**	Psychoeducational
2 G.P.A.	Open admission	**9**	Recommendations

Test Requirements:
Untimed SAT: **Yes** Untimed ACT: **Yes**
WAIS-R required: **Yes** Range accepted: **87+**
Documentation of LD required: **Yes**
Currency of diagnostic testing: **within 3 years**
Tests recommended: **Individualized IQ Test, Individualized Achievement Test**

Types of Disabilities Served
Speech/Lang • Reading • ADD with LD
Study skills • Spelling ADD without LD
• Written express • Math • ADHD with LD
Organizational • Fine Motor ADHD without LD
• Perceptual

Admissions Process

All application materials are reviewed by CAP staff to determine if an LD exists according to Tennessee State Guidelines, and the academic strength of the student.

High School Course Requirements:
English: **4** Math: **3** Science: **2** Foreign Language: **2**

Learning Disability Program

Program: Reinforces course work: **Yes**
Students mainstreamed **100** % of the day
Recommended credits per semester: **12-15**
Time required or recommended in learning center: **6-10 hours**
Services only for LD students: **Yes**
Counseling: Individual: **Yes** Group Counseling: **Yes** Vocational Counsel-

ing: **Yes**

Faculty:
Faculty: **5** Including Director: **Yes** Full time: **3** Part time: **2**
LD faculty with: BS/BA: **1** M.A.: **2** Ph.D.: **1**
Meets with instructor: **As needed**

Diagnostic Testing
ADD • Personality • Perceptual skills • Spelling
ADHD Organization• Fine motor skills • Reading
• I.Q. • Handwriting Spoken language Study skills
• Math Social skills• Written language

Tutoring:
Average size of group tutorials: **3**
Services rendered by:
•Graduates •Peers Faculty LD staff •Teacher trainees

Tutorials
Grp.	Ind.	Tutorials	Grp.	Ind.	Tutorials
	•	Math skills			Word processing
•	•	Study skills		•	Time management
	•	Language arts		•	Learning strategies
	•	Written express		•	Organizational skills

Academic Accommodations

Curriculum	Study Aids	Exams
• Priority registration	Typist	• Oral
Math waiver	• Reader	• Untimed
Foreign lang. waiver	• Notetaker	• Take home
Course substitution	• Proof reader	• With proctor
In Class	• Text on tape	• On computer
• Calculators	Early syllabus	• Extended time
• Tape recorder	Taped handouts	On tape
Word processor		Modified
• Priority seating		• Separate room

Graduation Requirements:
Course credits: **128 semester hours** GPA: **2.0** Years to complete degree: **No limit**

Program Strengths

Comprehensive in nature, 90% retention rate, 2.4 GPA overall, 130 students, 5 staff members, 30-40 tutors, early registration through CAP Office.

General Information:

University of Tennessee is a 4 year public university. Urban campus of 101 acres is Accessible by air or bus. 1% of students are foreign. 5 residential halls on campus. Housing is not guaranteed.

Accreditation:SACS

Expenses:
Tuition: In-state: Full year: $1,558.00. Part-time: Per credit:$72.00. Tuition: Out-of-state: Full year: $4,922.00. Part-time: Per credit:$195.00. Room and board: $1,554.00 (room) Cost of LD program:$1,000.00

Majors

• AREA STUDIES American • ARTS Dramatic Arts, Graphic Arts, Music • BUSINESS Business Administration, Economics • COMMUNICATIONS Communication • COMPUTER SCIENCE Computer Science • EDUCATION Early Childhood, Elementary, Music, Secondary, Special • HEALTH SCIENCES Medical Laboratory Technology, Nursing, Physical Therapy • HUMANITIES English/Writing/Literature, Humanities, Philosophy • LANGUAGES French, Greek, Latin, Spanish • MATHEMATICS Applied • SCIENCES Applied Mathematics, Biology, Chemistry, Geology, Mathematics, Physics • SOCIAL SCIENCES Criminal Justice, History, Human Service, Political Science, Psychology, Sociology • SPECIAL EDUCATION Gifted & Talented • VISUAL AND PERFORMING ARTS Art, Music, Theater

Sports/Activities

• SPORTS RELATED Cheerleading, Drum Major/Majorette, Marching Band, Pep Band • SPORTS-INTERCOLLEGIATE Basketball, Crew, Cross Country, Football (M), Golf, Tennis, Track and Field, Volleyball (F), Wrestling (M) • SPORTS-INTRAMURAL Basketball, Racquetball, Soccer, Softball (F), Swimming, Tennis, Volleyball, Weight Lifting • STUDENT LIFE ACTIVITIES Academic Clubs, Choral, Community Service, Concert Band, Dance, Drama Groups, Ethnic & Cultural Groups, Fraternities, Jazz Band, Music Groups, Musical Theater, Newsletter, Orchestra, Political Groups, Radio/TV station, Religious Organization, Sororities, Student Government, Symphony Orchestra, Yearbook

---

Highly Selective **Tennessee**

Vanderbilt University

401 24th Avenue South
Nashville, Tennessee 37212
(615) 322-2561

School Enrollment: **6,000** Male: **3,000** Female: **3,000**
LD Contact: **Anita Pulley, Special Services Coordinator**
Name of Program: **Students with Disabilities**
Telephone: **(615) 322-4705**

Admissions

Application Information:
Application deadline: **January 15th**
Notified when: **May 1st**

Secondary School Information
Most Important Criteria For Admissions (1-strongest)

2 SAT/ACT	**3** Application	**1** School transcript
2 Class rank	**1** Course selection	Personal statement
Interview	**3** Extra activities	Psychoeducational
1 G.P.A.	Open admission	**2** Recommendations

Test Requirements:
Diagnostic testing waived: **Yes**
Untimed SAT: **Yes** Untimed ACT: **Yes** Untimed ACH: **Yes**
Documentation of LD required: **Yes**

Types of Disabilities Served
• Speech/Lang • Reading • ADD with LD
• Study skills • Spelling   ADD without LD
• Written express • Math   ADHD with LD
• Organizational • Fine Motor   ADHD without LD
• Perceptual

Learning Disability Program

Counseling: Individual: **Yes**

Faculty:
Faculty: **2** Part time: **2**
Faculty advocate: **Yes** Meets with instructor: **When necessary**

Diagnostic Testing

ADD	Personality	Perceptual skills	Spelling
ADHD	Organization	Fine motor skills	Reading
I.Q.	Handwriting	Spoken language	Study skills
Math	Social skills	Written language	

Tutoring:
Average size of group tutorials: **2-5**
Services rendered by:
•Graduates •Peers Faculty LD staff Teacher trainees

Tutorials

Grp.	Ind.	Tutorials	Grp.	Ind.	Tutorials
•	•	Math skills	•	•	Word processing
•	•	Study skills	•	•	Time management
•	•	Language arts	•	•	Learning strategies
•	•	Written express	•	•	Organizational skills

Academic Accommodations

Curriculum	Study Aids	Exams
Priority registration	• Typist	• Oral
Math waiver	Reader	Untimed
• Foreign lang. waiver	• Notetaker	• Take home
• Course substitution	Proof reader	With proctor
In Class	• Text on tape	On computer
• Calculators	Early syllabus	• Extended time
• Tape recorder	Taped handouts	On tape
• Word processor		• Modified
Priority seating		Separate room

Program Strengths

Individual assistance is provided upon request to students with learning disabilities. The Opportunity Development Center's special services coordinator works with each student to determine appropriate accommodations, identify on-campus and off-campus resources, and provide additional support as necessary (i.e. advocate, counselor).

General Information:

Vanderbilt University is a 4 year private university. Urban campus of 330 acres is Accessible by air or bus. 2% of students are foreign. 30 residential halls on campus. Housing is guaranteed. Guaranteed through 1st year.

Accreditation: SACS

Class Rank:
About 55% of the present freshmen class were in the upper 20% of their high school class. 68% were in the top 40% of their class. 70% were in the top 60% of their class.

Expenses:
Tuition: In-state: Full year: $13,975.00. Room and board: $5,050.00

Majors

• AREA STUDIES Black/Afro-American, East Asian, European, Latin American, Russian/Slavic, Urban • BUSINESS Economics • COMMUNICATIONS Communication, English • COMPUTER SCIENCE Computer Science • EDUCATION Early Childhood, Elementary, Pre-Education, Secondary, Special • ENGINEERING Bio-medical, Bioengineering, Chemical, Civil/Environmental, Computer, Electrical, Engineering Science, Environmental/Water Resources, Materials, Mechanical • HUMANITIES Classics, Liberal Arts, Philosophy, Religion, Religious Studies • LANGUAGES French, German, Greek, Latin, Portuguese, Russian, Spanish • SCIENCES Astronomy, Biology, Chemistry, Geology, Mathematics, Molecular Biology, Physics • SOCIAL SCIENCES Anthropology, Government/Political, History, Human Service, Political Science, Psychology, Public Policy, Sociology • VISUAL AND PERFORMING ARTS Dramatic

Texas

Arts, Fine Arts, Music, Music Performance, Theater

Sports/Activities
• SPORTS RELATED Baton Twirling, Cheerleading, Chess, Drum Major/Majorette, Flying Team, Marching Band, Pep Band, Team Managers
• SPORTS-INTERCOLLEGIATE Baseball (M), Basketball, Cross Country, Diving (F), Football (M), Golf, Soccer, Swimming (F), Tennis, Track and Field • SPORTS-INTRAMURAL Badminton (F), Basketball, Bowling, Cross Country (M), Fencing, Field Hockey (F), Golf (M), Gymnastics, Hand Ball (M), Lacrosse (M), Ping-Pong, Racquetball, Rugby, Sailing, Skiing - Snow, Soccer, Squash (M), Swimming, Tennis, Track and Field, Volleyball, Water Polo (M), Wrestling (M) • STUDENT LIFE ACTIVITIES Academic Clubs, Choral, Concert Band, Dance, Debate, Drama Groups, Ethnic & Cultural Groups, Fraternities, Jazz Band, Magazine, Music Groups, Musical Theater, Newspaper, Opera, Political Groups, Radio/TV station, Religious Organization, Sororities, Student Government, Symphony Orchestra, Yearbook

Less Selective	Texas
	Services

Amarillo College
P. O. Box 447
Amarillo, Texas 79178
(806) 371-5030

School Enrollment: **5,300** Male: **2,200** Female: **3,100**

Admissions Contact: **Dennis McMillan, Registrar**
LD Contact: **Judy Johnson, Director Accessibility Services**
Name of Program: **Transitional Assistance**
Telephone:**(806) 371-5436**

Admissions

Application Information:
Separate application:**Yes**
Application deadline: **June 30th**
Applicant must apply **1** months in advance

Secondary School Information
Most Important Criteria For Admissions (1-strongest)

8 SAT/ACT	3 Application	5 School transcript
9 Class rank	6 Course selection	7 Personal statement
2 Interview	10 Extra activities	1 Psychoeducational
4 G.P.A.	1 Open admission	11 Recommendations

Test Requirements:
Diagnostic testing waived: **Yes**
Achievement tests required:**1**
WAIS-R required: **Yes** Range accepted: **85+**
Documentation of LD required: **Yes**
Currency of diagnostic testing: **Maximum of 3 years**
Tests recommended: **Woodcock-Johnson**

Types of Disabilities Served
• Speech/Lang
• Study skills
• Written express
• Organizational
• Perceptual
• Reading
• Spelling
• Math
• Fine Motor
• ADD with LD
• ADD without LD
• ADHD with LD
• ADHD without LD

Admissions Process
Amarillo College employs an open admission policy.

Learning Disability Program
Program: Reinforces course work: **Yes**
Students mainstreamed **100** % of the day
Time required or recommended in learning center: **None**
Counseling: Individual: **Yes** Group Counseling: **Yes**

Faculty:
Faculty: **2** Including Director: **Yes** Full time: **2** M.A.: **2**
Faculty advocate: **Yes** Meets with instructor: **As needed**

Diagnostic Testing
ADD	Personality	• Perceptual skills	Spelling
ADHD•	Organization	Fine motor skills	• Reading
• I.Q.	Handwriting	Spoken language	• Study skills
• Math	Social skills	• Written language	

Tutoring:
Average size of group tutorials: **2**
Services rendered by:
  Graduates •Peers •Faculty •LD staff Teacher trainees

Tutorials
Grp.	Ind.	Tutorials	Grp.	Ind.	Tutorials
•	•	Math skills	•	•	Word processing
•	•	Study skills	•	•	Time management
•	•	Language arts	•	•	Learning strategies
•	•	Written express	•	•	Organizational skills

Academic Accommodations
Curriculum	Study Aids	Exams
Priority registration	Typist	• Oral
Math waiver	• Reader	Untimed
Foreign lang. waiver	• Notetaker	Take home
• Course substitution	Proof reader	• With proctor
In Class	• Text on tape	• On computer
• Calculators	Early syllabus	• Extended time
• Tape recorder	Taped handouts	• On tape
• Word processor		• Modified
• Priority seating		• Separate room

General Information:
Amarillo College is a 2 year public college. Urban campus. Accessible by air or bus. Ski areas are 5-6 hours from campus. Beaches are 15 hours from campus. Housing is not guaranteed.

Accreditation: SACS

Expenses:
Tuition: In-state: Full year: $576.00. Part-time: Per credit:$54.00. Tuition: Out-of-state: Full year: $1,356.00. Part-time: Per credit:$214.00.

Majors
• BUSINESS Accounting, Banking, Business Administration, Business Management, Finance, Management, Marketing, Real Estate, Retailing • COMMUNICATIONS Advertising, Broadcasting, English, Journalism, Photography, Television/Radio/Film • COMPUTER SCIENCE Computer Science, Data Processing, Hardware Engineer, Programming, Software Engineer • CRAFTS AND DESIGN Graphic Design • EDUCATION Child Development • ENGINEERING Architectural, Chemical, Civil/Environmental, Engineering Science, Mechanical, Petroleum • HEALTH SCIENCES Medical Assistant, Medical Technology, Nursing, Occupational Therapy, Physical Therapy, Radiological Therapy • HUMANITIES Liberal

Arts, Philosophy, Religion • LANGUAGES French, German, Spanish
• PREPROFESSIONAL Architecture, Dentistry, Engineering, Law, Medi-
cine, Optometry, Pharmacy, Veterinarian • SCIENCES Biology, Chemistry,
Geology, Mathematics, Physical Science, Physics, Radiology • SOCIAL
SCIENCES Criminal Justice, Government/Political, History, Psychology,
Social Sciences, Sociology • VISUAL AND PERFORMING ARTS Dance,
Fine Arts, Music, Theater • VOCATIONAL Air Conditioning/Heating/Re-
fri, Automobile Technology, Business and Office, Court Reporting, Dental
Hygiene, Diesel Power Technology, Drafting, Electronics Technology,
Fashion Merchandising, Fire Science, Home Economics, Industrial Design,
Legal Secretary, Respiratory Therapy Technology, Secretarial, Veterinarian
Assistant, Welding, Word Processing

Sports/Activities

• SPORTS-INTRAMURAL Basketball, Bowling, Golf, Tennis • STU-
DENT LIFE ACTIVITIES Choral, Concert Band, Dance, Drama Groups,
Jazz Band, Magazine, Music Groups, Musical Theater, Newspaper, Opera,
Radio/TV station, Student Government

Less Selective

Texas
Services

El Paso Community College
P.O. Box 20500
El Paso, Texas 79998
(915) 594-2426

School Enrollment: **17,000**
LD Enrollment: **214**

Admissions Contact: **Ann Lemke, Director**
LD Contact: **Ann Lemke, Director, Handicapped Services**
Name of Program: **Educational Services for the Handicapped**
Address: **P.O. Box 20500**
Telephone:**(915) 594-2426**

Admissions

Application Information:
LD Students Applying: **196** Accepted: **196** Enrolled:**196**
Application deadline: **Approx. 6 weeks prior to semester**
Applicant must apply **6** months in advance

Secondary School Information
Most Important Criteria For Admissions (1-strongest)
7 SAT/ACT 1 Application 2 School transcript
10 Class rank 5 Course selection 9 Personal statement
4 Interview 11 Extra activities 3 Psychoeducational
8 G.P.A. Open admission 6 Recommendations

Test Requirements:
Diagnostic testing waived: **Yes**
Untimed SAT: **Yes** Untimed ACT: **Yes**
Documentation of LD required: **Yes**
Currency of diagnostic testing: **No specified time**
Tests recommended: **Intellectual, Achievement, Perceptual, Memo-
ry**

Types of Disabilities Served
• Speech/Lang • Reading • ADD with LD
• Study skills • Spelling • ADD without LD
• Written express • Math • ADHD with LD
• Organizational • Fine Motor • ADHD without LD
• Perceptual

Admissions Process

Application for admission, application fee ($10.00 citizen, $25.00
non-citizen). Transcripts to Admissions Office. Mandatory assessment in the Basic Skills. Separate application for CESH

High School Course Requirements:
English: **2** Math: **1/2** Science: **1** Foreign Language: **1**

Learning Disability Program
Special orientation for LD students: **Yes**
Students mainstreamed **100** % of the day
Recommended credits per semester: **varies**
Group Counseling: **Yes** Vocational Counseling: **Yes**
Support groups are available:**CESH group for students with non-vis-
ible disabilities.**

Faculty:
Faculty: **61** Including Director: **Yes** Full time: **12** Part time: **49**
LD faculty with: BS/BA: **3** M.A.: **4**
Faculty advocate: **Yes** Meets with instructor: **As needed**

Diagnostic Testing
ADD	Personality	Perceptual skills	Spelling
ADHD	Organization	Fine motor skills	Reading
I.Q.	Handwriting	Spoken language	Study skills
Math	Social skills	Written language	

Tutoring:
Average size of group tutorials: **1:1**
Services rendered by:
Graduates Peers Faculty •LD staff Teacher trainees

Tutorials
Grp.	Ind.	Tutorials	Grp.	Ind.	Tutorials
•	•	Math skills		•	Word processing
	•	Study skills		•	Time management
•	•	Language arts		•	Learning strategies
	•	Written express		•	Organizational skills

Academic Accommodations
Curriculum	Study Aids	Exams
• Priority registration	Typist	• Oral
Math waiver	• Reader	Untimed
Foreign lang. waiver	• Notetaker	• Take home
• Course substitution	• Proof reader	• With proctor
In Class	• Text on tape	• On computer
• Calculators	Early syllabus	• Extended time
• Tape recorder	• Taped handouts	• On tape
• Word processor		• Modified
• Priority seating		• Separate room

Graduation Requirements:
Course credits: **60** GPA: **2.0** Years to complete degree: **5 Maximum** Language waiver: **Yes**
Other requirements: **Texas Assessment Skills Program requirements must be satisfied. At least 6 hours of major course work
has to be taken at EPCC.**

Program Strengths
Adaptive equipment: Kurzweil Reading Machine, Dragon Dictate,
speech review on computers, expanded keyboards. Structured
multi-sensory approach, directive open-for higher level like computer
program-time established when students can meet with a tutor. Students come prepared with specific questions. Major emphasis on bilingual students learning to master a monolingual environment.

Texas

General Information:

El Paso Community College is a 2 year public college. Suburban campus Accessible by plane or bus Ski areas are 120 miles from campus. Beaches are 800 miles from campus. 1% of students are foreign. Housing is not guaranteed.

Accreditation:CCSACS

Expenses:

Tuition: In-state: Full year: $229.00 (12 hours), $271.00 (15 hours). Part-time: Per credit:$75.00 for first hour then $14.00 increase. Part-time: Per course: $103.00 for a 3 hour course, $89.00 for 2 hour. Tuition: Out-of-state: Full year: $740.00 (12 hours), $920.00 (15 hours). Part-time: Per credit:$200.00 for first 3 hours then $60.00 increase . Part-time: Per course:$200.00

Majors

• ARTS Art History, Commercial Art, Crafts, Dance, Design, Drafting, Dramatic Arts, Drawing, Fashion Design, Film & Video, Graphic Arts, Interior Design, Music, Music Performance, Painting, Photography, Sculpture, Theater Design • BUSINESS Accounting, Agricultural, Banking/Finance, Bookkeeping, Business Administration, Business Education, Business Management, Clerical, Commerce & Trade, Commercial Art, Data Processing, Education, Fashion Merchandising, Food Management, Hotel & Restaurant Management, Industrial Operations, Insurance, International Business, Management, Marketing, Marketing Research, Professional Communication, Real Estate, Retail Manufacturing, Retailing, Secretarial Science, Travel/Tourism Management • COMMUNICATIONS Advertising, Broadcasting, Commercial Design, Communication, Creative Writing, English, Graphic Design, Journalism, Literature, Photography, Printing, Television/Radio/Film • COMPUTER SCIENCE Business Data Programming, Computer Science, Data Processing, Medical Records Administration, Medical Records Technology, Programming, Robotics, Telecommunications • CRAFTS AND DESIGN Apparel Design, Ceramics, Graphic Design, Illustration Design, Industrial Design, Sculpture • EDUCATION Child Development, Early Childhood, Elementary, English, English As A Second Language, Foreign Language, Mathematics, Music, Psychology, Recreation/Youth Leadership, Secondary, Speech/Language • HEALTH SCIENCES Dental Assistant, Dental Hygiene, Dietary Manager, Health, Human Services, Medical Laboratory Technology, Medical Records Administration, Medical Secretary, Nuclear Medical Technology, Nursing, Nursing Assistant, Nutritional/Food, Ophthalmic Technology, Pharmacology, Physical Therapy Assistant, Radiological Therapy, Respiratory Therapy, Speech Therapy, Surgical Technology, Ultrasound Technology • HUMANITIES English/Writing/Literature, Fine Arts, Liberal Arts • LANGUAGES French, German, Russian, Spanish • PRE PROFESSIONAL Agriculture, Architecture, Business, Dentistry, Drafting, Engineering, Industrial Design, Landscaping, Law, Legal Assistant, Pharmacy, Recreation, Social Work • SCIENCES Anthropology, Astronomy, Biology, Chemistry, Computer Science, Geology, Horticultural, Mathematics, Physics • SOCIAL SCIENCES Anthropology, Criminal Justice, Criminology, Government/Political, History, Human Service, Law Enforcement, Political Science, Psychology, Social Science, Sociology • SPECIAL EDUCATION Deaf/Hearing Impaired • VISUAL AND PERFORMING ARTS Art, Art History, Dance, Dance Education, Dramatic Arts, Fine Arts, Music, Music Performance • VOCATIONAL Air Conditioning/Heating/Refri, Auto Body, Automobile Technology, Automotive Service, Building Construction, Business and Office, Dental Assistant, Dental Hygiene, Drafting, Electronics Technology, Fashion Design, Fashion Merchandising, Fire Science, Food Service, Legal Secretary, Office Administration, Painting, Paralegal, Paramedic, Radiological Technology, Respiratory Therapy Technology, Secretarial, Sign Language/Interpreter Prep, Textile and Clothing, Welding, Word Processing

Sports/Activities

• SPORTS-INTRAMURAL Archery, Badminton, Basketball, Bowling, Football, Golf, Gymnastics, Hand Ball, Martial Arts, Racquetball, Soccer, Softball, Swimming, Tennis, Track and Field, Volleyball, Weight Lifting, Wrestling • STUDENT LIFE ACTIVITIES Dance, Drama Groups, Music Groups, Newspaper, Student Government

---

North Harris Montgomery Community College District

2700 West Thorne Drive
Houston, Texas 77073
(713) 443-5481

School Enrollment: **13,000** Male: **5,000** Female: **8,000**
LD Enrollment: **200**
LD Contact: **Sandi Patton, Counselor**
Telephone:**(713) 443-5481**

Admissions

Application Information:

Application deadline: **Open**
Applicant must apply **1 semester** months in advance
Rolling Admissions: **Yes**Notified when: **Open**

Secondary School Information

Most Important Criteria For Admissions (1-strongest)

8	SAT/ACT	9	Application	3	School transcript
10	Class rank	4	Course selection	5	Personal statement
2	Interview	6	Extra activities	1	Psychoeducational
7	G.P.A.	1	Open admission		Recommendations

Test Requirements:

Standardized tests waived: **Yes**
Untimed SAT: **Yes** Untimed ACT: **Yes**
Documentation of LD required: **Yes**
Currency of diagnostic testing: **3 years**

Types of Disabilities Served

• Speech/Lang	• Reading	• ADD with LD
• Study skills	• Spelling	• ADD without LD
• Written express	• Math	• ADHD with LD
• Organizational	• Fine Motor	• ADHD without LD
• Perceptual		

Admissions Process

Open door policy

Learning Disability Program

Services available for all students: **Yes**
Counseling: Individual: **Yes**

Faculty:

Faculty: **3** Full time: **1** Part time: **2**

Diagnostic Testing

ADD	Personality	Perceptual skills	•	Spelling
ADHD	Organization	Fine motor skills	•	Reading
• I.Q.	Handwriting	Spoken language	•	Study skills
• Math	Social skills	• Written language		

Tutoring:

Services rendered by:
Graduates   •Peers   •Faculty   LD staff   Teacher trainees

Tutorials

Grp.	Ind.	Tutorials	Grp.	Ind.	Tutorials
•	•	Math skills	•	•	Word processing
•	•	Study skills	•	•	Time management
•	•	Language arts	•	•	Learning strategies
•	•	Written express	•	•	Organizational skills

Academic Accommodations

Curriculum	Study Aids	Exams
Priority registration	Typist	• Oral
Math waiver	• Reader	Untimed
Foreign lang. waiver	• Notetaker	Take home
Course substitution	Proof reader	With proctor
In Class	• Text on tape	On computer
• Calculators	Early syllabus	• Extended time
• Tape recorder	Taped handouts	• On tape
• Word processor		• Modified
• Priority seating		• Separate room

Program Strengths

We are a mainstreamed institution. Support services are provided on an individualized basis and are coordinated through Counseling Services. The diagnostician provides testing services and a diagnostic prescription of support services recommended. The counselor coordinates support services.

General Information:

North Harris Montgomery Community College District is a 2 year public college. Suburban campus 20 miles from Houston. Accessible by car. Beaches are 70 miles from campus. Housing is not guaranteed.

Accreditation: SACS

Expenses:

Tuition: In-state: Full year: $1,500.00, $800.00 (District residents). Part-time: Per credit: $35.00. Part-time: Per credit: $210.00.

Majors

• ARTS Art History, Drafting, Dramatic Arts, Drawing, Graphic Art, Interior Design, Music, Music Performance, Painting, Photography • BUSINESS Accounting, Banking/Finance, Business Management, Clerical, Data Processing, Economics, Food Management, Human Resources Management, Management, Marketing, Real Estate, Secretarial Science, Travel/Tourism Management • COMMUNICATIONS Communication, Creative Writing, English, Graphic Design, Journalism, Literature, Photography, Speech/Debate/Forensic • COMPUTER SCIENCE Business Data Programming, Computer Maintenance, Computer Technology, Data Processing, Programming, Systems Analysis • CRAFTS AND DESIGN Ceramic • EDUCATION Adult, Child Development, English As A Second Language • HEALTH SCIENCES Nursing, Veterinarian Assistant • HUMANITIES English/Writing/Literature, Fine Arts, Humanities, Liberal Arts, Philosophy • LANGUAGES English, French, German, Spanish • MATHEMATICS Applied • PREPROFESSIONAL Agriculture, Architecture, Business, Dentistry, Drafting, Engineering, Fisheries, Forestry, Industrial Design, Landscaping, Law, Legal Assistant, Medicine, Ministry, Natural Resources, Optometry, Pharmacy, Range Management, Recreation, Social Work, Sports Medicine, Urban Design, Veterinarian, Wildlife • RELIGIOUS STUDIES Philosophy • SCIENCES Anatomy, Anthropology, Applied Mathematics, Biology, Biotechnology, Botany, Chemistry, Computer Science, Geography, Geology, Human Biology, Inorganic Chemistry, Mathematics, Microbiology, Organic Chemistry, Physics • SOCIAL SCIENCES Anthropology, Criminal Justice, Criminology, Geography, Government/Political, History, Human Service, Law Enforcement, Political Science, Psychology, Social Science, Sociology • VISUAL AND PERFORMING ARTS Art, Art History, Dance, Dramatic Arts, Fine Arts, Music, Music Performance, Theater • VOCATIONAL Air Conditioning/Heating/Refri, Automobile Technology, Automotive Service, Aviation Maintenance, Business and Office, Cosmetology, Drafting, Electronics Technology, Food

Service, Interior Design, Legal Secretary, Office Administration, Paralegal, Respiratory Therapy Technology, Secretarial, Veterinarian Assistant, Welding, Word Processing

Sports/Activities

• STUDENT LIFE ACTIVITIES Academic Clubs, Choral, Community Service, Drama Groups, Ethnic & Cultural Groups, Magazine, Newspaper, Religious Organization

---

Less Selective   **Texas**
                                                            Services

North Lake College
5001 North MacArthur Boulevard
Irving, Texas 75038
(214) 659-5230

School Enrollment: **6,000**
LD Enrollment: **101**

Admissions Contact: **Steve Twenge, Registrar**
LD Contact: **Mary G. Ciminelli, Coordinator/Counselor**
Name of Program: **Special Services**
Telephone: **(214) 659-5237**

Admissions

Application Information:

LD Students Applying: **148** Accepted: **148** Enrolled: **101**
Application deadline: **ASAP**

Secondary School Information

Most Important Criteria For Admissions (1-strongest)

11	SAT/ACT	11	Application	8	School transcript
5	Class rank	5	Course selection	1	Personal statement
1	Interview	11	Extra activities	1	Psychoeducational
5	G.P.A.		Open admission	3	Recommendations

Test Requirements:

Standardized tests waived: **Yes**
Diagnostic testing waived: **Yes**
Untimed SAT: **Yes** Untimed ACT: **Yes** Untimed ACH: **Yes**
Documentation of LD required: **Yes**
Currency of diagnostic testing: **2 years**
Tests recommended: **WAIS-R and Woodcock-Johnson**

Types of Disabilities Served

• Speech/Lang	• Reading	• ADD with LD
• Study skills	• Spelling	• ADD without LD
• Written express	• Math	• ADHD with LD
• Organizational	• Fine Motor	• ADHD without LD
• Perceptual		

Admissions Process

Open admissions policy - no standardized cut off scores needed. LD student goes to Special Services upon acceptance, complete Intake Form, provide appropriate documentation. Counseling and guidance provided and accommodation for classroom are coordinated.

Learning Disability Program

Special orientation for LD students: **Yes**
Program: Remedial: **Yes**
Program: Reinforces course work: **Yes**
Program available through:**Upon request**
Students mainstreamed **95** % of the day
Recommended credits per semester: **9-12**
Counseling: Individual: **Yes** Vocational Counseling: **Yes**
Support groups are available:**If need indicated**

Faculty:
Faculty: **4** Including Director: **Yes** Full time: **1** Part time: **3** M.A.: **4**
Faculty advocate: **Yes** Meets with instructor: **When needed**

Diagnostic Testing
ADD	Personality	Perceptual skills	• Spelling
ADHD	Organization	Fine motor skills	• Reading
• I.Q.	Handwriting	Spoken language	• Study skills
• Math	Social skills	• Written language	

Tutoring:
Average size of group tutorials: **3-4**
Services rendered by:
•Graduates •Peers •Faculty •LD staff •Teacher trainees

Tutorials
Grp.	Ind.	Tutorials	Grp.	Ind.	Tutorials
•	•	Math skills	•	•	Word processing
•	•	Study skills	•	•	Time management
•	•	Language arts	•	•	Learning strategies
•	•	Written express	•	•	Organizational skills

Academic Accommodations

Curriculum	Study Aids	Exams
Priority registration	• Typist	• Oral
• Math waiver	• Reader	• Untimed
• Foreign lang. waiver	• Notetaker	• Take home
Course substitution	• Proof reader	• With proctor
In Class	• Text on tape	• On computer
• Calculators	Early syllabus	• Extended time
• Tape recorder	Taped handouts	• On tape
• Word processor		• Modified
• Priority seating		• Separate room

Graduation Requirements:
Course credits: **60** GPA: **2.0** Years to complete degree: **Unlimited**

General Information:

North Lake College is a 2 year public college. Suburban campus 10 miles from Dallas. Accessible by bus. Housing is not guaranteed.

Accreditation:SACS

Expenses:
Tuition: In-state: Full year: $174.00 (12 semester hours). Part-time: Per credit:$110.00 (1-3 semester hours). Part-time: Per course: Part-time: $52.00 (1-3 semester hours). Tuition: Out-of-state: Full year: $766.00 (12 semester hours). Part-time: Per credit:$210.00 (1-3 semester hours). Part-time: Per course:$210.00 (1-3 credit)

Majors

• BUSINESS Accounting, Business Data Processing, Management, Real Estate • COMPUTER SCIENCE Computer & Information Science, Data Processing • HUMANITIES Liberal/General • VISUAL AND PERFORMING ARTS Video • VOCATIONAL Business and Office, Carpentry, Electrical Construction, Electronics Technology, Secretarial

Sports/Activities

• SPORTS-INTERCOLLEGIATE Baseball (M) • SPORTS-INTRAMURAL Softball, Volleyball • STUDENT LIFE ACTIVITIES Drama Groups, Jazz Band, Music Ensemble, Newspaper, Student Government

Less Selective   **Texas**
                                      Program

Richland College
12800 Abrams Road
Dallas, Texas 75243-2199
(214) 238-6100

School Enrollment: **13,375** Male: **6,194** Female: **7,181**
LD Enrollment: **400**

Admissions Contact: **Gary Matney, Director of Admissions**
LD Contact: **Ann Straley, Director of LD Program**
Name of Program: **Learning Differences Program**
Address: **Special Services, 12800 Abrams Rd.**
Telephone:**(214) 238-6372**

Admissions

Application Information:
Accepted: **100** Enrolled:**100**
Separate application:**Yes**
LD on admissions committee:**Yes**
Applicant must apply **2** months in advance
Rolling Admissions: **Yes**

Secondary School Information
Most Important Criteria For Admissions (1-strongest)
12 SAT/ACT	**1** Application	**1** School transcript
12 Class rank	**12** Course selection	**12** Personal statement
1 Interview	**12** Extra activities	**1** Psychoeducational
12 G.P.A.	Open admission	**5** Recommendations

Test Requirements:
Standardized tests waived: **Yes**
Diagnostic testing waived: **Yes**
Untimed SAT: **Yes** Untimed ACT: **Yes** Untimed ACH: **Yes**
WAIS-R required: **Yes** Range accepted: **85+**
Documentation of LD required: **Yes**
Tests recommended: **Neuropsychological, Academic**

Types of Disabilities Served
• Speech/Lang	• Reading	• ADD with LD
• Study skills	• Spelling	• ADD without LD
• Written express	• Math	• ADHD with LD
• Organizational	• Fine Motor	• ADHD without LD
• Perceptual		

High School Course Requirements:
English: **1** Math: **1** Science: **1**
Waivers to standard high school courses
Foreign Language : **Yes** Course substitution: **Yes**

Learning Disability Program

Special orientation for LD students: **Yes**
Syllabus available during orientation:**Yes**
Program: Remedial: **Yes**
Program: Reinforces course work: **Yes**
Program available through:**Fall & Spring semesters**
Students mainstreamed **100** % of the day
Recommended credits per semester: **9-12**
Services only for LD students: **Yes**
Group Counseling: **Yes** Vocational Counseling: **Yes**
Support groups are available:**Yes**

Faculty:

Faculty: **8** Including Director: **Yes** Full time: **2** Part time: **6**
LD faculty with: BS/BA: **4** M.A.: **4**
Faculty advocate: **Yes** Meets with instructor: **As needed**

Diagnostic Testing

ADD	Personality	Perceptual skills	• Spelling
ADHD	Organization	Fine motor skills	• Reading
• I.Q.	Handwriting	Spoken language	Study skills
• Math	• Social skills	• Written language	

Tutoring:

Services rendered by:
•Graduates •Peers •Faculty •LD staff •Teacher trainees

Tutorials

Grp.	Ind.	Tutorials	Grp.	Ind.	Tutorials
•	•	Math skills	•	•	Word processing
•	•	Study skills	•	•	Time management
		Language arts	•	•	Learning strategies
•	•	Written express	•	•	Organizational skills

Academic Accommodations

Curriculum	Study Aids	Exams
• Priority registration	Typist	• Oral
Math waiver	• Reader	• Untimed
Foreign lang. waiver	• Notetaker	• Take home
Course substitution	Proof reader	• With proctor
In Class	• Text on tape	On computer
Calculators	• Early syllabus	• Extended time
• Tape recorder	• Taped handouts	• On tape
• Word processor		• Modified
• Priority seating		• Separate room

Program Strengths

The LD program of Richland College allows its students the option of registering in classes designed to meet their special needs. The LD curriculum includes instruction in basic reading, writing, and spelling skills; written expression; motivation and organization; multisensory math; career planning; and study skills. For students who need only minimal modification of courses in the regular college curriculum, Richland provides a full range of special services to augment regular classroom instruction.

General Information:

Richland College is a 2 year public college. Urban campus 8 miles from Dallas. Accessible by air, train or bus. 11% of students are foreign. Housing is not guaranteed.

Accreditation: State, Federal

Expenses:

Tuition: In-state: Full year: $179.00. Part-time: Per credit:$57.00. Tuition: Out-of-state: Full year: Part-time: Per credit: $200.00.

Majors

• AGRICULTURE Business, Education, Engineering, Horticultural
• AREA STUDIES American, Asian, Black/Afro-American, Ethnic/Cultural, European, Hispanic/American, International Studies, Mexican/American, Middle Eastern, Russian/Slavic, Urban, Women's Studies
• ARTS Art History, Crafts, Dance, Design, Drafting, Dramatic Arts, Drawing, Graphic Arts, Landscaping, Music, Music History, Music Performance, Painting, Photography, Sculpture • BUSINESS Accounting, Banking/Finance, Bookkeeping, Business Administration, Business Economics, Business Management, Business Statistics, Clerical, Construction, Data Processing, Economics, Education, Management, Marketing, Organizational Behavior, Real Estate, Secretarial Science • COMMUNICATIONS Broadcasting, Communication, Creative Writing, English, Graphic Design, Journalism, Literature, Photography, Public Relations • COMPUTER SCIENCE Business Data Programming, Computer Maintenance, Computer Science, Computer Technology, Data Processing, Programming, Robotics, Software Engineer, Systems Analysis • CRAFTS AND DESIGN Ceramics, Graphic Design, Jewelry, Sculpture • EDUCATION Art, Business, Child Development, English As A Second Language , Foreign Language, Mathematics, Music, Psychology, Reading, Religious, Social Studies, Technical, Vocational • ENGINEERING Drafting, Electrical, Engineering Science, Mechanical • HUMANITIES Classics, English/Writing/Literature, Fine Arts, Humanities, Liberal Arts , Philosophy, Religion
• LANGUAGES English, French, German, Spanish • PREPROFESSIONAL Business, Drafting, Engineering, Landscaping, Social Work • SCIENCES Anatomy, Anthropology, Applied Mathematics, Archeology, Astronomy, Biology, Botany, Chemistry, Computer Science, Horticultural, Human Biology, Inorganic Chemistry, Macrobiology, Marine Biology, Mathematics, Microbiology, Oceanography, Organic Chemistry, Physical Chemistry, Physical Science, Physics, Physiology, Statistics, Zoology
• SOCIAL SCIENCES Anthropology, Government/Political, History, International Studies, Library Science, Political Science, Psychology, Public Relations, Social Science, Sociology • SPECIAL EDUCATION Head Injured, Learning Disability • VISUAL AND PERFORMING ARTS Art, Art History, Dance, Dramatic Arts, Fine Arts, Music, Music Performance, Music Theatre, Studio Art, Theater • VOCATIONAL Building Construction, Business and Office, Chef Apprenticeship, Construction, Culinary Arts, Food Service, Office Administration, Secretarial

Sports/Activities

• SPORTS RELATED Cheerleading • SPORTS-INTERCOLLEGIATE Baseball , Basketball (M), Soccer (F), Soccer (M), Volleyball (F)
• SPORTS-INTRAMURAL Badminton, Badminton (F), Badminton (F), Badminton (M), Basketball , Basketball (F), Basketball (M), Bowling, Bowling (M), Canoeing, Canoeing (F), Canoeing (M), Cross Country, Cross Country (F), Cross Country (M), Field Hockey, Field Hockey (F), Field Hockey (M), Football, Football (F), Football (M), soccer Soccer (F), Soccer (M), softball Softball (F), Softball (M), Tennis, Tennis (F), Tennis (M), volleyball Volleyball (F), Volleyball (M), Weight Lifting, Weight Lifting (M) • STUDENT LIFE ACTIVITIES Drama Groups, Ethnic & Cultural Groups, Film, Jazz Band, Music Groups, Newspaper, Radio/TV station, Religious Organization

Selective

Texas
Services

Sam Houston State University
University Drive
Huntsville, Texas 77341
(409) 294-1056-(800) 232-7528

School Enrollment: **12,500** Male: **6,250** Female: **6,250**
LD Enrollment: **30**

Admissions Contact: **H.A. Bass, Director of Admissions**
LD Contact: **Patsy Copeland, Ph.D., Director Counseling Center**
Name of Program: **Academic Assistance**
Telephone:**(409) 294-1720**

Admissions

Application Information:
Rolling Admissions: **Yes**

Secondary School Information
Most Important Criteria For Admissions (1-strongest)

1 SAT/ACT	Application	School transcript
Class rank	Course selection	Personal statement
Interview	Extra activities	Psychoeducational
2 G.P.A.	Open admission	Recommendations

Test Requirements:
Diagnostic testing waived: **Yes**
Untimed SAT: **Yes** Untimed ACT: **Yes**
Documentation of LD required: **Yes**

Types of Disabilities Served
- Speech/Lang
- Study skills
- Written express
- Organizational
- Perceptual

- Reading
- Spelling
- Math
- Fine Motor

ADD with LD
ADD without LD
ADHD with LD
ADHD without LD

Learning Disability Program
Counseling: Individual: **Yes**

Faculty:
Faculty: **1** Part time: **1**

Diagnostic Testing

ADD	Personality	Perceptual skills	Spelling
ADHD	Organization	Fine motor skills	Reading
I.Q.	Handwriting	Spoken language	Study skills
Math	Social skills	Written language	

Services rendered by:
Graduates   Peers   Faculty   LD staff   Teacher trainees

Tutorials

Grp.	Ind.	Tutorials	Grp.	Ind.	Tutorials
		Math skills			Word processing
		Study skills			Time management
		Language arts			Learning strategies
		Written express			Organizational skills

Academic Accommodations

Curriculum	Study Aids	Exams
Priority registration	Typist	• Oral
Math waiver	Reader	Untimed
Foreign lang. waiver	• Notetaker	Take home
Course substitution	Proof reader	With proctor
In Class	• Text on tape	On computer
Calculators	Early syllabus	• Extended time
• Tape recorder	Taped handouts	On tape
• Word processor		Modified
Priority seating		Separate room

Program Strengths
* Each department finds tutors for those students who need assistance.

General Information:
Sam Houston State University is a 4 year public university. Accessible by bus. Beaches are 100 from campus. Housing is not guaranteed.10 % of students remain on campus for the weekends. 10 % of students join fraternities/sororities.

Accreditation:SACS

Expenses: Part-time: Per credit:$168.00 (1-2 hours), $204.00 (3 or more). Room and board: $1,600.00

Majors
• BUSINESS Accounting, Agricultural, Banking, Business Administration, Business Economics, Business Education, Business Management, Economics, Finance, International Business, Management, Marketing • COMMUNICATIONS Broadcasting, Communication, English, Graphic Design, Journalism, Photography, Speech, Television/Radio/Film • COMPUTER SCIENCE Computer Science, Programming • EDUCATION Agricultural, Art, Early Childhood, Elementary, Health, Industrial, Middle School, Music, Physical, School Psychology, Secondary, Special, Vocational • ENGINEERING Computer • HEALTH SCIENCES Health, Medical Technology, Nursing, Nutritional/Food, Physical Therapy • HUMANITIES Humanities, Philosophy • LANGUAGES French, German, Spanish • PRE-PROFESSIONAL Agriculture, Dentistry, Law, Medicine, Ministry, Pharmacy • SCIENCES Agricultural, Animal, Astronomy, Biochemistry, Biology, Botany, Chemistry, Earth, Geography, Geology, Horticultural, Marine Biology, Mathematics, Microbiology, Physical Chemistry, Physical Science, Physics, Zoology • SOCIAL SCIENCES Criminal Justice, Criminology, Government/Political, History, Psychology, Social Sciences, Sociology • VISUAL AND PERFORMING ARTS Art, Art History, Dance, Dramatic Arts, Fine Arts, Music, Music Performance, Studio Art, Theater • VOCATIONAL Business and Office, Fashion Design, Food Service, Home Economics, Interior Design

Sports/Activities
• SPORTS RELATED Cheerleading, Drill Team, Drum Major/Majorette, Marching Band, Pep Band • SPORTS-INTERCOLLEGIATE Baseball (M), Basketball, Cross Country (M), Football (M), Golf, Riflery, Soccer (M), Softball (F), Tennis, Volleyball (F) • SPORTS-INTRAMURAL Badminton, Basketball, Bowling, Diving, Golf, Hand Ball, Lacrosse (M), Racquetball, Softball, Swimming, Tennis, Volleyball, Water Polo • STUDENT LIFE ACTIVITIES Choral, Concert Band, Dance, Drama Groups, Fraternities, Jazz Band, Music Groups, Musical Theater, Newspaper, Opera, Radio/TV station, Sororities, Student Government, Symphony Orchestra, Yearbook

Less Selective

Texas
Services

San Antonio College
1300 San Pedro Avenue
San Antonio, Texas 78284
(512) 733-2300

School Enrollment: **20,800**
LD Enrollment: **325**

Admissions Contact: **Phyllis N. McCarley, Director of Admissions**
LD Contact: **Thomas C. Hoy, Coordinator**
Name of Program: **Disabled Student Services**
Address: **1300 San Pedro Ave.**
Telephone:**(512) 733-2352**

Admissions

Application Information:
Enrolled:**325**
Application deadline: **1 week prior to classes**

Secondary School Information
Most Important Criteria For Admissions (1-strongest)

SAT/ACT	Application	School transcript
Class rank	Course selection	Personal statement
Interview	Extra activities	Psychoeducational
G.P.A.	**1** Open admission	Recommendations

Test Requirements:
Diagnostic testing waived: **Yes**
Untimed SAT: **Yes** Untimed ACT: **Yes**
Documentation of LD required: **Yes**
Currency of diagnostic testing: **One week**
Tests recommended: **Any standardized battery recognized by AH-SSPPE, Coordinating Board of Texas (HE)**

Types of Disabilities Served
- Speech/Lang
- Study skills
- Written express
- Organizational
- Perceptual
- Reading
- Spelling
- Math
- Fine Motor
- ADD with LD
- ADD without LD
- ADHD with LD
- ADHD without LD

Admissions Process

Open door admissions (HS or GED), developmental courses required if ACT/SAT/ASSET Scores show a deficit.

Learning Disability Program

Syllabus available during orientation:**Yes**
Program: Remedial: **Yes**
Program: Reinforces course work: **Yes**
Program available through:**All times**
Students mainstreamed **100** % of the day
Recommended credits per semester: **12-14**
Counseling: Individual: **Yes** Group Counseling: **Yes** Vocational Counseling: **Yes**
Support groups are available:**LD Study Skills Group; LD Support Group**

Faculty:
Faculty: **3** Full time: **3** M.A.: **3**
Faculty advocate: **Yes** Meets with instructor: **As needed**

Diagnostic Testing
- ADD
- ADHD
- I.Q.
- Math

- Personality
- Organization
- Handwriting
- Social skills

- Perceptual skills
- Fine motor skills
- Spoken language
- Written language

- Spelling
- Reading
- Study skills

Tutoring:
Average size of group tutorials: **3-5**
Services rendered by:
Graduates •Peers Faculty LD staff Teacher trainees

Tutorials

Grp.	Ind.	Tutorials	Grp.	Ind.	Tutorials
•	•	Math skills	•	•	Word processing
•	•	Study skills	•	•	Time management
•	•	Language arts	•	•	Learning strategies
•	•	Written express	•	•	Organizational skills

Academic Accommodations

Curriculum	Study Aids	Exams
• Priority registration	• Typist	• Oral
• Math waiver	• Reader	Untimed
• Foreign lang. waiver	• Notetaker	Take home
• Course substitution	• Proof reader	• With proctor
In Class	• Text on tape	On computer
• Calculators	Early syllabus	• Extended time
• Tape recorder	Taped handouts	• On tape
• Word processor		• Modified
• Priority seating		• Separate room

Graduation Requirements:
Course credits: **66** GPA: **2.0** Years to complete degree: **Open**

Program Strengths

Students at San Antonio College who are learning disabled are mainstreamed in developmental, vocational, and/or academic classes according to entrance scores. The learning disability specialist evaluates the diagnostic LD tests to determine services to be provided through the Disabled Student Services Department. Notetaking, special testing, word processors, writers/readers, counseling, and other support services are made available.

General Information:

San Antonio College is a 2 year public college. Urban campus Accessible by air, train, or bus. Ski areas are 600 miles from campus. Beaches are 150 miles from campus. 1% of students are foreign. Housing is not guaranteed.

Accreditation: Regional and State

SAT/ACT Scores:
Scores for incoming freshmen: **ACT:** 94% below 20. 5% between 20 and 23. .05%between 24 and 25l. .05%between 26 and 28.

Expenses:
Tuition: In-state: Full year: $336.00. Part-time: Per credit:$14.00. Tuition: Out-of-state: Full year: $960.00. Part-time: Per credit:$40.00.

Majors

• BUSINESS Business Administration, Economics, Management, Real Estate • COMMUNICATIONS English, Journalism, Photography, Television/Radio/Film • COMPUTER SCIENCE Data Processing, Programming • EDUCATION Art, Physical • ENGINEERING Computer • HEALTH SCIENCES Medical Technology, Nursing • HUMANITIES Humanities,

Texas

Philosophy • PREPROFESSIONAL Architecture, Engineering, Law, Medicine • SCIENCES Biology, Chemistry, Geology, Mathematics, Physics • SOCIAL SCIENCES Criminal Justice, Government/Political, History, Sociology • VISUAL AND PERFORMING ARTS Art, Music, Theater

Sports/Activities

• SPORTS RELATED Team Managers • SPORTS-INTRAMURAL Baseball, Basketball, Cross Country, Diving, Fencing, Football, Soccer, Swimming, Tennis, Volleyball, Weight Lifting • STUDENT LIFE ACTIVITIES Debate, Drama Groups, Jazz Band, Music Groups, Newspaper, Radio/TV station, Religious Organization, Student Government

Selective   **Texas**
                                                                 Program

Schreiner College
Box 4503
Kerrville, Texas 78028
(512) 896-5411

School Enrollment: **540** Male: **250** Female: **290**
LD Enrollment: **80** Male: **60** Female: **20**

Admissions Contact: **Charles Tait, Admissions Counselor**
LD Contact: **Jude Gallik, Director**
Name of Program: **Learning Support Services**
Telephone:**(800) 343-4919**

Admissions

Application Information:
LD Students Applying: **80** Accepted: **41** Enrolled:**80**
Application deadline: **April 1st**
Applicant must apply **5** months in advance
Rolling Admissions: **Yes**

Secondary School Information
Most Important Criteria For Admissions (1-strongest)
5 SAT/ACT	**1** Application	**2**	School transcript
5 Class rank	**3** Course selection	**6**	Personal statement
4 Interview	**8** Extra activities	**3**	Psychoeducational
5 G.P.A.	Open admission	**7**	Recommendations

Test Requirements:
Standardized tests waived: **Yes**
Untimed SAT: **Yes** Untimed ACT: **Yes** Achievement tests required:**1**
WAIS-R required: **Yes** Range accepted: **Average+**
Documentation of LD required: **Yes**
Currency of diagnostic testing: **12 months**
Tests recommended: **WAIS-R, Individual Achievement Test, i.e. Woodcock-Johnson, that gives score in spelling, math, writing, and reading comprehension**

Types of Disabilities Served
• Speech/Lang   • Reading   • ADD with LD
• Study skills   • Spelling   • ADD without LD
• Written express   • Math   • ADHD with LD
• Organizational   • Fine Motor   • ADHD without LD
• Perceptual

Admissions Process

Student submits testing data; then has personal interview with LD staff member

High School Course Requirements:
English: **4** Math: **3** Science: **2**

Learning Disability Program
Special orientation for LD students: **Yes**
Program: Reinforces course work: **Yes**
Students mainstreamed **100** % of the day
Recommended credits per semester: **12-13**
Services available for all students: **Yes**
Counseling: Individual: **Yes** Group Counseling: **Yes** Vocational Counseling: **Yes**

Faculty:
Faculty: **4** Including Director: **Yes** Full time: **3** Part time: **1**
LD faculty with: BS/BA: **2** M.A.: **1** Ph.D.: **1**
Faculty advocate: **Yes** Meets with instructor: **As needed**

Diagnostic Testing
ADD	Personality	Perceptual skills	Spelling
ADHD	Organization	Fine motor skills	Reading
• I.Q.	Handwriting	Spoken language	• Study skills
Math	Social skills	Written language	

Tutoring:
Average size of group tutorials: **1-3**
Services rendered by:
Graduates   Peers   Faculty   •LD staff   Teacher trainees

Tutorials
Grp.	Ind.	Tutorials	Grp.	Ind.	Tutorials
•		Math skills		•	Word processing
•		Study skills	•		Time management
	•	Language arts	•		Learning strategies
	•	Written express	•		Organizational skills

Academic Accommodations
Curriculum	Study Aids	Exams
Priority registration	Typist	• Oral
Math waiver	Reader	Untimed
Foreign lang. waiver	Notetaker	• Take home
• Course substitution	• Proof reader	• With proctor
In Class	• Text on tape	On computer
Calculators	Early syllabus	• Extended time
Tape recorder	Taped handouts	On tape
• Word processor		Modified
Priority seating		Separate room

Graduation Requirements:
Course credits: **128** GPA: **2.0** Years to complete degree: **4**
Other requirements: **Special Interdisciplinary Studies Courses required (10 hours)**

Program Strengths
Schreiner College is a small liberal arts college with a faculty and staff strongly supportive of the Learning Support Services Program. There is much individual attention given to the students in the program. The program is structured but flexible enough to take into account the needs of the individual.

General Information:
Schreiner College is a 4 year private college. Suburban campus of 140 acres is 60 miles from San Antonio. Accessible by bus. Beaches are 240 miles from campus. 6 residential halls on campus. Housing is guaranteed.50 % of students remain on campus for the weekends.

Accreditation: SACS

SAT/ACT Scores:
Scores for incoming freshmen: **Verbal:** 95% below 500. 4% between 500 and 599. 1% between 600 and 699. **Math:** 95% below 500. 3% between 500 and 599. 2% between 600 and 699. **ACT:** 90% below 20. 8% between 20 and 23. 1% between 24 and 25l. 1% between 26 and 28.

Class Rank:
About 25% of the present freshmen class were in the upper 20% of their high school class. 75% were in the top 40% of their class. 80% were in the top 60% of their class. 100% were in the top 80% of their class.

Expenses:
Tuition: In-state: Full year: $7,385.00. Part-time: Per credit: $235.00. Room and board: $4,990.00 Cost of LD program: $2,390.00

Majors
• BUSINESS Accounting, Business Administration, Business Management, Economics, Real Estate • COMMUNICATIONS Creative Writing, English, Photography • COMPUTER SCIENCE Computer Science, Data Processing • EDUCATION Art, Elementary, English, Mathematics, Physical, Science, Secondary • ENGINEERING Engineering Science • HEALTH SCIENCES Fitness, Health, Medical Secretary, Nursing • HUMANITIES English/Writing/Literature, Liberal Arts, Philosophy, Religion • LANGUAGES French, German, Spanish • PREPROFESSIONAL Dentistry, Landscaping, Medicine, Ministry, Pharmacy, Social Work, Veterinarian • SCIENCES Biology, Chemistry, Mathematics, Physical Science, Physics • SOCIAL SCIENCES Government/Political, History, Psychology, Social Sciences • VISUAL AND PERFORMING ARTS Art, Dance, Fine Arts • VOCATIONAL Business and Office, Legal Secretary, Secretarial

Sports/Activities
• SPORTS-INTERCOLLEGIATE Baseball (M), Basketball, Cross Country, Golf (M), Soccer (M), Tennis, Volleyball (M) • SPORTS-INTRAMURAL Basketball, Bowling, Racquetball, Soccer (M), Swimming, Tennis, Track and Field, Volleyball • STUDENT LIFE ACTIVITIES Choral, Drama Groups, Magazine, Newspaper, Political Groups, Religious Organization, Student Government

Selective   **Texas**
                                 Services

Southern Methodist University
P. O. Box 355
Dallas, Texas 75275
(214) 692-2058-(800) 323-0672

School Enrollment: **8,566** Male: **4,283** Female: **4,283**
LD Enrollment: **100**

Admissions Contact: **Andrew Bryant, Director of Admissions**
LD Contact: **William McIntyre, Asst. Dean**
Telephone: **(214) 692-4560**

Admissions

Application Information:
Application deadline: **January 15th**
Rolling Admissions: **Yes** Notified when: **March 15th**

Secondary School Information
Most Important Criteria For Admissions (1-strongest)

3 SAT/ACT	Application	**2**	School transcript
2 Class rank	**1** Course selection	**4**	Personal statement
7 Interview	**6** Extra activities		Psychoeducational
2 G.P.A.	Open admission	**5**	Recommendations

Test Requirements:
Untimed SAT: **Yes** Untimed ACT: **Yes** Untimed ACH: **Yes**
Currency of diagnostic testing: **3 years**

Types of Disabilities Served
- Speech/Lang
- Study skills
- Written express
- Organizational
- Perceptual
- Reading
- Spelling
- Math
- Fine Motor
- ADD with LD
- ADD without LD
- ADHD with LD
- ADHD without LD

Learning Disability Program
Counseling: Individual: **Yes** Group Counseling: **Yes**

Faculty:
Faculty: **1**
Faculty advocate: **Yes** Meets with instructor: **As needed**

Diagnostic Testing
ADD	Personality	Perceptual skills	Spelling
ADHD	Organization	Fine motor skills	Reading
I.Q.	Handwriting	Spoken language	Study skills
Math	Social skills	Written language	

Tutoring:
Services rendered by:
• Graduates • Peers • Faculty • LD staff   Teacher trainees

Tutorials
Grp.	Ind.	Tutorials	Grp.	Ind.	Tutorials
•	•	Math skills			Word processing
•	•	Study skills	•	•	Time management
•	•	Language arts	•	•	Learning strategies
•	•	Written express	•	•	Organizational skills

Academic Accommodations
Curriculum	Study Aids	Exams
Priority registration	Typist	• Oral
Math waiver	Reader	Untimed
Foreign lang. waiver	Notetaker	• Take home
Course substitution	Proof reader	With proctor
In Class	• Text on tape	On computer
Calculators	Early syllabus	• Extended time
• Tape recorder	Taped handouts	On tape
• Word processor		• Modified
Priority seating		Separate room

Program Strengths
There is no separate program. All students are mainstreamed.

General Information:
Southern Methodist University is a 4 year private Methodist college. Urban campus. Accessible by air, train or bus. Ski areas are 400 miles from campus. Beaches are 40 miles from campus. 6.5% of students are foreign. Housing is not guaranteed. 90 % of students remain on campus for the weekends. 48 % of students join fraternities/sororities.

Texas

Accreditation: Regional

SAT/ACT Scores:
Scores for incoming freshmen: **Verbal:** 10% below 500. 60% between 500 and 599. 30% between 600 and 699. **Math:** 10% below 500. 60% between 500 and 599. 30% between 600 and 699.

Expenses:
Tuition: In-state: Full year: $10,816.00. Part-time: Per credit: $451.00. Room and board: $4,688.00

Majors

• AREA STUDIES African, Asian, Black/Afro-American, European, Latin American, Mexican/American, Russian/Slavic, Women's Studies • BUSINESS Accounting, Banking, Business Administration, Business Management, Economics, Finance, Insurance, Management, Marketing, Marketing Research, Personnel, Real Estate • COMMUNICATIONS Advertising, Broadcasting, English, Journalism, Photography, Public Relations, Television/Radio/Film • COMPUTER SCIENCE Computer Science, Data Processing, Programming, Systems Analysis, Telecommunications • EDUCATION Agricultural, Bilingual, Middle School, Music, Music Therapy, Physical, Secondary • ENGINEERING Bio-medical, Bioengineering, Civil/Environmental, Computer, Electrical, Engineering Science, Industrial, Mechanical • HEALTH SCIENCES Health • HUMANITIES English/Writing/Literature, Humanities, Philosophy, Religion • LANGUAGES French, German, Italian, Japanese, Latin, Russian, Spanish • PREPROFESSIONAL Dentistry, Engineering, Law, Medicine, Ministry, Natural Resources, Social Work • SCIENCES Anthropology, Biochemistry, Biology, Chemistry, Geology, Mathematics, Microbiology, Physical Chemistry, Physical Science, Physics • SOCIAL SCIENCES Anthropology, Criminal Justice, Government/Political, History, Psychology, Public Relations, Social Sciences, Sociology • VISUAL AND PERFORMING ARTS Art, Art History, Dramatic Arts, Music, Music History, Studio Art, Theater

Sports/Activities

• SPORTS RELATED Cheerleading, Chess, Drill Team, Drum Major/Majorette, Marching Band, Pep Band, Team Managers • SPORTS-INTERCOLLEGIATE Basketball, Cross Country, Diving, Golf, Soccer, Swimming, Tennis, Track and Field • SPORTS-INTRAMURAL Badminton, Basketball, Bowling, Ping-Pong, Racquetball, Rugby, Soccer, Softball, Swimming, Tennis, Volleyball, Water Polo • STUDENT LIFE ACTIVITIES Choral, Concert Band, Dance, Debate, Drama Groups, Ethnic & Cultural Groups, Film, Fraternities, Magazine, Music Groups, Newspaper, Opera, Radio/TV station, Religious Organization, Sororities, Student Government, Symphony Orchestra, Yearbook

Less Selective

Texas Services

St. Philip's College
1801 Martin Luther King
San Antonio, Texas 78203-2098
(512) 531-3200

School Enrollment: **6,000** Male: **3,000** Female: **3,000**
LD Enrollment: **750** Male: **400** Female: **350**

Admissions Contact: **Harry Stine, Dir., Admissions/Records**
LD Contact: **Rhonda Rapp, Learning Disabilities Specialist**
Name of Program: **LD Program/Special Needs Services**
Address: **1801 Martin Luther King**
Telephone: **(512) 531-3512**

Admissions

Application Information:
Application deadline: **Open**

Secondary School Information
Most Important Criteria For Admissions (1-strongest)

SAT/ACT	Application	School transcript
Class rank	Course selection	Personal statement
Interview	Extra activities	Psychoeducational
G.P.A.	**1** Open admission	Recommendations

Test Requirements:
Diagnostic testing waived: **Yes**
Untimed SAT: **Yes** Untimed ACT: **Yes**
WAIS-R required: **Yes**
Documentation of LD required: **Yes**
Currency of diagnostic testing: **Within 3 years**
Tests recommended: **Intelligence, Neurological, Achievement**

Types of Disabilities Served
• Speech/Lang • Reading • ADD with LD
• Study skills • Spelling • ADD without LD
• Written express • Math • ADHD with LD
• Organizational • Fine Motor • ADHD without LD
• Perceptual

Admissions Process

As an open door community college, students need to bring their high school diploma or G.E.D. scores and they are automatically admitted.

High School Course Requirements:
Waivers to standard high school courses
Course substitution: **Yes**

Learning Disability Program

Special orientation for LD students: **Yes**
Syllabus available during orientation: **Yes**
Program: Reinforces course work: **Yes**
Students mainstreamed **100 %** of the day
Recommended credits per semester: **9**
Time required or recommended in learning center: **As needed**
Services only for LD students: **Yes**
Services available for all students: **Yes**
Vocational Counseling: **Yes**

Faculty:
Faculty: **5** Full time: **1** Part time: **4**
LD faculty with: BS/BA: **2** M.A.: **2**
Faculty advocate: **Yes** Meets with instructor: **Every two weeks**

Diagnostic Testing
ADD Personality • Perceptual skills • Spelling
ADHD Organization • Fine motor skills • Reading
• I.Q. • Handwriting • Spoken language • Study skills
• Math • Social skills • Written language

Tutoring:
Average size of group tutorials: **Individual**
Services rendered by:
Graduates •Peers •Faculty •LD staff Teacher trainees

Tutorials

Grp.	Ind.	Tutorials	Grp.	Ind.	Tutorials
•	•	Math skills		•	Word processing
•	•	Study skills		•	Time management
•	•	Language arts	•		Learning strategies
•	•	Written express	•		Organizational skills

Academic Accommodations

Curriculum
- Priority registration
- Math waiver
- Foreign lang. waiver
- Course substitution

In Class
- Calculators
- Tape recorder
- Word processor
- Priority seating

Study Aids
- Typist
- Reader
- Notetaker
- Proof reader
- Text on tape
- Early syllabus
- Taped handouts

Exams
- Oral
- Untimed
- Take home
- With proctor
- On computer
- Extended time
- On tape
- Modified
- Separate room

Graduation Requirements:
Course credits: **60+** GPA: **2.0**

General Information:
St. Philip's College is a 2 year college. Urban campus 2 miles from San Antonio. Accessible by plane, train, or bus. Beaches are 2 hours from campus. .01% of students are foreign. Housing is not guaranteed.

Accreditation: SACS, TCUS, NAGAHP

SAT/ACT Scores:
Scores for incoming freshmen: **Verbal:** 98% below 500. **Math:** 95% below 500. **ACT:** 95% below 20.

Class Rank: 30% were in the top 80% of their class.

Expenses:
Tuition: In-state: Full year: $765.00. Part-time: Per credit: $75.00 plus $25.00 general fee. Part-time: Per course: $75.00 plus $25.00 general fee. Tuition: Out-of-state: Full year: Part-time: Per credit: $200.00 plus $75.00 general fee. Part-time: Per course: $200.00 plus fees

Majors
• AREA STUDIES Urban • ARTS Art History, Dance, Drafting, Drawing, Interior Design, Music, Music History, Music Performance, Painting, Sculpture • BUSINESS Accounting, Business Administration, Business Economics, Business Management, Clerical, Construction, Data Processing, Economics, Education, Food Management, Hotel & Restaurant Management, Management, Marketing, Real Estate, Retailing, Secretarial Science • COMMUNICATIONS English, Literature, Speech/Debate/Forensic • COMPUTER SCIENCE Computer Maintenance, Computer Science, Computer Technology, Data Processing, Hardware Engineer, Programming • CRAFTS AND DESIGN Ceramics, Crafts, Enameling, Sculpture, Textile/Weaving • EDUCATION Elementary • HEALTH SCIENCES Accounting, Fitness, Health, Medical Assistant, Medical Laboratory Technology, Medical Records Administration, Medical Secretary, Nursing, Nursing Assistant, Nutritional/Food, Occupational Therapy, Pharmacology, Physical Therapy, Practical Nursing, Radiological Therapy, Respiratory Therapy, Surgical Technology • HUMANITIES English/Writing/Literature, Fine Arts, Humanities, Liberal Arts , Philosophy • LANGUAGES English, Spanish • MATHEMATICS Applied, Theoretical • PRE PROFESSIONAL Business, Drafting, Engineering, Law, Medicine, Pharmacy, Social Work • SCIENCES Anatomy, Applied Mathematics, Biochemistry, Biology, Chemistry, Computer Science, Entomology, General, Gerontology, Human Biology, Inorganic Chemistry, Macrobiology, Mathematics, Microbiology, Molecular Biology, Organic Chemistry, Physical Science, Physics, Radiology • SOCIAL SCIENCES Geography, Government/Political, History, Political Science, Psychology, Social Science, Sociology • VISUAL AND PERFORMING ARTS Art, Art History, Dance, Dramatic Arts, Fine Arts, Music, Music Performance, Music Theatre, Studio Art,

Theater • VOCATIONAL Air Conditioning/Heating/Refri, Auto Body, Automobile Technology, Automotive Service, Building Construction, Business and Office, Carpentry, Chef Apprenticeship, Construction, Culinary Arts, Diesel Power Technology, Drafting, Electronics Technology, Fashion Merchandising, Food Service, Legal Secretary, Medical Laboratory Technology, Plumbing, Radiological Technology, Respiratory Therapy Technology, Secretarial, Textile and Clothing, Welding, Word Processing

Sports/Activities
• SPORTS-INTRAMURAL Basketball (F), Basketball (M), Swimming, Swimming (F), Swimming (M), Tennis, Tennis (F), Tennis (M), Volleyball, Volleyball (F), Volleyball (M), Weight Lifting, Weight Lifting (M) • STUDENT LIFE ACTIVITIES Academic Clubs, Choral, Community Service, Ethnic & Cultural Groups, Magazine, Music Groups, Musical Theater, Newspaper, Religious Organization, Student Government

---

Selective   **Texas**

Services

Tarleton State University
P. O. Box T-2003 Tarleton Station
Stephenville, Texas 76402
(817) 968-9125

School Enrollment: **6,300**

Admissions Contact: **Ms. Gail Mayfield, Dean of Admissions**
LD Contact: **Mary Ann Lipford, Dir., Teaching & Learning Center**
Name of Program: **Teaching & Learning Center**
Telephone: **(817) 968-9480**

Admissions

Application Information:
Application deadline: **August 7th**
Rolling Admissions: **Yes**

Secondary School Information
Most Important Criteria For Admissions (1-strongest)

3 SAT/ACT	1 Application	4 School transcript
2 Class rank	6 Course selection	11 Personal statement
11 Interview	11 Extra activities	11 Psychoeducational
5 G.P.A.	Open admission	11 Recommendations

Types of Disabilities Served
- Speech/Lang
- Study skills
- Written express
- Organizational
- Perceptual
- Reading
- Spelling
- Math
- Fine Motor
- ADD with LD
- ADD without LD
- ADHD with LD
- ADHD without LD

Learning Disability Program
Services available for all students: **Yes**
Counseling: Individual: **Yes**

Faculty:
Faculty: **1**

Diagnostic Testing

ADD	Personality	Perceptual skills	Spelling
ADHD	Organization	Fine motor skills	Reading
I.Q.	Handwriting	Spoken language	Study skills
Math	Social skills	Written language	

Services rendered by:

Texas

Tutorials

Grp.	Ind.	Tutorials	Grp.	Ind.	Tutorials
		Math skills			Word processing
		Study skills			Time management
		Language arts			Learning strategies
		Written express			Organizational skills

Academic Accommodations

Curriculum	Study Aids	Exams
Priority registration	Typist	Oral
Math waiver	Reader	Untimed
Foreign lang. waiver	Notetaker	Take home
Course substitution	Proof reader	With proctor
In Class	Text on tape	On computer
Calculators	Early syllabus	Extended time
Tape recorder	Taped handouts	On tape
Word processor		Modified
Priority seating		Separate room

Program Strengths

Presently, Tarleton State University does not have a Learning Disabilities Program per se. We do, however, provide support for students who have learning differences/disabilities in an effort to help them be successful in all their courses. The Director of the Teaching and Learning Center works with these students as they explore various techniques for learning.

General Information:

Tarleton State University is a 4 year public university. Rural campus of 1,923 acres is 67 miles from Fort Worth. Accessible by bus. 9 residential halls on campus. Housing is guaranteed.Guaranteed through 1st year. 55 % of students remain on campus for the weekends. 17 % of students join fraternities/sororities.

Accreditation:SACS

SAT/ACT Scores:
Scores for incoming freshmen:**Verbal:**88%below 500. 10%between 500 and 599. 2%between 600 and 699. **Math:**77% below 500. 19% between 500 and 599. 4% between 600 and 699. **ACT:** 52% below 20. 32% between 20 and 23. 16%between 26 and 28.

Class Rank:
About 28% of the present freshmen class were in the upper 20% of their high school class. 63% were in the top 40% of their class.

Expenses:
Tuition: In-state: Full year: $540.00. Part-time: Per credit:$18.00. Tuition: Out-of-state: Full year: $122.00. Room and board: $2,478.00

Majors

• BUSINESS Accounting, Business Administration, Business Education, Management, Marketing • COMMUNICATIONS Communication, English • COMPUTER SCIENCE Computer Science • EDUCATION Art, Early Childhood, Foreign Language, Industrial, Middle School, Music, Physical, Secondary, Special, Speech/Language • HEALTH SCIENCES Nursing • HUMANITIES English/Writing/Literature, Philosophy • LANGUAGES French, German, Spanish • MATHEMATICS Applied • PRE-PROFESSIONAL Dentistry, Engineering, Law, Medicine, Optometry, Pharmacy, Range Management, Social Work • SCIENCES Anthropology, Astronomy, Biology, Chemistry, Computer Science • SOCIAL SCIENCES Anthropology, Criminal Justice, Geography, History, Library Science, Political Science, Psychology, Sociology • SPECIAL EDUCATION Deaf/ Hearing Impaired, Learning Disability, Mentally Retarded • VISUAL AND PERFORMING ARTS Art, Dance, Music, Theater • VOCATIONAL Home Economics, Industrial Design, Secretarial

Sports/Activities

• SPORTS RELATED Baton Twirling, Cheerleading, Drill Team, Drum Major/Majorette, Marching Band, Pep Band, Team Managers • SPORTS-INTERCOLLEGIATE Baseball (M), Basketball, Cross Country, Football (M), Golf (M), Softball (F), Tennis • SPORTS-INTRAMURAL Basketball, Bowling, Football, Ping-Pong, Riflery, Soccer, Softball, Tennis, Volleyball • STUDENT LIFE ACTIVITIES Academic Clubs, Choral, Community Service, Concert Band, Dance, Debate, Drama Groups, Fraternities, Jazz Band, Music Groups, Musical Theater, Newspaper, Orchestra, Political Groups, Radio/TV station, Religious Organization, Sororities, Student Government

---

Selective　　　　　　　　　　　　　**Texas**
Accommodations

Texas A&I University
Campus Box 215
Kingsville, Texas 78363-8201
(512) 595-3300

School Enrollment: **5,937** Male: **2,997** Female: **2,940**

Admissions Contact: **Ruth Fletcher, Director of Admissions**
LD Contact: **Mary Jimenez, College I Reading Supervisor**
Name of Program: **General Program**
Telephone:**(512) 595-3300**

Admissions

Application Information:
Rolling Admissions: **Yes**

Secondary School Information
Most Important Criteria For Admissions (1-strongest)

1 SAT/ACT	1 Application	1 School transcript
1 Class rank	Course selection	Personal statement
Interview	Extra activities	Psychoeducational
G.P.A.	Open admission	Recommendations

Types of Disabilities Served

• Speech/Lang	• Reading	ADD with LD
• Study skills	• Spelling	ADD without LD
• Written express	• Math	ADHD with LD
• Organizational	Fine Motor	ADHD without LD
• Perceptual		

Admissions Process

Complete application with high school/college transcript, test scores, immunization records.

Learning Disability Program

Services available for all students: **Yes**
Counseling: Individual: **Yes** Group Counseling: **Yes**

Faculty:
Faculty: **1** Full time: **1** M.A.: **1**

Diagnostic Testing

ADD	Personality	Perceptual skills	Spelling
ADHD	Organization	Fine motor skills	Reading
I.Q.	Handwriting	Spoken language	Study skills
Math	Social skills	Written language	

Tutoring:

Services rendered by:
•Graduates •Peers •Faculty LD staff Teacher trainees

Tutorials

Grp.	Ind.	Tutorials	Grp.	Ind.	Tutorials
•	•	Math skills			Word processing
•	•	Study skills	•	•	Time management
•		Language arts		•	Learning strategies
•		Written express	•		Organizational skills

Academic Accommodations

Curriculum	Study Aids	Exams
Priority registration	Typist	Oral
Math waiver	Reader	Untimed
Foreign lang. waiver	• Notetaker	Take home
Course substitution	Proof reader	With proctor
In Class	Text on tape	On computer
Calculators	Early syllabus	• Extended time
• Tape recorder	Taped handouts	On tape
Word processor		Modified
Priority seating		Separate room

Graduation Requirements: GPA: **2.0** Language waiver: **Yes**

Program Strengths

Incoming freshmen register through College I. It is a program set up to make the transition easier for students just out of high school now seeking their goals through college. A college proficiency exam is required of all incoming freshmen. Tutors are available for students free of charge. Special help is given to students with learning disabilities so that they may be mainstreamed with their peers.

General Information:

Texas A&I University is a 4 year public university. Rural campus of 246 acres is 45 miles from Corpus Christi. Accessible by bus or plane. Beaches are 45 miles from campus. 4% of students are foreign. 5 residential halls on campus. Housing is guaranteed. 65 % of students remain on campus for the weekends. 2 % of students join fraternities/sororities.

Accreditation: SACS

SAT/ACT Scores:

Scores for incoming freshmen: **ACT:** 66% below 20. 20% between 20 and 23. 2% between 24 and 25l. 2% between 26 and 28. 1% above 28.

Expenses:

Tuition: In-state: Full year: $910.00. Part-time: Per credit: $121.00. Tuition: Out-of-state: Full year: $4,030.00. Part-time: Per credit: $143.00. Room and board: $2,624.00

Majors

• BUSINESS Accounting, Agricultural, Banking, Business Administration, Business Management, Economics, Finance, Food Management, Management, Marketing, Real Estate • COMMUNICATIONS Communication, English, Journalism • COMPUTER SCIENCE Computer Science, Data Processing • EDUCATION Agricultural, Art, Bilingual, Early Childhood, Elementary, Health, Music, Physical, Secondary, Special • ENGINEERING Chemical, Civil/Environmental, Computer, Mechanical, Natural Gas • HEALTH SCIENCES Nutritional/Food • LANGUAGES Spanish • PRE-PROFESSIONAL Agriculture, Dentistry, Engineering, Law, Medicine, Pharmacy, Range Management, Social Work, Veterinarian, Wildlife • SCIENCES Animal, Biology, Chemistry, Geography, Geology, Mathematics, Physics, Soil • SOCIAL SCIENCES Government/Political, History, Psychology, Public Relations, Sociology • VISUAL AND PERFORMING ARTS Fine Arts, Music, Theater • VOCATIONAL Home Economics, Industrial Technology, Interior Design, Textile and Clothing

Sports/Activities

• SPORTS RELATED Cheerleading, Drill Team, Drum Major/Majorette, Marching Band • SPORTS-INTERCOLLEGIATE Basketball, Football (M), Riflery, Tennis, Volleyball (F) • SPORTS-INTRAMURAL Badminton, Bowling, Diving, Fencing, Golf, Horseback Riding, Racquetball, Soccer, Softball, Swimming, Volleyball • STUDENT LIFE ACTIVITIES Choral, Concert Band, Debate, Ethnic & Cultural Groups, Jazz Band, Music Groups, Musical Theater, Newspaper, Radio/TV station, Religious Organization, Sororities, Student Government

---

Less Selective **Texas Services**

Texas Southmost College

80 Fort Brown
Brownsville, Texas 78520
(512) 544-8200

School Enrollment: **5,692** Male: **2,304** Female: **3,388**
LD Enrollment: **17**

Admissions Contact: **Alfonso Gutierrez, Director of Admissions**
LD Contact: **Steve Wilder, Counselor**
Name of Program: **Disabled Student Services**
Telephone: **(512) 544-8292**

Admissions

Secondary School Information

Most Important Criteria For Admissions (1-strongest)

SAT/ACT	Application	School transcript
Class rank	Course selection	Personal statement
Interview	Extra activities	Psychoeducational
G.P.A.	Open admission	Recommendations

Test Requirements:

Currency of diagnostic testing: **3 years**

Types of Disabilities Served

• Speech/Lang	• Reading	• ADD with LD
• Study skills	• Spelling	• ADD without LD
• Written express	• Math	• ADHD with LD
• Organizational	• Fine Motor	• ADHD without LD
• Perceptual		

Learning Disability Program

Counseling: Individual: **Yes**

Faculty:

Faculty: **1** Including Director: **1**

Diagnostic Testing

ADD	Personality	Perceptual skills	Spelling
ADHD	Organization	Fine motor skills	Reading
I.Q.	Handwriting	Spoken language	Study skills
Math	Social skills	Written language	

Tutoring:

Services rendered by:
  Graduates •Peers •Faculty •LD staff Teacher trainees

Tutorials

Grp.	Ind.	Tutorials	Grp.	Ind.	Tutorials
	•	Math skills	•		Word processing
•		Study skills	•		Time management
		Language arts	•		Learning strategies
•	•	Written express	•		Organizational skills

Academic Accommodations

Curriculum	Study Aids	Exams
Priority registration	Typist	Oral
Math waiver	Reader	Untimed
Foreign lang. waiver	• Notetaker	Take home
Course substitution	Proof reader	With proctor
In Class	• Text on tape	On computer
Calculators	Early syllabus	• Extended time
• Tape recorder	Taped handouts	On tape
• Word processor		• Modified
Priority seating		Separate room

General Information:

Texas Southmost College is a 2 year public college. Urban campus Accessible by bus. Beaches are 25 miles from campus. 2% of students are foreign. Housing is not guaranteed.

Accreditation:SACS

Expenses:

Tuition: In-state: Full year: $662.00. Part-time: Per course: $71.00. Tuition: Out-of-state: Full year: $2,372.00. Part-time: Per course:$242.00

Majors

• BUSINESS Accounting, Banking, Business Education, Management, Real Estate, Retailing • COMMUNICATIONS English, Journalism • COMPUTER SCIENCE Data Processing, Programming • EDUCATION Child Development • HEALTH SCIENCES Medical Technology, Nursing, Radiological Technology • LANGUAGES French, Italian, Spanish • SCIENCES Biology, Chemistry, Geology, Mathematics, Physical Science • SOCIAL SCIENCES Anthropology, Criminology, Government/Political, History, Psychology, Sociology • VISUAL AND PERFORMING ARTS Art, Music, Studio Art, Theater • VOCATIONAL Air Conditioning/Heating/Refri, Auto Body, Automobile Technology, Construction, Diesel Power Technology, Drafting, Fire Science, Machinist, Respiratory Therapy Technology, Secretarial, Welding

Sports/Activities

• SPORTS-INTERCOLLEGIATE Baseball, Basketball • SPORTS-INTRAMURAL Badminton, Golf, Ping-Pong, Sailing, Swimming, Tennis, Volleyball, Water Polo • STUDENT LIFE ACTIVITIES Jazz Band, Music Groups, Newspaper, Student Government, Yearbook

Texas Tech University
P.O. Box 42017
Lubbock, Texas 79409
(806) 742-2166

School Enrollment: **24,707** Male: **15,335** Female: **11,372**
LD Enrollment: **144**

Admissions Contact: **Dale Grusing, Director of Admissions**
LD Contact: **Trudy S. Puttect, Asst. Dean of Students**
Name of Program: **Disabled Student Services**
Address: **Box 45014**
Telephone:**(806) 742-2192**

Admissions

Secondary School Information
Most Important Criteria For Admissions (1-strongest)

1 SAT/ACT	**5** Application	**4** School transcript
2 Class rank	Course selection	Personal statement
Interview	Extra activities	Psychoeducational
3 G.P.A.	Open admission	Recommendations

Test Requirements:
Untimed SAT: **Yes** Untimed ACT: **Yes**
Documentation of LD required: **Yes**

Types of Disabilities Served

Speech/Lang	Reading	ADD with LD
Study skills	Spelling	ADD without LD
• Written express	Math	ADHD with LD
Organizational	Fine Motor	ADHD without LD
Perceptual		

High School Course Requirements:
English: **4** Math: **3** Science: **2** Foreign Language: **2**
Waivers to standard high school courses
Course substitution: **Yes**

Learning Disability Program
Students mainstreamed **100** % of the day
Recommended credits per semester: **varies**
Time required or recommended in learning center: **varies**
Services available for all students: **Yes**
Counseling: Individual: **Yes** Group Counseling: **Yes**
Support groups are available:**Yes, Association of Students with Learning Disabilities**

Faculty:
Faculty: **2** Including Director: **Yes** Full time: **1** Part time: **1**
Faculty advocate: **Yes** Meets with instructor: **As needed**

Diagnostic Testing

ADD	Personality	Perceptual skills	Spelling
ADHD	Organization	Fine motor skills	Reading
I.Q.	Handwriting	Spoken language	Study skills
Math	Social skills	Written language	

Tutoring:
Average size of group tutorials: **varies**
Services rendered by:

•Graduates •Peers Faculty LD staff Teacher trainees

Tutorials

Grp.	Ind.	Tutorials	Grp.	Ind.	Tutorials
•	•	Math skills	•	•	Word processing
•	•	Study skills	•	•	Time management
•	•	Language arts	•	•	Learning strategies
•	•	Written express	•	•	Organizational skills

Academic Accommodations

Curriculum	Study Aids	Exams
Priority registration	Typist	• Oral
Math waiver	• Reader	Untimed
Foreign lang. waiver	• Notetaker	Take home
Course substitution	• Proof reader	• With proctor
In Class	• Text on tape	• On computer
Calculators	Early syllabus	• Extended time
• Tape recorder	Taped handouts	On tape
Word processor		• Modified
Priority seating		• Separate room

General Information:

Texas Tech University is a 4 year public university. of 1,839 acres is Accessible by air or bus 3.5% of students are foreign. 18 residential halls on campus. Housing is guaranteed.Guaranteed through 4th year. 34 % of students join fraternities/sororities.

Accreditation:SACS

SAT/ACT Scores:

Scores for incoming freshmen:**Verbal:**75.1%below 500. 21.2%between 500 and 599. 3.3%between 600 and 699. 0.3%above 700. **Math:**46.7% below 500. 38.2% between 500 and 599. 13.5% between 600 and 699. 1.6%above 700.**ACT:** 30.5% below 20. 34.2% between 20 and 23. 22.7%between 24 and 251. 7.5%between 26 and 28. 5.0% above 28.

Expenses:

Tuition: In-state: Full year: $1,631.00. Part-time: Per credit:$20.00. Part-time: Per course: $100.00 . Tuition: Out-of-state: Full year: $4,471.00. Part-time: Per credit:$128.00. Room and board: $3,563.00

Majors

• AGRICULTURE Agricultural Economics, Business, Education, Engineering • AREA STUDIES Latin American • ARTS Music History • BUSINESS Accounting, Agricultural, Banking/Finance, Business Economics, Business Education, Business Management, Economics, Hotel & Restaurant Management, Human Environment and Housing, International Business, International Public Service, Management, Marketing • COMMUNICATIONS Advertising, Broadcasting, Journalism, Photo Communications, Speech/Debate/Forensic, Television/Radio/Film • COMPUTER SCIENCE Computer Science, Information Science and System, Management Information System, Telecommunications • EDUCATION Art, Child Development, Curriculum, Early Childhood, Elementary, Home Economics, Music, Physical, School Psychology, Secondary, Special • ENGINEERING Chemical, Civil/Environmental, Electrical, Engineering Science, Industrial, Mechanical, Petroleum, Physics, Radio/Television • HEALTH SCIENCES Environmental, Nutritional/Food, Occupational Therapy, Physical Therapy, Speech/Audiology and Speech • HUMANITIES Humanities, Liberal Arts , Philosophy • LANGUAGES English, French, German, Latin, Spanish • PRE PROFESSIONAL Architecture, Range Management, Social Work, Urban Design, Wildlife • SCIENCES Animal, Atmospheric, Biochemistry, Biology, Botany, Chemistry, Entomology, Geography, Geology, Geophysics & Seismology, Horticultural, Mathematics, Meteorology, Microbiology, Physics, Plant Pathology, Soil, Zoology • SOCIAL SCIENCES Family Counseling, Government/Political, History, Political Science, Public Relations, Sociology • SPECIAL EDUCATION Deaf/Hearing Impaired, Mentally Retarded • VISUAL AND PERFORMING ARTS Art History, Dance, Dramatic Arts, Music, Music Appreciation, Studio Art, Theater • VOCATIONAL Construction, Electronics Technology, Family Consumer Management, Fashion Design, Fashion Merchandising, Food Science, Home Economics, Individual & Family Development, Interior Design, Landscape Architecture, Park/Recreation, Secretarial, Textile and Clothing

Sports/Activities

• SPORTS RELATED Baton Twirling, Cheerleading, Drill Team, Drum Major/Majorette, Marching Band, Team Managers • SPORTS-INTERCOLLEGIATE Baseball (M), Basketball (F), Basketball (M), Cross Country (F), Cross Country (M), Football (M), Golf (F), Golf (M), Tennis (F), Tennis (M), Track and Field (F), Track and Field (M), Volleyball (F) • SPORTS-INTRAMURAL Archery (F), Archery (M), Badminton (F), Badminton (M), Boxing (M), Cycling, Football (M), Golf (M), Lacrosse (M), Ping-Pong (F), Ping-Pong (M), Racquetball (M), Rodeo, Rugby (M), Soccer (F), Soccer (M), Softball (F), Softball (M), Squash (F), Squash (M), Swimming (F), Swimming (M), Tennis (M), Track and Field (F), Track and Field (M), Trap and Skeet, Volleyball (F), Volleyball (M), Water Polo (F), Water Polo (M) • STUDENT LIFE ACTIVITIES Academic Clubs, Choral, Community Service, Concert Band, Dance, Debate, Drama Groups, Ethnic & Cultural Groups, Fraternities, Jazz Band, Musical Theater, Newspaper, Orchestra, Political Groups, Radio/TV station, Religious Organization, Sororities, Student Government, Symphony Orchestra, Yearbook

---

Less Selective   **Texas**
                                         Services

Tyler Jr. College
P. O. Box 9020
Tyler, Texas 75711-9020
(214) 510-2200

School Enrollment: **8,000**
LD Enrollment: **81**

Admissions Contact: **Kenneth Lewis, Dean of Admissions**
LD Contact: **Vickie Geisel, Director**
Name of Program: **Support Services**
Telephone:**(214) 510-2395**

Admissions

Application Information:
Application deadline: **Registration**

Secondary School Information
Most Important Criteria For Admissions (1-strongest)

	SAT/ACT	**1**	Application	**1**	School transcript
	Class rank		Course selection		Personal statement
1	Interview		Extra activities	**1**	Psychoeducational
	G.P.A.	**1**	Open admission	**1**	Recommendations

Test Requirements:
Diagnostic testing waived: **Yes**
WAIS-R required: **Yes**
Documentation of LD required: **Yes**

Types of Disabilities Served
• Speech/Lang	• Reading	• ADD with LD
• Study skills	• Spelling	• ADD without LD
• Written express	• Math	• ADHD with LD
• Organizational	• Fine Motor	• ADHD without LD
• Perceptual		

Learning Disability Program

Counseling: Individual: **Yes**

Faculty:

Faculty: **3** Full time: **1** Part time: **2**
Faculty advocate: **Yes** Meets with instructor: **Once a month**

Diagnostic Testing

ADD	Personality	Perceptual skills	Spelling
ADHD	Organization	Fine motor skills	Reading
I.Q.	Handwriting	Spoken language	Study skills
Math	Social skills	Written language	

Tutoring:

Services rendered by:
Graduates •Peers Faculty •LD staff Teacher trainees

Tutorials

Grp.	Ind.	Tutorials	Grp.	Ind.	Tutorials
•	•	Math skills			Word processing
•	•	Study skills			Time management
	•	Language arts			Learning strategies
	•	Written express			Organizational skills

Academic Accommodations

Curriculum	Study Aids	Exams
Priority registration	Typist	• Oral
Math waiver	Reader	Untimed
Foreign lang. waiver	• Notetaker	Take home
Course substitution	Proof reader	With proctor
In Class	• Text on tape	On computer
Calculators	Early syllabus	• Extended time
• Tape recorder	Taped handouts	On tape
Word processor		Modified
Priority seating		Separate room

Program Strengths

We have a transitional class for the learning disabled under the auspices of developmental reading. This class is designed to get at least some of these students together to work on school adjustment as well as to improve reading. We read about and discuss such things as: what are learning disabilities, how to study, and self advocacy. Thus we combine reading, improvement, and counseling for the disabled. We have found no other such program in the state.
* Seminar handouts are used to assist in the areas of Organizational Skills, Learning Strategies, Word Processing, and Time Management.

General Information:

Tyler Jr. College is a 2 year public college. 70 miles from Dallas. Accessible by air or bus. Ski areas are 1,000 miles from campus. Beaches are 200 miles from campus. 3% of students are foreign. Housing is not guaranteed.

Accreditation: SACS

Expenses:

Tuition: In-state: Full year: Part-time: Per credit: $21.00. Tuition: Out-of-state: Full year: Part-time: Per credit: $38.00. Room and board: $2,000.00

Majors

• BUSINESS Banking, Business Administration, Business Management, Economics, Finance, Management, Marketing, Real Estate • COMMUNICATIONS Communication, English, Graphic Design, Journalism, Photography, Television/Radio/Film • COMPUTER SCIENCE Computer Science, Data Processing, Programming • EDUCATION Art, Child Development, Elementary, Foreign Language, Health, Physical, Special • ENGINEERING Engineering Science • HEALTH SCIENCES Dental Hygiene, Medical Technology, Nursing, Practical Nursing, Speech/Audiology and Speech • HUMANITIES Humanities, Liberal Arts, Philosophy, Religion • LANGUAGES French, German, Spanish • PREPROFESSIONAL Agriculture, Architecture, Dentistry, Engineering, Law, Medicine, Pharmacy, Social Work, Veterinarian • SCIENCES Agricultural, Biology, Chemistry, Geology, Horticultural, Mathematics, Physics • SOCIAL SCIENCES Criminal Justice, Government/Political, History, Law Enforcement, Psychology, Social Sciences, Sociology • VISUAL AND PERFORMING ARTS Art, Dance, Fine Arts, Music, Theater • VOCATIONAL Air Conditioning/Heating/Refrig, Business and Office, Drafting, Fashion Design, Fashion Mechandizing, Fire Science, Home Economics, Park/Recreation, Precision Metal Work, Radiological Technology, Respiratory Therapy Technology

Sports/Activities

• SPORTS RELATED Marching Band • SPORTS-INTERCOLLEGIATE Basketball, Football (M), Tennis • SPORTS-INTRAMURAL Badminton, Basketball, Hand Ball, Ping-Pong, Racquetball, Softball, Tennis, Volleyball • STUDENT LIFE ACTIVITIES Choral, Concert Band, Dance, Fraternities, Music Groups, Musical Theater, Newspaper, Religious Organization, Sororities, Student Government, Symphony Orchestra

Very Selective　　　　　　　　　　**Texas Services**

University of Houston

4800 Calhoun 129 E. Cullen
Houston, Texas 77004
(713) 749-2321

School Enrollment: **33,500** Male: **16,750** Female: **16,750**
LD Enrollment: **75**

Admissions Contact: **Ann Reinig, Cord., Freshmen Admissions**
LD Contact: **Karen Waldman, M.Ed., Coordinator**
Name of Program: **Handicapped Student Services**
Address: **4800 Calhoun**
Telephone:**(713) 723-2067**

Admissions

Application Information:

Enrolled:**75**
Application deadline: **Varies with each semester**
Applicant must apply **3-4** months in advance

Secondary School Information

Most Important Criteria For Admissions (1-strongest)

SAT/ACT	Application	School transcript
Class rank	Course selection	Personal statement
Interview	Extra activities	Psychoeducational
G.P.A.	Open admission	Recommendations

Test Requirements:

Diagnostic testing waived: **Yes**
Untimed SAT **Yes** Untimed ACT: **Yes**
WAIS-R required: **Yes**
Documentation of LD required: **Yes**
Tests recommended: **WAIS-R and Woodcock-Johnson are required for LD students (only if they want to utilize our support services).**

Types of Disabilities Served
- Speech/Lang
- Study skills
- Written express
- Organizational
- Perceptual
- Reading
- Spelling
- Math
- Fine Motor
- ADD with LD
- ADD without LD
- ADHD with LD
- ADHD without LD

Admissions Process

Students with learning disabilities apply to the University of Houston just like everyone else. If denied admission based on low GPA or test scores, they may request an individualized review. At this time, they may explain any "extenuating circumstances" such as their disability.

High School Course Requirements:
English: **4** Math: **3** Science: **2**
Waivers to standard high school courses
Course substitution: **Yes**

Learning Disability Program
Program available through: **Each semester**
Students mainstreamed **100** % of the day
Recommended credits per semester: **9-12**
Counseling: Individual: **Yes** Vocational Counseling: **Yes**
Support groups are available: **Peer support groups**

Faculty: M.A.: **2**
Meets with instructor: **As needed**

Diagnostic Testing
- ADD
- ADHD
- I.Q.
- Math
- Personality
- Organization
- Handwriting
- Social skills
- Perceptual skills
- Fine motor skills
- Spoken language
- Written language
- Spelling
- Reading
- Study skills

Tutoring:
Average size of group tutorials: **5-8**
Services rendered by:
- Graduates
- Peers
- Faculty
- LD staff
- Teacher trainees

Tutorials

Grp.	Ind.	Tutorials	Grp.	Ind.	Tutorials
•	•	Math skills	•	•	Word processing
•	•	Study skills	•	•	Time management
•	•	Language arts	•	•	Learning strategies
•	•	Written express	•	•	Organizational skills

Academic Accommodations

Curriculum	Study Aids	Exams
• Priority registration	• Typist	• Oral
Math waiver	• Reader	• Untimed
• Foreign lang. waiver	• Notetaker	• Take home
• Course substitution	• Proof reader	• With proctor
In Class	• Text on tape	• On computer
• Calculators	• Early syllabus	• Extended time
• Tape recorder	• Taped handouts	• On tape
• Word processor		• Modified
• Priority seating		Separate room

Graduation Requirements:
Course credits: **120** GPA: **2.0** Years to complete degree: **No deadline**
Language waiver: **Yes**
Other requirements: **Vary with each major**

Program Strengths
Handicapped Student Services has an especially caring and dedicated staff. The University of Houston has a pretty understanding and helpful faculty who are usually more than happy to assist students with learning disabilities.

General Information:
University of Houston is a 4 year public university. Urban campus Accessible by air or bus. Beaches are 40 miles from campus. 4 residential halls on campus. Housing is not guaranteed.

Accreditation:

Expenses:
Tuition: In-state: Full year: $495.00. Part-time: Per credit:$20.00. Part-time: Per course: $60.00. Tuition: Out-of-state: Full year: $1,719.00. Part-time: Per credit:$122.00. Part-time: Per course:$366.00 Room and board: $3,800.00

Majors
• ARTS Graphic Arts, Painting, Photography, Sculpture • BUSINESS Accounting, Banking/Finance, Business Administration, Business Economics, Business Education, Business Management, Business Statistics, Economics, Hotel & Restaurant Management, Management, Organizational Behavior • COMMUNICATIONS Broadcasting, Communication Disorders, Creative Writing, English, Journalism, Photography, Television/Radio/Film • COMPUTER SCIENCE Computer Science, Computer Technology, Systems Analysis • CRAFTS AND DESIGN Ceramics, Jewelry, Printmaking • EDUCATION Bilingual, Early Childhood, English, Foreign Language, Health, Home Economics, Industrial, Mathematics, Music, Physical, Psychology, Reading, Science, Social Science, Social Studies, Special, Technical • ENGINEERING Chemical, Civil/Environmental, Computer, Electrical, Industrial, Mechanical, Nuclear • HEALTH SCIENCES Medical Laboratory Technology, Nuclear Medical Technology, Nursing, Nutritional/Food, Pharmacology, Speech/Audiology and Speech • HUMANITIES Classics, Fine Arts, Philosophy • LANGUAGES French, German, Spanish • MATHEMATICS Statistical • PRE PROFESSIONAL Architecture, Dentistry, Law, Medicine, Optometry, Pharmaceutical Chemistry, Veterinarian • SCIENCES Anthropology, Applied Mathematics, Biochemistry, Biology, Biophysics, Chemistry, Computer Science, Geology, Geophysics, Mathematics, Physics, Statistics • SOCIAL SCIENCES Family Counseling, Government/Political, History, Human Service, Political Science, Psychology, Sociology • VISUAL AND PERFORMING ARTS Art History, Dramatic Arts, Music, Music Appreciation, Music Performance, Studio Art • VOCATIONAL Drafting, Fashion Merchandising, Home Economics, Industrial Design, Jewelry-Metalsmithery, Manufacturing Technology, Surveying and Mapping

Sports/Activities
• SPORTS RELATED Marching Band • SPORTS-INTERCOLLEGIATE Baseball (M), Basketball (F), Basketball (M), Cross Country, Diving (F), Football (M), Golf (M), Swimming (F), Tennis (F), Track and Field, Volleyball (F) • SPORTS-INTRAMURAL Archery, Badminton, Baseball (M), Basketball, Bowling, Cross Country, Diving, Football, Golf, Hand Ball, Ping-Pong, Racquetball, Rugby, Soccer, Softball, Swimming, Tennis, Track and Field, Volleyball, Water Polo

Less Selective

University of Texas at Brownsville

80 Fort Brown
Brownsville, Texas 78520
(512) 544-8200

School Enrollment: **5,886** Male: **2,413** Female: **3,473**
LD Enrollment: **17**
LD Contact: **Steve Wilder, Counselor**
Name of Program: **Services for Students with Disabilities**
Telephone:**(512) 544-8292**

Admissions

Secondary School Information
Most Important Criteria For Admissions (1-strongest)

SAT/ACT	Application	School transcript
Class rank	Course selection	Personal statement
Interview	Extra activities	Psychoeducational
G.P.A.	**1** Open admission	Recommendations

Test Requirements:
Diagnostic testing waived: **Yes**
Documentation of LD required: **Yes**

Types of Disabilities Served
- Speech/Lang
- Study skills
- Written express
- Organizational
- Perceptual
- Reading
- Spelling
- Math
- Fine Motor
- ADD with LD
- ADD without LD
- ADHD with LD
- ADHD without LD

Admissions Process

Open admissions. All new students must take assessment test. Transfer students who have not taken college level English and/or math must take assessment test also. Results of assessment are used to place students at appropriate levels.

Learning Disability Program

Students mainstreamed **100** % of the day
Counseling: Individual: **Yes** Vocational Counseling: **Yes**

Faculty:
Faculty: **1** Full time: **1**

Diagnostic Testing

ADD	Personality	Perceptual skills	Spelling
ADHD	Organization	Fine motor skills	• Reading
• I.Q.	Handwriting	Spoken language	Study skills
• Math	Social skills	• Written language	

Tutoring:
Services rendered by:

Graduates	•Peers	•Faculty	LD staff	Teacher trainees

Tutorials

Grp.	Ind.	Tutorials	Grp.	Ind.	Tutorials
	•	Math skills		•	Word processing
•		Study skills		•	Time management
		Language arts		•	Learning strategies
•	•	Written express		•	Organizational skills

Academic Accommodations

Curriculum	Study Aids	Exams
Priority registration	Typist	Oral
Math waiver	Reader	Untimed
Foreign lang. waiver	• Notetaker	Take home
Course substitution	Proof reader	With proctor
In Class	• Text on tape	On computer
Calculators	Early syllabus	• Extended time
• Tape recorder	Taped handouts	On tape
• Word processor		• Modified
Priority seating		Separate room

Graduation Requirements:
Course credits: **124** GPA: **2.0**

General Information:

University of Texas at Brownsville is a 2 and 4 year public university. Urban campus of 55 acres is Accessible by bus. Beaches are 25 miles from campus. 2% of students are foreign. Housing is not guaranteed.

Accreditation:SACS

Expenses:
Tuition: In-state: Full year: $584.00 (lower division)-$810.00 (upper division). Tuition: Out-of-state: Full year: $3,042.00.

Majors

• BUSINESS Accounting, Business Administration, Business Management, Clerical, Construction, Management, Marketing, Secretarial Science, Travel/Tourism Management • COMMUNICATIONS English • COMPUTER SCIENCE Computer Science • EDUCATION English • HEALTH SCIENCES Fitness, Medical Laboratory Technology, Nursing, Practical Nursing, Radiological Therapy, Respiratory Therapy • LANGUAGES Spanish • PRE PROFESSIONAL Drafting • SCIENCES Biology, Mathematics • SOCIAL SCIENCES Criminal Justice, History, Political Science, Sociology • VOCATIONAL Air Conditioning/Heating/Refri, Auto Body, Automobile Technology, Construction, Drafting, Legal Secretary, Machinist, Medical Laboratory Technology, Radiological Technology, Respiratory Therapy Technology, secretarial Word Processing

Sports/Activities

• SPORTS-INTERCOLLEGIATE Baseball (M), Volleyball (F) • SPORTS-INTRAMURAL Badminton, Basketball, Golf, Ping-Pong, Racquetball, Sailing, Tennis, Volleyball • STUDENT LIFE ACTIVITIES Jazz Band, Music Groups, Newsletter, Student Government, Yearbook

Less Selective

Snow College
150 East College Avenue
Ephraim, Utah 84627
(801) 283-4021

School Enrollment: **1,450** Male: **700** Female: **750**
LD Enrollment: **156**

Admissions Contact: **G. Balli, Director of Admissions**
LD Contact: **Cindi Crabb, Director**
Name of Program: **Student Support Services**
Telephone:**Ext. 316**

Admissions

Secondary School Information
Most Important Criteria For Admissions (1-strongest)

SAT/ACT	Application	School transcript
Class rank	Course selection	Personal statement
Interview	Extra activities	Psychoeducational
G.P.A.	**1** Open admission	Recommendations

Test Requirements:
Diagnostic testing waived: **Yes**
Untimed ACT: **Yes**

Types of Disabilities Served
- Speech/Lang
- Study skills
- Written express
- Organizational
- Perceptual
- Reading
- Spelling
- Math
- Fine Motor
- ADD with LD
- ADD without LD
- ADHD with LD
- ADHD without LD

Learning Disability Program
Counseling: Individual: **Yes** Group Counseling: **Yes**

Faculty:
Faculty: **5** Full time: **3** Part time: **2**
Faculty advocate: **Yes** Meets with instructor: **As needed**

Diagnostic Testing

ADD	Personality	Perceptual skills	Spelling
ADHD	Organization	Fine motor skills	Reading
I.Q.	Handwriting	Spoken language	Study skills
Math	Social skills	Written language	

Tutoring:
Average size of group tutorials: **3**
Services rendered by:
Graduates •Peers •Faculty •LD staff Teacher trainees

Tutorials

Grp.	Ind.	Tutorials	Grp.	Ind.	Tutorials
•	•	Math skills	•	•	Word processing
•	•	Study skills	•	•	Time management
•	•	Language arts	•	•	Learning strategies
•	•	Written express	•	•	Organizational skills

Academic Accommodations

Curriculum	Study Aids	Exams
Priority registration	• Typist	• Oral
Math waiver	Reader	Untimed
Foreign lang. waiver	• Notetaker	• Take home
• Course substitution	• Proof reader	With proctor
In Class	• Text on tape	On computer
• Calculators	• Early syllabus	• Extended time
• Tape recorder	Taped handouts	On tape
• Word processor		• Modified
Priority seating		Separate room

Program Strengths
We have on campus a very good Student Support System, which includes help in math, English, study skills, and reading, as well as tutoring help for any class on campus. We also provide additional accommodations for learning disabled students such as, note takers, readers, and extended test time. We have a computer lab available for the students to use at any time.

General Information:
Snow College is a 2 year public college. Rural campus 85 miles from Provo. Ski areas are 100 miles from campus. Housing is not guaranteed.

Accreditation: Regional

Expenses:
Tuition: In-state: Full year: $1,005.00. Tuition: Out-of-state: Full year: $2,679.00.

Majors
• AREA STUDIES American, Latin American • BUSINESS Accounting, Business Administration, Business Economics, Business Management, Economics, Finance, Management, Marketing • COMMUNICATIONS Advertising, Communication, Creative Writing, English, Journalism • COMPUTER SCIENCE Data Processing, Programming, Systems Analysis • EDUCATION Art, Early Childhood, Elementary, Health, Industrial, Music, Physical, Vocational • ENGINEERING Computer • HEALTH SCIENCES Nursing, Nutritional/Food • HUMANITIES Humanities, Philosophy, Religion • LANGUAGES French, Spanish • PREPROFESSIONAL Agriculture, Architecture, Engineering, Law, Pharmacy • SCIENCES Biology, Botany, Chemistry, Geography, Geology, Macrobiology, Mathematics, Microbiology, Physical Chemistry, Physical Science, Physics, Physiology, Zoology • SOCIAL SCIENCES Anthropology, Criminal Justice, Government/Political, History, Political Science, Social Sciences, Sociology • VISUAL AND PERFORMING ARTS Art, Art History, Dance, Music, Studio Art, Theater

Sports/Activities
• SPORTS RELATED Cheerleading, Drill Team, Marching Band, Team Managers • SPORTS-INTRAMURAL Archery, Baseball, Basketball, Canoeing, Diving, Football, Golf, Gymnastics, Racquetball, Skiing - Snow, Softball, Swimming, Tennis, Volleyball, Weight Lifting • STUDENT LIFE ACTIVITIES Debate, Drama Groups, Ethnic & Cultural Groups, Jazz Band, Music Groups, Newspaper, Radio/TV station, Religious Organization, Student Government, Yearbook

Less Selective

Southern Utah University
P.O. Box 9375
Cedar City, Utah 84720
(801) 586-7771

School Enrollment: **4,280** Male: **1,890** Female: **2,390**

Admissions Contact: **Mr. Dale Orton, Director of Admissions**
LD Contact: **Pamela France, Counselor, Student Support**
Name of Program: **Student Support Services**
Telephone:**(801) 586-7848**

Admissions

Application Information:
Applicant must apply **2-3** months in advance
Rolling Admissions: **Yes**

Secondary School Information
Most Important Criteria For Admissions (1-strongest)

1 SAT/ACT	Application	School transcript
3 Class rank	Course selection	Personal statement
Interview	Extra activities	Psychocducational
2 G.P.A.	Open admission	Recommendations

Test Requirements:
Diagnostic testing waived: **Yes**
Untimed ACT: **Yes**
Documentation of LD required: **Yes**
Currency of diagnostic testing: **2-3 months**
Tests recommended: **We accept a wide variety and accept all students who show potential to succeed in our environment.**

Types of Disabilities Served
- Speech/Lang
- Study skills
- Written express
- Organizational
- Perceptual
- Reading
- Spelling
- Math
- Fine Motor
- ADD with LD
- ADD without LD
- ADHD with LD
- ADHD without LD

Admissions Process

Student fills out admissions and financial aid forms. Sends with official high school/college transcripts, copies of ACT scores and application fee ($25.00) to S.U.U. Admissions.

High School Course Requirements:
English: **4** Math: **2** Science: **2**

Learning Disability Program

Program: Reinforces course work: **Yes**
Program available through:**Fall, winter, spring**
Students mainstreamed **100** % of the day
Recommended credits per semester: **12**
Time required or recommended in learning center: **1 hour**
Counseling: Individual: **Yes** Vocational Counseling: **Yes**
Support groups are available:**Yes, administered by Academic Support Coordinator for all LD students.**

Faculty:
Faculty: **5** Including Director: **Yes** Full time: **5**

Diagnostic Testing
ADD	• Personality	• Perceptual skills	Spelling
ADHD	• Organization	Fine motor skills	• Reading
I.Q.	Handwriting	Spoken language	• Study skills
• Math	Social skills	• Written language	

Tutoring:
Average size of group tutorials: **2-3**
Services rendered by:
Graduates •Peers Faculty •LD staff Teacher trainees

Tutorials
Grp.	Ind.	Tutorials	Grp.	Ind.	Tutorials
•	•	Math skills			Word processing
•	•	Study skills	•		Time management
•	•	Language arts	•	•	Learning strategies
•	•	Written express	•		Organizational skills

Academic Accommodations

Curriculum	Study Aids	Exams
• Priority registration	• Typist	• Oral
Math waiver	• Reader	• Untimed
• Foreign lang. waiver	Notetaker	• Take home
Course substitution	• Proof reader	• With proctor
In Class	• Text on tape	On computer
• Calculators	• Early syllabus	• Extended time
• Tape recorder	Taped handouts	• On tape
• Word processor		Modified
• Priority seating		• Separate room

Graduation Requirements:
Course credits: **183 quarter hours** GPA: **2.0** Years to complete degree:
As many as needed Math waiver: **Yes**
Other requirements: **Some degree programs**

Program Strengths
Students are worked with and assisted on an individualized basis. Each student receives help in her/his area of need. Our retention and graduation rates are good. Students learn to advocate and take responsibility for themselves.

General Information:
Southern Utah University is a 2 and 4 year public university. Rural Campus of 116 acres is 180 miles from Las Vegas. Accessible by air or bus. Ski areas are 30 miles from campus. 1% of students are foreign. 3 residential halls on campus. Housing is not guaranteed.70 % of students remain on campus for the weekends. 1-2 % of students join fraternities/sororities.

Accreditation:NACS, UNBN

Expenses:
Tuition: In-state: Full year: $338.00 plus $112.00 fees. Part-time: Per credit:$59.00 plus $31.00 fees. Tuition: Out-of-state: Full year: $1,082.00 plus $112.00 fees. Part-time: Per credit:$191.00 plus $31.00 fees. Room and board: $800.00 per quarter

Majors
• BUSINESS Accounting, Agricultural, Business Administration, Business Education, Business Management, Economics, Finance, Management, Marketing, Real Estate • COMMUNICATIONS Advertising, Broadcasting, Communication, English, Journalism, Speech, Television/Radio/Film • COMPUTER SCIENCE Computer Science, Data Processing, Programming • EDUCATION Art, Curriculum, Early Childhood, Elementary, English, Industrial, Mathematics, Middle School, Music, Physical, School

Psychology, Secondary, Special, Speech/Language, Vocational • ENGINEERING Chemical, Mechanical • HEALTH SCIENCES Nursing, Practical Nursing • LANGUAGES French, German, Spanish • PREPROFESSIONAL Engineering, Forestry, Law, Medicine • SCIENCES Agricultural, Agronomy, Animal, Biology, Botany, Geology, Mathematics, Physical Science, Physics, Soil, Zoology • SOCIAL SCIENCES Government/Political, History, Law Enforcement, Library Science, Psychology, Public Relations, Social Sciences, Sociology • VISUAL AND PERFORMING ARTS Art, Dance, Music, Theater • VOCATIONAL Automobile Technology, Business and Office, Computer Assisted Drafting, Drafting, Forestry, Home Economics, Industrial Technology, Mechanical Design Technology, Precision Metal Work, Secretarial, Textile and Clothing, Wildlife Management

Sports/Activities

• SPORTS RELATED Bagpipe Band, Cheerleading, Drill Team, Drum Major/Majorette, Marching Band, Team Managers • SPORTS-INTERCOLLEGIATE Baseball, Basketball (F), Basketball (M), Football, Golf, Gymnastics (F), Rodeo, Track and Field (M) • SPORTS-INTRAMURAL Badminton, Baseball, Basketball, Cross Country, Football, Golf, Gymnastics, Gymnastics (F), Racquetball, Rodeo, Skiing - Cross Country, Skiing - Snow, Soccer, Softball, Swimming, Tennis, Track and Field, Volleyball, Weight Lifting • STUDENT LIFE ACTIVITIES Academic Clubs, Choral, Community Service, Concert Band, Dance, Debate, Drama Groups, Ethnic & Cultural Groups, Fraternities, Music Groups, Musical Theater, Newsletter, Orchestra, Political Groups, Radio/TV station, Religious Organization, Sororities, Student Government, Yearbook

Selective **Utah**
Services

University of Utah
160 Union
Salt Lake City, Utah 84112
(801) 581-8761

School Enrollment: 23,500
LD Enrollment: **200** Male: **130** Female: **70**

Admissions Contact: **Stayner Landward, Dir. of Admissions**
LD Contact: **Olga Nadeau, Director**
Name of Program: **Disabled Student Services**
Address: **160 Oplin Union Bldg.**
Telephone:**(801) 581-5020**

Admissions

Application Information:
Enrolled:**200**
Application deadline: **Quarterly deadline**

Secondary School Information
Most Important Criteria For Admissions (1-strongest)

1 SAT/ACT	Application	**2**	School transcript
Class rank	**2** Course selection		Personal statement
Interview	Extra activities	**3**	Psychoeducational
1 G.P.A.	Open admission	**3**	Recommendations

Test Requirements:
Diagnostic testing waived: **Yes**
Untimed ACT: **Yes**
WAIS-R required: **Yes**
Documentation of LD required: **Yes**
Currency of diagnostic testing: **3 years**
Tests recommended: **WAIS-R, Woodcock-Johnson Psychoeducational Battery**

Types of Disabilities Served
- Speech/Lang
- Study skills
- Written express
- Organizational
- Perceptual
- Reading
- Spelling
- Math
- Fine Motor
- ADD with LD
- ADD without LD
- ADHD with LD
- ADHD without LD

Admissions Process

Complete the application for admission and return with a $25.00 nonrefundable processing fee prior to the deadline dates listed in the application. If the student meets all the admission criteria, a letter of admission is sent from the Admission Office.

High School Course Requirements:
English: **4** Math: **3** Science: **2** Foreign Language: **2**
Waivers to standard high school courses
Foreign Language : **Yes** Math: **Yes**

Learning Disability Program
Services only for LD students: **Yes**
Counseling: Individual: **Yes**

Faculty:
Faculty: **2** Full time: **1** Part time: **1**
LD faculty with: BS/BA: **1** M.A.: **1**
Faculty advocate: **Yes** Meets with instructor: **As needed**

Diagnostic Testing
ADD • Personality	• Perceptual skills	• Spelling
ADHD• Organization	• Fine motor skills	• Reading
• I.Q. • Handwriting	• Spoken language	• Study skills
• Math • Social skills	• Written language	

Tutoring:
Average size of group tutorials: **1-10**
Services rendered by:
Graduates •Peers •Faculty •LD staff Teacher trainees

Tutorials
Grp.	Ind. Tutorials	Grp.	Ind. Tutorials
•	Math skills		Word processing
	Study skills	•	Time management
	Language arts	•	Learning strategies
•	Written express	•	Organizational skills

Academic Accommodations
Curriculum	Study Aids	Exams
• Priority registration	• Typist	• Oral
• Math waiver	• Reader	Untimed
• Foreign lang. waiver	• Notetaker	• Take home
• Course substitution	• Proof reader	• With proctor
In Class	• Text on tape	• On computer
• Calculators	Early syllabus	• Extended time
• Tape recorder	Taped handouts	On tape
Word processor		Modified
Priority seating		• Separate room

Graduation Requirements:
Course credits: **183** GPA: **2.0** Years to complete degree: **Varies** Math waiver: **Yes** Language waiver: **Yes**
Other requirements: **Meet the requirements for major**

Program Strengths
Disabled Student Services provides assistance with admissions and registration for classes, counseling services, liaison work with instructors, accommodations for taking exams, tape player loan ser-

Utah

vice, taped textbooks, adaptive computers, student group, and on and off campus LD assessments. Focus is on development of self reliance, independence and preparation for participating in all academic and nonacademic activities on an equal basis with other students.

General Information:

University of Utah is a 4 year public university. Urban campus. Accessible by air or bus Ski areas are 30 miles from campus. 4 residential halls on campus. Housing is not guaranteed.

Accreditation: Regional

Expenses:

Tuition: In-state: Full year: $1,884.00. Part-time: Per credit:$177.50. Part-time: Per course: $315.50. Tuition: Out-of-state: Full year: $5,310.00. Part-time: Per credit:$459.00. Part-time: Per course:$863.00 Room and board: $3,200.00

Majors

• AREA STUDIES Middle Eastern, Urban • BUSINESS Accounting, Banking, Business Administration, Business Economics, Business Management, Economics, Finance, Human Resources Management, Marketing • COMMUNICATIONS Communication, English, Journalism • EDUCATION Early Childhood, Elementary, Middle School, Physical, Secondary, Speech/Language • ENGINEERING Chemical, Computer, Geological, Industrial, Materials, Mechanical, Mining/Mineral, Petroleum • HEALTH SCIENCES Medical Technology, Nursing, Nutritional/Food, Physical Therapy, Speech/Audiology and Speech • HUMANITIES Liberal Arts, Philosophy • LANGUAGES Arabic, French, German, Greek, Latin, Linguistic, Russian, Spanish • PREPROFESSIONAL Pharmacy • SCIENCES Anthropology, Atmosphere, Biology, Chemistry, Geology, Geophysics & Seismology, Meteorology, Physics • SOCIAL SCIENCES Government/Political, History, Psychology, Social Sciences, Sociology • VISUAL AND PERFORMING ARTS Art History, Dance Education, Fine Arts, Music • VOCATIONAL Park/Recreation, Urban Design

Sports/Activities

• SPORTS RELATED Marching Band, Pep Band • SPORTS-INTERCOLLEGIATE Baseball (M), Basketball, Cross Country, Diving, Football (M), Golf (M), Gymnastics (F), Skiing - Snow, Softball (F), Swimming, Tennis, Track and Field, Volleyball (F), Water Polo (M) • SPORTS-INTRAMURAL Badminton, Basketball, Bowling, Cross Country, Golf, Hand Ball, Horseback Riding (M), Ice Hockey (M), Lacrosse (M), Racquetball, Skiing - Snow, Soccer, Softball (F), Squash, Swimming, Tennis, Track and Field, Volleyball, Wrestling • STUDENT LIFE ACTIVITIES Choral, Concert Band, Dance, Drama Groups, Ethnic & Cultural Groups, Fraternities, Jazz Band, Magazine, Music Groups, Musical Theater, Newspaper, Opera, Political Groups, Radio/TV station, Religious Organization, Sororities, Student Government, Symphony Orchestra

Selective	Utah
	Services

Utah State University
Logan, Utah 84322
(801) 750-1107

School Enrollment: **9,490**

Admissions Contact: **Rod Clark Director of Admissions**
LD Contact: **Diane Craig Baum Director**
Name of Program: **Disabled Student Center**
Telephone:**(801) 750-2444**

Admissions

Application Information:
Application deadline: **None**
Rolling Admissions: **Yes**

Secondary School Information
Most Important Criteria For Admissions (1-strongest)

1 SAT/ACT	**1** Application	**1** School transcript
Class rank	Course selection	Personal statement
Interview	Extra activities	Psychoeducational
G.P.A.	Open admission	Recommendations

Test Requirements:
Standardized tests waived: **Yes**
Diagnostic testing waived: **Yes**
WAIS-R required: **Yes**
Documentation of LD required: **Yes**

Types of Disabilities Served
• Speech/Lang	• Reading	• ADD with LD
• Study skills	• Spelling	• ADD without LD
• Written express	• Math	• ADHD with LD
• Organizational	• Fine Motor	• ADHD without LD
• Perceptual		

Diagnostic Testing
ADD	Personality	Perceptual skills	Spelling
ADHD	Organization	Fine motor skills	Reading
I.Q.	Handwriting	Spoken language	Study skills
Math	Social skills	Written language	

Tutoring:
Services rendered by:
•Graduates   •Peers   •Faculty   LD staff   Teacher trainees

Tutorials
Grp.	Ind.	Tutorials	Grp.	Ind.	Tutorials
•	•	Math skills	•	•	Word processing
•	•	Study skills	•	•	Time management
•	•	Language arts	•	•	Learning strategies
•	•	Written express	•	•	Organizational skills

Academic Accommodations

Curriculum	Study Aids	Exams
Priority registration	• Typist	• Oral
• Math waiver	Reader	Untimed
• Foreign lang. waiver	• Notetaker	• Take home
• Course substitution	• Proof reader	With proctor
In Class	• Text on tape	On computer
• Calculators	Early syllabus	• Extended time
• Tape recorder	Taped handouts	On tape
• Word processor		• Modified
Priority seating		Separate room

Program Strengths
Our services are highly individualized. We encourage our students to get as involved as possible and to use the Disabled Student Center to aid them in their academic endeavors.

General Information:
Utah State University is a 2 and 4 year public university. of 332 acres is 50 miles from Salt Lake City. Accessible by bus. Ski areas are 20 miles from campus. Beaches are 16 miles from campus. Housing is not guaranteed.

Accreditation: All major accreditation

SAT/ACT Scores:
Scores for incoming freshmen: **ACT:** 38% below 20. 22% between 20 and 23. 23% between 24 and 25l. 17% between 26 and 28.

Expenses:
Tuition: In-state: Full year: $1,500.00. Part-time: Per credit: $24.00. Tuition: Out-of-state: Full year: $4,131.00. Room and board: $2,445.00 Cost of LD program:

Majors
• AREA STUDIES American, Black/Afro-American, Latin American, Women's Studies • BUSINESS Accounting, Agricultural, Banking, Business Administration, Business Economics, Business Education, Business Management, Economics, Finance, Management, Marketing, Personnel • COMMUNICATIONS Advertising, Broadcasting, Communication, Creative Writing, English, Journalism, Photography, Speech, Television/Radio/Film • COMPUTER SCIENCE Computer Science, Data Processing, Programming, Systems Analysis, Telecommunications • EDUCATION Agricultural, Art, Early Childhood, Elementary, Health, Home Economics Education, Industrial, Marketing and Distributive Education, Mathematics, Middle School, Music, Music Therapy, Physical, Recreation and Youth Leadership, School Psychology, Secondary, Special, Speech/Language, Vocational • ENGINEERING Aerospace, Agricultural, Chemical, Civil/Environmental, Computer, Electrical, Environmental/Water Resources, Industrial, Irrigation, Mechanical • HEALTH SCIENCES Communication Disorders, Environmental, Health, Medical Technology, Nursing, Nutritional/Food, Occupational Therapy, Physical Therapy, Speech Therapy, Speech/Audiology and Speech • HUMANITIES Humanities, Liberal Arts, Philosophy • LANGUAGES Arabic, Chinese, French, German, Japanese, Latin, Russian, Spanish • PREPROFESSIONAL Agriculture, Architecture, Dentistry, Engineering, Forestry, Law, Medicine, Natural Resources, Range Management, Recreation, Social Work, Veterinarian • SCIENCES Agronomy, Animal, Astrophysics, Biochemistry, Biology, Botany, Chemistry, Earth, Ecology, Geography, Geology, Macrobiology, Marine Biology, Mathematics, Microbiology, Physical Chemistry, Physical Science, Physics, Physiology, Soil, Statistics, Zoology • SOCIAL SCIENCES Anthropology, Criminal Justice, Family Counseling, Geography, Government/Political, History, Political Science, Psychology, Social Sciences, Sociology • VISUAL AND PERFORMING ARTS Art, Art History, Dance, Dramatic Arts, Fine Arts, Music, Studio Art, Theater • VOCATIONAL Aviation Maintenance, Business and Office, Electronics Technology, Fishery Studies, Food Service, Forestry, Home Economics, Landscape Architecture, Medical Laboratory Technology, Park/Recreation, Textile and Clothing

Sports/Activities
• SPORTS RELATED Cheerleading, Drill Team, Drum Major/Majorette, Marching Band, Pep Band, Team Managers • SPORTS-INTERCOLLEGIATE Basketball (M), Cross Country (F), Football (M), Golf (M), Gymnastics (F), Softball (F), Tennis (M), Track and Field, Volleyball (F) • SPORTS-INTRAMURAL Archery (M), Badminton, Baseball, Basketball (M), Bowling, Hand Ball, Ping-Pong, Racquetball, Skiing - Snow, Soccer, Softball, Swimming, Tennis, Track and Field, Volleyball (F), Wrestling (M) • STUDENT LIFE ACTIVITIES Choral, Concert Band, Dance, Debate, Drama Groups, Ethnic & Cultural Groups, Fraternities, Jazz Band, Magazine, Music Groups, Musical Theater, Newspaper, Opera, Radio/TV station, Religious Organization, Sororities, Student Government, Symphony Orchestra

Burlington College
95 North Avenue
Burlington, Vermont 05401
(802) 862-9616

School Enrollment: **213**
LD Enrollment: **21**

Admissions Contact: **Larry Lewack, Director of Admissions**
LD Contact: **Laura Wisniewski, Director**
Name of Program: **Student Support Services**
Telephone: **(802) 862-9616**

Admissions

Application Information:
Application deadline: **Rolling**
Rolling Admissions: **Yes**

Secondary School Information
Most Important Criteria For Admissions (1-strongest)

SAT/ACT **1** Application		School transcript
Class rank	Course selection	Personal statement
1 Interview	Extra activities	Psychoeducational
G.P.A.	**1** Open admission	Recommendations

Test Requirements:
Standardized tests waived: **Yes**
Tests recommended: **We don't require results from any standardized tests as a condition of admission. LD students are asked to do assessment tests upon enrollment**

Types of Disabilities Served
• Speech/Lang • Reading • ADD with LD
• Study skills • Spelling • ADD without LD
• Written express • Math • ADHD with LD
• Organizational • Fine Motor • ADHD without LD
• Perceptual

Admissions Process

Our open admissions process requires applicants to complete and submit our 4-page application for admission, send us an official transcript proving high school graduation/GED test passing, and do an informal personal interview.

Learning Disability Program
Program: Remedial: **Yes**
Program: Reinforces course work: **Yes**
Students mainstreamed **100** % of the day
Recommended credits per semester:
Services available for all students: **Yes**
Counseling: Individual: **Yes** Vocational Counseling: **Yes**

Faculty:
Faculty: **6** Including Director: **Yes** Full time: **3** Part time: **3** M.A.: **2**
Meets with instructor: **As needed**

Vermont

Diagnostic Testing

ADD	Personality	Perceptual skills	Spelling
ADHD	Organization	Fine motor skills	• Reading
I.Q.	Handwriting	Spoken language	Study skills
Math	Social skills •	Written language	

Tutoring:
Services rendered by:
Graduates   •Peers   •Faculty   •LD staff   Teacher trainees

Tutorials

Grp.	Ind.	Tutorials	Grp.	Ind.	Tutorials
•	•	Math skills	•	•	Word processing
•	•	Study skills	•	•	Time management
		Language arts	•	•	Learning strategies
•	•	Written express	•	•	Organizational skills

Academic Accommodations

Curriculum	Study Aids	Exams
Priority registration	Typist	Oral
Math waiver	Reader	Untimed
Foreign lang. waiver	• Notetaker	• Take home
• Course substitution	Proof reader	• With proctor
In Class	Text on tape	On computer
• Calculators	• Early syllabus	Extended time
• Tape recorder	Taped handouts	On tape
• Word processor		• Modified
• Priority seating		Separate room

Graduation Requirements:
Course credits: **60** Years to complete degree: **Unlimited**

Program Strengths

Burlington College is a small, non-traditional school which is geared towards adult learners. Unique features helpful to the LD student include: small classes; individualized education; few tests; various modes of instruction. The LD program is quite small and part of Student Support Services, but it is very personalized and provides tutoring, counseling, advocacy, and support.

General Information:

Burlington College is a 4 year private college. Urban campus of 1 acres is Accessible by air or bus. Ski areas are 25 miles from campus. Beaches are 1 mile from campus. 2% of students are foreign. Housing is not guaranteed.

Accreditation: NEACS

Expenses:
Tuition: In-state: Full year: $6,750.00. Part-time: Per credit:$225.00. Tuition: Out-of-state: Full year: $6,750.00. Part-time: Per credit:$225.00.

Majors
• AREA STUDIES Women's Studies • COMMUNICATIONS Creative Writing, English, Literature • EDUCATION Early Childhood, Elementary, Middle School, Pre-Education, Secondary • HUMANITIES English/Writing/Literature, Humanities, Liberal Arts, Philosophy • SOCIAL SCIENCES History, Psychology, Social Sciences • VISUAL AND PERFORMING ARTS Fine Arts, Folklore & Mythology

Sports/Activities
• STUDENT LIFE ACTIVITIES Newspaper, Political Groups, Student Government

---

Community College of Vermont
P. O. Box 120
Waterbury, Vermont 05676
(802) 241-3535

School Enrollment: **4,400** Male: **880** Female: **3,520**
LD Contact: **Jack Anderson, Director**
Name of Program: **Student Support Services**

Admissions

Application Information:
Application deadline: **None**
Rolling Admissions: **Yes**

Secondary School Information
Most Important Criteria For Admissions (1-strongest)

SAT/ACT	Application	School transcript
Class rank	Course selection	Personal statement
Interview	Extra activities	Psychoeducational
G.P.A.	**1** Open admission	Recommendations

Test Requirements:
Standardized tests waived: **Yes**

Types of Disabilities Served
• Speech/Lang	• Reading	• ADD with LD
• Study skills	• Spelling	• ADD without LD
• Written express	• Math	• ADHD with LD
• Organizational	• Fine Motor	• ADHD without LD
• Perceptual		

Admissions Process

Open admissions

Learning Disability Program
Counseling: Individual: **Yes**

Faculty:
Faculty advocate: **Yes**

Diagnostic Testing

ADD	Personality	Perceptual skills	Spelling
ADHD	Organization	Fine motor skills	Reading
I.Q.	Handwriting	Spoken language	Study skills
Math	Social skills	Written language	

Tutoring:
Services rendered by:
•Graduates   •Peers   •Faculty   •LD staff   Teacher trainees

Tutorials

Grp.	Ind.	Tutorials	Grp.	Ind.	Tutorials
•	•	Math skills			Word processing
•		Study skills	•		Time management
		Language arts	•		Learning strategies
		Written express	•		Organizational skills

Academic Accommodations

Curriculum	Study Aids	Exams
Priority registration	Typist	• Oral
Math waiver	Reader	• Untimed
Foreign lang. waiver	Notetaker	Take home
• Course substitution	Proof reader	With proctor
In Class	Text on tape	On computer
Calculators	Early syllabus	• Extended time
• Tape recorder	Taped handouts	On tape
• Word processor		Modified
Priority seating		Separate room

Graduation Requirements:
Course credits: **60** Years to complete degree: **No limits**

Program Strengths

We are a community college and serve all students who choose to attend the best we can. We do not have an LD program but offer a lot of supportive services. Tutoring is for all students.

General Information:

Community College of Vermont is a 2 year public college. Rural campus 25 miles from Burlington. Accessible by train or bus. Housing is not guaranteed.

Accreditation:

Expenses:
Tuition: In-state: Full year: Part-time: Per credit: $61.00. Tuition: Out-of-state: Full year: Part-time: Per credit: $122.00.

Majors

• BUSINESS Accounting, Business Management, Management • COMPUTER SCIENCE Computer Science • EDUCATION Early Childhood, General, Teacher Aide • HEALTH SCIENCES Allied Health, Medical Technology • HUMANITIES Liberal Arts • SOCIAL SCIENCES Human Service • VOCATIONAL Automotive Service

---

Less Selective   **Vermont Program**

Landmark College
River Road Rural Route 1 Box 1000
Putney , Vermont 05346
(802) 387-4767

School Enrollment: **150** Male: **120** Female: **30**

Admissions Contact: **Carolyn Olivier, Director of Admissions**
LD Contact: **Carolyn Olivier, Director of Admissions**

Admissions

Application Information:
LD Students Applying: **120** Accepted: **105** Enrolled: **100**
Application deadline: **Rolling**
Applicant must apply **1** months in advance
Rolling Admissions: **Yes**

Secondary School Information
Most Important Criteria For Admissions (1-strongest)

SAT/ACT	**1** Application	School transcript
Class rank	Course selection **1**	Personal statement
1 Interview	**2** Extra activities	**1** Psychoeducational
G.P.A.	Open admission **1**	Recommendations

Test Requirements:
Standardized tests waived: **Yes**
Diagnostic testing waived: **Yes**
WAIS-R required: **Yes** Range accepted: **Average +**
Documentation of LD required: **Yes**
Currency of diagnostic testing: **2 years**
Tests recommended: **Diagnosis of dyslexia or specific learning disability**

Types of Disabilities Served
- Speech/Lang.
- Study skills
- Written express
- Organizational
- Perceptual
- Reading
- Spelling
- Math
- Fine Motor
- ADD with LD
- ADD without LD
- ADHD with LD
- ADHD without LD

Learning Disability Program
Program: Remedial: **Yes**
Program: Reinforces course work: **Yes**
Students mainstreamed **100** % of the day
Time required or recommended in learning center: **1 hour**
Counseling: Individual: **Yes** Group Counseling: **Yes**

Faculty:
Faculty: **70** Full time: **63** Part time: **7**
LD faculty with: BS/BA: **31** M.A.: **35** Ph.D.: **4**
Faculty advocate: **Yes** Meets with instructor: **As needed**

Diagnostic Testing
ADD	Personality	• Perceptual skills	• Spelling
ADHD	• Organization	• Fine motor skills	• Reading
• I.Q.	• Handwriting	• Spoken language	• Study skills
• Math	Social skills	• Written language	

Tutoring:
Average size of group tutorials:
Services rendered by:
Graduates   Peers   •Faculty   •LD staff   Teacher trainees

Tutorials
Grp.	Ind.	Tutorials	Grp.	Ind.	Tutorials
	•	Math skills		•	Word processing
	•	Study skills		•	Time management
	•	Language arts		•	Learning strategies
	•	Written express		•	Organizational skills

Academic Accommodations

Curriculum	Study Aids	Exams
Priority registration	Typist	Oral
Math waiver	Reader	Untimed
Foreign lang. waiver	Notetaker	• Take home
• Course substitution	Proof reader	With proctor
In Class	Text on tape	On computer
• Calculators	Early syllabus	• Extended time
Tape recorder	Taped handouts	On tape
• Word processor		• Modified
Priority seating		Separate room

Vermont

Program Strengths

Landmark College is an associate degree-granting institution which is exclusively for dyslexic or specific learning disabled students. It is the only accredited institution of its' kind in the country. Its goal is to prepare students to enter or return to non-specialized, bachelor degree-granting colleges or universities. Admission to Landmark College is based on a diagnosis of dyslexia or other specific learning disability, average to above-average intelligence, absence of primary emotional or behavioral disturbances, and high motivation to participate in the program.

General Information:

Landmark College is a 2 year private college. Rural campus of 128 acres is 100 miles from Boston. Accessible by air or bus. Ski areas are 15 miles from campus. Beaches are 2 hours from campus. 3 residential halls on campus. Housing is guaranteed.75 % of students remain on campus for the weekends.

Accreditation: Candidacy Status - NEACS

Expenses:

Tuition: In-state: Full year: $19,950.00. Room and board: $5,000.00

Majors

• HUMANITIES Liberal Arts

Sports/Activities

• SPORTS-INTERCOLLEGIATE Baseball (M), Basketball (M), Cross Country, Skiing - Snow, Soccer, Tennis, Volleyball, Wrestling (M)
• SPORTS-INTRAMURAL Archery, Badminton, Baseball, Basketball, Cross Country, Golf, Horseback Riding, Ping-Pong, Skiing - Snow, Soccer, Softball, Swimming, Tennis, Volleyball • STUDENT LIFE ACTIVITIES Choral, Community Service, Dance, Drama Groups, Newspaper, Radio/TV station, Student Government, Student Mentors

---

Special   Vermont
Services

New England Culinary Institute

250 Main Street
Montpelier, Vermont 05602
(802) 223-6324

School Enrollment: **275** Male: **183** Female: **92**
LD Enrollment: **9**

Admissions Contact: **Barry R. Vogel, Director of Admissions**
LD Contact: **Howard Fisher, Director**

Admissions

Application Information:
Rolling Admissions: **Yes**

Secondary School Information
Most Important Criteria For Admissions (1-strongest)

	SAT/ACT	**1** Application	**2** School transcript
7	Class rank	Course selection	**4** Personal statement
5	Interview	**8** Extra activities	Psychoeducational
6	G.P.A.	Open admission	**3** Recommendations

Test Requirements:
Standardized tests waived: **Yes**

Types of Disabilities Served

• Speech/Lang	• Reading	• ADD with LD
• Study skills	• Spelling	• ADD without LD
• Written express	• Math	• ADHD with LD
• Organizational	• Fine Motor	• ADHD without LD
• Perceptual		

Faculty:

Diagnostic Testing

ADD	Personality	Perceptual skills	Spelling
ADHD	Organization	Fine motor skills	Reading
I.Q.	Handwriting	Spoken language	Study skills
Math	Social skills	Written language	

Tutoring:
Services rendered by:
Graduates   •Peers   Faculty   LD staff   Teacher trainees

Tutorials

Grp.	Ind.	Tutorials	Grp.	Ind.	Tutorials
	•	Math skills			Word processing
		Study skills			Time management
	•	Language arts			Learning strategies
		Written express			Organizational skills

Academic Accommodations

Curriculum	Study Aids	Exams
Priority registration	Typist	• Oral
Math waiver	Reader	Untimed
Foreign lang. waiver	• Notetaker	• Take home
Course substitution	Proof reader	• With proctor
In Class	• Text on tape	On computer
• Calculators	Early syllabus	• Extended time
• Tape recorder	Taped handouts	On tape
• Word processor		• Modified
Priority seating		Separate room

Program Strengths

New England Culinary Institute provides small classes with a seven-to-one student-teacher ratio. Peer tutoring is available for all students. Resources within the community are made available to LD students.

General Information:

New England Culinary Institute is a 2 year private college. Rural campus 50 miles from Burlington. Accessible by air, train or bus. Ski areas are 25 miles from campus. Beaches are 10 miles from campus. 10 residential halls on campus. Housing is guaranteed.90 % of students remain on campus for the weekends.

Accreditation:CCA, State of Vermont, Award AOS degree.

Expenses:

Tuition: In-state: Full year: $15,200.00 includes room & board.

Majors

• BUSINESS Food Management • VOCATIONAL Culinary Arts, Food Service

Sports/Activities

• STUDENT LIFE ACTIVITIES Student Government, Yearbook

Selective **Vermont Services**

Norwich University
Northfield, Vermont 05663
(802) 485-2001

School Enrollment: **1,500** Male: **1,300** Female: **200**

Admissions Contact: **Jim Skinner, Director of Admissions**
LD Contact: **Paula A. Gills, Director**
Name of Program: **Learning Support Center**
Telephone:**(802) 485-2130**

Admissions

Application Information:
LD on admissions committee:**Yes**
Application deadline: **April 1st**
Rolling Admissions: **Yes**

Secondary School Information
Most Important Criteria For Admissions (1-strongest)

4 SAT/ACT	**10** Application	**3**	School transcript
5 Class rank	**2** Course selection	**8**	Personal statement
6 Interview	**9** Extra activities	**11**	Psychoeducational
1 G.P.A.	Open admission	**7**	Recommendations

Test Requirements:
Untimed SAT: **Yes** Untimed ACT: **Yes**
Documentation of LD required: **Yes**

Types of Disabilities Served
- Speech/Lang
- Study skills
- Written express
- Organizational
- Perceptual
- Reading
- Spelling
- Math
- Fine Motor
- ADD with LD
- ADD without LD
- ADHD with LD
- ADHD without LD

Admissions Process

Students apply, send grades, letters etc... Then speak with admissions personnel, LSC director reviews file, admissions personnel make final decision.

High School Course Requirements:
Waivers to standard high school courses
Course substitution: **Yes**

Learning Disability Program
Recommended credits per semester: **16-18**
Services available for all students: **Yes**
Counseling: Individual: **Yes**

Faculty:
Faculty: **3** Full time: **3**

Diagnostic Testing
ADD	Personality	Perceptual skills	Spelling
ADHD	Organization	Fine motor skills	Reading
I.Q.	Handwriting	Spoken language	Study skills
Math	Social skills	Written language	

Tutoring:
Services rendered by:
Graduates •Peers Faculty •LD staff Teacher trainees

Tutorials
Grp.	Ind.	Tutorials	Grp.	Ind.	Tutorials
•	•	Math skills		•	Word processing
•	•	Study skills	•	•	Time management
	•	Language arts	•	•	Learning strategies
	•	Written express	•	•	Organizational skills

Academic Accommodations
Curriculum	Study Aids	Exams
• Priority registration	• Typist	• Oral
• Math waiver	• Reader	• Untimed
• Foreign lang. waiver	• Notetaker	• Take home
• Course substitution	• Proof reader	• With proctor
In Class	• Text on tape	• On computer
• Calculators	Early syllabus	• Extended time
• Tape recorder	Taped handouts	• On tape
• Word processor		• Modified
Priority seating		• Separate room

General Information:
Norwich University is a 4 year public university. Rural campus of 1,000 acres is 40 miles from Burlington. Accessible by air, train or bus. Ski areas are 30 miles from campus. Beaches are 40 miles from campus. 2% of students are foreign. 12 residential halls on campus. Housing is guaranteed.50 % of students remain on campus for the weekends.

Accreditation: Regional

Expenses:
Tuition: In-state: Full year: $11,600.00. Room and board: $4,700.00

Majors
• ARTS Art Therapy • BUSINESS Accounting, Business Administration, Business Economics, Business Management, Economics, Marketing • COMMUNICATIONS Communication, English • COMPUTER SCIENCE Computer Science • EDUCATION Early Childhood, Elementary, Physical, Physics Education, Secondary • ENGINEERING Architectural, Civil/Environmental, Computer, Electrical, Mechanical • HEALTH SCIENCES Medical Technology, Nursing • HUMANITIES Humanities, Liberal Arts • LANGUAGES French, German, Russian, Spanish • MATHEMATICS Applied • SCIENCES Biology, Chemistry, Mathematics, Physics • SOCIAL SCIENCES Criminal Justice, Government/Political, History, International Studies, Physics, Psychology • VOCATIONAL Medical Laboratory Technology

Sports/Activities
• SPORTS RELATED Marching Band, Pep Band • SPORTS-INTERCOLLEGIATE Baseball (M), Basketball, Cross Country, Diving, Football (M), Golf, Ice Hockey (M), Lacrosse (M), Riflery, Rugby, Skiing - Snow, Soccer, Softball (F), Swimming, Tennis, Track and Field, Wrestling (M) • SPORTS-INTRAMURAL Baseball (M), Basketball, Boxing (M), Cross Country, Diving, Fencing, Golf, Hand Ball, Ice Hockey (M), Lacrosse (M), Racquetball, Riflery, Skiing - Snow, Softball (F), Swimming, Tennis, Track and Field, Volleyball, Water Polo • STUDENT LIFE ACTIVITIES Choral, Concert Band, Drama Groups, Ethnic & Cultural Groups, Jazz Band, Magazine, Music Groups, Musical Theater, Newspaper, Political Groups, Radio/TV station, Student Government, Symphony Orchestra, Yearbook

Very Selective	Vermont Accommodations

Saint Michael's College
Winooski Park
Colchester, Vermont 05439
(802) 654-2000

School Enrollment: **1,728** Male: **828** Female: **900**
LD Enrollment: **38** Male: **25** Female: **13**

Admissions Contact: **Jerry E. Flanagan, Dean of Admissions**
Telephone:**(802) 654-2516**

Admissions

Application Information:
Application deadline: **Rolling, priority to March 15th**
Rolling Admissions: **Yes**

Secondary School Information
Most Important Criteria For Admissions (1-strongest)

5 SAT/ACT	**7** Application	**1**	School transcript
4 Class rank	**2** Course selection	**11**	Personal statement
10 Interview	**8** Extra activities	**6**	Psychoeducational
3 G.P.A.	Open admission	**9**	Recommendations

Test Requirements:
Diagnostic testing waived: **Yes**
Untimed SAT: **Yes** Untimed ACT: **Yes**
Documentation of LD required: **Yes**

Types of Disabilities Served
Speech/Lang	Reading	ADD with LD
Study skills	Spelling	ADD without LD
Written express	Math	ADHD with LD
Organizational	Fine Motor	• ADHD without LD
Perceptual		

Admissions Process

Students are considered on the basis of high school record, rank in class, testing scores and personal qualities. Typical students are in the top 30% of their high school class, range between 950-1150 on the SAT and have been active in school/community organizations.

High School Course Requirements:
English: **4** Math: **3** Science: **3** Foreign Language: **2**
Waivers to standard high school courses
Foreign Language : **Yes**

Learning Disability Program
Students mainstreamed **100** % of the day
Services available for all students: **Yes**
Counseling: Individual: **Yes** Group Counseling: **Yes**
Support groups are available:**Once a month LD students get together**

Diagnostic Testing
ADD	Personality	Perceptual skills	Spelling
ADHD	Organization	Fine motor skills	Reading
I.Q.	Handwriting	Spoken language	Study skills
Math	Social skills	Written language	

Services rendered by:
Graduates	Peers	Faculty	LD staff	Teacher trainees

Tutorials
Grp.	Ind.	Tutorials	Grp.	Ind.	Tutorials
		Math skills			Word processing
		Study skills			Time management
		Language arts			Learning strategies
		Written express			Organizational skills

Academic Accommodations
Curriculum	Study Aids	Exams
• Priority registration	Typist	• Oral
Math waiver	Reader	• Untimed
• Foreign lang. waiver	• Notetaker	Take home
Course substitution	Proof reader	With proctor
In Class	• Text on tape	On computer
• Calculators	• Early syllabus	• Extended time
• Tape recorder	Taped handouts	On tape
Word processor		Modified
Priority seating		• Separate room

Graduation Requirements:
Course credits: **124** GPA: **2.0** Language waiver: **Yes**

Program Strengths
There are a small number of students enrolled who have diagnosed learning differences, and members of our student resource center work with these students on an individual and informal basis.

General Information:
Saint Michael's College is a 4 year private Roman Catholic college. Suburban campus of 430 acres is 3 miles from Burlington. Accessible by air, train or bus. Ski areas are 15 miles from campus. Beaches are 5 miles from campus. 4% of students are foreign. 8 residential halls on campus. Housing is guaranteed.Guaranteed through 4th year. 95 % of students remain on campus for the weekends.

Accreditation:NEASC

SAT/ACT Scores:
Scores for incoming freshmen:**Verbal:**64%below 500. 32%between 500 and 599. 4%between 600 and 699. **Math:**38% below 500. 45% between 500 and 599. 17% between 600 and 699.

Class Rank:
About 34% of the present freshmen class were in the upper 20% of their high school class. 82% were in the top 40% of their class. 99% were in the top 60% of their class. 100% were in the top 80% of their class.

Expenses:
Tuition: In-state: Full year: $11,800.00. Part-time: Per credit:$400.00. Tuition: Out-of-state: Full year: $11,800.00. Part-time: Per credit:$400.00. Part-time: Per course:$400.00 Room and board: $5,400.00

Majors
• AREA STUDIES American • BUSINESS Accounting, Business Administration, Business Management, Economics, Management • COMMUNICATIONS English, Journalism, Literature • COMPUTER SCIENCE Computer Science, Programming • EDUCATION Art, Elementary, English, Foreign Language, Mathematics, Music, Science, Secondary, Social Sciences • HUMANITIES Classics, English/Writing/Literature, Philoso-

phy, Religion • LANGUAGES Foreign Language, French, German, Greek, Italian, Japanese, Latin, Russian, Spanish • PREPROFESSIONAL Dentistry, Engineering, Law, Medicine, Pharmacy • SCIENCES Biochemistry, Biology, Chemistry, Mathematics, Physics • SOCIAL SCIENCES Government/Political, History, Political Science, Psychology, Sociology • VISUAL AND PERFORMING ARTS Art, Dance, Dramatic Arts, Fine Arts, Music, Studio Art

Sports/Activities

• SPORTS RELATED Campus Ministry, Team Managers • SPORTS-INTERCOLLEGIATE Baseball (M), Basketball (F), Basketball (M), Cross Country (F), Cross Country (M), Diving (F), Diving (M), Field Hockey (F), Golf, Ice Hockey (M), Lacrosse (F), Lacrosse (M), Rugby, Skiing - Cross Country, Skiing - Snow (F), Skiing - Snow (M), Soccer (F), Soccer (M), Softball (F), Swimming (F), Swimming (M), Tennis (F), Tennis (M), Volleyball (F) • STUDENT LIFE ACTIVITIES Academic Clubs, Choral, Community Service, Concert Band, Dance, Drama Groups, Ethnic & Cultural Groups, Film, Jazz Band, Magazine, Music Groups, Musical Theater, Newspaper, Political Groups, Radio/TV station, Religious Organization, Student Government, Yearbook

Less Selective	Vermont Program

Southern Vermont College
Monument Avenue Ext.
Bennington, Vermont 05201
(802) 442-5427

School Enrollment: **746**
LD Enrollment: **20**

Admissions Contact: **Mary Van Arsdale, Director**
LD Contact: **Virginia Sturtevant, LD Director**
Name of Program: **Special Services**
Telephone:**(802) 442-5427**

Admissions

Application Information:
LD Students Applying: **150** Accepted: **38** Enrolled:**20**
LD on admissions committee:**Yes**
Application deadline: **Rolling**
Rolling Admissions: **Yes**

Secondary School Information
Most Important Criteria For Admissions (1-strongest)

	SAT/ACT	Application		School transcript
3	Class rank	3	Course selection	Personal statement
2	Interview		Extra activities	1 Psychoeducational
3	G.P.A.		Open admission	Recommendations

Test Requirements:
Diagnostic testing waived: **Yes**
Untimed SAT: **Yes** Untimed ACT: **Yes** Untimed ACH: **Yes**
WAIS-R required: **Yes**
Documentation of LD required: **Yes**
Currency of diagnostic testing: **2 years**
Tests recommended: **Individually administered achievement tests in math, reading, writing, and spelling**

Types of Disabilities Served
- Speech/Lang
- Study skills
- Written express
- Organizational
- Perceptual
- Reading
- Spelling
- Math
- Fine Motor
- ADD with LD
- ADD without LD
- ADHD with LD
- ADHD without LD

High School Course Requirements:
English: **3** Math: **2**
Waivers to standard high school courses
Math: **Yes**

Learning Disability Program
Program: Reinforces course work: **Yes**
Students mainstreamed **100** % of the day
Time required or recommended in learning center: **1-4 hours**
Services only for LD students: **Yes**
Counseling: Individual: **Yes** Vocational Counseling: **Yes**

Faculty:
Faculty: **2** Including Director: **Yes** Full time: **2**
LD faculty with: BS/BA: **1** M.A.: **1**
Faculty advocate: **Yes** Meets with instructor: **As needed**

Diagnostic Testing
ADD	Personality	Perceptual skills	Spelling
ADHD	Organization	Fine motor skills	Reading
I.Q.	Handwriting	Spoken language	Study skills
Math	Social skills	Written language	

Tutoring:
Average size of group tutorials: **4**
Services rendered by:
Graduates •Peers •Faculty •LD staff Teacher trainees

Tutorials
Grp.	Ind.	Tutorials	Grp.	Ind.	Tutorials
	•	Math skills		•	Word processing
•	•	Study skills	•	•	Time management
	•	Language arts	•	•	Learning strategies
	•	Written express	•	•	Organizational skills

Academic Accommodations

Curriculum	Study Aids	Exams
Priority registration	• Typist	• Oral
• Math waiver	• Reader	• Untimed
Foreign lang. waiver	• Notetaker	Take home
Course substitution	• Proof reader	• With proctor
In Class	• Text on tape	• On computer
• Calculators	Early syllabus	• Extended time
• Tape recorder	Taped handouts	On tape
• Word processor		Modified
• Priority seating		• Separate room

Graduation Requirements:
Course credits: **120** Years to complete degree: **As many as needed** Math waiver: **Yes**

Program Strengths
Our program is very structured yet allows for flexibility in meeting individual needs. We do what we say we do, which gives us credibility. We follow through on our students. As part of the Special Services umbrella, we work with a number of sensitive, caring, and supportive individuals.

General Information:
Southern Vermont College is a 2 and 4 year private college. Rural campus

Vermont

of 371 acres is 41 miles from Albany, New York. Accessible by bus. Ski areas are 10 miles from campus. 2% of students are foreign. Housing is guaranteed.Guaranteed through 4th year. 75 % of students remain on campus for the weekends.

Accreditation:NEACS

Expenses:
Tuition: In-state: Full year: $7,740.00. Part-time: Per credit:$258.00. Tuition: Out-of-state: Full year: $7,740.00. Part-time: Per credit:$258.00.
Room and board: $4,180.00

Majors
• BUSINESS Accounting, Business Management • COMMUNICATIONS Communication, English • EDUCATION Child Development • ENVIRONMENTAL CONTROL Energy Conservation and Regula • HEALTH SCIENCES Environmental, Nursing • HUMANITIES Humanities • PRE-PROFESSIONAL Natural Resources, Social Work • SOCIAL SCIENCES Criminal Justice, Human Service, Law Enforcement, Social Sciences

Sports/Activities
• SPORTS-INTERCOLLEGIATE Baseball (M), Basketball, Soccer, Softball (F) • SPORTS-INTRAMURAL Baseball, Bowling, Cross Country, Football (M), Golf, Ice Hockey (M), Ping-Pong, Skiing - Snow, Soccer, Softball, Volleyball • STUDENT LIFE ACTIVITIES Drama Groups, Musical Theater, Newspaper, Student Government, Vermont Public Interest Research, Yearbook

Selective   **Vermont Program**

University of Vermont
146 South Williams Street
Burlington, Vermont 05405
(802) 656-3370

School Enrollment: **8,103** Male: **3,904** Female: **4,199**
LD Enrollment: **145**

Admissions Contact: **Debra Besetta, Admissions Counselor**
LD Contact: **Susan Krasnow, LD Specialist**
Name of Program: **Specialized Student Services**
Address: **A-170 Living/Learning Center**
Telephone:**(802) 656-7753**

Admissions

Application Information:
LD on admissions committee:**Yes**
Application deadline: **February 1st**
Notified when: **April 15th**

Secondary School Information
Most Important Criteria For Admissions (1-strongest)

7 SAT/ACT	**8** Application	**1** School transcript
3 Class rank	**5** Course selection	**9** Personal statement
10 Interview	**6** Extra activities	**4** Psychoeducational
2 G.P.A.	Open admission	**11** Recommendations

Test Requirements:
Diagnostic testing waived: **Yes**
Untimed SAT: **Yes** Untimed ACT: **Yes**
WAIS-R required: **Yes**
Documentation of LD required: **Yes**
Currency of diagnostic testing: **3 years**
Tests recommended: **Measure of cognitive functioning, measure of**

educational achievement in reading, math, written language.

Types of Disabilities Served

• Speech/Lang	• Reading	• ADD with LD
• Study skills	• Spelling	• ADD without LD
• Written express	• Math	• ADHD with LD
• Organizational	• Fine Motor	• ADHD without LD
• Perceptual		

Admissions Process

Students choose whether disability information is to be considered in the admission process. If so, diagnostic information is required. LD Program staff consult with Admissions Staff.

High School Course Requirements:
English: **4** Math: **3** Science: **2** Foreign Language: **2**
Waivers to standard high school courses
Foreign Language : **Yes** Math: **Yes** Course substitution: **Yes**

Learning Disability Program
Program: Reinforces course work: **Yes**
Program available through:**As needed**
Students mainstreamed **100** % of the day
Recommended credits per semester: **12**
Services only for LD students: **Yes**
Counseling: Individual: **Yes** Group Counseling: **Yes** Vocational Counseling: **Yes**
Support groups are available: **Yes**

Faculty:
Faculty: **3** Full time: **3** M.A.: **2** Ph.D.: **1**
Faculty advocate: **Yes**

Diagnostic Testing

ADD	Personality	• Perceptual skills	• Spelling
ADHD	Organization	• Fine motor skills	• Reading
• I.Q.	Handwriting	• Spoken language	Study skills
• Math	Social skills	• Written language	

Tutoring:
Services rendered by:

Graduates	•Peers	Faculty	•LD staff	Teacher trainees

Tutorials

Grp.	Ind.	Tutorials	Grp.	Ind.	Tutorials
	•	Math skills		•	Word processing
	•	Study skills		•	Time management
	•	Language arts		•	Learning strategies
	•	Written express		•	Organizational skills

Academic Accommodations

Curriculum	Study Aids	Exams
• Priority registration	Typist	Oral
• Math waiver	• Reader	• Untimed
• Foreign lang. waiver	• Notetaker	Take home
• Course substitution	• Proof reader	• With proctor
In Class	• Text on tape	• On computer
• Calculators	Early syllabus	• Extended time
• Tape recorder	Taped handouts	• On tape
• Word processor		• Modified
Priority seating		• Separate room

Graduation Requirements:
Course credits: **120** GPA: **Varies** Math waiver: **Yes** Language waiver: **Yes**

Program Strengths

We offer full diagnostics. We have an informed faculty and supportive administration.

General Information:

University of Vermont is a 4 year public university. Urban campus of 425 acres is Accessible by train, air or bus Ski areas are 45 mins. from campus. 1% of students are foreign. Housing is guaranteed.Guaranteed through 2nd year. 16 % of students join fraternities/sororities.

Accreditation:NCATE, ADA, AMA, AHEA, APTA, ASHA, NASM, APA

SAT/ACT Scores:

Scores for incoming freshmen:**Verbal:**49%below 500. 41%between 500 and 599. 9%between 600 and 699. 1%above 700. **Math:**18% below 500. 41% between 500 and 599. 35% between 600 and 699. 6%above 700.

Class Rank:

About 48.3% of the present freshmen class were in the upper 20% of their high school class. 36.6% were in the top 40% of their class. 13.1% were in the top 60% of their class. 2.0% were in the top 80% of their class.

Expenses:

Tuition: In-state: Full year: $4.900.00. Part-time: Per credit:$206.00. Tuition: Out-of-state: Full year: $13,500.00. Part-time: Per credit:$554.00. Room and board: $4,142.00

Majors

• AGRICULTURE Plant Science • ANIMAL SCIENCE Dairy • AREA STUDIES Asian, European, Latin American, Russian/Slavic • ARTS Art History, Dramatic Arts, Music, Music Performance • BUSINESS Business Administration • COMMUNICATIONS English • COMPUTER SCIENCE Computer Science • EDUCATION Child Development, Early Childhood, Elementary, English, Foreign Language, General, Health, Home Economics, Mathematics, Middle School, Music, Physical, Reading, Science, Secondary, Social Studies, Special • ENGINEERING Civil/Environmental, Computer, Electrical, Mathematical, Mechanical • HEALTH SCIENCES Communication Disorders, Dental Hygiene, Nursing, Physical Therapy, Radiological Therapy • HUMANITIES Classics, English/Writing/Literature, Fine Arts, Liberal Arts , Philosophy, Religion • LANGUAGES English, French, German, Greek, Latin, Russian, Spanish • MATHEMATICS Computer, Statistical • PRE PROFESSIONAL Dentistry, Law, Medicine, Veterinarian • SCIENCES Agricultural, Animal, Anthropology, Applied Mathematics, Biochemistry, Biology, Botany, Chemistry, Computer Science, Dairy, Geology, Mathematics, Microbiology, Physics, Soil, Statistics, Zoology • SOCIAL SCIENCES Anthropology, Geography, Government/Political, History, International Studies, Political Science, Psychology, Sociology • VISUAL AND PERFORMING ARTS Art, Art History, Dramatic Arts, Music, Music Performance, Studio Art, Theater • VOCATIONAL Dental Hygiene

Sports/Activities

• SPORTS RELATED Pep Band • SPORTS-INTERCOLLEGIATE Baseball (M), Basketball, Cross Country, Field Hockey (F), Golf (M), Gymnastics, Ice Hockey (M), Lacrosse (F), Skiing - Snow, Soccer, Softball (F), Swimming, Tennis, Track and Field, Volleyball (F) • SPORTS-INTRAMURAL Badminton, Basketball, Bowling, Football, Flag, Golf, Ice Hockey, Racquetball, Soccer, Softball, Squash, Volleyball, Water Polo • STUDENT LIFE ACTIVITIES Academic Clubs, Choral, Community Service, Dance, Debate, Drama Groups, Ethnic & Cultural Groups, Film, Fraternities, Music Groups, Newspaper, Political Groups, Radio/TV station, Religious Organization, Sororities, Student Government, Yearbook

---

Selective

Vermont Services

Vermont Technical College

Randolph Center, Vermont 05061
(802) 728-3391

School Enrollment: **767** Male: **614** Female: **153**
LD Enrollment: **50**

Admissions Contact: **Steve Waterman, Director of Admissions**
LD Contact: **Wendelyn Duquette, Disabilities Counselor**
Name of Program: **Disabled Student Services**

Admissions

Application Information:
Application deadline: **Rolling**
Rolling Admissions: **Yes**

Secondary School Information
Most Important Criteria For Admissions (1-strongest)

3 SAT/ACT	**7** Application	**1** School transcript
9 Class rank	**4** Course selection	Personal statement
8 Interview	**6** Extra activities	Psychoeducational
2 G.P.A.	Open admission	**5** Recommendations

Test Requirements:
Diagnostic testing waived: **Yes**
Untimed SAT: **Yes** Untimed ACT: **Yes**
WAIS-R required: **Yes**
Documentation of LD required: **Yes**
Tests recommended: **WAIS-R and Woodcock-Johnson (for provision of accommodations and for better counseling, not for Admissions)**

Types of Disabilities Served
• Speech/Lang	• Reading	• ADD with LD
• Study skills	• Spelling	• ADD without LD
• Written express	Math	• ADHD with LD
• Organizational	• Fine Motor	• ADHD without LD
• Perceptual		

High School Course Requirements:
English: **4** Math: **3** Science: **2**

Learning Disability Program

Program: Remedial: **Yes**
Program: Reinforces course work: **Yes**
Program available through:**Monday-Friday**
Students mainstreamed **100** % of the day
Recommended credits per semester: **Varies**
Counseling: Individual: **Yes** Vocational Counseling: **Yes**

Faculty:
Faculty: **3** Full time: **1** Part time: **2** M.A.: **2**
Faculty advocate: **Yes** Meets with instructor: **Semesters**

Diagnostic Testing
ADD	Personality	Perceptual skills	Spelling
ADHD	Organization	Fine motor skills	Reading
I.Q.	Handwriting	Spoken language	Study skills
Math	Social skills	Written language	

Virginia

Tutoring:
Average size of group tutorials: **5**
Services rendered by:
  Graduates   •Peers   •Faculty   •LD staff   Teacher trainees

Tutorials

Grp.	Ind.	Tutorials	Grp.	Ind.	Tutorials
•	•	Math skills	•	•	Word processing
•	•	Study skills	•	•	Time management
•	•	Language arts	•	•	Learning strategies
•	•	Written express	•	•	Organizational skills

Academic Accommodations

Curriculum	Study Aids	Exams
Priority registration	Typist	• Oral
Math waiver	Reader	Untimed
Foreign lang. waiver	• Notetaker	Take home
• Course substitution	• Proof reader	• With proctor
In Class	• Text on tape	• On computer
• Calculators	Early syllabus	• Extended time
• Tape recorder	Taped handouts	On tape
• Word processor		• Modified
Priority seating		• Separate room

Graduation Requirements:
Course credits: **72** GPA: **2.0**

Program Strengths
The counselor works with students having physical or learning disabilities to help them maximize the quality of their education. Services include: academic counseling; auxiliary aids, such as taped texts or interpreters; coordination of reasonable accommodations; and individualized instruction in reading strategies and study skills.

General Information:
Vermont Technical College is a 2 year public college. Rural campus 25 miles from Montpelier. Accessible by bus. Ski areas are 1 mile from campus. 5% of students are foreign. 4 residential halls on campus. Housing is guaranteed.Guaranteed through 2nd year. 30 % of students remain on campus for the weekends.

Accreditation: Regional plus ABET

SAT/ACT Scores:
Scores for incoming freshmen:**Verbal:**30%below 500. 60%between 500 and 599. 9%between 600 and 699. 1%above 700. **Math:**20% below 500. 70% between 500 and 599. 8% between 600 and 699. 2%above 700.

Class Rank:
About 10% of the present freshmen class were in the upper 20% of their high school class. 65% were in the top 40% of their class. 95% were in the top 60% of their class. 100% were in the top 80% of their class.

Expenses:
Tuition: In-state: Full year: $3,360.00. Part-time: Per credit:$140.00. Tuition: Out-of-state: Full year: $6,744.00. Part-time: Per credit:$210.00. Room and board: $4,290.00 Cost of LD program:$550.00

Majors
• AGRICULTURE Business, Horticultural, Plant Science • ANIMAL SCIENCE Dairy • ARTS Drafting, Landscaping • BUSINESS Agricultural, Business Management, Clerical, Secretarial Science • COMPUTER SCIENCE Computer Maintenance, Computer Technology • ENGINEERING Architectural, Automotive, Civil/Environmental, Computer, Electrical, Mechanical • HEALTH SCIENCES Veterinarian Assistant • SCIENCES Agricultural, Animal, Dairy, Horticultural • VOCATIONAL Building Construction

Sports/Activities
• SPORTS-INTERCOLLEGIATE Baseball (M), Basketball, Skiing - Cross Country, Skiing - Snow, Soccer, Softball (F), Volleyball (F) • SPORTS-INTRAMURAL Badminton, Basketball, Bowling, Football, Golf, Ice Hockey (M), Judo, Lacrosse (M), Ping-Pong, Racquetball, Riflery, Rugby, Skiing - Snow, Soccer, Softball, Swimming, Tennis, Volleyball, Water Polo • STUDENT LIFE ACTIVITIES Academic Clubs, Community Service, Drama Groups, Music Groups, Newspaper, Radio/TV station, Religious Organization, Student Government, Yearbook

---

Less Selective

Virginia
Accommodations

Blue Ridge Community College
P. O. Box 80
Weyers Cave, Virginia 24486-9989
(703) 234-9261

School Enrollment: **2,300**
LD Enrollment: **20**

Admissions Contact: **Kathy Hahn, Registrar**
LD Contact: **Emily Sterrett, Counselor**
Telephone:**(703) 234-9261**

Admissions

Application Information:
Application deadline: **End of August**
Rolling Admissions: **Yes**

Secondary School Information
Most Important Criteria For Admissions (1-strongest)

SAT/ACT	Application	School transcript
Class rank	Course selection	Personal statement
Interview	Extra activities	Psychoeducational
G.P.A.	1 Open admission	Recommendations

Test Requirements:
Standardized tests waived: **Yes**
Documentation of LD required: **Yes**
Tests recommended: **Placement testing - double time allowed**

Types of Disabilities Served
• Speech/Lang	• Reading	• ADD with LD
• Study skills	• Spelling	• ADD without LD
• Written express	• Math	• ADHD with LD
• Organizational	• Fine Motor	• ADHD without LD
• Perceptual		

Faculty:
Faculty: **1** Part time: **1** M.A.: **1**

Diagnostic Testing
ADD	Personality	Perceptual skills	Spelling
ADHD	Organization	Fine motor skills	Reading
I.Q.	Handwriting	Spoken language	Study skills
Math	Social skills	Written language	

Services rendered by:
  Graduates   Peers   Faculty   LD staff   Teacher trainees

Tutorials

Grp.	Ind.	Tutorials	Grp.	Ind.	Tutorials
•	•	Math skills			Word processing
		Study skills			Time management
•	•	Language arts			Learning strategies
		Written express			Organizational skills

Academic Accommodations

Curriculum	Study Aids	Exams
Priority registration	Typist	• Oral
Math waiver	Reader	Untimed
Foreign lang. waiver	• Notetaker	Take home
Course substitution	Proof reader	• With proctor
In Class	• Text on tape	On computer
• Calculators	Early syllabus	• Extended time
• Tape recorder	Taped handouts	On tape
• Word processor		• Modified
Priority seating		• Separate room

Program Strengths

We are a small 2-year school which is often a good way for students to bridge the gap between high school and a 4-year college. We try to treat each student as unique, meeting his or her individual needs. Our counselors assess students individually on time management and learning strategies.

General Information:

Blue Ridge Community College is a 2 year public college. Rural campus 15 miles from Harrisburg. Housing is not guaranteed.

Accreditation: SACS

Expenses:

Tuition: In-state: Full year: Part-time: Per credit: $35.00. Tuition: Out-of-state: Full year: Part-time: Per credit: $142.00. Part-time: Per credit: $142.00.

Majors

• BUSINESS Accounting, Banking, Business Administration, Business Management, Finance, Management, Marketing • COMPUTER SCIENCE Data Processing, Programming • ENGINEERING Mechanical • HEALTH SCIENCES Nursing • HUMANITIES Liberal Arts • PREPROFESSIONAL Veterinarian • SCIENCES Animal • SOCIAL SCIENCES Human Service, Law Enforcement • VOCATIONAL Business and Office, Electronics Technology, Secretarial, Veterinarian Technology

Sports/Activities

• SPORTS-INTRAMURAL Basketball, Softball, Volleyball • STUDENT LIFE ACTIVITIES Student Government

---

Selective　　　　　**Virginia**
　　　　　　　　　　Accommodations

Bluefield College

3000 College Drive
Bluefield, Virginia 24605
(703) 326-3682

School Enrollment: **370** Male: **190** Female: **180**
LD Enrollment: **6-8**

Admissions Contact: **Nina Wilburn**
LD Contact: **Ms. Mickey Pellillo, Director Learning Center**
Name of Program: **Learning Center**

Admissions

Application Information:
Rolling Admissions: **Yes**

Secondary School Information
Most Important Criteria For Admissions (1-strongest)

9 SAT/ACT	**5** Application	**3** School transcript
10 Class rank	**11** Course selection	**8** Personal statement
4 Interview	**7** Extra activities	**2** Psychoeducational
1 G.P.A.	Open admission	**6** Recommendations

Test Requirements:
Untimed SAT: **Yes** Untimed ACT: **Yes**

Types of Disabilities Served

Speech/Lang	• Reading	ADD with LD
• Study skills	• Spelling	ADD without LD
• Written express	• Math	ADHD with LD
• Organizational	Fine Motor	ADHD without LD
Perceptual		

High School Course Requirements:
English: **4** Math: **2** Science: **1**

Learning Disability Program

Services available for all students: **Yes**
Support groups are available: **Study group**

Faculty:
Faculty: **1** Including Director: **Yes** Full time: **1**

Diagnostic Testing

ADD	Personality	Perceptual skills	Spelling
ADHD	Organization	Fine motor skills	Reading
I.Q.	Handwriting	Spoken language	Study skills
Math	Social skills	Written language	

Tutoring:
Average size of group tutorials: **3-10**
Services rendered by:

Graduates	•Peers	•Faculty	LD staff	Teacher trainees

Tutorials

Grp.	Ind.	Tutorials	Grp.	Ind.	Tutorials
	•	Math skills		•	Word processing
	•	Study skills		•	Time management
	•	Language arts		•	Learning strategies
	•	Written express		•	Organizational skills

Academic Accommodations

Curriculum	Study Aids	Exams
Priority registration	Typist	• Oral
Math waiver	Reader	Untimed
Foreign lang. waiver	• Notetaker	Take home
Course substitution	Proof reader	With proctor
In Class	• Text on tape	On computer
Calculators	Early syllabus	Extended time
• Tape recorder	Taped handouts	On tape
Word processor		Modified
• Priority seating		• Separate room

Program Strengths

All freshmen are required to take a Freshman Seminar course which is designed to enhance the college experience by providing interdisciplinary resources and strategies to facilitate students' academic, vocational, social, and personal growth.

General Information:

Bluefield College is a 4 year independent Southern Baptist college. Rural campus of 55 acres is 120 miles from Roanoke. Accessible by air, train, or bus. Ski areas are 30 minutes from campus. Beaches are 7-8 hours from campus. 3 residential halls on campus. Housing is guaranteed.

Accreditation: SACS

Expenses:

Tuition: In-state: Full year: $5,940.00. Part-time: Per credit:$135.00. Tuition: Out-of-state: Full year: $5,940.00. Part-time: Per credit:$135.00. Room and board: $3,860.00

Majors

• ARTS Music, Religious Music • BUSINESS Accounting, Business Administration, Education, Human Resources Management • COMMUNICATIONS Communication, English • COMPUTER SCIENCE Computer Science • EDUCATION Business, Early Childhood, Elementary, English, Mathematics, Middle School, Music, Physical, Science, Secondary, Social Studies • HEALTH SCIENCES Fitness, Health, Medical Laboratory Technology, Medical Records Administration • HUMANITIES English/Writing/Literature, Fine Arts, Religion • PRE PROFESSIONAL Engineering, Law, Medicine, Pharmacy • RELIGIOUS STUDIES Religion & Philosophy • SCIENCES Biology, Computer Science, Equestrian Studies, Mathematics • SOCIAL SCIENCES Criminal Justice, History, Psychology, Social Studies • VISUAL AND PERFORMING ARTS Art, Fine Arts, Music, Theater

Sports/Activities

• SPORTS RELATED Cheerleading, Team Managers • SPORTS-INTERCOLLEGIATE Baseball (M), Basketball (F), Basketball (M), Golf (M), Softball (F), Volleyball (F) • SPORTS-INTRAMURAL Badminton (F), Badminton (M), Basketball, Football (M) • STUDENT LIFE ACTIVITIES Academic Clubs, Choral, Community Service, Dance, Drama Groups, Ethnic & Cultural Groups, Fraternities, Magazine, Music Groups, Newspaper, Religious Organization, Sororities, Student Government, Yearbook

Christopher Newport College

50 Shoe Lane
Newport News, Virginia 23606
(804) 594-7015

School Enrollment: **4,500**
LD Enrollment: **6**

Admissions Contact: **Robert LaVerriere, Assoc. Dean Admissions**
LD Contact: **Glen Vought, Coordinator**
Name of Program: **Services for Students w/Disabilities**
Telephone:**(804) 594-7047**

Admissions

Application Information:
Application deadline: **August 1st**
Rolling Admissions: **Yes**

Secondary School Information
Most Important Criteria For Admissions (1-strongest)

5 SAT/ACT	6 Application	3 School transcript
4 Class rank	1 Course selection	7 Personal statement
9 Interview	10 Extra activities	11 Psychoeducational
2 G.P.A.	Open admission	8 Recommendations

Test Requirements:
Untimed SAT: **Yes**
Documentation of LD required: **Yes**
Currency of diagnostic testing: **No more than 2 years**

Types of Disabilities Served
- Speech/Lang
- Study skills
- Written express
- Organizational
- Perceptual
- Reading
- Spelling
- Math
- Fine Motor
- ADD with LD
- ADD without LD
- ADHD with LD
- ADHD without LD

Admissions Process

When student indicates that she/he has a disability on admission application, the coordinator of Services for Students with Disabilities will send information and forms to declare disability. Professional documentation and recommendations for accommodations must also be provided.

Learning Disability Program

Program: Reinforces course work: **Yes**
Students mainstreamed **100** % of the day
Recommended credits per semester: **12-13**
Counseling: Individual: **Yes** Vocational Counseling: **Yes**

Faculty:
Faculty: **1** Full time: **1**
Faculty advocate: **Yes** Meets with instructor: **As needed**

Diagnostic Testing

ADD	Personality	Perceptual skills	Spelling
ADHD	Organization	Fine motor skills	Reading
I.Q.	Handwriting	Spoken language	Study skills
Math	Social skills	Written language	

Tutoring:

Services rendered by:
Graduates •Peers •Faculty LD staff Teacher trainees

Tutorials

Grp.	Ind.	Tutorials	Grp.	Ind.	Tutorials
	•	Math skills		•	Word processing
	•	Study skills		•	Time management
	•	Language arts		•	Learning strategies
	•	Written express		•	Organizational skills

Academic Accommodations

Curriculum	Study Aids	Exams
• Priority registration	• Typist	• Oral
• Math waiver	• Reader	Untimed
• Foreign lang. waiver	• Notetaker	• Take home
• Course substitution	• Proof reader	• With proctor
In Class	• Text on tape	On computer
• Calculators	Early syllabus	• Extended time
• Tape recorder	Taped handouts	• On tape
• Word processor		• Modified
• Priority seating		• Separate room

Graduation Requirements:

Course credits: **122** GPA: **2.0** Years to complete degree: **4**

Program Strengths

Several computers in computer lab are dedicated for the use of students who have declared a disability. One is fitted with a voice synthesizer and a scanner to enter printed material into computer.

General Information:

Christopher Newport College is a 4 year public college. Suburban campus of 75 acres is 25 miles from Norfolk. Accessible by air, train or bus. Ski areas are 3.5 hours from campus. Beaches are 30 minutes from campus. 2% of students are foreign. Housing is not guaranteed.

Accreditation: SACS

SAT/ACT Scores:

Scores for incoming freshmen: **Verbal:** 82% below 500. 15% between 500 and 599. 3% between 600 and 699. **Math:** 71% below 500. 23% between 500 and 599. 5% between 600 and 699. 1% above 700.

Expenses:

Tuition: In-state: Full year: $2,285.00. Part-time: Per credit: $96.00. Tuition: Out-of-state: Full year: $5,125.00. Part-time: Per credit: $213.00.

Majors

• AREA STUDIES Japanese, Urban • BUSINESS Accounting, Banking, Business Economics, Business Management, Economics, Finance, International Business, Marketing, Real Estate • COMMUNICATIONS Journalism, Literature • COMPUTER SCIENCE Computer Science • EDUCATION Early Childhood, Elementary, Middle School, Secondary • HEALTH SCIENCES Nursing • HUMANITIES English/Writing/Literature, Humanities, Liberal Arts, Philosophy, Religion • LANGUAGES Foreign, French, German, Spanish • PREPROFESSIONAL Dentistry, Engineering, Forestry, Law, Medicine, Ministry, Natural Resources, Pharmacy, Recreation, Social Work, Veterinarian, Wildlife • SCIENCES Biochemistry, Biology, Cell Biology, Horticultural, Mathematics, Microbiology, Physical Science, Physics • SOCIAL SCIENCES Criminal

Justice, Criminology, Government/Political, History, International Studies, Law Enforcement, Political Science, Psychology, Public Administration, Public Policy Studies, Social Sciences, Sociology • VISUAL AND PERFORMING ARTS Dance, Fine Arts, Music, Music Performance, Music Theory • VOCATIONAL Leisure Studies, Park/Recreation

Sports/Activities

• SPORTS-INTERCOLLEGIATE Baseball (M), Basketball, Cross Country, Golf, Sailing, Soccer (M), Softball (F), Tennis, Track and Field, Volleyball (F) • SPORTS-INTRAMURAL Badminton, Bowling, Fencing, Field Hockey (F), Gymnastics, Horseback Riding (F), Volleyball • STUDENT LIFE ACTIVITIES Choral, Drama Groups, Fraternities, Magazine, Music Groups, Newspaper, Sororities, Student Government, Yearbook

Highly Selective

Virginia Accommodations

College of William and Mary

Room 102 James Blair Hall
Williamsburg, Virginia 23185
(804) 253-4223

School Enrollment: **5,300**
LD Contact: **Carol Disque, Dean Student Affairs**
Name of Program: **Handicapped Services**
Telephone: **(804) 221-2305 or 2510**

Admissions

Application Information:
Application deadline: **January 15th**
Notified when: **April 1st**

Secondary School Information
Most Important Criteria For Admissions (1-strongest)

2 SAT/ACT	**3** Application	**1** School transcript
1 Class rank	**1** Course selection	**3** Personal statement
Interview	**2** Extra activities	Psychoeducational
1 G.P.A.	Open admission	**4** Recommendations

Test Requirements:
Standardized tests waived: **Yes**
Untimed SAT: **Yes**
Documentation of LD required: **Yes**
Currency of diagnostic testing: **3 years but we will test at no cost to the student**

Types of Disabilities Served
• Speech/Lang	• Reading	• ADD with LD
• Study skills	• Spelling	• ADD without LD
• Written express	• Math	• ADHD with LD
• Organizational	• Fine Motor	• ADHD without LD
• Perceptual		

Learning Disability Program
Counseling: Individual: **Yes**

Faculty:
Faculty: **2** Part time: **2** Ph.D.: **1**
Faculty advocate: **Yes** Meets with instructor: **As requested**

Diagnostic Testing
- ADD • Personality • Perceptual skills • Spelling
- ADHD Organization• Fine motor skills • Reading
- I.Q. Handwriting Spoken language • Study skills
- Math Social skills Written language

Tutoring:
Services rendered by:
•Graduates •Peers •Faculty LD staff Teacher trainees

Tutorials
Grp.	Ind.	Tutorials	Grp.	Ind.	Tutorials
		Math skills			Word processing
•		Study skills			Time management
•	•	Language arts	•		Learning strategies
•		Written express	•		Organizational skills

Academic Accommodations

Curriculum	Study Aids	Exams
• Priority registration	• Typist	Oral
Math waiver	• Reader	Untimed
Foreign lang. waiver	• Notetaker	• Take home
• Course substitution	• Proof reader	• With proctor
In Class	• Text on tape	On computer
• Calculators	Early syllabus	• Extended time
• Tape recorder	Taped handouts	On tape
• Word processor		• Modified
Priority seating		• Separate room

Graduation Requirements: GPA: **2.0**

Program Strengths
We offer a complete testing program and continuing liaison with individual faculty members so that the student does not have the task of informing each instructor about his disability. We try to provide the student with the help he or she needs to succeed.

General Information:
College of William and Mary is a 4 year public university. Suburban campus of 1,200 acres is 60 miles from Norfolk. Accessible by air, train or bus. Beaches are 20 miles from campus. Housing is guaranteed.Guaranteed through 3 out of 4 years . 35 % of students join fraternities/sororities.

Accreditation: Regional

SAT/ACT Scores:
Scores for incoming freshmen: 25%between 500 and 599. 45%between 600 and 699. 25%above 700.

Class Rank:
About 93% of the present freshmen class were in the upper 20% of their high school class.

Expenses:
Tuition: In-state: Full year: $3,500.00. Tuition: Out-of-state: Full year: $8,800.00. Room and board: $4,800.00

Majors
• AREA STUDIES African, American, Asian, Ethnic, Latin American, Russian/Slavic, Urban • BUSINESS Accounting, Business Administration, Business Management, Economics, Finance, Management, Marketing • COMMUNICATIONS English, Speech • COMPUTER SCIENCE Computer Science • EDUCATION Elementary, Physical, Secondary • HUMANITIES Classics, English/Writing/Literature, Humanities, Liberal Arts, Philosophy, Religion • LANGUAGES French, German, Greek, Italian, Japanese, Latin, Linguistics, Portuguese, Russian, Spanish • PREPROFESSIONAL Dentistry, Engineering, Forestry, Law, Medicine, Pharmacy

• SCIENCES Biology, Chemistry, Ecology, Geography, Geology, Marine Biology, Mathematics, Physical Science, Physics • SOCIAL SCIENCES Anthropology, Government/Political, History, International Studies, Political Science, Psychology, Social Sciences, Sociology • VISUAL AND PERFORMING ARTS Art, Art History, Dance, Fine Arts, Music, Theater

Sports/Activities
• SPORTS RELATED Marching Band, Pep Band • SPORTS-INTERCOLLEGIATE Baseball (M), Basketball, Cross Country, Diving, Fencing, Field Hockey (F), Football (M), Golf, Gymnastics, Lacrosse (F), Riflery, Soccer, Swimming, Tennis, Track and Field, Volleyball, Wrestling (M) • SPORTS-INTRAMURAL Archery, Badminton, Basketball, Bowling, Golf (M), Hand Ball (M), Softball, Swimming, Tennis, Track and Field, Volleyball, Wrestling (M) • STUDENT LIFE ACTIVITIES Choral, Community Service, Concert Band, Dance, Drama Groups, Ethnic & Cultural Groups, Fraternities, Jazz Band, Magazine, Music Groups, Musical Theater, Newspaper, Opera, Political Groups, Radio/TV station, Religious Organization, Sororities, Student Government, Symphony Orchestra, Yearbook

---

Less Selective **Virginia Services**

Dabney S. Lancaster Community College
P.O. Box 1000
Clifton Forge, Virginia 24422
(703) 862-4246

School Enrollment: **1,334** Male: **495** Female: **839**

Admissions Contact: **Ropy Tillery, Dir. of Student Services**
LD Contact: **Elizabeth Davis, Project Director**
Name of Program: **Student Support Services**
Address: **Room 343, Scott Hall**
Telephone: **(703) 862-4246**

Admissions

Application Information:
Application deadline: **None**

Secondary School Information
Most Important Criteria For Admissions (1-strongest)

SAT/ACT	Application	School transcript
Class rank	Course selection	Personal statement
Interview	Extra activities	Psychoeducational
G.P.A.	Open admission	Recommendations

Test Requirements:
Diagnostic testing waived: **Yes**
Documentation of LD required: **Yes**
Currency of diagnostic testing: **Advance testing not required**

Types of Disabilities Served
- Speech/Lang • Reading • ADD with LD
- Study skills • Spelling • ADD without LD
- Written express • Math • ADHD with LD
- Organizational • Fine Motor • ADHD without LD
- Perceptual

Admissions Process

Open door policy.

Learning Disability Program

Program: Remedial: **Yes**
Program: Reinforces course work: **Yes**
Students mainstreamed **100** % of the day
Recommended credits per semester: **12**
Counseling: Individual: **Yes** Vocational Counseling: **Yes**

Faculty:

Faculty: **5** Full time: **4** Part time: **1**
LD faculty with: BS/BA: **4** M.A.: **1**

Diagnostic Testing

ADD	Personality	Perceptual skills	Spelling
ADHD	Organization	Fine motor skills	Reading
I.Q.	Handwriting	Spoken language	Study skills
Math	Social skills	Written language	

Tutoring:

Average size of group tutorials: **1-3**
Services rendered by:
 Graduates •Peers Faculty •LD staff Teacher trainees

Tutorials

Grp.	Ind.	Tutorials	Grp.	Ind.	Tutorials
•		Math skills	•		Word processing
•		Study skills	•		Time management
•		Language arts	•		Learning strategies
•		Written express	•		Organizational skills

Academic Accommodations

Curriculum	Study Aids	Exams
Priority registration	Typist	• Oral
Math waiver	• Reader	Untimed
Foreign lang. waiver	• Notetaker	Take home
Course substitution	Proof reader	• With proctor
In Class	• Text on tape	On computer
Calculators	Early syllabus	• Extended time
• Tape recorder	Taped handouts	On tape
Word processor		Modified
Priority seating		• Separate room

General Information:

Dabney S. Lancaster Community College is a 2 year public college. Rural campus of 117 acres is 50 miles from Roanoke, VA. Accessible by train or bus. Ski areas are 70 miles from campus. Beaches are 250 miles from campus. .05% of students are foreign. Housing is not guaranteed.

Accreditation: SACS

Expenses:

Tuition: In-state: Full year: $424.80 per semester. Part-time: Per credit:$35.40. Part-time: Per course: $106.20. Tuition: Out-of-state: Full year: $1,708.80 per semester. Part-time: Per credit:$142.40. Part-time: Per course:$427.20

Majors

• AGRICULTURE • BUSINESS Business Administration, Business Management, Education • COMPUTER SCIENCE Computer Technology • HEALTH SCIENCES Nursing • HUMANITIES Liberal Arts

Sports/Activities

• SPORTS-INTERCOLLEGIATE Basketball (M) • SPORTS-INTRAMURAL Basketball, Bowling, Softball, Table Tennis, Volleyball

---

Selective

**Virginia
Accommodations**

George Mason University
4400 University Drive Rooms 205 & 119, Finley Build
Fairfax, Virginia 22030
(703) 993-2474

School Enrollment: **20,000** Male: **8,500** Female: **11,500**
LD Enrollment: **151**
LD Contact: **Paul Bonsel or Dorothy Mose, Advisor**
Name of Program: **Disabled Student Services**
Address: **Rooms 119 and 205, Finley Building**
Telephone:**(703) 993-2474**

Admissions

Application Information:
Enrolled:**151**
Application deadline: **February 1st**
Notified when: **April 1st**

Secondary School Information
Most Important Criteria For Admissions (1-strongest)

1 SAT/ACT	**1** Application	**1** School transcript
1 Class rank	Course selection	**1** Personal statement
Interview	**1** Extra activities	Psychoeducational
1 G.P.A.	Open admission	Recommendations

Test Requirements:
Standardized tests waived: **Yes**
Diagnostic testing waived: **Yes**
Untimed SAT: **Yes** Untimed ACT: **Yes** Untimed ACH: **Yes**
Documentation of LD required: **Yes**
Tests recommended: **Documentation of LD**

Types of Disabilities Served

• Speech/Lang	• Reading	• ADD with LD
• Study skills	• Spelling	• ADD without LD
• Written express	• Math	• ADHD with LD
• Organizational	• Fine Motor	• ADHD without LD
• Perceptual		

Learning Disability Program

Program: Reinforces course work: **Yes**
Students mainstreamed **100** % of the day
Recommended credits per semester: **12**
Services available for all students: **Yes**
Counseling: Individual: **Yes** Group Counseling: **Yes** Vocational Counseling: **Yes**

Faculty:

Faculty: **3** Including Director: **Yes** Full time: **2** Part time: **1**
Faculty advocate: **Yes** Meets with instructor: **As needed**

Diagnostic Testing

ADD	Personality	Perceptual skills	Spelling
ADHD	Organization	Fine motor skills	Reading
I.Q.	Handwriting	Spoken language	Study skills
Math	Social skills	Written language	

Tutoring:

Services rendered by:
•Graduates •Peers Faculty LD staff Teacher trainees

Tutorials

Grp.	Ind.	Tutorials	Grp.	Ind.	Tutorials
•	•	Math skills		•	Word processing
•		Study skills	•	•	Time management
	•	Language arts		•	Learning strategies
•		Written express		•	Organizational skills

Academic Accommodations

Curriculum	Study Aids	Exams
• Priority registration	Typist	Oral
Math waiver	• Reader	• Untimed
• Foreign lang. waiver	• Notetaker	Take home
• Course substitution	Proof reader	• With proctor
In Class	• Text on tape	• On computer
Calculators	Early syllabus	• Extended time
• Tape recorder	Taped handouts	• On tape
• Word processor		• Modified
Priority seating		• Separate room

Graduation Requirements:
Course credits: **120**

Program Strengths

We do not have a Learning Disability Student Center; we work with each student individually. Once a student is accepted to GMU, we ask him or her to provide us with documentation with regard to their disability and limitations. From then on we are in contact with them each semester through registration and newsletters as well as through services required. Tutoring is available to all students at an hourly cost.

General Information:

George Mason University is a 4 year public university. Urban campus of 583 acres is 15 miles from Washington, D.C. Accessible by air, train or bus. Housing is not guaranteed.5 % of students join fraternities/sororities.

Accreditation: State, Regional, National

Expenses:

Tuition: In-state: Full year: $2,988.00. Part-time: Per credit:$124.50. Tuition: Out-of-state: Full year: $7,464.00. Part-time: Per credit:$311.00.

Majors

• AREA STUDIES African, American, Asian, European, Latin American, Middle Eastern, Russian/Slavic, Women's Studies • ARTS Art History, Dance, Dramatic Arts, Drawing, Music, Music Performance, Painting, Theater Design • BUSINESS Accounting, Banking/Finance, Business Administration, Business Management, Economics, Human Resources Management, Management, Marketing • COMMUNICATIONS Broadcasting, English, Journalism, Literature • COMPUTER SCIENCE Business Data Programming, Computer Science, Computer Technology, Systems Analysis • ENGINEERING Civil/Environmental, Computer, Electrical • HEALTH SCIENCES Health, Nursing • HUMANITIES Classics, English/Writing/Literature, Philosophy, Religion • LANGUAGES English, French, German, Italian, Japanese, Latin, Russian, Spanish, Spanish • MATHEMATICS Applied, Theoretical • PREPROFESSIONAL Business, Law, Medicine, Social Work, Sports Medicine • RELIGIOUS STUDIES Philosophy, Religion and Theology • SCIENCES Anthropology, Applied Mathematics, Archeology, Behavioral, Biology, Chemistry, Computer Science, Ecology, Geography, Geology, Mathematics, Physics, Public Health, Statistics • SOCIAL SCIENCES Anthropology, Criminal Justice, Geography, Government/Political, History, Human Service, International Studies, Psychology, Sociology • VISUAL AND PERFORMING ARTS Art, Art History, Dance, Dramatic Arts, Music, Music Theatre, Studio Art, Theater • VOCATIONAL Park/Recreation

Sports/Activities

• SPORTS RELATED Pep Band • SPORTS-INTERCOLLEGIATE Baseball (M), Cross Country, Gymnastics, Riflery, Soccer, Softball (F), Tennis, Track and Field, Volleyball, Wrestling (M) • SPORTS-INTRAMURAL Basketball, Crew, Martial Arts, Racquetball, Rugby (M), Soccer, Softball, Tennis, Volleyball • STUDENT LIFE ACTIVITIES Academic Clubs, Choral, Community Service, Concert Band, Dance, Debate, Drama Groups, Ethnic & Cultural Groups, Fraternities, Jazz Band, Magazine, Music Groups, Musical Theater, Newspaper, Orchestra, Political Groups, Radio/TV station, Religious Organization, Sororities, Student Government, Symphony Orchestra, Yearbook

---

Highly Selective · Virginia

Accommodations

Hollins College
P.O. Box 9707
Roanoke, Virginia 24020
(703) 362-6226

School Enrollment: **852** Female: **852**

Admissions Contact: **Peggy Barker-Meise, Asso. Dir. Admissions**
LD Contact: **Mikie Haynes, Coordinator Counseling Services**
Name of Program: **Counseling Services**
Address: **P.O. Box 9541**
Telephone:**(703) 362-6226**

Admissions

Application Information:
Application deadline: **2**
Applicant must apply **7** months in advance
Rolling Admissions: **Yes** Notified when: **April 15th**

Secondary School Information
Most Important Criteria For Admissions (1-strongest)

4 SAT/ACT	**7** Application	**2** School transcript
5 Class rank	**1** Course selection	Personal statement
8 Interview	**9** Extra activities	Psychoeducational
3 G.P.A.	Open admission	**6** Recommendations

Test Requirements:
Diagnostic testing waived: **Yes**
Untimed SAT: **Yes** Untimed ACT: **Yes** Untimed ACH: **Yes**
Range accepted:
Documentation of LD required: **Yes**
Tests recommended: **L.D. documentation required**

Types of Disabilities Served

Speech/Lang	Reading	ADD with LD
Study skills	Spelling	ADD without LD
Written express	Math	ADHD with LD
Organizational	Fine Motor	• ADHD without LD
Perceptual		

Admissions Process

Students' applications are judged on school achievement record, school recommendation, test scores, writing ability, interview, school and community activities, personal characteristics, leadership skills, talent and special interests. Learning disability students must provide documentation.

High School Course Requirements:
English: **4** Math: **3** Science: **3** Foreign Language: **3**

Learning Disability Program

Students mainstreamed **100** % of the day
Services available for all students: **Yes**
Vocational Counseling: **Yes**
Support groups are available: Registrar **in Counseling Services Center**

Faculty:
Faculty advocate: **Yes**

Diagnostic Testing

ADD	Personality	Perceptual skills	Spelling
ADHD	Organization	Fine motor skills	Reading
I.Q.	Handwriting	Spoken language	Study skills
Math	Social skills	Written language	

Services rendered by:
Graduates   Peers   Faculty   LD staff   Teacher trainees

Tutorials

Grp.	Ind.	Tutorials	Grp.	Ind.	Tutorials
		Math skills			Word processing
		Study skills			Time management
		Language arts			Learning strategies
		Written express			Organizational skills

Academic Accommodations

Curriculum	Study Aids	Exams
Priority registration	Typist	• Oral
Math waiver	Reader	• Untimed
Foreign lang. waiver	Notetaker	• Take home
• Course substitution	Proof reader	• With proctor
In Class	Text on tape	• On computer
• Calculators	Early syllabus	• Extended time
• Tape recorder	Taped handouts	• On tape
Word processor		• Modified
• Priority seating		• Separate room

Graduation Requirements:
Course credits: **128** GPA: **2.0** Years to complete degree: **4**
Other requirements: **4 short terms (month of January)**

Program Strengths
Students must request their own special arrangements.

General Information:

Hollins College is a 4 year private college. Suburban campus of 475 acres is Accessible by plane, train or bus. Ski areas are 1.5 hours from campus. Beaches are 4 hours from campus. 2% of students are foreign. 9 residential halls on campus. Housing is guaranteed.Guaranteed through 4th year. 72 % of students remain on campus for the weekends.

Accreditation:SACS

SAT/ACT Scores:
Scores for incoming freshmen:**Verbal:**53%below 500. 32%between 500 and 599. 12%between 600 and 699. 3%above 700. **Math:**44% below 500. 42% between 500 and 599. 13% between 600 and 699. 1%above 700. **ACT:** 3% below 20. 60%between 24 and 25l. 37%between 26 and 28.

Class Rank:
About 48% of the present freshmen class were in the upper 20% of their high school class. 71% were in the top 40% of their class. 91% were in the top 60% of their class. 98% were in the top 80% of their class.

Expenses:
Tuition: In-state: Full year: $12,200.00. Part-time: Per credit:$339.00. Part-time: Per course: $1,356.00. Tuition: Out-of-state: Full year: $12,200.00.

Part-time: Per credit:$339.00. Part-time: Per course:$1,356.00 Room and board: $4,950.00.

Majors

• AREA STUDIES American • ARTS Art History, Music • BUSINESS Economics • COMMUNICATIONS Communication, Creative Writing, English, Film • HUMANITIES Classics, English/Writing/Literature, Philosophy, Religion • LANGUAGES French , German, Spanish • MATHEMATICS Applied, Computational Science, Statistical • RELIGIOUS STUDIES Philosophy, Religion & Theology • SCIENCES Biology, Chemistry, Physics • SOCIAL SCIENCES History, Political Science, Psychology, Sociology • VISUAL AND PERFORMING ARTS Art, Art History, Dramatic Arts, Studio Art, Theater

Sports/Activities

• SPORTS-INTERCOLLEGIATE Basketball (F), Fencing (F), Field Hockey (F), Horseback Riding (F), Lacrosse (F), Soccer (F), Swimming (F), Tennis (F), Volleyball (F) • STUDENT LIFE ACTIVITIES Academic Clubs, Choral, Dance, Drama Groups, Ethnic & Cultural Groups, Music Groups, Newspaper, Political Groups, Religious Organization, Student Government, Yearbook

---

Very Selective   **Virginia**
Services

James Madison University
Harrisonburg, Virginia 22807
(703) 568-6147

School Enrollment: **9,557**

Admissions Contact: **Alan Cerveny, Director of Admissions**
LD Contact: **Carole C. Grove, Coordinator**
Name of Program: **Office of Disability Services**
Telephone:**(703) 568-6705**

Admissions

Application Information:
Application deadline: **February 1st**
Notified when: **April 1st**

Secondary School Information
Most Important Criteria For Admissions (1-strongest)

3 SAT/ACT	Application	School transcript
2 Class rank	**1** Course selection **5**	Personal statement
Interview	**4** Extra activities	Psychoeducational
G.P.A.	Open admission **6**	Recommendations

Types of Disabilities Served
• Speech/Lang	• Reading	• ADD with LD
• Study skills	• Spelling	• ADD without LD
• Written express	• Math	ADHD with LD
• Organizational	• Fine Motor	ADHD without LD
• Perceptual		

Faculty:
Faculty: **1** Part time: **1**
Faculty advocate: **Yes** Meets with instructor: **As needed**

Virginia

Diagnostic Testing

ADD	Personality	Perceptual skills	Spelling
ADHD	Organization	Fine motor skills	Reading
I.Q.	Handwriting	Spoken language	Study skills
Math	Social skills	Written language	

Tutoring:

Services rendered by:
Graduates •Peers •Faculty •LD staff •Teacher trainees

Tutorials

Grp.	Ind.	Tutorials	Grp.	Ind.	Tutorials
	•	Math skills		•	Word processing
•	•	Study skills	•	•	Time management
	•	Language arts		•	Learning strategies
	•	Written express		•	Organizational skills

Academic Accommodations

Curriculum	Study Aids	Exams
Priority registration	• Typist	• Oral
Math waiver	Reader	Untimed
Foreign lang. waiver	• Notetaker	• Take home
• Course substitution	• Proof reader	With proctor
In Class	• Text on tape	On computer
• Calculators	Early syllabus	• Extended time
• Tape recorder	Taped handouts	On tape
• Word processor		• Modified
Priority seating		Separate room

Program Strengths

Students must meet the same criteria for admissions to programs as all other students. Students must supply appropriate written documentation of their learning disability in order to access services. Each student is considered an individual, and services are provided and planned on that basis. Course alternatives can be arranged when appropriate. Negotiations with instructors are arranged at the student's request. Registered learning disabled students receive priority registration to ensure workable academic schedules.

General Information:

James Madison University is a 4 year public university. Rural campus of 472 acres is 125 miles from Washington, D.C. Accessible by air, train, or bus. Ski areas are 10-15 miles from campus. Beaches are 4-5 hours from campus. 1% of students are foreign. 33 residential halls on campus. Housing is guaranteed.Guaranteed through 4th year. 36 % of students join fraternities/sororities.

Accreditation:SACS

SAT/ACT Scores:

Scores for incoming freshmen:**Verbal:**42%below 500. 44%between 500 and 599. 13%between 600 and 699. 1%above 700. **Math:**19% below 500. 42% between 500 and 599. 34% between 600 and 699. 5%above 700.

Class Rank:

About 67% of the present freshmen class were in the upper 20% of their high school class. 90% were in the top 40% of their class. 98% were in the top 60% of their class. 100% were in the top 80% of their class.

Expenses:

Tuition: In-state: Full year: $3,016.00. Part-time: Per credit:$92.00. Tuition: Out-of-state: Full year: $6,004.00. Part-time: Per credit:$191.00. Room and board: $3,908.00

Majors

• AREA STUDIES American, Latin American • BUSINESS Accounting, Business Education, Economics, Finance, Hotel and Restaurant Management, International Business, Management, Marketing • COMMUNICATIONS Communication, English, Journalism • COMPUTER SCIENCE Computer Science, Programming, Telecommunications • CRAFTS AND DESIGN Ceramics, Graphic Design • EDUCATION Art, Early Childhood, English, Middle School, Music, Physical, Secondary, Special • HEALTH SCIENCES Fitness, Health, Nursing, Speech/Audiology and Speech • LANGUAGES German, Russian • PREPROFESSIONAL Dentistry, Engineering, Law, Medicine, Social Work • SCIENCES Bacteriology, Biology, Chemistry, Geology, Gerontology, Microbiology, Molecular Biology, Physical Science, Physics • SOCIAL SCIENCES Anthropology, Criminal Justice, History, Political Science, Psychology, Public Relations, Sociology • VISUAL AND PERFORMING ARTS Art, Music, Studio Art, Theater • VOCATIONAL Home Economics, Interior Design, Office Administration

Sports/Activities

• SPORTS RELATED Band, Cheerleading, Marching Band • SPORTS-INTERCOLLEGIATE Archery, Baseball (M), Basketball, Cross Country, Diving, Fencing (F), Field Hockey (F), Football (M), Golf, Gymnastics, Lacrosse (F), Soccer, Swimming, Tennis, Track and Field, Volleyball (F), Wrestling (M) • SPORTS-INTRAMURAL Badminton, Basketball, Bowling, Cross Country, Diving, Golf, Ping-Pong, Racquetball, Rugby, Skiing - Snow, Soccer, Softball, Squash, Swimming, Tennis, Track and Field, Volleyball (F) • STUDENT LIFE ACTIVITIES Debate, Drama Groups, Ethnic & Cultural Groups, Film, Fraternities, Jazz Band, Magazine, Music Groups, Newspaper, Radio/TV station, Religious Organization, Sororities, Student Government, Symphony Orchestra, Yearbook

---

Less Selective **Virginia**
Accommodations

Liberty University

Box 20000
Lynchburg, Virginia 24506
(804) 582-2158

School Enrollment: **4,000** Male: **2,040** Female: **1,960**
LD Enrollment: **34** Male: **15** Female: **19**

Admissions Contact: **Barry Armstrong, Admissions Counselor**
LD Contact: **Denny McHaney, Faculty Advisor LD Students**
Name of Program: **Buckner Learning Center**
Telephone:**(804) 582-2226**

Admissions

Application Information:

Application deadline: **August 1st**
Rolling Admissions: **Yes**Notified when: **Within 2 weeks**

Secondary School Information

Most Important Criteria For Admissions (1-strongest)

5 SAT/ACT	**3** Application	**6**	School transcript
8 Class rank	Course selection	**1**	Personal statement
Interview	Extra activities	**4**	Psychoeducational
7 G.P.A.	Open admission	**2**	Recommendations

Test Requirements:

Untimed SAT: **Yes** Untimed ACT: **Yes**
Documentation of LD required: **Yes**

Types of Disabilities Served
- Speech/Lang
- Study skills
- Written express
- Organizational
- Perceptual
- Reading
- Spelling
- Math
- Fine Motor
- ADD with LD
- ADD without LD
- ADHD with LD
- ADHD without LD

Learning Disability Program
Time required or recommended in learning center: **Varies**
Services available for all students: **Yes**
Counseling: Individual: **Yes**

Faculty:
Faculty: **1** Full time: **1** M.A.: **1**
Faculty advocate: **Yes** Meets with instructor: **As needed**

Diagnostic Testing
ADD	Personality	Perceptual skills	Spelling
ADHD	Organization	Fine motor skills	Reading
I.Q.	Handwriting	Spoken language	Study skills
Math	Social skills	Written language	

Tutoring:
Services rendered by:
Graduates •Peers •Faculty LD staff Teacher trainees

Tutorials
Grp.	Ind.	Tutorials	Grp.	Ind.	Tutorials
	•	Math skills			Word processing
•	•	Study skills	•	•	Time management
	•	Language arts	•	•	Learning strategies
	•	Written express	•	•	Organizational skills

Academic Accommodations
Curriculum	Study Aids	Exams
• Priority registration	Typist	• Oral
Math waiver	Reader	• Untimed
• Foreign lang. waiver	Notetaker	Take home
• Course substitution	Proof reader	• With proctor
In Class	Text on tape	On computer
Calculators	Early syllabus	• Extended time
Tape recorder	Taped handouts	On tape
Word processor		• Modified
Priority seating		• Separate room

Graduation Requirements:
Course credits: **Varies** GPA: **2.0** Years to complete degree: **4+**

Program Strengths
Liberty does not have an organized LD program. However, Liberty does have a number of academic support services available under the direction of the Buckner Learning Center and a faculty advisor who is trained in working with LD students.

General Information:
Liberty University is a 4 year private Baptist university. Urban campus of 5,500 acres is 1 miles from Lynchburg. Accessible by air, train or bus. Ski areas are 60 miles from campus. Beaches are 200 miles from campus. Housing is guaranteed.70 % of students remain on campus for the weekends.

Accreditation:SACS

Expenses:
Tuition: In-state: Full year: $165.00 plus fees. Room and board: $3,970.00

Majors
• ARTS Fashion Design, Film & Video, Interior Design, Music, Music Performance, Religious Music, Theater Design • BUSINESS Accounting, Business Administration, Business Economics, Business Management, Economics, Fashion Merchandising, Food Management, Human Resources Management, Sports Management • COMMUNICATIONS Advertising, Broadcasting, English, Graphic Design, Journalism, Linguistics, Public Relations, Speech, Television/Radio/Film • COMPUTER SCIENCE Computer Science • CRAFTS AND DESIGN Apparel Design • EDUCATION Early Childhood, Elementary, English, Health, Home Economics, Mathematics, Middle School, Music, Physical, Recreation/Youth Leadership, Religion, Science, Secondary, Social Studies • HEALTH SCIENCES Health, Nursing, Public Health • HUMANITIES Philosophy, Religion • LANGUAGES English, French, German, Greek, Hebrew, Linguistics, Spanish • MATHEMATICS Applied • PREPROFESSIONAL Ministry, Recreation • RELIGIOUS STUDIES Bible, Philosophy, Religion and Theology, Religious Music • SCIENCES Biology, Chemistry, Computer Science, Public Health • SOCIAL SCIENCES Criminal Justice, Family Counseling, Government/Political, History, Law Enforcement, Political Science, Psychology, Public Relations, Social Sciences • VISUAL AND PERFORMING ARTS Dramatic Arts, Music, Music Performance • VOCATIONAL Fashion Merchandising, Food Service, Home Economics, Park/Recreation, Textile and Clothing

Sports/Activities
• SPORTS RELATED Cheerleading, Drill Team, Drum Major/Majorette, Marching Band, Pep Band, Team Managers • SPORTS-INTERCOLLEGIATE Baseball (M), Basketball, Cross Country, Football (M), Golf (M), Ice Hockey (M), Soccer (F), Soccer (M), Tennis (M), Track and Field, Volleyball (F), Wrestling (M) • SPORTS-INTRAMURAL Basketball (M), Football (M), Softball (M), Volleyball (F), Weight Lifting • STUDENT LIFE ACTIVITIES Academic Clubs, Choral, Concert Band, Concert Band, Debate, Drama Groups, Music Groups, Musical Theater, Newspaper, Political Groups, Radio/TV station, Religious Organization, Student Government, Yearbook

Less Selective	Virginia
	Accommodations

Lord Fairfax Community College
P. O. Box 47
Middletown, Virginia 22645
(703) 869-1120

School Enrollment: **1,357**
LD Enrollment: **4**

Admissions Contact: **C. T. Smith, Coordinator Admissions**
LD Contact: **Paula Dean, Coordinator, Learning Center**
Name of Program: **504 Program/ACT**
Telephone:**(703) 869-1120**

Admissions

Application Information:
LD Students Applying: **25** Accepted: **25** Enrolled:**20**
Application deadline: **Day semester begins**
Rolling Admissions: **Yes**

Secondary School Information
Most Important Criteria For Admissions (1-strongest)
SAT/ACT	**1**	Application	School transcript
Class rank		Course selection	Personal statement
Interview		Extra activities	Psychoeducational
G.P.A.	**1**	Open admission	Recommendations

Virginia

Test Requirements:
Range accepted:
Tests recommended: **WAIS-R recommended and achievements such as WRAT, Stanford.**

Types of Disabilities Served
- Speech/Lang
- Study skills
- Written express
- Organizational
- Perceptual
- Reading
- Spelling
- Math
- Fine Motor
- ADD with LD
- ADD without LD
- ADHD with LD
- ADHD without LD

Admissions Process

Open admission and placement testing in English, reading, and math. Counselor, academic advisor, or developmental advisor assigned depending on program.

Learning Disability Program
Program: Remedial: **Yes**
Program: Reinforces course work: **Yes**
Program available through: **Year round**
Students mainstreamed **100** % of the day
Recommended credits per semester: **12 or less**
Time required or recommended in learning center: **2-5 hours**
Services available for all students: **Yes**
Counseling: Individual: **Yes** Group Counseling: **Yes** Vocational Counseling: **Yes**

Faculty:
Faculty: **4** Part time: **4** M.A.: **3** Ph.D.: **1**
Faculty advocate: **Yes** Meets with instructor: **3-4 times per year**

Diagnostic Testing
ADD	Personality	Perceptual skills	Spelling
ADHD	Organization	Fine motor skills	• Reading
I.Q.	Handwriting	Spoken language	• Study skills
• Math	Social skills	• Written language	

Tutoring:
Average size of group tutorials: **1-3**
Services rendered by:
Graduates   •Peers   •Faculty   •LD staff   Teacher trainees

Tutorials
Grp.	Ind.	Tutorials	Grp.	Ind.	Tutorials
•	•	Math skills	•	•	Word processing
•	•	Study skills	•	•	Time management
•	•	Language arts	•	•	Learning strategies
•	•	Written express	•		Organizational skills

Academic Accommodations
Curriculum	Study Aids	Exams
Priority registration	• Typist	• Oral
Math waiver	Reader	• Untimed
Foreign lang. waiver	• Notetaker	Take home
• Course substitution	• Proof reader	• With proctor
In Class	• Text on tape	On computer
• Calculators	Early syllabus	• Extended time
• Tape recorder	Taped handouts	• On tape
• Word processor		• Modified
Priority seating		• Separate room

Graduation Requirements:
Course credits: **65** GPA: **2.0** Years to complete degree: **Unlimited** Math waiver: **Yes**

Program Strengths
We are working to build a team process to include each student's subject teachers in IEP development. We are forming a service area task force of secondary school and agency representatives to guide our program's development.

General Information:
Lord Fairfax Community College is a 2 year public college. Rural campus of 100 acres is 70 miles from Washington, DC. Ski areas are 40 miles from campus. Beaches are 4 miles from campus. Housing is not guaranteed.

Accreditation: SACS

Expenses:
Tuition: In-state: Full year: $1,230.00. Part-time: Per credit:$41.00. Tuition: Out-of-state: Full year: $4,350.00. Part-time: Per credit:$145.00.

Majors
• BUSINESS Accounting, Agricultural, Business Administration, Business Management, Management, Real Estate • COMMUNICATIONS Communication • COMPUTER SCIENCE Data Processing • EDUCATION General • ENGINEERING Mechanical • HEALTH SCIENCES Nursing • HUMANITIES Liberal Arts • PREPROFESSIONAL Agriculture, Natural Resources • SCIENCES Biology, Horticultural, Physical Science • VOCATIONAL Electronics Technology, Park/Recreation, Secretarial

Sports/Activities
• STUDENT LIFE ACTIVITIES Academic Clubs, Fraternities, Intramural, Student Government

---

Less Selective　　　　　　　　　　　**Virginia**
Services

New River Community College
Drawer 1127
Dublin, Virginia 24084
(703) 674-3600

School Enrollment: **1,389** Male: **627** Female: **762**
LD Enrollment: **100** Male: **75** Female: **25**

Admissions Contact: **Peggy Chrisley, Coordinator of Admissions**
LD Contact: **Jeananne Dixon, Coordinator**
Name of Program: **Center for the Learning Disabled**
Telephone:**(703) 674-3600**

Admissions

Application Information:
LD Students Applying: **35** Accepted: **35** Enrolled:**35**
Rolling Admissions: **Yes**

Secondary School Information
Most Important Criteria For Admissions (1-strongest)
SAT/ACT	Application	School transcript
Class rank	Course selection	Personal statement
Interview	Extra activities	Psychoeducational
G.P.A.	**1** Open admission	Recommendations

Test Requirements:
Standardized tests waived: **Yes**
Diagnostic testing waived: **Yes**
Documentation of LD required: **Yes**
Tests recommended: **Documentation of learning disability**

Types of Disabilities Served

- Speech/Lang
- Study skills
- Written express
- Organizational
- Perceptual
- Reading
- Spelling
- Math
- Fine Motor
- ADD with LD
- ADD without LD
- ADHD with LD
- ADHD without LD

Learning Disability Program

Program: Reinforces course work: **Yes**
Students mainstreamed **100** % of the day
Recommended credits per semester: **12**
Support groups are available:**Yes**

Faculty:

Faculty: **3** Full time: **2** Part time: **1**
LD faculty with: BS/BA: **1** M.A.: **2**

Diagnostic Testing

ADD	Personality	Perceptual skills	Spelling
ADHD	Organization	Fine motor skills	Reading
I.Q.	Handwriting	Spoken language	• Study skills
Math	Social skills	Written language	

Tutoring:

Average size of group tutorials: **1-3**
Services rendered by:
- Graduates
- Peers
- Faculty
- LD staff
- Teacher trainees

Tutorials

Grp.	Ind.	Tutorials	Grp.	Ind.	Tutorials
	•	Math skills	•	•	Word processing
•	•	Study skills	•	•	Time management
	•	Language arts	•	•	Learning strategies
	•	Written express	•	•	Organizational skills

Academic Accommodations

Curriculum	Study Aids	Exams
Priority registration	Typist	• Oral
Math waiver	Reader	Untimed
Foreign lang. waiver	• Notetaker	Take home
• Course substitution	• Proof reader	• With proctor
In Class	• Text on tape	On computer
• Calculators	Early syllabus	• Extended time
• Tape recorder	Taped handouts	On tape
• Word processor		• Modified
Priority seating		• Separate room

Program Strengths

The LD Center at New River Community College offers an extensive support system: a comprehensive schedule of reading, and tutoring; counseling to academic strengths; a summer prep program, and a student speakers group that addresses public schools, other colleges, and faculty.

General Information:

New River Community College is a 2 year public college. Rural campus of 100 acres is 50 miles from Roanoke. Ski areas are 1.5 miles from campus. Beaches are 5 miles from campus. 2% of students are foreign. Housing is not guaranteed.

Accreditation:Regional

Expenses:

Tuition: In-state: Full year: Part-time: Per credit: $28.00. Tuition: Out-of-state: Full year: Part-time: Per credit: $134.00.

Majors

• BUSINESS Business Administration, Business Management, Management, Marketing • COMPUTER SCIENCE Data Processing • EDUCATION Interpreter for Deaf • ENGINEERING Agricultural, Electrical, Industrial, Instrumentation Technology • HEALTH SCIENCES Nursing • HUMANITIES Liberal Arts • PREPROFESSIONAL Architecture • SCIENCES • VOCATIONAL Automobile Technology, Business and Office, Child Care, Community Services, Drafting, Electronics Technology, Fashion Merchandising, Industrial Equipment Maintenance, Machinist, Secretarial, Welding

Sports/Activities

• SPORTS-INTRAMURAL Basketball, Softball, Volleyball • STUDENT LIFE ACTIVITIES Choral, Ethnic & Cultural Groups, Newspaper, Sports Clubs, Student Government

---

Less Selective

Patrick Henry Community College

P.O. Drawer 5311
Martinsville, Virginia 24115-5311
(703) 638-8777

School Enrollment: **3,219** Male: **1,524** Female: **1,695**
LD Enrollment: **12** Male: **9** Female: **3**

Admissions Contact: **Graham Valentine, Admissions Counselor**
LD Contact: **Carolyn Byrd, Director**
Name of Program: **Student Support Services**

Admissions

Application Information:
Separate application:**Yes**

Secondary School Information
Most Important Criteria For Admissions (1-strongest)

SAT/ACT	Application	School transcript
Class rank	Course selection	Personal statement
Interview	Extra activities	Psychoeducational
G.P.A.	**1** Open admission	Recommendations

Test Requirements:
Standardized tests waived: **Yes**
Documentation of LD required: **Yes**

Types of Disabilities Served

- Speech/Lang
- Study skills
- Written express
- Organizational
- Perceptual
- Reading
- Spelling
- Math
- Fine Motor
- ADD with LD
- ADD without LD
- ADHD with LD
- ADHD without LD

Admissions Process

Open admissions.

Learning Disability Program

Counseling: Individual: **Yes**

Virginia

Faculty:
Faculty: **3** Full time: **2** Part time: **1**
Faculty advocate: **Yes** Meets with instructor: **As needed**

Diagnostic Testing
ADD	Personality	Perceptual skills	Spelling
ADHD	Organization	Fine motor skills	Reading
I.Q.	Handwriting	Spoken language	Study skills
Math	Social skills	Written language	

Tutoring:
Services rendered by:
Graduates •Peers •Faculty •LD staff Teacher trainees

Tutorials
Grp.	Ind.	Tutorials	Grp.	Ind.	Tutorials
•	•	Math skills	•	•	Word processing
•	•	Study skills	•	•	Time management
•	•	Language arts	•	•	Learning strategies
•	•	Written express	•	•	Organizational skills

Academic Accommodations
Curriculum	Study Aids	Exams
Priority registration	Typist	• Oral
Math waiver	Reader	Untimed
• Foreign lang. waiver	• Notetaker	Take home
• Course substitution	Proof reader	• With proctor
In Class	• Text on tape	On computer
• Calculators	Early syllabus	• Extended time
• Tape recorder	Taped handouts	On tape
• Word processor		• Modified
Priority seating		Separate room

Program Strengths
Patrick Henry Community College serves learning disabled students through the Student Support Services Program. A student must notify us of his or her handicap and apply to the program. Services are provided based on their handicapping condition. Presently, we hire peer tutors and notetakers for LD students. We do have a part-time LD specialist - approximately 10 hours per week. Professional counselor available - strong computer support.

General Information:
Patrick Henry Community College is a 2 year public college. Rural campus 50 miles from Roanoke. Ski areas are 3 hours from campus. Beaches are 5 hours from campus. 1% of students are foreign. Housing is not guaranteed.

Accreditation: SACS

Expenses:
Tuition: In-state: Full year: Part-time: Per credit: $41.00. Tuition: Out-of-state: Full year: Part-time: Per credit: $142.00.

Majors
• BUSINESS Accounting, Business Administration, Business Management, Management, Marketing • COMMUNICATIONS Communication, English, Journalism, Television/Radio/Film • COMPUTER SCIENCE Data Processing, Programming • HEALTH SCIENCES Nursing • HUMANITIES Liberal Arts • VISUAL AND PERFORMING ARTS Art, Theater • VOCATIONAL Automobile Technology, Aviation Administration, Business and Office, Electronics Technology, Home Economics, Industrial Equipment Maintenance, Secretarial

Sports/Activities
• SPORTS-INTERCOLLEGIATE Basketball (M) • SPORTS-INTRAMURAL Basketball, Ping-Pong, Soccer (M), Tennis • STUDENT LIFE ACTIVITIES Choral, Drama Groups, Ethnic & Cultural Groups, Fraternities, Musical Theater, Newspaper, Student Government

Paul D. Camp Community College
P.O. Box 737 College Drive
Franklin, Virginia 23851
(804) 562-2171

School Enrollment: **1,354** Male: **474** Female: **880**

Admissions Contact: **Dr. Jerry Standahl, Dir. Student Development**
LD Contact: **Mrs. Pat LeBlanc, Transition Division Chair**

Admissions

Application Information:
Application deadline: **Open**
Rolling Admissions: **Yes**

Secondary School Information
Most Important Criteria For Admissions (1-strongest)
SAT/ACT	Application	School transcript
Class rank	Course selection	Personal statement
Interview	Extra activities	Psychoeducational
G.P.A.	**1** Open admission	Recommendations

Test Requirements:
Documentation of LD required: **Yes**

Types of Disabilities Served
Speech/Lang.	• Reading	ADD with LD
• Study skills	Spelling	ADD without LD
Written express	• Math	ADHD with LD
Organizational	Fine Motor	ADHD without LD
Perceptual		

Faculty:

Diagnostic Testing
ADD	Personality	Perceptual skills	Spelling
ADHD	Organization	Fine motor skills	Reading
I.Q.	Handwriting	Spoken language	Study skills
Math	Social skills	Written language	

Tutoring:
Services rendered by:
Graduates •Peers Faculty LD staff Teacher trainees

Tutorials
Grp.	Ind.	Tutorials	Grp.	Ind.	Tutorials
	•	Math skills		•	Word processing
		Study skills			Time management
	•	Language arts			Learning strategies
		Written express		•	Organizational skills

Academic Accommodations

Curriculum	Study Aids	Exams
Priority registration	Typist	Oral
Math waiver	Reader	Untimed
Foreign lang. waiver	Notetaker	Take home
• Course substitution	Proof reader	With proctor
In Class	Text on tape	On computer
• Calculators	Early syllabus	Extended time
• Tape recorder	Taped handouts	On tape
• Word processor		Modified
Priority seating		Separate room

Graduation Requirements:
Course credits: **65** GPA: **2.0** Years to complete degree: **2 years**

Program Strengths

Paul D. Camp Community College does not have a specific program for LD students. It does have remedial classes in English, Reading, and Math. It also offers courses in study skills. The college has student support services and staff to assist with tutoring.

General Information:

Paul D. Camp Community College is a 2 year public college. Rural campus of 69 acres is 25 miles from Suffolk. Beaches are 45 miles from campus. 5% of students are foreign. Housing is not guaranteed.

Accreditation: SACS

Expenses:
Tuition: In-state: Full year: Part-time: Per credit: $41.00. Tuition: Out-of-state: Full year: Part-time: Per credit: $142.00.

Majors

• BUSINESS Business Administration, Business Management, Real Estate • COMPUTER SCIENCE Data Processing • HUMANITIES Humanities • LANGUAGES Spanish • PREPROFESSIONAL Dentistry • SCIENCES Mathematics • VOCATIONAL Drafting, Electronics Technology, Welding

Sports/Activities

• SPORTS RELATED Chess • SPORTS-INTRAMURAL Tennis, Volleyball • STUDENT LIFE ACTIVITIES Student Government

---

Selective

Virginia
Services

Radford University
P. O. Box 5705
Radford, Virginia 24142
(703) 831-5371

Admissions Contact: **Michael Walsh, Associate Director**
LD Contact: **Suzy Presson, Coordinator/Counselor**
Name of Program: **Disabled Student Services**
Telephone: **(703) 831-5226**

Admissions

Application Information:
Application deadline: **April 1st**
Rolling Admissions: **Yes**

Secondary School Information
Most Important Criteria For Admissions (1-strongest)

3	SAT/ACT	**5**	Application	**4** School transcript
2	Class rank	**1**	Course selection	Personal statement
7	Interview	**6**	Extra activities	**5** Psychoeducational
1	G.P.A.		Open admission	**6** Recommendations

Test Requirements:
Untimed SAT: **Yes** Untimed ACT: **Yes**
Documentation of LD required: **Yes**
Currency of diagnostic testing: **4 years**

Types of Disabilities Served
• Speech/Lang	• Reading	• ADD with LD
• Study skills	• Spelling	• ADD without LD
• Written express	• Math	• ADHD with LD
• Organizational	• Fine Motor	• ADHD without LD
• Perceptual		

Learning Disability Program
Counseling: Individual: **Yes** Group Counseling: **Yes**

Faculty:
Faculty: **1** Full time: **1**
Faculty advocate: **Yes** Meets with instructor: **As needed**

Diagnostic Testing
ADD	Personality	Perceptual skills	Spelling
ADHD	Organization	Fine motor skills	Reading
I.Q.	Handwriting	Spoken language	Study skills
Math	Social skills	Written language	

Tutoring:
Average size of group tutorials: **3-4**
Services rendered by:
• Graduates • Peers • Faculty • LD staff   Teacher trainees

Tutorials
Grp.	Ind.	Tutorials	Grp.	Ind.	Tutorials
		Math skills			Word processing
		Study skills	•	•	Time management
		Language arts	•	•	Learning strategies
		Written express	•	•	Organizational skills

Academic Accommodations

Curriculum	Study Aids	Exams
Priority registration	Typist	• Oral
Math waiver	Reader	Untimed
Foreign lang. waiver	• Notetaker	Take home
• Course substitution	Proof reader	With proctor
In Class	• Text on tape	On computer
Calculators	Early syllabus	• Extended time
• Tape recorder	Taped handouts	On tape
• Word processor		• Modified
Priority seating		Separate room

Program Strengths

Students with learning disabilities are registered with the Disabled Student Services Office by presenting testing documentation completed within the last 4 years. Students are then eligible for support services tailored to meet their individual needs. Although there is no structured program, the student is encouraged to meet with the coordinator on a regular basis to provide consistency to support services.

Virginia

General Information:

Radford University is a 4 year public university. 45 miles from Roanoke. Accessible by air or bus. Ski areas are 2 hours from campus. Beaches are 5 hours from campus. 3% of students are foreign. Housing is guaranteed.Guaranteed through 1st year. 70 % of students remain on campus for the weekends. 15 % of students join fraternities/sororities.

Accreditation:SACS

SAT/ACT Scores:

Scores for incoming freshmen:**Verbal:**67%below 500. 20%between 500 and 599. 10%between 600 and 699. 3%above 700. **Math:**52% below 500. 30% between 500 and 599. 15% between 600 and 699. 3%above 700.

Class Rank:

About 10% of the present freshmen class were in the upper 20% of their high school class. 60% were in the top 40% of their class. 90% were in the top 60% of their class. 100% were in the top 80% of their class.

Expenses:

Tuition: In-state: Full year: $2,300.00. Part-time: Per credit:$94.00. Tuition: Out-of-state: Full year: $4,900.00. Part-time: Per credit:$200.00. Room and board: $3,700.00

Majors

• AREA STUDIES Urban • BUSINESS Accounting, Banking, Business Administration, Business Management, Economics, Entrepreneur, Finance, Food Management, Hotel and Restaurant Management, Insurance, Management, Marketing, Swine Management • COMMUNICATIONS Broadcasting, Communication, English, Journalism, Speech, Television/Radio/Film • COMPUTER SCIENCE Computer Science, Systems Analysis • EDUCATION Art, Early Childhood, Elementary, Health, Music, Music Therapy, Physical, Pre-Education, Recreation and Youth Leadership, Secondary, Special • ENGINEERING Chemical • HEALTH SCIENCES Communication Disorders, Health, Medical Technology, Nursing, Nutritional/Food, Speech Therapy, Speech/Audiology and Speech • HUMANITIES Liberal Arts, Philosophy, Religion • LANGUAGES French, German, Italian, Latin, Spanish • PREPROFESSIONAL Dentistry, Law, Medicine, Pharmacy, Social Work, Sports Medicine • SCIENCES Biology, Chemistry, Earth, Geography, Geology, Mathematics, Physical Science, Statistics • SOCIAL SCIENCES Anthropology, Criminal Justice, Criminology, Family Counseling, Government/Political, History, International Studies, Political Science, Psychology, Public Relations, Social Sciences, Sociology • VISUAL AND PERFORMING ARTS Art, Dance, Dramatic Arts, Fine Arts, Music, Music Performance, Studio Art, Theater • VOCATIONAL Business and Office, Fashion Design, Fashion Mechandizing, Food Service, Interior Design, Park/Recreation, Secretarial, Textile and Clothing

Sports/Activities

• SPORTS RELATED Marching Band, Pep Band • SPORTS-INTERCOLLEGIATE Baseball (M), Basketball, Cross Country, Field Hockey (F), Golf (M), Gymnastics, Lacrosse (M), Soccer, Tennis, Volleyball (F) • SPORTS-INTRAMURAL Basketball, Bowling, Cross Country, Ping-Pong, Tennis, Volleyball, Water Polo • STUDENT LIFE ACTIVITIES Choral, Community Service, Concert Band, Dance, Drama Groups, Fraternities, Jazz Band, Magazine, Music Groups, Newspaper, Radio/TV station, Sororities, Student Government, Symphony Orchestra, Yearbook

Southern Seminary College
Buena Vista, Virginia 24416
(703) 261-8420

School Enrollment: **300** Female: **300**

Admissions Contact: **Beth Parker, Director of Admissions**
LD Contact: **Sue Coleman, Director**
Name of Program: **Academic Development**

Admissions

Application Information:
Application deadline: **May 1st**
Rolling Admissions: **Yes**

Secondary School Information
Most Important Criteria For Admissions (1-strongest)

3 SAT/ACT	Application	**1**	School transcript
Class rank	**1** Course selection		Personal statement
1 Interview	Extra activities	**1**	Psychoeducational
2 G.P.A.	Open admission		Recommendations

Test Requirements:
WAIS-R required: **Yes**
Documentation of LD required: **Yes**
Currency of diagnostic testing: **1 year**

Types of Disabilities Served
• Speech/Lang	• Reading	ADD with LD
• Study skills	• Spelling	ADD without LD
• Written express	• Math	ADHD with LD
• Organizational	Fine Motor	ADHD without LD
• Perceptual		

Learning Disability Program

Services available for all students: **Yes**

Diagnostic Testing
ADD	Personality	Perceptual skills	Spelling
ADHD	Organization	Fine motor skills	Reading
I.Q.	Handwriting	Spoken language	Study skills
Math	Social skills	Written language	

Tutoring:
Average size of group tutorials: **6-8**
Services rendered by:

Graduates	•Peers	•Faculty	LD staff	Teacher trainees

Tutorials
Grp.	Ind.	Tutorials	Grp.	Ind.	Tutorials
•	•	Math skills	•		Word processing
•		Study skills	•	•	Time management
•	•	Language arts	•		Learning strategies
•	•	Written express	•		Organizational skills

Academic Accommodations

Curriculum	Study Aids	Exams
Priority registration	Typist	Oral
Math waiver	Reader	Untimed
Foreign lang. waiver	• Notetaker	• Take home
Course substitution	• Proof reader	With proctor
In Class	• Text on tape	On computer
• Calculators	Early syllabus	• Extended time
• Tape recorder	Taped handouts	On tape
• Word processor		Modified
Priority seating		Separate room

Program Strengths

Our program is not clinically based. We work only with students who have experienced a regular classroom environment. We offer only support services to all students. There is no one area where they must go but we do all of our programming out of the Student Assistance Center. We serve the LD student who needs basic support for study skills development, reinforcement of positive academic discipline, self-discipline, and confidence building.

General Information:

Southern Seminary College is a 2 year private college. Rural campus of 100 acres is 50 miles from Roanoke. Accessible by air, train or bus. Ski areas are 1.5 miles from campus. Beaches are 5 miles from campus. 5% of students are foreign. Housing is guaranteed.

Accreditation:SACS

Expenses:

Tuition: In-state: Full year: $8,100.00. Room and board: $4,700.00.

Majors

• BUSINESS Business Administration • EDUCATION Early Childhood • HUMANITIES Liberal Arts • VOCATIONAL Interior Design

Sports/Activities

• SPORTS RELATED Team Managers • STUDENT LIFE ACTIVITIES Choral, Community Service, Dance, Drama Groups, Ethnic & Cultural Groups, Film, Magazine, Religious Organization, Student Government, Yearbook

---

Less Selective

Virginia
Services

Thomas Nelson Community College

P.O. Box 9407
Hampton, Virginia 23670
(804) 825-2827

School Enrollment: **11,777** Male: **5,155** Female: **6,622**
LD Enrollment: **6** Male: **4** Female: **2**

Admissions Contact: **J. McMillan, Director of Admissions**

LD Contact: **T. Kellen, Counselor**
Name of Program: **Disabled Student Services**
Telephone:**(804) 825-2827**

Admissions

Application Information:
LD Students Applying: **6** Accepted: **6** Enrolled:**6**
Separate application:**Yes**
Applicant must apply **1** months in advance
Rolling Admissions: **Yes**

Secondary School Information
Most Important Criteria For Admissions (1-strongest)

SAT/ACT	Application	School transcript
Class rank	Course selection	Personal statement
Interview	Extra activities	Psychoeducational
G.P.A.	**1** Open admission	Recommendations

Test Requirements:
Standardized tests waived: **Yes**
Diagnostic testing waived: **Yes**
Untimed SAT: **Yes** Untimed ACT: **Yes** Untimed ACH: **Yes**
Documentation of LD required: **Yes**
Currency of diagnostic testing: **At least 12 months**
Tests recommended: **WAIS-R, Woodcock-Johnson, WRAT, etc.**

Types of Disabilities Served
- Speech/Lang
- Study skills
- Written express
- Organizational
- Perceptual
- Reading
- Spelling
- Math
- Fine Motor
- ADD with LD
- ADD without LD
- ADHD with LD
- ADHD without LD

Admissions Process

We are an "open door" admissions institution.

High School Course Requirements:
English: **4**
Waivers to standard high school courses
  Course substitution: **Yes**

Learning Disability Program

Syllabus available during orientation:**Yes**
Program: Reinforces course work: **Yes**
Program available through:**Daily**
Students mainstreamed **100** % of the day
Recommended credits per semester: **9**
Services only for LD students: **Yes**
Counseling: Individual: **Yes** Vocational Counseling: **Yes**
Support groups are available:**Yes, from time to time**

Faculty:
Faculty: **1** M.A.: **1**
Faculty advocate: **Yes** Meets with instructor: **Periodically**

Diagnostic Testing

ADD	• Personality	Perceptual skills	Spelling
ADHD	Organization	Fine motor skills	• Reading
I.Q.	Handwriting	Spoken language	• Study skills
• Math	Social skills	• Written language	

Services rendered by:

Graduates	Peers	Faculty	LD staff	Teacher trainees

Tutorials

Grp.	Ind.	Tutorials	Grp.	Ind.	Tutorials
	•	Math skills		•	Word processing
•		Study skills		•	Time management
	•	Language arts		•	Learning strategies
	•	Written express	•		Organizational skills

Virginia

Academic Accommodations

Curriculum	Study Aids	Exams
• Priority registration	Typist	• Oral
Math waiver	Reader	• Untimed
Foreign lang. waiver	• Notetaker	Take home
• Course substitution	• Proof reader	• With proctor
In Class	• Text on tape	• On computer
• Calculators	• Early syllabus	• Extended time
• Tape recorder	Taped handouts	• On tape
• Word processor		Modified
• Priority seating		• Separate room

Graduation Requirements:
Course credits: **varies** GPA: **2.0** Years to complete degree: **Unlimited**
Math waiver: **Yes** Language waiver: **Yes**

General Information:
Thomas Nelson Community College is a 2 year public college. 30 miles from Norfolk. Accessible by plane, train or bus. Ski areas are 150 miles from campus. Beaches are 30 miles from campus. Housing is not guaranteed.

Accreditation:SACS

Expenses:
Tuition: In-state: Full year: $531.50 per semester. Part-time: Per credit:$35.00. Tuition: Out-of-state: Full year: $2,136.50. Part-time: Per credit:$142.00.

Majors
• ARTS Commercial Art, Photography • BUSINESS Accounting, Banking/Finance, Business Administration, Business Management, Data Processing, Food Management, Hotel & Restaurant Management, Retailing • COMPUTER SCIENCE Business Data Programming, Computer Maintenance, Computer Science, Data Processing, Programming • EDUCATION Early Childhood • ENGINEERING Air Conditioning Technology, Drafting, Electrical • HEALTH SCIENCES Medical Laboratory Technology, Nursing • PRE PROFESSIONAL Business, Dentistry, Engineering, Medicine, Pharmacy, Sports Medicine, Veterinarian • SCIENCES Biology, Chemistry, Computer Science, Physics • SOCIAL SCIENCES Government/Political, History, Human Service, Law Enforcement, Political Science, Psychology, Sociology • VISUAL AND PERFORMING ARTS Fine Arts • VOCATIONAL Air Conditioning/Heating/Refri, Building Construction, Drafting, Electronics Technology, Fire Science, Food Science, Medical Laboratory Technology, Secretarial, Word Processing

Sports/Activities
• SPORTS-INTRAMURAL Basketball (F), Basketball (M) • STUDENT LIFE ACTIVITIES Academic Clubs, Ethnic & Cultural Groups, Newspaper, Religious Organization

---

Most Selective

University of Virginia
P. O. Box 9017 University Station
Charlottesville, Virginia 22906
(804) 924-7751

School Enrollment: **11,199**
LD Enrollment: **250**

Admissions Contact: **Lee Morgan, Asst. Dean Admissions**
LD Contact: **E.C. Westhead, Ph.D.**
Name of Program: **Learning Needs & Evaluation Ctr.**
Address: **Bolz Brooks Hall, 22903**
Telephone:**(804) 924-3139**

Admissions

Application Information:
Enrolled:**250**
Application deadline: **January 2nd**
Applicant must apply **8** months in advance
Notified when: **April 1st**

Secondary School Information
Most Important Criteria For Admissions (1-strongest)

3 SAT/ACT	**4** Application	**2** School transcript
2 Class rank	**1** Course selection	**4** Personal statement
Interview	**4** Extra activities	**3** Psychoeducational
2 G.P.A.	Open admission	**5** Recommendations

Test Requirements:
Untimed SAT: **Yes** Achievement tests required:**3**
Documentation of LD required: **Yes**
Tests recommended: **Professional diagnosis, not specific tests**

Types of Disabilities Served
• Speech/Lang	• Reading	• ADD with LD
• Study skills	• Spelling	• ADD without LD
• Written express	• Math	• ADHD with LD
• Organizational	• Fine Motor	• ADHD without LD
• Perceptual		

High School Course Requirements:
English: **4** Math: **4** Science: **2** Foreign Language: **2**
Waivers to standard high school courses
Foreign Language : **Yes** Course substitution: **Yes**

Learning Disability Program
Special orientation for LD students: **Yes**
Program available through:**All year**
Counseling: Individual: **Yes** Group Counseling: **Yes** Vocational Counseling: **Yes**
Support groups are available:**Yes, several at The University Counseling Center and LNEC**

Faculty:
Faculty: **5** Including Director: **Yes** Full time: **5** M.A.: **3** Ph.D.: **1**

Diagnostic Testing

ADD	Personality	Perceptual skills	Spelling
ADHD	Organization	Fine motor skills	Reading
I.Q.	Handwriting	Spoken language	Study skills
Math	Social skills	Written language	

Tutoring:

Services rendered by:
•Graduates •Peers •Faculty •LD staff Teacher trainees

Tutorials

Grp.	Ind.	Tutorials	Grp.	Ind.	Tutorials
	•	Math skills		•	Word processing
	•	Study skills		•	Time management
	•	Language arts		•	Learning strategies
	•	Written express		•	Organizational skills

Academic Accommodations

Curriculum	Study Aids	Exams
• Priority registration	• Typist	• Oral
Math waiver	• Reader	Untimed
• Foreign lang. waiver	• Notetaker	• Take home
• Course substitution	• Proof reader	• With proctor
In Class	• Text on tape	• On computer
• Calculators	Early syllabus	• Extended time
• Tape recorder	• Taped handouts	• On tape
• Word processor		• Modified
Priority seating		• Separate room

Graduation Requirements:

Course credits: **120** GPA: **2.0** Language waiver: **Yes**
Other requirements: **Varies with field of study, undergraduate school (A&S, Engineering, Architecture, Commerce, Nursing)**

Program Strengths

The student with specific learning disabilities is not differentiated from those with any disability and is fully eligible for any relevant service. However, we also protect their right to fail. Once they know what is offered, they may choose to deny the need for assistance.

General Information:

University of Virginia is a 4 year public university. Suburban campus of 2,440 acres is 70 miles from Richmond. Accessible by air or bus. Ski areas are 3/4 of an hour from campus. Beaches are 2.5 hours from campus. 3% of students are foreign. 69 residential halls on campus. Housing is not guaranteed.70 % of students remain on campus for the weekends. 24 % of students join fraternities/sororities.

Accreditation:SACS

SAT/ACT Scores:

Scores for incoming freshmen:**Verbal:**2%below 500. **Math:**2% below 500.

Expenses:

Tuition: In-state: Full year: $3,354.00. Tuition: Out-of-state: Full year: $9,564.00. Room and board: $3,250.00

Majors

• AREA STUDIES African, American, Asian, Black/Afro-American, Latin American, Medieval Studies, Russian/Slavic, Urban, Women's Studies • BUSINESS Accounting, Banking, Business Administration, Business Management, Economics, Finance, Management, Marketing, Marketing Research, Personnel • COMMUNICATIONS Communication, Creative Writing, English, Journalism, Photography, Speech, Television/Radio/Film • COMPUTER SCIENCE Computer Science, Data Processing, Programming, Systems Analysis, Telecommunications • EDUCATION Curriculum, Early Childhood, Health, Middle School, Physical, Recreation and Youth Leadership, School Psychology, Secondary, Special, Speech/Language • ENGINEERING Aerospace, Chemical, Civil/Environmental, Computer, Electrical, Engineering Science, Mechanical, Nuclear • HEALTH SCIENCES Communication Disorders, Environmental, Health, Medical Technology, Nursing, Radiological Therapy, Speech Therapy, Speech/Audiology and Speech • HUMANITIES Classics, English/Writing/Literature, Humanities, Liberal Arts, Philosophy, Religion • LANGUAGES Chinese, French, German, Greek, Italian, Japanese, Latin, Russian, Spanish • PREPROFESSIONAL Architecture, Engineering, Law, Medicine, Pharmacy, Recreation • SCIENCES Astronomy, Astrophysics, Biochemistry, Biology, Chemistry, Earth, Ecology, Geology, Mathematics, Microbiology, Physics, Physiology, Radiology, Zoology • SOCIAL SCIENCES Anthropology, Government/Political, History, International Studies, Political Science, Psychology, Social Sciences, Sociology • VISUAL AND PERFORMING ARTS Art, Art History, Dramatic Arts, Music, Studio Art, Theater

Sports/Activities

• SPORTS RELATED Pep Band • SPORTS-INTERCOLLEGIATE Baseball (M), Basketball, Crew, Cross Country, Diving, Field Hockey (F), Football (M), Golf, Horseback Riding, Lacrosse, Rugby, Sailing, Soccer, Softball (F), Swimming, Tennis, Track and Field, Volleyball (F), Wrestling (M) • SPORTS-INTRAMURAL Archery, Badminton, Baseball (M), Basketball, Bowling, Boxing (M), Fencing, Field Hockey (F), Golf, Hand Ball, Horseback Riding, Lacrosse, Ping-Pong, Racquetball, Riflery, Skiing - Snow, Soccer, Softball, Squash, Swimming, Tennis, Track and Field, Volleyball, Water Polo • STUDENT LIFE ACTIVITIES Choral, Community Service, Concert Band, Dance, Debate, Ethnic & Cultural Groups, Film, Fraternities, Jazz Band, Magazine, Music Groups, Musical Theater, Newspaper, Political Groups, Radio/TV station, Religious Organization, Sororities, Student Government, Symphony Orchestra, Yearbook

Less Selective	Virginia
	Program

Virginia Highlands Community College

P. O. Box 828
Abingdon, Virginia 24210
(703) 628-6094

School Enrollment: **2,060** Male: **960** Female: **1,100**
LD Enrollment: **35** Male: **20** Female: **15**

Admissions Contact: **Edward A. Colley, Director of Admissions**
LD Contact: **Charlotte L. Faris, Director**
Name of Program: **Project EXCEL**
Address: **P.O. Box 828**
Telephone:**(703) 628-6094**

Admissions

Application Information:

LD Students Applying: **35** Accepted: **35** Enrolled:**35**
LD on admissions committee:**Yes**
Application deadline: **August 1st**

Secondary School Information

Most Important Criteria For Admissions (1-strongest)

SAT/ACT	Application	School transcript
Class rank	Course selection	Personal statement
Interview	Extra activities	Psychoeducational
G.P.A.	1 Open admission	Recommendations

Virginia

Test Requirements:
Diagnostic testing waived: **Yes**
Documentation of LD required: **Yes**
Currency of diagnostic testing: **Not over 3 years old**
Tests recommended: **WAIS-R, Woodcock-Johnson**

Types of Disabilities Served
- Speech/Lang
- Study skills
- Written express
- Organizational
- Perceptual
- Reading
- Spelling
- Math
- Fine Motor
- ADD with LD
- ADD without LD
- ADHD with LD
- ADHD without LD

Learning Disability Program
Program: Reinforces course work: **Yes**
Recommended credits per semester: **12**
Counseling: Individual: **Yes** Group Counseling: **Yes**

Faculty:
Faculty: **25** Including Director: **Yes** Full time: **3** Part time: **22**
LD faculty with: BS/BA: **16** M.A.: **12**
Faculty advocate: **Yes** Meets with instructor: **As needed**

Diagnostic Testing
- ADD
  ADHD
  I.Q.
- Math
- Personality
- Organization
- Handwriting
- Social skills
- Perceptual skills
- Fine motor skills
- Spoken language
- Written language
- Spelling
- Reading
- Study skills

Tutoring:
Average size of group tutorials: **1-3**
Services rendered by:
  Graduates •Peers •Faculty •LD staff •Teacher trainees

Tutorials

Grp.	Ind.	Tutorials	Grp.	Ind.	Tutorials
	•	Math skills		•	Word processing
•		Study skills		•	Time management
	•	Language arts		•	Learning strategies
	•	Written express		•	Organizational skills

Academic Accommodations

Curriculum	Study Aids	Exams
Priority registration	Typist	• Oral
• Math waiver	Reader	• Untimed
• Foreign lang. waiver	• Notetaker	Take home
Course substitution	• Proof reader	• With proctor
In Class	• Text on tape	On computer
• Calculators	Early syllabus	• Extended time
• Tape recorder	Taped handouts	On tape
Word processor		• Modified
Priority seating		• Separate room

Program Strengths
The Learning Disability Program is administered through Project EXCEL. Tutoring, notetaking, scribes, oral tests, untimed tests, and alternate locations on testing are the major services. There is no charge for the services available. Special application to Project EXCEL is required along with documentation of the disability.

General Information:
Virginia Highlands Community College is a 2 year public college. Rural campus of 100 acres is 15 miles from Bristol. Ski areas are 50 miles from campus. Beaches are 350 miles from campus. Housing is not guaranteed.

Accreditation: SACS

Expenses:
Tuition: In-state: Full year: Part-time: Per credit: $35.00. Part-time: Per course: $105.00. Tuition: Out-of-state: Full year: Part-time: Per credit: $142.00. Part-time: Per course:$426.00

Majors
• BUSINESS Accounting, Business Administration, Business Management, Clerical, Education, Secretarial Science • COMPUTER SCIENCE Business Data Programming, Computer Science • EDUCATION General • ENGINEERING Engineering Science • HEALTH SCIENCES Nursing, Physical Therapy, Radiological Therapy • PREPROFESSIONAL Engineering, Law • SCIENCES General, Radiology • SOCIAL SCIENCES Criminal Justice, Human Service • VOCATIONAL Air Conditioning/Heating/Refri, Drafting, Electronics Technology, Machinist

Sports/Activities
• SPORTS-INTERCOLLEGIATE Baseball, Basketball, Bowling, Cross Country, Cycling, Karate, Skiing - Snow, Softball, Tennis, Volleyball • STUDENT LIFE ACTIVITIES Drama Groups, Ethnic & Cultural Groups, Music Groups, Student Government

Selective	Virginia
	Services

Virginia Intermont College
1013 Moore Street
Bristol, Virginia 24201-4298
(703) 669-6101-(800) 451-1842

School Enrollment: **641** Male: **214** Female: **427**
LD Enrollment: **28**

Admissions Contact: **R. Lawton Blandford, Jr. Dean of Admissions**
LD Contact: **Talmage Dobbins, Dir. Student Support Services**
Name of Program: **Student Support Services**
Telephone:**Ext. 217**

Admissions

Application Information:
Application deadline: **August 31st**
Rolling Admissions: **Yes**

Secondary School Information
Most Important Criteria For Admissions (1-strongest)

4	SAT/ACT	7	Application	1	School transcript
5	Class rank	2	Course selection	6	Personal statement
11	Interview	10	Extra activities	8	Psychoeducational
3	G.P.A.		Open admission	9	Recommendations

Test Requirements:
Untimed SAT: **Yes** Untimed ACT: **Yes** Untimed ACH: **Yes**
Documentation of LD required: **Yes**
Currency of diagnostic testing: **3 years**
Tests recommended: **WAIS-R, Woodcock-Johnson**

Types of Disabilities Served
- Speech/Lang
- Study skills
- Written express
- Organizational
- Perceptual
- Reading
- Spelling
- Math
- Fine Motor
- ADD with LD
- ADD without LD
- ADHD with LD
- ADHD without LD

Admissions Process

Applicant must submit a completed application for admission, $15.00 application fee, official high school and college transcripts, and official SAT or ACT scores.

High School Course Requirements:
English: **4** Math: **2** Science: **1**

Learning Disability Program

Students mainstreamed **100** % of the day
Recommended credits per semester: **12-15**
Services only for LD students: **Yes**
Counseling: Individual: **Yes** Group Counseling: **Yes** Vocational Counseling: **Yes**
Support groups are available:**General LD support group, specialized topics based on student need and request.**

Faculty:
Faculty: **3** Including Director: **Yes** Full time: **2** Part time: **1** M.A.: **2**
Faculty advocate: **Yes** Meets with instructor: **As needed**

Diagnostic Testing
ADD	Personality •	Perceptual skills •	• Spelling
ADHD•	Organization•	Fine motor skills •	• Reading
• I.Q.	Handwriting•	Spoken language •	• Study skills
• Math	• Social skills•	Written language	

Tutoring:
Average size of group tutorials: **2-12**
Services rendered by:
Graduates •Peers   Faculty   •LD staff   Teacher trainees

Tutorials
Grp.	Ind.	Tutorials	Grp.	Ind.	Tutorials
	•	Math skills		•	Word processing
	•	Study skills		•	Time management
	•	Language arts		•	Learning strategies
	•	Written express		•	Organizational skills

Academic Accommodations
Curriculum	Study Aids	Exams
Priority registration	• Typist	• Oral
Math waiver	• Reader	Untimed
Foreign lang. waiver	• Notetaker	Take home
• Course substitution	• Proof reader	• With proctor
In Class	• Text on tape	• On computer
• Calculators	Early syllabus	• Extended time
• Tape recorder	Taped handouts	• On tape
• Word processor		• Modified
Priority seating		• Separate room

Graduation Requirements:
Course credits: **124** GPA: **2.0**
Other requirements: **Last 30 hours must be taken at Virginia Intermont**

Program Strengths
Student Support Services works with a variety of students including LD, so no labels are attached to utilizing services. There are two certified counselors who also serve as Director and Tutor Coordinator, a Learning Specialist who is currently certified as a School Psychologist, and a secretary. Peer tutoring is available, but most LD students receive individualized staff tutoring.

General Information:
Virginia Intermont College is a 4 year public Baptist college. Suburban campus of 16 acres is 110 miles from Knoxville. Accessible by air or bus. Ski areas are 2 miles from campus. Beaches are 7 miles from campus. 5% of students are foreign. 5 residential halls on campus. Housing is guaranteed.60 % of students remain on campus for the weekends.

Accreditation:SACS

Expenses:
Tuition: In-state: Full year: $7,320.00. Part-time: Per credit:$125.00 for 1-6 hours; $275.00 for 7-11hours. Tuition: Out-of-state: Full year: $7,320.00. Part-time: Per course:$125.00 Room and board: $3,980.00

Majors
• BUSINESS Business Administration, Business Management, Management • COMMUNICATIONS Creative Writing, English, Graphic Design, Photography • EDUCATION Art, Biology, Business, English, History/Political Science, Interdisciplinary, Music, Photography • HEALTH SCIENCES Health, Medical Technology • HUMANITIES Liberal Arts, Religion • PREPROFESSIONAL Dentistry, Law, Legal Assistant, Medicine, Ministry, Pharmacy, Social Work, Veterinarian • SCIENCES Biology, Equestrian Studies • SOCIAL SCIENCES History, Political Science, Psychology • VISUAL AND PERFORMING ARTS Art, Dance • VOCATIONAL Fashion Merchandising, Paralegal

Sports/Activities
• SPORTS-INTERCOLLEGIATE Baseball (M), Basketball, Horseback Riding, Tennis • SPORTS-INTRAMURAL Archery, Badminton, Basketball, Bowling, Horseback Riding, Ping-Pong, Skiing - Snow, Swimming, Tennis, Volleyball • STUDENT LIFE ACTIVITIES Choral, Drama Groups, Magazine, Religious Organization, Student Government, Yearbook

Very Selective   **Virginia Program**

Virginia Polytechnic Institute and State University
Smith House
Blacksburg, Virginia 24061-0202
(703) 231-3787

School Enrollment: **23,000** Male: **13,800** Female: **9,200**
LD Enrollment: **50** Male: **35**

Admissions Contact: **David Bousques, Director**
LD Contact: **Wayne Speer, Assistant Dean**
Name of Program: **Disabled Student Services**
Telephone:**(703) 231-3787**

Admissions

Application Information:
Application deadline: **February 1st**

Secondary School Information
Most Important Criteria For Admissions (1-strongest)
4 SAT/ACT	Application	School transcript
2 Class rank	**1** Course selection	**6** Personal statement
Interview	**5** Extra activities	Psychoeducational
3 G.P.A.	Open admission	**7** Recommendations

Virginia

Test Requirements:
Diagnostic testing waived: **Yes**
Untimed SAT: **Yes** Untimed ACT: **Yes** Untimed ACH: **Yes** Achievement tests required:**2**
WAIS-R required: **Yes**
Currency of diagnostic testing: **3 years**

Types of Disabilities Served

Speech/Lang	Reading	ADD with LD
• Study skills	Spelling	ADD without LD
• Written express	Math	ADHD with LD
• Organizational	Fine Motor	ADHD without LD
Perceptual		

Learning Disability Program
Program: Reinforces course work: **Yes**
Students mainstreamed **100** % of the day
Counseling: Individual: **Yes** Group Counseling: **Yes**

Faculty:
Faculty: **1** Full time: **1** M.A.: **1**
Faculty advocate: **Yes** Meets with instructor: **As needed**

Diagnostic Testing

ADD	Personality	Perceptual skills	Spelling
ADHD	Organization	Fine motor skills	Reading
I.Q.	Handwriting	Spoken language	Study skills
Math	Social skills	Written language	

Tutoring:
Services rendered by:
Graduates •Peers Faculty LD staff Teacher trainees

Tutorials

Grp.	Ind.	Tutorials	Grp.	Ind.	Tutorials
		Math skills			Word processing
•	•	Study skills	•	•	Time management
		Language arts		•	Learning strategies
	•	Written express		•	Organizational skills

Academic Accommodations

Curriculum	Study Aids	Exams
Priority registration	Typist	• Oral
Math waiver	• Reader	Untimed
• Foreign lang. waiver	• Notetaker	Take home
• Course substitution	• Proof reader	With proctor
In Class	Text on tape	On computer
Calculators	Early syllabus	• Extended time
• Tape recorder	Taped handouts	• On tape
• Word processor		• Modified
Priority seating		Separate room

General Information:
Virginia Polytechnic Institute and State University is a 4 year public university. Rural campus 40 miles from Roanoke. Accessible by bus. Ski areas are 2 hours from campus. Beaches are 7 hours from campus. Housing is not guaranteed.20 % of students join fraternities/sororities.

Accreditation:SACS

Class Rank:
About 71% of the present freshmen class were in the upper 20% of their high school class. 100% were in the top 40% of their class.

Expenses:
Tuition: In-state: Full year: $2,436.00. Tuition: Out-of-state: Full year: $5,820.00. Room and board: $2,672.00

Majors
• AREA STUDIES Urban • BUSINESS Accounting, Agricultural, Business Economics, Business Education, Business Management, Economics, Hotel and Restaurant Management, Management, Marketing • COMMUNICATIONS Communication, English • COMPUTER SCIENCE Computer Science • EDUCATION Agricultural, Early Childhood, Elementary, English, Foreign Language, Health, Industrial, Marketing and Distributive Education, Mathematics, Middle School, Physical, Pre-Education, Science, Secondary, Social Studies • ENGINEERING Aerospace, Agricultural, Chemical, Civil/Environmental, Computer, Electrical, Engineering Science, Industrial, Materials, Mechanical, Mining/Mineral, Ocean • HEALTH SCIENCES Nutritional/Food • HUMANITIES Liberal Arts, Philosophy, Religion • LANGUAGES French, German, Spanish • PRE-PROFESSIONAL Architecture, Dentistry, Medicine, Veterinarian • SCIENCES Agronomy, Animal, Biochemistry, Biology, Chemistry, Dairy, Geography, Geology, Geophysics and Seismology, Gerontology, Horticultural, Physics, Plant Sciences, Poultry, Statistics • SOCIAL SCIENCES Family Counseling, Government/Political, History, International Studies, Political Science, Psychology, Public Relations, Sociology • VISUAL AND PERFORMING ARTS Art History, Dramatic Arts, Music • VOCATIONAL Construction, Fashion Design, Forestry, Home Economics, Interior Design, Landscape Architecture, Textile and Clothing, Wildlife

Sports/Activities
• SPORTS RELATED Marching Band, Pep Band • SPORTS-INTERCOLLEGIATE Baseball (M), Basketball, Cross Country, Diving, Football (M), Golf (M), Horseback Riding, Soccer (M), Swimming, Tennis, Track and Field, Volleyball (F), Wrestling (M) • SPORTS-INTRAMURAL Archery, Badminton, Basketball, Bowling, Cross Country, Fencing, Field Hockey (F), Golf, Gymnastics, Hand Ball, Ice Hockey (M), Lacrosse, Racquetball, Rugby (M), Skiing - Snow, Soccer, Softball, Swimming, Tennis, Track and Field, Volleyball, Water Polo, Wrestling (M) • STUDENT LIFE ACTIVITIES Choral, Concert Band, Dance, Drama Groups, Ethnic & Cultural Groups, Film, Fraternities, Jazz Band, Magazine, Music Groups, Musical Theater, Newspaper, Radio/TV station, Sororities, Student Government, Symphony Orchestra, Yearbook

---

Very Selective **Virginia**
Accommodations

Virginia Wesleyan College
Wesleyan Drive
Norfolk, Virginia 23502
(804) 455-3200

School Enrollment: **1,200**
LD Enrollment: **10** Male: **8** Female: **2**

Admissions Contact: **W. Steve Stocks, V.P. for Admission**
LD Contact: **Fayne C. Pearson, Asst. to Academic Dean**
Name of Program: **Academic Skills Development**
Telephone:**(804) 455-3246**

Admissions

Application Information:
Application deadline: **March 1st**
Notified when: **April 1st**

Secondary School Information

Most Important Criteria For Admissions (1-strongest)

4	SAT/ACT	6 Application	1 School transcript
5	Class rank	3 Course selection	8 Personal statement
8	Interview	7 Extra activities	10 Psychoeducational
2	G.P.A.	Open admission	9 Recommendations

Types of Disabilities Served

- Speech/Lang
- Study skills
- Written express
- Organizational
- Perceptual
- Reading
- Spelling
- Math
- Fine Motor
- ADD with LD
- ADD without LD
- ADHD with LD
- ADHD without LD

Learning Disability Program

Special orientation for LD students: **Yes**
Syllabus available during orientation: **Yes**
Program available through: **Academic term**
Recommended credits per semester: **12-15**
Counseling: Individual: **Yes** Group Counseling: **Yes**

Faculty: M.A.: **1**
Faculty advocate: **Yes** Meets with instructor: **As needed**

Diagnostic Testing

ADD	Personality	Perceptual skills	• Spelling
ADHD	Organization	Fine motor skills	• Reading
• I.Q.	Handwriting	Spoken language	• Study skills
• Math	Social skills	• Written language	

Tutoring:

Services rendered by:

Graduates •Peers •Faculty •LD staff Teacher trainees

Tutorials

Grp.	Ind.	Tutorials	Grp.	Ind.	Tutorials
•	•	Math skills	•	•	Word processing
•		Study skills	•	•	Time management
		Language arts	•	•	Learning strategies
•	•	Written express	•	•	Organizational skills

Academic Accommodations

Curriculum	Study Aids	Exams
Priority registration	Typist	• Oral
Math waiver	Reader	Untimed
Foreign lang. waiver	• Notetaker	• Take home
• Course substitution	• Proof reader	• With proctor
In Class	• Text on tape	On computer
• Calculators	Early syllabus	• Extended time
• Tape recorder	Taped handouts	On tape
• Word processor		• Modified
Priority seating		Separate room

Graduation Requirements:

Course credits: **120** GPA: **2.0**

Program Strengths

We have a network for providing accommodations for LD students. We have tutorial support in peer tutors, a writing center, and an advocacy system.

General Information:

Virginia Wesleyan College is a 4 year private United Methodist college. Suburban campus of 300 acres is 10 miles from Norfolk. Accessible by air, train, or bus. Ski areas are 3 hours from campus. Beaches are 20 minutes from campus. 3% of students are foreign. 8 residential halls on campus. Housing is guaranteed. 80 % of students remain on campus for the weekends. 10 % of students join fraternities/sororities.

Accreditation: SACS

SAT/ACT Scores:
Scores for incoming freshmen: **Verbal:** 67% below 500. 24% between 500 and 599. 8% between 600 and 699. **Math:** 51% below 500. 34% between 500 and 599. 13% between 600 and 699. 2% above 700.

Class Rank:
About 26% of the present freshmen class were in the upper 20% of their high school class. 46% were in the top 40% of their class. 67% were in the top 60% of their class. 81% were in the top 80% of their class.

Expenses:
Tuition: In-state: Full year: $9,300.00. Part-time: Per credit: $338.00. Room and board: $4,100.00

Majors

• AREA STUDIES American, Urban • BUSINESS Accounting, Business Administration, Business Economics, Business Management, Economics, Entrepreneur, Human Resources Management, Insurance, Management, Marketing, Marketing Research • COMMUNICATIONS Broadcasting, Communication, Creative Writing, English, Literature, Speech, Television/Radio/Film • COMPUTER SCIENCE Computer Science, Data Processing, Programming, Systems Analysis, Telecommunications • EDUCATION Art, Early Childhood, Elementary, Foreign Language, General, Mathematics, Middle School, Music, Pre-Education, Science, Secondary, Social Science, Social Studies • HUMANITIES English/Writing/Literature, Humanities, Liberal Arts, Philosophy, Religion • LANGUAGES French, Spanish • PREPROFESSIONAL Dentistry, Law, Medicine, Ministry, Pharmacy, Recreation, Social Work, Veterinarian • SCIENCES Biochemistry, Biology, Chemistry, Geography, Mathematics, Physical Science • SOCIAL SCIENCES Anthropology, Criminal Justice, Government/Political, History, Human Service, International Studies, Law Enforcement, Political Science, Psychology, Public Relations, Social Sciences, Sociology • VISUAL AND PERFORMING ARTS Art, Art History, Dramatic Arts, Drawing, Fine Arts, Music, Studio Art, Theater • VOCATIONAL Painting, Park/Recreation

Sports/Activities

• SPORTS-INTERCOLLEGIATE Baseball (M), Basketball, Golf (M), Soccer, Softball (F), Tennis • SPORTS-INTRAMURAL Basketball, Golf (M), Ping-Pong, Soccer, Softball, Tennis, Volleyball • STUDENT LIFE ACTIVITIES Choral, Drama Groups, Fraternities, Magazine, Music Groups, Musical Theater, Newspaper, Radio/TV station, Sororities, Student Government, Yearbook

---

Less Selective

Virginia Services

Virginia Western Community College

P. O. Box 14007
Roanoke, Virginia 24036
(703) 982-7231

School Enrollment: **7,500**
LD Enrollment: **100**

Admissions Contact: **Gordon Hancock, Director of Admissions**
LD Contact: **Michael Henderson, Director**
Name of Program: **Student Support Services**
Telephone: **(703) 857-7286**

Washington

Admissions

Application Information:
LD Students Applying: **100** Accepted: **100**
Separate application:**Yes**
Application deadline: **None**
Applicant must apply **.5** months in advance
Rolling Admissions: **Yes**

Secondary School Information
Most Important Criteria For Admissions (1-strongest)

SAT/ACT	Application	School transcript
Class rank	Course selection	Personal statement
Interview	Extra activities	Psychoeducational
G.P.A.	**1** Open admission	Recommendations

Test Requirements:
Standardized tests waived: **Yes**
Documentation of LD required: **Yes**

Types of Disabilities Served
- Speech/Lang
- Study skills
- Written express
- Organizational
- Perceptual
- Reading
- Spelling
- Math
- Fine Motor
- ADD with LD
- ADD without LD
- ADHD with LD
- ADHD without LD

Admissions Process

Open admissions

Learning Disability Program

Program: Reinforces course work: **Yes**
Students mainstreamed **100** % of the day
Recommended credits per semester: **9**
Counseling: Individual: **Yes** Group Counseling: **Yes** Vocational Counseling: **Yes**
Support groups are available:**Peer support group**

Faculty:
Faculty: **3** Including Director: **Yes** Full time: **3** M.A.: **1**
Faculty advocate: **Yes** Meets with instructor: **As needed**

Diagnostic Testing

ADD	Personality	Perceptual skills	Spelling
ADHD	Organization	Fine motor skills	Reading
I.Q.	Handwriting	Spoken language	Study skills
Math	Social skills	Written language	

Tutoring:
Average size of group tutorials:
Services rendered by:
•Graduates   •Peers   •Faculty   •LD staff   Teacher trainees

Tutorials

Grp.	Ind.	Tutorials	Grp.	Ind.	Tutorials
	•	Math skills		•	Word processing
•	•	Study skills		•	Time management
	•	Language arts		•	Learning strategies
	•	Written express		•	Organizational skills

Academic Accommodations

Curriculum
- Priority registration
- Math waiver
  Foreign lang. waiver
- Course substitution

In Class
- Calculators
- Tape recorder
- Word processor
  Priority seating

Study Aids
- Typist
- Reader
- Notetaker
- Proof reader
- Text on tape
  Early syllabus
  Taped handouts

Exams
- Oral
- Untimed
- Take home
- With proctor
  On computer
- Extended time
- On tape
- Modified
- Separate room

Program Strengths
This program tries to tailor services and accommodations to individual student needs. There is a strong emphasis on personal counseling as an adjustment to other LD accommodations.

General Information:
Virginia Western Community College is a 2 year public college. Urban campus of 10 acres is Roanoke. Accessible by air, train or bus. Ski areas are 2 hours from campus. Beaches are 5 hours from campus. 2% of students are foreign. Housing is not guaranteed.

Accreditation:SACS

Expenses:
Tuition: In-state: Full year: $900.00. Part-time: Per credit:$35.00. Tuition: Out-of-state: Full year: $4,000.00.

Majors
• BUSINESS Accounting, Business Administration, Business Management, Management • COMMUNICATIONS Commercial Design, Television/Radio/Film • COMPUTER SCIENCE Data Processing • EDUCATION General • ENGINEERING Civil/Environmental, Engineering Science, Mechanical • HEALTH SCIENCES Dental Hygiene, Mental Health, Nursing, Radiological Therapy • PREPROFESSIONAL Architecture • SCIENCES Horticultural, Physical Science, Science Technology • SOCIAL SCIENCES Criminal Justice, Human Service • VISUAL AND PERFORMING ARTS Fine Arts • VOCATIONAL Auto Body, Electronics Technology, Radiological Technology, Secretarial, Word Processing

Sports/Activities
• SPORTS-INTRAMURAL Basketball (M) • STUDENT LIFE ACTIVITIES Choral, Drama Groups, Ethnic & Cultural Groups, Newspaper, Religious Organization, Student Government

---

Selective **Washington Services**

Central Washington University
Mitchell Hall
Ellensburg, Washington 98926
(509) 963-1211

School Enrollment: **6,200** Male: **3,000** Female: **3,200**

Admissions Contact: **James Maraviglia, Director of Admissions**
LD Contact: **Dave Brown, Coordinator**
Name of Program: **Disabled Student Services**
Telephone:**(509) 963-2171**

Admissions

Application Information:
Application deadline: **Rolling**
Rolling Admissions: **Yes** Notified when: **within a week**

Secondary School Information
Most Important Criteria For Admissions (1-strongest)

2 SAT/ACT	**1** Application	**4** School transcript
Class rank	**3** Course selection	Personal statement
5 Interview	Extra activities	Psychoeducational
1 G.P.A.	Open admission	Recommendations

Test Requirements:
Untimed SAT: **Yes** Untimed ACT: **Yes**

Types of Disabilities Served
- Speech/Lang
- Study skills
- Written express
- Organizational
- Perceptual
- Reading
- Spelling
- Math
- Fine Motor

ADD with LD
ADD without LD
ADHD with LD
ADHD without LD

Learning Disability Program
Counseling: Individual: **Yes**

Faculty:
Faculty: **1**
Faculty advocate: **Yes** Meets with instructor: **As needed**

Diagnostic Testing

ADD	Personality	Perceptual skills	Spelling
ADHD	Organization	Fine motor skills	Reading
I.Q.	Handwriting	Spoken language	Study skills
Math	Social skills	Written language	

Tutoring:
Average size of group tutorials: **3-5**
Services rendered by:
Graduates •Peers •Faculty •LD staff •Teacher trainees

Tutorials

Grp.	Ind.	Tutorials	Grp.	Ind.	Tutorials
•	•	Math skills		•	Word processing
•	•	Study skills	•	•	Time management
•	•	Language arts	•	•	Learning strategies
•	•	Written express	•	•	Organizational skills

Academic Accommodations

Curriculum	Study Aids	Exams
Priority registration	Typist	• Oral
Math waiver	Reader	Untimed
Foreign lang. waiver	• Notetaker	• Take home
Course substitution	• Proof reader	With proctor
In Class	• Text on tape	On computer
• Calculators	Early syllabus	• Extended time
• Tape recorder	Taped handouts	On tape
• Word processor		• Modified
Priority seating		Separate room

Program Strengths
Central Washington University does not have a "Learning Disability Program". Students with learning disabilities receive accommodations through Disabled Student Services. These accommodations help minimize the functional limitations of their disability. Central Washington University offers academic advising, tutoring, and peer support.

General Information:
Central Washington University is a 4 year public university. Rural campus of 350 acres is 100 miles from Seattle. Accessible by air or bus. Ski areas are 55 miles from campus. Beaches are 100 miles from campus. 2% of students are foreign. 21 residential halls on campus. Housing is guaranteed. Guaranteed through 4th year. 75 % of students remain on campus for the weekends.

Accreditation: NACS

SAT/ACT Scores:
Scores for incoming freshmen: **Verbal:** 80% below 500. 16% between 500 and 599. 4% between 600 and 699. 2% above 700. **Math:** 63% below 500. 28% between 500 and 599. 7% between 600 and 699. 1% above 700.

Expenses:
Tuition: In-state: Full year: $1,674.00. Part-time: Per credit: $54.00. Tuition: Out-of-state: Full year: $5,649.00. Part-time: Per credit: $188.00. Room and board: $2,993.00

Majors
• AREA STUDIES American Indian, Black/Afro-American, Latin American, Mexican/American • BUSINESS Accounting, Banking, Business Administration, Business Economics, Business Education, Business Management, Economics, Finance, International Business, Management, Marketing, Real Estate • COMMUNICATIONS Advertising, Broadcasting, Communication, English, Journalism, Speech, Television/Radio/Film • COMPUTER SCIENCE Artificial Intelligence, Computer Science, Data Processing, Programming, Telecommunications • CRAFTS AND DESIGN Graphic Design, Mechanical Design • EDUCATION Agricultural, Bilingual, Early Childhood, Elementary, English, Foreign Language, Health, Home Economics, Industrial, Mathematics, Middle School, Music, Physical, School Psychology, Science, Secondary, Social Science, Special, Speech/Language • ENGINEERING Manufacturing • ENVIRONMENTAL CONTROL • HEALTH SCIENCES Community Health Work, Emergency Medical Technician, Health, Medical Secretary, Nutritional/Food, Paramedics, Public Health Laboratory, Speech/Audiology and Speech • HUMANITIES Humanities, Liberal Arts, Philosophy, Religion • LANGUAGES French, German, Spanish • PREPROFESSIONAL Agriculture, Architecture, Dentistry, Engineering, Law, Medicine, Pharmacy • SCIENCES Anthropology, Biology, Botany, Chemistry, Earth, Geography, Geology, Gerontology, Mathematics, Physical Science, Physics, Zoology • SOCIAL SCIENCES Anthropology, Criminal Justice, Government/Political, History, Law Enforcement, Political Science, Psychology, Public Relations, Social Sciences, Sociology • VISUAL AND PERFORMING ARTS Art, Art History, Dance, Dramatic Arts, Fine Arts, Music, Music Performance, Music Theory & Composition, Theater • VOCATIONAL Aircraft Systems, Airline Piloting & Navigation, Airway Science Management, Aviation Maintenance, Business and Office, Construction, Electronics Technology, Fashion Mechandizing, Flight Officer, Flight Technology, Home Economics, Industrial Distribution, Industrial Supervision Technology, Manufacturing Technology, Medical Laboratory Technology, Office Administration, Operations Research, Park/Recreation, Secretarial, Textile and Clothing

Sports/Activities
• SPORTS RELATED Marching Band, Pep Band • SPORTS-INTERCOLLEGIATE Baseball (M), Basketball, Cross Country, Diving, Football (M), Golf (M), Soccer, Swimming, Tennis, Track and Field, Volleyball (F), Wrestling (M) • SPORTS-INTRAMURAL Basketball, Bowling, Rodeo, Skiing - Snow (M), Softball, Volleyball • STUDENT LIFE ACTIVITIES choral Concert Band, Dance, Ethnic & Cultural Groups, Jazz Band, Music Groups, Musical Theater, Newspaper, Opera, Political Groups, Radio/TV station, Religious Organization, Student Government, Student Handbook & Directory, Symphony Orchestra, Yearbook

Less Selective

Centralia College
600 West Locust
Centralia, Washington 98531
(206) 736-9391

School Enrollment: **3,184** Male: **1,288** Female: **1,896**
LD Enrollment: **80**

Admissions Contact: **Neena Stoskopf, Director of Admissions**
LD Contact: **Kay Odegaard, Coordinator**
Name of Program: **Special Needs**
Telephone:**(206) 736-9391**

Admissions

Application Information:
Application deadline: **Open**

Secondary School Information
Most Important Criteria For Admissions (1-strongest)

SAT/ACT	Application	School transcript
Class rank	Course selection	Personal statement
Interview	Extra activities	Psychoeducational
G.P.A.	**1** Open admission	Recommendations

Test Requirements:
Standardized tests waived: **Yes**
Diagnostic testing waived: **Yes**
Untimed SAT: **Yes**
Documentation of LD required: **Yes**
Currency of diagnostic testing: **3 years**
Tests recommended: **Some sort of I.Q. indication, Achievement testing and LD screening preferably with accommodation recommendations.**

Types of Disabilities Served
- Speech/Lang
- Study skills
- Written express
- Organizational
- Perceptual
- Reading
- Spelling
- Math
- Fine Motor
- ADD with LD
- ADD without LD
- ADHD with LD
- ADHD without LD

Admissions Process

"Open Door" Policy

Learning Disability Program

Special orientation for LD students: **Yes**
Program: Remedial: **Yes**
Program: Reinforces course work: **Yes**
Students mainstreamed **100** % of the day
Recommended credits per semester: **12**
Services available for all students: **Yes**
Counseling: Individual: **Yes** Vocational Counseling: **Yes**
Support groups are available:**Yes, LD support group**

Faculty:
Faculty: **1** Part time: **1**
LD faculty with: BS/BA: **1**
Faculty advocate: **Yes** Meets with instructor: **As requested**

Diagnostic Testing
ADD	Personality	Perceptual skills	• Spelling
ADHD	Organization	Fine motor skills	• Reading
I.Q.	Handwriting	Spoken language	• Study skills
• Math	Social skills	• Written language	

Tutoring:
Average size of group tutorials: **1**
Services rendered by:
Graduates •Peers •Faculty •LD staff Teacher trainees

Tutorials
Grp.	Ind.	Tutorials	Grp.	Ind.	Tutorials
	•	Math skills		•	Word processing
	•	Study skills		•	Time management
	•	Language arts		•	Learning strategies
	•	Written express		•	Organizational skills

Academic Accommodations

Curriculum	Study Aids	Exams
Priority registration	• Typist	• Oral
Math waiver	• Reader	• Untimed
Foreign lang. waiver	• Notetaker	• Take home
Course substitution	• Proof reader	• With proctor
In Class	• Text on tape	On computer
• Calculators	Early syllabus	• Extended time
• Tape recorder	Taped handouts	On tape
• Word processor		• Modified
• Priority seating		• Separate room

Graduation Requirements:
Course credits: **93** GPA: **2.0** Years to complete degree: **As needed**

Program Strengths

Learning disabled students are mainstreamed into all aspects of college life. Accommodation is made on an individual basis according to the "what works" method. The faculty is generally anxious to accommodate individual learning styles and to try anything that is reasonable. The Coordinator of Special Needs is learning disabled herself, so she has many experiences of her own to draw upon.

General Information:

Centralia College is a 2 year public college. Rural campus of 3 acres is 85 miles from Seattle. Accessible by train or bus. Ski areas are 50 miles from campus. Beaches are 85 miles from campus. Housing is not guaranteed.

Accreditation:NACS, SBCCE, SAATV, U.S. DOE

Expenses:
Tuition: In-state: Full year: $945.00. Part-time: Per credit:$31.50. Tuition: Out-of-state: Full year: $3,717.00. Part-time: Per credit:$123.90.

Majors

• ARTS Art History, Commercial Art, Dramatic Arts, Graphic Arts, Music Performance • BUSINESS Accounting, Bookkeeping, Business Administration, Business Education, Business Management, Clerical, Data Processing, Education, Marketing, Secretarial Science • COMMUNICATIONS Broadcasting, Communication, English, Graphic Design, Television/Radio/Film • EDUCATION Adult, General • ENGINEERING Engineering Science, General • HEALTH SCIENCES Medical Assistant, Nursing • HUMANITIES English/Writing/Literature, Fine Arts, Humanities, Liberal Arts , Philosophy • LANGUAGES German, Spanish • MATHEMATICS Applied, General, Theoretical • PREPROFESSIONAL Agriculture, Business, Dentistry, Engineering, Fisheries, Forestry, Law, Medicine, Natural Resources, Optometry, Pharmacy, Recreation, Social Work, Sports Medicine, Veterinarian, Wildlife • SCIENCES Anatomy, Applied Mathematics, Biology, Botany, Chemistry, General, Geology, Human Biology, Inorganic

Chemistry, Mathematics, Microbiology, Natural Science, Organic Chemistry, Zoology • SOCIAL SCIENCES Geography, History, Political Science, Psychology, Social Sciences, Sociology • VISUAL AND PERFORMING ARTS Art, Art History, Dramatic Arts, Fine Arts, Music, Theater • VOCATIONAL Diesel Power Technology, Electronics Technology, Forestry, Legal Secretary, Office Administration, Secretarial, Welding, Word Processing

Sports/Activities

• SPORTS-INTERCOLLEGIATE Baseball (M), Basketball (F), Basketball (M), Volleyball (F) • STUDENT LIFE ACTIVITIES Academic Clubs, Choral, Concert Band, Jazz Band, Music Groups, Newspaper, Radio/TV station, Student Government

---

Less Selective   **Washington Services**

Columbia Basin College

2600 North 20th Avenue
Pasco, Washington 99301
(509) 547-0511

School Enrollment: **6,640**
LD Enrollment: **112**

Admissions Contact: **Dr. John O. Startzel, Associate Dean**
LD Contact: **Peggy Buchmiller, Cord., Education Access Serv.**
Name of Program: **Educational Access Services**
Address: **Hawk Union Building**
Telephone:**(509) 547-0511 Ext. 252**

Admissions

Application Information:
Separate application:**Yes**
Application deadline: **August 1st**
Applicant must apply **2-3** months in advance

Secondary School Information
Most Important Criteria For Admissions (1-strongest)

SAT/ACT	Application	School transcript
Class rank	Course selection	Personal statement
Interview	Extra activities	Psychoeducational
G.P.A.	**1** Open admission	Recommendations

Test Requirements:
Diagnostic testing waived: **Yes**
Documentation of LD required: **Yes**
Currency of diagnostic testing: **within last 4 years**
Tests recommended: **Diagnosis from a Ph.D. certified in diagnosing learning disabilities.**

Types of Disabilities Served
• Speech/Lang   • Reading   • ADD with LD
• Study skills   • Spelling   • ADD without LD
• Written express   • Math   • ADHD with LD
• Organizational   • Fine Motor   • ADHD without LD
• Perceptual

Admissions Process

1) Contact Coordinator of EAS for interview, 2) Supply documentation of disability, 3) Take Asset Test (placement test).

Learning Disability Program

Special orientation for LD students: **Yes**
Program: Reinforces course work: **Yes**
Recommended credits per semester: **6-8 per quarter**
Time required or recommended in learning center: **Varies**
Counseling: Individual: **Yes** Vocational Counseling: **Yes**

Faculty:
Faculty: **1** Including Director: **Yes** Full time: **1**
LD faculty with: BS/BA: **1**
Faculty advocate: **Yes** Meets with instructor: **On demand**

Diagnostic Testing
ADD	Personality	• Perceptual skills	• Spelling
ADHD	Organization	Fine motor skills	• Reading
I.Q.	Handwriting	• Spoken language	Study skills
• Math	Social skills	• Written language	

Tutoring:
Services rendered by:
Graduates •Peers •Faculty •LD staff Teacher trainees

Tutorials
Grp.	Ind.	Tutorials	Grp.	Ind.	Tutorials
	•	Math skills		•	Word processing
	•	Study skills	•		Time management
	•	Language arts	•		Learning strategies
	•	Written express	•		Organizational skills

Academic Accommodations

Curriculum	Study Aids	Exams
• Priority registration	Typist	• Oral
Math waiver	• Reader	Untimed
Foreign lang. waiver	• Notetaker	Take home
• Course substitution	• Proof reader	• With proctor
In Class	• Text on tape	• On computer
• Calculators	Early syllabus	• Extended time
• Tape recorder	Taped handouts	• On tape
• Word processor		• Modified
Priority seating		• Separate room

Graduation Requirements:GPA: **2.0** Years to complete degree: **2+** Math waiver: **Yes** Language waiver: **Yes**

Program Strengths

Columbia Basin College's Educational Access Services provide assistance to ensure education opportunities for persons of disability. It serves individuals with learning disabilities or visual impairment as well as students who are deaf or physically challenged. Depending on needs, the following standard services are available: taped books, enlarged reprints of reference material, note takers, sign language interpreters, tutor referral, examination access, and use of auxiliary learning aids, such as a tone indexer tape recorder, closed circuit reading monitors and a reading machine. It is recognized there may be needs which are not addressed by standard access services. The Coordinator will be available on a one-half time basis to assist students with special needs.

General Information:

Columbia Basin College is a 2 year public college. Suburban campus 140 miles from Spokane. Accessible by air, train, or bus. Ski areas are 75 miles from campus. Beaches are 5 miles from campus. Housing is not guaranteed.

Accreditation: Regional

Expenses:
Tuition: In-state: Full year: $969.00. Part-time: Per credit:$31.50. Tuition:

Out-of-state: Full year: $3,741.00. Part-time: Per credit:$123.90.

Majors

• BUSINESS Accounting, Agricultural, Business Administration, Business Data Programming, Economics, Management, Marketing, Real Estate • COMMUNICATIONS English, Journalism, Television/Radio/Film • COMPUTER SCIENCE Computer Science, Computer Technology, Data Processing • CRAFTS AND DESIGN Graphic Art Technology • EDUCATION Early Childhood, Elementary, Health, Physical, Secondary, Special • ENGINEERING Civil/Environmental, Electrical, Engineering Science, Mechanical • HEALTH SCIENCES Medical Technology, Nursing, Practical Nursing • HUMANITIES Liberal Arts, Philosophy • LANGUAGES Foreign Language • PREPROFESSIONAL Agriculture, Architecture, Chiropractic, Dentistry, Engineering, Forestry, Law, Medicine, Ministry, Natural Resources, Optometry, Pharmacy, Recreation, Social Work, Veterinarian • SCIENCES Biology, Chemistry, General, Mathematics, Physical Science • SOCIAL SCIENCES Criminal Justice, History, Law Enforcement, Public Relations, Sociology • VISUAL AND PERFORMING ARTS Art, Dramatic Arts, Fine Arts, Music • VOCATIONAL Agricultural Production, Auto Body, Automobile Technology, Automotive Service, Business and Office, Carpentry, Diesel Power Technology, Drafting, Electronics Technology, Fire Science, Hazardous Materials Technology, Home Economics, Industrial Technology, Instrumentation Technology, Landscape Architecture, Machine Technology, Machine Tool Operation, Non-Destructive Evaluation, Nuclear Technology, Paralegal, Welding

Sports/Activities

• SPORTS RELATED Pep Band • SPORTS-INTERCOLLEGIATE Baseball (M), Basketball, Golf (M), Tennis, Volleyball (F) • SPORTS-INTRA-MURAL Basketball, Bowling, Softball, Volleyball • STUDENT LIFE ACTIVITIES Choral, Concert Band, Drama Groups, Jazz Band, Music Groups, Musical Theater, Newspaper, Student Government

Very Selective   **Washington Services**

Evergreen State College

Olympia, Washington 98505
(206) 866-6000

School Enrollment: **3,340** Male: **1,438** Female: **1,902**

Admissions Contact: **Doug Scrima, Ast. to Dean for Admissions**
LD Contact: **Linda Murphy, Access Coordinator**
Name of Program: **Affirmative Action**
Telephone:**Ext. 6368**

Admissions

Application Information:
Application deadline: **March 1st**
Notified when: **April 1st**

Secondary School Information
Most Important Criteria For Admissions (1-strongest)

1 SAT/ACT	1 Application	1	School transcript
1 Class rank	1 Course selection		Personal statement
Interview	1 Extra activities		Psychoeducational
1 G.P.A.	Open admission		Recommendations

Test Requirements:
Untimed SAT: **Yes** Untimed ACT: **Yes**

Types of Disabilities Served

Speech/Lang	Reading	ADD with LD
Study skills	Spelling	ADD without LD
Written express	Math	ADHD with LD
Organizational	Fine Motor	ADHD without LD
Perceptual		

High School Course Requirements:
English: **8** Math: **3** Science: **2** Foreign Language: **2**

Learning Disability Program
Program: Reinforces course work: **Yes**
Students mainstreamed **100** % of the day

Faculty:
Faculty: **2** Full time: **2**
LD faculty with: BS/BA: **1** Ph.D.: **1**
Faculty advocate: **Yes** Meets with instructor: **As needed**

Diagnostic Testing

ADD	Personality	Perceptual skills	Spelling
ADHD	Organization	Fine motor skills	Reading
I.Q.	Handwriting	Spoken language	Study skills
Math	Social skills	Written language	

Services rendered by:

Graduates	Peers	Faculty	LD staff	Teacher trainees

Tutorials

Grp.	Ind.	Tutorials	Grp.	Ind.	Tutorials
	•	Math skills		•	Word processing
	•	Study skills		•	Time management
	•	Language arts		•	Learning strategies
	•	Written express		•	Organizational skills

Academic Accommodations

Curriculum	Study Aids	Exams
Priority registration	• Typist	• Oral
Math waiver	Reader	Untimed
Foreign lang. waiver	• Notetaker	• Take home
Course substitution	• Proof reader	• With proctor
In Class	• Text on tape	On computer
• Calculators	Early syllabus	• Extended time
• Tape recorder	Taped handouts	On tape
• Word processor		• Modified
Priority seating		Separate room

Graduation Requirements:
Course credits: **180** Years to complete degree: **4**

Program Strengths
Fundamental to our approach in assisting students with learning disabilities: 1.) Based on reasonable accommodation; 2.) Design based on individual interview and student self-monitoring; 3.) Focus is on student's independence; 4.) We do not change standards for academic achievement but we can adjust the ways of meeting those standards.

General Information:
Evergreen State College is a 4 year public college. Rural campus of 1,000 acres is 5 miles from Olympia. Accessible by bus. Ski areas are 60 miles from campus. Beaches are 60 miles from campus. 1% of students are foreign. 18 residential halls on campus. Housing is not guaranteed.35 % of students remain on campus for the weekends.

Accreditation:NWACS

SAT/ACT Scores:
Scores for incoming freshmen:**Verbal:**40%below 500. 34%between 500 and 599. 23%between 600 and 699. 3%above 700. **Math:**39% below 500. 40% between 500 and 599. 17% between 600 and 699. 4%above 700.

Class Rank:
80% were in the top 40% of their class. 20% were in the top 60% of their class.

Expenses:
Tuition: In-state: Full year: $1,785.00. Part-time: Per credit:$59.50. Tuition: Out-of-state: Full year: $6,297.00. Part-time: Per credit:$209.90. Room and board: $4,000.00

Majors
• AREA STUDIES African, American, Asian, Black/Afro-American, European, Latin American, Russian/Slavic, Women's Studies • BUSINESS Agricultural, Business Administration, Business Management, Economics, Management, Marketing, Personnel • COMMUNICATIONS Broadcasting, Communication, Creative Writing, English, Journalism, Photography, Television/Radio/Film • COMPUTER SCIENCE Computer Maintenance, Programming, Systems Analysis • CRAFTS AND DESIGN Environmental Design • EDUCATION Art, Elementary, Middle School, Secondary • ENGINEERING Aerospace, Chemical, Civil/Environmental, Communication, Electrical, Mathematical • HEALTH SCIENCES Environmental, Health, Nutritional/Food • HUMANITIES Classics, English/Writing/Literature, Humanities, Liberal Arts, Philosophy, Religion • LANGUAGES Foreign, French, German, Greek, Italian, Japanese, Latin, Russian, Spanish • PREPROFESSIONAL Agriculture, Law, Medicine, Natural Resources, Social Work • SCIENCES Agricultural, Anatomy, Anthropology, Biochemistry, Biology, Cell Biology, Chemistry, Earth, Ecology, Environmental, Geography, Geology, Marine Biology, Mathematics, Microbiology, Molecular Biology, Oceanography, Physical Chemistry, Physical Science, Physics, Plant Psychology, Zoology • SOCIAL SCIENCES Anthropology, Counseling Psychology, Government/Political, History, Political Science, Psychology, Public Administration, Social Sciences, Sociology • VISUAL AND PERFORMING ARTS Art, Dance, Dramatic Arts, Music, Music History & Appreciation, Studio Art, Theater • VOCATIONAL City/Community/Regional Planning, Community Services, Park/Recreation

Sports
• SPORTS-INTERCOLLEGIATE Diving, Soccer, Swimming • SPORTS-INTRAMURAL Basketball, Crew, Cross Country, Fencing, Hand Ball, Ping-Pong, Racquetball, Sailing, Soccer, Swimming, Tennis, Volleyball • STUDENT LIFE ACTIVITIES Blue Grass Band, Choral, Dance, Drama Groups, Ethnic & Cultural Groups, Film, Jazz Band, Music Groups, Newspaper, Radio/TV station, Student Government

---

Less Selective   **Washington**

Lutheran Bible Institute of Seattle
4221 - 228th Avenue, S.E.
Issaquah, Washington 98027
(206) 392-0400

School Enrollment: **171** Male: **70** Female: **101**

Admissions Contact: **Beth Elness, Interim Director of Admissions**
LD Contact: **Rev. Robert Moylan, V.P. for Academic Affairs**
Name of Program: **Student Services**
Telephone:**(206) 392-0400**

Admissions

Application Information:
LD on admissions committee:**Yes**
Application deadline: **August 15th**
Rolling Admissions: **Yes**

Secondary School Information
Most Important Criteria For Admissions (1-strongest)

SAT/ACT	**1**	Application	**5** School transcript
Class rank		Course selection	Personal statement
Interview		Extra activities	Psychoeducational
4 G.P.A.		Open admission	**3** Recommendations

Test Requirements:
Standardized tests waived: **Yes**
Untimed SAT: **Yes** Untimed ACT: **Yes** Untimed ACH: **Yes**
Documentation of LD required: **Yes**

Types of Disabilities Served
Speech/Lang	Reading	ADD with LD
Study skills	Spelling	ADD without LD
Written express	Math	ADHD with LD
Organizational	Fine Motor	ADHD without LD
Perceptual		

Admissions Process

Personal application with brief essay, pastor's recommendation form, adult recommendation form, official transcripts.

Learning Disability Program
Students mainstreamed **100** % of the day
Recommended credits per semester: **12**
Time required or recommended in learning center: **Varies**
Services available for all students: **Yes**
Counseling: Individual: **Yes**

Faculty:
Faculty advocate: **Yes**

Diagnostic Testing
ADD •	Personality	Perceptual skills	Spelling
ADHD	Organization	Fine motor skills	Reading
I.Q.	Handwriting	Spoken language	Study skills
Math	Social skills	Written language	

Services rendered by:
Graduates	Peers	Faculty	LD staff	Teacher trainees

Tutorials
Grp.	Ind.	Tutorials	Grp.	Ind.	Tutorials
		Math skills			Word processing
		Study skills			Time management
		Language arts			Learning strategies
		Written express			Organizational skills

Academic Accommodations

Curriculum	Study Aids	Exams
Priority registration	Typist	• Oral
Math waiver	• Reader	• Untimed
Foreign lang. waiver	• Notetaker	Take home
Course substitution	Proof reader	With proctor
In Class	Text on tape	On computer
• Calculators	Early syllabus	• Extended time
• Tape recorder	Taped handouts	On tape
• Word processor		Modified
• Priority seating		Separate room

Graduation Requirements:
Course credits: **180** GPA: **2.0** Language waiver: **Yes**

General Information:
Lutheran Bible Institute of Seattle is a 2 and 4 year independent Lutheran college. Suburban campus of 40 acres is 18 miles from Seattle. Ski areas are 45 minutes from campus. Beaches are 3 miles from campus. 10% of students are foreign. 2 residential halls on campus. Housing is guaranteed.75 % of students remain on campus for the weekends.

Accreditation:NACS

Expenses:
Tuition: In-state: Full year: $2,000.00. Part-time: Per credit:$45.00. Tuition: Out-of-state: Full year: $2,00.00. Part-time: Per credit:$45.00. Room and board: $3,400.00

Majors
• EDUCATION Religious • RELIGIOUS STUDIES Bible, Missionary, Religion and Theology • SCIENCES Gerontology

Sports
• SPORTS-INTRAMURAL Band, Football, Flag, Golf, Softball, Tennis, Volleyball • STUDENT LIFE ACTIVITIES Community Service, Drama Groups, Film, Music Groups, Religious Organization, Student Government, Yearbook

---

Less Selective | **Washington Program**

Olympic College
1600 Chester Avenue
Bremerton, Washington 98310-1699
(206) 478-4504

School Enrollment: **8,000**
LD Enrollment: **35**
LD Contact: **Anna Hoey Dorsey, Program Manager**
Name of Program: **Supportive Services**
Telephone:**(206) 478-4607**

Admissions

Secondary School Information
Most Important Criteria For Admissions (1-strongest)

SAT/ACT	Application	School transcript
Class rank	Course selection	Personal statement
Interview	Extra activities	Psychoeducational
G.P.A.	**1** Open admission	Recommendations

Types of Disabilities Served
- Speech/Lang
- Study skills
- Written express
- Organizational
- Perceptual
- Reading
- Spelling
- Math
- Fine Motor
- ADD with LD
- ADD without LD
- ADHD with LD
- ADHD without LD

Learning Disability Program
Special orientation for LD students: **Yes**
Program: Reinforces course work: **Yes**
Students mainstreamed **100** % of the day
Counseling: Individual: **Yes**

Faculty:
Faculty: **3** Full time: **1** Part time: **2** M.A.: **1**

Diagnostic Testing

ADD	• Personality	• Perceptual skills	• Spelling
ADHD	• Organization	Fine motor skills	• Reading
I.Q.	Handwriting	Spoken language	• Study skills
• Math	Social skills	• Written language	

Tutoring:
Average size of group tutorials: **3-4**
Services rendered by:
Graduates • Peers • Faculty LD staff • Teacher trainees

Tutorials

Grp.	Ind.	Tutorials	Grp.	Ind.	Tutorials
	•	Math skills		•	Word processing
	•	Study skills		•	Time management
	•	Language arts		•	Learning strategies
	•	Written express		•	Organizational skills

Academic Accommodations

Curriculum	Study Aids	Exams
• Priority registration	• Typist	• Oral
Math waiver	• Reader	• Untimed
Foreign lang. waiver	• Notetaker	• Take home
• Course substitution	• Proof reader	• With proctor
In Class	• Text on tape	• On computer
• Calculators	Early syllabus	• Extended time
• Tape recorder	• Taped handouts	• On tape
• Word processor		• Modified
• Priority seating		Separate room

Graduation Requirements:Math waiver: **Yes** Language waiver: **Yes**

Program Strengths
Our program offers assistance to any student who is disadvantaged or handicapped. "Learning disability", as our definition words it, is a handicapping condition. We do not require psychological reports to verify that a student has a learning disability before he or she can enter our program. Students may come in and identify themselves or they may be referred by instructors or community agencies as perhaps having some learning disabilities.

General Information:
Olympic College is a 2 year public college. Urban campus of 21 acres is 85 miles from Seattle. Ski areas are 2 miles from campus. Beaches are 10-15 miles from campus. 1% of students are foreign. Housing is not guaranteed.

Accreditation: Regional

Expenses:
Tuition: In-state: Full year: $945.00. Part-time: Per credit:$63.00. Tuition: Out-of-state: Full year: $3,717.00. Part-time: Per credit:$248.00.

Majors

• BUSINESS Accounting, Banking, Business Administration, Business Data Programming, Business Economics, Business Education, Business Management, Economics, Finance, Insurance, Management, Marketing, Real Estate • COMMUNICATIONS Advertising, Communication, English, Journalism, Photography • COMPUTER SCIENCE Computer Science, Data Processing, Programming, Systems Analysis • EDUCATION Agricultural, Child Development, Early Childhood, General, Music, Psychology, Teacher Aid • ENGINEERING Computer, Engineering Science • HEALTH SCIENCES Health, Nursing • HUMANITIES English/Writing/Literature, Humanities, Liberal Arts, Philosophy • LANGUAGES French, German, Japanese, Russian, Spanish • PREPROFESSIONAL Engineering, Law • SCIENCES Anthropology, Astronomy, Biochemistry, Biology, Botany, Chemistry, Earth, Geography, Geology, Inorganic Chemistry, Macrobiology, Marine Biology, Mathematics, Microbiology, Oceanography, Organic Chemistry, Physical Chemistry, Physical Science, Physics, Statistics, Zoology • SOCIAL SCIENCES Anthropology, Criminal Justice, History, Law Enforcement, Political Science, Psychology, Social Sciences, Sociology • VISUAL AND PERFORMING ARTS Art, Music, Theater • VOCATIONAL Automobile Technology, Automotive Service, Business and Office, Construction, Culinary Arts, Electronics Technology, Fashion Merchandising, Fire Science, Legal Secretary, Medical Laboratory Technology, Secretarial, Welding

Sports/Activities

• SPORTS RELATED Pep Band • SPORTS-INTERCOLLEGIATE Baseball (M), Basketball, Softball (F), Volleyball (F) • STUDENT LIFE ACTIVITIES Choral, Concert Band, Drama Groups, Jazz Band, Musical Theater, Newspaper, Student Government, Symphony Orchestra

---

Less Selective　　　　**Washington**

Accommodations

Puget Sound Christian College

410 Fourth Avenue
Edmonds, Washington 98020-3171
(206) 775-8686

School Enrollment: 100 Male: **61** Female: **39**
LD Enrollment: 1 Male: **1**

Admissions Contact: **Delores Scarbrough, Admissions Officer**

Admissions

Application Information:
Rolling Admissions: **Yes**

Secondary School Information
Most Important Criteria For Admissions (1-strongest)

SAT/ACT **1**	Application **3**	School transcript
Class rank	Course selection	Personal statement
Interview	Extra activities	Psychoeducational
G.P.A.	Open admission **2**	Recommendations

Test Requirements:
Standardized tests waived: **Yes**
Untimed SAT: **Yes**

Types of Disabilities Served
• Speech/Lang	Reading	ADD with LD
• Study skills	Spelling	ADD without LD
• Written express	Math	ADHD with LD
Organizational	Fine Motor	ADHD without LD
Perceptual		

Admissions Process

Student submits application, receives Admission packet, submits three references, transcripts and medical questionnaire.

Diagnostic Testing
ADD	Personality	Perceptual skills	Spelling
ADHD	Organization	Fine motor skills	Reading
I.Q.	Handwriting	Spoken language	Study skills
Math	Social skills	Written language	

Services rendered by:
Graduates　　Peers　　Faculty　　LD staff　　Teacher trainees

Tutorials
Grp.	Ind.	Tutorials	Grp.	Ind.	Tutorials
		Math skills			Word processing
		Study skills			Time management
		Language arts			Learning strategies
		Written express			Organizational skills

Academic Accommodations

Curriculum	Study Aids	Exams
Priority registration	Typist	• Oral
Math waiver	Reader	Untimed
Foreign lang. waiver	Notetaker	• Take home
Course substitution	Proof reader	With proctor
In Class	Text on tape	On computer
Calculators	Early syllabus	• Extended time
• Tape recorder	Taped handouts	On tape
Word processor		Modified
Priority seating		Separate room

Graduation Requirements:
Course credits: **192** GPA: **2.0** Years to complete degree: **6**

Program Strengths
We offer individual help as needed, both from faculty and peers. We have a T.V. monitor for enlarging print for visually impaired.

General Information:
Puget Sound Christian College is a 4 year private Christian Church college. Suburban campus of 3.5 acres is 15 miles from Seattle. Accessible by plane, train or bus. Ski areas are 40 miles from campus. Beaches are 1 mile from campus. 1% of students are foreign. 1 residential halls on campus. Housing is guaranteed.25 % of students remain on campus for the weekends.

Accreditation: AABC

Expenses:
Tuition: In-state: Full year: $4,200.00. Part-time: Per credit:$140.00. Tuition: Out-of-state: Full year: $4,200.00. Part-time: Per credit:$140.00. Room and board: $3,000.00

Majors
• RELIGIOUS STUDIES Bible, Ministry & Church Administration, Religious Music

Sports/Activities

• SPORTS-INTERCOLLEGIATE Basketball (M) • SPORTS-INTRAMURAL Basketball (F) • STUDENT LIFE ACTIVITIES Choral, Drama Groups, Music Groups, Religious Organization, Student Government, Yearbook

Less Selective	Washington Services

Washington State University

342 French Administration Building
Pullman, Washington 99164
(509) 335-5586

School Enrollment: **14,589**
LD Enrollment: **80**

Admissions Contact: **Ms. Terry Flynn, Director of Admissions**
LD Contact: **Donna Wright**
Name of Program: **Disabled Student Services**
Telephone:**(509) 335-1566**

Admissions

Application Information:
Application deadline: **May 1st**

Secondary School Information
Most Important Criteria For Admissions (1-strongest)

1 SAT/ACT	Application	**1**	School transcript
Class rank	**1** Course selection		Personal statement
Interview	Extra activities		Psychoeducational
1 G.P.A.	Open admission	**2**	Recommendations

Test Requirements:
Diagnostic testing waived: **Yes**
Untimed SAT: **Yes** Untimed ACT: **Yes**
WAIS-R required: **Yes**
Documentation of LD required: **Yes**

Types of Disabilities Served
• Speech/Lang • Reading • ADD with LD
• Study skills • Spelling • ADD without LD
• Written express • Math • ADHD with LD
• Organizational Fine Motor • ADHD without LD
• Perceptual

Learning Disability Program

Counseling: Individual: **Yes** Group Counseling: **Yes**

Faculty:
Faculty: **3** Full time: **2** Part time: **1**
Faculty advocate: **Yes** Meets with instructor: **As needed**

Diagnostic Testing
ADD	Personality	Perceptual skills	Spelling
ADHD	Organization	Fine motor skills	Reading
I.Q.	Handwriting	Spoken language	Study skills
Math	Social skills	Written language	

Tutoring:
Average size of group tutorials: **4-5**
Services rendered by:
•Graduates   Peers   •Faculty   •LD staff   Teacher trainees

Tutorials

Grp.	Ind.	Tutorials	Grp.	Ind.	Tutorials
•	•	Math skills			Word processing
•	•	Study skills	•	•	Time management
	•	Language arts	•	•	Learning strategies
•	•	Written express	•	•	Organizational skills

Academic Accommodations

Curriculum	Study Aids	Exams
Priority registration	Typist	• Oral
Math waiver	Reader	Untimed
• Foreign lang. waiver	• Notetaker	Take home
• Course substitution	• Proof reader	With proctor
In Class	• Text on tape	On computer
Calculators	Early syllabus	• Extended time
Tape recorder	Taped handouts	On tape
• Word processor		• Modified
Priority seating		Separate room

General Information:

Washington State University is a 4 year public university. Rural campus of 620 acres is 80 miles from Spokane. Accessible by air or bus. Ski areas are 45 from campus. Beaches are 45 from campus. 6% of students are foreign. 2 residential halls on campus. Housing is guaranteed.80 % of students remain on campus for the weekends. 20 % of students join fraternities/sororities.

Accreditation:NWACS

Expenses:
Tuition: In-state: Full year: $1,954.00. Part-time: Per credit:$98.00. Tuition: Out-of-state: Full year: $5,434.00. Part-time: Per credit:$272.00. Room and board: $3,120.00

Majors

• AREA STUDIES American, Asian, Black/Afro-American, Mexican/American • BUSINESS Accounting, Agricultural, Banking, Business Administration, Business Economics, Business Management, Business Statistics, Economics, Finance, Hotel and Restaurant Management, Insurance, International Business, Management, Marketing, Marketing Research, Personnel, Real Estate • COMMUNICATIONS Advertising, Broadcasting, Communication, English, Journalism, Photography, Public Relations, Speech, Television/Radio/Film • COMPUTER SCIENCE Computer Science • EDUCATION Agricultural, Art, Bilingual, Early Childhood, Elementary, English, Foreign Language, Health, Home Economics, Mathematics, Music, Physical, Reading, School Psychology, Science, Secondary, Social Studies, Special, Speech/Language, Theater, Vocational • ENGINEERING Agricultural, Architectural, Chemical, Civil/Environmental, Communications, Computer, Electrical, Engineering Science, Environmental Health, Geological, Materials, Mechanical, Metallurgical, Resources • HEALTH SCIENCES Communication Disorders, Environmental, Human Environment and Housing, Nursing, Nutritional/Food, Physical Therapy, Speech Therapy, Speech/Audiology and Speech • HUMANITIES Humanities, Liberal Arts, Philosophy, Religion • LANGUAGES Foreign, French, German, Russian, Spanish • PREPROFESSIONAL Architecture, Dentistry, Law, Medicine, Pharmacy, Range Management, Social Work, Veterinarian, Wildlife • SCIENCES Agricultural, Agronomy, Animal, Bacteriology, Biochemistry, Biology, Chemistry, Entomology, Environmental, Geology, Horticultural, Mathematics, Microbiology, Physical Science, Physics, Public Health, Soil, Zoology • SOCIAL SCIENCES Anthropology, Criminal Justice, Government/Political, History, Law Enforcement, Political Science, Psychology, Public Relations, Social Sciences, Sociology • VISUAL AND PERFORMING ARTS Art, Fine Arts, Music, Theater • VOCATIONAL Food Science, Forestry, Home Economics, Interior Design, Landscape Architecture, Operations Research, Park/Recreation, Textile and Clothing

Sports/Activities

• SPORTS RELATED Marching Band, Pep Band • SPORTS-INTERCOLLEGIATE Baseball (M), Basketball, Cross Country, Diving (F), Football (M), Golf, Swimming (F), Tennis, Track and Field, Volleyball (F) • SPORTS-INTRAMURAL Badminton, Basketball, Bowling, Crew, Cross Country, Golf, Hand Ball, Lacrosse (M), Ping-Pong, Racquetball, Riflery, Rugby, Skiing - Snow, Soccer, Softball, Swimming, Synchronized Swimming, Tennis, Track and Field, Volleyball, Water Polo, Wrestling (M) • STUDENT LIFE ACTIVITIES Academic Clubs, Choral, Community Service, Concert Band, Dance, Drama Groups, Ethnic & Cultural Groups, Fraternities, Jazz Band, Magazine, Music Groups, Musical Theater, Newspaper, Opera, Political Groups, Radio/TV station, Religious Organization, Sororities, Student Government, Symphony Orchestra, Yearbook

---

Less Selective **Washington**
Services

Wenatchee Valley College

1300 Fifth Avenue
Wenatchee, Washington 98801
(509) 662-1651

School Enrollment: **3,387**

Admissions Contact: **Marlene Sinko, Registrar**
LD Contact: **Sharon A. Martin, Coordinator**
Name of Program: **Special Services**

Admissions

Secondary School Information
Most Important Criteria For Admissions (1-strongest)

SAT/ACT **1**	Application	School transcript
Class rank	Course selection	Personal statement
Interview	Extra activities	Psychoeducational
G.P.A.	Open admission	Recommendations

Types of Disabilities Served
• Speech/Lang • Reading • ADD with LD
• Study skills • Spelling • ADD without LD
• Written express • Math • ADHD with LD
• Organizational • Fine Motor • ADHD without LD
• Perceptual

Learning Disability Program

Counseling: Individual: **Yes**

Faculty:
Faculty: **1** Full time: **1**
Faculty advocate: **Yes** Meets with instructor: **Upon request**

Diagnostic Testing

ADD	Personality	Perceptual skills	Spelling
ADHD	Organization	Fine motor skills	Reading
I.Q.	Handwriting	Spoken language	Study skills
Math	Social skills	Written language	

Tutoring:
Services rendered by:
Graduates •Peers •Faculty •LD staff Teacher trainees

Tutorials

Grp.	Ind.	Tutorials	Grp.	Ind.	Tutorials
•		Math skills	•		Word processing
•		Study skills	•		Time management
•		Language arts	•		Learning strategies
•		Written express	•		Organizational skills

Academic Accommodations

Curriculum	Study Aids	Exams
Priority registration	• Typist	• Oral
Math waiver	Reader	Untimed
Foreign lang. waiver	• Notetaker	Take home
• Course substitution	• Proof reader	• With proctor
In Class	• Text on tape	On computer
• Calculators	Early syllabus	• Extended time
• Tape recorder	Taped handouts	On tape
• Word processor		• Modified
Priority seating		Separate room

Program Strengths

We do not have a formal program. We offer services to the LD student (and to other handicapped students). We attempt to help the student obtain an education in spite of learning disabilities by taping books, giving extended time, advocating and counseling.

General Information:

Wenatchee Valley College is a 2 year public college. Suburban campus of 35 acres is 140 miles from Seattle. Ski areas are 30 minutes from campus. Beaches are 4 hours from campus. 1 residential halls on campus. Housing is not guaranteed.

Accreditation:NWACS

Expenses:
Tuition: In-state: Full year: $822.00. Part-time: Per credit:$27.40. Tuition: Out-of-state: Full year: $3,234.00. Part-time: Per credit:$107.80. Room and board: $2,875.00

Majors

• BUSINESS Accounting, Agricultural, Business Administration, Business Education, Business Management, Marketing, Sports Management • COMMUNICATIONS Communication, Creative Writing, English, Speech, Technical and Business Writing • COMPUTER SCIENCE Computer Science, Data Processing, Medical Records Technology • EDUCATION Early Childhood, General, Teacher Aide • ENGINEERING Computer • HEALTH SCIENCES Chiropractic, Community Services, Medical Secretary, Medical Technology, Nursing, Physical Therapy, Radiograph Medical Technology, Radiological Therapy • HUMANITIES Humanities, Liberal Arts • LANGUAGES Spanish • PREPROFESSIONAL Agriculture, Dentistry, Forestry, Law, Medicine, Pharmacy, Recreation, Veterinarian • SCIENCES Agricultural, Biology, Chemistry, Mathematics, Physical Science, Radiology • SOCIAL SCIENCES History, Political Science, Psychology, Social Sciences, Sociology • VISUAL AND PERFORMING ARTS Drawing, Music, Music Performance, Studio Art, Theater, Visual and Performing Arts • VOCATIONAL Air Conditioning/Heating/Refri, Automobile Technology, Business and Office, Carpentry, Fire Science, Legal Secretary, Medical Laboratory Technology, Painting, Printing/Lithography, Secretarial, Welding

Sports/Activities

• SPORTS-INTERCOLLEGIATE Basketball, Skiing - Snow, Softball (F) • SPORTS-INTRAMURAL Basketball, Ping-Pong, Skiing - Snow, Soccer, Softball, Tennis, Volleyball • STUDENT LIFE ACTIVITIES Concert Band, Ethnic & Cultural Groups, Jazz Band, Music Groups, Newspaper, Radio/TV station, Student Government, Symphony Orchestra

Selective

Washington
Services

Whitworth College

Spokane, Washington 99251
(509) 466-3212

School Enrollment: **1,500** Male: **600** Female: **900**
LD Contact: **Gail Berg**

Admissions

Application Information:
Application deadline: **March 1st**
Rolling Admissions: **Yes**

Secondary School Information
Most Important Criteria For Admissions (1-strongest)

5 SAT/ACT	**2** Application	**1** School transcript
4 Class rank	**1** Course selection	**6** Personal statement
4 Interview	**5** Extra activities	**6** Psychoeducational
1 G.P.A.	Open admission	**4** Recommendations

Test Requirements:
Untimed SAT: **Yes** Untimed ACT: **Yes**

Types of Disabilities Served
- Speech/Lang
- Study skills
- Written express
- Organizational Perceptual
- Reading
- Spelling
- Math
- Fine Motor
- ADD with LD
- ADD without LD
- ADHD with LD
- ADHD without LD

Learning Disability Program
Counseling: Individual: **Yes**

Faculty:
Faculty: **1** Full time: **1**

Diagnostic Testing

ADD	Personality	Perceptual skills	Spelling
ADHD	Organization	Fine motor skills	Reading
I.Q.	Handwriting	Spoken language	Study skills
Math	Social skills	Written language	

Services rendered by:
Graduates   Peers   Faculty   LD staff   Teacher trainees

Tutorials

Grp.	Ind.	Tutorials	Grp.	Ind.	Tutorials
		Math skills			Word processing
		Study skills			Time management
		Language arts			Learning strategies
		Written express			Organizational skills

Academic Accommodations

Curriculum	Study Aids	Exams
Priority registration	Typist	• Oral
Math waiver	Reader	Untimed
Foreign lang. waiver	• Notetaker	Take home
Course substitution	• Proof reader	With proctor
In Class	• Text on tape	On computer
Calculators	Early syllabus	• Extended time
• Tape recorder	Taped handouts	On tape
• Word processor		Modified
Priority seating		Separate room

Program Strengths
The Whitworth College campus enrolls many students with some type of barrier to learning. It is part of the goal of Student Life to provide services and resources that will allow each student to pursue his or her education in the best manner possible.

General Information:
Whitworth College is a 4 year private Presbyterian college. Suburban campus of 200 acres is 300 miles from Seattle. Accessible by air, train or bus. Ski areas are 30 minutes from campus. Beaches are 5 hours from campus. 120 residential halls on campus. Housing is guaranteed.Guaranteed through 4th year. 90 % of students remain on campus for the weekends.

Accreditation:NASM, NCATE

SAT/ACT Scores:
Scores for incoming freshmen:**Verbal:**25%below 500. 75%between 500 and 599. **Math:**25% below 500. 75% between 500 and 599. **ACT:** 25% below 20. 75%between 24 and 25l.

Class Rank:
About 42% of the present freshmen class were in the upper 20% of their high school class. 76% were in the top 40% of their class. 92% were in the top 60% of their class. 99% were in the top 80% of their class.

Expenses:
Tuition: In-state: Full year: $9,200.00. Room and board: $3,700.00

Majors
• AREA STUDIES American, Peace • BUSINESS Accounting, Business Administration, Business Economics, Business Management, Economics, Finance, International Business, Management, Marketing • COMMUNICATIONS Advertising, Broadcasting, Communication, Creative Writing, English, Journalism • COMPUTER SCIENCE Computer Science, Programming • EDUCATION Art, Elementary, Health, Middle School, Music, Physical, Secondary • HEALTH SCIENCES Nursing • HUMANITIES English/Writing/Literature, Philosophy, Religion, Religious Studies • LANGUAGES Chinese, French, German, Italian, Japanese, Russian, Spanish • PREPROFESSIONAL Architecture, Dentistry, Forestry, Law, Medicine, Ministry, Pharmacy, Recreation, Social Work • SCIENCES Astronomy, Biochemistry, Biology, Botany, Chemistry, Earth, Geology, Health, Macrobiology, Mathematics, Physical Science, Physics • SOCIAL SCIENCES Government/Political, History, International Relations, Political Science, Psychology, Public Policy, Public Relations, Sociology • VISUAL AND PERFORMING ARTS Art, Art History, Art Management, Dramatic Arts, Music, Religious Music, Studio Art, Theater • VOCATIONAL Park/Recreation

Sports/Activities
• SPORTS-INTERCOLLEGIATE Baseball (M), Basketball, Cross Country, Diving, Football (M), Soccer, Swimming, Tennis, Track and Field, Volleyball (F) • SPORTS-INTRAMURAL Basketball, Football, Lacrosse (M), Ping-Pong, Rugby (M), Skiing - Snow, Soccer, Softball, Tennis, Volleyball, Water Polo • STUDENT LIFE ACTIVITIES Choral, Concert Band, Dance, Drama Groups, Ethnic & Cultural Groups, Film, Jazz Band, Magazine, Music Groups, Musical Theater, Newspaper, Political Groups, Radio/TV sta-

tion, Religious Organization, Student Government, Symphony Orchestra, Yearbook

---

Less Selective

Bluefield State College
219 Rock Street
Bluefield, West Virginia 24701
(304) 327-4000

School Enrollment: **2,487** Male: **1,422** Female: **1,065**
LD Contact: **Dr. Claudius Oni, Director**
Name of Program: **Student Support Services**
Telephone:**(304) 327-4098**

Admissions

Application Information:
Application deadline: **None**
Rolling Admissions: **Yes**

Secondary School Information
Most Important Criteria For Admissions (1-strongest)

2	SAT/ACT	**1**	Application	**3** School transcript
	Class rank	**2**	Course selection	Personal statement
	Interview	**5**	Extra activities	Psychoeducational
4	G.P.A.		Open admission	Recommendations

Test Requirements:
Diagnostic testing waived: **Yes**
Untimed SAT: **Yes** Untimed ACT: **Yes**
Documentation of LD required: **Yes**
Currency of diagnostic testing: **As soon as possible**

Types of Disabilities Served
- Speech/Lang
- Study skills
- Written express
- Organizational
- Perceptual
- Reading
- Spelling
- Math
- Fine Motor

ADD with LD
ADD without LD
ADHD with LD
ADHD without LD

High School Course Requirements:
English: **4** Math: **2** Science: **2**

Learning Disability Program
Services available for all students: **Yes**
Counseling: Individual: **Yes** Group Counseling: **Yes**

Faculty:
Faculty: **4** Including Director: **Yes** Full time: **1** Part time: **3**
Faculty advocate: **Yes** Meets with instructor: **As needed**

Diagnostic Testing

ADD	• Personality	Perceptual skills	• Spelling
ADHD	Organization	Fine motor skills	• Reading
I.Q.	Handwriting	Spoken language	• Study skills
• Math	Social skills	Written language	

Tutoring:
Average size of group tutorials: **3**
Services rendered by:
  Graduates • Peers • Faculty • LD staff • Teacher trainees

Tutorials

Grp.	Ind.	Tutorials	Grp.	Ind.	Tutorials
	•	Math skills		•	Word processing
•	•	Study skills	•	•	Time management
•	•	Language arts	•	•	Learning strategies
•	•	Written express	•	•	Organizational skills

Academic Accommodations

Curriculum	Study Aids	Exams
Priority registration	• Typist	• Oral
Math waiver	Reader	Untimed
Foreign lang. waiver	• Notetaker	• Take home
• Course substitution	• Proof reader	• With proctor
In Class	• Text on tape	On computer
• Calculators	Early syllabus	Extended time
• Tape recorder	Taped handouts	On tape
Word processor		• Modified
Priority seating		Separate room

Graduation Requirements:
Course credits: **128** GPA: **2.0** Years to complete degree: **4**

General Information:
Bluefield State College is a 2 and 4 year public college. Rural campus 90 miles from Charleston. Accessible by air or bus. Ski areas are 25 miles from campus. Beaches are 200 miles from campus. 3% of students are foreign. Housing is not guaranteed.10 % of students join fraternities/sororities.

Accreditation:NCACS, pending NCATE

Expenses:
Tuition: In-state: Full year: $600.00. Tuition: Out-of-state: Full year: $1,700.00.

Majors
• BUSINESS Accounting, Business Administration, Business Economics, Business Education, Business Management, Finance, Management, Marketing, Real Estate • COMMUNICATIONS English, Photography, Television/Radio/Film • COMPUTER SCIENCE Computer Science, Computer Technology, Data Processing, Programming • CRAFTS AND DESIGN Graphic Design • EDUCATION Early Childhood, Education of the Mentally Hand, Elementary, English, Mathematics, Middle School, Physical, Recreation and Youth Leadership, Science, Secondary, Social Studies • ENGINEERING Civil/Environmental, Computer, Electrical, Petroleum • HEALTH SCIENCES Dental Hygiene, Dental Technician, Nursing, Nursing Assistant, Practical Nursing, Radiograph Medical Technology, Radiological Therapy • HUMANITIES Liberal Arts • PREPROFESSIONAL Engineering, Law, Legal Assistant, Medicine, Recreation, Social Work • SCIENCES Agricultural, Animal, Biology, Botany, Chemistry, Mathematics, Physical Science, Physics • SOCIAL SCIENCES Criminal Justice, Government/Political, History, Law Enforcement, Social Sciences • VOCATIONAL Architectural Technology, Culinary Arts, Drafting, Mechanical Design, Office Administration, Park/Recreation, Respiratory Therapy Technology, Secretarial

Sports/Activities
• SPORTS RELATED Cheerleading, Chess, Pep Band • SPORTS-INTERCOLLEGIATE Baseball (M), Basketball, Golf, Softball (F) • SPORTS-INTRAMURAL Badminton, Ping-Pong, Soccer (M), Swimming, Tennis, Volleyball, Water Polo • STUDENT LIFE ACTIVITIES Choral, Fraternities, Jazz Band, Magazine, Newspaper, Radio/TV station, Sororities, Student Government, Yearbook

Davis and Elkins College
304 Albert Hall
Elkins, West Virginia 26241
(304) 636-1900

School Enrollment: **855** Male: **385** Female: **470**
LD Enrollment: **72**

Admissions Contact: **Kevin Chenoweth, Admissions Director**
LD Contact: **Dr. Margaret Turner, Director**
Name of Program: **LD Special Services**
Telephone:**(304) 636-1900 Ext. 384**

Admissions

Application Information:
LD Students Applying: **300** Accepted: **30** Enrolled:**72**
Applicant must apply **12** months in advance
Rolling Admissions: **Yes**

Secondary School Information
Most Important Criteria For Admissions (1-strongest)

SAT/ACT	**1**	Application	**1**	School transcript
Class rank	**1**	Course selection	**5**	Personal statement
1 Interview	**5**	Extra activities	**1**	Psychoeducational
1 G.P.A.		Open admission	**1**	Recommendations

Test Requirements:
Standardized tests waived: **Yes**
Diagnostic testing waived: **Yes**
Documentation of LD required: **Yes**
Tests recommended: **WAIS-R**

Types of Disabilities Served
- Speech/Lang
- Study skills
- Written express
- Organizational
- Perceptual
- Reading
- Spelling
- Math
- Fine Motor
- ADD with LD
- ADD without LD
- ADHD with LD
- ADHD without LD

High School Course Requirements:
English: **4** Math: **3** Science: **3** Foreign Language: **2**

Learning Disability Program
Special orientation for LD students: **Yes**
Syllabus available during orientation:**Yes**
Program: Reinforces course work: **Yes**
Students mainstreamed **100** % of the day
Recommended credits per semester: **12-14**
Time required or recommended in learning center: **1 hour**
Services only for LD students: **Yes**
Counseling: Individual: **Yes**

Faculty:
Faculty: **5** Including Director: **Yes** Full time: **3** Part time: **2** M.A.: **3** Ph.D.: **2**
Faculty advocate: **Yes** Meets with instructor: **weekly**

Diagnostic Testing

ADD •	Personality	Perceptual skills	Spelling
ADHD•	Organization	Fine motor skills	Reading
I.Q.	Handwriting	Spoken language	• Study skills
Math	Social skills	Written language	

Tutoring:
Services rendered by:
Graduates •Peers •Faculty •LD staff Teacher trainees

Tutorials
Grp.	Ind.	Tutorials	Grp.	Ind.	Tutorials
	•	Math skills		•	Word processing
	•	Study skills		•	Time management
	•	Language arts		•	Learning strategies
	•	Written express		•	Organizational skills

Academic Accommodations

Curriculum	Study Aids	Exams
Priority registration	• Typist	• Oral
Math waiver	• Reader	• Untimed
Foreign lang. waiver	• Notetaker	Take home
• Course substitution	• Proof reader	• With proctor
In Class	• Text on tape	• On computer
• Calculators	Early syllabus	• Extended time
• Tape recorder	Taped handouts	On tape
• Word processor		• Modified
Priority seating		• Separate room

Graduation Requirements: Years to complete degree: **4-5**

Program Strengths
The LD Program at Davis and Elkins College is designed to meet the needs of the individual. The LD students meet at scheduled times weekly with the staff one-to-one. The courses are examined using the measured strengths and weaknesses of the individual, and a Student Program Plan is developed each semester.

General Information:
Davis and Elkins College is a 4 year private Presbyterian college. Rural campus of 170 acres is 150 miles from Pittsburgh. Accessible by air. Ski areas are 35 miles from campus. 2% of students are foreign. 5 residential halls on campus. Housing is guaranteed.100 % of students remain on campus for the weekends. 15 % of students join fraternities/sororities.

Accreditation:NCACS

SAT/ACT Scores:
Scores for incoming freshmen:**Verbal:**90%below 500. 8%between 500 and 599. 2%between 600 and 699. **Math:**78% below 500. 21% between 500 and 599. 1% between 600 and 699. **ACT:** 60% below 20. 31% between 20 and 23. 2%between 24 and 251. 7%between 26 and 28.

Expenses:
Tuition: In-state: Full year: $8,050.00. Part-time: Per credit:0. Tuition: Out-of-state: Full year: $8,050.00. Room and board: $3,930.00 Cost of LD program:$2,150.00 per year

Majors
• AREA STUDIES Appalachian Studies • BUSINESS Accounting, Banking, Business Administration, Business Data Processing, Business Economics, Business Education, Business Management, Economics, Hotel Management, International Business, Management, Marketing, Marketing Research, Personnel, Real Estate, Resort Management, Sports Management, Travel/Tourism Management • COMMUNICATIONS Communication, Creative Writing, English, Journalism, Literature, Television/Radio/Film • COMPUTER SCIENCE Computer Mathematics, Computer Sci-

ence, Data Processing, Programming • EDUCATION Art, Curriculum, Elementary, General, Health, Industrial, Middle School, Music, Music Therapy, Physical, Recreation and Youth Leadership, School Psychology, Secondary, Special, Speech/Language, Vocational • ENGINEERING Engineering Science • HEALTH SCIENCES Health Care Administration, Mental Health, Nursing, Occupational Therapy, Physical Therapy, Practical Nursing • HUMANITIES Humanities, Liberal Arts, Philosophy, Religion, Religious Studies • LANGUAGES French, German, Japanese, Spanish • PREPROFESSIONAL Dentistry, Engineering, Forestry, Law, Medicine, Ministry, Pharmacy, Social Work • SCIENCES Biology, Chemistry, Environmental, Exercise, Geography, Mathematics, Physical Chemistry, Physical Science, Physics, Physiology, Public Health • SOCIAL SCIENCES Anthropology, Government/Political, History, Human Service, Political Science, Psychology, Social Sciences, Sociology • VISUAL AND PERFORMING ARTS Art, Art History, Dance, Dramatic Arts, Fine Arts, Music, Studio Art, Theater • VOCATIONAL Fashion Merchandising, Forestry, Hospitality and Recreation Mar, Painting, Park/Recreation, Secretarial, Word Processing

Sports/Activities

• SPORTS RELATED Team Managers • SPORTS-INTERCOLLEGIATE Baseball (M), Basketball, Cross Country, Field Hockey (F), Golf (M), Soccer (M), Softball (F), Tennis • SPORTS-INTRAMURAL Baseball (M), Basketball, Bowling, Football (M), Skiing - Snow, Soccer, Softball (F), Swimming, Volleyball • STUDENT LIFE ACTIVITIES Choral, Drama Groups, Fraternities, Jazz Band, Magazine, Newspaper, Radio/TV station, Religious Organization, Sororities, Student Government, Yearbook

---

Very Selective

West Virginia
Program

Marshall University
125 Old Main
Huntington, West Virginia 25755-2020
(304) 696-3160

School Enrollment: **12,400** Male: **6,200** Female: **6,200**
LD Enrollment: **150** Male: **125** Female: **25**

Admissions Contact: **James Harless, Ed.D., Director of Admissions**
LD Contact: **Barbara P. Guyer, Ed.D., Director**
Name of Program: **H.E.L.P.**
Address: **110 Jenkins Hall**
Telephone:**(304) 696-6252**

Admissions

Application Information:
LD Students Applying: **75** Accepted: **30** Enrolled:**30**
Application deadline: **December**
Applicant must apply **12 months** in advance
Rolling Admissions: **Yes** Notified when: **December 31st**

Secondary School Information
Most Important Criteria For Admissions (1-strongest)

6 SAT/ACT	5 Application	3 School transcript
11 Class rank	10 Course selection	7 Personal statement
1 Interview	8 Extra activities	2 Psychoeducational
4 G.P.A.	Open admission	9 Recommendations

Test Requirements:
Diagnostic testing waived: **Yes**
Untimed SAT: **Yes** Untimed ACT: **Yes**
WAIS-R required: **Yes** Range accepted: **90+**
Documentation of LD required: **Yes**
Currency of diagnostic testing: **1 year**
Tests recommended: **Reading, spelling, math, I.Q. (WAIS-R)**

Types of Disabilities Served
• Speech/Lang	• Reading	• ADD with LD
• Study skills	• Spelling	ADD without LD
• Written express	• Math	• ADHD with LD
• Organizational	• Fine Motor	ADHD without LD
• Perceptual		

Admissions Process

Interview required. Admissions Committee selects students for HELP.

High School Course Requirements:
English: **4** Math: **2** Science: **2**
Waivers to standard high school courses
Foreign Language : **Yes**

Learning Disability Program
Special orientation for LD students: **Yes**
Syllabus available during orientation:**Yes**
Program: Remedial: **Yes**
Program: Reinforces course work: **Yes**
Students mainstreamed **100** % of the day
Recommended credits per semester: **12**
Time required or recommended in learning center: **Varies**
Services only for LD students: **Yes**
Counseling: Individual: **Yes** Group Counseling: **Yes** Vocational Counseling: **Yes**
Support groups are available:**Yes through the psychology department**

Faculty:
Faculty: **43** Including Director: **Yes** Full time: **6** Part time: **37**
LD faculty with: BS/BA: **27** M.A.: **42** Ph.D.: **1**
Faculty advocate: **Yes** Meets with instructor: **As needed**

Diagnostic Testing
• ADD	• Personality	Perceptual skills	• Spelling
• ADHD	• Organization	Fine motor skills	• Reading
• I.Q.	• Handwriting	• Spoken language	• Study skills
• Math	• Social skills	• Written language	

Tutoring:
Average size of group tutorials: **3-5**
Services rendered by:
•Graduates   Peers   •Faculty   •LD staff   Teacher trainees

Tutorials
Grp.	Ind.	Tutorials	Grp.	Ind.	Tutorials
•	•	Math skills	•	•	Word processing
•	•	Study skills	•	•	Time management
•	•	Language arts	•	•	Learning strategies
•	•	Written express	•	•	Organizational skills

759

Academic Accommodations

Curriculum	Study Aids	Exams
• Priority registration	• Typist	• Oral
Math waiver	• Reader	Untimed
• Foreign lang. waiver	• Notetaker	Take home
Course substitution	• Proof reader	• With proctor
In Class	• Text on tape	• On computer
• Calculators	Early syllabus	• Extended time
• Tape recorder	Taped handouts	On tape
• Word processor		• Modified
Priority seating		• Separate room

Graduation Requirements:

Course credits: **Varies** GPA: **2.0** Years to complete degree: **Indefinite**
Language waiver: **Yes**

Program Strengths

H.E.L.P. (Higher Education for Learning Problems) is an individualized tutorial program for LD college students. Tutors are trained graduate assistants. Small study groups are also formed when several students are enrolled in the same class. Remediation is provided by Master's degree LD specialists in reading, spelling, and written language. Exceptions in testing are provided. 95% success rate with students in H.E.L.P. Students come from 30 states. H.E.L.P. main goal is to improve basic skills strategies and to prepare students for tests.

General Information:

Marshall University is a 4 year public college. Urban campus of 60 acres is 135 miles from Columbus, Ohio. Accessible by air, train, or bus. Ski areas are 2 hours from campus. Beaches are 8 miles from campus. 2% of students are foreign. 5 residential halls on campus. Housing is guaranteed.35 % of students remain on campus for the weekends. 10 % of students join fraternities/sororities.

Accreditation:NCACS

SAT/ACT Scores:

Scores for incoming freshmen: **ACT:** 62% below 20. 21% between 20 and 23. 9%between 24 and 25l. 5%between 26 and 28. 3% above 28.

Expenses:

Tuition: In-state: Full year: $1,487.00. Part-time: Per credit:$53.00. Tuition: Out-of-state: Full year: $3,557.00. Part-time: Per credit:$139.00. Room and board: $3,356.00

Majors

• AREA STUDIES American, Asian, Black/Afro-American, Hispanic/American, International Studies, Jewish/Judaism, Latin American, Middle Eastern, Russian/Slavic, Urban, Women's Studies • ARTS Art History, Art Therapy, Commercial Art, Crafts, Dance, Design, Drafting, Dramatic Arts, Drawing, Fashion Design, Film & Video, Graphic Arts, Music, Music History, Music Performance, Painting, Photography, Sculpture, Theater Design • BUSINESS Accounting, Actuarial, Banking/Finance, Bookkeeping, Business Administration, Business Economics, Business Management, Business Statistics, Clerical, Commerce & Trade, Commercial Art, Data Processing, Economics, Education, Fashion Merchandising, Food Management, Hotel & Restaurant Management, Industrial Operations, Insurance, International Business, Labor Relations, Management, Marketing, Marketing Research, Organizational Behavior, Personnel, Printing Manufacturing, Real Estate, Retail Manufacturing, Retailing, Secretarial Science, Sports Management, Taxation, Vocational Studies • COMMUNICATIONS Advertising, Broadcasting, Commercial Design, Communication, Creative Writing, English, Graphic Design, Journalism, Literature, Photography, Printing, Public Relations, Speech/Debate/Forensics, Television/Radio/Film • COMPUTER SCIENCE Business Data Programming, Computer Maintenance, Computer Mathematics, Computer Science, Computer Technology, Data Processing, Programming, Robotics, Software Engineer, Systems Analysis, Telecommunications • CRAFTS AND DESIGN Apparel

Design, Ceramic, Crafts, Enameling, Glass, Graphic Design, Illustration Design, Industrial Design, Jewelry, Printmaking, Sculpture, Textile/Weaving • EDUCATION Adult , Art, Art Therapy, Business, Child Development, Curriculum, Early Childhood, Elementary, English, Foreign Language, General, Health, Home Economics, Mathematics, Middle School, Music, Music Therapy, Outdoor, Physical, Psychology, Reading, Recreation/Youth Leadership, Science, Secondary, Social Studies, Special, Speech/Language, Vocational • HEALTH SCIENCES Biometrics/Biostatistics, Communication Disorders, Dental Assistant, Dental Hygiene, Dietary Manager, Environmental, Fitness, Health, Medical Assistant, Medical Laboratory Technology, Medical Records Administration, Medical Secretary, Nuclear Medical Technology, Nursing, Nursing Assistant, Nutritional/Food, Pharmacology, Rehabilitation, Speech Therapy, Speech/Audiology and Speech • HUMANITIES Classics, Fine Arts, Humanities, Liberal Arts , Philosophy, Religion • LANGUAGES English, French, German, Latin, Russian, Spanish • MATHEMATICS Actuarial, Applied, Computer, Statistical, Theoretical • PREPROFESSIONAL Business, Engineering, Law, Legal Assistant, Medicine, Ministry, Pharmacy, Physical Therapy, Recreation, Social Work, Sports Medicine • RELIGIOUS STUDIES Bible, Hebrew, Judaism & Jewish Studies, Philosophy • SCIENCES Anatomy, Anthropology, Astronomy, Biochemistry, Biology, Biomedical, Biophysics, Biostatistics, Botany, Cell Biology, Chemistry, Cognitive, Computer Science, General, Geography, Geology, Geophysics, Human Biology, Inorganic Chemistry, Mathematics, Natural , Organic Chemistry • SOCIAL SCIENCES Criminal Justice, Family Counseling, Geography, Government/Political, History, International Studies, Law Enforcement, Library Science, Political Science, Psychology, Public Relations, Social Sciences, Sociology • SPECIAL EDUCATION Emotionally Disturbed, Gifted & Talented, Learning Disability, Mentally Retarded, Physically Handicapped • VISUAL AND PERFORMING ARTS Art, Art History, Dance, Dance Education, Dramatic Arts, Fine Arts, Music, Music Theatre, Theater, Video • VOCATIONAL Fashion Design, Fashion Merchandising, Fishery Studies, Food Service, Home Economics, Legal Secretary, Library Assistant, Paralegal, Word Processing

Sports/Activities

• SPORTS RELATED Marching Band, Pep Band • SPORTS-INTERCOLLEGIATE Baseball (M), Basketball, Cross Country, Football (M), Golf (M), Soccer (M), Tennis (F), Track and Field, Volleyball (F) • SPORTS-INTRAMURAL Badminton, Baseball (M), Basketball, Bowling, Cross Country, Field Hockey, Football (M), Golf, Hand Ball, Ping-Pong, Racquetball, Soccer, Softball, Swimming, Tennis, Track and Field, Volleyball, Wrestling (M) • STUDENT LIFE ACTIVITIES Choral, Community Service, Concert Band, Dance, Drama Groups, Film, Fraternities, Jazz Band, Magazine, Music Groups, Musical Theater, Newspaper, Radio/TV station, Religious Organization, Sororities, Student Government, Symphony Orchestra, Yearbook

---

Less Selective   **West Virginia**
                                              Services

Potomac State College of W. Virginia
Keyser, West Virginia 26726
(304) 788-3011

School Enrollment: **1,133** Male: **612** Female: **521**
LD Enrollment: **17** Male: **9** Female: **8**

Admissions Contact: **Charles Uia, Director of Admissions**
LD Contact: **William Letrent, Director, Student Support Services**
Name of Program: **Student Support Services**
Telephone:**(304) 788-3011**

Admissions

Application Information:
LD Students Applying: **17** Accepted: **17** Enrolled:**9**
Separate application:**Yes**
LD on admissions committee:**Yes**
Application deadline: **One week after start of classes**
Rolling Admissions: **Yes**

Secondary School Information
Most Important Criteria For Admissions (1-strongest)

4 SAT/ACT	**1** Application	**3** School transcript
5 Class rank	**8** Course selection	**11** Personal statement
6 Interview	**10** Extra activities	**9** Psychoeducational
2 G.P.A.	Open admission	**7** Recommendations

Test Requirements:
Untimed SAT: **Yes** Untimed ACT: **Yes**
Documentation of LD required: **Yes**
Tests recommended: **Individual Education Plan along with most recent psychological report are preferred.**

Types of Disabilities Served
- Speech/Lang
- Study skills
- Written express
- Organizational
- Perceptual
- Reading
- Spelling
- Math
- Fine Motor
- ADD with LD
- ADD without LD
- ADHD with LD
- ADHD without LD

Admissions Process

Apply prior to start of classes.

Learning Disability Program

Special orientation for LD students: **Yes**
Syllabus available during orientation:**Yes**
Program: Reinforces course work: **Yes**
Program available through:**Daily and some evenings**
Students mainstreamed **100** % of the day
Recommended credits per semester: **12-15**
Time required or recommended in learning center: **Open**
Services available for all students: **Yes**
Counseling: Individual: **Yes** Group Counseling: **Yes** Vocational Counseling: **Yes**

Faculty:
Faculty: **5** Including Director: **Yes** Full time: **4** Part time: **1**
LD faculty with: BS/BA: **1** M.A.: **3**
Meets with instructor: **Weekly**

Diagnostic Testing

ADD	• Personality	Perceptual skills	Spelling
ADHD	Organization	Fine motor skills	Reading
I.Q.	Handwriting	Spoken language	• Study skills
Math	Social skills	Written language	

Tutoring:
Average size of group tutorials: **1 or 2; up to 5**
Services rendered by:
Graduates   Peers   Faculty   •LD staff   Teacher trainees

Tutorials

Grp.	Ind.	Tutorials	Grp.	Ind.	Tutorials
•	•	Math skills		•	Word processing
•	•	Study skills	•	•	Time management
	•	Language arts	•	•	Learning strategies
	•	Written express	•	•	Organizational skills

Academic Accommodations

Curriculum	Study Aids	Exams
Priority registration	Typist	• Oral
• Math waiver	• Reader	• Untimed
• Foreign lang. waiver	• Notetaker	• Take home
• Course substitution	• Proof reader	• With proctor
In Class	• Text on tape	• On computer
• Calculators	Early syllabus	• Extended time
• Tape recorder	Taped handouts	• On tape
Word processor		• Modified
• Priority seating		• Separate room

General Information:
Potomac State College of W. Virginia is a 2 year public college. Rural campus of 16 acres is 20 miles from Cumberland, Maryland. Accessible by air, train, or bus. Ski areas are 40 miles from campus. Beaches are 150 miles from campus. 4 residential halls on campus. Housing is not guaranteed.15 % of students remain on campus for the weekends.

Accreditation:

SAT/ACT Scores:
Scores for incoming freshmen:**Verbal:**94%below 500. 5%between 500 and 599. 1%between 600 and 699. **Math:**84% below 500. 12% between 500 and 599. 2% between 600 and 699. 1above 700. **ACT:** 70% below 20. 19% between 20 and 23. 2%between 24 and 25l. 4%between 26 and 28. 1% above 28.

Expenses:
Tuition: In-state: Full year: $1,350.00. Part-time: Per credit:$49.00. Part-time: Per course: $147.00. Tuition: Out-of-state: Full year: $3,750.00. Part-time: Per credit:$149.25. Part-time: Per course:$447.75 Room and board: $2,950.00

Majors
• AGRICULTURE Business, Education, Horticultural • ANIMAL SCIENCE Dairy, Poultry • ARTS Music, Music History, Music Performance • BUSINESS Accounting, Business Education, Business Management, Management, Marketing • COMMUNICATIONS Japanese • COMPUTER SCIENCE Business Data Programming, Computer Science • EDUCATION Business, Early Childhood, Elementary, English, Mathematics, Music, Physical, Secondary • ENGINEERING Civil/Environmental, Electrical, Mechanical • HEALTH SCIENCES Nursing, Physical Therapy • LANGUAGES French, German, Spanish • PRE PROFESSIONAL Law, Medicine, Pharmacy, Social Work, Veterinarian • SCIENCES Biology, Chemistry, Computer Science, Geology, Mathematics, Physical Science, Physics • SOCIAL SCIENCES Government/Political, History, Psychology, Sociology • VISUAL AND PERFORMING ARTS Art, Music, Music Performance • VOCATIONAL Business and Office, Surveying and Mapping

Sports/Activities
• SPORTS RELATED Cheerleading, Pep Band • SPORTS-INTERCOLLEGIATE Baseball (M), Basketball (F), Basketball (M), Football (M), Horseback Riding • STUDENT LIFE ACTIVITIES Choral, Concert Band, Jazz Band, Music Groups, Newspaper, Student Government

---

Less Selective   **West Virginia**
Services

West Virginia Northern Community College
College Square
Wheeling, West Virginia 26003
(304) 233-5900

School Enrollment: **2,806**

Admissions Contact: **Sharon Bungard, Dean, Educ. Support Serv.**
Name of Program: **Handicapped Student Services**

Admissions

Application Information:
Application deadline: **Rolling**
Rolling Admissions: **Yes**

Secondary School Information
Most Important Criteria For Admissions (1-strongest)

SAT/ACT	**1**	Application	**1**	School transcript
Class rank		Course selection		Personal statement
Interview		Extra activities		Psychoeducational
G.P.A.	**1**	Open admission		Recommendations

Test Requirements:
Untimed SAT: **Yes** Untimed ACT: **Yes**

Types of Disabilities Served
- Speech/Lang
- Study skills
- Written express
- Organizational
- Perceptual
- Reading
- Spelling
- Math
- Fine Motor

ADD with LD
ADD without LD
ADHD with LD
ADHD without LD

Learning Disability Program
Counseling: Individual: **Yes**

Faculty:
Faculty: **2** Part time: **2**

Diagnostic Testing

ADD	Personality	Perceptual skills	Spelling
ADHD	Organization	Fine motor skills	Reading
I.Q.	Handwriting	Spoken language	Study skills
Math	Social skills	Written language	

Tutoring:
Services rendered by:
Graduates   Peers   •Faculty   •LD staff   Teacher trainees

Tutorials

Grp.	Ind.	Tutorials	Grp.	Ind.	Tutorials
	•	Math skills			Word processing
•		Study skills		•	Time management
		Language arts		•	Learning strategies
	•	Written express		•	Organizational skills

Academic Accommodations

Curriculum	Study Aids	Exams
Priority registration	Typist	• Oral
Math waiver	Reader	Untimed
Foreign lang. waiver	• Notetaker	• Take home
• Course substitution	Proof reader	With proctor
In Class	• Text on tape	On computer
• Calculators	Early syllabus	• Extended time
• Tape recorder	Taped handouts	On tape
• Word processor		• Modified
Priority seating		Separate room

Program Strengths
West Virginia Northern Community College does not have an LD Program in place. We do have a Basic Skills Lab and a part-time Handicapped Services coordinator who works with LD students individually.

General Information:
West Virginia Northern Comm College is a 2 year public college. Urban campus 60 miles from Pittsburgh. Ski areas are 75 miles from campus. Beaches are 300 miles from campus. Housing is not guaranteed.

Accreditation: NCACS, NLN

Expenses:
Tuition: In-state: Full year: Part-time: Per credit: $39.00. Tuition: Out-of-state: Full year: Part-time: Per credit: $113.00.

Majors
• BUSINESS Accounting, Banking, Business Administration, Business Data Processing, Business Data Programming, Business Management, Finance, Real Estate • COMPUTER SCIENCE Computer Science, Data Processing, Programming • CRAFTS AND DESIGN Drafting and Design Technology • EDUCATION Education • HEALTH SCIENCES Nursing, Radiological Therapy, Surgical Technology • HUMANITIES Humanities, Liberal Arts • SCIENCES Biology, Physical Science • SOCIAL SCIENCES Criminal Justice, Human Service, Law Enforcement, Psychology, Social Sciences • VOCATIONAL Air Conditioning/Heating/Refrig, Aviation Technology, Business and Office, Drafting, Electromechanical Technology, Electronics Technology, Industrial Management, Medical Laboratory Technology, Respiratory Therapy Technology, Secretarial

Sports
• SPORTS-INTRAMURAL Basketball, Bowling, Golf, Ping-Pong, Softball, Volleyball • STUDENT LIFE ACTIVITIES Magazine, Newspaper, Student Government

---

Less Selective   **West Virginia**
Services

West Virginia State College
P. O. Box 1000 Campus Box 178
Institute, West Virginia 25112-0335
(304) 766-3221

School Enrollment: **5,200**
LD Enrollment: **27**

Admissions Contact: **Mr. Robin Green, Ast. Dir. of Admissions**
LD Contact: **Jacqueline Burns, Counselor Students with Disab.**
Telephone: **(304) 766-3083 (V/TDD)**

Admissions

Application Information:
LD Students Applying: **27**
Application deadline: **1 month prior to semester beginning**

Secondary School Information
Most Important Criteria For Admissions (1-strongest)

2 SAT/ACT	**1** Application	**3** School transcript
10 Class rank	**6** Course selection	**9** Personal statement
8 Interview	**7** Extra activities	**11** Psychoeducational
4 G.P.A.	**1** Open admission	**5** Recommendations

Test Requirements:
Untimed SAT: **Yes** Untimed ACT: **Yes** Untimed ACH: **Yes**
Documentation of LD required: **Yes**

Types of Disabilities Served
- Speech/Lang
- Study skills
- Written express
- Organizational
- Perceptual
- Reading
- Spelling
- Math
- Fine Motor
- ADD with LD
- ADD without LD
- ADHD with LD
- ADHD without LD

Admissions Process

WVSC is a state school with open admissions. Basically everyone is accepted.

High School Course Requirements:
English: **1-2** Math: **1-2** Science: **1** Foreign Language: **1**
Waivers to standard high school courses
Course substitution: **Yes**

Learning Disability Program

Special orientation for LD students: **Yes**
Students mainstreamed **100** % of the day
Recommended credits per semester: **12**
Services available for all students: **Yes**
Counseling: Individual: **Yes**

Faculty:
Faculty: **1** Full time: **1** M.A.: **1**
Faculty advocate: **Yes** Meets with instructor: **As necessary**

Diagnostic Testing

ADD	Personality	Perceptual skills	Spelling
ADHD	Organization	Fine motor skills	Reading
I.Q.	Handwriting	Spoken language	Study skills
Math	Social skills	Written language	

Tutoring:
Average size of group tutorials: **Less than 6**
Services rendered by:

Graduates	•Peers	Faculty	•LD staff	Teacher trainees

Tutorials

Grp.	Ind.	Tutorials	Grp.	Ind.	Tutorials
•	•	Math skills			Word processing
•	•	Study skills	•	•	Time management
•	•	Language arts	•	•	Learning strategies
•	•	Written express	•	•	Organizational skills

Academic Accommodations

Curriculum	Study Aids	Exams
Priority registration	• Typist	• Oral
• Math waiver	• Reader	Untimed
• Foreign lang. waiver	• Notetaker	• Take home
• Course substitution	Proof reader	• With proctor
In Class	• Text on tape	On computer
• Calculators	Early syllabus	• Extended time
• Tape recorder	Taped handouts	On tape
• Word processor		• Modified
Priority seating		• Separate room

Graduation Requirements:
Course credits: **130** Years to complete degree: **Unlimited**

General Information:
West Virginia State College is a 2 and 4 year public college. Suburban campus of 85 acres is 6 miles from Charleston. Accessible by bus. Ski areas are 50 miles from campus. Beaches are 450 miles from campus. 2% of students are foreign. 4 residential halls on campus. Housing is guaranteed.60-75 % of students remain on campus for the weekends. 50 % of students join fraternities/sororities.

Accreditation: Fully Accredited

Expenses:
Tuition: In-state: Full year: $789.00 per semester. Part-time: Per credit:$125.00. Part-time: Per course: $228.00. Tuition: Out-of-state: Full year: $1,844.00 per semester. Part-time: Per credit:$213.00. Part-time: Per course:$493.00 Room and board: $1,475.00

Majors
• AREA STUDIES African, American, Asian, Black/Afro-American, Jewish, Latin American, Urban • BUSINESS Accounting, Banking, Business Administration, Business Economics, Business Education, Business Management, Economics, Finance, Hotel and Restaurant Management, Insurance, Management, Marketing, Marketing Research, Personnel, Real Estate, Sports Management, Technical and Business Writing, Travel/Tourism Management • COMMUNICATIONS Advertising, Broadcasting, Communication, Creative Writing, English, Journalism, Photography, Television/Radio/Film • COMPUTER SCIENCE Data Processing, Programming, Systems Analysis • CRAFTS AND DESIGN Ceramics, Drafting and Design Technology, Graphic Design, Sculpture • EDUCATION Art, Curriculum, Early Childhood, Education of Exceptional Child, Elementary, English, Health, Industrial, Mathematics, Middle School, Music, Music Therapy, Physical, Recreation and Youth Leadership, School Psychology, Science, Secondary, Social Studies, Special, Speech/Language • HEALTH SCIENCES Medical Assistant, Nuclear Medical Technology, Recreational Therapy • HUMANITIES Humanities, Liberal Arts, Philosophy • LANGUAGES French, Spanish • PREPROFESSIONAL Engineering, Recreation, Social Work • SCIENCES Astronomy, Biology, Botany, Chemistry, Geography, Mathematics, Physical Science, Physics, Physiology, Zoology • SOCIAL SCIENCES Anthropology, Criminal Justice, Government/Political, History, Law Enforcement, Political Science, Psychology, Social Sciences, Sociology • VISUAL AND PERFORMING ARTS Fine Arts, Music • VOCATIONAL Architectural Technology, Chemical Manufacturing Technology, Chemical Technology, Construction, Drafting, Fashion Merchandising, Nuclear Technology, Painting, Park/Recreation Management, Printing/Lithography, Secretarial

Sports/Activities
• SPORTS RELATED Band, Cheerleading, Drum Major/Majorette • SPORTS-INTERCOLLEGIATE Baseball (M), Basketball, Cross Country, Football (M), Golf (M), Softball (F), Tennis, Track and Field • SPORTS-INTRAMURAL Baseball, Basketball, Bowling, Football (M), Ping-Pong, Softball, Tennis, Volleyball • STUDENT LIFE ACTIVITIES Choral, Concert Band, Drama Groups, Fraternities, Magazine, Music Ensembles, Newspaper, Radio/TV station, Religious Organization, Sororities, Student Government, Yearbook

Selective

**West Virginia
Services**

West Virginia University
215 Student Services
Morgantown, West Virginia 26506
(800) 344-WVU1

School Enrollment: **14,662**
LD Enrollment: **100**

Admissions Contact: **Dr. Glenn Carter, Director of Admissions**
LD Contact: **Gordon Kent, Ph.D., Coordinator**
Name of Program: **Disability Services**
Telephone:**(304) 293-6700**

Admissions

Application Information:
Application deadline: **May 1st**
Rolling Admissions: **Yes**Notified when: **within 3 weeks**

Secondary School Information
Most Important Criteria For Admissions (1-strongest)

1 SAT/ACT	Application	**1**	School transcript
Class rank	Course selection		Personal statement
Interview	Extra activities	**1**	Psychoeducational
1 G.P.A.	Open admission		Recommendations

Test Requirements:
Diagnostic testing waived: **Yes**
Untimed SAT: **Yes** Untimed ACT: **Yes**
WAIS-R required: **Yes**
Currency of diagnostic testing: **2 years**

Types of Disabilities Served
- Speech/Lang
- Study skills
- Written express
- Organizational
- Perceptual
- Reading
- Spelling
- Math
- Fine Motor
- ADD with LD
- ADD without LD
- ADHD with LD
- ADHD without LD

Faculty:
Faculty: **2** Full time: **2**
Faculty advocate: **Yes** Meets with instructor: **As needed**

Diagnostic Testing

ADD	Personality	Perceptual skills	Spelling
ADHD	Organization	Fine motor skills	Reading
I.Q.	Handwriting	Spoken language	Study skills
Math	Social skills	Written language	

Tutoring:
Average size of group tutorials: *
Services rendered by:

Graduates	Peers	Faculty	LD staff	Teacher trainees

Tutorials

Grp.	Ind.	Tutorials	Grp.	Ind.	Tutorials
		Math skills			Word processing
		Study skills			Time management
		Language arts			Learning strategies
		Written express			Organizational skills

Academic Accommodations

Curriculum	Study Aids	Exams
Priority registration	Typist	• Oral
• Math waiver	Reader	Untimed
• Foreign lang. waiver	• Notetaker	Take home
• Course substitution	Proof reader	With proctor
In Class	• Text on tape	On computer
Calculators	Early syllabus	• Extended time
• Tape recorder	Taped handouts	On tape
Word processor		• Modified
Priority seating		Separate room

Program Strengths
LD students at West Virginia University are mainstreamed and receive services to accommodate their needs. There are no programs for LD students. We receive many inquiries from parents/students and many LD students attend West Virginia University from up and down the eastern seaboard.
* We will help students find appropriate tutors.

General Information:
West Virginia University is a 4 year public university. Urban campus of 1,000 acres is Accessible by air or bus. 2% of students are foreign. 9 residential halls on campus. Housing is not guaranteed.16 % of students join fraternities/sororities.

Accreditation:NCACS

Expenses:
Tuition: In-state: Full year: $1,692.00. Tuition: Out-of-state: Full year: $4,222.00. Room and board: $3,389.00

Majors
• AREA STUDIES Appalachian Studies, Medieval Studies, Russian/Slavic • BUSINESS Accounting, Agricultural, Banking, Business Administration, Business Economics, Business Management, Economics, Finance, Marketing, Sports Management • COMMUNICATIONS Advertising, Broadcasting, Communication, English, Journalism, News/Editorial, Public Relations, Television/Radio/Film • COMPUTER SCIENCE Computer Science • CRAFTS AND DESIGN Ceramics, Graphic Design, Sculpture, Theater Design • EDUCATION Agricultural, Art, Communication Education, Driver and Safety Education, Early Childhood, Elementary, English, English As A Second Language (, Foreign Language, Health, Home Economics Education, Journalism Education, Mathematics, Music, Physical, Recreation and Youth Leadership, School Library Media, Science, Secondary, Speech/Language, Theater Education • ENGINEERING Aerospace, Chemical, Civil/Environmental, Communications, Computer, Electrical, Industrial, Mechanical, Mining/Mineral, Petroleum • ENVIRONMENTAL CONTROL Environmental Protection • HEALTH SCIENCES Athletic Training, Dental Hygiene, Mental Impairment, Mental Retardation, Nursing, Nutritional/Food, Occupational Therapy, Physical Therapy, Speech/Audiology and Speech, Sports and Exercise Studies • HUMANITIES Comparative Literature, Liberal Arts, Philosophy, Religion • LANGUAGES Foreign, French, German, Greek, Latin, Linguistic, Russian, Spanish • PREPROFESSIONAL Agriculture, Architecture, Engineering, Forestry, Law, Pharmacy, Social Work, Veterinarian • SCIENCES Agricultural, Agronomy, Animal, Anthropology, Biology, Chemistry, Ecology, Food Science, Geography, Geology, Horticultural, Mathematics, Physics, Plant Science, Soil, Statistics • SOCIAL SCIENCES Anthropology, Child Development and Family S, Geography, History, Human Service, International Studies, Political Science, Psychology, Public Relations, Sociology • VISUAL AND PERFORMING ARTS Art History, Dance, Dramatic Arts, Music, Music Performance, Music Theatre, Music Theory and Composition, Studio Art • VOCATIONAL Agricultural Mechanics, Fashion Mechandizing, Forestry, Home Economics, Interior Design, Landscape Architecture, Medical Laboratory Technology, Painting, Park/Recreation, Printing/Lithography, Resource Management, Textile and Clothing, Wildlife Management

Sports/Activities

• SPORTS RELATED band, Baton Twirling, Cheerleading, Chess, Drum Major/Majorette, Marching Band, Pep Band • SPORTS-INTERCOLLE-GIATE Baseball (M), Basketball, Cross Country, Football (M), Gymnastics (F), Riflery, Soccer (M), Swimming, Tennis, Track and Field, Volleyball, Wrestling (M) • SPORTS-INTRAMURAL Badminton, Basketball, Bowling, Field Hockey (M), Golf, Ping-Pong, Racquetball, Riflery, Soccer, Softball, Swimming, Tennis, Track and Field, Volleyball, Wrestling
• STUDENT LIFE ACTIVITIES Choral, Concert Band, Dance, Drama Groups, Fraternities, Jazz Band, Music Groups, Musical Theater, Newspaper, Opera, Radio/TV station, Sororities, Student Government, Symphony Orchestra

Very Selective	West Virginia Program

West Virginia Wesleyan College

College Avenue
Buckhannon, West Virginia 26201-9989
(304) 473-8510

School Enrollment: **1,529** Male: **738** Female: **791**
LD Enrollment: **225**

Admissions Contact: **Robert Skinner, Director of Admission**
LD Contact: **Phyllis Coston, Director Learning Center**
Name of Program: **Special Support Services**
Telephone:**(304) 473-8380**

Admissions

Application Information:
LD Students Applying: **300** Accepted: **125** Enrolled:**75**
LD on admissions committee:**Yes**
Application deadline: **March 1st**
Notified when: **March 20th**

Secondary School Information
Most Important Criteria For Admissions (1-strongest)

3	SAT/ACT	3	Application	1	School transcript
5	Class rank	1	Course selection	2	Personal statement
1	Interview	2	Extra activities	1	Psychoeducational
1	G.P.A.		Open admission	2	Recommendations

Test Requirements:
Diagnostic testing waived: **Yes**
Untimed SAT: **Yes** Untimed ACT: **Yes**
WAIS-R required: **Yes** Range accepted: **90+**
Documentation of LD required: **Yes**
Currency of diagnostic testing: **2 years**
Tests recommended: **WAIS, ACT or SAT, beginning 1993, Woodcock-Johnson**

Types of Disabilities Served
• Speech/Lang • Reading • ADD with LD
• Study skills • Spelling ADD without LD
• Written express • Math • ADHD with LD
• Organizational • Fine Motor ADHD without LD
• Perceptual

Admissions Process

Apply to Admission Office; interview with Learning Center and Admission staffs; joint decision by Admissions and Learning Center

- 2 rounds.

High School Course Requirements:
English: **4** Math: **3** Science: **3** Foreign Language:

Learning Disability Program

Special orientation for LD students: **Yes**
Program: Reinforces course work: **Yes**
Students mainstreamed **100** % of the day
Counseling: Individual: **Yes**

Faculty:
Faculty: **17** Including Director: **Yes** Full time: **12** Part time: **5**
LD faculty with: BS/BA: **3** M.A.: **14**
Faculty advocate: **Yes** Meets with instructor: **As needed**

Diagnostic Testing

ADD	•	Personality	Perceptual skills		Spelling
ADHD		Organization	Fine motor skills	•	Reading
I.Q.		Handwriting	Spoken language	•	Study skills
Math		Social skills	• Written language		

Tutoring:
Average size of group tutorials: **5**
Services rendered by:
•Graduates •Peers •Faculty •LD staff Teacher trainees

Tutorials

Grp.	Ind.	Tutorials	Grp.	Ind.	Tutorials
•	•	Math skills	•	•	Word processing
•	•	Study skills	•	•	Time management
•	•	Language arts	•	•	Learning strategies
•	•	Written express	•	•	Organizational skills

Academic Accommodations

Curriculum	Study Aids	Exams
• Priority registration	Typist	• Oral
Math waiver	• Reader	• Untimed
Foreign lang. waiver	• Notetaker	• Take home
• Course substitution	• Proof reader	• With proctor
In Class	• Text on tape	• On computer
• Calculators	Early syllabus	• Extended time
• Tape recorder	Taped handouts	• On tape
• Word processor		• Modified
Priority seating		• Separate room

Graduation Requirements:
Course credits: **128 hours**

Program Strengths

Our learning disability program is structured in the freshman year and works toward independence in the senior year. It is unique because it operates within the Learning Center that serves the entire campus. It is open from 8 a.m. to 11 p.m. There are twelve full-time staff members, two part-time, and 2 paraprofessionals.

General Information:

West Virginia Wesleyan College is a 4 year private United Methodist college. Rural campus of 80 acres is 30 miles from Clarksburg. Accessible by air or bus. Ski areas are 2 hours from campus. 5% of students are foreign. 10 residential halls on campus. Housing is guaranteed.90 % of students remain on campus for the weekends. 26 % of students join fraternities/sororities.

Wisconsin

Accreditation:NCACS

SAT/ACT Scores:
Scores for incoming freshmen:**Verbal:**72%below 500. 21%between 500 and 599. 6%between 600 and 699. .01%above 700. **Math:**52% below 500. 32% between 500 and 599. 14% between 600 and 699. .01%above 700. **ACT:** 22% below 20. 23% between 20 and 23. 12%between 24 and 25l. 18%between 26 and 28. 22% above 28.

Class Rank:
About 51% of the present freshmen class were in the upper 20% of their high school class. 73% were in the top 40% of their class. 86% were in the top 60% of their class. 97% were in the top 80% of their class.

Expenses:
Tuition: In-state: Full year: $12,605.00. Part-time: Per credit:$525.00. Tuition: Out-of-state: Full year: $12,605.00. Part-time: Per credit:$525.00. Room and board: $3,350.00 Cost of LD program:$750.00 - $3,700.00

Majors

• AREA STUDIES International Studies • ARTS Dramatic Arts, Music, Music Performance • BUSINESS Accounting, Banking/Finance, Business Administration, Business Management, Economics, Fashion Merchandising, Management, Marketing • COMMUNICATIONS Communication, Creative Writing, English, Public Relations, Speech • COMPUTER SCIENCE Computer Science, Data Processing, Management Information Systems, Programming, Systems Analysis • EDUCATION Art, Elementary, English, Health, Home Economics, Mathematics, Middle School, Music, Physical, Religious Education, Science, Secondary, Social Studies, Special, Speech/Language • ENGINEERING Aerospace, Aerospace, Communications, Physics • HEALTH SCIENCES Fitness, Health, Nursing, Nutritional/Food, Rehabilitation • HUMANITIES English/Writing/Literature, Humanities, Philosophy, Religion • PREPROFESSIONAL Dentistry, Engineering, Forestry, Law, Medicine, Ministry, Optometry, Pharmacy, Sports Medicine, Veterinarian • RELIGIOUS STUDIES Philosophy, Religion & Theology • SCIENCES Biology, Chemistry, Mathematics, Physics • SOCIAL SCIENCES Government/Political, History, International Studies, Political Science, Psychology, Public Relations, Social Sciences, Sociology • VISUAL AND PERFORMING ARTS Art, Dramatic Arts, Music, Music Performance, Studio Art, Theater • VOCATIONAL Fashion Merchandising, Forestry, Home Economics, Public Administration

Sports/Activities

• SPORTS RELATED Cheerleading, Pep Band, Team Managers • SPORTS-INTERCOLLEGIATE Baseball (M), Basketball, Cross Country, Diving, Football (M), Golf (M), Soccer, Softball (F), Swimming, Tennis, Track and Field, Volleyball (F) • SPORTS-INTRAMURAL Basketball, Bowling, Football, Ping-Pong, Racquetball, Racquetball, Softball, Tennis, Volleyball • STUDENT LIFE ACTIVITIES Academic Clubs, Choral, Community Service, Concert Band, Dance, Debate, Drama Groups, Ethnic & Cultural Groups, Fraternities, Jazz Band, Music Groups, Musical Theater, Newspaper, Political Groups, Radio, Religious Organization, Sororities, Student Government, Volunteerism, Yearbook

---

Beloit College
Beloit, Wisconsin 53511
(608) 363-2620

School Enrollment: **1,100** Male: **500** Female: **600**

Admissions Contact: **Tom Martin, Director of Admissions**
LD Contact: **Suzanne Bellrichard, Dir. Educ. Development Prog.**
Name of Program: **Educational Development Program**
Address: **700 College Street, Box137**
Telephone:**(608) 363-2620**

Admissions

Application Information:
Application deadline: **February 15th**
Rolling Admissions: **Yes**Notified when: **2 weeks**

Secondary School Information
Most Important Criteria For Admissions (1-strongest)

11 SAT/ACT	**4** Application	**3** School transcript
6 Class rank	**2** Course selection	**7** Personal statement
10 Interview	**8** Extra activities	**9** Psychoeducational
1 G.P.A.	Open admission	**5** Recommendations

Test Requirements:
Diagnostic testing waived: **Yes**
Untimed SAT: **Yes** Untimed ACT: **Yes** Untimed ACH: **Yes**
Documentation of LD required: **Yes**

Types of Disabilities Served

Speech/Lang	Reading	ADD with LD
Study skills	Spelling	ADD without LD
Written express	Math	ADHD with LD
Organizational	Fine Motor	ADHD without LD
Perceptual		

Admissions Process

We look for potential. Highly selective.

High School Course Requirements:
English: **4** Math: **3** Science: **3** Foreign Language: **2**

Learning Disability Program

Program: Reinforces course work: **Yes**
Students mainstreamed **100** % of the day
Recommended credits per semester: **4-4 hour courses**
Counseling: Individual: **Yes** Vocational Counseling: **Yes**
Support groups are available:**Dysfunctional family only**

Faculty:
Faculty: **1**

Diagnostic Testing

ADD	Personality	Perceptual skills	Spelling
ADHD	Organization	Fine motor skills	• Reading
I.Q.	Handwriting	Spoken language	Study skills
Math	Social skills	Written language	

Tutoring:
Average size of group tutorials: **Individual**
Services rendered by:
Graduates •Peers Faculty LD staff Teacher trainees

Tutorials

Grp.	Ind.	Tutorials	Grp.	Ind.	Tutorials
	•	Math skills			Word processing
•	•	Study skills	•	•	Time management
	•	Language arts		•	Learning strategies
	•	Written express	•	•	Organizational skills

Academic Accommodations

Curriculum	Study Aids	Exams
Priority registration	Typist	Oral
Math waiver	• Reader	Untimed
Foreign lang. waiver	• Notetaker	Take home
Course substitution	Proof reader	With proctor
In Class	Text on tape	On computer
Calculators	Early syllabus	• Extended time
Tape recorder	Taped handouts	On tape
Word processor		Modified
Priority seating		Separate room

Graduation Requirements:
Course credits: **31** GPA: **2.0** Years to complete degree: **4** Math waiver: **Yes**
Language waiver: **Yes**

General Information:
Beloit College is a 4 year independent college. Rural campus of 40 acres is 50 miles from Madison. Accessible by bus. Ski areas are 30 miles from campus. 10.2% of students are foreign. 14 residential halls on campus. Housing is guaranteed.Guaranteed through 3rd year. 80 % of students remain on campus for the weekends. 20 % of students join fraternities/sororities.

Accreditation:NCAC

Expenses:
Tuition: In-state: Full year: $12,900.00. Tuition: Out-of-state: Full year: $12,900.00. Room and board: $3,450.00

Majors
• ARTS Art History • BUSINESS Business Administration, Business Economics, Business Management, Economics • COMMUNICATIONS Broadcasting, Communication • COMPUTER SCIENCE Data Processing, Programming • EDUCATION Art, Child Development, Elementary, Middle School, Science, Secondary • HUMANITIES Classics, English/Writing/Literature, Philosophy, Religion • LANGUAGES Chinese, English, French, German, Greek, Japanese, Russian, Spanish • MATHEMATICS Computer, Statistical, Theoretical • PRE PROFESSIONAL Dentistry, Engineering, Forestry, Law, Medicine • SCIENCES Anthropology, Archeology, Astronomy, Biochemistry, Biology, Botany, Chemistry, Computer Science, Mathematics, Molecular Biology, Organic Chemistry, Physics, Zoology • SOCIAL SCIENCES Anthropology, Government/Political, History, International Studies, Political Science, Psychology, Sociology • VISUAL AND PERFORMING ARTS Art, Art History, Studio Art

Sports/Activities
• SPORTS RELATED Pep Band, Team Managers • SPORTS-INTERCOLLEGIATE Baseball (M), Basketball (F), Basketball (M), Bowling, Crew, Cross Country (F), Cross Country (M), Diving (F), Diving (M), Fencing, Football (M), Golf (M), Lacrosse (F), Lacrosse (M), Soccer (F), Soccer (M), Softball (F), Swimming (F), Swimming (M), Tennis (F), Tennis (M), Track and Field (F), Track and Field (M), Volleyball (F) • SPORTS-INTRAMURAL Basketball, Football, Flag, Racquetball, Volleyball • STUDENT LIFE ACTIVITIES Academic Clubs, Choral, Community Service, Drama Groups, Ethnic & Cultural Groups, Film, Fraternities, Jazz Band, Magazine, Music Groups, Newspaper, Orchestra, Political Groups, Radio/TV station, Religious Organization, Sororities, Student Government, Yearbook

---

Less Selective

Wisconsin Program

Chippewa Valley Technical College
620 West Clairemont
Eau Claire, Wisconsin 54701
(715) 833-6244

School Enrollment: **7,000**
LD Enrollment: **100**

Admissions Contact: **Gene Hinrichsen, Admissions Officer**
LD Contact: **Robert Benedict, Supervisor-Special Needs**
Name of Program: **Project SERVE**
Address: **620 W. Clairemont**
Telephone:**(715) 833-6280**

Admissions

Application Information:
LD Students Applying: **90** Accepted: **85** Enrolled:**80**
Application deadline: **Open**
Rolling Admissions: **Yes**

Secondary School Information
Most Important Criteria For Admissions (1-strongest)

SAT/ACT	**4**	Application	**5**	School transcript	
Class rank	**1**	Course selection		Personal statement	
2 Interview		Extra activities		Psychoeducational	
G.P.A.	**1**	Open admission	**3**	Recommendations	

Test Requirements:
Standardized tests waived: **Yes**
Documentation of LD required: **Yes**

Types of Disabilities Served
• Speech/Lang	• Reading	• ADD with LD
• Study skills	• Spelling	• ADD without LD
• Written express	• Math	• ADHD with LD
• Organizational	• Fine Motor	• ADHD without LD
• Perceptual		

Admissions Process

Open door with some majors having additional requirements.

Learning Disability Program
Program: Reinforces course work: **Yes**
Students mainstreamed **100** % of the day
Time required or recommended in learning center: **Optional**
Services available for all students: **Yes**
Counseling: Individual: **Yes** Vocational Counseling: **Yes**

Faculty:
Faculty: **3** Full time: **3** M.A.: **3**
Faculty advocate: **Yes** Meets with instructor: **As necessary**

Wisconsin

Diagnostic Testing

ADD	Personality	Perceptual skills	• Spelling
ADHD	Organization	Fine motor skills	• Reading
I.Q.	Handwriting	Spoken language	• Study skills
• Math	Social skills	Written language	

Tutoring:

Services rendered by:
•Graduates Peers •Faculty •LD staff •Teacher trainees

Tutorials

Grp.	Ind.	Tutorials	Grp.	Ind.	Tutorials
•	•	Math skills	•	•	Word processing
•	•	Study skills	•	•	Time management
•	•	Language arts	•	•	Learning strategies
•	•	Written express	•	•	Organizational skills

Academic Accommodations

Curriculum	Study Aids	Exams
• Priority registration	• Typist	• Oral
Math waiver	• Reader	• Untimed
Foreign lang. waiver	• Notetaker	Take home
• Course substitution	• Proof reader	• With proctor
In Class	• Text on tape	• On computer
• Calculators	Early syllabus	• Extended time
• Tape recorder	Taped handouts	On tape
• Word processor		• Modified
• Priority seating		• Separate room

Program Strengths

Individualized assistance - 100% mainstreamed with 100% placement.

General Information:

Chippewa Valley Technical College is a 2 year public college. Urban campus of 100 acres is 80 miles from Minneapolis. Accessible by air or bus. Ski areas are 60 miles from campus. 5% of students are foreign. Housing is not guaranteed.

Accreditation:

Expenses:

Tuition: In-state: Full year: $1,050.00. Part-time: Per credit:$41.00. Tuition: Out-of-state: Full year: $3,500.00. Room and board: $1,200.00

Majors

• BUSINESS Accounting, Agricultural, Business Data Processing, Business Data Programming, Business Management, Hotel and Restaurant Management, Insurance, Management, Marketing Management, Real Estate • COMPUTER SCIENCE Data Processing, Management Information System, Medical Records Administration, Medical Records Technology, Programming, Robotics • HEALTH SCIENCES Alcohol/Drug Abuse, Diagnostic Medical Scenography, Medical Secretary, Nursing, Radiograph Medical Technology, Radiological Therapy, Rehabilitation, Ultrasound Technology • PREPROFESSIONAL Agriculture, Architecture, Legal Assistant • SCIENCES Dairy • SOCIAL SCIENCES Law Enforcement • VOCATIONAL Agricultural Production, Air Conditioning/Heating/Refri, Architectural Technologies, Automobile Technology, Business and Office, Civil Technology, Drafting, Electrical/Electronics Repair, Electromechanical Technology, Electronics Technology, Fashion Merchandising, Food Management, Food Science, Histotechnology, Hospitality/Recreation Marketing, Industrial Technology, Legal Secretary, Machinist, Mechanical Design Technology, Medical Laboratory Technology, Paralegal, Precision Metal Work, Secretarial

Sports/Activities

• SPORTS-INTRAMURAL Basketball, Bowling, Football, Golf, Ping-Pong, Skiing - Snow, Softball, Tennis, Volleyball • STUDENT LIFE ACTIVITIES Academic Clubs, Choral, Community Service, Debate, Drama Groups, Ethnic & Cultural Groups, Music Groups, Newspaper, Student Government, Yearbook

---

Very Selective   **Wisconsin Program**

Edgewood College
855 Woodrow Street
Madison, Wisconsin 53711
(608) 257-4861

School Enrollment: **1,591** Male: **519** Female: **1,072**
LD Enrollment: **8**

Admissions Contact: **Kevin Kucera, Director of Admissions**
LD Contact: **Kathie Moran, Learning Center Coordinator**
Name of Program: **ASLD**

Admissions

Application Information:
LD Students Applying: **16** Accepted: **8** Enrolled:**8**
Separate application:**Yes**
Application deadline: **March 15th**
Applicant must apply **6** months in advance
Rolling Admissions: **Yes**Notified when: **May 1st**

Secondary School Information
Most Important Criteria For Admissions (1-strongest)

3 SAT/ACT	**4** Application	**1** School transcript
2 Class rank	**1** Course selection	**6** Personal statement
8 Interview	**5** Extra activities	**11** Psychoeducational
1 G.P.A.	Open admission	**7** Recommendations

Test Requirements:
Diagnostic testing waived: **Yes**
Untimed ACT: **Yes**
WAIS-R required: **Yes**
Documentation of LD required: **Yes**
Currency of diagnostic testing: **18 months**
Tests recommended: **Woodcock-Johnson Part I & II - submit all sub-test scores.**

Types of Disabilities Served

• Speech/Lang	• Reading	• ADD with LD
• Study skills	• Spelling	ADD without LD
• Written express	• Math	• ADHD with LD
• Organizational	• Fine Motor	ADHD without LD
• Perceptual		

Admissions Process

Student submits Edgewood and ASLD application along with supporting documentation.

Learning Disability Program

Special orientation for LD students: **Yes**
Program: Reinforces course work: **Yes**
Students mainstreamed **100** % of the day
Services available for all students: **Yes**
Counseling: Individual: **Yes** Group Counseling: **Yes**

Faculty:

Faculty: **1** Including Director: **Yes** Full time: **1** M.A.: **1**
Faculty advocate: **Yes** Meets with instructor: **As needed**

Diagnostic Testing

ADD	Personality	Perceptual skills	• Spelling
ADHD•	Organization	Fine motor skills	• Reading
I.Q.	Handwriting•	Spoken language	• Study skills
• Math	Social skills•	Written language	

Tutoring:

Services rendered by:
Graduates •Peers Faculty •LD staff Teacher trainees

Tutorials

Grp.	Ind.	Tutorials	Grp.	Ind.	Tutorials
•	•	Math skills	•	•	Word processing
•	•	Study skills	•	•	Time management
	•	Language arts	•	•	Learning strategies
	•	Written express	•	•	Organizational skills

Academic Accommodations

Curriculum	Study Aids	Exams
Priority registration	Typist	• Oral
Math waiver	Reader	Untimed
Foreign lang. waiver	• Notetaker	Take home
Course substitution	• Proof reader	• With proctor
In Class	• Text on tape	On computer
Calculators	Early syllabus	• Extended time
• Tape recorder	Taped handouts	On tape
Word processor		• Modified
• Priority seating		• Separate room

Program Strengths

The program is called Assistance to Students with Learning Differences (ASLD). Its purpose is to serve incoming freshman who have a demonstrated learning disability. Edgewood College has a long history of high quality instruction and attention to the individual, and we feel that this program builds upon that strong foundation.

General Information:

Edgewood College is a 4 year private Roman Catholic college. Urban campus of 55 acres is 90 miles from Milwaukee. Accessible by air or bus Ski areas are 20 mile from campus. Beaches are 1/2 mile from campus. 3.33% of students are foreign. 3 residential halls on campus. Housing is guaranteed.Guaranteed through 4th year.

Accreditation:NCACS

SAT/ACT Scores:

Scores for incoming freshmen: **ACT:** 15% below 20. 40% between 20 and 23. 30%between 24 and 25l. 12%between 26 and 28. 3% above 28.

Expenses:

Tuition: In-state: Full year: $6,950.00. Part-time: Per credit:$230.00. Tuition: Out-of-state: Full year: $6,950.00. Part-time: Per credit:$230.00. Room and board: $3,300.00

Majors

• AREA STUDIES American • ARTS Art Therapy • BUSINESS Accounting, Business Administration, Business Education, Business Management, Economics, Marketing • COMMUNICATIONS English • COMPUTER SCIENCE Computer Science • EDUCATION Art, Early Childhood, Education of Exceptional Child, Elementary, Middle School, Religious, Secondary, Special, Specific Learning Disabilities • HUMANITIES Humanities, Liberal Arts • LANGUAGES French, Spanish • PREPROFESSIONAL Chiropractic, Dentistry, Engineering, Law, Medicine, Phar-

macy, Veterinarian • SCIENCES Biology, Cytotechnology, Environmental, Mathematics, Physical Science • SOCIAL SCIENCES Criminal Justice, Government/Political, History, Political Science, Psychology, Public Administration, Social Sciences, Sociology • VISUAL AND PERFORMING ARTS Art, Music, Theater • VOCATIONAL Medical Laboratory Technology

Sports/Activities

• SPORTS RELATED Cheerleading • SPORTS-INTERCOLLEGIATE Baseball, Soccer (M), Tennis, Volleyball (F) • SPORTS-INTRAMURAL Badminton (M), Basketball, Ping-Pong, Skiing - Snow, Soccer, Softball, Swimming, Volleyball • STUDENT LIFE ACTIVITIES Academic Clubs, Choral, Community Service, Drama Groups, Ethnic & Cultural Groups, Music Groups, Newspaper, Religious Organization, Student Government, Yearbook

---

Less Selective	Wisconsin
	Services

Fox Valley Technical College

1825 North Bluemound Drive
Appleton, Wisconsin 54913-2277
(414) 735-5727

School Enrollment: **10,000** Male: **5,000** Female: **5,000**

Admissions Contact: **Ron Kautz, Registrar**
LD Contact: **Shary Schwabenlender, Instructor-Special Needs**
Name of Program: **Special Needs Services**
Telephone:**(414) 735-5679**

Admissions

Application Information:

Rolling Admissions: **Yes**

Secondary School Information

Most Important Criteria For Admissions (1-strongest)

11	SAT/ACT	**1**	Application	**3**	School transcript
7	Class rank	**1**	Course selection	**9**	Personal statement
4	Interview	**6**	Extra activities	**5**	Psychoeducational
2	G.P.A.		Open admission	**8**	Recommendations

Test Requirements:

Untimed ACT: **Yes** Untimed ACH: **Yes**

Types of Disabilities Served

• Speech/Lang	• Reading	• ADD with LD
• Study skills	• Spelling	• ADD without LD
• Written express	• Math	• ADHD with LD
• Organizational	• Fine Motor	• ADHD without LD
• Perceptual		

Learning Disability Program

Students mainstreamed **100** % of the day
Counseling: Individual: **Yes** Vocational Counseling: **Yes**

Faculty:

Faculty: **5** Full time: **3** Part time: **2**
LD faculty with: BS/BA: **5** M.A.: **2**
Faculty advocate: **Yes** Meets with instructor: **As needed**

Wisconsin

Diagnostic Testing

ADD	Personality	Perceptual skills	Spelling
ADHD	Organization	Fine motor skills	Reading
I.Q.	Handwriting	Spoken language	Study skills
Math	Social skills	Written language	

Tutoring:
Average size of group tutorials: **One-on-one**
Services rendered by:
  Graduates •Peers   •Faculty   •LD staff   Teacher trainees

Tutorials

Grp.	Ind.	Tutorials	Grp.	Ind.	Tutorials
	•	Math skills		•	Word processing
•	•	Study skills	•	•	Time management
		Language arts		•	Learning strategies
	•	Written express		•	Organizational skills

Academic Accommodations

Curriculum	Study Aids	Exams
Priority registration	• Typist	• Oral
Math waiver	Reader	Untimed
Foreign lang. waiver	• Notetaker	Take home
• Course substitution	Proof reader	• With proctor
In Class	• Text on tape	On computer
• Calculators	Early syllabus	• Extended time
• Tape recorder	Taped handouts	On tape
• Word processor		• Modified
Priority seating		Separate room

Program Strengths
We service handicapped and disadvantaged students by providing additional instructional support services and regular, on-going advisement and counseling. These services are tailored to meet the individualized educational needs of the student so that he or she can succeed in the course work.

General Information:
Fox Valley Technical College is a 2 year public college. Urban campus 100 miles from Milwaukee. Accessible by bus. Ski areas are 40-50 miles from campus. Beaches are 10 miles from campus. Housing is not guaranteed.

Accreditation: Regional

Expenses:
Tuition: In-state: Full year: $1,500.00-$2,000.00. Part-time: Per credit:$50.00.

Majors
• ARTS Drafting, Interior Design • BUSINESS Accounting, Banking/Finance, Clerical, Data Processing, Fashion Merchandising, Food Management, Hotel and Restaurant Management, Management, Marketing, Real Estate, Secretarial Science • COMPUTER SCIENCE Computer Science, Robotics, Telecommunications • HEALTH SCIENCES Dental Assistant, Nursing, Nursing Assistant, Occupational Therapy Assistant, Respiratory Therapy • PREPROFESSIONAL Natural Resources • VOCATIONAL Culinary Arts

Sports/Activities
• STUDENT LIFE ACTIVITIES Ethnic & Cultural Groups, Newspaper, Student Government

Gateway Technical College
3520 30th Avenue
Kenosha, Wisconsin 53144-1690
(414) 656-6911

School Enrollment: **10,000** Male: **4,000** Female: **6,000**
LD Enrollment: **365**

Admissions Contact: **Kurt Lehmann, Registrar**
LD Contact: **Jo Bailey, Learning Skills Specialist**
Name of Program: **Learning Skills**
Address: **1001 S. Main Street**
Telephone:**(414) 631-7360**

Admissions

Application Information:
LD Students Applying: **350**
Application deadline: **Late August and January**
Applicant must apply **2-6** months in advance
Rolling Admissions: **Yes**

Secondary School Information
Most Important Criteria For Admissions (1-strongest)

9	SAT/ACT	8	Application	7	School transcript
11	Class rank	5	Course selection	4	Personal statement
3	Interview	10	Extra activities	1	Psychoeducational
6	G.P.A.		Open admission	2	Recommendations

Test Requirements:
Standardized tests waived: **Yes**
Diagnostic testing waived: **Yes**
Untimed SAT: **Yes**
Documentation of LD required: **Yes**
Currency of diagnostic testing: **Just prior to**
Tests recommended: **Asset (intake) and/or IEP**

Types of Disabilities Served
• Speech/Lang	• Reading	• ADD with LD
• Study skills	• Spelling	• ADD without LD
• Written express	• Math	• ADHD with LD
• Organizational	• Fine Motor	• ADHD without LD
• Perceptual		

Admissions Process

Step one: See Jo Bailey in Student Services to write an EDP. Accommodations for testing and instruction are made from there.

High School Course Requirements:
Waivers to standard high school courses
  Course substitution: **Yes**

Learning Disability Program

Syllabus available during orientation:**Yes**
Program: Reinforces course work: **Yes**
Program available through:**At all times**
Students mainstreamed **100** % of the day
Recommended credits per semester: **6-12**
Services available for all students: **Yes**
Counseling: Individual: **Yes** Vocational Counseling: **Yes**
Support groups are available:**Ready, willing, able - advocacy**

Faculty:

Faculty: **4** Including Director: **1** Full time: **3** Part time: **1**
LD faculty with: BS/BA: **3** M.A.: **1**
Meets with instructor: **Daily**

Diagnostic Testing

- ADD
- ADHD
- I.Q.
- Math
- Personality
- Organization
- Handwriting
- Social skills
- Perceptual skills
- Fine motor skills
- Spoken language
- Written language
- Spelling
- Reading
- Study skills

Tutoring:

Average size of group tutorials: **1-5**
Services rendered by:
  Graduates • Peers • Faculty • LD staff   Teacher trainees

Tutorials

Grp.	Ind.	Tutorials	Grp.	Ind.	Tutorials
	•	Math skills		•	Word processing
	•	Study skills		•	Time management
	•	Language arts		•	Learning strategies
	•	Written express		•	Organizational skills

Academic Accommodations

Curriculum	Study Aids	Exams
• Priority registration	• Typist	• Oral
Math waiver	• Reader	• Untimed
• Foreign lang. waiver	• Notetaker	Take home
Course substitution	• Proof reader	With proctor
In Class	• Text on tape	• On computer
• Calculators	• Early syllabus	• Extended time
• Tape recorder	• Taped handouts	• On tape
• Word processor		• Modified
• Priority seating		• Separate room

Graduation Requirements:

Course credits: **Depends on program** GPA: **2.0** Years to complete degree: **1-7** Math waiver: **Yes**
Other requirements: **Attendance**

Program Strengths

Gateway Technical College welcomes students with disabilities. Ours is a mainstream approach. Help is available in the admission process, in planning the Gateway program, and in services during the disabled student's attendance at Gateway.

General Information:

Gateway Technical College is a 2 year public college. Rural campus of 3 acres is Accessible by bus. Ski areas are 15 miles from campus. Beaches are 2 miles from campus. Housing is not guaranteed.

Accreditation:NCACS

Expenses:

Tuition: In-state: Full year: $1,380.00, $3,300.00 for out of district. Tuition: Out-of-state: Full year: $8,400.00.

Majors

• BUSINESS Accounting, Aviation Management, Banking, Business Data Processing, Business Data Programming, Business Management, Finance, Hotel and Restaurant Management, Management, Marketing, Real Estate, Travel/Tourism Management • COMMUNICATIONS Broadcasting • COMPUTER SCIENCE Computer Technology • EDUCATION Child Development • HEALTH SCIENCES Medical Technology, Nursing • PREPROFESSIONAL Social Work • SCIENCES Botany, Horticultural • SOCIAL SCIENCES Human Service, Law Enforcement • VOCATIONAL Airline Piloting & Navigation, Automobile Technology, Automotive Service, Business and Office, Civil Technology, Court Reporting, Electrical Equipment Repair, Electromechanical Technology, Electronics Technology, Fashion Merchandising, Fire Science, Food Management, Industrial Technology, Interior Design, Manufacturing Technology, Mechanical Design Technology, Quality Control Technology, Radio/Television Technology, Secretarial, Surveying and Mapping

Sports/Activities

• STUDENT LIFE ACTIVITIES Community Service, Fraternities, Newspaper, Radio/TV station, Religious Organization, Sororities, Student Government

---

Highly Selective

Wisconsin
Services

Lawrence University

Box 599
Appleton, Wisconsin 54912
(414) 832-6530

School Enrollment: **1,138** Male: **564** Female: **574**

Admissions Contact: **Steven Syverson, Dean of Admissions**
LD Contact: **Martha Hemwall, Associate Dean**

Admissions

Application Information:

Application deadline: **February 15th**
Notified when: **April 1st**

Secondary School Information

Most Important Criteria For Admissions (1-strongest)

6 SAT/ACT	5 Application	1 School transcript
3 Class rank	4 Course selection	7 Personal statement
8 Interview	9 Extra activities	Psychoeducational
2 G.P.A.	Open admission	10 Recommendations

Test Requirements:

Untimed SAT: **Yes** Untimed ACT: **Yes** Untimed ACH: **Yes**
Documentation of LD required: **Yes**

Types of Disabilities Served

Speech/Lang	Reading	ADD with LD
Study skills	Spelling	ADD without LD
Written express	Math	ADHD with LD
Organizational	Fine Motor	ADHD without LD
Perceptual		

Admissions Process

Very holistic and humanistic. No "magic numbers". Consider each candidate based upon potential for success at Lawrence and likelihood of contribution to campus community. Environment from which candidate comes is carefully considered.

High School Course Requirements:
English: **4** Math: **3-4** Science: **3-4** Foreign Language: **2-3**

Learning Disability Program
Time required or recommended in learning center: **None**
Services only for LD students: **Yes**
Services available for all students: **Yes**

Diagnostic Testing
ADD	Personality	Perceptual skills	Spelling
ADHD	Organization	Fine motor skills	Reading
I.Q.	Handwriting	Spoken language	Study skills
Math	Social skills	Written language	

Tutoring:
Services rendered by:
Graduates	Peers	•Faculty	LD staff	Teacher trainees

Tutorials
Grp.	Ind.	Tutorials	Grp.	Ind.	Tutorials
	•	Math skills			Word processing
•		Study skills	•		Time management
		Language arts			Learning strategies
•	•	Written express	•		Organizational skills

Academic Accommodations
Curriculum	Study Aids	Exams
Priority registration	Typist	Oral
Math waiver	Reader	Untimed
Foreign lang. waiver	Notetaker	Take home
Course substitution	Proof reader	With proctor
In Class	Text on tape	On computer
Calculators	Early syllabus	Extended time
Tape recorder	Taped handouts	On tape
Word processor		Modified
Priority seating		Separate room

Graduation Requirements: GPA: **2.0**
Other requirements: **We have addressed waivers on an individual basis when a student's evaluation suggests this is appropriate.**

Program Strengths
Lawrence is a small selective college which demands a great deal of writing and analysis. However, our size allows us to address the specific needs of each individual student. The learning disabled student will work closely with an academic advisor and with the associate dean to identify appropriate accommodations. We assist students in discussions with instructors and staff about these accommodations. Academic support, such as tutoring is available to the entire student population and is not limited to the disabled students.

General Information:
Lawrence University is a 4 year independent college. of 1,250 acres is 80 miles from Milwaukee. Accessible by plane, train, or bus. 8% of students are foreign. Housing is guaranteed.Guaranteed through 4th year. 35 % of students join fraternities/sororities.

Accreditation: NCA

SAT/ACT Scores:
Scores for incoming freshmen: **Verbal:** 26%below 500. 43%between 500 and 599. 27%between 600 and 699. 4%above 700. **Math:** 14% below 500. 31% between 500 and 599. 45% between 600 and 699. 11%above 700. **ACT:** 2% below 20. 19% between 20 and 23. 14%between 24 and 25l.

37%between 26 and 28. 29% above 28.

Class Rank:
About 68% of the present freshmen class were in the upper 20% of their high school class. 94% were in the top 40% of their class. 99% were in the top 60% of their class. 100% were in the top 80% of their class.

Expenses:
Tuition: In-state: Full year: $15,342.00. Part-time: Per credit:$1,896.00 (1st credit), $1,692.00 (2nd credit), $1,536.00 (3rd credit). Tuition: Out-of-state: Full year: $15,342.00. Part-time: Per course:same as in state Room and board: $1,143.00

Majors
• ARTS Art History, Dramatic Arts • BUSINESS Economics • EDUCA-TION Art, English, Foreign Language, Mathematics, Music, Psychology, Science, Secondary, Social Studies • ENGINEERING Mathematical, Physics • HUMANITIES Classics, English/Writing/Literature, Philosophy • LANGUAGES Chinese, English, French, German, Greek, Latin, Linguistics, Russian, Spanish • MATHEMATICS Theoretical • PRE PROFESSIONAL Business, Engineering, Forestry, Law, Medicine • RELIGIOUS STUDIES Philosophy • SCIENCES Anthropology, Biology, Chemistry, Geology, Physics • SOCIAL SCIENCES Anthropology, Government/Political, History, Political Science, Psychology • VISUAL AND PERFORMING ARTS Art, Art History, Music, Music Performance, Studio Art, Theater

Sports/Activities
• SPORTS RELATED Cheerleading, Team Managers • SPORTS-INTER-COLLEGIATE Baseball, Baseball (M), Basketball, Basketball (F), Basketball (M), Crew, Crew (F), Crew (M), Diving, Diving (F), Diving (M), Fencing, Fencing (F), Fencing (M), Football, Football (M), Golf, Golf (M), Ice Hockey, Ice Hockey (M), Lacrosse, Rugby, Soccer, Soccer (F), Soccer (M), Softball, Softball (F), Swimming, Swimming (F), Swimming (M), Tennis, Tennis (F), Tennis (M), Track and Field, Track and Field (F), Track and Field (M), Volleyball, Volleyball (F), Wrestling, Wrestling (M) • SPORTS-INTRAMURAL Badminton, Badminton (M), Basketball, Basketball (F), Basketball (M), Bowling, Bowling (F), Bowling (M), Cross Country, Cross Country (M), Football, Football (F), Football (M), Racquetball, Racquetball (F), Racquetball (M), Soccer, Soccer (F), Soccer (M), Softball, Softball (F), Softball (M), Swimming, Swimming (F), Swimming (M), Tennis, Tennis (M), Track and Field, Track and Field (F), Track and Field (M), Volleyball, Volleyball (F), Volleyball (M), Water Polo, Water Polo (F), Water Polo (M) • STUDENT LIFE ACTIVITIES Academic Clubs, Choral, Community Service, Concert Band, Drama Groups, Ethnic & Cultural Groups, Film, Fraternities, Jazz Band, Magazine, Music Groups, Musical Theater, Newspaper, Orchestra, Political Groups, Radio, Religious Organization, Sororities, Student Government, Symphony Orchestra, Yearbook

Less Selective   **Wisconsin Services**

Marian College of Fond du Lac
45 South National Avenue
Fond du Lac, Wisconsin 54935-4699
(414) 923-7650

School Enrollment: **1,401** Male: **549** Female: **852**
LD Enrollment: **29** Male: **16** Female: **13**

Admissions Contact: **Carol Reichenberger, V.P. of Enrollment Serv**
LD Contact: **Gretchen Gall, Director, Academic Support Services**
Name of Program: **Academic Support Services**
Telephone: **(414) 923-8117**

Admissions

Application Information:
LD on admissions committee: **Yes**
Application deadline: **Rolling**
Applicant must apply **6-12** months in advance
Rolling Admissions: **Yes** Notified when: **within 1 month**

Secondary School Information
Most Important Criteria For Admissions (1-strongest)
4 SAT/ACT	**2** Application	**1** School transcript
3 Class rank	**4** Course selection	**4** Personal statement
1 Interview	**5** Extra activities	**1** Psychoeducational
1 G.P.A.	Open admission	**3** Recommendations

Test Requirements:
Diagnostic testing waived: **Yes**
Untimed SAT: **Yes** Untimed ACT: **Yes**
WAIS-R required: **Yes** Range accepted: **90+**
Documentation of LD required: **Yes**
Currency of diagnostic testing: **within 3 years**
Tests recommended: **DVR or current school M-Team**

Types of Disabilities Served
- Speech/Lang
- Study skills
- Written express
- Organizational
- Perceptual
- Reading
- Spelling
- Math
- Fine Motor
- ADD with LD
- ADD without LD
- ADHD with LD
- ADHD without LD

Admissions Process

Same for all students. High school GPA of 2.0, ACT composite of 18, completed high school in upper one-half of graduating class. Each applicant is treated as an individual - individual needs and qualifications are considered. Students may be accepted with provisions.

High School Course Requirements:
English: **3** Math: **2** Science: **1** Foreign Language: **1**

Learning Disability Program

Special orientation for LD students: **Yes**
Program: Reinforces course work: **Yes**
Students mainstreamed **100** % of the day
Recommended credits per semester: **12-15**
Time required or recommended in learning center: **None**
Services available for all students: **Yes**
Counseling: Individual: **Yes** Vocational Counseling: **Yes**
Support groups are available: **Yes**

Faculty:
Faculty: **2** Including Director: **Yes** Full time: **1** Part time: **1**
LD faculty with: BS/BA: **1** M.A.: **1**
Faculty advocate: **Yes** Meets with instructor: **Every 3-4 weeks**

Diagnostic Testing
ADD	Personality	Perceptual skills	Spelling
ADHD	Organization	Fine motor skills	Reading
I.Q.	Handwriting	Spoken language	Study skills
Math	Social skills	Written language	

Tutoring:
Average size of group tutorials: **3-10**
Services rendered by:
Graduates	•Peers	•Faculty	•LD staff	Teacher trainees

Tutorials
Grp.	Ind.	Tutorials	Grp.	Ind.	Tutorials
	•	Math skills			Word processing
	•	Study skills		•	Time management
	•	Language arts		•	Learning strategies
	•	Written express		•	Organizational skills

Academic Accommodations
Curriculum	Study Aids	Exams
Priority registration	Typist	• Oral
Math waiver	• Reader	• Untimed
Foreign lang. waiver	• Notetaker	Take home
• Course substitution	• Proof reader	• With proctor
In Class	• Text on tape	• On computer
• Calculators	• Early syllabus	• Extended time
• Tape recorder	Taped handouts	• On tape
• Word processor		• Modified
• Priority seating		• Separate room

Graduation Requirements:
Course credits: **128** GPA: **2.0** Years to complete degree: **4-5**

Program Strengths

Our program is individualized to meet the support needs of LD students. Students are most successful who know the supports they need and can advocate for themselves. Small teacher-student ratio (approximately 1-15) means faculty are open and supportive to all students. Math and Writing Labs as well as one-on-one peer tutoring and LD support is available.

General Information:

Marian College of Fond du Lac is a 4 year private Roman Catholic college. Urban campus 90 miles from Milwaukee. Accessible by air or bus. Ski areas are 40 mile from campus. Beaches are 1 mile from campus. 9% of students are foreign. 2 residential halls on campus. Housing is guaranteed. 65 % of students remain on campus for the weekends.

Accreditation: NCACS, NCATE, NLN, CSWE

Expenses:
Tuition: In-state: Full year: $7,400.00. Part-time: Per credit: $175.00. Tuition: Out-of-state: Full year: $7,400.00. Part-time: Per credit: $175.00. Room and board: $3,000.00

Majors

• BUSINESS Accounting, Business Education, Management, Marketing, Retailing, Sports Management • COMMUNICATIONS English • EDUCATION Art, Early Childhood, Elementary, English, Foreign Language, Mathematics, Middle School, Music, Religious, Secondary, Social Studies • HEALTH SCIENCES Medical Technology, Nursing, Radiological Technology • HUMANITIES Humanities, Liberal Arts • LANGUAGES Spanish • PREPROFESSIONAL Dentistry, Law, Medicine, Pharmacy, Veterinarian • SCIENCES Biology, Chemistry, Cytotechnology, Mathematics • SOCIAL SCIENCES Administration of Justice, History, Psychology, Social Work • VISUAL AND PERFORMING ARTS Art, Music

Sports/Activities

• SPORTS-INTERCOLLEGIATE Baseball (M), Basketball, Cross Country, Golf (M), Soccer (M), Softball (F), Volleyball (F) • SPORTS-INTRAMURAL Badminton, Baseball (M), Basketball (F), Basketball (M), Bowling, Cross Country (F), Cross Country (M), Football, Flag, Golf (M), Skiing - Snow, Soccer (F), Soccer (M), Softball (F), Softball (M), Tennis (F), Tennis (M), Volleyball, Volleyball (F) • STUDENT LIFE ACTIVITIES Choral, Concert Band, Drama Groups, Ethnic & Cultural Groups, Magazine, Music Groups, Newspaper, Religious Organization, Show Choir, Student Government, Symphony Orchestra, Yearbook

Very Selective	**Wisconsin Services**

Marquette University
1217 West Wisconsin Avenue
Milwaukee, Wisconsin 53233
(414) 288-7302

School Enrollment: **8,409** Male: **4,229** Female: **4,180**
LD Enrollment: **15-20**

Admissions Contact: **Leo B. Flynn, Director of Admissions**
LD Contact: **Patricia Almon, Coordinator**
Name of Program: **Disability Services**
Address: **Holthusen Hall, 1324 W. Wisconsin Ave.**
Telephone:**(414) 288-1645**

Admissions

Application Information:
Application deadline: **Dec. 15 for Physical Therapy, others rolling**
Rolling Admissions: **Yes**

Secondary School Information
Most Important Criteria For Admissions (1-strongest)

2 SAT/ACT	**6** Application	**3** School transcript
1 Class rank	**3** Course selection	Personal statement
Interview	Extra activities	Psychoeducational
1 G.P.A.	Open admission	**5** Recommendations

Test Requirements:
Diagnostic testing waived: **Yes**
Untimed SAT: **Yes** Untimed ACT: **Yes**
Documentation of LD required: **Yes**
Currency of diagnostic testing: **3-5 years**

Types of Disabilities Served

Speech/Lang	Reading	ADD with LD
Study skills	Spelling	ADD without LD
Written express	Math	ADHD with LD
Organizational	Fine Motor	ADHD without LD
Perceptual		

Admissions Process

The process for LD students at present is no different than for other academically qualified students.

High School Course Requirements:
English: **4** Math: **3** Science: **2** Foreign Language: **2**

Learning Disability Program
Students mainstreamed **100** % of the day
Recommended credits per semester: **12**
Services available for all students: **Yes**
Counseling: Individual: **Yes**

Faculty:
Faculty: **1** Including Director: **Yes** Full time: **1**
Faculty advocate: **Yes** Meets with instructor: **Depends on student**

Diagnostic Testing

ADD	Personality	Perceptual skills	Spelling
ADHD	Organization	Fine motor skills	Reading
I.Q.	Handwriting	Spoken language	Study skills
Math	Social skills	Written language	

Services rendered by:

Graduates	Peers	Faculty	LD staff	Teacher trainees

Tutorials

Grp.	Ind.	Tutorials	Grp.	Ind.	Tutorials
	•	Math skills		•	Word processing
•	•	Study skills		•	Time management
	•	Language arts			Learning strategies
	•	Written express			Organizational skills

Academic Accommodations

Curriculum	Study Aids	Exams
• Priority registration	Typist	Oral
Math waiver	Reader	Untimed
• Foreign lang. waiver	• Notetaker	Take home
• Course substitution	Proof reader	• With proctor
In Class	• Text on tape	On computer
• Calculators	Early syllabus	• Extended time
• Tape recorder	Taped handouts	On tape
• Word processor		Modified
Priority seating		Separate room

Graduation Requirements:
Course credits: **128** GPA: **2.0** Years to complete degree: **4 years if possible** Language waiver: **Yes**
Other requirements: **Course substitutes are available to fulfill course requirements.**

Program Strengths
Marquette does not have an LD program or specific LD-related services. We try to accommodate students as best we can with the resources available on the campus and in the community, on a case by case basis.
* Tutoring is offered on an as need basis.

General Information:
Marquette University is a 4 year private Roman Catholic university. Urban campus of 80 acres is Milwaukee. Accessible by air, train, or bus. Ski areas are 25 miles from campus. Beaches are 5 miles from campus. 4% of students are foreign. 9 residential halls on campus. Housing is guaranteed.Guaranteed through 4th year. 42 % of students remain on campus for the weekends. 10 % of students join fraternities/sororities.

Accreditation:NCACS

SAT/ACT Scores:
Scores for incoming freshmen:**Verbal:**55%below 500. 35%between 500 and 599. 9%between 600 and 699. 1%above 700. **Math:**28% below 500. 40% between 500 and 599. 27% between 600 and 699. 5%above 700. **ACT:** 6% below 20. 28% between 20 and 23. 23%between 24 and 251. 28%between 26 and 28. 15% above 28.

Class Rank:
About 57% of the present freshmen class were in the upper 20% of their high school class. 84% were in the top 40% of their class. 96% were in the top 60% of their class. 100% were in the top 80% of their class.

Expenses:
Tuition: In-state: Full year: $9,900.00-$10,400.00 (depends on study area). Part-time: Per credit:$235.00. Tuition: Out-of-state: Full year: $9,900.00-$10,400.00 (depends on study area). Part-time: Per credit:$235.00. Room and board: $4,350.00

Majors

• AREA STUDIES International Studies • BUSINESS Accounting, Business Administration, Business Economics, Business Management, Finance, Human Resources Management, International Business, Marketing • COMMUNICATIONS Advertising, Broadcasting, Communication, Journalism, Public Relations, Television/Radio/Film • COMPUTER SCIENCE Computer Mathematics, Computer Science • EDUCATION Bilingual, Elementary • ENGINEERING Biomedical, Civil/Environmental, Electrical, Industrial, Mechanical • HEALTH SCIENCES Dental Hygiene, Medical Laboratory Technology, Nursing, Physical Therapy, Speech Therapy, Speech/Audiology and Speech • HUMANITIES English/Writing/Literature, Philosophy • LANGUAGES French, German, Latin, Spanish • PRE-PROFESSIONAL Dentistry, Law, Medicine • RELIGIOUS STUDIES Religion and Theology • SCIENCES Biochemistry, Biology, Chemistry, Computer Science, Mathematics, Molecular Biology, Physics • SOCIAL SCIENCES Anthropology, Criminology, History, International Studies, Law Enforcement, Political Science, Psychology, Sociology • VISUAL AND PERFORMING ARTS Dramatic Arts, Theater

Sports/Activities

• SPORTS RELATED Cheerleading, Chess, Drill Team, Pep Band, Team Managers • SPORTS-INTERCOLLEGIATE Basketball, Cross Country, Golf (M), Soccer (M), Tennis, Track and Field, Volleyball (F) • SPORTS-INTRAMURAL Badminton, Baseball (M), Basketball, Bowling, Crew, Diving, Field Hockey, Football, Golf, Ice Hockey (M), Lacrosse (M), Racquetball, Rugby (M), Sailing, Skiing - Snow, Soccer, Softball (F), Squash, Swimming, Tennis, Volleyball, Water Polo • STUDENT LIFE ACTIVITIES Academic Clubs, Choral, Community Service, Concert Band, Dance, Drama Groups, Ethnic & Cultural Groups, Fraternities, Jazz Band, Magazine, Music Groups, Musical Theater, Newspaper, Orchestra, Political Groups, Radio/TV station, Religious Organization, Sororities, Student Government, Symphony Orchestra, Yearbook

Less Selective	Wisconsin Program

Milwaukee Area Technical College

700 West State Street
Milwaukee, Wisconsin 53233
(414) 278-6220

School Enrollment: **76,000**
LD Enrollment: **200**
LD Contact: **Brenda H. Benton, Guidance Counselor**
Name of Program: **Learning Impaired Program**
Telephone:**(414) 278-6594**

Admissions

Application Information:
LD Students Applying: **300** Accepted: **175** Enrolled:**175**
LD on admissions committee:**Yes**
Application deadline: **August**
Applicant must apply **10** months in advance
Rolling Admissions: **Yes**

Secondary School Information
Most Important Criteria For Admissions (1-strongest)

SAT/ACT		Application	1	School transcript	
Class rank	2	Course selection	11	Personal statement	
1	Interview	11	Extra activities	1	Psychoeducational
1	G.P.A.		Open admission	11	Recommendations

Test Requirements:
Standardized tests waived: **Yes**
Diagnostic testing waived: **Yes**
Untimed SAT: **Yes** Untimed ACT: **Yes**
WAIS-R required: **Yes**
Documentation of LD required: **Yes**
Currency of diagnostic testing: **1 year**

Types of Disabilities Served
• Speech/Lang	• Reading	• ADD with LD
• Study skills	• Spelling	• ADD without LD
• Written express	• Math	• ADHD with LD
• Organizational	• Fine Motor	• ADHD without LD
• Perceptual		

Admissions Process

Send application, high school or college transcript, and documentation of disability to guidance counselor. Counselor will notify student regarding admission test data.

Learning Disability Program

Program: Reinforces course work: **Yes**
Program available through:**Depends on schedule**
Students mainstreamed **100** % of the day
Recommended credits per semester: **9-12**
Services only for LD students: **Yes**
Counseling: Individual: **Yes** Vocational Counseling: **Yes**
Support groups are available:**Yes**

Faculty:
Faculty: **7** Full time: **5** Part time: **2**
LD faculty with: BS/BA: **4** M.A.: **2** Ph.D.: **1**
Faculty advocate: **Yes** Meets with instructor: **Regularly**

Diagnostic Testing
• ADD	• Personality	• Perceptual skills	• Spelling
• ADHD	• Organization	Fine motor skills	• Reading
• I.Q.	• Handwriting	• Spoken language	• Study skills
• Math	• Social skills	• Written language	

Tutoring:
Services rendered by:
•Graduates •Peers •Faculty •LD staff Teacher trainees

Tutorials
Grp.	Ind.	Tutorials	Grp.	Ind.	Tutorials
•	•	Math skills		•	Word processing
•	•	Study skills	•	•	Time management
•	•	Language arts	•	•	Learning strategies
•	•	Written express	•	•	Organizational skills

Academic Accommodations

Curriculum	Study Aids	Exams
• Priority registration	Typist	• Oral
Math waiver	• Reader	• Untimed
Foreign lang. waiver	• Notetaker	• Take home
• Course substitution	• Proof reader	• With proctor
In Class	• Text on tape	• On computer
• Calculators	Early syllabus	• Extended time
• Tape recorder	Taped handouts	On tape
• Word processor		• Modified
• Priority seating		• Separate room

Graduation Requirements:
Course credits: **varies** GPA: **2.0** Years to complete degree: **Varying**

Wisconsin

General Information:
Milwaukee Area Technical College is a 2 year public college. Urban campus Accessible by air, train or bus. Housing is not guaranteed.

Accreditation:

Expenses:
Tuition: In-state: Full year: Part-time: Per credit: $48.00.

Majors
• BUSINESS Accounting, Business Administration, Business Education, Business Management, Economics, Finance, Hotel and Restaurant Management, Marketing, Marketing Research, Real Estate, Travel/Tourism Management • COMMUNICATIONS Advertising, Communication, Creative Writing, English, Photography, Television/Radio/Film • COMPUTER SCIENCE Data Processing, Programming, Systems Analysis • EDUCATION Early Childhood, Health, Music, Vocational • HEALTH SCIENCES Health, Medical Secretary, Nursing, Nutritional/Food, Occupational Therapy, Physical Therapy, Radiological Therapy • HUMANITIES Humanities, Philosophy • PREPROFESSIONAL Agriculture, Architecture, Pharmacy, Social Work • SCIENCES Biology, Botany, Chemistry, Mathematics, Microbiology • SOCIAL SCIENCES Psychology, Social Sciences, Sociology

Sports/Activities
• STUDENT LIFE ACTIVITIES Music Groups, Newspaper, Radio/TV station, Student Government

Less Selective	Wisconsin
	Services

Moraine Park Technical Institute
235 North National Avenue
Fond du Lac, Wisconsin 54935
(414) 922-8611

School Enrollment: **8,033** Male: **3,778** Female: **4,255**

Admissions Contact: **Don Smeaton Counselor**
LD Contact: **Joel P. Newcomb Learning Specialist**
Name of Program: **Student Services**
Telephone:**(414) 922-8611 Ext. 296**

Admissions

Application Information:
Application deadline: **May 1st**
Rolling Admissions: **Yes**

Secondary School Information
Most Important Criteria For Admissions (1-strongest)

SAT/ACT	Application	School transcript
Class rank	Course selection	Personal statement
Interview	Extra activities	Psychoeducational
G.P.A.	Open admission	Recommendations

Test Requirements:
Documentation of LD required: **Yes**

Types of Disabilities Served
• Speech/Lang	• Reading	ADD with LD
• Study skills	• Spelling	ADD without LD
• Written express	• Math	ADHD with LD
• Organizational	• Fine Motor	ADHD without LD
• Perceptual		

Learning Disability Program
Services only for LD students: **Yes**

Faculty:
Faculty: **1** Full time: **1**
LD faculty with: BS/BA: **.5** M.A.: **1**

Diagnostic Testing
ADD	Personality	Perceptual skills	Spelling
ADHD	Organization	Fine motor skills	Reading
I.Q.	Handwriting	Spoken language	Study skills
Math	Social skills	Written language	

Tutoring:
Services rendered by:
•Graduates	Peers	Faculty	LD staff	Teacher trainees

Tutorials
Grp.	Ind.	Tutorials	Grp.	Ind.	Tutorials
	•	Math skills			Word processing
	•	Study skills		•	Time management
	•	Language arts	•	•	Learning strategies
•		Written express	•		Organizational skills

Academic Accommodations
Curriculum	Study Aids	Exams
Priority registration	Typist	Oral
Math waiver	Reader	Untimed
Foreign lang. waiver	• Notetaker	Take home
Course substitution	Proof reader	With proctor
In Class	• Text on tape	• On computer
• Calculators	Early syllabus	• Extended time
• Tape recorder	Taped handouts	On tape
• Word processor		Modified
Priority seating		Separate room

Program Strengths
Moraine Park Technical College has a Learning Specialist who will help students with learning problems through their program by: providing assistance to instructors on modifying teaching strategies; assessing and identifying students with learning problems; and coordinating existing resources.

General Information:
Moraine Park Technical Institute is a 2 year public college. Urban campus 60 miles from Milwaukee. Accessible by bus. Housing is not guaranteed.

Accreditation:

Expenses:
Tuition: In-state: Full year: Part-time: Per credit: $98.00. Tuition: Out-of-state: Full year: Part-time: Per credit: $321.00.

Majors
• BUSINESS Accounting, Business Data Processing, Business Data Programming, Business System Analysis, Marketing Communications • COMPUTER SCIENCE Computer Technology, Marketing Communications, Medical Records Technology, Programming • EDUCATION Child Development • ENVIRONMENTAL CONTROL Water and Wastewater Technology • HEALTH SCIENCES Medical Secretary, Nursing, Practical Nursing • SCIENCES Food • VOCATIONAL Auto Detailing, Civil Technology, Culinary Arts, Drafting, Electrical Equipment Repair, Electromechanical Technology, Food Service, Industrial Screen Printing, Industrial Technology, Legal Secretary, Mechanical Design Technology, Office Administration, Secretarial, Word Processing

Sports/Activities
• SPORTS-INTERCOLLEGIATE Golf • SPORTS-INTRAMURAL Basketball, Bowling, Softball, Table Tennis, Volleyball

Less Selective	Wisconsin Program

Northeast Wisconsin Technical College
P. O. Box 19042
Green Bay, Wisconsin 54307-9042
(414) 498-5600

School Enrollment: **4,500**
LD Enrollment: **75**

Admissions Contact: **Jerome L. Miller, Vocational Counselor**
LD Contact: **Julie Pullin, LD Instructor**
Name of Program: **Special Needs Services**
Address: **2740 West Mason**
Telephone: **(414) 498-5470**

Admissions

Application Information:
Applicant must apply **3-6** months in advance
Rolling Admissions: **Yes**

Secondary School Information
Most Important Criteria For Admissions (1-strongest)

7 SAT/ACT	6 Application	2 School transcript
4 Class rank	1 Course selection	9 Personal statement
1 Interview	8 Extra activities	3 Psychoeducational
5 G.P.A.	Open admission	9 Recommendations

Test Requirements:
Standardized tests waived: **Yes**
Diagnostic testing waived: **Yes**
Documentation of LD required: **Yes**
Currency of diagnostic testing: **6-12 months**
Tests recommended: **Timed/untimed reading/math evaluation**

Types of Disabilities Served
• Speech/Lang • Reading • ADD with LD
• Study skills • Spelling • ADD without LD
• Written express • Math • ADHD with LD
• Organizational • Fine Motor • ADHD without LD
• Perceptual

Learning Disability Program
Program: Remedial: **Yes**
Program: Reinforces course work: **Yes**
Students mainstreamed **100** % of the day
Services available for all students: **Yes**
Counseling: Individual: **Yes** Vocational Counseling: **Yes**

Faculty:
Faculty: **3** Full time: **2** Part time: **1**
LD faculty with: BS/BA: **1** M.A.: **2**
Faculty advocate: **Yes** Meets with instructor: **As needed**

Diagnostic Testing
• ADD • Personality • Perceptual skills • Spelling
  ADHD • Organization • Fine motor skills • Reading
  I.Q.   Handwriting   Spoken language • Study skills
• Math   Social skills • Written language

Tutoring:
Average size of group tutorials: **2-3**
Services rendered by:
•Graduates •Peers •Faculty •LD staff   Teacher trainees

Tutorials

Grp.	Ind.	Tutorials	Grp.	Ind.	Tutorials
•	•	Math skills		•	Word processing
•	•	Study skills		•	Time management
•	•	Language arts	•	•	Learning strategies
•	•	Written express	•	•	Organizational skills

Academic Accommodations

Curriculum	Study Aids	Exams
Priority registration	• Typist	• Oral
• Math waiver	• Reader	Untimed
Foreign lang. waiver	• Notetaker	Take home
Course substitution	Proof reader	• With proctor
In Class	• Text on tape	On computer
Calculators	Early syllabus	• Extended time
• Tape recorder	Taped handouts	On tape
• Word processor		• Modified
Priority seating		Separate room

Graduation Requirements:
Course credits: **Varies** GPA: **2.0** Years to complete degree: **1-5**

Program Strengths
Our utilization by LD students speaks to our quality.

General Information:
Northeast Wisconsin Technical College is a 2 year public college. Urban campus of 120 acres is Accessible by bus. Ski areas are 40 miles from campus. Beaches are 55 miles from campus. Housing is not guaranteed.

Accreditation: NCACS

Expenses:
Tuition: In-state: Full year: $1,325.00. Part-time: Per credit: $38.00. Tuition: Out-of-state: Full year: $7,440.00. Part-time: Per credit: $310.00.

Majors
• BUSINESS Accounting, Agricultural, Banking, Business Administration, Business Data Processing, Business Education, Business Management, Economics, Finance, Management, Marketing, Travel/Tourism Management • COMMUNICATIONS Advertising, Communication • COMPUTER SCIENCE Data Processing, Programming, Telecommunications • EDUCATION Vocational • ENGINEERING Civil/Environmental • HEALTH SCIENCES Dental Assistant, Medical Secretary, Medical Technology, Nursing, Physical Therapy • PREPROFESSIONAL Agriculture, Architecture, Legal Assistant • SOCIAL SCIENCES Law Enforcement • VOCATIONAL Automobile Technology, Automotive Service, Drafting, Electromechanical Technology, Fashion Merchandising, Fashion Merchandising, Fire Science, Instrumentation Technology, Legal Secretary, Machinist, Manufacturing Technology, Office Administration, Quality Control Technology, Respiratory Therapy Technology, Secretarial

Sports
• SPORTS-INTRAMURAL Baseball, Bowling, Golf, Softball, Tennis
• STUDENT LIFE ACTIVITIES Newspaper, Radio/TV station, Religious Organization, Student Government

| **Very Selective** | **Wisconsin Program** |

Ripon College
P.O. Box 248
Ripon, Wisconsin 54971
(414) 748-8107

School Enrollment: **800** Male: **400** Female: **400**
LD Enrollment: **25** Male: **19** Female: **6**

Admissions Contact: **Paul Weeks, Director**
LD Contact: **Dan Korhin, Director, Student Support Services**
Name of Program: **Educational Development Program**
Telephone:**(414) 748-8107**

Admissions

Application Information:
Application deadline: **March 15th**
Rolling Admissions: **Yes** Notified when: **After Jan. 1st**

Secondary School Information
Most Important Criteria For Admissions (1-strongest)

3 SAT/ACT	Application	School transcript
6 Class rank	**2** Course selection	**8** Personal statement
7 Interview	**5** Extra activities	**9** Psychoeducational
1 G.P.A.	Open admission	**4** Recommendations

Test Requirements:
Untimed SAT: **Yes** Untimed ACT: **Yes**
Documentation of LD required: **Yes**

Types of Disabilities Served
- Speech/Lang
- Reading
- ADD with LD
- Study skills
- Spelling
- ADD without LD
- Written express
- Math
- ADHD with LD
- Organizational
- Fine Motor
- ADHD without LD
- Perceptual

Admissions Process

Rolling after January 1st

High School Course Requirements:
English: **4** Math: **2**

Learning Disability Program

Program: Reinforces course work: **Yes**
Program available through:**during school session**
Students mainstreamed **100** % of the day
Recommended credits per semester: **15-16**
Services available for all students: **Yes**
Counseling: Individual: **Yes** Vocational Counseling: **Yes**
Support groups are available:**As needed depending on the student's academic performance**

Faculty:
Faculty: **2** Full time: **2**
LD faculty with: BS/BA: **2**

Diagnostic Testing
ADD	Personality	Perceptual skills	Spelling
ADHD	Organization	Fine motor skills	Reading
I.Q.	Handwriting	Spoken language	Study skills
Math	Social skills	Written language	

Tutoring:
Average size of group tutorials: **2-3**
Services rendered by:
Graduates •Peers Faculty LD staff Teacher trainees

Tutorials

Grp.	Ind.	Tutorials	Grp.	Ind.	Tutorials
	•	Math skills		•	Word processing
•	•	Study skills	•	•	Time management
	•	Language arts	•	•	Learning strategies
	•	Written express	•	•	Organizational skills

Academic Accommodations

Curriculum	Study Aids	Exams
Priority registration	• Typist	• Oral
Math waiver	Reader	• Untimed
• Foreign lang. waiver	• Notetaker	• Take home
Course substitution	• Proof reader	• With proctor
In Class	• Text on tape	• On computer
• Calculators	Early syllabus	• Extended time
• Tape recorder	Taped handouts	On tape
Word processor		• Modified
• Priority seating		• Separate room

Graduation Requirements:
Course credits: **123** GPA: **2.0** Language waiver: **Yes**
Other requirements: **A major with no required course having less than A**

Program Strengths
Very close working relationship with student, family, and faculty. Student Support Services Program staff easy access to services, high retention rate of LD students in past 16 years of program. We had an LD student selected in 1991 to give the commencement speech. Generous accommodations by faculty for evaluations.

General Information:
Ripon College is a 4 year independent United Church of Christ college. Rural campus of 200 acres is 22 miles from Oshkosh. Accessible by bus Ski areas are 30 miles from campus. Beaches are 10 miles from campus. 3% of students are foreign. 8 residential halls on campus. Housing is guaranteed.Guaranteed through 4th year. 90 % of students remain on campus for the weekends. 45 % of students join fraternities/sororities.

Accreditation:NCACS

SAT/ACT Scores:
Scores for incoming freshmen:**Verbal:**20%below 500. 39%between 500 and 599. 28%between 600 and 699. 13%above 700. **Math:**11% below 500. 54% between 500 and 599. 25% between 600 and 699. 10%above 700. **ACT:** 14% below 20. 32% between 20 and 23. 17%between 24 and 25l. 16%between 26 and 28. 21% above 28.

Class Rank:
About 54% of the present freshmen class were in the upper 20% of their high school class. 27% were in the top 40% of their class. 12% were in the top 60% of their class. 5% were in the top 80% of their class.

Expenses:
Tuition: In-state: Full year: $12,740.00. Tuition: Out-of-state: Full year: $12,740.00. Room and board: $3,150.00

Majors

• AREA STUDIES Women's Studies • ARTS Art History, Music • BUSINESS Business Management • COMMUNICATIONS English • COMPUTER SCIENCE Computer Science • HUMANITIES Classics, Philosophy, Religion • LANGUAGES French, German, Greek, Latin, Spanish • PRE PROFESSIONAL Business, Dentistry, Engineering, Forestry, Law, Medicine, Ministry, Optometry, Pharmacy, Social Work, Sports Medicine, Veterinarian • RELIGIOUS STUDIES Bible, Judaism & Jewish Studies • SCIENCES Anatomy, Anthropology, Archeology, Astronomy, Astrophysics, BiologY • SOCIAL SCIENCES Anthropology, History, Political Science, Psychology, Sociology

Sports/Activities

• SPORTS RELATED Cheerleading, Chess, Team Managers • SPORTS-INTERCOLLEGIATE Baseball (M), Basketball (F), Basketball (M), Cross Country (F), Cross Country (M), Football (F), Golf (F), Golf (M), Soccer (F), Soccer (M), Softball (F), Swimming (F), Swimming (M), Tennis (F), Tennis (M), Track and Field (F), Track and Field (M), Volleyball (F), WRESTLING(M) • SPORTS-INTRAMURAL Archery (F), Archery (M), Badminton (F), Badminton (M), Basketball (F), Basketball (M), Bowling (F), Bowling (M), Football, Golf (F), Golf (M), Ice Hockey (M), Judo, Lacrosse (F), Lacrosse (M), Martial Arts, Ping-Pong (F), Ping-Pong (M), Racquetball (F), Racquetball (M), Soccer (F), Soccer (M), Softball (F), Softball (M), Tennis (F), Tennis (M), Volleyball (F), Volleyball (M), Water Polo (F), Water Polo (M) • STUDENT LIFE ACTIVITIES Academic Clubs, Choral, Community Service, Dance, Debate, Drama Groups, Ethnic & Cultural Groups, Film, Fraternities, Magazine, Music Ensemble, Newspaper, Orchestra, Political Groups, Radio/TV station, Religious Organization, Sororities, Student Government, Symphony Orchestra, Yearbook

---

Selective   **Wisconsin**
                                 Services

University of Wisconsin - Milwaukee

P.O. Box 413
Milwaukee, Wisconsin 53201
(414) 229-3800

School Enrollment: **25,000** Male: **11,750** Female: **13,250**
LD Enrollment: **100**
LD Contact: **Laurie Gramatzki, Program Manager**
Name of Program: **Learning Disabilities Program**
Address: **Disabled Student Services**
Telephone:**(414) 229-6239**

Admissions

Application Information:
Application deadline: **June 30th-Fall - Nov. 15th - Spring**
Applicant must apply **6** months in advance
Rolling Admissions: **Yes**

Secondary School Information
Most Important Criteria For Admissions (1-strongest)
4 SAT/ACT **12** Application **10** School transcript
8 Class rank **6** Course selection **11** Personal statement
3 Interview **9** Extra activities **2** Psychoeducational
7 G.P.A. Open admission **5** Recommendations

Test Requirements:
Diagnostic testing waived: **Yes**
Untimed SAT: **Yes** Untimed ACT: **Yes** Achievement tests required:**3**
WAIS-R required: **Yes**
Documentation of LD required: **Yes**
Currency of diagnostic testing: **Within three years**
Tests recommended: **Psychoeducational including WAIS-R, Woodcock-Johnson Psycho Educational Battery Revised (tests of**

---

achievement), with academic recommendations.

Types of Disabilities Served

• Speech/Lang	• Reading	• ADD with LD
• Study skills	• Spelling	ADD without LD
• Written express	• Math	• ADHD with LD
• Organizational	• Fine Motor	ADHD without LD
• Perceptual		

Admissions Process

Regular admissions procedures with additional review and modified admissions standards. Documentation to be sent to LD program.

High School Course Requirements:
English: **4** Math: **2** Science: **2**
Waivers to standard high school courses
Course substitution: **Yes**

Learning Disability Program

Program: Remedial: **Yes**
Program: Reinforces course work: **Yes**
Program available through:**When needed**
Students mainstreamed **100** % of the day
Recommended credits per semester: **9-12**
Services only for LD students: **Yes**
Counseling: Individual: **Yes** Vocational Counseling: **Yes**
Support groups are available:**Students with a disability - student run support group, social support network**

Faculty:
Faculty: **1** Including Director: **Yes** Part time: **1** M.A.: **1**
Meets with instructor: **As needed**

Diagnostic Testing
ADD	Personality	• Perceptual skills	• Spelling
ADHD	• Organization	• Fine motor skills	• Reading
• I.Q.	Handwriting	• Spoken language	Study skills
• Math	Social skills	• Written language	

Tutoring:
Average size of group tutorials: **3**
Services rendered by:
•Graduates •Peers Faculty LD staff •Teacher trainees

Tutorials
Grp.	Ind.	Tutorials	Grp.	Ind.	Tutorials
•			•		Word processing
	•	Math skills		•	Time management
•	•	Study skills		•	Learning strategies
	•	Language arts		•	Organizational skills
	•	Written express			

Academic Accommodations

Curriculum	Study Aids	Exams
• Priority registration	Typist	• Oral
Math waiver	• Reader	Untimed
Foreign lang. waiver	• Notetaker	Take home
Course substitution	• Proof reader	• With proctor
In Class	• Text on tape	• On computer
Calculators	Early syllabus	• Extended time
• Tape recorder	Taped handouts	• On tape
• Word processor		• Modified
• Priority seating		• Separate room

Graduation Requirements:
Course credits: **Varies** GPA: **Varies** Years to complete degree: **4-5**
Other requirements: **Varies**

Wisconsin

Program Strengths

The Learning Disabilities Program is a component of Disabled Student Service which provides academic support services to students with learning disabilities. The University of Wisconsin-Milwaukee is well suited for those students who can basically function independently with some academic support available. If students are not regularly admissible to UWM, they will need to apply to DLSEO and take placement tests. It is the reading placement test that can have a deciding affect on admissions.

General Information:

University of Wisconsin - Milwaukee is a 4 year public university. Urban campus of 93 acres is Accessible by bus, train or air. Ski areas are 35 miles from campus. Beaches are 1 mile from campus. 1 residential halls on campus. Housing is not guaranteed.

Accreditation:

Expenses:

Tuition: In-state: Full year: $1,078.50. Part-time: Per credit:$137.60. Tuition: Out-of-state: Full year: $3,440.50. Part-time: Per credit:$334.35. Room and board: $2,300.00-$3,360.00

Majors

• AREA STUDIES Black/Afro-American, Women's Studies • ARTS Film Arts, Music, Music History, Music Performance • BUSINESS Accounting, Banking/Finance, Business Management, Economics, International Business, Labor Relations, Management, Marketing, Real Estate • COMMUNICATIONS Broadcasting, Communication, Creative Writing, Graphic Design, Journalism, Linguistics, Photography, Television/Radio/Film • COMPUTER SCIENCE Computer Science • EDUCATION Early Childhood, Elementary, English As A Second Language, Middle School, Secondary, Special • ENGINEERING Civil/Environmental, Electrical, Industrial, Material, Mechanical • HEALTH SCIENCES Health, Medical Records Administration, Nursing, Occupational Therapy, Speech/Audiology and Speech • HUMANITIES Classics, English/Writing/Literature, Fine Arts, Liberal Arts , Philosophy • LANGUAGES Entomology, French, German, Hebrew, Italian, Russian, Spanish • PRE PROFESSIONAL Architecture, Dentistry, Medicine, Pharmacy, Social Work • RELIGIOUS STUDIES Religion and Theology • SCIENCES Anthropology, Applied Mathematics, Biology, Botany, Chemistry, Geography, Geology, Mathematics, Physics, Statistics • SOCIAL SCIENCES Criminal Justice, Government/Political, History, International Studies, Polymer Science, Psychology, Sociology • SPECIAL EDUCATION Deaf/Hearing Impaired, Emotionally Disturbed, Learning Disability, Mentally Retarded • VISUAL AND PERFORMING ARTS Art History, Cinematography/Film, Dance, Dramatic Arts, Music

Sports/Activities

• SPORTS-INTERCOLLEGIATE Baseball (M), Basketball (F), Basketball (M), Cross Country (F), Cross Country (M), Soccer (F), Soccer (M), Swimming (F), Swimming (M), Tennis (F), Tennis (M), Track and Field, Track and Field (F), Volleyball (F), Volleyball (M) • SPORTS-INTRAMURAL Badminton, Baseball, Basketball, Bowling, Diving, Fencing, Football (M), Golf, Hand Ball, Racquetball, Rugby, Sailing, Soccer, Softball, Swimming, Tennis, Volleyball, Water Polo, Wrestling (M)

University of Wisconsin : Madison
750 University Avenue
Madison, Wisconsin 53706
(608) 262-3961

School Enrollment: **28,000**
LD Enrollment: **150**
LD Contact: **Cathleen M. Trueba, Learning Specialist**
Telephone:**(608) 263-2741**

Admissions

Application Information:
Rolling Admissions: **Yes**

Secondary School Information
Most Important Criteria For Admissions (1-strongest)

2 SAT/ACT	3 Application	1 School transcript
1 Class rank	2 Course selection	2 Personal statement
4 Interview	3 Extra activities	3 Psychoeducational
1 G.P.A.	Open admission	4 Recommendations

Test Requirements:
Diagnostic testing waived: **Yes**
Untimed SAT: **Yes** Untimed ACT: **Yes**
WAIS-R required: **Yes**
Documentation of LD required: **Yes**
Currency of diagnostic testing: **1 year**

Types of Disabilities Served
• Speech/Lang • Reading   • ADD with LD
• Study skills • Spelling   • ADD without LD
• Written express • Math   • ADHD with LD
• Organizational • Fine Motor   • ADHD without LD
• Perceptual

High School Course Requirements:
Waivers to standard high school courses
Course substitution: **Yes**

Faculty:
Faculty: **1** Full time: **1**

Diagnostic Testing

ADD	Personality	Perceptual skills	Spelling
ADHD	Organization	Fine motor skills	Reading
I.Q.	Handwriting	Spoken language	Study skills
Math	Social skills	Written language	

Tutoring:
Services rendered by:

Graduates	Peers	Faculty	•LD staff	Teacher trainees

Tutorials

Grp.	Ind.	Tutorials	Grp.	Ind.	Tutorials
•		Math skills	•	•	Word processing
•		Study skills	•	•	Time management
		Language arts	•		Learning strategies
	•	Written express	•		Organizational skills

Academic Accommodations

Curriculum	Study Aids	Exams
Priority registration	Typist	• Oral
Math waiver	Reader	Untimed
Foreign lang. waiver	• Notetaker	Take home
• Course substitution	Proof reader	With proctor
In Class	• Text on tape	On computer
• Calculators	Early syllabus	• Extended time
• Tape recorder	Taped handouts	On tape
• Word processor		• Modified
Priority seating		Separate room

Program Strengths

We offer minimal support services to LD students. The LD specialist acts as a resource and refers LD students to existing resources.

General Information:

University of Wisconsin : Madison is a 4 year public university. Urban campus of 900 acres is Housing is not guaranteed.

Accreditation: AACSB, ABET, ACEJMC, AHEA, ASLA, CSWE, NASAD, NASM

Expenses:

Tuition: In-state: Full year: $2,010.00. Tuition: Out-of-state: Full year: $6,090.00.

Majors

• AREA STUDIES African, American, Asian, Black/Afro-American, Jewish, Latin American, Urban • BUSINESS Accounting, Banking, Business Administration, Business Economics, Business Education, Business Management, Economics, Finance, Insurance, Labor Relations, Management, Marketing, Marketing Research, Personnel, Real Estate • COMMUNICATIONS Advertising, Broadcasting, Cinematography/Film, Communication, Comparative Literature, English, Graphic Design, Journalism, Photography, Television/Radio/Film • COMPUTER SCIENCE Computer Science, Data Processing, Medical Records Administration, Programming, Systems Analysis, Telecommunications • EDUCATION Art, Child Development, Early Childhood, Elementary, English As A Second Language (, Foreign Language, Health, Middle School, Physical, School Psychology, Secondary, Special, Specific Learning Disability, Speech/Language, Vocational • ENGINEERING Civil, Communication, Computer, Electrical, Engineering Science, Industrial, Materials, Mechanical • HEALTH SCIENCES Communication Disorders, Environmental, Medical Technology, Nursing, Nutritional/Food, Physical Therapy, Radiological Therapy, Speech Therapy, Speech/Audiology and Speech • HUMANITIES Classics, Liberal Arts, Philosophy, Religion • LANGUAGES Chinese, Danish, French, German, Greek, Hebrew, Italian, Latin, Linguistics, Russian, Spanish • PREPROFESSIONAL Agriculture, Architecture, Dentistry, Engineering, Forestry, Law, Medicine, Natural Resources, Pharmacy, Social Work • SCIENCES Anthropology, Astronomy, Astrophysics, Biochemistry, Biology, Botany, Chemistry, Ecology, Environmental, Geography, Geology, Macrobiology, Marine Biology, Mathematics, Oceanography, Physical Chemistry, Physical Science, Physics, Planetary, Radiology, Statistics, Zoology • SOCIAL SCIENCES Anthropology, Criminal Justice, Government/Political, History, International Relations, Political Science, Psychology, Social Sciences, Sociology • VISUAL AND PERFORMING ARTS Art, Art History, Dance, Dramatic Arts, Fine Arts, Music, Music History and Appreciation, Music Performance, Music Theory and Composition, Studio Art, Theater • VOCATIONAL Medical Laboratory Technology

Sports/Activities

• SPORTS RELATED Marching Band • SPORTS-INTERCOLLEGIATE Baseball (M), Basketball, Cross Country, Diving, Soccer, Swimming, Tennis, Track and Field, Volleyball (F) • SPORTS-INTRAMURAL Badminton, Baseball, Basketball, Bowling, Diving, Fencing, Football (M), Golf, Hand Ball, Racquetball, Rugby, Sailing, Skiing - Snow, Soccer, Softball, Swimming, Tennis, Volleyball, Water Polo, Wrestling (M) • STUDENT

LIFE ACTIVITIES Choral, Concert Band, Dance, Debate, Drama Groups, Film, Fraternities, Jazz Band, Magazine, Music Groups, Newspaper, Opera, Radio/TV station, Religious Organization, Sororities, Student Government, Symphony Orchestra, Yearbook

---

Less Selective **Wisconsin Accommodations**

University of Wisconsin Ctr: Waukesha

1500 University Drive
Waukesha, Wisconsin 53188-1628
(414) 521-5200

School Enrollment: **2,164**
LD Contact: **Janet V. Brown, Ph.D.**
Name of Program: **Disabled Student Services**

Admissions

Application Information:
Application deadline: **July 1st**

Secondary School Information
Most Important Criteria For Admissions (1-strongest)

3 SAT/ACT	Application	**2** School transcript
1 Class rank	Course selection	Personal statement
Interview	Extra activities	Psychoeducational
G.P.A.	Open admission	Recommendations

Test Requirements:
Untimed ACT: **Yes**
Documentation of LD required: **Yes**

Types of Disabilities Served
• Speech/Lang	• Reading	ADD with LD
• Study skills	• Spelling	ADD without LD
• Written express	• Math	ADHD with LD
• Organizational	Fine Motor	ADHD without LD
Perceptual		

High School Course Requirements:
English: **4** Math: **2** Science: **2**

Learning Disability Program

Services available for all students: **Yes**

Diagnostic Testing
ADD	Personality	Perceptual skills	Spelling
ADHD	Organization	Fine motor skills	Reading
I.Q.	Handwriting	Spoken language	Study skills
Math	Social skills	Written language	

Tutoring:
Services rendered by:
•Graduates   Peers   Faculty   LD staff   Teacher trainees

Tutorials
Grp.	Ind.	Tutorials	Grp.	Ind.	Tutorials
•	•	Math skills		•	Word processing
•	•	Study skills	•	•	Time management
•	•	Language arts	•	•	Learning strategies
•	•	Written express			Organizational skills

Wisconsin

Academic Accommodations

Curriculum	Study Aids	Exams
Priority registration	Typist	Oral
Math waiver	Reader	Untimed
Foreign lang. waiver	• Notetaker	Take home
Course substitution	• Proof reader	With proctor
In Class	• Text on tape	On computer
• Calculators	Early syllabus	• Extended time
• Tape recorder	Taped handouts	On tape
• Word processor		Modified
Priority seating		Separate room

General Information:

University of Wisconsin Ctr: Waukesha is a 2 year public university. Suburban campus 15 miles from Milwaukee. Accessible by bus. Ski areas are 10 minutes from campus. Beaches are 5 minutes from campus. 1% of students are foreign. Housing is not guaranteed.

Accreditation: Regional

SAT/ACT Scores:

Scores for incoming freshmen: **ACT:** 75% below 20. 8% between 20 and 23. 2% between 24 and 25l. 1% between 26 and 28. 1% above 28.

Expenses:

Tuition: In-state: Full year: $1,420.00. Part-time: Per credit:$58.55. Tuition: Out-of-state: Full year: $4,615.00. Part-time: Per credit:$192.30.

Majors

• HUMANITIES Liberal Arts

Sports/Activities

• SPORTS-INTERCOLLEGIATE Basketball, Cross Country, Fencing, Golf, Skiing - Snow, Soccer, Softball (F), Tennis, Volleyball (F) • SPORTS-INTRAMURAL Badminton, Basketball, Ping-Pong, Skiing - Snow, Softball, Tennis, Volleyball • STUDENT LIFE ACTIVITIES Academic Clubs, Community Service, Concert Band, Drama Groups, Ethnic & Cultural Groups, Jazz Band, Magazine, Music Groups, Musical Theater, Newspaper, Radio/TV station, Student Government

Very Selective

Wisconsin
Services

University of Wisconsin: LaCrosse
1725 State Street
La Crosse, Wisconsin 54601
(608) 785-8067

School Enrollment: **7,922** Male: **3,322** Female: **4,600**
LD Enrollment: **130**

Admissions Contact: **Tim Lewis, Director of Admissions**
LD Contact: **June Reinert, Coordinator**
Name of Program: **Students with Special Needs**
Address: **1725 State St.**
Telephone:**(608) 785-8535**

Admissions

Secondary School Information
Most Important Criteria For Admissions (1-strongest)

2 SAT/ACT	**3** Application	**4** School transcript
1 Class rank	**8** Course selection	**9** Personal statement
7 Interview	**10** Extra activities	**7** Psychoeducational
5 G.P.A.	Open admission	**6** Recommendations

Test Requirements:
Diagnostic testing waived: **Yes**
Untimed ACT: **Yes** Untimed ACH: **Yes**
WAIS-R required: **Yes**
Documentation of LD required: **Yes**
Currency of diagnostic testing: **3 years**

Types of Disabilities Served
• Speech/Lang	• Reading	• ADD with LD
• Study skills	• Spelling	• ADD without LD
• Written express	• Math	• ADHD with LD
• Organizational	• Fine Motor	• ADHD without LD
• Perceptual		

High School Course Requirements:
English: **4** Science: **3**

Learning Disability Program
Counseling: Individual: **Yes**

Faculty:
Faculty: **3** Full time: **3**
LD faculty with: BS/BA: **2** M.A.: **1**
Faculty advocate: **Yes** Meets with instructor: **As needed**

Diagnostic Testing
ADD	Personality	Perceptual skills	Spelling
ADHD	Organization	Fine motor skills	Reading
I.Q.	Handwriting	Spoken language	Study skills
Math	Social skills	Written language	

Tutoring:
Average size of group tutorials: **4**
Services rendered by:

Graduates	Peers	Faculty	•LD staff	Teacher trainees

Tutorials
Grp.	Ind.	Tutorials	Grp.	Ind.	Tutorials
•	•	Math skills		•	Word processing
•	•	Study skills	•	•	Time management
•	•	Language arts			Learning strategies
•	•	Written express	•	•	Organizational skills

Academic Accommodations

Curriculum	Study Aids	Exams
Priority registration	Typist	• Oral
Math waiver	Reader	Untimed
Foreign lang. waiver	• Notetaker	Take home
Course substitution	• Proof reader	• With proctor
In Class	• Text on tape	On computer
• Calculators	Early syllabus	• Extended time
• Tape recorder	Taped handouts	On tape
• Word processor		• Modified
Priority seating		Separate room

Program Strengths

Services for Special Needs Students provides accommodations for students with disabilities at the University.

General Information:

University of Wisconsin: LaCrosse is a 4 year public university. Urban campus 100 miles from Minneapolis. Accessible by air, train, or bus. Ski areas are 2 miles from campus. Beaches are 2 miles from campus. 11 residential halls on campus. Housing is not guaranteed.60 % of students remain on campus for the weekends. 10 % of students join fraternities/sororities.

Accreditation: Regional, AACSB, APTA, CSWE, NASM, NCATE

SAT/ACT Scores:

Scores for incoming freshmen: 100% between 20 and 23.

Class Rank: 100% were in the top 60% of their class.

Expenses:

Tuition: In-state: Full year: $2,070.00. Part-time: Per credit:$97.75. Tuition: Out-of-state: Full year: $6,256.00. Part-time: Per credit:$272.25. Room and board: $2,210.00

Majors

• BUSINESS Accounting, Banking, Business Administration, Business Economics, Business Education, Business Management, Economics, Finance, Insurance, Management, Marketing, Sports Management • COMMUNICATIONS Broadcasting, Communication, English, Journalism, Speech • COMPUTER SCIENCE Computer Science, Data Processing, Programming, Systems Analysis • EDUCATION Art, Early Childhood, Elementary, Health, Middle School, Music, Physical, Recreation and Youth Leadership, School Psychology, Secondary, Special • HEALTH SCIENCES Health, Medical Technology, Nuclear Medical Technology, Physical Therapy, Recreation Therapy • HUMANITIES Humanities, Liberal Arts, Philosophy • LANGUAGES French, German, Spanish • PREPROFESSIONAL Dentistry, Medicine, Pharmacy, Recreation, Social Work • SCIENCES Biochemistry, Biology, Botany, Chemistry, Earth, Geography, Macrobiology, Mathematics, Microbiology, Physical Chemistry, Physical Science, Physics, Statistics, Zoology • SOCIAL SCIENCES Anthropology, Government/Political, History, Political Science, Psychology, Public Administration, Social Sciences, Sociology • VISUAL AND PERFORMING ARTS Art, Art History, Dramatic Arts, Fine Arts, Music, Theater • VOCATIONAL Medical Laboratory Technology, Park/Recreation

Sports/Activities

• SPORTS RELATED Marching Band, Pep Band • SPORTS-INTERCOLLEGIATE Baseball (M), Basketball, Bowling, Cross Country, Diving, Football (M), Golf (M), Gymnastics, Softball (F), Swimming, Tennis, Track and Field, Volleyball (F), Wrestling (M) • SPORTS-INTRAMURAL Badminton, Basketball, Cross Country, Hand Ball, Racquetball, Rugby, Soccer, Softball, Swimming, Tennis, Volleyball • STUDENT LIFE ACTIVITIES Choral, Concert Band, Dance, Debate, Drama Groups, Ethnic & Cultural Groups, Film, Fraternities, Jazz Band, Magazine, Music Groups, Musical Theater, Newspaper, Opera, Radio/TV station, Religious Organization, Sororities, Student Government, Symphony Orchestra, Yearbook

---

Selective

Wisconsin Program

University of Wisconsin: Oshkosh

800 Algonna Boulevard
Oshkosh, Wisconsin 54901
(414) 424-0202

School Enrollment: **8,950** Male: **3,881** Female: **5,069**
LD Enrollment: **177**

Admissions Contact: **Rick Hillman, Admissions Counselor**
LD Contact: **Bill Kitz and /Robert Nash, Associate Directors**
Name of Program: **Project Success**
Telephone:**(414) 424-1033**

Admissions

Application Information:

LD Students Applying: **150** Accepted: **60** Enrolled:**50**
Application deadline: **None**
Applicant must apply **24** months in advance
Rolling Admissions: **Yes**

Secondary School Information

Most Important Criteria For Admissions (1-strongest)

5	SAT/ACT	Application	**2** School transcript
4	Class rank	Course selection	Personal statement
1	Interview	Extra activities	Psychoeducational
3	G.P.A.	Open admission	Recommendations

Test Requirements:

Diagnostic testing waived: **Yes**
Untimed SAT: **Yes** Untimed ACT: **Yes**
Tests recommended: **Student must come to campus for interview and testing.**

Types of Disabilities Served

- Speech/Lang
- Reading
- ADD with LD
- Study skills
- Spelling
- ADD without LD
- Written express
- Math
- ADHD with LD
- Organizational
- Fine Motor
- ADHD without LD
- Perceptual

Admissions Process

A student must request a Project Success application in writing. An on-campus interview and assessment is required with parent in attendance.

Learning Disability Program

Special orientation for LD students: **Yes**
Syllabus available during orientation:**Yes**
Program: Remedial: **Yes**
Program: Reinforces course work: **Yes**
Students mainstreamed **100** % of the day
Counseling: Individual: **Yes**

Faculty:

Faculty: **3** Including Director: **Yes** Full time: **3** M.A.: **1** Ph.D.: **2**
Faculty advocate: **Yes** Meets with instructor: **As necessary**

Wisconsin

Diagnostic Testing

ADD	Personality	Perceptual skills	•	Spelling
ADHD	Organization•	Fine motor skills	•	Reading
• I.Q.	• Handwriting	Spoken language		Study skills
• Math	Social skills•	Written language		

Tutoring:

Average size of group tutorials: **2-3**
Services rendered by:
•Graduates •Peers •Faculty •LD staff Teacher trainees

Tutorials

Grp.	Ind.	Tutorials	Grp.	Ind.	Tutorials
•	•	Math skills	•	•	Word processing
•	•	Study skills	•	•	Time management
•	•	Language arts	•	•	Learning strategies
•	•	Written express	•	•	Organizational skills

Academic Accommodations

Curriculum	Study Aids	Exams
Priority registration	Typist	Oral
Math waiver	Reader	• Untimed
• Foreign lang. waiver	Notetaker	Take home
• Course substitution	• Proof reader	• With proctor
In Class	Text on tape	On computer
• Calculators	Early syllabus	• Extended time
• Tape recorder	Taped handouts	On tape
• Word processor		Modified
Priority seating		Separate room

Graduation Requirements:

Course credits: **120** Years to complete degree: **4+**

Program Strengths

Project Success is a remedial program for dyslexic students with language deficits. An eight week summer program is mandatory for all entering students.

General Information:

University of Wisconsin: Oshkosh is a 4 year public university. Urban campus of 192 acres is 95 miles from Milwaukee. Accessible by air, train, or bus. Ski areas are 30 miles from campus. Beaches are 50 miles from campus. 12 residential halls on campus. Housing is guaranteed.80 % of students remain on campus for the weekends.

Accreditation:AASCB, ACEJMC, CSWE, NASM, NCATE, and NLN

Expenses:

Tuition: In-state: Full year: $1,900.00. Part-time: Per credit:$80.00. Tuition: Out-of-state: Full year: $5,700.00. Part-time: Per credit:$225.00. Room and board: $2,000.00

Majors

• AREA STUDIES Urban • BUSINESS Accounting, Banking, Business Administration, Business Economics, Business Management, Economics, Finance, Management, Marketing, Personnel • COMMUNICATIONS Advertising, English, Journalism, Speech, Television/Radio/Film • COMPUTER SCIENCE Computer Science, Data Processing, Management Information Systems, Programming, Systems Analysis • EDUCATION Art, Curriculum, Early Childhood, Elementary, Middle School, Music, Physical, School Psychology, Secondary, Special, Specific Learning Disabilities, Speech/Language • HEALTH SCIENCES Nursing • HUMANITIES Humanities, Liberal Arts, Philosophy, Religion • LANGUAGES French, German, Japanese, Spanish • PREPROFESSIONAL Law, Social Work • SCIENCES Anthropology, Biology, Botany, Chemistry, Earth, Geography, Geology, Marine Biology, Mathematics, Microbiology, Physics

• SOCIAL SCIENCES Anthropology, Criminal Justice, Government/Political, History, International Relations, Law Enforcement, Library Science, Political Science, Psychology, Social Sciences, Sociology • VISUAL AND PERFORMING ARTS Art, Art History, Fine Arts, Music, Music Performance, Music Theory and Composition, Studio Art, Visual and Performing Arts • VOCATIONAL Operations Research

Sports/Activities

• SPORTS RELATED Pep Band • SPORTS-INTERCOLLEGIATE Baseball (M), Basketball, Cross Country, Football (M), Gymnastics, Soccer (M), Softball (F), Swimming, Tennis, Track and Field, Volleyball (F), Wrestling (M) • SPORTS-INTRAMURAL Badminton, Basketball, Bowling, Sailing, Skiing - Snow, Softball, Volleyball • STUDENT LIFE ACTIVITIES Choral, Concert Band, Dance, Debate, Drama Groups, Ethnic & Cultural Groups, Film, Fraternities, Jazz Band, Magazine, Music Groups, Musical Theater, Newspaper, Radio/TV station, Religious Organization, Sororities, Student Government, Symphony Orchestra

---

Less Selective **Wisconsin Services**

University of Wisconsin: Platteville

1 University Plaza
Platteville, Wisconsin 53818
(608) 342-1125

School Enrollment: **5,213** Male: **3,440** Female: **1,773**
LD Enrollment: **15** Male: **10** Female: **5**

Admissions Contact: **Richard Schumacher, Asoc. Dean Admis.**
LD Contact: **Dale Bernhardt, Director**
Name of Program: **Special Services**
Telephone:**(608) 343-1816**

Admissions

Application Information:

Application deadline: **Open**

Secondary School Information

Most Important Criteria For Admissions (1-strongest)

1	SAT/ACT	1	Application	2	School transcript
1	Class rank	1	Course selection	10	Personal statement
10	Interview	5	Extra activities	2	Psychoeducational
3	G.P.A.		Open admission	5	Recommendations

Test Requirements:

Diagnostic testing waived: **Yes**
Untimed ACT: **Yes**
WAIS-R required: **Yes**
Documentation of LD required: **Yes**
Currency of diagnostic testing: **3 years**

Types of Disabilities Served

•	Speech/Lang	•	Reading	•	ADD with LD
•	Study skills	•	Spelling	•	ADD without LD
•	Written express	•	Math	•	ADHD with LD
•	Organizational	•	Fine Motor	•	ADHD without LD
•	Perceptual				

Learning Disability Program

Counseling: Individual: **Yes** Group Counseling: **Yes**

Faculty:

Faculty: **6** Full time: **4** Part time: **2**
Faculty advocate: **Yes** Meets with instructor: **As needed**

Diagnostic Testing

ADD	Personality	Perceptual skills	Spelling
ADHD	Organization	Fine motor skills	Reading
I.Q.	Handwriting	Spoken language	Study skills
Math	Social skills	Written language	

Tutoring:

Services rendered by:
Graduates •Peers Faculty •LD staff Teacher trainees

Tutorials

Grp.	Ind.	Tutorials	Grp.	Ind.	Tutorials
	•	Math skills		•	Word processing
	•	Study skills	•	•	Time management
	•	Language arts		•	Learning strategies
	•	Written express	•	•	Organizational skills

Academic Accommodations

Curriculum	Study Aids	Exams
Priority registration	Typist	• Oral
Math waiver	Reader	Untimed
Foreign lang. waiver	• Notetaker	Take home
Course substitution	• Proof reader	With proctor
In Class	• Text on tape	On computer
• Calculators	Early syllabus	• Extended time
• Tape recorder	Taped handouts	On tape
• Word processor		• Modified
Priority seating		Separate room

Program Strengths

The services at the University of Wisconsin: Platteville for learning disabled students were established to provide for the traditional age student a smooth transition from high school to college. Assistance with course selections, academic tutoring in 100-200 level courses, and personal counseling are available. The office can act as a liaison with the faculty to provide information about learning disabilities in general and how a specific student may need assistance.

General Information:

University of Wisconsin: Platteville is a 4 year public university. Rural campus of 400 acres is 60 miles from Madison. Accessible by bus. Ski areas are 25 miles from campus. Beaches are 150 miles from campus. .3% of students are foreign. Housing is guaranteed. 50 % of students remain on campus for the weekends. 17 % of students join fraternities/sororities.

Accreditation: ABET, NASM

Class Rank:

About 33% of the present freshmen class were in the upper 20% of their high school class. 68% were in the top 40% of their class. 91% were in the top 60% of their class. 99% were in the top 80% of their class.

Expenses:

Tuition: In-state: Full year: $1,811.00. Part-time: Per credit:$80.05. Tuition: Out-of-state: Full year: $5,155.00. Part-time: Per credit:$220.05. Room and board: $2,120.00

Majors

• BUSINESS Accounting, Agricultural, Business Administration, Business Economics, Business Management, Economics • COMMUNICATIONS Communication, English, Speech, Television/Radio/Film • COMPUTER SCIENCE Computer Science, Telecommunications • CRAFTS AND DESIGN Graphic Design Technology • EDUCATION Agricultural, Art, Driver and Safety Education, Early Childhood, Elementary, English, Foreign Language, Health, Industrial Arts, Mathematics, Middle School, Music, Physical, Reading, Science, Secondary, Social Studies, Trade and Industrial • ENGINEERING Agricultural, Civil/Environmental, Communications, Electrical, Industrial, Mechanical • HEALTH SCIENCES Occupational Health and Safety • HUMANITIES Humanities, Liberal Arts, Philosophy • LANGUAGES French, German, Spanish • SCIENCES Agricultural, Agronomy, Animal, Biology, Chemistry, Earth, Geography, Geology, Horticultural, Mathematics, Physical Science, Physics, Soil, Zoology • SOCIAL SCIENCES Criminal Justice, History, International Relations, Library Science, Political Science, Psychology, Social Sciences • VISUAL AND PERFORMING ARTS Fine Arts, Music • VOCATIONAL Construction, Industrial Technology

Sports/Activities

• SPORTS RELATED Marching Band, Pep Band • SPORTS-INTERCOLLEGIATE Baseball (M), Basketball, Cross Country, Football (M), Golf (M), Ice Hockey (M), Rugby (M), Tennis, Track and Field, Volleyball, Wrestling (M) • SPORTS-INTRAMURAL Baseball (M), Basketball, Bowling, Softball, Volleyball • STUDENT LIFE ACTIVITIES Choral, Concert Band, Drama Groups, Fraternities, Jazz Band, Magazine, Music Groups, Musical Theater, Newspaper, Radio/TV station, Sororities, Student Government, Symphony Orchestra, Yearbook

---

Selective **Wisconsin**
Services

University Wisconsin Center: Baraboo Sauk County

1006 Connie Road
Baraboo, Wisconsin 53913
(608) 356-8351

School Enrollment: **473** Male: **179** Female: **294**

Admissions Contact: **Tom Martin, Director Student Services**
LD Contact: **Jan Gerlach, Assistant Director**
Name of Program: **Office of Student Services**
Telephone:**(608) 356-8351**

Admissions

Application Information:

Application deadline: **August 31st**
Rolling Admissions: **Yes** Notified when: **2-3 Weeks**

Secondary School Information

Most Important Criteria For Admissions (1-strongest)

1 SAT/ACT	**2** Application	**2** School transcript
1 Class rank	**1** Course selection	Personal statement
Interview	Extra activities	Psychoeducational
3 G.P.A.	Open admission	Recommendations

Types of Disabilities Served

• Speech/Lang	• Reading	ADD with LD
• Study skills	• Spelling	ADD without LD
• Written express	• Math	ADHD with LD
• Organizational	Fine Motor	ADHD without LD
Perceptual		

High School Course Requirements:

English: **4** Math: **2** Science: **2**
Waivers to standard high school courses
Course substitution: **Yes**

Wisconsin

Learning Disability Program

Special orientation for LD students: **Yes**
Services available for all students: **Yes**
Vocational Counseling: **Yes**

Diagnostic Testing

ADD	Personality	Perceptual skills	Spelling
ADHD	Organization	Fine motor skills	Reading
I.Q.	Handwriting	Spoken language	Study skills
Math	Social skills	Written language	

Tutoring:

Average size of group tutorials: **10-15**
Services rendered by:
  Graduates   Peers   •Faculty   LD staff   •Teacher trainees

Tutorials

Grp.	Ind.	Tutorials	Grp.	Ind.	Tutorials
•	•	Math skills	•		Word processing
•	•	Study skills	•		Time management
	•	Language arts	•		Learning strategies
	•	Written express	•	•	Organizational skills

Academic Accommodations

Curriculum	Study Aids	Exams
Priority registration	• Typist	• Oral
Math waiver	Reader	Untimed
Foreign lang. waiver	• Notetaker	• Take home
• Course substitution	• Proof reader	• With proctor
In Class	• Text on tape	On computer
• Calculators	Early syllabus	• Extended time
• Tape recorder	Taped handouts	On tape
• Word processor		• Modified
• Priority seating		Separate room

Program Strengths

We offer students a great deal of individualization in the classroom and advising and serve the few disabled students we have in that way. The faculty is very willing to accommodate special needs and provide extra help to students. We have professional tutors in the areas of mathematics, reading, and composition available to our enrolled students free of charge.

General Information:

University Wisconsin Center: Baraboo Sauk County is a 2 year public university. Rural campus of 68 acres is 45 miles from Madison. Accessible by air. Ski areas are 4 miles from campus. Beaches are 2 miles from campus. 1% of students are foreign. Housing is not guaranteed.

Accreditation:NCACS

Expenses:

Tuition: In-state: Full year: $695.00 per semester. Part-time: Per credit:$57.80. Tuition: Out-of-state: Full year: $2,250.00 per semester. Part-time: Per credit:$187.50.

Majors

• HUMANITIES Liberal Arts

Sports/Activities

• SPORTS-INTERCOLLEGIATE Cross Country, Golf, Tennis • SPORTS-INTRAMURAL Basketball, Bowling, Ping-Pong, Softball, Tennis, Volleyball • STUDENT LIFE ACTIVITIES Choral, Concert Band, Drama Groups, Jazz Band, Music Groups, Musical Theater, Newspaper, Student Government

---

Less Selective	Wisconsin Program

University Wisconsin-Center Rock County

2909 Kellogg Avenue
Janesville, Wisconsin 53545
(608) 755-2823

School Enrollment: **971** Male: **409** Female: **562**
LD Enrollment: **12** Male: **6** Female: **6**

Admissions Contact: **Terry Borg, Student Services Director**
LD Contact: **Greg Smith, Director**
Name of Program: **Skills Development Program**
Telephone:**(608) 755-2819**

Admissions

Application Information:

Application deadline: **July 31st**
Applicant must apply **8** months in advance
Rolling Admissions: **Yes**Notified when: **August 14th**

Secondary School Information

Most Important Criteria For Admissions (1-strongest)

11 SAT/ACT	**3** Application	**4** School transcript
2 Class rank	**1** Course selection	**11** Personal statement
7 Interview	**10** Extra activities	**11** Psychoeducational
5 G.P.A.	Open admission	**6** Recommendations

Test Requirements:

Standardized tests waived: **Yes**
Diagnostic testing waived: **Yes**
Tests recommended: **ACT and institutional placement test**

Types of Disabilities Served

Speech/Lang	• Reading	ADD with LD
• Study skills	• Spelling	ADD without LD
• Written express	• Math	ADHD with LD
• Organizational	• Fine Motor	ADHD without LD
• Perceptual		

High School Course Requirements:

English: **4** Math: **2** Science: **2** Foreign Language: **0-3**

Learning Disability Program

Program: Remedial: **Yes**
Program: Reinforces course work: **Yes**
Students mainstreamed **100** % of the day

Faculty:

Faculty: **4** Including Director: **Yes** Full time: **1** Part time: **3** M.A.: **3** Ph.D.: **1**

Faculty advocate: **Yes** Meets with instructor: **As needed**

Diagnostic Testing

ADD	Personality	Perceptual skills	Spelling
ADHD	Organization	Fine motor skills	• Reading
I.Q.	Handwriting	Spoken language	• Study skills
• Math	Social skills •	Written language	

Tutoring:

Services rendered by:

Graduates •Peers Faculty •LD staff Teacher trainees

Tutorials

Grp.	Ind.	Tutorials	Grp.	Ind.	Tutorials
•	•	Math skills			Word processing
•	•	Study skills	•	•	Time management
		Language arts	•	•	Learning strategies
•	•	Written express	•	•	Organizational skills

Academic Accommodations

Curriculum	Study Aids	Exams
Priority registration	Typist	• Oral
Math waiver	Reader	Untimed
Foreign lang. waiver	• Notetaker	• Take home
• Course substitution	• Proof reader	• With proctor
In Class	• Text on tape	On computer
Calculators	Early syllabus	• Extended time
• Tape recorder	Taped handouts	On tape
• Word processor		• Modified
• Priority seating		• Separate room

Program Strengths

The Skills Development Center is a federally funded program designed to offer academic support services to disadvantaged students: first generation college, low income, physically disabled, or learning disabled. Services include career counseling, academic advising, individual tutoring, seminars, workshops, and remedial classes.

General Information:

University Wisconsin-Center Rock County is a 2 year public university. Suburban campus 40 miles from Madison. Accessible by bus. 1% of students are foreign. Housing is not guaranteed.

Accreditation: Regional

Class Rank:

About 13.8% of the present freshmen class were in the upper 20% of their high school class. 42.7% were in the top 40% of their class. 66.5% were in the top 60% of their class. 92.2% were in the top 80% of their class.

Expenses:

Tuition: In-state: Full year: $703.55. Part-time: Per credit:$59.20. Tuition: Out-of-state: Full year: $2,306.30. Part-time: Per credit:$192.70.

Majors

• HUMANITIES Liberal Arts

Sports/Activities

• SPORTS-INTERCOLLEGIATE Basketball, Tennis, Volleyball (F)
• SPORTS-INTRAMURAL Badminton, Basketball, Soccer, Volleyball
• STUDENT LIFE ACTIVITIES Choral, Concert Band, Jazz Band, Newspaper, Student Government

Selective

Viterbo College
815 South Ninth Street
La Crosse, Wisconsin 54601
(608) 791-0354

School Enrollment: **1,200** Male: **400** Female: **800**
LD Enrollment: **10** Male: **5** Female: **5**

Admissions Contact: **Dr. Rowland Nelson, Director**
LD Contact: **Jane Eddy, Project Director**
Name of Program: **Student Support Services**

Admissions

Application Information:
LD on admissions committee:**Yes**
Application deadline: **Negotiable**
Applicant must apply **6** months in advance

Secondary School Information
Most Important Criteria For Admissions (1-strongest)

2 SAT/ACT	Application	**6**	School transcript
3 Class rank	**5** Course selection		Personal statement
7 Interview	Extra activities		Psychoeducational
1 G.P.A.	Open admission	**4**	Recommendations

Test Requirements:
Diagnostic testing waived: **Yes**
Untimed SAT: **Yes** Untimed ACT: **Yes**
Documentation of LD required: **Yes**
Currency of diagnostic testing: **Anytime**

Types of Disabilities Served
• Speech/Lang • Reading ADD with LD
• Study skills • Spelling ADD without LD
• Written express • Math ADHD with LD
• Organizational • Fine Motor ADHD without LD
• Perceptual

Admissions Process

We look at ACT, high school grades and rank, and complete LD evaluation and recommendation. Based on all this criteria, we make a decision.

Learning Disability Program

Special orientation for LD students: **Yes**
Program: Reinforces course work: **Yes**
Program available through:**As needed**
Students mainstreamed **100** % of the day
Recommended credits per semester: **12-15**
Services available for all students: **Yes**
Counseling: Individual: **Yes**

Faculty:
Faculty: **8** Full time: **6** Part time: **2**
LD faculty with: BS/BA: **1** M.A.: **5** Ph.D.: **1**
Meets with instructor: **As needed**

Diagnostic Testing

ADD	Personality	Perceptual skills	Spelling
ADHD	Organization	Fine motor skills	Reading
I.Q.	Handwriting	Spoken language	Study skills
Math	Social skills	Written language	

Tutoring:

Average size of group tutorials: **1-5**
Services rendered by:
Graduates •Peers •Faculty •LD staff Teacher trainees

Tutorials

Grp.	Ind.	Tutorials	Grp.	Ind.	Tutorials
		Math skills			Word processing
		Study skills	•		Time management
•		Language arts	•		Learning strategies
•		Written express	•		Organizational skills

Academic Accommodations

Curriculum	Study Aids	Exams
Priority registration	Typist	• Oral
Math waiver	Reader	• Untimed
Foreign lang. waiver	Notetaker	Take home
• Course substitution	Proof reader	• With proctor
In Class	• Text on tape	On computer
• Calculators	Early syllabus	• Extended time
• Tape recorder	Taped handouts	On tape
Word processor		Modified
• Priority seating		• Separate room

Graduation Requirements:

Course credits: **128** GPA: **varies** Years to complete degree: **4-5**

Program Strengths

We are a small school and consequently can give individual attention.

General Information:

Viterbo College is a 4 year independent Roman Catholic college. Urban campus Accessible by air, train, or bus. Ski areas are 3 miles from campus. Beaches are 1/2 mile from campus. 3 residential halls on campus. Housing is not guaranteed.

Accreditation: NCACS, NASM, WSBN, NLN

SAT/ACT Scores:

Scores for incoming freshmen: **ACT:** 31% below 20. 33% between 20 and 23. 16% between 24 and 25l. 15% between 26 and 28. 7% above 28.

Class Rank:

About 31% of the present freshmen class were in the upper 20% of their high school class. 56% were in the top 40% of their class. 78% were in the top 60% of their class. 94% were in the top 80% of their class.

Expenses:

Tuition: In-state: Full year: $7,200.00. Part-time: Per credit:$160.00. Room and board: $2,800.00

Majors

• BUSINESS Accounting, Management, Marketing, Personnel • COMMUNICATIONS English • COMPUTER SCIENCE Computer Science, Computer Science & Information • EDUCATION Art, Business, Elementary, English, Mathematics, Middle School, Music, Religious, Secondary, Social Studies • HEALTH SCIENCES Dietary Dietetics, Nursing, Nutritional/Food • PRE PROFESSIONAL Business, Dentistry, Law, Medicine, Ministry, Optometry, Pharmacy, Social Work • RELIGIOUS STUDIES Philosophy, Religion & Theology, Religious Music • SCIENCES Biochemistry, Biology, Biomedical, Chemistry, Ecology, Molecular Biology • SOCIAL SCIENCES Human Service, Psychology, Sociology • VISUAL AND PERFORMING ARTS Art, Music, Music Performance, Music Theatre, Theater

Sports/Activities

• SPORTS-INTERCOLLEGIATE Baseball (M), Basketball (F), Basketball (M), Softball (F), Volleyball (F) • SPORTS-INTRAMURAL Baseball (F), Baseball (M), Basketball (F), Basketball (M), Football (M), Racquetball (F), Racquetball (M), Volleyball (F), Volleyball (M) • STUDENT LIFE ACTIVITIES Academic Clubs, Choral, Concert Band, Dance, Drama Groups, Jazz Band, Music Groups, Newspaper, Orchestra, Religious Organization, Student Government, Yearbook

---

Less Selective   **Wisconsin**
Services

Waukesha County Technical College

800 Main Street
Pewaukee, Wisconsin 53072
(414) 691-5200

School Enrollment: **5,500**
LD Enrollment: **500**

Admissions Contact: **Stan Goran, Director of Admissions**
LD Contact: **Elroy Harmelink, Special Needs Coordinator**
Name of Program: **Special Needs Academic Support**
Telephone:**(414) 691-5268**

Admissions

Application Information:

LD Students Applying: **75** Enrolled:**75**
Rolling Admissions: **Yes**

Secondary School Information

Most Important Criteria For Admissions (1-strongest)

11	SAT/ACT	6	Application	5	School transcript
9	Class rank	4	Course selection	8	Personal statement
1	Interview	10	Extra activities	2	Psychoeducational
7	G.P.A.		Open admission	3	Recommendations

Test Requirements:

Diagnostic testing waived: **Yes**
WAIS-R required: **Yes**
Documentation of LD required: **Yes**
Currency of diagnostic testing: **2 years**
Tests recommended: **Psychoeducational and academic**

Types of Disabilities Served

• Speech/Lang	• Reading	• ADD with LD
• Study skills	• Spelling	• ADD without LD
• Written express	• Math	• ADHD with LD
• Organizational	• Fine Motor	• ADHD without LD
• Perceptual		

Admissions Process

Special Population students are requested to meet with the Special Needs Counselor to assist in admission and vocational planning.

Learning Disability Program

Special orientation for LD students: **Yes**
Program: Remedial: **Yes**
Program: Reinforces course work: **Yes**
Students mainstreamed **98** % of the day
Recommended credits per semester: **Varies**
Time required or recommended in learning center: **varies**
Services available for all students: **Yes**
Counseling: Individual: **Yes** Vocational Counseling: **Yes**

Faculty:

Faculty: **7** Including Director: **Yes** Full time: **6** Part time: **1** M.A.: **7**
Faculty advocate: **Yes** Meets with instructor: **As needed**

Diagnostic Testing

ADD	Personality •	Perceptual skills	• Spelling
ADHD•	Organization	Fine motor skills	• Reading
• I.Q.	• Handwriting•	Spoken language	• Study skills
• Math	Social skills•	Written language	

Tutoring:

Average size of group tutorials: **5-7**
Services rendered by:
  Graduates   Peers   •Faculty   •LD staff   Teacher trainees

Tutorials

Grp.	Ind.	Tutorials	Grp.	Ind.	Tutorials
	•	Math skills	•		Word processing
•	•	Study skills	•	•	Time management
	•	Language arts	•		Learning strategies
	•	Written express	•		Organizational skills

Academic Accommodations

Curriculum	Study Aids	Exams
Priority registration	Typist	• Oral
Math waiver	Reader	• Untimed
Foreign lang. waiver	• Notetaker	Take home
• Course substitution	• Proof reader	• With proctor
In Class	Text on tape	On computer
• Calculators	Early syllabus	• Extended time
• Tape recorder	Taped handouts	On tape
• Word processor		• Modified
Priority seating		• Separate room

Graduation Requirements:

Course credits: **Varies**

Program Strengths

The Special Needs Program at Waukesha County Technical College includes three vocational training programs specifically designed for the needs of individuals who are handicapped or disadvantaged and a Special Needs Unit which provides academic support and tutoring to handicapped or disadvantaged students enrolled in vocational/technical programs or improving their basic skills. The unit also addresses the academic support needs of ESL students.

General Information:

Waukesha County Technical College is a 2 year public college. Urban campus of 66 acres is 20 miles from Milwaukee. Accessible by air, train, or bus. Ski areas are 15 minutes from campus. Beaches are 2 minutes from campus. 1% of students are foreign. Housing is not guaranteed.

Accreditation: NCACS

Expenses:

Tuition: In-state: Full year: Part-time: Per credit: $35.25. Tuition: Out-of-state: Full year: Part-time: Per credit: $105.75.

Majors

• BUSINESS Accounting, Business Data Processing, Business Data Programming, Business Management, Financial Planning Assistance, Hotel and Restaurant Management, Insurance, International Business, International Trade Association, Marketing, Real Estate, Taxation • COMPUTER SCIENCE Computer Science, Data Processing, Programming, Telecommunications • CRAFTS AND DESIGN Mechanical Design Technology • EDUCATION Child Development, Early Childhood, Instructional Assistant • ENGINEERING Engineering Science • HEALTH SCIENCES Health, Medical Assistant, Medical Technology, Nursing, Surgical Technology • SOCIAL SCIENCES Law Enforcement • VOCATIONAL Automobile Technology, Diesel Power Technology, Electronics Technology, Fashion Merchandising, Food Service, Industrial Technology, Precision Metal work, Secretarial

Sports/Activities

• SPORTS-INTERCOLLEGIATE Baseball, Basketball, Bowling, Cross Country, Golf, Soccer, Wrestling (M) • SPORTS-INTRAMURAL Baseball, Bowling, Golf, Racquetball, Skiing - Snow • STUDENT LIFE ACTIVITIES Newspaper, Student Government, Yearbook

---

Less Selective

Western Wisconsin Technical College

304 North 6th Street
La Crosse, Wisconsin 54602-0908
(608) 785-9200

School Enrollment: **7,815** Male: **3,337** Female: **4,478**
LD Enrollment: **25** Male: **15** Female: **10**

Admissions Contact: **Diane Rud, Admissions Manager**
Name of Program: **Special Needs**
Telephone: **(608) 785-9585**

Admissions

Application Information:

Application deadline: **None**

Secondary School Information

Most Important Criteria For Admissions (1-strongest)

8 SAT/ACT	**1** Application	**2**	School transcript
7 Class rank	**5** Course selection	**10**	Personal statement
3 Interview	**11** Extra activities	**9**	Psychoeducational
6 G.P.A.	Open admission	**4**	Recommendations

Test Requirements:

Documentation of LD required: **Yes**

Types of Disabilities Served

• Speech/Lang	• Reading	ADD with LD
• Study skills	• Spelling	ADD without LD
• Written express	• Math	ADHD with LD
• Organizational	• Fine Motor	• ADHD without LD
• Perceptual		

High School Course Requirements:

English: **1-2** Math: **1-2**

Wisconsin

Learning Disability Program

Program: Reinforces course work: **Yes**
Time required or recommended in learning center: **Optional**
Services available for all students: **Yes**
Counseling: Individual: **Yes** Vocational Counseling: **Yes**

Faculty:
Faculty: **2** Full time: **2**
LD faculty with: BS/BA: **1** M.A.: **1**
Faculty advocate: **Yes** Meets with instructor: **As needed**

Diagnostic Testing
ADD	Personality	Perceptual skills	Spelling
ADHD	Organization	Fine motor skills	• Reading
I.Q.	Handwriting	Spoken language	Study skills
• Math	Social skills	• Written language	

Tutoring:
Average size of group tutorials: **1-6**
Services rendered by:
Graduates   •Peers   •Faculty   LD staff   Teacher trainees

Tutorials
Grp.	Ind.	Tutorials	Grp.	Ind.	Tutorials
•	•	Math skills	•	•	Word processing
•	•	Study skills	•	•	Time management
•	•	Language arts	•	•	Learning strategies
•	•	Written express	•	•	Organizational skills

Academic Accommodations
Curriculum	Study Aids	Exams
Priority registration	• Typist	• Oral
Math waiver	Reader	Untimed
Foreign lang. waiver	• Notetaker	• Take home
• Course substitution	• Proof reader	• With proctor
In Class	• Text on tape	On computer
• Calculators	Early syllabus	• Extended time
• Tape recorder	Taped handouts	• On tape
• Word processor		• Modified
Priority seating		• Separate room

Graduation Requirements:
Course credits: **Varies with program** GPA: **2.0**

General Information:
Western Wisconsin Technical College is a 2 year public college. Urban campus 160 miles from Twin Cities. Accessible by air, train or bus. Ski areas are 7 miles from campus. Beaches are 3 miles from campus. 1 residential halls on campus. Housing is not guaranteed.

Accreditation: NCACS

Expenses:
Tuition: In-state: Full year: $1,500.00. Part-time: Per credit:$41.00. Tuition: Out-of-state: Full year: $9,500.00. Part-time: Per credit:$321.00. Room and board: $3,695.00

Majors
• AGRICULTURE Business • ARTS Commercial Art, Interior Design • BUSINESS Accounting, Banking/Finance, Business Management, Fashion Merchandising, Food Marketing, Marketing, Personnel, Retailing, Secretarial Science • COMMUNICATIONS Communication, Printing • COMPUTER SCIENCE Data Processing, Medical Records Technology • EDUCATION Child Development • ENGINEERING Air Conditioning Technology, Bio-medical, Drafting, Electrical • HEALTH SCIENCES Dental Assistant, Electroneurodiagnostic Tech, Health Unit Coordinator, Home Health Aide, Medical Assistant, Medical Laboratory Technology, Medical Secretary, Nursing, Nursing Assistant, Physical Therapy, Practical Nursing, Radiological Therapy, Respiratory Therapy, Surgical Technology • PREPROFESSIONAL Legal Assistant • SOCIAL SCIENCES Law Enforcement • VOCATIONAL Air Conditioning/Heating/Refri, Auto Body, Automobile Technology, Business and Office, Construction, Diesel Power Technology, Electrodiagnostic Technology, Electronics Technology, Food Service, Interior Design, Machinist, Secretarial, Welding

Sports/Activities
• SPORTS-INTERCOLLEGIATE Baseball (M), Basketball (F), Basketball (M), Bowling (F), Bowling (M), Volleyball (F) • SPORTS-INTRAMURAL Basketball (M), Bowling, Hand Ball, Ping-Pong, Racquetball, Swimming, Volleyball • STUDENT LIFE ACTIVITIES Academic Clubs, Newspaper, Radio/TV station, Student Government

---

Selective **Wisconsin Services**

Wisconsin Indianhead Technical College
Ashland Campus 2100 Beaser Avenue
Ashland, Wisconsin 54806
(715) 682-4591

School Enrollment: **325**
LD Enrollment: **25**

Admissions Contact: **Donald Mense, Student Services Coordinator**
LD Contact: **Lynn Reichert, Student Services Counselor**
Name of Program: **Learning Disabilities Program**
Telephone:**(715) 682-4591**

Admissions

Application Information:
Application deadline: **None**

Secondary School Information
Most Important Criteria For Admissions (1-strongest)
SAT/ACT **1**	Application	School transcript
Class rank	Course selection	Personal statement
Interview	Extra activities	Psychoeducational
G.P.A.	Open admission	Recommendations

Test Requirements:
Standardized tests waived: **Yes**
Diagnostic testing waived: **Yes**
Tests recommended: **Best suited to individual case**

Types of Disabilities Served
• Speech/Lang	• Reading	• ADD with LD
• Study skills	• Spelling	ADD without LD
• Written express	• Math	• ADHD with LD
• Organizational	• Fine Motor	ADHD without LD
• Perceptual		

Learning Disability Program
Program: Remedial: **Yes**
Program: Reinforces course work: **Yes**
Program available through:**Daily schedule**
Students mainstreamed **100** % of the day
Recommended credits per semester: **Varies**
Time required or recommended in learning center: **Varies**
Services available for all students: **Yes**
Counseling: Individual: **Yes** Group Counseling: **Yes** Vocational Counsel-

ing: **Yes**
Support groups are available:**Yes**

Faculty:
Faculty: **1** Including Director: **Yes** Full time: **1**
LD faculty with: BS/BA: **1**
Faculty advocate: **Yes** Meets with instructor: **Periodically**

Diagnostic Testing
ADD	Personality •	Perceptual skills	• Spelling
ADHD	Organization•	Fine motor skills	• Reading
I.Q. •	Handwriting	Spoken language	• Study skills
• Math	• Social skills•	Written language	

Tutoring:
Average size of group tutorials: **Varies**
Services rendered by:
Graduates　　Peers　•Faculty　　•LD staff　　Teacher trainees

Tutorials
Grp.	Ind.	Tutorials	Grp.	Ind.	Tutorials
•	•	Math skills			Word processing
•	•	Study skills			Time management
•	•	Language arts	•		Learning strategies
•		Written express	•		Organizational skills

Academic Accommodations
Curriculum	Study Aids	Exams
Priority registration	Typist	• Oral
• Math waiver	Reader	• Untimed
Foreign lang. waiver	Notetaker	Take home
• Course substitution	Proof reader	With proctor
In Class	• Text on tape	On computer
• Calculators	Early syllabus	• Extended time
• Tape recorder	Taped handouts	On tape
• Word processor		Modified
• Priority seating		• Separate room

Graduation Requirements:
Course credits: **Varies** GPA: **2.0** Years to complete degree: **Varies**

Program Strengths
Our Learning Disability Program takes a very personalized approach with students. The LD program staff works closely with instructors, counselors, and professionals in the area.

General Information:
Wisconsin Indianhead Technical College is a 2 year public college. Suburban campus of 15 acres is Accessible by air or bus. Ski areas are 30 miles from campus. Beaches are 1 mile from campus. Housing is not guaranteed.

Accreditation:NCACS

Expenses:
Tuition: In-state: Full year: $1,200.00. Part-time: Per credit:$38.00. Part-time: Per course: $200.00. Tuition: Out-of-state: Full year: $4,000.00. Part-time: Per credit:$170.00.

Majors
• BUSINESS Accounting, Administrative Assistant, Agricultural, Food Management, Hospitality and Recreation Mar, Office Secretarial, Travel/Tourism Management • COMPUTER SCIENCE Computer Repair, Computer Science, Data Processing • HEALTH SCIENCES Nursing, Nutritional/Food • PREPROFESSIONAL Architecture • VOCATIONAL Court Reporting, Culinary Arts, Industrial Technology, Machinist, Secretarial

Sports/Activities
• SPORTS-INTRAMURAL Baseball, Bowling, Boxing, Skiing - Snow, Softball, Volleyball • STUDENT LIFE ACTIVITIES Newspaper, Student Government, Yearbook

Less Selective　　　　　　　　**Wyoming
Services**

Casper College
125 College Drive
Casper, Wyoming 82601
(307) 268-2110

School Enrollment: **4,396** Male: **1,696** Female: **2,700**
LD Enrollment: **20** Male: **12** Female: **8**

Admissions Contact: **Linda King, Director of Admissions**
LD Contact: **Teresa Wallace, Special Populations Coordinator**
Telephone:**(307) 268-2200**

Admissions

Application Information:
LD Students Applying: **20** Accepted: **20** Enrolled:**20**
Application deadline: **August 1st**
Rolling Admissions: **Yes**Notified when: **Continuous**

Secondary School Information
Most Important Criteria For Admissions (1-strongest)
SAT/ACT **1**	Application **1**	School transcript
Class rank	Course selection	Personal statement
Interview	Extra activities	Psychoeducational
G.P.A.	Open admission	Recommendations

Test Requirements:
Range accepted:

Types of Disabilities Served
• Speech/Lang	• Reading	• ADD with LD
• Study skills	• Spelling	• ADD without LD
• Written express	• Math	• ADHD with LD
• Organizational	• Fine Motor	• ADHD without LD
• Perceptual		

Admissions Process

ACT scores are required for preregistration; otherwise, an application form must be completed and forwarded to the Admissions Office, along with official transcripts from previous educational institutions.

Learning Disability Program
Program: Remedial: **Yes**
Program: Reinforces course work: **Yes**
Students mainstreamed **100** % of the day
Recommended credits per semester: **Individual basis**
Services available for all students: **Yes**
Counseling: Individual: **Yes** Group Counseling: **Yes** Vocational Counseling: **Yes**
Support groups are available:**On request**

Wyoming

Faculty:
Faculty: **7** Full time: **5** Part time: **2**
LD faculty with: BS/BA: **1** M.A.: **5**

Diagnostic Testing
ADD • Personality • Perceptual skills • Spelling
ADHD Organization Fine motor skills • Reading
• I.Q. • Handwriting Spoken language Study skills
• Math Social skills • Written language

Tutoring:
Average size of group tutorials: **1-3**
Services rendered by:
Graduates •Peers Faculty LD staff Teacher trainees

Tutorials

Grp.	Ind.	Tutorials	Grp.	Ind.	Tutorials
•	•	Math skills	•	•	Word processing
•	•	Study skills	•	•	Time management
•	•	Language arts	•	•	Learning strategies
	•	Written express	•	•	Organizational skills

Academic Accommodations

Curriculum	Study Aids	Exams
• Priority registration	• Typist	• Oral
Math waiver	• Reader	• Untimed
Foreign lang. waiver	• Notetaker	• Take home
• Course substitution	• Proof reader	With proctor
In Class	Text on tape	• On computer
• Calculators	Early syllabus	• Extended time
• Tape recorder	Taped handouts	On tape
Word processor		Modified
• Priority seating		• Separate room

Graduation Requirements:
Course credits: **64** GPA: **2.0** Years to complete degree: **2**

General Information:
Casper College is a 2 year public college. Urban campus of 175 acres is 280 miles from Denver, Colorado. Accessible by air or bus. Ski areas are 15 minutes from campus. 1% of students are foreign. 3 residential halls on campus. Housing is not guaranteed.50 % of students remain on campus for the weekends.

Accreditation:NCACS, AMA CAHEA, NASM

Expenses:
Tuition: In-state: Full year: $744.00. Part-time: Per credit:$32.00. Part-time: Per course: $96.00 (3 credit hours). Tuition: Out-of-state: Full year: $1,992.00. Room and board: $2,150.00

Majors
• AGRICULTURE Business, Mechanics • AREA STUDIES Women's Studies • ARTS Commercial Art, Drafting, Music, Music Performance, Photography, Theater Design • BUSINESS Accounting, Business Administration, Business Education, Data Processing, Economics, Management, Marketing, Retailing, Secretarial Science • COMMUNICATIONS Communication, Journalism • COMPUTER SCIENCE Computer Science, Data Processing • EDUCATION Business, Early Childhood, Elementary, Music, Physical • ENGINEERING Engineering Science, Petroleum Technology • ENVIRONMENTAL CONTROL Water and Wastewater Technology • HEALTH SCIENCES Environmental, Medical Biology, Nursing, Physical Therapy • HUMANITIES English/Writing/Literature, Liberal Arts • LANGUAGES French, German, Italian, Spanish • PRE PROFESSIONAL Dentistry, Forestry, Law, Legal Assistant, Medicine, Optometry, Pharmacy, Social Work, Veterinarian, Wildlife • SCIENCES Biology, Chemistry, Geology, Mining , Physics • SOCIAL SCIENCES Addictions Specialist, Anthropology, Criminal Justice, History, International Studies,

Law Enforcement, Political Science, Psychology, Sociology • VISUAL AND PERFORMING ARTS Music, Music Performance, Theater • VOCATIONAL Automotive Service, Aviation Pilot, Business and Office, Construction, Diesel Power Mechanics, Drafting, Electronics Technology, Fire Science, Home Economics, Industrial Arts, Machinist, Office Administration, Radiological Technology, Secretarial, Welding

Sports/Activities
• SPORTS RELATED Cheerleading, Pep Band, Team Managers • SPORTS-INTERCOLLEGIATE Basketball (F), Basketball (M), Rodeo, Trap and Skeet, Volleyball (F) • SPORTS-INTRAMURAL Badminton (F), Badminton (M), Basketball (F), Basketball (M), Bowling, Football, Golf, Hand Ball, Ping-Pong, Racquetball, Racquetball (F), Racquetball (M), Skiing - Snow, Skiing - Snow (F), Skiing - Snow (M), Soccer, Softball, Tennis, Tennis (F), Tennis (M), Volleyball, Volleyball (F), Volleyball (M), Water Polo, Wrestling (M) • STUDENT LIFE ACTIVITIES Academic Clubs, Choral, Concert Band, Debate, Drama Groups, Ethnic & Cultural Groups, Jazz Band, Magazine, Music Groups, Musical Theater, Newspaper, Political Groups, Religious Organization, Student Government

---

Less Selective　　　　　　　　　　**Wyoming Program**

Central Wyoming College
Riverton, Wyoming 82501
(307) 856-9291

School Enrollment: **2,827**
LD Enrollment: **308**

Admissions Contact: **Linda Holladay, Asst. Dir. of Admissions**
LD Contact: **Janelle Pepper Chew, Dir. of Support Services**
Name of Program: **Student Support Services**

Admissions

Application Information:
Separate application:**Yes**
Application deadline: **Open**
Applicant must apply **6** months in advance

Secondary School Information
Most Important Criteria For Admissions (1-strongest)

SAT/ACT	**1**	Application	**2**	School transcript
Class rank	**3**	Course selection		Personal statement
Interview		Extra activities		Psychoeducational
G.P.A.	**1**	Open admission		Recommendations

Test Requirements:
Standardized tests waived: **Yes**

Types of Disabilities Served
• Speech/Lang • Reading ADD with LD
• Study skills • Spelling ADD without LD
• Written express • Math ADHD with LD
• Organizational • Fine Motor ADHD without LD
• Perceptual

Learning Disability Program
Program: Remedial: **Yes**
Program: Reinforces course work: **Yes**
Counseling: Individual: **Yes**

Faculty:

Faculty: **34** Including Director: **Yes** Full time: **4** Part time: **30**
Faculty advocate: **Yes** Meets with instructor: **3 times a week**

Diagnostic Testing

ADD	Personality	Perceptual skills	• Spelling
ADHD	Organization	Fine motor skills	• Reading
• I.Q.	Handwriting	Spoken language	Study skills
• Math	Social skills	• Written language	

Tutoring:

Services rendered by:
Graduates •Peers •Faculty •LD staff Teacher trainees

Tutorials

Grp.	Ind.	Tutorials	Grp.	Ind.	Tutorials
•	•	Math skills	•	•	Word processing
•	•	Study skills	•	•	Time management
•	•	Language arts	•	•	Learning strategies
•	•	Written express	•		Organizational skills

Academic Accommodations

Curriculum	Study Aids	Exams
Priority registration	• Typist	• Oral
Math waiver	Reader	Untimed
Foreign lang. waiver	• Notetaker	Take home
• Course substitution	• Proof reader	With proctor
In Class	• Text on tape	On computer
• Calculators	Early syllabus	• Extended time
• Tape recorder	Taped handouts	On tape
• Word processor		• Modified
Priority seating		Separate room

Program Strengths

Individualized attention and special adaptation of classroom materials and equipment enable CWC to serve the special student in ways that enable the student to succeed in a college education setting.

General Information:

Central Wyoming College is a 2 year public college. Rural campus of 200 acres is 125 miles from Casper. Accessible by air or auto. Ski areas are 130 miles from campus. 2% of students are foreign. 1 residential halls on campus. Housing is not guaranteed.50 % of students remain on campus for the weekends.

Accreditation:NCACS

Expenses:

Tuition: In-state: Full year: $652.00. Part-time: Per credit:$23.00. Tuition: Out-of-state: Full year: $1,390.00. Part-time: Per credit:$57.50. Room and board: $2,500.00

Majors

• BUSINESS Accounting, Agricultural, Business Administration, Business Data Processing, Business Management, Management, Marketing • COMMUNICATIONS Communication, English, Journalism, Television/Radio/Film • COMPUTER SCIENCE Computer Science, Data Processing, Programming • CRAFTS AND DESIGN Crafts • EDUCATION Elementary, General, Secondary • ENGINEERING Engineering Science • HEALTH SCIENCES Nursing • HUMANITIES Humanities, Liberal Arts • PRE-PROFESSIONAL Law, Natural Resources • SCIENCES Agricultural, Animal, Biology, Chemistry, Equestrian Studies, Geology, Mathematics, Physical Science, Science Technologies • SOCIAL SCIENCES Anthropology, Criminal Justice, Government/Political, Law Enforcement, Political Science, Psychology, Social Sciences, Sociology • VISUAL AND PERFORMING ARTS Dramatic Arts, Fine Arts, Music, Visual and Performing Arts • VOCATIONAL Automobile Technology, Automotive Service, Business and Office, Drafting, Electronic Equipment Repair, Electronics Technology, Secretarial, Welding, Word Processing

Sports/Activities

• SPORTS RELATED Pep Band • SPORTS-INTERCOLLEGIATE Basketball • SPORTS-INTRAMURAL Archery, Badminton, Baseball, Basketball, Bowling, Ping-Pong, Softball, Tennis, Volleyball • STUDENT LIFE ACTIVITIES Choral, Dance, Drama Groups, Jazz Band, Music Groups, Musical Theater, Newspaper, Radio/TV station, Student Government

---

Less Selective

Wyoming Program

Laramie County Community College

1400 East College Drive
Cheyenne, Wyoming 82007
(307) 778-5222

School Enrollment: **3,690**
LD Enrollment: **90**

Admissions Contact: **Dean Bartow**
LD Contact: **Caron Mellblom, LARC Coordinator**
Name of Program: **Learning Assistance Resource Center**

Admissions

Application Information:

Enrolled:**90**
Applicant must apply **2-3** months in advance
Rolling Admissions: **Yes**

Secondary School Information

Most Important Criteria For Admissions (1-strongest)

SAT/ACT	**1**	Application	**1**	School transcript
Class rank		Course selection		Personal statement
Interview		Extra activities	**1**	Psychoeducational
G.P.A.		Open admission		Recommendations

Test Requirements:

Standardized tests waived: **Yes**
Diagnostic testing waived: **Yes**
Untimed SAT: **Yes** Untimed ACT: **Yes** Untimed ACH: **Yes**
Tests recommended: **College-designed placement battery**

Types of Disabilities Served

• Speech/Lang	• Reading	• ADD with LD
• Study skills	• Spelling	• ADD without LD
• Written express	• Math	• ADHD with LD
• Organizational	• Fine Motor	• ADHD without LD
• Perceptual		

Learning Disability Program

Program: Remedial: **Yes**
Program: Reinforces course work: **Yes**
Students mainstreamed **100 %** of the day
Recommended credits per semester:
Counseling: Individual: **Yes** Group Counseling: **Yes**

Faculty:

Faculty: **9** Including Director: **Yes** Full time: **1** Part time: **8**
LD faculty with: BS/BA: **2** M.A.: **1**
Faculty advocate: **Yes** Meets with instructor: **As needed**

Wyoming

Diagnostic Testing

ADD	Personality	Perceptual skills	• Spelling
ADHD•	Organization	Fine motor skills	• Reading
I.Q.	Handwriting•	Spoken language	• Study skills
• Math	Social skills•	Written language	

Tutoring:
Average size of group tutorials: **2-5**
Services rendered by:
 Graduates Peers •Faculty •LD staff •Teacher trainees

Tutorials

Grp.	Ind.	Tutorials	Grp.	Ind.	Tutorials
•	•	Math skills	•	•	Word processing
•	•	Study skills	•	•	Time management
•	•	Language arts	•	•	Learning strategies
•	•	Written express	•	•	Organizational skills

Academic Accommodations

Curriculum	Study Aids	Exams
Priority registration	• Typist	• Oral
Math waiver	Reader	Untimed
Foreign lang. waiver	• Notetaker	Take home
• Course substitution	• Proof reader	• With proctor
In Class	• Text on tape	On computer
• Calculators	Early syllabus	• Extended time
• Tape recorder	Taped handouts	On tape
• Word processor		Modified
Priority seating		Separate room

Program Strengths

Any LARC (Learning Assistance Resource Center) student who needs help with reading, grammar, and math or who has been defined as learning disabled may find help in the LARC. All LARC services are free to LCCC students. The LARC provides tutoring, test-taking assistance, note-taking assistance, computer-aided instruction, adaptive equipment, and textbook taping services.

General Information:

Laramie County Community College is a 2 year public college. Urban campus of 170 acres is 90 miles from Denver. Accessible by air or bus. Ski areas are 1 hour from campus. 1% of students are foreign. 1 residential halls on campus. Housing is not guaranteed.

Accreditation: NCACS

Expenses:

Tuition: In-state: Full year: $640.00. Part-time: Per credit:$27.50. Tuition: Out-of-state: Full year: $1,172.00. Part-time: Per credit:$50.50. Room and board: $3,000.00 Cost of LD program:$640.00

Majors

• BUSINESS Accounting, Agricultural, Business Administration, Business Data Programming, Business Management, Marketing • COMMUNICATIONS English, Speech • COMPUTER SCIENCE Medical Records Technology • CRAFTS AND DESIGN Graphic Art Technology • EDUCATION General, Teacher Aide • ENGINEERING Engineering Science • HEALTH SCIENCES Nursing, Practical Nursing, Radiograph Medical Technology • HUMANITIES Humanities, Liberal Arts • SCIENCES Agricultural, Biology, Chemistry, Equestrian Studies, Mathematics, Physical Science • SOCIAL SCIENCES Law Enforcement, Psychology, Social Sciences • VISUAL AND PERFORMING ARTS Visual and Performing Arts • VOCATIONAL Automobile Technology, Business and Office, Chemical Manufacturing Technology, Diesel Engine Mechanics, Fire Science, Home Economics, Precision Metal Works, Secretarial

Sports/Activities

• SPORTS-INTERCOLLEGIATE Basketball, Golf, Volleyball • SPORTS-INTRAMURAL Archery, Badminton, Basketball, Bowling, Cross Country, Diving, Fencing, Golf, Gymnastics, Hand Ball, Ping-Pong, Racquetball, Riflery, Skiing - Snow, Soccer, Softball, Swimming, Tennis, Volleyball, Water Polo, Wrestling • STUDENT LIFE ACTIVITIES Choral, Drama Groups, Musical Theater, Newspaper, Student Government

---

Less Selective   **Wyoming Program**

Sheridan College
P. O. Box 1500
Sheridan, Wyoming 82801
(307) 674-6446

School Enrollment: **2,670**
LD Enrollment: **250**

Admissions Contact: **Ken Carlson, Dir. of Enrollment Management**
LD Contact: **Kerry Morgan, LD Consultant**
Name of Program: **Learning Center**
Telephone:**(307) 674-6446 Ext. 194**

Admissions

Secondary School Information
Most Important Criteria For Admissions (1-strongest)

7 SAT/ACT	**1** Application	**2** School transcript
5 Class rank	**4** Course selection	**10** Personal statement
11 Interview	**9** Extra activities	**6** Psychoeducational
3 G.P.A.	Open admission	**8** Recommendations

Test Requirements:
Standardized tests waived: **Yes**

Types of Disabilities Served
• Speech/Lang	• Reading	• ADD with LD
• Study skills	• Spelling	• ADD without LD
• Written express	• Math	• ADHD with LD
• Organizational	• Fine Motor	• ADHD without LD
• Perceptual		

Learning Disability Program
Program: Remedial: **Yes**
Program: Reinforces course work: **Yes**
Students mainstreamed **100** % of the day
Counseling: Individual: **Yes** Group Counseling: **Yes**

Faculty:
Faculty: **1** Including Director: **Yes** Full time: **1** M.A.: **1**
Faculty advocate: **Yes** Meets with instructor: **As needed**

Diagnostic Testing

ADD	Personality	Perceptual skills	Spelling
ADHD	Organization	Fine motor skills	Reading
I.Q.	Handwriting	Spoken language	Study skills
Math	Social skills	Written language	

Tutoring:
Average size of group tutorials: **5-8**
Services rendered by:
 Graduates •Peers •Faculty •LD staff •Teacher trainees

Tutorials

Grp.	Ind.	Tutorials	Grp.	Ind.	Tutorials
•		Math skills	•		Word processing
	•	Study skills		•	Time management
	•	Language arts		•	Learning strategies
	•	Written express		•	Organizational skills

Academic Accommodations

Curriculum
Priority registration
Math waiver
Foreign lang. waiver
Course substitution

In Class
Calculators
• Tape recorder
Word processor
Priority seating

Study Aids
Typist
Reader
• Notetaker
Proof reader
• Text on tape
Early syllabus
Taped handouts

Exams
• Oral
Untimed
Take home
• With proctor
On computer
• Extended time
On tape
Modified
Separate room

Program Strengths

Services provided are formal assessment, if recommended, in order to determine if a student has a learning disability. There is a Learning Disability Consultant/Instructor available to design an individualized program for the student. The Consultant/Instructor will monitor the services outlined in the individualized program.

General Information:

Sheridan College is a 2 year public college. Rural campus of 64 acres is 132 miles from Billings. Accessible by air or bus. Ski areas are 80 miles from campus. 1% of students are foreign. 6 residential halls on campus. Housing is not guaranteed.1 % of students remain on campus for the weekends.

Accreditation: NCACS

Expenses:

Tuition: In-state: Full year: $312.00. Part-time: Per credit:$32.00. Tuition: Out-of-state: Full year: $936.00. Part-time: Per credit:$86.50. Room and board: $1,115.00

Majors

• BUSINESS Accounting, Agricultural, Agricultural Production, Business Administration, Business Economics, Business Management, Marketing • COMMUNICATIONS Communication, English, Journalism • COMPUTER SCIENCE Computer Science • EDUCATION Elementary, General, Secondary • ENGINEERING Engineering Science, Engineering Technology • HEALTH SCIENCES Dental Hygiene, Health, Nursing • HUMANITIES Liberal Arts • LANGUAGES Spanish • PREPROFESSIONAL Range Management, Social Work • SCIENCES Agricultural, Animal, Biology, Botany, Chemistry, Mathematics • SOCIAL SCIENCES Government/Political, Political Science, Protective Services, Psychology, Public Relations, Social Sciences, Sociology • VISUAL AND PERFORMING ARTS Fine Arts, Music • VOCATIONAL Business and Office, Dental Assistant, Diesel Engine Mechanics, Electrical Power Technology, Electromechanical Technology, Electronics Technology, Machine Tool Technology, Mining and Petroleum Technology, Office Administration, Respiratory Therapy Technology, Secretarial, Welding, Welding Technology

Sports/Activities

• SPORTS RELATED Pep Band • SPORTS-INTERCOLLEGIATE Basketball, Riflery, Volleyball (F) • SPORTS-INTRAMURAL Basketball, Softball, Tennis, Volleyball • STUDENT LIFE ACTIVITIES Choral, Drama Groups, Jazz Band, Music Groups, Student Government

---

Selective   **Wyoming Services**

University of Wyoming
University Station Box 3435
Laramie, Wyoming 82071
(307) 766-5160

School Enrollment: **9,444** Male: **4,842** Female: **4,602**

Admissions Contact: **Rebecca Asplund, Ast. Dir. of Admissions**
LD Contact: **Chris Primus, Project Director**
Name of Program: **Disabled Student Services**
Telephone:**(307) 766-6189**

Admissions

Application Information:
Enrolled:**45**
Application deadline: **August 10th**
Applicant must apply **6 months** in advance

Secondary School Information
Most Important Criteria For Admissions (1-strongest)

2 SAT/ACT	Application	**1**	School transcript
3 Class rank	**3** Course selection	**5**	Personal statement
4 Interview	**5** Extra activities		Psychoeducational
1 G.P.A.	Open admission	**4**	Recommendations

Test Requirements:
Diagnostic testing waived: **Yes**
Untimed SAT: **Yes** Untimed ACT: **Yes**
Documentation of LD required: **Yes**
Tests recommended: **Diagnosis by a qualified professional is required.**

Types of Disabilities Served
• Speech/Lang	• Reading	• ADD with LD
• Study skills	• Spelling	• ADD without LD
• Written express	• Math	• ADHD with LD
• Organizational	• Fine Motor	• ADHD without LD
• Perceptual		

Learning Disability Program

Program: Reinforces course work: **Yes**
Students mainstreamed **100** % of the day
Counseling: Individual: **Yes**

Faculty:
Faculty: **2** Including Director: **Yes** Full time: **2** M.A.: **2**
Faculty advocate: **Yes** Meets with instructor: **Each semester**

Diagnostic Testing
ADD	Personality	Perceptual skills	Spelling
ADHD	Organization	Fine motor skills	Reading
I.Q.	Handwriting	Spoken language	Study skills
Math	Social skills	Written language	

Tutoring:
Average size of group tutorials: **2-8**
Services rendered by:
•Graduates   •Peers   Faculty   LD staff   •Teacher trainees

Wyoming

Tutorials

Grp.	Ind.	Tutorials	Grp.	Ind.	Tutorials
•	•	Math skills		•	Word processing
•	•	Study skills	•	•	Time management
	•	Language arts	•	•	Learning strategies
	•	Written express	•	•	Organizational skills

Academic Accommodations

Curriculum	Study Aids	Exams
• Priority registration	• Typist	• Oral
Math waiver	Reader	Untimed
Foreign lang. waiver	• Notetaker	Take home
• Course substitution	• Proof reader	• With proctor
In Class	• Text on tape	On computer
• Calculators	Early syllabus	• Extended time
• Tape recorder	Taped handouts	• On tape
• Word processor		• Modified
Priority seating		• Separate room

Graduation Requirements:
Course credits: **Varies** GPA: **2.0**

Program Strengths

Our learning disabilities program provides basic academic support and disability-related accommodations to University of Wyoming students with learning disabilities. Students must provide documentation of the learning disability, provided by a physician, psychologist, LD expert, or from school records in order to be eligible for program services.

General Information:

University of Wyoming is a 4 year public university. Rural campus of 785 acres is 129 miles from Accessible by air, train, or bus. Ski areas are 36 miles from campus. 2% of students are foreign. 6 residential halls on campus. Housing is not guaranteed. 12 % of students join fraternities/sororities.

Accreditation: NCACS

Expenses:
Tuition: In-state: Full year: $1,293.00. Part-time: Per credit: $60.25. Tuition: Out-of-state: Full year: $4,097.00. Part-time: Per credit: $178.20.
Room and board: $3,262.00

Majors

• AREA STUDIES American, International Studies • BUSINESS Accounting, Agricultural, Business Administration, Business Economics, Business Education, Business Management, Business Statistics, Economics, Fashion Merchandising, Finance, Marketing • COMMUNICATIONS Agricultural Communications, Communication, English, Journalism, Radio/Television • COMPUTER SCIENCE Computer Science, Management Information Systems • EDUCATION Agricultural, Art, Child Development, Early Childhood, Elementary, English, Foreign Language, Health, Home Economics, Industrial, Marketing Education, Mathematics, Middle School, Music, Physical, Reading, Science, Secondary, Social Studies, Special, Speech/Language, Theater, Trade • ENGINEERING Architectural, Bioengineering, Chemical, Civil/Environmental, Electrical, Engineering Science, Mechanical, Petroleum • HEALTH SCIENCES Dental Hygiene, Nursing, Speech Therapy, Speech/Audiology and Speech • HUMANITIES Humanities, Liberal Arts, Philosophy • LANGUAGES French, German, Russian, Spanish • PREPROFESSIONAL Dentistry, Medicine, Pharmacy, Range Management, Social Work, Veterinarian • SCIENCES Agricultural, Animal, Astronomy, Astrophysics, Biochemistry, Biology, Botany, Chemistry, Entomology, Food, Geography, Geology, Geophysics, International Agriculture, Mathematics, Microbiology, Physical Science, Physics, Physiology, Soil, Statistics, Zoology • SOCIAL SCIENCES Anthropology, Criminal Justice, History, International Relations, Political Science, Psychology, Social Sciences, Sociology • VISUAL AND PERFORMING ARTS Dance, Dramatic Arts, Fine Arts, Music, Music Performance, Music Theory and Composition, Visual and Performing Arts • VOCATIONAL Home Economics, Interior Design, Medical Laboratory Technology, Park/Recreation

Sports/Activities

• SPORTS RELATED Marching Band, Pep Band • SPORTS-INTERCOLLEGIATE Baseball (M), Basketball, Cross Country, Diving, Football (M), Golf, Riflery, Skiing - Snow, Swimming, Track and Field, Volleyball (F), Wrestling (M) • SPORTS-INTRAMURAL Badminton, Basketball, Bowling, Cross Country, Diving, Fencing, Hand Ball, Ice Hockey (M), Lacrosse, Ping-Pong, Racquetball, Riflery, Rugby (F), Rugby (M), Skiing - Snow, Soccer, Softball, Swimming, Tennis, Track and Field, Volleyball, Water Polo, Wrestling (M) • STUDENT LIFE ACTIVITIES Choral, Concert Band, Dance, Drama Groups, Fraternities, Jazz Band, Magazine, Music Groups, Musical Theater, Newspaper, Opera, Radio/TV station, Sororities, Student Government, Symphony Orchestra, Yearbook

Other Schools That Recognize Students With Learning Disabilities

Bishop State Community College
351 North Broad Street
Mobile, Alabama 36603
(800) 523-7235
Admissions Contact:Terry Hazzard
Title:Dean of Student Personnel
LD Contact: Ms. Carrie K. Moore
Title:Counselor

Brewer State Junior College
2631 Temple Avenue North
Fayette, Alabama 35555
(800) 526-5755
Admissions Contact:Nelda L. Oswalt
Title:Director of Admissions

Gadsden State Community College
P.O. Box 227
Gadsden, Alabama 35902
(205) 549-8201
Admissions Contact:Dr. Marie Luttrell
Title:Director of Admissions

George C. Wallace State Commmunity College at Selma
P.O. Drawer 1049
Selma, Alabama 36701
(205) 875-2634
Admissions Contact:W. D. Beaty
Title:Dean of Students

James H. Faulkner State Com. College
Hammond Circle
Bay Minette, Alabama 36507
(205) 037-9581
Admissions Contact:Linda Brown
Title:Director of Admissions
LD Contact: Ms. Lena Dexter
Title:Director
Telephone: (205) 937-9581

John C. Calhoun Community College
P.O. Box 2216
Decatur, Alabama 35609
(205) 353-3102
Admissions Contact:M. Wayne Tosh
Title:Director of Admissions

Reid State Technical College
P.O. Box 588
Evergreen, Alabama 36401
(205) 578-1313
Admissions Contact:Conrad Booker
Title:Financial Aid Officer

S.D. Bishop State Junior College
351 North Broad Street
Mobile, Alabama 36690
(205) 690-6164
Admissions Contact:Mr. Terry Hazzard
Title:Dean of Students
LD Contact: Carrie K. Moore
Title:Counselor
Name of Program: Student Services
Address: 351 N. Broad Street
Telephone: (205) 690-6423

Spring Hill College
4000 Dauphin Street
Mobile, Alabama 36608
(205) 460-2130
Admissions Contact:Tim Williams
Title:Director of Admissions

University of Montevallo
Station 6250
Montevallo, Alabama 35115
(205) 665-6030-(800) 292-4349
LD Contact: Maryann Darland

University of South Alabama
AHE Room 120
Mobile, Alabama 36688
(205) 460-6141-(800) 872-5247
LD Contact: Ms. Pat Edwards
Title:Coordinator

Alabama Agricultural and Mechanical University
P.O. Box 908
Normal, Alabama 35762
(800) 533-0816
Admissions Contact:James O. Heyward
Title:Director of Admissions

Arizona Western College
P.O. Box 929
Yuma, Arizona 85366
(602) 726-1050
Admissions Contact:Richard Lott
Title:Director of Admissions

Eastern Arizona College
600 Church Street
Thatcher, Arizona 85552
(602) 428-8244

Mesa Community College
1833 W. Southern Avenue
Mesa, Arizona 85202
(602) 461-7000
LD Contact: Judith Taussig
Title:Director

Northland Pioneer College
P.O. Box 610
Holbrook, Arizona 86025
(602) 524-1993
Admissions Contact:A. Daniel Simper
Title:Dean of Admissions

Paradise Valley Community College
1202 West Thomas Road
Phoenix, Arizona 85013
(602) 285-7500
Admissions Contact:Dr. Shirley Green
Title:Director of Admissions

Rio Salado Community College
640 North First Avenue
Phoenix, Arizona 85003
(602) 223-4001
Admissions Contact:Patricia Cardenas Adame
Title:Director of Admissions

Scottsdale Community College
9000 East Chaparral Road
Scottsdale, Arizona 85256
(602) 423-6000
LD Contact: Dee Duggan

South Mountain Community College
7050 South 24th Street
Phoenix, Arizona 85040
(602) 243-8123
Title:Director of Admissions
LD Contact: Bill Zepada

Yavapai College
1100 East Sheldon Street
Prescott, Arizona 86301
(602) 445-7300
Admissions Contact:Dr. Richard M. Boone
Title:Director of Admissions
LD Contact: Dr. Merrill Elastrom
Title:Director, Student Support Services
Name of Program: Student Support Services

East Arkansas Community College
Forest City, Arkansas 72335
(501) 633-4480
Admissions Contact:Janice Hurd
Title:Director of Admissions

Mississippi County Community College
P.O. Box 1109
Blytheville, Arkansas 72316
(501) 762-1020
LD Contact: Myles Jeffers
Title:Director Counseling Services

Ouachita Baptist University
OBU Box 3776
Arkadelphia, Arkansas 71998
(800) 342-5628
Admissions Contact:Michale L. Kolb
Title:Director of Admissions

Rich Mountain Community College
601 Bush Street
Mena, Arkansas 71953
(501) 394-5012
Admissions Contact:Dr. Robert Goldman
Title:Dean of Instruction

University of Arkansas
Office of Campus Access ARKU 113
Fayetteville, Arkansas 72701
(501) 575-5346-(800) 575-5346
LD Contact: Amy Bell

Allan Hancock College
800 South College Drive
Santa Maria , California 93454
(805) 922-6966
LD Contact: Debbie Vecente

Barstow College
2700 Barstow Road
Barstow, California 92311-9984
(619) 252-2411

California Polytechnic State University: San Luis
San Luis Obispo, California 93407
(805) 756-2311
Admissions Contact:Harriet Clendenen
Title:Coor/Special Admissions
LD Contact: Ann Fryer
Title:Learning Disability Specialist
Name of Program: Disabled Student Services
Telephone: (805) 756-1395

California State University, Hayward
Room L2177
Hayward, California 94542-3057
(510) 810-3811
LD Contact: Jeanne Reyes

California State University: San Marcos
820 Los Vallecitos Boulevard
San Marcos, California 92096
(619) 752-4800
Admissions Contact:Betty J. Huff
Title:Director of Admissions
LD Contact: John Segoria
Title:Coordinator of Student Support Services
Name of Program: Student Support Services
Telephone: (619) 752-4891

California State University: Stanislaus
801 West Monte Vista Avenue
Turlock, California 95380
(209) 667-3248
Admissions Contact:Chris Butzen
Title:Director of Admissions
LD Contact: Karen L. Mendonca
Title:Director
Name of Program: Academic Support Services
Telephone: (209) 667-3381

Cerro Coso Community College
3000 College Heights Boulevard
Ridgecrest, California 93555
(619) 375-5001
Admissions Contact:Dottie Cowan
Title:Registrar
LD Contact: Susan Smith
Title:Director of Special Services
Name of Program: Special Services Program
Telephone: (619) 375-5001 Ext. 248

Chapman University
333 North Glassell Street
Orange, California 92666
(714) 997-6711
LD Contact: Vi Champa

Christ College Irvine
1530 Concordia
Irvine, California 92715
(714) 854-8002-(800) 229-1200
LD Contact: Diane Vieselmeyer

Citrus College
1000 West Foothill Boulevard
Glendora, California 91740
(818) 914-8511
Admissions Contact:Melanie Cox
Title:Dean of Admissions

City College of San Francisco
50 Phelan Avenue
San Francisco, California 94112
(415) 239-3835
Admissions Contact:Mira D. Sinco
Title:Dean of Admissions

Coastline Community College
11460 Warner Avenue
Fountain Valley, California 92708
(714) 546-7600
Admissions Contact:James E. Garmon
Title:Vice President of Student Services
LD Contact: Gloria Kinnevey
Title:Staff Aide
Telephone: (714) 751-9776

College of the Desert
43-500 Monterey
Palm Desert, California 92260
(619) 346-9041
LD Contact: Michael O'Neill
Title:Learning Specialist

College of the Redwoods
7351 Tompkins Hill Road
Eureka, California 95501
(707) 445-6720
Admissions Contact:Paul Mendoza
Title:Dean of Student Services

Compton Community College
1111 East Artesia Boulevard
Compton, California 90221
(213) 637-2600
Admissions Contact:Dr. Essie French-Preston
Title:Associate Dean of Enrollment Services

Contra Costa College
2600 Mission Bell Drive
San Pablo, California 94806
(213) 637-2660
LD Contact: Pam Van Gilder

Cosumnes River College
8401 Center Parkway
Sacramento, California 95823
(916) 688-7410
Admissions Contact:Howard L. Harris
Title:Dean of Admission
LD Contact: Dave Aagaard
Title:Learning Disabilties Specialist
Name of Program: Learning Disabilities Pro.
Telephone: (916) 688-7330

Diablo Valley College
321 Golf Club Road
Pleasant Hill, California 94523
(415)685-1230
Admissions Contact:John Dravland
Title:Director of Admissions

Gavilan Community College
5055 Santa Teresa Boulevard
Gilroy, California 95020
(408) 848-1400
Admissions Contact:Joy Parker
Title:Director of Admissions
LD Contact: Dr. Carol Cooper
Title:Coordinator
Name of Program: Disabled Students Programs and Services
Telephone: (408) 848-4871

Grossmont Community College
8800 Grossmont College Drive
El Cajon, California 92020
(619) 465-1700
Admissions Contact:Jim Fenningham
Title:Director of Admissions

Holy Names College
3500 Mountain Boulevard
Oakland, California 94619-9989
(415) 436-1321
Admissions Contact:Mr. Tom Huff
Title:Assistant Director
LD Contact: Mary Lee Knapp
Title:Director
Name of Program: Raskob Learning Institute
Telephone: (415) 436-1275

Humphreys College
6650 Inglewood Avenue
Stockton, California 95207-3896
(209) 478-0800
Admissions Contact:Pamela Knapp
Title:Admissions/Pub. Relations

Irvine Valley College
5500 Irvine Center Drive
Irvine, California 92720
(714) 559-9300
LD Contact: William Hewitt

Lake Tahoe Community College
P.O. Box 14445
South Lake Tahoe, California 96151
(916) 541-1651
Admissions Contact:Linda M. Stevenson
Title:Director of Admissions

Lassen College
P.O. Box 3000
Susanville, California 96130
(916) 257-6181
Admissions Contact:Chris Alberico
Title:Registrar & Admissions Director

Los Angeles Pierce College
6201 Winnetka Avenue
Woodland Hills, California 91371
(818) 719-6404
Admissions Contact:Shelley Gerstl
Title:Coordinator of Admissions & Rcords
LD Contact: Mr. David Phoenix
Title:Specialist
Name of Program: Learning Disabilities Pro.
Telephone: (818) 719-6430

Los Medamos College
2700 East Leland Road
Pittsburg, California 94565
(510) 439-2188
Admissions Contact:Gail Newman
Title:Director
LD Contact: Ms. Dorrie Fisher
Title:Coordinator
Name of Program: Disabled Students Program and Services
Telephone: (510) 439-2181 Ext. 353

Marin Community College
835 College Avenue
Kentfield, California 94904
(415) 485-9411
LD Contact: Myles Mayo

Marymount College
30800 Palos Verdes Drive
Rachno Palos Verdes, California 90274
(310) 377-5501
Admissions Contact:Kenneth B. Mayer
Title:Director of Admissions

Mendocino College
1000 Hensley Creek
Ukiah, California 95482
(707) 468-3100
Admissions Contact:Kristie A. Taylor
Title:Registrar

Menlo College
1000 El Camino Real
Atherton, California 94027
(800) 55-MENLO
Admissions Contact:James Whitaker
Title:Dean Enrollment Management

Miracosta College
One Barnard Drive
Oceanside, California 92056
(619) 757-2121

Mission College
3000 Mission College Boulevard
Santa Clara, California 95054
(408) 748-2703
Admissions Contact:Dr. Glenn Hanley
Title:Assistant Dean of Student Services

Mount San Antonio College
1100 North Grand Avenue
Walnut, California 91789
(714) 594-5611
LD Contact: Dr. James Andrews

Napa Valley College
Napa Valley, California 94558
(707) 253-3000

Occidental College
1600 CampusRoad
Los Angeles, California 90041
(800) 825-5262
Admissions Contact:Charlene Liebau
Title:Dean of Admissions

Orange Coast College
2701 Fairview Road
Costa Mesa, California 92626
(714) 432-5772
Admissions Contact:Susan Brown
Title:Administrative Dean of Admissions
LD Contact: Dr. Ken Ortiz
Title:Dean

Oxnard College
4000 South Rose Avenue
Oxnard, California 93033
(805) 986-5810
LD Contact: Rosalie Souza

Pacific Union College
Angwin, California 94508
(707) 965-6673
Admissions Contact:Gary Clifford
Title:Director of Enrollment Services

Palomar College
1140 West Mission Road
San Marcos, California 92069
(619) 744-1150
Admissions Contact:Herman C. Lee
Title:Ronald Haines
LD Contact: Coordinator
Title:Disabled Student Programs & Services

Point Loma Nazarene College
3900 Lomaland Drive
San Diego, California 92106
(619) 221-2273
Admissions Contact:William J. Young
Title:Executive Director of Enrollment Ser

Rio Hondo
3600 Workman Mill road
Whittier, California 90608
(310) 692-0921
Admissions Contact:Tom Huffman
Title:Dean of Admissions and Records

Samuel Merritt College
370 Hawthorne Avenue
Oakland, California 94609
(510) 420-6076
Admissions Contact:CharisseHughen
Title:Director of Admissions

San Joaquin Delta College
5151 Pacific Avenue
Stockton, California 95207
(209) 474-5625
Admissions Contact:Cheryl L. Clark
Title:Registrar

San Jose City College
2100 Moorpark Avenue
San Jose, California 95128
(408) 298-2181
Admissions Contact:Robert L. Brown
Title:District Director of Admissions and
Records

Skyline College
3300 College Drive
San Bruno, California 94066
(415) 738-4251
Title:Director of Admissions
LD Contact: Linda Van Scivet

Solano Community College
4000 Suisun Valley Road
Suisun City, California 94585
(707) 864-7171
Title:Director of Admissions

Southwestern College
900 Otay Lakes Road
Chula Vista, California 92010
(619) 421-1189
LD Contact: Diane Branman

University of California: Irvine
245 Administration Building
Irvine, California 92717
(714) 856-6703
LD Contact: Dr. Ron Blosser

University of California: Los Angeles
405 Hilgard Avenue
Los Angeles, California 90024
(213) 825-3101
LD Contact: Arlene Halper

University of California: San Francisco
P.O. Box 0244
San Francisco, California 94143
(415) 476-4986
Admissions Contact:Robert D. Gibson
Title:Registrar

University of San Francisco
Ignatian Heights
San Francisco, California 94117-1080
(415) 666-6563-(800) 225-5873
Admissions Contact:Paula Podesta
Title:Admissions Counselor
LD Contact: Cally Salzman
Title:L.D. Specialist
Name of Program: Services/Learning Disabled
Telephone: (415) 666-6876

University of Southern California
666 Childs Way
Los Angeles, California 90080-0911
(213) 743-6741

University of the Pacific
3601 Pacific Avenue
Stockton, California 95211
(209) 946-2211
LD Contact: Howard Houck

Yuba College
2088 North Beale Road
Marysville, California 95901
(916) 741-6720
Admissions Contact:Susan Singhas
Title:Dean of Admissions

San Jose State University
One Washington Square
San Jose, California 95192
(408) 924-2009
Admissions Contact:Edgar Chambers
Title:Associate Vice President Admissions and
Records

Aims Community College
5401 West 20th Street
Greeley, Colorado 80632
(303) 330-8008
Admissions Contact:William D. Green
Title:Registrar

Fort Lewis College
Durango, Colorado 81301-3999
(303) 247-7184-(800) 826-6718
LD Contact: Tim Slane
Title:Coordinator

Lamar Community College
2401 South Main
Lamar, Colorado 81052
(719) 336-2248
LD Contact: Cindy Baer

Metropolitan State College of Denver
P.O. Box 173362
Denver, Colorado 80217
(303) 556-3018
Admissions Contact:Dr. Kenneth C. Curtis
Title:Dean of Admissions and Records

Trinidad State Junior College
600 Prospect
Trinidad, Colorado 81082
(719) 846-5621-(800) 621-8752
Title:Director of Admissions
LD Contact: Dr. Phyllis Brown

University of Northern Colorado
Greeley, Colorado 80639
(303) 351-2881
Admissions Contact:Gary O. Gullickson
Title:Director of Admissions
LD Contact: Dr. James K. Bowen
Title:Director
Name of Program: Disabled Student Services
Telephone: (303) 351-2289

University of Southern Colorado
2200 Bonforte Blvd.
Pueblo, Colorado 81001
(719) 549-2461-(800) 872-4769
LD Contact: Sam Clay

Asnuntuck Community College
170 Elm Street
Enfield, Connecticut 06082
(203) 253-3010
Admissions Contact:Vince Fulginiti
Title:Director of Admissions

Central Connecticut State University
1615 Stanley Street
New Britain, Connecticut 06050
(203) 827-7543
Admissions Contact:Dr. Hakim Salahu-Din
Title:Director of Admissions

Hartford State Technical College
401 Flatbush Avenue
Hartford, Connecticut 06106
(203) 527-4111
Admissions Contact:C. Raymond Hughes
Title:Director of Admissions

Housatonic Community College
510 Barnum Avenue
Bridgeport, Connecticut 06608
(203) 579-6475

Norwalk State Technical College
181 Richards Avenue
Norwalk, Connecticut 06854
(203) 855-6640

Quinnipac College
Mount Carmel Avenue
Hamden, Connecticut 06518
(203) 281-8600
Admissions Contact:David Tilley
Title:Dean of Admissions
LD Contact: Mr. David F. Blumenthal
Title:Associate Dean of Student Affairs
Telephone: (203) 281-8722

Sacred Heart University
5151 Park Avenue
Fairfield, Connecticut 06432
(203) 371-7880-(800) 333-8934
LD Contact: Dean Michael Bozzone

Southern Connecticut State University
501 Crescent Street
New Haven, Connecticut 06515
(203) 397-4450
Admissions Contact:Sharon Brennan Browne
Title:Director of Admissions
LD Contact: Kelly Johanan
Name of Program: Disabiltiy Resource Office

St. Joseph College
1678 Asylum Avenue
West Hartford, Connecticut 06117
(203) 232-4571
Admissions Contact:Mary C. Demo
Title:Director of Admissions

Trinity College
300 Summit Street
Hartford, Connecticut 06106
(203) 527-3151

University of Hartford
Bates House
West Hartford, Connecticut 06117-0395
(203) 243-4296
Admissions Contact:Richard A. Zeiser
Title:Director of Admissions
LD Contact: Helen Apthorp
Title:Director of Learning Plus
Name of Program: Learning Plus
Telephone: (203) 243-4522

Vista of Westbrook, Inc.
1356 Old Clinton Road
Westbrook, Connecticut 06498
(203) 399-8080
Admissions Contact:Helen K. Bosch
Title:Executive Director
Name of Program: Vista of Westbrook
Telephone: (203) 399-8080

Waterbury State Technical College
750 Chase Parkway
Waterbury, Connecticut 06708
(203) 575-8078
Admissions Contact:A. Robert McKnack
Title:Director of Admissions

Delaware State College
1200 N. Dupont Highway
Dover, Delaware 19901
(302) 736-4917
Admissions Contact:Jethro Williams
Title:Director of Admissions
LD Contact: Dr. Susan Iovino

Wesley College
120 North State Street
Dover, Delaware 19901
(302) 736-2400
Admissions Contact:Joseph R. Slights, Jr.
Title:Dean of Admissions

Georgetown University
1 Darnall Hall
Washington, District of Columbia 20057
(202) 687-3600
Title:Director of Admissions
LD Contact: Dr. Norma Jo Eitington
Title:Director
Name of Program: Learning Services

Howard University
2400 Sixth Street Northwest
Washington, District of Columbia 20059
(800) 822-6363
Admissions Contact:Emmett R. Griffin
Title:Director of Admissions

University of the District of Columbia
4200 Connecticut Avenue, NW
Washington, District of Columbia 20008
(202) 282-3200
Admissions Contact:Sandra Doldhin
Title:Director of Admissions/Registrar

Valencia Community College
P.O. Box 3028
Orlando, Flordia 32802
(407) 299-1506
Admissions Contact:Charles H. Drosin
Title:Direcotr of Admissions
LD Contact: Mr. Walter Johnson
Title:Counselor
Name of Program: Disabled Student Services
Address: 710 North Econlockhatchee Trail
Telephone: (407) 299-5000

Art Inst. of Ft. Lauderdale
1799 Southeast 17th Street
Fort Lauderdale, Florida 33316
(800) 275-7603

Broward Community College
225 East Las Olas Boulevard
Fort Lauderdale, Florida 33301
(305) 475-6500
Admissions Contact:Dr. Theodore D. Taylor
Title:Director of Admissions

Central Florida Community College
3001 SW College Avenue
Ocala, Florida 32678
(904) 237-2111
Admissions Contact:Sam Mitchell
Title:Associate VP of Student Services
LD Contact: Mr. Chuck Corcoran
Title:Coordinator
Name of Program: Disabled Student Services
Telephone: (904) 237-2111 Ext. 243

Daytona Beach Community College
P.O. Box 2811
Daytona Beach, Florida 32120
(904) 255-8131
Admissions Contact:Keith Kennedy
Title:Coordinator of Admissions

Florida International University
University Park
Miami, Florida 33199
(305) 348-2363
LD Contact: Peter Manheimer

Florida Keys Community College
5901 W. Junior College Road
Key West, Florida 33040
(305) 296-9081
Admissions Contact:Mitchell A. Grabois
Title:Admissions Coordinator

Hillsborough Community College
P.O. Box 31127
Tampa, Florida 33631
(813) 253-7004
Admissions Contact:Philip T. Dreier
Title:Registrar

Indian River Community College
3209 Virginia Av enue
Fort Pierce, Florida 34981
(407) 468-4740
Admissions Contact:Linda W. Hays
Title:Assistant Dean of Educational Services

Lake-Sumter Community College
9501 US Highway 441
Leesburg, Florida 34788
(904) 365-3573
Admissions Contact:Earl Evans
Title:Associate Dean of Students and Admissions

Manatee Community College
P.O. Box 1849
Bradenton, Florida 34206
(813) 755-1511
Admissions Contact:Gilbert W. McNeal
Title:Dean of Admissions and Records

Pensacola Junior College
1000 College Blvd.
Pensacola, Florida 32504
(904) 484-1600
LD Contact: Linda Shephred

Rollins College
1000 Holt Avenue
Winter Park, Florida 32789
(407) 646-2161
Admissions Contact:David G. Erdmann
Title:Dean of Admissions

St. Johns River Community College
5001 St. Johns Avenue
Palatka, Florida 32177-3897
(904) 328-1571

St. Thomas University
16400 Northwest 32nd Avenue
Miami, Florida 33054
(305) 628-6546
Admissions Contact:John M. Letvinchuk
Title:Director of Admissions

University of Central Florida
P.O. Box 25000
Orlando, Florida 32816
(407) 823-3000
Admissions Contact:Jeanne Rutenkroger
Title:Director of Admissions

University of Florida
Gainesville, Florida 32611
(904) 392-1365

University of North Florida
4657 St. Johns Bluff Road, South
Jacksonville, Florida 32216
(904) 646-2624

University of South Florida
4202 Fowler Avenue
Tampa, Florida 33620
(813) 974-3350
Admissions Contact:Vickie W. Ahrens
Title:Director of Admissions

Webber College
P.O. Box 96
Babson Park, Florida 33827
(813) 638-1431
Admissions Contact:Pam Bellamy
Title:Assistant Director of Admissions
LD Contact: Dr. Deborah Milliken
Title:Dean of Student Development
Name of Program: Tutorial Program
Telephone: (813) 638-1431 - Ext. 54

Abraham Baldwin Agricultrual College
AVAC Station Box 4
Tilton, Georgia 31794
(800) 733-3653
Admissions Contact:Garth L. Webb, Jr.
Title:Director of Admissions

Athens Area Technical Institute
U.S. Highway 29 North
Athens, Georgia 30610
(404) 542-8050
Admissions Contact:Carroll D. Humphries
Title:Vice President for Student Services

Atlanta Metropolitan College
1630 Stewart Avenue
Atlanta, Georgia 30310
(404) 756-4000
Admissions Contact:Verel V. Wilson
Title:Director of Admissions

Berry College
Mount Berry Station
Rome, Georgia 30149
(706) 236-2215-(800) MT-BERRY
LD Contact: Dr. Marshall Jenkins

Columbus College
3600 Algonquin
Columbus, Georgia 31993
(706) 568-2035
LD Contact: Dr. Thomas Wentland

DeVry Institute of Technology
250 North Arcadia
Decatur, Georgia 30030
(706) 292-2645-(800) 221-4771
LD Contact: Elaine Thornton

Georgia Southwestern College
800 Wheatly Street
Americus, Georgia 31709
(800) 338-0082
Admissions Contact:Diane Burns
Title:Director of Admissions

Kennesaw State College
P.O. Box 444
Marietta, Georgia 30061
(706)423-6300
Admissions Contact:Joe F. Head
Title:Director of Admissions

North Idaho College
1000 W. Garden AVenue
Coeur d'Alene, Idaho 83814
(208) 769-3311

Ricks College
Rexburg, Idaho 83460
(208) 356-1020
Admissions Contact:Gordon Westenkow

Belleville Area College
2500 Carlyle Road
Belleville, Illinois 62221
(800) 522-5131
Admissions Contact:Jann Haskins Florek
Title:Director of Admissions
LD Contact: Patricia Brian
Title:Director
Name of Program: Special Services Center
Telephone: (618) 235-2700 Ext. 333

Black Hawk College
6600 34 Avenue
Moline, Illinois 61265
(800) 798-1311
Admissions Contact:Barton Schiermeyer
Title:Director of Admissions

City Colleges of Chicago: Chicago City-Wide College
226 West Jackson Boulevard
Chicago, Illinois 60606
(312) 641-2595
Admissions Contact:Robert A. Reed
Title:Director of Admissions

City Colleges of Chicago: Kennedy King - College
6800 South Wentworth
Chicago, Illinois 60621
(312) 962-3200

City Colleges of Chicago: Richard J. Daley College
7500 South Pulaski Road
Chicago, Illinois 60652
(312) 735-3000
Admissions Contact:Walter A. Calgaro
Title:Director Recruitment & Marketing

City Colleges Chicago: Wright College
3400 North Austin Avenue
Chicago, Illinois 60634
(312) 794-3100
Admissions Contact:Michael P. Langley
Title:Dean of Student Services/Registrar

College of DuPage
22nd Street and Lambert Road
Glen Ellyn, Illinois 60137
(708) 858-2800
Admissions Contact:Charles D. ERickson
Title:Director of Admissions

College of Lake County
19351 West Washington Street
Grayslake, Illinois 60030
(708) 223-6601
Admissions Contact:Curtis Denny
Title:Director of Admissions

Eastern Illinois University
600 Lincoln - Old Main 117
Charleston, Illinois 61920
(800) 252-5711
Admissions Contact:Dale Wolf
Title:Director of Admissions

Illinois Eastern Community Colleges: Frontier Community College
Lot 2 Frontier Drive
Fairfield, Illinois 62837
(618) 842-3711
Admissions Contact:Suxanne Brooks
Title:Coordinator of Admissions and Records

Illinois Eastern Community Colleges: Lincoln Trail
Rural Route 3 Box 82A
Robinson, Illinois 62454-980 3
(618) 544-8657

Illinois Eastern Community Colleges: Wabash Valley
2200 College Drive
Mount Carmel, Illinois 62863
(618) 262-8641
Admissions Contact:Diana Spear
Title:Director of Admissions

Illinois Eastern Community Colleges: Lincoln Trail
Rural Route 3 Box 82A
Robinson, Illinois 62454
(618) 544-8657
Admissions Contact:Becky Mikeworth
Title:Director of Admissions
LD Contact: Ms. Seaaroba Mascher
Title:Director
Telephone: (618) 544-8657

Illinois Eatern Community Colleges: Olney Central
305 North West Street
Olney, Illinois 62450
(618) 395-4351
Admissions Contact:Chris Webber
Title:Director of Admissions

Illinois Wesleyan University
1312 North Park
Bloomington, Illinois 61702
(309) 556-3031
Admissions Contact:James Ruoti
Title:Dean of Admissions

John A. Logan College
Carterville, Illinois 62918
(618) 985-3741
Title:Director of Admissions
LD Contact: Tim williams

Joliet Junior College
1216 JHoubolt Avenue
Joliet, Illinois 60436
(815) 729-9020
Admissions Contact:Russell Corey
Title:Director of Enrollment Management
LD Contact: Ms. Jeanne Legan
Title:Special Needs Coordinator
Name of Program: Special Needs Program
Telephone: (815) 729-9020 Ext. 2230

Kishwaukee College
Route 38 and Malta Road
Malta, Illinois 60150
(815) 825-2086
LD Contact: Frances Loubere

Knox College
Box K109
Galesburg, Illinois 61410-4999
(309) 343-0112
Title:Director of Admissions
LD Contact: Karyn Halloran
Name of Program: Reading/Learning Center

Lewis and Clark Community College
5800 Godfrey Road
Godfrey, Illinois 62035
(618) 466-3411
Admissions Contact:Pete Basola
Title:Assistant Director of Admissions
LD Contact: Patricia Horn
Title:Asst. Director Special Services
Name of Program: Student Support Services
Telephone: (618) 466-3411 Ext. 310

Lewis University
Route 53
Romeoville, Illinois 60441-2298
(815) 838-0500

Montay College
3750 West Peterson
Chicago, Illinois 60659
(312) 539-1919
LD Contact: Linda Von Drasek

Morton College
3801 South Central Avenue
Cicero, Illinois 60650
(708) 656-8000
LD Contact: Patricia Valente

Northeastern Illinois University
5500 North St. Louis Avenue
Chicago, Illinois 60625
(312) 583-4050
Admissions Contact:Miriam rivera
Title:Director of Admissions
LD Contact: Victoria Amey-Flippin
Title:Coordinator
Name of Program: Student Support Services
Telephone: (312) 583-4050 Ext. 3135

Richland Community College
2425 Federal Drive
Decatur, Illinois 72526
(217) 875-7200
Admissions Contact:Jane Johnson
Title:Dean of Student Services
LD Contact: Teena Zindel-McWilliams
Title:Special Needs Coordinator
Name of Program: Special Needs Services

Rosary College
7900 West Division
River Forest, Illinois 60305
(708) 524-6800-(800) 828-8475
LD Contact: Dr. Therese Hogan

St. Xavier University
3700 West 103rd Street
Chicago, Illinois 60655
(312) 779-3300
Admissions Contact:Mary E. Hendry
Title:Dean of Admissions

University of Illinois at Chicago
P.O. Box 5220
Chicago, Illinois 60680
(312) 996-0998
Admissions Contact:Marilyn Fiduccia
Title:Executive Director Office of Admissions
LD Contact: Jean Gorman
Title:Coordinator
Name of Program: Disabled Student Services
Telephone: (312) 413-2183

University -Illinois:Urbana-Champaign
10 Administration Building
Urbana, Illinois 61801
(217) 333-0302
Admissions Contact:Patricia E. Askew
Title:Director of Admissions
Title:Cordinator
Name of Program: Services for Students with Disabilities
Telephone: (217) 333-4602

City Colleges of Chicago: Malcolm X
1900 West Van Buren Street
Chicago, Illinois 60612
(312) 738-5823
Admissions Contact:Anthony New
Title:Registrar

KAES College
5909 North Rogers Avenue
Chicago, Illinois 60646
(312) 725-1925
Admissions Contact:Dr. Shin T. Kang
Title:President

Ancilla College
Union Road
Donaldson, Indiana 46513
(219) 936-8898 Ext. 350
LD Contact: Admissions Office

Ball State University
2000 University Avenue
Muncie, Indiana 47306
(317) 285-8300
LD Contact: Richard Harris
Title:Director
Name of Program: Disabled Student Develop

Earlham College
National Road West
Richmond, Indiana 47374
(800) EARLHAM
Admissions Contact:Robert L. de Veer
Title:Dean of Admissions

Goshen College
1700 South Main Street
Goshen, Indiana 46526
(800) 348-7422
Admissions Contact:Martha Lehman Hooley
Title:Director of Admissions
LD Contact: Martha Hooley

Indiana State University
217 North Sixth Street
Terre Haute, Indiana 47809
(812) 237-2121
Admissions Contact:Richard Riehl
LD Contact: Richard Riehl

Indiana Vocational Technical College: Columbus
4475 Central Avenue
Columbus, Indiana 47203
(812) 372-9925
Admissions Contact:Kathleen Carmer
Title:Admissions Coordinator

Indiana Vocational Technical College: Southcentra
8204 Highway 31 West
Sellersburg, Indiana 47172
(812) 246-3301

Martin University
2171 Avondale
Indianapolis, Indiana 46218
(317) 543-3238
Admissions Contact:Bobbye Jean Craig
Title:Director of Admissions

St. Francis College
2701 Spring Street
Fort Wayne, Indiana 46808
(800) 729-4732
Admissions Contact:Debra A. Dotterer
Title:Director of Admissions

St. Joseph's College
P.O. Box 890
Rensselaer, Indiana 47978
(219)866-7111
Admissions Contact:Ken Rasp
Title:Director of Admissions
LD Contact: Diane Jennings
Title:Director of Counseling Services
Telephone: (219) 866-6170

Wabash College
P.O. Box 352
Crawfordsville, Indiana 47933
(800) 345-5385
Admissions Contact:Greg Birk
Title:Director of Admissions

Briar Cliff College
3303 Rebecca Street
Sioux City, Iowa 51104
(800) 662-3303
Admissions Contact:Patty White
Title:Director of Admissions

Iowa Lakes Community College
300 South 18th Street
Estherville, Iowa 51334
(712) 362-2604
Admissions Contact:John G. Nelson
Title:Director of Admissions

Iowa Western Community College
2700 College road
Council Bluffs, Iowa 51502
(712) 325-3200
Admissions Contact:Thomas O. Dutch
Title:Director of Admissions
LD Contact: Mary Pape
Title:Coordinator
Name of Program: Special Services Depart.
Telephone: (712) 325-3209

Kirkwood Community College
6301 Kirkwood Boulevard, SW
Cedar Rapids, Iowa 52406
(319) 398-5517
Admissions Contact:Jim Miller
Title:Director of Admissions

Luther College
Decorah, Iowa 52101-1042
(319) 387-1287
Title:Director of Admissions

North Iowa Area Community College
500 College Drive
Mason City, Iowa 50401
(515) 421-4253
Admissions Contact:Tom Dunn
Title:Enrollment Specialist
LD Contact: Sue Norton
Title:Special Needs Coordinator
Telephone: (515) 421-4365

Northeast Iowa Community College
P.O. Box 400
Calmar, Iowa 52132
(800) 728-2256
Admissions Contact:Martha Keune
Title:Coordinator of Admissions

Northwest Iowa Technical College
Highway 18 West
Sheldon, Iowa 51201
(800) 352-4907
Admissions Contact:Bonnie Brands
Title:Director of Admissions

Northwestern College
Orange City, Iowa 51041
(712) 737-4821
Title:Director of Admissions

St. Ambrose University
518 West Locust Street
Davenport, Iowa 52803
(800) 383-2627
Admissions Contact:Patrick O'Connor
Title:Dean of Admissions
LD Contact: Scott Howaldn
Title:Coordinator
Name of Program: Services for Students with Disabilities
Telephone: (319) 383-8920

Upper Iowa University
Carter Hall Box 1859
Fayette, Iowa 52142
(800) 553-4150
Admissions Contact:Debra Sanborn
Title:Director of Admissions

Baker University
Eighth and Grove Streets
Baldwin City, Kansas 66006
(800) 873-4282
Admissions Contact:John D. Haynes
Title:Director of Admissions

Barclay College
P.O. Box 288
Haviland, Kansas 67059
(316) 862-5252
Admissions Contact:Mr. Lonny Choate
Title:Director of Admissions

Butler County Community College
Towanda Avenue and Haverhill Road
Eldorado, Kansas 67042
(316) 321-5083
Admissions Contact:Neal Holting
Title:Director of Admissions
LD Contact: Lora Rozeboom
Title:Special Needs Director
Telephone: (316) 321-2222 Ext. 166

Colby Community College
1255 South Range
Colby, Kansas 67701
(913)462-3984
Admissions Contact:Theron Johnson
Title:Director of Admissions
LD Contact: Joyce Washburn
Title:Director of Academic Services
Telephone: (913) 462-3984

Donnelly College
608 North 18th Street
Kansas City, Kansas 66102
(913) 621-6070
Admissions Contact:Delia Marin
Title:Coordinator of College Relationships
LD Contact: Lee Stephenson
Title:Director
Name of Program: Student Support Services
Telephone: (913) 621-6070 Ext. 64

Fort Hays State University
600 Park Street
Hays, Kansas 67601
(913) 628-4222
Admissions Contact:Pat Mahon
Title:Director of Admissions Counseling

Hesston College
P.O. Box 3000
Hesston, Kansas 67062
(316) 327-4221
Admissions Contact:Diane Yoder
Title:Director of Admissions

Kansas Newman College
3100 McCormick Avenue
Wichita, Kansas 67213
(316) 942-4291-(800) 736-7585
Title:Director of Admissions
LD Contact: Kim Holdcraft

MidAmerica Nazarene College
P.O. Box 1776
Olathe, Kansas 66061
(913) 782-3750
Admissions Contact:Dennis Troyer
Title:Director of Admissions
LD Contact: Sue Moore
Title:Reading Specialist
Telephone: (913) 782-3750 Ext. 182

Pratt Community College
Highway 61
Pratt, Kansas 67124
(316) 672-5288
Admissions Contact:Lisa Miller
Title:Director of Admissions

Asbury College
l Macklem Drive
Wilmore, Kentucky 40390
(606) 858-3511
Admissions Contact:Stan F. Wiggam
Title:Dean of Admissions

Hazard Community College
One Community College Drive
Hazard, Kentucky 41701
(606) 436-5721

Madisonville Community College
College Drive
Madisonville, Kentucky 42431
(502) 821-2250
Admissions Contact:Robert Renn
Title:Admissions Officer

Northern Kentucky University
Highland Heights, Kentucky 41076
(606) 572-5220-(800) 637-9948
LD Contact: Dale Adams

Paducah Community College
P.O. Box 7380
Paducah, Kentucky 42002
(502) 554-9200
Admissions Contact:Jerry Anderson
Title:Student Services Officer

Spalding University
821 South Fourth Street
Louisville, Kentucky 40203
(502) 585-9911

University of Louisville
2211 South Brook Street
Louisville, Kentucky 40292
(502) 588-6166
LD Contact: Cathy Patus
Title:Student Development Specialist
Name of Program: Special Student Services
Telephone: (502) 588-6927

Louisiana State University at Eunice
P.O. Box 1129
Eunice , Louisiana 70535
(318) 457-7311
LD Contact: Jacquelyn Fruge

Loyola University
7214 St. Charles Avenue
New Orleans, Louisiana 70118
(504) 861-5888
Admissions Contact:Nan Massingill
Title:Director of Admissions

McNeese State University
P.O. Box 92495
Lake Charles, Louisiana 70609
(318) 475-5000
Admissions Contact:Kathy Bond
Title:Admissions Counselor

Nicholls State University
College Station
Thibodaux, Louisiana 70310
(504) 448-4139
Admissions Contact:Dr. Walker Allen
Title:Executive Director of Enrollment Servic

Northeast Louisiana University
700 University Avenue
Monroe, Louisiana 71209
(318) 342-5252
Admissions Contact:James Robertson
Title:Director of Admissions

University of New Orleans
Lakefornt
New Orleans, Louisiana 70148
(504) 286-6595
Admissions Contact:Roslyn Shelley
Title:Dean of Academic Services

Bates College
Lewiston, Maine 04240
(207) 786-6000
LD Contact: Virginia Harrison

Central Maine Technical College
1250 Turner Street
Auburn, Maine 04210
(207) 784-2385
Admissions Contact:Darcy Stevens
Title:Associate Director of Admissions

Husson College
Bangor, Maine 04401
(207) 947-1121
Admissions Contact:Jane Goodwin
Title:Director of Admissions

University of Maine at Augusta
University Heights
Augusta, Maine 04330
(207) 621-3175
Admissions Contact:Clayton Smith
Title:Director of Admissions

University of Maine at Farmington
102 Main Street
Farmington, Maine 04938
(207) 778-7052
Admissions Contact:J. Anthony McLaughlin
Title:Director of Admissions

University of Maine at Fort Kent
Pleasant Street
Fort Kent, Maine 94743
(207) 834-3162

University of Maine at Presque Isle
181 Main Street
Presque Isle, Maine 04769
(207) 764-0311
Admissions Contact:Dr. Gerald Wuori
Title:Director of Admissions

Allegany Community College
Willow Brook Road
Cumberland, Maryland 21502
(301) 724-7700
Admissions Contact:Gloria Stafford
Title:Director of Admissions

Anne Arundel Community College
101 College Parkway
Arnold, Maryland 21012
(301) 647-7100
Admissions Contact:Herbert Curkin
Title:Director of Admissions

Bowie State University
Jericho Park Road
Bowie, Maryland 20715
(301) 464-6570
Admissions Contact:Lawrence Waters
Title:Director of Admissions

Catonsville Community College
800 South Rolling Avenue
Catonsville, Maryland 21228
(301) 455-4304
Admissions Contact:Linda Emmerich
Title:Director of Admissions
LD Contact: Dr. Frank Babcock
Title:Director
Name of Program: Counseling
Telephone: (301) 455-4382

Dundalk Community College
7200 Sollers Point Road
Baltimore , Maryland 21222
(410) 282-6700
Admissions Contact:Karen McKenney
Title:Director of Admissions

Essex Community College
7201 Rossville Boulevard
Baltimore, Maryland 21237
(410) 522-1213
Admissions Contact:Daine C. Lane
Title:Director of Admissions

Frederick Community College
7932 Opossumtown Pike
Frederick, Maryland 21702
(301) 846-2430
Admissions Contact:Dr. James M. Holton
Title:Director of Admissions

Harford Community College
401 Thomas Run Road
Bel Air, Maryland 21015
(410) 836-4223
Admissions Contact:Jackie Strzelczyk
Title:Director of Admissions
LD Contact: Ms. Leigh W. Marshall
Title:Coordinator of special Services
Telephone: (410) 836-4414

Montgomery CollegeGermantown
20200 Observation Drive
Germantown, Maryland 20876
(301) 972-2000
Title:Director of Admissions
LD Contact: Janet Merrick

Montgomery College: Takoma Park Campus
Takoma Avenue and Fenton Street
Takoma Park, Maryland 20912
(301) 587-4090
Admissions Contact:Sherman Helberg
Title:Director of Admissions

Morgan State University
Cold spring Land and Hillen Road
Baltimore, Maryland 21239
(800) 332-6674
Admissions Contact:Chelseia Harold-Miller
Title:Director of Admissions

Salisbury State University
Camden and college Avenues
Salisbury, Maryland 21801
(800) 492-1175
Admissions Contact:M.P. Minton
Title:Dean of Admissions

St. Mary's College of Maryland
St. Mary's City, Maryland 20686
(800) 492-7181
Admissions Contact:James Antonio
Title:Cirector of Admissions

University Maryland Baltimore County
5401 Wilkins Avenue
Baltimore, Maryland 21228
(410) 455-2291
Title:Director of Admissions
LD Contact: Cynthia Hill

University of Maryland: College Park
Mitchell Building
College Park, Maryland 20742
(301) 314-8385
Admissions Contact:Dr. Linda M. Clement
Title:Director of Undergraduate Admissions
LD Contact: William R. Scales
Title:Director of Disability Support Services
Address: Shoemaker Bldg., Room 0126
Telephone: (301) 314-7682

Amherst College
P.O. Box 2231
Amherst, Massachusetts 01002
(413) 542-2328
LD Contact: Dean Francis Tuleja
Title:Dean of Students Office

Babson College
Wellesley, Massachusetts 02157
(617) 239-5521
LD Contact: Alix Jackson

Berkshire Community College
West Street
Pittsfield, Massachusetts 01201
(413) 499-4660
Admissions Contact:Adrienne A. Rulnick
Title:Director of Admissions

Bunker Hill Community College
Rutherford Avenue
Boston, Massachusetts 02129
(617) 241-8600
LD Contact: Kathleen Elcox
Title:Director Health & Handicap Serv.

Eastern Nazarene College
23 East Elm Avenue
Quincy, Massachusetts 02170
(617) 773-2373

Emerson College
100 Beacon Street
Boston, Massachusetts 02116
(617) 578-8600
LD Contact: Susan Wilcox

Emmanuel College
400 The Fenway
Boston, Massachusetts 02115
(617) 735-9715
Admissions Contact:Margaret Spillane Bonilla

Essex Agricultural & Technical Institute
562 Maple Street
Hathorne, Massachusetts 01937
(508) 774-0050
Admissions Contact:G. Don Glazier, Jr.
Title:Director of Admissions
LD Contact: Ms. Maura Pantageuus
Title: Counselor, Skills Development Center
Telephone: (617) 774-0050

Fitchburg State College
Pearl Street
Fitchburg, Massachusetts 01420
(508) 345-2151
Admissions Contact:Rudolph F. Jones
Title:Director of Admissions
LD Contact: Melanie Pallotta
Title:Coordinator

Framingham State College
Center for Academic Support Activities
Framingham, Massachusetts 01701
(508) 626-4500
LD Contact: Dr. Ava Ghosh

Greenfield Community College
1 College Drive
Greensfield, Massachusetts 01301
(413) 774-3131
Admissions Contact:Donald W. Brown
Title:Director of Admissions

Holyoke Community College
303 Homestead Avenue
Holyoke, Massachusetts 01040
(413) 538-7000
Admissions Contact:Therese Labine
Title:Director of Admissions

Lasell College
1844 Commonwealth Avenue
Newton, Massachusetts 02166
(617) 243-2225
Admissions Contact:Adrienne Asiaf
Title:Director of Admissions

Lesley College
29 Everett Street
Cambridge, Massachusetts 02138
(617) 868-9600
LD Contact: Sharon Lowenstein
Name of Program: Learning Center
Telephone: 617-349-8459

Newbury College
129 Fisher Avene
Brookline, Massachusetts 02146
(617) 730-7007
LD Contact: Don Cocci
Title:Dean Academic Support Seervices

Northern Essex Community College
Elliot Way
Haverhill, Massachusetts 01830
(508) 374-3900
Admissions Contact:Elizabeth Huntley Cole
Title:Director of Admissions

Quinsigamond Community College
670 West Boylston Street
Worcester, Massachusetts 01606
(508) 852-6365
Admissions Contact:Ronald Smith
Title:Director of Admissions

St. John's Seminary College
197 Foster Street
Brighton, Massachusetts 02135
(617) 254-2610
Admissions Contact:Rev. William F. Fay
Title:Dean of the College
LD Contact: Dr. Mark L. Noonan
Title:Adv., Students with Learning Disabilities
Telephone: (617) 254=2610

Suffolk University
Beacon Hill
Boston, Massachusetts 02108
(617) 573-8460
Admissions Contact:William F. Coughlin
Title:Director of Admissions
LD Contact: Ms. Zegenu Tsige
Title:Associate Dean of Students
Telephone: (617) 673-8239

University of Lowell
1 University Avenue
Lowell, Massachusetts 01854
(508) 452-5000

Wentworth Institute of Technology
550 Huntington Avenue
Boston, Massachusetts 02115
(617)442-9010
Admissions Contact:Thomas McGinn,III
Title:Dean of Enrollment Management

Westfield State College
Westfield, Massachusetts 01086
(413) 568-3311
LD Contact: Joe Shin

Williams College
P.O. Box 487
Williamstown, Massachusetts 01267
(413) 597-2211

New England Conservatory of Music
290 Huntington Avenue
Boston, Massachusetts 02115
(617) 262-1120
Admissions Contact:Robert L. Annis
Title:Dean of Enrollment Services

Andrews University
Berrien Springs, Michigan 49104
(616) 471-3353
Admissions Contact:Cyril Connelly
Title:Associate Vice President of Admissions

Calvin College
3201 Burton SE
Grand Rapids, Michigan 49546
(800) 748-0122
Admissions Contact:Thomas E. McWhertor
Title:Director of Admissions

Center for Creative Studies: College of Art amd Design
201 East Kirby
Detroit, Michigan 48202
(313) 872-3118

Eastern Michigan University
400 Pierce Hall
Ypsilanti, Michigan 48197
(800) 468-6368
Admissions Contact:M. Dolan Evanovich
Title:Dierctor of Admissions

Ferris State University
Starr 123
Big Rapids, Michigan 49307
(616) 592-2100
Admissions Contact:Donald Mullesn
Title:Assoc, Dean, Enrollment Services
LD Contact: Marcia Campbell
Title:Special Needs Coordinator

Grand Rapids Community College
143 Bostwick Northeast
Grand Rapids, Michigan 49503
(616) 771-4101
Admissions Contact:Diane DeFelice-Patrick
Title:Director of Admissions

Hillsdale College
Hillsdale, Michigan 49242
(517) 437-7341
Admissions Contact:Jeff Lantis
Title:Director of Admissions

Hope College
Holland, Michigan 49423
(616) 394-7850

Kirtland Community College
10775 North St. Helen road
Roscommon, Michigan 48653
(517) 275-5121
Admissions Contact:Cary Vajda
Title:Dean of Student Services

Macomb Community College
14500 Twelve Mile Road
Warren, Michigan 48093
(313) 445-7999
Admissions Contact:James W. Varty
Title:Dean of Academic Services

Madonna University
3600 Schoolcraft Road
Livonia, Michigan 48150
(313) 591-5052
Admissions Contact:Louis E. Brohl III
Title:Director Admissions

Marygrove College
8425 West McNichols Road
Detroit, Michigan 48221
(313) 862-5200
Admissions Contact:Karin Harabedian John
Title:Directgor of Admissions

Michigan State University
250 Administration Buidling
East Lansing, Michigan 48824
(517) 355-8332
Admissions Contact:William H. Turner, Ph.D.
Title:Director of Admissions

Northwestern Michigan College
1701 East Front Street
Traverse City, Michigan 49684
(619) 922-1054-(800) 748-0566
LD Contact: Mike Connolly

Oakland University
134 North Foundation Hall
Rochester, Michigan 48309
(313) 370-3360
LD Contact: Jean colburn

Saginaw Valley State University
2250 Pierce Road
University Center, Michigan 48710
(517) 790-4200
Admissions Contact:James P. Dwyer
Title:Director of Admissions

Southwestern Michigan College
58900 Cherry Grove Road
Dowagiac, Michigan 49047
(616) 782-5113
Admissions Contact:James D. Kensinger
Title:Associate Dean of Admissions

St. Clair County Community College
P.O. Box 5015
Port Huron, Michigan 48061
(313)984-3881
Admissions Contact:Michelle K. Mueller
Title:Associate Director of Admissions
LD Contact: Nancy Pecorilli
Title:Counselor
Telephone: (313) 984-3881 Ext. 425

University of Michigan: Dearborn
4901 Evergreen
Dearborn, Michigan 48128
(313) 593-5100
Admissions Contact:Carol Mack
Title:Director of Admissions

West Shore Community College
3000 North Stiles Road
Scottville, Michigan 49454
(616) 845-6211
Admissions Contact:Thomas Hoiles
Title:Director of Admissions

Bemidji State University
Bemidji, Minnesota 56601
(800) 475-2001
LD Contact: Phil Dahl

Bethel College
3900 Bethel Drive
St. Paul, Minnesota 55112
(612) 638-6242-(800) 255-8706

College of Associated Arts
344 Summit Avenue
St. Paul, Minnesota 55102
(612) 224-3416
Admissions Contact:Sherry Guggisberg
Title:Admissions Director
LD Contact: Barbara Davis
Title:Associate Professor
Telephone: (612) 224-3416

College of St. Benedict
37 South college Avenue
St. Joseph, Minnesota 56375
(800) 544-1489
Admissions Contact:Rick Smith
Title:Vice President for Admissions

College of St. Scholastica
1200 Kenwood Avenue
Duluth, Minnesota 55811-4199
(218) 723-6046

Concordia College: Moorhead
901 South Eighth Street
Moorhead, Minnesota 56562
(218) 299-3004
Admissions Contact:James Hausmann
Title:Vice President for Admissions

Inver Hills community College
8445 College Trail
Inver Grove Heights, Minnesota 55076
(612) 450-8500
Admissions Contact:Darlene Kalbler
Title:Admissions Officer

Macalester College
1600 Grand Avenue
St. Paul, Minnesota 55105
(612) 696-6357
LD Contact: Charles Norman

Mankato State University
PO MSU Box 55
Mankato, Minnesota 56002
(507) 389-1822
Admissions Contact:John M. Parkins
Title:Director of Admissions

Mesabi Community College:Arrowhead Region
Ninth Avenue and Chestnut Street
Virginia, Minnesota 55792
(218) 749-7700
Admissions Contact:Tracy Delich
Title:Director of Student Affairs

Minneapolis Community College
1501 Hennepin Avenue
Minneapolis, Minnesota 55403
(612) 341-7000
Admissions Contact:Bonnie Wiger
Title:Registrar
LD Contact: Dr. Melissa Russell
Title:Director, Office for Students with Disabilities
Telephone: (612) 341-7205

National Educa. Center: Brown Institute Campus
2225 East Lake Street
Minneapolis, Minnesota 55407
(612) 721-2481

Normandale Community College
9700 France Avenue, South
Bloomington, Minnesota 55431
(612)832-6320
Admissions Contact:Pam Smith Mentz
Title:Director of Admissions
LD Contact: Johy Orthey
Title:Student Needs Coordinator
Telephone: (612) 832-6422

Rainy River community College
Highway 11-71
International Falls, Minnesota 56649
(218) 285-7722
Admissions Contact:Sue Collins
Title:Director of Student Development
LD Contact: Carol Grim
Title:Disability Services Coordinator
Telephone: (218) 285-2238

St. Paul Technical College
235 Marshall Avenue
St. Paul, Minnesota 55102
(800) 227-6029
Admissions Contact:Milo Loken
Title:Vice President
LD Contact: Margie Warrington
Title:Transition Facilitator
Telephone: (612) 228-4300

University of Minnesota, Twin Cities
101Pleasant Street
Southeast, Minnesota 55455
(612) 625-2008-(800) 752-1000
Title:Director of Admissions
LD Contact: Susan Aase

Mary Holmes College
Highway 50 West
West Point, Mississippi 39773
(800) 634-2749
Admissions Contact:James Stewart
Title:Enrollment Marketing Manager

Mississippi State University
111Allen Hall
Mississippi State, Mississippi 39762
(601) 325-2224
Admissions Contact:Jerry Inmon
Title:Director of Admissions

Northeast Mississippi Commun College
Booneville, Mississippi 38829
(601) 728-7751
Admissions Contact:Ronald M. Sweeney
Title:Director of Admissions
LD Contact: Sarah Rhodes
Title:Director
Name of Program: Student Support Services
Telephone: (601) 728-7751

William Carey College
Box 181
Hattiesburg, Mississippi 39401
(601) 265-5352
LD Contact: Brenda Waldrip

Central Methodist College
411 Central Methodist Square
Fayette, Missouri 65248-1198
(816) 248-3391
Admissions Contact:Anthony J. Boes
Title:Dean of Students
LD Contact: Cara Garrison
Title:Director
Name of Program: Student Development Cen

East Central College
P.O. Box 529
Union, Missouri 63084
(314) 583-5193

Hannibal-LaGrange College
2800 Palmyra Road
Hannibal, Missouri 63401
(314) 221-3113
Admissions Contact:Bill Creech

Lindenwood College
St. Charles, Missouri 63301
(314) 949-2000

Mineral Area College
P.O. Box 1000
Flat River, Missouri 63601
(314) 431-4593
Admissions Contact:Barbara Boockenkamp
Title:Registrar/Counselor

Moberly Area Community College
College and rollins Streets
Moberly, Missouri 65270
(816) 263-4110
Admissions Contact:James C. Musick
Title:Dean of Student Services

Northwest Missouri State University
MC 205
Kirksville, Missouri 63501-9980
(816) 785-4114
Admissions Contact:Kathy Rieck
Title:Dean of Admissions and Records

Park College
Parkville, Missouri 64152
(800) 745-7275
Admissions Contact:Peter Pitts
Title:Director of Admissions

Penn Valley Community College
3201 Southwest Trafficway
Kansas City, Missouri 64111
(816) 932-7610

Southeast Missouri State University
Cape Girardeau, Missouri 63701
(314) 651-2255
LD Contact: Debra Mitchell-Braxton

Southwest Missouri State University
901 So. National Avenue
Springfield, Missouri 65804
(417) 836-5517-(800) 492-7900
LD Contact: Sylvia Buse, Ph.D.

St. Charles Community college
4601 Mid Rivers Mall Drive
St. Peters, Missouri 63376
(314) 922-8000
Admissions Contact:Jim Benedict
Title:Associates Dean of Students

Stephens College
1200 East Broadway
Columbia, Missouri 65215-9986
(314) 876-7207
Admissions Contact:Colleen Bevins
Title:Director of Admissions

Webster University
470 East Lockwood
St. Louis, Missouri 63119
(314) 968-7000-(800) 75-ENROL
LD Contact: Debra Dey

William Woods College
200 West Twelfth
Fulton, Missouri 65251-1098
(314) 592-4221
Admissions Contact:Leslie K. Krieger
Title:Director of Admissions

Dawson Community College
P.O. Box 421
Glendive, Montana 59330
(406) 365-3396
Admissions Contact:Jolene Myers
Title:Director of Admissions

Eastern Montana College
1500 North 30th Street
Billings, Montana 59101-0298
(406) 657-2211
Admissions Contact:Karen Everett
Title:Director of Admissions

Montana State University
Bozeman, Montana 59717-0016
(406) 994-2452
Admissions Contact:Jaynee Groseth
Title:Director of Admissions
LD Contact: Sandra Mandell
Title:Program Specialist
Name of Program: Disabled Student Services

University of Montana
Lodge 101
Missoula, Montana 59812
(406) 243-6266
Admissions Contact:Michael L. Akin
Title:Director of Admissions

Concordia Teachers College
800 No. Columbia Avenue
Seward, Nebraska 68434-9989
(402) 643-3651

McCook community College
1205 East Third
McCook, Nebraska 69001
(308) 345-6303
Admissions Contact:Rick Michaelsen
Title:Counselor

Metropolitan Community College
P.O. Box 3777
Omaha, Nebraska 68103-3777
(402) 449-8418
Admissions Contact:Randy Schmailzl
Title:Director of Enrollment Management

Northeast Community College
801 East Benjamin Avenue
Norfolk, Nebraska 68702-0469
(402) 371-2020
Admissions Contact:Eugene C. Hart
Title:Director of Admissions

Penn State College
Peru, Nebraska 68421
(800) 742-4412
Admissions Contact:Pam Sherwood-Cosgrove
Title:Director of Admissions

University of Nebraska-Lincoln
Room 106 Administration Building
Lincoln, Nebraska 68588
(402) 472-2023-(800) 742-8800
LD Contact: Christie Horn

Wayne State College
200 East Tenth Street
Wayne, Nebraska 68787
(402) 375-7234-(800) 228-9972
LD Contact: Tyrone Wrice

Community College Southern Nevada
3200 East Cheyenne Avenue
North Las Vegas, Nevada 89030
(702) 643-0830
Admissions Contact:Arlie J. Stops
Title:Director of Admissions

Western Nevada Community College
2201 West Nye Lane
Carson City, Nevada 89703
(702) 887-3138
Admissions Contact:Nick L. Paul
Title:Associate Dean, Student Services
LD Contact: Connie Capurro
Title:Counselor
Telephone: (702) 887-3092

Franklin Pierce College
College Road
Rindge, New Hampshire 03461
(603) 899-4050-(800) 437-0048
LD Contact: Judy Schriefer

Hesser College
3 Sundial Avenue
Manchester, New Hampshire 03103
(603) 668-6660-(800) 526-9231
LD Contact: Dr. Edward Clark

New Hampshire Technical: Berlin
2020 Riverside Drive
Berlin, New Hampshire 03570
(603) 752-1113-(800) 445-4525

Notre Dame College
2321 Elm Street
Manchester, New Hampshire 03104
(603) 669-4298
LD Contact: Jane O'Neil

Plymouth State College of the University System of New Hampshire
15 Holderness Road
Plymouth, New Hampshire 03264
(800) 842-6900
Admissions Contact:Donnie J. Scott
Title:Director of Admissions

University of New Hampshire at Manchester
220 Hackett Hill Road
Manchester, New Hampshire 03102
(603) 668-0700
Admissions Contact:James Washington, Jr.
Title:Director of Admissions

White Pines College
40 Chester Street
Chester, New Hampshire 03036
(603) 887-4401
Admissions Contact:Robert Fouquette
Title: Diirector of Admissions
LD Contact: John B. Hoar
Title:Dean
Telephone: (603) 887-4401

Atlantic Community College
Black Horse Pike
Mays Landing, New Jersey 08330-9888
(609) 343-4922
Admissions Contact:Bobby Royal
Title:Director of College Recruitment

Brookdale Community College
Newman Springs Road
Lincroft, New Jersey 07738
(908) 842-1900
Admissions Contact:Richard Pieffer
Title:Director of Enrollment Management
LD Contact: Sally Sorrell
Title:Learning Disabilities Specialist
Name of Program: Academic Skills workshops
Telephone: (908) 224-2786

Centenary College
400 Jefferson Street
Hackettstown, New Jersey 07840-9989
(908) 852-1400
Admissions Contact:Michael McGraw
Title:Vice President of Enrollment/Marketing
LD Contact: Michael McGraw
Title:Vice President for Enrollment Manag
Name of Program: Learning Differences Pro.
Telephone: (908) 852-1400 Ext. 217

Drew University
Madison Avenue
Madison, New Jersey -7940
(201) 408-3739
LD Contact: Dean Edwina Lawler

Essex County College
303 University Avenue
Newark, New Jersey 07102
(201) 877-3100
Admissions Contact:Vivian McCollough
Title:Associate Director of Admissions

Monmouth College
Cedar Avenue
West Long B each, New Jersey 07764-1898
(800) 543-9671
Admissions Contact:Barry Ward
Title:Director of Undergraduate Admissions

Princeton University
Box 430
Princeton, New Jersey 08544-0430
(609) 258) 3060
Admissions Contact:Fred Hargadon
Title:Dean of Admissions

Ramapo College of New Jersey
505 Ramapo Valley Road
Mahwah, New Jersey 07430-1680
(201) 529-7600
Admissions Contact:Nancy E. Jaeger
Title:Director of Admissions

Rider College
2083 Lawrenceville Road
Lawrenceville, New Jersey 08648-3099
(609) 896-5042
Admissions Contact:James F. Reilly
Title:Dean of Admissions

Rutgers-Camden College of Arts and Sciences
P.O. Box 93740
Camden, New Jersey 08101-3740
(609) 757-6104
Admissions Contact:Elizabeth Mitchell
Title:Assistant VP, Undergraduate Admissions

Rutgers- College of Engineering
P.O. Box 2101
New Brunswick, New Jersey 08903-2101
(908) 932-3770
Admissions Contact:Elizabeth Mitchell
Title:Assistant VP,University Undergradu

Rutgers- College of Nursing
P.O. Box 2101
New Brunswick, New Jersey 08903-2101
(908) 932-3770
Admissions Contact:Elizabeth Mitchell
Title:Assistant VP,University Undergradu

Rutgers- Cook College
P.O. Box 2101
New Brunswick, New Jersey 08903-2101
(908) 932-3770
Admissions Contact:Elizabeth Mitchell
Title:Assistant VP, University Undergradu

Rutgers- Douglass College
P.O. Box 2101
New Brunswick, New Jersey 08903-2101
(908) 932-3770
Admissions Contact:Elizabeth Mitchell
Title:Assistant VP, for University Undergradu

Rutgers- Livingstone College
P.O. B 2101
New Brunswick, New Jersey 08903-2101
(908) 932-3770
Admissions Contact:Elizabeth Mitchell
Title:Assistant VP University Undergradu

Rutgers- Mason Gross School
P.O. Box 2101
New Brunswick, New Jersey 08903-2101
(908) 932-3770
Admissions Contact:Elizabeth Mitchell
Title:Assistant VP University Undergradu

Rutgers- Rutgers College
P.O. Box 2101
New Brunswick, New Jersey 08903-2101
(908) 932-3770
Admissions Contact:Elizabeth Mitchell
Title:Assistant VP University Undergradu

Rutgers-New Brunswick
14 College Avenue
New Brunswick, New Jersey 08903
(908) 932-7346
Admissions Contact:S. Loretta Daniels
Title:Director of Admissions

Rutgers- University College:Newark
249 University Avenue
Newark, New Jersey 07102-1896
(201) 648-5205
Admissions Contact:Elizabeth Mitchell
Title:Assistant VP University Undergraduates

Seton Hall University
400 south Orange Avenue
South Orange, New Jersey 07079-2689
(800) THE-HALL
Admissions Contact:Patriia Burgh
Title:Dean of Enrollment Services

Stockton State College
Jimmy Leeds Road
Pomona, New Jersey 08240
(609) 652-4261
Admissions Contact:Sal Catalfamo
Title:Director of Admissions
LD Contact: Thomasa Gonzalez
Title:Director

Sussex County Community College
College Hill
Newton, New Jersey 07860
(201) 579-5400
Admissions Contact:Harold Damato
Title:Director Admissions/Registration

Trenton State College
Hillwood Lakes
Trenton, New Jersey 08650-4700
(609) 771-2131

Clovis Community College
417 Schepps Boulevard
Clovis, New Mexico 88101-8345
(505) 769-4025
Admissions Contact:Victoria Quintela
Title:Director of Enrollment Management

Dona Ana Branch Community College
Box 30001 Department 3DA
Las Cruces, New Mexico 88003
(505) 527-7500
Admissions Contact:Rosemary F. Gonzalez
Title:Admissions Technician

Eastern New Mexico University
Station 7
Portales, New Mexico 88130
(800) 367-3668
Admissions Contact:Larry Fuqua
Title:Director of Admissions

New Mexico Institute of Mining and Technology
Campus Station
Socorro, New Mexico 87801
(505) 835-4224-(800) 428-8324

New Mexico Junior College
Lovington Highway
Hobbs, New Mexico 88240
(505) 392-4510
Admissions Contact:Robert Snow
Title:Dean of Admissions

New Mexico State University
P.O. Box 3001 Department 3575
Las Cruces, New Mexico 88003
(505) 646-3121

New Mexico State University :Carlsbad
1500 University Drive
Carlsbad, New Mexico 88220
(505) 885-8831
Admissions Contact:Micahel J. Cleary
Title:Assistant Provost for Student Services

Northern New Mexico Comm. College
1002 North Onate Street
Espanola, New Mexico 87532
(505) 753-7141
Admissions Contact:Michael L. Costello
Title:Dir. of Adm., Recruiting and Records

Alfred University
26 North Main Street Bartlett Hall
Alfred, New York 14802
(607) 871-2115
Admissions Contact:Daniel L. Meyer
Title:Director of Admissions
LD Contact: Dr. Norman Pollard
Telephone: (607) 871-2164

Barnard College
3009 Broadway
New York, New York 10027-6598
(212) 854-2014
Admissions Contact:Doris Davis
Title:Directof of Admissions

Bramson ORT Technical Institute
6930 Austin Street
Forest Hills, New York 11375
(718) 261-5800
Admissions Contact:Lois Shallit
Title:Director of Admissions
LD Contact: Susan Davidovic
Title:Student Counselor
Telephone: (718) 26105800

City University of New York: Baruch College
P.O. Box 279 17 Lexington Avenue
New York , New York 10010
(212) 447-3750
Admissions Contact:John B. Fisher
Title:Deputy Dir.r of Enrollment Management

City University of New York: New York City Technical
300 Jay Street
Brooklyn , New York 11201-2983
(718) 260-5500
Admissions Contact:Arlene Floyd
Title:Director of Admissions

City Univ of NY: Queensborough
Springfield Boulevard and 56th Avenue
Bayside, New York 11364
(718) 631-6236
Admissions Contact:Mary Bryce
Title:Registrar
LD Contact: Elliot L. Rosman
Title:Director, Disabled Student Services
Telephone: (718) 631-6257

City University of NY:York College
94-20 Guy R. Brewer Boulevard
Jamaica, New York 11451-9989
(718) 262-2165
Admissions Contact:Sally Nelson
Title:Director of Admissions

College of Mount St. Vincent
6301 Riverdale Avenue
Riverdale, New York 10471
(212) 405-3400
Admissions Contact:Lenore Mott
Title:Director of Admissions

College of St. Rose
432 Western Avenue
Albany, New York 12203
(800) 637-8556
Admissions Contact:Mary M. O;Donnell
Title:Dean of Admissions

Columbia-Greene Community College
P.O. Box 1000
Hudson, New York 12534
(518) 828-4181
Admissions Contact:Patricia Hallenbeck
Title:Director of Admissions/Registrar
LD Contact: June D. Blake
Title:Cor.- Services to Students with Disabilit
Telephone: (518) 828-4181

Corning Community College
Spencer Hill
Corning, New York 14830
(607) 962-9220
Admissions Contact:David N. Biviano
Title:Director of Admissions
LD Contact: Deborah Cruise
Title:Director
Telephone: (607) 962-9459

Culinary Institute of America
651 South Albany Post Road
Hyde Park, New York 12538
(914) 452-9430-(800) 283-2433
Title:Director of Admissions
LD Contact: Fred Gairner

Eastman School of Music:University of Rochester
26 Gibbs Street
Rochester, New York 14604-2599
(716) 274-1060
Admissions Contact:Charles Krusensjerna
Title:Director of Admissions

Erie Community College, S. Campus
4140 Southwestern Boulevard
Orchard Park, New York 14127-2199
(716) 648-5400
Admissions Contact:B. Paul Hodan
Title:Assistant Director of Student Services
Title:Nancy Bailey
Name of Program: Counselor for the Disabled
Address: Main & Young Roads, Williamsville,
New York 14221
Telephone: (716) 851-1495

Genesee Community College
College Road
Batavia, New York 14020
(716) 343-0055
Admissions Contact:Malcolm Wormely
Title:Director of Admissions
LD Contact: Dr. Ann Marie Malachowski
Title:Director, Center for Academic Progress
Telephone: (716) 343-0055

Jamestown Community College
525 Falconer Street
Jamestown, New York 14701
(716) 665-5220
Admissions Contact:James A. Gallagher
Title:Director of Admissions
LD Contact: Nancy Callahan
Title:Co., Services for Students with Disabiliti
Telephone: (716) 665-5220 Ext. 558

King's College
150 Lodge Road
Briarcliff Manor, New York 10510-9985
(800) 344-4926
Admissions Contact:Cheryl Burcick
Title:Dean of Admissions

Kol Yaakov Torah Center
29 West Maple Avenue
Monsey, New York 10952
(914) 425-3863
Admissions Contact:Rabbi Aaron Parry
Title:Director of Admissions/Registrar

L.I. University: Brooklyn Campus
University Plaza
Brooklyn, New York 11201
(800) 548-7256
Admissions Contact:Alan B. Chaves
Title:Dean of Admissions and Financial Aid

Manhattan College
Manhattan College Parkway
Riverdale, New York 10471
(800) MC2-XCEL
Admissions Contact:John J. Brennan, Jr.
Title:Dean of Admissions
LD Contact: Dr. Sheila Meindl
Title:Administrator, Learning Disabilities Pro.
Telephone: (212) 920-0409

Manhattanville College
125 Purchase Street
Purchase, New York 10577
(914) 694-2200
Admissions Contact:James J. Skiff
Title:Dean of Admissions and Financial Aid

Marymount College
100 Marymount Avenue
Tarrytown, New York 10591-3796
(914) 332-8295
Admissions Contact:Gina R. Campbell
Title:Director of Admissions

Marymount Manhattan College
221 East 71st Street
New York, New York 10021
(212) 517-0555
Admissions Contact:Suzanne Murphy
Title:Director of Admissions
LD Contact: Dr. Joan Shapiro
Title:Director
Telephone: (212) 517-0501

Mount St. Mary College
330 Powell Avenue
Newburgh, New York 12550
(800) 558-0942
Admissions Contact:J. Randall Ognibene
Title:Director of Admissions

New York Institute of Technology
Central Islip, New York 11722
(516) 348-3000
Admissions Contact:Jim Rein
Title:Dean
LD Contact: David Finklestein
Title:Director
Name of Program: Vocational Independence
Address: Independence Hall
Telephone: (516) 348-3354

Niagara County Community College
3111 Saunders Settlement Road
Sanborn, New York 14132
(716) 731-3271
Admissions Contact:Ronald Mirabelli
Title:Dean of Enrollment Services

North Country Community College
20 Winona Avenue
Saranac Lake, New York 12983
(800) 541-1021
Admissions Contact:Tim Gerrish
Title:Director of Admissions and Treasurer
LD Contact: Jo Ann K. Branch
Title:Director, Learning Assistance Center
Telephone: (518) 891-2915 Ext. 210

Pratt Institute
200 WilloughbyAvenue
Brooklyn, New York 11205
(800) 331-0834
Admissions Contact:Judith Arrow
Title:Dean of Admissions

Rensselaer Polytechnic Institute
Troy, New York 12180
(518) 276-6216-(800) 448-6562
LD Contact: Debbie Hamilton

St. Francis College
180 Remsen Street
Brooklyn Heights, New York 11201
(718) 522-2300
Admissions Contact:Br. George Larkin, O.S.F.
Title:Dean of Admissions

State University of New York at Oswego
Culkin Hall 211
Oswego, New York 13126-3599
(315) 341-2250
Admissions Contact:Joseph F. Grant
Title:Dean of Admissions

State University of New York College of Agriculture and Tech. at Morrisville
Morrisville, New York 13408
(315) 684-6046
LD Contact: Kathy Sellers

State University of New York College of Agriculture and Tech. at Cobleskill
Cobleskill, New York 12043
95180 234-5525
LD Contact: John Ganio

State University of New York College at Alfred
Alfred, New York 14802
(6070 587-4215
LD Contact: Nadene Sharlow

State University of New York College at Brockport
101 Rakov Center
Brockport, New York 14420
(716) 395-27512
LD Contact: Karen Phelps

State University of New York College at Buffalo
1300 Elmwood Avenue
Buffalo, New York 14222
(716) 878-4017
LD Contact: Maryann Savino

State University of New York College at Potsdam
Pierrepoint Avenue
Potsdam, New York 13676-2294
(800) 458-1142
Admissions Contact:Mary Lou Retelle
Title:Director of Enrollment Management

State Univer. NY College of Agriculture
Cobleskill, New York 12043
(518) 234-5525
Admissions Contact:John Devney
Title:Director of Admissions
LD Contact: Wayne Morris
Title:Director of Counseling
Telephone: (518) 234-5211

State University of New York College of Technology
Alfred, New York 14802-1196
(607) 587-4215
Admissions Contact:Debroah J. Goodrich
Title:Director of Admissions
LD Contact: Kathryn Fosegan
Title:Coordinator, Project 5
Telephone: (607) 587-4122

State University of New York College at New Paltz
75 South Meanheim
New Paltz, New York 12561-2499
(914) 257-3200
Admissions Contact:Robert J. Seaman
Title:Dean of Admissions

State University of New York Institute of Technology
P.O. Box 3050
Utica, New York 13504-3050
(315) 797-7208
Admissions Contact:Roger Sullivan
Title:Director of Admissions

Suffolk County Community College
533 College Road
Selden, New York 11784
(516) 451-4033
Admissions Contact:Douglas Steele
Title:Director of Admissions

Suffolk County Community College: Eastern Campus
Speonk-Riverhead Road
Riverhead, New York 11901
(516) 369-2600
Admissions Contact:Charles Bartolotta
Title:Assistant Dir. of Admis./ Financial Aid
LD Contact: Judith Koodin
Title:Counselor/Co. for Disabled Students Ser.
Telephone: (516) 548-2525

Suffolk county Community College: Western Campus
Crooked Hill Road
Brentwood, New York 11717
(516) 434-6719
Admissions Contact:Douglas Steele
Title:Director of Admissions

Tobe-Coburn School for Fashion
8 East 40th Street
New York, New York 10016
(800) 451-5678
Admissions Contact:Patricia Nieme
Title:Director of Admissions

University of Rochester
Meliora Hall
Rochester, New York 14627-0251
(716) 275-3221
Admissions Contact:Wayne A. Locust
Title:Director of Admissions

Villa Maria College of Buffalo
240 Pine Ridge Road
Buffalo, New York 14225
(716) 896-0704
LD Contact: Bonnie Clark

Wagner College
631 Howard Avenue
Staten Island, New York 10301-4495
(800) 221-1010
Admissions Contact:Dr. Susan Robinson
Title:Dean of Admissions
LD Contact: Ruth Anna Perri
Title:Director, Academic Advisement Center
Telephone: (718) 390-3340

Asheville Buncombe Technical Com. College
340 Victoria Road
Asheville, North Carolina 28801
(704) 254-1921
Admissions Contact:Connie S. Buckner
Title:Director of Admissions

Beaufort County Community College
P.O. Box 1069
Washington, North Carolina 27889
(919) 946-6194
Admissions Contact:Gary R. Burbage
Title:Director of Admissions

Brunswick Community College
P.O. Box 30
Supply, North Carolina 28462
(919) 754-6900
Admissions Contact:H. Elizabeth McLean
Title:Dean of Student Services

Carteret Community College
3505 Arendell Street
Morehead City, North Carolina 28557-2989
(919) 247-4142
Admissions Contact:Don Thompson
Title:Director of Student Services

Chowan College
P.O. Box 1848
Murfreesboro, North Carolina 27855
(919) 398-4101-(800) 488-4101
Title:Director of Admissions
LD Contact: Bobbie Wooten

Duke University
2138 Campus Drive
Durham, North Carolina 27706
(919) 684-3214
Admissions Contact:Harold M. Wingood
Title:Director of Undergraduate Admissions

Durham Technical Community College
1637 Lawson Street
Durham, North Carolina 27703
(919) 598-9224
Admissions Contact:Dr. Ellen Austin
Title:Coordinator of Admissions and Financial Aid

Forsyth Technical Community College
2100 Silas Creek Parkway
Winston-Salem, North Carolina 27103
(919) 723-0371
Admissions Contact:George McLendon
Title:Director of Admissions/Career Guidance
LD Contact: Laura Wyatt
Title:Chairperson, Pre-Technical Program
Telephone: (919) 761-2399

Gaston College
201 Highway 321 South
Dallas, North Carolina 28034-1499
(704) 922-6200
Admissions Contact:Jackie Sumner
Title:Associate Dean ofEnrollment

Guilford College
5800 West Freindly Avenue
Greensboro, North Carolina 27410
(800) 992-7759
Admissions Contact:Larry M. West
Title:Director of Admissions

Hayward Community College
Freelander Drive
Clude, North Carolina 28721
(704) 627-4500
Admissions Contact:Carol Smith
Title:Director of Enrollment Management

Lenoir-Rhyne College
Hickory, North Carolina 28603
(704) 328-7300
Admissions Contact:Richard P. Thompson
Title:Director of Admissions
LD Contact: Dr. Donna Dewiggins
Title:Education Coordinator

Mayland Community College
P.O. Box 547
Spruce Pine, North Carolina 28777
(704) 765-7351
Admissions Contact:Dr. Loretta Church
Title:Dean of Academic Services
LD Contact: Nancy H. Goodwin
Title:Director of Special Services
Telephone: (704) 765-7351

Nash Community College
P.O. Box 7488
Rocky Mount, North Carolina 27804
(919) 443-4011
Admissions Contact:Mary R. Blount
Title:Admissions Officer

No. Carolina Agricultural and Technical State University
1601 East Market Street
Greensboro, North Carolina 27411
(919) 334-7946
Admissions Contact:John Smith
Title:Director of Admissions

North Carolina Wesleyan College
Wesleyan College Station
Rocky Mount, North Carolina 27804
(919) 977-7171

Piedmont Community College
1715 College Drive
Roxboro, North Carolina 27573
(919) 599-1181
Admissions Contact:Lizzie Hooker
Title:Admissions Officer

Pitt Community College
P.O. Drawer 7007
Greenville, North Carolina 27835-7007
(919) 355-4245
Admissions Contact:Kathy O kinlaw
Title:Registrar

Robeson Community College
P.O. Box 1420
Lumberton, North Carolina 28359
(919) 738-7101
Admissions Contact:Judith Revels
Title:Director of Admissions

Sampson Community College
P.O. Box 318
Clinton, North Carolina 28328
(919) 592-8084
Admissions Contact:William R. Jordan
Title:Director of Admissions

Sandhills Community College
2200 Airport Road
Pinehurst, North Carolina 28374
(919) 692-6185
Admissions Contact:Carol Ewign
Title:Director of Admissions

Southwestern Community College
275 Webster Road
Sylvia, North Carolina 28779
(704) 586-4091
Admissions Contact:Gary Corbin
Title:Director of Admissions and Recruitment
LD Contact: Drucilla P. Shelton
Title:Director, Student Support Services
Telephone: (704) 586-4091

St. Mary's College
900 Hillsborough Street
Raleigh, North Carolina 27603
(919) 839-4100

University of No. Carolina at Chapel Hill
05 Steele Building Campus Box 5100
Chapel Hill, North Carolina 27599-5100
(919) 966-3621
LD Contact: Laura Thomas

University of No. Carolina at Charlotte
University City Boulevard
Charlotte, North Carolina 28223
(704) 547-2213
LD Contact: Radhika Unnithan

Wake Technical Community College
9101 Fayetteville Road
Raleigh, North Carolina 27603
(919) 772-7500
Admissions Contact:Robert L. Brown
Title:Vice President of Student Services
LD Contact: Sheila L. Hite
Title:Dir. of Access Ser. for Disabled Students
Telephone: (919) 772-0551

Wayne Community College
Caller Box 8002
Goldsboro, North Carolina 27533-8002
(919) 735-5151
Admissions Contact:Susan M. Sasser
Title:Director of Admissions/Records

Western Carolina University
Cullowhee, North Carolina 28723
(704) 227-7317
LD Contact: Carol Mellen

Western Piedmont Community College
1001 Burkemont Avenue
Morganton, North Carolina 28655
(704) 438-6051
Admissions Contact:Jim A. Reed
Title:Director of Admissions

Wilson Technical Community College
P.O. Box 4305
Wilson, North Carolina 27893
(919) 291-1195
Admissions Contact:R. Williams Treadway
Title:Counselor

Bismarck State College
1500 Edwards Avenue
Bismarck, North Dakota 58501
(701) 224-5426
LD Contact: Jennifer Gladden

Little Hoop Community College
P.O. Box 269
Fort Totten, North Dakota 58335
(701) 766-4415
Admissions Contact:Dean Dauphinais
Title:Director of Admissions/Registrar

Standing Rock College
HC1 Box 4
Fort Yates, North Dakota 58538
(701) 854-3861
LD Contact: Janice Shields

University of North Dakota
P.O. Box 8070
Grand Forks, North Dakota 58022-8070
(701) 777-3821
Admissions Contact:Monty Nielsen
Title:Director of Admissions and Records

University of North Dakota: Williston
1426 University Avenue
Williston, North Dakota 58801-1326
(701) 774-4210
Admissions Contact:Phil Rabon
Title:Co. of Enrollment Services/Activities

Ashland University
401 College Avenue
Ashland, Ohio 44805-9981
(419) 289-5052
Admissions Contact:Carl Gerbasi
Title:Exec. Dir. of Admissions/Financial Aid

Baldwin-Wallace College
275 Eastland Road
Berea, Ohio 44107-2088
(216) 826-2222
Admissions Contact:Juliann K. Baker
Title:Director of Undergraduate Admissions

Chatfield College
20918 State Route 251
St. Martin, Ohio 45118-9705
(513) 875-3344
Admissions Contact:Rebecca Cluxton
Title:Dir. of Student Records/Financial Aid

Cincinnati College of Mortuary Science
3860 Pacific Avenue
Cincinnati, Ohio 45207-1033
(513) 745-3632
LD Contact: Patsy Leon
Title:Registrar
Telephone: (513) 745-3631

Cincinnati Technical College
3520 Central Parkway
Cincinnati, Ohio 45223
(513) 861-7700
Admissions Contact:John P. Wagner
Title:Dean of Admissions
LD Contact: David W. Cover
Title:Counselor/Special Needs
Telephone: (513) 569-1613

College of Wooster
Galpin Hall
Wooster, Ohio 44691-2363
(800) 877-9905
Admissions Contact:Hayden Schilling
Title:Dean ofAdmissions

Denison University
P.O. Box H
Granville, Ohio 43023
(614) 587-6276-(800) 336-4766
Title:Director of Admissions
LD Contact: Theron Snell

Heidelberg College
Tiffin, Ohio 44883
(419) 448-2330
Admissions Contact:Debralee Divers
Title:Director of Admissions

John Carroll University
20700 North Park Boulevard
University Heights, Ohio 44118-4581
(216) 397-4294
Admissions Contact:Laryn R/ Beacj
Title:Director of Admissions

Lakeland Community College
7700 Clocktower Drive
Mentor, Ohio 44060-7594
(216) 953-7100
Admissions Contact:William Kraus
Title:Director for Admissions/Registrar

Lorain County Community College
1005 North Abbe Road
Elyria, Ohio 44035-1697
(216) 365-4191
Admissions Contact:Dr. John Thrash, Jr.
Title:Director of Student Development
LD Contact: Ruth Porter
Title:Coordinator
Telephone: (216) 365-4191 Ext. 4058

Marion Technical College
1467 Mount Vernon Avenue
Marion, Ohio 43302-5694
(614) 389-4636
Admissions Contact:Joel Liles
Title:Director of Admissions/Career Services

Miami University
20 Campus Avenue Building
Oxford, Ohio 45056
(513) 529-2531
LD Contact: Lois Phillips

Miami University: Hamilton Campus
1601 Peck Boulevard
Hamilton, Ohio 45011
(513) 863-8833
Admissions Contact:T. Michael Smithson
Title:Director of Admissions

Ohio State Univer: Mansfield Campus
1680 University Drive
Mansifeld, Ohio 44906
(419) 755-4226
Admissions Contact:Henry Thomas
Title:Assistant Director

Ohio State University: Lima Campus
4240 Campus Drive
Lima, Ohio 45804-3596
(419) 221-1641
Admissions Contact:Melissa Green
Title:Assist ant Director
LD Contact: Jeanette Carter
Title:Learning disabilities Specialist
Telephone: (419) 221-1641

Ohio Wesleyan University
Sandusky Street
Delaware, Ohio 43015
(800) 922-8953
Admissions Contact:Donald C. Bishop
Title:Dean for Enrollment Management
LD Contact: Co. of Academic Advising
Telephone: (614) 368-3275

Shawnee State University
940 Second Street
Portsmouth, Ohio 45662
(614) 354-3205
Admissions Contact:Rosemary Poston
Title:Director of Admissions
LD Contact: Patty Gilmore
Title:Coordinator of Disability Services

Tiffin University
155 Miami Street
Tiffin, Ohio 44883
(419) 447-6443
Admissions Contact:Kristine Boyle
Title:Director of Admissions

University of Akron
381 Buchtel Common
Akron, Ohio 44325-2001
(216) 972-7100
Admissions Contact:Martha Boothe
Title:Associate Director of Admissions

University of Cincinnati
69 Beecher Hall
Cincinnati, Ohio 45221
(513) 556-1100
Title:Director of Admissions
LD Contact: Larry Goodall

University of Cincinnati:Clermont
25 College Drive
Batavia, Ohio 45103
(513) 732-5200
Admissions Contact:Kate Greenwald
Title:Admissions Officer

University of Findlay
1000 North Main Street
Findlay, Ohio 45840-3695
(800) 548-0932
Admissions Contact:Dr. Mary Ellen Klein
Title:Director of Admissions
LD Contact: Donna M. Smith
Title:Director, Supporting Skills System
Telephone: (419) 424-4822

University of Rio Grande
Rio Grande, Ohio 45674
(614) 245-5353
Admissions Contact:Mark Abell
Title:Executive Director of Admission

Urbana University
579 Collage Way
Urbana, Ohio 43978-2091
(513) 652-1301
Admissions Contact:Thomas A. Gallagher
Title:VP for Enrollment Management
LD Contact: Sheri Haines
Title:Director, Student Support Services
Telephone: (513) 652-1301

Virginia Marti College of Fashion and Art
11724 Detroit Avenue
Lakewood, Ohio 44107
(216) 221-8584
Admissions Contact:June James
Title:Director of Admissions

Wright State University
133 Student Service Lane
Dayton, Ohio 45435
(513) 873-2211
LD Contact: Ron Lofton

Xavier University
3800 Victory Parkway
Cincinnati, Ohio 45207-5311
(513) 745-3301
Admissions Contact:Jay Leienbecker
Title:Director of Admissions
LD Contact: Dr. Sally W. Pruden
Title:Coordinator
Telephone: (513) 745-3655

Youngstown State University
410 Wick Avenue
Youngstown, Ohio 44555-0001
(216) 742-3150
Admissions Contact:Dr. Harold Yiannaki
Title:Director of Enrollment Services

Bartlesville Wesleyan College
2201 Silver Lake Road
Bartlesville, Oklahoma 74006
(918) 333-6151
Admissions Contact:Peter Wood
Title:Enrollment Administrator
LD Contact: Kent Wade
Title:Placement/Testing Director

Cameron University
2800 West Gore Blvd.
Lawton, Oklahoma 73505
(405) 581-2230
LD Contact: Susan Aplin

Northeastern State University
Tahlequah, Oklahoma 74464
(918) 456-5511
Admissions Contact:Noel T. Smith
Title:Director of Admissions and Registrar

Oklahoma City University
2501 North Blackwelder
Oklahoma City, Oklahoma 73106
(800) 633-7242
Admissions Contact:Gary Whitcomb
Title:Director of Undergraduate Admissions

Oral Roberts University
7777 South Lewis Avenue
Tulsa, Oklahoma 74171
(918) 495-6518
Admissions Contact:Arthur E. Matzkvech
Title:Director of Admissions

Chemeketa Community College
P.O. Box 14007
Salem, Oregon 97309-7070
(503) 399-5006
Admissions Contact:Alan C. Scott
Title:Admissions Specialist

Columbia Christian College
9101 E. Burnside Street
Portland, Oregon 97216-1515
(503) 257-1202

George Fox College
414 North Meridian
Newberg, Oregon 97132
(503) 538-8383
LD Contact: Bonnie Jerke

Portland State University
P.O. Box 751
Portland, Oregon 97207-0751
(503) 725-3511
Admissions Contact:Jesse R. Welch
Title:Director of Admissions

Reed College
3202 S.E. Woodstock Blvd.
Portland, Oregon 97202-8199
(503) 777-7511-(800) 547-4750

Rogue Community College
3345 Redwood Highway
Grants Pass, Oregon 97527
(503) 479-5541
Admissions Contact:Valerie Moore
Title:Director Enrollment
LD Contact: Bonnie Long
Title:Coordinator
Name of Program: Vocational Special Services

Treasure Valley Community College
650 College Boulevard
Ontario, Oregon 97914
(503) 889-6493
Admissions Contact:Ron Kulm
Title:Director of Admissions
LD Contact: Mr. Cleo C. Dyer
Title:Dept. Chair, Developmental Education
Telephone: (503) 889-6493

University of Oregon: Robert Donal Clark Honors College
Eugene, Oregon 97403-1293
(503) 346-5414

Warner Pacific College
2219 Southeast 68th Street
Portland, Oregon 97215
(503) 775-4366
Admissions Contact:Kenneth S.T. Thomas
Title:Director of Admissions

Willamette University
900 State Street
Salem, Oregon 97301-3922
(503) 370-6303
Admissions Contact:James M. Summer
Title:Dean of Admissions

Allegheny College
Meadville, Pennsylvania 16335
(814) 332-4351
Admissions Contact:Gayle W. Pollock
Title:Director of Admissions

Bucks County Community College
Swamp Road
Newtown, Pennsylvania 18940
(215) 968-8100
Admissions Contact:Elizabeth M Kulick
Title:Dir. of Admissions, Records/Registration

Cedar Crest College
Allentown, Pennsylvania 18104
(215) 437-4471

Clarion University of Pennsylvania
Carlson Library Building
Clarion, Pennsylvania 16214
(814) 226-2306
Title:Director of Admissions
LD Contact: Gregory Ceary

Community College of Beaver County
One College Drive
Monaca, Pennsylvania 15061
(412) 775-8561
Admissions Contact:Scott Ensworth
Title:Director of Admissions

Dickinson College
P.O. Box 1773
Carlisle, Pennsylvania 17013-2896
(717) 245-1231
Admissions Contact:J. Larry Mench
Title:Dean of Admisions and Enrollment

Drexel University
32nd and Chestnut Streets
Philadelphia, Pennsylvania 19104
(215) 895-2400
LD Contact: Ina Ellen

Gannon University
University Square
Erie, Pennsylvania 16541-0001
(800) GANNON U
Admissions Contact:Joyce Scheid-Gilman
Title:Dir. of Freshmen/Transfer Admissions

Immaculata College
Route 353 and King Road
Immaculata, Pennsylvania 19345
(215) 647-4400
Admissions Contact:Sr. Claudine M. Hagerty
Title:Director of Admissions
LD Contact: Sr. Kathleen McKee
Title:Vice President for Academic Affairs

Indiana University of Pennsylvania
216 Pratt Hall
Indiana, Pennsylvania 15705-1088
(412) 357-2230
Admissions Contact:Nancy Newkerk
Title:Dean of Admissions
LD Contact: Catherine Dugan
Title:Director, Advising and Testing Center
Telephone: (412) 357-4067

Lafayette College
118 Markle Hall
Easton, Pennsylvania 18042-1770
(215) 250-5100
Admissions Contact:Carol A. Rowlands
Title:Director of Admissions

Lock Haven University
G5 Smith Hall
Lock Haven, Pennsylvania 17745
(717) 893-2027-(800) 233-8978
LD Contact: Nathan Hosley
Title:Director
Name of Program: Student Support Services

Lycoming College
Washington Blvd.
Williamsport, Pennsylvania 17701
(717) 321-4026-(800) 345-3920

Manor Junior College
Fox Chase & Forrest Aves.
Jenkintown, Pennsylvania 19046
(215) 885-2360

Marywood College
2300 Adams Avenue
Scranton, Pennsylvania 18509-9989
(717) 348-6234
Admissions Contact:Gary Sherman
Title:Director ofAdmissions

Millersville University of Pennsylvania
P.O. Box 1062
Millersville, Pennsylvania 17551-0302
(717) 872-3371
Admissions Contact:Darrell C. Davis
Title:Director of Admissions

Muhlenberg College
2400 Chew Street
Allentown, Pennsylvania 18104
(215) 821-3200
Admissions Contact:Chris Hooker-Haring
Title:Director of Admissions

Northampton County Area Community College
3835 Green Pond Road
Bethlehem, Pennsylvania 18017
(215) 861-5500
Admissions Contact:Mardi Closson
Title:Director of Admissions
LD Contact: Cheryl A. Ashcroft
Title:Director, Services for Disabled Students
Telephone: (215) 861-5346

Pennsylvania Institute of Technology
800 Manchester Avenue
Media, Pennsylvania 19063-4098
(215) 565-7900

Pittsburgh Technical Institute
635 Smithfield Street
Pittsburgh, Pennsylvania 15222
(412) 471-1011
Admissions Contact:Cathi Bost
Title:Vice President for Admissions

Shippensburg Univer. of Pennsylvania
Shippensburg, Pennsylvania 17257
(717) 532-1231
Admissions Contact:Doyle Bickers
Title:Dean of Admissions

Slippery Rock Univer.of Pennsylvania

Slippery Rock, Pennsylvania 16057
(412) 738-2015
Admissions Contact:David Collins
Title:Director of Admissions

Thomas Jefferson University: College of Allied Health
1020 Locust Street
Philadelphia, Pennsylvania 19107
(800) 247-6933
Admissions Contact:Thomas J. Coyne
Title:Dir. of Admissions and Enrollment Man.

University of Pennsylvania
1133 Blockley Hall 418 Service Drive
Philadelphia, Pennsylvania 19104-6201
(215) 898-7507
Title:Director of Admissions
LD Contact: Alice Nagle
Name of Program: Programs for People w\ith Disabilities

University of the Arts
Broad and Pine Streets
Philadelphia, Pennsylvania 19102
(215) 875-4808
Admissions Contact:Kenneth Stevenson
Title:Associate Provost for Enrollment Man.
LD Contact: Stephanie Bell
Title:Learning Specialist
Telephone: (215) 875-2254

West Chester Univer.of Pennsylvania
Messikomer Hall
West Chester, Pennsylvania 19383
(215) 436-3411
Admissions Contact:Marsha Haug
Title:Director of Admissions

Caribbean University College
P.O. Box 493
Bayamon, Puerto Rico 00960-0493
(809) 780-0070

University of Puerto Rico: Arecibo
P.O. Box 4010
Aercibo, Puerto Rico 00613
(809) 878-2830
Admissions Contact:Marharita Salenz
Title:Admissions Officer

University of the Sacred Heart
P.O. Box 12383
Santurce, Puerto Rico 00914
(809) 728-1602
Admissions Contact:Melvin Rosario
Title:Director of Admissions

New England Institute of Technology
2500 Post Road
Warwick, Rhode Island 02886
(800) 736-7744
Admissions Contact:Nick Azarone
Title:Director of Admissions
LD Contact: Jeanne Sjovall
Title:Director, Academic Skills Center
Telephone: (401) 738-5122

Providence College
River Avenue and Eaton Street
Providence, Rhode Island 02918-001
(401) 865-2535
Admissions Contact:Michael Backes
Title:Dean of Admissions

Rhode Island College
Providence, Rhode Island 02908
(401) 456-8234
Title:Director of Admissions
LD Contact: Sara Weiss

University of Rhode Island
Green Hall
Kingston, Rhode Island 02881-0806
(401) 792-9800
Admissions Contact:David G. Taggart
Title:Dean of Admissions and Financial Aid

Aiken Technical College
P.O. Drawer 696
Aiken, South Carolina 29802-0696
(803) 593-9231
LD Contact: Richard M. Wledon
Title:Director of Counseling Services
Telephone: (805) 593-9231

Clemson University
105 Sikes Hall
Clemson, South Carolina 29634-5124
(803) 656-2287
Admissions Contact:Michael R. Heintze
Title:Director of Admissions

College of Charleston
66 George Street
Charleston, South Carolina 29424
(803) 792-5670
LD Contact: Mary Burkehart

Columbia Jr. College of Business
3810 Main Street
Columbia, South Carolina 29203
(803) 799-9082

Converse College
580 East Main Street
Spartanburg, South Carolina 29302-0006
(803) 596-9040
Admissions Contact:Dr. Martha E. Rogers
Title:Dean of Admissions

Lander College
Greenwood , South Carolina 29646
(803) 229-8307-(800) 768-3600
Title:Director of Admissions
LD Contact: Betty Horne

North Greenville College
Tigerville, South Carolina 29688
(803) 895-1410
LD Contact: Dr. Chuch Burgess

The Citadel
Citadel Station
Charleston, South Carolina 29409
(803) 792-5230
Admissions Contact:Maj. Wallace West
Title:Director of Admissions
LD Contact: Dr. Wemme E. Walls
Title:Coordinator for Support Services for
Learning Disabled Students
Telephone: (803) 792-5097

Trident Technical College
P.O. Box 10367
Charleston, South Carolina 29411
(803) 572-6123
Admissions Contact:Cheryl A. Alston
Title:Director of Admissions
LD Contact: Vincent C. Ashby, Jr.
Title:Director
Telephone: (803) 572-6102

University of So. Carolina
1625 College Street
Columbia, South Carolina 29208
(803) 777-7700
Admissions Contact:Rosvelt Martain
Title:Assistant Dean
LD Contact: Debbie Haynes
Title:Dir. Academic Support Serv.
Name of Program: Learning Disability Pro.
Telephone: (803) 777-6142/0742

University of South Carolina at Aiken
171 University Parkway
Aiken, South Carolina 29801
(803) 641-3366
LD Contact: Randy Duckett

Dakota State University
Heston Hall
Madison, South Dakota 57042
(605) 256-5139
Admissions Contact:Mark Weiss
Title:Director of Admissions

Dakota Wesleyan University
1200 West University Boulevard
Mitchell, South Dakota 57301-4398
(800) 333-8506
Admissions Contact:Melinda Larson
Title:Director of Admissions

Mitchell Vocational Technical Institute
821 North Capital
Mitchell, South Dakota 57301
(800) 952-0042
Admissions Contact:Steve Kracht
Title:Director of Student Services

Mount Marty College
1105 West Eighth Street
Yankton, South Dakota 57078
(800) 658-4552
Admissions Contact:Paula Tacke
Title:Director of Admissions

National College
321 Kansas City Street
Rapid City, South Dakota 57701
(605) 394-4820-(800) 843-8892
LD Contact: Cynthia Howell

University of South Dakota
414 East Clark
Vermillion, South Dakota 57069-2390
(605) 677-5434
Admissions Contact:David Lorenz
Title:Director of Admissions

Western Dakota Vocational Techival Institute
1600 Sedivy Lane
Rapid City, South Dakota 57701
(605) 394-4034
Admissions Contact:Nancy Richter
Title:Assistant Director of Student Services

Chattanooga State Tech. Community Collage
4501 Amnicola Highway
Chattanooga, Tennessee 37406
(615) 697-4401
Admissions Contact:Ellis Forrester
Title:Director of Admissions

Lambuth College
702 Lambuth Blvd.
Jackson, Tennessee 38301
(901) 425-3223
Admissions Contact:Nancy Tipton
Title:Director of Admissions
LD Contact: Nancy Tipton

Memphis State University
215 Scates Hall
Memphis, Tennessee 38152
(901) 678-2101
Admissions Contact:David R. Wallace
Title:Associate Dean of Admissions
LD Contact: Dr. Donna Sprager

Nashville State Technical Institute
120 White Bridge Road
Nashville, Tennessee 37209
(615) 353-3215
Admissions Contact:Dr. Dorothy Huston
Title:Assistant Dean of Admissions

Tusculum College
Tusculum Station
Greeneville, Tennessee 37743
(800) 251-0256
Admissions Contact:Mark Stokes
Title:Dean of Enrollment Management
LD Contact: Annette Harmon
Title:Director
Telephone: (615) 636-7300

University of Tennessee, Knoxville
414 Student Services
Knoxville, Tennessee 37996
(615) 974-2184
LD Contact: Ms. Jan Scottby

Abilene Christian University
ACU Station Box 6000
Abilene, Texas 79699
(800) 888-0228
Admissions Contact:Clint Howeth
Title:Director of Admissions

Alvin Community College
3110 Mustang Road
Alvin, Texas 77511
(713) 388-4636
Admissions Contact:David N. Mclane
Title:Registrar
LD Contact: Eileen Cross
Title:LEAP Coordinator
Telephone: (713) 388-4636

Angelina College
P.O. Box 1768
Lufkin, Texas 75901
(409) 639-1301
LD Contact: Karen Foley

Austin Community College
Middle Fiskville Road
Austin, Texas 78714
(512) 483-7000
Admissions Contact:Clifton Van Dyke
Title:Director of Admissions

Brookhaven College
3939 Valley View Lane
Farmers Branch, Texas 75244
(214) 620-4700
Admissions Contact:Barbara Burke
Title:Director of Admissions and Registrar
LD Contact: Ms. Jweri Evans
Title:Director, Special Services
Telephone: (214) 620-4844

Central Texas College
Highway 190 West
Kiilleen, Texas 76541
(800) 792-3348
Admissions Contact:Bill Alexander
Title:Dean of Admissions and Counseling
LD Contact: Jose R. Aponte
Title:Counselor
Telephone: (817) 526-1339

Cisco Junior College
Route 3, Box 3
Cisco, Texas 76437
(817) 442-2567
LD Contact: Debra Robinson

College of the Mainland
1200 Amburn Road
Texas City, Texas 77591
(409) 938-1211
LD Contact: Maryann Urick

Collin County Community College Dist.
2200 West University
McKinney, Texas 75070-2906
(214) 548-6742
Admissions Contact:Toni P. Allen
Title:Dean of Enrollment Management
LD Contact: Audrey Newsome
Title:Director
Telephone: (214) 881-5898

Del Mar College
Baldwin and Syers Streets
Corpus Christi, Texas 78404-3897
(512) 886-1398
Admissions Contact:Joseph Estrada
Title:Registrar and Director of Admissions

East Texas Baptist University
1209 North Grove
Marshall, Texas 75670
(214) 935-7963

Eastfield College
3737 Motley Drive
Mesquite, Texas 75150
(214) 324-7100
LD Contact: Reva Rattan

El Centro College
Main & Lamar
Dallas, Texas 75202
(214) 746-2411
Admissions Contact:Bob Bennett
Title:Director
LD Contact: Jim Handy
Title:Director of Special Services
Name of Program: Special Services
Telephone: (214) 746-2411

Galveston College
4015 Avenue Q
Galveston, Texas 77550
(409) 763-6551
Admissions Contact:Gene Moore
Title:Dean of Admissions and Student Records
LD Contact: Dr. Gaynelle Hayes
Title:VP and Dean of Student Development

Hill College
P.O. Box 619
Hillsboro, Texas 76645
(817) 582-2555

Houston Community College
P.O. Box 7849
Houston, Texas 77270
(713) 868-0763
Admissions Contact:Mary Lemburg
Title:Registrar

Lamar University
P.O. Box 10043
Beaumont, Texas 77710
(409) 880-8345

Laredo Junior College
W. End Washinton Street
Laredo, Texas 78040
(512) 722-0521

Southwest Texas State University
601 University Drive
San Marcos, Texas 78666
(512) 245-2364
Title:Director of Admissions
LD Contact: Tom Hutson

St. Edward's University
3001 South Congress
Austin, Texas 78704
(512) 448-8500

St. Mary's University
One Camino Santa Maria
San Antonio, Texas 78284
(512) 436-3126
Admissions Contact:Richard Castillo
Title:Director of Admissions

Texas A & M University
College Station, Texas 77843-1257
(409) 845-1060
Admissions Contact:GALE WOOD
Title:Associate Director of Admissions
LD Contact: Gail Walters

Texas Woman's University
P.O. Box 22909 TWU Station
Denton, Texas 76204
(817) 898-3000
Title:Tricia Hurter

University of Texas at El Paso
500 West University Avenue
El Paso, Texas 79968
()915) 747-5576
LD Contact: Lois Bates

University of Texas: Pan American
1201 West University Drive
Edinburg, Texas 78539
(512) 381-2206
LD Contact: Art Ramos

West Texas State University
PO WT Box 907
Canyon, Texas 79016
(806) 656-2020
LD Contact: Kay Kropss

Brigham Young University
380 SWKT
Provo, Utah 84602
(801) 378-2507
LD Contact: Rodney Hansen

Westminster College of Salt Lake City
1840 South 1300 East
Salt Lake City, Utah 84105
(801) 488-4200
Admissions Contact:Brad Ericson
Title:Assoc. Dir. Admissions
LD Contact: Bill Simmons
Title:Director
Name of Program: Academic Advising
Telephone: (801) 488-4135

St. Michael's College
Winooski Park
Colchester, Vermont 05439
(802) 654-3000

Emory and Henry College
Emory, Virginia 24327
(703) 944-3121

Ferrum College
P.O. Box 2216
Ferrum, Virginia 24088
(703) 365-4290
LD Contact: Brenda Newcombs

Mary Baldwin College
Staunton, Virginia 24401
(703) 887-7019-(800) 826-0154
Admissions Contact:Elaine Liles
LD Contact: Beverly Askegaard
Title:Director

Randolph-Macon College
Ashland, Virginia 23005
(804) 752-7305

Randolph-Macon Women's College
2500 Rivermont Avenue
Lynchburg, Virginia 24503
(804) 846-7392
LD Contact: Paula Wallace

Clark College
1800 E. McLoughlin Blvd.
Vancouver, Washington 98663
(206) 699-0392
Title:Director of Admissions
LD Contact: Duane Henry

Eastern Washington University
117 Showalter Hall, MS-148
Cheney, Washington 90004
(509) 359-2397
LD Contact: Karen Raver

Highline Community College
P.O. Box 98000
Des Moines, Washington 98198-9800
(206) 878-3710

University of Washington
1400 Northeast Campus Parkway
Seattle, Washington 98195
(206) 543-9686
LD Contact: Judy Lonergan

Western Washington University
Old Main 200
Bellingham, Washington 98225
(206) 676-3440
LD Contact: Jane Bello-Brunson

Bethany College
Bethany, West Virginia 26032
(304) 829-7611-(800) 922-7611
LD Contact: Christine Sampson

Salem College
Main Street
Salem, West Virginia 26426
(304) 782-5336

University of Charleston
2300 Mac Corkle Avenue, S.E.
Charleston, West Virginia 25304
(304) 357-4748
Admissions Contact:Gloria E. Smith
Title:Director of Admissions

Carthage College
2001 Alford Drive
Kenosha, Wisconsin 53141
(414) 551-6000-(800) 351-4058
LD Contact: Laura Bush

Mid-State Technical College
500 32nd Street, North
Wisconsin Rapids, Wisconsin 54494
(715) 422-5500
LD Contact: Dr. William Lindroth

Northcentral Technical College
1000 Campus Drive
Wausau, Wisconsin 54401
(715) 675-3331
LD Contact: Grace Manthei

University of Wisconsin: Eau Claire
112 Schofield Hall
Eau Claire, Wisconsin 54702
(715) 836-5415
LD Contact: Tom Bouchard

University of Wisconsin: Whitewater
2019 Roseman Hall
Whitewater, Wisconsin 53190
(414) 472-1440
Admissions Contact:I.A. MADSEN
Title:Director of Admissions
LD Contact: Ken Anclam
Title:Director

	Application	Class Rank	Course Selection	Extra Activities	G.P.A.	Interview	Open Admissions	Personal Statement	Psychoeducational	Recommendations	SAT/ACT	School Transcript
Alabama												
Auburn University at Montgomery	9	10	7	5	8	2		4	1	6	11	3
Chattahoochee Valley Community College	2	6	1	1	6	1	1	1		1	1	1
Jacksonville State University							1					
Northeast Alabama State Junior College												
Troy State University at Dothan	3	6	4	9	1	8		11	7	10	2	5
UAB - Horizons Program			1			1		1	1			
University of Alabama					1						2	
University of Alabama at Birmingham					1						1	
Walker State Technical College	1				3						2	4
Alaska												
Sheldon Jackson College												
University of Alaska Anchorage	1				1		1			2		2
University of Alaska Fairbanks	1		2		2							
Arizona												
Arizona State University		1			1						1	
Glendale Community College												
Northern Arizona University	2	1	2		1				3		1	
Phoenix College							1					
Pima Community College												
University of Arizona	11	10	7	9	5	6		4	1	3	8	2
Arkansas												
Arkansas State University	1						1				2	3
Harding University	1	5	4	6	2					3	1	1
Henderson State University												
Southern Arkansas University												
University of Arkansas at Pine Bluff												
University of the Ozarks	4		7			2		6	1	3		5
California												
Antelope Valley College							1					
Bakersfield College	1											1
Biola University	10	7	8	9	1	5		3		4	2	6
Butte College							1					
Cabrillo College												
California State Polytechnic University					1						1	
California State University: Bakersfield	1		1		1						1	1
California State University: Chico					1	2			1	2	1	1
California State University: Dominguez Hills	2	5	11	10	1	7		8	9	6	3	4
California State University: Fullerton		2			1						3	
California State University: Northridge					1						1	

CRITERIA FOR ADMISSIONS

	Application	Class Rank	Course Selection	Extra Activities	G.P.A.	Interview	Open Admissions	Personal Statement	Psychoeducational	Recommendations	SAT/ACT	School Transcript
California State University: Sacramento			1	2						2	1	1
California State University: San Bernardino	1			7	6	3				5	4	2
Canada College	2		2			1	1					3
Cerritos Community College						1	1		1			
Chabot College							1					
Chaffey College							1					
College of Alameda							1					
College of San Mateo	2	4	6	7	1	8		10	11	9	5	3
College of the Canyons												
College of the Sequoias												
College of the Siskiyous							1					
Columbia College							1					
Crafton Hills College							1					
Cuesta College							1					
Cypress College												
De Anza College												
East Los Angeles College							1					
El Camino College	1											2
Evergreen Valley College							1					
Feather River College	1	11	7	10	4	2		8	6	9	3	5
Foothill College							1					
Fresno City College							1					
Fullerton College										1		1
Golden Gate University												
Golden West College												
Hartnell College	1					1	1		1			
Humboldt State University	1	5	2	6	1	3		3		4	2	1
Imperial Valley College							1		1			2
Kings River Community College	1											2
Laney College									1			
Long Beach City College	4					1	1		2	3		
Los Angeles City College							1					
Los Angeles Harbor College												
Los Angeles Mission College	2	7	5	10	7	8		5	4	8	5	4
Los Angeles Valley College	5	9	8	11	7	1		10	2	4	6	3
Merced College												
Merritt College							1					
Modesto Junior College							1					
Monterey Peninsula College	3	10	7	5	9	1		4	2	6	11	8
Mount San Jacinto College							1					

CRITERIA FOR ADMISSIONS

College	Application	Class Rank	Course Selection	Extra Activities	G.P.A.	Interview	Open Admissions	Personal Statement	Psychoeducational	Recommendation	School Transcript	SAT/ACT
Porterville College							1			1		
Rancho Santiago College	5	10	6	9	7	1		4	2	8	11	3
Saddleback College							1					
San Diego City College							1					
San Diego Mesa College	1					2	1		1			2
San Diego State University							1					
San Francisco State University						1					1	
Santa Barbara City College							1		1			
Santa Monica College												
Santa Rosa Junior College							1					1
Sierra College	1											
Sonoma State University						1					1	1
Stanford University		5	2	6	2	10		6	9	8	4	1
Taft College							1					
University of California: Berkeley	4	12	2	2	1			2	3	12	1	1
University of California: Davis	4	5	10	7	2	8		1	3	9	1	6
University of California: Riverside	1				1						1	
University of California: San Diego												
University of California: Santa Barbara	3	6	5	8	1	11		4	9	10	2	7
University of California: Santa Cruz	1		1	2	1			1		2	1	1
University of Redlands			1		1	4				3	2	
Ventura College							1	1		1		
Victor Valley College								1				2
West Hills College							2	1		1	3	
West Valley College												
Colorado												
Arapahoe Community College							1					
Colorado Northwestern Community College							1					
Colorado State University	1	1	2	3	1	3		2	2	3	1	1
Community College of Aurora							1					
Community College of Denver							1					
Front Range Community College							1					
Northeastern Junior College							1					
Pikes Peak Community College												
Pueblo Community College	1			4			1	3	5			2
Red Rocks Community College	1	5	3	5	4	5	1	5	5	5	5	2
Regis College	12	7	10	5	1	9		6	8	2	3	4
University of Colorado at Boulder	1		1		1	X				1	1	1
University of Denver	5	9	8	10	2	4		7	1	5	6	3
Western State College of Colorado	2	5	2	4	1	2		3	2	2	1	1

	Application	Class Rank	Course Selection	Extra Activities	G.P.A.	Interview	Open Admissions	Personal Statement	Psychoeducational	Recommendations	SAT/ACT	School Transcript
Connecticut												
Briarwood College												
Eastern Connecticut State University		1	1	5	1	3		5		3	3	1
Hartford College for Women	8	3	3	9	1	4		5	7	6	2	1
Mattatuck Community College							1					
Mitchell College	6	10	3	9	5	7		8	2	11	1	4
Northwestern Connecticut Community College							1					
Norwalk Community College		11	2	7	5	3		8	1	6	11	4
Paier College of Art	2	8	11	10	3	2		2	9	2	1	1
South Central Community College	1	10	6	9	3	5		7	4	8	11	2
Thames Valley State Technical College	8	4	2	9	3	5	1	10	11	6	7	1
University of Connecticut		4	2	6	1					3	5	
University of New Haven												
Wesleyan University	3	1	1	2	2	4				2	2	1
Western Connecticut State University	1	3	6	7	5			8			4	2
Yale University		1	1	4	1	5		4		2	3	1
Delaware												
Goldey Beacom College	11	5	10	7	1	6		8	9	4	3	2
University of Delaware	6	3	2	5	1			6		6	4	1
District of Columbia												
American University		4		6	1	11		4	2	5	1	2
Catholic University of America												
Gallaudet University												
George Washington University	3	2	2	5	1			4		4	3	1
Trinity College	1	7	2	9	3	8		10	11	6	5	4
Florida												
Beacon College	3			7		2		5	1	4		6
Brevard Community College	9	10	2	11	8	6		3	1	7	4	5
Chipola Junior College							1					
Edison Community College							1					
Embry-Riddle Aeronautical University		2		4	1	11		5		4	3	1
Florida Agricultural and Mechanical University	1			1	1	1		1	1	1	1	1
Florida Atlantic University		1	2		1						2	1
Florida Community College at Jacksonville							1					
Florida State University												
Gulf Coast Community College												
Lake City Community College	1	5	4	5	5	3		5	5	5	3	2
Miami-Dade Community College							1		2			1
Okaloosa-Walton Junior College							1					
Polk Community College	1						1					2

	Application	Class Rank	Course Selection	Extra Activities	G.P.A.	Interview	Open Admissions	Personal Statement	Psychoeducational	Recommendations	School Transcript	SAT/ACT
Saint Johns River Community College							1					
Santa Fe Community College							1					
Seminole Community College							1			1	2	3
Tallahassee Community College												
University of Tampa	8	4	7	6	1			9	10	5	2	3
Georgia												
Brenau Women's College			6		2	3		1		4	5	
Brunswick College	1		5		2						3	4
Clayton State College								2		3	1	
DeKalb College	5				1						1	1
East Georgia College	1		1		1						1	1
Emory University												
Georgia College	1	3	2	4	1	6		7	8	5	1	1
Georgia Institute of Technology	4		2		1						3	5
Georgia Southern University	3		4								2	1
Georgia State University			3	5	1	8		6	4	7	2	
Mercer University	6	5	1	6	1	2		8	7	4	3	1
Reinhardt College	6	12	2	8	3	7			4	9	5	1
South Georgia College	1		2		1						1	1
Southern College of Technology			2								1	
University of Georgia								1			2	
Valdosta State College												
West Georgia College								1			1	1
Hawaii												
Brigham Young University-Hawaii	2	6	8	7	3	4		5				3
University of Hawaii: Kapiolani Community College	1						1			1		
University of Hawaii: Leeward Community College							1					
Idaho												
Albertson College	1	6	5	10	2	7		8	11	9	4	3
Boise Bible College	1	5			4	7		3		2	8	6
University of Idaho	3	4	5		1						2	6
Illinois												
Barat College			1			1				1	1	1
Bradley University		2	3	7	3	5		5	2	6	4	1
City Colleges of Chicago: Harold Washington College												
City Colleges of Chicago: Harry S. Truman College	1											
DePaul University	2	1	1	4	1	3				3	1	1
Elgin Community College							1					
Governors State University	2							3				1
Highland Community College							1					

	Application	Class Rank	Course Selection	Extra Activities	G.P.A.	Interview	Open Admissions	Personal Statement	Psychoeducational	Recommendations	School Transcript	SAT/ACT
Illinois Central College	1											1
Illinois State University	4	2	7	8	3	10		9	11	6	1	5
Kendall College		3	1	7	8	3	1	6	5	2	4	3
Lake Land College							1		1			
Lincoln College	9	2	5	8	4	6				7	1	3
Moraine Valley Community College									1			
National-Louis University	1	2	1	2	2	1		2	2	1	2	1
Northern Illinois University		1	2		1	4		4	3	4	1	2
Oakton Community College	1	3					1					2
Roosevelt University	1					1		1	1	1		
School of the Art Institute of Chicago	2	6	10	11	6	5		2	4	2	3	2
Shawnee College												
Shimer College	7			6		1		2	4	3	8	5
Southeastern Illinois College									1			
Southern Illinois University at Carbondale		1									1	
Southern Illinois University at Edwardsville	1	1	5	7	6	11		11	11	8	1	4
Triton College									1			1
Waubonsee Community College	1	4	2	3	2	1	1	2	1	2	5	2
Western Illinois University	9	4	2	8	3	11		10	6	7	5	1
William Rainey Harper College	11	8	5	7	4	1	1	6	2	10	9	3
Indiana												
Anderson University		1		4	1	8		6		4	4	1
Indiana Institute of Technology		2	3	6	4	8				7	5	1
Indiana University Bloomington		3	1	7	4					8	6	2
Indiana University East												
Indiana University Northwest	1	2	2	7	1	3		6	5	4	1	1
Indiana UniversityPurdue Univeristy at Indianapolis		1	1							2	2	
Indiana Vocational Technical College Central Indiana									1			
Indiana Vocational Technical College: Eastcentral									1			
Indiana Vocational Technical College: Northcentral												1
Indiana Vocational Technical College: Northeast									1			
Indiana Vocational Technical College: Southwest									1		1	
Indiana Vocational Technical College: Whitewater	7		6		5	2	1		1	3		4
Indiana VocationalTechnical College Kokomo	1		3		4							2
Indiana Wesleyan University	6	3	5	7	1	10		4	9	8	1	2
Manchester College	9	3	3	11	1	6		10	5		8	4
Purdue University	7	2	4	9	2	5		8	10	6	3	1
University of Evansville	8	4	1	7	2	9		10	11	6	5	3
University of Indianapolis	7	3	5	10	4	6		11	9	8	2	1
University of Southern Indiana				8		10		9	11			

CRITERIA FOR ADMISSIONS

Institution	Application	Class Rank	Course Selection	Extra Activities	G.P.A.	Interview	Open Admissions	Personal Statement	Psychoeducational	Recommendations	SAT/ACT	School Transcript
Vincennes University												
Iowa												
Coe College	1	1	1	2	1	2				2	1	1
Cornell College		1	2	2	1	3		3		3	2	1
Graceland College	8	5	4	12	6	2		11	1	3	7	9
Grand View College		3	4	7	1	5				6	2	1
Hawkeye Institute of Technology	6	1	4		3	7				8	5	2
Indian Hills Community College	2					1			3			
Iowa Central Community College		3			2					4		1
Iowa State University of Science and Technology	4	1	1	9	3	8		10	7	6	2	5
Loras College	9	7	1	11	6	3		10	2	8	5	4
Scott Community College												
Southeastern Community College: North Campus	1		5						4			2
Southwestern Community College	4	5	4	10	6	8		7	2	3	9	1
University of Iowa	10	1	9	6	4	7			8	5	2	3
University of Northern Iowa	5	2	4	11	6	7		10	9	8	1	3
Waldorf College	1	5	4	11	2	8		10	9	7	6	3
Kansas												
Barton Community College									1			
Cowley County Community College	1		6		5				1			2
Emporia State University									1			
Hutchinson Community College									1			
Kansas City Kansas Community College									1			
Kansas State University		2	5	6	4	6		6	6	6	3	1
Pittsburg State University									1			
University of Kansas						1			1		1	
Wichita State University	1					3			1		4	2
Kentucky												
Cumberland College	1	3		4	2	6		1	7	5	1	1
Eastern Kentucky University									1			
Elizabethtown Community College									1			
Lexington Community College	3	9	6	10	5	7		11	2	8	4	1
Lindsey Wilson College									1			
Murray State University		3	1								2	
Prestonsburg Community College												
Thomas More College		2	1	3	1			3	1		2	1
University of Kentucky	7	7	7	7	1	11		11	11	11	1	7
Louisiana												
Louisiana College	11	10	6	4	9	7		3	1	5	2	8
Louisiana State University Agricultural and Mechanical Colle					4				3		2	1

CRITERIA FOR ADMISSIONS

	Application	Class Rank	Course Selection	Extra Activities	G.P.A.	Interview	Open Admissions	Personal Statement	Psychoeducational	Recommendations	SAT/ACT	School Transcript
Louisiana State University at Alexandria		1			1	1	1	1		1	1	1
University of Southwestern Louisiana	4	2	6	11	1	8		10	7	9	3	5
Maine												
Bowdoin College	6	2	1	7	3	11		8	3	5		2
Colby College	8	10	11	7	11					8	7	11
Southern Maine Technical College	6	4	1	10	3	11		8	9	5	7	2
St. Joseph's College	11	4	2	9	3	10		8	7	6	5	1
Unity College			4	5		1				2		3
University of Maine	8	10	10	8	10	10		8	10	8	8	10
University of Maine at Machias	5	4	3	8	2	7				6	5	1
University of New England	10	6	5	9	4	2		8	1	7	11	3
University of Southern Maine	1	2	1	4		2		1	1	2	3	1
Maryland												
Charles County Community College			1	1	1		1					1
Chesapeake College												
Frostburg State University	5	4	7	9	1	7		8	10	6	2	3
Hagerstown Junior College							1					
Howard Community College							1					
Johns Hopkins University	3	1	1	4	1	6		3	1	5	2	1
Montgomery Community College: Rockville Campus							1			1		
Towson State University	4			5	2	8		6	9	7	3	1
University of Maryland: Eastern Shore	5	3	6	9	1	7		11	10	8	4	2
Western Maryland College		5	4	10	3	8		7	1	6	9	2
Wor-Wic Tech Community College							1					
Massachusetts												
American International College	6	7	2	9	1	4			3	5	8	1
Anna Maria College for Men & Women	5	3	4	6	2	10		7	11	9	8	1
Aquinas College at Newton	1	2		3	1	2		3	2	1		1
Bentley College	3	1	2	3	1	3				3	2	1
Boston College	7	8	3	11	4	10		6	2	5	9	1
Boston University	1	1	1	4	1	5		3	3	3	2	1
Bradford College	9	6	3	10	8	4		7	1	5	11	2
Brandeis University		5	1	2	6	5		5		3	4	1
Bridgewater State College	10	5	2	7	4	9		8	3	6	11	1
Bristol Community College							1					
Cape Cod Community College							1					
Clark University	10	5	3	11	1	8		9	4	6	7	2
Curry College	1	5	2	4	2	4		3	1	3		1
Dean Junior College			5	6	4				2	4		4
Endicott College												1

	Application	Class Rank	Course Selection	Extra Activities	G.P.A.	Interview	Open Admissions	Personal Statement	Psychoeducational	Recommendations	SAT/ACT	School Transcript
Gordon College	11	3	7	9	8	5			10	6	4	1
Harvard University	2	2	2	2	1	2				2	2	2
Lesley College-Threshold												
Massachusetts Bay Community College												
Massachusetts College of Art		1	2	4	1	3		2	2	3	2	1
Massachusetts Institute of Technology	3	1	3	4	1	4				4	2	1
Massasoit Community College									1			
Merrimack College	6	2	5	8	3	9		10	11	7	4	1
Middlesex Community College						3	1		1	2		4
Mount Holyoke College	7	2	1	5	1	8		4		6	3	1
Mount Ida College	9	11	5	8		2		7	1	5	10	4
Mount Wachusett Community College	7	8	2	6	3	4		11	5	9	10	1
North Adams State College		4	3	5	1			7	2	6		1
Northeastern University										3	2	1
Pine Manor College	2	3	2	4	2	4		3		2	3	1
Simmons College			2	6					5	4		1
Smith College		2	1	4	1	5		3		4	3	1
Springfield Technical Community College									1			
Stonehill College	7	2	5	6	2	7		8	4	4	3	1
Tufts University	3	1	4	5	1	6		8	7	2	1	1
University of Massachusetts - Dartmouth			1	3	6	2			7	5	4	1
University of Massachusetts at Amherst			1		2				6	4	5	3
University of Massachusetts at Boston	1	5	1	6	2	4		3	1	3	5	2
Wellesley College	5	4	1	5	1	6				3	2	1
Wheaton College	1	5	2	9	4	10		7	11	8	6	3
Wheelock College		8	1	3	2	6			5	7		1
Worcester Polytechnic Institute												1
Michigan												
Adrian College		5	2	8	1	6		2	1	7	4	3
Albion College		3	1		3					4	2	1
Alma College	9	3	8	11	1	4		12	10	6	1	5
Aquinas College		3	4	5	1	6				7	2	
Central Michigan University		2	1	6	2	7				5		4
Charles Stewart Mott Community College												
Delta College												
Detroit College of Business	2											1
Glen Oaks Community College									1			
Grand Valley State University	1		1		1						1	1
Henry Ford Community College	1	9	4	10	8	3		6	1	2	7	5
Jackson Community College									1			

CRITERIA FOR ADMISSIONS

	Application	Class Rank	Course Selection	Extra Activities	G.P.A.	Interview	Open Admissions	Personal Statement	Psychoeducational	Recommendations	SAT/ACT	School Transcript
Kalamazoo College		3	1		5	2				6	4	
Kellogg Community College							1			1		
Lake Michigan College	1	9				7		11		8	10	2
Lake Superior State University	10	3	4	8	1				9	6	2	1
Lansing Community College	1						2			2		
Mercy College of Detroit												
Michigan Technological University		1	4	6	3	9		7	10	8	5	2
Mid Michigan Community College							1					
Montcalm Community College							1					
Northern Michigan University	5	2	1	5	1	3		5	4	3	1	4
Oakland Community College							1		1	3		2
Schoolcraft College							1					
Spring Arbor College		3		4	1	4				4	2	1
St. Mary's College					1	3					2	
Suomi College	11	12	5	7	9	4		3	2	1	8	6
University of Michigan	6	5	2	9	1	11		8	7	10	4	3
University of Michigan: Flint	11	6	3	8	1	7		9	10	5	4	2
Washtenaw Community College							1					
Wayne State University	3							1			2	4
Western Michigan University								2			1	
Minnesota												
Augsburg College				1		1			2	2		1
College of St. Catherine: St. Catherine Campus	2	2	1	3	1	3		3	3	3	2	1
Concordia College: St. Paul		2		7	3	6				4	1	5
Hamline University		3	2	5	1					4	4	1
Hibbing Community College	1						1					1
Itasca Community College: Arrowhead							1					
Lakewood Community College	1	10	6	8	7	3		5	2	9	11	4
Moorhead State University	9	1	4	11	8	10		6	7	5	2	3
Rochester Community College		0	3			4	2	1		1		
Saint Cloud State University												
Southwest State University	7	1	3	10	9	4		6	5	8	4	2
St. Cloud State University		1			3						2	
St. John's University		2		6	1			4		3	5	1
St. Mary's Campus of the College of St. Catherine	3	6	2					5	4	1		1
St. Olaf College	6	8	2	3	7	9		10	11	5	4	1
University of Minnesota: Duluth		1	3						4	5	2	1
University of Minnesota: Morris		1									1	
University of Minnesota: Crookston	1	3							1			2
Wilmar Community College	1	11	11	11	6	4	1	5	2	7	11	3

Institution	Application	Class Rank	Course Selection	Extra Activities	G.P.A.	Interview	Open Admissions	Personal Statement	Psychoeducational	Recommendations	SAT/ACT	School Transcript
Worthington Community College							1					
Mississippi												
Hinds Community College			4			2	1			5		3
University of Mississippi	1					1					1	1
Missouri												
Central Missouri State University		2				3					2	1
Evangel College	6	4	7	8	3	10		11	9	1	2	5
Jefferson College	2	1	3	7	1	5		8	9	6		
Kansas City Art Institute												
Longview Community College									1			
Maple Woods Community College												
Rockhurst College	1	1	1	2	1	2		3	4	1	1	1
Southwest Baptist University	6	3	5	7	2			11	9	1	4	
St. Louis Community College at Florissant	1						1					1
St. Louis Community College at Forest Park	11	6	8	10	4	2	1	9	1	3	7	5
St. Louis University		4	2			1					5	3
University of Missouri: Columbia		1								1	1	
University of Missouri: Rolla		1									1	1
Washington University	6	4	2	8	3			9	10	7	5	1
Westminster College	10	9	2	7	1	5		8	3	6	4	11
Montana												
Flathead Valley Community College									1			
Montana College of Mineral Science	7	4	2	8	3	9		10	11	6	1	5
Northern Montana College		4	1			2		1			3	
Rocky Mountain College		3				1				4	2	
Western Montana College University of Montana	1	5	11	8	3	6		10	9	7	2	4
Nebraska												
Dana College	11	2	4	7	1	5		9	8	6	3	10
Southeast Community College: Beatrice Campus		1				1				1	1	1
Southeast Community College: Lincoln Campus	1		3		4				1			2
Southeast Community College: Milford												
Union College			5		4	6		8	1	7	3	2
Western Nebraska Community College: Scottsbluff									1			
Nevada												
Truckee Meadows Community College												
University of Nevada: Las Vegas	1	3	4	5	1			6	7		2	1
University of Nevada: Reno	6	5	2	7	1	10		9	8	11	3	4
New Hampshire												
Dartmouth College	1	1	1	1	1	1		1		1	1	1
Keene State College	11	3	2		10	4	6	8	7	9	5	1

CRITERIA FOR ADMISSIONS

	Application	Class Rank	Course Selection	Extra Activities	G.P.A.	Interview	Open Admissions	Personal Statement	Psychoeducational	Recommendations	SAT/ACT	School Transcript
New England College			4			1				5	3	2
New Hampshire College	2	4	2	4	2	3		5		3	3	1
New Hampshire Technical College						1				4	3	2
New Hampshire Vocational-Technical	10	3	2	7	4	11		8	9	6	5	1
New Hampshire Vocational-Technical College: Laconia	10	11	5	6	8	4		9	1	2	7	3
University of New Hampshire												
New Jersey												
Caldwell College		1	3	5	1	4				3	2	
County College of Morris			2		5	6			1	4		3
Fairleigh Dickinson University	7	4	5	9	3				11	6	2	1
Georgian Court College		2	1	5	2	7		5	6	4	3	1
Gloucester County College	1	8	6	11	7	2		5	4	10	9	3
Jersey City State College	9	7	5	10	6	2		11	1	3	8	4
Middlesex County College	1		3	6		1		7	2	1		2
New Jersey Institute of Technology	8	2	5	6	1					7	4	3
Ocean County College							1					
William Paterson College of New Jersey		1									1	
New Mexico												
Albuquerque Technical-Vocational Institute	9	10	3	6	5	8		7	1	2	11	4
College of Santa Fe	3		8		10	1			7	4	2	5
Eastern New Mexico University: Roswell												
Institute of American Indian Arts	6	7	8	10	1	9		4	11	5	12	2
San Juan College												
Santa Fe Community College							1					
University of New Mexico	1	2	7	8	2			5	5	6	2	2
New York												
Adelphi University	12	10	2		12	11			3	7	12	1
Broome Community College							1					
Cazenovia College												1
City University New York: Brooklyn College	4	1	2		10	1		11		11	3	1
City University of New York: College of Staten Island												
City University of New York: City College		3			2	4						1
City University of New York: Borough of Manhattan Commur	2						1					1
City University of New York: John Jay-Criminal Justice	1	4	12	12	3	12		12	12	12	5	2
City University of NewYork: La Guardia Community College							1					
Clinton Community College	1		7	8	6	2		5	3	9		4
Community College of the Finger Lakes			1		1		1					
Cornell University	1	1	1		2	2				1	2	1
D'Youville College	8	2	3	5	2	4		7		6	2	1
Dowling College												

	Application	Class Rank	Course Selection	Extra Activities	G.P.A.	Interview	Open Admissions	Personal Statement	Psychoeducational	Recommendation	SAT/ACT	School Transcript
Dutchess Community College							1					
Eugene Lang College	6	6	2	7	3	2				5	4	1
Fashion Institute of Technology												
Fordham University	7	6	1	8	3	10		9	11	5	4	2
Fulton-Montgomery Community College	10	5	7	1	5	9		1	9	8	2	10
Herkimer County Community College	1	5	9	10	3	7	1	11	4	8	6	2
Hofstra University	3	5	3	1	5	11		11	11	11	3	8
Houghton College	5	4	2	10	3	9		1	8	7	6	1
Hudson Valley Community College							1					
Hunter College					1							1
Iona College - Seton School	8	9	4	12	7	1		11	2	6	10	5
Jefferson Community College							1					
Julliard School	2							4				3
Keuka College	11	5	4	9	2	8		6	10	7	3	1
Long Island University: C.W. Post Campus	10	3	6	7	1	9		8	5	11	2	4
Long Island University: Southampton Campus		9	1	8	3	6		7	10	5	4	2
Manhattan School of Music	9	10	8	6	3			7		5	4	2
Marist College	10	6	8	7	5	2		9	1	4	11	3
Medaille College	1					1				1		1
Mercy College	4	4	4	5	2	3		5	1	3	4	2
Mohawk Valley Community College							1					
Molloy College	3	4	8	9	1	5		7	10	6	1	2
Nassau Community College	2	1	3	8	5	9				7	6	4
New York Institute of Technology				4	1		1			3	2	
New York University		12	4	6	1	12			2	5	3	1
Niagara University		2								4	3	1
Onondaga Community College		4	3		2	6	1			7	5	1
Pace University: College of White Plain		3		8	1	7		6	9	4	2	5
Para-Educator Center for Young Adults	6		9	7					2	4		8
Paul Smith's College												
Rochester Institute of Technology	8	2	1	9	1	5		6	4	7	3	1
Rockland Community College	1							1		2		
Schenectady County Community College							1					
School of Visual Arts	5				6	2		4			7	3
Skidmore College	7	10	2	6	3	9		8	11	4	5	1
St. Bonaventure University	7	6	1	10	3			9	5	8	4	2
St. Lawrence University	3	2	1	3	2	3		3		2	3	2
St. Thomas Aquinas College			1	3	9	4		5	2	7	10	6
State University of New York at Albany		3	1		1						2	1
State University of New York at Binghamton	1	1	1	2	2	2		2	1	2	3	1

CRITERIA FOR ADMISSIONS

	Application	Class Rank	Course Selection	Extra Activities	G.P.A.	Interview	Open Admissions	Personal Statement	Psychoeducational	Recommendations	School Transcript	SAT/ACT
State University of New York at Buffalo		1			1						1	
State University of New York at Stony Brook												
State University of New York College at Oneonta		2	1	4	1			4		4	3	1
State University of New York College at Plattsburg	7	9	4	5	8	1		2	6	3	11	10
State University of New York College of Environmental Scie			1	11	3	10					4	2
State University of New York College of Technology at Cant	1	11	7	8	9	2		5	4	6	10	3
State University of New York College of Technology at Delhi	5	5	2	5	2	3		5	5	4	3	1
State University of New York College of Techology at Farmir	1		4		3							2
Syracuse University	1	1	1	1	1			1	1	1	1	1
Ulster County Community College	4	5	3		2							1
Utica College of Syracuse University	3	1	2	2	2	3		4	6	5	4	1
Westchester Community College	1	12	12	12	12	1	1	12	1	12	11	1
North Carolina												
Appalachian State University		1	1	1	1					1	1	1
Blue Ridge Community College							1					
Caldwell Community College and Technical Institute							1					
Catawba Valley Community College							1					
Central Piedmont Community College							1					
Craven Community College							1					
Davidson College	6	4	1	7	2			6		3	5	1
Davidson County Community College												1
East Carolina University	1	3	4		3						5	2
Guilford Technical Community College							1					
Halifax Community College							1					
Isothermal Community College							1					
Johnston Community College							1					
McDowell Technical Community College							1					
North Carolina State University		3	2	5	1			6		7	4	
Richmond Community College												
Surry Community College												
University of North Carolina: Greensboro		1	3		2	4					2	1
University of North Carolina: Wilmington	1	11	1	11	1	11		11	11	11	2	1
Wake Forest University	3	1	1	3	1			3	4	5	2	1
Wilkes Community College							1					
Wingate College	1	4	1	7	4	5		6	2	5	3	1
North Dakota												
Dickinson State University												
Mayville State University							1					
North Dakota State College of Science	1	7	2	9	4	6		11	8	10	5	3
North Dakota State University			1									1

Institution	Application	Class Rank	Course Selection	Extra Activities	G.P.A.	Interview	Open Admissions	Personal Statement	Psychoeducational	Recommendations	SAT/ACT	School Transcript
North Dakota State University: Bottineau	1	6	2	7	5	10		9	8	11	3	4
Ohio												
Bowling Green State University	5	4	7	6	2	10		8		9	1	3
Case Western Reserve University	7	3	1		5			8		2	6	4
Cedarville College	2	6	8	11	3	9		1	10	7	5	4
Central Ohio Technical College							1					
Cleveland State University											2	1
College of Mount St. Joseph	8	4	1	9	2	6		10	11	7	3	5
Columbus State Community College							1					
Cuyahoga Community College												
Defiance College	6	5	3	7	2	8				9	4	1
Edison State Community College							1					
Franklin University							1					
Hocking Technical College							1					
Jefferson Technical College												1
Kent State University: Ashtabula Regional Campus	3	5	4	7	1	9		11	8	10	2	6
Kent State University: Salem Regional	1						1					
Kenyon College	9	3	2	8	4	10		6	11	7	5	1
Malone College	4	6	2	9	3	7		8	11	10	5	1
Muskingum College	3	3	1	3	2	1		3	1	2	2	1
Oberlin College	8	1	2	3	1	6		5	7	4	1	2
Ohio State University Agricultural Technical Institute	1						1					1
Ohio State University: Columbus Campus		1	1	2				3		2	2	
Ohio State University: Marion Campus							1					
Ohio State University: Newark Campus		2	1				1					
Ohio University		1	1		3					4	2	1
Otterbein College	4	3	2	5	1	5		5	4	5	2	1
Owens Technical College							1					
Sinclair Community College	1											
The University of Akron - Wayne College	1	3			2						4	
University of Cincinnati: Raymond Walters College	1	3	5		4		1					2
University of Dayton	10	4	3	7	2	9		8	11	6	5	1
University of Toledo	6	5	3	7	2	10		8	11	9	4	1
Walsh College	11	3	5	10	1	6		7	8	9	2	4
Wilmington College		1	1		1	1		1	1			1
Oklahoma												
Carl Albert Junior College							1					
East Central University		2	4		2			1			1	3
Oklahoma State University	1	4			5	7		6			2	3
Rose State College							1					

CRITERIA FOR ADMISSIONS

	Application	Class Rank	Course Selection	Extra Activities	G.P.A.	Interview	Open Admissions	Personal Statement	Psychoeducational	Recommendations	SAT/ACT	School Transcript
Tulsa Junior College												
University of Oklahoma		1	3	4	1	2			2	2	1	2
Oregon												
Central Oregon Community College							1					
Clackamas Community College			3	5		1		1	2			4
Eastern Oregon State College	7	6	3	9	1			8	10	5	4	2
Lane Community College							1					
Linn-Benton Community College												1
Mount Hood Community College	1											
Oregon State University	1		3		2						4	3
Pacific University	5	10	3	9	2	6		8	11	7	4	1
Portland Community College							1					
Umpqua Community College	8	11	6	9	7	2	1	3	1	5	10	4
University of Oregon	6	9	4	10	5			7	2	8	1	3
Western Oregon State College	1		1	12	1				10	5	2	1
Pennsylvania												
Albright College	6	4	2	8	3	10		9		7	5	1
Bloomsburg University of Pennsylvania		1			1					2	1	1
Bryn Mawr College	3	2	1	4	2	4				3	3	1
California University of Pennsylvania	1	4	5	9	3	10		8		7	6	2
Carnegie Mellon University	10	2	4	7	3	8		9	11	6	5	1
Churchman Business School	11	9	1	6	1	3		8	5	7	10	4
College Misericordia	7	5	1	9	1	3		8	4	2	6	1
Community College of Allegheny College							1					
Community College of Philadelphia	1						1		1			1
Delaware County Community College	1						1					
Delaware Valley College	6	2	5	6	2	8		6	6	7	2	1
Duquesne University	1	1	1	3	1	3		3		3	2	1
Edinboro University of Pennsylvania												
Harcum Junior College	3	6	1	5	1	4			3	2		1
Kutztown University of Pennsylvania	4	1			2						3	5
Lehigh County Community College							1					
Lehigh University	11	4	2	6	3	10		7	8	9	5	1
Luzerne County Community College							1					
Mansfield University of Pennsylvania	4	2	1	7	1	5		6	5	6	3	1
Mercyhurst College	10	8	2	7	5	6		11	4	3	9	1
Peirce Junior College	8	3	2	11	1	6		9	10	7	5	4
Penn State Fayette Campus	1	10	3	11	8	5		6	7	2	9	4
Penn State Mont Alto Campus	5	4			1						3	2
Penn State University Park Campus					1						2	

CRITERIA FOR ADMISSIONS

Institution	Application	Class Rank	Course Selection	Extra Activities	G.P.A.	Interview	Open Admissions	Personal Statement	Psychoeducational	Recommendations	SAT/ACT	School Transcript
Penn State Worthington Scranton Campus												
Pinebrook Junior College							1			1		
Point Park College	12	3	4	8	2	6		9	10	7	5	1
Reading Area Community College							1					
Spring Garden College	10	8	6	9	4	1		11	2	3	7	5
University of Pittsburgh at Bradford		2	6	6	2	5		4	6	6	4	1
University of Pittsburgh: Pittsburgh Campus		2						5		4	3	1
Waynesburg College	6	4	3	7	2	8			10	9	5	1
Westmoreland County Community College							1					
Widener University	1	6	3	7	4	8		11	9	10	5	2
Puerto Rico												
American University of Puerto Rico	1							1				1
Inter American University of Puerto Rico	1							1				1
Rhode Island												
Brown University		1	1		3	1		5	2	2	4	1
Bryant College	5	4	2	7				8		6	3	1
Community College of Rhode Island							1	1				
Johnson and Wales University	3				2	1						
Rhode Island School of Design	3		3	4	2					4	3	1
Roger Williams College			3	3	2	6				5	4	1
South Carolina												
Central Wesleyan College	6	2	11	8	1	10		7	9	4	3	5
Francis Marion College	1	4	3	8	7	10		9	6	11	5	2
Midlands Technical College	1		1				1		1	1	1	1
University of South Carolina		1	4		3						2	1
South Dakota												
Black Hills State College	5	2	6	9	3	8		11	10	7	1	4
Huron University	11	9	3	4	2	5		7	6	8	10	1
Northern State University	1	4			3						2	
South Dakota State University	3	2		4	1	6			5		7	1
Tennessee												
Austin Peay State University		5	3		2						1	4
Freed-Hardeman University	4		5	7	2	8				6	3	1
Lee College	1		5	6	7	4	10	8	11	9	3	2
Martin Methodist College			1	1	1							1
Memphis College of Art	2	9			10	8		3	7	4	6	5
Middle Tennessee State University	2	7	9	4	1	5		6	8	3	1	1
Pellissippi State Technical Community College			3							4	2	1
Tennessee Technological University					2						1	
University of Tennessee	6	7	3	11	2	8		5	10	9	4	1

	Application	Class Rank	Course Selection	Extra Activities	G.P.A.	Interview	Open Admissions	Personal Statement	Psychoeducational	Recommendations	SAT/ACT	School Transcript
Vanderbilt University	3	2	1	3	1					2	2	1
Texas												
Amarillo College	3	9	6	10	4	2	1	7	1	11	8	5
El Paso Community College	1	10	5	11	8	4		9	3	6	7	2
North Harris Montgomery Community College District	9	10	4	6	7	2	1	5	1		8	3
North Lake College	11	5	5	11	5	1		1	1	3	11	8
Richland College	1	12	12	12	12	1		12	1	5	12	1
Sam Houston State University						2					1	
San Antonio College							1					
Schreiner College	1	5	3	8	5	4		6	3	7	5	2
Southern Methodist University		2	1	6	2	7		4		5	3	2
St. Philip's College							1					
Tarleton State University	1	2	6	11	5	11		11	11	11	3	4
Texas A&I University	1	1									1	1
Texas Southmost College												
Texas Tech University	5	2			3						1	4
Tyler Jr. College	1					1	1		1	1		1
University of Houston												
University of Texas at Brownsville							1					
Utah												
Snow College							1					
Southern Utah University		3			2						1	
University of Utah			2		1				3	3	1	2
Utah State University	1										1	1
Vermont												
Burlington College	1					1	1					
Community College of Vermont									1			
Landmark College	1			2		1		1	1	1		
New England Culinary Institute	1	7		8	6	5		4		3		2
Norwich University	10	5	2	9	1	6		8	11	7	4	3
Saint Michael's College	7	4	2	8	3	10		11	6	9	5	1
Southern Vermont College		3	3		3	2			1			
University of Vermont	8	3	5	6	2	10		9	4	11	7	1
Vermont Technical College	7	9	4	6	2	8				5	3	1
Virginia												
Blue Ridge Community College									1			
Bluefield College	5	10	11	7	1	4		8	2	6	9	3
Christopher Newport College	6	4	1	10	2	9		7	11	8	5	3
College of William and Mary	3	1	1	2	1			3		4	2	1
Dabney S. Lancaster Community College												

CRITERIA FOR ADMISSIONS

	Application	Class Rank	Course Selection	Extra Activities	G.P.A.	Interview	Open Admissions	Personal Statement	Psychoeducational	Recommendations	SAT/ACT	School Transcript
George Mason University	1	1		1	1			1			1	1
Hollins College	7	5	1	9	3	8				6	4	2
James Madison University		2	1	4				5		6	3	
Liberty University	3	8			7			1	4	2	5	6
Lord Fairfax Community College	1						1					
New River Community College							1					
Patrick Henry Community College							1					
Paul D. Camp Community College							1					
Radford University	5	2	1	6	1	7			5	6	3	4
Southern Seminary College			1			2	1			1	3	1
Thomas Nelson Community College							1					
University of Virginia	4	2	1	4	2			4	3	5	3	2
Virginia Highlands Community College							1					
Virginia Intermont College	7	5	2	10	3	11		6	8	9	4	1
Virginia Polytechnic Institute and State University		2	1	5	3			6		7	4	
Virginia Wesleyan College	6	5	3	7	2	8		8	10	9	4	1
Virginia Western Community College							1					
Washington												
Central Washington University	1		3		1	5					2	4
Centralia College							1					
Columbia Basin College							1					
Evergreen State College	1	1	1	1	1						1	1
Lutheran Bible Institute of Seattle	1				4					3		5
Olympic College							1					
Puget Sound Christian College	1									2		3
Washington State University			1		1					2	1	1
Wenatchee Valley College	1											
Whitworth College	2	4	1	5	1	4		6	6	4	5	1
West Virginia												
Bluefield State College	1		2	5	4						2	3
Davis and Elkins College	1		1	5	1	1		5	1	1		1
Marshall University	5	11	10	8	4	1		7	2	9	6	3
Potomac State College of W. Virginia	1	5	8	10	2	6		11	9	7	4	3
West Virginia Northern Comm College	1						1					1
West Virginia State College	1	10	6	7	4	8	1	9	11	5	2	3
West Virginia University					1					1	1	1
West Virginia Wesleyan College	3	5	1	2	1	1		2	1	2	3	1
Wisconsin												
Beloit College	4	6	2	8	1	10		7	9	5	11	3
Chippewa Valley Technical College	4		1			2	1			3		5

CRITERIA FOR ADMISSIONS

	Application	Class Rank	Course Selection	Extra Activities	G.P.A.	Interview	Open Admissions	Personal Statement	Psychoeducational	Recommendations	School Transcript	SAT/ACT
Edgewood College	4	2	1	5	1	8		6	11	7	3	1
Fox Valley Technical College	1	7	1	6	2	4		9	5	8	11	3
Gateway Technical College	8	11	5	10	6	3		4	1	2	9	7
Lawrence University	5	3	4	9	2	8		7		10	6	1
Marian College of Fond du Lac	2	3	4	5	1	1		4	1	3	4	1
Marquette University	6	1	3		1					5	2	3
Milwaukee Area Technical College			2	11	1	1		11	1	11		1
Moraine Park Technical Institute												
Northeast Wisconsin Technical College	6	4	1	8	5	1		9	3	9	7	2
Ripon College		6	2	5	1	7		8	9	4	3	
University of Wisconsin - Milwaukee	12	8	6	9	7	3		11	2	5	4	10
University of Wisconsin : Madison	3	1	2	3	1	4		2	3	4	2	1
University of Wisconsin Ctr: Waukesha		1									3	2
University of Wisconsin: LaCrosse	3	1	8	10	5	7		9	7	6	2	4
University of Wisconsin: Oshkosh		4			3	1					5	2
University of Wisconsin: Platteville	1	1	1	5	3	10		10	2	5	1	2
University Wisconsin Center: Baraboo Sauk County	2	1	1		3						1	2
University Wisconsin-Center Rock County	3	2	1	10	5	7		11	11	6	11	4
Viterbo College		3	5		1	7				4	2	6
Waukesha County Technical College	6	9	4	10	7	1		8	2	3	11	5
Western Wisconsin Technical College	1	7	5	11	6	3		10	9	4	8	2
Wisconsin Indianhead Technical College	1											
Wyoming												
Casper College	1											1
Central Wyoming College	1		3				1					2
Laramie County Community College	1									1		1
Sheridan College	1	5	4	9	3	11		10	6	8	7	2
University of Wyoming		3	3	5	1	4		5		4	2	1

	Speech/Language	Reading	Written Expression	Study Skills	Spelling	Organizational Skills	Math	Fine Motor	Perceptual	ADD without LD	ADD with LD	ADHD without LD	ADHD with LD
Alabama													
Auburn University at Montgomery	•	•	•	•	•	•	•	•	•	•	•	•	•
Chattahoochee Valley Community College	•	•	•	•	•	•	•	•	•	•	•	•	•
Jacksonville State University	•	•	•	•	•	•	•	•	•	•	•	•	•
Northeast Alabama State Junior College	•	•	•	•	•	•	•	•	•	•	•	•	•
Troy State University at Dothan	•	•	•	•	•	•	•	•	•	•	•	•	•
UAB - Horizons Program													
University of Alabama	•	•	•	•	•	•	•	•	•	•	•	•	•
University of Alabama at Birmingham	•	•	•	•	•	•	•	•	•	•	•	•	•
Walker State Technical College	•	•	•	•	•	•	•	•	•	•			
Alaska													
Sheldon Jackson College		•	•	•	•	•	•	•	•	•	•	•	•
University of Alaska Anchorage	•	•	•	•	•	•	•	•	•	•			
University of Alaska Fairbanks	•	•	•	•	•	•	•	•	•	•	•	•	•
Arizona													
Arizona State University	•	•	•	•	•	•	•	•	•	•	•	•	•
Glendale Community College													
Northern Arizona University	•	•	•	•	•	•	•	•	•	•	•	•	•
Phoenix College	•	•	•	•	•	•	•	•	•	•	•	•	•
Pima Community College	•	•	•	•	•	•	•	•		•	•	•	•
University of Arizona	•	•	•	•	•	•	•	•	•	•	•	•	•
Arkansas													
Arkansas State University	•	•	•	•	•	•	•	•	•	•	•		
Harding University	•	•	•	•	•	•	•	•	•	•	•	•	•
Henderson State University													
Southern Arkansas University	•	•	•	•	•	•	•	•	•	•	•	•	•
University of Arkansas at Pine Bluff	•	•	•	•	•	•	•	•	•	•	•		•
University of the Ozarks	•	•	•	•	•	•	•	•	•	•	•	•	•
California													
Antelope Valley College	•	•	•	•	•	•	•	•	•	•	•	•	•
Bakersfield College	•	•	•	•	•	•	•	•	•	•	•		•
Biola University	•	•	•	•	•	•	•	•	•				
Butte College	•	•	•	•	•	•	•	•	•	•	•	•	•
Cabrillo College	•	•	•	•	•	•	•	•	•	•	•	•	•
California State Polytechnic University	•	•	•	•	•	•	•	•	•	•	•	•	•
California State University: Bakersfield	•	•	•	•	•	•	•	•	•	•	•	•	•
California State University: Chico	•	•	•	•	•	•	•	•	•	•	•	•	•
California State University: Dominguez Hil	•	•	•	•	•	•	•	•	•	•	•	•	•
California State University: Fullerton	•	•	•	•	•	•	•	•	•	•	•	•	•
California State University: Northridge	•	•	•	•	•	•	•	•	•	•	•	•	•
California State University: Sacramento	•	•	•	•	•	•	•	•	•	•	•	•	•
California State University: San Bernardin	•	•	•	•	•	•	•	•	•	•	•		•
Canada College	•	•	•	•	•	•	•	•	•	•			
Cerritos Community College	•	•	•	•	•	•	•	•	•	•			•
Chabot College	•	•	•	•	•	•	•	•	•	•	•	•	•
Chaffey College	•	•	•	•	•	•	•	•	•	•	•	•	•
College of Alameda	•	•	•	•	•	•	•	•	•	•		•	

838

	Speech/Language	Reading	Written Expression	Study Skills	Organizational Skills	Spelling	Math	Fine Motor	Perceptual	ADD with LD	ADD without LD	ADHD with LD	ADHD without LD
College of San Mateo	•	•	•	•	•	•	•	•		•			
College of the Canyons													
College of the Sequoias	•	•	•	•	•	•	•	•	•	•		•	
College of the Siskiyous	•	•	•	•	•	•	•	•	•		•	•	•
Columbia College	•	•	•	•	•	•	•	•	•			•	•
Crafton Hills College	•	•	•	•	•	•	•	•	•			•	•
Cuesta College	•	•	•	•	•	•	•	•	•	•	•	•	
Cypress College	•	•	•	•	•	•	•	•	•	•	•	•	
De Anza College	•	•	•	•	•	•	•	•	•	•	•	•	
East Los Angeles College	•	•	•	•	•	•	•	•	•	•	•	•	•
El Camino College	•	•	•	•	•	•	•	•	•	•	•	•	•
Evergreen Valley College	•	•	•	•	•	•	•	•	•	•	•	•	•
Feather River College	•	•	•	•	•	•	•	•	•	•	•	•	•
Foothill College	•	•	•	•	•	•	•	•	•	•	•		
Fresno City College	•	•	•	•	•	•	•	•	•	•	•	•	•
Fullerton College	•	•	•	•	•	•	•	•	•	•	•	•	•
Golden Gate University	•	•			•	•	•	•	•	•			
Golden West College	•	•	•	•	•	•	•	•	•	•		•	
Hartnell College		•	•	•	•	•	•	•	•				
Humboldt State University	•	•	•	•	•	•	•	•	•	•	•	•	
Imperial Valley College	•	•	•	•	•	•	•	•	•	•			
Kings River Community College	•	•	•	•	•	•	•	•	•	•	•	•	•
Laney College		•	•	•	•	•	•	•					
Long Beach City College	•	•	•	•	•	•	•	•	•	•	•	•	•
Los Angeles City College	•	•	•	•	•	•	•	•	•	•	•	•	•
Los Angeles Harbor College	•	•	•	•	•	•	•	•	•	•	•	•	
Los Angeles Mission College	•	•	•	•	•	•	•	•	•	•	•	•	•
Los Angeles Valley College	•	•	•	•	•	•	•	•	•	•	•	•	•
Merced College													
Merritt College	•	•	•	•	•	•	•	•	•	•	•	•	•
Modesto Junior College	•	•	•	•	•	•	•	•	•	•	•	•	•
Monterey Peninsula College	•	•	•	•	•	•	•	•	•	•	•	•	•
Mount San Jacinto College	•	•	•	•	•	•	•	•	•	•		•	
Porterville College	•	•	•	•	•	•	•	•	•	•	•	•	
Rancho Santiago College	•	•	•	•	•	•	•	•	•	•	•	•	
Saddleback College	•	•	•	•	•	•	•	•	•	•	•	•	
San Diego City College	•	•	•	•	•	•	•	•	•	•	•	•	•
San Diego Mesa College	•	•	•	•	•	•	•	•	•	•	•	•	
San Diego State University	•	•	•	•	•	•	•	•	•	•	•	•	•
San Francisco State University	•	•	•	•	•	•	•	•	•	•	•	•	•
Santa Barbara City College	•	•	•	•	•	•	•	•	•	•	•	•	
Santa Monica College	•	•	•	•	•	•	•	•	•	•	•	•	
Santa Rosa Junior College	•	•	•	•	•	•	•	•	•	•	•	•	•
Sierra College	•	•	•	•	•	•	•	•	•	•	•	•	•
Sonoma State University	•	•	•	•	•	•	•	•	•	•			
Stanford University	•	•	•	•	•	•	•	•	•	•	•	•	•
Taft College	•	•	•	•	•	•	•	•	•	•	•	•	•
University of California: Berkeley	•	•	•	•	•	•	•	•	•	•	•	•	•

839

	Speech/Language	Reading	Written Expression	Study Skills	Spelling	Organizational Skills	Math	Fine Motor	Perceptual	ADD with LD	ADD without LD	ADHD with LD	ADHD without LD
University of California: Davis	•	•	•	•	•	•	•	•	•	•	•	•	•
University of California: Riverside	•	•	•	•	•	•	•		•	•	•	•	•
University of California: San Diego	•	•	•	•	•	•	•	•	•	•	•	•	•
University of California: Santa Barbara	•	•	•	•	•	•	•	•	•	•	•	•	•
University of California: Santa Cruz	•	•	•	•	•	•	•	•	•	•	•	•	•
University of Redlands		•	•	•	•	•	•						
Ventura College	•	•	•	•	•	•	•	•	•				•
Victor Valley College	•	•	•	•	•	•	•	•	•	•		•	
West Hills College	•	•	•	•	•	•	•	•	•	•	•		•
West Valley College	•	•	•	•	•	•	•	•	•	•	•		•
Colorado													
Arapahoe Community College	•	•	•	•	•	•	•	•	•	•	•	•	•
Colorado Northwestern Community College	•	•	•	•	•	•	•	•	•	•	•	•	•
Colorado State University	•	•	•	•	•	•	•	•	•	•	•	•	•
Community College of Aurora	•	•	•	•	•	•	•	•	•	•	•	•	•
Community College of Denver	•	•	•	•	•	•	•	•	•	•	•	•	•
Front Range Community College	•	•	•	•	•	•	•	•	•	•	•	•	•
Northeastern Junior College	•	•	•	•	•	•	•	•	•	•	•	•	•
Pikes Peak Community College	•	•	•	•	•	•	•	•	•	•	•		
Pueblo Community College	•	•	•	•	•	•	•	•	•	•	•		
Red Rocks Community College	•	•	•	•	•	•	•	•	•	•	•	•	•
Regis College	•	•	•	•	•	•	•	•	•				
University of Colorado at Boulder	•	•	•	•	•	•	•	•	•	•			
University of Denver	•	•	•	•	•	•	•	•	•			•	
Western State College of Colorado	•	•	•	•	•	•	•	•	•	•	•	•	•
Connecticut													
Briarwood College	•	•	•	•	•	•	•	•	•	•	•		•
Eastern Connecticut State University													
Hartford College for Women	•	•	•	•	•	•	•	•	•				
Mattatuck Community College	•	•	•	•	•	•	•	•	•	•	•	•	•
Mitchell College	•	•	•	•	•	•	•	•	•	•		•	
Northwestern Connecticut Community College	•	•	•	•	•	•	•	•	•	•	•	•	•
Norwalk Community College	•	•	•	•	•	•	•	•	•	•	•	•	•
Paier College of Art	•	•	•	•	•	•	•	•					
South Central Community College	•	•	•	•	•	•	•	•	•	•	•	•	•
Thames Valley State Technical College	•	•	•	•	•	•	•	•	•				
University of Connecticut	•	•	•	•	•	•	•	•	•	•	•	•	•
University of New Haven	•	•	•	•	•	•	•	•	•	•	•	•	•
Wesleyan University	•												
Western Connecticut State University	•	•	•	•	•	•	•		•				
Yale University	•	•	•	•	•	•	•	•	•	•		•	
Delaware													
Goldey Beacom College													
University of Delaware	•	•	•	•	•	•	•	•	•	•	•	•	•
District of Columbia													
American University	•	•	•	•	•	•	•	•	•	•	•	•	•
Catholic University of America	•	•	•	•	•	•	•	•	•	•	•	•	•

DISABILITIES SERVED

	Speech/Language	Reading	Written Expression	Study Skills	Organizational Skills	Spelling	Math	Fine Motor	Perceptual	ADD without LD	ADD with LD	ADHD without LD	ADHD with LD
Gallaudet University													
George Washington University		•	•	•	•	•	•						
Trinity College													
Florida													
Beacon College	•	•	•	•	•	•	•	•	•	•	•	•	•
Brevard Community College	•	•	•	•	•	•	•	•	•	•	•	•	•
Chipola Junior College	•	•	•	•	•	•	•	•	•	•	•	•	•
Edison Community College	•	•	•	•	•	•	•	•	•	•	•	•	•
Embry-Riddle Aeronautical University	•	•	•	•	•	•	•	•	•	•		•	•
Florida Agricultural and Mechanical Unive	•	•	•	•	•	•	•	•	•	•		•	
Florida Atlantic University	•	•	•	•	•	•	•	•	•	•	•		
Florida Community College at Jacksonville	•	•	•	•	•	•	•	•	•	•	•	•	•
Florida State University	•	•	•	•	•	•	•	•	•	•	•		
Gulf Coast Community College		•	•	•	•	•	•	•	•		•	•	
Lake City Community College	•	•	•	•	•	•	•	•	•	•	•	•	•
Miami-Dade Community College	•	•	•	•	•	•	•	•	•	•	•	•	•
Okaloosa-Walton Junior College	•	•	•	•	•	•	•	•	•	•	•	•	•
Polk Community College					•	•		•	•				
Saint Johns River Community College	•	•	•	•	•	•	•	•	•	•	•	•	•
Santa Fe Community College	•	•	•	•	•	•	•	•	•	•	•	•	•
Seminole Community College	•	•	•	•	•	•	•	•	•	•	•	•	•
Tallahassee Community College	•	•	•	•	•	•	•	•	•	•	•		
University of Tampa													
Georgia													
Brenau Women's College	•	•	•	•	•	•	•	•	•	•		•	
Brunswick College													
Clayton State College	•	•	•	•	•	•	•	•	•	•		•	
DeKalb College	•	•	•	•	•	•	•	•	•	•	•	•	•
East Georgia College	•								•				
Emory University	•	•	•	•	•	•	•	•	•	•	•	•	•
Georgia College	•	•	•	•	•	•	•	•	•	•	•	•	•
Georgia Institute of Technology	•	•	•	•	•	•	•	•	•	•	•	•	•
Georgia Southern University	•	•	•	•	•	•	•	•	•	•	•		
Georgia State University	•	•	•	•	•	•	•	•	•	•	•	•	•
Mercer University	•	•	•	•	•	•	•	•	•	•			
Reinhardt College	•	•	•	•	•	•	•	•	•	•	•	•	•
South Georgia College	•	•	•	•	•	•	•	•	•	•	•	•	•
Southern College of Technology	•	•	•					•					
University of Georgia	•	•	•	•	•	•	•	•	•	•			
Valdosta State College	•	•	•	•	•	•	•	•	•	•	•	•	•
West Georgia College	•	•	•	•	•	•	•	•	•	•	•	•	•
Hawaii													
Brigham Young University-Hawaii	•	•	•	•	•	•	•	•	•	•		•	
University of Hawaii: Kapiolani Community	•	•	•	•	•	•	•	•	•	•	•	•	•
University of Hawaii: Leeward Community	•	•	•	•	•	•	•	•		•			
Idaho													
Albertson College	•	•	•	•	•	•	•	•	•	•			

841

	Speech/Language	Reading	Written Expression	Study Skills	Spelling	Organizational Skills	Math	Fine Motor	Perceptual	ADD without LD	ADD with LD	ADHD without LD	ADHD with LD	ADHD without LD
Boise Bible College		•	•	•		•								
University of Idaho	•	•	•	•	•	•	•	•	•	•	•	•	•	•
Illinois														
Barat College	•	•	•	•	•	•	•	•	•	•		•		
Bradley University		•	•	•	•	•	•	•	•	•	•			•
City Colleges of Chicago: Harold Washing	•	•	•	•	•	•	•	•	•	•	•	•	•	•
City Colleges of Chicago: Harry S. Trumar	•	•	•	•	•	•	•	•	•	•	•			
DePaul University	•	•	•	•	•	•	•	•	•	•	•		•	
Elgin Community College	•	•	•	•	•	•	•	•	•	•	•	•	•	•
Governors State University	•	•	•	•	•	•	•	•	•	•	•	•	•	•
Highland Community College	•	•	•	•	•	•	•	•	•	•	•	•	•	•
Illinois Central College	•	•	•	•	•	•	•		•	•	•	•	•	•
Illinois State University	•	•	•		•	•		•	•	•	•	•	•	•
Kendall College		•	•	•	•	•	•	•	•					
Lake Land College	•	•	•	•	•	•	•	•	•	•	•		•	•
Lincoln College		•	•	•	•	•	•							
Moraine Valley Community College	•	•	•	•	•	•	•	•	•	•	•	•	•	•
National-Louis University	•	•	•	•	•	•	•	•	•	•				
Northern Illinois University	•	•	•	•	•	•	•	•	•	•	•	•		•
Oakton Community College	•	•	•	•	•	•	•	•	•	•	•	•	•	•
Roosevelt University	•	•	•	•	•	•	•	•	•	•				
School of the Art Institute of Chicago	•	•	•	•	•	•	•	•	•	•	•	•	•	•
Shawnee College														
Shimer College	•		•	•	•	•	•	•	•					
Southeastern Illinois College														
Southern Illinois University at Carbondale	•	•	•	•	•	•	•	•	•	•		•		
Southern Illinois University at Edwardsvill	•	•	•	•	•	•	•	•	•	•	•	•	•	•
Triton College	•	•	•	•	•	•		•	•	•				
Waubonsee Community College	•	•	•	•	•	•	•	•	•	•	•	•	•	•
Western Illinois University	•	•	•	•	•	•	•	•	•	•	•	•	•	•
William Rainey Harper College		•	•	•	•	•	•	•	•	•	•	•		
Indiana														
Anderson University														
Indiana Institute of Technology	•	•	•	•	•	•	•	•	•	•				
Indiana University Bloomington	•	•	•	•	•	•	•	•	•	•	•	•	•	•
Indiana University East	•	•	•	•	•	•	•							
Indiana University Northwest	•	•	•	•	•	•	•	•						
Indiana UniversityPurdue Univeristy at In														
Indiana Vocational Technical College Cer	•	•	•	•	•	•	•	•	•	•				
Indiana Vocational Technical College: Ea	•	•	•	•	•	•	•	•	•					
Indiana Vocational Technical College: No	•	•	•	•	•	•	•	•	•	•	•	•	•	•
Indiana Vocational Technical College: No	•	•	•	•	•	•	•	•	•	•	•	•	•	•
Indiana Vocational Technical College: So	•	•	•	•	•	•	•	•	•	•	•	•	•	•
Indiana Vocational Technical College: Wh	•	•	•	•	•	•	•	•	•	•	•	•	•	•
Indiana VocationalTechnical College Kok	•	•	•	•	•	•	•	•	•	•	•			
Indiana Wesleyan University	•	•	•	•	•	•	•	•	•	•	•	•	•	•
Manchester College	•	•	•	•	•	•	•	•	•	•				

	Speech/Language	Reading	Written Expression	Study Skills	Organizational Skills	Spelling	Math	Fine Motor	Perceptual	ADD with LD	ADD without LD	ADHD with LD	ADHD without LD
Purdue University	•	•	•	•	•	•	•	•	•			•	•
University of Evansville	•	•	•	•	•	•	•	•	•	•	•	•	•
University of Indianapolis		•			•			•	•				
University of Southern Indiana	•	•	•	•	•	•	•	•	•	•	•	•	•
Vincennes University													
Iowa													
Coe College	•	•	•	•	•	•	•	•	•	•			
Cornell College	•	•	•	•	•	•	•	•	•	•	•	•	•
Graceland College	•		•		•		•	•	•				
Grand View College	•	•	•	•	•	•	•	•	•	•	•	•	•
Hawkeye Institute of Technology	•	•	•	•	•	•	•	•	•	•			
Indian Hills Community College	•	•	•	•	•	•	•	•	•	•	•		•
Iowa Central Community College	•	•	•	•	•	•	•	•	•	•	•		
Iowa State University of Science and Tec	•	•	•	•	•	•	•	•	•	•	•	•	•
Loras College	•	•	•	•	•	•	•	•	•	•	•		•
Scott Community College	•	•	•	•	•	•	•	•	•	•	•	•	•
Southeastern Community College: North (	•	•	•	•	•	•	•	•	•	•	•	•	•
Southwestern Community College	•	•	•	•	•	•	•	•	•	•	•		
University of Iowa	•	•	•	•	•	•	•	•	•	•	•	•	•
University of Northern Iowa													
Waldorf College	•	•	•	•	•	•	•	•	•	•	•	•	•
Kansas													
Barton Community College	•	•	•	•	•	•	•	•	•	•	•	•	•
Cowley County Community College	•	•	•	•	•	•	•	•	•	•	•	•	•
Emporia State University	•	•	•	•	•	•	•	•	•	•	•	•	•
Hutchinson Community College	•	•	•	•	•	•	•	•	•	•	•	•	•
Kansas City Kansas Community College	•	•	•	•	•	•	•	•	•	•	•	•	•
Kansas State University	•	•	•	•	•	•	•	•	•	•	•	•	•
Pittsburg State University	•	•	•	•	•	•	•	•	•	•	•	•	•
University of Kansas	•	•	•	•	•	•	•	•	•	•	•	•	•
Wichita State University	•	•	•	•	•	•	•	•	•	•	•	•	•
Kentucky													
Cumberland College		•	•	•	•		•			•	•		
Eastern Kentucky University	•	•	•	•	•	•	•	•	•	•	•	•	•
Elizabethtown Community College	•	•	•	•	•	•	•	•	•	•	•	•	•
Lexington Community College	•	•	•	•	•	•	•	•	•	•	•	•	•
Lindsey Wilson College	•	•	•	•	•	•	•	•	•				
Murray State University		•	•		•		•		•	•	•	•	•
Prestonsburg Community College	•	•	•	•	•	•	•	•	•	•	•	•	•
Thomas More College	•	•	•	•	•	•	•	•	•	•	•	•	•
University of Kentucky	•	•	•	•	•	•	•	•	•	•	•	•	•
Louisiana													
Louisiana College	•	•	•	•	•	•	•	•	•	•	•		
Louisiana State University Agricultural an	•	•	•	•	•	•	•	•	•	•	•	•	•
Louisiana State University at Alexandria		•	•	•			•						
University of Southwestern Louisiana		•	•		•		•			•		•	
Maine													

843

DISABILITIES SERVED

Institution	Speech/Language	Reading	Written Expression	Study Skills	Spelling	Organizational Skills	Math	Fine Motor	Perceptual	ADD with LD	ADD without LD	ADHD with LD	ADHD without LD
Bowdoin College	•									•	•	•	•
Colby College		•	•				•	•					
Southern Maine Technical College													
St. Joseph's College													
Unity College	•			•	•		•			•			
University of Maine	•	•	•	•	•	•	•	•	•	•		•	•
University of Maine at Machias	•	•	•	•	•	•	•	•	•	•			
University of New England	•	•	•	•	•	•	•	•	•	•	•		•
University of Southern Maine	•	•	•	•	•	•	•	•	•	•			
Maryland													
Charles County Community College	•	•	•	•	•	•	•	•					
Chesapeake College	•	•	•	•	•	•	•	•					
Frostburg State University	•	•	•	•	•	•	•	•	•	•		•	•
Hagerstown Junior College	•	•	•	•	•	•	•	•		•			
Howard Community College	•	•	•	•	•	•	•	•	•	•	•	•	•
Johns Hopkins University	•	•	•	•	•	•	•	•	•	•	•	•	•
Montgomery Community College: Rockvill		•	•	•	•	•	•	•		•	•		
Towson State University	•	•	•	•	•	•	•	•	•	•		•	•
University of Maryland: Eastern Shore	•	•	•	•	•	•	•	•	•	•			
Western Maryland College	•	•	•	•	•	•	•	•	•				
Wor-Wic Tech Community College	•	•	•	•	•	•	•	•	•	•	•	•	•
Massachusetts													
American International College	•	•	•	•	•	•	•	•	•	•	•	•	
Anna Maria College for Men & Women	•	•	•	•	•	•	•	•	•	•			
Aquinas College at Newton	•	•	•	•	•	•	•	•	•	•	•	•	•
Bentley College													
Boston College	•	•	•	•	•	•	•	•	•	•	•	•	•
Boston University	•	•	•	•	•	•	•	•	•	•	•	•	•
Bradford College		•	•	•	•	•	•	•	•	•	•		•
Brandeis University	•	•	•	•	•	•	•	•	•	•	•		•
Bridgewater State College	•	•	•	•	•	•	•	•					
Bristol Community College	•	•	•	•	•	•	•	•	•	•	•		•
Cape Cod Community College	•	•	•	•	•	•	•	•	•	•	•		•
Clark University	•	•	•	•	•	•	•	•	•	•	•	•	•
Curry College													
Dean Junior College	•	•	•	•	•	•	•	•	•	•	•	•	•
Endicott College	•	•	•	•	•	•	•	•		•			
Gordon College	•	•	•	•	•	•	•	•	•	•	•	•	•
Harvard University	•	•	•	•	•	•	•	•	•	•	•	•	•
Lesley College-Threshold	•	•	•	•	•	•	•	•	•	•	•	•	•
Massachusetts Bay Community College	•	•	•	•	•	•	•	•	•	•	•	•	•
Massachusetts College of Art	•	•	•	•	•	•	•	•	•	•	•	•	•
Massachusetts Institute of Technology													
Massasoit Community College	•	•	•	•	•	•	•	•	•	•	•	•	•
Merrimack College													
Middlesex Community College	•	•	•	•	•	•	•	•	•	•	•	•	•
Mount Holyoke College	•	•	•	•	•	•	•	•	•	•	•	•	•

DISABILITIES SERVED

	Speech/Language	Reading	Written Expression	Study Skills	Organizational Skills	Spelling	Math	Fine Motor	Perceptual	ADD without LD	ADD with LD	ADHD without LD	ADHD with LD
Mount Ida College	•	•	•	•	•	•	•	•	•	•	•	•	•
Mount Wachusett Community College	•	•	•	•	•	•	•	•	•	•	•	•	•
North Adams State College	•	•	•	•	•	•	•	•	•				
Northeastern University	•	•	•	•	•	•	•	•	•	•	•	•	•
Pine Manor College	•	•	•	•	•	•	•	•	•	•	•	•	•
Simmons College	•	•							•	•		•	•
Smith College	•	•	•		•	•	•	•	•	•	•	•	•
Springfield Technical Community College													
Stonehill College	•	•	•	•	•	•	•	•	•	•	•	•	•
Tufts University	•	•	•	•	•	•	•	•	•	•	•	•	•
University of Massachusetts - Dartmouth	•	•	•	•	•	•	•	•	•	•	•	•	•
University of Massachusetts at Amherst	•	•	•	•	•	•	•	•	•	•	•	•	•
University of Massachusetts at Boston	•	•	•	•	•	•	•	•	•	•	•	•	•
Wellesley College	•	•	•		•	•	•		•	•	•	•	•
Wheaton College	•	•	•		•	•	•		•	•	•	•	•
Wheelock College													
Worcester Polytechnic Institute		•	•		•								
Michigan													
Adrian College	•	•	•	•	•	•	•		•	•	•	•	•
Albion College	•	•	•	•			•	•					
Alma College			•	•		•							
Aquinas College		•	•	•	•	•	•	•	•	•		•	
Central Michigan University													
Charles Stewart Mott Community College	•	•	•	•	•	•	•	•	•	•	•	•	•
Delta College	•	•	•	•	•	•	•	•	•	•	•	•	•
Detroit College of Business	•	•	•	•	•	•	•	•	•	•	•	•	•
Glen Oaks Community College	•	•	•	•	•	•	•	•	•				
Grand Valley State University	•	•	•	•	•	•	•	•	•	•	•	•	•
Henry Ford Community College	•	•	•	•	•	•	•	•	•	•	•	•	•
Jackson Community College	•	•	•	•	•	•	•		•	•	•	•	•
Kalamazoo College													
Kellogg Community College	•	•	•	•	•	•	•	•	•	•	•	•	•
Lake Michigan College	•	•	•	•	•	•	•	•	•	•	•	•	•
Lake Superior State University	•	•	•	•	•	•	•	•	•				
Lansing Community College	•	•	•	•	•	•	•	•	•	•	•	•	•
Mercy College of Detroit	•	•	•	•	•	•			•				
Michigan Technological University	•	•	•	•	•	•	•			•	•		
Mid Michigan Community College	•	•	•	•	•	•	•	•	•	•	•	•	•
Montcalm Community College	•	•	•	•	•	•	•	•	•	•	•	•	•
Northern Michigan University		•	•	•	•	•	•	•	•	•	•	•	•
Oakland Community College	•	•	•	•	•	•	•	•	•	•	•	•	•
Schoolcraft College	•	•	•	•	•	•	•	•	•	•	•		•
Spring Arbor College	•	•	•	•	•	•	•		•				
St. Mary's College	•	•	•	•	•	•	•		•				
Suomi College				•	•	•				•	•	•	•
University of Michigan	•	•	•	•	•	•			•				
University of Michigan: Flint	•	•	•	•	•	•	•	•	•	•	•	•	•
Washtenaw Community College	•	•	•	•	•	•	•	•	•	•	•	•	•

845

	Speech/Language	Reading	Written Expression	Study Skills	Organizational Skills	Spelling	Math	Fine Motor	Perceptual	ADD without LD	ADD with LD	ADHD without LD	ADHD with LD
Wayne State University	•	•	•	•	•	•	•	•	•	•	•	•	•
Western Michigan University	•	•	•	•	•	•	•	•	•	•	•		
Minnesota													
Augsburg College	•	•	•	•	•	•	•	•	•	•		•	
College of St. Catherine: St. Catherine Ca	•	•	•	•	•	•	•	•	•	•	•	•	•
Concordia College: St. Paul													
Hamline University	•	•	•	•	•	•	•	•	•	•	•	•	•
Hibbing Community College	•	•	•	•	•	•	•	•	•	•	•	•	•
Itasca Community College: Arrowhead													
Lakewood Community College	•	•	•	•	•	•	•	•	•	•	•	•	•
Moorhead State University	•	•	•	•	•	•	•	•	•	•	•	•	•
Rochester Community College	•	•	•	•	•	•	•	•	•	•	•	•	•
Saint Cloud State University	•	•	•	•	•	•	•	•	•	•	•	•	•
Southwest State University	•	•	•	•	•	•	•	•	•	•	•	•	•
St. Cloud State University	•	•	•	•	•	•	•	•	•	•	•	•	•
St. John's University	•	•	•	•	•	•	•	•	•	•	•	•	•
St. Mary's Campus of the College of St. C	•	•	•	•	•	•	•						
St. Olaf College		•	•	•	•	•	•						
University of Minnesota: Duluth	•	•	•	•	•	•	•	•	•	•	•	•	•
University of Minnesota: Morris	•	•	•	•	•	•	•	•	•	•	•	•	•
University of Minnesota: Crookston	•	•	•	•	•	•	•	•	•	•			
Wilmar Community College	•	•	•	•	•	•	•	•	•	•	•	•	•
Worthington Community College	•	•	•	•	•	•	•	•	•	•	•		
Mississippi													
Hinds Community College	•	•	•	•	•	•	•	•	•	•	•	•	•
University of Mississippi	•	•	•	•	•	•	•	•	•	•	•	•	•
Missouri													
Central Missouri State University	•	•	•	•	•	•	•						
Evangel College	•	•	•	•	•	•	•	•	•				
Jefferson College	•	•	•	•	•	•	•	•	•	•	•	•	•
Kansas City Art Institute		•	•	•	•	•	•						
Longview Community College	•	•	•	•	•	•	•	•	•	•		•	
Maple Woods Community College	•	•	•	•	•	•	•	•	•	•	•	•	•
Rockhurst College	•	•	•	•	•	•	•	•	•	•	•		
Southwest Baptist University	•	•	•	•	•	•	•						
St. Louis Community College at Florissant	•	•	•	•	•	•	•	•	•	•	•	•	•
St. Louis Community College at Forest Pa	•	•	•	•	•	•	•	•	•	•	•	•	•
St. Louis University	•	•	•	•	•	•	•	•	•	•	•		•
University of Missouri: Columbia	•	•	•			•		•					
University of Missouri: Rolla	•	•	•	•	•	•	•	•	•	•	•	•	•
Washington University													
Westminster College	•	•	•	•	•	•	•	•	•	•		•	
Montana													
Flathead Valley Community College	•	•	•	•	•	•	•	•	•	•	•	•	•
Montana College of Mineral Science													
Northern Montana College													
Rocky Mountain College	•	•	•	•	•	•	•	•	•	•	•	•	•

	Speech/Language	Reading	Written Expression	Study Skills	Spelling	Organizational Skills	Math	Fine Motor	Perceptual	ADD with LD	ADD without LD	ADHD with LD	ADHD without LD
Western Montana College University of M	•	•	•	•	•	•	•	•	•				
Nebraska													
Dana College		•	•	•	•	•	•	•					
Southeast Community College: Beatrice (	•	•	•	•	•	•	•			•	•		
Southeast Community College: Lincoln Ca	•		•	•	•	•							
Southeast Community College: Milford	•	•	•	•	•	•	•	•	•				
Union College	•	•	•	•	•	•	•	•					
Western Nebraska Community College: S	•	•	•	•	•	•	•	•					
Nevada													
Truckee Meadows Community College	•	•	•	•	•	•	•	•	•	•	•	•	•
University of Nevada: Las Vegas	•	•	•	•	•	•	•	•	•	•	•	•	•
University of Nevada: Reno	•	•	•	•	•	•	•	•	•	•	•	•	•
New Hampshire													
Dartmouth College	•	•	•	•	•	•	•	•	•	•	•	•	•
Keene State College	•	•	•	•	•	•	•	•	•	•	•		
New England College	•	•	•	•	•	•	•	•	•	•			
New Hampshire College	•		•	•	•	•	•	•					
New Hampshire Technical College													
New Hampshire Vocational-Technical													
New Hampshire Vocational-Technical Col	•	•	•	•	•	•	•	•	•	•	•	•	•
University of New Hampshire	•	•	•	•	•	•	•	•	•	•	•	•	•
New Jersey													
Caldwell College		•		•	•	•	•						
County College of Morris	•	•	•	•	•	•	•	•	•		•	•	
Fairleigh Dickinson University	•	•	•	•		•	•	•			•		
Georgian Court College	•	•	•	•	•	•	•	•	•		•	•	
Gloucester County College	•	•	•	•	•	•	•	•	•				
Jersey City State College	•	•	•	•	•	•	•	•	•		•		
Middlesex County College	•	•	•	•	•	•	•	•	•	•	•	•	•
New Jersey Institute of Technology													
Ocean County College	•	•	•	•	•	•	•	•	•	•	•	•	•
William Paterson College of New Jersey	•	•	•	•	•	•	•						
New Mexico													
Albuquerque Technical-Vocational Institu	•	•	•	•	•	•	•	•	•	•	•	•	•
College of Santa Fe	•	•	•	•	•	•	•	•	•	•	•	•	•
Eastern New Mexico University: Roswell	•	•	•	•	•	•	•	•	•	•	•	•	•
Institute of American Indian Arts		•	•	•	•		•						
San Juan College	•	•	•	•	•	•	•	•	•	•	•	•	•
Santa Fe Community College	•	•	•	•	•	•	•	•	•	•	•	•	•
University of New Mexico	•	•	•	•	•	•	•	•	•	•	•	•	•
New York													
Adelphi University	•	•	•	•	•	•	•	•	•	•	•	•	•
Broome Community College	•	•	•	•	•	•	•	•	•				
Cazenovia College	•	•	•	•	•	•	•	•	•	•	•	•	•
City University New York: Brooklyn College	•	•	•	•	•	•	•	•	•	•	•	•	•
City University of New York: College of S	•	•	•	•	•	•	•	•	•	•	•	•	•

847

	Speech/Language	Reading	Written Expression	Study Skills	Organizational Skills	Spelling	Math	Fine Motor	Perceptual	ADD without LD	ADD with LD	ADHD without LD	ADHD with LD
City University of New York: City College	•	•	•	•	•	•	•						
City University of New York: Borough of M	•	•	•	•	•	•	•	•	•	•	•	•	•
City University of New York: John Jay-Cri	•	•	•	•	•	•	•	•	•	•	•	•	•
City University of NewYork: La Guardia C(	•	•	•	•	•	•	•	•	•	•	•	•	•
Clinton Community College	•	•	•	•	•	•	•	•	•	•	•	•	•
Community College of the Finger Lakes	•	•	•	•	•	•	•	•	•	•	•	•	•
Cornell University	•	•	•	•	•	•	•	•	•	•	•	•	•
D'Youville College	•	•	•	•	•	•	•	•	•	•	•	•	•
Dowling College													
Dutchess Community College	•	•	•	•	•	•	•	•	•	•	•	•	•
Eugene Lang College													
Fashion Institute of Technology													
Fordham University													
Fulton-Montgomery Community College	•	•	•	•	•	•	•	•	•	•	•	•	•
Herkimer County Community College	•	•	•	•	•	•	•	•	•	•	•	•	•
Hofstra University	•	•	•	•	•	•	•	•	•	•	•	•	•
Houghton College	•	•	•	•	•	•	•	•	•	•	•	•	•
Hudson Valley Community College	•	•	•	•	•	•	•	•	•	•	•	•	•
Hunter College	•	•	•	•	•	•	•	•	•	•	•	•	•
Iona College - Seton School		•	•	•	•	•	•	•	•	•	•		•
Jefferson Community College	•	•	•	•	•	•	•	•	•	•	•	•	•
Julliard School													
Keuka College		•	•	•		•							
Long Island University: C.W. Post Campu	•	•	•	•	•	•	•	•	•	•	•		•
Long Island University: Southampton Car													
Manhattan School of Music	•	•	•	•	•	•							
Marist College	•	•	•	•	•	•	•	•	•	•	•	•	•
Medaille College		•	•	•	•	•	•	•	•	•			
Mercy College	•	•	•	•	•	•	•	•	•	•	•	•	•
Mohawk Valley Community College	•	•	•	•	•	•	•	•	•	•	•	•	•
Molloy College	•	•	•	•	•	•	•	•	•	•			
Nassau Community College	•	•	•	•	•	•	•	•	•	•	•		
New York Institute of Technology	•	•	•	•	•	•	•	•	•	•	•		
New York University	•	•	•	•	•	•	•	•	•	•	•	•	•
Niagara University		•	•		•		•						
Onondaga Community College	•	•	•	•	•	•	•	•	•	•	•	•	•
Pace University: College of White Plain													
Para-Educator Center for Young Adults	•	•	•	•	•	•	•	•	•	•	•		•
Paul Smith's College	•	•	•	•	•	•	•	•	•	•	•	•	•
Rochester Institute of Technology	•	•	•	•	•	•	•	•	•	•	•	•	•
Rockland Community College	•	•	•	•	•	•	•	•	•	•	•	•	•
Schenectady County Community College	•	•	•	•	•	•	•	•	•	•	•	•	•
School of Visual Arts													
Skidmore College	•	•	•	•	•	•	•	•	•	•	•	•	•
St. Bonaventure University	•	•	•	•	•	•	•	•	•	•	•	•	•
St. Lawrence University	•	•	•	•	•	•	•	•	•	•	•	•	•
St. Thomas Aquinas College	•	•	•	•	•	•	•	•	•	•	•		
State University of New York at Albany	•	•	•	•	•	•	•	•	•	•	•	•	•

DISABILITIES SERVED

	Speech/Language	Reading	Written Expression	Study Skills	Organizational Skills	Spelling	Math	Fine Motor	Perceptual	ADD with LD	ADD without LD	ADHD with LD	ADHD without LD
State University of New York at Binghamton	•	•	•	•	•	•	•	•	•	•	•	•	•
State University of New York at Buffalo	•			•		•							
State University of New York at Stony Brook													
State University of New York College at C	•	•	•	•	•	•	•	•	•	•	•	•	•
State University of New York College at F	•	•	•	•	•	•	•	•	•	•	•	•	•
State University of New York College of E	•	•	•	•	•	•	•	•	•	•	•	•	•
State University of New York College of T	•	•	•	•	•	•	•	•	•	•	•	•	•
State University of New York College of T·			•	•		•		•					
State University of New York College of T·	•	•	•	•	•	•	•	•	•	•	•		
Syracuse University	•	•	•	•	•	•	•	•	•	•	•	•	•
Ulster County Community College	•	•	•	•	•	•	•	•	•	•	•	•	•
Utica College of Syracuse University	•	•	•	•	•	•	•	•	•	•	•	•	•
Westchester Community College	•	•	•	•	•	•	•	•	•	•	•	•	•
North Carolina													
Appalachian State University													
Blue Ridge Community College	•	•	•	•	•	•	•	•	•	•	•	•	•
Caldwell Community College and Technic	•	•	•	•	•	•	•	•	•	•	•	•	•
Catawba Valley Community College	•	•	•	•	•	•	•	•	•	•	•		
Central Piedmont Community College	•	•	•	•	•	•	•	•	•	•	•	•	•
Craven Community College	•	•	•	•	•	•	•	•	•	•	•	•	•
Davidson College	•	•	•	•	•	•	•	•	•	•	•	•	•
Davidson County Community College	•	•	•	•	•	•	•	•	•	•	•	•	•
East Carolina University	•	•	•	•	•	•	•	•	•	•	•	•	•
Guilford Technical Community College	•	•	•	•	•	•	•	•	•	•	•	•	•
Halifax Community College	•	•	•	•	•	•	•	•	•	•	•	•	•
Isothermal Community College	•	•	•	•	•	•	•	•	•	•	•		
Johnston Community College	•	•	•	•	•	•	•	•	•	•	•		
McDowell Technical Community College	•	•	•	•	•	•	•	•	•	•	•	•	•
North Carolina State University	•	•	•	•	•	•	•	•	•	•	•	•	•
Richmond Community College													
Surry Community College													
University of North Carolina: Greensboro	•	•	•	•	•	•	•	•	•	•	•	•	•
University of North Carolina:Wilmington	•	•	•	•	•	•	•	•	•	•	•	•	•
Wake Forest University	•	•	•	•	•	•	•	•	•	•	•	•	•
Wilkes Community College	•	•	•	•	•	•	•	•	•	•	•	•	•
Wingate College			•	•		•							
North Dakota													
Dickinson State University													
Mayville State University	•	•	•	•	•	•	•	•	•	•	•	•	•
North Dakota State College of Science	•	•	•	•	•	•	•	•	•	•	•	•	•
North Dakota State University	•	•	•	•	•	•	•	•	•	•	•	•	
North Dakota State University: Bottineau													
Ohio													
Bowling Green State University	•	•	•		•	•	•	•	•	•	•	•	•
Case Western Reserve University	•	•	•			•		•	•				
Cedarville College													
Central Ohio Technical College	•	•	•	•	•	•	•	•	•		•		

849

	Speech/Language	Reading	Written Expression	Study Skills	Organizational Skills	Spelling	Math	Fine Motor	Perceptual	ADD with LD	ADD without LD	ADHD with LD	ADHD without LD
Cleveland State University	•	•	•	•	•	•	•	•	•	•	•	•	•
College of Mount St. Joseph	•	•	•	•	•	•	•			•		•	
Columbus State Community College	•	•	•	•	•	•	•	•	•	•	•	•	•
Cuyahoga Community College													
Defiance College	•	•	•	•	•	•	•	•	•				
Edison State Community College	•	•	•	•	•	•	•	•	•	•	•	•	•
Franklin University	•	•	•	•	•	•	•	•	•	•	•	•	•
Hocking Technical College	•	•	•	•	•	•	•	•	•	•	•	•	•
Jefferson Technical College		•		•		•		•					
Kent State University: Ashtabula Regiona	•	•	•	•	•	•	•	•	•				
Kent State University: Salem Regional													
Kenyon College													
Malone College	•	•	•	•	•	•	•	•	•	•	•	•	•
Muskingum College	•	•	•	•	•	•	•	•	•	•		•	
Oberlin College	•	•	•	•	•	•	•	•	•	•	•	•	•
Ohio State University Agricultural Techni	•	•	•	•	•	•	•	•	•	•	•	•	•
Ohio State University: Columbus Campus	•	•	•	•	•	•	•	•	•	•	•	•	•
Ohio State University: Marion Campus	•	•	•	•	•	•	•	•	•	•	•	•	•
Ohio State University: Newark Campus	•	•	•	•	•	•	•	•	•	•	•	•	•
Ohio University	•	•	•	•	•	•	•	•					
Otterbein College	•	•	•	•	•	•	•	•					
Owens Technical College		•			•		•	•					
Sinclair Community College	•	•	•	•	•	•	•	•	•	•	•		
The University of Akron - Wayne College	•	•	•	•	•	•	•	•	•	•	•	•	•
University of Cincinnati: Raymond Walter	•	•	•	•	•	•	•	•	•	•	•	•	•
University of Dayton	•	•	•	•	•	•	•	•	•	•	•	•	•
University of Toledo	•	•	•	•	•	•	•	•	•	•			
Walsh College	•	•	•	•	•	•	•	•	•	•	•	•	•
Wilmington College		•	•	•			•						
Oklahoma													
Carl Albert Junior College	•	•	•	•	•	•	•	•	•	•	•	•	•
East Central University	•	•	•	•	•	•	•	•	•				
Oklahoma State University													
Rose State College	•	•	•	•	•	•	•	•	•	•	•	•	•
Tulsa Junior College	•	•	•	•	•	•	•	•	•	•	•	•	•
University of Oklahoma	•	•	•	•	•	•	•	•	•	•	•	•	•
Oregon													
Central Oregon Community College	•	•	•	•	•	•	•	•	•	•	•	•	•
Clackamas Community College	•	•	•	•	•	•	•	•	•	•	•	•	•
Eastern Oregon State College	•	•	•	•	•	•	•	•	•				
Lane Community College	•	•	•	•	•	•	•	•	•	•	•	•	•
Linn-Benton Community College	•	•	•	•	•	•	•	•	•	•	•	•	•
Mount Hood Community College	•	•	•	•	•	•	•	•	•	•	•	•	•
Oregon State University	•	•	•	•	•	•	•	•	•	•		•	
Pacific University		•	•	•	•	•	•						
Portland Community College	•	•	•	•	•	•	•	•	•	•	•	•	•
Umpqua Community College	•	•	•	•	•	•	•	•	•	•	•	•	•

DISABILITIES SERVED

	Speech/Language	Reading	Written Expression	Study Skills	Organizational Skills	Spelling	Math	Fine Motor	Perceptual	ADD with LD	ADD without LD	ADHD with LD	ADHD without LD
University of Oregon	•	•	•	•	•	•	•	•	•	•	•	•	•
Western Oregon State College	•	•	•	•	•	•	•	•	•	•	•	•	•
Pennsylvania													
Albright College	•	•				•	•	•			•		
Bloomsburg University of Pennsylvania													
Bryn Mawr College	•	•	•	•	•	•	•	•		•	•	•	•
California University of Pennsylvania	•	•	•	•	•	•	•	•	•	•		•	
Carnegie Mellon University	•	•	•	•	•	•	•	•	•	•	•	•	•
Churchman Business School	•	•	•	•	•	•	•	•	•	•	•	•	•
College Misericordia		•	•	•	•	•	•	•		•		•	•
Community College of Allegheny College	•	•	•	•	•	•	•	•	•	•	•	•	•
Community College of Philadelphia	•	•	•	•	•	•	•	•	•	•	•		
Delaware County Community College	•	•	•	•	•	•	•	•	•	•	•	•	•
Delaware Valley College	•	•	•	•	•	•	•	•	•	•	•	•	•
Duquesne University	•	•	•	•	•	•	•		•	•	•	•	•
Edinboro University of Pennsylvania	•	•	•	•	•	•	•	•	•	•	•	•	•
Harcum Junior College	•	•	•	•	•	•	•	•	•	•	•	•	•
Kutztown University of Pennsylvania	•	•	•	•	•	•	•	•	•				
Lehigh County Community College	•	•	•	•	•	•	•	•	•	•	•	•	•
Lehigh University	•	•	•	•	•	•	•	•	•				•
Luzerne County Community College	•	•	•	•	•	•	•	•	•	•	•	•	•
Mansfield University of Pennsylvania	•	•	•	•	•	•	•	•	•	•	•	•	•
Mercyhurst College		•	•	•	•	•	•	•		•			
Peirce Junior College	•	•	•	•	•	•	•	•	•	•	•	•	•
Penn State Fayette Campus	•	•	•	•			•	•	•				
Penn State Mont Alto Campus	•	•	•	•	•	•	•	•	•	•	•	•	•
Penn State University Park Campus	•	•	•	•	•	•	•	•	•	•	•	•	•
Penn State Worthington Scranton Campus													
Pinebrook Junior College	•	•	•	•	•	•	•	•	•				
Point Park College	•	•	•	•	•	•	•			•			
Reading Area Community College	•	•	•	•	•	•	•	•	•	•	•	•	•
Spring Garden College	•	•	•	•	•	•	•	•	•	•	•	•	•
University of Pittsburgh at Bradford	•	•	•	•	•	•	•	•	•	•			
University of Pittsburgh: Pittsburgh Campus	•	•	•	•	•	•	•	•	•	•	•	•	•
Waynesburg College	•	•	•	•	•	•	•	•	•				
Westmoreland County Community College	•	•	•	•	•	•	•	•	•	•	•	•	•
Widener University	•	•	•	•	•	•	•	•	•	•	•		
Puerto Rico													
American University of Puerto Rico	•	•	•	•	•	•	•	•	•	•	•	•	
Inter American University of Puerto Rico													
Rhode Island													
Brown University	•	•	•	•	•	•	•	•	•	•	•	•	•
Bryant College				•		•		•	•	•	•	•	•
Community College of Rhode Island	•	•	•	•	•	•	•	•	•	•	•	•	•
Johnson and Wales University	•	•	•	•	•	•	•	•	•	•	•		
Rhode Island School of Design													
Roger Williams College													

851

	Speech/Language	Reading	Written Expression	Study Skills	Organizational Skills	Spelling	Fine Motor	Math	Perceptual	ADD without LD	ADD with LD	ADHD without LD	ADHD with LD
South Carolina													
Central Wesleyan College	•	•	•	•	•	•	•	•	•	•	•	•	•
Francis Marion College	•	•	•	•	•	•	•	•	•	•	•	•	•
Midlands Technical College	•	•	•	•	•	•	•	•	•	•	•		
University of South Carolina	•	•	•	•	•	•	•	•	•	•	•	•	•
South Dakota													
Black Hills State College	•	•	•	•	•	•	•	•	•	•	•		
Huron University	•	•	•	•	•	•	•	•	•				
Northern State University													
South Dakota State University	•	•	•	•	•	•	•	•	•	•	•		
Tennessee													
Austin Peay State University	•	•	•	•	•	•	•	•	•	•	•		
Freed-Hardeman University	•	•	•	•	•	•	•	•	•	•	•	•	•
Lee College	•	•	•	•	•	•	•	•	•	•	•		
Martin Methodist College													
Memphis College of Art	•	•	•	•	•	•	•	•	•				
Middle Tennessee State University	•	•	•	•	•	•	•	•	•	•	•	•	•
Pellissippi State Technical Community Co	•	•	•	•	•	•	•	•	•	•	•	•	•
Tennessee Technological University								•					
University of Tennessee		•	•		•		•	•	•	•		•	
Vanderbilt University	•	•	•	•	•	•	•	•	•	•	•		
Texas													
Amarillo College	•	•	•	•	•	•	•	•	•	•	•	•	•
El Paso Community College	•	•	•	•	•	•	•	•	•	•	•	•	•
North Harris Montgomery Community Coll	•	•	•	•	•	•	•	•	•	•	•	•	•
North Lake College	•	•	•	•	•	•	•	•	•	•	•	•	•
Richland College	•	•	•	•	•	•	•	•	•	•	•	•	•
Sam Houston State University	•	•	•	•	•	•	•	•	•	•			
San Antonio College	•	•	•	•	•	•	•	•	•	•	•	•	•
Schreiner College	•	•	•	•	•	•	•	•	•	•	•		
Southern Methodist University	•	•	•	•	•	•	•	•	•	•	•		
St. Philip's College	•	•	•	•	•	•	•	•	•	•	•	•	•
Tarleton State University	•	•	•	•	•	•	•	•		•	•	•	•
Texas A&I University	•	•	•	•	•	•	•	•		•			
Texas Southmost College	•	•	•	•	•	•	•	•	•	•	•	•	•
Texas Tech University			•										
Tyler Jr. College	•	•	•	•	•	•	•	•	•	•	•	•	•
University of Houston	•	•	•	•	•	•	•	•	•	•	•	•	•
University of Texas at Brownsville	•	•	•	•	•	•	•	•	•	•	•	•	•
Utah													
Snow College	•	•	•	•	•	•	•	•	•	•	•	•	•
Southern Utah University	•	•	•	•	•	•	•	•	•	•	•	•	•
University of Utah	•	•	•	•	•	•	•	•	•	•	•	•	•
Utah State University	•	•	•	•	•	•	•	•	•	•	•	•	•
Vermont													
Burlington College	•	•	•	•	•	•	•	•	•	•	•	•	•
Community College of Vermont	•	•	•	•	•	•	•	•	•	•	•	•	•

	Speech/Language	Reading	Written Expression	Study Skills	Spelling	Organizational Skills	Math	Fine Motor	Perceptual	ADD with LD	ADD without LD	ADHD with LD	ADHD without LD
Landmark College	•	•	•	•	•	•	•	•	•	•	•	•	•
New England Culinary Institute	•	•	•	•	•	•	•	•	•	•	•	•	•
Norwich University	•	•	•	•	•	•	•	•	•	•	•	•	•
Saint Michael's College													•
Southern Vermont College	•	•	•	•	•	•	•	•	•	•	•	•	
University of Vermont	•	•	•	•	•	•	•	•	•	•	•	•	•
Vermont Technical College	•	•	•	•	•	•		•	•	•	•	•	•
Virginia													
Blue Ridge Community College	•	•	•	•	•	•	•	•	•	•	•	•	•
Bluefield College		•	•	•	•	•	•						
Christopher Newport College	•	•	•	•	•	•	•	•	•	•	•	•	•
College of William and Mary	•	•	•	•	•	•	•	•	•	•	•	•	•
Dabney S. Lancaster Community College	•	•	•	•	•	•	•	•	•	•	•	•	•
George Mason University	•	•	•	•	•	•	•	•	•	•	•	•	•
Hollins College													•
James Madison University	•	•	•	•	•	•	•	•	•	•	•		
Liberty University	•	•	•	•	•	•	•	•	•	•	•	•	•
Lord Fairfax Community College	•	•	•	•	•	•	•	•	•	•	•	•	•
New River Community College	•	•	•	•	•	•	•	•	•	•	•	•	•
Patrick Henry Community College	•	•	•	•	•	•	•	•	•	•	•	•	•
Paul D. Camp Community College		•			•			•					
Radford University	•	•	•	•	•	•	•	•	•	•	•	•	•
Southern Seminary College	•	•	•	•	•	•	•		•				
Thomas Nelson Community College	•	•	•	•	•	•	•	•	•	•	•	•	•
University of Virginia	•	•	•	•	•	•	•	•	•	•	•	•	•
Virginia Highlands Community College	•	•	•	•	•	•	•	•	•	•	•	•	•
Virginia Intermont College	•	•	•	•	•	•	•	•	•	•	•	•	•
Virginia Polytechnic Institute and State U			•	•		•							
Virginia Wesleyan College	•	•	•	•	•	•	•	•	•	•	•		
Virginia Western Community College	•	•	•	•	•	•	•	•	•	•	•	•	•
Washington													
Central Washington University	•	•	•	•	•	•	•	•	•	•			
Centralia College	•	•	•	•	•	•	•	•	•	•	•	•	•
Columbia Basin College	•	•	•	•	•	•	•	•	•	•	•	•	•
Evergreen State College													
Lutheran Bible Institute of Seattle													
Olympic College	•	•	•	•	•	•	•	•	•	•	•	•	•
Puget Sound Christian College	•		•	•									
Washington State University	•	•	•	•	•	•	•		•	•	•	•	•
Wenatchee Valley College	•	•	•	•	•	•	•	•	•	•	•	•	•
Whitworth College	•	•	•	•	•	•	•	•		•	•	•	•
West Virginia													
Bluefield State College	•	•	•	•	•	•	•	•	•				
Davis and Elkins College	•	•	•	•	•	•	•	•	•	•		•	
Marshall University	•	•	•	•	•	•	•	•	•			•	
Potomac State College of W. Virginia	•	•	•	•	•	•	•	•	•	•	•	•	•
West Virginia Northern Comm College	•	•	•	•	•	•	•	•	•				

DISABILITIES SERVED

	Speech/Language	Reading	Written Expression	Study Skills	Spelling	Organizational Skills	Math	Fine Motor	Perceptual	ADD without LD	ADD with LD	ADHD without LD	ADHD with LD
West Virginia State College	•	•	•	•	•	•	•	•	•	•	•	•	•
West Virginia University	•	•	•	•	•	•	•	•	•	•	•	•	•
West Virginia Wesleyan College	•	•	•	•	•	•	•	•	•	•		•	
Wisconsin													
Beloit College													
Chippewa Valley Technical College	•	•	•	•	•	•	•	•	•	•	•	•	•
Edgewood College	•	•	•	•	•	•	•	•	•	•		•	
Fox Valley Technical College	•	•	•	•	•	•	•	•	•	•	•	•	•
Gateway Technical College	•	•	•	•	•	•	•	•	•	•	•	•	•
Lawrence University													
Marian College of Fond du Lac	•	•	•	•	•	•	•	•	•	•	•	•	•
Marquette University													
Milwaukee Area Technical College	•	•	•	•	•	•	•	•	•	•	•		•
Moraine Park Technical Institute	•	•	•	•	•	•	•	•	•				
Northeast Wisconsin Technical College	•	•	•	•	•	•	•	•	•	•	•	•	•
Ripon College	•	•	•	•	•	•	•	•	•	•	•	•	•
University of Wisconsin - Milwaukee	•	•	•	•	•	•	•	•	•	•	•		•
University of Wisconsin : Madison	•	•	•	•	•	•	•	•	•	•	•	•	•
University of Wisconsin Ctr: Waukesha	•	•	•	•	•	•	•	•					
University of Wisconsin: LaCrosse	•	•	•	•	•	•	•	•	•	•	•	•	•
University of Wisconsin: Oshkosh	•	•	•	•	•	•	•	•	•	•	•	•	•
University of Wisconsin: Platteville	•	•	•	•	•	•	•	•	•	•	•	•	•
University Wisconsin Center: Baraboo Sa	•	•	•	•	•	•	•	•		•			
University Wisconsin-Center Rock Count		•	•	•	•	•	•	•	•	•			
Viterbo College	•	•	•	•	•	•	•	•	•	•			
Waukesha County Technical College	•	•	•	•	•	•	•	•	•	•	•	•	•
Western Wisconsin Technical College	•	•	•	•	•	•	•	•	•	•			•
Wisconsin Indianhead Technical College	•	•	•	•	•	•	•	•	•	•	•		•
Wyoming													
Casper College	•	•	•	•	•	•	•	•	•	•	•	•	•
Central Wyoming College	•	•	•	•	•	•	•	•	•				
Laramie County Community College	•	•	•	•	•	•	•	•	•	•	•	•	•
Sheridan College	•	•	•	•	•	•	•	•	•	•	•	•	•
University of Wyoming	•	•	•	•	•	•	•	•	•	•	•	•	•

ACADEMIC ACCOMMODATIONS

Institution	Priority Registration	Math Waiver	Foreign Lang. Waiver	Course Substitution	Typist	Reader	Notetaker	Proof Reader	Text on Tape	Taped Handouts	Early Syllabus	Oral	Untimed	Take Home	With Proctor	On Computer	Extended Time	On Tape	Modified	Separate Room	Calculator	Tape Recorder	Word Processor	Priority Seating
Alabama																								
Auburn University at Montgomery	•			•	•	•	•	•	•	•	•	•	•	•	•	•	•	•	•	•	•	•	•	•
Chattahoochee Valley Community College								•	•								•	•			•			
Jacksonville State University				•			•	•	•								•	•		•		•	•	•
Northeast Alabama State Junior College				•				•				•	•				•	•	•	•	•	•	•	•
Troy State University at Dothan				•			•	•				•			•		•	•	•		•	•	•	•
UAB - Horizons Program									•	•	•						•	•	•	•		•	•	•
University of Alabama							•					•					•	•			•	•		
University of Alabama at Birmingham	•			•		•	•	•				•	•				•	•		•	•	•	•	•
Walker State Technical College																								
Alaska																								
Sheldon Jackson College				•	•	•	•					•	•	•			•	•	•	•	•	•	•	•
University of Alaska Anchorage				•			•		•		•				•				•				•	•
University of Alaska Fairbanks				•		•	•	•		•					•		•	•	•	•	•	•	•	•
Arizona																								
Arizona State University									•		•						•	•			•	•	•	
Glendale Community College	•				•	•	•		•	•	•		•	•	•	•	•	•	•		•	•	•	•
Northern Arizona University				•					•		•			•			•		•			•		
Phoenix College							•		•		•			•			•	•	•		•	•		
Pima Community College		•		•	•	•		•	•	•		•					•	•	•		•	•	•	•
University of Arizona		•	•	•		•		•				•			•		•	•	•	•	•	•		
Arkansas																								
Arkansas State University									•		•		•		•	•	•		•		•	•	•	
Harding University	•						•	•	•		•		•		•		•		•		•	•	•	
Henderson State University	•			•	•	•		•		•		•		•		•	•	•	•		•	•	•	•
Southern Arkansas University				•		•	•	•		•		•			•	•	•		•		•	•	•	•
University of Arkansas at Pine Bluff				•			•				•				•				•			•	•	•
University of the Ozarks			•	•	•	•		•	•	•		•		•	•	•	•	•	•		•	•	•	•
California																								
Antelope Valley College	•				•	•	•		•		•		•		•	•	•		•		•	•	•	•
Bakersfield College							•	•	•		•		•				•	•			•	•	•	•
Biola University		•	•				•		•		•		•		•		•		•		•	•	•	•
Butte College							•	•	•		•		•		•		•	•			•	•	•	•
Cabrillo College	•	•	•	•		•		•	•		•		•				•	•	•		•	•	•	•
California State Polytechnic University	•			•		•	•		•		•		•		•	•	•			•	•	•		•
California State University: Bakersfield				•		•	•	•		•		•		•	•	•	•			•	•	•		
California State University: Chico	•			•		•	•		•		•		•				•	•	•		•	•		
California State University: Dominguez Hil		•	•	•		•	•		•		•		•				•	•			•	•		
California State University: Fullerton					•	•	•		•		•		•		•		•	•			•	•		
California State University: Northridge					•		•	•	•		•		•				•	•			•	•	•	
California State University: Sacramento						•	•	•		•		•		•			•	•			•	•	•	
California State University: San Bernardin	•	•		•	•	•	•		•		•		•		•	•	•	•			•	•	•	•
Canada College	•			•		•	•	•		•		•	•			•			•		•	•	•	

855

ACADEMIC ACCOMMODATIONS

	Curriculum				Study Aids							Exams						In Class						
	Priority Registration	Math Waiver	Foreign Lang. Waiver	Course Substitution	Typist	Reader	Notetaker	Proof Reader	Text on Tape	Taped Handouts	Early Syllabus	Oral	Untimed	Take Home	With Proctor	On Computer	Extended Time	On Tape	Modified	Separate Room	Calculator	Tape Recorder	Word Processor	Priority Seating
Cerritos Community College					•	•		•	•									•	•			•	•	•
Chabot College							•		•			•						•	•			•	•	•
Chaffey College							•		•										•				•	•
College of Alameda						•		•	•	•		•		•				•	•		•		•	•
College of San Mateo						•		•	•	•	•	•	•	•	•	•	•	•	•	•	•	•	•	•
College of the Canyons	•					•	•		•				•					•	•	•	•		•	•
College of the Sequoias					•	•		•	•	•		•					•	•	•	•		•	•	•
College of the Siskiyous					•	•		•	•	•		•					•	•	•		•		•	•
Columbia College					•	•		•	•	•		•		•				•	•			•	•	•
Crafton Hills College						•		•	•	•		•		•				•	•			•	•	•
Cuesta College	•					•		•	•	•		•		•				•	•			•	•	•
Cypress College						•		•	•	•								•	•			•	•	
De Anza College												•				•		•	•			•	•	•
East Los Angeles College	•					•		•	•	•		•						•	•		•	•	•	•
El Camino College		•			•	•		•	•	•		•		•				•	•			•	•	•
Evergreen Valley College	•	•			•			•	•	•		•	•	•	•			•	•		•	•	•	•
Feather River College		•	•		•	•		•	•			•						•	•		•	•	•	•
Foothill College	•																						•	•
Fresno City College	•					•	•	•	•	•		•	•	•	•	•	•	•	•		•	•	•	•
Fullerton College	•				•		•	•	•			•						•	•	•	•	•	•	•
Golden Gate University												•	•	•	•	•	•	•	•	•	•	•	•	•
Golden West College	•					•	•		•			•	•		•							•		•
Hartnell College	•				•			•	•				•					•	•			•	•	•
Humboldt State University	•				•		•	•		•		•							•		•		•	•
Imperial Valley College	•				•	•		•	•	•			•					•	•			•	•	•
Kings River Community College		•	•		•	•		•	•	•		•		•				•	•		•		•	•
Laney College					•	•		•	•	•		•		•				•	•		•		•	•
Long Beach City College	•	•			•	•	•	•	•	•		•		•		•		•	•	•	•		•	•
Los Angeles City College	•	•	•		•		•	•	•			•		•		•		•	•	•	•	•	•	•
Los Angeles Harbor College								•	•		•		•					•	•		•		•	•
Los Angeles Mission College	•				•	•		•	•	•		•						•	•		•	•	•	•
Los Angeles Valley College	•							•	•			•		•				•	•			•	•	•
Merced College	•				•		•	•	•			•	•		•			•	•		•	•	•	•
Merritt College					•		•	•	•			•		•	•	•		•	•	•	•	•	•	•
Modesto Junior College							•		•	•		•						•	•			•	•	•
Monterey Peninsula College		•	•		•	•		•	•	•		•		•				•	•		•		•	•
Mount San Jacinto College	•						•	•		•		•		•				•	•		•		•	•
Porterville College						•		•	•			•						•	•		•	•	•	•
Rancho Santiago College	•				•	•	•	•		•		•	•	•	•	•	•	•	•	•	•	•	•	•
Saddleback College							•		•			•		•				•	•		•		•	•
San Diego City College			•		•			•	•	•		•						•	•		•		•	•
San Diego Mesa College	•					•		•	•	•		•		•				•	•		•	•	•	•
San Diego State University	•				•		•		•	•	•							•	•		•		•	•

856

ACADEMIC ACCOMMODATIONS

	Curriculum				Study Aids						Exams							In Class						
	Priority Registration	Math Waiver	Foreign Lang. Waiver	Course Substitution	Typist	Reader	Notetaker	Proof Reader	Text on Tape	Taped Handouts	Early Syllabus	Oral	Untimed	Take Home	With Proctor	On Computer	Extended Time	On Tape	Modified	Separate Room	Calculator	Tape Recorder	Word Processor	Priority Seating
San Francisco State University	•	•	•		•	•	•	•	•	•	•	•	•	•	•	•	•	•	•	•	•	•	•	•
Santa Barbara City College										•					•		•	•	•	•		•	•	•
Santa Monica College								•	•	•		•				•		•	•			•	•	•
Santa Rosa Junior College	•						•		•	•		•	•			•		•	•			•	•	•
Sierra College	•					•		•	•	•		•	•	•	•	•	•	•	•		•	•	•	•
Sonoma State University				•			•	•	•				•	•	•			•	•			•	•	
Stanford University	•		•	•	•	•	•	•	•	•	•	•	•	•	•	•	•	•	•	•	•	•	•	•
Taft College					•	•		•	•	•		•				•	•		•		•	•	•	
University of California: Berkeley	•	•	•	•	•	•	•	•	•	•	•	•	•	•	•	•	•	•	•	•	•	•	•	•
University of California: Davis	•			•	•	•	•	•	•	•			•		•		•	•	•			•	•	•
University of California: Riverside	•		•	•	•	•	•	•	•	•	•	•	•		•	•	•	•	•		•	•	•	•
University of California: San Diego	•		•	•	•	•	•		•	•	•		•		•	•	•	•	•		•	•	•	•
University of California: Santa Barbara	•		•			•	•	•	•	•			•		•	•	•	•	•		•	•	•	•
University of California: Santa Cruz		•	•	•	•	•	•		•	•				•		•	•	•	•			•	•	•
University of Redlands						•		•	•			•	•					•				•		
Ventura College		•	•	•		•	•		•	•		•		•	•	•	•	•	•		•	•	•	•
Victor Valley College										•		•						•				•	•	
West Hills College	•	•	•	•	•	•	•	•	•	•			•	•	•	•	•	•	•	•	•	•	•	•
West Valley College							•	•	•				•					•	•			•	•	•
Colorado																								
Arapahoe Community College		•	•	•		•	•	•			•		•		•			•	•			•	•	•
Colorado Northwestern Community College																						•	•	
Colorado State University	•	•	•	•			•	•	•	•		•			•		•	•	•		•	•	•	•
Community College of Aurora		•		•	•		•	•	•			•			•		•	•	•			•	•	•
Community College of Denver			•	•		•	•	•	•			•	•		•	•	•	•	•	•		•	•	•
Front Range Community College						•	•	•	•		•	•			•		•	•	•		•	•	•	•
Northeastern Junior College			•	•	•	•	•	•	•			•					•	•			•	•	•	•
Pikes Peak Community College		•	•	•	•		•	•	•			•			•			•	•			•	•	•
Pueblo Community College			•	•	•	•		•	•			•	•	•	•	•	•	•	•		•	•	•	•
Red Rocks Community College			•	•		•	•						•		•			•	•			•	•	
Regis College		•	•			•						•					•	•	•		•	•		
University of Colorado at Boulder	•												•	•	•	•	•	•	•		•	•	•	•
University of Denver	•			•			•	•	•			•		•	•	•	•	•	•		•	•	•	•
Western State College of Colorado					•	•	•	•	•			•			•			•	•		•	•	•	•
Connecticut																								
Briarwood College		•	•	•	•		•	•	•	•		•	•	•	•	•	•	•	•		•	•	•	•
Eastern Connecticut State University				•			•	•				•	•					•				•	•	•
Hartford College for Women			•															•	•			•	•	•
Mattatuck Community College	•							•		•			•	•		•	•	•	•			•	•	•
Mitchell College												•			•		•	•		•			•	•
Northwestern Connecticut Community College				•						•								•				•		
Norwalk Community College							•		•			•			•	•		•	•		•	•	•	•
Paier College of Art								•		•													•	

857

ACADEMIC ACCOMMODATIONS

	Curriculum				Study Aids							Exams						In Class						
	Priority Registration	Foreign Lang. Waiver	Math Waiver	Course Substitution	Typist	Reader	Notetaker	Proof Reader	Text on Tape	Early Syllabus	Taped Handouts	Oral	Untimed	Take Home	With Proctor	On Computer	Extended Time	On Tape	Separate Room	Modified	Calculator	Tape Recorder	Word Processor	Priority Seating
South Central Community College			•					•	•	•			•						•				•	•
Thames Valley State Technical College			•			•	•	•	•			•				•	•			•	•	•	•	•
University of Connecticut		•	•				•	•				•				•	•			•	•	•	•	
University of New Haven					•	•	•	•				•	•	•	•	•	•			•	•	•	•	•
Wesleyan University																								
Western Connecticut State University	•		•	•		•	•	•	•		•	•	•	•	•	•	•	•	•	•	•	•	•	•
Yale University			•	•	•		•	•	•		•	•	•	•	•	•	•	•	•	•	•	•	•	•
Delaware																								
Goldey Beacom College			•					•			•	•	•	•	•		•			•			•	
University of Delaware			•			•	•	•				•		•		•	•			•		•	•	•
District of Columbia																								
American University			•					•				•			•		•				•		•	•
Catholic University of America	•		•	•		•	•	•	•	•	•	•	•	•	•	•	•	•	•	•	•	•	•	•
Gallaudet University		•	•									•			•	•			•					
George Washington University		•	•	•			•	•				•			•	•				•		•	•	•
Trinity College				•								•	•	•			•		•					•
Florida																								
Beacon College			•				•	•	•			•			•	•	•		•	•	•	•	•	•
Brevard Community College	•	•	•	•	•		•	•	•			•			•	•	•		•	•	•	•	•	•
Chipola Junior College			•	•		•	•	•			•	•	•	•	•	•		•	•	•		•	•	•
Edison Community College						•	•	•			•					•			•				•	•
Embry-Riddle Aeronautical University	•		•				•				•	•	•	•	•	•	•	•		•			•	•
Florida Agricultural and Mechanical Unive		•	•	•	•		•	•	•			•		•		•	•	•		•		•	•	•
Florida Atlantic University			•			•	•	•			•			•		•	•		•	•		•	•	•
Florida Community College at Jacksonville			•			•					•		•	•		•	•		•	•		•	•	•
Florida State University		•	•	•	•		•	•	•			•		•		•	•		•	•		•	•	•
Gulf Coast Community College	•		•		•	•	•	•	•		•	•	•	•	•	•	•	•	•	•	•	•	•	•
Lake City Community College	•	•	•	•	•		•	•	•		•	•	•	•	•	•	•		•	•	•	•	•	•
Miami-Dade Community College		•		•			•	•			•					•			•	•			•	•
Okaloosa-Walton Junior College			•			•	•			•	•			•	•		•		•	•		•	•	•
Polk Community College			•				•	•	•			•			•	•			•	•		•	•	•
Saint Johns River Community College		•	•	•							•					•			•		•		•	
Santa Fe Community College		•	•	•			•	•	•			•				•	•		•	•		•	•	•
Seminole Community College			•			•	•	•			•				•	•			•	•		•	•	•
Tallahassee Community College	•	•	•	•		•	•	•	•			•	•	•		•	•		•	•		•	•	•
University of Tampa																								
Georgia																								
Brenau Women's College	•					•		•	•			•			•	•	•		•	•	•	•	•	•
Brunswick College								•				•					•		•			•	•	•
Clayton State College			•			•		•	•			•	•	•	•	•	•		•			•	•	•
DeKalb College	•		•	•			•	•	•			•			•	•	•		•	•	•	•	•	•
East Georgia College																			•				•	
Emory University	•				•	•	•	•	•	•			•	•		•	•	•	•	•		•	•	•

ACADEMIC ACCOMMODATIONS

	Curriculum				Study Aids							Exams									In Class			
	Priority Registration	Math Waiver	Foreign Lang. Waiver	Course Substitution	Typist	Notetaker	Reader	Proof Reader	Text on Tape	Taped Handouts	Early Syllabus	Oral	Untimed	Take Home	With Proctor	On Computer	Extended Time	On Tape	Modified	Separate Room	Calculator	Tape Recorder	Word Processor	Priority Seating
Georgia College										•		•					•	•			•	•		•
Georgia Institute of Technology	•					•	•	•	•	•	•	•	•	•	•	•	•	•	•	•	•	•	•	•
Georgia Southern University			•			•	•		•			•	•				•	•	•		•	•	•	
Georgia State University			•			•	•		•	•		•			•		•	•	•		•	•	•	
Mercer University												•		•			•		•					
Reinhardt College	•					•	•	•		•		•				•	•	•			•	•	•	
South Georgia College							•					•					•				•	•		
Southern College of Technology																	•				•	•		
University of Georgia						•	•	•		•		•		•			•	•		•		•	•	•
Valdosta State College	•					•	•	•	•		•	•	•	•	•	•	•	•		•	•	•	•	•
West Georgia College	•			•		•	•		•	•		•				•	•	•	•	•	•	•	•	•
Hawaii																								
Brigham Young University-Hawaii			•	•		•	•	•	•			•		•			•	•		•		•	•	
University of Hawaii: Kapiolani Community						•	•	•	•			•					•	•		•		•	•	
University of Hawaii: Leeward Community	•			•		•	•	•	•			•		•	•		•	•	•		•	•	•	•
Idaho																								
Albertson College							•					•					•	•		•		•	•	•
Boise Bible College																								
University of Idaho							•	•				•	•				•	•	•		•	•	•	•
Illinois																								
Barat College					•		•	•	•			•		•			•	•		•	•	•	•	•
Bradley University			•		•								•			•	•				•	•	•	
City Colleges of Chicago: Harold Washington					•	•					•		•		•		•			•		•	•	•
City Colleges of Chicago: Harry S. Truman	•	•	•		•	•	•		•		•		•	•		•	•					•	•	•
DePaul University	•	•	•	•		•	•	•	•	•		•	•		•	•	•	•	•	•	•	•	•	
Elgin Community College		•	•	•		•		•		•	•		•	•	•	•	•	•	•	•	•	•		•
Governors State University						•		•			•					•						•	•	
Highland Community College			•	•	•	•	•	•	•		•	•		•	•	•	•	•	•	•	•	•	•	•
Illinois Central College		•		•		•	•	•		•				•	•		•		•	•	•	•	
Illinois State University	•			•	•	•	•		•			•					•	•		•	•	•	
Kendall College		•		•							•			•	•				•	•	
Lake Land College		•		•	•	•	•	•	•	•		•	•		•	•	•	•	•	•	•	•	•	•
Lincoln College																								
Moraine Valley Community College			•	•		•	•		•			•	•		•		•	•			•	•	•	
National-Louis University	•			•	•	•	•	•	•	•	•	•	•	•	•	•	•	•	•	•	•	•	•	•
Northern Illinois University	•		•	•	•	•	•	•	•			•			•		•	•		•	•	•	•	•
Oakton Community College						•						•					•				•	•	•	
Roosevelt University						•	•	•			•		•			•			•					
School of the Art Institute of Chicago			•			•	•	•			•					•	•				•	•	
Shawnee College					•	•	•		•			•	•		•	•	•	•	•	•	•	•	•	•
Shimer College												•	•	•			•				•		•	
Southeastern Illinois College						•	•		•								•					•		•
Southern Illinois University at Carbondale		•				•	•	•	•			•			•		•			•		•	

859

	Curriculum				Study Aids					Exams								In Class						
	Priority Registration	Math Waiver	Foreign Lang. Waiver	Course Substitution	Typist	Reader	Notetaker	Proof Reader	Text on Tape	Early Syllabus	Taped Handouts	Oral	Untimed	Take Home	With Proctor	On Computer	Extended Time	On Tape	Modified	Separate Room	Calculator	Tape Recorder	Word Processor	Priority Seating
Southern Illinois University at Edwardsville	•					•	•	•	•	•	•	•			•	•	•	•	•	•		•	•	•
Triton College							•	•	•		•				•			•	•			•	•	•
Waubonsee Community College						•		•	•	•		•					•	•	•			•	•	•
Western Illinois University											•								•				•	
William Rainey Harper College				•			•	•		•		•			•		•	•	•		•	•	•	
Indiana																								
Anderson University				•		•	•	•	•	•		•	•		•	•		•	•		•	•	•	•
Indiana Institute of Technology					•			•			•		•	•	•	•		•	•			•	•	
Indiana University Bloomington		•	•	•				•	•				•			•		•		•		•	•	
Indiana University East				•	•	•	•	•	•		•		•	•	•	•		•	•		•	•	•	
Indiana University Northwest		•	•	•			•	•			•		•		•	•		•	•		•	•	•	
Indiana University Purdue Univeristy at In		•	•		•	•	•	•	•	•	•	•	•	•	•	•	•	•	•	•	•	•	•	
Indiana Vocational Technical College Cer					•			•			•				•	•			•	•	•	•	
Indiana Vocational Technical College: Ea	•			•			•		•	•		•	•	•	•	•	•	•	•	•	•	•	•	•
Indiana Vocational Technical College: No	•				•		•		•			•	•	•	•	•	•	•	•	•	•	•	•	•
Indiana Vocational Technical College: Nc							•						•	•		•	•	•	•		•	•	•	•
Indiana Vocational Technical College: So			•			•	•	•	•		•	•	•	•	•	•			•		•	•	•	
Indiana Vocational Technical College: Wt	•						•					•		•		•	•	•	•		•	•	•	•
Indiana Vocational Technical College Koke					•						•		•		•	•	•	•	•		•	•	•	
Indiana Wesleyan University				•				•					•			•					•	•	•	•
Manchester College					•	•	•	•	•		•	•	•		•	•		•	•		•	•	•	•
Purdue University		•	•	•		•	•	•	•		•		•	•	•	•		•	•		•	•	•	
University of Evansville				•			•	•		•	•		•		•			•		•		•	•	•
University of Indianapolis	•		•	•	•	•	•	•	•	•		•	•	•	•	•		•	•		•	•	•	•
University of Southern Indiana				•		•		•	•		•				•			•	•		•	•	•	•
Vincennes University											•	•		•	•	•	•	•	•	•	•	•	•	•
Iowa																								
Coe College	•	•	•		•	•			•	•		•		•	•		•	•		•	•	•	•	•
Cornell College		•	•		•	•		•	•		•		•		•			•		•		•	•	
Graceland College					•			•	•		•				•		•			•	•	•	•	•
Grand View College				•	•	•	•	•	•		•				•		•		•	•	•	•	•	
Hawkeye Institute of Technology						•		•		•	•		•		•			•		•	•	•	•	
Indian Hills Community College					•	•	•	•		•	•		•	•		•	•		•	•	•	•	•	•
Iowa Central Community College					•	•	•	•		•				•		•	•		•	•		•	•	
Iowa State University of Science and Tec		•	•	•				•			•		•	•		•		•		•		•	•	
Loras College		•			•		•	•	•		•		•		•	•		•	•		•	•	•	
Scott Community College	•						•	•	•		•	•		•	•		•	•	•	•	•	•	•	•
Southeastern Community College: North (				•		•	•	•		•			•						•				•	
Southwestern Community College		•	•	•			•			•				•					•				•	
University of Iowa	•	•	•	•	•	•	•	•		•		•		•	•	•	•	•	•	•	•	•	•	•
University of Northern Iowa	•				•			•		•				•				•	•	•	•	•	•	
Waldorf College				•	•	•		•	•	•		•		•			•	•	•	•	•	•	•	•
Kansas																								

ACADEMIC ACCOMMODATIONS

	Curriculum				Study Aids							Exams									In Class			
	Priority Registration	Math Waiver	Foreign Lang. Waiver	Course Substitution	Typist	Reader	Notetaker	Proof Reader	Text on Tape	Early Syllabus	Taped Handouts	Oral	Unlimited	Take Home	With Proctor	On Computer	Extended Time	On Tape	Modified	Separate Room	Calculator	Tape Recorder	Word Processor	Priority Seating
Barton Community College										•		•					•		•			•	•	•
Cowley County Community College									•		•	•			•		•		•			•	•	•
Emporia State University			•	•					•		•	•			•	•		•	•	•		•	•	•
Hutchinson Community College				•	•	•	•		•		•	•				•		•		•		•	•	•
Kansas City Kansas Community College			•	•			•		•		•	•			•	•	•	•	•		•	•	•	•
Kansas State University					•		•	•	•		•	•			•		•	•	•		•	•	•	•
Pittsburg State University					•			•									•					•		•
University of Kansas				•	•	•	•		•		•	•			•		•	•		•			•	•
Wichita State University		•	•		•		•		•		•	•				•		•	•		•	•	•	
Kentucky																								
Cumberland College		•	•									•												
Eastern Kentucky University							•		•		•	•					•		•			•		
Elizabethtown Community College			•						•		•	•		•			•		•			•		
Lexington Community College		•	•	•		•	•	•	•	•	•	•	•	•	•		•	•	•		•	•	•	•
Lindsey Wilson College									•			•	•		•			•	•		•	•	•	
Murray State University	•					•		•	•				•		•		•	•		•		•	•	•
Prestonsburg Community College					•	•	•	•	•	•	•	•	•	•	•	•	•	•	•		•	•	•	•
Thomas More College	•		•	•	•	•	•	•	•	•	•	•	•	•	•	•	•	•	•		•	•	•	•
University of Kentucky	•		•			•			•		•	•	•	•	•	•	•	•	•	•		•	•	•
Louisiana																								
Louisiana College			•		•	•	•	•		•	•	•	•	•	•		•	•	•		•	•	•	
Louisiana State University Agricultural an	•		•	•	•	•		•		•		•	•	•	•	•	•	•	•		•	•	•	•
Louisiana State University at Alexandria																						•		
University of Southwestern Louisiana		•	•	•			•		•		•				•			•				•	•	
Maine																								
Bowdoin College		•					•		•		•				•		•		•			•	•	
Colby College											•		•		•		•		•			•	•	
Southern Maine Technical College							•		•	•	•	•	•		•	•	•		•		•	•	•	•
St. Joseph's College																								
Unity College		•		•			•	•	•		•		•		•		•	•				•	•	
University of Maine		•	•	•			•		•		•	•		•	•	•	•	•	•		•	•	•	
University of Maine at Machias							•		•			•					•					•	•	
University of New England			•		•		•	•	•		•	•	•	•	•	•	•	•	•	•	•	•	•	•
University of Southern Maine			•	•		•	•	•		•		•			•		•	•			•	•	•	
Maryland																								
Charles County Community College							•	•	•		•		•	•	•	•	•	•	•	•	•	•	•	•
Chesapeake College																	•							
Frostburg State University		•	•	•		•	•		•		•			•		•	•	•		•		•	•	•
Hagerstown Junior College			•	•		•		•		•		•	•		•	•	•	•	•		•	•	•	
Howard Community College	•		•			•	•		•	•	•	•		•	•	•	•	•	•	•	•	•	•	
Johns Hopkins University			•	•		•	•	•		•	•	•	•	•	•	•			•	•		•	•	•
Montgomery Community College: Rockvill			•	•		•	•		•			•	•	•	•	•		•	•		•	•	•	
Towson State University				•	•		•		•		•	•			•			•			•	•	•	•

ACADEMIC ACCOMMODATIONS

	Curriculum				Study Aids							Exams									In Class			
	Priority Registration	Math Waiver	Foreign Lang. Waiver	Course Substitution	Typist	Reader	Notetaker	Proof Reader	Text on Tape	Early Syllabus	Taped Handouts	Oral	Untimed	Take Home	With Proctor	On Computer	Extended Time	On Tape	Modified	Separate Room	Calculator	Tape Recorder	Word Processor	Priority Seating
University of Maryland: Eastern Shore		•	•	•			•	•				•			•			•	•		•		•	•	•
Western Maryland College	•		•	•		•	•	•	•	•		•	•	•	•		•	•	•	•	•	•	•	•
Wor-Wic Tech Community College						•	•		•			•	•		•			•	•		•	•	•	•
Massachusetts																								
American International College			•				•	•		•		•		•			•	•		•		•	•	
Anna Maria College for Men & Women			•	•			•		•		•	•			•			•		•	•		•	•
Aquinas College at Newton				•			•	•		•	•	•	•	•	•		•	•		•	•	•	•	•
Bentley College	•			•			•		•	•		•	•	•	•	•		•	•	•	•	•	•	•
Boston College			•		•		•	•		•	•		•	•	•	•	•	•	•	•	•	•	•	•
Boston University				•	•	•	•	•		•		•		•	•	•	•	•	•	•	•	•	•	•
Bradford College							•	•					•		•		•		•		•	•	•	
Brandeis University		•	•	•				•		•	•	•	•	•	•		•	•		•	•	•	•	•
Bridgewater State College		•	•	•	•		•	•	•		•	•		•			•	•		•	•	•	•	
Bristol Community College				•			•	•		•		•	•		•		•	•		•		•		
Cape Cod Community College												•					•	•	•	•	•		•	
Clark University	•			•		•	•	•			•		•	•		•	•		•		•	•	•	•
Curry College			•						•	•			•	•			•	•		•	•		•	
Dean Junior College					•		•					•			•			•	•		•	•	•	
Endicott College												•	•		•	•		•	•		•	•		•
Gordon College	•		•	•	•	•	•	•	•	•	•	•	•	•	•	•	•	•	•	•	•	•	•	•
Harvard University			•				•	•		•		•		•				•		•			•	•
Lesley College-Threshold							•		•			•					•	•		•			•	•
Massachusetts Bay Community College							•		•				•			•	•	•	•	•	•	•	•	•
Massachusetts College of Art							•					•			•			•	•		•		•	•
Massachusetts Institute of Technology						•		•	•		•		•		•			•	•		•		•	
Massasoit Community College								•		•		•						•					•	•
Merrimack College								•							•			•				•		
Middlesex Community College				•		•	•	•	•		•	•	•	•	•		•	•		•	•	•	•	•
Mount Holyoke College			•	•		•	•	•	•	•	•	•	•	•	•		•	•		•	•	•	•	•
Mount Ida College	•	•	•	•	•		•	•	•		•	•			•			•	•		•	•	•	•
Mount Wachusett Community College				•			•	•		•		•		•	•		•	•			•	•	•	•
North Adams State College	•			•		•		•	•		•		•		•	•		•	•		•	•	•	•
Northeastern University			•	•	•		•	•	•	•		•	•	•	•	•	•	•	•	•	•	•	•	•
Pine Manor College									•						•			•	•		•	•	•	•
Simmons College			•	•				•		•		•			•			•	•		•	•	•	
Smith College	•						•	•	•	•	•	•			•			•	•	•	•	•	•	•
Springfield Technical Community College												•	•	•	•	•	•	•	•	•	•	•	•	
Stonehill College			•				•				•		•			•	•		•		•	•		
Tufts University		•	•	•	•		•	•	•		•		•		•	•		•			•		•	
University of Massachusetts - Dartmouth	•		•			•	•	•	•	•		•	•		•		•	•	•	•	•		•	•
University of Massachusetts at Amherst		•	•	•			•	•		•		•		•			•	•		•		•	•	•
University of Massachusetts at Boston		•	•	•	•		•	•		•		•		•			•	•		•		•	•	•
Wellesley College							•	•											•			•	•	•

ACADEMIC ACCOMMODATIONS

	Curriculum				Study Aids							Exams									In Class			
	Priority Registration	Math Waiver	Foreign Lang. Waiver	Course Substitution	Typist	Reader	Notetaker	Proof Reader	Text on Tape	Taped Handouts	Early Syllabus	Oral	Untimed	Take Home	With Proctor	On Computer	Extended Time	On Tape	Modified	Separate Room	Calculator	Tape Recorder	Word Processor	Priority Seating
Wheaton College				•					•									•	•	•		•	•	•	•
Wheelock College	•								•					•	•	•	•	•			•	•	•	•
Worcester Polytechnic Institute																		•		•		•		
Michigan																								
Adrian College				•	•	•	•	•	•			•	•		•		•		•	•	•	•		•	•
Albion College			•				•		•			•		•		•		•				•		
Alma College			•				•	•	•			•	•	•	•	•	•	•		•		•	•	•
Aquinas College							•					•	•			•		•		•	•		•	
Central Michigan University							•		•			•				•		•	•	•			•	•
Charles Stewart Mott Community College				•		•	•		•			•				•		•	•	•	•	•	•	•
Delta College							•	•	•			•				•		•	•	•		•	•	•
Detroit College of Business				•								•			•			•	•			•	•	•
Glen Oaks Community College				•	•		•	•	•			•				•		•	•			•	•	•
Grand Valley State University					•		•	•	•			•		•		•		•	•			•	•	•
Henry Ford Community College	•			•	•	•	•	•	•	•		•	•	•	•	•	•	•	•	•	•	•	•	•
Jackson Community College				•	•		•	•	•			•				•		•	•	•	•	•	•	•
Kalamazoo College				•					•						•	•			•	•	•	•	•	•
Kellogg Community College				•	•	•	•	•			•		•	•	•	•	•	•	•			•	•	•
Lake Michigan College				•		•	•				•			•		•	•					•	•	
Lake Superior State University							•					•				•		•				•		
Lansing Community College				•			•		•			•				•		•				•		
Mercy College of Detroit			•	•	•		•	•					•		•	•		•			•	•		
Michigan Technological University	•			•	•		•		•			•		•		•		•	•	•	•	•	•	
Mid Michigan Community College				•	•		•	•	•			•	•	•		•		•	•	•		•	•	
Montcalm Community College		•	•	•	•	•	•	•	•			•		•		•	•	•	•	•	•	•	•	•
Northern Michigan University				•	•	•	•		•	•		•	•		•	•	•	•	•	•	•	•	•	•
Oakland Community College				•	•	•	•	•		•	•	•	•		•	•				•	•	•	•	•
Schoolcraft College				•	•		•		•	•	•	•	•		•	•	•	•	•	•	•	•	•	•
Spring Arbor College				•	•		•		•					•		•			•					•
St. Mary's College												•				•		•		•		•		•
Suomi College	•			•			•	•	•	•		•	•	•	•	•	•	•	•	•	•	•	•	•
University of Michigan			•						•			•				•			•			•	•	
University of Michigan: Flint				•	•		•		•							•		•	•			•	•	
Washtenaw Community College							•		•			•				•		•				•		
Wayne State University	•	•	•		•	•	•		•			•				•		•	•			•		
Western Michigan University	•						•	•	•	•		•				•		•	•	•		•	•	
Minnesota																								
Augsburg College		•	•	•	•	•	•	•	•			•			•	•	•	•	•		•		•	•
College of St. Catherine: St. Catherine Ca		•	•	•								•			•			•	•	•		•	•	•
Concordia College: St. Paul									•							•		•	•	•		•	•	•
Hamline University					•		•		•			•			•			•		•		•		
Hibbing Community College					•	•	•		•	•	•	•				•	•	•	•	•	•	•	•	•
Itasca Community College: Arrowhead	•			•	•	•	•	•	•	•	•	•			•		•	•	•	•	•	•	•	•

ACADEMIC ACCOMMODATIONS

	Curriculum				Study Aids							Exams								In Class				
	Priority Registration	Math Waiver	Foreign Lang. Waiver	Course Substitution	Typist	Reader	Proof Reader	Notetaker	Text on Tape	Taped Handouts	Early Syllabus	Oral	Untimed	Take Home	With Proctor	On Computer	Extended Time	On Tape	Modified	Separate Room	Calculator	Tape Recorder	Word Processor	Priority Seating
Lakewood Community College		•		•			•			•			•		•		•	•		•		•	•	•
Moorhead State University	•	•	•	•		•	•			•	•	•	•	•	•	•	•		•	•	•	•	•	•
Rochester Community College	•					•	•	•	•			•			•	•		•	•	•	•	•	•	
Saint Cloud State University	•								•	•			•	•				•				•	•	•
Southwest State University	•	•	•	•	•	•		•	•	•	•	•	•	•	•		•	•	•	•	•	•	•	•
St. Cloud State University	•						•	•				•	•			•		•	•	•		
St. John's University	•	•	•	•					•			•	•	•	•	•	•	•	•			•	•	•
St. Mary's Campus of the College of St. C								•			•	•	•	•	•	•	•		•		
St. Olaf College					•	•		•	•		•	•	•	•	•	•		•	•	•	
University of Minnesota: Duluth			•	•	•	•	•		•			•	•	•	•	•	•	•	•	•	
University of Minnesota: Morris				•	•	•	•	•	•			•	•	•	•	•	•	•	•	•	
University of Minnesota: Crookston	•		•			•	•	•			•	•		•	•	•	•	•	•		•
Wilmar Community College	•				•		•		•			•		•	•	•	•	•	•	•	
Worthington Community College		•		•		•	•	•	•	•	•	•		•	•	•	•	•	•		
Mississippi																								
Hinds Community College	•		•			•	•	•			•			•	•		•		•	•	•	
University of Mississippi	•		•			•					•			•	•		•		•	•	•	•
Missouri																								
Central Missouri State University		•					•	•			•		•		•	•			•	•	•	
Evangel College		•					•	•			•			•				•	
Jefferson College		•	•	•	•	•	•	•	•	•	•	•	•	•	•	•	•	•	•	•	•	•
Kansas City Art Institute			•	•	•				•		•				•		•	•
Longview Community College	•			•	•	•	•	•			•	•	•	•	•	•	•	•	•	•	•
Maple Woods Community College				•						•	•	•	•	•	•	•	•
Rockhurst College								•									
Southwest Baptist University		•	•	•	•						•		•		•	•		•	•	•	
St. Louis Community College at Florissant			•	•	•	•	•	•		•	•	•	•	•	•	•	•	•	•	•	•
St. Louis Community College at Forest Pa	•		•			•	•	•		•	•		•	•	•	•	•	•	•	•	•
St. Louis University				•		•		•			•	•	•		•	•	•	•	•	•	•
University of Missouri: Columbia				•		•	•			•		•	•		•	•	•
University of Missouri: Rolla					•		•			•		•	•	•	•	•	•	•
Washington University					•	•	•	•			•	•	•	•	•	•	•	•	•	•
Westminster College					•	•	•			•		•	•	•	•	•	•
Montana																								
Flathead Valley Community College			•		•	•		•			•	•	•	•	•	•	•	•	
Montana College of Mineral Science			•	•		•			•	•	•	•	•
Northern Montana College				•	•		•				•	•	•	
Rocky Mountain College		•	•		•	•	•	•			•	•	•	•	•	•	•	•	•
Western Montana College University of M			•	•	•	•	•	•			•	•	•	•	•	•	•	•	•	•
Nebraska																								
Dana College	•	•	•		•	•	•	•	•		•			•		•	•	•	•	•
Southeast Community College: Beatrice C			•				•			•	•	•		•	•	•	•
Southeast Community College: Lincoln C		•		•		•	•		•		•	•	•	•	•	•	•	•	•

864

ACADEMIC ACCOMMODATIONS

Column groups: **Curriculum** (Priority Registration, Math Waiver, Foreign Lang. Waiver, Course Substitution) · **Study Aids** (Typist, Notetaker, Reader, Proof Reader, Text on Tape, Taped Handouts) · **Exams** (Early Syllabus, Oral, Untimed, Take Home, With Proctor, On Computer, Extended Time) · **In Class** (On Tape, Modified, Separate Room, Calculator, Tape Recorder, Word Processor, Priority Seating)

Institution	Priority Registration	Math Waiver	Foreign Lang. Waiver	Course Substitution	Typist	Notetaker	Reader	Proof Reader	Text on Tape	Taped Handouts	Early Syllabus	Oral	Untimed	Take Home	With Proctor	On Computer	Extended Time	On Tape	Modified	Separate Room	Calculator	Tape Recorder	Word Processor	Priority Seating
Southeast Community College: Milford							•		•		•	•		•		•	•	•	•		•	•	•	•
Union College			•	•		•	•	•		•		•		•	•		•	•		•		•	•	•
Western Nebraska Community College: S						•	•	•		•		•			•		•	•		•		•	•	•
Nevada																								
Truckee Meadows Community College			•			•		•									•					•		
University of Nevada: Las Vegas	•				•	•	•	•		•		•			•		•	•		•		•	•	
University of Nevada: Reno						•	•	•		•			•		•		•	•		•		•	•	
New Hampshire																								
Dartmouth College			•			•									•	•			•	•	•			
Keene State College	•		•			•	•	•		•		•	•		•	•		•	•	•	•			
New England College		•	•	•		•	•	•	•		•		•	•	•	•	•	•	•	•	•			
New Hampshire College		•	•						•	•		•	•		•	•	•	•						
New Hampshire Technical College	•				•	•	•	•	•	•	•	•		•	•	•	•	•	•	•	•	•	•	
New Hampshire Vocational-Technical								•	•	•	•	•	•	•	•	•	•	•	•	•	•			
New Hampshire Vocational-Technical Col				•	•	•	•		•	•		•	•	•	•	•	•	•	•	•	•			
University of New Hampshire			•			•		•			•		•		•	•		•	•	•				
New Jersey																								
Caldwell College						•	•			•		•	•	•		•		•	•		•			
County College of Morris	•				•	•	•	•		•	•	•	•	•	•	•	•	•	•	•	•	•	•	•
Fairleigh Dickinson University	•						•			•	•		•	•		•	•		•	•		•	•	
Georgian Court College	•				•	•	•	•	•	•	•	•	•	•	•	•	•	•	•	•	•		•	
Gloucester County College			•	•	•	•	•	•		•		•	•		•	•		•	•	•	•			
Jersey City State College						•			•		•		•	•		•	•		•	•	•			
Middlesex County College						•	•		•		•	•		•	•		•	•	•	•				
New Jersey Institute of Technology																								
Ocean County College		•	•			•	•	•		•		•	•	•		•	•		•	•				
William Paterson College of New Jersey		•	•			•		•		•		•		•		•		•	•					
New Mexico																								
Albuquerque Technical-Vocational Institu		•		•		•		•		•		•	•		•	•		•	•	•	•			
College of Santa Fe	•	•		•	•	•	•	•		•	•	•	•		•	•	•	•	•	•	•		•	
Eastern New Mexico University: Roswell											•	•							•					
Institute of American Indian Arts																								
San Juan College	•							•		•	•	•	•		•		•	•		•				
Santa Fe Community College						•	•		•		•		•	•	•	•	•	•	•				
University of New Mexico					•	•	•		•			•			•		•	•		•				
New York																								
Adelphi University	•				•	•	•	•	•		•		•		•	•	•	•		•	•	•	•	
Broome Community College	•	•	•	•	•	•	•	•		•	•	•	•	•	•	•	•	•	•	•	•	•		
Cazenovia College				•					•		•	•		•		•	•		•	•	•		•	
City University New York: Brooklyn Colleg	•		•	•	•	•	•	•	•		•	•		•	•	•	•		•	•	•	•	•	•
City University of New York: College of S			•	•		•	•	•		•		•	•		•	•		•	•		•	•	•	•
City University of New York: City College		•	•			•		•		•		•			•		•		•	•			•	•
City University of New York: Borough of N																								

865

ACADEMIC ACCOMMODATIONS

Institution	Priority Registration	Math Waiver	Foreign Lang. Waiver	Course Substitution	Typist	Reader	Notetaker	Proof Reader	Text on Tape	Early Syllabus	Taped Handouts	Oral	Untimed	Take Home	With Proctor	On Computer	Extended Time	On Tape	Modified	Separate Room	Calculator	Tape Recorder	Word Processor	Priority Seating
City University of New York: John Jay-Cri	•		•		•		•		•		•		•	•		•	•	•		•	•	•	•	
City University of New York: La Guardia Cc				•		•	•	•			•		•			•	•			•	•	•		
Clinton Community College	•		•	•	•	•	•	•	•				•	•	•	•	•	•		•		•	•	•
Community College of the Finger Lakes						•	•	•								•	•		•		•	•	•	
Cornell University	•		•		•	•	•	•	•		•		•		•	•		•		•	•	•	•	•
D'Youville College					•	•	•	•			•				•	•		•	•	•	•			
Dowling College																								
Dutchess Community College		•	•	•			•		•			•				•	•		•	•	•			
Eugene Lang College																								
Fashion Institute of Technology					•	•	•	•			•	•			•	•		•	•	•	•		•	
Fordham University		•		•			•						•	•		•	•		•	•	•		•	
Fulton-Montgomery Community College	•	•	•	•	•	•	•	•	•	•		•	•	•	•	•	•		•	•	•	•		•
Herkimer County Community College	•	•		•	•		•	•			•	•	•	•	•	•	•	•	•	•	•	•		•
Hofstra University		•		•			•		•		•		•	•		•	•		•	•	•	•		
Houghton College		•	•				•	•			•		•	•	•	•	•		•	•	•			
Hudson Valley Community College					•		•	•	•		•		•		•	•		•	•	•		•	•	
Hunter College	•	•		•		•	•				•	•		•	•	•	•	•	•	•	•	•	•	•
Iona College - Seton School	•	•	•	•	•	•	•	•	•	•	•	•	•	•	•	•	•	•	•	•	•	•	•	•
Jefferson Community College					•		•	•	•		•		•	•	•	•	•		•		•	•	•	
Julliard School																								
Keuka College				•							•		•		•	•	•		•		•		•	
Long Island University: C.W. Post Campu		•	•			•	•	•	•				•	•	•	•	•		•	•	•	•	•	
Long Island University: Southampton Car																	•							
Manhattan School of Music								•			•				•		•		•		•			
Marist College					•	•	•	•								•	•		•		•	•	•	
Medaille College				•	•	•	•			•	•	•	•	•	•			•	•	•	•	•		•
Mercy College			•			•	•	•			•				•	•		•	•	•	•			
Mohawk Valley Community College	•	•	•	•	•	•	•	•		•	•	•	•	•	•	•	•	•	•	•	•	•	•	•
Molloy College		•	•	•	•	•	•			•		•	•	•		•	•	•	•	•	•			
Nassau Community College		•		•		•	•	•			•	•		•	•		•		•	•	•			
New York Institute of Technology	•	•	•	•	•	•	•	•		•	•	•	•	•	•	•	•	•	•	•	•	•	•	
New York University		•	•	•		•			•					•	•		•	•		•	•	•	•	•
Niagara University								•							•	•			•	•	•			
Onondaga Community College				•		•	•	•			•		•	•		•	•	•	•		•	•		
Pace University: College of White Plain																								
Para-Educator Center for Young Adults																								
Paul Smith's College				•	•		•	•	•		•			•	•	•	•		•		•		•	
Rochester Institute of Technology			•		•		•	•	•		•		•		•	•		•	•	•		•	•	
Rockland Community College		•		•	•		•	•	•		•		•	•		•	•	•	•		•	•	•	
Schenectady County Community College							•									•	•		•		•	•	•	
School of Visual Arts																								
Skidmore College				•	•	•	•		•				•		•			•	•		•	•	•	•
St. Bonaventure University			•	•		•		•	•			•	•		•	•	•		•	•	•	•	•	•

ACADEMIC ACCOMMODATIONS

Institution	Priority Registration	Math Waiver	Foreign Lang. Waiver	Course Substitution	Typist	Reader	Notetaker	Proof Reader	Text on Tape	Early Syllabus	Taped Handouts	Oral	Untimed	Take Home	With Proctor	On Computer	Extended Time	On Tape	Modified	Separate Room	Calculator	Tape Recorder	Word Processor	Priority Seating
St. Lawrence University	•			•		•			•	•		•			•		•	•	•	•	•	•	•	•
St. Thomas Aquinas College	•					•	•	•	•			•	•		•		•	•	•	•				
State University of New York at Albany	•			•		•	•	•	•	•	•		•			•	•	•	•	•	•		•	
State University of New York at Binghamto			•	•	•	•	•	•	•	•	•		•		•		•	•	•	•	•		•	
State University of New York at Buffalo	•					•	•						•			•		•	•	•		•		
State University of New York at Stony Bro		•	•		•		•	•	•	•			•			•		•	•	•		•		
State University of New York College at C		•	•	•	•		•	•		•			•	•		•		•	•	•		•		
State University of New York College at F	•	•		•	•	•	•	•	•			•	•	•	•	•	•	•	•	•	•	•	•	•
State University of New York College of E							•	•	•			•			•		•	•	•		•	•		
State University of New York College of T				•	•	•			•	•	•		•			•		•	•	•		•		
State University of New York College of T.						•	•	•				•			•		•	•	•		•	•		
State University of New York College of T.						•	•	•				•	•	•	•	•	•	•	•		•	•		
Syracuse University		•	•	•	•		•			•			•		•	•	•	•	•		•		•	
Ulster County Community College				•	•	•	•		•			•			•		•	•	•		•	•	•	•
Utica College of Syracuse University				•	•				•	•		•			•		•	•	•		•	•	•	
Westchester Community College														•										
North Carolina																								
Appalachian State University	•						•		•			•			•		•	•			•	•	•	
Blue Ridge Community College						•	•		•			•	•	•	•		•	•	•		•	•	•	•
Caldwell Community College and Technic				•	•	•	•	•	•			•			•		•	•	•	•	•	•		
Catawba Valley Community College				•	•	•	•	•				•	•	•	•		•	•	•	•	•	•	•	
Central Piedmont Community College	•	•	•	•		•	•	•	•		•	•	•	•	•	•	•	•	•	•	•	•		•
Craven Community College				•			•		•			•					•	•	•		•	•	•	•
Davidson College		•	•	•		•	•	•	•	•	•	•			•		•	•	•	•	•		•	
Davidson County Community College		•	•	•		•	•		•						•						•	•	•	
East Carolina University			•				•	•	•			•			•		•	•	•		•	•	•	•
Guilford Technical Community College																	•	•			•	•	•	
Halifax Community College		•		•		•	•		•			•			•		•	•	•	•	•	•	•	•
Isothermal Community College					•	•	•	•	•	•		•			•		•	•	•		•	•	•	•
Johnston Community College									•						•									
McDowell Technical Community College				•	•		•	•	•			•	•		•		•	•	•		•	•	•	
North Carolina State University	•					•	•	•	•			•			•		•	•	•		•	•	•	•
Richmond Community College				•		•	•					•		•			•	•	•	•		•	•	•
Surry Community College				•																				
University of North Carolina: Greensboro				•		•			•	•	•		•			•		•	•		•	•	•	
University of North Carolina: Wilmington			•	•	•		•	•	•			•			•		•	•	•		•	•	•	
Wake Forest University				•					•	•	•		•			•		•	•		•	•	•	
Wilkes Community College						•	•	•	•			•	•	•	•		•	•	•		•	•	•	•
Wingate College			•	•					•				•			•		•	•		•	•		
North Dakota																								
Dickinson State University	•					•	•		•	•		•			•		•	•			•	•		
Mayville State University							•	•					•			•		•	•		•	•	•	
North Dakota State College of Science				•	•		•	•	•	•		•			•		•	•		•	•	•	•	•

867

ACADEMIC ACCOMMODATIONS

	Curriculum				Study Aids							Exams									In Class			
	Priority Registration	Math Waiver	Foreign Lang. Waiver	Course Substitution	Typist	Reader	Notetaker	Proof Reader	Text on Tape	Taped Handouts	Early Syllabus	Oral	Untimed	Take Home	With Proctor	On Computer	Extended Time	On Tape	Modified	Separate Room	Calculator	Tape Recorder	Word Processor	Priority Seating
North Dakota State University							•		•	•		•					•		•	•	•		•	•	•
North Dakota State University: Bottineau					•	•	•	•	•			•							•	•			•	•	•
Ohio																								
Bowling Green State University	•			•		•			•		•						•		•	•		•	•	•
Case Western Reserve University			•	•			•		•		•			•	•		•		•	•		•	•	•
Cedarville College																								
Central Ohio Technical College				•	•	•	•		•		•			•			•		•	•		•	•	•
Cleveland State University		•	•	•	•		•		•		•			•			•		•	•		•	•	•
College of Mount St. Joseph			•		•		•	•	•		•			•	•		•		•	•		•	•	•
Columbus State Community College	•			•	•	•	•		•		•			•			•	•	•	•		•	•	•
Cuyahoga Community College				•		•	•		•		•		•				•		•	•		•		•
Defiance College				•																		•		
Edison State Community College				•		•	•		•		•			•	•		•	•	•	•	•	•	•	•
Franklin University				•			•		•		•			•			•		•	•	•	•	•	•
Hocking Technical College		•	•	•			•		•		•			•			•		•	•		•	•	
Jefferson Technical College		•																						
Kent State University: Ashtabula Regiona		•					•							•			•		•	•		•	•	•
Kent State University: Salem Regional																								
Kenyon College						•			•	•					•		•	•			•	•	•	
Malone College	•			•	•	•	•	•	•	•		•			•		•	•	•	•	•	•	•	•
Muskingum College						•			•	•		•	•		•		•	•	•	•	•	•	•	•
Oberlin College			•	•		•	•		•		•		•		•		•		•			•	•	
Ohio State University Agricultural Techni		•	•	•		•	•		•		•			•			•		•	•		•	•	•
Ohio State University: Columbus Campus			•				•		•		•			•			•		•	•		•	•	•
Ohio State University: Marion Campus			•				•		•		•			•				•				•	•	
Ohio State University: Newark Campus	•		•	•	•	•	•		•		•			•			•	•	•	•	•	•	•	•
Ohio University									•					•				•	•	•		•	•	•
Otterbein College				•													•	•	•			•	•	
Owens Technical College							•	•	•		•			•			•	•	•			•	•	•
Sinclair Community College							•	•	•		•	•		•				•				•	•	
The University of Akron - Wayne College		•		•		•	•		•		•			•			•		•	•		•		•
University of Cincinnati: Raymond Walter	•					•	•	•						•	•		•	•	•	•	•	•	•	•
University of Dayton																	•	•				•		
University of Toledo	•		•	•			•	•	•		•		•	•	•		•	•	•	•		•	•	•
Walsh College											•						•	•			•	•	•	
Wilmington College									•									•						
Oklahoma																								
Carl Albert Junior College				•	•	•		•													•			
East Central University	•				•	•	•	•	•			•			•	•	•	•	•	•	•	•	•	•
Oklahoma State University	•	•	•	•			•	•	•			•			•		•	•			•		•	
Rose State College				•								•			•			•						
Tulsa Junior College							•		•			•			•	•	•	•	•	•	•	•	•	•
University of Oklahoma	•	•		•		•	•	•	•			•			•	•	•	•	•	•	•	•		

868

ACADEMIC ACCOMMODATIONS

Institution	Priority Registration	Math Waiver	Foreign Lang. Waiver	Course Substitution	Typist	Reader	Notetaker	Proof Reader	Text on Tape	Taped Handouts	Early Syllabus	Oral	Untimed	Take Home	With Proctor	On Computer	Extended Time	On Tape	Modified	Separate Room	Calculator	Tape Recorder	Word Processor	Priority Seating
Oregon																								
Central Oregon Community College																								
Clackamas Community College					•	•		•	•	•		•			•		•	•	•	•		•	•	•
Eastern Oregon State College									•	•	•				•		•	•	•			•	•	•
Lane Community College					•				•		•				•			•				•		
Linn-Benton Community College					•	•		•	•	•				•	•		•	•	•		•	•	•	•
Mount Hood Community College	•				•	•	•	•	•	•		•		•	•	•	•	•	•	•	•	•	•	•
Oregon State University	•	•	•	•		•	•		•		•		•		•	•	•	•	•	•	•	•	•	•
Pacific University											•					•		•		•		•		
Portland Community College	•	•	•	•		•	•	•	•	•	•	•	•	•	•	•	•	•	•	•	•	•	•	•
Umpqua Community College									•	•	•	•		•	•	•	•	•	•					
University of Oregon					•	•		•	•		•		•		•	•	•	•		•		•	•	
Western Oregon State College		•	•	•		•		•		•	•	•	•	•	•	•	•	•	•	•	•	•		•
Pennsylvania																								
Albright College	•	•	•	•		•	•	•	•	•		•	•		•	•	•	•	•	•	•	•	•	
Bloomsburg University of Pennsylvania					•			•	•	•		•			•	•	•	•	•			•	•	
Bryn Mawr College					•	•		•	•	•		•	•		•	•	•	•	•			•	•	
California University of Pennsylvania						•		•	•	•	•	•	•		•	•	•	•	•		•	•	•	•
Carnegie Mellon University						•		•	•	•		•	•		•	•	•	•	•		•	•	•	•
Churchman Business School															•									
College Misericordia	•				•	•	•	•	•	•		•	•		•	•	•	•	•	•	•	•	•	•
Community College of Allegheny College							•	•				•			•		•	•				•		
Community College of Philadelphia					•		•	•		•		•			•		•	•		•		•	•	
Delaware County Community College		•			•	•		•	•	•		•			•	•	•	•		•		•	•	
Delaware Valley College												•			•		•	•		•		•	•	
Duquesne University			•	•						•		•			•		•	•		•		•	•	
Edinboro University of Pennsylvania	•						•		•	•		•			•		•	•		•		•	•	
Harcum Junior College					•	•	•		•	•	•				•	•	•	•		•		•	•	
Kutztown University of Pennsylvania	•	•	•	•		•		•	•	•			•	•	•	•	•	•		•		•	•	
Lehigh County Community College					•		•	•	•	•			•	•			•	•		•	•	•	•	•
Lehigh University																								
Luzerne County Community College										•						•	•		•		•	•	•	
Mansfield University of Pennsylvania	•	•			•			•	•	•	•		•		•	•	•	•		•	•	•	•	•
Mercyhurst College	•									•					•		•			•		•	•	
Peirce Junior College										•					•	•		•	•		•	•	•	
Penn State Fayette Campus					•			•		•					•			•						
Penn State Mont Alto Campus			•		•				•		•			•	•		•	•		•	•	•	•	
Penn State University Park Campus	•				•		•		•		•				•		•	•		•		•	•	
Penn State Worthington Scranton Campus			•					•							•							•	•	
Pinebrook Junior College						•									•	•		•						
Point Park College								•							•			•				•		
Reading Area Community College					•		•	•	•	•		•	•		•	•	•	•	•	•		•	•	•
Spring Garden College							•								•			•	•		•	•	•	•

869

ACADEMIC ACCOMMODATIONS

	Curriculum				Study Aids							Exams									In Class			
	Priority Registration	Foreign Lang. Waiver	Math Waiver	Course Substitution	Typist	Reader	Notetaker	Proof Reader	Text on Tape	Early Syllabus	Taped Handouts	Oral	Untimed	Take Home	With Proctor	On Computer	Extended Time	On Tape	Separate Room	Modified	Calculator	Tape Recorder	Word Processor	Priority Seating
University of Pittsburgh at Bradford							•		•	•	•		•			•	•	•	•		•		•	•
University of Pittsburgh: Pittsburgh Camp		•	•	•		•	•		•				•		•	•	•	•	•		•	•	•	•
Waynesburg College			•				•	•				•			•	•			•		•	•	•	•
Westmoreland County Community College					•	•	•	•	•			•			•			•		•	•	•	•	•
Widener University	•			•			•	•				•			•			•		•	•	•	•	•
Puerto Rico																								
American University of Puerto Rico		•		•	•		•	•				•			•	•	•	•		•	•	•	•	•
Inter American University of Puerto Rico																								
Rhode Island																								
Brown University		•	•	•			•		•			•			•	•	•	•		•	•	•	•	•
Bryant College							•		•			•	•	•	•		•		•	•	•		•	
Community College of Rhode Island		•	•	•			•	•				•	•	•	•	•	•	•	•	•	•		•	
Johnson and Wales University		•	•				•	•				•	•	•	•	•		•	•	•	•	•	•	•
Rhode Island School of Design							•					•			•			•		•			•	
Roger Williams College					•	•	•					•	•			•	•		•	•	•	•	•	•
South Carolina																								
Central Wesleyan College												•	•			•					•		•	•
Francis Marion College							•					•				•							•	•
Midlands Technical College	•	•	•	•	•	•	•	•	•	•	•	•	•	•	•	•	•	•	•	•	•	•	•	•
University of South Carolina	•	•	•	•		•	•			•		•	•		•			•		•	•		•	•
South Dakota																								
Black Hills State College							•	•				•						•		•		•		
Huron University			•	•	•		•	•				•			•		•	•	•		•	•	•	•
Northern State University							•	•	•			•			•			•		•	•	•	•	•
South Dakota State University	•	•	•	•	•	•	•	•	•	•	•	•	•	•	•	•	•	•	•	•	•	•	•	•
Tennessee																								
Austin Peay State University	•					•	•		•			•			•			•		•		•	•	•
Freed-Hardeman University																	•				•	•		•
Lee College				•		•	•					•	•		•			•				•		•
Martin Methodist College			•	•					•									•	•					
Memphis College of Art				•																				
Middle Tennessee State University		•	•	•	•		•	•	•			•			•	•	•	•	•		•	•	•	•
Pellissippi State Technical Community Cc	•					•	•		•			•	•	•	•	•	•	•	•	•	•	•	•	•
Tennessee Technological University		•	•		•	•	•	•		•		•	•	•	•	•	•	•	•		•	•	•	•
University of Tennessee	•					•	•	•				•	•	•	•		•	•		•	•	•	•	•
Vanderbilt University		•	•	•		•			•			•			•		•	•		•		•	•	•
Texas																								
Amarillo College			•			•	•		•			•	•	•	•	•	•	•	•	•	•	•	•	•
El Paso Community College	•			•		•	•	•	•		•	•	•	•	•	•	•	•	•	•	•	•	•	•
North Harris Montgomery Community Coll						•	•		•			•			•	•	•	•	•	•	•	•	•	•
North Lake College		•	•	•	•	•	•	•	•		•	•	•	•	•	•	•	•	•	•	•	•	•	•
Richland College	•						•	•		•	•	•	•	•	•	•	•		•	•	•	•	•	•
Sam Houston State University							•		•			•						•				•	•	

ACADEMIC ACCOMMODATIONS

Institution	Priority Registration	Math Waiver	Foreign Lang. Waiver	Course Substitution	Typist	Reader	Proof Reader	Notetaker	Text on Tape	Taped Handouts	Early Syllabus	Oral	Untimed	Take Home	With Proctor	On Computer	Extended Time	On Tape	Modified	Separate Room	Calculator	Tape Recorder	Word Processor	Priority Seating
	Curriculum				**Study Aids**						**Exams**										**In Class**			
San Antonio College	•	•	•			•	•	•	•	•		•					•		•	•	•	•	•	•
Schreiner College							•		•	•		•		•	•		•		•				•	
Southern Methodist University							•			•		•		•			•		•		•		•	
St. Philip's College	•						•		•	•		•		•		•	•		•		•	•	•	•
Tarleton State University																								
Texas A&I University							•			•							•					•		
Texas Southmost College									•	•							•		•			•	•	
Texas Tech University							•		•	•		•		•			•				•	•	•	
Tyler Jr. College									•	•		•					•		•			•		
University of Houston	•			•		•	•	•	•	•	•	•	•	•	•	•	•	•	•	•	•		•	•
University of Texas at Brownsville									•	•		•					•		•			•		
Utah																								
Snow College						•	•		•	•	•	•					•		•	•	•	•	•	•
Southern Utah University	•		•			•	•		•	•	•	•		•	•	•	•	•	•	•		•	•	•
University of Utah	•	•	•			•	•		•	•	•	•		•		•	•	•		•		•	•	•
Utah State University		•	•			•	•		•	•	•	•					•		•	•		•	•	•
Vermont																								
Burlington College							•		•		•						•	•	•			•	•	•
Community College of Vermont							•						•	•	•				•				•	•
Landmark College																	•		•	•		•	•	•
New England Culinary Institute									•		•						•		•			•	•	
Norwich University	•	•	•		•	•	•		•	•	•						•	•	•	•	•	•	•	•
Saint Michael's College	•		•						•		•		•		•	•			•			•	•	•
Southern Vermont College		•					•	•	•	•	•			•			•		•			•	•	•
University of Vermont	•	•	•			•		•	•	•	•				•		•	•	•	•	•	•	•	
Vermont Technical College									•	•	•						•		•	•		•	•	•
Virginia																								
Blue Ridge Community College									•		•						•		•	•		•	•	•
Bluefield College									•		•						•					•	•	•
Christopher Newport College	•	•	•			•	•	•	•	•	•					•	•		•	•		•	•	•
College of William and Mary	•					•	•	•	•	•						•	•		•	•		•	•	•
Dabney S. Lancaster Community College								•	•		•						•		•			•	•	•
George Mason University	•		•			•		•	•		•					•		•	•	•		•	•	
Hollins College														•	•		•	•	•	•	•	•	•	•
James Madison University								•		•	•	•		•			•		•	•		•	•	•
Liberty University	•		•											•	•		•		•		•	•		
Lord Fairfax Community College							•	•	•		•	•		•			•		•	•		•	•	•
New River Community College									•	•	•						•		•	•		•	•	•
Patrick Henry Community College				•		•			•		•						•		•	•		•	•	•
Paul D. Camp Community College							•										•					•	•	•
Radford University									•								•		•			•	•	
Southern Seminary College							•		•	•						•			•			•	•	•
Thomas Nelson Community College	•					•			•	•	•		•	•	•		•		•	•		•	•	•

871

| | ACADEMIC ACCOMMODATIONS | | | | | | | | | | | | | | | | | | | | | | |
Institution	Priority Registration	Foreign Lang. Waiver	Math Waiver	Course Substitution	Typist	Notetaker	Reader	Proof Reader	Text on Tape	Early Syllabus	Taped Handouts	Oral	Untimed	Take Home	With Proctor	On Computer	Extended Time	On Tape	Modified	Separate Room	Calculator	Tape Recorder	Word Processor	Priority Seating
University of Virginia	•		•	•	•	•		•	•	•		•	•		•	•	•	•	•	•	•	•	•	
Virginia Highlands Community College		•	•	•				•	•	•			•	•			•	•	•		•	•	•	
Virginia Intermont College					•	•		•	•	•			•				•		•	•	•	•	•	
Virginia Polytechnic Institute and State U			•	•		•		•	•				•						•	•	•			
Virginia Wesleyan College								•	•				•				•		•		•			
Virginia Western Community College	•	•		•		•		•	•	•			•	•			•	•	•	•	•	•	•	
Washington																								
Central Washington University				•				•	•				•				•		•		•			
Centralia College					•	•		•	•				•	•		•	•	•	•		•	•	•	•
Columbia Basin College	•			•		•		•	•				•				•	•	•	•	•	•	•	
Evergreen State College						•		•	•				•				•		•					
Lutheran Bible Institute of Seattle						•		•					•		•		•		•					•
Olympic College	•				•	•		•	•	•		•	•	•	•		•	•	•	•		•	•	•
Puget Sound Christian College													•		•		•				•			
Washington State University			•	•				•	•				•				•		•		•		•	
Wenatchee Valley College					•	•		•	•				•		•		•	•	•		•	•	•	
Whitworth College								•	•				•				•					•	•	
West Virginia																								
Bluefield State College					•	•		•	•	•			•		•	•	•		•		•		•	•
Davis and Elkins College				•	•	•		•	•	•			•	•	•		•	•	•	•	•	•	•	
Marshall University	•		•	•	•	•		•	•				•				•		•		•	•	•	
Potomac State College of W. Virginia		•	•	•		•		•	•				•	•	•	•	•	•	•	•	•	•	•	•
West Virginia Northern Comm College				•				•		•			•		•		•	•			•	•	•	
West Virginia State College		•	•	•	•	•		•	•				•				•		•		•	•	•	
West Virginia University		•	•	•				•	•				•				•		•		•		•	
West Virginia Wesleyan College	•			•		•		•	•	•			•	•			•	•	•	•	•	•	•	
Wisconsin																								
Beloit College								•	•										•					
Chippewa Valley Technical College	•					•	•	•					•	•		•	•	•	•		•	•	•	•
Edgewood College						•		•	•	•			•			•	•		•		•		•	•
Fox Valley Technical College							•	•		•			•				•		•		•	•	•	
Gateway Technical College	•		•	•	•	•	•	•	•	•	•	•	•				•		•	•	•	•	•	•
Lawrence University																								
Marian College of Fond du Lac							•	•	•	•	•		•				•	•	•	•	•	•	•	•
Marquette University	•		•	•				•		•			•				•	•	•		•	•	•	
Milwaukee Area Technical College	•			•		•	•	•	•	•			•	•	•		•	•	•		•	•	•	•
Moraine Park Technical Institute								•	•				•				•	•			•	•	•	
Northeast Wisconsin Technical College		•		•	•	•	•	•		•			•				•		•		•		•	•
Ripon College		•					•	•	•	•			•	•			•	•	•	•	•		•	•
University of Wisconsin - Milwaukee	•			•			•	•	•				•				•		•	•	•	•	•	•
University of Wisconsin : Madison						•		•	•				•				•		•		•	•	•	•
University of Wisconsin Ctr: Waukesha								•	•	•									•	•		•	•	•
University of Wisconsin: LaCrosse					•			•	•	•			•				•		•		•	•	•	•

ACADEMIC ACCOMMODATIONS

	Curriculum				Study Aids					Exams											In Class			
	Priority Registration	Math Waiver	Foreign Lang. Waiver	Course Substitution	Typist	Reader	Proof Reader	Notetaker	Text on Tape	Early Syllabus	Taped Handouts	Oral	Untimed	Take Home	With Proctor	On Computer	Extended Time	On Tape	Modified	Separate Room	Calculator	Tape Recorder	Word Processor	Priority Seating
University of Wisconsin: Oshkosh			•						•				•				•	•	•			•	•	•
University of Wisconsin: Platteville						•	•	•			•					•				•		•	•	•
University Wisconsin Center: Baraboo Sa				•	•		•	•	•			•		•	•	•			•			•	•	•	•
University Wisconsin-Center Rock Count						•	•	•			•		•	•			•			•	•		•	•	•
Viterbo College							•			•	•		•	•	•				•			•
Waukesha County Technical College				•		•	•			•		•	•	•	•		•	•	•	•
Western Wisconsin Technical College					•		•	•	•		•		•	•	•	•	•	•	•	•
Wisconsin Indianhead Technical College		•		•			•		•	•		•	•	•	•	•	•
Wyoming																								
Casper College	•			•	•	•	•		•	•	•	•	•		•	•	•	•
Central Wyoming College				•	•	•	•	•		•	•	•	•	•	•	•
Laramie County Community College			•	•	•	•	•		•	•	•	•	•	•
Sheridan College				•		•		•	•	•
University of Wyoming	•		•	•	•	•	•		•	•	•	•	•	•	•	•	•	•

873

	Grp. - Math Skills	Ind. - Math Skills	Grp. - Study Skills	Ind. - Study Skills	Grp. - Language Arts	Ind. - Language Arts	Grp. - Written Express.	Ind. - Written Express.	Grp. - Word Processing	Ind. - Word Processing	Grp. - Time Manage.	Ind. - Time Manage.	Grp. - Learn. Strategies	Ind. - Learn. Strategies	Grp. - Organiz. Skills	Ind. - Organiz. Skills
Alabama																
Auburn University at Montgomery		•		•		•		•		•		•		•		•
Chattahoochee Valley Community College	•	•	•							•						
Jacksonville State University	•	•	•	•	•	•	•	•	•		•	•	•	•	•	
Northeast Alabama State Junior College		•							•							
Troy State University at Dothan	•	•	•	•		•	•	•	•	•	•	•	•	•	•	
UAB - Horizons Program																
University of Alabama		•				•										
University of Alabama at Birmingham	•	•	•	•	•	•	•	•	•	•	•	•	•	•	•	
Walker State Technical College																
Alaska																
Sheldon Jackson College	•	•	•	•	•	•	•	•	•	•	•	•	•	•	•	•
University of Alaska Anchorage	•	•	•	•	•	•	•	•	•	•	•	•	•	•	•	•
University of Alaska Fairbanks		•		•		•		•		•		•				•
Arizona																
Arizona State University		•		•				•		•						•
Glendale Community College		•		•	•		•				•		•			
Northern Arizona University	•	•	•		•	•						•		•		
Phoenix College		•		•		•		•		•	•		•		•	
Pima Community College		•		•		•		•		•		•		•		•
University of Arizona	•	•	•	•	•	•	•	•	•	•	•	•	•	•	•	•
Arkansas																
Arkansas State University	•	•	•	•								•	•			
Harding University	•	•	•	•	•	•	•	•	•	•	•	•	•	•	•	•
Henderson State University		•	•					•			•		•		•	
Southern Arkansas University		•					•		•							
University of Arkansas at Pine Bluff	•	•				•	•									
University of the Ozarks	•	•	•	•	•	•	•	•	•	•	•	•	•	•	•	•
California																
Antelope Valley College		•								•		•				•
Bakersfield College	•		•		•		•	•	•				•	•		
Biola University	•	•	•		•	•	•	•	•	•		•	•		•	•
Butte College		•		•		•		•		•		•		•		•
Cabrillo College	•		•		•	•	•	•	•		•			•	•	
California State Polytechnic University		•					•				•	•				
California State University: Bakersfield	•	•	•	•	•	•	•	•								
California State University: Chico			•	•			•	•	•	•	•	•	•	•		•
California State University: Dominguez Hills		•		•		•		•		•		•		•		•
California State University: Fullerton																
California State University: Northridge			•			•		•		•		•		•		•
California State University: Sacramento	•	•	•	•	•	•	•	•	•	•	•	•	•	•	•	•
California State University: San Bernardino		•		•		•		•		•		•		•		•
Canada College	•	•	•	•	•	•	•	•	•	•	•	•	•	•	•	•

	Grp. - Math Skills	Ind. - Math Skills	Grp. - Study Skills	Ind. - Study Skills	Grp. - Language Arts	Ind. - Language Arts	Grp. - Written Express.	Ind. - Written Express.	Grp. - Word Processing	Ind. - Word Processing	Grp. - Time Manage.	Ind. - Time Manage.	Grp. - Learn. Strategies	Ind. - Learn. Strategies	Grp. - Organiz. Skills	Ind. - Organiz. Skills
Cerritos Community College	•	•	•	•	•	•	•	•	•	•	•	•	•	•	•	•
Chabot College	•	•					•	•	•	•	•	•	•	•	•	•
Chaffey College	•	•	•	•	•	•	•	•		•	•	•	•	•	•	•
College of Alameda	•		•		•		•		•		•		•		•	
College of San Mateo		•					•								•	
College of the Canyons	•		•		•		•	•	•		•		•		•	
College of the Sequoias	•	•	•	•	•	•	•	•	•	•	•	•	•	•	•	•
College of the Siskiyous		•		•		•		•		•		•		•		•
Columbia College	•	•	•		•		•	•		•		•		•		•
Crafton Hills College		•		•		•		•		•		•		•		•
Cuesta College	•	•	•	•	•	•	•	•	•	•	•	•	•	•	•	•
Cypress College		•		•		•		•		•		•		•		•
De Anza College	•	•	•	•	•	•	•	•	•	•		•		•		•
East Los Angeles College	•	•	•	•	•	•	•	•	•		•		•	•	•	
El Camino College		•		•		•		•		•		•		•		•
Evergreen Valley College	•		•		•		•		•				•		•	
Feather River College	•	•		•	•	•	•	•	•	•			•		•	
Foothill College		•	•			•		•	•			•	•		•	
Fresno City College	•		•		•		•		•				•			
Fullerton College		•		•		•		•		•		•		•		•
Golden Gate University																
Golden West College		•		•		•		•							•	•
Hartnell College	•		•		•		•		•		•		•		•	
Humboldt State University	•	•	•	•	•		•	•			•		•			
Imperial Valley College	•	•	•	•	•	•	•	•	•	•	•	•	•	•	•	•
Kings River Community College	•	•	•	•		•		•		•		•		•		•
Laney College		•	•		•		•	•		•	•		•	•	•	
Long Beach City College		•	•	•		•		•		•		•		•		•
Los Angeles City College		•	•			•	•		•	•		•		•		•
Los Angeles Harbor College	•	•	•	•	•		•	•	•		•	•		•		•
Los Angeles Mission College		•	•			•		•	•		•					
Los Angeles Valley College		•	•	•	•	•	•	•		•	•	•	•	•	•	•
Merced College																
Merritt College	•	•	•		•	•	•	•	•		•		•	•	•	•
Modesto Junior College	•	•	•			•	•	•				•		•		•
Monterey Peninsula College	•	•	•	•	•	•	•	•	•	•	•	•	•	•	•	•
Mount San Jacinto College	•	•	•		•	•	•		•	•		•		•		
Porterville College	•	•	•		•	•	•		•	•	•					•
Rancho Santiago College		•		•		•		•		•		•		•		•
Saddleback College			•	•			•	•		•	•	•	•	•	•	•
San Diego City College	•	•	•		•		•	•	•	•		•		•	•	
San Diego Mesa College	•	•	•		•		•	•	•		•	•	•		•	
San Diego State University	•	•	•			•	•	•	•		•		•		•	

	TUTORIALS															
	Grp. - Math Skills	Ind. - Math Skills	Grp. - Study Skills	Ind. - Study Skills	Grp. - Language Arts	Ind. - Language Arts	Grp. - Written Express.	Ind. - Written Express.	Grp. - Word Processing	Ind. - Word Processing	Grp. - Time Manage.	Ind. - Time Manage.	Grp. - Learn. Strategies	Ind. - Learn. Strategies	Grp. - Organiz. Skills	Ind. - Organiz. Skills
San Francisco State University	•	•	•	•	•	•	•	•	•	•	•	•	•	•	•	•
Santa Barbara City College	•		•		•		•		•		•		•		•	
Santa Monica College	•	•	•	•	•	•	•	•	•		•		•	•	•	•
Santa Rosa Junior College	•	•	•	•	•	•	•		•		•		•	•		
Sierra College	•	•	•	•	•	•	•	•		•		•	•	•	•	•
Sonoma State University		•			•		•								•	
Stanford University		•		•		•		•		•		•		•		•
Taft College		•		•		•		•		•		•		•		•
University of California: Berkeley	•	•	•	•	•	•	•	•	•	•	•	•	•	•	•	•
University of California: Davis	•	•	•	•	•	•	•	•	•		•		•	•	•	•
University of California: Riverside	•			•			•				•			•		•
University of California: San Diego	•		•			•	•				•		•		•	
University of California: Santa Barbara	•		•			•		•			•		•		•	
University of California: Santa Cruz																
University of Redlands	•	•	•	•		•		•		•	•	•		•		•
Ventura College	•	•	•	•	•	•	•	•	•	•	•	•	•	•	•	•
Victor Valley College			•				•			•		•		•		
West Hills College	•	•	•	•			•	•		•			•			
West Valley College	•	•	•	•	•	•	•	•	•	•		•	•	•	•	•
Colorado																
Arapahoe Community College	•	•	•	•	•	•	•	•	•		•	•	•	•	•	•
Colorado Northwestern Community College	•			•		•	•		•	•	•				•	
Colorado State University	•	•	•		•		•	•		•	•			•	•	•
Community College of Aurora	•	•	•	•	•	•	•	•		•	•		•	•	•	•
Community College of Denver	•	•			•		•		•		•		•		•	•
Front Range Community College	•	•	•	•	•	•	•	•	•	•	•	•	•	•	•	•
Northeastern Junior College	•	•	•	•	•	•	•	•	•	•	•	•	•	•	•	•
Pikes Peak Community College	•	•	•			•		•			•		•		•	
Pueblo Community College	•	•	•	•	•	•	•			•	•		•	•	•	•
Red Rocks Community College		•	•	•		•		•		•	•		•		•	•
Regis College	•		•			•			•			•		•		•
University of Colorado at Boulder																
University of Denver		•		•		•		•			•	•		•		•
Western State College of Colorado		•	•	•		•		•		•	•		•	•	•	•
Connecticut																
Briarwood College		•		•		•		•		•		•		•		•
Eastern Connecticut State University	•		•		•		•		•		•		•		•	
Hartford College for Women	•	•	•	•			•	•	•	•	•	•	•	•	•	•
Mattatuck Community College		•	•	•	•	•	•		•		•		•		•	
Mitchell College	•	•	•	•	•	•	•	•	•	•	•	•	•	•	•	•
Northwestern Connecticut Community College			•	•						•	•			•	•	
Norwalk Community College	•	•		•		•		•		•	•		•		•	
Paier College of Art																

College	Grp. - Math Skills	Ind. - Math Skills	Grp. - Study Skills	Ind. - Study Skills	Grp. - Language Arts	Ind. - Language Arts	Grp. - Written Express.	Ind. - Written Express.	Grp. - Word Processing	Ind. - Word Processing	Grp. - Time Manage.	Ind. - Time Manage.	Grp. - Learn. Strategies	Ind. - Learn. Strategies	Grp. - Organiz. Skills	Ind. - Organiz. Skills
South Central Community College	•	•	•	•	•	•	•	•	•	•	•	•	•	•	•	•
Thames Valley State Technical College	•	•	•		•	•	•	•	•	•	•		•		•	
University of Connecticut		•		•		•	•				•		•		•	
University of New Haven	•	•	•	•			•	•	•	•	•	•	•	•	•	•
Wesleyan University																
Western Connecticut State University		•		•		•		•		•		•		•		
Yale University																
Delaware																
Goldey Beacom College		•	•	•		•		•		•		•		•	•	
University of Delaware		•		•		•		•		•		•		•		•
District of Columbia																
American University		•		•		•		•		•		•		•		•
Catholic University of America	•	•	•	•		•			•	•		•	•	•	•	•
Gallaudet University	•	•		•	•	•		•						•		•
George Washington University		•	•	•		•		•		•	•	•		•		
Trinity College	•	•	•	•	•	•	•	•	•	•	•	•	•			
Florida																
Beacon College	•	•	•	•	•	•	•	•		•	•		•	•	•	•
Brevard Community College	•	•	•	•	•	•	•	•		•	•		•	•	•	
Chipola Junior College		•		•		•		•		•		•		•		•
Edison Community College	•	•				•	•	•	•							
Embry-Riddle Aeronautical University	•			•	•			•	•		•	•	•	•	•	•
Florida Agricultural and Mechanical University	•	•						•	•	•			•	•	•	•
Florida Atlantic University		•		•		•		•		•		•		•		•
Florida Community College at Jacksonville	•				•											
Florida State University		•				•		•		•						
Gulf Coast Community College		•				•		•		•						
Lake City Community College		•		•		•		•		•		•		•		•
Miami-Dade Community College	•	•	•	•	•	•	•	•	•	•	•	•	•	•	•	•
Okaloosa-Walton Junior College																
Polk Community College		•		•								•				
Saint Johns River Community College	•		•		•			•		•		•		•		
Santa Fe Community College		•	•	•			•		•		•		•	•	•	
Seminole Community College	•	•	•	•		•		•					•		•	
Tallahassee Community College	•	•	•	•	•	•	•	•	•	•	•	•	•	•	•	•
University of Tampa	•	•	•	•			•			•	•		•	•	•	
Georgia																
Brenau Women's College		•		•		•		•		•		•		•		•
Brunswick College																
Clayton State College																
DeKalb College	•		•	•			•	•					•		•	
East Georgia College																
Emory University	•			•	•		•		•			•		•		•

TUTORIALS

	Grp. - Math Skills	Ind. - Math Skills	Grp. - Study Skills	Ind. - Study Skills	Grp. - Language Arts	Ind. - Language Arts	Grp. - Written Express.	Ind. - Written Express.	Grp. - Word Processing	Ind. - Word Processing	Grp. - Time Manage.	Ind. - Time Manage.	Grp. - Learn. Strategies	Ind. - Learn. Strategies	Grp. - Organiz. Skills	Ind. - Organiz. Skills
Georgia College			•	•											•	
Georgia Institute of Technology			•	•							•			•	•	•
Georgia Southern University	•	•			•	•	•	•								
Georgia State University		•	•			•	•			•	•		•		•	
Mercer University		•	•				•			•	•		•		•	
Reinhardt College	•	•			•	•										
South Georgia College		•	•		•		•	•			•		•	•	•	•
Southern College of Technology																
University of Georgia		•		•			•							•	•	
Valdosta State College		•		•		•		•		•		•		•	•	
West Georgia College	•		•				•								•	
Hawaii																
Brigham Young University-Hawaii	•	•			•	•	•	•		•	•		•		•	
University of Hawaii: Kapiolani Community College		•		•		•		•		•		•		•	•	
University of Hawaii: Leeward Community College		•		•		•		•		•		•		•	•	
Idaho																
Albertson College			•	•	•	•	•	•		•	•	•	•	•	•	•
Boise Bible College			•			•		•		•		•		•		
University of Idaho	•	•	•	•			•	•		•	•	•	•	•	•	
Illinois																
Barat College	•	•		•		•		•		•		•		•		•
Bradley University		•	•	•				•		•	•		•		•	•
City Colleges of Chicago: Harold Washington College																
City Colleges of Chicago: Harry S. Truman College	•	•	•	•	•	•	•	•	•	•	•	•	•	•	•	•
DePaul University		•		•		•		•		•		•				•
Elgin Community College		•	•			•		•		•						
Governors State University	•	•	•	•							•		•			
Highland Community College	•	•	•	•	•	•	•	•		•	•	•	•	•	•	•
Illinois Central College		•				•		•		•		•		•	•	
Illinois State University																
Kendall College	•	•	•	•	•		•		•		•		•	•	•	
Lake Land College	•	•	•	•	•	•	•	•	•	•	•	•	•	•	•	
Lincoln College		•		•		•		•		•		•		•		•
Moraine Valley Community College	•	•	•	•	•	•	•	•	•	•	•	•	•	•	•	
National-Louis University	•	•	•	•		•	•	•		•		•	•		•	
Northern Illinois University																
Oakton Community College	•	•	•	•	•	•	•	•		•	•	•	•	•	•	
Roosevelt University		•		•		•		•		•		•				•
School of the Art Institute of Chicago		•		•		•		•		•		•		•		•
Shawnee College																
Shimer College		•	•	•		•	•	•		•	•	•	•	•	•	
Southeastern Illinois College																
Southern Illinois University at Carbondale		•		•		•	•		•		•		•		•	

	Grp. - Math Skills	Ind. - Math Skills	Grp. - Study Skills	Ind. - Study Skills	Grp. - Language Arts	Ind. - Language Arts	Grp. - Written Express.	Ind. - Written Express.	Grp. - Word Processing	Ind. - Word Processing	Grp. - Time Manage.	Ind. - Time Manage.	Grp. - Learn. Strategies	Ind. - Learn. Strategies	Grp. - Organiz. Skills	Ind. - Organiz. Skills
Southern Illinois University at Edwardsville		•		•		•		•		•		•		•		•
Triton College		•	•			•		•						•		•
Waubonsee Community College	•	•	•	•	•	•	•	•	•	•	•	•	•	•	•	•
Western Illinois University	•	•	•	•		•		•				•	•			•
William Rainey Harper College		•	•	•		•		•			•	•				•
Indiana																
Anderson University		•	•			•		•			•	•		•		•
Indiana Institute of Technology	•	•	•	•	•	•	•	•	•	•	•	•	•	•	•	•
Indiana University Bloomington		•	•	•		•	•	•			•	•	•	•	•	•
Indiana University East	•	•	•	•	•	•	•	•	•	•	•	•	•	•	•	•
Indiana University Northwest	•	•	•	•	•	•	•	•	•	•	•	•	•	•	•	•
Indiana UniversityPurdue Univeristy at Indianapolis		•		•		•		•		•		•		•		•
Indiana Vocational Technical College Central Indiana		•		•		•		•						•		
Indiana Vocational Technical College: Eastcentral	•	•	•	•	•	•	•		•		•		•		•	
Indiana Vocational Technical College: Northcentral		•	•	•		•		•			•	•				•
Indiana Vocational Technical College: Northeast		•				•		•		•		•				
Indiana Vocational Technical College: Southwest		•	•	•		•		•	•	•	•	•	•	•	•	•
Indiana Vocational Technical College: Whitewater	•	•	•	•	•	•	•	•	•	•	•	•	•	•	•	•
Indiana VocationalTechnical College Kokomo		•	•		•		•		•		•		•		•	•
Indiana Wesleyan University		•	•	•	•	•	•	•		•	•	•	•	•	•	
Manchester College	•	•	•	•	•	•	•	•			•	•	•	•	•	•
Purdue University		•	•				•			•			•	•		•
University of Evansville		•								•						
University of Indianapolis	•	•	•	•	•	•	•	•	•	•	•	•	•	•	•	•
University of Southern Indiana	•			•			•				•	•	•		•	
Vincennes University		•		•		•					•					
Iowa																
Coe College		•	•	•		•		•					•		•	•
Cornell College				•		•		•					•		•	•
Graceland College																
Grand View College		•		•			•				•	•	•			
Hawkeye Institute of Technology	•	•		•	•	•	•	•		•			•	•	•	
Indian Hills Community College		•		•		•		•		•		•		•		•
Iowa Central Community College		•		•		•		•		•	•	•		•		•
Iowa State University of Science and Technology	•	•	•	•	•	•	•			•	•	•	•	•	•	•
Loras College	•	•	•	•	•	•	•	•	•	•	•	•	•	•	•	•
Scott Community College	•	•	•			•	•	•	•	•	•		•		•	
Southeastern Community College: North Campus	•	•	•	•	•	•	•	•	•	•	•	•	•	•	•	•
Southwestern Community College	•	•	•	•	•	•		•	•	•	•					
University of Iowa		•	•			•			•		•		•		•	•
University of Northern Iowa																
Waldorf College	•	•	•	•	•	•	•	•	•	•	•	•	•	•	•	•
Kansas																

	Grp. - Math Skills	Ind. - Math Skills	Grp. - Study Skills	Ind. - Study Skills	Grp. - Language Arts	Ind. - Language Arts	Grp. - Written Express.	Ind. - Written Express.	Grp. - Word Processing	Ind. - Word Processing	Grp. - Time Manage.	Ind. - Time Manage.	Grp. - Learn. Strategies	Ind. - Learn. Strategies	Grp. - Organiz. Skills	Ind. - Organiz. Skills
Barton Community College	•	•	•	•	•	•	•	•					•	•		
Cowley County Community College	•	•	•										•		•	
Emporia State University																
Hutchinson Community College	•	•	•	•	•	•	•	•	•	•	•	•	•	•	•	•
Kansas City Kansas Community College		•				•		•								
Kansas State University	•		•		•		•	•			•			•		
Pittsburg State University												•				•
University of Kansas		•	•			•					•			•		
Wichita State University	•	•	•	•	•	•	•	•	•	•	•	•	•	•	•	•
Kentucky																
Cumberland College	•	•					•	•								
Eastern Kentucky University																
Elizabethtown Community College		•		•		•		•		•		•		•		•
Lexington Community College	•	•	•	•	•	•	•	•		•		•	•	•		•
Lindsey Wilson College	•		•		•		•			•		•		•		
Murray State University		•	•					•		•		•		•		
Prestonsburg Community College			•	•							•	•	•	•		•
Thomas More College	•	•	•	•	•	•	•	•		•		•	•	•	•	•
University of Kentucky	•	•	•	•			•	•			•	•			•	•
Louisiana																
Louisiana College	•	•	•	•	•	•	•	•			•	•	•	•	•	•
Louisiana State University Agricultural and Mechanica	•	•	•			•	•	•			•		•		•	
Louisiana State University at Alexandria																
University of Southwestern Louisiana	•	•	•			•	•		•		•	•			•		•
Maine																
Bowdoin College		•		•		•		•		•		•		•		
Colby College				•				•	•	•		•		•		
Southern Maine Technical College		•		•		•		•		•		•		•		•
St. Joseph's College			•													
Unity College		•		•		•		•		•		•		•		•
University of Maine	•	•	•													
University of Maine at Machias	•	•	•	•		•	•	•		•	•	•	•	•	•	•
University of New England	•	•	•	•				•		•	•	•	•	•	•	•
University of Southern Maine		•	•			•		•		•	•		•		•	
Maryland																
Charles County Community College	•							•	•		•			•		•
Chesapeake College	•	•	•	•			•	•					•	•	•	•
Frostburg State University		•	•	•		•		•			•		•	•	•	•
Hagerstown Junior College	•					•					•					
Howard Community College	•	•	•	•	•	•	•	•	•	•	•	•	•	•	•	•
Johns Hopkins University		•		•		•		•			•		•		•	•
Montgomery Community College: Rockville Campus		•	•		•	•	•	•		•	•	•		•		•
Towson State University		•		•		•		•			•				•	

880

TUTORIALS

	Grp. - Math Skills	Ind. - Math Skills	Grp. - Study Skills	Ind. - Study Skills	Grp. - Language Arts	Ind. - Language Arts	Grp. - Written Express.	Ind. - Written Express.	Grp. - Word Processing	Ind. - Word Processing	Grp. - Time Manage.	Ind. - Time Manage.	Grp. - Learn. Strategies	Ind. - Learn. Strategies	Grp. - Organiz. Skills	Ind. - Organiz. Skills
University of Maryland: Eastern Shore		•	•				•				•	•			•	•
Western Maryland College	•	•	•	•		•		•	•	•	•	•	•	•	•	•
Wor-Wic Tech Community College																
Massachusetts																
American International College	•	•	•	•				•		•	•	•	•	•	•	•
Anna Maria College for Men & Women		•		•			•		•		•		•		•	
Aquinas College at Newton	•	•	•	•			•	•	•	•	•	•	•	•	•	•
Bentley College	•	•	•	•	•	•	•	•	•	•	•	•	•	•	•	•
Boston College	•		•		•		•		•		•		•		•	
Boston University		•		•		•		•		•		•		•		•
Bradford College	•	•	•	•	•	•	•	•	•	•	•	•	•	•	•	•
Brandeis University	•	•	•	•	•	•	•	•	•	•	•	•	•	•	•	•
Bridgewater State College		•		•		•		•				•		•		•
Bristol Community College						•	•	•	•							
Cape Cod Community College	•	•	•					•	•		•		•		•	
Clark University	•		•	•			•		•		•	•	•		•	
Curry College		•			•		•		•		•		•		•	
Dean Junior College		•		•		•		•		•		•		•		•
Endicott College	•	•	•	•	•	•	•	•			•	•	•	•	•	•
Gordon College																
Harvard University																
Lesley College-Threshold	•	•	•	•	•	•	•	•			•	•	•	•	•	•
Massachusetts Bay Community College	•	•	•		•		•	•	•	•	•		•		•	
Massachusetts College of Art																
Massachusetts Institute of Technology		•		•		•		•			•				•	
Massasoit Community College		•		•		•		•		•		•		•		•
Merrimack College	•	•					•	•								
Middlesex Community College		•		•		•		•		•		•		•		•
Mount Holyoke College		•	•	•	•	•	•	•		•	•	•	•	•	•	•
Mount Ida College		•	•	•		•		•		•		•	•	•	•	•
Mount Wachusett Community College	•	•	•	•	•	•	•	•	•	•	•	•	•	•	•	•
North Adams State College																
Northeastern University	•	•		•									•		•	•
Pine Manor College		•	•	•		•		•		•	•	•		•		•
Simmons College	•	•	•	•			•	•							•	•
Smith College		•		•		•		•		•		•		•		•
Springfield Technical Community College		•	•			•		•		•	•		•		•	
Stonehill College		•		•		•		•		•		•		•		•
Tufts University	•	•	•	•	•	•	•	•			•	•	•	•	•	•
University of Massachusetts - Dartmouth	•	•	•	•	•	•	•	•	•	•	•	•	•	•	•	•
University of Massachusetts at Amherst		•	•		•	•		•		•		•		•		•
University of Massachusetts at Boston	•	•	•	•	•	•		•	•	•	•	•	•	•	•	•
Wellesley College	•	•	•	•			•	•	•	•	•	•	•	•	•	•

	Grp. - Math Skills	Ind. - Math Skills	Grp. - Study Skills	Ind. - Study Skills	Grp. - Language Arts	Ind. - Language Arts	Grp. - Written Express.	Ind. - Written Express.	Grp. - Word Processing	Ind. - Word Processing	Grp. - Time Manage.	Ind. - Time Manage.	Grp. - Learn. Strategies	Ind. - Learn. Strategies	Grp. - Organiz. Skills	Ind. - Organiz. Skills
Wheaton College	•	•		•			•	•	•		•		•			•
Wheelock College		•				•		•			•		•			
Worcester Polytechnic Institute		•														
Michigan																
Adrian College	•	•	•	•	•	•	•	•	•	•	•	•	•	•	•	•
Albion College	•	•		•		•		•		•		•		•		•
Alma College	•	•	•	•			•	•	•	•	•	•	•	•	•	•
Aquinas College		•		•		•		•		•		•	•			•
Central Michigan University		•		•		•		•					•			•
Charles Stewart Mott Community College		•				•		•								
Delta College		•	•			•			•		•		•		•	
Detroit College of Business	•	•	•		•		•		•		•		•		•	
Glen Oaks Community College	•	•	•	•	•	•		•	•	•	•	•	•	•	•	•
Grand Valley State University		•		•	•	•	•	•		•		•		•		•
Henry Ford Community College	•	•	•	•	•	•	•	•	•	•	•	•	•	•	•	•
Jackson Community College		•	•	•				•		•		•		•		
Kalamazoo College																
Kellogg Community College	•	•	•	•	•	•	•	•	•	•	•	•	•	•	•	•
Lake Michigan College	•	•		•	•	•	•		•	•		•		•		•
Lake Superior State University		•	•					•			•		•		•	
Lansing Community College		•	•	•	•	•	•	•		•	•	•		•		•
Mercy College of Detroit	•	•	•	•	•	•				•	•	•	•	•	•	•
Michigan Technological University	•	•	•	•	•	•	•	•	•	•	•	•	•	•	•	•
Mid Michigan Community College	•	•	•	•	•	•	•	•	•	•	•	•		•	•	•
Montcalm Community College		•		•		•		•		•		•		•		•
Northern Michigan University		•		•	•	•		•		•		•		•		•
Oakland Community College	•	•	•	•		•		•		•	•	•		•		•
Schoolcraft College	•	•	•	•	•	•	•	•	•	•		•	•	•	•	•
Spring Arbor College	•	•	•	•	•	•	•	•	•	•	•	•	•	•	•	•
St. Mary's College																
Suomi College	•	•	•	•								•	•	•	•	•
University of Michigan	•	•	•	•	•	•	•	•	•	•	•	•	•	•	•	•
University of Michigan: Flint				•									•			
Washtenaw Community College		•	•		•		•		•		•		•		•	
Wayne State University	•	•	•	•			•	•		•		•	•	•	•	•
Western Michigan University		•	•			•		•		•		•	•		•	
Minnesota																
Augsburg College	•	•	•	•	•	•	•	•		•	•	•		•	•	•
College of St. Catherine: St. Catherine Campus		•	•	•		•	•	•		•	•	•	•	•	•	•
Concordia College: St. Paul			•				•			•						
Hamline University	•		•		•		•		•		•		•		•	
Hibbing Community College		•	•	•	•		•	•		•	•	•	•	•	•	•
Itasca Community College: Arrowhead	•	•		•		•	•	•	•	•		•		•		•

TUTORIALS

	Grp. Math Skills	Ind. Math Skills	Grp. Study Skills	Ind. Study Skills	Grp. Language Arts	Ind. Language Arts	Grp. Written Express.	Ind. Written Express.	Grp. Word Processing	Ind. Word Processing	Grp. Time Manage.	Ind. Time Manage.	Grp. Learn. Strategies	Ind. Learn. Strategies	Grp. Organiz. Skills	Ind. Organiz. Skills
Lakewood Community College	•	•	•	•	•	•	•	•	•	•	•	•	•	•	•	•
Moorhead State University																
Rochester Community College		•	•	•		•		•		•	•	•		•	•	•
Saint Cloud State University		•				•										
Southwest State University	•	•	•	•	•	•	•	•	•	•	•	•	•	•	•	•
St. Cloud State University		•				•										
St. John's University		•	•	•		•	•	•	•			•	•	•		•
St. Mary's Campus of the College of St. Catherine	•	•	•	•	•	•	•	•		•		•	•	•	•	•
St. Olaf College		•	•	•		•		•	•		•	•				
University of Minnesota: Duluth		•	•	•			•			•	•	•	•	•	•	•
University of Minnesota: Morris	•	•	•	•			•			•	•	•	•	•	•	
University of Minnesota: Crookston	•	•	•	•			•			•	•	•	•	•	•	
Wilmar Community College	•	•	•	•	•	•	•	•		•	•	•	•	•	•	•
Worthington Community College		•	•			•		•	•		•		•		•	
Mississippi																
Hinds Community College		•		•		•		•		•		•		•		•
University of Mississippi		•		•			•			•		•		•	•	
Missouri																
Central Missouri State University	•		•		•		•		•		•		•		•	
Evangel College		•		•		•		•			•		•			
Jefferson College	•	•	•	•	•		•	•	•	•	•	•	•		•	
Kansas City Art Institute		•	•		•		•		•	•	•	•	•	•	•	
Longview Community College	•	•	•	•		•	•	•	•	•	•	•	•	•	•	
Maple Woods Community College	•			•		•		•			•		•			
Rockhurst College	•	•	•	•		•	•	•	•	•	•	•	•	•	•	
Southwest Baptist University	•	•	•	•	•	•	•	•		•	•		•		•	
St. Louis Community College at Florissant	•	•		•		•	•	•		•	•		•			•
St. Louis Community College at Forest Park		•		•						•	•	•				
St. Louis University	•	•	•					•		•	•		•		•	
University of Missouri: Columbia	•	•		•	•	•		•		•	•		•		•	
University of Missouri: Rolla		•	•								•		•			
Washington University			•	•			•	•		•	•	•	•	•	•	
Westminster College	•	•	•	•		•	•	•	•	•		•		•		
Montana																
Flathead Valley Community College	•	•	•	•	•	•		•		•	•	•	•	•	•	
Montana College of Mineral Science																
Northern Montana College	•	•	•	•					•	•	•		•			
Rocky Mountain College	•	•	•	•	•		•	•	•		•	•	•	•	•	
Western Montana College University of Montana	•	•	•	•	•	•	•	•	•	•	•	•	•	•		•
Nebraska																
Dana College		•		•		•		•		•		•		•		•
Southeast Community College: Beatrice Campus		•		•		•		•		•		•		•		•
Southeast Community College: Lincoln Campus	•	•	•	•	•	•	•	•			•	•	•	•	•	•

	Grp. - Math Skills	Ind. - Math Skills	Grp. - Study Skills	Ind. - Study Skills	Grp. - Language Arts	Ind. - Language Arts	Grp. - Written Express.	Ind. - Written Express.	Grp. - Word Processing	Ind. - Word Processing	Grp. - Time Manage.	Ind. - Time Manage.	Grp. - Learn. Strategies	Ind. - Learn. Strategies	Grp. - Organiz. Skills	Ind. - Organiz. Skills
Southeast Community College: Milford	•			•		•		•		•		•		•		•
Union College	•	•	•	•	•	•	•	•	•	•	•	•	•	•	•	•
Western Nebraska Community College: Scottsbluff		•		•		•		•		•		•		•		•
Nevada																
Truckee Meadows Community College	•	•	•	•			•						•		•	
University of Nevada: Las Vegas				•			•			•		•		•		•
University of Nevada: Reno		•		•		•		•	•				•	•		•
New Hampshire																
Dartmouth College																
Keene State College		•		•		•		•		•		•		•		•
New England College		•		•		•		•	•		•		•		•	•
New Hampshire College	•	•	•	•	•	•	•	•	•	•	•	•	•	•	•	•
New Hampshire Technical College																
New Hampshire Vocational-Technical	•	•	•	•			•	•			•	•	•	•	•	•
New Hampshire Vocational-Technical College: Laconia		•		•		•		•		•		•		•		•
University of New Hampshire			•	•	•	•	•	•	•		•	•	•	•	•	•
New Jersey																
Caldwell College	•	•	•								•	•	•	•		
County College of Morris	•	•	•	•	•	•	•	•	•	•	•	•	•	•	•	•
Fairleigh Dickinson University	•	•	•	•	•	•	•	•	•	•	•	•	•	•	•	•
Georgian Court College		•		•		•		•	•			•		•		•
Gloucester County College	•	•	•	•	•	•	•	•	•			•		•		•
Jersey City State College		•		•		•	•	•		•	•	•	•	•	•	•
Middlesex County College	•	•	•	•	•	•	•	•	•	•	•	•	•	•	•	•
New Jersey Institute of Technology																
Ocean County College		•	•		•	•	•	•		•		•		•		
William Paterson College of New Jersey	•		•		•		•		•		•		•		•	
New Mexico																
Albuquerque Technical-Vocational Institute		•		•		•		•		•		•		•		•
College of Santa Fe	•	•	•	•	•	•	•	•	•	•	•	•	•	•	•	•
Eastern New Mexico University: Roswell	•	•			•	•	•	•	•							
Institute of American Indian Arts	•		•		•		•		•	•			•			
San Juan College																
Santa Fe Community College	•	•	•	•	•	•	•	•	•			•	•			
University of New Mexico		•					•									
New York																
Adelphi University		•	•	•		•		•	•	•		•		•		•
Broome Community College	•	•	•	•	•	•	•	•	•	•	•	•	•	•	•	•
Cazenovia College		•	•			•		•		•		•		•		
City University New York: Brooklyn College							•	•				•		•		•
City University of New York: College of Staten Islan		•		•		•		•		•		•		•		•
City University of New York: City College		•		•		•		•		•		•		•		•

	Grp. - Math Skills	Ind. - Math Skills	Grp. - Study Skills	Ind. - Study Skills	Grp. - Language Arts	Ind. - Language Arts	Grp. - Written Express.	Ind. - Written Express.	Grp. - Word Processing	Ind. - Word Processing	Grp. - Time Manage.	Ind. - Time Manage.	Grp. - Learn. Strategies	Ind. - Learn. Strategies	Grp. - Organiz. Skills	Ind. - Organiz. Skills
City University of New York: Borough of Manhattan C	•	•	•	•	•	•	•	•	•		•	•	•		•	•
City University of New York: John Jay-Criminal Jus		•		•			•	•		•		•		•		•
City University of NewYork: La Guardia Community C	•	•	•	•	•	•	•	•		•	•	•	•	•	•	•
Clinton Community College	•	•	•	•	•	•	•	•	•		•	•	•	•	•	
Community College of the Finger Lakes	•		•		•		•	•		•		•	•			•
Cornell University	•	•	•		•	•	•		•	•	•	•		•		•
D'Youville College	•	•	•		•		•	•								
Dowling College																
Dutchess Community College		•		•		•		•				•	•		•	•
Eugene Lang College																
Fashion Institute of Technology		•		•		•		•		•		•		•	•	•
Fordham University	•		•		•		•		•		•		•		•	
Fulton-Montgomery Community College	•	•	•	•	•	•	•	•	•	•	•	•	•	•	•	•
Herkimer County Community College	•	•	•	•	•	•	•	•	•	•	•	•	•	•	•	•
Hofstra University		•		•		•		•		•		•			•	
Houghton College	•	•	•	•			•	•			•	•	•		•	•
Hudson Valley Community College	•	•									•					
Hunter College											•					
Iona College - Seton School		•		•		•		•		•		•	•		•	
Jefferson Community College	•	•	•	•	•	•	•	•	•	•	•	•	•	•	•	•
Julliard School																
Keuka College	•	•	•	•	•	•	•	•	•	•	•	•	•	•	•	•
Long Island University: C.W. Post Campus	•	•	•	•	•	•	•	•		•	•	•	•	•	•	
Long Island University: Southampton Campus	•	•		•		•	•	•	•	•		•		•		•
Manhattan School of Music		•		•		•		•			•		•		•	
Marist College		•		•		•		•		•		•		•		•
Medaille College		•		•		•		•		•		•		•		•
Mercy College		•		•		•		•		•		•		•		•
Mohawk Valley Community College	•	•	•	•	•	•	•	•	•	•	•	•	•	•	•	•
Molloy College		•		•		•		•		•		•		•		•
Nassau Community College		•		•		•		•	•			•		•		•
New York Institute of Technology	•	•	•	•	•	•	•	•	•	•	•	•	•	•		•
New York University		•		•		•		•		•		•		•	•	
Niagara University																
Onondaga Community College		•		•		•		•		•		•		•		•
Pace University: College of White Plain																
Para-Educator Center for Young Adults		•	•	•	•	•		•	•	•	•	•	•	•	•	•
Paul Smith's College	•		•	•	•	•	•		•	•	•	•		•	•	•
Rochester Institute of Technology	•	•	•	•	•	•	•	•	•	•	•	•	•	•	•	•
Rockland Community College		•		•		•		•	•			•		•		•
Schenectady County Community College	•			•		•		•		•	•	•		•		•
School of Visual Arts																
Skidmore College		•							•							

885

	Grp. - Math Skills	Ind. - Math Skills	Grp. - Study Skills	Ind. - Study Skills	Grp. - Language Arts	Ind. - Language Arts	Grp. - Written Express.	Ind. - Written Express.	Grp. - Word Processing	Ind. - Word Processing	Grp. - Time Manage.	Ind. - Time Manage.	Grp. - Learn. Strategies	Ind. - Learn. Strategies	Grp. - Organiz. Skills	Ind. - Organiz. Skills
St. Bonaventure University		•		•				•		•		•		•		•
St. Lawrence University		•	•	•		•		•		•	•	•	•	•	•	•
St. Thomas Aquinas College			•	•				•	•	•		•	•	•	•	•
State University of New York at Albany			•						•		•		•		•	
State University of New York at Binghamton										•						
State University of New York at Buffalo			•								•		•			
State University of New York at Stony Brook		•		•		•		•		•		•		•		•
State University of New York College at Oneonta	•	•	•	•	•	•	•	•	•	•	•	•	•	•	•	•
State University of New York College at Plattsburg	•	•	•	•					•	•	•	•	•	•	•	•
State University of New York College of Environment:		•	•	•		•	•	•		•	•	•	•	•	•	•
State University of New York College of Technology a	•	•	•	•				•	•	•		•	•	•	•	
State University of New York College of Technology a	•	•	•	•			•	•	•	•		•	•	•	•	
State University of New York College of Techology at	•	•	•	•				•	•	•		•	•	•		
Syracuse University	•	•	•	•	•	•	•	•	•	•	•	•	•	•	•	
Ulster County Community College	•	•	•	•	•	•	•	•	•	•	•	•	•	•	•	
Utica College of Syracuse University		•	•	•		•	•	•				•		•	•	
Westchester Community College		•							•				•		•	
North Carolina																
Appalachian State University																
Blue Ridge Community College	•	•		•		•		•		•		•		•		•
Caldwell Community College and Technical Institute		•		•		•										
Catawba Valley Community College		•	•	•		•		•		•		•	•	•	•	
Central Piedmont Community College		•		•		•		•		•	•		•		•	
Craven Community College		•	•										•			
Davidson College																
Davidson County Community College	•	•	•	•	•	•		•	•					•		•
East Carolina University	•			•				•		•		•		•		•
Guilford Technical Community College		•					•		•		•			•		
Halifax Community College	•		•	•	•	•	•				•		•		•	•
Isothermal Community College		•		•		•		•		•		•		•		•
Johnston Community College		•		•				•					•		•	
McDowell Technical Community College	•	•	•	•	•	•		•	•	•		•			•	
North Carolina State University																
Richmond Community College	•	•	•	•							•	•	•	•	•	•
Surry Community College		•			•	•										
University of North Carolina: Greensboro	•	•		•		•		•		•	•	•	•	•	•	•
University of North Carolina:Wilmington		•	•	•		•		•		•	•	•	•	•	•	
Wake Forest University		•	•	•		•	•	•		•		•	•	•	•	
Wilkes Community College	•	•	•	•	•	•		•	•	•		•	•	•	•	•
Wingate College			•				•			•	•	•		•		
North Dakota																
Dickinson State University																
Mayville State University	•	•	•	•	•	•	•	•	•	•	•	•	•	•	•	•

886

	Math Skills		Study Skills		Language Arts		Written Express.		Word Processing		Time Manage.		Learn. Strategies		Organiz. Skills	
	Grp.	Ind.	Grp.	Ind.	Grp.	Ind.	Grp.	Ind.	Grp.	Ind.	Grp.	Ind.	Grp.	Ind.	Grp.	Ind.
North Dakota State College of Science	•	•	•	•	•	•	•	•	•	•	•	•	•	•	•	•
North Dakota State University		•	•	•		•		•		•	•	•	•	•	•	•
North Dakota State University: Bottineau		•	•	•	•	•		•			•	•	•	•	•	•
Ohio																
Bowling Green State University	•	•	•	•	•	•	•	•	•	•	•	•	•	•	•	•
Case Western Reserve University	•	•	•	•			•					•	•	•		•
Cedarville College																
Central Ohio Technical College		•	•	•		•		•		•		•		•		•
Cleveland State University	•	•	•		•	•	•	•			•				•	•
College of Mount St. Joseph	•	•	•	•			•			•	•	•	•	•		•
Columbus State Community College		•		•		•		•		•		•		•		•
Cuyahoga Community College		•		•		•		•		•		•		•		•
Defiance College	•	•	•	•			•			•		•		•		•
Edison State Community College	•	•	•	•	•	•	•	•	•	•	•	•	•	•	•	•
Franklin University	•	•		•		•	•									
Hocking Technical College		•	•	•		•		•				•	•	•	•	•
Jefferson Technical College		•		•		•				•						
Kent State University: Ashtabula Regional Campus		•		•		•		•					•	•		•
Kent State University: Salem Regional	•	•	•					•	•	•			•	•		
Kenyon College																
Malone College	•	•	•	•			•			•		•	•	•	•	•
Muskingum College	•	•	•	•	•	•	•	•	•	•	•	•	•	•	•	•
Oberlin College	•	•	•	•			•			•		•	•	•	•	•
Ohio State University Agricultural Technical Institute	•	•	•	•	•	•	•	•	•	•	•	•	•	•	•	•
Ohio State University: Columbus Campus	•		•	•						•	•	•	•	•	•	•
Ohio State University: Marion Campus	•	•	•	•	•			•	•	•	•	•		•		•
Ohio State University: Newark Campus	•	•	•	•	•	•	•	•	•	•	•	•	•	•	•	•
Ohio University	•	•	•	•	•	•		•		•	•	•	•	•	•	•
Otterbein College		•	•	•		•	•			•	•	•	•	•	•	•
Owens Technical College																
Sinclair Community College		•	•	•		•		•		•	•	•	•	•	•	•
The University of Akron - Wayne College	•	•	•	•			•	•	•	•	•	•	•	•	•	•
University of Cincinnati: Raymond Walters College		•	•	•		•		•			•	•		•		•
University of Dayton	•	•	•	•	•	•	•	•			•	•			•	•
University of Toledo	•	•	•	•	•	•	•	•	•	•	•	•	•	•	•	•
Walsh College	•	•	•	•	•	•	•	•	•	•	•	•	•	•	•	•
Wilmington College	•	•	•	•			•	•		•	•	•	•	•		•
Oklahoma																
Carl Albert Junior College	•	•		•	•	•			•	•						
East Central University	•	•	•	•				•	•	•		•	•	•	•	•
Oklahoma State University	•		•	•		•		•		•		•		•		•
Rose State College	•	•	•	•		•		•		•	•	•		•		
Tulsa Junior College																

	TUTORIALS															
	Grp. Math Skills	Ind. Math Skills	Grp. Study Skills	Ind. Study Skills	Grp. Language Arts	Ind. Language Arts	Grp. Written Express.	Ind. Written Express.	Grp. Word Processing	Ind. Word Processing	Grp. Time Manage.	Ind. Time Manage.	Grp. Learn. Strategies	Ind. Learn. Strategies	Grp. Organiz. Skills	Ind. Organiz. Skills
University of Oklahoma			•		•		•		•		•		•		•	•
Oregon																
Central Oregon Community College	•	•	•	•	•	•	•	•	•		•	•	•	•	•	•
Clackamas Community College	•	•	•	•	•	•	•	•		•	•	•	•	•	•	•
Eastern Oregon State College	•	•	•	•	•	•		•	•		•	•	•	•	•	•
Lane Community College	•	•	•	•	•		•	•				•	•	•	•	•
Linn-Benton Community College		•	•		•		•		•		•		•		•	
Mount Hood Community College	•	•	•	•	•		•		•		•	•	•	•	•	•
Oregon State University	•	•	•		•	•	•	•	•	•		•		•	•	•
Pacific University		•		•		•		•					•		•	
Portland Community College		•		•		•		•		•		•		•		•
Umpqua Community College		•	•		•		•		•		•	•		•		
University of Oregon	•	•	•	•	•	•	•	•					•	•		
Western Oregon State College																
Pennsylvania																
Albright College		•	•	•		•		•	•	•		•		•		•
Bloomsburg University of Pennsylvania	•	•	•	•	•	•		•	•	•	•	•		•		•
Bryn Mawr College	•	•	•	•	•	•	•	•	•	•	•	•	•	•	•	•
California University of Pennsylvania		•	•	•		•		•	•	•		•	•	•	•	•
Carnegie Mellon University			•				•		•			•		•		•
Churchman Business School		•		•				•			•		•		•	
College Misericordia	•	•	•	•		•	•	•	•		•	•	•	•		•
Community College of Allegheny College		•		•		•		•			•		•		•	
Community College of Philadelphia		•	•	•		•		•	•	•	•	•	•	•	•	•
Delaware County Community College	•	•	•	•	•	•	•	•	•	•	•	•	•	•	•	•
Delaware Valley College	•	•	•	•			•	•	•	•	•	•	•	•	•	•
Duquesne University		•	•			•		•		•		•		•		
Edinboro University of Pennsylvania		•	•	•	•	•	•	•	•	•	•	•	•	•	•	•
Harcum Junior College	•	•	•	•		•	•	•	•	•	•		•		•	
Kutztown University of Pennsylvania	•	•	•	•	•	•	•	•	•	•	•	•	•	•	•	•
Lehigh County Community College		•		•		•		•		•		•		•		•
Lehigh University																
Luzerne County Community College	•	•	•	•	•	•	•	•	•	•	•	•	•	•	•	•
Mansfield University of Pennsylvania	•	•	•	•	•	•	•	•	•	•	•	•	•	•	•	•
Mercyhurst College	•	•	•	•		•	•	•	•	•	•	•	•		•	
Peirce Junior College		•		•			•		•		•		•		•	
Penn State Fayette Campus	•	•	•	•	•	•	•	•	•	•	•	•	•	•	•	
Penn State Mont Alto Campus	•	•	•	•	•	•	•	•	•	•	•	•	•	•	•	
Penn State University Park Campus		•		•		•		•		•		•		•		
Penn State Worthington Scranton Campus	•	•	•	•				•	•	•	•	•	•	•	•	
Pinebrook Junior College																
Point Park College		•		•			•		•		•		•		•	
Reading Area Community College	•	•	•	•	•	•	•	•	•	•	•	•	•	•		•

	Grp. - Math Skills	Ind. - Math Skills	Grp. - Study Skills	Ind. - Study Skills	Grp. - Language Arts	Ind. - Language Arts	Grp. - Written Express.	Ind. - Written Express.	Grp. - Word Processing	Ind. - Word Processing	Grp. - Time Manage.	Ind. - Time Manage.	Grp. - Learn. Strategies	Ind. - Learn. Strategies	Grp. - Organiz. Skills	Ind. - Organiz. Skills
Spring Garden College	•	•	•	•		•		•	•	•		•	•	•	•	•
University of Pittsburgh at Bradford	•	•	•	•	•	•	•	•								
University of Pittsburgh: Pittsburgh Campus			•	•							•	•			•	•
Waynesburg College	•		•	•	•	•	•	•	•	•		•		•	•	•
Westmoreland County Community College	•	•		•		•	•	•	•	•			•		•	
Widener University	•	•	•	•	•	•	•	•	•		•	•		•	•	•
Puerto Rico																
American University of Puerto Rico																
Inter American University of Puerto Rico																
Rhode Island																
Brown University																
Bryant College	•	•	•	•					•		•	•	•	•		
Community College of Rhode Island	•	•	•	•		•	•	•	•	•			•			•
Johnson and Wales University	•	•	•	•	•	•	•	•	•	•	•	•	•	•	•	•
Rhode Island School of Design																
Roger Williams College																
South Carolina																
Central Wesleyan College																
Francis Marion College																
Midlands Technical College	•	•	•	•	•	•	•	•	•	•	•	•	•	•	•	•
University of South Carolina		•		•		•		•				•				•
South Dakota																
Black Hills State College	•	•	•	•	•	•	•	•		•	•	•	•	•	•	•
Huron University	•	•	•	•	•	•	•	•	•	•		•	•	•	•	•
Northern State University		•			•		•						•		•	
South Dakota State University		•		•		•		•		•		•		•		•
Tennessee																
Austin Peay State University		•		•		•		•				•		•		•
Freed-Hardeman University		•		•		•		•		•			•		•	
Lee College		•		•		•	•	•		•		•	•	•		
Martin Methodist College			•													
Memphis College of Art		•		•		•		•		•		•		•		•
Middle Tennessee State University	•	•	•	•	•	•	•	•	•	•	•	•	•	•	•	•
Pellissippi State Technical Community College		•		•		•	•			•						
Tennessee Technological University	•	•	•	•	•	•	•	•	•	•		•	•			
University of Tennessee		•	•	•		•		•			•		•		•	
Vanderbilt University	•	•	•	•		•	•	•	•	•	•	•	•	•	•	•
Texas																
Amarillo College	•	•	•	•	•	•	•	•	•	•	•	•	•	•	•	•
El Paso Community College	•	•		•		•		•		•		•		•		•
North Harris Montgomery Community College Distric	•	•	•	•	•	•	•	•	•	•	•	•	•	•	•	•
North Lake College	•	•	•	•	•	•	•	•	•	•	•	•	•	•	•	•

TUTORIALS

College	Grp. Math Skills	Ind. Math Skills	Grp. Study Skills	Ind. Study Skills	Grp. Language Arts	Ind. Written Express.	Grp. Word Processing	Ind. Word Processing	Grp. Time Manage.	Ind. Time Manage.	Grp. Learn. Strategies	Ind. Learn. Strategies	Grp. Organiz. Skills	Ind. Organiz. Skills		
Richland College	•	•	•	•		•	•	•	•	•	•	•	•	•	•	•
Sam Houston State University																
San Antonio College	•	•	•	•	•	•	•	•	•	•	•	•	•	•	•	•
Schreiner College	•	•		•		•		•		•	•		•		•	
Southern Methodist University	•	•	•	•	•	•	•		•	•		•		•	•	•
St. Philip's College	•	•	•	•	•	•	•	•	•	•		•		•		•
Tarleton State University											•					
Texas A&I University	•	•	•	•	•		•			•	•		•		•	
Texas Southmost College		•	•				•	•	•		•		•			•
Texas Tech University	•	•	•	•	•	•	•	•	•	•	•	•	•	•	•	•
Tyler Jr. College	•	•	•	•		•		•								
University of Houston	•	•	•	•	•	•	•	•	•	•	•	•	•	•	•	•
University of Texas at Brownsville		•	•			•	•	•		•		•			•	
Utah																
Snow College	•	•	•	•	•	•	•	•	•	•	•	•	•	•	•	•
Southern Utah University	•	•	•	•	•	•	•			•		•		•	•	
University of Utah	•		•			•				•		•		•		
Utah State University	•	•	•	•	•	•	•	•	•	•	•	•	•	•	•	•
Vermont																
Burlington College	•	•	•	•		•	•	•	•	•	•	•	•	•	•	•
Community College of Vermont	•	•	•							•		•		•		
Landmark College		•		•		•		•		•	•		•		•	
New England Culinary Institute		•				•										
Norwich University	•	•	•	•		•		•		•	•		•	•	•	•
Saint Michael's College																
Southern Vermont College		•	•	•		•		•		•	•	•	•	•	•	•
University of Vermont		•		•		•		•		•		•		•		•
Vermont Technical College	•	•	•	•	•	•	•	•	•	•	•	•	•	•	•	•
Virginia																
Blue Ridge Community College	•	•			•	•										
Bluefield College		•		•		•		•		•		•		•		•
Christopher Newport College		•		•		•		•		•		•		•		•
College of William and Mary			•		•	•	•						•		•	
Dabney S. Lancaster Community College	•		•		•		•		•		•		•		•	
George Mason University	•	•	•			•	•							•		
Hollins College																
James Madison University		•	•	•		•		•		•	•	•	•	•		•
Liberty University		•	•	•		•		•		•	•	•	•	•		•
Lord Fairfax Community College	•	•	•	•	•	•	•	•	•	•	•	•	•	•		•
New River Community College		•	•	•		•		•	•	•	•	•	•	•	•	•
Patrick Henry Community College	•	•	•	•	•	•	•	•	•	•	•	•	•	•		•
Paul D. Camp Community College		•				•		•			•					•
Radford University											•	•	•	•		•

890

	Grp. - Math Skills	Ind. - Math Skills	Grp. - Study Skills	Ind. - Study Skills	Grp. - Language Arts	Ind. - Language Arts	Grp. - Written Express.	Ind. - Written Express.	Grp. - Word Processing	Ind. - Word Processing	Grp. - Time Manage.	Ind. - Time Manage.	Grp. - Learn. Strategies	Ind. - Learn. Strategies	Grp. - Organiz. Skills	Ind. - Organiz. Skills
Southern Seminary College	•	•	•		•	•	•	•			•	•	•		•	
Thomas Nelson Community College		•	•			•		•	•		•		•		•	
University of Virginia		•		•		•		•		•		•		•		•
Virginia Highlands Community College		•	•	•		•		•		•	•	•	•		•	•
Virginia Intermont College		•		•		•	•		•		•		•		•	•
Virginia Polytechnic Institute and State University			•	•			•			•	•	•		•		
Virginia Wesleyan College	•	•	•				•	•	•	•	•	•	•		•	•
Virginia Western Community College		•	•	•		•		•		•		•		•		•
Washington																
Central Washington University	•	•	•	•	•	•	•	•		•		•	•		•	•
Centralia College		•		•		•		•		•		•		•		•
Columbia Basin College		•		•		•		•		•	•		•		•	
Evergreen State College		•		•		•		•		•		•		•		•
Lutheran Bible Institute of Seattle																
Olympic College		•		•		•		•		•		•		•		•
Puget Sound Christian College																
Washington State University	•	•	•	•		•	•	•	•			•	•	•	•	•
Wenatchee Valley College	•		•		•		•			•		•		•		•
Whitworth College																
West Virginia																
Bluefield State College		•	•	•	•	•	•	•		•	•		•		•	•
Davis and Elkins College		•		•		•		•		•		•		•		•
Marshall University	•	•	•	•	•	•	•	•	•	•	•	•	•	•	•	
Potomac State College of W. Virginia	•	•	•	•		•	•	•		•	•	•	•	•	•	•
West Virginia Northern Comm College		•	•					•		•		•		•		
West Virginia State College	•	•	•	•	•		•	•		•	•	•	•	•	•	
West Virginia University																
West Virginia Wesleyan College	•	•	•	•	•	•	•	•		•	•	•	•	•	•	
Wisconsin																
Beloit College		•	•	•		•		•			•	•		•	•	•
Chippewa Valley Technical College	•	•	•	•	•	•	•	•	•	•	•	•	•	•	•	•
Edgewood College	•	•	•	•		•		•	•	•	•	•	•	•	•	•
Fox Valley Technical College		•	•	•				•		•	•	•		•		•
Gateway Technical College		•		•		•		•		•		•		•		•
Lawrence University		•	•				•	•		•				•		
Marian College of Fond du Lac		•		•		•		•		•		•		•		•
Marquette University		•	•	•		•		•	•		•					
Milwaukee Area Technical College	•	•	•	•	•	•	•	•		•	•	•	•		•	•
Moraine Park Technical Institute		•		•		•	•			•	•	•	•			
Northeast Wisconsin Technical College	•	•	•	•	•	•	•	•		•		•	•	•	•	•
Ripon College		•	•	•		•		•		•	•	•	•		•	•
University of Wisconsin - Milwaukee	•		•	•	•		•	•		•		•		•		•
University of Wisconsin : Madison	•		•					•	•	•	•	•	•		•	

891

TUTORIALS

	Grp. Math Skills	Ind. Math Skills	Grp. Study Skills	Ind. Study Skills	Grp. Language Arts	Ind. Language Arts	Grp. Written Express.	Ind. Written Express.	Grp. Word Processing	Ind. Word Processing	Grp. Time Manage.	Ind. Time Manage.	Grp. Learn. Strategies	Ind. Learn. Strategies	Grp. Organiz. Skills	Ind. Organiz. Skills
University of Wisconsin Ctr: Waukesha	•	•	•	•	•	•	•	•		•	•	•	•	•	•	
University of Wisconsin: LaCrosse	•	•	•	•	•	•	•	•		•	•	•			•	•
University of Wisconsin: Oshkosh	•	•	•	•	•	•	•	•	•	•	•	•	•	•	•	•
University of Wisconsin: Platteville		•	•	•		•		•		•	•	•		•	•	•
University Wisconsin Center: Baraboo Sauk County	•	•	•	•		•		•	•		•		•		•	•
University Wisconsin-Center Rock County	•	•	•	•			•	•		•	•		•	•	•	•
Viterbo College						•		•		•		•		•		
Waukesha County Technical College		•	•	•		•		•	•		•	•		•		•
Western Wisconsin Technical College	•	•	•	•	•	•	•	•	•	•	•	•	•	•	•	•
Wisconsin Indianhead Technical College	•	•	•	•	•	•	•	•					•		•	
Wyoming																
Casper College	•	•	•	•	•	•			•	•	•	•	•	•	•	•
Central Wyoming College	•	•	•	•	•	•	•	•	•	•	•	•	•	•	•	
Laramie County Community College	•	•	•	•	•	•	•	•	•	•	•	•	•	•	•	•
Sheridan College	•			•	•			•	•		•		•		•	•
University of Wyoming	•	•	•	•		•		•		•	•	•	•	•	•	•

Alphabetical Listing of Colleges

895

896